Stephanie Christ

Human Anatomy & Physiology

SEVENTH EDITION

Elaine N. Marieb, R.N., Ph.D.
Holyoke Community College

Katja Hoehn, M.D., Ph.D.
Mount Royal College

PEARSON

Benjamin
Cummings

San Francisco Boston New York
Cape Town Hong Kong London Madrid Mexico City
Montreal Munich Paris Singapore Sydney Tokyo Toronto

Editor-in-Chief: Serina Beauparlant
Development Manager: Claire Alexander
Associate Project Editors: Karoliina Tuovinen
    and Sabrina Larson
Managing Editor: Wendy Earl
Production Supervisor: Michele Mangelli
Art Development Editor: Laura Southworth
Associate Media Editor: Ryan Shaw
Assistant Editor: Jessica Brunner
Editorial Assistant: Alex Streczyn

Text and Cover Designer: Frances Baca
Principal Artists: Imagineering STA Media Services Inc.
Art Coordinator: David Novak
Photo Researcher: Gillian Speeth
Copyeditor: Anita Wagner
Compositor: Techbooks/GTS
Indexer: Karen Hollister
Senior Manufacturing Buyer: Stacey Weinberger
Executive Marketing Manager: Lauren Harp

Cover Photograph: Seventh seed Serena Williams races to return a shot to compatriot and top seed Lindsay Davenport during their match at the 2005 Australian Open tennis final in Melbourne. © Adrees Latif/Reuters/Corbis..

Photo and illustration credits follow the Glossary.

Library of Congress Cataloging-in-Publication Data

Marieb, Elaine Nicpon
    Human anatomy & physiology / Elaine N. Marieb, Katja Hoehn.—7th ed.
    p. cm.
    Includes index.
    ISBN 0-8053-5910-9
    1. Human physiology. 2. Human anatomy. I. Hoehn, Katja. II. Title.

QP34.5.M265 2007
612–dc22   2005053535

ISBN 0-13-173297-8-(NASTA Edition)
2 3 4 5 6 7 8 9 10—DOW—09 08 07 06
www.aw-bc.com

About the Authors

We dedicate this work to our students both present and past, who always inspire us to "push the envelope."

Elaine N. Marieb

For Elaine N. Marieb, taking the student's perspective into account has always been an integral part of her teaching style. Dr. Marieb began her teaching career at Springfield College, where she taught anatomy and physiology to physical education majors. She then joined the faculty of the Biological Science Division of Holyoke Community College in 1969 after receiving her Ph.D. in zoology from the University of Massachusetts at Amherst. While teaching at Holyoke Community College, where many of her students were pursuing nursing degrees, she developed a desire to better understand the relationship between the scientific study of the human body and the clinical aspects of the nursing practice. To that end, while continuing to teach full time, Dr. Marieb pursued her nursing education, which culminated in a Master of Science degree with a clinical specialization in gerontology from the University of Massachusetts. It is this experience, along with stories from the field—including those of former students now in health careers—that has informed the development of the unique perspective and accessibility for which her texts and laboratory manuals are known.

In her ongoing commitment to students and her realization of the challenges they face, Dr. Marieb has given generously to provide opportunities for students to further their education. She contributes to the New Directions, New Careers Program at Holyoke Community College by providing several full-tuition scholarships each year for women who are returning to college after a hiatus or attending college for the first time and would be unable to continue their studies without financial support. She funds the E. N. Marieb Science Research Awards at Mount Holyoke College, which promotes research by undergraduate science majors, and has underwritten renovation and updating of one of the biology labs in Clapp Laboratory at that college. Dr. Marieb is also a contributor to the University of Massachusetts at Amherst where she generously provided funding for reconstruction and instrumentation of a cutting-edge cytology research laboratory that bears her name.

In 1994, Dr. Marieb received the Benefactor Award from the National Council for Resource Development, American Association of Community Colleges, which recognizes her ongoing sponsorship of student scholarships, faculty teaching awards, and other academic contributions to Holyoke Community College. In May 2000, the science building at Holyoke Community College was named in her honor.

Dr. Marieb is an active member of the Human Anatomy and Physiology Society (HAPS) and the American Association for the Advancement of Science (AAAS). Additionally, while actively engaged as an author, Dr. Marieb serves as a consultant for the Benjamin Cummings/A.D.A.M.® *InterActive Physiology*® CD-ROM series. This text—*Human Anatomy & Physiology*, Seventh Edition—is the latest expression of her commitment to the needs of students in their pursuit of the study of A&P.

When not involved in academic pursuits, Dr. Marieb is a world traveler and has vowed to visit every country on this planet. Shorter term, she serves on the board of directors of the famed Marie Selby Botanical Gardens and on the scholarship committee of the Women's Resource Center of Sarasota County. She is an enthusiastic supporter of the local arts and enjoys a competitive match of doubles tennis.

Katja Hoehn

Dr. Katja Hoehn is an instructor in the Department of Chemical, Biological, and Environmental Sciences at Mount Royal College in Calgary, Canada. Dr. Hoehn received her M.D. (with Distinction) from the University of Saskatchewan, and her Ph.D. in Pharmacology from Dalhousie University. Dr. Hoehn has been a contributor to several books and has written numerous research papers in Neuroscience and Pharmacology. In 1991, the Dalhousie Medical Research Foundation presented her with the Max Forman (Jr.) Prize for excellence in medical research. During her Ph.D. and postdoctoral studies, Dr. Hoehn pursued her love of teaching by presenting guest lectures to first- and second-year medical students at Dalhousie University and at the University of Calgary.

During her 11 years at Mount Royal College, Dr. Hoehn has received numerous awards including a PanCanadian Educational Technology Faculty Award (1999), a Teaching Excellence Award from the Student's Association of Mount Royal College (2001), and the Mount Royal College Distinguished Faculty Teaching Award (2004). She is also actively involved in the Human Anatomy and Physiology Society (HAPS). When not teaching, Dr. Hoehn likes to spend time outdoors with her husband and two boys, compete in triathlons, and play Irish flute.

CHAPTER

5

The Integumentary System

A chapter outline with student objectives prefaces each chapter and guides students to concepts that are most important to know.

The Skin (pp. 152–158)

1. Name the tissue types composing the epidermis and dermis. List the major layers of each and describe the functions of each layer.
2. Describe the factors that normally contribute to skin color. Briefly describe how changes in skin color may be used as clinical signs of certain disease states.

Appendages of the Skin (pp. 158–163)

3. Compare the structure and locations of sweat and oil glands. Also compare the composition and functions of their secretions.
4. Compare and contrast eccrine and apocrine glands.

5. List the parts of a hair follicle and explain the function of each part. Also describe the functional relationship of arrector pili muscles to the hair follicle.
6. Name the regions of a hair and explain the basis of hair color. Describe the distribution, growth, replacement, and changing nature of hair during the life span.
7. Describe the structure of nails.

Functions of the Integumentary System (pp. 163–165)

8. Describe how the skin accomplishes at least five different functions.

Homeostatic Imbalances of Skin (pp. 165–167, 170)

9. Summarize the characteristics of the three major types of skin cancers.
10. Explain why serious burns are life threatening. Describe how to determine the extent of a burn and differentiate first-, second-, and third-degree burns.

Developmental Aspects of the Integumentary System (pp. 170–171)

11. Describe and attempt to explain the causes of changes that occur in the skin from birth to old age.

Color-coded chapter and unit tabs help students find information quickly and easily.

9

Illustrated tables summarize complex information and serve as a "one-stop shopping" study tool.

314 UNIT 2 Covering, Support, and Movement of the Body

TABLE 9.3 Comparison of Skeletal, Cardiac, and Smooth Muscle

CHARACTERISTIC	SKELETAL	CARDIAC	SMOOTH
Body location	Attached to bones or (some facial muscles) to skin	Walls of the heart	Single-unit muscle in walls of hollow visceral organs (other than the heart); multiunit muscle in intrinsic eye muscles, airways, large arteries
Cell shape and appearance	Single, very long, cylindrical, multinucleate cells with obvious striations	Branching chains of cells; uni- or binucleate; striations	Single, fusiform, uninucleate; no striations
Connective tissue components	Epimysium, perimysium, and endomysium	Endomysium attached to fibrous skeleton of heart	Endomysium
Presence of myofibrils composed of sarcomeres	Yes	Yes, but myofibrils are of irregular thickness	No, but actin and myosin filaments are present throughout; dense bodies anchor actin filaments
Presence of T tubules and site of invagination	Yes; two in each sarcomere at A-I junctions	Yes; one in each sarcomere at Z disc; larger diameter than those of skeletal muscle	No; only caveolae

Meaningful analogies and jargon-free explanations. Drawing on her own unique experience as an A&P professor and former nursing student, Marieb presents anatomy and physiology as a "story" that can be more easily understood and remembered.

E very day the kidneys filter nearly 200 liters of fluid from the bloodstream, allowing toxins, metabolic wastes, and excess ions to leave the body in urine while returning needed substances to the blood. Much like a water purification plant that keeps a city's water drinkable and disposes of its wastes, the kidneys are usually unappreciated until they malfunction and body fluids become contaminated. Although the lungs and skin also participate in excretion, the kidneys are the major excretory organs.

As the kidneys perform these excretory functions, they also act as essential regulators of the volume and chemical makeup of the blood, maintaining the proper balance between water and salts and between acids and bases. Frankly, this would be tricky work for a chemical engineer, but the kidneys do it efficiently most of the time.

Other renal functions include

- Gluconeogenesis (see p. 966) during prolonged fasting.
- Producing the hormones renin and erythropoietin (see Chapter 16). *Renin* (re'nin; *ren* = kidney) acts as an enzyme to help regulate blood pressure and kidney function. *Erythropoietin* (ĕ-rith"ro-poi'ĕ-tin) stimulates red blood cell production.

Preface to the Instructor

As educators, clinically trained individuals, and perennial students, we are continually challenged by the learning mind. What works best to get students over conceptual hurdles and to help them apply new information to the world they personally understand? Our clinical backgrounds have served our teaching and writing purposes well. Perhaps even more important, our clinical experience has allowed us to view our presentations through our students' eyes and from the vantage points of their career interests.

For this edition, as for those preceding it, feedback from both student and instructor reviews indicated areas of the text that needed to be revised for clarity, timeliness, and just plain reduction of verbal meatiness. Overall, feedback was positive, verifying that the approach of explaining fundamental principles and unifying themes first as a strong base for all that comes later is still viable. Furthermore, it is clear that backing up these explanations with comfortable analogies and familiar examples enhances the students' understanding of the workings of the human body.

Unifying Themes

Three integrating themes that organized, unified, and set the tone of the first edition of this text continue to be valid and are retained in this edition. These themes are:

Interrelationships of body organ systems. The fact that nearly all regulatory mechanisms require interaction of several organ systems is continually emphasized. For example, Chapter 25, which deals with the structure and function of the urinary system, discusses the vital importance of the kidneys not only in maintaining adequate blood volume to ensure normal blood circulation, but also in continually adjusting the chemical composition of blood so that all body cells remain healthy. The unique *Making Connections* feature is the culmination of this approach and should help students think of the body as a dynamic community of interdependent parts rather than as a number of isolated structural units.

Homeostasis. The normal and most desirable condition of body functioning is homeostasis. Its loss or destruction always leads to some type of pathology—temporary or permanent. Pathological conditions are integrated with the text to clarify and illuminate normal functioning, not as an end in and of themselves. For example, Chapter 19, which deals with the structure and function of blood vessels, explains how the ability of healthy arteries to expand and recoil ensures continuous blood flow and proper circulation. The chapter goes on to discuss the effects on homeostasis when arteries lose their elasticity: high blood pressure and all of its attendant problems. These homeostatic imbalances are indicated visually by a purple symbol with a fulcrum.

Whenever students see the imbalance symbol in text, the concept of disease as a loss of homeostasis is reinforced.

Complementarity of structure and function. Students are encouraged to understand the structure of an organ, a tissue, or a cell as a prerequisite to comprehending its function. Concepts of physiology are explained and related to structural characteristics that promote or allow the various functions to occur. For example, the lungs can act as a gas exchange site because the walls of their air sacs present an incredibly thin barrier between blood and air.

Homeostasis icons alert the students to consequences of body systems not functioning optimally.

HOMEOSTATIC IMBALANCE

Pericarditis, inflammation of the pericardium, roughens the serous membrane surfaces. Consequently, as the beating heart rubs against its pericardial sac, it creates a creaking sound *(pericardial friction rub)* that can be heard with a stethoscope. Pericarditis is characterized by pain deep to the sternum. Over time, it may lead to adhesions in which the visceral and parietal pericardia stick together and impede heart activity. In severe cases, the situation ~~is~~ *large* amounts of inflammatory fluid ~~into the~~ pericardial cavity. This excess fluid ~~compresses th~~e heart, limiting its ability to pump ~~The co~~ndition in which the heart is com~~pressed by f~~luid is called *cardiac tamponade* ~~(tam'po-nād),~~ literally, "heart plug." Physicians ~~treat by inse~~rting a syringe into the pericardial cav~~ity and draining~~ off the excess fluid. ●

MAKING CONNECTIONS

SYSTEM CONNECTIONS: Homeostatic Interrelationships Between the Muscular System and Other Body Systems

Integumentary System
- Muscular exercise enhances circulation to skin and improves skin health
- Skin protects the muscles by external enclosure; helps dissipate heat generated by the muscles

Skeletal System
- Skeletal muscle activity maintains bone health and strength
- Bones provide levers for muscle activity

Nervous System
- Facial muscle activity allows emotions to be expressed

- Nervous system stimulates and regulates muscle activity

Endocrine System
- Growth hormone and androgens influence skeletal muscle strength and mass; other hormones help regulate cardiac and smooth muscle activity

Cardiovascular System
- Skeletal muscle activity increases efficiency of cardiovascular functioning; helps prevent atherosclerosis and causes cardiac hypertrophy
- Cardiovascular system delivers needed oxygen and nutrients to muscles

Lymphatic System/Immunity
- Physical exercise may enhance or depress immunity depending on its intensity
- Lymphatic vessels drain leaked tissue fluids; immune system protects muscles from disease

Respiratory System
- Muscular exercise increases respiratory capacity and efficiency of gas exchange
- Respiratory system provides oxygen ~~and disposes of~~ carbon dioxide

Digestive System
- Physical activity increases gastro~~intestinal motility and~~ elimination when at rest
- Digestive system provides nutrien~~ts needed for mus~~cle health; liver metabolizes lactic ~~acid~~

Urinary System
- Physical activity promotes normal v~~oiding;~~ skeletal muscle forms the voluntary ~~sphincter of the~~ urethra
- Urinary system disposes of nitroge~~nous wastes~~

Reproductive System
- Skeletal muscle helps support pel~~vic organs (e.g.,~~ uterus); assists erection of penis an~~d clitoris~~
- Testicular androgen promotes incre~~ased muscle size~~

As we age, the amount of connective tissue in our skeletal muscles increases, the number of muscle fibers decreases, and the muscles become stringier, or more sinewy. By the age of 30 even in healthy people, a gradual loss of muscle mass, called *sarcopenia* (sar-co-pe′ne-ah), begins to occur as muscle proteins start to degrade more rapidly than

they can be replaced. Just why t~~his happens is a good~~ question, but apparently the sa~~me signaling mole~~cules (transcription factors, e~~nzymes, growth factors,~~ and others) that promote musc~~le growth (where we~~ see this type of muscle atroph~~y and where skeletal~~ muscles form so much of th~~e total body~~ weight and muscle strength ~~...~~

CLOSER CONNECTIONS

THE MUSCULAR SYSTEM and Interrelationships with the Cardiovascular, Endocrine, Lymphatic/Immunity, and Skeletal Systems

Our skeletal muscles are a marvel. In the well conditioned, they ripple with energy. In those of us who are less athletic, they enable us to perform the rather remarkable tasks of moving and getting around. No one would argue that the nervous system is indispensable for activating muscles to contract and for keeping them healthy via tone. Let's look at how skeletal muscle activity affects other body systems from the vantage point of overall health and disease prevention.

Cardiovascular System

The single most important barometer of how "well" we age is the health of our cardiovascular system. More than any other factor, regular exercise helps to maintain that health. Anything that gets you huffing and puffing on a regular basis, be it racquetball or a vigorous walk, helps to keep heart muscle healthy and strong. It also keeps blood vessels clear, delaying atherosclerosis and helping to prevent the most common type of high blood pressure and hypertensive heart disease—ailments that can lead to the deterioration of heart muscle and the kidneys. Uncluttered blood vessels also stave off painful or disabling intermittent claudication in which muscle pain due to ischemia hinders walking. Furthermore, regular exercise boosts blood levels of clot-busting enzymes, helping to ward off heart attacks and strokes, other scourges of old age.

Endocrine System

Muscle has a high rate of metabolism, and even at rest it uses much more energy than does fat. Consequently, exercise that builds moderate muscle mass helps to keep weight down and prevents obesity. Obesity is one of the risk factors for development of age-related diabetes mellitus—the metabolic disorder in which body

cells are unresponsive to insulin (secreted by the pancreas) and, hence, unable to utilize glucose normally. Additionally, exercise helps to maintain normal cellular responses to insulin. On the other side of the coin, several hormones, including growth hormone, thyroid hormone, and sex hormones, are essential for normal development and maturation of the skeletal muscles.

Lymphatic System/Immunity

Physical exercise has a marked effect on immunity. Moderate or mild exercise causes a temporary rise in the number of phagocytes, T cells (a particular group of white blood cells), and antibodies, all of which populate lymphatic organs and mount the attack against infectious disease. By contrast, strenuous exercise depresses the immune system. The way in which exercise affects immunity—including these seemingly contradictory observations—is still a mystery, but the so-called stress hormones are definitely involved. Like major stressors such as surgery and serious burns, strenuous exercise increases blood levels of stress hormones such as epinephrine and glucocorticoids. These hormones depress the immune system during severe stress. This is thought to be a protective mechanism—a way of preventing large numbers of slightly damaged cells from being rejected.

Skeletal System

Last but not least, weight-bearing exercise of the skeletal muscles promotes skeletal strength and helps prevent osteoporosis. Since osteoporosis severely detracts from the quality of life by increasing risk of fractures, this is an extremely important interaction. But without their bony attachments, muscles would be ineffective in causing body movement.

CLINICAL CONNECTIONS

Muscular System

Case study: Let's continue our tale of Mrs. DeStephano's medical problems, this time looking at the notes made detailing observations of her skeletal musculature.

- Severe lacerations of the muscles of the right leg and knee
- Damage to the blood vessels serving the right leg and knee
- Transection of the sciatic nerve (the large nerve serving most of the lower limb), just above the right knee

Her physician orders daily passive range-of-motion (ROM) exercise and electrical stimulation for her right leg and a diet high in protein, carbohydrates, and vitamin C.

1. Describe the step-by-step process of wound healing that will occur in her fleshy (muscle) wounds, and note the consequences of the specific restorative process that occurs.

2. What complications in healing can be anticipated owing to vascular (blood vessel) damage in the right leg?

3. What complications in muscle structure and function result from transection of the sciatic nerve? Why are passive ROM and electrical stimulation of her right leg muscles ordered?

4. Explain the reasoning behind the dietary recommendations.

(Answers in Appendix G)

To help students understand the relationships between body systems, Marieb offers the focused, three-tiered presentation **Making Connections** at the end of each body system discussion:

- **Systems Connections** highlight the interrelationships between all of the body systems.
- **Closer Connections** focus in greater depth on selected systems interrelationships.
- **Clinical Connections** case studies encourage students to apply chapter concepts to a situation in a clinical setting.

Other hallmark features include:

- **Key questions** accompany selected figures and prod the student to interpret the concepts or illustrated processes, or to make predictions about what's next. Answers can be found upside-down on the same page.
- **Closer Look** boxes on timely subjects such as medical technology, new discoveries in medical research, and important societal issues broaden the students' horizons.
- **Related Clinical Terms** help students prepare for the clinical world.
- **Comprehensive Chapter Summaries** with page references provide excellent study aids.
- **Review Questions** help students to evaluate their progress in the subject.

PEDAGOGICALLY DRIVEN ART

Art plays a critical role in helping students visualize anatomical and physiological concepts. In science texts, where page count is always an important consideration, the tendency is to try to make each piece of art "say" as much as it can. Realizing this, an important aspect of the art conception for this text has been restraint—limiting the information to one or at most two major concepts to be taught or clarified by each piece. This prevents the student from being overwhelmed and confused by concept overload.

Size is also a consideration when crystallizing pedagogically effective art. Art that is too small lacks significance, and students tend to skip over or neglect it. Hence, our art program provides the largest visuals deemed possible to depict and elucidate a given concept.

Process art breaks down complex processes into a series of clear, easy-to-follow steps.

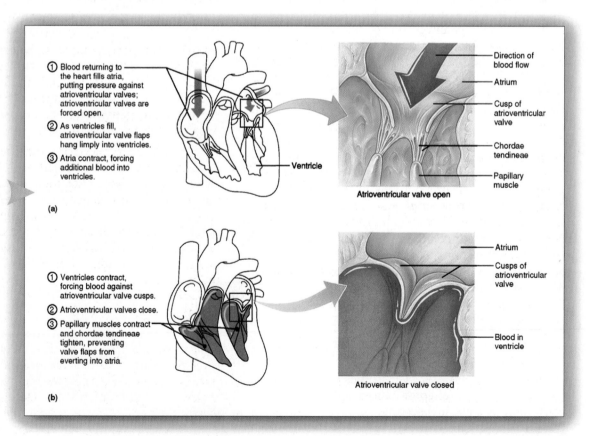

Upgraded Muscle Gallery art presents a more realistic view of muscles.

Labels on figure:
- Pectoralis major
- Serratus anterior
- Linea alba
- Tendinous intersection
- **Transversus abdominis**
- **Rectus abdominis**
- **Internal oblique**
- **External oblique**
- Aponeurosis of the external oblique
- Inguinal ligament (formed by free inferior border of the external oblique aponeurosis)

(a)

NEW TO THE SEVENTH EDITION

Factual material updates. A major undertaking of this edition, as in earlier editions, was to update the factual material and topic boxes in all subject areas—a monumental task that demands painstaking selectivity. Certain areas are updated in every edition—immunity, cell signaling, and the offerings of genetic engineering—and this edition is no exception. However, other subjects of study are also attended to as appropriate for the changing literature. Specific examples from nervous system Chapters 11 and 12 illustrate this trend: Information on neurotransmitters has been updated, the brain's processing of language now has its own section, and the structure of voltage-gated ion channels in figures is now depicted more realistically according to recent Nobel Prize–winning research. Chapter 12 also features a new *Closer Look* box on "mad cow" disease and its human equivalent, Creutzfeldt-Jakob disease. Chapters 24 (Nutrition, Metabolism, and Body Temperature Regulation) and 29 (Heredity) also received some substantial attention. In Chapter 24, current diets are compared and assessed and the long-term role of leptin in feeding behavior and satiety is explored. Chapter 29 now has a new section, Beyond DNA: Regulation of Gene Expression that showcases new research findings on the importance of chromatin proteins and small RNAs in directing our genetic heritage.

Throughout the book, figures of G protein–mediated second-messenger systems have been updated and each step numbered in sequence, enhancing their accessibility to students. Although information changes even as a textbook goes to press, be assured that this intent and responsibility was carried out to the best of our ability.

Reorganization of specific chapters and topics. Chapter 15 (The Special Senses) has been reorganized. Vision, smell, and taste, having similar transduction mechanisms, are discussed in sequence, beginning with vision, which is the best understood. In response to reviewers' comments, the sequence of physiological events in skeletal muscle contractions has been reordered in Chapter 9.

Revised art. Every piece of art in the book has been examined and the color palette has been revised to provide art that has richer, more organic color. Many pieces have been touched up to enhance their detail and many new views have been added. Many physiology figures have been rerendered to reflect recent research on functional processes. As before, the art has a consistent color protocol to encourage automatic learning. Every time you see an ATP starburst it is bright yellow; oxygen is red; cellular cytoplasm is routinely beige; and so on.

Photo usage. Additionally, there are many more photomicrographs and clinical photos in this edition, and many of those retained from earlier editions have been upsized. As pointed out by a conscientious reviewer, "If you can't see it clearly, then it's not worth having."

New! Marieb Media Manager (set of 7 CD-ROMs)   (0-8053-7376-4)

This powerful new tool combines all instructor and student media into a seven-CD-ROM library with a fold-out Quick Reference Guide. The CDs contain:

- All of the images from the textbook and *A Brief Atlas of the Human Body,* Second Edition, in labeled, unlabeled, and leaders-only versions.

- PowerPoint resources including customizable Label Edit and Step Edit art, chapter Art Presentations, Active Lecture ("Clicker") Questions, Lecture Outlines with animations, and new *InterActive Physiology*® (IP) links that make it easy to use IP animations in any presentation.

- Microsoft Word versions of the Test Bank and Instructor's Guide.

Slide 1

New! Step Edit art facilitates step-by-step presentation of complex topics. You can now customize each step by editing, removing, resizing, or highlighting the labels and leaders.

Slide 2

Slide 4

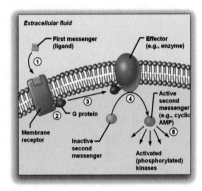

Slide 6

New! *InterActive Physiology®* **(IP) Links** make it easy to incorporate IP into any PowerPoint presentation. Following the built-in instructions, you can now link directly to IP from your PowerPoint presentation without the need for a web connection or other instructor CDs.

The Anatomy & Physiology Place Web Site

(www.anatomyandphysiology.com)
Each chapter of The A&P place contains relevant tutorials and exercises from *InterActive Physiology®*, Anatomy 360°™, and PhysioEx™ as well as links to the complete E-book version of the text. Students can also access the online component of *Get Ready for A&P* (please see a description under Supplements for the Student). In addition, The A&P Place includes self-study quizzes, anatomy labeling exercises, a new histology tutorial, animations, games and tutorials, case studies, a glossary, and flashcards. Instructors can now track student progress with the new Gradebook feature. An access kit is automatically packaged with each new copy of the text.

Instructor's Guide to Text and Media   (0-8053-7379-9)

This fully revised Guide includes detailed objectives, lecture outlines, activities, online media resources, answers to End-of-Chapter Questions, and *InterActive Physiology®* Exercise Sheets and answer key. All the illustrations from the text are indexed as thumbnails in the Visual Resource Guide so instructors can easily locate and make the best use of the available media.

Printed Test Bank   (0-8053-7378-0)
Computerized Test Bank   (0-8053-7381-0)

With more than 3600 test questions, this Test Bank has been updated with new and revised questions that cover all major topics at a range of difficulty levels. All questions in the printed Test Bank are available in electronic format through both the Media Manager CD-ROM, as Word files, and the TestGen-EQ CD-ROM. Both electronic options are cross-platform and allow instructors to easily generate and customize tests.

Transparency Acetates   (0-8053-7374-8)

This package includes all illustrations, photos, and tables from the text—approximately 800 images— with labels that have been enlarged for easy viewing in the classroom or lecture hall.

InterActive Physiology® 9-System Suite CD-ROM

Featuring a long-awaited ninth module on the Digestive System, *InterActive Physiology®* uses tutorials, animations, and engaging quizzes to help students advance beyond simple memorization to a genuine understanding of the most difficult concepts in the A&P course. This award-winning tutorial series is conveniently referenced in the appropriate end-of-chapter summaries. It is packaged free with each new copy of the text.

New! Anatomy 360°™

This easy-to-follow anatomy tutorial program helps students learn hundreds of anatomy terms, locations, and concepts. Based on real data from the Visible Human Project, Anatomy 360°™ features accurate, high-quality, rotatable images, engaging interactive exercises, and self-review questions. Students can also email their results from a wide variety of learning exercises to their instructor. Anatomy 360°™ is available via The Anatomy & Physiology Place.

A Brief Atlas of the Human Body, Second Edition   (0-8053-7373-X)

Revised for the seventh edition, this full-color atlas is bundled free with every new copy of the text, and includes 107 bone and 47 soft-tissue photographs with easy-to-read labels. This new edition of the atlas contains a brand-new, comprehensive histology photomicrograph section featuring over 50 slides of basic tissue and organ systems. Featuring photos taken by renowned biomedical photographer Ralph Hutchings, this high-quality photographic atlas makes an excellent resource for the classroom and laboratory, and is referenced in appropriate figure legends throughout the text.

Note: The following optional resources are available separately for qualified college adopters:

New! Get Ready for A&P
(0-8053-8284-4)

This new workbook and online component was created to help students be better prepared for their A&P course. This hands-on workbook helps students get up to speed in their knowledge of basic study skills, math review, basic chemistry, cell biology, anatomical terminology, and the human body. Features include pre-tests, guided explanations followed by interactive quizzes and exercises, and end-of-chapter cumulative tests. The online component includes a gradeable diagnostic pre-test and post-test, self-study quizzes with feedback, animations and links, a glossary, and flashcards. It is available via The Anatomy & Physiology Place.

Study Guide   (0-8053-7305-5)

Revised to accompany the Seventh Edition of *Human Anatomy & Physiology*, the study guide offers a wide variety of exercises that address different learning styles and call on students to develop their critical-thinking abilities. The three major sections, Building the Framework, Challenging Yourself, and Covering All Your Bases, help students build a base of knowledge using recall, reasoning, and imagination that can be applied to solving problems in both clinical and nonclinical situations.

Preface to the Student

This book is written for you. In a way, it is written by you (students) because it incorporates your suggestions, answers to questions most often asked, and explanations that have produced the greatest success in helping you learn about the human body. Human anatomy and physiology is more than just interesting—it is fascinating. To help get you involved in the study of this exciting subject, a number of special features are incorporated throughout the book.

The tone of this book is intentionally informal and unintimidating. There is absolutely no reason that you can't enjoy your learning task. This book is meant to be a guide to the understanding of your own body, not an encyclopedia of human anatomy and physiology. We have tried to be selective about the information included and have chosen facts that stress essential concepts. Physiological concepts are explained thoroughly; abundant analogies are used and examples are taken from familiar events whenever possible.

The illustrations and tables are designed with your learning needs in mind. The tables are summaries of important information in the text and should be valuable resources for reviewing for an exam. In all cases, the figures are referenced where their viewing would be most helpful in understanding the text. Those depicting physiological mechanisms often use the flowchart format so that you can see where you've been and where you're going. Additionally, many figures come equipped with questions that will help you to interpret the figures or to apply and integrate what you have learned. (Answers are provided at the bottom of the same page.) Special topic boxes, called *A Closer Look*, alert you to advances in medicine or present scientific information

that can be applied to your daily life. The *Making Connections* feature includes three elements to support your studies: *System Connections* recaps the information that you should know when you complete each body system; *Closer Connections* broadens your horizon and enriches your understanding of the system being studied—you may or may not have covered all of its concepts; and *Clinical Connections* challenges you to apply your learning to clinical situations. Please use this feature; it will help you to learn this subject.

Each chapter begins with an outline of its major topics (and their page references), with specific learning objectives listed for each topic. Important terms within the chapter text are bold-faced (in dark type), and phonetic spellings are provided for terms that are likely to be unfamiliar to you. To use these phonetic aids, you will need to remember the following rules:

1. Syllables are separated by dashes.

2. Accent marks follow stressed syllables. Primary stress is shown by ′ and secondary stress by ″.

3. Unless otherwise noted, assume that vowels at the ends of syllables are long. Assume that all other vowels are short unless a bar, indicating a long vowel sound, appears above them.

For example, the phonetic spelling of "thrombophlebitis" is throm″bo-fleh-bi′tis. The fourth syllable (bi′) receives the greatest stress, and the first syllable (throm″) gets the secondary stress. The "o" in the second syllable and "i" in the fourth syllable are long. Further explanation of the pronunciation system can be found at the beginning of the Glossary.

Any exam causes anxiety. To help you prepare for an exam or comprehend the material you have just read, thorough summaries complete with page references are found at the ends of the chapters, as are review questions that use a combination of testing techniques (multiple choice, matching, short answer essay, critical thinking, and clinical applications). Also remember that key figure questions are sprinkled throughout the chapter.

We hope that you enjoy *Human Anatomy & Physiology* and that this book makes learning about the body's structures and functions an exciting and rewarding process. Perhaps the best bit of advice we can give you is that memory depends on understanding. Thus, if you strive for understanding instead of rote memorization, your memory will not fail you often.

We would appreciate hearing from you about your experiences with this textbook or suggestions for improvements in future editions.

Elaine N. Marieb

Elaine N. Marieb

Katja Hoehn

Katja Hoehn

Elaine N. Marieb and Katja Hoehn
Anatomy and Physiology
Benjamin Cummings Science
1301 Sansome Street
San Francisco, CA 94111

Acknowledgments

Writing or revising a textbook is a lesson in lonely perseverance. Hence we could hardly express our joy at coming to the end of this Seventh Edition update. This revision, a major one, has consumed most of our day and night hours for over a year. Text has been streamlined, rewritten for currency, or reorganized, and art has been reconceived once again. As usual, it's been difficult to keep up to date in the very broad field of anatomy and physiology, and then a wrenching ordeal to decide how much of it to use in the new edition. We want our students to be informed intellectually, but how rich a diet that requires is a persistent question.

But, enough complaints or we'll be forced to give equal time to all of those who toiled with us, and they are numerous. The sponsoring editor for this edition, Serina Beauparlant, has supported every aspect of this revision—from money to doughnuts (at meetings). Like Daryl Fox, publisher for this and the past three editions who has gone on to grander venues (sob), Serina is insightful and dedicated to producing the best educational product possible (both text and multimedia). New to the position of project editor for this text is Karoliina Tuovinen. Learning the intricacies of team coordination, wrestling with schedule deadlines, picking up manuscript loose ends, and trying to make a surly old author and an anxious new author work more quickly have made her life this past year a nightmare, we are sure. But she survived and has learned an incredible amount in the process. Claire Alexander, development manager, provided a steadying anchor for Karoliina when the going got rough. Once again, Lauren Harp, the executive marketing manager, has efficiently kept us abreast of the pulse of the marketplace—keeping in touch with professors and students and providing feedback on what they do or don't like about the text and media products. Stacey Weinberger's expertise as manufacturing buyer has served us well. A resounding dollop of gratitude also goes to those on the editorial team with whom we have had little or no personal contact but who have provided valuable services for the revision: Ryan Shaw, associate media editor, Jessica Brunner, assistant editor and Alex Streczyn, editorial assistant for the Seventh Edition supplements.

We also want to thank numerous expert reviewers who shared their knowledge with us as the manuscript was being updated: Bonnie Blazer-Yost, Indiana University—Purdue University at Indianapolis; Sunny K. Boyd, University of Notre Dame; Eldon Braun, University of Arizona; Norma J. Criley, Illinois Wesleyan University; Michael Ferrari, University of Missouri—Kansas City; Kathleen French, University of California—San Diego; Bruce Johnson, Cornell University; John J. Lepri, University of North Carolina—Greensboro; Teresa Marcus, Chattanooga State Technical Community College; Kerry McDonald, University of Missouri—Columbia; Anthony Paganini, Michigan State University; John Rash, Colorado State University; Lauri J. Sammartano, Roane State Community College; Brian Tsukimura, Cal State Fresno; Larry Weiskirch, Onondaga Community College; and Elizabeth Weiss, University of Texas—Austin. Their input resulted in the continued excellence and accuracy of this text's presentations.

We are also grateful for our reviewers and colleagues from the United States and abroad who, over the past three years, have made helpful suggestions and offered constructive criticism to improve this work regarding readability and level, areas particularly important to student success. A complete list of reviewers follows these acknowledgments.

Additionally, we want to acknowledge Katja's colleagues at Mount Royal College (Janice Meeking, Izak Paul, Michael Pollock, Nishan Sharma, and Trevor Day) for stimulating discussions of the text, which they embraced as their own cause, providing feedback on changes and options.

Once again Wendy Earl Productions handled the production of this text. As always, Wendy Earl, the managing editor, selects highly qualified people to work with her. Michele Mangelli, production supervisor extraordinaire, guided us through the schedule with an expert hand. Her efficient management style and excellent problem-solving skills headed off many a storm, which the whole team appreciated. Laura Southworth, the art development editor, was charged with increasing the consistency of the art program to encourage automatic learning and helping to construct new pieces. All we had to say to Laura is "I don't like this piece of art; can't we do something to reconfigure it for more interest . . . more clarity . . . ?" Two days later there would be a mailer with a great new conceptualization of that figure. Laura is a dynamic, can-do woman! Recognition for a job well done is due Gillian Speeth, photo researcher, and David Novak, art coordinator. The talented artists at Imagineering generated the new art pieces conceived for this edition, and made any changes requested on existing art. It is their art that puts the zing in the book. The new modern text design is the handiwork of the talented Frances Baca, and the exciting cover image is a stunning photo of Serena Williams at the 2005 Australian Open. We feel that Serena's strength and power embody the spirit of our book. As always, a monumental thank-you goes to Anita Wagner, ultra-conscientious copyeditor. She edits with a light hand, all the while double-checking all statistics, drug names, and other technical data. We are also fortunate to have Martha Ghent returning as proofreader and Karen Hollister as indexer for this edition. As has been the practice with this text, Techbooks/GTS assembled the final pages with their customary expertise.

Once again, Harvey Howell, husband of Dr. Marieb for six years now, served as a sounding board for some of her ideas, manned the copy machine, and ran the manuscript to the UPS box daily with nary a complaint during the unbelievably busy days of the past year plus. Thanks also to Katja's husband, Dr. Lawrence W. Haynes, who as a fellow physiologist has provided invaluable assistance to her during the course of the revision. She also thanks her children, Eric and Stefan Haynes, who are an inspiration and a joy.

Well, our tenure on this edition is over, but there will be another edition three years hence. We would really appreciate hearing from you concerning your opinion—suggestions and constructive criticisms—of this text. It is this type of feedback that provides the basis of each revision, and underwrites its improvement.

Elaine N. Marieb

Elaine N. Marieb

Katja Hoehn

Katja Hoehn

Elaine N. Marieb and Katja Hoehn
Anatomy and Physiology
Benjamin Cummings Science
1301 Sansome Street
San Francisco, CA 94111

Reviewers for Human Anatomy & Physiology, Seventh Edition

Janet Frensilli
Sherwood High School, Sandy Spring, MD

Angel Hicks
Suwannee School District, Live Oak, FL

Karl Hoffman
Forest Hills High School, Forest Hills, NY

John Kernion
North Allegheny Senior High School, Wexford, PA

Patricia Ahanotu
Georgia Perimeter College, Clarkston Campus

Bonnie Blazer-Yost
Indiana University—Purdue University at Indianapolis

Sunny K. Boyd
University of Notre Dame

Edward Bradel
University of Cincinnati, Raymond Walters College

Eldon Braun
University of Arizona

Jackie Carnegie
University of Ottawa

Roger Choate
Oklahoma City Community College

Adrienne Coons
Camden County College

Norma J. Criley
Illinois Wesleyan University

Catherine Dallemagne
Queensland University of Technology

Leslie Day
Northeastern University

Ardath Egle
University of Texas—Pan American

Michael Ferrari
University of Missouri—Kansas City

Bruce Fisher
Roane State Community College

Kathleen French
University of California—San Diego

Maurice Heller
El Paso Community College

Mark J. Hubley
Prince George's Community College

Bruce Johnson
Cornell University

Sally Johnston
Community College of Southern Nevada

John J. Lepri
University of North Carolina—Greensboro

Barbara Mania-Farnell
Purdue University—Calumet

Teresa Marcus
Chattanooga State Technical Community College

Kerry McDonald
University of Missouri—Columbia

Jenny McFarland
Edmonds Community College

Mark Meade
Jacksonville State University

Maria Oehler
Florida Community College—Jacksonville

Anthony Paganini
Michigan State Univeristy

Mark Paternostro
Penn College of Technology

Lisa Plantefaber
Westfield State College

John Rash
Colorado State University

Lauri J. Sammartano
Roane State Community College

Andrea Scott
East Mississippi Community College

Michael Shipley
Midwestern State University

Harriet Tresham
Kennesaw State University

Brian Tsukimura
Cal State Fresno

Cinnamon VanPutte
Southwestern Illinois College

Amy Way
Lock Haven University

Larry Weiskirch
Onondaga Community College

Elizabeth Weiss
University of Texas—Austin

Willard Woodward
Parkland College

Nina Zanetti
Siena College

Contents

UNIT ONE   Organization of the Body

1 The Human Body: An Orientation   1

An Overview of Anatomy and Physiology   2
Topics of Anatomy • Topics of Physiology • Complementarity of Structure and Function

Levels of Structural Organization   3

Maintaining Life   4
Necessary Life Functions • Survival Needs

Homeostasis   8
Homeostatic Control Mechanisms • Homeostatic Imbalance

The Language of Anatomy   12
Anatomical Position and Directional Terms • Regional Terms • Anatomical Variability • Body Planes and Sections • Body Cavities and Membranes

A CLOSER LOOK   Medical Imaging: Illuminating the Body   20

2 Chemistry Comes Alive   24

PART 1: Basic Chemistry   25

Definition of Concepts: Matter and Energy   25
Matter • Energy

Composition of Matter: Atoms and Elements   27
Atomic Structure • Identifying Elements • Radioisotopes

How Matter Is Combined: Molecules and Mixtures   30
Molecules and Compounds • Mixtures • Distinguishing Mixtures from Compounds

Chemical Bonds   31
The Role of Electrons in Chemical Bonding • Types of Chemical Bonds

Chemical Reactions   36
Chemical Equations • Patterns of Chemical Reactions • Energy Flow in Chemical Reactions • Reversibility of Chemical Reactions • Factors Influencing the Rate of Chemical Reactions

PART 2: Biochemistry   40

Inorganic Compounds   40
Water • Salts • Acids and Bases

Organic Compounds   43
Carbohydrates • Lipids • Proteins • Nucleic Acids (DNA and RNA) • Adenosine Triphosphate (ATP)

A CLOSER LOOK   DNA Fingerprinting: Cracking Our Genetic "Barcode"   58

3 Cells: The Living Units   64

Overview of the Cellular Basis of Life   65

The Plasma Membrane: Structure   66
The Fluid Mosaic Model • Specializations of the Plasma Membrane

The Plasma Membrane: Functions   70
Membrane Transport • Generating and Maintaining a Resting Membrane Potential • Cell-Environment Interactions

The Cytoplasm   84
Cytoplasmic Organelles • Cellular Extensions

The Nucleus   95
The Nuclear Envelope • Nucleoli • Chromatin

Cell Growth and Reproduction   97
The Cell Life Cycle • Protein Synthesis • Other Roles of DNA • Cytosolic Protein Degradation

Extracellular Materials   111

Developmental Aspects of Cells   111

4 Tissue: The Living Fabric   117

Preparing Human Tissue for Microscopy   118

Epithelial Tissue   118
Special Characteristics of Epithelium • Classification of Epithelia • Glandular Epithelia

Connective Tissue   126
Common Characteristics of Connective Tissue • Structural Elements of Connective Tissue • Types of Connective Tissue

Nervous Tissue   139

Muscle Tissue   139

Covering and Lining Membranes   141
Cutaneous Membrane • Mucous Membranes • Serous Membranes

Tissue Repair   143
Steps of Tissue Repair • Regenerative Capacity of Different Tissues

Developmental Aspects of Tissues   145

A CLOSER LOOK   Cancer—The Intimate Enemy   146

UNIT TWO   Covering, Support, and Movement of the Body

5 The Integumentary System   151

The Skin   152
Epidermis • Dermis • Skin Color

Appendages of the Skin   158
Sweat (Sudoriferous) Glands • Sebaceous (Oil) Glands • Hairs and Hair Follicles • Nails

Functions of the Integumentary System   163
Protection • Body Temperature Regulation • Cutaneous Sensation • Metabolic Functions • Blood Reservoir • Excretion

Homeostatic Imbalances of Skin   165
Skin Cancer • Burns

Developmental Aspects of the Integumentary System   170

A CLOSER LOOK   Wrinkle Wrinkle Go Away—Or I'll Shoot You (with Botox)   156

MAKING CONNECTIONS   168

6 Bones and Skeletal Tissues   175

Skeletal Cartilages   176
Basic Structure, Types, and Locations • Growth of Cartilage

Classification of Bones   176

Functions of Bones   178

Bone Structure   179
Gross Anatomy • Microscopic Anatomy of Bone • Chemical Composition of Bone

Bone Development   184
Formation of the Bony Skeleton • Postnatal Bone Growth

Bone Homeostasis: Remodeling and Repair   187
Bone Remodeling • Bone Repair

Homeostatic Imbalances of Bone   193
Osteomalacia and Rickets • Osteoporosis • Paget's Disease

Developmental Aspects of Bones: Timing of Events   198

A CLOSER LOOK   Them Bones, Them Bones Goin' to Walk Around—Clinical Advances in Bone Repair   194

MAKING CONNECTIONS   196

7 The Skeleton   202

PART 1: The Axial Skeleton   203

The Skull   203
Overview of Skull Geography • Cranium • Facial Bones • Special Characteristics of the Orbits and Nasal Cavity • Paranasal Sinuses • The Hyoid Bone

The Vertebral Column   218
General Characteristics • General Structure of Vertebrae • Regional Vertebral Characteristics

The Thoracic Cage   226
Sternum • Ribs

PART 2: The Appendicular Skeleton   227

The Pectoral (Shoulder) Girdle   227
Clavicles • Scapulae

The Upper Limb   231
Arm • Forearm • Hand

The Pelvic (Hip) Girdle   237
Ilium • Ischium • Pubis • Pelvic Structure and Childbearing

The Lower Limb   239
Thigh • Leg • Foot

Developmental Aspects of the Skeleton   246

8 Joints   252

Classification of Joints   253

Fibrous Joints   253
Sutures • Syndesmoses • Gomphoses

Cartilaginous Joints   255
Synchondroses • Symphyses

Synovial Joints   255
General Structure • Bursae and Tendon Sheaths • Factors Influencing the Stability of Synovial Joints • Movements Allowed by Synovial Joints • Types of Synovial Joints • Selected Synovial Joints

Chapter 8, continued

Homeostatic Imbalances of Joints   272
Common Joint Injuries • Inflammatory and Degenerative
Conditions

Developmental Aspects of Joints   276

A CLOSER LOOK   Joints: From Knights in Shining Armor
to Bionic Humans   275

9 Muscles and Muscle Tissue   279

Overview of Muscle Tissues   280
Types of Muscle Tissue • Functional Characteristics of Muscle
Tissue • Muscle Functions

Skeletal Muscle   281
Gross Anatomy of a Skeletal Muscle • Microscopic Anatomy
of a Skeletal Muscle Fiber • Sliding Filament Model of
Contraction • Physiology of a Skeletal Muscle Fiber
• Contraction of a Skeletal Muscle • Muscle Metabolism
• Force of Muscle Contraction • Velocity and Duration of
Contraction • Effect of Exercise on Muscles

Smooth Muscle   309
Microscopic Structure of Smooth Muscle Fibers • Contraction
of Smooth Muscle • Types of Smooth Muscle

Developmental Aspects of Muscles   316

A CLOSER LOOK   Athletes Looking Good and Doing
Better with Anabolic Steroids?   308

MAKING CONNECTIONS   318

10 The Muscular System   324

Interactions of Skeletal Muscles in the Body   325
Naming Skeletal Muscles   325
Muscle Mechanics: Importance of Fascicle
Arrangement and Leverage   326
Arrangement of Fascicles • Lever Systems: Bone-Muscle
Relationships

Major Skeletal Muscles of the Body   330
Table 10.1 Muscles of the Head, Part I: Facial
Expression   335
Table 10.2 Muscles of the Head, Part II: Mastication
and Tongue Movement   338
Table 10.3 Muscles of the Anterior Neck and Throat:
Swallowing   340
Table 10.4 Muscles of the Neck and Vertebral Column:
Head and Trunk Movements   342
Table 10.5 Muscles of the Thorax: Breathing   346
Table 10.6 Muscles of the Abdominal Wall:
Trunk Movements and Compression of
Abdominal Viscera   348

Table 10.7 Muscles of the Pelvic Floor and Perineum:
Support of Abdominopelvic Organs   350
Table 10.8 Superficial Muscles of the Anterior and
Posterior Thorax: Movements of the Scapula   352
Table 10.9 Muscles Crossing the Shoulder Joint:
Movements of the Arm   354
Table 10.10 Muscles Crossing the Elbow Joint: Flexion
and Extension of the Forearm   357
Table 10.11 Muscles of the Forearm: Movements of the
Wrist, Hand, and Fingers   358
Table 10.12 Summary of the Actions of Muscles Acting
on the Arm, Forearm, and Hand   362
Table 10.13 Intrinsic Muscles of the Hand: Fine
Movements of the Fingers   364
Table 10.14 Muscles Crossing the Hip and Knee Joints:
Movements of the Thigh and Leg   367
Table 10.15 Muscles of the Leg: Movements of the
Ankle and Toes   373
Table 10.16 Summary of Actions of Muscles Acting on
the Thigh, Leg, and Foot   379
Table 10.17 Intrinsic Muscles of the Foot: Toe
Movement and Arch Support   381

UNIT THREE   **Regulation and Integration
of the Body**

11 Fundamentals of the Nervous System
and Nervous Tissue   387

Organization of the Nervous System   388
Histology of Nervous Tissue   389
Neuroglia • Neurons

Neurophysiology   397
Basic Principles of Electricity • The Resting Membrane
Potential • Membrane Potentials That Act as Signals • The
Synapse • Postsynaptic Potentials and Synaptic Integration
• Neurotransmitters and Their Receptors

Basic Concepts of Neural Integration   421
Organization of Neurons: Neuronal Pools • Types of Circuits
• Patterns of Neural Processing

Developmental Aspects of Neurons   423

A CLOSER LOOK   Pleasure Me, Pleasure Me!   424

12 The Central Nervous System   430

The Brain   431
Embryonic Development • Regions and Organization
• Ventricles • Cerebral Hemispheres • Diencephalon

• Brain Stem • Cerebellum • Functional Brain Systems

Higher Mental Functions   456
Brain Wave Patterns and the EEG • Consciousness • Sleep and Sleep-Wake Cycles • Language • Memory

Protection of the Brain   463
Meninges • Cerebrospinal Fluid • Blood-Brain Barrier • Homeostatic Imbalances of the Brain

The Spinal Cord   470
Embryonic Development • Gross Anatomy and Protection • Cross-Sectional Anatomy • Spinal Cord Trauma and Disorders

Diagnostic Procedures for Assessing CNS Dysfunction   481

Developmental Aspects of the Central Nervous System   481

A CLOSER LOOK   How Now Mad Cow   482

13   The Peripheral Nervous System and Reflex Activity   490

PART 1: Sensory Receptors and Sensation   491
Sensory Receptors   491
Classification by Stimulus Type • Classification by Location • Classification by Structural Complexity

Overview: From Sensation to Perception   494
General Organization of the Somatosensory System

PART 2: Transmission Lines: Nerves and Their Structure and Repair   498
Nerves and Associated Ganglia   498
Structure and Classification • Regeneration of Nerve Fibers

Cranial Nerves   500

Spinal Nerves   508
General Features • Innervation of Specific Body Regions

PART 3: Motor Endings and Motor Activity   519
Peripheral Motor Endings   519
Innervation of Skeletal Muscle • Innervation of Visceral Muscle and Glands

Overview of Motor Integration: From Intention to Effect   519
Levels of Motor Control

PART 4: Reflex Activity   521
The Reflex Arc   521
Components of a Reflex Arc

Spinal Reflexes   522
Stretch and Golgi Tendon Reflexes • The Flexor and Crossed-Extensor Reflexes • Superficial Reflexes

Developmental Aspects of the Peripheral Nervous System   527

A CLOSER LOOK   Pain: Sound the Alarm, But Pain Me Not!   496

14   The Autonomic Nervous System   532

Introduction   533
Comparison of the Somatic and Autonomic Nervous Systems • ANS Divisions

ANS Anatomy   535
Parasympathetic (Craniosacral) Division • Sympathetic (Thoracolumbar) Division • Visceral Reflexes

ANS Physiology   543
Neurotransmitters and Receptors • The Effects of Drugs • Interactions of the Autonomic Divisions • Control of Autonomic Functioning

Homeostatic Imbalances of the ANS   550

Developmental Aspects of the ANS   551

MAKING CONNECTIONS   548

15   The Special Senses   555

The Eye and Vision   556
Accessory Structures of the Eye • Structure of the Eyeball • Physiology of Vision

The Chemical Senses: Taste and Smell   578
The Olfactory Epithelium and the Sense of Smell • Taste Buds and the Sense of Taste • Homeostatic Imbalances of the Chemical Senses

The Ear: Hearing and Balance   583
Structure of the Ear • Physiology of Hearing • Homeostatic Imbalances of Hearing • Mechanisms of Equilibrium and Orientation

Developmental Aspects of the Special Senses   598
Taste and Smell • Vision • Hearing and Balance

16   The Endocrine System   604

The Endocrine System: An Overview   605

Hormones   606
The Chemistry of Hormones • Mechanisms of Hormone Action • Target Cell Specificity • Half-Life, Onset, and Duration of Hormone Activity • Interaction of Hormones at Target Cells • Control of Hormone Release

Major Endocrine Organs   612
The Pituitary Gland (Hypophysis) • The Thyroid Gland • The Parathyroid Glands • The Adrenal (Suprarenal) Glands • The Pancreas • The Gonads • The Pineal Gland • The Thymus

Chapter 16, continued

Other Hormone-Producing Structures   636

Developmental Aspects of the Endocrine System   639

A CLOSER LOOK   Sweet Revenge: Can Biotechnology
                 Tame the DM Monster?   636

MAKING CONNECTIONS   640

UNIT FOUR   Maintenance of the Body

17 Blood   646

Overview: Blood Composition and Functions   647
Components • Physical Characteristics and Volume
• Functions

Blood Plasma   648

Formed Elements   649
Erythrocytes • Leukocytes • Platelets

Hemostasis   663
Vascular Spasms • Platelet Plug Formation • Coagulation
• Clot Retraction and Repair • Fibrinolysis • Factors Limiting
Clot Growth or Formation • Disorders of Hemostasis

Transfusion and Blood Replacement   668
Transfusion of Red Blood Cells • Restoring Blood Volume

Diagnostic Blood Tests   671

Developmental Aspects of Blood   672

A CLOSER LOOK   Concocting Blood: Artificial Blood
                 Substitutes   672

18 The Cardiovascular System: The Heart   677

Heart Anatomy   678
Size, Location, and Orientation • Coverings of the Heart
• Layers of the Heart Wall • Chambers and Associated Great
Vessels • Pathway of Blood Through the Heart • Coronary
Circulation • Heart Valves

Properties of Cardiac Muscle Fibers   689
Microscopic Anatomy • Mechanism and Events of
Contraction • Energy Requirements

Heart Physiology   692
Electrical Events • Heart Sounds • Mechanical Events: The
Cardiac Cycle • Cardiac Output

Developmental Aspects of the Heart   705

A CLOSER LOOK   From "Oh, What a Beautiful Morning"
                 to Heart Boosters, Retreads, and
                 Replacements   706

19 The Cardiovascular System: Blood Vessels   713

PART 1: Overview of Blood Vessel
         Structure and Function   714

Structure of Blood Vessel Walls   714

Arterial System   716
Elastic (Conducting) Arteries • Muscular (Distributing)
Arteries • Arterioles

Capillaries   720
Types of Capillaries • Capillary Beds

Venous System   722
Venules • Veins

Vascular Anastomoses   723

PART 2: Physiology of Circulation   723

Introduction to Blood Flow, Blood Pressure, and
Resistance   723
Definition of Terms • Relationship Between Flow, Pressure,
and Resistance

Systemic Blood Pressure   724
Arterial Blood Pressure • Capillary Blood Pressure • Venous
Blood Pressure

Maintaining Blood Pressure   726
Short-Term Mechanisms: Neural Controls • Short-Term
Mechanisms: Hormonal Controls • Long-Term Mechanisms:
Renal Regulation • Monitoring Circulatory Efficiency
• Alterations in Blood Pressure

Blood Flow Through Body Tissues: Tissue
Perfusion   733
Velocity of Blood Flow • Autoregulation: Local Regulation of
Blood Flow • Blood Flow in Special Areas • Blood Flow
Through Capillaries and Capillary Dynamics • Circulatory
Shock

PART 3: Circulatory Pathways: Blood Vessels
         of the Body   742

The Two Main Circulations of the Body   742

Systemic Arteries and Veins: Differences in Pathways
and Courses   742

Principal Vessels of the Systemic Circulation   742

Developmental Aspects of the Blood Vessels   743

Table 19.3 Pulmonary and Systemic Circulations   744

Table 19.4 The Aorta and Major Arteries of the
Systemic Circulation   746

Table 19.5 Arteries of the Head and Neck   748

Table 19.6 Arteries of the Upper
Limbs and Thorax   750

Table 19.7 Arteries of the Abdomen   752

Table 19.8 Arteries of the Pelvis and
Lower Limbs   756

Table 19.9 The Venae Cavae and the
Major Veins of the Systemic Circulation   758

Table 19.10 Veins of the Head and Neck   760

Table 19.11 Veins of the Upper Limbs and Thorax   762

Table 19.12 Veins of the Abdomen   764

Table 19.13 Veins of the Pelvis
and Lower Limbs   766

A CLOSER LOOK   Atherosclerosis? Get Out the
Cardiovascular Drãno   718

MAKING CONNECTIONS   768

20 The Lymphatic System   773

Lymphatic Vessels   774
Distribution and Structure of Lymphatic Vessels • Lymph
Transport

Lymphoid Cells and Tissues   777
Lymphoid Cells • Lymphoid Tissue

Lymph Nodes   778
Structure of a Lymph Node • Circulation in the Lymph Nodes

Other Lymphoid Organs   779
Spleen • Thymus • Tonsils • Aggregates of Lymphoid
Follicles

Developmental Aspects of the Lymphatic System   783

MAKING CONNECTIONS   784

21 The Immune System: Innate and Adaptive Body Defenses   788

PART 1: Innate Defenses   789
Surface Barriers: Skin and Mucosae   789

Internal Defenses: Cells and Chemicals   790
Phagocytes • Natural Killer Cells • Inflammation: Tissue
Response to Injury • Antimicrobial Proteins • Fever

PART 2: Adaptive Defenses   798
Antigens   799
Complete Antigens and Haptens • Antigenic Determinants
• Self-Antigens: MHC Proteins

Cells of the Adaptive Immune System:
An Overview   800
Lymphocytes • Antigen-Presenting Cells

Humoral Immune Response   804
Clonal Selection and Differentiation of B Cells
• Immunological Memory • Active and Passive Humoral
Immunity • Antibodies

Cell-Mediated Immune Response   810
Clonal Selection and Differentiation of T Cells • Specific T
Cell Roles • Organ Transplants and Prevention of Rejection

Homeostatic Imbalances of Immunity   820
Immunodeficiencies • Autoimmune Diseases
• Hypersensitivities

Developmental Aspects of the
Immune System   825

A CLOSER LOOK   Too Clean for Our Own Good?   824

22 The Respiratory System   830

Functional Anatomy of the Respiratory System   831
The Nose and Paranasal Sinuses • The Pharynx • The Larynx
The Trachea • The Bronchi and Subdivisions: The Bronchial
Tree • The Lungs and Pleurae

Mechanics of Breathing   846
Pressure Relationships in the Thoracic Cavity • Pulmonary
Ventilation: Inspiration and Expiration • Physical Factors
Influencing Pulmonary Ventilation • Respiratory Volumes and
Pulmonary Function Tests • Nonrespiratory Air Movements

Gas Exchanges Between the Blood,
Lungs, and Tissues   854
Basic Properties of Gases • Composition of Alveolar Gas
• External Respiration: Pulmonary Gas Exchange • Internal
Respiration: Capillary Gas Exchange in the Body Tissues

Transport of Respiratory Gases by Blood   858
Oxygen Transport • Carbon Dioxide Transport

Control of Respiration   863
Neural Mechanisms and Generation of Breathing Rhythm
• Factors Influencing Breathing Rate and Depth

Respiratory Adjustments   869
Adjustments During Exercise • Adjustments at High Altitude

Homeostatic Imbalances of the
Respiratory System   870
Chronic Obstructive Pulmonary Disease • Asthma
• Tuberculosis • Lung Cancer

Developmental Aspects of the Respiratory System   873

A CLOSER LOOK   Dangerous Raptures of the Deep   868

MAKING CONNECTIONS   876

23 The Digestive System   882

PART 1: Overview of the Digestive System   883
Digestive Processes   884

Basic Functional Concepts   885

Digestive System Organs: Relationship and
Structural Plan   886
Relationship of the Digestive Organs to the Peritoneum •
Blood Supply: The Splanchnic Circulation • Histology of the
Alimentary Canal • Enteric Nervous System of the Alimentary
Canal

Chapter 23, continued

PART 2: Functional Anatomy of the Digestive System   889

The Mouth, Pharynx, and Esophagus   889
The Mouth and Associated Organs • The Pharynx • The Esophagus • Digestive Processes Occurring in the Mouth, Pharynx, and Esophagus

The Stomach   899
Gross Anatomy • Microscopic Anatomy • Digestive Processes Occurring in the Stomach

The Small Intestine and Associated Structures   908
The Small Intestine • The Liver and Gallbladder • The Pancreas • Digestive Processes Occurring in the Small Intestine

The Large Intestine   922
Gross Anatomy • Microscopic Anatomy • Bacterial Flora • Digestive Processes Occurring in the Large Intestine

PART 3: Physiology of Chemical Digestion and Absorption   927

Chemical Digestion   927
Mechanism of Chemical Digestion: Enzymatic Hydrolysis • Chemical Digestion of Specific Food Groups

Absorption   931
Absorption of Specific Nutrients • Malabsorption of Nutrients

Developmental Aspects of the Digestive System   933

MAKING CONNECTIONS   934

24 Nutrition, Metabolism, and Body Temperature Regulation   942

Nutrition   943
Carbohydrates • Lipids • Proteins • Vitamins • Minerals

Metabolism   956
Overview • Carbohydrate Metabolism • Lipid Metabolism • Protein Metabolism • Catabolic-Anabolic Steady State of the Body • Absorptive and Postabsorptive States • The Metabolic Role of the Liver

Energy Balance   981
Regulation of Food Intake • Metabolic Rate and Heat Production • Regulation of Body Temperature

Developmental Aspects of Nutrition and Metabolism   989

A CLOSER LOOK   Obesity: Magical Solution Wanted   990

25 The Urinary System   997

Kidney Anatomy   998
Location and External Anatomy • Internal Anatomy • Blood and Nerve Supply • Nephrons

Kidney Physiology: Mechanisms of Urine Formation   1007
Step 1: Glomerular Filtration • Step 2: Tubular Reabsorption • Step 3: Tubular Secretion • Regulation of Urine Concentration and Volume • Renal Clearance

Urine   1021
Physical Characteristics • Chemical Composition

Ureters   1023

Urinary Bladder   1024

Urethra   1026

Micturition   1027

Developmental Aspects of the Urinary System   1027

A CLOSER LOOK   Chronic Renal Disease: A National Health Crisis in the Making   1022

26 Fluid, Electrolyte, and Acid-Base Balance   1035

Body Fluids   1036
Body Water Content • Fluid Compartments • Composition of Body Fluids • Fluid Movement Among Compartments

Water Balance and ECF Osmolality   1039
Regulation of Water Intake • Regulation of Water Output • Influence of ADH • Disorders of Water Balance

Electrolyte Balance   1043
The Central Role of Sodium in Fluid and Electrolyte Balance • Regulation of Sodium Balance • Regulation of Potassium Balance • Regulation of Calcium and Phosphate Balance • Regulation of Anions

Acid-Base Balance   1049
Chemical Buffer Systems • Respiratory Regulation of H^+ • Renal Mechanisms of Acid-Base Balance • Abnormalities of Acid-Base Balance

Developmental Aspects of Fluid, Electrolyte, and Acid-Base Balance   1060

A CLOSER LOOK   Sleuthing: Using Blood Values to Determine the Cause of Acidosis or Alkalosis   1057

MAKING CONNECTIONS   1058

UNIT FIVE   **Continuity**

27 The Reproductive System   1065

Anatomy of the Male Reproductive System   1066
The Scrotum • The Testes • The Penis • The Male Duct System • Accessory Glands • Semen

Physiology of the Male Reproductive System   1072
Male Sexual Response • Spermatogenesis • Hormonal
Regulation of Male Reproductive Function

Anatomy of the Female Reproductive System   1082
The Ovaries • The Female Duct System • The External
Genitalia • The Mammary Glands

Physiology of the Female Reproductive System   1091
Oogenesis • The Ovarian Cycle • Hormonal Regulation of
the Ovarian Cycle • The Uterine (Menstrual) Cycle
• Extrauterine Effects of Estrogens and Progesterone • Female
Sexual Response

Sexually Transmitted Diseases   1100
Gonorrhea • Syphilis • Chlamydia • Trichomoniasis
• Genital Warts • Genital Herpes

Developmental Aspects of the Reproductive System:
Chronology of Sexual Development   1101
Embryological and Fetal Events • Puberty • Menopause

A CLOSER LOOK   Erectile Dysfunction and
                Passion Pills   1074

MAKING CONNECTIONS   1106

28 Pregnancy and Human Development   1113

From Egg to Zygote   1114
Accomplishing Fertilization

Events of Embryonic Development: Zygote to
Blastocyst Implantation   1117
Cleavage and Blastocyst Formation • Implantation
• Placentation

Events of Embryonic Development:
Gastrula to Fetus   1122
Formation and Roles of the Extraembryonic Membranes
• Gastrulation: Germ Layer Formation • Organogenesis:
Differentiation of the Germ Layers

Events of Fetal Development   1133

Effects of Pregnancy on the Mother   1133
Anatomical Changes • Metabolic Changes • Physiological
Changes

Parturition (Birth)   1135
Initiation of Labor • Stages of Labor

Adjustments of the Infant to Extrauterine Life   1137

Taking the First Breath and Transition • Occlusion of Special
Fetal Blood Vessels and Vascular Shunts

Lactation   1138

Assisted Reproductive Technology and Reproductive
Cloning   1139

A CLOSER LOOK   Contraception: To Be or Not to Be   1128

29 Heredity   1145

The Vocabulary of Genetics   1146
Gene Pairs (Alleles) • Genotype and Phenotype

Sexual Sources of Genetic Variation   1147
Chromosome Segregation and Independent Assortment
• Crossover of Homologues and Gene Recombination
• Random Fertilization

Types of Inheritance   1149
Dominant-Recessive Inheritance • Incomplete Dominance
• Multiple-Allele Inheritance • Sex-Linked Inheritance
• Polygene Inheritance

Environmental Factors in Gene Expression   1152

Nontraditional Inheritance   1153
Beyond DNA: Regulation of Gene Expression • Extranuclear
(Mitochondrial) Inheritance

Genetic Screening, Counseling, and Therapy   1154
Carrier Recognition • Fetal Testing • Human Gene Therapy

Appendices
A   The Metric System   1161
B   Functional Groups in Organic Molecules   1163
C   The Amino Acids   1164
D   Two Important Metabolic Pathways   1165
E   Periodic Table of the Elements   1168
F   Reference Values for Selected Blood and Urine
    Studies   1169
G   Answers to Clinical Connections, Multiple Choice,
    and Matching Questions   1174

Glossary   1177

Photo and Illustration Credits   1197

Index   1201

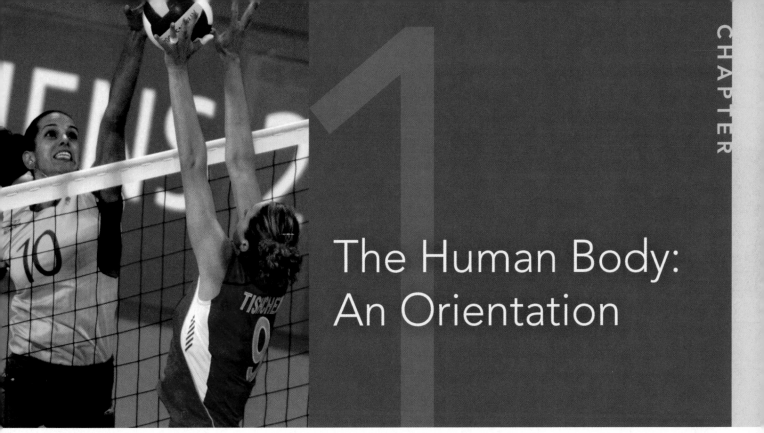

The Human Body: An Orientation

An Overview of Anatomy and Physiology (pp. 2–3)

1. Define anatomy and physiology and describe their subdivisions.

2. Explain the principle of complementarity.

Levels of Structural Organization (pp. 3–4, 6–7)

3. Name the different levels of structural organization that make up the human body, and explain their relationships.

4. List the 11 organ systems of the body, identify their components, and briefly explain the major function(s) of each system.

Maintaining Life (pp. 4–8)

5. List the functional characteristics necessary to maintain life in humans.

6. List the survival needs of the body.

Homeostasis (pp. 8–12)

7. Define homeostasis and explain its significance.

8. Describe how negative and positive feedback maintain body homeostasis.

9. Describe the relationship between homeostatic imbalance and disease.

The Language of Anatomy (pp. 12–19)

10. Describe the anatomical position.

11. Use correct anatomical terms to describe body directions, regions, and body planes or sections.

12. Locate and name the major body cavities and their subdivisions, and list the major organs contained within them.

13. Name the serous membranes and indicate their common function.

14. Name the nine regions or four quadrants of the abdominopelvic cavity and list the organs they contain.

As you make your way through this book, you will be learning about one of the most fascinating subjects possible—your own body. Such a study is not only highly personal, but timely as well. The current information blizzard brings news of some medical advance almost daily. If you are to appreciate emerging discoveries in genetic engineering, to understand new techniques for detecting and treating disease, and to make use of published facts on how to stay healthy, it is important to learn about the workings of your body. For those preparing for a career in the health sciences, the study of anatomy and physiology has added rewards because it provides the foundation needed to support your clinical experiences.

In this chapter we define and contrast anatomy and physiology and discuss how the human body is organized. Then we review needs and functional processes common to all living organisms. Three essential concepts—*the complementarity of structure and function, the hierarchy of structural organization,* and *homeostasis*—will unify and form the bedrock for your study of the human body. The final section of the chapter deals with the language of anatomy—terminology that anatomists use when they describe the body or its parts.

An Overview of Anatomy and Physiology

Two complementary branches of science—anatomy and physiology—provide the concepts that help us to understand the human body. **Anatomy** studies the *structure* of body parts and their relationships to one another. Anatomy has a certain appeal because it is concrete. Body structures can be seen, felt, and examined closely; it is not necessary to imagine what they look like. **Physiology** concerns the *function* of the body, in other words, how the body parts work and carry out their life-sustaining activities. When all is said and done, physiology is explainable only in terms of the underlying anatomy. To simplify the study of the body, most references to body structures and/or physiological values (body temperature, heart rate, and the like) assume that we are talking about a healthy young (22-year-old) male weighing about 155 lb (the *reference man*) or a healthy young female weighing about 125 lb (the *reference woman*).

Topics of Anatomy

Anatomy is a broad field with many subdivisions, each providing enough information to be a course in itself. **Gross,** or **macroscopic, anatomy** is the study of large body structures visible to the naked eye, such as the heart, lungs, and kidneys. Indeed, the term *anatomy* (derived from the Greek words meaning "to cut apart") relates most closely to gross anatomy because in such studies preserved animals or their organs are dissected (cut up) to be examined. Gross anatomy can be approached in different ways. In **regional anatomy,** all the structures (muscles, bones, blood vessels, nerves, etc.) in a particular region of the body, such as the abdomen or leg, are examined at the same time. In **systemic anatomy** (sis-tem'ik),* body structure is studied system by system. For example, when studying the cardiovascular system, you would examine the heart and the blood vessels of the entire body. Another subdivision of gross anatomy is **surface anatomy,** the study of internal structures as they relate to the overlying skin surface. You use surface anatomy when you identify the bulging muscles beneath a bodybuilder's skin, and clinicians use it to locate appropriate blood vessels in which to feel pulses and draw blood.

Microscopic anatomy deals with structures too small to be seen with the naked eye. For most such studies, exceedingly thin slices of body tissues are stained and mounted on slides to be examined under the microscope. Subdivisions of microscopic anatomy include **cytology** (si-tol'o-je), which considers the cells of the body, and **histology** (his-tol'o-je), the study of tissues.

Developmental anatomy traces structural changes that occur in the body throughout the life span. **Embryology** (em"bre-ol'o-je), a subdivision of developmental anatomy, concerns developmental changes that occur before birth.

Some highly specialized branches of anatomy are used primarily for medical diagnosis and scientific research. For example, *pathological anatomy* studies structural changes caused by disease. *Radiographic anatomy* studies internal structures as visualized by X-ray images or specialized scanning procedures. In *molecular biology,* the structure of biological molecules (chemical substances) is investigated. Molecular biology is actually a separate branch of biology, but it falls under the anatomy umbrella when we push anatomical studies to the subcellular level. As you can see, subjects of interest to anatomists range from easily seen structures down to the smallest molecule.

One essential tool for studying anatomy is a mastery of anatomical terminology. Others are observation, manipulation, and, in a living person, *palpation* (feeling organs with your hands) and *auscultation* (listening to organ sounds with a stethoscope). A simple example will illustrate how some of

---

*For the pronunciation guide rules, see the Preface to the Student.

these tools work together in an anatomical study. Let's assume that your topic is freely movable joints of the body. In the laboratory, you will be able to *observe* an animal joint, noting how its parts fit together. You can work the joint (*manipulate* it) to determine its range of motion. Using *anatomical terminology*, you can name its parts and describe how they are related so that other students (and your instructor) will have no trouble understanding you. The list of word roots (on the inside of the book cover) and the glossary will help you with this special vocabulary.

Although most of your observations will be made with the naked eye or with the help of a microscope, medical technology has developed a number of sophisticated tools that can peer into the body without disrupting it. These exciting medical imaging techniques are discussed in *A Closer Look* on pp. 20–21.

Topics of Physiology

Like anatomy, physiology has many subdivisions, most of which consider the operation of specific organ systems. For example, **renal physiology** concerns kidney function and urine production; **neurophysiology** explains the workings of the nervous system; and **cardiovascular physiology** examines the operation of the heart and blood vessels. While anatomy provides us with a static image of the body's architecture, physiology reveals the body's dynamic and animated nature.

Physiology often focuses on events at the cellular or molecular level. This is because the body's abilities depend on those of its individual cells, and cells' abilities ultimately depend on the chemical reactions that go on within them. Physiology also rests on principles of physics, which help to explain electrical currents, blood pressure, and the way muscles use bones to cause body movements, among other things. Basic chemical and physical principles are presented in Chapter 2 and throughout the book as needed to explain physiological topics.

Complementarity of Structure and Function

Although it is possible to study anatomy and physiology individually, they are really inseparable because function always reflects structure. That is, what a structure can do depends on its specific form. This is called the **principle of complementarity of structure and function.** For example, bones can support and protect body organs because they contain hard mineral deposits, and blood flows in one direction through the heart because the heart has valves that prevent backflow. Throughout this book, a description of a structure's anatomy is accompanied by an explanation of its function, and structural characteristics contributing to that function are emphasized.

Levels of Structural Organization

The human body has many levels of structural organization (Figure 1.1). The simplest level of the structural hierarchy is the **chemical level,** which we study in Chapter 2. At this level, *atoms,* tiny building blocks of matter, combine to form *molecules* such as water and proteins. Molecules, in turn, associate in specific ways to form *organelles,* basic components of the microscopic cells. *Cells* are the smallest units of living things. The **cellular level** is examined in Chapter 3. All cells have some common functions, but individual cells vary widely in size and shape, reflecting their unique functions in the body.

The simplest living creatures are composed of single cells, but in complex organisms such as human beings, the hierarchy continues on to the **tissue level.** *Tissues* are groups of similar cells that have a common function. The four basic tissue types in the human body are epithelium, muscle, connective tissue, and nervous tissue. Each tissue type has a characteristic role in the body, which we explore in Chapter 4. Briefly, epithelium covers the body surface and lines its cavities; muscle provides movement; connective tissue supports and protects body organs; and nervous tissue provides a means of rapid internal communication by transmitting electrical impulses.

An *organ* is a discrete structure composed of at least two tissue types (four is more common) that performs a specific function for the body. At the **organ level,** extremely complex functions become possible. Let's take the stomach for an example. Its lining is an epithelium that produces digestive juices; the bulk of its wall is muscle, which churns and mixes stomach contents (food); its connective tissue reinforces the soft muscular walls; and its nerve fibers increase digestive activity by stimulating the muscle to contract more vigorously and the glands to secrete more digestive juices. The liver, the brain, and a blood vessel are very different from the stomach, but they are organs as well. You can think of each organ of the body as a specialized functional center responsible for a necessary activity that no other organ can perform.

The next level of organization is the **organ system.** Organs that work together to accomplish a common purpose make up an *organ system.* For

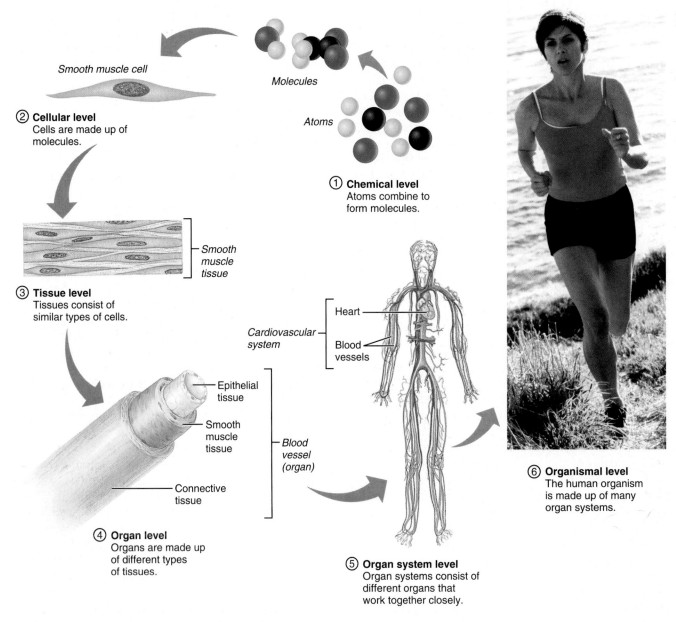

Smooth muscle cell

② **Cellular level**
Cells are made up of molecules.

Molecules

Atoms

① **Chemical level**
Atoms combine to form molecules.

Smooth muscle tissue

③ **Tissue level**
Tissues consist of similar types of cells.

Cardiovascular system

Heart

Blood vessels

Epithelial tissue

Smooth muscle tissue

Blood vessel (organ)

Connective tissue

④ **Organ level**
Organs are made up of different types of tissues.

⑥ **Organismal level**
The human organism is made up of many organ systems.

⑤ **Organ system level**
Organ systems consist of different organs that work together closely.

FIGURE 1.1 **Levels of structural organization.** Components of the cardio-vascular system illustrate the levels of structural organization in a human being.

example, the heart and blood vessels of the cardio-vascular system see to it that blood circulates continuously to carry oxygen and nutrients to all body cells. Besides the cardiovascular system, the other organ systems of the body are the integumentary, skeletal, muscular, nervous, endocrine, lymphatic, respiratory, digestive, urinary, and reproductive systems. Figure 1.3 on pp. 6 and 7 provides a brief overview of the 11 organ systems, which we study in more detail in Units 2–5.

The highest level of organization is the *organism*, the living human being. The **organismal** level represents the sum total of all structural levels working together to promote life.

Maintaining Life

Necessary Life Functions

Now that you know the structural levels composing the human body, the question that naturally follows is: What does this highly organized human body do? Like all complex animals, human beings maintain their boundaries, move, respond to environmental changes, take in and digest nutrients, carry out metabolism, dispose of wastes, reproduce themselves, and grow. We will discuss each of these necessary life functions briefly here and in more detail in later chapters.

It cannot be emphasized too strongly that the multicellular state and parceling out of vital body functions to different organ systems result in interdependence of all body cells. Organ systems do not work in isolation; they work cooperatively to promote the well-being of the entire body. This theme is emphasized throughout the book, and some of the organ systems making major contributions to selected functional processes are identified in Figure 1.2. Also, as you read this section you will want to refer to the more detailed descriptions of the organ systems in Figure 1.3.

Maintaining Boundaries Every living organism must **maintain its boundaries** so that its internal environment (inside) remains distinct from the external environment surrounding it (outside). In single-celled organisms, the external boundary is a limiting membrane that encloses its contents and admits needed substances while restricting entry of potentially damaging or unnecessary substances. Similarly, all the cells of our body are surrounded by a selectively permeable membrane. Additionally, the body as a whole is enclosed and protected by the integumentary system, or skin, which protects our internal organs from drying out (a fatal change), bacteria, and the damaging effects of heat, sunlight, and an unbelievable number of chemicals in the external environment.

Movement **Movement** includes the activities promoted by the muscular system, such as propelling ourselves from one place to another by running or swimming, and manipulating the external environment with our nimble fingers. The skeletal system provides the bony framework that the muscles pull on as they work. Movement also occurs when substances such as blood, foodstuffs, and urine are propelled through internal organs of the cardiovascular, digestive, and urinary systems, respectively. On the cellular level, the muscle cell's ability to move by shortening is more precisely called **contractility.**

Responsiveness **Responsiveness,** or **irritability,** is the ability to sense changes (stimuli) in the environment and then respond to them. For example, if you cut your hand on broken glass, a withdrawal reflex occurs—you involuntarily pull your hand away from the painful stimulus (the broken glass). It is not necessary to think about it; it just happens! Likewise, when carbon dioxide in your blood

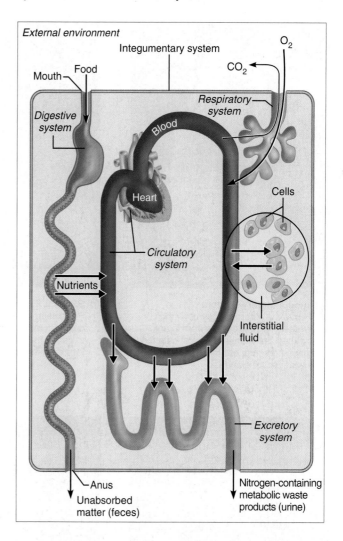

FIGURE 1.2 Examples of interrelationships among body organ systems. The integumentary system protects the body as a whole from the external environment. The digestive and respiratory systems, in contact with the external environment, take in nutrients and oxygen, respectively, which are then distributed by the blood to all body cells. Elimination of metabolic wastes is accomplished by the urinary and respiratory systems.

rises to dangerously high levels, chemical sensors respond by sending messages to brain centers controlling respiration, and your breathing rate speeds up.

Because nerve cells are highly irritable and communicate rapidly with each other via electrical impulses, the nervous system is most involved with responsiveness. However, all body cells are irritable to some extent.

Digestion **Digestion** is the breaking down of ingested foodstuffs to simple molecules that can be absorbed into the blood. The nutrient-rich blood is

1

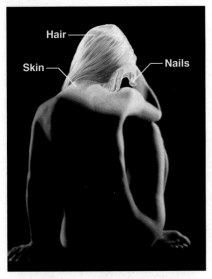

(a) Integumentary System
Forms the external body covering; protects deeper tissues from injury; synthesizes vitamin D; site of cutaneous (pain, pressure, etc.) receptors, and sweat and oil glands.

(b) Skeletal System
Protects and supports body organs; provides a framework the muscles use to cause movement; blood cells are formed within bones; stores minerals.

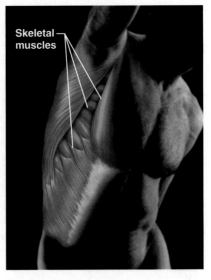

(c) Muscular System
Allows manipulation of the environment, locomotion, and facial expression; maintains posture; produces heat.

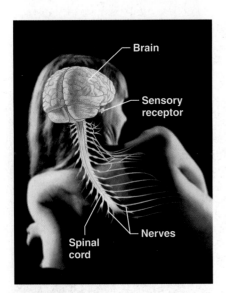

(d) Nervous System
Fast-acting control system of the body; responds to internal and external changes by activating appropriate muscles and glands.

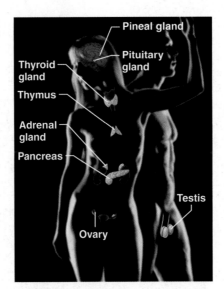

(e) Endocrine System
Glands secrete hormones that regulate processes such as growth, reproduction, and nutrient use (metabolism) by body cells.

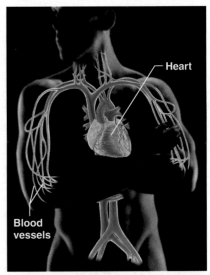

(f) Cardiovascular System
Blood vessels transport blood, which carries oxygen, carbon dioxide, nutrients, wastes, etc.; the heart pumps blood.

FIGURE 1.3 **Summary of the body's organ systems.** The structural components of each system are illustrated, and its major functions are listed below.

then distributed to all body cells by the cardiovascular system. In a simple, one-celled organism such as an amoeba, the cell itself is the "digestion factory," but in the multicellular human body, the digestive system performs this function for the entire body.

Metabolism Metabolism (mĕ-tab'o-lizm; "a state of change") is a broad term that includes all chemical reactions that occur within body cells. It includes breaking down substances into their simpler building blocks (more specifically called *catabolism*), synthesizing more complex cellular structures from

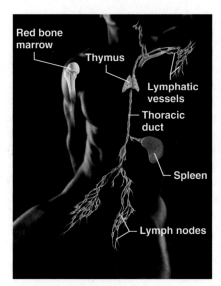

(g) Lymphatic System/Immunity
Picks up fluid leaked from blood vessels and returns it to blood; disposes of debris in the lymphatic stream; houses white blood cells (lymphocytes) involved in immunity. The immune response mounts the attack against foreign substances within the body.

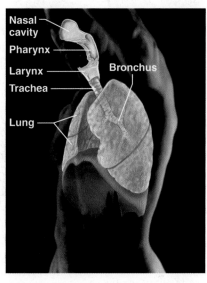

(h) Respiratory System
Keeps blood constantly supplied with oxygen and removes carbon dioxide; the gaseous exchanges occur through the walls of the air sacs of the lungs.

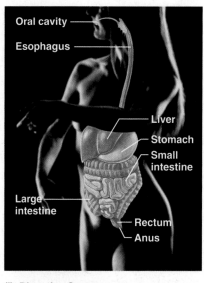

(i) Digestive System
Breaks down food into absorbable units that enter the blood for distribution to body cells; indigestible foodstuffs are eliminated as feces.

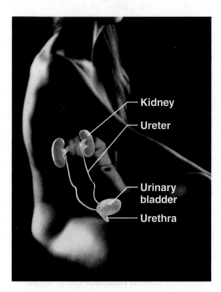

(j) Urinary System
Eliminates nitrogenous wastes from the body; regulates water, electrolyte and acid-base balance of the blood.

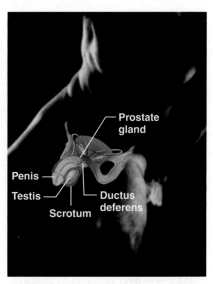

(k) Male Reproductive System
Overall function is production of offspring. Testes produce sperm and male sex hormone; ducts and glands aid in delivery of sperm to the female reproductive tract. Ovaries produce eggs and female sex hormones; remaining structures serve as sites for fertilization and development of the fetus. Mammary glands of female breasts produce milk to nourish the newborn.

(l) Female Reproductive System

simpler substances *(anabolism)*, and using nutrients and oxygen to produce (via *cellular respiration*) ATP, the energy-rich molecules that power cellular activities. Metabolism depends on the digestive and respiratory systems to make nutrients and oxygen available to the blood and on the cardiovascular system to distribute these needed substances throughout the body. Metabolism is regulated largely by hormones secreted by endocrine system glands.

Excretion   **Excretion** is the process of removing *excreta* (ek-skre'tah), or wastes, from the body. If the body is to operate as we expect it to, it must get rid of nonuseful substances produced during digestion and metabolism. Several organ systems participate in excretion. For example, the digestive system rids the body of indigestible food residues in feces, and the urinary system disposes of nitrogen-containing metabolic wastes, such as urea, in urine. Carbon dioxide, a by-product of cellular respiration, is carried in the blood to the lungs, where it leaves the body in exhaled air.

Reproduction   **Reproduction** can occur at the cellular or organismal level. In cellular reproduction the original cell divides, producing two identical daughter cells that may then be used for body growth or repair. Reproduction of the human organism, or making a whole new person, is the major task of the reproductive system. When a sperm unites with an egg, a fertilized egg forms, which then develops into a baby within the mother's body. The reproductive system is directly responsible for producing offspring, but its function is exquisitely regulated by hormones of the endocrine system.

Because males produce sperm and females produce eggs (ova), there is a division of labor in the reproductive process, and the reproductive organs of males and females are different (see Figure 1.3). Additionally, the female's reproductive structures provide the site for fertilization of eggs by sperm, then protect and nurture the developing fetus until birth.

Growth   **Growth** is an increase in size of a body part or the organism. It is usually accomplished by increasing the number of cells. However, individual cells also increase in size when not dividing. For true growth to occur, constructive activities must occur at a faster rate than destructive ones.

Survival Needs

The ultimate goal of all body systems is to maintain life. However, life is extraordinarily fragile and requires that several factors be present. These factors, which we will call *survival needs*, include nutrients (food), oxygen, water, and appropriate temperature and atmospheric pressure.

Nutrients, taken in via the diet, contain the chemical substances used for energy and cell building. Most plant-derived foods are rich in carbohydrates, vitamins, and minerals, whereas most animal foods are richer in proteins and fats. Carbohydrates are the major energy fuel for body cells. Proteins, and to a lesser extent fats, are essential for building cell structures. Fats also provide a reserve of energy-rich fuel. Selected minerals and vitamins are required for the chemical reactions that go on in cells and for oxygen transport in the blood. The mineral calcium helps to make bones hard and is required for blood clotting.

All the nutrients in the world are useless unless **oxygen** is also available. Because the chemical reactions that release energy from foods are *oxidative* reactions that require oxygen, human cells can survive for only a few minutes without oxygen. Approximately 20% of the air we breathe is oxygen. It is made available to the blood and body cells by the cooperative efforts of the respiratory and cardiovascular systems.

Water accounts for 60–80% of body weight and is the single most abundant chemical substance in the body. It provides the watery environment necessary for chemical reactions and the fluid base for body secretions and excretions. Water is obtained chiefly from ingested foods or liquids and is lost from the body by evaporation from the lungs and skin and in body excretions.

If chemical reactions are to continue at life-sustaining rates, **normal body temperature** must be maintained. As body temperature drops below 37°C (98.6°F), metabolic reactions become slower and slower, and finally stop. When body temperature is too high, chemical reactions occur at a frantic pace and body proteins lose their characteristic shape and stop functioning. At either extreme, death occurs. Most body heat is generated by the activity of the muscular system.

Atmospheric pressure is the force that air exerts on the surface of the body. Breathing and gas exchange in the lungs depend on *appropriate* atmospheric pressure. At high altitudes, where atmospheric pressure is lower and the air is thin, gas exchange may be inadequate to support cellular metabolism.

The mere presence of these survival factors is not sufficient to sustain life. They must be present in *appropriate* amounts; excesses and deficits may be equally harmful. For example, oxygen is essential, but excessive amounts are toxic to body cells. Similarly, the food we eat must be of high quality and in proper amounts; otherwise, nutritional disease, obesity, or starvation is likely. Also, while the needs listed above are the most crucial, they do not even begin to encompass all of the body's needs. For example, we can live without gravity if we must, but the quality of life suffers.

Homeostasis

When you think about the fact that your body contains trillions of cells in nearly constant activity, and that remarkably little usually goes wrong with

③ Input:
Information
sent along
afferent
pathway to

Control center

④ Output:
Information sent
along efferent
pathway to

Receptor (sensor)

Effector

② Change
detected
by receptor

⑤ Response of
effector feeds
back to influence
magnitude of
stimulus and
returns variable to
homeostasis

① Stimulus:
Produces
change
in variable

Imbalance

Variable (in homeostasis)

Imbalance

FIGURE 1.4 **The elements of a homeostatic control system.** Communication between the receptor, control center, and effector is essential for normal operation of the control system.

it, you begin to appreciate what a marvelous machine your body is. Walter Cannon, an American physiologist of the early twentieth century, spoke of the "wisdom of the body," and he coined the word **homeostasis** (ho″me-o-sta′sis) to describe its ability to maintain relatively stable internal conditions even though the outside world changes continuously. Although the literal translation of homeostasis is "unchanging," the term does not really mean a static, or unchanging, state. Rather, it indicates a *dynamic* state of equilibrium, or a balance, in which internal conditions vary, but always within relatively narrow limits. In general, the body is in homeostasis when its needs are adequately met and it is functioning smoothly.

Maintaining homeostasis is more complicated than it appears at first glance. Virtually every organ system plays a role in maintaining the constancy of the internal environment. Adequate blood levels of vital nutrients must be continuously present, and heart activity and blood pressure must be constantly monitored and adjusted so that the blood is propelled to all body tissues. Also, wastes must not be allowed to accumulate, and body temperature must be precisely controlled. A wide variety of chemical, thermal, and neural factors act and interact in complex ways—sometimes helping and sometimes hindering the body as it works to maintain its "steady rudder."

Homeostatic Control Mechanisms

Communication within the body is essential for homeostasis. Communication is accomplished chiefly by the nervous and endocrine systems, which use neural electrical impulses or bloodborne hormones, respectively, as information carriers. The details of how these two great regulating systems operate are covered in later chapters, but the basic characteristics of control systems that promote homeostasis are explained here.

Regardless of the factor or event being regulated—the **variable**—all homeostatic control mechanisms have at least three interdependent components (Figure 1.4). The first component, the **receptor,** is some type of sensor that monitors the environment and responds to changes, called *stimuli,* by sending information (input) to the second component, the *control center.* Input flows from the receptor to the control center along the so-called *afferent pathway*. The **control center,** which determines the *set point* (the level or range at which a variable is to be maintained), analyzes the input it receives and then determines the appropriate response or course of action.

The third component, the **effector,** provides the means for the control center's response (output) to the stimulus. Information flows from the control center to the effector along the *efferent pathway*. The results of the response then *feed back* to influence the stimulus, either depressing it (negative feedback) so that the whole control mechanism is shut off or enhancing it (positive feedback) so that the reaction continues at an even faster rate. (To help you remember the difference between "afferent" and "efferent," you might note that information traveling along the afferent pathway **a**pproaches the control center and **e**fferent information **e**xits from the control center.)

Negative Feedback Mechanisms

Most homeostatic control mechanisms are **negative feedback mechanisms.** In these systems, the output shuts off the original stimulus or reduces its intensity. These mechanisms cause the variable to change in a direction *opposite* to that of the initial change, returning it to its "ideal" value; thus the name "negative" feedback mechanisms.

A good example of a nonbiological negative feedback system is a home heating system connected to a temperature-sensing thermostat (Figure 1.5). The thermostat houses both the receptor (thermometer) and the control center. If the thermostat is set at 20°C (68°F), the heating system (effector) is triggered ON when the house temperature drops below that setting. As the furnace produces heat and warms the air, the temperature rises, and when it reaches 20°C or slightly higher, the thermostat triggers the furnace OFF. This process results in a cycling of "furnace-ON" and "furnace-OFF" so that the temperature in the house stays very near the desired temperature of 20°C. Your body "thermostat," located in a part of your brain called the hypothalamus, operates in a similar fashion.

Regulation of body temperature is only one of the many ways the nervous system maintains the constancy of the internal environment. Another type of neural control mechanism is seen in the *withdrawal reflex* referred to earlier, in which the hand is jerked away from a painful stimulus such as broken glass. The endocrine system is equally important in maintaining homeostasis, however, and a good example of a hormonal negative feedback mechanism is the control of blood volume by antidiuretic hormone (ADH). As blood volume drops, the hypothalamus of the brain (the control center) is stimulated to release ADH to the blood. This in turn prompts the kidneys to reabsorb more water and return it to the bloodstream. The rising blood volume then ends the stimulus for ADH release.

The body's ability to regulate its internal environment is fundamental, and all negative feedback mechanisms have the same goal: preventing sudden severe changes within the body. Body temperature and blood volume are only two of the variables that need to be regulated. There are hundreds! Other negative feedback mechanisms regulate heart rate, blood pressure, the rate and depth of breathing, and blood levels of oxygen, carbon dioxide, and minerals. Now, let's take a look at the other type of feedback control mechanism—positive feedback.

Positive Feedback Mechanisms

In **positive feedback mechanisms,** the result or response enhances the original stimulus so that the activity (output) is accelerated. This feedback mechanism is "positive" because the change that occurs proceeds in the *same* direction as the initial disturbance, causing the variable to deviate further and further from its original value or range. In contrast to negative feedback controls, which maintain some physiological function or keep blood chemicals within narrow ranges, positive feedback mechanisms usually control infrequent events that do not require continuous adjustments. Typically, they set off a series of events that may be self-perpetuating and that, once initiated, have an amplifying or waterfall effect. Because of these characteristics, positive feedback mechanisms are often referred to as *cascades* (from the Italian word meaning "to fall"). Positive feedback mechanisms are likely to race out of control, and so they are rarely used to promote the moment-to-moment well-being of the body. However, two familiar examples of their use as homeostatic mechanisms are the enhancement of labor contractions during birth and blood clotting.

The positive feedback mechanism in which oxytocin, a hypothalamic hormone, intensifies labor contractions during the birth of a baby is described in Chapter 28 (see Figure 28.16). Oxytocin causes the contractions to become both more frequent and more powerful. The increased contractions cause more oxytocin to be released, which causes more contractions and so on until the baby is finally born, an event that ends the stimulus for oxytocin release and shuts off the positive feedback mechanism.

Blood clotting is a normal response to a break in the lining of a blood vessel and is an excellent

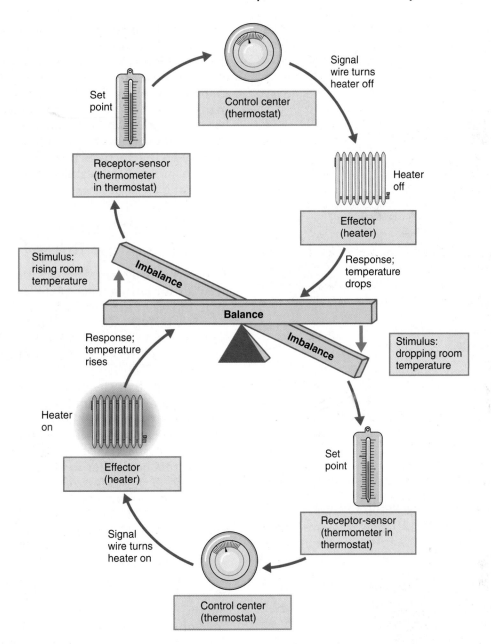

FIGURE 1.5   **Regulation of room temperature by a negative feedback mechanism.**

example of an important body function controlled by positive feedback. Basically, once vessel damage has occurred, blood elements called platelets immediately begin to cling to the injured site and release chemicals that attract more platelets. This rapidly growing pileup of platelets initiates the sequence of events that finally forms a clot (Figure 1.6).

Homeostatic Imbalance

Homeostasis is so important that most disease can be regarded as a result of its disturbance, a condition called **homeostatic imbalance.** As we age, our body's control systems become less efficient, and our internal environment becomes less and less stable. These events increase our risk for illness and produce the changes we associate with aging.

Another important source of homeostatic imbalance occurs when the usual negative feedback mechanisms are overwhelmed and destructive positive feedback mechanisms take over. Some instances of heart failure reflect this phenomenon.

Examples of homeostatic imbalance are provided throughout this book to enhance your understanding of normal physiological mechanisms. These homeostatic imbalance sections are preceded by the

1

Q *(1) Why is this control mechanism called a "positive feedback mechanism"? (2) What event ends the cascade or chain reaction seen in this positive feedback control mechanism?*

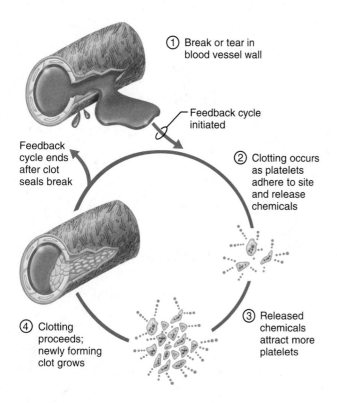

① Break or tear in blood vessel wall

Feedback cycle initiated

Feedback cycle ends after clot seals break

② Clotting occurs as platelets adhere to site and release chemicals

④ Clotting proceeds; newly forming clot grows

③ Released chemicals attract more platelets

FIGURE 1.6   **Summary of the positive feedback mechanism regulating blood clotting.**

symbol ◤◥ to alert you to the fact that an abnormal condition is being described.

The Language of Anatomy

Although most of us are naturally curious about our bodies, our interest sometimes dwindles when we are confronted with the terminology used in the study of anatomy and physiology. Let's face it—you can't just pick up an anatomy and physiology book and read it as though it were a novel. Unfortunately, confusion is inevitable without such specialized

A *(1) Because the response leads to an even greater response (i.e., platelets cling to damaged vessels and release chemicals that attract more platelets, which release more chemicals, etc.) rather than shutting off the stimulus, it involves positive feedback. (2) When the clot seals the break in the vessel, the cascade ends.*

terminology. For example, if you are looking at a ball, "above" always means the area over the top of the ball. Other directional terms can also be used consistently because the ball is a totally symmetrical object, a sphere. The human body, of course, has many bends and protrusions. Thus, the question becomes: above what? To prevent misunderstanding, anatomists use universally accepted terms to identify body structures precisely and with a minimum of words. This language of anatomy is presented and explained next.

Anatomical Position and Directional Terms

To describe body parts and position accurately, we need an initial reference point and must indicate direction. The anatomical reference point is a standard body position called the **anatomical position.** In the anatomical position, the body is erect with feet slightly apart. This position is easy to remember because it resembles "standing at attention," except that the palms face forward and the thumbs point away from the body. You can see the anatomical position in Table 1.1 (top) and Figure 1.7a. It is essential to understand the anatomical position because most of the directional terms used in this book refer to the body *as if it were in this position, regardless of its actual position.* Another point to remember is that the terms "right" and "left" refer to those sides of the person or the cadaver (deceased person) being viewed—not those of the observer.

Directional terms allow us to explain where one body structure is in relation to another. For example, we could describe the relationship between the ears and the nose informally by stating, "The ears are located on each side of the head to the right and left of the nose." Using anatomical terminology, this condenses to, "The ears are lateral to the nose." Clearly, using anatomical terms saves words and is less ambiguous. Commonly used orientation and directional terms are defined and illustrated in Table 1.1. Many of these terms are also used in everyday conversation, but keep in mind that their anatomical meanings are very precise.

Regional Terms

The two fundamental divisions of our body are its *axial* and *appendicular* (ap″en-dik′u-lar) parts. The **axial part,** which makes up the main *axis* of our body, includes the head, neck, and trunk. The **appendicular part** consists of the *appendages,* or *limbs,* which are attached to the body's axis.

TABLE 1.1	Orientation and Directional Terms		
TERM	**DEFINITION**	**EXAMPLE**	
Superior (cranial)	Toward the head end or upper part of a structure or the body; above		The head is superior to the abdomen
Inferior (caudal)	Away from the head end or toward the lower part of a structure or the body; below		The navel is inferior to the chin
Ventral (anterior)*	Toward or at the front of the body; in front of		The breastbone is anterior to the spine
Dorsal (posterior)*	Toward or at the back of the body; behind		The heart is posterior to the breastbone
Medial	Toward or at the midline of the body; on the inner side of		The heart is medial to the arm
Lateral	Away from the midline of the body; on the outer side of		The arms are lateral to the chest
Intermediate	Between a more medial and a more lateral structure		The collarbone is intermediate between the breastbone and shoulder
Proximal	Closer to the origin of the body part or the point of attachment of a limb to the body trunk		The elbow is proximal to the wrist
Distal	Farther from the origin of a body part or the point of attachment of a limb to the body trunk		The knee is distal to the thigh
Superficial (external)	Toward or at the body surface		The skin is superficial to the skeletal muscles
Deep (internal)	Away from the body surface; more internal		The lungs are deep to the skin

*The terms *ventral* and *anterior* are synonymous in humans, but this is not the case in four-legged animals. Whereas *anterior* refers to the leading portion of the body (abdominal surface in humans, head in a cat), *ventral* specifically refers to the "belly" of a vertebrate animal and thus is the inferior surface of four-legged animals. Likewise, although the dorsal and posterior surfaces are the same in humans, the term *dorsal* specifically refers to an animal's back. Thus, the dorsal surface of four-legged animals is their superior surface.

Q *As you study this figure, determine precisely where you would be injured if you (1) pulled a muscle in your inguinal region, (2) cracked a bone in your olecranal region, and (3) received a cut on the fibular region.*

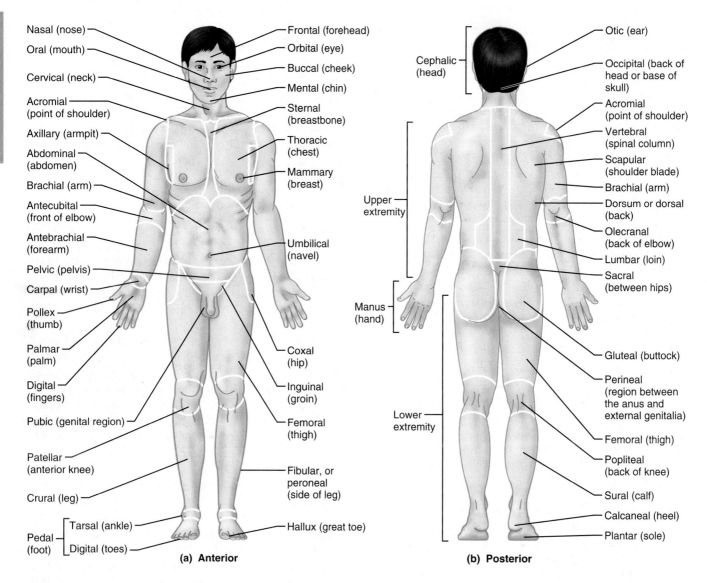

Nasal (nose)
Oral (mouth)
Cervical (neck)
Acromial (point of shoulder)
Axillary (armpit)
Abdominal (abdomen)
Brachial (arm)
Antecubital (front of elbow)
Antebrachial (forearm)
Pelvic (pelvis)
Carpal (wrist)
Pollex (thumb)
Palmar (palm)
Digital (fingers)
Pubic (genital region)
Patellar (anterior knee)
Crural (leg)
Pedal (foot) — Tarsal (ankle), Digital (toes)

Frontal (forehead)
Orbital (eye)
Buccal (cheek)
Mental (chin)
Sternal (breastbone)
Thoracic (chest)
Mammary (breast)
Umbilical (navel)
Coxal (hip)
Inguinal (groin)
Femoral (thigh)
Fibular, or peroneal (side of leg)
Hallux (great toe)

(a) Anterior

Cephalic (head)
Upper extremity
Manus (hand)
Lower extremity

Otic (ear)
Occipital (back of head or base of skull)
Acromial (point of shoulder)
Vertebral (spinal column)
Scapular (shoulder blade)
Brachial (arm)
Dorsum or dorsal (back)
Olecranal (back of elbow)
Lumbar (loin)
Sacral (between hips)
Gluteal (buttock)
Perineal (region between the anus and external genitalia)
Femoral (thigh)
Popliteal (back of knee)
Sural (calf)
Calcaneal (heel)
Plantar (sole)

(b) Posterior

FIGURE 1.7 **Regional terms used to designate specific body areas. (a)** The anatomical position. **(b)** The heels are raised slightly to show the plantar surface of the foot, which is actually on the inferior surface of the body.

Regional terms used to designate specific areas within the major body divisions are indicated in Figure 1.7. The common term for each of these body regions is also provided (in parentheses).

A *(1) Your groin. (2) Posterior aspect of the elbow. (3) The side of your leg.*

Anatomical Variability

Although we use common directional and regional terms to refer to all human bodies, we know from observing the faces and body shapes of people around us that we humans differ in our external anatomy. The same kind of variability holds for our internal organs as well. In some bodies, for example, a nerve or blood vessel may be somewhat out of place, or a small muscle may be missing. Nonetheless, well over 90% of all structures present in any human body match the textbook descriptions. Extreme anatomical variations are seldom seen because they are incompatible with life.

Body Planes and Sections

For anatomical studies, the body is often *sectioned* (cut) along a flat surface called a plane. The most frequently used body planes are sagittal, frontal, and transverse planes, which lie at right angles to one another (Figure 1.8). A section is named for the plane along which it is cut. Thus, a cut along a sagittal plane produces a sagittal section.

A **sagittal plane** (saj'ĭ-tal; "arrow") is a vertical plane that divides the body into right and left parts. A sagittal plane that lies exactly in the midline is the **median plane,** or **midsagittal plane** (Figure 1.8c). All other sagittal planes, offset from the midline, are **parasagittal planes** (*para* = near).

Frontal planes, like sagittal planes, lie vertically. Frontal planes, however, divide the body into anterior and posterior parts (Figure 1.8a). A frontal plane is also called a **coronal plane** (kŏ-ro'nal; "crown").

A **transverse,** or **horizontal, plane** runs horizontally from right to left, dividing the body into superior and inferior parts (Figure 1.8b). Of course, many different transverse planes exist, at every possible level from head to foot. A transverse section is also called a **cross section.** Cuts made diagonally between the horizontal and the vertical planes are called **oblique sections.** Such sections are often confusing and difficult to interpret and are seldom used.

The ability to interpret sections made through the body, especially transverse sections, is important in the clinical sciences. New medical imaging devices (pp. 20–21) produce sectional images rather than three-dimensional images. It can be difficult to decipher an object's overall shape from sectioned material. A cross section of a banana, for example, looks like a circle and gives no indication of the whole banana's crescent shape. Likewise, sectioning the body or an organ along different planes often results in very different views. For example, a transverse section of the body trunk at the level of the kidneys would show kidney structure in cross section very nicely; a frontal section of the body trunk would show a different view of kidney anatomy; and a midsagittal section would miss the kidneys completely. With practice, you will gradually learn to relate two-dimensional sections to three-dimensional shapes.

Body Cavities and Membranes

Anatomy and physiology textbooks typically describe two sets of internal body cavities called the dorsal and ventral body cavities. These cavities are closed to the outside and provide different degrees of protection to the organs contained within them.

Because these two cavities differ in their mode of embryonic development, and their lining membranes, the dorsal body cavity is not recognized as such in many anatomical references. However, the idea of two sets of internal body cavities is a useful learning concept and is used here.

Dorsal Body Cavity

The **dorsal body cavity,** which protects the fragile nervous system organs (Figure 1.9), has two subdivisions. The **cranial cavity,** in the skull, encases the brain. The **vertebral,** or **spinal, cavity,** which runs within the bony vertebral column, encloses the delicate spinal cord. The spinal cord is essentially a continuation of the brain, and the cranial and spinal cavities are continuous with one another.

Ventral Body Cavity

The more anterior and larger of the closed body cavities is the **ventral body cavity** (see Figure 1.9). Like the dorsal cavity, it has two major subdivisions, the *thoracic cavity* and the *abdominopelvic cavity.* The ventral body cavity houses internal organs collectively called the **viscera** (vis'er-ah; *viscus* = an organ in a body cavity), or visceral organs.

The superior subdivision, the **thoracic cavity** (tho-ras'ik), is surrounded by the ribs and muscles of the chest. The thoracic cavity is further subdivided into lateral **pleural cavities** (ploo'ral), each enveloping a lung, and the medial **mediastinum** (me"de-ah-sti'num). The mediastinum contains the **pericardial cavity** (per"ĭ-kar'de-al), which encloses the heart, and it also surrounds the remaining thoracic organs (esophagus, trachea, and others).

The thoracic cavity is separated from the more inferior **abdominopelvic cavity** (ab-dom'ĭ-no-pel'vic) by the diaphragm, a dome-shaped muscle important in breathing. The abdominopelvic cavity, as its name suggests, has two parts. However, these regions are not physically separated by a muscular or membrane wall. Its superior portion, the **abdominal cavity,** contains the stomach, intestines, spleen, liver, and other organs. The inferior part, the **pelvic cavity,** lies in the bony pelvis and contains the bladder, some reproductive organs, and the rectum. The abdominal and pelvic cavities are not aligned with each other. Instead, the bowl-shaped pelvis tips away from the perpendicular.

◤ HOMEOSTATIC IMBALANCE

When the body is subjected to physical trauma (as often happens in an automobile accident), the abdominopelvic organs are most vulnerable. This is because the walls of the abdominal cavity are formed only by trunk muscles and are not reinforced by bone. The pelvic organs receive a somewhat greater degree of protection from the bony pelvis. ●

Q *Which of these planes would separate the woman's arms?*

Frontal plane

Median (midsagittal) plane

Transverse plane

(a) Frontal section through torso

(b) Transverse section through torso (superior view)

(c) Median (midsagittal) section

Posterior

Left and right lung   Liver   Heart   Stomach   Spleen

Liver   Spinal cord   Aorta   Stomach   Spleen

Subcutaneous fat layer

Rectum   Vertebral column   Intestines

Pubic symphysis

FIGURE 1.8   **Planes of the body—frontal, transverse, and median (midsagittal) with corresponding magnetic resonance imaging (MRI) scans.**

A *Median or midsagittal.*

Cranial cavity
(contains brain)

Dorsal body cavity

Vertebral cavity
(contains spinal cord)

Key:

☐ Dorsal body cavity

■ Ventral body cavity

Thoracic cavity (contains heart and lungs)

Diaphragm

Abdominal cavity (contains digestive viscera)

Pelvic cavity (contains bladder, reproductive organs, and rectum)

(a) Lateral view

Cranial cavity

Vertebral cavity

Superior mediastinum

Pleural cavity

Pericardial cavity within the mediastinum

Abdomino-pelvic cavity

Ventral body cavity (thoracic and abdominopelvic cavities)

(b) Anterior view

FIGURE 1.9 **Dorsal and ventral body cavities and their subdivisions.**

Membranes in the Ventral Body Cavity The walls of the ventral body cavity and the outer surfaces of the organs it contains are covered by a thin, double-layered membrane, the **serosa** (se-ro'sah), or **serous membrane.** The part of the membrane lining the cavity walls is called the **parietal serosa** (pah-ri'ĕ-tal; *parie* = wall). It folds in on itself to form the **visceral serosa,** covering the organs in the cavity.

You can visualize the relationship between the serosal layers by pushing your fist into a limp balloon (Figure 1.10a). The part of the balloon that clings to your fist can be compared to the visceral serosa clinging to the organ's external surface. The outer wall of the balloon then represents the parietal serosa that lines the walls of the cavity. (However, unlike the balloon, it is never exposed but is always fused to the cavity wall.) In the body, the serous membranes are separated not by air but by a thin layer of lubricating fluid, called **serous fluid,** which is secreted by both membranes. Although there is a potential space between the two membranes, the barely present, slit-like cavity is filled with serous fluid.

The slippery serous fluid allows the organs to slide without friction across the cavity walls and one another as they carry out their routine functions. This freedom of movement is especially important

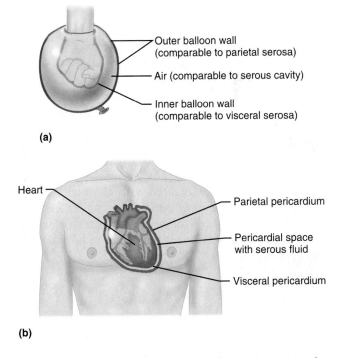

Outer balloon wall (comparable to parietal serosa)

Air (comparable to serous cavity)

Inner balloon wall (comparable to visceral serosa)

(a)

Heart

Parietal pericardium

Pericardial space with serous fluid

Visceral pericardium

(b)

FIGURE 1.10 **Serous membrane relationships. (a)** A fist is thrust into a flaccid balloon to demonstrate the relationship between the parietal and visceral serous membrane layers. **(b)** The serosae associated with the heart. The parietal pericardium is the outer layer lining the pericardial cavity; the visceral pericardium clings to the external heart surface.

(a)

Diaphragm

Liver

Gallbladder

Ascending colon of large intestine

Small intestine

Cecum

Appendix

Stomach

Transverse colon of large intestine

Descending colon of large intestine

Initial part of sigmoid colon

Urinary bladder

(b)

FIGURE 1.11 **The nine abdominopelvic regions. (a)** Division of the abdominopelvic cavity into nine regions delineated by four planes. The superior transverse plane is just inferior to the ribs; the inferior transverse plane is just superior to the hip bones; and the parasagittal planes lie just medial to the nipples. **(b)** Anterior view of the abdominopelvic cavity showing the superficial organs.

for mobile organs such as the pumping heart and the churning stomach.

The serous membranes are named for the specific cavity and organs with which they are associated. For example, as shown in Figure 1.10b, the *parietal pericardium* lines the pericardial cavity and reflects back as the *visceral pericardium*, which covers the heart. Likewise, the *parietal pleura* (ploo'rah) lines the walls of the thoracic cavity, and the *visceral pleura* covers the lungs. The *parietal peritoneum* (per"ĭ-to-ne'um) is associated with the walls of the abdominopelvic cavity, while the *visceral peritoneum* covers most of the organs within that cavity. (The pleural and peritoneal serosae are illustrated in Figure 4.12c on p. 142.)

HOMEOSTATIC IMBALANCE

When serous membranes are inflamed, their normally smooth surfaces become roughened. This leads to excruciating pain as the organs stick together and drag across one another, as anyone who has experienced *pleurisy* (inflammation of the pleurae) or *peritonitis* (inflammation of the peritonea) knows. ●

Abdominopelvic Regions and Quadrants

Because the abdominopelvic cavity is large and contains several organs, it helps to divide it into smaller areas for study. One division method, used primarily by anatomists, uses two transverse and two parasagittal planes. These planes, positioned like a tic-tac-toe grid on the abdomen, divide the cavity into nine regions (Figure 1.11):

- The **umbilical region** is the centermost region deep to and surrounding the umbilicus (navel).

- The **epigastric region** is located superior to the umbilical region (*epi* = upon, above; *gastri* = belly).

- The **hypogastric (pubic) region** is located inferior to the umbilical region (*hypo* = below).

- The **right** and **left iliac,** or **inguinal, regions** (ing'gwĭ-nal) are located lateral to the hypogastric region (*iliac* = superior part of the hip bone).

- The **right** and **left lumbar regions** lie lateral to the umbilical region (*lumbus* = loin).

- The **right** and **left hypochondriac regions** flank the epigastric region laterally (*chondro* = cartilage).

Medical personnel usually use a simpler scheme to localize the abdominopelvic cavity organs

(Figure 1.12). In this scheme, one transverse and one median sagittal plane pass through the umbilicus at right angles. The resulting quadrants are named according to their positions from the subject's point of view: the **right upper quadrant (RUQ)**, **left upper quadrant (LUQ)**, **right lower quadrant (RLQ)**, and **left lower quadrant (LLQ)**.

Other Body Cavities

In addition to the large closed body cavities, there are several smaller body cavities (Figure 1.13). Most of these are in the head and most open to the body exterior:

1. Oral and digestive cavities. The oral cavity, commonly called the mouth, contains the teeth and tongue. This cavity is part of and continuous with the cavity of the digestive organs, which opens to the exterior at the anus.

2. Nasal cavity. Located within and posterior to the nose, the nasal cavity is part of the respiratory system passageways.

3. Orbital cavities. The orbital cavities (orbits) in the skull house the eyes and present them in an anterior position.

4. Middle ear cavities. The middle ear cavities carved into the skull lie just medial to the eardrums. These cavities contain tiny bones that transmit sound vibrations to the hearing receptors in the inner ears.

5. Synovial cavities (sĭ-no′ve-al). Synovial cavities are joint cavities. They are enclosed within fibrous capsules that surround freely movable joints of the

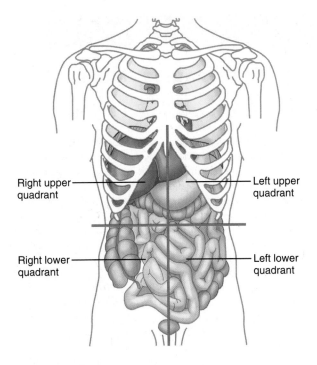

FIGURE 1.12   **The four abdominopelvic quadrants.** In this scheme, the abdominopelvic cavity is divided into four quadrants by two planes. The figure shows superficial organs within each quadrant.

body (such as the elbow and knee joints). Like the serous membranes, membranes lining synovial cavities secrete a lubricating fluid that reduces friction as the bones move across one another.

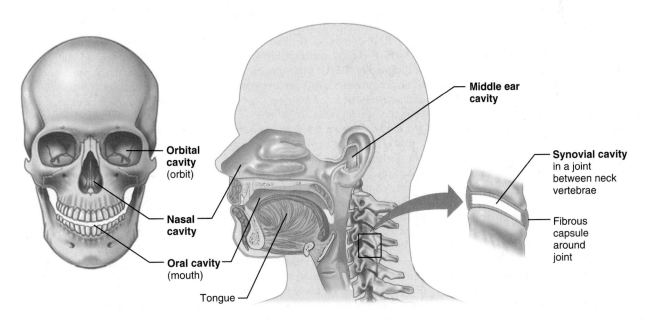

FIGURE 1.13   **Other body cavities.** The oral, nasal, orbital, and middle ear cavities are located in the head and open to the body exterior. Synovial cavities are found in the joints between many bones, such as the vertebrae of the spine.

A CLOSER LOOK

Medical Imaging: Illuminating the Body

Until 50 years ago, the magical but murky X ray was the only nonsurgical means to extract information from within a living body. Produced by directing *X rays*, electromagnetic waves of very short wavelength, at the body, an **X ray** or **radiograph** is essentially a shadowy negative of internal structures. Dense structures absorb the X rays most and so appear as light areas on the radiograph. Hollow air-containing organs and fat, which absorb the X rays less, show up as dark areas. What X rays do best is visualize hard, bony structures and locate abnormally dense structures (tumors, tuberculosis nodules) in the lungs.

The 1950s saw the advent of nuclear medicine, which uses radioisotopes to scan the body, and ultrasound techniques. The 1970s brought CT, PET, and MRI scans. These technologies not only reveal the structure of our "insides" but also wring out information about the private, and until then secret, workings of their molecules.

Computed tomography (CT, formerly called **computerized axial tomography, CAT**) utilizes a refined version of X-ray equipment. As the patient is slowly moved through the doughnut-shaped CT machine, its X-ray tube rotates around the body and sends beams from all directions to a specific level of the patient's body. Because at any moment its beam is confined to a "slice" of the body about as thick as a dime, CT ends the confusion resulting from overlapping structures seen in conventional X rays. The device's computer translates this information into a detailed, cross-sectional picture of each body region scanned. CT scans are at the forefront for evaluating most problems that affect the brain and abdomen [see photo (a)], and their clarity has all but eliminated exploratory surgery. Some found it troubling, when, in the early 2000s, CT-screening centers sprung up like weeds in many United States cities. The lure of these centers goes something like this: "You think you're healthy, right? So did Joe So-and-So until he died of a heart attack. Have a whole body scan to save yourself from life-threatening conditions." Most people that use CT-screening centers do so without medical consultation and then take the results to a doctor. Although such scans may save some lives, they also turn up anomalies that are not medically dangerous, resulting in unnecessary surgery and/or hospital stays at considerable expense. The assumption that there was a huge market of people willing to dip into their pockets has proven untrue and this "medical bubble" has rapidly deflated.

Xenon CT is a CT brain scan enhanced with xenon, a radioactive gas, to quickly trace blood flow. Inhaled xenon rapidly enters the bloodstream and distributes to different body tissues in proportion to their blood flow. Absence of xenon from part of the brain indicates that a stroke is occurring there, information that aids treatment.

Dynamic spatial reconstruction (DSR) uses ultrafast CT scanners to provide three-dimensional images of body organs from any angle, and scrutinize their movements and changes in their internal volumes at normal speed, in slow motion, and at a specific moment. DSR's greatest value has been to visualize the heart beating and blood flowing through blood vessels, allowing clinicians to evaluate heart defects, constricted or blocked blood vessels, and the status of coronary bypass grafts.

Another computer-assisted X-ray technique, **digital subtraction angiography (DSA)** (*angiography* = "vessel pictures"), provides an unobstructed view of small arteries. Conventional radiographs are taken before and after a contrast medium is injected into an artery. The computer subtracts the "before" image from the "after" image, eliminating all traces of body structures that obscure the vessel. DSA is often used to identify blockages in the arteries that supply the heart wall [photo (b)] and brain.

Just as the X ray spawned "big brothers," so too did nuclear medicine in the form of **positron emission tomography (PET)**. PET excels in observing *metabolic processes*. The patient is given an injection of radioisotopes tagged to biological molecules (such as glucose) and is then positioned in the PET scanner. As the radioisotopes are absorbed by the most active brain cells, high-energy gamma rays are produced. The computer analyzes the gamma-ray emission and produces a live-action picture of the brain's biochemical activity in vivid colors. PET's greatest value has been its ability to provide insights into brain activity in people affected by mental illness, stroke, Alzheimer's disease, and epilepsy. One of its most exciting uses has been to determine which areas of the healthy brain are most active during certain tasks (e.g., speaking, listening to music, or figuring out a mathematical problem), providing direct evidence of the functions of specific brain regions.

Sonography, or **ultrasound imaging,** has some distinct advantages over the approaches examined so far. The equipment is inexpensive and ultrasound used as its energy source seems to be safer than the ionizing forms of radiation used in nuclear medicine. The body is probed with pulses of sound waves that cause echoes when reflected and scattered by body tissues. A computer analyzes these echoes to construct somewhat blurry outlines of body organs. A single easy to use handheld device emits the sound and picks up the echoes, so sections can be scanned from many different body planes.

Because of its safety, ultrasound is the imaging technique of choice in obstetrics for determining fetal age and position and locating the placenta. However, sound waves have low penetrating power and rapidly dissipate in air, so sonography is of little value for looking at air-filled structures (the lungs) or those surrounded by bone (the brain and spinal cord).

Magnetic resonance imaging (MRI) produces high-contrast images of our soft tissues, an area in which X rays and CT scans are weak. As initially developed, MRI primarily maps the element hydrogen in the body, most of which is in water. The technique subjects the body to magnetic fields up to 60,000 times stronger than that of the earth to pry information from the body's molecules. The patient lies in a chamber within a huge magnet. Hydrogen molecules act like tiny magnets, spinning like tops in the magnetic field.

Their energy is further enhanced by radio waves and when the radio waves are turned off, the energy released is translated into a visual image.

MRI distinguishes body tissues based on their water content, so it can differentiate between the fatty white matter and the more watery gray matter of the brain. Because dense structures do not show up at all in MRI, it peers easily into the skull and vertebral column, enabling the delicate nerve fibers of the spinal cord to be seen. MRI is also particularly good at detecting tumors and degenerative disease. Multiple sclerosis plaques do not show up well in CT scans, but are dazzlingly clear in MRI scans. MRI can also tune in on metabolic reactions, such as processes that generate energy-rich ATP molecules. Until recently, trying to diagnose asthma and other lung problems has been off limits to MRI scans because the lungs have a low water content. However, an alternate tack—filling the lungs with a gas that can be magnetized (hyperpolarized helium-3 or xenon-129)—has yielded spectacular pictures of the lungs in just the few seconds it takes the patient to inhale, hold the breath briefly, and then exhale—a distinct improvement over the hours required for conventional MRI. This technique has the additional advantage of using a magnetic field as little as one-tenth that of the conventional MRI.

Newer variations of MRI include **magnetic resonance spectroscopy (MRS),** which maps the distribution of elements other than hydrogen to reveal more about how disease changes body chemistry. Other advances in computer techniques display MRI scans in three dimensions to guide laser surgery. The **functional MRI** tracks blood flow into the brain in real time. Matching thoughts, deeds, and disease to brain activity has been the sole domain of PET. Because functional MRI does not require injections of tracers and can pinpoint much smaller brain areas than PET, it may provide a desirable alternative.

Despite its advantages, the powerful magnets of the clanging, claustrophobia-inducing MRI present some thorny problems. For example, they can "suck" metal objects, such as implanted pacemakers and loose tooth fillings, through the body. Moreover, although such strong magnetic fields are currently

(a) A CT scan through the superior abdomen.

Left · Right · Pancreas · Left kidney · Spleen · Vertebra · Liver

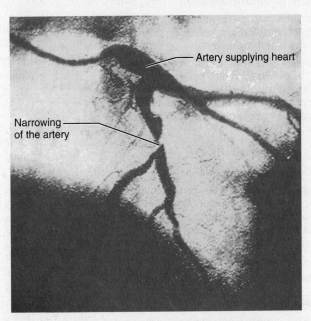

(b) A (DSA) image of the arteries that supply the heart.

Artery supplying heart · Narrowing of the artery

considered safe, there is no convincing evidence that they are risk free.

Although stunning, medical images other than straight X rays are abstractions assembled within the "mind" of a computer. They are artificially enhanced for sharpness and artificially colored to increase contrast (all their colors are "phony"). The images are several steps removed from direct observation.

As you can see, medical science offers remarkable diagnostic tools. Consider the M2A Swallowable Imaging Capsule, a tiny camera that is swallowed like a pill, then excreted normally 8–72 hours later. As the M2A travels through the digestive tract, it photographs the small intestine and beams the color images to a Walkman-sized receiver. A study found the device to be 60% effective at detecting intestinal problems, compared to a 35% success rate with other imaging techniques. At present the M2A can provide images only of the small intestine because the battery gives out before it enters the large intestine.

New imaging technologies also make long-distance surgery possible. Visual images of a diseased organ travel via fiber-optic cable to surgeons at another location (even a different country), who manipulate delicate robotic instruments to remove the organ. ■

Chapter Summary

An Overview of Anatomy and Physiology (pp. 2–3)

1. Anatomy is the study of body structures and their relationships. Physiology is the science of how body parts function.

Topics of Anatomy (pp. 2–3)

2. Major subdivisions of anatomy include gross anatomy, microscopic anatomy, and developmental anatomy.

Topics of Physiology (p. 3)

3. Typically, physiology concerns the functioning of specific organs or organ systems. Examples include cardiac physiology, renal physiology, and muscle physiology.

4. Physiology is explained by chemical and physical principles.

Complementarity of Structure and Function (p. 3)

5. Anatomy and physiology are inseparable: What a body can do depends on the unique architecture of its parts. This is called the complementarity of structure and function.

Levels of Structural Organization (pp. 3–4)

1. The levels of structural organization of the body, from simplest to most complex, are: chemical, cellular, tissue, organ, organ system, and organismal.

2. The 11 organ systems of the body are the integumentary, skeletal, muscular, nervous, endocrine, cardiovascular, lymphatic, respiratory, digestive, urinary, and reproductive systems. The immune system is a functional system closely associated with the lymphatic system. (For functions of these systems see pp. 6–7.)

Maintaining Life (pp. 4–8)

Necessary Life Functions (pp. 4–8)

1. All living organisms carry out certain vital functional activities necessary for life, including maintenance of boundaries, movement, responsiveness, digestion, metabolism, excretion, reproduction, and growth.

Survival Needs (p. 8)

2. Survival needs include nutrients, water, oxygen, and appropriate body temperature and atmospheric pressure.

Homeostasis (pp. 9–12)

1. Homeostasis is a dynamic equilibrium of the internal environment. All body systems contribute to homeostasis, but the nervous and endocrine systems are most important. Homeostasis is necessary for health.

Homeostatic Control Mechanisms (pp. 9–11)

2. Control systems of the body contain at least three elements: receptor(s), control center, and effector(s).

3. Negative feedback mechanisms reduce the original stimulus, and are essential for maintaining homeostasis. Body temperature, heart rate, breathing rate and depth, and blood levels of glucose and certain ions are regulated by negative feedback mechanisms.

4. Positive feedback mechanisms intensify the initial stimulus, leading to an enhancement of the response. They rarely contribute to homeostasis, but blood clotting and labor contractions are regulated by such mechanisms.

Homeostatic Imbalance (pp. 11–12)

5. With age, the efficiency of negative feedback mechanisms declines, and positive feedback mechanisms occur more frequently. These changes underlie certain disease conditions.

The Language of Anatomy (pp. 12–19)

Anatomical Position and Directional Terms (p. 12)

1. In the anatomical position, the body is erect, facing forward, feet together, arms at sides with palms forward.

2. Directional terms allow body parts to be located precisely. Terms used to describe body directions and orientation include: superior/inferior; anterior/posterior; ventral/dorsal; medial/lateral; intermediate; proximal/distal; and superficial/deep.

Regional Terms (pp. 12–14)

3. Regional terms are used to designate specific areas of the body (see Figure 1.7).

Anatomical Variability (pp. 14–15)

4. People vary internally as well as externally, although extreme variations are rare.

Body Planes and Sections (p. 15)

5. The body or its organs may be cut along planes, or imaginary lines, to produce different types of sections. Frequently used planes are sagittal, frontal, and transverse.

Body Cavities and Membranes (pp. 15, 17–19)

6. The body contains two major closed cavities. The dorsal cavity, subdivided into the cranial and spinal cavities, contains the brain and spinal cord. The ventral cavity is subdivided into the thoracic cavity, which houses the heart and lungs, and the abdominopelvic cavity, which contains the liver, digestive organs, and reproductive structures.

7. The walls of the ventral cavity and the surfaces of the organs it contains are covered with thin membranes, the parietal and visceral serosae, respectively. The serosae produce a thin fluid that decreases friction during organ functioning.

8. The abdominopelvic cavity may be divided by four planes into nine abdominal regions (epigastric, umbilical, hypogastric, right and left iliac, right and left lumbar, and right and left hypochondriac), or by two planes into four quadrants. (For boundaries and organs contained see Figures 1.11 and 1.12.)

9. There are several smaller body cavities. Most of these are in the head and open to the exterior.

Review Questions

Multiple Choice/Matching

(Some questions have more than one correct answer. Select the best answer or answers from the choices given.)

1. The correct sequence of levels forming the structural hierarchy is (a) organ, organ system, cellular, chemical, tissue, organismal; (b) chemical, cellular, tissue, organismal, organ, organ system; (c) chemical, cellular, tissue, organ, organ system, organismal; (d) organismal, organ system, organ, tissue, cellular, chemical.

2. The structural and functional unit of life is (a) a cell, (b) an organ, (c) the organism, (d) a molecule.

3. Which of the following is a *major* functional characteristic of all organisms? (a) movement, (b) growth, (c) metabolism, (d) responsiveness, (e) all of these.

4. Two of these organ systems bear the *major* responsibility for ensuring homeostasis of the internal environment. Which two? (a) nervous system, (b) digestive system, (c) cardiovascular system, (d) endocrine system, (e) reproductive system.

5. In (a)–(e), a directional term [e.g., distal in (a)] is followed by terms indicating different body structures or locations (e.g., the elbow/the wrist). In each case, choose the structure or organ that matches the given directional term.

   (a) distal: the elbow/the wrist
   (b) lateral: the hip bone/the umbilicus
   (c) superior: the nose/the chin
   (d) anterior: the toes/the heel
   (e) superficial: the scalp/the skull

6. Assume that the body has been sectioned along three planes: (1) a median sagittal plane, (2) a frontal plane, and (3) a transverse plane made at the level of each of the organs listed below. Which organs would not be visible in all three cases? (a) urinary bladder, (b) brain, (c) lungs, (d) kidneys, (e) small intestine, (f) heart.

7. Relate each of the following conditions or statements to either the dorsal body cavity or the ventral body cavity.

   (a) surrounded by the bony skull and the vertebral column
   (b) includes the thoracic and abdominopelvic cavities
   (c) contains the brain and spinal cord
   (d) contains the heart, lungs, and digestive organs

8. Which of the following relationships is *incorrect*?

   (a) visceral peritoneum/outer surface of small intestine
   (b) parietal pericardium/outer surface of heart
   (c) parietal pleura/wall of thoracic cavity

9. Which ventral cavity subdivision has no bony protection? (a) thoracic cavity, (b) abdominal cavity, (c) pelvic cavity.

10. Terms that apply to the backside of the body in the anatomical position include:

   (a) ventral; anterior
   (b) back; rear
   (c) posterior; dorsal
   (d) medial; lateral

Short Answer Essay Questions

11. According to the principle of complementarity, how does anatomy relate to physiology?

12. Construct a table that lists the 11 systems of the body, names two organs of each system (if appropriate), and describes the overall or major function of each system.

13. List and describe briefly five external factors that must be present or provided to sustain life.

14. Define homeostasis.

15. Compare and contrast the operation of negative and positive feedback mechanisms in maintaining homeostasis. Provide two examples of variables controlled by negative feedback mechanisms and one example of a process regulated by a positive feedback mechanism.

16. Describe and assume the anatomical position. Why is an understanding of this position important? What is the importance of directional terms?

17. Define plane and section.

18. Provide the anatomical term that correctly names each of the following body regions: (a) arm, (b) thigh, (c) chest, (d) fingers and toes, (e) anterior aspect of the knee.

19. Use as many directional terms as you can to describe the relationship between the elbow's olecranal region and your palm.

20. (a) Make a diagram showing the nine abdominopelvic regions, and name each region. Name two organs (or parts of organs) that could be located in each of the named regions. (b) Make a similar sketch illustrating how the abdominopelvic cavity may be divided into quadrants, and name each quadrant.

Critical Thinking and Clinical Application Questions

1. John has been suffering agonizing pain with each breath and has been informed by the physician that he has pleurisy. (a) Specifically, what membranes are involved in this condition? (b) What is their usual role in the body? (c) Explain why John's condition is so painful.

2. At the clinic, Harry was told that blood would be drawn from his antecubital region. What body part was Harry asked to hold out? Later, the nurse came in and gave Harry a shot of penicillin in the area just distal to his acromial region. Did Harry take off his shirt or drop his pants to receive the injection? Before Harry left, the nurse noticed that Harry had a nasty bruise on his gluteal region. What part of his body was black and blue?

3. A man is behaving abnormally, and his physician suspects that he has a brain tumor. Which of the following medical imaging devices would best localize the tumor in the man's brain (and why)? Conventional X ray, DSA, PET, sonography, MRI.

4. When we become dehydrated, we usually feel thirsty, which causes us to drink fluids. Decide whether the thirst sensation is part of a negative or positive feedback control system and defend your choice.

5. Mr. Harvey, a computer programmer, has been complaining of numbness and pain in his right hand. The nurse practitioner diagnosed his problem as carpal tunnel syndrome and prescribed use of a splint. Where will Mr. Harvey apply the splint?

Chemistry Comes Alive

PART 1: BASIC CHEMISTRY

Definition of Concepts: Matter and Energy (pp. 25–26)

1. Differentiate between matter and energy and between potential energy and kinetic energy.
2. Describe the major energy forms.

Composition of Matter: Atoms and Elements (pp. 27–30)

3. Define chemical element and list the four elements that form the bulk of body matter.
4. Define atom. List the subatomic particles; describe their relative masses, charges, and positions in the atom.
5. Define atomic number, atomic mass, atomic weight, isotope, and radioisotope.

How Matter Is Combined: Molecules and Mixtures (pp. 30–31)

6. Distinguish between a compound and a mixture. Define molecule.
7. Compare solutions, colloids, and suspensions.

Chemical Bonds (pp. 31–36)

8. Explain the role of electrons in chemical bonding and in relation to the octet rule.
9. Differentiate among ionic, covalent, and hydrogen bonds.
10. Compare and contrast polar and nonpolar compounds.

Chemical Reactions (pp. 36–40)

11. Define the three major types of chemical reactions: synthesis, decomposition, and exchange. Comment on the nature of oxidation-reduction reactions and their importance.
12. Explain why chemical reactions in the body are often irreversible.
13. Describe factors that affect chemical reaction rates.

PART 2: BIOCHEMISTRY

Inorganic Compounds (pp. 40–43)

14. Explain the importance of water and salts to body homeostasis.
15. Define acid and base, and explain the concept of pH.

Organic Compounds (pp. 43–59)

16. Describe and compare the building blocks, general structures, and biological functions of carbohydrates, lipids, proteins, and nucleic acids.
17. Explain the role of dehydration synthesis and hydrolysis in the formation and breakdown of organic molecules.
18. Describe the four levels of protein structure.
19. Describe the general mechanism of enzyme activity.
20. Describe the function of molecular chaperones.
21. Compare and contrast DNA and RNA.
22. Explain the role of ATP in cell metabolism.

Why study chemistry in an anatomy and physiology course? The answer is simple. Your entire body is made up of chemicals, thousands of them, continuously interacting with one another at an incredible pace. Although it is possible to study anatomy without much reference to chemistry, chemical reactions underlie all physiological processes—movement, digestion, the pumping of your heart, and even your thoughts. This chapter presents the basic chemistry and biochemistry (the chemistry of living material) needed to understand body functions.

PART 1: BASIC CHEMISTRY

Definition of Concepts: Matter and Energy

Matter

Matter is the "stuff" of the universe. More precisely, **matter** is anything that occupies space and has mass. With some exceptions, it can be seen, smelled, and felt. For all practical purposes, we can consider mass to be the same as weight. However, this usage is not quite accurate. The *mass* of an object, which is equal to the actual amount of matter in the object, remains constant wherever the object is. In contrast, weight varies with gravity. So while your mass is the same at sea level and on a mountaintop, you weigh just slightly less on that mountaintop. The science of chemistry studies the nature of matter, especially how its building blocks are put together and interact.

States of Matter

Matter exists in *solid, liquid,* and *gaseous states.* Examples of each state are found in the human body. Solids, like bones and teeth, have a definite shape and volume. Liquids such as blood plasma have a definite volume, but they conform to the shape of their container. Gases have neither a definite shape nor a definite volume. The air we breathe is a gas.

Energy

Compared with matter, energy is less tangible. It has no mass, does not take up space, and can be measured only by its effects on matter. **Energy** is defined as the capacity to do work, or to put matter into motion. The greater the work done, the more energy is used doing it. A baseball player who has just hit the ball over the fence uses much more energy than a batter who just bunts the ball back to the pitcher.

Kinetic Versus Potential Energy

Energy exists in two forms, or work capacities, each transformable to the other. **Kinetic energy** (ki-net′ik) is energy in action. Kinetic energy is seen in the constant movement of the tiniest particles of matter (atoms) as well as in larger objects (a bouncing ball). It does work by moving objects, which in turn can do work by moving or pushing on other objects. For example, a push on a swinging door sets it into motion.

Potential energy is stored energy, that is, inactive energy that has the *potential,* or capability, to do work but is not presently doing so. The batteries in an unused toy have potential energy, as do your leg muscles when you sit still on the couch. When potential energy is released, it becomes kinetic energy and so is capable of doing work. For example, dammed water becomes a rushing torrent when the dam is opened, and that rushing torrent can move a turbine at a hydroelectric plant, or charge a battery.

Actually, energy is a topic of physics, but matter and energy are inseparable. Matter is the substance, and energy is the mover of the substance. All living things are composed of matter and they all require energy to grow and function. It is the release and use of energy by living systems that gives us the elusive quality called life. Thus, it is worth taking a brief detour to introduce the forms of energy used by the body as it does its work.

Forms of Energy

▪ **Chemical energy** is the form stored in the bonds of chemical substances. When chemical reactions occur that rearrange the atoms of the chemicals in a certain way, the potential energy is unleashed and becomes kinetic energy, or energy in action.

For example, some of the energy in the foods you eat is eventually converted into the kinetic energy of your moving arm. However, food fuels cannot be used to energize body activities directly. Instead, some of the food energy is captured temporarily in the bonds of a chemical called *adenosine triphosphate (ATP)* (ah-den′o-sēn tri″fos′fāt). Later, ATP's bonds are broken and the stored energy is released as needed to do cellular work. Chemical energy in the form of ATP is the most useful form of energy in living systems because it is used to run all functional processes.

▪ **Electrical energy** results from the movement of charged particles. In your home, electrical energy is found in the flow of electrons along the household wiring. In your body, electrical currents are generated when charged particles called *ions* move along or across cell membranes. The nervous system uses electrical currents, called *nerve impulses*, to transmit messages from one part of the body to another.

TABLE 2.1	Common Elements Composing the Human Body*		
ELEMENT	ATOMIC SYMBOL	APPROX. % BODY MASS†	FUNCTIONS
MAJOR (96.1%)			
Oxygen	O	65.0	A major component of both organic (carbon-containing) and inorganic (non-carbon-containing) molecules; as a gas, it is needed for the production of cellular energy (ATP)
Carbon	C	18.5	A primary component of all organic molecules, which include carbohydrates, lipids (fats), proteins, and nucleic acids
Hydrogen	H	9.5	A component of all organic molecules; as an ion (proton), it influences the pH of body fluids
Nitrogen	N	3.2	A component of proteins and nucleic acids (genetic material)
LESSER (3.9%)			
Calcium	Ca	1.5	Found as a salt in bones and teeth; its ionic (Ca^{2+}) form is required for muscle contraction, conduction of nerve impulses, and blood clotting
Phosphorus	P	1.0	Part of calcium phosphate salts in bones and teeth; also present in nucleic acids; part of ATP
Potassium	K	0.4	Its ion (K^+) is the major positive ion (cation) in cells; necessary for conduction of nerve impulses and muscle contraction
Sulfur	S	0.3	Component of proteins, particularly muscle proteins
Sodium	Na	0.2	As an ion (Na^+), sodium is the major positive ion found in extracellular fluids (fluids outside of cells); important for water balance, conduction of nerve impulses, and muscle contraction
Chlorine	Cl	0.2	Ionic chlorine (Cl^-) is the most abundant negative ion (anion) in extracellular fluids
Magnesium	Mg	0.1	Present in bone; also an important cofactor in a number of metabolic reactions
Iodine	I	0.1	Needed to make functional thyroid hormones
Iron	Fe	0.1	Component of hemoglobin (which transports oxygen within red blood cells) and some enzymes

TRACE (LESS THAN 0.01%)

Chromium (Cr); cobalt (Co); copper (Cu); fluorine (F); manganese (Mn); molybdenum (Mo); selenium (Se); silicon (Si); tin (Sn); vanadium (V); zinc (Zn)

These elements are referred to as *trace elements* because they are required in very minute amounts; many are found as part of enzymes or are required for enzyme activation.

*A listing of the elements by ascending order of atomic number appears in the periodic table, Appendix E.
†Percentage of "wet" body mass; includes water.

Electrical currents traveling across the heart stimulate it to contract (beat) and pump blood. (This is why a strong electrical shock, which interferes with such currents, can cause death.)

- **Mechanical energy** is energy *directly* involved in moving matter. When you ride a bicycle, your legs provide the mechanical energy that moves the pedals.

- **Radiant energy,** or **electromagnetic energy** (e-lek"tro-mag-net'ik), is energy that travels in waves. These waves, which vary in length, are col-lectively called the *electromagnetic spectrum* and include visible light, infrared waves, radio waves, ultraviolet waves, and X rays. Light energy, which stimulates the retinas of our eyes, is important in vision. Ultraviolet waves cause sunburn, but they also stimulate our body to make vitamin D.

Energy Form Conversions

With few exceptions, energy is easily converted from one form to another. For example, chemical energy (gasoline) that powers the motor of a speedboat is converted into the mechanical energy of the whirling propeller that allows the boat to skim across the water. Energy conversions are quite inefficient; some of the initial energy supply is always "lost" to the environment as heat. (It is not really lost because energy cannot be created or destroyed, but that part given off as heat is at least partly *unusable.*) It is easy to demonstrate this principle. Electrical energy is converted into light energy in a lightbulb. But if you touch a lit bulb, you will soon discover that some of the electrical energy is producing heat instead. Likewise, all energy conversions that occur in the body liberate heat. This heat contributes to our relatively high body temperature, which has an important influence on body functioning. For example, when matter is heated, the kinetic energy of its particles increases and they begin to move more quickly. The higher the temperature, the faster the body's chemical reactions occur. We will learn more about this later.

Composition of Matter: Atoms and Elements

All matter is composed of **elements,** unique substances that cannot be broken down into simpler substances by ordinary chemical methods. Among the well-known elements are oxygen, carbon, gold, silver, copper, and iron. At present, 112 elements are known with certainty (and numbers 113, 114, 115, and 116 are alleged). Of these, 92 occur in nature. The rest are made artificially in particle accelerator devices. Four elements—carbon, oxygen, hydrogen, and nitrogen—make up about 96% of body weight; 20 others are present in the body, some in trace amounts. The elements contributing to body mass and their importance are given in Table 2.1. A kind of odd-shaped checkerboard called the **periodic table** provided in Appendix E provides a more complete listing of the known elements.

Each element is composed of more or less identical particles or building blocks, called **atoms.** The smallest atoms are less than 0.1 nanometer (nm) in diameter, and the largest are only about five times as large. [1 nm = 0.0000001 (or 10^{-7}) centimeter (cm), or 40 billionths of an inch!]

Every element's atoms differ from those of all other elements and give the element its unique physical and chemical properties. *Physical properties* are those we can detect with our senses (such as color and texture) or measure (such as boiling point and freezing point). *Chemical properties* pertain to the way atoms interact with other atoms (bonding behavior) and account for the facts that iron rusts, animals can digest their food, and so on.

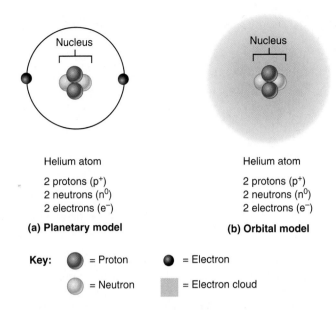

Key: = Proton = Electron = Neutron = Electron cloud

FIGURE 2.1 **The structure of an atom.** The dense central nucleus contains the protons and neutrons. **(a)** In the planetary model of atomic structure, the electrons move around the nucleus in fixed orbits. **(b)** In the orbital model, electrons are shown as a cloud of negative charge (electron cloud).

Each element is designated by a one- or two-letter chemical shorthand called an **atomic symbol,** usually the first letter(s) of the element's name. For example, C stands for carbon, O for oxygen, and Ca for calcium. In a few cases, the atomic symbol is taken from the Latin name for the element. For example, sodium is indicated by Na, from the Latin word *natrium.*

Atomic Structure

The word *atom* comes from the Greek word meaning "indivisible." However, we now know that atoms are clusters of even smaller particles called protons, neutrons, and electrons and that even those subatomic particles can be subdivided with high-technology tools. Even so, the old idea of atomic indivisibility is still helpful because an atom loses the unique properties of its element when it is split into its subatomic particles.

An atom's subatomic particles differ in mass, electrical charge, and position in the atom. An atom has a central **nucleus** containing protons and neutrons tightly bound together. The nucleus, in turn, is surrounded by orbiting electrons (Figure 2.1). **Protons** (p^+) bear a positive electrical charge, and **neutrons** (n^0) are neutral. Thus, the nucleus is positively charged overall. Protons and neutrons are heavy particles and have approximately the same

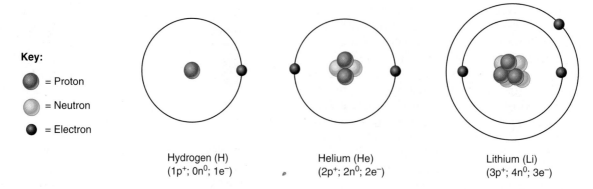

Key:

= Proton

= Neutron

= Electron

Hydrogen (H)
($1p^+$; $0n^0$; $1e^-$)

Helium (He)
($2p^+$; $2n^0$; $2e^-$)

Lithium (Li)
($3p^+$; $4n^0$; $3e^-$)

FIGURE 2.2   **Atomic structure of the three smallest atoms.**

mass, arbitrarily designated as 1 **atomic mass unit** (1 amu). Since all of the heavy subatomic particles are concentrated in the nucleus, the nucleus is fantastically dense and accounts for nearly the entire mass (99.9%) of the atom. The tiny **electrons** (e^-) bear a negative charge equal in strength to the positive charge of the proton. However, an electron has only about 1/2000 the mass of a proton, and the mass of an electron is usually designated as 0 amu.

All atoms are electrically neutral because the number of protons in an atom is precisely balanced by its number of electrons (the + and − charges will then cancel the effect of each other). Thus, hydrogen has one proton and one electron, and iron has 26 protons and 26 electrons. For any atom, the number of protons and electrons is always equal.

The **planetary model,** illustrated in Figure 2.1a, is a simplified (and now outdated) model of atomic structure. As you can see, it depicts electrons moving around the nucleus in fixed, generally circular orbits. But we can never determine the exact location of electrons at a particular time because they jump around following unknown trajectories. So, instead of speaking of specific orbits, chemists talk about **orbitals**—regions around the nucleus in which a given electron or electron pair is likely to be found most of the time. This more modern model of atomic structure, called the **orbital model,** is more useful for predicting the chemical behavior of atoms. As illustrated in Figure 2.1b, the orbital model depicts *probable* regions of greatest electron density by denser shading (this haze is called the *electron cloud*). However, because of the simplicity of the planetary model, most descriptions of atomic structure in this text will use that model.

Hydrogen, with just one proton and one electron, is the simplest atom. You can visualize the spatial relationships in the hydrogen atom by imagining it enlarged until its diameter equals the length of a football field. In that case, the nucleus could be represented by a lead ball the size of a gumdrop in the exact center of the sphere and its lone electron pictured as a fly buzzing about unpredictably within the sphere. Though not completely accurate, this mental picture should serve as a reminder that most of the volume of an atom is empty space, and nearly all of its mass is concentrated in the central nucleus.

Identifying Elements

All protons are alike, regardless of the atom considered. The same is true of all neutrons and all electrons. So what determines the unique properties of each element? The answer is that atoms of different elements are composed of *different numbers* of protons, neutrons, and electrons.

The simplest and smallest atom, hydrogen, has one proton, one electron, and no neutrons (Figure 2.2). Next in size is the helium atom, with two protons, two neutrons, and two orbiting electrons. Lithium follows with three protons, four neutrons, and three electrons. If we continued this step-by-step progression, we would get a graded series of atoms containing from 1 to 112 protons, an equal number of electrons, and a slightly larger number of neutrons at each step. However, all we really need to know to identify a particular element are its atomic number, mass number, and atomic weight. Taken together, these provide a fairly complete picture of each element.

Atomic Number

The **atomic number** of any atom is equal to the number of protons in its nucleus and is written as a subscript to the left of its atomic symbol. Hydrogen, with one proton, has an atomic number of 1 ($_1$H); helium, with two protons, has an atomic number of 2 ($_2$He); and so on. The number of protons is always equal to the number of electrons in an atom, so the atomic number *indirectly* tells us the number of electrons in the atom as well. As explained shortly,

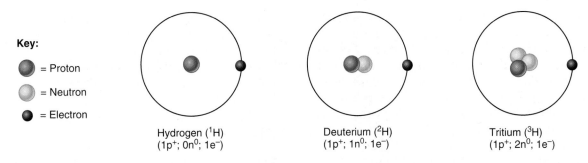

Key:

⬤ = Proton

◯ = Neutron

● = Electron

Hydrogen (^{1}H)
(1p$^+$; 0n^0; 1e$^-$)

Deuterium (^{2}H)
(1p$^+$; 1n^0; 1e$^-$)

Tritium (^{3}H)
(1p$^+$; 2n^0; 1e$^-$)

FIGURE 2.3 **Isotopes of hydrogen.**

this is important information indeed, because electrons determine the chemical behavior of atoms.

Mass Number and Isotopes

The **mass number** of an atom is the sum of the masses of its protons and neutrons. (The mass of the electrons is so small that it is ignored.) Recall that protons and neutrons have a mass of 1 amu. Hydrogen has only one proton in its nucleus, so its atomic and mass numbers are the same: 1. Helium, with two protons and two neutrons, has a mass number of 4. The mass number is usually indicated by a superscript to the left of the atomic symbol. Thus, helium is $^4_2$He. This simple notation allows us to deduce the total number and kinds of subatomic particles in any atom because it indicates the number of protons (the atomic number), the number of electrons (equal to the atomic number), and the number of neutrons (mass number minus atomic number).

From what we have said so far, it may appear as if each element has one, and only one, type of atom representing it. This is not the case. Nearly all known elements have two or more structural variations called **isotopes** (i'so-tōps), which have the same number of protons (and electrons), but differ in the number of neutrons they contain. Earlier, when we said that hydrogen has a mass number of 1, we were speaking of ^{1}H, its most abundant isotope. Some hydrogen atoms have a mass of 2 or 3 amu (atomic mass units), which means that they have one proton and, respectively, one or two neutrons (Figure 2.3). Carbon has several isotopic forms. The most abundant of these are ^{12}C, ^{13}C, and ^{14}C. Each of the carbon isotopes has six protons (otherwise it would not be carbon), but ^{12}C has six neutrons, ^{13}C has seven, and ^{14}C has eight. Isotopes are also written with the mass number following the symbol: C-14, for example.

Atomic Weight

It would seem that atomic weight should be the same as atomic mass, and this would be so if atomic weight referred to the weight of a single atom. However, **atomic weight** is an average of the relative weights (mass numbers) of *all* the isotopes of an element, taking into account their relative abundance in nature. As a rule, the atomic weight of an element is approximately equal to the mass number of its most abundant isotope. For example, the atomic weight of hydrogen is 1.008, which reveals that its lightest isotope (^{1}H) is present in much greater amounts in our world than its ^{2}H or ^{3}H forms.

Radioisotopes

The heavier isotopes of many elements are unstable, and their atoms decompose spontaneously into more stable forms. This process of atomic decay is called *radioactivity*, and isotopes that exhibit this behavior are called **radioisotopes** (ra"de-o-i'so-tōps). The disintegration of a radioactive nucleus may be compared to a tiny explosion. It occurs when subatomic *alpha* (α) *particles* (packets of 2p + 2n), *beta* (β) *particles* (electron-like negative particles), or *gamma* (γ) *rays* (electromagnetic energy) are ejected from the atomic nucleus. Why this happens is complex, and you only need to know that the dense nuclear particles are composed of even smaller particles called *quarks* that associate in one way to form protons and in another way to form neutrons. Apparently, the "glue" that holds these nuclear particles together is weaker in the heavier isotopes. When disintegration occurs, the element may transform to a different element.

Radioisotopes gradually lose their radioactive behavior. The time required for a radioisotope to lose one-half of its activity is called its *half-life*. The half-lives of radioisotopes vary dramatically from hours to thousands of years.

Because radioactivity can be detected with scanners, and radioactive isotopes share the same chemistry as their more stable isotopes, radioisotopes are valuable tools for biological research and medicine. Most radioisotopes used in the clinical setting are used for diagnosis, that is, to localize and illuminate damaged or cancerous tissues. For example, iodine-131 is used to determine the size and activity of the thyroid gland and to detect thyroid cancer. The sophisticated PET scans described in *A Closer Look* in Chapter 1 use radioisotopes to probe the workings of molecules deep within our bodies. All types of radioactivity, regardless of the purpose for which they are used, damage living tissue.

Alpha emission has the lowest penetrating power and is least damaging to living tissue. Nonetheless, inhaled alpha particles from decaying radon are second only to smoking as a cause of lung cancer. (Radon results naturally from decay of uranium in the ground.) Gamma emission has the greatest penetrating power. Radium-226, cobalt-60, and certain other radioisotopes that decay by gamma emission are used to destroy localized cancers. Contrary to what some believe, ionizing radiation does not damage organic molecules directly. Instead, it knocks electrons out of other atoms and sends them flying, like bowling balls smashing through pins all along their path. It is the electron energy and the unstable molecules left behind that do the damage.

How Matter Is Combined: Molecules and Mixtures

Molecules and Compounds

Most atoms do not exist in the free state, but instead are chemically combined with other atoms. Such a combination of two or more atoms held together by chemical bonds is called a **molecule.**

If two or more atoms of the *same* element combine, the resulting substance is called a *molecule of that element.* When two hydrogen atoms bond, the product is a molecule of hydrogen gas and is written as H_2. Similarly, when two oxygen atoms combine, a molecule of oxygen gas (O_2) is formed. Sulfur atoms commonly combine to form sulfur molecules containing eight sulfur atoms (S_8).

When two or more *different* kinds of atoms bind, they form molecules of a **compound.** Two hydrogen atoms combine with one oxygen atom to form the compound water (H_2O), and four hydrogen atoms combine with one carbon atom to form the compound methane (CH_4). Notice again that molecules of methane and water are compounds, but molecules of hydrogen gas are not, because compounds always contain atoms of at least two different elements.

Compounds are chemically pure, and all of their molecules are identical. Thus, just as an atom is the smallest particle of an element that still exhibits the properties of the element, a molecule is the smallest particle of a compound that still displays the specific characteristics of the compound. This is an important concept because the properties of compounds are usually very different from those of the atoms they contain. Indeed, it is next to impossible to tell what atoms are in a compound without analyzing it chemically.

Mixtures

Mixtures are substances composed of two or more components *physically intermixed.* Although most matter in nature exists in the form of mixtures, there are only three basic types: *solutions, colloids,* and *suspensions.*

Solutions

Solutions are *homogeneous* mixtures of components that may be gases, liquids, or solids. Examples include the air we breathe (a mixture of gases) and seawater (a mixture of salts, which are solids, and water). The substance present in the greatest amount is called the **solvent** (or dissolving medium). Solvents are usually liquids. Substances present in smaller amounts are called **solutes.**

Water is the body's chief solvent. Most solutions in the body are *true solutions* containing gases, liquids, or solids dissolved in water. True solutions are usually transparent. Examples are saline solution [table salt (NaCl) and water] and a mixture of glucose and water. The solutes of true solutions are minute, usually in the form of individual atoms and molecules. Consequently, they are not visible to the naked eye, do not settle out, and do not scatter light. If a beam of light is passed through a true solution, you will not see the path of light.

Concentration of Solutions   True solutions are described in terms of their *concentration*, which may be indicated in various ways. Solutions used in a college laboratory or a hospital are often described in terms of the **percent** (parts per 100 parts) of the solute in the total solution. This designation always refers to the solute percentage, and unless otherwise noted, water is assumed to be the solvent. Milligrams per deciliter (mg/dl) is another common concentration measurement. (A dl is 100 ml or 0.1 L.)

Still another way to express the concentration of a solution is in terms of its **molarity** (mo-lar′ĭ-te), or moles per liter, indicated by *M*. This method is more complicated but much more useful. To understand molarity, you must first understand what a mole is. A **mole** of any element or compound is equal to its atomic weight or **molecular weight** (sum of the atomic weights) weighed out in grams. This concept is easier than it seems, as illustrated by the following example.

Glucose is $C_6H_{12}O_6$, which indicates that it has 6 carbon atoms, 12 hydrogen atoms, and 6 oxygen atoms. To compute the molecular weight of glucose, you would look up the atomic weight of each of its atoms in the periodic table (see Appendix E) and compute its molecular weight as follows:

Atom	Number of Atoms		Atomic Weight		Total Atomic Weight
C	6	$\times$	12.011	=	72.066
H	12	$\times$	1.008	=	12.096
O	6	$\times$	15.999	=	95.994
					180.156

Then, to make a *one-molar* solution of glucose, you would weigh out 180.156 grams (g), called a gram molecular weight, of glucose and add enough water to make 1 liter (L) of solution. Thus, a one-molar solution (abbreviated 1.0 *M*) of a chemical substance is one gram molecular weight of the substance (or one gram atomic weight in the case of elemental substances) in 1 L (1000 ml) of solution.

The beauty of using the mole as the basis of preparing solutions is its precision. One mole of any substance always contains exactly the same number of solute particles, that is, 6.02×10^{23}. This number is called **Avogadro's number** (av"o-gad'rōz). So whether you weigh out 1 mole of glucose (180 g) or 1 mole of water (18 g) or 1 mole of methane (16 g), in each case you will have 6.02×10^{23} molecules of that substance.* This allows almost mind-boggling precision to be achieved. Because solute concentrations in body fluids tend to be quite low, those values are usually reported in terms of millimoles (m*M*; 1/1000 mole).

Colloids

Colloids (kol'oidz), also called *emulsions*, are *heterogeneous* mixtures that often appear translucent or milky. Although the solute particles are larger than those in true solutions, they still do not settle out. However, they do scatter light, and so the path of a light beam shining through a colloidal mixture is visible.

Colloids have many unique properties, including the ability of some to undergo **sol-gel transformations,** that is, to change reversibly from a fluid (sol) state to a more solid (gel) state. Jell-O, or any gelatin

product, is a familiar example of a nonliving colloid that changes from a sol to a gel when refrigerated (and that will liquefy again if placed in the sun). Cytosol, the semifluid material in living cells, is also a colloid, largely because of its dispersed proteins, and its sol-gel changes underlie many important cell activities, such as cell division.

Suspensions

Suspensions are *heterogeneous* mixtures with large, often visible solutes that tend to settle out. An example of a suspension is a mixture of sand and water. So is blood, in which the living blood cells are suspended in the fluid portion of blood (blood plasma). If left to stand, the suspended cells will settle out unless some means—mixing, shaking, or circulation in the body—is used to keep them in suspension.

As you can see, all three types of mixtures are found in both living and nonliving systems. In fact, living material is the most complex mixture of all, since it contains all three kinds of mixtures interacting with one another.

Distinguishing Mixtures from Compounds

Now we are ready to zero in on how to distinguish mixtures and compounds from one another. Mixtures differ from compounds in several important ways:

1. The chief difference between mixtures and compounds is that no chemical bonding occurs between the components of a mixture. The properties of atoms and molecules are not changed when they become part of a mixture. Remember they are only physically intermixed.

2. Depending on the mixture, its components can be separated by physical means—straining, filtering, evaporation, and so on. Compounds, by contrast, can be separated into their constituent atoms only by chemical means (breaking bonds).

3. Some mixtures are homogeneous, whereas others are heterogeneous. To say that a substance is *homogeneous* means that a sample taken from any part of the substance has exactly the same composition (in terms of the atoms or molecules it contains) as any other sample. A bar of 100% pure (elemental) iron is homogeneous, as are all compounds. *Heterogeneous* substances vary in their makeup from place to place. For example, iron ore is a heterogeneous mixture that contains iron and many other elements.

Chemical Bonds

As noted earlier, when atoms combine with other atoms, they are held together by **chemical bonds.** A chemical bond is not a physical structure like a pair

---

* The important exception to this rule concerns molecules that ionize and break up into charged particles (ions) in water, such as salts, acids, and bases (see p. 41). For example, simple table salt (sodium chloride) breaks up into two types of charged particles; therefore, in a 1.0-*M* solution of sodium chloride, there are actually *2 moles* of solute particles in solution.

of handcuffs linking two people together. Instead, it is an energy relationship between the electrons of the reacting atoms, and it is made or broken in less than a trillionth of a second.

The Role of Electrons in Chemical Bonding

Electrons forming the electron cloud around the nucleus of an atom occupy regions of space called **electron shells** that consecutively surround the atomic nucleus. The atoms known so far can have electrons in seven shells (numbered 1 to 7 from the nucleus outward), but the actual number of electron shells occupied in a given atom depends on the number of electrons that atom has. Each electron shell contains one or more orbitals.

It is important to understand that each electron shell represents a different **energy level**, because this prompts you to think of electrons as particles with a certain amount of potential energy. In general, the terms *electron shell* and *energy level* are used interchangeably.

The amount of potential energy an electron has depends on the energy level it occupies, because the attraction between the positively charged nucleus and negatively charged electrons is greatest closest to the nucleus and falls off with increasing distance. This statement explains why electrons farthest from the nucleus (1) have the greatest potential energy (it takes more energy to overcome the nuclear attraction and reach the more distant energy levels), and (2) are most likely to interact chemically with other atoms (they are the least tightly held by their own atomic nucleus and the most easily influenced by other atoms and molecules).

Each electron shell can hold a specific number of electrons. Shell 1, the shell immediately surrounding the nucleus, accommodates only 2 electrons. Shell 2 holds a maximum of 8; shell 3 has room for 18. Subsequent shells hold larger and larger numbers of electrons, and the shells tend to be filled with electrons consecutively. For example, shell 1 is completely filled before any electrons appear in shell 2.

When considering bonding behavior, the only electrons that are important are those in the atom's outermost energy level. Inner electrons usually do not take part in bonding because they are more tightly held by the atomic nucleus. When the outermost energy level of an atom is filled to capacity or contains eight electrons, the atom is stable. Such atoms are *chemically inert*, that is, unreactive. A group of elements called the *noble gases*, which include helium and neon, typify this condition (Figure 2.4a). On the other hand, atoms in which the outer-

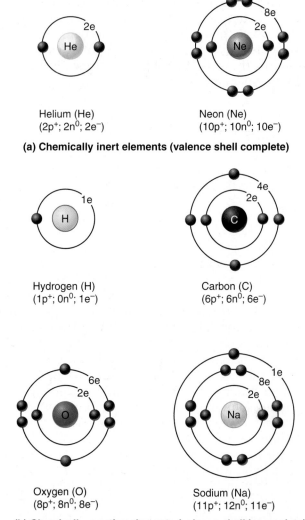

Helium (He)
(2p$^+$; 2n^0; 2e$^-$)

Neon (Ne)
(10p$^+$; 10n^0; 10e$^-$)

(a) Chemically inert elements (valence shell complete)

Hydrogen (H)
(1p$^+$; 0n^0; 1e$^-$)

Carbon (C)
(6p$^+$; 6n^0; 6e$^-$)

Oxygen (O)
(8p$^+$; 8n^0; 8e$^-$)

Sodium (Na)
(11p$^+$; 12n^0; 11e$^-$)

(b) Chemically reactive elements (valence shell incomplete)

FIGURE 2.4   **Chemically inert and reactive elements.** **(a)** Helium and neon are chemically inert because in each case the outermost energy level (valence shell) is fully occupied by electrons. **(b)** Elements in which the valence shell is incomplete are chemically reactive. Such atoms tend to react with other atoms to gain, lose, or share electrons to fill their valence shells. (*Note:* For simplicity, each atomic nucleus is shown as a sphere with the atom's symbol; individual protons and neutrons are not shown.)

most energy level contains fewer than eight electrons (Figure 2.4b) tend to gain, lose, or share electrons with other atoms to achieve stability.

A possible point of confusion must be addressed here. In atoms that have more than 20 electrons, the energy levels beyond shell 2 can contain *more* than eight electrons. However, the number of electrons that can participate in bonding is still limited to a total of eight. The term **valence shell** (va'lens) is used specifically to indicate an atom's outermost energy level *or that portion of it* containing

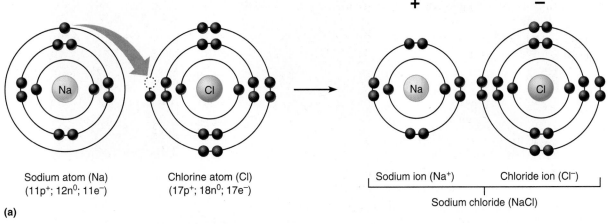

Sodium atom (Na)
(11p$^+$; 12n^0; 11e$^-$)

Chlorine atom (Cl)
(17p$^+$; 18n^0; 17e$^-$)

(a)

Sodium ion (Na$^+$)

Chloride ion (Cl$^-$)

Sodium chloride (NaCl)

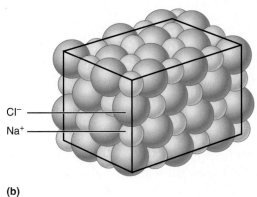

Cl$^-$

Na$^+$

(b)

FIGURE 2.5 **Formation of an ionic bond. (a)** Both sodium and chlorine atoms are chemically reactive because their valence shells are incompletely filled. Sodium gains stability by losing one electron, whereas chlorine becomes stable by gaining one electron. After electron transfer, sodium becomes a sodium ion (Na$^+$), and chlorine becomes a chloride ion (Cl$^-$). The oppositely charged ions attract each other. **(b)** Large numbers of Na$^+$ and Cl$^-$ ions associate to form salt (NaCl) crystals.

the electrons that are chemically reactive. Hence, the key to chemical reactivity is the **octet rule** (ok-tet′), or **rule of eights.** Except for shell 1, which is full when it has two electrons, atoms tend to interact in such a way that they have eight electrons in their valence shell.

Types of Chemical Bonds

Three major types of chemical bonds—*ionic, covalent,* and *hydrogen bonds*—result from attractive forces between atoms.

Ionic Bonds

Atoms are electrically neutral. However, electrons can be transferred from one atom to another, and when this happens, the precise balance of + and − charges is lost so that charged particles called **ions** are formed. An **ionic bond** (i-on′ik) is a chemical bond between atoms formed by the transfer of one or more electrons from one atom to the other. The atom that gains one or more electrons, the *electron acceptor,* acquires a net negative charge and is called an **anion** (an′i-on). The atom that loses electrons (the *electron donor*) acquires a net positive charge and is called a **cation** (kat′i-on). (It might help to think of the "t" in "cation" as a + sign.) Both anions

and cations are formed whenever electron transfer between atoms occurs. Because opposite charges attract, these ions tend to stay close together, resulting in an ionic bond.

One example of ionic bonding is the formation of sodium chloride (NaCl), by interaction of sodium and chlorine atoms (Figure 2.5). Sodium, with an atomic number of 11, has only one valence shell electron, and it would be very difficult to attempt to fill this shell by adding seven more. However, if this single electron is lost, shell 2 with eight electrons becomes the valence shell (outermost energy level containing electrons) and is full. Thus, by losing the lone electron in its third energy level, sodium achieves stability and becomes a cation (Na$^+$). On the other hand, chlorine, atomic number 17, needs only one electron to fill its valence shell. By accepting an electron, chlorine becomes an anion and achieves stability. When these two atoms interact, this is exactly what happens. Sodium donates an electron to chlorine, and the ions created in this exchange attract each other, forming sodium chloride. Ionic bonds are commonly formed between atoms with one or two valence shell electrons (the metallic elements, such as sodium, calcium, and potassium) and atoms with seven valence shell electrons (such as chlorine, fluorine, and iodine).

Sodium   Chlorine   Sodium chloride

FIGURE 2.6   **Properties of a compound differ from those of its atoms.** In this example, the metal sodium combines with the poisonous gas chlorine to form the edible compound sodium chloride, or table salt.

Most ionic compounds fall in the chemical category called *salts.* In the dry state, salts such as sodium chloride do not exist as individual molecules. Instead, they form **crystals,** large arrays of cations and anions held together by ionic bonds (see Figure 2.5b).

Sodium chloride is an excellent example of the difference in properties between a compound and its constituent atoms (Figure 2.6). Sodium is a silvery white metal, and chlorine in its molecular state is a poisonous green gas used to make bleach. However, sodium chloride is a white crystalline solid that we sprinkle on our food.

Covalent Bonds

Electrons do not have to be completely transferred for atoms to achieve stability. Instead, they may be *shared* so that each atom is able to fill its outer electron shell at least part of the time. Electron sharing produces molecules in which the shared electrons occupy a single orbital common to both atoms and constitute **covalent bonds** (ko-va'lent).

Hydrogen with its single electron can fill its only shell (shell 1) by sharing a pair of electrons with another atom. When it shares with another hydrogen atom, a molecule of hydrogen gas is formed. The shared electron pair orbits around the molecule as a whole, satisfying the stability needs of each atom. Hydrogen can also share an electron pair with different kinds of atoms to form a compound (Figure 2.7a). Carbon has four electrons in its outermost shell, but needs eight to achieve stability, whereas hydrogen has one electron, but needs two. When a methane molecule (CH_4) is formed, carbon shares four pairs of electrons with four hydrogen atoms (one pair with each hydrogen). Again, the shared electrons orbit and "belong to" the whole molecule, ensuring the stability of each atom. When two atoms share one pair of electrons, a *single covalent bond* is formed (indicated by a single line connecting the atoms, such as H—H). In some cases, atoms share two or three electron pairs (Figure 2.7b and c), resulting in *double* or *triple covalent bonds* (indicated by double or triple connecting lines such as $O=O$ or $N\equiv N$).

Polar and Nonpolar Molecules   In the covalent bonds discussed thus far, the shared electrons are shared equally between the atoms of the molecule for the most part. The molecules formed are electrically balanced and are called **nonpolar molecules** (because they do not have separate + and − poles of charge). This is not always the case. When covalent bonds are formed, the resulting molecule always has a specific three-dimensional shape, with the bonds formed at definite angles. A molecule's shape helps determine what other molecules or atoms it can interact with; it may also result in unequal electron pair sharing and **polar molecules.** This is especially true in nonsymmetrical molecules that have atoms with different electron-attracting abilities. In general, *small* atoms with six or seven valence shell electrons, such as oxygen, nitrogen, and chlorine, are electron-hungry and attract electrons very strongly, a capability called **electronegativity.** Conversely, most atoms with only one or two valence shell electrons tend to be **electropositive;** that is, their electron-attracting ability is so low that they usually lose *their* valence shell electrons to other atoms. Potassium and sodium, each with one valence shell electron, are good examples of electropositive atoms.

Carbon dioxide and water illustrate how molecular shape and the relative electron-attracting abilities of atoms determine whether a covalently bonded molecule is nonpolar or polar. In carbon dioxide (CO_2), carbon shares four electron pairs with two oxygen atoms (two pairs are shared with each oxygen). Oxygen is very electronegative and so attracts the shared electrons much more strongly than does

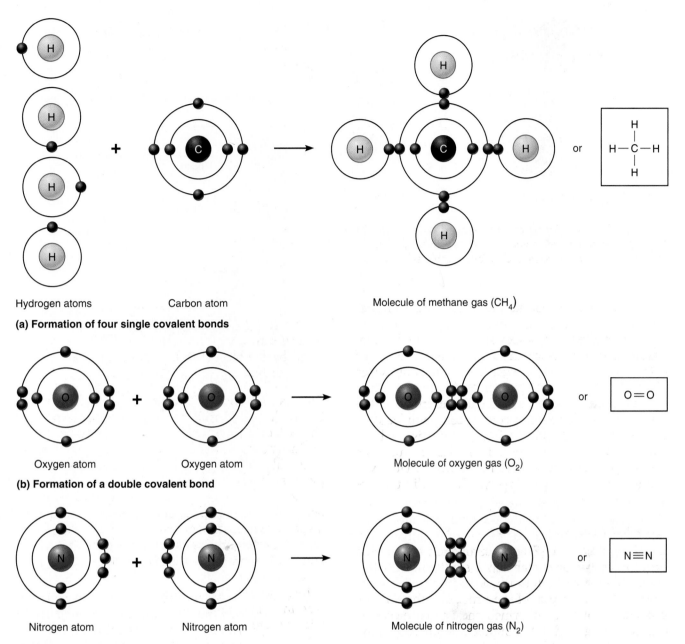

Hydrogen atoms   Carbon atom   Molecule of methane gas (CH$_4$)

(a) Formation of four single covalent bonds

Oxygen atom   Oxygen atom   Molecule of oxygen gas (O$_2$)

(b) Formation of a double covalent bond

Nitrogen atom   Nitrogen atom   Molecule of nitrogen gas (N$_2$)

(c) Formation of a triple covalent bond

FIGURE 2.7   Formation of covalent bonds. Left, the electron-sharing patterns of interacting atoms; center, the resulting molecules; right, the structural formula shows each covalent bond as a single line between the atoms that share an electron pair.

carbon. However, because the carbon dioxide molecule is linear and symmetrical (Figure 2.8a), the electron-pulling ability of one oxygen atom is offset by that of the other, like a standoff between equally strong teams in a game of tug-of-war. As a result, the shared electrons orbit the entire molecule and carbon dioxide is a nonpolar compound.

In contrast, a water molecule (H$_2$O) is V shaped (Figure 2.8b). The two hydrogen atoms are located at the same end of the molecule, and oxygen is at the opposite end. This arrangement allows oxygen to pull the shared electrons toward itself and away from

the two hydrogen atoms. In this case, the electron pairs are *not* shared equally, but spend more time in the vicinity of oxygen. Because electrons are negatively charged, the oxygen end of the molecule is slightly more negative (the charge is indicated with a delta and minus as δ^-) and the hydrogen end slightly more positive (indicated by δ^+). Because water has two poles of charge, it is a *polar molecule*, or **dipole** (di′pōl). Polar molecules orient themselves toward other dipoles or toward charged particles (such as ions and some proteins), and they play essential roles in chemical reactions in body cells. The polarity

(a) Carbon dioxide (CO$_2$)

$$O=C=O$$

(b) Water (H$_2$O)

FIGURE 2.8 **Molecular models of carbon dioxide and water molecules.**

of water is particularly significant, as you will see later in this chapter.

Different molecules exhibit different degrees of polarity, and we can see a gradual change from ionic to nonpolar covalent bonding as summarized in Figure 2.9. Ionic bonds (complete electron transfer) and nonpolar covalent bonds (equal electron sharing) are the extremes of a continuum, with various degrees of unequal electron sharing in between.

Hydrogen Bonds

Unlike the stronger ionic and covalent bonds, hydrogen bonds are more like attractions than true bonds. Hydrogen bonds form when a hydrogen atom, already covalently linked to one electronegative atom (usually nitrogen or oxygen), is attracted by another electron-hungry atom, so that a "bridge" forms between them. Hydrogen bonding is common between dipoles such as water molecules, because the slightly negative oxygen atoms of one molecule attract the slightly positive hydrogen atoms of other molecules (Figure 2.10). The tendency of water molecules to cling together and form films, referred to as *surface tension*, helps explain why water beads up into spheres when it sits on a hard surface and why water striders can walk on a pond's surface.

Although hydrogen bonds are too weak to bind atoms together to form molecules, they are important as *intramolecular bonds*, which bind different parts of a single large molecule together into a specific three-dimensional shape. Some large biological molecules, such as proteins and DNA, have numerous hydrogen bonds that help maintain and stabilize their structures.

Chemical Reactions

As noted earlier, all particles of matter are in constant motion because of their kinetic energy. Movement of atoms or molecules in a solid is usually lim-

Q *Assume imaginary compound XY has a polar covalent bond. How does its charge distribution differ from that of XX molecules?*

Ionic bond	Polar covalent bond	Nonpolar covalent bond
Complete transfer of electrons	Unequal sharing of electrons	Equal sharing of electrons
Separate ions (charged particles) form	Slight negative charge (δ^-) at one end of molecule, slight positive charge (δ^+) at other end	Charge balanced among atoms
Na$^+$ Cl$^-$		$O=C=O$
Sodium chloride	Water	Carbon dioxide

FIGURE 2.9 **Comparison of ionic, polar covalent, and nonpolar covalent bonds.** This display compares the status of electrons involved in bonding and the electrical charge distribution in the molecules formed.

ited to vibration because the particles are united by fairly rigid bonds. But in liquids or gases, particles dart about randomly, sometimes colliding with one another and interacting to undergo chemical reactions. A **chemical reaction** occurs whenever chemical bonds are formed, rearranged, or broken.

Chemical Equations

Chemical reactions can be written in symbolic form as **chemical equations.** For example, joining two hydrogen atoms to form hydrogen gas is indicated as

$$H + H \rightarrow H_2 \text{ (hydrogen gas)}$$
(reactants)   (product)

A *Because X and Y are different atoms, one is bound to be more electronegative than the other. Consequently, there will be a separation of charge in XY, which is a dipole. In XX, the two atoms are the same and there will be equal e⁻ sharing; no dipole is formed.*

Hydrogen bonds

(a)

(b)

FIGURE 2.10 **Hydrogen bonding between polar water molecules. (a)** The slightly positive ends (indicated by δ^+) of the water molecules become aligned with the slightly negative ends (indicated by δ^-) of other water molecules. **(b)** The high surface tension of water, a result of the combined strength of its hydrogen bonds, allows a water strider to walk on a pond without breaking its surface.

and combining four hydrogen atoms and one carbon atom to form methane is written

$$4H + C \rightarrow CH_4 \text{ (methane)}$$

Notice that a number written as a *subscript* indicates that the atoms are joined by chemical bonds. But a number written as a *prefix* denotes the number of *unjoined* atoms or molecules. Hence, CH_4 reveals

that four hydrogen atoms are bonded together with carbon to form the methane molecule, but 4H signifies four unjoined hydrogen atoms.

A chemical equation is like a sentence describing what happens in a reaction. It contains the following information: the number and kinds of reacting substances, or **reactants;** the chemical composition of the **product(s);** and in balanced equations, the relative proportion of each reactant and product. In the examples used above, the reactants are atoms, as indicated by their atomic symbols (H, C). The product in each case is a molecule, as represented by its **molecular formula** (H_2, CH_4). The equation for the formation of methane may be read as *either* "four hydrogen atoms plus one carbon atom yield one molecule of methane" *or* "four moles of hydrogen atoms plus one mole of carbon yield one mole of methane." Using moles is more practical because it is impossible to measure out one atom or one molecule of anything!

Patterns of Chemical Reactions

Most chemical reactions exhibit one of three recognizable patterns: they are either *synthesis, decomposition,* or *exchange reactions.*

When atoms or molecules combine to form a larger, more complex molecule, the process is a **synthesis,** or **combination, reaction.** A synthesis reaction, which always involves bond formation, can be represented (using arbitrary letters) as

$$A + B \rightarrow AB$$

Synthesis reactions are the basis of constructive, or **anabolic,** activities in body cells, such as joining small molecules called amino acids into large protein molecules (Figure 2.11a). Synthesis reactions are conspicuous in rapidly growing tissues.

A **decomposition reaction** occurs when a molecule is broken down into smaller molecules or its constituent atoms:

$$AB \rightarrow A + B$$

Essentially, decomposition reactions are reverse synthesis reactions; bonds are broken. Decomposition reactions underlie all degradative, or **catabolic,** processes that occur in body cells. For example, the bonds of glycogen molecules are broken to release simpler molecules of glucose sugar (Figure 2.11b).

Exchange, or **displacement, reactions** involve both synthesis and decomposition; bonds are both made and broken. In an exchange reaction, parts of the reactant molecules change partners, so to speak, producing different product molecules:

$$AB + C \rightarrow AC + B \quad \text{and} \quad AB + CD \rightarrow AD + CB$$

Q *Which of the reaction types depicted occurs when fats are digested in your small intestine?*

Amino acids   Protein molecule

(a) Example of a synthesis reaction: amino acids are joined to form a protein molecule

Glycogen   Glucose molecules

(b) Example of a decomposition reaction: breakdown of glycogen to release glucose units

Glucose   Adenosine triphosphate (ATP)

Glucose   Adenosine diphosphate (ADP)
phosphate

(c) Example of an exchange reaction: ATP transfers its terminal phosphate group to glucose to form glucose-phosphate

FIGURE 2.11   **Patterns of chemical reactions. (a)** In synthesis reactions, smaller particles are bonded together to form larger, more complex molecules. **(b)** Decomposition reactions involve bond breaking. **(c)** In exchange, or displacement, reactions, bonds are both made and broken.

An exchange reaction occurs when ATP reacts with glucose and transfers its end phosphate group (indicated by a circled P in Figure 2.11c) to glucose, forming glucose-phosphate. At the same time, the ATP becomes ADP. This important reaction occurs whenever glucose enters a body cell and it effectively traps the glucose fuel molecule inside the cell.

Another group of important chemical reactions in living systems is **oxidation-reduction reactions—**

A *Digestion of fats (triglycerides) to their fatty acid and glycerol building blocks is an example of (b) a decomposition reaction.*

redox reactions for short. Oxidation-reduction reactions are decomposition reactions in that they are the basis of all reactions in which food fuels are catabolized for energy (that is, in which ATP is produced). They are also a special type of exchange reaction because electrons are exchanged between the reactants. The reactant losing the electrons is referred to as the *electron donor* and is said to be **oxidized;** the reactant taking up the transferred electrons is called the *electron acceptor* and is said to become **reduced.**

Redox reactions also occur when ionic compounds are formed. Recall that in the formation of NaCl (see Figure 2.5), sodium loses an electron to chlorine. Consequently, sodium is oxidized and becomes a sodium ion, and chlorine is reduced and becomes a chloride ion. However, not all oxidation-reduction reactions involve *complete transfer* of electrons—some simply change the pattern of electron sharing in covalent bonds. For example, a substance is oxidized both by losing hydrogen atoms and by combining with oxygen. The common factor in these events is that electrons that formerly "belonged" to the reactant molecule are lost, either entirely (as hydrogen is removed and takes its electron with it) or relatively (the shared electrons spend more time in the vicinity of the very electronegative oxygen atom).

To understand the importance of oxidation-reduction reactions in living systems, take a look at the overall equation for *cellular respiration,* which represents the major pathway by which glucose is broken down for energy in body cells:

$$C_6H_{12}O_6 + 6O_2 \rightarrow 6CO_2 + 6H_2O + ATP$$

glucose   oxygen   carbon   water   cellular
dioxide   energy

As you can see, it is an oxidation-reduction reaction. Glucose is oxidized to carbon dioxide as it loses hydrogen atoms, and oxygen is reduced to water as it accepts the hydrogen atoms. This reaction is described in detail in Chapter 24, along with other topics of cellular metabolism.

Energy Flow in Chemical Reactions

Because all chemical bonds represent stored chemical energy, all chemical reactions ultimately result in net absorption or release of energy. Reactions that release energy are called **exergonic reactions.** These reactions yield products with less energy than the initial reactants, along with energy that can be harvested for other uses. With a few exceptions, catabolic and oxidative reactions are exergonic.

In contrast, the products of energy-absorbing, or **endergonic,** reactions contain more potential energy in their chemical bonds than did the reactants. Anabolic reactions are typically energy-absorbing endergonic reactions. Essentially this is a case of "one hand washing the other"—the energy released when fuel molecules are broken down (oxidized) is captured in ATP molecules and then used to synthesize the complex biological molecules the body needs to sustain life.

Reversibility of Chemical Reactions

All chemical reactions are theoretically reversible. If chemical bonds can be made, they can be broken, and vice versa. Reversibility is indicated by a double arrow. When the arrows differ in length, the longer arrow indicates the major direction in which the reaction proceeds:

$$A + B \rightleftharpoons AB$$

In this example, the forward reaction (reaction going to the right) predominates. Over time, the product (AB) accumulates and the reactants (A and B) decrease in amount.

When the arrows are of equal length, as in

$$A + B \rightleftharpoons AB$$

neither the forward reaction nor the reverse reaction is dominant; that is, for each molecule of product (AB) formed, one product molecule breaks down, releasing the reactants A and B. Such a chemical reaction is said to be in a state of **chemical equilibrium.** Once chemical equilibrium is reached, there is no further *net change* in the amounts of reactants and products unless more of either are added to the mix. Product molecules are still formed and broken down, but the situation established when equilibrium was reached (such as greater numbers of product molecules) remains unchanged. This is analogous to the admission scheme used by many large museums in which tickets are sold according to time of entry. If 300 tickets are issued for the 9 AM admission, 300 people will be admitted when the doors open. Thereafter, when 6 people leave, 6 are admitted, and when another 15 people leave, 15 more are allowed in. Although there is a continual turnover, the museum contains about 300 art lovers throughout the day.

Although all chemical reactions are reversible, many biological reactions show so little tendency to go in the reverse direction that they are irreversible for all practical purposes. Chemical reactions that release energy when going in one direction will not go in the opposite direction unless energy is put back into the system. For example, when our cells break down glucose via the reactions of cellular respiration to yield carbon dioxide and water, some of the energy released is trapped in the bonds of ATP. Because the cells need ATP's energy for various functions (and more glucose will be along with the next meal), this particular reaction is never reversed in our cells. Furthermore, if a product of a reaction is continuously removed from the reaction site, it is unavailable to take part in the reverse reaction. This situation occurs when the carbon dioxide that is released during glucose breakdown leaves the cell, enters the blood, and is eventually removed from the body by the lungs.

Factors Influencing the Rate of Chemical Reactions

For atoms and molecules to react chemically, they must *collide* with enough force to overcome the repulsion between their electrons. Interactions between valence shell electrons—the basis of bond making and breaking—cannot occur long distance. The force of collisions depends on how fast the particles are moving. Solid, forceful collisions between rapidly moving particles in which valence shells overlap are much more likely to cause reactions than are those in which the particles graze each other lightly.

Temperature Increasing the temperature of a substance increases the kinetic energy of its particles and the force of their collisions. Therefore, chemical reactions proceed quicker at higher temperatures.

Concentration Chemical reactions progress most rapidly when the reacting particles are present in high numbers, because the chance of successful collisions is greater. As the concentration of the reactants declines, chemical equilibrium eventually occurs unless additional reactants are added or products are removed from the reaction site.

Particle Size Smaller particles move faster than larger ones (at the same temperature) and tend to collide more frequently and more forcefully. Hence, the smaller the reacting particles, the faster a chemical reaction goes at a given temperature and concentration.

Catalysts Although many chemical reactions in nonliving systems can be speeded up simply by heating, drastic increases in body temperature are life threatening because important biological molecules are destroyed. Still, at normal body temperatures, most chemical reactions would proceed far too slowly to maintain life were it not for the presence of catalysts. **Catalysts** (kat′ah-lists) are substances that increase the rate of chemical reactions without themselves becoming chemically changed or part of the product. Biological catalysts are called *enzymes* (en′zīmz). The mode of action of enzymes is described later in this chapter.

PART 2: BIOCHEMISTRY

Biochemistry is the study of the chemical composition and reactions of living matter. All chemicals in the body fall into one of two major classes: organic or inorganic compounds. **Organic compounds** contain carbon. All organic compounds are covalently bonded molecules, and many are large.

All other chemicals in the body are considered **inorganic compounds.** These include water, salts, and many acids and bases. Organic and inorganic compounds are equally essential for life. Trying to decide which is more valuable is like trying to decide whether the ignition system or the engine is more essential to run your car!

Inorganic Compounds

Water

Water is the most abundant and important inorganic compound in living material. It makes up 60–80% of the volume of most living cells. Among the properties that make water vital are its

1. High heat capacity. Water has a high heat capacity; that is, it absorbs and releases large amounts of heat before changing appreciably in temperature itself. This prevents sudden changes in temperature caused by external factors, such as sun or wind exposure, or by internal conditions that release heat rapidly, such as vigorous muscle activity. As part of blood, water redistributes heat among body tissues, ensuring temperature homeostasis.

2. High heat of vaporization. When water evaporates, or vaporizes, it changes from a liquid to a gas (water vapor). This transformation requires that large amounts of heat be absorbed to break the hydrogen bonds that hold water molecules together. This property is extremely beneficial when we sweat. As perspiration (mostly water) evaporates from our skin, large amounts of heat are removed from the body, providing an efficient cooling mechanism.

3. Polar solvent properties. Water is an unparalleled solvent; indeed, it is often called the **universal solvent.** Biochemistry is "wet chemistry." Biological molecules do not react chemically unless they are in solution, and virtually all chemical reactions occurring in the body depend on water's solvent properties.

Because of their polar nature, water molecules orient themselves with their slightly negative ends toward the positive ends of the solutes, and vice

FIGURE 2.12 **Dissociation of a salt in water.** The slightly negative ends of the water molecules (δ^-) are attracted to Na^+, whereas the slightly positive ends of water molecules (δ^+) orient toward Cl^-, causing the ions to be pulled off the crystal lattice.

versa, first attracting them, then surrounding them. This property of water explains why ionic compounds and other small reactive molecules (such as acids and bases) *dissociate* in water, their ions separating from each other and becoming evenly scattered in the water, forming true solutions (Figure 2.12). Water also forms **hydration layers** (layers of water molecules) around large charged molecules such as proteins, shielding them from the effects of other charged substances in the vicinity and preventing them from settling out of solution. Such protein-water mixtures are *biological colloids*. Cerebrospinal fluid and blood are examples of colloids.

Water is the body's major transport medium because it is such an excellent solvent. Nutrients, respiratory gases, and metabolic wastes carried throughout the body are dissolved in blood plasma, and many metabolic wastes are excreted from the body in urine, another watery fluid. Specialized molecules that lubricate the body (e.g., mucus) also use water as their dissolving medium.

4. Reactivity. Water is an important *reactant* in many chemical reactions. For example, foods are digested to their building blocks by adding a water molecule to each bond to be broken. Such decomposition reactions are more specifically called **hydrolysis reactions** (hi-drol'ĭ-sis; "water splitting"). Conversely, when large carbohydrate or protein molecules are synthesized from smaller molecules, a water molecule is removed for every bond formed, a reaction called **dehydration synthesis.**

5. Cushioning. By forming a resilient cushion around certain body organs, water helps protect them from physical trauma. The cerebrospinal fluid surrounding the brain exemplifies water's cushioning role.

Salts

A **salt** is an ionic compound containing cations other than H^+ and anions other than the hydroxyl ion (OH^-). As already noted, when salts are dissolved in water, they dissociate into their component ions (Figure 2.12). For example, sodium sulfate (Na_2SO_4) dissociates into two Na^+ ions and one SO_4^{2-} ion. This occurs easily because the ions are already formed. All that remains is for water to overcome the attraction between the oppositely charged ions. All ions are **electrolytes** (e-lek'tro-līts), substances that conduct an electrical current in solution. (Note that groups of atoms that bear an overall charge, such as sulfate, are called *polyatomic ions.*)

Salts commonly found in the body include NaCl, $CaCO_3$ (calcium carbonate), and KCl (potassium chloride). However, the most plentiful salts are the calcium phosphates that make bones and teeth hard. In their ionized form, salts play vital roles in body function. For instance, the electrolyte properties of sodium and potassium ions are essential for nerve impulse transmission and muscle contraction. Ionic iron forms part of the hemoglobin molecules that transport oxygen within red blood cells, and zinc and copper ions are important to the activity of some enzymes. Other important functions of the elements found in body salts are summarized in Table 2.1.

▲ HOMEOSTATIC IMBALANCE

Maintaining proper ionic balance in our body fluids is one of the most crucial homeostatic roles of the kidneys. When this balance is severely disturbed, virtually nothing in the body works. All the physiological activities listed above and thousands of others are disrupted and grind to a stop. ●

Acids and Bases

Like salts, acids and bases are electrolytes; that is, they ionize and dissociate in water and can then conduct an electrical current.

Acids

Acids have a sour taste, can react with (dissolve) many metals, and "burn" a hole in your rug. But for our purposes the most useful definition of an acid is a substance that releases **hydrogen ions** (H^+) in detectable amounts. Because a hydrogen ion is just a hydrogen nucleus, or "naked" proton, acids are also defined as **proton donors.**

When acids dissolve in water, they release hydrogen ions (protons) and anions. It is the concentration of protons that determines the acidity of a solution. The anions have little or no effect on acidity. For example, hydrochloric acid (HCl), an acid produced by stomach cells that aids digestion, dissociates into a proton and a chloride ion:

$$HCl \rightarrow \underset{\text{proton}}{H^+} + \underset{\text{anion}}{Cl^-}$$

Other acids found or produced in the body include acetic acid $(HC_2H_3O_2$, commonly abbreviated as HAc), which is the acidic portion of vinegar; and carbonic acid (H_2CO_3). The molecular formula for an acid is easy to recognize because the hydrogen is written first.

Bases

Bases have a bitter taste, feel slippery, and are **proton acceptors**—that is, they take up hydrogen ions (H^+) in detectable amounts. Common inorganic bases include the *hydroxides* (hi-drok'sīds), such as magnesium hydroxide (milk of magnesia) and sodium hydroxide (lye). Like acids, hydroxides dissociate when dissolved in water, but in this case **hydroxyl ions (OH^-)** (hi-drok'sil) and cations are liberated. For example, ionization of sodium hydroxide (NaOH) produces a hydroxyl ion and a sodium ion; the hydroxyl ion then binds to (accepts) a proton present in the solution. This produces water and simultaneously reduces the acidity (hydrogen ion concentration) of the solution:

$$NaOH \rightarrow \underset{\text{cation}}{Na^+} + \underset{\substack{\text{hydroxyl} \\ \text{ion}}}{OH^-}$$

and then

$$OH^- + H^+ \rightarrow \underset{\text{water}}{H_2O}$$

Bicarbonate ion (HCO_3^-), an important base in the body, is particularly abundant in blood. **Ammonia (NH_3),** a common waste product of protein breakdown in the body, is also a base. It has one pair of unshared electrons that strongly attracts

Q *Which ion is responsible for increasing acidity?*

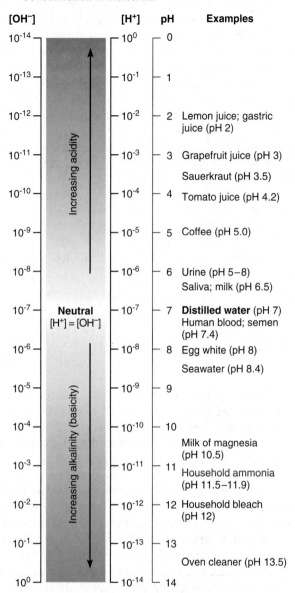

Concentration in moles/liter

[OH⁻]	[H⁺]	pH	Examples
10^{-14}	10^{0}	0	
10^{-13}	10^{-1}	1	
10^{-12}	10^{-2}	2	Lemon juice; gastric juice (pH 2)
10^{-11}	10^{-3}	3	Grapefruit juice (pH 3)
			Sauerkraut (pH 3.5)
10^{-10}	10^{-4}	4	Tomato juice (pH 4.2)
10^{-9}	10^{-5}	5	Coffee (pH 5.0)
10^{-8}	10^{-6}	6	Urine (pH 5–8) Saliva; milk (pH 6.5)
10^{-7}	10^{-7}	7	**Distilled water** (pH 7) Human blood; semen (pH 7.4)
10^{-6}	10^{-8}	8	Egg white (pH 8) Seawater (pH 8.4)
10^{-5}	10^{-9}	9	
10^{-4}	10^{-10}	10	
10^{-3}	10^{-11}	11	Milk of magnesia (pH 10.5) Household ammonia (pH 11.5–11.9)
10^{-2}	10^{-12}	12	Household bleach (pH 12)
10^{-1}	10^{-13}	13	Oven cleaner (pH 13.5)
10^{0}	10^{-14}	14	

Increasing acidity

Neutral [H⁺] = [OH⁻]

Increasing alkalinity (basicity)

FIGURE 2.13 The pH scale and pH values of representative substances. The pH scale is based on the number of hydrogen ions in solution. The actual concentration of hydrogen ions, [H⁺], and hydroxyl ions, [OH⁻], in moles per liter are indicated for each pH value noted. At a pH of 7, the concentrations of hydrogen and hydroxyl ions are equal and the solution is neutral.

protons. By accepting a proton, ammonia becomes an ammonium ion:

$$NH_3 + H^+ \rightarrow NH_4^+$$

ammonium
ion

A *Hydrogen ion.*

pH: Acid-Base Concentration

The more hydrogen ions in a solution, the more acidic the solution is. Conversely, the greater the concentration of hydroxyl ions (the lower the concentration of H⁺), the more basic, or *alkaline* (al'kuh-līn), the solution becomes. The relative concentration of hydrogen ions in various body fluids is measured in concentration units called **pH units** (pe-āch').

The idea for a pH scale was devised by a Danish biochemist and part-time beer brewer named Sören Sörensen in 1909. He was searching for a convenient means of checking the acidity of his alcoholic product to prevent its spoilage by bacterial action. (Many bacteria are inhibited by acidic conditions.) The pH scale that resulted is based on the concentration of hydrogen ions in a solution, expressed in terms of moles per liter, or molarity. The pH scale runs from 0 to 14 and is logarithmic; that is, each successive change of one pH unit represents a tenfold change in hydrogen ion concentration (Figure 2.13). The pH of a solution is thus defined as the negative logarithm of the hydrogen ion concentration [H⁺] in moles per liter or −log[H⁺]. (Note that brackets [ ] indicate concentration of a substance.)

At a pH of 7 (at which [H⁺] is 10^{-7} M), the number of hydrogen ions exactly equals the number of hydroxyl ions (pH = pOH), and the solution is *neutral*—neither acidic nor basic. Absolutely pure (distilled) water has a pH of 7. Solutions with a pH below 7 are acidic; the hydrogen ions outnumber the hydroxyl ions. The lower the pH, the more acidic the solution. A solution with a pH of 6 has ten times as many hydrogen ions as a solution with a pH of 7.

Solutions with a pH higher than 7 are alkaline, and the relative concentration of hydrogen ions decreases by a factor of 10 with each higher pH unit. Thus, solutions with pH values of 8 and 12 have, respectively, 1/10 and 1/100,000 (1/10 × 1/10 × 1/10 × 1/10 × 1/10) as many hydrogen ions as a solution of pH 7. Notice that as the hydrogen ion concentration decreases, the hydroxyl ion concentration rises, and vice versa. The approximate pH of several body fluids and of a number of common substances also appears in Figure 2.13.

Neutralization

When acids and bases are mixed, they react with each other in displacement reactions to form water and a salt. For example, when hydrochloric acid and sodium hydroxide interact, sodium chloride (a salt) and water are formed.

$$HCl + NaOH \rightarrow NaCl + H_2O$$

acid   base   salt   water

This type of reaction is called a **neutralization reaction,** because the joining of H⁺ and OH⁻ to form water neutralizes the solution. Although the salt produced is written in molecular form (NaCl), remember that it actually exists as dissociated sodium and chloride ions when dissolved in water.

Buffers

Living cells are extraordinarily sensitive to even slight changes in the pH of the environment. In high concentrations, acids and bases are extremely damaging to living tissue. (Imagine what would happen to all those hydrogen bonds in biological molecules with large numbers of free H^+ running around.) Homeostasis of acid-base balance is carefully regulated by the kidneys and lungs and by chemical systems (proteins and other types of molecules) called **buffers.** Buffers resist abrupt and large swings in the pH of body fluids by releasing hydrogen ions (acting as acids) when the pH begins to rise and by binding hydrogen ions (acting as bases) when the pH drops. Because blood comes into close contact with nearly every body cell, regulation of its pH is particularly critical. Normally, blood pH varies within a very narrow range (7.35 to 7.45). If blood pH varies from these limits by more than a few tenths of a unit, it may be fatal.

To comprehend how chemical buffer systems operate, you must thoroughly understand strong and weak acids and bases. The first important concept is that the acidity of a solution reflects *only* the free hydrogen ions, not those still bound to anions. Consequently, acids that dissociate completely and irreversibly in water are called **strong acids,** because they can dramatically change the pH of a solution. Examples are hydrochloric acid and sulfuric acid. If we could count out 100 hydrochloric acid molecules and place them in 1 ml of water, we could expect to end up with 100 H^+, 100 Cl^-, and no undissociated hydrochloric acid molecules in that solution.

Acids that do not dissociate completely, like carbonic acid (H_2CO_3) and acetic acid (HAc), are **weak acids.** If we were to place 100 acetic acid molecules in 1 ml of water, the reaction would be something like this:

$$100 \text{ HAc} \rightarrow 90 \text{ HAc} + 10 \text{ H}^+ + 10 \text{ Ac}^-$$

Because undissociated acids do not affect pH, the acetic acid solution is much less acidic than the HCl solution. Weak acids dissociate in a predictable way, and molecules of the intact acid are in dynamic equilibrium with the dissociated ions. Consequently, the dissociation of acetic acid may also be written as

$$\text{HAc} \rightleftharpoons \text{H}^+ + \text{Ac}^-$$

This viewpoint allows us to see that if H^+ (released by a strong acid) is added to the acetic acid solution, the equilibrium will shift to the left and some H^+ and Ac^- will recombine to form HAc. On the other hand, if a strong base is added and the pH begins to rise, the equilibrium shifts to the right and more HAc molecules dissociate to release H^+. This characteristic of weak acids allows them to play important roles in the chemical buffer systems of the body.

The concept of strong and weak bases is more easily explained. Remember that bases are proton acceptors. Thus, **strong bases** are those, like hydroxides, that dissociate easily in water and quickly tie up H^+. On the other hand, sodium bicarbonate (commonly known as baking soda) ionizes incompletely and reversibly. Because it accepts relatively few protons, its released bicarbonate ion is considered a **weak base.**

Now let's examine how one buffer system helps to maintain pH homeostasis of the blood. Although there are other chemical blood buffers, the **carbonic acid–bicarbonate system** is a major one. Carbonic acid (H_2CO_3) dissociates reversibly releasing bicarbonate ions (HCO_3^-) and protons (H^+):

$$\underset{\substack{\text{H}^+ \text{ donor} \\ \text{(weak acid)}}}{\text{H}_2\text{CO}_3} \underset{\text{Response to drop in pH}}{\overset{\text{Response to rise in pH}}{\rightleftharpoons}} \underset{\substack{\text{H}^+ \text{ acceptor} \\ \text{(weak base)}}}{\text{HCO}_3^-} + \underset{\text{proton}}{\text{H}^+}$$

The chemical equilibrium between carbonic acid (a weak acid) and bicarbonate ion (a weak base) resists changes in blood pH by shifting to the right or left as H^+ ions are added to or removed from the blood. As blood pH rises (i.e., becomes more alkaline due to the addition of a strong base), the equilibrium shifts to the right, forcing more carbonic acid to dissociate. Similarly, as blood pH begins to drop (i.e., becomes more acidic due to the addition of a strong acid), the equilibrium shifts to the left as more bicarbonate ions begin to bind with protons. As you can see, strong bases are replaced by a weak base (bicarbonate ion) and protons released by strong acids are tied up in a weak one (carbonic acid). In either case, the blood pH changes much less than it would in the absence of the buffering system. Acid-base balance and buffers are discussed in more detail in Chapter 26.

Organic Compounds

Molecules unique to living systems—proteins, carbohydrates, lipids (fats), and nucleic acids—all contain carbon and hence are organic compounds. Although organic compounds are distinguished by the fact that they contain carbon and inorganic compounds are defined as compounds that lack carbon, there are a few irrational exceptions to this generalization that you should be aware of. Carbon dioxide, carbon monoxide, and carbides, for example, all contain carbon but are considered inorganic compounds. For the most part, organic molecules are very large molecules and their interactions with other molecules typically involve only small, reactive parts of their structure called *functional groups* (acid groups, amines, and others). The most important functional groups involved in biochemical reactions are illustrated in Appendix B.

What makes carbon so special that "living" chemistry depends on its presence? To begin with, no other *small* atom is so precisely **electroneutral.** The consequence of its electroneutrality is that carbon never loses or gains electrons; it always shares them. Furthermore, with four valence shell electrons, carbon forms four covalent bonds with other elements, as well as with other carbon atoms. As a result, carbon is found in long, chainlike molecules (common in fats), ring structures (typical of carbohydrates and steroids), and many other structures that are uniquely suited for specific roles in the body.

Carbohydrates

Carbohydrates, a group of molecules that includes sugars and starches, represent 1–2% of cell mass. Carbohydrates contain carbon, hydrogen, and oxygen, and generally the hydrogen and oxygen atoms occur in the same 2:1 ratio as in water. This ratio is reflected in the word *carbohydrate* ("hydrated carbon").

A carbohydrate can be classified according to size and solubility as a monosaccharide ("one sugar"), disaccharide ("two sugars"), or polysaccharide ("many sugars"). Monosaccharides are the structural units, or building blocks, of the other carbohydrates. In general, the larger the carbohydrate molecule, the less soluble it is in water.

Monosaccharides

Monosaccharides (mon"o-sak'ah-rīdz), or *simple sugars*, are single-chain or single-ring structures containing from three to seven carbon atoms (Figure 2.14a). Usually the carbon, hydrogen, and oxygen atoms occur in the ratio 1:2:1, so a general formula for a monosaccharide is $(CH_2O)n$, where n is the number of carbons in the sugar. Glucose, for example, has six carbon atoms, and its molecular formula is $C_6H_{12}O_6$. Ribose, with five carbons, is $C_5H_{10}O_5$.

Monosaccharides are named generically according to the number of carbon atoms they contain. Most important in the body are the pentose (five-carbon) and hexose (six-carbon) sugars. For example, the pentose *deoxyribose* (de-ok"sĭ-ri'bōs) is part of DNA, and *glucose*, a hexose, is blood sugar. Two other hexoses, *galactose* and *fructose*, are **isomers** (i'so-mers) of glucose. That is, they have the same molecular formula ($C_6H_{12}O_6$), but their atoms are

arranged differently, giving them different chemical properties.

Disaccharides

A **disaccharide** (di-sak'ah-rīd), or *double sugar,* is formed when two monosaccharides are joined by *dehydration synthesis* (Figure 2.14b). In this synthesis reaction, a water molecule is lost as the bond is made, as illustrated by the synthesis of sucrose (soo'krōs):

$$2C_6H_{12}O_6 \rightarrow C_{12}H_{22}O_{11} + H_2O$$

glucose + fructose   sucrose   water

Notice that the molecular formula for sucrose contains two hydrogen atoms and one oxygen atom less than the total number of hydrogen and oxygen atoms in glucose and fructose, because a water molecule is released during bond formation.

Important disaccharides in the diet are *sucrose* (glucose + fructose), which is cane or table sugar; *lactose* (glucose + galactose), found in milk; and *maltose* (glucose + glucose), also called malt sugar (see Figure 2.14b). Disaccharides are too large to pass through cell membranes, so they must be digested to their simple sugar units to be absorbed from the digestive tract into the blood. This decomposition process, called *hydrolysis*, is essentially the reverse of dehydration synthesis. A water molecule is added to each bond, breaking the bonds and releasing the simple sugar units.

Polysaccharides

Polysaccharides (pol"e-sak'ah-rīdz) are long chains of simple sugars linked together by dehydration synthesis. Such chainlike molecules made of many similar units are called **polymers.** Because polysaccharides are large, fairly insoluble molecules, they are ideal storage products. Another consequence of their large size is that they lack the sweetness of the simple and double sugars. Only two polysaccharides are of major importance to the body: starch and glycogen. Both are polymers of glucose. Only their degree of branching differs.

---

*Notice that in Figure 2.14 the carbon (C) atoms present at the angles of the carbohydrate ring structures are not illustrated and in Figure 2.14c only the oxygen atoms are shown. For example, the illustrations below show the full structure of glucose on the left and the shorthand structure on the right. This type of shorthand is used for nearly all organic ringlike structures illustrated in this chapter.

Glucose   Fructose   Galactose   Deoxyribose   Ribose

(a) Monosaccharides

Glucose   Fructose   Dehydration synthesis H_2O Hydrolysis H_2O Sucrose

Glucose   Glucose   Galactose   Glucose

Maltose   Lactose

(b) Disaccharides

Glycogen

(c) Portion of a polysaccharide molecule (glycogen)

FIGURE 2.14 **Carbohydrate molecules.*** **(a)** Monosaccharides important to the body. The hexose sugars glucose, fructose, and galactose are isomers: They have the same molecular formula ($C_6H_{12}O_6$), but the arrangement of their atoms differs, as shown here. Deoxyribose and ribose are pentose sugars. **(b)** Disaccharides are two monosaccharides linked together by dehydration synthesis. Formation of sucrose ($C_{12}H_{22}O_{11}$) from glucose and fructose molecules is illustrated. In the reverse reaction (hydrolysis), sucrose is broken down to glucose and fructose. Other important disaccharides are maltose and lactose (both $C_{12}H_{22}O_{11}$). **(c)** Simplified representation of part of a glycogen molecule, a polysaccharide formed from glucose units.

* See footnote on facing page concerning the complete structure of these sugars.

Starch is the storage carbohydrate formed by plants. The number of glucose units composing a starch molecule is high and variable. When we eat starchy foods such as grain products and potatoes, the starch must be digested for its glucose units to be absorbed. We are unable to digest *cellulose*, another polysaccharide found in all plant products. However, it is important in providing the *bulk* (one form of fiber) that helps move feces through the colon.

Glycogen (gli′ko-jen), the storage carbohydrate of animal tissues, is stored primarily in skeletal muscle and liver cells. Like starch, it is highly branched and is a very large molecule (see Figure 2.14c). When blood sugar levels drop sharply, liver cells break down glycogen and release its glucose units to the blood. Since there are many branch endings from which glucose can be released simultaneously, body cells have almost instant access to glucose fuel.

Carbohydrate Functions

The major function of carbohydrates in the body is to provide a ready, easily used source of cellular fuel. Most cells can use only a few simple sugars, and glucose is at the top of the "cellular menu." As described in our earlier discussion of oxidation-reduction reactions (p. 38), glucose is broken down and oxidized within cells. During these chemical reactions, electrons are transferred. This relocation of electrons releases the bond energy stored in glucose, and this energy is used to synthesize ATP. When ATP supplies are sufficient, dietary carbohydrates are converted to glycogen or fat and stored. Those of us who have gained weight from eating too many carbohydrate-rich snacks have personal experience with this conversion process!

Only small amounts of carbohydrates are used for structural purposes. For example, some sugars are found in our genes. Others are attached to the external surfaces of cells where they act as "road signs" to guide cellular interactions.

Lipids

Lipids are insoluble in water but dissolve readily in other lipids and in organic solvents such as alcohol and ether. Like carbohydrates, all lipids contain carbon, hydrogen, and oxygen, but the proportion of oxygen in lipids is much lower. In addition, phosphorus is found in some of the more complex lipids. Lipids include *triglycerides*, *phospholipids* (fos″fo-lip′idz), *steroids* (stĕ′roidz), and a number of other lipoid substances. Table 2.2 on page 48 gives the locations and functions of some lipids found in the body.

Triglycerides (Neutral Fats)

Triglycerides (tri-glis′er-īdz), also called **neutral fats,** are commonly known as *fats* when solid or *oils* when liquid. A triglyceride is composed of two types of building blocks, **fatty acids** and **glycerol** (glis′er-ol), in a 3:1 ratio of fatty acids to glycerol (Figure 2.15a). Fatty acids are linear chains of carbon and hydrogen atoms (hydrocarbon chains) with an organic acid group (—COOH) at one end. Glycerol is a modified simple sugar (a sugar alcohol). Fat synthesis involves attaching three fatty acid chains to a single glycerol molecule by dehydration synthesis; the result is an E-shaped molecule. The glycerol backbone is the same in all triglycerides, but the fatty acid chains vary, resulting in different kinds of fats and oils. These are large molecules, often consisting of hundreds of atoms, and ingested fats and oils must be broken down to their building blocks before they can be absorbed. Their hydrocarbon chains make the triglycerides nonpolar molecules. Because polar and nonpolar molecules do not interact, oil (or fats) and water do not mix. Consequently, triglycerides provide the body's most efficient and compact form of stored energy, and when they are oxidized, they yield large amounts of energy.

Deposits of triglycerides are found mainly beneath the skin, where they insulate the deeper body tissues from heat loss and protect them from mechanical trauma. Women are usually more successful English Channel swimmers than men. This is due partly to their thicker subcutaneous fatty layer, which helps insulate them from the bitterly cold water of the Channel.

The length of a triglyceride's fatty acid chains and their degree of saturation with H atoms determine how solid the molecule is at a given temperature. Fatty acid chains with only single covalent bonds between carbon atoms are referred to as **saturated.** Their fatty acid chains are straight and, at room temperature, the molecules of a saturated fat are packed closely together, forming a solid. Fatty acids that contain one or more double bonds between carbon atoms are said to be **unsaturated** (**monounsaturated** and **polyunsaturated,** respectively). The double bonds cause the fatty acid chains to kink so that they cannot be packed closely enough to solidify. Hence, triglycerides with short fatty acid chains or unsaturated fatty acids are oils (liquid at room temperature) and are typical of plant lipids. Examples include olive and peanut oils (rich in monounsaturated fats) and corn, soybean, and safflower oils, which contain a high percentage of polyunsaturated fatty acids. Longer fatty acid chains and more saturated fatty acids are common in animal fats such as butterfat and the fat of meats, which are solid at room temperature. Of the two types of fatty acids, the unsaturated variety, especially olive oil, is said to be more "heart healthy."

Trans fats, common in many margarines and baked products, are oils that have been solidified by

(a) Formation of a triglyceride

(b) Phospholipid molecule (phosphatidylcholine)

(c) Cholesterol

FIGURE 2.15 **Lipids. (a)** The triglycerides, or neutral fats, are synthesized by dehydration synthesis. **(b)** Structure of a typical phospholipid molecule. Two fatty acid chains and a phosphorus-containing group are attached to the glycerol backbone. In the commonly used schematic to the right, the polar end ("head") is depicted as a sphere, and the nonpolar end ("tail") is depicted as two wavy lines. **(c)** The generalized structure of cholesterol. Cholesterol is the basis for all steroids formed in the body.

addition of H atoms at sites of double carbon bonds. They have recently been branded as increasing the risk of heart disease even more than the solid animal fats. Conversely, the **omega-3 fatty acids,** found naturally in cold-water fish, appear to decrease the risk of heart disease and some inflammatory diseases.

Phospholipids

Phospholipids are modified triglycerides, that is, they are diglycerides with a phosphorus-containing group and two, rather than three, fatty acid chains (Figure 2.15b). The phosphorus-containing group gives phospholipids their distinctive chemical properties. Although the hydrocarbon portion (the "tail") of the molecule is nonpolar and interacts only with nonpolar molecules, the phosphorus-containing part (the "head") is polar and attracts other polar or charged particles, such as water or ions. Molecules

that have both polar and nonpolar regions are *amphipathic* (am-fe-path'ik). As you will see in Chapter 3, cells use this unique characteristic of phospholipids in building their membranes. Some biologically important phospholipids and their functions are listed in Table 2.2.

Steroids

Structurally, steroids differ quite a bit from fats and oils. **Steroids** are basically flat molecules made of four interlocking hydrocarbon rings. Like triglycerides, steroids are fat soluble and contain little oxygen. The single most important molecule in our steroid chemistry is *cholesterol* (ko-les'ter-ol) (Figure 2.15c). We ingest cholesterol in animal products such as eggs, meat, and cheese, and our liver produces some.

2

TABLE 2.2	Representative Lipids Found in the Body
LIPID TYPE	**LOCATION/FUNCTION**
Triglycerides (Neutral Fats)	In fat deposits (subcutaneous tissue and around organs); protect and insulate body organs; the major source of *stored* energy in the body
Phospholipids (phosphatidylcholine; cephalin; others)	Chief component of cell membranes; may participate in the transport of lipids in plasma; prevalent in nervous tissue
Steroids	
Cholesterol	The structural basis for manufacture of all body steroids
Bile salts	Breakdown products of cholesterol; released by the liver into the digestive tract, where they aid fat digestion and absorption
Vitamin D	A fat-soluble vitamin produced in the skin on exposure to UV radiation; necessary for normal bone growth and function
Sex hormones	Estrogen and progesterone (female hormones) and testosterone (a male hormone) are produced in the gonads and are necessary for normal reproductive function
Adrenocortical hormones	Cortisol, a glucocorticoid, is a metabolic hormone necessary for maintaining normal blood glucose levels; aldosterone helps to regulate salt and water balance of the body by targeting the kidneys
Other Lipoid Substances	
Fat-soluble vitamins:	
A	Found in orange-pigmented vegetables and fruits; converted in the retina to retinal, a part of the photoreceptor pigment involved in vision
E	Found in plant products such as wheat germ and green leafy vegetables; claims have been made (but not proved in humans) that it promotes wound healing, contributes to fertility; and may help to neutralize highly reactive particles called free radicals believed to be involved in triggering some types of cancer
K	Made available to humans largely by the action of intestinal bacteria; also prevalent in a wide variety of foods; necessary for proper clotting of blood
Eicosanoids (prostaglandins; leukotrienes; thromboxanes)	Group of molecules derived from fatty acids found in all cell membranes; the potent prostaglandins have diverse effects, including stimulation of uterine contractions, regulation of blood pressure, control of gastrointestinal tract motility, and secretory activity; both prostaglandins and leukotrienes are involved in inflammation; thromboxanes are powerful vasoconstrictors
Lipoproteins	Lipoid and protein-based substances that transport fatty acids and cholesterol in the bloodstream; major varieties are high-density lipoproteins (HDLs) and low-density lipoproteins (LDLs)

Cholesterol has earned bad press because of its role in arteriosclerosis, but it is essential for human life. Cholesterol is found in cell membranes and is the raw material of vitamin D, steroid hormones, and bile salts. Although steroid hormones are present in the body in only small quantities, they are vital to homeostasis. Without sex hormones, reproduction would be impossible, and a total lack of the corticosteroids produced by the adrenal glands is fatal.

Eicosanoids

The **eicosanoids** (i-ko′sah-noyds) are diverse lipids chiefly derived from a 20-carbon fatty acid (arachidonic acid) found in all cell membranes. Most important of these are the *prostaglandins* and their relatives, which play roles in various body processes (see Table 2.2) including blood clotting, inflammation, and labor contractions.

Proteins

The full set of proteins made by the body, called the *proteome,* and the way those proteins network in the body or change with disease, is a matter of intense biotech research.

Protein composes 10–30% of cell mass and is the basic structural material of the body. However, not all

FIGURE 2.16 **Amino acid structures.** **(a)** Generalized structure of amino acids. All amino acids have both an amine (—NH$_2$) group and an acid (—COOH) group; they differ only in the atomic makeup of their R groups (green). **(b–e)** Specific structures of four amino acids. **(b)** The simplest (glycine) has an R group consisting of a single hydrogen atom. **(c)** An acid group in the R group, as in aspartic acid, makes the amino acid more acidic. **(d)** An amine group in the R group, as in lysine, makes the amino acid more basic. **(e)** The presence of a sulfhydryl (—SH) group in the R group of cysteine suggests that this amino acid is likely to participate in intramolecular bonding.

proteins are construction materials; many play vital roles in cell function. Proteins, which include enzymes (biological catalysts), hemoglobin of the blood, and contractile proteins of muscle, have the most varied functions of any molecules in the body. All proteins contain carbon, oxygen, hydrogen, and nitrogen, and many contain sulfur and phosphorus as well.

Amino Acids and Peptide Bonds

The building blocks of proteins are molecules called **amino acids,** of which there are 20 common types (see Appendix C). All amino acids have two important functional groups: a basic group called an *amine* (ah'mēn) *group* (—NH$_2$), and an organic *acid group* (—COOH). An amino acid may therefore act either as a base (proton acceptor) or an acid (proton donor). In fact, all amino acids are identical except for a single group of atoms called their *R group*. Differences in the R group make each amino acid chemically unique (Figure 2.16).

Proteins are long chains of amino acids joined together by dehydration synthesis, with the amine end of one amino acid linked to the acid end of the next.

The resulting bond produces a characteristic arrangement of linked atoms called a **peptide bond** (Figure 2.17). Two united amino acids form a *dipeptide,* three a *tripeptide,* and ten or more a *polypeptide.* Although polypeptides containing more than 50 amino acids are called proteins, most proteins are **macromolecules,** large, complex molecules containing from 100 to over 10,000 amino acids.

Because each type of amino acid has distinct properties, the sequence in which they are bound together produces proteins that vary widely in both structure and function. We can think of the 20 amino acids as a 20-letter "alphabet" used in specific combinations to form "words" (proteins). Just as a change in one letter can produce a word with an entirely different meaning (flour → floor) or that is nonsensical (flour → fllur), changes in the kinds or positions of amino acids can yield proteins with different functions or proteins that are nonfunctional. Nevertheless, there are thousands of different proteins in the body, each with distinct functional properties, and all constructed from different combinations of the 20 common amino acids.

FIGURE 2.17 **Amino acids are linked together by dehydration synthesis.** The acid group of one amino acid is bonded to the amine group of the next, with loss of a water molecule. The bond formed is called a peptide bond. Peptide bonds are broken when water is added to the bond (i.e., during hydrolysis).

Structural Levels of Proteins

Proteins can be described in terms of four structural levels. The linear sequence of amino acids composing the polypeptide chain is called the *primary structure* of a protein. This structure, which resembles a strand of amino acid "beads," is the backbone of the protein molecule (Figure 2.18a).

Proteins do not normally exist as simple, linear chains of amino acids. Instead, they twist or bend upon themselves to form a more complex *secondary structure*. The most common type of secondary structure is the **alpha (α)-helix,** which resembles a Slinky toy or the coils of a telephone cord (Figure 2.18b). The α-helix, formed by coiling of the primary chain, is stabilized by hydrogen bonds formed between NH and CO groups in amino acids in the primary chain which are approximately four amino acids apart. Hydrogen bonds in α-helices always link different parts of the *same* chain together. In another type of secondary structure, the **beta (β)-pleated sheet,** the primary polypeptide chains do not coil, but are linked side by side by hydrogen bonds to form a pleated, ribbonlike structure (Figure 2.18c) that resembles an accordion. Notice that in this type of secondary structure, the hydrogen bonds may link together *different polypeptide chains* as well as *different parts* of the same chain that has folded back on itself. A single polypeptide chain may exhibit both types of secondary structure at various places along its length.

Many proteins have *tertiary structure* (ter'she-a"re), the next higher level of complexity, which is superimposed on secondary structure. Tertiary structure is achieved when α-helical or β-pleated regions of the polypeptide chain fold upon one another to produce a compact ball-like, or globular, molecule. The tertiary structure (and underlying secondary structure) of a beta polypeptide chain of hemoglobin, the oxygen-binding protein found in red blood cells, is shown in Figure 2.18d. This unique structure is maintained by both covalent and hydrogen bonds between amino acids that are often far apart in the primary chain. When two or more polypeptide chains aggregate in a regular manner to form a complex protein, the protein has *quaternary structure* (kwah'ter-na"re). Hemoglobin (Figure 2.18e) exhibits this structural level.

Although a protein with tertiary or quaternary structure looks a bit like a clump of congealed pasta, the ultimate overall structure of any protein is very specific and is dictated by its primary structure. This reflects the fact that the types and relative positions of amino acids in the protein backbone determine where bonds can form to produce the complex coiled or folded structures that keep water-loving amino acids near the surface and water-fleeing amino acids

buried in the protein's core. In addition, cells decorate many proteins by attaching sugars or fatty acids to them in ways that are difficult to imagine or predict.

Fibrous and Globular Proteins

The overall structure of a protein determines its biological function. In general, proteins are classified according to their overall appearance and shape as either fibrous or globular.

Fibrous proteins are extended and strandlike. Many exhibit only secondary structure, but some have quaternary structure as well. For example, *collagen* (kol'ah-jen) is a composite of the helical tropocollagen molecules packed together side by side to form a strong ropelike structure. Fibrous proteins are insoluble in water, and very stable—qualities ideal for providing mechanical support and tensile strength to the body's tissues. Besides collagen, which is the single most abundant protein in the body, the fibrous proteins include keratin, elastin, and certain contractile proteins of muscle (Table 2.3). Because fibrous proteins are the chief building materials of the body, they are also known as **structural proteins.**

Globular proteins are compact, spherical proteins that have at least tertiary structure; some also exhibit quaternary structure. The globular proteins are water soluble, chemically active molecules, and they play crucial roles in virtually all biological processes. Consequently, this group is also called **functional proteins.** Some (antibodies) help to provide immunity, others (protein-based hormones) regulate growth and development, and still others (enzymes) are catalysts that oversee just about every chemical reaction in the body. The roles of these and selected other proteins found in the body are summarized in Table 2.3.

Protein Denaturation

Fibrous proteins are stable, but globular proteins are quite the opposite. The activity of a protein depends on its specific three-dimensional structure, and intramolecular bonds, particularly hydrogen bonds, are important in maintaining that structure. However, hydrogen bonds are fragile and easily broken by many chemical and physical factors, such as excessive acidity or temperature. Although individual proteins vary in their sensitivity to environmental conditions, hydrogen bonds begin to break when the pH drops or the temperature rises above normal (physiological) levels, causing proteins to unfold and lose their specific three-dimensional shape. In this condition, a protein is said to be **denatured.** Fortunately, the disruption is reversible in most cases, and the "scrambled" protein regains its native structure

(a) Primary structure (polypeptide strand)

(b) Secondary structure (α-helix)

(c) Secondary structure (β-pleated sheet)

α-Helix

(d) Tertiary structure

Heme group

(e) Quaternary structure (hemoglobin molecule)

FIGURE 2.18 **Levels of protein structure. (a)** Primary structure. Amino acids are linked together to form a polypeptide strand. **(b)** Secondary structure— the α-helix. The primary chain is coiled upon itself to form a spiral structure that is maintained by hydrogen bonds (indicated by dotted lines). **(c)** Secondary structure— the β-pleated sheet. Two or more primary chains are linked side by side by hydrogen bonds to form an undulating ribbonlike structure. **(d)** Tertiary structure is super- imposed on secondary structure (in this example on α-helical regions) to form a basically spherical molecule that is maintained by intramolecular bonds. The molecule shown is a beta chain, one of the four polypeptide chains of hemoglobin. **(e)** Quaternary structure of hemoglobin. Hemoglobin is formed from four poly- peptide chains that are linked together in a specific manner.

TABLE 2.3	Representative Types of Proteins in the Body	

CLASSIFICATION ACCORDING TO

OVERALL STRUCTURE	GENERAL FUNCTION	EXAMPLES FROM THE BODY
Fibrous	Structural framework/ mechanical support	*Collagen,* found in all connective tissues, is the single most abundant protein in the body. It is responsible for the tensile strength of bones, tendons, and ligaments.
		Keratin is the structural protein of hair and nails and a waterproofing material of skin.
		Elastin is found, along with collagen, where durability and flexibility are needed, such as in the ligaments that bind bones together.
		Spectrin internally reinforces and stabilizes the surface membrane of some cells, particularly red blood cells. *Dystrophin* reinforces and stabilizes the surface membrane of muscle cells. *Titin* helps organize the intracellular structure of muscle cells and accounts for the elasticity of skeletal muscles.
	Movement	*Actin and myosin,* contractile proteins, are found in substantial amounts in muscle cells, where they cause muscle cell shortening (contraction); they also function in cell division in all cell types. Actin is important in intracellular transport, particularly in nerve cells.
Globular	Catalysis	Protein enzymes are essential to virtually every biochemical reaction in the body; they increase the rates of chemical reactions by at least a millionfold. Examples include salivary amylase (in saliva), which catalyzes the breakdown of starch, and oxidase enzymes, which act to oxidize food fuels.
	Transport	*Hemoglobin* transports oxygen in blood, and *lipoproteins* transport lipids and cholesterol. Other transport proteins in the blood carry iron, hormones, or other substances. Some globular proteins in plasma membranes are involved in membrane transport (as carriers or channels).
	Regulation of pH	Many plasma proteins, such as *albumin,* function reversibly as acids or bases, thus acting as buffers to prevent wide swings in blood pH.
	Regulation of metabolism	*Peptide* and *protein hormones* help to regulate metabolic activity, growth, and development. For example, *growth hormone* is an anabolic hormone necessary for optimal growth; *insulin* helps regulate blood sugar levels.
	Body defense	*Antibodies* (immunoglobulins) are specialized proteins released by immune cells that recognize and inactivate foreign substances (bacteria, toxins, some viruses). *Complement proteins,* which circulate in blood, enhance both immune and inflammatory responses.
		Molecular chaperones aid folding of new proteins in both healthy and damaged cells and transport of metal ions into and within the cell. They also promote breakdown of damaged proteins.

when desirable conditions are restored. However, if the temperature or pH change is so extreme that protein structure is damaged beyond repair, the protein is *irreversibly denatured.* The coagulation of egg white (primarily albumin protein) that occurs when you boil or fry an egg is an example of irreversible protein denaturation. There is no way to restore the white, rubbery protein to its original translucent form.

When globular proteins are denatured, they can no longer perform their physiological roles because their function depends on the presence of specific arrangements of atoms, called **active sites,** on their surfaces. The active sites are regions that fit and interact chemically with other molecules of complementary shape and charge. Because atoms contributing to an active site may actually be far apart in the primary chain, dis-

ruption of intramolecular bonds separates them and destroys the active site (Figure 2.19). Hemoglobin becomes totally unable to bind and transport oxygen when blood pH is too acidic, because the structure needed for its function has been destroyed.

Most body proteins are described in conjunction with the organ systems or functional processes to which they are closely related. However, two groups of proteins—*molecular chaperones* and *enzymes*—are intimately involved in the normal functioning of all cells, and so these incredibly complex molecules are considered here.

Molecular Chaperones

In addition to the ubiquitous enzymes, all cells contain a class of unrelated globular proteins called

Q *What event, which is possible in situation (a), can no longer occur in situation (b)?*

(a)

(b)

FIGURE 2.19 **Denaturation of a globular protein such as an enzyme. (a)** The molecule's globular structure is maintained by intramolecular bonds. Atoms composing the active site of the enzyme are shown as stalked particles. The substrate, or interacting molecule, has a corresponding binding site, and the two sites fit together precisely. **(b)** Breaking the intramolecular bonds that maintain the secondary and tertiary structure of the enzyme results in a linear molecule, with atoms of the former active site widely separated. Enzyme-substrate binding can no longer occur.

molecular chaperones, or **chaperonins,** which, among other things, help proteins to achieve their functional three-dimensional structure. Although its amino acid sequence determines the precise way a protein folds, the folding process also requires the help of molecular chaperones to ensure that the folding is quick and accurate. Apparently, molecular

A *The substrate can no longer bind to the enzyme's active site in (b) because the atoms composing the active site are no longer in their functional relationship to one another.*

chaperones have numerous protein-related roles to play. For example, specific chaperonins

- Prevent accidental, premature, or incorrect folding of polypeptide chains or their association with other polypeptides
- Aid the desired folding and association process
- Help to translocate proteins and certain metal ions (copper, iron, zinc) across cell membranes
- Promote the breakdown of damaged or denatured proteins

The first such proteins discovered were called *heat shock proteins (hsp)* because they seemed to protect cells from the destructive effects of heat. It was later found that these proteins are produced in response to a variety of traumatizing stimuli—for example, in the oxygen-deprived cells of a heart attack patient—and the name *stress proteins* replaced hsp for that particular group of chaperonins. It is now clear that chaperonins are vitally important to cell function in all types of stressful circumstances.

Enzymes and Enzyme Activity

Characteristics of Enzymes **Enzymes** are globular proteins that act as biological catalysts. *Catalysts* are substances that regulate and accelerate the rate of biochemical reactions but are not used up or changed in those reactions. More specifically, enzymes can be thought of as chemical traffic cops that keep our metabolic pathways flowing. Enzymes cannot force chemical reactions to occur between molecules that would not otherwise react; they can only increase the speed of reaction. Without enzymes, biochemical reactions proceed so slowly that for practical purposes they do not occur at all.

Some enzymes are purely protein. In other cases, the functional enzyme consists of two parts, collectively called a **holoenzyme:** an **apoenzyme** (the protein portion) and a **cofactor.** Depending on the enzyme, the cofactor may be an ion of a metal element such as copper or iron, or an organic molecule needed to assist the reaction in some particular way. Most organic cofactors are derived from vitamins (especially the B complex vitamins); this type of cofactor is more precisely called a **coenzyme.**

Each enzyme is chemically specific. Some enzymes control only a single chemical reaction. Others exhibit a broader specificity in that they can bind with similar (but not identical) molecules and thus regulate a small group of related reactions. The presence of specific enzymes thus determines not only which reactions will be speeded up, but also which reactions will occur—no enzyme, no reaction. This also means that unwanted or unnecessary chemical reactions do not occur. Most enzymes are named for the type of reaction they catalyze. *Hydrolases*

(a) Noncatalyzed reaction

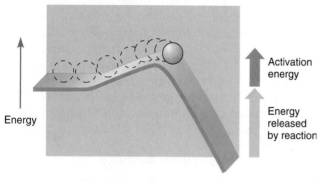

(b) Enzyme-catalyzed reaction

FIGURE 2.20 **Enzymes lower the energy barrier for a reaction. (a)** The reacting particles, indicated by the ball, must achieve a certain energy level before they can interact. The amount of energy that must be absorbed to reach that state is the activation energy. **(b)** The energy barrier and thus the activation energy is lower in the same reaction catalyzed by an enzyme.

(hi′druh-lās-es) add water during hydrolysis reactions; *oxidases* (ok′sĭ-dās-es) add oxygen; and so on. Most enzyme names can be recognized by the suffix *-ase.*

In many cases, enzymes are part of cellular membranes in a bucket-brigade type of arrangement; that is, the product of one enzyme-catalyzed reaction becomes the substrate of the abutting enzyme, and so on. Some enzymes are produced in an inactive form and must be activated in some way before they can function, often by a change in the pH of their surroundings. For example, digestive enzymes produced in the pancreas are activated in the small intestine, where they actually do their work. If they were produced in active form, the pancreas would digest itself. Sometimes, enzymes are inactivated immediately after they have performed their catalytic function. This is true of enzymes that promote blood clot formation when the wall of a blood vessel is damaged. Once clotting is triggered, those enzymes are inactivated. Otherwise, you would have blood vessels full of solid blood instead of one protective blood clot.

Mechanism of Enzyme Activity How do enzymes perform their catalytic role? Every chemical reaction requires that a certain amount of energy, called **activation energy,** be absorbed to prime the reaction. The activation energy is the amount of energy required to break the bonds of the reactants so that they can rearrange themselves and become the product. It is present when kinetic energy pushes the reactants to an energy level where their random collisions are forceful enough to ensure interaction. This is true regardless of whether the overall reaction is ultimately energy absorbing or energy releasing.

One obvious way to increase kinetic energy is to increase the temperature, but in living systems this would denature proteins. (This is why a high fever can be a serious event.) Enzymes allow reactions to occur at normal body temperature by decreasing the amount of activation energy required (Figure 2.20). Exactly how enzymes accomplish this remarkable feat is not fully understood. However, we know that, due to structural and electrostatic factors, they decrease the randomness of reactions by binding the reacting molecules temporarily to the enzyme surface and presenting them to each other in the proper position for chemical interaction to occur.

Three basic steps appear to be involved in the mechanism of enzyme action (Figure 2.21).

① The enzyme's active site must first bind with the substance(s) on which it acts. These substances are called the **substrates** of the enzyme. Substrate binding causes the active site to change shape so that the substrate and the active site fit together precisely. Although enzymes are specific for particular substrates, other (nonsubstrate) molecules may act as *enzyme inhibitors* if their structure is similar enough to occupy or block the enzyme's active site.

② The enzyme-substrate complex undergoes internal rearrangements that form the product.

③ The enzyme releases the product of the reaction. This step shows the catalytic role of an enzyme: If the enzyme became part of the product, it would be a reactant and not a catalyst.

Because the unaltered enzymes can act again and again, cells need only small amounts of each enzyme. Catalysis occurs with incredible speed; most enzymes can catalyze millions of reactions per minute.

Nucleic Acids (DNA and RNA)

The **nucleic acids** (nu-kle′ic), composed of carbon, oxygen, hydrogen, nitrogen, and phosphorus, are the largest molecules in the body. Their structural units, called **nucleotides,** are quite complex. Each nucleotide

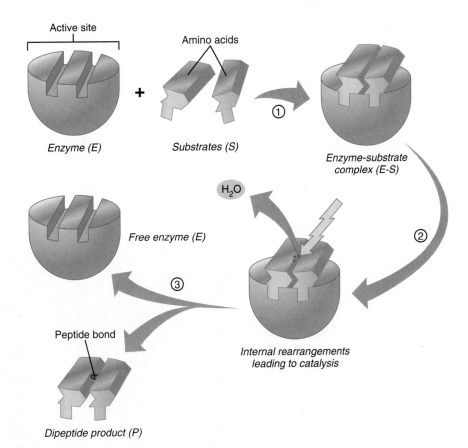

FIGURE 2.21 **Mechanism of enzyme action.** In this example, the enzyme catalyzes the formation of a dipeptide from specific amino acids. ① The enzyme-substrate complex (E-S) is formed. ② Internal rearrangements occur. In this case, energy is absorbed (indicated by the yellow arrow) as a water molecule is removed and a peptide bond is formed. ③ The enzyme releases the product (P) of the reaction, the dipeptide. The free enzyme has not changed in the course of the reaction and is now available to catalyze another such reaction.
Summary: E + S → E-S → P + E

consists of three components (Figure 2.22a): a nitrogen-containing base, a pentose sugar, and a phosphate group. Five major varieties of nitrogen-containing bases can contribute to nucleotide structure: **adenine,** abbreviated **A** (ad'ĕ-nēn); **guanine, G** (gwan'ēn); **cytosine, C** (si'to-sēn); **thymine, T** (thi'mēn); and **uracil, U** (u'rah-sil). Adenine and guanine are large, two-ring bases (called purines), whereas cytosine, thymine, and uracil are smaller, single-ring bases (called pyrimidines).

The stepwise synthesis of a nucleotide involves the attachment of a base to the pentose sugar to form first a *nucleoside,* named for the nitrogenous base it contains. The nucleotide is formed when a phosphate group is bonded to the sugar of the nucleoside.

The nucleic acids include two major classes of molecules, **deoxyribonucleic acid (DNA)** (de-ok"sĭ-ri"bo-nu-kle'ik) and **ribonucleic acid (RNA).** Although DNA and RNA are both composed of nucleotides, they differ in many respects. Typically, DNA is found in the nucleus (control center) of the cell, where it constitutes the *genetic material,* also called the *genes,* or more recently the *genome.* DNA has two fundamental roles: It replicates (reproduces) itself before a cell divides, ensuring that the genetic information in the descendant cells is identical, and it provides the basic instructions for building every protein in the body. By providing the information for protein synthesis, DNA determines what type of organism you will be—frog, human, oak tree—and directs your growth and development. Although we have said that enzymes govern all chemical reactions, remember that enzymes, too, are proteins formed at the direction of DNA. RNA is located chiefly outside the nucleus and can be considered a "molecular slave" of DNA. That is, RNA carries out the orders for protein synthesis issued by DNA. [Viruses in which RNA (rather than DNA) is the genetic material are an exception to this generalization.]

DNA is a long, double-stranded polymer—a double chain of nucleotides (Figure 2.22b and c). The bases in DNA are A, G, C, and T, and its pentose sugar is *deoxyribose* (as reflected in its name). Its two nucleotide chains are held together by hydrogen

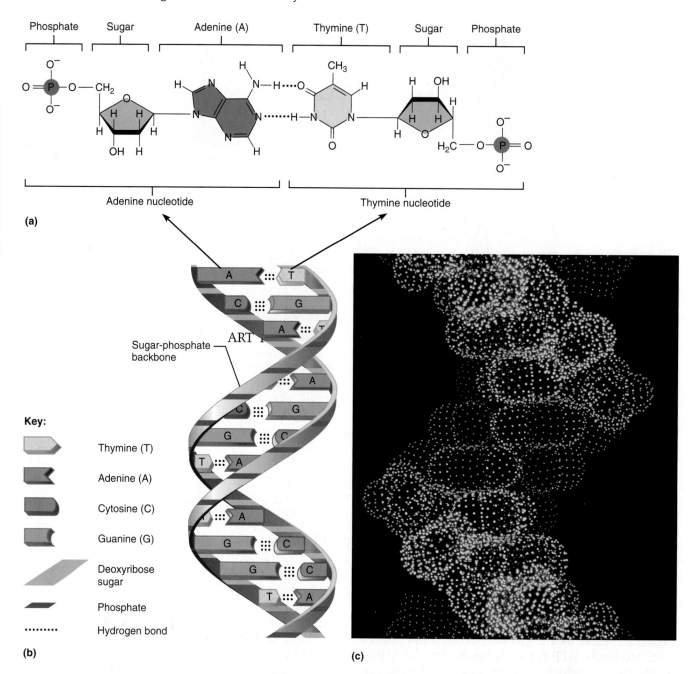

(a)

(b)

Key:

Thymine (T)

Adenine (A)

Cytosine (C)

Guanine (G)

Deoxyribose sugar

Phosphate

Hydrogen bond

(c)

FIGURE 2.22 **Structure of DNA.**
(a) The unit of DNA is the nucleotide, which is composed of a deoxyribose sugar molecule linked to a phosphate group, with a base attached to the sugar. Two nucleotides, linked by hydrogen bonds between their complementary bases, are illustrated. **(b)** DNA is a coiled double polymer of nucleotides (a double helix). The backbones of the ladderlike molecule are formed by alternating sugar and phosphate units. The rungs are formed by the binding together of complementary bases (A-T and G-C) by hydrogen bonds (shown by dotted lines). **(c)** Computer-generated image of a DNA molecule.

bonds between the bases, so that a ladderlike molecule is formed. Alternating sugar and phosphate molecules of each chain form the *backbones* or "uprights" of the "ladder," and the joined bases form the "rungs." The whole molecule is coiled into a spiral staircase–like structure called a **double helix.** Bonding of the bases is very specific: A always bonds to T, and G always bonds to C. A and T are therefore called **complementary bases,** as are C and G. Hence, ATGA on one nucleotide strand would necessarily be bonded to TACT (a complementary base sequence) on the other strand.

RNA molecules are single strands of nucleotides. RNA bases include A, G, C, and U (U replaces the T found in DNA), and its sugar is *ribose* instead of deoxyribose (Table 2.4). The three major

TABLE 2.4 Comparison of DNA and RNA

CHARACTERISTIC	DNA	RNA
Major cellular site	Nucleus	Cytoplasm (cell area outside the nucleus)
Major functions	Is the genetic material; directs protein synthesis; replicates itself before cell division	Carries out the genetic instructions for protein synthesis
Sugar	Deoxyribose	Ribose
Bases	Adenine, guanine, cytosine, thymine	Adenine, guanine, cytosine, uracil
Structure	Double strand coiled into a double helix	Single strand, straight or folded

varieties of RNA (messenger RNA, ribosomal RNA, and transfer RNA) are distinguished by their relative size and shape, and each has a specific role to play in carrying out DNA's instructions for protein synthesis. In addition to these three RNAs, there are small RNA molecules called *microRNAs (miRNAs)* that appear to control genetic expression by shutting down genes or altering their expression. We discuss DNA replication and the relative roles of DNA and RNA in protein synthesis in Chapter 3. DNA can also help solve forensic mysteries, as described in *A Closer Look* on pages 58 and 59.

Adenosine Triphosphate (ATP)

Although glucose is the most important cellular fuel, none of the chemical energy contained in its bonds is used directly to power cellular work. Instead, energy released during glucose catabolism is coupled to **adenosine triphosphate (ATP)** synthesis—that is, it is captured and stored as small packets of energy in the bonds of ATP. ATP, in turn, acts as a chemical "drive shaft" to provide a form of energy that is immediately usable by all body cells.

Structurally, ATP is an adenine-containing RNA nucleotide to which two additional phosphate groups have been added (Figure 2.23). Chemically, the triphosphate tail of ATP can be compared to a tightly coiled spring ready to uncoil with tremendous energy when the catch is released. Actually, ATP is a very unstable energy-storing molecule because its three negatively charged phosphate groups are closely packed and repel each other. When its terminal high-energy phosphate bonds are broken (hydrolyzed), the chemical "spring" relaxes and the molecule as a whole becomes more stable. Cells tap ATP's bond energy during coupled reactions by using enzymes to transfer the terminal phosphate groups from ATP to other compounds. The newly *phosphorylated* molecules are said to be "primed" and temporarily become more energetic and capable of performing some type of cellular work. In the

process of doing their work, they lose the phosphate group. The amount of energy released and transferred during ATP hydrolysis corresponds closely to that needed to drive most biochemical reactions. As a result, cells are protected from excessive energy release that might be damaging, and energy squandering is kept to a minimum.

Cleaving the terminal phosphate bond of ATP yields a molecule with two phosphate groups— *adenosine diphosphate (ADP)*—and an inorganic

FIGURE 2.23 **Structure of ATP (adenosine triphosphate).** ATP is an adenine nucleotide to which two additional phosphate groups have been attached during breakdown of food fuels. (The phosphate bonds that can be hydrolyzed to liberate energy are indicated by the wavy red lines.) When the terminal phosphate group is cleaved off, energy is released to do useful work and ADP (adenosine diphosphate) is formed. When the terminal phosphate group is cleaved off ADP, a similar amount of energy is released and AMP (adenosine monophosphate) is formed.

A CLOSER LOOK

DNA Fingerprinting: Cracking Our Genetic "Barcode"

The terrorist attacks on New York City's World Trade Center left nearly 3000 people dead, their bodies buried in tons of rubble. As the weeks passed, it became clear that even if victims could be recovered from the wreckage, their bodies would probably be mangled, crushed, burned, or decomposed to a point where even family members would not recognize them.

In a situation like this, how can we identify individuals with any certainty? The New York Medical Examiner's Office turned to **DNA fingerprinting,** a technique for analyzing minuscule samples of DNA taken from semen, skin, blood, or other body tissues. DNA fingerprinting is based on the fact that no two members of a species, except for identical twins, possess identical sets of genetic material. In effect, DNA fingerprinting creates a unique genetic "barcode" that distinguishes each of us from all other humans. Let's see how it works.

Creating a DNA Profile

Recall that DNA contains four nucleotides—A, G, T, and C—that form complementary base pairs. In members of

DNA electrophoresis. *A scientist looking at DNA fragments in an electrophoresis gel. The fragments have been stained with ethidium bromide. This fluoresces under ultraviolet light and makes the positions of the fragments easier to see. A face visor has to be worn to protect the eyes against the UV light.*

the same species, 99.9% of the DNA is identical. This means that only 0.1% of your DNA differs from that of other humans—but this is enough to make you genetically unique. In a DNA string 3 billion units long, that 0.1% translates into 3 million variations that differ slightly from everyone else's—even close relatives. Unless you are an identical sibling, your set of DNA is yours alone. DNA fingerprinting involves analyzing an individual's DNA, mapping its unique pattern, and comparing it to other DNA profiles to determine whether there's a match.

A standard technique for creating a DNA profile focuses on 13 specific sites on our chromosomes. At these sites, short segments of nuclear DNA are arranged in a repeating sequence. Individuals vary greatly in the number of repetitions, from 1 to 30 sets or more. While it is theoretically possible that unrelated people could have identical repeats at all 13 sites, the odds are less than one in 1 trillion.

Sometimes it can be difficult to obtain sufficient nuclear DNA for analysis. DNA samples recovered from crime scenes, for example, are often contaminated with dirt, fibers, and debris. Many body parts recovered from the World Trade Center are charred, ground into dust, or badly decomposed, limiting the amount of testable tissue. DNA retrieval can become a race against time as microbes, enzymes, insects, and environmental factors such as heat and humidity accelerate the decomposition process. However, mitochondria also contain DNA, some of which can survive in bones, teeth, and hair. Mitochondrial DNA too can be profiled to find a match, and sometimes it can be combined with a partial nuclear profile to give a positive identification.

Sorting and Identifying DNA

For DNA to be profiled, it must first be cut into manageable fragments by *restriction enzymes,* enzymes that "recognize" a specific base sequence and cleave the DNA at that location. This

breaks down chromosomes into millions of different-sized pieces, which are then subjected to *gel electrophoresis* (see the photo), a technique that separates them by length. The DNA is placed on a gel and positioned in an electric field. The negatively charged DNA fragments are attracted to the positively charged electrode and migrate toward it. Because the smaller pieces move through the gel faster than their larger cousins, the fragments end up sorted by size.

To locate a specific repeating sequence, researchers make a DNA *probe* with a complementary sequence and tag it with a radioactive compound. The probe binds to the complementary site and when the product is exposed to X-ray film, the image shows dark bands where the probe bound to the DNA. A victim's DNA profile is then compared with known references to find one that matches. In the case of the World Trade Center attack, DNA references were obtained from victim's personal effects such as toothbrushes and combs, entered into a computer, and sorted to find a match.

DNA Fingerprinting and Forensics

DNA fingerprinting has become a vital tool in forensic medicine (the application of medical knowledge to questions of law). For example, DNA fingerprinting is used to identify "John and Jane Doe's" unknown human remains. The U.S. military takes blood and saliva samples from every recruit so that it can identify soldiers killed in the line of duty. DNA fingerprinting can also identify victims of mass disasters such as airplane crashes. The World Trade Center tragedy called for genetic analysis on an unprecedented scale—some 1 million DNA tests were necessary to identify all the missing. DNA fingerprinting can prove that a suspect was actually at the scene of a crime, and in the United States, some communities require criminal offenders to provide DNA samples, which are phosphate group, indicated by P_i, accompanied by a transfer of energy:

$$ATP \xrightleftharpoons[H_2O]{H_2O} ADP + P_i + energy$$

As ATP is hydrolyzed to provide energy for cellular needs, ADP accumulates. Cleavage of the terminal phosphate bond of ADP liberates a similar amount of energy and produces adenosine monophosphate (AMP). ATP supplies are replenished as glucose and other fuel molecules are oxidized and their bond energy is released. The same amount of energy that is liberated when ATP's terminal phosphates are cleaved off must be captured and used to reverse the reaction to reattach phosphates and re-form the energy-transferring phosphate bonds. Without ATP, molecules cannot be made or degraded, cells cannot transport substances across their membrane boundaries, muscles cannot shorten to tug on other structures, and life processes cease (Figure 2.24).

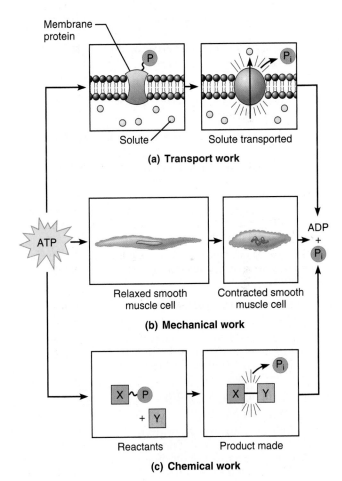

FIGURE 2.24 **Three examples of how ATP drives cellular work.** The high-energy bonds of ATP are like coiled springs that release energy for use by the cell when they are broken. **(a)** ATP drives the transport of certain solutes (amino acids, for example) across cell membranes. **(b)** ATP activates contractile proteins in muscle cells so that the cells can shorten and perform mechanical work. **(c)** ATP provides the energy to drive endergonic (energy-absorbing) chemical reaction

Related Clinical Terms

Acidosis (as″ĭ-do′sis; *acid* = sour, sharp) A condition of acidity or low pH (below 7.35) of the blood; high hydrogen ion concentration.

Alkalosis (al″kah-lo′sis) A condition of basicity or high pH (above 7.45) of the blood; low hydrogen ion concentration.

Heavy metals Metals with toxic effects on the body, including arsenic, mercury, and lead. Iron, also included in this group, is toxic in high concentrations.

Ionizing radiation Radiation that causes atoms to ionize; for example, radioisotope emissions and X rays.

Ketosis (ke-to′sis) A form of acidosis resulting from excessive ketones (breakdown products of fats) in the blood; common during starvation and acute attacks of diabetes mellitus.

Radiation sickness Disease resulting from exposure of the body to radioactivity; digestive system organs are most affected.

Chapter Summary

Media study tools that could provide you additional help in reviewing specific key topics of Chapter 2 are referenced below.
IP = *InterActive Physiology*

PART 1: BASIC CHEMISTRY

Definition of Concepts: Matter and Energy (pp. 25–26)

Matter (p. 25)

1. Matter is anything that takes up space and has mass.

Energy (pp. 25–26)

2. Energy is the capacity to do work or put matter into motion.

3. Energy exists as potential energy (stored energy or energy of position) and kinetic energy (active or working energy).

4. Forms of energy involved in body functioning are chemical, electrical, radiant, and mechanical. Of these, chemical (bond) energy is most important.

5. Energy may be converted from one form to another, but some energy is always unusable (lost as heat) in such transformations.

Composition of Matter: Atoms and Elements (pp. 27–30)

1. Elements are unique substances that cannot be decomposed into simpler substances by ordinary chemical methods. Four elements (carbon, hydrogen, oxygen, and nitrogen) make up 96% of body weight.

Atomic Structure (pp. 27–28)

2. The building blocks of elements are atoms.

3. Atoms are composed of positively charged protons, negatively charged electrons, and uncharged neutrons. Protons and neutrons are located in the atomic nucleus, constituting essentially the atom's total mass; electrons are outside the nucleus in the electron shells. In any atom, the number of electrons equals the number of protons.

Identifying Elements (p. 28)

4. Atoms may be identified by their atomic number (p^+) and mass number ($p^+ + n^0$). The notation $^4_2$He means that helium (He) has an atomic number of 2 and a mass number of 4.

5. Isotopes of an element differ in the number of neutrons they contain. The atomic weight of any element is approximately equal to the mass number of its most abundant isotope.

Radioisotopes (pp. 29–30)

6. Many heavy isotopes are unstable (radioactive). These so-called radioisotopes decompose to more stable forms by emitting alpha or beta particles or gamma rays. Radioisotopes are useful in medical diagnosis and treatment and in biochemical research.

How Matter Is Combined: Molecules and Mixtures (pp. 30–31)

Molecules and Compounds (p. 30)

1. A molecule is the smallest unit resulting from the chemical bonding of two or more atoms. If the atoms are different, they form a molecule of a compound.

Mixtures (pp. 30–31)

2. Mixtures are physical combinations of solutes in a solvent. Mixture components retain their individual properties.

3. The types of mixtures, in order of increasing solute size, are solutions, colloids, and suspensions.

4. Solution concentrations are typically designated in terms of percent or molarity.

Distinguishing Mixtures from Compounds (p. 31)

5. Compounds are homogeneous; their elements are chemically bonded. Mixtures may be homogeneous or heterogeneous; their components are physically combined and separable.

Chemical Bonds (pp. 31–36)

The Role of Electrons in Chemical Bonding (pp. 32–33)

1. Electrons of an atom occupy areas of space called electron shells or energy levels. Electrons in the shell farthest from the nucleus (valence shell) are most energetic.

2. Chemical bonds are energy relationships between valence shell electrons of the reacting atoms. Atoms with a full valence shell or eight valence shell electrons are chemically unreactive (inert); those with an incomplete valence shell interact with other atoms to achieve stability.

Types of Chemical Bonds (pp. 33–36)

3. Ionic bonds are formed when valence shell electrons are completely transferred from one atom to another.

4. Covalent bonds are formed when atoms share electron pairs. If the electron pairs are shared equally, the molecule is nonpolar; if they are shared unequally, it is polar (a dipole).

5. Hydrogen bonds are weak bonds formed between hydrogen and nitrogen or hydrogen and oxygen. They bind together different molecules (e.g., water molecules) or different parts of the same molecule (as in protein molecules).

Chemical Reactions (pp. 36–40)

Chemical Equations (pp. 36–37)

1. Chemical reactions involve the formation, breaking, or rearrangement of chemical bonds.

Patterns of Chemical Reactions (pp. 37–38)

2. Chemical reactions include synthesis, decomposition, and exchange reactions. Oxidation-reduction reactions may be considered a special type of exchange (or catabolic) reaction.

Energy Flow in Chemical Reactions (p. 38–39)

3. Bonds are energy relationships and there is a net loss or gain of energy in every chemical reaction.

4. In exergonic reactions, energy is liberated; in endergonic reactions, energy is absorbed.

Reversibility of Chemical Reactions (p. 39)

5. If reaction conditions remain unchanged, all chemical reactions eventually reach a state of chemical equilibrium in which the reaction proceeds in both directions at the same rate.

6. All chemical reactions are theoretically reversible, but many biological reactions go in only one direction because of energy requirements or the removal of reaction products.

Factors Influencing the Rate of Chemical Reactions (pp. 39–40)

7. Chemical reactions occur only when particles collide and valence shell electrons interact.

8. The smaller the reacting particles, the greater their kinetic energy and the faster the reaction rate. Higher temperature or reactant concentration, as well as the presence of catalysts, increases chemical reaction rates.

PART 2: BIOCHEMISTRY

Inorganic Compounds (pp. 40–43)

1. Most inorganic compounds do not contain carbon. Those found in the body include water, salts, and inorganic acids and bases.

Water (pp. 40–41)

2. Water is the single most abundant compound in the body. It absorbs and releases heat slowly, acts as a universal solvent, participates in chemical reactions, and cushions body organs.

Salts (p. 41)

3. Salts are ionic compounds that dissolve in water and act as electrolytes. Calcium and phosphorus salts contribute to the hardness of bones and teeth. Ions of salts are involved in many physiological processes.

Acids and Bases (pp. 41–43)

4. Acids are proton donors; in water, they ionize and dissociate, releasing hydrogen ions (which account for their properties) and anions.

 IP Fluid, Electrolyte and Acid/Base Balance; Topic: Acid Base Homeostasis, pp. 1–12, 16, 17.

5. Bases are proton acceptors. The most important inorganic bases are the hydroxides; bicarbonate ion and ammonia are important bases in the body.

6. pH is a measure of hydrogen ion concentration of a solution (in moles per liter). A pH of 7 is neutral; a higher pH is alkaline, and a lower pH is acidic. Normal blood pH is 7.35–7.45. Buffers help to prevent excessive changes in the pH of body fluids.

 IP Fluid, Electrolyte and Acid/Base Balance; Topic: Introduction to Body Fluids, pp. 1–8.

Organic Compounds (pp. 43–59)

1. Organic compounds contain carbon. Those found in the body include carbohydrates, lipids, proteins, and nucleic acids, all of which are synthesized by dehydration synthesis and digested by hydrolysis. All of these biological molecules contain C, H, and O. Proteins and nucleic acids also contain N.

Carbohydrates (pp. 44–46)

2. Carbohydrate building blocks are monosaccharides, the most important of which are hexoses (glucose, fructose, galactose) and pentoses (ribose, deoxyribose).

3. Disaccharides (sucrose, lactose, maltose) and polysaccharides (starch, glycogen) are composed of linked monosaccharide units.

4. Carbohydrates, particularly glucose, are the major energy fuel for forming ATP. Excess carbohydrates are stored as glycogen or converted to fat for storage.

Lipids (pp. 46–48)

5. Lipids dissolve in fats or organic solvents, but not in water.

6. Triglycerides are composed of fatty acid chains and glycerol. They are found chiefly in fatty tissue where they provide insulation and reserve body fuel. Unsaturated fatty acid chains produce oils; saturated fatty acids produce solid fats typical of animal fats.

7. Phospholipids are modified phosphorus-containing triglycerides that have polar and nonpolar portions. They are found in all plasma membranes.

8. The steroid cholesterol is found in cell membranes and is the basis of steroid hormones, bile salts, and vitamin D.

Proteins (pp. 48–54)

9. The unit of proteins is the amino acid; 20 common amino acids are found in the body.

10. Many amino acids joined by peptide bonds form a polypeptide. A protein (one or more polypeptides) is distinguished by the number and sequence of amino acids in its chain(s) and by the complexity of its three-dimensional structure.

11. Fibrous proteins, such as keratin and collagen, have secondary (α-helix or β-pleated sheet) and perhaps quaternary structure. Fibrous proteins are used as structural materials.

12. Globular proteins achieve tertiary or quaternary structure and are generally spherical, soluble molecules. Globular proteins (e.g., enzymes, some hormones, antibodies, hemoglobin) perform special functional roles for the cell (e.g., catalysis, molecule transport).

13. Proteins are denatured by extremes of temperature or pH. Denatured globular proteins are unable to perform their usual function.

14. Molecular chaperones assist in folding proteins into their functional 3-D shape. They are synthesized in greater amounts when cells are stressed by environmental factors and begin to accumulate denatured proteins.

15. Enzymes are biological catalysts; they increase the rate of chemical reactions by decreasing the amount of activation energy needed. They do this by combining with the reactants and holding them in the proper position to interact. Many enzymes require cofactors to function.

Nucleic Acids (DNA and RNA) (pp. 54–57)

16. Nucleic acids include deoxyribonucleic acid (DNA) and ribonucleic acid (RNA). The structural unit of nucleic acids is the nucleotide, which consists of a nitrogenous base (adenine, guanine, cytosine, thymine, or uracil), a sugar (ribose or deoxyribose), and a phosphate group.

17. DNA is a double-stranded helix: it contains deoxyribose and the bases A, G, C, and T. DNA specifies protein structure and replicates itself exactly before cell division.

18. RNA is single-stranded; it contains ribose and the bases A, G, C, and U. RNAs involved in carrying out DNA's instructions for protein synthesis include messenger, ribosomal, and transfer RNA.

Review Questions

Multiple Choice/Matching

(Some questions have more than one correct answer. Select the best answer or answers from the choices given.)

1. Which of the following forms of energy are in use during vision? (a) chemical, (b) electrical, (c) mechanical, (d) radiant.

2. All of the following are examples of the four major elements contributing to body mass except (a) hydrogen, (b) carbon, (c) nitrogen, (d) sodium, (e) oxygen.

3. The mass number of an atom is (a) equal to the number of protons it contains, (b) the sum of its protons and neutrons, (c) the sum of all of its subatomic particles, (d) the average of the mass numbers of all of its isotopes.

4. A deficiency in this element can be expected to reduce the hemoglobin content of blood: (a) Fe, (b) I, (c) F, (d) Ca, (e) K.

5. Which set of terms best describes a proton? (a) negative charge, massless, in the orbital; (b) positive charge, 1 amu, in the nucleus; (c) uncharged, 1 amu, in the nucleus.

6. The subatomic particles responsible for the chemical behavior of atoms are (a) electrons, (b) ions, (c) neutrons, (d) protons.

7. In the body, carbohydrates are stored in the form of (a) glycogen, (b) starch, (c) cholesterol, (d) polypeptides.

8. Which of the following does *not* describe a mixture? (a) properties of its components are retained, (b) chemical bonds are formed, (c) components can be separated physically, (d) includes both heterogeneous and homogeneous examples.

9. In a beaker of water, the water-water bonds can properly be called (a) ionic bonds, (b) polar covalent bonds, (c) nonpolar covalent bonds, (d) hydrogen bonds.

10. When a pair of electrons is shared between two atoms, the bond formed is called (a) a single covalent bond, (b) a double covalent bond, (c) a triple covalent bond, (d) an ionic bond.

11. Molecules formed when electrons are shared unequally are (a) salts, (b) polar molecules, (c) nonpolar molecules.

12. Which of the following covalently bonded molecules are polar?

(a) H—Cl (b) H—C—H (c) Cl—C—Cl (d) N≡N

13. Identify each reaction as (a) a synthesis reaction, (b) a decomposition reaction, or (c) an exchange reaction.

(1) $2Hg + O_2 \rightarrow 2HgO$
(2) $HCl + NaOH \rightarrow NaCl + H_2O$

Adenosine Triphosphate (ATP) (pp. 56–59)

19. ATP is the universal energy compound of body cells. Some of the energy liberated by the breakdown of glucose and other food fuels is captured in the bonds of ATP molecules and transferred via coupled reactions to energy-consuming reactions.

14. Factors that accelerate the rate of chemical reactions include all but (a) the presence of catalysts, (b) increasing the temperature, (c) increasing the particle size, (d) increasing the concentration of the reactants.

15. Which of the following molecules is an inorganic molecule? (a) sucrose, (b) cholesterol, (c) collagen, (d) sodium chloride.

16. Water's importance to living systems reflects (a) its polarity and solvent properties, (b) its high heat capacity, (c) its high heat of vaporization, (d) its chemical reactivity, (e) all of these.

17. Acids (a) release hydroxyl ions when dissolved in water, (b) are proton acceptors, (c) cause the pH of a solution to rise, (d) release protons when dissolved in water.

18. A chemist, during the course of an analysis, runs across a chemical composed of carbon, hydrogen, and oxygen in the proportion 1:2:1 and having a six-sided molecular shape. It is probably (a) a pentose, (b) an amino acid, (c) a fatty acid, (d) a monosaccharide, (e) a nucleic acid.

19. A triglyceride consists of (a) glycerol plus up to three fatty acids, (b) a sugar-phosphate backbone to which two amino groups are attached, (c) two to several hexoses, (d) amino acids that have been thoroughly saturated with hydrogen.

20. A chemical has an amine group and an organic acid group. It does not, however, have any peptide bonds. It is (a) a monosaccharide, (b) an amino acid, (c) a protein, (d) a fat.

21. The lipid(s) used as the basis of vitamin D, sex hormones, and bile salts is/are (a) triglycerides, (b) cholesterol, (c) phospholipids, (d) prostaglandin.

22. Enzymes are organic catalysts that (a) alter the direction in which a chemical reaction proceeds, (b) determine the nature of the products of a reaction, (c) increase the speed of a chemical reaction, (d) are essential raw materials for a chemical reaction that are converted into some of its products.

Short Answer Essay Questions

23. Define or describe energy, and explain the relationship between potential and kinetic energy.

24. Some energy is lost in every energy conversion. Explain the meaning of this statement. (Direct your response to answering the question: Is it really lost? If not, what then?)

25. Provide the atomic symbol for each of the following elements: (a) calcium, (b) carbon, (c) hydrogen, (d) iron, (e) nitrogen, (f) oxygen, (g) potassium, (h) sodium.

26. Consider the following information about three atoms:

$^{12}_6C \quad ^{13}_6C \quad ^{14}_6C$

(a) How are they similar to one another? (b) How do they differ from one another? (c) What are the members of such a group of atoms called? (d) Using the planetary model, draw the atomic configuration of $^{12}_{6}C$ showing the relative position and numbers of its subatomic particles.

27. How many moles of aspirin, $C_9H_8O_4$, are in a bottle containing 450 g by weight? (*Note:* The approximate atomic weights of its atoms are C = 12, H = 1, and O = 16.)

28. Given the following types of atoms, decide which type of bonding, ionic or covalent, is most likely to occur: (a) two oxygen atoms; (b) four hydrogen atoms and one carbon atom; (c) a potassium atom ($^{39}_{19}K$) and a fluorine atom ($^{19}_{9}F$).

29. What are hydrogen bonds and how are they important in the body?

30. The following equation, which represents the oxidative breakdown of glucose by body cells, is a reversible reaction.

Glucose + oxygen → carbon dioxide + water + ATP

(a) How can you indicate that the reaction is reversible? (b) How can you indicate that the reaction is in chemical equilibrium? (c) Define chemical equilibrium.

31. (a) Differentiate clearly between primary, secondary, and tertiary protein structure. (b) What level of structure do most fibrous proteins achieve? (c) How do globular proteins relate to the structural levels?

32. Dehydration and hydrolysis reactions are essentially opposite reactions. How are they related to the synthesis and degradation (breakdown) of biological molecules?

33. Describe the mechanism of enzyme activity. In your discussion, explain how enzymes decrease activation energy requirements.

34. Explain the importance of molecular chaperones.

35. Explain why, if you pour water into a glass very carefully, you can "stack" the water slightly above the rim of the glass.

36. Water is a precious natural resource in Florida and it is said that supplies are dwindling. Desalinizing (removing salt from) ocean water has been recommended as a solution to the problem. Why shouldn't we drink salt water?

Critical Thinking and Clinical Application Questions

1. As Ben jumped on his bike and headed for the freshwater lake, his mother called after him, "Don't swim if we have an electrical storm—it looks threatening." This was a valid request. Why?

2. Some antibiotics act by binding to certain essential enzymes in the target bacteria. (a) How might these antibiotics influence the chemical reactions controlled by the enzymes? (b) What is the anticipated effect on the bacteria? On the person taking the antibiotic prescription?

3. Mrs. Roberts, in a diabetic coma, has just been admitted to Noble Hospital. Her blood pH indicates that she is in severe acidosis, and measures are quickly instituted to bring her blood pH back within normal limits. (a) Define pH and note the normal pH of blood. (b) Why is severe acidosis problematic?

4. Jimmy, a 12-year-old boy, was awakened suddenly by a loud crash. As he sat up in bed, straining to listen, his fright was revealed by his rapid breathing (hyperventilation), a breathing pattern effective in ridding the blood of CO_2. At this point, was his blood pH rising or falling?

LOOKING FOR MORE STUDY HELP?

A wide variety of quiz questions, tutorials, and learning exercises are available online at the Anatomy & Physiology Place (www.anatomyandphysiology.com) and, if your instructor has provided you with a MyA&P Course ID number, in MyA&P (www.myaandp.com).

2

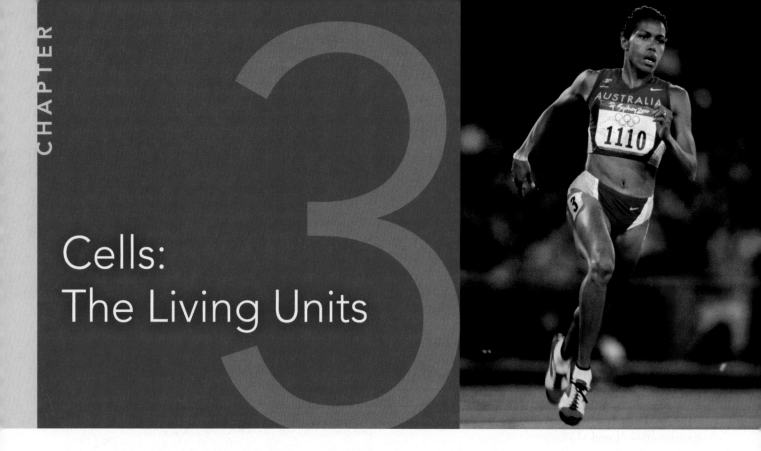

CHAPTER 3

Cells:
The Living Units

Overview of the Cellular Basis of Life (pp. 65–66)

1. Define cell.
2. List the three major regions of a generalized cell and indicate the function of each.

The Plasma Membrane: Structure (pp. 66–70)

3. Describe the chemical composition of the plasma membrane and relate it to membrane functions.
4. Compare the structure and function of tight junctions, desmosomes, and gap junctions.

The Plasma Membrane: Functions (pp. 70–84)

5. Relate plasma membrane structure to active and passive transport mechanisms. Differentiate between these transport processes relative to energy source, substances transported, direction, and mechanism.
6. Define membrane potential and explain how the resting membrane potential is maintained.

7. Describe the role of the glycocalyx when cells interact with their environment.
8. List several roles of membrane receptors and that of voltage-sensitive membrane channel proteins.

The Cytoplasm (pp. 84–95)

9. Describe the composition of the cytosol; define inclusions and list several types.
10. Discuss the structure and function of mitochondria.
11. Discuss the structure and function of ribosomes, the endoplasmic reticulum, and the Golgi apparatus including functional interrelationships among these organelles.
12. Compare the functions of lysosomes and peroxisomes.
13. Name and describe the structure and function of cytoskeletal elements.
14. Describe the roles of centrioles in mitosis and in formation of cilia and flagella.

The Nucleus (pp. 95–97)

15. Outline the structure and function of the nuclear envelope, nucleolus, and chromatin.

Cell Growth and Reproduction (pp. 97–111)

16. List the phases of the cell life cycle and describe the key events of each phase.
17. Describe the process of DNA replication.
18. Define gene and genetic code and explain the function of genes.
19. Name the two phases of protein synthesis and describe the roles of DNA, mRNA, tRNA, and rRNA in each phase. Contrast triplets, codons, and anticodons.
20. Describe the importance of ubiquitin degradation of soluble proteins.

Extracellular Materials (p. 111)

21. Name and describe the composition of extracellular materials.

Developmental Aspects of Cells (pp. 111–112)

22. Discuss some theories of cell differentiation and aging.

Just as bricks and timbers are the structural units of a house, **cells** are the structural units of all living things, from one-celled "generalists" like amoebas to complex multicellular organisms such as humans, dogs, and trees. The human body has 50 to 100 trillion of these tiny building blocks.

This chapter focuses on structures and functions shared by all cells. Specialized cells and their unique functions are addressed in later chapters.

Overview of the Cellular Basis of Life

The English scientist Robert Hooke first observed plant cells with a crude microscope in the late 1600s. However, it was not until the 1830s that two German scientists, Matthias Schleiden and Theodor Schwann, were bold enough to insist that all living things are composed of cells. The German pathologist Rudolf Virchow extended this idea by contending that cells arise only from other cells. Virchow's proclamation was revolutionary because it openly challenged the widely accepted *theory of spontaneous generation*, which held that organisms arise spontaneously from garbage or other nonliving matter. Since the late 1800s, cell research has been exceptionally fruitful and provided us with four concepts collectively known as the **cell theory:**

1. A cell is the basic structural and functional unit of living organisms. So when you define cell properties you are in fact defining the properties of life.

2. The activity of an organism depends on both the individual and the collective activities of its cells.

3. According to the *principle of complementarity*, the biochemical activities of cells are dictated by the relative number of their specific subcellular structures.

4. Continuity of life has a cellular basis.

We will expand on all of these concepts as we progress. Let us begin with the idea that the cell is the smallest living unit. Whatever its form, however it behaves, the cell is the microscopic package that contains all the parts necessary to survive in an ever-changing world. It follows then that loss of cellular homeostasis underlies virtually every disease.

The trillions of cells in the human body include over 200 different cell types that vary greatly in shape, size, and function (Figure 3.1). The spherical fat cells, disc-shaped red blood cells, branching nerve cells, and cubelike cells of kidney tubules are just a few examples of the shapes cells take. Depending on type, cells also vary greatly in length—ranging from 2 micrometers (1/12,000 of an inch) in the smallest

Erythrocytes

Fibroblasts

Epithelial cells

(a) Cells that connect body parts, form linings, or transport gases

Skeletal muscle cell

Smooth muscle cells

(b) Cells that move organs and body parts

Fat cell

Macrophage

(c) Cell that stores nutrients   **(d) Cell that fights disease**

Nerve cell

(e) Cell that gathers information and controls body functions

Sperm

(f) Cell of reproduction

FIGURE 3.1 **Cell diversity.**

cells to over a meter in the nerve cells that cause you to wiggle your toes. A cell's shape reflects its function. For example, the flat, tilelike epithelial cells that line the inside of your cheek fit closely together, forming a living barrier that protects underlying tissues from bacterial invasion.

Regardless of type, all cells are composed chiefly of carbon, hydrogen, nitrogen, oxygen, and trace

3

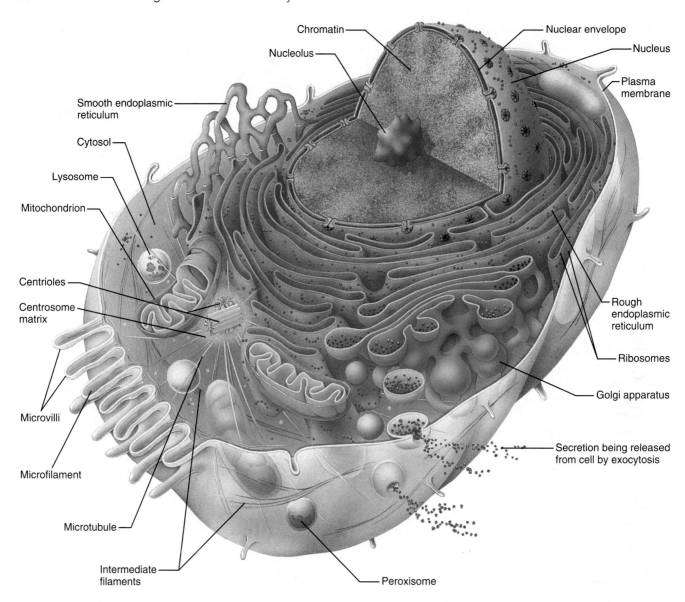

Smooth endoplasmic reticulum

Cytosol

Lysosome

Mitochondrion

Centrioles

Centrosome matrix

Microvilli

Microfilament

Microtubule

Intermediate filaments

Chromatin

Nucleolus

Nuclear envelope

Nucleus

Plasma membrane

Rough endoplasmic reticulum

Ribosomes

Golgi apparatus

Secretion being released from cell by exocytosis

Peroxisome

FIGURE 3.2 **Structure of the generalized cell.** No cell is exactly like this one, but this composite illustrates features common to many human cells. Note that not all of the organelles are drawn to the same scale in this illustration.

amounts of several other elements. In addition, all cells have the same basic parts and some common functions. Thus, it is possible to speak of a **generalized,** or **composite, cell** (Figure 3.2). Human cells have three main parts: the plasma membrane, the cytoplasm, and the nucleus. The *plasma membrane,* a fragile barrier, is the outer boundary of the cell. Internal to this membrane is the *cytoplasm* (si'to-plazm), the intracellular fluid that is packed with organelles, small structures that perform specific cell functions. The *nucleus* (nu'kle-us) controls cellular activities and lies near the cell's center. These cell structures are summarized in Table 3.3 (pp. 94–95) and are described next.

The Plasma Membrane: Structure

The flexible **plasma membrane** defines the extent of a cell, thereby separating two of the body's major fluid compartments—the *intracellular* fluid within cells and the *extracellular* fluid outside cells. The term *cell membrane* is commonly used as a synonym for plasma membrane, but because nearly all cellular organelles are enclosed in a membrane, in this book we will always refer to the cell's surface or outer limiting membrane as the plasma membrane. The plasma membrane is much more than a passive envelope. As you will see, its unique structure allows it to play a dynamic role in many cellular activities.

Q *Some membrane proteins float freely in the lipid phase of the membrane. Others are secured in specific locations. According to this diagram, what would serve as the anchoring structures in the latter case?*

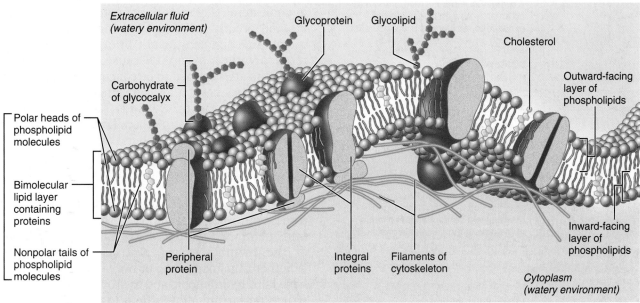

FIGURE 3.3 **Structure of the plasma membrane according to the fluid mosaic model.**

The Fluid Mosaic Model

The **fluid mosaic model** of membrane structure (Figure 3.3) depicts the plasma membrane as an exceedingly thin (7–10 nm) structure composed of a double layer, or bilayer, of lipid molecules with protein molecules dispersed in it. The proteins, many of which float in the fluid *lipid bilayer,* form a constantly changing mosaic pattern; hence the name of the model.

The lipid bilayer, which forms the basic "fabric" of the membrane, is constructed largely of *phospholipids,* with smaller amounts of *cholesterol* and *glycolipids.* Each lollipop-shaped phospholipid molecule has a polar "head" that is charged and is **hydrophilic** (*hydro* = water, *philic* = loving), and an uncharged, nonpolar "tail" that is made of two fatty acid chains and is **hydrophobic** (*phobia* = hating). The polar heads are attracted to water—the main constituent of both the intracellular and extracellular fluids—and so they lie on both the inner and outer surfaces of the membrane. The nonpolar tails, being hydrophobic, avoid water and line up in the center of the membrane. The result is that all biological membranes share a common sandwich-like structure: They are composed of two parallel sheets of phospholipid molecules lying tail to tail, with their polar heads exposed to water inside and outside the cell. This self-orienting property of phospholipids encourages biological membranes to self-assemble into closed, generally spherical, structures and to reseal themselves quickly when torn. It also enables scientists to suck out and replace a cell's nucleus in *cloning experiments,* a hot scientific area today.

The inward-facing and outward-facing surfaces of the plasma membrane differ in the kinds and amounts of lipids they contain. The majority of membrane phospholipids are unsaturated (like phosphatidylcholine), a condition which kinks their tails (increasing the space between them) and increases membrane fluidity. **Glycolipids** (gli"ko-lip'idz), phospholipids with attached sugar groups, are found only on the outer plasma membrane surface and account for about 5% of the total membrane lipid. Their sugar

A *Filaments of the cytoskeleton.*

3

Transport
(a) A protein that spans the membrane may provide a hydrophilic channel across the membrane that is selective for a particular solute. **(b)** Some transport proteins hydrolyze ATP as an energy source to actively pump substances across the membrane.

Enzymatic activity
A protein built into the membrane may be an enzyme with its active site exposed to substances in the adjacent solution. In some cases, several enzymes in a membrane act as a team that catalyzes sequential steps of a metabolic pathway as indicated (right to left) here.

Receptors for signal transduction
A membrane protein exposed to the outside of the cell may have a binding site with a specific shape that fits the shape of a chemical messenger, such as a hormone. The external signal may cause a conformational change in the protein that initiates a chain of chemical reactions in the cell.

Intercellular joining
Membrane proteins of adjacent cells may be hooked together in various kinds of intercellular junctions. Some membrane proteins (CAMs) of this group provide temporary binding sites that guide cell migration and other cell-to-cell interactions.

Cell-cell recognition
Some glycoproteins (proteins bonded to short chains of sugars) serve as identification tags that are specifically recognized by other cells.

Attachment to the cytoskeleton and extracellular matrix (ECM)
Elements of the cytoskeleton (cell's internal supports) and the extracellular matrix (ECM) may be anchored to membrane proteins, which help maintain cell shape and fix the location of certain membrane proteins. Others play a role in cell movement or bind adjacent cells together.

groups, like the phosphate-containing groups of phospholipids, make that end of the glycolipid molecule polar, whereas the fatty acid tails are nonpolar. Some 20% of membrane lipid is cholesterol, which wedges its platelike hydrocarbon rings between the phospholipid tails, decreasing their orderliness and increasing the mobility of the phospholipids.

About 20% of the outer membrane surface contains **lipid rafts,** dynamic assemblies of saturated phospholipids (which pack together tightly) associated with unique lipids called sphingolipids and lots of cholesterol. These quiltlike patches are more stable and orderly and less fluid than the rest of the membrane, and can include or exclude specific proteins to various extents. Because of these qualities, lipid rafts are assumed to be concentrating platforms for molecules needed for cell signaling. (Cell signaling is discussed on pp. 83–84.)

There are two distinct populations of membrane proteins, integral and peripheral (see Figure 3.3). Proteins make up about half of the plasma membrane by mass and are responsible for most of the specialized membrane functions (Figure 3.4). **Integral proteins** are firmly inserted into the lipid bilayer. Some protrude from one membrane face only, but most are *transmembrane proteins* that span the entire width of the membrane and protrude on both sides. Whether transmembrane or not, all integral proteins have both hydrophobic and hydrophilic regions. This structural feature allows them to interact both with the nonpolar lipid tails buried in the membrane and with water inside and outside the cell. Transmembrane proteins are mainly involved in transport. Some cluster together to form *channels,* or pores, through which small, water-soluble molecules or ions can move, thus bypassing the lipid part of the membrane. Others act as *carriers* that bind to a substance and then move it through the membrane. Still others are receptors for hormones or other chemical messengers and relay messages to the cell interior (a process called *signal transduction*).

Peripheral proteins, in contrast, are not embedded in the lipid. Instead, they attach rather loosely to integral proteins or membrane lipids and are easily removed without disrupting the membrane. Peripheral proteins include a network of filaments that helps support the membrane from its cytoplasmic side. Some peripheral proteins are enzymes. Others are involved in mechanical functions, such as changing cell shape during cell division and muscle cell contraction, or linking cells together.

Many of the proteins that abut the extracellular space are glycoproteins that sport branching sugar

FIGURE 3.4   Some functions of membrane proteins. A single protein may perform some combination of these tasks.

groups. The term **glycocalyx** (gli"ko-kal'iks; "sugar covering") is used to describe the fuzzy, sticky carbohydrate-rich area at the cell surface. You can think of your cells as sugar-coated. The glycocalyx that clings to each cell's surface is enriched both by glycolipids and by glycoproteins secreted by the cell.

Because every cell type has a different pattern of sugars in its glycocalyx, the glycocalyx provides highly specific biological markers by which approaching cells recognize each other. For example, a sperm recognizes an ovum (egg cell) by the ovum's unique glycocalyx, and cells of the immune system identify a bacterium by binding to certain membrane glycoproteins in the bacterial glycocalyx.

◤ HOMEOSTATIC IMBALANCE

Definite changes in the glycocalyx occur in a cell that is becoming cancerous. In fact, a cancer cell's glycocalyx may change almost continuously, allowing it to keep ahead of immune system recognition mechanisms and avoid destruction. (Cancer is discussed on pp. 146–147.) ●

The plasma membrane is a dynamic fluid structure that is in constant flux. Its consistency is like that of olive oil. The lipid molecules of the bilayer move freely from side to side, parallel to the membrane surface, but their polar-nonpolar interactions prevent them from flip-flopping or moving from one leaflet (half of the bilayer) to the other. Some of the proteins float freely. Others, particularly the peripheral proteins, are restricted in their movements because they are "tethered" to intracellular structures that make up the *cytoskeleton* (see Figure 3.4).

Specializations of the Plasma Membrane

Microvilli

Microvilli (mi"kro-vil'i; "little shaggy hairs") are minute, fingerlike extensions of the plasma membrane that project from a free, or exposed, cell surface (Figures 3.2 and 3.5). They increase the plasma membrane surface area tremendously and are most often found on the surface of absorptive cells such as intestinal and kidney tubule cells. Microvilli have a core of actin filaments. Actin is a contractile protein, but in microvilli it appears to function as a mechanical "stiffener."

Membrane Junctions

Although certain cell types—blood cells, sperm cells, and some phagocytic cells—are "footloose" in the body, many other types, particularly epithelial cells, are knit into tight communities. Typically, three factors act to bind cells together:

1. Glycoproteins in the glycocalyx act as an adhesive.
2. Wavy contours of the membranes of adjacent cells fit together in a tongue-and-groove fashion.
3. Special membrane junctions are formed (Figure 3.5). Because this last factor is the most important let us look more closely at the various types of junctions.

Tight Junctions   In a **tight junction,** a series of integral protein molecules (including occludins and claudins) in the plasma membranes of adjacent cells fuse together, forming an *impermeable junction* that encircles the cell (Figure 3.5a). Tight junctions help prevent molecules from passing through the extracellular space between adjacent cells. For example, tight junctions between epithelial cells lining the digestive tract keep digestive enzymes and microorganisms in the intestine from seeping into the bloodstream. (Although called "impermeable" junctions, some tight junctions are somewhat leaky and may allow certain types of ions to pass.)

Desmosomes   **Desmosomes** (des'mo-sōmz; "binding bodies") are *anchoring junctions*—mechanical couplings scattered like rivets along the sides of abutting cells that prevent their separation (Figure 3.5b). On the cytoplasmic face of each plasma membrane is a buttonlike thickening called a *plaque*. Adjacent cells are held together by thin linker protein filaments (cadherins) that extend from the plaques and interdigitate like the teeth of a zipper in the intercellular space. Thicker protein filaments (intermediate filaments, which form part of the cytoskeleton) extend from the cytoplasmic side of the plaque across the width of the cell to anchor to the plaque on the cell's opposite side. Thus, desmosomes not only bind neighboring cells together, they also contribute to a continuous internal network of strong "guy-wires." This arrangement distributes tension throughout a cellular sheet and reduces the chance of tearing when it is subjected to pulling forces. Desmosomes are abundant in tissues subjected to great mechanical stress, such as skin and heart muscle.

Gap Junctions   A **gap junction,** or *nexus* (nek'sus; "bond"), is a communicating junction between adjacent cells. At gap junctions the adjacent plasma membranes are very close, and the cells are connected by hollow cylinders called *connexons* (kŏ-nek'sonz), composed of transmembrane proteins. The many different types of connexon proteins vary the selectivity of the gap junction channels. Ions, simple sugars, and other small molecules pass through these water-filled channels from one cell to the next (Figure 3.5c). Gap junctions are present in electrically excitable tissues, such as the heart and smooth muscle, where ion passage from cell to cell helps synchronize their electrical activity and contraction.

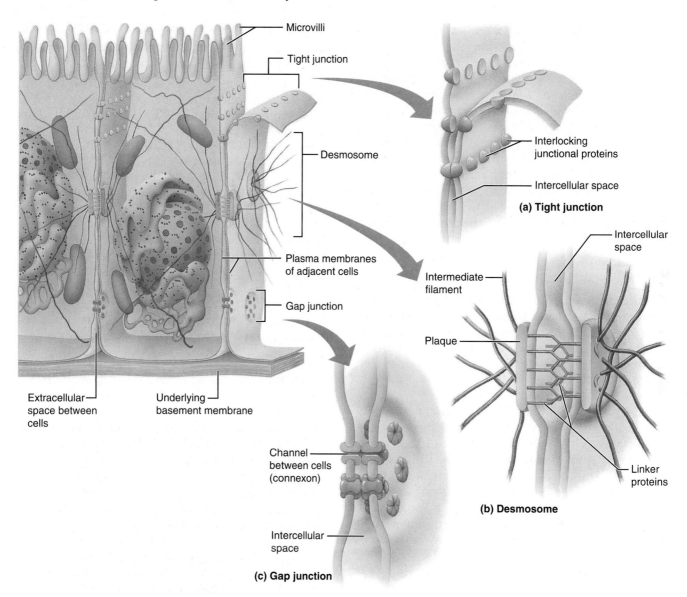

FIGURE 3.5 **Cell junctions.** An epithelial cell is shown joined to adjacent cells by three common types of cell junctions: **(a)** tight junctions, **(b)** desmosomes, and **(c)** gap junctions. (Note: Except for epithelia, it is unlikely that a single cell will have all three junction types.)

The Plasma Membrane: Functions

Membrane Transport

Our cells are bathed in an extracellular fluid called **interstitial fluid** (in"ter-stish'al) that is derived from the blood. Interstitial fluid is like a rich, nutritious "soup." It contains thousands of ingredients, including amino acids, sugars, fatty acids, vitamins, regulatory substances such as hormones and neurotransmitters, salts, and waste products. To remain healthy, each cell must extract from this mix the exact amounts of the substances it needs at specific times.

Although there is continuous traffic across the plasma membrane, it is a **selectively,** or **differentially, permeable** barrier, meaning that it allows some substances to pass while excluding others. Thus, it allows nutrients to enter the cell, but keeps many undesirable substances out. At the same time, it keeps valuable cell proteins and other substances in the cell, but allows wastes to exit.

Substances move through the plasma membrane in essentially two ways—passively or actively. In **passive processes,** substances cross the membrane without any energy input from the cell. In **active processes,** the cell provides the metabolic energy (ATP) needed to move substances across the membrane. The various transport processes that occur in cells are summarized in Table 3.1 on p. 75 and Table 3.2 on p. 80. Let's examine each of these types of membrane transport.

⚠ HOMEOSTATIC IMBALANCE

Selective permeability is a characteristic of healthy, intact cells. When a cell (or its plasma membrane) is severely damaged, the membrane becomes permeable to virtually everything, and substances flow into and out of the cell freely. This phenomenon is evident when someone has been severely burned. Precious fluids, proteins, and ions "weep" from the dead and damaged cells. ●

Passive Processes

The two main types of passive transport in cells are *diffusion* (di-fu'zhun) and *filtration*. Diffusion is an important means of passive membrane transport for every cell of the body. By contrast, filtration generally occurs only across capillary walls.

Diffusion   **Diffusion** is the tendency of molecules or ions to scatter evenly throughout the environment (Figure 3.6). Recall that all molecules possess kinetic energy and are in constant motion (see p. 25). As molecules move about randomly at high speeds, they collide and ricochet off one another, changing direction with each collision. The overall effect of this erratic movement is that molecules move away from areas where they are in higher concentration to areas where their concentration is lower, so we say that molecules diffuse *along*, or *down*, their **concentration gradient.** The greater the difference in concentration between the two areas, the faster the net diffusion of the particles.

Because the driving force for diffusion is the kinetic energy of the molecules themselves, the speed of diffusion is influenced by molecular *size* (the smaller, the faster) and by *temperature* (the warmer, the faster). In a closed container, diffusion eventually produces a uniform mixture of molecules. In other words, the system reaches equilibrium, with molecules moving equally in all directions (no *net* movement). Examples of diffusion are familiar to everyone. When you peel onions, you get teary-eyed because the cut onion releases volatile substances that diffuse through the air, dissolve in the fluid film covering your eyes, and form irritating sulfuric acid.

Because of its hydrophobic core, the plasma membrane is a physical barrier to free diffusion. However, a molecule *will* diffuse through the membrane if the molecule is (1) lipid soluble, (2) small enough to pass through membrane channels, or (3) assisted by a carrier molecule. The unassisted diffusion of lipid-soluble or very small particles is called **simple diffusion.** A special name, *osmosis*, is given

(a)   **(b)**

FIGURE 3.6   **Diffusion.** Molecules in solution move continuously and collide constantly with other molecules. As a result, molecules tend to move away from areas of their highest concentration and become evenly distributed. **(a)** Diagram of dye molecules diffusing from a dye pellet into the surrounding water. **(b)** Dye molecules from pellet have diffused evenly throughout the water.

to the unassisted diffusion of a solvent (usually water) through a membrane. Assisted diffusion is known as *facilitated diffusion.*

1. Simple diffusion. Nonpolar and lipid-soluble substances diffuse directly through the lipid bilayer (Figure 3.7a). Such substances include oxygen, carbon dioxide, and fat-soluble vitamins. Because oxygen concentration is always higher in the blood than in tissue cells, oxygen continuously diffuses from the blood into the cells, whereas carbon dioxide (in higher concentration within the cells) diffuses from tissue cells into the blood.

2. Facilitated diffusion. Certain molecules, notably glucose and other sugars, amino acids, and ions are transported passively even though they are unable to pass through the lipid bilayer. Instead they move through the membrane by a passive transport process called **facilitated diffusion** in which the transported substance either (1) binds to protein carriers in the membrane and is ferried across or (2) moves through water-filled protein channels.

▪ **Carriers.** A **carrier** is a transmembrane integral protein that shows specificity for molecules of a certain polar substance or class of substances that are too large to pass through membrane channels, such as sugars and amino acids. Although it was initially believed that the integral proteins that act as carriers either flip-flopped or physically crossed the membrane like ferryboats, the most popular model for this process indicates that changes in the shape of the carrier allow it to first envelop and then release the

3

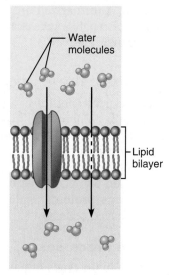

Extracellular fluid

Lipid-soluble solutes

Lipid-insoluble solutes

Small lipid-insoluble solutes

Water molecules

Lipid bilayer

Cytoplasm

(a) Simple diffusion directly through the phospholipid bilayer

(b) Carrier-mediated facilitated diffusion via protein carrier specific for one chemical; binding of substrate causes shape change in transport protein

(c) Channel-mediated facilitated diffusion through a channel protein; mostly ions selected on basis of size and charge

(d) Osmosis, diffusion through a specific channel protein (aquaporin) or through the lipid bilayer

FIGURE 3.7 **Diffusion through the plasma membrane. (a)** In simple diffusion, fat-soluble molecules diffuse directly through the lipid bilayer of the plasma membrane, in which they can dissolve. **(b)** In facilitated diffusion using protein carriers, large, lipid-insoluble molecules (e.g., glucose) are moved across the membrane via a transport protein. **(c)** In facilitated diffusion via membrane channels, small polar or charged particles diffuse through membrane channels constructed by channel proteins. **(d)** In osmosis, water moves across the plasma membrane via specific channels (aquaporins) or diffuses directly through the lipid portion of the membrane.

transported substance, shielding it en route from the nonpolar regions of the membrane (Figure 3.7b). Essentially, the binding site is moved from one face of the membrane to the other by changes in the conformation of the carrier protein.

Just as in any simple diffusion process, a substance transported by carrier-mediated facilitated diffusion, like glucose, moves down its concentration gradient. Glucose is normally in higher concentrations in the blood than in the cells, where it is rapidly used for ATP synthesis. So, within the body glucose transport is *typically* unidirectional—into the cells. However, carrier-mediated transport is limited by the number of receptors present. For example, when all the glucose carriers are "engaged," they are said to be *saturated,* and glucose transport is occurring at its maximum rate.

• **Channels. Channels** are transmembrane proteins that serve to transport substances, usually ions or water, through aqueous channels from one side of the membrane to the other (Figure 3.7c and d). Binding or association sites exist within the channels, and the channels are selective due to pore size and the charges of the amino acids lining the channel. Some channels, the so-called leakage channels, are always open and simply allow ion or water fluxes according to concentration gradients. Others are gated and controlled (opened or closed) by various chemical or electrical signals.

Like carriers, many channels can be inhibited by certain molecules, show saturation, and tend to be specific. Substances moving through them also honor the concentration gradient (always moving down the gradient). When a substance crosses the membrane by simple diffusion, the rate of diffusion is not controllable because the lipid solubility of the membrane is not immediately changeable. By contrast, the rate of facilitated diffusion *is* controllable because the permeability of the membrane can be altered by regulating the activity or number of individual carriers or channels.

Oxygen, water, glucose, and various ions are vitally important to cellular homeostasis. Thus, their passive transport by diffusion (either simple or facilitated) represents a tremendous saving of cellular energy. Indeed, if these substances had to be transported actively, cell expenditures of ATP would increase exponentially!

3. Osmosis. The diffusion of a solvent, such as water, through a selectively permeable membrane is **osmosis** (oz-mo'sis; *osmos* = pushing). Even though water is highly polar, it passes via osmosis through the lipid bilayer (Figure 3.7d). This is surprising

(a) Membrane permeable to both solute molecules and water

(b) Membrane impermeable to solute molecules, permeable to water

FIGURE 3.8   **Influence of membrane permeability on diffusion and osmosis. (a)** In this system, the membrane is permeable to both water and solute (sugar) molecules. Water moves from the solution with lower osmolarity (left compartment) to the solution with greater osmolarity (right compartment). The solute moves along its own concentration gradient in the opposite direction. When the system comes to equilibrium (right), the solutions have the same osmolarity and volume. **(b)** This system is identical to that in (a) except that the membrane is impermeable to the solute. Water moves by osmosis from the left to the right compartment, until its concentration and that of the solutions are identical. Because the solute is prevented from moving, the volume of the solution in the right compartment increases.

because you'd expect it to be repelled by the hydrophobic lipid tails. Although still hypothetical, one explanation is that random movements of the membrane lipids open small gaps between their wiggling tails, allowing water to slip and slide its way through the membrane by moving from gap to gap. Water also moves freely and reversibly through water-specific channels constructed by transmembrane proteins called **aquaporins (AQP).** Although aquaporins are believed to be present in all cell types, they are particularly abundant in red blood cells and in cells involved in water balance such as kidney tubule cells.

Osmosis occurs whenever the water concentration differs on the two sides of a membrane. If distilled water is present on both sides of a selectively permeable membrane, no *net* osmosis occurs, even though water molecules move in both directions through the membrane. If the solute concentration on the two sides of the membrane differs, water concentration differs as well (as solute concentration increases, water concentration decreases). The extent to which water's concentration is decreased by solutes depends on the *number,* not the *type,* of solute particles, because one molecule or one ion of solute (theoretically) displaces one water molecule. The total concentration of all solute particles in a solution is referred to as the solution's **osmolarity** (oz″mo-lar′ĭ-te). When equal volumes of aqueous solutions of different osmolarity are separated by a membrane that is *permeable to all molecules* in the system, net diffusion of both solute and water occurs, each moving down its own concentration gradient (Figure 3.8a). Eventually, equilibrium is reached when the water concentration on the left equals that on the right, and the solute concentration on both sides is the same. If we consider the same system, but make the membrane *impermeable to solute molecules,* we see quite a different result (Figure 3.8b). Water quickly diffuses from the left to the right compartment and continues to do so until its concentration is the same on the two sides of the membrane. Notice that in this case equilibrium results from the movement of water alone (the solutes are prevented from moving). Notice also that the movement of water leads to dramatic changes in the volumes of the two compartments.

The last example mimics osmosis across plasma membranes of living cells, with one major difference. In our examples, the volumes of the compartments are infinitely expandable and the effect of pressure exerted by the added weight of the higher fluid column is not considered. In living plant cells, which have rigid cell walls external to their plasma membranes, this is not the case. As water diffuses into the cell, the point is finally reached where the **hydrostatic pressure** (the back pressure exerted by water against the membrane) within the cell is equal to its **osmotic pressure**—the cell's tendency to resist further (net) water entry. As a rule, the higher the amount of nondiffusible (or nonpenetrating) solutes in a cell, the higher the osmotic pressure and the greater the hydrostatic pressure that must be developed to resist further net water entry.

(a)

(b)

(c)

FIGURE 3.9 **The effect of solutions of varying tonicities on living red blood cells. (a)** In isotonic solutions (same solute/water concentrations as inside cells), cells retain their normal size and shape. **(b)** In a hypertonic solution (containing more solutes than are present inside the cells), the cells lose water and shrink (crenate). **(c)** In a hypotonic solution (containing fewer solutes than are present inside the cell), the cells take in water by osmosis until they become bloated and burst (lyse).

However, such major changes in hydrostatic (and osmotic) pressures do not occur in living animal cells, which lack rigid cell walls. Osmotic imbalances cause animal cells to swell or shrink (due to net water gain or loss) until either the solute concentration is the same on both sides of the plasma membrane, or the membrane is stretched to its breaking point.

This leads us to the important concept of *tonicity* (to-nis'ĭ-te). As noted, many molecules, particularly intracellular proteins and selected ions, are prevented from diffusing through the plasma membrane. Consequently, any change in their concentration alters the water concentration on the two sides of the membrane and results in a net loss or gain of water by the cell.

The ability of a solution to change the shape or tone of cells by altering their internal water volume is called **tonicity** (*tono* = tension). Solutions with the same concentrations of nonpenetrating solutes as those found in cells (0.9% saline or 5% glucose) are **isotonic** ("the same tonicity"). Cells exposed to such solutions retain their normal shape, and exhibit no net loss or gain of water (Figure 3.9a). As you might expect, the body's extracellular fluids and most intravenous solutions (solutions infused into the body via a vein) are isotonic. Solutions with a higher concentration of nonpenetrating solutes than seen in the cell (for example, a strong saline solution) are **hypertonic.** Cells immersed in hypertonic solutions lose water and shrink, or *crenate* (kre'nāt) (Figure 3.9b). Solutions that are more dilute (contain a lower concentration of nonpenetrating solutes) than cells are called **hypotonic.** Cells placed in a hypotonic solution plump up rapidly as water rushes into them (Figure 3.9c). Distilled water represents the most extreme example of hypotonicity. Because

it contains *no* solutes, water continues to enter cells until they finally burst or *lyse.*

Notice that osmolarity and tonicity are not the same thing. A solution's osmolarity is based solely on its total solute concentration; its tonicity is based on how the solution affects cell volume, which depends on (1) solute concentration and (2) solute permeability of the plasma membrane. Osmolarity is expressed as osmoles per liter (osmol/L) where 1 osmol is equal to 1 mole of nonionizing molecules.* A 0.3-osmol/L solution of NaCl is isotonic because sodium ions are usually prevented from diffusing through the plasma membrane. But if the cell is immersed in a 0.3-osmol/L solution of a penetrating solute, the solute will enter the cell and water will follow. The cell will swell and burst, just as if it had been placed in pure water.

Osmosis is extremely important in determining distribution of water in the various fluid-containing compartments of the body (in cells, in blood, and so on). In general, osmosis continues until osmotic and hydrostatic pressures acting at the membrane are equal. For example, water is forced out of capillary blood by the hydrostatic pressure of the blood against the capillary wall, but the presence in blood of solutes that are too large to cross the capillary membrane draws water back into the bloodstream. As a result, very little net loss of plasma fluid occurs.

Simple diffusion and osmosis occurring directly through the plasma membrane are not selective processes. In those processes, whether a molecule can

---

*Osmolarity (Osm) is determined by multiplying molarity (moles per liter, or *M*) by the number of particles resulting from ionization. For example, since NaCl ionizes to Na⁺ + Cl⁻, a 1-*M* solution of NaCl is a 2-Osm solution. For substances that do not ionize (e.g., glucose), molarity and osmolarity are the same.

TABLE 3.1	Passive Membrane Transport Processes			
PROCESS	**ENERGY SOURCE**	**DESCRIPTION**		**EXAMPLES**
DIFFUSION				
Simple diffusion	Kinetic energy	Net movement of particles (ions, molecules, etc.) from an area of their higher concentration to an area of their lower concentration, that is, along their concentration gradient		Movement of fats, oxygen, carbon dioxide through the lipid portion of the membrane
Facilitated diffusion	Kinetic energy	Same as simple diffusion, but the diffusing substance is attached to a lipid-soluble membrane carrier protein or moves through a membrane channel		Movement of glucose and some ions into cells
Osmosis	Kinetic energy	Simple diffusion of water through a selectively permeable membrane		Movement of water into and out of cells directly through the lipid phase of the membrane or via membrane pores (aquaporins)
FILTRATION				
	Hydrostatic pressure	Movement of water and solutes through a semipermeable membrane (either through the plasma membrane or between cells) from a region of higher hydrostatic pressure to a region of lower hydrostatic pressure, that is, along a pressure gradient		Movement of water, nutrients, and gases through a capillary wall; formation of kidney filtrate

pass through the membrane depends chiefly on its size or its solubility in lipid, not on its unique structure. Facilitated diffusion, on the other hand, *is* often highly selective. The carrier for glucose, for example, combines specifically with glucose, in much the same way an enzyme binds to its specific substrate and ion channels allow only selected ions to pass.

 HOMEOSTATIC IMBALANCE

Hypertonic solutions are sometimes infused intravenously into the bloodstream of edematous patients (those swollen because water is retained in their tissues) to draw excess water out of the extracellular space and move it into the bloodstream so that it can be eliminated by the kidneys. Hypotonic solutions may be used (with care) to rehydrate the tissues of extremely dehydrated patients. In less extreme cases of dehydration, drinking hypotonic fluids (colas, apple juice, and sports drinks) usually does the trick. ●

Filtration   **Filtration** is the process that forces water and solutes through a membrane or capillary wall by *fluid*, or *hydrostatic*, pressure. Like diffusion, filtration is a passive transport process and involves a gradient. However, the gradient for filtration is a **pressure gradient** that pushes solute-containing fluid (filtrate)

from a higher-pressure area to a lower-pressure area. As already mentioned, in the body hydrostatic pressure exerted by the blood forces fluid out of the capillaries, and this fluid contains solutes that are vital to the tissues. Filtration also provides the fluid ultimately excreted by the kidneys as urine. Filtration is not selective; only blood cells and protein molecules too large to pass through membrane pores or the paracellular path (between cells) are held back. Table 3.1 summarizes passive membrane transport processes.

Active Processes

Whenever a cell uses the bond energy of ATP to move solutes across the membrane, the process is referred to as *active*. Substances moved actively across the plasma membrane are usually unable to pass in the necessary direction by passive transport processes. The substance may be too large to pass through the channels, incapable of dissolving in the lipid bilayer, or unable to move down its concentration gradient. There are two major mechanisms of active membrane transport: active transport and vesicular transport.

Active Transport   **Active transport,** like carrier-mediated facilitated diffusion, requires carrier proteins that combine *specifically* and *reversibly*

Q *(1) What happens when the pump protein is phosphory-lated? (2) What happens when potassium binds to the pump protein?*

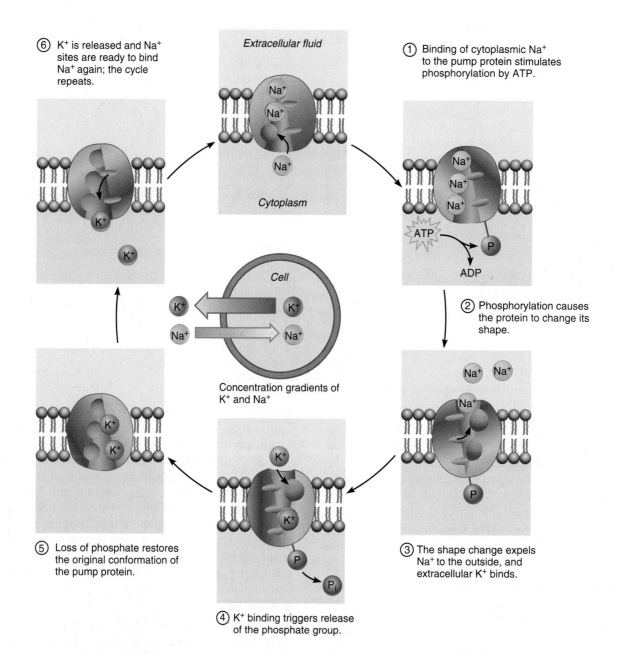

⑥ K⁺ is released and Na⁺ sites are ready to bind Na⁺ again; the cycle repeats.

Extracellular fluid

Cytoplasm

① Binding of cytoplasmic Na⁺ to the pump protein stimulates phosphorylation by ATP.

ATP

ADP

P

② Phosphorylation causes the protein to change its shape.

Cell

Concentration gradients of K⁺ and Na⁺

⑤ Loss of phosphate restores the original conformation of the pump protein.

④ K⁺ binding triggers release of the phosphate group.

③ The shape change expels Na⁺ to the outside, and extracellular K⁺ binds.

FIGURE 3.10 **Operation of the sodium-potassium pump, an antiport pump (Na⁺-K⁺ ATPase).** Hydrolysis of a molecule of ATP provides energy for an antiport "pump" protein to move three sodium ions out of the cell and two potassium ions into the cell. Both ions are moved against their concentration gradients, indicated in the center diagram by colored arrows moving through the membrane (yellow arrow = Na⁺ gradient; green arrow = K⁺ gradient).

A *(1) The protein changes shape, expelling sodium to the extracellular fluid and loading potassium ions. (2) The cleaved phosphate group is released.*

with the transported substances. However, facilitated diffusion always honors concentration gradients because its driving force is kinetic energy. In contrast, the active transporters or **solute pumps** move solutes, most importantly ions (such as Na^+, K^+, and Ca^{2+}), "uphill" *against* a concentration gradient. To do this work, cells must expend the energy of ATP.

Active transport processes are distinguished according to their source of energy. In *primary active transport*, the energy to do work comes directly from hydrolysis of ATP. In *secondary active transport*, transport is driven indirectly by energy stored in ionic gradients created by operation of primary active transport pumps. Secondary active transport systems are all *coupled systems*; that is, they move more than one substance at a time. If the two transported substances are moved in the same direction, the system is a **symport system** (*sym* = same). If the transported substances "wave to each other" as they cross the membrane in opposite directions, the system is an **antiport system** (*anti* = opposite, against). Let's examine these processes more carefully.

1. Primary active transport. In primary active transport, hydrolysis of ATP results in the phosphorylation of the transport protein, a step that causes the protein to change its conformation in such a manner that it "pumps" the bound solute across the membrane.

The most investigated example of a primary active transport system is the operation of the **sodium-potassium pump** (Figure 3.10), for which the carrier is an enzyme called **Na^+-K^+ ATPase.** The concentration of K^+ inside the cell is some 10 times higher than that outside, and the reverse is true of Na^+. These ionic concentration differences are essential for excitable cells like muscle and nerve cells to function normally and for all body cells to maintain their normal fluid volume. Because Na^+ and K^+ leak slowly but continuously through leakage channels in the plasma membrane along their concentration gradient (and cross more rapidly in stimulated muscle and nerve cells), the Na^+-K^+ pump operates more or less continuously as an antiporter to simultaneously drive Na^+ out of the cell against a steep concentration gradient and pump K^+ back in. Other examples of primary active transport include the calcium pumps that actively sequester ionic calcium from the intracellular fluid into specific organelles or eject it from the cell.

2. Secondary active transport. A single ATP-powered pump, such as the Na^+-K^+ pump, can indirectly drive the secondary active transport of several other solutes (Figure 3.11). By moving sodium across the plasma membrane against its concentration gradient, the pump stores energy (in the ion gradient). Then, just as water pumped uphill can do

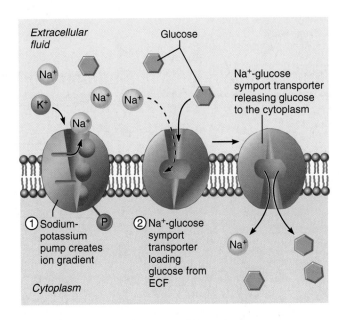

FIGURE 3.11   Secondary active transport. In this example, ① the ATP-driven Na^+-K^+ pump stores energy by creating a steep concentration gradient for Na^+ entry into the cell. ② As Na^+ diffuses back across the membrane through a membrane cotransporter protein, it drives glucose against its concentration gradient into the cell. (ECF = extracellular fluid)

work as it flows back down (turn a turbine or water wheel), a substance pumped across a membrane can do work as it leaks back, propelled downhill along its concentration gradient. Thus, as sodium moves back into the cell with the help of a carrier protein (facilitated diffusion), other substances are "dragged along" or cotransported by a common carrier protein. For example, some sugars, amino acids, and many ions are cotransported in this way into cells lining the small intestine. Though the cotransported substances both move passively, Na^+ has to be pumped back out into the lumen (cavity) of the intestine to maintain its diffusion gradient. Ion gradients can also be used to drive antiport systems such as those that help to regulate intracellular pH by using the sodium gradient to expel hydrogen ions.

Regardless of whether the energy is provided directly (primary active transport) or indirectly (secondary active transport), each membrane pump or cotransporter transports only specific substances. Hence, active transport systems provide a way for the cell to be very selective in cases where substances cannot pass by diffusion. (No pump—no transport.)

Vesicular Transport   Large particles, macromolecules, and fluids are transported across plasma and intracellular membranes by **vesicular transport.** Vesicular transport is the mechanism used for **exocytosis** (ek"so-si-to'sis; "out of the cell"),

Extracellular fluid

Plasma membrane SNARE

Vesicle SNARE

Molecules to be secreted

Secretory vesicle

Cytoplasm

(a)

FIGURE 3.12   **Exocytosis. (a)** The membrane-bounded vesicle containing the substance to be secreted migrates to the plasma membrane. There, proteins at the vesicle surface called v-SNAREs bind with t-SNAREs (plasma membrane proteins), and the membranes fuse. The fused site opens and releases the contents of the secretory vesicle into the intercellular space. **(b)** Photograph of a secretory vesicle releasing its contents to the cell exterior (60,000×).

(b)

moving substances from the cell interior to the extracellular space; and **endocytosis** (en"do-si-to'sis; "within the cell"), moving substances across the plasma membrane into the cell from the extracellular environment.

Vesicular transport is also used for combination processes such as *transcytosis,* moving substances into, across, and then out of the cell; and *substance,* or *vesicular, trafficking,* moving substances from one area (or organelle) in the cell to another.

Like solute pumping, vesicular transport processes are energized by ATP (or in some cases *GTP*—guanosine triphosphate, another energy-rich compound).

1. Exocytosis. This mechanism, typically stimulated by a cell-surface signal such as binding of a hormone to a membrane receptor, accounts for hormone secretion, neurotransmitter release, mucus secretion, and in some cases, ejection of wastes. The substance to be removed from the cell is first enclosed in a membranous sac called a **vesicle.** In most cases, the vesicle migrates to the plasma membrane, fuses with it, and then ruptures, spilling the sac contents out of the cell (Figure 3.12). The mechanism involves a "docking" process in which transmembrane proteins on the vesicles, fancifully called v-SNAREs (*v* for vesicle), recognize certain plasma membrane proteins, called t-SNAREs (*t* for target),

and bind with them. This causes the membranes to "corkscrew" together, rearranging the lipid monolayers without mixing them. As described shortly, membrane material added by exocytosis is removed by endocytosis—the reverse process.

In selected cases (particularly in cases of neurotransmitter secretion by some neurons of the brain), the membranes do not fuse. Instead, a fusion pore flickers open, part of the vesicle contents are released, and then the fusion pore closes. Called "kiss and run," this mechanism of exocytosis saves energy. Because the vesicles do not collapse into the plasma membrane, they can be reused.

2. Endocytosis, transcytosis, and vesicular trafficking. Virtually all the remaining forms of vesicular transport involve the use of an assortment of protein-coated vesicles of three types and, with some exceptions, all are mediated by membrane receptors. Let's look at the specialties of each type of coated vesicular transport.

▪ *Clathrin-coated vesicles.* Clathrin-coated vesicles provide the main route for endocytosis and transcytosis of bulk solids, most macromolecules, and fluids. These vesicles are also hijacked on occasion by pathogens seeking entry into a cell. Basically, the substance to be taken into the cell by endocytosis is progressively enclosed by an infolding portion of the plasma membrane called a *coated pit,* a term that

Q Phagocytic cells gather in the air sacs of the lungs, especially in the lungs of smokers. What is the connection?

(a) Clathrin-mediated endocytosis

(b) Phagocytosis

(c) Receptor-mediated endocytosis

FIGURE 3.13 **Clathrin-mediated endocytosis. (a)** Events of clathrin-mediated endocytosis, including three possible fates for the vesicle and its contents. **(b)** Phagocytosis. **(c)** Receptor-mediated endocytosis.

refers to the bristlelike **clathrin** (kla'thrin; "lattice clad") protein coating on the cytoplasmic face of the vesicle (Figure 3.13a). The clathrin coat (clathrin and some accessory proteins) acts both in cargo selection and in deforming the membrane to produce the vesicle.

Once inside, the vesicle loses its fuzzy coat and then typically fuses with a processing and sorting vesicle called an *endosome*. As shown in Figure 3.13a, contents of the endosome may be ① recycled back to the plasma membrane (applies to many receptors and membrane components), ② combined with a *lysosome* (li'so-some), a specialized cell structure containing digestive enzymes, where the ingested substance is degraded or released (if iron or cholesterol), or ③ transported completely across the cell and released by exocytosis on the opposite side *(transcytosis)*. Transcytosis is common in the endothelial cells lining blood vessels because it provides a quick means to get substances from the blood to the interstitial fluid. Based on the nature and quantity of material taken up and the mechanism of uptake, three types of endocytosis that use clathrin-coated vesicles are recognized: phagocytosis, pinocytosis, and receptor-mediated endocytosis.

Phagocytosis (fag"o-si-to'sis; "cell eating") is the type of endocytosis in which some relatively large or solid material, such as a clump of bacteria or cell debris, is engulfed by the cell. When a particle binds to receptors on the cell's surface, cytoplasmic extensions called pseudopods (soo'do-pahdz; *pseudo* = false, *pod* = foot) form and flow around the particle and engulf it (Figure 3.13b). The endocytotic vesicle thus formed is called a **phagosome** (fag'o-sōm; "eaten body"). In most cases, the phagosome then fuses with a lysosome and its contents are digested.

In the human body only macrophages and certain white blood cells are "experts" at phagocytosis. They help police and protect the body by ingesting and disposing of bacteria, other foreign substances, and dead tissue cells. The disposal of dying cells is

A Lungs, open to the external environment, collect dust and other airborne debris. In the lungs of smokers, carbon particles are added to this debris.

3

TABLE 3.2	Active Membrane Transport Processes		
PROCESS	**ENERGY SOURCE**	**DESCRIPTION**	**EXAMPLES**
ACTIVE TRANSPORT			
Primary active transport	ATP	Transport of substances against a concentration (or electrochemical) gradient; across the plasma membrane by a solute pump; directly uses energy of ATP hydrolysis	Ions (Na^+, K^+, H^+, Ca^{2+}, and others)
Secondary active transport	Ion concentration gradient maintained with ATP	Cotransport (coupled transport) of two solutes across the membrane; energy is supplied by the ion gradient created by a primary active solute pump (indirectly); symporters move the transported substances in the same direction; antiporters move transported substances in opposite directions across the membrane	Movement of polar or charged solutes, e.g., amino acids (into cell by symporters); Ca^{2+}, H^+ (out of cells via antiporters)
VESICULAR TRANSPORT			
Exocytosis	ATP	Secretion or ejection of substances from a cell; the substance is enclosed in a membranous vesicle, which fuses with the plasma membrane and ruptures, releasing the substance to the exterior	Secretion of neurotransmitters, hormones, mucus, etc.; ejection of cell wastes
Endocytosis • Via clathrin-coated vesicles	ATP		
Phagocytosis	ATP	"Cell eating": A large external particle (proteins, bacteria, dead cell debris) is surrounded by a "seizing foot" and becomes enclosed in a vesicle (phagosome)	In the human body, occurs primarily in protective phagocytes (some white blood cells and macrophages)
Pinocytosis (fluid-phase endocytosis)	ATP	Plasma membrane sinks beneath an external fluid droplet containing small solutes; membrane edges fuse, forming a fluid-filled vesicle; clathrin-coated vesicles formed	Occurs in most cells; important for taking in dissolved solutes by absorptive cells of the kidney and intestine
Receptor-mediated endocytosis	ATP	Selective endocytosis and transcytosis; external substance binds to membrane receptors, and clathrin-coated pits are formed	Means of intake of some hormones, cholesterol, iron, and most macromolecules
• Via caveolin-coated vesicles (caveolae)	ATP	Selective endocytosis (and transcytosis); external substance binds to membrane receptors (often associated with lipid rafts); caveolin-coated vesicles formed	Roles not fully known; proposed roles include cholesterol regulation and trafficking; platforms for signal transduction
Intracellular vesicular trafficking • Via coatomer-coated vesicles	ATP	Vesicles coated with coatomer proteins pinch off from organelles and travel to other organelles to deliver their cargo	Accounts for nearly all intracellular trafficking of molecules

crucial, because dead cell remnants trigger inflammation in the surrounding area or may stimulate an undesirable immune response. Most phagocytes move about by **amoeboid motion** (ah-me′boyd; "changing shape"); that is, the flowing of their cytoplasm into temporary pseudopods allows them to creep along.

In **pinocytosis** ("cell drinking"), also called **fluid-phase endocytosis,** a bit of infolding plasma membrane surrounds a very small volume of extracellular fluid containing dissolved molecules. This droplet enters the cell and fuses with an endosome. Unlike phagocytosis, pinocytosis is a routine activity of most cells, affording them a nonselective way of sampling the extracellular fluid. It is particularly important in cells that absorb nutrients, such as cells that line the intestines.

As mentioned, bits of the plasma membrane are removed when the membranous sacs are internalized. However, these membranes are recycled back to the plasma membrane by exocytosis, so the surface area of the plasma membrane remains remarkably constant.

Receptor-mediated endocytosis is the main mechanism for the specific endocytosis and transcytosis of most macromolecules by body cells, and it is exquisitely selective (Figure 3.13c). The receptors for this process are plasma membrane proteins that bind only with certain substances. Both the receptors and attached molecules are internalized in a clathrin-coated pit and then dealt with in one of the ways discussed above. Substances taken up by receptor-mediated endocytosis include enzymes, insulin (and some other hormones), low-density lipoproteins (such as cholesterol attached to a transport protein), and iron. Unfortunately, flu viruses, diptheria, and cholera toxins use this route to enter and attack our cells.

▪ *Non-clathrin-coated vesicles.* *Caveolae* (ka"ve-o'le; "little caves"), tubular or flask-shaped inpocketings of the plasma membrane seen in many cell types, also seem to be involved in a kind of receptor-mediated endocytosis. Like clathrin-coated pits, they capture specific molecules (folate, tetanus toxin) from the extracellular fluid in coated vesicles and participate in some forms of transcytosis. However, caveolae are smaller than clathrin-coated vesicles. Additionally, their coat is thinner and composed of a different protein called **caveolin** (Figure 3.14). Because of the close association of caveolae with lipid rafts that are platforms for signaling molecules such as G proteins, receptors for hormones (e.g., insulin), and enzymes involved in cell regulation, these vesicles may provide important sites for cell signaling and cross talk between the same or different signaling pathways. Their precise role in the cell is still being worked out.

Virtually all intracellular *vesicular trafficking,* in which vesicles pinch off from organelles and travel to other organelles to unload their contents [for example, proteins made at the endoplasmic reticulum are sent to the Golgi apparatus (see Figure 3.20, p. 88)], uses vesicles coated with **coatomer (COP1 and COP2) proteins.**

Table 3.2 summarizes active membrane transport processes.

Generating and Maintaining a Resting Membrane Potential

As you're now aware, the selective permeability of the plasma membrane can lead to dramatic osmotic flows, but that is not its only consequence. An

FIGURE 3.14   Clathrin-coated versus caveolin-coated vesicles. Structural differences between the two vesicle types are shown in electron micrographs of cells that have been sheared open by freeze-fracturing. The larger photo shows the inner surface of the plasma membrane, upon which many polygonal lattices are visible. Some lattices are relatively flat (these are the clathrin-coated pits pointed out by the yellow arrow); others curve around a vesicle (clathrin-coated vesicle indicated by the white arrow). The clathrin lattices are easily distinguished from the striped coats of caveolin protein that characterize caveolae (seen in the inset).

equally important result is the generation of a **membrane potential,** or voltage, across the membrane. A *voltage* is electrical potential energy resulting from the separation of oppositely charged particles. In cells, the oppositely charged particles are ions, and the barrier that keeps them apart is the plasma membrane.

In their resting state, all body cells exhibit a **resting membrane potential** that typically ranges from −50 to −100 millivolts (mV), depending on cell type. Hence, all cells are said to be **polarized.** The minus sign before the voltage indicates that the *inside* of the cell is negative compared to its outside. This voltage (or charge separation) exists only at the

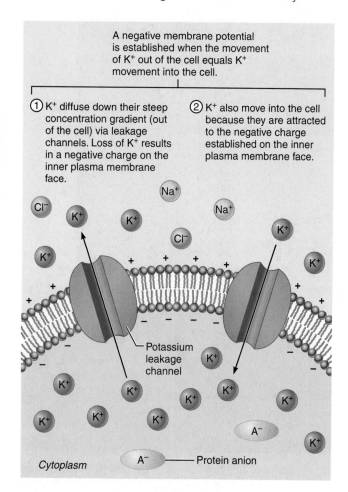

A negative membrane potential is established when the movement of K^+ out of the cell equals K^+ movement into the cell.

① K^+ diffuse down their steep concentration gradient (out of the cell) via leakage channels. Loss of K^+ results in a negative charge on the inner plasma membrane face.

② K^+ also move into the cell because they are attracted to the negative charge established on the inner plasma membrane face.

Potassium leakage channel

A^- —— Protein anion

Cytoplasm

FIGURE 3.15   **The role of K^+ in generating the resting membrane potential.** The resting membrane potential is largely determined by K^+ because the membrane is much more permeable to K^+ than to Na^+ at rest. K^+ moves more easily across the membrane by diffusing through membrane leakage channels. The net effect of this K^+ movement is that the outside membrane face becomes more electrically positive (more positive ions build up) than the inside, which is relatively more negative. The active transport of sodium and potassium ions (in a ratio of 3:2) by the Na^+-K^+ pump maintains these conditions.

membrane. If we were to add up all the negative and positive charges in the cytoplasm, we would find that the cell interior is electrically neutral. Likewise, the positive and negative charges in the extracellular fluid balance each other exactly.

So how does the resting membrane potential come about, and how is it maintained? Although many kinds of ions are found both inside cells and in the extracellular fluid, the resting membrane potential is determined mainly by the concentration gradient of K^+, and by the differential permeability of the plasma membrane to K^+ and other ions. As mentioned, K^+ and protein anions predominate inside body cells and the extracellular fluid contains relatively more Na^+, which is largely balanced by

Cl^-. The unstimulated plasma membrane is somewhat permeable to K^+ because of leakage channels, but impermeable to the protein anions. Potassium therefore diffuses out of the cell along its concentration gradient but the protein anions are unable to follow, so loss of positive charges makes the membrane interior more negative (Figure 3.15). As more and more K^+ leaves the cell, the negativity of the inner membrane face becomes great enough to attract K^+ back toward and even into the cell. At the point where potassium's concentration gradient is balanced by the membrane potential (-90 mV), one K^+ enters the cell as one leaves.

In many cells, sodium also contributes to the resting membrane potential. Sodium is strongly attracted to the cell interior by its concentration gradient, bringing the resting membrane potential to -70 mV. However, potassium still largely determines the resting membrane potential because the membrane is much more permeable to K^+ than to Na^+. In most cells, Cl^- does not contribute to the resting membrane potential because, even though the membrane is permeable to Cl^-, its entry is resisted by the negative charge of the interior. Although it is tempting to believe that massive flows of K^+ ions are needed to generate the resting potential, this is not the case. Surprisingly, the number of ions producing the membrane potential is so small that it does not change ion concentrations in any significant way.

In a cell at rest, very few ions cross its plasma membrane. However, Na^+ and K^+ are not at equilibrium and there is some net movement of K^+ out of the cell and of Na^+ into the cell because of its strong pull into the cell by both its concentration gradient and the interior negative charge. If only passive forces were at work, these ion concentrations would eventually become equal inside and outside the cell.

Instead, the cell exhibits a *steady state* in which diffusion causes ionic imbalances that polarize the membrane, and active transport processes *maintain* that membrane potential. The rate of active transport is equal to, and depends on, the rate of Na^+ diffusion into the cell. If more Na^+ enters, more is pumped out. (This is like being in a leaky boat. The more water that comes in, the faster you bail!) The Na^+-K^+ pump couples sodium and potassium transport and, on average, each "turn" of the pump ejects $3Na^+$ out of the cell and carries $2K^+$ back in (see Figure 3.10). Because the membrane is always 50 to 100 times more permeable to K^+, the ATP-dependent Na^+-K^+ pump maintains both the membrane potential and the osmotic balance. Indeed, were Na^+ not continuously removed from cells, in time so much would accumulate intracellularly that the osmotic gradient would draw water into the cells, causing them to burst.

Now that we've introduced the membrane potential, we can add a detail or two to our discussion of diffusion. Earlier we said that solutes diffuse down their concentration gradient. This is true for uncharged solutes, but only partially true for ions. The negatively and positively charged faces of the plasma membrane can help or hinder diffusion of ions driven by a concentration gradient. It is more correct to say that ions diffuse according to **electrochemical gradients,** thereby recognizing the effect of both electrical and concentration (chemical) forces. Consequently, although diffusion of K^+ across the plasma membrane is aided by the membrane's greater permeability to it and by the ion's concentration gradient, its diffusion is resisted somewhat by the positive charge on the cell exterior. In contrast, Na^+ is drawn into the cell by a steep electrochemical gradient; the limiting factor is the membrane's relative impermeability to it. As we will describe in detail in later chapters, "upsetting" the resting membrane potential by transient opening of Na^+ and K^+ channels in the plasma membrane is a normal means of activating neurons and muscle cells.

Cell-Environment Interactions

Cells are biological minifactories and, like other factories, they receive and send orders from and to the outside community. But *how* does a cell interact with its environment, and what activates it to carry out its homeostatic functions?

Although cells sometimes interact directly with other cells, this is not always the case. In many cases cells respond to extracellular chemicals, such as hormones and neurotransmitters distributed in body fluids. Cells also interact with molecules in the substratum that act as signposts to guide cell migration during development and repair.

Whether cells interact directly or indirectly, however, the glycocalyx is always involved. The best understood of the participating glycocalyx molecules fall into two large families—cell adhesion molecules and plasma membrane receptors (see Figure 3.4). Another group of membrane proteins, the voltage-sensitive channel proteins, are important in cells that respond to electrical signals.

Roles of Cell Adhesion Molecules

Thousands of **cell adhesion molecules (CAMs)** are found on almost every cell in the body. They play key roles in embryonic development and wound repair (situations where cell mobility is important) and in immunity. These sticky glycoproteins (*cadherins* and *integrins*) act as

1. The molecular "Velcro" that cells use to anchor themselves to molecules in the extracellular space and to each other (see desmosome discussion on p. 69)

2. The "arms" that migrating cells use to haul themselves past one another

3. SOS signals sticking out from the blood vessel lining that rally protective white blood cells to a nearby infected or injured area

4. Mechanical sensors that respond to local tension at the cell surface by stimulating synthesis or degradation of adhesive membrane junctions

5. Transmitters of intracellular signals that direct cell migration, proliferation, and specialization.

Roles of Membrane Receptors

A huge and diverse group of integral proteins and glycoproteins that serve as binding sites are collectively known as **membrane receptors.** Some function in contact signaling, and others in chemical signaling. Let's take a look.

Contact Signaling *Contact signaling,* the actual coming together and touching of cells, is the means by which cells recognize one another. It is particularly important for normal development and immunity. Some bacteria and other infectious agents use contact signaling to identify "preferred" target tissues or organs.

Chemical Signaling Most plasma membrane receptors are involved in *chemical signaling,* and this group will receive the bulk of our attention. Signaling chemicals that bind specifically to plasma membrane receptors are called **ligands.** Among these ligands are most *neurotransmitters* (nervous system signals), *hormones* (endocrine system signals), and *paracrines* (chemicals that act locally and are rapidly destroyed). Different cells respond in different ways to the same ligand. Acetylcholine, for instance, stimulates skeletal muscle cells to contract, but inhibits heart muscle. Thus, a target cell's response depends on the internal machinery that the receptor is linked to, not the specific ligand that binds to it.

Though cell responses to receptor binding vary widely, there is a fundamental similarity. When a ligand binds to a membrane receptor, the receptor's structure changes, and cell proteins are altered in some way; for example, muscle proteins change shape to generate force. Some of these membrane receptor proteins are *catalytic proteins* that function as enzymes. Others, such as the *chemically-gated channel-linked receptors* common in muscle and nerve cells, respond to ligands by transiently opening or closing ion gates or channels, which in turn changes the excitability of the cell. Still other receptors are coupled to enzymes or ion channels by a regulatory molecule called a G protein. Because nearly every cell in the body displays at least some of these receptors, we will spend a bit more time with them. The lipid rafts mentioned earlier group together many receptor-mediated elements, thus facilitating cell signaling.

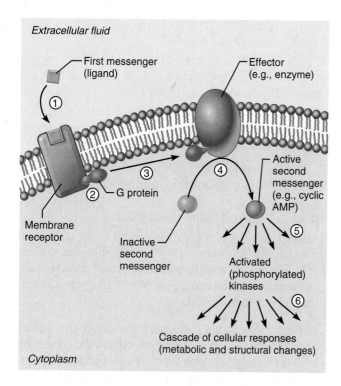

FIGURE 3.16   **Model of the operation of a G protein–linked receptor.** In this simplified diagram, ① an extracellular molecule (ligand) is a first messenger that binds to a specific receptor protein. ② The receptor activates a G protein that acts as a relay to ③ stimulate an effector protein. ④ The effector is an enzyme that produces a second messenger inside the cell. ⑤ The second messenger, cyclic AMP in this model, activates kinase enzymes. ⑥ The kinase enzymes can activate a whole series of enzymes that trigger the various responses of the cell.

G protein–linked receptors exert their effect indirectly through a **G protein,** which acts as a middleman or relay to activate (or inactivate) a membrane-bound enzyme or ion channel (Figure 3.16). As a result, one or more intracellular chemical signals, commonly called **second messengers,** are generated and connect plasma membrane events to the internal metabolic machinery of the cell. Two very important second messengers are **cyclic AMP** and ionic calcium, both of which typically activate protein kinase enzymes. By transferring phosphate groups from ATP to other proteins, the protein kinases can activate a whole series of enzymes that bring about the desired cellular activity. Because a single enzyme can catalyze hundreds of reactions, the amplification effect of such a chain of events is tremendous. These and other receptor systems are described in greater detail in Chapter 16.

One more signaling molecule must be mentioned, even though it doesn't fit any of the mechanisms described. *Nitric oxide (NO),* made of a single atom of nitrogen and one of oxygen, is one of nature's simplest molecules, an environmental pollutant, and the first gas known to act as a biological messenger. Because of its tiny size, it slips into and out of cells easily. Its unpaired electron makes it a highly reactive free radical that reacts with head-spinning speed with other key molecules to spur cells into a broad array of activities. You will be hearing more about NO later (in the neural, cardiovascular, and immune system chapters).

Role of Voltage-Sensitive Membrane Channel Proteins

Electrical Signaling   In the process known as *electrical signaling,* certain plasma membrane proteins are channel proteins that respond to changes in membrane potential by opening or closing the channel. Such voltage-gated channels are common in excitable tissues like neural and muscle tissues, and are indispensable to their normal functioning.

The Cytoplasm

Cytoplasm ("cell-forming material") is the cellular material between the plasma membrane and the nucleus. It is the site where most cellular activities are accomplished. Although early microscopists thought that the cytoplasm was a structureless gel, the electron microscope has revealed that it consists of three major elements: the cytosol, organelles, and inclusions.

The **cytosol** (si'to-sol) is the viscous, semitransparent fluid in which the other cytoplasmic elements are suspended. It is a complex mixture with properties of both a colloid and a true solution. Dissolved in the cytosol, which is largely water, are proteins, salts, sugars, and a variety of other solutes.

The **cytoplasmic organelles** are the metabolic machinery of the cell. Each type of organelle is "engineered" to carry out a specific function for the cell—some synthesize proteins, others package those proteins, and so on.

Inclusions are chemical substances that may or may not be present, depending on cell type. Examples include stored nutrients, such as the glycogen granules abundant in liver and muscle cells; lipid droplets common in fat cells; pigment (melanin) granules seen in certain cells of skin and hair; water-containing vacuoles; and crystals of various types.

Cytoplasmic Organelles

The cytoplasmic organelles ("little organs") are specialized cellular compartments, each performing its own job to maintain the life of the cell. Some organelles, the *nonmembranous organelles,* lack membranes. Examples are the cytoskeleton, centrioles, and ribosomes. However, most organelles are bounded by a membrane similar in composition to the plasma membrane (minus the glycocalyx), and this membrane enables such *membranous organelles* to maintain an internal environment different from that of the surrounding cytosol. This compartmentalization is crucial to cell functioning. Without it, thousands of enzymes would be randomly mixed and biochemical activity would be chaotic. The cell's membranous organelles include the mitochondria, peroxisomes, lysosomes, endoplasmic reticulum, and Golgi apparatus. Besides providing "splendid isolation," an organelle's membrane often unites it with the rest of an interactive intracellular system called the *endomembrane system* (see pp. 89–90). Now, let us consider what goes on in each of the workshops of our cellular factory.

Mitochondria

Mitochondria (mi″to-kon′dre-ah) are threadlike (*mitos* = thread) or sausage-shaped membranous organelles (Figure 3.17). In living cells they squirm, elongate, and change shape almost continuously. They are the power plants of a cell, providing most of its ATP supply. The density of mitochondria in a particular cell reflects that cell's energy requirements, and mitochondria are generally clustered where the action is. Busy cells like kidney and liver cells have hundreds of mitochondria, whereas relatively inactive cells (such as unchallenged lymphocytes) have just a few.

Mitochondria are enclosed by *two* membranes, each with the general structure of the plasma membrane. The outer membrane is smooth and featureless, but the inner membrane folds inward, forming shelflike **cristae** (krī′ste; "crests") that protrude into the *matrix*, the gel-like substance within the mitochondrion. Intermediate products of food fuels (glucose and others) are broken down to water and carbon dioxide by teams of enzymes, some dissolved in the mitochondrial matrix and others forming part of the crista membrane.

As the metabolites are broken down and oxidized, some of the energy released is captured and used to attach phosphate groups to ADP molecules to form ATP. This multistep mitochondrial process (described in Chapter 24) is generally referred to as *aerobic cellular respiration* (a-er-o′bik) because it requires oxygen.

Mitochondria are complex organelles: They contain their own DNA and RNA and are able to reproduce themselves. Mitochondrial genes (some 37 of them) direct the synthesis of some 5% of the proteins required for mitochondrial function, and the DNA of the cell's nucleus encodes the remaining proteins needed to carry out cellular respiration. When cellular requirements for ATP increase, the

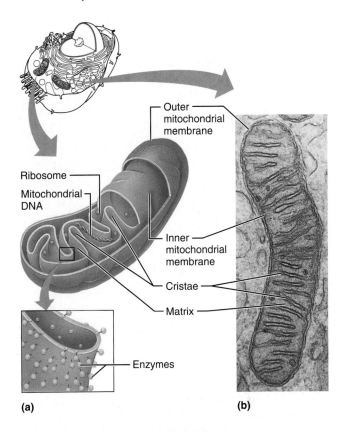

FIGURE 3.17   **Mitochondrion. (a)** Diagrammatic view of a longitudinally sectioned mitochondrion. **(b)** Electron micrograph of a mitochondrion (28,400×).

mitochondria synthesize more cristae or simply pinch in half (a process called *fission*) to increase their number, then grow to their former size.

Intriguingly, mitochondria are similar to a specific group of bacteria (the purple bacteria phylum), and mitochondrial DNA is similar to that found in bacterial cells. It is now widely believed that mitochondria arose from bacteria that invaded the ancient ancestors of plant and animal cells.

Ribosomes

Ribosomes (ri′bo-sōmz) are small, dark-staining granules composed of proteins and a variety of RNA called *ribosomal RNA*. Each ribosome has two globular subunits that fit together like the body and cap of an acorn (Figure 3.18c). Ribosomes are sites of protein synthesis, a function we discuss in detail later in this chapter.

Some ribosomes float freely in the cytoplasm; others are attached to membranes, forming a complex called the *rough endoplasmic reticulum*. These two ribosomal populations appear to divide the chore of protein synthesis. *Free ribosomes* make soluble proteins that function in the cytosol. *Membrane-bound ribosomes* synthesize proteins destined either for incorporation into cell membranes or for export

3

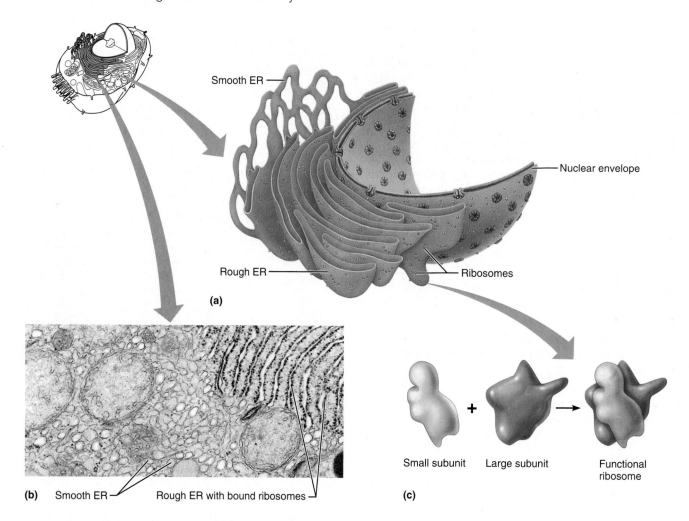

Smooth ER

Nuclear envelope

Rough ER

Ribosomes

(a)

(b) Smooth ER — Rough ER with bound ribosomes

Small subunit + Large subunit → Functional ribosome

(c)

FIGURE 3.18 **The endoplasmic reticulum (ER) and ribosomes. (a)** Diagram of the rough ER and smooth ER in a cell. **(b)** Electron micrograph of smooth and rough endoplasmic reticulum (15,000×). **(c)** Diagram of a functional ribosome made from small and large subunits.

from the cell. Ribosomes can switch back and forth between these two functions, attaching to and detaching from the membranes of the endoplasmic reticulum, according to the type of protein they are making at a given time.

Endoplasmic Reticulum

The **endoplasmic reticulum (ER)** (en"do-plaz'mik re-tik'u-lum; "network within the cytoplasm") is an extensive system of interconnected tubes and parallel membranes enclosing fluid-filled cavities, or **cisternae** (sis-ter'ne), that coils and twists through the cytosol. The ER is continuous with the nuclear membrane and accounts for about half of the cell's membranes. There are two distinct varieties of ER: rough ER and smooth ER.

Rough Endoplasmic Reticulum The external surface of the **rough ER** is studded with ribosomes (Figure 3.18a). Proteins assembled on these ribosomes thread their way into the fluid-filled interior of the ER cisternae, where various fates await them (as described shortly). The rough ER has several functions. Its ribosomes manufacture all proteins secreted from cells. Thus, the rough ER is particularly abundant and well developed in most secretory cells, antibody-producing plasma cells, and liver cells, which produce most blood proteins. It is also the cell's "membrane factory" because integral proteins and phospholipids that form part of all cellular membranes are manufactured there. The enzymes needed to catalyze lipid synthesis have their active sites on the external (cytosolic) face of the ER membrane, where the needed substrates are readily available.

As mentioned, ribosomes attach to and detach from the rough ER. When a short "leader" peptide called a **signal sequence** is present in a protein being synthesized, the associated ribosome attaches to the membrane of the rough ER. This signal sequence, with its attached "cargo" of ribosome and messenger RNA (mRNA), is guided to the appropriate receptor sites on the ER membrane by a **signal-recognition particle (SRP)**, which cycles between the ER and the cytosol. The subsequent events occurring at the ER are detailed in Figure 3.19.

Smooth Endoplasmic Reticulum The **smooth ER** (see Figures 3.2 and 3.18) is in communication with the rough ER and consists of tubules arranged in a looping network. Its enzymes (all integral proteins forming part of its membranes) play no role in protein synthesis. Instead, they catalyze reactions involved with the following processes:

1. Lipid metabolism, cholesterol synthesis, and synthesis of the lipid components of lipoproteins (in liver cells)

2. Synthesis of steroid-based hormones such as sex hormones (testosterone-synthesizing cells of the testes are full of smooth ER)

3. Absorption, synthesis, and transport of fats (in intestinal cells)

4. Detoxification of drugs, certain pesticides, and carcinogens (in liver and kidneys)

5. Breakdown of stored glycogen to form free glucose (in liver cells especially)

Additionally, skeletal and cardiac muscle cells have an elaborate smooth ER (called the sarcoplasmic reticulum) that plays an important role in calcium ion storage and release during muscle contraction. Except for the examples given above, most body cells contain little, if any, true smooth ER.

Golgi Apparatus

The **Golgi apparatus** (gol'je) consists of stacked and flattened membranous sacs, shaped like hollow dinner plates, associated with swarms of tiny membranous vesicles (Figure 3.20). The Golgi apparatus is the principal "traffic director" for cellular proteins. Its major function is to modify, concentrate, and package the proteins and lipids made at the rough ER. The transport vesicles that bud off from the rough ER move to and fuse with the membranes at its convex *cis face,* the "receiving" side of the Golgi apparatus. Inside the apparatus, the proteins are modified: Some sugar groups are trimmed while others are added, and in some cases, phosphate groups are added. The various proteins are "tagged" for delivery to a specific address, sorted, and packaged in at least three types of vesicles that bud from the concave *trans face* (the "shipping" side) of the Golgi stack.

Q *The transport vesicle shown has a coatamer protein coat. How does that differ from the protein coat of a vesicle taken in by receptor-mediated endocytosis?*

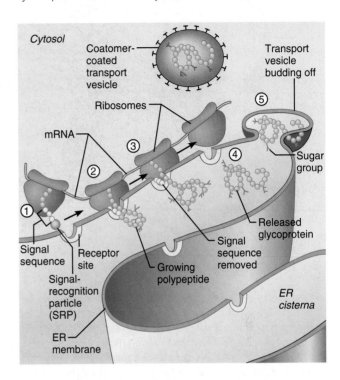

FIGURE 3.19 **The signal mechanism targets ribosomes to the ER for protein synthesis.** Steps in the signal mechanism of protein synthesis: ① Presence of a short signal sequence on a newly forming protein causes the signal-recognition particle (SRP) to direct the mRNA-ribosome complex to the rough ER. The SRP binds to the protein-translocation site (a receptor site that includes a pore and an enzyme to clip the signal sequence). ② Once attached to the ER receptor site, the SRP is released and the growing polypeptide snakes through the ER membrane into the cisterna. ③ The signal sequence initially remains attached to the receptor but is soon clipped off by an enzyme. As protein synthesis continues, sugar groups may be added to the protein. ④ In this example, the completed protein is released from the ribosome and folds into its 3-D conformation, a process aided by molecular chaperones (see p. 53). Transmembrane proteins are only partially translocated and remain embedded in the membrane. ⑤ The protein is enclosed within a coatamer-coated transport vesicle that pinches off the ER. The transport vesicles make their way to the Golgi apparatus, where further processing of the proteins occurs (see Figure 3.20).

Vesicles containing proteins destined for export pinch off from the trans face as **secretory vesicles,** or **granules,** which migrate to the plasma membrane and discharge their contents from the cell by exocytosis (pathway 1, Figure 3.21). Specialized secretory cells,

A *The protein coating on the endocytosed vesicle would be clathrin protein.*

3

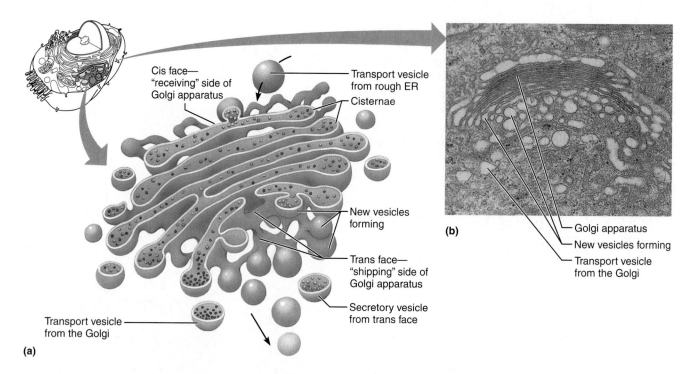

(a)

(b)

FIGURE 3.20   **Golgi apparatus. (a)** Diagrammatic view of the Golgi apparatus.
(b) Electron micrograph of the Golgi apparatus (28,000×). Notice the vesicles in the
process of pinching off from the membranous Golgi apparatus. (The various and
abundant vesicles shown would have coatomer proteins on their external surfaces;
these proteins have been omitted from the diagram for simplicity.)

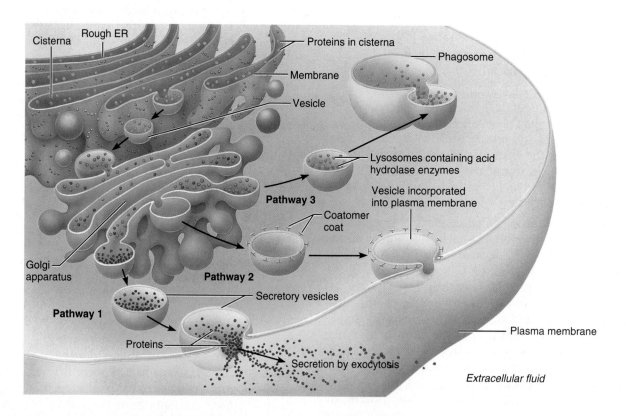

FIGURE 3.21   **The sequence of events from protein synthesis on the rough ER
to the final distribution of those proteins.** Protein-containing vesicles pinch off the
rough ER and migrate to fuse with the membranes of the Golgi apparatus. Within the
Golgi compartments, the proteins are modified; they are then packaged within different
Golgi vesicle types, depending on their ultimate destination (pathways 1–3 as shown).

such as the enzyme-producing cells of the pancreas, have a very prominent Golgi apparatus. Besides its packaging-for-release function, the Golgi apparatus pinches off vesicles containing lipids and transmembrane proteins destined for a "home" in the plasma membrane (pathway 2, Figure 3.21) or other membranous organelles. It also packages digestive enzymes into membranous lysosomes that remain in the cell (pathway 3 in Figure 3.21, and discussed next).

Lysosomes

Lysosomes ("disintegrator bodies") are spherical membranous organelles containing digestive enzymes (Figure 3.22). As you might guess, lysosomes are large and abundant in phagocytes, the cells that dispose of invading bacteria and cell debris. Lysosomal enzymes can digest almost all kinds of biological molecules. They work best in acidic conditions and thus are called *acid hydrolases* (hi"drah-la'siz). The lysosomal membrane is adapted to serve lysosomal functions in two important ways: (1) It contains H^+ (proton) "pumps," ATPases that gather hydrogen ions from the surrounding cytosol to maintain the organelle's acidic pH, and (2) it retains the dangerous acid hydrolases while permitting the final products of digestion to escape so that they can be used by the cell or excreted. Hence, lysosomes provide sites where digestion can proceed *safely* within a cell.

Lysosomes function as a cell's "demolition crew" by

- Digesting particles taken in by endocytosis, particularly ingested bacteria, viruses, and toxins

- Degrading worn-out or nonfunctional organelles

- Performing metabolic functions, such as glycogen breakdown and release

- Breaking down nonuseful tissues, such as the webs between the fingers and toes of a developing fetus and the uterine lining during menstruation

- Breaking down bone to release calcium ions into the blood

Some unique lysosomes called *secretory lysosomes* are found mainly in white blood cells, immune cells, and melanocytes (pigment-producing cells). They appear to have the ability to store and then secrete by exocytosis newly synthesized proteins in response to external stimuli.

The lysosomal membrane is ordinarily quite stable, but it becomes fragile when the cell is injured or deprived of oxygen and when excessive amounts of vitamin A are present. Lysosomal rupture results in self-digestion of the cell, a process called **autolysis** (aw"tol'ĭ-sis). Autolysis is the basis for desirable destruction of cells (see fourth bullet point above).

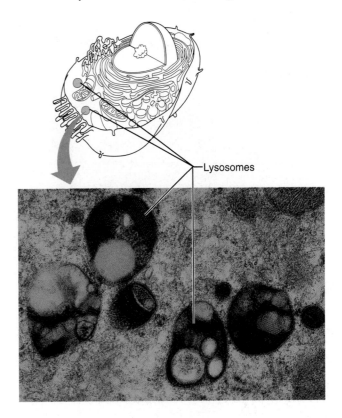

FIGURE 3.22 Lysosomes. Electron micrograph of a cell containing lysosomes (90,000×).

⚠ HOMEOSTATIC IMBALANCE

Glycogen and certain lipids in the brain are degraded by lysosomes at a relatively constant rate. In *Tay-Sachs disease*, an inherited condition seen mostly in Jews from Central Europe, the lysosomes lack an enzyme needed to break down a glycolipid abundant in nerve cell membranes. As a result, the nerve cell lysosomes swell with the undigested lipids, which interfere with nervous system functioning. Affected infants typically have doll-like features and pink translucent skin. At 3 to 6 months of age, the first signs of disease appear (listlessness, motor weakness). These progress to mental retardation, seizures, blindness, and ultimately death within 18 months. ●

Summary of Interactions in the Endomembrane System

The **endomembrane system** (Figure 3.23) is a system of organelles (most described above) that work together mainly (1) to produce, store, and export biological molecules, and (2) to degrade potentially harmful substances. It includes the ER, Golgi apparatus, secretory vesicles, and lysosomes, as well as the nuclear membrane—that is, all of the membranous organelles or elements that are either structurally continuous or arise via forming or fusing

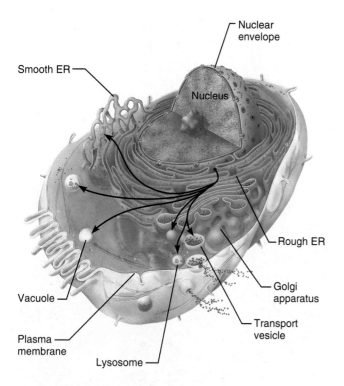

Smooth ER

Nuclear envelope

Nucleus

Rough ER

Golgi apparatus

Transport vesicle

Vacuole

Plasma membrane

Lysosome

FIGURE 3.23   **The endomembrane system.**

transport vesicles. There are continuities between the nuclear envelope (itself an extension of the rough ER) and the rough and smooth ER. The plasma membrane, though not actually an *endo* membrane, is also functionally part of this system. Besides these direct structural relationships, a wide variety of indirect interactions (indicated by arrows in Figure 3.23) occur among the members of the system. Some of the vesicles "born" in the ER migrate to and fuse with the Golgi apparatus or the plasma membrane, and vesicles arising from the Golgi apparatus can become part of the plasma membrane, secretory vesicles, or lysosomes.

Peroxisomes

Peroxisomes (pĕ-roks'ĭ-sōmz; "peroxide bodies") are membranous sacs containing a variety of powerful enzymes, the most important of which are oxidases and catalases. Oxidases use molecular oxygen (O_2) to detoxify harmful substances, including alcohol and formaldehyde. However, their most important function is to neutralize dangerous **free radicals,** highly reactive chemicals with unpaired electrons that can scramble the structure of biological molecules. Oxidases convert free radicals to hydrogen peroxide, which is also reactive and dangerous but is quickly converted to water by catalase enzymes. Free radicals and hydrogen peroxide are normal by-products of cellular metabolism,

but they have devastating effects on cells if allowed to accumulate. Peroxisomes are especially numerous in liver and kidney cells, which are very active in detoxification.

Although peroxisomes look like small lysosomes (see Figure 3.2), they are self-replicating organelles formed by a simple pinching in half of preexisting peroxisomes. Unlike lysosomes, they do not arise by budding from the Golgi apparatus.

Cytoskeleton

The **cytoskeleton,** literally, "cell skeleton," is an elaborate series of rods running through the cytosol. This network acts as a cell's "bones," "muscles," and "ligaments" by supporting cellular structures and providing the machinery to generate various cell movements. The three types of rods in the cytoskeleton are *microtubules, microfilaments,* and *intermediate filaments*. None of these is membrane covered.

Microtubules (mi"kro-tu'būlz), the elements with the largest diameter, are hollow tubes made of spherical protein subunits called *tubulins* (Figure 3.24c). Most microtubules radiate from a small region of cytoplasm near the nucleus called the *centrosome* or *cell center* (see Figure 3.26). These stiff but bendable microtubules determine the overall shape of the cell, as well as the distribution of cellular organelles. Mitochondria, lysosomes, and secretory granules attach to the microtubules like ornaments hanging from tree branches. These attached organelles are continually pulled along the microtubules and repositioned by tiny protein machines called **motor proteins** (*kinesins, dyneins,* and others) that act like train engines by inching along or moving "hand-over-hand" like an orangutan on the microtubular "railroad tracks" (see Figure 3.25a). Microtubules are remarkably dynamic organelles, constantly growing out from the centrosome, disassembling, and then reassembling.

Microfilaments (mi"kro-fil'ah-ments), the thinnest elements of the cytoskeleton, are strands of the protein *actin* ("ray"). Each cell has its own unique arrangement of microfilaments; thus no two cells are alike. However, nearly all cells have a fairly dense cross-linked network of microfilaments (Figure 3.24a) attached to the cytoplasmic side of their plasma membrane that strengthens the cell surface. Most microfilaments are involved in cell motility or changes in cell shape. You could say that cells move when they get their act(in) together. For example, actin microfilaments interact with another protein, **unconventional myosin** (mi'o-sin), to generate contractile forces in a cell (Figure 3.25b) and to form the cleavage furrow that pinches one cell into two during cell division.

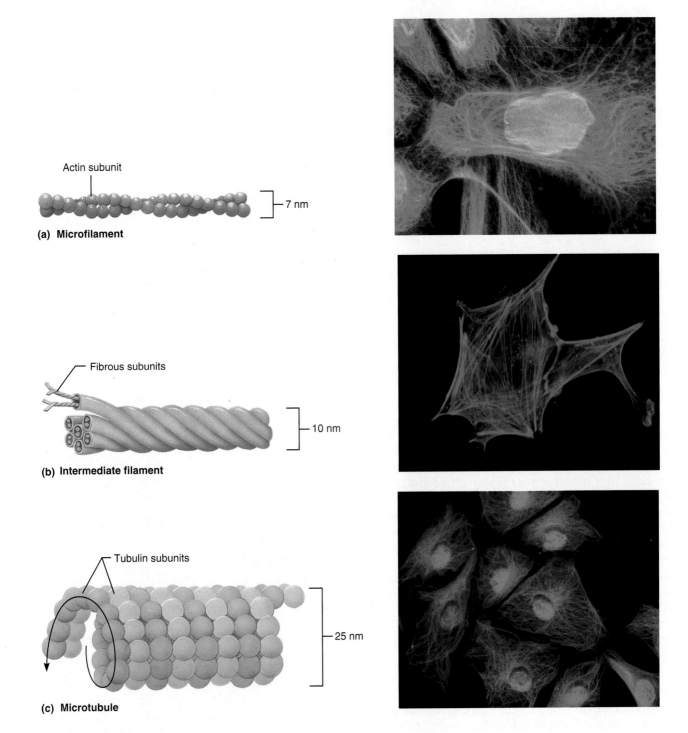

Actin subunit

7 nm

(a) Microfilament

Fibrous subunits

10 nm

(b) Intermediate filament

Tubulin subunits

25 nm

(c) Microtubule

FIGURE 3.24 **Cytoskeleton.** Diagrammatic views (left) and photos (right) of the cytoskeletal elements. **(a)** Microfilaments show up as green strands. **(b)** Intermediate filaments form a red batlike network in this view. **(c)** Microtubules appear as green networks surrounding the cells' blue nuclei.

Microfilaments attached to CAMs (see Figure 3.4) are responsible for the crawling movements of amoeboid motion, and for the membrane changes that accompany endocytosis and exocytosis. Except in muscle cells, where they are highly developed, stable, and long-lived, actin filaments are constantly breaking down and re-forming from

smaller subunits whenever and wherever their services are needed.

Intermediate filaments are tough, insoluble protein fibers that have a diameter between those of microfilaments and microtubules (Figure 3.24b). Constructed like woven ropes, intermediate filaments are the most stable and permanent of the

(a)

(b)

FIGURE 3.25   **Interaction of motor molecules (motor proteins) with cytoskeletal elements.** Microtubules and microfilaments function in motility by interacting with protein complexes called motor molecules. The various motor molecules, all powered by ATP, work by changing their shapes, moving back and forth something like

microscopic legs. With each cycle of shape changes, the motor molecule releases at its free end and grips at a site farther along the microtubule or microfilament. **(a)** Motor molecules can attach to receptors on organelles, such as mitochondria or ribosomes, and "walk" the organelles along the microtubules of the cytoskeleton.

(b) In some types of cell motility, motor molecules attached to one element of the cytoskeleton can cause it to slide over another element. For example, the sliding of one set of microfilaments past another underlies muscle contraction, and the sliding of neighboring microtubules moves cilia.

cytoskeletal elements and have high tensile strength. Unlike microtubules and microfilaments, intermediate filaments do not bind ATP or serve as "tracks" for molecular motors to transport intracellular substances. They attach to desmosomes, and their main job is to act as internal guy-wires to resist pulling forces exerted on the cell. Because the protein composition of intermediate filaments varies in different cell types, there are numerous names for these cytoskeletal elements—for example, they are called neurofilaments in nerve cells and keratin filaments in epithelial cells.

Centrosome and Centrioles

As mentioned, microtubules are anchored at one end in a region near the nucleus called the **centrosome.** The centrosome, which acts as a *microtubule organizing center,* has few distinguishing marks other than a granular-looking *matrix* that contains paired **centrioles,** small, barrel-shaped organelles oriented at right angles to each other (Figure 3.26). The centrosome matrix is best known for its generation of microtubules and its role of organizing the mitotic

FIGURE 3.26   **Centrioles. (a, b)** Three-dimensional views of a centriole pair oriented at right angles, as they are usually seen in the cell. The centrioles are located in an inconspicuous region to one side of the nucleus called the centrosome, or cell center. **(c)** An electron micrograph showing a cross section of a centriole (180,000×). Notice that it is composed of nine microtubule triplets.

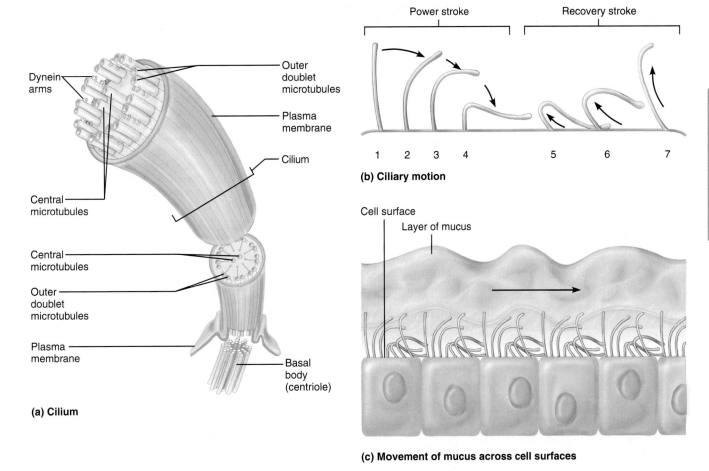

(a) Cilium

(b) Ciliary motion

(c) Movement of mucus across cell surfaces

FIGURE 3.27 **Cilia structure and function. (a)** Three-dimensional diagram of a cross section through a cilium, showing its nine pairs of peripheral microtubules and one central microtubule pair. **(b)** Diagram of the phases of ciliary motion. 1–4 are part of the power (propulsive) stroke; 5–7 are phases of the recovery (nonpropulsive) stroke when the cilium is resuming its initial position. **(c)** A representation of the traveling wave created by the activity of many cilia acting together to propel mucus across the cell surfaces.

spindle (see Figure 3.32 on pp. 102–103) in cell division. Each centriole consists of a pinwheel array of nine *triplets* of microtubules, arranged to form a hollow tube. Centrioles also form the bases of cilia and flagella.

Cellular Extensions

Cilia and Flagella

Cilia (sil′e-ah; "eyelashes") are whiplike, motile cellular extensions (Figure 3.27) that occur, typically in large numbers, on the exposed surfaces of certain cells. Ciliary action moves substances in one direction across cell surfaces. For example, ciliated cells that line the respiratory tract propel mucus laden with dust particles and bacteria upward away from the lungs.

When a cell is about to form cilia, the centrioles multiply and line up beneath the plasma membrane at the free cell surface. Microtubules then begin to "sprout" from each centriole, form-

ing the ciliary projections by exerting pressure on the plasma membrane. When the projections formed by centrioles are substantially longer, they are called **flagella** (flah-jel′ah). The single example of a flagellated cell in the human body is a sperm, which has one propulsive flagellum, commonly called a tail. Notice that cilia *propel other substances* across a cell's surface, whereas a flagellum *propels the cell itself.*

Centrioles forming the bases of cilia and flagella are commonly referred to as **basal bodies** (ba′sal) (Figure 3.27a) because they were thought to be different from the structures seen in the centrosome. We now know that centrioles and basal bodies are identical. However, the pattern of microtubules in the cilium or flagellum itself (nine *doublets,* or pairs, of microtubules encircling one central pair) differs slightly from that of a centriole (nine microtubule *triplets*).

Just how cilia activity is coordinated is not fully understood, but microtubules are definitely involved. Extending from the microtubule doublets are arms

TABLE 3.3   **Parts of the Cell: Structure and Function**

CELL PART	STRUCTURE	FUNCTIONS
PLASMA MEMBRANE (FIGURE 3.3)		
	Membrane made of a double layer of lipids (phospholipids, cholesterol, and so on) within which proteins are embedded; proteins may extend entirely through the lipid bilayer or protrude on only one face; externally facing proteins and some lipids have attached sugar groups	Serves as an external cell barrier; acts in transport of substances into or out of the cell; maintains a resting potential that is essential for functioning of excitable cells; externally facing proteins act as receptors (for hormones, neurotransmitters, and so on) and in cell-to-cell recognition
CYTOPLASM		
	Cellular region between the nuclear and plasma membranes; consists of fluid **cytosol,** containing dissolved solutes, **organelles** (the metabolic machinery of the cytoplasm), and **inclusions** (stored nutrients, secretory products, pigment granules)	
Cytoplasmic Organelles		
■ Mitochondria (Figure 3.17)	Rodlike, double-membrane structures; inner membrane folded into projections called cristae	Site of ATP synthesis; powerhouse of the cell
■ Ribosomes (Figures 3.18, 3.19)	Dense particles consisting of two subunits, each composed of ribosomal RNA and protein; free or attached to rough endoplasmic reticulum	The sites of protein synthesis
■ Rough endoplasmic reticulum (Figures 3.18, 3.19)	Membrane system enclosing a cavity, the cisterna, and coiling through the cytoplasm; externally studded with ribosomes	Sugar groups are attached to proteins within the cisternae; proteins are bound in vesicles for transport to the Golgi apparatus and other sites; external face synthesizes phospholipids
■ Smooth endoplasmic reticulum (Figure 3.18)	Membranous system of sacs and tubules; free of ribosomes	Site of lipid and steroid (cholesterol) synthesis, lipid metabolism, and drug detoxification
■ Golgi apparatus (Figures 3.20, 3.21)	A stack of smooth membrane sacs and associated vesicles close to the nucleus	Packages, modifies, and segregates proteins for secretion from the cell, inclusion in lysosomes, and incorporation into the plasma membrane
■ Lysosomes (Figure 3.22)	Membranous sacs containing acid hydrolases	Sites of intracellular digestion
■ Peroxisomes (Figure 3.2)	Membranous sacs of oxidase enzymes	The enzymes detoxify a number of toxic substances; the most important enzyme, catalase, breaks down hydrogen peroxide
■ Microtubules (Figures 3.24–3.27)	Cylindrical structures made of tubulin proteins	Support the cell and give it shape; involved in intracellular and cellular movements; form centrioles and cilia and flagella, if present
■ Microfilaments (Figures 3.24, 3.25)	Fine filaments of the contractile protein actin	Involved in muscle contraction and other types of intracellular movement; help form the cell's cytoskeleton
■ Intermediate filaments (Figure 3.24)	Protein fibers; composition varies	The stable cytoskeletal elements; resist mechanical forces acting on the cell
■ Centrioles (Figure 3.26)	Paired cylindrical bodies, each composed of nine triplets of microtubules	Organize a microtubule network during mitosis to form the spindle and asters; form the bases of cilia and flagella
Inclusions	Varied; includes stored nutrients such as lipid droplets and glycogen granules, protein crystals, pigment granules	Storage for nutrients, wastes, and cell products

TABLE 3.3 *(continued)*

CELL PART	STRUCTURE	FUNCTIONS
CELLULAR EXTENSIONS		
▪ Cilia (Figure 3.27)	Short, cell surface projections; each cilium composed of nine pairs of microtubules surrounding a central pair	Move in unison, creating a unidirectional current that propels substances across cell surfaces
▪ Flagella	Like cilium, but longer; only example in humans is the sperm tail	Propels the cell
▪ Microvilli (Figure 3.2)	Tubular extensions of the plasma membrane; contain a bundle of actin filaments	Increase surface area for absorption
NUCLEUS (FIGURE 3.28)		
	Largest organelle; surrounded by the nuclear envelope; contains fluid nucleoplasm, nucleoli, and chromatin	Control center of the cell; responsible for transmitting genetic information and providing the instructions for protein synthesis
▪ Nuclear envelope (Figure 3.28)	Double-membrane structure; pierced by pores; outer membrane continuous with the endoplasmic reticulum	Separates the nucleoplasm from the cytoplasm and regulates passage of substances to and from the nucleus
▪ Nucleoli (Figure 3.28)	Dense spherical (non-membrane-bounded) bodies; composed of ribosomal RNA and proteins	Site of ribosome subunit manufacture
▪ Chromatin (Figures 3.28, 3.29)	Granular, threadlike material composed of DNA and histone proteins	DNA constitutes the genes

composed of the motor protein *dynein*. Cilia move when the dynein side arms grip adjacent doublets and start to crawl along their length, much like cats dig in their claws to climb a tree. The collective bending action of all the doublets causes the cilium to bend.

As a cilium moves, it alternates rhythmically between a propulsive *power stroke*, when it is nearly straight and moves in an arc, and a *recovery stroke*, when it bends and returns to its initial position (Figure 3.27b). With these two strokes, the cilium produces a pushing motion in a single direction that is repeated some 10 to 20 times per second. The activity of cilia in a particular region is coordinated so that the bending of one cilium is quickly followed by the bending of the next and then the next, creating a current at the cell surface that brings to mind the traveling waves that pass across a field of grass on a windy day (Figure 3.27c).

The Nucleus

Anything that works, works best when it is controlled. For cells, the control center is the gene-containing **nucleus** (*nucle* = pit, kernel). The nucleus can be compared to a computer, design department, construction boss, and board of directors—all rolled into one. As the genetic library, it contains the instructions needed to build nearly all the body's proteins. Additionally, it dictates the kinds and amounts of proteins to be synthesized at any one time in response to signals acting on the cell.

Most cells have only one nucleus, but some, including skeletal muscle cells, bone destruction cells, and some liver cells, are **multinucleate** (mul″tĭ-nu′kle-āt); that is, they have many nuclei. The presence of more than one nucleus usually signifies that a larger-than-usual cytoplasmic mass must be regulated. With one exception, all of our body cells are nucleated. The exception is mature red blood cells, whose nuclei are ejected before the cells enter the bloodstream. These **anucleate** (a-nu′kle-āt; *a* = without) cells cannot reproduce and therefore live in the bloodstream for only three to four months before they begin to deteriorate. Without a nucleus, a cell cannot produce mRNA to make proteins, and when its enzymes and cell structures start to break down (as all eventually do), they cannot be replaced.

The nucleus, averaging 5 μm in diameter, is larger than any of the cytoplasmic organelles. Although most often spherical or oval, its shape usually conforms to the shape of the cell. The nucleus has three recognizable regions or structures: the *nuclear envelope*

Q *Methylene blue binds to DNA. What nuclear structure would be stained by this dye?*

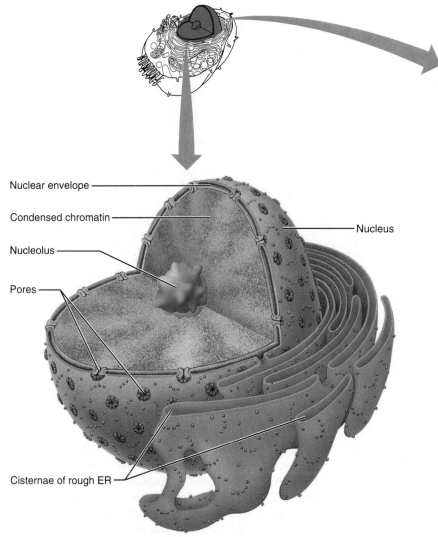

Nuclear envelope

Condensed chromatin

Nucleolus

Pores

Nucleus

Cisternae of rough ER

(a)

FIGURE 3.28   **The nucleus. (a)** Three-dimensional diagrammatic view of the nucleus, showing the continuity of its double membrane with the ER. **(b)** From top to bottom, freeze-fracture electron micrographs of the outer face of the nuclear envelope, the nuclear pore complexes, and the nuclear lamina on the inner face of the nuclear envelope.

Surface of nuclear envelope.
TEM prepared by freeze-fracture. A, inner membrane; B, outer membrane; NP, nuclear pore (pore complex); White arrows, fracture lines of outer membrane.

Pore complexes (TEM). Each pore is ringed by protein particles.

Nuclear lamina (TEM). The netlike lamina composed of intermediate filaments called lamins lines the inner surface of the nuclear envelope.

(b)

A *The chromatin, which contains DNA complexed with histone proteins.*

(membrane), nucleoli, and chromatin (Figure 3.28). Besides these structures, there are several distinct compartments (a splicing factor compartment and others) rich in specific sets of proteins. These are not limited by membranes and are in a constant state of dynamic flux. Much remains to be learned about them.

The Nuclear Envelope

The nucleus is bounded by the **nuclear envelope,** a *double* membrane barrier separated by a fluid-filled space (similar to the mitochondrial membrane). The outer nuclear membrane is continuous with the rough ER of the cytoplasm and is studded with ribosomes on its external face. The inner nuclear membrane is lined by the *nuclear lamina,* a network of *lamins* (rod-shaped proteins of the intermediate filament class), that maintains the shape of the nucleus and acts as a scaffold to organize DNA in the nucleus.

At various points, the two layers of the nuclear envelope interconnect to form the edges of **nuclear pores.** An intricate complex of proteins, called a *pore complex,* lines each pore forming an aqueous transport channel and regulating the entry and exit of large particles into and out of the nucleus.

Like other cell membranes, the nuclear envelope is selectively permeable, but here passage of substances is much freer than elsewhere. Protein molecules imported from the cytoplasm and RNA molecules exported from the nucleus pass easily through the relatively large nuclear pore complexes, transported in an energy-dependent process by soluble transport proteins (importins and others).

The nuclear envelope encloses a jellylike fluid called *nucleoplasm* (nu'kle-o-plazm) in which other nuclear elements are suspended. Like the cytosol, the nucleoplasm contains dissolved salts, nutrients, and other essential solutes.

Nucleoli

Nucleoli (nu-kle'o-li; "little nuclei") are the dark-staining spherical bodies found within the nucleus. They are not membrane bounded. Typically, there are one or two nucleoli per nucleus, but there may be more. Because they are sites where ribosome subunits are assembled, nucleoli are usually large in growing cells that are making large amounts of tissue proteins. Nucleoli are associated with *nucleolar organizer regions,* which contain the DNA that issues genetic instructions for synthesizing ribosomal RNA (rRNA). As molecules of rRNA are synthesized, they are combined with proteins to form the two kinds of ribosomal subunits. (The proteins are manufactured on ribosomes in the cytoplasm and "imported" into the nucleus.) Most of these subunits leave the nucleus through the nuclear pores and enter the cytoplasm, where they join to form functional ribosomes.

Chromatin

Seen through a light microscope, **chromatin** (kro'mah-tin) appears as a fine, unevenly stained network, but special techniques reveal it as a system of bumpy threads weaving their way through the nucleoplasm (Figure 3.29a). Chromatin is composed of about 30% **DNA,** which is traditionally called our genetic material, about 60% globular **histone proteins** (his'tōn), and about 10% RNA chains, newly formed or forming. The fundamental units of chromatin, **nucleosomes** (nu'kle-o-sōmz; "nuclear bodies"), consist of flattened disc-shaped cores or clusters of eight histone proteins connected like beads on a string by a DNA molecule. The DNA winds (like a ribbon of Velcro) twice around each nucleosome and continues on to the next cluster via *linker DNA* segments (Figure 3.29a). In addition to providing a physical means for packing the very long DNA molecules in a compact, orderly way, the histones play an important role in gene regulation. In a nondividing cell, for example, the presence of methyl groups on histone proteins shuts down the nearby DNA, and attachment of a phosphate group to a particular histone protein may indicate that the cell is about to commit suicide. On the other hand, addition of acetyl groups to histone exposes different DNA segments, or genes, so that they can dictate the specifications for protein synthesis or for various small RNA species. Such active chromatin segments, referred to as *extended chromatin,* are not usually visible under the light microscope. The generally inactive *condensed chromatin* segments are darker staining and so are more easily detected. Understandably, the most active body cells have much larger amounts of extended chromatin.

When a cell is preparing to divide, the chromatin threads coil and condense enormously to form short, barlike bodies called **chromosomes** ("colored bodies") (Figure 3.29b). Chromosome compactness avoids entanglement and breakage of the delicate chromatin strands during the movements that occur during cell division. The functions of DNA and the events of cell division are described in the next section.

Cell Growth and Reproduction

The Cell Life Cycle

The **cell life cycle,** the series of changes a cell goes through from the time it is formed until it reproduces, encompasses two major periods: *interphase,*

(a)

① DNA double helix (2-nm diameter)

Histones

② Chromatid ("beads on a string") structure

Linker DNA

Nucleosome (10-nm diameter)

③ Tight helical fiber (30-nm diameter)

④ Supercoiled structure (200-nm diameter)

⑤ Chromatid (700-nm diameter)

Metaphase chromosome

(b)

FIGURE 3.29 **Chromatin and chromosome structure.** **(a)** Electron micrograph of chromatin fibers (10,000×). **(b)** DNA packing in a chromosome. The levels of increasing structural complexity (coiling) from the DNA helix to the metaphase chromosome are indicated in numerical order. (Metaphase is a stage of nuclear division that occurs before the genetic material is distributed to the daughter cells.) Notice the structure of the nucleosomes, the fundamental units of chromatin that give it the "beads on a string" appearance. Each nucleosome is composed of a flattened disc-like core of eight histone proteins wrapped by two winds of the DNA helix.

in which the cell grows and carries on its usual activities, and *cell division*, or the *mitotic phase*, during which it divides into two cells (Figure 3.30).

Interphase

Interphase is the period from cell formation to cell division. Early cytologists, unaware of the constant molecular activity in cells and impressed by the obvious movements of cell division, called interphase the resting phase of the cell cycle. (The term *interphase* reflects this idea of a stage *between* cell divisions.) However, this image is grossly misleading because during interphase a cell is carrying out all its routine activities and is "resting" only from dividing. Perhaps a more accurate name for this phase would be *metabolic phase* or *growth phase.*

Subphases In addition to carrying on its life-sustaining reactions, an interphase cell prepares for the next cell division. Interphase is divided into G_1, S, and G_2 subphases (the Gs stand for gaps before and after the S phase; S is for synthetic). In all three subphases, the cell grows by producing proteins and organelles; however, chromatin is reproduced only during the S subphase. During **G_1 (gap 1),** the cell is metabolically active, synthesizing proteins rapidly and growing vigorously. This is the most variable phase in terms of length. In cells that divide rapidly, G_1 typically lasts several minutes to hours; in those that divide slowly, it may last for days or even years. Cells that permanently cease dividing are said to be in the **G_0 phase.** For most of G_1, virtually no activities directly related to cell division occur. However, as G_1 ends, the centrioles start to replicate in preparation for cell division.

During the **S phase**, DNA is replicated, ensuring that the two future cells being created will receive identical copies of the genetic material. New histones are made and assembled into chromatin. One thing is sure: Without a proper S phase, there can be no correct mitotic phase. (We will describe DNA replication next.)

The final phase of interphase, called G_2, is brief. Enzymes and other proteins needed for division are synthesized and moved to their proper sites. By the end of G_2, centriole replication (begun in G_1) is complete. The cell is now ready to divide. Throughout S and G_2, the cell continues to grow and carries on with business as usual.

DNA Replication Before a cell can divide, its DNA must be replicated exactly, so that identical copies of the cell's genes can be passed on to each of its offspring. Replication begins simultaneously on several chromatin threads and continues until all the DNA has been replicated.

This process, still being studied, appears to involve the following events:

1. The DNA helices begin unwinding from the nucleosomes.

2. A *helicase* enzyme untwists the double helix and gradually separates the DNA molecule into two complementary nucleotide chains, exposing the nitrogenous bases. The site of separation is called the *replication bubble;* the Y-shaped region at each end of the replication bubble is called the *replication fork.* Figure 3.31b shows a replication fork at one end of a replication bubble.

3. Each nucleotide strand then serves as a *template,* or set of instructions, for building a new complementary nucleotide strand from free DNA precursors dissolved in the nucleoplasm.

Recall from Chapter 2 that nucleotide base pairing is always complementary: *adenine (A)* bonds to *thymine (T),* and *guanine (G)* bonds to *cytosine (C).* Hence the order of the nucleotides on the template strand determines the order on the strand being built. For example, a TACTGC sequence on a template strand would bond to new nucleotides with the order ATGACG.

4. At sites where DNA synthesis is to occur, the needed "machinery" gradually accumulates until several different proteins (mostly enzymes) are present in a large complex called a **replisome.** The actual initiation of DNA synthesis requires formation of short (about ten bases long) **RNA primers** by primase enzymes which are part of the replisome (Figure 3.31a).

5. Once the primer is in place, **DNA polymerase III** comes into the picture. Continuing from the primer, it positions complementary nucleotides along the template strand and then covalently links them together. DNA polymerase works only in one direction. Consequently, one strand, the *leading strand,* is synthesized continuously (once primed by the RNA primer) following the movement of the replication fork. The other strand, called the *lagging strand,* is constructed in segments in the opposite direction and requires that a primer initiate replication of each segment. These primers are eventually erased and replaced with DNA nucleotides by DNA polymerases (Figure 3.31a).

6. The short segments of DNA are then spliced together by **DNA ligase.** The end result is that two DNA molecules are formed from the original DNA helix and are identical to it. Each new molecule consists of one old and one new nucleotide strand. This mechanism of DNA replication is referred to as **semiconservative replication** (Figure 3.31b). Replication also involves the generation of two new telomeres (*tel* = end; *mer* = piece), snugly fitting nu-

FIGURE 3.30 **The cell cycle.** During G_1, cells grow rapidly and carry out their routine functions. The S phase is the period of DNA synthesis. In G_2, materials needed for cell division are synthesized and growth continues. During the M phase (cell division), mitosis and cytokinesis occur, producing two daughter cells. Important checkpoints at which mitosis may be prevented from occurring are found throughout interphase; two are shown on the diagram.

cleoprotein caps that prevent degradation of the ends of the chromatin strands.

7. As soon as replication ends, histones (synthesized in the cytoplasm and imported into the nucleus) associate with the DNA, completing the formation of two new chromatin strands. The chromatin strands, united by a buttonlike centromere (a stretch of repetitive DNA), condense to form **chromatids** (see Figure 3.29b). The chromatids remain attached, held together by the centromere and a protein complex called *cohesin,* until the cell enters the anaphase stage of mitotic cell division (see p. 103). They are then distributed to the daughter cells, as described next, ensuring that each cell has identical genetic information.

Cell Division

Cell division is essential for body growth and tissue repair. Cells that continually wear away, such as cells of the skin and intestinal lining, reproduce themselves almost continuously. Others, such as liver cells, divide more slowly (to maintain the particular size of the organ they compose) but retain the ability to reproduce quickly if the organ is damaged. Most

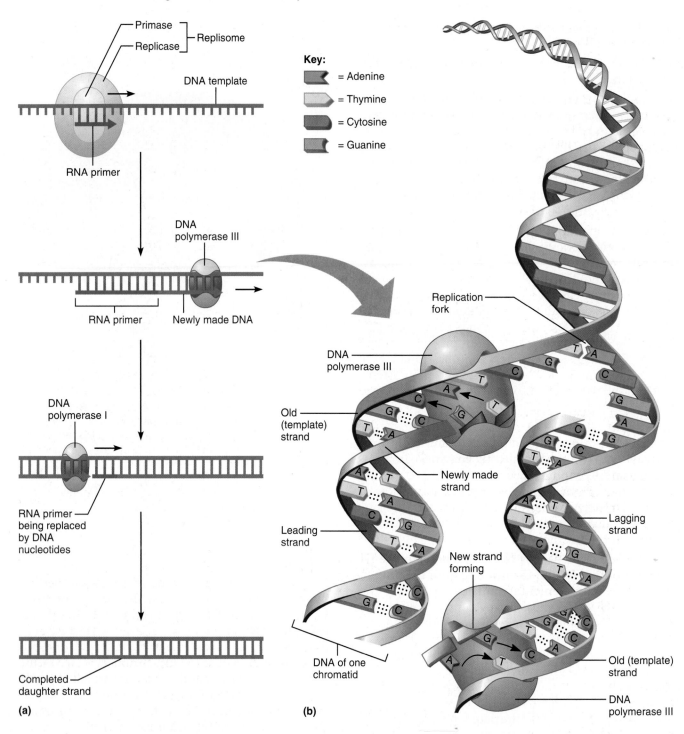

Key:
= Adenine
= Thymine
= Cytosine
= Guanine

FIGURE 3.31 **Replication of DNA.** **(a)** Role of the RNA primer. The RNA primer initiates DNA synthesis. The primer is synthesized by primase, an RNA polymerase, that is part of a protein complex called a replisome and that uses a single strand of DNA as its template. When a short stretch of RNA is available, DNA polymerase III is able to initiate DNA synthesis. The primer is eventually removed by DNA polymerase I, which replaces the ribonucleotides with deoxyribonucleotides. **(b)** Sequential events of DNA synthesis. The DNA helix uncoils, and the hydrogen bonds between its base pairs are broken. Then each nucleotide strand of the DNA acts as a template for the construction of a complementary strand, as illustrated in the bottom portion of the diagram. DNA polymerases work in one direction only, so the two new strands (leading and lagging) are synthesized in opposite directions. For simplicity, the DNA ligase enzymes that join the DNA fragments on the lagging strand are not illustrated. Each DNA molecule formed consists of one old (template) strand and one newly assembled strand and constitutes a chromatid of a chromosome.

cells of nervous tissue, skeletal muscle, and heart muscle lose their ability to divide when they are fully mature, and repairs are made with scar tissue (a fibrous type of connective tissue).

Events of Cell Division
In most body cells, cell division, which is called the **M (mitotic) phase** of the cell life cycle (see Figure 3.30), involves two distinct events: **mitosis** (mi-to'sis; *mit* = thread; *osis* = process), or division of the nucleus, and **cytokinesis** (si-to-kĭ-ne'sis; *kines* = movement), or division of the cytoplasm. A somewhat different process of nuclear division called *meiosis* (mi-o'sis) produces sex cells (ova and sperm) with only half the number of genes found in other body cells. The details of meiosis are discussed in Chapter 27. Here we concentrate on mitotic cell division.

Mitosis
Mitosis is the series of events that parcel out the replicated DNA of the mother cell to two daughter cells (Figure 3.32). It is described in terms of four phases: **prophase, metaphase, anaphase,** and **telophase,** but it is actually a continuous process, with one phase merging smoothly into the next. Its duration varies according to cell type, but in human cells it typically lasts about an hour or less from start to finish.

Cytokinesis
Cytokinesis, or the division of the cytoplasm, begins during late anaphase and is completed after mitosis ends. The plasma membrane over the center of the cell (the spindle equator) is drawn inward to form a **cleavage furrow** by the activity of a *contractile ring* made of actin filaments. The furrow deepens until the cytoplasmic mass is pinched into two parts, so that at the end of cytokinesis there are two daughter cells. Each is smaller and has less cytoplasm than the mother cell, but is *genetically* identical to it. The daughter cells then enter the interphase portion of the life cycle until it is their turn to divide.

Control of Cell Division
The signals that prod cells to divide are poorly understood, but we know that the ratio of cell surface area to cell volume is important. The amount of nutrients a growing cell requires is directly related to its volume. Volume increases with the cube of cell radius, whereas surface area increases with the square of the radius. Thus, for example, a 64-fold (4^3) increase in cell volume is accompanied by only a 16-fold (4^2) increase in surface area. Consequently, the surface area of the plasma membrane becomes inadequate for nutrient and waste exchange when a cell reaches a certain critical size. Cell division solves this problem because the smaller daughter cells have a favorable surface-area-to-volume ratio. These surface-volume relationships help explain why most cells are microscopic in size.

Two other mechanisms that influence when cells divide are chemical signals (growth factors, hormones, and others) released by other cells and the availability of space. Normal cells stop proliferating when they begin touching, a phenomenon called *contact inhibition.* Cancer cells lack many of the normal controls and therefore divide wildly, which makes them dangerous to their host.

The cell life cycle is controlled by a system that has been compared to an automatic washer's timer control. Like that timer, the cell life cycle control system is driven by a built-in clock. However, just as the washer's cycle is subject to adjustments (by regulating the flow from the faucet, say, or by an internal water-level sensor), the cell cycle is regulated by both internal and external factors.

Although triggers for cell division are still being researched, we do know that throughout interphase a number of "switches" and checkpoints are involved. Thus far, two groups of proteins appear crucial to the ability of a cell to accomplish the S phase and enter mitosis—**cyclins** (regulatory proteins whose levels rise and fall during each life cycle) and **Cdks (cyclin-dependent kinases),** which are present in a constant concentration in the cell and are activated by binding to particular cyclins. In response to specific signals, a new batch of cyclins accumulates during each interphase. Subsequent joining of specific Cdk and cyclin proteins initiates enzymatic cascades that phosphorylate histones and other proteins needed for the various stages of cell division. At the end of mitosis, the cyclins are abruptly destroyed by proteasomes.

As mentioned, a number of crucial checkpoints occur throughout interphase. These built-in stop signals halt the cell cycle until overridden by internal or external go-ahead signals. In many cells, a G_1 checkpoint (see Figure 3.30), called the *restriction point*, seems to be most important. If the cell is diverted from dividing at this checkpoint, it enters the nondividing state (G_0). Another important checkpoint, and the first to be understood, occurs late in G_2, when a threshold amount of a protein complex called **MPF (M-phase promoting factor)** is required to give the okay signal to pass the G_2 checkpoint and enter the M phase. Later in M phase, MPF is inactivated.

Protein Synthesis

In addition to directing its own replication, DNA serves as the master blueprint for protein synthesis. Although cells also make lipids and carbohydrates, DNA does not dictate their structure. Historically,

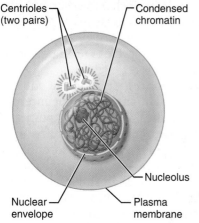

Centrioles (two pairs) — Condensed chromatin

Nuclear envelope — Nucleolus — Plasma membrane

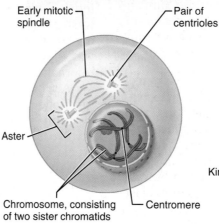

Early mitotic spindle — Pair of centrioles

Aster

Chromosome, consisting of two sister chromatids — Centromere

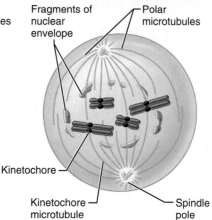

Fragments of nuclear envelope — Polar microtubules

Kinetochore —

Kinetochore microtubule — Spindle pole

Interphase ➤

Interphase is the period of a cell's life when it is carrying out its normal metabolic activities and growing. During interphase, the chromosomal material is seen in the form of extended and condensed chromatin, and the nuclear envelope and nucleolus are intact and visible. Microtubule arrays (asters) are seen extending from the centrosomes. During various periods of this phase, the centrioles begin replicating (G_1 through G_2), DNA is replicated (S), and the final preparations for mitosis are completed (G_2). The centriole pair finishes replicating into two pairs during G_2.

Early prophase ➤

As mitosis begins, microtubule arrays called *asters* ("stars") are seen extending from the centrosome matrix around the centrioles. Early in *prophase,* the first and longest phase of mitosis, the chromatin threads coil and condense, forming barlike *chromosomes* that are visible with a light microscope. Since DNA replication has occurred during interphase, each chromosome is actually made up of two identical chromatin threads, now called *chromatids.* The chromatids of each chromosome are held together by a small, buttonlike body called a *centromere* and a protein complex called cohesin. (After the chromatids separate, each is considered a new chromosome.)

As the chromosomes appear, the nucleoli disappear, and the cytoskeletal microtubules disassemble. The centriole pairs separate from one another. The centrioles act as focal points for growth of a new assembly of microtubules called the **mitotic spindle.** As these microtubules lengthen, they push the centrioles farther and farther apart, propelling them toward opposite ends (poles) of the cell.

Late prophase ➤

While the centrioles are still moving away from each other, the nuclear envelope fragments and is dispersed to the ER, allowing the spindle to occupy the center of the cell and to interact with the chromosomes. Meanwhile, some of the growing spindle microtubules attach to special protein-DNA complexes, called *kinetochores* (ki-ne′to-korz), at each chromosome's centromere. Such microtubules are called *kinetochore microtubules.* The remaining spindle microtubules, which do not attach to any chromosomes, are called *polar microtubules.* The tips of the polar microtubules are linked near the center; these push against each other, forcing the poles apart. Meanwhile, the kinetochore microtubules pull on each chromosome from both poles in a tug-of-war that ultimately draws the chromosomes to the middle of the cell.

FIGURE 3.32 **The stages of mitosis.** The light micrographs show dividing lung cells from a newt. The chromosomes appear blue and the microtubules green. (The red fibers are intermediate filaments.) The schematic drawings show details not visible in the micrographs. For simplicity, only four chromosomes are drawn.

3

Metaphase plate

Spindle

Daughter chromosomes

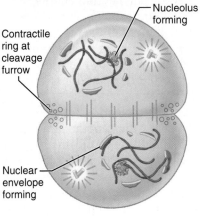

Nucleolus forming

Contractile ring at cleavage furrow

Nuclear envelope forming

Metaphase

Metaphase is the second phase of mitosis. The chromosomes cluster at the middle of the cell, with their centromeres precisely aligned at the exact center, or *equator,* of the spindle. This arrangement of the chromosomes along a plane midway between the poles is called the *metaphase* plate.

An enzyme called *separase* cleaves cohesin, triggering separation of the chromatids at the metaphase-anaphase transition.

Anaphase

Anaphase, the third phase of mitosis, begins abruptly as the centromeres of the chromosomes split, and each chromatid now becomes a chromosome in its own right. The kinetochore fibers, moved along by motor proteins in the kinetochores, rapidly disassemble at their kinetochore ends by removing tubulin subunits, and gradually pull each chromosome toward the pole it faces. By contrast the polar microtubules slide past each other and lengthen (a process presumed to be driven by kinesin motor molecules), and push the two poles of the cell apart, causing the cell to elongate. Anaphase is easy to recognize because the moving chromosomes look V-shaped. The centromeres, which are attached to the kinetochore microtubules, lead the way, and the chromosomal "arms" dangle behind them. Anaphase is the shortest stage of mitosis; it typically lasts only a few minutes.

This process of moving and separating the chromosomes is helped by the fact that the chromosomes are short, compact bodies. Diffuse threads of extended chromatin would tangle, trail, and break, which would damage the genetic material and result in its imprecise "parceling out" to the daughter cells.

Telophase and cytokinesis

Telophase begins as soon as chromosomal movement stops. This final phase is like prophase in reverse. The identical sets of chromosomes at the opposite poles of the cell uncoil and resume their threadlike extended-chromatin form. A new nuclear envelope, derived from components of the original nuclear envelope stored temporarily in the rough ER, re-forms around each chromatin mass. Nucleoli reappear within the nuclei, and the spindle breaks down and disappears. Mitosis is now ended. The cell, for just a brief period, is binucleate (has two nuclei) and each new nucleus is identical to the original mother nucleus.

As a rule, as mitosis draws to a close, *cytokinesis* completes the division of the cell into two daughter cells. Cytokinesis occurs as a contractile ring of peripheral microfilaments forms at the *cleavage furrow* and squeezes the cells apart. Cytokinesis actually begins during late anaphase and continues through and beyond telophase.

DNA is said to specify *only* the structure of protein molecules, including the enzymes that catalyze the synthesis of all classes of biological molecules. Most of the metabolic machinery of the cell is concerned in some way with protein synthesis. This is not surprising, seeing as structural proteins constitute most of the dry cell material, and functional proteins direct almost all cellular activities. Essentially, cells are miniature protein factories that synthesize the huge variety of proteins that determine the chemical and physical nature of cells—and therefore of the whole body.

Proteins, you will recall from Chapter 2, are composed of polypeptide chains, which in turn are made up of amino acids. For purposes of this discussion, we can define a **gene** as a segment of a DNA molecule that carries instructions for creating one polypeptide chain (however, some genes specify the structure of certain varieties of RNA as their final product).

The four nucleotide bases (A, G, T, and C) are the "letters" of the genetic dictionary, and the information of DNA is found in the sequence of these bases. Each sequence of three bases, called a **triplet**, can be thought of as a "word" that specifies a particular amino acid. For example, the triplet AAA calls for the amino acid phenylalanine, and CCT calls for glycine. The sequence of triplets in each gene forms a "sentence" that tells exactly how a particular polypeptide is to be made; it specifies the number, kinds, and order of amino acids needed to build a particular polypetide. Variations in the arrangement of A, T, C, and G allow our cells to make all the different kinds of proteins needed. Even an unusually "small" gene has an estimated 210 base pairs in sequence. Because the ratio between DNA bases in the gene and amino acids in the polypeptide is 3:1, the polypeptide specified by such a gene would be expected to contain 70 amino acids. Additionally, most genes of higher organisms contain **exons,** amino acid–specifying informational sequences, separated by **introns,** which are noncoding, often repetitive, segments that range from 60 to 100,000 nucleotides. Once considered a type of "junk DNA," intron DNA is now believed to represent a genome scrapyard that provides a reservoir of ready-to-use DNA segments for genome evolution, as well as a rich source of a large variety of small RNA molecules.

The Role of RNA

By itself, DNA is like a strip of magnetic recording tape: The information it contains cannot be used without a decoding mechanism. Furthermore, most polypeptides are manufactured at ribosomes in the cytoplasm, but in interphase cells, DNA never leaves the nucleus. So, DNA requires not only a decoder, but a messenger as well. The decoding and messenger functions are carried out by RNA, the second type of nucleic acid.

As you learned in Chapter 2, RNA differs from DNA in being single stranded and in having the sugar ribose instead of deoxyribose and the base uracil (U) instead of thymine (T). Three forms of RNA typically act together to carry out DNA's instructions for polypeptide synthesis:

1. **Transfer RNA (tRNA),** small, roughly cloverleaf-shaped molecules
2. **Ribosomal RNA (rRNA),** part of the ribosomes
3. **Messenger RNA (mRNA),** relatively long nucleotide strands resembling "half-DNA" molecules, or one of the two strands of a DNA molecule coding for protein structure

All types of RNA are formed on the DNA in the nucleus in much the same way as DNA replicates itself: The DNA helix separates and one of its strands serves as a template for synthesizing a complementary RNA strand. Once formed, the RNA molecule is released from the DNA template and migrates into the cytoplasm. Its job done, the DNA simply recoils into its helical, inactive form. Approximately 2% of the nuclear DNA codes for the synthesis of short-lived mRNA, so named because it carries, from gene to ribosome, the "message" containing the instructions for building a polypeptide. DNA in the nucleolar organizer regions (mentioned previously) codes for the synthesis of rRNA, which is long-lived and stable, as is tRNA coded by other DNA sequences. Because rRNA and tRNA do not transport codes for synthesizing other molecules, they are the final products of the genes that code for them. Ribosomal RNA and tRNA act together to "translate" the message carried by mRNA.

The rules by which the base sequence of a gene is translated into an amino acid sequence are called the **genetic code.** Essentially, polypeptide synthesis involves two major steps: (1) *transcription,* in which DNA's information is encoded in mRNA, and (2) *translation,* in which the information carried by mRNA is decoded and used to assemble polypeptides. These steps are shown in simplified form in Figure 3.33 and described in more detail next.

Transcription

A transcriptionist converts a message from a recording or shorthand notes into a word-processed or electronic copy. In other words, the same information is transformed, or transferred, from one form or format to another. In cells, **transcription** involves the transfer of information from a DNA gene's base sequence to the complementary base sequence of an

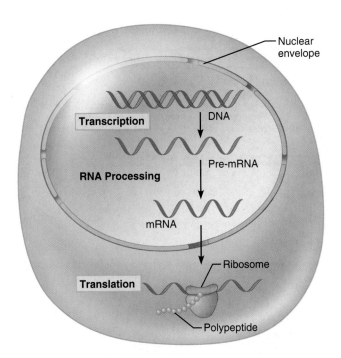

FIGURE 3.33 **Simplified scheme of information flow from the DNA gene to protein structure.** Information flows from DNA to mRNA during transcription. (The RNA is first synthesized as pre-mRNA, which is processed by enzymes before leaving the nucleus.) During translation, information flows from mRNA to synthesize a protein as amino acids are joined together in the designated order.

mRNA molecule. The form is different, but the same information is being conveyed. Once the mRNA molecule is made, it detaches and leaves the nucleus via a nuclear pore.

Let us follow the transcription process when a particular polypeptide is to be made.

Making the mRNA Complement   Transcription cannot begin until a gene-activating chemical called a *transcription factor* stimulates loosening of the histones at the site-to-be of gene transcription and then binds to the promoter. The **promoter** is a special DNA sequence adjacent to the *start point* of the structural gene that specifies where mRNA synthesis starts and which DNA strand is going to serve as the *template strand* (Figure 3.34a). Once gene activation has occurred, transcription is ready to begin.

The transcription factor mediates the binding of **RNA polymerase,** the enzyme that oversees the synthesis of mRNA. Once bound, the polymerase unwinds 16 to 18 base pairs of the DNA helix at a time (Figure 3.34b). Then, using incoming ribonucleoside triphosphates as substrates, it aligns them with complementary DNA bases on the template strand and joins the RNA nucleotides together. For exam-

ple, if a particular DNA triplet is AGC, the mRNA sequence synthesized at that site will be UCG. [The uncoiled DNA strand not used as a template is called the *coding strand* because the mRNA to be built will have the same (coded) sequence except for the use of U instead of T in mRNA.] As RNA polymerase elongates the mRNA strand one base at a time, it unwinds the DNA helix in front of it, and rewinds the helix behind it so that only a small region—the *DNA-RNA hybrid* (Figure 3.34b)—of the template DNA and mRNA is united at any one time. When the polymerase codes a special sequence called a *termination signal*, transcription ends and the newly formed messenger pulls off the DNA template.

For each triplet, or three-base sequence, on DNA, the corresponding three-base sequence on mRNA is called a **codon.** Since there are four kinds of RNA (or DNA) nucleotides, there are 4^3, or 64, possible codons. Three of these 64 codons are "stop signs" that call for termination of a polypeptide. All the rest code for amino acids. Because there are only about 20 amino acids, some are specified by more than one codon. This redundancy in the genetic code helps protect against problems due to transcription (and translation) errors. The genetic code and a complete codon list is found in Figure 3.35.

Editing of mRNA   Although it would appear that translation can begin as soon as the mRNA is made, the process is a bit more complex. As mentioned before, mammalian DNA like ours has coding regions (exons) separated by non-protein-coding regions (introns). Because the DNA gene is transcribed sequentially, the mRNA initially made, called *pre-mRNA* or *primary transcript,* is littered with intron "junk" or "nonsense." Before the newly formed RNA can be used as a messenger, it must be edited or processed—that is, sections corresponding to introns must be removed. This job is done by *spliceosomes,* large RNA-protein complexes that snip out the introns and splice together the remaining exon-coded sections in the order in which they occurred in the DNA gene, producing the functional mRNA that directs translation at the ribosome.

Although many introns naturally degrade, some contain active segments (such as microRNAs) that can function to control, interfere with, or silence other genes. Additionally, before the edited mRNA can become involved in protein synthesis, a number of specific RNA-binding proteins, called *mRNA complex proteins,* must become associated with it. These mRNA complex proteins guide its export from the nucleus, determine its localization, translation, and stability, and check it for premature termination codons.

3

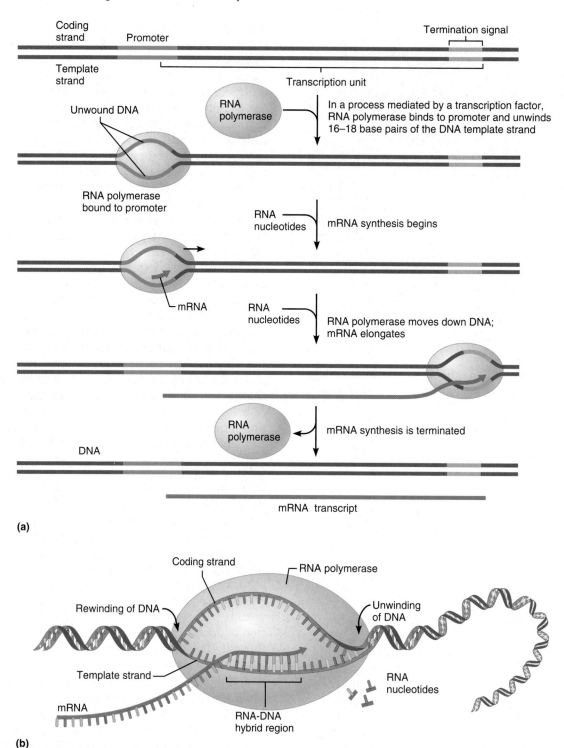

(a)

(b)

FIGURE 3.34 **An overview of transcription.** **(a)** Transcription of DNA occurs in these stages: binding of RNA polymerase to a DNA promoter; initiation of transcription on the template DNA strand; elongation of the mRNA chain; and termination of transcription accompanied by the release of RNA polymerase and the completed mRNA from the DNA template. **(b)** Elongation of mRNA. During mRNA elongation, RNA polymerase binds to about 30 base pairs of DNA. At any given moment, 16 to 18 base pairs of DNA are unwound, and the most recently synthesized mRNA is still hydrogen-bonded to the DNA, forming a short RNA-DNA hybrid. This hybrid is up to about 12 base pairs long.

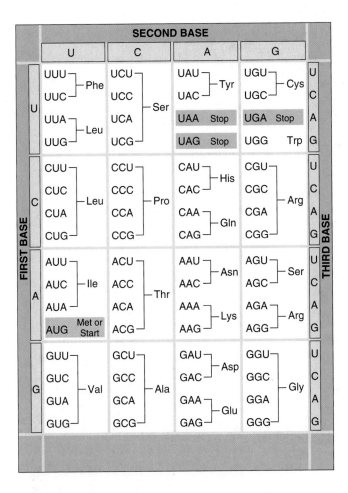

FIGURE 3.35 **The genetic code.** The three bases in an mRNA codon are designated as the first, second, and third, starting at the 5' end. Each set of three specifies a particular amino acid, represented here by a three-letter abbreviation (see list below). The codon AUG (which specifies the amino acid methionine) is the usual start signal for protein synthesis. The word *stop* indicates the codons that serve as signals to terminate protein synthesis.

Abb.*	Amino acid	Abb.*	Amino acid
Ala	alanine	Leu	leucine
Arg	arginine	Lys	lysine
Asn	asparagine	Met	methionine
Asp	aspartic acid	Phe	phenylalanine
Cys	cysteine	Pro	proline
Glu	glutamic acid	Ser	serine
Gln	glutamine	Thr	threonine
Gly	glycine	Trp	tryptophan
His	histidine	Tyr	tyrosine
Ile	isoleucine	Val	valine

* Abbreviation for the amino acid

Translation

A translator takes a message in one language and restates it in another. In the **translation** step of protein synthesis, the language of nucleic acids (base sequence) is translated into the language of pro-

teins (amino acid sequence). The process of translation occurs in the cytoplasm and involves the mRNAs, tRNAs, and rRNAs mentioned above (Figure 3.36).

When it reaches the cytoplasm, the mRNA molecule carrying instructions for a particular protein binds to a small ribosomal subunit by base pairing to rRNA. Then tRNA comes into the picture, its job being to *transfer* amino acids, dissolved in the cytosol, to the ribosome. There are approximately 45 different types of tRNA, each capable of binding with a specific amino acid. The attachment process is controlled by a synthetase enzyme and is activated by ATP. Once its amino acid is loaded, the tRNA migrates to the ribosome, where it maneuvers the amino acid into the proper position, as specified by the mRNA codons.

Shaped like a handheld drill, tRNA is well suited to its dual function. The amino acid is bound to one end of tRNA, at a region called the stem. At the other end, the head, is its **anticodon** (an"ti-ko'don), a three-base sequence complementary to the mRNA codon calling for the amino acid carried by that particular tRNA. Anticodons form hydrogen bonds with complementary codons, meaning that a tRNA is the link between the language of nucleic acids and the language of proteins. Thus, if the mRNA codon is UUU, which specifies phenylalanine, the tRNAs carrying phenylalanine will have the anticodon AAA, which can bind to the correct codons.

The ribosome is more than just a passive attachment site for mRNA and tRNA. Besides its binding site for mRNA, it has three binding sites for tRNA: an A (aminoacyl) site for incoming tRNA, a P (peptidyl) site for the tRNA holding the growing polypeptide chain, and an E (exit) site for outgoing tRNA. Like a vise, the ribosome holds the tRNA and mRNA close together to coordinate the coupling of codons and anticodons, and positions the next (incoming) amino acid for addition to the growing polypeptide chain.

Initiation of translation requires that a number of events occur. The newly formed mRNA attaches to the small ribosomal subunit by a *leader sequence* of bases that functions only to make this attachment. As a methionine-charged **initiator tRNA** also binds, a large ribosomal subunit attaches to the smaller one, forming a functional ribosome, with the mRNA positioned in the "groove" between the two ribosomal particles. The ribosome scans along the leader sequence until it reaches the "start" codon (AUG) which is recognized and bound by the anticodon (UAC) of the initiator tRNA. This initiation process requires the help of a number of initiation factors and is energized by GTP.

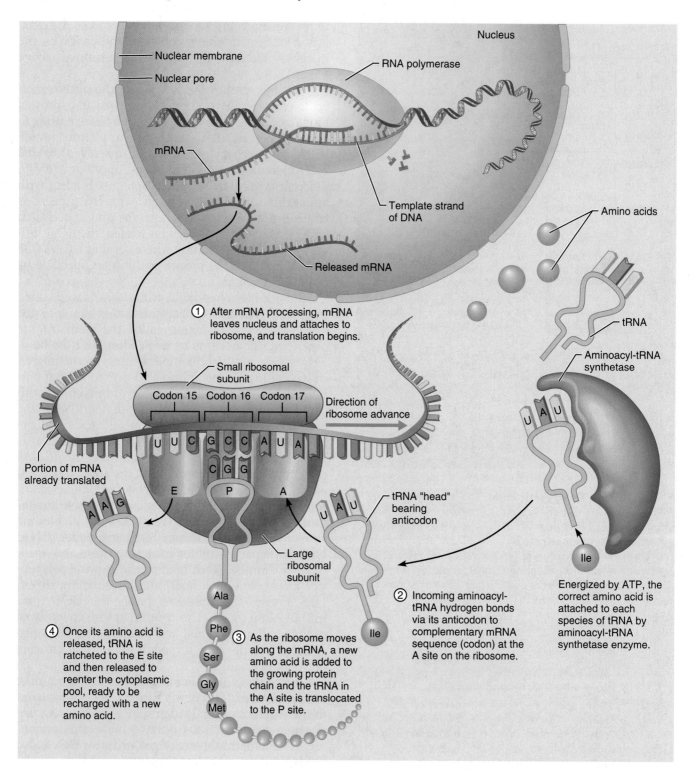

FIGURE 3.36 Translation. Once transcription of a DNA segment, or gene, has occurred in the nucleus and a complementary mRNA is formed, translation can begin. ① The messenger RNA attaches to a small ribosomal subunit in the cytoplasm. ② Transfer RNA transports its amino acid to the mRNA strand and recognizes the mRNA codon calling for its amino acid by base pairing to it (via its anticodon) at the A site. ③ The ribosome moves along the mRNA strand and each codon is read in sequence. As each successive amino acid is bound to the next by a peptide bond, its tRNA is translocated to the P site. ④ Once its amino acid is released, tRNA is ratcheted from the P site to the E site and then released. The polypeptide is released when the stop codon is read.

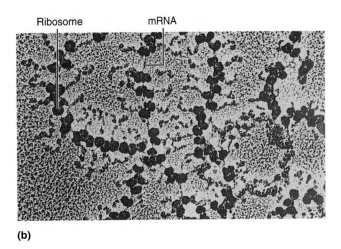

(b)

FIGURE 3.37 **Polyribosomes.** Each polyribosome consists of one strand of mRNA that is being read by several ribosomes simultaneously. **(a)** In this diagram, the mRNA is moving through the ribosome to the left and the "oldest" functional ribosome is farthest to the right. Polyribosome arrays allow a single strand of mRNA to produce hundreds of the same polypeptide molecules in a short time. **(b)** Micrograph (120,000×).

When the initiator tRNA binds to the mRNA, it occupies the P site on the ribosome and the A and E sites are vacant. Now the ribosome slides the mRNA strand along, bringing the next codon into position to be "read" by an aminoacyl-tRNA coming into the A site. It is at this point that the ribosome does a little "proofreading" to make sure of the codon-anticodon match. That accomplished, a catalytic component in the large ribosomal particle peptide-bonds the amino acid of the initiator tRNA to that of the tRNA at the A site. The ribosome then translocates the tRNA that is now carrying two amino acids to the P site, and ratchets the initiator tRNA to the E site, from which it moves away from the ribosome.

This kind of "musical chairs" situation continues: the peptidyl-tRNAs transferring their polypeptide cargo to the aminoacyl-tRNAs, and then the P-site-to-E-site, and A-site-to-P-site movements of the tRNAs (Figure 3.36). As mRNA is progressively read, its initial portion passes through the ribosome and may become attached successively to several other ribosomes, all reading the same message simultaneously and sequentially. Such a multiple ribosome-mRNA complex is called a *polyribosome* (Figure 3.37), and it provides an efficient system for producing many copies of the same protein. The mRNA strand continues to be read sequentially until its last codon, the *stop codon* (one

of UGA, UAA, or UAG) enters the ribosomal groove. The stop codon is the "period" at the end of the mRNA sentence that tells the ribosome that translation of that mRNA is finished. The completed polypeptide chain is then released from the ribosome (Figure 3.37), and the ribosome separates into its two subunits.

The genetic information of a cell is translated into the production of proteins via a sequence of information transfer that is completely directed by complementary base pairing (Figure 3.38). Thus, the transfer of information goes from DNA base sequence (triplets) to the complementary base sequence of mRNA (codons) and then to the tRNA base sequence (anticodons), which replicates that of DNA except for the substitution of uracil (U) for thymine (T).

Other Roles of DNA

The story of DNA doesn't end with the production of proteins encoded by exons. Scientists are finding that other intron or "junk" DNA actually codes for a surprising variety of active RNA species, including:

- **Antisense RNAs,** made on the DNA strand complementary to the protein coding strand, can intercept and bind to the protein-coding mRNA strand and prevent it from being translated into protein.

3

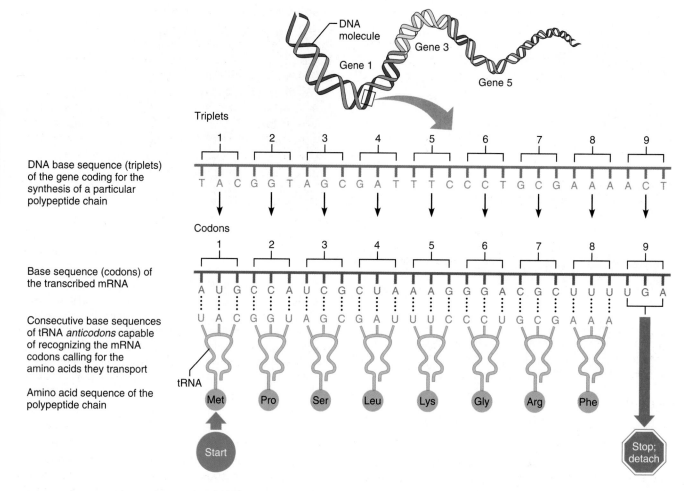

DNA base sequence (triplets) of the gene coding for the synthesis of a particular polypeptide chain

Base sequence (codons) of the transcribed mRNA

Consecutive base sequences of tRNA *anticodons* capable of recognizing the mRNA codons calling for the amino acids they transport

Amino acid sequence of the polypeptide chain

FIGURE 3.38 **Information transfer from DNA to RNA.** Information is transferred from the DNA of the gene to the complementary messenger RNA molecule, whose codons are then "read" by transfer RNA anticodons. Notice that the "reading" of the mRNA by tRNA anticodons reestablishes the base (triplet) sequence of the DNA genetic code (except that T is replaced by U).

- **MicroRNAs** are small RNAs that can use RNA interference machinery to interfere with and suppress mRNAs made by certain exons, thus effectively silencing them.

- **Riboswitches** are folded RNAs that code, like mRNA, for a particular protein. What sets them apart from other mRNAs is a region that acts as a switch to turn protein synthesis on or off in response to specific changes in the environment, such as temperature shifts or changes in the concentration of vitamins, amino acids, or other small molecules in the cell. When it senses these changes, the riboswitch changes shape, thereby stopping or starting production of the protein it specifies.

We still have much to learn about these versatile RNA species that arise from intron and "junk" DNA and appear to play a role in heredity. This topic is saved for Chapter 29.

Cytosolic Protein Degradation

To carry out their physiological roles, proteins must be in the right place at the right time and in the right amounts. Like everythng else, proteins outlive their usefulness and are eventually degraded. Organelle proteins are digested by lysosomes, but lysosomal enzymes do not have access to misfolded, damaged, or unneeded soluble proteins in the cytosol that need to be disposed of. For example, these might include some proteins used only in cell division, or short-lived transcription factors. To prevent such proteins from accumulating while preventing wholesale destruction of virtually all soluble proteins by the cytosolic enzymes, doomed proteins are marked for attack (proteolysis) by attachment of proteins called *ubiquitins* (u-bĭ′kwĭ-tin) by ubiquitin ligases in an ATP-dependent reaction. The tagged proteins are hydrolyzed to small peptides by soluble enzymes or by giant "waste disposal" complexes composed of protein-digesting enzymes called *proteasomes*, and the ubiquitin is recycled. (Structurally, proteasomes are remarkably similar to one variety of molecular chaperone and may in fact be members of that protein group.)

Extracellular Materials

Extracellular materials are any substances contributing to body mass that are found outside the cells. One class of extracellular materials is *body fluids*, mainly interstitial fluid, blood plasma, and cerebrospinal fluid. These fluids are important transport and dissolving media. *Cellular secretions*, also extracellular materials, include substances that aid in digestion (intestinal and gastric fluids) and some that act as lubricants (saliva, mucus, and serous fluids).

By far the most abundant extracellular material is the *extracellular matrix*. Most body cells are in contact with a jellylike substance composed of proteins and polysaccharides. These molecules are secreted by the cells and self-assemble into an organized mesh in the extracellular space, where they serve as a universal "cell glue" that helps to hold body cells together. The extracellular matrix is particularly abundant in connective tissues—so much so, in some cases, that it (rather than living cells) accounts for the bulk of that tissue type. Depending on the structure to be formed, the extracellular matrix in connective tissue ranges from soft to rock-hard.

Developmental Aspects of Cells

We all begin life as a single cell, the fertilized egg, from which arise all the cells of our body. Very early in development, cells begin to specialize; some become liver cells, some nerve cells, and so on. All our cells carry the same genes, so how can one cell be so different from another? This is a fascinating question. Apparently, cells in various regions of the embryo are exposed to different chemical signals that channel them into specific pathways of development. When the embryo consists of just a few cells (these are the embryonic *stem cells* you keep hearing about) the major signals may be nothing more than slight differences in oxygen and carbon dioxide concentrations between the more superficial and the deeper cells. But as development continues, cells release chemicals that influence development of neighboring cells by triggering processes that switch some genes "off." Some genes are active in all cells. For example, genes for protein and ATP synthesis are "on" in all cells, but genes for synthesizing the en-

zymes needed to produce thyroxine are "on" only in cells that are going to be part of the thyroid gland. Hence, the secret of cell specialization lies in the kinds of proteins made and reflects differential gene activation in different cell types.

Cell specialization leads to *structural* variation—different organelles come to predominate in different cells. For example, muscle cells make large amounts of actin and myosin, and their cytoplasm fills with microfilaments. Liver and phagocytic cells produce more lysosomes. The development of specific and distinctive features in cells is called **cell differentiation.**

During early development, cell death and destruction are normal events. Nature takes few chances. More cells than are needed are produced and excesses are eliminated later in a type of programmed cell death called **apoptosis** (ap"o-to'sis; "falling away"). This process of controlled cellular suicide eliminates cells that are stressed, unneeded, excessive, or aged. In response to damaged macromolecules within the cell or to some extracellular signal, a series of intracellular enzymes is activated. These enzymes, called *caspases*, destroy the cell's DNA, cytoskeleton, and so on, producing a quick, neat death. The apoptotic cell shrinks without leaking its contents into the surrounding tissue, detaches from other cells, and rounds up. Because the dying cell releases the chemical lysophosphatidylcholine, which attracts macrophages, and sprouts "eat me" signals, it is immediately phagocytized. Cancer cells do not undergo apoptosis, but oxygen-starved cells do so excessively (heart-muscle and brain cells during heart attacks and strokes, for example). Apoptosis is particularly common in the developing nervous system and is also responsible for "carving out" fingers and toes from their embryonic precursors.

Most organs are well formed and functional long before birth, but the body continues to grow and enlarge by forming new cells throughout childhood and adolescence. Once adult size has been reached, cell division is important mainly to replace short-lived cells and repair wounds.

During young adulthood, cell numbers remain fairly constant. However, local changes in the rate of cell division are common. For example, when one is anemic, bone marrow undergoes **hyperplasia** (hi"per-pla'ze-ah), or accelerated growth (*hyper* = over; *plas* = grow), so that red blood cells are produced at a faster rate. If the anemia is remedied, the excessive marrow activity ceases. **Atrophy** (at'ro-fe), a decrease in size of an organ or body tissue, can result from loss of normal stimulation. Muscles that lose their nerve supply atrophy and waste away, and lack of exercise leads to thinned, brittle bones.

Cell aging occurs and it accounts for most problems associated with old age. Cell aging is a complicated process with many causes. The *wear-and-tear theory* attributes aging to little chemical insults and formation of free radicals, both of which have cumulative effects. For example, environmental toxins such as pesticides, alcohol, and bacterial toxins may damage cell membranes, poison enzyme systems, or cause "mistakes" in DNA replication. Temporary lack of oxygen, which occurs increasingly with age as our blood vessels clog with fatty materials, leads to accelerated rates of cell death throughout the body. Most free radicals are produced in the mitochondria, because these organelles have the highest metabolic rate. This finding implies that diminished energy production by radical-damaged mitochondria, due perhaps to an increasing burden of mutations in mitochondrial DNA, weakens (and ages) cells. X rays and other types of radiation, and some chemicals, also generate huge numbers of free radicals, which can overwhelm the peroxisomal enzymes. Vitamins C and E act as antioxidants in the body and may help to prevent excessive free radical formation. With age, glucose (blood sugar) becomes party to cross-linking proteins together, a condition that severely disrupts protein function and accelerates the course of arteriosclerosis.

Another theory attributes cell aging to progressive disorders in the immune system. According to this theory, cell damage results from (1) autoimmune responses, which means the immune system turns against one's own tissues, and (2) a progressive weakening of the immune response, so that the body is less and less able to get rid of cell-damaging pathogens.

Perhaps the most widely accepted theory of cell aging is the *genetic theory*, which suggests that cessation of mitosis and cell aging are "programmed into our genes." One interesting notion here is that a *telomere clock* determines the number of times a cell can divide. **Telomeres** (*telo* = end; *mer* = piece) are strings of nucleotides that cap the end of chromosomes, protecting them from fraying or fusing with other chromosomes. In human telomeres, the base sequence TTAGGG is repeated a thousand times or more (like a DNA stutter). Though telomeres carry no genes, they appear to be vital for chromosomal survival, because each time DNA is replicated, 50 to 100 of the end nucleotides are lost and the telomeres get a bit shorter. When telomeres reach a certain minimum length, the stop-division signal is given. The idea that cell longevity depends on telomere integrity was supported by the discovery of *telomerase,* an enzyme that protects telomeres from degrading. Pegged as the "immortality enzyme," telomerase is found in germ line cells (cells that give rise to sperm and ova), but it is barely detectable or absent in other adult cell types.

■ ■ ■

We have described here the structure and function of the generalized cell. One of the wonders of the cell is the disparity between its minute size and its extraordinary activity, which reflects the amazing diversity of its organelles. The evidence for division of labor and functional specialization among organelles is inescapable. Only ribosomes synthesize proteins, while protein packaging is the bailiwick of the Golgi apparatus. Membranes compartmentalize most organelles, allowing them to work without hindering or being hindered by other cell activities, and the plasma membrane regulates molecular traffic across the cell's boundary. Now that you know what cells have in common, you are ready to explore how they differ in the various body tissues.

Related Clinical Terms

Anaplasia (an"ah-pla'ze-ah; *an* = without, not; *plas* = to grow) Abnormalities in cell structure; for example, cancer cells typically lose the appearance of the parent cells and come to resemble undifferentiated or embryonic cells.

Dysplasia (dis-pla'ze-ah; *dys* = abnormal) A change in cell size, shape, or arrangement due to chronic irritation or inflammation (infections, etc.).

Hypertrophy (hi-per'tro-fe) Growth of an organ or tissue due to an increase in the size of its cells. Hypertrophy is a normal response of skeletal muscle cells when they are challenged to lift excessive weight; differs from hyperplasia, which is an increase in size due to an increase in cell number.

Liposomes (lip'o-sōmz) Hollow microscopic sacs formed of phospholipids that can be filled with a variety of drugs. Serve as multipurpose vehicles for drugs, genetic material, and cosmetics.

Mutation A change in DNA base sequence leading to incorporation of incorrect amino acids in particular positions in the resulting protein; the affected protein may remain unimpaired or may function abnormally or not at all, leading to disease.

Necrosis (ně-kro'sis; *necros* = death; *osis* = process) Death of a cell or group of cells due to injury or disease. Acute injury causes the cells to swell and burst, and induces the inflammatory response. (This is *uncontrolled* cell death, in contrast to apoptosis described in the text.)

Chapter Summary

Media study tools that could provide you additional help in reviewing specific key topics of Chapter 3 are referenced below.
IP = *InterActive Physiology*

Overview of the Cellular Basis of Life (pp. 65–66)

1. All living organisms are composed of cells—the basic structural and functional units of life. Cells vary widely in both shape and size.

2. The principle of complementarity states that the biochemical activity of cells reflects the operation of organelles.

3. The generalized cell is a concept that typifies all cells. The generalized cell has three major regions—the nucleus, cytoplasm, and plasma membrane.

The Plasma Membrane: Structure (pp. 66–70)

1. The plasma membrane encloses cell contents, mediates exchanges with the extracellular environment, and plays a role in cellular communication.

The Fluid Mosaic Model (pp. 67–69)

2. The fluid mosaic model depicts the plasma membrane as a fluid bilayer of lipids (phospholipids, cholesterol, and glycolipids) within which proteins are inserted.

3. The lipids have both hydrophilic and hydrophobic regions that organize their aggregation and self-repair. The lipids form the structural part of the plasma membrane.

4. Most proteins are integral transmembrane proteins that extend entirely through the membrane. Some, appended to the integral proteins, are peripheral proteins.

5. Proteins are responsible for most specialized membrane functions: some are enzymes, some are receptors, and others mediate membrane transport functions. Externally facing glycoproteins contribute to the glycocalyx.

Specializations of the Plasma Membrane (p. 69)

6. Microvilli are extensions of the plasma membrane that increase its surface area for absorption.

7. Membrane junctions join cells together and may aid or inhibit movement of molecules between or past cells. Tight junctions are impermeable junctions; desmosomes mechanically couple cells into a functional community; gap junctions allow joined cells to communicate.

The Plasma Membrane: Functions (pp. 70–84)

Membrane Transport (pp. 70–81)

1. The plasma membrane acts as a selectively permeable barrier. Substances move across the plasma membrane by passive processes, which depend on the kinetic energy of molecules or on pressure gradients, and by active processes, which depend on the use of cellular energy (ATP).

2. Diffusion is the movement of molecules (driven by kinetic energy) down a concentration gradient. Fat-soluble solutes can diffuse directly through the membrane by dissolving in the lipid.

3. Facilitated diffusion is the passive movement of certain solutes across the membrane either by their binding with a membrane carrier protein or by their moving through a membrane channel. As with other diffusion processes, it is driven by kinetic energy, but the carriers and channels are selective.

4. Osmosis is the diffusion of a solvent, such as water, through a selectively permeable membrane. Water diffuses through membrane pores (aquaporins) or directly through the lipid portion of the membrane from a solution of lesser osmolarity to a solution of greater osmolarity.

5. The presence of solutes unable to permeate the plasma membrane leads to changes in cell tone that may cause the cell to swell or shrink. Net osmosis ceases when the solute concentration on both sides of the plasma membrane reaches equilibrium.

6. Solutions that cause a net loss of water from cells are hypertonic; those causing net water gain are hypotonic; those causing neither gain nor loss of water are isotonic.

7. Filtration occurs when a filtrate is forced across a membrane by hydrostatic pressure. It is nonselective and limited only by pore size. The pressure gradient is the driving force.

8. Active transport (solute pumping) depends on a carrier protein and ATP. Substances transported move against concentration or electrical gradients. In primary active transport, such as that provided by the Na^+-K^+ pump, ATP directly provides the energy. In secondary active transport, the energy of an ion gradient (produced by a primary active transport process) is used to transport a substance passively. Many active transport systems are coupled; cotransported substances move in either the same (symport) or opposite (antiport) directions across the membrane.

9. Vesicular transport also requires ATP. Exocytosis, which uses SNAREs to anchor the vesicles to the plasma membrane, ejects substances (hormones, wastes, secretions) from the cell. Endocytosis brings substances into the cell in protein-coated vesicles. If the substance is particulate, the process is called phagocytosis; if the substance is dissolved molecules, the process is pinocytosis. Receptor-mediated endocytosis is selective; engulfed particles attach to receptors on the membrane before endocytosis occurs.

10. Most endocytosis (and transcytosis) is mediated by clathrin-coated vesicles. Caveolin-coated vesicles engulf some substances but appear to be more important as sites that accumulate receptors involved in cell signaling. Coatomer-coated vesicles mediate substance (vesicular) trafficking within the cell.

Generating and Maintaining a Resting Membrane Potential (pp. 81–83)

11. All cells in the resting stage exhibit a voltage across their membrane, called the resting membrane potential. Because of the membrane potential, both concentration and electrical gradients determine the ease of an ion's diffusion.

12. The resting membrane potential is generated by concentration gradients of and differential permeability of the plasma membrane to ions, particularly potassium ions. Sodium is in high extracellular–low intracellular concentration, and the membrane is poorly permeable to it. Potassium is in high concentration in the cell and low concentration in the extracellular fluid. The membrane is more permeable to potassium than to sodium. Protein anions in the cell are too large to cross the membrane and Cl^-, the main anion in extracellular fluid, is repelled by the negative charge on the inner membrane face.

13. Essentially, a negative membrane potential is established when the movement of K^+ out of the cell equals K^+ movement into the cell. Na^+ movements across the membrane contribute minimally to establishing the membrane potential. The greater outward diffusion of potassium (than inward diffusion of sodium) leads to a charge separation at the membrane (inside negative). This charge separation is maintained by the operation of the sodium-potassium pump.

IP Nervous System I; Topics: Ion Channels, pp. 3, 8, 9; The Membrane Potential, pp. 1–17.

Cell-Environment Interactions (pp. 83–84)

14. Cells interact directly and indirectly with other cells. Indirect interactions involve extracellular chemicals carried in body fluids or forming part of the extracellular matrix.

15. Molecules of the glycocalyx are intimately involved in cell-environment interactions. Most are cell adhesion molecules or membrane receptors.

16. Activated membrane receptors act as catalysts, regulate channels, or, like G protein–linked receptors, act through second messengers such as cyclic AMP and Ca^{2+}. Ligand binding results in changes in protein structure or function within the targeted cell.

The Cytoplasm (pp. 84–95)

1. The cytoplasm, the cellular region between the nuclear and plasma membranes, consists of the cytosol (fluid cytoplasmic environment), inclusions (nonliving nutrient stores—lipid droplets, glycosomes—pigment granules, crystals, etc.), and cytoplasmic organelles.

Cytoplasmic Organelles (pp. 84–93)

2. The cytoplasm is the major functional area of the cell. These functions are mediated by cytoplasmic organelles.

3. Mitochondria, organelles limited by a double membrane, are sites of ATP formation. Their internal enzymes carry out the oxidative reactions of cellular respiration.

4. Ribosomes, composed of two subunits containing ribosomal RNA and proteins, are the sites of protein synthesis. They may be free or attached to membranes.

5. The rough endoplasmic reticulum is a ribosome-studded membrane system. Its cisternae act as sites for protein modification. Its external face acts in phospholipid synthesis. Vesicles pinched off from the ER transport the proteins to other cell sites.

6. The smooth endoplasmic reticulum synthesizes lipid and steroid molecules. It also acts in fat metabolism and in drug detoxification. In muscle cells, it is a calcium ion depot.

7. The Golgi apparatus is a membranous system close to the nucleus that packages protein secretions for export, packages enzymes into lysosomes for cellular use, and modifies proteins destined to become part of cellular membranes.

8. Lysosomes are membranous sacs of acid hydrolases packaged by the Golgi apparatus. Sites of intracellular digestion, they degrade worn-out organelles, and tissues that are no longer useful, and release ionic calcium from bone.

9. Peroxisomes are membranous sacs containing oxidase enzymes that protect the cell from the destructive effects of free radicals and other toxic substances by converting them first to hydrogen peroxide and then water.

10. The cytoskeleton includes microfilaments, intermediate filaments, and microtubules. Microfilaments, formed of contractile proteins, are important in cell motility or movement of cell parts. Microtubules organize the cytoskeleton and are important in intracellular transport. Motility functions involve motor proteins. Intermediate filaments help cells resist mechanical stress and connect other elements.

Cellular Extensions (pp. 93–95)

11. Centrioles form the mitotic spindle and are the basis of cilia and flagella.

The Nucleus (pp. 95–97)

1. The nucleus is the control center of the cell. Most cells have a single nucleus. Without a nucleus, a cell cannot divide or synthesize more proteins; thus, it is destined to die.

2. The nucleus is surrounded by the nuclear envelope, a double membrane penetrated by fairly large pores.

3. Nucleoli are nuclear sites of ribosome subunit synthesis.

4. Chromatin is a complex network of slender threads containing histone proteins and DNA. The chromatin units are called nucleosomes. When a cell begins to divide, the chromatin coils and condenses, forming chromosomes.

Cell Growth and Reproduction (pp. 97–111)

The Cell Life Cycle (pp. 97–101)

1. The cell life cycle is the series of changes that a cell goes through from the time it is formed until it divides.

2. Interphase is the nondividing phase of the cell life cycle. Interphase consists of G_1, S, and G_2 subphases. During G_1, the cell grows and centriole replication begins; during the S phase, DNA replicates; and during G_2, the final preparations for division are made. Many checkpoints occur during interphase at which the cell gets the go-ahead signal to go through mitosis or is prevented from continuing to mitosis.

3. DNA replication occurs before cell division; it ensures that all daughter cells have identical genes. The DNA helix uncoils, and each DNA nucleotide strand acts as a template for the formation of a complementary strand. Base pairing provides the guide for the proper positioning of nucleotides.

4. The products of the semiconservative replication of a DNA molecule are two DNA molecules identical to the parent molecule, each formed of one "old" and one "new" strand.

5. Cell division, essential for body growth and repair, occurs during the M phase. Cell division is stimulated by certain chemicals (including growth factors and some hormones) and increasing cell size. Lack of space and inhibitory chemicals deter cell division. Cell division is regulated by cyclin-Cdk complexes, of which one example is MPF. Cell division consists of two distinct phases: mitosis and cytokinesis.

6. Mitosis, consisting of prophase, metaphase, anaphase, and telophase, results in the parceling out of the replicated chromosomes to two daughter nuclei, each genetically identical to the mother nucleus. Cytokinesis, which begins late in mitosis, divides the cytoplasmic mass into two parts.

Protein Synthesis (pp. 101–109)

7. A gene is defined as a DNA segment that provides the instructions for the synthesis of one polypeptide chain. Since the major structural materials of the body are proteins, and all enzymes are proteins, this amply covers the synthesis of all biological molecules.

8. The base sequence of exon DNA provides the information for protein structure. Each three-base sequence (triplet) calls for a particular amino acid to be built into a polypeptide chain.

9. The RNA molecules acting in protein synthesis are synthesized on single strands of the DNA template. RNA nucleotides are joined following base-pairing rules.

10. Ribosomal RNA forms part of the protein synthesis sites; messenger RNA carries instructions for making a polypeptide chain from the DNA to the ribosomes;

transfer RNA ferries amino acids to the ribosomes and recognizes codons on the mRNA strand specifying its amino acid.

11. Protein synthesis involves (1) transcription, synthesis of a complementary mRNA, and (2) translation, "reading" of the mRNA by tRNA and peptide bonding of the amino acids into the polypeptide chain. Ribosomes coordinate translation.

Other Roles of DNA (pp. 109–110)

12. Intron and other junk DNA encodes many RNA species that may interfere with or promote the function of specific genes.

Cytosolic Protein Degradation (pp. 110–111)

13. Soluble proteins that are damaged or no longer needed are targeted for destruction by attachment of ubiquitin. Such proteins are degraded by cytosolic enzymes or proteasomes.

Extracellular Materials (p. 111)

1. Extracellular materials are substances found outside the cells. These include body fluids, cellular secretions, and extracellular matrix. Extracellular matrix is particularly abundant in connective tissues.

Developmental Aspects of Cells (pp. 111–112)

1. The first cell of an organism is the fertilized egg. Early in development, cell specialization begins and reflects differential gene activation.

2. Apoptosis is programmed cell death. Its function is to dispose of damaged or unnecessary cells.

3. During adulthood, cell numbers remain fairly constant; cell division occurs primarily to replace lost cells.

4. Cellular aging may reflect chemical insults, progressive disorders of immunity, or a genetically programmed decline in the rate of cell division with age.

Review Questions

Multiple Choice/Matching

(Some questions have more than one correct answer. Select the best answer or answers from the choices given.)

1. The smallest unit capable of life by itself is (a) the organ, (b) the organelle, (c) the tissue, (d) the cell, (e) the nucleus.

2. The major types of lipid found in the plasma membranes are (choose two) (a) cholesterol, (b) triglycerides, (c) phospholipids, (d) fat-soluble vitamins.

3. Membrane junctions that allow nutrients or ions to flow from cell to cell are (a) desmosomes, (b) gap junctions, (c) tight junctions, (d) all of these.

4. A person drinks a six-pack of beer and has to make several trips to the bathroom. This increase in urination reflects an increase in what process occurring in the kidneys? (a) diffusion, (b) osmosis, (c) solute pumping, (d) filtration.

5. The term used to describe the type of solution in which cells will lose water to their environment is (a) isotonic, (b) hypertonic, (c) hypotonic, (d) catatonic.

6. Osmosis always involves (a) a selectively permeable membrane, (b) a difference in solvent concentration, (c) diffusion, (d) active transport, (e) a, b, and c.

7. A physiologist observes that the concentration of sodium inside a cell is decidedly lower than that outside the cell. Yet sodium does diffuse easily across the plasma membrane of such cells when they are dead, but *not* when they are alive. Which of the following terms applies best to this cellular function that is lacking in dead cells? (a) osmosis, (b) diffusion, (c) active transport (solute pumping), (d) dialysis.

8. The solute-pumping type of active transport is accomplished by (a) exocytosis, (b) phagocytosis, (c) electrical forces in the cell membrane, (d) conformational-positional changes in carrier molecules in the plasma membrane.

9. The endocytotic process in which a sampling of particulate matter is engulfed and brought into the cell is called (a) phagocytosis, (b) fluid-phase endocytosis, (c) exocytosis.

10. The nuclear substance composed of histone proteins and DNA is (a) chromatin, (b) the nucleolus, (c) nuclear sap, or nucleoplasm, (d) nuclear pores.

11. The information sequence that determines the nature of a protein is the (a) nucleotide, (b) gene, (c) triplet, (d) codon.

12. Mutations may be caused by (a) X rays, (b) certain chemicals, (c) radiation from ionizing radioisotopes, (d) all of these.

13. The phase of mitosis during which centrioles reach the poles and chromosomes attach to the spindle is (a) anaphase, (b) metaphase, (c) prophase, (d) telophase.

14. Final preparations for cell division are made during the life cycle subphase called (a) G_1, (b) G_2, (c) M, (d) S.

15. The RNA synthesized on one of the DNA strands is (a) mRNA, (b) tRNA, (c) rRNA, (d) all of these.

16. The RNA species that carries the coded message, specifying the sequence of amino acids in the protein to be made, from the nucleus to the cytoplasm is (a) mRNA, (b) tRNA, (c) rRNA, (d) all of these.

17. If DNA has a sequence of AAA, then a segment of mRNA synthesized on it will have a sequence of (a) TTT, (b) UUU, (c) GGG, (d) CCC.

18. A nerve cell and a lymphocyte are presumed to differ in their (a) specialized structure, (b) suppressed genes and embryonic history, (c) genetic information, (d) a and b, (e) a and c.

19. A pancreas cell makes proteins (enzymes) which it releases to the small intestine. Which of the following best describes the path of these proteins from synthesis to exocytosis at the pancreatic cell's plasma membrane (PM)? (a) Golgi → rough ER → PM, (b) smooth ER → Golgi → lysosome → PM, (c) rough ER → Golgi → PM, (d) nucleus → Golgi → PM.

Short Answer Essay Questions

20. (a) Name the organelle that is the major site of ATP synthesis. (b) Name three organelles involved in protein synthesis or modification or both. (c) Name two organelles that contain enzymes, and describe their relative functions.

21. Explain why mitosis can be thought of as cellular immortality.

22. If a cell loses or ejects its nucleus, what is its fate and why?

23. The external faces of some of the proteins in the plasma membrane have carbohydrate groups attached to them. What role do such "sugar-coated" proteins play in the life of the cell?

24. Cells are living units. However, three classes of nonliving substances are found outside the cells. What are these classes, and what functional roles do they play?

25. Comment on the role of the sodium-potassium pump in maintaining a cell's resting membrane potential.

26. Differentiate clearly between primary and secondary active transport processes.

Critical Thinking and Clinical Application Questions

1. Explain why limp celery becomes crisp and the skin of your fingertips wrinkles when placed in tap water. (The principle is exactly the same.)

2. A "red-hot" bacterial infection of the intestinal tract irritates the intestinal cells and interferes with digestion. Such a condition is often accompanied by diarrhea, which causes loss of body water. On the basis of what you have learned about osmotic water flows, explain why diarrhea may occur.

3. Two examples of chemotherapeutic drugs (drugs used to treat cancer) and their cellular actions are listed below. Explain why each drug could be fatal to a cell.

- Vincristine: damages the mitotic spindle
- Adriamycin: binds to DNA and blocks mRNA synthesis

4. The normal function of one tumor-suppressor gene is to prevent cells with damaged chromosomes and DNA from "progressing from G_1 to S," whereas another tumor-suppressor gene prevents "passage from G_2 to M." When these tumor-suppressor genes fail to work, cancer can result. Explain what the phrases in quotations mean.

5. In their anatomy lab, many students are exposed to the chemical preservatives phenol, formaldehyde, and alcohol. Our cells break down these toxins very effectively. What cellular organelle is responsible for this?

6. Dynein is missing from the cilia and flagella of individuals with a specific inherited disorder. These individuals have severe respiratory problems and, if males, are sterile. What is the structural connection between these two symptoms?

7. Explain why alcoholics are likely to have much more smooth ER than teetotalers.

LOOKING FOR MORE STUDY HELP?

A wide variety of quiz questions, tutorials, and learning exercises are available online at the Anatomy & Physiology Place (www.anatomyandphysiology.com) and, if your instructor has provided you with a MyA&P Course ID number, in MyA&P (www.myaandp.com).

3

CHAPTER 4

Tissue: The Living Fabric

Preparing Human Tissue for Microscopy (p. 118)

1. List the steps involved in preparing animal tissue for microscopic viewing.

Epithelial Tissue (pp. 118–126)

2. List several structural and functional characteristics of epithelial tissue.

3. Name, classify, and describe the various types of epithelia; also indicate their chief function(s) and location(s).

4. Define gland. Differentiate between exocrine and endocrine glands and multicellular and unicellular glands.

5. Describe how multicellular exocrine glands are classified structurally and functionally.

Connective Tissue (pp. 126–139)

6. Indicate common characteristics of connective tissue, and list and describe its structural elements.

7. Describe the types of connective tissue found in the body, and indicate their characteristic functions.

Nervous Tissue (p. 139)

8. Indicate the general characteristics of nervous tissue.

Muscle Tissue (pp. 139–141)

9. Compare and contrast the structures and body locations of the three types of muscle tissue.

Covering and Lining Membranes (pp. 141–143)

10. Describe the structure and function of cutaneous, mucous, and serous membranes.

Tissue Repair (pp. 143–145)

11. Outline the process of tissue repair involved in normal healing of a superficial wound.

Developmental Aspects of Tissues (p. 145)

12. Indicate the embryonic origin of each tissue class.

13. Briefly describe tissue changes that occur with age.

Amoebas and other unicellular (one-cell) organisms are rugged individualists. Each cell alone obtains and digests its food, ejects its wastes, and carries out all the other activities necessary to keep itself alive and "buzzin' around on all cylinders." But in the multicellular human body, cells do not operate independently. Instead, they form tight cell communities that live and work together.

Individual body cells are specialized, with each type performing specific functions that help maintain homeostasis and benefit the body as a whole. Cell specialization is obvious: How muscle cells look and act differs greatly from skin cells, which in turn are easy to distinguish from brain cells. Cell specialization allows the body to function in sophisticated ways, but division of labor has certain hazards. When a particular group of cells is indispensable, its loss or injury can severely disable or even destroy the body.

Groups of cells that are similar in structure and perform a common or related function are called **tissues** (*tissu* = woven). Four primary tissue types interweave to form the "fabric" of the body. These basic tissues are epithelial (ep"i-the'le-ul), connective, muscle, and nervous tissue, and each has numerous subclasses or varieties. If we had to assign a single term to each primary tissue type that would best describe its general role, the terms would most likely be *covering* (epithelial), *support* (connective), *movement* (muscle), and *control* (nervous). However, these terms reveal only a fraction of the functions that each tissue performs.

As explained in Chapter 1, tissues are organized into organs such as the kidneys and the heart. Most organs contain all four tissue types, and their arrangement determines the organ's structure and capabilities. The study of tissues, or **histology,** complements the study of gross anatomy. Together they provide the structural basis for understanding organ physiology.

Preparing Human Tissue for Microscopy

Elaborate steps are taken to prepare human or animal tissue for microscopic viewing. The specimen must be **fixed** (preserved) and then cut into **sections** (slices) thin enough to transmit light or electrons. Finally the specimen must be stained to enhance contrast. The stains used in light microscopy are beautifully colored organic dyes, most of which were originally developed by clothing manufacturers in the mid-1800s. Many dyes consist of negatively or positively charged molecules (acidic and basic stains respectively) that bind within the tissue to macromolecules of the opposite charge. Because different parts of cells and tissues take up different dyes, the stains distinguish different anatomical structures.

For transmission electron microscopy, tissue sections are "stained" with heavy metal salts. These metals deflect electrons in the beam to different extents, providing contrast in the image. Electron-microscope images are in shades of gray because color is a property of light, not of electron waves, but the image may be artificially colored to enhance contrast. Another kind of electron microscopy, scanning electron microscopy (SEM), provides three-dimensional pictures of an unsectioned tissue surface. These striking images are scattered throughout this book.

Preserved tissue seen under the microscope has been exposed to many procedures that alter its original condition and introduce minor distortions called **artifacts.** Hence, keep in mind that most microscopic structures we view are not exactly like those in living tissue.

Epithelial Tissue

Epithelial tissue, or an **epithelium** (plural: epithelia), is a sheet of cells that covers a body surface or lines a body cavity (*epithe* = laid on, covering). It occurs in the body as (1) *covering and lining epithelium* and (2) *glandular epithelium*. Covering and lining epithelium forms the outer layer of the skin, dips into and lines the open cavities of the cardiovascular, digestive, and respiratory systems, and covers the walls and organs of the closed ventral body cavity. Glandular epithelium fashions the glands of the body.

Epithelia form boundaries between different environments. For example, the epidermis of the skin lies between the inside and the outside of the body, and epithelium lining the urinary bladder separates underlying cells of the bladder wall from urine. Furthermore, nearly all substances received or given off by the body must pass through an epithelium.

In its role as an interface tissue, epithelium accomplishes many functions, including (1) protection, (2) absorption, (3) filtration, (4) excretion, (5) secretion, and (6) sensory reception. Each of these functions is described in detail later, but to illustrate these functions briefly: The epithelium of the skin protects underlying tissues from mechanical and chemical injury and bacterial invasion and contains nerve endings that respond to various stimuli acting at the skin surface (pressure, heat, etc.). The epithelium lining the digestive tract is specialized to absorb substances; and that found in the kidneys performs nearly the whole functional "menu"—excretion, absorption, secretion, and filtration. Secretion is the specialty of glands.

Special Characteristics of Epithelium

Epithelial tissues have many characteristics that distinguish them from other tissue types.

1. **Polarity.** All epithelia have an **apical surface,** an upper free surface exposed to the body exterior or the cavity of an internal organ, and a lower attached **basal surface.** Hence, all epithelia exhibit *apical-basal polarity,* meaning that cell regions near the apical surface differ from those near the basal surface in both structure and function, a situation maintained, at least in part, by the highly ordered cytoskeleton of epithelial cells.

Although some apical surfaces are smooth and slick, most have **microvilli,** fingerlike extensions of the plasma membrane. Microvilli tremendously increase the exposed surface area, and in epithelia that absorb or secrete substances (those lining the intestine or kidney tubules, for instance), the microvilli are often so dense that the cell apices have a fuzzy appearance called a *brush border.* Some epithelia, such as that lining the trachea, have motile **cilia** that propel substances along their free surface.

Lying adjacent to the basal surface of an epithelium is a thin supporting sheet called the **basal lamina** (lam′ĭ-nah; "sheet"). This noncellular, adhesive sheet consists largely of glycoproteins secreted by the epithelial cells. The basal lamina acts as a selective filter that determines which molecules diffusing from the underlying connective tissue are allowed to enter the epithelium. The basal lamina also acts as a scaffolding along which epithelial cells can migrate to repair a wound.

2. **Specialized contacts.** Except for glandular epithelia (discussed on pp. 124–125), epithelial cells fit close together to form continuous sheets. Adjacent cells are bound together at many points by lateral contacts, including *tight junctions* and *desmosomes* (see Chapter 3). The tight junctions help keep proteins in the apical region of the plasma membrane from diffusing into the basal region, and thus help to maintain epithelial polarity.

3. **Supported by connective tissue.** All epithelial sheets rest upon and are supported by connective tissue. Just deep to the basal lamina is the **reticular lamina,** a layer of extracellular material containing a fine network of collagen protein fibers that "belongs to" the underlying connective tissue. Together the two laminae form the **basement membrane.** The basement membrane reinforces the epithelial sheet, helping it to resist stretching and tearing forces, and defines the epithelial boundary.

HOMEOSTATIC IMBALANCE

An important characteristic of cancerous epithelial cells is their failure to respect this boundary, which they penetrate to invade the tissues beneath. ●

4. **Avascular but innervated.** Although epithelium is *innervated* (supplied by nerve fibers), it is *avascular* (contains no blood vessels). Epithelial cells are nourished by substances diffusing from blood vessels in the underlying connective tissue.

5. **Regeneration.** Epithelium has a high regenerative capacity. Some epithelia are exposed to friction and their surface cells rub off. Others are damaged by hostile substances in the external environment (bacteria, acids, smoke). If and when their apical-basal polarity and lateral contacts are destroyed, epithelial cells begin to reproduce themselves rapidly. As long as epithelial cells receive adequate nutrition, they can replace lost cells by cell division.

Classification of Epithelia

Each epithelium is given two names. The first name indicates the number of cell layers present; the second describes the shape of its cells (Figure 4.1). Based on the number of cell layers, there are simple and stratified epithelia. **Simple epithelia** are composed of a single cell layer. They are typically found where absorption and filtration occur and a thin epithelial barrier is desirable. **Stratified epithelia,** consisting of two or more cell layers stacked one on top of the other, are common in high-abrasion areas where protection is important, such as the skin surface and the lining of the mouth.

In cross section, all epithelial cells have six (somewhat irregular) sides, and an apical surface view of an epithelial sheet looks like a honeycomb. This polyhedral shape allows the cells to be closely packed. However, epithelial cells vary in height, and on that basis, there are three common shapes of epithelial cells. **Squamous cells** (skwa′mus) are flattened and scalelike (*squam* = scale); **cuboidal cells** (ku-boi′dahl) are boxlike, approximately as tall as they are wide; and **columnar cells** (kŏ-lum′nar) are tall and column shaped. In each case, the shape of the nucleus conforms to that of the cell. The nucleus of a squamous cell is a flattened disc; that of a cuboidal cell is spherical; and a columnar cell nucleus is elongated from top to bottom and usually located close to the cell base. Keep nuclear shape in mind when you attempt to identify epithelial types.

Simple epithelia are easy to classify by cell shape because all cells in the layer usually have the same shape. In stratified epithelia, however, the cell shapes usually differ among the different cell layers. To avoid ambiguity, stratified epithelia are named according to the shape of the cells in the *apical* layer. This naming system will become clearer as we explore the specific epithelial types.

As you read about the epithelial classes, study Figure 4.2. Using the photomicrographs, try to pick out the individual cells within each epithelium. This

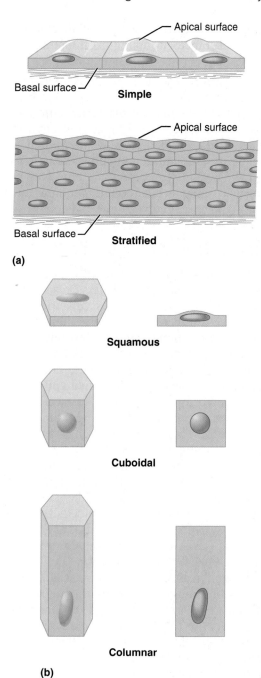

FIGURE 4.1 **Classification of epithelia. (a)** Classification on the basis of number of layers. **(b)** Classification on the basis of cell shape. For each category, a whole cell is shown on the left and a longitudinal section is shown on the right.

is not always easy, because the boundaries between epithelial cells often are indistinct. Furthermore, the nucleus of a particular cell may or may not be visible, depending on the precise plane of the cut made to prepare the tissue slides.

Simple Epithelia

The simple epithelia are most concerned with absorption, secretion, and filtration. Because they consist of a single cell layer and are usually very thin, protection is not one of their specialties.

Simple Squamous Epithelium The cells of a **simple squamous epithelium** are flattened laterally, and their cytoplasm is sparse (Figure 4.2a). In a surface view, the close-fitting cells resemble a tiled floor. When the cells are cut perpendicular to their free surface, they resemble fried eggs seen from the side, with their cytoplasm wisping out from the slightly bulging nucleus. Thin and often permeable, this epithelium is found where filtration or the exchange of substances by rapid diffusion is a priority. In the kidneys, simple squamous epithelium forms part of the filtration membrane; in the lungs, it forms the walls of the air sacs across which gas exchange occurs.

Two simple squamous epithelia in the body have special names that reflect their location. **Endothelium** (en"do-the'le-um; "inner covering") provides a slick, friction-reducing lining in lymphatic vessels and in all hollow organs of the cardiovascular system—blood vessels and the heart. Capillaries consist exclusively of endothelium, and its exceptional thinness encourages the efficient exchange of nutrients and wastes between the bloodstream and surrounding tissue cells. **Mesothelium** (mez"o-the'le-um; "middle covering") is the epithelium found in serous membranes lining the ventral body cavity and covering its organs.

Simple Cuboidal Epithelium Simple **cuboidal epithelium** consists of a single layer of cells as tall as they are wide (Figure 4.2b). The spherical nuclei stain darkly, causing the cell layer to look like a string of beads when viewed microscopically. Important functions of simple cuboidal epithelium are secretion and absorption. This epithelium forms the walls of the smallest ducts of glands and of many kidney tubules.

Simple Columnar Epithelium Simple **columnar epithelium** is seen as a single layer of tall, closely packed cells, aligned like soldiers in a row (Figure 4.2c). It lines the digestive tract from the stomach through the rectum. Columnar cells are mostly associated with absorption and secretion, and the digestive tract lining has two distinct modifications that make it ideal for that dual function: (1) dense microvilli on the apical surface of absorptive cells and (2) **goblet cells** that secrete a protective lubricating mucus. The goblet cells are named for their goblet-shaped "cups" of mucus that occupy most of the apical cell volume (see Figures 4.2d and 4.3). Some simple columnar epithelia display cilia on their free surfaces, which help to move substances or cells through an internal passageway.

(a) Simple squamous epithelium

Description: Single layer of flattened cells with disc-shaped central nuclei and sparse cytoplasm; the simplest of the epithelia.

Function: Allows passage of materials by diffusion and filtration in sites where protection is not important; secretes lubricating substances in serosae.

Location: Kidney glomeruli; air sacs of lungs; lining of heart, blood vessels, and lymphatic vessels; lining of ventral body cavity (serosae).

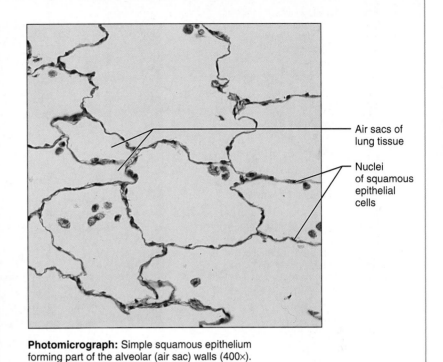

Air sacs of lung tissue

Nuclei of squamous epithelial cells

Photomicrograph: Simple squamous epithelium forming part of the alveolar (air sac) walls (400×).

(b) Simple cuboidal epithelium

Description: Single layer of cubelike cells with large, spherical central nuclei.

Function: Secretion and absorption.

Location: Kidney tubules; ducts and secretory portions of small glands; ovary surface.

Simple cuboidal epithelial cells

Basement membrane

Connective tissue

Photomicrograph: Simple cuboidal epithelium in kidney tubules (400×).

FIGURE 4.2 **Epithelial tissues. (a)** and **(b)** Simple epithelium.

(c) Simple columnar epithelium

Description: Single layer of tall cells with *round* to *oval* nuclei; some cells bear cilia; layer may contain mucus-secreting unicellular glands (goblet cells).

Function: Absorption; secretion of mucus, enzymes, and other substances; ciliated type propels mucus (or reproductive cells) by ciliary action.

Location: Nonciliated type lines most of the digestive tract (stomach to anal canal), gallbladder, and excretory ducts of some glands; ciliated variety lines small bronchi, uterine tubes, and some regions of the uterus.

Simple columnar epithelial cell

Basement membrane

Photomicrograph: Simple columnar epithelium of the stomach mucosa (1300×).

(d) Pseudostratified columnar epithelium

Description: Single layer of cells of differing heights, some not reaching the free surface; nuclei seen at different levels; may contain goblet cells and bear cilia.

Function: Secretion, particularly of mucus; propulsion of mucus by ciliary action.

Location: Nonciliated type in male's sperm-carrying ducts and ducts of large glands; ciliated variety lines the trachea, most of the upper respiratory tract.

Trachea

Cilia

Mucus of goblet cell

Pseudo-stratified epithelial layer

Basement membrane

Connective tissue

Photomicrograph: Pseudostratified ciliated columnar epithelium lining the human trachea (400×).

FIGURE 4.2 **Epithelial tissues.** *(continued)*   **(c)** and **(d)** Simple epithelium.

(e) Stratified squamous epithelium

Description: Thick membrane composed of several cell layers; basal cells are cuboidal or columnar and metabolically active; surface cells are flattened (squamous); in the keratinized type, the surface cells are full of keratin and dead; basal cells are active in mitosis and produce the cells of the more superficial layers.

Function: Protects underlying tissues in areas subjected to abrasion.

Location: Nonkeratinized type forms the moist linings of the esophagus, mouth, and vagina; keratinized variety forms the epidermis of the skin, a dry membrane.

Stratified squamous epithelium

Nuclei

Basement membrane

Connective tissue

Photomicrograph: Stratified squamous epithelium lining the esophagus (425×).

FIGURE 4.2 *(continued)*   **(e)** Stratified epithelium.

Pseudostratified Columnar Epithelium   The cells of **pseudostratified columnar epithelium** (soo″do-stră′tĭ-fīd) vary in height (Figure 4.2d). All of its cells rest on the basement membrane, but only the tallest reach the free surface of the epithelium. Because the cell nuclei lie at different levels above the basement membrane, the tissue gives the false (pseudo) impression that several cell layers are present; hence "pseudostratified." The short cells are relatively unspecialized and give rise to the taller cells. This epithelium, like the simple columnar variety, secretes or absorbs substances. A ciliated version containing goblet cells lines most of the respiratory tract. Here the motile cilia propel sheets of dust-trapping mucus superiorly away from the lungs.

Stratified Epithelia

Stratified epithelia contain two or more cell layers. They regenerate from below; that is, the basal cells divide and push apically to replace the older surface cells. Considerably more durable than the simple epithelia, the major (but not the only) role of stratified epithelia is protection.

Stratified Squamous Epithelium   Stratified squamous epithelium is the most widespread of the stratified epithelia (Figure 4.2e). Composed of several layers, it is thick and well suited for its protective role in the body. Its free surface cells are squamous; cells of the deeper layers are cuboidal or columnar. This epithelium is found in areas subjected to wear and tear, and its surface cells are constantly being rubbed away and replaced by division of its basal cells. Because epithelium depends on diffusion of nutrients from a deeper connective tissue layer, the epithelial cells farther from the basement membrane are less viable and those at the apical surface are often flattened and atrophied.

To avoid memorizing all its locations simply remember that this epithelium forms the external part of the skin and extends a short distance into every body opening that is directly continuous with the skin. The outer layer, or *epidermis*, of the skin is *keratinized* (ker′ah-tin″īzd), meaning its surface cells contain *keratin*, a tough protective protein. (The epidermis is discussed in Chapter 5.) The other stratified squamous epithelia of the body are *nonkeratinized*.

Stratified Cuboidal and Columnar Epithelia
Stratified cuboidal epithelium is quite rare in the body, mostly found in the ducts of some of the larger glands (sweat glands, mammary glands). It typically has two layers of cuboidal cells.

4

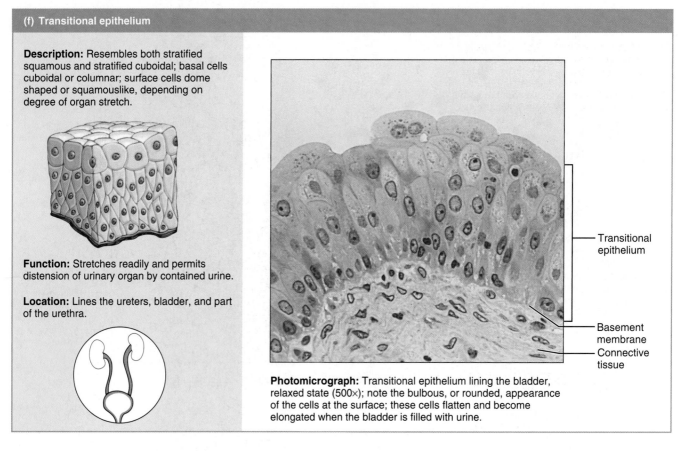

(f) Transitional epithelium

Description: Resembles both stratified squamous and stratified cuboidal; basal cells cuboidal or columnar; surface cells dome shaped or squamouslike, depending on degree of organ stretch.

Function: Stretches readily and permits distension of urinary organ by contained urine.

Location: Lines the ureters, bladder, and part of the urethra.

Transitional epithelium

Basement membrane

Connective tissue

Photomicrograph: Transitional epithelium lining the bladder, relaxed state (500×); note the bulbous, or rounded, appearance of the cells at the surface; these cells flatten and become elongated when the bladder is filled with urine.

FIGURE 4.2 **Epithelial tissues.** *(continued)* **(f)** Stratified epithelium.

Stratified columnar epithelium also has a limited distribution in the body. Small amounts are found in the pharynx, the male urethra, and lining some glandular ducts. This epithelium also occurs at transition areas or junctions between two other types of epithelia. Only its apical layer of cells is columnar. Because of their relative scarcity in the body, these two stratified epithelia are not illustrated in Figure 4.2.

Transitional Epithelium **Transitional epithelium** forms the lining of hollow urinary organs, which stretch as they fill with urine (Figure 4.2f). Cells of its basal layer are cuboidal or columnar. The apical cells vary in appearance, depending on the degree of distension of the organ. When the organ is distended with urine, the transitional epithelium thins from about six cell layers to three, and its domelike apical cells flatten and become squamouslike. The ability of transitional cells to change their shape (undergo "transitions") allows a greater volume of urine to flow through a tubelike organ. In the bladder, it allows more urine to be stored.

Glandular Epithelia

A **gland** consists of one or more cells that make and secrete (export) a particular product. This product, called a **secretion,** is an aqueous (water-based) fluid that usually contains proteins, but there is variation—for example, some glands release a lipid- or steroid-rich secretion. Secretion is an active process; glandular cells obtain needed substances from the blood and transform them chemically into a product that is then discharged from the cell. Notice that the term *secretion* can refer to both the gland's *product* and the *process* of making and releasing that product.

Glands are classified as *endocrine* ("internally secreting") or *exocrine* ("externally secreting") depending on where they release their product, and as *unicellular* ("one-celled") or *multicellular* ("many-celled") based on the relative cell number making up the gland. Unicellular glands are scattered within epithelial sheets. By contrast, most multicellular epithelial glands form by invagination (inward growth) or evagination (outward growth) from an epithelial sheet and, at least initially, most have *ducts,* tubelike connections to the epithelial sheets.

Endocrine Glands

Because **endocrine glands** eventually lose their ducts, they are often called *ductless glands.* They produce **hormones,** regulatory chemicals that they secrete by exocytosis directly into the extracellular space. From there the hormones enter the blood or lymphatic fluid and travel to specific target organs. Each hormone prompts its target organ(s) to respond in some characteristic way. For example, hormones produced by certain intestinal cells cause the pancreas to release enzymes that help digest food in the digestive tract.

Endocrine glands are structurally diverse, so one description does not fit all. Although most endocrine glands are compact multicellular organs, some individual hormone-producing cells are scattered in the digestive tract mucosa and in the brain, giving rise to their collective description as the *diffuse endocrine system*. Their secretions are also varied, ranging from modified amino acids to peptides, glycoproteins, and steroids. Since not all endocrine glands are epithelial derivatives, we defer consideration of their structure and function to Chapter 16.

Exocrine Glands

Exocrine glands are numerous, and many of their products are familiar. All exocrine glands secrete their products onto body surfaces (skin) or into body cavities—the unicellular glands directly (by exocytosis) and the multicellular glands via an epithelium-walled duct that transports the secretion to the epithelial surface. Exocrine glands are a diverse lot. They include mucous, sweat, oil, and salivary glands, the liver (which secretes bile), the pancreas (which synthesizes digestive enzymes), and many others.

Unicellular Exocrine Glands   The only important example of a **unicellular** (or one-celled) **gland** is the *goblet cell*. True to its name, a goblet cell is shaped like a goblet (a drinking glass with a stem). Goblet cells are sprinkled in the epithelial linings of the intestinal and respiratory tracts amid columnar cells with other functions (see Figures 4.3 and 4.2d). In humans, all such glands produce **mucin** (mu'sin), a complex glycoprotein that dissolves in water when secreted. Once dissolved, mucin forms **mucus**, a slimy coating that both protects and lubricates surfaces.

Multicellular Exocrine Glands   Compared to the unicellular glands, **multicellular exocrine glands** are structurally more complex. They have two basic parts: an epithelium-derived *duct* and a *secretory unit (acinus)* consisting of secretory cells. In all but the simplest glands, *supportive connective tissue* surrounds the secretory unit and supplies it with blood vessels and nerve fibers, and forms a *fibrous capsule* that extends into the gland proper and divides the gland into *lobes*.

- **Structural classification.** On the basis of their duct structures, multicellular exocrine glands are either simple or compound (Figure 4.4). **Simple glands** have an unbranched duct, whereas **compound glands** have

(a)

(b)

FIGURE 4.3   **Goblet cells (unicellular exocrine glands). (a)** Photomicrograph of a mucus-secreting goblet cell in the simple columnar epithelium lining the small intestine (approx. 2000×). **(b)** Diagram of a goblet cell. Notice the secretory vesicles and well-developed rough ER and Golgi apparatus.

a branched duct. The glands are further categorized by their secretory units as (1) **tubular** if the secretory cells form tubes; (2) **alveolar** (al-ve'o-lar) if the secretory cells form small, flasklike sacs (*alveolus* = "small hollow cavity"); and (3) **tubuloalveolar** if they have both types of secretory units. Note that the term **acinar** (as'ĭ-nar; "berrylike") is used interchangeably with alveolar.

4

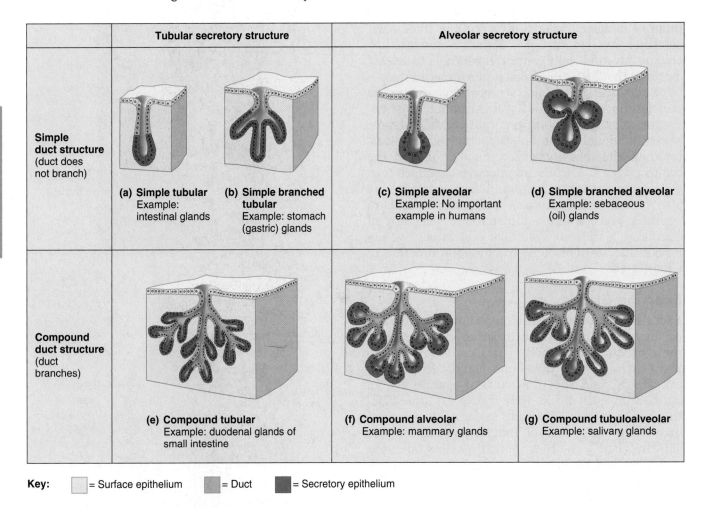

	Tubular secretory structure		Alveolar secretory structure	
Simple duct structure (duct does not branch)	**(a) Simple tubular** Example: intestinal glands	**(b) Simple branched tubular** Example: stomach (gastric) glands	**(c) Simple alveolar** Example: No important example in humans	**(d) Simple branched alveolar** Example: sebaceous (oil) glands
Compound duct structure (duct branches)	**(e) Compound tubular** Example: duodenal glands of small intestine		**(f) Compound alveolar** Example: mammary glands	**(g) Compound tubuloalveolar** Example: salivary glands

Key: ☐ = Surface epithelium   ☐ = Duct   ■ = Secretory epithelium

FIGURE 4.4   **Types of multicellular exocrine glands.** Multicellular glands are classified according to duct type (simple or compound) and the structure of their secretory units (tubular, alveolar, or tubuloalveolar).

▪ **Modes of secretion.** Multicellular exocrine glands secrete their products in different ways, so they can also be described functionally. Most are **merocrine glands** (mer′o-krin), which secrete their products by exocytosis as they are produced. The secretory cells are not altered in any way. The pancreas, most sweat glands, and salivary glands belong to this class (Figure 4.5a).

Secretory cells of **holocrine glands** (hol′o-krin) accumulate their products within them until they rupture. (They are replaced by the division of underlying cells.) Because holocrine gland secretions include the synthesized product plus dead cell fragments (*holos* = all), you could say that their cells "die for their cause." Sebaceous (oil) glands of the skin are the only true example of holocrine glands (Figure 4.5b).

Although *apocrine glands* (ap′o-krin) are definitely present in other animals, there is some controversy over whether humans have this third gland type. Like holocrine glands, apocrine glands accu-

mulate their products, but in this case only just beneath the free surface. Eventually, the apex of the cell pinches off (*apo* = from, off), releasing the secretory granules and a small amount of cytoplasm. The cell repairs its damage and the process repeats again and again. The best possibility in humans is the release of lipid droplets by the mammary glands, but most histologists classify mammary glands as merocrine glands because this is the means by which milk proteins are secreted.

Connective Tissue

Connective tissue is found everywhere in the body. It is the most abundant and widely distributed of the primary tissues, but its amount in particular organs varies. For example, skin consists primarily of connective tissue, while the brain contains very little. There are four main classes of connective tissue and several subclasses. The main classes are (1) *connective tissue proper* (which includes fat and the fibrous tissue of ligaments), (2) *cartilage,* (3) *bone tissue,* and (4) *blood.*

Connective tissue does much more than just *connect* body parts; it has many forms and functions. Its major functions include (1) *binding and support,* (2) *protection,* (3) *insulation,* and as blood, (4) *transportation* of substances within the body. For example, bone and cartilage support and protect body organs by providing the hard underpinnings of the skeleton; fat cushions insulate and protect body organs and provide reserve energy fuel.

Common Characteristics of Connective Tissue

Despite their many and diverse functions in the body, connective tissues have some common properties that set them apart from other primary tissues:

1. Common origin. All connective tissues arise from *mesenchyme* (an embryonic tissue) and hence have a common kinship (Figure 4.6).

2. Degrees of vascularity. Connective tissues run the entire gamut of vascularity. Cartilage is avascular; dense connective tissue is poorly vascularized; and the other types of connective tissue have a rich supply of blood vessels.

3. Extracellular matrix. Whereas all other primary tissues are composed mainly of cells, connective tissues are largely nonliving **extracellular matrix** (ma'triks; "womb"), which separates, often widely, the living cells of the tissue. Because of its matrix, connective tissue is able to bear weight, withstand great tension, and endure abuses, such as physical trauma and abrasion, that no other tissue would be able to tolerate.

Structural Elements of Connective Tissue

Connective tissues have three main elements: *ground substance, fibers,* and *cells.* Ground substance and fibers make up the extracellular matrix. (Note that some authors use the term *matrix* to indicate the ground substance only.)

The properties of the cells and the composition and arrangement of extracellular matrix elements vary tremendously. The result is an amazing diversity of connective tissues, each adapted to perform its specific function in the body. For example, the matrix can be delicate and fragile to form a soft "packing" around an organ, or it can form "ropes" (tendons and ligaments) of incredible strength. Nonetheless, connective tissues have a common structural plan, and we use *areolar connective tissue* (ah-re'o-lar) as our *prototype,* or model, for this

Q *Which of the gland types illustrated would have the highest rate of cellular mitosis? Why?*

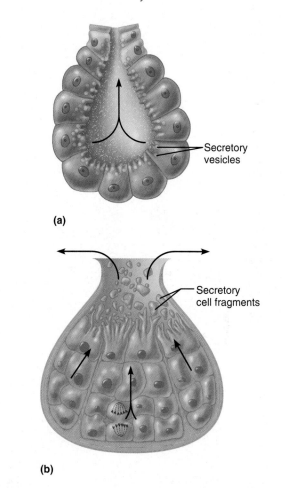

(a)

(b)

FIGURE 4.5 **Chief modes of secretion in human exocrine glands. (a)** Merocrine glands secrete their products by exocytosis. **(b)** In holocrine glands, the entire secretory cell ruptures, releasing secretions and dead cell fragments.

group of tissues (see Figure 4.8). All other subclasses are simply variants of this common tissue type.

Ground Substance

Ground substance is the unstructured material that fills the space between the cells and contains the fibers. It is composed of *interstitial (tissue) fluid, cell adhesion proteins,* and *proteoglycans* (pro"te-o-gli'kanz). Cell adhesion proteins (*fibronectin, laminin,* and others) serve mainly as a connective tissue glue that allows connective tissue cells to attach themselves to matrix elements. The proteoglycans consist

A The holocrine gland, because cells that are fragmented and secreted have to be replaced.

4

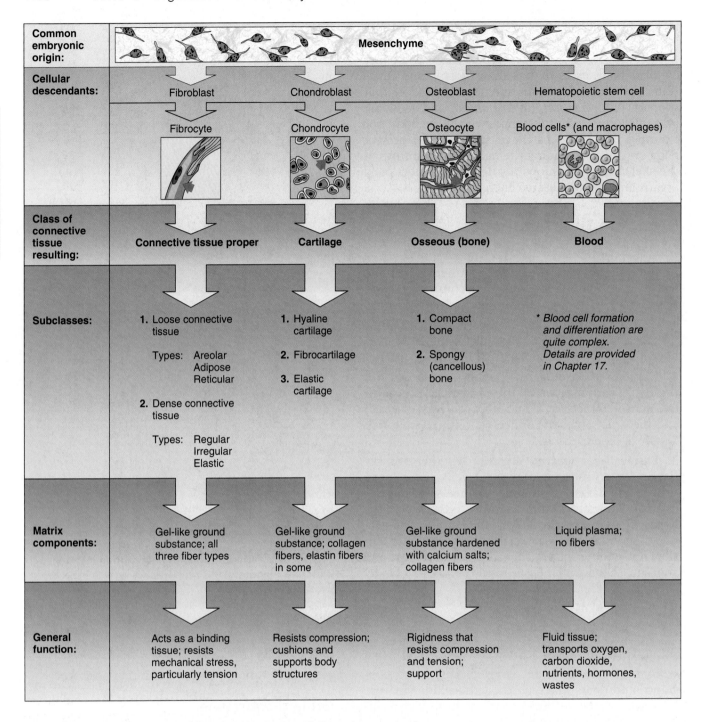

Common embryonic origin:	Mesenchyme			
Cellular descendants:	Fibroblast	Chondroblast	Osteoblast	Hematopoietic stem cell
	Fibrocyte	Chondrocyte	Osteocyte	Blood cells* (and macrophages)
Class of connective tissue resulting:	**Connective tissue proper**	**Cartilage**	**Osseous (bone)**	**Blood**

Subclasses:	1. Loose connective tissue
	
	  Types: Areolar
	      Adipose
	      Reticular
	
	2. Dense connective tissue
	
	  Types: Regular
	      Irregular
	      Elastic
		1. Hyaline cartilage
		
		2. Fibrocartilage
		
		3. Elastic cartilage
			1. Compact bone
			
			2. Spongy (cancellous) bone
				Blood cell formation and differentiation are quite complex. Details are provided in Chapter 17.

Matrix components:	Gel-like ground substance; all three fiber types	Gel-like ground substance; collagen fibers, elastin fibers in some	Gel-like ground substance hardened with calcium salts; collagen fibers	Liquid plasma; no fibers
General function:	Acts as a binding tissue; resists mechanical stress, particularly tension	Resists compression; cushions and supports body structures	Rigidity that resists compression and tension; support	Fluid tissue; transports oxygen, carbon dioxide, nutrients, hormones, wastes

FIGURE 4.6   Major classes of connective tissue. All these classes arise from the same embryonic tissue type (mesenchyme).

of a protein core to which *glycosaminoglycans* (GAGs) (gli″kos-ah-me″no-gli′kanz) are attached. The strandlike GAGs are large, negatively charged polysaccharides that stick out from the core protein like the fibers of a bottle brush (Figure 4.7). Important examples of GAGs in connective tissues include *chondroitin* and *keratan sulfates* and *hyaluronic acid*

(hi″ah-lu-ron′ik). The proteoglycans tend to form huge aggregates (often attached to a hyaluronic acid molecule). The GAGs intertwine and trap water, forming a substance that varies from a fluid to a viscous gel; in general, the higher the GAG content, the more viscous the ground substance.

The ground substance holds large amounts of fluid and functions as a molecular sieve, or medium, through which nutrients and other dissolved substances can diffuse between the blood capillaries and the cells. The fibers embedded in the ground substance make it less pliable and impede diffusion somewhat.

Fibers

The *fibers* of connective tissue provide support. Three types of fibers are found in connective tissue matrix: collagen, elastic, and reticular fibers. Of these, collagen fibers are by far the strongest and most abundant.

Collagen fibers are constructed primarily of the fibrous protein *collagen*. Collagen molecules are secreted into the extracellular space, where they assemble spontaneously into cross-linked fibrils, which in turn are bundled together into the thick collagen fibers seen with a microscope. Because of the cross-linking of their fibrils, collagen fibers are extremely tough and provide high tensile strength (that is, the ability to resist longitudinal stress) to the matrix. Indeed, stress tests show that collagen fibers are stronger than steel fibers of the same size! When fresh, they have a glistening white appearance; they are therefore also called *white fibers*.

Elastic fibers are long, thin fibers that form branching networks in the extracellular matrix. These fibers contain a rubberlike protein, *elastin*, that allows them to stretch and recoil like rubber bands. Connective tissue can stretch only so much before its thick, ropelike collagen fibers become taut. Then, when the tension lets up, elastic fibers snap the connective tissue back to its normal length and shape. Elastic fibers are found where greater elasticity is needed, for example, in the skin, lungs, and blood vessel walls. Because fresh elastic fibers appear yellow, they are sometimes called *yellow fibers*.

Reticular fibers are short, fine, collagenous fibers (with a slightly different chemistry and form) and are continuous with collagen fibers. They branch extensively, forming delicate networks (*reticul* = network) that surround small blood vessels and support the soft tissue of organs. They are particularly abundant where connective tissue abuts other tissue types, for example, in the basement membrane of epithelial tissues, and around capillaries, where they form fuzzy "nets" that allow more "give" than the larger collagen fibers.

Cells

Each major class of connective tissue has a fundamental cell type that exists in immature and mature forms (see Figure 4.6). The undifferentiated cells, in-

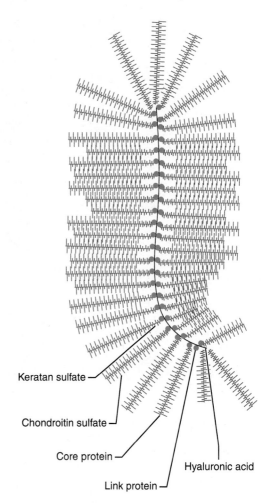

Keratan sulfate

Chondroitin sulfate

Core protein

Link protein

Hyaluronic acid

FIGURE 4.7 **Proteoglycan aggregate in cartilage.** A schematic drawing of the GAGs keratan sulfate and chondroitin sulfate linked to core protein molecules, forming proteoglycans, which in turn attach to a long hyaluronic acid molecule with the aid of a link protein to form the aggregate.

dicated by the suffix *blast* (literally, "bud" or "sprout," but the suffix means "forming"), are actively mitotic cells that secrete the ground substance and the fibers characteristic of their particular matrix. The primary blast cell types by connective tissue class are (1) connective tissue proper: **fibroblast;** (2) cartilage: **chondroblast** (kon'dro-blast"); (3) bone: **osteoblast** (os'te-o-blast"); and (4) blood: **hematopoietic stem cell** (hem"ah-to-poy-et'ik). Although the hematopoietic stem cell is an undifferentiated blast cell that produces blood cells, it differs from the other blast cells in that it is not located in "its" tissue (blood) and does not make the fluid matrix (plasma) of that tissue.

Once they synthesize the matrix, the blast cells assume their less active, mature mode, indicated by the suffix *cyte* (see Figure 4.6). The mature cells

4

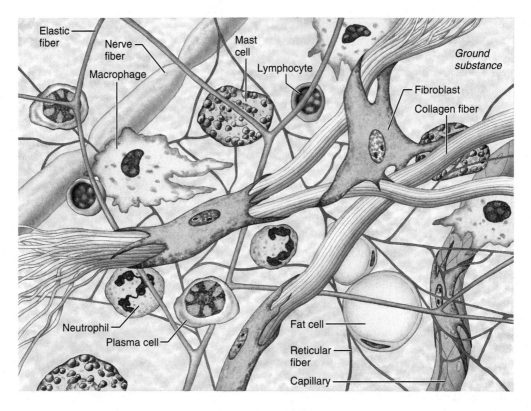

FIGURE 4.8   **Areolar connective tissue: A prototype (model) connective tissue.** This tissue underlies epithelia and surrounds capillaries. Note the various cell types and the three classes of fibers (collagen, reticular, elastic) embedded in the ground substance. (See Figure 4.9a for a less idealized version.)

maintain the health of the matrix. However, if the matrix is injured, they can easily revert to their more active state to repair and regenerate the matrix. (The blood-forming hematopoietic stem cell found in bone marrow is always actively mitotic.)

Additionally, connective tissue is home to an assortment of other cell types, such as nutrient-storing *fat cells* and mobile cells that migrate into the connective tissue matrix from the bloodstream. The latter include defensive **white blood cells** (neutrophils, eosinophils, lymphocytes) and other cell types concerned with tissue response to injury, such as *mast cells*, *macrophages* (mak′ro-fāj-es), and antibody-producing **plasma cells.** This wide variety of cells is particularly obvious in our prototype, areolar connective tissue (Figure 4.8).

All of these accessory cell types are described in later chapters, but mast cells and macrophages are so important to overall body defense that they deserve a brief mention here. The oval **mast cells** typically cluster along blood vessels. These cells act as sensitive sentinels to detect foreign substances (e.g., bacteria, fungi) and initiate local inflammatory responses against them. In the mast cell cytoplasm are conspicuous secretory granules (mast = "stuffed full of granules") containing several chemicals that

mediate inflammation, especially in severe allergies. These include (1) *heparin* (hep′ah-rin), an anticoagulant chemical that prevents blood clotting when free in the bloodstream (but in human mast cells it appears to bind to and regulate the action of other mast cell chemicals); (2) *histamine* (his′tah-mēn), a substance that makes capillaries leaky; and (3) *proteases* (protein-degrading enzymes).

Macrophages (*macro* = large; *phago* = eat) are large, irregularly shaped cells that avidly phagocytize a broad variety of foreign materials, ranging from foreign molecules to entire bacteria to dust particles. These "big eaters" also dispose of dead tissue cells, and they are central actors in the immune system. In connective tissues, they may be attached to connective tissue fibers (fixed) or may migrate freely through the matrix.

Macrophages are peppered throughout loose connective tissue, bone marrow, and lymphatic tissue. Those in certain sites are given specific names; for example, those in the lungs are called dust cells. Some macrophages have selective appetites; for example, those of the spleen primarily dispose of aging red blood cells, but they will not turn down other "delicacies" that come their way.

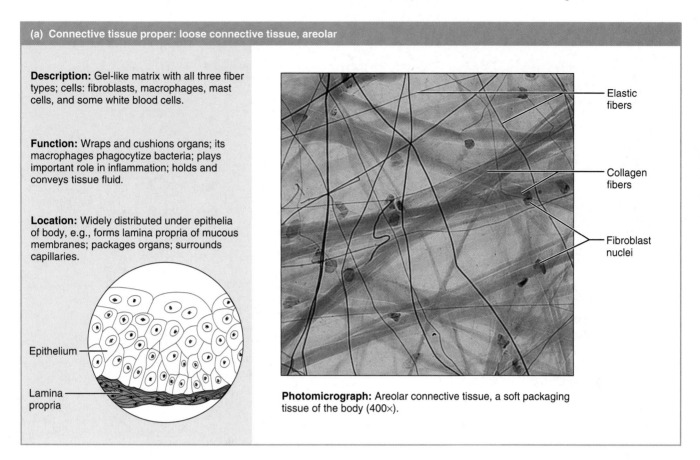

(a) Connective tissue proper: loose connective tissue, areolar

Description: Gel-like matrix with all three fiber types; cells: fibroblasts, macrophages, mast cells, and some white blood cells.

Function: Wraps and cushions organs; its macrophages phagocytize bacteria; plays important role in inflammation; holds and conveys tissue fluid.

Location: Widely distributed under epithelia of body, e.g., forms lamina propria of mucous membranes; packages organs; surrounds capillaries.

Elastic fibers

Collagen fibers

Fibroblast nuclei

Epithelium

Lamina propria

Photomicrograph: Areolar connective tissue, a soft packaging tissue of the body (400×).

4

FIGURE 4.9 **Connective tissues. (a)** Connective tissue proper.

Types of Connective Tissue

As noted, all classes of connective tissue consist of living cells surrounded by a matrix. Their major differences reflect cell type, and fiber types and relative amounts, as summarized in Figure 4.6. The connective tissues described in this section are illustrated in Figure 4.9. Mature connective tissues arise from a common embryonic tissue, called **mesenchyme** (meh'zin-kīm), derived from embryonic mesoderm (see Figure 4.14, p. 145). Mesenchyme has a fluid ground substance containing fine sparse fibers and star-shaped *mesenchymal cells* (see the top bar of Figure 4.6). It arises during the early weeks of embryonic development and eventually differentiates (specializes) into all other connective tissue cells. However, some mesenchymal cells remain and provide a source of new cells in mature connective tissues.

Connective Tissue Proper

Connective tissue proper has two subclasses: the **loose connective tissues** (areolar, adipose, and reticular) and **dense connective tissues** (dense regular, dense irregular, and elastic). Except for bone, cartilage, and blood, all mature connective tissues belong to this class.

Areolar Connective Tissue   The functions of **areolar connective tissue,** shared by some but not all connective tissues, include (1) supporting and binding other tissues (the job of the fibers); (2) holding body fluids (the ground substance's role); (3) defending against infection (via the activity of white blood cells and macrophages); and (4) storing nutrients as fat (in fat cells) (Figure 4.9a).

Fibroblasts, flat, branching cells that appear spindle shaped in profile, predominate, but numerous macrophages are also seen and present a formidable barrier to invading microorganisms. Fat cells appear singly or in clusters, and occasional mast cells are identified easily by the large, darkly stained cytoplasmic granules that often obscure their nuclei. Other cell types are scattered throughout.

The most obvious structural feature of this tissue is the loose arrangement of its fibers; hence, its classification as a *loose* connective tissue is fitting. The rest of the matrix, occupied by ground substance, appears to be empty space when viewed through the microscope; in fact, the Latin term *areola* means "a small open space." Because of its loose nature, areolar connective tissue provides a reservoir of water and salts for surrounding body tissues, always holding approximately as much fluid as

(b) Connective tissue proper: loose connective tissue, adipose

Description: Matrix as in areolar, but very sparse; closely packed adipocytes, or fat cells, have nucleus pushed to the side by large fat droplet.

Function: Provides reserve food fuel; insulates against heat loss; supports and protects organs.

Location: Under skin; around kidneys and eyeballs; within abdomen; in breasts.

Vacuole containing fat droplet

Nuclei of fat cells

Photomicrograph: Adipose tissue from the subcutaneous layer under the skin (450×).

FIGURE 4.9 **Connective tissues.** *(continued)* **(b)** Connective tissue proper.

there is in the entire bloodstream. Essentially all body cells obtain their nutrients from and release their wastes into this "tissue fluid." However, its high content of hyaluronic acid makes the ground substance quite viscous, like molasses, which may hinder the movement of cells through it. Some white blood cells, which protect the body from disease-causing microorganisms, secrete the enzyme hyaluronidase to liquefy the ground substance and ease their passage. (Unhappily, some potentially harmful bacteria have the same ability.) When a body region is inflamed, the areolar tissue in the area soaks up excess fluids like a sponge, and the affected area swells and becomes puffy, a condition called **edema** (ĕ-de'mah).

Areolar connective tissue is the most widely distributed connective tissue in the body and it serves as a kind of universal packing material between other tissues. It binds body parts together while allowing them to move freely over one another; wraps small blood vessels and nerves; surrounds glands; and forms the subcutaneous tissue, which cushions and attaches the skin to underlying structures. It is present in all mucous membranes as the *lamina propria.* (Mucous membranes line body cavities open to the exterior.)

Adipose (Fat) Tissue Adipose tissue (ad'ĭ-pōs) is similar to areolar tissue in structure and function but its nutrient-storing ability is much greater. Consequently, **adipocytes** (ad'ĭ-po-sītz), commonly called *adipose* or *fat cells*, predominate and account for 90% of this tissue's mass. The matrix is scanty and the cells are packed closely together, giving a chicken wire appearance to the tissue. A glistening oil droplet (almost pure triglyceride) occupies most of a fat cell's volume and displaces the nucleus to one side so that only a thin rim of surrounding cytoplasm is seen (Figure 4.9b). Mature adipocytes are among the largest cells in the body. As they take up or release fat, they become plumper or more wrinkled looking, respectively.

Adipose tissue is richly vascularized, indicating its high metabolic activity. Without the fat stores in our adipose tissue, we could not live for more than a few days without eating. Adipose tissue is certainly abundant: It constitutes 18% of an average person's body weight. Indeed, a chubby person's body can be 50% fat without being considered morbidly obese.

Adipose tissue may develop almost anywhere areolar tissue is plentiful, but it usually accumulates in subcutaneous tissue, where it also acts as a

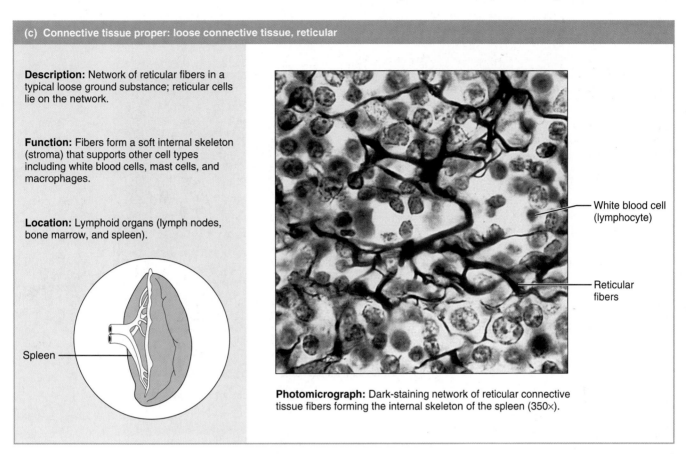

(c) Connective tissue proper: loose connective tissue, reticular

Description: Network of reticular fibers in a typical loose ground substance; reticular cells lie on the network.

Function: Fibers form a soft internal skeleton (stroma) that supports other cell types including white blood cells, mast cells, and macrophages.

Location: Lymphoid organs (lymph nodes, bone marrow, and spleen).

Spleen

White blood cell (lymphocyte)

Reticular fibers

Photomicrograph: Dark-staining network of reticular connective tissue fibers forming the internal skeleton of the spleen (350×).

FIGURE 4.9 *(continued)*   **(c)** Connective tissue proper.

shock absorber, as insulation, and as an energy storage site. Because fat is a poor conductor of heat, it helps prevent heat loss from the body. Other sites where fat accumulates include surrounding the kidneys, behind the eyeballs, and at genetically determined fat depots such as the abdomen and hips.

Whereas the abundant fat beneath the skin serves the general nutrient needs of the entire body, smaller depots of fat serve the local nutrient needs of highly active organs. Such depots occur around the hard-working heart and around lymph nodes (where cells of the immune system are furiously fighting infection), within some muscles, and as individual fat cells in the bone marrow, where new blood cells are produced at a rapid rate. Many of these local depots are highly enriched in special lipids.

The adipose tissue just described is sometimes called *white fat,* or *white adipose tissue,* to distinguish it from **brown fat,** or **brown adipose tissue.** Whereas white fat stores nutrients, brown fat adipose cells contain abundant mitochondria, which use the lipid fuels to heat the bloodstream to warm the body rather than to produce ATP molecules. The richly vascular brown fat occurs only in babies who

(as yet) lack the ability to produce body heat by shivering. Most such deposits are located between the shoulder blades, on the anterolateral neck, and on the anterior abdominal wall.

Reticular Connective Tissue   **Reticular connective tissue** resembles areolar connective tissue, but the only fibers in its matrix are reticular fibers, which form a delicate network along which fibroblasts called **reticular cells** lie scattered (Figure 4.9c). Although reticular *fibers* are widely distributed in the body, reticular *tissue* is limited to certain sites. It forms a labyrinth-like **stroma** (literally, "bed" or "mattress"), or internal framework, that can support many free blood cells (largely lymphocytes) in lymph nodes, the spleen, and bone marrow.

Dense Regular Connective Tissue   **Dense regular connective tissue** (Figure 4.9d) is one variety of the dense connective tissues, all of which have fibers as their predominant element. For this reason, the dense connective tissues are often referred to as **fibrous connective tissues.**

Dense regular connective tissue contains closely packed bundles of collagen fibers running in the same direction, parallel to the direction of pull.

4

(d) Connective tissue proper: dense connective tissue, dense regular

Description: Primarily parallel collagen fibers; a few elastin fibers; major cell type is the fibroblast.

Function: Attaches muscles to bones or to muscles; attaches bones to bones; withstands great tensile stress when pulling force is applied in one direction.

Location: Tendons, most ligaments, aponeuroses.

Shoulder joint

Ligament

Tendon

Collagen fibers

Nuclei of fibroblasts

Photomicrograph: Dense regular connective tissue from a tendon (1000×).

(e) Connective tissue proper: dense connective tissue, dense irregular

Description: Primarily irregularly arranged collagen fibers; some elastic fibers; major cell type is the fibroblast.

Function: Able to withstand tension exerted in many directions; provides structural strength.

Location: Dermis of the skin; submucosa of digestive tract; fibrous capsules of organs and of joints.

Fibrous joint capsule

Nuclei of fibroblasts

Collagen fibers

Photomicrograph: Dense irregular connective tissue from the dermis of the skin (400×).

FIGURE 4.9   **Connective tissues.** *(continued)*   **(d)** and **(e)** Connective tissue proper.

This results in white, flexible structures with great resistance to tension (pulling forces) where the tension is exerted in a single direction. Crowded between the collagen fibers are rows of fibroblasts that continuously manufacture the fibers and scant ground substance. As seen in Figure 4.9d, collagen fibers are slightly wavy. This allows the tissue to stretch a little, but once the fibers are straightened out by a pulling force, there is no further "give" to this tissue. Unlike our model (areolar) connective tissue, this tissue has few cells other than fibroblasts and it is poorly vascularized.

With its enormous tensile strength, dense regular connective tissue forms the *tendons*, which are cords that attach muscles to bones, and flat, sheet-like tendons called *aponeuroses* (ap"o-nu-ro'sēz) that attach muscles to other muscles or to bones. It also forms fascia (fash'e-ah; "a bond"), a fibrous membrane that wraps around muscles, groups of muscles, blood vessels, and nerves, binding those structures together like plastic sandwich wrap; and the ligaments that bind bones together at joints. Ligaments contain more elastic fibers than tendons and are slightly more stretchy. A few ligaments, such as the *ligamenta nuchae* and *flava* connecting adjacent vertebrae, are very elastic, so much so that the connective tissue in those structures is referred to as *elastic connective tissue*.

Dense Irregular Connective Tissue **Dense irregular connective tissue** has the same structural elements as the regular variety. However, the bundles of collagen fibers are much thicker and they are arranged irregularly; that is, they run in more than one plane (Figure 4.9e). This type of tissue forms sheets in body areas where tension is exerted from many different directions. It is found in the skin as the leathery *dermis*, and it forms fibrous joint capsules and the fibrous coverings that surround some organs (kidneys, bones, cartilages, muscles, and nerves).

Cartilage

Cartilage (kar'tĭ-lij), which stands up to both tension *and* compression, has qualities intermediate between dense connective tissue and bone. It is tough but flexible, providing a resilient rigidity to the structures it supports. Cartilage lacks nerve fibers and is avascular. It receives its nutrients by diffusion from blood vessels located in the connective tissue membrane (perichondrium) surrounding it. Its ground substance contains large amounts of the GAGs chrondroitin sulfate and hyaluronic acid, firmly bound collagen fibers (and in some cases elastic fibers), and is quite firm. Cartilage matrix also contains an exceptional amount of tissue fluid; in fact, cartilage is up to 80% water! The movement of tissue fluid in its matrix enables cartilage to rebound after being compressed and also helps to nourish the cartilage cells.

Chondroblasts, the predominant cell type in growing cartilage, produce new matrix until the skeleton stops growing at the end of adolescence. The firmness of the cartilage matrix prevents the cells from becoming widely separated, so **chondrocytes,** or mature cartilage cells, are typically found in small groups within cavities called *lacunae* (lah-ku'ne; "pits").

◢ HOMEOSTATIC IMBALANCE

Because cartilage is avascular and aging cartilage cells lose their ability to divide, cartilages heal slowly when injured. This phenomenon is excruciatingly familiar to those who have experienced sports injuries. During later life, cartilages tend to calcify or even ossify (become bony). In such cases, the chondrocytes are poorly nourished and die. ●

There are three varieties of cartilage: *hyaline cartilage, elastic cartilage,* and *fibrocartilage,* each dominated by a particular fiber type.

Hyaline Cartilage **Hyaline cartilage** (hi'ah-lĭn), or *gristle,* is the most abundant cartilage type in the body. Although it contains large numbers of collagen fibers, they are not apparent and the matrix appears amorphous and glassy (*hyalin* = glass) blue-white when viewed by the unaided eye (Figure 4.9f). Chondrocytes account for only 1–10% of the cartilage volume.

Hyaline cartilage provides firm support with some pliability. It covers the ends of long bones as *articular cartilage,* providing springy pads that absorb compression at joints. Hyaline cartilage also supports the tip of the nose, connects the ribs to the sternum, and supports most of the respiratory system passages. Most of the embryonic skeleton is formed of hyaline cartilage before bone is formed. Skeletal hyaline cartilage persists during childhood as the *epiphyseal plates* (e"pĭ-fis'e-ul), actively growing regions near the end of long bones that provide for continued growth in length.

4

(f) Cartilage: hyaline

Description: Amorphous but firm matrix; collagen fibers form an imperceptible network; chondroblasts produce the matrix and when mature (chondrocytes) lie in lacunae.

Function: Supports and reinforces; has resilient cushioning properties; resists compressive stress.

Location: Forms most of the embryonic skeleton; covers the ends of long bones in joint cavities; forms costal cartilages of the ribs; cartilages of the nose, trachea, and larynx.

Costal cartilages

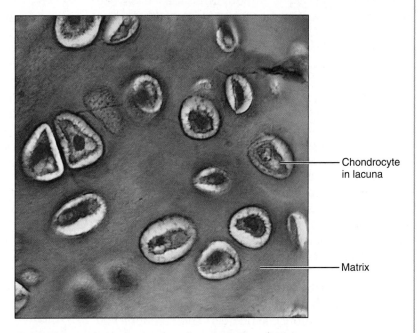

Chondrocyte in lacuna

Matrix

Photomicrograph: Hyaline cartilage from the trachea (300×).

(g) Cartilage: elastic

Description: Similar to hyaline cartilage, but more elastic fibers in matrix.

Function: Maintains the shape of a structure while allowing great flexibility.

Location: Supports the external ear (pinna); epiglottis.

Chondrocyte in lacuna

Matrix

Photomicrograph: Elastic cartilage from the human ear pinna; forms the flexible skeleton of the ear (640×).

FIGURE 4.9 **Connective tissues.** *(continued)* **(f)** and **(g)** Cartilage.

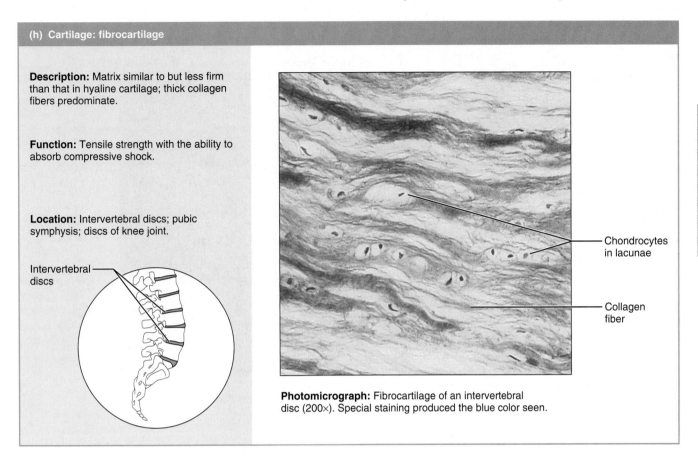

(h) Cartilage: fibrocartilage

Description: Matrix similar to but less firm than that in hyaline cartilage; thick collagen fibers predominate.

Function: Tensile strength with the ability to absorb compressive shock.

Location: Intervertebral discs; pubic symphysis; discs of knee joint.

Intervertebral discs

Chondrocytes in lacunae

Collagen fiber

Photomicrograph: Fibrocartilage of an intervertebral disc (200×). Special staining produced the blue color seen.

FIGURE 4.9 *(continued)* **(h)** Cartilage.

Elastic Cartilage Histologically, **elastic cartilage** (Figure 4.9g) is nearly identical to hyaline cartilage. However, there are many more elastin fibers in elastic cartilage. Found where strength and exceptional stretchability are needed, elastic cartilage forms the "skeletons" of the external ear and the epiglottis. (The epiglottis is the flap that covers the opening to the respiratory passageway when we swallow, preventing food or fluids from entering the lungs.)

Fibrocartilage **Fibrocartilage** is a perfect structural intermediate between hyaline cartilage and dense regular connective tissues. Its rows of chondrocytes (a cartilage feature) alternate with rows of thick collagen fibers (a feature of dense regular connective tissue) (Figure 4.9h). Because it is compressible and resists tension well, fibrocartilage is found where strong support and the ability to withstand heavy pressure are required. For example, the intervertebral discs (resilient cushions between the bony vertebrae) and the spongy cartilages of the knee (menisci) are fibrocartilage structures (see Figure 6.1, p. 177).

Bone (Osseous Tissue)

Because of its rocklike hardness, **bone,** or **osseous tissue** (os′e-us), has an exceptional ability to support and protect body structures. Bones of the skeleton also provide cavities for fat storage and synthesis of blood cells. Bone matrix is similar to that of cartilage but is harder and more rigid because, in addition to its more abundant collagen fibers, bone has an added matrix element—inorganic calcium salts (bone salts).

Osteoblasts produce the organic portion of the matrix; then bone salts are deposited on and between the fibers. Mature bone cells, or **osteocytes,** reside in the lacunae within the matrix they have made (Figure 4.9i). In cross section, bone tissue is seen as closely packed structural units called *osteons* formed of concentric rings of bony matrix (lamellae) surrounding central canals containing the blood vessels and nerves serving the bone. Unlike cartilage, the next firmest connective tissue, bone is well supplied by invading blood vessels.

Blood

Blood, the fluid within blood vessels, is the most atypical connective tissue. It does *not* connect things or give mechanical support. It is classified as a connective tissue because it develops from mesenchyme and consists of blood *cells,* surrounded by a nonliving fluid matrix called *blood plasma* (Figure 4.9j).

4

(i) Others: bone (osseous tissue)

Description: Hard, calcified matrix containing many collagen fibers; osteocytes lie in lacunae. Very well vascularized.

Function: Bone supports and protects (by enclosing); provides levers for the muscles to act on; stores calcium and other minerals and fat; marrow inside bones is the site for blood cell formation (hematopoiesis).

Location: Bones

Central canal

Lacunae

Lamella

Photomicrograph: Cross-sectional view of bone (70×).

(j) Others: blood

Description: Red and white blood cells in a fluid matrix (plasma).

Function: Transport of respiratory gases, nutrients, wastes, and other substances.

Location: Contained within blood vessels.

Plasma

Neutrophil

Red blood cells

Lymphocyte

Photomicrograph: Smear of human blood (1500×); two white blood cells (neutrophil in upper left and lymphocyte in lower right) are seen surrounded by red blood cells.

FIGURE 4.9 **Connective tissues.** *(continued)*   **(i)** Bone. **(j)** Blood.

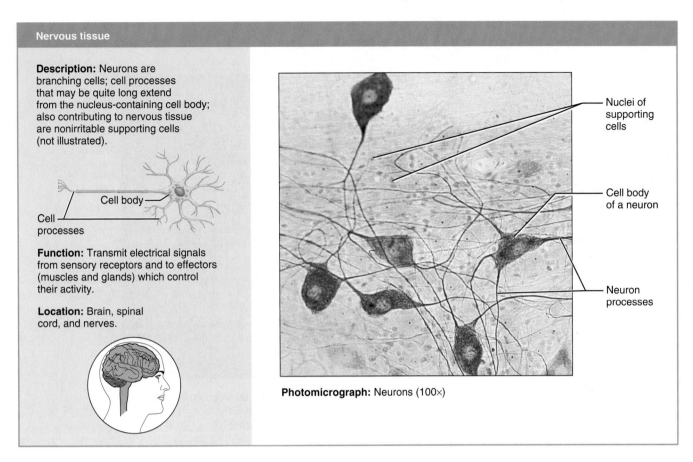

Nervous tissue

Description: Neurons are branching cells; cell processes that may be quite long extend from the nucleus-containing cell body; also contributing to nervous tissue are nonirritable supporting cells (not illustrated).

Cell body

Cell processes

Function: Transmit electrical signals from sensory receptors and to effectors (muscles and glands) which control their activity.

Location: Brain, spinal cord, and nerves.

Nuclei of supporting cells

Cell body of a neuron

Neuron processes

Photomicrograph: Neurons (100×)

FIGURE 4.10 **Nervous tissue.**

The vast majority of blood cells are red blood cells or erythrocytes, but scattered white blood cells (neutrophils, lymphocytes, monocytes, eosinophils, basophils) are also seen. The "fibers" of blood are soluble protein molecules that precipitate, forming large visible fiberlike structures during blood clotting. Blood functions as the transport vehicle for the cardiovascular system, carrying nutrients, wastes, respiratory gases, and many other substances throughout the body.

Nervous Tissue

Nervous tissue is the main component of the nervous system—the brain, spinal cord, and nerves—which regulates and controls body functions. It contains two major cell types. **Neurons** are highly specialized nerve cells that generate and conduct nerve impulses (Figure 4.10). Typically, they are branching cells with cytoplasmic extensions or processes. Their processes allow them to respond to stimuli (a role of *dendrites*) and to transmit electrical impulses over substantial distances within the body (the job of *axons*, which may be very long and myelinated, that is, covered with a fatty sheath that increases the speed of nerve transmission). The balance of nervous tissue consists of various types of supporting cells, nonconducting

cells that support, insulate, and protect the delicate neurons. A more complete discussion of nervous tissue appears in Chapter 11.

Muscle Tissue

Muscle tissues are highly cellular, well-vascularized tissues that are responsible for most types of body movement. Muscle cells possess **myofilaments,** elaborate versions of the *actin* and *myosin* filaments that bring about movement or contraction in all cell types. There are three kinds of muscle tissue: skeletal, cardiac, and smooth.

Skeletal muscle tissue is packaged by connective tissue sheets into organs called *skeletal muscles* that are attached to the bones of the skeleton. These muscles form the flesh of the body, and as they contract, they pull on bones or skin, causing body movements. Skeletal muscle cells, also called **muscle fibers,** are long, cylindrical cells that contain many nuclei. Their obvious banded, or *striated*, appearance reflects the precise alignment of their myofilaments (Figure 4.11a).

Cardiac muscle is found only in the wall of the heart. Its contractions help propel blood through the blood vessels to all parts of the body. Like skeletal muscle cells, cardiac muscle cells are striated.

(a) Skeletal muscle

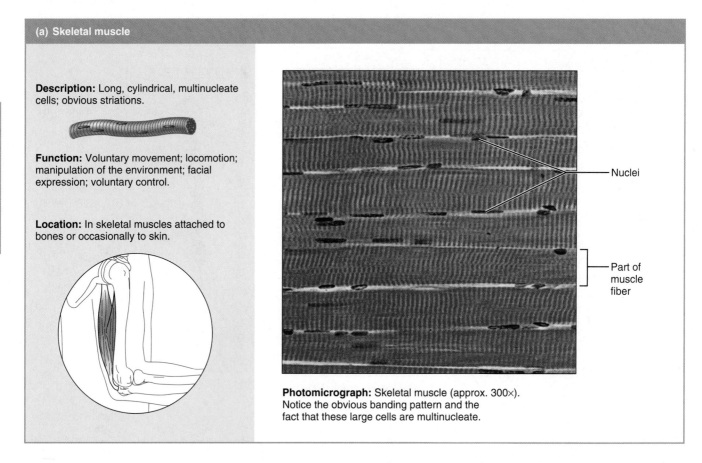

Description: Long, cylindrical, multinucleate cells; obvious striations.

Function: Voluntary movement; locomotion; manipulation of the environment; facial expression; voluntary control.

Location: In skeletal muscles attached to bones or occasionally to skin.

Nuclei

Part of muscle fiber

Photomicrograph: Skeletal muscle (approx. 300×). Notice the obvious banding pattern and the fact that these large cells are multinucleate.

(b) Cardiac muscle

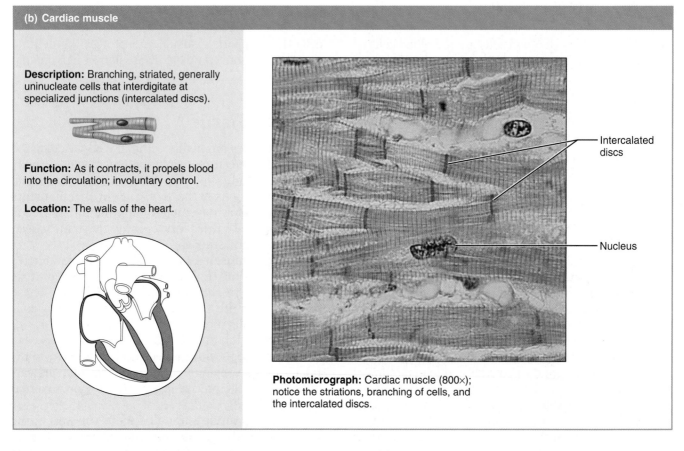

Description: Branching, striated, generally uninucleate cells that interdigitate at specialized junctions (intercalated discs).

Function: As it contracts, it propels blood into the circulation; involuntary control.

Location: The walls of the heart.

Intercalated discs

Nucleus

Photomicrograph: Cardiac muscle (800×); notice the striations, branching of cells, and the intercalated discs.

FIGURE 4.11   **Muscle tissues. (a)** Skeletal muscle tissue. **(b)** Cardiac muscle tissue.

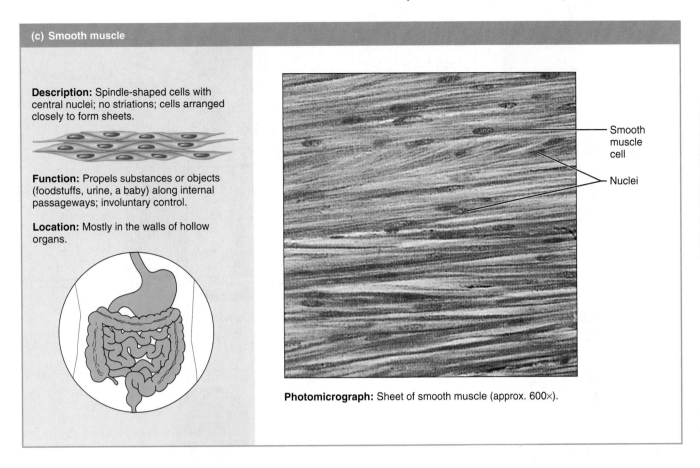

(c) Smooth muscle

Description: Spindle-shaped cells with central nuclei; no striations; cells arranged closely to form sheets.

Function: Propels substances or objects (foodstuffs, urine, a baby) along internal passageways; involuntary control.

Location: Mostly in the walls of hollow organs.

Smooth muscle cell

Nuclei

Photomicrograph: Sheet of smooth muscle (approx. 600×).

FIGURE 4.11 *(continued)* **(c)** Smooth muscle tissue.

However, they differ structurally in that cardiac cells (1) are uninucleate and (2) are branching cells that fit together tightly at unique junctions called **intercalated discs** (in-ter′kah-la″ted) (Figure 4.11b).

Smooth muscle is so named because its cells have no visible striations. Individual smooth muscle cells are spindle shaped and contain one centrally located nucleus (Figure 4.11c). Smooth muscle is found mainly in the walls of hollow organs other than the heart (digestive and urinary tract organs, uterus, and blood vessels). It acts to squeeze substances through these organs by alternately contracting and relaxing.

Because skeletal muscle contraction is under our conscious control, skeletal muscle is often called **voluntary muscle,** and the other two types are called **involuntary muscle.** Skeletal muscle and smooth muscle are described in detail in Chapter 9; cardiac muscle is discussed in Chapter 18.

Covering and Lining Membranes

Now that we have described all four primary tissues, we can consider the body's membranes that incorporate more than one type of tissue. The covering and lining membranes are of three types: *cutaneous, mucous,* or *serous.* Essentially they all are continu-

ous multicellular sheets composed of at least two primary tissue types: an epithelium bound to an underlying layer of connective tissue proper. Hence, these membranes are simple organs. The *synovial membranes,* which line joint cavities and consist of connective tissue only, are described in Chapter 8.

Cutaneous Membrane

The **cutaneous membrane** (ku-ta′ne-us; *cutis* = skin) is your skin (Figure 4.12a). It is an organ system consisting of a keratinized stratified squamous epithelium (epidermis) firmly attached to a thick layer of dense irregular connective tissue (dermis). Unlike other epithelial membranes, the cutaneous membrane is exposed to the air and is a dry membrane. Chapter 5 is devoted to this unique organ system.

Mucous Membranes

Mucous membranes, or **mucosae** (mu-ko′se), line body cavities that open to the exterior, such as those of the hollow organs of the digestive, respiratory, and urogenital tracts (Figure 4.12b). In all cases, they are "wet," or moist, membranes bathed by secretions or, in the case of the urinary mucosa, urine. Notice that the term *mucosa* refers to the location of the membrane, *not* its cell composition, which varies.

4

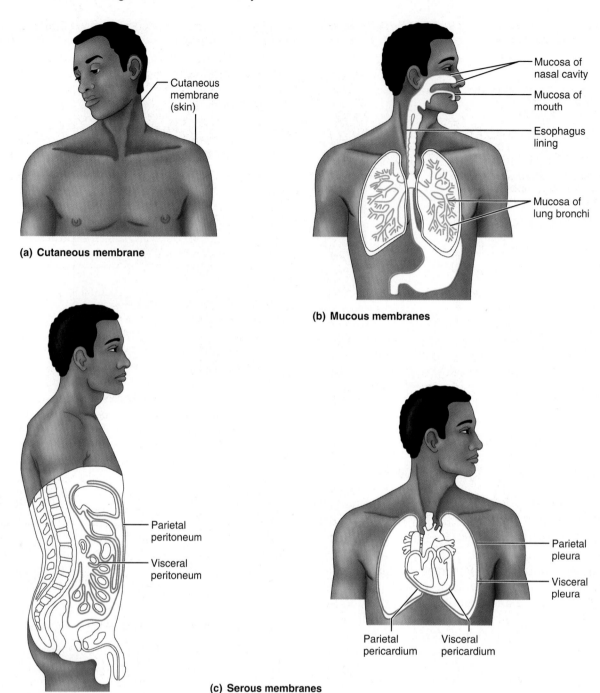

(a) Cutaneous membrane

Cutaneous
membrane
(skin)

Mucosa of
nasal cavity

Mucosa of
mouth

Esophagus
lining

Mucosa of
lung bronchi

(b) Mucous membranes

Parietal
peritoneum

Visceral
peritoneum

Parietal
pleura

Visceral
pleura

Parietal
pericardium

Visceral
pericardium

(c) Serous membranes

FIGURE 4.12   **Classes of membranes. (a)** Cutaneous membrane, or skin.
(b) Mucous membranes line body cavities that are open to the exterior. **(c)** Serous
membranes line ventral body cavities that are closed to the exterior.

However, most mucosae contain either stratified
squamous or simple columnar epithelia. The epithelial sheet is directly underlain by a layer of loose connective tissue called the **lamina propria** (lam'ĭ-nah
pro'pre-ah; "one's own layer"). In some mucosae,
the lamina propria rests on a third (deeper) layer of
smooth muscle cells.

Mucous membranes are often adapted for absorption and secretion. Although many mucosae secrete mucus, this is not a requirement. The mucosae
of both the digestive and respiratory tracts secrete

copious amounts of lubricating mucus; that of the
urinary tract does not.

Serous Membranes

Serous membranes, or **serosae** (se-ro'se), introduced in Chapter 1, are the moist membranes
found in closed ventral body cavities (Figure 4.12c).
A serous membrane consists of simple squamous
epithelium (a mesothelium) resting on a thin layer

of loose connective (areolar) tissue. The mesothelial cells enrich the fluid that filters from the capillaries in the associated connective tissue with hyaluronic acid. The result is the thin, clear *serous fluid* that lubricates the facing surfaces of the parietal and visceral layers, so that they slide across each other easily.

The serosae are named according to their site and specific organ associations. For example, the serosa lining the thoracic wall and covering the lungs is the **pleura;** that enclosing the heart is the **pericardium;** and those of the abdominopelvic cavity and viscera are the **peritoneums.**

Tissue Repair

The body has many techniques for protecting itself from uninvited "guests" or injury. Intact mechanical barriers such as the skin and mucosae, the cilia of epithelial cells lining the respiratory tract, and the strong acid (chemical barrier) produced by stomach glands represent three defenses exerted at the body's external boundaries. When tissue injury occurs, these barriers are penetrated; this stimulates the body's inflammatory and immune responses, which wage their battles largely in the connective tissues of the body. The inflammatory response is a relatively nonspecific reaction that develops quickly wherever tissues are injured, while the immune response is extremely specific, but takes longer to swing into action. The inflammatory and immune responses are considered in detail in Chapter 21.

Steps of Tissue Repair

Tissue repair requires that cells divide and migrate, activities that are initiated by growth factors (wound hormones) released by injured cells. Repair occurs in two major ways: by regeneration and by fibrosis. Which of these occurs depends on (1) the type of tissue damaged and (2) the severity of the injury. **Regeneration** is replacement of destroyed tissue with the same kind of tissue, whereas **fibrosis** involves proliferation of fibrous connective tissue called **scar tissue.** In skin, the tissue we will use as our example, repair involves both activities.

1. Inflammation sets the stage. Let us briefly examine the inflammatory events that tissue injury sets into motion. First, the tissue trauma causes injured tissue cells, macrophages, mast cells, and others to release inflammatory chemicals, which cause the capillaries to dilate and become very permeable. This allows white blood cells (neutrophils, monocytes) and plasma fluid rich in clotting proteins, antibodies, and other substances to seep into the injured area. The leaked clotting proteins construct a clot, which stops the loss of blood, holds the edges of

the wound together, and effectively walls in, or isolates, the injured area, preventing bacteria, toxins, or other harmful substances from spreading to surrounding tissues (Figure 4.13a). The part of the clot exposed to air quickly dries and hardens, forming a *scab.* The inflammatory events leave excess fluid, bits of destroyed cells, and other debris in the area, which are eventually removed via lymphatic vessels or phagocytized by macrophages.

2. Organization restores the blood supply. Even while the inflammatory process is going on, **organization,** the first phase of tissue repair, begins. During organization the blood clot is replaced by granulation tissue (Figure 4.13b). **Granulation tissue** is a delicate pink tissue composed of several elements. It contains capillaries that grow in from nearby areas and lay down a new capillary bed. Granulation tissue is actually named for these capillaries, which protrude nublike from its surface, giving it a granular appearance. These capillaries are fragile and bleed freely, as demonstrated when someone picks at a scab. Proliferating fibroblasts in granulation tissue produce growth factors as well as new collagen fibers to bridge the gap. Some of these fibroblasts have contractile properties that pull the margins of the wound together. As organization proceeds, macrophages digest the original blood clot and collagen fiber deposit continues. The granulation tissue, destined to become scar tissue (a permanent fibrous patch), is highly resistant to infection because it produces bacteria-inhibiting substances. As a rule, wound healing is a self-limited response. Once enough matrix has accumulated in the injured area, the fibroblasts either revert to the resting stage or undergo apoptosis.

3. Regeneration and fibrosis effect permanent repair. During organization, the surface epithelium begins to *regenerate* (see Figure 4.13b), growing under the scab, which soon detaches. As the fibrous tissue beneath matures and contracts, the regenerating epithelium thickens until it finally resembles that of the adjacent skin (Figure 4.13c). The end result is a fully regenerated epithelium, and an underlying area of scar tissue. The scar may be invisible, or visible as a thin white line, depending on the severity of the wound.

The repair process described above follows healing of a wound (cut, scrape, puncture) that breaches an epithelial barrier. In simple *infections* (a pimple or sore throat), healing is solely by regeneration. There is usually no clot formation or scarring. Only severe (destructive) infections lead to scarring.

Regenerative Capacity of Different Tissues

The capacity for regeneration varies widely among the different tissues. Epithelial tissues, bone, areolar connective tissue, dense irregular connective tissue,

Q *(1) What is the makeup of granulation tissue formed at the injured site? (2) Where do the new capillaries that invade the injured area come from? (3) How would this pictorial series look different if repair by regeneration was not possible?*

(a)

(b)

(c)

FIGURE 4.13 **Tissue repair of a nonextensive skin wound: regeneration and fibrosis. (a)** Severed blood vessels bleed. Inflammatory chemicals are released, and local blood vessels dilate and become more permeable, allowing white blood cells, fluid, clotting proteins, and other plasma proteins to invade the injured site. Clotting proteins initiate clotting; surface dries and forms a scab. **(b)** Granulation tissue is formed. Capillaries invade the clot, restoring a vascular supply. Fibroblasts secrete soluble collagen, which constructs collagen fibers that bridge the gap. Macrophages phagocytize dead and dying cell debris. Surface epithelial cells proliferate and migrate over the granulation tissue. **(c)** Approximately one week later, the fibrosed area (scar) has contracted and regeneration of the epithelium is in progress.

and blood-forming tissue regenerate extremely well. Smooth muscle and dense regular connective tissue have a moderate capacity for regeneration, but skeletal muscle and cartilage have a weak regenerative capacity. Cardiac muscle and the nervous tissue in the brain and spinal cord have virtually no *functional* regenerative capacity, and they are routinely replaced by scar tissue. However, recent studies have shown that some unexpected (and highly selective) cellular division occurs in both these tissues after damage,

A *(1) Budding capillaries and loose connective tissue. (2) They bud from uninjured blood vessels in the area. (3) The epidermis would not be continuous. The tissue in the injured region would be totally replaced by scar tissue.*

and efforts are under way to coax them to regenerate better.

In nonregenerating tissues and in exceptionally severe wounds, fibrosis totally replaces the lost tissue. Over a period of months, the fibrous mass shrinks and becomes more and more compact. The resulting scar appears as a pale, often shiny area composed mostly of collagen fibers. Scar tissue is strong, but it lacks the flexibility and elasticity of most normal tissues. Also, it cannot perform the normal functions of the tissue it has replaced.

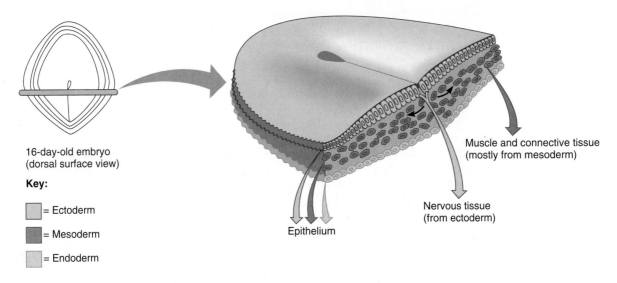

16-day-old embryo
(dorsal surface view)

Key:

◻ = Ectoderm

◼ = Mesoderm

◻ = Endoderm

Muscle and connective tissue
(mostly from mesoderm)

Nervous tissue
(from ectoderm)

Epithelium

FIGURE 4.14 **Embryonic germ layers and the primary tissue types they produce.** The three embryonic layers collectively form the very early embryonic body.

HOMEOSTATIC IMBALANCE

Scar tissue that forms in the wall of the urinary bladder, heart, or other muscular organ may severely hamper the function of that organ. The normal shrinking of the scar reduces the internal volume of an organ and may hinder or even block movement of substances through a hollow organ. Scar tissue hampers muscle's ability to contract and may interfere with its normal excitation by the nervous system. In the heart, these problems may lead to progressive heart failure. In irritated visceral organs, particularly following abdominal surgery, *adhesions* may form as the newly forming scar tissue connects adjacent organs together. Such adhesions can prevent the normal shifting about (churning) of loops of the intestine, dangerously obstructing the flow of foodstuffs through it. Adhesions can also restrict heart movements and immobilize joints. ●

Developmental Aspects of Tissues

One of the first events of embryonic development is the formation of the three **primary germ layers,** which lie one atop the next like a three-layered cellular pancake. From superficial to deep, these layers are the **ectoderm, mesoderm** (mez′o-derm), and **endoderm.** As shown in Figure 4.14, these primary germ layers then specialize to form the four primary tissues from which all body organs are derived.

By the end of the second month of development, the primary tissues have appeared, and all major organs are in place. In general, tissue cells remain mitotic and produce the rapid growth that occurs before birth. The division of nerve cells, however, stops or nearly stops during the fetal period. After birth, the cells of most other tissues continue to divide until adult body size is achieved. Cellular division then slows greatly, although many tissues retain the ability to regenerate. In adults, only epithelia and blood-forming tissues are highly mitotic. Some tissues that regenerate through life, such as the glandular cells of the liver, do so through division of their mature (specialized) cells. Others, like the epidermis of the skin and cells lining the intestine, have abundant *stem cells,* relatively undifferentiated cells that divide as necessary to produce new cells.

Given good nutrition, good circulation, and relatively infrequent wounds and infections, our tissues normally function efficiently through youth and middle age. But with increasing age, epithelia thin and are more easily breached. Tissue repair is less efficient, and bone, muscle, and nervous tissues begin to atrophy. These events are due partly to decreased circulatory efficiency, which reduces delivery of nutrients to the tissues, but in some cases, diet is a contributing factor. As income declines or as chewing becomes more difficult, older people tend to eat soft foods, which may be low in protein and vitamins. As a result, tissue health suffers.

Another problem of aging tissues is the likelihood of DNA mutations in the most actively mitotic cells, which increases the risk of cancer (as indicated in the *Closer Look Box* on p. 146).

■ ■ ■

Cancer—The Intimate Enemy

The word *cancer* elicits dread in everyone. Why does cancer strike some and not others?

Although once perceived as disorganized cell growth, this disease is now known to be a logical, coordinated process in which a precise sequence of tiny alterations changes a normal cell into a killer. Let's take a closer look at what cancer really is.

When cells fail to honor normal controls of cell division and multiply excessively, an abnormal mass of proliferating cells called a *neoplasm* (ne'o-plazm, "new growth") results. Neoplasms are classified as **benign** ("kindly") or **malignant** ("bad"). A benign neoplasm is strictly a local affair. Its cells remain compacted, are often encapsulated, tend to grow slowly, and seldom kill their hosts if they are removed before they compress vital organs. In contrast, cancers are malignant neoplasms, nonencapsulated masses that grow relentlessly and may become killers. Their cells resemble immature cells, and they invade their surroundings rather than pushing them aside, as reflected in the name *cancer*, from the Latin word for "crab." Whereas normal cells become fatally "homesick" and die when they lose contact with the surrounding matrix, malignant cells tend to break away from the parent mass, the primary tumor, and travel via blood or lymph to other body organs, where they survive and form *secondary cancer masses*. This capability for traveling to other parts of the body, called **metastasis** (mĕ-tas'tah-sis), probably has a lot to do with cell surface glycoproteins the cancer cells bear. For example, a carbohydrate called sialyl Lewis X binds to adhesion molecules on epithelial cells and platelets. Metastasis and invasiveness distinguish cancer cells from the cells of benign neoplasms. Cancer cells consume an exceptional amount of the body's nutrients, leading to weight loss and tissue wasting that contribute to death.

Mechanisms of Carcinogenesis

Autopsies on individuals aged 50–70 who died of another cause have revealed that most of them (us) have microscopic (but dormant) in situ neoplasms. So what causes a normal cell to **transform** or change into a cancerous one? Some physical factors (radiation, mechanical trauma), certain viral infections, chronic inflammations, and many chemicals (tobacco tars, saccharine, some natural food chemicals) can act as **carcinogens** (cancer-causers). What these factors have in common: They all cause *mutations*—changes in DNA that alter the expression of certain genes. However, not all carcinogens do damage because most are eliminated by peroxisomal or lysosomal enzymes or by the immune system. Furthermore, one mutation usually isn't enough; it takes several genetic changes to transform a normal cell into a cancerous cell.

A clue to the role of genes in cancer was provided by the discovery of **oncogenes** (Greek *onco* = tumor), or cancer-causing genes, in rapidly spreading cancers. **Proto-oncogenes,** benign forms of oncogenes in normal cells, were discovered later. Proto-oncogenes code for proteins that are essential for cell division, growth, and cellular adhesion, among other things. Many have fragile sites that break when exposed to carcinogens, converting them to oncogenes. Failure to code for certain proteins may lead to loss of an enzyme that controls an important metabolic process. Oncogenes, now known to number over 100, may also "switch on" dormant genes that allow cells to become invasive and metastasize.

Oncogenes have been detected in only 15–20% of human cancers, so investigators were not too surprised by the discovery of **tumor suppressor genes,** or **antioncogenes,** which suppress cancer by inactivating carcinogens, aiding DNA repair, or enhancing the immune system's counterattack. In fact, over half of all cancers involve malfunction or loss of just two of the 15 identified tumor suppressor genes—*p53* and *p16*. This is not surprising when you learn that *p53* prompts most cells to make proteins that put the brakes on cell division in stressed cells by promoting apoptosis or cell cycle arrest. Hence, its impairment invites un-controlled division and cancer. Furthermore, although each type of cancer is genetically distinct, human cancers appear to share a common master set of genes—an activated group of 67 genes—and almost all cancer cells have gained or lost entire chromosomes. Whatever genetic factors are at work, the "seeds" of cancer do appear to be in our own genes. Thus, cancer is an intimate enemy indeed.

The illustration depicts some of the mutations involved in colorectal cancer, one of the best-understood human cancers. As with most cancers, a metastasis develops gradually. One of the first signs is a polyp, a small benign growth consisting of apparently normal mucosa cells. As cell division continues, the growth enlarges, becoming an adenoma. As various tumor-suppressor genes are inactivated and the *K-ras* oncogene is mobilized, the mutations pile up and the adenoma becomes increasingly abnormal. The final consequence is colon carcinoma, a form of cancer that metastasizes quickly.

Cancer Prevalence

Almost half of all Americans develop cancer in their lifetime and a fifth of us will die of it. Cancer can arise from almost any cell type, but the most common cancers originate in the skin, lung, colon, breast, and prostate gland. Although stomach and colon cancer incidence is down, skin and lymphoid cancer rates are up.

Many cancers are preceded by observable lumps or other structural changes in tissue—for instance, *leukoplakia,* white patches in the mouth caused by the chronic irritation of ill-fitting dentures or heavy smoking. Although these lesions sometimes progress to cancer, in many cases they remain stable or even revert to normal if the environmental stimulus is removed.

Diagnosis and Staging

Screening procedures are vital for early detection. Examples include *mammography,* examining breasts or testicles for lumps, and checking fecal samples for blood. Unfortunately, most cancers are diagnosed only after symptoms have already appeared. In this case the diagnostic method is usually a **biopsy:** removing a tissue sample surgically and examining it microscopically for malignant cells. Increasingly, diagnosis is made by chemical or genetic analysis of the sample. Typing cancer cells by what genes are switched on or off tells clinicians which drugs to use. For example, taxol, quite successful with breast and ovarian cancer, works only against tumors with a specific genetic makeup. Medical imaging techniques (MRI, CT) can detect large tumors.

Several techniques (physical and histological examinations, lab tests, and imaging techniques) are used to determine the extent of the disease (size of the neoplasm, degree of metastasis, etc.). Then, the cancer is assigned a **stage** from 1 to 4 according to the probability of cure (stage 1 has the best probability, stage 4 the worst).

Cancer Treatments

Most cancers are removed surgically if possible. To destroy metastasized cells, surgery is commonly followed by radiation therapy (X irradiation and/or treatment with radioisotopes) and chemotherapy (treatment with cytotoxic drugs). Chemotherapy is beset with the problem of resistance. Some cancer cells can eject the drugs in tiny bubbles or flattened vesicles dubbed exosomes, and these cells proliferate, forming new tumors that are invulnerable to chemotherapy. Furthermore, anticancer drugs have unpleasant side effects—nausea, vomiting, hair loss—because they kill all rapidly dividing cells, including normal tissues and cells. X rays also have side effects because, in passing through the body, they destroy healthy tissue in their path as well as cancer cells.

Promising New Therapies

Traditional cancer treatments—"cut, burn, and poison"—are widely recognized as crude and painful. Promising new therapies focus on

- Targeted drugs that interrupt the signaling pathways which fuel the cancer's growth. Examples include imatinib (Gleevec), which incapacitates a mutated enzyme that triggers uncontrolled division of cells in two rare blood and digestive system cancers,

and trastuzumab (Herceptin), used to treat breast cancer patients. These drugs have been strikingly successful in providing a few extra weeks of life, before their protective effects wear off and the disease progresses again.

- Delivering drugs more precisely to the cancer while sparing normal tissue. One approach is to inject the patient with tiny drug-coated metal beads, which are guided to the tumor by a powerful magnet positioned over the body site. Or, a patient might take light-sensitive drugs that are drawn naturally into rapidly dividing cancer cells. Exposure to certain frequencies of laser light sets off a series of reactions that kill the malignant cells.

- Starving cancer cells by cutting off their blood supply. For instance, researchers are testing a drug, called the "icon molecule," that attacks endothelial cells lining the blood vessels in tumors. However, several clinical studies have found that hypoxic cancer cells sometimes go into a protective mode that produces angiogenic proteins to attract new blood vessels and prompts the cancer cells to become more aggressive.

Other experimental treatments seek to fix defective tumor-suppressor genes and oncogenes, destroy cancer cells with viruses, or signal cancer cells to commit suicide by apoptosis. One promising technique extracts and then infuses handpicked immune cells (T cells) that have shown an enhanced ability to attack the cancer cells. Additionally, a cancer vaccine (TRICOM) still in clinical studies, contains genetically engineered viruses carrying genes for a cancer protein called carcinoembryonic antigen (CEA). When these proteins are delivered into the patient's body they stimulate an immune response which then orchestrates an attack on all CEA-bearing cancer cells.

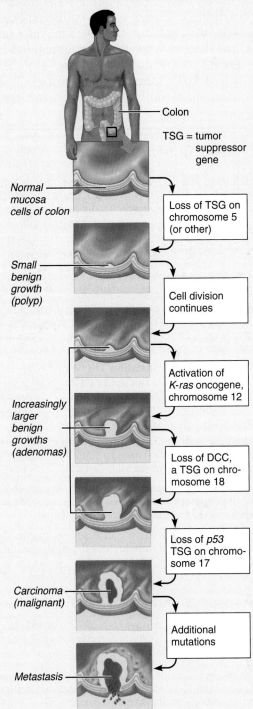

Colon

TSG = tumor suppressor gene

Normal mucosa cells of colon

Small benign growth (polyp)

Increasingly larger benign growths (adenomas)

Carcinoma (malignant)

Metastasis

Loss of TSG on chromosome 5 (or other)

Cell division continues

Activation of *K-ras* oncogene, chromosome 12

Loss of DCC, a TSG on chromosome 18

Loss of *p53* TSG on chromosome 17

Additional mutations

Development of colon cancer.

At present, about half of all cancer cases are cured. Although average survival rates have not increased, the quality of life of cancer patients has improved in the last decade. We can offer better treatments for cancer-associated pain, and antinausea drugs and other helpful medicines can soothe the side effects of chemotherapy. ■

As we have seen, body cells combine to form four discrete tissue types: epithelial, connective, muscle, and nervous tissues. The cells making up each of these tissues share certain features but are by no means identical. They "belong" together because they have basic functional similarities. The connective tissues assume many guises, but perhaps the most versatile cells are those of epithelium: They protect our outer and inner surfaces, permit us to obtain oxygen, absorb vital nutrients into the blood, and allow our kidneys to excrete wastes. The important concept to carry away with you is that tissues, despite their unique abilities, cooperate to keep the body safe, healthy, and whole.

Related Clinical Terms

Adenoma (ad″ĕ-no′mah; *aden* = gland, *oma* = tumor) Any neoplasm of glandular epithelium, benign or malignant. The malignant type is more specifically called *adenocarcinoma*.

Autopsy (aw′top-se) Examination of the body, its organs, and its tissues after death to determine the actual cause of death; also called postmortem examination and necropsy.

Carcinoma (kar″sĭ-no′mah; *karkinos* = crab, cancer) Cancer arising in an epithelium; accounts for 90% of human cancers.

Healing by first intention The simplest type of healing; occurs when the edges of the wound are brought together by sutures, staples, or other means used to close surgical incisions. Only small amounts of granulation tissue need be formed.

Healing by second intention The wound edges remain separated, and the gap is bridged by relatively large amounts of granulation tissue; the manner in which unattended wounds heal. Healing is slower than in wounds in which the edges are brought together, and larger scars result.

Keloid (ke′loid) Abnormal proliferation of connective tissue during healing of skin wounds; results in large, unsightly mass of scar tissue at the skin surface.

Lesion (le′zhun; "wound") Any injury, wound, or infection that affects tissue over an area of a definite size (as opposed to being widely spread throughout the body).

Marfan's syndrome Genetic disease resulting in abnormalities of connective tissues due to a defect in fibrillin, a protein that is associated with elastin in elastic fibers. Clinical signs include loose-jointedness, long limbs and spiderlike fingers and toes, visual problems, and weakened blood vessels (especially the aorta) due to poor connective tissue reinforcement.

Pathology (pah-thol′o-je) Scientific study of changes in organs and tissues produced by disease.

Pus A collection of tissue fluid, bacteria, dead and dying tissue cells, white blood cells, and macrophages in an inflamed area.

Sarcoma (sar-ko′mah; *sarkos* = flesh; *oma* = tumor) Cancer arising in the mesenchyme-derived tissues, that is, in connective tissues and muscle.

Scurvy A nutritional deficiency caused by lack of adequate vitamin C needed to synthesize collagen; signs and symptoms include blood vessel disruption, delay in wound healing, weakness of scar tissue, and loosening of teeth.

VAC (vacuum-assisted closure) Innovative healing process for open-skin wounds and skin ulcers. Often induces healing when all other methods fail. Involves covering the wound with a special sponge, and then applying suction through the sponge. In response to the subsequent skin stretching, fibroblasts in the wound form more collagen tissue and new blood vessels proliferate, bringing more blood into the injured area, which also promotes healing.

Chapter Summary

Media study tools that could provide you additional help in reviewing specific key topics of Chapter 4 are referenced below.
IP = *InterActive Physiology*

Tissues are collections of structurally similar cells with related functions. The four primary tissues are epithelial, connective, muscle, and nervous tissues.

Preparing Human Tissue for Microscopy (p. 118)

1. Preparation of tissues for microscopic examination involves the use of dyes to stain the tissue, and knives to cut thin sections of the tissue. Artifacts result from modifications introduced by the tissue preparation process.

Epithelial Tissue (pp. 118–126)

1. Epithelial tissue is the covering, lining, and glandular tissue of the body. Its functions include protection, absorption, excretion, filtration, secretion, and sensory reception.

Special Characteristics of Epithelium (pp. 118–119)

2. Epithelial tissues exhibit specialized contacts, polarity, avascularity, support from connective tissue, and high regenerative capacity.

Classification of Epithelia (pp. 119–124)

3. Epithelium is classified by arrangement as simple (one layer) or stratified (more than one) and by cell shape as squamous, cuboidal, or columnar. The terms denoting cell shape and arrangement are combined to describe the epithelium fully.

4. Simple squamous epithelium is a single layer of squamous cells. Highly adapted for filtration and exchange of substances, it forms walls of air sacs of the lungs and lines blood vessels. It contributes to serosae as mesothelium and lines all hollow circulatory system organs as endothelium.

5. Simple cuboidal epithelium, commonly active in secretion and absorption, is found in glands and in kidney tubules.

6. Simple columnar epithelium, specialized for secretion and absorption, consists of a single layer of tall columnar cells that exhibit microvilli and often goblet cells. It lines most of the digestive tract.

7. Pseudostratified columnar epithelium is a simple columnar epithelium that appears stratified. Its ciliated variety, rich in goblet cells, lines most of the upper respiratory passages.

8. Stratified squamous epithelium is multilayered; cells at the free edge are squamous. It is adapted to resist abrasion.

It lines the esophagus and vagina; its keratinized variety forms the skin epidermis.

9. Stratified cuboidal epithelia are rare in the body, and are found chiefly in ducts of large glands. Stratified columnar epithelium has a very limited distribution, found mainly in the male urethra and at transition areas between other epithelia types.

10. Transitional epithelium is a modified stratified squamous epithelium, adapted for responding to stretch. It lines hollow urinary system organs.

Glandular Epithelia   (pp. 124–126)

11. A gland is one or more cells specialized to secrete a product.

12. On the basis of site of product release, glands are classified as exocrine or endocrine. Glands are classified structurally as multicellular or unicellular.

13. Unicellular glands, also called goblet cells, are mucus-secreting single-celled glands.

14. Multicellular exocrine glands are classified according to duct structure as simple or compound, and according to the structure of their secretory parts as tubular, alveolar, or tubuloalveolar.

15. Multicellular exocrine glands of humans are classified functionally as merocrine or holocrine.

Connective Tissue   (pp. 126–139)

1. Connective tissue is the most abundant and widely distributed tissue of the body. Its functions include support, protection, binding, insulation, and transportation (blood).

Common Characteristics of Connective Tissue   (p. 127)

2. Connective tissues originate from embryonic mesenchyme and exhibit matrix. Depending on type, a connective tissue may be well vascularized (most), poorly vascularized (dense connective tissue), or avascular (cartilage).

Structural Elements of Connective Tissue   (pp. 127–130)

3. The structural elements of all connective tissues are extracellular matrix and cells.

4. Extracellular matrix consists of ground substance and fibers (collagen, elastic, and reticular). It may be fluid, gel-like, or firm.

5. Each connective tissue type has a primary cell type that can exist as a mitotic, matrix-secreting cell (blast) or as a mature cell (cyte) responsible for maintaining the matrix. The chief cell type of connective tissue proper is the fibroblast; that of cartilage is the chondroblast; that of bone is the osteoblast; and that of blood-forming tissue is the hematopoietic stem cell.

Types of Connective Tissue   (pp. 131–139)

6. Embryonic connective tissue is called mesenchyme.

7. Connective tissue proper consists of loose and dense varieties. The loose connective tissues are
- Areolar: semifluid ground substance; all three fiber types loosely interwoven; a variety of cells; forms the lamina propria and soft packing around body organs; the prototype.
- Adipose: consists largely of adipocytes; scant matrix; insulates and protects body organs; provides reserve energy fuel. Brown fat, present only in infants, is more important for generating body heat.
- Reticular: finely woven reticular fibers in soft ground substance; the stroma of lymphoid organs and bone marrow.

8. Dense connective tissue proper includes
- Dense regular: dense parallel bundles of collagen fibers; few cells, little ground substance; high tensile strength; forms tendons, ligaments, aponeuroses; in cases where this tissue also contains numerous elastic fibers it is called elastic connective tissue.
- Dense irregular: like regular variety, but fibers are arranged in different planes; resists tension exerted from many different directions; forms the dermis of the skin and organ capsules.

9. Cartilage exists as
- Hyaline: firm ground substance containing collagen fibers; resists compression well; found in fetal skeleton, at articulating surfaces of bones, and trachea; most abundant type.
- Elastic cartilage: elastic fibers predominate; provides flexible support of the external ear and epiglottis.
- Fibrocartilage: coarse parallel collagen fibers; provides support with compressibility; forms intervertebral discs and knee cartilages.

10. Bone (osseous tissue) consists of a hard, collagen-containing matrix embedded with calcium salts; forms the bony skeleton.

11. Blood consists of blood cells in a fluid matrix (plasma).

Nervous Tissue   (p. 139)

1. Nervous tissue forms organs of the nervous system. It is composed of neurons and supporting cells.

2. Neurons are branching cells that receive and transmit electrical impulses; they are involved in body regulation.

IP Nervous System I; Topic: Anatomy Review, pp. 1, 3.

Muscle Tissue   (pp. 139–141)

1. Muscle tissue consists of elongated cells specialized to contract and cause movement.

2. Based on structure and function, the muscle tissues are
- Skeletal muscle: attached to and moves the bony skeleton; cells are cylindrical and striated.
- Cardiac muscle: forms the walls of the heart; pumps blood; cells are branched and striated.
- Smooth muscle: in the walls of hollow organs; propels substances through the organs; cells are spindle shaped and lack striations.

Covering and Lining Membranes   (pp. 141–143)

1. Membranes are simple organs, consisting of an epithelium bound to an underlying connective tissue layer. They include mucosae, serosae, and the cutaneous membrane.

Tissue Repair   (pp. 143–145)

1. Inflammation is the body's response to injury. Tissue repair begins during the inflammatory process. It may lead to regeneration, fibrosis, or both.

2. Tissue repair begins with organization, during which the blood clot is replaced by granulation tissue. If the wound is small and the damaged tissue is actively mitotic, the tissue will regenerate and cover the fibrous tissue. When a wound is extensive or the damaged tissue amitotic, it is repaired only by fibrous connective (scar) tissue.

Developmental Aspects of Tissues   (p. 145)

1. Epithelium arises from all three primary germ layers (ectoderm, mesoderm, endoderm); muscle and connective tissue from mesoderm; and nervous tissue from ectoderm.

2. The decrease in mass and viability seen in most tissues during old age often reflects circulatory deficits or poor nutrition.

Review Questions

Multiple Choice/Matching

(Some questions have more than one correct answer. Select the best answer or answers from the choices given.)

1. Use the key to classify each of the following described tissue types into one of the four major tissue categories.

Key: (a) connective tissue (c) muscle
     (b) epithelium (d) nervous tissue

____ (1) Tissue type composed largely of nonliving extracellular matrix; important in protection and support
____ (2) The tissue immediately responsible for body movement
____ (3) The tissue that enables us to be aware of the external environment and to react to it
____ (4) The tissue that lines body cavities and covers surfaces

2. An epithelium that has several layers, with an apical layer of flattened cells, is called (choose all that apply): (a) ciliated, (b) columnar, (c) stratified, (d) simple, (e) squamous.

3. Match the epithelial types named in column B with the appropriate description(s) in column A.

Column A	Column B
____ (1) Lines most of the digestive tract	(a) pseudostratified ciliated columnar
____ (2) Lines the esophagus	(b) simple columnar
____ (3) Lines much of the respiratory tract	(c) simple cuboidal
____ (4) Forms the walls of the air sacs of the lungs	(d) simple squamous
____ (5) Found in urinary tract organs	(e) stratified columnar
____ (6) Endothelium and mesothelium	(f) stratified squamous
	(g) transitional

4. The gland type that secretes products such as milk, saliva, bile, or sweat through a duct is (a) an endocrine gland, (b) an exocrine gland.

5. The membrane which lines body cavities that open to the exterior is a(n) (a) endothelium, (b) cutaneous membrane, (c) mucous membrane, (d) serous membrane.

6. Scar tissue is a variety of (a) epithelium, (b) connective tissue, (c) muscle tissue, (d) nerve tissue, (e) all of these.

Short Answer Essay Questions

7. Define tissue.

8. Name four important functions of epithelial tissue and provide at least one example of a tissue that exemplifies each function.

9. Describe the criteria used to classify covering and lining epithelia.

10. Explain the functional classification of multicellular exocrine glands and supply an example for each class.

11. Name four important functions of connective tissue and provide examples from the body that illustrate each function.

12. Name the primary cell type in connective tissue proper; in cartilage; in bone.

13. Name the two major components of matrix and, if applicable, subclasses of each component.

14. Matrix is extracellular. How does the matrix get to its characteristic position?

15. Name the specific connective tissue type found in the following body locations: (a) forming the soft packing around organs, (b) supporting the ear pinna, (c) forming "stretchy" ligaments, (d) first connective tissue in the embryo, (e) forming the intervertebral discs, (f) covering the ends of bones at joint surfaces, (g) main component of subcutaneous tissue.

16. What is the function of macrophages?

17. Differentiate clearly between the roles of neurons and the supporting cells of nervous tissue.

18. Compare and contrast skeletal, cardiac, and smooth muscle tissue relative to structure, body location, and specific function.

19. Describe the process of tissue repair, making sure you indicate factors that influence this process.

20. Name the three embryonic germ layers, and indicate which primary tissue classes derive from each layer.

21. Cell division typically yields two daughter cells, each with one nucleus. How is the multinucleate condition of a skeletal muscle cell explained?

Critical Thinking and Clinical Application Questions

1. John has sustained a severe injury during football practice and is told that he has a torn knee cartilage. Can he expect a quick, uneventful recovery? Explain your response.

2. The epidermis (epithelium of the cutaneous membrane or skin) is a keratinized stratified squamous epithelium. Explain why that epithelium is much better suited for protecting the body's external surface than a mucosa consisting of a simple columnar epithelium would be.

3. Your friend is trying to convince you that if the ligaments binding the bones together at your freely movable joints (such as your knee, shoulder, and hip joints) contained more elastic fibers, you would be much more flexible. Although there is *some* truth to this statement, such a condition would present serious problems. Why?

4. In adults, over 90% of all cancers are either adenomas (adenocarcinomas) or carcinomas. (See Related Clinical Terms for this chapter.) In fact, cancers of the skin, lung, colon, breast, and prostate are all in these categories. Which one of the four basic tissue types gives rise to most cancers? Why do you think this is so?

5. Cindy, an overweight high school student, is overheard telling her friend that she's going to research how she can transform some of her white fat to brown fat. What is her rationale here (assuming it is possible)?

6. Mrs. Delancy went to the local meat market and bought a beef tenderloin (cut from the loin, the region along the steer's vertebral column) and some tripe (cow's stomach). What type of muscle was she preparing to eat in each case?

LOOKING FOR MORE STUDY HELP?
A wide variety of quiz questions, tutorials, and learning exercises are available online at the Anatomy & Physiology Place (www.anatomyandphysiology.com) and, if your instructor has provided you with a MyA&P Course ID number, in MyA&P (www.myaandp.com).

The Integumentary System

The Skin (pp. 152–158)

1. Name the tissue types composing the epidermis and dermis. List the major layers of each and describe the functions of each layer.

2. Describe the factors that normally contribute to skin color. Briefly describe how changes in skin color may be used as clinical signs of certain disease states.

Appendages of the Skin (pp. 158–163)

3. Compare the structure and locations of sweat and oil glands. Also compare the composition and functions of their secretions.

4. Compare and contrast eccrine and apocrine glands.

5. List the parts of a hair follicle and explain the function of each part. Also describe the functional relationship of arrector pili muscles to the hair follicle.

6. Name the regions of a hair and explain the basis of hair color. Describe the distribution, growth, replacement, and changing nature of hair during the life span.

7. Describe the structure of nails.

Functions of the Integumentary System (pp. 163–165)

8. Describe how the skin accomplishes at least five different functions.

Homeostatic Imbalances of Skin (pp. 165–167, 170)

9. Summarize the characteristics of the three major types of skin cancers.

10. Explain why serious burns are life threatening. Describe how to determine the extent of a burn and differentiate first-, second-, and third-degree burns.

Developmental Aspects of the Integumentary System (pp. 170–171)

11. Describe and attempt to explain the causes of changes that occur in the skin from birth to old age.

Would you be enticed by an advertisement for a coat that is waterproof, stretchable, washable, and permanent-press, that automatically repairs small cuts, rips, and burns, and that is guaranteed to last a lifetime with reasonable care? Sounds too good to be true, but you already have such a coat—your skin. The skin and its derivatives (sweat and oil glands, hairs, and nails) make up a complex set of organs that serves several functions, mostly protective. Together, these organs form the **integumentary system** (in-teg"u-men'tar-e).

The Skin

The skin ordinarily receives little respect from its inhabitants, but architecturally it is a marvel. It covers the entire body, has a surface area of 1.2 to 2.2 square meters, weighs 4 to 5 kilograms (4–5 kg = 9–11 lb), and accounts for about 7% of total body weight in the average adult. Also called the integument, which simply means "covering," the skin's functions go well beyond serving as a large, opaque bag for the body contents. It is pliable yet tough, allowing it to take constant punishment from external agents. Without our skin, we would quickly fall prey to bacteria and perish from water and heat loss.

The skin, which varies in thickness from 1.5 to 4.0 millimeters (mm) or more in different parts of the body, is composed of two distinct regions, the *epidermis* (ep"ĭ-der'mis) and the *dermis* (Figure 5.1). The epidermis (*epi* = upon), composed of epithelial cells, is the outermost protective shield of the body. The underlying dermis, making up the bulk of the skin, is a tough, leathery layer composed of fibrous connective tissue. Only the dermis is vascularized. Nutrients reach the epidermis by diffusing through the tissue fluid from blood vessels in the dermis.

The subcutaneous tissue just deep to the skin is known as the **hypodermis** (Figure 5.1). Strictly speaking, the hypodermis is not really part of the skin, but it shares some of the skin's protective functions. The hypodermis, also called **superficial fascia** because it is superficial to the tough connective tissue wrapping (fascia) of the skeletal muscles, consists mostly of adipose tissue. Besides storing fat, the hypodermis anchors the skin to the underlying structures (mostly to muscles), but loosely enough that the skin can slide relatively freely over those structures. Sliding skin protects us by ensuring that many blows just glance off our bodies. Because of its fatty composition, the hypodermis also acts as a shock absorber and an insulator that prevents heat loss from the body. The hypodermis thickens markedly when one gains weight. In females, this "extra" subcutaneous fat accumulates first in the thighs and breasts, but in males it first collects in the anterior abdomen (as a "beer belly").

Epidermis

Structurally, the **epidermis** is a keratinized stratified squamous epithelium consisting of four distinct cell types and four or five distinct layers.

Cells of the Epidermis

The cells populating the epidermis include *keratinocytes, melanocytes, Merkel cells,* and *Langerhans' cells* (Figure 5.2). Most epidermal cells are keratinocytes, so we will consider them first. The chief role of **keratinocytes** (kĕ-rat'ĭ-no-sītz"; "keratin cells") is to produce **keratin,** the fibrous protein that helps give the epidermis its protective properties (Greek *kera* = horn). Tightly connected to one another by desmosomes, the keratinocytes arise in the deepest part of the epidermis from a layer of cells (stratum basale) that undergo almost continuous mitosis. As these cells are pushed upward by the production of new cells beneath them, they make the keratin that eventually dominates their cell contents. By the time the keratinocytes reach the free surface of the skin, they are dead, scalelike structures that are little more than keratin-filled plasma membranes. Millions of these dead cells rub off every day, giving us a totally new epidermis every 25 to 45 days. In body areas regularly subjected to friction, such as the hands and feet, both cell production and keratin formation are accelerated. Persistent friction (from a poorly fitting shoe, for example) causes a thickening of the epidermis called a *callus.*

Melanocytes (mel'ah-no-sītz), the spider-shaped epithelial cells that synthesize the pigment **melanin** (mel'ah-nin; *melan* = black), are found in the deepest layer of the epidermis (Figure 5.2). As melanin is made, it is accumulated in membrane-bound granules called *melanosomes* that are moved along actin filaments by motor proteins to the ends of the melanocyte's processes (the "spider arms") from where they are taken up by nearby keratinocytes. The melanin granules accumulate on the superficial, or "sunny," side of the keratinocyte nucleus, forming a pigment shield that protects the nucleus from the damaging effects of ultraviolet (UV) radiation in sunlight.

The star-shaped **Langerhans' cells** (lahng'er-hanz) arise from bone marrow and migrate to the epidermis. Also called **epidermal dendritic cells,** they are phagocytes that ingest foreign substances and help to activate our immune system, as described later in this chapter. Their slender processes extend among the surrounding keratinocytes, forming a more or less continuous network (Figure 5.2).

Occasional **Merkel cells** are present at the epidermal-dermal junction. Shaped like a spiky hemisphere (Figure 5.2), each Merkel cell is intimately

Q *What cell component of the hypodermis makes it a good shock absorber and insulator?*

FIGURE 5.1 **Skin structure.** Three-dimensional view of the skin and underlying subcutaneous tissue. The epidermal and dermal layers have been pulled apart at the right corner to reveal the dermal papillae.

associated with a disclike sensory nerve ending. The combination, called a *Merkel disc*, functions as a sensory receptor for touch.

Layers of the Epidermis

Variation in epidermal thickness determines if skin is *thick* or *thin*. In **thick skin,** which covers the palms, fingertips, and soles of the feet, the epidermis consists of five layers, or *strata* (stra'tah; "bed sheets"). From deep to superficial, these layers are

stratum basale, stratum spinosum, stratum granulosum, stratum lucidum, and stratum corneum. In thin skin, which covers the rest of the body, the stratum lucidum appears to be absent and the other strata are thinner (Figure 5.2).

Stratum Basale (Basal Layer)   The **stratum basale** (stra'tum ba-sǎ'le), the deepest epidermal layer, is attached to the underlying dermis along a wavy borderline that reminds one of corrugated cardboard. For the most part, it consists of a single row of cells—a continually renewing cell population—representing the youngest keratinocytes. The many mitotic nuclei

A *Adipose cells.*

Q *(1) Why are the desmosomes connecting the keratinocytes so important? (2) Given that epithelia are avascular, which epidermal layer would be expected to have the best-nourished cells?*

Keratinocytes
Desmosomes   Langerhans' cell

Stratum corneum — Cells are dead; represented only by flat membranous sacs filled with keratin. Glycolipids in extracellular space.

Stratum granulosum — Cells are flattened; organelles deteriorating; cytoplasm full of lamellated granules (release lipids) and keratohyaline granules.

Cells contain thick bundles of intermediate filaments made of pre-keratin.

Stratum spinosum

Cells are actively mitotic stem cells; some newly formed cells become part of the more superficial layers.

Stratum basale — Merkel cell — Dermis

Dermis — Melanocytes Melanin granules Sensory nerve ending

(a) (b)

FIGURE 5.2 The main structural features in skin epidermis. (a) Photomicrograph of the four major epidermal layers. **(b)** Diagram showing the layers and relative distribution of the different cell types. The keratinocytes (tan) form the bulk of the epidermis. Less numerous are the melanocytes (gray), which produce the pigment melanin; Langerhans' cells (blue), which function as immune cells; and Merkel cells (purple). A sensory nerve ending (yellow), extending to the Merkel cell from the dermis (pink), is shown associated with the Merkel cell forming a Merkel disc (touch receptor). Notice that the keratinocytes, but not the other cell types, are joined by numerous desmosomes. The stratum lucidum, present in thick skin, is not illustrated here. Only a portion of the stratum corneum is illustrated in each case.

seen in this layer reflect the rapid division of these cells and account for its alternate name, **stratum germinativum** (jer′mĭ-nă″tiv-um; "germinating layer").

Some 10–25% of the cells in the stratum basale are melanocytes, and their branching processes extend among the surrounding cells, reaching well into the more superficial stratum spinosum layer. Occasional Merkel cells are also seen in this stratum.

Stratum Spinosum (Prickly Layer) The **stratum spinosum** (spi′no-sum; "prickly") is several cell layers thick. These cells contain a weblike system of intermediate filaments, mainly tension-resisting bundles of pre-keratin filaments, which span their cytosol to attach to desmosomes. The keratinocytes

A *(1) The desmosomes connecting the keratinocytes are important to maintain continuity of the epidermis which is subjected to frequent friction. (2) The stratum basale or basal layer of the epidermis.*

in this layer appear irregular (spiny) in shape, causing them to be called *prickle cells*. The spines do not exist in the living cells; they are artifacts that arise during tissue preparation when these cells shrink but their numerous desmosomes hold tight. Scattered among the keratinocytes are melanin granules and Langerhans' cells, which are most abundant in this epidermal layer.

Stratum Granulosum (Granular Layer)   The thin **stratum granulosum** (gran"u-lo'sum) consists of three to five cell layers in which keratinocyte appearance changes drastically. These cells flatten, their nuclei and organelles begin to disintegrate, and they accumulate two types of granules: The *keratohyaline granules* (ker"ah-to-hi'ah-lin) help to form keratin in the upper layers, as we will see. The *lamellated granules* (lam'ĭ-la-ted; "plated") contain a waterproofing glycolipid that is spewed into the extracellular space and is a major factor in slowing water loss across the epidermis. The plasma membranes of these cells thicken as cytosol proteins bind to the inner membrane face and lipids released by the lamellated granules coat their external surfaces. This makes them more resistant to destruction, so you might say that the keratinocytes are "toughening up" to make the outer strata the strongest skin region.

Like all epithelia, the epidermis relies on capillaries in the underlying connective tissue (the dermis in this case) for its nutrients. Above the stratum granulosum, the epidermal cells are too far from the dermal capillaries, so they die. This is a completely normal sequence of events.

Stratum Lucidum (Clear Layer)   Through the light microscope, the **stratum lucidum** (loo'sid-um; "light") appears as a thin translucent band just above the stratum granulosum. It consists of a few rows of clear, flat, dead keratinocytes with indistinct boundaries. Here, or in the stratum corneum above, the gummy substance of the keratohyaline granules clings to the keratin filaments in the cells, causing them to aggregate in parallel arrays. As mentioned before, the stratum lucidum is visible only in thick skin.

Stratum Corneum (Horny Layer)   The outermost **stratum corneum** (kor'ne-um) is a broad zone 20 to 30 cell layers thick that accounts for up to three-quarters of the epidermal thickness. Keratin and the thickened plasma membranes of cells in this stratum protect the skin against abrasion and penetration, and the glycolipid between its cells waterproofs this layer. Hence, the stratum corneum provides a durable "overcoat" for the body, protecting deeper cells from the hostile external environment (air) and from water loss, and rendering the body relatively insensitive to biological, chemical, and physical assaults. It is amazing that a layer of dead cells can still play so many roles.

The shingle-like cell remnants of the stratum corneum are referred to as *cornified*, or *horny*, *cells* (*cornu* = horn). They are familiar to everyone as the dandruff shed from the scalp and the flakes that slough off dry skin. [The average person sheds 18 kg (40 lb) of these skin flakes in a lifetime, providing a lot of fodder for the dust mites that inhabit our homes and bed linens.] The common saying "Beauty is only skin deep" is especially interesting in light of the fact that nearly everything we see when we look at someone is dead!

Dermis

The **dermis** (*derm* = skin), the second major skin region, is strong, flexible connective tissue. Its cells are typical of those found in any connective tissue proper: fibroblasts, macrophages, and occasional mast cells and white blood cells, and its semifluid matrix is heavily embedded with fibers. The dermis binds the entire body together like a body stocking. It is your "hide" and corresponds exactly to animal hides used to make leather products.

The dermis is richly supplied with nerve fibers, blood vessels, and lymphatic vessels. The major portions of hair follicles, as well as oil and sweat glands, are derived from epidermal tissue but reside in the dermis.

The dermis has two layers: the papillary and reticular. The thin superficial **papillary layer** (pap'il-er-e) is areolar connective tissue in which the collagen and elastin fibers form a loosely woven mat that is heavily invested with blood vessels. Its superior surface is thrown into peglike projections called **dermal papillae** (pah-pil'e; *papill* = nipple) that indent the overlying epidermis (see Figure 5.1). Many dermal papillae contain capillary loops (of the *subcapillary plexus*); others house free nerve endings (pain receptors) and touch receptors called *Meissner's corpuscles* (mīs'nerz kor'pus-lz). On the palms of the hands and soles of the feet, these papillae lie atop larger mounds called *dermal ridges*, which in turn cause the overlying epidermis to form *epidermal ridges* that increase friction and enhance the gripping ability of the fingers and feet. Epidermal ridge patterns are genetically determined and unique to each of us. Because sweat pores open along their crests, our fingertips leave identifying films of sweat called *fingerprints* on almost anything they touch.

The deeper **reticular layer,** accounting for about 80% of the thickness of the dermis, is dense irregular connective tissue. The network of blood vessels that nourishes this layer, the *cutaneous plexus*, lies between this layer and the hypodermis. Its extracellular

A CLOSER LOOK

Wrinkle Wrinkle Go Away—Or I'll Shoot You (with Botox)

When it comes to staving off wrinkles, it helps to have good genes, to not smoke, to use a good sunscreen, and to think pleasant thoughts. Good genes speak for themselves—it's partly the luck of the draw whether you look your age or not. Smoking ages the skin by increasing production of an enzyme referred to as MMP, which destroys collagen. Collagen supports the skin and provides it with resilience and elasticity. So with less of it, wrinkles appear. UV radiation damage to the skin from too much unprotected exposure to the sun is covered on p. 157. Treatment with an Alexandrite laser, more commonly used to lighten skin pigmentation, heats up the dermis, which causes collagens to reorganize, thus reducing wrinkling to some extent. For those wrinkled by years of smoking and sun damage, a surgical face-lift that removes the excess and sagging skin followed by laser resurfacing or microdermabrasion to lift out the remaining small wrinkles seems to be the only way the wrinkles can be banished.

However, for those who sport frown lines, furrowed brows, or crow's feet due not to skin damage but to frequent and repetitive facial expressions, cosmetic injections of Botox may be the answer to regaining younger-looking skin. Botulinum toxin type A, more familiarly called Botox Cosmetic, is a toxin produced by the bacterium *Clostridium botulinum*, which causes botulism, a dreaded form of food poisoning. Used in a medical setting in injectable doses (considerably less than the amount that would induce botulism), the purified toxin helps

Woman receiving Botox injection.

regulate acetylcholine (ACh) release by nerve cells. (ACh plays a key role in relaying messages from nerves to muscles.) By selectively inhibiting the underlying muscles' ability to contract, existing lines or furrows are smoothed out and nearly invisible in a week.

Botox was first approved in 1989 to treat two eye muscle disorders—blepharospasm (uncontrollable blinking) and strabismus (misaligned eyes). In 2000, Botox was approved to treat muscle dystonia, painful neuromuscular disorders leading to sustained and disabling muscle spasms that cause abnormal body twisting or postures. The discovery that Botox could be used cosmetically was serendipitous—physicians using the toxin to counter abnormal eye contractions noticed that

the vertical frown lines between the eyes (which make people look tired, angry, or displeased) had softened.

The recent rise in popularity of Botox "shots" has led to changes in the way it is marketed. Some physicians buy the toxin in bulk and arrange "Botox parties" or "Botox happy hours," get-togethers for 10 to 15 people which make the treatment both more relaxed and more affordable. One by one, as their names are called, each "guest" slips away for about 15 minutes to a private examining room to be injected with Botox Cosmetic. Anesthesia is rarely needed, but sedatives and numbing agents are usually available. The U.S. Food and Drug Administration is concerned that gathering as many patients as possible may trivialize a medical treatment and has the potential for being abused as unqualified people begin to dispense the toxin in salons, gyms, and other retail establishments.

Although there is no chance of contracting botulism from the injections, the process has some risks. If too much toxin is injected or injected into the wrong area, a person can end up with droopy eyelid muscles for weeks, or temporary muscle weakness. The effects of Botox Cosmetic last only three to six months; still, battling the signs of age in a noninvasive way is appealing to many. Also, the fact that there is little or no recovery time allows one to be treated during a lunch hour. The attraction of Botox to physicians is both professional (a new tool to fight wrinkles) and monetary (truly dedicated patients are back for injections every three to six months). Vanity pays! ∎

---

matrix contains thick bundles of interlacing collagen fibers that run in various planes; however, most run parallel to the skin surface. Separations, or less dense regions, between these bundles form *cleavage,* or *tension, lines,* in the skin. These externally invisible lines tend to run longitudinally in the skin of the head and limbs and in circular patterns around the neck and trunk. Cleavage lines are important to both surgeons and their patients. When an incision is made *parallel* to these lines, the skin gapes less and

heals more readily than when the incision is made *across* cleavage lines.

The collagen fibers of the dermis give skin strength and resiliency that prevent most jabs and scrapes from penetrating the dermis. In addition, collagen binds water, helping to keep skin hydrated. Elastin fibers provide the stretch-recoil properties of skin.

In addition to the epidermal ridges and cleavage lines, a third type of skin marking, *flexure lines,* reflects dermal modifications. Flexure lines are dermal folds that occur at or near joints, where the dermis is tightly secured to deeper structures (notice the deep creases on your palms). Since the skin cannot slide easily to accommodate joint movement in such regions, the dermis folds and deep skin creases form. Flexure lines are also visible on the wrists, fingers, soles, and toes.

HOMEOSTATIC IMBALANCE

Extreme stretching of the skin, such as occurs during pregnancy, can tear the dermis. Dermal tearing is indicated by silvery white scars called *striae* (stri′e; "streaks"), commonly called "stretch marks." Short-term but acute trauma (as from a burn or wielding a hoe) can cause a *blister,* the separation of the epidermal and dermal layers by a fluid-filled pocket. ●

Skin Color

Three pigments contribute to skin color: melanin, carotene, and hemoglobin. Of these, only melanin is made in the skin. **Melanin,** a polymer made of tyrosine amino acids, ranges in color from yellow to reddish-brown to black. Its synthesis depends on an enzyme in melanocytes called tyrosinase (ti-ro′sĭ-nās) and, as noted earlier, it passes from melanocytes to the basal keratinocytes.

Human skin comes in different colors. However, distribution of those colors is not random—populations of darker-skinned people tend to be found nearer the equator (where greater protection from the sun is needed), whereas those with the lightest skin are found closer to the poles. Since all humans have the same relative number of melanocytes, individual and racial differences in skin coloring reflect the relative kind and amount of melanin made and retained. Melanocytes of black- and brown-skinned people produce many more and darker melanosomes than those of fair-skinned individuals, and their keratinocytes retain it longer. *Freckles* and *pigmented moles* are local accumulations of melanin.

Melanocytes are stimulated to greater activity when we expose our skin to sunlight. Prolonged sun exposure causes a substantial melanin buildup, which helps protect the DNA of viable skin cells from UV radiation by absorbing the light and dissipating the energy as heat. Indeed, the initial signal for speeding up melanin synthesis seems to be a faster rate of repair of photodamaged DNA. In all but the darkest people, this response causes visible darkening of the skin (a tan).

HOMEOSTATIC IMBALANCE

Despite melanin's protective effects, excessive sun exposure eventually damages the skin. It causes clumping of elastin fibers, which results in leathery skin; temporarily depresses the immune system; and can alter the DNA of skin cells and in this way lead to skin cancer. The fact that dark-skinned people get skin cancer less often than fair-skinned people and get it in areas with less pigment—the soles of the feet and nail beds—attests to melanin's effectiveness as a natural sunscreen.

Ultraviolet radiation has other consequences as well. It destroys the body's folate stores necessary for DNA synthesis, which can have serious consequences, particularly in pregnant women because the deficit may impair the development of the embryo's nervous system. Many chemicals induce photosensitivity; that is, they heighten the skin's sensitivity to UV radiation, setting sun worshippers up for an unsightly skin rash. Such substances include some antibiotic and antihistamine drugs, and many chemicals in perfumes and detergents. Small, itchy, blisterlike lesions erupt all over the body; then the peeling begins, in sheets! ●

Carotene (kar′o-tēn) is a yellow to orange pigment found in certain plant products such as carrots. It tends to accumulate in the stratum corneum and in fatty tissue of the hypodermis. Its color is most obvious in the palms and soles, where the stratum corneum is thickest (for example the skin of the heels), and most intense when large amounts of carotene-rich foods are eaten. However, the yellowish tinge of the skin of some Asian peoples is due to variations in melanin, as well as to carotene.

The pinkish hue of fair skin reflects the crimson color of oxygenated **hemoglobin** (he′mo-glo″bin) in the red blood cells circulating through the dermal capillaries. Because Caucasian skin contains only small amounts of melanin, the epidermis is nearly transparent and allows hemoglobin's color to show through.

HOMEOSTATIC IMBALANCE

When hemoglobin is poorly oxygenated, both the blood and the skin of Caucasians appear blue, a condition called *cyanosis* (si″ah-no′sis; *cyan* = dark blue). Skin often becomes cyanotic during heart failure and severe respiratory disorders. In dark-skinned individuals, the skin does not appear cyanotic because of the masking effects of melanin, but cyanosis is apparent in their mucous membranes and nail beds (the same sites where the red cast of normally oxygenated blood is visible).

Many alterations in skin color signal certain disease states, and in many people emotional states:

• *Redness,* or *erythema* (er″ĭ-the′mah): Reddened skin may indicate embarrassment (blushing), fever, hypertension, inflammation, or allergy.

- *Pallor,* or *blanching:* During fear, anger, and certain other types of emotional stress, some people become pale. Pale skin may also signify anemia or low blood pressure.

- *Jaundice* (jawn'dis), or *yellow cast:* An abnormal yellow skin tone usually signifies a liver disorder, in which yellow bile pigments accumulate in the blood and are deposited in body tissues. [Normally, the liver cells secrete the bile pigments (bilirubin) as a component of bile.]

- *Bronzing:* A bronze, almost metallic appearance of the skin is a sign of Addison's disease, hypofunction of the adrenal cortex.

- *Black-and-blue marks,* or *bruises:* Black-and-blue marks reveal where blood escaped from the circulation and clotted beneath the skin. Such clotted blood masses are called *hematomas* (he"mah-to'mah; "blood swelling"). ●

Appendages of the Skin

Along with the skin itself, the integumentary system includes several derivatives of the epidermis. These **skin appendages** include the nails, sweat glands, sebaceous (oil) glands, and hair follicles and hair. Each of these plays a unique role in maintaining body homeostasis. A key step in beginning to form any of the skin's appendages is formation of an epithelial bud. This is stimulated by a reduced production of cell adhesion factor (cadherin). Once the cell-to-cell attractions are broken, the cells can move about and rearrange themselves, allowing an epithelial bud to form.

Sweat (Sudoriferous) Glands

Sweat glands, also called **sudoriferous glands** (su"do-rif'er-us; *sudor* = sweat), are distributed over the entire skin surface except the nipples and parts of the external genitalia. Their number is staggering—up to 3 million of them per person. There are two types of sweat glands: eccrine and apocrine.

Eccrine sweat glands (ek'rin; "secreting"), also called **merocrine sweat glands,** are far more numerous and are particularly abundant on the palms, soles of the feet, and forehead. Each is a simple, coiled, tubular gland. The secretory part lies coiled in the dermis; the duct extends to open in a funnel-shaped *pore* (*por* = channel) at the skin surface (see Figure 5.3b). (These sweat pores are different from the so-called pores of one's complexion, which are actually the external outlets of hair follicles.)

Eccrine gland secretion, commonly called sweat, is a hypotonic filtrate of the blood that passes through the secretory cells of the sweat glands and is released by exocytosis. It is 99% water, with some salts (mostly sodium chloride), vitamin C, antibodies, a microbe-killing peptide dubbed *dermicidin,* and traces of metabolic wastes (urea, uric acid, and ammonia). The exact composition depends on heredity and diet. Small amounts of ingested drugs may also be excreted by this route. Normally, sweat is acidic with a pH between 4 and 6.

Sweating is regulated by the sympathetic division of the autonomic nervous system, over which we have little control. Its major role is to prevent overheating of the body. Heat-induced sweating begins on the forehead and then spreads inferiorly over the remainder of the body. Emotionally induced sweating—the so-called "cold sweat" brought on by fright, embarrassment, or nervousness—begins on the palms, soles, and axillae (armpits) and then spreads to other body areas.

Apocrine sweat glands* (ap'o-krin), approximately 2000 of them, are largely confined to the axillary and anogenital areas. They are larger than eccrine glands, and their ducts empty into hair follicles. Apocrine secretion contains the same basic components as true sweat, plus fatty substances and proteins. Consequently, it is quite viscous and sometimes has a milky or yellowish color. The secretion is odorless, but when its organic molecules are decomposed by bacteria on the skin, it takes on a musky and generally unpleasant odor, the basis of body odor.

Apocrine glands begin functioning at puberty under the influence of androgens and have little role to play in thermoregulation. Their precise function is not yet known, but they are activated by sympathetic nerve fibers during pain and stress. Because their activity is increased by sexual foreplay, and they enlarge and recede with the phases of a woman's menstrual cycle, they may be the human equivalent of the sexual scent glands of other animals.

Ceruminous glands (sĕ-roo'mĭ-nus; *cera* = wax) are modified apocrine glands found in the lining of the external ear canal. They secrete a sticky, bitter substance called *cerumen,* or earwax, that is thought to deter insects and block entry of foreign material.

Mammary glands, another variety of specialized sweat glands, secrete milk. Although they are properly part of the integumentary system, we consider the mammary glands in Chapter 27, along with female reproductive organs.

---

* The term *apocrine sweat glands* is a misnomer. These glands were originally thought to release their product by the apocrine mode (in which the apical surface pinches off) and were named accordingly. Subsequent studies proved them to be merocrine glands, which release their product by exocytosis like the eccrine sweat glands.

(a) Sectioned sebaceous gland

(b) Sectioned eccrine gland

FIGURE 5.3 **Cutaneous glands. (a)** Photomicrograph of a sebaceous gland (160×). **(b)** Photomicrograph of eccrine sweat glands (250×).

Sebaceous (Oil) Glands

The **sebaceous glands** (se-ba'shus; "greasy"), or **oil glands** (see Figure 5.3a), are simple branched alveolar glands that are found all over the body except on the palms and soles. They are small on the body trunk and limbs, but quite large on the face, neck, and upper chest. These glands secrete an oily secretion called **sebum** (se'bum). The central cells of the alveoli accumulate oily lipids until they become so engorged that they burst, so functionally these glands are *holocrine glands* (see p. 126). The accumulated lipids and cell fragments constitute sebum. Sebum is secreted into a hair follicle, or occasionally to a pore on the skin surface. Sebum softens and lubricates the hair and skin, prevents hair from becoming brittle, and slows water loss from the skin when the external humidity is low. Perhaps even more important is its *bactericidal* (bacterium-killing) action.

The secretion of sebum is stimulated by hormones, especially androgens. These glands are relatively inactive during childhood but are activated in both sexes during puberty, when androgen production begins to rise.

◤ HOMEOSTATIC IMBALANCE

If a sebaceous gland duct is blocked by accumulated sebum, a *whitehead* appears on the skin surface. If the material oxidizes and dries, it darkens to form a *blackhead. Acne* is an active inflammation of the se-baceous glands accompanied by "pimples" (pustules or cysts) on the skin. It is usually caused by bacterial infection, particularly by staphylococcus, and can be mild or extremely severe, leading to permanent scarring. Seborrhea (seb"o-re'ah; "fast-flowing sebum"), known as "cradle cap" in infants, is caused by overactive sebaceous glands. It begins on the scalp as pink, raised lesions that gradually become yellow to brown and begin to slough off oily scales. ●

Hairs and Hair Follicles

Hair is an important part of our body image—consider, for example, the spiky hair style of punk rockers and the flowing, glossy manes of some high-fashion models. Millions of hairs are distributed over our entire skin surface except our palms, soles, lips, nipples, and parts of the external genitalia (the head of the penis, for instance). Although hair helps to keep other mammals warm, our sparse body hair is far less luxuriant and useful. Its main function in humans is to sense insects on the skin before they bite or sting us. Hair on the scalp guards the head against physical trauma, heat loss, and sunlight. Eyelashes shield the eyes, and nose hairs filter large particles like lint and insects from the air we inhale.

Structure of a Hair

Hairs, or **pili** (pi'li), are flexible strands produced by hair follicles and consist largely of dead, keratinized

5

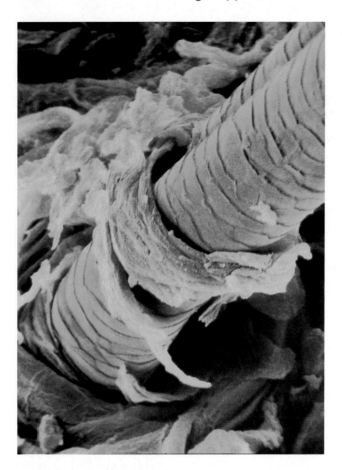

FIGURE 5.4 **Hair shaft emerging from a follicle at the epidermal surface.** Notice how the scalelike cells of the cuticle overlap one another (scanning electron micrograph, 1300×).

The most heavily keratinized part of the hair, the cuticle provides strength and helps keep the inner layers tightly compacted. Because it is subjected to the most abrasion, the cuticle tends to wear away at the tip of the hair shaft, allowing the keratin fibrils in the cortex and medulla to frizz out, creating "split ends."

Hair pigment is made by melanocytes at the base of the hair follicle and transferred to the cortical cells. Various proportions of melanins of different colors (yellow, rust, brown, and black) combine to produce hair color from blond to pitch black. Additionally, red hair is colored by the iron-containing pigment called *trichosiderin*. Gray or white hair results from decreased melanin production (mediated by delayed-action genes) and from the replacement of melanin by air bubbles in the hair shaft.

Structure of a Hair Follicle

Hair follicles (*folli* = bag) fold down from the epidermal surface into the dermis. In the scalp, they may even extend into the hypodermis. The deep end of the follicle, located about 4 mm (1/6 in.) below the skin surface, is expanded, forming a **hair bulb** (Figure 5.5c and d). A knot of sensory nerve endings called a **hair follicle receptor,** or **root hair plexus,** wraps around each hair bulb (see Figure 5.1), and bending the hair stimulates these endings. Consequently, our hairs act as sensitive touch receptors.

▪ Feel the tickle as you run your hand over the hairs on your forearm.

A *hair papilla*, a nipplelike bit of dermal tissue, protrudes into the hair bulb. This papilla contains a knot of capillaries that supplies nutrients to the growing hair and signals it to grow. Except for its specific location, this papilla is similar to the dermal papillae underlying other epidermal regions.

The wall of a hair follicle is composed of an outer **connective tissue root sheath,** derived from the dermis; a thickened basement membrane called the *glassy membrane;* and an inner **epithelial root sheath,** derived mainly from an invagination of the epidermis (Figure 5.5c and d). The epithelial root sheath, which has external and internal parts, thins as it approaches the hair bulb, so that only a single layer of epithelial cells covers the papilla. However, the cells that compose the **hair matrix,** or actively dividing area of the hair bulb that produces the hair, originate in a region called the *hair bulge* located a fraction of a millimeter above the hair bulb. When chemical signals diffusing from the papilla reach the hair bulge, some of its cells migrate toward the papilla, where they divide to produce the hair cells. As new hair cells are produced

cells. The *hard keratin* that dominates hairs and nails has two advantages over the *soft keratin* found in typical epidermal cells: (1) It is tougher and more durable, and (2) its individual cells do not flake off.

The chief regions of a hair are the *shaft*, which projects from the skin (Figure 5.4), and the *root*, the part embedded in the skin (Figure 5.5). If the shaft is flat and ribbonlike in cross section, the hair is kinky; if it is oval, the hair is silky and wavy; if it is perfectly round, the hair is straight and tends to be coarse.

A hair has three concentric layers of keratinized cells (Figure 5.5a and b). Its central core, the *medulla* (mĕ-dul'ah; "middle"), consists of large cells and air spaces. The medulla is absent in fine hairs. The *cortex*, a bulky layer surrounding the medulla, consists of several layers of flattened cells. The outermost **cuticle** is formed from a single layer of cells that overlap one another from below like shingles on a roof (Figure 5.4). This arrangement helps to keep neighboring hairs apart so that the hair does not mat. (Hair conditioners smooth out the rough surface of the cuticle and make our hair look shiny.)

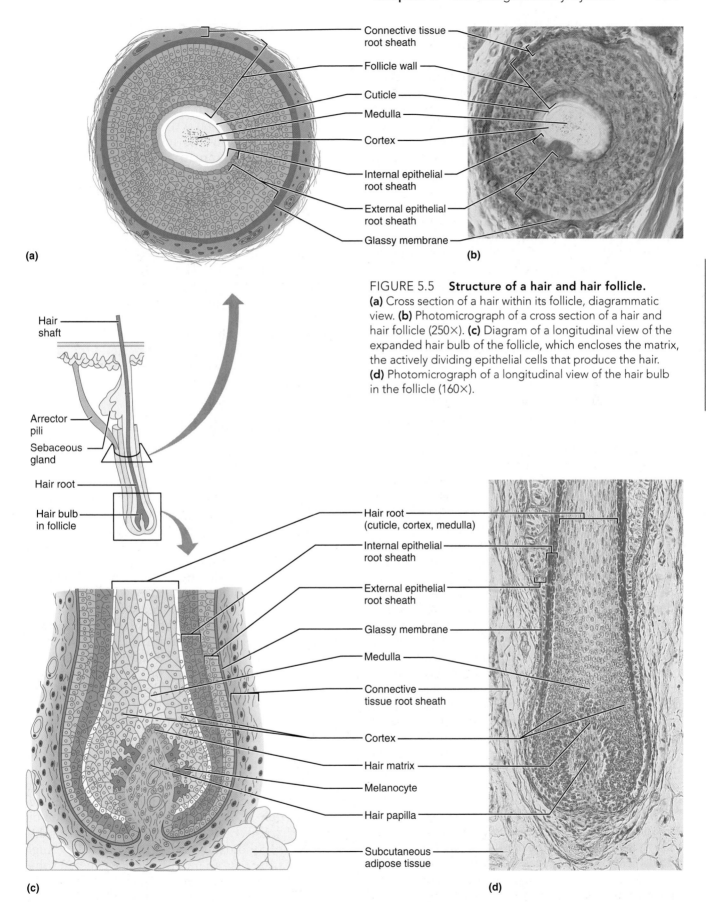

(a)

Connective tissue root sheath
Follicle wall
Cuticle
Medulla
Cortex
Internal epithelial root sheath
External epithelial root sheath
Glassy membrane

(b)

FIGURE 5.5 **Structure of a hair and hair follicle.**
(a) Cross section of a hair within its follicle, diagrammatic view. **(b)** Photomicrograph of a cross section of a hair and hair follicle (250×). **(c)** Diagram of a longitudinal view of the expanded hair bulb of the follicle, which encloses the matrix, the actively dividing epithelial cells that produce the hair. **(d)** Photomicrograph of a longitudinal view of the hair bulb in the follicle (160×).

Hair shaft
Arrector pili
Sebaceous gland
Hair root
Hair bulb in follicle

Hair root (cuticle, cortex, medulla)
Internal epithelial root sheath
External epithelial root sheath
Glassy membrane
Medulla
Connective tissue root sheath
Cortex
Hair matrix
Melanocyte
Hair papilla
Subcutaneous adipose tissue

(c)

(d)

by the matrix, the older part of the hair is pushed upward, and its fused cells become increasingly keratinized and die.

Associated with each hair follicle is a bundle of smooth muscle cells called an **arrector pili** (ah-rek'tor pi'li; "raiser of hair") muscle. As you can see in Figure 5.1, most hair follicles approach the skin surface at a slight angle. The arrector pili muscles are attached in such a way that their contraction pulls the hair follicle into an upright position and dimples the skin surface to produce goose bumps in response to cold external temperatures or fear. This "hair-raising" response is not very useful to humans, with our short sparse hairs, but it is an important heat retention and protection mechanism in other animals. Furry animals can stay warmer by trapping a layer of insulating air in their fur; and a scared animal with its hair on end looks larger and more formidable to its enemy.

Types and Growth of Hair

Hairs come in various sizes and shapes, but as a rule, they can be classified as vellus or terminal. The body hair of children and adult females is of the pale, fine **vellus hair** (vel'us; *vell* = wool, fleece) variety. The coarser, longer hair of the eyebrows and scalp is **terminal hair**; terminal hair may also be darker. At puberty, terminal hairs appear in the axillary and pubic regions of both sexes and on the face and chest (and typically the arms and legs) of males. These terminal hairs grow in response to the stimulating effects of male sex hormones called *androgens* (of which *testosterone* is the most important), and when male hormones are present in large amounts, terminal hair growth is luxuriant.

Hair growth and density are influenced by many factors, but most importantly by nutrition and hormones. Poor nutrition means poor hair growth, whereas conditions that increase local dermal blood flow (such as chronic physical irritation or inflammation) may enhance local hair growth. Many old-time bricklayers who carried their hod on one shoulder all the time developed one hairy shoulder. Undesirable hair growth (such as on a woman's upper lip) may be arrested by *electrolysis* or laser treatments, which use electricity or light energy, respectively, to destroy the hair roots.

◤ HOMEOSTATIC IMBALANCE

In women, small amounts of androgens are normally produced by both the ovaries and the adrenal glands. Excessive hairiness, or *hirsutism* (her'soot-izm; *hirsut* = hairy), as well as other signs of masculinization, may result from an adrenal gland or ovarian tumor that secretes abnormally large amounts of androgens. Since few women want a beard or hairy chest, such tumors are surgically removed as soon as possible. ●

The rate of hair growth varies from one body region to another and with sex and age, but it averages 2.5 mm per week. Each follicle goes through *growth cycles*. In each cycle, an active growth phase, ranging from weeks to years, is followed by a regressive phase, when the hair matrix cells die and the follicle base and hair bulb shrivel somewhat. The follicle then enters a resting phase for one to three months. After the resting phase, the matrix proliferates again and forms a new hair to replace the old one that has fallen out or will be pushed out by the new hair.

The life span of hairs varies and appears to be under the control of a slew of proteins. The follicles of the scalp remain active for six to ten years before becoming inactive for a few months. Because only a small percentage of the hair follicles are shed at any one time, we lose an average of 90 scalp hairs daily. The follicles of the eyebrow hairs remain active for only three to four months, which explains why your eyebrows are never as long as the hairs on your head.

Hair Thinning and Baldness

A follicle has only a limited number of cycles in it. Given ideal conditions, hair grows fastest from the teen years to the 40s; then its growth slows. The fact that hairs are not replaced as fast as they are shed leads to hair thinning and some degree of baldness, or **alopecia** (al"o-pe'she-ah), in both sexes. Much less dramatic in women, the process usually begins at the anterior hairline and progresses posteriorly. Coarse terminal hairs are replaced by vellus hairs, and the hair becomes increasingly wispy.

True, or *frank*, *baldness* is a different story entirely. The most common type, **male pattern baldness,** is a genetically determined, sex-influenced condition. It is thought to be caused by a delayed-action gene that "switches on" in adulthood and changes the response of the hair follicles to DHT (dihydrotestosterone), a metabolite of testosterone. As a result, the follicular growth cycles become so short that many hairs never even emerge from their follicles before shedding, and those that do are fine vellus hairs that look like peach fuzz in the "bald" area. Until recently, the only cure for male pattern baldness was drugs that inhibit testosterone production, but they also cause loss of sex drive—a trade-off few men would choose. Quite by accident, it was discovered that minoxidil, a drug used to reduce high blood pressure, has an interesting side effect in some bald men; it stimulates hair regrowth. Although its results are variable, minoxidil is available over the counter in dropper bottles or spray form for application to the scalp. Finasteride, according to some the

FIGURE 5.6 **Structure of a nail.** **(a)** Surface view of the distal part of a finger. **(b)** Sagittal section of the fingertip. The nail matrix that forms the nail lies beneath the lunula.

most promising cure ever developed for male pattern baldness, hit pharmacy shelves in early 1998 and has had moderate success. Available only by prescription in once-a-day pill form, it must be taken for the rest of one's life. Once the patient stops taking it, all of the new growth falls out, and so does what remains of the "old" hair.

HOMEOSTATIC IMBALANCE

Hair thinning can be induced by a number of factors that upset the normal balance between hair loss and replacement. Outstanding examples are acutely high fever, surgery, severe emotional trauma, and certain drugs (excessive vitamin A, some antidepressants and blood thinners, anabolic steroids, and most chemotherapy drugs). Protein-deficient diets and lactation lead to hair thinning because new hair growth stops when protein needed for keratin synthesis is not available or is being used for milk production. In all of these cases, hair regrows if the cause of thinning is removed or corrected. In the rare condition called *alopecia areata* the follicles are attacked by the immune system and the hair falls out in patches. But again, the follicles survive. However, hair loss due to severe burns, excessive radiation, or other factors that eliminate the follicles is permanent. ●

Nails

A **nail** is a scalelike modification of the epidermis that forms a clear protective covering on the dorsal surface of the distal part of a finger or toe (Figure 5.6). Nails, which correspond to the hooves or claws of other animals, are particularly useful as "tools" to help pick up small objects and to scratch an itch. As noted, in contrast to *soft keratin* of the epider-

mis, nails contain *hard keratin*. Each nail has a *free edge*, a *body* (visible attached portion), and a proximal *root* (embedded in the skin). The deeper layers of the epidermis extend beneath the nail as the *nail bed*; the nail itself corresponds to the superficial keratinized layers. The thickened proximal portion of the nail bed, called the **nail matrix,** is responsible for nail growth. As the nail cells produced by the matrix become heavily keratinized, the nail body slides distally over the nail bed.

Nails normally appear pink because of the rich bed of capillaries in the underlying dermis. However, the region that lies over the thick nail matrix appears as a white crescent called the *lunula* (lu'nu-lah; "little moon"). The proximal and lateral borders of the nail are overlapped by skin folds, called **nail folds.** The proximal nail fold projects onto the nail body as the **cuticle** or **eponychium** (ep"o-nik'e-um; "on the nail"). The region beneath the free edge of the nail where dirt and debris tend to accumulate is the **hyponychium** ("below nail"), informally called the quick.

Functions of the Integumentary System

The skin and its derivatives perform a variety of functions that affect body metabolism and prevent external factors from upsetting body homeostasis. Given its superficial location it is our most vulnerable organ system, exposed to bacteria, abrasion, temperature extremes, and harmful chemicals.

Protection

The skin constitutes at least three types of barriers: chemical, physical, and biological.

Chemical Barriers

The chemical barriers include skin secretions and melanin. Although the skin's surface teems with bacteria, the low pH of skin secretions, or the so-called **acid mantle,** retards their multiplication. In addition, many bacteria are killed outright by bactericidal substances in sebum. Skin cells also secrete a natural antibiotic called *human defensin* that literally punches holes in bacteria, making them look like sieves. Wounded skin releases large quantities of protective peptides called *cathelicidins* that are particularly effective in preventing infection by group A streptococcus bacteria. As discussed earlier, melanin provides a chemical pigment shield to prevent UV damage to the viable skin cells.

Physical/Mechanical Barriers

Physical, or mechanical, barriers are provided by the continuity of skin and the hardness of its keratinized cells. As a physical barrier, the skin is a remarkable compromise. A thicker epidermis would be more impenetrable, but we would pay the price in loss of suppleness and agility. Epidermal continuity works hand in hand with the acid mantle to ward off bacterial invasion. The waterproofing glycolipids of the epidermis block the diffusion of water and water-soluble substances between cells, preventing both their loss from and entry into the body through the skin. Substances that *do* penetrate the skin in limited amounts include (1) *lipid-soluble substances,* such as oxygen, carbon dioxide, fat-soluble vitamins (A, D, E, and K), and steroids; (2) *oleoresins* (o"le-o-rez'inz) of certain plants, such as poison ivy and poison oak; (3) *organic solvents,* such as acetone, dry-cleaning fluid, and paint thinner, which dissolve the cell lipids; (4) *salts of heavy metals,* such as lead and mercury; and (5) drug agents called *penetration enhancers* that help ferry other drugs into the body.

 HOMEOSTATIC IMBALANCE

Organic solvents and heavy metals are devastating to the body and can be lethal. Passage of organic solvents through the skin into the blood can cause the kidneys to shut down and can also cause brain damage. Absorption of lead results in anemia and neurological defects. These substances should never be handled with bare hands. ●

Biological Barriers

Biological barriers include the Langerhans' (dendritic) cells of the epidermis, macrophages in the dermis, and DNA itself. Langerhans' cells are active elements of the immune system. For the immune response to be activated, the foreign substances, or *antigens,* must be presented to specialized white blood cells called lymphocytes. In the epidermis, it is the Langerhans' cells that play this role. Dermal macrophages constitute a second line of defense to dispose of viruses and bacteria that have managed to penetrate the epidermis. They, too, act as antigen "presenters." Although melanin provides a fairly good chemical sunscreen, DNA itself is a remarkably effective biologically based sunscreen. Electrons in DNA molecules absorb UV radiation and transfer it to the atomic nuclei, which heat up and vibrate vigorously. However, since the heat dissipates to surrounding water molecules instantaneously, the DNA converts potentially destructive radiation into harmless heat.

Body Temperature Regulation

The body works best when its temperature remains within homeostatic limits. Like car engines, we need to get rid of the heat generated by our internal reactions. As long as the external temperature is lower than body temperature, the skin surface loses heat to the air and to cooler objects in its environment, just as a car radiator loses heat to the air and other nearby engine parts.

Under normal resting conditions, and as long as the environmental temperature is below 31–32°C (88–90°F), sweat glands continuously secrete unnoticeable amounts of sweat [about 500 ml (0.5 L) of sweat per day]. When body temperature rises, dermal blood vessels dilate and the sweat glands are stimulated into vigorous secretory activity. Sweat becomes noticeable and can account for the loss of up to 12 L of body water in one day. Evaporation of sweat from the skin surface dissipates body heat and efficiently cools the body, thus preventing overheating.

When the external environment is cold, dermal blood vessels constrict. This causes the warm blood to bypass the skin temporarily and allows skin temperature to drop to that of the external environment. Once this has happened, passive heat loss from the body is slowed, thus conserving body heat. Body temperature regulation is discussed in greater detail in Chapter 24.

Cutaneous Sensation

The skin is richly supplied with **cutaneous sensory receptors,** which are actually part of the nervous system. The cutaneous receptors are classified as *exteroceptors* (ek"ster-o-sep'torz) because they respond to stimuli arising outside the body. For example, Meissner's corpuscles (in the dermal papillae) and Merkel discs allow us to become aware of a caress or the feel of our clothing against our skin, whereas Pacinian corpuscles (in the deeper dermis or hypodermis) alert us to bumps or contacts involving deep pressure. Hair follicle receptors report on wind blowing through our hair and a playful tug on a pigtail. Painful stimuli (irritating chemicals, extreme heat or cold, and others) are sensed by free nerve endings that meander throughout the skin. Detailed discussion of these cutaneous receptors is deferred to Chapter 13, but those mentioned above are illustrated in Figure 5.1. One, a Merkel disc, is also shown in Figure 5.2b.

Metabolic Functions

When sunlight bombards the skin, modified cholesterol molecules circulating through dermal blood vessels are converted to a vitamin D precursor, and transported via the blood to other body areas to play various roles in calcium metabolism. For example, calcium cannot be absorbed from the digestive tract without vitamin D.

Besides synthesizing the vitamin D precursor, the epidermis has a host of other metabolic functions. It makes chemical conversions that supplement those of the liver—for example, keratinocyte enzymes can (1) "disarm" many cancer-causing chemicals that penetrate the epidermis; (2) convert some harmless chemicals into carcinogens; and (3) activate some steroid hormones; for instance, they can transform cortisone applied to irritated skin into hydrocortisone, a potent anti-inflammatory drug. Skin cells also make several biologically important proteins, including collagenase, an enzyme that aids the natural turnover of collagen (and deters wrinkles).

Blood Reservoir

The dermal vascular supply is extensive and can hold large volumes of blood (about 5% of the body's entire blood volume). When other body organs, such as vigorously working muscles, need a greater blood supply, the nervous system constricts the dermal blood vessels. This shunts more blood into the general circulation, making it available to the muscles and other body organs.

Excretion

Limited amounts of nitrogen-containing wastes (ammonia, urea, and uric acid) are eliminated from the body in sweat, although most such wastes are excreted in urine. Profuse sweating is an important avenue for water and salt (sodium chloride) loss.

Homeostatic Imbalances of Skin

When skin rebels, it is quite a visible revolution. Loss of homeostasis in body cells and organs reveals itself on the skin, sometimes in startling ways. The skin can develop more than 1000 different conditions and ailments. The most common skin disorders are bacterial, viral, or yeast infections. A number of these are summarized in Related Clinical Terms on p. 171. Less common, but far more damaging to body well-being, are skin cancer and burns, considered next.

Skin Cancer

One in five Americans develop skin cancer at some point. Most tumors that arise in the skin are benign and do not spread (metastasize) to other body areas. (A wart, a neoplasm caused by a virus, is one example.) However, some skin tumors are malignant, or cancerous, and invade other body areas. A crucial risk factor for skin cancer is overexposure to the UV radiation in sunlight, which damages DNA bases. Adjacent pyrimidine bases often respond by fusing, forming lesions called *dimers*. UV radiation also appears to disable a tumor suppressor gene [*p53* or the patched (*ptc*) gene]. In limited numbers of cases, however, frequent irritation of the skin by infections, chemicals, or physical trauma seems to be a predisposing factor.

Interestingly, sunburned skin accelerates its production of Fas, a protein that causes genetically damaged skin cells to commit suicide, thus reducing the risk of mutations that will cause sun-linked skin cancer. It is the death of these gene-damaged cells that causes the skin to peel after a sunburn. Good news for sun worshippers is the newly developed skin lotions that can fix damaged DNA before the involved cells can develop into cancer cells. These lotions contain tiny oily vesicles (liposomes) filled with enzymes that initiate repair of the DNA mutations most commonly caused by sunlight. The liposomes penetrate the epidermis and enter the keratinocytes, ultimately making their way into the nuclei to bind to specific sites where two DNA bases have fused. There, by selective cutting of the DNA strands, they begin a DNA repair process that is completed by cellular enzymes.

Basal Cell Carcinoma

Basal cell carcinoma (kar″sĭ-no′mah) is the least malignant and most common skin cancer; over 30% of all white people get it in their lifetime. Stratum basale cells proliferate, invading the dermis and hypodermis. The cancer lesions occur most often on sun-exposed areas of the face and appear as shiny, dome-shaped nodules that later develop a central ulcer with a pearly, beaded edge (Figure 5.7a). Basal cell carcinoma is relatively slow-growing, and metastasis seldom occurs before it is noticed. Full cure by surgical excision is the rule in 99% of cases.

5

(a)

(b)

(c)

FIGURE 5.7   **Photographs of skin cancers. (a)** Basal cell carcinoma.
(b) Squamous cell carcinoma. **(c)** Melanoma.

Squamous Cell Carcinoma

Squamous cell carcinoma arises from the keratinocytes of the stratum spinosum. The lesion appears as a scaly reddened papule (small, rounded elevation) that arises most often on the head (scalp,
ears, and lower lip), and hands (Figure 5.7b). It tends
to grow rapidly and metastasize if not removed. If it
is caught early and removed surgically or by radiation therapy, chance of complete cure is good.

Melanoma

Melanoma (mel″ah-no′mah), cancer of melanocytes,
is the most dangerous skin cancer because it is highly
metastatic and resistant to chemotherapy. It accounts for only about 5% of skin cancers, but its incidence is increasing rapidly (by 3–8% per year in the
United States). Melanoma can begin wherever there
is pigment. Most such cancers appear spontaneously; about one-third develop from preexisting
moles. It usually appears as a spreading brown to
black patch (Figure 5.7c) that metastasizes rapidly
to surrounding lymph and blood vessels. The key to
surviving melanoma is early detection. The chance
of survival is poor if the lesion is over 4 mm thick.
The usual therapy for melanoma is wide surgical

excision accompanied by immunotherapy (immu-
nizing the body against its cancer cells).

The American Cancer Society suggests that sun
worshippers regularly examine their skin for new
moles or pigmented spots and apply the **ABCD rule**
for recognizing melanoma. **A. Asymmetry:** The two
sides of the pigmented spot or mole do not match.
B. Border irregularity: The borders of the lesion
exhibit indentations. **C. Color:** The pigmented spot
contains several colors (blacks, browns, tans, and
sometimes blues and reds). **D. Diameter:** The spot
is larger than 6 mm in diameter (the size of a pencil
eraser). Some experts have found that adding an **E,**
for elevation above the skin surface, improves diagnosis, so they use the ABCD(E) rule.

Burns

Burns are a devastating threat to the body primarily
because of their effects on the skin. A **burn** is tissue
damage inflicted by intense heat, electricity, radiation, or certain chemicals, all of which denature cell
proteins and cause cell death in the affected areas.

The immediate threat to life resulting from severe
burns is a catastrophic loss of body fluids containing
proteins and electrolytes, resulting in dehydration

Q *Although the anterior head and face represent a very small proportion of the body surface, burns to this region are often much more serious than burns to the trunk. Why?*

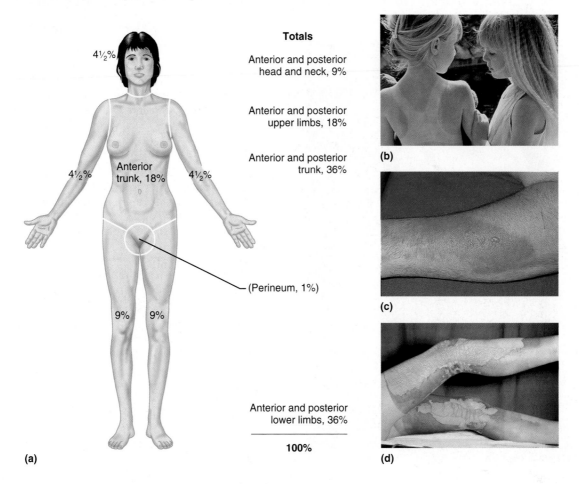

Totals

Anterior and posterior head and neck, 9%

Anterior and posterior upper limbs, 18%

Anterior and posterior trunk, 36%

— (Perineum, 1%)

Anterior and posterior lower limbs, 36%

100%

4½%

4½% — Anterior trunk, 18% — 4½%

9% 9%

(a)

(b)

(c)

(d)

FIGURE 5.8 Estimating the extent and severity of burns. (a) The extent of burns is estimated by using the rule of nines. Surface area values for the anterior body surface are indicated on the human figure. Total surface area (anterior and posterior body surfaces) for each body region is indicated to the right of the figure. Severity of burns depends on the depth of tissue damage. **(b)** In first-degree burns only the epidermis is destroyed. **(c)** In second-degree burns, the epidermis and part of the dermis are involved and blistering occurs. **(d)** In third-degree burns the epidermis and dermis (and often part of the hypodermis) are destroyed.

and electrolyte imbalance. These, in turn, lead to renal shutdown and circulatory shock (inadequate blood circulation due to reduced blood volume). To save the patient, the lost fluids must be replaced immediately via the intravenous (IV) route. In adults, the volume of fluid lost can be estimated by computing the percentage of body surface burned (extent of the burns) using the **rule of nines.** This method divides the body into 11 areas, each accounting for 9% of total body area, plus an additional area surrounding the genitals accounting for 1% of body surface area (Figure 5.8). This method is only approximate, so special tables are used when greater accuracy is desired.

Burn patients also need thousands of extra food calories daily to replace lost proteins and allow tissue repair. No one can eat enough food to provide these calories, so burn patients are given supplementary nutrients through gastric tubes and IV lines. After the initial crisis has passed, infection becomes the main threat and is the leading cause of death in burn victims. Burned skin is sterile for about 24 hours. Thereafter, bacteria, fungi, and other pathogens easily invade areas where the skin barrier is destroyed, and they multiply rapidly in the nutrient-rich environment of dead tissues. Adding to this problem is the fact that the immune system becomes deficient within one to two days after severe burn injury.

A *Burn injury to the facial area may burn the respiratory passages, putting the patient at risk for suffocation as the burned tissues swell.*

(Text continues on p. 170.)

MAKING CONNECTIONS

SYSTEM CONNECTIONS: Homeostatic Interrelationships Between the Integumentary System and Other Body Systems

Endocrine System

- Skin protects endocrine organs; converts some hormones to their active forms
- Androgens produced by the endocrine system activate sebaceous glands and are involved in regulation of hair growth

Cardiovascular System

- Skin protects cardiovascular organs; prevents fluid loss from body; serves as blood reservoir
- Cardiovascular system transports oxygen and nutrients to skin and removes wastes from skin; provides substances needed by skin glands to make their secretions

Lymphatic System/Immunity

- Skin protects lymphatic organs; prevents pathogen invasion; Langerhans' cells and macrophages help activate the immune system
- Lymphatic system prevents edema by picking up excessive leaked fluid; immune system protects skin cells

Respiratory System

- Skin protects respiratory organs
- Respiratory system furnishes oxygen to skin cells and removes carbon dioxide via gas exchange with blood

Digestive System

- Skin protects digestive organs; provides vitamin D needed for calcium absorption; performs some of the same chemical conversions as liver cells
- Digestive system provides needed nutrients to the skin

Urinary System

- Skin protects urinary organs; excretes salts and some nitrogenous wastes in sweat
- Urinary system activates vitamin D precursor made by keratinocytes; disposes of nitrogenous wastes of skin metabolism

Reproductive System

- Skin protects reproductive organs; cutaneous receptors respond to erotic stimuli; highly modified sweat glands (mammary glands) produce milk. During pregnancy, skin stretches to accommodate growing fetus; changes in skin pigmentation may occur

Skeletal System

- Skin protects bones; skin synthesizes vitamin D that bones need for normal calcium absorption and deposit of bone (calcium) salts, which make bones hard
- Skeletal system provides support for skin

Muscular System

- Skin protects muscles
- Active muscles generate large amounts of heat, which increases blood flow to the skin and may promote activation of sweat glands of skin

Nervous System

- Skin protects nervous system organs; cutaneous sensory receptors located in skin (see Figure 5.1)
- Nervous system regulates diameter of blood vessels in skin; activates sweat glands, contributing to thermoregulation; interprets cutaneous sensation; activates arrector pili muscles

THE INTEGUMENTARY SYSTEM and Interrelationships with the Nervous, Cardiovascular, and Lymphatic/Immune Systems

First and foremost, our skin is a barrier. Like the skin of a grape, it keeps its contents juicy and whole. The skin, however, is a master at self (wound) repair, and interacts intimately with other body systems by making vitamin D (necessary for hard bones) and other potent molecules, all the while protecting deeper tissues from damaging external agents. Perhaps the most crucial roles of the skin in terms of overall body homeostasis are those it plays with the nervous, cardiovascular, and lymphatic systems. These interactions are detailed next.

Nervous System

The skin houses the tiny sensory receptors that provide a great deal of information about our external environment—its temperature, the pressure exerted by objects, and the presence of dangerous substances. What if we stepped on broken glass or hot pavement but did not have neural monitors in our skin? If we did not actually see, hear, taste, or smell such a damaging event, no reports would be sent to the nervous system. Consequently, the nervous system would be left "in the dark," unable to evaluate the need for a response and to order the steps needed to protect us from further damage or to get first aid. Thus, the whole body benefits from the skin's interaction with the nervous system.

Nervous and Cardiovascular System

Skin provides the site both for sensing external temperature and for responding to temperature changes. Dermal blood vessels (cardiovascular system organs) and sweat glands (controlled by the nervous system) play crucial roles in thermoregulation. So too do blood and the hot and cold receptors in the skin. When we are chilled, our blood loses heat to internal organs and cools. This alerts the nervous system to retain heat by constricting blood vessels. When body and blood temperature rises, dermal vessels dilate and sweating begins.

Thermoregulation is vital: When the body overheats, life-threatening changes occur. Chemical reactions speed up, and if excessive, they destroy vital proteins and cells die. Cold has the opposite effect; cellular activity slows and ultimately stops.

Lymphatic System/Immunity

The role of the skin in immunity is complex. Keratinocytes in the skin manufacture interferons (proteins that block viral infection) and other proteins important to the immune response. Langerhans' cells in the skin interact with antigens (foreign substances) that have penetrated the stratum corneum. The Langerhans' cells then migrate to lymphatic organs, where they present bits of the antigens to cells that will mount the immune response against them. This "messenger" function alerts the immune system early on to the presence of pathogens in the body.

Even a mild sunburn disrupts the normal immune response because UV radiation disables the skin's presenter cells. This may explain why many people infected by the cold sore virus tend to have a cold sore eruption after sun exposure.

Integumentary System

A terrible collision between a trailer truck and a bus has occurred on Route 91. Several of the passengers are rushed to area hospitals for treatment. We will follow a few of these people in clinical case studies that will continue through the book from one organ system to the next.

Case Study: Examination of Mrs. DeStephano, a 45-year-old woman, reveals several impairments of homeostasis. Relative to her integumentary system, the following comments are noted on her chart:

- Epidermal abrasions of the right arm and shoulder
- Severe lacerations of the right cheek and temple
- Cyanosis apparent

The lacerated areas are cleaned, sutured, and bandaged by the emergency room (ER) personnel, and Mrs. DeStephano is admitted for further tests.

Relative to her signs:

1. What protective mechanisms are impaired or deficient in the abraded areas?

2. Assuming that bacteria are penetrating the dermis in these areas, what remaining skin defense mechanisms might act to prevent further bacterial invasion?

3. What benefit is conferred by suturing the lacerations? (Hint: see Chapter 4, p. 148.)

4. Mrs. DeStephano's cyanotic skin may hint at what additional problem (and impairment of what body systems or functions)?

(Answers in Appendix G)

Burns are classified according to their severity (depth) as first-, second-, or third-degree burns (Figure 5.8b–d). In **first-degree burns,** only the epidermis is damaged. Symptoms include localized redness, swelling, and pain. First-degree burns tend to heal in two to three days without special attention. Sunburn is usually a first-degree burn. **Second-degree burns** injure the epidermis and the upper region of the dermis. Symptoms mimic those of first-degree burns, but blisters also appear. Skin regeneration occurs with little or no scarring within three to four weeks if care is taken to prevent infection. First- and second-degree burns are referred to as *partial-thickness* burns.

Third-degree burns are *full-thickness* burns, involving the entire thickness of the skin. The burned area appears gray-white, cherry red, or blackened, and initially there is little or no edema. Since the nerve endings in the area have been destroyed, the burned area is not painful. Although skin regeneration might eventually occur by proliferation of epithelial cells at the edges of the burn or from stem cells in hair follicles, it is usually impossible to wait that long because of fluid loss and infection. Thus, skin grafting is usually necessary.

To prepare the burned area for grafting, the *eschar* (es'kar), or burned skin, must first be debrided (removed). To prevent infection and fluid loss, the area is then flooded with antibiotics and covered temporarily with a synthetic membrane, animal (pig) skin, cadaver skin, or "living bandage" made from the thin amniotic sac membrane that surrounds a fetus. Then healthy skin is transplanted to the burned site. Unless the graft is taken from the patient (an autograft), however, there is a good chance that it will be rejected by the patient's immune system (see p. 815 in Chapter 21). Even if the graft "takes," extensive scar tissue often forms in the burned areas.

An exciting technique is eliminating many of the traditional problems of skin grafting and rejection. Synthetic skin made of a silicone "epidermis" bound to a spongy "dermal" layer composed of collagen and ground cartilage is applied to the debrided area. In time, the patient's own dermal tissue replaces and absorbs the artificial one. Then the silicone sheet is peeled off and replaced with a network of epidermal cells cultured from the patient's own skin. The artificial skin is not rejected by the body, saves lives, and results in minimal scarring. However, it is more likely to become infected than is an autograft.

In general, burns are considered critical if any of the following conditions exists: (1) over 25% of the body has second-degree burns, (2) over 10% of the body has third-degree burns, or (3) there are third-degree burns of the face, hands, or feet. Facial burns introduce the possibility of burned respiratory passageways, which can swell and cause suffocation. Burns at joints are also troublesome because scar tissue formation can severely limit joint mobility.

Developmental Aspects of the Integumentary System

The epidermis develops from the embryonic ectoderm, and the dermis and hypodermis develop from mesoderm. By the end of the fourth month of development, the skin is fairly well formed: The epidermis has all its strata, dermal papillae are obvious, and rudimentary epidermal derivatives are present. During the fifth and sixth months, the fetus is covered with a downy coat of delicate hairs called the *lanugo coat* (lah-nu'go; "wool"). This hairy cloak is shed by the seventh month, and vellus hairs make their appearance.

When a baby is born, its skin is covered with *vernix caseosa* (ver'niks kă-se-o'sah; "varnish of cheese"), a white, cheesy-looking substance produced by the sebaceous glands that protects the fetus's skin within the water-filled amnion. The newborn's skin is very thin and often has accumulations in the sebaceous glands on the forehead and nose that appear as small white spots called *milia* (mil'e-ah). These normally disappear by the third week after birth. During infancy and childhood, the skin thickens, and more subcutaneous fat is deposited. Although we all have approximately the same number of sweat glands, the number that begin to function increases in the first two years after birth and is determined by climate. Hence, people who grow up in hot climates have more active sweat glands than those raised in cooler areas of the world.

During adolescence, the skin and hair become oilier as sebaceous glands are activated, and acne may appear. Acne generally subsides in early adulthood, and skin reaches its optimal appearance when we reach our 20s and 30s. Thereafter, the skin starts to show the effects of cumulative environmental assaults (abrasion, wind, sun, chemicals). Scaling and various kinds of skin inflammation, or **dermatitis** (der"mah-ti'tis), become more common.

As old age approaches, the rate of epidermal cell replacement slows, the skin thins, and its susceptibility to bruises and other types of injury increases. All of the lubricating substances produced by the skin glands that make young skin so soft start to become deficient. As a result, the skin becomes dry and itchy. However, those with naturally oily skin seem to postpone this dryness until later in life. Elastic fibers clump, and collagen fibers become fewer and stiffer. The subcutaneous fat layer diminishes, leading to the intolerance to cold so common in elderly people. The decreasing elasticity of the skin, along with the loss of subcutaneous tissue, inevitably leads to wrinkling. (See the *Closer Look* box on p. 156.) Decreasing numbers of melanocytes and Langerhans' cells enhance the risk and incidence of skin cancer in this age group. As a rule, redheads and fair-skinned individuals, who have less melanin to begin with, show age-related changes more rapidly than do those with darker skin and hair.

By the age of 50 years, the number of active hair follicles has declined by two-thirds and continues to fall, resulting in hair thinning. Hair loses its luster in old age, and the delayed-action genes responsible for graying and male pattern baldness become active.

Although there is no known way to avoid the aging of the skin, one of the best ways to slow the process is to shield your skin from the sun with sunscreens and protective clothing. Remember, the same sunlight that produces that fashionable tan also causes the sagging, blotchy, wrinkled skin of old age complete with pigmented "liver spots." (It is instructive to note that aged skin that has been protected from the sun has lost some elasticity and is thinned as noted, but it remains unwrinkled and unmarked.) Much of this havoc is due to UV activation of enzymes called matrix metalloproteinases, which degrade collagen and other dermal components. A drug called tretinoin, related to vitamin A, inhibits these enzymes and is now being used in some skin creams to slow photo-aging. Good nutrition, plenty of fluids, and cleanliness may also delay the process.

■ ■ ■

The skin is only about as thick as a paper towel—not too impressive as organ systems go. Yet, when it is severely damaged, nearly every body system reacts. Metabolism accelerates or may be impaired, immune system changes occur, bones may soften, the cardiovascular system may fail—the list goes on and on. On the other hand, when the skin is intact and performing its functions, the body as a whole benefits. Homeostatic interrelationships between the integumentary system and other organ systems are summarized in *Making Connections* on pp. 168–169.

Related Clinical Terms

Albinism (al'bĭ-nizm; *alb* = white) Inherited condition in which melanocytes do not synthesize melanin owing to a lack of tyrosinase. An albino's skin is pink, the hair pale or white, and the irises of the eyes unpigmented or poorly so.

Boils and carbuncles (kar'bung-klz; "little glowing embers") Inflammation of hair follicles and sebaceous glands in which an infection has spread to the underlying hypodermis; common on the dorsal neck. Carbuncles are composite boils. A common cause is bacterial infection.

Cold sores (fever blisters) Small fluid-filled blisters that itch and smart; usually occur around the lips and in the mucosa of the mouth; caused by a herpes simplex infection. The virus localizes in a cutaneous nerve, where it remains dormant until activated by emotional upset, fever, or UV radiation.

Contact dermatitis Itching, redness, and swelling, progressing to blister formation; caused by exposure of the skin to chemicals (e.g., poison ivy oleoresin) that provoke an allergic response in sensitive individuals.

Decubitus ulcer (de-ku'bĭ-tus) Localized breakdown and ulceration of skin due to interference with its blood supply. Usually occurs over a bony prominence, such as the hip or heel, that is subjected to continuous pressure; also called a bedsore.

Dermatology The branch of medicine that studies and treats disorders of the skin.

Epidermolysis bullosa (EB) A group of hereditary disorders characterized by inadequate or faulty synthesis of keratin, collagen, and/or basement membrane "cement" that results in lack of cohesion between layers of the skin and mucosa; a simple touch causes layers to separate and blister. For this reason, EB victims are called "touch-me-nots." In severe cases fatal blistering occurs in major vital organs. Because the blisters rupture easily, victims suffer frequent infections; treatments are aimed at relieving the symptoms and preventing infection.

Impetigo (im"pĕ-ti'go; *impet* = an attack) Pink, fluid-filled, raised lesions (common around the mouth and nose) that develop a yellow crust and eventually rupture. Caused by staphylococcus infection, contagious, and common in school-age children.

Mongolian spot Blue-black spot appearing in the skin of the sacral region, which results from the unusual presence of a cluster of melanocytes in the dermis; the light-scattering effect of the epidermis causes these dermal melanin-containing regions to appear blue. Disappears by age 3 or 4.

Porphyria (por-fer'e-ah; "purple") An inherited condition in which certain enzymes essential to form the heme of hemoglobin of blood are lacking. Without these enzymes, metabolic intermediates of the heme pathway called porphyrins build up, spill into the circulation, and eventually cause lesions throughout the body, especially when exposed to sunlight. The skin becomes lesioned and scarred; fingers, toes, and nose are disfigured; gums degenerate and teeth become prominent; thus it's believed to be the basis of folklore about vampires.

Psoriasis (so-ri'ah-sis) A chronic condition characterized by raised, reddened epidermal lesions covered with dry silvery scales that itch, burn, crack, and sometimes bleed or become infected. When severe, it may be disfiguring and debilitating. Autoimmune attack in affected regions is suspect; attacks are often triggered by trauma, infection, hormonal changes, and stress. Phototherapy with UV light in conjunction with chemotherapeutic drugs provides some relief.

Vitiligo (vit"ĭ-li'go; *viti* = a vine, winding) The most prevalent skin pigmentation disorder, characterized by a loss of melanocytes and uneven dispersal of melanin, i.e., unpigmented skin regions (light spots) surrounded by normally pigmented areas. Probably an autoimmune disorder.

Chapter Summary

The Skin (pp. 152–158)

1. The skin, or integument, is composed of two discrete tissue layers, an outer epidermis and a deeper dermis, resting on subcutaneous tissue, the hypodermis.

Epidermis (pp. 152–155)

2. The epidermis is an avascular, keratinized sheet of stratified squamous epithelium. Most epidermal cells are keratinocytes. Scattered among the keratinocytes in the deepest epidermal layers are melanocytes, Merkel cells, and Langerhans' cells.

3. From deep to superficial, the strata, or layers of the epidermis, are the basale, spinosum, granulosum, lucidum, and corneum. The stratum lucidum is absent in thin skin. The actively mitotic stratum basale is the source of new cells for epidermal growth. The most superficial layers are increasingly keratinized and less viable.

Dermis (pp. 155–157)

4. The dermis, composed mainly of dense, irregular connective tissue, is well supplied with blood vessels, lymphatic vessels, and nerves. Cutaneous receptors, glands, and hair follicles reside within the dermis.

5. The more superficial papillary layer exhibits dermal papillae that protrude into the epidermis above, as well as dermal ridges, and the epidermal ridges that produce fingerprints.

6. In the deeper, thicker reticular layer, the connective tissue fibers are much more densely interwoven. Less dense regions between the collagen bundles produce cleavage, or tension, lines in the skin. Points of tight dermal attachment to the hypodermis produce dermal folds, or flexure lines.

Skin Color (pp. 157–158)

7. Skin color reflects the amount of pigments (melanin and carotene) in the skin and the oxygenation level of hemoglobin in blood.

8. Melanin production is stimulated by exposure to ultraviolet radiation in sunlight. Melanin, produced by melanocytes and transferred to keratinocytes, protects the keratinocyte nuclei from the damaging effects of UV radiation.

9. Skin color is affected by emotional state. Alterations in normal skin color (jaundice, bronzing, erythema, and others) may indicate certain disease states.

Appendages of the Skin (pp. 158–163)

1. Skin appendages, which derive from the epidermis, include hairs and hair follicles, nails, and glands (sweat and sebaceous).

Sweat (Sudoriferous) Glands (pp. 158–159)

2. Eccrine (merocrine) sweat glands, with a few exceptions, are distributed over the entire body surface. Their primary function is thermoregulation. They are simple coiled tubular glands that secrete a salt solution containing small amounts of other solutes. Their ducts usually empty to the skin surface via pores.

3. Apocrine sweat glands, which may function as scent glands, are found primarily in the axillary and anogenital areas. Their secretion is similar to eccrine secretion, but it also contains proteins and fatty substances on which bacteria thrive.

Sebaceous (Oil) Glands (p. 159)

4. Sebaceous glands occur all over the body surface except for the palms and soles. They are simple alveolar glands; their oily holocrine secretion is called sebum. Sebaceous gland ducts usually empty into hair follicles.

5. Sebum lubricates the skin and hair, prevents water loss from the skin, and acts as a bactericidal agent. Sebaceous glands are activated (at puberty) and controlled by androgens.

Hairs and Hair Follicles (pp. 159–163)

6. A hair, produced by a hair follicle, consists of heavily keratinized cells. A typical hair has a central medulla, a cortex, and an outer cuticle and root and shaft portions. Hair color reflects the amount and kind of melanin present.

7. A hair follicle consists of an inner epithelial root sheath, enclosing the matrix (region of the hair bulb that produces the hair), and an outer connective tissue root sheath derived from the dermis. A hair follicle is richly vascularized and well supplied with nerve fibers. Arrector pili muscles pull the follicles into an upright position and produce goose bumps.

8. Except for hairs of the scalp and around the eyes, hairs formed initially are fine vellus hairs; at puberty, under the influence of androgens, coarser, darker terminal hairs appear in the axillae and genital region.

9. The rate of hair growth varies in different body regions and with sex and age. Differences in life span of hairs account for differences in length on different body regions. Hair thinning reflects factors that lengthen follicular resting periods, age-related atrophy of hair follicles, and a delayed-action gene.

Nails (p. 163)

10. A nail is a scalelike modification of the epidermis that covers the dorsum of a finger (or toe) tip. The actively growing region is the nail matrix.

Functions of the Integumentary System (pp. 163–165)

1. Protection. The skin protects by chemical barriers (the antibacterial nature of sebum, human defensin, cathelicidins, the acid mantle, and the UV shield of melanin), physical barriers (the hardened keratinized and lipid-rich surface), and biological barriers (Langerhans' cells, macrophages, and DNA).

2. Body temperature regulation. The skin vasculature and sweat glands, regulated by the nervous system, play an important role in maintaining body temperature homeostasis.

3. Cutaneous sensation. Cutaneous sensory receptors respond to temperature, touch, pressure, and pain stimuli.

4. Metabolic functions. Vitamin D is synthesized from cholesterol by epidermal cells. Skin cells also play a role in some chemical conversions.

5. Blood reservoir. The extensive vascular supply of the dermis allows the skin to act as a blood reservoir.

6. Excretion. Sweat contains small amounts of nitrogenous wastes and plays a minor role in excretion.

Homeostatic Imbalances of Skin (pp. 165–167, 170)

1. The most common skin disorders result from infections.

Skin Cancer (pp. 165–166)

2. The most common cause of skin cancer is exposure to ultraviolet radiation.

3. Basal cell carcinoma and squamous cell carcinoma are cured if they are removed before metastasis. Melanoma, a cancer of melanocytes, is less common but dangerous.

Burns (pp. 166–167, 170)

4. In severe burns, the initial threat is loss of protein- and electrolyte-rich body fluids, which may lead to circulatory collapse. The second threat is overwhelming bacterial infection.

5. The extent of a burn may be evaluated by using the rule of nines. The severity of burns is indicated by the terms first degree, second degree, and third degree. Third-degree burns require grafting for successful recovery.

Developmental Aspects of the Integumentary System (pp. 170–171)

1. The epidermis develops from embryonic ectoderm; the dermis (and hypodermis) develop from mesoderm.

2. The fetus exhibits a downy lanugo coat. Fetal sebaceous glands produce vernix caseosa, which helps protect the fetus's skin from its watery environment.

3. A newborn's skin is thin. During childhood the skin thickens and more subcutaneous fat is deposited. At puberty, sebaceous glands are activated and terminal hairs appear in greater numbers.

4. In old age, the rate of epidermal cell replacement declines and the skin and hair thin. Skin glands become less active. Loss of collagen and elastin fibers and subcutaneous fat leads to wrinkling; delayed-action genes cause graying and balding. Photodamage is a major cause of skin aging.

Review Questions

Multiple Choice/Matching

(Some questions have more than one correct answer. Select the best answer or answers from the choices given.)

1. Which epidermal cell type is most numerous? (a) keratinocyte, (b) melanocyte, (c) Langerhans' cell, (d) Merkel cell.

2. Which cell functions as part of the immune system? (a) a keratinocyte, (b) a melanocyte, (c) a Langerhans' cell, (d) a Merkel cell.

3. The epidermis provides a physical barrier due largely to the presence of (a) melanin, (b) carotene, (c) collagen, (d) keratin.

4. Skin color is determined by (a) the amount of blood, (b) pigments, (c) oxygenation level of the blood, (d) all of these.

5. The sensations of touch and pressure are picked up by receptors located in (a) the stratum germinativum, (b) the dermis, (c) the hypodermis, (d) the stratum corneum.

6. Which is not a true statement about the papillary layer of the dermis? (a) It produces the pattern for fingerprints, (b) it is most responsible for the toughness of the skin, (c) it contains nerve endings that respond to stimuli, (d) it is highly vascular.

7. Skin surface markings that reflect points of tight dermal attachment to underlying tissues are called (a) tension lines, (b) papillary ridges, (c) flexure lines, (d) epidermal papillae.

8. Which of the following is not an epidermal derivative? (a) hair, (b) sweat gland, (c) sensory receptor, (d) sebaceous gland.

9. You can cut hair without feeling pain because (a) there are no nerves associated with hair, (b) the shaft of the hair consists of dead cells, (c) hair follicles develop from epidermal cells and the epidermis lacks a nerve supply, (d) hair follicles have no source of nourishment and therefore cannot respond.

10. An arrector pili muscle (a) is associated with each sweat gland, (b) can cause a hair to stand up straight, (c) enables each hair to be stretched when wet, (d) provides new cells for continued growth of its associated hair.

11. The product of this type of sweat gland includes protein and lipid substances that become odoriferous as a result of bacterial action: (a) apocrine gland, (b) eccrine gland, (c) sebaceous gland, (d) pancreatic gland.

12. Sebum (a) lubricates the surface of the skin and hair, (b) consists of dead cells and fatty substances, (c) in excess may cause seborrhea, (d) all of these.

13. The rule of nines is helpful clinically in (a) diagnosing skin cancer, (b) estimating the extent of a burn, (c) estimating how serious a cancer is, (d) preventing acne.

Short Answer Essay Questions

14. Which epidermal cells are also called prickle cells? Which contain keratohyaline and lamellated granules?

15. Is a bald man really hairless? Explain.

16. Both newborn infants and aged individuals have very little subcutaneous tissue. How does this affect their sensitivity to cold environmental temperature?

17. You go to the beach to swim on an extremely hot, sunny summer afternoon. Describe two ways in which your integumentary system acts to preserve homeostasis during your outing.

18. Distinguish clearly between first-, second-, and third-degree burns.

19. Describe the process of hair formation, and list several factors that may influence (a) growth cycles and (b) hair texture.

20. What is cyanosis and what does it reflect?

21. Why does skin wrinkle and what factors accelerate the wrinkling process?

22. Explain each of these familiar phenomena in terms of what you learned in this chapter: (a) pimples, (b) dandruff, (c) greasy hair and "shiny nose," (d) stretch marks from gaining weight, (e) freckles, (f) leaving fingerprints.

23. Count Dracula, the most famous vampire, rumored to have killed at least 200,000 people, was based on a real person who lived in eastern Europe about 600 years ago. He was indeed a "monster," although he was not a real vampire. The historical Count Dracula may have suffered from which of the following? (a) porphyria, (b) EB, (c) halitosis, (d) vitiligo. Explain your answer.

24. Why are there no skin cancers that originate from stratum corneum cells?

25. A man got his finger caught in a machine at the factory. The damage was less serious than expected, but the entire nail was torn off his right index finger. The parts lost were the body, root, bed, matrix, and eponychium of the nail. First, define each of these parts. Then, tell if this nail is likely to grow back.

26. On a diagram of the human body, mark off various regions according to the rule of nines. What percentage of the total body surface is affected if the skin over the following body parts is burned? (a) the entire posterior trunk and buttocks, (b) an entire lower limb, (c) the entire front of the left upper limb.

Critical Thinking and Clinical Application Questions

1. Dean, a 40-year-old aging beach boy, is complaining to you that although his suntan made him popular when he was young, now his face is all wrinkled, and he has several darkly pigmented moles that are growing rapidly and are as big as large coins. He shows you the moles, and immediately you think "ABCD." What does that mean and why should he be concerned?

2. Victims of third-degree burns demonstrate the loss of vital functions performed by the skin. What are the two most important problems encountered clinically with such patients? Explain each in terms of the absence of skin.

3. Thelma, 30-year-old resident of a mental hospital, has an abnormal growth of hair on the dorsum of her right index finger. The orderly comments that she gnaws on that finger

continuously. What do you think is the relationship between Thelma's gnawing activity and her hairy finger?

4. A model is concerned about a new scar on her abdomen. She tells her surgeon that there is practically no scar from the appendix operation done when she was 16, but this new gallbladder scar is "gross." Her appendectomy scar is small and obliquely located on the inferior abdominal surface—it is very indistinct. By contrast, the gallbladder scar is large and lumpy and runs at right angles to the central axis of the body trunk. Can you explain why the scars are so different?

5. Mrs. Gaucher received second-degree burns on her abdomen when she dropped a kettle of boiling water. She asked her doctor (worriedly) if she would need to have a skin graft. What do you think he told her?

LOOKING FOR MORE STUDY HELP?
A wide variety of quiz questions, tutorials, and learning exercises are available online at the Anatomy & Physiology Place (www.anatomyandphysiology.com) and, if your instructor has provided you with a MyA&P Course ID number, in MyA&P (www.myaandp.com).

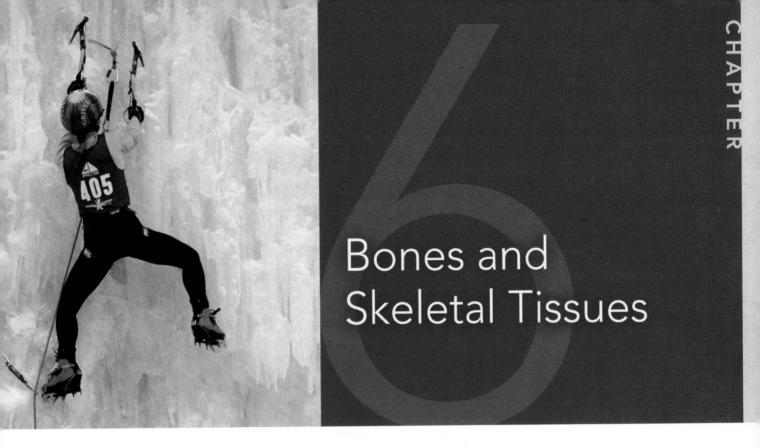

6 Bones and Skeletal Tissues

Skeletal Cartilages (p. 176)

1. Describe the functional properties of the three types of cartilage tissue.
2. Locate the major cartilages of the adult skeleton.
3. Explain how cartilage grows.

Classification of Bones (pp. 176–178)

4. Name the major regions of the skeleton and describe their relative functions.
5. Compare and contrast the structure of the four bone classes and provide examples of each class.

Functions of Bones (pp. 178–179)

6. List and describe five important functions of bones.

Bone Structure (pp. 179–184)

7. Describe the gross anatomy of a typical long bone and a flat bone. Indicate the locations and functions of red and yellow marrow, articular cartilage, periosteum, and endosteum.
8. Indicate the functional importance of bone markings.

9. Describe the histology of compact and spongy bone.
10. Discuss the chemical composition of bone and the relative advantages conferred by the organic and inorganic components.

Bone Development (pp. 184–187)

11. Compare and contrast intramembranous ossification and endochondral ossification.
12. Describe the process of long bone growth that occurs at the epiphyseal plates.

Bone Homeostasis: Remodeling and Repair (pp. 187–193)

13. Compare the locations and remodeling functions of the osteoblasts, osteocytes, and osteoclasts.
14. Explain how hormones and physical stress regulate bone remodeling.
15. Describe the steps of fracture repair.

Homeostatic Imbalances of Bone (pp. 193–195, 198)

16. Contrast the disorders of bone remodeling seen in osteoporosis, osteomalacia, and Paget's disease.

Developmental Aspects of Bones: Timing of Events (p. 198)

17. Describe the timing and cause of changes in bone architecture and bone mass throughout life.

6

All of us have heard the expressions "bone tired" and "bag of bones"—rather unflattering and inaccurate images of one of our most phenomenal tissues and our main skeletal elements. Our brains, not our bones, convey feelings of fatigue. As for "bag of bones," they are indeed more prominent in some of us, but without bones to form our internal skeleton we would all creep along the ground like slugs, lacking any definite shape or form. Along with its bones, the skeleton contains resilient cartilages, which we briefly discuss in this chapter. However, our major focus is the structure and function of bone tissue and the dynamics of its formation and remodeling throughout life.

Skeletal Cartilages

Although the human skeleton is initially made up of cartilages and fibrous membranes, most of these early supports are soon replaced by bone. The few cartilages that remain in adults are found mainly in regions where flexible skeletal tissue is needed.

Basic Structure, Types, and Locations

A **skeletal cartilage** is made of some variety of *cartilage tissue*, which consists primarily of water. The high water content of cartilage accounts for its resilience, that is, its ability to spring back to its original shape after being compressed. The cartilage, which contains no nerves or blood vessels, is surrounded by a layer of dense irregular connective tissue, the *perichondrium* (per″ĭ-kon′dre-um; "around the cartilage"). The perichondrium acts like a girdle to resist outward expansion when the cartilage is compressed. Additionally, the perichondrium contains the blood vessels from which nutrients diffuse through the matrix to reach the cartilage cells. This mode of nutrient delivery limits cartilage thickness.

As described in Chapter 4, there are three types of cartilage tissue in the body: hyaline, elastic, and fibrocartilage. All three types have the same basic components—cells called *chondrocytes*, encased in small cavities (lacunae) within an *extracellular matrix* containing a jellylike ground substance and fibers. The skeletal cartilages contain representatives from all three types (Figure 6.1).

Hyaline cartilages, which look like frosted glass when freshly exposed, provide support with flexibility and resilience. They are the most abundant skeletal cartilages. When viewed under the microscope, their chondrocytes appear spherical (see Figure 4.9f). The only fiber type in their matrix is fine collagen fibers (which, however, are not detectable microscopically). Skeletal hyaline cartilages include (1) *articular cartilages*, which cover the ends of most bones at movable joints; (2) *costal cartilages*, which connect the ribs to the sternum (breastbone); (3) *respiratory cartilages*, which form the skeleton of the *larynx (voicebox)*, and reinforce other respiratory passageways; and (4) *nasal cartilages*, which support the external nose.

Elastic cartilages look very much like hyaline cartilages (see Figure 4.9g), but they contain more stretchy elastic fibers and so are better able to stand up to repeated bending. They are found in only two skeletal locations (Figure 6.1)—the external ear and the epiglottis (the flap that bends to cover the opening of the larynx each time we swallow).

Fibrocartilages are highly compressible and have great tensile strength. The perfect intermediate between hyaline and elastic cartilages, fibrocartilages consist of roughly parallel rows of chondrocytes alternating with thick collagen fibers (see Figure 4.9h). Fibrocartilages occur in sites that are subjected to both heavy pressure and stretch, such as the padlike cartilages (menisci) of the knee and the discs between vertebrae (Figure 6.1).

Growth of Cartilage

Unlike bone, which has a hard matrix, cartilage has a flexible matrix which can accommodate mitosis. Hence, it is the ideal tissue to use to lay down the embryonic skeleton and to provide for new skeletal growth. Cartilage grows in two ways. In **appositional growth** (ap″o-zish′un-al; "growth from outside"), cartilage-forming cells in the surrounding perichondrium secrete new matrix against the external face of the existing cartilage tissue. In **interstitial growth** (in″ter-stish′al; "growth from inside"), the lacunae-bound chondrocytes divide and secrete new matrix, expanding the cartilage from within. Typically, cartilage growth ends during adolescence when the skeleton stops growing.

Under certain conditions—during normal bone growth in youth and during old age—calcium salts may be deposited in the matrix and cause it to harden, a process called calcification. Note, however, that calcified cartilage is *not* bone; cartilage and bone are always distinct tissues.

Classification of Bones

The 206 named bones of the human skeleton are divided into two groups: axial and appendicular. The **axial skeleton** forms the long axis of the body and includes the bones of the skull, vertebral column, and rib cage. Generally speaking these bones are most involved in protecting, supporting, or carrying other body parts. The **appendicular skeleton** (ap″en-dik′u-lar) consists of the bones of the upper and lower limbs

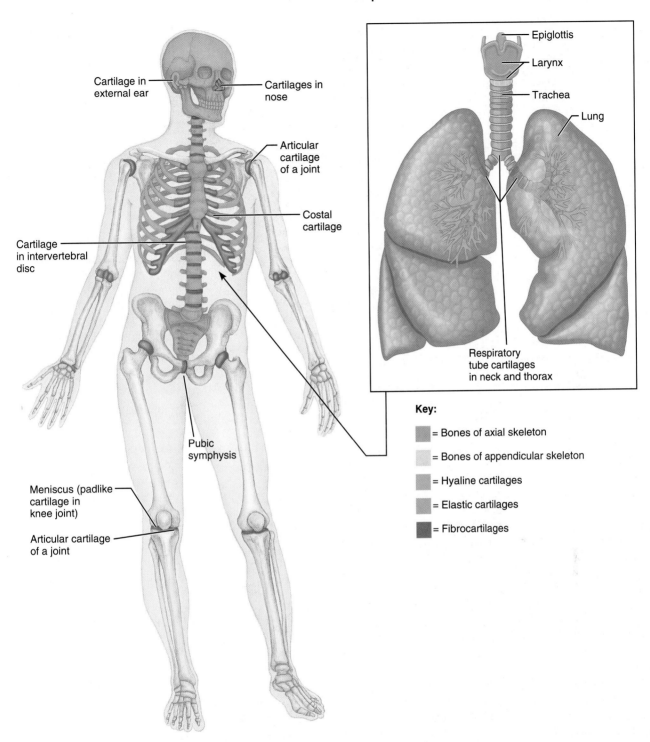

Key:

= Bones of axial skeleton

= Bones of appendicular skeleton

= Hyaline cartilages

= Elastic cartilages

= Fibrocartilages

FIGURE 6.1 **The bones and cartilages of the human skeleton.**

and the girdles (shoulder bones and hip bones) that attach the limbs to the axial skeleton. Bones of the limbs help to get us from place to place (locomotion) and to manipulate our environment. An overview of the human skeleton appears in Figure 6.1.

Bones come in many sizes and shapes. For example, the pisiform bone of the wrist is the size and shape of a pea, whereas the femur (thigh bone) is nearly 2 feet long in some people and has a large ball-shaped head. The unique shape of each bone fulfills a particular need. The femur, for example, withstands great weight and pressure, and its hollow-cylinder design provides maximum strength with minimum weight.

For the most part, bones are classified by their shape as long, short, flat, and irregular (Figure 6.2).

6

(a) Long bone (humerus)

(b) Short bone (triquetral)

(c) Flat bone (sternum)

(d) Irregular bone (vertebra),
left lateral view

FIGURE 6.2 **Classification of bones on the basis of shape.**

1. **Long bones,** as their name suggests, are considerably longer than they are wide. A long bone has a shaft plus two ends. All limb bones except the patella (kneecap) and the wrist and ankle bones are long bones. Notice that these bones are named for their elongated shape, *not* their overall size. The three bones in each of your fingers are long bones, even though they are very small.

2. **Short bones** are roughly cube shaped. The bones of the wrist and ankle are examples.

  Sesamoid bones (ses'ah-moid; "shaped like a sesame seed") are a special type of short bone that form in a tendon (for example, the patella). They vary in size and number in different individuals. Some sesamoid bones clearly act to alter the direction of pull of a tendon; the function of others is not known.

3. **Flat bones** are thin, flattened, and usually a bit curved. The sternum (breastbone), scapulae (shoulder blades), ribs, and most skull bones are flat bones.

4. **Irregular bones** have complicated shapes that fit none of the preceding classes. Examples include the vertebrae and the hip bones.

Functions of Bones

Besides contributing to body shape and form, our bones perform several important functions:

1. **Support.** Bones provide a framework that supports the body and cradles its soft organs. For example, bones of lower limbs act as pillars to support the body trunk when we stand, and the rib cage supports the thoracic wall.

2. Protection. The fused bones of the skull protect the brain. The vertebrae surround the spinal cord, and the rib cage helps protect the vital organs of the thorax.

3. Movement. Skeletal muscles, which attach to bones by tendons, use bones as levers to move the body and its parts. As a result, we can walk, grasp objects, and breathe. The design of joints determine the types of movement possible.

4. Mineral and growth factor storage. Bone is a reservoir for minerals, most importantly calcium and phosphate. The stored minerals are released into the bloodstream as needed for distribution to all parts of the body. Indeed, "deposits" and "withdrawals" of minerals to and from the bones go on almost continuously. Additionally, mineralized bone matrix stores important growth factors such as insulin-like growth factors, transforming growth factor, bone morphogenic proteins, and others.

5. Blood cell formation. Most blood cell formation, or *hematopoiesis* (hem"ah-to-poi-e′sis), occurs in the marrow cavities of certain bones.

Bone Structure

Because they contain various types of tissue, bones are *organs*. (Recall that an organ contains several different tissues.) Although bone (osseous) tissue dominates bones, they also contain nervous tissue in their nerves, cartilage in their articular cartilages, fibrous connective tissue lining their cavities, and muscle and epithelial tissues in their blood vessels. We will consider bone structure at three levels: gross, microscopic, and chemical.

Gross Anatomy

Bone Markings

The external surfaces of bones are rarely smooth and featureless. Instead, they display projections, depressions, and openings that serve as sites of muscle, ligament, and tendon attachment, as joint surfaces, or as conduits for blood vessels and nerves. These **bone markings** are named in different ways. Projections (bulges) that grow outward from the bone surface include heads, trochanters, spines, and others, each having distinguishing features and functions. In most cases, bone projections are indications of the stresses created by muscles attached to and pulling on them or are modified surfaces where bones meet and form joints. Depressions and openings include fossae, sinuses, foramina, and grooves; these usually serve to allow passage of nerves and blood vessels. The most important types of bone markings are described in Table 6.1. You should familiarize yourself with these terms because you will meet them again as identifying marks of the individual bones studied in the lab.

TABLE 6.1	Bone Markings
NAME OF BONE MARKING	**DESCRIPTION**
PROJECTIONS THAT ARE SITES OF MUSCLE AND LIGAMENT ATTACHMENT	
Tuberosity (too"bĕ-ros′ĭ-te)	Large rounded projection; may be roughened
Crest	Narrow ridge of bone; usually prominent
Trochanter (tro-kan′ter)	Very large, blunt, irregularly shaped process (the only examples are on the femur)
Line	Narrow ridge of bone; less prominent than a crest
Tubercle (too′ber-kl)	Small rounded projection or process
Epicondyle (ep″ĭ-kon′dĭl)	Raised area on or above a condyle
Spine	Sharp, slender, often pointed projection
Process	Any bony prominence
PROJECTIONS THAT HELP TO FORM JOINTS	
Head	Bony expansion carried on a narrow neck
Facet	Smooth, nearly flat articular surface
Condyle (kon′dĭl)	Rounded articular projection
Ramus (ra′mus)	Armlike bar of bone
DEPRESSIONS AND OPENINGS ALLOWING BLOOD VESSELS AND NERVES TO PASS	
Meatus (me-a′tus)	Canal-like passageway
Sinus	Cavity within a bone, filled with air and lined with mucous membrane
Fossa (fos′ah)	Shallow, basinlike depression in a bone, often serving as an articular surface
Groove	Furrow
Fissure	Narrow, slitlike opening
Foramen (fo-ra′men)	Round or oval opening through a bone

Bone Textures: Compact and Spongy Bone

Every bone has a dense outer layer that looks smooth and solid to the naked eye. This external layer is **compact bone** (Figures 6.3 and 6.4). Internal to this is **spongy bone** (also called *cancellous bone*), a honeycomb of small needle-like or flat pieces called

FIGURE 6.3   **The structure of a long bone (humerus of arm). (a)** Anterior view with bone sectioned frontally to show the interior at the proximal end. **(b)** Enlarged view of spongy bone and compact bone of the epiphysis of (a). **(c)** Enlarged cross-sectional view of the shaft (diaphysis) of (a). Note that the external surface of the diaphysis is covered by periosteum, but the articular surface of the epiphysis is covered with hyaline cartilage.

trabeculae (trah-bek'u-le; "little beams"). In living bones the open spaces between trabeculae are filled with red or yellow bone marrow.

Structure of a Typical Long Bone

With few exceptions, all long bones have the same general structure (Figure 6.3).

Diaphysis   A tubular **diaphysis** (di-af'ĭ-sis; *dia* = through, *physis* = growth), or shaft, forms the long axis of the bone. It is constructed of a relatively thick *collar* of compact bone that surrounds a central **medullary cavity** (med'u-lar-e; "middle") or *marrow cavity*. In adults, the medullary cavity contains fat (yellow marrow) and is called the **yellow bone marrow cavity.**

Epiphyses   The **epiphyses** (e-pif'ĭ-sēz; singular: epiphysis) are the bone ends (*epi* = upon). In many

cases, they are more expanded than the diaphysis. Compact bone forms the exterior of epiphyses; their interior contains spongy bone. The joint surface of each epiphysis is covered with a thin layer of articular (hyaline) cartilage, which cushions the opposing bone ends during joint movement and absorbs stress. Between the diaphysis and each epiphysis of an adult long bone is an **epiphyseal line,** a remnant of the **epiphyseal plate,** a disc of hyaline cartilage that grows during childhood to lengthen the bone. The region where the diaphysis and epiphysis meet, whether it is the epiphyseal plate or line, is sometimes called the *metaphysis.*

Membranes   A third structural feature of long bones is membranes. The external surface of the entire bone except the joint surfaces is covered by a glistening white, double-layered membrane called the **periosteum** (per"e-os'te-um; *peri* = around, *osteo* = bone). The outer *fibrous layer* is dense irregular connective tissue. The inner *osteogenic layer,* abutting the bone surface, consists primarily of bone-forming cells, **osteoblasts** (os′te-o-blasts; "bone germinators"), and bone-destroying cells, **osteoclasts** ("bone breakers").

The periosteum is richly supplied with nerve fibers, lymphatic vessels, and blood vessels, which enter the diaphysis via a **nutrient foramen** (fo-ra′min; "opening").

The periosteum is secured to the underlying bone by *perforating (Sharpey's) fibers* (Figure 6.3), tufts of collagen fibers that extend from its fibrous layer into the bone matrix. The periosteum also provides anchoring points for tendons and ligaments. At these points the perforating fibers are exceptionally dense.

Internal bone surfaces are covered with a delicate connective tissue membrane called the **endosteum** (en-dos′te-um; "within the bone"). The endosteum (Figure 6.3) covers the trabeculae of spongy bone and lines the canals that pass through the compact bone. Like the periosteum, the endosteum contains both osteoblasts and osteoclasts.

Structure of Short, Irregular, and Flat Bones

Short, irregular, and flat bones share a simple design: They all consist of thin plates of periosteum-covered compact bone on the outside and endosteum-covered spongy bone within. However, these bones are not cylindrical and so they have no shaft or epiphyses. They contain bone marrow (between their trabeculae), but no significant marrow cavity is present.

Figure 6.4 shows a typical flat bone of the skull. In flat bones, the spongy bone is called the **diploë** (dip′lo-e; "folded") and the whole arrangement resembles a stiffened sandwich.

Location of Hematopoietic Tissue in Bones

Hematopoietic tissue, **red marrow,** is typically found within the trabecular cavities of spongy bone of long bones and in the diploë of flat bones. For this reason, both these cavities are often referred to as **red marrow cavities.** In newborn infants, the medullary cavity of the diaphysis and all areas of spongy bone contain red bone marrow. In most adult long bones, the fat-containing medullary cavity extends well into the epiphysis, and little red marrow is present in the spongy bone cavities. Hence, blood cell production in adult long bones routinely occurs only in the heads of the femur and humerus (the long bone of the arm). The red marrow found in the diploë of flat bones (such as the sternum) and in some irregular bones (such as the hip bone) is much more active in hematopoiesis, and these are the sites routinely used for obtaining red marrow samples when problems with the blood-forming tissue are suspected. However,

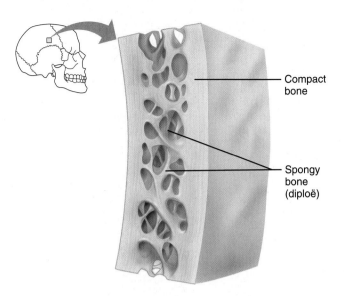

FIGURE 6.4 **Structure of a flat bone.** Flat bones consist of a layer of spongy bone (the diploë) sandwiched between two thin layers of compact bone.

— Compact bone

— Spongy bone (diploë)

yellow marrow in the medullary cavity can revert to red marrow if a person becomes very anemic and needs enhanced red blood cell production.

Microscopic Anatomy of Bone

Essentially, four major cell types populate bone tissue: osteogenic cells, osteoblasts, osteocytes, and osteoclasts. These, like other connective tissue cells, are surrounded by an extracellular matrix of their making. The **osteogenic cells,** also called **osteoprogenitor cells,** are actively mitotic stem cells found in the membranous periosteum and endosteum. Some of their progeny differentiate into osteoblasts (bone-forming cells) while others persist as bone stem cells to provide osteoblasts in the future. The structure and function of the remaining three types of bone cells are described below.

Compact Bone

Although compact bone looks dense and solid, a microscope reveals that it is riddled with passageways that serve as conduits for nerves, blood vessels, and lymphatic vessels (see Figure 6.6). The structural unit of compact bone is called either the **osteon** (os′te-on) or the **Haversian system** (ha-ver′zhen). Each osteon is an elongated cylinder oriented parallel to the long axis of the bone. Functionally, osteons are tiny weight-bearing pillars. As shown in the "exploded" view in Figure 6.5, an osteon is a group of hollow tubes of bone matrix, one placed outside the next like the growth rings of a tree trunk. Each matrix tube is a **lamella** (lah-mel′ah; "little plate"), and for this reason compact bone is often called **lamellar**

Structures
in the
central
canal

Artery with
capillaries

Vein

Nerve fiber

Lamellae

Collagen
fibers

Twisting
force

FIGURE 6.5 **A single osteon.** The osteon is drawn as if pulled out like a telescope to illustrate the individual lamellae. The slanted lines in each lamella indicate the direction of its collagen fibers.

bone. Although all of the collagen fibers in a particular lamella run in a single direction, the collagen fibers in adjacent lamellae always run in opposite directions. This alternating pattern is beautifully designed to withstand torsion stresses—the adjacent lamellae reinforce one another to resist twisting. You can think of the osteon's design as a "twister resister." Collagen fibers are not the only part of bone lamellae that are beautifully ordered. The tiny crystals of bone salts align with the collagen fibers and thus also alternate their direction in adjacent lamellae.

Running through the core of each osteon is the **central,** or **Haversian, canal** containing small blood vessels and nerve fibers that serve the needs of the osteon's cells. Canals of a second type called **perforating canals,** or **Volkmann's canals** (folk'mahnz), lie at right angles to the long axis of the bone and connect the blood and nerve supply of the periosteum to those in the central canals and the medullary cavity (Figure 6.6a). Like all other internal bone cavities, these canals are lined with endosteum.

Spider-shaped **osteocytes** (mature bone cells) occupy **lacunae** (*lac* = hollow; *una* = little) at the junctions of the lamellae. Hairlike canals called **canaliculi** (kan"ah-lik'u-li) connect the lacunae to each other and to the central canal. The manner in which canaliculi are formed is interesting. When bone is being formed, the osteoblasts secreting bone matrix surround blood vessels and maintain contact with one another by tentacle-like projections containing gap junctions. Then, as the newly secreted

matrix hardens and the maturing cells become trapped within it, a system of tiny canals—the canaliculi, filled with tissue fluid and containing the osteocyte extensions—is formed. The canaliculi tie all the osteocytes in an osteon together, permitting nutrients and wastes to be relayed from one osteocyte to the next throughout the osteon. Although bone matrix is hard and impermeable to nutrients, its canaliculi and cell-to-cell relays (via gap junctions) allow bone cells to be well nourished. One function of osteocytes is to maintain the bone matrix. If they die, the surrounding matrix is resorbed. The osteocytes also act as stress or strain "sensors" in cases of bone deformation or other damaging stimuli. They communicate this information to the cells responsible for bone remodeling (osteoblasts and osteoclasts) so that countermeasures can be taken or repairs made. The bone-destroying osteoclast is discussed on p. 188 in conjunction with the topic of bone remodeling.

Not all the lamellae in compact bone are part of osteons. Lying between intact osteons are incomplete lamellae called **interstitial lamellae** (in"ter-stish'al) (Figure 6.6c). These either fill the gaps between forming osteons or are remnants of osteons that have been cut through by bone remodeling (discussed later). **Circumferential lamellae,** located just deep to the periosteum and just superficial to the endosteum, extend around the entire circumference of the diaphysis (Figure 6.6a) and effectively resist twisting of the long bone.

Spongy Bone

In contrast to compact bone, spongy bone looks like a poorly organized, even haphazard, tissue (Figure 6.4 and Figure 6.3b). However, the trabeculae in spongy bone align precisely along lines of stress and help the bone resist stress as much as possible. Thus, these tiny bone struts are as carefully positioned as the flying buttresses of a Gothic cathedral.

Only a few cells thick, trabeculae contain irregularly arranged lamellae and osteocytes interconnected by canaliculi. No osteons are present. Nutrients reach the osteocytes of spongy bone by diffusing through the canaliculi from capillaries in the endosteum surrounding the trabeculae.

Chemical Composition of Bone

Bone has both organic and inorganic components. Its *organic components* include the cells (osteogenic cells, osteoblasts, osteocytes, and osteoclasts) and **osteoid** (os'te-oid), the organic part of the matrix. Osteoid, which makes up approximately one-third of the matrix, includes ground substance (composed of proteoglycans and glycoproteins) and collagen fibers,

Q *What membrane lines the internal canals and covers the trabeculae of spongy bone?*

FIGURE 6.6 **Microscopic anatomy of compact bone. (a)** Diagrammatic view of a pie-shaped segment of compact bone. **(b)** Close-up of a portion of one osteon. Note the position of osteocytes in the lacunae. **(c)** Photomicrograph of a cross-sectional view of an osteon (140×).

both of which are made and secreted by osteoblasts. These organic substances, particularly collagen, contribute not only to a bone's structure but also to the flexibility and great tensile strength that allow the bone to resist stretch and twisting. Bone's exceptional toughness and tensile strength has been the subject of intense research. It now appears that this resilience comes from the presence of *sacrificial bonds* in or between collagen molecules that break easily on impact, dissipating energy to prevent the force from rising to a fracture value. In the absence of continued or additional trauma, most of the sacrificial bonds re-form.

The balance of bone tissue (65% by mass) consists of inorganic *hydroxyapatites* (hi-drok″se-ap′ah-tītz), or *mineral salts*, largely calcium phosphates present in the form of tiny, tightly packed crystals in and around the collagen fibers in the extracellular matrix. The crystals account for the most notable characteristic of bone—its exceptional hardness, which allows it to resist compression.

A *Endosteum.*

(1) An ossification center appears in the fibrous connective tissue membrane.

- Selected centrally located mesenchymal cells cluster and differentiate into osteoblasts, forming an ossification center.

(2) Bone matrix (osteoid) is secreted within the fibrous membrane.

- Osteoblasts begin to secrete osteoid, which is mineralized within a few days.
- Trapped osteoblasts become osteocytes.

(3) Woven bone and periosteum form.

- Accumulating osteoid is laid down between embryonic blood vessels, which form a random network. The result is a network (instead of lamellae) of trabeculae.
- Vascularized mesenchyme condenses on the external face of the woven bone and becomes the periosteum.

(4) Bone collar of compact bone forms and red marrow appears.

- Trabeculae just deep to the periosteum thicken, forming a woven bone collar that is later replaced with mature lamellar bone.
- Spongy bone (diploë), consisting of distinct trabeculae, persists internally and its vascular tissue becomes red marrow.

The proper combination of organic and inorganic matrix elements allows bones to be exceedingly durable and strong without being brittle. Healthy bone is half as strong as steel in resisting compression and fully as strong as steel in resisting tension.

Because of the salts they contain, bones last long after death and provide an enduring "monument." In fact, skeletal remains many centuries old have revealed the shapes and sizes of ancient peoples, the kinds of work they did, and many of the ailments they suffered from (arthritis, for example).

Bone Development

Ossification and **osteogenesis** (os"te-o-jen'ĕ-sis) are synonyms meaning the process of bone formation (*os* = bone, *genesis* = beginning). In embryos this process leads to the *formation of the bony skeleton*. Later another form of ossification known as *bone growth* goes on until early adulthood as the body continues to increase in size. Bones are capable of growing in thickness throughout life. However, ossification in adults serves mainly for bone *remodeling* and repair.

Formation of the Bony Skeleton

Before week 8, the skeleton of a human embryo is constructed entirely from fibrous membranes and hyaline cartilage. Bone tissue begins to develop at about this time and eventually replaces most of the existing fibrous or cartilage structures. When a bone develops from a fibrous membrane, the process is *intramembranous ossification,* and the bone is called a **membrane bone.** Bone development by replacing hyaline cartilage is called *endochondral ossification* (*endo* = within, *chondro* = cartilage), and the resulting bone is called a **cartilage,** or **endochondral, bone.** The beauty of using structures (membranes and cartilages) that are flexible and resilient to fashion the embryonic skeleton is that they can accommodate mitosis. Were the early skeleton composed of bone tissue from the onset, growth would be much more difficult.

Intramembranous Ossification

Intramembranous ossification (Figure 6.7) results in the formation of cranial bones of the skull (frontal, parietal, occipital, and temporal bones) and the clavicles. All bones formed by this process are flat bones. Fibrous connective tissue membranes

FIGURE 6.7 **Intramembranous ossification.** Diagrams (3) and (4) represent much lower magnification than diagrams (1) and (2).

Q *What is the composition of the periosteal bud?*

FIGURE 6.8 **Endochondral ossification in a long bone.** Stages ①–③ occur during the fetal period (week 9 to month 9 of development). Stage ④ represents the situation shortly before or just after birth. Stage ⑤ is the process of long bone growth during childhood and adolescence.

formed by *mesenchymal cells* are the supporting structures on which ossification begins at about week 8 of development. Essentially, the process involves the four major steps depicted in Figure 6.7.

Endochondral Ossification

Except for the clavicles, essentially all bones of the skeleton below the base of the skull form by **endochondral ossification** (en"do-kon'dral). This process, which begins in the second month of development, uses hyaline cartilage "bones" formed earlier as models, or patterns, for bone construction. It is more complex than intramembranous ossification because the hyaline cartilage must be broken down as ossification proceeds. We will use a forming long bone as our example.

The formation of a long bone typically begins in the center of the hyaline cartilage shaft at a region called the **primary ossification center.** First, the perichondrium covering the hyaline cartilage "bone" is infiltrated with blood vessels, converting it to a vascularized periosteum. As a result of this change

in nutrition, the underlying mesenchymal cells specialize into osteoblasts. The stage is now set for ossification to begin, as illustrated in Figure 6.8.

① **A bone collar forms around the diaphysis of the hyaline cartilage model.** Osteoblasts of the newly converted periosteum secrete osteoid against the hyaline cartilage diaphysis, encasing it in a bone collar.

② **Cartilage in the center of the diaphysis calcifies and then cavitates.** As the bone collar forms, chondrocytes within the shaft hypertrophy (enlarge) and signal the surrounding cartilage matrix to calcify. Because calcified cartilage matrix is impermeable to diffusing nutrients, the chondrocytes die and the matrix begins to deteriorate. Although this deterioration opens up cavities, the hyaline cartilage model is stabilized by the bone collar. Elsewhere, the cartilage remains healthy and continues to grow briskly, causing the cartilage model to elongate.

③ **The periosteal bud invades the internal cavities and spongy bone forms.** In month 3, the forming cavities are invaded by a collection of elements called the **periosteal bud,** which contains a nutrient artery and vein, lymphatics, nerve fibers, red marrow elements, osteoblasts, and osteoclasts. The entering osteoclasts partially erode the calcified cartilage matrix, and the osteoblasts secrete osteoid

A *Blood vessels, nerve fibers, lymph vessels, osteoblasts, osteoclasts, and red marrow elements.*

- **Resting (quiescent) zone**

- **Growth (proliferation) zone**
  Cartilage cells undergo mitosis

- **Hypertrophic zone**
  Older cartilage cells enlarge

- **Calcification zone**
  Matrix becomes calcified; cartilage cells die; matrix begins deteriorating

- **Ossification (osteogenic) zone**
  New bone formation is occurring

Calcified cartilage spicule

Osteoblast depositing bone matrix

Osseous tissue (bone) covering cartilage spicules

FIGURE 6.9   **Growth in length of a long bone.** The side of the epiphyseal plate facing the epiphysis (distal face) contains resting cartilage cells. The cells of the epiphyseal plate proximal to the resting cartilage area are arranged in four zones—growth, hypertrophic, calcification, and ossification (80×).

around the remaining fragments of hyaline cartilage, forming bone-covered cartilage trabeculae. In this way, the earliest version of spongy bone in a developing long bone forms.

④ **The diaphysis elongates and a medullary cavity forms.** As the primary ossification center enlarges, osteoclasts break down the newly formed spongy bone and open up a medullary cavity in the center of the diaphysis. Throughout the fetal period, the rapidly growing epiphyses consist only of cartilage, and the hyaline cartilage models continue to elongate by division of viable cartilage cells at the epiphyses. Because cartilage is calcifying, being eroded, and then being replaced by bony spicules on the epiphyseal surfaces facing the medullary cavity, ossification "chases" cartilage formation along the length of the shaft.

⑤ **The epiphyses ossify.** When we are born, most of our long bones have a bony diaphysis surrounding

remnants of spongy bone, a widening medullary cavity, and two cartilaginous epiphyses. Shortly before or after birth, **secondary ossification centers** appear in one or both epiphyses, and the epiphyses gain bony tissue. (Typically, the large long bones form secondary centers in both epiphyses, whereas the small long bones form only one secondary ossification center.) The cartilage in the center of the epiphysis calcifies and deteriorates, opening up cavities that allow a periosteal bud to enter. Then bone trabeculae appear, just as they did earlier in the primary ossification center. (In short bones, only the primary ossification center is formed. Most irregular bones develop from several distinct ossification centers.)

Secondary ossification reproduces almost exactly the events of primary ossification, except that the spongy bone in the interior is retained and no medullary cavity forms in the epiphyses. When secondary ossification is complete, hyaline cartilage remains only at two places: (1) on the epiphyseal surfaces, as the *articular cartilages*, and (2) at the junction of the diaphysis and epiphysis, where it forms the *epiphyseal plates*.

Postnatal Bone Growth

During infancy and youth, long bones lengthen entirely by interstitial growth of the epiphyseal plates, and all bones grow in thickness by appositional growth. Most bones stop growing during adolescence; however, some facial bones, such as those of the nose and lower jaw, continue to grow almost imperceptibly throughout life.

Growth in Length of Long Bones

Longitudinal bone growth mimics many of the events of endochondral ossification. On the side of the epiphyseal plate facing the epiphysis, a region called the *resting* or *quiescent zone*, the cartilage is relatively inactive. But the epiphyseal plate cartilage abutting the diaphysis organizes into a pattern that allows fast, efficient growth. The cartilage cells here form tall columns, like coins in a stack. The cells at the "top" (epiphysis-facing side) of the stack abutting the resting zone comprise the *growth zone* (Figure 6.9). These cells divide quickly, pushing the epiphysis away from the diaphysis, causing the entire long bone to lengthen.

Meanwhile, the older chondrocytes in the stack, which are closer to the diaphysis (*hypertrophic zone* in Figure 6.9), hypertrophy, and their lacunae erode and enlarge. Subsequently, the surrounding cartilage matrix calcifies and these chondrocytes die and deteriorate, producing the *calcification zone*. This leaves long spicules of calcified cartilage at the epiphysis-diaphysis junction, which look like stalactites hanging from the roof of a cave. These calcified spicules ultimately become part of the *ossification* or *osteogenic zone*, and are invaded by marrow elements from the medullary cavity. The cartilage spicules are partly eroded by osteoclasts and then quickly covered with bone matrix by osteoblasts, forming spongy bone. The spicule tips are eventually digested by osteoclasts; thus, the medullary cavity also grows longer as the long bone lengthens. During growth, the epiphyseal plate maintains a constant thickness because the rate of cartilage growth on its epiphysis-facing side is balanced by its replacement with bony tissue on its diaphysis-facing side.

Longitudinal growth is accompanied by almost continuous remodeling of the epiphyseal ends to maintain the proper proportions between the diaphysis and epiphyses (Figure 6.10). Bone remodeling, involving both new bone formation and bone resorption (destruction), is described in more detail below in conjunction with the changes that occur in adult bones.

As adolescence draws to an end, the chondroblasts of the epiphyseal plates divide less often and the plates become thinner and thinner until they are entirely replaced by bone tissue. Longitudinal bone growth ends when the bone of the epiphysis and diaphysis fuses. This process, called *epiphyseal plate closure*, happens at about 18 years of age in females and 21 years of age in males. However, as noted earlier, an adult bone can still increase in diameter or thickness by appositional growth if stressed by excessive muscle activity or body weight.

Growth in Width (Thickness)

Growing bones widen as they lengthen. As with cartilages, bones increase in thickness or, in the case of long bones, diameter, by appositional growth. Osteoblasts beneath the periosteum secrete bone matrix on the external bone surface as osteoclasts on the endosteal surface of the diaphysis remove bone (see Figure 6.10). However, there is normally slightly less breaking down than building up. This unequal process produces a thicker, stronger bone but prevents it from becoming too heavy.

Hormonal Regulation of Bone Growth

The growth of bones that occurs until young adulthood is exquisitely controlled by a symphony of hormones. During infancy and childhood, the single most important stimulus of epiphyseal plate activity is *growth hormone* released by the anterior pituitary gland. Thyroid hormones modulate the activity of growth hormone, ensuring that the skeleton has proper proportions as it grows. At puberty, male and female sex hormones (testosterone and estrogens, respectively) are released in increasing amounts.

Q *What would a long bone look like at the end of adolescence if remodeling did not occur?*

FIGURE 6.10 **Long bone growth and remodeling during youth.** The events at the left depict endochondral ossification that occurs at the articular cartilages and epiphyseal plates as the bone grows in length. Events at the right show bone remodeling during long bone growth to maintain proper bone proportions.

Initially these sex hormones promote the growth spurt typical of adolescence, as well as the masculinization or feminization of specific parts of the skeleton. Later the hormones induce epiphyseal plate closure, ending longitudinal bone growth.

Excesses or deficits of any of these hormones can result in obviously abnormal skeletal growth. For example, hypersecretion of growth hormone in children results in excessive height (gigantism), and deficits of growth hormone or thyroid hormone produce characteristic types of dwarfism.

Bone Homeostasis: Remodeling and Repair

Bones appear to be the most lifeless of body organs, and may even summon images of a graveyard. But as you have just learned, appearances can be deceiving. Bone is a dynamic and active tissue, and small-scale changes in bone architecture occur continually. Every week we recycle 5–7% of our bone mass, and as much as half a gram of calcium may enter or leave the adult skeleton each day! Spongy bone is replaced every three to four years; compact bone, every ten years or so. This is fortunate because when bone

A *Its shaft would still be its original length, and it would have two very elongated and expanded ends (epiphyses).*

remains in place for long periods the calcium crystallizes and becomes more brittle—ripe conditions for fracture. And when we break bones—the most common disorder of bone homeostasis—they undergo a remarkable process of self-repair.

Bone Remodeling

In the adult skeleton, bone deposit and bone resorption (removal) occur both at the surface of the periosteum and the surface of the endosteum. Together, the two processes constitute **bone remodeling,** and they are coupled and coordinated by "packets" of adjacent osteoblasts and osteoclasts called *remodeling units* (with help from the stress-sensing osteocytes). In healthy young adults, total bone mass remains constant, an indication that the rates of bone deposit and resorption are essentially equal. Remodeling does not occur uniformly, however. For example, the distal part of the femur, or thigh bone, is fully replaced every five to six months, whereas its shaft is altered much more slowly.

Bone deposit occurs wherever bone is injured or added bone strength is required. For optimal bone deposit, a healthy diet rich in proteins, vitamin C, vitamin D, vitamin A, and several minerals (calcium, phosphorus, magnesium, and manganese, to name a few) is essential.

New matrix deposits by osteocytes are marked by the presence of an *osteoid seam*, an unmineralized band of gauzy-looking bone matrix 10–12 μm wide. Between the osteoid seam and the older mineralized bone, there is an abrupt transition called the *calcification front*. Because the osteoid seam is always of constant width and the change from unmineralized to mineralized matrix is sudden, it seems that the osteoid must mature for about a week before it can calcify. The precise trigger for calcification is still controversial. However, one critical factor is the product of the local concentrations of calcium and phosphate (P_i) ions (the $Ca^{2+} \cdot P_i$ product). When this product reaches a certain level, tiny crystals of hydroxyapatite form spontaneously and then catalyze further crystallization of calcium salts in the area. Other factors involved are matrix proteins that bind and concentrate calcium, and the enzyme *alkaline phosphatase* (shed by the osteoblasts), which is essential for mineralization. Once proper conditions are present, calcium salts are deposited all at once and with great precision throughout the "matured" matrix.

Bone resorption is accomplished by osteoclasts, giant multinucleate cells that arise from the same hematopoietic stem cells that differentiate into macrophages. Osteoclasts move along a bone surface, digging grooves as they break down the bone matrix. The part of the osteoclast that touches the bone is highly folded to form a ruffled membrane that clings tightly to the bone, sealing off the area of bone destruction. The ruffled border secretes (1) *lysosomal enzymes* that digest the organic matrix and (2) *hydrochloric acid* that converts the calcium salts into soluble forms that pass easily into solution. Osteoclasts may also phagocytize the demineralized matrix and dead osteocytes. The digested matrix end products, growth factors, and dissolved minerals are then endocytosed, transported across the osteoclast (by transcytosis), and released at the opposite side where they enter first the interstitial fluid and then the blood. Although there is much to learn about osteoclast activation, proteins secreted by T cells of the immune system appear to be important.

Control of Remodeling

The remodeling that goes on continuously in the skeleton is regulated by two control loops that serve different "masters." One is a negative feedback hormonal mechanism that maintains Ca^{2+} homeostasis in the blood. The other involves responses to mechanical and gravitational forces acting on the skeleton.

The hormonal mechanism becomes much more meaningful when you understand calcium's importance in the body. Ionic calcium is necessary for an amazing number of physiological processes, including transmission of nerve impulses, muscle contraction, blood coagulation, secretion by glands and nerve cells, and cell division. The human body contains 1200–1400 g of calcium, more than 99% present as bone minerals. Most of the remainder is in body cells. Less than 1.5 g is present in blood, and the hormonal control loop normally maintains blood Ca^{2+} within the very narrow range of 9–11 mg per dl (100 ml) of blood. Calcium is absorbed from the intestine under the control of vitamin D metabolites. The daily calcium requirement is 400–800 mg from birth until the age of 10, and 1200–1500 mg from ages 11 to 24.

Hormonal Mechanism The hormonal mechanism primarily involves **parathyroid hormone (PTH),** produced by the parathyroid glands. To a much lesser extent it involves **calcitonin** (kal"sĭ-to'nin), produced by parafollicular cells (C cells) of the thyroid gland (Figure 6.11). PTH is released when blood levels of ionic calcium decline. The increased PTH level stimulates osteoclasts to resorb bone, releasing calcium to the blood. Osteoclasts are no respecters of matrix age. When activated, they break down both old and new matrix. Only osteoid, which lacks calcium salts, escapes digestion. As blood concentrations of calcium rise, the stimulus for PTH release ends. The decline of PTH reverses its effects and causes blood Ca^{2+} levels to fall.

Q *What is the result of the negative feedback of calcitonin (particularly in children)?*

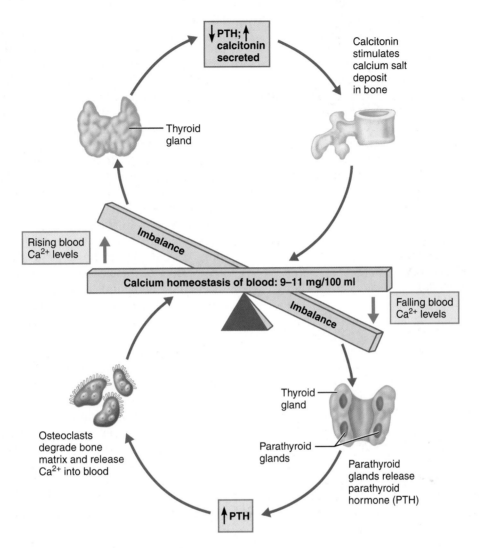

PTH; ↑ calcitonin secreted

Calcitonin stimulates calcium salt deposit in bone

Thyroid gland

Rising blood Ca²⁺ levels

Imbalance

Calcium homeostasis of blood: 9–11 mg/100 ml

Imbalance

Falling blood Ca²⁺ levels

Thyroid gland

Parathyroid glands

Parathyroid glands release parathyroid hormone (PTH)

Osteoclasts degrade bone matrix and release Ca²⁺ into blood

↑ PTH

FIGURE 6.11 **Hormonal control of blood calcium levels.** PTH and to a lesser extent calcitonin operate in negative feedback fashion to control blood calcium levels.

Calcitonin, secreted when blood calcium levels rise, inhibits bone resorption and encourages calcium salt deposit in bone matrix, effectively reducing blood calcium levels. As blood calcium levels fall, calcitonin release wanes. Calcitonin is most effective in reducing blood Ca²⁺ levels in children. In adults, its effects appear to be negligible.

These hormonal controls act not to preserve the skeleton's strength or well-being but rather to maintain blood calcium homeostasis. In fact, if blood calcium levels are low for an extended time, the bones become so demineralized that they develop large, punched-out-

looking holes. Thus, the bones serve as a storehouse from which ionic calcium is drawn as needed.

 HOMEOSTATIC IMBALANCE

Minute changes from the homeostatic range for blood calcium can lead to severe neuromuscular problems ranging from hyperexcitability (when blood Ca²⁺ levels are too low) to nonresponsiveness and inability to function (with high blood Ca²⁺ levels). In addition, sustained high blood levels of Ca²⁺, a condition known as *hypercalcemia* (hi″per-kal-se′me-ah), can lead to undesirable deposits of calcium salts in the blood vessels, kidneys, and other soft organs, which may hamper the functioning of these organs. ●

A *Calcium salts are deposited in bone, and blood Ca²⁺ levels fall.*

FIGURE 6.12 Bone anatomy and stress. When loaded, bones are subjected to bending stress. In this example using the femur of the thigh, body weight transmitted to the head of the femur threatens to bend the bone along the indicated arc. This bending compresses the bone on one side (converging arrows), and stretches it on the other side (diverging arrows). Because these two forces cancel each other internally, much less bone material is needed internally than superficially.

In addition to the hormones that regulate bone remodeling in response to blood calcium levels, it is now established that *leptin*, a fat-derived hormone, plays a role in regulating bone density. Best known for its effects on weight and energy balance (see pp. 982–983), in animal studies leptin appears to inhibit osteoblasts through an additional pathway mediated by the hypothalamus which activates sympathetic nerves serving bones. However, the full scope of leptin's bone-modifying activity in humans is still being worked out.

Response to Mechanical Stress The second set of controls regulating bone remodeling, bone's response to mechanical stress (muscle pull) and gravity, serves the needs of the skeleton by keeping the bones strong where stressors are acting. *Wolff's law* holds that a bone grows or remodels in response to the demands placed on it. The first thing to under-

stand is that a bone's anatomy reflects the common stresses it encounters. For example, a bone is loaded (stressed) whenever weight bears down on it or muscles pull on it. This loading is usually off center, however, and tends to *bend* the bone. Bending compresses the bone on one side and subjects it to tension (stretching) on the other (Figure 6.12). But both forces are minimal toward the center of the bone (they cancel each other out), so a bone can "hollow out" for lightness (using spongy bone instead of compact bone) without jeopardy.

Other observations explained by Wolff's law include these: (1) Long bones are thickest midway along the diaphysis, exactly where bending stresses are greatest (bend a stick and it will split near the middle); (2) curved bones are thickest where they are most likely to buckle; (3) the trabeculae of spongy bone form trusses, or struts, along lines of compression; and (4) large, bony projections occur where heavy, active muscles attach. (The bones of weight lifters have enormous thickenings at the attachment sites of the most used muscles.) Wolff's law also explains the featureless bones of the fetus and the atrophied bones of bedridden people—situations in which bones are not stressed.

How do mechanical forces communicate with the cells responsible for remodeling? Although the mechanisms by which bone responds to mechanical stimuli are still uncertain, we do know that deforming a bone produces an electrical current. Because compressed and stretched regions are oppositely charged, it has been suggested that electrical signals direct remodeling. This principle and some of the devices currently used to speed bone repair and the healing of fractures are discussed in *A Closer Look* (pp. 194–195).

The skeleton is continuously subjected to both hormonal influences and mechanical forces. At the risk of constructing too large a building on too small a foundation, we can speculate that the hormonal loop determines *whether* and *when* remodeling occurs in response to changing blood calcium levels, and mechanical stress determines *where* it occurs. For example, when bone must be broken down to increase blood calcium levels, PTH is released and targets the osteoclasts. However, mechanical forces determine *which* osteoclasts are most sensitive to PTH stimulation, so that bone in the *least* stressed areas (which is temporarily dispensable) is broken down.

Bone Repair

Despite their remarkable strength, bones are susceptible to **fractures,** or breaks. During youth, most fractures result from exceptional trauma that twists or smashes the bones (sports injuries, automobile

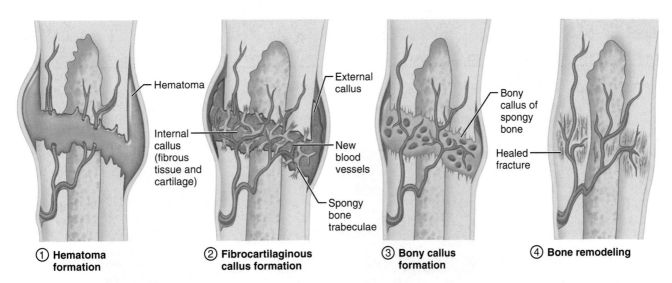

① **Hematoma formation**

② **Fibrocartilaginous callus formation**

③ **Bony callus formation**

④ **Bone remodeling**

FIGURE 6.13 **Stages in the healing of a bone fracture.**

accidents, and falls, for example). Excessive intake of vitamin A and elevated blood levels of the protein homocysteine (a known risk factor for atherosclerosis) appear to increase fracture risk in some people. In old age, most fractures occur as bones thin and weaken.

Fractures may be classified by

1. Position of the bone ends after fracture. In *nondisplaced fractures* the bone ends retain their normal position; in *displaced fractures* the bone ends are out of normal alignment.

2. Completeness of the break. If the bone is broken through, the fracture is a *complete fracture*; if not, it is an *incomplete fracture.*

3. Orientation of the break relative to the long axis of the bone. If the break parallels the long axis, the fracture is *linear*; if the break is perpendicular to the bone's long axis, it is *transverse.*

4. Whether the bone ends penetrate the skin. If so, the fracture is an *open (compound) fracture*; if not it is a *closed (simple) fracture.*

In addition to these four either-or classifications, all fractures can be described in terms of the location of the fracture, the external appearance of the fracture, and/or the nature of the break. Table 6.2 summarizes the various descriptions.

A fracture is treated by *reduction*, the realignment of the broken bone ends. In *closed* or *external reduction*, the bone ends are coaxed into position by the physician's hands. In *open (internal) reduction*, the bone ends are secured together surgically with pins or wires. After the broken bone is reduced, it is immobilized either by a cast or traction to allow the healing process to begin. For a simple fracture the healing time is six to eight weeks for small or medium-sized bones in young adults, but it is much

longer for large, weight-bearing bones and for bones of elderly people (because of their poorer circulation).

Repair in a simple fracture involves four major stages (Figure 6.13).

① **Hematoma formation.** When a bone breaks, blood vessels in the bone and periosteum, and perhaps in surrounding tissues, are torn and hemorrhage. As a result, a **hematoma** (he″mah-to′mah), a mass of clotted blood, forms at the fracture site. Soon, bone cells deprived of nutrition die, and the tissue at the site becomes swollen, painful, and inflamed.

② **Fibrocartilaginous callus formation.** Within a few days, several events lead to the formation of soft *granulation tissue,* also called the *soft callus* (kal′us; "hard skin"). Capillaries grow into the hematoma and phagocytic cells invade the area and begin cleaning up the debris. Meanwhile, fibroblasts and osteoblasts invade the fracture site from the nearby periosteum and endosteum and begin reconstructing the bone. The fibroblasts produce collagen fibers that span the break and connect the broken bone ends, and some differentiate into chondroblasts that secrete cartilage matrix. Within this mass of repair tissue, osteoblasts begin forming spongy bone, but those farthest from the capillary supply secrete an externally bulging cartilaginous matrix that later calcifies. This entire mass of repair tissue, now called the **fibrocartilaginous callus,** splints the broken bone.

③ **Bony callus formation.** Within a week, new bone trabeculae begin to appear in the fibrocartilaginous callus and gradually convert it to a **bony (hard) callus** of spongy bone. Bony callus formation continues until a firm union is formed about two months later.

TABLE 6.2	Common Types of Fractures

FRACTURE TYPE	DESCRIPTION AND COMMENTS	FRACTURE TYPE	DESCRIPTION AND COMMENTS
Comminuted	Bone fragments into three or more pieces Particularly common in the aged, whose bones are more brittle	*Compression*	Bone is crushed Common in porous bones (i.e., osteoporotic bones) subjected to extreme trauma, as in a fall

Crushed vertebra

FRACTURE TYPE	DESCRIPTION AND COMMENTS	FRACTURE TYPE	DESCRIPTION AND COMMENTS
Spiral	Ragged break occurs when excessive twisting forces are applied to a bone Common sports fracture	*Epiphyseal*	Epiphysis separates from the diaphysis along the epiphyseal plate Tends to occur where cartilage cells are dying and calcification of the matrix is occurring

FRACTURE TYPE	DESCRIPTION AND COMMENTS	FRACTURE TYPE	DESCRIPTION AND COMMENTS
Depressed	Broken bone portion is pressed inward Typical of skull fracture	*Greenstick*	Bone breaks incompletely, much in the way a green twig breaks. Only one side of the shaft breaks; the other side bends Common in children, whose bones have relatively more organic matrix and are more flexible than those of adults

④ **Bone remodeling.** Beginning during bony callus formation and continuing for several months after, the bony callus is remodeled. The excess material on the diaphysis exterior and within the medullary cavity is removed, and compact bone is laid down to reconstruct the shaft walls. The final structure of the remodeled area resembles that of the original unbroken bony region because it responds to the same set of mechanical stressors.

Homeostatic Imbalances of Bone

Imbalances between bone deposit and bone resorption underlie nearly every disease that affects the adult skeleton.

Osteomalacia and Rickets

Osteomalacia (os"te-o-mah-la'she-ah; "soft bones") includes a number of disorders in which the bones are inadequately mineralized. Osteoid is produced, but calcium salts are not deposited, so bones soften and weaken. The main symptom is pain when weight is put on the affected bones.

Rickets is the analogous disease in children. Because young bones are still growing rapidly, rickets is much more severe than adult osteomalacia. Bowed legs and deformities of the pelvis, skull, and rib cage are common. Because the epiphyseal plates cannot be calcified, they continue to widen, and the ends of long bones become visibly enlarged and abnormally long.

Osteomalacia and rickets are caused by insufficient calcium in the diet or by a vitamin D deficiency. Hence, drinking vitamin D–fortified milk and exposing the skin to sunlight (which spurs the body to form vitamin D) usually cure these disorders. Although the seeming elimination of rickets in the United States has been heralded as a public health success, rickets still rears its head in isolated situations. For example, if a mother who breastfeeds her infant becomes vitamin D deficient because of dreary winter weather, the infant too will be vitamin D deficient and will develop rickets.

Osteoporosis

For most of us, the phrase "bone problems of the elderly" brings to mind the stereotype of a victim of osteoporosis—a hunched-over old woman shuffling behind her walker. **Osteoporosis** (os"te-o-po-ro'sis) refers to a group of diseases in which bone resorption outpaces bone deposit. The bones become so fragile that something as simple as a hearty sneeze or stepping off a curb can cause them to break. The compo-

(a)

(b)

FIGURE 6.14 **Normal versus osteoporotic bone.** The contrasting architecture of **(a)** normal bone and **(b)** osteoporotic bone as shown in scanning electron micrographs (both 300×).

sition of the matrix remains normal but bone mass is reduced, and the bones become porous and light (Figure 6.14). Even though osteoporosis affects the entire skeleton, the spongy bone of the spine is most vulnerable, and compression fractures of the vertebrae are common. The femur, particularly its neck, is also very susceptible to fracture (called a *broken hip*) in people with osteoporosis.

Osteoporosis occurs most often in the aged, particularly in postmenopausal women. Although men develop it to a lesser degree, 30% of American women have osteoporosis between the ages of 60 and 70; 70% have it by age 80. Moreover, 30% of all Caucasian women (the most susceptible group) will experience a bone fracture due to osteoporosis. Sex hormones, particularly estrogen help to maintain the health and normal density of the skeleton by restraining osteoclast activity and by promoting deposit of new bone. After menopause, however, estrogen secretion wanes and estrogen deficiency is strongly implicated in osteoporosis in older women. Other factors that contribute to osteoporosis include a petite body form, insufficient exercise to stress the bones, a diet poor in calcium and protein, abnormal vitamin D receptors, smoking (which reduces estrogen levels), and hormone-related conditions (such as

A CLOSER LOOK

Them Bones, Them Bones Goin' to Walk Around—Clinical Advances in Bone Repair

Although bones have remarkable self-regenerative powers, some conditions frustrate even their most heroic efforts. Outstanding examples include massive shattering (as in automobile accidents), poor circulation in old bones, and certain birth defects. However, recent medical advances address healing problems that bones cannot handle themselves. Let's take a look.

■ **Electrical stimulation.** In large or slowly healing fractures, electrical stimulation of the fracture site dramatically increases the speed of healing. A lesson from geology notes that minute electrical currents are produced when minerals are stressed, a phenomenon called the *piezo-electric effect*. Bone tissue is deposited in regions of negative electrical charge (stressed areas) and absorbed in areas of positive charge, but the process by which applied electricity promotes healing is poorly understood. One theory is that the electrical fields prevent PTH from stimulating the bone-absorbing osteoclasts at the fracture site, thus allowing increased accumulation of bony tissue. Another theory holds that the electrical fields induce production of growth factors that stimulate the osteoblasts.

■ **Ultrasound treatments.** Daily exposure to pulsed low-intensity ultrasound waves reduces the healing time of broken arms and shinbones by 35–45%. This treatment seems to stimulate cartilage cells to make callus.

■ **Free vascular fibular graft.** This technique uses pieces of the fibula (the sticklike bone of the leg) to replace missing or severely damaged bone. In the past, extensive bone grafts (typically using pieces of bone from the hip) usually failed because blood could not reach their interior, necessitating eventual amputation. This new technique grafts normal blood vessels along with the bone section. Subsequent remodeling leads to a good replica of the bone normally present.

Although bone implants have proved effective in adults, they have been less desirable for children with growing bones because of the limb-length discrepancy that results. This problem has been partially resolved, at least for knee replacement candidates, with *self-extending endoprostheses*. The telescopic sleeve of these devices (see the figure) undergoes continual automatic limb elongation enforced by knee bending. Over-lengthening of the prosthesis is prevented by tension in the surrounding soft tissue, which increases after each elongation and then gradually decreases as the soft tissue grows.

■ **Vascular endothelial growth factor (VEGF).** VEGF is a protein that stimulates the growth of blood vessels. Researchers have been exploring its potential to create new arteries in people with heart disease, and more recently they began studying VEGF as a way to build new bone tissue. Experiments on mice with bone fractures show that VEGF stimulates the formation of osteoblasts and proteins associated with bone growth.

■ **Nanobiotechnology.** Researchers are experimenting with *nanostructures* (Greek *nanos* = dwarf) that mimic the structure of bone at a microscopic level. Scientists at Northwestern University assembled molecules of synthetic materials into a network of tiny fibers—each 10,000 times narrower than a human hair—similar to the collagen framework of bone tissue. When exposed to calcium and phosphate ions, the fibers developed crystalline deposits similar to those that form bone. Although still in the experimental stage, these fibers could someday be incorporated into a gel and packed into fracture sites to speed healing.

■ **Bone substitutes.** Desperate for bone fillers, surgeons have traditionally resorted to using crushed bone from cadavers or synthetic materials. Crushed bone induces the body to

hyperthyroidism, low blood levels of thyroid stimulating hormone (better known for its role in stimulating the secretion of thyroid hormones), and diabetes mellitus). In addition, osteoporosis can occur at any age as a result of immobility.

Osteoporosis has traditionally been treated with calcium and vitamin D supplements, weight-bearing exercise, and *hormone (estrogen) replacement therapy (HRT)*. Frustratingly, HRT only slows the loss of bone; it does not reverse it. Additionally, because of the increased risk of heart attack, stroke, and breast cancer associated with estrogen replacement therapy, it is a controversial treatment these days. Newer drugs are available. These include alendronate, a drug that suppresses osteoclast activity and shows

promise in reversing osteoporosis in the spine; and selective estrogen receptor modulators (SERMs), such as raloxifene, dubbed "estrogen light" because it mimics estrogen's beneficial bone-sparing properties without targeting the uterus or breast. Additionally, *statins*, drugs used by tens of thousands of people to lower cholesterol levels, have been shown to have an unexpected side effect of increasing bone mineral density up to 8% over four years. Although not a substitute for HRT, estrogenic compounds in soy protein (principally the isoflavones daidzein and genistein) offer a good addition or adjunct for some patients.

Osteoporosis can be prevented (or at least delayed). The first requirement is to get enough calcium while your bones are still increasing in density (bones form new bone of its own. When mixed with water, it can be molded to the shape of the desired bone or packed into small, difficult-to-reach spaces. Thus, it avoids the often painful and time-consuming procedure of bone grafting. The same can be said for most synthetic bone substitutes, but both approaches have shortcomings. Cadaveric bone carries a small (but real) risk of hepatitis or HIV infection. Additionally, as foreign tissue, it may be rejected by the immune system. Synthetics tend to cause inflammation which hinders healing and promotes infection.

Pro Osteon (made from coral) avoids both problems. The coral is heat-treated to kill the living coral cells and convert its mineral structure to hydroxyapatite, the salt in bone. The brittle coral graft is then carved to the desired shape, sterilized by irradiation with gamma rays, and coated with *bone morphogenic protein (BMP)*, a natural substance that enhances bone growth. Osteoblasts and blood vessels migrate from the adjacent natural bone into the coral implant, gradually replacing it with living bone.

Research has also produced several types of artificial bone. One is TCP, a biodegradable ceramic substance soft enough to be shaped, but not very strong. TCP's biggest application has been to replace parts of non-weight-bearing bones, such as skull bones.

Norian SRS, a bone cement made of calcium phosphate, provides immediate structural support to fractured or osteoporotic sites. Mixed at the time of surgery, Norian SRS starts out as a paste that can be injected into damaged areas to create an "internal cast." The paste hardens in minutes and cures into a substance with greater compressive strength than spongy bone. Because its crystalline structure and chemistry are the same as that of natural bone, it is gradually remodeled and replaced by host bone cells. A limitation is that Norian SRS can be used only on the ends of long bones, because it cannot resist the twisting and flexing experienced by the central shaft. ■

(a)

Telescopic/extension portion

(b)

The self-extending endoprosthesis (leg implant). *Lengthening occurs at the telescopic/extension portion.*

reach their peak density during early adulthood). Second, drinking fluoridated water hardens bones (as well as teeth); conversely, excessive intake of carbonated beverages leaches minerals from bone and decreases bone density. Finally, getting plenty of weight-bearing exercise (walking, jogging, tennis, etc.) throughout life will increase bone mass above normal values and provide a greater buffer against age-related bone loss.

Paget's Disease

Often discovered by accident when X rays are taken for some other reason, **Paget's disease** (paj'ets) is characterized by excessive and haphazard bone deposit and resorption. The newly formed bone, called *Pagetic bone*, is hastily made and has an abnormally high ratio of spongy bone to compact bone. This, along with reduced mineralization, causes a spotty weakening of the bones. Late in the disease, osteoclast activity wanes, but osteoblasts continue to work, often forming irregular bone thickenings or filling the marrow cavity with Pagetic bone.

Paget's disease may affect any part of the skeleton, but it is usually a localized condition. The spine, pelvis, femur, and skull are most often involved and become increasingly deformed and painful. It rarely occurs before the age of 40, and it affects about 3% of North American elderly people.

SYSTEM CONNECTIONS: Homeostatic Interrelationships Between the Skeletal System and Other Body Systems

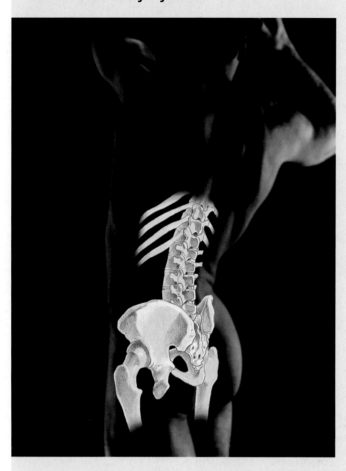

Integumentary System
- Skeletal system provides support for body organs including the skin
- Skin provides vitamin D needed for proper calcium absorption and use

Muscular System
- Skeletal system provides levers plus ionic calcium for muscle activity
- Muscle pull on bones increases bone strength and viability; helps determine bone shape

Nervous System
- Skeletal system protects brain and spinal cord; provides depot for calcium ions needed for neural function
- Nerves innervate bone and joint capsules, providing for pain and joint sense

Endocrine System
- Skeletal system provides some bony protection; stores calcium needed for second-messenger signaling mechanisms
- Hormones regulate uptake and release of calcium from bone; promote long bone growth and maturation

Cardiovascular System
- Bone marrow cavities provide site for blood cell formation; matrix stores calcium needed for cardiac muscle activity
- Cardiovascular system delivers nutrients and oxygen to bones; carries away wastes

Lymphatic System/Immunity
- Skeletal system provides some protection to lymphatic organs; bone marrow is site of origin for lymphocytes involved in immune response
- Lymphatic system drains leaked tissue fluids; immune cells protect against pathogens

Respiratory System
- Skeletal system protects lungs by enclosure (rib cage)
- Respiratory system provides oxygen; disposes of carbon dioxide

Digestive System
- Skeletal system provides some bony protection to intestines, pelvic organs, and liver
- Digestive system provides nutrients needed for bone health and growth

Urinary System
- Skeletal system protects pelvic organs (bladder, etc.)
- Urinary system activates vitamin D; disposes of nitrogenous wastes

Reproductive System
- Skeletal system protects some reproductive organs by enclosure
- Gonads produce hormones that influence form of skeleton and epiphyseal closure

6

THE SKELETAL SYSTEM and Interrelationships with the Muscular, Endocrine, and Integumentary Systems

Our skeleton supports us, protects our "innards" (the protection our brain gets from the skull is indispensable), gives us stature (for some reason, tall people get more respect), contributes to our shape (women *are* shaped differently than men), and allows us to move. Obviously, the skeletal system has important interactions with many other body systems, not the least of which are the endocrine and integumentary systems. However, its most intimate and mutually beneficial relationship is with the muscular system, so we will consider that first.

Muscular System

The codependence of the skeletal and muscular systems is striking—as one system goes, so goes the other. If we participate in weight-bearing exercise (run, play tennis, do aerobics) regularly, our muscles become more efficient and exert more force on our bones. As a result, our bones stay healthy and strong and increase their mass to assume the added stress.

Since both spongy and compact bone reach peak density during midlife, weight-bearing exercise during youth is important, especially in females who have less bone mass than males and lose it faster.

Regular exercise also stretches the connective tissues binding bones to muscles and to other bones, and reinforcing joints. Since this increases overall flexibility, we have fewer injuries, allowing us to stay active well into old age. (Pain makes couch potatoes.)

Endocrine System

Although mechanical factors are undeniably important in shaping the skeleton and helping to keep it strong, hormones acting individually and in concert direct skeletal growth during youth, and enhance (or impair) skeletal strength in adults. Growth hormone is essential for normal skeletal growth and maintenance throughout life, whereas thyroid and sex hormones ensure that normal skeletal proportions are established during childhood and adolescence. Conversely, PTH and calcitonin serve not the skeleton but a different master—homeostasis of blood calcium levels. Any interference with normal hormonal functioning is soon apparent as a skeletal abnormality or malproportion.

Integumentary System

The skeletal system is absolutely dependent on the integumentary system (the skin) for the calcium that keeps the bones hard and strong. The relationship is indirect to be sure: In the presence of sunlight, a vitamin D precursor is produced in the dermal capillary blood. It is activated elsewhere, and (among its other roles) it regulates the carrier system that absorbs calcium from ingested foods into the blood. Because calcium is required for so many body functions, and bones provide the "calcium bank," the bones become increasingly soft and weak in the absence of vitamin D because no daily rations of calcium are allowed to enter the blood from the digestive tract.

6

Skeletal System

Case study: Remember Mrs. DeStephano? When we last heard about her she was being admitted for further studies. Relative to her skeletal system, the following notes have been added to her chart.

- Fracture of superior right tibia (shinbone of leg); skin lacerated; area cleaned and protruding bone fragments subjected to internal (open) reduction and casted
- Nutrient artery of tibia damaged
- Medial meniscus (hyaline cartilage disc) of right knee joint crushed; knee joint inflamed and painful

Relative to these notes:

1. What type of fracture does Mrs. DeStephano have?

2. What problems can be predicted with such fractures and how are they treated?

3. What is internal reduction? Why was a cast applied?

4. Given an uncomplicated recovery, approximately how long should it take before Mrs. DeStephano has a good solid bony callus?

5. What complications might be predicted by the fact that the nutrient artery is damaged?

6. What new techniques might be used to enhance fracture repair if healing is delayed or impaired?

7. How likely is it that Mrs. DeStephano's knee cartilage will regenerate? Why?

(Answers in Appendix G)

FIGURE 6.15 **Fetal primary ossification centers at 12 weeks.** The darker areas indicate primary ossification centers in the skeleton of a 12-week-old fetus.

Its cause is unknown, but it may be initiated by a virus. Drug therapies include calcitonin (now administered by a nasal inhaler), and the newer bisphosphonates (etidronate, alendronate, and others) which have shown success in preventing bone breakdown.

Developmental Aspects of Bones: Timing of Events

Bones are on a precise schedule from the time they form until death. The mesoderm germ layer gives rise to embryonic mesenchymal cells, which in turn produce the membranes and cartilages that form the embryonic skeleton. These structures then ossify according to an amazingly predictable timetable that allows fetal age to be determined easily from either X rays or sonograms. Although each bone has its own developmental schedule, most long bones begin ossifying by 8 weeks after conception and have obvious primary ossification centers by 12 weeks (Figure 6.15).

At birth, most long bones of the skeleton are well ossified except for their epiphyses. After birth, secondary ossification centers develop in a predictable sequence. The epiphyseal plates persist and provide for long bone growth during childhood and the sex hormone–mediated growth spurt at adolescence. By the age of 25 years, nearly all bones are completely ossified and skeletal growth ceases.

In children and adolescents, bone formation exceeds bone resorption; in young adults, these processes are in balance; in old age, resorption predominates. Despite the environmental factors (listed above) that influence bone density, genetics still plays the major role in determining how much one's bone density will change over a lifetime. A single gene that codes for vitamin D's cellular docking site helps determine both the tendency to accumulate bone mass during early life and one's risk of osteoporosis later in life. Beginning in the fourth decade of life, bone mass decreases with age; the only exception appears to be in bones of the skull. Among young adults, skeletal mass is generally greater in males than in females, and greater in blacks than in whites. Age-related bone loss is faster in whites than in blacks (who have greater bone density to begin with) and faster in females than in males. Qualitative changes also occur: More osteons remain incompletely formed, mineralization is less complete, and the amount of nonviable bone increases, reflecting a diminished blood supply to the bones in old age.

■ ■ ■

Skeletal cartilages and bones—their architecture, composition, and dynamic nature—have been examined in this chapter. We have also discussed the role of bones in maintaining overall body homeostasis, as summarized in *Making Connections*. Now we are ready to look at the individual bones of the skeleton and how they contribute to its functions, both collectively and individually.

Related Clinical Terms

Achondroplasia (a-kon"dro-pla'ze-ah; *a* = without; *chondro* = cartilage; *plasi* = mold, shape) A congenital condition involving defective cartilage and endochondral bone growth so that the limbs are too short but the membrane bones are of normal size; a type of dwarfism.

Bony spur Abnormal projection from a bone due to bony overgrowth; common in aging bones.

Ostealgia (os"te-al'je-ah; *algia* = pain) Pain in a bone.

Osteitis (os"te-i'tis; *itis* = inflammation) Inflammation of bony tissue.

Osteogenesis imperfecta Also called brittle bone disease, a disorder in which the bone matrix contains inadequate amounts of collagen, putting it at risk for shattering.

Osteomyelitis (os"te-o-mi"ĕ-l-li'tis) Inflammation of bone and bone marrow caused by pus-forming bacteria that enter the body via a wound (e.g., compound bone fracture), or spread from an infection near the bone. Commonly affects the long bones, causing acute pain and fever. May result in joint stiffness, bone destruction, and shortening of a limb. Treatment involves antibiotic therapy, draining of any abscesses (local collections of pus) formed, and removal of dead bone fragments (which prevent healing).

Osteosarcoma (os"te-o-sar-ko'mah) A form of bone cancer typically arising in a long bone of a limb and most often in those 10–25 years of age. Grows aggressively, painfully eroding the bone; tends to metastasize to the lungs and cause secondary lung tumors. Usual treatment is amputation of the affected bone or limb, followed by chemotherapy and surgical removal of any metastases. Survival rate is about 50% if detected early.

Pathologic fracture Fracture in a diseased bone involving slight (coughing or a quick turn) or no physical trauma. For example, a hip bone weakened by osteoporosis may break and cause the person to fall, rather than breaking because of the fall.

Traction ("pulling") Placing sustained tension on a body region to keep the parts of a fractured bone in proper alignment; also prevents spasms of skeletal muscles, which would separate the fractured bone ends or crush the spinal cord in the case of vertebral column fractures.

Chapter Summary

Skeletal Cartilages (p. 176)

Basic Structure, Types, and Locations (p. 176)

1. A skeletal cartilage exhibits chondrocytes housed in lacunae (cavities) within the extracellular matrix (ground substance and fibers). It contains large amounts of water (which accounts for its resilience), lacks nerve fibers, is avascular, and is surrounded by a fibrous perichondrium that resists expansion.

2. Hyaline cartilages appear glassy; the fibers are collagenic. They provide support with flexibility and resilience and are the most abundant skeletal cartilages, accounting for the articular, costal, respiratory, and nasal cartilages.

3. Elastic cartilages contain abundant elastic fibers, in addition to collagen fibers, and are more flexible than hyaline cartilages. They support the outer ear and epiglottis.

4. Fibrocartilages, which contain thick collagen fibers, are the most compressible cartilages and are resistant to stretch. They form vertebral discs and knee joint cartilages.

Growth of Cartilage (p. 176)

5. Cartilages grow from within (interstitial growth) and by addition of new cartilage tissue at the periphery (appositional growth).

Classification of Bones (pp. 176–178)

1. Bones are classified as long, short, flat, or irregular on the basis of their shape and their proportion of compact or spongy bone.

Functions of Bones (pp. 178–179)

1. Bones give the body shape; protect and support body organs; provide levers for muscles to pull on; store calcium and other minerals; and are the site of blood cell production.

Bone Structure (pp. 179–184)

Gross Anatomy (pp. 179–181)

1. Bone markings are important anatomical landmarks that reveal sites of muscle attachment, points of articulation, and sites of blood vessels and nerve passage.

2. A long bone is composed of a diaphysis (shaft) and epiphyses (ends). The medullary cavity of the diaphysis contains yellow marrow; the epiphyses contain spongy bone. The epiphyseal line is the remnant of the epiphyseal plate. Periosteum covers the diaphysis; endosteum lines inner bone cavities. Hyaline cartilage covers joint surfaces.

3. Flat bones consist of two thin plates of compact bone enclosing a diploë (spongy bone layer). Short and irregular bones resemble flat bones structurally.

4. In adults, hematopoietic tissue is found within the diploë of flat bones and occasionally within the epiphyses of long bones. In infants red marrow is also found in the medullary cavity.

Microscopic Anatomy of Bone (pp. 181–182)

5. The structural unit of compact bone, the osteon, consists of a central canal surrounded by concentric lamellae of bone matrix. Osteocytes, embedded in lacunae, are connected to each other and the central canal by canaliculi.

6. Spongy bone has slender trabeculae containing irregular lamellae, which enclose red marrow–filled cavities.

Chemical Composition of Bone (pp. 182–184)

7. Bone is composed of living cells (osteogenic cells, osteoblasts, osteocytes, and osteoclasts) and matrix. The matrix includes osteoid, organic substances that are secreted by osteoblasts and give the bone tensile strength. Its inorganic components, the hydroxyapatites (calcium salts), make bone hard.

Bone Development (pp. 184–187)

Formation of the Bony Skeleton (pp. 184–186)

1. Intramembranous ossification forms the clavicles and most skull bones. The ground substance of the bone matrix is deposited between collagen fibers within the fibrous membrane to form spongy bone. Eventually, compact bone plates enclose the diploë.

2. Most bones are formed by endochondral ossification of a hyaline cartilage model. Osteoblasts beneath the periosteum secrete bone matrix on the cartilage model, forming the bone collar. Deterioration of the cartilage model internally opens up cavities, allowing periosteal bud entry. Bone matrix is deposited around the cartilage remnants but is later broken down.

Postnatal Bone Growth (pp. 186–187)

3. Long bones increase in length by interstitial growth of the epiphyseal plate cartilage and its replacement by bone.

4. Appositional growth increases bone diameter/thickness.

Bone Homeostasis: Remodeling and Repair (pp. 187–193)

Bone Remodeling (pp. 188–190)

1. New bone is continually deposited and resorbed in response to hormonal and mechanical stimuli. Together these processes constitute bone remodeling.

2. An osteoid seam appears at areas of new bone deposit; calcium salts are deposited a few days later.

3. Osteoclasts release lysosomal enzymes and acids on bone surfaces to be resorbed. The dissolved products are transcytosed to the opposite face of the osteoclast for release to the extracellular fluid.

4. The hormonal mechanism of bone remodeling serves blood calcium homeostasis. When blood calcium levels decline, PTH is released and stimulates osteoclasts to digest bone matrix, releasing ionic calcium. When blood calcium levels rise, calcitonin is released, stimulating removal of calcium from the blood. Mechanical stress and gravity acting on the skeleton help maintain skeletal strength. Bones thicken, develop heavier prominences, or rearrange their trabeculae in sites where stressed.

Bone Repair (pp. 190–193)

5. Fractures are treated by open or closed reduction. The healing process involves formation of a hematoma, a fibrocartilaginous callus, a bony callus, and bone remodeling, in succession.

Homeostatic Imbalances of Bone (pp. 193–195, 198)

1. Imbalances between bone formation and resorption underlie all skeletal disorders.

2. Osteomalacia and rickets occur when bones are inadequately mineralized. The bones become soft and deformed. The most frequent cause is inadequate vitamin D.

3. Osteoporosis is any condition in which bone breakdown outpaces bone formation, causing bones to become weak and porous. Postmenopausal women are particularly susceptible.

4. Paget's disease is characterized by excessive and abnormal bone remodeling.

Developmental Aspects of Bones: Timing of Events (p. 198)

1. Osteogenesis is predictable and precisely timed.

2. Longitudinal long bone growth continues until the end of adolescence. Skeletal mass increases dramatically during puberty and adolescence, when formation exceeds resorption.

3. Bone mass is fairly constant in young adulthood, but beginning in the 40s, bone resorption exceeds formation.

Review Questions

Multiple Choice/Matching

(Some questions have more than one correct answer. Select the best answer or answers from the choices given.)

1. Which is a function of the skeletal system? (a) support, (b) hematopoietic site, (c) storage, (d) providing levers for muscle activity, (e) all of these.

2. A bone with approximately the same width, length, and height is most likely (a) a long bone, (b) a short bone, (c) a flat bone, (d) an irregular bone.

3. The shaft of a long bone is properly called the (a) epiphysis, (b) periosteum, (c) diaphysis, (d) compact bone.

4. Sites of hematopoiesis include all but (a) red marrow cavities of spongy bone, (b) the diploë of flat bones, (c) medullary cavities in bones of infants, (d) medullary cavities in bones of a healthy adult.

5. An osteon has (a) a central canal carrying blood vessels, (b) concentric lamellae, (c) osteocytes in lacunae, (d) canaliculi that connect lacunae to the central canal, (e) all of these.

6. The organic portion of matrix is important in providing all but (a) tensile strength, (b) hardness, (c) ability to resist stretch, (d) flexibility.

7. The flat bones of the skull develop from (a) areolar tissue, (b) hyaline cartilage, (c) fibrous connective tissue, (d) compact bone.

8. The remodeling of bone is a function of which cells? (a) chondrocytes and osteocytes, (b) osteoblasts and osteoclasts, (c) chondroblasts and osteoclasts, (d) osteoblasts and osteocytes.

9. Bone growth during childhood and in adults is regulated and directed by (a) growth hormone, (b) thyroid hormones, (c) sex hormones, (d) mechanical stress, (e) all of these.

10. Where within the epiphyseal plate are the *dividing* cartilage cells located? (a) nearest the shaft, (b) in the marrow cavity, (c) farthest from the shaft, (d) in the primary ossification center.

11. Wolff's law is concerned with (a) calcium homeostasis of the blood, (b) the thickness and shape of a bone being determined by mechanical and gravitational stresses placed on it, (c) the electrical charge on bone surfaces.

12. Formation of the bony callus in fracture repair is followed by (a) hematoma formation, (b) fibrocartilaginous callus formation, (c) bone remodeling to convert woven bone to compact bone, (d) formation of granulation tissue.

13. The fracture type in which the bone ends are incompletely separated is (a) greenstick, (b) compound, (c) simple, (d) comminuted, (e) compression.

14. The disorder in which bones are porous and thin but bone composition is normal is (a) osteomalacia, (b) osteoporosis, (c) Paget's disease.

Short Answer Essay Questions

15. Compare bone to cartilage tissue relative to its resilience, speed of regeneration, and access to nutrients.

16. Describe in proper order the events of endochondral ossification.

17. Compare compact and spongy bone in macroscopic appearance, microscopic structure, and relative location.

18. As we grow, our long bones increase in diameter, but the thickness of the bony collar of the shaft remains relatively constant. Explain this phenomenon.

19. Describe the process of new bone formation in an adult bone. Use the terms *osteoid seam* and *calcification front* in your discussion.

20. Compare and contrast controls of bone remodeling exerted by hormones and by mechanical and gravitational forces relative to the actual purpose of each control system and changes in bone architecture that might occur.

21. (a) During what period of life does skeletal mass increase dramatically? Begin to decline? (b) Why are fractures most common in elderly individuals? (c) Why are greenstick fractures most common in children?

22. Yolanda is asked to review a bone slide that her professor has set up under the microscope. She sees concentric layers surrounding a central cavity. Is this bone section taken from the diaphysis or the epiphseal plate of the specimen?

Critical Thinking and Clinical Application Questions

1. Following a motorcycle accident, a 22-year-old man was rushed to the emergency room. X rays revealed a spiral fracture of his right tibia (main bone of the leg). Two months later, X rays revealed good bony callus formation. What is bony callus?

2. Mrs. Abbruzzo brought her 4-year-old daughter to the doctor, complaining that she didn't "look right." The child's forehead was enlarged, her rib cage was knobby, and her lower limbs were bent and deformed. X rays revealed very thick epiphyseal plates. Mrs. Abbruzzo was advised to increase dietary amounts of vitamin D and milk and to "shoo" the girl outside to play in the sun. Considering the child's signs and symptoms, what disease do you think she has? Explain the doctor's instructions.

3. You overhear some anatomy students imagining out loud what their bones would look like if they had compact bone on the inside and spongy bone on the outside, instead of the other way around. You tell them that such imaginary bones would be poorly designed mechanically and would break easily. Explain your reason for saying this.

4. Why do you think wheelchair-bound people with paralyzed lower limbs have thin, weak leg and thigh bones?

5. Jay Beckenstein went to weight-lifting camp in the summer between seventh and eighth grade. He noticed that the camp trainer put tremendous pressure on him and his friends to improve their strength. After an especially vigorous workout, Jay's arm felt extremely sore and weak around the elbow. He went to the camp doctor, who took X rays and then told him that the injury was serious, for the "end of his upper arm bone was starting to twist off." What had happened? Could the same thing happen to Jay's 23-year-old sister, Trixie, who was also starting a program of weight lifting? Why or why not?

6. After splashdown in the Atlantic Ocean, the American astronaut team was brought to the Naval Hospital for checkups. X rays revealed decreased bone mass in all of them. Isn't this surprising in view of the fact that they exercised regularly in the space capsule? Explain.

7. Old Norse stories tell of a famous Viking named Egil, who lived around 900 AD. His skull was greatly enlarged and misshapen, and the cranial bones were thickened (6 cm, more than 2 inches, thick). After he died, his skull was dug up and it withstood the blow of an ax without damage. In life, he had headaches from the pressure exerted by enlarged vertebrae on his spinal cord. So much blood was diverted to his bones to support their extensive remodeling that his fingers and toes always felt cold and his heart was damaged through overexertion. What bone disorder did Egil probably have?

8. The serving arm of many tennis players is often significantly larger (thicker) than the other arm. Explain this phenomenon.

LOOKING FOR MORE STUDY HELP?

A wide variety of quiz questions, tutorials, and learning exercises are available online at the Anatomy & Physiology Place (www.anatomyandphysiology.com) and, if your instructor has provided you with a MyA&P Course ID number, in MyA&P (www.myaandp.com).

1. Name the major parts of the axial and appendicular skeletons and describe their relative functions.

PART 1: THE AXIAL SKELETON

The Skull (pp. 203–218)

2. Name, describe, and identify the skull bones. Identify their important markings.

3. Compare and contrast the major functions of the cranium and the facial skeleton.

4. Define the bony boundaries of the orbits, nasal cavity, and paranasal sinuses.

The Vertebral Column (pp. 218–225)

5. Describe the structure of the vertebral column, list its components, and describe its curvatures.

6. Indicate a common function of the spinal curvatures and the intervertebral discs.

7. Discuss the structure of a typical vertebra and describe regional features of cervical, thoracic, and lumbar vertebrae.

The Thoracic Cage (pp. 226–228)

8. Name and describe the bones of the thoracic cage (bony thorax).

9. Differentiate true from false ribs.

PART 2: THE APPENDICULAR SKELETON

The Pectoral (Shoulder) Girdle (pp. 229–231)

10. Identify bones forming the pectoral girdle and relate their structure and arrangement to the function of this girdle.

11. Identify important bone markings on the pectoral girdle.

The Upper Limb (pp. 231–237)

12. Identify or name the bones of the upper limb and their important markings.

The Pelvic (Hip) Girdle (pp. 237–239)

13. Name the bones contributing to the os coxa and relate the pelvic girdle's strength to its function.

14. Describe differences in the male and female pelves and relate these to functional differences.

The Lower Limb (pp. 239–246)

15. Identify the lower limb bones and their important markings.

16. Name the arches of the foot and explain their importance.

Developmental Aspects of the Skeleton (pp. 246–248)

17. Define fontanels and indicate their significance.

18. Describe how skeletal proportions change through life.

19. Discuss how age-related skeletal changes may affect health.

The word *skeleton* comes from the Greek word meaning "dried-up body" or "mummy," a rather unflattering description. Nonetheless, the human skeleton is a triumph of design and engineering that puts most skyscrapers to shame. It is strong, yet light, and almost perfectly adapted for the protective, locomotor, and manipulative functions it performs.

The **skeleton,** or **skeletal system,** composed of bones, cartilages, joints, and ligaments, accounts for about 20% of body mass (about 30 pounds in a 160-pound person). Bones make up most of the skeleton. Cartilages occur only in isolated areas, such as the nose, parts of the ribs, and the joints. Ligaments connect bones and reinforce joints, allowing required movements while restricting motions in other directions. Joints, the junctions between bones, provide for the remarkable mobility of the skeleton. Joints and ligaments are discussed separately in Chapter 8.

PART 1: THE AXIAL SKELETON

As described in Chapter 6, the skeleton is divided into *axial* and *appendicular* portions (see Figure 6.1) for descriptive purposes. The **axial skeleton** is structured from 80 bones segregated into three major regions: the *skull, vertebral column,* and *thoracic cage* (Figure 7.1). This part of the skeleton supports the head, neck, and trunk, and it protects the brain, spinal cord, and the organs in the thorax.

The Skull

The **skull** is the body's most complex bony structure. It is formed by *cranial* and *facial bones,* 22 in all. The cranial bones, or **cranium** (kra′ne-um), enclose and protect the fragile brain and furnish attachment sites for head and neck muscles. The facial bones (1) form the framework of the face, (2) contain cavities for the special sense organs of sight, taste, and smell, (3) provide openings for air and food passage, (4) secure the teeth, and (5) anchor the facial muscles of expression, which we use to show our feelings. As you will see, the individual skull bones are well suited to their assignments.

Most skull bones are flat bones. Except for the mandible, which is connected to the rest of the skull by a freely movable joint, all bones of the adult skull are firmly united by interlocking joints called **sutures** (soo′cherz). The suture lines have a saw-toothed or serrated appearance. The major skull sutures, the *coronal, sagittal, squamous,* and *lambdoid sutures,* connect cranial bones (Figures 7.2b and 7.3a). Most other skull sutures connect facial bones and are named according to the specific bones they connect.

Overview of Skull Geography

It is worth surveying basic skull "geography" before describing the individual bones. With the lower jaw removed, the skull resembles a lopsided, hollow, bony sphere. The facial bones form its anterior aspect, and the cranium forms the rest of the skull (see Figure 7.3a). The cranium can be divided into a vault and a base. The *cranial vault,* also called the *calvaria* (kal-va′re-ah; "bald part of skull"), forms the superior, lateral, and posterior aspects of the skull, as well as the forehead. The *cranial base,* or *floor,* forms the skull's inferior aspect. Internally, prominent bony ridges divide the base into three distinct "steps" or fossae—the *anterior, middle,* and *posterior cranial fossae* (see Figure 7.4c on p. 208). The brain sits snugly in these cranial fossae, completely enclosed by the cranial vault. Overall, the brain is said to occupy the *cranial cavity.*

In addition to the large cranial cavity, the skull has many smaller cavities. These include the middle and internal ear cavities (carved into the lateral side of its base) and, anteriorly, the nasal cavity and the orbits (see Figure 1.13, p. 19). The *orbits* house the eyeballs. Several bones of the skull contain air-filled sinuses, which lighten the skull.

The skull also has about 85 named openings (foramina, canals, fissures, etc.). The most important of these provide passageways for the spinal cord, the major blood vessels serving the brain, and the 12 pairs of cranial nerves (numbered I through XII), which transmit impulses to and from the brain.

As you read about the bones of the skull, locate each bone on the different skull views in Figures 7.2, 7.3, and 7.4. The skull bones and their important markings are also summarized in Table 7.1 (pp. 216–217). The color-coded boxes before a bone's name in the text and in Table 7.1 correspond to the color of that bone in the figures.

Cranium

The eight cranial bones are the paired parietal and temporal bones and the unpaired frontal, occipital, sphenoid, and ethmoid bones. Together, these construct the brain's protective bony "helmet." Because its superior aspect is curved, the cranium is self-bracing. This allows the bones to be thin, and, like an eggshell, the cranium is remarkably strong for its weight.

▢ Frontal Bone

The shell-shaped **frontal bone** (Figures 7.2a, 7.3, and 7.4b) forms the anterior cranium. It articulates posteriorly with the paired parietal bones via the prominent *coronal suture.*

Anterior view

Posterior view

FIGURE 7.1 **Bones of the axial skeleton.** The three major subdivisions are the skull, thoracic cage (sternum and ribs), and vertebral column (vertebrae, sacrum, and coccyx).

The most anterior part of the frontal bone is the vertical *frontal squama*, commonly called the *forehead*. The frontal squama ends inferiorly at the **supraorbital margins,** the thickened superior margins of the orbits that lie under the eyebrows. From here, the frontal bone extends posteriorly, forming the superior wall of the *orbits* and most of the **anterior cranial fossa** (Figure 7.4b and c). This fossa supports the frontal lobes of the brain. Each supraorbital margin is pierced by a **supraorbital foramen (notch),** which allows the supraorbital artery and nerve to pass to the forehead.

The smooth portion of the frontal bone between the orbits is the **glabella** (glah-bel'ah). Just inferior to this the frontal bone meets the nasal bones at the *frontonasal suture* (Figure 7.2a). The areas lateral to the glabella are riddled internally with sinuses, called the **frontal sinuses** (Figures 7.3b and 7.11).

Q *(1) Which of the bones illustrated in view (a) are cranial bones? (2) Which two terms are used interchangeably to indicate the entire group of cranial bones?*

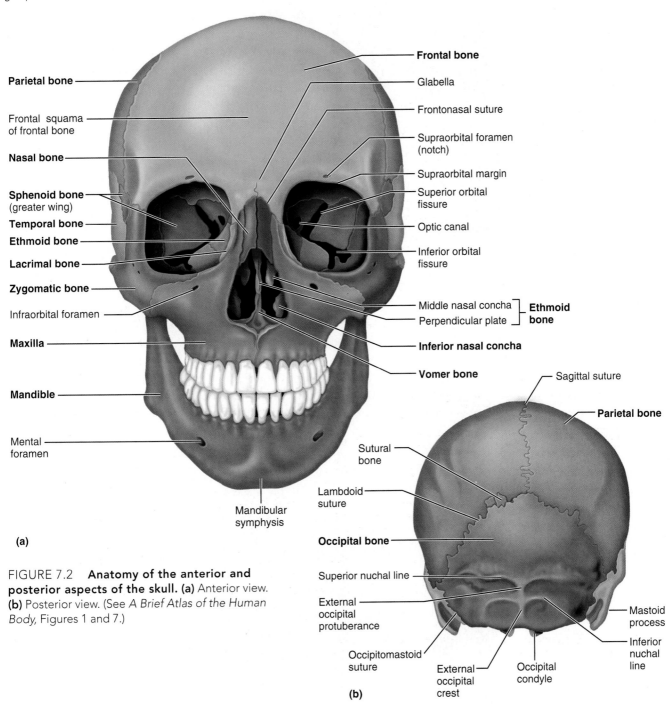

FIGURE 7.2 **Anatomy of the anterior and posterior aspects of the skull. (a)** Anterior view. **(b)** Posterior view. (See *A Brief Atlas of the Human Body*, Figures 1 and 7.)

7

A *(1) The temporals, parietals, frontal, ethmoid, and sphenoid are all cranial bones. (2) The cranial vault or calvaria.*

Parietal Bones and the Major Sutures

The two large **parietal bones** are curved, rectangular bones that form most of the superior and lateral aspects of the skull; hence they form the bulk of the

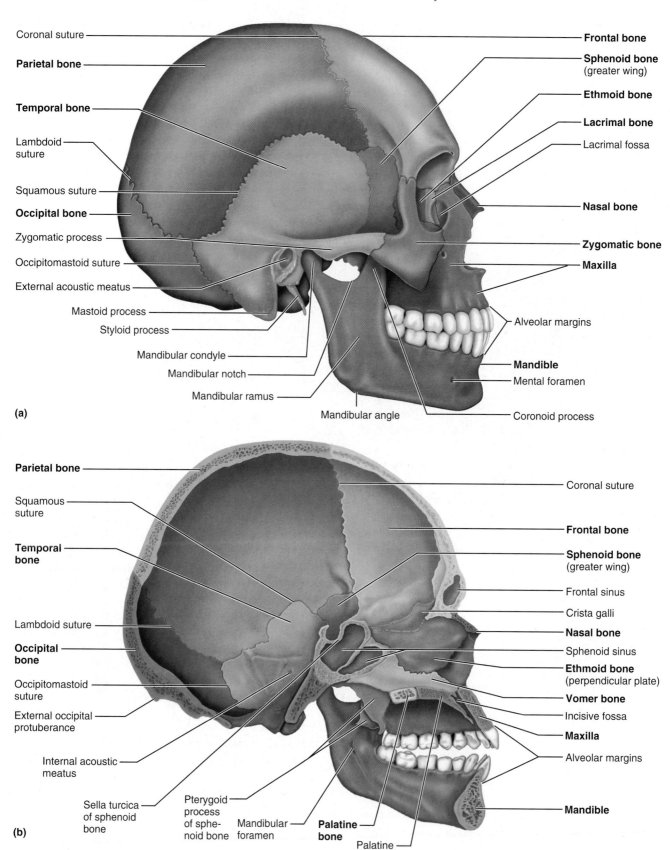

(a)

Coronal suture
Parietal bone
Temporal bone
Lambdoid suture
Squamous suture
Occipital bone
Zygomatic process
Occipitomastoid suture
External acoustic meatus
Mastoid process
Styloid process
Mandibular condyle
Mandibular notch
Mandibular ramus
Mandibular angle

Frontal bone
Sphenoid bone (greater wing)
Ethmoid bone
Lacrimal bone
Lacrimal fossa
Nasal bone
Zygomatic bone
Maxilla
Alveolar margins
Mandible
Mental foramen
Coronoid process

(b)

Parietal bone
Squamous suture
Temporal bone
Lambdoid suture
Occipital bone
Occipitomastoid suture
External occipital protuberance
Internal acoustic meatus
Sella turcica of sphenoid bone
Pterygoid process of sphenoid bone
Mandibular foramen
Palatine bone
Palatine process of maxilla

Coronal suture
Frontal bone
Sphenoid bone (greater wing)
Frontal sinus
Crista galli
Nasal bone
Sphenoid sinus
Ethmoid bone (perpendicular plate)
Vomer bone
Incisive fossa
Maxilla
Alveolar margins
Mandible

FIGURE 7.3 **Anatomy of the lateral aspects of the skull. (a)** External anatomy of the right lateral aspect of the skull. **(b)** Midsagittal view of the skull showing the internal anatomy of the left side of the skull. (See *A Brief Atlas of the Human Body*, Figures 2 and 3.)

cranial vault. The four largest sutures occur where the parietal bones articulate (form a joint) with other cranial bones:

1. The **coronal suture** (ko-ro′nul), where the parietal bones meet the frontal bone anteriorly (Figure 7.3)

2. The **sagittal suture**, where the parietal bones meet superiorly at the cranial midline (Figure 7.2b)

3. The **lambdoid suture** (lam′doid), where the parietal bones meet the occipital bone posteriorly (see Figures 7.2b and 7.3)

4. The **squamous** (or **squamosal**) **suture** (one on each side), where a parietal and temporal bone meet on the lateral aspect of the skull (see Figure 7.3)

Occipital Bone

The **occipital bone** (ok-sip′ĭ-tal) forms most of the skull's posterior wall and base. It articulates anteriorly with the paired parietal and temporal bones via the *lambdoid* and *occipitomastoid sutures*, respectively (Figure 7.3). It also joins with the sphenoid bone in the cranial floor via a plate called the *basioccipital*, which bears a midline projection called the *pharyngeal tubercle* (fah-rin′je-ul) (Figure 7.4a).

Internally, the occipital bone forms the walls of the **posterior cranial fossa** (Figure 7.4b and c), which supports the cerebellum of the brain. In the base of the occipital bone is the **foramen magnum** ("large hole") through which the inferior part of the brain connects with the spinal cord. The foramen magnum is flanked laterally by two occipital condyles (Figure 7.4a). The rockerlike **occipital condyles** articulate with the first vertebra of the spinal column in a way that permits a nodding movement of the head. Hidden medially and superiorly to each occipital condyle is a **hypoglossal canal** (Figure 7.4b), through which a nerve of the same name passes.

Just superior to the foramen magnum is a median protrusion called the **external occipital protuberance** (see Figures 7.2b, 7.3b, and 7.4a). You can feel this knoblike projection just below the most bulging part of your posterior skull. A number of inconspicuous ridges, the *external occipital crest* and the *superior* and *inferior nuchal lines* (nu′kal), mark the occipital bone near the foramen magnum. The external occipital crest secures the *ligamentum nuchae* (lig″ah-men′tum noo′ke; *nucha* = back of the neck), an elastic ligament that connects the vertebrae of the neck to the skull. The nuchal lines, and the bony regions between them, anchor many neck and back muscles. The superior nuchal line marks the upper limit of the neck.

Temporal Bones

The two **temporal bones** are best viewed on the lateral skull surface (see Figure 7.3). They lie inferior to the parietal bones and meet them at the squamous sutures. The temporal bones form the inferolateral aspects of the skull and parts of the cranial floor. The use of the terms *temple* and *temporal*, from the Latin word *temporum*, meaning "time," came about because gray hairs, a sign of time's passing, usually appear first in the temple areas.

Each temporal bone has a complicated shape and is described in terms of its four major areas, the *squamous, tympanic, mastoid,* and *petrous regions.* The flaring **squamous region** abuts the squamous suture. It has a barlike **zygomatic process** that meets the zygomatic bone of the face anteriorly. Together, these two bony structures form the **zygomatic arch,** which you can feel as the projection of your cheek (*zygoma* = cheekbone). The small, oval **mandibular fossa** (man-dib′u-lar) on the inferior surface of the zygomatic process receives the condyle of the mandible (lower jawbone), forming the freely movable *temporomandibular joint.*

The **tympanic region** (tim-pan′ik; "eardrum") (Figure 7.5) of the temporal bone surrounds the **external acoustic meatus,** or external ear canal, through which sound enters the ear. The external acoustic meatus and the eardrum at its deep end are part of the *external ear.* In a dried skull, the eardrum has been removed; thus, part of the middle ear cavity deep to the external meatus can also be seen. Below the external acoustic meatus is the needle-like **styloid process** (sti′loid; "stakelike"), an attachment point for several tongue and neck muscles and for a ligament that secures the hyoid bone of the neck to the skull (see Figure 7.12).

The **mastoid region** (mas′toid; "breast") of the temporal bone exhibits the conspicuous **mastoid process,** an anchoring site for some neck muscles (see Figures 7.3a, 7.4a, and 7.5). The mastoid process can be felt as a lump just posterior to the ear. The **stylomastoid foramen,** between the styloid and mastoid processes, allows cranial nerve VII (the facial nerve) to leave the skull (Figure 7.4a).

HOMEOSTATIC IMBALANCE

The mastoid process is full of air cavities, the **mastoid sinuses,** or **air cells.** Its position adjacent to the middle ear cavity (a high-risk area for infections spreading from the throat) puts it at risk for infection itself. A mastoid sinus infection, or *mastoiditis,* is notoriously difficult to treat. Since the mastoid air cells are separated from the brain by only a very thin bony plate, mastoid infections may spread to the brain as well. Surgical removal of the mastoid process was once the best way to prevent life-threatening brain inflammations in people susceptible to repeated bouts of mastoiditis. Today, antibiotic therapy is the treatment of choice. ●

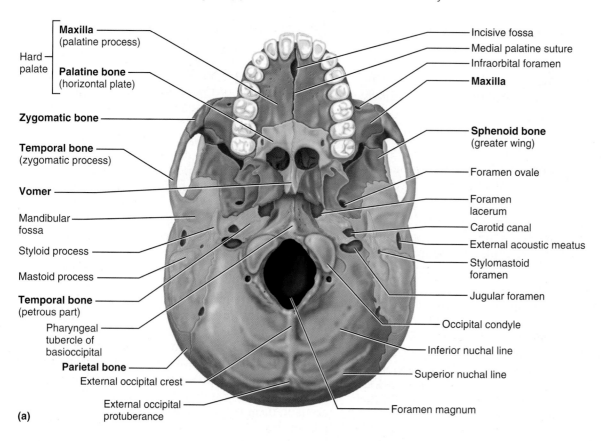

Maxilla
(palatine process)

Hard palate

Palatine bone
(horizontal plate)

Zygomatic bone

Temporal bone
(zygomatic process)

Vomer

Mandibular fossa

Styloid process

Mastoid process

Temporal bone
(petrous part)

Pharyngeal tubercle of basioccipital

Parietal bone

External occipital crest

External occipital protuberance

Incisive fossa

Medial palatine suture

Infraorbital foramen

Maxilla

Sphenoid bone
(greater wing)

Foramen ovale

Foramen lacerum

Carotid canal

External acoustic meatus

Stylomastoid foramen

Jugular foramen

Occipital condyle

Inferior nuchal line

Superior nuchal line

Foramen magnum

(a)

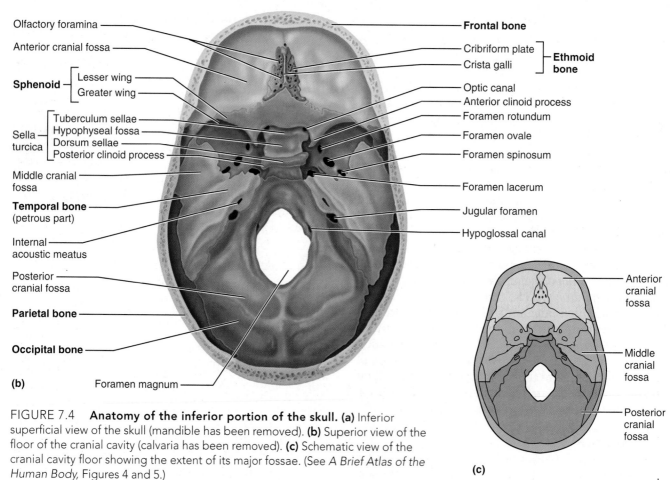

Olfactory foramina

Anterior cranial fossa

Sphenoid — Lesser wing / Greater wing

Sella turcica — Tuberculum sellae / Hypophyseal fossa / Dorsum sellae / Posterior clinoid process

Middle cranial fossa

Temporal bone
(petrous part)

Internal acoustic meatus

Posterior cranial fossa

Parietal bone

Occipital bone

Foramen magnum

Frontal bone

Cribriform plate / Crista galli — Ethmoid bone

Optic canal

Anterior clinoid process

Foramen rotundum

Foramen ovale

Foramen spinosum

Foramen lacerum

Jugular foramen

Hypoglossal canal

(b)

Anterior cranial fossa

Middle cranial fossa

Posterior cranial fossa

(c)

FIGURE 7.4 **Anatomy of the inferior portion of the skull. (a)** Inferior superficial view of the skull (mandible has been removed). **(b)** Superior view of the floor of the cranial cavity (calvaria has been removed). **(c)** Schematic view of the cranial cavity floor showing the extent of its major fossae. (See *A Brief Atlas of the Human Body*, Figures 4 and 5.)

7

The deep **petrous** (pet′rus) part of the temporal bone contributes to the cranial base (Figure 7.4). It looks like a miniature mountain ridge (*petrous* = rocky) between the occipital bone posteriorly and the sphenoid bone anteriorly. The posterior slope of this ridge lies in the posterior cranial fossa; the anterior slope is in the middle cranial fossa. Together, the sphenoid bone and the petrous portions of the temporal bones construct the **middle cranial fossa** (see Figure 7.4b and c), which supports the temporal lobes of the brain. Housed in the petrous are the *middle* and *internal ear cavities*, which contain sensory receptors for hearing and balance.

Several foramina penetrate the bone of the petrous region (Figure 7.4a). The large **jugular foramen** at the junction of the occipital and petrous temporal bones allows passage of the internal jugular vein and three cranial nerves. The **carotid canal** (kar-rot′id), just anterior to the jugular foramen, transmits the internal carotid artery into the cranial cavity. The two internal carotid arteries supply blood to over 80% of the cerebral hemispheres of the brain; their closeness to the internal ear cavities explains why, during excitement or exertion, we sometimes hear our rapid pulse as a thundering sound in the head. The **foramen lacerum** (la′ser-um) is a jagged opening (*lacerum* = torn or lacerated) between the petrous temporal bone and the sphenoid bone. It is almost completely closed by cartilage in a living person, but it is conspicuous in a dried skull, and students usually ask its name. The **internal acoustic meatus**, positioned superolateral to the jugular foramen (Figures 7.3b and 7.4b), transmits cranial nerves VII and VIII.

Sphenoid Bone

The butterfly-shaped **sphenoid bone** (sfe′noid; *sphen* = wedge) spans the width of the middle cranial fossa (Figure 7.4b). The sphenoid is considered the keystone of the cranium because it forms a central wedge that articulates with all other cranial bones. It is a challenging bone to study because of its complex shape. As shown in Figure 7.6, it consists of a central body and three pairs of processes: the greater wings, lesser wings, and pterygoid processes (ter′ĭ-goid). Within the **body** of the sphenoid are the paired **sphenoid sinuses** (see Figures 7.3b and 7.11).

The superior surface of the body bears a saddle-shaped prominence, the **sella turcica** (sel′ah ter′sĭ-kah), meaning "Turk's saddle." The seat of this saddle, called the **hypophyseal fossa**, forms a snug enclosure for the pituitary gland (hypophysis). This fossa is abutted anteriorly and posteriorly by the **tuberculum sellae** and the **dorsum sellae**, respectively. The dorsum sellae terminates laterally in the **posterior clinoid processes.**

The **greater wings** project laterally from the body, forming parts of (1) the middle cranial fossa

FIGURE 7.5 **The temporal bone.** Right lateral view. (See *A Brief Atlas of the Human Body,* Figures 3 and 8.)

(see Figure 7.4b and c), (2) the dorsal walls of the orbits (see Figure 7.2a), and (3) the external wall of the skull, where they are seen as flag-shaped, bony areas medial to the zygomatic arch (see Figure 7.3). The hornlike **lesser wings** form part of the floor of the anterior cranial fossa (Figure 7.4b and c) and part of the medial walls of the orbits. These terminate medially in the **anterior clinoid processes,** which provide an anchoring site for securing the brain within the skull.

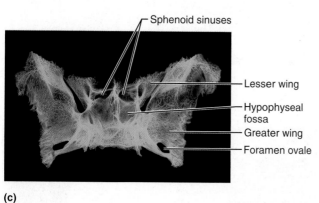

Chiasmatic groove

Optic canal

Lesser wing

Greater wing

Anterior clinoid process

Foramen rotundum

Foramen ovale

Foramen spinosum

Dorsum sellae

Body of sphenoid

Greater wing

Hypophyseal fossa of sella turcica

Posterior clinoid process

(a) Superior view

Posterior clinoid process

Body of sphenoid

Greater wing

Lesser wing

Superior orbital fissure

Foramen rotundum

Pterygoid processes

(b) Posterior view

Sphenoid sinuses

Lesser wing

Hypophyseal fossa

Greater wing

Foramen ovale

(c)

FIGURE 7.6　**The sphenoid bone. (a)** Superior view.
(b) Posterior view. **(c)** High-resolution microradiograph of the sphenoid bone, superior view. Note in particular its body, contained sinuses, the greater and lesser wings, and the pterygoid processes. (See *A Brief Atlas of the Human Body,* Figures 3 and 9.)

The trough-shaped **pterygoid processes** project inferiorly from the junction of the body and greater wings (see Figure 7.6b). They anchor the pterygoid muscles, which are important in chewing.

A number of openings in the sphenoid bone are visible in Figures 7.4b and 7.6. The **optic canals,** connected by the *chiasmatic groove,* lie anterior to the sella turcica; they allow the optic nerves to pass to the eyes. On each side of the sphenoid body is a crescent-shaped row of four openings. The anterior-most of these, the **superior orbital fissure,** is a long slit between the greater and lesser wings. It allows cranial nerves that control eye movements (III, IV, VI) to enter the orbit. This fissure is most obvious in

an anterior view of the skull (see Figure 7.2). The **foramen rotundum** and **foramen ovale** (o-vă′le) provide passageways for branches of cranial nerve V (the maxillary and mandibular nerves, respectively) to reach the face. The foramen rotundum is in the medial part of the greater wing and is usually oval, despite its name meaning "round opening." The foramen ovale, a large, oval foramen posterior to the foramen rotundum, is visible in an inferior view of the skull (see Figure 7.4a). Posterolateral to the foramen ovale is the small **foramen spinosum** (Figure 7.4b); it transmits the *middle meningeal artery,* which serves the internal faces of some of the cranial bones.

Ethmoid Bone

Like the temporal and sphenoid bones, the delicate **ethmoid bone** has a complex shape (Figure 7.7). Lying between the sphenoid and the nasal bones of the face, it is the most deeply situated bone of the skull. It forms most of the bony area between the nasal cavity and the orbits.

The superior surface of the ethmoid is formed by the paired horizontal **cribriform plates** (krib′rĭ-form) (see also Figure 7.4b), which help form the roof of the nasal cavities and the floor of the anterior cranial fossa. The cribriform plates are punctured by tiny holes (*cribr* = sieve) called *olfactory foramina* that allow the olfactory nerves to pass from the smell receptors in the nasal cavities to the brain. Projecting superiorly between the cribriform plates is

Q *Of what importance is the crista galli?*

Olfactory foramina — Crista galli — Cribriform plate

Orbital plate

Ethmoid sinuses

Left lateral mass

Perpendicular plate — Middle nasal concha

FIGURE 7.7   **The ethmoid bone.** Anterior view. (See *A Brief Atlas of the Human Body*, Figures 3 and 10.)

a triangular process called the **crista galli** (kris'tah gah'le; "rooster's comb"). The outermost covering of the brain (the dura mater) attaches to the crista galli and helps secure the brain in the cranial cavity.

The **perpendicular plate** of the ethmoid bone projects inferiorly in the median plane and forms the superior part of the nasal septum, which divides the nasal cavity into right and left halves (see Figure 7.3b). Flanking the perpendicular plate on each side is a **lateral mass** riddled with the **ethmoid sinuses** (Figures 7.7 and 7.11) for which the bone itself is named (*ethmos* = sieve). Extending medially from the lateral masses are the delicately coiled **superior** and **middle nasal conchae** (kong'ke; *concha* = shell), or **turbinates,** which protrude into the nasal cavity (Figures 7.7 and 7.10a). The lateral surfaces of the ethmoid's lateral masses are called **orbital plates** because they contribute to the medial walls of the orbits.

Sutural Bones

Sutural bones are tiny irregularly shaped bones or bone clusters that appear within sutures, most often in the lambdoid suture (see Figure 7.2b). Structurally unimportant, their number varies, and not all skulls exhibit them. Sutural bones represent additional ossification centers that appeared when the skull was expanding rapidly during fetal development.

Facial Bones

The facial skeleton is made up of 14 bones (see Figures 7.2a and 7.3a), of which only the mandible and the vomer are unpaired. The maxillae, zygomatics, nasals, lacrimals, palatines, and inferior conchae are paired bones. As a rule, the facial skeleton of men is more elongated than that of women; therefore, women's faces tend to be rounder and less angular.

■ Mandible

The U-shaped **mandible** (man'dĭ-bl), or lower jawbone (Figures 7.2, 7.3, and 7.8a), is the largest, strongest bone of the face. It has a *body,* which forms the chin, and two upright *rami* (*rami* = branches). Each ramus meets the body posteriorly at a **mandibular angle.** At the superior margin of each ramus are two processes separated by the **mandibular notch.** The anterior **coronoid process** (kor'o-noid; "crown-shaped") is an insertion point for the large temporalis muscle that elevates the lower jaw during chewing. The posterior **mandibular condyle** articulates with the mandibular fossa of the temporal bone, forming the *temporomandibular joint* on the same side.

The mandibular **body** anchors the lower teeth. Its superior border, called the **alveolar margin** (al-ve'o-lar), contains the sockets (*alveoli*) in which the teeth are embedded. In the midline of the mandibular body is a slight depression, the **mandibular symphysis** (sim'fih-sis), indicating where the two mandibular bones fused during infancy (see Figure 7.2a).

Large **mandibular foramina,** one on the medial surface of each ramus, permit the nerves

A *It is the site to which the membranes surrounding the brain attach to secure the brain in the cranial cavity.*

Q *Which of the bones illustrated is the keystone of the facial skeleton?*

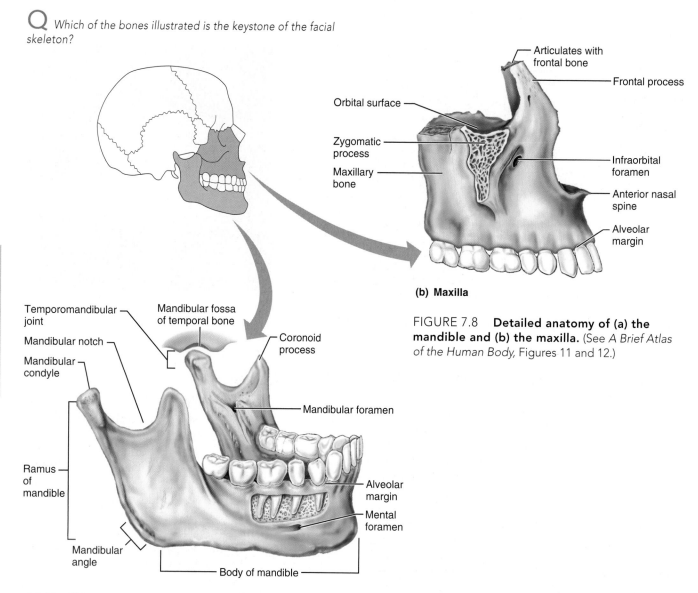

(b) Maxilla

FIGURE 7.8 **Detailed anatomy of (a) the mandible and (b) the maxilla.** (See *A Brief Atlas of the Human Body,* Figures 11 and 12.)

(a) Mandible

responsible for tooth sensation to pass to the teeth in the lower jaw. Dentists inject lidocaine into these foramina to prevent pain while working on the lower teeth. The **mental foramina,** openings on the lateral aspects of the mandibular body, allow blood vessels and nerves to pass to the skin of the chin (*ment* = chin) and lower lip.

Maxillary Bones

The **maxillary bones,** or **maxillae** (mak-sil'le; "jaws") (see Figures 7.2 to 7.4 and 7.8b), are fused medially.

They form the upper jaw and the central portion of the facial skeleton. All facial bones except the mandible articulate with the maxillae. Hence, the maxillae are considered the keystone bones of the facial skeleton.

The maxillae carry the upper teeth in their **alveolar margins.** Just inferior to the nose the maxillae meet medially, forming the pointed **anterior nasal spine** at their junction. The **palatine processes** (pă'lah-tīn) of the maxillae project posteriorly from the alveolar margins and fuse medially, forming the anterior two-thirds of the hard palate, or bony roof of the mouth (see Figures 7.3b and 7.4a). Just posterior to the teeth is a midline foramen, called the **incisive fossa,** which serves as a passageway for blood vessels and nerves.

A *The maxilla is the keystone of the facial skeleton and forms the anterior portion of the hard palate.*

The **frontal processes** extend superiorly to the frontal bone, forming part of the lateral aspects of the bridge of the nose (see Figures 7.2a and 7.8b). The regions that flank the nasal cavity laterally contain the **maxillary sinuses** (Figure 7.11), the largest of the paranasal sinuses. They extend from the orbits to the roots of the upper teeth. Laterally, the maxillae articulate with the zygomatic bones via their **zygomatic processes.**

The **inferior orbital fissure** is located deep within the orbit (see Figure 7.2a) at the junction of the maxilla with the greater wing of the sphenoid. It permits the zygomatic nerve, the maxillary nerve (a branch of cranial nerve V), and blood vessels to pass to the face. Just below the eye socket on each side is an **infraorbital foramen** that allows the infraorbital nerve (a continuation of the maxillary nerve) and artery to reach the face.

Zygomatic Bones

The irregularly shaped **zygomatic bones** (see Figures 7.2a, 7.3a, and 7.4a) are commonly called the cheekbones (*zygoma* = cheekbone). They articulate with the zygomatic processes of the temporal bones posteriorly, the zygomatic process of the frontal bone superiorly, and with the zygomatic processes of the maxillae anteriorly. The zygomatic bones form the prominences of the cheeks and part of the inferolateral margins of the orbits.

Nasal Bones

The thin, basically rectangular **nasal bones** (na'zal) are fused medially, forming the bridge of the nose (see Figures 7.2a and 7.3a). They articulate with the frontal bone superiorly, the maxillary bones laterally, and the perpendicular plate of the ethmoid bone posteriorly. Inferiorly they attach to the cartilages that form most of the skeleton of the external nose.

Lacrimal Bones

The delicate fingernail-shaped **lacrimal bones** (lak'rĭ-mal) contribute to the medial walls of each orbit (see Figures 7.2a and 7.3a). They articulate with the frontal bone superiorly, the ethmoid bone posteriorly, and the maxillae anteriorly. Each lacrimal bone contains a deep groove that helps form a **lacrimal fossa.** The lacrimal fossa houses the *lacrimal sac,* part of the passageway that allows tears to drain from the eye surface into the nasal cavity (*lacrima* = tears).

Palatine Bones

Each L-shaped **palatine bone** is fashioned from two bony plates, the *horizontal* and *perpendicular* (Figures 7.10a and 7.4a), and has three important articular processes, the *pyramidal, sphenoidal,* and *orbital.* The **horizontal plates** complete the poste-

rior portion of the hard palate. The superiorly projecting **perpendicular (vertical) plates** form part of the posterolateral walls of the nasal cavity and a small part of the orbits.

Vomer

The slender, plow-shaped **vomer** (vo'mer; "plow") lies in the nasal cavity, where it forms part of the nasal septum (see Figures 7.2a and 7.10b). It is discussed below in connection with the nasal cavity.

Inferior Nasal Conchae

The paired **inferior nasal conchae** are thin, curved bones in the nasal cavity. They project medially from the lateral walls of the nasal cavity, just inferior to the middle nasal conchae of the ethmoid bone (see Figures 7.2a and 7.10a). They are the largest of the three pairs of conchae and, like the others, they form part of the lateral walls of the nasal cavity.

Special Characteristics of the Orbits and Nasal Cavity

Two restricted skull regions, the orbits and the nasal cavity, are formed from an amazing number of bones. Thus, even though the individual bones forming these structures have been described, a brief summary is provided here to pull the parts together.

The Orbits

The **orbits** are bony cavities in which the eyes are firmly encased and cushioned by fatty tissue. The muscles that move the eyes and the tear-producing lacrimal glands are also housed in the orbits. The walls of each orbit are formed by parts of seven bones—the frontal, sphenoid, zygomatic, maxilla, palatine, lacrimal, and ethmoid bones. Their relationships are shown in Figure 7.9. Also seen in the orbits are the superior and inferior orbital fissures and the optic canals, described earlier.

The Nasal Cavity

The **nasal cavity** is constructed of bone and hyaline cartilage (Figure 7.10a). The *roof* of the nasal cavity is formed by the cribriform plate of the ethmoid. The *lateral walls* are largely shaped by the superior and middle conchae of the ethmoid bone, the perpendicular plates of the palatine bones, and the inferior nasal conchae. The depressions under cover of the conchae on the lateral walls are called *meatuses* (*meatus* = passage), so there are superior, middle, and inferior meatuses. The *floor* of the nasal cavity is formed by the palatine processes of the maxillae and the palatine bones. The nasal cavity is divided into right and left parts by the *nasal septum.* The bony

(a)

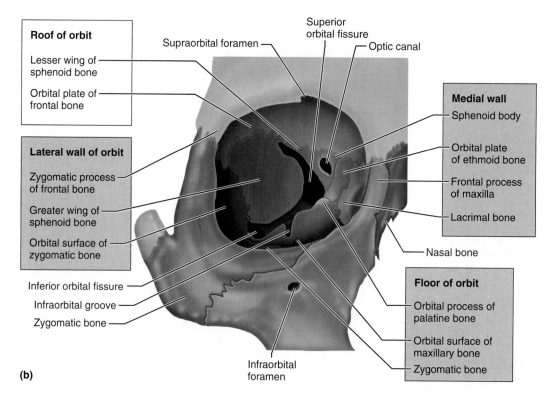

Roof of orbit

Lesser wing of sphenoid bone

Orbital plate of frontal bone

Lateral wall of orbit

Zygomatic process of frontal bone

Greater wing of sphenoid bone

Orbital surface of zygomatic bone

Inferior orbital fissure

Infraorbital groove

Zygomatic bone

Supraorbital foramen

Superior orbital fissure

Optic canal

Medial wall

Sphenoid body

Orbital plate of ethmoid bone

Frontal process of maxilla

Lacrimal bone

Nasal bone

Floor of orbit

Orbital process of palatine bone

Orbital surface of maxillary bone

Zygomatic bone

Infraorbital foramen

(b)

FIGURE 7.9 **Special anatomical characteristics of the orbits.** The contribution of each of the seven bones forming the right orbit is illustrated. **(a)** Photograph. **(b)** Diagrammatic view. (See *A Brief Atlas of the Human Body,* Figure 14.)

portion of the septum is formed by the vomer inferiorly and the perpendicular plate of the ethmoid bone superiorly (Figure 7.10b). A sheet of cartilage called the *septal cartilage* completes the septum anteriorly.

The nasal septum and conchae are covered with a mucus-secreting mucosa that moistens and warms the entering air and helps cleanse it of debris. The scroll-shaped conchae increase the turbulence of air flowing through the nasal cavity. This swirling forces more of the inhaled air into contact with the warm, damp mucosa and encourages trapping of airborne particles (dust, pollen, bacteria) in the sticky mucus.

Paranasal Sinuses

Five skull bones—the frontal, sphenoid, ethmoid, and paired maxillary bones—contain mucosa-lined, air-filled sinuses that give them a rather moth-eaten appearance in an X-ray image. These particular

(Text continues on p. 218.)

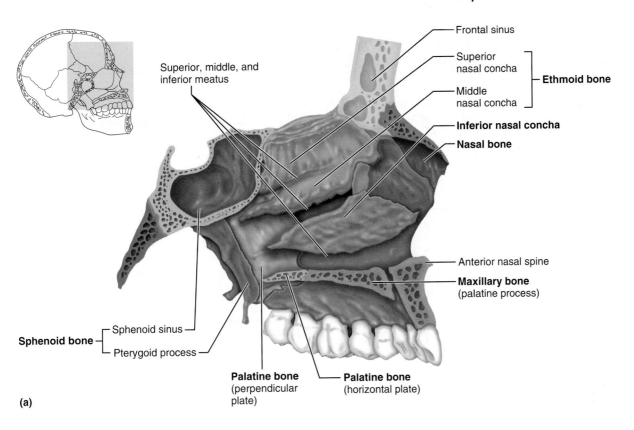

(a)

- Superior, middle, and inferior meatus
- Frontal sinus
- Superior nasal concha — **Ethmoid bone**
- Middle nasal concha
- **Inferior nasal concha**
- **Nasal bone**
- Anterior nasal spine
- **Maxillary bone** (palatine process)
- **Sphenoid bone** — Sphenoid sinus — Pterygoid process
- **Palatine bone** (perpendicular plate)
- **Palatine bone** (horizontal plate)

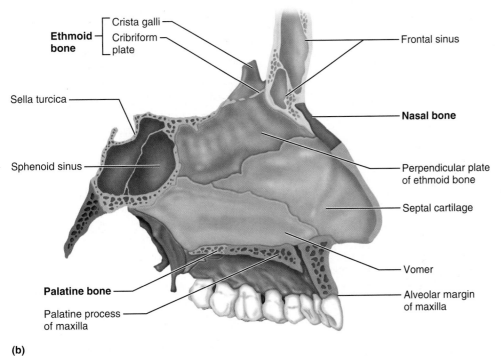

(b)

- **Ethmoid bone** — Crista galli — Cribriform plate
- Frontal sinus
- Sella turcica
- **Nasal bone**
- Sphenoid sinus
- Perpendicular plate of ethmoid bone
- Septal cartilage
- Vomer
- Alveolar margin of maxilla
- **Palatine bone**
- Palatine process of maxilla

FIGURE 7.10 **Special anatomical characteristics of the nasal cavity.**
(a) Bones forming the left lateral wall of the nasal cavity (nasal septum removed).
(b) Nasal cavity with nasal septum in place, showing the contribution of the ethmoid, vomer, and cartilage to the nasal septum. (See *A Brief Atlas of the Human Body,* Figure 15.)

7

TABLE 7.1 **Bones of the Skull**

BONE*	COMMENTS	IMPORTANT MARKINGS†
CRANIAL BONES		
☐ **Frontal** (1) (Figures 7.2a, 7.3, and 7.4b)	Forms forehead; superior part of orbits and anterior cranial fossa; contains sinuses	**Supraorbital foramen (notch) (2):** allows the supraorbital arteries and nerves to pass
☐ **Parietal** (2) (Figures 7.2 and 7.3)	Forms most of the superior and lateral aspects of the skull	
☐ **Occipital** (1) (Figures 7.2b, 7.3, and 7.4)	Forms posterior aspect and most of the base of the skull	**Foramen magnum:** allows the spinal cord to issue from the brain stem to enter the vertebral canal
		Hypoglossal canal (2): allows passage of the hypoglossal nerve (cranial nerve XII)
		Occipital condyle (2): articulates with the atlas (first vertebra)
		External occipital protuberance and **nuchal lines:** sites of muscle attachment
		External occipital crest: attachment site of ligamentum nuchae
☐ **Temporal** (2) (Figures 7.3, 7.4, and 7.5)	Forms inferolateral aspects of the skull and contributes to the middle cranial fossa; has squamous, mastoid, tympanic, and petrous regions	**Zygomatic process:** helps to form the zygomatic arch, which forms the prominence of the cheek
		Mandibular fossa: articular point of the mandibular condyle
		External acoustic meatus: canal leading from the external ear to the eardrum
		Styloid process: attachment site for hyoid bone and several neck muscles
		Mastoid process: attachment site for several neck and tongue muscles
		Stylomastoid foramen: allows cranial nerve VII (facial nerve) to pass
		Jugular foramen: allows passage of the internal jugular vein and cranial nerves IX, X, and XI
		Internal acoustic meatus: allows passage of cranial nerves VII and VIII
		Carotid canal: allows passage of the internal carotid artery
☐ **Sphenoid** (1) (Figures 7.2a, 7.3, 7.4, and 7.6)	Keystone of the cranium; contributes to the middle cranial fossa and orbits; main parts are the body, greater wings, lesser wings, and pterygoid processes	**Sella turcica:** hypophyseal fossa portion is the seat of the pituitary gland
		Optic canal (2): allows passage of cranial nerve II and the ophthalmic arteries
		Superior orbital fissure (2): allows passage of cranial nerves III, IV, VI, part of V (ophthalmic division), and ophthalmic vein
		Foramen rotundum (2): allows passage of the maxillary division of cranial nerve V
		Foramen ovale (2): allows passage of the mandibular division of cranial nerve V
		Foramen spinosum (2): allows passage of the middle meningeal artery

*The color code beside each bone name corresponds to the bone's color in Figures 7.2 to 7.10. The number in parentheses ( ) following the bone name denotes the total number of such bones in the body.
†A (2) following the name of a marking indicates a pair of markings in an unpaired bone.

TABLE 7.1 (continued)

BONE*	COMMENTS	IMPORTANT MARKINGS†
CRANIAL BONES		
Ethmoid (1) (Figures 7.2a, 7.3, 7.4b, 7.7, and 7.10)	Helps to form the anterior cranial fossa; forms part of the nasal septum and the lateral walls and roof of the nasal cavity; contributes to the medial wall of the orbit	**Crista galli:** attachment point for the falx cerebri, a dural membrane **Cribriform plate (2):** allows passage of nerve filaments of the olfactory nerves (cranial nerve I) **Superior** and **middle nasal conchae (2):** forms part of lateral walls of nasal cavity; increase turbulence of air flow
Auditory ossicles (malleus, incus, and stapes) (2 each)	Found in middle ear cavity; involved in sound transmission; see Chapter 15	
FACIAL BONES		
Mandible (1) (Figures 7.2a, 7.3, and 7.8a)	The lower jaw	**Coronoid process (2):** insertion point for the temporalis muscle **Mandibular condyle (2):** articulates with the temporal bones in freely movable joints (temporomandibular joints) of the jaw **Mandibular symphysis:** medial fusion point of the mandibular bones **Alveoli:** sockets for the teeth **Mandibular foramen (2):** permits the inferior alveolar nerves to pass **Mental foramen (2):** allows blood vessels and nerves to pass to the chin and lower lip
Maxilla (2) (Figures 7.2a, 7.3, 7.4a, and 7.8b)	Keystone bones of the face; form the upper jaw and parts of the hard palate, orbits, and nasal cavity walls	**Alveoli:** sockets for the teeth **Zygomatic process:** helps form the zygomatic arch **Palatine process:** forms the anterior hard palate; processes meet in medial palatine suture **Frontal process:** forms part of lateral aspect of bridge of nose **Incisive fossa:** permits blood vessels and nerves to pass through hard palate (fused palatine processes) **Inferior orbital fissure:** permits maxillary branch of cranial nerve V, the zygomatic nerve, and blood vessels to pass **Infraorbital foramen:** allows passage of infraorbital nerve to skin of face
Zygomatic (2) (Figures 7.2a, 7.3a, and 7.4a)	Forms the cheek and part of the orbit	
Nasal (2) (Figures 7.2a and 7.3)	Constructs the bridge of the nose	
Lacrimal (2) (Figures 7.2a and 7.3a)	Forms part of the medial orbit wall	**Lacrimal fossa:** houses the lacrimal sac, which helps to drain tears into the nasal cavity
Palatine (2) (Figures 7.3b, 7.4a, and 7.10)	Forms posterior part of the hard palate and a small part of nasal cavity and orbit wall	
Vomer (1) (Figures 7.2a, 7.3b, and 7.10)	Part of the nasal septum	
Inferior nasal concha (2) (Figures 7.2a and 7.10a)	Forms part of the lateral wall of the nasal cavity	

7

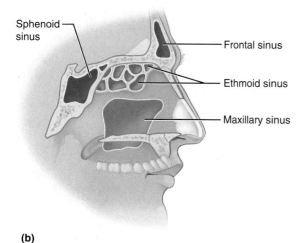

(a)

(b)

FIGURE 7.11 **Paranasal sinuses. (a)** Anterior aspect. **(b)** Medial aspect.

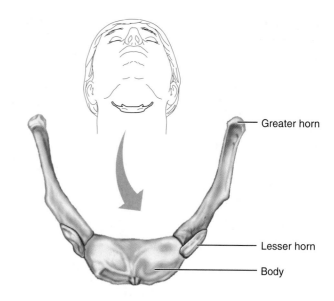

FIGURE 7.12 **The hyoid bone.** The hyoid bone is suspended in the mid-anterior neck by ligaments attached to the lesser horns (cornua) and the styloid processes of the temporal bones.

sinuses are called **paranasal sinuses** because they cluster around the nasal cavity (Figure 7.11). Small openings connect the sinuses to the nasal cavity and act as "two-way streets"; air enters the sinuses from the nasal cavity, and mucus formed by the sinus mucosae drains into the nasal cavity. The mucosae of the sinuses also help to warm and humidify inspired air. The paranasal sinuses lighten the skull and enhance the resonance of the voice.

The Hyoid Bone

Though not really part of the skull, the **hyoid bone** (hi'oid; "U-shaped") lies just inferior to the mandible in the anterior neck, and looks like a miniature version of it (Figure 7.12). The hyoid bone is unique in that it is the only bone of the body that does not articulate directly with any other bone. Instead, it is anchored by the narrow *stylohyoid ligaments* to the styloid processes of the

temporal bones. Horseshoe-shaped, with a *body* and two pairs of *horns*, or *cornua*, the hyoid bone acts as a movable base for the tongue. Its body and greater horns are attachment points for neck muscles that raise and lower the larynx during swallowing and speech.

The Vertebral Column

General Characteristics

Some people think of the **vertebral column** as a rigid supporting rod, but this is inaccurate. Also called the **spine,** the vertebral column is formed from 26 irregular bones connected in such a way that a flexible, curved structure results (Figure 7.13). Serving as the axial support of the trunk, the spine extends from the skull to the pelvis, where it transmits the weight of the trunk to the lower limbs. It also surrounds and protects the delicate spinal cord and provides attachment points for the ribs and for the muscles of the back and neck. In the fetus and infant, the vertebral column consists of 33 separate bones, or **vertebrae** (ver'tĕ-bre). Inferiorly, nine of these eventually fuse to form two composite bones, the sacrum and the tiny coccyx. The remaining 24 bones persist as individual vertebrae separated by intervertebral discs.

Divisions and Curvatures

The vertebral column is about 70 cm (28 inches) long in an average adult and has five major divisions (Figure 7.13). The seven vertebrae of the neck are the **cervical vertebrae** (ser'vi-kal), the next 12 are the **thoracic vertebrae** (tho-ras'ik), and the five supporting the lower back are the **lumbar vertebrae** (lum'bar). Remembering common meal times— 7 AM, 12 noon, and 5 PM—will help you recall the number of bones in these three regions of the spine. The vertebrae become progressively larger from the cervical to the lumbar region, as they must support greater and greater weight.

Inferior to the lumbar vertebrae is the **sacrum** (sa'krum), which articulates with the hip bones of the pelvis. The terminus of the vertebral column is the tiny **coccyx** (kok'siks). All of us have the same number of cervical vertebrae. Variations in numbers of vertebrae in other regions occur in about 5% of people.

When you view the vertebral column from the side, you can see the four curvatures that give it its S, or sinusoid, shape. The **cervical** and **lumbar curvatures** are concave posteriorly; the **thoracic** and **sacral curvatures** are convex posteriorly. These curvatures increase the resilience and flexibility of the spine, allowing it to function like a spring rather than a rigid rod.

◤ HOMEOSTATIC IMBALANCE

There are several types of abnormal spinal curvatures. Some are congenital (present at birth); others result from disease, poor posture, or unequal muscle pull on the spine. *Scoliosis* (sko"le-o'sis), literally, "twisted disease," is an abnormal *lateral* curvature that occurs most often in the thoracic region. It is quite common during late childhood, particularly in girls, for some unknown reason. Other, more severe cases result from abnormal vertebral structure, lower limbs of unequal length, or muscle paralysis. If muscles on one side of the body are nonfunctional, those of the opposite side exert an unopposed pull on the spine and force it out of alignment. Scoliosis is treated (with body braces or surgically) before growth ends to prevent permanent deformity and breathing difficulties due to a compressed lung.

Kyphosis (ki-fo'sis), or hunchback, is a *dorsally* exaggerated *thoracic* curvature. It is particularly common in elderly people because of osteoporosis, but may also reflect tuberculosis of the spine, rickets, or osteomalacia. *Lordosis*, or swayback, is an accentuated *lumbar* curvature. It, too, can result from spinal tuberculosis or osteomalacia. Temporary lordosis is common in those carrying a large load up front, such as men with "potbellies" and pregnant women. In an attempt to preserve their center of gravity, these individuals automatically throw back their shoulders, accentuating their lumbar curvature. ●

Q *Why would it be anatomically "stupid" to have the sturdiest vertebrae in the cervical instead of the lumbar region of the spine?*

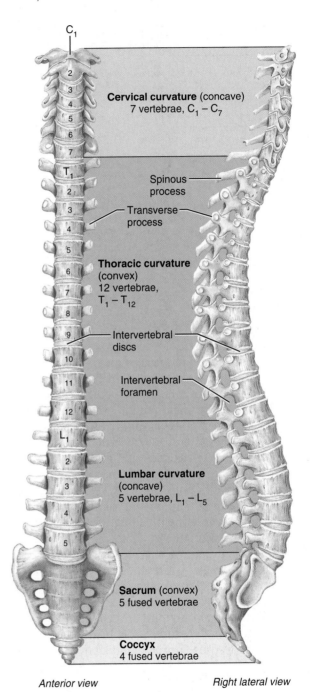

FIGURE 7.13 **The vertebral column.** Notice the curvatures in the lateral view. (The terms *convex* and *concave* refer to the curvature of the posterior aspect of the vertebral column.) (See *A Brief Atlas of the Human Body,* Figure 17.)

A *Because the lumbar region bears the greatest weight, its vertebrae are the sturdiest.*

(a)

(b)

FIGURE 7.14 **Ligaments and fibrocartilage discs uniting the vertebrae.**
(a) Median section of three vertebrae, illustrating the composition of the discs and
the ligaments. **(b)** Superior view of a sectioned herniated disc (slipped disc).

Ligaments

Like a tall, tremulous TV transmitting tower, the vertebral column cannot possibly stand upright by itself. It must be held in place by an elaborate system of cablelike supports. In the case of the vertebral column, straplike ligaments and the trunk muscles assume this role. The major supporting ligaments are the **anterior** and **posterior longitudinal ligaments** (Figure 7.14). These run as continuous bands down the front and back surfaces of the spine from the neck to the sacrum. The broad anterior ligament is strongly attached to both the bony vertebrae and the discs. Along with its supporting role, it prevents hyperextension of the spine (bending too far backward). The posterior ligament, which resists hyperflexion of the spine (bending too sharply forward), is narrow and relatively weak. It attaches only to the discs. However, the *ligamentum flavum*, which contains elastic connective tissue, is especially strong. It stretches as we bend forward and then recoils when we resume an erect posture. Short ligaments connect each vertebra to those immediately above and below.

Intervertebral Discs

Each **intervertebral disc** is a cushionlike pad composed of two parts. The inner gelatinous **nucleus pulposus** (pul-po'sus; "pulp") acts like a rubber ball, giving the disc its elasticity and compressibility. Surrounding the nucleus pulposus is a strong collar composed of collagen fibers superficially and fibrocartilage internally, the **anulus fibrosus** (an'u-lus fibro'sus; "ring of fibers") (see Figure 7.14a). The anulus fibrosus limits the expansion of the nucleus pulposus when the spine is compressed. It also acts like a woven strap to bind successive vertebrae together, withstands twisting forces, and resists tension in the spine.

The intervertebral discs act as shock absorbers during walking, jumping, and running, and they allow the spine to flex and extend, and to a lesser extent to bend laterally. At points of compression, the discs flatten and bulge out a bit between the vertebrae. The discs are thickest in the lumbar and cervical regions, which enhances the flexibility of these regions. Collectively the discs account for about 25% of the height of the vertebral column. They flatten somewhat during the course of the day, so we are always a few centimeters shorter at night than when we awake in the morning.

◤ HOMEOSTATIC IMBALANCE

Severe or sudden physical trauma to the spine—for example, from bending forward while lifting a heavy object—may result in herniation of one or more discs. A **herniated (prolapsed) disc** (commonly called a *slipped disc*) usually involves rupture of the anulus fibrosus followed by protrusion of the spongy nucleus pulposus through the anulus (see Figure 7.14b). If the protrusion presses on the spinal cord or on spinal nerves exiting from the cord, numbness or excruciating pain may result. Herniated discs are generally treated with moderate exercise, massage, heat therapy, and painkillers. If this fails, the protruding disc may have to be removed surgically and a bone graft done to fuse the adjoining vertebrae. For those preferring to avoid general anesthesia, the disc can be partially vaporized with a laser in an outpatient procedure called percutaneous laser disc decompression that takes only 30 to 40 minutes. The patient leaves with only an adhesive bandage to mark the spot. ●

General Structure of Vertebrae

All vertebrae have a common structural pattern (Figure 7.15). Each vertebra consists of a **body,** or **centrum,** anteriorly and a **vertebral arch** posteriorly. The disc-shaped body is the weight-bearing region. Together, the body and vertebral arch enclose an opening called the **vertebral foramen.** Successive vertebral foramina of the articulated vertebrae form the long **vertebral canal,** through which the spinal cord passes.

The vertebral arch is a composite structure formed by two pedicles and two laminae. The **pedicles** (ped′ĭ-kelz; "little feet"), short bony pillars projecting posteriorly from the vertebral body, form the sides of the arch. The **laminae** (lam′ĭ-ne), flattened plates that fuse in the median plane, complete the arch posteriorly. Seven processes project from the vertebral arch. The **spinous process** is a median posterior projection arising at the junction of the two laminae. A **transverse process** extends laterally from each side of the vertebral arch. The spinous and transverse processes are attachment sites for muscles that move the vertebral column and for ligaments that stabilize it. The paired **superior** and **inferior articular processes** protrude superiorly and inferiorly, respectively, from the pedicle-lamina junctions. The smooth joint surfaces of the articular processes, called *facets* ("little faces"), are covered with hyaline cartilage. The inferior articular processes of each vertebra form movable joints with the superior articular processes of the vertebra immediately below. Thus, successive vertebrae join both at their bodies and at their articular processes.

The pedicles have notches on their superior and inferior borders, providing lateral openings between adjacent vertebrae called **intervertebral foramina** (see Figure 7.13). The spinal nerves issuing from the spinal cord pass through these foramina.

Regional Vertebral Characteristics

Beyond their common structural features, vertebrae exhibit variations that allow different regions of the spine to perform slightly different functions and movements. In general, movements that can occur between vertebrae are (1) flexion and extension (anterior bending and posterior straightening of the spine), (2) lateral flexion (bending the *upper body* to the right or left), and (3) rotation (in which vertebrae rotate on one another in the longitudinal axis of the spine). The regional vertebral characteristics described in this section are illustrated and summarized in Table 7.2 on p. 224.

Q *What structural parts of the vertebra are sites of muscle attachment?*

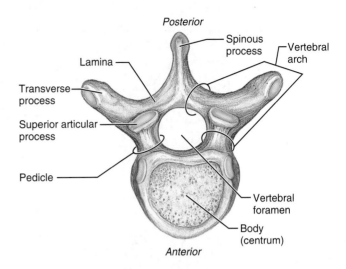

FIGURE 7.15 **Structure of a typical vertebra.** Superior view (inferior articulating surfaces not shown).

Cervical Vertebrae

The seven cervical vertebrae, identified as C_1–C_7, are the smallest, lightest vertebrae. The first two (C_1 and C_2) are unusual and we will skip them for the moment. The "typical" cervical vertebrae (C_3–C_7) have the following distinguishing features:

1. The body is oval—wider from side to side than in the anteroposterior dimension.

2. Except in C_7, the spinous process is short, projects directly back, and is *bifid* (bi′fid), or split at its tip.

3. The vertebral foramen is large and generally triangular.

4. Each transverse process contains a **transverse foramen** through which the vertebral arteries pass to service the brain.

The spinous process of C_7 is not bifid and is much larger than those of the other cervical vertebrae (see Figure 7.17a). Because its spinous process is visible through the skin, C_7 can be used as a landmark for counting the vertebrae and is called the **vertebra prominens** ("prominent vertebra").

The first two cervical vertebrae, the atlas and the axis, have no intervertebral disc between them, and they are highly modified, reflecting their special functions. The **atlas** (C_1) has no body and no spinous process (Figure 7.16a and b). Essentially, it is a ring of bone consisting of *anterior* and *posterior arches* and a *lateral mass* on each side. Each lateral

A *The spinous and transverse processes are sites of muscle attachment.*

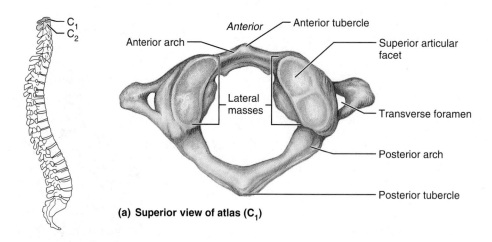

(a) Superior view of atlas (C$_1$)

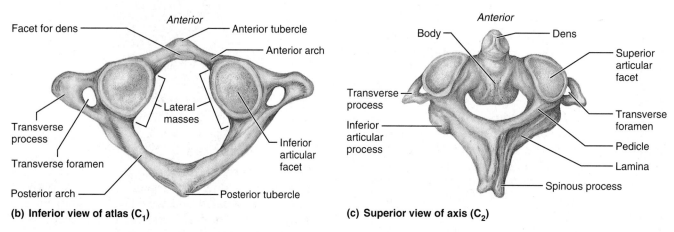

(b) Inferior view of atlas (C$_1$)

(c) Superior view of axis (C$_2$)

FIGURE 7.16   **The first and second cervical vertebrae.** (See *A Brief Atlas of the Human Body*, Figure 18.)

mass has articular facets on both its superior and inferior surfaces. The superior articular facets receive the occipital condyles of the skull; thus, they "carry" the skull, just as Atlas supported the heavens in Greek mythology. These joints allow you to nod "yes." The inferior articular facets form joints with the axis (C$_2$) below.

The **axis**, which has a body, spine, and the other typical vertebral processes, is not as specialized as the atlas. In fact, its only unusual feature is the knoblike **dens** (denz; "tooth"), or **odontoid process** (o-don'toid), projecting superiorly from its body. The dens is actually the "missing" body of the atlas, which fuses with the axis during embryonic development. Cradled in the anterior arch of the atlas by the transverse ligaments (Figure 7.17a), the dens acts as a pivot for the rotation of the atlas. Hence, this joint allows you to rotate your head from side to side to indicate "no."

Thoracic Vertebrae

The 12 thoracic vertebrae (T$_1$–T$_{12}$) all articulate with the ribs (see Table 7.2 and Figure 7.17b). The first looks much like C$_7$, and the last four show a

progression toward lumbar vertebral structure. The thoracic vertebrae increase in size from the first to the last. Unique characteristics of these vertebrae include the following:

1. The body is roughly heart shaped. It typically bears two small *facets*, commonly called *demifacets* (half-facets), on each side, one at the superior edge (the *superior costal facet*) and the other at the inferior edge (the *inferior costal facet*). The demifacets receive the heads of the ribs. (The bodies of T$_{10}$–T$_{12}$ vary from this pattern by having only a single facet to receive their respective ribs.)

2. The vertebral foramen is circular.

3. The spinous process is long and points sharply downward.

4. With the exception of T$_{11}$ and T$_{12}$, the transverse processes have facets, the *transverse costal facets*, that articulate with the *tubercles* of the ribs.

5. The superior and inferior articular facets lie mainly in the frontal plane, a situation that prevents flexion and extension, but which allows rotation of this region of the spine.

Dens of axis
Transverse ligament of atlas
C_1 (atlas)
C_2 (axis)
C_3
Inferior articular process
Bifid spinous process
Transverse processes
C_7 (vertebra prominens)

(a) Cervical vertebrae

Transverse process
Superior articular process
Transverse costal facet (for tubercle of rib)
Lamina
Pedicle
Intervertebral disc
Body
Spinous process
Inferior costal facet (for head of rib)
Inferior articular process

(b) Thoracic vertebrae

Superior articular process
Transverse process
Pedicle
Body
Intervertebral disc
Inferior articular process
Spinous process

(c) Lumbar vertebrae

FIGURE 7.17 **Posterolateral views of articulated vertebrae.** Notice the bulbous tip on the spinous process of C_7, the vertebra prominens. (See *A Brief Atlas of the Human Body*, Figures 19, 20, and 21.)

Lumbar Vertebrae

The lumbar region of the vertebral column, commonly referred to as the small of the back, receives the most stress. The enhanced weight-bearing function of the five lumbar vertebrae (L_1–L_5) is reflected in their sturdier structure. Their bodies are massive and kidney shaped in a superior view (see Table 7.2 and Figure 7.17c). Other characteristics typical of these vertebrae:

1. The pedicles and laminae are shorter and thicker than those of other vertebrae.

2. The spinous processes are short, flat, and hatchet shaped and are easily seen when a person bends forward. These processes are robust and project directly backward, adaptations for the attachment of the large back muscles.

3. The vertebral foramen is triangular.

4. The orientation of the facets of the articular processes of the lumbar vertebrae differs substantially from that of the other vertebra types (see Table 7.2). These modifications lock the lumbar vertebrae together and provide stability by preventing rotation of the lumbar spine.

TABLE 7.2	Regional Characteristics of Cervical, Thoracic, and Lumbar Vertebrae		
CHARACTERISTIC	**CERVICAL (3–7)**	**THORACIC**	**LUMBAR**
Body	Small, wide side to side	Larger than cervical; heart shaped; bears two costal facets	Massive; kidney shaped
Spinous process	Short; bifid; projects directly posteriorly	Long; sharp; projects inferiorly	Short; blunt; projects directly posteriorly
Vertebral foramen	Triangular	Circular	Triangular
Transverse processes	Contain foramina	Bear facets for ribs (except T_{11} and T_{12})	Thin and tapered
Superior and inferior articulating processes	Superior facets directed superoposteriorly	Superior facets directed posteriorly	Superior facets directed posteromedially (or medially)
	Inferior facets directed inferoanteriorly	Inferior facets directed anteriorly	Inferior facets directed anterolaterally (or laterally)
Movements allowed	Flexion and extension; lateral flexion; rotation; the spine region with the greatest range of movement	Rotation; lateral flexion possible but limited by ribs; flexion and extension prevented	Flexion and extension; some lateral flexion; rotation prevented

CERVICAL (3–7)	**THORACIC**	**LUMBAR**

SUPERIOR VIEW

RIGHT LATERAL VIEW

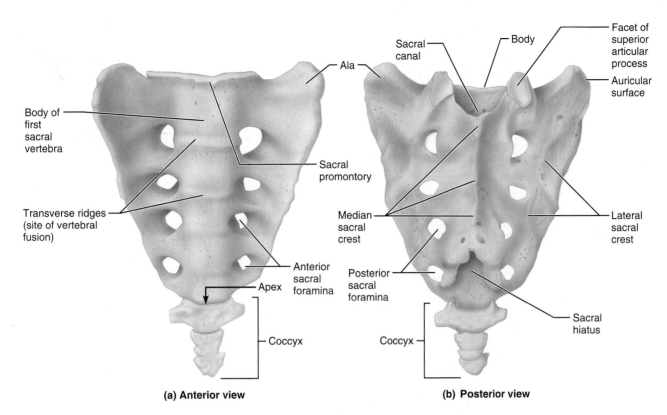

FIGURE 7.18 **The sacrum and coccyx.** (See *A Brief Atlas of the Human Body*, Figure 22.)

Sacrum

The triangular sacrum (Figure 7.18), which shapes the posterior wall of the pelvis, is formed by five fused vertebrae (S_1–S_5) in adults. It articulates superiorly (via its **superior articular processes**) with L_5 and inferiorly with the coccyx. Laterally, the sacrum articulates, via its **auricular surfaces,** with the two hip bones to form the **sacroiliac joints** (sa″kro-il′e-ak) of the pelvis.

The **sacral promontory** (prom′on-tor″e; "high point of land projecting into the sea"), the antero-superior margin of the first sacral vertebra, bulges anteriorly into the pelvic cavity. The body's center of gravity lies about 1 cm posterior to this landmark. Four ridges, the **transverse ridges,** cross its concave anterior aspect, marking the lines of fusion of the sacral vertebrae. The **anterior sacral foramina** penetrate the sacrum at the lateral ends of these ridges and transmit blood vessels and anterior rami of the sacral spinal nerves. The regions lateral to these foramina expand superiorly as the winglike **alae.**

In its posterior midline the sacral surface is roughened by the **median sacral crest** (the fused spinous processes of the sacral vertebrae). This is flanked laterally by the **posterior sacral foramina,** which transmit the posterior rami of the sacral spinal nerves, and then the **lateral sacral crests** (remnants of the transverse processes of S_1–S_5).

The vertebral canal continues inside the sacrum as the **sacral canal.** Since the laminae of the fifth (and sometimes the fourth) sacral vertebrae fail to fuse medially, an enlarged external opening called the **sacral hiatus** (hi-a′tus; "gap") is obvious at the inferior end of the sacral canal.

Coccyx

The coccyx, our tailbone, is a small triangular bone (Figure 7.18). It consists of four (or in some cases three or five) vertebrae fused together. The coccyx articulates superiorly with the sacrum. (The name *coccyx* is from the Greek word meaning "cuckoo" and was so named because of its fancied resemblance to a bird's beak.) Except for the slight support the coccyx affords the pelvic organs, it is a nearly useless bone. Occasionally, a baby is born with an unusually long coccyx. In most such cases, this bony "tail" is discreetly snipped off by the physician.

■ ■ ■

The characteristics of the regional vertebrae are summarized in Table 7.2.

Q   *Which ribs are also known as vertebrosternal ribs?*

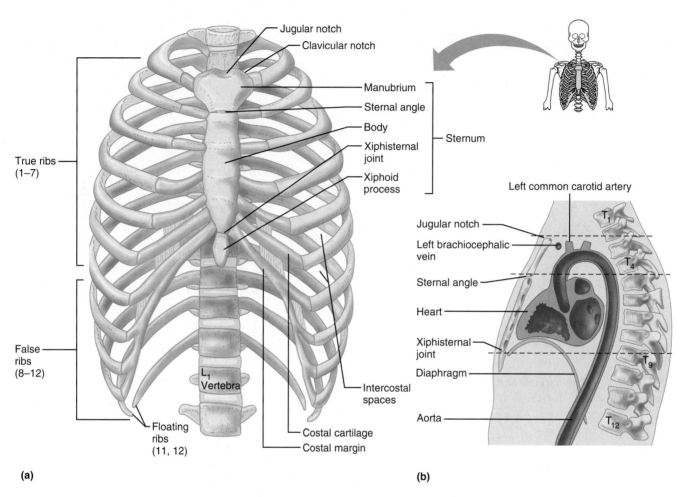

FIGURE 7.19   **The thoracic cage. (a)** Skeleton of the thoracic cage, anterior view (costal cartilages are shown in blue). **(b)** Left lateral view of the thorax, illustrating the relationship of the surface anatomical landmarks of the thorax to the vertebral column (thoracic portion). (See *A Brief Atlas of the Human Body,* Figure 23.)

The Thoracic Cage

Anatomically, the thorax is the chest, and its bony underpinnings are called the **thoracic cage** or **bony thorax.** Elements of the thoracic cage include the thoracic vertebrae dorsally, the ribs laterally, and the sternum and costal cartilages anteriorly. The costal cartilages secure the ribs to the sternum (Figure 7.19a). Roughly cone shaped with its broad dimension positioned inferiorly, the bony thorax forms a protective cage around the vital organs of the thoracic cavity (heart, lungs, and great blood vessels), supports the shoulder girdles and upper limbs, and provides attachment points for many muscles of the neck, back, chest, and shoulders. The *intercostal spaces* between

the ribs are occupied by the intercostal muscles, which lift and depress the thorax during breathing.

Sternum

The **sternum** (breastbone) lies in the anterior midline of the thorax. Vaguely resembling a dagger, it is a flat bone approximately 15 cm (6 inches) long, resulting from the fusion of three bones: the manubrium, the body, and the xiphoid process. The **manubrium** (mah-nu'bre-um), the superior portion shaped like the knot in a necktie, articulates via its **clavicular notches** (klah-vik'u-lar) with the clavicles (collarbones) laterally. It also articulates with the first two pairs of ribs. The **body,** or midportion, forms the bulk of the sternum. The sides of the body are notched where it articulates with the cartilages of the second to seventh ribs. The **xiphoid process**

7

(zif'oid; "swordlike") forms the inferior end of the sternum. This small, variably shaped process is a plate of hyaline cartilage in youth, but it is usually ossified in adults. The xiphoid process articulates only with the sternal body and serves as an attachment point for some abdominal muscles.

The sternum has three important anatomical landmarks: the jugular notch, the sternal angle, and the xiphisternal joint (see Figure 7.19). The easily palpated **jugular** (*suprasternal*) **notch** is the central indentation in the superior border of the manubrium. It is generally in line with the disc between the second and third thoracic vertebrae and the point where the left common carotid artery issues from the aorta (see Figure 7.19b). The **sternal angle** is felt as a horizontal ridge across the front of the sternum, where the manubrium joins the sternal body. This cartilaginous joint acts like a hinge, allowing the sternal body to swing forward when we inhale. The sternal angle is in line with the disc between the fourth and fifth thoracic vertebrae and at the level of the second pair of ribs. It is a handy reference point for finding the second rib and thus for counting the ribs during a physical examination and for listening to sounds made by specific heart valves. The **xiphisternal joint** (zif"ĭ-ster'nul) is the point where the sternal body and xiphoid process fuse. It lies opposite the ninth thoracic vertebra.

Ribs

Twelve pairs of **ribs** form the flaring sides of the thoracic cage (Figure 7.19a). All ribs attach posteriorly to the thoracic vertebrae (bodies and transverse processes) and curve inferiorly toward the anterior body surface. The superior seven rib pairs attach directly to the sternum by individual costal cartilages (bars of hyaline cartilage). These are **true** or **vertebrosternal ribs** (ver"tĕ-bro-ster'nal). (Notice that the anatomical name indicates the two attachment points of a rib—the posterior attachment given first.)

The remaining five pairs of ribs are called **false ribs;** they either attach indirectly to the sternum or entirely lack a sternal attachment. Rib pairs 8–10 attach to the sternum indirectly; each joins the costal cartilage immediately above it. These ribs are also called **vertebrochondral ribs** (ver"tĕ-bro-kon'dral). The inferior margin of the rib cage, or **costal margin,** is formed by the costal cartilages of ribs 7–10. Rib pairs 11 and 12 are called **vertebral ribs** or **floating ribs** because they have no anterior attachments. Instead, their costal cartilages lie embedded in the muscles of the lateral body wall. The ribs increase in length from pair 1 to pair 7, then decrease in length from pair 8 to pair 12. Except for the first rib, which lies deep to the clavicle, the ribs are easily felt in people of normal weight.

A typical rib is a bowed flat bone (Figure 7.20). The bulk of a rib is simply called the *shaft*. Its superior border is smooth, but its inferior border is sharp and thin and has a *costal groove* on its inner face that lodges the intercostal nerves and blood vessels. In addition to the shaft, each rib has a head, neck, and tubercle. The wedge-shaped *head*, the posteriormost end, articulates with the vertebral bodies by two facets: One joins the body of the same-numbered thoracic vertebra, the other articulates with the body of the vertebra immediately superior. The *neck* is the constricted portion of the rib just beyond the head. Lateral to this, the knoblike *tubercle* articulates with the costal facet of the transverse process of the same-numbered thoracic vertebra. Beyond the tubercle, the shaft angles sharply forward (at the angle of the rib) and then extends to attach to its costal cartilage anteriorly. The costal cartilages provide secure but flexible rib attachments to the sternum.

The first pair of ribs is quite atypical. They are flattened superiorly to inferiorly and are quite broad, forming a horizontal table that supports the subclavian blood vessels that serve the upper limbs. There are also other exceptions to the typical rib pattern. Rib 1 and ribs 10–12 articulate with only one vertebral body, and ribs 11 and 12 do not articulate with a vertebral transverse process.

PART 2: THE APPENDICULAR SKELETON

Bones of the limbs and their girdles are collectively called the **appendicular skeleton** because they are *appended to* the axial skeleton that forms the longitudinal axis of the body (see Figure 7.21). The yoke-like *pectoral girdles* (pek'tor-al; "chest") attach the upper limbs to the body trunk. The more sturdy *pelvic girdle* secures the lower limbs. Although the bones of the upper and lower limbs differ in their functions and mobility, they have the same fundamental plan: Each limb is composed of three major segments connected by movable joints.

The appendicular skeleton enables us to carry out the movements typical of our freewheeling and manipulative lifestyle. Each time we take a step, throw a ball, or pop a caramel into our mouth, we are making good use of our appendicular skeleton.

The Pectoral (Shoulder) Girdle

The **pectoral,** or **shoulder, girdle** consists of the *clavicle* (klav'ĭ-kl) anteriorly and the *scapula* (skap'u-lah) posteriorly (Figure 7.22 and Table 7.3 on p. 236).

(a)

(b)

(c)

FIGURE 7.20 **Ribs. (a)** Vertebral and sternal articulations of a typical true rib. **(b)** Superior view of the articulation between a rib and a thoracic vertebra. **(c)** A typical rib (rib 6, right), posterior view. All ribs illustrated in this figure are right ribs. (See *A Brief Atlas of the Human Body*, Figure 23e and f.)

The paired pectoral girdles and their associated muscles form your shoulders. Although the term *girdle* usually signifies a beltlike structure encircling the body, a single pectoral girdle, or even the pair, does not quite satisfy this description. Anteriorly, the medial end of each clavicle joins the sternum; the distal ends of the clavicles meet the scapulae laterally. However, the scapulae fail to complete the ring posteriorly, because their medial borders do not join each other or the axial skeleton. Instead, the scapulae are attached to the thorax and vertebral column only by the muscles that clothe their surfaces.

The pectoral girdles attach the upper limbs to the axial skeleton and provide attachment points for many of the muscles that move the upper limbs. These girdles are very light and allow the upper limbs a degree of mobility not seen anywhere else in the body. This mobility is due to the following factors:

1. Because only the clavicle attaches to the axial skeleton, the scapula can move quite freely across the thorax, allowing the arm to move with it.

2. The socket of the shoulder joint (the scapula's glenoid cavity) is shallow and poorly reinforced, so it does not restrict the movement of the humerus (arm bone). Although this arrangement is good for flexibility, it is bad for stability: Shoulder dislocations are fairly common.

Clavicles

The **clavicles** ("little keys"), or collarbones, are slender, doubly curved long bones that can be felt along their entire course as they extend horizontally across the superior thorax (Figures 7.22a–c and 7.25). Each clavicle is cone shaped at its medial **sternal end,** which attaches to the sternal manubrium, and flattened at its lateral **acromial end** (ah-kro′me-al), which articulates with the scapula. The medial two-thirds of the clavicle is convex anteriorly; its lateral third is concave anteriorly. Its superior surface is smooth, but the inferior surface is ridged and grooved by ligaments and by the action of the muscles that attach to it. The *conoid tubercle*, for example, is an anchoring point for a ligament which runs to attach to the first rib.

Besides anchoring many muscles, the clavicles act as braces: They hold the scapulae and arms out laterally, away from the narrower superior part of the thorax. This bracing function becomes obvious when a clavicle is fractured: The entire shoulder region collapses medially. The clavicles also transmit compression forces from the upper limbs to the axial skeleton, as when someone pushes a car to a gas station.

The clavicles are not very strong and are likely to fracture, for example, when a person uses outstretched arms to break a fall. The curves in the clavicle ensure that it usually fractures anteriorly (outward). If it were to collapse posteriorly (inward), bone splinters would damage the subclavian artery, which passes just deep to the clavicle to serve the upper limb. The clavicles are exceptionally sensitive to muscle pull and become noticeably larger and stronger in those who perform manual labor or athletics involving the shoulder and arm muscles.

Scapulae

The **scapulae,** or *shoulder blades,* are thin, triangular flat bones (Figures 7.22d–f and 7.25). Interestingly, their name derives from a word meaning "spade" or "shovel," for ancient cultures made spades from the shoulder blades of animals. The scapulae lie on the dorsal surface of the rib cage, between ribs 2 and 7. Each scapula has three borders. The *superior border* is the shortest, sharpest border. The *medial,* or *vertebral, border* parallels the vertebral column. The thick *lateral,* or *axillary, border* abuts the armpit and ends superiorly in a small, shallow fossa, the **glenoid cavity** (gle′noid). This cavity articulates with the humerus of the arm, forming the shoulder joint.

Like all triangles, the scapula has three corners or *angles.* The superior scapular border meets the medial border at the *superior angle* and the lateral border at the *lateral angle.* The medial and lateral borders join at the *inferior angle.* The inferior angle moves extensively as the arm is raised and lowered, and is an important landmark for studying scapular movements.

The anterior, or costal, surface of the scapula is concave and relatively featureless. Its posterior surface bears a prominent **spine** that is easily felt through the skin. The spine ends laterally in an

Q The skeleton shown here is incomplete. What major bony regions are missing?

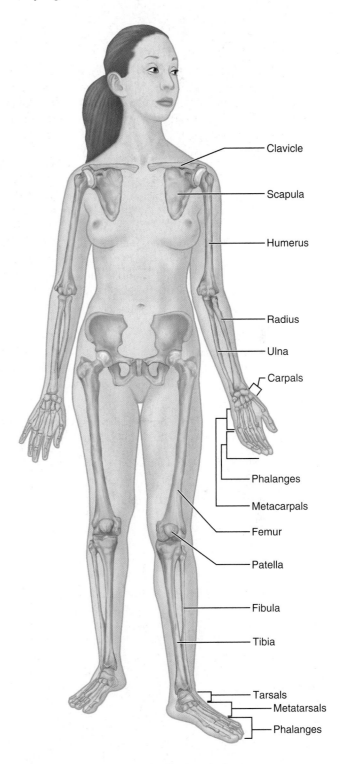

FIGURE 7.21 **The appendicular skeleton.**

A The skull, the thoracic cage, and the vertebral column, all parts of the axial skeleton.

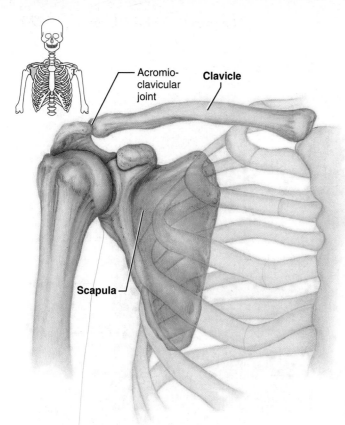

Acromio-clavicular joint

Clavicle

Scapula

(a) Articulated pectoral girdle

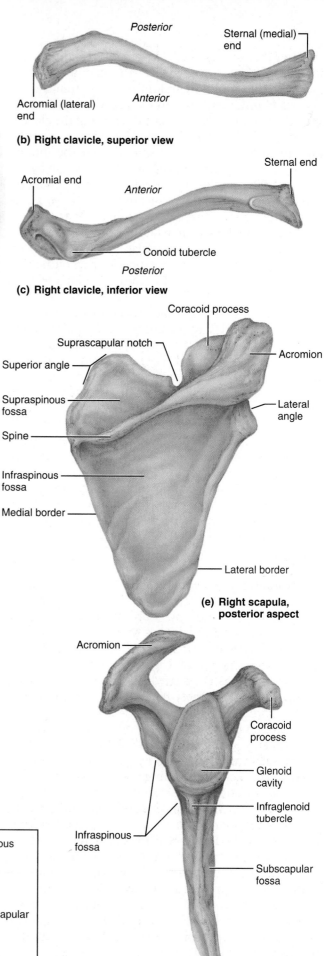

Posterior

Sternal (medial) end

Acromial (lateral) end

Anterior

(b) Right clavicle, superior view

Acromial end

Anterior

Sternal end

Conoid tubercle

Posterior

(c) Right clavicle, inferior view

Coracoid process

Suprascapular notch

Superior angle

Acromion

Supraspinous fossa

Lateral angle

Spine

Infraspinous fossa

Medial border

Lateral border

(e) Right scapula, posterior aspect

Acromion

Coracoid process

Glenoid cavity

Infraglenoid tubercle

Infraspinous fossa

Subscapular fossa

Inferior angle

(f) Right scapula, lateral aspect

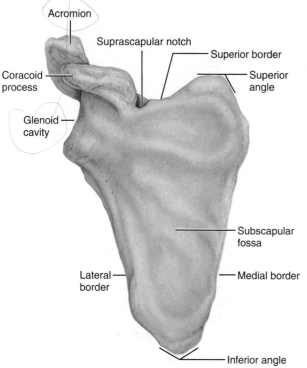

Acromion

Suprascapular notch

Superior border

Coracoid process

Superior angle

Glenoid cavity

Subscapular fossa

Lateral border

Medial border

Inferior angle

(d) Right scapula, anterior aspect

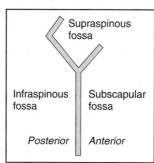

Supraspinous fossa

Infraspinous fossa

Subscapular fossa

Posterior

Anterior

FIGURE 7.22 **Bones of the pectoral girdle.** In view **(a)**, the scapula is positioned posterior to the ribs. View **(f)** is accompanied by a schematic representation of its orientation. (See *A Brief Atlas of the Human Body*, Figure 24.)

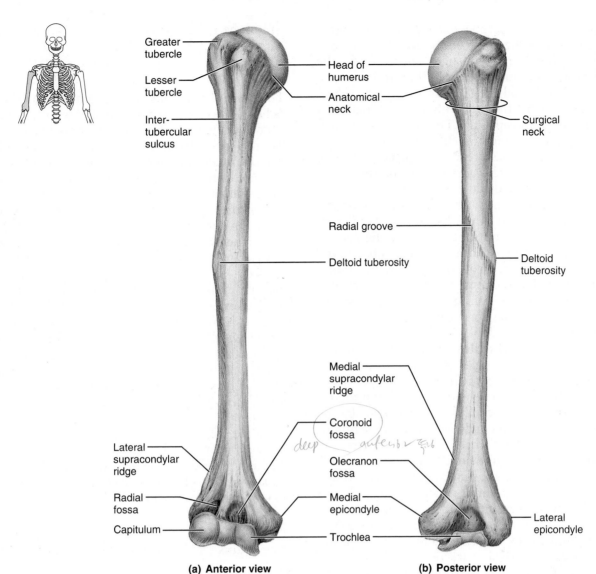

Greater tubercle

Lesser tubercle

Inter-tubercular sulcus

Head of humerus

Anatomical neck

Surgical neck

Radial groove

Deltoid tuberosity

Deltoid tuberosity

Medial supracondylar ridge

Coronoid fossa

deep   anterior 部分

Lateral supracondylar ridge

Radial fossa

Capitulum

Olecranon fossa

Medial epicondyle

Trochlea

Lateral epicondyle

(a) Anterior view

(b) Posterior view

FIGURE 7.23   **The humerus of the right arm.** (See *A Brief Atlas of the Human Body*, Figure 25.)

7

enlarged, roughened triangular projection called the **acromion** (ah-kro′me-on; "point of the shoulder"). The acromion articulates with the acromial end of the clavicle, forming the **acromioclavicular joint.**

Projecting anteriorly from the superior scapular border is the **coracoid process** (kor′ah-coid); *corac* means "beaklike," but this process looks more like a bent little finger. The coracoid process helps anchor the biceps muscle of the arm. It is bounded by the **suprascapular notch** (a nerve passage) medially and by the glenoid cavity laterally.

Several large fossae appear on both sides of the scapula and are named according to location. The *infraspinous* and *supraspinous fossae* are respectively inferior and superior to the spine. The *subscapular fossa* is the shallow concavity formed by the entire anterior scapular surface.

The Upper Limb

Thirty separate bones form the bony framework of each upper limb (see Figures 7.23 to 7.26, and Table 7.3 on p. 236). Each of these bones may be described regionally as a bone of the arm, forearm, or hand. (Keep in mind that anatomically the "arm" is only that part of the upper limb between the shoulder and elbow.)

Arm

The **humerus** (hu′mer-us), the sole bone of the arm, is a typical long bone (Figures 7.23 and 7.25). The largest, longest bone of the upper limb, it articulates with the scapula at the shoulder and with the radius and ulna (forearm bones) at the elbow.

At the proximal end of the humerus is its smooth, hemispherical **head,** which fits into the glenoid cavity of the scapula in a manner that allows the arm to hang freely at one's side. Immediately inferior to the head is a slight constriction, the **anatomical neck.** Just inferior to this are the lateral **greater tubercle** and the more medial **lesser tubercle,** separated by the **intertubercular sulcus,** or *bicipital groove* (bi-sip′ĭ-tal). The tubercles are sites of attachment of the rotator cuff muscles. The intertubercular sulcus guides a tendon of the biceps muscle of the arm to its attachment point at the rim of the glenoid cavity. Just distal to the tubercles is the **surgical neck,** so named because it is the most frequently fractured part of the humerus. About midway down the shaft on its lateral side is the **deltoid tuberosity,** the roughened attachment site for the deltoid muscle of the shoulder. Nearby, the **radial groove** runs obliquely down the posterior aspect of the shaft, marking the course of the radial nerve, an important nerve of the upper limb.

At the distal end of the humerus are two condyles, a medial **trochlea** (trok′le-ah; "pulley"), which looks like an hourglass tipped on its side, and the lateral ball-like **capitulum** (kah-pit′u-lum). These condyles articulate with the ulna and the radius, respectively. The condyle pair is flanked by the **medial** and **lateral epicondyles** (muscle attachment sites). Directly above these epicondyles are the **medial** and **lateral supracondylar ridges.** The ulnar nerve runs behind the medial epicondyle and is responsible for the painful, tingling sensation you experience when you hit your "funny bone."

Superior to the trochlea on the anterior surface is the **coronoid fossa;** on the posterior surface is the deeper **olecranon fossa** (o-lek′rah-non). These two depressions allow the corresponding processes of the ulna to move freely when the elbow is flexed and extended. A small **radial fossa,** lateral to the coronoid fossa, receives the head of the radius when the elbow is flexed.

Forearm

Two parallel long bones, the radius and the ulna, form the skeleton of the forearm, or *antebrachium* (an″te-bra′ke-um) (Figures 7.24 and 7.25). Unless a person's forearm muscles are very bulky, these bones are easily palpated along their entire length. Their proximal ends articulate with the humerus; their distal ends form joints with bones of the wrist. The radius and ulna articulate with each other both proximally and distally at small **radioulnar joints** (ra″de-o-ul′nar), and they are connected along their entire length by a flat, flexible ligament, the **interosseous membrane** (in″ter-os′e-us; "between the bones"). In the anatomical position, the radius lies laterally (on the thumb side) and the ulna medially. However, when you rotate your forearm so that the palm faces posteriorly (a movement called pronation), the distal end of the radius crosses over the ulna and the two bones form an X.

Ulna

The **ulna** (ul′nah; "elbow") is slightly longer than the radius. It has the main responsibility for forming the elbow joint with the humerus. Its proximal end looks like the adjustable end of a monkey wrench; it bears two prominent processes, the **olecranon** (elbow) and **coronoid processes,** separated by a deep concavity, the **trochlear notch** (see Figures 7.24 and 7.25). Together, these two processes grip the trochlea of the humerus, forming a hinge joint that allows the forearm to be bent upon the arm (flexed), then straightened again (extended). When the forearm is fully extended, the olecranon process "locks" into the olecranon fossa, keeping the forearm from hyperextending (moving posteriorly beyond the elbow joint). The posterior olecranon process forms the angle of the elbow when the forearm is flexed and is the bony part that rests on the table when you lean on your elbows. On the lateral side of the coronoid process is a small depression, the **radial notch,** where the ulna articulates with the head of the radius.

Distally the ulnar shaft narrows and ends in a knoblike **head.** Medial to the head is a **styloid process,** from which a ligament runs to the wrist. The ulnar head is separated from the bones of the wrist by a disc of fibrocartilage and plays little or no role in hand movements.

Radius

The **radius** ("rod") is thin at its proximal end and wide distally—the opposite of the ulna. The **head** of the radius is shaped somewhat like the head of a nail (see Figures 7.24 and 7.25). The superior surface of this head is concave, and it articulates with the capitulum of the humerus. Medially, the head articulates with the radial notch of the ulna. Just inferior to the head is the rough **radial tuberosity,** which anchors the biceps muscle of the arm. Distally, where the radius is expanded, it has a medial **ulnar notch,** which articulates with the ulna, and a lateral **styloid process** (an anchoring site for ligaments that run to the wrist). Between these two markings, the radius is concave where it articulates with carpal bones of the wrist. While the ulna contributes more heavily to the elbow joint, the radius is the major forearm bone contributing to the wrist joint. When the radius moves, the hand moves with it.

◤ HOMEOSTATIC IMBALANCE

Colle's fracture is a break in the distal end of the radius. It is a common fracture when a falling person attempts to break his or her fall with outstretched hands (see Figure 7.24c). ●

Q *(1) Which of these bones "carries" the hand? (2) Which plays the major role in forming the elbow joint with the humerus?*

Radial notch

Head

Neck

Radial tuberosity

flat

Olecranon process

Trochlear notch *anterior*

Coronoid process

Proximal radioulnar joint

Head of radius

Neck of radius

Interosseous membrane

Ulna

pinky side

Colle's fracture

Radius

lateral out thumb

Radius

Ulnar notch

Head of ulna

Styloid process of ulna *little bump*

Distal radioulnar joint

Styloid process of radius

Styloid process of radius

(a) Anterior view

(b) Posterior view

(c)

FIGURE 7.24 **Radius and ulna of the right forearm. (a, b)** Anterior and posterior views, respectively. **(c)** X ray of Colle's fracture of the radius. (See *A Brief Atlas of the Human Body*, Figure 26.)

Hand

The skeleton of the hand (Figure 7.26) includes the bones of the *carpus* (wrist); the bones of the *metacarpus* (palm); and the *phalanges* (bones of the fingers).

Carpus (Wrist)

A "wrist" watch is actually worn on the distal forearm (over the lower ends of the radius and ulna), not on the wrist at all. The true wrist, or **carpus,** is the proximal part of the structure we generally call our "hand." The carpus consists of a group of eight marble-size short bones, or **carpals** (kar′palz), closely united by ligaments. Because gliding movements occur between these bones, the carpus as a whole is quite flexible. The carpals are arranged in two irregular rows of four bones each (Figure 7.26). In the proximal row (lateral to medial) are the **scaphoid** (skaf′oid; "boat-shaped"),

A *(1) The radius carries the hand. (2) The ulna forms the elbow joint with the humerus.*

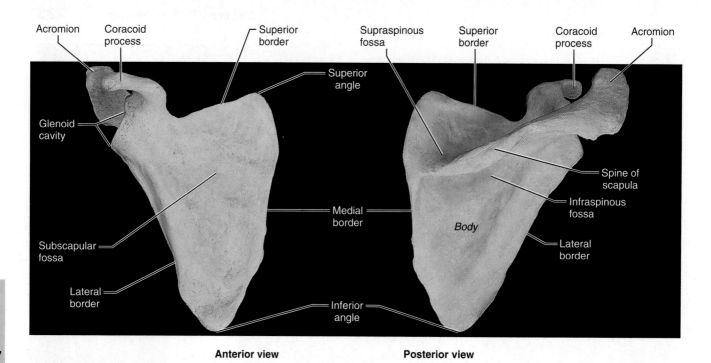

Acromion — Coracoid process — Superior border — Supraspinous fossa — Superior border — Coracoid process — Acromion

Glenoid cavity

Superior angle

Subscapular fossa

Medial border

Spine of scapula

Infraspinous fossa

Body

Lateral border

Lateral border

Inferior angle

Anterior view   **Posterior view**

Scapula

Posterior

Sternal (medial) end

Acromial (lateral) end

Anterior

Right clavicle, superior view

Anterior

Acromial end   Sternal end

Conoid tubercle   Impression for costoclavicular ligament

Posterior

Right clavicle, inferior view

Greater tubercle — Lesser tubercle
Intertubercular sulcus — Head
Anatomical neck
Surgical neck
Shaft
Deltoid tuberosity
Lateral epicondyle — Coronoid fossa
Capitulum — Trochlea — Medial epicondyle

Humerus, anterior view

Coronoid process — Olecranon process
Head of radius — Trochlear notch
Neck of radius — Radial notch
Radial tuberosity
Radius — Ulna
Location of interosseous membrane
Distal radioulnar joint
Styloid process of radius — Ulnar head

Radius (left) and ulna (right), anterior view

FIGURE 7.25   **Photographs of selected bones of the pectoral girdle and right upper limb.** (See *A Brief Atlas of the Human Body*, Figures 24, 25, and 26.)

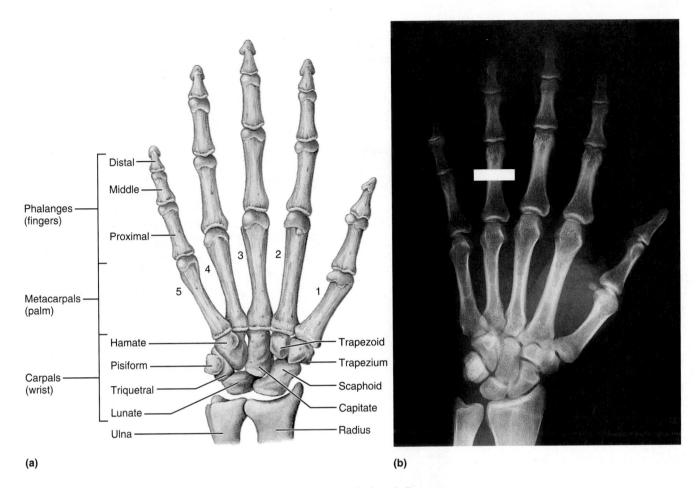

FIGURE 7.26 **Bones of the hand. (a)** Anterior view of the right hand, illustrating the carpals, metacarpals, and phalanges. **(b)** X ray of the right hand. Notice the white bar on the proximal phalanx of finger 4, showing the position at which a ring would be worn. (See *A Brief Atlas of the Human Body,* Figure 27.)

lunate (lu'nāt; "moonlike"), **triquetral** (tri-kwe'trul; "triangular"), and **pisiform** (pi'sĭ-form; "pea-shaped"). Only the scaphoid and lunate articulate with the radius to form the wrist joint. The carpals of the distal row (lateral to medial) are the **trapezium** (trah-pe'ze-um; "little table"), **trapezoid** (tra'peh-zoid; "four-sided"), **capitate** ("head-shaped"), and **hamate** (ham'āt; "hooked"). There are numerous memory-jogging phrases to help you recall the carpals in the order given above. If you don't have one, try: **S**ally **l**eft **t**he **p**arty **t**o **t**ake **C**athy **h**ome. As with all such memory jogs, the first letter of each word is the first letter of the term you need to remember.

◣ HOMEOSTATIC IMBALANCE

The arrangement of its bones is such that the carpus is concave anteriorly and a ligament roofs over this concavity, forming the notorious *carpal tunnel.* Besides the median nerve (which supplies the lateral side of the hand), several long muscle tendons crowd into this tunnel. Overuse and inflammation of the tendons cause them to swell, compressing the me-dian nerve, which causes tingling and numbness of the areas served. Pain is greatest at night. Those who repeatedly flex their wrists and fingers, such as those who work at computer keyboards all day, are particularly susceptible to this nerve impairment, called *carpal tunnel syndrome.* This condition is treated by splinting the wrist during sleep or by surgery. ●

Metacarpus (Palm)

Five **metacarpal bones** radiate from the wrist like spokes to form the palm of the hand (*meta* = beyond). These small long bones are not named, but instead are numbered 1 to 5 from thumb to little finger. The **bases** of the metacarpals articulate with the carpals proximally and each other medially and laterally (see Figure 7.26). Their bulbous **heads** articulate with the proximal phalanges of the fingers. When you clench your fist, the heads of the metacarpals become prominent as your *knuckles.*

Metacarpal 1, associated with the thumb, is the shortest and most mobile. It occupies a more anterior position than the other metacarpals. Consequently, the

TABLE 7.3	Bones of the Appendicular Skeleton Part 1: Pectoral Girdle and Upper Limb			
BODY REGION	**BONES***	**ILLUSTRATION**	**LOCATION**	**MARKINGS**
Pectoral girdle (Figures 7.22, 7.25)	Clavicle (2)		Clavicle is in superoanterior thorax; articulates medially with sternum and laterally with scapula	Acromial end; sternal end
	Scapula (2)		Scapula is in posterior thorax; forms part of the shoulder; articulates with humerus and clavicle	Glenoid cavity; spine; acromion; coracoid process; infraspinous, supraspinous, and subscapular fossae
Free upper limb Arm (Figures 7.23, 7.25)	Humerus (2)		Humerus is the sole bone of arm; between scapula and elbow	Head; greater and lesser tubercles; intertubercular sulcus; deltoid tuberosity; trochlea; capitulum; coronoid and olecranon fossae; radial groove; epicondyles
Forearm (Figures 7.24, 7.25)	Ulna (2)		Ulna is the medial bone of forearm between elbow and wrist; forms elbow joint	Coronoid process; olecranon process; radial notch; trochlear notch; styloid process; head
	Radius (2)		Radius is lateral bone of forearm; carries wrist	Radial tuberosity; styloid process; head; ulnar notch
Hand (Figure 7.26)	8 Carpals (16) • scaphoid • lunate • triquetral • pisiform • trapezium • trapezoid • capitate • hamate		Carpals form a bony crescent at the wrist; arranged in two rows of four bones each	
	5 Metacarpals (10)		Metacarpals form the palm; one in line with each digit	
	14 Phalanges (28) • distal • middle • proximal		Phalanges form the fingers; three in digits 2–5; two in digit 1 (the thumb)	

Anterior view of pectoral girdle and upper limb

*The number in parentheses ( ) following the bone name denotes the total number of such bones in the body.

7

joint between metacarpal 1 and the trapezium is a unique saddle joint that allows *opposition,* the action of touching your thumb to the tips of your other fingers.

Phalanges (Fingers)

The **fingers,** or **digits** of the upper limb, are numbered 1 to 5 beginning with the thumb, or **pollex** (pol'eks). In most people, the third finger is the longest. Each hand contains 14 miniature long bones called **phalanges** (fah-lan'jēz). Except for the thumb, each finger has three phalanges: *distal, middle,* and *proximal.* The thumb has no middle phalanx. [Phalanx (fa'langks; "a closely knit row of soldiers") is the singular term for phalanges.]

The Pelvic (Hip) Girdle

The **pelvic girdle,** or **hip girdle,** attaches the lower limbs to the axial skeleton, transmits the weight of the upper body to the lower limbs, and supports the visceral organs of the pelvis (Figures 7.27 and 7.30 and Table 7.4, p. 240). Whereas the pectoral girdle is sparingly attached to the thoracic cage, the pelvic girdle is secured to the axial skeleton by some of the strongest ligaments in the body. And whereas the glenoid cavity of the scapula is shallow, the corresponding sockets of the pelvic girdle are deep and cuplike and firmly secure the head of the femur in place. Thus, even though both the shoulder and hip joints are ball-and-socket joints, very few of us can wheel or swing our legs about with the same degree of freedom as our arms. The pelvic girdle lacks the mobility of the pectoral girdle but is far more stable.

The pelvic girdle is formed by a pair of **hip bones** (Figure 7.27), each also called an **os coxae** (ahs kok'se), or **coxal bone** (*coxa* = hip). Each hip bone unites with its partner anteriorly and with the sacrum posteriorly. The deep, basinlike structure formed by the hip bones, together with the sacrum and coccyx, is called the **bony pelvis.**

Each large, irregularly shaped hip bone consists of three separate bones during childhood: the ilium, ischium, and pubis. In adults, these bones are firmly fused and their boundaries are indistinguishable. Their names are retained, however, to refer to different regions of the composite hip bone. At the point of fusion of the ilium, ischium, and pubis is a deep hemispherical socket called the **acetabulum** (as"ĕ-tab'u-lum; "wine cup") on the lateral surface of the pelvis (see Figure 7.27b). The acetabulum receives the head of the femur, or thigh bone, at this *hip joint.*

Ilium

The **ilium** (il'e-um; "flank") is a large flaring bone that forms the superior region of a coxal bone. It consists of a **body** and a superior winglike portion called the **ala** (a'lah). When you rest your hands on your hips, you are resting them on the thickened superior margins of the alae, the **iliac crests.** Thickest at the **tubercle of the iliac crest,** each iliac crest ends anteriorly in the blunt **anterior superior iliac spine** and posteriorly in the sharp **posterior superior iliac spine.** Located below these are the less prominent **anterior** and **posterior inferior iliac spines.** All of these spines are attachment points for the muscles of the trunk, hip, and thigh. The anterior superior iliac spine is an especially important anatomical landmark. It is easily felt through the skin and is visible in thin people. The posterior superior iliac spine is difficult to palpate, but its position is revealed by a skin dimple in the sacral region.

Just inferior to the posterior inferior iliac spine, the ilium indents deeply to form the **greater sciatic notch** (si-at'ik), through which the thick cordlike sciatic nerve passes to enter the thigh. The broad posterolateral surface of the ilium, the **gluteal surface** (gloo'te-al), is crossed by three ridges, the **posterior, anterior,** and **inferior gluteal lines,** to which the gluteal (buttock) muscles attach.

The internal surface of the iliac ala exhibits a concavity called the **iliac fossa.** Posterior to this, the roughened **auricular surface** (aw-rik'u-lar; "ear-shaped") articulates with the same-named surface of the sacrum, forming the *sacroiliac joint.* The weight of the body is transmitted from the spine to the pelvis through the sacroiliac joints. Running inferiorly and anteriorly from the auricular surface is a robust ridge called the **arcuate line** (ar'ku-at; "bowed"). The arcuate line helps define the **pelvic brim,** the superior margin of the *true pelvis,* which we will discuss shortly. Anteriorly, the body of the ilium joins the pubis; inferiorly it joins the ischium.

Ischium

The **ischium** (is'ke-um; "hip") forms the posteroinferior part of the hip bone (Figures 7.27 and 7.30). Roughly L- or arc-shaped, it has a thicker, superior **body** adjoining the ilium and a thinner, inferior **ramus** (*ramus* = branch). The ramus joins the pubis anteriorly. The ischium has three important markings. Its **ischial spine** projects medially into the pelvic cavity and serves as a point of attachment of the *sacrospinous ligament* running from the sacrum. Just inferior to the ischial spine is the **lesser sciatic notch.** A number of nerves and blood vessels pass through this notch to supply the anogenital area. The inferior surface of the ischial body is rough and grossly thickened as the **ischial tuberosity.** When we sit, our weight is borne entirely by the ischial tuberosities, which are the strongest parts of the hip bones. A massive ligament runs from the sacrum to

Q *What bone marking identified in Figure 7.27 allows passage of the sciatic nerve and artery?*

Coxal bone
(os coxae or hip bone)

Ilium

Pubic bone

Ischium

Base of sacrum

Iliac crest

Sacroiliac joint

Iliac fossa

Sacral promontory

Pelvic brim

Ischial spine

Acetabulum

Pubic crest

Pubic symphysis

Sacrum

Coccyx

Pubic arch

(a)

Tubercle of the iliac crest

Anterior gluteal line

Posterior gluteal line

Posterior superior iliac spine

Posterior inferior iliac spine

Greater sciatic notch

Ischial body

Ischial spine

Lesser sciatic notch

Ischial tuberosity

Ischium

Ischial ramus

Ala

Ilium

Iliac crest

Anterior superior iliac spine

Inferior gluteal line

Anterior inferior iliac spine

Acetabulum

Pubic body

Pubis

Inferior ramus of pubis

(b)

Ilium

Iliac fossa

Posterior superior iliac spine

Posterior inferior iliac spine

Body

Auricular surface

Ischial spine

Obturator foramen

Ischium

Ischial ramus

Arcuate line

Superior ramus of pubis

Pubic tubercle

Pubic crest

Articular surface of pubis (at pubic symphysis)

(c)

FIGURE 7.27 **Bones of the bony pelvis. (a)** Articulated pelvis showing the two hip (coxal) bones (which together form the pelvic girdle) and the sacrum. **(b)** Lateral view of right hip bone showing the point of fusion of the ilium (gold), ischium (gray-blue), and pubic (red) bones at the acetabulum. **(c)** Right hip bone, medial view. (See *A Brief Atlas of the Human Body*, Figure 28.)

A Greater sciatic notch.

each ischial tuberosity. This *sacrotuberous ligament* (not illustrated) helps hold the pelvis together. The ischial tuberosity is also a site of attachment of the large hamstring muscles of the posterior thigh.

Pubis

The **pubis** (pu'bis; "sexually mature"), or **pubic bone,** forms the anterior portion of the hip bone (Figures 7.27 and 7.30). In the anatomical position, it lies nearly horizontally and the urinary bladder rests upon it. Essentially, the pubis is V shaped with **superior** and **inferior rami** issuing from a flattened medial **body.** The body of the pubis lies medially and its anterior border is thickened to form a **pubic crest.** At the lateral end of the pubic crest is the **pubic tubercle,** one of the attachments for the inguinal ligament. As the two rami of the pubic bone run laterally to join with the body and ramus of the ischium, they define a large opening in the hip bone, the **obturator foramen** (ob"tu-ra'tor), through which a few blood vessels and nerves pass. Although the obturator foramen is large, it is nearly closed by a fibrous membrane in life (*obturator* = closed up).

The bodies of the two pubic bones are joined by a fibrocartilage disc, forming the midline **pubic symphysis joint.** Inferior to this joint, the inferior pubic rami angle laterally, forming an inverted V-shaped arch called the **pubic arch** or **subpubic angle.** The acuteness of this arch helps to differentiate the male and female pelves.

Pelvic Structure and Childbearing

So striking are the differences between the male and female pelves that a trained anatomist can immediately determine the sex of a skeleton from a casual examination of the pelvis. The female pelvis is modified for childbearing: It tends to be wider, shallower, lighter, and rounder than that of a male. The female pelvis not only accommodates a growing fetus, but it must be large enough to allow the infant's relatively large head to exit at birth. The major differences between the typical male and female pelves are summarized and illustrated in Table 7.4.

The pelvis is said to consist of a false (greater) pelvis and a true (lesser) pelvis separated by the **pelvic brim,** a continuous oval ridge that runs from the pubic crest through the arcuate line and sacral promontory (Figure 7.27a). The false pelvis, that portion superior to the pelvic brim, is bounded by the alae of the ilia laterally and the lumbar vertebrae posteriorly. The **false pelvis** is really part of the abdomen and helps support the abdominal viscera. It does not restrict childbirth in any way. The **true pelvis** is the region inferior to the pelvic brim that is almost entirely surrounded by bone. It forms a deep bowl containing the pelvic organs. Its dimensions,

particularly those of its *inlet* and *outlet*, are critical to the uncomplicated delivery of a baby, and they are carefully measured by an obstetrician.

The **pelvic inlet** *is* the pelvic brim, and its widest dimension is from right to left along the frontal plane. As labor begins, an infant's head typically enters the inlet with its forehead facing one ilium and its occiput facing the other. A sacral promontory that is particularly large can impair the infant's entry into the true pelvis. The **pelvic outlet,** illustrated in the photos at the bottom of Table 7.4, is the inferior margin of the true pelvis. It is bounded anteriorly by the pubic arch, laterally by the ischia, and posteriorly by the sacrum and coccyx. Both the coccyx and the ischial spines protrude into the outlet opening, so a sharply angled coccyx or unusually large spines can interfere with delivery. The largest dimension of the outlet is the anteroposterior diameter. Generally, after the baby's head passes through the inlet, it rotates so that the forehead faces posteriorly and the occiput anteriorly. Thus, during birth, the infant's head makes a quarter turn to follow the widest dimensions of the true pelvis.

The Lower Limb

The lower limbs carry the entire weight of the erect body and are subjected to exceptional forces when we jump or run. Thus, it is not surprising that the bones of the lower limbs are thicker and stronger than comparable bones of the upper limbs. The three segments of each lower limb are the thigh, the leg, and the foot (see Table 7.5 on p. 246).

Thigh

The **femur** (fe'mur; "thigh"), the single bone of the thigh (Figures 7.28 and 7.30), is the largest, longest, strongest bone in the body. Its durable structure reflects the fact that the stress on the femur during vigorous jumping can reach 280 kg/cm^2 (about 2 tons per square inch)! The femur is clothed by bulky muscles that prevent us from palpating its course down the length of the thigh. Its length is roughly one-quarter of a person's height.

Proximally, the femur articulates with the hip bone and then courses medially as it descends toward the knee. This arrangement allows the knee joints to be closer to the body's center of gravity and provides for better balance. The medial course of the two femurs is more pronounced in women because of their wider pelvis.

The ball-like **head** of the femur has a small central pit called the **fovea capitis** (fo've-ah kă'pǐ-tis; "pit of the head"). The short *ligament of the head of the femur* runs from this pit to the acetabulum, where it helps secure the femur. The head is carried on a *neck* that angles *laterally* to join the shaft. This

TABLE 7.4	Comparison of the Male and Female Pelves	
CHARACTERISTIC	FEMALE	MALE
General structure and functional modifications	Tilted forward; adapted for childbearing; true pelvis defines the birth canal; cavity of the true pelvis is broad, shallow, and has a greater capacity	Tilted less far forward; adapted for support of a male's heavier build and stronger muscles; cavity of the true pelvis is narrow and deep
Bone thickness	Less; bones lighter, thinner, and smoother	Greater; bones heavier and thicker, and markings are more prominent
Acetabula	Smaller; farther apart	Larger; closer
Pubic arch/angle	Broader (80–90°); more rounded	More acute (50–60°)
Anterior view		
Sacrum	Wider; shorter; sacral curvature is accentuated	Narrow; longer; sacral promontory more ventral
Coccyx	More movable; straighter	Less movable; curves ventrally
Left lateral view		
Pelvic inlet (brim)	Wider; oval from side to side	Narrow; basically heart shaped
Pelvic outlet	Wider; ischial tuberosities shorter, farther apart and everted	Narrower; ischial tuberosities longer, sharper, and point more medially
Posteroinferior view		

Pelvic brim

Pubic arch

7

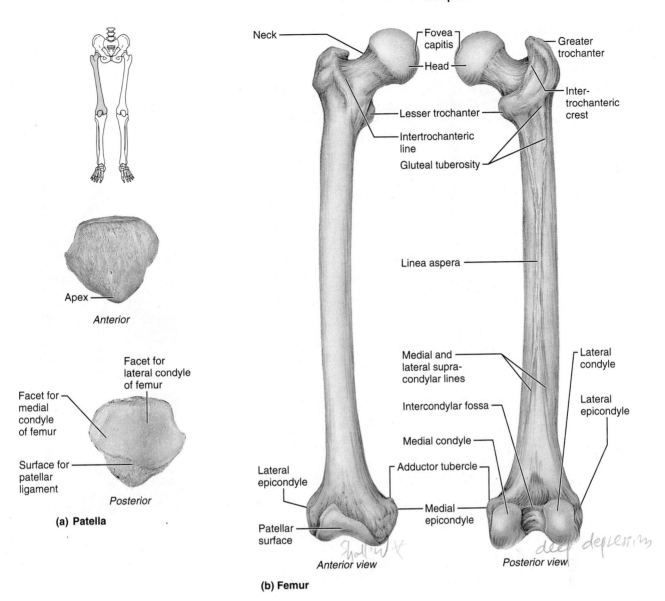

FIGURE 7.28 **Bones of the right thigh and knee. (a)** The patella (kneecap). **(b)** The femur (thigh bone). (See *A Brief Atlas of the Human Body*, Figure 29.)

arrangement reflects the fact that the femur articulates with the lateral aspect (rather than the inferior region) of the pelvis. The neck is the weakest part of the femur and is often fractured, an injury commonly called a broken hip. At the junction of the shaft and neck are the lateral **greater trochanter** (tro-kan'ter) and posteromedial **lesser trochanter.** These projections serve as sites of attachment for thigh and buttock muscles. The two trochanters are connected by the **intertrochanteric line** anteriorly and by the prominent **intertrochanteric crest** posteriorly.

Inferior to the intertrochanteric crest on the posterior shaft is the **gluteal tuberosity,** which blends into a long vertical ridge, the **linea aspera** (lin'e-ah as'per-ah; "rough line"), inferiorly. Distally, the linea aspera diverges, forming the **medial** and **lateral**

supracondylar lines. All of these markings are sites of muscle attachment. Except for the linea aspera, the femur shaft is smooth and rounded.

Distally, the femur broadens and ends in the wheel-like **lateral** and **medial condyles,** which articulate with the tibia of the leg. The **medial** and **lateral epicondyles** (sites of muscle attachment) flank the condyles superiorly. On the superior part of the medial epicondyle is a bump, the **adductor tubercle.** The smooth **patellar surface,** between the condyles on the anterior femoral surface, articulates with the *patella* (pah-tel'ah), or kneecap (see Figures 7.28a, 7.30, and 7.21).

Between the condyles on the posterior aspect of the femur is the deep, U-shaped **intercondylar fossa,** and superior to that on the shaft is the smooth popliteal surface.

FIGURE 7.29   **The tibia and fibula of the right leg. (a)** Anterior view.
(b) Posterior view. **(c)** X ray of Pott's fracture of the fibula. (See *A Brief Atlas of the Human Body*, Figure 30.)

The **patella** ("small pan") is a triangular sesamoid bone enclosed in the (quadriceps) tendon that secures the anterior thigh muscles to the tibia. It protects the knee joint anteriorly and improves the leverage of the thigh muscles acting across the knee.

Leg

Two parallel bones, the tibia and fibula, form the skeleton of the leg, the region of the lower limb between the knee and the ankle (Figures 7.29 and 7.30). These two bones are connected by an *interosseous membrane* and articulate with each other both proximally and distally. However, unlike the joints between the radius and ulna of the forearm, the *tibiofibular joints* (tib"e-o-fib'u-lar) of the leg allow essentially no movement. The bones of the leg thus form a less flexible but stronger and more stable limb than those of the forearm. The medial tibia articulates proximally with the femur to form the modified

hinge joint of the knee and distally with the talus bone of the foot at the ankle. The fibula, by contrast, does not contribute to the knee joint and merely helps stabilize the ankle joint.

Tibia

The **tibia** (tib'e-ah; "shinbone") receives the weight of the body from the femur and transmits it to the foot. It is second only to the femur in size and strength. At its broad proximal end are the concave **medial** and **lateral condyles,** which look like two huge checkers lying side by side. These are separated by an irregular projection, the **intercondylar eminence.** The tibial condyles articulate with the corresponding condyles of the femur. The inferior region of the lateral tibial condyle bears a facet that indicates the site of the *proximal tibiofibular joint.* Just inferior to the condyles, the tibia's anterior surface displays the rough **tibial tuberosity,** to which the patellar ligament attaches.

(a) Lateral view   **Right hip bone**   **(b) Medial view**

Anterior gluteal line
Posterior gluteal line
Posterior superior iliac spine
Posterior inferior iliac spine
Greater sciatic notch
Ischial spine
Lesser sciatic notch
Ischial tuberosity
Ischial ramus
Obturator foramen

Iliac crest
Anterior superior iliac spine
Anterior inferior iliac spine
Inferior gluteal line
Acetabulum
Pubic body
Superior ramus of pubis
Pubic tubercle
Inferior ramus of pubis

Auricular surface
Iliac fossa
Arcuate line
Posterior superior iliac spine
Posterior inferior iliac spine
Greater sciatic notch
Ischial spine
Lesser sciatic notch
Ischial tuberosity
Ischial ramus
Pubic symphysis (symphyseal surface)

Right femur, anterior surface

Neck
Head
Greater trochanter
Intertrochanteric line
Lesser trochanter
Patellar surface
Adductor tubercle
Lateral epicondyle
Medial epicondyle
Lateral condyle
Medial condyle

Right tibia and fibula, anterior view

Lateral condyle of tibia
Intercondylar eminence
Medial condyle of tibia
Head of fibula
Tibial tuberosity
Anterior border
Fibula
Tibia
Distal tibiofibular joint
Medial malleolus
Lateral malleolus of fibula
Inferior articular surface

Proximal right tibia, posterior view

Lateral condyle
Fibula articulates here

FIGURE 7.30 **Photographs of selected bones of the pelvic girdle and lower limb.** (See *A Brief Atlas of the Human Body,* Figures 28, 29, and 30.)

7

The tibial shaft is triangular in cross section. Neither the tibia's sharp **anterior border** nor its medial surface is covered by muscles, so they can be felt just deep to the skin along their entire length. The anguish of a "bumped" shin is an experience familiar to nearly everyone. Distally the tibia is flat where it articulates with the talus bone of the foot. Medial to that joint surface is an inferior projection, the **medial malleolus** (mah-le'o-lus; "little hammer"), which forms the medial bulge of the ankle. The **fibular notch,** on the lateral surface of the tibia, participates in the *distal tibiofibular joint.*

Fibula

The **fibula** (fib'u-lah; "pin") is a sticklike bone with slightly expanded ends. It articulates proximally and distally with the lateral aspects of the tibia. Its proximal end is its **head;** its distal end is the **lateral malleolus.** The lateral malleolus forms the conspicuous lateral ankle bulge and articulates with the talus. The fibular shaft is heavily ridged and appears to have been twisted a quarter turn. The fibula does not bear weight, but several muscles originate from it.

 HOMEOSTATIC IMBALANCE

A *Pott's fracture* occurs at the distal end of the fibula, the tibia, or both. It is a common sports injury. (See Figure 7.29c.) ●

Foot

The skeleton of the foot includes the bones of the *tarsus,* the bones of the *metatarsus,* and the *phalanges,* or toe bones (Figure 7.31). The foot has two important functions: It supports our body weight, and it acts as a lever to propel the body forward when we walk and run. A single bone could serve both purposes, but it would adapt poorly to uneven ground. Segmentation makes the foot pliable, avoiding this problem.

Tarsus

The **tarsus** is made up of seven **tarsal bones** (tar'sal) that form the posterior half of the foot. It corresponds to the carpus of the hand. Body weight is carried primarily by the two largest, most posterior tarsals: the **talus** (ta'lus; "ankle"), which articulates with the tibia and fibula superiorly, and the strong **calcaneus** (kal-ka'ne-us; "heel bone"), which forms the heel of the foot and carries the talus on its superior surface. The thick *calcaneal,* or *Achilles, tendon* of the calf muscles attaches to the posterior surface of the calcaneus. The part of the calcaneus that touches the ground is the **calcaneal tuberosity,** and its shelflike projection that supports part of the talus is the **sustentaculum tali** (sus"ten-tak'u-lum ta'le; "supporter of the talus") or

talar shelf. The tibia articulates with the talus at the *trochlea* of the talus. The remaining tarsals are the lateral **cuboid,** the medial **navicular** (nah-vik'u-lar), and the anterior **medial, intermediate,** and **lateral cuneiform bones** (ku-ne'i-form; "wedge-shaped"). The cuboid and cuneiform bones articulate with the metatarsal bones anteriorly.

Metatarsus

The **metatarsus** consists of five small, long bones called **metatarsal bones.** These are numbered 1 to 5 beginning on the medial (great toe) side of the foot. The first metatarsal is short and thick and its plantar surface rests on paired sesamoid bones (not shown), which play an important role in supporting body weight. The arrangement of the metatarsals is more parallel than that of the metacarpals of the hands. Distally, where the metatarsals articulate with the proximal phalanges of the toes, the enlarged head of the first metatarsal forms the "ball" of the foot.

Phalanges (Toes)

The 14 phalanges of the toes are a good deal smaller than those of the fingers and thus are less nimble. But their general structure and arrangement are the same. There are three phalanges in each digit except for the great toe, the **hallux.** The hallux has only two, proximal and distal.

Arches of the Foot

A segmented structure can hold up weight only if it is arched. The foot has three arches: two *longitudinal arches* (*medial* and *lateral*) and one *transverse arch* (Figure 7.32), which account for its awesome strength. These arches are maintained by the interlocking shapes of the foot bones, by strong ligaments, and by the pull of some tendons during muscle activity. The ligaments and muscle tendons provide a certain amount of springiness. In general, the arches "give" or stretch slightly when weight is applied to the foot and spring back when the weight is removed, which makes walking and running more economical in terms of energy use than would otherwise be the case.

If you examine your wet footprints, you will see that the medial margin from the heel to the head of the first metatarsal leaves no print. This is because the **medial longitudinal arch** curves well above the ground. The talus is the keystone of this arch, which originates at the calcaneus, rises to the talus, and then descends to the three medial metatarsals. The **lateral longitudinal arch** is very low. It elevates the lateral part of the foot just enough to redistribute some of the weight to the calcaneus and the head of the fifth metatarsal (to the ends of the arch). The cuboid is the keystone bone of this arch. The two longitudinal arches serve as pillars for the **transverse**

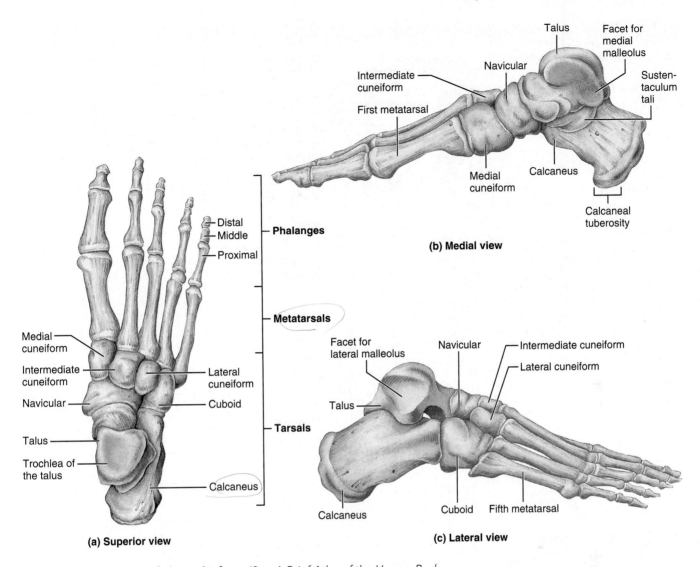

Phalanges
- Distal
- Middle
- Proximal

Metatarsals

Medial cuneiform

Intermediate cuneiform

Navicular

Talus

Trochlea of the talus

Calcaneus

Lateral cuneiform

Cuboid

Tarsals

(a) Superior view

Intermediate cuneiform

First metatarsal

Navicular

Talus

Facet for medial malleolus

Sustentaculum tali

Medial cuneiform

Calcaneus

Calcaneal tuberosity

(b) Medial view

Facet for lateral malleolus

Talus

Navicular

Intermediate cuneiform

Lateral cuneiform

Calcaneus

Cuboid

Fifth metatarsal

(c) Lateral view

FIGURE 7.31   Bones of the right foot. (See *A Brief Atlas of the Human Body*, Figure 31a, c, and d.)

arch, which runs obliquely from one side of the foot to the other, following the line of the joints between the tarsals and metatarsals. Together, the arches of the foot form a half-dome that distributes about half of a person's standing and walking weight to the heel bones and half to the heads of the metatarsals.

HOMEOSTATIC IMBALANCE

Standing immobile for extended periods places excessive strain on the tendons and ligaments of the feet (because the muscles are inactive) and can result in fallen arches, or "flat feet," particularly if one is overweight. Running on hard surfaces can also cause arches to fall unless one wears shoes that give proper arch support. ●

• • •

The bones of the thigh, leg, and foot are summarized in Table 7.5.

Medial longitudinal arch

Transverse arch

Lateral longitudinal arch

FIGURE 7.32   Arches of the foot.

TABLE 7.5   Bones of the Appendicular Skeleton Part 2: Pelvic Girdle and Lower Limb

BODY REGION	BONES*	ILLUSTRATION	LOCATION	MARKINGS
Pelvic girdle (Figures 7.27, 7.30)	Coxal (2) (hip)		Each hip bone is formed by the fusion of an ilium, an ischium, and a pubic bone; the hip bones fuse anteriorly at the pubic symphysis and form sacroiliac joints with the sacrum posteriorly; girdle consisting of both hip bones is basinlike	Iliac crest; anterior and posterior iliac spines; auricular surface; greater and lesser sciatic notches; obturator foramen; ischial tuberosity and spine; acetabulum; pubic arch; pubic crest; pubic tubercle
Free lower limb Thigh (Figures 7.28b, 7.30)	Femur (2)		Femur is the only bone of thigh; between hip joint and knee; largest bone of the body	Head; greater and lesser trochanters; neck; lateral and medial condyles and epicondyles; adductor tubercle; gluteal tuberosity; linea aspera
Kneecap (Figure 7.28a)	Patella (2)		Patella is a sesamoid bone lodged in the tendon of the quadriceps (anterior thigh) muscles	
Leg (Figures 7.29, 7.30)	Tibia (2)		Tibia is the larger and more medial bone of leg; between knee and foot	Medial and lateral condyles; tibial tuberosity; anterior border; medial malleolus
	Fibula (2)		Fibula is the lateral bone of leg; sticklike	Head; lateral malleolus
Foot (Figure 7.31)	7 Tarsals (14) • talus • calcaneus • navicular • cuboid • lateral cuneiform • intermediate cuneiform • medial cuneiform		Seven tarsal bones form the proximal part of the foot; the talus articulates with the leg bones at the ankle joint; the calcaneus, the largest tarsal, forms the heel	
	5 Metatarsals (10)		Metatarsals are five bones numbered 1–5 from the great toe	
	14 Phalanges (28) • distal • middle • proximal		Phalanges form the toes; three in digits 2–5, two in digit 1 (the great toe)	

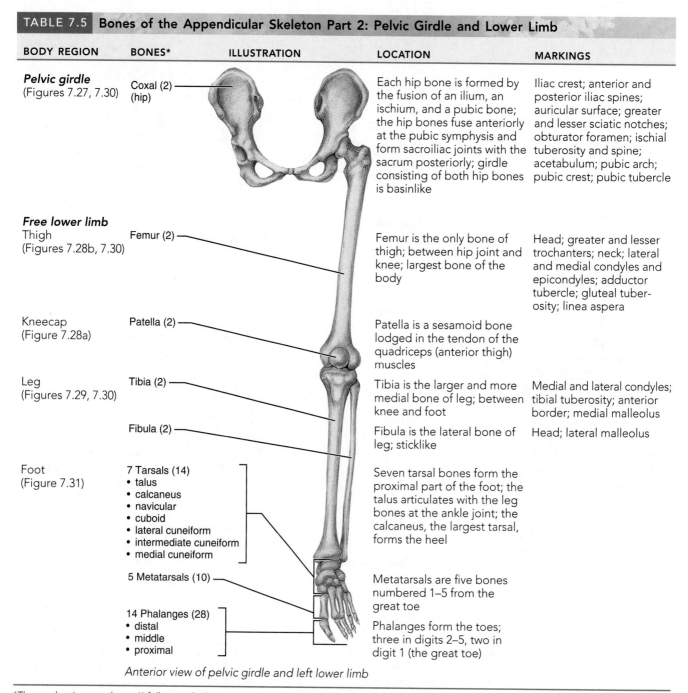

Anterior view of pelvic girdle and left lower limb

*The number in parentheses ( ) following the bone name denotes the total number of such bones in the body.

Developmental Aspects of the Skeleton

The membrane bones of the skull start to ossify late in the second month of development. The rapid deposit of bone matrix at the ossification centers produces cone-shaped protrusions in the developing bones. At birth, the skull bones are still incomplete and are connected by as yet unossified remnants of fibrous membranes called **fontanels** (fon"tah-nelz') (Figure 7.33). The fontanels allow the infant's head to be compressed slightly during birth, and they accommodate brain growth in the fetus and infant. A baby's pulse can be felt surging in these "soft spots"; hence their name (*fontanel* = little fountain). The large, diamond-shaped *anterior fontanel* is palpable for 1½ to 2 years after birth. The others are replaced by bone by the end of the first year.

 HOMEOSTATIC IMBALANCE

Several congenital abnormalities may distort the skull. Most common is *cleft palate,* a condition in which the right and left halves of the palate fail to

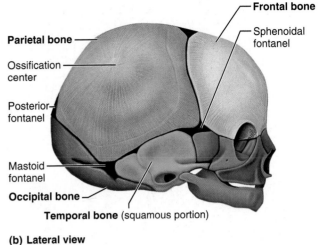

(a) Superior view

Frontal suture
Frontal bone
Anterior fontanel
Ossification center
Posterior fontanel
Parietal bone
Occipital bone

(b) Lateral view

Frontal bone
Parietal bone
Sphenoidal fontanel
Ossification center
Posterior fontanel
Mastoid fontanel
Occipital bone
Temporal bone (squamous portion)

FIGURE 7.33 **The fetal skull.** Notice that the infant's skull has more bones than that of an adult. (See *A Brief Atlas of the Human Body,* Figure 16.)

fuse medially (Figure 7.34). The persistent opening between the oral and nasal cavities interferes with sucking and can lead to aspiration (inhalation) of food into the lungs and *aspiration pneumonia.* ●

The skeleton changes throughout life, but the changes in childhood are most dramatic. At birth, the baby's cranium is huge relative to its face, and several bones are still unfused (e.g., the mandible and frontal bones). The maxillae and mandible are foreshortened, and the contours of the face are flat (Figure 7.35). By 9 months after birth, the cranium is already half of its adult size (volume) because of the rapid growth of the brain. By 8 to 9 years, the cranium has almost reached adult proportions. Between the ages of 6 and 13, the head appears to enlarge substantially as the face literally grows out from the skull. The jaws, cheekbones, and nose become more prominent. These facial changes are correlated with the expansion of the nose and paranasal sinuses, and development of the permanent teeth. Figure 7.35 tracks how differential bone growth alters body proportions throughout life.

Only the thoracic and sacral curvatures are well developed at birth. These so-called **primary curvatures** are convex posteriorly, and an infant's spine arches, like that of a four-legged animal. The **secondary curvatures**—cervical and lumbar—are convex anteriorly and are associated with a child's development. They result from reshaping of the intervertebral discs rather than from modifications of the vertebrae. The cervical curvature is present before birth but is not pronounced until the baby starts to lift its head (at about 3 months). The lumbar curvature develops when the baby begins to walk (at about 12 months). The lumbar curvature positions the weight of the trunk over the body's center of gravity, providing optimal balance when standing.

Vertebral problems (scoliosis or lordosis) may appear during the early school years, when rapid growth of the limb bones stretches many muscles. During the preschool years, lordosis is often present, but this is usually rectified as the abdominal muscles become stronger and the pelvis tilts forward. The thorax grows wider, but a true "military posture" (head erect, shoulders back, abdomen in, and chest out) does not develop until adolescence.

HOMEOSTATIC IMBALANCE

The appendicular skeleton can also suffer from a number of congenital abnormalities. One that is fairly common (4% of infants) and quite severe is *dysplasia of the hip* (dis-pla′ze-ah; "bad formation"). The acetabulum forms incompletely or the ligaments of the hip joint are loose, so the head of the femur slips out of its socket. Early treatment (a splint or harness to hold the femur in place or

FIGURE 7.34 **A baby born with a cleft lip and palate.**

Human newborn   Human adult

(a)

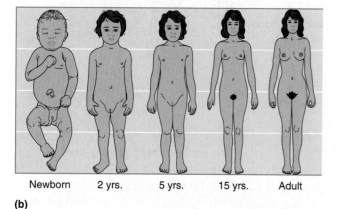

Newborn   2 yrs.   5 yrs.   15 yrs.   Adult

(b)

FIGURE 7.35 **Different growth rates of body parts determine body proportions. (a)** Differential growth transforms the rounded, foreshortened skull of a newborn to the sloping skull characteristic of adults. **(b)** During growth of a human, the arms and legs grow faster than the head and trunk, as can be seen in this conceptualization of different-aged individuals all drawn at the same height.

surgery to tighten hip ligaments) is essential to prevent permanent crippling. ●

During youth, growth of the skeleton not only increases overall body height but also changes body proportions (Figure 7.35). At birth, the head and trunk are approximately 1½ times as long as the lower limbs. The lower limbs grow more rapidly than the trunk

from this time on, and by the age of 10, the head and trunk are approximately the same height as the lower limbs, a condition that persists thereafter. During puberty, the female pelvis broadens in preparation for childbearing, and the entire male skeleton becomes more robust. Once adult height is reached, a healthy skeleton changes very little until late middle age.

Old age affects many parts of the skeleton, especially the spine. As the discs become thinner, less hydrated, and less elastic, the risk of disc herniation increases. By 55 years, a loss of several centimeters in stature is common. Further shortening can be produced by osteoporosis of the spine or by kyphosis (called "dowager's hump" in the elderly). What was done during youth may be undone in old age as the vertebral column gradually resumes its initial arc shape.

The thorax becomes more rigid with age, largely because the costal cartilages ossify. This loss of rib cage elasticity causes shallow breathing, which leads to less efficient gas exchange.

All bones, you will recall, lose mass with age. Cranial bones lose less mass than most, but changes in facial contours with age are common. As the bony tissue of the jaws declines, the jaws look small and childlike once again. If the elderly person loses his or her teeth, this loss of bone from the jaws is accelerated, because the alveolar region bone is resorbed. As bones become more porous, they are more likely to fracture, especially the vertebrae and the neck of the femur.

■ ■ ■

Our skeleton is a marvelous substructure, to be sure, but it is much more than that. It is a protector and supporter of other body systems, and without it (and the joints considered in Chapter 8), our muscles would be almost useless. The homeostatic relationships between the skeletal system and other body systems are illustrated in *Making Connections* in Chapter 6 (pp. 196–197).

Related Clinical Terms

Chiropractic (ki″ro-prak′tik) A system of treating disease by manipulating the vertebral column based on the theory that most diseases are due to pressure on nerves caused by faulty bone alignment; a specialist in this field is a chiropractor.

Clubfoot A relatively common congenital defect (1 in 700 births) in which the soles of the feet face medially and the toes point inferiorly; may be genetically induced or reflect an abnormal position of the foot during fetal development.

Laminectomy Surgical removal of a vertebral lamina; most often done to relieve the symptoms of a ruptured disc.

Orthopedist (or″tho-pe′dist) or **orthopedic surgeon** A physician who specializes in restoring lost skeletal system function or repairing damage to bones and joints.

Pelvimetry Measurement of the dimensions of the inlet and outlet of the pelvis, usually to determine whether the pelvis is of adequate size to allow normal delivery of a baby.

Spina bifida (spi′nah bĭ′fi-dah; "cleft spine") Congenital defect of the vertebral column in which one or more of the vertebral arches are incomplete; ranges in severity from inconsequential to severe conditions that impair neural functioning and encourage nervous system infections.

Spinal fusion Surgical procedure involving insertion of bone chips (or crushed bone) to immobilize and stabilize a specific region of the vertebral column, particularly in cases of vertebral fracture and herniated discs.

Chapter Summary

1. The axial skeleton forms the longitudinal axis of the body. Its principal subdivisions are the skull, vertebral column, and bony thorax. It provides support and protection (by enclosure).

2. The appendicular skeleton consists of the bones of the pectoral and pelvic girdles and the limbs. It allows mobility for manipulation and locomotion.

PART 1: THE AXIAL SKELETON

The Skull   (pp. 203–218)

1. The skull is formed by 22 bones. The cranium forms the vault and base of the skull, which protect the brain. The facial skeleton provides openings for the respiratory and digestive passages and attachment points for facial muscles.

2. Except for the temporomandibular joints, all bones of the adult skull are joined by immovable sutures.

3. **Cranium.** The eight bones of the cranium include the paired parietal and temporal bones and the single frontal, occipital, ethmoid, and sphenoid bones (see Table 7.1, pp. 216–217).

4. **Facial bones.** The 14 bones of the face include the paired maxillae, zygomatics, nasals, lacrimals, palatines, and inferior conchae and the single mandible and vomer bones (Table 7.1).

5. **Orbits and nasal cavity.** Both the orbits and the nasal cavities are complicated bony regions formed of several bones.

6. **Paranasal sinuses.** Paranasal sinuses occur in the frontal, ethmoid, sphenoid, and maxillary bones.

7. **Hyoid bone.** The hyoid bone, supported in the neck by ligaments, serves as an attachment point for tongue and neck muscles.

The Vertebral Column   (pp. 218–225)

1. **General characteristics.** The vertebral column includes 24 movable vertebrae (7 cervical, 12 thoracic, and 5 lumbar) and the sacrum and coccyx.

2. The fibrocartilage intervertebral discs act as shock absorbers and provide flexibility to the vertebral column.

3. The primary curvatures of the vertebral column are the thoracic and sacral; the secondary curvatures are the cervical and lumbar. Curvatures increase spine flexibility.

4. **General structure of vertebrae.** With the exception of C_1 and C_2, all vertebrae have a body, two transverse processes, two superior and two inferior articular processes, a spinous process, and a vertebral arch.

5. **Regional vertebral characteristics.** Special features distinguish the regional vertebrae (see Table 7.2, p. 224).

The Thoracic Cage   (pp. 226–228)

1. The bones of the thoracic cage include the 12 rib pairs, the sternum, and the thoracic vertebrae. The thoracic cage protects the organs of the thoracic cavity.

2. **Sternum.** The sternum consists of the fused manubrium, body, and xiphoid process.

3. **Ribs.** The first seven rib pairs are called true ribs; the rest are called false ribs. Ribs 11 and 12 are floating ribs.

PART 2: THE APPENDICULAR SKELETON

The Pectoral (Shoulder) Girdle*   (pp. 229–231)

1. Each pectoral girdle consists of one clavicle and one scapula. The pectoral girdles attach the upper limbs to the axial skeleton.

2. **Clavicles.** The clavicles hold the scapulae laterally away from the thorax. The sternoclavicular joints are the only attachment points of the pectoral girdle to the axial skeleton.

3. **Scapulae.** The scapulae articulate with the clavicles and with the humerus bones of the arms.

The Upper Limb*   (pp. 231–237)

1. Each upper limb consists of 30 bones and is specialized for mobility.

2. **Arm/forearm/hand.** The skeleton of the arm is composed solely of the humerus; the skeleton of the forearm is composed of the radius and ulna; and the skeleton of the hand consists of the carpals, metacarpals, and phalanges.

The Pelvic (Hip) Girdle*   (pp. 237–239)

1. The pelvic girdle, a heavy structure specialized for weight bearing, is composed of two hip bones that secure the lower limbs to the axial skeleton. Together with the sacrum, the hip bones form the basinlike bony pelvis.

2. Each hip bone consists of three fused bones: ilium, ischium, and pubis; the acetabulum occurs at the point of fusion.

3. **Ilium/ischium/pubis.** The ilium is the superior flaring portion of the hip bone. Each ilium forms a secure joint with the sacrum posteriorly. The ischium is a curved bar of bone; we sit on the ischial tuberosities. The V-shaped pubic bones articulate anteriorly at the pubic symphysis.

4. **Pelvic structure and childbearing.** The male pelvis is deep and narrow with larger, heavier bones than those of the female. The female pelvis, which forms the birth canal, is shallow and wide.

The Lower Limb*   (pp. 239–246)

1. Each lower limb consists of the thigh, leg, and foot and is specialized for weight bearing and locomotion.

2. **Thigh.** The femur is the only bone of the thigh. Its ball-shaped head articulates with the acetabulum.

3. **Leg.** The bones of the leg are the tibia, which participates in forming both the knee and ankle joints, and the fibula.

4. **Foot.** The bones of the foot include the tarsals, metatarsals, and phalanges. The most important tarsals are the calcaneus (heel bone) and the talus, which articulates with the tibia superiorly.

5. The foot is supported by three arches (lateral, medial, and transverse) that distribute body weight to the heel and ball of the foot.

Developmental Aspects of the Skeleton (pp. 246–248)

1. Fontanels, which allow brain growth and ease birth passage, are present in the skull at birth. Growth of the cranium after birth is related to brain growth; increase in size of the facial skeleton follows tooth development and enlargement of nose and sinus cavities.

---

*For associated bone markings, see the pages indicated in the section heads.

2. The vertebral column is C shaped at birth (thoracic and sacral curvatures are present); the secondary curvatures form when the baby begins to lift its head and walk.

3. Long bones continue to grow in length until late adolescence. The head and torso, initially 1½ times the length of the lower limbs, equal their length by the age of 10.

4. Changes in the female pelvis (preparatory for childbirth) occur during puberty.

5. Once at adult height, the skeleton changes little until late middle age. With old age, the intervertebral discs thin; this, along with osteoporosis, leads to a gradual loss in height and increased risk of disc herniation. Loss of bone mass increases the risk of fractures, and thoracic cage rigidity promotes breathing difficulties.

Review Questions

Multiple Choice/Matching

(Some questions have more than one correct answer. Select the best answer or answers from the choices given.)

1. Using the letters from column B, match the bone descriptions in column A. (Note that some require more than a single choice.)

Column A	Column B
_____ (1) connected by the coronal suture	(a) ethmoid
_____ (2) keystone bone of cranium	(b) frontal
	(c) mandible
_____ (3) keystone bone of the face	(d) maxillary
_____ (4) form the hard palate	(e) occipital
_____ (5) allows the spinal cord to pass	(f) palatine
	(g) parietal
_____ (6) forms the chin	(h) sphenoid
_____ (7) contain paranasal sinuses	(i) temporal
_____ (8) contains mastoid sinuses	

2. Match the key terms with the bone descriptions that follow.

Key: (a) clavicle   (b) ilium   (c) ischium
     (d) pubis   (e) sacrum   (f) scapula
     (g) sternum

_____ (1) bone of the axial skeleton to which the pectoral girdle attaches
_____ (2) markings include glenoid cavity and acromion
_____ (3) features include the ala, crest, and greater sciatic notch
_____ (4) doubly curved; acts as a shoulder strut
_____ (5) pelvic girdle bone that articulates with the axial skeleton
_____ (6) the "sit-down" bone
_____ (7) anteriormost bone of the pelvic girdle
_____ (8) part of the vertebral column

3. Use key choices to identify the bone descriptions that follow.

Key: (a) carpals   (b) femur   (c) fibula
     (d) humerus   (e) radius   (f) tarsals
     (g) tibia   (h) ulna

_____ (1) articulates with the acetabulum and the tibia
_____ (2) forms the lateral aspect of the ankle
_____ (3) bone that "carries" the hand
_____ (4) the wrist bones
_____ (5) end shaped like a monkey wrench
_____ (6) articulates with the capitulum of the humerus
_____ (7) largest bone of this "group" is the calcaneus

Short Answer Essay Questions

4. Name the cranial and facial bones and compare and contrast the functions of the cranial and facial skeletons.

5. How do the relative proportions of the cranium and face of a fetus compare with those of an adult skull?

6. Name and diagram the normal vertebral curvatures. Which are primary and which are secondary curvatures?

7. List at least two specific anatomical characteristics each for typical cervical, thoracic, and lumbar vertebrae that would allow *anyone* to identify each type correctly.

8. (a) What is the function of the intervertebral discs? (b) Distinguish between the anulus fibrosus and nucleus pulposus regions of a disc. (c) Which provides durability and strength? (d) Which provides resilience? (e) Which part is involved in a "slipped" disc?

9. Name the major components of the thoracic cage.

10. (a) What is a true rib? A false rib? (b) Is a floating rib a true rib or a false rib? (c) Why are floating ribs easily broken?

11. The major function of the shoulder girdle is flexibility. What is the major function of the pelvic girdle? Relate these functional differences to anatomical differences seen in these girdles.

12. List three important differences between the male and female pelves.

13. Describe the function of the arches of the foot.

14. Briefly describe the anatomical characteristics and impairment of function seen in cleft palate and hip dysplasia.

15. Compare a young adult skeleton to that of an extremely aged person relative to bone mass in general and the bony structure of the skull, thorax, and vertebral column in particular.

16. Peter Howell, a teaching assistant in the anatomy class, picked up a hip bone and pretended it was a telephone. He held the big hole in this bone right up to his ear and said, "Hello, obturator, obturator (operator, operator)." Name the structure he was helping the student to learn.

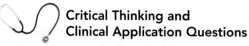

Critical Thinking and Clinical Application Questions

1. Justiniano worked in a poultry-packing plant where his job was cutting open chickens and stripping out their visceral organs. After work, he typed for long hours on his computer keyboard, writing a book about his work in the plant. Soon, his wrist and hand began to hurt whenever he flexed it, and he began to awaken at night with pain and tingling on the thumb-half of his hand. What condition did he probably have?

2. Ralph had polio as a boy and was partially paralyzed in one lower limb for over a year. Although no longer paralyzed, he now has a severe lateral curvature of the lumbar spine. Explain what has happened and identify his condition.

3. Mary's grandmother slipped on a scatter rug and fell heavily to the floor. Her left lower limb was laterally rotated and noticeably shorter than the right, and when she attempted to get up, she winced with pain. Mary surmised that her grandmother might have "fractured her hip," which later proved to be true. What bone was probably fractured and at what site? Why is a "fractured hip" a common type of fracture in the elderly?

4. Mrs. Shea came up with what she considered to be a clever idea to bypass the long lines at Disney World. She had her husband rent a wheelchair and he wheeled her around from one exhibit to another for the better part of three days. As they sat on the plane, waiting to take off for Chicago, she complained to him that she had two sore spots on her buttocks. Why? What do you suppose would happen (to her buttocks) if she was wheeled around for a few more days?

LOOKING FOR MORE STUDY HELP?

A wide variety of quiz questions, tutorials, and learning exercises are available online at the Anatomy & Physiology Place (www.anatomyandphysiology.com) and, if your instructor has provided you with a MyA&P Course ID number, in MyA&P (www.myaandp.com).

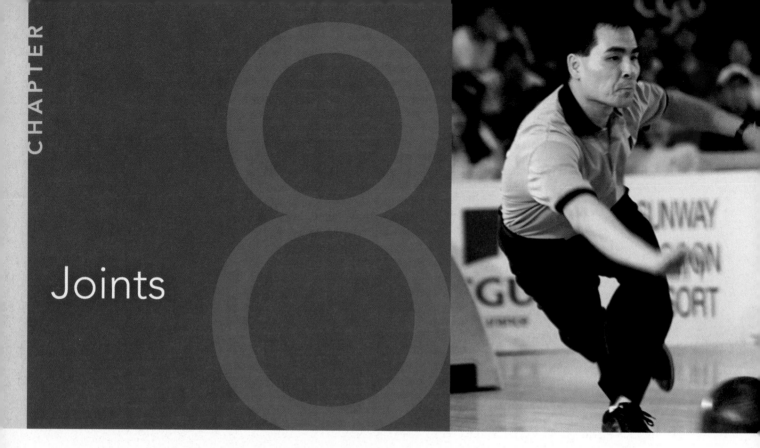

CHAPTER 8

Joints

1. Define joint or articulation.

Classification of Joints (p. 253)

2. Classify joints structurally and functionally.

Fibrous Joints (pp. 253–254)

3. Describe the general structure of fibrous joints. Name and give an example of each of the three common types of fibrous joints.

Cartilaginous Joints (p. 255)

4. Describe the general structure of cartilaginous joints. Name and give an example of each of the two common types of cartilaginous joints.

Synovial Joints (pp. 255–272)

5. Describe the structural characteristics of synovial joints.

6. List three natural factors that stabilize synovial joints.

7. Compare the structures and functions of bursae and tendon sheaths.

8. Name and describe (or perform) the common body movements.

9. Name and provide examples of the six types of synovial joints based on the movement(s) allowed.

10. Describe the elbow, knee, hip, jaw, and shoulder joints relative to articulating bones, anatomical characteristics of the joint, movements allowed, and joint stability.

Homeostatic Imbalances of Joints (pp. 272–274, 276)

11. Name the most common joint injuries and discuss the symptoms and problems associated with each.

12. Compare and contrast the common types of arthritis.

Developmental Aspects of Joints (p. 276)

13. Discuss factors that promote or disturb joint homeostasis.

The graceful movements of ballet dancers and the rough-and-tumble grapplings of football players demonstrate the great variety of motion allowed by **joints,** or **articulations**—the sites where two or more bones meet. Our joints have two fundamental functions: They give our skeleton mobility, and they hold it together, sometimes playing a protective role in the process.

Joints are the weakest parts of the skeleton. Nonetheless, their structure resists various forces, such as crushing or tearing, that threaten to force them out of alignment.

Classification of Joints

Joints are classified by structure and by function. The *structural classification* focuses on the material binding the bones together and whether or not a joint cavity is present. Structurally, there are *fibrous, cartilaginous,* and *synovial joints* (Table 8.1 on p. 256).

The *functional classification* is based on the amount of movement allowed at the joint. On this basis, there are **synarthroses** (sin″ar-thro′sēz; *syn* = together, *arthro* = joint), which are immovable joints; **amphiarthroses** (am″fe-ar-thro′sēz; *amphi* = on both sides), slightly movable joints; and **diarthroses** (di″ar-thro′sēz; *dia* = through, apart), or freely movable joints. Freely movable joints predominate in the limbs; immovable and slightly movable joints are largely restricted to the axial skeleton.

In general, fibrous joints are immovable, and synovial joints are freely movable. However, cartilaginous joints have both rigid and slightly movable examples. Since the structural categories are more clear-cut, we will use the structural classification in this discussion, indicating functional properties where appropriate.

Fibrous Joints

In **fibrous joints,** the bones are joined by fibrous tissue; no joint cavity is present. The amount of movement allowed depends on the length of the connective tissue fibers uniting the bones. Although a few are slightly movable, most fibrous joints are immovable. The three types of fibrous joints are *sutures, syndesmoses,* and *gomphoses.*

Sutures

Sutures, literally "seams," occur only between bones of the skull (Figure 8.1a). The wavy articulating bone edges interlock, and the junction is completely filled by a minimal amount of very short connective tissue fibers that are continuous with the periosteum. The result is nearly rigid splices that bind the bones

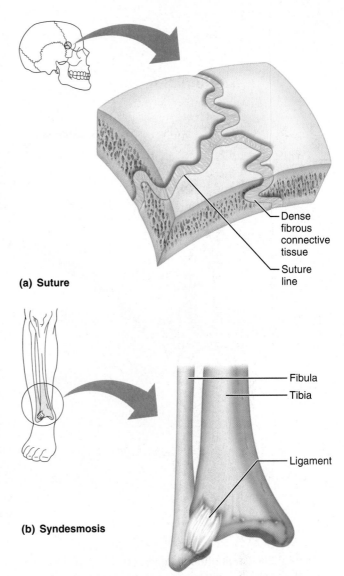

(a) Suture

(b) Syndesmosis

FIGURE 8.1   **Fibrous joints. (a)** Sutures of the skull have interconnecting connective tissue fibers that are very short, and the bone edges interlock so that the joint is immovable (synarthrotic). **(b)** In the syndesmosis at the distal tibiofibular joint, the fibrous tissue (ligament) connecting the bones is longer than that in sutures.

tightly together, yet allow the bones to grow at their edges during youth. During middle age, the fibrous tissue ossifies and the skull bones fuse into a single unit. At this stage, the sutures are more precisely called **synostoses** (sin″os-to′sēz), literally, "bony junctions." Because movement of the cranial bones would damage the brain, the immovable nature of sutures is a protective adaptation.

Syndesmoses

In **syndesmoses** (sin″des-mo′sēz), the bones are connected by a *ligament* (*syndesmos* = ligament), a cord

Q *Which one of the joint types shown here has the greatest flexibility and why?*

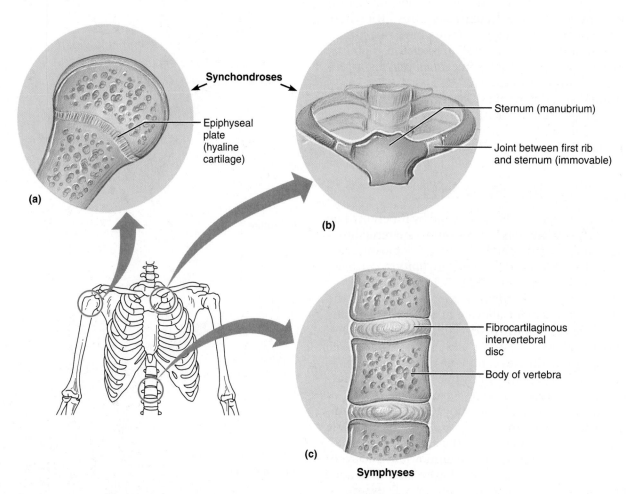

Synchondroses

Epiphyseal plate (hyaline cartilage)

(a)

Sternum (manubrium)

Joint between first rib and sternum (immovable)

(b)

Fibrocartilaginous intervertebral disc

Body of vertebra

(c)

Symphyses

FIGURE 8.2 **Cartilaginous joints. (a)** The epiphyseal plate in a growing long bone is a temporary synchondrosis; the shaft and epiphysis are connected by hyaline cartilage that is later completely ossified. **(b)** The sternocostal joint between rib 1 and the manubrium of the sternum is an immovable hyaline cartilage joint, or synchondrosis. **(c)** The intervertebral joints, in which the vertebrae are connected by fibrocartilaginous discs, are symphyses.

or band of fibrous tissue. Although the connecting fibers are always longer than those in sutures, they vary quite a bit in length. The amount of movement allowed depends on the length of the connecting fibers, and slight to considerable movement is possible. For example, the ligament connecting the distal ends of the tibia and fibula is short (Figure 8.1b), and this joint allows only slightly more movement than a suture, a characteristic best described as "give." True movement is still prevented, so the joint is classed functionally as an immovable joint, or synarthrosis. (Note, however, that some authorities classify this joint as an amphiarthrosis.) On the other hand, the fibers of the ligament-like interosseous membrane connecting the radius and ulna along their length (Figure 7.24, p. 233) are long enough to permit rotation of the radius around the ulna.

Gomphoses

A **gomphosis** (gom-fo′sis) is a peg-in-socket fibrous joint. The only example is the articulation of a tooth with its bony alveolar socket. The term *gomphosis* comes from the Greek *gompho*, meaning "nail" or "bolt," and refers to the way teeth are embedded in their sockets (as if hammered in). The fibrous connection in this case is the short **periodontal ligament** (Figure 23.11, p. 894).

A The symphyses, represented by the intervertebral joints in (c), are most flexible because the uniting cartilage in this joint type is the resilient fibrocartilage, versus the hyaline cartilage seen in (a) and (b).

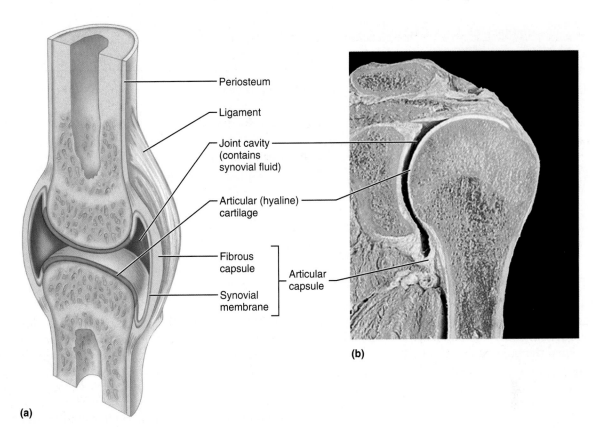

(a)

(b)

FIGURE 8.3   **General structure of a synovial joint. (a)** The articulating bone ends are covered with articular cartilage and enclosed within an articular capsule which is typically reinforced by ligaments externally. Internally, the fibrous capsule is lined with a smooth synovial membrane that secretes synovial fluid. **(b)** Photo of frontally sectioned shoulder joint.

Cartilaginous Joints

In **cartilaginous joints** (kar″ti-laj′ĭ-nus), the articulating bones are united by cartilage. Like fibrous joints, they lack a joint cavity. The two types of cartilaginous joints are *synchondroses* and *symphyses*.

Synchondroses

A bar or plate of *hyaline cartilage* unites the bones at a **synchondrosis** (sin″kon-dro′sis; "junction of cartilage"). Virtually all synchondroses are synarthrotic.

The most common examples of synchondroses are the epiphyseal plates connecting the diaphysis and epiphysis regions in long bones of children (Figure 8.2a). Epiphyseal plates are temporary joints and eventually become synostoses. Another example of a synchondrosis is the immovable joint between the costal cartilage of the first rib and the manubrium of the sternum (Figure 8.2b).

Symphyses

In **symphyses** (sim′fih-sēz; "growing together") the articular surfaces of the bones are covered with articular (hyaline) cartilage, which in turn is fused to an intervening pad, or plate, of *fibrocartilage*. Since fibrocartilage is compressible and resilient, it acts as a shock absorber and permits a limited amount of movement at the joint. Symphyses are amphiarthrotic joints designed for strength with flexibility. Examples include the intervertebral joints (Figure 8.2c) and the pubic symphysis of the pelvis (see Table 8.2 on p. 258).

Synovial Joints

Synovial joints are those in which the articulating bones are separated by a fluid-containing joint cavity. This arrangement permits substantial freedom of movement, and all synovial joints are freely movable diarthroses. All joints of the limbs—indeed, most joints of the body—fall into this class.

General Structure

Synovial joints have five distinguishing features (Figure 8.3a):

1. Articular cartilage. Glassy-smooth hyaline cartilage covers the opposing bone surfaces as **articular**

TABLE 8.1	Summary of Joint Classes		
STRUCTURAL CLASS	**STRUCTURAL CHARACTERISTICS**	**TYPES**	**MOBILITY**
Fibrous	Bone ends/parts united by collagenic fibers	Suture (short fibers)	Immobile (synarthrosis)
		Syndesmosis (longer fibers)	Slightly mobile (amphiarthrosis) and immobile
		Gomphosis (periodontal ligament)	Immobile
Cartilaginous	Bone ends/parts united by cartilage	Synchondrosis (hyaline cartilage)	Immobile
		Symphysis (fibrocartilage)	Slightly movable
Synovial	Bone ends/parts covered with articular cartilage and enclosed within an articular capsule lined with synovial membrane	Plane Condyloid Hinge Saddle Pivot Ball and socket	Freely movable (diarthrosis; movements depend on design of joint)

cartilage. These thin (1 mm or less) but spongy cushions absorb compression placed on the joint and thereby keep the bone ends from being crushed.

2. Joint (synovial) cavity. A feature unique to synovial joints, the **joint cavity** is really just a potential space that contains a small amount of synovial fluid.

3. Articular capsule. The joint cavity is enclosed by a two-layered **articular capsule,** or *joint capsule.* The external layer is a tough **fibrous capsule,** composed of dense irregular connective tissue, that is continuous with the periostea of the articulating bones. It strengthens the joint so that the bones are not pulled apart. The inner layer of the joint capsule is a **synovial membrane** composed of loose connective tissue. Besides lining the fibrous capsule internally, it covers all internal joint surfaces that are not hyaline cartilage.

4. Synovial fluid. A small amount of slippery **synovial fluid** occupies all free spaces within the joint capsule. This fluid is derived largely by filtration from blood flowing through the capillaries in the synovial membrane. Synovial fluid has a viscous, egg-white consistency (*synovi* = joint egg) due to hyaluronic acid secreted by cells in the synovial membrane, but it thins, becoming less viscous, as it warms during joint activity. Synovial fluid, which is also found *within* the articular cartilages, provides a slippery weight-bearing film that reduces friction between the cartilages. The synovial fluid is forced from the cartilages when a joint is compressed; then as pressure on the joint is relieved, synovial fluid seeps back into the articular cartilages like water into a sponge, ready to be squeezed out again the next time the joint is loaded (put under pressure). This mechanism, called *weeping lubrication,* lubricates the free surfaces of the cartilages and nourishes their cells. Synovial fluid also contains phagocytic cells that rid the joint cavity of microbes and cellular debris.

5. Reinforcing ligaments. Synovial joints are reinforced and strengthened by a number of bandlike **ligaments.** Most often, these are **capsular,** or **intrinsic, ligaments;** that is, they are thickened parts of the fibrous capsule. In other cases, they remain distinct and are found outside the capsule (**extracapsular ligaments**) or deep to it (**intracapsular ligaments**). Since intracapsular ligaments are covered with synovial membrane, they do not actually lie *within* the joint cavity.

People said to be double-jointed amaze the rest of us by placing both heels behind their neck. However, they have the normal number of joints; it's just that their joint capsules and ligaments are more stretchy and looser than average.

The articular capsule and ligaments are richly supplied with sensory nerve endings that monitor joint position and help to maintain muscle tone. Stretching these structures sends nerve impulses to the central nervous system, resulting in reflexive contraction of muscles surrounding the joint. Synovial joints are also richly supplied with blood vessels, most of which supply the synovial membrane.

Besides the basic components described above, certain synovial joints have other structural features. Some, such as the hip and knee joints, have cushioning **fatty pads** between the fibrous capsule and the synovial membrane or bone. Others have discs or wedges of fibrocartilage separating the articular surfaces. Where present, these so-called **articular discs,** or **menisci** (mĕ-nis′ki; "crescents"), extend inward from the articular capsule and partially or completely divide the synovial cavity in two (see the menisci in Figure 8.8). Articular discs improve the fit between articulating bone ends, making the joint more stable and minimizing wear and tear on the joint surfaces. Articular discs occur in the knee, jaw, and a few other joints (see Table 8.2).

(a)

Labels on figure (a):
- Acromion of scapula
- Coracoacromial ligament
- Subacromial bursa
- Fibrous articular capsule
- Tendon sheath
- Tendon of long head of biceps brachii muscle
- Glenoid cavity containing synovial fluid
- Hyaline cartilage
- Synovial membrane
- Fibrous capsule
- Humerus

Labels on figure (b):
- Coracoacromial ligament
- Subacromial bursa
- Cavity in bursa containing synovial fluid

(b)

FIGURE 8.4 **Friction-reducing structures: Bursae and tendon sheaths. (a)** Frontal section through the right shoulder joint showing a bursa and a tendon sheath around a muscle tendon. **(b)** Enlargement showing how a bursa eliminates friction where a tendon (or other structure) would rub against a bone.

Bursae and Tendon Sheaths

Bursae and tendon sheaths are not strictly part of synovial joints, but they are often found closely associated with them (Figure 8.4). Essentially bags of lubricant, they act as "ball bearings" to reduce friction between adjacent structures during joint activity. **Bursae** (ber′se; "purse") are flattened fibrous sacs lined with synovial membrane and containing a thin film of synovial fluid. They are common where ligaments, muscles, skin, tendons, or bones rub together.

A **tendon sheath** is essentially an elongated bursa that wraps completely around a tendon subjected to friction, like a bun around a hot dog.

Factors Influencing the Stability of Synovial Joints

Because joints are constantly stretched and compressed, they must be stabilized so that they do not dislocate (come out of alignment). The stability of a synovial joint depends chiefly on three factors: the shapes of the articular surfaces; the number and positioning of ligaments; and muscle tone.

Articular Surfaces

The shapes of articular surfaces determine what movements are possible at a joint, but surprisingly, articular surfaces play only a minor role in joint stability. Many joints have shallow sockets or noncomplementary articulating surfaces ("misfits") that actually hinder joint stability. But when articular surfaces are large and fit snugly together, or when the socket is deep, stability is vastly improved. The ball and deep socket of the hip joint provide the best example of a joint made extremely stable by the shape of its articular surfaces.

Ligaments

The capsules and ligaments of synovial joints unite the bones and prevent excessive or undesirable motion. As a rule, the more ligaments a joint has, the stronger it is. However, when other stabilizing factors are inadequate, undue tension is placed on the ligaments and they stretch. Stretched ligaments stay stretched, like taffy, and a ligament can stretch only about 6% of its length before it snaps. Thus, when ligaments are the major means of bracing a joint, the joint is not very stable.

Muscle Tone

For most joints, the muscle tendons that cross the joint are the most important stabilizing factor. These tendons are kept taut at all times by the tone of their muscles. (Muscle tone is defined as low levels of contractile activity in relaxed muscles that keep the muscles healthy and ready to react to stimulation.) Muscle tone is extremely important in

TABLE 8.2	Structural and Functional Characteristics of Body Joints			
ILLUSTRATION	**JOINT**	**ARTICULATING BONES**	**STRUCTURAL TYPE***	**FUNCTIONAL TYPE; MOVEMENTS ALLOWED**
	Skull	Cranial and facial bones	Fibrous; suture	Synarthrotic; no movement
	Temporo-mandibular	Temporal bone of skull and mandible	Synovial; modified hinge† (contains articular disc)	Diarthrotic; gliding and uniaxial rotation; slight lateral movement, elevation, depression, protraction, and retraction of mandible
	Atlanto-occipital	Occipital bone of skull and atlas	Synovial; condyloid	Diarthrotic; biaxial; flexion, extension, lateral flexion, circumduction of head on neck
	Atlantoaxial	Atlas (C_1) and axis (C_2)	Synovial; pivot	Diarthrotic; uniaxial; rotation of the head
	Intervertebral	Between adjacent vertebral bodies	Cartilaginous; symphysis	Amphiarthrotic; slight movement
	Intervertebral	Between articular processes	Synovial; plane	Diarthrotic; gliding
	Vertebrocostal	Vertebrae (transverse processes or bodies) and ribs	Synovial; plane	Diarthrotic; gliding of ribs
	Sternoclavicular	Sternum and clavicle	Synovial; shallow saddle (contains articular disc)	Diarthrotic; multiaxial (allows clavicle to move in all axes)
	Sternocostal	Sternum and rib 1	Cartilaginous; synchondrosis	Synarthrotic; no movement
	Sternocostal	Sternum and ribs 2–7	Synovial; double plane	Diarthrotic; gliding
	Acromio-clavicular	Acromion of scapula and clavicle	Synovial; plane (contains articular disc)	Diarthrotic; gliding and rotation of scapula on clavicle
	Shoulder (glenohumeral)	Scapula and humerus	Synovial; ball and socket	Diarthrotic; multiaxial; flexion, extension, abduction, adduction, circumduction, rotation of humerus
	Elbow	Ulna (and radius) with humerus	Synovial; hinge	Diarthrotic; uniaxial; flexion, extension of forearm
	Radioulnar (proximal)	Radius and ulna	Synovial; pivot	Diarthrotic; uniaxial; rotation of radius around long axis of forearm to allow pronation and supination
	Radioulnar (distal)	Radius and ulna	Synovial; pivot (contains articular disc)	Diarthrotic; uniaxial; rotation (convex head of ulna rotates in ulnar notch of radius)
	Wrist (radiocarpal)	Radius and proximal carpals	Synovial; condyloid	Diarthrotic; biaxial; flexion, extension, abduction, adduction, circumduction of hand
	Intercarpal	Adjacent carpals	Synovial; plane	Diarthrotic; gliding
	Carpometacarpal of digit 1 (thumb)	Carpal (trapezium) and metacarpal 1	Synovial; saddle	Diarthrotic; biaxial; flexion, extension, abduction, adduction, circumduction, opposition of metacarpal 1
	Carpometacarpal of digits 2–5	Carpal(s) and metacarpal(s)	Synovial; plane	Diarthrotic; gliding of metacarpals
	Knuckle (metacarpo-phalangeal)	Metacarpal and proximal phalanx	Synovial; condyloid	Diarthrotic; biaxial; flexion, extension, abduction, adduction, circumduction of fingers
	Finger (interphalangeal)	Adjacent phalanges	Synovial; hinge	Diarthrotic; uniaxial; flexion, extension of fingers

TABLE 8.2	(continued)			
ILLUSTRATION	**JOINT**	**ARTICULATING BONES**	**STRUCTURAL TYPE***	**FUNCTIONAL TYPE; MOVEMENTS ALLOWED**
	Sacroiliac	Sacrum and coxal bone	Synovial; plane in childhood, increasingly fibrous in adult	Diarthrotic in child; amphiarthrotic in adult; (more movement during pregnancy)
	Pubic symphysis	Pubic bones	Cartilaginous; symphysis	Amphiarthrotic; slight movement (enhanced during pregnancy)
	Hip (coxal)	Hip bone and femur	Synovial; ball and socket	Diarthrotic; multiaxial; flexion, extension, abduction, adduction, rotation, circumduction of thigh
	Knee (tibiofemoral)	Femur and tibia	Synovial; modified hinge† (contains articular discs)	Diarthrotic; biaxial; flexion, extension of leg, some rotation allowed
	Knee (femoropatellar)	Femur and patella	Synovial; plane	Diarthrotic; gliding of patella
	Tibiofibular	Tibia and fibula (proximally)	Synovial; plane	Diarthrotic; gliding of fibula
	Tibiofibular	Tibia and fibula (distally)	Fibrous; syndesmosis	Synarthrotic; slight "give" during dorsiflexion
	Ankle	Tibia and fibula with talus	Synovial; hinge	Diarthrotic; uniaxial; dorsiflexion, and plantar flexion of foot
	Intertarsal	Adjacent tarsals	Synovial; plane	Diarthrotic; gliding; inversion and eversion of foot
	Tarsometatarsal	Tarsal(s) and metatarsal(s)	Synovial; plane	Diarthrotic; gliding of metatarsals
	Metatarso-phalangeal	Metatarsal and proximal phalanx	Synovial; condyloid	Diarthrotic; biaxial; flexion, extension, abduction, adduction, circumduction of great toe
	Toe (interphalangeal)	Adjacent phalanges	Synovial; hinge	Diarthrotic; uniaxial; flexion; extension of toes

*__Fibrous joints__ indicated by orange circles; __cartilaginous joints__ by blue circles; __synovial joints__ by purple circles.
†These modified hinge joints are structurally bicondylar.

reinforcing the shoulder and knee joints and the arches of the foot.

Movements Allowed by Synovial Joints

Every skeletal muscle of the body is attached to bone or other connective tissue structures at no fewer than two points. The muscle's **origin** is attached to the immovable (or less movable) bone. Its other end, the **insertion,** is attached to the movable bone. Body movement occurs when muscles contract across joints and their insertion moves toward their origin. The movements can be described in directional terms relative to the lines, or *axes,* around which body part moves and the planes of space along which the movement occurs, that is, along the transverse, frontal, or sagittal plane. (These planes were described in Chapter 1.)

Range of motion allowed by synovial joints varies from **nonaxial movement** (slipping movements only, since there is no axis around which movement can occur) to **uniaxial movement** (movement in one plane) to **biaxial movement** (movement in two planes) to **multiaxial movement** (movement in or around all three planes of space and axes). Range of motion varies greatly in different people. In some, such as trained gymnasts or acrobats, range of joint movement may be extraordinary. The ranges of motion at the major joints are given in Table 8.2.

There are three general types of movements: *gliding, angular movements,* and *rotation.* The most common body movements allowed by synovial joints are described next and illustrated in Figure 8.5.

8

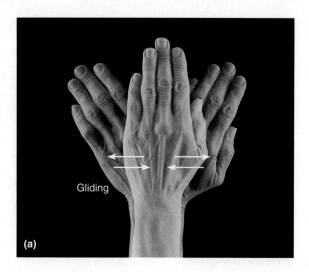

FIGURE 8.5   **Movements allowed by synovial joints.**
(a) Gliding movements.

Gliding Movements

Gliding movements (Figure 8.5a), also known as *translation*, are the simplest joint movements. One flat, or nearly flat, bone surface glides or slips over another (back-and-forth and side-to-side) without appreciable angulation or rotation. Gliding move- ments occur at the intercarpal and intertarsal joints, and between the flat articular processes of the verte- brae, as well as in combination with other move- ments (see Table 8.2).

Angular Movements

Angular movements (Figure 8.5b–f) increase or decrease the angle between two bones. These move- ments may occur in any plane of the body and include flexion, extension, hyperextension, abduc- tion, adduction, and circumduction.

Flexion   **Flexion** (flek'shun) is a bending move- ment, usually along the sagittal plane, that *decreases the angle* of the joint and brings the articulating bones closer together. Examples include bending the head forward on the chest (Figure 8.5d) and bending the body trunk or the knee from a straight to an angled position (Figure 8.5b and c). As a less obvious example, the arm is flexed at the shoulder when the arm is lifted in an anterior direction (Figure 8.5b).

Extension   **Extension** is the reverse of flexion and occurs at the same joints. It involves movement along the sagittal plane that *increases the angle* be- tween the articulating bones, such as straightening a

FIGURE 8.5 *(continued)*   **Movements allowed by synovial joints. (b)** Angular movements.

FIGURE 8.5 *(continued)* **Movements allowed by synovial joints. (c–e)** Angular movements

flexed neck, body trunk, elbow, or knee (Figure 8.5b–d). Bending the head backward beyond its straight (upright) position is called **hyperextension.** At the shoulder and hip, extension carries the limb to a point posterior to the shoulder joint.

Dorsiflexion and Plantar Flexion of the Foot
The up-and-down movements of the foot at the ankle joint are given more specific names (Figure 8.5e). Lifting the foot so that its superior surface approaches the shin is **dorsiflexion** (corresponds to wrist extension), whereas depressing the foot (pointing the toes) is **plantar flexion** (corresponds to wrist flexion).

Abduction   **Abduction** ("moving away") is movement of a limb *away* from the midline or median plane of the body, along the frontal plane. Raising the arm laterally is an example of abduction (Figure 8.5f). When the term is used to indicate the movement of the fingers or toes, it means spreading them apart. In this case "midline" is the longest digit: the third finger or second toe. Notice, however, that lateral bending of the trunk away from the body midline in the frontal plane is called *lateral flexion,* not abduction.

Adduction   **Adduction** ("moving toward") is the opposite of abduction, so it is the movement of a limb *toward* the body midline or, in the case of the digits, toward the midline of the hand or foot (Figure 8.5f).

Circumduction   **Circumduction** (Figure 8.5f) is moving a limb so that it describes a cone in space (*circum* = around; *duco* = to draw). The distal end of the limb moves in a circle, while the point of the cone (the shoulder or hip joint) is more or less stationary. A pitcher winding up to throw a ball is actually circumducting his or her pitching arm. Because circumduction consists of flexion, abduction, extension, and adduction performed in succession, it is the quickest way to exercise the many muscles that move the hip and shoulder ball-and-socket joints.

Rotation

Rotation is the turning of a bone around its own long axis. It is the only movement allowed between

8

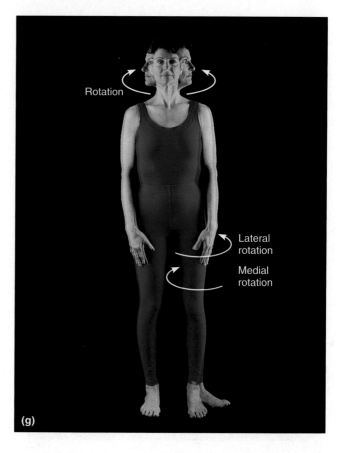

FIGURE 8.5 *(continued)*   **Movements allowed by synovial joints. (f)** Angular movements, continued. **(g)** Rotation.

the first two cervical vertebrae and is common at the hip (Figure 8.5g) and shoulder joints. Rotation may be directed toward the midline or away from it. For example, in *medial rotation* of the thigh, the femur's anterior surface moves toward the median plane of the body; *lateral rotation* is the opposite movement.

Special Movements

Certain movements do not fit into any of the above categories and occur at only a few joints. Some of these special movements are illustrated in Figure 8.6.

Supination and Pronation   The terms **supination** (soo″pĭ-na′shun; "turning backward") and **pronation** (pro-na′shun; "turning forward") refer to the movements of the radius around the ulna (Figure 8.6a). Rotating the forearm laterally so that the palm faces anteriorly or superiorly is supination. In the anatomical position, the hand is supinated and the radius and ulna are parallel. In pronation, the forearm rotates medially and the palm faces posteriorly or inferiorly. Pronation moves the distal end of the radius across the ulna so that the two bones form an X. This is the forearm's position when we are

standing in a relaxed manner. Pronation is a much weaker movement than supination.

A trick to help you keep these terms straight: A *pro* basketball player pronates his or her forearm to dribble the ball.

Inversion and Eversion   **Inversion** and **eversion** are special movements of the foot (Figure 8.6b). In inversion, the sole of the foot turns medially. In eversion, the sole faces laterally.

Protraction and Retraction   Nonangular anterior and posterior movements in a transverse plane are called **protraction** and **retraction**, respectively (Figure 8.6c). The mandible is protracted when you jut out your jaw and retracted when you move it back to its original position.

Elevation and Depression   **Elevation** means lifting a body part superiorly (Figure 8.6d). For example, the scapulae are elevated when you shrug your shoulders. Moving the elevated part inferiorly is **depression.** During chewing, the mandible is alternately elevated and depressed.

Opposition   The saddle joint between metacarpal 1 and the carpals allows a movement called

Q *Which hand position—pronation or supination—is characteristic of the anatomical position?*

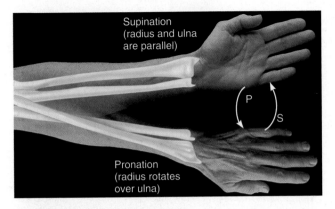

Supination
(radius and ulna
are parallel)

P

S

Pronation
(radius rotates
over ulna)

(a) Supination (S) and pronation (P)

Inversion

Eversion

(b) Inversion and eversion

Protraction
of mandible

Retraction
of mandible

(c) Protraction and retraction

FIGURE 8.6 **Special body movements.**

Elevation
of mandible

Depression
of mandible

(d) Elevation and depression

Opposition

(e) Opposition

opposition of the thumb (Figure 8.6e). This movement is the action taken when you touch your thumb to the tips of the other fingers on the same hand. It is opposition that makes the human hand such a fine tool for grasping and manipulating objects.

Types of Synovial Joints

Although all synovial joints have structural features in common, they do not have a common structural plan. Based on the shape of their articular surfaces, which in turn determine the movements allowed, synovial joints can be classified further into six major categories—plane, hinge, pivot, condyloid, saddle, and ball-and-socket joints.

Plane Joints

In **plane joints** (Figure 8.7a) the articular surfaces are essentially flat, and they allow only short gliding or translational movements. Examples are the gliding joints introduced earlier—the intercarpal and intertarsal joints, and the joints between vertebral

A *Supination.*

FIGURE 8.7 **Types of synovial joints.** Dashed lines indicate the articulating bones. **(a)** Plane joint (e.g., intercarpal and intertarsal joints). **(b)** Hinge joint (e.g., elbow joints and interphalangeal joints). **(c)** Pivot joint (e.g., proximal radioulnar joint). **(d)** Condyloid joint (e.g., metacarpophalangeal joints). **(e)** Saddle joint (e.g., carpometacarpal joint of the thumb). **(f)** Ball-and-socket joint (e.g., shoulder joint).

Nonaxial
Uniaxial
Biaxial
Multiaxial

a Plane joint

b Hinge joint

e Saddle joint

f Ball-and-socket joint

c Pivot joint

d Condyloid joint

articular processes. Gliding does not involve rotation around any axis, and gliding joints are the only examples of nonaxial joints.

Hinge Joints

In **hinge joints** (Figure 8.7b), a cylindrical projection of one bone fits into a trough-shaped surface on another. Motion is along a single plane and resembles that of a mechanical hinge. The uniaxial hinge joints permit flexion and extension only, typified by bending and straightening the elbow and interphalangeal joints.

Pivot Joints

In a **pivot joint** (Figure 8.7c), the rounded end of one bone protrudes into a "sleeve" or ring composed of bone (and possibly ligaments) of another. The only movement allowed is uniaxial rotation of one bone around its own long axis. An example is the joint between the atlas and dens of the axis, which allows you to move your head from side to side to indicate "no." Another is the proximal radioulnar joint, where the head of the radius rotates within a ringlike ligament secured to the ulna.

Condyloid Joints

In **condyloid joints** (kon′dĭ-loid; "knuckle-like"), or **ellipsoidal joints**, the oval articular surface of one bone fits into a complementary depression in another (Figure 8.7d). The important characteristic is that both articulating surfaces are oval. The biaxial condyloid joints permit all *angular* motions, that is, flexion and extension, abduction and adduction, and circumduction. The radiocarpal (wrist) joints and the metacarpophalangeal (knuckle) joints are typical condyloid joints.

Saddle Joints

Saddle joints (Figure 8.7e) resemble condyloid joints, but they allow greater freedom of movement. Each articular surface has *both* concave and convex areas; that is, it is shaped like a saddle. The articular surfaces then fit together, concave to convex surfaces. The most clear-cut examples of saddle joints in the body are the carpometacarpal joints of the thumbs, and the movements allowed by these joints are clearly demonstrated by twiddling your thumbs.

Ball-and-Socket Joints

In **ball-and-socket joints** (Figure 8.7f), the spherical or hemispherical head of one bone articulates with the cuplike socket of another. These joints are multiaxial and the most freely moving synovial joints. Universal movement is allowed (that is, in all axes and planes, including rotation). The shoulder and hip joints are examples.

Selected Synovial Joints

In this section, we examine five joints [knee, shoulder, hip, elbow, and temporomandibular (jaw) joint] in detail. All of these joints have the five distinguishing characteristics of synovial joints, and we will not discuss these common features again. Instead, we will emphasize the unique structural features, functional abilities, and, in certain cases, functional weaknesses of each of these joints.

Knee Joint

The knee joint is the largest and most complex joint in the body (Figure 8.8). It allows extension, flexion, and some rotation. Despite its single joint cavity, the knee consists of three joints in one: an intermediate one between the patella and the lower end of the femur (the **femoropatellar joint**), and lateral and medial joints (collectively known as the **tibiofemoral joint**) between the femoral condyles above and the C-shaped **menisci**, or *semilunar cartilages*, of the tibia below. Besides deepening the shallow tibial articular surfaces, the menisci help prevent side-to-side rocking of the femur on the tibia and absorb shock transmitted to the knee joint. However, the menisci are attached only at their outer margins and are frequently torn free.

The tibiofemoral joint acts primarily as a hinge, permitting flexion and extension. However, structurally it is a bicondylar joint. Some rotation is possible when the knee is partly flexed, but when it is extended, side-to-side movements and rotation are strongly resisted by ligaments and the menisci. The femoropatellar joint is a plane joint, and the patella glides across the distal end of the femur during knee movements.

The knee joint is unique in that its joint cavity is only partially enclosed by a capsule. The relatively thin articular capsule is present only on the sides and posterior aspects of the knee, where it covers the bulk of the femoral and tibial condyles. Anteriorly, where the capsule is absent, three broad ligaments run from the patella to the tibia below. These are the **patellar ligament** flanked by the **medial** and **lateral patellar retinacula** (ret″ĭ-nak′u-lah; "retainers"), which merge imperceptibly into the articular capsule on each side (Figure 8.8c). The patellar ligament and retinacula are actually continuations of the tendon of the bulky quadriceps muscle of the anterior thigh. Physicians tap the patellar ligament to test the knee-jerk reflex.

The synovial cavity of the knee joint has a complicated shape, with several extensions that lead into "blind alleys." At least a dozen bursae are associated

8

(a)

Tendon of quadriceps femoris
Suprapatellar bursa
Patella
Subcutaneous prepatellar bursa
Synovial cavity
Lateral meniscus
Infrapatellar fat pad
Deep infrapatellar bursa
Patellar ligament

Femur
Articular capsule
Posterior cruciate ligament
Lateral meniscus
Anterior cruciate ligament
Tibia

(b)

Posterior cruciate ligament
Medial condyle
Tibial collateral ligament
Anterior cruciate ligament
Medial meniscus
Patellar ligament
Patella
Quadriceps tendon

Fibular collateral ligament
Lateral condyle of femur
Lateral meniscus
Tibia
Fibula

(c)

Quadriceps femoris muscle
Tendon of quadriceps femoris muscle
Patella
Lateral patellar retinaculum
Fibular collateral ligament
Fibula

Medial patellar retinaculum
Tibial collateral ligament
Patellar ligament
Tibia

(d)

Medial femoral condyle
Anterior cruciate ligament
Medial meniscus on medial tibial condyle

(e)

Tendon of adductor magnus
Medial head of gastrocnemius muscle
Popliteus muscle
Tendon of semimembranosus muscle

Femur
Articular capsule
Oblique popliteal ligament
Lateral head of gastrocnemius muscle
Bursa
Fibular collateral ligament
Arcuate popliteal ligament
Tibia

FIGURE 8.8 **Knee joint. (a)** Midsagittal section of right knee. **(b)** Anterior view of slightly flexed right knee joint showing the cruciate ligaments. Articular capsule removed; quadriceps tendon is cut and reflected distally. **(c)** Anterior view of right knee. **(d)** Photograph of an opened knee joint corresponds to view in (b). **(e)** Posterior superficial view of the ligaments clothing the knee joint.

with this joint, some of which are shown in Figure 8.8a. For example, notice the *subcutaneous prepatellar bursa*, which is often injured when the knee is bumped.

All three types of joint ligaments stabilize and strengthen the capsule of the knee joint. The ligaments of two of the types, capsular and extracapsular, all act to prevent hyperextension of the knee and are stretched taut when the knee is extended. These include the following:

1. The extracapsular **fibular** and **tibial collateral ligaments** are also critical in preventing lateral or medial rotation when the knee is extended. The broad, flat tibial collateral ligament runs from the medial epicondyle of the femur to the medial condyle of the tibial shaft below and is fused to the medial meniscus.

2. The **oblique popliteal ligament** (pop″lĭ-te′al) is actually part of the tendon of the semimembranosus muscle that fuses with the capsule and stabilizes the posterior aspect of the knee joint (Figure 8.8e).

3. The **arcuate popliteal ligament** arcs superiorly from the head of the fibula over the popliteus muscle and reinforces the joint capsule posteriorly.

The knee's *intracapsular ligaments* are called *cruciate ligaments* (kroo′she-āt) because they cross each other, forming an X (*cruci* = cross) in the notch between the femoral condyles. They help prevent anterior-posterior displacement of the articular surfaces and secure the articulating bones when we stand (see Figure 8.8b). Although these ligaments are in the joint capsule, they are *outside* the synovial cavity, and synovial membrane nearly covers their surfaces. Note that the two cruciate ligaments both run up to the femur and are named for their *tibial* attachment site. The **anterior cruciate ligament** attaches to the *anterior* intercondylar area of the tibia. From there it passes posteriorly, laterally, and upward to attach to the femur on the medial side of its lateral condyle. This ligament prevents forward sliding of the tibia on the femur and checks hyperextension of the knee. It is somewhat lax when the knee is flexed, and taut when the knee is extended. The stronger **posterior cruciate ligament** is attached to the *posterior* intercondylar area of the tibia and passes anteriorly, medially, and upward to attach to the lateral side of the medial femoral condyle. This ligament prevents backward displacement of the tibia or forward sliding of the femur.

The knee capsule is heavily reinforced by muscle tendons. Most important are the strong tendons of the quadriceps muscles of the anterior thigh and the tendon of the semimembranosus muscle posteriorly. The greater the strength and tone of these muscles, the less the chance of knee injury.

The knees have a built-in locking device that provides steady support for the body in the standing position. As we begin to stand up, the wheel-shaped femoral condyles roll like ball bearings across the flat

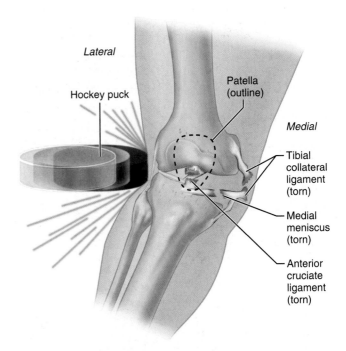

FIGURE 8.9 A common knee injury. Anterior view of a knee being hit by a hockey puck. By separating the femur from the tibia medially, such blows to the lateral side tear both the tibial collateral ligament and the medial meniscus because the two are attached. The anterior cruciate ligament also tears.

condyles of the tibia and the flexed leg begins to extend at the knee. Because the lateral femoral condyle stops rolling before the medial condyle stops, the femur *spins* (rotates) medially on the tibia, until all major ligaments of the knee are twisted and taut and the menisci are compressed. The tension in the ligaments effectively locks the joint into a rigid structure that cannot be flexed again until it is unlocked. This unlocking is accomplished by the popliteus muscle (see Figure 8.8 and Table 10.15, p. 373), which rotates the femur laterally on the tibia, causing the ligaments to become untwisted and slack.

HOMEOSTATIC IMBALANCE

Of all body joints, the knees are most susceptible to sports injuries because of their high reliance on nonarticular factors for stability and the fact that they carry the body's weight. The knee can absorb a vertical force equal to nearly seven times body weight. However, it is very vulnerable to *horizontal* blows, such as those that occur during blocking and tackling in football. When thinking of common knee injuries, remember the 3 Cs: collateral ligaments, cruciate ligaments, and cartilages (menisci). Most dangerous are *lateral* blows to the extended knee. These forces tear the tibial collateral ligament and the medial meniscus attached to it, as well as the anterior cruciate ligament (Figure 8.9). It is estimated that 50% of all professional football players have serious knee injuries during their careers.

8

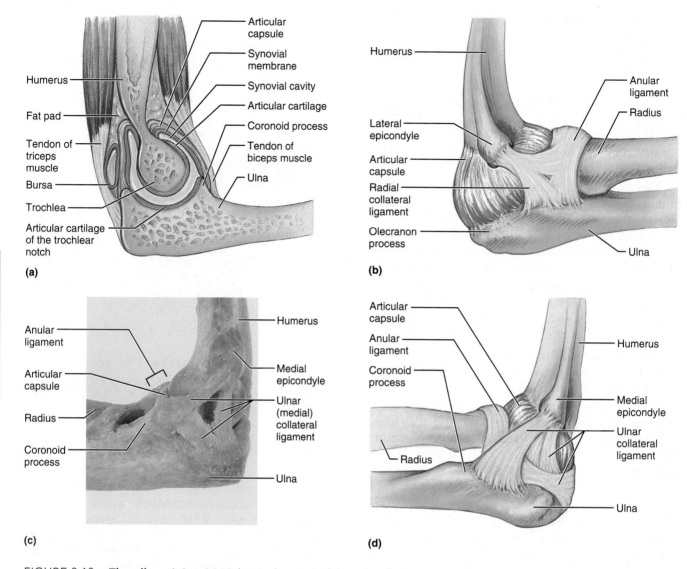

FIGURE 8.10 **The elbow joint. (a)** Midsagittal section of the right elbow joint.
(b) Lateral view. **(c)** Cadaver photograph of the right elbow joint, medial view.
(d) Diagram corresponding to view (c).

Although less devastating than the injury just described, injuries that affect only the anterior cruciate ligament (ACL) are becoming more common, particularly as women's sports become more vigorous and competitive. Most ACL injuries occur when a runner changes direction quickly, twisting a hyperextended knee. A torn ACL heals poorly, so repair usually requires a ligament graft using connective tissue taken from one of the larger ligaments (e.g., patellar, Achilles, or semitendinosus). ●

Elbow Joint

Our upper limbs are flexible extensions that permit us to reach out and manipulate things in our environment. Besides the shoulder joint, the most prominent of the upper limb joints is the elbow. The elbow joint provides a stable and smoothly operating hinge that allows flexion and extension only (Figure 8.10). Within the joint, both the radius and ulna articulate

with the condyles of the humerus, but it is the close gripping of the trochlea by the ulna's trochlear notch that forms the "hinge" and stabilizes this joint. A relatively lax articular capsule extends inferiorly from the humerus to the ulna and to the **anular ligament** (an'u-lar) surrounding the head of the radius.

Anteriorly and posteriorly, the articular capsule is thin and allows substantial freedom for elbow flexion and extension. However, side-to-side movements are restricted by two strong capsular ligaments: the **ulnar collateral ligament** medially, and the **radial collateral ligament,** a triangular ligament on the lateral side. Additionally, tendons of several arm muscles, such as the biceps and triceps, cross the elbow joint and provide security.

The radius is a passive "onlooker" in the angular elbow movements. However, its head rotates within the anular ligament during supination and pronation of the forearm.

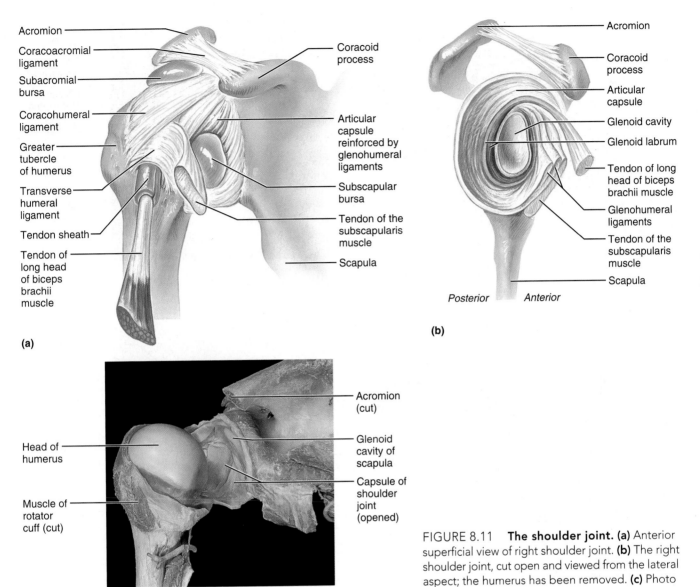

(a)

Acromion

Coracoacromial ligament

Subacromial bursa

Coracohumeral ligament

Greater tubercle of humerus

Transverse humeral ligament

Tendon sheath

Tendon of long head of biceps brachii muscle

Coracoid process

Articular capsule reinforced by glenohumeral ligaments

Subscapular bursa

Tendon of the subscapularis muscle

Scapula

(b)

Acromion

Coracoid process

Articular capsule

Glenoid cavity

Glenoid labrum

Tendon of long head of biceps brachii muscle

Glenohumeral ligaments

Tendon of the subscapularis muscle

Scapula

Posterior   Anterior

(c)

Head of humerus

Muscle of rotator cuff (cut)

Acromion (cut)

Glenoid cavity of scapula

Capsule of shoulder joint (opened)

FIGURE 8.11   **The shoulder joint. (a)** Anterior superficial view of right shoulder joint. **(b)** The right shoulder joint, cut open and viewed from the lateral aspect; the humerus has been removed. **(c)** Photo of an opened shoulder joint, anterior view.

Shoulder (Glenohumeral) Joint

In the shoulder joint, stability has been sacrificed to provide the most freely moving joint of the body. The shoulder joint is a ball-and-socket joint. The large hemispherical head of the humerus fits in the small, shallow glenoid cavity of the scapula (Figures 8.4 and 8.11), like a golf ball sitting on a tee. Although the glenoid cavity is slightly deepened by a rim of fibrocartilage, the **glenoid labrum** (*labrum* = lip), it is only about one-third the size of the humeral head and contributes little to joint stability.

The articular capsule enclosing the joint cavity (from the margin of the glenoid cavity to the anatomical neck of the humerus) is remarkably thin and loose, qualities that contribute to this joint's freedom of movement. The few ligaments reinforcing the shoulder joint are located primarily on its anterior aspect. The superiorly located **coracohumeral ligament** (kor'ah-ko-hu'mer-ul) provides the only strong thickening of the capsule and helps support the weight of the upper limb. Three **glenohumeral ligaments** (glĕ″no-hu′mer-ul) strengthen the front of the capsule somewhat but are weak and may even be absent.

Muscle tendons that cross the shoulder joint contribute most to this joint's stability. The "superstabilizer" is the tendon of the long head of the biceps brachii muscle of the arm (Figure 8.11a). This tendon attaches to the superior margin of the glenoid labrum, travels through the joint cavity, and then runs within the intertubercular sulcus of the humerus. It secures the head of the humerus against the glenoid cavity. Four other tendons (and the associated muscles) make up the **rotator cuff.** This cuff encircles the shoulder joint and blends with the articular capsule. The muscles include the subscapularis, supraspinatus, infraspinatus, and teres minor. (The rotator cuff muscles are illustrated in Figure 10.14, p. 356.) The rotator cuff can be severely

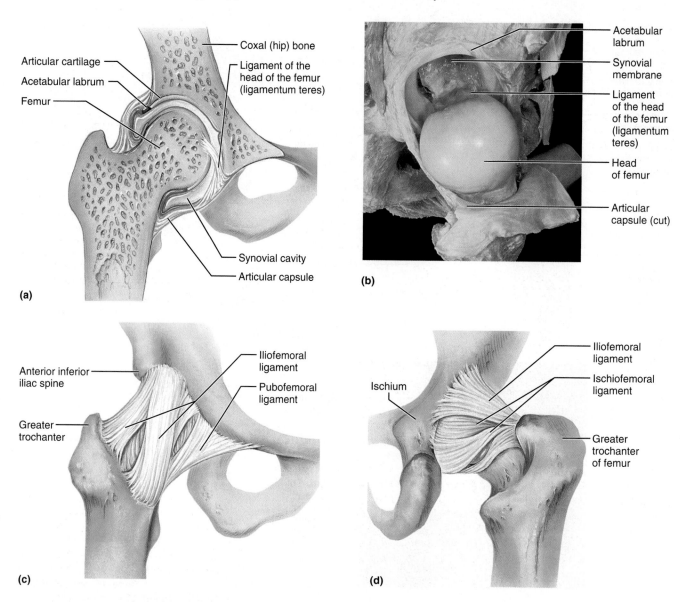

FIGURE 8.12 **The hip joint. (a)** Frontal section through the right hip joint. **(b)** Photograph of the joint, interior lateral view. **(c)** Anterior superficial view of the right hip joint. **(d)** Posterior superficial view.

stretched when the arm is vigorously circumducted; this is a common injury of baseball pitchers. As noted in Chapter 7, shoulder dislocations are fairly common. Because the shoulder's reinforcements are weakest anteriorly and inferiorly, the humerus tends to dislocate in the forward and downward direction.

Hip (Coxal) Joint

The hip joint, like the shoulder joint, is a ball-and-socket joint. It has a good range of motion, but not nearly as wide as the shoulder's range. Movements occur in all possible planes but are limited by the joint's strong ligaments and its deep socket. The hip joint is formed by the articulation of the spherical head of the femur with the deeply cupped acetabulum of the hip

bone (Figure 8.12). The depth of the acetabulum is enhanced by a circular rim of fibrocartilage called the **acetabular labrum** (as″ĕ-tab′u-lar) (Figure 8.12a and b). The labrum's diameter is less than that of the head of the femur, and these articular surfaces fit snugly together, so hip joint dislocations are rare.

The thick articular capsule extends from the rim of the acetabulum to the neck of the femur and completely encloses the joint. Several strong ligaments reinforce the capsule of the hip joint. These include the **iliofemoral ligament** (il″e-o-fem′o-ral), a strong V-shaped ligament anteriorly; the **pubofemoral ligament** (pu″bo-fem′o-ral), a triangular thickening of the inferior part of the capsule; and the **ischiofemoral ligament** (is″ke-o-fem′o-ral), a spiraling

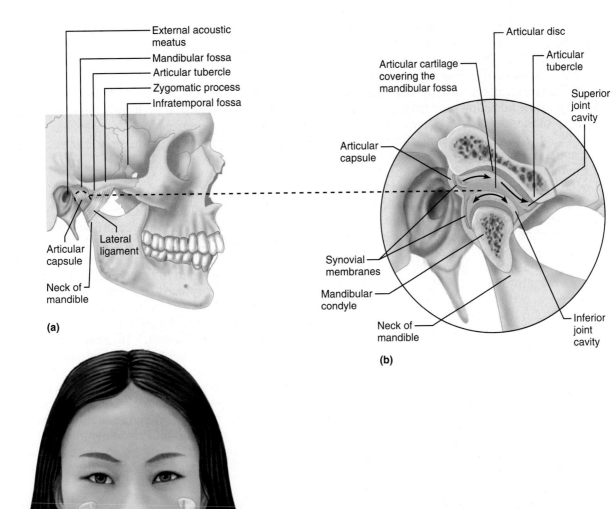

(a)

(b)

(c) Lateral excursion

FIGURE 8.13 **The temporomandibular (jaw) joint. (a)** Location of the joint in the skull showing important surrounding structures. **(b)** Enlargement of a sagittal section through the joint, showing the articular disc, the superior and inferior compartments of the joint cavity, and two movements that occur (arrows). The inferior joint cavity allows the mandibular condyle to rotate in opening and closing the mouth, whereas the superior joint cavity lets the mandibular condyle move forward to brace against the articular tubercle when the mouth opens wide. **(c)** Lateral movements of the mandible.

posterior ligament. These ligaments are arranged in such a way that they "screw" the femur head into the acetabulum when a person stands up straight, thereby providing more stability.

The **ligament of the head of the femur,** also called the **ligamentum teres,** is a flat intracapsular band that runs from the femur head to the lower lip of the acetabulum. This ligament is slack during most hip movements, so it is not important in stabilizing the joint. In fact, its mechanical function (if any) is unclear, but it does contain an artery that helps supply the head of the femur. Damage to this artery may lead to severe arthritis of the hip joint.

Muscle tendons that cross the joint and the bulky hip and thigh muscles that surround it contribute to its stability and strength. However, the deep socket that securely encloses the femoral head and the strong ligaments contribute most to the stability of the hip joint.

Temporomandibular Joint

The **temporomandibular joint (TMJ),** or jaw joint, lies just anterior to the ear. At this joint, the mandibular condyle articulates with the inferior surface of the squamous temporal bone (Figure 8.13). The mandibular condyle is egg-shaped, whereas the articular surface of the temporal bone has a more complex shape. Posteriorly, it forms the concave mandibular fossa; anteriorly it forms a dense knob called the **articular tubercle.** The lateral aspect of the loose articular capsule that encloses the joint is thickened into a **lateral ligament**. Within the capsule, an articular disc divides the synovial cavity into superior and inferior compartments (Figure 8.13).

Two distinct kinds of movement occur at the TMJ. First, the concave inferior disc surface receives the mandibular condyle and allows the familiar hinge-like movement of depressing and elevating the mandible while opening and closing the mouth. Second, the superior disc surface glides anteriorly along with the mandibular condyle when the mouth is opened wide. This anterior movement braces the condyle against the articular tubercle, so that the mandible is not forced through the thin roof of the mandibular fossa when one bites hard foods such as nuts or hard candies. The superior compartment also allows this joint to glide from side to side. As the posterior teeth are drawn into occlusion during grinding, the mandible moves with a side-to-side movement called *lateral excursion* (Figure 8.13). This lateral jaw movement is unique to mammals and it is readily apparent in horses and cows as they chew.

HOMEOSTATIC IMBALANCE

Because of its shallow socket, the TMJ is the most easily dislocated joint in the body. Even a deep yawn can dislocate it. This joint almost always dislocates anteriorly, the mandibular condyle ending up in a skull region called the infratemporal fossa (see Figure 8.13a). In such cases, the mouth remains wide open. To realign a dislocated TMJ, the physician places his or her thumbs in the patient's mouth between the lower molars and the cheeks, and then pushes the mandible inferiorly and posteriorly.

At least 5% of Americans suffer from painful temporomandibular disorders, the most common symptoms of which are pain in the ear and face, tenderness of the jaw muscles, popping sounds when the mouth opens, and joint stiffness. Usually caused by painful spasms of the chewing muscles, TMJ disorders often afflict people who grind their teeth; however, it can also result from jaw trauma or from poor occlusion of the teeth. Treatment usually focuses on getting the jaw muscles to relax by using massage, applying moist heat or ice, muscle-relaxant drugs, and adopting stress reduction tehniques. For tooth grinders, use of a bite plate during sleep is generally recommended. ●

Homeostatic Imbalances of Joints

Few of us pay attention to our joints unless something goes wrong with them. Joint pain and malfunction can be caused by a number of factors, but most joint problems result from injuries and inflammatory or degenerative conditions.

Common Joint Injuries

For most of us, sprains and dislocations are the most common trauma-induced joint injuries, but cartilage injuries are equally threatening to athletes.

Sprains

In a **sprain,** the ligaments reinforcing a joint are stretched or torn. The lumbar region of the spine, the ankle, and the knee are common sprain sites. Partially torn ligaments will repair themselves, but they heal slowly because ligaments are so poorly vascularized. Sprains tend to be painful and immobilizing. Completely ruptured ligaments require prompt surgical repair because inflammation in the joint will break down the neighboring tissues and turn the injured ligament to "mush." Surgical repair can be difficult: A ligament consists of hundreds of fibrous strands, and sewing one back together has been compared to trying to sew two hairbrushes together.

When important ligaments are too severely damaged to be repaired, they must be removed and replaced with grafts or substitute ligaments. For example, a piece of tendon from a muscle, or woven collagen bands, can be stapled to the articulating bones.

Cartilage Injuries

Many aerobics devotees, encouraged to "feel the burn" during their workout, may feel the snap and pop of their overstressed cartilage instead. Although most cartilage injuries involve tearing of the knee menisci, overuse damage to the articular cartilages of other joints is becoming increasingly common in competitive young athletes.

Cartilage is avascular and it rarely can obtain sufficient nourishment to repair itself; thus, it usually stays torn. Cartilage fragments (called *loose bodies*) can interfere with joint function by causing the joint to lock or bind, so most sports physicians recommend that the central (nonvascular) part of a damaged cartilage be removed. Today, this can be done by **arthroscopic surgery** (ar-thro-skop'ik; "looking into joints"), a procedure that enables patients to be out of the hospital the same day. The arthroscope, a small instrument bearing a tiny lens and fiber-optic light source, enables the surgeon to view the joint interior (Figure 8.14), repair a ligament, or remove cartilage fragments through one or more tiny slits, minimizing tissue damage and scarring. Removal of part of a meniscus does not severely impair knee joint mobility, but the joint is definitely less stable.

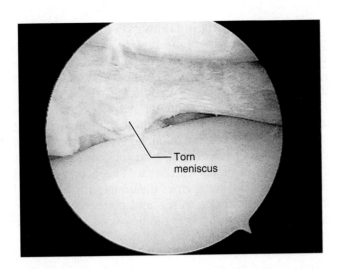

FIGURE 8.14   **Arthroscopic photograph of a torn medial meniscus** (Courtesy of the author's tennis game).

Dislocations

A **dislocation (luxation)** occurs when bones are forced out of alignment. It is usually accompanied by sprains, inflammation, and joint immobilization. Dislocations may result from serious falls and are common contact sports injuries. Joints of the jaw, shoulders, fingers, and thumbs are most commonly dislocated. Like fractures, dislocations must be *reduced*; that is, the bone ends must be returned to their proper positions by a physician. *Subluxation* is a partial dislocation of a joint.

Repeat dislocations of the same joint are common because the initial dislocation stretches the joint capsule and ligaments. The resulting loose capsule provides poor reinforcement for the joint.

Inflammatory and Degenerative Conditions

Inflammatory conditions that affect joints include bursitis, tendonitis, and various forms of arthritis.

Bursitis and Tendonitis

Bursitis is inflammation of a bursa and is usually caused by a blow or friction. Falling on one's knee may result in a painful bursitis of the prepatellar bursa, known as *housemaid's knee* or *water on the knee*. Prolonged leaning on one's elbows may damage the bursa close to the olecranon process, producing *student's elbow*, or *olecranon bursitis*. Severe cases are treated by injecting anti-inflammatory drugs into the bursa. If excessive fluid accumulates, removing some fluid by needle aspiration may relieve the pressure.

Tendonitis is inflammation of tendon sheaths, typically caused by overuse. Its symptoms (pain and swelling) and treatment (rest, ice, and anti-inflammatory drugs) mirror those of bursitis.

Arthritis

The term **arthritis** describes over 100 different types of inflammatory or degenerative diseases that damage the joints. In all its forms, arthritis is the most widespread crippling disease in the United States. One out of seven Americans suffers its ravages. To a greater or lesser degree, all forms of arthritis have the same initial symptoms: pain, stiffness, and swelling of the joint.

Acute forms of arthritis usually result from bacterial invasion and are treated with antibiotics. The synovial membrane thickens and fluid production decreases, causing increased friction and pain. Chronic forms of arthritis include osteoarthritis, rheumatoid arthritis, and gouty arthritis.

Osteoarthritis   **Osteoarthritis (OA)** is the most common chronic arthritis. A chronic (long-term) degenerative condition, OA is often called "wear-and-tear arthritis." OA is most prevalent in the aged and is probably related to the normal aging process (although it is seen occasionally in younger people and some forms have a genetic basis). More women than men are affected, but 85% of all Americans develop this condition.

Current theory holds that normal joint use prompts the release of (metalloproteinase) enzymes that break down articular cartilage, especially its collagen fibrils. In healthy individuals, this damaged cartilage is eventually replaced, but in people with OA, more cartilage is destroyed than replaced. Although its specific cause is unknown, OA may reflect the cumulative effects of years of compression and abrasion acting at joint surfaces, causing excessive amounts of the cartilage-destroying enzymes to be released. The result is softened, roughened, pitted, and eroded articular cartilages. Because this process occurs most where an uneven orientation of forces cause extensive microdamage, badly aligned or overworked joints are likely to develop OA.

As the disease progresses, the exposed bone tissue thickens and forms bony spurs (osteophytes) that enlarge the bone ends and may restrict joint movement. Patients complain of stiffness on arising that lessens somewhat with activity. The affected joints may make a crunching noise, called *crepitus* (krep'ĭ-tus), as they move and the roughened articular surfaces rub together. The joints most often affected are those of the cervical and lumbar spine and the fingers, knuckles, knees, and hips.

The course of osteoarthritis is usually slow and irreversible. In many cases, its symptoms are controllable with a mild pain reliever like aspirin or acetaminophen, along with moderate activity to keep the joints mobile. Rubbing a hot-pepper-like substance

FIGURE 8.15 **X ray of a hand deformed by rheumatoid arthritis.**

8

called capsaicin on the skin over the painful joints helps lessen the pain of OA. Glucosamine and chondroitin sulfate, nutritional supplements consisting of macromolecules normally present in cartilage, appear to decrease pain and inflammation in some people and may help to preserve the articular cartilage. Osteoarthritis is rarely crippling, but it can be, particularly when the hip or knee joints are involved.

Rheumatoid Arthritis **Rheumatoid arthritis (RA)** (roo'mah-toid) is a chronic inflammatory disorder with an insidious onset. Though it usually arises between the ages of 40 and 50, it may occur at any age. It affects three times as many women as men. While not as common as osteoarthritis, rheumatoid arthritis causes disability in millions (Figure 8.15). It occurs in more than 1% of Americans.

In the early stages of RA, joint tenderness and stiffness are common. Many joints, particularly the small joints of the fingers, wrists, ankles, and feet, are afflicted at the same time and bilaterally. For example, if the right elbow is affected, most likely the left elbow is also affected. The course of RA is variable and marked by flare-ups (exacerbations) and remissions (*rheumat* = susceptible to change). Other manifestations may include anemia, osteoporosis, muscle atrophy, and cardiovascular problems.

RA is an *autoimmune disease*—a disorder in which the body's immune system attacks its own tissues. The initial trigger for this reaction is unknown, but the streptococcus bacterium and viruses have been suspect. Perhaps these microorganisms bear molecules similar to some naturally present in the joints (possibly glucosaminoglycans, complex carbohydrates found in cartilage, joint fluid, and other connective tissues) and the immune system, once activated, attempts to destroy both.

RA begins with inflammation of the synovial membrane (*synovitis*) of the affected joints. Inflammatory cells (lymphocytes, neutrophils, and others) migrate into the joint cavity from the blood and unleash a deluge of inflammatory chemicals that destroy body tissues when released inappropriately in large amounts as in RA. Synovial fluid accumulates, causing joint swelling and in time, the inflamed synovial membrane thickens into a **pannus** ("rag"), an abnormal tissue that clings to the articular cartilages. The pannus erodes the cartilage (and sometimes the underlying bone) and eventually scar tissue forms and connects the bone ends. Later this scar tissue ossifies and the bone ends fuse together, immobilizing the joint. This end condition, called *ankylosis* (ang″ki-lo′sis; "stiff condition"), often produces bent, deformed fingers (see Figure 8.15). Not all cases of RA progress to the severely crippling ankylosis stage, but all cases do involve restriction of joint movement and extreme pain.

A wonder drug for RA sufferers is still undiscovered. Currently the pendulum is swinging from conservative RA therapy utilizing aspirin, long-term antibiotic therapy, and physical therapy to a more progressive treatment course using immunosuppressants such as methotrexate, or anti-inflammatory drugs. Particularly promising are etanercept (Enbrel) and infliximab (Remicade), the first in a class of drugs called *biologic response modifiers* that neutralize some of the harmful properties of the inflammatory chemicals. Unexpected success has been achieved in clinical studies using a tandem drug therapy approach (methotrexate in combination with etanercept). The arthritis of 35% of those treated went into remission and the arthritic joints of some patients actually improved after a year of therapy. Joint prostheses, if available, are the last resort for severely crippled RA patients (see *A Closer Look*).

Gouty Arthritis Uric acid, a normal waste product of nucleic acid metabolism, is ordinarily excreted in urine without any problems. However, when blood levels of uric acid rise excessively (due to its excessive production or slow excretion), it may be deposited as needle-shaped urate crystals in the soft tissues of joints. An inflammatory response follows, leading into an agonizingly painful attack of **gouty arthritis** (gow'te), or gout. The initial attack typically affects one joint, often at the base of the great toe.

Gout is far more common in males than in females because males naturally have higher blood levels of uric acid (perhaps because estrogens increase the rate of its excretion). Because gout seems to run in families, genetic factors are definitely implicated.

Untreated gout can be very destructive; the articulating bone ends fuse and immobilize the joint. Fortunately, several drugs (colchicine, nonsteroidal

A CLOSER LOOK

Joints: From Knights in Shining Armor to Bionic Humans

The technology for fashioning joints in medieval suits of armor developed over centuries. The technology for creating the prostheses (artificial joints) used in medicine today developed, in relative terms, in a flash. The history of joint prostheses dates to the 1940s and 1950s, when World War II and the Korean War left large numbers of wounded who needed artificial limbs. Today, over a third of a million Americans receive total joint replacements each year, mostly because of the destructive effects of osteoarthritis or rheumatoid arthritis.

To produce durable, mobile joints requires a substance that is strong, nontoxic, and resistant to the corrosive effects of organic acids in blood. In 1963, Sir John Charnley, an English orthopedic surgeon, performed the first total hip replacement and revolutionized the therapy of arthritic hips. His device consisted of a metal ball on a stem and a cup-shaped polyethylene plastic socket anchored to the pelvis by methyl methacrylate cement. This cement proved to be exceptionally strong and relatively problem free. Hip prostheses were followed by knee prostheses, but not until ten years later did smoothly operating total knee joint replacements become a reality. Today, the metal parts of the prostheses are strong cobalt and titanium alloys, and the number of knee replacements equals the number of hip replacements.

Replacements are now available for many other joints, including fingers, elbows, and shoulders. Total hip and knee replacements last about 10 to 15 years in elderly patients who do not excessively stress the joint. Most such operations are done to reduce pain and restore about 80% of original joint function.

Replacement joints are not yet strong or durable enough for young, active people, but making them so is a major goal. The problem is that the prostheses work loose over time, so researchers are seeking to enhance the

A hip prosthesis.

fit between implant and bone. One solution is to strengthen the cement that binds them (simply eliminating air bubbles from the cement increases its durability). Another solution currently being tested is a robotic surgeon, ROBODOC, to drill a better-fitting hole for the femoral prosthesis in hip surgery. In cementless prostheses, researchers are exploring ways to get the bone to grow so that it binds strongly to the implant. A supersmooth titanium coating seems to encourage direct bony on-growth.

Dramatic changes are also occurring in the way artificial joints are made. CAD/CAM (computer-aided design and computer-aided manufacturing) techniques have significantly reduced the time and cost of creating individualized joints. Fed the patient's X rays and medical information, the computer draws from a database of hundreds of normal joints and generates possible designs and modifications for a prosthesis. Once the best design is selected, the computer produces a program to direct the machines that shape it.

Joint replacement therapy is coming of age, but equally exciting are techniques that call on the ability of

X ray of right knee showing total knee replacement prosthesis (Co-designed by Kenneth Gustke M.D. of Florida Orthopedic Institute).

the patient's own tissues to regenerate, such as

- Osteochondral grafting: Healthy bone and cartilage are removed from one part of the body and transplanted to the injured joint.

- Autologous chondrocyte implantation: Healthy chondrocytes are removed from the body, cultivated in the lab, and implanted at the damaged joint.

- Mesenchymal stem cell regeneration: Undifferentiated mesenchymal cells are removed from bone marrow and placed in a gel, which is packed into an area of eroded cartilage.

These techniques offer hope for younger patients, since they could stave off the need for a joint prosthesis for several years.

And so, through the centuries, the focus has shifted from jointed armor to artificial joints that can be put inside the body to restore lost function. Modern technology has accomplished what the armor designers of the Middle Ages never dreamed of. ■

anti-inflammatory drugs, glucocorticoids, and others) that terminate or prevent gout attacks are available. Patients are advised to drink plenty of water and to avoid alcohol excess (which promotes uric acid overproduction), and foods high in purine-containing nucleic acids, such as liver, kidneys, and sardines.

Developmental Aspects of Joints

As bones form from mesenchyme in the embryo, the joints develop in parallel. By week 8, the synovial joints resemble adult joints in form and arrangement.

Injuries aside, relatively few interferences with joint function occur until late middle age. Eventually advancing years take their toll and ligaments and tendons shorten and weaken. The intervertebral discs become more likely to herniate, and osteoarthritis rears its ugly head. Virtually everyone has osteoarthritis to some degree by the time they are in their 70s. The middle years also see an increased incidence of rheumatoid arthritis.

Exercise that coaxes joints through their full range of motion, such as regular stretching and aerobics, is the key to postponing the immobilizing effects of aging on ligaments and tendons, to keeping cartilages well nourished, and to strengthening the muscles that stabilize the joints. The key word for exercising is "prudently," because excessive or abusive use of the joints guarantees early onset of osteoarthritis. The buoyancy of water relieves much of the stress on weight-bearing joints, and people who swim or exercise in a pool often retain good joint function as long as they live. As with so many medical problems, it is easier to prevent joint problems than to cure or correct them.

■ ■ ■

The importance of joints is obvious: The skeleton's ability to protect other organs and to move smoothly reflects their presence. Now that we are familiar with joint structure and with the movements that joints allow, we are ready to consider how the muscles attached to the skeleton cause body movements by acting across its joints.

Related Clinical Terms

Ankylosing spondylitis (ang′kĭ-lōz″ing spon″dĭ-li′tis; *ankyl* = crooked, bent; *spondyl* = vertebra) A variant of rheumatoid arthritis that chiefly affects males; it usually begins in the sacroiliac joints and progresses superiorly along the spine. The vertebrae become interconnected by fibrous tissue, causing the spine to become rigid ("poker back").

Arthrology (ar-throl′o-je; *logos* = study) The study of joints.

Chondromalacia patellae (kon-dro-mal-a′sĭ-ah; "softening of cartilage by the patella") Damage and softening of the articular cartilages on the posterior patellar surface and the anterior surface of the distal femur; most often seen in adolescent athletes. Produces a sharp pain in the knee when the leg is extended (in climbing stairs, for example). May result when the quadriceps femoris, the main group of muscles on the anterior thigh, pulls unevenly on the patella, persistently rubbing it against the femur in the knee joint; often corrected by exercises that strengthen weakened parts of the quadriceps muscles.

Lyme disease An inflammatory disease caused by spirochetes, bacteria transmitted by the bites of ticks that live on mice and deer. It often results in joint pain and arthritis, especially in the knees, and is characterized by a skin rash, flulike symptoms, and foggy thinking. If untreated, neurological disorders and irregular heartbeat may ensue. Because symptoms vary from person to person, the disease is hard to diagnose. Antibiotic therapy is the usual treatment, but it takes a long time to kill the infecting bacteria.

Rheumatism A term used by laypeople to indicate disease involving muscle or joint pain; consequently may be used to apply to arthritis, bursitis, etc.

Synovitis (sin″o-vi′tis) Inflammation of the synovial membrane of a joint. In healthy joints, only small amounts of synovial fluid are present, but synovitis causes copious amounts to be produced, leading to swelling and limitation of joint movement.

Chapter Summary

1. Joints, or articulations, are sites where bones meet. Their functions are to hold bones together and to allow various degrees of skeletal movement.

Classification of Joints (p. 253)

1. Joints are classified structurally as fibrous, cartilaginous, or synovial. They are classed functionally as synarthrotic, amphiarthrotic, or diarthrotic.

Fibrous Joints (pp. 253–254)

1. Fibrous joints occur where bones are connected by fibrous tissue; no joint cavity is present. Nearly all fibrous joints are synarthrotic.

2. **Sutures/syndesmoses/gomphoses.** The major types of fibrous joints are sutures, syndesmoses, and gomphoses.

Cartilaginous Joints (p. 255)

1. In cartilaginous joints, the bones are united by cartilage; no joint cavity is present.

2. Synchondroses/symphyses. Cartilaginous joints include synchondroses and symphyses. Synchondroses are synarthrotic; all symphyses are amphiarthrotic.

Synovial Joints   (pp. 255–272)

1. Most body joints are synovial joints, all of which are diarthrotic.

General Structure   (pp. 255–256)

2. All synovial joints have a joint cavity enclosed by a fibrous capsule lined with synovial membrane and reinforced by ligaments; articulating bone ends covered with articular cartilage; and synovial fluid in the joint cavity. Some (e.g., the knee) contain fibrocartilage discs that absorb shock.

Bursae and Tendon Sheaths   (p. 257)

3. Bursae are fibrous sacs lined with synovial membrane and containing synovial fluid. Tendon sheaths are similar to bursae but are cylindrical structures that surround muscle tendons. Both allow adjacent structures to move smoothly over one another.

Factors Influencing the Stability of Synovial Joints (pp. 257–259)

4. Articular surfaces providing the most stability have large surfaces and deep sockets and fit snugly together.

5. Ligaments prevent undesirable movements and reinforce the joint.

6. The tone of muscles whose tendons cross the joint is the most important stabilizing factor in many joints.

Movements Allowed by Synovial Joints   (pp. 259–263)

7. When a skeletal muscle contracts, the insertion (movable attachment) moves toward the origin (immovable attachment). Three common types of movements can occur when muscles contract across joints: (a) gliding movements, (b) angular movements (which include flexion, extension, abduction, adduction, and circumduction), and (c) rotation.

8. Special movements include supination and pronation, inversion and eversion, protraction and retraction, elevation and depression, and opposition.

Types of Synovial Joints   (pp. 263–265)

9. Synovial joints differ in their range of motion. Motion may be nonaxial (gliding), uniaxial (in one plane), biaxial (in two planes), or multiaxial (in all three planes).

10. The six major categories of synovial joints are plane joints (nonaxial movement), hinge joints (uniaxial), pivot joints (uniaxial, rotation permitted), condyloid joints (biaxial with angular movements in two planes), saddle joints (biaxial, like condyloid joints, but with freer movement), and ball-and-socket joints (multiaxial and rotational movement).

Selected Synovial Joints   (pp. 265–272)

11. The knee joint is the largest joint in the body. It is a hinge joint formed by the articulation of the tibial and femoral condyles (and anteriorly by the patella and patellar surface of the femur). Extension, flexion, and (some) rotation are allowed. Its articular surfaces are shallow and condyloid. C-shaped menisci deepen the articular surfaces. The joint cavity is enclosed by a capsule only on the sides and posterior aspects. Several ligaments help prevent displacement of the joint surfaces. Muscle tone of the quadriceps and semimembranosus muscles is important in knee stability.

12. The elbow is a hinge joint in which the ulna (and radius) articulates with the humerus, allowing flexion and extension. Its articular surfaces are highly complementary and are the most important factor contributing to joint stability.

13. The shoulder joint is a ball-and-socket joint formed by the glenoid cavity of the scapula and the humeral head. The most freely movable joint of the body, it allows all angular and rotational movements. Its articular surfaces are shallow. Its capsule is lax and poorly reinforced by ligaments. The tendons of the biceps brachii and rotator cuff muscles help to stabilize it.

14. The hip joint is a ball-and-socket joint formed by the acetabulum of the coxal bone and the femoral head. It is highly adapted for weight bearing. Its articular surfaces are deep and secure. Its capsule is heavy and strongly reinforced by ligaments.

15. The temporomandibular joint is formed by (1) the mandibular condyle and (2) the mandibular fossa and articular tubercle of the temporal bone. This joint allows both a hingelike opening and closing of the mouth and an anterior gliding of the mandible. It often dislocates anteriorly and exhibits a number of TMJ disorders.

Homeostatic Imbalances of Joints (pp. 272–274, 276)

Common Joint Injuries   (p. 272–273)

1. Sprains involve stretching or tearing of joint ligaments. Because ligaments are poorly vascularized, healing is slow.

2. Cartilage injuries, particularly of the knee, are common in contact sports and may result from excessive twisting or high pressure. The avascular cartilage is unable to repair itself.

3. Dislocations involve displacement of the articular surfaces of bones. They must be reduced.

Inflammatory and Degenerative Conditions (pp. 273–274, 276)

4. Bursitis and tendonitis are inflammations of a bursa and a tendon sheath, respectively.

5. Arthritis is joint inflammation or degeneration accompanied by stiffness, pain, and swelling. Acute forms generally result from bacterial infection. Chronic forms include osteoarthritis, rheumatoid arthritis, and gouty arthritis.

6. Osteoarthritis is a degenerative condition most common in the aged. Weight-bearing joints are most affected.

7. Rheumatoid arthritis, the most crippling arthritis, is an autoimmune disease involving severe inflammation of the joints.

8. Gouty arthritis, or gout, is joint inflammation caused by the deposit of urate salts in soft joint tissues.

Developmental Aspects of Joints   (p. 276)

1. Joints form from mesenchyme and in tandem with bone development in the embryo.

2. Excluding traumatic injury, joints usually function well until late middle age, at which time symptoms of connective tissue stiffening and osteoarthritis begin to appear. Prudent exercise delays these effects, whereas excessive exercise promotes the early onset of arthritis.

8

Review Questions

Multiple Choice/Matching

(Some questions have more than one correct answer. Select the best answer or answers from the choices given.)

1. Match the key terms to the appropriate descriptions.

Key: **(a)** fibrous joints   **(c)** synovial joints
     (b) cartilaginous joints

_____ **(1)** exhibit a joint cavity
_____ **(2)** types are sutures and syndesmoses
_____ **(3)** bones connected by collagen fibers
_____ **(4)** types include synchondroses and symphyses
_____ **(5)** all are diarthrotic
_____ **(6)** many are amphiarthrotic
_____ **(7)** bones connected by a disc of hyaline cartilage or fibrocartilage
_____ **(8)** nearly all are synarthrotic
_____ **(9)** shoulder, hip, jaw, and elbow joints

2. Freely movable joints are (a) synarthroses, (b) diarthroses, (c) amphiarthroses.

3. Anatomical characteristics of a synovial joint include (a) articular cartilage, (b) a joint cavity, (c) an articular capsule, (d) all of these.

4. Factors that influence the stability of a synovial joint include (a) shape of articular surfaces, (b) presence of strong reinforcing ligaments, (c) tone of surrounding muscles, (d) all of these.

5. The description "Articular surfaces deep and secure; capsule heavily reinforced by ligaments and muscle tendons; extremely stable joint" best describes (a) the elbow joint, (b) the hip joint, (c) the knee joint, (d) the shoulder joint.

6. Ankylosis means (a) twisting of the ankle, (b) tearing of ligaments, (c) displacement of a bone, (d) immobility of a joint due to fusion of its articular surfaces.

7. An autoimmune disorder in which joints are affected bilaterally and which involves pannus formation and gradual joint immobilization is (a) bursitis, (b) gout, (c) osteoarthritis, (d) rheumatoid arthritis.

Short Answer Essay Questions

8. Define joint.

9. Discuss the relative value (to body homeostasis) of immovable, slightly movable, and freely movable joints.

10. Compare the structure, function, and common body locations of bursae and tendon sheaths.

11. Joint movements may be nonaxial, uniaxial, biaxial, or multiaxial. Define what each of these terms means.

12. Compare and contrast the paired movements of flexion and extension with adduction and abduction.

13. How does rotation differ from circumduction?

14. Name two types of uniaxial, biaxial, and multiaxial joints.

15. What is the specific role of the menisci of the knee? of the anterior and posterior cruciate ligaments?

16. The knee has been called "a beauty and a beast." Provide several reasons that might explain the negative (beast) part of this description.

17. Why are sprains and cartilage injuries a particular problem?

18. List the functions of the following elements of a synovial joint: fibrous part of the capsule, synovial fluid, articular disc.

Critical Thinking and Clinical Application Questions

1. Sophie worked cleaning homes for 30 years so she could send her two children to college. Several times, she had been forced to call her employers to tell them she could not come in to work because one of her kneecaps was swollen and painful. What is Sophie's condition, and what probably caused it?

2. As Harry was jogging down the road, he tripped and his left ankle twisted violently to the side. When he picked himself up, he was unable to put any weight on that ankle. The diagnosis was severe dislocation and sprains of the left ankle. The orthopedic surgeon stated that she would perform a closed reduction of the dislocation and attempt ligament repair by using arthroscopy. (a) Is the ankle joint normally a stable joint? (b) What does its stability depend on? (c) What is a closed reduction? (d) Why is ligament repair necessary? (e) What does arthroscopy entail? (f) How will the use of this procedure minimize Harry's recuperation time (and suffering)?

3. Mrs. Bell, a 45-year-old woman, appeared at her physician's office complaining of unbearable pain in the distal interphalangeal joint of her right great toe. The joint was red and swollen. When asked about previous episodes, she recalled a similar attack two years earlier that disappeared as suddenly as it had come. Her diagnosis was arthritis. (a) What type? (b) What is the precipitating cause of this particular type of arthritis?

4. Grace heard on the evening TV news that the deer population in her state had been increasing rapidly in the past few years and it was common knowledge that deer walked the streets at night. After the program, she suddenly exclaimed, "So that's why those three boys in my son's class got Lyme disease last year." Explain what she meant by that comment.

5. Tony Bowers, an exhausted biology student, was attending a lecture. After 30 minutes or so, he lost interest and began to doze. As the lecture ended, the hubbub aroused him and he let go with a tremendous yawn. To his great distress, he couldn't close his mouth—his lower jaw was "stuck" open. What do you think had happened?

LOOKING FOR MORE STUDY HELP?

A wide variety of quiz questions, tutorials, and learning exercises are available online at the Anatomy & Physiology Place (www.anatomyandphysiology.com) and, if your instructor has provided you with a MyA&P Course ID number, in MyA&P (www.myaandp.com).

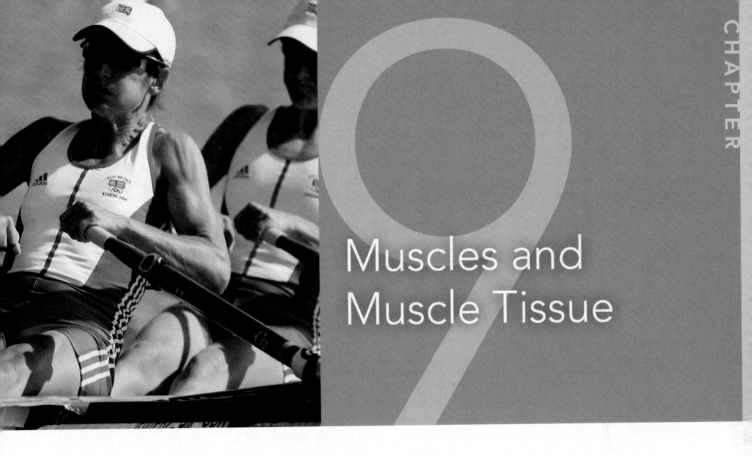

Muscles and Muscle Tissue

Overview of Muscle Tissues (pp. 280–281)

1. Compare and contrast the basic types of muscle tissue.
2. List four important functions of muscle tissue.

Skeletal Muscle (pp. 281–309)

3. Describe the gross structure of a skeletal muscle.
4. Describe the microscopic structure and functional roles of the myofibrils, sarcoplasmic reticulum, and T tubules of muscle fibers (cells).
5. Explain the sliding filament mechanism.
6. Define motor unit and explain how muscle fibers are stimulated to contract.
7. Define muscle twitch and describe the events occurring during its three phases.

8. Explain how smooth, graded contractions of a skeletal muscle are produced.
9. Differentiate between isometric and isotonic contractions.
10. Describe three ways in which ATP is regenerated during skeletal muscle contraction.
11. Define oxygen debt and muscle fatigue. List possible causes of muscle fatigue.
12. Describe factors that influence the force, velocity, and duration of skeletal muscle contraction.
13. Describe three types of skeletal muscle fibers and explain the relative value of each type.
14. Compare and contrast the effects of aerobic and resistance exercise on skeletal muscles and on other body systems.

Smooth Muscle (pp. 309–316)

15. Compare the gross and microscopic anatomy of smooth muscle cells to that of skeletal muscle cells.
16. Compare and contrast the contractile mechanisms and the means of activation of skeletal and smooth muscles.
17. Distinguish between single-unit and multiunit smooth muscle structurally and functionally.

Developmental Aspects of Muscles (pp. 316–318, 320)

18. Describe embryonic development of muscle tissues and the changes that occur in skeletal muscles with age.

Because flexing muscles look like mice scurrying beneath the skin, some scientist long ago dubbed them *muscles*, from the Latin *mus* meaning "little mouse." Indeed, the rippling muscles of professional boxers or weight lifters are often the first thing that comes to mind when one hears the word *muscle*. But muscle is also the dominant tissue in the heart and in the walls of other hollow organs. In all its forms, muscle tissue makes up nearly half the body's mass. The most distinguishing functional characteristic of muscles is their ability to transform chemical energy (ATP) into directed mechanical energy. In so doing, they become capable of exerting force.

Overview of Muscle Tissues

Types of Muscle Tissue

The three types of muscle tissue are *skeletal, cardiac,* and *smooth.* Before exploring their characteristics, however, let us introduce some terminology. First, skeletal and smooth muscle cells (but not cardiac muscle cells) are elongated and, for this reason, are called **muscle fibers.** Second, muscle contraction depends on two kinds of *myofilaments,* which are the muscle equivalents of the actin- or myosin-containing microfilaments described in Chapter 3. As you will recall, these two proteins play a role in motility and shape changes in virtually every cell in the body, but this property reaches its highest development in the contractile muscle fibers. Third, whenever you see the prefixes **myo** or **mys** (both are word roots meaning "muscle") or **sarco** (flesh), the reference is to muscle. For example, the plasma membrane of muscle fibers is called the *sarcolemma* (sar"ko-lem'ah), literally "muscle" (sarco) "husk" (lemma), and muscle fiber cytoplasm is called *sarcoplasm.* Now we are ready to describe the three types of muscle tissue.

Skeletal muscle tissue is packaged into the *skeletal muscles,* organs that attach to and cover the bony skeleton. Skeletal muscle fibers are the longest muscle cells; they have obvious stripes called *striations* and can be controlled voluntarily. Although it is often activated by reflexes, skeletal muscle is called **voluntary muscle** because it is the *only type subject to* conscious control. Therefore, when you think of skeletal muscle tissue, the key words to keep in mind are *skeletal, striated,* and *voluntary.* Skeletal muscle is responsible for overall body mobility. It can contract rapidly, but it tires easily and must rest after short periods of activity. Nevertheless, it can exert tremendous power, a fact revealed by reports of people lifting cars to save their loved ones. Skeletal muscle is also remarkably adaptable. For example, your hand muscles can exert a force of a fraction of an ounce to pick up a dropped paper clip and the same muscles can exert a force of about 70 pounds to pick up this book!

Cardiac muscle tissue occurs only in the heart (the body's blood pump), where it constitutes the bulk of the heart walls. Like skeletal muscle cells, cardiac muscle cells are striated, but cardiac muscle is not voluntary. Most of us have no conscious control over how fast our heart beats. Key words to remember for this muscle type are *cardiac, striated,* and *involuntary.* Cardiac muscle usually contracts at a fairly steady rate set by the heart's pacemaker, but neural controls allow the heart to "shift into high gear" for brief periods, as when you race across the tennis court to make that overhead smash.

Smooth muscle tissue is found in the walls of hollow visceral organs, such as the stomach, urinary bladder, and respiratory passages. Its role is to force fluids and other substances through internal body channels. It has no striations, and like cardiac muscle, it is not subject to voluntary control. We can describe smooth muscle tissue most precisely as *visceral, nonstriated,* and *involuntary.* Contractions of smooth muscle fibers are slow and sustained.

Skeletal and smooth muscles are discussed in this chapter. Cardiac muscle is discussed in Chapter 18 (The Heart). Table 9.3 on pp. 314–315 summarizes the most important characteristics of each type of muscle tissue.

Functional Characteristics of Muscle Tissue

Muscle tissue is endowed with some special functional properties that enable it to perform its duties.

Excitability, also termed **responsiveness** or **irritability,** is the ability to receive and respond to a stimulus, that is, any change in the environment whether inside or outside the body. In the case of muscle, the stimulus is usually a chemical—for example, a neurotransmitter released by a nerve cell, or a local change in pH. The response is generation of an electrical impulse that passes along the sarcolemma (plasma membrane) of the muscle cell and causes the cell to contract.

Contractility is the ability to shorten forcibly when adequately stimulated. This property sets muscle apart from all other tissue types.

Extensibility is the ability to be stretched or extended. Muscle fibers shorten when contracting, but they can be stretched, even beyond their resting length, when relaxed.

Elasticity is the ability of a muscle fiber to recoil and resume its resting length after being stretched.

Muscle Functions

Muscle performs four important functions for the body: It produces movement, maintains posture, stabilizes joints, and generates heat.

Producing Movement

Just about all movements of the human body and its parts are a result of muscle contraction. Skeletal muscles are responsible for all locomotion and manipulation. They enable you to respond quickly to changes in the external environment—for example, by jumping out of the way of a runaway car, directing your eyeballs, and smiling or frowning.

The coursing of blood through your body is evidence of the work of the rhythmically beating cardiac muscle of your heart and the smooth muscle in the walls of your blood vessels, which helps maintain blood pressure. Smooth muscle in organs of the digestive, urinary, and reproductive tracts propels, or squeezes, substances (foodstuffs, urine, a baby) through the organs and along the tract.

Maintaining Posture

We are rarely aware of the workings of the skeletal muscles that maintain body posture. Yet these muscles function almost continuously, making one tiny adjustment after another that enables us to maintain an erect or seated posture despite the never-ending downward pull of gravity.

Stabilizing Joints

Even as muscles pull on bones to cause movements, they stabilize and strengthen the joints of the skeleton (Chapter 8).

Generating Heat

Muscles generate heat as they contract. This heat is vitally important in maintaining normal body temperature. Because skeletal muscle accounts for at least 40% of body mass, it is the muscle type most responsible for generating heat.

Although not usually cited as a major muscle function, skeletal muscles also protect more fragile internal organs (the viscera) by enclosure. Also, smooth muscle, in particular, forms valves to regulate the passage of substances through internal body openings.

■ ■ ■

In the following section, we examine the structure and function of skeletal muscle in detail. Then we consider smooth muscle more briefly, largely by comparing it with skeletal muscle. Because cardiac muscle is described in Chapter 18, its treatment in this chapter is limited to the summary of its characteristics provided in Table 9.3.

Skeletal Muscle

The levels of skeletal muscle organization, gross to microscopic, are summarized in Table 9.1.

FIGURE 9.1 **Photomicrograph of the capillary network surrounding skeletal muscle fibers.** The arterial supply was injected with dark red gelatin to demonstrate the capillary bed. The long muscle fibers are stained orange (30×).

Gross Anatomy of a Skeletal Muscle

Each **skeletal muscle** is a discrete organ, made up of several kinds of tissues. Although skeletal muscle fibers predominate, blood vessels, nerve fibers, and substantial amounts of connective tissue are also present. A skeletal muscle's shape and its attachments in the body can be examined easily without the help of a microscope.

Nerve and Blood Supply

In general, each muscle is served by one nerve, an artery, and by one or more veins, all of which enter or exit near the central part of the muscle and branch profusely through its connective tissue sheaths (described below). Unlike cells of cardiac and smooth muscle tissues, which can contract in the absence of nerve stimulation, each skeletal muscle fiber is supplied with a nerve ending that controls its activity.

Contracting muscle fibers use huge amounts of energy, a situation that requires more or less continuous delivery of oxygen and nutrients via the arteries. Muscle cells also give off large amounts of metabolic wastes that must be removed through veins if contraction is to remain efficient. Muscle capillaries, the smallest of the body's blood vessels, are long and winding and have numerous cross-links, features that accommodate changes in muscle length (Figure 9.1). They straighten when the muscle is stretched and contort when the muscle contracts.

Connective Tissue Sheaths

In an intact muscle, the individual muscle fibers are wrapped and held together by several different connective tissue sheaths. Together these connective tissue sheaths support each cell and reinforce the muscle as

TABLE 9.1 Structure and Organizational Levels of Skeletal Muscle

STRUCTURE AND ORGANIZATIONAL LEVEL	DESCRIPTION	CONNECTIVE TISSUE WRAPPINGS
Muscle (organ) Epimysium　Fascicle　Muscle　Tendon	Consists of hundreds to thousands of muscle cells, plus connective tissue wrappings, blood vessels, and nerve fibers	Covered externally by the epimysium
Fascicle (a portion of the muscle) Part of a fascicle　Muscle fiber (cell)　Perimysium	Discrete bundle of muscle cells, segregated from the rest of the muscle by a connective tissue sheath	Surrounded by a perimysium
Muscle fiber (cell) Nucleus　Sarcolemma surrounded by endomysium　Myofibril　Part of a muscle fiber　Striations	Elongated multinucleate cell; has a banded (striated) appearance	Surrounded by the endomysium
Myofibril or fibril (complex organelle composed of bundles of myofilaments) Sarcomere　Myofibril	Rodlike contractile element; myofibrils occupy most of the muscle cell volume; composed of sarcomeres arranged end to end; appear banded, and bands of adjacent myofibrils are aligned	
Sarcomere (a segment of a myofibril) Sarcomere　Thin (actin) filament　Thick (myosin) filament	The contractile unit, composed of myofilaments made up of contractile proteins	
Myofilament or filament (extended macromolecular structure) Thin filament　Actin molecules　Thick filament　Head of myosin molecule	Contractile myofilaments are of two types—thick and thin: the thick filaments contain bundled myosin molecules; the thin filaments contain actin molecules (plus other proteins); the sliding of the thin filaments past the thick filaments produces muscle shortening. Elastic filaments (not shown here) maintain the organization of the A band and provide for elastic recoil when muscle contraction ends	

Q *Consider the term epimysium. What is the meaning of epi? Of mys? How do these word stems relate to the role and position of this connective tissue sheath?*

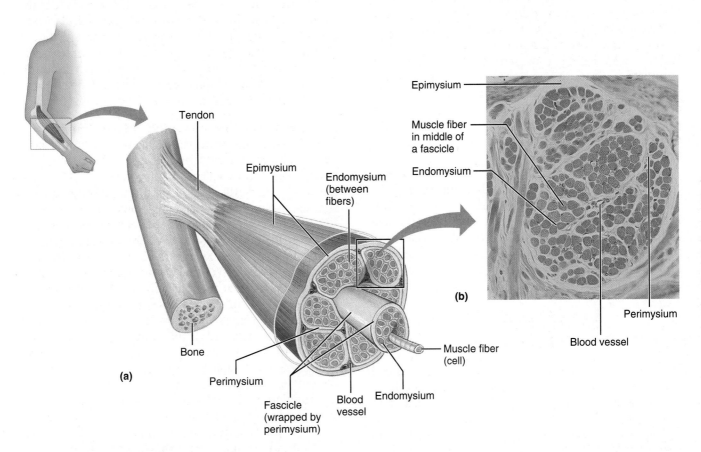

FIGURE 9.2 **Connective tissue sheaths of skeletal muscle. (a)** Each muscle fiber is wrapped with a delicate connective tissue sheath, the endomysium. Bundles, or fascicles, of muscle fibers are bound by a collagenic sheath called a perimysium. The entire muscle is strengthened and wrapped by a coarse epimysium sheath. **(b)** Photomicrograph of a cross section of part of a skeletal muscle (90×).

a whole, preventing the bulging muscles from bursting during exceptionally strong contractions. We will consider these from internal to external (Figure 9.2).

1. Endomysium. Each individual muscle fiber is surrounded by a fine sheath of connective tissue consisting of areolar and reticular fibers. This is the endomysium (en"do-mis'e-um; "within the muscle").

2. Perimysium and **fascicles.** Within each skeletal muscle, the endomysium-wrapped muscle fibers are grouped into fascicles (fas'i-klz; "bundles") that resemble bundles of sticks. Surrounding each fascicle is a layer of fibrous connective tissue called perimysium [per"i-mis'e-um; "around the muscle (fascicles)"].

3. Epimysium. An "overcoat" of dense irregular connective tissue surrounds the whole muscle. This coat is the epimysium (ep"i-mis'e-um), a name that means "outside the muscle." Sometimes the epimysium blends with the deep fascia that lies between neighboring muscles or the superficial fascia deep to the skin.

As shown in Figure 9.2, all of these connective tissue sheaths are continuous with one another as well as with the tendons that join muscles to bones. Therefore, when muscle fibers contract, they pull on these sheaths, which in turn transmit the pulling force to the bone to be moved. They also contribute to the natural elasticity of muscle tissue, and for this reason these elements are sometimes referred to collectively as the *series elastic components.* The wrappings also provide entry and exit routes for the blood vessels and nerve fibers that serve the muscle.

Attachments

Recall from Chapter 8 that (1) most skeletal muscles span joints and are attached to bones (or other structures) in at least two places and (2) when a muscle contracts, the movable bone, the muscle's **insertion,**

A Epi = outer; mys = muscle. The epimysium covers the external surface of the muscle.

moves toward the immovable or less movable bone, the muscle's **origin.** In the muscles of the limbs, the origin typically lies proximal to the insertion.

Muscle attachments, whether origin or insertion, may be direct or indirect. In **direct, or fleshy, attachments,** the epimysium of the muscle is fused to the periosteum of a bone or perichondrium of a cartilage. In **indirect attachments,** the muscle's connective tissue wrappings extend beyond the muscle either as a ropelike **tendon** or as a sheetlike **aponeurosis** (ap″o-nu-ro′sis). The tendon or aponeurosis anchors the muscle to the connective tissue covering of a skeletal element (bone or cartilage) or to the fascia of other muscles.

Of the two, indirect attachments are much more common because of their durability and small size. Tendons are mostly tough collagenic fibers so they can cross rough bony projections that would tear apart the more delicate muscle tissues. Because of their relatively small size, more tendons than fleshy muscles can pass over a joint—thus, tendons also conserve space.

Microscopic Anatomy of a Skeletal Muscle Fiber

Each skeletal muscle fiber is a long cylindrical cell with multiple oval nuclei arranged just beneath its **sarcolemma,** or plasma membrane (see Figure 9.3a). Skeletal muscle fibers are huge cells. Their diameter typically ranges from 10 to 100 μm—up to ten times that of an average body cell—and their length is phenomenal, some up to 30 cm long. Their large size and the fact that they are multinucleate are not surprising once you learn that each fiber is produced by the fusion of hundreds of embryonic cells.

The **sarcoplasm** of a muscle fiber is similar to the cytoplasm of other cells, but it contains unusually large amounts of *glycosomes* (granules of stored glycogen) and **myoglobin,** a red pigment that stores oxygen and is similar to hemoglobin, the pigment that transports oxygen in blood. The usual organelles are present, along with some that are highly modified in muscle fibers: myofibrils and the sarcoplasmic reticulum. T tubules are unique modifications of the sarcolemma. Let's look at these special structures more closely.

Myofibrils

Each muscle fiber contains many rodlike **myofibrils** that run parallel to its length (see Figure 9.3b). The myofibrils, each 1–2 μm in diameter, are so densely packed in the fiber that mitochondria and other organelles appear to be squeezed between them. Hundreds to thousands of myofibrils are in a single muscle fiber, depending on its size, and they account for about 80% of cellular volume. The myofibrils contain the contractile elements of skeletal muscle cells.

Striations, Sarcomeres, and Myofilaments

Striations, a repeating series of dark **A bands** and light **I bands,** are evident along the length of each myofibril. In an intact muscle fiber, the A and I bands are nearly perfectly aligned with one another, giving the cell as a whole its striped (striated) appearance.

As illustrated in Figure 9.3c, each A band has a lighter stripe in its midsection called the **H zone** (*H* for *helle;* "bright"). Each H zone is bisected vertically by a dark line called the **M line** (*M* for middle). The I bands also have a midline interruption, a darker area called the **Z disc** (or Z line). A **sarcomere** (sar′ko-měr; literally, "muscle segment") is the region of a myofibril between two successive Z discs, that is, it contains an A band flanked by half an I band at each end (see Figure 9.3c). Averaging 2 μm long, the sarcomere is the smallest contractile unit of a muscle fiber. Thus, the *functional units* of skeletal muscle are sarcomeres aligned end-to-end like boxcars in a myofibril "train."

If we examine the *banding pattern* of a myofibril at the molecular level, we see that it arises from an orderly arrangement of two types of even smaller structures, called **myofilaments** or **filaments,** within the sarcomeres (Figure 9.3d). The central **thick filaments** extend the entire length of the A band. The more lateral **thin filaments** extend across the I band and partway into the A band. The Z disc, a coin-shaped sheet composed largely of the protein alpha actinin, anchors the thin filaments. Intermediate (desmin) filaments extending from the Z disc connect each myofibril to the next throughout the width of the muscle cell. The H zone of the A band appears less dense because the thin filaments do not extend into this region. The M line in the center of the H zone is slightly darker because of the presence there of fine protein strands that hold adjacent thick filaments together. The third type of myofilament illustrated in Figure 9.3d, the *elastic*

FIGURE 9.3 **Microscopic anatomy of a skeletal muscle fiber.** **(a)** Photomicrograph of portions of two isolated muscle fibers (700×). Notice the obvious striations (alternating light and dark bands). **(b)** Diagram of part of a muscle fiber showing the myofibrils. One myofibril extends from the cut end of the fiber. **(c)** A small portion of one myofibril enlarged to show the myofilaments responsible for the banding pattern. Each sarcomere extends from one Z disc to the next. **(d)** Enlargement of one sarcomere (sectioned lengthwise). Notice the myosin heads on the thick filaments. **(e)** Cross-sectional view of a sarcomere cut through in different areas.

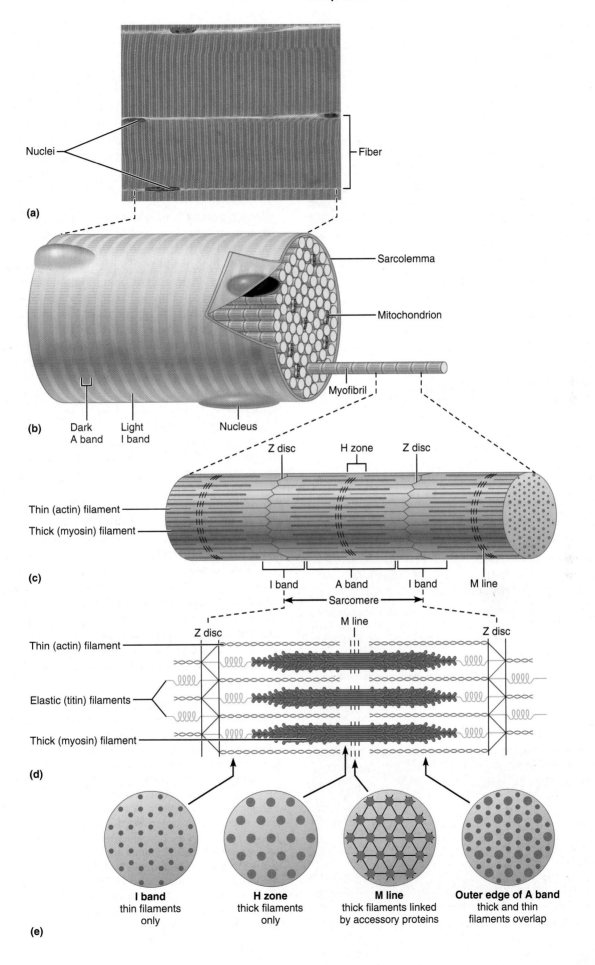

(a)

Nuclei

Fiber

(b)

Sarcolemma

Mitochondrion

Myofibril

Dark
A band

Light
I band

Nucleus

(c)

Z disc

H zone

Z disc

Thin (actin) filament

Thick (myosin) filament

I band

A band

I band

M line

Sarcomere

(d)

M line

Z disc

Z disc

Thin (actin) filament

Elastic (titin) filaments

Thick (myosin) filament

(e)

I band
thin filaments
only

H zone
thick filaments
only

M line
thick filaments linked
by accessory proteins

Outer edge of A band
thick and thin
filaments overlap

(a) Myosin molecule

Tail

Heads

Flexible hinge region

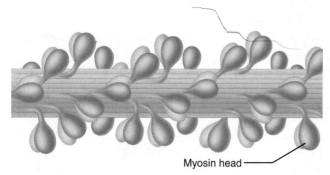

Myosin head

(b) Portion of a thick filament

Troponin complex   Tropomyosin   Actin

(c) Portion of a thin filament

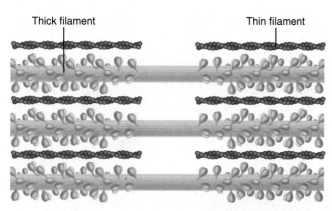

Thick filament   Thin filament

(d) Longitudinal section of filaments within one sarcomere of a myofibril

Thin filament (actin)   Myosin heads   Thick filament (myosin)

(e) Transmission electron micrograph of part of a sarcomere

filament, is described in the next section. The myofilaments are connected to the sarcolemma at the Z discs and the M lines.

A longitudinal view of the myofilaments, such as that in Figure 9.3d, is a bit misleading because it gives the impression that each thick filament interdigitates with only four thin filaments. In areas where thick and thin filaments overlap, each thick filament is actually surrounded by a hexagonal arrangement of six thin filaments, and each thin filament is enclosed by three thick filaments (Figure 9.3e).

Ultrastructure and Molecular Composition of the Myofilaments   Thick filaments (about 16 nm in diameter) are composed primarily of the protein **myosin** (Figure 9.4a). Each myosin molecule has a rodlike *tail* terminating via a flexible hinge in two globular *heads.* The tail consists of two interwoven helical polypeptide chains. Its globular heads are the "business end" of myosin; they link the thick and thin filaments together (form **cross bridges**) and swivel around their point of attachment during contraction. As explained shortly, these cross bridges act as motors to generate the tension developed by a contracting muscle cell. Each thick filament contains about 300 myosin molecules bundled together with their tails forming the central part of the thick filament and their heads facing outward and in opposite directions at each end (Figure 9.4b and d). As a result, the central portion of a thick filament is smooth, but its ends are studded with a staggered array of myosin heads. Besides bearing actin binding sites, the heads contain ATPase enzymes that split ATP to generate energy for muscle contraction.

The thin filaments (7–8 nm thick) are composed chiefly of the protein **actin** (Figure 9.4c). The kidney-shaped polypeptide subunits of actin, called *globular actin* or *G actin,* bear the active sites to which the myosin heads attach during contraction. G actin monomers are polymerized into long actin filaments called *fibrous,* or *F, actin.* The backbone of each thin

FIGURE 9.4   **Composition of thick and thin filaments.** **(a)** An individual myosin molecule has a rodlike tail, from which two "heads" protrude. **(b)** Each thick filament consists of many myosin molecules, whose heads protrude at opposite ends of the filament, as shown in (d). **(c)** A thin filament contains two strands of actin subunits twisted into a helix. Tropomyosin molecules coil around the actin filaments, helping to reinforce them. A troponin complex is attached to each tropomyosin molecule. **(d)** Arrangement of the filaments in a sarcomere (longitudinal view). In the center of the sarcomere, the thick filaments are devoid of myosin heads, but at points of thick and thin filament overlap, myosin heads extend toward the actin, with which they interact during contraction. **(e)** Transmission electron micrograph of part of a sarcomere clearly showing the myosin heads forming cross bridges that generate the contractile force.

filament appears to be formed by two intertwined actin filaments that look like a twisted double strand of pearls.

Several regulatory proteins are also present in the thin filament. Two strands of **tropomyosin** (tro"po-mi'o-sin), a rod-shaped protein, spiral about the actin core and help stiffen it. Successive tropomyosin molecules are arranged end-to-end along the actin filaments, and in a relaxed muscle fiber, they block myosin binding sites on actin so that the myosin heads cannot bind to the thin filaments. The other major protein in the thin filament, **troponin** (tro'po-nin), is a three-polypeptide complex. One of these polypeptides (TnI) is an inhibitory subunit that binds to actin; another (TnT) binds to tropomyosin and helps position it on actin. The third (TnC) binds calcium ions. Both troponin and tropomyosin help control the myosin-actin interactions involved in contraction.

The discoveries of additional types of muscle filaments during the past decade or so demanded that the established view of striated muscle as a two-filament system be rewritten. One of these newly discovered filament types, the **elastic filament** referred to earlier, is composed of the giant protein **titin**, which extends from the Z disc to the thick filament, and then runs within the latter to attach to the M line. Acting as a kind of molecular ruler, it has two basic functions: (1) holding the thick filaments in place, thus maintaining the organization of the A band, and (2) assisting the muscle cell to spring back into shape after being stretched or shortening. (The part of the titin that spans the I bands is extensible, unfolding when the muscle is stretched and recoiling when the tension is released.) Titin does not resist stretching in the ordinary range of extension, but it stiffens as it uncoils, helping the muscle to resist excessive stretching, which might pull the sarcomeres apart. Another important structural protein is **dystrophin**, which links the thin filaments to the integral proteins of the sarcolemma (which in turn are anchored to the extracellular matrix). Other proteins that act to bind filaments or sarcomeres together include *nebulin, myomesin,* and *vimentin.*

Sarcoplasmic Reticulum and T Tubules

Skeletal muscle fibers (cells) contain two sets of intracellular tubules that participate in regulation of muscle contraction: (1) the sarcoplasmic reticulum and (2) the T tubules (Figure 9.5).

Sarcoplasmic Reticulum   The **sarcoplasmic reticulum (SR)** is an elaborate smooth endoplasmic reticulum (see p. 88). Its interconnecting tubules surround each myofibril the way the sleeve of a loosely crocheted sweater surrounds your arm. Most of these tubules run longitudinally along the myofibril. Others form larger, perpendicular cross channels

at the A band–I band junctions. These channels are called **terminal cisternae** ("end sacs") and they always occur in pairs.

The major role of the SR is to regulate intracellular levels of ionic calcium: It stores calcium and releases it on demand when the muscle fiber is stimulated to contract. As you will see, calcium provides the final "go" signal for contraction.

T Tubules   At each A band–I band junction, the sarcolemma of the muscle cell penetrates into the cell interior, forming an elongated tube called the **T tubule** (T for "transverse"). Possibly the result of fusing tubelike caveolae (inpocketings of the sarcolemma), the lumen of the T tubule is continuous with the extracellular space. As each T tubule protrudes deep into the cell, it runs between the paired terminal cisternae of the SR so that **triads,** successive groupings of the three membranous structures (terminal cisterna, T tubule, and terminal cisterna), are formed (Figure 9.5). As they pass from one myofibril to the next, the T tubules also encircle each sarcomere.

Muscle contraction is ultimately controlled by nerve-initiated electrical impulses that travel along the sarcolemma. Because T tubules are continuations of the sarcolemma, they can and do conduct impulses to the deepest regions of the muscle cell and to every sarcomere. These impulses signal for the release of calcium from the adjacent terminal cisternae. Thus, the T tubules can be thought of as a rapid telegraph system that ensures that every myofibril in the muscle fiber contracts at virtually the same time.

Triad Relationships   The roles of the T tubules and SR in providing signals for contraction are tightly linked. At the triads, where these organelles come into closest contact, something that resembles a *double zipper* of integral proteins protrudes into the intermembrane spaces. The protruding integral proteins of the T tubule (DHP receptors) act as voltage sensors; and those of the SR, called *foot proteins,* (or ryanodine receptors) form channels through which Ca^{2+} can be released form the SR cisternae. We will return to consider their interaction shortly.

Sliding Filament Model of Contraction

Although we almost always think "shortening" when we hear the word **contraction,** to physiologists the term refers only to the activation of myosin's cross bridges, which are the force-generating sites. Shortening occurs when the tension generated by the cross bridges on the thin filaments exceeds the forces opposing shortening. Contraction ends when the cross bridges become inactive and the tension generated declines, inducing *relaxation* of the muscle

Q *Which of the following structures shown in this diagram would contain the highest concentration of Ca²⁺ in a resting muscle cell: T tubule, mitochondrion, or SR?*

FIGURE 9.5 **Relationship of the sarcoplasmic reticulum and T tubules to myofibrils of skeletal muscle.** The tubules of the SR encircle each myofibril like a "holey" sleeve. The tubules fuse to form communicating channels at the level of the H zone and abutting the A-I junctions, where the saclike elements called terminal cisternae are formed. The T tubules, inward invaginations of the sarcolemma, run deep into the cell between the terminal cisternae. Sites of close contact of these three elements (terminal cisterna, T tubule, and terminal cisterna) are called triads.

fiber. The **sliding filament theory of contraction** states that during contraction the thin filaments slide past the thick ones so that the actin and myosin filaments overlap to a greater degree (Figure 9.6). In a relaxed muscle fiber, the thick and thin filaments overlap only at the ends of the A band. But when muscle fibers are stimulated by the nervous system, the myosin heads latch on to myosin binding sites on actin in the thin filaments, and the sliding begins. These cross bridge attachments are formed and broken several times during a contraction, acting like tiny ratchets to generate tension and propel the thin filaments toward the center of the sarcomere. As this event occurs simultaneously in sarcomeres throughout the cell, the muscle cell shortens. Notice that as the thin filaments slide centrally, the Z discs to which they are attached are pulled *toward* the thick filaments. Overall, the I bands shorten, the distance between successive Z discs is reduced, the H zones disappear, and the contiguous A bands move closer together but do not change in length.*

A *The SR, which is a calcium storage depot.*

Physiology of a Skeletal Muscle Fiber

For a skeletal muscle fiber to contract, it must be stimulated by a nerve ending and must propagate an electrical current, or **action potential,** along its sarcolemma. This electrical event causes the short-lived rise in intracellular calcium ion levels that is the final trigger for contraction. The series of events linking the electrical signal to contraction is called *excitation-contraction coupling.* Let's consider these events in order.

The Nerve Stimulus and Events at the Neuromuscular Junction

Skeletal muscle cells are stimulated by *motor neurons*[†] of the somatic nervous system. Although these motor neurons "reside" in the brain or spinal cord,

---

* These changes in the banding pattern apply to a muscle contraction that produces shortening (an isotonic contraction, not an isometric contraction; see p. 300).

† Somatic motor neurons are nerve cells that activate skeletal muscle cells.

their long threadlike extensions called *axons* travel, bundled within nerves, to the muscle cells they serve. The axon of each motor neuron divides profusely as it enters the muscle, and each axon ending gives off several short, curling branches that form an elliptical **neuromuscular junction** with a single muscle fiber (Figure 9.7). As a rule, each muscle fiber has only one neuromuscular junction, located approximately midway along the fiber's length. Although the axon terminal and the muscle fiber are exceedingly close (1–2 nm apart), they remain separated by a space, the **synaptic cleft,** which is filled with a gel-like extracellular substance rich in glycoproteins and collagen fibers. Within the flattened moundlike axon terminal are **synaptic vesicles,** small membranous sacs containing the neurotransmitter **acetylcholine** (as"ĕ-til-ko'lēn), or **ACh.** The **motor end plate,** the troughlike part of the muscle fiber's sarcolemma that helps form the neuromuscular junction, is highly folded. These *junctional folds* provide a large surface area for the millions of **ACh receptors** located there.

When a nerve impulse reaches the end of an axon, voltage-gated calcium channels in its membrane open, allowing Ca^{2+} (propelled by its electrochemical gradient) to flow in from the extracellular fluid. The presence of calcium inside the axon terminal causes some of the synaptic vesicles to fuse with the axonal membrane and release ACh into the synaptic cleft by *exocytosis*. ACh diffuses across the cleft and attaches to ACh receptors on the sarcolemma. The electrical events triggered in a sarcolemma when ACh binds are similar to those that take place in excited nerve cell membranes (see Chapter 11).

After ACh binds to the ACh receptors, it is swiftly broken down to its building blocks, acetic acid and choline, by **acetylcholinesterase** (as"ĕ-til-ko"lin-es'ter-ās), an enzyme located in the synaptic cleft (Figure 9.7c). This destruction of ACh prevents continued muscle fiber contraction in the absence of additional nervous system stimulation.

◥ HOMEOSTATIC IMBALANCE

Many toxins, drugs, and diseases interfere with events at the neuromuscular junction. For example, *myasthenia gravis* (*asthen* = weakness; *gravi* = heavy), a disease characterized by drooping upper eyelids, difficulty swallowing and talking, and generalized muscle weakness, involves a shortage of ACh receptors. Serum analysis reveals antibodies to ACh receptors, suggesting that myasthenia gravis is an autoimmune disease. Although normal numbers of receptors are initially present, they appear to be destroyed as the disease progresses. ●

FIGURE 9.6 Sliding filament model of contraction. The numbers indicate a sequence of events, with ① being relaxed and ③ fully contracted. At full contraction, the Z discs abut the thick filaments and the thin filaments overlap each other. The photomicrographs (top view in each case) show enlargements of 25,000×.

(a)

(b)

(c)

FIGURE 9.7 **The neuromuscular junction.**
(a) Axon terminal of a motor neuron forming a neuromuscular junction with a muscle fiber. (b) Each axon terminal contains vesicles filled with the neurotransmitter acetylcholine (ACh), which is released when the action potential reaches the axon terminal. The sarcolemma is highly folded adjacent to the synaptic cleft, and ACh receptors are present in these junctional folds. (c) ACh diffuses across the synaptic cleft and attaches to receptors on the sarcolemma, opening ion channels and initiating depolarization of the sarcolemma.

Generation of an Action Potential Across the Sarcolemma

Like the plasma membranes of all cells, a resting sarcolemma is *polarized*. That is, a voltmeter would show there is a potential difference (voltage) across the membrane and the inside is negative relative to the outer membrane face. (The resting membrane potential is described in Chapter 3.) Binding of ACh molecules to ACh receptors at the motor end plate opens the *chemically (ligand) gated ion channels* (p. 83) housed in the ACh receptors and allows both Na^+ and K^+ to pass (Figure 9.7). Because more Na^+ diffuses in than K^+ diffuses out, a transient change in membrane potential occurs such that the interior of the sarcolemma becomes slightly less negative, an event called **depolarization.**

Initially, depolarization is a local electrical event called an *end plate potential*, but it ignites the action potential that spreads in all directions from the neuromuscular junction across the sarcolemma, just as ripples move away from pebbles dropped into a stream.

The action potential (AP) is the result of a predictable sequence of electrical changes that once initi-

ated occurs along the entire length of the sarcolemma (Figure 9.8). Essentially three steps are involved.

1. First the membrane areas adjacent to the depolarized motor end plate are depolarized by local currents that spread to them from the neuromuscular junction. This opens *voltage-gated* (p. 84) sodium channels there, so Na^+ enters, following its electrochemical gradient, and initiates the action potential (Figure 9.9).

2. During step 2, the action potential is propagated (moves along the length of the sarcolemma) as the local depolarization wave spreads to adjacent areas of the sarcolemma and opens voltage-gated sodium channels there (see Figure 9.8c). Again, sodium ions, normally restricted from entering, diffuse into the cell following their electrochemical gradient.

3. Step 3 is **repolarization,** which restores the sarcolemma to its initial polarized state. The repolarization wave, which quickly follows the depolarization wave, is a consequence of Na^+ channels closing and voltage-gated K^+ channels opening. Since the potassium ion concentration is substantially higher inside the cell than in the extracellular fluid, K^+ diffuses rapidly out of the muscle fiber (Figures 9.8d and 9.9).

[Na⁺] [K⁺]

[K⁺] [Na⁺]

(a)

↑ Na⁺
Stimulus

(b)

(c)

K⁺

(d)

(a) Electrical conditions of a resting (polarized) sarcolemma.
The outside face is positive, while the inside face is negative. The predominant extracellular ion is sodium (Na⁺); the predominant intracellular ion is potassium (K⁺). The sarcolemma is relatively impermeable to both ions.

(b) Step 1: Depolarization and generation of the action potential.
Production of an end plate potential at the motor end plate causes adjacent areas of the sarcolemma to become permeable to sodium (voltage-gated sodium channels open). As sodium ions diffuse rapidly into the cell, the resting potential is decreased (i.e., depolarization occurs). If the stimulus is strong enough, an action potential is initiated.

(c) Step 2: Propagation of the action potential.
The positive charge inside the initial patch of sarcolemma changes the permeability of an adjacent patch, opening voltage-gated Na⁺ channels there. Consequently the membrane potential in that region decreases and depolarization occurs there as well. Thus, the action potential travels rapidly over the entire sarcolemma.

(d) Step 3: Repolarization.
Immediately after the depolarization wave passes, the sarcolemma's permeability changes once again: Na⁺ channels close and K⁺ channels open, allowing K⁺ to diffuse from the cell. This restores the electrical conditions of the resting (polarized) state. Repolarization occurs in the same direction as depolarization, and must occur before the muscle fiber can be stimulated again. The ionic concentrations of the resting state are restored later by the sodium-potassium pump.

FIGURE 9.8 **An action potential in a skeletal muscle fiber.** Events in the generation and propagation of an action potential are summarized.

During repolarization, a muscle fiber is said to be in a **refractory period,** because the cell cannot be stimulated again until repolarization is complete. Notice that repolarization restores only the *electrical conditions* of the resting (polarized) state. The ATP-dependent Na⁺-K⁺ pump restores the ionic conditions of the resting state, but hundreds of contractions can occur before ionic imbalances interfere with contractile activity.

Once initiated, the action potential is unstoppable and ultimately results in contraction of the muscle cell. Although the action potential itself is very brief [1–2 milliseconds (ms)], the contraction phase of a muscle fiber may persist for 100 ms or more and far outlasts the electrical event that triggers it because active transport of Ca^{2+} back into the SR takes substantially longer than its release.

Excitation-Contraction Coupling

Excitation-contraction (E-C) coupling is the sequence of events by which transmission of an action potential along the sarcolemma leads to the sliding of myofilaments. The action potential is brief and

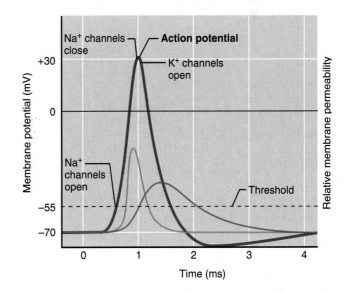

FIGURE 9.9 **Action potential scan showing changing sarcolemma permeability to Na⁺ and K⁺ ions.** (Na⁺ permeability = yellow scan line; K⁺ permeability = green scan line; action potential = blue scan line)

Q *(1)* Why is Ca^{2+} called the final *trigger* for contraction?
(2) What constitutes the initial *trigger*?

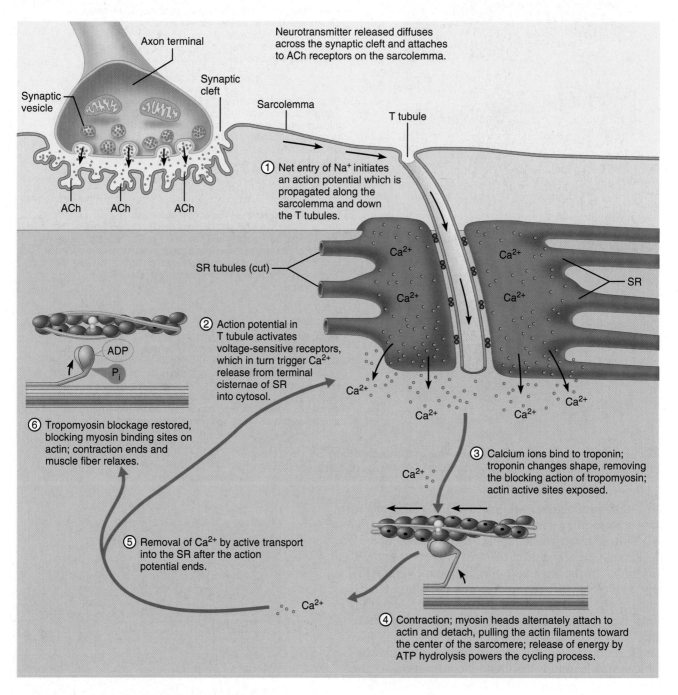

Neurotransmitter released diffuses across the synaptic cleft and attaches to ACh receptors on the sarcolemma.

Axon terminal

Synaptic cleft

Synaptic vesicle

ACh   ACh   ACh

Sarcolemma

T tubule

① Net entry of Na^+ initiates an action potential which is propagated along the sarcolemma and down the T tubules.

SR tubules (cut)

Ca^{2+} Ca^{2+}

Ca^{2+} Ca^{2+}

SR

② Action potential in T tubule activates voltage-sensitive receptors, which in turn trigger Ca^{2+} release from terminal cisternae of SR into cytosol.

Ca^{2+} Ca^{2+} Ca^{2+} Ca^{2+}

ADP

P_i

⑥ Tropomyosin blockage restored, blocking myosin binding sites on actin; contraction ends and muscle fiber relaxes.

③ Calcium ions bind to troponin; troponin changes shape, removing the blocking action of tropomyosin; actin active sites exposed.

Ca^{2+}

⑤ Removal of Ca^{2+} by active transport into the SR after the action potential ends.

Ca^{2+}

④ Contraction; myosin heads alternately attach to actin and detach, pulling the actin filaments toward the center of the sarcomere; release of energy by ATP hydrolysis powers the cycling process.

FIGURE 9.10 **Excitation-contraction coupling.** Events ① through ⑤ indicate the sequence of events in the coupling process. Contraction continues until ⑥ the calcium signal ends.

A *(1)* Because calcium binding to troponin frees the actin active sites to bind with myosin heads. *(2)* The initial trigger is neurotransmitter binding, which initiates generation of an action potential along the sarcolemma.

ends well before any signs of contraction are obvious. The events of excitation-contraction coupling occur during the *latent period* (*laten* = hidden), between action potential initiation and the beginning of mechanical activity (shortening). As you will see, the electrical signal does not act directly on the myofilaments; rather, it causes the rise in intracellular calcium ion concentration that allows the filaments to slide.

Excitation-contraction coupling consists of the following steps illustrated in (Figure 9.10):

① The action potential propagates along the sarcolemma and down the T tubules.

② Transmission of the action potential in the T tubules of the triads causes the terminal cisternae of the SR to release Ca^{2+} into the sarcoplasm, where it becomes available to the myofilaments. The "double zippers" (p. 287) at the T-SR junctions of the triads are involved in this action as follows: The T tubule proteins (DHP receptors) are sensitive to voltage and change shape in response to the arrival of the action potential. This voltage-regulated change is communicated to the linked SR foot proteins, which in turn undergo shape changes that open their calcium-release channels (and perhaps other mechanically linked Ca^{2+} channels nearby). Because these events occur at every triad in the cell, within 1 ms massive amounts of Ca^{2+} flood into the sarcoplasm from the SR cisternae.

③ Some of this calcium binds to troponin, which changes shape and removes the blocking action of tropomyosin.

④ When the intracellular calcium level is about 10^{-5} M, the myosin heads attach and pull the thin filaments toward the center of the sarcomere. At this point you can say the muscle cell is in the active state.

⑤ The short-lived Ca^{2+} signal ends, usually within 30 ms after the action potential is over. The fall in Ca^{2+} levels reflects the operation of a continuously active, ATP-dependent calcium pump that moves Ca^{2+} back into the SR to be stored once again.

⑥ The inactive state occurs when intracellular Ca^{2+} levels drop too low for the amount of Ca^{2+} needed for contraction to bind to troponin, so the tropomyosin blockade is reestablished, and myosin-actin interaction is inhibited. Cross bridge activity ends and relaxation occurs.

This sequence of events is repeated when another nerve impulse arrives at the neuromuscular junction. When the impulses are delivered rapidly, intracellular Ca^{2+} levels increase greatly due to successive "puffs" or rounds of Ca^{2+} released from the SR. In such cases, the muscle cells do not completely relax between successive stimuli and contraction is stronger and more sustained (within limits) until nervous stimulation ceases.

Summary of Roles of Ionic Calcium in Muscle Contraction

Except for the brief period following muscle cell excitation, calcium ion concentrations in the sarcoplasm are kept almost undetectably low. There is a reason for this: ATP provides the cell's energy source and its hydrolysis yields inorganic phosphate (P_i). If the intracellular level of Ca^{2+} were always high, calcium and phosphate ions would combine to form hydroxyapatite crystals, the stony-hard salts found in bone matrix. Such calcified cells would die. Also, because calcium's physiological roles are so vital (besides triggering neurotransmitter secretion and sliding of the myofilaments, it promotes breakdown of glycogen and ATP synthesis), its cytoplasmic concentration is exquisitely regulated by intracellular proteins. These include **calsequestrin** (found within the SR cisternae) and **calmodulin,** which can alternately bind and release calcium to provide a metabolic signal.

Muscle Fiber Contraction

As noted, cross bridge formation (attachment of myosin heads to actin) requires Ca^{2+}. When intracellular calcium levels are low, the muscle cell is relaxed, and the active (myosin binding) sites on actin are physically blocked by tropomyosin molecules (Figure 9.11a). As Ca^{2+} levels rise, the ions bind to regulatory sites on troponin TnC (Figure 9.11b), causing it to change shape. This event moves tropomyosin deeper into the groove of the actin helix and away from the myosin binding sites (Figure 9.11c and d). Thus, the tropomyosin "blockade" is removed when sufficient calcium is present.

Once binding sites on actin are exposed, the following events occur in rapid succession (Figure 9.12):

① **Cross bridge formation.** The activated myosin heads are strongly attracted to the exposed binding sites on actin, and cross bridges form.

② **The power (working) stroke.** As a myosin head binds, phosphate (P_i) generated during the prior contraction cycle is released, initiating the power stroke. During the power stroke the myosin head pivots (moves through an angle of about 70°), changing from its high-energy configuration to its bent, low-energy shape, which pulls on the thin filament, sliding it toward the center of the sarcomere. At the same time, ADP generated during the *prior* contraction cycle is released. Each working stroke of myosin produces a movement or step of 5–15 nm.

③ **Cross bridge detachment.** As a new ATP molecule binds to the myosin head, myosin's hold on actin loosens and the cross bridge detaches from actin.

④ **"Cocking" of the myosin head.** The ATPase in the myosin head hydrolyzes ATP to ADP and P_i which provides the energy needed to return the myosin head to its prestroke high-energy, or "cocked," position. This provides the potential energy needed for its *next* sequence of attachment and power stroke. (The ADP and P_i remain attached to the myosin head during this phase.)

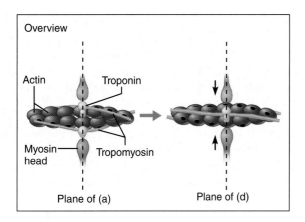

FIGURE 9.11 **Role of ionic calcium in the contraction mechanism.** Views (a–d) are cross-sectional views of the thin (actin) filament. **(a)** At low intracellular Ca^{2+} concentration, tropomyosin blocks the binding sites on actin, preventing attachment of myosin heads and enforcing the relaxed muscle state. **(b)** At higher intracellular Ca^{2+} concentrations, additional calcium binds to TnC of troponin. **(c)** Calcium-activated troponin undergoes a conformational change that moves the tropomyosin away from actin's binding sites. **(d)** This displacement allows the myosin heads to bind and cycle, and contraction (sliding of the thin filaments by the myosin cross bridges) begins.

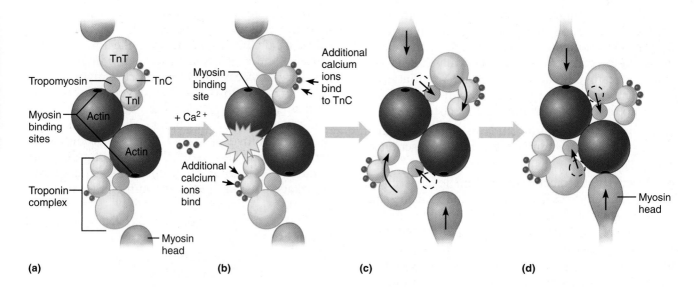

At this point, the cycle is back where it started. The myosin head is in its upright high-energy configuration, ready to take another "step" and attach to an actin site farther along the thin filament. This "walking" of the myosin heads along the adjacent thin filaments during muscle shortening is much like a centipede's gait. Because some myosin heads ("legs") are always in contact with actin (the "ground"), the thin filaments cannot slide backward as the cycle is repeated again and again.

A single power stroke of all the cross bridges in a muscle results in a shortening of only about 1%. Because contracting muscles routinely shorten by 30–35% of their total resting length, each myosin cross bridge must attach and detach many times during a single contraction. It is likely that only half of the myosin heads of a thick filament are pulling at the same instant; the balance are randomly seeking their next binding site. Sliding of thin filaments continues as long as the calcium signal and adequate ATP are present. As the Ca^{2+} pumps of the SR reclaim calcium ions from the sarcoplasm and troponin again changes shape, actin's myosin-binding sites are covered by tropomyosin, the contraction ends, and the muscle fiber relaxes.

HOMEOSTATIC IMBALANCE

Rigor mortis (death rigor) illustrates the fact that cross bridge detachment is ATP driven. Most muscles begin to stiffen 3 to 4 hours after death. Peak rigidity occurs at 12 hours and then gradually dissipates over the next 48 to 60 hours. Dying cells are unable to exclude calcium (which is in higher concentration in the extracellular fluid), and the calcium influx into muscle cells promotes formation of myosin cross bridges. Shortly after breathing stops, ATP synthesis ceases, but it continues to be consumed and cross bridge detachment is impossible. Actin and myosin become irreversibly cross-linked, producing the stiffness of rigor mortis, which gradually disappears as muscle proteins break down after death. ●

Q *What would happen if the muscle fiber suddenly ran out of ATP when the sarcomeres had only partially contracted?*

① Myosin head attaches to the actin myofilament, forming a cross bridge.

② Inorganic phosphate (P_i) generated in the previous contraction cycle is released, initiating the power (working) stroke. The myosin head pivots and bends as it pulls on the actin filament, sliding it toward the M line. Then ADP is released.

③ As new ATP attaches to the myosin head, the link between myosin and actin weakens, and the cross bridge detaches.

④ As ATP is split into ADP and P_i, the myosin head is energized (cocked into the high-energy conformation).

FIGURE 9.12   The cross bridge cycle. A small section of adjacent thick and thin filaments is used to illustrate the interactions between the two types of myofilaments during contraction. These events occur only in the presence of ionic calcium (Ca^{2+}), which releases tropomyosin's blockade of actin's active sites.

A *The sarcomeres would remain in their partially contracted state.*

Contraction of a Skeletal Muscle

In its relaxed state, a muscle is soft and unimpressive; not what you would expect of a prime mover of the body. However, within a few milliseconds, it can contract to become a hard elastic structure with dynamic characteristics that intrigue not only biologists but engineers and physicists as well.

Before we consider muscle contraction on the organ level, let's review a few principles of muscle mechanics.

1. The principles governing contraction of a muscle fiber (cell) and of a skeletal muscle consisting of a huge number of cells are pretty much the same.

2. The force exerted by a contracting muscle on an object is called **muscle tension**, and the opposing

(a)

FIGURE 9.13 **A motor unit consists of a motor neuron and all the muscle fibers it innervates. (a)** Schematic view of portions of two motor units. The cell bodies of the motor neurons reside in the spinal cord, and their axons extend to the muscle. In the muscle, each axon divides into a number of axon terminals that are distributed to muscle fibers scattered throughout the muscle. **(b)** Photomicrograph of a portion of a motor unit (80×). Notice the diverging axon terminals and the neuromuscular junctions formed by the terminals and muscle fibers.

force exerted on the muscle by the weight of the object to be moved is called the **load.**

3. A contracting muscle does not always shorten and move the load. If muscle tension develops but the load is not moved, the contraction is called *isometric* ("same measure"). If the muscle tension developed overcomes the load and muscle shortening occurs, the contraction is *isotonic*. These major types of contraction will be described in detail shortly, but for now the important thing to remember when reading the accompanying graphs is that *increasing muscle tension* is measured in isometric contractions, whereas the *amount of shortening* (distance in millimeters) is measured in isotonic contractions.

4. A skeletal muscle contracts with varying force and for different periods of time in response to stim-uli of varying frequencies and intensities. To understand how this occurs, we must first look at the nerve-muscle functional unit called a *motor unit*. This is our next topic.

The Motor Unit

Each muscle is served by at least one motor nerve, which contains axons (fibrous extensions) of up to hundreds of motor neurons. As an axon enters a muscle, it branches into a number of terminals, each of which forms a neuromuscular junction with a single muscle fiber. A motor neuron and all the muscle fibers it supplies is called a **motor unit** (Figure 9.13). When a motor neuron fires (transmits an electrical impulse), all the muscle fibers it innervates contract. The number of muscle fibers per motor unit may be as high as several hundred or as few as four. Muscles that exert fine control (such as those controlling the fingers and eyes) have small motor units. By contrast, large, weight-bearing muscles, whose movements are less precise (such as the hip muscles), have large motor units. The muscle fibers in a single motor unit are not clustered together but are spread throughout the muscle. As a result, stimulation of a single motor unit causes a weak contraction of the *entire* muscle.

The Muscle Twitch

Muscle contraction is easily investigated in the laboratory using an isolated muscle. The muscle is attached to an apparatus that produces a **myogram,** a graphic recording of contractile activity. (The line recording the activity is called a *tracing.*)

The response of a motor unit to a single action potential of its motor neuron is called a **muscle twitch.** The muscle fibers contract quickly and then relax. Every twitch myogram has three distinct phases (Figure 9.14a).

1. Latent period. The **latent period** is the first few milliseconds following stimulation when excitation-contraction coupling is occurring. During this period, muscle tension is beginning to increase but no response is seen on the myogram.

2. Period of contraction. The period of contraction is when cross bridges are active, from the onset to the peak of tension development, and the myogram tracing rises to a peak. This period lasts 10–100 ms. If the tension (pull) becomes great enough to overcome the resistance of a load, the muscle shortens.

3. Period of relaxation. The period of contraction is followed by the period of relaxation. This final phase, lasting 10–100 ms, is initiated by reentry of Ca^{2+} into the SR. Because contractile force is no longer being generated, muscle tension decreases to zero and the tracing returns to the baseline. If the muscle shortened during contraction, it now returns to its initial length.

As you can see in Figure 9.14b, twitch contractions of some muscles are rapid and brief, as with the muscles controlling eye movements. In contrast, the fibers of fleshy calf muscles (gastrocnemius and soleus) contract more slowly and remain contracted for much longer periods. These differences between muscles reflect metabolic properties of the myofibrils and enzyme variations.

Graded Muscle Responses

Although *muscle twitches*—like those single, jerky contractions provoked in a laboratory—may result from certain neuromuscular problems, this is *not* the way our muscles normally operate. Instead, healthy muscle contractions are relatively smooth and vary in strength as different demands are placed

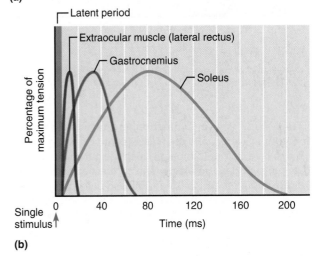

FIGURE 9.14 **The muscle twitch. (a)** Myogram of an isometric twitch contraction, showing its three phases: the latent period, the period of contraction, and the period of relaxation. **(b)** Comparison of the relative duration of twitch responses of extraocular, gastrocnemius, and soleus muscles.

on them. These variations (an obvious requirement for proper control of skeletal movement) are referred to as **graded muscle responses.** In general, muscle contraction can be graded in two ways: (1) by changing the frequency of stimulation and (2) by changing the strength of the stimulus.

Muscle Response to Changes in Stimulation Frequency The nervous system achieves greater muscular force by increasing the firing rate of motor neurons. For example, if two identical stimuli (electrical shocks or nerve impulses) are delivered to a muscle in rapid succession, the second twitch will be stronger than the first. On a myogram the second twitch will appear to ride on the shoulders of the first (Figure 9.15). This phenomenon, called **wave summation,** occurs because the second contraction occurs before the muscle has completely relaxed. Because the muscle is already partially contracted when the next

Q *If the second stimulus in part 2 was delayed by a few milliseconds, would the second peak be higher or lower? Why?*

① **Twitch** ② **Wave summation** ③ **Unfused (incomplete) tetanus** ④ **Fused (complete) tetanus**

FIGURE 9.15 **Wave summation and tetanus in a whole muscle.** ① A single stimulus is delivered, and the muscle contracts and relaxes (twitch contraction). ② Stimuli are delivered more frequently, so that the muscle does not have adequate time to relax completely, and contraction force increases (wave summation). ③ More complete twitch fusion (unfused or incomplete tetanus) occurs as stimuli are delivered more rapidly. ④ In fused or complete tetanus, a smooth, continuous contraction without any evidence of relaxation occurs.

stimulus arrives and more calcium is being released to replace that being reclaimed by the SR, muscle tension produced during the second contraction causes more shortening than the first. In other words, the contractions are summed. (However, the refractory period is *always* honored. Thus, if a second stimulus is delivered before repolarization is complete, no summation occurs.) If the stimulus strength is held constant and the muscle is stimulated at an increasingly faster rate, the relaxation time between the twitches becomes shorter and shorter, the concentration of Ca^{2+} in the sarcoplasm higher and higher, and the degree of summation greater and greater, progressing to a sustained but quivering contraction referred to as **unfused** or **incomplete tetanus.** Finally, as the stimulation frequency continues to increase, muscle tension increases until a maximal tension is reached. At this point all evidence of muscle relaxation disappears and the contractions fuse into a smooth, sustained contraction plateau called **fused** or **complete tetanus** (tet'ah-nus; *tetan* = rigid, tense). (This term is often confused with the bacterial disease called tetanus that causes severe involuntary contractions.)

Vigorous muscle activity cannot continue indefinitely. Prolonged tetanus inevitably leads to *muscle fatigue*, a situation in which the muscle is unable to contract and its tension drops to zero.

Muscle Response to Stronger Stimuli Although wave summation contributes to contractile force, its primary function is to produce smooth, continuous muscle contractions by rapidly stimulating a specific number of muscle cells. The force of contraction is controlled more precisely by **recruitment,** also called **multiple motor unit summation** (Figure 9.16). In the laboratory this phenomenon is achieved by delivering shocks of increasing voltage to the muscle, calling more and more muscle fibers into play. The stimulus at which the first observable contraction occurs is called the **threshold stimulus.** Beyond this point, the muscle contracts more and more vigorously as the stimulus strength is increased (Figure 9.16). The **maximal stimulus** is the strongest stimulus that produces increased contractile force. It represents the point at which all the muscle's motor units are recruited. Increasing the stimulus intensity beyond the maximal stimulus does not produce a stronger contraction. In the body, the same phenomenon is caused by neural activation of an

A *The second peak would be lower, more like the first peak because more of the muscle cells would have had time to relax.*

FIGURE 9.16 **Relationship between stimulus intensity (graph at top) and muscle tension (tracing below).** Below threshold voltage, no muscle response is seen on the tracing (1 and 2). Once threshold (3) is reached, increases in voltage excite (recruit) more and more motor units until the maximal stimulus is reached (7). Further increases in stimulus voltage produce no further increase in contractile strength.

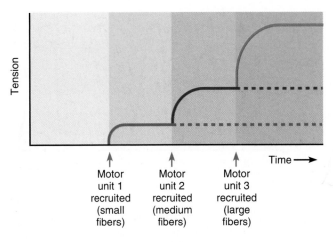

FIGURE 9.17 **The size principle.** Recruitment of motor neurons controlling skeletal muscle fibers is orderly—small motor neurons are generally recruited more readily than large ones. This phenomenon is referred to as the *size principle*. In weaker contractions, small motor neurons controlling motor units containing small-diameter muscle fibers are recruited. As contractile strength increases, larger and larger motor neurons are activated, which in turn stimulate motor units containing larger numbers of increasingly larger diameter muscle fibers. Consequently, the contractions get stronger and stronger in a disproportionate and predictable way.

increasingly large number of motor units serving the muscle.

The recruitment process is not random; instead it is dictated by the *size principle*. In any muscle, motor units with the smallest muscle fibers are controlled by small, highly excitable motor neurons, and these motor units tend to be activated first. As the contractile strength increases, motor units with larger and larger muscle fibers begin to be excited. The largest motor units, containing large, coarse muscle fibers have as much as 50 times the contractile force of the smallest ones. They are controlled by the largest, least excitable (highest-threshold) neurons and are activated only when the most powerful contraction is necessary (Figure 9.17). The size principle is important because it allows the increases in force during weak contractions (for example, those that maintain posture or slow movements) to occur in small steps, whereas gradations in muscle force are progressively greater when large amounts of force are needed for vigorous activities such as jumping or running. This explains how the same hand that pats your cheek can deliver a stinging slap.

Although *all* the motor units of a muscle may be recruited simultaneously to produce an exceptionally strong contraction, motor units are more commonly activated asynchronously in the body. At a given instant, some are in tetanus (usually unfused tetanus) while others are resting and recovering. This technique helps prolong a strong contraction by preventing or delaying fatigue. It also explains how weak contractions promoted by infrequent stimuli can remain smooth.

Treppe: The Staircase Effect When a muscle begins to contract after a long period of rest, its initial contractions may be only half as strong as those that occur later in response to stimuli of the same strength. During these periods, a tracing shows a staircase pattern called **treppe** (trep′ĕ) (Figure 9.18). Treppe probably reflects the increasing availability of Ca^{2+} in the sarcoplasm; more Ca^{2+} ions expose more active sites on the thin filaments for cross bridge attachment. Additionally, as the muscle begins to work and liberates heat, its enzymes become more efficient and the muscle becomes more pliable. Together, these factors produce a slightly stronger contraction with each successive stimulus during the initial phase of muscle activity. This is the basis of the warm-up period used by athletes.

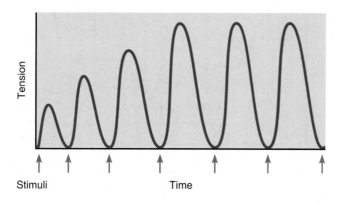

FIGURE 9.18 **Myogram of treppe.** Notice that although the stimuli are of the same intensity and the muscle is not being stimulated rapidly, the first few contractile responses get stronger and stronger.

Muscle Tone

Skeletal muscles are described as voluntary, but even relaxed muscles are almost always slightly contracted, a phenomenon called **muscle tone.** This is due to spinal reflexes that activate first one group of motor units and then another in response to activation of stretch receptors in the muscles. Muscle tone does not produce active movements, but it keeps the muscles firm, healthy, and ready to respond to stimulation. Skeletal muscle tone also helps stabilize joints and maintain posture.

Isotonic and Isometric Contractions

As noted earlier, there are two main categories of contractions—*isotonic* and *isometric.* In **isotonic contractions** (*iso* = same; *ton* = tension), muscle length changes (decreasing the angle at the joint) and moves the load. Once sufficient tension has developed to move the load, the tension remains relatively constant through the rest of the contractile period (Figure 9.19a).

Isotonic contractions come in two "flavors"—*concentric* and *eccentric.* **Concentric contractions** in which the muscle *shortens* and does work—picking up a book or kicking a ball, for instance—are probably more familiar. However, **eccentric contractions,** in which the muscle generates force as it *lengthens,* are equally important for coordination and purposeful movements. Eccentric contractions occur in your calf muscle, for example, as you walk up a steep hill. Eccentric contractions are about 50% more forceful than concentric ones at the same load and more often cause delayed-onset muscle soreness. (Consider how your calf muscles *feel* the day after hiking up that hill.) Just why this is so is unclear, but it may be that the muscle stretching that occurs during such contractions causes microtears in the muscles.

Squats, or deep knee bends, provide a simple example of how concentric and eccentric contractions work together in our everyday activities. As the knees flex, the powerful quadriceps muscles of the anterior thigh lengthen (are stretched), but at the same time they also contract (eccentrically) to counteract the force of gravity and control the descent of the torso ("muscle braking") and prevent joint injury. Raising the body back to its starting position requires that the same muscles contract concentrically as they shorten to extend the knees again. As you can see, eccentric contractions put the body in position to contract concentrically. All jumping and throwing activities involve both types of contraction.

In **isometric contractions** (*metric* = measure), tension may build to the muscle's peak tension-producing capacity, but the muscle *neither shortens nor lengthens* (Figure 9.19b). Isometric contractions occur when a muscle attempts to move a load that is greater than the force (tension) the muscle is able to develop—think of trying to lift a piano singlehandedly. Muscles contract isometrically when they act primarily to maintain upright posture or to hold joints in stationary positions while movements occur at other joints. In our knee bend example, the quadriceps muscles contract isometrically when the squat position is held for a few seconds to hold the knee in the flexed position. They also contract isometrically when we begin to rise to the upright position until their tension exceeds the load (weight of the upper body). At that point muscle shortening (concentric contraction) begins. So the quadriceps contractile sequence for a deep knee bend from start to finish is (1) flex knee (eccentric), (2) hold squat position (isometric), (3) extend knee (isometric, then concentric). Of course, this does not even begin to consider the isometric contractions of the posterior thigh muscles or of the trunk muscles that maintain a relatively erect trunk posture during the movement.

Electrochemical and mechanical events occurring within a muscle are identical in both isotonic and isometric contractions. However, the result is different. In isotonic contractions, the thin filaments are sliding; in isometric contractions, the cross bridges are generating force but are *not* moving the thin filaments, so there is no change in the banding pattern from that of the resting state. (You could say that they are "spinning their wheels" on the same actin binding sites.)

Muscle Metabolism

Providing Energy for Contraction

Now let's look at the mechanisms by which the body provides the energy needed for contraction.

Stored ATP As a muscle contracts, ATP provides the energy for cross bridge movement and detachment

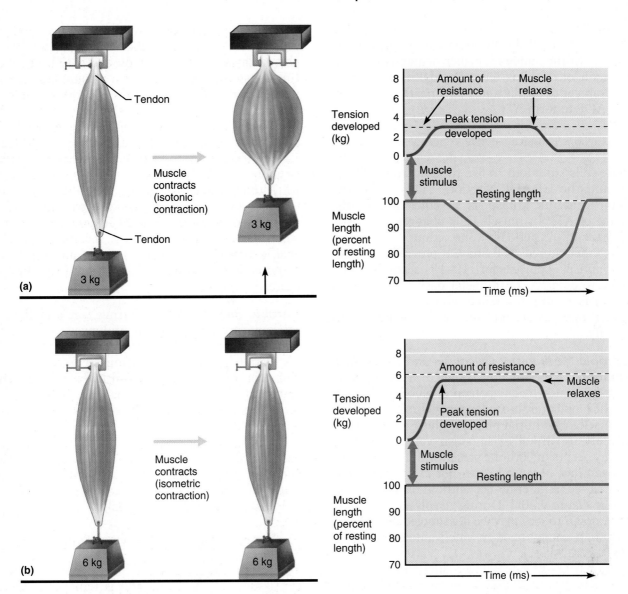

FIGURE 9.19 **Isotonic (concentric) and isometric contractions. (a)** On stimulation, this muscle develops enough tension (force) to lift the load (weight). Once the resistance is overcome, tension remains constant for the rest of the contraction and the muscle shortens. This is a concentric isotonic contraction. **(b)** This muscle is attached to a weight that exceeds the muscle's peak tension-developing capabilities. When stimulated, the tension increases to the muscle's peak tension-developing capability, but the muscle does not shorten. This is an isometric contraction.

and for operation of the calcium pump. Surprisingly, muscles store very limited reserves of ATP—4 to 6 seconds' worth at most, just enough to get you going.

Because ATP is the *only* energy source used directly for contractile activities, it must be regenerated as fast as it is broken down if contraction is to continue. Fortunately, after ATP is hydrolyzed to ADP and inorganic phosphate, it is regenerated within a fraction of a second by three pathways (Figure 9.20): (1) by interaction of ADP with creatine phosphate, (2) from stored glycogen via the anaero-

bic pathway called glycolysis, and (3) by aerobic respiration. The second and third of these metabolic pathways, which are used to produce ATP in all body cells, are just touched on here, as they are described in detail in Chapter 24.

Direct Phosphorylation of ADP by Creatine Phosphate As we begin to exercise vigorously, the demand for ATP soars and the ATP stored in working muscles is consumed within a few twitches. Then **creatine phosphate (CP)** (kre'ah-tin), a unique high-energy molecule stored in muscles, is tapped to regenerate ATP while the metabolic pathways are adjusting to the suddenly higher demands for ATP. The result of coupling CP with ADP is almost instant transfer of energy and a phosphate group from CP to ADP to form ATP:

Creatine phosphate + ADP → creatine + ATP

Muscle cells store four to five times as much CP as ATP, and the CP-ADP reaction, catalyzed by the enzyme **creatine kinase,** is so efficient that the amount of ATP in muscle cells changes very little during the initial period of contraction.

Together, stored ATP and CP provide for maximum muscle power for 10–15 seconds—long enough to energize a 100-meter dash. The coupled reaction is readily reversible, and to keep CP "on tap," CP reserves are replenished during periods of inactivity.

Anaerobic Mechanism: Glycolysis and Lactic Acid Formation

As stored ATP and CP are used, more ATP is generated by catabolism of glucose obtained from the blood or by breakdown of glycogen stored in the muscle. The initial phase of glucose respiration is **glycolysis** (gli-kol′ĭ-sis; "sugar splitting"). This pathway occurs in both the presence *and* the absence of oxygen, but because it does not *use* oxygen, it is an *anaerobic* (an-a′er-ob-ik; "without oxygen") pathway (see Figure 9.20b). During glycolysis, glucose is broken down to two *pyruvic acid* molecules, releasing enough energy to form small amounts of ATP (2 ATPs per glucose).

Ordinarily, pyruvic acid produced in glycolysis then enters the mitochondria and reacts with oxygen to produce still more ATP in the oxygen-using pathway called aerobic respiration, described shortly. But when muscles contract vigorously and contractile activity reaches about 70% of the maximum possible (e.g., running 600 meters with maximal effort), the bulging muscles compress the blood vessels within them, impairing blood flow and hence oxygen delivery. Under these anaerobic conditions, most of the pyruvic acid produced during glycolysis is converted into **lactic acid,** and the overall process is referred to as **anaerobic glycolysis.** Thus, during oxygen deficit, lactic acid is the end product of cellular metabolism of glucose. Most of the lactic acid diffuses out of the muscles into the bloodstream and is gone from the muscle tissue within 30 minutes after exercise stops. Subsequently, the lactic acid is picked up by liver, heart, or kidney cells, which can use it as an energy source. Additionally, liver cells can reconvert it to pyruvic acid or glucose and release it back into the bloodstream for muscle use, or convert it to glycogen for storage.

The anaerobic pathway harvests only about 5% as much ATP from each glucose molecule as the aerobic pathway; however, it produces ATP about 2½ times faster. Thus, when large amounts of ATP are needed for moderate periods (30–40 seconds) of strenuous muscle activity, glycolysis can provide most of the ATP needed as long as the required fuels and enzymes are available. Together, stored ATP and CP and the glycolysis–lactic acid system can support strenuous muscle activity for nearly a minute.

Although anaerobic glycolysis readily fuels spurts of vigorous exercise, it has shortcomings. Huge amounts of glucose are used to produce relatively small harvests of ATP, and the accumulating lactic acid contributes to muscle fatigue and is partially responsible for muscle soreness during intense exercise.

Aerobic Respiration

During rest and light to moderate exercise, even if prolonged, 95% of the ATP used for muscle activity comes from aerobic respiration. **Aerobic respiration** occurs in the mitochondria, requires oxygen, and involves a sequence of chemical reactions in which the bonds of fuel molecules are broken and the energy released is used to make ATP.

During aerobic respiration, which includes glycolysis and the reactions that take place in the mitochondria, glucose is broken down entirely, yielding water, carbon dioxide, and large amounts of ATP as the final products (Figure 9.20c).

Glucose + oxygen → carbon dioxide + water + ATP

The carbon dioxide released diffuses out of the muscle tissue into the blood and is removed from the body by the lungs.

As exercise begins, muscle glycogen provides most of the fuel. Shortly thereafter, bloodborne glucose, pyruvic acid from glycolysis, and free fatty acids are the major sources of fuels for oxidation. After about 30 minutes, fatty acids become the major energy fuels. Aerobic respiration provides a high yield of ATP (about 38 ATPs per glucose), but it is relatively sluggish because of its many steps and it requires continuous delivery of oxygen and nutrient fuels to keep it going.

Energy Systems Used During Sports Activities

As long as it has enough oxygen, a muscle cell will form ATP by aerobic reactions. When ATP demands are within the capacity of the aerobic pathway, light to moderate muscular activity can continue for several hours in well-conditioned individuals. However, when exercise demands begin to exceed the ability of the muscle cells to carry out the necessary reactions quickly enough, glycolysis begins to contribute more

Q *Which of these energy-producing pathways would predominate in the leg muscles of a long-distance cyclist?*

(a) Direct phosphorylation [coupled reaction of creatine phosphate (CP) and ADP]	(b) Anaerobic mechanism (glycolysis and lactic acid formation)	(c) Aerobic mechanism (aerobic cellular respiration)
Energy source: CP	Energy source: glucose	Energy source: glucose; pyruvic acid; free fatty acids from adipose tissue; amino acids from protein catabolism
Oxygen use: None Products: 1 ATP per CP, creatine Duration of energy provision: 15 s.	Oxygen use: None Products: 2 ATP per glucose, lactic acid Duration of energy provision: 30–60 s.	Oxygen use: Required Products: 38 ATP per glucose, CO_2, H_2O Duration of energy provision: Hours

FIGURE 9.20 **Methods of regenerating ATP during muscle activity.** The fastest mechanism is direct phosphorylation (**a**); the slowest is the aerobic mechanism (**c**).

and more of the total ATP generated. The length of time a muscle can continue to contract using aerobic pathways is called **aerobic endurance,** and the point at which muscle metabolism converts to anaerobic glycolysis is called **anaerobic threshold.**

Exercise physiologists have been able to estimate the relative importance of each energy-producing system to athletic performance. Activities that require a surge of power but last only a few seconds, such as weight lifting, diving, and sprinting, rely entirely on ATP and CP stores. The more on-and-off or burstlike activities of tennis, soccer, and a 100-meter swim appear to be fueled almost entirely by anaerobic glycolysis. Prolonged activities such as marathon runs and jogging, where endurance rather than power is the goal, depend mainly on aerobic respiration.

Muscle Fatigue

Muscle fatigue is a state of *physiological inability to contract* even though the muscle still may be receiving stimuli. This is quite different from *psychological,* or *central, fatigue,* in which the flesh is still able to perform but we feel tired.

Although many factors appear to contribute to fatigue, its specific causes are not fully understood. Most experimental evidence indicates that fatigue is due to a problem in excitation-contraction coupling or within the muscle cells themselves. Hence, physiological fatigue is a peripheral mechanism (rather than a central mechanism). Availability of ATP declines during contraction and a total lack of ATP results in **contractures,** states of continuous contraction because the cross bridges are unable to detach (not unlike what happens in rigor mortis). Writer's cramp is a familiar example of temporary contractures. However, ATP is not a fatigue-producing limiting factor in moderate exercise.

Although excessive intracellular accumulation of lactic acid (which causes the muscles to ache and raises H^+) alters contractile proteins, it seems to be more important in provoking central fatigue than physiological fatigue. pH is normally regulated within normal limits in all but the greatest degree of exertion. Other ionic imbalances also contribute to muscle

A (c) *The aerobic pathway.*

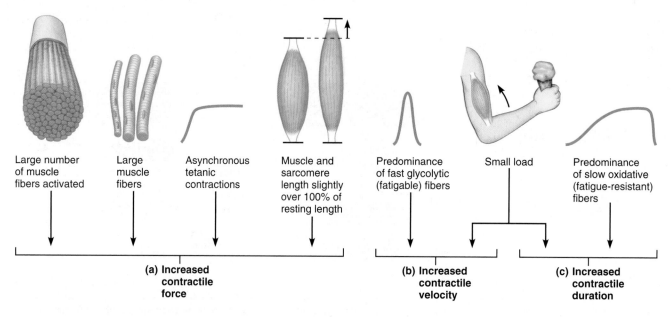

| Large number of muscle fibers activated | Large muscle fibers | Asynchronous tetanic contractions | Muscle and sarcomere length slightly over 100% of resting length | Predominance of fast glycolytic (fatigable) fibers | Small load | Predominance of slow oxidative (fatigue-resistant) fibers |

(a) Increased contractile force

(b) Increased contractile velocity

(c) Increased contractile duration

FIGURE 9.21   **Factors influencing force, velocity, and duration of skeletal muscle contraction.**

fatigue. As action potentials are transmitted, potassium is lost from the muscle cells, and the Na$^+$-K$^+$ pumps are insufficient to reverse the ionic imbalances quickly, so K$^+$ accumulates in the fluids of the T tubules. This disturbs the membrane potential of the muscle cell and halts Ca^{2+} release from the SR. Theoretically, an accumulation of inorganic phosphate (P$_i$) from CP and ATP breakdown may interfere with calcium release or alternatively with the release of P$_i$ from myosin and thus hamper myosin's power strokes.

In general, intense exercise of short duration produces fatigue rapidly via ionic disturbances that alter E-C coupling, but recovery is also rapid. In contrast to short-duration exercise, the slow-developing fatigue of prolonged low-intensity exercise may require several hours for complete recovery. It appears that this type of exercise damages the SR, interfering with Ca^{2+} regulation and release, and therefore with muscle activation.

Oxygen Debt

Whether or not fatigue occurs, vigorous exercise causes a muscle's chemistry to change dramatically. For a muscle to return to its resting state, its oxygen reserves must be replenished, the accumulated lactic acid must be reconverted to pyruvic acid, glycogen stores must be replaced, and ATP and creatine phosphate reserves must be resynthesized. Additionally, the liver must convert any lactic acid persisting in blood to glucose or glycogen. During anaerobic muscle contraction, all of these oxygen-requiring activities occur more slowly and are (at least partially) deferred until oxygen is again available. Thus, we say an *oxygen debt* is incurred, which must be repaid.

Oxygen debt is defined as the extra amount of oxygen that the body must take in for these restorative processes. It represents the difference between the amount of oxygen needed for totally aerobic muscle activity and the amount actually used. All nonaerobic sources of ATP used during muscle activity contribute to this debt.

Heat Production During Muscle Activity

Only about 40% of the energy released during muscle contraction is converted to useful work (still, this is significantly higher than that of many mechanical devices). The rest is given off as heat, which has to be dealt with if body homeostasis is to be maintained. When you exercise vigorously, you start to feel hot as your blood is warmed by the liberated heat. Ordinarily, heat buildup is prevented from reaching dangerous levels by several homeostatic mechanisms, including sweating and radiation of heat from the skin surface. Shivering represents the opposite side of homeostatic balance, in which muscle contractions are used to produce more heat.

Force of Muscle Contraction

The force of muscle contraction is affected by (1) the number of muscle fibers stimulated, (2) the relative size of the fibers, (3) frequency of stimulation, and (4) the degree of muscle stretch (Figure 9.21a). Let's briefly examine the role of each of these factors.

Number of Muscle Fibers Stimulated

As already discussed, the more motor units that are recruited, the greater the muscle force will be.

FIGURE 9.22   **Length-tension relationships in skeletal muscles.** Maximum force is generated when the muscle is between 80 and 120% of its resting length. Increases and decreases beyond this optimal range result in decreased force and inability to generate tension. Depicted here is the relative sarcomere length in a muscle that is **(a)** greatly shortened, **(b)** at normal resting length, and **(c)** excessively stretched.

Size of the Muscle Fibers Stimulated

The bulkier the muscle (the greater its cross-sectional area), the more tension it can develop and the greater its strength, but there is more to it than this. As noted earlier, the large fibers of large motor units are very effective in producing the most powerful movements. Regular exercise increases muscle force by causing muscle cells to *hypertrophy* (hi-per'tro-fe), or increase in size.

Frequency of Stimulation

As a muscle begins to contract, the force generated by the cross bridges (myofibrils)—the **internal tension**—stretches the series elastic (noncontractile) components. These in turn become taut and transfer their tension, called the **external tension,** to the load (muscle insertion), and when the contraction ends, their recoil helps to return the muscle to its resting length.

The point is that time is required to take up slack and stretch the series elastic components, and while this is happening, the internal tension is already declining. So, in brief twitch contractions, the external tension is always less than the internal tension. However, when a muscle is stimulated rapidly, contractions are summed up, becoming stronger and more vigorous and ultimately producing tetanus. During tetanic contractions more time is available to stretch the series elastic components, and external tension approaches the internal tension. So, the more rapidly a muscle is stimulated, the greater the force it exerts.

Degree of Muscle Stretch

The optimal resting length for muscle fibers is the length at which they can generate maximum force (Figures 9.21a and 9.22). Within a sarcomere, the ideal **length-tension relationship** occurs when a muscle is slightly stretched and the thin and thick filaments overlap optimally, because this permits sliding along nearly the entire length of the thin filaments. If a muscle fiber is stretched to the extent

that the filaments do not overlap (Figure 9.22c), the myosin heads have nothing to attach to and cannot generate tension. Alternatively, if the sarcomeres are so compressed and cramped that the Z discs abut the thick myofilaments, and the thin filaments touch and interfere with one another (Figure 9.22a), little or no further shortening can occur.

Identical relationships exist in a whole muscle. If you stretch a muscle to various extents and then stimulate it tetanically, the active tension the muscle can generate varies with length as shown in Figure 9.22. A severely stretched muscle (say one at 180% of its optimal length) cannot develop tension. Likewise, at 75% of a muscle's resting length, force generation (or shortening) is limited. Muscles, like muscle fibers, are at optimal operational length from about 80% to about 120% of their normal resting length. In the body, skeletal muscles are maintained near that optimum by the way they are attached to bones; that is, the joints normally prevent bone movements that would stretch attached muscles beyond their optimal range.

Velocity and Duration of Contraction

Muscles vary in how fast they can contract and in how long they can continue to contract before they fatigue. These characteristics are influenced by muscle fiber type, load, and recruitment.

Muscle Fiber Type

There are several ways of classifying muscle fibers, but learning about these classes will be easier if you initially pay attention to just two major functional characteristics:

- **Speed of contraction.** On the basis of speed of shortening, or contraction, there are **slow fibers** and **fast fibers.** The difference in their speed reflects how fast their myosin ATPases split ATP, and on the pattern of electrical activity of their motor neurons.

TABLE 9.2 **Structural and Functional Characteristics of the Three Types of Skeletal Muscle Fibers**

	SLOW OXIDATIVE FIBERS	FAST OXIDATIVE FIBERS	FAST GLYCOLYTIC FIBERS
METABOLIC CHARACTERISTICS			
Speed of contraction	Slow	Fast	Fast
Myosin ATPase activity	Slow	Fast	Fast
Primary pathway for ATP synthesis	Aerobic	Aerobic (some anaerobic glycolysis)	Anaerobic glycolysis
Myoglobin content	High	High	Low
Glycogen stores	Low	Intermediate	High
Recruitment order	First	Second	Third
Rate of fatigue	Slow (fatigue-resistant)	Intermediate (moderately fatigue-resistant)	Fast (fatigable)
ACTIVITIES BEST SUITED FOR			
	Endurance-type activities—e.g., running a marathon; maintaining posture (antigravity muscles)	Sprinting, walking	Short-term intense or powerful movements, e.g., hitting a baseball
STRUCTURAL CHARACTERISTICS			
Color	Red	Red to pink	White (pale)
Fiber diameter	Small	Intermediate	Large
Mitochondria	Many	Many	Few
Capillaries	Many	Many	Few

- **The major pathways for forming ATP.** The cells that rely mostly on the oxygen-using aerobic pathways for ATP generation are **oxidative fibers;** those that rely more on anaerobic glycolysis are **glycolytic fibers.**

On the basis of these two criteria, we can classify skeletal muscle cells as being **slow oxidative fibers, fast oxidative fibers,** or **fast glycolytic fibers.** Details about each group are given in Table 9.2, but a word to the wise: Do not approach this information by rote memorization—you'll just get frustrated. Instead, start with what you know for any category and see how the characteristics listed support that. For example, a *slow oxidative fiber*

- Contracts relatively *slowly* because its myosin ATPases are slow (a criterion)

- Depends on oxygen delivery and aerobic mechanisms (*high oxidative capacity*—a criterion)

- Is fatigue resistant and has high endurance (typical of fibers that depend on aerobic metabolism)

- Is thin (a large amount of cytoplasm impedes diffusion of O_2 and nutrients from the blood)

- Has relatively little power (a thin cell can contain only a limited number of myofibrils)

- Has many mitochondria (actual sites of oxygen use)

- Has a rich capillary supply (the better to deliver bloodborne O_2)

- Is red (its color stems from an abundant supply of myoglobin, muscle's oxygen-binding pigment that stores O_2 reserves in the cell and aids diffusion of O_2 through the cell)

Conversely, a *fast glycolytic fiber* contracts rapidly (Figure 9.21b), depends on plentiful glycogen reserves for fuel rather than on a blood-delivered glucose or fatty acids, and does not use oxygen (Table 9.2). Compared to an oxidative cell, it has few mitochondria, little myoglobin and low capillary density (and so is white), and is a much larger cell (because it doesn't depend on continuous oxygen and nutrient diffusion from the blood). Because glycogen reserves are short-lived and lactic acid accumulates quickly in these cells, they tire quickly and hence are fatigable fibers. However, their large diameter reflects their plentiful contractile myofilaments that allow them to contract powerfully before they "poop out." Thus, the fast glycolytic fibers are best suited for short-term, rapid, intense movements (moving furniture across the room, for example). Intermediate muscle fiber types, called fast oxidative fibers, have many characteristics (fiber diameter and power for example) intermediate between the other two types (Table 9.2). Like fast glycolytic fibers, they contract quickly; like slow oxidative fibers, they are oxygen dependent and have a rich supply of myoglobin and capillaries.

Although some muscles have a predominance of one fiber type, most contain a mixture of fiber types, which gives them a range of contractile speeds and fatigue resistance. For example, a calf muscle can propel us in a sprint (using mostly its white fast glycolytic fibers), or a long-distance race (making good use of its intermediate fast oxidative fibers), or may simply help maintain a standing posture (using slow oxidative fibers). As might be expected, all muscle fibers in a particular motor unit are of the same type.

Although everyone's muscles contain mixtures of the three fiber types, some people have relatively more of one variety. These differences are genetically initiated, but are modified by exercise and no doubt determine athletic capabilities (endurance versus strength) to a large extent. For example, muscles of marathon runners have a high percentage of slow oxidative fibers (about 80%), while those of sprinters contain a higher percentage (about 60%) of fast oxidative fibers. Weight lifters appear to have approximately equal amounts of both. However, fiber type interconversion of the "fast" fiber types does occur as a result of specific exercise regimes, as described below.

Load   Because muscles are attached to bones, they are always pitted against some resistance, or load, when they contract. As you might expect, they contract fastest when there is no added load on them. The greater the load, the longer the latent period, the slower the contraction, and the shorter the duration of contraction (Figure 9.23). If the load exceeds the muscle's maximum tension, the speed of shortening is zero and the contraction is isometric.

Recruitment   Just as many hands on a project can get a job done more quickly and also can keep working longer, the more motor units that are contracting, the faster and more prolonged the contraction.

Effect of Exercise on Muscles

The amount of work a muscle does is reflected in changes in the muscle itself. When used actively or strenuously, muscles may increase in size or strength or become more efficient and fatigue resistant. Muscle inactivity, on the other hand, *always* leads to muscle weakness and wasting.

Adaptations to Exercise

Aerobic, or **endurance, exercise** such as swimming, jogging, fast walking, and biking results in several recognizable changes in skeletal muscles. There is an increase in the number of capillaries surrounding the

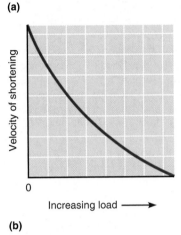

FIGURE 9.23   **Influence of load on contraction velocity and duration. (a)** Relationship of load to degree and duration of contraction (shortening). **(b)** Relationship of load to velocity of shortening. As the load increases, the velocity of shortening decreases.

muscle fibers, and in the number of mitochondria within them, and the fibers synthesize more myoglobin. These changes occur in all fiber types, but are most dramatic in slow oxidative fibers, which depend primarily on aerobic pathways. The changes result in more efficient muscle metabolism and in greater endurance, strength, and resistance to fatigue. Additionally, regular endurance exercise may convert fast glycolytic fibers into fast oxidative fibers.

The moderately weak but sustained muscle activity required for endurance exercise does not promote significant skeletal muscle hypertrophy, even though the exercise may go on for hours. Muscle hypertrophy, illustrated by the bulging biceps and chest muscles of a professional weight lifter, results mainly from high-intensity **resistance exercise** (typically under anaerobic conditions) such as weight lifting or isometric exercise, in which the muscles are pitted against high-resistance or immovable forces. Here strength, not stamina, is important; a few minutes every other day is sufficient to allow a

A CLOSER LOOK

Athletes Looking Good and Doing Better with Anabolic Steroids?

Society loves a winner and top athletes reap large social and monetary rewards. Thus, it is not surprising that some will grasp at anything that might increase their performance—including "juice" (anabolic steroids). Anabolic steroids, variants of the male sex hormone testosterone engineered by pharmaceutical companies, were introduced in the 1950s to treat anemia and certain muscle-wasting diseases and to prevent muscle atrophy in patients immobilized after surgery. Testosterone is responsible for the increase in muscle and bone mass and other physical changes that occur during puberty and converts boys into men.

Convinced that megadoses of steroids could produce enhanced masculinizing effects in grown men, many athletes and bodybuilders were using them by the early 1960s, and this is still going on. Investigations of the so-called Balco Scandal have stunned fans of major league baseball players with revelations in 2004 of rampant steroid use by Barry Bonds, of the San Francisco Giants, and others. Steroid use today is not confined to athletes. Indeed, it is estimated that nearly one in every ten young men has tried them, and the practice is also growing rapidly among young women.

It is difficult to determine the extent of anabolic steroid use because most international competitions ban the use of drugs. Users (and prescribing physicians or drug dealers) are naturally reluctant to talk about it, and users stop doping before the event, aware that evidence of drug use is hard to find a week after its use is stopped. Additionally, "underground" suppliers of performance-enhancing drugs keep producing new versions of designer steroids that evade standard antidoping tests. Indeed, the Olympic Analytical Laboratory in Los Angeles rocked the sports world in November of 2003 when it revealed that a number of elite athletes tested positive for tetrahydrogestrinone (THG), a designer steroid not previously known or

tested for. Nonetheless, there is little question that many professional bodybuilders and athletes competing in events that require muscle strength (e.g., shot put, discus throwing, and weight lifting) are heavy users. Sports figures such as football players have also admitted to using steroids as an adjunct to training, diet, and psychological preparation for games. These athletes claim that anabolic steroids enhance muscle mass and strength, and raise oxygen-carrying capability owing to greater red blood cell volume.

Typically, bodybuilders who use steroids combine high doses (up to 200 mg/day) via injection or transdermal skin patches with heavy resistance training. Intermittent use begins several months before an event, and commonly entails the use of many anabolic steroid supplements (a method called stacking). Doses are increased gradually as the competition nears.

Do the drugs do all that is claimed? Research studies report increased isometric strength and body weight in steroid users. While these are results weight lifters dream about, for runners and others requiring fine muscle coordination and endurance this may not translate into improved performance. The "jury is still out" on this question.

Do the alleged advantages of steroids outweigh their risks? Absolutely not. Physicians say they cause bloated faces (Cushingoid sign of steroid excess); acne and hair loss; shriveled testes and infertility; damage to the liver that promotes liver cancer; and changes in blood cholesterol levels that may predispose users to coronary heart disease. In addition, females can develop masculine characteristics such as smaller breasts, enlarged clitoris, excess body hair, and thinning scalp hair. The psychiatric hazards of anabolic steroid use may be equally threatening: Recent studies indicate that one-third of users suffer serious mental problems. Depression, delusions, and manic behavior—in which users undergo

Jekyll-and-Hyde personality swings and become extremely violent (termed 'roid rage)—are all common.

A more recent arrival on the scene, sold over the counter as a "nutritional performance-enhancer," is androstenedione, which is converted to testosterone in the body. Though it is taken orally (and much of it is destroyed by the liver soon after ingestion), the few milligrams that survive temporarily boost testosterone levels. Reports of its use by baseball great Mark McGwire before he retired, and of athletic wanna-bes from the fifth grade up sweeping the supplement off the drugstore shelves, are troubling, particularly since it is not regulated by the U.S. Food and Drug Administration (FDA) and its long-term effects are unpredictable and untested. A study at Massachusetts General Hospital found that males who took androstenedione developed higher levels of the female hormone estrogen as well as testosterone, raising their risk of feminizing effects such as enlarged breasts. Youths with elevated levels of estrogen or testosterone may enter puberty early, stunting bone growth and leading to shorter-than-normal adult height. Some people admit to a willingness to try almost anything to win, short of killing themselves. Are they unwittingly doing this as well? ■

proverbial weakling to put on 50% more muscle within a year. The increased muscle bulk largely reflects increases in the size of individual muscle fibers (particularly the fast glycolytic variety) rather than an increased number of muscle fibers. [However, some of the increased muscle size may result either from longitudinal splitting or tearing of the fibers and subsequent growth of these "split" cells, or from the proliferation and fusion of satellite cells (see p. 317). The controversy is still raging.] Vigorously stressed muscle fibers contain more mitochondria, form more myofilaments and myofibrils, and store more glycogen. The amount of connective tissue between the cells also increases. Collectively these changes promote significant increases in muscle strength and size. Fast oxidative fibers can be shifted to fast glycolytic fibers in response to resistance activities. However, if the specific exercise routine is discontinued, the fibers previously converted revert to their original metabolic properties.

Resistance training can produce magnificently bulging muscles, but if done unwisely, some muscles may develop more than others. Because muscles work in antagonistic pairs (or groups), opposing muscles must be equally strong to work together smoothly. When muscle training is not balanced, individuals can become *muscle-bound*, which means they lack flexibility, have a generally awkward stance, and are unable to make full use of their muscles.

Whatever the activity, exercise gains adhere to the *overload principle*. Forcing a muscle to work hard promotes increased muscle strength and endurance, and as muscles adapt to the increased demands, they must be overloaded even more to produce further gains. To become faster, you must train at an increasingly fast pace. A heavy-workout day should be followed by one of rest or an easy workout to allow the muscles to recover and repair themselves. Doing too much too soon, or ignoring the warning signs of muscle or joint pain, increases the risk of **overuse injuries** that may prevent future sports activities, or even lead to lifetime disability.

Endurance and resistance exercises produce different patterns of muscular response, so it is important to know what your exercise goals are. Lifting weights will not improve your endurance for a triathlon. By the same token, jogging will do little to improve your muscle definition or to enhance your strength for moving furniture. A program that alternates aerobic activities with anaerobic ones provides the best program for optimal health.

◤ HOMEOSTATIC IMBALANCE

To remain healthy, muscles must be active. Complete immobilization due to enforced bed rest or loss of neural stimulation results in *disuse atrophy* (degeneration and loss of mass), which begins almost as soon as the muscles are immobilized. Under such conditions, muscle strength can decrease at the rate of 5% per day!

As noted earlier, even at rest, muscles receive weak intermittent stimuli from the nervous system. When totally deprived of neural stimulation, a paralyzed muscle may atrophy to one-quarter of its initial size. Lost muscle tissue is replaced by fibrous connective tissue, making muscle rehabilitation impossible. Atrophy of a denervated muscle may be delayed by electrically stimulating the muscle periodically while waiting to see whether the damaged nerve fibers regenerate. ●

Smooth Muscle

Except for the heart, which is made of cardiac muscle, the muscle in the walls of all the body's hollow organs is almost entirely smooth muscle. Although the chemical and mechanical events of contraction are essentially the same in all muscle tissues, smooth muscle is distinctive in several ways (see Table 9.3).

Microscopic Structure of Smooth Muscle Fibers

Smooth muscle fibers are spindle-shaped cells, each with one centrally located nucleus (Figure 9.24). Typically, they have a diameter of 5–10 μm and are 30–200 μm long. Skeletal muscle fibers are some 10 times wider and thousands of times longer.

Smooth muscle lacks the coarse connective tissue sheaths seen in skeletal muscle. However, a small amount of fine connective tissue (endomysium), secreted by the smooth muscles themselves and containing blood vessels and nerves, is found between smooth muscle fibers. Most smooth muscle is organized into sheets of closely apposed fibers. These sheets occur in the walls of all but the smallest blood vessels and in the walls of hollow organs of the respiratory, digestive, urinary, and reproductive tracts. In most cases, two sheets of smooth muscle are present, with their fibers oriented at right angles to each other (Figure 9.24). In the *longitudinal layer*, the muscle fibers run parallel to the long axis of the organ. Consequently, when the muscle contracts, the organ dilates and shortens. In the *circular layer*, the fibers run around the circumference of the organ. Contraction of this layer constricts the lumen (cavity) of the organ and causes the organ to elongate. The alternating contraction and relaxation of these opposing layers mixes substances in the lumen and squeezes them through the organ's internal pathway. This phenomenon is called **peristalsis** (per"i-stal'sis; "around contraction"). Contraction of smooth muscle

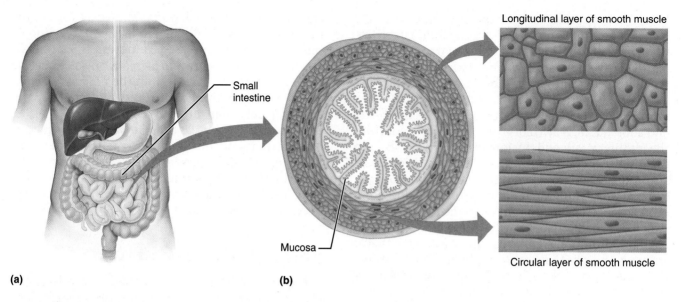

Longitudinal layer of smooth muscle

Small intestine

Mucosa

Circular layer of smooth muscle

(a) **(b)**

FIGURE 9.24 **Arrangement of smooth muscle in the walls of hollow organs.** Simplified cross-sectional view of the intestine showing two smooth muscle layers (one circular and the other longitudinal) running at right angles to each other.

in the rectum, urinary bladder, and uterus helps those organs to expel their contents. Smooth muscle contraction also accounts for the constricted breathing of asthma and for stomach cramps.

Smooth muscle lacks the highly structured, specific neuromuscular junctions of skeletal muscle. Instead, the innervating nerve fibers, which are part of the autonomic nervous system, have numerous bulbous swellings, called **varicosities** (Figure 9.25). The varicosities release neurotransmitter into a wide synaptic cleft in the general area of the smooth muscle cells. Such junctions are called **diffuse junctions.** Comparing the specificity of neural input to skeletal and smooth muscles, you could say that skeletal muscle gets priority mail while smooth muscle gets bulk mailings.

The sarcoplasmic reticulum of smooth muscle fibers is much less developed than that of skeletal muscle and lacks a specific pattern relative to the myofilaments. Some SR tubules of smooth muscle touch the sarcolemma at several sites, forming what resembles half-triads that may couple the action potential to calcium release from the SR. T tubules are notably absent, but the sarcolemma of the smooth muscle fiber has multiple caveolae, pouchlike infoldings that sequester bits of extracellular fluid containing a high concentration of Ca^{2+} close to the membrane. Consequently, when calcium channels open, Ca^{2+} influx occurs rapidly. Although the SR *does* release some of the calcium ions that trigger contraction, most gain entry via calcium channels directly from the extracellular space. Contraction ends when calcium is actively transported into the SR and out of the cell. This is quite different from what we see

in skeletal muscle, which does not depend on extracellular Ca^{2+} for excitation-contraction coupling.

There are no striations, as the name *smooth muscle* indicates, and no sarcomeres. Smooth muscle fibers *do* contain interdigitating thick and thin filaments, but they are much longer than those in skeletal muscle and the type of myosin contained differs in smooth muscle. The proportion and organization of the myofilaments are also different:

1. The ratio of thick to thin filaments is much lower in smooth muscle than in skeletal muscle (1:13 compared to 1:2). However, thick filaments of smooth muscle contain actin-gripping heads along their *entire length*, a feature that allows smooth muscle to be as powerful as a skeletal muscle of the same size.

2. As opposed to skeletal muscle, no troponin complex is present in smooth muscle.

3. Smooth muscle thick and thin filaments are arranged diagonally within the cell so that they spiral down the long axis of the cell like the stripes on a barber pole. Because of this arrangement, the smooth muscle cells contract in a twisting way so that they look like tiny corkscrews (Figure 9.26b).

4. Smooth muscle fibers contain a lattice-like arrangement of noncontractile *intermediate filaments* that resist tension. These attach at regular intervals to structures called **dense bodies.** The dense bodies, which are also tethered to the sarcolemma, act as anchoring points for thin filaments and therefore correspond to Z discs of skeletal muscle. The intermediate filament–dense body network forms a strong, cablelike intracellular cytoskeleton that harnesses the pull generated by the sliding of the thick

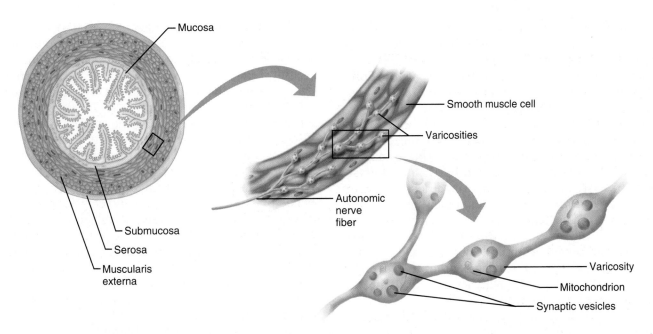

FIGURE 9.25 **Innervation of smooth muscle.** Most smooth muscle cells are innervated by autonomic nervous system fibers that release their neurotransmitters from varicosities into a wide synaptic cleft (a diffuse junction).

and thin filaments (Figure 9.26). During contraction, areas of the sarcolemma between the dense bodies bulge outward, giving the cell a puffy appearance (see Figure 9.26b). Dense bodies at the sarcolemma surface also bind the muscle cell to the connective tissue fibers outside the cell (endomysium) and to adjacent cells, an arrangement that transmits the pulling force to the surrounding connective tissue and that partly accounts for the synchronous contraction of most smooth muscle.

Contraction of Smooth Muscle

Mechanism and Characteristics of Contraction

In most cases, adjacent smooth muscle fibers exhibit slow, synchronized contractions, the whole sheet responding to a stimulus in unison. This phenomenon reflects electrical coupling of smooth muscle cells by *gap junctions*, specialized cell connections described in Chapter 3. Skeletal muscle fibers are electrically isolated from one another, each stimulated to contract by its own neuromuscular junction. By contrast, gap junctions allow smooth muscles to transmit action potentials from fiber to fiber. Some smooth muscle fibers in the stomach and small intestine are *pacemaker cells* and, once excited, act as "drummers" to set the contractile pace for the entire muscle sheet. Additionally, these pacemakers have fluctuating membrane potentials and are self-excitatory, that is, they depolarize spontaneously in the absence of external stimuli. However, both the

rate and the intensity of smooth muscle contraction may be modified by neural and chemical stimuli.

The contraction mechanism in smooth muscle is like that in skeletal muscle in the following ways: (1) actin and myosin interact by the sliding filament mechanism; (2) the final trigger for contraction is a rise in the intracellular calcium ion level; and (3) the sliding process is energized by ATP.

(a) Relaxed smooth muscle cell

(b) Contracted smooth muscle cell

FIGURE 9.26 **Intermediate filaments and dense bodies of smooth muscle fibers harness the pull generated by the activity of myosin cross bridges.** Intermediate filaments attach to dense bodies scattered throughout the sarcoplasm and occasionally anchor to the sarcolemma. **(a)** A relaxed smooth muscle cell. **(b)** A contracted smooth muscle cell. [Caveolae are not illustrated in (b).]

During excitation-contraction coupling, Ca^{2+} is released by the tubules of the SR, but, as mentioned above, it also moves into the cell from the extracellular space. By binding to troponin, calcium ions trigger myosin activity in all striated muscle types, but in smooth muscle, they activate myosin by interacting with a regulatory molecule called **calmodulin,** a cytoplasmic calcium-binding protein. Calmodulin, in turn, interacts with a kinase enzyme called **myosin kinase** or **myosin light chain kinase** which phosphorylates the myosin heads. The thin filaments lack troponin and so are always ready for contraction. The sequence of events that occurs is depicted in Figure 9.27. [Note that this is just one mechanism of smooth muscle activation. There are others. For example, in some smooth muscles, regulatory proteins associated with actin (caldesmon and others) appear to play a role as well.]

As in skeletal muscle, smooth muscle relaxes when intracellular Ca^{2+} levels drop, but getting smooth muscle to cease its contractile activity is quite a bit more complex in smooth muscle. Events known to be involved include calcium detachment from calmodulin, active transport of Ca^{2+} into the SR and the extracellular fluid, and dephosphorylation of the myosin heads by a phosphorylase enzyme, which reduces the activity of the myosin ATPases.

Smooth muscle takes 30 times longer to contract and relax than does skeletal muscle and can maintain the same contractile tension for prolonged periods at less than 1% of the energy cost. If skeletal muscle is like a speedy windup car that quickly runs down, then smooth muscle is like a steady, heavy-duty engine that lumbers along tirelessly. Part of the striking energy economy of smooth muscle is the sluggishness of its ATPases compared to those in skeletal muscle. Moreover, smooth muscle myofilaments may latch together during prolonged contractions, saving energy in that way as well. Smooth muscle cells may maintain that *latch state* even after dephosphorylation of the myosin heads.

The ATP-efficient contraction of smooth muscle is extremely important to overall body homeostasis. The smooth muscle in small arterioles and other visceral organs routinely maintains a moderate degree of contraction, called *smooth muscle tone,* day in and day out without fatiguing. Smooth muscle has low energy requirements. Typically, enough ATP is made via aerobic pathways to keep up with the demand.

Regulation of Contraction

Neural Regulation

In some cases, the activation of smooth muscle by a neural stimulus is identical to that in skeletal muscle: An action potential is generated by neurotransmitter binding, and is coupled to a rise in calcium ions in the sarcoplasm. However, some types of smooth muscle respond to neural stimulation with graded potentials (local electrical signals) only.

All somatic nerve endings, that is, nerve endings that serve skeletal muscle, release acetylcholine, which excites the skeletal muscle. However, different autonomic nerves serving the smooth muscle of visceral organs release different neurotransmitters, each of which may excite or inhibit a particular group of smooth muscle cells. The effect of a specific neurotransmitter on a given smooth muscle cell depends on the type of receptor molecules on its sarcolemma. For example, when acetylcholine binds to ACh receptors on smooth muscle in the bronchioles (small air passageways of the lungs), the muscle contracts strongly, narrowing the bronchioles. When norepinephrine, released by a different type of autonomic nerve fiber, binds to norepinephrine receptors on the *same* smooth muscle cells, the effect is inhibitory; the muscle relaxes, dilating the air passageways. However, when norepinephrine binds to smooth muscle in the walls of most blood vessels, it stimulates the smooth muscle cells to contract and constrict the vessel.

Hormones and Local Factors

Not all smooth muscle activation results from neural signals. Some smooth muscle layers have no nerve supply at all; instead they depolarize spontaneously or in response to chemical stimuli that bind to G protein–linked receptors. Others respond to both neural and chemical stimuli. Chemical factors that cause smooth muscle contraction or relaxation without an action potential (by enhancing or inhibiting Ca^{2+} entry into the sarcoplasm) include certain hormones, lack of oxygen, histamine, excess carbon dioxide, and low pH. The direct response to these chemical stimuli alters smooth muscle activity according to local tissue needs and probably is most responsible for smooth muscle tone. For example, the hormone gastrin stimulates contraction of stomach smooth muscle so that it can churn foodstuffs more efficiently. We will consider how the smooth muscle of specific organs is activated as we discuss each organ in subsequent chapters.

Special Features of Smooth Muscle Contraction

Smooth muscle is intimately involved in the functioning of most hollow organs and has a number of unique characteristics. Some of these—smooth muscle tone; slow, prolonged contractile activity; and low energy requirements—have already been considered. But smooth muscle also responds differently to stretch and can shorten more than other muscle types. Let's take a look.

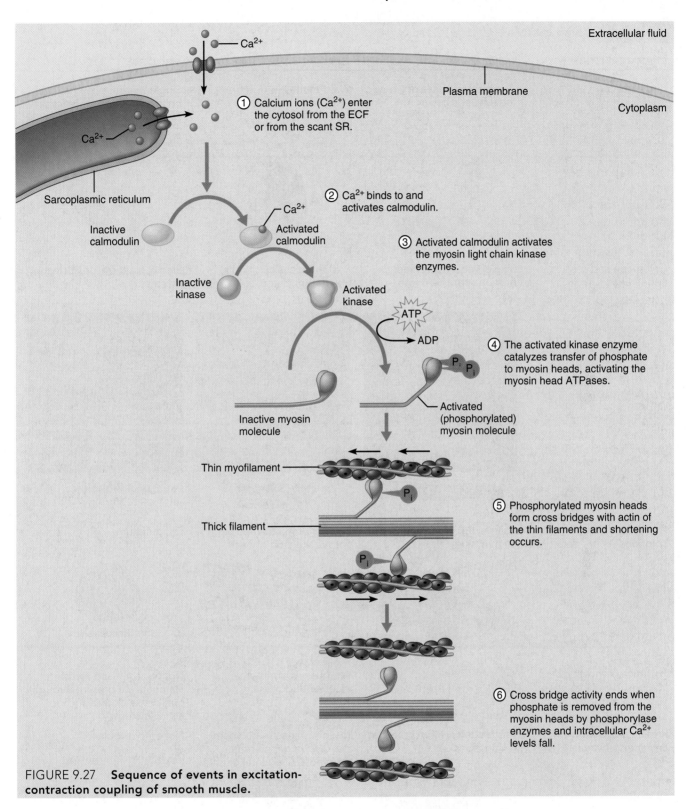

FIGURE 9.27 **Sequence of events in excitation-contraction coupling of smooth muscle.**

Within the figure:

Extracellular fluid

Ca²⁺

Plasma membrane

Cytoplasm

① Calcium ions (Ca²⁺) enter the cytosol from the ECF or from the scant SR.

Ca²⁺

Sarcoplasmic reticulum

Inactive calmodulin

Ca²⁺

Activated calmodulin

② Ca²⁺ binds to and activates calmodulin.

③ Activated calmodulin activates the myosin light chain kinase enzymes.

Inactive kinase

Activated kinase

ATP

ADP

④ The activated kinase enzyme catalyzes transfer of phosphate to myosin heads, activating the myosin head ATPases.

Pᵢ Pᵢ

Inactive myosin molecule

Activated (phosphorylated) myosin molecule

Thin myofilament

Pᵢ

Thick filament

⑤ Phosphorylated myosin heads form cross bridges with actin of the thin filaments and shortening occurs.

Pᵢ

⑥ Cross bridge activity ends when phosphate is removed from the myosin heads by phosphorylase enzymes and intracellular Ca²⁺ levels fall.

Response to Stretch When cardiac muscle is stretched, it responds with more vigorous contractions. So does skeletal muscle up to a point (about 120% of resting length). Stretching of smooth muscle also provokes contraction, which automatically moves substances along an internal tract. However, the increased tension persists only briefly; soon the muscle adapts to its new length and relaxes, while still retaining the ability to contract on demand. This **stress-relaxation response** allows a hollow organ to fill or expand slowly (within certain limits) to accommodate a greater volume without promoting

(*Text continues on p. 316.*)

TABLE 9.3 **Comparison of Skeletal, Cardiac, and Smooth Muscle**

CHARACTERISTIC	SKELETAL	CARDIAC	SMOOTH
Body location	Attached to bones or (some facial muscles) to skin	Walls of the heart	Single-unit muscle in walls of hollow visceral organs (other than the heart); multiunit muscle in intrinsic eye muscles, airways, large arteries
Cell shape and appearance	Single, very long, cylindrical, multinucleate cells with obvious striations	Branching chains of cells; uni- or binucleate; striations	Single, fusiform, uninucleate; no striations
Connective tissue components	Epimysium, perimysium, and endomysium	Endomysium attached to fibrous skeleton of heart	Endomysium
Presence of myofibrils composed of sarcomeres	Yes	Yes, but myofibrils are of irregular thickness	No, but actin and myosin filaments are present throughout; dense bodies anchor actin filaments
Presence of T tubules and site of invagination	Yes; two in each sarcomere at A-I junctions	Yes; one in each sarcomere at Z disc; larger diameter than those of skeletal muscle	No; only caveolae
Elaborate sarcoplasmic reticulum	Yes	Less than skeletal muscle (1–8% of cell volume); scant terminal cisternae	Equivalent to cardiac muscle (1–8% of cell volume); some SR contacts the sarcolemma

Epimysium — Endomysium
— Cells
— Perimysium

Endomysium

Endomysium

T tubule — SR
I band · A band · I band

Z disc

TABLE 9.3 *(continued)*			
CHARACTERISTIC	**SKELETAL**	**CARDIAC**	**SMOOTH**
Presence of gap junctions	No	Yes; at intercalated discs	Yes; in single-unit muscle
Cells exhibit individual neuromuscular junctions	Yes	No	Not in single-unit muscle; yes in multiunit muscle
Regulation of contraction	Voluntary via axon terminals of the somatic nervous system	Involuntary; intrinsic system regulation; also autonomic nervous system controls; hormones; stretch	Involuntary; autonomic nerves, hormones, local chemicals; stretch
Source of Ca^{2+} for calcium pulse	Sarcoplasmic reticulum (SR)	SR and from extracellular fluid	SR and from extracellular fluid
Site of calcium regulation	Troponin on actin-containing thin filaments	Troponin on actin-containing thin filaments	Calmodulin in the sarcoplasm
Presence of pacemaker(s)	No	Yes	Yes (in single-unit muscle only)
Effect of nervous system stimulation	Excitation	Excitation or inhibition	Excitation or inhibition
Speed of contraction	Slow to fast	Slow	Very slow
Rhythmic contraction	No	Yes	Yes in single-unit muscle
Response to stretch	Contractile strength increases with degree of stretch (to a point)	Contractile strength increases with degree of stretch	Stress-relaxation response
Respiration	Aerobic and anaerobic	Aerobic	Mainly aerobic

strong contractions that would expel their contents. This is an important attribute, because organs such as the stomach and intestines must be able to store their contents temporarily to provide sufficient time for digestion and absorption of the nutrients. Likewise, your urinary bladder must be able to store the continuously made urine until it is convenient to empty your bladder, or you would spend all your time in the bathroom.

Length and Tension Changes   Smooth muscle stretches much more than skeletal muscle and generates more tension than skeletal muscles stretched to a comparable extent. As Figure 9.22c shows, precise, highly organized sarcomeres limit how far a skeletal muscle can be stretched before it is unable to generate force. In contrast, the lack of sarcomeres and the irregular, overlapping arrangement of smooth muscle filaments allow them to generate considerable force, even when they are substantially stretched. The total length change that skeletal muscles can undergo and still function efficiently is about 60% (from 30% shorter to 30% longer than resting length), but smooth muscle can contract when it is anywhere from twice to half its resting length—a total length change of 150%. This allows hollow organs to tolerate tremendous changes in volume without becoming flabby when they empty.

Hyperplasia   Besides the ability to hypertrophy (increase in cell size), which is common to all muscle cells, certain smooth muscle fibers can divide to increase their numbers, that is, they undergo *hyperplasia* (hi"per-pla′ze-ah). One example is the response of the uterus to estrogen. At puberty, girls' plasma estrogen levels rise. As estrogen binds to uterine smooth muscle receptors, it stimulates the synthesis of more uterine smooth muscle, causing the uterus to grow to adult size. During pregnancy, high blood levels of estrogen stimulate uterine hyperplasia to accommodate the growing fetus.

Types of Smooth Muscle

The smooth muscle in different body organs varies substantially in its (1) fiber arrangement and organization, (2) responsiveness to various stimuli, and (3) innervation. For simplicity, however, smooth muscle is usually categorized into two major types: *single-unit* and *multiunit*.

Single-Unit Smooth Muscle

Single-unit smooth muscle, commonly called **visceral muscle** because it is in the walls of all hollow organs except the heart, is far more common. Its cells (1) contract rhythmically and as a unit, (2) are

electrically coupled to one another by *gap junctions*, and (3) often exhibit spontaneous action potentials. All the smooth muscle characteristics described so far pertain to single-unit smooth muscle. Thus, the cells of single-unit smooth muscle are arranged in opposing sheets, exhibit the stress-relaxation response, and so on.

In single-unit smooth muscle, contractile force is related to the amount of calcium that enters the cells during excitation-contraction coupling. Because the cells are united by gap junctions, the number of muscle fibers activated is not variable. Thus, recruitment is not an option in this type of smooth muscle.

Multiunit Smooth Muscle

The smooth muscles in the large airways to the lungs and in large arteries, the arrector pili muscles attached to hair follicles, and the internal eye muscles that adjust pupil size and allow the eye to focus visually are all examples of **multiunit smooth muscle.**

In contrast to what we see in single-unit muscle, gap junctions are rare, and spontaneous synchronous depolarizations are infrequent. Like skeletal muscle, multiunit smooth muscle

1. Consists of muscle fibers that are structurally independent of one another

2. Is richly supplied with nerve endings, each of which forms a motor unit with a number of muscle fibers

3. Responds to neural stimulation with graded contractions that involve recruitment

However, while skeletal muscle is served by the somatic (voluntary) division of the nervous system, multiunit smooth muscle (like single-unit smooth muscle) is innervated by the autonomic (involuntary) division and is also responsive to hormonal controls.

Developmental Aspects of Muscles

With rare exceptions, all muscle tissues develop from embryonic mesoderm cells called **myoblasts.** Multinucleate skeletal muscle fibers form by the fusion of several myoblasts to form multinuclear *myotubes*, a process guided by the integrins (cell adhesion proteins) forming part of the myoblast membranes. Soon functional sarcomeres are present, and skeletal muscle fibers are contracting by week 7 when the embryo is only about 1 inch long. Initially, ACh receptors "sprout" over the entire surface of the developing myoblasts. As spinal nerves invade the muscle masses, the nerve endings target individual myoblasts and release the growth factor *agrin*, which stimulates clustering and maintenance of ACh receptors at the newly forming motor end plate in each muscle fiber. Then, the nerve endings provide an independent chemical signal that disperses the receptor sites not innervated and stabilized by agrin. Electrical activity in the neurons serving the muscle fibers also plays a critical role in muscle fiber maturation. As the muscle fibers are brought under the control of the somatic nervous system, the number of fast and slow contractile fiber types is determined.

Myoblasts producing cardiac and smooth muscle cells do not fuse. However, both develop gap junctions at a very early embryonic stage. Cardiac muscle is pumping blood just 3 weeks after fertilization.

Specialized skeletal and cardiac muscle cells become amitotic early on but retain the ability to lengthen and thicken in a growing child and to hypertrophy in adults. However, *satellite cells,* myoblast-like cells associated with skeletal muscle, help repair injured fibers and allow *very limited* regeneration of dead skeletal muscle fibers. Cardiac muscle was thought to have no regenerative capability whatsoever, but recent studies suggest that cardiac cells do divide at a modest rate. Nonetheless, injured heart muscle is repaired mostly by scar tissue. Smooth muscles have a good ability to regenerate throughout life.

At birth, a baby's movements are uncoordinated and largely reflexive. Muscular development reflects the level of neuromuscular coordination, which develops in a head-to-toe and proximal-to-distal direction. In other words, a baby can lift its head before it can walk, and gross movements precede fine ones. All through childhood, our control of our skeletal muscles becomes more and more sophisticated. By midadolescence, we reach the peak of our *natural* neural control of muscles, and can either accept that level of development or improve it by athletic or other types of training.

A frequently asked question is whether the difference in strength between women and men has a biological basis. It does. Individuals vary, but on average, women's skeletal muscles make up approximately 36% of body mass, whereas men's account for about 42%. Men's greater muscular development is due primarily to the effects of testosterone on skeletal muscle, not to the effects of exercise. Body strength per unit muscle mass, however, is the same in both sexes. Strenuous muscle exercise causes more muscle enlargement in males than in females, again because of the influence of testosterone. Some athletes take large doses of synthetic male sex hormones ("steroids") to increase their muscle mass. This illegal and physiologically dangerous practice is discussed in *A Closer Look* (p. 308).

Because of its rich blood supply, skeletal muscle is amazingly resistant to infection throughout life and, given good nutrition and moderate exercise, relatively few problems afflict skeletal muscles. However, muscular dystrophy, the world's most common genetic disorder, is a serious condition that deserves more than a passing mention.

HOMEOSTATIC IMBALANCE

The term **muscular dystrophy** refers to a group of inherited muscle-destroying diseases that generally appear during childhood. The affected muscles initially enlarge due to fat and connective tissue deposit, but the muscle fibers atrophy and degenerate.

The most common and serious form is **Duchenne muscular dystrophy (DMD),** which is inherited as a sex-linked recessive disease: Females carry and transmit the abnormal gene, but it is expressed almost exclusively in males (one in every 3500 births). This tragic disease is usually diagnosed when the boy is between 2 and 7 years old. Active, normal-appearing children become clumsy and fall frequently as their skeletal muscles weaken. The disease progresses relentlessly from the extremities upward, finally affecting the head and chest muscles and cardiac muscle of the heart. Victims rarely live beyond their early 20s, dying of respiratory failure.

Recent research has pinned down the cause of DMD: The diseased muscle fibers lack *dystrophin,* a cytoplasmic protein that links the cytoskeleton to the extracellular matrix and, like a girder, helps stabilize the sarcolemma. The fragile sarcolemma of DMD patients tears during contraction allowing entry of excess Ca^{2+}. The deranged calcium homeostasis damages the contractile fibers which then breakdown, and inflammatory cells (macrophages and lymphocytes) accumulate in the surrounding connective tissue. As the regenerative capacity of the muscle is lost, and damaged cells undergo apoptosis, muscle mass drops.

There is still no cure for DMD, and thus far the only medication that has improved muscle strength and function is the steroid prednisone. One initially promising technique, *myoblast transfer therapy,* involves injecting diseased muscle with healthy myoblast cells that fuse with the unhealthy ones. The idea is that the normal gene provided would allow the fiber to produce dystrophin and so to grow normally. The therapy has shown some success in mice but human trials have been disappointing. The large size of the dystrophin gene and of human muscles presents a huge challenge to that therapy. On the other hand, injection of adeno-associated viruses carrying pared-down microdystrophin genes has produced a striking reversal of disease symptoms in dystrophic mice. A different approach being tested is coaxing dystrophic muscles to produce more *utrophin,* a similar protein present in low amounts in adults but at much higher levels in fetal muscles. In mice at least, utrophin can compensate for dystrophin deficiency. ●

MAKING CONNECTIONS

SYSTEM CONNECTIONS: Homeostatic Interrelationships Between the Muscular System and Other Body Systems

- Nervous system stimulates and regulates muscle activity

Endocrine System

- Growth hormone and androgens influence skeletal muscle strength and mass; other hormones help regulate cardiac and smooth muscle activity

Cardiovascular System

- Skeletal muscle activity increases efficiency of cardiovascular functioning; helps prevent atherosclerosis and causes cardiac hypertrophy
- Cardiovascular system delivers needed oxygen and nutrients to muscles

Lymphatic System/Immunity

- Physical exercise may enhance or depress immunity depending on its intensity
- Lymphatic vessels drain leaked tissue fluids; immune system protects muscles from disease

Respiratory System

- Muscular exercise increases respiratory capacity and efficiency of gas exchange
- Respiratory system provides oxygen and disposes of carbon dioxide

Digestive System

- Physical activity increases gastrointestinal motility and elimination when at rest
- Digestive system provides nutrients needed for muscle health; liver metabolizes lactic acid

Urinary System

- Physical activity promotes normal voiding behavior; skeletal muscle forms the voluntary sphincter of the urethra
- Urinary system disposes of nitrogenous wastes

Reproductive System

- Skeletal muscle helps support pelvic organs (e.g., uterus); assists erection of penis and clitoris
- Testicular androgen promotes increased skeletal muscle

Integumentary System

- Muscular exercise enhances circulation to skin and improves skin health
- Skin protects the muscles by external enclosure; helps dissipate heat generated by the muscles

Skeletal System

- Skeletal muscle activity maintains bone health and strength
- Bones provide levers for muscle activity

Nervous System

- Facial muscle activity allows emotions to be expressed

As we age, the amount of connective tissue in our skeletal muscles increases, the number of muscle fibers decreases, and the muscles become stringier, or more sinewy. By the age of 30 even in healthy people, a gradual loss of muscle mass, called *sarcopenia* (sar-co-pe'ne-ah), begins to occur as muscle proteins start to degrade more rapidly than they can be replaced. Just why this happens is still a question, but apparently the same regulatory molecules (transcription factors, enzymes, hormones, and others) that promote muscle growth also oversee this type of muscle atrophy. Because skeletal muscles form so much of the body mass, body weight and muscle strength decline in tandem.

THE MUSCULAR SYSTEM and Interrelationships with the Cardiovascular, Endocrine, Lymphatic/Immunity, and Skeletal Systems

Our skeletal muscles are a marvel. In the well conditioned, they ripple with energy. In those of us who are less athletic, they enable us to perform the rather remarkable tasks of moving and getting around. No one would argue that the nervous system is indispensable for activating muscles to contract and for keeping them healthy via tone. Let's look at how skeletal muscle activity affects other body systems from the vantage point of overall health and disease prevention.

Cardiovascular System

The single most important barometer of how "well" we age is the health of our cardiovascular system. More than any other factor, regular exercise helps to maintain that health. Anything that gets you huffing and puffing on a regular basis, be it racquetball or a vigorous walk, helps to keep heart muscle healthy and strong. It also keeps blood vessels clear, delaying atherosclerosis and helping to prevent the most common type of high blood pressure and hypertensive heart disease—ailments that can lead to the deterioration of heart muscle and the kidneys. Uncluttered blood vessels also stave off painful or disabling intermittent claudication in which muscle pain due to ischemia hinders walking. Furthermore, regular exercise boosts blood levels of clot-busting enzymes, helping to ward off heart attacks and strokes, other scourges of old age.

Endocrine System

Muscle has a high rate of metabolism, and even at rest it uses much more energy than does fat. Consequently, exercise that builds moderate muscle mass helps to keep weight down and prevents obesity. Obesity is one of the risk factors for development of age-related diabetes mellitus—the metabolic disorder in which body cells are unresponsive to insulin (secreted by the pancreas) and, hence, unable to utilize glucose normally. Additionally, exercise helps to maintain normal cellular responses to insulin. On the other side of the coin, several hormones, including growth hormone, thyroid hormone, and sex hormones, are essential for normal development and maturation of the skeletal muscles.

Lymphatic System/Immunity

Physical exercise has a marked effect on immunity. Moderate or mild exercise causes a temporary rise in the number of phagocytes, T cells (a particular group of white blood cells), and antibodies, all of which populate lymphatic organs and mount the attack against infectious disease. By contrast, strenuous exercise depresses the immune system. The way in which exercise affects immunity—including these seemingly contradictory observations—is still a mystery, but the so-called stress hormones are definitely involved. Like major stressors such as surgery and serious burns, strenuous exercise increases blood levels of stress hormones such as epinephrine and glucocorticoids. These hormones depress the immune system during severe stress. This is thought to be a protective mechanism—a way of preventing large numbers of slightly damaged cells from being rejected.

Skeletal System

Last but not least, weight-bearing exercise of the skeletal muscles promotes skeletal strength and helps prevent osteoporosis. Since osteoporosis severely detracts from the quality of life by increasing risk of fractures, this is an extremely important interaction. But without their bony attachments, muscles would be ineffective in causing body movement.

Muscular System

Case study: Let's continue our tale of Mrs. DeStephano's medical problems, this time looking at the notes made detailing observations of her skeletal musculature.

■ Severe lacerations of the muscles of the right leg and knee

■ Damage to the blood vessels serving the right leg and knee

■ Transection of the sciatic nerve (the large nerve serving most of the lower limb), just above the right knee

Her physician orders daily passive range-of-motion (ROM) exercise and electrical stimulation for her right leg and a diet high in protein, carbohydrates, and vitamin C.

1. Describe the step-by-step process of wound healing that will occur in her fleshy (muscle) wounds, and note the consequences of the specific restorative process that occurs.

2. What complications in healing can be anticipated owing to vascular (blood vessel) damage in the right leg?

3. What complications in muscle structure and function result from transection of the sciatic nerve? Why are passive ROM and electrical stimulation of her right leg muscles ordered?

4. Explain the reasoning behind the dietary recommendations.

(Answers in Appendix G)

Muscle strength has usually decreased by about 50% by the age of 80 years. This "flesh wasting" condition has serious health implications for the elderly, particularly because falling becomes a common event. But we don't have to slow up during old age; muscle is responsive to exercise throughout life. Regular exercise helps reverse sarcopenia, and frail elders who begin to "pump iron" (lift leg and hand weights) can rebuild muscle mass and dramatically increase their strength. Performing those lifting exercises rapidly can improve one's ability to carry out the "explosive" movements needed to rise from a chair or catch one's balance. Even moderate activity, like taking a walk daily, results in improved neuromuscular functioning and enhances independent living.

Muscles can also suffer indirectly. Aging of the cardiovascular system affects nearly every organ in the body, and muscles are no exception. As atherosclerosis takes its toll and begins to block distal arteries, a circulatory condition called *intermittent claudication* (klaw″dĭ-ka′shun; "limping") occurs in some individuals. This condition restricts blood delivery to the legs, leading to excruciating pains in the leg muscles during walking, which forces the person to stop and rest to get relief.

Smooth muscle is remarkably trouble free. The few problems that impair its functioning stem from external irritants. In the gastrointestinal tract, irritation might result from ingestion of excess alcohol, spicy foods, or bacterial infection. Under such conditions, smooth muscle motility increases in an attempt to rid the body of irritating agents, and diarrhea or vomiting occurs.

■ ■ ■

The capacity for movement is a property of all cells but, with the exception of muscle, these movements are largely restricted to intracellular events. Skeletal muscles, the major focus of this chapter, permit us to interact with our external environment in an amazing number of ways, and they also contribute to our internal homeostasis as summarized in *Making Connections* (pp. 318–319). In this chapter we have covered muscle anatomy from the gross level to the molecular level and have considered muscle physiology in some detail. Chapter 10 continues from this point to explain how muscles interact with bones and with each other, and then describes the individual skeletal muscles that make up the muscular system of the body.

Related Clinical Terms

Fibromyositis (*fibro* = fiber; *itis* = inflammation) Also known as **fibromyalgia**, a group of conditions involving chronic inflammation of a muscle, its connective tissue coverings and tendons, and capsules of nearby joints. Symptoms are nonspecific and involve varying degrees of tenderness associated with specific trigger points, as well as fatigue and frequent awakening from sleep.

Hernia Protrusion of an organ through its body cavity wall; may be congenital (owing to failure of muscle fusion during development), but most often is caused by heavy lifting or obesity and subsequent muscle weakening.

Myalgia (mi-al′je-ah; *algia* = pain) Muscle pain resulting from any muscle disorder.

Myofascial pain syndrome Pain caused by a tightened band of muscle fibers, which twitch when the skin over them is touched. Mostly associated with overused or strained postural muscles.

Myopathy (mi-op′ah-the; *path* = disease, suffering) Any disease of muscle.

Myotonic dystrophy A form of muscular dystrophy that is less common than DMD; in the U.S. it affects about 14 of 100,000 people. Symptoms include a gradual reduction in muscle mass and control of the skeletal muscles, abnormal heart rhythm, and diabetes mellitus. May appear at any time; not sex-linked. Underlying genetic defect is multiple repeats of a particular gene on chromosome 19. Because the number of repeats tends to increase from generation to generation, subsequent generations develop more severe symptoms. No effective treatment.

RICE Acronym for *rest, ice, compression*, and *elevation*, the standard treatment for a pulled muscle, or excessively stretched tendons or ligaments.

Spasm A sudden, involuntary twitch in smooth or skeletal muscle ranging in severity from merely irritating to very painful; may be due to chemical imbalances. In spasms of the eyelid or facial muscles, called tics, psychological factors have been implicated. Stretching and massaging the affected area may help to end the spasm. A cramp is a prolonged spasm; usually occurs at night or after exercise.

Strain Commonly called a "pulled muscle," a strain is excessive stretching and possible tearing of a muscle due to muscle overuse or abuse; the injured muscle becomes painfully inflamed (myositis), and adjacent joints are usually immobilized.

Tetanus (1) A state of sustained contraction of a muscle that is a normal aspect of skeletal muscle functioning. (2) An acute infectious disease caused by the anaerobic bacterium *Clostridium tetani* and resulting in persistent painful spasms of some of the skeletal muscles. Progresses to fixed rigidity of the jaws (lockjaw) and spasms of trunk and limb muscles; usually fatal due to respiratory failure.

Chapter Summary

Media study tools that could provide you additional help in reviewing specific key topics of Chapter 9 are referenced below.
IP *= InterActive Physiology*

Overview of Muscle Tissues   (pp. 280–281)

Types of Muscle Tissue   (p. 280)

1. Skeletal muscle is attached to the skeleton, is striated, and can be controlled voluntarily.

2. Cardiac muscle forms the heart, is striated, and is controlled involuntarily.

3. Smooth muscle, located chiefly in the walls of hollow organs, is controlled involuntarily. Its fibers are not striated.

Functional Characteristics of Muscle Tissue   (p. 280)

4. Special functional characteristics of muscle include excitability, contractility, extensibility, and elasticity.

Muscle Functions   (pp. 280–281)

5. Muscles move internal and external body parts, maintain posture, stabilize joints, generate heat, and protect some visceral organs.

Skeletal Muscle   (pp. 281–309)

Gross Anatomy of a Skeletal Muscle   (pp. 281–284)

1. Skeletal muscle fibers (cells) are protected and strengthened by connective tissue coverings. Deep to superficial, these are endomysium, perimysium, and epimysium.

2. Skeletal muscle attachments (origins/insertions) may be direct or indirect via tendons or aponeuroses. Indirect attachments withstand friction better.

Microscopic Anatomy of a Skeletal Muscle Fiber (pp. 284–287)

3. Skeletal muscle fibers are long, striated, and multinucleate.

4. Myofibrils are contractile elements that occupy most of the cell volume. Their banded appearance results from a regular alternation of dark (A) and light (I) bands. Myofibrils are chains of sarcomeres; each sarcomere contains thick (myosin) and thin (actin) myofilaments arranged in a regular array. The heads of myosin molecules form cross bridges that interact with the thin filaments.

5. The sarcoplasmic reticulum (SR) is a system of membranous tubules surrounding each myofibril. Its function is to release and then sequester calcium ions.

6. T tubules are invaginations of the sarcolemma that run between the terminal cisternae of the SR. They allow the electrical stimulus to be delivered quickly to deep cell regions.

Sliding Filament Model of Contraction   (pp. 287–288)

7. According to the sliding filament theory, the thin filaments are pulled toward the sarcomere centers by cross bridge (myosin head) activity of the thick filaments.

Physiology of a Skeletal Muscle Fiber   (pp. 288–294)

8. Regulation of skeletal muscle cell contraction involves (a) generation and transmission of an action potential along the sarcolemma and (b) excitation-contraction coupling.

9. An end plate potential is set up when acetylcholine released by a nerve ending binds to ACh receptors on the sarcolemma, causing changes in membrane permeability which allow ion flows that depolarize the membrane at the motor end plate. Once initiated, the action potential is self-propagating and unstoppable.

10. Current flows from the motor end plate depolarize the adjacent area of the sarcolemma, opening voltage-gated Na^+ channels which allow Na^+ influx. Then Na^+ channels close and K^+ voltage-gated channels open, repolarizing the membrane. These events generate the action potential.

11. In excitation-contraction coupling, the action potential is propagated down the T tubules, causing calcium to be released from the SR into the cell interior.

12. Sliding of the filaments is triggered by a rise in intracellular calcium ion levels. Troponin binding of calcium moves tropomyosin away from myosin binding sites on actin, allowing cross bridge binding. Myosin ATPases split ATP, which energizes the power strokes and is necessary for cross bridge detachment. Cross bridge activity ends when calcium is pumped back into the SR.

IP Muscular System; Topic: Sliding Filament Theory, pp. 18–29.

Contraction of a Skeletal Muscle   (pp. 295–300)

13. A motor unit is one motor neuron and all the muscle cells it innervates. The neuron's axon has several branches, each of which forms a neuromuscular junction with one muscle cell.

14. A motor unit's response to a single brief threshold stimulus is a twitch. A twitch has three phases: the latent period (preparatory events occurring), the period of contraction (the muscle tenses and may shorten), and the period of relaxation (muscle tension declines and the muscle resumes its resting length).

15. Graded responses of muscles to rapid stimuli are wave summation and unfused and fused tetanus. A graded response to increasingly strong stimuli is multiple motor unit summation or recruitment. The type and order of motor unit recruitment follows the size principle.

16. Isotonic contractions occur when the muscle shortens (concentric contraction) or lengthens (eccentric contraction) as the load is moved. Isometric contractions occur when muscle tension produces neither shortening nor lengthening.

IP Muscular System; Topic: Contraction of Motor Units, pp. 1–11.

Muscle Metabolism   (pp. 300–304)

17. The energy source for muscle contraction is ATP, obtained from a coupled reaction of creatine phosphate with ADP and from aerobic and anaerobic metabolism of glucose.

18. When ATP is produced by nonaerobic pathways, lactic acid accumulates and ionic imbalances disturb the membrane potential; an oxygen debt occurs. To return the muscles to their resting state, ATP must be produced aerobically and used to regenerate creatine phosphate, glycogen reserves must be restored, and accumulated lactic acid must be oxidized.

19. Only about 40% of energy released during ATP hydrolysis powers contractile activity. The rest is liberated as heat.

IP Muscular System; Topic: Muscle Metabolism, pp. 1–7.

Force of Muscle Contraction   (pp. 304–305)

20. The force of muscle contraction is affected by the number and size of contracting muscle cells (the more and the larger the cells, the greater the force), the frequency of stimulation, and the degree of muscle stretch.

21. In twitch contractions, the external tension exerted on the load is always less than the internal tension. When a muscle is tetanized, the external tension equals the internal tension.

22. When the thick and thin filaments are optimally overlapping, the muscle can generate maximum force. With excessive increase or decrease in muscle length, force declines.

Velocity and Duration of Contraction (pp. 305–307)

23. Factors determining the velocity and duration of muscle contraction include the load (the greater the load, the slower the contraction) and muscle fiber types.

24. There are three types of muscle fibers: (1) fast glycolytic (fatigable) fibers, (2) slow oxidative (fatigue-resistant) fibers, and (3) intermediate fast oxidative (fatigue-resistant) fibers. Most muscles contain a mixture of fiber types. The fast muscle fiber types are interconvertible with certain exercise regimens.

Effect of Exercise on Muscles (pp. 307–309)

25. Regular aerobic exercise results in increased efficiency, endurance, strength, and resistance to fatigue of skeletal muscles.

26. Resistance exercises cause skeletal muscle hypertrophy and large gains in skeletal muscle strength.

27. Immobilization of muscles leads to muscle weakness and severe atrophy.

28. Improper training and excessive exercise result in overuse injuries, which may be disabling.

Smooth Muscle (pp. 309–316)

Microscopic Structure of Smooth Muscle Fibers (pp. 309–311)

1. Smooth muscle fibers are spindle shaped and uninucleate; they display no striations.

2. Smooth muscle cells are most often arranged in sheets. They lack elaborate connective tissue coverings.

3. The SR is poorly developed; T tubules are absent. Actin and myosin filaments are present, but sarcomeres are not. Intermediate filaments and dense bodies form an intracellular network that harnesses the pull generated during cross bridge activity and transfers it to the extracellular matrix.

Contraction of Smooth Muscle (pp. 311–316)

4. Smooth muscle fibers may be electrically coupled by gap junctions, and the pace of contraction may be set by pacemaker cells.

5. Smooth muscle contraction is energized by ATP and is activated by a calcium pulse. However, calcium binds to calmodulin rather than to troponin (which is not present in smooth muscle fibers), and the myosin heads must be phosphorylated to become active in contraction.

6. Smooth muscle contracts for extended periods at low energy cost and without fatigue.

7. Neurotransmitters of the autonomic nervous system may inhibit or stimulate smooth muscle fibers. Smooth muscle contraction may also be initiated by pacemaker cells, hormones, or other local chemical factors that influence intracellular calcium levels, and by mechanical stretch.

8. Special features of smooth muscle contraction include the stress-relaxation response, the ability to generate large amounts of force when extensively stretched, and hyperplasia under certain conditions.

Types of Smooth Muscle (p. 316)

9. Single-unit smooth muscle has electrically coupled fibers that contract synchronously and often spontaneously.

10. Multiunit smooth muscle has independent, well-innervated fibers that lack gap junctions and pacemaker cells. Stimulation is via autonomic nerves (or hormones). Multiunit muscle contractions are rarely synchronous.

Developmental Aspects of Muscles (pp. 316–318, 320)

1. Muscle tissue develops from embryonic mesoderm cells called myoblasts. Skeletal muscle fibers are formed by the fusion of several myoblasts. Smooth and cardiac cells develop from single myoblasts and display gap junctions.

2. For the most part, specialized skeletal and cardiac muscle cells lose their ability to divide but retain the ability to hypertrophy. Smooth muscle regenerates well and undergoes hyperplasia.

3. Skeletal muscle development reflects maturation of the nervous system and occurs in cephalocaudal and proximal-to-distal directions. Peak development of natural neuromuscular control is achieved in midadolescence.

4. Women's muscles account for about 36% of their total body weight and men's for about 42%, a difference due chiefly to the effects of male hormones on skeletal muscle growth.

5. Skeletal muscle is richly vascularized and quite resistant to infection, but in old age, skeletal muscles become fibrous, decline in strength, and atrophy unless an appropriate exercise regimen is followed.

Review Questions

Multiple Choice/Matching

(Some questions have more than one correct answer. Select the best answer or answers from the choices given.)

1. The connective tissue covering that encloses the sarcolemma of an individual muscle fiber is called the (a) epimysium, (b) perimysium, (c) endomysium, (d) periosteum.

2. A fascicle is a (a) muscle, (b) bundle of muscle fibers enclosed by a connective tissue sheath, (c) bundle of myofibrils, (d) group of myofilaments.

3. Thick and thin myofilaments have different compositions. For each descriptive phrase, indicate whether the filament is (a) thick or (b) thin.

_____ **(1)** contains actin
_____ **(2)** contains ATPases
_____ **(3)** attaches to the Z disc
_____ **(4)** contains myosin
_____ **(5)** contains troponin
_____ **(6)** does not lie in the I band

4. The function of the T tubules in muscle contraction is to (a) make and store glycogen, (b) release Ca^{2+} into the cell interior and then pick it up again, (c) transmit the action potential deep into the muscle cells, (d) form proteins.

5. The sites where the motor nerve impulse is transmitted from the nerve endings to the skeletal muscle cell membranes are the (a) neuromuscular junctions, (b) sarcomeres, (c) myofilaments, (d) Z discs.

6. Contraction elicited by a single brief stimulus is called (a) a twitch, (b) wave summation, (c) multiple motor unit summation, (d) fused tetanus.

7. A smooth, sustained contraction resulting from very rapid stimulation of the muscle, in which no evidence of relaxation is seen, is called (a) a twitch, (b) wave summation, (c) multiple motor unit summation, (d) fused tetanus.

8. Characteristics of isometric contractions include all but (a) shortening, (b) increased muscle tension throughout the contraction phase, (c) absence of shortening, (d) use in resistance training.

9. During muscle contraction, ATP is provided by (a) a coupled reaction of creatine phosphate with ADP, (b) aerobic respiration of glucose, and (c) anaerobic glycolysis.

____ (1) Which provides ATP fastest?
____ (2) Which does (do) not require that oxygen be available?
____ (3) Which provides the highest yield of ATP per glucose molecule?
____ (4) Which results in the formation of lactic acid?
____ (5) Which has carbon dioxide and water products?
____ (6) Which is most important in endurance sports?

10. The neurotransmitter released by somatic motor neurons is (a) acetylcholine, (b) acetylcholinesterase, (c) norepinephrine.

11. The ions that enter the muscle cell during action potential generation are (a) calcium ions, (b) chloride ions, (c) sodium ions, (d) potassium ions.

12. Myoglobin has a special function in muscle tissue. It (a) breaks down glycogen, (b) is a contractile protein, (c) holds a reserve supply of oxygen in the muscle.

13. Aerobic exercise results in all of the following except (a) increased cardiovascular system efficiency, (b) more mitochondria in the muscle cells, (c) increased size and strength of existing muscle cells, (d) increased neuromuscular system coordination.

14. The smooth muscle type found in the walls of digestive and urinary system organs and that exhibits gap junctions and pacemaker cells is (a) multiunit, (b) single-unit.

Short Answer Essay Questions

15. Name and describe the four special functional characteristics of muscle that are the basis for muscle response.

16. Distinguish between (a) direct and indirect muscle attachments and (b) a tendon and an aponeurosis.

17. (a) Describe the structure of a sarcomere and indicate the relationship of the sarcomere to the myofilament. (b) Explain the sliding filament theory of contraction using appropriately labeled diagrams of a relaxed and a contracted sarcomere.

18. What is the importance of acetylcholinesterase in muscle cell contraction?

19. Explain how a slight (but smooth) contraction differs from a vigorous contraction of the same muscle; use the concepts of multiple motor unit summation.

20. Explain what is meant by the term excitation-contraction coupling.

21. Define motor unit.

22. Describe the three distinct types of skeletal muscle fibers.

23. True or false: Most muscles contain a predominance of one skeletal muscle fiber type. Explain the reasoning behind your choice.

24. Describe the cause(s) of muscle fatigue and define this term clearly.

25. Define oxygen debt.

26. Name four factors that influence contractile force and two that influence velocity and duration of contraction.

27. Smooth muscle has some unique properties, such as low energy usage, ability to maintain contraction over long periods, and the stress-relaxation response. Tie these properties to the function of smooth muscle in the body.

Critical Thinking and Clinical Application Questions

1. Diego was seriously out of shape the day he joined his friends for a game of touch football. While he was running pell-mell for the ball, his left calf began to hurt. He went to the clinic the next day and was told he had a strain. Diego insisted that this must be wrong, because his joints did not hurt. Clearly, Diego was confusing a *strain* with a *sprain*. Explain the difference.

2. Jim Fitch decided that his physique left much to be desired, so he joined a local health club and began to "pump iron" three times weekly. After three months of training, during which he was able to lift increasingly heavier weights, he noticed that his arm and chest muscles were substantially larger. Explain the structural and functional basis of these changes.

3. When a suicide victim was found, the coroner was unable to remove the drug vial clutched in his hand. Explain the reasons for this. If the victim had been discovered three days later, would the coroner have had the same difficulty? Explain.

4. Muscle-relaxing drugs are administered to a patient during major surgery. Which of the two chemicals described next would be a good skeletal muscle relaxant and why?
- Chemical A binds to and blocks ACh receptors of muscle cells
- Chemical B floods the muscle cells' cytoplasm with Ca^{2+}

5. When Eric returned from jogging, he was breathing heavily, sweating profusely, and complained that his legs ached and felt weak. His wife poured him a sports drink and urged him to take it easy until he could "catch his breath." On the basis of what you have learned about muscle energy metabolism, respond to the following questions.
- Why is Eric breathing heavily?
- What ATP harvesting pathway have his working muscles been using that leads to such a breathing pattern?
- What metabolic product(s) might account for his sore muscles and his feeling of muscle weakness?

LOOKING FOR MORE STUDY HELP?
A wide variety of quiz questions, tutorials, and learning exercises are available online at the Anatomy & Physiology Place (www.anatomyandphysiology.com) and, if your instructor has provided you with a MyA&P Course ID number, in MyA&P (www.myaandp.com).

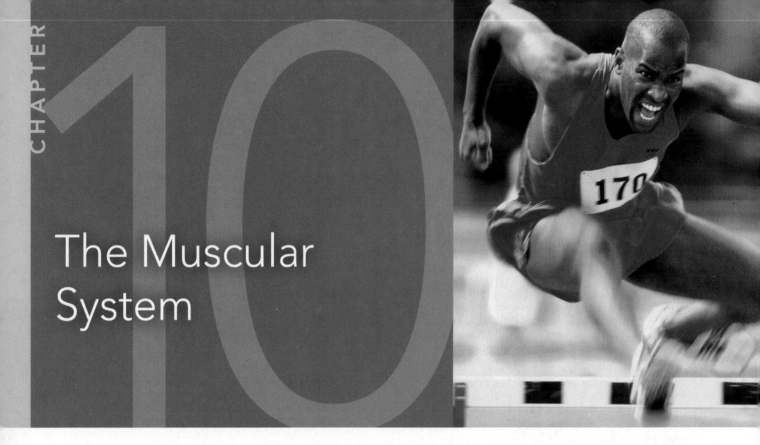

The Muscular System

10

Interactions of Skeletal Muscles in the Body (p. 325)

1. Describe the function of prime movers, antagonists, synergists, and fixators.

Naming Skeletal Muscles (pp. 325–326)

2. List the criteria used in naming muscles. Provide an example to illustrate the use of each criterion.

Muscle Mechanics: Importance of Fascicle Arrangement and Leverage (pp. 326–330)

3. Name the common patterns of muscle fascicle arrangement and relate these to power generation.

4. Define lever, and explain how a lever operating at a mechanical advantage differs from one operating at a mechanical disadvantage.

5. Name the three types of lever systems and indicate the arrangement of effort, fulcrum, and load in each. Also note the advantages of each type of lever system.

Major Skeletal Muscles of the Body (pp. 330–383)

6. Name and identify the muscles described in Tables 10.1 to 10.17. State the origin, insertion, and action of each.

The human body enjoys an incredibly wide range of movements. The gentle blinking of your eye, standing on tiptoe, and wielding a sledgehammer are just a small sample of different activities promoted by the muscular system. Although muscle tissue includes all contractile tissues (skeletal, cardiac, and smooth muscle), when we study the muscular system, **skeletal muscles** take center stage. These muscular "machines" that enable us to perform so many different activities are the focus of this chapter. Before describing the individual muscles in detail, we will describe the manner in which muscles "play" with or against each other to bring about movements, consider the criteria used for naming muscles, and explain the principles of leverage.

Interactions of Skeletal Muscles in the Body

The arrangement of body muscles permits them to work either together or in opposition to achieve a wide variety of movements. As you eat, for example, you alternately raise your fork to your lips and lower it to your plate, and both sets of actions are accomplished by your arm and hand muscles. But muscles can only *pull*; they never *push*. Generally as a muscle shortens, its *insertion* (attachment on the movable bone) moves toward its *origin* (its fixed or immovable point of attachment). Thus, whatever one muscle or muscle group can do, there is another muscle or group of muscles that "undoes" the action.

Muscles can be classified into four *functional* groups: prime movers, antagonists, synergists, and fixators. A muscle that provides the major force for producing a specific movement is a **prime mover,** or **agonist** (ag′o-nist; "leader"), of that movement. The biceps brachii muscle, which fleshes out the anterior arm (and inserts on the radius), is a prime mover of elbow flexion.

Muscles that oppose, or reverse, a particular movement are called **antagonists** (an-tag′o-nists). When a prime mover is active, the antagonist muscles are often stretched and may be relaxed. Antagonists can also help to regulate the action of a prime mover by contracting to provide some resistance, thus helping to prevent overshoot or to slow or stop the movement. As you might expect, a prime mover and its antagonist are located on opposite sides of the joint across which they act. Antagonists can also be prime movers in their own right. For example, flexion of the forearm by the biceps brachii muscle of the arm is antagonized by the triceps brachii, the prime mover for extending the forearm.

In addition to agonists and antagonists, most movements involve the action of one or more **synergists** (sin′er-jists; *syn* = together, *erg* = work).

Synergists help prime movers by (1) adding a little extra force to the same movement or (2) reducing undesirable or unnecessary movements that might occur as the prime mover contracts. This latter function deserves more explanation. When a muscle crosses two or more joints, its contraction causes movement at all of the spanned joints unless other muscles act as joint stabilizers. For example, the finger flexor muscles cross both the wrist and the phalangeal joints, but you can make a fist without bending your wrist because synergistic muscles stabilize the wrist. Additionally, as some flexors act, undesirable rotatory movements occur; synergists can prevent this, allowing all of the prime mover's force to be exerted in the desired direction.

When synergists immobilize a bone, or a muscle's origin, they are more specifically called **fixators** (fik′sa-terz). Recall from Chapter 7 that the scapula is held to the axial skeleton only by muscles and is quite freely movable. The fixator muscles that run from the axial skeleton to the scapula can immobilize the scapula so that only the desired movements occur at the mobile shoulder joint. Additionally, muscles that help to maintain upright posture are fixators.

In summary, although prime movers seem to get all the credit for causing certain movements, antagonistic and synergistic muscles are also important in producing smooth, coordinated, and precise movements. Furthermore, a muscle may act as a prime mover in one movement, an antagonist for another movement, a synergist for a third movement, and so on.

Naming Skeletal Muscles

Skeletal muscles are named according to a number of criteria, each of which describes the muscle in some way. Paying attention to these cues can simplify the task of learning muscle names and actions.

1. Location of the muscle. Some muscle names indicate the bone or body region with which the muscle is associated. For example, the temporalis (tem″por-ā′lis) muscle overlies the temporal bone, and intercostal (*costal* = rib) muscles run between the ribs.

2. Shape of the muscle. Some muscles are named for their distinctive shapes. For example, the deltoid (del′toid) muscle is roughly triangular (*deltoid* = triangle), and together the right and left trapezius (trah-pe′ze-us) muscles form a trapezoid.

3. Relative size of the muscle. Terms such as *maximus* (largest), *minimus* (smallest), *longus* (long), and *brevis* (short) are often used in muscle names—as in gluteus maximus and gluteus minimus (the large and small gluteus muscles, respectively).

4. Direction of muscle fibers. The names of some muscles reveal the direction in which their fibers (and fascicles) run in reference to some imaginary line, usually the midline of the body or the longitudinal axis of a limb bone. In muscles with the term *rectus* (straight) in their names, the fibers run parallel to that imaginary line (axis), whereas the terms *transversus* and *oblique* indicate that the muscle fibers run respectively at right angles and obliquely to that line. Specific examples include the rectus femoris (straight muscle of the thigh, or femur) and transversus abdominis (transverse muscle of the abdomen).

5. Number of origins. When *biceps*, *triceps*, or *quadriceps* forms part of a muscle's name, you can assume that the muscle has two, three, or four origins, respectively. For example, the biceps brachii (bra'ke-i) muscle of the arm has two origins, or *heads*.

6. Location of the attachments. Some muscles are named according to their points of origin and insertion. The origin is always named first. For instance, the sternocleidomastoid (ster"no-kli"do-mas'toid) muscle of the neck has a dual origin on the sternum (*sterno*) and clavicle (*cleido*), and it inserts on the *mastoid* process of the temporal bone.

7. Action. When muscles are named for their action, action words such as *flexor*, *extensor*, or *adductor* appear in the muscle's name. For example, the adductor longus, located on the medial thigh, brings about thigh adduction, and the supinator (soo'pĭ-na"tor) muscle supinates the forearm.

Often, several criteria are combined in the naming of a muscle. For instance, the name *extensor carpi radialis longus* tells us the muscle's action (extensor), what joint it acts on (*carpi* = wrist), and that it lies close to the radius of the forearm (radialis); it also hints at its size (longus) relative to other wrist extensor muscles. Unfortunately, not all muscle names are this descriptive.

Muscle Mechanics: Importance of Fascicle Arrangement and Leverage

Most factors contributing to muscle force and speed (load, fiber type, etc.) have already been covered in Chapter 9 with two important exceptions—the patterns of fascicle arrangement in muscles and lever systems. These are attended to next.

Arrangement of Fascicles

All skeletal muscles consist of fascicles, but fascicle arrangements vary, resulting in muscles with different shapes and functional capabilities. The most common patterns of fascicle arrangement are parallel, pennate, convergent, and circular (Figure 10.1).

The fascicular pattern is **circular** when the fascicles are arranged in concentric rings (Figure 10.1a). Muscles with this arrangement surround external body openings, which they close by contracting. A general term for such muscles is *sphincters* ("squeezers"). Examples are the orbicularis muscles surrounding the eyes and the mouth.

A **convergent** muscle has a broad origin, and its fascicles *converge* toward a single tendon of insertion. Such a muscle is triangular or fan shaped like the pectoralis major muscle of the anterior thorax (Figure 10.1b).

In a **parallel** arrangement, the long axes of the fascicles run parallel to the long axis of the muscle. Such muscles are either *straplike* (Figure 10.1c), or spindle shaped with an expanded belly (midsection), like the biceps brachii muscle of the arm (Figure 10.1f). However, some authorities classify the spindle-shaped muscles into a separate class as **fusiform muscles.** This is the approach used here.

In a **pennate** (pen'āt) pattern, the fascicles are short and they attach obliquely (*penna* = feather) to a central tendon that runs the length of the muscle. If, as seen in the extensor digitorum muscle of the leg, the fascicles insert into only one side of the tendon, the muscle is *unipennate* (Figure 10.1d). If the fascicles insert into the tendon from opposite sides, so that the muscle's "grain" resembles a feather, the arrangement is *bipennate* (Figure 10.1g). The rectus femoris of the thigh is bipennate. A *multipennate* arrangement looks like many feathers situated side by side, with all their quills inserted into one large tendon. The deltoid muscle, which forms the roundness of the shoulder, is multipennate (Figure 10.1e).

The arrangement of a muscle's fascicles determines its range of motion and power. Because skeletal muscle fibers shorten to about 70% of their resting length when they contract, the longer and the more nearly parallel the muscle fibers are to a muscle's long axis, the more the muscle can shorten. Muscles with parallel fascicle arrangement shorten the most, but they are not usually very powerful. Muscle power depends more on the total number of muscle cells in the muscle; the greater the number, the greater the power. The stocky bipennate and multipennate muscles, which "pack in" the most fibers, shorten very little but are very powerful.

Lever Systems: Bone-Muscle Relationships

The operation of most skeletal muscles involves the use of leverage and **lever systems** (partnerships between the *muscular* and skeletal systems). A **lever** is a rigid bar that moves on a fixed point, or **fulcrum,** when a force is applied to it. The applied force, or **effort,** is used to move a resistance, or **load.** In your

Q *Of the muscles illustrated, which could shorten most? Which two would probably be most powerful? Why?*

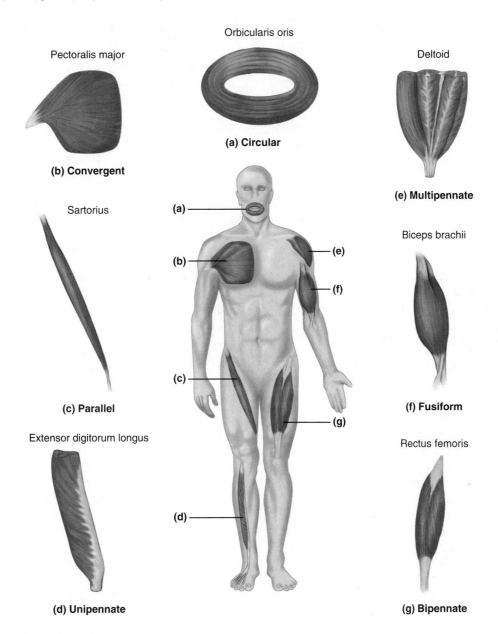

Orbicularis oris

(a) Circular

Pectoralis major

(b) Convergent

Deltoid

(e) Multipennate

Sartorius

(c) Parallel

Biceps brachii

(f) Fusiform

Extensor digitorum longus

(d) Unipennate

Rectus femoris

(g) Bipennate

FIGURE 10.1 **Relationship of fascicle arrangement to muscle structure.**

body, your joints are the fulcrums, and your bones act as levers. Muscle contraction provides the effort which is applied at the muscle's insertion point on a bone. The load is the bone itself, along with overlying tissues and anything else you are trying to move with that lever.

A *The biceps brachii and sartorius could shorten most because they have the longest fibers and fibers that run generally parallel to the long axis of the bone with which it is closely associated. The pectoralis major, deltoid, and rectus femoris would be the most powerful because they are the most fleshy.*

A lever allows a given effort to move a heavier load, or to move a load farther or faster, than it otherwise could. If, as shown in Figure 10.2a, the load is close to the fulcrum and the effort is applied far from the fulcrum, a small effort exerted over a relatively large distance can be used to move a large load over a small distance. Such a lever is said to operate at a **mechanical advantage** and is commonly called a *power lever.* For example, as shown to the right in Figure 10.2a, a person can lift a car with such a lever, in this case, a jack. The car moves up only a small distance with each downward "push" of the jack handle, but relatively little muscle effort is needed. If, on the other

Effort × length of effort arm = load × length of load arm
(force × distance) = (resistance × distance)

$10 \times 25 = 1000 \times 0.25$
$250 = 250$

(a)

$100 \times 25 = 50 \times 50$
$2500 = 2500$

(b)

FIGURE 10.2 **Lever systems operating at a mechanical advantage and a mechanical disadvantage.** The equation at the top expresses the relationships among the forces and distances in any lever system. **(a)** 10 kg of force (the effort) is used to lift a 1000-kg car (the load). This lever system, which employs a jack, operates at a mechanical advantage: The load lifted is greater than the applied muscular effort. **(b)** Using a shovel to lift dirt is an example of a lever system that operates at a mechanical disadvantage. A muscular force (effort) of 100 kg is used to lift 50 kg of dirt (the load). Levers operating at a mechanical disadvantage are common in the body.

hand, the load is far from the fulcrum and the effort is applied near the fulcrum, the force exerted by the muscle must be greater than the load moved or supported (Figure 10.2b). This lever system operates at a **mechanical disadvantage** and is a *speed lever.* These levers are useful because they provide rapid contractions with a wide range of motion. Wielding a shovel is an example. As you can see, small differences in the site of a muscle's insertion (relative to the fulcrum or joint) can translate into large differences in the amount of force a muscle must generate to move a given load or resistance. Regardless of type, all levers follow the same basic principle: effort farther than load from fulcrum = mechanical advantage; effort nearer than load to fulcrum = mechanical disadvantage.

Depending on the relative position of the three elements—effort, fulcrum, and load—a lever belongs to one of three classes. In **first-class levers,** the effort is applied at one end of the lever and the load is at the other, with the fulcrum somewhere between (Figure 10.3a). Seesaws and scissors are first-class levers. First-class leverage also occurs when you lift your head off your chest. Some first-class levers in the body operate at a mechanical advantage, but others, such as the action of the triceps muscle in extending the forearm against resistance, operate at a mechanical disadvantage.

In a **second-class lever,** the effort is applied at one end of the lever and the fulcrum is located at the

other, with the load between them (Figure 10.3b). A wheelbarrow demonstrates this type of lever system. Second-class levers are uncommon in the body; the best example is the act of standing on your toes. All second-class levers in the body work at a mechanical advantage because the muscle insertion is always farther from the fulcrum than is the load to be moved. Second-class levers are levers of strength, but speed and range of motion are sacrificed for that strength.

In **third-class levers,** the effort is applied between the load and the fulcrum (Figure 10.3c). These levers operate with great speed and *always* at a mechanical disadvantage. Tweezers or forceps provide this type of leverage. Most skeletal muscles of the body act in third-class lever systems; an example is the activity of the biceps muscle of the arm, lifting the distal forearm and anything carried in the hand. Third-class lever systems permit a muscle to be inserted very close to the joint across which movement occurs, which allows rapid, extensive movements with relatively little shortening of the muscle. Muscles involved in third-class levers tend to be thicker and more powerful.

In conclusion, differences in the positioning of the three elements modify muscle activity with respect to (1) speed of contraction, (2) range of movement, and (3) the weight of the load that can be lifted. In lever systems that operate at a mechanical disadvantage (speed levers), force is lost but speed and range of movement are gained, and this can be a

Q *Which of these lever systems as demonstrated at far left in the diagrams would be the fastest lever?*

(a) First-class lever

(b) Second-class lever

(c) Third-class lever

FIGURE 10.3 **Lever systems. (a)** In a first-class lever, the arrangement of the elements is load-fulcrum-effort. Scissors are in this lever class. In the body, a first-class lever system is activated when you raise your head off your chest. The posterior neck muscles provide the effort, the atlanto-occipital joint is the fulcrum, and the weight to be lifted is the facial skeleton. **(b)** In second-class levers, the arrangement is fulcrum-load-effort, as exemplified by a wheelbarrow. In the body, second-class leverage is exerted when you stand on tiptoe. The joints of the ball of the foot are the fulcrum, the weight of the body is the load, and the effort is exerted by the calf muscles pulling upward on the heel (calcaneus) of the foot. **(c)** In a third-class lever, the arrangement is load-effort-fulcrum. A pair of tweezers or forceps uses this type of leverage. The operation of the biceps brachii muscle in flexing the forearm exemplifies third-class leverage. The load is the hand and distal end of the forearm, the effort is exerted on the proximal radius of the forearm, and the fulcrum is the elbow joint.

A *(c) The third-class lever.*

Q *Which two muscles identified in (a) are used to do biceps curls (flex the elbow)? Which would be active during abdominal crunches (sit-ups)?*

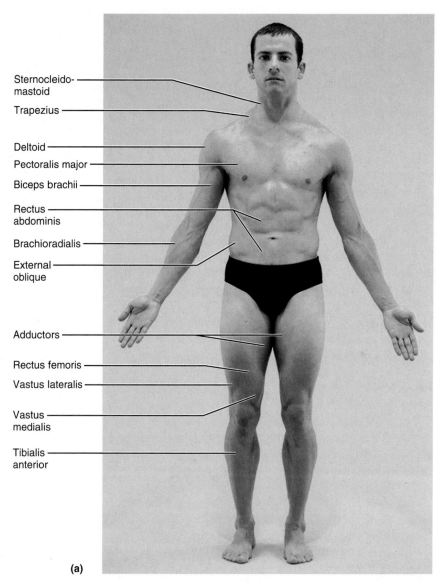

Sternocleido-
mastoid

Trapezius

Deltoid

Pectoralis major

Biceps brachii

Rectus
abdominis

Brachioradialis

External
oblique

Adductors

Rectus femoris

Vastus lateralis

Vastus
medialis

Tibialis
anterior

FIGURE 10.4 **Anterior view of superficial muscles of the body.** **(a)** Photograph of surface anatomy. **(b)** Diagrammatic view. The abdominal surface has been partially dissected on the right side to show somewhat deeper muscles. (See *A Brief Atlas of the Human Body*, Figure 33.)

(a)

distinct benefit. Systems that operate at a mechanical advantage (power levers) are slower, more stable, and used where strength is a priority.

Major Skeletal Muscles of the Body

The grand plan of the muscular system is all the more impressive because of the sheer number of skeletal muscles in the body—there are over 600 of them (many more than are shown in Figures 10.4

and 10.5 combined)! Obviously, trying to remember all the names, locations, and actions of these muscles is a monumental task. Take heart; only the principal muscles (approximately 125 pairs of them) are considered here. Although this number is far fewer than 600, the job of learning about all these muscles will still require a concerted effort on your part. Memorization will be easier if you can apply what you have learned in a practical, or clinical, way; that is, with a *functional anatomy focus*. Once you are satisfied that you have learned the name of a muscle and can identify it on a cadaver, model, or diagram, you must then flesh out your learning by asking yourself, "What does it do?" [It might be a good idea to review body movements (pp. 259–263) before you get to this point.]

A *Brachioradialis and biceps brachii would be used to do curls. The external obliques and rectus abdominis muscle would be working during crunches.*

Facial
- Epicranius, frontal belly
- Orbicularis oculi
- Zygomaticus
- Orbicularis oris

Facial
- Temporalis
- Masseter

Platysma

Shoulder
- Trapezius
- Deltoid

Arm
- Triceps brachii
- Biceps brachii
- Brachialis

Forearm
- Pronator teres
- Brachioradialis
- Flexor carpi radialis
- Palmaris longus

Pelvis/thigh
- Iliopsoas
- Pectineus

Thigh
- Rectus femoris
- Vastus lateralis
- Vastus medialis

Leg
- Fibularis longus
- Extensor digitorum longus
- Tibialis anterior

Neck
- Sternohyoid
- Sternocleidomastoid

Thorax
- Pectoralis minor
- Pectoralis major
- Serratus anterior
- Intercostals

Abdomen
- Rectus abdominis
- External oblique
- Internal oblique
- Transversus abdominis

Thigh
- Tensor fasciae latae
- Sartorius
- Adductor longus
- Gracilis

Leg
- Gastrocnemius
- Soleus

10

(b)

Q *Which muscles would you contract to shrug your shoulders? To retract your scapulae?*

10

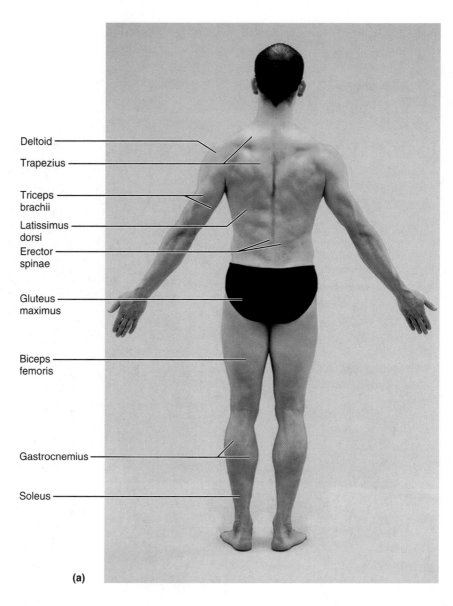

Deltoid

Trapezius

Triceps brachii

Latissimus dorsi

Erector spinae

Gluteus maximus

Biceps femoris

Gastrocnemius

Soleus

(a)

FIGURE 10.5 **Posterior view of superficial muscles of the body.** **(a)** Photograph of surface anatomy. **(b)** Diagrammatic view. (See *A Brief Atlas of the Human Body*, Figures 32, 35, and 36.)

In the tables that follow, the muscles of the body have been grouped by function and by location, roughly from head to foot. Each table is keyed to a particular figure or group of figures illustrating the muscles it describes. The legend at the beginning of each table provides an overview of the types of movements effected by the muscles listed and gives pointers on the way those muscles interact with one another. The table itself describes each muscle's shape, location relative to other muscles, origin and inser-

tion, primary actions, and innervation. (Because some instructors want students to defer learning the muscle innervations until the nervous system has been studied, you might want to check on what is expected of you in this regard.)

As you consider each muscle, be alert to the information its name provides. After reading its entire description, identify the muscle on the corresponding figure and, in the case of superficial muscles, also on Figure 10.4 or 10.5. This will help you to link the descriptive material in the table to a visual image of the muscle's location in the body. Also try to relate a muscle's attachments and location to its actions. This will focus your attention on functional

A *The trapezius. The trapezius and rhomboids.*

Neck
- Epicranius, occipital belly
- Sternocleidomastoid
- Trapezius

Shoulder
- Deltoid
- Infraspinatus
- Teres major

Rhomboid major

Latissimus dorsi

Arm
- Triceps brachii
- Brachialis

Forearm
- Brachioradialis
- Extensor carpi radialis longus
- Flexor carpi ulnaris
- Extensor carpi ulnaris
- Extensor digitorum

Hip
- Gluteus medius
- Gluteus maximus

Thigh
- Adductor magnus
- Hamstrings:
  - Biceps femoris
  - Semitendinosus
  - Semimembranosus

Iliotibial tract

Leg
- Gastrocnemius
- Soleus
- Fibularis longus
- Calcaneal (Achilles) tendon

10

(b)

details that often escape student awareness. For example, both the elbow and knee joints are hinge joints that allow flexion and extension. However, the knee flexes to the dorsum of the body (the calf moves toward the posterior thigh), whereas elbow flexion carries the forearm toward the anterior aspect of the arm. Therefore, leg flexors are located on the posterior thigh, while forearm flexors are found on the anterior aspect of the humerus.

Finally, keep in mind that the *best* way to learn muscle actions is to act out their movements yourself while feeling for the muscles contracting (bulging) beneath your skin.

The following list summarizes the organization and sequence of the tables in this chapter:

- **Table 10.1** Muscles of the Head, Part I: Facial Expression (Figure 10.6); pp. 335–337.

- **Table 10.2** Muscles of the Head, Part II: Mastication and Tongue Movement (Figure 10.7); pp. 338–339.

- **Table 10.3** Muscles of the Anterior Neck and Throat: Swallowing (Figure 10.8); pp. 340–341.

- **Table 10.4** Muscles of the Neck and Vertebral Column: Head and Trunk Movements (Figure 10.9); pp. 342–345.

- **Table 10.5** Muscles of the Thorax: Breathing (Figure 10.10); pp. 346–347.

- **Table 10.6** Muscles of the Abdominal Wall: Trunk Movements and Compression of Abdominal Viscera (Figure 10.11); pp. 348–349.

- **Table 10.7** Muscles of the Pelvic Floor and Perineum: Support of Abdominopelvic Organs (Figure 10.12); pp. 350–351.

- **Table 10.8** Superficial Muscles of the Anterior and Posterior Thorax: Movements of the Scapula (Figure 10.13); pp. 352–353.

- **Table 10.9** Muscles Crossing the Shoulder Joint: Movements of the Arm (Figure 10.14); pp. 354–356.

- **Table 10.10** Muscles Crossing the Elbow Joint: Flexion and Extension of the Forearm (Figure 10.14); p. 357.

- **Table 10.11** Muscles of the Forearm: Movements of the Wrist, Hand, and Fingers (Figures 10.15 and 10.16); pp. 358–361.

- **Table 10.12** Summary of Actions of Muscles Acting on the Arm, Forearm, and Hand (Figure 10.17); pp. 362–363.

- **Table 10.13** Intrinsic Muscles of the Hand: Fine Movements of the Fingers (Figure 10.18); pp. 364–366.

- **Table 10.14** Muscles Crossing the Hip and Knee Joints: Movements of the Thigh and Leg (Figures 10.19 and 10.20); pp. 367–372.

- **Table 10.15** Muscles of the Leg: Movements of the Ankle and Toes (Figures 10.21 to 10.23); pp. 373–378.

- **Table 10.16** Summary of Actions of Muscles Acting on the Thigh, Leg, and Foot (Figure 10.24); pp. 379–380.

- **Table 10.17** Intrinsic Muscles of the Foot: Toe Movement and Arch Support (Figure 10.25); pp. 381–383.

MUSCLE GALLERY TABLE 10.1   **Muscles of the Head, Part I: Facial Expression (Figure 10.6)**

The muscles that promote facial expression lie in the scalp and face just deep to the skin. They are thin and variable in shape and strength, and adjacent muscles tend to be fused. They are unusual muscles in that they insert into skin (or other muscles), not bones. In the scalp, the main muscle is the **epicranius,** which has distinct anterior and posterior parts; the lateral scalp muscles are vestigial in humans. Muscles clothing the facial bones lift the eyebrows, flare the nostrils, open and close the eyes and mouth, and provide one of the

best tools for influencing others—the smile. The tremendous importance of facial muscles in nonverbal communication becomes especially clear when they are paralyzed, as in some stroke victims. All muscles listed in this table are innervated by *cranial nerve VII,* the *facial nerve* (see Table 13.2). The external muscles of the eyes, which act to direct the eyeballs, and the levator palpebrae superioris muscles that raise the eyelids are described in Chapter 15.

MUSCLE	DESCRIPTION	ORIGIN (O) AND INSERTION (I)	ACTION	NERVE SUPPLY
Muscles of the Scalp				
Epicranius (occipitofrontalis) (ep″ĭ-kra′ne-us; ok-sip″ĭ-to-fron-ta′lis) (*epi* = over; *cran* = skull)	Bipartite muscle consisting of the frontal and occipital bellies connected by a cranial aponeurosis, the galea aponeurotica; the alternate actions of these two muscles pull scalp forward and backward			
▪ **Frontal belly** (fron′tal) (*front* = forehead)	Covers forehead and dome of skull; no bony attachments	O—galea aponeurotica I—skin of eyebrows and root of nose	With aponeurosis fixed, raises the eyebrows (as in surprise); wrinkles forehead skin horizontally	Facial nerve (cranial VII)
▪ **Occipital belly** (ok-sip″ĭ-tal′) (*occipito* = base of skull)	Overlies posterior occiput; by pulling on the galea, fixes origin of frontalis	O—occipital and temporal bones I—galea aponeurotica	Fixes aponeurosis and pulls scalp posteriorly	Facial nerve
Muscles of the Face				
Corrugator supercilii (kor′ah-ga-ter soo″per-sĭ′le-i) (*corrugo* = wrinkle; *supercilium* = eyebrow)	Small muscle; activity associated with that of orbicularis oculi	O—arch of frontal bone above nasal bone I—skin of eyebrow	Draws eyebrows together and inferiorly; wrinkles skin of forehead vertically (as in frowning)	Facial nerve
Orbicularis oculi (or-bik′u-lar-is ok′u-li) (*orb* = circular; *ocul* = eye)	Thin, tripartite sphincter muscle of eyelid; surrounds rim of the orbit	O—frontal and maxillary bones and ligaments around orbit I—tissue of eyelid	Protects eyes from intense light and injury; various parts can be activated individually; produces blinking, squinting, and draws eyebrows inferiorly	Facial nerve

MUSCLE GALLERY TABLE 10.1	Muscles of the Head, Part I: Facial Expression (Figure 10.6) *(continued)*			
MUSCLE	**DESCRIPTION**	**ORIGIN (O) AND INSERTION (I)**	**ACTION**	**NERVE SUPPLY**
Zygomaticus—major and minor (zi-go-mat'ĭ-kus) (*zygomatic* = cheekbone)	Muscle pair extending diagonally from cheekbone to corner of mouth	O—zygomatic bone I—skin and muscle at corner of mouth	Raises lateral corners of mouth upward (smiling muscle)	Facial nerve
Risorius (ri-zor'e-us) (*risor* = laughter)	Slender muscle inferior and lateral to zygomaticus	O—lateral fascia associated with masseter muscle I—skin at angle of mouth	Draws corner of lip laterally; tenses lips; synergist of zygomaticus	Facial nerve
Levator labii superioris (lĕ-va'tor la'be-i soo-per"e-or'is) (*leva* = raise; *labi* = lip; *superior* = above, over)	Thin muscle between orbicularis oris and inferior eye margin	O—zygomatic bone and infraorbital margin of maxilla I—skin and muscle of upper lip	Opens lips; raises and furrows the upper lip	Facial nerve
Depressor labii inferioris (de-pres'or la'be-i in-fer"e-or'is) (*depressor* = depresses; *infer* = below)	Small muscle running from mandible to lower lip	O—body of mandible lateral to its midline I—skin and muscle of lower lip	Draws lower lip inferiorly (as in a pout)	Facial nerve
Depressor anguli oris (ang'gu-li or-is) (*angul* = angle, corner; *or* = mouth)	Small muscle lateral to depressor labii inferioris	O—body of mandible below incisors I—skin and muscle at angle of mouth below insertion of zygomaticus	Zygomaticus antagonist; draws corners of mouth downward and laterally (as in a "tragedy mask" grimace)	Facial nerve
Orbicularis oris	Complicated, multilayered muscle of the lips with fibers that run in many different directions; most run circularly	O—arises indirectly from maxilla and mandible; fibers blended with fibers of other facial muscles associated with the lips I—encircles mouth; inserts into muscle and skin at angles of mouth	Closes lips; purses and protrudes lips; kissing and whistling muscle	Facial nerve
Mentalis (men-ta'lis) (*ment* = chin)	One of the muscle pair forming a V-shaped muscle mass on chin	O—mandible below incisors I—skin of chin	Protrudes lower lip; wrinkles chin	Facial nerve
Buccinator (bu'sĭ-na"ter) (*bucc* = cheek or "trumpeter")	Thin, horizontal cheek muscle; principal muscle of cheek; deep to masseter (see also Figure 10.7)	O—molar region of maxilla and mandible I—orbicularis oris	Draws corner of mouth laterally; compresses cheek (as in whistling and sucking); holds food between teeth during chewing; well developed in nursing infants	Facial nerve
Platysma (plah-tiz'mah) (*platy* = broad, flat)	Unpaired, thin, sheetlike superficial neck muscle; not strictly a head muscle, but plays a role in facial expression	O—fascia of chest (over pectoral muscles and deltoid) I—lower margin of mandible, and skin and muscle at corner of mouth	Helps depress mandible; pulls lower lip back and down, i.e., produces downward sag of mouth; tenses skin of neck (e.g., during shaving)	Facial nerve

FIGURE 10.6   Lateral view of muscles of the scalp, face, and neck.

MUSCLE GALLERY TABLE 10.2	**Muscles of the Head, Part II: Mastication and Tongue Movement (Figure 10.7)**

Four pairs of muscles are involved in mastication (chewing and biting) activities, and all are innervated by the *mandibular branch* of *cranial nerve V* (the *trigeminal nerve*). The prime movers of jaw closure (and biting) are the powerful **masseter** and **temporalis** muscles, which can be palpated easily when the teeth are clenched. Grinding movements are brought about by the **pterygoid** muscles. The **buccinator** muscles (see Table 10.1) also play a role in chewing. Normally, gravity is sufficient to depress the mandible, but if there is resistance to jaw opening, neck muscles such as the digastric and mylohyoid muscles (see Table 10.3) are activated. In 1996, researchers claimed to have discovered a tiny new muscle (not illustrated) extending from the lateral sphenoid to the medial aspect of the mandibular ramus and coronoid process. It is still uncertain whether this *sphenomandibular muscle* is a chewing muscle or actually part of the temporalis or lateral pterygoid.

The tongue is composed of muscle fibers that curl, squeeze, and fold the tongue during speaking and chewing. These **intrinsic tongue muscles,** arranged in several planes, change the shape of the tongue and contribute to its exceptional nimbleness, but they do not really move the tongue. They are considered in Chapter 23 with the digestive system. Only the **extrinsic tongue muscles,** which anchor and move the tongue, are considered in this table. All extrinsic tongue muscles are innervated by *cranial nerve XII,* the *hypoglossal nerve* (see Table 13.2).

MUSCLE	DESCRIPTION	ORIGIN (O) AND INSERTION (I)	ACTION	NERVE SUPPLY
Muscles of Mastication				
Masseter (mah-se′ter) (*maseter* = chewer)	Powerful muscle that covers lateral aspect of mandibular ramus	O—zygomatic arch and maxilla I—angle and ramus of mandible	Prime mover of jaw closure; elevates mandible	Trigeminal nerve (cranial V)
Temporalis (tem″por-ă′lis) (*tempora* = time; pertaining to the temporal bone)	Fan-shaped muscle that covers parts of the temporal, frontal, and parietal bones	O—temporal fossa I—coronoid process of mandible via a tendon that passes deep to zygomatic arch	Closes jaw; elevates and retracts mandible; synergist of pterygoids (see below) in side-to-side movements; maintains position of the mandible at rest	Trigeminal nerve
Medial pterygoid (me′de-ul ter′ĭ-goid) (*medial* = toward median plane; *pterygoid* = winglike)	Deep two-headed muscle that runs along internal surface of mandible and is largely concealed by that bone	O—medial surface of lateral pterygoid plate of sphenoid bone, maxilla, and palatine bone I—medial surface of mandible near its angle	Synergist of temporalis and masseter muscles in elevation of the mandible; acts with the lateral pterygoid muscle to protrude mandible and to promote side-to-side (grinding) movements	Trigeminal nerve
Lateral pterygoid (*lateral* = away from median plane)	Deep two-headed muscle; lies superior to medial pterygoid muscle	O—greater wing and lateral pterygoid plate of sphenoid bone I—condyle of mandible and capsule of temporomandibular joint	Protrudes mandible (pulls it anteriorly); provides forward sliding and side-to-side grinding movements of the lower teeth	Trigeminal nerve
Buccinator	See Table 10.1	See Table 10.1	Trampoline-like action of buccinator muscles helps keep food between grinding surfaces of teeth during chewing	Facial nerve (cranial VII)

MUSCLE	DESCRIPTION	ORIGIN (O) AND INSERTION (I)	ACTION	NERVE SUPPLY
Muscles Promoting Tongue Movements (Extrinsic Muscles)				
Genioglossus (je"ne-o-glah'sus) (*geni* = chin; *glossus* = tongue)	Fan-shaped muscle; forms bulk of inferior part of tongue; its attachment to mandible prevents tongue from falling backward and obstructing respiration	O—internal surface of mandible near symphysis I—inferior aspect of the tongue and body of hyoid bone	Primarily protrudes tongue, but can depress or act in concert with other extrinsic muscles to retract tongue	Hypoglossal nerve (cranial XII)
Hyoglossus (hi'o-glos"us) (*hyo* = pertaining to hyoid bone)	Flat, quadrilateral muscle	O—body and greater horn of hyoid bone I—inferolateral tongue	Depresses tongue and draws its sides downward	Hypoglossal nerve
Styloglossus (sti-lo-glah'sus) (*stylo* = pertaining to styloid process)	Slender muscle running superiorly to and at right angles to hyoglossus	O—styloid process of temporal bone I—inferolateral tongue	Retracts (and elevates) tongue	Hypoglossal nerve

(a)

(b)

FIGURE 10.7 **Muscles promoting mastication and tongue movements.**
(a) Lateral view of the temporalis, masseter, and buccinator muscles.
(b) Lateral view of the deep chewing muscles, the medial and lateral pterygoid muscles.
(c) Extrinsic muscles of the tongue. Some suprahyoid muscles of the throat are also illustrated.

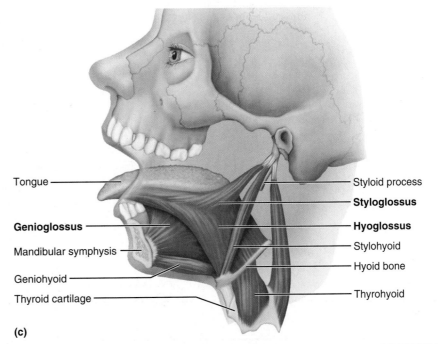

(c)

The neck is divided into two triangles (anterior and posterior) by the sternocleidomastoid muscle (Figure 10.8a). This table considers the muscles of the *anterior* triangle, which are divided into **suprahyoid** and **infrahyoid muscles** (above and below the hyoid bone respectively). Most of these muscles are deep (throat) muscles involved in swallowing.

Swallowing begins when the tongue and buccinator muscles of the cheeks squeeze the food back along the roof of the mouth toward the pharynx. Then a rapid series of muscular movements in the posterior mouth and pharynx complete the process. Events of swallowing include: (1) Widening the pharynx to receive the food, and closing the respiratory passageway (larynx) anteriorly to prevent aspiration of food, is accomplished by the *suprahyoid muscles,* which pull the hyoid bone upward and forward toward the mandible. Since the hyoid bone is attached by the thyrohyoid membrane to the larynx, the larynx is also pulled upward and forward, a maneuver that widens the pharynx and closes the respiratory passageway. (2) Closing off the nasal passages to prevent food from entering the superior nasal cavity is accomplished by small muscles that elevate the soft palate. (These muscles, the *tensor* and *levator veli palatini,* are not described in the table but are illustrated in Figure 10.8b.) (3) Food is propelled through the pharynx into the esophagus inferiorly by the **pharyngeal constrictor muscles.** (4) Returning the hyoid bone and larynx to their more inferior positions after swallowing is promoted by the *infrahyoid muscles.*

MUSCLE	DESCRIPTION	ORIGIN (O) AND INSERTION (I)	ACTION	NERVE SUPPLY
Suprahyoid Muscles (soo"prah-hi'oid)	Muscles that help form floor of oral cavity, anchor tongue, elevate hyoid, and move larynx superiorly during swallowing; lie superior to hyoid bone			
Digastric (di-gas'trik) (*di* = two; *gaster* = belly)	Consists of two bellies united by an intermediate tendon, forming a V shape under the chin	O—lower margin of mandible (anterior belly) and mastoid process of the temporal bone (posterior belly) I—by a connective tissue loop to hyoid bone	Acting in concert, the digastric muscles elevate hyoid bone and steady it during swallowing and speech; acting from behind, they open mouth and depress mandible	Mandibular branch of trigeminal nerve (cranial V) for anterior belly; facial nerve (cranial VII) for posterior belly
Stylohyoid (sti"lo-hi'oid) (also see Figure 10.7)	Slender muscle below angle of jaw; parallels posterior belly of diagastric muscle	O—styloid process of temporal bone I—hyoid bone	Elevates and retracts hyoid, thereby elongating floor of mouth during swallowing	Facial nerve
Mylohyoid (mi"lo-hi'oid) (*myle* = molar)	Flat, triangular muscle just deep to digastric muscle; this muscle pair forms a sling that forms the floor of the anterior mouth	O—medial surface of mandible I—hyoid bone and median raphe	Elevates hyoid bone and floor of mouth, enabling tongue to exert backward and upward pressure that forces food bolus into pharynx	Mandibular branch of trigeminal nerve
Geniohyoid (je'ne-o-hy"oid) (also see Figure 10.7) (*geni* = chin)	Narrow muscle in contact with its partner medially; runs from chin to hyoid bone deep to mylohyoid	O—inner surface of mandibular symphysis I—hyoid bone	Pulls hyoid bone superiorly and anteriorly, shortening floor of mouth and widening pharynx for receiving food	First cervical spinal nerve via hypoglossal nerve (cranial XII)
Infrahyoid Muscles	Straplike muscles that depress the hyoid bone and larynx during swallowing and speaking (see also Figure 10.9c)			
Sternohyoid (ster"no-hi'oid) (*sterno* = sternum)	Most medial muscle of the neck: thin; superficial except inferiorly, where covered by sternocleidomastoid	O—manubrium and medial end of clavicle I—lower margin of hyoid bone	Depresses larynx and hyoid bone if mandible is fixed; may also flex skull	Cervical spinal nerves 1–3 (C_1–C_3) through ansa cervicalis (slender nerve root in cervical plexus)
Sternothyroid (ster"no-thi'roid) (*thyro* = thyroid cartilage)	Lateral and deep to sternohyoid	O—posterior surface of manubrium of sternum I—thyroid cartilage	Pulls thyroid cartilage (plus larynx and hyoid bone) inferiorly	As for sternohyoid

10

MUSCLE	DESCRIPTION	ORIGIN (O) AND INSERTION (I)	ACTION	NERVE SUPPLY
Omohyoid (o"mo-hi'oid) (*omo* = shoulder)	Straplike muscle with two bellies united by an intermediate tendon; lateral to sternohyoid	O—superior surface of scapula I—hyoid bone, lower border	Depresses and retracts hyoid bone	As for sternohyoid
Thyrohyoid (thi"ro-hi'oid) (also see Figure 10.7)	Appears as a superior continuation of sternothyroid muscle	O—thyroid cartilage I—hyoid bone	Depresses hyoid bone and elevates larynx if hyoid is fixed	First cervical nerve via hypoglossal
Pharyngeal constrictor muscles—superior, middle, and inferior (far-rin'je-al)	Composite of three paired muscles whose fibers run circularly in pharynx wall; superior muscle is innermost and inferior one is outermost; substantial overlap	O—attached anteriorly to mandible and medial pterygoid plate (superior), hyoid bone (middle), and laryngeal cartilages (inferior) I—posterior median raphe of pharynx	Working as a group and in sequence, all constrict pharynx during swallowing, which propels a food bolus to esophagus (via a massagelike action called peristalsis)	Pharyngeal plexus [branches of vagus (X)]

10

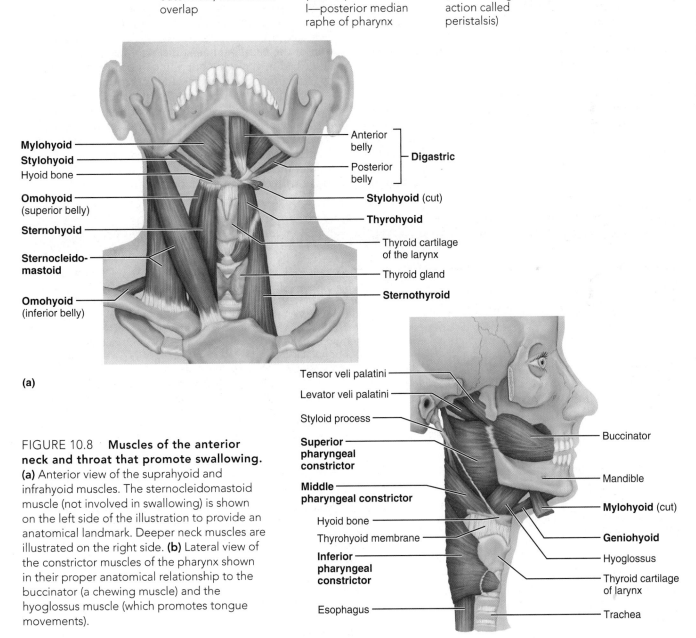

(a)

FIGURE 10.8 **Muscles of the anterior neck and throat that promote swallowing.** **(a)** Anterior view of the suprahyoid and infrahyoid muscles. The sternocleidomastoid muscle (not involved in swallowing) is shown on the left side of the illustration to provide an anatomical landmark. Deeper neck muscles are illustrated on the right side. **(b)** Lateral view of the constrictor muscles of the pharynx shown in their proper anatomical relationship to the buccinator (a chewing muscle) and the hyoglossus muscle (which promotes tongue movements).

(b)

Head movements. The head is moved by muscles originating from the axial skeleton. The major head flexors are the **sternocleidomastoid muscles,** but the suprahyoid and infrahyoid muscles described in Table 10.3 act as synergists in this action. Lateral head movements are effected by the sternocleidomastoids and a number of deeper neck muscles, including the **scalenes,** and by several straplike muscles of the vertebral column at the back of the neck. Head extension is aided by the superficial trapezius muscles of the back, but the **splenius** muscles deep to the trapezius muscles bear most of the responsibility for head extension.

Trunk movements. Trunk extension is effected by the *deep* or *intrinsic back muscles* associated with the bony vertebral column. As opposed to these deep back muscles, superficial back muscles are concerned primarily with movements of the shoulder girdle and upper limbs (see Tables 10.8 and 10.9).

The deep muscles of the back form a broad, thick column extending from the sacrum to the skull. Many muscles of varying length contribute to this mass. It helps to regard each of these individual muscles as a string that when pulled causes one or several vertebrae to extend or to rotate on the vertebrae below. The largest of the deep back muscle groups is the **erector** spinae ("spine erectors"). Since the origins and insertions of the different muscle groups overlap extensively, entire regions of the vertebral column can be moved simultaneously and smoothly. Acting in concert, the deep back muscles extend (or hyperextend) the spine, but contraction of the muscles on only one side causes lateral bending of the back, neck, or head. Lateral flexion is automatically accompanied by some degree of rotation of the vertebral column. During vertebral movements, the articular facets of the vertebrae glide on each other.

In addition to the long back muscles, a number of short muscles extend from one vertebra to the next (Figure 10.9e). These small muscles (the rotatores, multifidus, interspinales, and intertransversarii muscles) act primarily as synergists in extension and rotation of the spine and as spine stabilizers. They are not described in the table but you can deduce their actions by examining their origins and insertions in the figure.

Trunk muscles also maintain the normal curvatures of the spine, acting as postural muscles. It is these deep trunk *extensors* that are considered in this table. The more superficial muscles, which have other functions, are considered in subsequent tables. For example, the anterior muscles of the abdominal wall that cause trunk *flexion* are described in Table 10.6.

MUSCLE	DESCRIPTION	ORIGIN (O) AND INSERTION (I)	ACTION	NERVE SUPPLY
Anterolateral Neck Muscles (Figure 10.9a and c)				
Sternocleidomastoid (ster"no-kli"do-mas'toid) (*sterno* = breastbone; *cleido* = clavicle; *mastoid* = mastoid process)	Two-headed muscle located deep to platysma on anterolateral surface of neck; fleshy parts on either side of neck delineate limits of anterior and posterior triangles; key muscular landmark in neck; spasms of one of these muscles may cause torticollis (wryneck)	O—manubrium of sternum and medial portion of clavicle I—mastoid process of temporal bone and superior nuchal line of occipital bone	Prime mover of active head flexion; simultaneous contraction of both muscles causes neck flexion, generally against resistance as when one raises head when lying on back; acting alone, each muscle rotates head toward shoulder on opposite side and tilts or laterally flexes head to its own side	Accessory nerve (cranial nerve XI) and branches of cervical spinal nerves C_2 and C_3 (ventral rami)
Scalenes (ska'lēnz)— anterior, middle, and posterior (*scalene* = uneven)	Located more laterally than anteriorly on neck; deep to platysma and sternocleidomastoid	O—transverse processes of cervical vertebrae I—anterolaterally on first two ribs	Elevate first two ribs (aid in inspiration); flex and rotate neck	Cervical spinal nerves

MUSCLE GALLERY TABLE 10.4 (continued)

MUSCLE	DESCRIPTION	ORIGIN (O) AND INSERTION (I)	ACTION	NERVE SUPPLY
Intrinsic Muscles of the Back (Figure 10.9b, d, e)				
Splenius (sple'ne-us)—capitis and cervicis portions (kah-pit'us; ser-vis'us) (*splenion* = bandage; *caput* = head; *cervi* = neck) (Figures 10.9b and 10.6)	Broad bipartite superficial muscle (capitis and cervicis parts) extending from upper thoracic vertebrae to skull; capitis portion known as "bandage muscle" because it covers and holds down deeper neck muscles	O—ligamentum nuchae,* spinous processes of vertebrae C_7–T_6 I—mastoid process of temporal bone and occipital bone (capitis); transverse processes of C_2–C_4 vertebrae (cervicis)	Act as a group to extend or hyperextend head; when splenius muscles on one side are activated, head is rotated and bent laterally toward same side	Cervical spinal nerves (dorsal rami)

(a) Anterior

(b) Posterior

FIGURE 10.9 **Muscles of the neck and vertebral column causing movements of the head and trunk. (a)** Muscles of the anterolateral neck. The superficial platysma muscle and the deeper neck muscles have been removed to show the origins and insertions of the sternocleidomastoid and scalene muscles. **(b)** Deep muscles of the posterior neck; superficial muscles have been removed. **(c)** Photograph of the anterior and lateral regions of the neck. (*Figure continues on p. 345.*)

(c)

*The ligamentum nuchae (lig"ah-men'tum noo'ke) is a strong, elastic ligament extending from the occipital bone of the skull along the tips of the spinous processes of the cervical vertebrae. It binds the cervical vertebrae together and inhibits excessive head and neck flexion, thus preventing damage to the spinal cord in the vertebral canal.

10

MUSCLE GALLERY TABLE 10.4	Muscles of the Neck and Vertebral Column: Head and Trunk Movements (Figure 10.9) *(continued)*			
MUSCLE	**DESCRIPTION**	**ORIGIN (O) AND INSERTION (I)**	**ACTION**	**NERVE SUPPLY**
Erector spinae (e-rek'tor spi'ne) Also called **sacrospinalis** (Figure 10.9d, left side)	Prime mover of back extension. Each side consists of three columns—the iliocostalis, longissimus, and spinalis muscles—forming intermediate layer of intrinsic back muscles. Erector spinae provide resistance that helps control action of bending forward at the waist and act as powerful extensors to promote return to erect position. During full flexion (i.e., when touching fingertips to floor), erector spinae are relaxed and strain is borne entirely by ligaments of back; on reversal of the movement, these muscles are initially inactive, and extension is initiated by hamstring muscles of thighs and gluteus maximus muscles of buttocks. As a result of this peculiarity, lifting a load or moving suddenly from a bent-over position is potentially dangerous (in terms of possible injury) to muscles and ligaments of back and intervertebral discs; erector spinae muscles readily go into painful spasms following injury to back structures.			
▪ **Iliocostalis** (il"e-o-kos-tă'lis)— lumborum, thoracis, and cervicis portions (lum'bor-um; tho-ra'sis) (*ilio* = ilium; *cost* = rib; *thorac* = thorax)	Most lateral muscle group of erector spinae muscles; extend from pelvis to neck	O—iliac crests (lumborum); inferior 6 ribs (thoracis); ribs 3 to 6 (cervicis) I—angles of ribs (lumborum and thoracis); transverse processes of cervical vertebrae C_6–C_4 (cervicis)	Extend vertebral column, maintain erect posture; acting on one side, bend vertebral column to same side	Spinal nerves (dorsal rami)
▪ **Longissimus** (lon-jis'ĭ-mus)— thoracis, cervicis, and capitis parts (*longissimus* = longest)	Intermediate tripartite muscle group of erector spinae; extend by many muscle slips from lumbar region to skull; mainly pass between transverse processes of the vertebrae	O—transverse processes of lumbar through cervical vertebrae I—transverse processes of thoracic or cervical vertebrae and to ribs superior to origin as indicated by name; capitis inserts into mastoid process of temporal bone	Thoracis and cervicis act together to extend vertebral column and acting on one side, bend it laterally; capitis extends head and turns the face toward same side	Spinal nerves (dorsal rami)
▪ **Spinalis** (spi-nă'lis)— thoracis and cervicis parts (*spin* = vertebral column, spine)	Most medial muscle column of erector spinae; cervicis usually rudimentary and poorly defined	O—spines of upper lumbar and lower thoracic vertebrae I—spines of upper thoracic and cervical vertebrae	Extends vertebral column	Spinal nerves (dorsal rami)
Semispinalis (sem'e-spĭ-nă'lis)— thoracis, cervicis, and capitis regions (*semi* = half) (Figure 10.9d, right side)	Composite muscle forming part of deep layer of intrinsic back muscles; extends from thoracic region to head	O—transverse processes of C_7–T_{12} I—occipital bone (capitis) and spinous processes of cervical (cervicis) and thoracic vertebrae T_1–T_4 (thoracis)	Extends vertebral column and head and rotates them to opposite side; acts synergistically with sternocleidomastoid muscles of opposite side	Spinal nerves (dorsal rami)
Quadratus lumborum (kwod-ra'tus lum-bor'um) (*quad* = four-sided; *lumb* = lumbar region) (See also Figure 10.19a)	Fleshy muscle forming part of posterior abdominal wall	O—iliac crest and lumbar fascia I—transverse processes of upper lumbar vertebrae and lower margin of 12th rib	Flexes vertebral column laterally when acting separately; when pair acts jointly, lumbar spine is extended and 12th rib is fixed; maintains upright posture; assists in forced inspiration	T_{12} and upper lumbar spinal nerves (ventral rami)

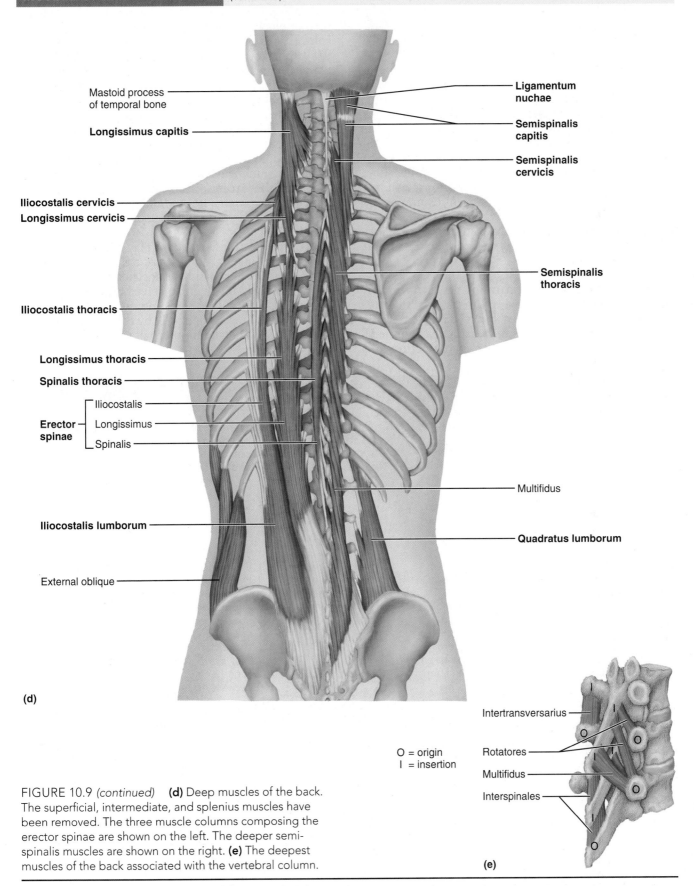

Mastoid process
of temporal bone

Longissimus capitis

**Ligamentum
nuchae**

**Semispinalis
capitis**

**Semispinalis
cervicis**

Iliocostalis cervicis

Longissimus cervicis

**Semispinalis
thoracis**

Iliocostalis thoracis

Longissimus thoracis

Spinalis thoracis

**Erector
spinae** — Iliocostalis

Longissimus

Spinalis

Multifidus

Iliocostalis lumborum

Quadratus lumborum

External oblique

(d)

O = origin
I = insertion

Intertransversarius

Rotatores

Multifidus

Interspinales

FIGURE 10.9 *(continued)*   **(d)** Deep muscles of the back.
The superficial, intermediate, and splenius muscles have
been removed. The three muscle columns composing the
erector spinae are shown on the left. The deeper semispinalis muscles are shown on the right. **(e)** The deepest
muscles of the back associated with the vertebral column.

(e)

10

The primary function of the deep muscles of the thorax is to promote movements necessary for breathing. Breathing consists of two phases—inspiration, or inhaling, and expiration, or exhaling—caused by cyclic changes in the volume of the thoracic cavity.

Two main layers of muscles help form the anterolateral wall of the thorax. The thoracic muscles are very short, most extending only from one rib to the next. On contraction, they draw the somewhat flexible ribs closer together. The **external intercostal muscles,** considered inspiratory muscles, form the more superficial layer. They lift the rib cage, an action that increases the anterior to posterior and side-to-side dimensions of the thorax. The **internal intercostal muscles** form the deeper layer and aid active (forced) expiration by depressing the rib cage. (However, quiet expiration is largely a passive phenomenon, resulting from relaxation of the external intercostals and diaphragm and elastic recoil of the lungs.)

The **diaphragm,** the most important muscle of inspiration, forms a muscular partition between the thoracic and abdominopelvic cavities. In the relaxed state, the diaphragm is dome shaped, but when it contracts it moves inferiorly and flattens, increasing the volume of the thoracic cavity. The alternating contraction and relaxation of the diaphragm causes pressure changes in the abdominopelvic cavity below that facilitate the return of blood to the heart. In addition to its rhythmic contractions during respiration, one can also contract the diaphragm voluntarily to push down on the abdominal viscera and increase the pressure in the abdominal cavity to help evacuate pelvic organ contents (urine, feces, or a baby) or during weight lifting. When one takes a deep breath to fix the diaphragm, the abdomen becomes a firm pillar that will not buckle under the weight being lifted. Needless to say, it is important to have good control of the bladder and anal sphincters during such maneuvers.

With the exception of the diaphragm, which is served by the *phrenic nerves,* the muscles listed in this table are served by the *intercostal nerves,* which run between the ribs.

Forced breathing calls into play a number of other muscles that insert into the ribs; e.g., during forced inspiration the scalene and sternocleidomastoid muscles of the neck help lift the ribs. Forced expiration is aided by muscles that pull the ribs inferiorly and those that push the diaphragm superiorly by compressing the abdominal contents (abdominal wall muscles).

MUSCLE	DESCRIPTION	ORIGIN (O) AND INSERTION (I)	ACTION	NERVE SUPPLY
External intercostals (in"ter-kos'talz) (*external* = toward the outside; *inter* = between; *cost* = rib)	11 pairs lie between ribs; fibers run obliquely (down and forward) from each rib to rib below; in lower intercostal spaces, fibers are continuous with external oblique muscle, forming part of abdominal wall	O—inferior border of rib above I—superior border of rib below	With first ribs fixed by scalene muscles, pull ribs toward one another to elevate rib cage; aid in inspiration; synergists of diaphragm	Intercostal nerves
Internal intercostals (*internal* = toward the inside, deep)	11 pairs lie between ribs; fibers run deep to and at right angles to those of external intercostals (i.e., run downward and posteriorly); lower internal intercostal muscles are continuous with fibers of internal oblique muscle of abdominal wall	O—superior border of rib below I—inferior border (costal groove) of rib above	With 12th ribs fixed by quadratus lumborum, muscles of posterior abdominal wall, and oblique muscles of the abdominal wall, they draw ribs together and depress rib cage; aid in forced expiration; antagonistic to external intercostals	Intercostal nerves
Diaphragm (di'ah-fram) (*dia* = across; *phragm* = partition)	Broad muscle pierced by the aorta, inferior vena cava, and esophagus, forms floor of thoracic cavity; in relaxed state is dome shaped; fibers converge from margins of thoracic cage toward a boomerang-shaped central tendon	O—inferior, internal surface of rib cage and sternum, costal cartilages of last six ribs and lumbar vertebrae I—central tendon	Prime mover of inspiration; flattens on contraction, increasing vertical dimensions of thorax; when strongly contracted, dramatically increases intra-abdominal pressure	Phrenic nerves

FIGURE 10.10 **Muscles of respiration. (a)** Deep muscles of the thorax. The external intercostals (inspiratory muscles) are shown on the left and the internal intercostals (expiratory muscles) are shown on the right. These two muscle layers run obliquely and at right angles to each other. **(b)** Inferior view of the diaphragm, the prime mover of inspiration. Notice that its muscle fibers converge toward a central tendon, an arrangement that causes the diaphragm to flatten and move inferiorly as it contracts. **(c)** Photograph of the diaphragm, superior view. (See *A Brief Atlas of the Human Body,* Figure 63.)

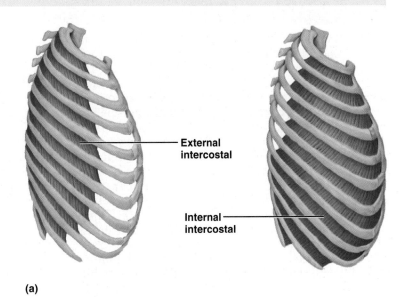

External intercostal

Internal intercostal

(a)

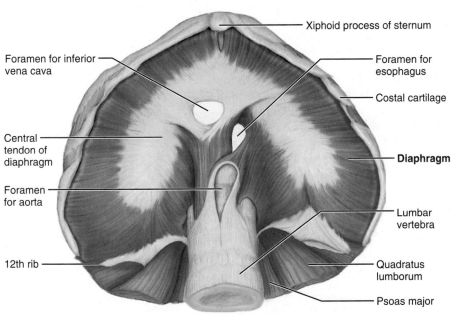

Xiphoid process of sternum

Foramen for inferior vena cava

Foramen for esophagus

Costal cartilage

Central tendon of diaphragm

Diaphragm

Foramen for aorta

Lumbar vertebra

12th rib

Quadratus lumborum

Psoas major

(b)

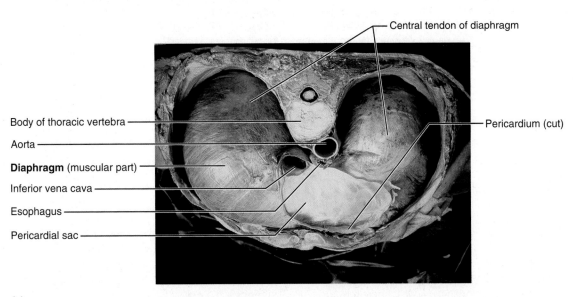

Central tendon of diaphragm

Body of thoracic vertebra

Aorta

Diaphragm (muscular part)

Inferior vena cava

Esophagus

Pericardial sac

Pericardium (cut)

(c)

Unlike the thorax, the anterior and lateral abdominal wall has no bony reinforcements (ribs). Instead, it is a composite of four paired muscles, their investing fasciae, and aponeuroses. Three broad flat muscle pairs, layered one atop the next, form the lateral abdominal walls: The fibers of the **external oblique muscle** run inferomedially and at right angles to those of the **internal oblique,** which immediately underlies it. The fibers of the deep **transversus abdominis muscle** run horizontally across the abdomen at an angle to both. This alternation of fascicle directions is similar to the construction of plywood (which is made of sheets with different grains) and provides great strength. These three muscles blend into broad insertion aponeuroses anteriorly. The aponeuroses, in turn, enclose a fourth muscle pair medially, the straplike **rectus abdominis muscles,** and then fuse, forming the **linea alba** ("white line"), a tendinous raphe (seam) that runs from the sternum to the pubic symphysis. Enclosure of the rectus abdominis muscles within the aponeuroses prevents them from "bowstringing" (protruding anteriorly). The quadratus lumborum muscles of the *posterior* abdominal wall are covered in Table 10.4.

The abdominal muscles protect and support the viscera most effectively when they are well toned. When weak or severely stretched (as during pregnancy), they allow the abdomen to become pendulous (i.e., to form a potbelly). Additional functions include lateral flexion and rotation of the trunk and anterior flexion of the trunk against resistance (as in sit-ups). During inspiration, the abdominal muscles relax, allowing the abdominal viscera to be pushed inferiorly by the descending diaphragm. When all these abdominal muscles contract in unison, several different activities may be effected. For example, when they contract simultaneously, the ribs are pulled inferiorly and the abdominal contents compressed. This pushes the visceral organs upward on the diaphragm, aiding forced expiration. When the abdominal muscles contract with the diaphragm and the glottis is closed (an action called the Valsalva maneuver), the increased intra-abdominal pressure helps to promote urination, defecation, childbirth, vomiting, coughing, screaming, sneezing, burping, and nose blowing. (Next time you perform one of these activities, feel your abdominal muscles contract under your skin.) These muscles also contract during heavy lifting—sometimes so forcefully that hernias result. Contraction of the abdominal muscles along with contraction of the deep back muscles helps prevent hyperextension of the spine and splints the entire body trunk.

MUSCLE	DESCRIPTION	ORIGIN (O) AND INSERTION (I)	ACTION	NERVE SUPPLY
Muscles of the Anterior and Lateral Abdominal Wall				
Rectus abdominis (rek'tus ab-dom' ĭ-nis) (*rectus* = straight; *abdom* = abdomen)	Medial superficial muscle pair; extend from pubis to rib cage; ensheathed by aponeuroses of lateral muscles; segmented by 3 tendinous intersections	O—pubic crest and symphysis I—xiphoid process and costal cartilages of ribs 5–7	Flex and rotate lumbar region of vertebral column; fix and depress ribs, stabilize pelvis during walking, increase intra-abdominal pressure; used in sit-ups, curls	Intercostal nerves (T_6 or T_7–T_{12})
External oblique (o-blēk') (*external* = toward outside; *oblique* = running at an angle)	Largest and most superficial of the three lateral muscles; fibers run downward and medially (same direction outstretched fingers take when hands put into pants pockets); aponeurosis turns under inferiorly, forming inguinal ligament	O—by fleshy strips from outer surfaces of lower eight ribs I—most fibers insert anteriorly via a broad aponeurosis into linea alba; some into pubic crest and tubercle and iliac crest	When pair contract simultaneously, aid rectus abdominis muscles in flexing vertebral column and in compressing abdominal wall and increasing intra-abdominal pressure; acting individually, aid muscles of back in trunk rotation and lateral flexion; used in oblique curls	Intercostal nerves (T_7–T_{12})
Internal oblique (*internal* = toward the inside; deep)	Most fibers run upward and medially; however, the muscle fans so its inferior fibers run downward and medially	O—lumbar fascia, iliac crest, and inguinal ligament I—linea alba, pubic crest, last three or four ribs, and costal margin	As for external oblique	Intercostal nerves (T_7–T_{12}) and L_1
Transversus abdominis (trans-ver'sus) (*transverse* = running straight across)	Deepest (innermost) muscle of abdominal wall; fibers run horizontally	O—inguinal ligament, lumbar fascia, cartilages of last six ribs; iliac crest I—linea alba, pubic crest	Compresses abdominal contents	Intercostal nerves (T_7–T_{12}) and L_1

FIGURE 10.11   Muscles of the abdominal wall. (a) Anterior view of the muscles forming the anterolateral abdominal wall. The superficial muscles have been partially cut away to reveal the deeper muscles. **(b)** Lateral view of the trunk, illustrating the fiber direction and attachments of the external and internal obliques, and transversus abdominis muscles. Although shown in the same view, the rectus abdominis is deep to the fascia of the internal oblique muscle. **(c)** Transverse section through the anterolateral abdominal wall (midregion), showing how the aponeuroses of the lateral abdominal muscles contribute to the rectus abdominis sheath.

Muscles of the Pelvic Floor and Perineum: Support of Abdominopelvic Organs (Figure 10.12)

Two paired muscles, the **levator ani** and **coccygeus**, form the funnel-shaped pelvic floor, or **pelvic diaphragm.** These muscles (1) seal the inferior outlet of the pelvis, (2) support the pelvic floor and elevate it to release feces, and (3) resist increased intra-abdominal pressure (which would expel contents of the bladder, rectum, and uterus). The pelvic diaphragm is pierced by the rectum and urethra (urinary tube), and by the vagina in females. The body region inferior to the pelvic diaphragm is the *perineum*. The relationships of the perineum are worth explaining. Inferior to the muscles of the pelvic floor, and stretching between the two sides of the pubic arch in the anterior half of the perineum, is

the **urogenital diaphragm.** This thin triangular sheet of muscle contains the **external urethral sphincter,** a sphincter muscle that surrounds the urethra and allows voluntary control of urination. Superficial to the urogenital diaphragm, and covered by the skin of the perineum, is the *superficial space*, which contains muscles (**ischiocavernosus** and **bulbospongiosus**) that help maintain erection of the penis and clitoris. In the posterior half of the perineum encircling the anus is the **external anal sphincter,** which allows voluntary control of defecation. Just anterior to this sphincter is the **central tendon of the perineum,** a strong tendon into which many of the perineal muscles insert.

MUSCLE	DESCRIPTION	ORIGIN (O) AND INSERTION (I)	ACTION	NERVE SUPPLY
Muscles of the Pelvic Diaphragm (Figure 10.12a)				
Levator ani (lĕ-va′tor a′ne) (*levator* = raises; *ani* = anus)	Broad, thin, tripartite muscle (pubococcygeus, puborectalis, and iliococcygeus parts); its fibers extend inferomedially, forming a muscular "sling" around male prostate (or female vagina), urethra, and anorectal junction before meeting in the median plane	O—extensive linear origin inside pelvis from pubis to ischial spine I—inner surface of coccyx, levator ani of opposite side, and (in part) into the structures that penetrate it	Supports and maintains position of pelvic viscera; resists downward thrusts that accompany rises in intrapelvic pressure during coughing, vomiting, and expulsive efforts of abdominal muscles; forms sphincters at anorectal junction and vagina; lifts anal canal during defecation	S_4 and inferior rectal nerve (branch of pudendal nerve)
Coccygeus (kok-sij′e-us) (*coccy* = coccyx)	Small triangular muscle lying posterior to levator ani; forms posterior part of pelvic diaphragm	O—spine of ischium I—sacrum and coccyx	Supports pelvic viscera; supports coccyx and pulls it forward after it has been reflected posteriorly by defecation and childbirth	S_4 and S_5
Muscles of the Urogenital Diaphragm (Figure 10.12b)				
Deep transverse perineal muscle (per″ĭ-ne′al) (*deep* = far from surface; *transverse* = across; *perine* = near anus)	Together the pair spans distance between ischial rami; in females, lies posterior to vagina	O—ischial rami I—midline central tendon of perineum; some fibers into vaginal wall in females	Supports pelvic organs; steadies central tendon	Pudendal nerve
External urethral sphincter (*sphin* = squeeze)	Muscle encircling urethra and vagina (female)	O—ischiopubic rami I—midline raphe	Constricts urethra; helps support pelvic organs	Pudendal nerve
Muscles of the Superficial Space (Figure 10.12c)				
Ischiocavernosus (is′ke-o-kav′ern-o′sus) (*ischi* = hip; *caverna* = hollow chamber)	Runs from pelvis to base of penis or clitoris	O—ischial tuberosities I—crus of corpus cavernosa of male penis or female clitoris	Retards venous drainage and maintains erection of penis or clitoris	Pudendal nerve
Bulbospongiosus (bul″bo-spun″je-o′sus) (*bulbon* = bulb; *spongio* = sponge)	Encloses base of penis (bulb) in males and lies deep to labia in females	O—central tendon of perineum and midline raphe of penis I—anteriorly into corpus cavernosa of penis or clitoris	Empties male urethra; assists in erection of penis and of clitoris	Pudendal nerve
Superficial transverse perineal muscles (*superficial* = closer to surface)	Paired muscle bands posterior to urethral (and in females, vaginal) opening; variable; sometimes absent	O—ischial tuberosity I—central tendon of perineum	Stabilizes and strengthens midline tendon of perineum	Pudendal nerve

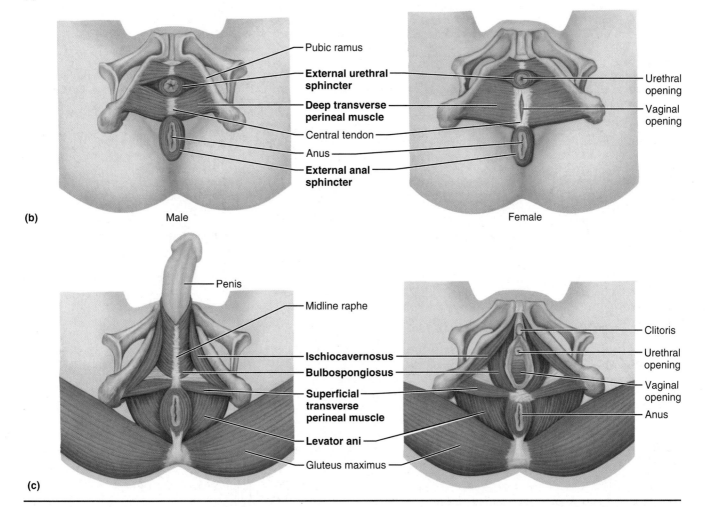

FIGURE 10.12 **Muscles of the pelvic floor and perineum.** **(a)** Superior view of muscles of the pelvic diaphragm (levator ani and coccygeus) in a female pelvis. **(b)** Inferior view of muscles of the urogenital diaphragm of the perineum (external urethral sphincter and deep transverse perineus). **(c)** Inferior view of muscles of the superficial space of the perineum (ischiocavernosus, bulbospongiosus, and superficial transverse perineal muscle), which lie just deep to the skin of the perineum. Note that a raphe is a seam of fibrous tissue.

(a) panel labels:
Anterior
Levator ani — Pubococcygeus, Iliococcygeus
Symphysis pubis
Urogenital diaphragm
Urethra
Vagina
Anal canal
Obturator internus
Coccyx
Piriformis
Coccygeus
Levator ani — **Pelvic diaphragm**
Posterior

(b) panel labels:
Pubic ramus
External urethral sphincter
Deep transverse perineal muscle
Central tendon
Anus
External anal sphincter
Urethral opening
Vaginal opening
Male
Female

(c) panel labels:
Penis
Midline raphe
Ischiocavernosus
Bulbospongiosus
Superficial transverse perineal muscle
Levator ani
Gluteus maximus
Clitoris
Urethral opening
Vaginal opening
Anus

Most superficial thorax muscles are *extrinsic shoulder muscles*, which run from the ribs and vertebral column to the shoulder girdle. They fix the scapula to the wall of the thorax; they also move it to increase the range of arm movements. The muscles of the anterior thorax include the **pectoralis major, pectoralis minor, serratus anterior,** and **subclavius.** Except for the pectoralis major, which inserts into the humerus, all muscles of the anterior group insert into the pectoral girdle. Extrinsic muscles of the posterior thorax include the **latissimus dorsi** and **trapezius muscles** superficially and the underlying **levator scapulae** and **rhomboids.** The latissimus dorsi, like the pectoralis major muscles anteriorly, insert into the humerus and are more concerned with movements of the arm than of the scapula. We will defer consideration of these two muscle pairs to Table 10.9 (arm-moving muscles).

The important movements of the pectoral girdle involve displacements of the scapula, i.e., its elevation and depression, rotation, lateral (forward) movements, and medial (backward) movements. The clavicles rotate around their own axes to provide both stability and precision to scapular movements.

Except for the serratus anterior, the anterior muscles stabilize and depress the shoulder girdle. Thus, most scapular movements are promoted by the serratus anterior muscles anteriorly and by posterior muscles. The arrangement of muscle attachments to the scapula is such that one muscle cannot bring about a simple (linear) movement on its own. To effect scapular movements, several muscles must act in combination.

The prime movers of shoulder elevation are the trapezius and levator scapulae. When acting together to shrug the shoulder, their opposite rotational effects counterbalance each other. The scapula is depressed largely by gravity (weight of the arm), but when it is depressed against resistance, the trapezius and serratus anterior (along with the latissimus dorsi, Table 10.9) are active. Forward movements (abduction) of the scapula on the thorax wall, as in pushing or punching movements, mainly reflect serratus anterior activity. Retraction (adduction) of the scapula is effected by the trapezius and rhomboids. Although the serratus anterior and trapezius muscles are antagonists in forward/backward movements of the scapulae, they act together to coordinate *rotational* scapular movements.

MUSCLE	DESCRIPTION	ORIGIN (O) AND INSERTION (I)	ACTION	NERVE SUPPLY
Muscles of the Anterior Thorax (Figure 10.13a)				
Pectoralis minor (pek"to-ra'lis mi'nor) (*pectus* = chest, breast; *minor* = lesser)	Flat, thin muscle directly beneath and obscured by pectoralis major	O—anterior surfaces of ribs 3–5 (or 2–4) I—coracoid process of scapula	With ribs fixed, draws scapula forward and downward; with scapula fixed, draws rib cage superiorly	Medial and lateral pectoral nerves $(C_6–C_8)$
Serratus anterior (ser-a'tus) (*serratus* = saw)	Fan-shaped muscle; lies deep to scapula, beneath and inferior to pectoral muscles on lateral rib cage; forms medial wall of axilla; origins have serrated, or sawtooth, appearance; paralysis results in "winging" of vertebral border of scapula away from chest wall, making arm elevation impossible	O—by a series of muscle slips from ribs 1–8 (or 9) I—entire anterior surface of vertebral border of scapula	Prime mover to protract and hold scapula against chest wall; rotates scapula so that its inferior angle moves laterally and upward; raises point of shoulder; important role in abduction and raising of arm and in horizontal arm movements (pushing, punching); called "boxer's muscle"	Long thoracic nerve $(C_5–C_7)$
Subclavius (sub-kla've-us) (*sub* = under, beneath; *clav* = clavicle)	Small cylindrical muscle extending from rib 1 to clavicle	O—costal cartilage of rib 1 I—groove on inferior surface of clavicle	Helps stabilize and depress pectoral girdle	Nerve to subclavius $(C_5$ and $C_6)$
Muscles of the Posterior Thorax (Figure 10.13b)				
Trapezius (trah-pe'ze-us) (*trapezion* = irregular four-sided figure)	Most superficial muscle of posterior thorax; flat, and triangular in shape; upper fibers run inferiorly to scapula; middle fibers run horizontally to scapula; lower fibers run superiorly to scapula	O—occipital bone, ligamentum nuchae, and spines of C_7 and all thoracic vertebrae I—a continuous insertion along acromion and spine of scapula and lateral third of clavicle	Stabilizes, raises, retracts, and rotates scapula; middle fibers retract (adduct) scapula; superior fibers elevate scapula (as in shrugging the shoulders) or can help extend head with scapula fixed; inferior fibers depress scapula (and shoulder)	Accessory nerve (cranial nerve XI); C_3 and C_4

10

MUSCLE	DESCRIPTION	ORIGIN (O) AND INSERTION (I)	ACTION	NERVE SUPPLY
Levator scapulae (skap'u-le) (*levator* = raises)	Located at back and side of neck, deep to trapezius; thick, straplike muscle	O—transverse processes of C_1–C_4 I—medial border of the scapula, superior to the spine	Elevates/adducts scapula in concert with superior fibers of trapezius; tilts glenoid cavity downward when scapula is fixed, flexes neck to same side	Cervical spinal nerves and dorsal scapular nerve (C_3–C_5)
Rhomboids (rom'boidz)—major and minor (*rhomboid* = diamond shaped)	Two rectangular muscles lying deep to trapezius and inferior to levator scapulae; rhomboid minor is the more superior muscle	O—spinous processes of C_7 and T_1 (minor) and spinous processes of T_2–T_5 (major) I—medial border of scapula	Act together (and with middle trapezius fibers) to retract scapula, thus "squaring shoulders"; rotate glenoid cavity of scapula downward (as when arm is lowered against resistance; e.g., paddling a canoe); stabilize scapula	Dorsal scapular nerve (C_4 and C_5)

Sternocleidomastoid
Deltoid
Pectoralis major
Sternum
Biceps brachii
(a)

Subclavius
Clavicle
Subscapularis
Pectoralis minor
Coracobrachialis
Serratus anterior
Humerus

FIGURE 10.13 **Superficial muscles of the thorax and shoulder acting on the scapula and arm. (a)** Anterior view. The superficial muscles, which effect arm movements, are shown on the left side of the illustration. These muscles are removed on the right to show the muscles that stabilize or move the pectoral girdle. **(b)** Posterior view. The superficial muscles are shown for the left side of the illustration, with a corresponding photograph. The superficial muscles are removed on the right side to reveal the deeper muscles acting on the scapula, and the rotator cuff muscles that help stabilize the shoulder joint.

Trapezius
Deltoid
Rhomboid minor
Rhomboid major
Teres major
Latissimus dorsi
(b)

Levator scapulae
Supraspinatus
Clavicle
Spine of scapula
Infraspinatus
Teres minor
Humerus

10

Muscles Crossing the Shoulder Joint: Movements of the Arm (Figure 10.14)

Recall that the ball-and-socket shoulder joint is the most flexible joint in the body, but pays the price of instability. A total of nine muscles cross each shoulder joint to insert on the humerus. All muscles acting on the humerus originate from the pectoral girdle; however, the latissimus dorsi and pectoralis major primarily originate on the axial skeleton.

Of these nine muscles, only the superficial **pectoralis major, latissimus dorsi,** and **deltoid muscles** are prime movers of arm movements. The remaining six are synergists and fixators. Four of these, the **supraspinatus, infraspinatus, teres minor,** and **subscapularis,** are known as *rotator cuff muscles.* They originate on the scapula, and their tendons blend with the fibrous capsule of the shoulder joint en route to the humerus. Although the rotator cuff muscles act as synergists in the angular and rotational movements of the arm, their main function is to reinforce the capsule of the shoulder joint to prevent dislocation of the humerus. The remaining two muscles, the small **teres major** and **coracobrachialis,** cross the shoulder joint but do not contribute to its reinforcement.

Generally speaking, muscles that originate *anterior* to the shoulder joint (pectoralis major, coracobrachialis, and anterior fibers of the deltoid) *flex* the arm, i.e., lift it anteriorly. The prime mover of arm flexion is the pectoralis major. The biceps brachii of the arm (see Table 10.10) also assists in this action. Muscles originating *posterior* to the shoulder joint extend the arm. These include the latissimus dorsi and posterior fibers of the deltoid muscles (both prime movers of arm extension) and the teres major. Thus, the latissimus dorsi and pectoralis muscles are *antagonists* of one another in the flexion-extension movements of the arm.

The middle region of the fleshy deltoid muscle of the shoulder is the prime mover of arm abduction. The main adductors are the pectoralis major anteriorly and latissimus dorsi posteriorly. The small muscles acting on the humerus promote lateral and medial rotation of the shoulder joint. Since the interactions of these nine muscles are complex and each muscle contributes to more than a single movement, a summary of muscles contributing to the various angular and rotational movements of the humerus is provided in Table 10.12 (Part I).

MUSCLE	DESCRIPTION	ORIGIN (O) AND INSERTION (I)	ACTION	NERVE SUPPLY
Pectoralis major (pek"to-ra'lis ma'jer) (*pectus* = breast, chest; *major* = larger)	Large, fan-shaped muscle covering upper portion of chest; forms anterior axillary fold; divided into clavicular and sternal parts	O—sternal end of clavicle, sternum, cartilage of ribs 1–6 (or 7), and aponeurosis of external oblique muscle I—fibers converge to insert by a short tendon into greater tubercle of humerus	Prime mover of arm flexion; rotates arm medially; adducts arm against resistance; with scapula (and arm) fixed, pulls rib cage upward, thus can help in climbing, throwing, pushing, and in forced inspiration	Lateral and medial pectoral nerves (C_5–C_8, and T_1)
Latissimus dorsi (lah-tis'ĭ-mus dor'si) (*latissimus* = widest; *dorsi* = back)	Broad, flat, triangular muscle of lower back (lumbar region); extensive superficial origins; covered by trapezius superiorly; contributes to the posterior wall of axilla	O—indirect attachment via lumbodorsal fascia into spines of lower six thoracic vertebrae, lumbar vertebrae, lower 3 to 4 ribs, and iliac crest I—spirals around teres major to insert in floor of intertubercular sulcus of humerus	Prime mover of arm extension; powerful arm adductor; medially rotates arm at shoulder; depresses scapula; because of its power in these movements, it plays an important role in bringing the arm down in a power stroke, as in striking a blow, hammering, swimming, and rowing; with arms fixed overhead, it pulls the rest of the body upward and forward	Thoracodorsal nerve (C_6–C_8)

10

MUSCLE	DESCRIPTION	ORIGIN (O) AND INSERTION (I)	ACTION	NERVE SUPPLY
Deltoid (del'toid)) (*delta* = triangular)	Thick, multipennate muscle forming rounded shoulder muscle mass; responsible for roundness of shoulder; a site commonly used for intramuscular injection, particularly in males, where it tends to be quite fleshy	O—embraces insertion of the trapezius; lateral third of clavicle; acromion and spine of scapula I—deltoid tuberosity of humerus	Prime mover of arm abduction when all its fibers contract simultaneously; antagonist of pectoralis major and latissimus dorsi, which adduct the arm; if only anterior fibers are active, can act powerfully in flexion and medial rotation of humerus, therefore synergist of pectoralis major; if only posterior fibers are active, effects extension and lateral rotation of arm; active during rhythmic arm swinging movements during walking	Axillary nerve (C$_5$ and C$_6$)
Subscapularis (sub-scap"u-lar'is) (*sub* = under; *scapular* = scapula)	Forms part of posterior wall of axilla; tendon of insertion passes in front of shoulder joint; a rotator cuff muscle	O—subscapular fossa of scapula I—lesser tubercle of humerus	Chief medial rotator of humerus; assisted by pectoralis major; helps to hold head of humerus in glenoid cavity, thereby stabilizing shoulder joint	Subscapular nerves (C$_5$–C$_7$)
Supraspinatus (soo"prah-spi-nah'tus) (*supra* = above, over; *spin* = spine)	Named for its location on posterior aspect of scapula; deep to trapezius; a rotator cuff muscle	O—supraspinous fossa of scapula I—superior part of greater tubercle of humerus	Stabilizes shoulder joint; helps to prevent downward dislocation of humerus, as when carrying a heavy suitcase; assists in abduction	Suprascapular nerve
Infraspinatus (in"frah-spi-nah'tus) (*infra* = below)	Partially covered by deltoid and trapezius; named for its scapular location; a rotator cuff muscle	O—infraspinous fossa of scapula I—greater tubercle of humerus posterior to insertion of supraspinatus	Helps to hold head of humerus in glenoid cavity, stabilizing the shoulder joint; rotates humerus laterally	Suprascapular nerve
Teres minor (te'rēz) (*teres* = round; *minor* = lesser)	Small, elongated muscle; lies inferior to infraspinatus and may be inseparable from that muscle; a rotator cuff muscle	O—lateral border of dorsal scapular surface I—greater tubercle of humerus inferior to infraspinatus insertion	Same action(s) as infraspinatus muscle; adducts arm	Axillary nerve
Teres major	Thick, rounded muscle; located inferior to teres minor; helps to form posterior wall of axilla (along with latissimus dorsi and subscapularis)	O—posterior surface of scapula at inferior angle I—intertubercular sulcus of the humerus; insertion tendon fused with that of latissimus dorsi	Posteromedially extends, medially rotates, and adducts humerus; synergist of latissimus dorsi	Lower subscapular nerve (C$_6$ and C$_7$)
Coracobrachialis (kor"ah-ko-bra"ke-al'is) (*coraco* = coracoid; *brachi* = arm)	Small, cylindrical muscle	O—coracoid process of scapula I—medial surface of humerus shaft	Flexion and adduction of the humerus; synergist of pectoralis major	Musculocutaneous nerve (C$_5$–C$_7$)

10

10

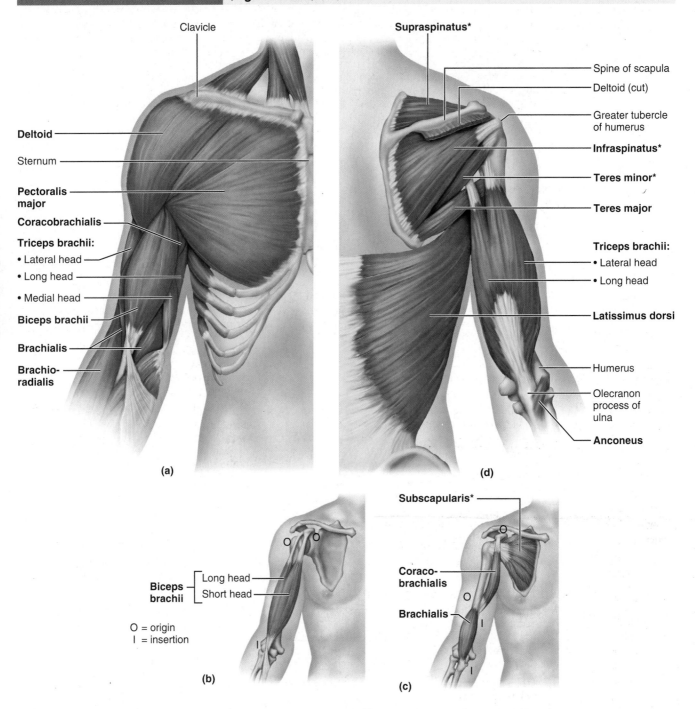

FIGURE 10.14   **Muscles crossing the shoulder and elbow joint, respectively causing movements of the arm and forearm. (a)** Superficial muscles of the anterior thorax, shoulder, and arm, anterior view. (See *A Brief Atlas* *of the Human Body,* Figures 35 and 36.) **(b)** The biceps brachii muscle of the anterior arm, shown in isolation. **(c)** The brachialis muscle and the coraco-brachialis and subscapularis muscles shown in isolation. **(d)** The extent of the triceps brachii muscle of the posterior arm, shown in relation to the deep scapular muscles. The deltoid muscle of the shoulder has been removed.

* Rotator cuff muscles

Muscles fleshing out the arm cross the elbow joint to insert on the forearm bones. Since the elbow is a hinge joint, movements promoted by these muscles are limited almost entirely to flexion and extension of the forearm. Walls of fascia divide the arm into two muscle compartments—the *posterior extensors* and *anterior flexors*. The prime mover of forearm extension is the bulky **triceps brachii** muscle, which forms nearly the entire musculature of the posterior compartment. It is assisted (minimally) by the tiny **anconeus** muscle, which just about spans the elbow joint posteriorly.

All anterior arm muscles cause elbow flexion. In order of decreasing strength, these are the **brachialis, biceps brachii,** and **brachioradialis.** The brachialis and biceps insert (respectively) into the ulna and radius and contract simultaneously during flexion; they are the chief forearm flexors. The biceps brachii, a muscle that bulges when the forearm is flexed, is familiar to almost everyone; the brachialis, which lies deep to the biceps, is less known, but is as important in flexing the elbow. The biceps muscle also supinates the forearm and is ineffective in flexing the elbow when the forearm *must* stay pronated. (This is why doing chin-ups with palms facing anteriorly is harder than with palms facing posteriorly.) Since the brachioradialis arises from the distal humerus and inserts on the distal forearm, it resides mainly in the forearm (rather than in the arm). Because its force is exerted far from the fulcrum, the brachioradialis is a weak forearm flexor. It becomes active only when the elbow has been partially flexed and is semipronated.

The actions of the muscles described here are summarized in Table 10.12 (Part II).

MUSCLE	DESCRIPTION	ORIGIN (O) AND INSERTION (I)	ACTION	NERVE SUPPLY
Posterior Muscles				
Triceps brachii (tri′seps bra″ke-i) (*triceps* = three heads; *brachi* = arm)	Large fleshy muscle; the only muscle of posterior compartment of arm; three-headed origin; long and lateral heads lie superficial to medial head	O—long head: infraglenoid tubercle of scapula; lateral head: posterior shaft of humerus; medial head: posterior humeral shaft distal to radial groove I—by common tendon into olecranon process of ulna	Powerful forearm extensor (prime mover, particularly medial head); antagonist of forearm flexors; long and lateral heads mainly active in extension against resistance; long head tendon may help stabilize shoulder joint and assist in arm adduction	Radial nerve (C$_6$–C$_8$)
Anconeus (an-ko′ne-us) (*ancon* = elbow) (see Figure 10.16)	Short triangular muscle; closely associated (blended) with distal end of triceps on posterior humerus	O—lateral epicondyle of humerus I—lateral aspect of olecranon process of ulna	Abducts ulna during forearm pronation; synergist of triceps brachii in elbow extension	Radial nerve
Anterior Muscles				
Biceps brachii (bi′seps) (*biceps* = two heads)	Two-headed fusiform muscle; bellies unite as insertion point is approached; tendon of long head helps stabilize shoulder joint	O—short head: coracoid process; long head: tubercle above and lip of glenoid cavity; tendon of long head runs within capsule and into intertubercular sulcus of humerus I—by common tendon into radial tuberosity	Flexes elbow joint and supinates forearm; these actions usually occur at same time (e.g., when you open a bottle of wine, it turns the corkscrew and pulls the cork); weak flexor of arm at shoulder	Musculocutaneous nerve (C$_5$ and C$_6$)
Brachialis (bra′ke-al-is)	Strong muscle that is immediately deep to biceps brachii on distal humerus	O—front of distal humerus; embraces insertion of deltoid muscle I—coronoid process of ulna	A major forearm flexor (lifts ulna as biceps lifts the radius)	Musculocutaneous nerve
Brachioradialis (bra″ke-o-ra″de-al′is) (*radi* = radius, ray) (also see Figure 10.15)	Superficial muscle of lateral forearm; forms lateral boundary of antecubital fossa; extends from distal humerus to distal forearm	O—lateral supracondylar ridge at distal end of humerus I—base of styloid process of radius	Synergist in forearm flexion; acts to best advantage when forearm is partially flexed and semi-pronated; during rapid flexion *and* extension, stabilizes the elbow	Radial nerve (an important exception: the radial nerve typically serves extensor muscles)

10

The forearm muscles are functionally divided into two approximately equal groups: those causing wrist movements and those moving the fingers and thumb. In most cases, their fleshy portions contribute to the roundness of the proximal forearm and then they taper to long insertion tendons. Their insertions are securely anchored by strong ligaments called **flexor** and **extensor retinacula** ("retainers"). These "wrist bands" keep the tendons from jumping outward when tensed. Crowded together in the wrist and palm, the muscle tendons are surrounded by slippery tendon sheaths that minimize friction as they slide against one another.

Although many forearm muscles arise from the humerus (and thus cross both the elbow and wrist joints), their actions on the elbow are slight. Flexion and extension are the movements typically effected at both the wrist and finger joints. In addition, the wrist can be abducted and adducted.

The forearm muscles are subdivided by fascia into two main compartments (the *anterior flexors* and *posterior extensors*), each with superficial and deep muscle layers. Most flexors in the anterior compartment arise from a common tendon on the humerus and are innervated largely by the median nerve. Two

anterior compartment muscles are not flexors but pronators, the **pronator teres** and **pronator quadratus.** Pronation is one of the most important forearm movements.

Muscles of the posterior compartment extend the wrist and fingers. An exception is the **supinator** muscle, which assists the biceps brachii muscle of the arm in supinating the forearm. (Also residing in the posterior compartment is the **brachioradialis** muscle, the weak elbow flexor considered in Table 10.10.) Like those of the anterior compartment, most muscles of the posterior compartment arise from a common origin tendon on the humerus. All posterior forearm muscles are supplied by the radial nerve.

As described above, most muscles that move the hand are located in the forearm and "operate" the fingers via their long tendons, like operating a puppet by strings. This design makes the hand less bulky and enables it to perform finer movements. The hand movements promoted by the forearm muscles are assisted and made more precise by the small *intrinsic* muscles of the hand (see Table 10.13). A summary of the actions of the forearm muscles is provided in Table 10.12 (Parts II and III).

MUSCLE	DESCRIPTION	ORIGIN (O) AND INSERTION (I)	ACTION	NERVE SUPPLY
Part I: Anterior Muscles (Figure 10.15)	These eight muscles of the anterior fascial compartment are listed from the lateral to the medial aspect. Most arise from a common flexor tendon attached to the medial epicondyle of the humerus and have additional origins as well. Most of the tendons of insertion of these flexors are held in place at the wrist by a thickening of deep fascia called the *flexor retinaculum*.			
Superficial Muscles				
Pronator teres (pro-na'tor te'rēz) (*pronation* = turning palm posteriorly, or down; *teres* = round)	Two-headed muscle; seen in superficial view between proximal margins of brachioradialis and flexor carpi radialis; forms medial boundary of antecubital fossa	O—medial epicondyle of humerus; coronoid process of ulna I—by common tendon into lateral radius, midshaft	Pronates forearm; weak flexor of elbow	Median nerve
Flexor carpi radialis (flek'sor kar'pe ra"de-a'lis) (*flex* = decrease angle between two bones; *carpi* = wrist; *radi* = radius)	Runs diagonally across forearm; midway, its fleshy belly is replaced by a flat tendon that becomes cordlike at wrist	O—medial epicondyle of humerus I—base of second and third metacarpals; insertion tendon easily seen and provides guide to position of radial artery (used for pulse taking) at wrist	Powerful flexor of wrist; abducts hand; weak synergist of elbow flexion	Median nerve
Palmaris longus (pahl-ma'ris lon'gus) (*palma* = palm; *longus* = long)	Small fleshy muscle with a long insertion tendon; often absent; may be used as guide to find median nerve that lies lateral to it at wrist	O—medial epicondyle of humerus I—palmar aponeurosis; skin and fascia of palm	Weak wrist flexor; tenses skin and fascia of palm during hand movements; weak synergist for elbow flexion	Median nerve
Flexor carpi ulnaris (ul-na'ris) (*ulnar* = ulna)	Most medial muscle of this group; two-headed; ulnar nerve lies lateral to its tendon	O—medial epicondyle of humerus; olecranon process and posterior surface of ulna I—pisiform and hamate bones and base of fifth metacarpal	Powerful flexor of wrist; also adducts hand in concert with extensor carpi ulnaris (posterior muscle); stabilizes wrist during finger extension	Ulnar nerve (C_7 and C_8)

10

MUSCLE	DESCRIPTION	ORIGIN (O) AND INSERTION (I)	ACTION	NERVE SUPPLY
Flexor digitorum superficialis (dǐ"ji-tor'um soo"per-fish"e-a'lis) (*digit* = finger, toe; *superficial* = close to surface)	Two-headed muscle; more deeply placed (therefore, actually forms an intermediate layer); overlain by muscles above but visible at distal end of forearm	O—medial epicondyle of humerus, coronoid process of ulna; shaft of radius I—by four tendons into middle phalanges of fingers 2–5	Flexes wrist and middle phalanges of fingers 2–5; the important finger flexor when speed and flexion against resistance are required	Median nerve (C₇, C₈, and T₁)

Deep Muscles

MUSCLE	DESCRIPTION	ORIGIN (O) AND INSERTION (I)	ACTION	NERVE SUPPLY
Flexor pollicis longus (pah'lǐ-kis) (*pollix* = thumb)	Partly covered by flexor digitorum superficialis; parallels flexor digitorum profundus laterally	O—anterior surface of radius and interosseous membrane I—distal phalanx of thumb	Flexes distal phalanx of thumb	Branch of median nerve (C₈, T₁)
Flexor digitorum profundus (pro-fun'dus) (*profund* = deep)	Extensive origin; overlain entirely by flexor digitorum superficialis	O—coronoid process, anteromedial surface of ulna, and interosseous membrane I—by four tendons into distal phalanges of fingers 2–5	Slow-acting flexor of any or all fingers; assists in flexing wrist; the only muscle that can flex distal interphalangeal joints	Medial half by ulnar nerve; lateral half by median nerve

10

FIGURE 10.15 **Muscles of the anterior compartment of the forearm acting on the right wrist and fingers. (a)** Superficial view. **(b)** The brachioradialis, flexors carpi radialis and ulnaris, and palmaris longus muscles have been removed to reveal the position of the flexor digitorum superficialis. **(c)** Deep muscles of the anterior compartment. The lumbricals and thenar muscles (intrinsic hand muscles) are also illustrated. (See *A Brief Atlas of the Human Body*, Figure 37.)

MUSCLE	DESCRIPTION	ORIGIN (O) AND INSERTION (I)	ACTION	NERVE SUPPLY
Pronator quadratus (kwod-ra′tus) (*quad* = square, four-sided)	Deepest muscle of distal forearm; passes downward and laterally; only muscle that arises solely from ulna and inserts solely into radius	O—distal portion of anterior ulnar shaft I—distal surface of anterior radius	Prime mover of forearm pronation; acts with pronator teres; also helps hold ulna and radius together	Median nerve (C_8 and T_1)
Part II: Posterior Muscles (Figure 10.16)	These muscles of the posterior fascial compartment are listed from the lateral to the medial aspect. They are all innervated by the radial nerve or its branches. More than half of the posterior compartment muscles arise from a common extensor origin tendon attached to the posterior surface of the lateral epicondyle of the humerus and adjacent fascia. The extensor tendons are held in place at the posterior aspect of the wrist by the *extensor retinaculum*, which prevents "bowstringing" of these tendons when the wrist is hyperextended. The extensor muscles of the fingers end in a broad hood over the dorsal side of the digits, the extensor expansion.			

Superficial Muscles

MUSCLE	DESCRIPTION	ORIGIN (O) AND INSERTION (I)	ACTION	NERVE SUPPLY
Brachioradialis (see Table 10.10)				
Extensor carpi radialis longus (ek-sten′sor) (*extend* = increase angle between two bones)	Parallels brachioradialis on lateral forearm, and may blend with it	O—lateral supracondylar ridge of humerus I—base of second metacarpal	Extends wrist in conjunction with the extensor carpi ulnaris and abducts wrist in conjunction with the flexor carpi radialis	Radial nerve (C_6 and C_7)
Extensor carpi radialis brevis (brē′vis) (*brevis* = short)	Somewhat shorter than extensor carpi radialis longus and lies deep to it	O—lateral epicondyle of humerus I—base of third metacarpal	Extends and abducts wrist; acts synergistically with extensor carpi radialis longus to steady wrist during finger flexion	Deep branch of radial nerve
Extensor digitorum	Lies medial to extensor carpi radialis brevis; a detached portion of this muscle, called *extensor digiti minimi*, extends little finger	O—lateral epicondyle of humerus I—by four tendons into extensor expansions and distal phalanges of fingers 2–5	Prime mover of finger extension; extends wrist; can abduct (flare) fingers	Posterior interosseous nerve, a branch of radial nerve (C_5 and C_6)
Extensor carpi ulnaris	Most medial of superficial posterior muscles; long, slender muscle	O—lateral epicondyle of humerus and posterior border of ulna I—base of fifth metacarpal	Extends wrist in conjunction with the extensor carpi radialis and adducts wrist in conjunction with flexor carpi ulnaris	Posterior interosseous nerve

Deep Muscles

MUSCLE	DESCRIPTION	ORIGIN (O) AND INSERTION (I)	ACTION	NERVE SUPPLY
Supinator (soo″pĭ-na′tor) (*supination* = turning palm anteriorly or upward)	Deep muscle at posterior aspect of elbow; largely concealed by superficial muscles	O—lateral epicondyle of humerus; proximal ulna I—proximal end of radius	Assists biceps brachii to forcibly supinate forearm; works alone in slow supination; antagonist of pronator muscles	Posterior interosseous nerve
Abductor pollicis longus (ab-duk′tor) (*abduct* = movement away from median plane)	Lateral and parallel to extensor pollicis longus; just distal to supinator	O—posterior surface of radius and ulna; interosseous membrane I—base of first metacarpal and trapezium	Abducts and extends thumb; abducts wrist	Posterior interosseous nerve
Extensor pollicis brevis and longus	Deep muscle pair with a common origin and action; overlain by extensor carpi ulnaris	O—dorsal shaft of radius and ulna; interosseous membrane I—base of proximal (brevis) and distal (longus) phalanx of thumb	Extends thumb	Posterior interosseous nerve

MUSCLE	DESCRIPTION	ORIGIN (O) AND INSERTION (I)	ACTION	NERVE SUPPLY
Extensor indicis (in'dĭ-kis) (*indicis* = index finger)	Tiny muscle arising close to wrist	O—posterior surface of distal ulna; interosseous membrane I—extensor expansion of index finger; joins tendon of extensor digitorum	Extends index finger and assists in wrist extension	Posterior interosseous nerve

(a)

Brachioradialis

Insertion of triceps brachii

Anconeus

Flexor carpi ulnaris

Extensor carpi ulnaris

Extensor digit minimi

Extensor indicis

Tendons of extensor carpi radialis brevis and longus

Extensor carpi radialis longus

Extensor carpi radialis brevis

Extensor digitorum

Abductor pollicis longus

Extensor pollicis brevis

Extensor pollicis longus

Tendons of extensor digitorum

Extensor expansion

(b)

Olecranon process of ulna

Anconeus

Supinator

Abductor pollicis longus

Extensor pollicis longus

Extensor pollicis brevis

Extensor indicis

Interossei

(c)

Extensor carpi radialis brevis
Abductor pollicis longus
Extensor pollicis brevis
Extensor pollicis longus

Brachioradialis

Extensor carpi radialis longus

Olecranon process

Extensor digitorum

Extensor carpi ulnaris

Extensor digiti minimi

Tendons of extensor digitorum

FIGURE 10.16 **Muscles of the posterior compartment of the right forearm acting on the wrist and fingers. (a)** Superficial muscles, posterior view. (See *A Brief Atlas of the Human Body,* Figure 37b.) **(b)** Deep posterior muscles, superficial muscles removed. The interossei, the deepest layer of intrinsic hand muscles, are also illustrated. **(c)** Photograph of the posterior muscles.

10

MUSCLE GALLERY TABLE 10.12 Summary of Actions of Muscles Acting on the Arm, Forearm, and Hand (Figure 10.17)

Part I: Muscles Acting on the Arm (Humerus) (PM = prime mover)

	ACTIONS AT THE SHOULDER					
	Flexion	Extension	Abduction	Adduction	Medial Rotation	Lateral Rotation
Pectoralis	X (PM)			X (PM)	X	
Latissimus dorsi		X (PM)		X (PM)	X	
Deltoid	X (PM) (anterior fibers)	X (PM) (posterior fibers)	X (PM)		X (anterior fibers)	X (posterior fibers)
Subscapularis					X (PM)	
Supraspinatus			X			
Infraspinatus				X		X (PM)
Teres minor				X (weak)		X (PM)
Teres major		X		X	X	
Coracobrachialis	X			X		
Biceps brachii	X					
Triceps brachii				X		

Part II: Muscles Acting on the Forearm

	ACTIONS			
	Elbow Flexion	Elbow Extension	Pronation	Supination
Biceps brachii	X (PM)			X
Triceps brachii		X (PM)		
Anconeus		X		
Brachialis	X (PM)			
Brachioradialis	X			
Pronator teres	X (weak)		X	
Pronator quadratus			X (PM)	
Supinator				X

Part III: Muscles Acting on the Wrist and Fingers

	ACTIONS ON THE WRIST				ACTIONS ON THE FINGERS	
	Flexion	Extension	Abduction	Adduction	Flexion	Extension
Anterior Compartment						
Flexor carpi radialis	X (PM)		X			
Palmaris longus	X (weak)					
Flexor carpi ulnaris	X (PM)			X		
Flexor digitorum superficialis	X (PM)				X	
Flexor pollicis longus					X (thumb)	
Flexor digitorum profundus	X				X	
Posterior Compartment						
Extensor carpi radialis longus and brevis		X	X			
Extensor digitorum		X (PM)				X (and abducts)
Extensor carpi ulnaris		X		X		
Abductor pollicis longus			X		(abducts thumb)	
Extensor pollicis longus and brevis						X (thumb)
Extensor indicis		X				X (index finger)

10

Key:

= Extensors

= Flexors

= Others

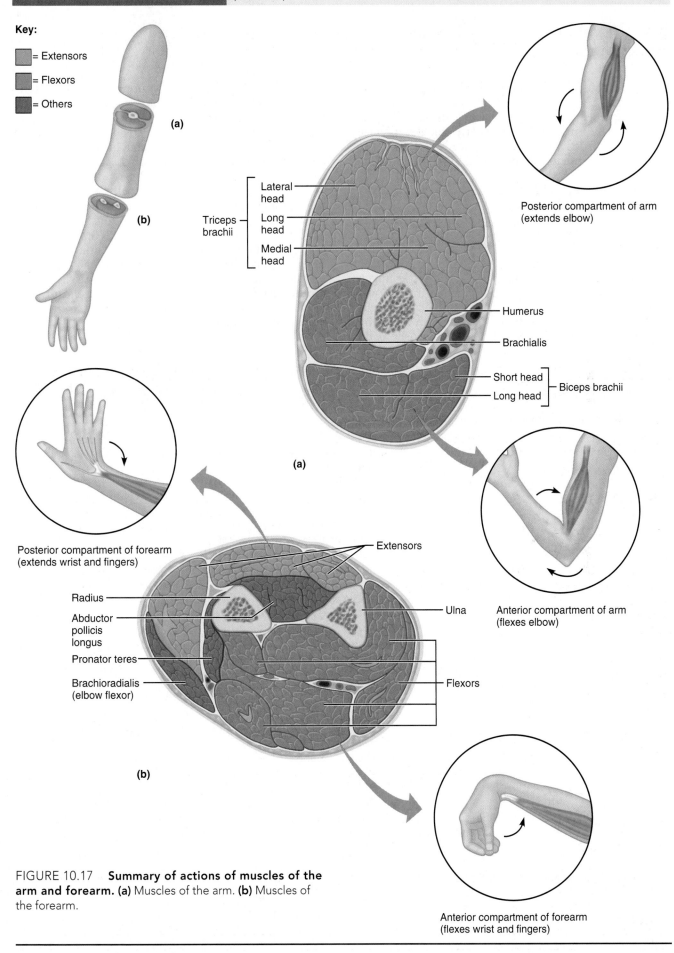

(a)

(b)

Triceps
brachii
- Lateral head
- Long head
- Medial head

Humerus

Brachialis

Short head
Long head — Biceps brachii

(a)

Posterior compartment of arm
(extends elbow)

Anterior compartment of arm
(flexes elbow)

Posterior compartment of forearm
(extends wrist and fingers)

Extensors

Radius

Abductor pollicis longus

Pronator teres

Brachioradialis
(elbow flexor)

Ulna

Flexors

(b)

Anterior compartment of forearm
(flexes wrist and fingers)

10

FIGURE 10.17 **Summary of actions of muscles of the arm and forearm. (a)** Muscles of the arm. **(b)** Muscles of the forearm.

This table considers the small muscles that lie entirely in the hand. All are in the palm, none on the hand's dorsal side. All move the metacarpals and fingers. Small, weak muscles, they mostly control precise movements (such as threading a needle), leaving the powerful movements of the fingers ("power grip") to the forearm muscles.

The intrinsic muscles include the main abductors and adductors of the fingers, as well as muscles that produce the movement of opposition—moving the thumb toward the little finger—that enables one to grip objects in the palm (the handle of a hammer, for example). Many palm muscles are specialized to move the thumb, and surprisingly many move the little finger. Thumb movements are defined differently from movements of other fingers because the thumb lies at a right angle to the rest of the hand. The thumb flexes by bending medially along the palm, not anteriorly, as do the other fingers. (Start with your hand in the anatomical position or this will not be clear!) The thumb extends by pointing laterally (as in hitchhiking), not posteriorly, as do the other fingers. To abduct the fingers is to splay them laterally, but to abduct the thumb is to point it anteriorly. Adduction of the thumb brings it back posteriorly.

The intrinsic muscles of the palm are divided into three groups, those in (1) the *thenar eminence* (ball of the thumb); (2) the *hypothenar eminence* (ball of the little finger); and (3) the midpalm. Thenar and hypothenar muscles are almost mirror images of each other, each containing a small flexor, an abductor, and an opponens muscle. The midpalmar muscles, called **lumbricals** and **interossei**, extend our fingers at the interphalangeal joints. The interossei are also the main finger abductors and adductors.

MUSCLE	DESCRIPTION	ORIGIN (O) AND INSERTION (I)	ACTION	NERVE SUPPLY
Thenar Muscles in Ball of Thumb (the'nar) (*thenar* = palm)				
Abductor pollicis brevis (*pollex* = thumb)	Lateral muscle of thenar group; superficial	O—flexor retinaculum and nearby carpals I—lateral base of thumb's proximal phalanx	Abducts thumb (at carpometacarpal joint)	Median nerve (C_8, T_1)
Flexor pollicis brevis	Medial and deep muscle of thenar group	O—flexor retinaculum and trapezium I—lateral side of base of proximal phalanx of thumb	Flexes thumb (at carpometacarpal and metacarpophalangeal joints)	Median (or occasionally ulnar) nerve (C_8, T_1)
Opponens pollicis (o-pōn'enz) (*opponens* = opposition)	Deep to abductor pollicis brevis, on metacarpal 1	O—flexor retinaculum and trapezium I—whole anterior side of metacarpal 1	Opposition: moves thumb to touch tip of little finger	Median (or occasionally ulnar) nerve
Adductor pollicis	Fan-shaped with horizontal fibers; distal to other thenar muscles; oblique and transverse heads	O—capitate bone and bases of metacarpals 2–4; front of metacarpal 3 I—medial side of base of proximal phalanx of thumb	Adducts and helps to oppose thumb	Ulnar nerve (C_8, T_1)
Hypothenar Muscles in Ball of Little Finger				
Abductor digiti minimi (dĭ'jĭ-ti min'ĭ-mi) (*digiti minimi* = little finger)	Medial muscle of hypothenar group; superficial	O—pisiform bone I—medial side of proximal phalanx of little finger	Abducts little finger at metacarpophalangeal joint	Ulnar nerve
Flexor digiti minimi brevis	Lateral deep muscle of hypothenar group	O—hamate bone and flexor retinaculum I—same as abductor digiti minimi	Flexes little finger at metacarpophalangeal joint	Ulnar nerve
Opponens digiti minimi	Deep to abductor digiti minimi	O—same as flexor digiti minimi brevis I—most of length of medial side of metacarpal 5	Helps in opposition: brings metacarpal 5 toward thumb to cup the hand	Ulnar nerve

MUSCLE GALLERY TABLE 10.13 *(continued)*

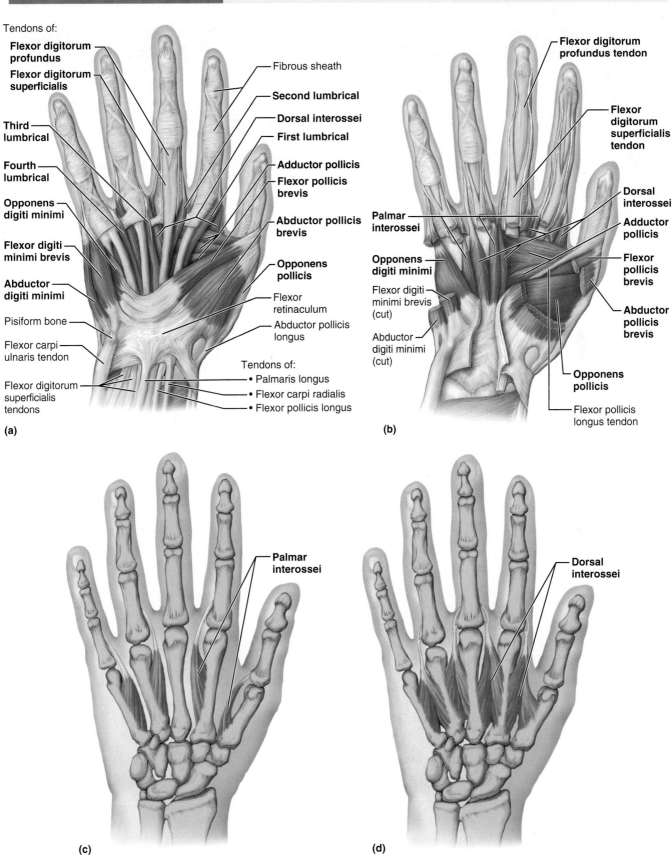

Tendons of:
Flexor digitorum profundus
Flexor digitorum superficialis
Third lumbrical
Fourth lumbrical
Opponens digiti minimi
Flexor digiti minimi brevis
Abductor digiti minimi
Pisiform bone
Flexor carpi ulnaris tendon
Flexor digitorum superficialis tendons

Fibrous sheath
Second lumbrical
Dorsal interossei
First lumbrical
Adductor pollicis
Flexor pollicis brevis
Abductor pollicis brevis
Opponens pollicis
Flexor retinaculum
Abductor pollicis longus
Tendons of:
• Palmaris longus
• Flexor carpi radialis
• Flexor pollicis longus

(a)

Flexor digitorum profundus tendon
Flexor digitorum superficialis tendon
Palmar interossei
Opponens digiti minimi
Flexor digiti minimi brevis (cut)
Abductor digiti minimi (cut)
Dorsal interossei
Adductor pollicis
Flexor pollicis brevis
Abductor pollicis brevis
Opponens pollicis
Flexor pollicis longus tendon

(b)

Palmar interossei

(c)

Dorsal interossei

(d)

FIGURE 10.18 **Hand muscles, ventral views of right hand. (a)** First superficial layer. **(b)** Second layer. **(c)** Palmar interossei (isolated). **(d)** Dorsal interossei (isolated).

MUSCLE GALLERY TABLE 10.13	Intrinsic Muscles of the Hand: Fine Movements of the Fingers (Figure 10.18) *(continued)*			
MUSCLE	**DESCRIPTION**	**ORIGIN (O) AND INSERTION (I)**	**ACTION**	**NERVE SUPPLY**
Midpalmar Muscles				
Lumbricals (lum′brĭ-klz) (*lumbric* = earthworm)	Four worm-shaped muscles in palm, one to each finger (except thumb); unusual because they originate from the tendons of another muscle	O—lateral side of each tendon of flexor digitorum profundus in palm I—lateral edge of extensor expansion on first phalanx of fingers 2–5	Flex fingers at metacarpophalangeal joints but extend fingers at interphalangeal joints	Median nerve (lateral two) and ulnar nerve (medial two)
Palmar interossei (in″ter-os′e-i) (*interossei* =between bones)	Four long, cone-shaped muscles in the spaces between the metacarpals; lie ventral to the dorsal interossei	O—the side of each metacarpal that faces the midaxis of the hand (metacarpal 3) but absent from metacarpal 3 I—extensor expansion on first phalanx of each finger (except finger 3), on side facing midaxis of hand	Adductors of fingers: pull fingers in toward third digit; act with lumbricals to extend fingers at interphalangeal joints and flex them at metacarpophalangeal joints	Ulnar nerve
Dorsal interossei	Four bipennate muscles filling spaces between the metacarpals; deepest palm muscles, also visible on dorsal side of hand (Figure 10.16b)	O—sides of metacarpals I—extensor expansion over first phalanx of fingers 2–4 on side opposite midaxis of hand (finger 3), but on *both* sides of finger 3	Abduct (diverge) fingers; extend fingers at interphalangeal joints and flex them at metacarpophalangeal joint	Ulnar nerve

| **MUSCLE GALLERY** TABLE 10.14 | Muscles Crossing the Hip and Knee Joints: Movements of the Thigh and Leg (Figures 10.19 and 10.20) |

The muscles fleshing out the thigh are difficult to segregate into groups on the basis of action. Some thigh muscles act only at the hip joint, others only at the knee, while still others act at both joints. Attempts to classify these muscles solely on the basis of location are equally frustrating because different muscles in a particular location often have very different actions. However, the *most anterior* muscles of the hip and thigh flex the femur at the hip and extend the leg at the knee—producing the foreswing phase of walking. The *posterior* muscles of the hip and thigh, by contrast, mostly extend the thigh and flex the leg—the backswing phase of walking. The third group of muscles in this region, the *medial*, or *adductor*, muscles, all adduct the thigh; they have no effect on the leg. In the thigh, the anterior, posterior, and adductor muscles are separated by walls of fascia into *anterior, posterior,* and *medial compartments* (see Figure 10.24a). The deep fascia of the thigh, the *fascia lata,* surrounds and encloses all three groups of muscles like a support stocking.

Movements of the thigh (occurring at the hip joint) are accomplished largely by muscles anchored to the pelvic girdle. Like the shoulder joint, the hip joint is a ball-and-socket joint permitting flexion, extension, abduction, adduction, circumduction, and rotation. Muscles effecting these movements of the thigh are among the most powerful muscles of the body. For the most part, the thigh *flexors* pass in front of the hip joint. The most important of these are the **iliopsoas, tensor fasciae latae,** and **rectus femoris.** They are assisted in this action by the **adductor muscles** of the medial thigh and the straplike **sartorius.** The prime mover of thigh flexion is the iliopsoas.

Thigh *extension* is effected primarily by the massive **hamstring muscles** of the posterior thigh. However, during forceful extension, the **gluteus maximus** of the buttock is activated. Buttock muscles that lie lateral to the hip joint (**gluteus medius** and **minimus**) *abduct* the thigh. Thigh adduction is the role of the adductor muscles of the medial thigh. Abduction and adduction of the thighs are extremely important during walking to keep the body's weight balanced over the limb that is on the ground. Many different muscles bring about medial and lateral rotation of the thigh.

At the knee joint, flexion and extension are the main movements. The sole knee *extensor* is the **quadriceps femoris** muscle of the anterior thigh, the most powerful muscle in the body. The quadriceps is antagonized by the hamstrings of the posterior compartment, which are prime movers of knee flexion.

The actions of the muscles presented here are further summarized in Table 10.16 (Part I).

MUSCLE	DESCRIPTION	ORIGIN (O) AND INSERTION (I)	ACTION	NERVE SUPPLY
Part I: Anterior and Medial Muscles (Figure 10.19)				
Origin on the Pelvis				
Iliopsoas (il″e-o-so′us)	Iliopsoas is a composite of two closely related muscles (iliacus and psoas major) whose fibers pass under the inguinal ligament [see Table 10.6 (external oblique muscle) and Figure 10.11] to insert via a common tendon on the femur.			
■ **Iliacus** (il-e-ak′us) (*iliac* = ilium)	Large, fan-shaped, more lateral muscle	O—iliac fossa and crest, lateral sacrum I—femur on and immediately below lesser trochanter of femur via iliopsoas tendon	Iliopsoas is the prime mover for flexing thigh or for flexing trunk on thigh during a bow	Femoral nerve (L_2 and L_3)
■ **Psoas major** (so′us) (*psoa* = loin muscle; *major* = larger)	Longer, thicker, more medial muscle of the pair (butchers refer to this muscle as the tenderloin)	O—by fleshy slips from transverse processes, bodies, and discs of lumbar vertebrae and T_{12} I—lesser trochanter of femur via iliopsoas tendon	As above; also effects lateral flexion of vertebral column; important postural muscle	Ventral rami L_1–L_3
Sartorius (sar-tor′e-us) (*sartor* = tailor)	Straplike superficial muscle running obliquely across anterior surface of thigh to knee; longest muscle in body; crosses both hip and knee joints	O—anterior superior iliac spine I—winds around medial aspect of knee and inserts into medial aspect of proximal tibia	Flexes, abducts, and laterally rotates thigh; flexes knee (weak) as in a soccer kick; known as "tailor's muscle" because it helps effect cross-legged position in which tailors are often depicted	Femoral nerve

10

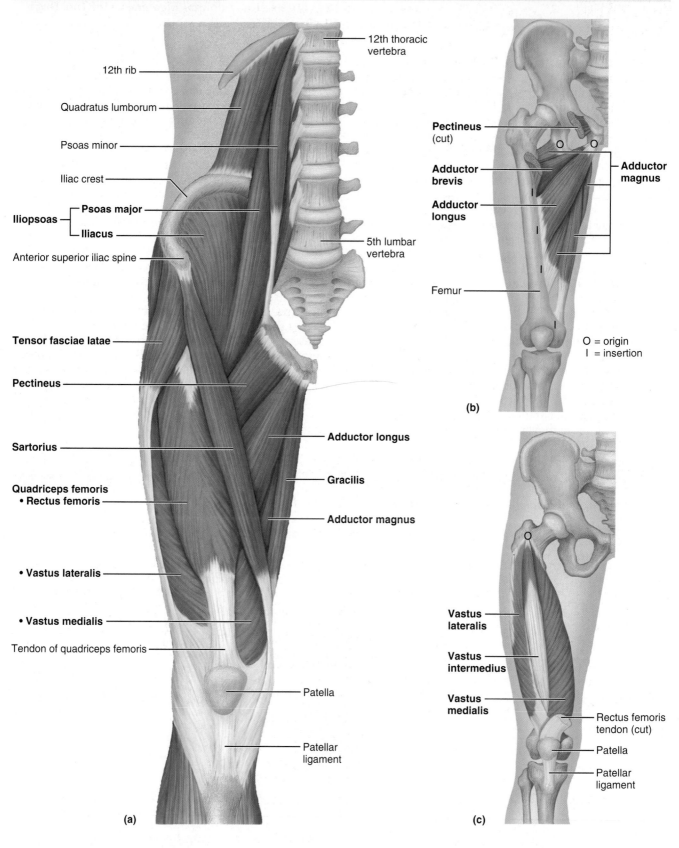

12th thoracic vertebra

12th rib

Quadratus lumborum

Psoas minor

Iliac crest

Psoas major

Iliopsoas

Iliacus

Anterior superior iliac spine

5th lumbar vertebra

Tensor fasciae latae

Pectineus

Sartorius

Quadriceps femoris
• **Rectus femoris**

• **Vastus lateralis**

• **Vastus medialis**

Tendon of quadriceps femoris

Patella

Patellar ligament

Adductor longus

Gracilis

Adductor magnus

(a)

Pectineus (cut)

Adductor brevis

Adductor longus

O   O

Adductor magnus

I

I

I

Femur

I

I

O = origin
I = insertion

(b)

O

Vastus lateralis

Vastus intermedius

Vastus medialis

Rectus femoris tendon (cut)

Patella

Patellar ligament

(c)

FIGURE 10.19 **Anterior and medial muscles promoting movements of the thigh and leg. (a)** Anterior view of the deep muscles of the pelvis and superficial muscles of the right thigh. (See *A Brief Atlas of the Human Body*, Figure 40.) **(b)** Adductor muscles of the medial compartment of the thigh isolated. **(c)** The vastus muscles of the quadriceps group. The rectus femoris muscle of the quadriceps group and surrounding muscles have been removed.

MUSCLE	DESCRIPTION	ORIGIN (O) AND INSERTION (I)	ACTION	NERVE SUPPLY
Muscles of the Medial Compartment of the Thigh				
Adductors (ah-duk'torz)	Large muscle mass consisting of three muscles (magnus, longus, and brevis) forming medial aspect of thigh; arise from inferior part of pelvis and insert at various levels on femur; all used in movements that press thighs together, as when astride a horse; important in pelvic tilting movements that occur during walking and in fixing the hip when the knee is flexed and the foot is off the ground; entire group innervated by obturator nerve. Strain or stretching of this muscle group is called a "pulled groin."			
▪ **Adductor magnus** (mag'nus) (*adduct* = move toward midline; *magnus* = large)	A triangular muscle with a broad insertion; is a composite muscle that is part adductor and part hamstring in action	O—ischial and pubic rami and ischial tuberosity I—linea aspera and adductor tubercle of femur	Anterior part adducts and medially rotates and flexes thigh; posterior part is a synergist of hamstrings in thigh extension	Obturator nerve and sciatic nerve (L$_2$–L$_4$)
▪ **Adductor longus** (*longus* = long)	Overlies middle aspect of adductor magnus; most anterior of adductor muscles	O—Pubis near pubic symphysis I—linea aspera	Adducts, flexes, and medially rotates thigh	Anterior division of obturator nerve (L$_2$–L$_4$)
▪ **Adductor brevis** (*brevis* = short)	In contact with obturator externus muscle; largely concealed by adductor longus and pectineus	O—body and inferior ramus of pubis I—linea aspera above adductor longus	Adducts and medially rotates thigh	Obturator nerve
Pectineus (pek-tin'e-us) (*pecten* = comb)	Short, flat muscle; overlies adductor brevis on proximal thigh; abuts adductor longus medially	O—pectineal line of pubis (and superior ramus) I—inferior from lesser trochanter to the linea aspera of posterior aspect of femur	Adducts, flexes, and medially rotates thigh	Femoral and sometimes obturator nerve
Gracilis (grah-sĭ'lis) (*gracilis* = slender)	Long, thin, superficial muscle of medial thigh	O—inferior ramus and body of pubis and adjacent ischial ramus I—medial surface of tibia just inferior to its medial condyle	Adducts thigh, flexes and medially rotates thigh, especially during walking; flexes knee	Obturator nerve
Muscles of the Anterior Compartment of the Thigh				
Quadriceps femoris (kwod'rĭ-seps fem'o-ris)	Quadriceps femoris arises from four separate heads (*quadriceps* = four heads) that form the flesh of front and sides of thigh; these heads (rectus femoris, and lateral, medial, and intermediate vastus muscles) have a common insertion tendon, the quadriceps tendon, which inserts into the patella and then via the patellar ligament into tibial tuberosity. The quadriceps is a powerful knee extensor used in climbing, jumping, running, and rising from seated position; group is innervated by femoral nerve; the tone of quadriceps plays important role in strengthening knee joint.			
▪ **Rectus femoris** (rek'tus) (*rectus* = straight; *femoris* = femur)	Superficial muscle of anterior thigh; runs straight down thigh; longest head and only muscle of group to cross hip joint	O—anterior inferior iliac spine and superior margin of acetabulum I—patella and tibial tuberosity via patellar ligament	Extends knee and flexes thigh at hip	Femoral nerve (L$_2$–L$_4$)
▪ **Vastus lateralis** (vas'tus lat"er-a'lis) (*vastus* = large; *lateralis* = lateral)	Largest head of the group, forms lateral aspect of thigh; a common intramuscular injection site, particularly in infants (who have poorly developed buttock and arm muscles)	O—greater trochanter, intertrochanteric line, linea aspera I—as for rectus femoris	Extends and stabilizes knee	Femoral nerve
▪ **Vastus medialis** (me"de-a'lis) (*medialis* = medial)	Forms inferomedial aspect of thigh	O—linea aspera, intertrochanteric line I—as for rectus femoris	Extends knee; inferior fibers stabilize patella	Femoral nerve

10

MUSCLE	DESCRIPTION	ORIGIN (O) AND INSERTION (I)	ACTION	NERVE SUPPLY
▪ **Vastus intermedius** (in″ter-me′de-us) (*intermedius* = intermediate)	Obscured by rectus femoris; lies between vastus lateralis and vastus medialis on anterior thigh	O—anterior and lateral surfaces of proximal femur shaft I—as for rectus femoris	Extends knee	Femoral nerve
Tensor fasciae latae (ten′sor fă′she-e la′te) (*tensor* = to make tense; *fascia* = band; *lata* = wide)	Enclosed between fascia layers of anterolateral aspect of thigh; functionally associated with medial rotators and flexors of thigh	O—anterior aspect of iliac crest and anterior superior iliac spine I—iliotibial tract*	Flexes and abducts thigh (thus a synergist of the iliopsoas and gluteus medius and minimus muscles); rotates thigh medially; steadies the knee and trunk on thigh by making iliotibial tract taut	Superior gluteal nerve (L_4 and L_5)

Part II: Posterior Muscles (Figure 10.20)

Gluteal Muscles—Origin on Pelvis

MUSCLE	DESCRIPTION	ORIGIN (O) AND INSERTION (I)	ACTION	NERVE SUPPLY
Gluteus maximus (gloo′te-us mak′sĭ-mus) (*glutos* = buttock; *maximus* = largest)	Largest and most superficial of gluteus muscles; forms bulk of buttock mass; fibers are thick and coarse; important site of intramuscular injection (dorsal gluteal site); overlies large sciatic nerve; covers ischial tuberosity only when standing; when sitting, moves superiorly, leaving ischial tuberosity exposed in the subcutaneous position	O—dorsal ilium, sacrum, and coccyx I—gluteal tuberosity of femur; iliotibial tract	Major extensor of thigh; complex, powerful, and most effective when thigh is flexed and force is necessary, as in rising from a forward flexed position and in thrusting the thigh posteriorly in climbing stairs and running; generally inactive during standing and walking; laterally rotates and abducts thigh	Inferior gluteal nerve (L_5, S_1, and S_2)
Gluteus medius (me′de-us) (*medius* = middle)	Thick muscle largely covered by gluteus maximus; important site for intramuscular injections (ventral gluteal site); considered safer than dorsal gluteal site because there is less chance of injuring sciatic nerve	O—between anterior and posterior gluteal lines on lateral surface of ilium I—by short tendon into lateral aspect of greater trochanter of femur	Abducts and medially rotates thigh; steadies pelvis; its action is extremely important in walking; e.g., muscle of limb planted on ground tilts or holds pelvis in abduction so that pelvis on side of swinging limb does not sag; the foot of swinging limb can thus clear the ground	Superior gluteal nerve (L_5, S_1)
Gluteus minimus (mĭ″nĭ-mus) (*minimus* = smallest)	Smallest and deepest of gluteal muscles	O—between anterior and inferior gluteal lines on external surface of ilium I—anterior border of greater trochanter of femur	As for gluteus medius	Superior gluteal nerve (L_5, S_1)

Lateral Rotators

MUSCLE	DESCRIPTION	ORIGIN (O) AND INSERTION (I)	ACTION	NERVE SUPPLY
Piriformis (pir′ĭ-form-is) (*piri* = pear; *forma* = shape)	Pyramidal muscle located on posterior aspect of hip joint; inferior to gluteus minimus; issues from pelvis via greater sciatic notch	O—anterolateral surface of sacrum (opposite greater sciatic notch) I—superior border of greater trochanter of femur	Rotates extended thigh laterally; since inserted above head of femur, can also assist in abduction of thigh when hip is flexed; stabilizes hip joint	S_1 and S_2, L_5

*The iliotibial tract is a thickened lateral portion of the *fascia lata* (the fascia that ensheathes all the muscles of the thigh). It extends as a tendinous band from the iliac crest to the knee (see Figure 10.20a).

MUSCLE	DESCRIPTION	ORIGIN (O) AND INSERTION (I)	ACTION	NERVE SUPPLY
Obturator externus (ob"tu-ra'tor ek-ster'-nus) (*obturator* = obturator foramen; *externus* = outside)	Flat, triangular muscle deep in superomedial aspect of thigh	O—outer surfaces of obturator membrane, pubis, and ischium, margins of obturator foramen I—by a tendon into trochanteric fossa of posterior femur	As for piriformis	Obturator nerve

FIGURE 10.20 **Posterior muscles of the right hip and thigh. (a)** Superficial view showing the gluteus muscles of the buttock and hamstring muscles of the thigh. **(b)** Deep muscles of the gluteal region, which act primarily to rotate the thigh laterally. The superficial gluteus maximus and medius have been removed. **(c)** Anterior view of the isolated obturator externus muscle.

| MUSCLE GALLERY TABLE 10.14 | Muscles Crossing the Hip and Knee Joints: Movements of the Thigh and Leg (Figures 10.19 and 10.20) *(continued)* | | | |

MUSCLE	DESCRIPTION	ORIGIN (O) AND INSERTION (I)	ACTION	NERVE SUPPLY
Obturator internus (in-ter'nus) (*internus* = inside)	Surrounds obturator foramen within pelvis; leaves pelvis via lesser sciatic notch and turns acutely forward to insert in femur	O—inner surface of obturator membrane, greater sciatic notch, and margins of obturator foramen I—greater trochanter in front of piriformis	As for piriformis	L_5 and S_1
Gemellus (jĕ-mĕ'lis)— superior and inferior (*gemin* = twin, double; *superior* = above; *inferior* = below)	Two small muscles with common insertions and actions; considered extrapelvic portions of obturator internus	O—ischial spine (superior); ischial tuberosity (inferior) I—greater trochanter of femur	As for piriformis	L_5 and S_1
Quadratus femoris (*quad* = four-sided square)	Short, thick muscle; most inferior of lateral rotator muscles; extends laterally from pelvis	O—ischial tuberosity I—trochanteric crest of femur	Rotates thigh laterally and stabilizes hip joint	L_5 and S_1

Muscles of the Posterior Compartment of the Thigh

Hamstrings	The hamstrings are fleshy muscles of the posterior thigh (biceps femoris, semitendinosus, and semimembranosus). They cross both the hip and knee joints and are prime movers of thigh extension and knee flexion. Group has a common origin site and is innervated by sciatic nerve (actually two nerves, the tibial and common fibular nerves wrapped in a common sheath). Ability of hamstrings to act on one of the two joints spanned depends on which joint is fixed; i.e., if knee is fixed (extended), they promote hip extension; if hip is extended, they promote knee flexion. However, when hamstrings are stretched, they tend to restrict full accomplishment of antagonistic movements; e.g., if knees are fully extended, it is difficult to flex the hip fully (and touch your toes), and when the thigh is fully flexed as in kicking a football, it is almost impossible to extend the knee fully at the same time (without considerable practice). Name of this muscle group comes from old butchers' practice of using their tendons to hang hams for smoking. "Pulled hamstrings" are common sports injuries in those who run very hard, e.g., football halfbacks.			
▪ **Biceps femoris** (*biceps* = two heads)	Most lateral muscle of the group; arises from two heads	O—ischial tuberosity (long head); linea aspera and distal femur (short head) I—common tendon passes downward and laterally (forming lateral border of popliteal fossa) to insert into head of fibula and lateral condyle of tibia	Extends thigh and flexes knee; laterally rotates leg, especially when knee is flexed	Sciatic nerve— tibial nerve to long head, common fibular nerve to short head (L_5–S_2)
▪ **Semitendinosus** (sem"e-ten"dĭ-no'sus) (*semi* = half; *tendinosus* = tendon)	Lies medial to biceps femoris; although its name suggests that this muscle is largely tendinous, it is quite fleshy; its long slender tendon begins about two-thirds of the way down thigh	O—ischial tuberosity in common with long head of biceps femoris I—medial aspect of upper tibial shaft	Extends thigh at hip; flexes knee; with semimembranosus, medially rotates leg	Sciatic nerve— tibial nerve portion (L_5–S_2)
▪ **Semimembranosus** (sem"e-mem"-brah- no'sus) (*membranosus* = membrane)	Deep to semitendinosus	O—ischial tuberosity I—medial condyle of tibia; via oblique popliteal ligament to lateral condyle of femur	Extends thigh and flexes knee; medially rotates leg	Sciatic nerve— tibial nerve portion (L_5–S_2)

The deep fascia of the leg is continuous with the fascia lata that ensheathes the thigh. Like a snug knee sock beneath the skin, the leg fascia binds the leg muscles tightly, helping to prevent excessive swelling of muscles during exercise and aiding venous return. Its inward extensions segregate the leg muscles into *anterior, lateral,* and *posterior compartments* (see Figure 10.24b), each with its own nerve and blood supply. Distally the leg fascia thickens to form the **flexor, extensor,** and **fibular** (or **peroneal**) **retinaculae,** "ankle brackets" that hold the tendons in place where they run to the foot.

The various muscles of the leg promote movements at the ankle joint (dorsiflexion and plantar flexion), the intertarsal joints (inversion and eversion of the foot), and/or the toes (flexion and extension). Muscles in the *anterior extensor compartment of the leg*—**tibialis anterior, extensor digitorum longus, extensor hallucis longus,** and **fibularis tertius**—are primarily toe extensors and ankle dorsiflexors. Although dorsiflexion is not a powerful movement, it is important in preventing the toes from dragging during walking. Lateral compartment muscles are the **fibular,** formerly **peroneal** (*peron* = fibula), **muscles** that plantar flex and evert the foot. Muscles of the *posterior flexor compartment*—**gastrocnemius, soleus, tibialis posterior, flexor digitorum longus,** and **flexor hallucis longus**—primarily plantar flex the foot and flex the toes. Plantar flexion is the most powerful movement of the ankle (and foot) because it lifts the entire weight of our body. It is essential for standing on tiptoe and provides the forward thrust when walking and running. The **popliteus muscle,** which crosses the knee, "unlocks" the extended knee in preparation for flexion.

The tiny intrinsic muscles of the sole of the foot (lumbricals, interossei, and others) are considered separately in Table 10.17.

The actions of the muscles in this table are summarized in Table 10.16 (Part II).

MUSCLE	DESCRIPTION	ORIGIN (O) AND INSERTION (I)	ACTION	NERVE SUPPLY
Part I: Muscles of the Anterior Compartment (Figures 10.21 and 10.22)	All muscles of the anterior compartment are dorsiflexors of the ankle and have a common innervation, the deep fibular nerve. Paralysis of the anterior muscle group causes *foot drop,* which requires that the leg be lifted unusually high during walking to prevent tripping over one's toes. "Shin splints" is a painful inflammatory condition of the muscles of the anterior compartment.			
Tibialis anterior (tib"e-a'lis) (*tibial* = tibia; *anterior* = toward the front)	Superficial muscle of anterior leg; laterally parallels sharp anterior margin of tibia	O—lateral condyle and upper 2/3 of tibial shaft; interosseous membrane I—by tendon into inferior surface of medial cuneiform and first metatarsal bone	Prime mover of dorsiflexion; inverts foot; assists in supporting medial longitudinal arch of foot	Deep fibular nerve (L_4 and L_5)
Extensor digitorum longus (*extensor* = increases angle at a joint; *digit* = finger or toe; *longus* = long)	Unipennate muscle on anterolateral surface of leg; lateral to tibialis anterior muscle	O—lateral condyle of tibia; proximal 3/4 of fibula; interosseous membrane I—middle and distal phalanges of toes 2–5 via extensor expansion	Prime mover of toe extension (acts mainly at metatarsophalangeal joints); dorsiflexes foot (in conjunction with the tibialis anterior and extensor hallucis longus)	Deep fibular nerve (L_5 and S_1)
Fibularis (peroneus) tertius (fib-u-lar'ris ter'shus) (*fibular* = fibula; *tertius* = third)	Small muscle; usually continuous and fused with distal part of extensor digitorum longus; not always present	O—distal anterior surface of fibula and interosseous membrane I—tendon inserts on dorsum of fifth metatarsal	Dorsiflexes and everts foot	Deep fibular nerve (L_5 and S_1)
Extensor hallucis longus (hal'yu-kis) (*hallux* = great toe)	Deep to extensor digitorum longus and tibialis anterior; narrow origin	O—anteromedial fibula shaft and interosseous membrane I—tendon inserts on distal phalanx of great toe	Extends great toe; dorsiflexes foot	Deep fibular nerve (L_5 and S_1)

10

10

Fibularis longus

Gastrocnemius

Tibia

Tibialis anterior

Extensor digitorum longus

Soleus

Extensor hallucis longus

Fibularis tertius

Superior and inferior extensor retinacula

Extensor hallucis brevis

Extensor digitorum brevis

(a)

Extensor hallucis longus

Fibularis tertius

O

O

I

I

(c)

Tibialis anterior

O

I

(b)

Extensor digitorum longus

O

O = origin
I = insertion

I

(d)

FIGURE 10.21   **Muscles of the anterior compartment of the right leg.**
(a) Superficial view of anterior leg muscles. **(b–d)** Some of the same muscles shown
in isolation to allow visualization of their origins and insertions.

O = origin
I = insertion

FIGURE 10.22   **Muscles of the lateral compartment of the right leg.**
(a) Superficial view of lateral aspect of the leg, illustrating positions of lateral
compartment muscles (fibularis longus and brevis) relative to anterior and posterior
leg muscles. **(b)** Isolated view of fibularis longus; inset illustrates the insertion of the
fibularis longus on the plantar surface of the foot. **(c)** Isolated view of the fibularis
brevis muscle. (See *A Brief Atlas of the Human Body,* Figure 42.)

10

MUSCLE	DESCRIPTION	ORIGIN (O) AND INSERTION (I)	ACTION	NERVE SUPPLY

Part II: Muscles of the Lateral Compartment (Figures 10.22 and 10.23) These muscles have a common innervation, the superficial fibular nerve. Besides plantar flexion and foot eversion, these muscles stabilize the lateral ankle and lateral longitudinal arch of the foot.

MUSCLE	DESCRIPTION	ORIGIN (O) AND INSERTION (I)	ACTION	NERVE SUPPLY
Fibularis (peroneus) longus (See also Figure 10.21)	Superficial lateral muscle; overlies fibula	O—upper portion of lateral fibula I—by long tendon that curves under foot to first metatarsal and medial cuneiform	Plantar flexes and everts foot; may help keep foot flat on ground	Superficial fibular nerve (L_5–S_2)
Fibularis (peroneus) brevis (*brevis* = short)	Smaller muscle; deep to fibularis longus; enclosed in a common sheath	O—distal fibula shaft I—by tendon running behind lateral malleolus to insert on proximal end of fifth metatarsal	Plantar flexes and everts foot	Superficial fibular nerve (L_5–S_2)

Part III: Muscles of the Posterior Compartment (Figure 10.23) The muscles of the posterior compartment have a common innervation, the tibial nerve. They act in concert to plantar flex the ankle.

Superficial Muscles

MUSCLE	DESCRIPTION	ORIGIN (O) AND INSERTION (I)	ACTION	NERVE SUPPLY
Triceps surae (tri"seps sur'e) (See also Figure 10.22)	Refers to muscle pair (gastrocnemius and soleus) that shapes the posterior calf and inserts via a common tendon into the calcaneus of the heel; this calcaneal or Achilles tendon is the largest tendon in the body. Prime movers of ankle plantar flexion.			
■ **Gastrocnemius** (gas"truk-ne'me-us) (*gaster* = belly; *kneme* = leg)	Superficial muscle of pair; two prominent bellies that form proximal curve of calf	O—by two heads from medial and lateral condyles of femur I—posterior calcaneus via calcaneal tendon	Plantar flexes foot when knee is extended; since it also crosses knee joint, it can flex knee when foot is dorsiflexed	Tibial nerve (S_1, S_2)
■ **Soleus** (so'le-us) (*soleus* = fish)	Broad, flat muscle, deep to gastrocnemius on posterior surface of calf	O—extensive origin from superior tibia, fibula, and interosseous membrane I—as for gastrocnemius	Plantar flexes foot; important locomotor and postural muscle during walking, running, and dancing	Tibial nerve
Plantaris (plan-tar'is) (*planta* = sole of foot)	Generally a small, feeble muscle, but varies in size and extent; may be absent	O—posterior femur above lateral condyle I—via a long, thin tendon into calcaneus or its tendon	Assists in knee flexion and plantar flexion of foot	Tibial nerve

Deep Muscles

MUSCLE	DESCRIPTION	ORIGIN (O) AND INSERTION (I)	ACTION	NERVE SUPPLY
Popliteus (pop-lit'e-us) (*poplit* = back of knee)	Thin, triangular muscle at posterior knee; passes inferomedially to tibial surface	O—lateral condyle of femur and lateral meniscus I—proximal tibia	Flexes and rotates leg medially to unlock extended knee; with tibia fixed, rotates thigh laterally	Tibial nerve (L_4–S_1)
Flexor digitorum longus (*flexor* = decreases angle at a joint)	Long, narrow muscle; runs medial to and partially overlies tibialis posterior	O—extensive origin on the posterior tibia I—tendon runs behind medial malleolus and inserts into distal phalanges of toes 2–5	Plantar flexes and inverts foot; flexes toes; helps foot "grip" ground	Tibial nerve (S_2 and S_3)
Flexor hallucis longus (See also Figure 10.22)	Bipennate muscle; lies lateral to inferior aspect of tibialis posterior	O—midshaft of fibula; interosseous membrane I—tendon runs under foot to distal phalanx of great toe	Plantar flexes and inverts foot; flexes great toe at all joints; "push off" muscle during walking	Tibial nerve (S_2 and S_3)
Tibialis posterior (*posterior* = toward the back)	Thick, flat muscle deep to soleus; placed between posterior flexors	O—extensive origin from superior tibia and fibula and interosseous membrane I—tendon passes behind medial malleolus and under arch of foot; inserts into several tarsals and metatarsals 2–4	Prime mover of foot inversion; plantar flexes foot; stabilizes medial longitudinal arch of foot (as during ice skating)	Tibial nerve (L_4 and L_5)

10

Plantaris

Lateral
head
(cut)

**Gastroc-
nemius**

Medial
head
(cut)

Plantaris

Popliteus

Head of fibula

Plantaris

**Gastroc-
nemius**

Medial
head

Lateral
head

Soleus

Tendon of
plantaris

Fibularis longus

Tendon of
gastrocnemius

Fibularis brevis

Calcaneal
tendon

Medial
malleolus

Lateral
malleolus

Tendon of tibialis
posterior

Calcaneus

(a)

(b)

10

FIGURE 10.23   **Muscles of the posterior compartment of the right leg.**
(a) Superficial view of the posterior leg. **(b)** The gastrocnemius has been removed to
show the soleus immediately deep to it.

Muscles of the Leg: Movements of the Ankle and Toes (Figures 10.21 to 10.23) *(continued)*

O = origin
I = insertion

Plantaris (cut)

Gastrocnemius lateral head (cut)

Gastroc-nemius medial head (cut)

Popliteus

Soleus (cut)

Tibialis posterior

Fibula

Fibularis longus

Flexor digitorum longus

Flexor hallucis longus

Fibularis brevis

Tendon of tibialis posterior

Medial malleolus

Calcaneal tendon (cut)

Calcaneus

(c)

Tibialis posterior

(d)

Flexor digitorum longus

(e)

Popliteus

Flexor hallucis longus

(f)

FIGURE 10.23 *(continued)* **Muscles of the posterior compartment of the right leg. (c)** The triceps surae has been removed to show the deep muscles of the posterior compartment. **(d–f)** Individual deep muscles are shown in isolation.

10

Summary of Actions of Muscles Acting on the Thigh, Leg, and Foot (Figure 10.24)

Part I: Muscles Acting on the Thigh and Leg (PM = prime mover)

	ACTIONS AT THE HIP JOINT						ACTIONS AT THE KNEE	
	Flexion	Extension	Abduction	Adduction	Medial Rotation	Lateral Rotation	Flexion	Extension
Anterior and Medial Muscles								
Iliopsoas	× (PM)							
Sartorius	×		×				×	
Adductor magnus	×	×		×	×			
Adductor longus	×			×	×			
Adductor brevis	×			×	×			
Pectineus	×			×	×			
Gracilis	×			×	×		×	
Rectus femoris	×							× (PM)
Vastus muscles								× (PM)
Tensor fasciae latae	×		×		×			
Posterior Muscles								
Gluteus maximus		× (PM)	×			×		
Gluteus medius			× (PM)		×			
Gluteus minimus			×		×			
Piriformis			×			×		
Obturator internus			×			×		
Obturator externus			×			×		
Gemelli			×			×		
Quadratus femoris						×		
Biceps femoris		× (PM)				×	× (PM)	
Semitendinosus		×					× (PM) (and rotates leg medially)	
Semimembranosus		×					× (PM)	
Gastrocnemius							×	
Plantaris							×	
Popliteus						×	× (and rotates leg medially)	

Part II: Muscles Acting on the Ankle and Toes

	ACTIONS AT THE ANKLE JOINT				ACTIONS AT THE TOES	
	Plantar Flexion	Dorsiflexion	Inversion	Eversion	Flexion	Extension
Anterior Compartment						
Tibialis anterior		× (PM)	×			
Extensor digitorum longus		×				× (PM)
Fibularis tertius		×		×		
Extensor hallucis longus		×	× (weak)			× (great toe)
Lateral Compartment						
Fibularis longus and brevis	×			×		
Posterior Compartment						
Gastrocnemius	× (PM)					
Soleus	× (PM)					
Plantaris	×					
Flexor digitorum longus	×		×		× (PM)	
Flexor hallucis longus	×		×		× (great toe)	
Tibialis posterior	×		× (PM)			

FIGURE 10.24 **Summary of actions of muscles of the thigh and leg.**
(a) Muscles of the thigh. **(b)** Muscles of the leg.

The intrinsic muscles of the foot help to flex, extend, abduct, and adduct the toes. Collectively, along with the tendons of some leg muscles that enter the sole, the foot muscles help support the arches of the foot. There is a single muscle on the foot's dorsum (supe-rior aspect), and several muscles on the plantar aspect (the sole). The plantar muscles occur in four layers, from superficial to deep. Overall, the foot muscles are remarkably similar to those in the palm of the hand.

MUSCLE	DESCRIPTION	ORIGIN (O) AND INSERTION (I)	ACTION	NERVE SUPPLY
Muscle on Dorsum of Foot				
Extensor digitorum brevis (Figures 10.21a and 10.22a)	Small, four-part muscle on dorsum of foot; deep to the tendons of extensor digitorum longus; corresponds to the extensor indicis muscle of forearm. Its most medial muscle slip corresponds to the extensor pollicis of the forearm and is some-times called the extensor hallucis brevis.	O—anterior part of calcaneus bone; extensor retinaculum I—base of proximal phalanx of great toe; extensor expansions on toes 2–5	Helps extend toes at metatarsophalangeal joints	Deep fibular nerve (S_1 and S_2)
Muscles on Sole of Foot—First Layer (Most Superficial) (Figure 10.25)				
Flexor digitorum brevis	Bandlike muscle in middle of sole; corre-sponds to flexor digitorum superficialis of forearm and inserts into digits in the same way	O—calcaneal tuberosity I—middle phalanx of toes 2–4	Helps flex toes	Medial plantar nerve (S_2 and S_3)
Abductor hallucis (hal'yu-kis) (*hallux* = great toe)	Lies medial to flexor digitorum brevis (recall the similar thumb muscle, abductor pollicis brevis)	O—calcaneal tuberosity and flexor retinaculum I—proximal phalanx of great toe, medial side, in the tendon of flexor hallucis brevis (see below)	Abducts great toe	Medial plantar nerve
Abductor digiti minimi	Most lateral of the three superficial sole muscles; (recall similar abductor muscle in palm)	O—calcaneal tuberosity I—lateral side of base of little toe's proximal phalanx	Abducts and flexes little toe	Lateral plantar nerve (S_2 and S_3)
Muscles on Sole of Foot—Second Layer				
Flexor accessorius (quadratus plantae)	Rectangular muscle just deep to flexor digitorum brevis in posterior half of sole; two heads (see also Figure 10.25c)	O—medial and lateral sides of calcaneus I—tendon of flexor digitorum longus in midsole	Straightens out the oblique pull of flexor digitorum longus	Lateral plantar nerve
Lumbricals	Four little "worms" (like lumbricals in hand)	O—from each tendon of flexor digitorum longus I—extensor expansion on proximal phalanx of toes 2–5, medial side	By pulling on extensor expansion, flex toes at metatarsophalangeal joints and extend toes at interphalangeal joints	Medial plantar nerve (first lumbrical) and lateral plantar nerve (second to fourth lumbrical)

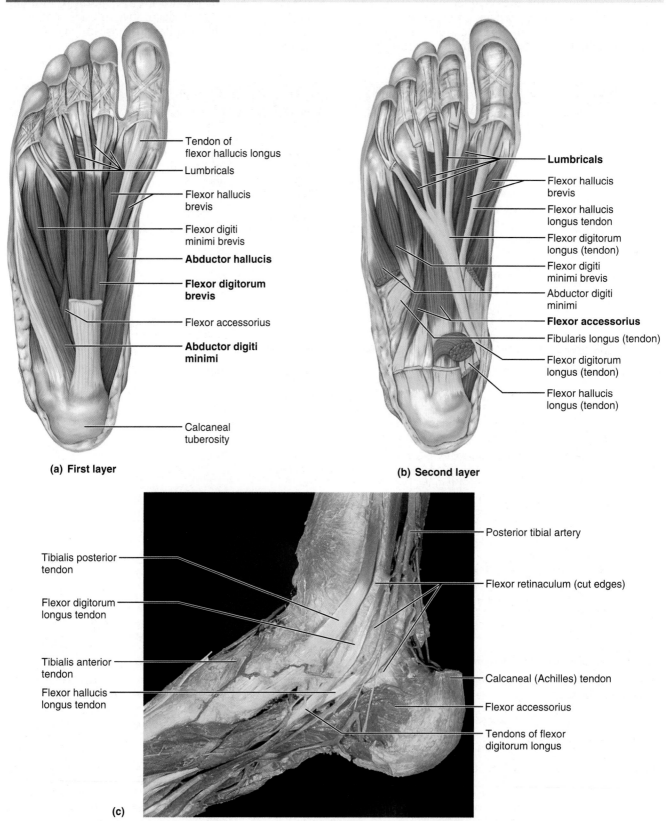

Tendon of flexor hallucis longus

Lumbricals

Flexor hallucis brevis

Flexor digiti minimi brevis

Abductor hallucis

Flexor digitorum brevis

Flexor accessorius

Abductor digiti minimi

Calcaneal tuberosity

(a) First layer

Lumbricals

Flexor hallucis brevis

Flexor hallucis longus tendon

Flexor digitorum longus (tendon)

Flexor digiti minimi brevis

Abductor digiti minimi

Flexor accessorius

Fibularis longus (tendon)

Flexor digitorum longus (tendon)

Flexor hallucis longus (tendon)

(b) Second layer

Tibialis posterior tendon

Flexor digitorum longus tendon

Tibialis anterior tendon

Flexor hallucis longus tendon

Posterior tibial artery

Flexor retinaculum (cut edges)

Calcaneal (Achilles) tendon

Flexor accessorius

Tendons of flexor digitorum longus

(c)

FIGURE 10.25   **Muscles of the right foot, plantar and medial aspects.**

MUSCLE	DESCRIPTION	ORIGIN (O) AND INSERTION (I)	ACTION	NERVE SUPPLY
Muscles on Sole of Foot—Third Layer				
Flexor hallucis brevis	Covers metatarsal 1; splits into two bellies—recall flexor pollicis brevis of thumb	O—lateral cuneiform and cuboid bones I—via two tendons onto base of the proximal phalanx of great toe	Flexes great toe's metatarsophalangeal joint	Medial plantar nerve
Adductor hallucis	Oblique and transverse heads; deep to lumbricals (recall adductor pollicis in thumb)	O—from bases of metatarsals 2–4 and from fibularis longus tendon sheath (oblique head); from a ligament across metatarsophalangeal joints (transverse head) I—base of proximal phalanx of great toe, lateral side	Helps maintain the transverse arch of foot; weak adductor of great toe	Lateral plantar nerve (S_2 and S_3)
Flexor digiti minimi brevis	Covers metatarsal 5 (recall same muscle in hand)	O—base of metatarsal 5 and tendon sheath of fibularis longus I—base of proximal phalanx of toe 5	Flexes little toe at metatarsophalangeal joint	Lateral plantar nerve
Muscles on Sole of Foot—Fourth Layer (Deepest)				
Plantar (3) and dorsal interossei (4)	Similar to the palmar and dorsal interossei of hand in locations, attachments, and actions; however, the long axis of foot around which these muscles orient is the second digit, not the third	See palmar and dorsal interossei (Table 10.13)	See palmar and dorsal interossei (Table 10.13)	Lateral plantar nerve

(d) Third layer

(e) Fourth layer: plantar interossei

(f) Fourth layer: dorsal interossei

FIGURE 10.25 (continued)   **Muscles of the right foot, plantar aspect.**

Related Clinical Terms

Charley horse A muscle contusion, i.e., tearing of muscle followed by bleeding into the tissues (hematoma) and severe, prolonged pain; a common contact sports injury; a charley horse of the quadriceps muscle of the thigh occurs frequently in football players.

Electromyography Recording and interpretation of graphic records of the electrical activity of contracting muscles. Electrodes inserted into the muscles record the impulses that pass over muscle-cell membranes to stimulate contraction. The best and most important technique for determining the functions of muscles and muscle groups.

Hernia An abnormal protrusion of abdominal contents (typically coils of the small intestine) through a weak point in the muscles of the abdominal wall. Most often caused by increased intra-abdominal pressure during lifting or straining. The hernia penetrates the muscle wall but not the skin and so appears as a visible bulge in the body surface. Common abdominal hernias include the inguinal and umbilical hernias.

Quadriceps and hamstring strains Also called quad and hamstring pulls, these conditions involve tearing of these muscles or their tendons; happen mainly in athletes who do not warm up properly and then fully extend their hip (quad pull) or knee (hamstring pull) quickly or forcefully (e.g., sprinters, tennis players); not painful at first, but pain intensifies within three to six hours (30 minutes if the tearing is severe). After a week of rest, stretching is the best therapy.

Rupture of the calcaneal tendon Although the calcaneal (Achilles) tendon is the largest, strongest tendon in the body, its rupture is surprisingly common, particularly in older people as a result of stumbling and in young sprinters when the tendon is traumatized during the takeoff. The rupture is followed by abrupt pain; a gap is seen just above the heel, and the calf bulges as the triceps surae are released from their insertion. Plantar flexion is weak or impossible, but dorsiflexion is exaggerated. Surgical repair of the tendon is necessary.

Shin splints Common term for pain in the anterior compartment of the leg caused by irritation of the tibialis anterior muscle as might follow extreme or unusual exercise without adequate prior conditioning. Because it is tightly wrapped by fascia, the inflamed tibialis anterior cuts off its own circulation as it swells and presses painfully on its own nerves.

Tennis elbow Tenderness due to trauma or overuse of the tendon of origin of the forearm extensor muscles at the lateral epicondyle of the humerus. Caused and aggravated when these muscles contract forcefully to extend the hand at the wrist—as in executing a tennis backhand or lifting a loaded snow shovel. Despite its name, tennis elbow does not involve the elbow joint; most cases caused by work activities.

Torticollis (tor″tĭ-kol′is; *tort* = twisted) A twisting of the neck in which there is a chronic rotation and tilting of the head to one side, due to injury of the sternocleidomastoid muscle on one side; also called wryneck. Sometimes present at birth when the muscle fibers are torn during difficult delivery. Exercise that stretches the affected muscle is the usual treatment.

Chapter Summary

Interactions of Skeletal Muscles in the Body (p. 325)

1. Skeletal muscles are arranged in opposing groups across body joints so that one group can reverse or modify the action of the other.

2. Muscles are classified as prime movers, or agonists (bear the chief responsibility for producing movement); antagonists (reverse, or oppose, the action of another muscle); synergists (aid a prime mover by effecting the same action, stabilizing joints, or preventing undesirable movements); and fixators (function to immobilize a bone or a muscle's origin).

Naming Skeletal Muscles (pp. 325–326)

1. Criteria used to name muscles include a muscle's location, shape, relative size, fiber (fascicle) direction, number of origins, attachment sites (origin/insertion), and action. Several criteria are combined to name some muscles.

Muscle Mechanics: Importance of Fascicle Arrangement and Leverage (pp. 326–330)

1. Common patterns of fascicle arrangement are parallel, fusiform, pennate, convergent, and circular. Muscles with fibers that run parallel to the long axis of the muscle shorten most; stocky pennate muscles shorten little but are the most powerful muscles.

2. A lever is a bar that moves on a fulcrum. When an effort is applied to the lever, a load is moved. In the body, bones are the levers, joints are the fulcrums, and the effort is exerted by skeletal muscles at their insertions.

3. When the effort is farther from the fulcrum than is the load, the lever operates at a mechanical advantage (is slow and strong). When the effort is exerted closer to the fulcrum than is the load, the lever operates at a mechanical disadvantage (is fast and promotes a large degree of movement).

4. First-class levers (effort-fulcrum-load) may operate at a mechanical advantage or disadvantage. Second-class levers (fulcrum-load-effort) all operate at a mechanical advantage. Third-class levers (fulcrum-effort-load) always operate at a mechanical disadvantage.

Major Skeletal Muscles of the Body (pp. 330–383)

1. Muscles of the head that produce facial expression tend to be small and to insert into soft tissue (skin and other muscles) rather than into bone. These muscles open and close the eyes and mouth, compress the cheeks, allow smiling and other types of facial language (see Table 10.1*).

2. Muscles of the head involved in mastication include the masseter and temporalis that elevate the mandible and two deep muscle pairs that promote grinding and sliding jaw movements (see Table 10.2*). Extrinsic muscles of the tongue anchor the tongue and control its movements.

---

*See specific table cited for detailed description of each muscle in the group.

3. Deep muscles of the anterior neck promote swallowing movements, including elevation/depression of the hyoid bone, closure of the respiratory passages, and peristalsis of the pharynx (see Table 10.3*).

4. Neck muscles and deep muscles of the vertebral column promote head and trunk movements (see Table 10.4*). The deep muscles of the posterior trunk can extend large regions of the vertebral column (and head) simultaneously. Head flexion and rotation are effected by the anteriorly located sternocleidomastoid and scalene muscles.

5. Movements of quiet breathing are promoted by the diaphragm and the external intercostal muscles of the thorax (see Table 10.5*). Downward movement of the diaphragm increases intra-abdominal pressure.

6. The four muscle pairs forming the abdominal wall are layered like plywood to form a natural muscular girdle that protects, supports, and compresses abdominal contents. These muscles also flex and laterally rotate the trunk (see Table 10.6*).

7. Muscles of the pelvic floor and perineum (see Table 10.7*) support the pelvic viscera, resist increases in intra-abdominal pressure, inhibit urination and defecation, and aid erection.

8. Except for the pectoralis major and the latissimus dorsi, the superficial muscles of the thorax act to fix or promote movements of the scapula (see Table 10.8*). Scapular movements are effected primarily by posterior thoracic muscles.

9. Nine muscles cross the shoulder joint to effect movements of the humerus (see Table 10.9*). Of these, seven originate on the scapula and two arise from the axial skeleton. Four muscles contribute to the "rotator cuff" helping to stabilize the multiaxial shoulder joint. Generally speaking, muscles located anteriorly flex, rotate, and adduct the arm.

Those located posteriorly extend, rotate, and adduct the arm. The deltoid muscle of the shoulder is the prime mover of shoulder abduction.

10. Muscles causing movements of the forearm form the flesh of the arm (see Table 10.10*). Anterior arm muscles are forearm flexors; posterior muscles are forearm extensors.

11. Movements of the wrist, hand, and fingers are effected mainly by muscles originating on the forearm (see Table 10.11*). Except for the two pronator muscles, the anterior forearm muscles are wrist and/or finger flexors; those of the posterior compartment are wrist and finger extensors.

12. The intrinsic muscles of the hand aid in precise movements of the fingers (Table 10.13*) and in opposition, which helps us grip things in our palms. These small muscles are divided into thenar, hypothenar, and midpalmar groups.

13. Muscles crossing the hip and knee joints effect thigh and leg movements (see Table 10.14*). Anteromedial muscles include thigh flexors and/or adductors and knee extensors. Muscles of the posterior gluteal region extend and rotate the thigh. Posterior thigh muscles extend the hip and flex the knee.

14. Muscles in the leg act on the ankle and toes (see Table 10.15*). Anterior compartment muscles are largely ankle dorsiflexors. Lateral compartment muscles are plantar flexors and foot everters. Those of the posterior leg are plantar flexors.

15. The intrinsic muscles of the foot (Table 10.17*) support the foot arches and help move the toes. Most occur in the sole, arranged in four layers. They resemble the small muscles in the palm of the hand.

---

*See specific table cited for detailed description of each muscle in the group.

Review Questions

Multiple Choice/Matching

(Some questions have more than one correct answer. Select the best answer or answers from the choices given.)

1. A muscle that assists an agonist by causing a like movement or by stabilizing a joint over which an agonist acts is (a) an antagonist, (b) a prime mover, (c) a synergist, (d) an agonist.

2. A muscle in which the fibers are arranged at an angle to a central longitudinal tendon has a _____ arrangement. (a) circular, (b) longitudinal, (c) pennate, (d) parallel.

3. Match the muscle names in column B to the facial muscles described in column A.

Column A	Column B
____ (1) squints the eyes	(a) corrugator supercilii
____ (2) raises the eyebrows	(b) depressor anguli oris
____ (3) smiling muscle	(c) frontal belly of epicranius
____ (4) puckers the lips	(d) occipital belly of epicranius
____ (5) pulls the scalp posteriorly	(e) orbicularis oculi
	(f) orbicularis oris
	(g) zygomaticus

4. The prime mover of inspiration is the (a) diaphragm, (b) internal intercostals, (c) external intercostals, (d) abdominal wall muscles.

5. The arm muscle that both flexes the elbow and supinates the forearm is the (a) brachialis, (b) brachioradialis, (c) biceps brachii, (d) triceps brachii.

6. The chewing muscles that protrude the mandible and produce side-to-side grinding movements are the (a) buccinators, (b) masseters, (c) temporalis, (d) pterygoids.

7. Muscles that depress the hyoid bone and larynx include all but the (a) sternohyoid, (b) omohyoid, (c) geniohyoid, (d) sternothyroid.

8. Intrinsic muscles of the back that promote extension of the spine (or head) include all but (a) splenius muscles, (b) semispinalis muscles, (c) scalene muscles, (d) erector spinae.

9. Several muscles act to move and/or stabilize the scapula. Which of the following are small rectangular muscles that square the shoulders as they act together to retract the scapula? (a) levator scapulae, (b) rhomboids, (c) serratus anterior, (d) trapezius.

10. The quadriceps include all but (a) vastus lateralis, (b) vastus intermedius, (c) vastus medialis, (d) biceps femoris, (e) rectus femoris.

11. A prime mover of hip flexion is the (a) rectus femoris, (b) iliopsoas, (c) vasti muscles, (d) gluteus maximus.

12. The prime mover of hip extension *against* resistance is the (a) gluteus maximus, (b) gluteus medius, (c) biceps femoris, (d) semimembranosus.

10

13. Muscles that cause plantar flexion include all but the (a) gastrocnemius, (b) soleus, (c) tibialis anterior, (d) tibialis posterior, (e) fibularis muscles.

14. In walking, which two lower limb muscles keep the forward-swinging foot from dragging on the ground? (a) pronator teres and popliteus, (b) flexor digitorum longus and popliteus, (c) adductor longus and abductor digiti minimi in foot, (d) gluteus medius and tibialis anterior.

15. What criterion (or criteria) are used in naming the gluteus medius? (a) relative size, (b) muscle location, (c) muscle shape, (d) action, (e) number of origins.

16. Which of the following is a large, deep muscle that protracts the scapula during punching? (a) serratus anterior, (b) rhomboids, (c) levator scapulae, (d) subscapularis.

Short Answer Essay Questions

17. Name four criteria used in naming muscles, and provide an example (other than those used in the text) that illustrates each criterion.

18. Differentiate between the arrangement of elements (load, fulcrum, and effort) in first-, second-, and third-class levers.

19. What does it mean when we say that a lever operates at a mechanical disadvantage, and what benefits does such a lever system provide?

20. What muscles act to propel a food bolus down the length of the pharynx to the esophagus?

21. Name and describe the action of muscles used to shake your head no. To nod yes.

22. (a) Name the four muscle pairs that act in unison to compress the abdominal contents. (b) How does their arrangement (fiber direction) contribute to the strength of the abdominal wall? (c) Which of these muscles can effect lateral rotation of the spine? (d) Which can act alone to flex the spine?

23. List all (six) possible movements that can occur at the shoulder joint and name the prime mover(s) of each movement. Then name their antagonists.

24. (a) Name two forearm muscles that are powerful extensors and abductors of the wrist. (b) Name the sole forearm muscle that can flex the distal interphalangeal joints.

25. Name the muscles usually grouped together as the lateral rotators of the hip.

26. Name three thigh muscles that help you keep your seat astride a horse.

27. (a) Name three muscles or muscle groups used as sites for intramuscular injections. (b) Which of these is used most often in infants, and why?

28. Name two muscles in each of the following compartments or regions: (a) thenar eminence (ball of thumb), (b) posterior compartment of forearm, (c) anterior compartment of forearm—deep muscle group, (d) anterior muscle group in the arm, (e) muscles of mastication, (f) third muscle layer of the foot, (g) posterior compartment of leg, (h) medial compartment of thigh, (i) posterior compartment of thigh.

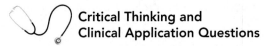

Critical Thinking and Clinical Application Questions

1. Assume you have a 10-lb weight in your right hand. Explain why it is easier to flex the right elbow when your forearm is supinated than when it is pronated.

2. When Mrs. O'Brien returned to her doctor for a follow-up visit after childbirth, she complained that she was having problems controlling her urine flow (was incontinent) when she sneezed. The physician asked his nurse to give Mrs. O'Brien instructions on how to perform exercises to strengthen the muscles of the pelvic floor. To what muscles was he referring?

3. Mr. Ahmadi, an out-of-shape 45-year-old man, was advised by his physician to lose weight and to exercise on a regular basis. He followed his diet faithfully and began to jog daily. One day, while on his morning jog, he heard a snapping sound that was immediately followed by a severe pain in his right lower calf. When his leg was examined, a gap was seen between his swollen upper calf region and his heel, and he was unable to plantar flex that ankle. What do you think happened? Why was the upper part of his calf swollen?

4. As Peter watched Sue walk down the runway at the fashion show, he contracted his right orbicularis oculi muscle, raised his arm, and contracted his opponens pollicis. Was he pleased or displeased with her performance? How do you know?

5. What type of lever is described by the following activities? (a) The soleus muscle plantar flexes the foot. (b) The deltoid abducts the arm. (c) The triceps brachii is strained while doing pushups.

6. While riding an unusually large horse, Chao Jung had to spread her thighs widely to span its back and she pulled the muscles in her medial thighs. Which muscles were these and what might this condition be called?

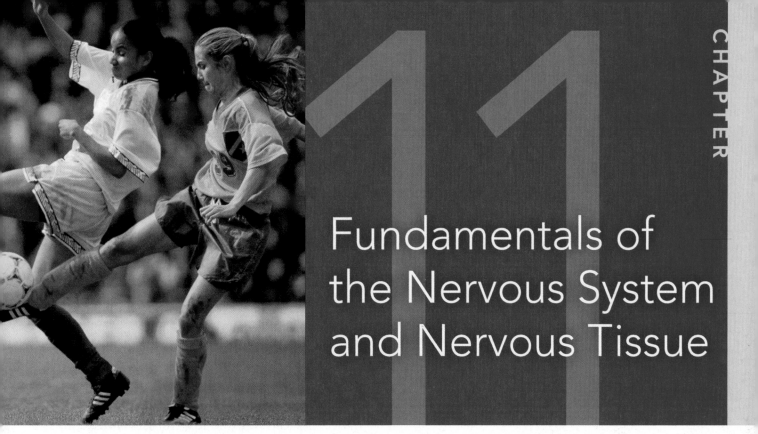

11

CHAPTER

Fundamentals of the Nervous System and Nervous Tissue

1. List the basic functions of the nervous system.

Organization of the Nervous System (pp. 388–389)

2. Explain the structural and functional divisions of the nervous system.

Histology of Nervous Tissue (pp. 389–397)

3. List the types of neuroglia and cite their functions.

4. Define neuron, describe its important structural components, and relate each to a functional role.

5. Differentiate between a nerve and a tract, and between a nucleus and a ganglion.

6. Explain the importance of the myelin sheath and describe how it is formed in the central and peripheral nervous systems.

7. Classify neurons structurally and functionally.

Neurophysiology (pp. 397–421)

8. Define resting membrane potential and describe its electrochemical basis.

9. Compare and contrast graded and action potentials.

10. Explain how action potentials are generated and propagated along neurons.

11. Define absolute and relative refractory periods.

12. Define saltatory conduction and contrast it to conduction along unmyelinated fibers.

13. Define synapse. Distinguish between electrical and chemical synapses structurally and in their mechanisms of information transmission.

14. Distinguish between excitatory and inhibitory postsynaptic potentials.

15. Describe how synaptic events are integrated and modified.

16. Define neurotransmitter and name several classes of neurotransmitters.

Basic Concepts of Neural Integration (pp. 421–423)

17. Describe common patterns of neuronal organization and processing.

18. Distinguish between serial and parallel processing.

Developmental Aspects of Neurons (pp. 423–425)

19. Describe the role of astrocytes and nerve cell adhesion molecules in neuronal differentiation.

You are driving down the freeway, and a horn blares to your right. You immediately swerve to your left. Charlie leaves a note on the kitchen table: "See you later. Have the stuff ready at 6." You know the "stuff" is chili with taco chips. You are dozing but you awaken instantly as your infant son makes a soft cry. What do these three events have in common? They are all everyday examples of the functioning of your nervous system, which has your body cells humming with activity nearly all the time.

The **nervous system** is the master controlling and communicating system of the body. Every thought, action, and emotion reflects its activity. Its cells communicate by electrical and chemical signals, which are rapid and specific, and usually cause almost immediate responses.

The nervous system has three overlapping functions (Figure 11.1): (1) It uses its millions of sensory receptors to monitor changes occurring both inside and outside the body. The gathered information is called **sensory input.** (2) It processes and interprets sensory input and decides what should be done at each moment—a process called **integration.** (3) It causes a *response*, called **motor output,** by activating *effector organs.* For example, when you are driving and see a red light ahead (sensory input), your nervous system integrates this information (red light means "stop"), and your foot goes for the brake (motor output).

This chapter begins with a brief overview of the organization of the nervous system. It then focuses on the functional anatomy of nervous tissue, especially that of nerve cells, or *neurons*, which are the key to neural communication.

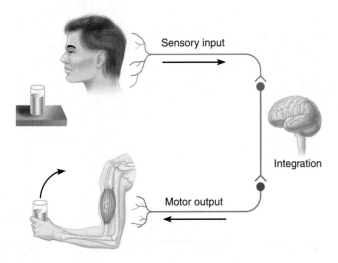

FIGURE 11.1 **The nervous system's functions.**

Organization of the Nervous System

We have only one highly integrated nervous system. However, for convenience, it can be divided into two principal parts (Figure 11.2). The **central nervous system (CNS)** consists of the *brain* and *spinal cord*, which occupy the dorsal body cavity. The CNS is the integrating and command center of the nervous system. It interprets sensory input and dictates motor responses based on past experience, reflexes, and current conditions. The **peripheral nervous system (PNS),** the part of the nervous system *outside* the CNS, consists mainly of the nerves (bundles of axons) that extend from the brain and spinal cord. *Spinal nerves* carry impulses to and from the spinal cord; *cranial nerves* carry impulses to and from the brain. These peripheral nerves serve as the communication lines that link all parts of the body to the CNS.

The PNS has two functional subdivisions (see Figure 11.2). The **sensory,** or **afferent, division** (af'er-ent; "carrying toward") consists of nerve fibers that convey impulses to the central nervous system from sensory receptors located throughout the body. Sensory fibers conveying impulses from the skin, skeletal muscles, and joints are called *somatic afferent fibers* (*soma* = body), and those transmitting impulses from the visceral organs (organs within the ventral body cavity) are called *visceral afferent fibers.* The sensory division keeps the CNS constantly informed of events going on both inside and outside the body.

The **motor,** or **efferent, division** (ef'er-ent; "carrying away") of the PNS transmits impulses *from* the CNS to effector organs, which are the muscles and glands. These impulses activate muscles to contract and glands to secrete; that is, they *effect* (bring about) a motor response.

The motor division also has two main parts:

1. The **somatic nervous system** is composed of somatic motor nerve fibers (axons) that conduct impulses from the CNS to skeletal muscles. It is often referred to as the **voluntary nervous system** because it allows us to consciously control our skeletal muscles.

2. The **autonomic nervous system (ANS)** consists of visceral motor nerve fibers that regulate the activity of smooth muscles, cardiac muscles, and glands. *Autonomic* means "a law unto itself," and because we generally cannot control such activities as the pumping of our heart or the movement of food through our digestive tract, the ANS is also referred to as the **involuntary nervous system.** As indicated in Figure 11.2 and described in Chapter 14, the ANS has two functional subdivisions, the **sympathetic**

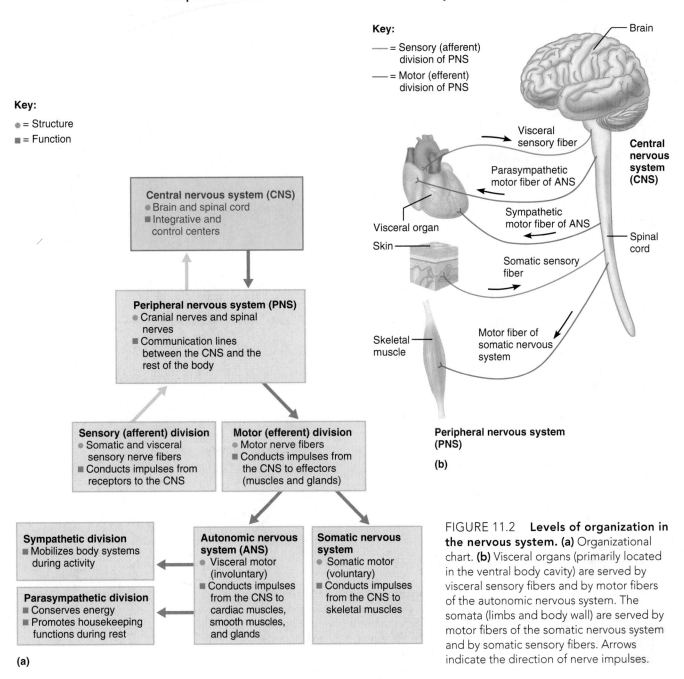

Key:

● = Structure

■ = Function

Key:

—— = Sensory (afferent) division of PNS

—— = Motor (efferent) division of PNS

Central nervous system (CNS)
- ● Brain and spinal cord
- ■ Integrative and control centers

Peripheral nervous system (PNS)
- ● Cranial nerves and spinal nerves
- ■ Communication lines between the CNS and the rest of the body

Sensory (afferent) division
- ● Somatic and visceral sensory nerve fibers
- ■ Conducts impulses from receptors to the CNS

Motor (efferent) division
- ● Motor nerve fibers
- ■ Conducts impulses from the CNS to effectors (muscles and glands)

Sympathetic division
- ■ Mobilizes body systems during activity

Parasympathetic division
- ■ Conserves energy
- ■ Promotes housekeeping functions during rest

Autonomic nervous system (ANS)
- ● Visceral motor (involuntary)
- ■ Conducts impulses from the CNS to cardiac muscles, smooth muscles, and glands

Somatic nervous system
- ● Somatic motor (voluntary)
- ■ Conducts impulses from the CNS to skeletal muscles

(a)

Brain

Visceral sensory fiber

Parasympathetic motor fiber of ANS

Central nervous system (CNS)

Visceral organ

Skin

Sympathetic motor fiber of ANS

Somatic sensory fiber

Spinal cord

Skeletal muscle

Motor fiber of somatic nervous system

Motor fiber of somatic nervous system

Peripheral nervous system (PNS)

(b)

FIGURE 11.2 **Levels of organization in the nervous system. (a)** Organizational chart. **(b)** Visceral organs (primarily located in the ventral body cavity) are served by visceral sensory fibers and by motor fibers of the autonomic nervous system. The somata (limbs and body wall) are served by motor fibers of the somatic nervous system and by somatic sensory fibers. Arrows indicate the direction of nerve impulses.

11

and the **parasympathetic,** which typically work in opposition to each other—what one subdivision stimulates, the other inhibits.

Histology of Nervous Tissue

The nervous system consists mostly of nervous tissue, which is highly cellular. For example, less than 20% of the CNS is extracellular space, which means that the cells are densely packed and tightly intertwined. Although it is very complex, nervous tissue is made up of just two principal types of cells: (1) *supporting cells*, smaller cells that surround and wrap the more delicate neurons, and (2) *neurons*, the excitable nerve cells that transmit electrical signals.

Neuroglia

Neurons associate closely with much smaller cells called **neuroglia** (nu-rog′le-ah; "nerve glue") or simply **glial cells** (gle′al). There are six types of neuroglia—four in the CNS and two in the PNS (Figure 11.3). Each type has a unique function, but in general, these cells provide a supportive scaffolding for neurons. Some produce chemicals that guide young neurons to the proper connections, and

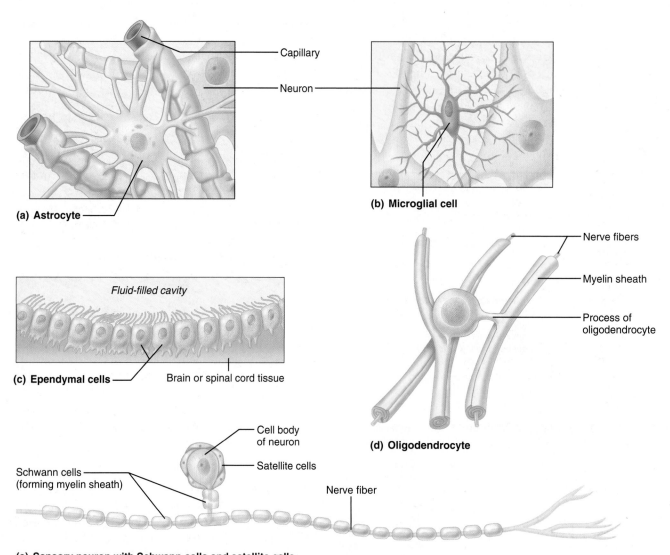

(a) Astrocyte

Capillary

Neuron

(b) Microglial cell

Fluid-filled cavity

(c) Ependymal cells

Brain or spinal cord tissue

Nerve fibers

Myelin sheath

Process of oligodendrocyte

(d) Oligodendrocyte

Cell body of neuron

Satellite cells

Schwann cells (forming myelin sheath)

Nerve fiber

(e) Sensory neuron with Schwann cells and satellite cells

FIGURE 11.3 **Neuroglia. (a–d)** Types of neuroglia found in the CNS. Notice in (d) that it is the processes of the oligodendrocytes that form the myelin sheaths around CNS nerve fibers. **(e)** The relationships of Schwann cells (myelinating cells) and satellite cells to a sensory neuron (nerve cell) in the peripheral nervous system.

promote neuron health and growth. Others wrap around and insulate neuronal processes to speed up action potential conduction.

Neuroglia in the CNS

Neuroglia in the CNS include *astrocytes, microglia, ependymal cells,* and *oligodendrocytes.* Like neurons, most glial cells have branching processes (extensions) and a central cell body (Figure 11.3a–d). Neuroglia can be distinguished, however, by their much smaller size and by their darker-staining nuclei. They outnumber neurons in the CNS by about 10 to 1, and make up about half the mass of the brain.

Shaped like delicate branching sea anemones, **astrocytes** (as′tro-sītz; "star cells") are the most abun-

dant and most versatile glial cells. Their numerous radiating processes cling to neurons and their synaptic endings, and cover nearby capillaries, supporting and bracing the neurons and anchoring them to their nutrient supply lines, the blood capillaries (Figure 11.3a). Astrocytes have a role in making exchanges between capillaries and neurons, in guiding the migration of young neurons, in synapse formation, and in helping to determine capillary permeability. They also control the chemical environment around neurons, where their most important job is "mopping up" leaked potassium ions and recapturing (and recycling) released neurotransmitters. Furthermore, astrocytes connected by gap junctions have been shown to respond to nearby nerve impulses and released

11

neurotransmitters by taking in calcium and signaling one another both by slow-paced intracellular calcium pulses (calcium sparks) and extracellular chemical messengers. According to recent research, astrocytes also influence neuronal functioning and therefore participate in information processing in the brain.

Microglia (mi-kro′gle-ah) are small ovoid cells with relatively long "thorny" processes (Figure 11.3b). Their processes touch nearby neurons, monitoring their health, and when they sense that certain neurons are injured or in other trouble, the microglia migrate toward them. Where invading microorganisms or dead neurons are present, the microglia transform into a special type of macrophage that phagocytizes the microorganisms or neuronal debris. This protective role of the microglia is important because cells of the immune system are denied access to the CNS.

Ependymal cells (ĕ-pen′dĭ-mul; "wrapping garment") range in shape from squamous to columnar, and many are ciliated. They line the central cavities of the brain and the spinal cord, where they form a fairly permeable barrier between the cerebrospinal fluid that fills those cavities and the tissue fluid bathing the cells of the CNS. The beating of their cilia helps to circulate the cerebrospinal fluid that cushions the brain and spinal cord (Figure 11.3c).

Though they also branch, the **oligodendrocytes** (ol″ĭ-go-den′dro-sīts) have fewer processes (oligo = few; dendr = branch) than astrocytes. Oligodendrocytes line up along the thicker neuron fibers in the CNS and wrap their processes tightly around the fibers, producing insulating coverings called myelin sheaths (Figure 11.3d).

Neuroglia in the PNS

The two kinds of PNS neuroglia—satellite cells and Schwann cells—differ mainly in location. **Satellite cells** surround neuron cell bodies located in the peripheral neurons system (Figure 11.3e), but their function is still largely unknown. Their name comes from a fancied resemblance to the moons (satellites) around a planet.

Schwann cells (also called neurolemmocytes) surround and form myelin sheaths around the larger nerve fibers in the peripheral nervous system (Figures 11.3e and 11.4b). Hence, they are functionally similar to oligodendrocytes. (The formation of myelin sheaths is described later in this chapter.) Schwann cells are vital to regeneration of damaged peripheral nerve fibers.

Neurons

The billions of **neurons,** also called **nerve cells,** are the structural units of the nervous system. They are highly specialized cells that conduct messages in the form of nerve impulses from one part of the body to another. Besides their ability to conduct nerve impulses, neurons have some other special characteristics:

1. They have extreme longevity. Given good nutrition, neurons can function optimally for a lifetime (over 100 years).

2. They are amitotic. As neurons assume their roles as communicating links of the nervous system, they lose their ability to divide. We pay a high price for this neuron feature because they cannot be replaced if destroyed. There are exceptions to this rule. For example, olfactory epithelium and some hippocampal regions contain stem cells that can produce new neurons throughout life. (The hippocampus is a brain region involved in memory.)

3. They have an exceptionally high metabolic rate and require continuous and abundant supplies of oxygen and glucose. Neurons cannot survive for more than a few minutes without oxygen.

Neurons are typically large, complex cells. Although they vary in structure, they all have a cell body from which one or more slender processes project (Figure 11.4). The plasma membrane of neurons is the site of electrical signaling, and it plays a crucial role in cell-to-cell interactions that occur during development.

Cell Body

The **neuron cell body** consists of a transparent, spherical nucleus with a conspicuous nucleolus surrounded by cytoplasm. Also called the **perikaryon** (peri = around, kary = nucleus) or **soma,** the cell body ranges in diameter from 5 to 140 μm. The cell body is the major biosynthetic center of a neuron. Except for centrioles, it contains the usual organelles. (Centrioles play an important role in forming the mitotic spindle. Their apparent absence reflects the amitotic nature of most neurons.)

The neuron cell body's protein- and membrane-making machinery, consisting of clustered free ribosomes and rough endoplasmic reticulum (ER), is probably the most active and best developed in the body. This rough ER, referred to as **Nissl bodies** (nis′l) or **chromatophilic substance** (chromatophilic = "color loving"), stains darkly with basic dyes. The Golgi apparatus is also well developed and forms an arc or a complete circle around the nucleus. Mitochondria are scattered among the other organelles. Microtubules and **neurofibrils,** bundles of intermediate filaments (neurofilaments), which are important in maintaining cell shape and integrity, form a network throughout the cell body. The cell body of some neurons also contains pigment inclusions. For example, some contain a black melanin, a red iron-containing pigment, or a golden-brown pigment

11

Q *Neurons with the longest axons tend to have large cell bodies, while those with short axons usually have small cell bodies. Can you think of an explanation for this relationship?*

(a)

(b)

FIGURE 11.4 **Structure of a motor neuron. (a)** Scanning electron micrograph showing the cell body and dendrites with obvious dendritic spines (6000×). **(b)** Diagrammatic view.

called *lipofuscin* (lip"o-fu'sin). Lipofuscin, a harmless by-product of lysosomal activity, is sometimes called the "aging pigment" because it accumulates in neurons of elderly individuals.

The cell body is the focal point for the outgrowth of neuron processes during embryonic development. In most neurons, the plasma membrane of the cell body also acts as *part of the receptive region* (Table 11.1, pp. 396–397) that receives information from other neurons.

Most neuron cell bodies are located in the CNS, where they are protected by the bones of the skull

and vertebral column. Clusters of cell bodies in the CNS are called **nuclei,** whereas those that lie along the nerves in the PNS are called **ganglia** (gang'gle-ah; *ganglion* = "knot on a string," "swelling").

Processes

Armlike **processes** extend from the cell body of all neurons. The brain and spinal cord (CNS) contain both neuron cell bodies and their processes. The PNS, for the most part, consists chiefly of neuron processes. Bundles of neuron processes are called **tracts** in the CNS and **nerves** in the PNS.

The two types of neuron processes, *dendrites* and *axons* (ak'sonz), differ from each other in the structure and function of their plasma membranes. The convention is to describe these processes using

A *A longer axon requires more supporting "machinery" in the cell body to service it.*

a motor neuron as an example of a typical neuron. We shall follow this practice, but keep in mind that many sensory neurons and some tiny CNS neurons differ from the "typical" pattern we present here.

Dendrites   **Dendrites** of motor neurons are short, tapering, diffusely branching extensions. Typically, motor neurons have hundreds of twiglike dendrites clustering close to the cell body. Virtually all organelles present in the cell body also occur in dendrites. Dendrites are the main **receptive** or **input regions** (see Table 11.1). They provide an enormous surface area for receiving signals from other neurons. In many brain areas, the finer dendrites are highly specialized for information collection. They bristle with thorny appendages having bulbous or spiky ends called *dendritic spines* (Figure 11.4a), which represent points of close contact (synapses) with other neurons. Dendrites convey incoming messages *toward* the cell body. These electrical signals are usually *not* action potentials (nerve impulses) but are short-distance signals called *graded potentials*, as described shortly.

The Axon   Each neuron has a single **axon** (*axo* = axis, axle). The initial region of the axon arises from a cone-shaped area of the cell body called the **axon hillock** ("little hill") and then narrows to form a slender process that is uniform in diameter for the rest of its length (Figure 11.4). In some neurons, the axon is very short or absent; in others it is long and accounts for nearly the entire length of the neuron. For example, axons of the motor neurons controlling the skeletal muscles of your great toe extend from the lumbar region of your spine to your foot, a distance of a meter or more (3–4 feet), making them among the longest cells in the body. Any long axon is called a **nerve fiber.**

Each neuron has only one axon, but axons may have occasional branches along their length. These branches, called **axon collaterals,** extend from the axon at more or less right angles. Whether an axon is undivided or has collaterals, it usually branches profusely at its end (terminus): 10,000 or more **terminal branches,** or **telodendria,** per neuron is not unusual. The knoblike distal endings of the terminal branches are variously called **axon terminals, synaptic knobs,** or **boutons** (boo-tonz; "buttons"). Take your pick!

Functionally, the axon is the **conducting region** of the neuron (Table 11.1). It *generates nerve impulses* and *transmits them*, typically away from the cell body. In motor neurons, the nerve impulse is generated at the junction of the axon hillock and axon (which is therefore called the *trigger zone*) and conducted along the axon to the axon terminals, which are the **secretory region** of the neuron. When the impulse reaches the axon terminals, it causes *neurotransmitters*, signaling chemicals stored in vesicles there, to be released into the extracellular space. The neurotransmitters either excite or inhibit neurons (or effector cells) with which the axon is in close contact. Because each neuron both receives signals from and sends signals to scores of other neurons, it carries on "conversations" with many different neurons at the same time.

An axon contains the same organelles found in the dendrites and cell body with two important exceptions—it lacks Nissl bodies and a Golgi apparatus, the structures involved with protein synthesis and packaging. Consequently, an axon depends (1) on its cell body to renew the necessary proteins and membrane components, and (2) on efficient transport mechanisms to distribute them. Axons quickly decay if cut or severely damaged.

Because axons are often very long, moving molecules along their length might appear to be a problem. However, through the cooperative effort of several types of cytoskeletal elements (microtubules, actin filaments, and so on), substances travel continuously along the axon both away from and toward the cell body. Movement toward the axon terminals is *anterograde movement*, and that in the opposite direction is *retrograde movement*.

Substances moved in the anterograde direction include mitochondria, cytoskeletal elements, membrane components used to renew the axon plasma membrane, or **axolemma** (ak"so-lem'ah), and enzymes needed for synthesis of certain neurotransmitters. (Some neurotransmitters are synthesized in the cell body and then transported to the axon terminals.)

Substances transported through the axon in the retrograde direction are mostly organelles being returned to the cell body for degradation or recycling. Retrograde transport is also an important means of intracellular communication for "advising" the cell body of conditions at the axon terminals, and for delivering to the cell body vesicles containing signal molecules (like nerve growth factor, which activates certain nuclear genes promoting growth).

A single bidirectional transport mechanism appears to be responsible for axonal transport. It uses ATP-dependent "motor" proteins such as kinesin, dynein, and myosin. These proteins propel cellular components along the microtubules like trains along tracks at speeds up to 40 cm (15 inches) per day.

HOMEOSTATIC IMBALANCE

Certain viruses and bacterial toxins that damage neural tissues use retrograde axonal transport to reach the cell body. This transport mechanism has

11

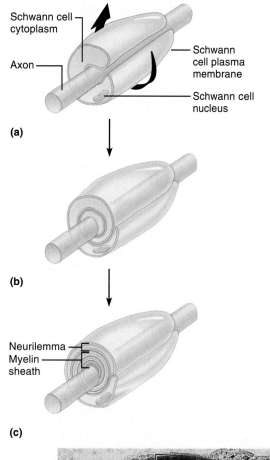

Schwann cell cytoplasm

Axon

Schwann cell plasma membrane

Schwann cell nucleus

(a)

(b)

Neurilemma
Myelin sheath

(c)

Myelin sheath

Schwann cell cytoplasm

Neurilemma

Axon

(d)

FIGURE 11.5   **Relationship of Schwann cells to axons in the PNS. (a–c)** Myelination of a nerve fiber (axon). As illustrated, a Schwann cell envelops an axon in a trough. It then rotates around the axon, enveloping the axon loosely in successive layers of its plasma membrane. Eventually, the Schwann cell cytoplasm is forced from between the membranes and comes to lie peripherally just beneath the exposed portion of the Schwann cell plasma membrane. The tight membrane wrappings surrounding the axon form the myelin sheath; the area of Schwann cell cytoplasm and its exposed membrane is referred to as the neurilemma. **(d)** Electron micrograph of a myelinated axon, cross-sectional view (20,000×).

been demonstrated for polio, rabies, and herpes simplex viruses and for tetanus toxin. Its use as a tool to treat genetic diseases by introducing viruses containing "corrected" genes is under investigation. ●

Myelin Sheath and Neurilemma   Many nerve fibers, particularly those that are long or large in diameter, are covered with a whitish, fatty (protein-lipoid), segmented **myelin sheath** (mi′ĕ-lin). Myelin protects and electrically insulates fibers, and it increases the speed of transmission of nerve impulses. **Myelinated fibers** (axons bearing a myelin sheath) conduct nerve impulses rapidly, whereas **unmyelinated fibers** conduct impulses quite slowly. Note that myelin sheaths are associated only with axons. Dendrites are *always* unmyelinated.

Myelin sheaths in the PNS are formed by Schwann cells, which indent to receive an axon and then wrap themselves around it in a jelly roll fashion (Figure 11.5). Initially the wrapping is loose, but the Schwann cell cytoplasm is gradually squeezed from between the membrane layers. When the wrapping process is complete, many concentric layers of Schwann cell plasma membrane enclose the axon, much like gauze wrapped around an injured finger. This tight coil of wrapped membranes is the myelin sheath, and its thickness depends on the number of spirals. Plasma membranes of myelinating cells contain much less protein than the plasma membranes of most body cells. Channel and carrier proteins are notably absent, a characteristic that makes myelin sheaths exceptionally good electrical insulators. Another unique characteristic of these membranes is the presence of specific protein molecules that interlock to form a sort of molecular Velcro between adjacent myelin membranes.

The nucleus and most of the cytoplasm of the Schwann cell end up as a bulge just external to the myelin sheath. This portion of the Schwann cell, which includes the exposed part of its plasma membrane, is called the **neurilemma** ("neuron husk"). Adjacent Schwann cells along an axon do not touch one another, so there are gaps in the sheath. These gaps, called **nodes of Ranvier** (ran′vē-ā″) or **neurofibril nodes,** occur at regular intervals (about 1 mm apart) along the myelinated axon. It is at these nodes that axon collaterals can emerge from the axon.

Sometimes Schwann cells surround peripheral nerve fibers but the coiling process does not occur. In such instances, a single Schwann cell can partially enclose 15 or more axons, each of which occupies a separate recess in the Schwann cell surface. Nerve fibers associated with Schwann cells in this manner are said to be *unmyelinated* and are typically thin fibers.

Both myelinated and unmyelinated axons are also found in the central nervous system. However, it is oligodendrocytes that form CNS myelin sheaths (Figure 11.3d). In contrast to Schwann cells, each of which forms only one segment (internode) of a myelin sheath, oligodendrocytes have multiple flat processes that can coil around as many as 60 axons at the same time. Nodes of Ranvier are present, but are more widely spaced than in the PNS. CNS myelin sheaths lack a neurilemma because cell extensions are doing the coiling and the squeezed-out cytoplasm is forced not peripherally but back toward the centrally located nucleus. As in the PNS, the smallest-diameter axons are unmyelinated. These unmyelinated axons are covered by the long extensions of adjacent glial cells.

Regions of the brain and spinal cord containing dense collections of myelinated fibers are referred to as **white matter** and are primarily fiber tracts. **Gray matter** contains mostly nerve cell bodies and unmyelinated fibers.

Classification of Neurons

Neurons are classified both structurally and functionally. We describe both classifications here but use the functional classification in most discussions.

Structural Classification   Neurons are grouped structurally according to the number of processes extending from their cell body. Three major neuron groups make up this classification: multipolar (*polar = end, pole*), bipolar, and unipolar neurons (Table 11.1).

Multipolar neurons have three or more processes. They are the most common neuron type in humans (more than 99% of neurons belong to this class) and the major neuron type in the CNS.

Bipolar neurons have two processes—an axon and a dendrite—that extend from opposite sides of the cell body. These rare neurons are found in some of the special sense organs. Examples include some neurons in the retina of the eye and in the olfactory mucosa.

Unipolar neurons have a single short process that emerges from the cell body and divides T-like into proximal and distal branches. The more distal process, which is often associated with a sensory receptor, is the **peripheral process,** whereas that entering the CNS is the **central process** (Table 11.1). Unipolar neurons are more accurately called **pseudounipolar neurons** (*pseudo = false*) because they originate as bipolar neurons. Then, during early embryonic development, the two processes converge and partially fuse to form the short single process that issues from the cell body. Unipolar neurons are found chiefly in ganglia in the PNS, where they function as sensory neurons.

The fact that the fused peripheral and central processes of unipolar neurons are continuous and function as a single fiber might make you wonder whether they are axons or dendrites. The central process is definitely an axon because it conducts impulses away from the cell body (one definition of axon). However, the peripheral process is perplexing. Three facts favor classifying it as an axon: (1) it generates and conducts an impulse (functional definition of axon); (2) when large, it is heavily myelinated; and (3) it has a uniform diameter and is indistinguishable microscopically from an axon. However, the older definition of a dendrite as a process that transmits impulses *toward* the cell body interferes with that conclusion. So which is it? In this book, we have chosen to emphasize the newer definition of an axon as generating and transmitting an impulse. Hence, *for unipolar neurons,* we will refer to the combined length of the peripheral and central process as an axon. In place of "dendrites," unipolar neurons have *receptive endings* (sensory terminals) at the end of the peripheral process.

Functional Classification   This scheme groups neurons according to the direction in which the nerve impulse travels relative to the central nervous system. Based on this criterion, there are sensory neurons, motor neurons, and interneurons (Table 11.1).

Sensory, or **afferent, neurons** transmit impulses from sensory receptors in the skin or internal organs *toward* or *into* the central nervous system. Except for certain neurons found in some special sense organs, virtually all sensory neurons are unipolar, and their cell bodies are located in sensory ganglia *outside* the CNS. Only the most distal parts of these unipolar neurons act as impulse receptor sites, and the peripheral processes are often very long. For example, fibers carrying sensory impulses from the skin of your great toe travel for more than a meter before they reach their cell bodies in a ganglion close to the spinal cord.

Although the receptive endings of some sensory neurons are naked, in which case those terminals themselves function as sensory receptors, many bear receptors that include other cell types. The various types of general sensory receptor end organs, such as those of the skin, are described in Chapter 13. The special sensory receptors (of the ear, eye, etc.) are the topic of Chapter 15.

Motor, or **efferent, neurons** carry impulses *away from* the CNS to the effector organs (muscles and glands) of the body periphery. Motor neurons are multipolar, and except for some neurons of the autonomic nervous system, their cell bodies are located in the CNS.

Interneurons, or **association neurons,** lie between motor and sensory neurons in neural

11

TABLE 11.1	Comparison of Structural Classes of Neurons	
	NEURON TYPE	
MULTIPOLAR	**BIPOLAR**	**UNIPOLAR (PSEUDOUNIPOLAR)**

STRUCTURAL CLASS: NEURON TYPE ACCORDING TO THE NUMBER OF PROCESSES EXTENDING FROM THE CELL BODY

Many processes extend from the cell body; all are dendrites except for a single axon.	Two processes extend from the cell body: one is a fused dendrite, the other is an axon.	One process extends from the cell body and forms central and peripheral processes, which together comprise an axon.
		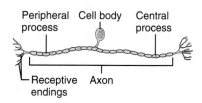

RELATIONSHIP OF ANATOMY TO THE THREE FUNCTIONAL REGIONS

▢ = Receptive region (receives stimulus). Plasma membrane exhibits chemically gated ion channels.	▢ = Conducting region (generates/ transmits action potential). Plasma membrane exhibits voltage-gated Na^+ and K^+ channels.	▢ = Secretory region (axon terminals release neurotransmitters). Plasma membrane exhibits voltage-gated Ca^+ channels.
	(Many bipolar neurons do not generate action potentials and, in those that do, the location of the trigger zone is not universal.)	

RELATIVE ABUNDANCE AND LOCATION IN HUMAN BODY

Most abundant in body. Major neuron type in the CNS.	Rare. Found in some special sensory organs (olfactory mucosa, eye, ear).	Found mainly in the PNS. Common only in dorsal root ganglia of the spinal cord and sensory ganglia of cranial nerves.

STRUCTURAL VARIATIONS

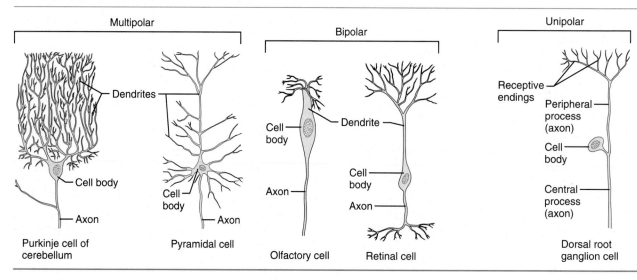

TABLE 11.1	*(continued)*

NEURON TYPE		
MULTIPOLAR	**BIPOLAR**	**UNIPOLAR (PSEUDOUNIPOLAR)**

FUNCTIONAL CLASS: NEURON TYPE ACCORDING TO DIRECTION OF IMPULSE CONDUCTION

1. Most multipolar neurons are **interneurons (association neurons)** that conduct impulses within the CNS, integrating sensory input or motor output; may be one of a chain of CNS neurons, or a single neuron connecting sensory and motor neurons. **2.** Some multipolar neurons are **motor neurons** that conduct impulses along the efferent pathways from the CNS to an effector (muscle/gland).	Essentially all bipolar neurons are **sensory neurons** that are located in some special sense organs. For example, bipolar cells of the retina are involved with the transmission of visual inputs from the eye to the brain (via an intermediate chain of neurons).	Most unipolar neurons are **sensory neurons** that conduct impulses along afferent pathways to the CNS for interpretation. (These sensory neurons are called primary or first-order sensory neurons.)

pathways and shuttle signals through CNS pathways where integration occurs. Most interneurons are confined within the CNS. They make up over 99% of the neurons of the body, including most of those in the CNS. Almost all interneurons are multipolar, but there is considerable diversity in both size and fiber-branching patterns. The Purkinje and pyramidal cells illustrated as structural variations in Table 11.1 are just two examples of their variety.

Neurophysiology

Neurons are highly *irritable* (responsive to stimuli). When a neuron is adequately stimulated, an electrical impulse is generated and conducted along the length of its axon. This response, called the *action potential (nerve impulse)*, is always the same, regardless of the source or type of stimulus, and it underlies virtually all functional activities of the nervous system.

In this section, we will consider how neurons become excited or inhibited and how they communicate with other cells. First, however, we need to explore some basic principles of electricity and revisit the resting membrane potential.

Basic Principles of Electricity

The human body is electrically neutral; it has the same number of positive and negative charges. However, there are areas where one type of charge predominates, making such regions positively or negatively charged. Because opposite charges attract each other, energy must be used (work must be done) to separate them. On the other hand, the coming together of opposite charges liberates energy that can be used to do work. Thus, situations in which there are separated electrical charges of opposite sign have potential energy.

Some Definitions: Voltage, Resistance, Current

The measure of potential energy generated by separated charge is called **voltage** and is measured in either *volts* or *millivolts* (1 mV = 0.001 V). Voltage is always measured between two points and is called the **potential difference** or simply the **potential** between the points. The greater the difference in charge between two points, the higher the voltage.

The flow of electrical charge from one point to another is called a **current**, and it can be used to do

11

work—for example, to power a flashlight. The amount of charge that moves between the two points depends on two factors: voltage and resistance. **Resistance** is the hindrance to charge flow provided by substances through which the current must pass. Substances with high electrical resistance are called *insulators*; those with low resistance are called *conductors*.

The relationship between voltage, current, and resistance is given by **Ohm's law:**

$$\text{Current } (I) = \frac{\text{voltage } (V)}{\text{resistance } (R)}$$

which tells us that current (*I*) is directly proportional to voltage: The greater the voltage (potential difference), the greater the current. This relationship also tells us there is no net current flow between points that have the same potential, as you can see by inserting a value of 0 V into the equation. A third thing Ohm's law tells us is that current is inversely related to resistance: The greater the resistance, the smaller the current.

In the body, electrical currents reflect the flow of ions (rather than free electrons) across cellular membranes. (Unlike the electrons flowing along your house wiring, there are no free electrons "running around" in a living system.) As described in Chapter 3, there is a slight difference in the numbers of positive and negative ions on the two sides of cellular plasma membranes (there is a charge separation), so there is a potential across those membranes. The resistance to current flow is provided by the plasma membranes.

Role of Membrane Ion Channels

Plasma membranes are peppered with a variety of membrane proteins that act as *ion channels*. These channels are large proteins, often with several subunits, whose amino acid chains snake back and forth across the membrane. In many channels, part of the protein forms a molecular "gate" that changes shape to open and close the channel in response to specific signals. These are called *gated* channels (Figure 11.6). **Chemically gated,** or **ligand-gated, channels** open when the appropriate chemical (in this case a neurotransmitter) binds. **Voltage-gated channels** open and close in response to changes in the membrane potential. **Mechanically gated channels** open in response to physical deformation of the receptor (seen in sensory receptors for touch and pressure)—more on this later. Other channels, **leakage** or **nongated channels,** do not respond to these signals and are always open. Each type of channel is selective as to the type of ion (or ions) it allows to pass. For example, a potassium ion channel allows only potassium ions to pass.

When gated ion channels are open, ions diffuse quickly across the membrane following their electrochemical gradients, creating electrical currents and

11

Q *For an open channel, what factors determine in which direction ions will flow through that channel?*

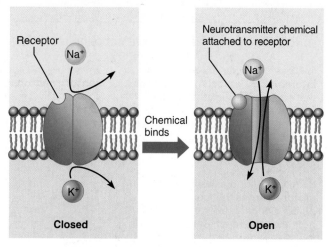

(a) Chemically gated ion channel

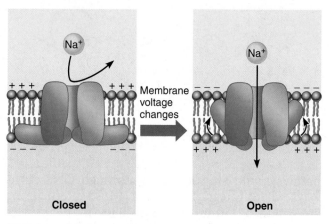

(b) Voltage-gated ion channel

FIGURE 11.6 **Operation of gated channels.** **(a)** Chemically (ligand) gated channels (a Na⁺-K⁺ channel in this example) open when the appropriate neurotransmitter binds to the receptor, allowing simultaneous movement of Na⁺ and K⁺ through the channel. **(b)** Voltage-gated channels open or close in response to changes in membrane voltage. In this example, a Na⁺ channel opens as the membrane interior changes from negative to positive.

voltage changes across the membrane according to the rearranged Ohm's law equation:

$$\text{Voltage } (V) = \text{current } (I) \times \text{resistance } (R)$$

Ions move along chemical *concentration gradients* when they diffuse passively from an area of their higher concentration to an area of lower concentration,

The concentration gradient and the electrical gradient— together called the electrochemical gradient. A

and along *electrical gradients* when they move toward an area of opposite electrical charge. Together, electrical and concentration gradients constitute the **electrochemical gradient.** It is ion flows along electrochemical gradients that underlie all electrical phenomena in neurons.

The Resting Membrane Potential

The potential difference between two points is measured with a voltmeter (Figure 11.7). When one microelectrode of the voltmeter is inserted into the neuron and the other is in the extracellular fluid, a voltage across the membrane of approximately −70 mV is recorded. The minus sign indicates that the cytoplasmic side (inside) of the membrane is negatively charged relative to the outside. This potential difference in a resting neuron (V_r) is called the **resting membrane potential,** and the membrane is said to be **polarized.** The value of the resting membrane potential varies (from −40 mV to −90 mV) in different types of neurons.

The resting potential exists only across the membrane; that is, the bulk solutions inside and outside the cell are electrically neutral. As shown in Figure 11.8, the resting membrane potential is generated by differences in the ionic makeup of the intracellular and extracellular fluids and the differential permeability of the plasma membrane to those ions. The cell cytosol contains a lower concentration of Na^+ and a higher concentration of K^+ than the extracellular

FIGURE 11.7 Measuring membrane potential in neurons. The potential across the membrane of a neuron (membrane potential) can be recorded by inserting an electrode inside a neuron. The potential difference between this electrode and the ground electrode outside the cell is approximately −70 mV (inside negative).

fluid. In the extracellular fluid, the positive charges of sodium and other cations are balanced chiefly by chloride ions (Cl^-). Negatively charged (anionic) proteins (A^-) help to balance the positive charges of intracellular cations (primarily K^+). Although there are many other solutes (glucose, urea, and other ions) in both fluids, potassium plays the most important role in generating the membrane potential.

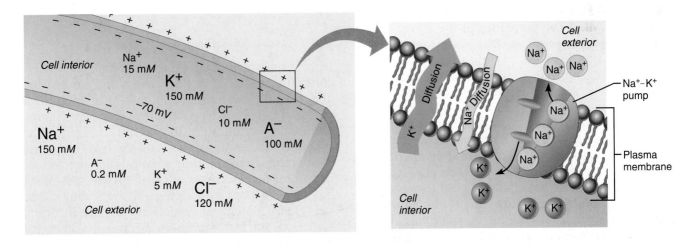

FIGURE 11.8 The basis of the resting membrane potential. Approximate concentrations of major ions in mammalian cells are indicated in millimoles per liter (m*M*). Steady diffusion of K^+ to the cell exterior through leakage channels is strongly promoted by its concentration gradient. Na^+ is strongly attracted to the cell interior by its concentration gradient, but it is far less able to cross the cell membrane because of the near lack of Na^+ leakage channels. The relative membrane permeability to Na^+ and K^+ through such leakage channels is indicated by diffusion arrows of different thickness. The resulting net outward diffusion of positive charge (K^+) leads to a state of relative negativity on the inner membrane face. This membrane potential (−70 mV, inside negative) is maintained indirectly by the sodium-potassium pump, which transports three Na^+ out of the cell for each two K^+ transported back into the cell. The electrochemical gradient thus maintained resists K^+ efflux but enhances the drive for Na^+ influx.

Q Hyper *means greater than or more than. When we say the membrane becomes hyperpolarized, what value has increased or become greater?*

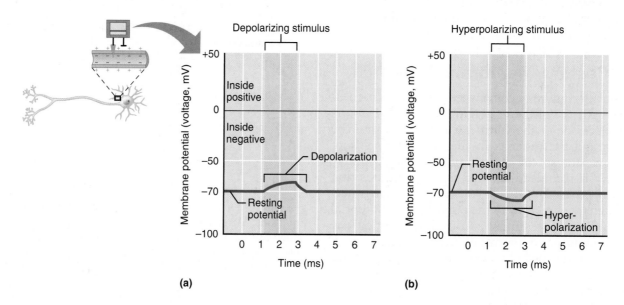

(a)

(b)

FIGURE 11.9 **Depolarization and hyperpolarization of the membrane.** The resting membrane potential is approximately −70 mV (inside negative) in neurons. Changes in this potential are called depolarization or hyperpolarization of the membrane. **(a)** In depolarization, the membrane potential moves toward 0 mV, the inside becoming less negative (more positive). **(b)** In hyperpolarization, the membrane potential increases, the inside becoming more negative.

At rest the membrane is impermeable to the large anionic cytoplasmic proteins, very slightly permeable to sodium, approximately 75 times more permeable to potassium than to sodium, and quite freely permeable to chloride ions. These resting permeabilities reflect the properties of the leakage ion channels in the membrane. Potassium ions diffuse out of the cell along their *concentration gradient* much more easily than sodium ions can enter the cell along theirs. K^+ flowing out of the cell causes the cell to become more negative inside. Na^+ trickling into the cell makes the cell just slightly more positive than it would be if only K^+ flowed. Therefore, at resting membrane potential, the negative interior of the cell is due to much greater diffusion of K^+ out of the cell than Na^+ diffusion into the cell.

Because some K^+ is always leaking out of the cell and some Na^+ is always leaking in, you might think that the concentration gradients would eventually "run down," resulting in equal concentrations of Na^+ and K^+ inside and outside the cell. This does not happen, because the ATP-driven sodium-potassium pump first ejects three Na^+ from the cell and then transports two K^+ back into the cell. Thus,

the sodium-potassium pump stabilizes the resting membrane potential by maintaining the concentration gradients for sodium and potassium.

Membrane Potentials That Act as Signals

Neurons use changes in their membrane potential as communication signals for receiving, integrating, and sending information. A change in membrane potential can be produced by (1) anything that changes membrane permeability to any ion or (2) anything that alters ion concentrations on the two sides of the membrane. However, only permeability changes are important for information transfer. Two types of signals are produced by a change in membrane potential: *graded potentials*, which are usually incoming signals operating over short distances, and *action potentials*, which are long-distance signals of axons.

The terms *depolarization* and *hyperpolarization* are used in the following sections to describe membrane potential changes *relative to resting membrane potential*, so it is important to understand these terms clearly. **Depolarization** is a reduction in membrane potential: The inside of the membrane becomes *less negative* (moves closer to zero) than the resting potential (Figure 11.9a). For instance, a

A *The negativity of the internal membrane surface.*

change in resting potential from −70 mV to −65 mV is a depolarization. By convention, depolarization also includes events in which the membrane potential reverses and moves above zero to become positive.

Hyperpolarization occurs when the membrane potential increases, becoming *more negative* than the resting potential. For example, a change from −70 mV to −75 mV is hyperpolarization (Figure 11.9b). As described shortly, depolarization increases the probability of producing nerve impulses, whereas hyperpolarization reduces this probability.

Graded Potentials

Graded potentials are short-lived, localized changes in membrane potential that can be either depolarizations or hyperpolarizations. These changes cause current flows that decrease in magnitude with distance. Graded potentials are called "graded" because their magnitude varies directly with stimulus strength. The stronger the stimulus, the more the voltage changes and the farther the current flows.

Graded potentials are triggered by some change (a stimulus) in the neuron's environment that causes gated ion channels to open. Graded potentials are given different names, depending on where they occur and the functions they perform. When the receptor of a sensory neuron is excited by some form of energy (heat, light, or other), the resulting graded potential is called a *receptor potential* or *generator potential*. These types of graded potentials are considered in Chapter 13. When the stimulus is a neurotransmitter released by another neuron, the graded potential is called a *postsynaptic potential*, because the neurotransmitter is released into a fluid-filled gap called a synapse and influences the neuron beyond (post) the synapse.

Fluids inside and outside cells are fairly good conductors, and current, carried by ions, flows through these fluids whenever voltage changes occur. Let us assume that a small area of a neuron's plasma membrane has been depolarized by a stimulus (Figure 11.10a). Current will flow on both sides of the membrane between the depolarized (active) membrane area and the adjacent polarized (resting) areas. Positive ions migrate toward more negative areas (the direction of cation movement is the direction of current flow), and negative ions simultaneously move toward more positive areas (Figure 11.10b). Thus, inside the cell, positive ions (mostly K⁺) move away from the depolarized area and accumulate on the neighboring membrane areas, where they neutralize negative ions. Meanwhile, positive ions on the outer membrane face are moving toward the region of reversed membrane polarity (the depolarized region), which is momentarily less positive. As these positive ions move, their "places" on the membrane become occupied by negative ions (such as Cl^- and HCO_3^-), sort of like ionic

(a) Depolarization

(b) Spread of depolarization

FIGURE 11.10   **The mechanism of a graded potential.** **(a)** A small patch of the membrane has become depolarized, resulting in a change in polarity at that point. **(b)** As positive ions flow toward negative areas (and negative ions flow toward adjacent more positive areas), local currents are created that depolarize adjacent membrane areas and allow the wave of depolarization to spread.

musical chairs. Thus, at regions abutting the depolarized region, the inside becomes less negative and the outside becomes less positive; that is, the neighboring membrane is, in turn, depolarized.

To simplify the explanation, virtually all diagrams that illustrate local currents give the impression that the circuit is completed by ions passing into and out of the cell through the membrane. This is *not* the case. Only the inward current across the membrane is caused by the flow of ions through gated channels. The outward current, the so-called *capacitance current*, reflects changes in the charge distribution as the ions migrate *along* the two membrane faces as described above. The capacitance current reflects the fact that the fatty membrane interior is a poor conductor of current. That is, it is a *capacitor* (an insulating element surrounded by a conducting surface) that *temporarily* stores the charge, forcing the ions of opposite charge to

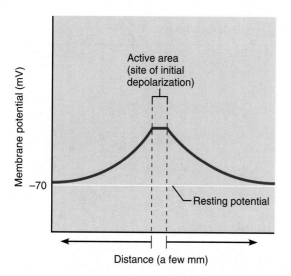

FIGURE 11.11   **Changes in membrane potential produced by a depolarizing graded potential.** Such voltage changes are decremental because the current is quickly dissipated by loss of ions through the "leaky" plasma membrane. Consequently, graded potentials are short-distance signals.

accumulate opposite one another on either side of the membrane.

As just explained, the flow of current to adjacent membrane areas changes the membrane potential there as well. However, the plasma membrane is permeable like a leaky water hose, and most of the charge is quickly lost through leakage channels. Consequently, the current is *decremental*; that is, it dies out within a few millimeters of its origin (Figure 11.11). Because the current dissipates quickly and dies out with increasing distance from the site of initial depolarization, graded potentials can act as signals only over very short distances. Nonetheless, they are essential in initiating action potentials, the long-distance signals.

Action Potentials

The principal way neurons send signals over long distances is by generating and propagating **action potentials (APs)**, and for the most part, only cells with *excitable membranes*—neurons and muscle cells—can generate action potentials. As illustrated in the graph in Figure 11.12, an action potential is a brief reversal of membrane potential with a total amplitude (change in voltage) of about 100 mV (from −70 mV to +30 mV). A depolarization phase is followed by a repolarization phase and often a short period of hyperpolarization. The whole event is over in a few milliseconds. Unlike graded potentials, action potentials do not decrease in strength with distance.

The events of action potential generation and transmission are identical in skeletal muscle cells

and neurons. In a neuron, an AP is also called a **nerve impulse,** and is typically generated *only in axons*. A neuron transmits a nerve impulse only when it is adequately stimulated. The stimulus changes the permeability of the neuron's membrane by opening specific voltage-gated channels on the axon. These channels open and close in response to changes in the membrane potential and are activated by local currents (graded potentials) that spread toward the axon along the dendritic and cell body membranes. In many neurons, the transition from local graded potential to action potential takes place at the axon hillock. In sensory neurons, the action potential is generated by the peripheral (axonal) process just proximal to the receptor region. However, for simplicity, we will just use the term *axon* in our discussion.

Generation of an Action Potential   Generating an action potential involves three consecutive but overlapping changes in membrane permeability resulting from the opening and closing of voltage-gated ion channels, all induced by depolarization of the axon membrane (Figure 11.12). These permeability changes are a transient increase in Na^+ permeability, followed by restoration of Na^+ impermeability, and then a short-lived increase in K^+ permeability. The first two permeability changes mark the beginning and the end of the *depolarization phase* of action potential generation, indicated by the upward-rising part of the AP curve or spike of Figure 11.12. The third permeability change is responsible for both the *repolarization* (the downward part of the AP spike) and *hyperpolarization phases* shown in the Figure 11.12 graph. Let's examine each of these phases more carefully, starting with a neuron in the resting (polarized) state.

① **Resting state: Voltage-gated channels closed.** Virtually all the voltage-gated Na^+ and K^+ channels are closed. Only the leakage channels are open, maintaining resting membrane potential.

Each Na^+ channel has two gates: a voltage-sensitive *activation gate* that is closed at rest and responds to depolarization by opening, and an *inactivation gate* that blocks the channel once it is open. Thus, *depolarization opens and then inactivates sodium channels.* Both gates must be open in order for Na^+ to enter, but the closing of *either* gate effectively closes the channel. By contrast, each active potassium channel has a single voltage-sensitive gate; it is closed in the resting state and opens slowly in response to depolarization.

② **Depolarizing phase: Increase in Na^+ permeability and reversal of membrane potential.** As the axon membrane is depolarized by local currents, the sodium channels open and Na^+ rushes into the cell. This influx of positive charge depolarizes that local

Q *The green line on the graph, representing K⁺ permeability, starts to increase at about the peak of the action potential. Relative to channels, what does an increase in K⁺ permeability mean?*

② **Depolarizing phase: Na⁺ channels open**

③ **Repolarizing phase: Na⁺ channels inactivating, K⁺ channels open**

① **Resting state: All gated Na⁺ and K⁺ channels closed** (Na⁺ activation gates closed; inactivation gates open)

④ **Hyperpolarization: K⁺ channels remain open; Na⁺ channels resetting**

FIGURE 11.12 **Phases of the action potential and the role of voltage-gated ion channels.** The center graph shows the intracellular voltage during the action potential (red) together with the membrane permeability changes to Na⁺ (P_{Na}, orange) and K⁺ (P_K, green) which underlie the voltage changes during the action potential. The outer diagrams show the motion of the gates within the voltage-gated channels during the course of the action potential. In each case, the arrows show the gate movement just completed. ① Resting state: Neither channel is open. (Sodium inactivation gates are open, but activation gates are closed.) ② Depolarizing phase of the action potential: Sodium activation gates open, but potassium channels remain closed. ③ Repolarizing phase of the action potential: Sodium inactivation gates block the sodium channels, and potassium channels open. ④ Hyperpolarization: Potassium channels remain open temporarily because they have not had time to respond to repolarization. Sodium channels begin resetting, opening their inactivation gates and closing their activation gates. Within another millisecond or two, the resting state ① is restored, and the system is ready to respond to the next stimulus.

A *An increase in K⁺ permeability means that K⁺ channels have opened.*

"patch" of membrane further, opening more Na$^+$ channels so that the cell interior becomes progressively less negative. When depolarization at the stimulation site reaches a certain critical level called **threshold** (often between −55 and −50 mV), depolarization becomes self-generating, urged on by positive feedback. That is, after being initiated by the stimulus, depolarization is driven by the ionic currents created by Na$^+$ influx. As more Na$^+$ enters, the membrane depolarizes further and opens still more channels until all Na$^+$ channels are open. At this point, Na$^+$ permeability is about 1000 times greater than in a resting neuron. As a result, the membrane potential becomes less and less negative and then overshoots to about +30 mV as Na$^+$ rushes in along its electrochemical gradient. This rapid depolarization and polarity reversal produces the sharply upward *spike* of the action potential (see the Figure 11.12 graph).

Earlier, we stated that membrane potential depends on membrane permeability, but here we are saying that membrane permeability depends on membrane potential. Can both statements be true? Yes, because these two relationships establish a *positive feedback* cycle (increased Na$^+$ permeability due to increased channel openings leads to greater depolarization, which leads to increased Na$^+$ permeability, and so on). It is this explosive positive feedback cycle that is responsible for the rising (depolarizing) phase of action potentials and is the property that puts the "action" in the action potential.

③ **Repolarizing phase: Decrease in Na$^+$ permeability.** The explosively rising phase of the action potential persists for only about 1 ms. It is self-limiting because the slow inactivation gates of the Na$^+$ channels begin to close at this point. As a result, the membrane permeability to Na$^+$ declines to resting levels, and the net influx of Na$^+$ stops completely. Consequently, the AP spike stops rising and reverses direction.

Repolarizing phase: Increase in K$^+$ permeability. As Na$^+$ entry declines, the slow voltage-gated K$^+$ channels open and K$^+$ rushes out of the cell, following its electrochemical gradient. Consequently, internal negativity of the resting neuron is restored, an event called **repolarization** (see the Figure 11.12 graph). Both the abrupt decline in Na$^+$ permeability and the increased permeability to K$^+$ contribute to repolarization.

④ **Hyperpolarization: K$^+$ permeability continues.** The period of increased K$^+$ permeability typically lasts longer than needed to restore the resting state. As a result of the excessive K$^+$ efflux, an **after-hyperpolarization**, also called the *undershoot*, is seen on the AP curve as a slight dip following the spike (and before the potassium gates close). Also at this point, the Na$^+$ channels begin to reset back to their original position by changing shape to reopen their inactivation gates and close their activation gates.

Although repolarization restores resting electrical conditions, it does *not* restore resting ionic conditions. The ion redistribution is accomplished by the **sodium-potassium pump** following repolarization. While it might appear that tremendous numbers of Na$^+$ and K$^+$ ions change places during action potential generation, this is not the case. Only small amounts of sodium and potassium cross the membrane. (The Na$^+$ influx required to reach threshold produces only a 0.012% change in intracellular Na$^+$ concentration.) Because an axon membrane has thousands of Na$^+$-K$^+$ pumps, these small ionic changes are quickly corrected.

Propagation of an Action Potential If it is to serve as the neuron's signaling device, an AP must be **propagated** (sent or transmitted) along the axon's entire length (Figure 11.13). As we have seen, the AP is generated by the influx of Na$^+$ through a given area of the membrane. This establishes local currents that depolarize adjacent membrane areas in the forward direction (away from the origin of the nerve impulse), which opens voltage-gated channels and triggers an action potential there. Because the area where the AP originated has just generated an AP, the sodium channels in that area are inactivated and no new AP is generated there. Thus, the AP propagates away from its point of origin. (If an *isolated* axon is stimulated by an electrode, the nerve impulse will move away from the point of stimulus in *all* directions along the membrane.) In the body, APs are initiated at one end of the axon and conducted away from that point toward the axon's terminals. Once initiated, an AP is *self-propagating* and continues along the axon at a constant velocity—something like a domino effect.

Following depolarization, each segment of axon membrane repolarizes, which restores the resting membrane potential in that region. Because these electrical changes also set up local currents, the repolarization wave chases the depolarization wave down the length of the axon. The propagation process just described occurs on unmyelinated axons. Propagation that occurs along myelinated axons, called *saltatory conduction*, is described shortly.

Although the phrase *conduction of a nerve impulse* is commonly used, nerve impulses are not really conducted in the same way that an insulated wire conducts current. In fact, neurons are fairly poor conductors, and as noted earlier, local current flows decline with distance because the charges leak through the membrane. The expression *propagation of a nerve impulse* is more accurate, because the AP

Q *The action potential shown will not get smaller as it propagates along the axon. Why not?*

(a) Time = 0 ms   **(b) Time = 2 ms**   **(c) Time = 4 ms**

☐ Resting potential

■ Peak of action potential

■ Hyperpolarization

FIGURE 11.13 Propagation of an action potential (AP). Recordings at three successive times as an AP propagates along an axon (from left to right). The arrows show the direction of local current flow generated by the movement of positive ions. This current brings the resting membrane at the leading edge of the AP to threshold, propagating the AP forward. Local current flow at the trailing edge of the AP (not shown) does not initiate another AP because the voltage-gated Na^+ channels there are inactivated.

11

is *regenerated anew* at each membrane patch, and every subsequent AP is identical to that generated initially.

Threshold and the All-or-None Phenomenon

Not all local depolarization events produce APs. The depolarization must reach threshold values if an axon is to "fire." What determines the *threshold point*? One explanation is that threshold is the membrane potential at which the outward current created by K^+ movement is exactly equal to the inward current created by Na^+ movement. Threshold is typically reached when the membrane has been depolarized by 15 to 20 mV from the resting value. This depolarization status seems to represent an unstable equilibrium state at which one of two

things can happen. If one more Na^+ enters, further depolarization occurs, opening more Na^+ channels and allowing more Na^+ entry. If, on the other hand, one more K^+ leaves, the membrane potential is driven away from threshold, Na^+ channels close, and K^+ continues to diffuse outward until the potential returns to its resting value.

Recall that local depolarizations are graded potentials and that their magnitude increases with increasing stimulus intensity. Brief weak stimuli (*subthreshold stimuli*) produce subthreshold depolarizations that are not translated into nerve impulses. On the other hand, stronger *threshold stimuli* produce depolarizing currents that push the membrane potential toward and beyond the threshold voltage. As a result, Na^+ permeability is increased to such an extent that entering sodium ions "swamp" (exceed) the outward movement of K^+, allowing the positive feedback cycle to become established and generating an AP. The critical factor here is the total amount of current that flows through the membrane during a stimulus (electrical charge × time). Strong stimuli depolarize

A *Once the membrane reaches threshold, a positive feedback cycle is initiated that results in all available Na^+ channels opening, and this is true for each new piece of membrane that depolarizes.*

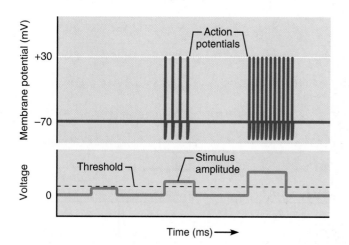

FIGURE 11.14   **Relationship between stimulus strength and action potential frequency.** APs are shown as vertical lines in the upper trace. The lower trace shows the intensity of the applied stimulus. A subthreshold stimulus does not generate an AP, but once threshold voltage is reached, the stronger the stimulus, the more frequently APs are generated.

the membrane to threshold quickly. Weaker stimuli must be applied for longer periods to provide the crucial amount of current flow. Very weak stimuli do not trigger an AP because the local current flows they produce are so slight that they dissipate long before threshold is reached.

The AP is an **all-or-none phenomenon;** it either happens completely or doesn't happen at all. Generation of an AP can be compared to lighting a match under a small dry twig. The changes occurring where the twig is heated are analogous to the change in membrane permeability that initially allows more Na$^+$ to enter the cell. When that part of the twig becomes hot enough (when enough Na$^+$ has entered the cell), the flash point (threshold) is reached and the flame consumes the entire twig, even if you blow out the match (the AP is generated and propagated whether or not the stimulus continues). But if the match is extinguished just before the twig has reached the critical temperature, ignition will not take place. Likewise, if the number of Na$^+$ entering the cell is too low to achieve threshold, no AP will occur.

Coding for Stimulus Intensity

Once generated, all APs are independent of stimulus strength, and all APs are alike. So how can the CNS determine whether a particular stimulus is intense or weak—information it needs to initiate an appropriate response? The answer is really quite simple: Strong stimuli cause nerve impulses to be generated more *often* in a given time interval than do weak stimuli (Figure 11.14). Thus, stimulus intensity is coded for

Q *What causes after-hyperpolarization?*

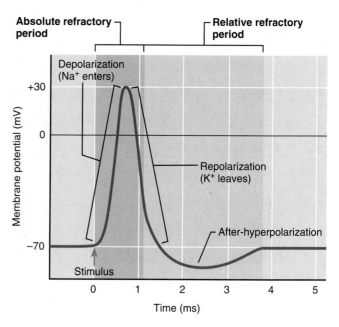

FIGURE 11.15   **Refractory periods in an AP.** This recording of an action potential indicates the timing of the absolute and relative refractory periods.

by the number of impulses generated per second—that is, by the *frequency of action potentials*—rather than by increases in the strength (amplitude) of the individual APs.

Refractory Periods

When a patch of neuron membrane is generating an AP and its voltage-gated sodium channels are open, the neuron cannot respond to another stimulus, no matter how strong. This period from the opening of the Na$^+$ channels until the Na$^+$ channels begin to reset to their original resting state, called the **absolute refractory period** (Figure 11.15), ensures that each AP is a separate, *all-or-none event* and enforces one-way transmission of the AP.

The **relative refractory period** is the interval following the absolute refractory period. During the relative refractory period, most Na$^+$ channels have returned to their resting state, some K$^+$ channels are still open, and repolarization is occurring. During this time, the axon's threshold for AP generation is substantially elevated. A stimulus that would normally have generated an AP is no longer sufficient, but an exceptionally strong stimulus can reopen the Na$^+$

A *After-hyperpolarization occurs because potassium channel gates are slow to respond to changes in the membrane voltage. Hence more K$^+$ leaves the cell than is absolutely necessary to restore the neuron to its resting membrane potential.*

Q *How does the location of voltage-gated Na⁺ channels differ in a myelinated axon (as depicted here) and in an unmyelinated axon?*

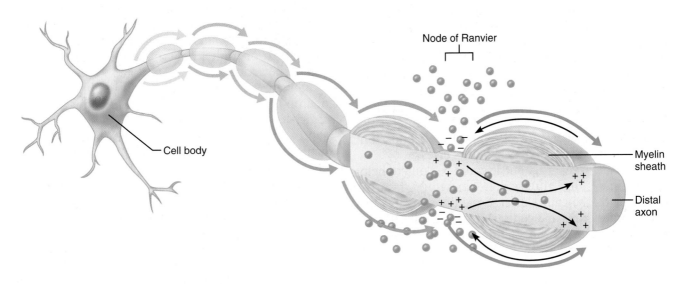

FIGURE 11.16　Saltatory conduction in a myelinated axon. In myelinated nerve fibers, local currents (thin black arrows) give rise to a propagated AP (pink and red arrows) that appears to jump from node to node. Notice that while APs are generated only at the nodes, the current flows along the axon from node to node.

channels that have already returned to their resting state and allow another AP to be generated. Thus, by intruding into the relative refractory period, strong stimuli cause more frequent generation of APs.

Conduction Velocity　Conduction velocities of neurons vary widely. Nerve fibers that transmit impulses most rapidly (100 m/s or more) are found in neural pathways where speed is essential, such as those that mediate some postural reflexes. Axons that conduct impulses more slowly typically serve internal organs (the gut, glands, blood vessels), where slower responses are not a handicap. The rate of impulse propagation depends largely on two factors:

1. Axon diameter. Axons vary considerably in diameter and, as a rule, the larger the axon's diameter, the faster it conducts impulses. This is because larger axons offer less resistance to the flow of local currents, and so adjacent areas of the membrane can more quickly be brought to threshold.

2. Degree of myelination. On unmyelinated axons, APs are generated at sites immediately adjacent to each other and conduction is relatively slow, a type of AP propagation called **continuous conduction.** The presence of a myelin sheath dramatically increases the rate of AP propagation because myelin acts as an insulator, both preventing almost all leakage of charge from the axon and allowing the membrane voltage to change more rapidly. Current can pass through the membrane of a myelinated axon *only* at the nodes of Ranvier, where the myelin sheath is interrupted and the axon is bare, and essentially all the voltage-gated Na⁺ channels are concentrated at the nodes. Thus, when an AP is generated in a myelinated fiber, the local depolarizing current does not dissipate through the adjacent (nonexcitable) membrane regions but instead is maintained and moves rapidly to the next node, a distance of approximately 1 mm, where it triggers another AP. Consequently, APs are triggered only at the nodes, a type of conduction called **saltatory conduction** (*saltare* = to leap) because the electrical signal jumps from node to node along the axon (Figure 11.16). Saltatory conduction is about 30 times faster than continuous conduction.

◤◢ HOMEOSTATIC IMBALANCE

The importance of myelin to nerve transmission is painfully clear to those with demyelinating diseases such as **multiple sclerosis (MS).** This autoimmune disease affects mostly young adults. Common symptoms are visual disturbances (including blindness), problems controlling muscles (weakness, clumsiness,

A *In a myelinated axon, voltage-gated sodium channels are located only at the nodes of Ranvier, instead of along the entire length of an unmyelinated axon.*

and ultimately paralysis), speech disturbances, and urinary incontinence. In this disease, myelin sheaths in the CNS are gradually destroyed, reduced to nonfunctional hardened lesions called *scleroses*. The loss of myelin (a result of the immune system's attack on myelin proteins) causes such substantial shunting and short-circuiting of the current that successive nodes are excited more and more slowly, and eventually impulse conduction ceases. However, the axons themselves are not damaged and growing numbers of Na^+ channels appear spontaneously in the demyelinated fibers. This may account for the remarkably variable cycles of relapse (disability) and remission (symptom-free periods) typical of this disease.

Until a few years ago, little could be done to help MS victims. This situation is changing with the advent of the so-called disease-modifying drugs including interferons and glatiramer (Copaxone). These drugs seem to hold the symptoms at bay, reducing complications and the disability that often occurs with MS. ●

Nerve fibers may be classified based on diameter, degree of myelination, and conduction speed. **Group A fibers** are mostly somatic sensory and motor fibers serving the skin, skeletal muscles, and joints. They have the largest diameter and thick myelin sheaths, and conduct impulses at speeds ranging up to 150 m/s (over 300 miles per hour). Autonomic nervous system motor fibers serving the visceral organs; visceral sensory fibers; and the smaller somatic sensory fibers transmitting afferent impulses from the skin (such as pain and small touch fibers) belong in the B and C fiber groups. **Group B fibers,** lightly myelinated fibers of intermediate diameter, transmit impulses at an average rate of 15 m/s (about 40 mi/h). **Group C fibers** have the smallest diameter and are unmyelinated. Hence, they are incapable of saltatory conduction and conduct impulses at a leisurely pace—1 m/s (2 mi/h) or less.

◩ HOMEOSTATIC IMBALANCE

A number of chemical and physical factors impair impulse propagation. Local anesthetics like those used by your dentist act by blocking voltage-gated Na^+ channels. As we have seen, no Na^+ entry—no AP.

Cold and continuous pressure interrupt blood circulation (and hence the delivery of oxygen and nutrients) to neuron processes, impairing their ability to conduct impulses. For example, your fingers get numb when you hold an ice cube for more than a few seconds, and your foot "goes to sleep" when you sit on it. When you remove the cold object or pressure, impulses are transmitted again, leading to an unpleasant prickly feeling. ●

The Synapse

The operation of the nervous system depends on the flow of information through chains of neurons functionally connected by synapses. A **synapse** (sin'aps), from the Greek *syn*, "to clasp or join," is a junction that mediates information transfer from one neuron to the next or from a neuron to an effector cell—it's where the action is.

Synapses between the axon endings of one neuron and the dendrites of other neurons are **axodendritic synapses** (Figure 11.17). Those between axon endings of one neuron and cell bodies of other neurons are **axosomatic synapses**. Less common (and far less understood) are synapses between axons (*axoaxonic*), between dendrites (*dendrodendritic*), or between dendrites and cell bodies (*dendrosomatic*).

The neuron conducting impulses toward the synapse is the **presynaptic neuron,** and the neuron transmitting the electrical signal away from the synapse is the **postsynaptic neuron.** At a *given* synapse, the presynaptic neuron is the information sender, and the postsynaptic neuron is the information receiver. As you might anticipate, most neurons function as both presynaptic and postsynaptic neurons. Neurons have anywhere from 1000 to 10,000 axon terminals making synapses and are stimulated by an equal number of other neurons. In the body periphery, the postsynaptic cell may be either another neuron or an effector cell (a muscle cell or gland cell).

There are two varieties of synapses: *electrical* and *chemical*. These are described next.

Electrical Synapses

Electrical synapses, the less common variety, correspond to the gap junctions found between certain other body cells. They contain protein channels, made of connexin subunits, that intimately connect the cytoplasm of adjacent neurons and allow ions and small molecules to flow directly from one neuron to the next. Neurons joined in this way are said to be *electrically coupled*, and transmission across these synapses is very rapid. Depending on the nature of the synapse, communication may be unidirectional or bidirectional.

A key feature of electrical synapses between neurons is that they provide a simple means of synchronizing the activity of all interconnected neurons. In adults, electrical synapses are found in regions of the brain responsible for certain stereotyped movements, such as the normal jerky movements of the eyes, and in axoaxonic synapses in the hippocampus, a region intimately involved in emotions and memory. They are far more abundant in embryonic nervous tissue, where they permit exchange of guiding clues during early neuronal development so that neurons can connect properly with one another. As

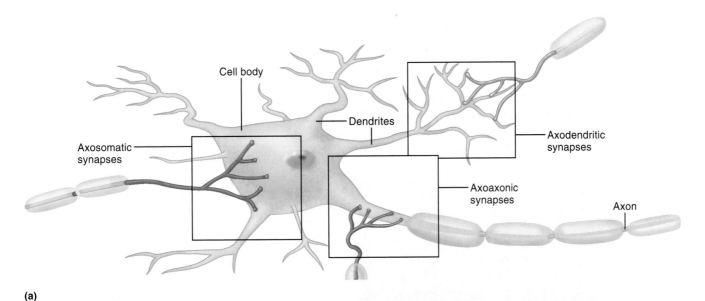

(a)

FIGURE 11.17 **Synapses. (a)** Axodendritic, axosomatic, and axoaxonic synapses. **(b)** Scanning electron micrograph of incoming fibers at axosomatic synapses (4000×).

(b)

the nervous system develops, some electrical synapses are replaced by chemical synapses. Gap junctions also exist between glial cells of the CNS.

Chemical Synapses

In contrast to electrical synapses, which are specialized to allow the flow of ions between neurons, **chemical synapses** are specialized for release and reception of chemical neurotransmitters. A typical chemical synapse is made up of two parts: (1) a knoblike *axon terminal* of the presynaptic neuron, which contains many tiny, membrane-bounded sacs called **synaptic vesicles,** each containing thousands of neurotransmitter molecules; and (2) a neurotransmitter *receptor region* on the membrane of a dendrite or the cell body of the postsynaptic neuron.

Although close to each other, presynaptic and postsynaptic membranes are always separated by the **synaptic cleft,** a fluid-filled space approximately 30 to 50 nm (about one-millionth of an inch) wide. (If an electrical synapse is like the threshold of a doorway between neurons, a synaptic cleft is like a good-size lake intervening between them.) Because the current from the presynaptic membrane dissipates in the fluid-filled cleft, chemical synapses effectively prevent a nerve impulse from being *directly* transmitted from one neuron to another. Instead, transmission of signals across these synapses is a *chemical event* that depends on the release, diffusion, and receptor binding of neurotransmitter molecules and results in *unidirectional communication* between neurons. Thus, while transmission of nerve impulses along an axon and across electrical synapses is a purely electrical event, chemical synapses convert the electrical signals to chemical

signals (neurotransmitters) that travel across the synapse to the postsynaptic cells, where they are converted back into electrical signals.

Information Transfer Across Chemical Synapses

When a nerve impulse reaches the axon terminal, it sets into motion a chain of events that triggers neurotransmitter release. The neurotransmitter crosses the synaptic cleft and, on binding to receptors on the postsynaptic membrane, causes changes in the postsynaptic membrane permeability. The steps are shown in Figure 11.18:

① **Calcium channels open in the presynaptic axon terminal.** When the nerve impulse reaches the axon terminal, membrane depolarization opens not only Na^+ channels but voltage-gated Ca^{2+} channels as well. During the brief time the Ca^{2+} channels are open, Ca^{2+} floods down its electrochemical gradient into the terminal from the extracellular fluid.

Q *Why may such axon terminals be referred to as "biological transducers"?*

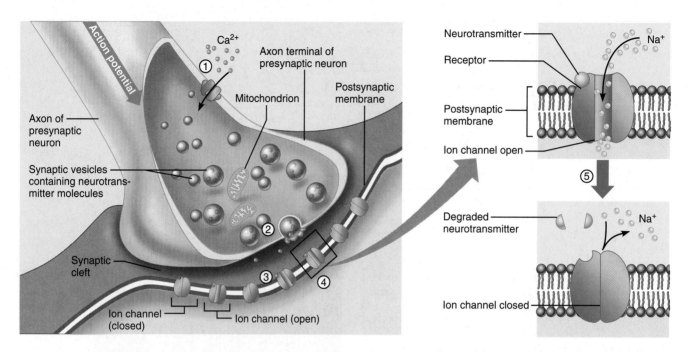

FIGURE 11.18 **Events at a chemical synapse in response to depolarization.** ① Arrival of the depolarization wave (action potential) opens voltage-gated calcium channels and allows Ca^{2+} influx into the axon terminal. ② Synaptic vesicles fuse with the presynaptic membrane and neurotransmitter is released into the synapse.

③ The neurotransmitter diffuses across the synaptic cleft and attaches to receptors on the postsynaptic membrane. ④ Binding of neurotransmitter opens ion channels in the postsynaptic membrane, resulting in graded potentials in that membrane. In this example of an excitatory synapse,

chemically gated ion channels are opened, leading to depolarization. ⑤ Neurotransmitter is quickly destroyed by enzymes present at the synapse or taken back into the presynaptic terminal; depletion of neurotransmitter closes the ion channels and terminates the synaptic response.

② **Neurotransmitter is released.** The surge of Ca^{2+} into the axon terminal acts as an intracellular messenger, directing synaptic vesicles to fuse with the axon membrane and empty their contents by exocytosis into the synaptic cleft. Ca^{2+} is then quickly removed from the terminal, either taken up into the mitochondria or ejected from the neuron by an active Ca^{2+} pump. The precise Ca^{2+} sensor that initiates neurotransmitter exocytosis is still a question, but a Ca^{2+}-binding protein called *synaptotagmin* found in the synaptic vesicles seems a likely candidate.

③ **Neurotransmitter binds to postsynaptic receptors.** The neurotransmitter diffuses across the synaptic cleft and binds reversibly to specific protein receptors clustered on the postsynaptic membrane.

④ **Ion channels open in the postsynaptic membrane.** When neurotransmitter binds to the receptor

protein, this receptor changes its three-dimensional shape. This in turn causes ion channels to open and creates graded potentials. Postsynaptic membranes often contain receptor proteins and ion channels packaged together as chemically gated ion channels. Depending on the receptor protein to which the neurotransmitter binds and the type of channel the receptor controls, the postsynaptic neuron may be either excited or inhibited.

For each nerve impulse reaching the presynaptic terminal, many vesicles (perhaps 300) are emptied into the synaptic cleft. The higher the impulse frequency (that is, the more intense the stimulus), the greater the number of synaptic vesicles that fuse and spill their contents, and the greater the effect on the postsynaptic cell.

⑤ **Neurotransmitter effects are terminated.** As long as it is bound to a postsynaptic receptor, a neurotransmitter continues to affect membrane permeability and to block reception of additional signals from presynaptic neurons. Thus, some means of "wiping the postsynaptic slate clean" is necessary.

A *Because they change the signal from an electrical current to a chemical signal (neurotransmitter), which in turn initiates an electrical current in the postsynaptic neuron.*

The effects of neurotransmitters generally last a few milliseconds before being terminated by one of three mechanisms. Depending on the particular neurotransmitter, the terminating mechanism may be

1. Degradation by enzymes associated with the postsynaptic membrane or present in the synapse, as with acetylcholine

2. Reuptake by astrocytes or the presynaptic terminal, where the neurotransmitter is stored or destroyed by enzymes, as with norepinephrine

3. Diffusion away from the synapse

Synaptic Delay   Although an impulse may travel at speeds of up to 150 m/s (300 mi/h) down an axon, neural transmission across a chemical synapse is comparatively slow and reflects the time required for neurotransmitter release, diffusion across the synapse, and binding to receptors. Typically, this **synaptic delay**, which lasts 0.3–5.0 ms, is the *rate-limiting* (slowest) step of neural transmission. Synaptic delay helps explain why transmission along neural pathways involving only two or three neurons occurs rapidly, but transmission along multisynaptic pathways typical of higher mental functioning occurs much more slowly. However, in practical terms these differences are not noticeable.

Postsynaptic Potentials and Synaptic Integration

Many receptors present on postsynaptic membranes at chemical synapses are specialized to open ion channels, thereby converting chemical signals to electrical signals. Unlike the voltage-gated ion channels responsible for APs, however, these chemically gated channels are relatively insensitive to changes in membrane potential. Consequently, channel opening at postsynaptic membranes cannot possibly become self-amplifying or self-generating. Instead, neurotransmitter receptors mediate graded potentials—local changes in membrane potential that are *graded* according to the amount of neurotransmitter released and the time it remains in the area. APs are compared with postsynaptic potentials in Table 11.2.

Chemical synapses are either excitatory or inhibitory, depending on how they affect the membrane potential of the postsynaptic neuron.

Excitatory Synapses and EPSPs

At excitatory synapses, neurotransmitter binding causes depolarization of the postsynaptic membrane. However, in contrast to what happens on axon membranes, a single type of *chemically gated* ion channel opens on postsynaptic membranes (those of dendrites and neuronal cell bodies). This channel allows Na^+ and K^+ to diffuse *simultaneously* through the membrane in opposite directions. Although this two-way cation flow may appear to be self-defeating when depolarization is the goal, remember that the electrochemical gradient for sodium is much steeper than that for potassium. Hence, Na^+ influx is greater than K^+ efflux, and *net* depolarization occurs.

If enough neurotransmitter binds, depolarization of the postsynaptic membrane can successfully reach 0 mV, which is well above an axon's threshold (about -50 mV) for "firing off" an AP. However, *postsynaptic membranes generally do not generate APs; axons* (with their voltage-gated channels) *do have this capability*. The dramatic polarity reversal seen in axons never occurs in membranes containing *only* chemically gated channels because the opposite movements of K^+ and Na^+ prevent accumulation of excessive positive charge inside the cell. Hence, instead of APs, local graded depolarization events called **excitatory postsynaptic potentials (EPSPs)** occur at excitatory postsynaptic membranes (Figure 11.19a). Each EPSP lasts a few milliseconds and then the membrane returns to its resting potential. The only function of EPSPs is to help trigger an AP distally at the axon hillock of the postsynaptic neuron. Although currents created by individual EPSPs decline with distance, they can and often *do* spread all the way to the axon hillock. If currents reaching the hillock are strong enough to depolarize the axon to threshold, axonal voltage-gated channels open and an AP is generated.

Inhibitory Synapses and IPSPs

Binding of neurotransmitters at inhibitory synapses *reduces* a postsynaptic neuron's ability to generate an AP. Most inhibitory neurotransmitters induce hyperpolarization of the postsynaptic membrane by making the membrane more permeable to K^+ or Cl^-. Sodium ion permeability is not affected. If K^+ channels are opened, K^+ moves out of the cell; if Cl^- channels are opened, Cl^- moves in. In either case, the charge on the inner face of the membrane becomes more negative. As the membrane potential increases and is driven farther from the axon's threshold, the postsynaptic neuron becomes less and less likely to "fire" and larger depolarizing currents are required to induce an AP. Such changes in potential are called **inhibitory postsynaptic potentials (IPSPs)** (Figure 11.19b).

Integration and Modification of Synaptic Events

Summation by the Postsynaptic Neuron   A single EPSP cannot induce an AP in the postsynaptic neuron. But if thousands of excitatory axon terminals are firing on the same postsynaptic membrane,

11

(a) Excitatory postsynaptic potential (EPSP)

(b) Inhibitory postsynaptic potential (IPSP)

FIGURE 11.19 **Postsynaptic potentials. (a)** An excitatory postsynaptic potential (EPSP) is a local depolarization of the postsynaptic membrane that brings the neuron closer to threshold for AP generation. It is mediated by neurotransmitter binding that opens chemically gated channels allowing the simultaneous passage of Na$^+$ and K$^+$ through the postsynaptic membrane. **(b)** An inhibitory postsynaptic potential results in hyperpolarization of the postsynaptic neuron and drives the neuron away from the threshold for firing. It is mediated by neurotransmitter binding that opens K$^+$ or Cl$^-$ channels. The red vertical arrows represent stimulation.

or if a smaller number of terminals are delivering impulses rapidly, the probability of reaching threshold depolarization increases greatly. Thus, EPSPs can add together, or **summate,** to influence the activity of a postsynaptic neuron (Figure 11.20). Nerve impulses would never be initiated if this were not so.

Two types of summation occur. **Temporal summation** (*temporal* = time) occurs when one or more presynaptic neurons transmit impulses in rapid-fire order and bursts of neurotransmitter are released in quick succession. The first impulse produces a small EPSP, and before it dissipates, successive impulses trigger more EPSPs. These summate, producing a much greater depolarization of the postsynaptic membrane than would result from a single EPSP.

Spatial summation occurs when the postsynaptic neuron is stimulated at the same time by a large number of terminals from the same or, more commonly, different neurons. Huge numbers of its receptors bind neurotransmitter and simultaneously initiate EPSPs, which summate and dramatically enhance depolarization.

Although we have focused on EPSPs here, IPSPs also summate, both temporally and spatially. In this case, the postsynaptic neuron is inhibited to a greater degree.

Most neurons receive both excitatory and inhibitory inputs from thousands of other neurons. Additionally, the same fiber may form different types of synapses (in terms of biochemical and electrical characteristics) with different types of target neurons. How is all this conflicting information sorted out? Each neuron's axon hillock keeps a running account of all the signals it receives (Figure 11.20d). Not only do EPSPs summate and IPSPs summate, but also EPSPs summate with IPSPs. If the stimulatory effects of EPSPs dominate the membrane potential enough to reach threshold, the neuron will fire. If summation yields only subthreshold depolarization or hyperpolarization, the neuron fails to generate an AP. However, partially depolarized neurons are **facilitated**—that is, more easily excited by successive depolarization events—because they are already near threshold. Thus, axon hillock membranes function as *neural integrators,* and their potential at any time reflects the sum of all incoming neural information.

Because EPSPs and IPSPs are graded potentials that diminish in strength the farther they spread, this means that the most effective synapses are those closest to the axon hillock. As a result, inhibitory synapses are most effective when placed between the site of excitatory inputs and the site of action potential generation (the axon hillock). In general, inhibitory synapses occur most often on the cell body and excitatory synapses occur most often on the dendrites.

Synaptic Potentiation Repeated or continuous use of a synapse (even for short periods) enhances the presynaptic neuron's ability to excite the postsynaptic neuron, producing larger-than-expected postsynaptic potentials. This phenomenon is called **synaptic potentiation.** The presynaptic terminals at such synapses contain relatively high Ca^{2+} concentrations, a condition that (presumably) triggers the release of more neurotransmitter, which in turn produces larger EPSPs. Furthermore, synaptic potentiation brings about Ca^{2+} influx via dendritic spines into the postsynaptic neuron as well. Brief high-frequency stimulation partially depolarizes the postsynaptic membrane. This causes certain chemically gated channels called *NMDA (N-methyl-D-aspartate)*

Q *Graphs b and c show an action potential on the axon of this neuron. Why don't APs generally occur on neuronal cell bodies and dendrites?*

(a) Subthreshold, no summation

(b) Temporal summation

(c) Spatial summation

(d) Spatial summation of EPSP and IPSP

FIGURE 11.20 **Neural integration of EPSPs and IPSPs.** Synapses E_1 and E_2 are excitatory; synapse I_1 is inhibitory. Each individual impulse is subthreshold. **(a)** Synapse E_1 is stimulated and then stimulated again shortly thereafter. The two EPSPs do not overlap in time, so no summation occurs; threshold is not reached in the axon of the postsynaptic neuron. **(b)** Synapse E_1 is stimulated a second time before the initial EPSP has died away; temporal summation occurs, and the axon's threshold is reached, causing an AP to be generated. **(c)** Synapses E_1 and E_2 are stimulated simultaneously (spatial summation), resulting in a threshold depolarization. **(d)** Synapse I_1 is stimulated, resulting in a short-lived IPSP (hyperpolarization). When E_1 and I_1 are simultaneously stimulated, the changes in potential cancel each other.

receptors to allow Ca^{2+} entry, something that only happens when the membrane is depolarized. As Ca^{2+} floods into the cell, it activates certain kinase enzymes that promote changes that result in more effective responses to subsequent stimuli. In some neurons, APs generated at the axon hillock propagate back up into the dendrites. This current flow may alter the effectiveness of synapses by causing voltage-gated Ca^{2+} channels to open, again allowing Ca^{2+} into the dendrites and promoting synaptic potentiation.

Synaptic potentiation can be viewed as a learning process that increases the efficiency of neurotransmission along a particular pathway. Indeed, the hippocampus of the brain, which plays a special role in memory and learning, exhibits an important type of synaptic plasticity called *long-term potentiation* (LTP).

Presynaptic Inhibition Postsynaptic activity can also be influenced by events occurring at the presynaptic membrane. **Presynaptic inhibition** occurs when the release of excitatory neurotransmitter by one neuron is inhibited by the activity of another neuron via an axoaxonic synapse. More than one mechanism is involved, but the end result is that less neurotransmitter is released and bound, and smaller EPSPs are formed. Notice that this is the opposite of what we see with synaptic potentiation. In contrast to postsynaptic inhibition by IPSPs, which decreases the excitability of the postsynaptic neuron, presynaptic inhibition is more like a functional synaptic "pruning." Events at the presynaptic neuron reduce excitatory stimulation of the postsynaptic neuron.

Neurotransmitters and Their Receptors

Neurotransmitters, along with electrical signals, are the "language" of the nervous system—the means by which each neuron communicates with others to

A *Cell bodies and dendrites generally don't have enough voltage-gated Na^+ channels to generate APs.*

TABLE 11.2   Comparison of Action Potentials with Postsynaptic Potentials

CHARACTERISTIC	ACTION POTENTIAL (AP)	POSTSYNAPTIC POTENTIAL (A TYPE OF GRADED POTENTIAL)	
		EXCITATORY (EPSP)	INHIBITORY (IPSP)
Function	Long-distance signaling; constitutes the nerve impulse	Short-distance signaling; depolarization that spreads to axon hillock; moves membrane potential *toward* threshold for generation of AP	Short-distance signaling; hyperpolarization that spreads to axon hillock; moves potential *away from* threshold for generation of AP
Stimulus for opening of ionic gates	Voltage (depolarization)	Chemical (neurotransmitter)	Chemical (neurotransmitter)
Initial effect of stimulus	First opens Na^+ channels, then K^+ channels	Opens channels that allow simultaneous Na^+ and K^+ fluxes	Opens K^+ or Cl^- channels
Repolarization	Voltage-regulated; inactivation of Na^+ channels together with opening of K^+ channels	Voltage independent; occurs when neurotransmitter is no longer present	
Conduction distance	Not conducted by local current flows; continually regenerated (propagated) along entire axon; intensity does not decline with distance	0.1–1 mm; local electrical events; intensity declines with distance	
Positive feedback cycle	Present	Absent	Absent
Peak membrane potential	+30 to +50 mV	Becomes depolarized; moves toward 0 mV	Becomes hyperpolarized; moves toward −90 mV
Summation	None; an all-or-none phenomenon	Present; temporal or spatial	Present; temporal or spatial
Refractory period	Present	Absent	Absent

process and send messages to the rest of the body. Sleep, thought, rage, hunger, memory, movement, and even your smile reflect the "doings" of these versatile molecules. Most factors that affect synaptic transmission do so by enhancing or inhibiting neurotransmitter release or destruction, or by blocking their binding to receptors. Just as speech defects may hinder interpersonal communication, interferences with neurotransmitter activity may short-circuit the brain's "conversations" or internal talk (see *A Closer Look* on pp. 424–425).

At present, more than 50 neurotransmitters or neurotransmitter candidates have been identified. Although some neurons produce and release only one kind of neurotransmitter, most make two or more and may release any one or all of them. It appears that in most cases, different neurotransmitters are released at different stimulation frequencies, a restriction that avoids producing a jumble of nonsense messages. However, co-release of two

neurotransmitters from the same vesicles has been documented. The coexistence of more than one neurotransmitter in a single neuron makes it possible for that cell to exert several influences rather than one discrete effect.

Neurotransmitters are classified chemically and functionally. Table 11.3 provides a fairly detailed overview of neurotransmitters, some of which are described here. No one expects you to memorize this table at this point, but it will be a handy reference for you to look back at when neurotransmitters are mentioned in subsequent chapters.

Classification of Neurotransmitters by Chemical Structure

Neurotransmitters fall into several chemical classes based on molecular structure.

Acetylcholine   Acetylcholine (ACh) (as"ĕ-til-ko'lēn) was the first neurotransmitter identified. It is still the best understood because it is released at

TABLE 11.3 **Neurotransmitters and Neuromodulators**

NEUROTRANSMITTER	FUNCTIONAL CLASSES	SITES WHERE SECRETED	COMMENTS
ACETYLCHOLINE			
• At *nicotinic ACh receptors* (on skeletal muscles, autonomic ganglia, and in the CNS)	Excitatory Direct action	CNS: widespread throughout cerebral cortex, hippocampus, and brain stem	Effects prolonged, leading to tetanic muscle spasms, when AChE blocked by nerve gas and organophosphate insecticides (malathion). Release inhibited by botulinum toxin; binding to nicotinic ACh receptors inhibited by curare (a muscle paralytic agent) and some snake venoms, and to muscarinic ACh receptors by atropine. ACh levels decreased in certain brain areas in Alzheimer's disease; nicotinic ACh receptors destroyed in myasthenia gravis. Binding of nicotine to nicotinic receptors in the brain enhances dopamine release, which may account for the behavioral effects of nicotine in smokers
• At *muscarinic ACh receptors* (on visceral effectors and in the CNS)	Excitatory or inhibitory depending on subtype of muscarinic receptor Indirect action via second messengers	PNS: all neuromuscular junctions with skeletal muscle; some autonomic motor endings (all preganglionic and parasympathetic postganglionic fibers)	

$$H_3C-\overset{\overset{\displaystyle O}{\|}}{C}-O-CH_2-CH_2-\overset{+}{N}-(CH_3)_3$$

NEUROTRANSMITTER	FUNCTIONAL CLASSES	SITES WHERE SECRETED	COMMENTS
BIOGENIC AMINES			
Norepinephrine	Excitatory or inhibitory, depending on receptor type bound Indirect action via second messengers	CNS: brain stem, particularly in the locus coeruleus of the midbrain; limbic system; some areas of cerebral cortex PNS: main neurotransmitter of ganglion neurons in the sympathetic nervous system	A "feeling good" neurotransmitter; release enhanced by amphetamines; removal from synapse blocked by tricyclic antidepressants [amitriptyline (Elavil) and others] and cocaine; brain levels reduced by reserpine (an antihypertensive drug), leading to depression
Dopamine	Excitatory or inhibitory depending on the receptor type bound Indirect action via second messengers	CNS: substantia nigra of midbrain; hypothalamus; is the principal neurotransmitter of extrapyramidal system PNS: some sympathetic ganglia	A "feeling good" neurotransmitter; release enhanced by L-dopa and amphetamines; reuptake blocked by cocaine; deficient in Parkinson's disease; may be involved in pathogenesis of schizophrenia
Serotonin (5-HT)	Mainly inhibitory Indirect action via second messengers; direct action at 5-HT$_3$ receptors	CNS: brain stem, especially midbrain; hypothalamus; limbic system; cerebellum; pineal gland; spinal cord	Activity blocked by LSD and enhanced by ecstasy (MDMA); may play a role in sleep, appetite, nausea, migraine headaches, and regulation of mood; drugs that block its uptake [fluoxetine (Prozac)] relieve anxiety and depression
Histamine	Indirect action via second messengers	CNS: hypothalamus	Increases acid secretion in the stomach; acid secretion blocked by histamine H$_2$ receptor blockers (cimetidine); also released by mast cells during inflammation and acts as powerful vasodilator

TABLE 11.3	**Neurotransmitters and Neuromodulators** (continued)		
NEUROTRANSMITTER	**FUNCTIONAL CLASSES**	**SITES WHERE SECRETED**	**COMMENTS**
PURINES			
ATP	Excitatory or inhibitory depending on receptor type bound	CNS: basal nuclei, induces Ca^{2+} wave propagation in astrocytes	ATP released by sensory neurons (as well as that released by injured cells) provokes pain sensation
	Direct and indirect actions via second messengers	PNS: dorsal root ganglion neurons	
Adenosine	Inhibitory neuromodulator	Throughout CNS	
	Indirect action via second messengers		Caffeine (coffee), theophylline (tea), and theobromine (chocolate) stimulate by blocking brain adenosine receptors; may be involved in sleep-wake cycle and terminating seizures. Dilates arterioles, increasing blood flow to heart and other tissues as needed

Adenosine / ATP structure

AMINO ACIDS			
GABA (γ-aminobutyric acid)	Generally inhibitory	CNS: cerebral cortex, hypothalamus, Purkinje cells of cerebellum, spinal cord, granule cells of olfactory bulb, retina	Principal inhibitory neurotransmitter in the brain; important in presynaptic inhibition at axoaxonic synapses. GABA-dependent neural communication declines with age in visual and auditory systems. Inhibitory effects augmented by alcohol, antianxiety drugs of the benzodiazepine class (e.g., Valium), and barbiturates, resulting in impaired motor coordination. Substances that block its synthesis, release, or action induce convulsions
	Direct and indirect actions via second messengers		

$$H_2N-CH_2-CH_2-CH_2-COOH$$

| Glutamate | Generally excitatory | CNS: spinal cord; widespread in brain where it represents the major excitatory neurotransmitter | Important in learning and memory. The "stroke neurotransmitter": excessive release produces excitotoxicity—neurons literally stimulated to death; most commonly caused by ischemia (oxygen deprivation, usually due to a blocked blood vessel). When released by gliomas, aids tumor advance |
| | Direct action | | |

$$H_2N-CH-CH_2-CH_2-COOH$$
$$|$$
$$COOH$$

| Glycine | Generally inhibitory | CNS: spinal cord and brain stem, retina | Principal inhibitory neurotransmitter of the spinal cord. Strychnine blocks glycine receptors, resulting in uncontrolled convulsions and respiratory arrest |
| | Direct action | | |

$$H_2N-CH_2-COOH$$

TABLE 11.3 (continued)			
NEUROTRANSMITTER	**FUNCTIONAL CLASSES**	**SITES WHERE SECRETED**	**COMMENTS**
PEPTIDES			
Endorphins, e.g., dynorphin, enkephalins (illustrated) (Tyr)(Gly)(Gly)(Phe)(Met)	Generally inhibitory Indirect action via second messengers	CNS: widely distributed in brain; hypothalamus; limbic system; pituitary; spinal cord	Natural opiates; inhibit pain by inhibiting substance P; effects mimicked by morphine, heroin, and methadone
Tachykinins: Substance P (illustrated), neurokinin A (NKA) (Arg)(Pro)(Lys)(Pro)(Gln)(Gln)(Phe)(Phe)(Gly)(Leu)(Met)	Excitatory Indirect action via second messengers	CNS: basal nuclei, midbrain, hypothalamus, cerebral cortex PNS: certain sensory neurons of dorsal root ganglia (pain afferents)	Substance P mediates pain transmission in the PNS; in the CNS tachykinins are involved in respiratory and cardiovascular controls and in mood
Somatostatin (Ala)(Gly)(Cys)(Lys)(Asn)(Phe)(Phe)(Trp) (Cys)(Ser)(Thr)(Phe)(Thr)(Lys)	Generally inhibitory Indirect action via second messengers	CNS: hypothalamus, retina, and other parts of brain Pancreas	Inhibits release of growth hormone; a gut-brain peptide
Cholecystokinin (CCK) (Asp)(Tyr)(Met)(Gly)(Trp)(Met)(Asp)(Phe) SO$_4$	Possible neurotransmitter	Cerebral cortex Small intestine	May be related to feeding behaviors; a gut-brain peptide
DISSOLVED GASES			
Nitric oxide (NO)	Excitatory Indirect action via second messengers	CNS: brain, spinal cord PNS: adrenal gland; nerves to penis	Its release potentiates stroke damage; some types of male impotence treated by enhancing NO action [e.g., with sildenafil (Viagra)]
Carbon monoxide (CO)	Excitatory Indirect action via second messengers	Brain and some neuromuscular and neuroglandular synapses	

neuromuscular junctions, which are much easier to study than synapses buried in the CNS. ACh is synthesized and enclosed in synaptic vesicles in axon terminals in a reaction catalyzed by the enzyme *choline acetyltransferase*. Acetic acid is bound to coenzyme A (CoA) to form acetyl CoA, which then combines with choline. Then coenzyme A is released.

$$\text{Acetyl CoA} + \text{choline} \xrightarrow[\text{acetyltransferase}]{\text{choline}} \text{ACh} + \text{CoA}$$

Once released by the presynaptic terminal, ACh binds to the postsynaptic receptors briefly. Then it is released and degraded to acetic acid and choline by the enzyme **acetylcholinesterase (AChE),** located in the synaptic cleft and on postsynaptic membranes. The released choline is recaptured by the presynaptic terminals and reused to synthesize more ACh.

ACh is released by all neurons that stimulate skeletal muscles and by some neurons of the autonomic nervous system. ACh-releasing neurons are also found in the CNS.

11

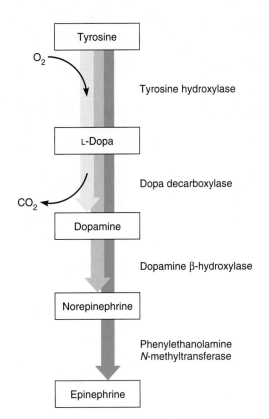

FIGURE 11.21 **Common pathway for synthesis of dopamine, norepinephrine, and epinephrine.** How far synthesis proceeds along the pathway depends on the enzymes present in the cell.

Biogenic Amines The **biogenic amines** (bi″o-jen′ik) include the **catecholamines** (kat″ĕ-kol′ah-mēnz), such as dopamine, norepinephrine (NE), and epinephrine, and the **indolamines**, which include serotonin and histamine. As illustrated in Figure 11.21, *dopamine* and *NE* are synthesized from the amino acid tyrosine in a common pathway consisting of several steps. Apparently, neurons contain only the enzymes needed to produce their own neurotransmitter(s). Thus, the sequence stops at dopamine in dopamine-releasing neurons but continues on to NE in NE-releasing neurons. The same pathway is used by the epinephrine-releasing cells of the brain and the adrenal medulla. *Serotonin* is synthesized from the amino acid tryptophan. *Histamine* is synthesized from the amino acid histidine.

Biogenic amine neurotransmitters are broadly distributed in the brain, where they play a role in emotional behavior and help regulate the biological clock. Additionally, catecholamines (particularly NE) are released by some motor neurons of the autonomic nervous system. Imbalances of these neurotransmitters

are associated with mental illness; for example, overactive dopamine signaling occurs in schizophrenia. Additionally, certain psychoactive drugs (LSD and mescaline) can bind to biogenic amine receptors and induce hallucinations.

Amino Acids It is difficult to prove a neurotransmitter role when the suspect is an *amino acid*, because amino acids occur in all cells of the body and are important in many biochemical reactions. The amino acids for which a neurotransmitter role is certain include **gamma (γ)-aminobutyric acid (GABA)**, **glycine**, **aspartate**, and **glutamate**, but there may be others.

Peptides The **neuropeptides**, essentially strings of amino acids, include a broad spectrum of molecules with diverse effects. For example, a neuropeptide called **substance P** is an important mediator of pain signals. By contrast, **endorphins**, which include **beta endorphin**, **dynorphin**, and **enkephalins** (en-kef′ah-linz), act as natural opiates, reducing our perception of pain under certain stressful conditions. Enkephalin activity increases dramatically in pregnant women in labor. Endorphin release is enhanced when an athlete gets a so-called second wind and is probably responsible for the "runner's high." Additionally, some researchers claim that the placebo effect is due to endorphin release. These painkilling neurotransmitters remained undiscovered until investigators began to ask why morphine and other opiates reduce anxiety and pain, and found that these drugs attach to the same receptors that bind natural opiates, producing similar but stronger effects.

Some neuropeptides, such as somatostatin and cholecystokinin, are also produced by nonneural body tissues and are widespread in the gastrointestinal tract. Such peptides are commonly referred to as **gut-brain peptides.**

Purines Like amino acids, another ubiquitous cellular component, **adenosine triphosphate (ATP**, the universal form of energy), is now recognized as a major neurotransmitter (perhaps the most primitive one) in both the CNS and PNS. Like glutamate and acetylcholine, it produces a fast excitatory response at certain receptors. Depending on the ATP receptor type it binds to, ATP can mediate fast excitatory responses or trigger slow, second-messenger responses. Upon binding to receptors in astrocytes, it mediates Ca^{2+} influx.

In addition to the neurotransmitter action of extracellular ATP, **adenosine,** a part of ATP, also acts outside of cells on adenosine receptors. Adenosine is a potent inhibitor in the brain. Caffeine's well-known stimulatory effects result from its block of these adenosine receptors. Four subtypes of adenosine receptors have now been recognized, all of which act indirectly via second messengers.

Dissolved Gases Just a short while ago, it would have been scientific suicide to suggest that nitric oxide and carbon monoxide—two ubiquitous molecules—might be neurotransmitters. Nonetheless, the discovery of these unlikely messengers has opened up a whole new chapter in the story of neurotransmission.

Nitric oxide (NO), a short-lived toxic gas, defies all the official descriptions of neurotransmitters in that rather than being stored in vesicles and released by exocytosis, it is synthesized on demand and diffuses out of the cells making it. Instead of attaching to surface receptors, it zooms through the plasma membrane of nearby cells to bind with a peculiar intracellular receptor—iron in *guanylyl cyclase,* the enzyme that makes the second messenger *cyclic GMP.* The precise role of NO in the brain has been hard to pin down, but when the neurotransmitter glutamate binds to NMDA receptors, Ca^{2+} channels open to allow an influx of Ca^{2+} into the cell. The Ca^{2+} triggers reactions that activate *nitric oxide synthase (NOS),* the enzyme needed for NO synthesis. Many believe NO is the retrograde messenger involved in long-term potentiation (learning and memory)—that is, it may travel back from the postsynaptic neuron to the presynaptic neuron where it activates guanylyl cyclase. Excessive release of NO contributes to much of the brain damage seen in stroke patients (see pp. 468–469). In the myenteric plexus of the intestine, NO causes intestinal smooth muscle to relax.

It may be that NO is just the first of a soon-to-be-discovered class of signaling gases that pass swiftly into cells, bind briefly to metal-containing enzymes, and then vanish. **Carbon monoxide (CO)**, another airy messenger, also stimulates synthesis of cyclic GMP, and some researchers speculate that CO is the main regulator of cyclic GMP levels in the brain. Though NO and CO are found in different brain regions and appear to act in different pathways, their mode of action is similar.

Classification of Neurotransmitters by Function

This text cannot begin to describe the incredible diversity of functions that neurotransmitters mediate. Therefore, we limit our discussion to two broad ways of classifying neurotransmitters according to function; more details will be added as appropriate in subsequent chapters.

Effects: Excitatory Versus Inhibitory We can summarize this classification scheme by saying that some neurotransmitters are excitatory (cause depolarization), some are inhibitory (cause hyperpolarization), and others exert both effects, depending on the specific receptor types with which they

interact. For example, the amino acids GABA and glycine are usually inhibitory, whereas glutamate is typically excitatory (see Table 11.3). On the other hand, ACh and NE each bind to at least two receptor types that cause opposite effects. For example, acetylcholine is excitatory at neuromuscular junctions in skeletal muscle and inhibitory in cardiac muscle.

Mechanism of Action: Direct Versus Indirect Neurotransmitters that bind to and open ion channels are said to act *directly.* These neurotransmitters provoke rapid responses in postsynaptic cells by promoting changes in membrane potential. ACh and the amino acid neurotransmitters typically act as direct-acting neurotransmitters.

Neurotransmitters that act *indirectly* tend to promote broader, longer-lasting effects by acting through intracellular *second-messenger* molecules [typically via G protein mechanisms (see Figure 3.16)]. In this way their mechanism of action is similar to that of many hormones. The biogenic amines, neuropeptides, and the dissolved gases are indirect neurotransmitters.

Neuromodulator is a term used to describe a chemical messenger released by a neuron that does not directly cause EPSPs or IPSPs but does affect the strength of synaptic transmission. A neuromodulator may act presynaptically to influence the synthesis, release, degradation, or reuptake of neurotransmitter. Alternatively, a neuromodulator may act postsynaptically by altering the sensitivity of the postsynaptic membrane to neurotransmitter. Receptors for neuromodulators are not necessarily found at a synapse. Instead, a neuromodulator may be released from one cell to act at many cells in its vicinity in the manner typical of paracrines (chemical messengers that act locally and are quickly destroyed). The distinction between neurotransmitters and neuromodulators is fuzzy, but chemical messengers such as NO and a number of neuropeptides are often referred to as neuromodulators.

Neurotransmitter Receptors

In Chapter 3, we introduced the various receptors involved in cell signaling. Now we are ready to pick up that thread again as we examine the action of receptors that bind neurotransmitters. For the most part, neurotransmitter receptors are either channel-linked receptors, which mediate fast synaptic transmission, or G protein–linked receptors, which oversee slow synaptic responses.

Mechanism of Action of Channel-Linked Receptors **Channel-linked receptors** are ligand-gated ion channels that mediate direct transmitter action.

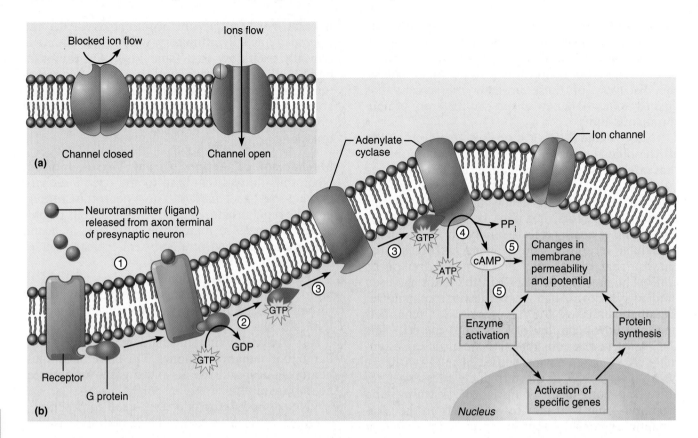

FIGURE 11.22 **Neurotransmitter receptor mechanism. (a)** Channel-linked receptors open in response to binding of ligand (ACh in this case). When no ligand is bound, the channel is closed and no current passes through it. As soon as ligand binds, the channel opens and ions flow through it. The precise ion current is determined by the structure and charge of the channel proteins. (In ACh channels, Na^+, K^+, and Ca^{2+} pass, resulting in a depolarizing current.) **(b)** A G protein–linked receptor. ① A neurotransmitter (ligand, first messenger) binds to its receptor. ② Binding of the neurotransmitter to the receptor results in receptor–G protein interaction and activation of the G protein. Once GTP replaces GDP in the G protein complex, ③ the G protein can interact with and activate adenylate cyclase. ④ Activated adenylate cyclase catalyzes the formation of cyclic AMP (cAMP) from ATP. ⑤ cAMP, acting as an intracellular second messenger, mediates events which activate enzymes that bring about the postsynaptic neuron's response (changes in membrane potential, protein synthesis, etc.).

Also called *ionotropic receptors*, they are composed of several protein subunits arranged in a "rosette" around a central pore. As the ligand binds to one (or more) receptor subunits, the proteins change shape. This event opens the central channel and allows ions to pass (Figure 11.22a), altering the membrane potential of the target cell. Channel-linked receptors are always located precisely opposite sites of neurotransmitter release, and their ion channels open instantly upon ligand binding and remain open 1 ms or less while the ligand is bound. At excitatory receptor sites (nicotinic ACh channels and receptors for glutamate, aspartate, and ATP), the channel-linked receptors are cation channels that allow small cations (Na^+, K^+, Ca^{2+}) to pass, but Na^+ entry contributes most to membrane depolarization. Channel-linked receptors that respond to GABA and glycine, and allow Cl^- to pass, mediate fast inhibition (hyperpolarization).

Mechanism of Action of G Protein–Linked Receptors

Unlike responses to neurotransmitter binding at channel-linked receptors, which are immediate, simple, and brief, the activity mediated by **G protein–linked receptors** is indirect, slow (hundreds of milliseconds or more), complex, and often prolonged—ideal as a basis for some types of learning. Receptors that fall into this class are transmembrane protein complexes and include muscarinic ACh receptors and those that bind the biogenic amines and neuropeptides. When a neurotransmitter binds to a G protein–linked receptor, the G protein is activated (Figure 11.22b). (You might like to refer back to the simpler G protein explanation in Figure 3.16 on p. 84 to orient yourself.) Activated G proteins typically work by controlling the production of second messengers such as **cyclic AMP, cyclic GMP, diacylglycerol,** or **Ca^{2+}.** These, in turn, act as go-betweens to regulate (open or close) ion channels or activate kinase enzymes that initiate a cascade of enzymatic reactions in the target cells. Some of these second messengers modify (activate or inactivate) other proteins, including channel proteins, by attaching phosphate groups to them. Others interact with nuclear proteins that activate genes and induce synthesis of new proteins in the target cell. Because the effects produced tend to bring about widespread metabolic changes, G protein–linked receptors are commonly called *metabotropic receptors*.

Basic Concepts of Neural Integration

Until now, we have been concentrating on the activities of individual neurons; however, neurons function in groups, and each group contributes to still broader neural functions. Thus, the organization of the nervous system is hierarchical, or ladderlike.

Any time you have a large number of *anything*— people included—there must be *integration*; that is, the parts must be fused into a smoothly operating whole. In this section, we begin to ascend the ladder of **neural integration,** dealing only with the first rung, *neuronal pools* and their patterns of communicating with other parts of the nervous system. Chapter 13 picks up the thread of neural integration to examine how sensory inputs interface with motor activity. The highest levels of neural integration— how we think and remember—are discussed in Chapter 12.

Organization of Neurons: Neuronal Pools

The millions of neurons in the CNS are organized into **neuronal pools,** functional groups of neurons that integrate incoming information received from receptors or different neuronal pools and then forward the processed information to other destinations.

In a simple type of neuronal pool, shown in Figure 11.23, one incoming presynaptic fiber branches profusely as it enters the pool and then synapses with several different neurons in the pool. When the incoming fiber is excited, it will excite some postsynaptic neurons and facilitate others. Neurons most likely to generate impulses are those closely associated with the incoming fiber, because they receive the bulk of the synaptic contacts. Those neurons are said to be in the *discharge zone* of the pool. Neurons farther from the center are not usually excited to threshold by EPSPs induced by the incoming fiber, but they are facilitated

Presynaptic (input) fiber

| Facilitated zone | Discharge zone | Facilitated zone |

FIGURE 11.23 **Simple neuronal pool.** This simplified representation shows the relative position of postsynaptic neurons in the discharge and facilitated zones. Notice that the presynaptic fiber makes more synapses per neuron with neurons in the discharge zone.

and can easily be brought to threshold by stimuli from another source. Thus, the periphery of the pool is the *facilitated zone*. Keep in mind, however, that our figure is a gross oversimplification. Most neuronal pools consist of thousands of neurons and include inhibitory as well as excitatory neurons.

Types of Circuits

Individual neurons in a neuronal pool both send and receive information, and synaptic contacts may cause either excitation or inhibition. The patterns of synaptic connections in neuronal pools are called **circuits,** and they determine the pool's functional capabilities. Four basic circuit patterns are shown in simplified form in Figure 11.24.

In **diverging circuits,** one incoming fiber triggers responses in ever-increasing numbers of neurons farther and farther along in the circuit. Thus, diverging circuits are often *amplifying* circuits. Divergence can occur along a single pathway or along several (Figure 11.24a and b). These circuits are common in both sensory and motor systems. For example, impulses traveling from a single neuron of the brain can activate a hundred or more motor neurons in the spinal cord and, consequently, thousands of skeletal muscle fibers.

The pattern of **converging circuits** is opposite that of diverging circuits, but they too are common in both sensory and motor pathways. In a converging circuit, the pool receives inputs from several presynaptic neurons, and the circuit has a funneling, or *concentrating*, effect. Incoming stimuli may converge from one area or from many different

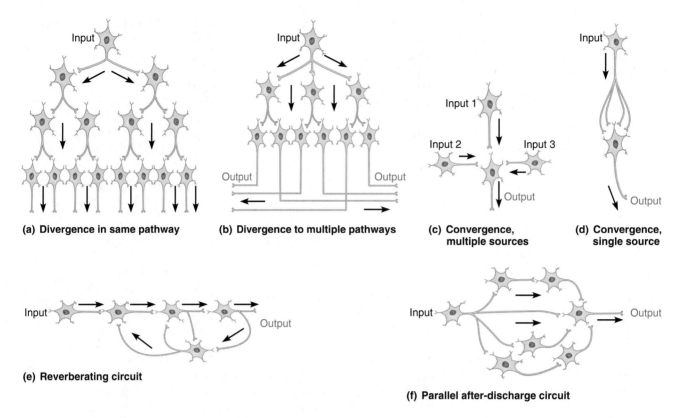

(a) Divergence in same pathway

(b) Divergence to multiple pathways

(c) Convergence, multiple sources

(d) Convergence, single source

(e) Reverberating circuit

(f) Parallel after-discharge circuit

FIGURE 11.24 **Types of circuits in neuronal pools.**

areas (Figure 11.24c and d), which results in strong stimulation or inhibition. The former condition helps explain how different types of sensory stimuli can have the same ultimate effect. For instance, seeing the smiling face of their infant, smelling the baby's freshly powdered skin, or hearing the baby gurgle can all trigger a flood of loving feelings in parents.

In **reverberating,** or **oscillating, circuits** (Figure 11.24e), the incoming signal travels through a chain of neurons, each of which makes collateral synapses with neurons in a previous part of the pathway. As a result of the positive feedback, the impulses *reverberate* (are sent through the circuit again and again), giving a continuous output signal until one neuron in the circuit fails to fire. Reverberating circuits are involved in control of rhythmic activities, such as the sleep-wake cycle, breathing, and certain motor activities (such as arm swinging when walking). Some researchers believe that such circuits underlie short-term memory. Depending on the specific circuit, reverberating circuits may continue to oscillate for seconds, hours, or (in the case of the circuit controlling the rhythm of breathing) a lifetime.

In **parallel after-discharge circuits,** the incoming fiber stimulates several neurons arranged in parallel arrays that eventually stimulate a common output cell (Figure 11.24f). Impulses reach the output cell at different times, creating a burst of impulses called an *after-discharge* that lasts 15 ms or more after the initial input has ended. This type of circuit has no positive feedback, and once all the neurons have fired, circuit activity ends. Parallel after-discharge circuits may be involved in complex, exacting types of mental processing.

Patterns of Neural Processing

Input processing is both *serial* and *parallel*. In serial processing, the input travels along one pathway to a specific destination. In parallel processing, the input travels along several different pathways to be integrated in different CNS regions. Each mode has unique advantages in the overall scheme of neural functioning, but as an information processor, the brain derives its power from its ability to process in parallel.

Serial Processing

In **serial processing,** the whole system works in a predictable all-or-nothing manner. One neuron stimulates the next, which stimulates the next, and so on, eventually causing a specific, anticipated response. The most clear-cut examples of serial processing are spinal reflexes, but straight-through

FIGURE 11.25   **A simple reflex arc.** Receptors detect changes in the internal or external environment. Effectors are muscles or glands.

sensory pathways from receptors to the brain are also examples. Because reflexes are the functional units of the nervous system, it is important that you understand them early on.

Reflexes are rapid, automatic responses to stimuli, in which a particular stimulus always causes the *same* response. Reflex activity, which produces the simplest of behaviors, is stereotyped and dependable. For example, jerking away your hand after touching a hot object is the norm, and an object approaching the eye triggers a blink. Reflexes occur over neural pathways called **reflex arcs** that have five essential components—receptor, sensory neuron, CNS integration center, motor neuron, and effector (Figure 11.25).

Parallel Processing

In **parallel processing,** inputs are segregated into many pathways, and information delivered by each pathway is dealt with simultaneously by different parts of the neural circuitry. For example, smelling a pickle (the input) may cause you to remember picking cucumbers on a farm; or it may remind you that you don't like pickles or that you must buy some at the market; or perhaps it will call to mind *all* these thoughts. For each person, parallel processing triggers some pathways that are unique. The same stimulus—pickle smell, in our example—promotes many responses beyond simple awareness of the smell. Parallel processing is not repetitious because the circuits do different things with the information, and each "channel" is decoded in relation to all the others to produce a total picture.

Think, for example, about what happens when you step on something sharp while walking barefoot. The serially processed withdrawal reflex causes instantaneous removal of your injured foot from the sharp object (painful stimulus). At the same time, pain and pressure impulses are speeding up to the brain along parallel pathways that allow you to

decide whether to simply rub the hurt spot to soothe it or to seek first aid.

Parallel processing is extremely important for higher level mental functioning—for putting the parts together to understand the whole. For example, you can recognize a dollar bill in a split second, a task that takes a serial-based computer a fairly long time. This is because you use parallel processing, which allows a single neuron to send information along several pathways instead of just one, so a large amount of information is processed much more quickly.

Developmental Aspects of Neurons

The nervous system is covered in several chapters, so we limit our attention here to the development of neurons, beginning with the questions, How do nerve cells originate? and How do they mature?

The nervous system originates from a dorsal *neural tube* and the *neural crest* (see Figure 12.1, p. 431), formed from surface ectoderm. The neural tube, whose walls begin as a layer of *neuroepithelial* cells, becomes the CNS. The neuroepithelial cells then begin a three-phase process of differentiation, which occurs largely in the second month of development. (1) They *proliferate* to produce the appropriate number of cells needed for nervous system development. (2) The potential neurons, **neuroblasts,** become amitotic and *migrate* externally into their characteristic positions. (3) The neuroblasts sprout axons to *connect with* their functional targets and in so doing become neurons.

How does a neuroblast's growing axon "know" where to go—and once it gets there, where to make the proper connection? This question has been a topic of intense research over the past decade. We now know a great deal about how axons find their correct targets. The growth of an axon toward an appropriate target requires multiple steps and is guided by multiple signals. The growing tip of an axon, called a **growth cone,** is a prickly, fanlike structure that gives an axon the ability to interact with its environment. Extracellular and cell surface adhesion proteins such as laminin, integrin, and *nerve cell adhesion molecule (N-CAM)* provide anchor points for the growth cone, saying, "It's okay to grow here." *Neurotropins* are chemicals that signal to the growth cone "come this way" (netrin) or "go away" (ephrin) or "stop here" (semaphorin). Throughout this growth and development, neurotrophic factors such as *nerve growth factor (NGF)* must be present to keep the neuroblast alive. Failure of any of these guiding signals results in catastrophic developmental problems. For example, lack of N-CAM action causes developing

11

A CLOSER LOOK

Pleasure Me, Pleasure Me!

Sex! Drugs! Rock 'n' roll! Eat, drink and be merry! Why do we find these activities so compelling? Our brains are wired to give us pleasurable rewards when we engage in behavior that is necessary for our own and our species' survival. This reward system consists of dopamine-releasing neurons in areas of the brain called the *ventral tegmental area* (VTA), the *nucleus accumbens,* and the *amygdala.*

Our ability to "feel good" involves brain neurotransmitters in this reward system. For example, the ecstasy of romantic love may be just a brain bath of glutamate and norepinephrine, which act on the reward system to release dopamine. Cole Porter knew what he was talking about when he wrote "I get a kick out of you," because these neurotransmitters are chemical cousins of the amphetamines. People who use "crystal meth" (methamphetamine) artificially stimulate their brains to provide their highly addictive pleasure flush. However, their pleasure is short-lived, because when the brain is flooded with neurotransmitter-like chemicals from the outside, it makes less of its own (why bother?).

Unfortunately, this powerful system can be subverted by drugs of abuse. Cocaine, another reward system titillater, has been around since ancient times. Once a toy of the rich, its granular form is inhaled, or "snorted." The laws of supply and demand have now brought cheaper cocaine to the masses, notably "crack"—a cheaper, more potent, smokable form of cocaine. For ten dollars or so, a novice user can experience a rush of intense pleasure. But crack is treacherous and

PET scans show that normal levels of brain activity (yellow and red) are depressed in cocaine users long after drug use has stopped.

Normal

Abuser: 10 days without cocaine

Abuser: 100 days without cocaine

intensely addictive. It produces not only a higher high than the inhaled form of cocaine, but also a deeper crash that leaves the user desperate for more.

How does cocaine produce its effects? Basically, the drug stimulates the reward system and then "squeezes it dry." Cocaine produces its rush by hooking up to the dopamine reuptake transporter protein, thus blocking the reabsorption of dopamine. The neurotransmitter remains in the synapse and

stimulates the postsynaptic receptor cells again and again, allowing the body to feel its effects over a prolonged period. This sensation is accompanied by increases in heart rate, blood pressure, and sexual appetite. As dopamine uptake continues to be blocked by repeated doses of cocaine, the system releases less and less dopamine and the reward system effectively goes dry. The cocaine user becomes anxious and, in a very real

---

neural tissue to fall into a tangled, spaghetti-like mass and hopelessly impairs neural function.

The growth cone gropes along like an amoeba, with oozing processes called *filopodia* which detect the guiding signals in the surrounding environment. Receptors for these signals generate various second messengers that cause the filopodia to move by rearranging their actin protein cores. Once the axon has reached its target area, it must select the right site on the target cell to form a synapse, an event that requires

signaling by both presynaptic and postsynaptic cells. This process is not yet well understood, but involves clustering postsynaptic neurotransmitter receptors while the postsynaptic cell tells the presynaptic cell what neurotransmitters to make. In the brain and spinal cord, astrocytes seem to provide both physical support and the cholesterol essential for constructing synapses. Both dendrites and astrocytes are active partners in the process of synapse formation. In the presence of thrombospondin released by astrocytes, sense, unable to experience pleasure without the drug. Consequently, the postsynaptic cells become hypersensitive and sprout new receptors in a desperate effort to pick up dopamine signals. A vicious cycle of addiction begins: Cocaine is needed to experience pleasure, but using it suppresses dopamine release even more.

The dopamine effect alone is not enough to establish addiction. Another neurotransmitter, glutamate, which plays an important role in learning, is required to maintain addiction. Glutamate signaling seems to cause more permanent changes in the brain (synaptic potentiation) that lead to compulsive drug-seeking behaviors elicited by external cues. Take, for example, mice genetically engineered to lack a particular glutamate receptor (GluR5). These mice are perfectly willing to try cocaine but never become addicted. (Of course, they're none too bright, either.)

Current thinking, then, is that the rush of pleasure on taking cocaine is due to dopamine. Glutamate, on the other hand, is thought to be responsible for the learning that makes true the perception "once an addict, always an addict." So strong is the combined dopamine and glutamate system that, even years later, certain settings can trigger intense cravings for the drug.

These out-of-control, desperate cravings are notoriously difficult to manage. Drug abusers call it "jonesing." Traditional antiaddiction drugs take so long to reduce the cravings that users commonly drop out of treatment programs. How can we break this cycle of addiction? One way is to prevent cocaine from ever reaching the brain. Researchers have created a vaccine that prevents cocaine from entering the brain, and clinical trials on this vaccine are ongoing. Another approach to breaking the addiction cycle is to even out the highs and lows experienced by the drug user. Clinical trials are under way with a drug (vanoxerine) that slowly binds the dopamine reuptake transporter and inhibits it in a more long-lasting manner than cocaine does. This results in a leveling-out of brain dopamine levels and keeps the user from "crashing" so badly. A final approach to breaking the addiction cycle is to interrupt the learned reinforcement that brings on cravings. An effective ancient African folk remedy called ibogaine may do exactly this. However, ibogaine itself is too toxic for clinical use, as some unfortunate "underground" users have discovered. A close synthetic cousin, 18-methoxycoronaridine (18-MC) is much less toxic and promises to be effective against not only cocaine but also a number of other abused drugs. Future studies will show if it is truly effective.

The craving for drugs has made some who depend on them into very creative home pharmacologists, willing to experiment with practically anything, no matter how toxic or dangerous, to get the "buzz" they need. A cheap mixture of cold medications, match heads, and iodine in acetone yields crystal meth—the highly addictive and once-again popular drug that wreaks people's lives and often explodes their home laboratories. Another creative mixture, with the street name of "ill face" or "illy," involves dipping marijuana in formaldehyde, drying and then smoking it. Other remarkable combinations are the "H-bomb" (ecstasy mixed with heroin), "A-bomb" (marijuana with heroin or opium), "sextasy" [ecstasy mixed with sildenafil (Viagra)], "octane" (PCP laced with gasoline), and "ozone" (marijuana, PCP, and crack in a cigarette). Formaldehyde is a known cancer-causing agent and gasoline damages the liver, but the real damage comes from the drugs themselves. Take, for example, ecstasy, a drug that many of its users believe to be innocuous. In reality, ecstasy (MDMA) targets serotonin-releasing neurons. The "rush" of pleasure and energy that users feel is due to release of serotonin and other neurotransmitters. However, it damages and may destroy these neurons, causing the loss of verbal and spatial memory. Depression, sleeplessness, and memory problems may be permanent consequences—a high price for a few moments of pleasure!

People who want pure, effective, and "safe" drugs of abuse don't get them on the street. They get them from doctors or "pill ladies" [female senior citizens who sell oxycodone (OxyContin), a powerful prescription opioid with effects similar to heroin]. Even those who would never dream of taking the illicit drugs can be caught in the addictive cycle of prescription drugs. Prescribed legitimately to relieve severe pain, oxycodone is meant to be swallowed whole. Abusers crush the tablets and snort the powder or dissolve it in water and inject the solution. Oxycodone abuse is spreading rapidly. Medical examiners across North America report soaring rates of oxycodone-related emergency room visits and deaths.

The brain, with its complex biochemistry, always circumvents attempts to keep it in a euphoric haze. Perhaps this means that pleasure must be transient by nature, experienced only against a background of its absence. ■

11

dendrites actually reach out and grasp migrating axons, and synapses begin sprouting.

Neurons that fail to make appropriate or functional synaptic contacts act as if they have been deprived of some essential nutrient and die. Besides cell death resulting from unsuccessful synapse formation, *apoptosis* (programmed cell death) also appears to be a normal part of the developmental process. Of the neurons formed during the embryonic period, perhaps two-thirds die before we are born. Those that remain constitute most of our neural endowment for life. The generally amitotic nature of neurons is important because their activity depends on the synapses they've formed; if neurons were to divide, their connections might be hopelessly disrupted. This aside, there *do* appear to be some specific neuronal populations where stem cells are found and new neurons can be formed—notably olfactory neurons and some cells of the hippocampus, a brain region involved in learning and memory.

■ ■ ■

In this chapter, we have examined how the amazingly complex neurons, via electrical and chemical signals, serve the body in a variety of ways: Some serve as "lookouts," others process information for immediate use or for future reference, and still others stimulate the body's muscles and glands into activity. With this background, we are ready to study the most sophisticated mass of neural tissue in the entire body—the brain (and its continuation, the spinal cord), the focus of Chapter 12.

Related Clinical Terms

Neuroblastoma (nu″ro-blas-to′mah; *oma* = tumor) A malignant tumor in children; arises from cells that retain a neuroblast-like structure. These tumors sometimes arise in the brain, but most occur in the peripheral nervous system.

Neurologist (nu-rol′o-jist) A medical specialist in the study of the nervous system, its functions, and its disorders.

Neuropathy (nu-rop′ah-the) Any disease of nervous tissue, but particularly degenerative disease of nerves.

Neuropharmacology (nu″ro-far″mah-kol′o-je) Scientific study of the effects of drugs on the nervous system.

Neurotoxin Substance that is poisonous or destructive to nervous tissue, e.g., botulinum and tetanus toxins.

Rabies (*rabies* = madness) A viral infection of the nervous system transmitted by the bite of an infected mammal (such as a dog, bat, or skunk). After entry, the virus travels via axonal transport in peripheral nerve axons to the CNS, where it causes brain inflammation, delirium, and death. A vaccine- and antibody-based treatment is effective if given before symptoms appear; rabies in humans is very rare in the United States.

Shingles (herpes zoster) A viral infection of sensory neurons serving the skin. Characterized by scaly, painful blisters usually confined to a narrow strip of skin, often on one side of the body trunk. Caused by the varicella-zoster virus, which causes chicken pox (generally during childhood); during this initial infection the virus is transported from the skin lesions to the sensory cell bodies in the sensory ganglia. Typically, the virus is held in check by the immune system and remains dormant until the immune system is weakened, often by stress. Then viral particles multiply and travel back to the skin, producing the characteristic rash. Attacks last several weeks, alternating between periods of healing and relapse. Seen mostly in those over 50 years old.

Chapter Summary

Media study tools that could provide you additional help in reviewing specific key topics of Chapter 11 are referenced below.

IP = *InterActive Physiology*

1. The nervous system bears a major responsibility for maintaining body homeostasis. Its chief functions are to monitor, integrate, and respond to information in the environment.

Organization of the Nervous System   (pp. 388–389)

1. The nervous system is divided anatomically into the central nervous system (brain and spinal cord) and the peripheral nervous system (cranial and spinal nerves).

2. The major functional divisions of the nervous system are the sensory (afferent) division, which conveys impulses to the CNS, and the motor (efferent) division, which conveys impulses from the CNS.

3. The efferent division includes the somatic (voluntary) system, which serves skeletal muscles, and the autonomic (involuntary) system, which innervates smooth and cardiac muscle and glands.

Histology of Nervous Tissue   (pp. 389–397)

Neuroglia   (pp. 389–391)

1. Neuroglia (supporting cells) segregate and insulate neurons and assist neurons in various other ways.

2. CNS neuroglia include astrocytes, microglia, ependymal cells, and oligodendrocytes. Schwann cells and satellite cells are neuroglia found in the PNS.

Neurons   (pp. 391–397)

3. Neurons have a cell body and cytoplasmic processes called axons and dendrites.

4. A bundle of nerve fibers is called a tract in the CNS and a nerve in the PNS. A collection of cell bodies is called a nucleus in the CNS and a ganglion in the PNS.

5. The cell body is the biosynthetic (and receptive) center of the neuron. Except for those found in ganglia, cell bodies are found in the CNS.

6. Some neurons have many dendrites, receptive sites that conduct signals from other neurons toward the nerve cell body. With few exceptions, all neurons have one axon, which generates and conducts nerve impulses away from the nerve cell body. Terminal endings of axons release neurotransmitter.

7. Bidirectional transport along axons uses ATP-dependent motor proteins "walking" along microtubule tracks. It moves vesicles, mitochondria, and cytosolic proteins toward the axon terminals and conducts substances destined for degradation back to the cell body. It involves microtubules and motor proteins.

8. Large nerve fibers (axons) are myelinated. The myelin sheath is formed in the PNS by Schwann cells and in the CNS by oligodendrocytes. The sheath has gaps called nodes of Ranvier. Unmyelinated fibers are surrounded by supporting cells, but the membrane-wrapping process does not occur.

9. Anatomically, neurons are classified according to the number of processes issuing from the cell body as multipolar, bipolar, or unipolar.

10. Functionally, neurons are classified according to the direction of nerve impulse conduction. Sensory neurons conduct impulses toward the CNS, motor neurons conduct away from the CNS, and interneurons (association neurons) lie between sensory and motor neurons in the neural pathways.

IP Nervous System I; Topic: Anatomy Review, pp. 1–12.

Neurophysiology (pp. 397–421)

Basic Principles of Electricity (pp. 397–399)

1. The measure of the potential energy of separated electrical charges is called voltage (*V*) or potential. Current (*I*) is the flow of electrical charge from one point to another. Resistance (*R*) is hindrance to current flow. The relationship among these is given by Ohm's law: $I = V/R$.

2. In the body, electrical charges are provided by ions; cellular plasma membranes provide resistance to ion flow. The membranes contain leakage channels (nongated, always open) and gated channels.

IP Nervous System I; Topic: Ion Channels, pp. 1–10.

The Resting Membrane Potential (pp. 399–400)

3. A resting neuron exhibits a resting membrane potential, which is −70 mV (inside negative). It is due to both differences in sodium and potassium ion concentrations inside and outside the cell and differences in permeability of the membrane to these ions.

4. The ionic concentration differences result from the operation of the sodium-potassium pump, which ejects $3Na^+$ from the cell for each $2K^+$ transported in.

IP Nervous System I; Topic: The Membrane Potential, pp. 1–16.

Membrane Potentials That Act as Signals (pp. 400–408)

5. Depolarization is a reduction in membrane potential (inside becomes less negative); hyperpolarization is an increase in membrane potential (inside becomes more negative).

6. Graded potentials are small, brief, local changes in membrane potential that act as short-distance signals. The current produced dissipates with distance.

7. An action potential (AP), or nerve impulse, is a large, but brief, depolarization signal (and polarity reversal) that underlies long-distance neural communication. It is an all-or-none phenomenon.

8. An AP has three underlying changes in membrane permeability: (1) Increase in sodium permeability: Local depolarization opens voltage-gated Na^+ channels; at threshold, depolarization becomes self-generating (driven by Na^+ influx). The membrane potential is reversed to approximately +30 mV (inside positive). (2) Decrease in sodium permeability. (3) Increase in potassium permeability. Repolarization occurs during phases 2 and 3.

9. In nerve impulse propagation, each AP provides the depolarizing stimulus for triggering an AP in the next membrane patch. Regions that have just generated APs are refractory; hence, the nerve impulse is propagated in one direction only.

10. If threshold is reached, an AP is generated; if not, depolarization remains local.

11. APs are independent of stimulus strength: strong stimuli cause APs to be generated more frequently but not with greater amplitude.

12. During the absolute refractory period, a neuron cannot respond to another stimulus because it is already generating an AP. During the relative refractory period the neuron's threshold is elevated because repolarization is ongoing.

13. In unmyelinated fibers, APs are produced in a wave all along the axon, that is, by continuous conduction. In myelinated fibers, APs are generated only at nodes of Ranvier and are propagated more rapidly by saltatory conduction.

IP Nervous System I; Topic: The Action Potential, pp. 1–18.

The Synapse (pp. 408–411)

14. A synapse is a functional junction between neurons. The information-transmitting neuron is the presynaptic neuron; the information-receiving neuron is the postsynaptic neuron.

15. Electrical synapses allow ions to flow directly from one neuron to another; the cells are electrically coupled.

16. Chemical synapses are sites of neurotransmitter release and binding. When the impulse reaches the presynaptic axon terminals, voltage-gated Ca^{2+} channels open, and Ca^{2+} enters the cell and mediates neurotransmitter release. Neurotransmitters diffuse across the synaptic cleft and attach to postsynaptic membrane receptors, opening ion channels. After binding, the neurotransmitters are removed from the synapse by enzymatic breakdown or by reuptake into the presynaptic terminal or astrocytes.

IP Nervous System II; Topics: Anatomy Review, pp. 1–9, Ion Channels, pp. 1–8, Synaptic Transmission, pp. 1–7.

Postsynaptic Potentials and Synaptic Integration (pp. 411–413)

17. Binding of neurotransmitter at excitatory chemical synapses results in local graded potentials called EPSPs, caused by the opening of channels that allow simultaneous passage of Na^+ and K^+.

18. Neurotransmitter binding at inhibitory chemical synapses results in hyperpolarizations called IPSPs, caused by the opening of K^+ or Cl^- channels. IPSPs drive the membrane potential farther from threshold.

19. EPSPs and IPSPs summate temporally and spatially. The membrane of the axon hillock acts as a neuronal integrator.

20. Synaptic potentiation, in which the postsynaptic neuron's response is enhanced, is produced by intense repeated stimulation. Ionic calcium appears to mediate such effects, which may be the basis of learning.

21. Presynaptic inhibition is mediated by axoaxonic synapses that reduce the amount of neurotransmitter released by the inhibited neuron.

IP Nervous System II; Topic: Synaptic Potentials and Cellular Integration, pp. 1–10.

Neurotransmitters and Their Receptors (pp. 413–421)

22. The major classes of neurotransmitters based on chemical structure are acetylcholine, biogenic amines, amino acids, peptides, purines, and dissolved gases.

23. Functionally, neurotransmitters are classified as (1) inhibitory or excitatory (or both) and (2) direct or indirect. Direct-acting neurotransmitters bind to and open ion channels. Indirect-acting neurotransmitters act through second messengers. Neuromodulators also act indirectly presynaptically or postsynaptically to change synaptic strength.

24. Neurotransmitter receptors are either channel-linked receptors that open ion channels, leading to fast changes in membrane potential, or G protein–linked receptors that oversee slow synaptic responses mediated by G proteins and intracellular second messengers. Second messengers most often activate kinases, which in turn act on ion channels or activate other proteins.

IP Nervous System II; Topic: Synaptic Transmission pp. 6–15.

11

Basic Concepts of Neural Integration (pp. 421–423)

Organization of Neurons: Neuronal Pools (p. 421)

1. CNS neurons are organized into several types of neuronal pools, each with distinguishing patterns of synaptic connections called circuits.

Types of Circuits (pp. 421–422)

2. The four basic circuit types are diverging, converging, reverberating, and parallel after-discharge.

Patterns of Neural Processing (pp. 422–423)

3. In serial processing, one neuron stimulates the next in sequence, producing specific, predictable responses, as in spinal reflexes. A reflex is a rapid, involuntary motor response to a stimulus.

4. Reflexes are mediated over neural pathways called reflex arcs. The minimum number of elements in a reflex arc is five: receptor, sensory neuron, integration center, motor neuron, and effector.

5. In parallel processing, which underlies complex mental functions, impulses are sent along several pathways to different integration centers.

Developmental Aspects of Neurons (pp. 423–425)

1. Neuron development involves proliferation, migration, and cellular differentiation. Cellular differentiation entails neuron specialization, specific neurotransmitter synthesis, and synapse formation.

2. Axon outgrowth and synapse formation are guided by other neurons, glial fibers, and chemicals (such as N-CAM and nerve growth factor). Neurons that do not make appropriate synapses die, and approximately two-thirds of neurons formed in the embryo undergo programmed cell death before birth.

Review Questions

Multiple Choice/Matching

(Some questions have more than one correct answer. Select the best answer or answers from the choices given.)

1. Which of the following structures is not part of the central nervous system? (a) the brain, (b) a nerve, (c) the spinal cord, (d) a tract.

2. Match the names of the supporting cells found in column B with the appropriate descriptions in column A.

Column A	Column B
____ (1) myelinates nerve fibers in the CNS	(a) astrocyte
____ (2) lines brain cavities	(b) ependymal cell
____ (3) myelinates nerve fibers in the PNS	(c) microglia
____ (4) CNS phagocytes	(d) oligodendrocyte
____ (5) helps regulate the ionic composition of CNS extracellular fluid	(e) satellite cell
	(f) Schwann cell

3. What type of current flows through the axolemma during the steep phase of repolarization? (a) chiefly a sodium current, (b) chiefly a potassium current, (c) sodium and potassium currents of approximately the same magnitude.

4. Assume that an EPSP is being generated on the dendritic membrane. Which will occur? (a) specific Na^+ channels will open, (b) specific K^+ channels will open, (c) a single type of channel will open, permitting simultaneous flow of Na^+ and K^+, (d) Na^+ channels will open first and then close as K^+ channels open.

5. The velocity of nerve impulse conduction is greatest in (a) heavily myelinated, large-diameter fibers, (b) myelinated, small-diameter fibers, (c) unmyelinated, small-diameter fibers, (d) unmyelinated, large-diameter fibers.

6. Chemical synapses are characterized by all of the following except (a) the release of neurotransmitter by the presynaptic membranes, (b) postsynaptic membranes bearing receptors that bind neurotransmitter, (c) ions flowing through protein channels from the presynaptic to the postsynaptic neuron, (d) a fluid-filled gap separating the neurons.

7. Biogenic amine neurotransmitters include all but (a) norepinephrine, (b) acetylcholine, (c) dopamine, (d) serotonin.

8. The neuropeptides that act as natural opiates are (a) substance P, (b) somatostatin, (c) cholecystokinin, (d) enkephalins.

9. Inhibition of acetylcholinesterase by poisoning blocks neurotransmission at the neuromuscular junction because (a) ACh is no longer released by the presynaptic terminal, (b) ACh synthesis in the presynaptic terminal is blocked, (c) ACh is not degraded, hence prolonged depolarization is enforced on the postsynaptic neuron, (d) ACh is blocked from attaching to the postsynaptic ACh receptors.

10. The anatomical region of a multipolar neuron that has the lowest threshold for generating an AP is the (a) soma, (b) dendrites, (c) axon hillock, (d) distal axon.

11. An IPSP is inhibitory because (a) it hyperpolarizes the postsynaptic membrane, (b) it reduces the amount of neurotransmitter released by the presynaptic terminal, (c) it prevents calcium ion entry into the presynaptic terminal, (d) it changes the threshold of the neuron.

12. Identify the neuronal circuits described by choosing the correct response from the key.

Key: (a) converging
    (b) diverging
    (c) parallel after-discharge
    (d) reverberating

____ (1) Impulses continue around and around the circuit until one neuron stops firing.
____ (2) One or a few inputs ultimately influence large numbers of neurons.
____ (3) Many neurons influence a few neurons.
____ (4) May be involved in exacting types of mental activity.

Short Answer Essay Questions

13. Explain both the anatomical and functional divisions of the nervous system. Include the subdivisions of each.

14. (a) Describe the composition and function of the cell body. (b) How are axons and dendrites alike? In what ways (structurally and functionally) do they differ?

15. (a) What is myelin? (b) How does the myelination process differ in the CNS and PNS?

16. (a) Contrast unipolar, bipolar, and multipolar neurons structurally. (b) Indicate where each is most likely to be found.

17. What is the polarized membrane state? How is it maintained? (Note the relative roles of both passive and active mechanisms.)

18. Describe the events that must occur to generate an AP. Relate the sequence of changes in permeability to changes in the ion channels, and explain why the AP is an all-or-none phenomenon.

19. Since all APs generated by a given nerve fiber have the same magnitude, how does the CNS "know" whether a stimulus is strong or weak?

20. (a) Explain the difference between an EPSP and an IPSP. (b) What specifically determines whether an EPSP or IPSP will be generated at the postsynaptic membrane?

21. Since at any moment a neuron is likely to have thousands of neurons releasing neurotransmitters at its surface, how is neuronal activity (to fire or not to fire) determined?

22. The effects of neurotransmitter binding are very brief. Explain.

23. During a neurobiology lecture, a professor repeatedly refers to group A and group B fibers, absolute refractory period, and nodes of Ranvier. Define these terms.

24. Distinguish between serial and parallel processing.

25. Briefly describe the three stages of neuron development.

26. What factors appear to guide the outgrowth of an axon and its ability to make the "correct" synaptic contacts?

Critical Thinking and Clinical Application Questions

1. Mr. Miller is hospitalized for cardiac problems. Somehow, medical orders are mixed up and Mr. Miller is infused with a K^+-enhanced intravenous solution meant for another patient who is taking potassium-wasting diuretics (i.e., drugs that cause excessive loss of potassium from the body in urine). Mr. Miller's potassium levels are normal before the IV is administered. What do you think will happen to Mr. Miller's resting membrane potentials? To his neurons' ability to generate APs?

2. Local anesthetics block voltage-gated Na^+ channels. General anesthetics are thought to activate chemically gated Cl^- channels, thereby rendering the nervous system quiescent while surgery is performed. What specific process do anesthetics impair, and how does this interfere with nerve transmission?

3. When admitted to the emergency room, John was holding his right hand, which had a deep puncture hole in its palm. He explained that he had fallen on a nail while exploring a barn. John was given an antitetanus shot to prevent neural complications. Tetanus bacteria fester in deep, dark wounds, but how do they travel in neural tissue?

4. Rochelle developed multiple sclerosis when she was 27. After eight years she had lost a good portion of her ability to control her skeletal muscles. How did this happen?

5. In the Netherlands a young man named Jan was admitted to the emergency room. He and his friends had been to a rave. His friends say he started twitching and having muscle spasms which progressed until he was "stiff as a board." On examination, staff found a marked increase in muscle tone and hyperreflexia involving facial and limb muscles. In his pocket, he had unmarked dark yellow tablets with dark flecks. Analysis of the tablets showed them to contain a mixture of ecstasy and strychnine. Ecstasy would not cause this clinical picture, but strychnine, which blocks glycine receptors, could. Explain how.

LOOKING FOR MORE STUDY HELP?

A wide variety of quiz questions, tutorials, and learning exercises are available online at the Anatomy & Physiology Place (www.anatomyandphysiology.com) and, if your instructor has provided you with a MyA&P Course ID number, in MyA&P (www.myaandp.com).

11

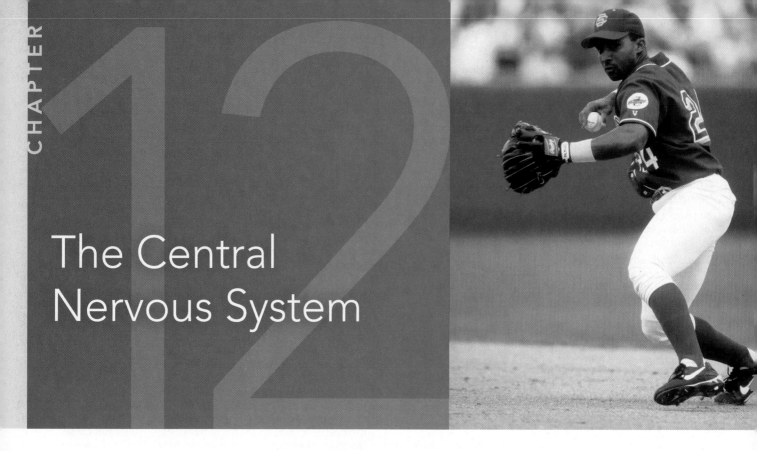

CHAPTER 12

The Central Nervous System

The Brain (pp. 431–456)

1. Describe the process of brain development.
2. Name the major regions of the adult brain.
3. Name and locate the ventricles of the brain.
4. List the major lobes, fissures, and functional areas of the cerebral cortex.
5. Explain lateralization of hemisphere function.
6. Differentiate between commissures, association fibers, and projection fibers.
7. Describe the general function of the basal nuclei (basal ganglia).
8. Describe the location of the diencephalon, and name its subdivisions.
9. Identify the three major regions of the brain stem, and note the functions of each area.
10. Describe the structure and function of the cerebellum.
11. Locate the limbic system and the reticular formation, and explain the role of each functional system.

Higher Mental Functions (pp. 456–463)

12. Define EEG and distinguish between alpha, beta, theta, and delta brain waves.
13. Compare and contrast the events and importance of slow-wave and REM sleep, and indicate how their patterns change through life.
14. Describe consciousness clinically.
15. Compare and contrast the stages and categories of memory.
16. Describe the relative roles of the major brain structures believed to be involved in declarative and procedural memories.

Protection of the Brain (pp. 463–470)

17. Describe how meninges, cerebrospinal fluid, and the blood-brain barrier protect the CNS.
18. Describe the formation of cerebrospinal fluid, and follow its circulatory pathway.
19. Describe the cause (if known) and major signs and symptoms of cerebrovascular accidents, Alzheimer's disease, Huntington's disease, and Parkinson's disease.

The Spinal Cord (pp. 470–481)

20. Describe the embryonic development of the spinal cord.
21. Describe the gross and microscopic structure of the spinal cord.
22. List the major spinal cord tracts, and classify each as a motor or sensory tract.
23. Distinguish between flaccid and spastic paralysis and between paralysis and paresthesia.

Diagnostic Procedures for Assessing CNS Dysfunction (p. 481)

24. List and explain several techniques used to diagnose brain disorders.

Developmental Aspects of the Central Nervous System (pp. 481–484)

25. Indicate several maternal factors that can impair development of the nervous system in an embryo.
26. Explain the effects of aging on the brain.

Historically, the **central nervous system (CNS)**—brain and spinal cord—has been compared to the central switchboard of a telephone system that interconnects and directs a dizzying number of incoming and outgoing calls. Nowadays, many people compare it to a supercomputer. These analogies may explain some workings of the spinal cord, but neither does justice to the fantastic complexity of the human brain. Whether we view the brain as an evolved biological organ, an impressive computer, or simply a miracle, it is one of the most amazing things known.

During the course of animal evolution, **cephalization** (sĕ″fah-lĭ-za′shun) has occurred. That is, there has been an elaboration of the rostral ("toward the snout"), or anterior, portion of the CNS, along with an increase in the number of neurons in the head. This phenomenon reaches its highest level in the human brain.

In this chapter, we examine the structure of the CNS and the functions associated with its various regions. Complex integrative functions, such as sleep-wake cycles and memory, are also touched on.

The Brain

The unimpressive appearance of the human **brain** gives few hints of its remarkable abilities. It is about two good fistfuls of quivering pinkish gray tissue, wrinkled like a walnut, and somewhat the consistency of cold oatmeal. The average adult man's brain has a mass of about 1600 g (3.5 lb); that of a woman averages 1450 g (3.2 lb). In terms of brain mass per body mass, however, males and females have equivalent brain sizes.

Embryonic Development

We begin our study of the brain with brain embryology, as the terminology used for the structural divisions of the adult brain is easier to follow when you understand brain development.

The earliest phase of brain development is shown in Figure 12.1. Starting in the three-week-old embryo, the ectoderm (cell layer at the dorsal surface) thickens along the dorsal midline axis of the embryo to form the **neural plate.** The neural plate then invaginates, forming a groove flanked by **neural folds.** As this **neural groove** deepens, the superior edges of the neural folds fuse, forming the **neural tube,** which soon detaches from the surface ectoderm and sinks to a deeper position. The neural tube, formed by the fourth week of pregnancy, differentiates rapidly into the CNS. The brain forms anteriorly (rostrally) and the spinal cord develops from the caudal ("toward the tail") or posterior portion of the neural tube. Small

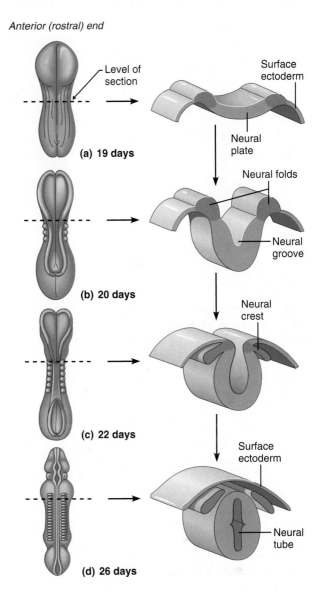

Anterior (rostral) end

(a) 19 days

(b) 20 days

(c) 22 days

(d) 26 days

FIGURE 12.1 **Development of the neural tube from embryonic ectoderm.** Left: dorsal surface views of the embryo; right: transverse sections. **(a)** Formation of the neural plate from surface ectoderm. **(b–d)** Development of neural plate into neural groove (flanked by neural folds) and then neural tube. The neural tube forms CNS structures; neural crest cells form some PNS structures.

groups of neural fold cells migrate laterally from between the surface ectoderm and the neural tube, forming the **neural crest** (Figure 12.1c). Neural crest cells give rise (among other things) to some neurons destined to reside in ganglia.

As soon as the neural tube forms, its anterior end immediately begins to expand and constrictions appear that mark off the three **primary brain vesicles** (Figure 12.2): the **prosencephalon** (pros″en-sef′ah-lon), or **forebrain;** the **mesencephalon** (mes″en-sef′ah-lon), or **midbrain;** and the **rhombencephalon** (romb″en-sef′ah-lon), or **hindbrain.** (Note

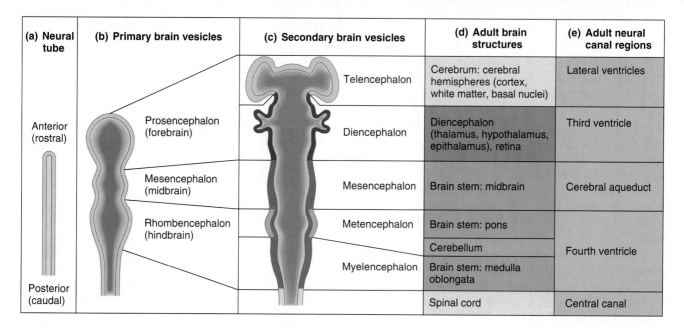

(a) Neural tube	(b) Primary brain vesicles	(c) Secondary brain vesicles		(d) Adult brain structures	(e) Adult neural canal regions
Anterior (rostral)	Prosencephalon (forebrain)		Telencephalon	Cerebrum: cerebral hemispheres (cortex, white matter, basal nuclei)	Lateral ventricles
			Diencephalon	Diencephalon (thalamus, hypothalamus, epithalamus), retina	Third ventricle
	Mesencephalon (midbrain)		Mesencephalon	Brain stem: midbrain	Cerebral aqueduct
	Rhombencephalon (hindbrain)		Metencephalon	Brain stem: pons	Fourth ventricle
				Cerebellum	
Posterior (caudal)			Myelencephalon	Brain stem: medulla oblongata	
				Spinal cord	Central canal

FIGURE 12.2 **Embryonic development of the human brain. (a)** Formed by week 4, the neural tube quickly subdivides into **(b)** the primary brain vesicles, which subsequently form **(c)** the secondary brain vesicles by week 5. These five vesicles differentiate into **(d)** the adult brain structures. **(e)** The adult structures derived from the neural canal.

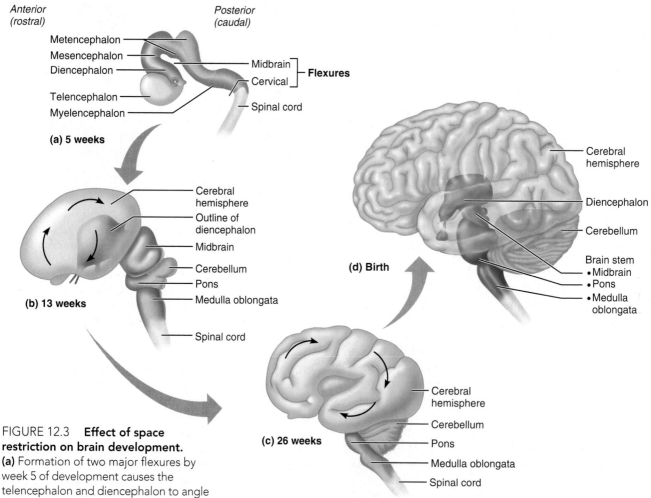

FIGURE 12.3 **Effect of space restriction on brain development.**
(a) Formation of two major flexures by week 5 of development causes the telencephalon and diencephalon to angle toward the brain stem. Development of the cerebral hemispheres at **(b)** 13 weeks, **(c)** 26 weeks, and **(d)** birth. Initially, the cerebral surface is smooth; the folding begins in month 6, and convolutions become more obvious as development continues. The posterolateral growth of the cerebral hemispheres ultimately encloses the diencephalon and superior aspect of the brain stem (seen through the cerebral hemispheres in this see-through view).

that *encephalo* means "brain.") The remainder of the neural tube becomes the spinal cord (discussed later in the chapter).

In week 5, the primary vesicles give rise to the **secondary brain vesicles.** The forebrain divides into the **telencephalon** ("endbrain") and **diencephalon** ("interbrain"), and the hindbrain constricts, forming the **metencephalon** ("afterbrain") and **myelencephalon** ("spinal brain"). The midbrain remains undivided. Each of the five secondary vesicles then develops rapidly to produce the major structures of the adult brain (Figure 12.2d). The greatest change occurs in the telencephalon, which sprouts two lateral swellings that look like Mickey Mouse's ears. These become the two *cerebral hemispheres*, referred to collectively as the **cerebrum** (ser'ĕ-brum). The diencephalon part of the forebrain specializes to form the *hypothalamus* (hi"po-thal'ah-mus), *thalamus, epithalamus,* and *retina* of the eye. Less dramatic changes occur in the mesencephalon, metencephalon, and myelencephalon as these regions are transformed into the *midbrain,* the *pons* and *cerebellum,* and the *medulla oblongata,* respectively. All these midbrain and hindbrain structures, except the cerebellum, form the **brain stem.** The central cavity of the neural tube remains continuous and enlarges in four areas to form the fluid-filled *ventricles* (*ventr* = little belly) of the brain. The ventricles are described shortly.

Because the brain grows more rapidly than the membranous skull that contains it, two major flexures develop—the *midbrain* and *cervical flexures*—which bend the forebrain toward the brain stem (Figure 12.3a). A second consequence of restricted space is that the cerebral hemispheres are forced to take a horseshoe-shaped course and grow posteriorly and laterally (indicated by black arrows in Figure 12.3b and c). As a result, they grow back over and almost completely envelop the diencephalon and midbrain. By week 26, the continued growth of the cerebral hemispheres causes their surfaces to crease and fold (Figure 12.3c and d), producing *convolutions* and increasing their surface area, which allows more neurons to occupy the limited space.

Regions and Organization

Some textbooks discuss brain anatomy in terms of the *embryonic scheme* (see Figure 12.2c), but in this text, we will consider the brain in terms of the medical scheme and the adult brain regions shown in Figure 12.3d: (1) cerebral hemispheres, (2) diencephalon, (3) brain stem (midbrain, pons, and medulla), and (4) cerebellum.

The basic pattern of the CNS consists of a central cavity surrounded by a gray matter core, external to which is white matter (myelinated fiber tracts).

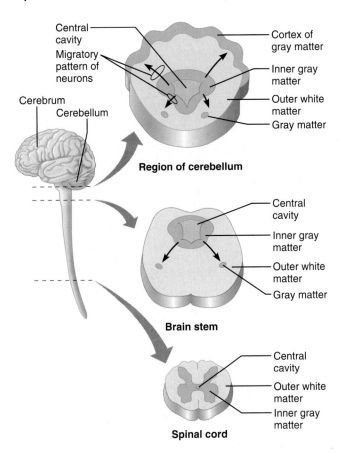

FIGURE 12.4 Arrangement of gray and white matter in the CNS (highly simplified). Cross sections at three CNS levels. In each section, the dorsal aspect is at the top. In general, white matter lies external to gray matter; however, collections of gray matter migrate externally into the white matter in the developing brain (see black arrows). The cerebrum resembles the cerebellum in its external cortex of gray matter.

The brain exhibits this basic design but has additional regions of gray matter not present in the spinal cord (Figure 12.4). Both the cerebral hemispheres and the cerebellum have an outer layer or "bark" of gray matter consisting of neuron cell bodies called a *cortex.* This pattern changes with descent through the brain stem—the cortex disappears, but scattered gray matter nuclei are seen within the white matter. At the caudal end of the brain stem, the basic pattern is evident.

Ventricles

As noted earlier, the brain **ventricles** arise from expansions of the lumen of the embryonic neural tube. They are continuous with one another and with the central canal of the spinal cord (Figure 12.5). The hollow ventricular chambers are filled with cerebrospinal fluid and lined by *ependymal cells,* a type of neuroglia (see Figure 11.3c on p. 390).

Q *Why are the lateral ventricles horn-shaped rather than vertically erect like the third and fourth ventricles?*

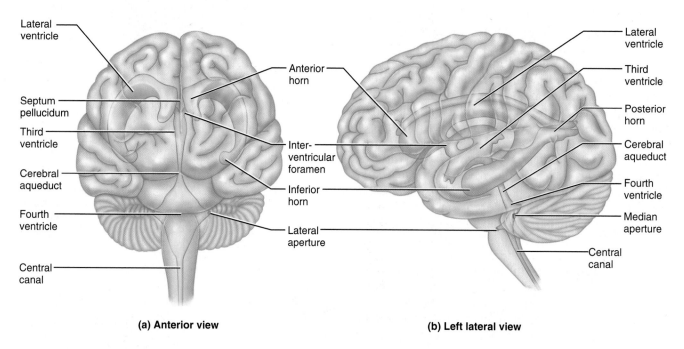

(a) Anterior view

(b) Left lateral view

FIGURE 12.5 **Ventricles of the brain.** Note that different regions of the large lateral ventricles are indicated by the terms anterior horn, posterior horn, and inferior horn.

The paired **lateral ventricles,** one deep within each cerebral hemisphere, are large C-shaped chambers that reflect the pattern of cerebral growth. Anteriorly, the lateral ventricles lie close together, separated only by a thin median membrane called the **septum pellucidum** (pĕ-lu'sid-um; "transparent wall"). (See Figure 12.12, p. 445.) Each lateral ventricle communicates with the narrow **third ventricle** in the diencephalon via a channel called an **interventricular foramen** (*foramen of Monro*). The third ventricle is continuous with the **fourth ventricle** via the canal-like **cerebral aqueduct** that runs through the midbrain. The fourth ventricle lies in the hindbrain dorsal to the pons and superior medulla. It is continuous with the central canal of the spinal cord inferiorly. Three openings mark the walls of the fourth ventricle: the paired **lateral apertures** in its side walls and the **median aperture** in its roof. These apertures connect the ventricles to the *subarachnoid space* (sub"ah-rak'noid), a fluid-filled space surrounding the brain.

A *Because their growth is restricted by the forming embryonic skull, the cerebral hemispheres are forced to grow posteriorly and inferiorly. Hence their cavities (ventricles) become horn-shaped.*

Cerebral Hemispheres

The **cerebral hemispheres** form the superior part of the brain (Figure 12.6). Together they account for about 83% of total brain mass and are the most conspicuous parts of an intact brain. Picture how a mushroom cap covers the top of its stalk, and you have a fairly good idea of how the paired cerebral hemispheres cover and obscure the diencephalon and the top of the brain stem (see Figure 12.3d).

Nearly the entire surface of the cerebral hemispheres is marked by elevated ridges of tissue called **gyri** (ji'ri; "twisters"), separated by shallow grooves called **sulci** (sul'ki; "furrows"). The singular forms of these terms are *gyrus* and *sulcus*. Deeper grooves, called **fissures,** separate large regions of the brain. The more prominent gyri and sulci are similar in all people and are important anatomical landmarks. The median **longitudinal fissure** separates the cerebral hemispheres (Figure 12.6c). Another large fissure, the **transverse cerebral fissure,** separates the cerebral hemispheres from the cerebellum below (see Figure 12.6a).

Several sulci divide each hemisphere into five lobes—frontal, parietal, temporal, occipital, and insula—all but the last named for the cranial bones that overlie them (Figure 12.6a). The **central sulcus,**

FIGURE 12.6 **Lobes and fissures of the cerebral hemispheres. (a)** Diagram of the lobes and major sulci and fissures of the brain. **(b)** The frontal and temporal lobes have been pulled back (retracted) to reveal the cortex of the insula below. **(c)** Superior surface of the cerebral hemispheres. Arachnoid has been removed on right half of the brain. **(d)** Photograph of the left lateral view of the brain.

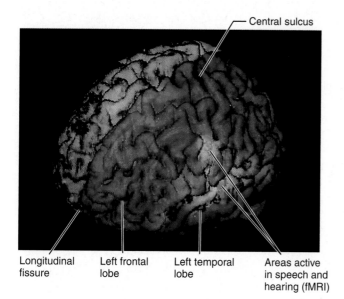

Central sulcus

Longitudinal fissure | Left frontal lobe | Left temporal lobe | Areas active in speech and hearing (fMRI)

FIGURE 12.7   **Functional neuroimaging of the cerebral cortex.** The rostral direction is to the left. Functional magnetic resonance image (fMRI) of the cerebral cortex of a person speaking and hearing reveals activity (blood flow) in the posterior frontal and superior temporal lobes, respectively.

which lies in the frontal plane, separates the **frontal lobe** from the **parietal lobe.** Bordering the central sulcus are the **precentral gyrus** anteriorly and the **postcentral gyrus** posteriorly. More posteriorly, the **occipital lobe** is separated from the parietal lobe by the **parieto-occipital sulcus** (pah-ri″ĕ-to-ok-sip′ĭ-tal), located on the medial surface of the hemisphere.

The deep **lateral sulcus** outlines the flaplike **temporal lobe** and separates it from the parietal and frontal lobes. A fifth lobe of the cerebral hemisphere, the **insula** (in′su-lah; "island"), is buried deep within the lateral sulcus and forms part of its floor (Figure 12.6b). The insula is covered by portions of the temporal, parietal, and frontal lobes.

The cerebral hemispheres fit snugly in the skull. Rostrally, the frontal lobes lie in the anterior cranial fossa. The anterior parts of the temporal lobes fill the middle cranial fossa. The posterior cranial fossa, however, houses the brain stem and cerebellum; the occipital lobes are located well superior to that cranial fossa.

Each cerebral hemisphere has three basic regions: a superficial *cortex* of gray matter, which looks gray in fresh brain tissue; an internal *white matter*; and the *basal nuclei*, islands of gray matter situated deep within the white matter. We consider these regions next.

Cerebral Cortex

The **cerebral cortex** is the "executive suite" of the nervous system, where our *conscious mind* is found. It enables us to be aware of ourselves and our sensations, to communicate, remember, and understand, and to initiate voluntary movements. The cerebral cortex is composed of gray matter: neuron cell bodies, dendrites, associated glia and blood vessels, but no fiber tracts. It contains billions of neurons arranged in six layers. Although it is only 2–4 mm (about 1/8 inch) thick, it accounts for roughly 40% of total brain mass. Its many convolutions effectively triple its surface area.

In the late 1800s, anatomists mapped subtle variations in the thickness and structure of the cerebral cortex. Most successful in these efforts was K. Brodmann, who in 1906 produced an elaborate numbered mosaic of 52 cortical areas, now called **Brodmann areas.** With a structural map emerging, early neurologists were eager to localize *functional* regions of the cortex as well. Modern imaging techniques—PET scans to show maximal metabolic activity in the brain, or functional MRI scans to reveal blood flow (Figure 12.7)—have shown that specific motor and sensory functions are localized in discrete cortical areas called *domains*. However, many higher mental functions, such as memory and language, appear to have overlapping domains and are spread over large areas of the cortex. Some of the most important Brodmann areas are numbered in Figure 12.8.

Before we examine the functional regions of the cerebral cortex, let's consider some generalizations about this region of the brain:

1. The cerebral cortex contains three kinds of functional areas: *motor areas, sensory areas,* and *association areas.* As you read about these areas, do not confuse the sensory and motor areas of the cortex with sensory and motor neurons. All neurons in the cortex are interneurons.

2. Each hemisphere is chiefly concerned with the sensory and motor functions of the opposite (contralateral) side of the body.

3. Although largely symmetrical in structure, the two hemispheres are not entirely equal in function. Instead, there is a lateralization (specialization) of cortical functions.

4. The final, and perhaps most important, generalization to keep in mind is that our approach is a gross oversimplification; no functional area of the cortex acts alone, and conscious behavior involves the entire cortex in one way or another.

Motor Areas   As shown in Figure 12.8a, the following **motor areas** of the cortex, which control voluntary movement, lie in the posterior part of the frontal lobes: primary motor cortex, premotor cortex, Broca's area, and the frontal eye field.

Q *What anatomical landmark separates motor areas of the cerebral cortex from sensory areas?*

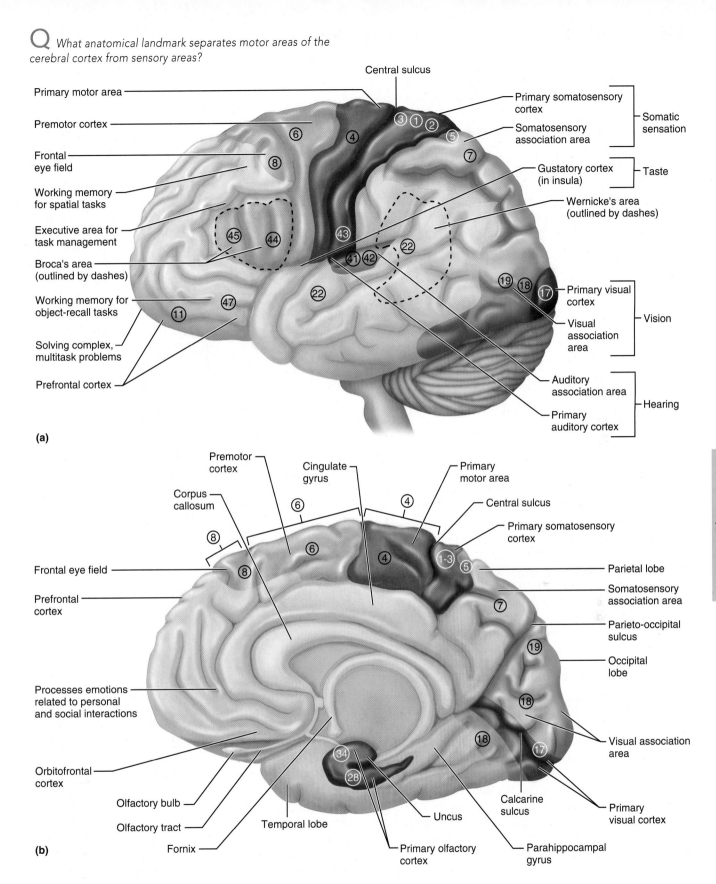

(a)

(b)

FIGURE 12.8 Functional and structural areas of the cerebral cortex. (a) Lateral view, left cerebral hemisphere. Different colors define functional regions of the cortex. Dark colors show primary motor (red) or sensory (blue) cortex and lighter colors show association cortices. Violet shows multimodal association cortex. The olfactory area, which is deep to the temporal lobe on the medial hemispheric surface, is not identified. Numbers indicate Brodmann structural areas. **(b)** Parasagittal view, right hemisphere.

A *Central sulcus.*

12

Q *Why are the motor and sensory homunculi anatomically "deformed"?*

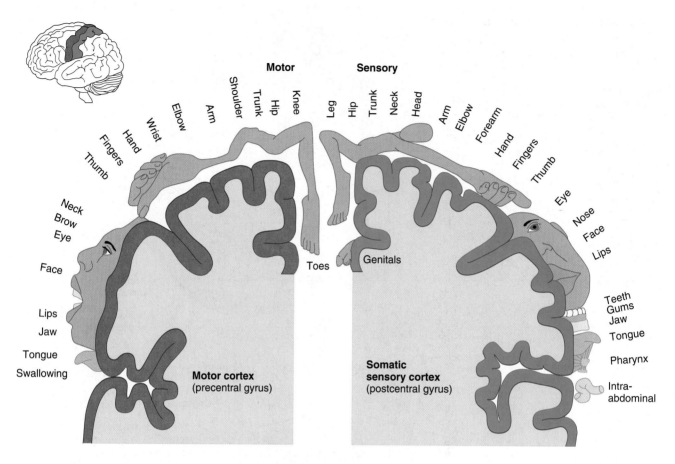

FIGURE 12.9 **Motor and sensory areas of the cerebral cortex.** The relative amount of cortical tissue devoted to each function is indicated by the amount of the gyrus occupied by the body diagrams. The primary motor cortex in the precentral gyrus is represented on the left, and the somatic sensory cortex in the postcentral gyrus is represented on the right.

1. Primary (somatic) motor cortex. The primary motor cortex is located in the precentral gyrus of the frontal lobe of each hemisphere (Brodmann area 4). Large neurons, called **pyramidal cells,** in these gyri allow us to consciously control the precise or skilled voluntary movements of our skeletal muscles. Their long axons, which project to the spinal cord, form the massive voluntary motor tracts called the **pyramidal tracts,** or **corticospinal tracts** (kor″tĭ-ko-spi′nal). All other descending motor tracts issue from brain stem nuclei and consist of chains of two or more neurons.

The entire body is represented spatially in the primary motor cortex of each hemisphere. In other

words, the pyramidal cells that control foot movements are in one place and those that control hand movements are in another. Such a mapping of the body in CNS structures is called **somatotopy** (so″mah-to-to′pe). As illustrated in Figure 12.9, the body is typically represented upside down—with the head at the inferolateral part of the precentral gyrus, and the toes at the superomedial end. Most of the neurons in these gyri control muscles in body areas having the most precise motor control—that is, the face, tongue, and hands. Consequently, these regions of the caricature-like **motor homunculi** (ho-mung′ku-li; singular: homunculus; "little man") drawn in Figure 12.9 are disproportionately large. The motor innervation of the body is contralateral; that is, the left primary motor gyrus controls muscles on the right side of the body, and vice versa.

A *Because the relative size of each body area in the drawing represents the relative amount of the cerebral cortex dedicated to that body area.*

The *motor homunculus* view of the primary motor cortex, shown at the left in Figure 12.9, implies a one-to-one correspondence between certain cortical neurons and the muscles they control, but this is somewhat misleading. Current research indicates that a given muscle is controlled by multiple spots on the cortex and that individual cortical neurons actually send impulses to more than one muscle. In other words, individual pyramidal motor neurons control muscles that work together in a synergistic way to perform a given movement. For example, reaching forward with one arm involves some muscles acting at the shoulder and some acting at the elbow. Thus, instead of the discrete map offered by the motor homunculus, the primary motor cortex map is an orderly but fuzzy map with neurons arranged in useful ways to control and coordinate sets of muscles. Neurons controlling the arm, for instance, are intermingled and overlap with those controlling the hand and shoulder. However, neurons controlling unrelated movements, such as those controlling the arm and those controlling body trunk muscles, do not cooperate in motor activity. Thus, the motor homunculus is useful to show that broad areas of the primary cortex are devoted to the leg, arm, torso, and head, but neuron organization within those broad areas is much more diffuse than initially imagined.

2. Premotor cortex. Just anterior to the precentral gyrus in the frontal lobe (Brodmann area 6) is the premotor cortex (see Figure 12.8). This region controls learned motor skills of a repetitive or patterned nature, such as playing a musical instrument and typing. The premotor cortex coordinates the movement of several muscle groups either simultaneously or sequentially, mainly by sending activating impulses to the primary motor cortex. However, the premotor cortex also influences motor activity more directly by supplying about 15% of pyramidal tract fibers. Think of this region as the memory bank for skilled motor activities.

This region also appears to be involved in planning movements. Using highly processed sensory information received from other cortical areas, it can control voluntary actions that depend on sensory feedback, such as moving an arm through a maze to grasp a hidden object.

3. Broca's area (bro'kahz). Broca's area lies anterior to the inferior region of the premotor area and overlaps Brodmann areas 44 and 45. It has long been considered to be (1) present in one hemisphere only (usually the left) and (2) a special *motor speech area* that directs the muscles involved in speech production. However, recent studies using PET scans to watch active areas of the brain "light up" indicate that Broca's area also becomes active as we prepare to speak and even as we think about (plan) many voluntary motor activities other than speech.

4. Frontal eye field. The frontal eye field is located partially in and anterior to the premotor cortex and superior to Broca's area. This cortical region controls voluntary movement of the eyes.

◤ HOMEOSTATIC IMBALANCE

Damage to localized areas of the *primary motor cortex* (as from a stroke) paralyzes the body muscles controlled by those areas. If the lesion is in the right hemisphere, the left side of the body will be paralyzed. Only *voluntary* control is lost, however, as the muscles can still contract reflexively.

Destruction of the *premotor cortex*, or part of it, results in a loss of the motor skill(s) programmed in that region, but muscle strength and the ability to perform the discrete individual movements are not hindered. For example, if the premotor area controlling the flight of your fingers over a computer keyboard were damaged, you couldn't type with your usual speed, but you could still make the same movements with your fingers. Reprogramming the skill into another set of premotor neurons would require practice, just as the initial learning process did. ●

Sensory Areas   Areas concerned with conscious awareness of sensation, the **sensory areas** of the cortex, occur in the parietal, insular, temporal, and occipital lobes (see Figure 12.8).

1. Primary somatosensory cortex. This cortex resides in the postcentral gyrus of the parietal lobe, just posterior to the primary motor cortex (Brodmann areas 1–3). Neurons in this gyrus receive information from the general (somatic) sensory receptors in the skin and from proprioceptors (position sense receptors) in skeletal muscles, joints, and tendons. The neurons then identify the body region being stimulated, an ability called **spatial discrimination.** As with the primary motor cortex, the body is represented spatially and upside-down according to the site of stimulus input, and the right hemisphere receives input from the left side of the body. The amount of sensory cortex devoted to a particular body region is related to that region's sensitivity (that is, to how many receptors it has), not to the size of the body region. In humans, the face (especially the lips) and fingertips are the most sensitive body areas; hence these are the largest parts of the **somatosensory homunculus** shown in the right half of Figure 12.9.

2. Somatosensory association cortex. The somatosensory association cortex lies just posterior to the primary somatosensory cortex and has many connections with it. The major function of this area is to integrate sensory inputs (temperature, pressure, and so forth) relayed to it via the primary somatosensory cortex to produce an understanding of an object being felt: its size, texture, and the relationship of its parts. For example, when you reach into your pocket, your somatosensory association cortex draws upon stored memories of past sensory experiences to perceive the objects you feel as coins or keys. Someone with damage to this area could not recognize these objects without looking at them.

3. **Visual areas.** The **primary visual (striate) cortex** is seen on the extreme posterior tip of the occipital lobe, but most of it is buried deep in the *calcarine sulcus* (Figure 12.8b) in the medial aspect of the occipital lobe. The largest of all cortical sensory areas, the primary visual cortex receives visual information that originates on the retina of the eye. There is a contralateral map of visual space on the primary visual cortex, analogous to the body map on the somatosensory cortex.

The **visual association area** surrounds the primary visual cortex and covers much of the occipital lobe. Communicating with the primary visual cortex, the visual association area uses past visual experiences to interpret visual stimuli (color, form, and movement), enabling us to recognize a flower or a person's face and to appreciate what we are seeing. We do our "seeing" with these cortical neurons. However, recent experiments on monkeys indicate that complex visual processing involves the entire posterior half of the cerebral hemispheres. Particularly important are two visual "streams"—one running along the top of the brain and handling spatial relationships and object location, the other taking the lower road and focusing on object identity (recognizing faces, words, and objects).

4. **Auditory areas.** Each **primary auditory cortex** is located in the superior margin of the temporal lobe abutting the lateral sulcus. Sound energy exciting the inner ear hearing receptors causes impulses to be transmitted to the primary auditory cortex, where they are interpreted as pitch, loudness, and location.

The more posterior **auditory association area** then permits the perception of the sound stimulus, which we "hear" as speech, a scream, music, thunder, noise, and so on. Memories of sounds heard in the past appear to be stored here for reference. Wernicke's area, described later, includes parts of the auditory cortex.

5. **Olfactory (smell) cortex.** The primary olfactory cortex lies on the medial aspect of the temporal lobe in a small region called the *piriform lobe* which is dominated by the hooklike *uncus* (Figure 12.8b). Afferent fibers from smell receptors in the superior nasal cavities send impulses along the olfactory tracts that are ultimately relayed to the olfactory

cortices. The outcome is conscious awareness of different odors.

The olfactory cortex is part of the primitive **rhinencephalon** (ri"nen-sef'ah-lon; "nose brain"), which includes all parts of the cerebrum that receive olfactory signals—the orbitofrontal cortex, the uncus and associated regions located on or in the medial aspects of the temporal lobes, and the protruding olfactory tracts and bulbs that extend to the nose. During the course of evolution, most of the "old" rhinencephalon has taken on new functions concerned chiefly with emotions and memory. This "newer" emotional brain, called the *limbic system*, is considered later in this chapter. The only portions of the human rhinencephalon still devoted to smell are the olfactory bulbs and tracts (described in Chapter 13) and the greatly reduced olfactory cortices.

6. **Gustatory (taste) cortex.** The gustatory cortex (gus'tah-tor-e) (see Figure 12.8a), a region involved in the perception of taste stimuli, is located in the insula just deep to the temporal lobe.

7. **Visceral sensory area.** The cortex of the insula just posterior to the gustatory cortex is involved in conscious perception of visceral sensations. These include upset stomach, full bladder, and the feeling that your lungs will burst when you hold your breath too long.

8. **Vestibular (equilibrium) cortex.** It has been difficult to pin down the part of the cortex responsible for conscious awareness of balance, that is, of the position of the head in space. However, medical imaging studies now locate this region in the posterior part of the insula, deep to the temporal lobe.

HOMEOSTATIC IMBALANCE

Damage to the primary visual cortex (Figure 12.8) results in functional blindness. By contrast, those with damage to the visual association area can see, but they do not comprehend what they are looking at. ●

Multimodal Association Areas The association areas that you have considered so far (colored light red or blue in Figure 12.8) have all been tightly tied to one kind of primary sensory or motor cortex (colored dark red or blue). Most of the cortex, though, is more complexly connected, receiving inputs from multiple senses and sending outputs to multiple areas. We call these areas **multimodal association areas** (colored violet in Figure 12.8).

In general, information flows from sensory receptors to the appropriate primary sensory cortex, then to a sensory association cortex and then on to the multimodal association cortex. Multimodal association cortex allows us to give meaning to the information that we receive, store it in memory if needed, tie it to previous experience and knowledge, and decide what action to take. Once the course of action has been decided, those decisions are relayed to the premotor cortex, which in turn communicates with the motor cortex. The multimodal association cortex seems to be where sensations, thoughts, and emotions become conscious and is what makes us who we are.

Suppose, for example, you drop a bottle of acid in the chem lab and it splashes on you. You see the bottle shatter; hear the crash; feel your skin burning; and smell the acid fumes. These individual perceptions come together in the multimodal association areas. Along with feelings of panic, these perceptions are woven into a seamless whole, which (hopefully) recalls instructions about what to do in this situation. As a result your premotor and primary motor cortices direct your legs to propel you to the safety shower. The multimodal association areas can be broadly divided into three parts, which are described next.

1. Anterior association area. The anterior association area in the frontal lobe (Figure 12.8b), also called the **prefrontal cortex,** is the most complicated cortical region of all. It is involved with intellect, complex learning abilities (called cognition), recall, and personality. It contains working memory, necessary for the production of abstract ideas, judgment, reasoning, persistence, and planning. That these qualities develop slowly in children implies that the prefrontal cortex matures slowly and is heavily dependent on positive and negative feedback from one's social environment.

2. Posterior association area. The posterior association area is a large region encompassing parts of the temporal, parietal, and occipital lobes. This area plays a role in recognizing patterns and faces, localizing us and our surroundings in space, and in binding different sensory inputs into a coherent whole. In the spilled acid example above, your awareness of the entire scene originates from this area. Attention to an area of space or an area of one's own body is also a function of this part of the brain. This is strikingly demonstrated by the experiences of some patients with lesions in the right posterior parietal region of this area who refuse to wash or dress the left side of their body because "that doesn't belong to me." Many parts of this area (including Wernicke's area, Figure 12.8a) are also involved in understanding written and spoken language.

3. Limbic association area. The limbic association area, which includes the cingulate gyrus, the parahippocampal gyrus, and the hippocampus, is part of the limbic system (described later). The limbic association area provides the emotional impact, which makes a scene important to us. In our exam-ple above, it provides the sense of "danger" when the acid splashes on our legs. The hippocampus (Figure 12.18) establishes memories that allow us to remember this incident. More on this later.

Lateralization of Cortical Functioning We use both cerebral hemispheres for almost every activity, and the hemispheres appear nearly identical. Nonetheless, there is a division of labor, and each hemisphere has unique abilities not shared by its partner. This phenomenon is called **lateralization.** Although one cerebral hemisphere or the other "dominates" each task, the term **cerebral dominance** designates the hemisphere that is *dominant for language.* In most people (about 90%), the left hemisphere has greater control over language abilities, math, and logic. This so-called dominant hemisphere is working when we compose a sentence, balance a checkbook, and memorize a list. The other hemisphere (usually the right) is more free-spirited, involved in visual-spatial skills, intuition, emotion, and artistic and musical skills. It is the poetic, creative, and the "Ah-ha!" (insightful) side of our nature, and it is far better at recognizing faces. Most individuals with left cerebral dominance are right-handed.

In the remaining 10% of people, the roles of the hemispheres are reversed or the hemispheres share their functions equally. Typically, right-cerebral-dominant people are left-handed and male. Some "lefties" who have a cerebral cortex that functions bilaterally are ambidextrous. In other cases, however, this phenomenon may also result in cerebral confusion ("Is it your turn, or mine?") and learning disabilities, such as the reading disorder *dyslexia,* in which otherwise intelligent people reverse the order of letters in words (and the order of words in sentences).

The two cerebral hemispheres have perfect and almost instantaneous communication with one another via connecting fiber tracts, as well as complete functional integration. Furthermore, although lateralization means that each hemisphere is better than the other at certain functions, neither side is better at everything.

Cerebral White Matter

The second of the three basic regions of each cerebral hemisphere is the internal **cerebral white matter.** From what has already been described, it is clear that communication within the brain is extensive. The white matter (Figure 12.10) deep to the cortical gray matter is responsible for communication between cerebral areas and between the cerebral cortex and lower CNS centers. White matter consists largely of myelinated fibers bundled into large tracts. These fibers and tracts are classified according to the

Q *How can you explain the observation that the two cerebral hemispheres have instantaneous communication with each other when it is obvious from diagram (c) that the projection fibers are part of crossed pathways and that information flows from each side of the body to only one (the opposite) hemisphere?*

(a)

(b)

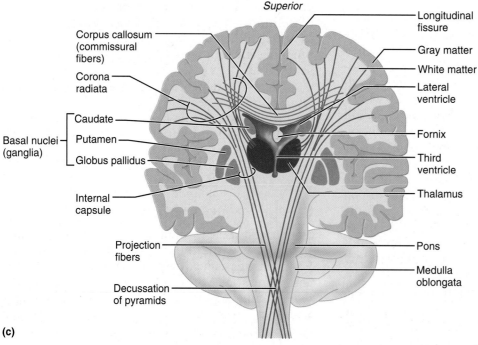

(c)

FIGURE 12.10 **Types of fiber tracts in white matter. (a)** Parasagittal view of the right cerebral hemisphere showing the association tract fibers (tracts connecting different parts of the same hemisphere), and the corpus callosum, a commissure that connects the hemispheres. **(b)** Photo of the same view as (a). **(c)** Frontal section showing commissural fibers and projection fibers running between the cerebrum and lower CNS centers. Notice the tight band of projection fibers called the internal capsule that passes between the thalamus and the basal nuclei, and then fans out as the corona radiata.

A *Commissures allow the cerebral hemispheres to "talk to each other."*

direction in which they run as *commissural, association,* or *projection.*

Commissures (kom'ĭ-shūrz), composed of **commissural fibers,** connect corresponding gray areas of the two hemispheres, enabling them to function as a coordinated whole. The largest commissure is the **corpus callosum** (kah-lo'sum; "thickened body"), which lies superior to the lateral ventricles, deep within the longitudinal fissure. Less prominent examples are the **anterior** and **posterior commissures** (see Figure 12.12, p. 445).

Association fibers connect different parts of the same hemisphere. Short association fibers connect adjacent gyri. Long association fibers are bundled into tracts and connect different cortical lobes.

Projection fibers are those that enter the cerebral hemispheres from lower brain or cord centers, and those that leave the cortex to travel to lower areas. They tie the cortex to the rest of the nervous system and to the body's receptors and effectors. In contrast to commissural and association fibers, which run horizontally, projection fibers run vertically as Figure 12.10c shows.

At the top of the brain stem, the projection fibers on each side form a compact band, the **internal capsule,** that passes between the thalamus and some of the basal nuclei. Beyond that point, the fibers radiate fanlike through the cerebral white matter to the cortex. This distinctive arrangement of projection tract fibers is known as the **corona radiata** ("radiating crown").

Basal Nuclei

Deep within the cerebral white matter is the third basic region of each hemisphere, a group of subcortical nuclei called the **basal nuclei** or **basal ganglia.** * Although the definition of the precise structures forming the basal nuclei is controversial, most anatomists agree that the **caudate nucleus** (kaw'dāt), **putamen** (pu-ta'men), and **globus pallidus** (glo'bis pal'ĭ-dus) constitute most of the mass of each group of basal nuclei (Figure 12.11). Together, the putamen ("pod") and globus pallidus ("pale globe") form a lens-shaped mass, the **lentiform nucleus,** that flanks the internal capsule laterally. The comma-shaped caudate nucleus arches superiorly over the diencephalon. Collectively, the lentiform and caudate nuclei are called the **corpus striatum** (stri-a'tum) because the fibers of the internal capsule that course past and through

them give them a striped appearance. The basal nuclei are functionally associated with the *subthalamic nuclei* (located in the lateral "floor" of the diencephalon) and the *substantia nigra* of the midbrain (see Figure 12.16a).

The nuclei of the corpus striatum receive input from the entire cerebral cortex, as well as from other subcortical nuclei and each other. Via relays through the thalamus, the output nuclei of the basal nuclei (globus pallidus and the substantia nigra) project to the premotor and prefrontal cortices and so influence muscle movements directed by the primary motor cortex. The basal nuclei have no direct access to motor pathways.

The precise role of the basal nuclei has been elusive because of their inaccessible location and because their functions overlap with those of the cerebellum. Their role in motor control is complex and there is evidence they play a part in regulating attention and in cognition. The basal nuclei are particularly important in starting, stopping, and monitoring the intensity of movements executed by the cortex, especially those that are relatively slow or stereotyped, such as arm-swinging during walking. Additionally, they inhibit antagonistic or unnecessary movements; thus their input seems necessary to our ability to perform several activities at once. Disorders of the basal nuclei result in either too much or too little movement as exemplified by Huntington's chorea and Parkinson's disease, respectively (see pp. 469–470).

Diencephalon

Forming the central core of the forebrain and surrounded by the cerebral hemispheres, the **diencephalon** consists largely of three paired structures—the thalamus, hypothalamus, and epithalamus. These gray matter areas collectively enclose the third ventricle (Figure 12.12).

Thalamus

The **thalamus** consists of bilateral egg-shaped nuclei, which form the superolateral walls of the third ventricle (Figures 12.10 and 12.12). In most people, the nuclei are connected at the midline by an **interthalamic adhesion (intermediate mass).** *Thalamus* is a Greek word meaning "inner room," which well describes this deep, well-hidden brain region that makes up 80% of the diencephalon.

The thalamus contains a large number of nuclei, most named according to their relative location (Figure 12.13a). Each nucleus has a functional specialty, and each projects fibers to and receives fibers from a specific region of the cerebral cortex. Afferent impulses from all senses and all parts of

---

* Because a nucleus is a collection of nerve cell bodies within the CNS, the term *basal nuclei* is technically correct. The more frequently used but misleading historical term *basal ganglia* is a misnomer and should be abandoned, because ganglia are PNS structures.

Q *Why are the lentiform nucleus and caudate nucleus collectively referred to as the corpus striatum?*

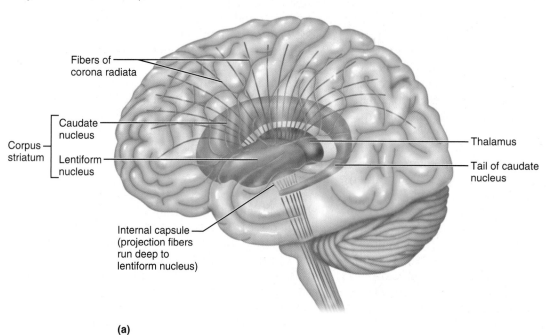

Fibers of corona radiata

Corpus striatum
- Caudate nucleus
- Lentiform nucleus

Internal capsule (projection fibers run deep to lentiform nucleus)

Thalamus

Tail of caudate nucleus

(a)

FIGURE 12.11 **Basal nuclei. (a)** Three-dimensional view of the basal nuclei (basal ganglia), showing their position in the cerebrum. **(b)** Transverse section of cerebrum and diencephalon showing the relationship of the basal nuclei to the thalamus and the lateral and third ventricles.

Anterior

Cerebral cortex

Cerebral white matter

Corpus callosum

Anterior horn of lateral ventricle

Caudate nucleus

Third ventricle

Putamen

Globus pallidus

Lentiform nucleus

Thalamus

Inferior horn of lateral ventricle

(b) *Posterior*

A *Because the fibers of the corona radiata running through them make them appear striped.*

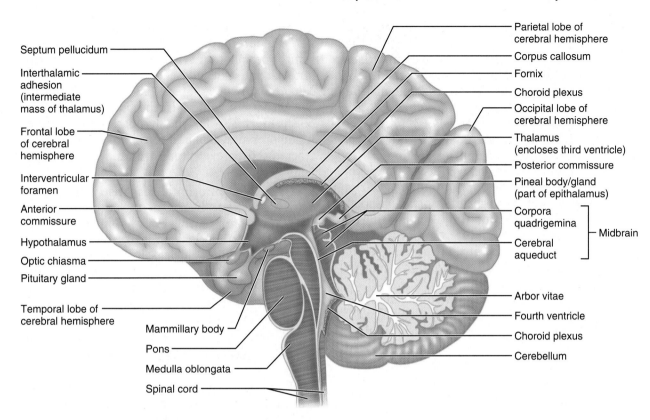

Septum pellucidum

Interthalamic adhesion (intermediate mass of thalamus)

Frontal lobe of cerebral hemisphere

Interventricular foramen

Anterior commissure

Hypothalamus

Optic chiasma

Pituitary gland

Temporal lobe of cerebral hemisphere

Mammillary body

Pons

Medulla oblongata

Spinal cord

Parietal lobe of cerebral hemisphere

Corpus callosum

Fornix

Choroid plexus

Occipital lobe of cerebral hemisphere

Thalamus (encloses third ventricle)

Posterior commissure

Pineal body/gland (part of epithalamus)

Corpora quadrigemina — Midbrain

Cerebral aqueduct

Arbor vitae

Fourth ventricle

Choroid plexus

Cerebellum

FIGURE 12.12   Midsagittal section of the brain illustrating the diencephalon and brain stem.

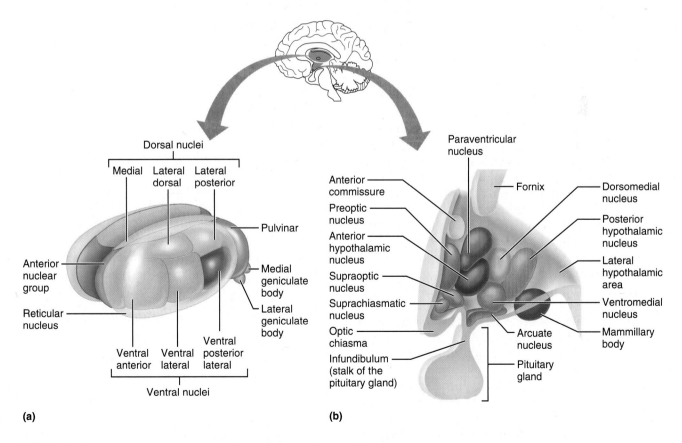

Dorsal nuclei

Medial   Lateral dorsal   Lateral posterior

Pulvinar

Medial geniculate body

Lateral geniculate body

Anterior nuclear group

Reticular nucleus

Ventral anterior   Ventral lateral   Ventral posterior lateral

Ventral nuclei

(a)

Paraventricular nucleus

Anterior commissure

Preoptic nucleus

Anterior hypothalamic nucleus

Supraoptic nucleus

Suprachiasmatic nucleus

Optic chiasma

Infundibulum (stalk of the pituitary gland)

Fornix

Dorsomedial nucleus

Posterior hypothalamic nucleus

Lateral hypothalamic area

Ventromedial nucleus

Mammillary body

Arcuate nucleus

Pituitary gland

(b)

FIGURE 12.13   Selected structures of the diencephalon. (a) Thalamus showing the main thalamic nuclei. (The reticular nuclei that "cap" the thalamic nuclei laterally are depicted as curving translucent structures.) **(b)** Main hypothalamic nuclei.

12

the body converge on the thalamus and synapse with at least one of its nuclei. For example, the *ventral posterior lateral nucleus* receives impulses from the general somatic sensory receptors (touch, pressure, pain, etc.), and the *lateral* and *medial geniculate bodies* (jĕ-nik'u-lāt; "knee shaped") are important visual and auditory relay centers, respectively. Within the thalamus, information is sorted out and "edited." Impulses having to do with similar functions are relayed as a group via the internal capsule to the appropriate area of the sensory cortex as well as to specific cortical association areas. As the afferent impulses reach the thalamus, we have a crude recognition of the sensation as pleasant or unpleasant. However, specific stimulus localization and discrimination occur in the cerebral cortex.

In addition to sensory inputs, virtually *all* other inputs ascending to the cerebral cortex funnel through thalamic nuclei. These include impulses participating in the regulation of emotion and visceral function from the hypothalamus (via the anterior nuclei), and impulses that help direct the activity of the motor cortices from the cerebellum and basal nuclei (via the ventral lateral and ventral anterior nuclei, respectively). Several thalamic nuclei (pulvinar, lateral dorsal, and lateral posterior nuclei) are involved in integration of sensory information and project to specific association cortices. Thus the thalamus plays a key role in mediating sensation, motor activities, cortical arousal, learning, and memory. It is truly the gateway to the cerebral cortex.

Hypothalamus

Named for its position below (*hypo*) the thalamus, the **hypothalamus** caps the brain stem and forms the inferolateral walls of the third ventricle (Figure 12.12). Merging into the midbrain inferiorly, the hypothalamus extends from the optic chiasma (crossover point of the optic nerves) to the posterior margin of the mammillary bodies. The **mammillary bodies** (mam'mil-er-e; "little breast"), paired pealike nuclei that bulge anteriorly from the hypothalamus, are relay stations in the olfactory pathways. Between the optic chiasma and mammillary bodies is the **infundibulum** (in"fun-dib'u-lum), a stalk of hypothalamic tissue that connects the **pituitary gland** to the base of the hypothalamus. Like the thalamus, the hypothalamus contains many functionally important nuclei (Figure 12.13b).

Despite its small size, the hypothalamus is the main visceral control center of the body and is vitally important to overall body homeostasis. Few tissues in the body escape its influence. Its chief homeostatic roles are summarized next.

1. **Autonomic control center.** As you will remember, the autonomic nervous system (ANS) is a system of peripheral nerves that regulates cardiac and smooth muscle and secretion by the glands. The hypothalamus regulates ANS activity by controlling the activity of centers in the brain stem and spinal cord. In this role, the hypothalamus influences blood pressure, rate and force of heartbeat, digestive tract motility, eye pupil size, and many other visceral activities.

2. **Center for emotional response.** The hypothalamus lies at the "heart" of the limbic system (the emotional part of the brain). Nuclei involved in the perception of pleasure, fear, and rage, as well as those involved in biological rhythms and drives (such as the sex drive), are found in the hypothalamus.

The hypothalamus acts through ANS pathways to initiate most physical expressions of emotion. For example, a fearful person has a pounding heart, high blood pressure, pallor, sweating, and a dry mouth.

3. **Body temperature regulation.** The body's thermostat is in the hypothalamus. Hypothalamic neurons monitor blood temperature and receive input from other thermoreceptors in the brain and body periphery. Accordingly, the hypothalamus initiates cooling (sweating) or heat-generating mechanisms (shivering) as needed to maintain a relatively constant body temperature.

4. **Regulation of food intake.** In response to changing blood levels of certain nutrients (glucose and perhaps amino acids) or hormones [cholecystokinin (CCK) and others], the hypothalamus regulates feelings of hunger and satiety.

5. **Regulation of water balance and thirst.** When body fluids become too concentrated, hypothalamic neurons called *osmoreceptors* are activated. These neurons excite hypothalamic nuclei that trigger the release of antidiuretic hormone (ADH) from the posterior pituitary. ADH causes the kidneys to retain water. The same conditions also stimulate hypothalamic neurons in the *thirst center*, causing us to feel thirsty and, therefore, to drink more fluids.

6. **Regulation of sleep-wake cycles.** Acting with other brain regions, the hypothalamus helps regulate sleep. Through the operation of its *suprachiasmatic nucleus* (our biological clock), it sets the timing of the sleep cycle in response to daylight-darkness cues received from the visual pathways.

7. **Control of endocrine system functioning.** The hypothalamus acts as the helmsman of the endocrine system in two important ways. First, its *releasing hormones* control the secretion of hormones by the anterior pituitary gland. Second, its *supraoptic* and *paraventricular nuclei* produce the hormones ADH and oxytocin.

Q *What part of the brain lies between the optic chiasma and the mammillary bodies?*

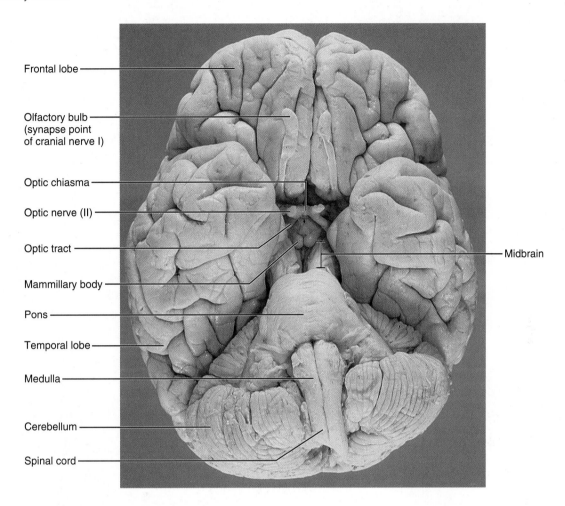

FIGURE 12.14 **Ventral aspect of the human brain, showing the three regions of the brain stem.** Only a small portion of the midbrain can be seen; the rest is surrounded by other brain regions.

Labels (left side, top to bottom):
Frontal lobe
Olfactory bulb (synapse point of cranial nerve I)
Optic chiasma
Optic nerve (II)
Optic tract
Mammillary body
Pons
Temporal lobe
Medulla
Cerebellum
Spinal cord

Label (right side):
Midbrain

12

HOMEOSTATIC IMBALANCE

Hypothalamic disturbances cause a number of disorders including severe body wasting, obesity, sleep disturbances, dehydration, and a broad range of emotional imbalances. For example, infants deprived of a warm, nurturing relationship may develop *failure to thrive,* a clinical term describing a delay in a child's growth or development. ●

Epithalamus

The **epithalamus** is the most dorsal portion of the diencephalon and forms the roof of the third ventricle. Extending from its posterior border and visible externally is the **pineal gland** or **body** (pin′e-al; "pine cone shaped") (see Figures 12.12 and 12.15). The pineal gland secretes the hormone *melatonin* (a sleep-inducing signal and antioxidant; see Chapter 16) and, along with hypothalamic nuclei, helps regulate the sleep-wake cycle.

Brain Stem

From superior to inferior, the brain stem regions are midbrain, pons, and medulla oblongata (Figures 12.12, 12.14, and 12.15). Each roughly an inch long, collectively they account for only 2.5% of total brain mass. Histologically, the organization of the brain stem is similar (but not identical) to that of the spinal cord—deep gray matter surrounded by white matter fiber tracts (see Figure 12.4). However, the brain stem has nuclei of gray matter embedded in the white matter, a feature not found in the spinal cord.

A *The hypothalamus.*

FIGURE 12.15 **Relationship of the brain stem and the diencephalon.**
(a) Ventral view. **(b)** Lateral view.

Brain stem centers produce the rigidly programmed, automatic behaviors necessary for survival. Positioned between the cerebrum and the spinal cord, the brain stem also provides a pathway for fiber tracts running between higher and lower neural centers. Additionally, brain stem nuclei are associated with 10 of the 12 pairs of cranial nerves (described in Chapter 13), so it is heavily involved with innervation of the head.

Midbrain

The **midbrain** is located between the diencephalon and the pons (Figures 12.14 and 12.15). On its ventral

aspect two bulging **cerebral peduncles** (pĕ-dung′klz) form vertical pillars that seem to hold up the cerebrum, hence their name meaning "little feet of the cerebrum." These peduncles contain the large pyramidal (corticospinal) motor tracts descending toward the spinal cord. The *superior cerebellar peduncles,* also fiber tracts, connect the midbrain to the cerebellum dorsally.

Running through the midbrain is the hollow *cerebral aqueduct* (Figures 12.12 and 12.16a), which connects the third and fourth ventricles, and delineates the cerebral peduncles ventrally from the *tectum,* the midbrain's roof. Surrounding the

(c) Dorsal view

FIGURE 12.15 *(continued)* **Relationship of the brain stem and the diencephalon. (c)** Dorsal view. Cerebral hemispheres have been removed.

aqueduct is the *periaqueductal gray matter,* which is involved in pain suppression and serves as the link between the fear-perceiving amygdala and ANS pathways that control the "fight-or-flight" response. The periaqueductal gray matter also includes nuclei that control two cranial nerves, the *oculomotor* and the *trochlear nuclei* (trok'le-ar).

Nuclei are also scattered in the surrounding white matter of the midbrain. The largest of these are the **corpora quadrigemina** (kor'por-ah kwod"ri-jem'i-nah; "quadruplets"), which raise four dome-like protrusions on the dorsal midbrain surface (Figures 12.12 and 12.15). The superior pair, the **superior colliculi** (kŏ-lik'u-li), are visual reflex centers that coordinate head and eye movements when we visually follow a moving object, even if we are not consciously looking at the object. The **inferior colliculi** are part of the auditory relay from the hearing receptors of the ear to the sensory cortex. They also act in reflexive responses to sound, such as in the *startle reflex,* which causes you to turn your head toward an unexpected sound.

Also embedded in each side of the midbrain white matter are two pigmented nuclei, the substantia nigra and red nucleus (Figure 12.16a). The band-like **substantia nigra** (sub-stan'she-ah ni'grah) is located deep to the cerebral peduncle. Its dark (*nigr* = black) color reflects a high content of melanin pigment, a precursor of the neurotransmitter (dopamine)

released by these neurons. The substantia nigra is functionally linked to the basal nuclei (its axons project to the globus pallidus), and is considered part of the basal nuclear complex by many authorities. Degeneration of the dopamine-releasing neurons of the substantia nigra is the ultimate cause of Parkinson's disease.

The oval **red nucleus** lies deep to the substantia nigra. Its reddish hue is due to its rich blood supply and to the presence of iron pigment in its neurons. The red nuclei are relay nuclei in some descending motor pathways that effect limb flexion, and they are embedded in the *reticular formation,* a system of small nuclei scattered through the core of the brain stem (see pp. 455–456).

Pons

The **pons** is the bulging brain stem region wedged between the midbrain and the medulla oblongata (see Figures 12.12, 12.14, and 12.15). Dorsally, it forms part of the anterior wall of the fourth ventricle.

As its name suggests (*pons* = bridge), the pons is chiefly composed of conduction tracts that course in two directions. The deep projection fibers run longitudinally and complete the pathway between higher brain centers and the spinal cord. The more superficial ventral fibers issue from numerous *pontine nuclei,* which act as relays for "conversations" between

Q *Just what are the pyramids of the medulla?*

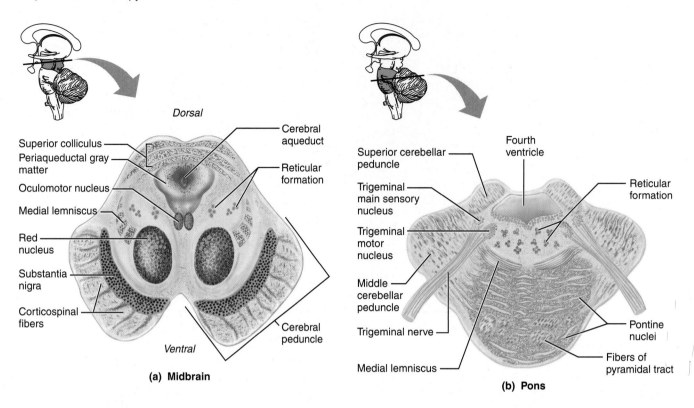

Superior colliculus
Periaqueductal gray matter
Oculomotor nucleus
Medial lemniscus
Red nucleus
Substantia nigra
Corticospinal fibers

Dorsal

Cerebral aqueduct
Reticular formation

Cerebral peduncle

Ventral

(a) Midbrain

Superior cerebellar peduncle
Trigeminal main sensory nucleus
Trigeminal motor nucleus
Middle cerebellar peduncle
Trigeminal nerve
Medial lemniscus

Fourth ventricle

Reticular formation

Pontine nuclei

Fibers of pyramidal tract

(b) Pons

Hypoglossal nucleus
Dorsal motor nucleus of vagus
Inferior cerebellar peduncle

Fourth ventricle
Choroid plexus

Solitary nucleus
Vestibular nuclear complex
Cochlear nuclei

Reticular formation
Lateral nuclear group
Medial nuclear group
Raphe nucleus

Medial lemniscus

Nucleus ambiguus

Inferior olivary nucleus

Pyramid

(c) Medulla oblongata

FIGURE 12.16   **Important brain stem nuclei.** Horizontal sections through **(a)** midbrain at the level of superior colliculi, **(b)** pons at the level of its trigeminal nerve nuclei, **(c)** superior medulla oblongata.

12

A *The corticospinal (pyramidal) tracts. The large voluntary motor tracts descending from the motor cortex.*

the motor cortex and cerebellum. These fibers are oriented transversely and dorsally as the *middle cerebellar peduncles* (Figure 12.15) and connect the pons bilaterally with the two sides of the cerebellum dorsally.

Several cranial nerve pairs issue from pons nuclei (Figure 12.16b), including the *trigeminal* (tri-jem′ĭ-nal), the *abducens* (ab-du′senz), and *facial nerves*. The cranial nerves and their functions are discussed in Chapter 13. Other important pons nuclei are part of the reticular formation and some help the medulla maintain the normal rhythm of breathing.

Medulla Oblongata

The conical **medulla oblongata** (me-dul′ah ob″long-gah′tah), or simply **medulla,** is the most inferior part of the brain stem. It blends imperceptibly into the spinal cord at the level of the foramen magnum of the skull (Figures 12.12 and 12.14). The central canal of the spinal cord continues upward into the medulla, where it broadens out to form the cavity of the fourth ventricle. Thus, both the medulla and the pons help form the ventral wall of the fourth ventricle. [The dorsal ventricular wall is formed by a thin capillary-rich membrane called a choroid plexus which abuts the cerebellum dorsally (Figure 12.12).]

Flanking the midline on the medulla's ventral aspect are two longitudinal ridges called **pyramids,** formed by the large pyramidal (corticospinal) tracts descending from the motor cortex (Figure 12.16c). Just above the medulla–spinal cord junction, most of these fibers cross over to the opposite side before continuing into the spinal cord. This crossover point is called the **decussation of the pyramids** (de″kus-sa′shun; "a crossing"). As mentioned earlier, the consequence of this crossover is that each cerebral hemisphere chiefly controls the voluntary movements of muscles on the opposite side of the body.

Also obvious externally are several other structures. The *inferior cerebellar peduncles* are fiber tracts that connect the medulla to the cerebellum dorsally. Situated lateral to the pyramids, the **olives** are oval swellings (which *do* resemble olives) produced mainly by the underlying **inferior olivary nuclei,** wavy folds of gray matter (Figure 12.16c). These nuclei relay sensory information on the state of stretch of muscles and joints to the cerebellum. The rootlets of the *hypoglossal nerves* emerge from the groove between the pyramid and olive on each side of the brain stem. Other cranial nerves associated with the medulla are the *glossopharyngeal nerves* and *vagus nerves*, and portions of the accessory nerves. Additionally, the fibers of the *vestibulocochlear nerves* (ves-tib″u-lo-kok′le-ar) synapse

with the **cochlear nuclei** (auditory relays), and with numerous vestibular nuclei in both the pons and medulla. Collectively, the vestibular nuclei, called the **vestibular nuclear complex,** mediate responses that maintain equilibrium.

Also housed in the medulla are several nuclei associated with ascending sensory tracts. The most prominent are the dorsally located **nucleus gracilis** (grah-sĭ′lis) and **nucleus cuneatus** (ku′ne-āt-us), associated with the *medial lemniscal tract*. These serve as relay nuclei in a pathway by which general somatic sensory information ascends from the spinal cord to the somatosensory cortex.

The small size of the medulla belies its crucial role as an autonomic reflex center involved in maintaining body homeostasis. Important visceral motor nuclei found in the medulla include the following:

1. **Cardiovascular center.** This includes the *cardiac center*, which adjusts the force and rate of heart contraction to meet the body's needs, and the *vasomotor center*, which changes blood vessel diameter to regulate blood pressure.

2. **Respiratory centers.** These control the rate and depth of breathing and (in concert with pons centers) maintain respiratory rhythm.

3. **Various other centers.** Additional centers regulate such activities as vomiting, hiccuping, swallowing, coughing, and sneezing.

Notice that many functions listed above were also attributed to the hypothalamus (p. 446). The overlap is easily explained. The hypothalamus exerts its control over many visceral functions by relaying its instructions through medullary reticular centers, which carry them out.

Cerebellum

The cauliflower-like **cerebellum** (ser″ĕ-bel′um; "small brain"), exceeded in size only by the cerebrum, accounts for about 11% of total brain mass. The cerebellum is located dorsal to the pons and medulla (and to the intervening fourth ventricle). It protrudes under the occipital lobes of the cerebral hemispheres, from which it is separated by the transverse cerebral fissure (see Figure 12.6d).

By processing inputs received from the cerebral motor cortex, various brain stem nuclei, and sensory receptors, the cerebellum provides the precise timing and appropriate patterns of skeletal muscle contraction for smooth, coordinated movements and agility needed for our daily living—driving, typing, and for some of us, playing the tuba. Cerebellar activity occurs subconsciously; that is, we have no awareness of its functioning.

Q *The cerebellum is primarily involved in motor control. What type of sensory information do you think is relayed to the sensory areas of the cerebellum?*

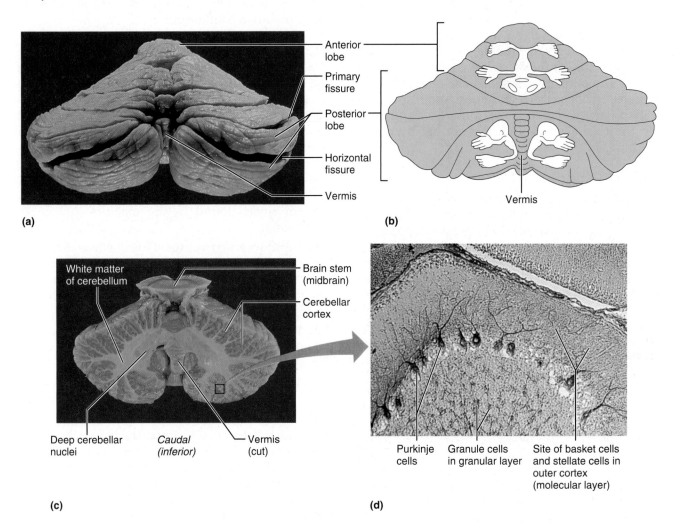

(a)

(b)

(c)

(d)

FIGURE 12.17   Cerebellum. (a) Photograph of the posterior aspect of the cerebellum. The flocculonodular lobe, which lies deep to the vermis, is not visible in this view. **(b)** Positioning of overlapping motor and sensory maps of the body (in the form of three homunculi). **(c)** Posterior view sectioned frontally to reveal the three cerebellar layers. **(d)** Photomicrograph of a small portion of the cerebellar cortex showing the relative positions of granule cells, Purkinje cells, and stellate and basket cells (200×).

Anatomy

The cerebellum is bilaterally symmetrical; its two apple-sized **cerebellar hemispheres** are connected medially by the wormlike **vermis** (Figure 12.17). Its surface is heavily convoluted, with fine, transversely oriented pleatlike gyri known as **folia** ("leaves"). Deep fissures subdivide each hemisphere into **anterior, posterior,** and **flocculonodular lobes** (flok"u-lo-nod'u-lar). The small propeller-shaped flocculonodular lobes, situated deep to the vermis and posterior lobe, cannot be seen in a surface view.

Like the cerebrum, the cerebellum has a thin outer cortex of gray matter, internal white matter, and small, deeply situated, paired masses of gray matter, the most familiar of which are the *dentate nuclei.* Several types of neurons populate the cerebellar cortex, including stellate, basket, granule, and Purkinje cells (Figure 12.17d). Of these, the large **Purkinje cells,** with their extensively branched dendrites, are the only cortical neurons that send axons through the white matter to synapse with the central nuclei of the cerebellum. The distinctive pattern of

A *Position sense (proprioception), for example from muscle and tendon stretch receptors (see Figure 12.34a).*

TABLE 12.1	Functions of Major Brain Regions

REGION	FUNCTION

CEREBRAL HEMISPHERES (pp. 434–443)

Cortical gray matter localizes and interprets sensory inputs, controls voluntary and skilled skeletal muscle activity, and functions in intellectual and emotional processing; basal nuclei (ganglia) are subcortical motor centers important in initiation of skeletal muscle movements

DIENCEPHALON (pp. 443–447)

Thalamic nuclei are relay stations in conduction of (1) sensory impulses to cerebral cortex for interpretation, and (2) impulses to and from cerebral motor cortex and lower (subcortical) motor centers, including cerebellum; thalamus is also involved in memory processing

Hypothalamus is chief integration center of autonomic (involuntary) nervous system; it functions in regulation of body temperature, food intake, water balance, thirst, and biological rhythms and drives; regulates hormonal output of anterior pituitary gland and is an endocrine organ in its own right (produces ADH and oxytocin); part of limbic system

Limbic system (pp. 454–455)

A functional system involving cerebral and diencephalon structures that mediates emotional response; also involved in memory processing

BRAIN STEM (pp. 447–451)

Midbrain: Conduction pathway between higher and lower brain centers (e.g., cerebral peduncles contain the fibers of the pyramidal tracts); its superior and inferior colliculi are visual and auditory reflex centers; substantia nigra and red nuclei are subcortical motor centers; contains nuclei for cranial nerves III and IV

Pons: Conduction pathway between higher and lower brain centers; pontine nuclei relay information from the cerebrum to the cerebellum; its respiratory nuclei cooperate with the medullary respiratory centers to control respiratory rate and depth; houses nuclei of cranial nerves V–VII

Medulla oblongata: Conduction pathway between higher brain centers and spinal cord; site of decussation of the pyramidal tracts; houses nuclei of cranial nerves VIII–XII; contains nuclei cuneatus and gracilis (synapse points of ascending sensory pathways transmitting sensory impulses from skin and proprioceptors), and visceral nuclei controlling heart rate, blood vessel diameter, respiratory rate, vomiting, coughing, etc.; its inferior olivary nuclei provide the sensory relay to the cerebellum

Reticular formation (pp. 455–456)

A functional brain stem system that maintains cerebral cortical alertness (reticular activating system) and filters out repetitive stimuli; its motor nuclei help regulate skeletal and visceral muscle activity

CEREBELLUM (pp. 451–454)

Processes information from cerebral motor cortex and from proprioceptors and visual and equilibrium pathways, and provides "instructions" to cerebral motor cortex and subcortical motor centers that result in proper balance and posture and smooth, coordinated skeletal muscle movements

white matter in the cerebellum resembles a branching tree, a pattern fancifully called the **arbor vitae** (ar'bor vi'te; "tree of life").

The anterior and posterior lobes of the cerebellum, which coordinate body movements, have completely overlapping sensory and motor maps of the entire body as indicated by the three homunculi in Figure 12.17b. The medial portions influence the motor activities of the trunk and girdle muscles. The intermediate parts of each hemisphere are more concerned with the distal parts of the limbs and skilled movements. The lateralmost parts of each hemisphere integrate information from the association areas of the cerebral cortex and appear to play a role in planning rather than executing movements. The flocculonodular lobes receive inputs from the equilibrium apparatus of the inner ears, and adjust posture to maintain balance.

Cerebellar Peduncles

As noted earlier, three paired fiber tracts—the cerebellar peduncles—connect the cerebellum to the brain stem (see Figure 12.15). Unlike the contralateral fiber distribution to and from the cerebral cortex, virtually all fibers entering and leaving the cerebellum are **ipsilateral** (*ipsi* = same)—from and to the same side of the body. The **superior cerebellar peduncles** connecting cerebellum and midbrain carry instructions from neurons in the deep cerebellar nuclei to the cerebral motor cortex via thalamic relays. Like the basal nuclei, the cerebellum has no *direct* connections to the cerebral cortex.

The **middle cerebellar peduncles** carry one-way communication from the pons to the cerebellum, advising the cerebellum of voluntary motor activities initiated by the motor cortex (via relays in the pontine nuclei). The **inferior cerebellar peduncles** connect medulla and cerebellum. These peduncles convey sensory information to the cerebellum from (1) muscle proprioceptors throughout the body and (2) the vestibular nuclei of the brain stem, which are concerned with equilibrium and balance.

Cerebellar Processing

The functional scheme of cerebellar processing for motor activity seems to be as follows:

1. The motor areas of the cerebral cortex, via relay nuclei in the brain stem, notify the cerebellum of their intent to initiate voluntary muscle contractions.

2. At the same time, the cerebellum receives information from proprioceptors throughout the body (regarding tension in the muscles and tendons, and joint position) and from visual and equilibrium pathways. This information enables the cerebellum to evaluate body position and momentum, that is, where the body is and where it is going.

3. The cerebellar cortex calculates the best way to coordinate the force, direction, and extent of muscle contraction to prevent overshoot, maintain posture, and ensure smooth, coordinated movements.

4. Then, via the superior peduncles, the cerebellum dispatches to the cerebral motor cortex its "blueprint" for coordinating movement. Cerebellar fibers also send information to brain stem nuclei, which in turn influence motor neurons of the spinal cord.

Just as its automatic pilot compares a plane's instrument settings with the planned course, the cerebellum continually compares the higher brain's intention with the body's performance and sends out messages to initiate the appropriate corrective measures. Cerebellar injury results in loss of muscle tone and clumsy, unsure movements.

Cognitive Function of the Cerebellum

Functional imaging studies indicate that the cerebellum plays a role in cognition. The cerebellum recognizes and predicts sequences of events so that it may adjust for the multiple forces exerted on a limb during complex movements involving several joints. Some nonmotor functions, including word association and puzzle solving, also appear to involve the cerebellum.

Functional Brain Systems

Functional brain systems are networks of neurons that work together but span relatively large distances in the brain, so they cannot be localized to specific brain regions. The *limbic system* and the *reticular formation* are excellent examples (Table 12.1).

The Limbic System

The **limbic system** is a group of structures located on the medial aspect of each cerebral hemisphere and diencephalon. Its cerebral structures encircle (*limbus* = ring) the upper part of the brain stem (Figure 12.18), and include parts of the rhinencephalon (*septal nuclei, cingulate gyrus, parahippocampal gyrus, dentate gyrus,* and C-shaped *hippocampus*), and the **amygdala** (ah-mig′dah-lah), an almond-shaped nucleus that sits on the tail of the caudate nucleus. In the diencephalon, the main limbic structures are the *hypothalamus* and the *anterior thalamic nuclei.* The **fornix** ("arch") and other fiber tracts link these limbic system regions together.

The limbic system is our *emotional,* or *affective* (feelings), *brain.* Two parts seem especially important in emotions—the amygdala and the anterior part of the **cingulate gyrus.** The former recognizes angry or fearful facial expressions, assesses danger, and elicits the fear response. The latter plays a role in expressing our emotions through gestures and in resolving mental conflicts when we are frustrated.

Odors often trigger emotional reactions and memories; this reflects the origin of much of the limbic system in the primitive "smell brain" (rhinencephalon). Our reactions to odors are rarely neutral (a skunk smells *bad* and repulses us), and odors often recall memories of emotion-laden events.

Extensive connections between the limbic system and lower and higher brain regions allow the system to integrate and respond to a variety of environmental stimuli. Most limbic system output is relayed through the hypothalamus. Because the

FIGURE 12.18   The limbic system. Lateral view of the brain, showing some of the structures of the limbic system, the emotional-visceral brain. The brain stem is not illustrated.

hypothalamus is the neural clearinghouse for both autonomic (visceral) function and emotional response, it is not surprising that some people under acute or unrelenting emotional stress fall prey to visceral illnesses, such as high blood pressure and heartburn. Such emotion-induced illnesses are called **psychosomatic illnesses.**

Because the limbic system interacts with the prefrontal lobes, there is an intimate relationship between our feelings (mediated by the emotional brain) and our thoughts (mediated by the cognitive brain). As a result, we (1) react emotionally to things we consciously understand to be happening, and (2) are consciously aware of the emotional richness of our lives. Communication between the cerebral cortex and limbic system explains why emotions sometimes override logic and, conversely, why reason can stop us from expressing our emotions in inappropriate situations. Particular limbic system structures—the **hippocampus** and amygdala—also play a role in memory.

The Reticular Formation

The **reticular formation** extends through the central core of the medulla oblongata, pons, and midbrain (Figure 12.19). It is composed of loosely clustered neurons in what is otherwise white matter. These neurons form three broad columns along the length of the brain stem (Figure 12.16c): (1) the midline **raphe nuclei** (ra′fe; *raphe* = seam or crease), which are flanked laterally by (2) the **medial (large cell) group** and then (3) the **lateral (small cell) group of nuclei.**

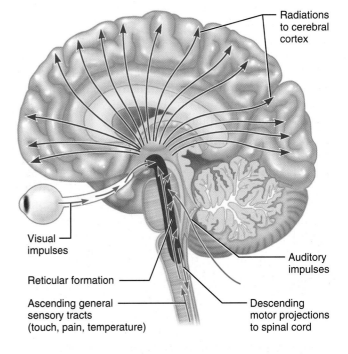

FIGURE 12.19   The reticular formation. The reticular formation extends the length of the brain stem. A portion of this formation, the reticular activating system, maintains alert wakefulness of the cerebral cortex. Ascending arrows indicate input of sensory systems to the RAS and then reticular output (some via thalamic relays) to the cerebral cortex. Other reticular nuclei are involved in muscle coordination. Their output is indicated by the red arrow descending the brain stem.

The outstanding feature of the reticular neurons is their far-flung axonal connections. Individual reticular neurons project to the hypothalamus, thalamus, cerebellum, and spinal cord, making reticular neurons ideal for governing the arousal of the brain as a whole. For example, certain reticular neurons, unless inhibited by other brain areas, send a continuous stream of impulses (via thalamic relays) to the cerebral cortex, which keeps the cortex alert and conscious and enhances its excitability. This arm of the reticular formation is known as the **reticular activating system (RAS)**. Impulses from all the great ascending sensory tracts synapse with RAS neurons, keeping them active and enhancing their arousing effect on the cerebrum. (This may explain why many students, stimulated by a bustling environment, like to study in a crowded cafeteria.) The RAS also acts like a filter for this flood of sensory inputs. Repetitive, familiar, or weak signals are filtered out, but unusual, significant, or strong impulses do reach consciousness. For example, you are probably unaware of your watch encircling your wrist, but would immediately notice it if the clasp broke. Between them, the RAS and the cerebral cortex disregard perhaps 99% of all sensory stimuli as unimportant. If this did not occur, the sensory overload would drive us crazy. The drug LSD interferes with these sensory dampers, promoting an often overwhelming sensory overload.

- Take a moment to become aware of all the stimuli in your environment. Notice all the colors, shapes, odors, sounds, and so on. How many of these sensory stimuli are you usually aware of?

The RAS is inhibited by sleep centers located in the hypothalamus and other neural regions, and is depressed by alcohol, sleep-inducing drugs, and tranquilizers. Severe injury to this system, as might follow a knockout punch that twists the brain stem, results in permanent unconsciousness (irreversible *coma*). Although the RAS is central to wakefulness, some of its nuclei are also involved in sleep, which we will discuss later in this chapter.

The reticular formation also has a *motor* arm. Some of its motor nuclei project to motor neurons in the spinal cord via the *reticulospinal tracts*, and help control skeletal muscles during coarse limb movements. Other reticular motor nuclei, such as the vasomotor, cardiac, and respiratory centers of the medulla, are autonomic centers that regulate visceral motor functions.

Higher Mental Functions

During the last four decades, an exciting exploration of our "inner space," or what we commonly call *the mind,* has been going on. But researchers in the field of cognition are still struggling to understand how the mind's presently incomprehensible qualities might spring from living tissue and electrical impulses. Souls and synapses are hard to reconcile!

Because brain waves reflect the electrical activity on which higher mental functions are based, we will consider them first, along with the related topics of consciousness and sleep. We will then examine language and (hesitantly) memory, an area in which we are still forced to hypothesize or speculate about what must (or should) happen.

Brain Wave Patterns and the EEG

Normal brain function involves continuous electrical activity of neurons. An **electroencephalogram** (e-lek″tro-en-sef′ah-lo-gram), or **EEG,** records some aspects of this activity. An EEG is made by placing electrodes on the scalp and then connecting the electrodes to an apparatus that measures electrical potential differences between various cortical areas (Figure 12.20a). The patterns of neuronal electrical activity recorded, called **brain waves,** are generated by synaptic activity at the surface of the cortex, rather than by action potentials in the white matter.

Each of us has a brain wave pattern that is as unique as our fingerprints. For simplicity, however, we can group brain waves into the four frequency classes shown in Figure 12.20b. Each wave is a continuous train of peaks and troughs, and the wave frequency, expressed in hertz (Hz), is the number of peaks in one second. A frequency of 1 Hz means that one peak occurs each second.

- **Alpha waves** (8–13 Hz) are relatively regular and rhythmic, low-amplitude, synchronous waves. In most cases, they indicate a brain that is "idling"—a calm, relaxed state of wakefulness.

- **Beta waves** (14–30 Hz) are also rhythmic, but they are not as regular as alpha waves and have a higher frequency. Beta waves occur when we are mentally alert, as when concentrating on some problem or visual stimulus.

- **Theta waves** (4–7 Hz) are still more irregular. Though common in children, theta waves are abnormal in awake adults.

- **Delta waves** (4 Hz or less) are high-amplitude waves seen during deep sleep and when the reticular activating system is damped, such as during anesthesia. In awake adults, they indicate brain damage.

The amplitude or intensity of any wave is represented by how high the wave peaks rise and how low the troughs dip. The amplitude of brain waves reflects the synchronous activity of many neurons and not the degree of electrical activity of individual neurons. Usually, brain waves are complex and low amplitude. During some stages of sleep, neurons tend to fire synchronously, producing similar, high-amplitude brain waves.

(a)

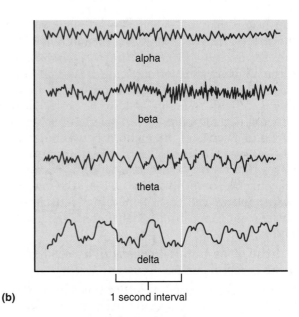

(b)

1 second interval

FIGURE 12.20 **Electroencephalog-raphy and brain waves. (a)** To obtain a recording of brain wave activity (an EEG), electrodes are positioned on the patient's scalp and attached to a recording device called an electroen-cephalograph. **(b)** Typical EEGs. Alpha waves are typical of the awake but relaxed state; beta waves occur in the awake, alert state; theta waves are common in children but not adults; delta waves occur during deep sleep.

Brain waves change with age, sensory stimuli, brain disease, and the chemical state of the body. EEGs are used for research on sleep, and for diagnosing epilepsy and many types of brain lesions. Interference with cerebral cortical functions is suggested when brain waves are too fast or too slow, and unconsciousness occurs at both extremes. Because spontaneous brain waves are always present, even during unconsciousness and coma, their absence—called a "flat EEG"—is clinical evidence of brain death.

HOMEOSTATIC IMBALANCE

Almost without warning, a victim of epilepsy may lose consciousness and fall stiffly to the ground, body wracked by uncontrollable jerking. These **epileptic seizures** reflect a torrent of electrical discharges of groups of brain neurons, and while their uncontrolled activity is occurring, no other messages can get through. Epilepsy, manifested by one out of 100 of us, is not associated with, nor does it cause, intellectual impairment. Some cases of epilepsy are induced by genetic factors, but it can also result from brain injuries caused by blows to the head, stroke, infections, high fever, or tumors.

Epileptic seizures can vary tremendously in their expression and severity. *Absence seizures,* formerly known as *petit mal,* are mild forms in which the expression goes blank for a few seconds as consciousness disappears. These are typically seen in young children and usually disappear by the age of 10. In the most severe, convulsive form of epileptic seizures, *tonic-clonic* (formerly called *grand mal*), the person loses consciousness. Bones are often broken during the intense convulsions, showing the incredible strength of the muscle contractions that occur. Loss of bowel and bladder control and severe biting of the tongue are common. The seizure lasts for a few minutes, then the muscles relax and the person awakens but remains disoriented for several minutes. Many seizure sufferers experience a sensory hallucination, such as a taste, smell, or flashes of light, just before the seizure begins. This phenomenon, called an **aura,** is helpful because it gives the person time to lie down and avoid falling to the floor.

Epilepsy can usually be controlled by anticonvulsive drugs. Newer on the scene is the *vagus nerve stimulator,* which is implanted under the skin of the chest and delivers pulses via the vagus nerve to the brain at predetermined intervals to keep the electrical activity of the brain from becoming chaotic. A current line of research seeks to use implanted electrodes programmed to detect coming seizures in time to deliver customized drug or shock therapy. ●

Consciousness

Consciousness encompasses conscious perception of sensations, voluntary initiation and control of movement, and capabilities associated with higher mental processing (memory, logic, judgment, perseverance, and so on). Clinically, consciousness is defined on a continuum that grades behavior in response to stimuli as (1) *alertness*, (2) *drowsiness* or *lethargy* (which proceeds to sleep), (3) *stupor*, and (4) *coma*. Alertness is the highest state of consciousness and cortical activity, and coma the most depressed. Consciousness is difficult to define. And to be perfectly frank, reducing our response to the palette of a Key West sunset to a series of interactions between dendrites, axons, and neurotransmitters does not capture what makes that event so special. A sleeping person obviously lacks something that he or she has when awake, and we call this "something" consciousness. The current suppositions about consciousness are as follows:

1. **It involves simultaneous activity of large areas of the cerebral cortex.**

2. **It is superimposed on other types of neural activity.** At any time, specific neurons and neuronal pools are involved both in localized activities (such as motor control) and in cognition.

3. **It is holistic and totally interconnected.** Information for "thought" can be claimed from many locations in the cerebrum simultaneously. For example, retrieval of a specific memory can be triggered by several routes—a smell, a place, a particular person, and so on.

◤ HOMEOSTATIC IMBALANCE

Except when a person is sleeping, unconsciousness is always a signal that brain function is impaired. A brief loss of consciousness is called **fainting** or **syncope** (sing'ko-pe; "cut short"). Most often, it indicates inadequate cerebral blood flow due to low blood pressure, as might follow hemorrhage or sudden emotional stress.

Total unresponsiveness to sensory stimuli for an extended period is called **coma.** Coma is *not* deep sleep. During sleep, the brain is active and oxygen consumption resembles that of the waking state. In coma patients, in contrast, oxygen use is always below normal resting levels.

Blows to the head may induce coma by causing widespread cerebral or brain stem trauma. Coma may also be produced by tumors or infections that invade the brain stem. Metabolic disturbances such as hypoglycemia (abnormally low blood sugar levels), drug overdose, or liver or kidney failure interfere with overall brain function and can result in coma. Cerebral infarctions, unless massive and accompanied by extreme swelling of the brain, rarely cause coma.

When the brain has suffered irreparable damage, irreversible coma occurs, even though life-support measures may have restored vitality to other body organs. The result is **brain death,** a dead brain in an otherwise living body. Because life support can be removed only after death, physicians must determine whether a patient in an irreversible coma is legally alive or dead. ●

Sleep and Sleep-Wake Cycles

Sleep is defined as a state of partial unconsciousness from which a person can be aroused by stimulation. This distinguishes sleep from *coma*, a state of unconsciousness from which a person *cannot* be aroused by even the most vigorous stimuli. For the most part, cortical activity is depressed during sleep, but brain stem functions, such as control of respiration, heart rate, and blood pressure, continue. Even environmental monitoring continues to some extent, as illustrated by the fact that strong stimuli ("things that go bump in the night") immediately arouse us. In fact, people who sleepwalk can avoid objects and navigate stairs while truly asleep.

Types of Sleep

The two major types of sleep, which alternate through most of the sleep cycle, are **non–rapid eye movement (NREM) sleep** and **rapid eye movement (REM) sleep,** defined in terms of their EEG patterns. During the first 30 to 45 minutes of the sleep cycle, we pass through the four stages of NREM sleep (Figure 12.21), culminating in **slow-wave sleep.** As we pass through these stages and slip into deeper and deeper sleep, the frequency of the EEG waves declines, but their amplitude increases.

About 90 minutes after sleep begins, once NREM stage 4 has been achieved, the EEG pattern changes abruptly. It becomes very irregular and appears to backtrack quickly through the stages until alpha waves (more typical of the awake state) appear, indicating the onset of REM sleep. This brain wave change is coupled with increases in heart rate, respiratory rate, and blood pressure and a decrease in gastrointestinal motility. Oxygen use by the brain is tremendous during REM—greater than during the awake state.

Although the eyes move rapidly under the lids during REM, most of the body's skeletal muscles are actively inhibited and go limp. This temporary paralysis prevents us from acting out our dreams. Most dreaming occurs during REM sleep, and some suggest that the flitting eye movements are following the visual imagery of our dreams. (Note, however, that most nightmares and night terrors occur during NREM stages 3 and 4.) In adolescents and adults, REM episodes are frequently associated with erection of the penis or engorgement of the clitoris.

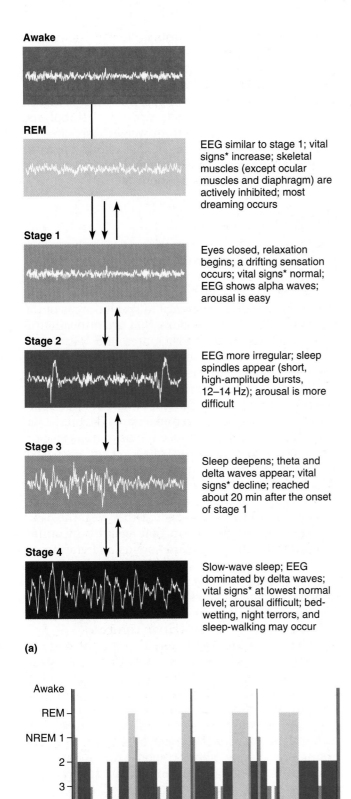

Awake

REM

EEG similar to stage 1; vital signs* increase; skeletal muscles (except ocular muscles and diaphragm) are actively inhibited; most dreaming occurs

Stage 1

Eyes closed, relaxation begins; a drifting sensation occurs; vital signs* normal; EEG shows alpha waves; arousal is easy

Stage 2

EEG more irregular; sleep spindles appear (short, high-amplitude bursts, 12–14 Hz); arousal is more difficult

Stage 3

Sleep deepens; theta and delta waves appear; vital signs* decline; reached about 20 min after the onset of stage 1

Stage 4

Slow-wave sleep; EEG dominated by delta waves; vital signs* at lowest normal level; arousal difficult; bed-wetting, night terrors, and sleep-walking may occur

(a)

(b)

FIGURE 12.21   **Types and stages of sleep. (a)** The progression from the waking state through the four stages of non–rapid eye movement (NREM) sleep and REM sleep is shown. Each stage is characterized by a particular EEG pattern. **(b)** The bar graph shows the time spent during each of these stages in a typical 7½-hour sleep period for a young adult.

*Vital signs refer to heart rate and blood pressure only.

Sleep Patterns

The alternating cycles of sleep and wakefulness reflect a natural *circadian*, or 24-hour, *rhythm*. In the awake state, alertness of the cerebral cortex is mediated by the RAS (see Figure 12.19). When RAS activity declines, cerebral cortical activity declines as well; thus, lesions of the RAS nuclei result in unconsciousness. However, sleep is much more than simply turning off the arousal (RAS) mechanism. RAS centers not only help maintain the awake state but also mediate some sleep stages, especially dreaming sleep. The hypothalamus is responsible for the timing of the sleep cycle: Its *suprachiasmatic nucleus* (a biological clock) regulates its *preoptic nucleus* (a sleep-inducing center).

In young and middle-aged adults, a typical night's sleep alternates between REM and NREM sleep with occasional partial arousals. Following each REM episode, the sleeper descends to stage 4 again. REM recurs about every 90 minutes, with each REM period getting longer. The first REM of the night lasts 5–10 minutes and the final one 20 to 50 minutes (Figure 12.21). Hence, our longest dreams occur just before we wake. When certain neurons of the midbrain reticular formation fire at maximal rates, we awaken for the day.

The slow theta and delta waves of deep sleep are the result of synchronized firing of thalamic neurons that is normally inhibited during wakefulness by the RAS of the pons. Some pontine neurons of the reticular formation control the transition from NREM sleep to REM sleep, and others suppress motor activity, inducing paralysis. A large number of chemical substances in the body cause sleepiness, but the relative importance of these various sleep-inducing substances is not known.

Importance of Sleep

Slow-wave (NREM stage 4) and REM sleep seem to be important in different ways. Slow-wave sleep is presumed to be restorative—the time when most neural mechanisms can wind down to basal levels. When deprived of sleep, we spend more time than usual in slow-wave sleep during the next sleep episode.

A person persistently deprived of REM sleep becomes moody and depressed, and exhibits various personality disorders. REM sleep may give the brain an opportunity to analyze the day's events and to work through emotional problems in dream imagery.

12

Another idea is that REM sleep is reverse learning. According to this hypothesis, accidental, repetitious, and meaningless communications continually occur, and they must be eliminated from the neural networks by dreaming if the cortex is to remain a well-behaved and efficient thinking system. In other words, we dream to forget.

Alcohol and some sleep medications (barbiturates and others) suppress REM sleep but not slow-wave sleep. On the other hand, certain tranquilizers, such as diazepam (Valium) reduce slow-wave sleep much more than REM sleep.

Whatever its importance, the daily sleep requirement declines steadily from 16 hours or so in infants to approximately 7½ to 8½ hours in early adulthood. It then levels off before declining once again in old age. Sleep patterns also change throughout life. REM sleep occupies about half the total sleeping time in infants and then declines until the age of 10 years, when it stabilizes at about 25%. In contrast, stage 4 sleep declines steadily from birth and often disappears completely in those over 60.

◢◣ HOMEOSTATIC IMBALANCE

People with **narcolepsy** lapse abruptly into REM sleep from the awake state. These sleep episodes last about 15 minutes, can occur without warning at any time, and are often triggered by a pleasurable event—a good joke, a game of poker. In most patients with narcolepsy, an emotionally intense experience can also trigger *cataplexy*, a sudden loss of voluntary muscle control similar to that seen during REM sleep. During cataplectic attacks, lasting seconds to minutes, the patient remains fully conscious but unable to move. Obviously this can be extremely hazardous when one is driving a car or swimming! It appears that the brains of patients with narcolepsy have fewer cells in the hypothalamus that secrete chemicals called hypocretins. This finding may be a key to future treatments.

Insomnia is a chronic inability to obtain the *amount* or *quality* of sleep needed to function adequately during the day. Sleep requirements vary from four to nine hours a day in healthy people, so there is no way to determine the "right" amount. Insomniacs tend to overestimate the extent of their sleeplessness, and some come to rely on hypnotics (sleep medications), which can exacerbate the problem.

True insomnia often reflects normal age-related changes, but perhaps the most common cause is psychological disturbance. We have difficulty falling asleep when we are anxious or upset, and depression is often accompanied by early awakening.

Sleep apnea, a temporary cessation of breathing during sleep, is scary. The victim awakes abruptly due to hypoxia (lack of oxygen)—a condition that may occur repeatedly throughout the night. Obstructive sleep apnea, the most common form, occurs when the loss of muscle tone during sleep allows excess fatty tissue or other structural abnormalities to block the upper airway. It is associated with obesity and made worse by alcohol and other depressants. Aside from weight loss, effective treatments are either a mask that allows air to be blown in through the nose, keeping the airway open, or surgery to correct the problem. ●

Language

Language is such an important part of the brain that practically all of the association cortex on the left side is involved in one way or another. Pioneering studies of patients with *aphasias* (the loss of language abilities due to damage to specific areas of the brain) pointed to two regions that are critically important for language, Broca's area and Wernicke's area. Patients with lesions involving **Broca's area** (Figure 12.8a) can understand language but have difficulty speaking (and sometimes cannot write or type or use sign language). On the other hand, patients with lesions involving **Wernicke's area** (Figure 12.8a) are able to speak but produce a type of nonsense often referred to as a "word salad." They also have great difficulty understanding language. Recent functional studies of the brain indicate that this picture is clinically useful, but oversimplified. In fact, Broca's and Wernicke's areas together with the basal nuclei form a single system that analyzes incoming and produces outgoing word sounds and grammatical structures. A surrounding set of cortical areas forms a bridge between this language implementation system and the regions of cortex that hold concepts and ideas, which are distributed throughout the remainder of the association cortices.

The corresponding areas in the right or non-language-dominant hemisphere are involved in "body language"—the nonverbal emotional (affective) components of language. These areas allow the lilt or tone of our voice and our gestures to express our emotions when we speak, and permit us to comprehend the emotional content of what we hear. For example, a soft, melodious response to your question conveys quite a different meaning than a sharp reply.

Memory

Memory is the storage and retrieval of information. Memories are essential for learning and incorporating our experiences into behavior and are part and parcel of our consciousness. Stored somewhere in your 3 pounds of wrinkled brain are zip codes, the face of your grandfather, and the taste of yesterday's pizza. Your memories reflect your lifetime.

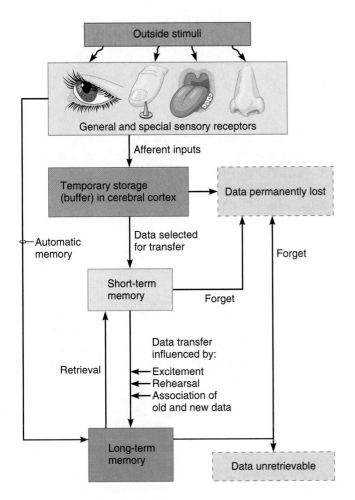

FIGURE 12.22 Memory processing. Sensory inputs are processed by the cerebral cortex (indicated as the temporary storage area), which selects what is to be sent to short-term memory. Rehearsal and other factors help the transfer of information from short-term memory to long-term memory. For long-term memory to become permanent, consolidation must occur. Some information not consciously attended to goes directly into long-term memory (automatic memory).

Stages of Memory

Memory storage involves two distinct stages: short-term memory and long-term memory (Figure 12.22). **Short-term memory (STM),** also called *working memory,* is the preliminary step, as well as the power that lets you look up a telephone number, dial it, and then never think of it again. The capacity of STM is limited to seven or eight chunks of information, such as the digits of a telephone number or the sequence of words in an elaborate sentence.

In contrast to STM, **long-term memory (LTM)** seems to have a limitless capacity. Although our STM devices cannot recall numbers much longer than a telephone number, we can remember scores of telephone numbers by committing them to LTM. However, our ability to store and to retrieve information declines with aging. Thus, long-term memories

too can be forgotten, and our memory bank continually changes with time.

We do not remember or even consciously notice much of what is going on around us. As sensory inputs flood into our cerebral cortex, they are processed, and some 5% of this information is selected for transfer to STM (Figure 12.22). STM serves as a sort of temporary holding bin for data that we may or may not want to retain. The transfer of information from STM to LTM is affected by many factors, including

1. **Emotional state.** We learn best when we are alert, motivated, surprised, and aroused. For example, when we witness shocking events, transferal is almost immediate. Norepinephrine, a neurotransmitter involved in memory processing of emotionally charged events, is released when we are excited or "stressed out," which helps to explain this phenomenon.

2. **Rehearsal.** Rehearsal or repetition of the material enhances memory.

3. **Association.** Tying "new" information to "old" information already stored in LTM appears to be important in remembering facts.

4. **Automatic memory.** Not all impressions that become part of LTM are consciously formed. A student concentrating on a lecturer's speech may record an automatic memory of the pattern of the lecturer's tie.

Memories transferred to LTM take time to become permanent. The process of **memory consolidation** apparently involves fitting new facts into the various categories of knowledge already stored in the cerebral cortex.

Categories of Memory

The brain distinguishes between factual knowledge and skills, and we process and store these different kinds of information in different ways. **Declarative (fact) memory** entails learning explicit information, such as names, faces, words, and dates. It is related to our conscious thoughts and our ability to manipulate symbols and language. When fact memories are committed to LTM, they are usually filed along with the context in which they were learned. For instance, when you think of your new acquaintance Joe, you probably picture him at the basketball game where you met him.

Nondeclarative memory is less conscious or even unconscious learning. Categories of nondeclarative memory are **procedural (skills) memory** (piano playing), **motor memory** (riding a bike), and **emotional memory** (your pounding heart when you hear a rattlesnake nearby). These kinds of memory are acquired through experience and usually repetition. They do not preserve the circumstances of learning; in fact, they are best remembered in the doing. You do not have to think through how to tie

12

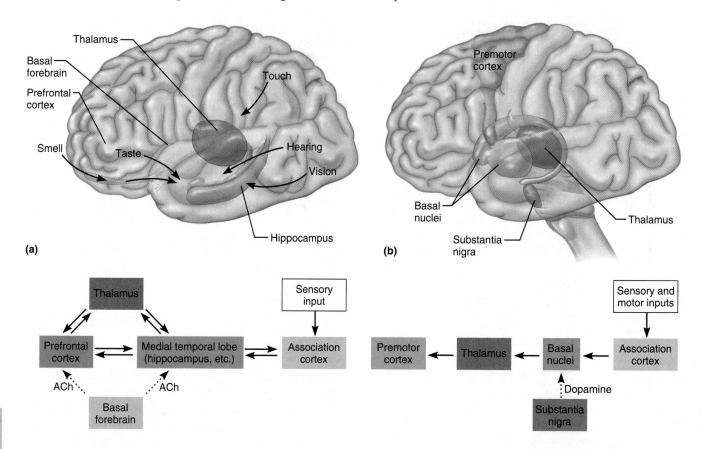

FIGURE 12.23 **Proposed memory circuits. (a)** Essential structures of declarative memory circuits. The flowchart below indicates how these structures may interact in memory formation. Information from association cortices flows to the medial temporal lobe (including the hippocampus), which communicates with the thalamus and prefrontal cortex. The medial temporal lobe structures then feed back to the association cortices. Acetylcholine, released from the basal forebrain, is necessary for this circuit to function. **(b)** Essential structures of procedural (skills) memory. Sensory and motor input flows through the association cortices and is relayed via the basal nuclei through the thalamus to the premotor cortex. Dopamine, released from the substantia nigra, is necessary for this circuit to function.

your shoes. Once learned, nondeclarative memories are hard to unlearn.

Brain Structures Involved in Memory

Much of what scientists know about learning and memory comes from experiments with macaque monkeys, and studies of amnesia and functional imaging in humans. Such studies have revealed that different brain structures are involved in the two categories of memory.

It appears that specific pieces of each memory are stored near regions of the brain that need them so that new inputs can be quickly associated with the old. Accordingly, visual memories are stored in the occipital cortex, memories of music in the temporal cortex, and so on.

But how do we create new memories? It seems that different types of memory are created in different parts of the brain. A proposed scheme of information flow for declarative memory is shown in Figure 12.23a. When sensory input is processed in the association cortices, the cortical neurons dispatch impulses to the medial temporal lobe, which includes the hippocampus and surrounding temporal cortical areas. These temporal lobe areas play a major role in memory consolidation and memory access by communicating with the thalamus and the prefrontal cortex. The prefrontal cortex and medial temporal lobe receive input from acetylcholine-releasing neurons in the basal forebrain. The sprinkling of acetylcholine onto these structures is thought to prime them to allow the formation of memories. The loss of this cholinergic input, for example in Alzheimer's disease, seems to disrupt both the formation of new memories and the retrieval of old ones. Memories are retrieved when the same sets of neurons that were initially involved in memory formation are stimulated.

▲ HOMEOSTATIC IMBALANCE

Damage to the hippocampus and surrounding medial temporal lobe structures on either side results in only slight memory loss, but bilateral destruction causes widespread amnesia. Consolidated memories are not lost, but new sensory inputs cannot be associated with old, and the person lives in the here and now from that point on. This phenomenon is called *anterograde amnesia* (an′ter-o-grād″), in contrast to *retrograde amnesia*, which is the loss of memories formed in the distant past. You could carry on an animated conversation with a person with anterograde amnesia, excuse yourself, return five minutes later, and that person would not remember you. ●

Individuals suffering from anterograde amnesia can still learn skills such as drawing, which means a different learning circuit must be used for procedural memory (Figure 12.23b). Like the medial temporal lobe for declarative memory, the basal nuclei are the key players for procedural memory. Sensory and motor inputs passing through the cortex to the basal nuclei are then relayed via the thalamus back to the premotor cortex. The basal nuclei receive input from dopamine-releasing neurons in the substantia nigra of the midbrain. Just as acetylcholine is necessary for declarative memory, dopamine appears to be necessary for this procedural memory circuit to function. The loss of this dopamine input, as in Parkinson's disease, interferes with procedural memory.

The two other kinds of nondeclarative memory involve yet other brain regions. The cerebellum is involved in motor memory, while the amygdala (see Figure 12.18) is crucial for emotional memory. These will not be described further here.

Mechanisms of Memory

Human memory is notoriously difficult to study. Animal experimental studies reveal that during learning, (1) neuronal RNA content is altered and newly synthesized mRNAs are delivered to axons and dendrites, (2) dendritic spines change shape, (3) unique extracellular proteins are deposited at synapses involved in LTM, (4) the number and size of presynaptic terminals may increase, and (5) more neurotransmitter is released by the presynaptic neurons.

Each one of these changes is an aspect of *long-term potentiation (LTP)*, which has been shown to be crucial for memory formation. LTP refers to a persistent increase in synaptic strength, first identified in hippocampal neurons that use the amino acid glutamate as a neurotransmitter. One kind of glutamate receptor, the **NMDA receptor,** can act as a calcium channel and initiate the cellular changes that bring about LTP.

Normally, NMDA receptors are blocked so that calcium entry is prevented. When the postsynaptic terminal is depolarized by binding of glutamate to different receptors, as would happen upon the rapid arrival of action potentials at the synapse, this NMDA block is removed and calcium flows into the postsynaptic cell. Calcium influx triggers activation of enzymes that carry out two main tasks. First, they modify the proteins in the postsynaptic terminal, and also in the presynaptic terminal via retrograde messengers such as nitric oxide, which strengthens the response to subsequent stimuli. Second, they cause the activation of genes in the postsynaptic neuron's nucleus, which leads to synthesis of synaptic proteins. The molecular messenger that brings the news to the nucleus that more protein is needed is a molecule called CREB (cAMP response-element binding protein). A neurotrophic factor called BDNF (brain-derived neurotrophic factor) is required for the protein synthesis phase of LTP. These changes create long-lasting increases in synaptic strength that are believed to underlie memory.

The mechanisms underlying memory at a cellular level suggest several approaches to enhancing memory acquisition. Currently several drugs to improve memory are undergoing clinical trials. Among these are drugs that enhance CREB production—the more CREB, the more protein synthesis and the stronger the synapse becomes.

Protection of the Brain

Nervous tissue is soft and delicate, and neurons are injured by even slight pressure. However, the brain is protected by bone (the skull), membranes (the meninges), and a watery cushion (cerebrospinal fluid). Furthermore, the brain is protected from harmful substances in the blood by the blood-brain barrier. We described the cranium, the brain's bony encasement, in Chapter 7. Here we will attend to the other protective devices.

Meninges

The **meninges** (mĕ-nin′jēz; *mening* = membrane) are three connective tissue membranes that lie just external to the CNS organs. They (1) cover and protect the CNS, (2) protect blood vessels and enclose venous sinuses, (3) contain cerebrospinal fluid, and (4) form partitions in the skull. From external to internal, the meninges (singular: **meninx**) are the dura mater, arachnoid mater, and pia mater (Figure 12.24).

Dura Mater

The leathery **dura mater** (du′rah ma′ter), meaning "tough mother," is the strongest meninx. Where it

12

(a)

(b)

FIGURE 12.24 **Meninges. (a)** Frontal section showing the relationship of the dura mater, arachnoid, and pia mater. The meningeal dura forms the falx cerebri fold. A dural sinus, the superior sagittal sinus, is enclosed by the dural membranes superiorly. Arachnoid villi, which return cerebrospinal fluid to the dural sinus, are also shown. **(b)** Posterior view of the brain in place, surrounded by the dura mater and sinuses.

surrounds the brain, it is a two-layered sheet of fibrous connective tissue. The more superficial *periosteal layer* is attached to the inner surface of the skull (the periosteum). (There is no dural periosteal layer surrounding the spinal cord.) The deeper *meningeal layer* forms the true external covering of the brain and continues caudally in the vertebral canal as the dural sheath of the spinal cord. The brain's two dural layers are fused together except in certain areas, where they separate to enclose **dural sinuses** that collect venous blood from the brain and direct it into the internal jugular veins of the neck.

In several places, the meningeal dura mater extends inward to form flat partitions that subdivide the cranial cavity. These **dural septa,** which limit excessive movement of the brain within the cranium, include the following (Figure 12.25):

- **Falx cerebri** (falks ser'ĕ-bri). A large sickle-shaped (*falks* = sickle) fold that dips into the longitudinal fissure between the cerebral hemispheres. Anteriorly, it attaches to the crista galli of the ethmoid bone.
- **Falx cerebelli** (ser″ĕ-bel′i). Continuing inferiorly from the posterior falx cerebri, this small midline partition runs along the vermis of the cerebellum.
- **Tentorium cerebelli** (ten-to′re-um; "tent"). Resembling a tent over the cerebellum, this nearly horizontal dural fold extends into the transverse fissure between the cerebral hemispheres (which it helps to support) and the cerebellum.

Arachnoid Mater

The middle meninx, the **arachnoid mater,** or simply the **arachnoid** (ah-rak′noid), forms a loose brain covering, never dipping into the sulci at the cerebral surface. It is separated from the dura mater by a narrow serous cavity, the **subdural space,** which contains a film of fluid. Beneath the arachnoid membrane is the wide **subarachnoid space.** Weblike extensions span this space and secure the arachnoid mater to the underlying pia mater. (*Arachnida* means "spider," and this membrane was named for its weblike extensions.) The subarachnoid space is filled with cerebrospinal fluid and also contains the largest blood vessels serving the brain. Because the arachnoid is fine and elastic, these blood vessels are poorly protected.

Knoblike projections of the arachnoid mater called **arachnoid villi** (vil'i) protrude superiorly through the dura mater and into the superior sagittal sinus (see Figure 12.24a). Cerebrospinal fluid is absorbed into the venous blood of the sinus by these valvelike villi.

Pia Mater

The **pia mater** (pi'ah), meaning "gentle mother," is composed of delicate connective tissue and is richly invested with tiny blood vessels. It is the only meninx that clings tightly to the brain, following its every convolution. Small arteries entering the brain tissue carry ragged sheaths of pia mater inward with them for short distances.

◤ HOMEOSTATIC IMBALANCE

Meningitis, inflammation of the meninges, is a serious threat to the brain because a bacterial or viral meningitis may spread to the CNS. This condition of brain inflammation is called *encephalitis* (en'sef-ah-li'tis). Meningitis is usually diagnosed by obtaining a sample of cerebrospinal fluid via a lumbar tap (see Figure 12.30) and examining it for microbes. ●

Cerebrospinal Fluid

Cerebrospinal fluid (CSF), found in and around the brain and spinal cord, forms a liquid cushion that gives buoyancy to the CNS structures. By floating the jellylike brain, the CSF effectively reduces brain weight by 97% and prevents the brain from crushing under its own weight. CSF also protects the brain and spinal cord from blows and other trauma. Additionally, although the brain has a rich blood supply, CSF helps nourish the brain, and there is some evidence that it carries chemical signals (such as hormones and sleep- and appetite-inducing molecules) from one part of the brain to another.

CSF is a watery "broth" similar in composition to blood plasma, from which it is formed. However, it contains less protein than plasma and its ion concentrations are different. For example, CSF contains

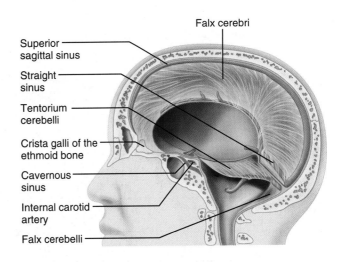

FIGURE 12.25 **Partitioning folds of dura mater in the cranial cavity.** Some dural sinuses are also shown.

more Na$^+$, Cl$^-$, and H$^+$ than does blood plasma, and less Ca^{2+} and K$^+$. CSF composition, particularly its pH, is important in the control of cerebral blood flow and breathing.

The **choroid plexuses** that hang from the roof of each ventricle form CSF (Figure 12.26a). These plexuses are frond-shaped clusters of broad, thin-walled capillaries (*plex* = interwoven) enclosed first by pia mater and then by a layer of ependymal cells lining the ventricles. These capillaries are fairly permeable, and tissue fluid filters continuously from the bloodstream. However, the choroid plexus ependymal cells are joined by tight junctions and have ion pumps that allow them to modify this filtrate by actively transporting only certain ions across their membranes into the CSF pool. This sets up ionic gradients that cause water to diffuse into the ventricles as well. In adults, the total CSF volume of about 150 ml (about half a cup) is replaced every 8 hours or so; hence about 500 ml of CSF is formed daily. The choroid plexuses also help cleanse the CSF by removing waste products and unnecessary solutes.

Once produced, CSF moves freely through the ventricles. Some CSF circulates into the central canal of the spinal cord, but most enters the subarachnoid space via the lateral and median apertures in the walls of the fourth ventricle (Figure 12.26b). The constant motion of the CSF is aided by movement of the long cilia of the ependymal cells lining the ventricles. In the subarachnoid space, CSF bathes the outer surfaces of the brain and spinal cord and then returns to the blood in the dural sinuses via the arachnoid villi.

◤ HOMEOSTATIC IMBALANCE

Ordinarily, CSF is produced and drained at a constant rate. However, if something (such as a tumor)

Q *What structures return CSF to the bloodstream?*

Superior sagittal sinus
Superior cerebral vein
Choroid plexus
Cerebrum covered with pia mater
Septum pellucidum
Corpus callosum
Interventricular foramen
Third ventricle
Pituitary gland

Cerebral aqueduct
Lateral aperture
Fourth ventricle
Median aperture

Arachnoid villus
Subarachnoid space
Arachnoid mater
Meningeal dura mater
Periosteal dura mater
Great cerebral vein
Tentorium cerebelli
Straight sinus
Confluence of sinuses
Cerebellum
Choroid plexus
Cerebellar vessels that supply choroid plexus
Central canal of spinal cord
Spinal dura mater
Inferior end of spinal cord
Filum terminale (inferior end of pia mater)

(b)

Ependymal cells
Capillary
Connective tissue of pia mater
Section of choroid plexus
Cavity of ventricle
Wastes and unnecessary solutes absorbed
Filtrate containing glucose, oxygen, vitamins, and ions (Na$^+$, Cl$^-$, Mg^{2+}, etc.)

(a)

FIGURE 12.26 **Formation, location, and circulation of CSF. (a)** Choroid plexuses form CSF. Each choroid plexus consists of a knot of porous capillaries surrounded by a single layer of ependymal cells joined by tight junctions and bearing long cilia with blunted ends. Although the filtrate moves easily from the capillaries, it must move through and be processed by the ependymal cells before it is allowed to enter the ventricles as cerebrospinal fluid. **(b)** Location and circulatory pattern of CSF. Direction of circulation is indicated by the arrows. (The relative position of the right lateral ventricle is indicated by the pale bluish green area deep to the corpus callosum and septum pellucidum.)

12

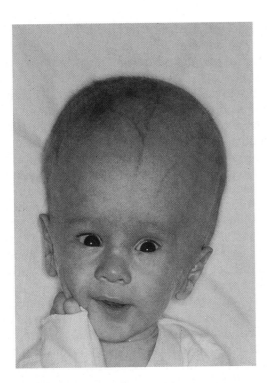

FIGURE 12.27 **Hydrocephalus in a newborn.**

obstructs its circulation or drainage, it accumulates and exerts pressure on the brain. This condition is called *hydrocephalus* ("water on the brain"). Hydrocephalus in a newborn baby causes its head to enlarge (Figure 12.27); this is possible because the skull bones have not yet fused. In adults, however, hydrocephalus is likely to result in brain damage because the skull is rigid and hard, and accumulating fluid compresses blood vessels serving the brain and crushes the soft nervous tissue. Hydrocephalus is treated by inserting a shunt into the ventricles to drain the excess fluid into a vein in the neck. ●

Blood-Brain Barrier

The **blood-brain barrier** is a protective mechanism that helps maintain a stable environment for the brain. No other body tissue is so absolutely dependent on a constant internal milieu as is the brain. In other body regions, the extracellular concentrations of hormones, amino acids, and ions are in constant flux, particularly after eating or exercise. If the brain were exposed to such chemical variations, the neurons would fire uncontrollably, because some hormones and amino acids serve as neurotransmitters and certain ions (particularly K^+) modify the threshold for neuronal firing.

Bloodborne substances in the brain's capillaries are separated from the extracellular space and neurons by (1) the continuous endothelium of the capillary wall, (2) a relatively thick basal lamina surrounding

the external face of each capillary, and (3) the bulbous "feet" of the astrocytes clinging to the capillaries. The capillary endothelial cells are almost seamlessly joined all around by *tight junctions* (Chapter 19), making them the least permeable capillaries in the body, a characteristic that constitutes most (if not all) of the blood-brain barrier. Although the astrocytes' feet contribute to the blood-brain barrier, it now appears that their major role is to provide the signals that stimulate the capillary endothelial cells to *form* the tight junctions characteristic of the blood-brain barrier.

The blood-brain barrier is selective, rather than absolute. Nutrients such as glucose, essential amino acids, and some electrolytes move passively by facilitated diffusion through the endothelial cell membranes. Bloodborne metabolic wastes, proteins, certain toxins, and most drugs are denied entry to brain tissue. Small nonessential amino acids and potassium ions not only are prevented from entering the brain, but also are actively pumped from the brain across the capillary endothelium.

The barrier is ineffective against fats, fatty acids, oxygen, carbon dioxide, and other fat-soluble molecules that diffuse easily through all plasma membranes. This explains why bloodborne alcohol, nicotine, and anesthetics can affect the brain.

The structure of the blood-brain barrier is not completely uniform. The capillaries of the choroid plexuses are very porous, but the ependymal cells surrounding them have tight junctions. In some brain areas surrounding the third and fourth ventricles, the blood-brain barrier is entirely absent and the capillary endothelium is quite permeable, allowing bloodborne molecules easy access to the neural tissue. One such region is the vomiting center of the brain stem, which monitors the blood for poisonous substances. Another is in the hypothalamus, which regulates water balance, body temperature, and many other metabolic activities; lack of a blood-brain barrier here is essential to allow the hypothalamus to sample the chemical composition of the blood. The barrier is incomplete in newborn and premature infants, and potentially toxic substances can enter the CNS and cause problems not seen in adults.

Injury to the brain, whatever the cause, may result in a localized breakdown of the blood-brain barrier. Most likely, this reflects some change in the capillary endothelial cells or their tight junctions.

Homeostatic Imbalances of the Brain

Brain dysfunctions are unbelievably varied and extensive. We have mentioned some of them already, and one family of transmissible brain disorders is described in *A Closer Look* on p. 482. Here, we will focus on traumatic brain injuries, cerebrovascular accidents, and degenerative brain disorders.

Traumatic Brain Injury

Head injuries are a leading cause of accidental death in North America. Consider, for example, what happens if you forget to fasten your seat belt and then rear-end another car. Your head is moving and then is suddenly stopped as it hits the windshield. Brain damage is caused not only by localized injury at the site of the blow (the *coup* injury), but also by the ricocheting effect as the brain hits the opposite end of the skull (the *contrecoup* injury).

A **concussion** is an alteration in brain function, usually temporary, following a blow to the head. The victim may be dizzy or lose consciousness. Although typically mild and short lived, even a seemingly mild concussion can be damaging, and multiple concussions over time have been shown to produce cumulative damage. More serious concussions can cause bruising of the brain and permanent neurological damage, a condition called a **contusion.** In cortical contusions, the individual may remain conscious, but severe brain stem contusions always cause coma, lasting from hours to a lifetime because of injury to the reticular activating system.

Following a head blow, death may result from **subdural** or **subarachnoid hemorrhage** (bleeding from ruptured vessels into those spaces). Individuals who are initially lucid and then begin to deteriorate neurologically are, in all probability, hemorrhaging intracranially. Blood accumulating in the skull increases intracranial pressure and compresses brain tissue. If the pressure forces the brain stem inferiorly through the foramen magnum, control of blood pressure, heart rate, and respiration is lost. Intracranial hemorrhages are treated by surgical removal of the hematoma (localized blood mass) and repair of the ruptured vessels.

Another consequence of traumatic head injury is **cerebral edema,** swelling of the brain. Anti-inflammatory drugs are routinely administered to head injury patients in an attempt to prevent cerebral edema from aggravating brain injury.

Cerebrovascular Accidents

The single most common nervous system disorder and the third leading cause of death in North America are **cerebrovascular accidents (CVAs)** (ser″ĕ-bro-vas′ku-lar), also called *strokes.* CVAs occur when blood circulation to a brain area is blocked and brain tissue dies. [Deprivation of blood supply to any tissue is called **ischemia** (is-ke′me-ah; "to hold back blood") and results in deficient oxygen and nutrient delivery to cells.] The most common cause of CVA is blockage of a cerebral artery by a blood clot. Other causes include compression of brain tissue by hemorrhage or edema and narrowing of brain vessels by atherosclerosis.

Those who survive a CVA are typically paralyzed on one side of the body *(hemiplegia).* Many exhibit sensory deficits or have difficulty in understanding or vocalizing speech. Whatever the cause, fewer than 35% of patients who survive a CVA are alive three years later. Even so, the picture is not hopeless. Some patients recover at least part of their lost faculties, because undamaged neurons sprout new branches that spread into the injured area and take over some lost functions. Physical therapy is usually started as soon as possible to prevent muscle contractures (abnormal shortening of muscles due to differences in strength between opposing muscle groups).

Not all strokes are "completed." Temporary episodes of reversible cerebral ischemia, called **transient ischemic attacks (TIAs),** are common. TIAs last from 5 to 50 minutes and are characterized by temporary numbness, paralysis, or impaired speech. While these deficits are not permanent, TIAs do constitute "red flags" that warn of impending, more serious CVAs.

CVAs are like undersea earthquakes. It's not the initial temblor that does most of the damage, it's the tsunami that floods the coast later. Similarly, the initial vascular blockage during a stroke is not usually disastrous because there are many blood vessels in the brain that can pick up the slack; it's the events that lead to killing of neurons not in the initial ischemic zone that wreak the most havoc.

Experimental evidence indicates that the main culprit is *glutamate,* an excitatory neurotransmitter also involved in learning and memory. Normally, glutamate binding to NMDA receptors opens NMDA channels that allow Ca^{2+} to enter the stimulated neuron. After brain injury, neurons totally deprived of oxygen begin to disintegrate, unleashing the cellular equivalent of "buckets" of glutamate. Under these conditions, glutamate acts as an *excitotoxin,* literally exciting surrounding cells to death. The initial events in excitotoxicity are identical to those in LTP—Ca^{2+} flows in through NMDA receptor channels (see p. 463). In excitotoxicity, however, the amount of Ca^{2+} swamps the cell's ability to cope and Ca^{2+} homeostasis breaks down. High levels of Ca^{2+} lead to cell death in two ways. First, Ca^{2+} damages mitochondria, causing them to produce the free radical superoxide, which can damage cells directly and also cause programmed cell death (apoptosis). Second, Ca^{2+} turns on the synthesis of certain proteins. Some of these promote apoptosis while others are enzymes that produce the free radical NO and other powerful inflammatory agents.

Although the NMDA receptor and the enzyme that makes NO are attractive targets for drug therapies to decrease damage around the stroke epicenter, clinical trials so far have all failed. At present, the only approved treatment for stroke is tissue plasminogen activator (tPA), which dissolves blood clots in the brain. Various mechanical devices to retrieve clots are currently undergoing clinical trials, and two other approaches are being studied. One method implants immature neurons into stroke-damaged brain regions in the hope that they will take on properties of the nearby mature neurons. Another tries to coax adult brain stem cells to replace damaged neurons. Mice with strokes can generate new tissue and recover motor function when treated with a combination of growth factors during a critical time following injury. Hopefully, this will be true for humans, too.

Degenerative Brain Disorders

Alzheimer's Disease   **Alzheimer's disease (AD)** (altz'hi-merz) is a progressive degenerative disease of the brain that ultimately results in dementia (mental deterioration). Alzheimer's patients represent nearly half of the people living in nursing homes. Between 5 and 15% of people over 65 develop this condition, and for up to half of those over 85 it is a major contributing cause in their deaths.

Its victims exhibit memory loss (particularly for recent events), shortened attention span, disorientation, and eventual language loss. Over a period of several years, formerly good-natured people may become irritable, moody, and confused. Ultimately, hallucinations occur.

Examinations of brain tissue reveal senile plaques littering the brain like shrapnel between the neurons. The plaques consist of extracellular aggregations of *beta amyloid peptide*, which has been cut from a normal membrane precursor protein (APP) by enzymes. One form of Alzheimer's disease is caused by an inherited mutation in APP, which suggests that beta amyloid may be toxic. Some researchers believe that small clusters of these protein fragments kill cells by forming holes in their plasma membranes. Unfortunately, clinical trials of vaccines to stimulate an immune response to clear away beta amyloid protein have not been successful.

Another hallmark of Alzheimer's disease is the presence of *neurofibrillary tangles* inside neurons. These involve a protein called tau, which functions like railroad ties to bind microtubule "tracks" together. In the brains of AD victims, tau abandons its microtubule-stabilizing role and grabs onto other tau molecules, forming spaghetti-like neurofibrillary tangles, which kill the neurons by disrupting their transport mechanisms.

As the brain cells die, the brain shrinks. Particularly vulnerable brain areas include the hippocampus and the basal forebrain, regions involved in thinking and memory (Figure 12.23). Loss of neurons in the basal forebrain is associated with a shortage of the neurotransmitter acetylcholine, and drugs that inhibit breakdown of acetylcholine slightly enhance cognitive function in AD patients. Interestingly, a drug that blocks NMDA receptors, memantine, also seems to improve thinking in AD victims, suggesting that glutamate excitotoxicity is also involved in this disease.

Parkinson's Disease   Typically striking people in their 50s and 60s, **Parkinson's disease** results from a degeneration of the dopamine-releasing neurons of the substantia nigra. As those neurons deteriorate, the dopamine-deprived basal nuclei they target become overactive, causing the well-known symptoms of the disease. Afflicted individuals have a persistent tremor at rest (exhibited by head nodding and a "pill-rolling" movement of the fingers), a forward-bent walking posture and shuffling gait, and a stiff facial expression, and they are slow in initiating and executing movement.

The cause of Parkinson's disease is still unknown, although recent evidence points to mitochondrial malfunction leading to the death of dopamine-releasing neurons. The drug L-dopa often helps to alleviate some symptoms; it passes through the blood-brain barrier and is then converted into dopamine. However, it is not curative, and as more and more neurons die off, L-dopa becomes ineffective. Mixing L-dopa with drugs that inhibit the breakdown of dopamine (for example, deprenyl), can prolong the effectiveness of L-dopa. In addition, deprenyl by itself, early in the disease, slows the neurological deterioration to some extent and delays the need to administer L-dopa for up to 18 months.

Deep brain stimulation via implanted electrodes shuts down abnormal brain activity and has proved helpful in alleviating tremors. This treatment (for patients who no longer respond to drug therapy) is delicate, expensive, and risky. Another possibility is to use gene therapy to insert genes into adult brain cells, causing them to secrete the inhibitory neurotransmitter GABA. GABA then inhibits the abnormal brain activity just as the electrical stimulation does. In the past, implantation of embryonic or fetal cells has shown limited success. However, the use of embryonic or fetal tissue is controversial and riddled with ethical and legal roadblocks.

Huntington's Disease   **Huntington's disease** is a fatal hereditary disorder that strikes during middle age. Mutant *huntingtin* protein accumulates in brain cells and the tissue dies, leading to massive degeneration of the basal nuclei and later of the cerebral cortex. Its initial symptoms in many are wild, jerky, almost continuous "flapping" movements called *chorea* (Greek for "dance"). Although the movements appear to be voluntary they are not. Late in the disease, marked mental deterioration occurs. Huntington's disease is progressive and usually fatal within 15 years of onset of symptoms.

The hyperkinetic manifestations of Huntington's disease are essentially the opposite of those of Parkinson's disease (overstimulation rather than inhibition of the motor drive), and Huntington's is usually treated with drugs that block, rather than enhance, dopamine's effects. As with Parkinson's disease, fetal tissue implants may provide promise for its treatment in the future.

The Spinal Cord

Embryonic Development

The spinal cord develops from the caudal portion of the embryonic neural tube (see Figure 12.2 on p. 432). By the sixth week, each side of the developing cord has two recognizable clusters of neuroblasts that have migrated outward from the original neural tube: a dorsal **alar plate** (a'lar) and a ventral **basal plate** (Figure 12.28).

Alar plate neuroblasts become interneurons. The basal plate neuroblasts develop into motor neurons and sprout axons that grow out to the effector organs. Axons that emerge from alar plate cells (and some basal plate cells) form the white matter of the cord by growing along the length of the cord. As development progresses, these plates expand dorsally and ventrally to produce the H-shaped central mass of gray matter of the adult spinal cord. Neural crest cells that come to lie alongside the cord form the *dorsal root ganglia* containing sensory neuron cell bodies; these send their axons into the dorsal aspect of the cord.

Gross Anatomy and Protection

The spinal cord, enclosed in the vertebral column, extends from the foramen magnum of the skull to the level of the first or second lumbar vertebra, just inferior to the ribs (Figure 12.29). About 42 cm (17 inches) long and 1.8 cm (3/4 of an inch) thick, the glistening-white **spinal cord** provides a two-way conduction pathway to and from the brain. It is a major reflex center: Spinal reflexes are initiated and completed at the spinal cord level. We discuss reflex functions and motor activity of the cord in subsequent chapters. In this section we focus on the

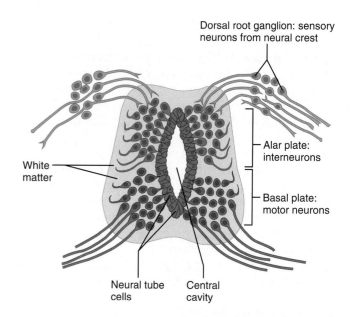

FIGURE 12.28 Structure of the embryonic spinal cord. At six weeks of development, aggregations of gray matter called the alar plates (future interneurons) and basal plates (future motor neurons) have formed, and dorsal root ganglia (future sensory neurons) have arisen from neural crest cells.

anatomy of the cord and on the location and naming of its ascending and descending tracts.

Like the brain, the spinal cord is protected by bone, meninges, and cerebrospinal fluid. The single-layered **spinal dura mater** (Figure 12.26) is not attached to the bony walls of the vertebral column. Between the bony vertebrae and the dural sheath is an **epidural space** filled with a soft padding of fat and a network of veins (see Figure 12.31a). Cerebrospinal fluid fills the subarachnoid space between the *arachnoid* and *pia mater* meninges. Inferiorly, the dural and arachnoid membranes extend to the level of S_2, well beyond the end of the spinal cord. The spinal cord typically ends between L_1 and L_2 (Figure 12.29a). Thus, the subarachnoid space within the meningeal sac inferior to that point provides a nearly ideal spot for removing cerebrospinal fluid for testing, a procedure called a **lumbar puncture** or **tap** (Figure 12.30). Because the spinal cord is absent there and the delicate nerve roots drift away from the point of needle insertion, there is little or no danger of damaging the cord (or spinal roots) beyond L_3.

Inferiorly, the spinal cord terminates in a tapering cone-shaped structure called the **conus medullaris** (ko'nus me"dul-ar'is). The **filum terminale** (fi'lum ter"mĭ-nah'le; "terminal filament"), a fibrous extension of the conus covered by pia mater, extends inferiorly from the conus medullaris to the posterior surface of the coccyx, where it anchors the spinal cord in place so it is not jostled by body movements (Figure 12.29d). Furthermore, the spinal cord is

Q *What is the explanation for the cervical and lumbar enlargements of the cord?*

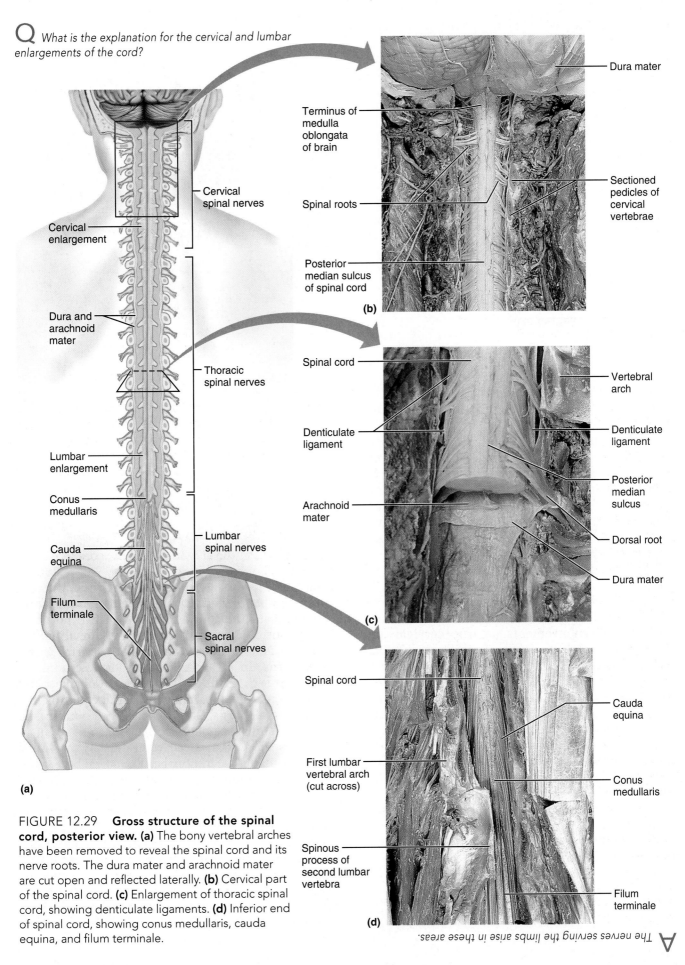

Dura mater

Terminus of medulla oblongata of brain

Spinal roots

Posterior median sulcus of spinal cord

Sectioned pedicles of cervical vertebrae

(b)

Cervical spinal nerves

Cervical enlargement

Dura and arachnoid mater

Thoracic spinal nerves

Lumbar enlargement

Conus medullaris

Cauda equina

Filum terminale

Lumbar spinal nerves

Sacral spinal nerves

Spinal cord

Denticulate ligament

Arachnoid mater

Vertebral arch

Denticulate ligament

Posterior median sulcus

Dorsal root

Dura mater

(c)

Spinal cord

First lumbar vertebral arch (cut across)

Spinous process of second lumbar vertebra

Cauda equina

Conus medullaris

Filum terminale

(d)

(a)

FIGURE 12.29   **Gross structure of the spinal cord, posterior view. (a)** The bony vertebral arches have been removed to reveal the spinal cord and its nerve roots. The dura mater and arachnoid mater are cut open and reflected laterally. **(b)** Cervical part of the spinal cord. **(c)** Enlargement of thoracic spinal cord, showing denticulate ligaments. **(d)** Inferior end of spinal cord, showing conus medullaris, cauda equina, and filum terminale.

12

A *The nerves serving the limbs arise in these areas.*

Q *What information would you get by performing a lumbar tap?*

FIGURE 12.30 **Diagrammatic view of a lumbar tap.**

secured to the tough dura mater meninx throughout its length by saw-toothed shelves of pia mater called **denticulate ligaments** (den-tik'u-lāt; "toothed") (Figure 12.29c).

In humans, 31 pairs of *spinal nerves* attach to the cord by paired roots. Each nerve exits from the vertebral column by passing superior to its corresponding vertebra via the intervertebral foramina, and travels to the body region it serves. While each nerve pair defines a segment of the cord, the spinal cord is, in fact, continuous throughout its length and its internal structure changes gradually.

The spinal cord is about the width of a thumb for most of its length, but it has obvious enlargements in the cervical and lumbosacral regions, where the nerves serving the upper and lower limbs arise. These enlargements are the **cervical** and **lumbar enlargements,** respectively (Figure 12.29a). Because the cord does not reach the end of the vertebral column, the lumbar and sacral spinal nerve roots angle sharply downward and travel inferiorly through the vertebral canal for some distance before reaching their intervertebral foramina. The collection of nerve roots at the inferior end of the vertebral canal is named the **cauda equina** (kaw'da e-kwi'nuh) because of its resemblance to a horse's tail. This strange arrangement reflects the fact that during fetal development, the vertebral column grows faster than the spinal cord, forcing the lower spinal nerve roots to "chase" their exit points inferiorly through the vertebral canal.

A *Obtaining a sample of CSF allows you to check for CNS infection, inflammation, or the presence of abnormal cells.*

Cross-Sectional Anatomy

The spinal cord is somewhat flattened from front to back and two grooves mark its surface: the **anterior median fissure** and the shallower **posterior median sulcus** (see Figure 12.31b). These grooves run the length of the cord and partially divide it into right and left halves. The gray matter of the cord is located in its core, the white matter outside.

Gray Matter and Spinal Roots

In cross section the gray matter of the cord looks like the letter H or like a butterfly (Figure 12.31b). It consists of mirror-image lateral gray masses connected by a cross-bar of gray matter, the **gray commissure,** that encloses the central canal. The two posterior projections of the gray matter are the **dorsal (posterior) horns;** the anterior pair are the **ventral (anterior) horns.** In 3-D, these horns form columns of gray matter that run the entire length of the spinal cord. An additional pair of gray matter columns, the small **lateral horns,** is present in the thoracic and superior lumbar segments of the cord.

All neurons whose cell bodies are in the spinal cord gray matter are multipolar. The dorsal horns consist entirely of interneurons. The ventral horns have some interneurons but mainly house cell bodies of somatic motor neurons. These send their axons out via the **ventral roots** of the spinal cord (Figure 12.31b) to the skeletal muscles (their effector organs). The amount of ventral gray matter present at a given level of the spinal cord reflects the amount of skeletal muscle innervated at that level. Thus, the ventral horns are largest in the limb-innervating cervical and lumbar regions of the cord and are responsible for the cord enlargements seen in those regions.

Q *Which spaces in this figure are filled with CSF?*

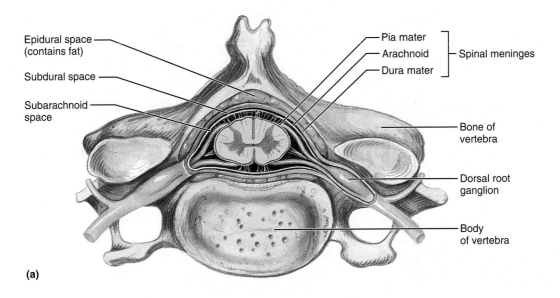

Epidural space (contains fat)

Subdural space

Subarachnoid space

Pia mater

Arachnoid

Dura mater

Spinal meninges

Bone of vertebra

Dorsal root ganglion

Body of vertebra

(a)

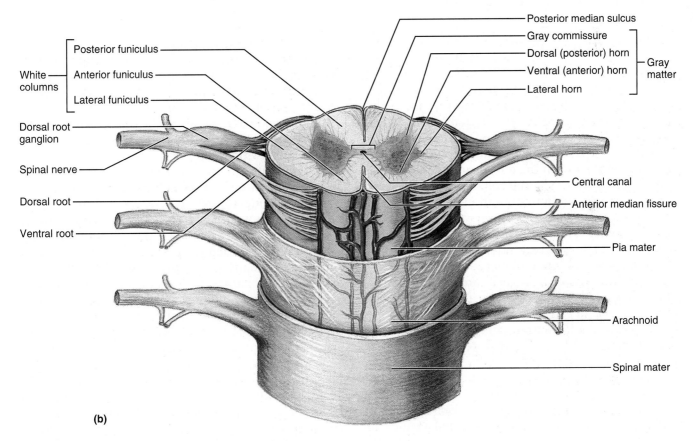

Posterior median sulcus

Gray commissure

Dorsal (posterior) horn

Ventral (anterior) horn

Lateral horn

Gray matter

White columns

Posterior funiculus

Anterior funiculus

Lateral funiculus

Dorsal root ganglion

Spinal nerve

Dorsal root

Ventral root

Central canal

Anterior median fissure

Pia mater

Arachnoid

Spinal mater

(b)

FIGURE 12.31   **Anatomy of the spinal cord. (a)** Cross section through the spinal cord illustrating its relationship to surrounding vertebral column. **(b)** Three-dimensional view of the adult spinal cord and its meningeal coverings.

A *Subarachnoid space and central canal of the spinal cord.*

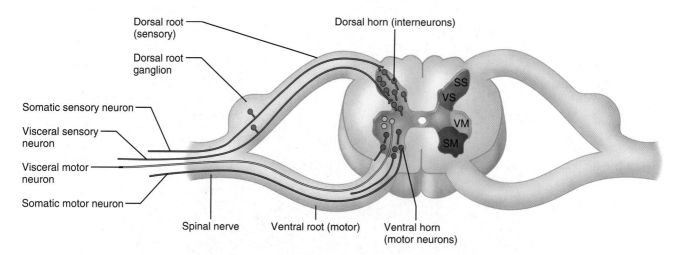

FIGURE 12.32 **Organization of the gray matter of the spinal cord.** The gray matter of the spinal cord is divided into a sensory half dorsally and a motor half ventrally. SS: interneurons receiving input from somatic sensory neurons. VS: interneurons receiving input from visceral sensory neurons. VM: visceral motor (autonomic) neurons. SM: somatic motor neurons. Note that the dorsal and ventral roots are part of the PNS, not of the spinal cord.

The lateral horn neurons are autonomic (sympathetic division) motor neurons that serve visceral organs. Their axons leave the cord via the ventral root along with those of the somatic motor neurons. Because the ventral roots contain both somatic and autonomic efferents, they serve both motor divisions of the peripheral nervous system (Figure 12.32).

Afferent fibers carrying impulses from peripheral sensory receptors form the **dorsal roots** of the spinal cord (Figure 12.31). The cell bodies of the associated sensory neurons are found in an enlarged region of the dorsal root called the **dorsal root ganglion** or **spinal ganglion.** After entering the cord, the axons of these neurons may take a number of routes. Some enter the posterior white matter of the cord directly and travel to synapse at higher cord or brain levels. Others synapse with interneurons in the dorsal horns of the spinal cord gray matter at their entry level.

The dorsal and ventral roots are very short and fuse laterally to form the **spinal nerves.** The spinal nerves, which are part of the peripheral nervous system, are considered further in Chapter 13.

The spinal gray matter can be divided further according to its neurons' relative involvement in the innervation of the somatic and visceral regions of the body. The following four zones are evident within this gray matter (Figure 12.32): **somatic sensory (SS), visceral** (autonomic) **sensory (VS), visceral motor (VM), somatic motor (SM).**

White Matter

The white matter of the spinal cord is composed of myelinated and unmyelinated nerve fibers that allow communication between different parts of the spinal cord and between the cord and brain. These fibers run in three directions: (1) *ascending*—up to higher centers (sensory inputs), (2) *descending*—down to the cord from the brain or within the cord to lower levels (motor outputs), and (3) *transversely*—across from one side of the cord to the other (commissural fibers). Ascending and descending tracts make up most of the white matter.

The white matter on each side of the cord is divided into three **white columns,** or **funiculi** (fu-nik'u-li; "long ropes"), named according to their position as **posterior, lateral,** and **anterior funiculi** (Figure 12.31b). Each funiculus contains several fiber tracts, and each tract is made up of axons with similar destinations and functions. With a few exceptions, the names of the spinal tracts reveal both their origin and destination. The principal ascending and descending tracts of the spinal cord are illustrated schematically in the cross-sectional view of the spinal cord in Figure 12.33.

All major spinal tracts are *part of multineuron pathways* that connect the brain to the body periphery. These great ascending and descending pathways contain not only spinal cord neurons but also parts of peripheral neurons and neurons in the brain. Before we get specific about the individual tracts, we will make some generalizations about them and the pathways to which they contribute:

1. Most pathways cross from one side of the CNS to the other (decussate) at some point along their journey.

2. Most consist of a chain of two or three neurons that contribute to successive tracts of the pathway.

Q *What is a tract?*

Ascending tracts

Dorsal white column
- Fasciculus gracilis
- Fasciculus cuneatus

Posterior spinocerebellar tract

Anterior spinocerebellar tract

Lateral spinothalamic tract

Anterior spinothalamic tract

Anterior white commissure

Descending tracts

Lateral reticulospinal tract

Lateral corticospinal tract

Rubrospinal tract

Medial reticulospinal tract

Anterior corticospinal tract

Vestibulospinal tract

Tectospinal tract

Key:
- ■ Descending tracts
- ■ Ascending tracts

FIGURE 12.33 **Major ascending (sensory) and descending (motor) tracts of the spinal cord, cross-sectional view.**

3. Most exhibit *somatotopy,* a precise spatial relationship among the tract fibers that reflects the orderly mapping of the body. For example, in an ascending sensory tract, somatotopy refers to the fact that fibers transmitting inputs from sensory receptors in the superior parts of the body lie lateral to those conveying sensory information from inferior body regions.

4. All pathways and tracts are paired (right and left) with a member of the pair present on each side of the spinal cord or brain.

Ascending Pathways to the Brain

Neuronal Composition   The ascending pathways conduct sensory impulses upward, typically through chains of three successive neurons (first-, second-, and third-order neurons) to various areas of the brain (Figure 12.34). (Note that both second- and third-order neurons are interneurons.)

- **First-order neurons,** whose cell bodies reside in a ganglion (dorsal root or cranial), conduct impulses from the cutaneous receptors of the skin and from proprioceptors to the spinal cord or brain stem, where they synapse with second-order neurons. Impulses from the facial area are transmitted by cranial

nerves; spinal nerves conduct somatic sensory impulses from the rest of the body to the CNS.

- **Second-order neurons,** whose cell bodies reside in the dorsal horn of the spinal cord or in medullary nuclei, transmit impulses to the thalamus or to the cerebellum where they synapse.

- **Third-order neurons,** whose cell bodies reside in the thalamus, conduct impulses to the somatosensory cortex of the cerebrum. (There are no third-order neurons in the cerebellum.)

The Main Ascending Pathways   In general, somatosensory information is conveyed along three main pathways on each side of the spinal cord. Two of these pathways (the *nonspecific* and *specific ascending pathways*) transmit impulses to the sensory cortex. Collectively the inputs of these sister tracts provide *discriminative touch* and *conscious proprioception.* Both pathways decussate—the first in the spinal cord and the second in the medulla.

The third pathway, consisting of the *spinocerebellar tracts,* tracks to the cerebellum, and hence does not contribute to sensory perception. Let's examine these pathways more closely.

1. Nonspecific ascending pathways. The evolutionarily older **nonspecific ascending pathways** receive inputs from many different types of sensory receptors and make multiple synapses in the brain stem. These pathways, also called the **anterolateral pathways** (because they are located in the anterior

A *A collection of axons in the CNS, having the same origin and termination.*

12

12

Somatosensory cortex

Axons of third-order neurons

Thalamus

Cerebrum

Midbrain

Cerebellum

Pons

Posterior spinocerebellar tract (axons of second-order neurons)

Medial lemniscal tract (axons of second-order neurons)

Nucleus gracilis

Nucleus cuneatus

Medulla oblongata

Fasciculus cuneatus (axon of first-order sensory neuron)

Joint stretch receptor (proprioceptor)

Cervical spinal cord

Fasciculus gracilis (axon of first-order sensory neuron)

Lumbar spinal cord

Axon of first-order neuron

Muscle spindle (proprioceptor)

Touch receptor

Spinocerebellar pathway

(a)

Medial lemniscal pathway

Lateral spinothalamic tract (axons of second-order neurons)

Pain receptors

Axons of first-order neurons

Temperature receptors

Spinothalamic pathway

(b)

FIGURE 12.34 **Pathways of selected ascending spinal cord tracts.** Cross sections up to the cerebrum, which is shown in frontal section. **(a)** Right: Specific pathways for discriminative touch and conscious proprioception in the fasciculus gracilis and fasciculus cuneatus tracts and their continuation, the medial lemniscal tracts. Left: Posterior spinocerebellar tract (extends only to cerebellum). **(b)** Nonspecific pathways for pain, temperature, and crude touch in the lateral spinothalamic tract of the anterolateral pathways. The entire ascending pathway is shown in each case.

TABLE 12.2	Major Ascending (Sensory) Pathways and Spinal Cord Tracts			
SPINAL CORD TRACT	**LOCATION (FUNICULUS)**	**ORIGIN**	**TERMINATION**	**FUNCTION**
SPECIFIC ASCENDING (LEMNISCAL) PATHWAYS				
Fasciculus cuneatus and fasciculus gracilis (dorsal white column)	Posterior	Central axons of sensory (first-order) neurons enter dorsal root of the spinal cord and branch; branches enter dorsal white column on same side without synapsing	By synapse with second-order neurons in nucleus cuneatus and nucleus gracilis in medulla; fibers of medullary neurons cross over and ascend in medial lemniscal tracts to thalamus, where they synapse with third-order neurons; thalamic neurons then transmit impulses to somato-sensory cortex	Both tracts transmit sensory impulses from general sensory receptors of skin and proprioceptors, which are interpreted as discriminative touch, pressure, and "body sense" (limb and joint position) in opposite somatosensory cortex. Cuneatus transmits afferent impulses from upper limbs, upper trunk, and neck; it is not present in spinal cord below level of T_6. Gracilis carries impulses from lower limbs and inferior body trunk
NONSPECIFIC ASCENDING (ANTEROLATERAL) PATHWAYS				
Lateral spinothalamic	Lateral	Interneurons (second-order neurons) of dorsal horn; fibers cross to opposite side before ascending	By synapse with third-order neurons in thalamus; impulses then conveyed to somatosensory cortex by thalamic neurons	Transmits impulses concerned with pain and temperature to opposite side of brain; eventually inter-preted in somatosensory cortex
Anterior spinothalamic	Anterior	Interneurons (second-order neurons) in dorsal horns; fibers cross to opposite side before ascending	By synapse with third-order neurons in thalamus; impulses eventually conveyed to somatosensory cortex by thalamic neurons	Transmits impulses concerned with crude touch and pressure to opposite side of brain for interpretation by somatosensory cortex
SPINOCEREBELLAR PATHWAYS				
Posterior spinocerebellar*	Lateral (posterior part)	Interneurons (second-order neurons) in dorsal horn on same side of cord; fibers ascend without crossing	By synapse in cerebellum	Transmits impulses from trunk and lower limb proprioceptors on one side of body to same side of cerebellum; subconscious proprioception
Anterior spinocerebellar*	Lateral (anterior part)	Interneurons (second-order neurons) of dorsal horn; contains crossed fibers that cross back to the opposite side in the pons	By synapse in cerebellum	Transmits impulses from the trunk and lower limb on the same side of body to cerebellum; subconscious proprioception

*The posterior and anterior spinocerebellar tracts carry information from the lower limbs and trunk only. The corresponding tracts for the upper limb and neck (rostral spinocerebellar and others) are beyond the scope of this book.

and lateral white columns of the spinal cord), are largely formed by the **lateral** and **anterior spinotha-lamic tracts** (see Figure 12.34b and Table 12.2). Crossover of fibers occurs in the spinal cord.

Most of the fibers in these pathways transmit pain, temperature, and coarse touch impulses, sensations that we are aware of but have difficulty localizing precisely on the body surface.

12

2. Specific ascending pathways. Also called the **medial lemniscal system** (lem-nis'kul; *lemnisc* = a ribbon), the **specific ascending pathways** mediate precise, straight-through transmission of inputs from a single type (or a few related types) of sensory receptor that *can* be localized precisely on the body surface, such as discriminative touch and vibrations. These pathways are formed by the paired tracts of the **dorsal white column—fasciculus cuneatus** and **fasciculus gracilis—**of the spinal cord and the **medial lemniscal tracts.** The latter arise in the medulla and terminate in the *ventral posterior nuclei* of the thalamus (see Figure 12.34a and Table 12.2). From the thalamus, impulses are forwarded to specific areas of the somatosensory cortex.

3. Spinocerebellar tracts. The last pair of ascending pathways, the **anterior** and **posterior spinocerebellar tracts,** convey information about muscle or tendon stretch to the cerebellum, which uses this information to coordinate skeletal muscle activity. As noted earlier, these pathways do not contribute to conscious sensation. The fibers of the spinocerebellar pathways either do not decussate or else cross over twice (thus "undoing" the decussation).

Descending Pathways and Tracts

The descending tracts that deliver efferent impulses from the brain to the spinal cord are divided into two groups: (1) the *direct pathways* equivalent to the pyramidal tracts and (2) the *indirect pathways,* essentially all others. Motor pathways involve two neurons, referred to as the upper and lower motor neurons. The pyramidal cells of the motor cortex, as well as the neurons in subcortical motor nuclei that give rise to other descending motor pathways, are called *upper motor neurons.* The ventral horn motor neurons, which actually innervate the skeletal muscles (their effectors), are called *lower motor neurons.* These tracts are briefly overviewed here; more information is provided in Table 12.3.

The Direct (Pyramidal) System   The direct pathways originate mainly with the pyramidal neurons located in the precentral gyri. These neurons send impulses through the brain stem via the large **pyramidal (corticospinal) tracts** (Figure 12.35a). The direct pathways are so called because their axons descend without synapsing from the pyramidal neurons to the spinal cord. There they synapse either with interneurons or with ventral horn motor neurons. Stimulation of the ventral horn neurons activates the skeletal muscles with which they are associated. The direct pathway primarily regulates fast and fine (or skilled) movements such as doing needlework and writing.

The Indirect (Extrapyramidal) System   The indirect system includes brain stem motor nuclei and *all motor pathways except* the pyramidal pathways. These tracts were formerly lumped together as the **extrapyramidal system** because their nuclei of origin were presumed to be independent of ("extra to") the pyramidal tracts. This term is still widely used clinically; however, pyramidal tract neurons are now known to project to and influence the activity of most "extrapyramidal" nuclei, so modern anatomists prefer to use the term **indirect,** or **multineuronal, pathways,** or even just the names of the individual motor pathways.

These motor pathways are complex and multisynaptic. They are most involved in regulating (1) the axial muscles that maintain balance and posture, (2) the muscles controlling coarse limb movements, and (3) head, neck, and eye movements that follow objects in the visual field. Many of the activities controlled by subcortical motor nuclei are heavily dependent on reflex activity. One of these tracts, the rubrospinal tract, is illustrated in Figure 12.35b.

Overall, the **reticulospinal** and **vestibulospinal tracts** (see Table 12.3) maintain balance by varying the tone of postural muscles. The **rubrospinal tracts** control flexor muscles, whereas the **tectospinal tracts** and the *superior colliculi* mediate head movements in response to visual stimuli.

Spinal Cord Trauma and Disorders

Spinal Cord Trauma

The spinal cord is elastic, stretching with every turn of the head or bend of the trunk, but it is exquisitely sensitive to direct pressure. Any localized damage to the spinal cord or its roots leads to some functional loss, either **paralysis** (loss of motor function) or sensory loss. Severe damage to ventral root or ventral horn cells results in a **flaccid paralysis** (flak'sid) of the skeletal muscles served. Nerve impulses do not reach these muscles, which consequently cannot move either voluntarily or involuntarily. Without stimulation, the muscles atrophy. When only the upper motor neurons of the primary motor cortex are damaged, **spastic paralysis** occurs. In this case, the spinal motor neurons remain intact and the muscles continue to be stimulated irregularly by spinal reflex activity. Thus, the muscles remain healthy longer, but their movements are no longer subject to voluntary control. In many such cases, the muscles become permanently shortened.

Transection (cross sectioning) of the spinal cord at any level results in total motor and sensory loss in body regions inferior to the site of damage. If the transection occurs between T_1 and L_1, both lower limbs are affected, resulting in **paraplegia**

TABLE 12.3	Major Descending (Motor) Pathways and Spinal Cord Tracts			
SPINAL CORD TRACT	**LOCATION (FUNICULUS)**	**ORIGIN**	**TERMINATION**	**FUNCTION**
DIRECT (PYRAMIDAL)				
Lateral corticospinal	Lateral	Pyramidal neurons of motor cortex of the cerebrum; decussate in pyramids of medulla	By synapse directly with ventral horn motor neurons and with ventral horn interneurons that influence motor neurons	Transmits motor impulses from cerebrum to spinal cord motor neurons (which activate skeletal muscles on opposite side of body); voluntary motor tract
Anterior corticospinal	Anterior	Pyramidal neurons of motor cortex; fibers cross over at the spinal cord level	Ventral horn (as above)	Same as lateral corticospinal tract
INDIRECT (EXTRAPYRAMIDAL) PATHWAYS				
Tectospinal	Anterior	Superior colliculus of midbrain of brain stem (fibers cross to opposite side of cord)	By synapse with ventral horn interneurons that influence motor neurons	Transmits motor impulses from midbrain that are important for coordinated movement of head and eyes toward visual targets
Vestibulospinal	Anterior	Vestibular nuclei in medulla of brain stem (fibers descend without crossing)	By synapse, directly with ventral horn motor neurons and with ventral horn interneurons that influence motor neurons	Transmits motor impulses that maintain muscle tone and activate ipsilateral limb and trunk extensor muscles and muscles that move head; in this way helps maintain balance during standing and moving
Rubrospinal	Lateral	Red nucleus of midbrain of brain stem (fibers cross to opposite side just inferior to the red nucleus)	Ventral horn (as above)	In experimental animals, transmits motor impulses concerned with muscle tone of distal limb muscles (mostly flexors) on opposite side of body; in humans, functions largely assumed by corticospinal tracts except for some upper limb movement
Reticulospinal (anterior, medial, and lateral)	Anterior and lateral	Reticular formation of brain stem (medial nuclear group of pons and medulla); both crossed and uncrossed fibers	Ventral horn (as above)	Transmits impulses concerned with muscle tone and many visceral motor functions; may control most unskilled movements

(par"ah-ple′je-ah; *para* = beside, *plegia* = a blow). If the injury occurs in the cervical region, all four limbs are affected and the result is **quadriplegia.** *Hemiplegia,* paralysis of one side of the body, usually reflects brain injury rather than spinal cord injury.

Anyone with traumatic spinal cord injury must be watched for symptoms of **spinal shock,** a transient period of functional loss that follows the injury. Spinal shock results in immediate depression of all reflex activity caudal to the lesion site. Bowel and bladder reflexes stop, blood pressure falls, and all muscles (somatic and visceral alike) below the injury are paralyzed and insensitive. Neural function usually returns within a few hours following injury. If function does not resume within 48 hours, paralysis is permanent in most cases.

Upper motor neurons

Primary motor area of cerebral cortex

Internal capsule

Cerebrum

Red nucleus

Cerebral peduncle

Midbrain

Cerebellum

Pons

Rubrospinal tract

Medulla oblongata

Pyramids

Decussation of pyramid

Anterior corticospinal tract

Lateral corticospinal tract

Cervical spinal cord

Skeletal muscle

Lumbar spinal cord

Lower motor neurons

(a) Pyramidal (lateral and anterior corticospinal) tracts

(b) Rubrospinal tract (an extrapyramidal tract)

FIGURE 12.35 **Pathways of selected descending spinal cord tracts.** Cross sections up to the cerebrum, which is shown in frontal section. **(a)** Direct pathways, that is, the pyramidal tracts (lateral and anterior corticospinal tracts), carrying motor impulses to skeletal muscles. **(b)** The rubrospinal tract, one of the indirect or extrapyramidal tracts, helps regulate tone of muscles on opposite side of body.

Poliomyelitis

Poliomyelitis (po"le-o-mi"ĕ-li'tis; *polio* = gray matter; *myelitis* = inflammation of the spinal cord) results from destruction of ventral horn motor neurons by the poliovirus. Early symptoms include fever, headache, muscle pain and weakness, and loss of certain somatic reflexes. Later, paralysis develops and the muscles served atrophy. The victim may die from paralysis of the respiratory muscles or from cardiac arrest if neurons in the medulla oblongata are destroyed. In most cases, the poliovirus enters the body in feces-contaminated water (such as might occur in a public swimming pool), and the incidence of the disease has traditionally been highest in children and during the summer months. Fortunately, vaccines have nearly eliminated this disease and a global effort is ongoing to eradicate it completely from the world.

However, many of the "recovered" survivors of the great polio epidemic of the late 1940s and 1950s have begun to experience extreme lethargy, sharp burning pains in their muscles, and progressive muscle weakness and atrophy. Initially dismissed as the flu or psychosomatic illness, these disturbing symptoms are now referred to as **postpolio syndrome.** The cause of postpolio syndrome is not known, but a likely explanation is that its victims, like the rest of us, continue to lose neurons throughout life. While a healthy nervous system can recruit nearby neurons to compensate for the losses, polio survivors have already drawn on that "pool" and have few neurons left to take over. Ironically, those who worked hardest to overcome their disease are its newest victims.

Amyotrophic Lateral Sclerosis

Amyotrophic lateral sclerosis (ALS) (ah-mi"o-trof'ik), also called Lou Gehrig's disease, is a devastating neuromuscular condition that involves progressive destruction of ventral horn motor neurons and fibers of the pyramidal tract. As the disease progresses, the sufferer loses the ability to speak, swallow, and breathe. Death typically occurs within five years. For 90% of cases, the cause of ALS is unknown, although ALS patients appear to have excess extracellular glutamate. Researchers now believe that motor neurons are killed as a result of glutamate excitotoxicity, attack by the immune system, or possibly a combination of the two. Riluzole, the only advance in pharmacological treatment of ALS in 50 years, prolongs life, apparently by inhibiting glutamate release.

Diagnostic Procedures for Assessing CNS Dysfunction

Anyone who has had a routine physical examination is familiar with the reflex tests done to assess neural function. A tap with a reflex hammer stretches your quadriceps tendon and your anterior thigh muscles contract, which results in the knee-jerk response. This response shows that the spinal cord and upper brain centers are functioning normally. Abnormal reflex test responses may indicate such serious disorders as intracranial hemorrhage, multiple sclerosis, or hydrocephalus and suggest that more sophisticated neurological tests are needed to identify the problem.

New imaging techniques have revolutionized the diagnosis of brain lesions (see *A Closer Look*, pp. 20–21). Together the various *CT* and *MRI scanning techniques* allow most tumors, intracranial lesions, multiple sclerosis plaques, and areas of dead brain tissue (infarcts) to be identified quickly. PET scans can localize brain lesions that generate seizures (epileptic tissue) and diagnose Alzheimer's disease.

Take, for example, a patient arriving in emergency with a stroke. A race against time to save the affected area of the patient's brain begins. The first step is to determine if the stroke is due to a clot or a bleed by imaging the brain, most often with CT. If the stroke is due to a clot, then the clot-busting drug tPA can be used, but only within the first hours. tPA is usually given intravenously, but a longer time window can be obtained if tPA is applied directly to the clot using a catheter guided into position. In order to visualize the location of the catheter with respect to the clot, dye is injected to make arteries stand out in an X ray, a procedure called *cerebral angiography*.

Cerebral angiography is also used for patients who have had a warning stroke or TIA. The carotid arteries of the neck feed most of the cerebral vessels and often become narrowed with age, which can lead to strokes. Cheaper and less invasive than angiography, ultrasound can be used to quickly examine the carotid arteries and even measure the flow of blood through them.

Developmental Aspects of the Central Nervous System

Induced by several organizer centers and established during the first month of development, the brain and spinal cord continue to grow and mature throughout the prenatal period. During development, gender-specific areas appear in both the brain and the spinal cord. For example, certain hypothalamic nuclei concerned with regulating typical male sexual behavior and clusters of neurons in the spinal cord that serve the external genitals are much larger in males. Females have a larger corpus callosum, and gender differences are seen in the language and auditory area of the cerebral cortex. The key to this CNS gender-specific development is whether or not testosterone is being secreted by the fetus. If it is, the male pattern develops.

12

A CLOSER LOOK

How Now Mad Cow

Sarah, a 19-year-old from Carlisle, U.K., was first in her high school graduating class of 1996. She loved the university, but during her second term she began having problems. During the Easter break, her parents were distressed by her slovenly appearance and by the amount of time she spent in her room crying. She complained of being persecuted, had trouble remembering things, and lashed out angrily at her younger brother. Her doctor diagnosed depression and prescribed an antidepressant. Sarah did not return to the university and over the next several months, she became increasingly withdrawn. She grew uncharacteristically aggressive, pushing and swearing at her parents, and was admitted to the psychiatric ward of the district hospital. When she developed difficulty in walking, the medical staff attributed it to "acting out" or a side effect of the various psychiatric medications that had been tried. Confined to a wheelchair, she had lost bowel and bladder control and could no longer speak or feed herself. Her parents feared a brain tumor and insisted on a neurological consultation. Over the next months, many tests were done while her condition steadily deteriorated. Finally, spinal fluid was obtained and abnormal proteins, called **prion proteins** (prē′on), were found. Sarah had **variant Creutzfeldt-Jakob disease (vCJD).** She died shortly thereafter.

On autopsy, Sarah's brain was found to be riddled with sponge-like holes (see photomicrograph), characteristic of a group of diseases called **transmissible spongiform encephalopathies**

(TSEs). TSEs include bovine spongiform encephalopathy (BSE, mad cow disease), scrapie in sheep, and a number of conditions in humans, most notably kuru. Kuru ("to tremble with fear") was a mysterious disease that threatened the survival of the Fore people in Papua New Guinea in the 1960s.

Kuru was transmitted from person to person primarily by the ritual cannibalistic practice of eating the brains of affected relatives. Similarly, vCJD seems to be acquired by eating beef contaminated with neural tissue from "mad" cows. What factor is transmitted to cause this disease? The most likely candidates were thought to be viruses or bacteria, but these were ruled out by treating brain extracts with agents that destroy DNA and RNA. Stanley Prusiner (Nobel Prize, 1997) proposed that the infectious factor is in fact a protein, for which he coined the name "prion" (**pr**oteinaceous **in**fectious particle). The idea that a protein, all by itself, could cause an infection was at first viewed with great skepticism. How could a protein possibly cause infection?

Prions are unusual proteins—they are almost indestructible. Cooking, digestion with protein-hydrolyzing enzymes (proteases), even autoclaving, does not destroy them; formaldehyde just makes them more stable. In fact, not even burning to ash at 600°C or burying in the ground for up to three years completely destroys them. Infectious prions are extremely stable, which explains why cooking meat did not protect victims of vCJD and kuru.

Unlike viruses, which take over the cell's protein-making machinery to make more viruses, prions can't program our cells to make new protein. So how do they wreak such havoc in our brains? Prions are, in fact, abnormally folded versions of proteins that are normally found throughout the animal kingdom, and even in yeasts. The function of the normally folded protein, abundant in brain synapses, is still unknown. We do know that it is a glycoprotein attached to the outside of plasma membranes and that it binds copper, suggesting that it plays a role in copper metabolism. To find out what prion protein does, researchers have genetically engineered a strain of mice without it. These mice survive, but some reports show subtle abnormalities in synaptic function and circadian rhythm. They are also completely immune to infection by infectious prions.

Although the amino acid sequence of the normally folded protein and the infectious prion are the same, the molecules have very different shapes. The prion is thought to act as a template that catalyzes a shape conversion in the normal protein, resulting in a shape with many more beta sheets than alpha helices (see p. 50). Once a normal protein has taken on the abnormal shape, it can convert many more of the normal proteins into the abnormal prion shape.

Not all prions are identical. Differences in amino acid sequences between species can make it difficult for prions infecting one species to successfully infect another species. In fact, the prion that causes scrapie in sheep has never been transmitted to humans

Maternal exposure to radiation, various drugs (alcohol, opiates, and others), and infections can harm a developing infant's nervous system, particularly during the initial formative stages. For example, rubella (German measles) often leads to deafness and other types of CNS damage in the newborn. Smoking decreases the amount of oxygen in the blood, and lack of oxygen for even a few minutes causes death of neurons. Hence, a smoking mother may be sentencing her infant to some degree of brain damage.

◤ HOMEOSTATIC IMBALANCE

In difficult deliveries, a temporary lack of oxygen may lead to **cerebral palsy,** but any of the factors listed above may also be a cause. Cerebral palsy is a neuromuscular disability in which the voluntary muscles are poorly controlled or paralyzed as a result of brain damage. In addition to spasticity, speech difficulties, and other motor impairments, about half of cerebral palsy victims have seizures, half are mentally retarded, even though it has been around for at least 200 years. Within a species, different strains of prions cause different clinical manifestations. A strain is determined by exactly how the protein is misfolded and how many sugars it has attached to it. In humans, these differences between strains gives rise to a number of distinct diseases: Creutzfeldt-Jakob disease (CJD), vCJD, kuru, Gerstmann-Sträussler-Scheinker disease (GSS), and fatal familial insomnia (FFI).

CJD and other TSEs are unique in that they can be acquired in three different ways: spontaneously (*sporadic* CJD), by inheritance (*familial* CJD), or by infection. The sporadic form of this disease occurs in people with no family history of the illness and no exposure to infected meat. Occurring in about one per million people per year, *sporadic* CJD is thought to arise from a spontaneous conversion of prion protein from the normal to the infective shape, which then alters the shape of its neighbors, and so on. CJD can also be inherited. This *familial* form of CJD arises from mutations in the gene which codes for the prion protein, making it more susceptible to misfolding. Tissue from a person with either one of these forms of CJD can *infect* another person. Infection via exposure to human tissue has occurred via corneal transplants, dural meningeal patches, contaminated surgical instruments, and of course, by eating as in kuru.

Some people appear to be more prone to acquiring the infective form of CJD than others. Like all proteins, prion protein in a human population exhibits a certain amount of normal variability in its amino acid sequence. Some of these variants make the pro-

Spongiform degeneration (holes)

Plaques of aggregated prion protein

Brain tissue affected by variant Creutzfeldt-Jakob disease. *Photomicrograph of human brain showing spongiform degeneration (holes) associated with vCJD (200×). Prions, once formed, tend to aggregate, forming protein plaques.*

tein more susceptible to conversion to the abnormal shape. Unfortunately, Sarah and all of the other victims of vCJD diagnosed so far, had a particular sequence of prion protein that left them vulnerable to the abnormal prion from cows with BSE.

Although there is no cure or even an approved treatment for prion diseases, a treatment being used on an emergency basis in the U.K. may prove helpful. Direct injection of pentosan polysulfate into the brain is thought to block conversion of the prion protein to its abnormal form. Another approach, still at the research stage, is to create small protein fragments called "beta breakers" that destabilize the beta sheet conformation of the abnormal protein, making it less likely to convert normal proteins. Genetically engineered dimers of the normal prion

protein seem able, at least in mice, to "soak up" abnormal prion proteins and slow the onset of neuronal damage.

Sarah and others like her were infected with vCJD by eating meat from a cow with BSE. Cows acquired BSE from eating infected feed containing the rendered remains of other cows and sheep. Cannibalistic cows don't roam the range, but it was once common practice to use rendered animal carcasses as a cheap source of feed protein, allowing cows to grow bigger, faster, cheaper. Recent laws in countries around the world have abolished the practice of supplementing feed of ruminants in this way. In the Fore people kuru virtually disappeared one generation after they stopped their cannibalistic rituals. We can hope the same will be true for vCJD. ■

12

and about a third have some degree of deafness. Visual impairments are also common. Cerebral palsy does not get worse over time, but its deficits are irreversible. It is the largest single cause of physical disability in children, affecting three out of every thousand births.

The CNS is plagued by a number of other congenital malformations triggered by genetic or environmental factors during early development. The most serious are congenital hydrocephalus (discussed previously), anencephaly, and spina bifida.

In **anencephaly** (an"en-sef'ah-le; "without brain") the cerebrum and part of the brain stem never develop, presumably because the neural folds fail to fuse rostrally. The child is totally vegetative, unable to see, hear, or process sensory inputs. Muscles are flaccid, and no voluntary movement is possible. Mental life as we know it does not exist. Mercifully, death occurs soon after birth.

Spina bifida (spi'nah bif'ĭ-dah; "forked spine") results from incomplete formation of the vertebral

FIGURE 12.36   **Newborn with a lumbar myelomeningocele.**

arches and typically involves the lumbosacral region. The technical definition is that laminae and spinous processes are missing on at least one vertebra. If the condition is severe, neural deficits occur as well. *Spina bifida occulta*, the least serious type, involves one or only a few vertebrae and causes no neural problems. Other than a small dimple or tuft of hair over the site of nonfusion, it has no external manifestations. In the more common and severe form, *spina bifida cystica*, a saclike cyst protrudes dorsally from the child's spine. The cyst may contain meninges and cerebrospinal fluid [a *meningocele* (mĕ-ning′go-sēl)], or even portions of the spinal cord and spinal nerve roots (a *myelomeningocele*, "spinal cord in a meningeal sac," see Figure 12.36). The larger the cyst and the more neural structures it contains, the greater the neurological impairment. In the worst case, where the inferior spinal cord is functionless, bowel incontinence, bladder muscle paralysis (which predisposes the infant to urinary tract infection and renal failure), and lower limb paralysis occur. Problems with infection are continual because the cyst wall is thin and porous and tends to rupture or leak. Spina bifida cystica is accompanied by hydrocephalus in 90% of all cases.

Up to 70% of cases of spina bifida are caused by inadequate amounts of the B vitamin folate in the maternal diet, a finding that has led to folate supplementation of all bread, flour, and pasta products sold in the United States. ●

One of the last CNS areas to mature is the hypothalamus. Since the hypothalamus contains body temperature regulatory centers, premature babies have problems controlling their loss of body heat and must be kept in temperature-controlled environments. PET scans have revealed that the thalamus and somatosensory cortex are active in a 5-day-old baby, but that the visual cortex is not. This explains why infants of this age respond to touch but have poor vision. By 11 weeks, more of the cortex is active, and the baby can reach for a rattle. By 8 months, the cortex is very active and the child can think about what he or she sees. Growth and maturation of the nervous system continue throughout childhood and largely reflect progressive myelination. As described in Chapter 9, neuromuscular coordination progresses in a superior-to-inferior direction and in a proximal-to-distal direction, and we know that myelination also occurs in this sequence.

The brain reaches its maximum weight in the young adult. Over the next 60 years or so, neurons are damaged and die, and brain weight and volume steadily decline. However, the number of neurons lost over the decades is normally only a small percentage of the total, and the remaining neurons can change their synaptic connections, providing for continued learning throughout life.

Although age brings some cognitive declines in spatial ability, speed of perception, decision making, reaction time, and working memory, these losses are not significant in the *healthy individual* until after the seventh decade. Then the brain becomes increasingly fragile, presumably due to an increase in the density of Ca^{2+} channels in aging neurons (as we have seen, elevated Ca^{2+} levels are neurotoxic), and a fairly rapid decline occurs in some, but not all, of these abilities. Ability to build on experience, mathematical skills, and verbal fluency do not decline with age, and many people continue to enjoy intellectual lives and to work at mentally demanding tasks their entire life. Fewer than 5% of people over 65 demonstrate true dementia. Sadly, many cases of "reversible dementia" are caused by prescription drug effects, low blood pressure, poor nutrition, hormone imbalances, depression, and/or dehydration that go undiagnosed. The best way to maintain one's mental abilities in old age may be to seek regular medical checkups throughout life.

Although eventual shrinking of the brain is normal and accelerates in old age, alcoholics and professional boxers hasten the process. Whether a boxer wins the match or not, the likelihood of brain damage and atrophy increases with every blow. Everyone recognizes that alcohol profoundly affects both the mind and the body. CT scans of alcoholics reveal a reduction in brain size and density appearing at a fairly early age. Both boxers and alcoholics exhibit signs of mental deterioration unrelated to the aging process.

■ ■ ■

The human cerebral hemispheres—our "thinking caps"—are awesome in their complexity. But no less amazing are the brain regions that oversee our subconscious, autonomic body functions—the diencephalon and brain stem—particularly when you consider their relatively insignificant size. The spinal cord, which acts as a reflex center and a communication link between the brain and body periphery, is equally important to body homeostasis.

A good deal of new terminology has been introduced in this chapter, and much of it will come up again in one or more of the remaining nervous system chapters. Chapter 13, your next challenge, considers the structures of the peripheral nervous system that work hand in hand with the CNS to keep it informed and to deliver its orders to the effectors of the body.

Related Clinical Terms

Autism A complex developmental neurological disorder that typically appears in the first three years of life and is characterized by difficulty in communicating, forming relationships with others, and responding appropriately to the environment. No single cause has been determined although a number of genes are thought to play a role and structural brain abnormalities are present. Occurs in about 2 per 1000 people, and early behavioral intervention is beneficial.

Cordotomy (kor-dot'o-me) A procedure in which a tract in the spinal cord is severed surgically; usually done to relieve unremitting pain.

Encephalopathy (en-sef"ah-lop'ah-the; *enceph* = brain; *path* = disease) Any disease or disorder of the brain.

Functional brain disorders Psychological disorders for which no structural cause can be found; include *neuroses* and *psychoses* (see entries in this list).

Hypersomnia (*hyper* = excess; *somnus* = sleep) A condition in which affected individuals sleep as much as 15 hours daily.

Microcephaly (mi"kro-sef'ah-le; *micro* = small) Congenital condition involving the formation of a small brain, as evidenced by reduced skull size; most microcephalic children are retarded.

Myelitis (mi"ĕ-li'tis; *myel* = spinal cord; *itis* = inflammation) Inflammation of the spinal cord.

Myelogram (*gram* = recording) X ray of the spinal cord after injection of a contrast medium.

Myoclonus (mi"o-klo'nus; *myo* = muscle; *clon* = violent motion, tumult) Sudden contraction of a muscle or muscle part, usually involving muscles of the limbs. Myoclonal jerks occurring in normal individuals as they are falling asleep are thought to reflect a fleeting reactivation of the RAS; others may be due to diseases of the reticular formation or cerebellum.

Neuroses (nu-ro'sēs) A less debilitating class of mental illness; examples include severe anxiety (panic attacks), phobias (irrational fears), and obsessive-compulsive behaviors (e.g., washing one's hands every few minutes); the affected individual, however, retains contact with reality.

Pallidectomy ("cutting the pallidus") Surgically lesioning part of the globus pallidus of the basal nuclei to relieve some symptoms of Parkinson's disease.

Psychoses (si-ko'sēs) A class of severe mental illness in which affected individuals lose touch with reality and exhibit bizarre behaviors; the *legal* word for psychotic behavior is *insanity*; the psychoses include *schizophrenia* (skit-so-fre'ne-ah), *manic-depressive disease*, and some forms of *depression*.

Chapter Summary

The Brain   (pp. 431–456)

1. The brain provides for voluntary movements, interpretation and integration of sensation, consciousness, and cognitive function.

Embryonic Development   (pp. 431–433)

2. The brain develops from the rostral portion of the embryonic neural tube.

3. Early brain development yields the three primary brain vesicles: the prosencephalon (cerebral hemispheres and diencephalon), mesencephalon (midbrain), and rhombencephalon (pons, medulla, and cerebellum).

4. Cephalization results in the envelopment of the diencephalon and superior brain stem by the cerebral hemispheres.

Regions and Organization   (p. 433)

5. In a widely used system, the adult brain is divided into the cerebral hemispheres, diencephalon, brain stem, and cerebellum.

6. The cerebral hemispheres and cerebellum have gray matter nuclei surrounded by white matter and an outer cortex of gray matter. The diencephalon and brain stem lack a cortex.

Ventricles   (pp. 433–434)

7. The brain contains four ventricles filled with cerebrospinal fluid. The lateral ventricles are in the cerebral hemispheres; the third ventricle is in the diencephalon; the fourth ventricle is in the brain stem and connects with the central canal of the spinal cord.

Cerebral Hemispheres   (pp. 434–443)

8. The two cerebral hemispheres exhibit gyri, sulci, and fissures. The longitudinal fissure partially separates the hemispheres; other fissures or sulci subdivide each hemisphere into lobes.

9. Each cerebral hemisphere consists of the cerebral cortex, the cerebral white matter, and basal nuclei (ganglia).

10. Each cerebral hemisphere receives sensory impulses from, and dispatches motor impulses to, the opposite side of the body. The body is represented in an upside-down fashion in the sensory and motor cortices.

11. Functional areas of the cerebral cortex include (1) motor areas: primary motor and premotor areas of the frontal lobe, the frontal eye field, and Broca's area in the frontal lobe of one hemisphere (usually the left); (2) sensory areas: primary somatosensory cortex and somatosensory association cortex in the parietal lobe; visual areas in the occipital lobe; olfactory and auditory areas in the temporal lobe; gustatory, visceral, and vestibular areas in the insula; (3) association areas: anterior association area in the frontal lobe, and posterior and limbic association areas spanning several lobes.

12

12. The cerebral hemispheres show lateralization of cortical function. In most people, the left hemisphere is dominant (i.e., specialized for language and mathematical skills); the right hemisphere is more concerned with visual-spatial skills and creative endeavors.

13. Fiber tracts of the cerebral white matter include commissures, association fibers, and projection fibers.

14. The paired basal nuclei (also called basal ganglia) include the lentiform nucleus (globus pallidus and putamen) and caudate nucleus. The basal nuclei are subcortical nuclei that help control muscular movements. Functionally they are closely associated with the substantia nigra of the midbrain.

Diencephalon   (pp. 443–447)

15. The diencephalon includes the thalamus, hypothalamus, and epithalamus and encloses the third ventricle.

16. The thalamus is the major relay station for (1) sensory impulses ascending to the sensory cortex, (2) inputs from subcortical motor nuclei and the cerebellum traveling to the cerebral motor cortex, and (3) impulses traveling to association cortices from lower centers.

17. The hypothalamus is an important autonomic nervous system control center and a pivotal part of the limbic system. It maintains water balance and regulates thirst, eating behavior, gastrointestinal activity, body temperature, and the activity of the anterior pituitary gland.

18. The epithalamus includes the pineal gland, which secretes the hormone melatonin.

Brain Stem   (pp. 447–451)

19. The brain stem includes the midbrain, pons, and medulla oblongata.

20. The midbrain contains the corpora quadrigemina (visual and auditory reflex centers), the red nucleus (subcortical motor centers), and the substantia nigra. The periaqueductal gray matter is involved in pain suppression and contains the motor nuclei of cranial nerves III and IV. The cerebral peduncles on its ventral face house the pyramidal fiber tracts. The midbrain surrounds the cerebral aqueduct.

21. The pons is mainly a conduction area. Its nuclei contribute to regulation of respiration and cranial nerves V–VII.

22. The pyramids (descending corticospinal tracts) form the ventral face of the medulla oblongata; these fibers cross over (decussation of the pyramids) before entering the spinal cord. Important nuclei in the medulla regulate respiratory rhythm, heart rate, and blood pressure and serve cranial nerves VIII–XII. The olivary nuclei and cough, sneezing, swallowing, and vomiting centers are also in the medulla.

Cerebellum   (pp. 451–454)

23. The cerebellum consists of two hemispheres, marked by convolutions and separated by the vermis. It is connected to the brain stem by superior, middle, and inferior peduncles.

24. The cerebellum processes and interprets impulses from the motor cortex and sensory pathways and coordinates motor activity so that smooth, well-timed movements occur. It also plays a poorly understood role in cognition.

Functional Brain Systems   (pp. 454–456)

25. The limbic system consists of numerous structures that encircle the brain stem. It is the "emotional-visceral brain." It also plays a role in memory.

26. The reticular formation is a diffuse network of neurons and nuclei spanning the length of the brain stem. It maintains the alert state of the cerebral cortex (RAS), and its motor nuclei serve both somatic and visceral motor activities.

Higher Mental Functions   (pp. 456–463)

Brain Wave Patterns and the EEG   (pp. 456–457)

1. Patterns of electrical activity of the brain are called brain waves; a record of this activity is an electroencephalogram (EEG). Brain wave patterns, identified by their frequencies, include alpha, beta, theta, and delta waves.

2. Epilepsy results from abnormal electrical activity of brain neurons. Involuntary muscle contractions and sensory auras are typical during such seizures.

Consciousness   (pp. 457–458)

3. Consciousness is described clinically on a continuum from alertness to drowsiness to stupor and finally to coma.

4. Human consciousness is thought to involve holistic information processing, which is (1) not localizable, (2) superimposed on other types of neural activity, and (3) totally interconnected.

5. Fainting (syncope) is a temporary loss of consciousness that usually reflects inadequate blood delivery to the brain. Coma is loss of consciousness in which the victim is unresponsive to stimuli.

Sleep and Sleep-Wake Cycles   (pp. 458–460)

6. Sleep is a state of partial consciousness from which one can be aroused by stimulation. The two major types of sleep are non–rapid eye movement (NREM) sleep and rapid eye movement (REM) sleep.

7. During stages 1–4 of NREM sleep, brain wave frequency decreases and amplitude increases until delta wave sleep (stage 4) is achieved. REM sleep is indicated by a return to a stage 1 EEG. During REM, the eyes move rapidly under the lids. NREM and REM sleep alternate throughout the night.

8. Slow-wave sleep (stage 4 of NREM) appears to be restorative. REM sleep is important for emotional stability.

9. REM occupies half of an infant's sleep time and then declines to about 25% of sleep time by the age of 10 years. Time spent in slow-wave sleep declines steadily throughout life.

10. Narcolepsy is involuntary lapses into REM sleep that occur without warning during waking periods. Insomnia is a chronic inability to obtain the amount or quality of sleep needed to function adequately. Sleep apnea is a temporary cessation of breathing during sleep, causing hypoxia.

Language   (p. 460)

11. In most people language is controlled by the left hemisphere. The language implementation system, which includes Broca's and Wernicke's areas and the basal nuclei, analyzes incoming and produces outgoing language. The opposite hemisphere deals with the emotional content of language.

Memory   (pp. 460–463)

12. Memory is the ability to recall one's thoughts. It is essential for learning and is part of consciousness.

13. Memory storage has two stages: short-term memory (STM) and long-term memory (LTM). Transfer of information from STM to LTM takes minutes to hours, but more time is required for LTM consolidation.

14. Declarative memory is the ability to learn and consciously remember information. Procedural memory is the learning of motor skills, which are then performed without conscious thought.

15. Declarative memory appears to involve the medial temporal lobe (hippocampus and surrounding temporal cortical areas), thalamus, basal forebrain, and prefrontal cortex. Skill memory (a type of procedural memory) relies on the basal nuclei.

16. The nature of memory traces in the human brain is not fully known, but NMDA receptors (essentially calcium channels), activated by depolarization and glutamate binding, play a major role in long-term potentiation (LTP). The calcium influx that follows NMDA receptor activation mobilizes enzymes that mediate events necessary for memory consolidation.

Protection of the Brain   (pp. 463–470)

Meninges   (pp. 463–465)

1. The brain is protected by bone, meninges, cerebrospinal fluid, and the blood-brain barrier.

2. The meninges from superficial to deep are the dura mater, the arachnoid mater, and the pia mater. They enclose the brain and spinal cord and their blood vessels. Inward folds of the inner layer of the dura mater secure the brain to the skull.

Cerebrospinal Fluid   (pp. 465–467)

3. Cerebrospinal fluid (CSF), formed by the choroid plexuses from blood plasma, circulates through the ventricles and into the subarachnoid space. It returns to the dural venous sinuses via the arachnoid villi. CSF supports and cushions the brain and cord and helps to nourish them.

Blood-Brain Barrier   (p. 467)

4. The blood-brain barrier reflects the relative impermeability of the epithelium of capillaries of the brain. It allows water, respiratory gases, essential nutrients, and fat-soluble molecules to enter the neural tissue, but prevents entry of other, water-soluble, potentially harmful substances.

Homeostatic Imbalances of the Brain   (pp. 467–470)

5. Head trauma may cause brain injuries called concussions or, in severe cases, contusions (bruising). When the brain stem is affected, unconsciousness (temporary or permanent) occurs. Trauma-induced brain injuries may be aggravated by intracranial hemorrhage or cerebral edema, both of which compress brain tissue.

6. Cerebrovascular accidents (strokes) result when blood circulation to brain neurons is impaired and brain tissue dies. The result may be hemiplegia, sensory deficits, or speech impairment.

7. Alzheimer's disease is a degenerative brain disease in which beta amyloid peptide deposits and neurofibrillary tangles appear. Marked by a deficit of ACh, it results in slow, progressive loss of memory and motor control and increasing dementia.

8. Parkinson's disease and Huntington's disease are neurodegenerative disorders of the basal nuclei. Both involve abnormalities of the neurotransmitter dopamine (too little or too much secreted) and are characterized by abnormal movements.

The Spinal Cord   (pp. 470–481)

Embryonic Development   (p. 470)

1. The spinal cord develops from the neural tube. Its gray matter forms from the alar and basal plates. Fiber tracts form the outer white matter. The neural crest forms the sensory (dorsal root) ganglia.

Gross Anatomy and Protection   (pp. 470–472)

2. The spinal cord, a two-way impulse conduction pathway and a reflex center, resides within the vertebral column and is protected by meninges and cerebrospinal fluid. It extends from the foramen magnum to the end of the first lumbar vertebra.

3. Thirty-one pairs of spinal nerve roots issue from the cord. The cord is enlarged in the cervical and lumbar regions, where spinal nerves serving the limbs arise.

Cross-Sectional Anatomy   (pp. 472–478)

4. The central gray matter of the cord is H shaped. Ventral horns mainly contain somatic motor neurons. Lateral horns contain visceral (autonomic) motor neurons. Dorsal horns contain interneurons.

5. Axons of neurons of the lateral and ventral horns emerge in common from the cord via the ventral roots. Axons of sensory neurons (with cell bodies located in the dorsal root ganglion) enter the posterior aspect of the cord and form the dorsal roots. The ventral and dorsal roots combine to form the spinal nerves.

6. Each side of the white matter of the cord has posterior, lateral, and anterior columns (funiculi), and each funiculus contains a number of ascending and descending tracts. All tracts are paired and most decussate.

7. Ascending (sensory) tracts include the fasciculi gracilis and cuneatus, spinothalamic tracts, and spinocerebellar tracts.

8. The specific sensory pathway consists of the dorsal white column (fasciculus cuneatus, fasciculus gracilis) and the medial lemniscal tracts, which are concerned with straight-through, precise transmission of one or a few related sensory modalities. The nonspecific pathway (the spinothalamic tracts) is a multimodal pathway that permits brain stem processing of ascending impulses. The spinocerebellar tracts, which terminate in the cerebellum, serve muscle sense, not conscious sensory perception.

9. Descending tracts include the pyramidal tracts (anterior and lateral corticospinal tracts) and a number of motor tracts originating from subcortical motor nuclei. These descending fibers issue from the brain stem motor areas [indirect (extrapyramidal) system] and cortical motor areas [direct (pyramidal) system].

Spinal Cord Trauma and Disorders   (pp. 478–481)

10. Injury to the ventral horn neurons or the ventral roots results in flaccid paralysis. (Injury to the upper motor neurons in the brain results in spastic paralysis.) If the dorsal roots or sensory tracts are damaged, paresthesias occur.

11. Poliomyelitis results from inflammation and destruction of the ventral horn neurons by the poliovirus. Paralysis and muscle atrophy ensue.

12. Amyotrophic lateral sclerosis results from destruction of the ventral horn neurons and the pyramidal tract. The victim eventually loses the ability to swallow, speak, and breathe. Death generally occurs within five years.

Diagnostic Procedures for Assessing CNS Dysfunction   (p. 481)

1. Diagnostic procedures used to assess neurological condition and function range from routine reflex testing to sophisticated techniques such as cerebral angiography, CT scans, MRI scans, and PET scans.

Developmental Aspects of the Central Nervous System   (pp. 481–484)

1. Maternal and environmental factors may impair embryonic brain development, and oxygen deprivation destroys brain cells. Severe congenital brain diseases include cerebral palsy, anencephaly, hydrocephalus, and spina bifida.

2. Premature babies have trouble regulating body temperature because the hypothalamus is one of the last brain areas to mature prenatally.

3. Development of motor control indicates progressive myelination and maturation of a child's nervous system.

4. Brain growth ends in young adulthood. Neurons die throughout life and most are not replaced; thus, brain weight and volume decline with age.

5. Healthy elders maintain nearly optimal intellectual function. Disease—particularly cardiovascular disease—is the major cause of declining mental function with age.

Review Questions

Multiple Choice/Matching

(Some questions have more than one correct answer. Select the best answer or answers from the choices given.)

1. The primary motor cortex, Broca's area, and the premotor area are located in which lobe? (a) frontal, (b) parietal, (c) temporal, (d) occipital.

2. The innermost layer of the meninges, delicate and closely apposed to the brain tissue, is the (a) dura mater, (b) corpus callosum, (c) arachnoid, (d) pia mater.

3. Cerebrospinal fluid is formed by (a) arachnoid villi, (b) the dura mater, (c) choroid plexuses, (d) all of these.

4. A patient has suffered a cerebral hemorrhage that has caused dysfunction of the precentral gyrus of his right cerebral cortex. As a result, (a) he cannot voluntarily move his left arm or leg, (b) he feels no sensation on the left side of his body, (c) he feels no sensation on his right side.

5. Choose the proper term from the key to respond to the statements describing various brain areas.

Key:

(a) cerebellum   (d) corpus striatum   (g) midbrain
(b) corpora quadrigemina (e) hypothalamus   (h) pons
(c) corpus callosum   (f) medulla   (i) thalamus

_____ (1) basal nuclei involved in fine control of motor activities

_____ (2) region where there is a gross crossover of fibers of descending pyramidal tracts

_____ (3) control of temperature, autonomic nervous system reflexes, hunger, and water balance

_____ (4) houses the substantia nigra and cerebral aqueduct

_____ (5) relay stations for visual and auditory stimuli input; found in midbrain

_____ (6) houses vital centers for control of the heart, respiration, and blood pressure

_____ (7) brain area through which all the sensory input is relayed to get to the cerebral cortex

_____ (8) brain area most concerned with equilibrium, body posture, and coordination of motor activity

6. Which of the following tracts convey vibration and other specific sensations that can be precisely localized? (a) pyramidal tract, (b) medial lemniscal tract, (c) lateral spinothalamic tract, (d) reticulospinal tract.

7. Destruction of the ventral horn cells of the spinal cord results in loss of (a) integrating impulses, (b) sensory impulses, (c) voluntary motor impulses, (d) all of these.

8. Fiber tracts that allow neurons within the same cerebral hemisphere to communicate are (a) association tracts, (b) commissures, (c) projection tracts.

9. A number of brain structures are listed below. If an area is primarily gray matter, write **a** in the answer blank; if mostly white matter, respond with **b**.

_____ (1) cerebral cortex

_____ (2) corpus callosum and corona radiata

_____ (3) red nucleus

_____ (4) medial and lateral nuclear groups

_____ (5) medial lemniscal tract

_____ (6) cranial nerve nuclei

_____ (7) spinothalamic tract

_____ (8) fornix

_____ (9) cingulate and precentral gyri

10. A professor unexpectedly blew a loud horn in his anatomy and physiology class. The students looked up, startled. The reflexive movements of their eyes were mediated by the (a) cerebral cortex, (b) inferior olives, (c) raphe nuclei, (d) superior colliculi, (e) nucleus gracilis.

11. Identify the stage of sleep described by using choices from the key. (Note that responses a–d refer to NREM sleep.)

Key: (a) stage 1 (b) stage 2 (c) stage 3 (d) stage 4 (e) REM

_____ (1) the stage when vital signs (blood pressure and heart rate) reach their lowest levels

_____ (2) indicated by movement of the eyes under the lids; dreaming occurs

_____ (3) when sleepwalking is likely to occur

_____ (4) when the sleeper is very easily awakened; EEG shows alpha waves

Short Answer Essay Questions

12. Make a diagram showing the three primary (embryonic) brain vesicles. Name each and then use clinical terminology to name the resulting adult brain regions.

13. (a) What is the advantage of having a cerebrum that is highly convoluted? (b) What term is used to indicate its grooves? Its outward folds? (c) What groove divides the cerebrum into two hemispheres? (d) What divides the parietal from the frontal lobe? The parietal from the temporal lobe?

14. (a) Make a rough drawing of the lateral aspect of the left cerebral hemisphere. (b) You may be thinking, "But I just can't draw!" So, name the hemisphere involved with most people's ability to draw. (c) On your drawing, locate the following areas and provide the major function of each: primary motor cortex, premotor cortex, somatosensory association area, primary sensory area, visual and auditory areas, prefrontal cortex, Wernicke's and Broca's areas.

15. (a) What does lateralization of cortical functioning mean? (b) Why is the term cerebral dominance a misnomer?

16. (a) What is the function of the basal nuclei? (b) Which basal nuclei form the lentiform nucleus? (c) Which arches over the diencephalon?

17. (a) Explain how the cerebellum is physically connected to the brain stem. (b) List ways in which the cerebellum is very similar to the cerebrum.

18. Describe the role of the cerebellum in maintaining smooth, coordinated skeletal muscle activity.

19. (a) Where is the limbic system located? (b) What structures make up this system? (c) How is the limbic system important in behavior?

20. (a) Localize the reticular formation in the brain. (b) What does RAS mean, and what is its function?

21. What is an aura?

22. How do sleep patterns, extent of sleeping time, and amount of time spent in REM and NREM sleep change through life?

23. Compare and contrast short-term memory (STM) and long-term memory (LTM) relative to storage capacity and duration of the memory.

24. (a) Name several factors that can enhance transfer of information from STM to LTM. (b) Define memory consolidation.

25. Compare and contrast declarative and procedural memory relative to the types of things remembered and the importance of conscious retrieval.

26. List four ways in which the CNS is protected.

27. (a) How is cerebrospinal fluid formed and drained? Describe its pathway within and around the brain. (b) What happens if CSF is not drained properly? Why is this consequence more harmful in adults?

28. What constitutes the blood-brain barrier?

29. A brain surgeon is about to make an incision. Name all the tissue layers that she cuts through from the skin to the brain.

30. (a) Define concussion and contusion. (b) Why does severe brain stem injury result in unconsciousness?

31. Describe the spinal cord, depicting its extent, its composition of gray and white matter, and its spinal roots.

32. All of the following descriptions refer to specific ascending pathways except one: (a) they include the fasciculus gracilis and fasciculus cuneatus, which terminate in the thalamus; (b) they include a chain of three neurons; (c) their connections are diffuse and polymodal; (d) they are concerned with precise transmission of one or a few related sensory modalities.

33. Describe the functional problems that would be experienced by a person in which these fiber tracts have been cut: (a) lateral spinothalamic, (b) anterior and posterior spinocerebellar, (c) tectospinal.

34. Differentiate between spastic and flaccid paralysis.

35. How do the conditions paraplegia, hemiplegia, and quadriplegia differ?

36. (a) Define cerebrovascular accident or CVA. (b) Describe its possible causes and consequences.

37. (a) What factors account for brain growth after birth? (b) List some structural brain changes observed with aging.

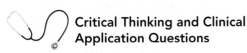

Critical Thinking and Clinical Application Questions

1. A 10-month-old infant has an enlarging head circumference and delayed overall development. She has a bulging anterior fontanel and her CSF pressure is elevated. Based on these findings, answer the following questions: (a) What are the possible cause(s) of an enlarged head? (b) What tests might be helpful in obtaining information about this infant's problem? (c) Assuming the tests conducted showed the cerebral aqueduct to be constricted, which ventricles or CSF-containing areas would you expect to be enlarged?

Which would likely not be visible? Respond to the same questions based on a finding of obstructed arachnoid villi.

2. Mrs. Jones has had a progressive decline in her mental capabilities in the last five or six years. At first her family attributed her occasional memory lapses, confusion, and agitation to grief over her husband's death six years earlier. When examined, Mrs. Jones was aware of her cognitive problems and was shown to have an IQ score approximately 30 points less than would be predicted by her work history. A CT scan showed diffuse cerebral atrophy. The physician prescribed an acetylcholinesterase inhibitor and Mrs. Jones showed slight improvement. What is Mrs. Jones's problem? Why did the acetylcholinesterase inhibitor help?

3. Robert, a brilliant computer analyst, suffered a blow to his anterior skull from a falling rock while mountain climbing. Shortly thereafter, it was obvious to his co-workers that his behavior had undergone a dramatic change. Although previously a smart dresser, he was now unkempt. One morning, he was observed defecating into the wastebasket. His supervisor ordered Robert to report to the company's doctor immediately. What region of Robert's brain was affected by the cranial blow?

4. Mrs. Adams is ready to deliver her first baby. Unfortunately, the baby appears to have a myelomeningocele. Would a vaginal or surgical (C-section) delivery be more appropriate and why?

5. The medical chart of a 68-year-old man includes the following notes: "Slight tremor of right hand at rest; stony facial expression; difficulty in initiating movements." (a) Based on your present knowledge, what is the diagnosis? (b) What brain areas are most likely involved in this man's disorder, and what is the deficiency? (c) How is this condition currently treated?

6. Cynthia, a 16-year-old girl, was rushed to the hospital after taking a bad spill off the parallel bars. After she had a complete neurological workup, her family was told that she would be permanently paralyzed from the waist down. The neurologist then outlined for Cynthia's parents the importance of preventing complications in such cases. Common complications include urinary infection, bed sores, and muscular spasms. Using your knowledge of neuroanatomy, explain the underlying reasons for these complications.

7. Mrs. Herrera suffered a stroke two weeks ago. Initially she was unable to move her right arm and the right side of her face, but her paralysis has decreased markedly. However, she still has a great deal of difficulty speaking. Mrs. Herrera's speech consists of very few words. She struggles to produce these words and they are distorted and separated by long pauses. Her comprehension of written and spoken language is unaltered. She is fully aware of what happened to her and is tearful much of the time. Which side of the brain and which particular area of the brain was affected by Mrs. Herrera's stroke?

8. Five-year-old Amy wakes her parents up at 3 AM crying and complaining of a sore neck, a severe headache, and feeling sick to her stomach. She has a temperature of 40°C (104°F) and hides her eyes, saying that the lights are too bright. The emergency physician suspects meningitis and performs a lumbar tap. Using your knowledge of neuroanatomy, explain into which space and at what level of the vertebral column the needle will be inserted to perform this test. Which fluid is being obtained and why?

12

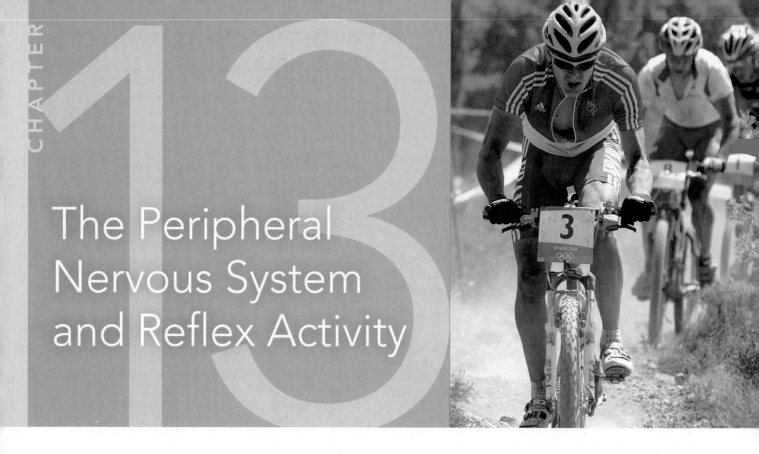

1. Define peripheral nervous system and list its components.

PART 1: SENSORY RECEPTORS AND SENSATION

Sensory Receptors (pp. 491–494)

2. Classify general sensory receptors by structure, stimulus detected, and body location.

Overview: From Sensation to Perception (pp. 494–498)

3. Outline the events that lead to sensation and perception.
4. Describe receptor and generator potentials and sensory adaptation.
5. Describe the main aspects of sensory perception.

PART 2: TRANSMISSION LINES: NERVES AND THEIR STRUCTURE AND REPAIR

Nerves and Associated Ganglia (pp. 498–500)

6. Define ganglion and indicate the general body location of ganglia.

7. Describe the general structure of a nerve, and follow the process of nerve regeneration.

Cranial Nerves (pp. 500–508)

8. Name the 12 pairs of cranial nerves; indicate the body region and structures innervated by each.

Spinal Nerves (pp. 508–518)

9. Describe the formation of a spinal nerve and the general distribution of its rami.
10. Define plexus. Name the major plexuses and describe the distribution and function of the peripheral nerves arising from each plexus.

PART 3: MOTOR ENDINGS AND MOTOR ACTIVITY

Peripheral Motor Endings (p. 519)

11. Compare and contrast the motor endings of somatic and autonomic nerve fibers.

Overview of Motor Integration: From Intention to Effect (pp. 519–521)

12. Outline the three levels of the motor hierarchy.

13. Compare the roles of the cerebellum and basal nuclei in controlling motor activity.

PART 4: REFLEX ACTIVITY

The Reflex Arc (pp. 521–522)

14. Name the components of a reflex arc and distinguish between autonomic and somatic reflexes.

Spinal Reflexes (pp. 522–527)

15. Compare and contrast stretch, flexor, crossed-extensor, and Golgi tendon reflexes.

Developmental Aspects of the Peripheral Nervous System (p. 527)

16. List changes that occur in the sensory system with aging.
17. Describe the developmental relationship between the segmented arrangement of peripheral nerves, skeletal muscles, and skin dermatomes.

The human brain, for all its sophistication, would be useless without its links to the outside world. In one experiment that illustrates this point, blindfolded volunteers suspended in warm water in a sensory deprivation tank (a situation that limits sensory inputs) hallucinated. One saw charging pink and purple elephants. Another heard a chorus, still others had taste hallucinations. Our very sanity depends on a continuous flow of information from the outside.

No less important to our well-being are the orders sent from the CNS to voluntary muscles and other effectors of the body, which allow us to move and to take care of our own needs. The **peripheral nervous system (PNS)** provides these links from and to the world outside our bodies. Ghostly white nerves thread through virtually every part of the body, enabling the CNS to receive information and to carry out its decisions.

The PNS includes all neural structures outside the brain and spinal cord, that is, the *sensory receptors*, peripheral *nerves* and their associated *ganglia*, and efferent *motor endings*. Its basic components are diagrammed in Figure 13.1. The first portion of this chapter deals with the functional anatomy of each PNS element. Then we consider the components of reflex arcs and some important somatic reflexes, played out almost entirely in PNS structures, that help to maintain homeostasis.

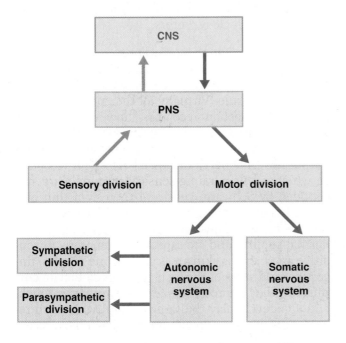

FIGURE 13.1 **Place of the PNS in the structural organization of the nervous system.**

PART 1: SENSORY RECEPTORS AND SENSATION

Sensory Receptors

Sensory receptors are specialized to respond to changes in their environment; such environmental changes are called **stimuli.** Typically, activation of a sensory receptor by an adequate stimulus results in graded potentials that in turn trigger nerve impulses along the afferent PNS fibers coursing to the CNS. *Sensation* (awareness of the stimulus) and *perception* (interpretation of the meaning of the stimulus) occur in the brain. But we are getting ahead of ourselves here. For now, let us just examine how sensory receptors are classified. Basically, there are three ways to classify sensory receptors: (1) by the type of stimulus they detect; (2) by their body location; and (3) by their structural complexity.

Classification by Stimulus Type

The receptor classes named according to the activating stimulus are easy to remember because the class name usually indicates the stimulus.

1. Mechanoreceptors generate nerve impulses when they, or adjacent tissues, are deformed by a mechanical force such as touch, pressure (including blood pressure), vibration, and stretch.

2. Thermoreceptors are sensitive to temperature changes.

3. Photoreceptors, such as those of the retina of the eye, respond to light energy.

4. Chemoreceptors respond to chemicals in solution (molecules smelled or tasted, or changes in blood or interstitial fluid chemistry).

5. Nociceptors (no″se-sep′torz; *noci* = harm) respond to potentially damaging stimuli that result in pain. For example, searing heat, extreme cold, excessive pressure, and inflammatory chemicals are all interpreted as painful. These signals stimulate subtypes of thermoreceptors, mechanoreceptors, and chemoreceptors.

Classification by Location

Three receptor classes are recognized according to either their location or the location of the activating stimulus.

1. Exteroceptors (ek″ster-o-sep′torz) are sensitive to stimuli arising outside the body (*extero* = outside), so most exteroceptors are near or at the body surface. They include touch, pressure, pain, and temperature receptors in the skin and most receptors of the

13

special senses (vision, hearing, equilibrium, taste, smell).

2. **Interoceptors** (in"ter-o-sep'torz), also called **visceroceptors,** respond to stimuli within the body (*intero*=inside), such as from the internal viscera and blood vessels. They monitor a variety of stimuli, including chemical changes, tissue stretch, and temperature. Sometimes their activity causes us to feel pain, discomfort, hunger, or thirst. However, we are usually unaware of their workings.

3. **Proprioceptors** (pro"pre-o-sep'torz), like interoceptors, respond to internal stimuli; however, their location is much more restricted. Proprioceptors occur in skeletal muscles, tendons, joints, and ligaments and in connective tissue coverings of bones and muscles. (Some authorities include the equilibrium receptors of the inner ear in this class.) Proprioceptors constantly advise the brain of our body movements (*propria* = one's own) by monitoring how much the organs containing these receptors are stretched.

Classification by Structural Complexity

On the basis of overall receptor structure, there are **simple** and **complex receptors,** but the overwhelming majority are simple. The simple receptors are modified dendritic endings of sensory neurons. They are found throughout the body and monitor most types of general sensory information. Complex receptors are actually **sense organs,** localized collections of cells (usually of many types) associated with the **special senses** (vision, hearing, equilibrium, smell, and taste). For example, the sense organ we know as the eye is composed not only of sensory neurons but also of nonneural cells that form its supporting wall, lens, and other associated structures. Though the complex sense organs are most familiar to us, the simple sensory receptors associated with the **general senses** are no less important, and we will concentrate on their structure and function in this chapter. The special senses are the topic of Chapter 15.

Simple Receptors of the General Senses

The widely distributed **general sensory receptors** are involved in tactile sensation (a mix of touch, pressure, stretch, and vibration), temperature monitoring, and pain, as well as the "muscle sense" provided by proprioceptors. Anatomically, these receptors are either *unencapsulated (free) nerve endings* or *encapsulated nerve endings.* The general sensory receptors are illustrated and classified in Table 13.1.

Unencapsulated Dendritic Endings   **Free,** or **naked, nerve endings** of sensory neurons are present nearly everywhere in the body, but they are particularly abundant in epithelia and connective tissues. Most of these sensory fibers are unmyelinated, small-diameter C fibers, and their distal endings (the sensory terminals) usually have small knoblike swellings. They respond chiefly to temperature and painful stimuli, but some respond to tissue movements caused by pressure as well. Nerve endings that respond to cold (10–40°C) are located in the superficial dermis; those responding to heat (32–48°C) are found deeper in the dermis.

Heat or cold outside the range of thermoreceptors activates nociceptors and is perceived as painful. Nociceptors also respond to pinch and chemicals released from damaged tissue. A recently discovered receptor *(vanilloid receptor)* in the plasma membrane of nociceptive free nerve endings is an ion channel that is opened by heat, low pH, and the substance found in red peppers called capsaicin.

Another sensation mediated by free nerve endings is itch. Located in the dermis, the itch receptor escaped detection until 1997 because of its thin diameter. A number of chemicals—notably histamine—present at inflamed sites activate these nerve endings.

Certain free nerve endings associate with enlarged, disc-shaped epidermal cells *(Merkel cells)* to form **Merkel (tactile) discs,** which lie in the deeper layers of the epidermis and function as light touch receptors. **Hair follicle receptors,** free nerve endings that wrap basketlike around hair follicles, are light touch receptors that detect bending of hairs. The tickle of a mosquito landing on your skin is mediated by hair follicle receptors.

Encapsulated Dendritic Endings   All **encapsulated dendritic endings** consist of one or more fiber terminals of sensory neurons enclosed in a connective tissue capsule. Virtually all the encapsulated receptors are mechanoreceptors; however, they vary greatly in shape, size, and distribution in the body.

The encapsulated receptors known as **Meissner's corpuscles** (mīs'nerz kor'pus"lz) are small receptors in which a few spiraling sensory terminals are surrounded by Schwann cells and then by a thin egg-shaped connective tissue capsule. Meissner's corpuscles are found just beneath the epidermis in the dermal papillae and are especially numerous in sensitive and hairless skin areas such as the nipples, fingertips, and soles of the feet. Also called **tactile corpuscles,** they are receptors for discriminative touch, and apparently play the same role in light touch reception in hairless skin as do the hair follicle receptors in hairy skin.

Pacinian corpuscles, also called **lamellated corpuscles,** are scattered deep in the dermis, and in subcutaneous tissue underlying the skin. Although they are mechanoreceptors stimulated by deep pressure, they respond only when the pressure is first applied,

STRUCTURAL CLASS	ILLUSTRATION	FUNCTIONAL CLASSES ACCORDING TO LOCATION (L) AND STIMULUS TYPE (S)	BODY LOCATION
UNENCAPSULATED			
Free nerve endings of sensory neurons		L: Exteroceptors, interoceptors, and proprioceptors S: Thermoreceptors (warm and cool), chemoreceptors (itch, pH, etc.), mechanoreceptors (pressure), nociceptors (pain, hot, cold, pinch, and chemicals)	Most body tissues; most dense in connective tissues (ligaments, tendons, dermis, joint capsules, periostea) and epithelia (epidermis, cornea, mucosae, and glands)
Modified free nerve endings: Merkel discs (tactile discs)		L: Exteroceptors S: Mechanoreceptors (light pressure); slowly adapting	Basal layer of epidermis of skin
Hair follicle receptors		L: Exteroceptors S: Mechanoreceptors (hair deflection); rapidly adapting	In and surrounding hair follicles
ENCAPSULATED			
Meissner's corpuscles (tactile corpuscles)		L: Exteroceptors S: Mechanoreceptors (light pressure, discriminative touch, vibration of low frequency); rapidly adapting	Dermal papillae of hairless skin, particularly nipples, external genitalia, fingertips, soles of feet, eyelids
Pacinian corpuscles (lamellated corpuscles)		L: Exteroceptors, interoceptors, and some proprioceptors S: Mechanoreceptors (deep pressure, stretch, vibration of high frequency); rapidly adapting	Dermis and hypodermis; periostea, mesentery, tendons, ligaments, joint capsules; most abundant on fingers, soles of feet, external genitalia, nipples
Ruffini endings		L: Exteroceptors and proprioceptors S: Mechanoreceptors (deep pressure and stretch); slowly or nonadapting	Deep in dermis, hypodermis, and joint capsules
Muscle spindles	Intrafusal fibers	L: Proprioceptors S: Mechanoreceptors (muscle stretch, length)	Skeletal muscles, particularly those of the extremities
Golgi tendon organs		L: Proprioceptors S: Mechanoreceptors (tendon stretch, tension)	Tendons
Joint kinesthetic receptors	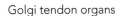	L: Proprioceptors S: Mechanoreceptors and nociceptors	Joint capsules of synovial joints

13

and thus are best suited to monitoring vibration (an "on/off" pressure stimulus). They are the largest corpuscular receptors. Some are over 3 mm long and half as wide and are visible to the naked eye as white, egg-shaped bodies. In section, a Pacinian corpuscle resembles a cut onion. Its single dendrite is surrounded by a capsule containing up to 60 layers of collagen fibers and flattened supporting cells.

Ruffini endings, which lie in the dermis, subcutaneous tissue, and joint capsules, contain a spray of receptor endings enclosed by a flattened capsule. They bear a striking resemblance to Golgi tendon organs (which monitor tendon stretch) and probably play a similar role in other dense connective tissues where they respond to deep and *continuous* pressure.

Muscle spindles are fusiform (spindle-shaped) proprioceptors found throughout the perimysium of a skeletal muscle. Each muscle spindle consists of a bundle of modified skeletal muscle fibers, called *intrafusal fibers* (in"trah-fu'zal), enclosed in a connective tissue capsule (Table 13.1). They detect muscle stretch and initiate a reflex that resists the stretch. Details of muscle spindle innervation are considered later when the stretch reflex is described (see pp. 523–525).

Golgi tendon organs are proprioceptors located in tendons, close to the skeletal muscle insertion. They consist of small bundles of tendon (collagen) fibers enclosed in a layered capsule, with sensory terminals coiling between and around the fibers. When the tendon fibers are stretched by muscle contraction, the nerve endings are activated by compression. When Golgi tendon organs are activated, the contracting muscle is inhibited, which causes it to relax.

Joint kinesthetic receptors (kin"es-thet'ik) are proprioceptors that monitor stretch in the articular capsules that enclose synovial joints. At least four receptor types (Pacinian corpuscles, Ruffini endings, free nerve endings, and receptors resembling Golgi tendon organs) contribute to this receptor category. Together these receptors provide information on joint position and motion (*kines* = movement), a sensation of which we are highly conscious.

- Close your eyes and flex and extend your fingers—you can *feel* exactly which joints are moving.

Overview: From Sensation to Perception

Our survival depends not only on **sensation** (awareness of changes in the internal and external environments) but also on **perception** (conscious interpretation of those stimuli). For example, a pebble kicked up into my shoe causes the *sensation* of localized deep pressure, but my *perception* of it is an awareness of discomfort. Perception in turn determines how we will respond to stimuli. In the case of the pebble-in-my-shoe example, I'm taking off my shoe to get rid of the pesky pebble in a hurry.

General Organization of the Somatosensory System

The **somatosensory system,** or that part of the sensory system serving the body wall and limbs, receives inputs from exteroceptors, proprioceptors, and interoceptors; consequently, it transmits information about several different sensory modalities.

There are three main levels of neural integration in the somatosensory (or any sensory) system (Figure 13.2):

① **Receptor level:** sensory receptors
② **Circuit level:** ascending pathways
③ **Perceptual level:** neuronal circuits in the cerebral cortex

Although sensory input is generally relayed toward the head, it is also processed along the way.

Let's examine the events that must occur at each level along the pathway.

Processing at the Receptor Level

For sensation to occur, a stimulus must excite a receptor. For this to happen:

- The stimulus energy must match the *specificity* of the receptor. For example, a given touch receptor may be sensitive to mechanical pressure, stretch, and vibration, but not to light energy (which is the province of receptors in the eye). The more complex the sensory receptor, the greater its specificity.

- The stimulus must be applied within a sensory receptor's *receptive field,* the particular area monitored by the receptor. Typically, the smaller the receptive field, the greater the ability of the brain to accurately localize the stimulus site.

- The stimulus energy must be converted into the energy of a *graded potential* called a **receptor potential,** a process called **transduction.** This may be a depolarizing or hyperpolarizing graded potential similar to the EPSPs or IPSPs generated at postsynaptic membranes in response to neurotransmitter binding. Membrane depolarizations that summate and directly lead to generation of action potentials in an afferent fiber are called **generator potentials.** When the receptor region is part of a sensory neuron (as with free dendrites or the encapsulated receptors of most general sense receptors), the terms receptor potential and generator potential are synonymous. When the receptor is a separate (nonneuron) cell, the receptor and generator potentials are completely separate events. Upon stimulation, such a depolarizing receptor cell produces a receptor potential, which (if strong enough) causes it to release a neurotransmitter that in turn excites the associated afferent neuron.

- A generator potential in the associated sensory neuron (a first-order neuron) must reach threshold so that voltage-gated sodium channels on the axon (these are usually just proximal to the receptor membrane, often at the first node of Ranvier) are opened and nerve impulses are generated and propagated to the CNS.

Information about the stimulus—its strength, duration, and pattern—is encoded in the frequency of nerve impulses (the greater the frequency, the stronger the stimulus). Many but not all sensory receptors exhibit **adaptation,** a change in sensitivity (and nerve impulse generation) in the presence of a constant stimulus. For example, when you step into bright sunlight from a darkened room, your eyes are initially dazzled, but your photoreceptors rapidly adapt, allowing you to see both bright areas and dark areas in the scene. **Phasic receptors** are *fast adapting* often giving bursts of impulses at the beginning and at the end of the stimulus. These act mainly to report changes in the internal or external environment. Examples of phasic receptors are Pacinian and Meissner's corpuscles. **Tonic receptors** provide a sustained response with little or no adaptation. Nociceptors and most proprioceptors are tonic receptors because of the protective importance of their information. Pain and its modulation are discussed in more detail in *A Closer Look* (pp. 496–497).

Processing at the Circuit Level

The task at the circuit level is to deliver impulses to the appropriate region of the cerebral cortex for stimulus localization and perception. Recall from Chapter 12 (p. 475) that ascending sensory pathways typically consist of a chain of three neurons called first-, second-, and third-order sensory neurons. The axons of first-order sensory neurons, whose cell bodies are in the dorsal root or cranial ganglia, link the receptor and circuit levels of processing. Central processes of first-order neurons branch diffusely when they enter the spinal cord. Some branches take part in local spinal cord reflexes; others synapse with second-order sensory neurons, which then synapse with the third-order sensory neurons that take the message to the cortex of the cerebrum.

Impulses ascending in the specific and nonspecific ascending pathways (see p. 476) reach conscious awareness in the sensory cortex. In general, fibers in the nonspecific ascending pathways transmit pain, temperature, and coarse touch impulses. They give off numerous branches to the reticular formation and thalamus on the way up; and information sent to "headquarters" is fairly general, nondiscriminatory, and heavily involved in emotional aspects of perception (pleasure, pain, etc.).

Identify the neurons in this figure as first-, second-, and third-order sensory neurons.

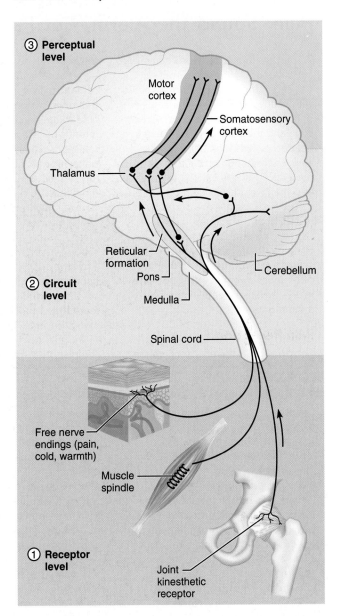

FIGURE 13.2 General organization of the somatosensory system. The three basic levels of neural integration are ① the receptor level, ② the circuit level, and ③ the perceptual level. The circuit level involves noncortical CNS centers, while the perceptual level involves cortical sensory centers.

The specific ascending pathways are more involved in the discriminative aspects of touch (tactile discrimination), vibration, pressure, and conscious proprioception (limb and joint position).

The first-order neurons are at the bottom of the figure and include the sensory receptors. The third-order neurons are the uppermost neurons in the figure, with cell bodies in the thalamus and terminals in the somatosensory cortex. Second-order neurons connect the first- and third-order neurons.

A CLOSER LOOK

Pain: Sound the Alarm, But Pain Me Not!

Pain is a four-letter word that means suffering. It is also a primitive experience that we humans share with nearly all animals. Almost everyone has suffered the smart of a bee sting and the cruel persistence of a headache. Although pain warns of actual or impending tissue damage, its protective value is difficult to appreciate when we are its victims.

Clinically, pain is measured by roundabout techniques, such as tapping the painful spot and observing the patient's degree of wincing. This seems a bit strange, given that the other most common sign of disease or injury—fever—is readily measured with a thermometer.

Pain Reception

The principal pain receptors are the several million bare sensory nerve endings that weave through all the tissues and organs of the body (except the brain) and respond to noxious stimuli—a catchall term for anything damaging to tissues. Wherever body tissue is injured, the damaged cells release an "inflammatory soup" of chemicals including prostaglandins and bradykinins, among the most potent pain-producing chemicals known. This begins an avalanche of inflammatory chemicals, such as histamine, potassium, and ATP, that ubiquitous energy source for all cells. These chemicals activate specific receptors on small-diameter C fibers, thus initiating pain signals.

Pain Transmission and Perception

Clinically, pain is classified as *somatic* or *visceral*. Somatic pain, arising from the skin, muscles, or joints, can be either superficial or deep. Superficial somatic pain is a sharp, pricking pain that often causes us to cry out. Localizable to the skin epidermis or mucosae, it tends to be brief. This type of pain is transmitted along finely myelinated A delta (δ) fibers at the rate of 4–36 m/s (up to 120 ft/s). Deep somatic pain is more likely to burn or ache; it results from stimulation of pain receptors in joints, muscles, or deep skin layers. Deep somatic pain is more diffuse than superficial somatic pain, lasts longer, and *always* indicates tissue destruction. Impulses from the deep pain receptors are transmitted slowly (from 0.4 to more than 1 m/s, or up to 3.5 ft/s) along the small, unmyelinated C fibers.

Visceral pain results from noxious stimulation of receptors in the organs of the thorax and abdominal cavity. Like deep somatic pain, it is usually a sensation of dull aching, gnawing, or vague burning. Important stimuli for visceral pain are extreme stretching of tissue, ischemia, irritating chemicals, and muscle spasms. Because visceral pain inputs follow the same pathways as somatic pain (convergence), projection by the brain may cause visceral pain to be perceived as somatic in origin. Chapter 14 describes this phenomenon of *referred pain*.

Both the superficial somatic pain fibers and deep somatic/visceral pain fibers synapse with interneurons in the dorsal horns of the spinal cord (see the figure). Transmission of pain impulses to the CNS along the sensory neurons causes release of glutamate and *substance P,* the pain neurotransmitter, into the synaptic cleft. Glutamate, of course, depolarizes the postsynaptic neurons,

relaying the pain message to the brain. Substance P, on the other hand, acts more diffusely as a neuromodulator to sensitize adjacent neurons.

The axons of most pain-relaying interneurons cross the cord and enter ventrolateral ascending tracts. Some fibers form an "express" pathway (the lateral spinothalamic tract) that ascends directly to the thalamus, which relays to the cortex. This allows the sensory cortex to rapidly analyze exactly what hurts and how much. Other pain messages "take the local," a set of smaller-diameter, slower fibers that make abundant synapses in the brain stem, hypothalamus, and other limbic system structures before reaching the thalamus. This second set of pathways mediates arousal and emotional reactions to pain, and has longer-lasting effects on the CNS.

We all have the same **pain threshold;** that is, we perceive it at the same stimulus intensity. For example, heat is perceived as painful at 44–46°C, the range at which it begins to damage tissue. However, reactions to pain, or pain tolerance, vary widely and are heavily influenced by persistent pain stimuli (they decrease it) as well as cultural and psychological factors. When we say that someone is "sensitive to pain," we are referring to that person's **pain tolerance** rather than pain threshold. Pain tolerance seems to increase with age, and is modified by emotions and mental state. In a disaster, many who feel no pain while struggling to help others may actually be severely injured.

Normally a steady state is maintained that correlates injury and pain. However, long-lasting or very intense pain inputs, such as limb amputation,

---

Proprioceptive impulses conducted via the *spinocerebellar tracts* end at the cerebellum, which uses this information to coordinate skeletal muscle activity. These tracts do not contribute to conscious sensation.

Processing at the Perceptual Level

Interpretation of sensory input occurs in the cerebral cortex. The ability to identify and appreciate sensations depends on the specific location of the target neurons in the sensory cortex, not on the nature of the message (which is, after all, just an action potential). Each sensory fiber is analogous to a "labeled line" that tells the brain "who" is calling—a taste bud or a pressure receptor—and from "where." The brain always interprets the activity of a specific sensory receptor ("who") as a specific sensation, no matter how it is activated. For example, pressing on your eyeball activates photoreceptors, but what you "see" is light.

can disrupt this system, leading to **hyperalgesia** (pain amplification), chronic pain, and phantom limb pain. Intense or long-duration pain causes activation of **NMDA receptors,** the same receptors that strengthen neural connections during certain kinds of learning. Essentially, the spinal cord *learns* hyperalgesia. In light of this, it is crucial that pain is effectively managed early to prevent the establishment of chronic pain. *Phantom limb pain* (pain perceived in tissue that is no longer present) is a curious example of hyperalgesia. Until recently, surgical limb amputations were conducted under general anesthesia only and the spinal cord still experienced the pain of amputation. Blocking neurotransmission in the spinal cord by additionally using epidural anesthetics greatly reduces the incidence of phantom limb pain.

Pain Modulation and Analgesia

As everyone knows, rubbing that aching knee somehow makes it feel better. The body has its own mechanisms for modulating the intensity of pain. Massage, acupuncture, and transcutaneous electrical nerve stimulation (TENS) activate larger-diameter touch fibers that interfere with pain transmission in the spinal cord. These phenomena underlie the *gate control theory of pain* developed by Melzack and Wall in 1965. Threshold stimulation of the large touch fibers (as in massaging your knee) causes a burst of firing in certain dorsal horn cells, followed by a brief period of inhibited pain transmission, essentially closing the "gate" on pain.

Descending projections from the brain also modulate pain. When we're in pain, the brain activates these pathways to dull our pain perception. The

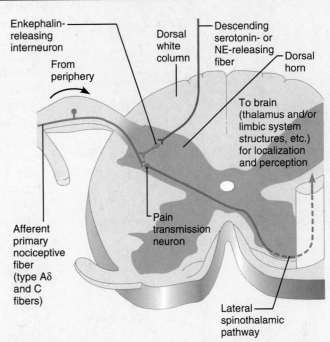

Pain signals and analgesia. *When group A delta and group C pain fibers transmit via interneurons to the spinothalamic pathway, pain impulses travel to the cerebral cortex. Descending control of pain transmission (analgesia) is mediated by descending CNS fibers which synapse with small enkephalin-releasing interneurons in the dorsal horn that make inhibitory synapses with the afferent pain fibers, preventing their release of substance P.*

periaqueductal gray matter, a crucial way station in this descending control of pain, contains many receptors for the body's own opiates called *endorphins* and *enkephalins.* Together with the periventricular nucleus of the hypothalamus, it oversees descending pain suppressor fibers that synapse in the dorsal horns. Hypnosis, natural childbirth techniques, morphine, and electrical stimulation of the periaqueductal gray matter all tap into these natural opiate pathways.

Descending pain suppressor fibers don't release opiates. Instead, they release either norepinephrine or serotonin onto dorsal horn neurons, either inhibiting pain transmission directly

or activating enkephalin-releasing interneurons (see the diagram). This released enkephalin acts both presynaptically on synaptic terminals of nociceptor fibers to decrease their release of substance P (a pain neurotransmitter), and postsynaptically to inhibit action potential generation. For centuries physicians have made use of the juice of the opium poppy to relieve pain. Now we know that opiates such as morphine work because of their ability to mimic the actions of our own endorphins and enkephalins. You could say that such pain-reducing techniques—drugs, electrical stimulation, and massage—work because the body allows it! ∎

13

The exact point in the cortex that is activated always refers to the same "where," regardless of how it is activated, a phenomenon called **projection**. Electrically stimulating a particular spot in the visual cortex causes you to "see" light in a particular place.

The main aspects of sensory perception include the following:

- **Perceptual detection** is the ability to detect that a stimulus has occurred; this is the simplest level of perception. As a general rule, several receptor impulses must be summed for perceptual detection to occur.

- **Magnitude estimation** is the ability to detect how *intense* the stimulus is. Because of frequency coding, perception increases as stimulus intensity increases (see Figure 11.14).

- **Spatial discrimination** allows us to identify the site or pattern of stimulation. A common tool for studying this quality in the laboratory is the

(a)

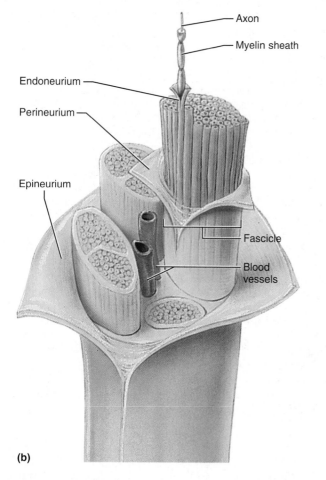

(b)

FIGURE 13.3   **Structure of a nerve. (a)** Scanning electron micrograph of a cross section of a portion of a nerve (500×). (© R. G. Kessel and R. H. Kardon, *Tissues and Organs: A Text-Atlas of Scanning Electron Microscopy,* W. H. Freeman and Company, 1979, all rights reserved.) **(b)** Three-dimensional view of a portion of a nerve, showing connective tissue wrappings.

two-point discrimination test. The test determines how close together two points on the skin can be and still be perceived as two points rather than as one. This test provides a crude map of the density of tactile receptors in the various regions of the skin. The distance between perceived points varies from less than 5 mm on highly sensitive body areas (tip of the tongue) to more than 50 mm on less sensitive areas (back).

- **Feature abstraction** is the mechanism by which a neuron or circuit is tuned to one feature in preference to others. Sensation usually involves an interplay of several stimulus properties or features. For example, one touch tells us that velvet is warm, compressible, and smooth but not completely continuous, each a feature that contributes to our perception of "velvet." Feature abstraction enables us to identify more complex aspects of a sensation.

- **Quality discrimination** is the ability to differentiate the submodalities of a particular sensation. Each sensory modality has several **qualities,** or submodalities. For example, the submodalities of taste include sweet and bitter.

- **Pattern recognition** is the ability to take in the scene around us and recognize a familiar pattern, an unfamiliar one, or one that has special significance for us. For example, a figure made of dots may be recognized as a familiar face, and when we listen to music, we hear the melody, not just a string of notes.

PART 2: TRANSMISSION LINES: NERVES AND THEIR STRUCTURE AND REPAIR

Nerves and Associated Ganglia

Structure and Classification

A **nerve** is a cordlike organ that is part of the peripheral nervous system. Nerves vary in size, but every nerve consists of parallel bundles of peripheral axons (some myelinated and some not) enclosed by successive wrappings of connective tissue (Figure 13.3).

Within a nerve, each axon is surrounded by **endoneurium** (en"do-nu're-um), a delicate layer of loose connective tissue that also encloses the fiber's associated myelin sheath or neurilemma. Groups of fibers are bound into bundles or **fascicles** by a coarser connective tissue wrapping, the **perineurium.** Finally, all the fascicles are enclosed by a tough fibrous sheath, the **epineurium,** to form the nerve. Axons constitute only a small fraction of a nerve's bulk. The balance consists chiefly of myelin, the protective connective tissue wrappings, blood vessels, and lymphatic vessels.

Recall that the PNS is divided into *sensory* (afferent) and *motor* (efferent) divisions. Hence, nerves are classified according to the direction in which they transmit impulses. Nerves containing both sensory and motor fibers and transmitting impulses both to and from the central nervous system are called **mixed nerves.** Those that carry impulses only toward the CNS are **sensory (afferent) nerves;** and those carrying impulses only away from the CNS are **motor (efferent) nerves.** Most nerves are mixed. Pure sensory or motor nerves are rare.

Because mixed nerves often carry both somatic and autonomic (visceral) nervous system fibers, the fibers in them may be classified according to the region they innervate as *somatic afferent, somatic efferent, visceral afferent,* and *visceral efferent.*

For convenience, the peripheral nerves are classified as *cranial* or *spinal* depending on whether they arise from the brain or the spinal cord. Although autonomic efferents of cranial nerves are mentioned, this chapter focuses on somatic functions. The discussion of the autonomic nervous system and the visceral functions it serves is deferred to Chapter 14.

Ganglia are collections of neuron cell bodies associated with nerves in the PNS. Ganglia associated with *afferent* nerve fibers contain cell bodies of sensory neurons. (These are the *dorsal root ganglia* studied in Chapter 12.) Ganglia associated with *efferent* nerve fibers mostly contain cell bodies of autonomic motor neurons. These more complicated ganglia are described in Chapter 14.

Regeneration of Nerve Fibers

Damage to nervous tissue is serious because, as a rule, mature neurons do not divide. If the damage is severe or close to the cell body, the entire neuron may die, and other neurons that are normally stimulated by its axon may die as well. However, if the cell body remains intact, cut or compressed axons of peripheral nerves can regenerate successfully.

Almost immediately after a peripheral axon has been severed or crushed, the separated ends seal themselves off and then swell as substances being transported along the axon begin to accumulate in the sealed ends (Figure 13.4a). Within a few hours, the axon and its myelin sheath distal to the injury site begin to disintegrate because they cannot receive nutrients from the cell body. This process, **Wallerian degeneration,** spreads distally from the injury site, completely fragmenting the axon (Figure 13.4b). Generally, the entire axon distal to the injury is degraded by phagocytes within a week, but the neurilemma remains intact within the endoneurium. After the debris has been disposed of, surviving Schwann cells proliferate in response to mitosis-stimulating chemicals released by the macrophages, and migrate into the injury site. Once

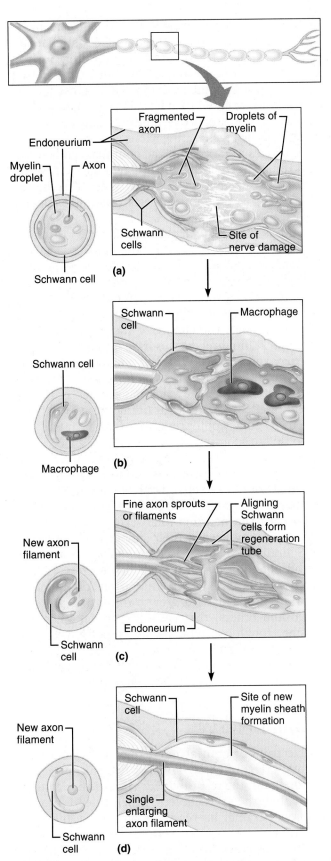

FIGURE 13.4 Regeneration of a nerve fiber in a peripheral nerve. (a) Fragmentation of the axon at the injury site. **(b)** Macrophages destroy the axon distal to the injury. **(c)** Axon filaments grow within a regeneration tube formed by Schwann cells. **(d)** Regenerated axon and the formation of a new myelin sheath.

13

there, they release growth factors and begin to express cell adhesion molecules (CAMs) that encourage axonal growth. Additionally, they form a *regeneration tube*, a system of cellular cords that guide the regenerating axon "sprouts" across the gap and to their original contacts (Figure 13.4c and d). The same Schwann cells protect, support, and remyelinate the regenerating axons.

Changes also occur in the neuronal cell body after axonal destruction. Within two days, its chromatophilic substance breaks apart, and then the cell body swells as protein synthesis revs up to support regeneration of its axon.

Axons regenerate at the approximate rate of 1.5 mm a day. The greater the distance between the severed endings, the less the chance of recovery because adjacent tissues block growth by protruding into the gaps, and axonal sprouts fail to find the regeneration tube. Neurosurgeons align cut nerve endings surgically to enhance the chance of successful regeneration, and scaffolding devices have been successful in guiding axon growth. Whatever the measures taken, post-trauma axon regrowth never exactly matches what existed before the injury, and much of the recovery protocol involves retraining the nervous system to respond appropriately so that stimulus and response are coordinated.

Unlike peripheral nerve fibers, most CNS fibers never regenerate. Consequently, damage to the brain or spinal cord has been viewed as irreversible. This difference in regenerative capacity seems to have less to do with the neurons themselves than with the "company they keep"—their supporting cells. After CNS injury, "cleanup" is much slower. Moreover, the oligodendrocytes surrounding the injured fibers fail to guide fiber regrowth. Indeed, the oligodendrocytes are studded with growth-inhibiting proteins (Nogo and others) that act on neuronal receptors, causing growth cone collapse and repulsion. Experiments neutralizing the myelin-bound growth inhibitors with antibodies or blocking their receptors have resulted in useful fiber regeneration.

Cranial Nerves

Twelve pairs of **cranial nerves** are associated with the brain (Figure 13.5). The first two pairs attach to the forebrain; the rest originate from the brain stem. Other than the vagus nerves, which extend into the abdomen, cranial nerves serve only head and neck structures.

In most cases, the names of the cranial nerves reveal either the structures they serve or their functions. The nerves are also numbered (using Roman numerals) from the most rostral to the most caudal. A mini-introduction to the cranial nerves follows.

I. Olfactory. These are the tiny sensory nerves (filaments) of smell, which run from the nasal mucosa to synapse with the olfactory bulbs. Note that the olfactory bulbs and tracts, shown in Figure 13.5a, are brain structures and not part of cranial nerve I. (See Table 13.2 art for the olfactory nerve filaments.)

II. Optic. Because this sensory nerve of vision develops as an outgrowth of the brain, it is really a brain tract.

III. Oculomotor. This nerve has a name meaning "eye mover" because it supplies four of the six extrinsic muscles that move the eyeball in the orbit.

IV. Trochlear. This nerve's name means "pulley" and it innervates an extrinsic eye muscle that loops through a pulley-shaped ligament in the orbit.

V. Trigeminal. Three *(tri)* branches spring from this, the largest of the cranial nerves. It supplies sensory fibers to the face and motor fibers to the chewing muscles.

VI. Abducens. This nerve controls the extrinsic eye muscle that *abducts* the eyeball (turns it laterally).

VII. Facial. A large nerve that innervates muscles of *facial* expression (among other things).

VIII. Vestibulocochlear. This sensory nerve for hearing and balance was formerly called the *auditory nerve.*

IX. Glossopharyngeal. Its name, meaning "tongue and pharynx," reveals the structures it helps to innervate.

X. Vagus. This nerve's name means "wanderer" or "vagabond," and it is the only cranial nerve to extend beyond the head and neck to the thorax and abdomen.

XI. Accessory. Considered an *accessory* part of the vagus nerve, this nerve was formerly called the *spinal accessory nerve.*

XII. Hypoglossal. This nerve runs inferior to the tongue and innervates some tongue-moving muscles, as reflected by its name meaning "under the tongue."

You might make up your own saying to remember the first letters of the cranial nerves in order, or use the following memory jog sent to me by a student: "**O**n **o**ccasion, **o**ur **t**rusty **t**ruck **a**cts **f**unny— **v**ery **g**ood **v**ehicle **a**ny**h**ow."

In the last chapter, we described how spinal nerves are formed by the fusion of ventral (motor) and dorsal (sensory) roots. Cranial nerves, on the other hand, vary markedly in their composition. Most cranial nerves are mixed nerves as shown in Figure 13.5b. However, two nerve pairs (the olfactory and optic) associated with special sense organs, are

(a)

Cranial nerves I – VI	Sensory function	Motor function	PS* fibers
I Olfactory	Yes (smell)	No	No
II Optic	Yes (vision)	No	No
III Oculomotor	No	Yes	Yes
IV Trochlear	No	Yes	No
V Trigeminal	Yes (general sensation)	Yes	No
VI Abducens	No	Yes	No

Cranial nerves VII – XII	Sensory function	Motor function	PS* fibers
VII Facial	Yes (taste)	Yes	Yes
VIII Vestibulocochlear	Yes (hearing and balance)	Some	No
IX Glossopharyngeal	Yes (taste)	Yes	Yes
X Vagus	Yes (taste)	Yes	Yes
XI Accessory	No	Yes	No
XII Hypoglossal	No	Yes	No

(b) *PS = parasympathetic

FIGURE 13.5 **Location and function of cranial nerves. (a)** Ventral view of the human brain, showing the cranial nerves. **(b)** Summary of cranial nerves by function. Two cranial nerves (I and II) have sensory function only, no motor function. Four nerves (III, VII, IX, and X) carry parasympathetic fibers that serve visceral muscles and glands. All cranial nerves that innervate muscles also carry afferent fibers from proprioceptors in the muscles served; only sensory functions other than proprioception are indicated.

generally considered purely sensory. The cell bodies of the sensory neurons of the olfactory and optic nerves are located *within* their respective special sense organs. In other cases of sensory neurons contributing to cranial nerves (V, VII, IX, and X) the cell bodies are located in **cranial sensory ganglia** just outside the brain. Some cranial nerves have a single sensory ganglion, others have several, and still others have none.

Several of the mixed cranial nerves contain both somatic and autonomic motor fibers and hence serve both skeletal muscles and visceral organs. Except for some autonomic motor neurons located in ganglia, the cell bodies of motor neurons contributing to the cranial nerves are located in the ventral gray matter regions (nuclei) of the brain stem.

Having read this overview, you are now ready to tackle Table 13.2, which provides a more detailed

(Text continues on p. 508.)

TABLE 13.2   **Cranial Nerves**

I THE OLFACTORY NERVES (ol-fak'to-re)

Origin and course: Olfactory nerve fibers arise from olfactory receptor cells located in olfactory epithelium of nasal cavity and pass through cribriform plate of ethmoid bone to synapse in olfactory bulb. Fibers of olfactory bulb neurons extend posteriorly as olfactory tract, which runs beneath frontal lobe to enter cerebral hemispheres and terminates in primary olfactory cortex. See also Figure 15.21.

Function: Purely sensory; carry afferent impulses for sense of smell

Clinical testing: Person is asked to sniff aromatic substances, such as oil of cloves and vanilla, and to identify each.

Homeostatic imbalance: Fracture of ethmoid bone or lesions of olfactory fibers may result in partial or total loss of smell, a condition known as *anosmia* (an-oz'me-ah). ●

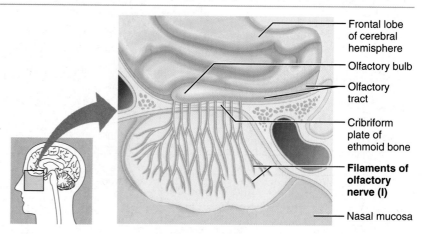

- Frontal lobe of cerebral hemisphere
- Olfactory bulb
- Olfactory tract
- Cribriform plate of ethmoid bone
- **Filaments of olfactory nerve (I)**
- Nasal mucosa

II THE OPTIC NERVES

Origin and course: Fibers arise from retina of eye to form optic nerve, which passes through optic canal of orbit. The optic nerves converge to form the optic chiasma (ki-az'mah) where fibers partially cross over, continue on as optic tracts, enter thalamus, and synapse there. Thalamic fibers run (as the optic radiation) to occipital (visual) cortex, where visual interpretation occurs. See also Figure 15.19.

Function: Purely sensory; carry afferent impulses for vision

Clinical testing: Vision and visual field are determined with eye chart and by testing the point at which the person first sees an object (finger) moving into the visual field. Fundus of eye viewed with ophthalmoscope to detect papilledema (swelling of optic disc, the site where the optic nerve leaves the eyeball), as well as for routine examination of the optic disc and retinal blood vessels.

Homeostatic imbalance: Damage to optic nerve results in blindness in eye served by nerve; damage to visual pathway beyond the optic chiasma results in partial visual losses; visual defects are called *anopsias* (ah-nop'se-ahz). ●

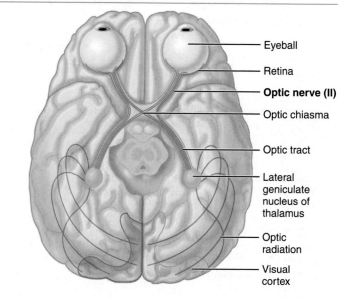

- Eyeball
- Retina
- **Optic nerve (II)**
- Optic chiasma
- Optic tract
- Lateral geniculate nucleus of thalamus
- Optic radiation
- Visual cortex

13

TABLE 13.2 *(continued)*

III THE OCULOMOTOR NERVES (ok"u-lo-mo'tor)

Origin and course: Fibers extend from ventral midbrain (near its junction with pons) and pass through bony orbit, via superior orbital fissure, to eye.

Function: Chiefly motor nerves (*oculomotor* = motor to the eye); contain a few proprioceptive afferents; each nerve includes

- Somatic motor fibers to four of the six extrinsic eye muscles (inferior oblique and superior, inferior, and medial rectus muscles) that help direct eyeball, and to levator palpebrae superioris muscle, which raises upper eyelid

- Parasympathetic (autonomic) motor fibers to sphincter pupillae (circular muscles of iris), which cause pupil to constrict, and to ciliary muscle, controlling lens shape for visual focusing; some parasympathetic cell bodies are in the ciliary ganglia

- Sensory (proprioceptor) afferents, which run from same four extrinsic eye muscles to midbrain

Clinical testing: Pupils are examined for size, shape, and equality. Pupillary reflex is tested with penlight (pupils should constrict when illuminated). Convergence for near vision is tested, as is subject's ability to follow objects with the eyes.

Homeostatic imbalance: In oculomotor nerve paralysis, eye cannot be moved up, down, or inward, and at rest, eye rotates laterally [*external strabismus* (strah-biz'mus)] because the actions of the two extrinsic eye muscles not served by cranial nerve III are unopposed; upper eyelid droops *(ptosis),* and the person has double vision and trouble focusing on close objects. ●

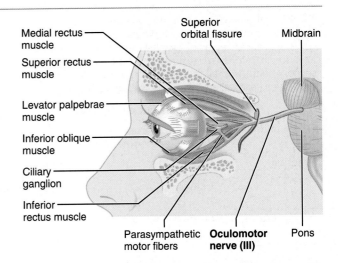

IV THE TROCHLEAR NERVES (trok'le-ar)

Origin and course: Fibers emerge from dorsal midbrain and course ventrally around midbrain to enter orbit through superior orbital fissure along with oculomotor nerves.

Function: Primarily motor nerves; supply somatic motor fibers to (and carry proprioceptor fibers from) one of the extrinsic eye muscles, the superior oblique muscle

Clinical testing: Tested in common with cranial nerve III.

Homeostatic imbalance: Trauma to, or paralysis of, a trochlear nerve results in double vision and reduced ability to rotate eye inferolaterally. ●

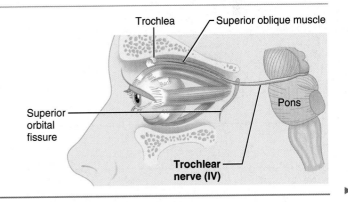

TABLE 13.2 **Cranial Nerves** (continued)

V THE TRIGEMINAL NERVES

Largest of cranial nerves; fibers extend from pons to face, and form three divisions (*trigemina* = threefold): ophthalmic, maxillary, and mandibular divisions. As major general sensory nerves of face, transmit afferent impulses from touch, temperature, and pain receptors. Cell bodies of sensory neurons of all three divisions are located in large *trigeminal* (also called *semilunar* or *gasserian*) *ganglion*.

The mandibular division also contains motor fibers that innervate chewing muscles.

Dentists desensitize upper and lower jaws by injecting local anesthetic (such as Novocain) into alveolar branches of maxillary and mandibular divisions, respectively; since this blocks pain-transmitting fibers of teeth, the surrounding tissues become numb.

	Ophthalmic division (V$_1$)	Maxillary division (V$_2$)	Mandibular division (V$_3$)
Origin and course	Fibers run from face to pons via superior orbital fissure	Fibers run from face to pons via foramen rotundum	Fibers pass through skull via foramen ovale
Function	Conveys sensory impulses from skin of anterior scalp, upper eyelid, and nose, and from nasal cavity mucosa, cornea, and lacrimal gland	Conveys sensory impulses from nasal cavity mucosa, palate, upper teeth, skin of cheek, upper lip, lower eyelid	Conveys sensory impulses from anterior tongue (except taste buds), lower teeth, skin of chin, temporal region of scalp; supplies motor fibers to, and carries proprioceptor fibers from, muscles of mastication
Clinical testing	Corneal reflex tested: touching cornea with wisp of cotton should elicit blinking	Sensations of pain, touch, and temperature are tested with safety pin and hot and cold objects	Motor branch assessed by asking person to clench his teeth, open mouth against resistance, and move jaw side to side

Homeostatic imbalance: *Tic douloureux* (tik doo"loo-roo'; *tic* = twitch, *douloureux* = painful), or *trigeminal neuralgia* (nu-ral'je-ah), caused by inflammation of trigeminal nerve, is widely considered to produce most excruciating pain known; the stabbing pain lasts for a few seconds to a minute, but it can be relentless, occurring a hundred times a day. Usually provoked by some sensory stimulus, such as brushing teeth or even a passing breeze hitting the face. It seems to be caused by pressure on the trigeminal nerve root. Analgesics and carbamazepine (an anticonvulsant) are only partially effective. In severe cases, nerve is cut proximal to trigeminal ganglion; this relieves the agony, but also results in loss of sensation on that side of face. ●

13

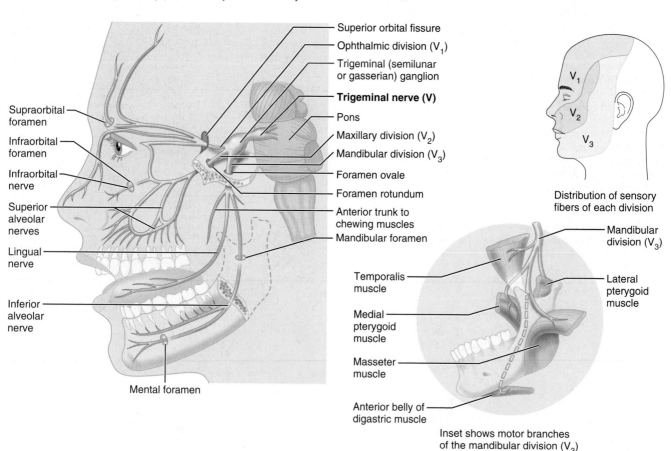

Superior orbital fissure
Ophthalmic division (V$_1$)
Trigeminal (semilunar or gasserian) ganglion
Trigeminal nerve (V)
Pons
Maxillary division (V$_2$)
Mandibular division (V$_3$)
Foramen ovale
Foramen rotundum
Anterior trunk to chewing muscles
Mandibular foramen

Supraorbital foramen
Infraorbital foramen
Infraorbital nerve
Superior alveolar nerves
Lingual nerve
Inferior alveolar nerve
Mental foramen

Distribution of sensory fibers of each division

V$_1$
V$_2$
V$_3$

Mandibular division (V$_3$)
Lateral pterygoid muscle
Temporalis muscle
Medial pterygoid muscle
Masseter muscle
Anterior belly of digastric muscle

Inset shows motor branches of the mandibular division (V$_3$)

TABLE 13.2 *(continued)*

VI THE ABDUCENS NERVES (ab-du'senz)

Origin and course: Fibers leave inferior pons and enter orbit via superior orbital fissure to run to eye.
Function: Primarily motor; supply somatic motor fibers to lateral rectus muscle, an extrinsic muscle of the eye; convey proprioceptor impulses from same muscle to brain.
Clinical testing: Tested in common with cranial nerve III.

⚠ Homeostatic imbalance: In abducens nerve paralysis, eye cannot be moved laterally; at rest, affected eyeball rotates medially *(internal strabismus)*. ●

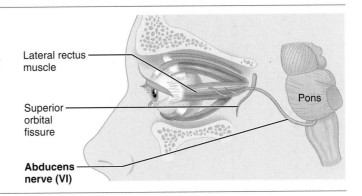

VII THE FACIAL NERVES

Origin and course: Fibers issue from pons, just lateral to abducens nerves (see Figure 13.5), enter temporal bone via *internal acoustic meatus,* and run within bone (and through inner ear cavity) before emerging through *stylomastoid foramen;* nerve then courses to lateral aspect of face.
Function: Mixed nerves that are the chief motor nerves of face; have five major branches: temporal, zygomatic, buccal, mandibular, and cervical (see **c**)

- Convey motor impulses to skeletal muscles of face (muscles of facial expression), except for chewing muscles served by trigeminal nerves, and transmit proprioceptor impulses from same muscles to pons (see **b**)

- Transmit parasympathetic (autonomic) motor impulses to lacrimal (tear) glands, nasal and palatine glands, and submandibular and sublingual salivary glands. Some of the cell bodies of these parasympathetic motor neurons are in *pterygopalatine* (ter"eh-go-pal'ah-tīn) and *submandibular ganglia* on the trigeminal nerve (see **a**)

- Convey sensory impulses from taste buds of anterior two-thirds of tongue; cell bodies of these sensory neurons are in *geniculate ganglion* (see **a**)

Clinical testing: Anterior two-thirds of tongue is tested for ability to taste sweet (sugar), salty, sour (vinegar), and bitter (quinine) substances. Symmetry of face is checked. Subject is asked to close eyes, smile, whistle, and so on. Tearing is assessed with ammonia fumes.

⚠ Homeostatic imbalance: *Bell's palsy,* characterized by paralysis of facial muscles on affected side and partial loss of taste sensation, may develop rapidly (often overnight). Most often caused by herpes simplex I viral infection, which causes swelling and inflammation of facial nerve. Lower eyelid droops, corner of mouth sags (making it difficult to eat or speak normally), tears drip continuously from eye and eye cannot be completely closed (conversely, dry-eye syndrome may occur). Condition may disappear spontaneously without treatment. ●

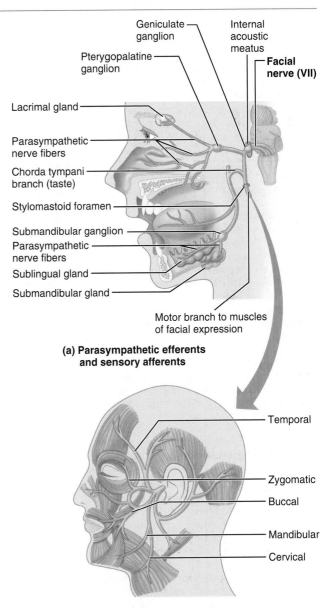

(a) Parasympathetic efferents and sensory afferents

(b) Motor branches to muscles of facial expression and scalp muscles

13

TABLE 13.2   Cranial Nerves (continued)

VII THE FACIAL NERVES (continued)

(c) A simple method of remembering the courses of the five major motor nerves of the face

---

VIII THE VESTIBULOCOCHLEAR NERVES (ves-tib"u-lo-kok'le-ar)

Origin and course: Fibers arise from hearing and equilibrium apparatus located within inner ear of temporal bone and pass through internal acoustic meatus to enter brain stem at pons-medulla border. Afferent fibers from hearing receptor in cochlea form the *cochlear division*; those from equilibrium receptors in semicircular canals and vestibule form the *vestibular division* (vestibular nerve); the two divisions merge to form vestibulocochlear nerve. See also Figure 15.27.

Function: Mostly sensory. Vestibular branch transmits afferent impulses for sense of equilibrium, and sensory nerve cell bodies are located in *vestibular ganglia.* Cochlear branch transmits afferent impulses for sense of hearing, and sensory nerve cell bodies are located in *spiral ganglion* within cochlea. Some motor fibers from the pons innervate the outer hair cells of the cochlea. See also Figure 15.28c

Clinical testing: Hearing is checked by air and bone conduction using tuning fork.

◥ **Homeostatic imbalance:** Lesions of cochlear nerve or cochlear receptors result in *central* or *nerve deafness*, whereas damage to vestibular division produces dizziness, rapid involuntary eye movements, loss of balance, nausea, and vomiting. ●

IX THE GLOSSOPHARYNGEAL NERVES (glos"o-fah-rin'je-al)

Origin and course: Fibers emerge from medulla and leave skull via *jugular foramen* to run to throat.

Function: Mixed nerves that innervate part of tongue and pharynx. Provide somatic motor fibers to, and carry proprioceptor fibers from, a superior pharyngeal muscle called the *stylopharyngeus,* which elevates the pharynx in swallowing. Provide parasympathetic motor fibers to parotid salivary glands (some of the nerve cell bodies of these parasympathetic motor neurons are located in *otic ganglion*).

13

TABLE 13.2 *(continued)*

IX THE GLOSSOPHARYNGEAL NERVES *(continued)*

Sensory fibers conduct taste and general sensory (touch, pressure, pain) impulses from pharynx and posterior tongue, from chemoreceptors in the carotid body (which monitor O_2 and CO_2 levels in the blood and help regulate respiratory rate and depth), and from baroreceptors of carotid sinus (which monitor blood pressure). Sensory neuron cell bodies are located in *superior* and *inferior ganglia*.

Clinical testing: Position of the uvula is checked. Gag and swallowing reflexes are checked. Subject is asked to speak and cough. Posterior third of tongue may be tested for taste.

Homeostatic imbalance: Injury or inflammation of glossopharyngeal nerves impairs swallowing and taste. ●

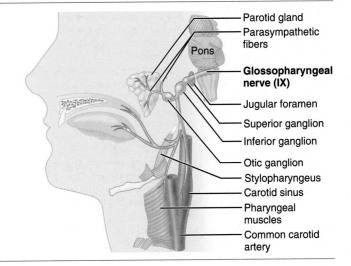

X THE VAGUS NERVES (va'gus)

Origin and course: The only cranial nerves to extend beyond head and neck region. Fibers emerge from medulla, pass through skull via jugular foramen, and descend through neck region into thorax and abdomen. See also Figure 14.4.

Function: Mixed nerves; nearly all motor fibers are parasympathetic efferents, except those serving skeletal muscles of pharynx and larynx (involved in swallowing). Parasympathetic motor fibers supply heart, lungs, and abdominal viscera and are involved in regulation of heart rate, breathing, and digestive system activity. Transmit sensory impulses from thoracic and abdominal viscera, from the aortic arch baroreceptors (for blood pressure) and the carotid and aortic bodies (chemoreceptors for respiration), and taste buds of posterior tongue and pharynx. Carry proprioceptor fibers from muscles of larynx and pharynx.

Clinical testing: As for cranial nerve IX (IX and X are tested in common, since they both innervate muscles of throat and mouth).

Homeostatic imbalance: Since nearly all muscles of the larynx ("voice box") are innervated by laryngeal branches of the vagus, vagal nerve paralysis can lead to hoarseness or loss of voice; other symptoms are difficulty swallowing and impaired digestive system motility. Total destruction of both vagus nerves is incompatible with life, because these parasympathetic nerves are crucial in maintaining normal state of visceral organ activity; without their influence, the activity of the sympathetic nerves, which mobilize and accelerate vital body processes (and shut down digestion), would be unopposed. ●

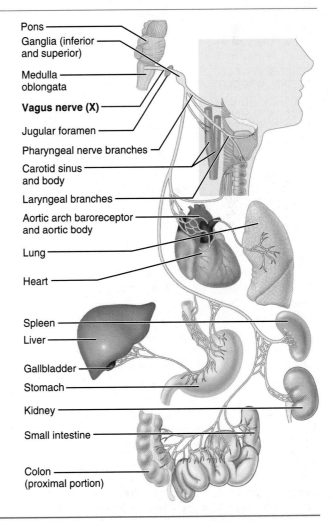

TABLE 13.2   **Cranial Nerves** (continued)

XI THE ACCESSORY NERVES

Origin and course: Unique in that they are formed by union of a *cranial root* and a *spinal root*. Cranial root emerges from lateral aspect of medulla of brain stem; spinal root arises from superior region (C_1–C_5) of spinal cord. Spinal portion passes upward along spinal cord, enters skull via foramen magnum, and temporarily joins cranial root; the resulting accessory nerve exits from skull through *jugular foramen*. Cranial and spinal fibers then diverge; cranial root fibers join vagus nerve, and spinal root runs to the largest neck muscles.

Function: Mixed nerves, but primarily motor in function. Cranial division joins with fibers of vagus nerve (X) to supply motor fibers to larynx, pharynx, and soft palate. Spinal root supplies motor fibers to trapezius and sternocleidomastoid muscles, which together move head and neck, and conveys proprioceptor impulses from same muscles.

Clinical testing: Sternocleidomastoid and trapezius muscles are checked for strength by asking person to rotate head and shrug shoulders against resistance.

🔺 **Homeostatic imbalance:** Injury to the spinal root of one accessory nerve causes head to turn toward injury side as result of sternocleidomastoid muscle paralysis; shrugging of that shoulder (role of trapezius muscle) becomes difficult. ●

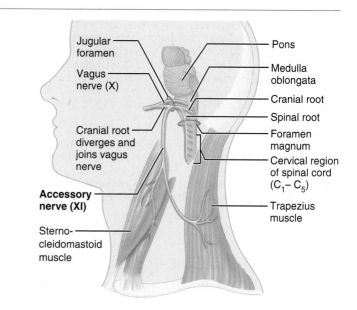

XII THE HYPOGLOSSAL NERVES (hi″po-glos′al)

Origin and course: As their name implies (*hypo* = beneath; *glossal* = tongue), hypoglossal nerves mainly serve the tongue. Fibers arise by a series of roots from medulla and exit from skull via *hypoglossal canal* to travel to tongue. See also Figure 13.5.

Function: Mixed nerves, but primarily motor in function. Carry somatic motor fibers to intrinsic and extrinsic muscles of tongue, and proprioceptor fibers from same muscles to brain stem. Hypoglossal nerve control allows not only food mixing and manipulation by tongue during chewing, but also tongue movements that contribute to swallowing and speech.

Clinical testing: Person is asked to protrude and retract tongue. Any deviations in position are noted.

🔺 **Homeostatic imbalance:** Damage to hypoglossal nerves causes difficulties in speech and swallowing; if both nerves are impaired, the person cannot protrude tongue; if only one side is affected, tongue deviates (points) toward affected side; eventually paralyzed side begins to atrophy. ●

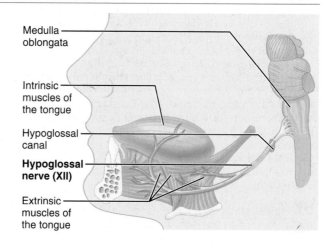

description of the origin, course, and function of the cranial nerves. Notice that the pathways of the purely or mostly sensory nerves (I, II, and VIII) are described from the receptors to the brain, while those of the other nerves are described in the opposite direction (from the brain distally). Remembering the primary functions of the cranial nerves (as sensory, **m**otor, or **b**oth) can be a problem; this sentence might help: "**S**ome **s**ay **m**arry **m**oney, **b**ut **m**y **b**rother **b**elieves (it's) **b**ad **b**usiness (to) **m**arry **m**oney."

Spinal Nerves

General Features

Thirty-one pairs of **spinal nerves,** each containing thousands of nerve fibers, arise from the spinal cord and supply all parts of the body except the head and some areas of the neck. All are mixed nerves. As illustrated in Figure 13.6, these nerves are named according to their point of issue from the spinal cord.

Q *Why are the lumbar and cervical regions of the spinal cord enlarged?*

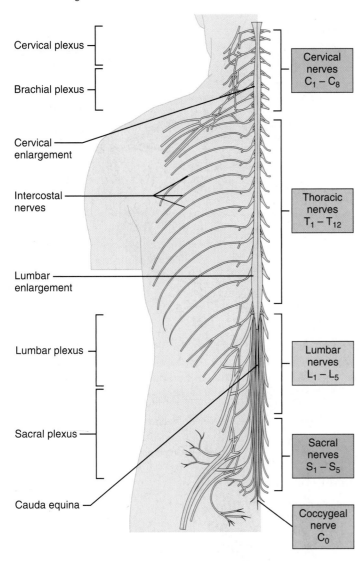

Cervical plexus

Brachial plexus

Cervical enlargement

Intercostal nerves

Lumbar enlargement

Lumbar plexus

Sacral plexus

Cauda equina

Cervical nerves $C_1 - C_8$

Thoracic nerves $T_1 - T_{12}$

Lumbar nerves $L_1 - L_5$

Sacral nerves $S_1 - S_5$

Coccygeal nerve C_0

FIGURE 13.6 **Distribution of spinal nerves.** Distribution of spinal nerves, posterior view. Note that the spinal nerves are named according to their points of issue.

There are 8 pairs of cervical spinal nerves (C_1–C_8), 12 pairs of thoracic nerves (T_1–T_{12}), 5 pairs of lumbar nerves (L_1–L_5), 5 pairs of sacral nerves (S_1–S_5), and 1 pair of tiny coccygeal nerves (C_0).

Notice that there are eight pairs of cervical nerves but only seven cervical vertebrae. This "discrepancy" is easily explained. The first seven pairs exit the vertebral canal *superior to* the vertebrae for which they are named, but C_8 emerges *inferior to* the seventh cervical vertebra (between C_7 and T_1). Below

A *The peripheral nerves serving the limbs arise in the lumbar and cervical regions.*

the cervical level, each spinal nerve leaves the vertebral column *inferior to* the same-numbered vertebra.

As mentioned in Chapter 12, each spinal nerve connects to the spinal cord by a dorsal root and a ventral root. Each root forms from a series of **rootlets** that attach along the length of the corresponding spinal cord segment (Figure 13.7). The **ventral roots** contain *motor* (efferent) fibers that arise from ventral horn motor neurons and extend to and innervate the skeletal muscles. (Autonomic nervous system efferents also contained in the ventral roots are described in Chapter 14.) **Dorsal roots** contain *sensory* (afferent) fibers that arise from sensory neurons in the dorsal root ganglia and conduct impulses from peripheral receptors to the spinal cord.

The spinal roots pass laterally from the cord and unite just distal to the dorsal root ganglion to form a spinal nerve before emerging from the vertebral column via their respective intervertebral foramina. Because motor and sensory fibers mingle in a spinal nerve, it contains both efferent and afferent fibers. The length of the spinal roots increases progressively from the superior to the inferior aspect of the cord. In the cervical region, the roots are short and run horizontally, but the roots of the lumbar and sacral nerves extend inferiorly for some distance through the lower vertebral canal as the *cauda equina* before exiting the vertebral column (Figure 13.6).

A spinal nerve is quite short (only 1–2 cm) because almost immediately after emerging from its foramen, it divides into a small **dorsal ramus**, a larger **ventral ramus** (ra'mus; "branch"), and a tiny **meningeal branch** (mĕ-nin'je-al) that reenters the vertebral canal to innervate the meninges and blood vessels within. Each ramus, like the spinal nerve itself, is mixed. Finally, joined to the base of the ventral rami of the thoracic spinal nerves are special rami called **rami communicantes**, which contain autonomic (visceral) nerve fibers.

Innervation of Specific Body Regions

The spinal nerve rami and their main branches supply the entire somatic region of the body (voluntary muscles and skin) from the neck down. The dorsal rami supply the posterior body trunk. The thicker ventral rami supply the rest of the trunk and the limbs. To be clear, let's review the difference between roots and rami: Roots lie medial to and form the spinal nerves, and each root is strictly sensory *or* motor. Rami lie distal to and are lateral branches of the spinal nerves and, like spinal nerves, carry both sensory and motor fibers.

Before getting into the specifics of how the body is innervated, some important points about the ventral rami of the spinal nerves need to be understood.

13

FIGURE 13.7 **Formation of spinal nerves and rami distribution. (a)** A diagrammatic view of a spinal cord segment, illustrating the formation of one pair of spinal nerves by the union of the ventral and dorsal roots of the spinal cord. **(b)** Cross-sectional view of the left side of the body at the level of the thorax, showing the distribution of the dorsal and ventral rami of the spinal nerve. In the thorax, each ventral ramus continues as an intercostal nerve. Notice also the rami communicantes branches of the spinal nerve. (The small meningeal branch is not illustrated.)

(a)

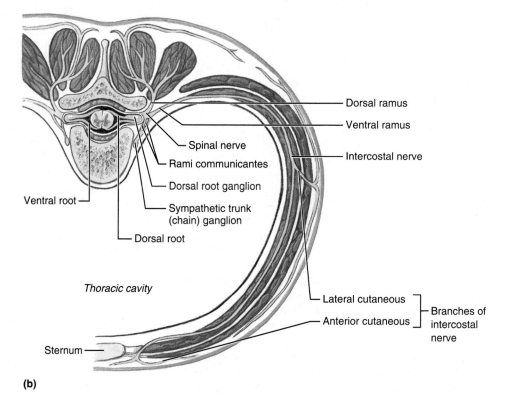

Thoracic cavity

(b)

Except for T_2–T_{12}, all ventral rami branch and join one another lateral to the vertebral column, forming complicated **nerve plexuses** (Figure 13.6). Such interlacing nerve networks occur in the cervical, brachial, lumbar, and sacral regions and primarily serve the limbs. Notice that *only ventral rami form plexuses*. Within a plexus, fibers from the various ventral rami crisscross one another and become redistributed so that (1) each resulting branch of the plexus contains fibers from several spinal nerves and (2) fibers from each ventral ramus travel to the body periphery via several routes. Thus, each muscle in a limb receives its nerve supply from more than one spinal nerve. An advantage of this fiber regrouping is that damage to one spinal segment or root cannot completely paralyze any limb muscle.

Throughout this section, we mention major groups of skeletal muscles served. For more specific information on muscle innervations, see Tables 10.1–10.17.

TABLE 13.3	Branches of the Cervical Plexus (See Figure 13.8)		
NERVES	**SPINAL ROOTS (VENTRAL RAMI)**	**STRUCTURES SERVED**	
CUTANEOUS BRANCHES (SUPERFICIAL)			
Lesser occipital	C_2 (C_3)	Skin on posterolateral aspect of neck	
Greater auricular	C_2, C_3	Skin of ear, skin over parotid gland	
Transverse cutaneous (cervical)	C_2, C_3	Skin on anterior and lateral aspect of neck	
Supraclavicular (medial, intermediate, and lateral)	C_3, C_4	Skin of shoulder and clavicular region	
MOTOR BRANCHES (DEEP)			
Ansa cervicalis (superior and inferior roots)	C_1–C_3	Infrahyoid muscles of neck (omohyoid, sternohyoid, and sternothyroid)	
Segmental and other muscular branches	C_1–C_5	Deep muscles of neck (geniohyoid and thyrohyoid) and portions of scalenes, levator scapulae, trapezius, and sternocleidomastoid muscles	
Phrenic	C_3–C_5	Diaphragm (sole motor nerve supply)	

Back

The innervation of the posterior body trunk by the dorsal rami follows a neat, segmented plan. Via its several branches (see Figure 13.7), each dorsal ramus innervates the narrow strip of muscle (and skin) in line with its emergence point from the spinal column.

Anterolateral Thorax and Abdominal Wall

Only in the thorax are the ventral rami arranged in a simple segmental pattern corresponding to that of the dorsal rami. The ventral rami of T_1–T_{12} mostly course anteriorly, deep to each rib, as the **intercostal nerves.** Along their course, these nerves give off *cutaneous branches* to the skin (Figures 13.6 and 13.7b). Two thoracic nerves are unusual: the tiny T_1 (most fibers enter the brachial plexus) and T_{12}, which lies inferior to the twelfth rib, making it a **subcostal nerve.** The intercostal nerves and their branches supply the intercostal muscles lying between the ribs, the muscle and skin of the anterolateral thorax, and most of the abdominal wall.

Cervical Plexus and the Neck

Buried deep in the neck under the sternocleidomastoid muscle, the looping **cervical plexus** is formed by the ventral rami of the first four cervical nerves (Figure 13.8). Its branches are summarized in Table 13.3. Most branches are **cutaneous nerves** (nerves that supply only the skin) that transmit sensory impulses from the skin of the neck, the ear area, the back of the head, and the shoulder. Other branches innervate muscles of the anterior neck.

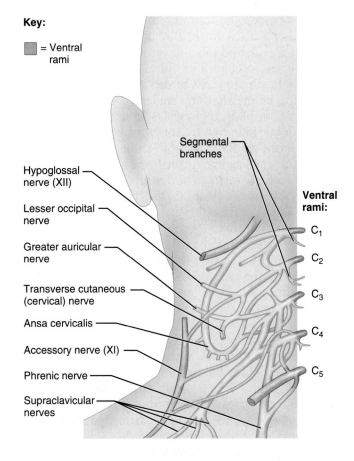

Key:

▨ = Ventral rami

Hypoglossal nerve (XII)
Lesser occipital nerve
Greater auricular nerve
Transverse cutaneous (cervical) nerve
Ansa cervicalis
Accessory nerve (XI)
Phrenic nerve
Supraclavicular nerves

Segmental branches

Ventral rami:
C_1
C_2
C_3
C_4
C_5

FIGURE 13.8 The cervical plexus. The nerves colored gray connect to the plexus but do not belong to it. See Table 13.3 for structures served.

13

The single most important nerve from this plexus is the **phrenic nerve** (fren'ik) (which receives its major input from C_3 and C_4). The phrenic nerve runs inferiorly through the thorax and supplies both motor and sensory fibers to the diaphragm (*phren* = diaphragm), which is the chief muscle causing breathing movements.

HOMEOSTATIC IMBALANCE

Irritation of the phrenic nerve causes spasms of the diaphragm, or hiccups. If both phrenic nerves are severed, or if the C_3–C_5 region of the spinal cord is crushed or destroyed, the diaphragm is paralyzed and respiratory arrest occurs. Victims are kept alive by mechanical respirators that force air into their lungs and do their breathing for them. ●

Brachial Plexus and Upper Limb

The large, important **brachial plexus,** situated partly in the neck and partly in the axilla, gives rise to virtually all the nerves that innervate the upper limb (Table 13.4). It can be palpated (felt) in a living person just superior to the clavicle at the lateral border of the sternocleidomastoid muscle.

This plexus is formed by intermixing of ventral rami of C_5–C_8 and most of the T_1 ramus. Additionally, it often receives fibers from C_4 or T_2 or both.

The brachial plexus is very complex (some consider it to be the anatomy student's nightmare). Perhaps the simplest approach is to master the terms used for its four major groups of branches (Figure 13.9). From medial to lateral, these are (1) the ventral rami, misleadingly called *roots*, which form (2) *trunks*, which form (3) *divisions*, which form (4) *cords*. You might want to use the saying "**R**eally **t**ired? **D**rink **c**offee" to help you remember this branching sequence.

The five **roots** (ventral rami C_5–T_1) of the brachial plexus lie deep to the sternocleidomastoid muscle. At the lateral border of that muscle, these roots unite to form **upper, middle,** and **lower trunks,** each of which divides almost immediately into an **anterior** and a **posterior division.** These divisions, which generally indicate which fibers serve the front or back of the limb, pass deep to the clavicle and enter the axilla, where they give rise to three large fiber bundles called the **lateral, medial,** and **posterior cords.** (The cords are named for their relationship to the axillary artery, which runs through the axilla; see Figure 19.22.) All along the plexus, small nerves branch off. These supply the muscles and skin of the shoulder and superior thorax.

HOMEOSTATIC IMBALANCE

Injuries to the brachial plexus are common; when severe, they cause weakness or paralysis of the entire upper limb. Such injuries may occur when the upper limb is pulled hard and the plexus is stretched (as when a football tackler yanks the arm of the running back), and by blows to the top of the shoulder that force the humerus inferiorly (as when a cyclist is pitched headfirst off a motorcycle and his shoulder grinds into the pavement). ●

The brachial plexus ends in the axilla, where its three cords wind along the axillary artery and then give rise to the main nerves of the upper limb (Figure 13.9c). Five of these nerves are especially important: the axillary, musculocutaneous, median, ulnar, and radial nerves. Their distribution and targets are described briefly here, and in more detail in Table 13.4.

The **axillary nerve** branches off the posterior cord and runs posterior to the surgical neck of the humerus. It innervates the deltoid and teres minor muscles and the skin and joint capsule of the shoulder.

The **musculocutaneous nerve,** the major end branch of the lateral cord, courses inferiorly in the anterior arm, supplying motor fibers to the biceps brachii and brachialis muscles. Distal to the elbow, it provides for cutaneous sensation of the lateral forearm.

The **median nerve** descends through the arm to the anterior forearm, where it gives off branches to the skin and to most flexor muscles. On reaching the hand, it innervates five intrinsic muscles of the lateral palm. The median nerve activates muscles that pronate the forearm, flex the wrist and fingers, and oppose the thumb.

HOMEOSTATIC IMBALANCE

Median nerve injury makes it difficult to use the pincer grasp (opposed thumb and index finger) to pick up small objects. Because this nerve runs down the midline of the forearm and wrist, it is a frequent casualty of wrist-slashing suicide attempts. In carpal tunnel syndrome (see p. 235), the median nerve is compressed. ●

The **ulnar nerve** branches off the medial cord of the plexus. It descends along the medial aspect of the arm toward the elbow, swings behind the medial epicondyle, and then follows the ulna along the medial forearm. There it supplies the flexor carpi ulnaris and the medial part of the flexor digitorum profundus (the flexors not supplied by the median nerve). It continues into the hand, where it innervates most intrinsic hand muscles and the skin of the medial aspect of the hand. It produces wrist and finger flexion

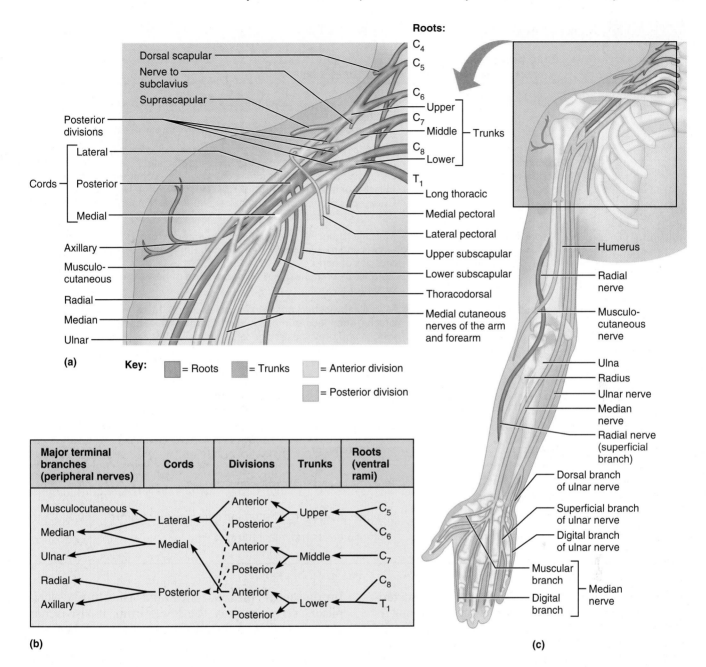

FIGURE 13.9 **The brachial plexus. (a)** Roots, trunks, divisions, and cords. **(b)** Flowchart of consecutive branches formed in the brachial plexus from the spinal roots (ventral rami) to the major nerves formed from the cords. **(c)** Distribution of the major peripheral nerves of the upper limb. (See Table 13.4.)

and (with the median nerve) adduction and abduction of the medial fingers.

 HOMEOSTATIC IMBALANCE

Where it takes a superficial course, the ulnar nerve is very vulnerable to injury. Striking the "funny bone"—the spot where this nerve rests against the medial epicondyle—causes tingling of the little finger. Severe or chronic damage can lead to sensory loss, paralysis, and muscle atrophy. Affected individ-

uals have trouble making a fist and gripping objects. As the little and ring fingers become hyperextended at the knuckles and flexed at the distal interphalangeal joints, the hand contorts into a *clawhand*. ●

The **radial nerve,** the largest branch of the brachial plexus, is a continuation of the posterior cord. This nerve wraps around the humerus (in the radial groove), and then runs anteriorly around the lateral epicondyle at the elbow. There it divides into a superficial branch that follows the lateral edge of the radius to the hand

TABLE 13.4	Branches of the Brachial Plexus (See Figure 13.9)	
NERVES	**CORD AND SPINAL ROOTS (VENTRAL RAMI)**	**STRUCTURES SERVED**
Musculocutaneous	Lateral cord (C_5–C_7)	Muscular branches: flexor muscles in anterior arm (biceps brachii, brachialis, coracobrachialis) Cutaneous branches: skin on anterolateral forearm (extremely variable)
Median	By two branches, one from medial cord (C_8, T_1) and one from the lateral cord (C_5–C_7)	Muscular branches to flexor group of anterior forearm (palmaris longus, flexor carpi radialis, flexor digitorum superficialis, flexor pollicis longus, lateral half of flexor digitorum profundus, and pronator muscles); intrinsic muscles of lateral palm and digital branches to the fingers Cutaneous branches: skin of lateral two-thirds of hand, palm side and dorsum of fingers 2 and 3
Ulnar	Medial cord (C_8, T_1)	Muscular branches: flexor muscles in anterior forearm (flexor carpi ulnaris and medial half of flexor digitorum profundus); most intrinsic muscles of hand Cutaneous branches: skin of medial third of hand, both anterior and posterior aspects
Radial	Posterior cord (C_5–C_8, T_1)	Muscular branches: posterior muscles of arm, forearm, and hand (triceps brachii, anconeus, supinator, brachioradialis, extensors carpi radialis longus and brevis, extensor carpi ulnaris, and several muscles that extend the fingers) Cutaneous branches: skin of posterolateral surface of entire limb (except dorsum of fingers 2 and 3)
Axillary	Posterior cord (C_5, C_6)	Muscular branches: deltoid and teres minor muscles Cutaneous branches: some skin of shoulder region
Dorsal scapular	Branches of C_5 rami	Rhomboid muscles and levator scapulae
Long thoracic	Branches of C_5–C_7 rami	Serratus anterior muscle
Subscapular	Posterior cord; branches of C_5 and C_6 rami	Teres major and subscapular muscles
Suprascapular	Upper trunk (C_5, C_6)	Shoulder joint; supraspinatus and infraspinatus muscles
Pectoral (lateral and medial)	Branches of lateral and medial cords (C_5–T_1)	Pectoralis major and minor muscles

and a deep branch (not illustrated) that runs posteriorly. It supplies the posterior skin of the limb along its entire course. Its motor branches innervate essentially all the extensor muscles of the upper limb. The radial nerve produces elbow extension, forearm supination, wrist and finger extension, and thumb abduction.

 HOMEOSTATIC IMBALANCE

Trauma to the radial nerve results in *wrist drop*, an inability to extend the hand at the wrist. Improper use of a crutch or "Saturday night paralysis," in which an intoxicated person falls asleep with an arm draped over the back of a chair or sofa edge, causes radial nerve compression and ischemia (deprivation of blood supply). ●

Lumbosacral Plexus and Lower Limb

The sacral and lumbar plexuses overlap substantially, and because many fibers of the lumbar plexus contribute to the sacral plexus via the **lumbosacral trunk,** the two plexuses are often referred to as the **lumbosacral plexus.** Although the lumbosacral plexus serves mainly the lower limb, it also sends some branches to the abdomen, pelvis, and buttock.

Lumbar Plexus The **lumbar plexus** arises from the spinal nerves L_1–L_4 (Figure 13.10) and lies within the psoas major muscle. Its proximal branches innervate parts of the abdominal wall muscles and the psoas muscle, but its major branches descend to innervate the anterior and medial thigh. The **femoral nerve,** the largest terminal nerve of this plexus, runs deep to the inguinal ligament to enter the thigh and then divides into several large branches. The motor branches innervate anterior thigh muscles (quadriceps), which are the principal thigh flexors and knee extensors. The cutaneous branches serve the skin of the anterior thigh and the medial surface of the leg from knee to foot. The **obturator nerve** (ob"tu-ra'tor) enters the medial thigh via the obturator foramen and innervates the adductor muscles. These and other smaller branches of the lumbar plexus are summarized in Table 13.5.

13

TABLE 13.5	Branches of the Lumbar Plexus (See Figure 13.10)	

NERVES	SPINAL ROOTS (VENTRAL RAMI)	STRUCTURES SERVED
Femoral	L_2–L_4	Skin of anterior and medial thigh via *anterior femoral cutaneous* branch; skin of medial leg and foot, hip and knee joints via *saphenous* branch; motor to anterior muscles (quadriceps and sartorius) of thigh and to pectineus, iliacus
Obturator	L_2–L_4	Motor to adductor magnus (part), longus, and brevis muscles, gracilis muscle of medial thigh, obturator externus; sensory for skin of medial thigh and for hip and knee joints
Lateral femoral cutaneous	L_2, L_3	Skin of lateral thigh; some sensory branches to peritoneum
Iliohypogastric	L_1	Skin of lower abdomen, lower back, and hip; muscles of anterolateral abdominal wall (obliques and transversus) and pubic region
Ilioinguinal	L_1	Skin of external genitalia and proximal medial aspect of the thigh; inferior abdominal muscles
Genitofemoral	L_1, L_2	Skin of scrotum in males, of labia majora in females, and of anterior thigh inferior to middle portion of inguinal region; cremaster muscle in males

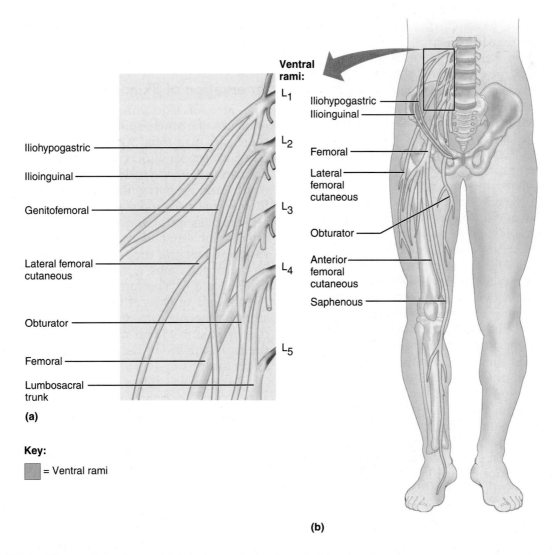

FIGURE 13.10 **The lumbar plexus. (a)** Spinal roots (ventral rami) and major branches. **(b)** Distribution of the major peripheral nerves in the lower limb (anterior view). (See Table 13.5.)

HOMEOSTATIC IMBALANCE

Compression of the spinal roots of the lumbar plexus, as by a herniated disc, results in gait problems because the femoral nerve serves the prime movers of both hip flexion and knee extension. Anesthesia of the anterior thigh and pain in the medial thigh occur if the obturator nerve is impaired. ●

Sacral Plexus The **sacral plexus** arises from spinal nerves L₄–S₄ and lies immediately caudal to the lumbar plexus (Figure 13.11). Some fibers of the lumbar plexus contribute to the sacral plexus via the *lumbosacral trunk,* as mentioned earlier. The sacral plexus has about a dozen named branches. About half of these serve the buttock and lower limb; the others innervate pelvic structures and the perineum. The most important branches are described here. Table 13.6 summarizes all but the smallest ones.

The largest branch of the sacral plexus is the **sciatic nerve** (si-at'ik), the thickest and longest nerve in the body. It supplies the entire lower limb, except the anteromedial thigh.

Actually two nerves (the tibial and common fibular) wrapped in a common sheath, the sciatic nerve leaves the pelvis via the greater sciatic notch. It courses deep to the gluteus maximus muscle and enters the posterior thigh just medial to the hip joint (*sciatic* = of the hip). There it gives off motor branches to the hamstring muscles (all thigh extensors and knee flexors) and to the adductor magnus. Immediately above the knee, the two divisions of the sciatic nerve diverge.

The **tibial nerve** courses through the popliteal fossa (the region just posterior to the knee joint) and supplies the posterior compartment muscles of the leg and the skin of the posterior calf and sole of the foot. In the vicinity of the knee, the tibial nerve gives off the **sural nerve,** which serves the skin of the posterolateral leg, and at the ankle the tibial nerve divides into the **medial** and **lateral plantar nerves,** which serve most of the foot. The **common fibular (peroneal) nerve** descends from its point of origin, wraps around the head of the fibula (fibula = *perone*), and then divides into superficial and deep branches. These branches innervate the knee joint, skin of the lateral calf and dorsum of the foot, and muscles of the anterolateral leg (the extensors that dorsiflex the foot).

The next largest sacral plexus branches are the **superior** and **inferior gluteal nerves.** Together, they innervate the buttock (gluteal) and tensor fasciae latae muscles. The **pudendal nerve** (pu-den'dal; "shameful") innervates the muscles and skin of the perineum, mediates the act of erection, and is involved in voluntary control of urination (see Table 10.7). Other branches of the sacral plexus supply the thigh rotators and muscles of the pelvic floor.

 HOMEOSTATIC IMBALANCE

Injury to the proximal part of the sciatic nerve, as might follow a fall, disc herniation, or improper administration of an injection into the buttock, results in a number of lower limb impairments, depending on the precise nerve roots injured. *Sciatica* (si-at'ĭ-kah), characterized by stabbing pain radiating over the course of the sciatic nerve, is common. When the nerve is transected, the leg is nearly useless. The leg cannot be flexed (because the hamstrings are paralyzed), and all foot and ankle movement is lost. The foot drops into plantar flexion (it dangles), a condition called *footdrop.* Recovery from sciatic nerve injury is usually slow and incomplete.

If the lesion occurs below the knee, thigh muscles are spared. When the tibial nerve is injured, the paralyzed calf muscles cannot plantar flex the foot and a shuffling gait develops. The common fibular nerve is susceptible to injury largely because of its superficial location at the head and neck of the fibula. Even a tight leg cast, or remaining too long in a side-lying position on a firm mattress, can compress this nerve and cause footdrop. ●

Innervation of Skin: Dermatomes

The area of skin innervated by the cutaneous branches of a single spinal nerve is called a **dermatome** (der'mah-tōm; "skin segment"). Every spinal nerve except C₁ innervates dermatomes. Adjacent dermatomes on the body trunk are fairly uniform in width, almost horizontal, and in direct line with their spinal nerves (Figure 13.12). The dermatome arrangement in the limbs is less obvious. (It is also more variable and different clinicians have mapped a variety of areas for the same dermatomes.) The skin of the upper limbs is supplied by ventral rami of C₅–T₁ (or T₂). The lumbar nerves supply most of the anterior surfaces of the thighs and legs, and the sacral nerves serve most of the posterior surfaces of the lower limbs. (This distribution basically reflects the areas supplied by the lumbar and sacral plexuses, respectively.)

Dermatome regions are not as cleanly separated as a typical dermatome map indicates. Because those of the trunk overlap considerably (about 50%), destruction of a single spinal nerve will not result in complete numbness anywhere. In the limbs, the overlap is less complete and some skin regions are innervated by just one spinal nerve.

Innervation of Joints

The easiest way to remember which nerves serve which synovial joint is to use **Hilton's law,** which says: *Any nerve serving a muscle that produces movement at a joint also innervates the joint and*

TABLE 13.6	Branches of the Sacral Plexus (See Figure 13.11)	
NERVES	**SPINAL ROOTS (VENTRAL RAMI)**	**STRUCTURES SERVED**
Sciatic nerve	L_4, L_5, S_1–S_3	Composed of two nerves (tibial and common fibular) in a common sheath; they diverge just proximal to the knee
▪ Tibial (including sural, medial and lateral plantar, and medial calcaneal branches)	L_4–S_3	Cutaneous branches: to skin of posterior surface of leg and sole of foot Motor branches: to muscles of back of thigh, leg, and foot [hamstrings (except short head of biceps femoris), posterior part of adductor magnus, triceps surae, tibialis posterior, popliteus, flexor digitorum longus, flexor hallucis longus, and intrinsic muscles of foot]
▪ Common fibular (superficial and deep branches)	L_4–S_2	Cutaneous branches: to skin of anterior surface of leg and dorsum of foot Motor branches: to short head of biceps femoris of thigh, fibular muscles of lateral compartment of leg, tibialis anterior, and extensor muscles of toes (extensor hallucis longus, extensors digitorum longus and brevis)
Superior gluteal	L_4, L_5, S_1	Motor branches: to gluteus medius and minimus and tensor fasciae latae
Inferior gluteal	L_5–S_2	Motor branches: to gluteus maximus
Posterior femoral cutaneous	S_1–S_3	Skin of buttock, posterior thigh, and popliteal region; length variable; may also innervate part of skin of calf and heel
Pudendal	S_2–S_4	Supplies most of skin and muscles of perineum (region encompassing external genitalia and anus and including clitoris, labia, and vaginal mucosa in females, and scrotum and penis in males); external anal sphincter

Ventral rami:

Superior gluteal
Lumbosacral trunk
Inferior gluteal
Common fibular
Tibial
Posterior femoral cutaneous
Pudendal
Sciatic

L_4
L_5
S_1
S_2
S_3
S_4
S_5
C_0

(a)

Key:

▢ = Ventral rami

Superior gluteal
Inferior gluteal
Pudendal
Sciatic
Posterior femoral cutaneous
Common fibular
Tibial
Sural
Deep fibular
Superficial fibular
Plantar branches

(b)

FIGURE 13.11   The sacral plexus. (a) The spinal roots (ventral rami) and major branches. **(b)** Distribution of the major peripheral nerves in the lower limb (posterior view). (See Table 13.6.)

13

Q *In what way are dermatomes clinically significant in patients with spinal cord injury?*

FIGURE 13.12   **Dermatomes.** Each dermatome is the skin segment innervated by the cutaneous sensory branches of a single spinal nerve. All spinal nerves but C₁ participate in the innervation of the dermatomes. **(a)** Anterior view. **(b)** Posterior view.

the skin over the joint. Hence, once you learn which nerves serve the various major muscles and muscle groups, no *new* learning is necessary. For example, the knee is crossed by the quadriceps, gracilis, and hamstring muscles. The nerves to these muscles are the femoral nerve anteriorly and branches of the sciatic and obturator nerves posteriorly. Consequently, these nerves innervate the knee joint as well.

A *The distribution of dermatomes affected can help the physician determine which nerves are damaged and localize the injured region of the spinal cord.*

PART 3: MOTOR ENDINGS AND MOTOR ACTIVITY

Peripheral Motor Endings

So far we have covered the structure of sensory receptors that detect stimuli, and that of nerves containing the afferent and efferent fibers that deliver impulses to and from the CNS. We now turn to **motor endings,** the PNS elements that activate effectors by releasing neurotransmitters. Because we discussed that topic earlier with the innervation of body muscles, all we need to do here is recap. To balance the overview of sensory function provided earlier in the chapter, this will be followed by a brief overview of motor integration.

Innervation of Skeletal Muscle

As illustrated in Figure 9.7 (p. 290), the terminals of somatic motor fibers that innervate voluntary muscles form elaborate **neuromuscular junctions** with their effector cells. As each axon branch reaches its target, a single muscle fiber, the ending splits into a cluster of *axon terminals (boutons)* that branch treelike over the motor end plate of the muscle fiber. The axon terminals contain mitochondria and synaptic vesicles filled with the neurotransmitter acetylcholine (ACh). When a nerve impulse reaches an axon terminal, ACh is released by exocytosis, diffuses across the fluid-filled synaptic cleft (about 50 nm wide), and attaches to ACh receptors on the highly infolded sarcolemma at the junction. ACh binding results in the opening of ligand-gated channels that allow both Na^+ and K^+ to pass. Because more Na^+ enters the cell than K^+ leaves, the muscle cell interior at that point depolarizes, producing a type of graded potential called an end plate potential. The end plate potential spreads to adjacent areas of the membrane where it triggers the opening of voltage-gated sodium channels. This event leads to propagation of an action potential along the sarcolemma that stimulates the muscle fiber to contract. The synaptic cleft at somatic neuromuscular junctions is filled with a glycoprotein-rich basal lamina (a structure not seen at other synapses). The basal lamina contains *acetylcholinesterase,* the enzyme that breaks down ACh almost immediately after it binds.

Innervation of Visceral Muscle and Glands

The junctions between autonomic motor endings and their effectors (which are smooth and cardiac muscle and glands) are much simpler than the junctions formed between somatic fibers and skeletal muscle cells. The autonomic motor axons branch repeatedly, each branch forming *synapses en passant* with its effector cells. Instead of a cluster of bulblike terminals, an axon ending serving smooth muscle or a gland (but not cardiac muscle) has a series of **varicosities,** knoblike swellings containing mitochondria and synaptic vesicles, that make it look like a string of beads (see Figure 9.25). The autonomic synaptic vesicles typically contain either acetylcholine or norepinephrine, both of which act indirectly on their targets via second messengers. Consequently, the visceral motor responses tend to be slower than those induced by somatic motor fibers, which directly open ion channels.

Overview of Motor Integration: From Intention to Effect

In the motor system, we have motor endings serving effectors (muscle fibers) instead of sensory receptors, descending efferent circuits instead of ascending afferent circuits, and motor behavior instead of perception. However, like sensory systems, the basic mechanisms of motor systems operate at three levels.

Levels of Motor Control

The cerebral cortex is at the highest level of the conscious motor pathways, but it is *not* the ultimate planner and coordinator of complex motor activities. The cerebellum and basal nuclei (ganglia) play this role and are therefore put at the top of the motor control hierarchy. Motor control exerted by lower levels is mediated by *reflex arcs* in some cases, but complex motor behavior, such as walking and swimming, appears to depend on more complex patterns. Currently, we define three levels of motor control: the *segmental level*, the *projection level*, and the *precommand level* (Figure 13.13).

The Segmental Level

The lowest level of the motor hierarchy, the **segmental level,** consists of the spinal cord circuits. A segmental circuit activates a network of ventral horn neurons in a group of cord segments, causing them to stimulate specific groups of muscles. Those circuits that control locomotion and other specific and oft-repeated motor activities are called **central pattern generators (CPGs).** CPGs consist of networks of oscillating inhibitory and excitatory neurons, which set crude rhythms and alternating patterns of movement.

FIGURE 13.13   **Hierarchy of motor control.**

The Projection Level

The spinal cord is under the direct control of the **projection level** of motor control. The projection level consists of *upper motor neurons* of the motor cortex, which initiate the *direct (pyramidal) system,* and of brain stem motor areas, which oversee the *indirect (multineuronal) system* (see Table 12.3 and p. 478). Axons of the direct system neurons produce discrete voluntary movements of the skeletal muscles. Axons of the indirect system help control reflex and CPG-controlled motor actions, modifying and controlling the activity of the segmental apparatus.

Projection motor pathways convey information to lower motor neurons, and send a copy of that information *(internal feedback)* back to higher command levels, continually informing them of what is happening. The direct and indirect systems provide separate and parallel pathways for controlling the spinal cord, but these systems are interrelated at all levels.

The Precommand Level

Two other systems of brain neurons, located in the cerebellum and basal nuclei, regulate motor activity. They precisely start or stop movements, coordinate movements with posture, block unwanted movements, and monitor muscle tone. Collectively called

precommand areas, these systems *control the outputs* of the cortex and brain stem motor centers and stand at the highest level of the motor hierarchy.

The key center for "online" sensorimotor integration and control is the **cerebellum.** Remember the cerebellum is a target of ascending proprioceptor, tactile, equilibrium, and visual inputs—feedback that it needs for rapid correction of "errors" in motor activity. It also receives information via branches from descending pyramidal tracts, and from various brain stem nuclei. The cerebellum lacks direct connections to the spinal cord; it acts on motor pathways through the projection areas of the brain stem and on the motor cortex via the thalamus to fine-tune motor activity.

The **basal nuclei** receive inputs from *all* cortical areas and send their output back mainly to premotor and prefrontal cortical areas via the thalamus. Compared to the cerebellum, the basal nuclei appear to be involved in more complex aspects of motor control. Under resting conditions, the basal nuclei inhibit various motor centers of the brain, but when the motor centers are released from inhibition, coordinated motions can begin. Cells in both the basal nuclei and the cerebellum are involved in this unconscious planning and discharge *in advance* of willed movements. When you actually move your fingers, both the precommand areas and the primary motor cortex

FIGURE 13.14 **The basic components of all human reflex arcs.** The reflex arc illustrated is polysynaptic.

are active. At the risk of oversimplifying, it appears that the cortex says, "I want to do this," and then lets the precommand areas take over to provide the proper timing and patterns to execute the movements desired. The precommand areas control the motor cortex and provide its readiness to initiate a voluntary act. The conscious cortex then chooses to act or not act, but the groundwork has already been laid.

PART 4: REFLEX ACTIVITY

The Reflex Arc

Many of the body's control systems belong to a general category known as reflexes, which can be either inborn or learned. In the most restricted sense, an *inborn*, or *intrinsic, reflex* is a rapid, predictable motor response to a stimulus. It is unlearned, unpremeditated, and involuntary, and may be considered as built into our neural anatomy. Reflexes prevent us from having to *think* about all the little details of staying upright, intact, and alive—helping us maintain posture, avoid pain, and control visceral activites.

One example of an inborn reflex is what happens when you splash a pot of boiling water on your arm; you are likely to drop the pot instantly and involuntarily even before feeling any pain. This response is triggered by a spinal reflex without any help from the brain. In many cases we are aware of the final response of a basic reflex activity (you know you've dropped the pot of boiling water). In other cases, reflex activities go on without any awareness on our part. This is typical of many visceral reflexes, which are regulated by the subconscious lower regions of the CNS, specifically the brain stem and spinal cord.

In addition to these basic, inborn types of reflexes, there are *learned,* or *acquired, reflexes* that result from practice or repetition. Take, for instance, the complex sequence of reactions that occurs when an experienced driver drives a car. The process is largely automatic, but only because substantial time and effort were expended to acquire the driving skill. In reality, the distinction between inborn and learned reflexes is not clear-cut and most inborn reflex actions are subject to modification by learning and conscious effort. For instance, if a 3-year-old child was standing by your side when you scalded your arm, you most likely would set the pot down (rather than just letting go) because of your conscious recognition of the danger to the child.

Recall the discussion in Chapter 11 about serial and parallel processing of sensory input. What happens when you scald your arm is a good example of how these two processing mechanisms work together. You drop the pot before feeling any pain, but the pain signals picked up by the interneurons of the spinal cord are quickly transmitted to the brain, so that within the next few seconds you *do* become aware of pain, and you also know what happened to cause it. The withdrawal reflex is serial processing mediated by the spinal cord, and pain awareness reflects simultaneous parallel processing of the sensory input.

Components of a Reflex Arc

As you learned in Chapter 11, reflexes occur over highly specific neural paths called **reflex arcs,** all of which have five essential components (Figure 13.14):

① **Receptor:** Site of the stimulus action.

② **Sensory neuron:** Transmits afferent impulses to the CNS.

③ **Integration center:** In simple reflex arcs, may be a single synapse between a sensory neuron and a motor neuron (**monosynaptic reflex).** More complex reflex arcs involve multiple synapses with chains of interneurons (**polysynaptic reflex).** The integration center is always within the CNS.

④ **Motor neuron:** Conducts efferent impulses from the integration center to an effector organ.

⑤ **Effector:** Muscle fiber or gland cell that responds to the efferent impulses (by contracting or secreting).

Reflexes are classified functionally as **somatic reflexes** if they activate skeletal muscle, or as **autonomic (visceral) reflexes** if they activate visceral

Q *There is a major difference in the functions of the intrafusal and extrafusal muscle fibers. What is it?*

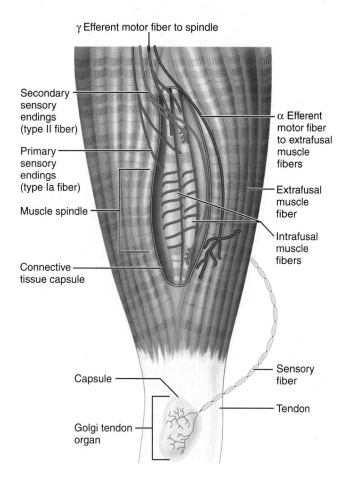

γ Efferent motor fiber to spindle

Secondary sensory endings (type II fiber)

Primary sensory endings (type Ia fiber)

Muscle spindle

Connective tissue capsule

α Efferent motor fiber to extrafusal muscle fibers

Extrafusal muscle fiber

Intrafusal muscle fibers

Capsule

Sensory fiber

Golgi tendon organ

Tendon

FIGURE 13.15 **Anatomy of the muscle spindle and Golgi tendon organ.** Notice the afferent fibers from and efferent fibers to the muscle spindle.

effectors (smooth or cardiac muscle or glands). Here we describe some common somatic reflexes mediated by the spinal cord. Autonomic reflexes are considered in later chapters with the visceral processes they help to regulate.

Spinal Reflexes

Somatic reflexes mediated by the spinal cord are called **spinal reflexes.** Many spinal reflexes occur without the direct involvement of higher brain centers. Generally, these reflexes are present in decerebrate animals (those in which the brain has been de-

stroyed) as long as the spinal cord is functional. However, the brain is "advised" of most spinal reflex activity and can facilitate, inhibit, or adapt it, depending on the circumstances (as described in the above example of the hot water–filled pot). Moreover, continuous facilitating signals from the brain are required for normal spinal reflex activity because, as noted in Chapter 12, if the spinal cord is transected, *spinal shock* occurs (all functions controlled by the cord are immediately depressed).

Testing of somatic reflexes is important clinically to assess the condition of the nervous system. Exaggerated, distorted, or absent reflexes indicate degeneration or pathology of specific nervous system regions, often before other signs are apparent.

Stretch and Golgi Tendon Reflexes

In order to smoothly coordinate skeletal muscular activity, your nervous system needs two types of information about the current state of a muscle. First, it needs to know the amount of tension in the muscle and its associated tendons. This information is provided by the *Golgi tendon organs.* Second, it needs to know the length of the muscle. This information is provided by the *muscle spindles.* These two types of proprioceptors play an important role in spinal reflexes and also provide essential feedback to the cerebral cortex and cerebellum.

Functional Anatomy of Muscle Spindles

Each muscle spindle consists of three to ten **intrafusal muscle fibers** (*intra* = within; *fusal* = the spindle) enclosed in a connective tissue capsule (Figure 13.15). These modified skeletal muscle fibers are less than one-quarter the size of **extrafusal muscle fibers** (the effector fibers of the muscle). The central regions of the intrafusal fibers, which lack myofilaments and are noncontractile, are the receptive surfaces of the spindle. These regions are wrapped by two types of afferent endings that send sensory inputs to the CNS. The **primary sensory endings** of large **type Ia fibers,** which innervate the spindle center, are stimulated by both the rate and degree of stretch. The **secondary sensory endings** of small **type II fibers** supply the spindle ends and are stimulated only by degree of stretch. The contractile regions of the intrafusal muscle fibers are limited to their ends because these are the only areas that contain actin and myosin myofilaments. These regions are innervated by **gamma (γ) efferent fibers** that arise from small motor neurons in the ventral horn of the spinal cord. These γ motor fibers, which maintain spindle sensitivity (as described shortly), are distinct from the **alpha (α) efferent fibers** of the large **alpha (α) motor neurons** that stimulate the extrafusal muscle fibers to contract.

A *The extrafusal muscle fibers are effectors; when adequately stimulated, they contract, shortening the muscle. The intrafusal fibers are part of a receptor apparatus that provides input for regulation of the activity of the muscle.*

13

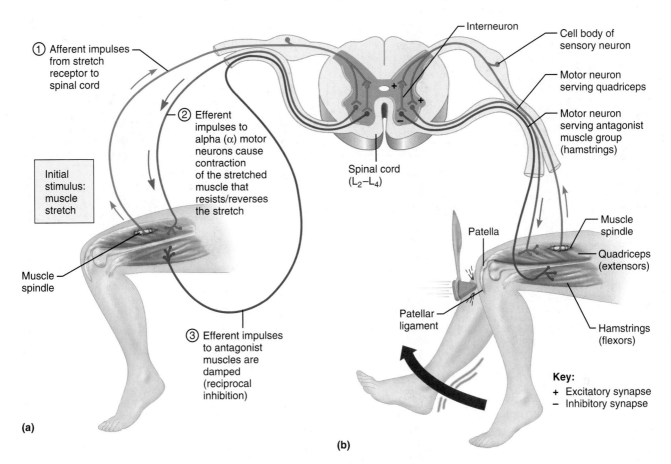

FIGURE 13.16 **The stretch reflex.**
(a) Events of the stretch reflex by which muscle stretch is damped. The events are shown in circular fashion. **(b)** The patellar reflex. Tapping the patellar tendon excites muscle spindles in the quadriceps muscle. Afferent impulses travel to the spinal cord, where synapses occur with motor neurons and interneurons. The motor neurons send activating impulses to the quadriceps causing it to contract, which causes extension of the knee and forward movement of the foot, counteracting the initial stretch. The interneurons make inhibitory synapses with ventral horn neurons that serve the antagonistic muscle group (hamstrings), thus preventing the hamstrings from resisting the contraction.

The muscle spindle is stretched (and excited) in one of two ways: (1) by applying an external force that lengthens the entire muscle, such as occurs when we carry a heavy weight or when antagonistic muscles contract (external stretch); or (2) by activating the γ motor neurons that stimulate the distal ends of the intrafusal fibers to contract, thus stretching the middle of the spindle (internal stretch).

The Stretch Reflex

By sending commands to the motor neurons, the brain essentially sets a muscle's length. The **stretch reflex** makes sure that the muscle stays at that length (Figure 13.16). For example, the **patellar** (pah-tel'ar) or **knee-jerk reflex** (Figure 13.16b) helps keep your knees from buckling when you are standing upright. As your knees begin to buckle and the quadriceps lengthens, the stretch reflex causes the quadriceps to contract without your having to think about it. The stretch reflex is important for maintaining muscle tone and adjusting it reflexively. It is most important in the large extensor muscles that sustain upright posture and in postural muscles of the trunk. For example, contractions of the postural muscles of the spine are almost continuously regulated by stretch reflexes initiated first on one side of the spine and then on the other.

Let's look at how the stretch reflex works. When muscle spindles are activated by stretch, the associated sensory neurons transmit impulses at a higher frequency to the spinal cord (Figure 13.17b). There the sensory neurons synapse directly with α motor neurons, which rapidly excite the extrafusal muscle fibers of the stretched muscle (Figure 13.16a). The reflexive muscle contraction that follows (an example of serial processing) resists further muscle

Muscle spindle
Intrafusal muscle fiber
Primary sensory (Ia) nerve fiber
Extrafusal muscle fiber

Time ⟶

(a) Unstretched muscle; AP frequency constant

(b) Stretched muscle; AP frequency increased

(c) α Motor neuron stimulation only; no APs, unable to signal length changes

(d) α–γ Neuron coactivation; AP frequency constant

FIGURE 13.17 **Operation of the muscle spindle. (a)** Action potentials (APs) in unstretched muscle are generated at a constant rate in the associated sensory (Ia) fiber. **(b)** Stretching the muscle activates the muscle spindle, increasing the rate of AP generation. **(c)** Activation of α motor neurons alone causes contraction of extrafusal muscle fibers only. The muscle spindle becomes slack and unable to signal further length changes. **(d)** Coactivation of both α and γ motor neurons causes contraction of both extrafusal and intrafusal muscle fibers, maintaining tension on the muscle spindle. The muscle spindle can still signal changes in muscle length.

13

stretching. Branches of the afferent fibers also synapse with interneurons that inhibit motor neurons controlling antagonistic muscles (parallel processing), and the resulting inhibition is called **reciprocal inhibition.** Consequently, the stretch stimulus causes the antagonists to relax so that they cannot resist the shortening of the "stretched" muscle caused by the main reflex arc. While this spinal reflex is occurring, information on muscle length and the speed of muscle shortening is being relayed (mainly via the dorsal white columns) to higher brain centers (more parallel processing).

The most familiar clinical example of a stretch reflex is the knee-jerk reflex we have just described. Stretch reflexes can be elicited in any skeletal muscle by a sudden jolt to the tendon or the muscle itself. All stretch reflexes are **monosynaptic** and **ipsilateral;** that is, they involve a single synapse and motor activity on the same side of the body. Although stretch reflexes *themselves* are monosynaptic, the reflex arcs that inhibit the motor neurons serving the antagonistic muscles are polysynaptic.

A positive knee jerk (or a positive result for any other stretch reflex test) provides two important pieces of information. First, it proves that the sensory and motor connections between that muscle and the spinal cord are intact. Second, the vigor of the response indicates the degree of excitability of the spinal cord. When the spinal motor neurons are highly facilitated by impulses descending from higher centers, just touching the muscle tendon produces a vigorous reflex response. On the other hand, when the lower motor neurons are bombarded by inhibitory signals, even pounding on the tendon may fail to cause the reflex response.

HOMEOSTATIC IMBALANCE

Stretch reflexes tend to be either hypoactive or absent in cases of peripheral nerve damage or ventral horn injury involving the tested area. These reflexes are absent in those with chronic diabetes mellitus or neurosyphilis and during coma. However, they are hyperactive when lesions of the corticospinal tract reduce the inhibitory effect of the brain on the spinal cord (as in stroke patients). ●

Adjusting Muscle Spindle Sensitivity

During voluntary skeletal muscle contraction, the muscle shortens. If the intrafusal muscle fibers didn't contract along with the extrafusal fibers, then the muscle spindle would go slack and cease generating action potentials (Figure 13.17c). At this point it would be unable to signal further changes in muscle length, so it would be useless. Fortunately, **α-γ coactivation** prevents this from happening. Descending fibers of motor pathways synapse with both α and γ motor neurons, and motor impulses are simultaneously sent to the large extrafusal fibers and to muscle spindle intrafusal fibers. Stimulating the intrafusal fibers maintains the spindle's tension (and sensitivity) during muscle contraction, so that the brain continues to be notified of conditions in the muscle. Without such a system, information on changes in muscle length would cease to flow from contracting muscles.

The motor supply to the muscle spindle also allows the brain to voluntarily modify the stretch reflex response and the firing rate of α motor neurons. When the γ neurons are vigorously stimulated by impulses from the brain, the spindle is stretched and highly sensitive, and muscle contraction force is maintained or increased. When the γ motor neurons are inhibited, the spindle resembles a loose rubber band and is non-responsive, and the extrafusal muscles relax.

The ability to modify the stretch reflex is important in many situations. As the speed and difficulty of a movement increases, the brain increases γ motor output to increase the sensitivity of the muscle spindles. For example, a gymnast on a balance beam needs to have highly sensitive muscle spindles or she'll fall off. On the other hand, if you want to wind up to pitch a baseball, it is essential to suppress the stretch reflex so that your muscles can produce a large degree of motion (i.e., circumduct your pitching arm). Other athletes who require movements of maximum force learn to stretch muscles as much and as quickly as possible just before the movement. This advantage is demonstrated by the crouch that athletes assume just before jumping or running.

As we have seen, muscle tone and smooth coordination of movement depends upon having intact stretch reflex pathways. Both afferent and efferent fibers to the muscle spindle are vitally important. If either afferent or efferent fibers are cut, the muscle immediately loses its tone and becomes flaccid.

The Golgi Tendon Reflex

Whereas stretch reflexes cause muscle contraction in response to increased muscle length (stretch), the polysynaptic **Golgi tendon reflexes** produce exactly the opposite effect: muscle relaxation and lengthening in response to tension (Figure 13.18). When muscle tension increases substantially during contraction or passive stretching, high-threshold Golgi tendon organs in the tendon may be activated, and afferent impulses are transmitted to the spinal cord,

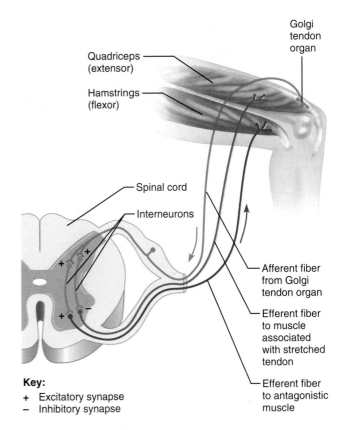

Key:
+ Excitatory synapse
− Inhibitory synapse

FIGURE 13.18 **The Golgi tendon reflex.** When the quadriceps muscle of the thigh contracts strongly, the tension in the patellar region increases, activating Golgi tendon organs in the tendon. Afferent neurons associated with the Golgi tendon organs synapse with interneurons in the spinal cord that inhibit motor neurons serving the contracting muscle and stimulate motor neurons activating the antagonistic muscle groups (the hamstrings). As a result, the contracting muscle relaxes and lengthens as the antagonist contracts and shortens.

and then to the cerebellum, where the information is used to adjust muscle tension. Simultaneously, motor neurons in spinal cord circuits supplying the contracting muscle are inhibited and antagonist muscles are activated, a phenomenon called **reciprocal activation.** As a result, the contracting muscle relaxes as its antagonist is activated.

Golgi tendon organs help avoid tearing of muscles and tendons subjected to possibly damaging stretching force. Golgi tendon organs also function at normal muscle tensions. In the normal range, Golgi tendon organs help to ensure smooth onset and termination of muscle contraction.

The Flexor and Crossed-Extensor Reflexes

The **flexor,** or **withdrawal, reflex** is initiated by a painful stimulus and causes automatic withdrawal of the threatened body part from the stimulus

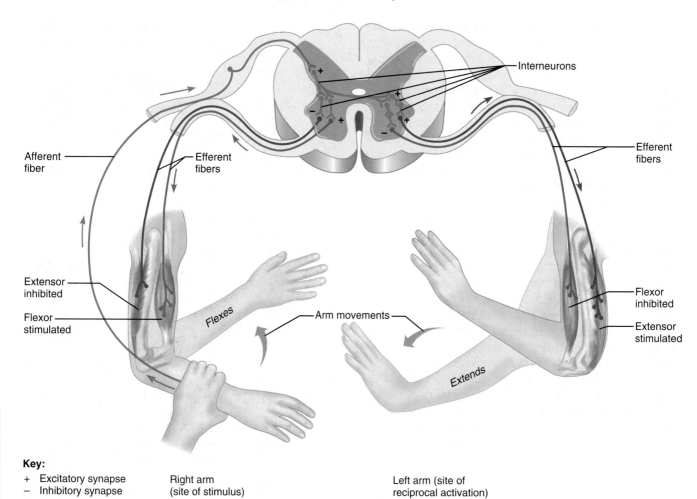

Key:
+ Excitatory synapse
− Inhibitory synapse

Right arm
(site of stimulus)

Left arm (site of
reciprocal activation)

FIGURE 13.19   **The crossed-extensor reflex.** A noxious stimulus causes a flexor reflex on the same side, withdrawing that limb, as shown on the left side of the diagram. At the same time, the extensor muscles on the opposite side are activated. In the example illustrated, a stranger suddenly grasps one arm, which is reflexively withdrawn while the opposite arm reflexively extends and pushes the stranger away.

(Figure 13.19). The response that occurs when you prick your finger is a good example. Flexor reflexes are ipsilateral and polysynaptic, the latter a necessity when several muscles must be recruited to withdraw the injured body part. Because flexor reflexes are protective reflexes important to our survival, they override the spinal pathways and prevent any other reflexes from using them at the same time. However, this reflex, like other spinal reflexes, can be overridden by descending signals from the brain. This happens when you are expecting a painful stimulus, for example a skin prick as a lab technician prepares to draw blood from a vein.

The **crossed-extensor reflex** often accompanies the flexor reflex in weight-bearing limbs and is particularly important in maintaining balance. It is a complex spinal reflex consisting of an ipsilateral withdrawal reflex and a contralateral extensor reflex. Incoming afferent fibers synapse with interneurons that control the flexor withdrawal response on the same side of the body and with other interneurons that control the extensor muscles on the opposite side. This reflex is obvious when you step barefoot on broken glass. The ipsilateral response causes rapid lifting of the cut foot, while the contralateral response activates the extensor muscles of the opposite leg to support the weight suddenly shifted to it. The withdrawal reflex is also seen when someone unexpectedly grabs your arm. The grasped arm is withdrawn as the opposite arm pushes you away from the attacker (Figure 13.19).

Superficial Reflexes

Superficial reflexes are elicited by gentle cutaneous stimulation, such as that produced by stroking the skin with a tongue depressor. These clinically important reflexes depend both on functional upper motor pathways and on cord-level reflex arcs. The best known of these are the plantar and abdominal reflexes.

The **plantar reflex** tests the integrity of the spinal cord from L_4 to S_2 and indirectly determines if the corticospinal tracts are functioning properly. It is elicited by drawing a blunt object downward along the lateral aspect of the plantar surface (sole) of the foot. The normal response is a downward flexion (curling) of the toes. However, if the primary motor cortex or corticospinal tract is damaged, the plantar reflex is replaced by an abnormal reflex called **Babinski's sign,** in which the great toe dorsiflexes and the smaller toes fan laterally. Infants exhibit Babinski's sign until they are about a year old because their nervous systems are incompletely myelinated. Despite its clinical significance, the physiological mechanism of Babinski's sign is not understood.

Stroking the skin of the lateral abdomen above, to the side, or below the umbilicus induces a reflex contraction of the abdominal muscles in which the umbilicus moves toward the stimulated site. These reflexes, called **abdominal reflexes,** check the integrity of the spinal cord and ventral rami from T_8 to T_{12}. The abdominal reflexes vary in intensity from one person to another. They are absent when corticospinal tract lesions are present.

Developmental Aspects of the Peripheral Nervous System

Most skeletal muscles derive from paired blocks of mesoderm (somites) distributed segmentally down the posteromedial aspect of the embryo. The spinal nerves branch from the developing spinal cord and adjacent neural crest and exit between the forming vertebrae, and each nerve becomes associated with the adjacent muscle mass. The spinal nerves supply both sensory and motor fibers to the developing muscles and help direct their maturation. Cranial nerves innervate muscles of the head in a comparable manner.

The distribution of cutaneous nerves to the skin follows a similar pattern. Most of the scalp and facial skin is innervated by the trigeminal nerves. Spinal nerves supply cutaneous branches to specific (adjacent) dermatomes that eventually become dermal segments. Thus, the distribution and growth of the spinal nerves correlate with the segmented body plan, which is established by the fourth week of embryonic development.

Growth of the limbs and unequal growth of other body areas result in an adult pattern of dermatomes with unequal sizes and shapes and varying degrees of overlap. Because embryonic muscle cells migrate extensively, much of the early segmental pattern is lost. Understanding the general pattern of sensory nerve distribution is critical for physicians. For example, in areas of substantial dermatome overlap, two or three spinal nerves must be blocked to perform local surgery.

Sensory receptors atrophy to some degree with age, and there is some lessening of muscle tone in the face and neck. Reflexes occur a bit more slowly during old age. This deterioration seems to reflect a general loss of neurons, fewer synapses per neuron, and a slowdown in central processing rather than any major changes in the peripheral nerve fibers. In fact, the peripheral nerves remain viable and normally functional throughout life unless subjected to traumatic injury or ischemia. The most common symptom of ischemia is a tingling sensation or numbness in the affected region.

■ ■ ■

The PNS is an essential part of any functional nervous system. Without it, the CNS would lack its rich bank of information about events of the external and internal environments. Now that we have connected the CNS to both of these environments, we are ready to consider the autonomic nervous system, the topic of Chapter 14.

Related Clinical Terms

Analgesia (an"al-je'zeah; *an* = without; *algos* = pain) Reduced ability to feel pain, not accompanied by loss of consciousness. An analgesic is a pain-relieving drug.

Dysarthria (dis-ar'thre-ah) Difficulty in speech articulation due to motor pathway disorders that result in weakness, uncoordinated motion, or altered respiration or rhythm. For example, lesions of cranial nerves IX, X, and XII result in nasal, breathy speech, and lesions in upper motor pathways produce a hoarse, strained voice. Not to be confused with *dysphasia* or *aphasia*, which are disorders of language processing.

Dystonia (dis-to'ne-ah) Impairment of muscle tone.

Nerve conduction studies Diagnostic tests that assess nerve integrity as indicated by their conduction velocities; the nerve is stimulated at one point, activity is recorded at a second point a known distance away, and the time required for the response to reach the recording electrode is measured; used to assess suspected peripheral neuropathies.

Neuralgia (nu-ral'je-ah; *neuro* = nerve) Sharp spasmlike pain along the course of one or more nerves; may be caused by inflammation or injury to the nerve(s) (for example, trigeminal neuralgia).

13

Neuritis (nu-ri′tis) Inflammation of a nerve; there are many forms with different effects (e.g., increased or decreased nerve sensitivity, paralysis of structure served, and pain).

Paresthesia (par″es-the′ze-ah) An abnormal sensation (burning, numbness, tingling) in the absence of stimuli; caused by a sensory nerve disorder.

Tabes dorsalis (ta′bēz dor-sa′lis) A slowly progressive condition caused by deterioration of the posterior tracts (gracilis and cuneatus) and associated dorsal roots; a late sign of the neurological damage caused by the syphilis bacterium. Because joint proprioceptor tracts are destroyed, affected individuals have poor muscle coordination and an unstable gait. Bacterial invasion of the sensory (dorsal) roots results in pain, which ends when dorsal root destruction is complete.

Chapter Summary

1. The peripheral nervous system consists of sensory receptors, nerves conducting impulses to and from the CNS, their associated ganglia, and motor endings.

PART 1: SENSORY RECEPTORS AND SENSATION

Sensory Receptors (pp. 491–494)

1. Sensory receptors are specialized to respond to environmental changes (stimuli).

2. Sensory receptors include the simple (general) receptors for pain, touch, pressure, and temperature found in the skin, as well as those found in skeletal muscles and tendons and in the visceral organs. Complex receptors (sense organs), consisting of sensory receptors and other cells, serve the special senses (vision, hearing, equilibrium, smell, and taste).

3. Receptors are classified according to stimulus detected as mechanoreceptors, thermoreceptors, photoreceptors, chemoreceptors, and nociceptors, and according to location as exteroceptors, interoceptors, and proprioceptors.

4. The general sensory receptors are classified structurally as free or encapsulated nerve (receptor) endings of sensory neurons. The free endings are mainly receptors for temperature and pain, although two are for light touch (Merkel discs and hair follicle receptors). The encapsulated endings, which are mechanoreceptors, include Meissner's corpuscles, Pacinian corpuscles, Ruffini endings, muscle spindles, Golgi tendon organs, and joint kinesthetic receptors.

Overview: From Sensation to Perception (pp. 494–498)

1. Sensation is awareness of internal and external stimuli; perception is conscious interpretation of those stimuli.

2. The three levels of sensory integration are the receptor, circuit, and perceptual levels. These levels are functions of the sensory receptors, the ascending pathways, and the cerebral cortex, respectively.

3. Sensory receptors transduce (convert) stimulus energy via receptor or generator potentials into action potentials. Stimulus strength is frequency coded. Adaptation (decreased response to a continuous or unchanging stimulus) is seen in all general receptors except pain and proprioceptors.

4. Some sensory fibers entering the spinal cord act in local reflex arcs. Some synapse with the dorsal horn neurons (nonspecific ascending pathways), and others continue upward to synapse in medullary nuclei (specific ascending pathways). Second-order neurons of both specific and nonspecific ascending pathways terminate in the thalamus.

5. Perception—the internal, conscious image of the stimulus that serves as the basis for response—is the result of cortical processing.

6. The main aspects of sensory perception are detection, magnitude estimation, spatial discrimination, feature abstraction, quality discrimination, and pattern recognition.

PART 2: TRANSMISSION LINES: NERVES AND THEIR STRUCTURE AND REPAIR

Nerves and Associated Ganglia (pp. 498–500)

1. A nerve is a bundle of axons in the PNS. Each fiber is enclosed by an endoneurium, fascicles of fibers are wrapped by a perineurium, and the whole nerve is bundled by the epineurium.

2. Nerves are classified according to the direction of impulse conduction as sensory, motor, or mixed; most nerves are mixed. The efferent fibers may be somatic or autonomic.

3. Ganglia are collections of neuron cell bodies associated with nerves in the PNS. Examples are the dorsal root (sensory) ganglia and autonomic (motor) ganglia.

4. Injured PNS fibers may regenerate if macrophages enter the area, phagocytize the debris, and promote Schwann cell proliferation. Schwann cells then form a channel and secrete chemicals to guide axon sprouts to their original contacts. Fibers in the CNS do not normally regenerate because the oligodendrocytes inhibit axonal sprouting and regrowth.

Cranial Nerves (pp. 500–508)

1. Twelve pairs of cranial nerves originate from the brain and issue through the skull to innervate the head and neck. Only the vagus nerves extend into the thoracic and abdominal cavities.

2. Cranial nerves are numbered from anterior to posterior in order of emergence from the brain. Their names reflect structures served or function or both. The cranial nerves include
- The olfactory nerves (I): purely sensory; concerned with the sense of smell.
- The optic nerves (II): purely sensory; transmit visual impulses from the retina to the thalamus.
- The oculomotor nerves (III): primarily motor; emerge from the midbrain and serve four extrinsic eye muscles, the levator palpebrae superioris of the eyelid, and the intrinsic ciliary muscle of the eye and constrictor fibers of the iris. Also carry proprioceptive impulses from the skeletal muscles served.
- The trochlear nerves (IV): primarily motor; emerge from the dorsal midbrain and carry motor and proprioceptor impulses to and from superior oblique muscles of the eyeballs.
- The trigeminal nerves (V): mixed nerves; emerge from the lateral pons as the major general sensory nerves of the face. Each has three sensory divisions: ophthalmic, maxillary, and mandibular; the mandibular branch also contains motor fibers that innervate the chewing muscles.

- The abducens nerves (VI): primarily motor; emerge from the pons and serve the motor and proprioceptive functions of the lateral rectus muscles of the eyeballs.
- The facial nerves (VII): mixed nerves; emerge from the pons as the major motor nerves of the face. Also carry sensory impulses from the taste buds of anterior two-thirds of the tongue.
- The vestibulocochlear nerves (VIII): mostly sensory; transmit impulses from the hearing and equilibrium receptors of the inner ears.
- The glossopharyngeal nerves (IX): mixed nerves; issue from the medulla. Transmit sensory impulses from the taste buds of the posterior tongue, from the pharynx, and from chemo- and baroreceptors of the carotid bodies and sinuses. Innervate some pharyngeal muscles and parotid glands.
- The vagus nerves (X): mixed nerves; arise from the medulla. Almost all motor fibers are autonomic parasympathetic fibers; motor efferents to, and sensory fibers from, the pharynx, larynx, and visceral organs of the thoracic and abdominal cavities.
- The accessory nerves (XI): primarily motor; consist of a cranial root arising from the medulla and a spinal root arising from the cervical spinal cord. Cranial root supplies motor fibers to the pharynx and larynx; spinal root supplies somatic efferents to the trapezius and sternocleidomastoid muscles of the neck and carries proprioceptor afferents from the same muscles.
- The hypoglossal nerves (XII): primarily motor; issue from the medulla and carry somatic motor efferents to, and proprioceptive fibers from, the tongue muscles.

Spinal Nerves   (pp. 508–518)

1. The 31 pairs of spinal nerves (all mixed nerves) are numbered successively according to the region of the spinal cord from which they issue.

2. Spinal nerves are formed by the union of dorsal and ventral roots of the spinal cord and are short, confined to the intervertebral foramina.

3. Branches of each spinal nerve include dorsal and ventral rami, and a meningeal branch, and in the thoracic region, rami communicantes (ANS branches).

4. Ventral rami, except T_2–T_{12}, form plexuses that serve the limbs.

5. Dorsal rami serve the muscles and skin of the posterior body trunk. T_1–T_{12} ventral rami give rise to intercostal nerves that serve the thorax wall and abdominal surface.

6. The cervical plexus (C_1–C_4) innervates the muscles and skin of the neck and shoulder. Its phrenic nerve serves the diaphragm.

7. The brachial plexus serves the shoulder, some thorax muscles, and the upper limb. It arises primarily from C_5–T_1. Proximal to distal, the brachial plexus has roots, trunks, divisions, and cords. The main nerves arising from the cords are the axillary, musculocutaneous, median, radial, and ulnar nerves.

8. The lumbar plexus (L_1–L_4) provides the motor supply to the anterior and medial thigh muscles and the cutaneous supply to the anterior thigh and part of the leg. Its chief nerves are the femoral and obturator.

9. The sacral plexus (L_4–S_4) supplies the posterior muscles and skin of the lower limb. Its principal nerve is the large sciatic nerve composed of the tibial and common fibular nerves.

10. Joints are innervated by the same nerves that serve the muscles acting at the joint. All spinal nerves except C_1 innervate specific segments of the skin called dermatomes.

PART 3: MOTOR ENDINGS AND MOTOR ACTIVITY

Peripheral Motor Endings   (p. 519)

1. Motor endings of somatic nerve fibers (axon terminals) help to form elaborate neuromuscular junctions with skeletal muscle cells. Axon terminals contain synaptic vesicles filled with acetylcholine, which (when released) signals the muscle cell to contract. An elaborate basal lamina fills the synaptic cleft.

2. Autonomic motor endings, called varicosities, are functionally similar, but structurally simpler, beaded terminals that innervate smooth muscle and glands. They do not form specialized neuromuscular junctions and generally a wider synaptic cleft separates them from their effector cells.

Overview of Motor Integration: From Intention to Effect   (pp. 519–521)

1. Motor mechanisms operate at the level of the effectors (muscle fibers), descending circuits, and control levels of motor behavior.

2. The motor control hierarchy consists of the segmental level, the projection level, and the precommand level.

3. The segmental level is the spinal cord circuitry that activates ventral horn motor neurons to stimulate the muscles. It consists of reflexes and central pattern generators (CPGs), segmental circuits controlling locomotion.

4. The projection level consists of descending fibers that project to and control the segmental level. These fibers issue from the brain stem motor areas [indirect (extrapyramidal) system] and cortical motor areas [direct (pyramidal) system]. Command neurons in the brain stem appear to turn CPGs on and off, or to modulate them.

5. The cerebellum and basal nuclei constitute the precommand areas that subconsciously integrate mechanisms mediated by the projection level.

PART 4: REFLEX ACTIVITY

The Reflex Arc   (pp. 521–522)

1. A reflex is a rapid, involuntary motor response to a stimulus. The reflex arc has five elements: receptor, sensory neuron, integration center, motor neuron, and effector.

Spinal Reflexes   (pp. 522–527)

1. Testing of somatic spinal reflexes provides information on the integrity of the reflex pathway and the degree of excitability of the spinal cord.

2. Somatic spinal reflexes include stretch, Golgi tendon, flexor, crossed-extensor, and superficial reflexes.

3. A stretch reflex, initiated by stretching of muscle spindles, causes contraction of the stimulated muscle and inhibits its antagonist. It is monosynaptic and ipsilateral. Stretch reflexes maintain muscle tone and body posture.

4. Golgi tendon reflexes, initiated by stimulation of Golgi tendon organs by excessive muscle tension, are polysynaptic reflexes. They cause relaxation of the stimulated muscle and contraction of its antagonist to prevent muscle and tendon damage.

13

5. Flexor reflexes are initiated by painful stimuli. They are polysynaptic, ipsilateral reflexes that are protective in nature.

6. Crossed-extensor reflexes consist of an ipsilateral flexor reflex and a contralateral extensor reflex.

7. Superficial reflexes (e.g., the plantar and abdominal reflexes) are elicited by cutaneous stimulation. They require functional cord reflex arcs and corticospinal pathways.

Developmental Aspects of the Peripheral Nervous System (p. 527)

1. Each spinal nerve provides the sensory and motor supply of an adjacent muscle mass (destined to become skeletal muscles) and the cutaneous supply of a dermatome (skin segment).

2. Reflexes decline in speed with age; this probably reflects neuronal loss or sluggish CNS integration circuits.

Review Questions

Multiple Choice/Matching

(Some questions have more than one correct answer. Select the best answer or answers from the choices given.)

1. The large onion-shaped receptors that are found deep in the dermis and in subcutaneous tissue and that respond to deep pressure are (a) Merkel discs, (b) Pacinian corpuscles, (c) free nerve endings, (d) muscle spindles.

2. Proprioceptors include all of the following except (a) muscle spindles, (b) Golgi tendon organs, (c) Merkel discs, (d) joint kinesthetic receptors.

3. The aspect of sensory perception by which the cerebral cortex identifies the site or pattern of stimulation is (a) perceptual detection, (b) feature abstraction, (c) pattern recognition, (d) spatial discrimination.

4. The neural machinery of the spinal cord is at the (a) precommand level, (b) projection level, (c) segmental level.

5. Dorsal root ganglia contain (a) cell bodies of somatic motor neurons, (b) axon terminals of somatic motor neurons, (c) cell bodies of autonomic motor neurons, (d) axon terminals of sensory neurons, (e) cell bodies of sensory neurons.

6. The connective tissue sheath that surrounds a fascicle of nerve fibers is the (a) epineurium, (b) endoneurium, (c) perineurium, (d) neurilemma.

7. Match the receptor type from column B to the correct description in column A.

Column A	Column B
____ (1) pain, itch, and temperature receptors	(a) Ruffini endings
____ (2) contains intrafusal fibers and type Ia and II sensory endings	(b) Golgi tendon organ
	(c) muscle spindle
	(d) free nerve endings
____ (3) discriminative touch receptor in hairless skin (fingertips)	(e) Pacinian corpuscle
	(f) Meissner's corpuscle
____ (4) contains receptor endings wrapped around thick collagen bundles	
____ (5) rapidly adapting deep-pressure receptor	
____ (6) slowly adapting deep-pressure receptor	

8. Match the names of the cranial nerves in column B to the appropriate description in column A.

Column A	Column B
____ (1) causes pupillary constriction	(a) abducens
____ (2) is the major sensory nerve of the face	(b) accessory
	(c) facial
____ (3) serves the sternocleidomastoid and trapezius muscles	(d) glossopharyngeal
	(e) hypoglossal
____ (4) are purely sensory (two nerves)	(f) oculomotor
	(g) olfactory
____ (5) serves the tongue muscles	(h) optic
____ (6) allows you to chew your food	(i) trigeminal
	(j) trochlear
____ (7) is impaired in Bell's palsy	(k) vagus
____ (8) helps to regulate heart activity	(l) vestibulocochlear
____ (9) helps you to hear and to maintain your balance	
____, ____, ____, ____ (10) contain parasympathetic motor fibers (four nerves)	

9. For each of the following muscles or body regions, identify the plexus and the peripheral nerve(s) (or branch of one) involved. Use choices from keys A and B.

	Key A: Plexuses
____; ____ (1) the diaphragm	(a) brachial
____; ____ (2) muscles of the posterior leg	(b) cervical
____; ____ (3) anterior thigh muscles	(c) lumbar
	(d) sacral
____; ____ (4) medial thigh muscles	**Key B: Nerves**
____; ____ (5) anterior arm muscles that flex the forearm	(1) common fibular
	(2) femoral
____; ____ (6) muscles that flex the wrist and digits (two nerves)	(3) median
	(4) musculocutaneous
____; ____ (7) muscles that extend the wrist and digits	(5) obturator
	(6) phrenic
____; ____ (8) skin and extensor muscles of the posterior arm	(7) radial
	(8) tibial
____; ____ (9) fibularis muscles, tibialis anterior, and toe extensors	(9) ulnar
____; ____, ____, ____, ____ (10) elbow joint	

10. Characterize each receptor activity described below by choosing the appropriate letter and number(s) from keys A and B.

____, ____ **(1)** You are enjoying an ice cream cone.

____, ____ **(2)** You have just scalded yourself with hot coffee.

____, ____ **(3)** The retinas of your eyes are stimulated.

____, ____ **(4)** You bump (lightly) into someone.

____, ____ **(5)** You are in a completely dark room and reaching toward the light switch.

____, ____ **(6)** You feel uncomfortable after a large meal.

Key A:
(a) exteroceptor
(b) interoceptor
(c) proprioceptor

Key B:
(1) chemoreceptor
(2) mechanoreceptor
(3) nociceptor
(4) photoreceptor
(5) thermoreceptor

11. A reflex that causes reciprocal activation of the antagonist muscle is the (a) crossed-extensor, (b) flexor, (c) Golgi tendon, (d) muscle stretch.

Short Answer Essay Questions

12. What is the functional relationship of the peripheral nervous system to the central nervous system?

13. List the structural components of the peripheral nervous system, and describe the function of each component.

14. Differentiate clearly between sensation and perception.

15. Central pattern generators (CPGs) are found at the segmental level of motor control. (a) What is the job of the CPGs? (b) What controls them, and where is this control localized?

16. Make a diagram of the hierarchy of motor control. Position the CPGs, the command neurons, and the cerebellum and basal nuclei in this scheme.

17. How do the types of motor activity controlled by the direct (pyramidal) and indirect systems differ?

18. Describe the functional problems that would be experienced by a person in which these fiber tracts have been cut: (a) lateral spinothalamic, (b) anterior and posterior spinocerebellar, (c) tectospinal.

19. Why are the cerebellum and basal nuclei called *pre*command areas?

20. Explain why damage to peripheral nerve fibers is often reversible, whereas damage to CNS fibers rarely is.

21. (a) Describe the formation and composition of a spinal nerve. (b) Name the branches of a spinal nerve (other than the rami communicantes), and indicate their distribution.

22. (a) Define plexus. (b) Indicate the spinal roots of origin of the four major nerve plexuses, and name the general body regions served by each.

23. Differentiate between ipsilateral and contralateral reflexes.

24. What is the homeostatic value of flexor reflexes?

25. Compare and contrast flexor and crossed-extensor reflexes.

26. Explain how a crossed-extensor reflex exemplifies both serial and parallel processing.

27. What clinical information can be gained by conducting somatic reflex tests?

28. What is the structural and functional relationship between spinal nerves, skeletal muscles, and dermatomes?

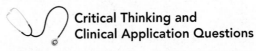 **Critical Thinking and Clinical Application Questions**

1. In 1962 a boy playing in a train yard fell under a train. His right arm was cut off cleanly by the train wheel. Surgeons reattached the arm, sewing nerves and vessels back together. The boy was told he should eventually regain the use of his arm but that it would never be strong enough to pitch a baseball. Explain why full recovery of strength was unlikely.

2. Jefferson, a football quarterback, suffered torn menisci in his right knee joint when tackled from the side. The same injury crushed his common fibular nerve against the head of the fibula. What locomotor problems did Jefferson have after this?

3. As Harry fell off a ladder, he grabbed a tree branch with his right hand, but unfortunately lost his grip and fell heavily to the ground. Days later, Harry complained that his upper limb was numb. What was damaged in his fall?

4. Mr. Frank, a former stroke victim who had made a remarkable recovery, suddenly began to have problems reading. He complained of seeing double and also had problems navigating steps. He was unable to move his left eye downward and laterally. What cranial nerve was the site of lesion? (Right or left?)

5. One of a group of rabbit hunters was accidentally sprayed with buckshot in both of his gluteal prominences. When his companions saw that he would survive, they laughed and joked about where he had been shot. They were horrified and ashamed a week later when it was announced that their friend would be permanently paralyzed and without sensation in both legs from the knee down, as well as on the back of his thighs. What had happened?

6. You are at a party at Mary's house. After you are blindfolded, an object (a key *or* a rabbit's foot) is placed in your hand. What spinal tracts carry the signals to the cortex that will allow you to differentiate between these objects, and what aspects of sensory perception are operating?

7. Fumiko, a 19-year-old nursing student, had had a runny nose and sore throat for several days. Upon waking, her face felt "twisted." When she examined her face in the mirror, she noticed that the right side looked "droopy" and she was unable to move the facial muscles on that side. This made it difficult to eat or speak clearly. Which cranial nerve was affected and on which side? What is a common cause of this condition?

13

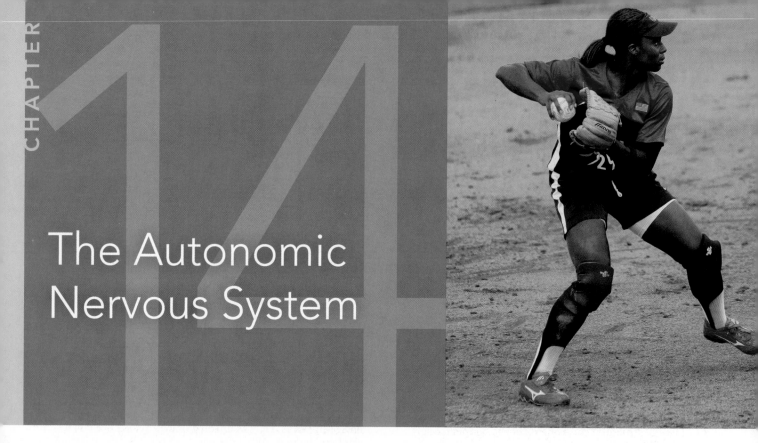

The Autonomic Nervous System

Introduction (pp. 533–535)

1. Define autonomic nervous system and explain its relationship to the peripheral nervous system.

2. Compare the somatic and autonomic nervous systems relative to effectors, efferent pathways, and neurotransmitters released.

3. Compare and contrast the functions of the parasympathetic and sympathetic divisions.

ANS Anatomy (pp. 535–543)

4. For the parasympathetic and sympathetic divisions, describe the site of CNS origin, locations of ganglia, and general fiber pathways.

ANS Physiology (pp. 543–547, 550)

5. Define cholinergic and adrenergic fibers, and list the different types of their receptors.

6. Describe the clinical importance of drugs that mimic or inhibit adrenergic or cholinergic effects.

7. State the effects of the parasympathetic and sympathetic divisions on the following organs: heart, blood vessels, gastrointestinal tract, lungs, adrenal medulla, and external genitalia.

8. Describe autonomic nervous system controls.

Homeostatic Imbalances of the ANS (pp. 550–551)

9. Explain the relationship of some types of hypertension, Raynaud's disease, and autonomic dysreflexia to disorders of autonomic functioning.

Developmental Aspects of the ANS (p. 551)

10. Describe some effects of aging on the autonomic nervous system.

The human body is exquisitely sensitive to changes in its internal environment, and engages in a lifelong struggle to balance competing demands for resources under ever-changing conditions. Although all body systems contribute, the stability of our internal environment depends largely on the **autonomic nervous system (ANS),** the system of motor neurons that innervates smooth and cardiac muscle and glands (Figure 14.1). At every moment, signals stream from visceral organs into the CNS, and autonomic nerves make adjustments as necessary to ensure optimal support for body activities. In response to changing conditions, the ANS shunts blood to "needy" areas, speeds or slows heart rate, adjusts blood pressure and body temperature, and increases or decreases stomach secretions.

Most of this fine-tuning occurs without our awareness or attention. Can you tell when your arteries are constricting or when your pupils are dilating? Probably not, but if you've ever been stuck in a checkout line, and your full bladder was contracting as if it had a mind of its own, you've been very aware of a visceral activity. These functions, both those we're aware of and those that occur without our awareness or attention, are controlled by the ANS. Indeed, as the term *autonomic* (*auto* = self; *nom* = govern) implies, this motor subdivision of the peripheral nervous system has a certain amount of functional independence. The ANS is also called the **involuntary nervous system,** which reflects its subconscious control, or the **general visceral motor system,** which indicates the location of most of its effectors.

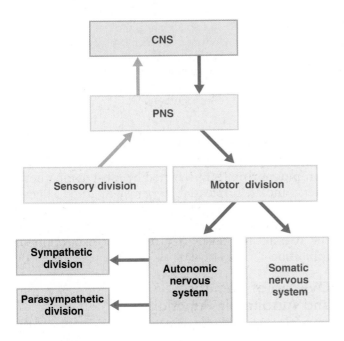

FIGURE 14.1   **Place of the ANS in the structural organization of the nervous system.**

Introduction

Comparison of the Somatic and Autonomic Nervous Systems

Our previous discussions of motor nerves have focused largely on the activity of the somatic nervous system. So, before describing autonomic nervous system anatomy, we will point out the major differences between the somatic and autonomic systems as well as some areas of functional overlap. Although both systems have motor fibers, the somatic and autonomic nervous systems differ (1) in their effectors, (2) in their efferent pathways, and (3) to some degree in target organ responses to their neurotransmitters. The differences are summarized in Figure 14.2.

Effectors

The somatic nervous system stimulates skeletal muscles, whereas the ANS innervates cardiac and smooth muscle and glands. Differences in the physiology of the effector organs account for most of the remaining differences between somatic and autonomic effects on their target organs.

Efferent Pathways and Ganglia

In the somatic nervous system, the motor neuron cell bodies are in the CNS, and their axons extend in spinal or cranial nerves all the way to the skeletal muscles they activate. Somatic motor fibers are typically thick, heavily myelinated group A fibers that conduct nerve impulses rapidly.

In contrast, the ANS uses a *two-neuron chain* to its effectors. The cell body of the first neuron, the **preganglionic neuron,** resides in the brain or spinal cord. Its axon, the **preganglionic axon,** synapses with the second motor neuron, the **ganglionic neuron,** in an **autonomic ganglion** outside the CNS. The axon of the ganglionic neuron, called the **postganglionic axon,** extends to the effector organ. If you think about the meanings of all these terms while referring to Figure 14.2, understanding the rest of the chapter will be much easier. Preganglionic axons are lightly myelinated, thin fibers; postganglionic axons are even thinner and are unmyelinated. Consequently, conduction through the autonomic efferent chain is slower than conduction in the somatic motor system. For most of their course, many pre- and postganglionic fibers are incorporated into spinal or cranial nerves.

Keep in mind that autonomic ganglia are *motor* ganglia, containing the cell bodies of motor neurons. Technically, they are sites of synapse and information transmission from preganglionic to ganglionic neurons. Also, remember that the somatic motor

Q *Why are the axons of the first and second neurons of the two-neuron motor autonomic chain named the preganglionic and postganglionic axons respectively?*

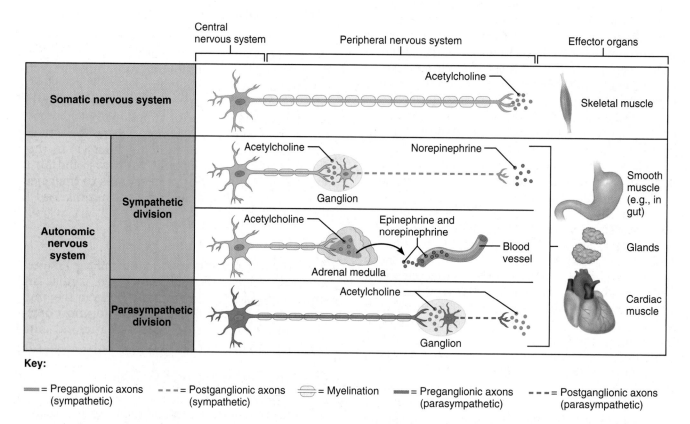

FIGURE 14.2   Comparison of somatic and autonomic nervous systems. *Somatic Division:* Axons of somatic motor neurons extend from the CNS to their effectors (skeletal muscle cells). These axons are typically heavily myelinated. Somatic motor neurons release acetylcholine, and the effect is always stimulatory.
Autonomic Division: Axons of most preganglionic neurons run from the CNS to synapse in a peripheral autonomic ganglion with a ganglionic neuron. A few sympathetic preganglionic axons synapse with cells of the adrenal medulla. Postganglionic axons run from the ganglion to effectors (cardiac and smooth muscle fibers and glands). Preganglionic axons are lightly myelinated; postganglionic axons are unmyelinated. All preganglionic fibers release acetylcholine; all parasym- pathetic postganglionic fibers release acetylcholine; most sympathetic postganglionic fibers release norepinephrine. Stimulated adrenal medullary cells release norepinephrine and epinephrine into the blood. Autonomic effects are stimulatory or inhibitory, depending on the postganglionic neurotransmitter released and the receptor types on the effector organs.

division *lacks* ganglia entirely. The dorsal root ganglia are part of the sensory, not the motor, division of the PNS.

Neurotransmitter Effects

All somatic motor neurons release **acetylcholine (ACh)** at their synapses with skeletal muscle fibers. The effect is always *excitatory,* and if stimulation reaches threshold, the muscle fibers contract.

Neurotransmitters released onto visceral effector organs by postganglionic autonomic fibers include **norepinephrine (NE)** secreted by most sympathetic fibers, and ACh released by parasympathetic fibers. Depending on the type of receptors present on the target organ (Figure 14.2 and Table 14.3 on p. 544), the organ's response may be either excitation or inhibition.

Overlap of Somatic and Autonomic Function

Higher brain centers regulate and coordinate both somatic and autonomic motor activities, and nearly all spinal nerves (and many cranial nerves) contain

A *The axon of the preganglionic neuron spans the distance between the CNS and the autonomic ganglion, whereas the ganglionic neuron's axon lies distal to ("post") the ganglion.*

both somatic and autonomic fibers. Moreover, most of the body's adaptations to changing internal and external conditions involve both skeletal muscle activity and enhanced responses of certain visceral organs. For example, when skeletal muscles are working hard, they need more oxygen and glucose and so autonomic control mechanisms speed up heart rate and dilate airways to meet these needs and maintain homeostasis. The ANS is only one part of our highly integrated nervous system, but according to convention we will consider it an individual entity and describe its role in isolation in the sections that follow.

ANS Divisions

The two arms of the ANS, the *parasympathetic* and *sympathetic divisions*, generally serve the same visceral organs but cause essentially opposite effects. If one division stimulates certain smooth muscles to contract or a gland to secrete, the other division inhibits that action. Through this **dual innervation,** the two divisions counterbalance each other's activities to keep body systems running smoothly. The sympathetic division mobilizes the body during activity, whereas the parasympathetic arm promotes maintenance functions and conserves body energy. Let's elaborate on these functional differences by focusing briefly on extreme situations in which each division is exerting primary control.

Role of the Parasympathetic Division

The **parasympathetic division,** sometimes called the "resting and digesting" system, keeps body energy use as low as possible, even as it directs vital "housekeeping" activities like digestion and elimination of feces and urine. (This explains why it is a good idea to relax after a heavy meal: so that digestion is not interfered with by sympathetic activity.) Parasympathetic activity is best illustrated in a person who relaxes after a meal and reads the newspaper. Blood pressure and heart rate are regulated at low normal levels, and the gastrointestinal tract is actively digesting food. In the eyes, the pupils are constricted and the lenses are accommodated for close vision to improve the clarity of the close-up image.

Role of the Sympathetic Division

The **sympathetic division** is often referred to as the "fight-or-flight" system. Its activity is evident when we are excited or find ourselves in emergency or threatening situations, such as being frightened by street toughs late at night. A rapidly pounding heart; deep breathing; dry mouth; cold, sweaty skin; and dilated eye pupils are sure signs of sympathetic nervous system mobilization. Not as obvious, but equally characteristic, are changes in brain wave patterns and in the electrical resistance of the skin (galvanic skin resistance)—events that are recorded during lie detector examinations.

During any type of vigorous physical activity, the sympathetic division also promotes a number of other adjustments. Visceral (and sometimes cutaneous) blood vessels are constricted, and blood is shunted to active skeletal muscles and the vigorously working heart. The bronchioles in the lungs dilate, increasing ventilation (and ultimately increasing oxygen delivery to body cells), and the liver releases more glucose into the blood to accommodate the increased energy needs of body cells. At the same time, temporarily nonessential activities, such as gastrointestinal tract motility, are damped. If you are running from a mugger, digesting lunch can wait! It is far more important that your muscles be provided with everything they need to get you out of danger.

In such active situations, the sympathetic division generates a head of steam that enables the body to cope with situations that threaten homeostasis. Its function is to provide the optimal conditions for an appropriate response to some threat, whether that response is to run, to see better, or to think more clearly.

We have just looked at two extreme situations in which one or the other branch of the ANS dominates. An easy way to remember the most important roles of the two ANS divisions is to think of the parasympathetic division as the **D** division [digestion, defecation, and diuresis (urination)], and the sympathetic division as the **E** division (exercise, excitement, emergency, embarrassment). A more detailed summary of the effects of each division is presented in Table 14.5 (p. 546). Remember, however, while it is easiest to think of the two ANS divisions as working in an all-or-none fashion as described above, this is rarely the case. A dynamic antagonism exists between the divisions, and fine adjustments are made continuously by both.

ANS Anatomy

The sympathetic and parasympathetic divisions are distinguished by

1. Their unique origin sites: Parasympathetic fibers emerge from the brain and sacral spinal cord (are craniosacral); sympathetic fibers originate in the thoracolumbar region of the spinal cord.

2. The relative lengths of their fibers: The parasympathetic division has long preganglionic and short postganglionic fibers; the sympathetic division has the opposite condition.

3. The location of their ganglia: Most parasympathetic ganglia are located in the visceral effector organs; sympathetic ganglia lie close to the spinal cord.

These and other differences are summarized in Table 14.1 and illustrated in Figure 14.3.

TABLE 14.1	Anatomical and Physiological Differences Between the Parasympathetic and Sympathetic Divisions	
CHARACTERISTIC	**PARASYMPATHETIC**	**SYMPATHETIC**
Origin	Craniosacral outflow: brain stem nuclei of cranial nerves III, VII, IX, and X; spinal cord segments S_2-S_4	Thoracolumbar outflow: lateral horn of gray matter of spinal cord segments T_1-L_2
Location of ganglia	Ganglia in (intramural) or close to visceral organ served	Ganglia within a few centimeters of CNS: alongside vertebral column (sympathetic trunk, or chain, ganglia) and anterior to vertebral column (collateral, or prevertebral, ganglia)
Relative length of pre- and postganglionic fibers	Long preganglionic; short postganglionic	Short preganglionic; long postganglionic
Rami communicantes	None	Gray and white rami communicantes. White rami contain myelinated preganglionic fibers; gray contain unmyelinated postganglionic fibers
Degree of branching of preganglionic fibers	Minimal	Extensive
Functional role	Maintenance functions; conserves and stores energy	Prepares body for activity
Neurotransmitters	All fibers release ACh (cholinergic fibers)	All preganglionic fibers release ACh; most postganglionic fibers release norepinephrine (adrenergic fibers); postganglionic fibers serving sweat glands and some blood vessels of skeletal muscles release ACh; neurotransmitter activity augmented by release of adrenal medullary hormones (norepinephrine and epinephrine)

14

Parasympathetic (Craniosacral) Division

We begin our exploration of the ANS with the anatomically simpler parasympathetic division. Because its preganglionic fibers spring from opposite ends of the CNS—the brain stem and the sacral region of the spinal cord—the parasympathetic division is also called the **craniosacral division** (Figure 14.4). The preganglionic axons extend from the CNS nearly all the way to the structures to be innervated. There the axons synapse with ganglionic neurons located in **terminal ganglia** that lie very close to or within the target organs. Very short postganglionic axons issue from the terminal ganglia and synapse with effector cells in their immediate area.

FIGURE 14.3 **Overview of the subdivisions of the ANS.** Sites of origin of their nerves and major organs served are indicated. Synapse sites indicate the relative locations of the sympathetic and parasympathetic ganglia.

*Although sympathetic innervation to the skin is mapped to the cervical region here, all nerves to the periphery carry postganglionic sympathetic fibers.

Cranial Outflow

Preganglionic fibers run in the oculomotor, facial, glossopharyngeal, and vagus cranial nerves. Their cell bodies lie in associated motor cranial-nerve nuclei in the brain stem (see Figures 12.15 and 12.16). The precise locations of the neurons of the cranial parasympathetics are described next.

1. Oculomotor nerves (III). The parasympathetic fibers of the oculomotor nerves innervate smooth muscles in the eyes that cause the pupils to constrict and the lenses to bulge—actions needed to focus on close objects. The preganglionic axons found in the oculomotor nerves issue from the *accessory oculomotor (Edinger-Westphal) nuclei* in the midbrain. The cell bodies of the ganglionic neurons are in the **ciliary ganglia** within the eye orbits (see Table 13.2, p. 503).

2. Facial nerves (VII). The parasympathetic fibers of the facial nerves stimulate many large glands in the head. Fibers that activate the nasal glands and the lacrimal glands of the eyes originate in the *lacrimal nuclei* of the pons. The preganglionic fibers synapse with ganglionic neurons in the **pterygopalatine ganglia** (ter″eh-go-pal′ah-tīn) just posterior to the maxillae. The preganglionic neurons that stimulate the submandibular and sublingual salivary glands originate in the *superior salivatory nuclei* of the pons and synapse with ganglionic neurons in the **submandibular ganglia**, deep to the mandibular angles (see Table 13.2, p. 505).

3. Glossopharyngeal nerves (IX). The parasympathetics in the glossopharyngeal nerves originate in the *inferior salivatory nuclei* of the medulla and synapse in the **otic ganglia**, located just inferior to the foramen ovale of the skull. The postganglionic fibers course to and activate the parotid salivary glands anterior to the ears (see Table 13.2, p. 507).

Cranial nerves III, VII, and IX supply the entire parasympathetic innervation of the head; however, only the *preganglionic fibers* lie within these three pairs of cranial nerves—postganglionic fibers do not. The distal ends of the preganglionic fibers "jump over" to branches of the *trigeminal nerves (V)* to synapse; then the postganglionic fibers travel in the trigeminal nerves to reach the face. This "hitchhiking" takes advantage of the fact that the trigeminal nerves have the broadest facial distribution of all the cranial nerves and are well suited for this "delivery" role to the widely separated glands and smooth muscles in the head.

4. Vagus nerves (X). The remaining and major portion of the parasympathetic cranial outflow is via the vagus (X) nerves. Between them, the two vagus nerves account for about 90% of all preganglionic parasympathetic fibers in the body. They provide fibers to the

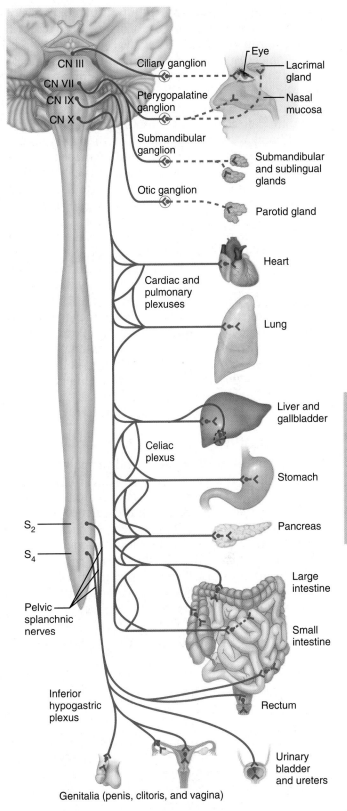

FIGURE 14.4 Parasympathetic (craniosacral) division of the ANS. Solid lines indicate preganglionic nerve fibers. Dashed lines indicate postganglionic fibers. Terminal ganglia of the vagus and pelvic splanchnic nerve fibers are not shown; most of these ganglia are located in or on the target organ. (Note: CN = cranial nerve.)

neck and to nerve plexuses (interweaving networks of nerves) that serve virtually every organ in the thoracic and abdominal cavities. The vagal nerve fibers (preganglionic axons) arise mostly from the *dorsal motor nuclei* of the medulla and synapse in terminal ganglia usually located in the walls of the target organ. Most terminal ganglia are not individually named; instead they are collectively called *intramural ganglia,* literally, "ganglia within the walls." As the vagus nerves pass into the thorax, they send branches to the **cardiac plexuses** supplying fibers to the heart that slow heart rate, the **pulmonary plexuses** serving the lungs and bronchi, and the **esophageal plexuses** (ĕ-sof"ah-je'al) supplying the esophagus.

When the main trunks of the vagus nerves reach the esophagus, their fibers intermingle, forming the **anterior** and **posterior vagal trunks,** each containing fibers from both vagus nerves. These vagal trunks then "ride" the esophagus down to the abdominal cavity. There they send fibers *through* the large **aortic plexus** [formed by a number of smaller plexuses (e.g., *celiac, superior mesenteric,* and *hypogastric*) that run along the aorta] before giving off branches to the abdominal viscera. The vagus nerves innervate the liver, gallbladder, stomach, small intestine, kidneys, pancreas, and the proximal half of the large intestine.

Sacral Outflow

The rest of the large intestine and the pelvic organs are served by the sacral outflow, which arises from neurons located in the lateral gray matter of spinal cord segments S_2–S_4. Axons of these neurons run in the ventral roots of the spinal nerves to the ventral rami and then branch off to form the **pelvic splanchnic nerves** (Figure 14.4), which pass through the **inferior hypogastric (pelvic) plexus** in the pelvic floor. Some preganglionic fibers synapse with ganglia in this plexus, but most synapse in intramural ganglia in the walls of the following organs: distal half of the large intestine, urinary bladder, ureters, and reproductive organs.

Sympathetic (Thoracolumbar) Division

The sympathetic division is more complex than the parasympathetic division, partly because it innervates more organs. It supplies not only the visceral organs in the internal body cavities but also all visceral structures in the superficial (somatic) part of the body. This sounds impossible, but there is an explanation—some glands and smooth muscle structures in the soma (sweat glands and the hair-raising arrector pili muscles of the skin) require autonomic innervation and are served only by sympathetic fibers. Moreover, all arteries and veins (be they deep or superficial) have smooth muscle in their walls that is innervated by sympathetic fibers. But these matters will be explained later—let us get on with the anatomy of the sympathetic division.

All preganglionic fibers of the sympathetic division arise from cell bodies of preganglionic neurons in spinal cord segments T_1 through L_2 (Figure 14.5). For this reason, the sympathetic division is also referred to as the **thoracolumbar division** (tho"rah-ko-lum'bar). The presence of numerous preganglionic sympathetic neurons in the gray matter of the spinal cord produces the **lateral horns**—the so-called **visceral motor zones** (see Figures 12.31b, p. 473, and 12.32, p. 474). The lateral horns are just posterolateral to the ventral horns that house somatic motor neurons. (Parasympathetic preganglionic neurons in the sacral cord are far less abundant than the comparable sympathetic neurons in the thoracolumbar regions, and *lateral horns are absent* in the sacral region of the spinal cord. This is a major anatomical difference between the two divisions.)

After leaving the cord via the ventral root, preganglionic sympathetic fibers pass through a **white ramus communicans** [plural: **rami communicantes** (kom-mu"nĭ-kan"tēz)] to enter an adjoining **sympathetic trunk (chain) ganglion** forming part of the **sympathetic trunk** or **chain** (Figure 14.6). Looking like strands of glistening white beads, the sympathetic trunks flank each side of the vertebral column. These ganglia are also called *paravertebral ganglia,* named for their location.

Although the sympathetic *trunks* extend from neck to pelvis, sympathetic *fibers* arise only from the thoracic and lumbar cord segments, as shown in Figure 14.5. The ganglia vary in size, position, and number, but typically there are 23 in each sympathetic trunk—3 cervical, 11 thoracic, 4 lumbar, 4 sacral, and 1 coccygeal.

Once a preganglionic axon reaches a trunk ganglion, one of three things can happen to the axon, as shown by the three numbered pathways in Figure 14.6:

① It can synapse with a ganglionic neuron in the same trunk ganglion.

② It can ascend or descend the sympathetic trunk to synapse in another trunk ganglion. (It is these fibers running from one ganglion to another that connect the ganglia into the sympathetic trunk.)

③ It can pass through the trunk ganglion and emerge from the sympathetic trunk without synapsing.

Preganglionic fibers following pathway ③ help form the **splanchnic nerves** (splank'nik) that synapse in **collateral,** or **prevertebral, ganglia** located anterior to the vertebral column. Unlike sympathetic trunk (chain) ganglia, the prevertebral ganglia are neither paired nor segmentally arranged and occur only in the abdomen and pelvis.

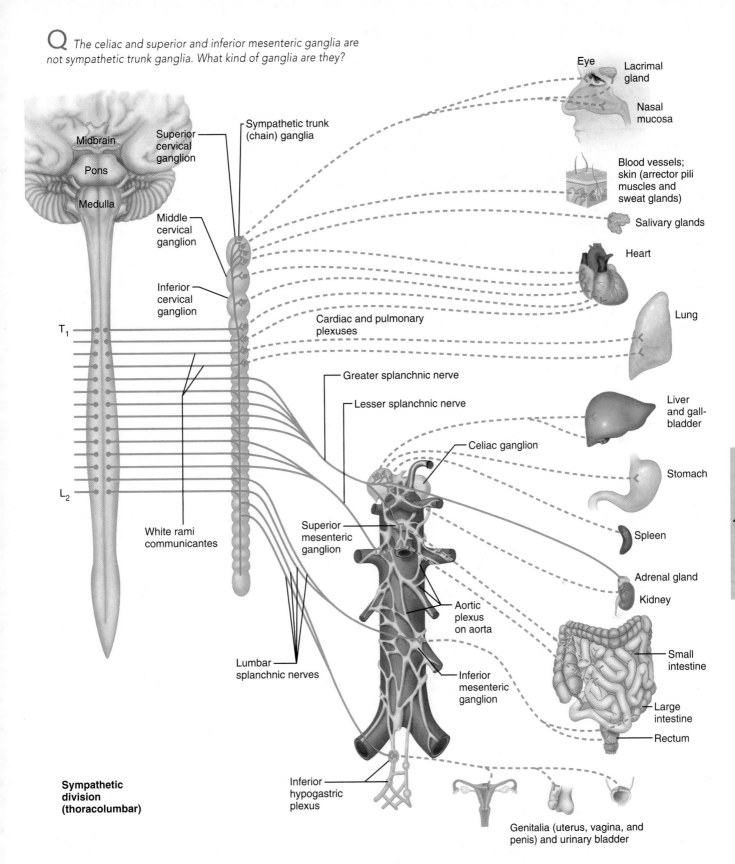

Q The celiac and superior and inferior mesenteric ganglia are not sympathetic trunk ganglia. What kind of ganglia are they?

Eye
Lacrimal gland
Nasal mucosa
Midbrain
Pons
Medulla
Superior cervical ganglion
Sympathetic trunk (chain) ganglia
Blood vessels; skin (arrector pili muscles and sweat glands)
Middle cervical ganglion
Salivary glands
Inferior cervical ganglion
Heart
Lung
T₁
Cardiac and pulmonary plexuses
Greater splanchnic nerve
Lesser splanchnic nerve
Liver and gall-bladder
Celiac ganglion
L₂
Stomach
Superior mesenteric ganglion
Spleen
White rami communicantes
Adrenal gland
Kidney
Aortic plexus on aorta
Small intestine
Inferior mesenteric ganglion
Large intestine
Lumbar splanchnic nerves
Rectum
Sympathetic division (thoracolumbar)
Inferior hypogastric plexus
Genitalia (uterus, vagina, and penis) and urinary bladder

14

FIGURE 14.5 **Sympathetic (thoracolumbar) division of the ANS.** Solid lines indicate preganglionic fibers; dashed lines indicate postganglionic fibers. Sympathetic innervation to peripheral structures (blood vessels, glands, and arrector pili muscles) is shown only in the cervical area, but occurs in all areas. The least thoracic and sacral splanchnic nerves are not shown.

A Collateral (prevertebral) ganglia.

Q *On what basis are the rami communicantes distinguished as gray or white?*

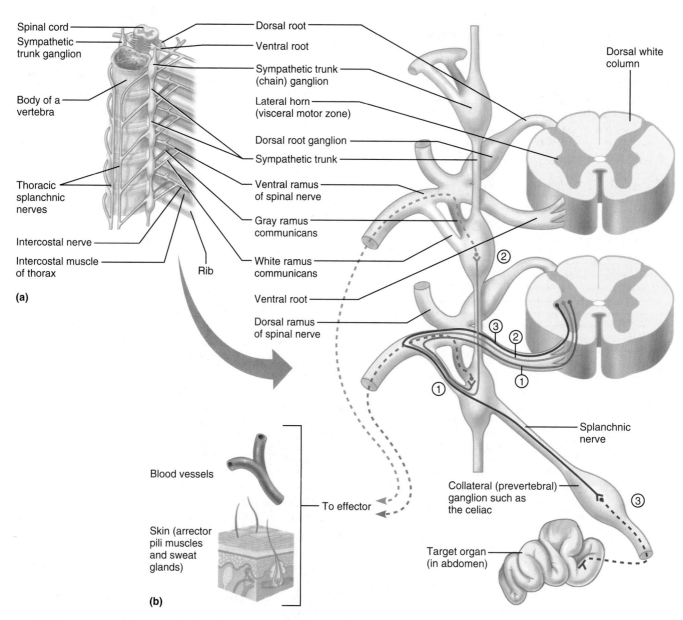

FIGURE 14.6   **Sympathetic trunks and pathways. (a)** Diagram of the left sympathetic trunk in the posterior thorax, along the side of the vertebral column. **(b)** Three sympathetic pathways. ① Synapse in a sympathetic trunk (chain) ganglion at same level (red). ② Synapse in a sympathetic trunk ganglion at a different level (green). ③ Synapse in a collateral (prevertebral) ganglion anterior to the vertebral column (purple).

Regardless of where the synapse occurs, all sympathetic ganglia are close to the spinal cord, and their postganglionic fibers are typically much longer than their preganglionic fibers. Recall that the oppo-site condition exists in the parasympathetic division, an anatomical distinction that is functionally important.

Pathways with Synapses in Trunk Ganglia

When synapses are made in sympathetic trunk ganglia, the postganglionic axons enter the ventral (or dorsal) ramus of the adjoining spinal nerves by way

A *The gray rami are unmyelinated. The white rami are myelin-ated, which gives them a distinguishing white color.*

of communicating branches called **gray rami communicantes** (Figure 14.6). From there they travel via branches of the rami to their effectors, including sweat glands and arrector pili muscles of the skin. Anywhere along their path, the postganglionic axons may transfer over to nearby blood vessels and innervate the vascular smooth muscle all the way to their final branches.

Notice that the naming of the rami communicantes as *white* or *gray* reflects their appearance, revealing whether or not their fibers are myelinated (and has *no* relationship to the white and gray matter of the CNS). Preganglionic fibers composing the white rami are myelinated. Postganglionic axons forming the gray rami are not.

The white rami, which carry preganglionic axons to the sympathetic trunks, are found only in the T_1–L_2 cord segments, regions of sympathetic outflow. However, gray rami carrying postganglionic fibers headed for the periphery issue from *every* trunk ganglion from the cervical to the sacral region, allowing sympathetic output to reach all parts of the body. Because parasympathetic fibers never run in spinal nerves, *rami communicantes are associated only with the sympathetic division.*

Pathways to the Head Sympathetic preganglionic fibers serving the head emerge from spinal cord segments T_1–T_4 and ascend the sympathetic trunk to synapse with ganglionic neurons in the **superior cervical ganglion.** This ganglion contributes sympathetic fibers that run in several cranial nerves and with the upper three or four cervical spinal nerves. Besides serving the skin and blood vessels of the head, its fibers stimulate the dilator muscles of the irises of the eyes, inhibit the nasal and salivary glands (the reason your mouth goes dry when you are scared), and innervate the smooth (tarsal) muscle that lifts the upper eyelid. The superior cervical ganglion also sends direct branches to the heart.

Pathways to the Thorax Sympathetic preganglionic fibers innervating the thoracic organs originate at T_1–T_6. From there the preganglionic fibers run to synapse in the cervical trunk ganglia. Postganglionic fibers emerging from the **middle** and **inferior cervical ganglia** enter cervical nerves C_4–C_8. Some of these fibers innervate the heart via the cardiac plexus, and some innervate the thyroid gland, but most serve the skin. Additionally, some T_1–T_6 preganglionic fibers synapse in the nearest trunk ganglion, and the postganglionic fibers pass directly to the organ served. Fibers to the heart, aorta, lungs, and esophagus take this direct route. Along the way, they run into the plexuses associated with those organs. Sympathetic innervation by spinal cord segment is summarized in Table 14.2.

TABLE 14.2	Segmental Sympathetic Supplies
SPINAL CORD SEGMENT	**ORGANS SERVED**
T_1–T_5	Head and neck, heart
T_2–T_4	Bronchi and lungs
T_2–T_5	Upper limb
T_5–T_6	Esophagus
T_6–T_{10}	Stomach, spleen, pancreas
T_7–T_9	Liver
T_9–T_{10}	Small intestine
T_{10}–L_1	Kidney, reproductive organs (uterus, testis, ovary, etc.)
T_{10}–L_2	Lower limb
T_{11}–L_2	Large intestine, ureter, urinary bladder

Pathways with Synapses in Collateral Ganglia

The preganglionic fibers from T_5 down synapse in collateral ganglia; thus these fibers enter and leave the sympathetic trunks without synapsing. They form several nerves called splanchnic nerves, including the thoracic **splanchnic nerves** (greater, lesser, and least) and the **lumbar** and **sacral splanchnic nerves.** The splanchnic nerves contribute to a number of interweaving nerve plexuses known collectively as the **abdominal aortic plexus** (a-or'tik), which clings to the surface of the abdominal aorta (Figure 14.5). This complex plexus contains several ganglia that together serve the abdominopelvic viscera (*splanchni* = viscera). From superior to inferior, the most important of these ganglia (and related subplexuses) are the **celiac, superior mesenteric, inferior mesenteric,** and **inferior hypogastric,** named for the arteries with which they most closely associate. Postganglionic fibers issuing from these ganglia generally travel to their target organs in the company of the arteries serving these organs.

Pathways to the Abdomen Sympathetic innervation of the abdomen is via preganglionic fibers from T_5 to L_2, which travel in the thoracic *splanchnic nerves* to synapse mainly at the celiac and superior mesenteric ganglia. Postganglionic fibers issuing from these ganglia serve the stomach, intestines (except the distal half of the large intestine), liver, spleen, and kidneys.

Pathways to the Pelvis Preganglionic fibers innervating the pelvis originate from T_{10} to L_2 and then descend in the sympathetic trunk to the lumbar and sacral trunk ganglia. Some fibers synapse there, but most go directly out from the cord via the

Q *According to the figure legend, the afferent neuron shown in this diagram reaches the CNS via a spinal nerve. How would you know that if it was not mentioned?*

FIGURE 14.7 **Visceral reflexes.** Visceral reflexes have the same elements as somatic reflexes, but the efferent response occurs over a two-motor-neuron efferent pathway. The integration center may involve a dorsal horn interneuron, or it may just be a synapse with a preganglionic neuron (as shown). The visceral afferent fibers are found both in spinal nerves (as depicted here) and in autonomic nerves.

lumbar and *sacral splanchnic nerves,* which send the bulk of their fibers to the inferior mesenteric and inferior hypogastric ganglia. From these ganglia issue postganglionic fibers serving the distal half of the large intestine, the urinary bladder, and the reproductive organs. For the most part, sympathetic fibers *inhibit* the activity of the muscles and glands in these visceral organs.

Pathways with Synapses in the Adrenal Medulla

Some fibers traveling in the thoracic splanchnic nerves pass through the celiac ganglion without synapsing and terminate by synapsing with the hormone-producing medullary cells of the adrenal gland (Figure 14.5). When stimulated by preganglionic fibers, the medullary cells secrete NE and *epinephrine* (also called *noradrenaline* and *adrenaline,* respectively) into the blood, producing the excitatory effects we have all felt as a "surge of adrenaline." Embryologically, sympathetic ganglia and the adrenal

medulla arise from the same tissue. For this reason, the adrenal medulla is sometimes viewed as a "misplaced" sympathetic ganglion, and its hormone-releasing cells, although lacking nerve processes, are considered equivalent to ganglionic sympathetic neurons.

Visceral Reflexes

Because most anatomists consider the ANS to be a visceral motor system, the presence of sensory fibers (mostly visceral pain afferents) is often overlooked. However, **visceral sensory neurons,** which send information concerning chemical changes, stretch, and irritation of the viscera, are the first link in autonomic reflexes. **Visceral reflex arcs** have essentially the same components as somatic reflex arcs—receptor, sensory neuron, integration center, motor neuron, effector—except that a visceral reflex arc has *two* neurons in its motor component (Figure 14.7).

Nearly all the sympathetic and parasympathetic fibers described thus far are accompanied by afferent fibers conducting sensory impulses from glands or muscles. Thus, peripheral processes of visceral sensory neurons are found in cranial nerves VII, IX, and X, splanchnic nerves, and the sympathetic trunk, as well as in spinal nerves. Like sensory neurons serving somatic structures (skeletal muscles and skin), the cell bodies of visceral sensory neurons are located either in the sensory ganglia of associated cranial nerves or in dorsal root ganglia of the spinal cord. Visceral sensory neurons are also found in sympathetic ganglia where preganglionic neurons synapse. Furthermore, complete three-neuron reflex arcs (with sensory, inter-, and motor neurons) exist entirely within the walls of the gastrointestinal tract. Neurons composing these reflex arcs make up the *enteric nervous system,* which plays an important role in controlling gastrointestinal tract activity. We will discuss the enteric nervous system in more detail in Chapter 23.

The fact that visceral pain afferents travel along the same pathways as somatic pain fibers helps explain the phenomenon of **referred pain,** in which pain stimuli arising in the viscera are perceived as somatic in origin. For example, a heart attack may produce a sensation of pain that radiates to the superior thoracic wall and along the medial aspect of the left arm. Because the same spinal segments (T_1–T_5) innervate both the heart and the regions to which pain signals from heart tissue are referred, the brain interprets most such inputs as coming from the more common somatic pathway. Cutaneous areas to which visceral pain is commonly referred are shown in Figure 14.8. (Somatic and visceral pain are described in more detail in *A Closer Look* in Chapter 13.)

A *The visceral afferent fiber enters the spinal cord via a dorsal root ganglion, found only on the dorsal root of spinal nerves.*

ANS Physiology

Neurotransmitters and Receptors

Acetylcholine and *norepinephrine* are the major neurotransmitters released by ANS neurons. ACh, the same neurotransmitter secreted by somatic motor neurons, is released by (1) all ANS preganglionic axons and (2) all parasympathetic postganglionic axons at synapses with their effectors. ACh-releasing fibers are called **cholinergic fibers** (ko″lin-er′jik).

In contrast, most sympathetic postganglionic axons release NE and are classified as **adrenergic fibers** (ad″ren-er′jik). Some exceptions are sympathetic postganglionic fibers innervating sweat glands and some blood vessels in skeletal muscles; these fibers secrete ACh.

Unfortunately for memorization purposes, the effects of ACh and NE on their effectors are not consistently either excitation or inhibition. The response of visceral effectors to these neurotransmitters depends not only on the neurotransmitter but also on the receptor to which it attaches. The two or more kinds of receptors for each autonomic neurotransmitter allows it to exert different effects (activation or inhibition) at different body targets (Table 14.3).

Cholinergic Receptors

The two types of receptors that bind ACh are named for drugs that bind to them and mimic acetylcholine's effects. The first of these receptors identified were the **nicotinic receptors** (nik″o-tin′ik). A mushroom poison, *muscarine* (mus′kah-rin), activates a different set of ACh receptors, named **muscarinic receptors.** All ACh receptors are either nicotinic or muscarinic.

Nicotinic receptors are found on (1) motor end plates of skeletal muscle cells (which, however, are somatic and not autonomic targets), (2) *all* ganglionic neurons, both sympathetic and parasympathetic, and (3) the hormone-producing cells of the adrenal medulla. Just as at the motor end plate of skeletal muscle (examined in Chapter 9), ACh binding to any nicotinic receptor directly opens ion channels, depolarizing the postsynaptic cell. Thus, the effect of ACh binding to nicotinic receptors anywhere is *always* stimulatory.

Muscarinic receptors occur on all effector cells stimulated by postganglionic cholinergic fibers—that is, all parasympathetic target organs and a few sympathetic targets, such as eccrine sweat glands and some blood vessels of skeletal muscles. The effect of ACh binding to muscarinic receptors can be either inhibitory or stimulatory, depending on the subclass of muscarinic receptor found on the target organ. For example, binding of ACh to cardiac muscle receptors slows heart activity, whereas ACh binding

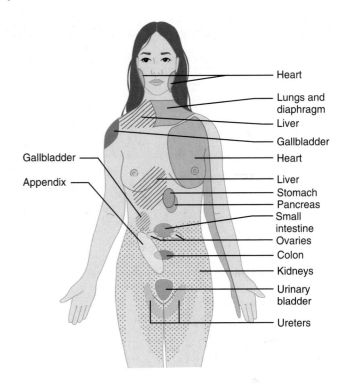

FIGURE 14.8 **Referred pain.** Anterior cutaneous areas to which pain from certain visceral organs is referred.

to receptors on smooth muscle of the gastrointestinal tract increases its motility.

Adrenergic Receptors

There are also two major classes of adrenergic (NE-binding) receptors: **alpha** (α) and **beta** (β). These receptors are further divided into subclasses (α_1 and α_2; β_1, β_2, and β_3). Organs that respond to NE (or epinephrine) have one or more of these receptor subtypes. NE or epinephrine can have either excitatory or inhibitory effects on target organs depending on which subclass of receptor predominates in that organ. For example, binding of NE to the β_1 receptors of cardiac muscle prods the heart into more vigorous activity, whereas epinephrine binding to β_2 receptors in bronchiole smooth muscle causes it to relax, dilating the bronchiole. An overview of the locations and effects of these receptor subclasses is provided in Table 14.3.

The Effects of Drugs

Knowing the locations of the cholinergic and adrenergic receptor subtypes allows specific drugs to be prescribed to obtain the desired inhibitory or stimulatory effects on selected target organs. For example, atropine, an anticholinergic drug that blocks muscarinic ACh receptors, is routinely administered before surgery to prevent salivation and to dry up respiratory system secretions. It is also used by ophthalmologists to dilate the pupils for eye examination.

14

TABLE 14.3 Cholinergic and Adrenergic Receptors

NEUROTRANSMITTER	RECEPTOR TYPE	MAJOR LOCATIONS*	EFFECT OF BINDING
Acetylcholine	**Cholinergic**		
	Nicotinic	All ganglionic neurons; adrenal medullary cells (also neuromuscular junctions of skeletal muscle)	Excitation
	Muscarinic	All parasympathetic target organs	Excitation in most cases; inhibition of cardiac muscle
		Limited sympathetic targets:	
		■ Eccrine sweat glands	Activation
		■ Blood vessels in skeletal muscles	Vasodilation (may not occur in humans)
Norepinephrine (and epinephrine released by adrenal medulla)	**Adrenergic**		
	β_1	Heart predominantly, but also kidneys and adipose tissue	Increases heart rate and strength; stimulates renin release by kidneys
	β_2	Lungs and most other sympathetic target organs; abundant on blood vessels serving the heart, liver and skeletal muscle	Effects mostly inhibitory; dilates blood vessels and bronchioles; relaxes smooth muscle walls of digestive and urinary visceral organs; relaxes uterus
	β_3	Adipose tissue	Stimulates lipolysis by fat cells
	α_1	Most importantly blood vessels serving the skin, mucosae, abdominal viscera, kidneys, and salivary glands; also, virtually all sympathetic target organs except heart	Constricts blood vessels and visceral organ sphincters; dilates pupils of the eyes
	α_2	Membrane of adrenergic axon terminals; pancreas; blood platelets	Inhibits NE release from adrenergic terminals; inhibits insulin secretion by pancreas; promotes blood clotting

*Note that all of these receptor subtypes are also found in the CNS.

The anticholinesterase drug *neostigmine* inhibits acetylcholinesterase, thus preventing enzymatic breakdown of ACh and allowing it to accumulate in the synapses. This drug is used to treat myasthenia gravis, a condition in which skeletal muscle activity is impaired for lack of ACh stimulation.

As described in Chapter 11, NE is one of our "feeling good" neurotransmitters, and drugs that prolong the activity of NE on the postsynaptic membrane help to relieve depression. Hundreds of over-the-counter drugs used to treat colds, coughs, allergies, and nasal congestion contain sympathomimetics (phenylephrine and others), sympathetic-mimicking drugs that stimulate α-adrenergic receptors. Much pharmaceutical research is directed toward finding drugs that affect only one subclass of receptor without upsetting the whole adrenergic or cholinergic system. An important breakthrough was finding drugs that mainly activate β_2 receptors. People with asthma use such β_2 activators to dilate their lung bronchioles without activating β_1 receptors, which would increase their heart rate. Selected drug classes that influence ANS activity are summarized in Table 14.4.

Interactions of the Autonomic Divisions

As mentioned earlier, most visceral organs receive *dual innervation*. Normally, both ANS divisions are partially active, producing a dynamic antagonism that allows visceral activity to be precisely controlled. However, one division or the other usually exerts the predominant effects in given circumstances, and in a few cases, the two divisions actually cooperate with each other. The major effects of the two divisions are summarized in Table 14.5.

Antagonistic Interactions

Antagonistic effects, described earlier, are most clearly seen on the activity of the heart, respiratory system, and gastrointestinal organs. In a fight-or-flight situation, the sympathetic division increases heart rate, dilates airways, and inhibits digestion and elimination. When the emergency is over, the parasympathetic division restores heart rate and airway diameter to resting levels and then attends to processes that refuel body cells and discard wastes.

TABLE 14.4	Selected Drug Classes That Influence the Activity of the Autonomic Nervous System			
DRUG CLASS	**RECEPTOR BOUND**	**EFFECTS**	**EXAMPLE**	**CLINICAL USE**
Nicotinic agents (little therapeutic value, but important because of presence of nicotine in tobacco)	Nicotinic ACh receptors on all ganglionic neurons and in CNS	Typically stimulation of sympathetic effects; heart rhythm becomes less regular; blood pressure increases	Nicotine	Used in smoking cessation products
Parasympathomimetic agents (muscarinic agents)	Muscarinic ACh receptors	Mimics effects of ACh, enhances PNS effects	Pilocarpine	Glaucoma (opens aqueous humor drainage pores)
			Bethanechol	Difficulty urinating (increases bladder contraction)
Acetylcholinesterase inhibitors	None; binds to the enzyme (AChE) that degrades ACh	Indirect effect at all ACh receptors; prolongs the effect of ACh	Neostigmine	Myasthenia gravis, (increases availability of ACh)
			Sarin	Used as chemical warfare agent (similar to widely used insecticides)
Sympathomimetic agents	Adrenergic receptors	Enhances sympathetic activity by increasing NE release or binding to adrenergic receptors	Albuterol (Ventolin)	Asthma (dilates bronchioles by binding to β_2 receptors)
			Phenylephrine	Colds (nasal decongestant, binds to α_1 receptors)
Sympatholytic agents	Adrenergic receptors	Decreases sympathetic activity by blocking adrenergic receptors or inhibiting NE release	Propranolol	Hypertension (member of a class of drugs called β *blockers* that decrease heart rate and blood pressure)

14

Sympathetic and Parasympathetic Tone

Although we have described the parasympathetic division as the "resting and digesting" division, the sympathetic division is the major actor in controlling blood pressure, even at rest. With few exceptions, the vascular system is entirely innervated by sympathetic fibers that keep the blood vessels in a continual state of partial constriction called **sympathetic** or **vasomotor tone.** When a higher blood pressure is needed to maintain blood flow, the sympathetic fibers fire more rapidly, causing blood vessels to constrict and blood pressure to rise. When blood pressure is to be decreased, the vessels are prompted to dilate. *Alpha-blocker drugs* that interfere with the activity of these **vasomotor fibers** are sometimes used to treat hypertension. During circulatory shock (inadequate blood delivery to body tissues), or when more blood is needed to meet the increased needs of working skeletal muscles, blood vessels serving the skin and abdominal viscera are strongly constricted. This blood "shunting" helps maintain circulation to vital organs or enhance blood delivery to skeletal muscles.

On the other hand, parasympathetic effects normally dominate the heart and the smooth muscle of digestive and urinary tract organs. Thus, these organs exhibit **parasympathetic tone.** The parasympathetic division slows the heart and dictates the normal activity levels of the digestive and urinary tracts. However, the sympathetic division can override these parasympathetic effects during times of stress. Drugs that block parasympathetic responses increase heart rate and cause fecal and urinary retention. Except for the adrenal glands and sweat glands of the skin, most glands are activated by parasympathetic fibers.

Cooperative Effects

The best example of cooperative ANS effects is seen in controls of the external genitalia. Parasympathetic stimulation causes vasodilation of blood vessels in the external genitalia and is responsible for erection of the male penis or female clitoris during sexual excitement. (This may explain why sexual performance is sometimes impaired when people

TABLE 14.5	Effects of the Parasympathetic and Sympathetic Divisions on Various Organs	
TARGET ORGAN OR SYSTEM	**PARASYMPATHETIC EFFECTS**	**SYMPATHETIC EFFECTS**
Eye (iris)	Stimulates sphincter pupillae muscles; constricts pupils	Stimulates dilator pupillae muscles; dilates pupils
Eye (ciliary muscle)	Stimulates muscles, which results in bulging of the lens for close vision	Weakly inhibits muscles, which results in flattening of the lens for far vision
Glands (nasal, lacrimal, gastric, pancreas)	Stimulates secretory activity	Inhibits secretory activity; causes vasoconstriction of blood vessels supplying the glands
Salivary glands	Stimulates secretion of watery saliva	Stimulates secretion of thick, viscous saliva
Sweat glands	No effect (no innervation)	Stimulates copious sweating (cholinergic fibers)
Adrenal medulla	No effect (no innervation)	Stimulates medulla cells to secrete epinephrine and norepinephrine
Arrector pili muscles attached to hair follicles	No effect (no innervation)	Stimulates to contract (erects hairs and produces "goosebumps")
Heart muscle	Decreases rate; slows heart	Increases rate and force of heartbeat
Heart: coronary blood vessels	Weakly dilates coronary vessels	Causes vasodilation*
Bladder/urethra	Causes contraction of smooth muscle of bladder wall; relaxes urethral sphincter; promotes voiding	Causes relaxation of smooth muscle of bladder wall; constricts urethral sphincter; inhibits voiding
Lungs	Constricts bronchioles	Dilates bronchioles*
Digestive tract organs	Increases motility (peristalsis) and amount of secretion by digestive organs; relaxes sphincters to allow movement of foodstuffs along tract	Decreases activity of glands and muscles of digestive system and constricts sphincters (e.g., anal sphincter)
Liver	No effect (no innervation)	Stimulates release of glucose to blood*
Gallbladder	Excites (gallbladder contracts to expel bile)	Inhibits (gallbladder is relaxed)
Kidney	No effect (no innervation)	Causes vasoconstriction; decreases urine output; promotes renin release
Penis	Causes erection (vasodilation)	Causes ejaculation
Vagina/clitoris	Causes erection (vasodilation) of clitoris	Causes contraction of vagina; increases mucus secretion
Blood vessels	Little or no effect	Constricts most vessels and increases blood pressure; constricts vessels of abdominal viscera and skin to divert blood to muscles, brain, and heart when necessary; NE constricts most vessels when necessary; epinephrine dilates vessels of the skeletal muscles during exercise*
Blood coagulation	No effect (no innervation)	Increases coagulation*
Cellular metabolism	No effect (no innervation)	Increases metabolic rate*
Adipose tissue	No effect (no innervation)	Stimulates lipolysis (fat breakdown)*

*Effects are mediated by epinephrine release into the bloodstream from the adrenal medulla.

are anxious or upset and the sympathetic division is in charge.) Sympathetic stimulation then causes ejaculation of semen by the penis or reflex contractions of a female's vagina.

Unique Roles of the Sympathetic Division

The adrenal medulla, sweat glands and arrector pili muscles of the skin, the kidneys, and most blood vessels receive only sympathetic fibers. It is easy to remember that the sympathetic system innervates these structures because most of us sweat under stress, our scalp "prickles" during fear, and our blood pressure skyrockets (from widespread vasoconstriction) when we get excited. We have already described how sympathetic control of blood vessels regulates blood pressure and shunting of blood in the vascular system. We will now mention several other uniquely sympathetic functions.

Thermoregulatory Responses to Heat The sympathetic division mediates reflexes that regulate body temperature. For example, applying heat to the skin causes reflexive dilation of blood vessels in that area. When systemic body temperature is elevated, sympathetic nerves cause the skin's blood vessels to dilate, allowing the skin to become flushed with warm blood, and activate the sweat glands to help cool the body. When body temperature falls, skin blood vessels are constricted, and, as a result, blood is restricted to deeper, more vital organs.

Release of Renin from the Kidneys Sympathetic impulses stimulate the kidneys to release renin, an enzyme that promotes an increase in blood pressure. This renin-angiotensin mechanism is described in Chapter 25.

Metabolic Effects Through both direct neural stimulation and release of adrenal medullary hormones, the sympathetic division promotes a number of metabolic effects not reversed by parasympathetic activity. It (1) increases the metabolic rate of body cells; (2) raises blood glucose levels; and (3) mobilizes fats for use as fuels. These medullary hormones also cause skeletal muscle to contract more strongly and quickly. As a side effect, muscle spindles are stimulated more often and, consequently, nerve impulses traveling to the muscles occur more synchronously. These neutral bursts, which put muscle contractions on a "hair trigger," are great if you have to make a quick jump or run, but they can be embarrassing or even disabling to the nervous musician or surgeon.

Localized Versus Diffuse Effects

In the parasympathetic division, one preganglionic neuron synapses with one (or at most a few) ganglionic neurons. Additionally, all parasympathetic fibers release ACh, which is quickly destroyed (hydrolyzed) by acetylcholinesterase. Consequently, the parasympathetic division exerts short-lived, highly localized control over its effectors. In contrast, preganglionic sympathetic axons branch profusely as they enter the sympathetic trunk, and they synapse with ganglionic neurons at several levels. Thus, when the sympathetic division is activated, it responds in a diffuse and highly interconnected way. Indeed, the literal translation of sympathetic (*sym* = together; *pathos* = feeling) relates to the bodywide mobilization this division provokes. Nevertheless, parts of the sympathetic nervous system can be activated individually. For example, just because your eye pupils dilate in dim light doesn't necessarily mean that your heart rate speeds up.

Effects produced by sympathetic activation are much longer lasting than parasympathetic effects. In contrast to the parasympathetic system's ACh, NE is inactivated more slowly because it must be taken back up into the presynaptic ending before being hydrolyzed (or stored). More importantly, NE and epinephrine are secreted into the blood by adrenal medullary cells when the sympathetic division is mobilized. Although epinephrine is more potent at increasing heart rate and raising blood glucose levels and metabolic rate, these hormones have essentially the same effects as NE released by sympathetic neurons. In fact, circulating adrenal medullary hormones produce 25–50% of all the sympathetic effects acting on the body at a given time. These effects continue for several minutes until the hormones are destroyed by the liver. Thus, although sympathetic nerve impulses act only briefly, the hormonal effects they provoke linger. The widespread and prolonged effect of sympathetic activation helps explain why we need time to "come down" after an extremely stressful experience.

Control of Autonomic Functioning

Although the ANS is not usually considered to be under voluntary control, its activity *is* regulated by CNS controls in the spinal cord, brain stem, hypothalamus, and cerebral cortex (Figure 14.9). In general, the

FIGURE 14.9 **Levels of ANS control.** The hypothalamus stands at the top of the control hierarchy as the integrator of ANS activity. However, subconscious cerebral inputs via limbic lobe connections influence hypothalamic functioning.

SYSTEM CONNECTIONS: Homeostatic Interrelationships Between the Nervous System and Other Body Systems

Endocrine System

- Sympathetic division of the ANS activates the adrenal medulla; hypothalamus helps regulate the activity of the anterior pituitary gland and produces the two posterior pituitary hormones
- Hormones influence neuronal metabolism

Cardiovascular System

- ANS helps regulate heart rate and blood pressure
- Cardiovascular system provides blood containing oxygen and nutrients to the nervous system and carries away wastes

Lymphatic System/Immunity

- Nerves innervate lymphoid organs; the brain plays a role in regulating immune function
- Lymphatic vessels carry away leaked tissue fluids from tissues surrounding nervous system structures; immune elements protect all body organs from pathogens (CNS has additional mechanisms as well)

Respiratory System

- Nervous system initiates and regulates respiratory rhythm and depth
- Respiratory system provides life-sustaining oxygen; disposes of carbon dioxide

Digestive System

- ANS (particularly the parasympathetic division) regulates digestive motility and glandular activity
- Digestive system provides nutrients needed for neuronal health

Urinary System

- ANS regulates bladder emptying and renal blood pressure
- Kidneys help to dispose of metabolic wastes and maintain proper electrolyte composition and pH of blood for neural functioning

Reproductive System

- ANS regulates sexual erection and ejaculation in males; erection of the clitoris in females
- Testosterone causes masculinization of the brain and underlies sex drive and aggressive behavior

Integumentary System

- Sympathetic division of the ANS regulates sweat glands and blood vessels of skin (therefore heat loss/retention)
- Skin serves as heat loss surface

Skeletal System

- Nerves innervate bones and joints, providing for pain and joint sense
- Bones serve as depot for calcium needed for neural function; skeletal system protects CNS structures

Muscular System

- Somatic division of nervous system activates skeletal muscles; maintains muscle health
- Skeletal muscles are the effectors of the somatic division

THE NERVOUS SYSTEM and Interrelationships with the Muscular, Respiratory, and Digestive Systems

The nervous system pokes its figurative nose into the activities of virtually every organ system of the body. Hence, trying to choose the most significant interactions comes pretty close to a lesson in futility. Which is more important: digestion, elimination of wastes, or motility? Your answer probably depends on whether you are hungry or need to make a "pit stop" at the bathroom when you read this. Since neural interactions with several other systems are thoroughly plumbed in chapters to come, here we will look at the all-important interactions between the nervous system and the muscular, respiratory, and digestive systems.

Muscular System

Most simply said, the muscular system would cease to function without the nervous system. Unlike visceral or cardiac muscles, both of which have other controlling systems, somatic motor fibers are *it* for skeletal muscle activation and regulation. Somatic nerve fibers "tell" skeletal muscles not only when to contract but also how strongly. Additionally, as the nervous system makes its initial synapses with skeletal muscle fibers, it determines their fate as fast or slow fibers, which forever after affects our potential for muscle speed and endurance. The interactions of the various brain regions (basal nuclei, cerebellum, premotor cortex, etc.) and inputs of stretch receptors also determine our grace—how smooth and coordinated we are. Nonetheless, keep in mind that as long as the skeletal muscle effector cells are healthy, they help determine the viability of the neurons synapsing with them. The relationship is truly synergistic.

Respiratory System

Another system that depends entirely on the nervous system for its function is the respiratory system, which continuously refreshes the blood with oxygen and unloads the carbon dioxide waste to the sea of air that surrounds us. Neural centers in the medulla and pons both initiate and maintain the tidelike rhythm of air flushing into and out of our lungs by activating skeletal muscles that change the volume (thus the gas pressure) within the lungs. Peripheral receptors supply information about gas concentrations, lung stretch and skeletal muscle activity to these CNS respiratory centers.

Digestive System

Although the digestive system responds to many different types of controls—for example, hormones, local pH, and irritating chemicals—the parasympathetic nervous system is crucial to its normal functioning. Without the parasympathetic inputs, sympathetic neural activity, which inhibits normal digestion would be unopposed. So important are parasympathetic controls that some of the parasympathetic neurons are actually located in the walls of the digestive organs, in what are called intrinsic plexuses. Thus, even if all extrinsic controls are severed, the intrinsic mechanisms can still maintain this crucial body function. The role the digestive system plays for the nervous system is the same one it offers to all body systems—it sees that ingested foodstuff gets digested and loaded into the blood for cell use.

CLINICAL CONNECTIONS

Nervous System

Case study: On arrival at Holyoke Hospital, Jimmy Chin, a 10-year-old boy, is immobilized on a rigid stretcher so that he is unable to move his head or trunk. The paramedics report that when they found him some 50 feet from the bus, he was awake and alert, but crying and complaining that he couldn't "get up to find his mom" and that he had a "wicked headache." He has severe bruises on his upper back and head, and lacerations of his back and scalp. His blood pressure is low, body temperature is below normal, lower limbs are paralyzed, and he is insensitive to painful stimuli below the nipples. Although still alert on arrival, Jimmy soon begins to drift in and out of unconsciousness.

Jimmy is immediately scheduled for a CT scan, an operating room is reserved, and an intravenous infusion of dexamethasone, an anti-inflammatory steroid, is started.

Relative to Jimmy's condition:

1. Why were his head and torso immobilized for transport to the hospital?

2. What do his worsening neurological signs (drowsiness, incoherence, etc.) probably indicate? (Relate this to the type of surgery that will be performed.)

3. Why was dexamethasone ordered?

4. Assuming that Jimmy's sensory and motor deficits are due to a spinal cord injury, at what level do you expect to find a spinal cord lesion?

5. Two days after his surgery, Jimmy is alert and his MRI scan shows no residual brain injury, but pronounced swelling and damage to the spinal cord at T_4. On physical examination, Jimmy shows no reflex activity below the level of the spinal cord injury. His blood pressure is still low. Why are there no reflexes in his lower limbs and abdomen?

6. Over the next few days, his reflexes return in his lower limbs and become exaggerated. He is incontinent. Why is Jimmy hyperreflexive and incontinent?

On one occasion, Jimmy complains of a massive headache and his blood pressure is way above normal. On examination, he is sweating intensely above the nipples but has cold, clammy skin below the nipple and his heart rate is very slow.

7. What is this condition called and what precipitates it?

8. How does Jimmy's excessively high blood pressure put him at risk?

(Answers in Appendix G)

hypothalamus is the integrative center at the top of the ANS control hierarchy. From there, orders flow to lower and lower CNS centers for execution. Although the cerebral cortex may modify the workings of the ANS, it does so at the subconscious level and by acting through limbic system structures on hypothalamic centers.

Brain Stem and Spinal Cord Controls

The hypothalamus is the "boss," but the brain stem reticular formation appears to exert the most *direct* influence over autonomic functions. For example, certain motor centers in the ventrolateral medulla (*cardiac* and *vasomotor centers*) reflexively regulate heart rate and blood vessel diameter. Other medullary regions oversee gastrointestinal activities. Most sensory impulses involved in eliciting these autonomic reflexes reach the brain stem via vagus nerve afferents. Although not considered part of the ANS, the medulla and pons also contain respiratory centers that mediate involuntary control of respiration and receive inputs from the hypothalamus. Midbrain centers (*oculomotor nuclei*) control the muscles concerned with pupil diameter and lens focus. Defecation and micturition reflexes that promote emptying of the rectum and bladder are integrated at the spinal cord level but are subject to conscious inhibition. All of these autonomic reflexes are described in later chapters in relation to the organ systems they serve.

Hypothalamic Controls

As noted, the main integration center of the autonomic nervous system is the hypothalamus. In general, anterior hypothalamic regions direct parasympathetic functions, whereas posterior areas direct sympathetic functions. These centers exert their effects both directly and via relays through the *reticular formation*, which in turn influences the preganglionic motor neurons in the brain stem and spinal cord (Figure 14.9). The hypothalamus contains centers that coordinate heart activity, blood pressure, body temperature, water balance, and endocrine activity. It also contains centers that mediate various emotional states (rage, pleasure) and biological drives (thirst, hunger, sex).

Via its associations with the periaqueductal gray matter and the amygdala, the hypothalamus also mediates our reactions to fear. Emotional responses of the limbic system of the cerebrum to danger and stress signal the hypothalamus to activate the sympathetic system to fight-or-flight status. Thus, the hypothalamus serves as the keystone of the emotional and visceral brain, and through its centers emotions influence ANS functioning and behavior.

Cortical Controls

It was originally believed that the ANS is not subject to voluntary controls. However, we have all had occasions when remembering a frightening event made our heart race (sympathetic response) or just the thought of a favorite food, pecan pie for example, made our mouth water (a parasympathetic response). These inputs converge on the hypothalamus through its connections to the limbic lobe.

Additionally, studies have shown that voluntary cortical control of visceral activities is possible—a capability untapped by most people.

Influence of Biofeedback on Autonomic Function

During **biofeedback training**, subjects are connected to monitoring devices that provide an awareness of what is happening in their body. This awareness is called **biofeedback.** The devices detect and amplify changes in physiological processes such as heart rate and blood pressure, and these data are "fed back" in the form of flashing lights or audible tones. Subjects are asked to try to alter or control some "involuntary" function by concentrating on calming, pleasant thoughts. The monitor allows them to identify changes in the desired direction, so they can recognize the feelings associated with these changes and learn to produce the changes at will.

Biofeedback techniques have been successful in helping individuals plagued by migraine headaches. They are also used by cardiac patients to manage stress and reduce their risk of heart attack. However, biofeedback training is time-consuming and often frustrating, and the training equipment is expensive and difficult to use.

Homeostatic Imbalances of the ANS

Because the ANS is involved in nearly every important process that goes on in the body, it is not surprising that abnormalities of autonomic functioning can have far-reaching effects and threaten life itself. Most autonomic disorders reflect exaggerated or deficient controls of smooth muscle activity. Of these, the most devastating involve blood vessels and include conditions such as hypertension, Raynaud's disease, and autonomic dysreflexia.

Hypertension, or high blood pressure, may result from an overactive sympathetic vasoconstrictor response promoted by continuous high levels of stress. Hypertension is always serious because it increases the workload on the heart, which may precipitate heart disease, and increases the wear and tear on artery walls. Stress-induced hypertension can be treated with adrenergic receptor–blocking drugs.

Raynaud's disease is characterized by intermittent attacks causing the skin of the fingers and toes to become pale, then cyanotic and painful. Commonly provoked by exposure to cold or emotional stress, it is an exaggerated vasoconstriction response. The severity of this disease ranges from merely uncomfortable to such severe blood vessel constriction that ischemia and gangrene (tissue death) results. Vasodilators (for example, adrenergic blockers) usually suffice, but to treat very severe cases, preganglionic sympathetic fibers serving the affected regions are severed (a procedure called *sympathectomy*). The involved vessels then dilate, reestablishing adequate blood delivery to the region.

Autonomic dysreflexia is a life-threatening condition involving uncontrolled activation of autonomic neurons. It occurs in a majority of individuals with quadriplegia and in others with spinal cord injuries above the T_6 level, usually in the first year after injury. The usual trigger is a painful stimulus to the skin or overfilling of a visceral organ, such as the bladder. Arterial blood pressure skyrockets to life-threatening levels, which may rupture a blood vessel in the brain, precipitating stroke. This may be accompanied by a headache, flushed face, sweating above the level of the injury, and cold, clammy skin below. The precise mechanism of autonomic dysreflexia is not yet clear.

Developmental Aspects of the ANS

ANS preganglionic neurons derive from the embryonic *neural tube,* as do somatic motor neurons. ANS structures in the PNS—ganglionic neurons, the adrenal medulla, and all autonomic ganglia—derive from the *neural crest* (along with all sensory neurons). Neural crest cells reach their ultimate destinations by migrating along growing axons. Forming ganglia receive axons from preganglionic neurons in the cord or brain and send their axons to synapse with their effector cells in the body periphery. This process depends upon the presence of **nerve growth factor,** and is guided by a number of signaling chemicals similar to those acting in the CNS.

During youth, impairments of ANS function are usually due to injuries to the spinal cord or autonomic nerves. In old age the efficiency of the ANS begins to decline. At least part of the problem appears to be due to structural changes (bloating) of some preganglionic axon terminals, which become congested with neurofilaments.

Many elderly people complain of constipation (a result of reduced gastrointestinal tract motility), and of dry eyes and frequent eye infections (both a result of a diminished ability to form tears). Additionally, when they stand up they may have fainting episodes due to **orthostatic hypotension** (*ortho* = straight; *stat* = standing), a form of low blood pressure that occurs because the aging pressure receptors respond less to changes in blood pressure following changes in position, and because of slowed responses by aging sympathetic vasoconstrictor centers. These problems are distressing, but not usually life threatening, and most can be managed by lifestyle changes or artificial aids. For example, changing position slowly gives the sympathetic nervous system time to adjust the blood pressure; and eye drops (artificial tears) are available for the dry-eye problem.

∎ ∎ ∎

In this chapter, we have described the structure and function of the ANS, one arm of the motor division of the peripheral nervous system. Because virtually every organ system still to be considered depends on autonomic controls, you will be hearing more about the ANS in chapters that follow. Now that we have explored most of the nervous system, this is a good time to examine how it interacts with the rest of the body as summarized in the *Making Connections* feature, pp. 548–549.

Related Clinical Terms

Atonic bladder (ah-ton'ik; *a* = without; *ton* = tone, tension) A condition in which the urinary bladder becomes flaccid and overfills, allowing urine to dribble through the sphincters; results from temporary loss of the micturition reflex following spinal cord injury.

Horner's syndrome A condition due to damage to the superior sympathetic trunk on one side of the body; the affected person exhibits drooping of the upper eyelid (ptosis) and constricted pupil, and does not sweat on the affected side of the head.

Vagotomy (va-got'o-me) Cutting or severing of the vagus nerve to decrease secretion of gastric juice in those with peptic ulcers that do not respond to medication.

Vasovagal syncope Vasovagal syncope, also called *neurocardiogenic syncope,* is the most common cause of fainting. Although it may be provoked by emotional stress, pain, or dehydration, it typically occurs during prolonged standing. Fainting is due to a drop in blood pressure, which decreases blood flow to the brain and results in loss of consciousness.

Chapter Summary

Media study tools that could provide you additional help in reviewing specific key topics of Chapter 14 are referenced below.

IP = InterActive Physiology

1. The autonomic nervous system (ANS) is the motor division of the PNS that controls visceral activities, with the goal of maintaining internal homeostasis.

Introduction (pp. 533–535)

Comparison of the Somatic and Autonomic Nervous Systems (pp. 533–535)

1. The somatic (voluntary) nervous system provides motor fibers to skeletal muscles. The autonomic (involuntary or visceral motor) nervous system provides motor fibers to smooth and cardiac muscles and glands.

2. In the somatic division, a single motor neuron forms the efferent pathway from the CNS to the effectors. The efferent pathway of the autonomic division consists of a two-neuron chain: the preganglionic neuron in the CNS and the ganglionic neuron in a ganglion.

3. Acetylcholine, the neurotransmitter of somatic motor neurons, is stimulatory to skeletal muscle fibers. Neurotransmitters released by autonomic motor neurons (acetylcholine and norepinephrine) may cause excitation or inhibition.

IP Nervous System II; Topic: Synaptic Transmission, pp. 8–11.

ANS Divisions (p. 535)

4. The ANS consists of two divisions, the parasympathetic and sympathetic, which normally exert antagonistic effects on many of the same target organs.

5. The parasympathetic division (the resting-digesting system) conserves body energy and maintains body activities at basal levels.

6. Parasympathetic effects include pupillary constriction, glandular secretion, increased digestive tract motility, and smooth muscle activity leading to elimination of feces and urine.

7. The sympathetic division prepares the body for activity and is called the fight-or-flight system.

8. Sympathetic responses include dilated pupils, increased heart rate, increased blood pressure, dilation of the bronchioles of the lungs, increased blood glucose levels, and sweating. During exercise, sympathetic vasoconstriction shunts blood from the skin and digestive viscera to the heart, brain, and skeletal muscles.

ANS Anatomy (pp. 535–543)

Parasympathetic (Craniosacral) Division (pp. 536–538)

1. Parasympathetic preganglionic neurons arise from the brain stem and from the sacral (S_2–S_4) region of the cord.

2. Preganglionic fibers synapse with ganglionic neurons in terminal ganglia located in (intramural ganglia) or close to their effector organs. Preganglionic fibers are long; postganglionic fibers are short.

3. Cranial fibers arise in the brain stem nuclei of cranial nerves III, VII, IX, and X and synapse in ganglia of the head, thorax, and abdomen. The vagus nerves serve virtually all organs of the thoracic and abdominal cavities.

4. Sacral fibers (S_2–S_4) issue from the lateral region of the cord and form pelvic splanchnic nerves that innervate the pelvic viscera. The preganglionic axons do not travel within rami communicantes or spinal nerves.

Sympathetic (Thoracolumbar) Division (pp. 538–542)

5. Preganglionic sympathetic neurons arise from the lateral horn of the spinal cord from the level of T_1 to L_2.

6. Preganglionic axons leave the cord via white rami communicantes and enter the sympathetic trunk (chain) ganglia in the sympathetic trunk. An axon may synapse in a trunk ganglion at the same or at a different level, or it may issue from the sympathetic trunk without synapsing. Preganglionic fibers are short; postganglionic fibers are long.

7. When the synapse occurs in a trunk ganglion, the postganglionic fiber may enter the spinal nerve ramus via the gray ramus communicans to travel to the body periphery. Postganglionic fibers issuing from the cervical ganglia also serve visceral organs and blood vessels of the head, neck, and thorax.

8. When synapses do not occur in the trunk ganglia, the preganglionic fibers form splanchnic nerves (thoracic, lumbar, and sacral). Most splanchnic nerve fibers synapse in collateral ganglia, and the postganglionic fibers serve the abdominal viscera. Some splanchnic nerve fibers synapse with cells of the adrenal medulla.

Visceral Reflexes (p. 542)

9. Visceral reflex arcs have the same components as somatic reflexes.

10. Cell bodies of visceral sensory neurons are located in dorsal root ganglia, sensory ganglia of cranial nerves, or autonomic ganglia. Visceral afferents are found in spinal nerves and in virtually all autonomic nerves.

ANS Physiology (pp. 543–547, 550)

Neurotransmitters and Receptors (p. 543)

1. Two major neurotransmitters, acetylcholine (ACh) and norepinephrine (NE), are released by autonomic motor neurons. On the basis of the neurotransmitter released, the fibers are classified as cholinergic or adrenergic.

2. ACh is released by all preganglionic fibers and all parasympathetic postganglionic fibers. NE is released by all sympathetic postganglionic fibers except those serving the sweat glands of the skin, and some blood vessels within skeletal muscles.

3. Neurotransmitter effects depend on the receptors to which the transmitter binds. Cholinergic (ACh) receptors are classified as nicotinic or muscarinic. Adrenergic (NE) receptors are classified as α_1 or α_2, or β_1, β_2, or β_3.

IP Nervous System II; Topic: Synaptic Transmission, pp. 8–11, 14.

The Effects of Drugs (pp. 543–544)

4. Drugs that mimic, enhance, or inhibit the action of ANS neurotransmitters are used to treat conditions caused by excessive, inadequate, or inappropriate ANS functioning. Some drugs bind with only one receptor subtype, allowing specific ANS-mediated activities to be enhanced or blocked.

Interactions of the Autonomic Divisions (pp. 544–547)

5. Most visceral organs are innervated by both divisions; they interact in various ways but usually exert a dynamic antagonism. Antagonistic interactions mainly involve the heart, respiratory system, and gastrointestinal organs. Sympathetic activity increases heart and respiratory system activity and depresses gastrointestinal activity. Parasympathetic activity reverses these effects.

6. Most blood vessels are innervated only by sympathetic fibers and exhibit vasomotor tone. Parasympathetic activity dominates the heart and muscles of the gastrointestinal tract (which normally exhibit parasympathetic tone) and glands.

7. The two ANS divisions exert cooperative effects on the external genitalia.

8. Roles unique to the sympathetic division are blood pressure regulation, shunting of blood in the vascular system, thermoregulatory responses, stimulation of renin release by the kidneys, and metabolic effects.

9. Activation of the sympathetic division can cause widespread, long-lasting mobilization of the fight-or-flight response. Parasympathetic effects are highly localized and short lived.

Control of Autonomic Functioning (pp. 547, 550)

10. Autonomic function is controlled at several levels: (1) Reflex activity is mediated by the spinal cord and brain stem (particularly medullary) centers; (2) hypothalamic integration centers interact with both higher and lower centers to orchestrate autonomic, somatic, and endocrine responses; and (3) cortical centers influence autonomic functioning via connections with the limbic system; conscious controls of autonomic function are rare but possible, as illustrated by biofeedback training.

Homeostatic Imbalances of the ANS (pp. 550–551)

1. Most autonomic disorders reflect problems with smooth muscle control. Abnormalities in vascular control, such as occur in hypertension, Raynaud's disease, and autonomic dysreflexia, are most devastating.

Developmental Aspects of the ANS (p. 551)

1. Preganglionic neurons develop from the neural tube; ganglionic neurons develop from the embryonic neural crest.

2. The efficiency of the autonomic nervous system declines in old age, as reflected by decreased glandular secretory activity, decreased gastrointestinal motility, and slowed sympathetic vasomotor responses to changes in position.

Review Questions

Multiple Choice/Matching

(Some questions have more than one correct answer. Select the best answer or answers from the choices given.)

1. All of the following characterize the ANS except (a) two-neuron efferent chain, (b) presence of nerve cell bodies in the CNS, (c) presence of nerve cell bodies in the ganglia, (d) innervation of skeletal muscles.

2. Relate each of the following terms or phrases to either the sympathetic (S) or parasympathetic (P) division of the autonomic nervous system:

_____ **(1)** short preganglionic, long postganglionic fibers
_____ **(2)** intramural ganglia
_____ **(3)** craniosacral outflow
_____ **(4)** adrenergic fibers
_____ **(5)** cervical ganglia
_____ **(6)** otic and ciliary ganglia
_____ **(7)** generally short duration action
_____ **(8)** increases heart rate and blood pressure
_____ **(9)** increases gastric motility and secretion of lacrimal, salivary, and digestive juices
_____ **(10)** innervates blood vessels
_____ **(11)** most active when you are swinging in a hammock
_____ **(12)** active when you are running in the Boston Marathon

3. Preganglionic neurons develop from (a) neural crest cells, (b) neural tube cells, (c) alar plate cells, (d) endoderm.

4. The white rami communicantes contain what kind of fibers? (a) preganglionic parasympathetic, (b) postganglionic parasympathetic, (c) preganglionic sympathetic, (d) postganglionic sympathetic.

5. Prevertebral sympathetic ganglia are involved with the innervation of the (a) abdominal organs, (b) thoracic organs, (c) head, (d) arrector pili, (e) all of these.

Short Answer Essay Questions

6. Briefly explain why the following terms are sometimes used to refer to the autonomic nervous system: involuntary nervous system and emotional-visceral system.

7. Describe the anatomical relationship of the white and gray rami to the spinal nerve, and indicate the kind of fibers found in each ramus type.

8. Indicate the results of sympathetic activation of the following structures: sweat glands, eye pupils, adrenal medulla, heart, lungs, liver, blood vessels of vigorously working skeletal muscles, blood vessels of digestive viscera, salivary glands.

9. Which of the effects listed in response to question 8 would be reversed by parasympathetic activity?

10. Which ANS fibers release acetylcholine? Which release norepinephrine?

11. Describe the meaning and importance of sympathetic tone and parasympathetic tone.

12. List the receptor subtypes for ACh and NE, and indicate the major sites where each type is found.

13. What area of the brain is most directly involved in mediating autonomic reflexes?

14. Describe the importance of the hypothalamus in controlling the autonomic nervous system.

15. Describe the basis and uses of biofeedback training.

16. What manifestations of decreased autonomic nervous system efficiency are seen in elderly individuals?

17. Ganglionic neurons were initially called postganglionic neurons. Why is this a misnomer?

 Critical Thinking and Clinical Application Questions

1. Mr. Johnson has been suffering from functional urinary retention and a hypoactive urinary bladder. Bethanechol, a drug that mimics acetylcholine's autonomic effects, is prescribed to manage his problem. First explain the rationale for prescribing bethanechol, and then predict which of the following adverse effects Mr. Johnson might experience while taking this drug (select all that apply): dizziness, low blood pressure, deficient tear formation, wheezing, increased mucus production in bronchi, deficient salivation, diarrhea, cramping, excessive sweating, undesirable erection of penis.

2. Mr. Jake was admitted to the hospital with excruciating pain in his left shoulder and arm. He was found to have suffered a heart attack. Explain the phenomenon of referred pain as exhibited by Mr. Jake.

3. A 32-year-old woman complains that she has been experiencing aching pains in the medial two fingers of both hands and that during such episodes, the fingers become blanched and then blue. Her history is taken, and it is noted that she is a heavy smoker. The physician advises her that she must stop smoking and states that he will not prescribe any medication until she has discontinued smoking for a month. What is this woman's problem, and why was she told to stop smoking?

4. Tiffany, a 21-year-old college student, had been having trouble sleeping, crying frequently, and having recurrent thoughts of suicide. She was prescribed an antidepressant. Like many such drugs, this antidepressant has anticholiner-gic side effects. What side effects might Tiffany experience in the first week of treatment?

5. As the aroma of freshly brewed coffee drifted by dozing Henry's nose, his mouth started to water and his stomach began to rumble. Explain his reactions in terms of ANS activity.

6. Which clinical condition has the classic signs of blue fingertips that later turn red?

LOOKING FOR MORE STUDY HELP?

A wide variety of quiz questions, tutorials, and learning exercises are available online at the Anatomy & Physiology Place (www.anatomyandphysiology.com) and, if your instructor has provided you with a MyA&P Course ID number, in MyA&P (www.myaandp.com).

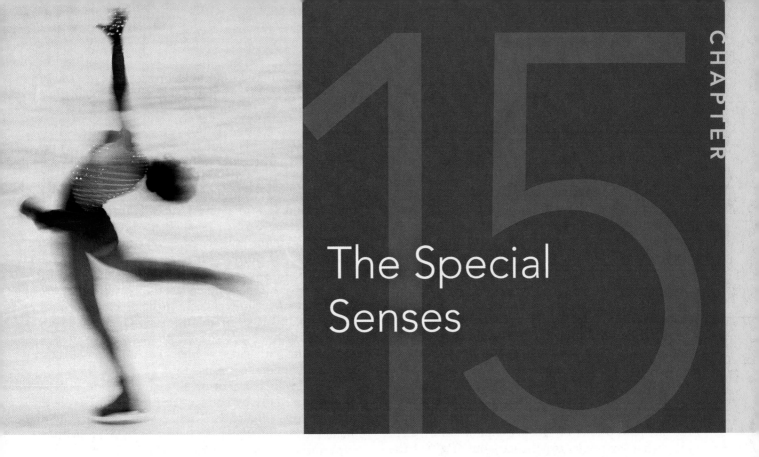

The Special Senses

The Eye and Vision (pp. 556–578)

1. Describe the structure and function of accessory eye structures, eye layers, the lens, and humors of the eye.

2. Trace the pathway of light through the eye to the retina, and explain how light is focused for distant and close vision.

3. Describe the events involved in the stimulation of photoreceptors by light, and compare and contrast the roles of rods and cones in vision.

4. Note the cause and consequences of astigmatism, cataract, glaucoma, hyperopia, myopia, presbyopia, and color blindness.

5. Compare and contrast light and dark adaptation.

6. Trace the visual pathway to the visual cortex, and briefly describe the steps in visual processing.

The Chemical Senses: Taste and Smell (pp. 578–583)

7. Describe the location, structure, and afferent pathways of taste and smell receptors, and explain how these receptors are activated.

The Ear: Hearing and Balance (pp. 583–598)

8. Describe the structure and general function of the outer, middle, and internal ears.

9. Describe the sound conduction pathway to the fluids of the internal ear, and follow the auditory pathway from the spiral organ (of Corti) to the temporal cortex.

10. Explain how one is able to differentiate pitch and loudness and localize the source of sounds.

11. Explain how the balance organs of the semicircular canals and the vestibule help maintain dynamic and static equilibrium.

12. List possible causes and symptoms of otitis media, deafness, Ménière's syndrome, and motion sickness.

Developmental Aspects of the Special Senses (pp. 598–599)

13. List changes that occur in the special sense organs with aging.

People are responsive creatures. The aroma of freshly baked bread makes our mouths water. A sudden clap of thunder makes us jump. These stimuli and many others continually greet us and are interpreted by our nervous systems.

We are usually told that we have five senses: touch, taste, smell, sight, and hearing. Actually, touch reflects the activity of the general senses that we considered in Chapter 13. The other four traditional senses—*smell, taste, sight,* and *hearing*—are called **special senses.** Receptors for a fifth special sense, *equilibrium,* are housed in the ear, along with the organ of hearing. In contrast to the widely distributed general receptors (most of which are modified nerve endings of sensory neurons), the **special sensory receptors** are distinct *receptor cells.* These receptor cells are confined to the head region and are highly localized, either housed within complex sensory organs (eyes and ears) or in distinct epithelial structures (taste buds and olfactory epithelium).

This chapter considers the functional anatomy of each of the five special senses. But keep in mind that our perceptions of sensory inputs are overlapping. What we finally experience—our "feel" of the world—is a blending of stimulus effects.

The Eye and Vision

Vision is our dominant sense: Some 70% of all the sensory receptors in the body are in the eyes, and nearly half of the cerebral cortex is involved in some aspect of visual processing.

The adult **eye** is a sphere with a diameter of about 2.5 cm (1 inch). Only the anterior one-sixth of the eye's surface is visible (Figure 15.1); the rest is enclosed and protected by a cushion of fat and the walls of the bony orbit. The fat pad occupies nearly all of the orbit not occupied by the eye itself. The eye is a complex structure and only a small portion of its tissues are actually involved in photoreception. Before turning our attention to the eye itself, let us consider the accessory structures that protect it or aid its functioning.

Accessory Structures of the Eye

The **accessory structures** of the eye include the eyebrows, eyelids, conjunctiva, lacrimal apparatus, and extrinsic eye muscles.

Eyebrows

The **eyebrows** are short, coarse hairs that overlie the supraorbital margins of the skull (Figure 15.1). They help shade the eyes from sunlight and prevent perspiration trickling down the forehead from reaching the eyes. Deep to the skin of the eyebrows are parts of the orbicularis oculi and corrugator muscles. Contraction of the orbicularis muscle depresses the eyebrow, whereas the corrugator moves the eyebrow medially.

Eyelids

Anteriorly, the eyes are protected by the mobile **eyelids** or **palpebrae** (pal'pĕ-bre). The eyelids are separated by the **palpebral fissure** ("eyelid slit") and meet at the medial and lateral angles of the eye—the **medial** and **lateral commissures (canthi),** respectively (Figure 15.1a). The medial canthus sports a fleshy elevation called the **lacrimal caruncle** (kar'ung-kl; "a bit of flesh"). The caruncle contains sebaceous and sweat glands and produces the whitish, oily secretion (fancifully called the Sandman's eye-sand) that sometimes collects at the medial canthus, especially during sleep. In most Asian peoples, a vertical fold of skin called the *epicanthic fold* commonly appears on both sides of the nose and sometimes covers the medial commissure.

The eyelids are thin, skin-covered folds supported internally by connective tissue sheets called **tarsal plates** (Figure 15.1b). The tarsal plates also anchor the orbicularis oculi and **levator palpebrae superioris** muscles that run within the eyelid. The orbicularis muscle encircles the eye; when it contracts, the eye closes. Of the two eyelids, the larger, upper one is much more mobile, mainly because of the levator palpebrae superioris muscle, which raises that eyelid to open the eye. The eyelid muscles are activated reflexively to cause blinking every 3–7 seconds and to protect the eye when it is threatened by foreign objects. Reflex blinking helps prevent drying of the eyes because each time we blink, accessory structure secretions (oil, mucus, and saline solution) are spread across the eyeball surface.

Projecting from the free margin of each eyelid are the **eyelashes.** The follicles of the eyelash hairs are richly innervated by nerve endings (hair follicle receptors), and anything that touches the eyelashes (even a puff of air) triggers reflex blinking.

Several types of glands are associated with the eyelids. The **tarsal glands** (*Meibomian glands;* mi-bo'me-an) are embedded in the tarsal plates (see Figure 15.1b), and their ducts open at the eyelid edge just posterior to the eyelashes. These modified sebaceous glands produce an oily secretion that lubricates the eyelid and the eye and prevents the eyelids from sticking together. Associated with the eyelash follicles are a number of smaller, more typical sebaceous glands, and modified sweat glands called *ciliary glands* lie between the hair follicles (*cilium* = eyelash).

◤ **HOMEOSTATIC IMBALANCE**

Infection of a tarsal gland results in an unsightly cyst called a *chalazion* (kah-la'ze-on; "swelling"). Inflammation of any of the smaller glands is called a *sty.* ●

FIGURE 15.1 **The eye and associated accessory structures.**
(a) Surface anatomy of the right eye. The eyelids are open more widely than normal to show the entire iris.
(b) Lateral view; some structures are shown in sagittal section.

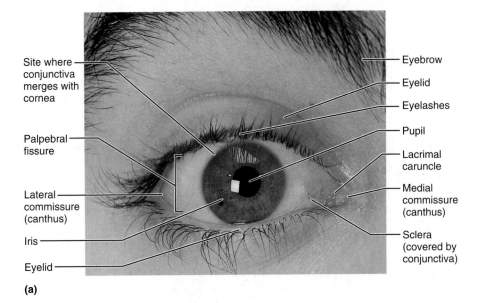

Site where conjunctiva merges with cornea

Palpebral fissure

Lateral commissure (canthus)

Iris

Eyelid

Eyebrow

Eyelid

Eyelashes

Pupil

Lacrimal caruncle

Medial commissure (canthus)

Sclera (covered by conjunctiva)

(a)

Conjunctiva

The **conjunctiva** (kon″junk-ti′vah; "joined together") is a transparent mucous membrane. It lines the eyelids as the **palpebral conjunctiva** and reflects (folds back) over the anterior surface of the eyeball as the **bulbar conjunctiva** (see Figure 15.1b). The latter covers only the white of the eye, not the cornea (the clear "window" over the iris and pupil). The bulbar conjunctiva is very thin, and blood vessels are clearly visible beneath it. (They are even more visible in irritated "bloodshot" eyes.) When the eye is closed, a slitlike space occurs between the conjunctiva-covered eyeball and eyelids. This so-called **conjunctival sac** is where a contact lens lies, and eye medications are often administered into its inferior recess. The major function of the conjunctiva is to produce a lubricating mucus that prevents the eyes from drying out.

 HOMEOSTATIC IMBALANCE

Inflammation of the conjunctiva, called *conjunctivitis*, results in reddened, irritated eyes. *Pinkeye*, a conjunctival infection caused by bacteria or viruses, is highly contagious. ●

Lacrimal Apparatus

The **lacrimal apparatus** (lak′rĭ-mal; "tear") consists of the lacrimal gland and the ducts that drain excess lacrimal secretions into the nasal cavity (Figure 15.2). The **lacrimal gland** lies in the orbit above the lateral end of the eye and is visible through the conjunctiva when the lid is everted. It continually releases a dilute saline solution called **lacrimal secretion**—or, more commonly, **tears**—into the superior part of the conjunctival sac through several small excretory ducts. Blinking spreads the tears

Levator palpebrae superioris muscle

Orbicularis oculi muscle

Eyebrow

Tarsal plate

Palpebral conjunctiva

Tarsal glands

Cornea

Palpebral fissure

Eyelashes

Bulbar conjunctiva

Conjunctival sac

Orbicularis oculi muscle

15

(b)

downward and across the eyeball to the medial commissure, where they enter the paired **lacrimal canaliculi** via two tiny openings called **lacrimal puncta** (literally, "prick points"), visible as tiny red dots on the medial margin of each eyelid. From the lacrimal canaliculi, the tears drain into the **lacrimal sac** and then into the **nasolacrimal duct,** which empties into the nasal cavity at the inferior nasal meatus.

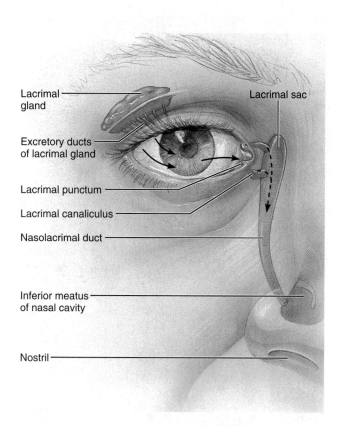

Lacrimal gland

Lacrimal sac

Excretory ducts of lacrimal gland

Lacrimal punctum

Lacrimal canaliculus

Nasolacrimal duct

Inferior meatus of nasal cavity

Nostril

FIGURE 15.2   The lacrimal apparatus. Arrows indicate the direction of flow of lacrimal fluid (tears) after its secretion by the lacrimal gland.

Lacrimal fluid contains mucus, antibodies, and **lysozyme,** an enzyme that destroys bacteria. Thus, it cleanses and protects the eye surface as it moistens and lubricates it. When lacrimal secretion increases substantially, tears spill over the eyelids and fill the nasal cavities, causing congestion and the "sniffles." This happens when the eyes are irritated and when we are emotionally upset. In the case of eye irritation, enhanced tearing serves to wash away or dilute the irritating substance. The importance of emotionally induced tears is poorly understood.

HOMEOSTATIC IMBALANCE

Because the nasal cavity mucosa is continuous with that of the lacrimal duct system, a cold or nasal inflammation often causes the lacrimal mucosa to become inflamed and swell. This constricts the ducts and prevents tears from draining from the eye surface, causing "watery" eyes. ●

Extrinsic Eye Muscles

The movement of each eyeball is controlled by six straplike **extrinsic eye muscles,** which originate from the bony orbit and insert into the outer surface of the eyeball (Figure 15.3). These muscles allow the eyes to follow a moving object, and provide external "guy-wires" that help to maintain the shape of the eyeball and hold it in the orbit.

The four *rectus muscles* originate from a common tendinous ring, the **annular ring,** at the back of the orbit and run straight to their insertion on the eyeball. Their locations and the movements that they promote are clearly indicated by their names: **superior, inferior, lateral,** and **medial rectus muscles.** The actions of the two *oblique muscles* are less easy to deduce because they take rather strange paths through the orbit. They move the eye in the vertical plane when the eyeball is already turned medially by the rectus muscle. The **superior oblique muscle** originates in common with the rectus muscles, runs along the medial wall of the orbit, and then makes a right-angle turn and passes through a fibrocartilaginous loop suspended from the frontal bone called the **trochlea** (trok'le-ah; "pulley") before inserting on the superolateral aspect of the eyeball. It rotates the eye downward and somewhat laterally. The **inferior oblique muscle** originates from the medial orbit surface and runs laterally and obliquely to insert on the inferolateral eye surface. It rotates the eye up and laterally.

The four rectus muscles would seem to provide all the eye movements we require—medial, lateral, superior, and inferior—so why the two oblique muscles? The simplest way to answer this question is to point out that the superior and inferior recti cannot elevate or depress the eye *without also turning it medially* because they approach the eye from a posteromedial direction. For an eye to be *directly* elevated or depressed, the lateral pull of the oblique muscles is necessary to cancel the medial pull of the superior and inferior recti.

Except for the lateral rectus and superior oblique muscles, which are innervated respectively by the *abducens* and *trochlear nerves,* all extrinsic eye muscles are served by the *oculomotor nerves.* The actions and nerve supply of these muscles are summarized in Figure 15.3c. The courses of the associated cranial nerves are illustrated in Table 13.2.

The extrinsic eye muscles are among the most precisely and rapidly controlled skeletal muscles in the entire body. This reflects their high axon-to-muscle-fiber ratio: The motor units of these muscles contain only 8 to 12 muscle cells and in some cases as few as two or three.

HOMEOSTATIC IMBALANCE

When movements of the external muscles of the two eyes are not perfectly coordinated, a person cannot properly focus the images of the same area of the visual field from each eye and so sees two images instead of one. This condition is called **diplopia**

Q *Which three extrinsic eye muscles turn the eyeball laterally?*

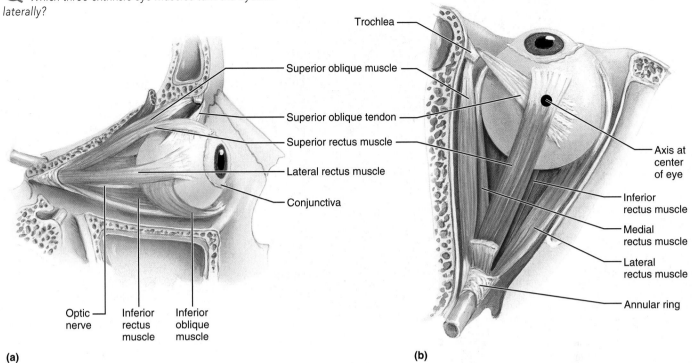

FIGURE 15.3 **Extrinsic eye muscles.**
(a) Lateral view of the right eye.
(b) Superior view of the right eye.
(c) Summary of innervating cranial nerves and muscle actions.

Name	Action	Controlling cranial nerve
Lateral rectus	Moves eye laterally	VI (abducens)
Medial rectus	Moves eye medially	III (oculomotor)
Superior rectus	Elevates eye and turns it medially	III (oculomotor)
Inferior rectus	Depresses eye and turns it medially	III (oculomotor)
Inferior oblique	Elevates eye and turns it laterally	III (oculomotor)
Superior oblique	Depresses eye and turns it laterally	IV (trochlear)

15

(dǐ-plo'pe-ah), or *double vision.* It can result from paralysis or weakness of certain extrinsic muscles, or it may be a temporary consequence of acute alcohol intoxication.

Congenital weakness of the external eye muscles may cause **strabismus** (strah-biz'mus; "cross-eyed"), a condition in which the affected eye rotates medially or laterally. To compensate, the eyes may alternate in focusing on objects. In other cases, only the controllable eye is used, and the brain begins to disregard inputs from the deviant eye, which then becomes functionally blind. Strabismus is treated either with eye exercises to strengthen the weak muscles or by temporarily placing a patch on the stronger eye, which forces the child to use the weaker eye. Surgery is needed for unyielding conditions. ●

A *The lateral rectus and the superior and inferior obliques.*

Structure of the Eyeball

The eye itself, commonly called the **eyeball**, is a slightly irregular hollow sphere (Figure 15.4). Because the eyeball is shaped roughly like the globe of the earth, it is said to have poles. Its most anterior point is the **anterior pole**; its most posterior point, the **posterior pole**. Its wall is composed of three layers (formerly called tunics): the fibrous, vascular, and sensory layers. Its internal cavity is filled with fluids called *humors* that help to maintain its shape. The lens, the adjustable focusing apparatus of the eye, is supported vertically within the internal cavity, dividing it into *anterior* and *posterior segments*, or *cavities*.

Layers Forming the Wall of the Eyeball

The Fibrous Layer The outermost coat of the eye, the **fibrous layer**, is composed of dense avascular

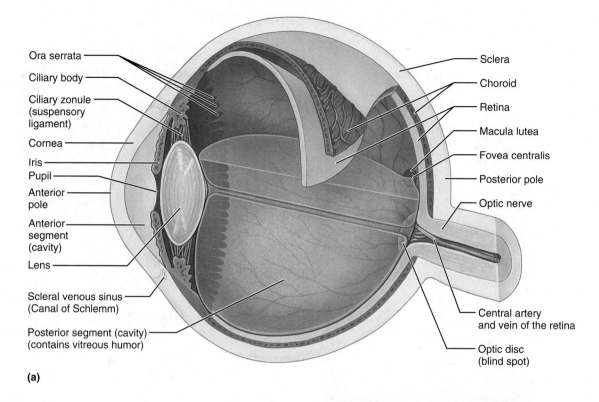

Ora serrata
Ciliary body
Ciliary zonule (suspensory ligament)
Cornea
Iris
Pupil
Anterior pole
Anterior segment (cavity)
Lens
Scleral venous sinus (Canal of Schlemm)
Posterior segment (cavity) (contains vitreous humor)

Sclera
Choroid
Retina
Macula lutea
Fovea centralis
Posterior pole
Optic nerve
Central artery and vein of the retina
Optic disc (blind spot)

(a)

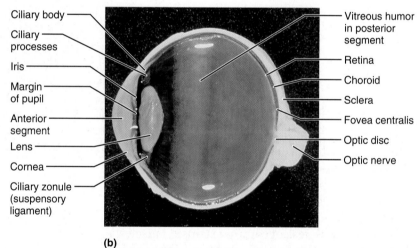

Ciliary body
Ciliary processes
Iris
Margin of pupil
Anterior segment
Lens
Cornea
Ciliary zonule (suspensory ligament)

Vitreous humor in posterior segment
Retina
Choroid
Sclera
Fovea centralis
Optic disc
Optic nerve

(b)

FIGURE 15.4 **Internal structure of the eye (sagittal section). (a)** Diagrammatic view. The vitreous humor is illustrated only in the bottom half of the eyeball. **(b)** Photograph of the human eye.

connective tissue. It has two obviously different regions: the sclera and the cornea. The **sclera** (skle'rah), forming the posterior portion and the bulk of the fibrous layer, is glistening white and opaque. Seen anteriorly as the "white of the eye," the tough, tendonlike sclera (*sclera* = hard) protects and shapes the eyeball and provides a sturdy anchoring site for the extrinsic eye muscles. Posteriorly, where the sclera is pierced by the optic nerve, it is continuous with the dura mater of the brain. The anterior sixth of the fibrous layer is modified to form the transparent **cornea,** which bulges anteriorly from its junction with the sclera. The crystal-clear cornea

forms a window that lets light enter the eye, and is a major part of the light-bending apparatus of the eye.

The cornea is covered by epithelial sheets on both faces. The external sheet, a stratified squamous epithelium that helps protect the cornea from abrasion, merges with the bulbar conjunctiva at the sclera-cornea junction. Epithelial cells that continually renew the cornea are located here. The deep *corneal endothelium,* composed of simple squamous epithelium, lines the inner face of the cornea. Its cells have active sodium pumps that maintain the clarity of the cornea by keeping the water content of the cornea low.

The cornea is well supplied with nerve endings, most of which are pain receptors. (For this reason, some people can never adjust to wearing contact lenses.) When the cornea is touched, blinking and increased tearing occur reflexively. Even so, the cornea is the most exposed part of the eye and is very vulnerable to damage from dust, slivers, and the like. Luckily, its capacity for regeneration and repair is extraordinary. Furthermore, the cornea is the only tissue in the body that can be transplanted from one person to another with little or no possibility of rejection. Because it has no blood vessels, it is beyond the reach of the immune system.

The Vascular Layer (Uvea) The **vascular layer,** or middle coat of the eyeball, is also called the **uvea** (u've-ah; "grape"). The pigmented uvea has three regions: choroid, ciliary body, and iris (see Figure 15.4).

The **choroid** is a highly vascular, dark brown membrane (*choroids* = membranelike) that forms the posterior five-sixths of the uvea. Its blood vessels provide nutrition to all eye layers. Its brown pigment, produced by melanocytes, helps absorb light, preventing it from scattering and reflecting within the eye (which would cause visual confusion). The choroid is incomplete posteriorly where the optic nerve leaves the eye. Anteriorly, it becomes the **ciliary body,** a thickened ring of tissue that encircles the lens. The ciliary body consists chiefly of interlacing smooth muscle bundles called **ciliary muscles,** which are important in controlling lens shape. Near the lens, its posterior surface is thrown into radiating folds called **ciliary processes,** which contain the capillaries that secrete the fluid that fills the cavity of the anterior segment of the eyeball. The **ciliary zonule** *(suspensory ligament)* extends from the ciliary processes to the lens; this halo of fine fibers encircles and helps hold the lens in its upright position in the eye.

The **iris,** the visible colored part of the eye, is the most anterior portion of the uvea. Shaped like a flattened doughnut, it lies between the cornea and the lens and is continuous with the ciliary body posteriorly. Its round central opening, the **pupil,** allows light to enter the eye. The iris is made up of two smooth muscle layers with bunches of sticky elastic fibers that congeal into a random pattern before birth. Its muscle fibers allow it to act as a reflexively activated diaphragm to vary pupil size (Figure 15.5). In close vision and bright light, the *sphincter pupillae* (circular muscles) contract and the pupil constricts. In distant vision and dim light, the *dilator pupillae* (radial muscles) contract and the pupil dilates, allowing more light to enter the eye. Pupillary dilation and constriction are controlled by sympathetic and parasympathetic fibers, respectively.

Changes in pupil size may also reflect our interests and emotional reactions to what we are seeing.

FIGURE 15.5 **Pupil dilation and constriction, anterior view.** Activation of parasympathetic fibers to sphincter pupillae (circular) muscles of the iris causes them to contract, decreasing pupil size. Activation of sympathetic fibers to dilator pupillae (radial) muscles of the iris causes them to contract, increasing pupil size.

Pupil dilation often occurs when the subject matter is appealing, in response to fear, and during problem solving. (Computing your taxes should make your pupils get bigger and bigger.) On the other hand, boredom or subject matter that is personally repulsive causes pupil constriction.

Although irises come in different colors (*iris* = rainbow), they contain only brown pigment. When they have a lot of pigment, the eyes appear brown or black. If the amount of pigment is small and restricted to the posterior surface of the iris, the shorter wavelengths of light are scattered from the unpigmented parts, and the eyes appear blue, green, or gray. Most newborn babies' eyes are slate gray or blue because their iris pigment is not yet developed.

The Inner Layer (Retina) The innermost layer of the eyeball is the delicate, two-layered **retina** (ret'ĭ-nah). Its outer **pigmented layer,** a single-cell-thick lining, abuts the choroid, and extends anteriorly to cover the ciliary body and the posterior face of the iris. These pigmented epithelial cells, like those of the choroid, absorb light and prevent it from scattering in the eye. They also act as phagocytes to remove dead or damaged photoreceptor cells, and store vitamin A needed by the photoreceptor cells. The transparent inner **neural layer** extends anteriorly to the posterior margin of the ciliary body. This junction is called the **ora serrata,** literally, the saw-toothed margin (see Figure 15.4). Originating as an outpocketing of the brain, the retina contains millions of photoreceptors that transduce light energy, other neurons involved in the processing of light stimuli, and glia. Although the pigmented and neural layers are very close together, they are not fused. Only the neural layer of the retina plays a direct role in vision.

From posterior to anterior, the neural layer is composed of three main types of neurons: **photoreceptors,**

15

Q *Which retinal cells are the output cells?*

(a)

Pigmented layer of retina

Horizontal cell

Rod

Cone

Bipolar cells

Amacrine cell

Ganglion cells

Pathway of light

(c)

Choroid

Pigmented layer of retina

Outer segments of rods and cones

Axons of ganglion cells

Nuclei of rods and cones

Nuclei of ganglion cells

Nuclei of bipolar cells

FIGURE 15.6 **Microscopic anatomy of the retina.** **(a)** Schematic view of the photoreceptors, bipolar cells, and ganglion cells composing the neural layer of the retina. Notice that light (indicated by the yellow arrow) passes through the retina to excite the photoreceptor cells (rods and cones). The flow of information occurs in the opposite direction. **(b)** Schematic view of the posterior aspect of the eyeball illustrating how the axons of the ganglion cells form the optic nerve, which leaves the back of the eyeball at the optic disc. **(c)** Photomicrograph of the retina (500×).

Pigmented layer of retina

Neural layer of retina

Central artery and vein of retina

Optic disc

Sclera

Optic nerve

Choroid

(b)

A *Ganglion cells.*

bipolar cells, and ganglion cells (Figure 15.6). Signals are produced in response to light and spread from the photoreceptors (abutting the pigmented layer) to the bipolar neurons and then to the innermost ganglion cells, where action potentials are generated. The ganglion cell axons make a right-angle turn at the inner face of the retina, then leave the posterior aspect of the eye as the thick optic nerve. The retina also contains other types of neurons—horizontal cells and amacrine cells—which play a role in visual processing. The **optic disc,** where the optic nerve exits the eye, is a weak spot in the **fundus** (posterior wall) of the eye because it is not reinforced by the sclera. The optic disc is also called the **blind spot** because it lacks photoreceptors, so light focused on it cannot be seen. Nonetheless, we do not usually notice these gaps in our vision because the brain uses a sophisticated process called *filling in* to deal with absence of input.

The quarter-billion photoreceptors found in the neural retinas are of two types: rods and cones. The more numerous **rods** are our dim-light and peripheral vision receptors. They are far more sensitive to light than cones are, but they do not provide either sharp images or color vision. This is why colors are indistinct and edges of objects appear fuzzy in dim light and at the edges of our visual field. **Cones,** by contrast, operate in bright light and provide high-acuity color vision. Lateral to the blind spot of each eye, and located precisely at the eye's posterior pole, is an oval region called the **macula lutea** (mak′u-lah lu′te-ah; "yellow spot") with a minute (0.4 mm) pit in its center called the **fovea centralis** (see Figure 15.4). In this region, the retinal structures abutting the vitreous humor are displaced to the sides. This allows light to pass almost directly to the photoreceptors rather than through several retinal layers, greatly enhancing visual acuity. The fovea contains only cones; the macula contains mostly cones; and from the edge of the macula toward the retina periphery, cone density declines gradually. The retina periphery contains mostly rods, which continuously decrease in density from there to the macula. Only the foveae (plural of fovea) have a sufficient cone density to provide detailed color vision, so anything we wish to view critically is focused on the foveae. Because each fovea is only about the size of the head of a pin, not more than a thousandth of the entire visual field is in *hard focus* (foveal focus) at a given moment. Consequently, for us to visually comprehend a scene that is rapidly changing (as when we drive in traffic), our eyes must flick rapidly back and forth to provide the foveae with images of different parts of the visual field.

The neural retina receives its blood supply from two sources. The outer third (containing photoreceptors) is supplied by vessels in the choroid. The inner two-thirds is served by the **central artery** and **central vein of the retina,** which enter and leave the eye through the center of the optic nerve. Radiating outward from the optic disc, these vessels give rise to a rich vascular network that is clearly seen when the eyeball interior is examined with an ophthalmoscope (Figure 15.7). The fundus of the eye is the only place in the body where small blood vessels can be observed directly in a living person.

HOMEOSTATIC IMBALANCE

The pattern of vascularization of the retina makes it susceptible to *retinal detachment*. This condition, in

Which of the areas shown here would have the highest cone density?

FIGURE 15.7 Part of the posterior wall (fundus) of the right eye as seen with an ophthalmoscope. Note the optic disc from which the retinal blood vessels radiate.

which the pigmented and neural layers separate (detach) and allow the jellylike vitreous humor to seep between them, can cause permanent blindness because it deprives the photoreceptors of their nutrient source. It usually happens when the retina is torn during a traumatic blow to the head or when the head stops moving suddenly and then is jerked in the opposite direction (as in bungee jumping). The symptom that victims most often describe is "a curtain being drawn across the eye," but some people see sootlike spots or light flashes. If diagnosed early, it is often possible to reattach the retina with a laser before photoreceptor damage becomes permanent. ●

Internal Chambers and Fluids

As noted earlier, the lens and its halolike ciliary zonule divide the eye into two segments, the anterior segment in front of the lens and the larger posterior segment behind it (Figure 15.4a). The **posterior segment** (cavity) is filled with a clear gel called **vitreous humor** (*vitre* = glassy) that binds tremendous amounts of water. Vitreous humor (1) transmits light, (2) supports the posterior surface of the lens and holds the neural retina firmly against the pigmented layer, and (3) contributes to intraocular pressure,

FIGURE 15.8 Circulation of aqueous humor. The anterior segment in front of the lens is incompletely divided into anterior and posterior chambers, which are continuous through the pupil. Aqueous humor fills the chambers and diffuses freely through the vitreous humor in the posterior segment. It is formed by filtration from capillaries in the ciliary processes and is reabsorbed into the venous blood by the scleral venous sinus. The arrows indicate the circulation pathway.

helping to counteract the pulling force of the extrinsic eye muscles.

The **anterior segment** (cavity) is partially subdivided by the iris into the **anterior chamber** (between the cornea and the iris) and the **posterior chamber** (between the iris and the lens) (Figure 15.8). The *entire* anterior segment is filled with **aqueous humor,** a clear fluid similar in composition to blood plasma. Unlike the vitreous humor, which forms in the embryo and lasts for a lifetime, aqueous humor forms and drains continually and is in constant motion. It filters from the capillaries of the ciliary processes into the posterior chamber and a portion of it freely diffuses through the vitreous humor in the posterior segment while the remainder flows into the anterior segment. After flowing through the pupil into the anterior chamber, it drains into the venous blood via the **scleral venous sinus** *(canal of Schlemm),* an unusual venous channel that encir-

cles the eye in the angle at the sclera-cornea junction. Normally, aqueous humor is produced and drained at the same rate, maintaining a constant intraocular pressure of about 16 mm Hg, which helps to support the eyeball internally. Aqueous humor supplies nutrients and oxygen to the lens and cornea and to some cells of the retina, and it carries away their metabolic wastes.

HOMEOSTATIC IMBALANCE

If the drainage of aqueous humor is blocked, fluid backs up like in a clogged sink. Pressure within the eye may increase to dangerous levels and compress the retina and optic nerve—a condition called **glaucoma** (glaw-ko'mah). The eventual result is blindness *(glaucoma = vision growing gray)* unless the condition is detected early. Unfortunately, many forms of glaucoma steal sight so slowly and painlessly that people do not realize they have a problem until the damage is done. Late signs include seeing halos around lights and blurred vision. The glaucoma examination is simple. The intraocular pressure is determined by directing a puff of air at the cornea and measuring the amount of corneal deformation it causes. This exam should be done yearly after the age of 40. The most common treatment is eye drops that increase the rate of aqueous humor drainage or decrease its production. Laser therapy or surgery can also be used. ●

Lens

The **lens** is a biconvex, transparent, flexible structure that can change shape to allow precise focusing of light on the retina. It is enclosed in a thin, elastic capsule and held in place just posterior to the iris by the ciliary zonule (Figure 15.8). Like the cornea, the lens is avascular; blood vessels interfere with transparency.

The lens has two regions: the **lens epithelium** and the lens fibers. The lens epithelium, confined to the anterior lens surface, consists of cuboidal cells that eventually differentiate into the **lens fibers** that form the bulk of the lens. The lens fibers, which are packed tightly together like the layers in an onion, contain no nuclei and few organelles. They do, however, contain transparent, precisely folded proteins called **crystallins** that form the body of the lens. Since new lens fibers are continually added, the lens enlarges throughout life, becoming denser, more convex, and less elastic, all of which gradually impair its ability to focus light properly.

◤ HOMEOSTATIC IMBALANCE

A **cataract** ("waterfall") is a clouding of the lens that causes the world to appear distorted, as if seen through frosted glass (Figure 15.9). Some cataracts are congenital, but most result from age-related hardening and thickening of the lens or are a secondary consequence of diabetes mellitus. Heavy smoking and frequent exposure to intense sunlight increase the risk for cataracts, whereas long-term dietary supplementation with vitamin C may decrease the risk. Whatever the promoting factors, the *direct* cause of cataracts seems to be inadequate delivery of nutrients to the deeper lens fibers. The metabolic changes that result promote clumping of the crystallin proteins. Fortunately, the offending lens can be surgically removed and an artificial lens implanted to save the patient's sight. ●

Physiology of Vision

Overview: Light and Optics

To really comprehend the function of the eye as a photoreceptor organ, we need to have some understanding of the properties of light.

FIGURE 15.9 **Photograph of a cataract due to a clouded lens.**

Wavelength and Color   Electromagnetic radiation includes all energy waves, from long radio waves (with wavelengths measured in meters) to very short gamma (γ) waves and X rays with wavelengths of 1 nm and less. Our eyes respond to the part of the spectrum called **visible light,** which has a wavelength range of approximately 400–700 nm (Figure 15.10a). (1 nm = 10^{-9} m, or one-billionth of a meter.) Visible light travels in the form of waves, and its wavelengths can be measured very accurately. However, light can also be envisioned as small particles or packets of energy called **photons** or **quanta.** Attempts to reconcile these two findings have led to the present concept of light as packets of energy (photons) traveling in a wavelike fashion at very high speeds (300,000 km/s or about 186,000 mi/s). Thus, light can be thought of as a vibration of pure energy ("a bright wiggle") rather than a material substance.

When visible light passes through a prism, each of its component waves bends to a different degree, so that the beam of light is dispersed and a **visible spectrum,** or band of colors, is seen (Figure 15.10b). (In the same manner, the rainbow seen during a summer shower represents the collective prismatic effects of all the tiny water droplets suspended in air.) Red wavelengths are the longest and have the lowest energy, whereas the violet wavelengths are the shortest and most energetic. Objects have color because they absorb some wavelengths and reflect others. Things that look white reflect all wavelengths of light, whereas black objects absorb them all. A red apple reflects mostly red light; grass reflects more of the green.

Refraction and Lenses   Light travels in straight lines and is easily blocked by any non-transparent object. Like sound, light can reflect, or bounce, off a surface. **Reflection** of light by objects

15

(a)

(b)

FIGURE 15.11 **A spoon standing in a glass of water appears to be broken at the water-air interface.** This phenomenon occurs because light is bent toward the perpendicular when it travels from a less dense to a more dense medium (air to water in this example).

FIGURE 15.10 **The electromagnetic spectrum and photoreceptor sensitivities. (a)** The electromagnetic spectrum extends from the very short gamma waves to the long radio waves. The wavelengths of the electromagnetic spectrum are indicated in nanometers. The spectrum of visible light constitutes only a small portion of this energy range. **(b)** Sensitivities of rods and the three cone types to the different wavelengths of the visible spectrum.

in our environment accounts for most of the light reaching our eyes.

When light is traveling in a given medium, its speed is constant. But when it passes from one transparent medium into another with a different density, its speed changes. Light speeds up as it passes into a less dense medium and slows as it passes into a denser medium. Because of these changes in speed, bending or **refraction** of a light ray occurs when it meets the surface of a different medium at an oblique angle rather than at a right angle (perpendicular). The greater the incident angle, the greater the amount of bending. Figure 15.11 demonstrates the consequence of light refraction when a spoon is placed in a half-full glass of water: The spoon appears to break at the air-water interface.

A lens is a transparent object curved on one or both surfaces. Since light hits the curve at an angle, it is refracted. If the lens surface is convex, that is, thickest in the center like a camera lens, the light rays are bent so that they converge (come together) or intersect at a single point called the **focal point** (Figure 15.12). In general, the thicker (more convex) the lens, the more the light is bent and the shorter the focal distance (distance between the lens and focal point). The image formed by a convex lens, called a **real image,** is upside down and reversed from left to right. Concave lenses, which are thicker at the edges than at the center, diverge the light (bend it outward) so that the light rays move away from each other. Consequently, concave lenses prevent light from focusing and extend the focal distance.

Focusing of Light on the Retina

As light passes from air into the eye, it moves sequentially through the cornea, aqueous humor, lens, and vitreous humor, and then passes *through the entire thickness of the neural layer of the retina* to excite the photoreceptors that abut the pigmented layer (see Figures 15.4 and 15.6). During its passage, light is bent three times: as it enters the cornea and on entering and leaving the lens. The refractory power of the humors and cornea is constant. On the

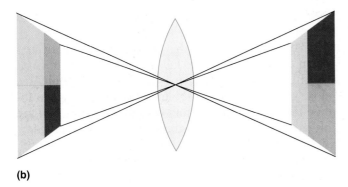

(a)

(b)

FIGURE 15.12 **Bending of light points by a convex lens. (a)** How two light points are focused on the opposite side of the lens. **(b)** Formation of an image by a convex lens. Notice that the image is upside down and reversed from right to left.

other hand, the lens is highly elastic, and its curvature and light-bending power can be actively changed to allow fine focusing of the image.

Focusing for Distant Vision   Our eyes are best adapted ("preset to focus") for distant vision. To look at distant objects, we need only aim our eyeballs so that they are both fixated on the same spot. The **far point of vision** is that distance beyond which no change in lens shape (accommodation) is needed for focusing. For the normal or **emmetropic** (em″ĕ-tro′pik) eye, the far point is 6 m (20 feet).

Any object being viewed can be said to consist of many small points, with light radiating outward in all directions from each point. However, because distant objects appear smaller, light from an object at or beyond the far point of vision approaches the eyes as nearly parallel rays and is focused precisely on the retina by the fixed refractory apparatus (cornea and humors) and the at-rest lens (Figure 15.13a). During distant vision, the ciliary muscles are completely relaxed, and the lens (stretched flat by tension in the ciliary zonule) is as thin as it gets. Consequently, the lens is at its lowest refractory power. The ciliary muscles relax when sympathetic input to them increases and parasympathetic decreases.

(a) Lens is flattened for distant vision

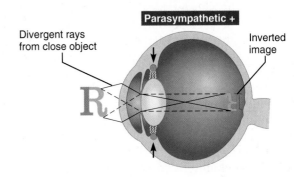

(b) Lens bulges for close vision

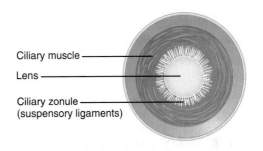

(c) Anterior segment viewed from behind

FIGURE 15.13 **Focusing for distant and close vision. (a)** For distant vision, the sympathetic nervous system relaxes the ciliary muscle, tightening the ciliary zonule (suspensory ligament) and flattening the lens. Light from distant objects (over 6 m away) approaches as parallel rays and is focused on the retina by the flattened lens. **(b)** For close vision, the parasympathetic nervous system stimulates the ciliary muscle, allowing the ciliary zonule to become less taut and the lens to bulge. Light from close objects (less than 6 m away) tends to diverge and lens convexity must be increased (accommodation) for proper focusing. Notice in both cases that the image formed on the retina is inverted and reversed from left to right (i.e., it is a real image). **(c)** Anterior segment as viewed from within the eye showing the ciliary muscles and ciliary zonule arranged sphincterlike around the lens.

Focusing for Close Vision   Light from objects less than 6 m away diverges as it approaches the eyes and it comes to a focal point farther from the lens. Thus, close vision demands that the eye make active adjustments. To restore focus, three processes—accommodation of the lenses, constriction of the pupils, and convergence of the eyeballs—must occur simultaneously. The signal that induces this trio of reflex responses appears to be a blurring of the retinal image.

1. Accommodation of the lenses. Accommodation is the process that increases the refractory power of the lens. As the ciliary muscles contract, the ciliary body is pulled anteriorly and inward toward the pupil and releases tension in the ciliary zonule. No longer stretched, the elastic lens recoils and bulges, providing the shorter focal length needed to focus the image of a close object on the retina (Figure 15.13b). Contraction of the ciliary muscles is controlled mainly by the parasympathetic fibers of the oculomotor nerves.

The closest point on which we can focus clearly is called the **near point of vision,** and it represents the maximum bulge the lens can achieve. In young adults with emmetropic vision, the near point is 10 cm (4 inches) from the eye. However, it is closer in children and gradually recedes with age, explaining why children can hold their books very close to their faces while many elderly people must hold the newspaper at arm's length. The gradual loss of accommodation with age reflects the lens's decreasing elasticity. In many people over the age of 50, the lens is nonaccommodating, a condition known as **presbyopia** (pres″be-o′pe-ah), literally "old person's vision."

2. Constriction of the pupils. The sphincter pupillae muscles of the iris enhance the effect of accommodation by reducing the size of the pupil (see Figure 15.5) toward 2 mm. This **accommodation pupillary reflex,** mediated by parasympathetic fibers of the oculomotor nerves, prevents the most divergent light rays from entering the eye. Such rays would pass through the extreme edge of the lens and would not be focused properly, and so would cause blurred vision.

3. Convergence of the eyeballs. The visual goal is always to keep the object being viewed focused on the retinal foveae. When we look at distant objects, both eyes are directed either straight ahead or to one side to the same degree, but when we fixate on a close object, our eyes converge. **Convergence,** controlled by somatic motor fibers of the oculomotor nerves, is medial rotation of the eyeballs by the medial rectus muscles so that each is directed toward the object being viewed. The closer that object, the greater the degree of convergence required; when you focus on the tip of your nose, you "go cross-eyed."

Reading or other close work requires almost continuous accommodation, pupillary constriction, and convergence. This is why prolonged periods of reading tire the eye muscles and can result in *eyestrain.* When you read for an extended time, it is helpful to look up and stare into the distance occasionally to relax the intrinsic eye muscles.

◢ HOMEOSTATIC IMBALANCES

Theoretically, visual problems related to refraction could result from a hyperrefractive (overconverging) or hyporefractive (underconverging) lens or from structural abnormalities of the eyeball. In practice, 99% of refractive problems are related to eyeball shape—either too long or too short.

Myopia (mi-o′pe-ah; "short vision") occurs when distant objects are focused not on, but in front of, the retina (Figure 15.14b). Myopic people see close objects without problems because they can focus them on the retina, but distant objects are blurred. The common name for myopia is *near-sightedness.* (Notice that this terminology names the aspect of vision that is *unimpaired.*) Myopia typically results from an eyeball that is too long. Correction has traditionally involved use of concave lenses that diverge the light before it enters the eye, but procedures to flatten the cornea slightly—a 10-minute surgery called *radial keratotomy,* or PRK and LASIK procedures using a laser—have offered other treatment options.

Hyperopia (hy′per-o″pe-ah; "far vision"), or *far-sightedness,* occurs when the parallel light rays from distant objects are focused *behind* the retina (Figure 15.14c). Hyperopic individuals can see distant objects perfectly well because their ciliary muscles contract almost continuously to increase the light-bending power of the lens, which moves the focal point forward onto the retina. However, diverging light rays from *nearby* objects are focused so far behind the retina that the lens cannot bring the focal point onto the retina even at its full refractory power. Thus, close objects appear blurry, and convex corrective lenses are needed to converge the light more strongly for close vision. Hyperopia usually results from an eyeball that is too short.

Unequal curvatures in different parts of the cornea or lens lead to blurry images. This refractory problem is **astigmatism** (*astigma* = not a point). Special cylindrically ground lenses, corneal implants, or laser procedures are used to correct this problem. ●

Phototransduction

Once light is focused on the retina, the photoreceptors come into play. First, we will describe the functional anatomy of photoreceptor cells, then the chemistry and response of their visual pigments to

FIGURE 15.14   **Problems of refraction. (a)** In the emmetropic eye, light from both near and distant objects is focused properly on the retina. **(b)** In a myopic eye, light from a distant object comes to a focal point before reaching the retina and then diverges again. **(c)** In the hyperopic eye, light from a near object comes to a focal point behind (past) the retina. (Refractory effect of the cornea is ignored.)

light, and finally, photoreceptor activation and phototransduction. **Phototransduction** is the process by which light energy is converted into a graded receptor potential.

Functional Anatomy of the Photoreceptors

Although photoreceptors are modified neurons, structurally they resemble tall epithelial cells turned upside down with their "tips" immersed in the pigmented layer of the retina (Figure 15.15a). Moving from the pigmented layer into the neural layer, both the rods and cones have an **outer segment** (the receptor region) joined to an **inner segment** by a connecting cilium. The inner segment connects to the *cell body*, which is continuous with an *inner fiber* bearing *synaptic terminals*. The outer segment of the rods is slender and rod shaped (hence their name) and their inner segment connects to the cell body by the *outer fiber*. By contrast, the cones have a short conical outer segment and the inner segment directly joins the cell body.

The outer segments contain an elaborate array of **visual pigments (photopigments)** that change shape as they absorb light. These pigments are embedded in areas of the plasma membrane that form discs. Folding the plasma membrane into discs magnifies the surface area available for trapping light (Figure 15.15b). In rods, the discs are discontinuous—stacked like a row of pennies in a coin wrapper. In cones, the disc membranes are continuous with the plasma membrane; thus, the interiors of the cone discs are continuous with the extracellular space.

The photoreceptor cells are highly vulnerable to damage and immediately begin to degenerate if the retina becomes detached. They are also destroyed by intense light, the very energy they are designed to detect. How is it, then, that we do not all gradually go blind? The answer lies in the photoreceptors' unique system for renewing their light-trapping outer segment. In rods, new discs are assembled at the proximal end of the outer segment from materials

15

15

(a)

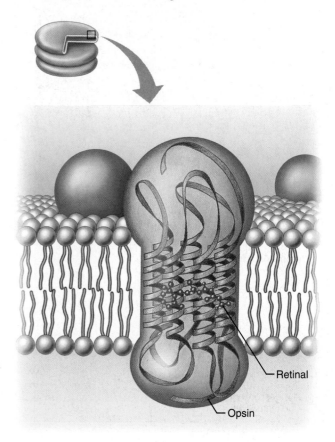

(b)

FIGURE 15.15   Photoreceptors of the retina.
(a) Diagram of the photoreceptors (rods and cones). The relationship of the outer segments of the photoreceptors to the pigmented layer of the retina is also illustrated. **(b)** Diagram of a small section of the membrane of a visual pigment–containing disc of the outer segment of a rod cell. The visual pigments consist of a light-absorbing molecule called retinal bound to an opsin protein. Each type of photoreceptor has a characteristic kind of opsin protein, which affects the absorption spectrum of the retinal. In rods, the pigment-opsin complex is called rhodopsin. Notice that the light-absorbing retinal occupies the core of the rhodopsin molecule.

synthesized in the cell body at the end of each night. As new discs are made, they push the others peripherally. The discs at the tip of the outer segment continually fragment off and are phagocytized by cells of the pigmented layer. The tips of the outer segments of cones are also removed and renewed (but at the end of each day).

A *Because the photopigment is in the membrane, folding the membrane increases the amount of pigment able to catch light.*

Because the rods and each of the three cone types contain unique visual pigments, they absorb different wavelengths of light. Rods and cones also have different thresholds for activation. Rods, for example, (1) are very sensitive (respond to very dim light—a single photon), making them best suited for night vision and peripheral vision, and (2) contain a single kind of visual pigment so their inputs are perceived only in gray tones. Cones (1) need bright light for activation (have low sensitivity), but (2) have one of three different pigments that furnish a vividly colored view of the world.

Rods and cones are also "wired" differently to other retinal neurons. Rods participate in converging pathways, and as many as 100 rods may ultimately feed into each ganglion cell. As a result, rod effects are summated and considered collectively, resulting in vision that is fuzzy and indistinct. (The visual cortex has no way of knowing exactly *which* rods of the large number influencing a particular ganglion cell are actually activated.) In contrast, each cone in the fovea (or at most a few) has a straight-through pathway via its "own personal bipolar cell" to a ganglion cell (see Figure 15.6a). Hence, each cone essentially has its own "labeled line" to the higher visual centers. This accounts for the detailed, high-resolution views of very small areas of the visual field provided by cones.

Because rods are absent from the foveae and cones do not respond to low-intensity light, we see dimly lit objects best when we do not look at them directly, and recognize them best when they move. If you doubt this, go out into your backyard on a moonlit evening and see how much you can actually discriminate.

The Chemistry of Visual Pigments

How does light affect the photoreceptors so that it is ultimately translated into electrical signals? The key is a light-absorbing molecule called **retinal** that combines with proteins called **opsins** to form four types of visual pigments. Depending on the type of opsin to which it is bound, retinal preferentially absorbs different wavelengths of the visible spectrum. Retinal is chemically related to vitamin A and is made from it. The liver stores vitamin A and releases it as needed by the photoreceptors to make their visual pigments. The cells of the pigmented layer of the retina absorb vitamin A from the blood and serve as the local vitamin A depot for the rods and cones.

Retinal can assume a variety of distinct three-dimensional forms, each form called an isomer. When bound to opsin, retinal has a bent, or kinked, shape called the **11-cis isomer** (Figure 15.16). However, when the pigment is struck by light and absorbs photons, retinal twists and snaps into a new configuration, its **all-trans isomer**, which causes opsin to

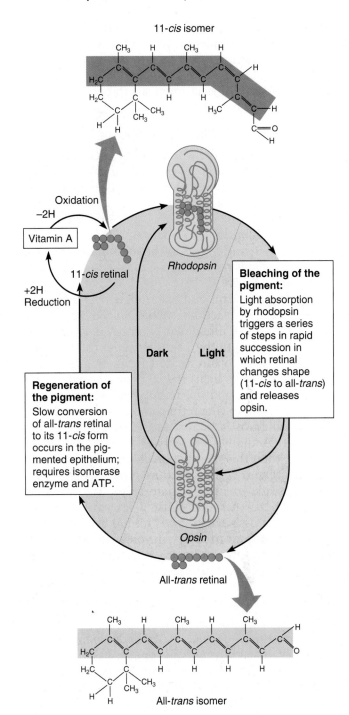

FIGURE 15.16 **Sequence of chemical events in the formation and breakdown of rhodopsin.** When struck by light, rhodopsin breaks down and is converted to its precursors via a number of intermediate steps. Absorption of light converts 11-*cis* retinal to all-*trans* retinal, an event that is responsible for transduction of the light stimulus and which bleaches the pigment. Eventually, all-*trans* retinal separates from opsin. The 11-*cis* retinal is regenerated in energy (ATP)-requiring reactions by enzymatic action from all-*trans* retinal or from vitamin A and recombined with opsin to form rhodopsin.

change shape and assume its activated form. This is the *only* light-dependent stage, and this simple photochemical event initiates a whole chain of chemical and electrical reactions in rods and cones that ultimately causes electrical impulses to be transmitted along the optic nerve.

Stimulation of the Photoreceptors

1. Excitation of rods. The visual pigment of rods is a deep purple pigment called **rhodopsin** (ro-dop′sin; *rhodo* = rose, *opsis* = vision). (Do you suppose the person who coined the expression "looking at the world through rose-colored glasses" knew the meaning of "rhodopsin"?) Rhodopsin molecules are arranged in a single layer in the membranes of each of the thousands of discs in the rods' outer segments (see Figure 15.15b).

Rhodopsin forms and accumulates in the dark in the sequence of reactions shown on the left side of Figure 15.16. As illustrated, vitamin A is oxidized (and isomerized) to the 11-*cis* retinal form and then combined with opsin to form rhodopsin. When rhodopsin absorbs light, retinal changes shape to its all-*trans* isomer, and the retinal-opsin combination breaks down, allowing retinal and opsin to separate. This breakdown is known as the **bleaching of the pigment.** Actually, the story is a good deal more complex than this, and the breakdown of rhodopsin that triggers the transduction process involves a rapid cascade of intermediate steps (right side of Figure 15.16) that takes just a few milliseconds. Once the light-struck all-*trans* retinal detaches from opsin, it is reconverted by enzymes within the pigmented epithelium to its 11-*cis* isomer in an ATP-requiring process. Then, retinal heads "homeward" again to the photoreceptor cells' outer segments. Rhodopsin is regenerated when 11-*cis* retinal is rejoined to opsin.

2. Excitation of cones. The breakdown and regeneration of visual pigments in cones is essentially the same as for rhodopsin. However, cones are about a hundred times less sensitive than rods, which means that it takes higher-intensity (brighter) light to activate cones.

Visual pigments of the three types of cones, like those of rods, are a combination of retinal and opsins. However, the cone opsins differ both from the opsin of the rods and from one another. The naming of cones reflects the colors (that is, wavelengths) of light that each cone variety absorbs best. The blue cones respond maximally to wavelengths around 420 nm, the green cones to wavelengths of 530 nm, and the red cones to wavelengths at or close to 560 nm (see Figure 15.10b). However, their absorption spectra overlap, and perception of intermediate hues, such as orange, yellow, and purple, results from differential activation of more than one type of cone at the same time. For example, yellow light stimulates both red and green cone receptors, but if the red cones are stimulated more strongly than the green cones, we see orange instead of yellow. When all cones are stimulated equally, we see white.

▲ HOMEOSTATIC IMBALANCE

Color blindness is due to a congenital lack of one or more of the cone types. Inherited as an X-linked condition, it is far more common in males than in females. As many as 8–10% of males have some form of color blindness. The most common type is red-green color blindness, resulting from a deficit or absolute absence of either red or green cones. Red and green are seen as the same color—either red or green, depending on the cone type present. Many color-blind people are unaware of their condition because they have learned to rely on other cues—such as differences in intensities of the same color—to distinguish something green from something red, such as traffic signals. ●

Light Transduction Reactions   How is the capture of light by visual pigments that we've just described converted into an electrical event, that is, a change in membrane potential? In the dark, **cyclic GMP (cGMP)** binds to cation channels in the outer segments, holding them open. Consequently, Na^+ and Ca^{2+} continually enter the outer segment, producing a *dark current* that maintains a transmembrane potential (a *dark potential*) of about −40 mV. This depolarizing current keeps the Ca^{2+} channels *at the photoreceptor synaptic terminals* open. Thus, in the dark there is continuous neurotransmitter (glutamate) release by the photoreceptors at their synapses with the bipolar cells (Figure 15.17a).

When light triggers pigment breakdown, the net effect is to "turn off" cation entry. That is, an enzymatic cascade occurs that ultimately destroys the cGMP that keeps the channels open in the dark. In this process, described in more detail in Figure 15.18, light-activated rhodopsin (metarhodopsin II) activates a G protein called **transducin.** Transducin, in turn, activates *PDE (phosphodiesterase),* the enzyme that breaks down cGMP, and the cation channels close. Cation influx in the outer segment now decreases dramatically but potassium channels in the inner segment remain open, so the photoreceptors develop a *hyperpolarizing receptor potential* (−70 mV) that inhibits their release of neurotransmitter (Figure 15.17b). This is bewildering, to say the least. Here we have receptors built to detect light that depolarize in the dark and hyperpolarize when exposed to light! Nevertheless, turning off neurotransmitter release

(a)   **(b)**

FIGURE 15.17 **Signal transmission in the retina. (a)** In the dark, ① photoreceptors are depolarized to about −40 mV by a continuous influx of cations through cGMP-gated channels. ② In the synaptic terminals of the photoreceptors, voltage-gated Ca²⁺ channels opened by depolarization cause ③ continuous release of neurotransmitter. ④ This neuro-transmitter hyperpolarizes the bipolar cells (by producing inhibitory postsynaptic potentials, IPSPs), and ⑤ inhibits release of their neurotransmitter. Signal transmission stops at this point. ⑥ There are no excitatory postsynaptic potentials (EPSPs) in the ganglion cells, and ⑦ no action potentials are generated. **(b)** ① Light causes the photoreceptors to hyperpolarize, ② closing the Ca²⁺ channels in the synaptic terminals, and ③ inhibiting neurotransmitter release. ④ In the absence of IPSPs, the bipolar cell is disinhibited. It depolarizes and ⑤ releases neurotransmitter, which ⑥ depolarizes the ganglion cell (EPSPs). ⑦ Action potentials are generated and propagate along the optic nerve.

by hyperpolarization conveys information as effectively as depolarization.

The photoreceptors do not generate action potentials and neither do the bipolar cells that lie between them and the ganglion cells. The ganglion cells do, however, generate action potentials, which is consistent with their function as the output neurons of the retina. In all other cases, only local currents (graded potentials) are produced. This is not surprising if you remember that the primary function of action potentials

Q *Assume that everything is proceeding normally in the scheme illustrated, but then a metabolic poison that interferes with the Na⁺-K⁺ pump is introduced. What would happen and why?*

FIGURE 15.18 **Events of phototransduction.** A portion of photoreceptor disc membrane showing the events in phototransduction. ① Light (photons) isomerizes retinal to its all-*trans* form, activating the visual pigment, which in turn ② activates transducin (G protein). ③ Transducin activates the enzyme phosphodiesterase (PDE), which ④ converts cGMP into GMP. ⑤ As the concentration of cGMP falls, cGMP-gated cation channels close, leading to the hyperpolarization of the photoreceptor. The G protein conversion of GTP to GDP has been omitted for clarity. For simplicity, the cGMP-gated channels are shown on the same membrane as the visual pigment instead of in the plasma membrane.

15

is to carry information rapidly over long distances. Retinal cells are small cells that are very close together, so graded potentials can serve quite adequately as signals to regulate neurotransmitter release.

Light and Dark Adaptation Rhodopsin is amazingly sensitive; even starlight causes some of the molecules to become bleached. As long as the light is low intensity, relatively little rhodopsin is bleached and the retina continues to respond to light stimuli. However, in high-intensity light there is wholesale bleaching of the pigment, and rhodopsin is bleached as fast as it is re-formed. At this point, the rods are nonfunctional, but cones still respond. Hence, retinal sensitivity automatically adjusts to the amount of light present.

Light adaptation occurs when we move from darkness into bright light, as when leaving a movie matinee. We are momentarily dazzled—all we see is white light—because the sensitivity of the retina is still "set" for dim light. Both rods and cones are strongly stimulated, and large amounts of the visual pigments are broken down almost instantaneously, producing a flood of signals that accounts for the glare. Under such conditions, compensations occur. The rod system essentially turns off, while the cone system and other retinal neurons rapidly adapt, so that retinal sensitivity decreases dramatically. Within about 60 seconds, the cones, initially overexcited by the bright light, are sufficiently desensitized to take over. Visual acuity and color vision continue to improve over the next 5–10 minutes. Thus, during light adaptation, retinal sensitivity (rod function) is lost, but visual acuity (the ability to resolve detail) is gained.

Dark adaptation, essentially the reverse of light adaptation, occurs when we go from a well-lit area into a dark one. Initially, we see nothing but velvety blackness because (1) our cones stop functioning in low-intensity light, and (2) our rod pigments have been bleached out by the bright light, and the rods are still turned off. But once we are in the dark, rhodopsin accumulates and retinal sensitivity increases. Dark adaptation is much slower than light adaptation and can go on for hours. However, there

A *The whole process will come to a halt because excitation depends on having the proper ionic concentrations on the two sides of the membrane.*

is usually enough rhodopsin within 20–30 minutes to allow adequate dim-light vision.

During these adaptations, reflexive changes also occur in pupil size. Bright light shining in one or both eyes causes both pupils to constrict (elicits the *consensual* and *pupillary light reflexes*). These pupillary reflexes are mediated by the pretectal nucleus of the midbrain and by parasympathetic fibers. In dim light, the pupils dilate, allowing more light to enter the eye interior.

◢ HOMEOSTATIC IMBALANCE

Night blindness, or *nyctalopia* (nic″tă-lo′pe-uh), is a condition in which rod function is seriously hampered, impairing one's ability to drive safely at night. In countries where malnutrition is common, the most common cause of night blindness is prolonged vitamin A deficiency, which leads to rod degeneration. Vitamin A supplements restore function if they are administered early. In countries where nutrition isn't a problem, a group of degenerative retinal diseases called *retinitis pigmentosa*, in which rods are selectively destroyed, are the most common causes of night blindness. Retinitis pigmentosa is a result of the pigment epithelial cells being unable to recycle the tips of the rods as they get sloughed off. ●

The Visual Pathway to the Brain

As described earlier, the axons of the retinal ganglion cells issue from the back of the eyeballs in the **optic nerves** (Figure 15.19). At the X-shaped **optic chiasma** (*chiasm* = cross), fibers from the medial aspect of each eye cross over to the opposite side and then continue on via the **optic tracts.** Thus, each optic tract (1) contains fibers from the lateral (temporal) aspect of the eye on the same side and fibers from the medial (nasal) aspect of the opposite eye, and (2) carries all the information from the same half of the visual field. Notice that, because the lens system of each eye reverses all images, the medial half of each retina receives light rays from the *temporal* (lateralmost) part of the visual field (that is, from the far left or far right rather than from straight ahead), and the lateral half of each retina receives an image of the *nasal* (central) part of the visual field. Consequently, the left optic tract carries (and sends on) a complete representation of the right half of the visual field, and the opposite is true for the right optic tract.

The paired optic tracts sweep posteriorly around the hypothalamus and send most of their axons to synapse with neurons in the **lateral geniculate body** of the thalamus, which maintains the fiber separation established at the chiasma, but balances and combines the retinal input for delivery to the visual cortex. Axons of the thalamic neurons project through the internal capsule to form the **optic radi-** **ation** of fibers in the cerebral white matter. These fibers project to the **primary visual cortex** in the occipital lobes, where conscious perception of visual images (seeing) occurs.

Some nerve fibers in the optic tracts send branches to the midbrain. These fibers end in the **superior colliculi,** visual reflex centers controlling the extrinsic muscles of the eyes. A small subset of neurons donating fibers to the visual pathway contain the visual pigment *melanopsin*, dubbed the circadian pigment, and respond directly to light stimuli independent of vision. These project to the **pretectal nuclei,** which mediate pupillary light reflexes, and to the **suprachiasmatic nucleus** of the hypothalamus, which functions as the "timer" to set our daily biorhythms.

Notice that although both eyes are set anteriorly and look in approximately the same direction, their visual fields, each about 170 degrees, overlap to a considerable extent, and each eye sees a slightly different view (see Figure 15.19). Cortical "fusion" of the slightly different images delivered by the two eyes provides us with **depth perception,** an accurate means of locating objects in space. This faculty is also called **three-dimensional vision.** In contrast, many animals (pigeons, rabbits, and others) have *panoramic vision.* Their eyes are placed more laterally on the head, so that the visual fields overlap very little, and crossover of the optic nerve fibers is almost complete. Consequently, each visual cortex receives input principally from a single eye and a totally different visual field.

Depth perception depends on the two eyes working together. If only one eye is used, depth perception is lost, and the person must learn to judge an object's position based on learned cues (for example, nearer objects appear larger, and parallel lines converge with distance).

◢ HOMEOSTATIC IMBALANCE

The relationships described above explain patterns of blindness that follow damage to different visual structures. Loss of an eye or destruction of one optic nerve eliminates true depth perception, and peripheral vision is lost on the side of damage. For example, if the "left eye" in Figure 15.19 was lost in a hunting accident, nothing would be seen in the visual field area colored yellow in that figure. If neural destruction occurs beyond the optic chiasma—in an optic tract, the thalamus, or visual cortex—then part or all of the opposite half of the visual field is lost. For example, a stroke affecting the left visual cortex leads to blindness in the right half of the visual field, but since the right (undamaged) visual cortex still receives inputs from both eyes, depth perception in the remaining half of the visual field is retained. ●

15

Q *Where on the retina of the right eye would light from an object in the nasal portion of its visual field be projected?*

Fixation point

Right eye

Left eye

Supra-chiasmatic nucleus

Pretectal nucleus

Optic nerve

Optic chiasma

Optic tract

Lateral geniculate body

Superior colliculus (sectioned)

Uncrossed (ipsilateral) fiber

Crossed (contralateral) fiber

Optic radiation

Lateral geniculate body of thalamus

Superior colliculus

Occipital lobe (visual cortex)

Corpus callosum

(a)

(b)

FIGURE 15.19   **Visual fields of the eyes and visual pathway to the brain, inferior view. (a)** Diagram. **(b)** Photograph of human brain. The right side has been dissected to reveal internal structures. In (a) notice that the visual fields of the two eyes overlap considerably. Also notice the retinal sites at which a real image would be focused when both eyes are fixated on a close, pointlike object. The full lateral extension of the visual fields is not illustrated here.

Visual Processing

How does information received by the rods and cones become vision? In the past few years, a tremendous amount of research has been devoted to

this question. Some of the more basic information that has come out of these studies is presented here.

Retinal Processing   The retinal ganglion cells generate action potentials at a fairly steady rate (20–30 per second), even in the dark. Surprisingly, illuminating the entire retina evenly has no effect on

A *On the temporal portion of the retina.*

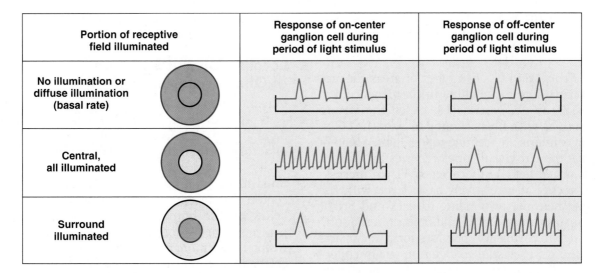

Portion of receptive field illuminated	Response of on-center ganglion cell during period of light stimulus	Response of off-center ganglion cell during period of light stimulus
No illumination or diffuse illumination (basal rate)		
Central, all illuminated		
Surround illuminated		

FIGURE 15.20 **Responses of on-center and off-center retinal ganglion cells to different types of illumination.** Intermediate amounts of illumination of the central and surround regions lead to intermediate rates of impulse transmission.

that basal rate. However, the activity of individual ganglion cells changes dramatically when a tiny spot of light falls just on certain portions of their receptive field. The *receptive field* of a ganglion cell consists of the area of the retina that, when stimulated, influences the activity of that ganglion cell (via the rods or cones that funnel their impulses to it).

When researchers mapped the receptive fields of ganglion cells receiving inputs only from rods, they found two types of doughnut-shaped (circle-within-a-circle) receptive fields (Figure 15.20). These are called **on-center** and **off-center fields,** based on what happens to the ganglion cell when the center of its receptive field is illuminated with a spot of light. Ganglion cells with on-center fields are stimulated (depolarized) by light hitting the field center (the "doughnut hole") and are inhibited by light hitting rods in the periphery (the doughnut itself). The opposite situation occurs in ganglion cells with off-center fields. Equal illumination of "on" and "off" regions causes little change in the basal rate of ganglion cell firing.

The mechanisms of retinal processing as currently understood can be summarized briefly as follows:

1. The action of light on photoreceptors hyperpolarizes them.

2. Bipolar neurons in the "on" regions are excited (depolarize) and excite the associated ganglion cell when the rods feeding into them are illuminated (and hyperpolarized). Bipolar neurons in the "off" regions are inhibited (hyperpolarize) and inhibit the ganglion cell when the rods feeding into them are stimulated. The opposite responses of the bipolar

neurons in the "on" versus the "off" regions reflect the fact that they have different receptor types for glutamate.

3. Bipolar neurons receiving signals from cones feed directly into excitatory synapses on ganglion cells. Hence, cone inputs are perceived as sharp and clear (and in color).

4. Bipolar neurons receiving inputs from rods excite amacrine cells via gap junctions. These local integrator neurons modify rod inputs and ultimately direct excitatory inputs to appropriate ganglion cells. Thus, rod inputs are not only summated but are subject to "detours" before reaching the output (ganglion) cells. Together these factors provide a more smeary picture than cone inputs.

5. Inputs are also modified and subjected to lateral inhibition by synaptic (gap junction) contacts with horizontal cells. Inputs from these local integrator cells allow the retina to convert inputs that are points of light into perceptually more meaningful contour information by accentuating bright/dark or color contrasts (edges).

6. Two common varieties of ganglion cells are identified. P cells, the target of cone input, relay information about small nonmoving objects in the center of the visual field—their color and details. M cells, which also receive rod input, respond best to large, moving objects at the edge of the image.

Thalamic Processing The lateral geniculate nuclei (LGN) of the thalamus relay information on movement, segregate the retinal axons in preparation for depth perception, emphasize visual inputs from the cones, and sharpen the contrast information

15

received from the retina. The separation of signals from the two eyes is relayed accurately to the visual cortex.

Cortical Processing   Two types of areas for processing retinal inputs are found in the visual cortex. The *primary visual cortex,* also called the **striate cortex,** is thick with fibers coming in from the LGN. This area contains an accurate topographical map of the retina; the left visual cortex receives input from the right visual field and vice versa. Visual processing here occurs at a relatively basic level, with the processing neurons responding to dark and bright edges (contrast information) and object orientation.

The striate cortex also provides form, color, and motion inputs to *visual association areas* collectively called the **prestriate cortices.** The more anterior prestriate cortices are occipital lobe centers that continue the processing of visual information concerned with form, color, and movement. Functional neuroimaging of humans has revealed that complex visual processing extends well forward into the temporal, parietal, and frontal lobes via two main streams: (1) The "what" processing stream extends through the ventral part of the temporal lobe and specializes in the identification of objects in the visual field. (2) The "where" processing stream takes a dorsal path through the parietal cortex all the way to the postcentral gyrus and uses information from the primary visual cortex to assess the spatial location of objects. Output from both these regions then appears to pass to the frontal cortex, which uses that information to direct activities that, among other things, can guide movements such as reaching for a juicy peach.

The Chemical Senses: Taste and Smell

Taste and smell are gritty, primitive senses that alert us to whether that "stuff" nearby (or in our mouth) is to be savored or avoided. The receptors for taste (gustation) and smell (olfaction) are **chemoreceptors** (respond to chemicals in an aqueous solution); they complement each other and respond to different classes of chemicals. Taste receptors are excited by food chemicals dissolved in saliva; smell receptors, by airborne chemicals that dissolve in fluids coating nasal membranes.

The Olfactory Epithelium and the Sense of Smell

Although our olfactory sense (*olfact* = to smell) is far less acute than that of many other animals, the human nose is still no slouch in picking up small differences in odors. Some people capitalize on this ability by becoming wine tasters.

Localization and Structure of Olfactory Receptors

Olfaction detects chemicals (*odorants*) in solution. The organ of smell is a yellow-tinged patch (about 5 cm^2) of pseudostratified epithelium, called the **olfactory epithelium,** located in the roof of the nasal cavity (Figure 15.21). Air entering the nasal cavity must make a hairpin turn to stimulate olfactory receptors before entering the respiratory passageway below, so the human olfactory epithelium is in a poor position for doing its job. (This is why sniffing, which draws more air superiorly across the olfactory epithelium, intensifies the sense of smell.) The olfactory epithelium covers the superior nasal concha on each side of the nasal septum, and contains millions of bowling pin–shaped **olfactory receptor cells.** These are surrounded and cushioned by columnar **supporting cells,** which make up the bulk of the penny-thin epithelial membrane (Figure 15.21). The supporting cells contain a yellow-brown pigment similar to lipofuscin, which gives the olfactory epithelium its yellow hue. At the base of the epithelium lie the short **basal cells.**

The olfactory receptor cells are unusual bipolar neurons. Each has a thin apical dendrite that terminates in a knob from which several long cilia radiate. These **olfactory cilia,** which substantially increase the receptive surface area, typically lie flat on the nasal epithelium and are covered by a coat of thin mucus produced by the supporting cells and by olfactory glands in the underlying connective tissue. This mucus is a solvent that "captures" and dissolves airborne odorants. Unlike other cilia in the body, which beat rapidly and in a coordinated manner, olfactory cilia are largely nonmotile. The slender, unmyelinated axons of the olfactory receptor cells are gathered into small fascicles that collectively form the **filaments of the olfactory nerve** (cranial nerve I). They project superiorly through the openings in the cribriform plate of the ethmoid bone, where they synapse in the overlying olfactory bulbs.

Olfactory receptor cells are unique in that they are one of the few types of *neurons* that undergo noticeable turnover throughout adult life. Their superficial location puts them at risk for damage and their typical life span is 30–60 days, after which they are replaced by differentiation of the basal cells in the olfactory epithelium.

Specificity of the Olfactory Receptors

Smell is difficult to research because any given odor (say, tobacco smoke) may be made up of hundreds of different chemicals. Taste has been neatly packaged

Q *What is the importance of the layer of mucus that coats the olfactory epithelium surface?*

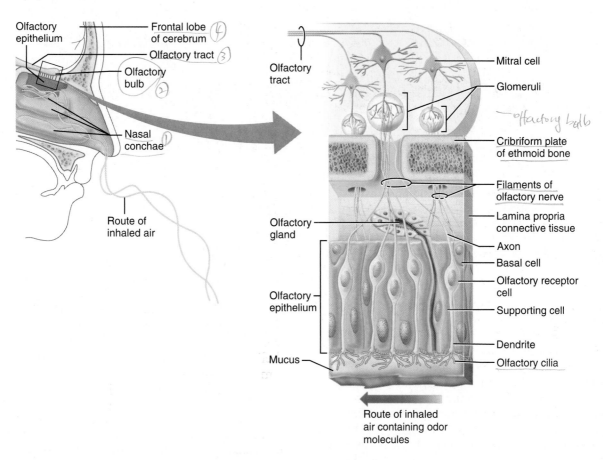

FIGURE 15.21 **Olfactory receptors.** Site of olfactory epithelium in the superior nasal cavity is shown on the left. On the right is an enlarged view of the olfactory epithelium and the course of the fibers (filaments) of the olfactory nerve (I) through the ethmoid bone to synapse in the overlying olfactory bulb. The glomeruli and mitral cells (output cells) within the olfactory bulb are also shown.

into four or five taste qualities, but science has yet to discover any similar means for classifying smell. Humans can distinguish 10,000 or so odors, but research suggests that our olfactory receptors are stimulated by different combinations of a more limited number of olfactory qualities. Most promising in throwing light on this matter are the studies done in the early 1990s suggesting that there are at least 1000 "smell genes" that are active only in the nose. Each such gene encodes a unique receptor protein, and it appears that each of the receptor proteins responds to several different odors and each odor binds to several different receptor types. However, each receptor cell has only one type of receptor protein.

Olfactory neurons are exquisitely sensitive—in some cases, just a few molecules activate them.

Some of what we call smell is really pain. The nasal cavities contain pain receptors that respond to irritants such as the sharpness of ammonia, the hotness of chili peppers, and the "chill" of menthol. Impulses from these pain receptors reach the central nervous system via afferent fibers of the trigeminal nerves.

Physiology of Smell

Activation of the Olfactory Receptors For us to smell a particular odorant, it must be *volatile*—that is, it must be in the gaseous state as it enters the nasal cavity. Additionally, it must dissolve in the fluid coating the olfactory epithelium. The dissolved odorants stimulate the olfactory receptors by binding to protein receptors in the olfactory cilium membranes and opening cation channels. This leads to a receptor potential and ultimately (assuming threshold

A *It serves as a dissolving medium for odor molecules.*

FIGURE 15.22 **Olfactory transduction process.** A portion of olfactory cilium membrane showing the events in olfactory transduction. ① Olfactory transduction occurs when an odorant chemical binds to its receptor. ② The receptor activates G protein (G_{olf}), which ③ activates adenylate cyclase. ④ Adenylate cyclase converts ATP to cAMP, which in turn ⑤ directly opens a cation channel allowing the influx of Na^+ and Ca^{2+}, depolarizing the cell.

stimulation) to an action potential that is conducted to the first relay station in the olfactory bulb.

Mechanism of Smell Transduction Transduction of odorants uses a receptor linked to a G protein (Figure 15.22). The events following odorant binding will be easy for you to remember if you compare them to what you already know: general mechanisms of receptors and G proteins (see Figure 11.22) and phototransduction (Figure 15.18). In olfactory transduction, an odorant binds to a receptor, which activates G protein (G_{olf}), which activates enzymes (adenylate cyclases) that synthesize cyclic AMP as a second messenger. Cyclic AMP acts directly on a plasma membrane cation channel (as in photoreceptors), causing it to open and allowing Na^+ and Ca^{2+} to enter. Na^+ influx leads to depolarization and impulse transmission. Ca^{2+} influx causes the transduction mechanism to adapt, decreasing its response to a sustained stimulus. This *olfactory adaptation* helps explain how a person working in a paper mill or sewage treatment plant can still enjoy lunch!

The Olfactory Pathway

As noted above, axons of the olfactory receptor cells constitute the olfactory nerves that synapse in the overlying **olfactory bulbs,** the distal ends of the olfactory tracts (see Table 13.2). There, the filaments of the olfactory nerves synapse with **mitral cells** (mi'tral), which are second-order neurons, in complex structures called **glomeruli** (glo-mer'u-li; "little balls") (see Figure 15.21). Axons from neurons bearing the same kind of receptor converge on a given type of glomerulus. Hence, each glomerulus represents a "file" that receives only one type of odor signal, and different odors (which would excite a variety of receptor types) would

be expected to activate different subsets of glomeruli. The mitral cells refine the signal, amplify it, and then relay it. The olfactory bulbs also house *granule cells,* GABA-releasing cells that inhibit mitral cells (via dendrodendritic synapses), so that only highly excitatory olfactory impulses are transmitted.

When the mitral cells are activated, impulses flow from the olfactory bulbs via the **olfactory tracts** (composed mainly of mitral cell axons) to two main destinations. The first pathway travels to the piriform lobe of the olfactory cortex and the part of the frontal lobe just above the orbit, where smells are consciously interpreted and identified. Each olfactory cortical neuron receives input from up to 100 receptors to analyze. The second pathway flows via the subcortical route to the hypothalamus, amygdala, and other regions of the limbic system, which elicits emotional responses to odors. Smells associated with danger—smoke, cooking gas, or skunk scent—trigger the sympathetic fight-or-flight response. Appetizing odors cause increased salivation and stimulation of the digestive tract, and unpleasant odors can trigger protective reflexes such as sneezing and choking.

Taste Buds and the Sense of Taste

The word *taste* comes from the Latin *taxare,* meaning "to touch, estimate, or judge." When we taste things, we are in fact intimately testing or judging our environment, and the sense of taste is considered by many to be the most pleasurable of the special senses.

Localization and Structure of Taste Buds

The **taste buds,** the sensory receptor organs for taste, are located primarily in the oral cavity. Of our 10,000

Q *Think back to your studies of the cranial nerves as you view Part (a). Sensitivity from which part of the tongue would be most impaired by injury to the glossopharyngeal nerve?*

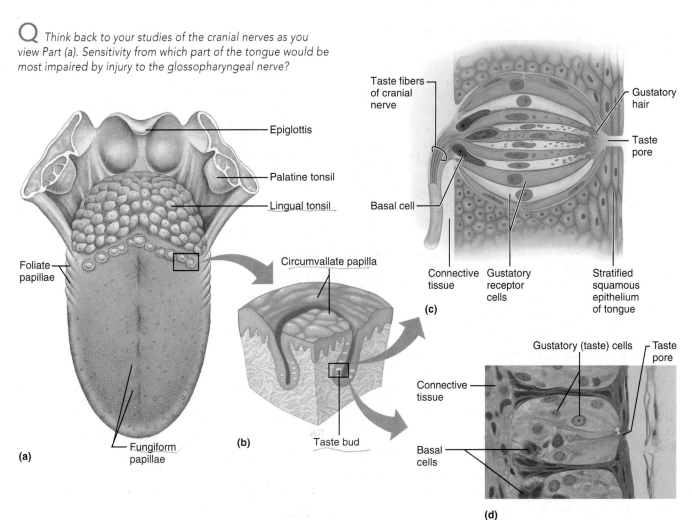

FIGURE 15.23 **Location and structure of taste buds on the tongue. (a)** Taste buds on the tongue are associated with fungiform, foliate, and vallate (circumvallate) papillae, peglike projections of the tongue mucosa. (See *A Brief Atlas of the Human Body,* Figure 62.) **(b)** A sectioned circumvallate papilla shows the positioning of the taste buds in its lateral walls. **(c)** An enlarged view of one taste bud, illustrating gustatory (taste) and basal cells. **(d)** Photomicrograph of a taste bud.

or so taste buds, most are on the tongue. A few taste buds are scattered on the soft palate, inner surface of the cheeks, pharynx, and epiglottis of the larynx, but most are found in **papillae** (pah-pil′e), peglike projections of the tongue mucosa that give the tongue surface a slightly abrasive feel. Taste buds are located mainly on the tops of the mushroom-shaped **fungiform papillae** (fun′jĭ-form) (which are scattered over the entire tongue surface) and in the epithelium of the side walls of the **foliate papillae** and of the large round **circumvallate** (ser″kum-val′āt), or simply **vallate, papillae.** The vallate papillae are the largest and least numerous papillae; 7 to 12 of these form an inverted V at the back of the tongue (see Figure 15.23a).

Each flask-shaped taste bud consists of 50 to 100 *epithelial cells* of two major types: **gustatory,** or **taste cells,** and basal cells (Figure 15.23c). Long microvilli called **gustatory hairs** project from the tips of all gustatory cells and extend through a **taste pore** to the surface of the epithelium, where they are bathed by saliva. The gustatory hairs are the sensitive portions *(receptor membranes)* of the gustatory cells. Coiling intimately around the gustatory cells are sensory dendrites that represent the initial part of the gustatory pathway to the brain. Each afferent fiber receives signals from several receptor cells within the taste bud. Because of their location, taste bud cells are subjected to huge amounts of friction and are routinely burned by hot foods. Luckily, they are among the most dynamic cells in the body, and they are replaced every seven to ten days. The **basal**

A *Posterior tongue.*

cells act as stem cells, dividing and differentiating into new gustatory cells.

Basic Taste Sensations

Normally, our taste sensations are complicated mixtures of qualities. However, when taste is tested with pure chemical compounds, taste sensations can all be grouped into one of five basic qualities: *sweet, sour, salty, bitter,* and *umami.* The sweet taste is elicited by many organic substances including sugars, saccharin, alcohols, some amino acids, and some lead salts (such as those found in lead paint). Sour taste is produced by acids, specifically their hydrogen ions (H^+) in solution. Salty taste is produced by metal ions (inorganic salts); table salt (sodium chloride) tastes the "saltiest." The bitter taste is elicited by alkaloids (such as quinine, nicotine, caffeine, morphine, and strychnine) as well as a number of nonalkaloid substances, such as aspirin. Umami (u-mam'e; "delicious"), a new taste discovered by the Japanese, is elicited by the amino acids glutamate and aspartate, which appear to be responsible for the "beef taste" of steak, the characteristic tang of aging cheese, and the flavor of the food additive monosodium glutamate. However, these differences are not absolute: Most taste buds respond to two or more taste qualities, and many substances produce a mixture of the basic taste sensations.

Taste maps that spatially assign sweet receptors to the tip of the tongue, salty and sour receptors to the sides, bitter receptors to the back, and umami receptors to the pharynx are common in the literature. However, researchers have known for years that these mapped areas are misrepresentations, or are dubious at the very least. In reality, there are only slight differences in the localization of specific taste receptors in different regions of the tongue, and all modalities of taste can be elicited from all areas that contain taste buds.

Taste likes and dislikes have homeostatic value. Umami guides the intake of proteins, and a liking for sugar and salt helps satisfy the body's need for carbohydrates and minerals (as well as some amino acids). Many sour, naturally acidic foods (such as oranges, lemons, and tomatoes) are rich sources of vitamin C, an essential vitamin. Because many natural poisons and spoiled foods are bitter, our dislike for bitterness is protective.

Physiology of Taste

Activation of Taste Receptors For a chemical to be tasted it must dissolve in saliva, diffuse into the taste pore, and contact the gustatory hairs. The gustatory cells contain synaptic vesicles, and binding of the food chemical, or *tastant,* to the receptors in the gustatory cell membrane induces a graded depolariz-

ing potential that causes the release of the synaptic vesicle contents, neurotransmitter. Binding of the neurotransmitter to the associated sensory dendrites triggers generator potentials that elicit action potentials in these fibers.

The different gustatory cells have different thresholds for activation. The bitter receptors (in line with their protective nature) detect substances present in minute amounts; the other receptors are less sensitive. Taste receptors adapt rapidly, with partial adaptation in 3–5 seconds and complete adaptation in 1–5 minutes.

Mechanism of Taste Transduction The mechanisms of taste transduction are only partly known—each taste quality has its own special mechanism. However, all of these mechanisms ultimately cause an increase in intracellular Ca^{2+}, which increases neurotransmitter release. Salty taste is due to Na^+ influx through apically located Na^+ channels, which directly depolarizes the gustatory cell. Sour is mediated by H^+, which appears to act on a taste cell in one of three ways—by directly entering the cell through a channel, by opening channels that allow other cations to enter, or by blockade of K^+ channels. Bitter, sweet, and umami responses are mediated by G protein–dependent mechanisms that act via second messengers. Bitter causes Ca^{2+} release from intracellular stores, whereas sweet causes closure of K^+ channels, thereby depolarizing the cell. The G protein that mediates transduction of bitter tastes has recently been identified and named *gustducin.*

The Gustatory Pathway

Afferent fibers carrying taste information from the tongue are found primarily in two cranial nerve pairs. A branch of the **facial nerve** (VII), the *chorda tympani,* transmits impulses from taste receptors in the anterior two-thirds of the tongue, whereas the lingual branch of the **glossopharyngeal nerve** (IX) services the posterior third and the pharynx just behind. Taste impulses from the few taste buds in the epiglottis and the lower pharynx are conducted primarily by the **vagus nerve** (X). These afferent fibers synapse in the **solitary nucleus** of the medulla (Figure 15.24), and from there impulses stream to the thalamus and ultimately to the gustatory cortex in the insula. Fibers also project to the hypothalamus and limbic system structures, regions that determine our appreciation of what we are tasting.

An important role of taste is to trigger reflexes involved in digestion. As taste impulses pass through the solitary nucleus, they initiate reflexes (via synapses with parasympathetic nuclei) that increase saliva secretion into the mouth and gastric juice into the stomach. Saliva contains mucus that moistens food and digestive enzymes that begin the digestion of starch. Acidic foods are particularly strong stimulants of the salivary reflex. Additionally, when we eat revolting or foul-tasting substances, gagging or even reflexive vomiting may be initiated.

Influence of Other Sensations on Taste

Taste is 80% smell. When the olfactory receptors in the nasal cavity are blocked by nasal congestion (or pinching your nostrils), food is bland. Without smell, our morning coffee would lack its richness and simply taste bitter.

The mouth also contains thermoreceptors, mechanoreceptors, and nociceptors, and the temperature and texture of foods can enhance or detract from their taste. "Hot" foods such as chili peppers actually bring about their pleasurable effects by exciting pain receptors in the mouth.

Homeostatic Imbalances of the Chemical Senses

Most olfactory disorders, or *anosmias* (an-oz'me-ahz; "without smells"), result from head injuries that tear the olfactory nerves, the aftereffects of nasal cavity inflammation, and aging. Brain disorders can distort the sense of smell. Some people have *uncinate fits* (uns'ih-nāt), olfactory hallucinations during which they experience a particular (usually unpleasant) odor, such as rotting meat. Some such cases are undeniably psychological, but many result from irritation of the olfactory pathway by brain surgery or head trauma. *Olfactory auras* experienced by some epileptics just before they have a seizure are transient uncinate fits.

Taste disorders are less common than disorders of smell, in part because the taste receptors are served by three different nerves and thus are less likely to be "put out of business" completely. Causes of taste disorders include upper respiratory tract infections, head injuries, chemicals or medications, or head and neck radiation for cancer treatment. Zinc supplements have been found to help in some cases of radiation-induced taste disorders.

The Ear: Hearing and Balance

At first glance, the machinery for hearing and balance appears very crude. Fluids must be stirred to stimulate the mechanoreceptors of the internal ear. Nevertheless, our hearing apparatus allows us to hear an extraordinary range of sound, and our equilibrium receptors keep the nervous system continually informed of head movements and position. Although the organs serving these two senses are structurally interconnected within the ear, their receptors respond to different stimuli and are activated independently of one another.

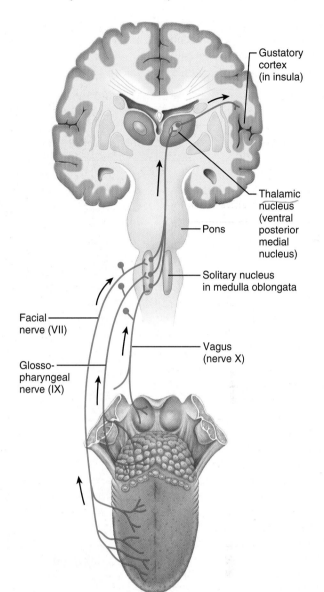

FIGURE 15.24 **The gustatory pathway.** From the taste buds on the tongue and elsewhere, taste impulses travel to the gustatory area of the cerebral cortex.

Structure of the Ear

The ear is divided into three major areas: external ear, middle ear, and internal ear (Figure 15.25). The external and middle ear structures are involved with hearing only and are rather simply engineered. The internal ear functions in both equilibrium and hearing and is extremely complex.

The External (Outer) Ear

The **external (outer) ear** consists of the auricle and the external acoustic meatus. The **auricle**, or **pinna**, is what most people call the ear—the shell-shaped projection surrounding the opening of the external

Q Besides the bony boundaries, what structure separates the external from the middle ear?

FIGURE 15.25 Structure of the ear. (a) The three regions of the ear. **(b)** Enlarged view of the middle and internal ear. Notice that the semicircular canals, vestibule, and cochlea of the internal ear form the bony labyrinth.

A *The tympanic membrane.*

acoustic meatus. The auricle is composed of elastic cartilage covered with thin skin and an occasional hair. Its rim, the **helix,** is somewhat thicker, and its fleshy, dangling **lobule** ("earlobe") lacks supporting cartilage. The function of the auricle is to direct sound waves into the external acoustic meatus.

The **external acoustic meatus** (auditory canal) is a short, curved tube (about 2.5 cm long by 0.6 cm wide) that extends from the auricle to the eardrum. Near the auricle, its framework is elastic cartilage; the remainder of the canal is carved into the temporal bone. The entire canal is lined with skin bearing hairs, sebaceous glands, and modified apocrine sweat glands called **ceruminous glands** (sĕ-roo'mĭ-nus). These glands secrete yellow-brown waxy **cerumen,** or earwax (*cere* = wax), which provides a sticky trap for foreign bodies and repels insects. In many people, the ear is naturally cleansed as the cerumen dries and then falls out of the external acoustic meatus. (Jaw movements as a person eats, talks, and so on, create an unnoticeable conveyor-belt effect that moves the wax out.) In others, cerumen builds up excessively and becomes compacted, a condition that can impair hearing.

Sound waves entering the external acoustic meatus eventually hit the **tympanic membrane,** or **eardrum** (*tympanum* = drum), the boundary between the outer and middle ears. The eardrum is a thin, translucent, connective tissue membrane, covered by skin on its external face and by a mucosa internally. It is shaped like a flattened cone, with its apex protruding medially into the middle ear. Sound waves make the eardrum vibrate. The eardrum, in turn, transfers the sound energy to the tiny bones of the middle ear and sets them into vibration.

The Middle Ear

The **middle ear,** or **tympanic cavity,** is a small, air-filled, mucosa-lined cavity in the petrous portion of the temporal bone. It is flanked laterally by the eardrum and medially by a bony wall with two openings, the superior **oval (vestibular) window** and the inferior **round (cochlear) window.** Superiorly the tympanic cavity arches upward as the **epitympanic recess,** the "roof" of the middle ear cavity. The **mastoid antrum,** a canal in the posterior wall of the tympanic cavity, allows it to communicate with *mastoid air cells* housed in the mastoid process. The anterior wall of the middle ear abuts the internal carotid artery (the main artery supplying the brain) and contains the opening of the **pharyngotympanic (auditory) tube.** This tube, formerly called the eustachian tube, runs obliquely downward to link the middle ear cavity with the nasopharynx (the superiormost part of the throat), and the mucosa of the middle ear is continuous with that lining the pharynx (throat).

Normally, the pharyngotympanic tube is flattened and closed, but swallowing or yawning opens it briefly to equalize pressure in the middle ear cavity with external air pressure. This is important because the eardrum vibrates freely only if the pressure on both of its surfaces is the same; otherwise sounds are distorted. The ear-popping sensation of the pressures equalizing is familiar to anyone who has flown in an airplane.

HOMEOSTATIC IMBALANCE

Otitis media (me'de-ah), or middle ear inflammation, is a fairly common result of a sore throat, especially in children, whose pharyngotympanic tubes are shorter and run more horizontally. Otitis media is the most frequent cause of hearing loss in children. In acute infectious forms, the eardrum bulges and becomes inflamed and red. Most cases of otitis media are treated with antibiotics. When large amounts of fluid or pus accumulate in the cavity, an emergency *myringotomy* (lancing of the eardrum) may be required to relieve the pressure, and a tiny tube implanted in the eardrum permits pus to drain into the external ear. The tube falls out by itself within the year. ●

The tympanic cavity is spanned by the three smallest bones in the body: the **auditory ossicles** (see Figures 15.25 and 15.26). These bones, named for their shape, are the **malleus** (mal'e-us; "hammer"); the **incus** (ing'kus; "anvil"); and the **stapes**

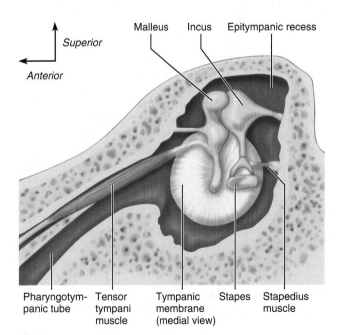

FIGURE 15.26 **The three auditory ossicles in the right middle ear.** Ossicles are seen as if viewed from the oval window looking outward (medial view).

Semicircular ducts in semicircular canals:
- Anterior
- Posterior
- Lateral

Cristae ampullares in the ampullae

Utricle in vestibule

Saccule in vestibule

Stapes in oval window

Temporal bone

Facial nerve

Vestibular nerve

Superior vestibular ganglion

Inferior vestibular ganglion

Cochlear nerve

Maculae

Spiral organ (of Corti)

Cochlear duct in cochlea

Round window

FIGURE 15.27 **Membranous labyrinth of the internal ear.** The membranous labyrinth (blue), is shown in relation to the chambers of the bony labyrinth (orange). The sensory organs for hearing [spiral organ (of Corti)] and equilibrium (maculae and cristae ampullares) are also shown.

(sta'pēz; "stirrup"). The "handle" of the malleus is secured to the eardrum, and the base of the stapes fits into the oval window.

Tiny ligaments suspend the ossicles, and mini synovial joints link them together into a chain that spans the middle ear cavity. The incus articulates with the malleus laterally and the stapes medially. The ossicles transmit the vibratory motion of the eardrum to the oval window, which in turn sets the fluids of the internal ear into motion, eventually exciting the hearing receptors.

Two tiny skeletal muscles are associated with the ossicles (Figure 15.26). The **tensor tympani** (ten'sor tim'pah-ni) arises from the wall of the pharyngotympanic tube and inserts on the malleus. The **stapedius** (stah-pe'de-us) runs from the posterior wall of the middle ear cavity to the stapes. When the ears are assaulted by very loud sounds, these muscles contract reflexively to prevent damage to the hearing receptors. Specifically, the tensor tympani tenses the eardrum by pulling it medially; the stapedius checks vibration of the whole ossicle chain and limits the movement of the stapes in the oval window.

The Internal (Inner) Ear

The **internal (inner) ear** is also called the **labyrinth** ("maze") because of its complicated shape (see Figure 15.25). It lies deep in the temporal bone behind the eye socket and provides a secure site for all of the delicate receptor machinery housed there. The internal ear has two major divisions: the bony labyrinth and the membranous labyrinth. The **bony,** or **osseous, labyrinth** is a system of tortuous channels worming through the bone. Its three regions are the *vestibule,* the *cochlea* (kok'le-ah), and the *semicircular canals.* The views of the bony labyrinth typically seen in textbooks, including this one, are somewhat misleading because we are talking about a *cavity* here. The representation seen in Figure 15.25 can be compared to a plaster of paris cast of the cavity or hollow space inside the bony labyrinth. The **membranous labyrinth** is a continuous series of membranous sacs and ducts contained within the bony labyrinth and (more or less) following its contours (Figure 15.27).

The bony labyrinth is filled with **perilymph,** a fluid similar to cerebrospinal fluid and continuous with it. The membranous labyrinth is suspended in the surrounding perilymph; its interior contains **endolymph,** which is chemically similar to K^+-rich intracellular fluid. These two fluids conduct the sound vibrations involved in hearing and respond to the mechanical forces occurring during changes in body position and acceleration.

The Vestibule The **vestibule** is the central egg-shaped cavity of the bony labyrinth. It lies posterior to the cochlea, anterior to the semicircular canals, and flanks the middle ear medially. In its lateral wall is the oval window. Suspended in its perilymph and united by a small duct are two membranous labyrinth sacs, the **saccule** and **utricle** (u'tri-kl) (Figure 15.27). The smaller saccule is continuous with the membranous labyrinth extending anteriorly into the cochlea (the *cochlear duct*), whereas the utricle is continuous with the semicircular ducts extending into the semicircular canals posteriorly. The saccule and utricle house equilibrium receptor regions called *maculae* that respond to the pull of gravity and report on changes of head position.

The Semicircular Canals   The **semicircular canals** lie posterior and lateral to the vestibule, and each of these canals defines about two-thirds of a circle. The cavities of the bony semicircular canals project from the posterior aspect of the vestibule, each oriented in one of the three planes of space. Accordingly, there is an *anterior, posterior,* and *lateral* semicircular canal in each internal ear. The anterior and posterior canals are oriented at right angles to each other in the vertical plane, whereas the lateral canal lies horizontally (see Figure 15.27). Snaking through each semicircular canal is a corresponding membranous **semicircular duct,** which communicates with the utricle anteriorly. Each of these ducts has an enlarged swelling at one end called an **ampulla,** which houses an equilibrium receptor region called a *crista ampullaris* (literally, crest of the ampulla). These receptors respond to angular (rotational) movements of the head.

The Cochlea   The **cochlea,** from the Latin "snail," is a spiral, conical, bony chamber about the size of a split pea. It extends from the anterior part of the vestibule and coils for about 2½ turns around a bony pillar called the **modiolus** (mo-di'o-lus) (Figure 15.28a). Running through its center like a wedge-shaped worm is the membranous **cochlear duct,** which ends blindly at the cochlear apex. The cochlear duct houses the **spiral organ (of Corti),** the receptor organ for hearing (Figures 15.27 and 15.28b). The cochlear duct and the **osseous spiral lamina,** a thin shelflike extension of bone that spirals up the modiolus like the thread on a screw, together divide the cavity of the bony cochlea into three separate chambers or **scalae** (*scala* = ladder). The **scala vestibuli** (ska'lah věs-tǐ'bu-li), which lies superior to the cochlear duct, is continuous with the vestibule and abuts the oval window. The middle **scala media** is the cochlear duct itself. The **scala tympani,** which terminates at the round window, is inferior to the cochlear duct. Since the scala media is part of the membranous labyrinth, it is filled with endolymph. The scala vestibuli and the scala tympani, both part of the bony labyrinth, contain perilymph. The perilymph-containing chambers are continuous with each other at the cochlear apex, a region called the **helicotrema** (hel"ĭ-ko-tre'mah; "the hole in the spiral").

The "roof" of the cochlear duct, separating the scala media from the scala vestibuli, is the **vestibular membrane** (see Figure 15.28b). Its external wall, the **stria vascularis,** is composed of an unusual richly vascularized mucosa that secretes endolymph. The "floor" of the cochlear duct is composed of the bony spiral lamina and the flexible, fibrous **basilar membrane,** which supports the spiral organ (of Corti). (We will describe the spiral organ when we discuss the mechanism of hearing.) The basilar membrane, which plays a critical role in sound reception, is narrow and thick near the oval window and gradually widens and thins as it approaches the cochlear apex. The *cochlear nerve,* a division of the *vestibulocochlear* (eighth cranial) *nerve,* runs from the spiral organ through the modiolus on its way to the brain.

Physiology of Hearing

The mechanics of human hearing can be summed up in a single sprawling sentence: Sounds set up vibrations in air that beat against the eardrum that pushes a chain of tiny bones that press fluid in the internal ear against membranes that set up shearing forces that pull on the tiny hair cells that stimulate nearby neurons that give rise to impulses that travel to the brain, which interprets them—and you hear. Before we unravel this intriguing sequence, let us describe sound, the stimulus for hearing.

Overview: Properties of Sound

Light can be transmitted through a vacuum (for instance, outer space), but sound depends on an *elastic* medium for its transmission. Sound also travels much more slowly than light. Its speed in dry air is only about 331 m/s (0.2 mi/s), as opposed to the about 300,000 km/s (186,000 mi/s) of light. A lightning flash is almost instantly visible, but the sound it creates (thunder) reaches our ears much more slowly. (For each second between the lightning bolt and the roll of thunder, the storm is 1/5 mile farther away.) The speed of sound is constant in a given medium. It is greatest in solids and lowest in gases, including air.

Sound is a pressure disturbance—alternating areas of high and low pressure—produced by a vibrating object and propagated by the molecules of the medium. Consider a sound arising from a vibrating tuning fork (Figure 15.29a). If the tuning fork is struck on the left, its prongs will move first to the right, creating an area of high pressure by compressing the air molecules there. Then, as the prongs rebound to the left, the air on the left will be compressed, and the region on the right will be a rarefied, or low-pressure, area (since most of its air molecules

Q *Which scala contains endolymph?*

FIGURE 15.28   **Anatomy of the cochlea. (a)** A section through the cochlea (superior half removed). The area containing the helicotrema is the apex of the cochlea. **(b)** Magnified cross-sectional view of one turn of the cochlea, showing the relationship of the three scalae. The scalae vestibuli and tympani contain perilymph; the cochlear duct (scala media) contains endolymph. **(c)** Detailed structure of the spiral organ (of Corti). **(d)** Electron micrograph of cochlear hair cells (2000×).

have been pushed farther to the right). As the fork vibrates alternately from right to left, it produces a series of compressions and rarefactions, collectively called a *sound wave*, which moves outward in all directions (Figure 15.29b). However, the individual air molecules just vibrate back and forth for short dis-

tances as they bump other molecules and rebound. Because the outward-moving molecules give up kinetic energy to the molecules they bump, energy is always transferred in the direction the sound wave is traveling. Thus, with time and distance, the energy of the wave declines, and the sound dies a natural death.

We can illustrate a sound wave as an S-shaped curve, or *sine wave*, in which the compressed areas are crests and the rarefied areas are troughs (Figure

A   *The scala media.*

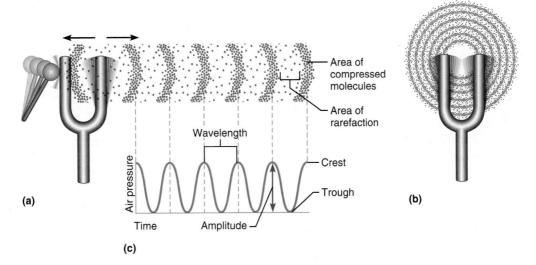

(a)

(b)

(c)

Wavelength

Air pressure

Time   Amplitude

Area of compressed molecules

Area of rarefaction

Crest

Trough

FIGURE 15.29 Sound: source and propagation. The source of sound is a vibrating object. **(a)** A tuning fork is struck on the left with a mallet. Its tines move to the right, compressing the air molecules in that region. (The tine movement is shown on the right side only and is exaggerated.) Then the tines move in the opposite direction, compressing the air there and leaving a rarefied area to the right side of the tuning fork. **(b)** In this way, sound waves, consisting of alternate areas of compression and rarefaction, are set up and radiate outward in all directions from the sound source. **(c)** The sound wave may be depicted as a sine wave. The peaks of the wave represent areas of high pressure (compressed areas), and the troughs represent areas of low pressure (rarefied areas). For any tone, the distance between two corresponding points on the wave (two crests or two troughs) is called the wavelength. The height (amplitude) of the crests is related to the energy, or intensity, of the sound wave.

15.29c). Sound can be described in terms of two physical properties inferred from this sine wave graph: frequency and amplitude.

Frequency is defined as the number of waves that pass a given point in a given time. The sine wave of a pure tone is *periodic;* that is, its crests and troughs repeat at definite distances. The distance between two consecutive crests (or troughs) is called the **wavelength** of the sound and is constant for a particular tone. The shorter the wavelength, the higher the frequency of the sound (Figure 15.30a).

The frequency range of human hearing is from 20 to 20,000 waves per second, or *hertz (Hz)*. Our ears are most sensitive to frequencies between 1500 and 4000 Hz and, in that range, we can distinguish frequencies differing by only 2–3 Hz. We perceive different sound frequencies as differences in **pitch:** The higher the frequency, the higher the pitch. A tuning fork produces a *tone*, a pure (but bland) sound with a single frequency, but most sounds are mixtures of several frequencies. It is this characteristic of sound, called **quality**, that enables us to distinguish between the same musical note—say, high C—sung by a soprano and played on a piano or clarinet, and that provides the richness and complexity of sounds (and music) that we hear.

The **amplitude**, or height, of the sine wave crests reveals a sound's intensity, which is related to its energy, or the pressure differences between its compressed and rarefied areas (Figure 15.30b).

Loudness refers to our subjective interpretation of sound intensity. Because we can hear such an enormous range of intensities, from the proverbial pin drop to a steam whistle 10 million times as intense, sound intensity (and loudness) is measured in logarithmic units called **decibels (dB)** (des′ĭ-belz). On a clinical audiometer, the decibel scale is arbitrarily set to begin at 0 dB, which is the threshold of hearing (barely audible sound) for normal ears. Each 10-dB increase represents a tenfold increase in sound intensity. A sound of 10 dB has 10 times more energy than one of 0 dB, and a 20-dB sound has 100 times (10×10) more energy than one of 0 dB. However, the same 10-dB increase represents only a twofold increase in loudness. In other words, most people would report that a 20-dB sound seems about twice as loud as a 10-dB sound. The normal range of hearing (from barely audible to the loudest sound we can process without excruciating pain) extends over a range of 120 dB. (The threshold of pain is 130 dB.)

Severe hearing loss occurs with frequent or prolonged exposure to sounds with intensities greater than 90 dB, and in the U.S., employees exposed to occupational noise over that range must wear ear (hearing) protection. This figure becomes more meaningful when you realize that a normal conversation is in the 50-dB range, a noisy restaurant has 70-dB levels, and amplified rock music is 120 dB or more, far above the 90-dB danger zone.

15

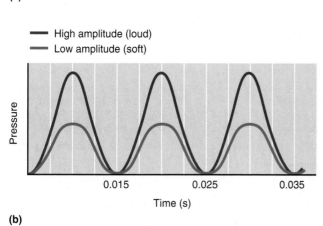

FIGURE 15.30   **Frequency and amplitude of sound waves. (a)** The wave shown in red has a shorter wavelength, and thus a greater frequency, than that shown in blue. The frequency of sound is perceived as pitch. **(b)** The wave shown in purple has a greater amplitude (intensity) than that shown in green and is perceived as being louder.

Transmission of Sound to the Internal Ear

Hearing occurs when the auditory area of the temporal lobe cortex is stimulated. However, before this can happen, sound waves must be propagated through air, membranes, bones, and fluids to reach and stimulate receptor cells in the spiral organ (of Corti) (Figure 15.31).

Airborne sound entering the external acoustic meatus strikes the tympanic membrane and sets it vibrating at the same frequency. The greater the intensity, the farther the membrane is displaced in its vibratory motion. The motion of the tympanic membrane is amplified and transferred to the oval window by the ossicle lever system, which acts much like a hydraulic press or piston to transfer the same total force hitting the eardrum to the oval window. Because the tympanic membrane is 17–20 times larger than the oval window, the pressure (force per unit area) actually exerted on the oval window is about 20 times that on the tympanic membrane. This increased pressure overcomes the stiffness and inertia of cochlear fluid and sets it into wave motion. This situation can be roughly compared to the difference in pressure relayed to the floor by the broad rubber heels of a man's shoes and a woman's tiny spike heels. The man's weight—say, 70 kg (about 150 pounds)—is spread over several square inches, and his heels will not make dents in a pliable vinyl floor. But spike heels will concentrate the same 70-kg force in an area of about 2.5 cm^2 (1 square inch) and *will* dent the floor.

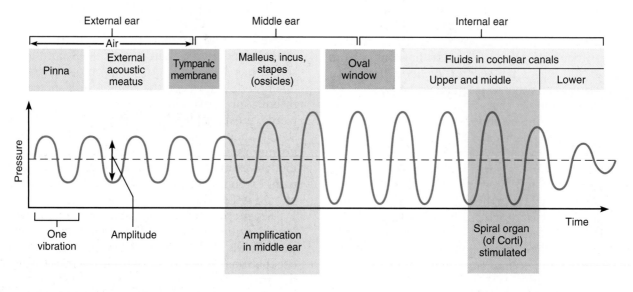

FIGURE 15.31   **Route of sound waves through the ear.** To excite the hair cells in the spiral organ (of Corti) in the internal ear, sound wave vibrations must pass through air, membranes, bones, and fluids. Note that the amplification of pressure in the middle ear is actually much larger than shown here.

Resonance of the Basilar Membrane

As the stapes rocks back and forth against the oval window, it sets the perilymph in the scala vestibuli into a similar back-and-forth motion, and a pressure wave travels through the perilymph from the basal end toward the helicotrema, much as a piece of rope held horizontally can be set into wave motion by movements initiated at one end. Sounds of very low frequency (below 20 Hz) create pressure waves that take the complete route through the cochlea—up the scala vestibuli, around the helicotrema, and back toward the round window through the scala tympani (Figure 15.32a). Such sounds do not activate the spiral organ (are below the threshold of hearing). But sounds of higher frequency (and shorter wavelengths) create pressure waves that take a "shortcut" and are transmitted through the cochlear duct into the perilymph of the scala tympani. Fluids are incompressible. Think of what happens when you sit on a water bed—you sit "here" and it bulges over "there." Thus, each time the fluid adjacent to the oval window is forced medially by the stapes, the membrane of the round window bulges laterally into the middle ear cavity and acts as a pressure valve.

As a pressure wave descends through the flexible cochlear duct, it sets the entire basilar membrane into vibration. Maximal displacement of the membrane occurs where the fibers of the basilar membranes are "tuned" to a particular sound frequency (Figure 15.32b). (This characteristic of many natural substances is called *resonance*.) The fibers of the basilar membrane span its width like the strings of a harp. The fibers near the oval window (cochlear base) are short and stiff, and they resonate in response to high-frequency pressure waves (Figure 15.32b). The longer, more floppy basilar membrane fibers near the cochlear apex resonate in time with lower-frequency pressure waves. Thus, sound signals are mechanically processed by the resonance of the basilar membrane, before ever reaching the receptors.

Excitation of Hair Cells in the Spiral Organ

The spiral organ (of Corti), which rests atop the basilar membrane, is composed of supporting cells and hearing receptor cells called *cochlear hair cells*. The hair cells are arranged functionally—specifically, one row of **inner hair cells** and three rows of **outer hair cells**—sandwiched between the tectorial and basilar membranes. Afferent fibers of the **cochlear nerve** [a division of the vestibulocochlear nerve (VIII)] are coiled about the bases of the hair cells. The hair cells have numerous *stereocilia* (actually long microvilli) and a single *kinocilium* (a true cilium) protruding from their apices. The "hairs" (stereocilia) of the hair cells are stiffened by actin filaments and linked

(a)

(b)

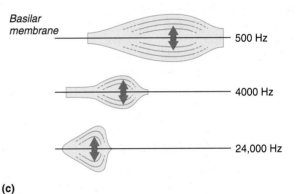

(c)

FIGURE 15.32 **Resonance of the basilar membrane and activation of the cochlear hair cells.** **(a)** The cochlea is depicted as if uncoiled. Sound waves with frequencies below the level of hearing travel through the helicotrema without exciting hair cells. Higher-frequency sounds result in pressure waves that penetrate through the cochlear duct, setting up vibrations in the basilar membrane. The basilar membrane vibrates maximally in specific areas corresponding to specific frequencies of sound. **(b)** Fibers span the width of the basilar membrane. These fibers vary in length and stiffness, being shorter and stiffer near the base of the membrane and longer and floppier near its apex. The stiffness of the fibers "tunes" specific regions of the basilar membrane to vibrate at specific frequencies. **(c)** Different frequencies of pressure waves in the cochlea cause specific places along the basilar membrane to vibrate, stimulating particular hair cells and sensory neurons. The differential stimulation of hair cells is perceived in the brain as sound of a certain pitch.

FIGURE 15.33 **Photo of cochlear hair cells with their precise arrays of stereocilia.** White arrows point to tip-links.

together by fine fibers called *tip-links* (Figure 15.33). They protrude into the K^+-rich endolymph, and the longest of them are enmeshed in the overlying, stiff gel-like **tectorial membrane** (see Figure 15.28c).

Transduction of sound stimuli occurs after the trapped stereocilia of the hair cells are "tweaked" or deflected by localized movements of the basilar membrane. Bending the cilia toward the tallest cilium (the kinocilium) puts tension on the tip-links, which in turn opens cation channels in the adjacent shorter stereocilia. This results in an inward K^+ (and Ca^{2+}) current and a graded depolarization (receptor potential). Bending the cilia away from the tallest cilium relaxes the tip-links, closes the mechanically gated ion channels, and allows repolarization and even a graded hyperpolarization. Depolarization increases intracellular Ca^{2+} and so increases the hair cells' release of neurotransmitter (glutamate), which causes the afferent cochlear fibers to transmit a faster stream of impulses to the brain for auditory interpretation. Hyperpolarization produces the exact opposite effect. As you might guess, activation of the hair cells occurs at points of vigorous basilar membrane vibration.

The outer hair cells, more numerous than the inner hair cells, send little information to the brain. Instead, they act on the basilar membrane itself. When outer hair cells depolarize and hyperpolarize as the basilar membrane moves, they contract and stretch in a type of cellular boogie called *fast motility*. Their strange behavior changes the stiffness of the basilar membrane, which alters its motion and amplifies the responsiveness of the inner hair cells—kind of a cochlear tuning. Outer hair cell mobility is also responsible for producing ear sounds *(otoacoustic emissions)* that are so audible in some people that they can actually be heard by others. In clinical pedi-

atrics, the ability to detect a stimulated otoacoustic emission has proven a quick, inexpensive way to screen newborns for hearing defects.

The vast majority of the sensory fibers of the spiral ganglia (90–95%) service the inner hair cells, which shoulder nearly the entire responsibility for sending auditory messages to the brain. By contrast, most fibers coiling around the outer hair cells are *efferent* fibers that convey messages from brain to ear. What is the brain "telling" the outer hair cells? Loud sounds activate a feedback loop from the brain stem to the outer hair cells that dampens the motion of the outer hair cells and causes the sound energy to be spread over a wider area of the basilar membrane. This may help protect the inner hair cells from damage by loud noise.

The Auditory Pathway to the Brain

The ascending auditory pathways to the brain involve several brain stem nuclei, but here we will stress only the major way stations. Impulses generated in the cochlea pass through the **spiral ganglion,** where the auditory bipolar neurons reside, and along the afferent fibers of the cochlear nerve to the **cochlear nuclei** of the medulla (Figure 15.34). From

FIGURE 15.34 **Simplified diagram of the auditory pathway to the auditory cortex of the brain.** For clarity, only the pathway from the right ear is illustrated.

there, impulses are sent on to the **superior olivary nucleus** and then via the **lateral lemniscal tract** to the **inferior colliculus** (auditory reflex center in the midbrain) and the **auditory cortex** (which provides for conscious awareness of sound) in the temporal lobe. Relays also communicate with the **medial geniculate body** of the thalamus and the **superior colliculus** of the midbrain. The colliculi act together to initiate auditory reflexes to sound, such as the startle reflex and head turning. The auditory pathway is unusual in that not all of the fibers from each ear decussate (cross over); therefore each auditory cortex receives impulses from both ears.

Auditory Processing

If you are at a Broadway musical, the sound of the instruments, the actors' voices, rustling of clothing, and closing of doors are all intermingled in your sound awareness. Yet, the auditory cortex can distinguish the separate parts of this auditory jumble. Whenever the difference between sound wavelengths is sufficient for discrimination, you hear two separate and distinct tones. In fact, the analytic powers of the auditory cortex are so great that we are able to pick single instruments out of a whole orchestra.

Cortical processing of sound stimuli is complex. For example, certain cortical cells depolarize at the beginning of a particular tone, and others depolarize when the tone ends. Some cortical cells depolarize continuously, and others appear to have high thresholds (low sensitivity), and so on. Here we will concentrate on the more straightforward aspects of cortical perception of pitch, loudness, and sound location.

Perception of Pitch   As explained, hair cells in different positions along the length of the basilar membrane are activated by sound waves of different frequencies, and impulses from specific hair cells are interpreted as specific pitches. When the sound is composed of tones of many frequencies, several populations of cochlear hair cells and cortical cells are activated simultaneously, resulting in the perception of multiple tones.

Detection of Loudness   Louder sounds cause larger movements of the tympanic membrane, auditory ossicles, and oval window, and pressure waves of greater amplitude in the fluid of the cochlea. This in turn causes larger movements of the basilar membrane, larger deflections of the hairs on the hair cells, and larger graded potentials of the hair cells. As a result, more neurotransmitter is released and action potentials are generated more frequently. The brain interprets this as increased loudness. In addition, as the release of neurotransmitter increases, more of the ten or so bipolar cells connected to a given hair cell are recruited to fire action potentials.

Localization of Sound   Several brain stem nuclei (most importantly the superior olivary nuclei) help us localize a sound's source in space by means of two cues: the *relative intensity* and the *relative timing* of sound waves reaching the two ears. If the sound source is directly in front, in back, or over the midline of the head, the intensity and timing cues are the same for both ears. However, when sound comes from one side, the receptors of the nearer ear are activated slightly earlier and more vigorously (because of the greater intensity of the sound waves entering that ear).

Homeostatic Imbalances of Hearing

Deafness

Any hearing loss, no matter how slight, is **deafness** of some sort. Deafness is classified as conduction or sensorineural deafness, according to its cause.

Conduction deafness occurs when something hampers sound conduction to the fluids of the internal ear, for example, impacted earwax blocking the external acoustic meatus or a *perforated (ruptured)* eardrum, which prevents sound conduction from the eardrum to the ossicles. But the most common causes of conduction deafness are middle ear inflammations (otitis media) and **otosclerosis** (o"to-sklĕ-ro'sis) of the ossicles. Otosclerosis ("hardening of the ear") occurs when overgrowth of bony tissue fuses the stapes foot plate to the oval window or welds the ossicles to one another. In such cases, sound is conducted to the receptors of that ear through vibrations of the skull bones, which is far less satisfactory. Otosclerosis is treated surgically.

Sensorineural deafness results from damage to neural structures at any point from the cochlear hair cells to and including the auditory cortical cells. This type of deafness typically results from the gradual loss of the hair cells throughout life. These cells can also be destroyed at an earlier age by a single explosively loud noise or prolonged exposure to high-intensity sounds, such as rock bands or airport noise, which literally tears off their cilia. Degeneration of the cochlear nerve, cerebral infarcts, and tumors in the auditory cortex are other causes. For congenital defects or age- or noise-related cochlear damage, cochlear implants (devices that convert sound energy into electrical signals) can be inserted into a drilled recess in the temporal bone. The original cochlear implants made human voices sound tinny and robotlike, but modern versions are so effective that even children born deaf can hear well enough to learn to speak well.

15

Tinnitus

Tinnitus (tĭ-ni′tus) is a ringing or clicking sound in the ears in the absence of auditory stimuli. It is more a symptom of pathology than a disease. For example, tinnitus is one of the first symptoms of cochlear nerve degeneration. It may also result from inflammation of the middle or internal ears and is a side effect of some medications, such as aspirin. Recent evidence suggests that tinnitus is analogous to phantom limb pain; that is, it is "phantom cochlear noise" caused by destruction of some neurons of the auditory pathway and the subsequent ingrowth of nearby neurons whose signals are interpreted as noise by the CNS.

Ménière's Syndrome

Classic **Ménière's syndrome** (men″ĕ-ār′z) is a labyrinth disorder that seems to affect all three parts of the internal ear. The afflicted person has repeated attacks of vertigo, nausea, and vomiting. Balance is so disturbed that standing erect is nearly impossible. A "howling" tinnitus is common, so hearing is impaired (and ultimately lost) as well. The cause is uncertain, but it may result from distortion of the membranous labyrinth by excessive endolymph accumulation, or rupture of membranes which allows the perilymph and endolymph to mix. Mild cases can usually be managed by antimotion drugs or a low-salt diet and diuretics to decrease endolymph fluid volume. In severe cases, draining the excess endolymph from the internal ear may help. A last resort is removal of the entire malfunctioning labyrinth, which is usually deferred until hearing loss is complete.

Mechanisms of Equilibrium and Orientation

The equilibrium sense is not easy to describe because it does not "see," "hear," or "feel," but responds (frequently without our awareness) to various head movements. Furthermore, this sense depends not only on inputs from the internal ear but also on vision and on information from stretch receptors of muscles and tendons. Under normal conditions the equilibrium receptors in the semicircular canals and vestibule, collectively called the **vestibular apparatus,** send signals to the brain that initiate reflexes needed to make the simplest changes in position as well as to serve a tennis ball precisely to the right spot (your opponent's backhand). The equilibrium receptors of the internal ear can be divided into two functional arms, with the receptors in the vestibule and semicircular canals monitoring **static** and **dynamic equilibrium,** respectively.

The Maculae and Static Equilibrium

The sensory receptors for static equilibrium are the **maculae** (mak′u-le; "spots"), one in each saccule wall and one in each utricle wall. These receptors monitor the position of the head in space, and in so doing, they play a key role in control of posture. They respond to *linear* acceleration forces, that is, straight-line changes in speed and direction, but not to rotation.

Anatomy of the Maculae   Each macula is a flat epithelial patch containing **hair cells** whose structure and function are basically the same as the hair cells of the cochlea. These scattered receptor cells are surrounded by **supporting cells** (Figure 15.35). The "hairs" of the hair cells are embedded in the overlying **otolithic membrane** (o′to-lith-ik), a jellylike mass studded with tiny stones (calcium carbonate

FIGURE 15.35   **Structure of a macula.** The "hairs" of the receptor cells of a macula project into the gelatinous otolithic membrane. Vestibular nerve fibers surround the base of the hair cells.

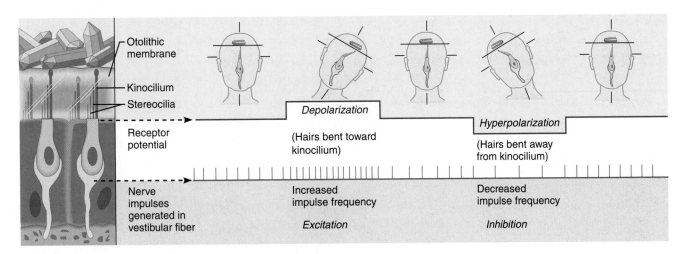

FIGURE 15.36 **The effect of gravitational pull on a macula receptor cell in the utricle.** When movement of the otolithic membrane bends the hair cells in the direction of the kinocilium, the vestibular nerve fibers depolarize and generate action potentials more rapidly. When the hairs are bent in the direction away from the kinocilium, the hair cells become hyperpolarized, and the nerve fibers send impulses at a reduced rate (i.e., below the resting rate of discharge).

crystals) called **otoliths** ("ear stones"). The otoliths, though small, are dense and they increase the membrane's weight and its inertia (resistance to change in motion). In the utricle, the macula is horizontal (Figure 15.35), and the hairs are vertically oriented when the head is upright. Thus, the utricular maculae respond best to acceleration in the horizontal plane and tilting the head to the side, because vertical (up-down) movements do not displace their horizontal otolithic membrane. In the saccule, the macula is nearly vertical, and the hairs protrude horizontally into the otolithic membrane. The saccular maculae respond best to vertical movements, such as the sudden acceleration of an elevator. The hair cells synapse with fibers of the **vestibular nerve,** whose endings coil around their bases. [Like the cochlear nerve, the vestibular nerve is a subdivision of the vestibulocochlear nerve (VIII)]. The cell bodies of the sensory neurons are located in the nearby **superior** and **inferior vestibular ganglia** (Figure 15.27).

Activating Maculae Receptors   Let's look more closely at the happenings in the maculae that lead to sensory transduction. When your head starts or stops moving in a linear direction, inertia causes the otolithic membrane to slide backward or forward like a greased plate over the hair cells, bending the hairs. For example, when you start to run, the otolithic membranes of the utricle maculae lag behind, bending the hairs backward. When you suddenly stop, the otolithic membrane slides abruptly forward (just as you slide forward in your car when you brake), bending the hair cells forward. Likewise, when you nod your head or fall, the otoliths roll inferiorly, bending the hairs of the maculae in the saccules. The hair cells release neuro-

transmitter continuously but movement of their hairs modifies the amount they release. When the hairs are bent *toward the kinocilium*, the hair cells depolarize, stepping up their pace of neurotransmitter release, and a faster stream of impulses travels up the vestibular nerve to the brain (Figure 15.36). When the hairs are bent in the opposite direction, the receptors hyperpolarize, and neurotransmitter release and impulse generation decline. In either case, the brain is informed of the changing position of the head in space.

It is important to understand that the maculae respond *only to changes* in acceleration or velocity of head movement. Because the hair cells adapt quickly (resuming their basal level of neurotransmitter release), they do not report on unchanging head positions. Thus, the maculae help us to maintain normal head position with respect to gravity. They also contribute to dynamic equilibrium by responding to changes in linear acceleration.

The Crista Ampullaris and Dynamic Equilibrium

The receptor for dynamic equilibrium, called the **crista ampullaris,** or simply *crista,* is a minute elevation in the ampulla of each semicircular canal (see Figure 15.27). Like the maculae, the cristae are excited by head movement (acceleration and deceleration), but in this case the major stimuli are rotatory (angular) movements. When you twirl on the dance floor or suffer through a rough boat ride, these gyroscope-like receptors are working overtime. Since the semicircular canals are located in all three planes of space, all rotatory movements of the head disturb one or another *pair* of cristae (one in each ear).

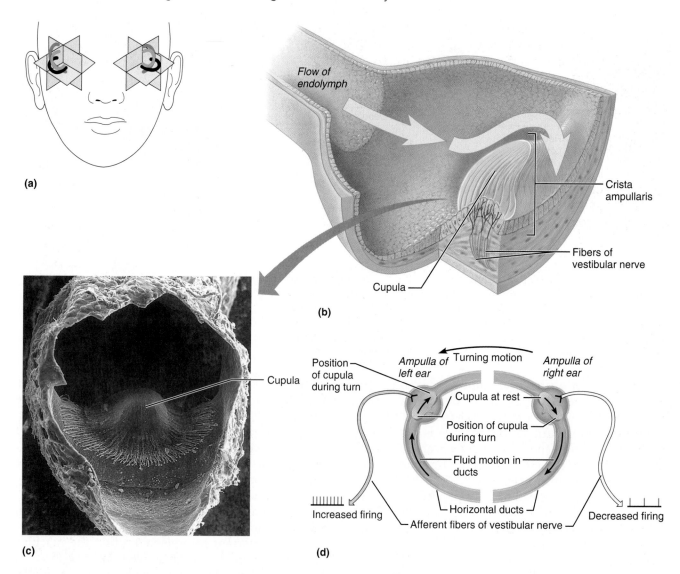

FIGURE 15.37   Location and structure of a crista ampullaris. (a) Location of the semicircular canals within the temporal bones of the skull. **(b)** The ampulla of a semicircular duct has been sectioned to show the position of a crista ampullaris receptor. **(c)** Scanning electron micrograph of a crista ampullaris (1000×). **(d)** View of the horizontal ducts from above shows how paired semicircular canals work together to provide bilateral information on rotatory head movement. Notice that the cupula bends in the direction of fluid flow, which is opposite to the direction of head movement.

Anatomy of the Crista Ampullaris   Each crista is composed of supporting cells and hair cells. These hair cells, like all those of the internal ear, have stereocilia plus one kinocilium that project into a gel-like mass. In this case, the gelled mass is a **cupula** (ku'pu-lah), which resembles a pointed cap (Figure 15.37b and c). The cupula is a delicate, loosely organized network of gelatinous strands that radiate outward to contact the "hairs" of each hair cell. Dendrites of vestibular nerve fibers encircle the base of the hair cells.

Activating Crista Ampullaris Receptors   The cristae respond to *changes* in the velocity of rotatory movements of the head. Because of its inertia, the endolymph in the semicircular ducts moves briefly in

the direction *opposite* the body's rotation, deforming the crista in the duct. As the hairs are bent, the hair cells depolarize and impulses reach the brain at a faster rate. Bending the cilia in the opposite direction causes hyperpolarization and reduces impulse generation. Because the axes of the hair cells in the complementary semicircular ducts are opposite, rotation in a given direction causes depolarization of the receptors in one ampulla of the pair, and hyperpolarization of the receptors in the other (Figure 15.37d).

   If the body continues to rotate at a constant rate, the endolymph eventually comes to rest—it moves along at the same speed as the body and stimulation of the hair cells ends. Consequently, if we are blindfolded, we cannot tell whether we are moving at a constant speed or not moving at all after the first few seconds of rotation. However, when we suddenly stop moving, the endolymph keeps on going, in effect reversing its direction within the canal. This sudden reversal in the direction of hair bending results in membrane voltage changes in the receptor cells and modifies the rate of impulse transmission, which tells the brain that we have slowed or stopped.

The key point to remember when considering both types of equilibrium receptors is that the rigid bony labyrinth moves with the body, while the fluids (and gels) within the membranous labyrinth are free to move at various rates, depending on the forces (gravity, acceleration, and so on) acting on them.

Impulses transmitted from the semicircular canals are particularly important to reflex movements of the eyes. **Vestibular nystagmus** is a complex of rather strange eye movements that occurs during and immediately after rotation. As you rotate, your eyes slowly drift in the opposite direction, as though fixed on some object in the environment. This reaction relates to the backflow of endolymph in the semicircular canals. Then, because of CNS compensating mechanisms, the eyes jump rapidly toward the direction of rotation to establish a new fixation point. These alternating eye movements continue until the endolymph comes to rest. When you stop rotating, at first your eyes continue to move in the direction of the previous spin, and then they jerk rapidly in the opposite direction. This sudden change is caused by the change in the direction in which the cristae are bent after you stop. Nystagmus is often accompanied by vertigo.

The Equilibrium Pathway to the Brain

Our responses to body imbalance, such as during stumbling, must be fast and reflexive. By the time we "thought about" correcting our fall, we would already be on the ground. Hence, information from the balance receptors goes directly to reflex centers in the brain stem, rather than to the cerebral cortex as with the other special senses. However, the nerve pathways connecting the vestibular apparatus with the brain are complex and poorly traced. The transmission sequence begins when the hair cells in the vestibular apparatus are activated. As depicted in Figure 15.38, impulses travel initially to one of two destinations: the **vestibular nuclear complex** in the brain stem or the **cerebellum.** The vestibular nuclei, the major integrative center for balance, also receive inputs from the visual and somatic receptors, particularly from proprioceptors in neck muscles that report on the position of the head. They integrate this information and then send commands to brain stem motor centers that control the extrinsic eye muscles (cranial nerve nuclei III, IV, and VI) and reflex movements of the neck, limb, and trunk muscles (via the

FIGURE 15.38   **Pathways of the balance and orientation system.** The three modes of input—vestibular, visual, and somatic (skin, muscle, and joint) receptors—transmit impulses to two major processing areas: the vestibular nuclei of the brain stem and the cerebellum. (The pathways to and the precise function of the reticular nuclei are unclear.) After vestibular nuclear processing, impulses are sent to one of two major output regions—areas controlling eye movements (oculomotor control) or those controlling the skeletal muscles of the neck (spinal motor control).

vestibulospinal tracts). The ensuing reflex movements of the eyes and body allow us to remain focused on the visual field and to quickly adjust our body position to maintain or regain balance.

The cerebellum also integrates inputs from the eyes and somatic receptors (as well as from the cerebrum). It coordinates skeletal muscle activity and regulates muscle tone so that head position, posture, and balance are maintained, often in the face of rapidly changing inputs. Its "specialty" is fine control of delicate postural movements and timing. Inputs from the eyes and somatic receptors also reach the reticular nuclei, but their precise function in equilibrium is unclear.

Notice that the vestibular apparatus does *not automatically compensate* for forces acting on the body. Its job is to send warning signals to the central nervous system, which initiates the appropriate compensations

15

(righting) to keep your body balanced, your weight evenly distributed, and your eyes focused on what you were looking at when the disturbance occurred.

◥ HOMEOSTATIC IMBALANCE

Responses to equilibrium signals are totally reflexive, and usually we are aware of vestibular apparatus activity only when its functioning is impaired. Equilibrium problems are usually obvious and unpleasant. Nausea, dizziness, and loss of balance are common and there may be nystagmus in the absence of rotational stimuli.

Motion sickness has been difficult to explain, but it appears to be due to sensory input mismatch. For example, if you are inside a ship during a storm, visual inputs indicate that your body is fixed with reference to a stationary environment (your cabin). But as the ship is tossed about by the rough seas, your vestibular apparatus detects movement and sends impulses that disagree with the visual information. The brain thus receives conflicting information, and its "confusion" somehow leads to motion sickness. Warning signals, which precede nausea and vomiting, include excessive salivation, pallor, rapid deep breathing, and profuse sweating. Removal of the stimulus usually ends the symptoms. Over-the-counter anti-motion drugs, such as meclizine (Bonine), depress vestibular inputs and help alleviate the symptoms. They are most effective when taken "before the fact." Scopolamine-containing timed-release skin patches are also used to head off motion sickness. ●

Developmental Aspects of the Special Senses

Taste and Smell

All the special senses are functional, to a greater or lesser degree, at birth. Smell and taste are sharp, and infants relish food that adults consider bland or tasteless. Some researchers claim that smell is just as important as touch in guiding newborn infants to their mother's breast. However, very young children seem indifferent to odors and can play happily with their own feces.

There are few problems with the chemical senses during childhood and young adulthood. Women generally have a more acute sense of smell than men, and nonsmokers have a sharper sense of smell than smokers. Beginning in the fourth decade of life, our ability to taste and smell declines due to the gradual loss of receptors, which are replaced more slowly than in younger people. More than half of people over the age of 65 years have serious problems detecting odors, which may explain their tendency to douse themselves with large amounts of cologne, or their inattention to formerly disagreeable odors. Additionally, their sense of taste is poor. This along with the decline in the sense of smell makes food taste bland and results in loss of appetite.

Vision

By the fourth week of development, the beginnings of the eyes are seen in the **optic vesicles** that protrude from the diencephalon (see Figure 12.2c on p. 432). Soon these hollow vesicles indent to form double-layered **optic cups,** and their stalks form the optic nerves and provide a pathway for blood vessels to reach the eye interior. Once an optic vesicle reaches the overlying surface ectoderm, it induces the ectoderm to thicken and then form a **lens vesicle** that pinches off into the cavity of the optic cup, where it becomes the lens. The lining (internal layer) of the optic cup becomes the neural retina, and the outer layer forms the pigmented layer of the retina. The rest of the eye tissues and the vitreous humor are formed by mesenchymal cells derived from the mesoderm that surrounds the optic cup.

In the darkness of the uterus, the fetus cannot see. Nonetheless, even before the light-sensitive portions of the photoreceptors develop, the central nervous system connections have been made and are functional. During infancy, synaptic connections are fine-tuned, and the typical cortical fields that allow binocular vision are established.

◥ HOMEOSTATIC IMBALANCE

Congenital problems of the eyes are relatively uncommon, but their incidence is dramatically increased by certain maternal infections, particularly rubella (German measles), occurring during the critical first three months of pregnancy. Common rubella sequels include blindness and cataracts. ●

As a rule, vision is the only special sense not fully functional at birth. Because the eyeballs are foreshortened, most babies are hyperopic. The newborn infant sees only in gray tones, eye movements are uncoordinated, and often only one eye at a time is used. The lacrimal glands are not completely developed until about two weeks after birth, so babies are tearless for this period, even though they may cry lustily. By 5 months, infants can follow moving objects with their eyes, but visual acuity is still poor (20/200). By the age of 5 years, depth perception is present and color vision is well developed. Because the eyeball has grown, visual acuity has improved to about 20/30, providing a readiness to begin reading. By first grade, the initial hyperopia has usually been replaced by emmetropia, and the eye reaches its adult size at 8–9 years of age. Emmetropia usually continues until presbyopia begins to set in around age 40 owing to decreasing lens elasticity.

With age, the lens loses its crystal clarity and discolors. As a result, it begins to scatter light, causing a glare that is distressing when driving at night. The dilator pupillae muscles become less efficient, so the pupils stay partly constricted. These two changes together decrease the amount of light reaching the retina, and visual acuity is dramatically lower in people over 70. In addition, the lacrimal glands are less active and the eyes tend to be dry and more susceptible to infection. Elderly persons are also at risk for certain conditions that cause blindness, such as macular degeneration, glaucoma, cataracts, arteriosclerosis, and diabetes mellitus.

Hearing and Balance

Development of the ear begins in the three-week embryo. The internal ears develop first, from thickenings of the surface ectoderm called the **otic placodes** (o'tik), which lie lateral to the hindbrain on each side. The otic placode invaginates, forming the **otic pit** and then the **otic vesicle,** which detaches from the surface epithelium. The otic vesicle develops into the membranous labyrinth. The surrounding mesenchyme forms the bony labyrinth.

The middle ear cavity and pharyngotympanic tube of the middle ear develop from **pharyngeal pouches,** lateral outpocketings of the endoderm lining the pharynx. The auditory ossicles develop from neural crest cells.

The external acoustic meatus and external face of the tympanic membrane of the external ear differentiate from the **branchial groove** (brang'ke-al), an indentation of the surface ectoderm, and the auricle develops from swellings of the surrounding tissue.

Newborn infants can hear, but early responses to sound are mostly reflexive—for example, crying and clenching the eyelids in response to a startling noise. By the fourth month, infants will turn to the voices of family members. Critical listening begins as toddlers increase their vocabulary, and good language skills are closely tied to the ability to hear well.

> ## HOMEOSTATIC IMBALANCE

Congenital abnormalities of the ears are fairly common. Examples include partly or completely missing pinnae and closed or absent external acoustic meatuses. Maternal rubella during the first trimester commonly results in sensorineural deafness. ●

Except for ear inflammations, mostly due to infections, few problems affect the ears during childhood and adult life. By the 60s, however, deterioration of the spiral organ becomes noticeable. We are born with approximately 40,000 hair cells, but their number decreases when they are damaged or destroyed by loud noises, disease, or drugs. The hair cells *are* replaced, but at such a slow rate that there really is no functional regeneration. It is estimated that if we were to live 140 years, we would have lost all of our hearing receptors.

The ability to hear high-pitched sounds leaves us first. This condition, called **presbycusis** (pres"bĭ-ku'sis), is a type of sensorineural deafness. Although presbycusis is considered a disability of old age, it is becoming much more common in younger people as our world grows noisier. Since noise is a stressor, one of its physiological consequences is vasoconstriction, and when delivery of blood to the ear is reduced, the ear becomes even more sensitive to the damaging effects of noise.

■ ■ ■

Our abilities to see, hear, taste, and smell—and some of our responses to the effects of gravity—are largely the work of our brain. However, as we have discovered in this, the last of the nervous system chapters, the large and often elaborate sensory receptor organs that serve the special senses are works of art in and of themselves.

The final chapter of this unit describes how the body's functions are controlled by chemicals called hormones in a manner quite different from what we have described for neural control.

Related Clinical Terms

Ageusia (ah-gu'ze-ah) Loss or impairment of the taste sense.

Age-related macular degeneration (ARMD) Progressive deterioration of the retina that affects the macula lutea and leads to loss of central vision; the main cause of vision loss in those over age 65. Early stages and mild forms involve the buildup of pigments in the macula and impaired functioning of the pigmented epithelium. Continued accumulation of pigment leads to the "dry" form of ARMD, in which many pigment epithelial cells and macular photoreceptors die. Less common is the "wet" form in which an overgrowth of new blood vessels invades the retina from the choroid. Leakage of blood and fluids from these vessels causes scarring

and detachment of the retina. The cause is unknown and ARMD is largely untreatable, although laser treatment can destroy some of the growing vessels in the "wet" form.

Blepharitis (blef"ah-ri'tis; *blephar* = eyelash; *itis* = inflammation) Inflammation of the margins of the eyelids.

Enucleation (e-nu"kle-a'shun) Surgical removal of an eyeball.

Exophthalmos (ek"sof-thal'mos; *exo* = out; *phthalmo* = the eye) Anteriorly bulging eyeballs; this condition is seen in some cases of hyperthyroidism.

Labyrinthitis Inflammation of the labyrinth.

Ophthalmology (of"thal-mol'o-je) The science that studies the eye and eye diseases. An ophthalmologist is a medical doctor who specializes in treating eye disorders.

Optometrist A licensed nonphysician who measures vision and prescribes corrective lenses.

Otalgia (o-tal'je-ah; *algia* = pain) Earache.

Otitis externa Inflammation and infection of the external acoustic meatus, caused by bacteria or fungi that enter the canal from outside, especially when the canal is moist (e.g., after swimming).

Papilledema (pap"il-ĕ-de'mah; *papill* = nipple; *edema* = swelling) Protrusion of the optic disc into the eyeball, which can be observed by ophthalmoscopic examination; caused by conditions that increase intracranial pressure.

Scotoma (sko-to'mah; *scoot* = darkness) A blind spot other than the normal (optic disc) blind spot; many causes, including the presence of a brain tumor pressing on fibers of the visual pathway, and stroke.

Trachoma (trah-ko'mah; *trach* = rough) A highly contagious bacterial (chlamydial) infection of the conjunctiva and cornea. Common worldwide, it blinds millions of people in poor countries of Africa and Asia; treated with eye ointments containing antibiotic drugs.

Weber's test Hearing test during which a sounding tuning fork is held to the forehead. In those with normal hearing, the tone is heard equally in both ears. The tone will be heard best in the "good" ear if sensorineural deafness is present, and in the "bad" ear if conduction deafness is present.

Chapter Summary

The Eye and Vision (pp. 556–578)

1. The eye is enclosed in the bony orbit and cushioned by fat.

Accessory Structures of the Eye (pp. 556–559)

2. Eyebrows help to shade and protect the eyes.

3. Eyelids protect and lubricate the eyes by reflex blinking. Within the eyelids are the orbicularis oculi and levator palpebrae muscles, and modified sebaceous and sweat glands.

4. The conjunctiva is a mucosa that lines the eyelids and covers the anterior eyeball surface. Its mucus lubricates the eyeball surface.

5. The lacrimal apparatus consists of the lacrimal gland (which produces a saline solution containing mucus, lysozyme, and antibodies), the lacrimal canaliculi, the lacrimal sac, and the nasolacrimal duct.

6. The extrinsic eye muscles (superior, inferior, lateral, and medial rectus and superior and inferior oblique) move the eyeballs.

Structure of the Eyeball (pp. 559–565)

7. The wall of the eyeball is made up of three layers. The outermost fibrous layer consists of the sclera and the cornea. The sclera protects the eye and gives it shape; the cornea allows light to enter the eye.

8. The middle, pigmented vascular layer (uvea) consists of the choroid, the ciliary body, and the iris. The choroid provides nutrients to the eye and prevents light scattering within the eye. The ciliary muscles of the ciliary body control lens shape; the iris controls the size of the pupil.

9. The sensory layer, or retina, consists of an outer pigmented layer and an inner neural layer. The neural layer contains photoreceptors (rods and cones), bipolar cells, and ganglion cells. Ganglion cell axons form the optic nerve, which exits via the optic disc ("blind spot").

10. The outer segments of the photoreceptors contain the light-absorbing pigment in membrane-bounded discs.

11. The posterior segment of the eyeball, behind the lens, contains vitreous humor, which helps support the eyeball and keep the retina in place. The anterior segment, anterior to the lens, is filled with aqueous humor, formed by capillaries in the ciliary processes and drained into the scleral venous sinus. Aqueous humor is a major factor in maintaining intraocular pressure.

12. The biconvex lens is suspended within the eye by the ciliary zonule attached to the ciliary body. It is the only adjustable refractory structure of the eye.

Physiology of Vision (pp. 565–578)

13. Light is made up of those wavelengths of the electromagnetic spectrum that excite the photoreceptors.

14. Light is refracted (bent) when passing from one transparent medium to another of different density. Concave lenses disperse light; convex lenses converge light and bring its rays to a focal point. The greater the lens curvature, the more light bends.

15. As light passes through the eye, it is bent by the cornea and the lens and focused on the retina. The cornea accounts for most of the refraction, but the lens allows active focusing for different distances.

16. Focusing for distance vision requires no special movements of the eye structures. Focusing for close-up vision requires accommodation (bulging of the lens), pupillary constriction, and convergence of the eyeballs. All three reflexes are controlled by cranial nerve III.

17. Refractory problems include presbyopia, myopia, hyperopia, and astigmatism.

18. Rods respond to low-intensity light and provide night and peripheral vision. Cones are bright-light, high-discrimination receptors that provide for color vision. Anything that must be viewed precisely is focused on the cone-rich fovea centralis.

19. The light-absorbing molecule retinal is combined with various opsins in the visual pigments. When struck by light, retinal changes shape (11-*cis* to all-*trans*) and activates opsin. Activated opsin activates transducin (a G protein) which in turn activates PDE, an enzyme that breaks down cGMP, allowing the cation channels to close. This results in hyperpolarization of the receptor cells and inhibits their release of neurotransmitter.

20. Rod visual pigment, rhodopsin, is a combination of retinal and opsin. The light-triggered changes in retinal cause hyperpolarization of the rods. Photoreceptors and bipolar cells generate graded potentials only; action potentials are generated by the ganglion cells.

21. The three types of cones all contain retinal, but each has a different type of opsin. Each cone type responds maximally to one color of light: red, blue, or green. The chemistry of cone function is similar to that of rods.

22. During light adaptation, photopigments are bleached and rods are inactivated; then, as cones decrease their light sensitivity, high-acuity vision ensues. In dark adaptation, cones cease functioning, and visual acuity decreases; rod function begins when sufficient rhodopsin has accumulated.

23. The visual pathway to the brain begins with the optic nerve fibers (ganglion cell axons) from the retina. At the optic chiasma, fibers from the medial half of each retina cross over and continue on in the optic tracts to the thalamus. Thalamic neurons project to the visual cortex via the optic radiation. Fibers also project from the retina to the midbrain pretectal nuclei and the superior colliculi, and to the suprachiasmatic nucleus of the hypothalamus.

24. Each eye receives a slightly different view of the visual field. These views are fused by the visual cortices to provide for depth perception.

25. Retinal processing involves the selective destruction of inputs so as to emphasize bright/dark or color contrasts (edges). (The horizontal cells and amacrine cells are local integrator cells of the retina that modify and process inputs to the ganglion cells.) Thalamic processing subserves high-acuity color vision and depth perception. Cortical processing involves neurons of the striate (primary) cortex, which receive inputs from the retinal ganglion cells, and neurons of the prestriate (association) cortices, which receive inputs from striate cortical cells and mostly integrate inputs concerned with color, form, and movement. Visual processing also proceeds anteriorly in the "what" and "where" processing streams via the temporal and parietal lobes, respectively.

The Chemical Senses: Taste and Smell (pp. 578–583)

The Olfactory Epithelium and the Sense of Smell (pp. 578–580)

1. The olfactory epithelium is located in the roof of the nasal cavity. The receptor cells are ciliated bipolar neurons. Their axons are the filaments of the olfactory nerve (cranial nerve I).

2. Individual olfactory neurons show a range of responsiveness to different chemicals. Olfactory cells bearing the same odorant receptors synapse in the same glomerulus type.

3. Olfactory neurons are excited by volatile chemicals that bind to receptors in the olfactory cilia.

4. Action potentials of the olfactory nerve filaments are transmitted to the olfactory bulb where the filaments synapse with mitral cells. The mitral cells send impulses via the olfactory tract to the olfactory cortex. Fibers carrying impulses from the olfactory receptors also project to the limbic system.

Taste Buds and the Sense of Taste (pp. 580–583)

5. The taste buds are scattered in the oral cavity and pharynx but are most abundant on the tongue papillae.

6. Gustatory cells, the epithelial receptor cells of the taste buds, have gustatory hairs (microvilli) that serve as the receptor regions. The gustatory cells are excited by the binding of tastants (food chemicals) to receptors on their microvilli.

7. The five basic taste qualities are sweet, sour, salty, bitter, and umami.

8. The taste sense is served by cranial nerves VII, IX, and X, which send impulses to the solitary nucleus of the medulla. From there, impulses are sent to the thalamus and the taste cortex.

Homeostatic Imbalances of the Chemical Senses (p. 583)

9. Most chemical sense dysfunctions are olfactory disorders (anosmias). Common causes are nasal damage or obstruction.

The Ear: Hearing and Balance (pp. 583–598)

Structure of the Ear (pp. 583–587)

1. The auricle and external acoustic meatus compose the external ear. The tympanic membrane, the boundary between the outer and middle ears, transmits sound waves to the middle ear.

2. The middle ear is a small chamber within the temporal bone, connected by the pharyngotympanic tube to the nasopharynx. The ossicles, which help to amplify sound, span the middle ear cavity and transmit sound vibrations from the eardrum to the oval window.

3. The internal ear consists of the bony labyrinth, within which the membranous labyrinth is suspended. The bony labyrinth chambers contain perilymph; the membranous labyrinth ducts and sacs contain endolymph.

4. The vestibule contains the saccule and utricle. The semicircular canals extend posteriorly from the vestibule in three planes. They contain the semicircular ducts.

5. The cochlea houses the cochlear duct (scala media), containing the spiral organ (of Corti), the receptor organ for hearing. Within the cochlear duct, the hair (receptor) cells rest on the basilar membrane, and their hairs project into the gelatinous tectorial membrane.

Physiology of Hearing (pp. 587–593)

6. Sound originates from a vibrating object and travels in waves consisting of alternating areas of compression and rarefaction of the medium.

7. The distance from crest to crest on a sine wave is the sound's wavelength; the shorter the wavelength, the higher the frequency (measured in hertz). Frequency is perceived as pitch.

8. The amplitude of sound is the height of the peaks of the sine wave, which reflect the sound's intensity. Sound intensity is measured in decibels. Intensity is perceived as loudness.

9. Sound passing through the external acoustic meatus sets the eardrum into vibration at the same frequency. The ossicles amplify and deliver the vibrations to the oval window.

10. Pressure waves in cochlear fluids set specific locations on the basilar membrane into resonance. At points of maximal membrane vibration, the hair cells of the spiral organ are alternately depolarized and hyperpolarized by the vibratory motion. Movements of the stereocilia toward the kinocilium depolarize the hair cells and increase the rate of impulse generation in the auditory nerve fibers. Movements away from the kinocilium have the opposite effect. High-frequency sounds stimulate hair cells near the oval window; low-frequency sounds stimulate hair cells near the apex. Most auditory inputs are sent to the brain by inner hair cells. Outer hair cells amplify responsiveness of the inner hair cells.

11. Impulses generated along the cochlear nerve travel to the cochlear nuclei of the medulla and from there through several brain stem nuclei to the medial geniculate body of the thalamus and then the auditory cortex. Each auditory cortex receives impulses from both ears.

12. Auditory processing is analytic; each tone is perceived separately. Perception of pitch is related to the position of the excited hair cells along the basilar membrane. Intensity perception reflects the fact that as sound intensity increases, basilar membrane mobility is increased and the frequency of impulse transmission to the cortex is enhanced. Cues for sound localization include the intensity and timing of sound arriving at each ear.

Homeostatic Imbalances of Hearing (pp. 593–594)

13. Conduction deafness results from interference with conduction of sound vibrations to the fluids of the internal ear. Sensorineural deafness reflects damage to neural structures.

14. Tinnitus is an early sign of sensorineural deafness; it may also result from the use of certain drugs.

15

15. Ménière's syndrome is a disorder of the membranous labyrinth. Symptoms include tinnitus, deafness, and vertigo. Excessive endolymph accumulation is the suspected cause.

Mechanisms of Equilibrium and Orientation (pp. 594–598)

16. The equilibrium receptor regions of the internal ear are called the vestibular apparatus.

17. The receptors for static equilibrium are the maculae of the saccule and utricle. A macula consists of hair cells with stereocilia and a kinocilium embedded in an overlying otolithic membrane. Linear movements cause the otolithic membrane to move, pulling on the hair cells and changing the rate of impulse generation in the vestibular nerve fibers.

18. The dynamic equilibrium receptor, the crista ampullaris within each semicircular duct, responds to angular or rotatory movements in one plane. It consists of a tuft of hair cells whose microvilli are embedded in the gelatinous cupula. Rotatory movements cause the endolymph to flow in the opposite direction, bending the cupula and either exciting or inhibiting the hair cells.

19. Impulses from the vestibular apparatus are sent via vestibular nerve fibers mainly to the vestibular complex of the brain stem and the cerebellum. These centers initiate responses that fix the eyes on objects and activate muscles to maintain balance.

Developmental Aspects of the Special Senses (pp. 598–599)

Taste and Smell (pp. 598)

1. The chemical senses are sharpest at birth and gradually decline with age as replacement of the receptor cells becomes more sluggish.

Vision (pp. 598–599)

2. Congenital eye problems are uncommon, but maternal rubella can cause blindness.

3. The eye starts as an optic vesicle, an outpocketing of the diencephalon that invaginates to form the optic cup, which becomes the retina. Overlying ectoderm folds to form the lens vesicle, which gives rise to the lens. The remaining eye tissues and the accessory structures are formed by mesenchyme.

4. The eye is foreshortened at birth and reaches adult size at the age of 8–9 years. Depth perception and color vision develop during early childhood.

5. With age, the lens loses its elasticity and clarity, there is a decline in the ability of the iris to dilate, and visual acuity decreases. The elderly are at risk for eye problems resulting from dry eyes and disease.

Hearing and Balance (pp. 599)

6. The membranous labyrinth develops from the otic placode, an ectodermal thickening lateral to the hindbrain. Mesenchyme forms the surrounding bony structures. Pharyngeal pouch endoderm, in conjunction with mesenchyme, forms most middle ear structures; the external ear is formed largely by ectoderm.

7. Congenital ear problems are fairly common. Maternal rubella can cause deafness.

8. Response to sound in infants is reflexive. By 5 months, an infant can locate sound. Critical listening develops in toddlers.

9. Deterioration of the spiral organ (of Corti) occurs throughout life as noise, disease, and drugs destroy cochlear hair cells. Age-related loss of hearing (presbycusis) occurs in the 60s and 70s.

Review Questions

Multiple Choice/Matching

(Some questions have more than one correct answer. Select the best answer or answers from the choices given.)

1. The accessory glands that produce an oily secretion are the (a) conjunctiva, (b) lacrimal glands, (c) tarsal glands.

2. The portion of the fibrous layer that is white and opaque is the (a) choroid, (b) cornea, (c) retina, (d) sclera.

3. Which sequence best describes a normal route for the flow of tears from the eyes into the nasal cavity? (a) lacrimal canaliculi, nasolacrimal ducts, nasal cavity; (b) lacrimal ducts, lacrimal canaliculi, nasolacrimal ducts; (c) nasolacrimal ducts, lacrimal canaliculi, lacrimal sacs.

4. Four refractory media of the eye, listed in the sequence in which they refract light, are (a) vitreous humor, lens, aqueous humor, cornea; (b) cornea, aqueous humor, lens, vitreous humor; (c) cornea, vitreous humor, lens, aqueous humor; (d) lens, aqueous humor, cornea, vitreous humor.

5. Damage to the medial recti muscles would probably affect (a) accommodation, (b) refraction, (c) convergence, (d) pupil constriction.

6. The phenomenon of light adaptation is best explained by the fact that (a) rhodopsin does not function in dim light, (b) rhodopsin breakdown occurs slowly, (c) rods exposed to intense light need time to generate rhodopsin, (d) cones are stimulated to function by bright light.

7. Blockage of the scleral venous sinus might result in (a) a sty, (b) glaucoma, (c) conjunctivitis, (d) a cataract.

8. Nearsightedness is more properly called (a) myopia, (b) hyperopia, (c) presbyopia, (d) emmetropia.

9. Of the neurons in the retina, the axons of which of these form the optic nerve? (a) bipolar neurons, (b) ganglion cells, (c) cone cells, (d) horizontal cells.

10. Which sequence of reactions occurs when a person looks at a distant object? (a) pupils constrict, ciliary zonule (suspensory ligament) relaxes, lenses become less convex; (b) pupils dilate, ciliary zonule becomes taut, lenses become less convex; (c) pupils dilate, ciliary zonule becomes taut, lenses become more convex; (d) pupils constrict, ciliary zonule relaxes, lenses become more convex.

11. During embryonic development, the lens of the eye forms (a) as part of the choroid coat, (b) from the surface ectoderm overlying the optic cup, (c) as part of the sclera, (d) from mesodermal tissue.

12. The blind spot of the eye is (a) where more rods than cones are found, (b) where the macula lutea is located, (c) where only cones occur, (d) where the optic nerve leaves the eye.

13. Olfactory tract damage would probably affect your ability to (a) see, (b) hear, (c) feel pain, (d) smell.

14. Sensory impulses transmitted over the facial, glossopharyngeal, and vagus nerves are involved in the sensation of (a) taste, (b) touch, (c) equilibrium, (d) smell.

15. Taste buds are found on the (a) anterior part of the tongue, (b) posterior part of the tongue, (c) palate, (d) all of these.

16. Gustatory cells are stimulated by (a) movement of otoliths, (b) stretch, (c) substances in solution, (d) photons of light.

17. Cells in the olfactory bulb that act as local "integrators" of olfactory inputs are the (a) hair cells, (b) granule cells, (c) basal cells, (d) mitral cells, (e) supporting cells.

18. Olfactory nerve filaments are found (a) in the optic bulbs, (b) passing through the cribriform plate of the ethmoid bone, (c) in the optic tracts, (d) in the olfactory cortex.

19. Conduction of sound from the middle ear to the internal ear occurs via vibration of the (a) malleus against the tympanic membrane, (b) stapes in the oval window, (c) incus in the round window, (d) stapes against the tympanic membrane.

20. The transmission of sound vibrations through the internal ear occurs chiefly through (a) nerve fibers, (b) air, (c) fluid, (d) bone.

21. Which of the following statements does not correctly describe the spiral organ (of Corti)? (a) sounds of high frequency stimulate hair cells at the basal end, (b) the "hairs" of the receptor cells are embedded in the tectorial membrane, (c) the basilar membrane acts as a resonator, (d) the more numerous outer hair cells are largely responsible for our perception of sound.

22. Pitch is to frequency of sound as loudness is to (a) quality, (b) intensity, (c) overtones, (d) all of these.

23. The structure that allows pressure in the middle ear to be equalized with atmospheric pressure is the (a) pinna, (b) pharyngotympanic tube, (c) tympanic membrane, (d) oval window.

24. Which of the following is important in maintaining the balance of the body? (a) visual cues, (b) semicircular canals, (c) the saccule, (d) proprioceptors, (e) all of these.

25. Static equilibrium receptors that report the position of the head in space relative to the pull of gravity are (a) spiral organ, (b) maculae, (c) cristae ampullares, (d) otoliths.

26. Which of the following is *not* a possible cause of conduction deafness? (a) impacted cerumen, (b) middle ear infection, (c) cochlear nerve degeneration, (d) otosclerosis.

27. Which of the following are intrinsic eye muscles? (a) superior rectus, (b) orbicularis oculi, (c) smooth muscles of the iris and ciliary body, (d) levator palpebrae superioris.

28. Which lies closest to the exact posterior pole of the eye? (a) optic nerve, (b) optic disc, (c) macula lutea, (d) point of entry of central artery into the eye.

29. Otoliths (ear stones) are (a) a cause of deafness, (b) a type of hearing aid, (c) important in equilibrium, (d) the rock-hard petrous temporal bones.

Short Answer Essay Questions

30. Name the five primary taste qualities and the cranial nerves that serve the sense of taste.

31. Where are the olfactory receptors, and why is that site poorly suited for their job?

32. Why do you often have to blow your nose after crying?

33. How do rods and cones differ functionally?

34. Where is the fovea centralis, and why is it important?

35. Describe the response of rhodopsin to light stimuli. What is the outcome of this cascade of events?

36. Since there are only three types of cones, how can you explain the fact that we see many more colors?

37. Describe the effect of aging on the special sense organs.

38. Each olfactory cell responds to a single odorant molecule. True or false? Explain your choice.

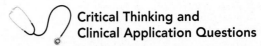

Critical Thinking and Clinical Application Questions

1. During an ophthalmoscopic examination, Mrs. James was found to have bilateral papilledema. Further investigation indicated that this condition resulted from a rapidly growing intracranial tumor. First, define papilledema. Then, explain its presence in terms of Mrs. James's diagnosis.

2. Sally, a 9-year-old girl, told the clinic physician that her "ear lump hurt" and she kept "getting dizzy and falling down." As she told her story, she pointed to her mastoid process. An otoscopic examination of the external acoustic meatus revealed a red, swollen eardrum, and her throat was inflamed. Her condition was described as mastoiditis with secondary labyrinthitis (inflammation of the labyrinth). Describe the most likely route of infection and the infected structures in Sally's case. Also explain the cause of her dizziness and falling.

3. Mr. Gaspe appeared at the eye clinic complaining of a chip of wood in his eye. No foreign body was found, but the conjunctiva was obviously inflamed. What name is given to this inflammatory condition, and where would you look for a foreign body that has been floating around on the eye surface for a while?

4. Mrs. Orlando has been noticing flashes of light and tiny specks in her right visual field. When she begins to see a "veil" floating before her right eye, she makes an appointment to see the eye doctor. What is your diagnosis? Is the condition serious? Explain.

5. David Norris, an engineering student, has been working in a disco to earn money to pay for his education. After about eight months, he notices that he is having problems hearing high-pitched tones. What is the cause-and-effect relationship here?

6. Assume that a tumor in the pituitary gland or hypothalamus is protruding inferiorly and compressing the optic chiasma. What could be the visual outcome?

7. Four-year-old Gary Zammer is brought to the ophthalmologist for a routine checkup on his vision. Gary is an albino. How do you think albinism affects vision?

8. Right before Jan, a senior citizen, had a large plug of earwax cleaned from her ear, she developed a constant howling sound in her ear that would not stop. It was very annoying and stressful, and she had to go to counseling to learn how to live with this awful noise. What was her condition called?

9. During an anatomy and physiology lab exercise designed to teach the use of the ophthalmoscope, you notice that your lab partner has difficulty seeing objects in the darkened room. Upon examining her retina through the ophthalmoscope, you observe streaks and patches of dark pigmentation at the back of the eye. What might this condition be?

10. Henri, a chef in a five-star French restaurant, has been diagnosed with leukemia. He is about to undergo chemotherapy, which will kill rapidly dividing cells in his body. He needs to continue working between bouts of chemotherapy. What consequences of chemotherapy would you predict that might affect his job as a chef?

LOOKING FOR MORE STUDY HELP?
A wide variety of quiz questions, tutorials, and learning exercises are available online at the Anatomy & Physiology Place (www.anatomyandphysiology.com) and, if your instructor has provided you with a MyA&P Course ID number, MyA&P (www.myaandp.com).

15

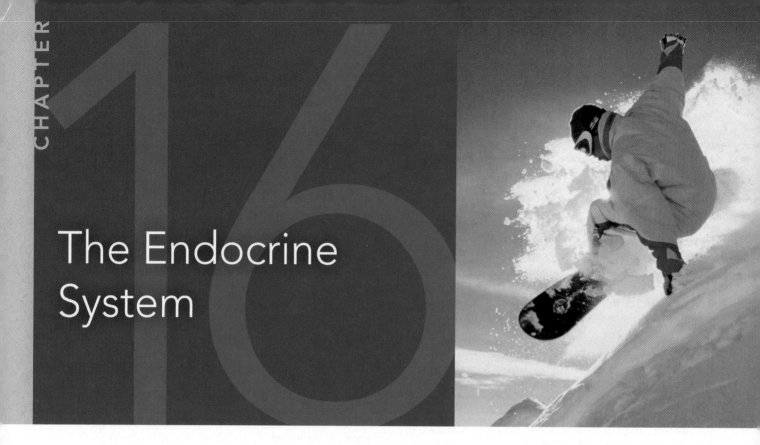

The Endocrine System

1. Indicate important differences between hormonal and neural controls of body functioning.

The Endocrine System: An Overview (pp. 605–606)

2. List the major endocrine organs, and describe their body locations.
3. Distinguish between hormones, paracrines, and autocrines.

Hormones (pp. 606–612)

4. Describe how hormones are classified chemically.
5. Describe the two major mechanisms by which hormones bring about their effects on their target tissues.
6. List three kinds of interaction of different hormones acting on the same target cell.
7. Explain how hormone release is regulated.

Major Endocrine Organs (pp. 612–636)

8. Describe structural and functional relationships between the hypothalamus and the pituitary gland.
9. List and describe the chief effects of adenohypophyseal hormones.
10. Discuss the structure of the neurohypophysis, and describe the effects of the two hormones it releases.
11. Describe important effects of the two groups of hormones produced by the thyroid gland. Follow the process of thyroxine formation and release.
12. Indicate general functions of parathyroid hormone.
13. List hormones produced by the adrenal gland, and cite their physiological effects.

14. Compare and contrast the effects of the two major pancreatic hormones.
15. Describe the functional roles of hormones of the testes and ovaries.
16. Briefly describe the importance of thymic and pineal hormones.

Other Hormone-Producing Structures (p. 636–638)

17. Name a hormone produced by the heart, and localize enteroendocrine cells.
18. Briefly explain the hormonal functions of the placenta, kidney, skin, and adipose tissue.

Developmental Aspects of the Endocrine System (p. 639)

19. Describe the effects of aging on endocrine system functioning.

You don't have to watch *CSI* to experience action-packed drama. Molecules and cells inside your body have dynamic adventures on microscopic levels all the time. For instance, when insulin molecules, carried passively along in the blood, attach to protein receptors of nearby cells, the response is dramatic: Glucose molecules begin to disappear from the blood into the cells, and cellular activity accelerates. Such is the power of the second great control system of the body, the **endocrine system,** which interacts with the nervous system to coordinate and integrate the activity of body cells.

The means of control and the speed of the endocrine system are very different from those of the nervous system, however. The nervous system regulates the activity of muscles and glands via electrochemical impulses delivered by neurons, and those organs respond within milliseconds. The endocrine system influences metabolic activity by means of **hormones** (*hormon* = to excite), which are chemical messengers released into the blood to be transported throughout the body. Binding of a hormone to cellular receptors initiates responses that typically occur after a lag period of seconds or even days. But, once initiated, those responses tend to be much more prolonged than those induced by the nervous system.

Hormonal targets ultimately include most cells of the body, and hormones have widespread and diverse effects. The major processes controlled and integrated by these "mighty molecules" are reproduction; growth and development; mobilization of body defenses; maintenance of electrolyte, water, and nutrient balance of the blood; and regulation of cellular metabolism and energy balance. As you can see, the endocrine system orchestrates processes that go on for relatively long periods, in some instances continuously. The scientific study of hormones and the endocrine organs is called **endocrinology.**

The Endocrine System: An Overview

Compared with other organs of the body, those of the endocrine system are small and unimpressive. Indeed, to collect 1 kg (2.2 lb) of hormone-producing tissue, you would need to collect *all* the endocrine tissue from eight or nine adults! In addition, the anatomical continuity typical of most organ systems does not exist in the endocrine system. Instead, endocrine organs are widely scattered about the body.

As explained in Chapter 4, there are two kinds of glands. *Exocrine glands* produce nonhormonal substances, such as sweat and saliva, and have ducts through which these substances are routed to a membrane surface. **Endocrine glands,** also called

FIGURE 16.1 **Location of the major endocrine organs of the body.**

ductless glands, produce hormones and lack ducts. They release their hormones into the surrounding tissue fluid (*endo* = within; *crine* = to secrete), and they typically have a rich vascular and lymphatic drainage that receives their hormones. Most of the hormone-producing cells in endocrine glands are arranged in cords and branching networks—a situation that maximizes contact between them and the capillaries surrounding them.

The endocrine glands include the pituitary, thyroid, parathyroid, adrenal, pineal, and thymus glands (Figure 16.1). The hypothalamus, along with its neural functions, produces and releases hormones, so we can consider the hypothalamus a **neuroendocrine organ.** In addition, several organs contain discrete areas of endocrine tissue and produce hormones as well as exocrine products. Such organs, which include the pancreas and gonads (ovaries and testes), are also major endocrine glands.

Besides the major endocrine organs, various other tissues and organs produce hormones. For example, adipose cells release leptin, and pockets of hormone-producing cells are found in the walls of the small intestine, stomach, kidneys, and heart—organs whose chief functions have little to do with hormone production. These other hormone-producing structures are described on pp. 636–638.

Although some physiologists include local chemical messengers—autocrines and paracrines—as part of the realm of the endocrine system, that is not the consensus. Hormones are long-distance chemical signals that travel in blood or lymph throughout the body. **Autocrines** are chemicals that exert their effects on the same cells that secrete them. For example, certain prostaglandins released by smooth muscle cells cause those smooth muscle cells to contract. **Paracrines** also act locally but affect cell types other than those releasing the paracrine chemicals. For example, somatostatin released by one population of pancreatic cells inhibits the release of insulin by a different population of pancreatic cells.

◢ HOMEOSTATIC IMBALANCE

Certain tumor cells, such as those of some cancers of the lung or pancreas, synthesize hormones identical to those made in normal endocrine glands. However, they do so in an excessive and uncontrolled fashion leading to problems due to hormone-mediated pathology. ●

Hormones

The Chemistry of Hormones

Hormones are chemical substances, secreted by cells into the extracellular fluids, that regulate the metabolic function of other cells in the body. Although a large variety of hormones are produced, nearly all of them can be classified chemically as either amino acid based or steroids.

Most hormones are **amino acid based.** Molecular size varies widely in this group—from simple amino acid derivatives (which include amines and thyroxine constructed from the amino acid tyrosine), to peptides (short chains of amino acids), to proteins (long polymers of amino acids). The **steroids** are synthesized from cholesterol. Of the hormones produced by the major endocrine organs, only gonadal and adrenocortical hormones are steroids.

If we also consider the **eicosanoids** (i-ko'să-noyds), which include *leukotrienes* and *prostaglandins*, we must add a third chemical class. These biologically active lipids (made from arachidonic acid) are released by nearly all cell membranes. Leukotrienes are signaling chemicals that mediate inflammation and some allergic reactions. Prostaglandins have multiple targets and effects, ranging from raising blood pressure and increasing the expulsive uterine contractions of birth to enhancing blood clotting, pain, and inflammation. Because the effects of eicosanoids are typically highly localized, affecting only nearby cells, they generally act as

paracrines and autocrines and do not fit the definition of the true *hormones*, which influence distant targets. Hence, this class of hormonelike chemicals will not be considered here. Instead, their important effects are considered in later chapters as appropriate.

Mechanisms of Hormone Action

Even though all major hormones circulate to virtually all tissues, a given hormone influences the activity of only certain tissue cells, referred to as its **target cells.** Hormones bring about their characteristic effects on target cells by *altering* cell activity; that is, they increase or decrease the rates of normal cellular processes. The precise response depends on the target cell type. For example, when the hormone epinephrine binds to certain smooth muscle cells in blood vessel walls, it stimulates them to contract. Epinephrine binding to cells other than muscle cells may have a different effect, but it does *not* cause those cells to contract.

A hormonal stimulus typically produces one or more of the following changes:

1. Alters plasma membrane permeability or membrane potential, or both, by opening or closing ion channels

2. Stimulates synthesis of proteins or regulatory molecules such as enzymes within the cell

3. Activates or deactivates enzymes

4. Induces secretory activity

5. Stimulates mitosis

Two main mechanisms account for how a hormone communicates with its target cell, that is, how hormone receptor binding is harnessed to the intracellular machinery needed for hormone action. The mechanism used depends on the chemical nature of the hormone and the cellular location of the receptor. *Water-soluble hormones* (all amino acid–based hormones except thyroid hormone) act on *receptors in the plasma membrane* coupled via regulatory molecules called G proteins to one or more intracellular second messengers which mediate the target cell's response. *Lipid-soluble hormones* (steroid and thyroid hormones) act on *intracellular receptors*, directly activating genes. This will be easy for you to remember if you think about *why* this must be so: Receptors for water-soluble hormones must be in the plasma membrane since these hormones *cannot* enter the cell; receptors for lipid-soluble steroid and thyroid hormones are inside the cell because these hormones *can* enter the cell. Of course, things are not quite that clear-cut. Recent research has shown that steroid hormones exert some of their more immediate effects via plasma membrane receptors, and the second messengers of some hydrophilic hormones can turn genes on.

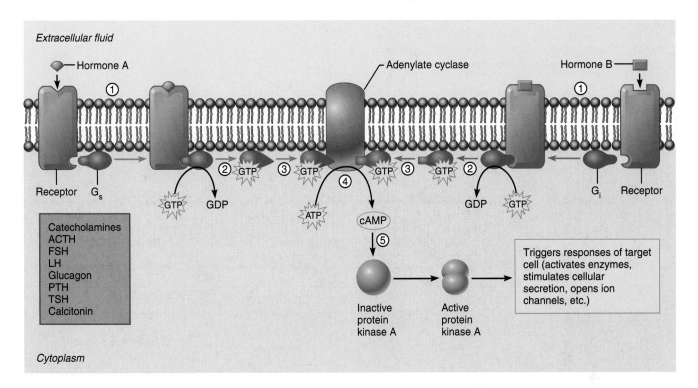

FIGURE 16.2 **Cyclic AMP second-messenger mechanism of amino acid–based hormones.** Mechanisms that generate cyclic AMP by activation of adenylate cyclase are mediated by G_s proteins, which are activated when a hormone (the first messenger, A in this case) binds to plasma membrane receptors (①–③ on left of effector enzyme, green arrows). Cyclic AMP (the second messenger, ④) acts intracellularly to activate protein kinase A enzymes (⑤) that mediate the cell's responses to the hormone. Notice that not all hormones provoke the activation of the effector enzyme. As depicted on the right, binding of hormone B to a membrane receptor is inhibitory because it activates a different G protein (G_i, ①–③ on right of effector enzyme, red arrows). Examples of hormones that act through these mechanisms are listed.

Plasma Membrane Receptors and Second-Messenger Systems

With the exception of thyroid hormone, all amino acid–based hormones exert their signaling effects through intracellular **second messengers** generated when a hormone binds to a receptor on the plasma membrane. You are already familiar with one of these second messengers, **cyclic AMP,** which is used by neurotransmitters (Chapter 11) and olfactory and gustatory receptors (Chapter 15).

The Cyclic AMP Signaling Mechanism As you recall, this mechanism involves the interaction of three plasma membrane components to determine intracellular levels of cyclic AMP (cAMP)—a hormone receptor, a signal transducer (a G protein), and an effector enzyme (adenylate cyclase).

① The hormone, acting as the **first messenger,** binds to its receptor (Figure 16.2).

② Hormone binding causes the receptor to change shape, allowing it to bind a nearby inactive **G protein.** The G protein is activated as the guanosine diphosphate (GDP) bound to it is displaced by the high-energy compound *guanosine triphosphate (GTP).*

The G protein behaves like a light switch; it is "off" when GDP is bound to it, and "on" when GTP is bound.

③ The activated G protein (moving along the membrane) binds to the effector enzyme **adenylate cyclase.** Some G proteins (G_s) *stimulate* adenylate cyclase (left side of Figure 16.2); others (G_i) *inhibit* adenylate cyclase (right side of Figure 16.2). Eventually, the GTP bound to the G protein is hydrolyzed to GDP and the G protein becomes inactive once again. (The G protein possesses GTPase activity and cleaves the terminal phosphate group off GTP in much the same way that ATPase enzymes hydrolyze ATP.)

④ If activated, adenylate cyclase generates the second-messenger cAMP from ATP.

⑤ cAMP, which is free to diffuse throughout the cell, triggers a cascade of chemical reactions beginning with the activation of *protein kinase A.* **Protein kinases** are enzymes that *phosphorylate* (add a phosphate group to) various proteins, many of which are other enzymes. Because phosphorylation activates some of these proteins and inhibits others, a variety of reactions may occur in the same target cell at the same time.

Q *Which of the membrane proteins acts as the signal transducer in Figures 16.2 and 16.3? Why are reactions initiated by second-messenger mechanisms called cascades?*

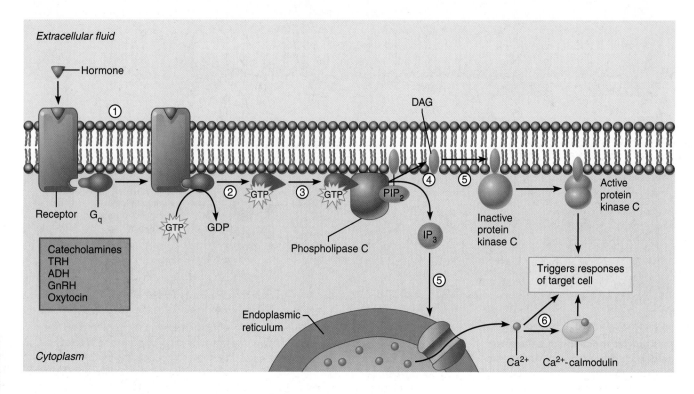

FIGURE 16.3 **PIP second-messenger mechanism of amino acid–based hormones.** Some G protein–coupled receptors use DAG, IP$_3$, and Ca^{2+} as intracellular messengers. ①–③ The activated G protein (G$_q$) stimulates the effector molecule, phospholipase C, to ④ cleave PIP$_2$ into two fragments—diacylglycerol (DAG) and inositol triphosphate (IP$_3$), which act as intracellular second messengers to ⑤ activate protein kinases and increase the cytoplasmic concentration of Ca^{2+}. ⑥ Ca^{2+} also acts as a second messenger to modify the activity of cellular proteins. Examples of hormones that act through these mechanisms are listed.

This type of intracellular enzymatic cascade has a huge amplification effect. Each activated adenylate cyclase generates large numbers of cAMP molecules, and a single kinase enzyme can catalyze hundreds of reactions. Hence, as the reaction cascades through one enzyme intermediate after another, the number of product molecules increases dramatically at each step. Theoretically, receptor binding of a single hormone molecule could generate millions of final product molecules!

The sequence of reactions set into motion by cAMP depends on the type of target cell, the specific protein kinases it contains, and the substrates within that cell available for phosphorylation by the protein kinase. For example, in thyroid cells, binding of thyroid-stimulating hormone promotes synthesis of the thyroid hormone thyroxine; in bone and muscle cells, binding of growth hormone activates anabolic reactions in which amino acids are built into tissue proteins. Since some G proteins inhibit rather than activate adenylate cyclase, thereby reducing the cytoplasmic concentration of cAMP, even slight changes in levels of antagonistic hormones can influence a target cell's activity.

Because cAMP is rapidly degraded by the intracellular enzyme **phosphodiesterase,** its action persists only briefly. While at first glance this may appear to be a problem, it is quite the opposite. Because of the amplification effect, most hormones need to be present only briefly to cause the desired results. Continued production of hormones then prompts continued cellular activity; no extracellular controls are necessary to stop the activity.

The PIP-Calcium Signal Mechanism
Although cyclic AMP is the activating second messenger in some tissues for at least ten amino acid–based hormones, some of the same hormones (e.g.,

A *The signal transducer is the G protein(s). Because each step in the pathway has a huge amplification effect and the number of product molecules increases dramatically at each step, a single signal has a cascade effect.*

epinephrine) act through a different second-messenger system in other tissues. In one such mechanism, called the PIP-calcium signal mechanism, intracellular calcium ions act as the final mediator. Let's follow this process (Figure 16.3).

① Hormone binding to the receptor causes it to change shape.

② The receptor binds the G protein, which is activated as GTP binds, displacing GDP.

③ The activated G protein (G_q) then binds to and activates membrane-bound **phospholipase C** (the effector enzyme).

④ Phospholipase C splits a plasma-membrane phospholipid called **PIP$_2$** (**p**hosphatidyl **i**nositol bis**p**hosphate) into **diacylglycerol (DAG)** and **inositol triphosphate (IP$_3$)**. Both these molecules act as second messengers.

⑤ DAG activates *protein kinase C*, and IP$_3$ triggers the release of Ca^{2+} from the endoplasmic reticulum and other intracellular storage sites.

⑥ The liberated Ca^{2+} takes on a second-messenger role, either by directly altering the activity of specific enzymes and plasma membrane Ca^{2+} channels or by binding to the intracellular regulatory protein **calmodulin.** Once Ca^{2+} binds to calmodulin, enzymes are activated that amplify the cellular response.

Other Signaling Mechanisms Examples of hormones known to act on their target cells via G protein receptors and the cAMP or PIP mechanisms are listed in Figures 16.2 and 16.3. Other hormones that bind plasma membrane receptors act on their target cells through different (and in some cases, unknown) mechanisms. For example, cyclic guanosine monophosphate (cGMP) is a second messenger for selected hormones. Insulin (and other growth factors) appear to work without second messengers. The insulin receptor is a *tyrosine kinase* enzyme that is activated by autophosphorylation (addition of phosphate to several of its own tyrosines) when insulin binds. The activated insulin receptor provides docking sites for intracellular *relay proteins* that, in turn, initiate a series of protein phosphorylations that trigger specific cell responses. In certain instances, any of the second messengers mentioned—and the hormone receptor itself—can cause changes in intracellular Ca^{2+} levels.

Intracellular Receptors and Direct Gene Activation

Being lipid soluble, steroid hormones (and, strangely, thyroid hormone, a small iodinated amine) diffuse into their target cells where they bind to an intracellular receptor that is activated by the coupling (Figure 16.4). The activated hormone-receptor

Q *What is the crucial difference between the signaling mechanism depicted here and those shown in Figures 16.2 and 16.3?*

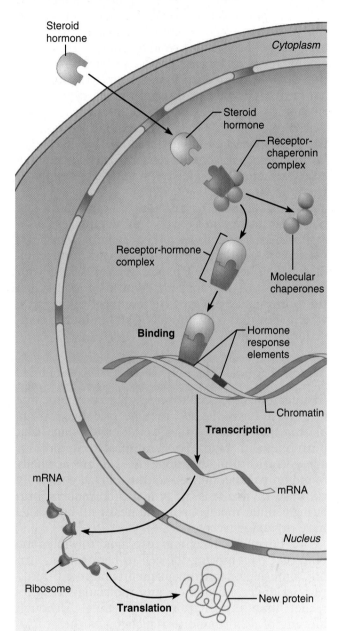

FIGURE 16.4 Direct gene activation mechanism of steroid hormones. A lipid-soluble hormone (steroid or thyroid hormone) diffuses through the plasma membrane of the target cell and binds to a receptor-chaperonin complex in the nucleus. Once hormone is bound, the chaperonin dissociates from the receptor and the hormone-receptor complex binds to a specific sequence on the DNA, initiating transcription of a certain gene. The messenger RNA formed migrates into the cytoplasm, where it directs synthesis of a specific protein.

A *Here, the hormone can enter the cell (because it is soluble in the plasma membrane lipids) and directly stimulates the desired effect by acting on DNA to cause transcription. In the Figures 16.2 and 16.3 mechanisms, the hormone cannot enter the cell because it is insoluble in membrane lipids.*

complex then makes its way to the nuclear chromatin, where the hormone receptor binds to a region of DNA (a *hormone response element*) specific for it. (The exception to these generalizations is that thyroid hormone receptors are always bound to DNA even in the absence of thyroid hormone.) This interaction "turns on" a gene, that is, prompts transcription of DNA to produce a messenger RNA (mRNA). The mRNA is then translated on the cytoplasmic ribosomes, producing specific protein molecules. These proteins include enzymes that promote the metabolic activities induced by that particular hormone and, in some cases, promote synthesis of either structural proteins or proteins to be exported from the target cell.

In the absence of hormone, the receptors are bound up in receptor-chaperonin complexes, associations that seem to keep the receptors from binding to DNA and perhaps protect them from proteolysis. (Check back to Chapter 2, pp. 52–53, if your recall of molecular chaperones needs a jog.) When the hormone *is* present, the complex dissociates, which allows it to bind to DNA and influence transcription.

Target Cell Specificity

In order for a target cell to respond to a hormone, the cell must have *specific* protein receptors on its plasma membrane or in its interior to which that hormone can bind. For example, receptors for adrenocorticotropic hormone (ACTH) are normally found only on certain cells of the adrenal cortex. By contrast, thyroxine is the principal hormone stimulating cellular metabolism, and nearly all body cells have thyroxine receptors.

A hormone receptor responds to hormone binding by prompting the cell to perform, or turn on, some gene-determined "preprogrammed" function. Hence, hormones are molecular triggers rather than informational molecules. Although binding of a hormone to a receptor is the crucial first step, target cell activation by hormone-receptor interaction depends equally on three factors: (1) blood levels of the hormone, (2) relative numbers of receptors for that hormone on or in the target cells, and (3) *affinity* (strength) of the bond between the hormone and the receptor. All three factors change rapidly in response to various stimuli and changes within the body. As a rule, for a given level of hormone in the blood, a large number of high-affinity receptors produces a pronounced hormonal effect, and a smaller number of low-affinity receptors results in reduced target cell response or outright endocrine dysfunction.

Receptors are dynamic structures. In some instances, target cells form more receptors in response to rising blood levels of the specific hormones to which they respond, a phenomenon called **up-regulation.** In other cases, prolonged exposure to high hormone concentrations desensitizes the target cells, so that they respond less vigorously to hormonal stimulation. This **down-regulation** involves loss of receptors and prevents the target cells from overreacting to persistently high hormone levels. Hormones influence the number and affinity not only of their own receptors but also of receptors that respond to other hormones. For example, progesterone induces a loss of estrogen receptors in the uterus, thus antagonizing estrogen's actions. On the other hand, estrogen causes the same cells to produce more progesterone receptors, enhancing their ability to respond to progesterone.

Half-Life, Onset, and Duration of Hormone Activity

Hormones are potent chemicals, and they exert profound effects on their target organs at very low concentrations. Hormones circulate in the blood in two forms—free or bound to a protein carrier. In general, lipid-soluble hormones (steroids and thyroid hormone) travel in the bloodstream attached to plasma proteins. Most others circulate unencumbered by carriers. The concentration of a circulating hormone in blood at any time reflects (1) its rate of release, and (2) the speed at which it is inactivated and removed from the body. Some hormones are rapidly degraded by enzymes in their target cells, but most are removed from the blood by the kidneys or liver, and their breakdown products are excreted from the body in urine or, to a lesser extent, in feces. As a result, the length of time for a hormone's blood level to be decreased by half, referred to as its **half-life,** varies from a fraction of a minute to a week, with the water-soluble hormones exhibiting the shortest half-lives.

The time required for hormone effects to appear also varies greatly. Some hormones provoke target organ responses almost immediately, while others, particularly the steroid hormones, require hours to days before their effects are seen. Additionally, some hormones are secreted in a relatively inactive form and must be activated in the target cells.

The duration of hormone action is limited, ranging from 10 seconds to several hours, depending on the hormone. Effects may disappear rapidly as blood levels drop, or they may persist for hours after very low hormone levels have been reached. Because of these many variations, hormonal blood levels must be precisely and individually controlled to meet the continuously changing needs of the body.

Interaction of Hormones at Target Cells

Understanding hormonal effects is a bit more complicated than you might expect because multiple hormones may act on the same target cells at the same time and in many cases the result of such an interaction is not predictable even when you know the effects of the individual hormones. Here we will look at three types of hormone interaction—permissiveness, synergism, and antagonism.

Permissiveness is the situation when one hormone cannot exert its full effects without another hormone being present. For example, the development of the reproductive system is largely regulated by reproductive system hormones, as we might expect. However, thyroid hormone is necessary (has a permissive effect) for normal *timely* development of reproductive structures; without thyroid hormone, reproductive system development is delayed.

Synergism of hormones occurs in situations where more than one hormone produces the same effects at the target cell and their combined effects are amplified. For example, both glucagon (produced by the pancreas) and epinephrine cause the liver to release glucose to the blood; when they act together, the amount of glucose released is about 150% of what is released when each hormone acts alone.

When one hormone opposes the action of another hormone, the interaction is called **antagonism.** For example, insulin, which lowers blood glucose levels, is antagonized by the action of glucagon, which acts to raise blood glucose levels. Antagonists may compete for the same receptors, act through different metabolic pathways, or even, as noted in the progesterone-estrogen interaction at the uterus, cause down-regulation of the receptors for the antagonistic hormone.

Control of Hormone Release

The synthesis and release of most hormones are regulated by some type of **negative feedback system** (see Chapter 1). In such a system, hormone secretion is triggered by some internal or external stimulus. As hormone levels rise, they cause target organ effects and inhibit further hormone release. As a result, blood levels of many hormones vary only within a narrow range.

Endocrine Gland Stimuli

Endocrine glands are stimulated to manufacture and release their hormones by three major types of stimuli: *humoral* (hu'mer-ul), *neural*, and *hormonal.*

Humoral Stimuli Some endocrine glands secrete their hormones in direct response to changing blood levels of certain critical ions and nutrients. These stimuli are called *humoral stimuli* to distinguish them from hormonal stimuli, which are also blood-borne chemicals. The term *humoral* harks back to the ancient use of the term *humor* to refer to various body fluids (blood, bile, and others). This is the simplest of the endocrine control systems. For example, cells of the parathyroid glands monitor blood Ca^{2+} levels, and when they detect a decline from normal values, they secrete parathyroid hormone (PTH). Because PTH acts by several routes to reverse that decline, blood Ca^{2+} levels soon rise, ending the initiative for PTH release (Figure 16.5a). Other hormones released in response to humoral stimuli include insulin, produced by the pancreas, and aldosterone, one of the adrenal cortex hormones.

Neural Stimuli In a few cases, nerve fibers stimulate hormone release. The classic example of neural stimuli is sympathetic nervous system stimulation of the adrenal medulla to release catecholamines (norepinephrine and epinephrine) during periods of stress (Figure 16.5b).

Hormonal Stimuli Finally, many endocrine glands release their hormones in response to hormones produced by other endocrine organs, and the stimuli in these cases are called hormonal stimuli. For example, release of most anterior pituitary hormones is regulated by releasing and inhibiting hormones produced by the hypothalamus, and many anterior pituitary hormones in turn stimulate other endocrine organs to release their hormones (Figure 16.5c). As blood levels of the hormones produced by the final target glands increase, they inhibit the release of anterior pituitary hormones and thus their own release. This hypothalamic-pituitary-target endocrine organ feedback loop lies at the very core of endocrinology, and it will come up many times in this chapter. Hormonal stimuli promote rhythmic hormone release, with hormone blood levels rising and falling in a specific pattern.

Although these three mechanisms typify most systems that control hormone release, they are by no means all-inclusive or mutually exclusive, and some endocrine organs respond to multiple stimuli.

Nervous System Modulation

Both "turn-on" factors (hormonal, humoral, and neural stimuli) and "turn-off" factors (feedback inhibition and others) may be modified by the nervous system. Without this added safeguard, endocrine system activity would be strictly mechanical, much like a household thermostat. A thermostat can maintain the temperature at or around its set value, but it cannot sense that your grandmother visiting from Florida feels cold at that temperature and reset

① Capillary blood contains low concentration of Ca²⁺, which stimulates…

Capillary (low Ca²⁺ in blood)

Thyroid gland (posterior view)

Parathyroid glands

Parathyroid glands

PTH

② …secretion of parathyroid hormone (PTH) by parathyroid glands

(a) Humoral

① Preganglionic SNS fiber stimulates adrenal medulla cells…

CNS (spinal cord)

Preganglionic SNS fiber

Medulla of adrenal gland

Capillary

② …to secrete catecholamines

(b) Neural

① The hypothalamus secretes hormones that…

Hypothalamus

② …stimulate the anterior pituitary gland to secrete hormones that…

Pituitary gland

Thyroid gland   Adrenal cortex   Gonad (Testis)

③ …stimulate other endocrine glands to secrete hormones

(c) Hormonal

FIGURE 16.5 **Three types of endocrine gland stimuli. (a)** Humoral stimulus: Low blood calcium levels trigger parathyroid hormone release from the parathyroid glands, which causes blood Ca²⁺ levels to rise by stimulating release of Ca²⁺ from bone. **(b)** Neural stimulus: The stimulation of adrenal medullary cells by sympathetic nervous system (SNS) fibers triggers the release of catecholamines to the blood. **(c)** Hormonal stimulus: Hormones released by the hypothalamus stimulate the anterior pituitary to release hormones that stimulate other endocrine organs to secrete hormones.

itself accordingly. *You* must make that adjustment. In your body, it is the nervous system that makes certain adjustments to maintain homeostasis by overriding normal endocrine controls. For example, the action of insulin and several other hormones normally keeps blood glucose levels in the range of 90–110 mg/100 ml of blood. However, when the body is under severe stress, blood glucose levels rise because the hypothalamus and sympathetic nervous system centers are strongly activated. This ensures that body cells have sufficient fuel for the more vigorous activity required during such periods.

Major Endocrine Organs

The Pituitary Gland (Hypophysis)

Securely seated in the sella turcica of the sphenoid bone, the tiny **pituitary gland,** or **hypophysis** (hi-pof′ĭ-sis; "to grow under"), secretes at least nine hor-mones. Usually said to be the size and shape of a pea, this gland is more accurately described as a pea on a stalk. Its stalk, the funnel-shaped **infundibulum,** connects the gland to the hypothalamus superiorly (Figure 16.1). In humans, the pituitary gland has two major lobes; one is neural tissue and the other glandular. The **posterior pituitary** (lobe) (Figure 16.6) is composed largely of pituicytes (glia-like supporting cells) and nerve fibers. It releases **neurohormones** (hormones secreted by neurons) received ready-made from the hypothalamus. Thus, this lobe is a hormone-storage area and not a true endocrine gland in the precise sense. The posterior lobe plus the infundibulum make up the region called the **neurohypophysis** (nu″ro-hi-pof′ĭ-sis), a term commonly used (incorrectly) to indicate the posterior lobe alone. The **anterior pituitary** (lobe), or **adenohypophysis** (ad″ĕ-no-hi-pof′ĭ-sis), is composed of glandular tissue (*adeno* = gland), and it manufactures and releases a number of hormones (Table 16.1 on pp. 618–619).

Q *What do you think is the advantage of having the hypophyseal portal system as compared to having the usual arrangement of blood vessels?*

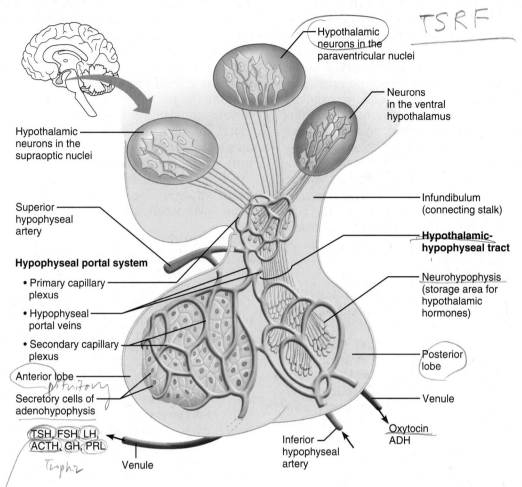

TSRF

FIGURE 16.6   **Relationships of the pituitary gland and hypothalamus.** Hypothalamic neurons in the supraoptic and paraventricular nuclei synthesize ADH and oxytocin, which are transported along the hypothalamic-hypophyseal tract to the neurohypophysis for storage. Neurons in the ventral hypothalamus have short axons that discharge releasing and inhibiting hormones to the capillaries of the hypophyseal portal system, which runs to the adenohypophysis. These hormones influence the adenohypophyseal secretory cells to release (or not release) their hormones.

Arterial blood is delivered to the pituitary via hypophyseal branches of the internal carotid arteries. The veins leaving the pituitary drain into the dural sinuses.

Pituitary-Hypothalamic Relationships

The contrasting histology of the two pituitary lobes reflects the dual origin of this tiny gland. The posterior lobe is actually part of the brain. It derives from a downgrowth of hypothalamic tissue and maintains its neural connection with the hypothalamus via a nerve bundle called the **hypothalamic-hypophyseal tract,** which runs through the infundibulum (Figure 16.6). This tract arises from neurons in the **supraoptic** and **paraventricular nuclei** of the hypothalamus. These neurosecretory cells synthesize two neurohormones and transport them along their axons to the posterior pituitary. Oxytocin (ok″sĭ-to′sin) is made primarily by the paraventricular neurons, and antidiuretic hormone (ADH) primarily by the supraoptic neurons. When these hypothalamic neurons fire, they release the stored hormones into a capillary bed in the posterior pituitary for distribution throughout the body.

The glandular anterior lobe originates from a superior outpocketing of the oral mucosa (*Rathke's*

A *The portal system allows releasing and inhibiting hormones from the hypothalamus to reach the anterior pituitary more quickly than they would otherwise. They are also less diluted, so they can be released in smaller quantities.*

16

pouch) and is formed from epithelial tissue. After touching the posterior lobe, the anterior lobe loses its connection with the oral mucosa and adheres to the neurohypophysis. There is no direct neural connection between the anterior lobe and hypothalamus, but there is a vascular connection. Specifically, the **primary capillary plexus** in the infundibulum communicates inferiorly via the small **hypophyseal portal veins** with a **secondary capillary plexus** in the anterior lobe. The primary and secondary capillary plexuses and the intervening hypophyseal portal veins make up the **hypophyseal portal system*** (Figure 16.6). Via this portal system, **releasing** and **inhibiting hormones** secreted by neurons in the ventral hypothalamus circulate to the adenohypophysis, where they regulate secretion of its hormones. All these hypothalamic regulatory hormones are amino acid based, but they vary in size from a single amine to peptides to proteins.

Adenohypophyseal Hormones

Although the adenohypophysis has traditionally been called the "master endocrine gland" because of its numerous hormonal products, many of which regulate the activity of other endocrine glands, it has in recent years been dethroned by the hypothalamus, which is now known to control anterior pituitary activity. Researchers have identified six distinct adenohypophyseal hormones, all of them proteins (Table 16.1). In addition, a large molecule with the tongue-twisting name **pro-opiomelanocortin (POMC)** (pro"o"pe-o-mah-lan′o-kor"tin) has been isolated from the anterior pituitary. POMC is a *prohormone*, that is, a large precursor molecule that can be split enzymatically into one or more active hormones. POMC is the source of adrenocorticotropic hormone, two natural opiates (an enkephalin and a beta endorphin, described in Chapter 11), and *melanocyte-stimulating hormone (MSH)*. In amphibians, reptiles, and other animals MSH stimulates melanocytes to increase synthesis of melanin pigment, but this is not an important function of MSH in humans. In humans and other animals, MSH is a CNS neurotransmitter involved in the control of appetite. Although low levels of MSH are found in plasma, its role in the periphery is not yet well understood.

When the adenohypophysis receives an appropriate chemical stimulus from the hypothalamus, one or more of its hormones are released by certain of its cells. Although many different hormones pass from the hypothalamus to the anterior lobe, each target cell in the anterior lobe distinguishes the messages directed to it and responds in kind—secreting the proper hormone in response to specific releasing hormones, and shutting off hormone release in response to specific inhibiting hormones. In general, the hypothalamic releasing hormones are more important than the inhibiting hormones as regulatory factors, because only very little hormone is stored by secretory cells of the anterior lobe.

Four of the six anterior pituitary hormones—thyroid-stimulating hormone, adrenocorticotropic hormone, follicle-stimulating hormone, and luteinizing hormone—are **tropins** or **tropic hormones** (*tropi* = turn on, change), which are hormones that regulate the secretory action of other endocrine glands. Except for growth hormone, all affect their target cells via a cyclic AMP second-messenger system.

Growth Hormone   Growth hormone (GH) is produced by cells called **somatotrophs** of the anterior lobe (Figure 16.7). Although GH stimulates most body cells to increase in size and divide, its major targets are the bones and skeletal muscles. Stimulation of the epiphyseal plate leads to long bone growth; stimulation of skeletal muscles promotes increased muscle mass.

Essentially an anabolic (tissue-building) hormone, GH promotes protein synthesis, and it encourages the use of fats for fuel, thus conserving glucose. Most growth-promoting effects of GH are mediated indirectly by **insulin-like growth factors (IGFs)**, also known as **somatomedins** (so"mah-to-me′dinz), a family of growth-promoting proteins produced by the liver, skeletal muscle, bone, and other tissues. Specifically, IGFs (1) stimulate uptake of amino acids from the blood and their incorporation into cellular proteins throughout the body; and (2) stimulate uptake of sulfur (needed for the synthesis of chondroitin sulfate) into cartilage matrix. Acting directly, GH mobilizes fats from fat depots for transport to cells, increasing blood levels of fatty acids. It also decreases the rate of glucose uptake and metabolism. In the liver, it encourages glycogen breakdown and release of glucose to the blood. The elevation in blood glucose levels that occurs as a result of this *glucose sparing* is called the *diabetogenic effect* of GH, because it mimics the high blood glucose levels typical of diabetes mellitus.

Secretion of GH is regulated chiefly by two hypothalamic hormones with antagonistic effects. **Growth hormone–releasing hormone (GHRH)** stimulates GH release, while **growth hormone–inhibiting hormone (GHIH)**, also called **somatostatin** (so"mah-to-stat′in), inhibits it. GHIH release is (presumably) triggered by the feedback of GH and IGFs. Rising levels of GH also feed back to inhibit its own release. As indicated in Table 16.1, a number of

---

*A portal system is an unusual arrangement of blood vessels in which a capillary bed feeds into veins, which in turn feed into another capillary bed.

Feedback mechanism

→ Inhibits GHRH release
  Stimulates GHIH release

→ Inhibits GH synthesis and release

Hypothalamus secretes growth hormone–releasing hormone (GHRH), and somatostatin (GHIH)

Anterior pituitary

Growth hormone

Direct effects

Liver and other tissues

Insulin-like growth factors (IGFs)

Indirect growth-promoting actions

Anti-insulin actions

Skeletal effects

Extraskeletal effects

Fat

Carbohydrate metabolism

Increased cartilage formation and skeletal growth

Increased protein synthesis, and cell growth and proliferation

Increased lipolysis

Increased blood glucose and other anti-insulin effects

Key:

← Increases, stimulates

← Reduces, inhibits

☐ Initial stimulus

☐ Physiological response

☐ Result

FIGURE 16.7 **Metabolic actions of growth hormone (GH).** The direct actions of GH on target cells stimulate liver, skeletal muscle, bone, and cartilage cells to produce and release insulin-like growth factors, which mediate the indirect, largely anabolic effects of GH. GH acts directly on other tissue cells to promote fat breakdown (lipolysis) and release from adipose tissues and to hinder glucose uptake from the blood by tissue cells. (Because these actions antagonize those of the pancreatic hormone insulin, they are referred to as anti-insulin or glucose-sparing actions.) Elevated levels of GH and IGF feed back to promote GHIH release (and depress GHRH release) by the hypothalamus and to inhibit GH release by the anterior pituitary gland.

16

secondary triggers also influence GH release. Typically, GH secretion has a daily cycle, with the highest levels occurring during evening sleep, but the total amount secreted daily peaks during adolescence and then declines with age.

Besides inhibiting growth hormone secretion, GHIH blocks the release of thyroid-stimulating hormone. GHIH is also produced in various locations in the gut, where it inhibits the release of virtually all gastrointestinal and pancreatic secretions—both endocrine and exocrine.

◢ HOMEOSTATIC IMBALANCE

Both hypersecretion and hyposecretion of GH may result in structural abnormalities. Hypersecretion in children results in **gigantism** as the still-active epiphyseal (growth) plates are targeted by GH. The person becomes abnormally tall, often reaching a height of 2.4 m (8 feet), but has relatively normal body proportions. If excessive amounts of GH are secreted after the epiphyseal plates have closed, **acromegaly** (ak″ro-meg′ah-le) results. Literally translated as "enlarged extremities," this condition is characterized by overgrowth of bony areas still responsive to GH, namely bones of the hands, feet, and face. Hypersecretion usually results from an adenohypophyseal tumor that churns out excessive amounts of GH and the usual treatment is surgical removal of the tumor; however, anatomical changes that have already occurred are not reversible.

Hyposecretion of GH in adults usually causes no problems. GH deficiency in children results in slowed long bone growth, a condition called **pituitary dwarfism.** Such individuals attain a maximum height of 1.2 m (4 feet), but usually have fairly normal body proportions. Lack of GH is often accompanied by deficiencies of other adenohypophyseal hormones, and if thyroid-stimulating hormone and gonadotropins are lacking, the individual will be malproportioned and will fail to mature sexually as well. Fortunately, human GH is produced commercially by genetic engineering techniques and when pituitary dwarfism is diagnosed before puberty, growth hormone replacement therapy can promote nearly normal somatic growth.

The availability of synthetic GH also has a downside. Athletes and the elderly have been tempted to use GH for its body-building properties, and some parents have used GH in an attempt to give their children additional height. However, while muscle mass increases, there is no evidence for an increase in muscle strength in either athletes or the elderly, and only minimal increases in stature occur in normal children. Moreover, taking GH can lead to fluid retention, joint and muscle pain, diabetes, and may promote cancer. •

Thyroid-Stimulating Hormone Thyroid-stimulating hormone (TSH), or **thyrotropin,** is a tropic hormone that stimulates normal development and secretory activity of the thyroid gland. TSH release from cells of the anterior pituitary called **thyrotrophs** is triggered by the hypothalamic peptide **thyrotropin-releasing hormone (TRH).** Rising blood levels of thyroid hormones act on both the pituitary and the hypothalamus to inhibit TSH secretion. The hypothalamus, in response, releases GHIH, which reinforces the blockade of TSH release.

Adrenocorticotropic Hormone Adrenocorticotropic hormone (ACTH) (ah-dre"no-kor"tĭ-ko-trōp'ik), or **corticotropin,** is secreted by the **corticotrophs** of the adenohypophysis. ACTH stimulates the adrenal cortex to release corticosteroid hormones, most importantly glucocorticoids that help the body to resist stressors. ACTH release, elicited by hypothalamic **corticotropin-releasing hormone (CRH),** has a daily rhythm, with levels peaking in the morning, shortly before awakening. Rising levels of glucocorticoids feed back and block secretion of CRH and consequently ACTH release. Internal and external factors that alter the normal ACTH rhythm by triggering CRH release include fever, hypoglycemia, and stressors of all types.

Gonadotropins Follicle-stimulating hormone (FSH) and **luteinizing hormone (LH)** (lu'te-in-

īz"ing), referred to collectively as **gonadotropins,** regulate the function of the gonads (ovaries and testes). In both sexes, FSH stimulates gamete (sperm or egg) production and LH promotes production of gonadal hormones. In females, LH works with FSH to cause maturation of an egg-containing ovarian follicle. LH then independently triggers ovulation and promotes synthesis and release of ovarian hormones. In males, LH stimulates the interstitial cells of the testes to produce the male hormone testosterone.

Gonadotropins are virtually absent from the blood of prepubertal boys and girls. During puberty, the **gonadotrophs** of the adenohypophysis are activated and gonadotropin levels begin to rise, causing the gonads to mature. In both sexes, gonadotropin release by the adenohypophysis is prompted by **gonadotropin-releasing hormone (GnRH)** produced by the hypothalamus. Gonadal hormones, produced in response to the gonadotropins, feed back to suppress FSH and LH release.

Prolactin Prolactin (PRL) is a protein hormone structurally similar to GH. Produced by the **lactotrophs,** PRL stimulates the gonads of some animals (other than humans) and is considered a gonadotropin by some researchers. Its only well-documented effect in humans is to stimulate milk production by the breasts (*pro* = for; *lact* = milk). The role of prolactin in males is not well understood.

As with GH, PRL release is controlled by hypothalamic releasing and inhibiting hormones, but in this case it is the inhibitory hormone that plays the dominant role. **Prolactin-inhibiting hormone (PIH),** now known to be *dopamine (DA),* prevents prolactin secretion. Decreased PIH secretion leads to a surge in PRL release. The exact nature of **prolactin-releasing hormone (PRH)** is unknown, but it may be a combination of several releasing factors. In females, prolactin levels rise and fall in rhythm with estrogen blood levels. Estrogen stimulates prolactin release, both directly and indirectly. A brief rise in prolactin levels just before the menstrual period partially accounts for the breast swelling and tenderness some women experience at that time, but because this PRL stimulation is so brief, the breasts do not produce milk. In pregnant women, PRL blood levels rise dramatically toward the end of pregnancy, and milk production becomes possible. After birth, the infant's suckling stimulates PRH release in the mother, encouraging continued milk production and availability.

◤ HOMEOSTATIC IMBALANCE

Hypersecretion of prolactin is more common than hyposecretion (which is not a problem in anyone except women who choose to nurse). In fact, hyperprolactinemia is the most frequent abnormality of adenohypophyseal tumors. Clinical signs include inappropriate lactation, lack of menses, infertility in females, and breast enlargement and impotence in males. ●

The Posterior Pituitary and Hypothalamic Hormones

The posterior pituitary, made largely of the axons of hypothalamic neurons, stores antidiuretic hormone (ADH) and oxytocin that have been synthesized and forwarded by hypothalamic neurons of the supraoptic and paraventricular nuclei. These hormones are later released "on demand" in response to nerve impulses from the same hypothalamic neurons.

ADH and oxytocin, each composed of nine amino acids, are almost identical. They differ in only two amino acids, and yet they have dramatically different physiological effects (Table 16.1). ADH influences body water balance, and oxytocin stimulates contraction of smooth muscle, particularly that of the uterus and breasts.

Oxytocin   A strong stimulant of uterine contraction, **oxytocin** is released in significantly higher amounts during childbirth (*ocytocia* = childbirth) and in nursing women. The number of oxytocin receptors in the uterus peaks near the end of pregnancy, and uterine smooth muscle becomes more and more sensitive to the hormone's stimulatory effects. Stretching of the uterus and cervix as birth nears dispatches afferent impulses to the hypothalamus, which responds by synthesizing oxytocin and triggering its release from the neurohypophysis. Oxytocin acts via the PIP-Ca^{2+} second-messenger system to mobilize Ca^{2+}, allowing stronger contractions. As blood levels of oxytocin rise, the expulsive contractions of labor gain momentum and finally end in birth.

Oxytocin also acts as the hormonal trigger for milk ejection (the "letdown" reflex) in women whose breasts are producing milk in response to prolactin. Suckling causes a reflex-initiated release of oxytocin, which targets specialized myoepithelial cells surrounding the milk-producing glands. As these cells contract, milk is forced from the breast into the infant's mouth. Both of these mechanisms are *positive feedback mechanisms* and are described in more detail in Chapter 28.

Both natural and synthetic oxytocic drugs are used to induce labor or to hasten normal labor that is progressing slowly. Less frequently, oxytocics are used to stop postpartum bleeding (by compressing ruptured blood vessels at the placental site) and to stimulate the milk ejection reflex.

Until recently, oxytocin's role in males and nonpregnant, nonlactating females was unknown, but new studies reveal that this potent peptide plays a role in sexual arousal and orgasm when the body is already primed for reproduction by sex hormones. Then, it may be responsible for the feeling of sexual satisfaction that results from that interaction. In nonsexual relationships, it is thought to promote nurturing and affectionate behavior, that is, it acts as a "cuddle hormone."

Antidiuretic Hormone   *Diuresis* (di"u-re′sis) is urine production. Thus, an *antidiuretic* is a substance that inhibits or prevents urine formation. **Antidiuretic hormone (ADH)** prevents wide swings in water balance, helping the body avoid dehydration and water overload. Hypothalamic neurons, called *osmoreceptors*, continually monitor the solute concentration (and thus the water concentration) of the blood. When solutes threaten to become too concentrated (as might follow excessive perspiration or inadequate fluid intake), the osmoreceptors transmit excitatory impulses to the hypothalamic neurons, which synthesize and release ADH. Liberated into the blood by the neurohypophysis, ADH targets the kidney tubules via cAMP. The tubule cells respond by reabsorbing more water from the forming urine and returning it to the bloodstream. As a result, less urine is produced and blood volume increases. As the solute concentration of the blood declines, the osmoreceptors stop depolarizing, effectively ending ADH release. Other stimuli triggering ADH release include pain, low blood pressure, and such drugs as nicotine, morphine, and barbiturates.

Drinking alcoholic beverages inhibits ADH secretion and causes copious urine output. The dry mouth and intense thirst of the "morning after" reflect this dehydrating effect of alcohol. As might be expected, ADH release is also inhibited by drinking excessive amounts of water. *Diuretic drugs* antagonize the effects of ADH and cause water to be flushed from the body. These drugs are used to manage some cases of hypertension and the edema (water retention in tissues) typical of congestive heart failure.

At high blood concentrations, ADH causes vasoconstriction, primarily of the visceral blood vessels, a response that indicates targeting of different receptors found on vascular smooth muscle. Under certain conditions, such as severe blood loss, exceptionally large amounts of ADH are released, causing a rise in blood pressure. The alternative name for this hormone, **vasopressin,** reflects this particular effect.

◤ HOMEOSTATIC IMBALANCE

One result of ADH deficiency is **diabetes insipidus,** a syndrome marked by the output of huge amounts of urine and intense thirst. The name of this condition (*diabetes* = overflow; *insipidus* = tasteless)

TABLE 16.1	Pituitary Hormones: Summary of Regulation and Effects		
HORMONE (CHEMICAL STRUCTURE AND CELL TYPE)	**REGULATION OF RELEASE**	**TARGET ORGAN AND EFFECTS**	**EFFECTS OF HYPOSECRETION ↓ AND HYPERSECRETION ↑**

ANTERIOR PITUITARY HORMONES

Growth hormone (GH) (Protein, somatotroph)	**Stimulated** by GHRH* release, which is triggered by low blood levels of GH as well as by a number of secondary triggers including hypoglycemia, increases in blood levels of amino acids, low levels of fatty acids, exercise, other types of stressors, and estrogens **Inhibited** by feedback inhibition exerted by GH and IGFs, and by hyperglycemia, hyperlipidemia, obesity, and emotional deprivation via either increased GHIH* (somatostatin) or decreased GHRH* release	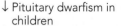 Liver, muscle, bone, cartilage, and other tissues: anabolic hormone; stimulates somatic growth; mobilizes fats; spares glucose Most effects mediated indirectly by IGFs	↓ Pituitary dwarfism in children ↑ Gigantism in children; acromegaly in adults
Thyroid-stimulating hormone (TSH) (Glycoprotein, thyrotroph)	**Stimulated** by TRH* and indirectly by pregnancy and (in infants) cold temperature **Inhibited** by feedback inhibition exerted by thyroid hormones on anterior pituitary and hypothalamus and by GHIH*	 Thyroid gland: stimulates thyroid gland to release thyroid hormone	↓ Cretinism in children; myxedema in adults ↑ Hyperthyroidism; effects similar to those of Graves' disease, in which antibodies mimic TSH
Adrenocorticotropic hormone (ACTH) (Polypeptide of 39 amino acids, corticotroph)	**Stimulated** by CRH*; stimuli that increase CRH release include fever, hypoglycemia, and other stressors **Inhibited** by feedback inhibition exerted by glucocorticoids	 Adrenal cortex: promotes release of glucocorticoids and androgens (mineralocorticoids to a lesser extent)	↓ Rare ↑ Cushing's disease
Follicle-stimulating hormone (FSH) (Glycoprotein, gonadotroph)	**Stimulated** by GnRH* **Inhibited** by feedback inhibition exerted by inhibin, and estrogen in females and testosterone in males	 Ovaries and testes: in females, stimulates ovarian follicle maturation and estrogen production; in males, stimulates sperm production	↓ Failure of sexual maturation ↑ No important effects

distinguishes it from diabetes mellitus (*mel =* honey), in which insulin deficiency causes large amounts of blood glucose to be lost in the urine. At one time, urine was tasted to determine which type of diabetes the patient was suffering from.

Diabetes insipidus can be caused by a blow to the head that damages the hypothalamus or the posterior pituitary. In either case, ADH release is deficient. Though inconvenient, the condition is not serious when the thirst center is operating

TABLE 16.1	*(continued)*		
HORMONE (CHEMICAL STRUCTURE AND CELL TYPE)	**REGULATION OF RELEASE**	**TARGET ORGAN AND EFFECTS**	**EFFECTS OF HYPOSECRETION ↓ AND HYPERSECRETION ↑**
Luteinizing hormone (LH) (Glycoprotein, gonadotroph)	**Stimulated** by GnRH* **Inhibited** by feedback inhibition exerted by estrogen and progesterone in females and testosterone in males	 Ovaries and testes: in females, triggers ovulation and stimulates ovarian production of estrogen and progesterone; in males, promotes testosterone production	As for FSH
Prolactin (PRL) (Protein, lactotroph)	**Stimulated** by decreased PIH* and increased PRH*; release enhanced by estrogens, birth control pills, breast-feeding, and dopamine-blocking drugs **Inhibited** by PIH* (dopamine)	 Breast secretory tissue: promotes lactation	↓ Poor milk production in nursing women ↑ Inappropriate milk production (galactorrhea); cessation of menses in females; impotence and breast enlargement (gynecomastia) in males

 POSTERIOR PITUITARY HORMONES (MADE BY HYPOTHALAMIC NEURONS AND STORED IN POSTERIOR PITUITARY)

Oxytocin (Peptide mostly from neurons in paraventricular nucleus of hypothalamus)	**Stimulated** by impulses from hypothalamic neurons in response to cervical/uterine stretching and suckling of infant at breast **Inhibited** by lack of appropriate neural stimuli	 Uterus: stimulates uterine contractions; initiates labor; breast: initiates milk ejection	Unknown
Antidiuretic hormone (ADH) or **vasopressin** (Peptide, mostly from neurons in supraoptic nucleus of hypothalamus)	**Stimulated** by impulses from hypothalamic neurons in response to increased osmolality of blood or decreased blood volume; also stimulated by pain, some drugs, low blood pressure **Inhibited** by adequate hydration of the body and by alcohol	 Kidneys: stimulates kidney tubule cells to reabsorb water	↓ Diabetes insipidus ↑ Syndrome of inappropriate ADH secretion (SIADH)

*Indicates hypothalamic releasing and inhibiting hormones: GHRH = growth hormone–releasing hormone; GHIH = growth hormone–inhibiting hormone; TRH = thyrotropin-releasing hormone; CRH = corticotropin-releasing hormone; GnRH = gonadotropin-releasing hormone; PRH = prolactin-releasing hormone; PIH = prolactin-inhibiting hormone

properly and the person drinks enough water to prevent dehydration. However, it can be life threatening in unconscious or comatose patients, so accident victims with head trauma must be carefully monitored.

Hypersecretion of ADH occurs in children with meningitis, may follow neurosurgery or hypothalamic injury, or results from ectopic ADH secretion by cancer cells (particularly pulmonary cancers). It also may occur after general anesthesia or administration

Q *Which of the cell populations shown in view (b) produces calcitonin?*

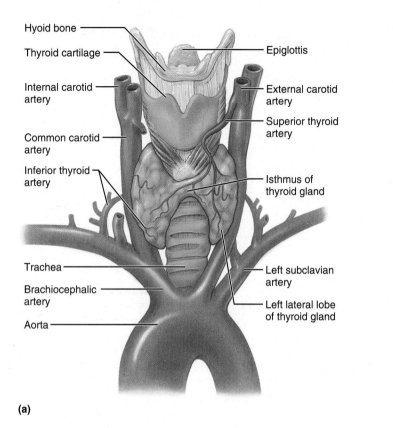

Hyoid bone
Thyroid cartilage
Internal carotid artery
Common carotid artery
Inferior thyroid artery
Trachea
Brachiocephalic artery
Aorta

Epiglottis
External carotid artery
Superior thyroid artery
Isthmus of thyroid gland
Left subclavian artery
Left lateral lobe of thyroid gland

(a)

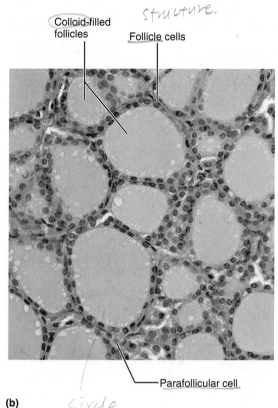

Colloid-filled follicles
Follicle cells
Parafollicular cell

(b)

FIGURE 16.8 **Gross and microscopic anatomy of the thyroid gland.**
(a) Location and arterial blood supply of the thyroid gland, anterior view.
(b) Photomicrograph of the thyroid gland follicles (250×).

of certain drugs. The resulting condition, *syndrome of inappropriate ADH secretion (SIADH),* is marked by retention of fluid, headache and disorientation due to brain edema, weight gain, and hypo-osmolarity of the blood. SIADH management requires fluid restriction and careful monitoring of blood sodium levels. ●

The Thyroid Gland

Location and Structure

The butterfly-shaped **thyroid gland** is located in the anterior neck, on the trachea just inferior to the larynx (Figures 16.1 and 16.8a). Its two lateral *lobes* are connected by a median tissue mass called the *isthmus.* The thyroid gland is the largest pure endocrine gland in the body. Its prodigious blood sup-

ply (from the *superior* and *inferior thyroid arteries*) makes thyroid surgery a painstaking (and bloody) endeavor.

Internally, the gland is composed of hollow, spherical **follicles** (Figure 16.8b). The walls of each follicle are formed largely by cuboidal or squamous epithelial cells called *follicle cells,* which produce the glycoprotein **thyroglobulin** (thi″ro-glob′u-lin). The central cavity, or lumen, of the follicle stores **colloid,** an amber-colored, sticky material consisting of thyroglobulin molecules with attached iodine atoms. *Thyroid hormone* is derived from this iodinated thyroglobulin. The *parafollicular cells,* another population of endocrine cells in the thyroid gland, produce *calcitonin,* an entirely different hormone. The parafollicular cells lie in the follicular epithelium but protrude into the soft connective tissue that separates and surrounds the thyroid follicles.

Thyroid Hormone

Often referred to as the body's major metabolic hormone, **thyroid hormone (TH)** is actually two iodine-containing amine hormones, **thyroxine** (thi-rok′sin),

A *The parafollicular cells.*

TABLE 16.2	Major Effects of Thyroid Hormone (T_4 and T_3) in the Body		
PROCESS OR SYSTEM AFFECTED	**NORMAL PHYSIOLOGICAL EFFECTS**	**EFFECTS OF HYPOSECRETION**	**EFFECTS OF HYPERSECRETION**
Basal metabolic rate (BMR)/ temperature regulation	Promotes normal oxygen use and BMR; calorigenesis; enhances effects of sympathetic nervous system	BMR below normal; decreased body temperature and cold intolerance; decreased appetite; weight gain; reduced sensitivity to catecholamines	BMR above normal; increased body temperature and heat intolerance; increased appetite; weight loss
Carbohydrate/lipid/protein metabolism	Promotes glucose catabolism; mobilizes fats; essential for protein synthesis; enhances liver's synthesis of cholesterol	Decreased glucose metabolism; elevated cholesterol/ triglyceride levels in blood; decreased protein synthesis; edema	Enhanced catabolism of glucose, proteins, and fats; weight loss; loss of muscle mass
Nervous system	Promotes normal development of nervous system in fetus and infant; promotes normal adult nervous system function	In infant, slowed/deficient brain development, retardation; in adult, mental dulling, depression, paresthesias, memory impairment, hypoactive reflexes	Irritability, restlessness, insomnia, personality changes, exophthalmos (in Graves' disease)
Cardiovascular system	Promotes normal functioning of the heart	Decreased efficiency of pumping action of the heart; low heart rate and blood pressure	Increased sensitivity to catecholamines leads to rapid heart rate and possible palpitations; high blood pressure; if prolonged, heart failure
Muscular system	Promotes normal muscular development and function	Sluggish muscle action; muscle cramps; myalgia	Muscle atrophy and weakness
Skeletal system	Promotes normal growth and maturation of the skeleton	In child, growth retardation, skeletal stunting and retention of child's body proportions; in adult, joint pain	In child, excessive skeletal growth initially, followed by early epiphyseal closure and short stature; in adult, demineralization of skeleton
Gastrointestinal system	Promotes normal GI motility and tone; increases secretion of digestive juices	Depressed GI motility, tone, and secretory activity; constipation	Excessive GI motility; diarrhea; loss of appetite
Reproductive system	Promotes normal female reproductive ability and lactation	Depressed ovarian function; sterility; depressed lactation	In females, depressed ovarian function; in males, impotence
Integumentary system	Promotes normal hydration and secretory activity of skin	Skin pale, thick, and dry; facial edema; hair coarse and thick	Skin flushed, thin, and moist; hair fine and soft; nails soft and thin

16

or T_4, and **triiodothyronine** (tri"i-o"do-thi'ro-nēn), or T_3. T_4 is the major hormone secreted by the thyroid follicles; most T_3 is formed at the target tissues by conversion of T_4 to T_3. Very much like one another, the hormones are constructed from two linked tyrosine amino acids. The principal difference is that T_4 has four bound iodine atoms, and T_3 has three (thus, T_4 and T_3).

Except for the adult brain, spleen, testes, uterus, and the thyroid gland itself, TH affects virtually every cell in the body (Table 16.2). By stimulating enzymes concerned with glucose oxidation, it increases basal metabolic rate and body heat production; this is known as the hormone's **calorigenic effect** (*calorigenic* = heat producing). Because TH provokes an increase in the number of adrenergic receptors in blood vessels, it plays an important role in maintaining blood pressure. Additionally, it is an important regulator of tissue growth and development. It is especially critical for normal skeletal and nervous system development and maturation and for reproductive capabilities.

Synthesis Thyroid hormone synthesis involves six interrelated processes that begin when TSH secreted by the anterior pituitary binds to follicle cell receptors. The following numbers correspond to steps 1–6 in Figure 16.9:

① **Formation and storage of thyroglobulin.** After being synthesized on the ribosomes, thyroglobulin is

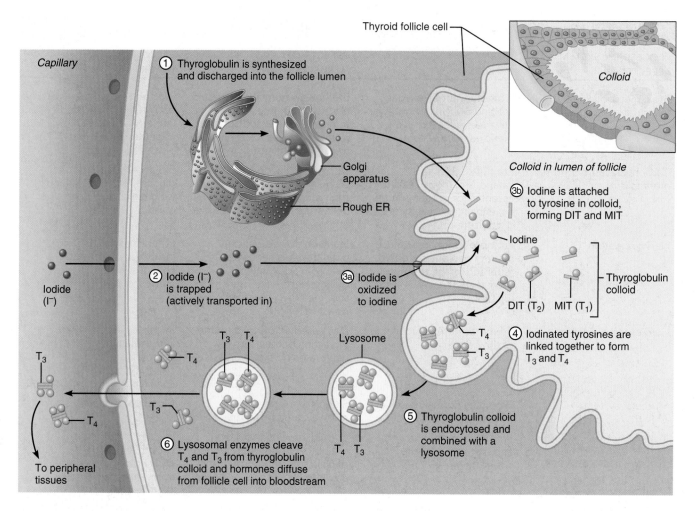

Thyroid follicle cell

Capillary

① Thyroglobulin is synthesized
and discharged into the follicle lumen

Colloid

Golgi
apparatus

Rough ER

Colloid in lumen of follicle

③b Iodine is attached
to tyrosine in colloid,
forming DIT and MIT

Iodine

Iodide
(I⁻)

② Iodide (I⁻)
is trapped
(actively transported in)

③a Iodide is
oxidized
to iodine

DIT (T₂)   MIT (T₁)

Thyroglobulin
colloid

T_3 T_4

T_4

Lysosome

T_4

T_3

④ Iodinated tyrosines are
linked together to form
T_3 and T_4

T_3

T_3

T_4

T_4 T_3

⑤ Thyroglobulin colloid
is endocytosed and
combined with a
lysosome

To peripheral
tissues

⑥ Lysosomal enzymes cleave
T_4 and T_3 from thyroglobulin
colloid and hormones diffuse
from follicle cell into bloodstream

T_4 T_3

FIGURE 16.9   Synthesis of thyroid hormone. Binding of TSH to follicle cell receptors (not illustrated) stimulates synthesis of the thyroglobulin colloid and the release of thyroxine (T_4) and triiodothyronine (T_3) from the cell in the six steps illustrated here. (Only a few of the thyroglobulins in the colloid are illustrated. The rest of the colloid is represented by the unstructured yellow substance.)

16

transported to the Golgi apparatus, where sugar residues are attached and the molecules are packed into vesicles. These transport vesicles move to the apex of the follicle cell, where their contents are discharged into the follicle lumen and become part of the stored colloid.

② **Iodide trapping.** To produce the functional iodinated hormones, the follicle cells must accumulate iodides (anions of iodine, I⁻) from the blood. Because the intracellular concentration of I⁻ is over 30 times higher than that in blood, iodide trapping depends on active transport. Once trapped inside the follicle cell, iodide then moves into the follicle lumen by facilitated diffusion.

③ **Oxidation to iodine and iodination.** At the border of the follicle cell and colloid, iodides are oxidized (by removal of electrons) and converted to iodine (I_2). Once formed, iodine is attached to tyrosine amino acids that form part of the thyroglobulin colloid. This

iodination reaction occurs at the junction of the follicle cell apex and the colloid and is mediated by peroxidase enzymes. Attachment of one iodine to a tyrosine produces **monoiodotyrosine (MIT or T₁);** attachment of two iodines produces **diiodotyrosine (DIT or T₂).**

④ **Coupling of T₂ and T₁.** Next, enzymes in the colloid link T_1 and T_2 together. Two linked DITs result in T_4; coupling of MIT and DIT produces T_3. At this point, the hormones are still part of the thyroglobulin colloid.

⑤ **Colloid endocytosis.** Hormone secretion requires that the follicle cells reclaim iodinated thyroglobulin by endocytosis and combine the vesicles with lysosomes.

⑥ **Cleavage of the hormones for release.** In the lysosomes, the hormones are cleaved out of the colloid by lysosomal enzymes. The hormones then diffuse from the follicle cells into the bloodstream. The

(a)

(b)

FIGURE 16.10   **Thyroid disorders. (a)** An enlarged thyroid (goiter) of a Bangladeshi boy. **(b)** Exophthalmos of Graves' disease.

main hormonal product secreted is T_4. Some T_4 is converted to T_3 before secretion, but most T_3 is generated in the peripheral tissues.

Although we have followed TH synthesis from beginning to end (secretion), the *initial response* to TSH binding is secretion of thyroid hormone. Then more colloid is synthesized to "restock" the follicle lumen. As a general rule, TSH levels are lower during the day, peak just before sleep, and remain high during the night.

The thyroid gland is unique among the endocrine glands in its ability to store its hormone extracellularly and in large quantities. In the normal thyroid gland, the amount of stored colloid remains relatively constant and is sufficient to provide normal levels of hormone release for two to three months.

Transport and Regulation   Most released T_4 and T_3 immediately binds to transport proteins, most importantly *thyroxine-binding globulins (TBGs)* produced by the liver. Both T_4 and T_3 bind to target tissue receptors, but T_3 binds much more avidly and is about ten times more active. Most peripheral tissues have the enzymes needed to convert T_4 to T_3, a process that entails enzymatic removal of one iodine atom.

Several mechanisms of TH activity probably exist. However, what we know for sure is that, like steroids, TH enters a target cell and binds to intracellular receptors within the cell's nucleus and initiates transcription of mRNA.

Falling TH blood levels trigger release of *thyroid-stimulating hormone (TSH)*, and ultimately of more TH. Rising TH levels feed back to inhibit the hypothalamic-adenohypophyseal axis, temporarily shutting off the stimulus for TSH release. Conditions that increase body energy requirements, such as

pregnancy and exposure of infants to cold, stimulate the hypothalamus to secrete *thyrotropin-releasing hormone (TRH)*, which triggers TSH release, and in such instances, TRH overcomes the negative feedback controls. As the thyroid gland releases larger amounts of thyroid hormones, body metabolism and heat production are enhanced. Factors that inhibit TSH release include somatostatin, and rising levels of glucocorticoids. Excessively high blood iodide concentrations inhibit TH release.

◥ HOMEOSTATIC IMBALANCE

Both overactivity and underactivity of the thyroid gland can cause severe metabolic disturbances. Hypothyroid disorders may result from some thyroid gland defect or secondarily from inadequate TSH or TRH release. They also occur when the thyroid gland is removed surgically and when dietary iodine is inadequate.

In adults, the full-blown hypothyroid syndrome is called **myxedema** (mik″sĕ-de′mah; "mucous swelling"). Symptoms include a low metabolic rate; feeling chilled; constipation; thick, dry skin and puffy eyes; edema; lethargy; and mental sluggishness (but not mental retardation). If myxedema results from lack of iodine, the thyroid gland enlarges and protrudes, a condition called **endemic** (en-dem′ik), or *colloidal*, **goiter** (Figure 16.10a). The follicle cells produce colloid but cannot iodinate it or make functional hormones. The pituitary gland secretes increasing amounts of TSH in a futile attempt to stimulate the thyroid to produce TH, but the only result is that the follicles accumulate more and more *unusable* colloid. Untreated, the thyroid cells eventually "burn out" from frantic activity, and the gland atrophies. Before the marketing of iodized salt, parts

(a)

(b)

FIGURE 16.11 **The parathyroid glands. (a)** Location of the parathyroid glands on the posterior aspect of the thyroid gland. These tiny glands may be more inconspicuous than depicted. **(b)** Micrograph of a section of the parathyroid gland (1500×).

a short, disproportionately sized body and a thick tongue and neck. Cretinism may reflect a genetic deficiency of the fetal thyroid gland or maternal factors, such as lack of dietary iodine. It is preventable by thyroid hormone replacement therapy if diagnosed early enough, but once developmental abnormalities and mental retardation appear, they are not reversible.

The most common (and puzzling) hyperthyroid pathology is **Graves' disease.** Because the serum of patients with this condition often contains abnormal antibodies that mimic TSH and continuously stimulate TH release, Graves' disease is believed to be an autoimmune disease. Typical symptoms include an elevated metabolic rate; sweating; rapid, irregular heartbeat; nervousness; and weight loss despite adequate food intake. *Exophthalmos*, protrusion of the eyeballs, may occur if the tissue behind the eyes becomes edematous and then fibrous (Figure 16.10b). Treatments include surgical removal of the thyroid gland or ingestion of radioactive iodine (^{131}I), which selectively destroys the most active thyroid cells. ●

Calcitonin

Calcitonin is a polypeptide hormone produced by the **parafollicular,** or **C, cells** of the thyroid gland. Because its most important effect is to lower blood Ca^{2+} levels, calcitonin is a direct antagonist of parathyroid hormone, produced by the parathyroid glands. Calcitonin targets the skeleton, where it (1) inhibits osteoclast activity and hence bone resorption and release of Ca^{2+} from the bony matrix and (2) stimulates Ca^{2+} uptake and incorporation into bone matrix. Thus, calcitonin has a bone-sparing effect.

Excessive blood levels of Ca^{2+} (approximately 20% above normal) act as a humoral stimulus for calcitonin release, whereas declining blood Ca^{2+} levels inhibit C cell secretory activity. Calcitonin regulation of blood Ca^{2+} levels is short lived but extremely rapid.

Calcitonin appears to be important only in childhood, when the skeleton grows quickly and the bones are changing dramatically in mass, size, and shape. In adults, it is at best a weak hypocalcemic agent.

The Parathyroid Glands

The tiny, yellow-brown **parathyroid glands** are nearly hidden from view in the posterior aspect of the thyroid gland (Figure 16.11a). There are usually four of these glands, but the precise number varies from one individual to another. As many as eight have been reported, and some may be located in other regions of the neck or even in the thorax. The parathyroid's glandular cells are arranged in thick,

of the midwestern United States were called the "goiter belt." Because these areas had iodine-poor soil and no access to iodine-rich shellfish, goiters were common there. Depending on the cause, myxedema can be reversed by iodine supplements or hormone replacement therapy.

Like many other hormones, the important effects of TH depend on one's age and development. Severe hypothyroidism in infants is called **cretinism** (kre'tĭ-nizm). The child is mentally retarded and has branching cords containing scattered *oxyphil cells* and large numbers of smaller **chief cells** (Figure 16.11b). The chief cells secrete PTH. The function of the oxyphil cells is unclear.

Discovery of the parathyroid glands was accidental. Years ago, surgeons were baffled by the observation that while most patients recovered uneventfully after partial (or even total) thyroid gland removal, others suffered uncontrolled muscle spasms and severe pain, and subsequently died. It was only after several such tragic deaths that the parathyroid glands were discovered and their hormonal function, quite different from that of the thyroid gland hormones, became known.

Parathyroid hormone (PTH), or **parathormone**, the protein hormone of these glands, is the single most important hormone controlling the calcium balance of the blood. PTH release is triggered by falling blood Ca^{2+} levels and inhibited by hypercalcemia. PTH increases Ca^{2+} levels in blood by stimulating three target organs: the skeleton (which contains considerable amounts of calcium salts in its matrix), the kidneys, and the intestine (Figure 16.12).

PTH release (1) stimulates osteoclasts (bone-resorbing cells) to digest some of the bony matrix and release ionic calcium and phosphates to the blood; (2) enhances reabsorption of Ca^{2+} (and excretion of PO_4^{3-}) by the kidneys; and (3) increases absorption of Ca^{2+} by the intestinal mucosal cells. PTH's effect on calcium absorption by the intestine is indirect via its effect on vitamin D activation. Vitamin D is required for absorption of Ca^{2+} from ingested food, but the form in which the vitamin is ingested or produced by the skin is inactive. For vitamin D to exert its physiological effects, it must first be converted by the kidneys to its active vitamin D_3 form, *calcitriol* (1,25-dihydroxycholecalciferol), a transformation stimulated by PTH.

Because plasma calcium ion homeostasis is essential for so many functions, including transmission of nerve impulses, muscle contraction, and blood clotting, precise control of Ca^{2+} levels is critical.

⬥ HOMEOSTATIC IMBALANCE

Hyperparathyroidism is rare and usually the result of a parathyroid gland tumor. When it occurs, calcium is leached from the bones, and the bones soften and deform as their mineral salts are replaced by fibrous connective tissue. In *osteitis fibrosa cystica*, a severe example of this disorder, the bones have a moth-eaten appearance on X rays and tend to fracture spontaneously. The resulting abnormally elevated blood Ca^{2+} level (hypercalcemia) has many outcomes, but the two most notable are (1) depression of the nervous system, which leads to abnormal reflexes and weakness of the skeletal

Key:

$\therefore$ = Ca^{2+} ions

▸▴ = PTH molecules

FIGURE 16.12   Effect of parathyroid hormone on bone, the intestine, and the kidneys. The effect on the intestine is indirect via activated vitamin D.

muscles, and (2) formation of kidney stones as excess calcium salts precipitate in the kidney tubules. Calcium deposits may also form in soft tissues throughout the body and severely impair vital organ functioning, a condition called *metastatic calcification*.

Hypoparathyroidism, or PTH deficiency, most often follows parathyroid gland trauma or removal during thyroid surgery. However, an extended deficiency of dietary magnesium (required for PTH secretion) can cause functional hypoparathyroidism. The resulting hypocalcemia increases the excitability of neurons and accounts for the classical symptoms of *tetany* such as loss of sensation, muscle twitches, and convulsions. Untreated, the symptoms progress to respiratory paralysis and death. ●

Q *Suppose your lab professor springs a "pop" quiz and has adrenal cortical tissue under the microscope for identification. What information about the cell arrangements would help you in this quiz?*

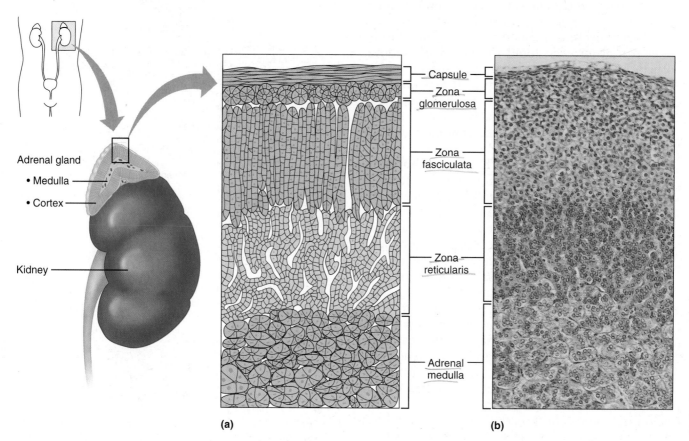

FIGURE 16.13 **Microscopic structure of the adrenal gland. (a)** Diagram and **(b)** photomicrograph of the zona glomerulosa, zona fasciculata, and zona reticularis of the adrenal cortex, and part of the adrenal medulla (200×).

The Adrenal (Suprarenal) Glands

The paired **adrenal glands** are pyramid-shaped organs perched atop the kidneys (*ad* = near; *renal* = kidney), where they are enclosed in a fibrous capsule and a cushion of fat (see Figures 16.1 and 16.13). They are also often referred to as the **suprarenal glands** (*supra* = above).

Each adrenal gland is structurally and functionally two endocrine glands. The inner **adrenal medulla,** more like a knot of nervous tissue than a gland, is part of the sympathetic nervous system. The outer **adrenal cortex,** encapsulating the medullary region and forming the bulk of the gland, is glandular tissue derived from embryonic mesoderm. Each region produces its own set of hormones (Table 16.3), but all adrenal hormones help us cope with stressful situations.

A *Zona glomerulosa cells are in clusters, zona fasciculata cells are in parallel cords, and zona reticularis cells have a netlike arrangement.*

The Adrenal Cortex

Well over two dozen steroid hormones, collectively called **corticosteroids,** are synthesized from cholesterol by the adrenal cortex. The pathway is multistep and involves varying intermediates depending on the hormone being formed. Unlike the amino acid–based hormones, steroid hormones are not stored in cells. Therefore, their rate of release in response to stimulation depends on their rate of synthesis. The structures of several corticosteroids are illustrated in Table 16.3.

The large, lipid-laden cortical cells are arranged in three layers or zones (Figure 16.13). The cell clusters forming the superficial **zona glomerulosa** (zo'nah glo-mer"u-lo'sah) produce mineralocorticoids, hormones that help control the balance of minerals and water in the blood. The principal products of the middle **zona fasciculata** (fah-sik"u-la'tah) cells, arranged in more or less linear cords, are the metabolic hormones called glucocorticoids. The cells of the innermost **zona reticularis** (rĕ-tik'u-lar-is), abutting the adrenal medulla, have a netlike arrangement. These cells mainly produce

TABLE 16.3	Adrenal Gland Hormones: Summary of Regulation and Effects		
HORMONE, STRUCTURE	**REGULATION OF OF RELEASE**	**TARGET ORGAN AND EFFECTS**	**EFFECTS OF HYPERSECRETION ↑ AND HYPOSECRETION ↓**
ADRENOCORTICAL HORMONES			
Mineralocorticoids (chiefly aldosterone) Aldosterone	Stimulated by renin-angiotensin mechanism (activated by decreasing blood volume or blood pressure), elevated K⁺ or low Na⁺ blood levels, and ACTH (minor influence); inhibited by increased blood volume and pressure, increased Na⁺ and decreased K⁺ blood levels	Kidneys: increase blood levels of Na^+ and decrease blood levels of K^+; since water reabsorption accompanies sodium retention, blood volume and blood pressure rise	↑ Aldosteronism ↓ Addison's disease
Glucocorticoids (chiefly cortisol) Cortisol	Stimulated by ACTH; inhibited by feedback inhibition exerted by cortisol	Body cells: promote gluconeogenesis and hyperglycemia; mobilize fats for energy metabolism; stimulate protein catabolism; assist body to resist stressors; depress inflammatory and immune responses	↑ Cushing's syndrome ↓ Addison's disease
Gonadocorticoids (chiefly androgens, converted to testosterone or estrogens after release) Testosterone	Stimulated by ACTH; mechanism of inhibition incompletely understood, but feedback inhibition not seen	Insignificant effects in males; responsible for female libido; development of pubic and axillary hair in females; source of estrogen after menopause	↑ Virilization of females (adrenogenital syndrome) ↓ No effects known
ADRENAL MEDULLARY HORMONES			
Catecholamines (epinephrine and norepinephrine) Epinephrine	Stimulated by preganglionic fibers of the sympathetic nervous system	Sympathetic nervous system target organs: effects mimic sympathetic nervous system activation; increase heart rate and metabolic rate; increase blood pressure by promoting vasoconstriction	↑ Prolonged fight-or-flight response; hypertension ↓ Unimportant

small amounts of adrenal sex hormones, or gonadocorticoids. Note, however, that the two innermost layers of the adrenal cortex share production of glucocorticoids and gonadocorticoids, although each layer is the predominant producer of one type.

Mineralocorticoids   The essential function of **mineralocorticoids** is regulation of the electrolyte (mineral salt) concentrations in extracellular fluids, particularly of Na^+ and K^+. The single most abundant cation in extracellular fluid is Na^+, and although this ion is vital to homeostasis, excessive sodium intake and retention may promote high blood pressure (hypertension) in susceptible individuals. Although there are several mineralocorticoids, **aldosterone** (al-dos′ter-ōn) is the most potent and

16

Q   *In controlling blood pressure, how do the response times compare for this hormonal mechanism and the action of sympathetic nerves?*

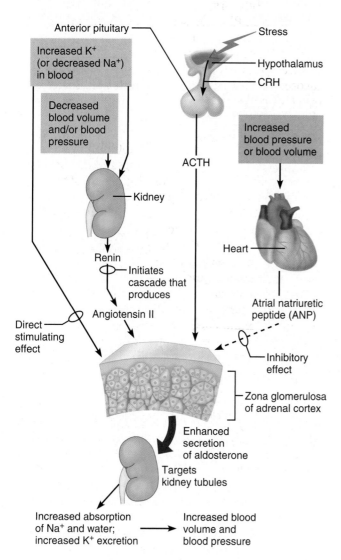

FIGURE 16.14   **Major mechanisms controlling aldosterone release from the adrenal cortex.**

accounts for more than 95% of the mineralocorticoids produced. As you might guess, maintaining sodium ion balance is aldosterone's primary job.

Aldosterone reduces excretion of Na^+ from the body. Its primary target is the distal parts of the kidney tubules, where it stimulates Na^+ reabsorption from the forming urine and its return to the bloodstream. Aldosterone also enhances Na^+ reabsorption from perspiration, saliva, and gastric juice. The

mechanism of aldosterone activity involves the synthesis and activation of proteins required for Na^+ transport such as Na^+-K^+ ATPase, the sodium pump that exchanges K^+ for Na^+.

Regulation of a number of other ions, including K^+, H^+, HCO_3^- (bicarbonate), and Cl^- (chloride), is coupled to that of Na^+; and where Na^+ goes, water follows—an event that leads to changes in blood volume and blood pressure. Hence, Na^+ regulation is crucial to overall body homeostasis. Briefly, aldosterone's effects on the renal tubules cause sodium and water retention accompanied by elimination of K^+ and, in some instances, alterations in the acid-base balance of the blood (by H^+ excretion). Because aldosterone's regulatory effects are brief (lasting approximately 20 minutes), plasma electrolyte balance can be precisely controlled and modified continuously.

Although this discussion represents the major roles of bloodborne aldosterone produced by the adrenal cortex, aldosterone is also secreted by cardiovascular organs, where it is a paracrine and plays a completely different role in cardiac regulation.

Aldosterone secretion is stimulated by rising blood levels of K^+, low blood levels of Na^+, and decreasing blood volume and blood pressure. The reverse conditions inhibit aldosterone secretion. Four mechanisms regulate aldosterone secretion (Figure 16.14); these mechanisms are described next.

1. The renin-angiotensin mechanism (re'nin an"je-o-ten'sin). The renin-angiotensin mechanism, the major regulator of aldosterone release, influences both blood volume and blood pressure. Specialized cells of the *juxtaglomerular apparatus* in the kidneys become excited when blood pressure (or blood volume) declines. These cells respond by releasing **renin** into the blood. Renin cleaves off part of the plasma protein **angiotensinogen** (an"je-o-ten'sin-o-gen), triggering an enzymatic cascade leading to the formation of **angiotensin II,** a potent stimulator of aldosterone release by the glomerulosa cells. However, the renin-angiotensin mechanism does much more than trigger aldosterone release, and all of its effects are ultimately involved in raising the blood pressure. These additional effects are described in detail in Chapters 25 and 26.

2. Plasma concentrations of potassium and sodium ions. Fluctuating blood levels of K^+ directly influence the zona glomerulosa cells. Increased K^+ stimulates, whereas decreased K^+ inhibits aldosterone release. Large decreases in Na^+ directly cause a slight increase in aldosterone release.

3. ACTH. Under normal circumstances, ACTH released by the anterior pituitary has little or no effect on aldosterone release. However, when a person is severely stressed, the hypothalamus secretes more corticotropin-releasing hormone (CRH), and the rise in ACTH blood levels that follows steps up the rate

A   *The hormonal response is much slower because the "messengers" are bloodborne hormones instead of nerve impulses and neurotransmitters.*

of aldosterone secretion to a small extent. The increase in blood volume and blood pressure that results helps ensure adequate delivery of nutrients and respiratory gases during the stressful period.

4. Atrial natriuretic peptide (ANP). Atrial natriuretic peptide, a hormone secreted by the heart when blood pressure rises, fine-tunes blood pressure and sodium-water balance of the body. Its major effect is to inhibit the renin-angiotensin mechanism: It blocks renin and aldosterone secretion and inhibits other angiotensin-induced mechanisms that enhance water and Na^+ reabsorption. Consequently, ANP's overall influence is to decrease blood pressure by allowing Na^+ (and water) to flow out of the body in urine (*natriuretic* = producing salty urine).

▲ HOMEOSTATIC IMBALANCE

Hypersecretion of aldosterone, a condition called *aldosteronism*, typically results from adrenal neoplasms. Two major sets of problems result: (1) hypertension and edema due to excessive Na^+ and water retention and (2) accelerated excretion of potassium ions. If K^+ loss is extreme, neurons become nonresponsive and muscle weakness (and eventually paralysis) occurs. *Addison's disease*, a hyposecretory disease of the adrenal cortex, generally involves a deficient output of both mineralocorticoids and glucocorticoids, as described shortly. ●

Glucocorticoids   Essential to life, the **glucocorticoids** influence the energy metabolism of most body cells and help us to resist stressors. Under normal circumstances, they help the body adapt to intermittent food intake by keeping blood glucose levels fairly constant, and maintain blood pressure by increasing the action of vasoconstrictors. However, severe stress due to hemorrhage, infection, or physical or emotional trauma evokes a dramatically higher output of glucocorticoids, which helps the body negotiate the crisis. Glucocorticoid hormones include **cortisol (hydrocortisone)** (see Table 16.3), **cortisone**, and **corticosterone**, but only cortisol is secreted in significant amounts in humans. As for all steroid hormones, the basic mechanism of glucocorticoid activity on target cells is to modify gene activity.

Glucocorticoid secretion is regulated by negative feedback. Cortisol release is promoted by ACTH, triggered in turn by the hypothalamic releasing hormone CRH. Rising cortisol levels feed back to act on both the hypothalamus and the anterior pituitary, preventing CRH release and shutting off ACTH and cortisol secretion. Cortisol secretory bursts, driven by patterns of eating and activity, occur in a definite pattern throughout the day and night. Cortisol blood levels peak shortly before we arise in the morning. The lowest levels occur in the evening just before

and shortly after we fall asleep. The normal cortisol rhythm is interrupted by acute stress of any variety as the sympathetic nervous system overrides the (usually) inhibitory effects of elevated cortisol levels and triggers CRH release. The resulting increase in ACTH blood levels causes an outpouring of cortisol from the adrenal cortex.

Stress results in a dramatic rise in blood levels of glucose, fatty acids, and amino acids, all provoked by cortisol. Cortisol's prime metabolic effect is to provoke *gluconeogenesis*, that is, the formation of glucose from fats and proteins. In order to "save" glucose for the brain, cortisol mobilizes fatty acids from adipose tissue and encourages their increased use for energy. Under cortisol's influence, stored proteins are broken down to provide building blocks for repair or for making enzymes to be used in metabolic processes. Cortisol enhances epinephrine's vasoconstrictive effects, and the rise in blood pressure and circulatory efficiency that results helps ensure that these nutrients are quickly distributed to the cells.

Although *ideal amounts of glucocorticoids promote normal function*, significant anti-inflammatory and anti-immune effects are associated with cortisol excess. Excessive levels of glucocorticoids (1) depress cartilage and bone formation, (2) inhibit inflammation by decreasing the release of inflammatory chemicals and preventing vasodilation, (3) depress the immune system, and (4) promote changes in cardiovascular, neural, and gastrointestinal function. Recognition of the effects of glucocorticoid hypersecretion has led to widespread use of glucocorticoid drugs to control symptoms of many chronic inflammatory disorders, such as rheumatoid arthritis or allergic responses. However, these potent drugs are a double-edged sword. Although they relieve some of the symptoms of these disorders, they also cause the undesirable effects of excessive levels of these hormones.

▲ HOMEOSTATIC IMBALANCE

The pathology of glucocorticoid excess, **Cushing's syndrome**, may be caused by an ACTH-releasing pituitary tumor (in which case, it is called **Cushing's disease**); by an ACTH-releasing malignancy of the lungs, pancreas, or kidneys; or by a tumor of the adrenal cortex. However, it most often results from the clinical administration of pharmacological doses (doses higher than those found in the body) of glucocorticoid drugs. The syndrome is characterized by persistent hyperglycemia *(steroid diabetes)*, dramatic losses in muscle and bone protein, and water and salt retention, leading to hypertension and edema. The so-called *cushingoid signs* (Figure 16.15) include a swollen "moon" face, redistribution of fat to the abdomen and the posterior neck (causing a "buffalo hump"), a tendency to bruise, and poor wound

16

(a)

(b)

FIGURE 16.15 **A patient (a) before and (b) during Cushing's disease.** In (b), the characteristic "buffalo hump" of fat on the upper back is indicated by a white arrow.

healing. Because of enhanced anti-inflammatory effects, infections may become overwhelmingly severe before producing recognizable symptoms. Eventually, muscles weaken and spontaneous fractures force the person to become bedridden. The only treatment is removal of the cause—be it surgical removal of the offending tumor or discontinuation of the drug.

Addison's disease, the major hyposecretory disorder of the adrenal cortex, usually involves deficits in both glucocorticoids and mineralocorticoids. Its victims tend to lose weight; their plasma glucose and sodium levels drop and potassium levels rise. Severe dehydration and hypotension are common. Corticosteroid replacement therapy at physiological doses (doses typical of those normally found in the body) is the usual treatment. ●

Gonadocorticoids (Sex Hormones)   The bulk of the **gonadocorticoids** secreted by the adrenal cortex are weak **androgens,** or male sex hormones, such as *androstenedione* and *dehydroepiandrosterone (DHEA).* These are converted to the more potent male hormone, *testosterone,* in the tissue cells or to estrogens (female sex homones) in females (see Table 16.3). The adrenal cortex also makes small amounts of female hormones (estradiol and other estrogens). The amount of gonadocorticoids produced by the adrenal cortex is insignificant compared with the

amounts made by the gonads during late puberty and adulthood. The exact role of the adrenal sex hormones is still in question, but because adrenal androgen levels rise continuously between the ages of 7 and 13 in both boys and girls, it is assumed that these hormones contribute to the onset of puberty and the appearance of axillary and pubic hair during that time. In adult women adrenal androgens are thought to be responsible for the sex drive, and they may account for the estrogens produced after menopause when ovarian estrogens are no longer produced. Control of gonadocorticoid secretion is not completely understood. Release seems to be stimulated by ACTH, but the gonadocorticoids do not appear to exert feedback inhibition on ACTH release.

HOMEOSTATIC IMBALANCE

Since androgens predominate, hypersecretion of gonadocorticoids causes *adrenogenital syndrome* (masculinization). In adult males, these effects of elevated gonadocorticoid levels may be obscured, since testicular testosterone has already produced virilization; but in prepubertal males and in females, the results can be dramatic. In the young man, maturation of the reproductive organs and appearance of the secondary sex characteristics occur rapidly, and the sex drive emerges with a vengeance. Females develop a beard

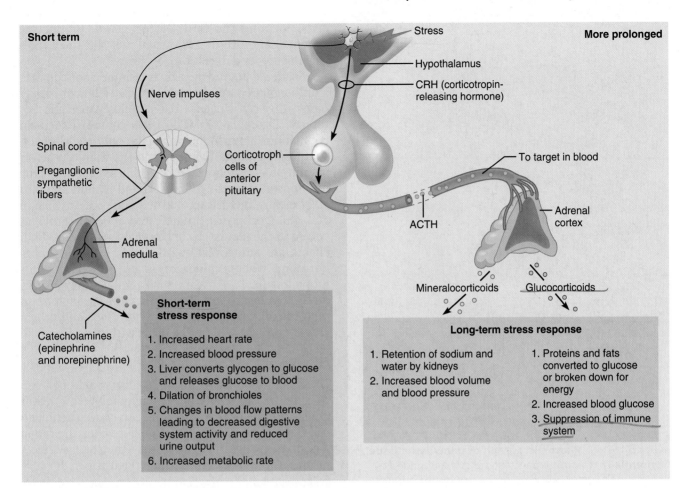

Short term   **More prolonged**

Stress

Nerve impulses

Hypothalamus

CRH (corticotropin-releasing hormone)

Spinal cord

Preganglionic sympathetic fibers

Corticotroph cells of anterior pituitary

To target in blood

ACTH

Adrenal cortex

Adrenal medulla

Catecholamines (epinephrine and norepinephrine)

Mineralocorticoids   Glucocorticoids

Short-term stress response

1. Increased heart rate
2. Increased blood pressure
3. Liver converts glycogen to glucose and releases glucose to blood
4. Dilation of bronchioles
5. Changes in blood flow patterns leading to decreased digestive system activity and reduced urine output
6. Increased metabolic rate

Long-term stress response

1. Retention of sodium and water by kidneys
2. Increased blood volume and blood pressure

1. Proteins and fats converted to glucose or broken down for energy
2. Increased blood glucose
3. Suppression of immune system

FIGURE 16.16 **Stress and the adrenal gland.** Stressful stimuli cause the hypothalamus to activate the adrenal medulla via sympathetic nerve impulses and the adrenal cortex via hormonal signals. The medulla mediates short-term responses to stress by secreting epinephrine and norepinephrine. The cortex controls more prolonged responses by secreting steroid hormones.

and a masculine pattern of body hair distribution, and the clitoris grows to resemble a small penis. ●

The Adrenal Medulla

Because it is discussed in Chapter 14 as part of the autonomic nervous system, the adrenal medulla is covered only briefly here. Its spherical **chromaffin cells** (kro-maf'in), which crowd around blood-filled capillaries and sinusoids, are modified ganglionic sympathetic neurons that synthesize the *catecholamines* **epinephrine** and **norepinephrine (NE)** via a molecular sequence from tyrosine to dopamine to NE to epinephrine (see Figure 11.21).

When the body is activated to fight-or-flight status by some short-term stressor, the sympathetic nervous system is mobilized: Blood glucose levels rise, blood vessels constrict and the heart beats faster (together raising the blood pressure), blood is diverted from temporarily nonessential organs to the heart and skeletal muscles, and preganglionic sym-

pathetic nerve endings weaving through the adrenal medulla signal for release of catecholamines, which reinforce and prolong the fight-or-flight response.

Unequal amounts of the two hormones are stored and released; approximately 80% is epinephrine and 20% norepinephrine. With a few exceptions, the two hormones exert the same effects (Table 14.3, p. 544). Epinephrine is the more potent stimulator of metabolic activities, bronchial dilation, and increased blood flow to skeletal muscles and the heart, but norepinephrine has the greater influence on peripheral vasoconstriction and blood pressure. Epinephrine is used clinically as a heart stimulant and to dilate the bronchioles during acute asthmatic attacks.

Unlike the adrenocortical hormones, which promote long-lasting body responses to stressors, catecholamines cause fairly brief responses. The interrelationships of the adrenal hormones and the hypothalamus, the "director" of the stress response, are depicted in Figure 16.16.

Pancreatic acinar cells (exocrine)

α (Glucagon-producing) cells

β (Insulin-producing) cells

Pancreatic islet (of Langerhans)

FIGURE 16.17 **Photomicrograph of pancreatic tissue, differentially stained.** A pancreatic islet is surrounded by blue-gray acinar cells, which produce the exocrine product (enzyme-rich pancreatic juice). In this preparation, the β cells of the islets that produce insulin are stained pale pink, and the α cells that produce glucagon are stained bright pink (150×).

HOMEOSTATIC IMBALANCE

Because hormones of the adrenal medulla merely intensify activities set into motion by the sympathetic nervous system neurons, a deficiency of these hormones is not a problem. Unlike glucocorticoids, adrenal catecholamines are not essential for life. However, hypersecretion of catecholamines, sometimes arising from a chromaffin cell tumor called a *pheochromocytoma* (fe-o-kro"mo-si-to'mah), produces symptoms of uncontrolled sympathetic nervous system activity—hyperglycemia, increased metabolic rate, rapid heartbeat and palpitations, hypertension, intense nervousness, and sweating. ●

The Pancreas

Located partially behind the stomach in the abdomen, the soft, triangular **pancreas** is a mixed gland composed of both endocrine and exocrine gland cells (Figure 16.1). Along with the thyroid and parathyroids, it develops as an outpocketing of the epithelial lining of the gastrointestinal tract. *Acinar*

cells, forming the bulk of the gland, produce an enzyme-rich juice that is ducted into the small intestine during food digestion.

Scattered among the acinar cells are approximately a million **pancreatic islets** (also called **islets of Langerhans**), tiny cell clusters that produce pancreatic hormones (Figure 16.17). The islets contain two major populations of hormone-producing cells, the glucagon-synthesizing **alpha (α) cells** and the more numerous insulin-producing **beta (β) cells**. These cells act as tiny fuel sensors, secreting glucagon and insulin appropriately during the fasting and fed states. Thus insulin and glucagon are intimately but independently involved in the regulation of blood glucose levels. Their effects are antagonistic: Insulin is a *hypoglycemic* hormone, whereas glucagon is a *hyperglycemic* hormone (Figure 16.18). Some islet cells also synthesize other peptides in small amounts. These include *somatostatin, pancreatic polypeptide (PP)*, and others. However, these will not be dealt with here.

Glucagon

Glucagon (gloo'kah-gon), a 29-amino-acid polypeptide, is an extremely potent hyperglycemic agent. One molecule of this hormone can cause the release of 100 million molecules of glucose into the blood! The major target of glucagon is the liver, where it promotes the following actions (Figure 16.18):

1. Breakdown of glycogen to glucose (*glycogenolysis*)

2. Synthesis of glucose from lactic acid and from noncarbohydrate molecules (*gluconeogenesis*)

3. Release of glucose to the blood by liver cells, which causes blood glucose levels to rise

A secondary effect is a fall in the amino acid concentration in the blood as the liver cells sequester these molecules to make new glucose molecules.

Secretion of glucagon by the alpha cells is prompted by humoral stimuli, mainly falling blood glucose levels. However, sympathetic nervous system stimulation and rising amino acid levels (as might follow a protein-rich meal) are also stimulatory. Glucagon release is suppressed by rising blood glucose levels, insulin, and somatostatin.

Insulin

Insulin is a small (51-amino-acid) protein consisting of two amino acid chains linked by disulfide (–S–S–) bonds. It is synthesized as part of a larger polypeptide chain called **proinsulin.** The middle portion of this chain is then excised by enzymes, releasing functional insulin. This "clipping" process occurs in the secretory vesicles just before insulin is released from the beta cell.

Insulin's effects are most obvious when we have just eaten. Its main effect is to lower blood glucose

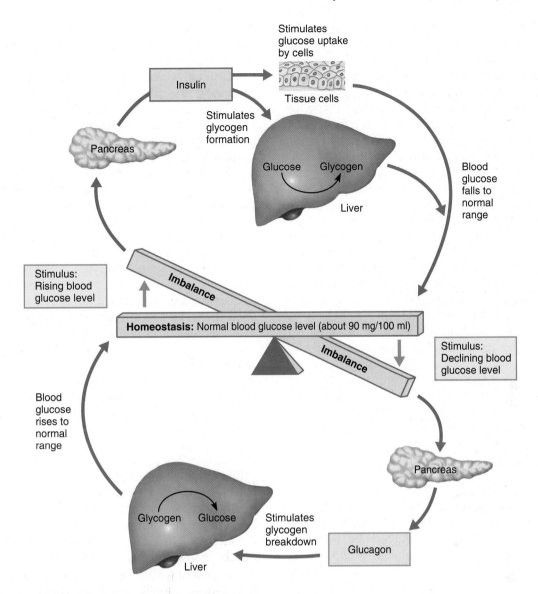

FIGURE 16.18 Regulation of blood glucose levels by insulin and glucagon.
When blood glucose levels are high, the pancreas releases the hypoglycemic hormone insulin, which stimulates glucose uptake by cells and glycogen formation in the liver, so that blood glucose levels are lowered. When blood glucose levels are low, the pancreas releases the hyperglycemic hormone glucagon, which stimulates glycogen breakdown and thereby increases the amount of blood glucose.

levels (Figure 16.18), but it also influences protein and fat metabolism. Circulating insulin lowers blood glucose levels by enhancing membrane transport of glucose (and other simple sugars) into body cells, especially muscle and fat cells. (It does *not* accelerate glucose entry into liver, kidney, and brain* tissue, all of which have easy access to blood glucose regardless of insulin levels.) Insulin inhibits the breakdown of glycogen to glucose and the conversion of amino acids or fats to glucose; thus, it counters any metabolic

activity that would increase plasma levels of glucose. At the cellular level, insulin activates its receptor (a tyrosine kinase enzyme), which phosphorylates specific proteins, beginning the cascade that leads to increased glucose uptake and insulin's other effects.

After glucose enters a target cell, insulin binding triggers enzymatic activities that

1. Catalyze the oxidation of glucose for ATP production

2. Join glucose molecules together to form glycogen

3. Convert glucose to fat (particularly in adipose tissue)

*However, insulin does have important roles in the brain. It participates in neuronal development, feeding behavior, and learning and memory.

As a rule, energy needs are met first, followed by glycogen formation. Finally, if excess glucose is still available, it is converted to fat. Insulin also stimulates amino acid uptake and protein synthesis in muscle tissue. In summary, insulin sweeps glucose out of the blood, causing it to be used for energy or converted to other forms (glycogen or fats), and it promotes protein synthesis and fat storage.

Pancreatic beta cells are stimulated to secrete insulin chiefly by elevated blood glucose levels, but rising plasma levels of amino acids and fatty acids, and release of acetylcholine by parasympathetic nerve fibers, also trigger insulin release. As body cells take up glucose and other nutrients, and plasma levels of these substances drop, insulin secretion is suppressed. Other hormones also influence insulin release. For example, any hyperglycemic hormone (such as glucagon, epinephrine, growth hormone, thyroxine, or glucocorticoids) called into action as blood glucose levels drop indirectly stimulates insulin release by promoting glucose entry into the bloodstream. Somatostatin depresses insulin release. Thus, blood glucose levels represent a balance of humoral and hormonal influences. Insulin and (indirectly) somatostatin are the hypoglycemic factors that counterbalance the many hyperglycemic hormones.

◤ HOMEOSTATIC IMBALANCE

Diabetes mellitus (DM) results from either hyposecretion or hypoactivity of insulin. When insulin is absent or deficient, blood glucose levels remain high after a meal because glucose is unable to enter most tissue cells. Ordinarily, when blood glucose levels rise, hyperglycemic hormones are not released, but when hyperglycemia becomes excessive, the person begins to feel nauseated, which precipitates the fight-or-flight response. This results, inappropriately, in all the reactions that normally occur in the hypoglycemic (fasting) state to make glucose available—that is, glycogenolysis, lipolysis (breakdown of fat), and gluconeogenesis. Thus, the already high blood glucose levels soar even higher, and excesses of glucose begin to be lost from the body in the urine *(glycosuria)*.

When sugars cannot be used as cellular fuel, more fats are mobilized, resulting in high fatty acid levels in the blood, a condition called lipidemia or lipemia. In severe cases of diabetes mellitus, blood levels of fatty acids and their metabolites (acetoacetic acid, acetone, and others) rise dramatically. The fatty acid metabolites, collectively called **ketones** (ke'tōnz) or **ketone bodies,** are organic acids. When they accumulate in the blood, the blood pH drops, resulting in **ketoacidosis,** and ketone bodies

begin to spill into the urine *(ketonuria).* Severe ketoacidosis is life threatening. The nervous system responds by initiating rapid deep breathing (hyperpnea) to blow off carbon dioxide from the blood and increase blood pH. (The physiological basis of this mechanism is explained in Chapter 22.) If untreated, ketoacidosis disrupts heart activity and oxygen transport, and severe depression of the nervous system leads to coma and death.

The three cardinal signs of diabetes mellitus are polyuria, polydipsia, and polyphagia. The excessive glucose in the kidney filtrate acts as an osmotic diuretic (that is, it inhibits water reabsorption by the kidney tubules), resulting in **polyuria,** a huge urine output that leads to decreased blood volume and dehydration. Serious electrolyte losses also occur as the body rids itself of excess ketone bodies. Ketone bodies are negatively charged and carry positive ions out with them; as a result, sodium and potassium ions are also lost from the body. Because of the electrolyte imbalance, the person gets abdominal pains and may vomit, and the stress reaction spirals even higher. Dehydration stimulates hypothalamic thirst centers, causing **polydipsia,** or excessive thirst. The final sign, **polyphagia,** refers to excessive hunger and food consumption, a sign that the person is "starving in the land of plenty." Although plenty of glucose is available, it cannot be used, and the body starts to utilize its fat and protein stores for energy metabolism. Figure 16.19 summarizes the consequences of insulin deficiency. DM is discussed in greater detail in *A Closer Look* on pp. 636–637.

Hyperinsulinism, or excessive insulin secretion, results in low blood glucose levels, or **hypoglycemia.** This condition triggers the release of hyperglycemic hormones, which cause anxiety, nervousness, tremors, and weakness. Insufficient glucose delivery to the brain causes disorientation, progressing to convulsions, unconsciousness, and even death. In rare cases, hyperinsulinism results from an islet cell tumor. More commonly, it is caused by an overdose of insulin and is easily treated by ingesting some sugar. ●

The Gonads

The male and female **gonads** (see Figure 16.1) produce steroid sex hormones, identical to those produced by adrenal cortical cells. The major distinction is the source and relative amounts produced. The paired *ovaries* are small, oval organs located in the female's abdominopelvic cavity. Besides producing ova, or eggs, the ovaries produce several hormones, most importantly **estrogens** and **progesterone** (pro-jes'té-rōn). Alone, the estrogens are

Organs/tissue involved	Organ/tissue responses to insulin deficiency	Resulting conditions:		Signs and symptoms
		In blood	In urine	
	Decreased glucose uptake and utilization	Hyperglycemia	Glycosuria	Polyuria (and dehydration, soft eyeballs)
	Glycogenolysis		Osmotic diuresis	Polydipsia (and fatigue, weight loss)
	Protein catabolism and gluconeogenesis			Polyphagia
	Lipolysis and ketogenesis	Lipidemia and ketoacidosis	Ketonuria	Acetone breath
				Hyperpnea
			Loss of Na+, K+; electrolyte and acid-base imbalances	Nausea/vomiting/ abdominal pain
				Cardiac irregularities
				Central nervous system depression; coma

= Muscle   = Adipose tissue   = Liver

FIGURE 16.19 **Symptomatic results of insulin deficit (diabetes mellitus).**

responsible for maturation of the reproductive organs and the appearance of the secondary sex characteristics of females at puberty. Acting with progesterone, estrogens promote breast development and cyclic changes in the uterine mucosa (the menstrual cycle).

The male *testes*, located in an extra-abdominal skin pouch called the scrotum, produce sperm and male sex hormones, primarily **testosterone** (testos'té-rōn). During puberty, testosterone initiates the maturation of the male reproductive organs and the appearance of secondary sex characteristics and sex drive. In addition, testosterone is necessary for normal sperm production and maintains the reproductive organs in their mature functional state in adult males.

The release of gonadal hormones is regulated by gonadotropins, as described earlier. We will discuss the roles of the gonadal, placental, and gonadotropic hormones in detail in Chapters 27 and 28, where we consider the reproductive system and pregnancy.

The Pineal Gland

The tiny, pine cone–shaped **pineal gland** hangs from the roof of the third ventricle in the diencephalon (see Figure 16.1). Its secretory cells, called **pinealocytes,** are arranged in compact cords and clusters. Lying between pinealocytes in adults are dense particles containing calcium salts ("brain-sand" or "pineal sand"). These salts are radiopaque; hence, the pineal gland is a handy landmark for determining brain orientation in X rays.

The endocrine function of the pineal gland is still somewhat of a mystery. Although many peptides and amines have been isolated from this minute gland, its only major secretory product is **melatonin** (mel"ah-to'nin), a powerful antioxidant and amine hormone derived from serotonin. Melatonin concentrations in the blood rise and fall in a diurnal (daily) cycle. Peak levels occur during the night and make us drowsy; lowest levels occur around noon.

The pineal gland indirectly receives input from the visual pathways (retina → suprachiasmatic nucleus of hypothalamus → superior cervical ganglion → pineal gland) concerning the intensity and duration of daylight. In some animals, mating behavior and gonadal size vary with changes in the relative lengths of light and dark periods, and melatonin mediates these effects. In children, melatonin may have an antigonadotropic effect, that is, it may inhibit precocious (too early) sexual maturation and thus affect the timing of puberty.

The *suprachiasmatic nucleus* of the hypothalamus, an area referred to as our "biological clock," is richly supplied with melatonin receptors, and exposure to bright light (known to suppress melatonin secretion) can reset the clock timing. Hence, changing melatonin levels may also be a means by which the day/night cycles influence physiological processes

A CLOSER LOOK

Sweet Revenge: Can Biotechnology Tame the DM Monster?

Few medical breakthroughs have been as electrifying as the discovery of insulin in 1921, an event that changed diabetes mellitus from a death sentence to a survivable disease. Nonetheless, DM is still a huge health problem: Determining blood glucose levels accurately and maintaining desirable levels sorely challenge our present biotechnology. Let's take a closer look at the characteristics and challenges of type 1 and type 2, the major forms of diabetes mellitus.

More than 1 million Americans have **type 1 diabetes mellitus,** formerly called *insulin-dependent diabetes mellitus (IDDM).* Symptoms appear suddenly, usually before age 15. However, a long asymptomatic period during which the beta cells are systemically destroyed by an autoimmune response precedes these symptoms.

Type 1 diabetes susceptibility genes have been localized on several chromosomes, indicating that type 1 diabetes is an example of a multigene autoimmune response. However, some investigators believe that *molecular mimicry* is at least part of the problem: Some foreign substance (for example, a virus) has entered the body and is so similar to certain self (beta cell) proteins that the immune system attacks the beta cells as well as the invader.

Indeed, elegant studies on certain strains of diabetic mice, stressed by infections or other irritants, demonstrated that they produced increasing amounts of a particular stress protein (heat shock protein 60) and also churned out antibodies against that stress protein. When fragments of the stress protein called p277 were injected into other mice showing early signs of diabetes, the beta cells were spared from the autoimmune attack. This study was extended to newly diagnosed human diabetic subjects, who received the fragment as a drug called DiaPep277. By the end of the study, those receiving DiaPep277 hardly needed outside insulin while those receiving the placebo needed an increasing amount as time went on.

Type 1 diabetics totally lack insulin activity, and their disease is difficult to control. Typically they develop long-term vascular and neural problems. The lipidemia and high blood cholesterol levels typical of the disease can lead to severe vascular complications including atherosclerosis, strokes, heart attacks, renal shutdown, gangrene, and blindness. Consequences of neuropathies include loss of sensation, impaired bladder function, and impotence. Female type 1 diabetics also tend to have lumpy breasts and to undergo premature menopause, which increases their risk for cardiac

problems. Some diabetics can delay renal damage by taking drugs to manage high blood pressure.

Previously, the protocol was insulin injections once or twice daily to manage ketoacidosis and, to a lesser extent, hyperglycemia. Currently, more frequent insulin injections (up to four times daily, or better yet, by a continuous infusion pump) are recommended to reduce vascular and renal complications. Add a glucose sensor and a small computer to an insulin pump and you could have an artificial pancreas that would dispense insulin as needed. Such devices are being tested, but problems with glucose sensing and calculating the amount of insulin to dispense have so far confined such devices to the laboratory. A number of alternative insulin delivery methods are also in clinical trials, including insulin mist inhalers and insulin patches.

Pancreatic islet cell transplants have become increasingly successful in helping type 1 diabetics, with 84% of patients needing no injected insulin after three years. The need for long-term immunosuppression, however, limits this treatment to only those diabetics who cannot control their blood glucose by any other means.

Over 90% of known DM cases are **type 2 diabetes mellitus,** formerly called *non-insulin-dependent*

that show rhythmic variations, such as body temperature, sleep, and appetite.

The Thymus

Located deep to the sternum in the thorax is the lobulated **thymus gland.** Large and conspicuous in infants and children, the thymus diminishes in size throughout adulthood. By old age, it is composed largely of adipose and fibrous connective tissues.

The major hormonal product of the thymic epithelial cells is a family of peptide hormones, including **thymopoietins, thymic factor,** and **thymosins**

(thi′mo-sinz), which appear to be essential for the normal development of *T lymphocytes* and the immune response. Thymic hormones are described in Chapter 21 with the discussion of the immune system.

Other Hormone-Producing Structures

Other hormone-producing cells occur in various organs of the body, including the following (see Table 16.4):

diabetes mellitus (NIDDM), which grows increasingly common with age. About 12 million people in the U.S. have been diagnosed with type 2 diabetes, and roughly half as many are believed to be undiagnosed victims. Although ketoacidosis is not a major problem for type 2 diabetics, they are at risk for the same complications as type 1 diabetics—heart disease, amputations, kidney failure, and blindness.

Heredity or a familial predisposition is particularly striking in this diabetic group. An estimated 25–30% of Americans carry a gene that predisposes them to type 2 diabetes, with nonwhites affected to a much greater extent. If an identical twin has type 2 diabetes mellitus, the probability that the other twin will have the disease is 100%. Most type 2 diabetics produce insulin, but for some reason the insulin receptors are unable to respond to it, a phenomenon called **insulin resistance.** Mutations in any one of several genes could lead to insulin resistance. For example, a particular mutation in the PC-1 membrane protein gene causes PC-1 to interact more strongly with the insulin receptor, preventing receptor activation.

Lifestyle factors also play a role: Type 2 diabetics are almost always overweight and sedentary. Adipose cells of obese people overproduce a number of hormonelike chemicals including _tumor necrosis factor alpha_ and _adiponectin_, which may alter the

enzymatic cascade triggered by insulin binding. The Diabetes Prevention Program, a major clinical trial, showed that weight loss and regular exercise can lower the risk of type 2 diabetes dramatically, even for people at high risk.

In many cases type 2 diabetes can be managed solely by exercise, weight loss, and a healthy diet. Some type 2 diabetics also benefit from oral medications that enhance insulin release [like tolbutamide (Orinase), which has been around for decades]. Other medications are _insulin resistance reducers_, such as rosiglitazone (Avandia). If the disease is not controlled, however, most type 2 diabetics must eventually inject insulin (today manufactured by recombinant DNA techniques or produced by animals, usually pigs). Today nearly all pharmaceutical companies are vying to find _the_ drug to treat type 2 diabetes—not only to conquer insulin resistance but also to decrease the neurological and vascular consequences of the disease.

The race is also on to find an easier, preferably bloodless, method of measuring blood glucose. Promising products include the following:

- GlucoWatch, worn like a wristwatch, which uses a mild electric current to extract glucose painlessly onto a transdermal pad. It is approved for use in the U.S. for supplemental but not primary use, because its accuracy is limited.

- Diasensor, a printer-sized device approved in Europe, which shines an infrared beam on the skin to measure blood glucose.

- A battery-operated device that bombards skin pores with ultrasound shock waves, enlarging them so that insulin's large molecules can be absorbed from a transdermal patch.

Biotechnology is on the threshold of taking on the monster and looks like a good bet to win that battle soon. ∎

16

1. Heart. The atria contain some specialized cardiac muscle cells that secrete **atrial natriuretic peptide.** By signaling the kidneys to increase their production of salty urine and by inhibiting aldosterone release by the adrenal cortex, ANP reduces blood volume, blood pressure, and blood sodium concentration (see Figure 16.14).

2. Gastrointestinal tract. _Enteroendocrine cells_ are hormone-secreting cells sprinkled in the mucosa of the gastrointestinal (GI) tract. These scattered cells release several peptide hormones that help regulate a wide variety of digestive functions, some of which are summarized in Table 16.4. Enteroendocrine cells also release amines such as serotonin,

which act as paracrines, diffusing to and influencing nearby target cells without first entering the bloodstream. Because they are similar in certain ways to neurons and many of their hormones and paracrines are chemically identical to neurotransmitters, enteroendocrine cells are sometimes referred to as _paraneurons._

3. Placenta. Besides sustaining the fetus during pregnancy, the placenta secretes several steroid and protein hormones that influence the course of pregnancy. Placental hormones include estrogens and progesterone (hormones more often associated with the ovary), and human chorionic gonadotropin (hCG).

TABLE 16.4	Selected Examples of Hormones Produced by Organs Other Than the Major Endocrine Organs			
SOURCE	**HORMONE**	**CHEMICAL COMPOSITION**	**TRIGGER**	**TARGET ORGAN AND EFFECTS**
GI tract mucosa				
▪ Stomach	Gastrin	Peptide	Secreted in response to food	Stomach: stimulates glands to release hydrochloric acid (HCl)
▪ Duodenum of small intestine	Intestinal gastrin	Peptide	Secreted in response to food, especially fats	Stomach: stimulates HCl secretion and gastrointestinal tract motility
▪ Duodenum	Secretin	Peptide	Secreted in response to food	Pancreas and liver: stimulates release of bicarbonate-rich juice; stomach: inhibits secretory activity
▪ Duodenum	Cholecystokinin (CCK)	Peptide	Secreted in response to food	Pancreas: stimulates release of enzyme-rich juice; gallbladder: stimulates expulsion of stored bile; sphincter of Oddi: causes sphincter to relax, allowing bile and pancreatic juice to enter duodenum
Kidney	Erythropoietin (EPO)	Glycoprotein	Secreted in response to hypoxia	Bone marrow: stimulates production of red blood cells
Kidney	Renin	Peptide	Secreted in response to low blood pressure or plasma volume, or sympathetic stimulation	Initiates renin-angiotensin mechanism of aldosterone release; returns blood pressure to normal
Skin (epidermal cells)	Cholecalciferol (provitamin D_3)	Steroid	Activated by the kidneys to active vitamin D_3 (calcitriol) in response to parathyroid hormone	Intestine: stimulates active transport of dietary calcium across intestinal cell membranes
Heart (atria)	Atrial natriuretic peptide	Peptide	Secreted in response to stretching of atria (by rising blood pressure)	Kidney: inhibits sodium ion reabsorption and renin release; adrenal cortex: inhibits secretion of aldosterone; decreases blood pressure
Adipose tissue	Leptin	Peptide	Secretion proportional to fat stores; increased by nutrient uptake	Brain: suppresses appetite; increases energy expenditure
Adipose tissue	Resistin	Peptide	Unknown	Fat, muscle, liver: antagonizes insulin's action on liver cells

4. Kidneys. Interstitial cells in the kidneys secrete **erythropoietin** (ĕ-rith″ro-poi′ĕ-tin; "red-maker"), a protein hormone that signals the bone marrow to increase production of red blood cells. The kidneys also release *renin*, the hormone that initiates the renin-angiotensin mechanism of aldosterone release described earlier.

5. Skin. The skin produces **cholecalciferol,** an inactive form of vitamin D_3, when modified cholesterol molecules in epidermal cells are exposed to ultraviolet radiation. This compound then enters the blood via the dermal capillaries, is modified in the liver, and becomes fully activated in the kidneys. The active form of vitamin D_3, **calcitriol,** is an essential regulator of the carrier system that intestinal cells use to absorb Ca^{2+} from ingested food. Without this vitamin, the bones become weak and soft.

6. Adipose tissue. Adipose cells release **leptin** following their uptake of glucose, which they store as fat. As described in Chapter 24, leptin binds to CNS neurons concerned with appetite control, producing a sensation of satiety, and appears to stimulate increased energy expenditure. *Resistin,* also secreted by adipose cells, is an insulin antagonist.

Developmental Aspects of the Endocrine System

Hormone-producing glands arise from all three embryonic germ layers. Endocrine glands derived from mesoderm produce steroid hormones. All others produce amines, peptides, or protein hormones.

Though not usually considered important when describing hormone effectiveness, exposure to many pesticides, industrial chemicals, arsenic, dioxin, and other soil and water pollutants has been shown to disrupt endocrine function. Thus far, sex hormones, thyroid hormone, and glucocorticoids have proved vulnerable to the effects of such pollutants. Interference with glucocorticoids, which turn on many genes that may suppress cancer, may help to explain the high cancer rates in certain areas of the country.

Barring exposure to environmental pollutants, and hypersecretory and hyposecretory disorders, most endocrine organs operate smoothly throughout life until old age. Aging may bring about changes in the rates of hormone secretion, breakdown, and excretion, or in the sensitivity of target cell receptors. Endocrine functioning in the elderly is difficult to research, however, because it is frequently altered by the chronic illnesses common in that age group.

Structural changes in the anterior pituitary occur with age; the amount of connective tissue increases, vascularization decreases, and the number of hormone-secreting cells declines. This may or may not affect hormone production. In women, for example, blood levels and the release rhythm of ACTH remain constant, but levels of gonadotropins increase with age. GH levels decline in both sexes, which partially explains muscle atrophy in old age.

The adrenal gland also shows structural changes with age, but normal controls of cortisol appear to persist as long as a person is healthy and not stressed. Chronic stress, on the other hand, drives up blood levels of cortisol and appears to contribute to hippocampal (and memory) deterioration. Plasma levels of aldosterone are reduced by half in old age; however, this may reflect a decline in renin release by the kidneys, which become less responsive to renin-evoking stimuli. No age-related differences have been found in the release of catecholamines by the adrenal medulla.

The gonads, particularly the ovaries, undergo significant changes with age. In late middle age, the ovaries decrease in size and weight, and they become unresponsive to gonadotropins. As female hormone production declines dramatically, the ability to bear children ends, and problems associated with estrogen deficiency, such as arteriosclerosis and osteoporosis, begin to occur. Testosterone production by the testes also wanes with age, but this effect usually is not seen until very old age.

Glucose tolerance (the ability to dispose of a glucose load effectively) begins to deteriorate as early as the fourth decade of life. Blood glucose levels rise higher and return to resting levels more slowly in the elderly than in young adults. The fact that near-normal amounts of insulin continue to be secreted by the islet cells leads researchers to conclude that decreasing glucose tolerance with age may reflect declining receptor sensitivity to insulin (pre–type 2 diabetes).

Thyroid hormone synthesis and release diminish somewhat with age. Typically, the follicles are loaded with colloid in the elderly, and fibrosis of the gland occurs. Basal metabolic rate declines with age. Mild hypothyroidism is only one cause of this decline. The increase in body fat relative to muscle is equally important, because muscle tissue is more actively metabolically than fat.

The parathyroid glands change little with age, and PTH levels remain fairly normal throughout life. Estrogens protect women against the demineralizing effects of PTH, but estrogen production wanes after menopause, leaving older women vulnerable to the bone-demineralizing effects of PTH and osteoporosis.

■ ■ ■

In this chapter, we have covered the general mechanisms of hormone action and have provided an overview of the major endocrine organs, their chief targets, and their most important physiological effects, as summarized in *Making Connections* on p. 640. However, every one of the hormones discussed here comes up in at least one other chapter, where its actions are described as part of the functional framework of a particular organ system. For example, the effects of PTH and calcitonin on bone mineralization are described in Chapter 6 along with the discussion of bone remodeling.

SYSTEM CONNECTIONS: Homeostatic Interrelationships Between the Endocrine System and Other Body Systems

Integumentary System

- Androgens cause activation of sebaceous glands; estrogen increases skin hydration
- Skin produces cholecalciferol (provitamin D)

Skeletal System

- PTH and calcitonin regulate calcium blood levels; growth hormone, T_3, T_4, and sex hormones are necessary for normal skeletal development
- The skeleton provides some protection to endocrine organs, especially to those in the brain, chest, and pelvis

Muscular System

- Growth hormone is essential for normal muscular development; other hormones (thyroxine and catecholamines) influence muscle metabolism
- Muscular system mechanically protects some endocrine glands; muscular activity elicits catecholamine release

Nervous System

- Many hormones (growth hormone, thyroxine, sex hormones) influence normal maturation and function of the nervous system
- Hypothalamus controls anterior pituitary function and produces two hormones

Cardiovascular System

- Several hormones influence blood volume, blood pressure, and heart contractility; erythropoietin stimulates red blood cell production
- Blood is the main transport medium of hormones; heart produces atrial natriuretic peptide

Lymphatic System/Immunity

- Lymphocytes "programmed" by thymic hormones seed the lymph nodes; glucocorticoids depress the immune response and inflammation
- Chemical messengers of the immune system stimulate the release of cortisol and ACTH; lymph provides a route for transport of hormones

Respiratory System

- Epinephrine influences ventilation (dilates bronchioles)
- Respiratory system provides oxygen; disposes of carbon dioxide; converting enzyme in lungs converts angiotensin I to angiotensin II

Digestive System

- GI hormones and paracrines influence GI function; activated vitamin D necessary for absorption of calcium from diet; catecholamines influence digestive motility and secretory activity
- Digestive system provides nutrients to endocrine organs

Urinary System

- Aldosterone and ADH influence renal function; erythropoietin released by kidneys influences red blood cell formation
- Kidneys activate vitamin D (considered a hormone)

Reproductive System

- Hypothalamic, anterior pituitary, and gonadal hormones direct reproductive system development and function; oxytocin and prolactin involved in birth and breast-feeding
- Gonadal hormones feed back to influence endocrine system function

16

THE ENDOCRINE SYSTEM and Interrelationships with the Nervous and Reproductive Systems

Like most body systems, the endocrine system performs many functions that benefit the body as a whole. For example, without insulin, thyroxine, and various other metabolic hormones, body cells would be unable to get or use glucose, and would die. Likewise, total body growth is beholden to the endocrine system, which coordinates the growth spurts with increases in skeletal and muscular mass so that we don't look out of proportion most of the time. But the interactions that are most noticeable and crucial are those that the endocrine system has with the nervous and the reproductive systems, and they begin before birth.

Nervous System

The influence of hormones on behavior is striking. While we are still in the wet darkness of our mother's uterus, testosterone—or lack of it—is determining the "sex" of our brain. If testosterone is produced by the exceedingly tiny male testes, then certain areas of the brain enlarge, develop large numbers of androgen receptors, and thereafter determine the so-called masculine aspects of behavior (aggressiveness, etc.). Conversely, in the absence of testosterone, the brain is feminized. At puberty, Mom and Dad's "little angels," driven by raging hormones, turn into strangers. The surge of androgens—produced first by the adrenal cortices, and then by the maturing gonads—produces an often thoughtless aggressiveness and galloping sex drive, typically long before the cognitive abilities of the brain can rein them in.

Neural involvement in hormonal affairs is no less striking. Not only is the hypothalamus an endocrine organ in its own right, it also effectively regulates the bulk of hormonal activity via its hormonal or neural controls of the pituitary and adrenal medulla. And that's just on a normal day. The effects of trauma on the hypothalamic-pituitary axis can be far-reaching. Lack of loving care to a newborn baby results in failure to thrive; exceptionally vigorous athletic training in the pubertal female can result in bone wasting and infertility. The shadow the nervous system casts over the endocrine system is long indeed.

Reproductive System

The reproductive system is totally dependent on hormones to "order up the right organs" to match our genetic sex. Testosterone secretion by the testes of male embryos directs formation of the male reproductive tract and external genitalia. Without testosterone, female structures develop—regardless of gonadal sex. The next crucial period is puberty, when gonadal sex hormone production rises and steers maturation of the reproductive organs, bringing them to their adult structure and function. Without these hormonal signals, the reproductive organs remain childlike and the person cannot produce offspring. Pregnancy invites more endocrine system interactions with the reproductive system. The placenta, a temporary endocrine organ, churns out estrogens and progesterone, which help maintain the pregnancy and prepare the mother's breasts for lactation, as well as a number of other hormones that influence maternal metabolism. During and after birth, oxytocin and prolactin take center stage to promote labor and delivery, and then milk production and ejection. Other than feedback inhibition exerted by its sex hormones on the hypothalamic-pituitary axis, the influence of reproductive organs on the endocrine system is negligible.

Endocrine System

Case study: We have a new patient to consider today. Mr. Gutteman, a 70-year-old male, was brought into the ER in a comatose state and has yet to come out of it. It is obvious that he suffered severe head trauma—his scalp was badly lacerated, and he has an impacted skull fracture. His initial lab tests (blood and urine) were within normal limits. His fracture was repaired and the following orders (and others) were given:

- Check qh (every hour) and record: spontaneous behavior, level of responsiveness to stimulation, movements, pupil size and reaction to light, speech, and vital signs.
- Turn patient q4h and maintain meticulous skin care and dryness.

1. Explain the rationale behind these orders.

On the second day of his hospitalization, the aide reports that Mr. Gutteman is breathing irregularly, his skin is dry and flaccid, and that she has emptied his urine reservoir several times during the day. Upon receiving this information, the physician ordered

- Blood and urine tests for presence of glucose and ketones
- Strict I&O (fluid intake and output recording)

Mr. Gutteman is found to be losing huge amounts of water in urine and the volume lost is being routinely replaced (via IV line). Mr. Gutteman's blood and urine tests are negative for glucose and ketones.

Relative to these findings:

2. What would you say Mr. Gutteman's hormonal problem is and what do you think caused it?
3. Is it life threatening? (Explain your answer.)

(Answers in Appendix G)

Related Clinical Terms

Hirsutism (her'soot-izm; *hirsut* = hairy, rough) Excessive hair growth; usually refers to this phenomenon in women and reflects excessive androgen production.

Hypophysectomy (hi-pof'i-sek'to-me) Surgical removal of the pituitary gland.

Prolactinoma (pro-lak"tĭ-no'mah; *oma* = tumor) The most common type (30–40% or more) of pituitary gland tumor; evidenced by hypersecretion of prolactin and menstrual disturbances in women.

Psychosocial dwarfism Dwarfism (and failure to thrive) resulting from stress and emotional disorders that suppress hypothalamic release of growth hormone–releasing hormone and thus anterior pituitary secretion of growth hormone.

Thyroid storm (thyroid crisis) A sudden and dangerous increase in all of the symptoms of hyperthyroidism due to excessive amounts of circulating TH. Symptoms of this hypermetabolic state include fever, rapid heart rate, high blood pressure, dehydration, nervousness, and tremors. Precipitating factors include stressful situations, excessive intake of TH supplements, and trauma.

Chapter Summary

Media study tools that could provide you additional help in reviewing specific key topics of Chapter 16 are referenced below.
IP = *InterActive Physiology*

1. The nervous and endocrine systems are the major controlling systems of the body. The nervous system exerts rapid controls via nerve impulses; the endocrine system's effects are mediated by hormones and are more prolonged.

2. Hormonally regulated processes include reproduction; growth and development; mobilization of body defenses; maintaining electrolyte, water, and nutrient balance; and regulating cellular metabolism and energy balance.

The Endocrine System: An Overview (pp. 605–606)

1. Endocrine organs are ductless, well-vascularized glands that release hormones directly into the blood or lymph. They are small and widely separated in the body.

2. The major endocrine organs are the pituitary, thyroid, parathyroid, adrenal, pineal, and thymus glands, as well as the pancreas and gonads. The hypothalamus is a neuroendocrine organ.

3. Local chemical messengers, not generally considered part of the endocrine system, include autocrines, which act on the cells that secrete them, and paracrines, which act on a different cell type nearby.

IP Endocrine System; Topic: Endocrine System Review, p. 3.

Hormones (pp. 606–612)

The Chemistry of Hormones (p. 606)

1. Most hormones are steroids or amino acid based.

IP Endocrine System; Topic: Biochemistry, Secretion, and Transport of Hormones, p. 3.

Mechanisms of Hormone Action (pp. 606–610)

2. Hormones alter cell activity by stimulating or inhibiting characteristic cellular processes of their target cells.

3. Cell responses to hormone stimulation may involve changes in membrane permeability; enzyme synthesis, activation, or inhibition; secretory activity; gene activation; and mitosis.

4. Second-messenger mechanisms employing intracellular messengers and transduced by G proteins are a common means by which amino acid–based hormones interact with their target cells. In the cyclic AMP system, the hormone binds to a plasma membrane receptor that couples to a G protein. When the G protein is activated it, in turn, couples to adenylate cyclase, which catalyzes the synthesis of cyclic AMP from ATP. Cyclic AMP initiates reactions that activate protein kinases and other enzymes, leading to cellular response. The PIP-calcium signal mechanism, involving phosphatidyl inositol, is another important second-messenger system. Other second messengers are cyclic GMP and calcium.

IP Endocrine System; Topic: The Actions of Hormones on Target Cells, pp. 3–7.

5. Steroid hormones (and thyroid hormone) enter their target cells and effect responses by activating DNA, which initiates messenger RNA formation leading to protein synthesis.

Target Cell Specificity (p. 610)

6. The ability of a target cell to respond to a hormone depends on the presence of receptors, within the cell or on its plasma membrane, to which the hormone can bind.

7. Hormone receptors are dynamic structures. Changes in number and sensitivity of hormone receptors may occur in response to high or low levels of stimulating hormones.

IP Endocrine System; Topic: The Actions of Hormones on Target Cells, p. 3.

Half-Life, Onset, and Duration of Hormone Activity (p. 610)

8. Blood levels of hormones reflect a balance between secretion and degradation/excretion. The liver and kidneys are the major organs that degrade hormones; breakdown products are excreted in urine and feces.

9. Hormone half-life and duration of activity are limited and vary from hormone to hormone.

Interaction of Hormones at Target Cells (p. 611)

10. Permissiveness is the situation in which a hormone cannot exert its full effects without the presence of another hormone.

11. Synergism occurs when two or more hormones produce the same effects in a target cell and their results are amplified.

12. Antagonism occurs when a hormone opposes or reverses the effect of another hormone.

Control of Hormone Release (pp. 611–612)

13. Endocrine organs are activated to release their hormones by humoral, neural, or hormonal stimuli. Negative

feedback is important in regulating hormone levels in the blood.

14. The nervous system, acting through hypothalamic controls, can in certain cases override or modulate hormonal effects.

IP Endocrine System; Topic: The Hypothalamic–Pituitary Axis, pp. 4 and 5.

Major Endocrine Organs (pp. 612–636)

The Pituitary Gland (Hypophysis) (pp. 612–620)

1. The pituitary gland hangs from the base of the brain by a stalk and is enclosed by bone. It consists of a hormone-producing glandular portion (anterior pituitary) and a neural portion (posterior pituitary), which is an extension of the hypothalamus.

2. The hypothalamus (a) regulates the hormonal output of the anterior pituitary via releasing and inhibiting hormones and (b) synthesizes two hormones that it exports to the posterior pituitary for storage and later release.

3. Four of the six adenohypophyseal hormones are tropic hormones that regulate the function of other endocrine organs. Most anterior pituitary hormones exhibit a diurnal rhythm of release, which is subject to modification by stimuli influencing the hypothalamus.

4. Growth hormone (GH) is an anabolic hormone that stimulates growth of all body tissues but especially skeletal muscle and bone. It may act directly, or indirectly via insulin-like growth factors (IGFs). GH mobilizes fats, stimulates protein synthesis, and inhibits glucose uptake and metabolism. Secretion is regulated by growth hormone–releasing hormone (GHRH) and growth hormone–inhibiting hormone (GHIH), or somatostatin. Hypersecretion causes gigantism in children and acromegaly in adults; hyposecretion in children causes pituitary dwarfism.

5. Thyroid-stimulating hormone (TSH) promotes normal development and activity of the thyroid gland. Thyrotropin-releasing hormone (TRH) stimulates its release; negative feedback of thyroid hormone inhibits it.

6. Adrenocorticotropic hormone (ACTH) stimulates the adrenal cortex to release corticosteroids. ACTH release is triggered by corticotropin-releasing hormone (CRH) and inhibited by rising glucocorticoid levels.

7. The gonadotropins—follicle-stimulating hormone (FSH) and luteinizing hormone (LH)—regulate the functions of the gonads in both sexes. FSH stimulates sex cell production; LH stimulates gonadal hormone production. Gonadotropin levels rise in response to gonadotropin-releasing hormone (GnRH). Negative feedback of gonadal hormones inhibits gonadotropin release.

8. Prolactin (PRL) promotes milk production in humans. Its secretion is prompted by prolactin-releasing hormone (PRH) and inhibited by prolactin-inhibiting hormone (PIH).

9. The neurohypophysis stores and releases two hypothalamic hormones, oxytocin and antidiuretic hormone (ADH).

10. Oxytocin stimulates powerful uterine contractions, which trigger labor and delivery of an infant, and milk ejection in nursing women. Its release is mediated reflexively by the hypothalamus and represents a positive feedback mechanism.

11. Antidiuretic hormone stimulates the kidney tubules to reabsorb and conserve water, resulting in small volumes of highly concentrated urine and decreased plasma osmolality. ADH is released in response to high solute concentrations in the blood and inhibited by low solute concentrations in the blood. Hyposecretion results in diabetes insipidus.

The Thyroid Gland (pp. 620–624)

12. The thyroid gland is located in the anterior throat. Thyroid follicles store colloid containing thyroglobulin, a glycoprotein from which thyroid hormone is derived.

13. Thyroid hormone (TH) includes thyroxine (T_4) and triiodothyronine (T_3), which increase the rate of cellular metabolism. Consequently, oxygen use and heat production rise.

14. Secretion of thyroid hormone, prompted by TSH, requires reuptake of the stored colloid by the follicle cells and splitting of the hormones from the colloid for release. Rising levels of thyroid hormone feed back to inhibit the pituitary and hypothalamus.

15. Most T_4 is converted to T_3 (the more active form) in the target tissues. These hormones act by turning on gene transcription and protein synthesis.

16. Graves' disease is the most common cause of hyperthyroidism; hyposecretion causes cretinism in infants and myxedema in adults.

17. Calcitonin, produced by the parafollicular (C) cells of the thyroid gland in response to rising blood calcium levels, depresses blood calcium levels by inhibiting bone matrix resorption and enhancing calcium deposit in bone.

IP Endocrine System; Topic: The Hypothalamic–Pituitary Axis, p. 6.

The Parathyroid Glands (pp. 624–625)

18. The parathyroid glands, located on the dorsal aspect of the thyroid gland, secrete parathyroid hormone (PTH), which causes an increase in blood calcium levels by targeting bone, the intestine, and the kidneys. PTH is the antagonist of calcitonin.

19. PTH release is triggered by falling blood calcium levels and is inhibited by rising blood calcium levels.

20. Hyperparathyroidism results in hypercalcemia and all its effects and in extreme bone wasting. Hypoparathyroidism leads to hypocalcemia, evidenced by tetany and respiratory paralysis.

The Adrenal (Suprarenal) Glands (pp. 626–632)

21. The paired adrenal (suprarenal) glands sit atop the kidneys. Each adrenal gland has two functional portions, the cortex and the medulla.

22. Three groups of steroid hormones are produced by the cortex from cholesterol.

23. Mineralocorticoids (primarily aldosterone) regulate sodium ion reabsorption and potassium ion excretion by the kidneys. Sodium ion reabsorption leads to water reabsorption, and increases in blood volume and blood pressure. Release of aldosterone is stimulated by the renin-angiotensin mechanism, rising potassium ion or falling sodium levels in the blood, and ACTH. Atrial natriuretic peptide inhibits aldosterone release.

24. Glucocorticoids (primarily cortisol) are important metabolic hormones that help the body resist stressors by increasing blood glucose, fatty acid and amino acid levels, and blood pressure. High levels of glucocorticoids depress the immune system and the inflammatory response. ACTH is the major stimulus for glucocorticoid release.

25. Gonadocorticoids (mainly androgens) are produced in small amounts throughout life.

26. Hypoactivity of the adrenal cortex results in Addison's disease. Hypersecretion can result in aldosteronism, Cushing's syndrome, and adrenogenital syndrome.

16

27. The adrenal medulla produces catecholamines (epinephrine and norepinephrine) in response to sympathetic nervous system stimulation. Its catecholamines enhance and prolong the fight-or-flight response to short-term stressors. Hypersecretion leads to symptoms typical of sympathetic nervous system overactivity.

IP Endocrine System; Topic: Response to Stress, pp. 5–8.

The Pancreas (pp. 632–634)

28. The pancreas, located in the abdomen close to the stomach, is both an exocrine and an endocrine gland. The endocrine portion (pancreatic islets) releases insulin and glucagon and smaller amounts of other hormones to the blood.

29. Glucagon, released by alpha (α) cells when blood levels of glucose are low, stimulates the liver to release glucose to the blood.

30. Insulin is released by beta (β) cells when blood levels of glucose (and amino acids) are rising. It increases the rate of glucose uptake and metabolism by most body cells. Hyposecretion of insulin results in diabetes mellitus; cardinal signs are polyuria, polydipsia, and polyphagia.

IP Endocrine System; Topic: The Actions of Hormones on Target Cells, pp. 5 and 8.

The Gonads (pp. 634–635)

31. The ovaries of the female, located in the pelvic cavity, release two main hormones. Secretion of estrogens by the ovarian follicles begins at puberty under the influence of FSH. Estrogens stimulate maturation of the female reproductive system and development of the secondary sex characteristics. Progesterone is released in response to high blood levels of LH. It works with estrogens in establishing the menstrual cycle.

32. The testes of the male begin to produce testosterone at puberty in response to LH. Testosterone promotes maturation

of the male reproductive organs, development of secondary sex characteristics, and production of sperm by the testes.

The Pineal Gland (pp. 635–636)

33. The pineal gland is located in the diencephalon. Its primary hormone is melatonin, which influences daily rhythms and may have an antigonadotropic effect in humans.

The Thymus (p. 636)

34. The thymus gland, located in the upper thorax, declines in size and function with age. Its hormones, thymosins, thymic factor, and thymopoietins, are important to the normal development of the immune response.

Other Hormone-Producing Structures (pp. 636–638)

1. Many body organs not normally considered endocrine organs contain isolated cell clusters that secrete hormones. Examples include the heart (atrial natriuretic peptide); gastrointestinal tract organs (gastrin, secretin, and others); the placenta (hormones of pregnancy—estrogen, progesterone, and others); the kidneys (erythropoietin and renin); skin (cholecalciferol); and adipose tissue (leptin and resistin).

Developmental Aspects of the Endocrine System (p. 639)

1. Endocrine glands derive from all three germ layers. Those derived from mesoderm produce steroidal hormones; the others produce the amino acid–based hormones.

2. The natural decrease in function of the female's ovaries during late middle age results in menopause.

3. The efficiency of all endocrine glands seems to decrease gradually as aging occurs. This leads to a generalized increase in the incidence of diabetes mellitus and a lower metabolic rate.

Review Questions

Multiple Choice/Matching

(Some questions have more than one correct answer. Select the best answer or answers from the choices given.)

1. The major stimulus for release of parathyroid hormone is (a) hormonal, (b) humoral, (c) neural.

2. The anterior pituitary secretes all but (a) antidiuretic hormone, (b) growth hormone, (c) gonadotropins, (d) TSH.

3. A hormone not involved in glucose metabolism is (a) glucagon, (b) cortisone, (c) aldosterone, (d) insulin.

4. Parathyroid hormone (a) increases bone formation and lowers blood calcium levels, (b) increases calcium excretion from the body, (c) decreases calcium absorption from the gut, (d) demineralizes bone and raises blood calcium levels.

5. Choose from the following key to identify the hormones described.

Key: (a) aldosterone   (e) oxytocin
     (b) antidiuretic hormone   (f) prolactin
     (c) growth hormone   (g) T₄ and T₃
     (d) luteinizing hormone   (h) TSH

_____ **1.** important anabolic hormone; many of its effects mediated by IGFs

_____ **2.** involved in water balance; cause the kidneys to conserve water (two choices)

_____ **3.** stimulates milk production

_____ **4.** tropic hormone that stimulates the gonads to secrete sex hormones

_____ **5.** increases uterine contractions during birth

_____ **6.** major metabolic hormone(s) of the body

_____ **7.** causes reabsorption of sodium ions by the kidneys

_____ **8.** tropic hormone that stimulates the thyroid gland to secrete thyroid hormone

_____ **9.** secreted by the neurohypophysis (two choices)

_____ **10.** the only steroid hormone in the list

6. A hypodermic injection of epinephrine would (a) increase heart rate, increase blood pressure, dilate the bronchi of the lungs, and increase peristalsis, (b) decrease heart rate, decrease blood pressure, constrict the bronchi, and increase peristalsis, (c) decrease heart rate, increase blood pressure, constrict the bronchi, and decrease peristalsis, (d) increase heart rate, increase blood pressure, dilate the bronchi, and decrease peristalsis.

7. Testosterone is to the male as what hormone is to the female? (a) luteinizing hormone, (b) progesterone, (c) estrogen, (d) prolactin.

8. If anterior pituitary secretion is deficient in a growing child, the child will (a) develop acromegaly, (b) become a dwarf but have fairly normal body proportions, (c) mature sexually at an earlier than normal age, (d) be in constant danger of becoming dehydrated.

9. If there is adequate carbohydrate intake, secretion of insulin results in (a) lower blood glucose levels, (b) increased cell utilization of glucose, (c) storage of glycogen, (d) all of these.

10. Hormones (a) are produced by exocrine glands, (b) are carried to all parts of the body in blood, (c) remain at constant concentration in the blood, (d) affect only non-hormone-producing organs.

11. Some hormones act by (a) increasing the synthesis of enzymes, (b) converting an inactive enzyme into an active enzyme, (c) affecting only specific target organs, (d) all of these.

12. Absence of thyroxine would result in (a) increased heart rate and increased force of heart contraction, (b) depression of the CNS and lethargy, (c) exophthalmos, (d) high metabolic rate.

13. Chromaffin cells are found in the (a) parathyroid gland, (b) anterior pituitary gland, (c) adrenal gland, (d) pineal gland.

14. Atrial natriuretic peptide secreted by the heart has exactly the opposite function of this hormone secreted by the zona glomerulosa: (a) antidiuretic hormone, (b) epinephrine, (c) calcitonin, (d) aldosterone, (e) androgens.

Short Answer Essay Questions

15. Define hormone.

16. Which type of hormone receptor—plasma membrane bound or intracellular—would be expected to provide the most long-lived response to hormone binding and why?

17. (a) Describe the body location of each of the following endocrine organs: anterior pituitary, pineal gland, pancreas, ovaries, testes, and adrenal glands. (b) List the hormones produced by each organ.

18. Name two endocrine glands (or regions) that are important in the stress response, and explain why they are important.

19. The anterior pituitary is often referred to as the master endocrine organ, but it, too, has a "master." What controls the release of anterior pituitary hormones?

20. The posterior pituitary is not really an endocrine gland. Why not? What is it?

21. A colloidal, or endemic, goiter is not really the result of malfunction of the thyroid gland. What does cause it?

22. List some problems that elderly people might have as a result of decreasing hormone production.

23. Name a hormone secreted by a muscle cell and two hormones secreted by neurons.

24. How are the hyperglycemia and lipidemia of insulin deficiency linked?

Critical Thinking and Clinical Application Questions

1. Richard Neis had symptoms of excessive secretion of PTH (high blood calcium levels), and his physicians were certain he had a parathyroid gland tumor. Yet when surgery was performed on his neck, the surgeon could not find the parathyroid glands at all. Where should the surgeon look next to find the tumorous parathyroid gland?

2. Mary Morgan has just been brought into the emergency room of City General Hospital. She is perspiring profusely and is breathing rapidly and irregularly. Her breath smells like acetone (sweet and fruity), and her blood glucose tests out at 650 mg/100 ml of blood. She is in acidosis. What hormone drug should be administered, and why?

3. Johnny, a 5-year-old boy, has been growing by leaps and bounds; his height is 100% above normal for his age. He has been complaining of headaches and vision problems. A CT scan reveals a large pituitary tumor. (a) What hormone is being secreted in excess? (b) What condition will Johnny exhibit if corrective measures are not taken? (c) What is the probable cause of his headaches and visual problems?

4. Sean, a 42-year-old single father, goes to his physician complaining of nausea and chronic fatigue. He reports having felt fatigued and listless for about half a year, but he had attributed this to stress. He has lost considerable weight and, strangely, his skin has a healthy tan, even though he spends long hours at work and rarely ventures outside. His doctor finds very low blood pressure and a rapid, weak pulse. Blood tests show that Sean does not have anemia, but his plasma glucose, cortisol, and Na^+ are low, and his plasma K^+ is high. His doctor orders an ACTH stimulation test, in which Sean's secretion of cortisol is measured after he is given a synthetic form of ACTH. (a) What would account for Sean's low plasma Na^+ and high plasma K^+? (b) What is the reason for doing an ACTH stimulation test? (c) What gland is primarily affected if ACTH *does not* cause a normal elevation of cortisol secretion? What is this abnormality called? (d) What gland is primarily affected if ACTH *does* cause an elevation of cortisol secretion?

5. Roger Proulx has severe arthritis and has been taking prednisone (a glucocorticoid) for two months. He isn't feeling well, complains of repeated "colds," and is extremely "puffy" (edematous). Explain the reason for these symptoms.

16

Overview: Blood Composition and Functions (pp. 647–648)

1. Describe the composition and physical characteristics of whole blood. Explain why it is classified as a connective tissue.
2. List six functions of blood.

Blood Plasma (pp. 648–649)

3. Discuss the composition and functions of plasma.

Formed Elements (pp. 649–662)

4. Describe the structure, function, and production of erythrocytes.
5. Describe the chemical makeup of hemoglobin.
6. List the classes, structural characteristics, and functions of leukocytes. Also describe leukocyte genesis.

7. Describe the structure and function of platelets.
8. Give examples of disorders caused by abnormalities of each of the formed elements. Explain the mechanism of each disorder.

Hemostasis (pp. 663–668)

9. Describe the process of hemostasis. List factors that limit clot formation and prevent undesirable clotting.
10. Give examples of hemostatic disorders. Indicate the cause of each condition.

Transfusion and Blood Replacement (pp. 668–671)

11. Describe the ABO and Rh blood groups. Explain the basis of transfusion reactions.

12. Describe fluids used to replace blood volume and the circumstances for their use.

Diagnostic Blood Tests (pp. 671–672)

13. Explain the diagnostic importance of blood testing.

Developmental Aspects of Blood (pp. 672–673)

14. Describe changes in the sites of blood production and in the type of hemoglobin produced after birth.
15. Name some blood disorders that become more common with age.

Blood is the river of life that surges within us, transporting nearly everything that must be carried from one place to another. Long before modern medicine, blood was viewed as magical—an elixir that held the mystical force of life—because when it drained from the body, life departed as well. Today, centuries later, blood still has enormous importance in the practice of medicine. Clinicians examine it more often than any other tissue when trying to determine the cause of disease in their patients.

In this chapter, we describe the composition and functions of this life-sustaining fluid that serves as a transport "vehicle" for the organs of the cardiovascular system. To get started, we need a brief overview of blood circulation, which is initiated by the pumping action of the heart. Blood exits the *heart* via *arteries*, which branch repeatedly until they become tiny *capillaries*. By diffusing across the capillary walls, oxygen and nutrients leave the blood and enter the body tissues, and carbon dioxide and wastes move from the tissues to the bloodstream. As oxygen-deficient blood leaves the capillary beds, it flows into *veins*, which return it to the heart. The returning blood then flows from the heart to the lungs, where it picks up oxygen and then returns to the heart to be pumped throughout the body once again. Now let us look more closely at the nature of blood.

Overview: Blood Composition and Functions

Components

Blood is the only fluid tissue in the body. Although blood appears to be a thick, homogeneous liquid, the microscope reveals that it has both cellular and liquid components. Blood is a specialized type of connective tissue in which living blood cells, the *formed elements*, are suspended in a nonliving fluid matrix called *plasma* (plaz'mah). The collagen and elastic fibers typical of other connective tissues are absent from blood, but dissolved fibrous proteins become visible as fibrin strands during blood clotting.

If a sample of blood is spun in a centrifuge, the heavier formed elements are packed down by centrifugal force and the less dense plasma remains at the top (Figure 17.1). Most of the reddish mass at the bottom of the tube is *erythrocytes* (ĕ-rith'ro-sīts; *erythro* = red), the red blood cells that transport oxygen. A thin, whitish layer called the **buffy coat** is present at the erythrocyte-plasma junction. This layer contains *leukocytes* (*leuko* = white), the white blood cells that act in various ways to protect the body, and *platelets*, cell fragments that help stop bleeding. Erythrocytes normally constitute about 45% of the total volume of a blood sample, a percentage known as the **hematocrit** (he-mat'o-krit;

Q *Which of the percentages given in this figure represents the measurement called the hematocrit?*

① Withdraw blood and place in tube ② Centrifuge

Plasma (55% of whole blood)

Buffy coat: leukocytes and platelets (<1% of whole blood)

Erythrocytes (45% of whole blood)

Formed elements

FIGURE 17.1 **The major components of whole blood.** When a blood sample is centrifuged, it separates into layers, the heaviest particles (erythrocytes) moving to the bottom of the test tube. The least dense component is plasma, which is the top layer.

A *45%, the percentage of the erythrocytes.*

"blood fraction"). Normal hematocrit values vary. In healthy males the norm is 47% ± 5%; in females it is 42% ± 5%. Leukocytes and platelets contribute less than 1% of blood volume. Plasma makes up most of the remaining 55% of whole blood.

Physical Characteristics and Volume

Blood is a sticky, opaque fluid with a characteristic metallic taste. As children, we discover its saltiness the first time we stick a cut finger into our mouth. Depending on the amount of oxygen it is carrying, the color of blood varies from scarlet (oxygen rich) to dark red (oxygen poor). Blood is more dense than water and about five times more viscous, largely because of its formed elements. Blood is slightly alkaline, with a pH between 7.35 and 7.45, and its temperature (38°C or 100.4°F) is always slightly higher than body temperature.

Blood accounts for approximately 8% of body weight. Its average volume in healthy adult males is 5–6 L (about 1.5 gallons), somewhat greater than in healthy adult females (4–5 L).

Functions

Blood performs a number of functions, all concerned in one way or another with substance distribution, regulating blood levels of particular substances, or body protection.

Distribution

Distribution functions of blood include

- Delivering oxygen from the lungs and nutrients from the digestive tract to all body cells.
- Transporting metabolic waste products from cells to elimination sites (to the lungs for elimination of carbon dioxide, and to the kidneys for disposal of nitrogenous wastes in urine).
- Transporting hormones from the endocrine organs to their target organs.

Regulation

Regulatory functions of blood include

- Maintaining appropriate body temperature by absorbing and distributing heat throughout the body and to the skin surface to encourage heat loss.
- Maintaining normal pH in body tissues. Many blood proteins and other bloodborne solutes act as buffers to prevent excessive or abrupt changes in blood pH that could jeopardize normal cell activities. Additionally, blood acts as the reservoir for the body's "alkaline reserve" of bicarbonate atoms.

- Maintaining adequate fluid volume in the circulatory system. Salts (sodium chloride and others) and blood proteins act to prevent excessive fluid loss from the bloodstream into the tissue spaces. As a result, the fluid volume in the blood vessels remains ample to support efficient blood circulation to all parts of the body.

Protection

Protective functions of blood include

- Preventing blood loss. When a blood vessel is damaged, platelets and plasma proteins initiate clot formation, halting blood loss.
- Preventing infection. Drifting along in blood are antibodies, complement proteins, and white blood cells, all of which help defend the body against foreign invaders such as bacteria and viruses.

Blood Plasma

Blood **plasma** is a straw-colored, sticky fluid (see Figure 17.1). Although it is mostly water (about 90%), plasma contains over 100 different dissolved solutes, including nutrients, gases, hormones, wastes and products of cell activity, ions, and proteins. Table 17.1 summarizes the major plasma components.

Plasma proteins, accounting for about 8% by weight of plasma volume, are the most abundant plasma solutes. Except for hormones and gamma globulins, most plasma proteins are produced by the liver. Plasma proteins serve a variety of functions, but they are *not* taken up by cells to be used as fuels or metabolic nutrients as are most other plasma solutes, such as glucose, fatty acids, and amino acids. **Albumin** (al-bu'min) accounts for some 60% of plasma protein. It acts as a carrier to shuttle certain molecules through the circulation, is an important blood buffer, and is the major blood protein contributing to the plasma osmotic pressure (the pressure that helps to keep water in the bloodstream). (Sodium ions are the other major solute contributing to blood osmotic pressure.)

The makeup of plasma varies continuously as cells remove or add substances to the blood. However, assuming a healthy diet, plasma composition is kept relatively constant by various homeostatic mechanisms. For example, when blood protein levels drop undesirably, the liver makes more proteins; and when the blood starts to become too acidic (acidosis), both the respiratory system and the kidneys are called into action to restore plasma's normal, slightly alkaline pH. Body organs make dozens of adjustments, day in and day out, to maintain the many plasma solutes at life-sustaining levels. In addition to transporting various solutes around the

TABLE 17.1 Composition of Plasma

CONSTITUENT	DESCRIPTION AND IMPORTANCE
Water	90% of plasma volume; dissolving and suspending medium for solutes of blood; absorbs heat
Solutes Plasma proteins	8% (by weight) of plasma volume; all contribute to osmotic pressure, maintaining water balance in blood and tissues; all have other functions (transport, enzymatic, etc.)
▪ Albumin	60% of plasma proteins; produced by liver; main contributor to osmotic pressure
▪ Globulins	36% of plasma proteins
alpha, beta	Produced by liver; mostly transport proteins that bind to lipids, metal ions, and fat-soluble vitamins
gamma	Antibodies released by plasma cells during immune response
▪ Fibrinogen	4% of plasma proteins; produced by liver; forms fibrin threads of blood clot
Nonprotein nitrogenous substances	By-products of cellular metabolism, such as urea, uric acid, creatinine, and ammonium salts
Nutrients (organic)	Materials absorbed from digestive tract and transported for use throughout body; include glucose and other simple carbohydrates, amino acids (digestion products of proteins), fatty acids, glycerol and triglycerides (fat products), cholesterol, and vitamins
Electrolytes	Cations include sodium, potassium, calcium, magnesium; anions include chloride, phosphate, sulfate, and bicarbonate; help to maintain plasma osmotic pressure and normal blood pH
Respiratory gases	Oxygen and carbon dioxide; oxygen mostly bound to hemoglobin inside RBCs; carbon dioxide transported bound to hemoglobin in RBCs or dissolved in plasma as bicarbonate ion or CO_2
Hormones	Steroid and thyroid hormones carried by plasma proteins

body, plasma distributes heat (a by-product of cellular metabolism) throughout the body.

Formed Elements

The **formed elements** of blood, *erythrocytes, leukocytes,* and *platelets,* have some unusual features. (1) Two of the three are not even true cells: Erythrocytes have no nuclei or organelles, and platelets are cell fragments. Only leukocytes are complete cells. (2) Most of the formed elements survive in the blood-

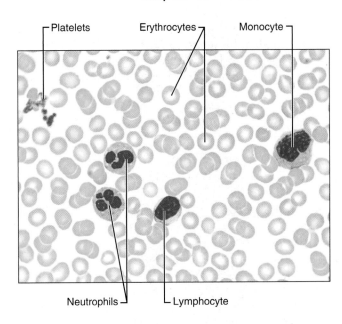

FIGURE 17.2 **Photomicrograph of a human blood smear stained with Wright's stain.**

stream for only a few days. (3) Most blood cells do not divide. Instead, they are continuously renewed by division of cells in bone marrow, where they originate.

If you examine a stained smear of human blood under the light microscope, you will see disc-shaped red blood cells, a variety of gaudily stained spherical white blood cells, and some scattered platelets that look like debris (Figure 17.2). Erythrocytes vastly outnumber the other types of formed elements. Table 17.2 on p. 658 summarizes the important characteristics of the formed elements.

Erythrocytes

Structural Characteristics

Erythrocytes or **red blood cells (RBCs)** are small cells, about 7.5 µm in diameter. Shaped like biconcave discs—flattened discs with depressed centers (Figure 17.3)—they appear lighter in color at their thin centers than at their edges. Consequently, erythrocytes look like miniature doughnuts when viewed with a microscope. Mature erythrocytes are bound by a plasma membrane, but lack a nucleus (are *anucleate*) and have essentially no organelles. In fact, they are little more than "bags" of *hemoglobin (Hb),* the RBC protein that functions in gas transport. Other proteins are present, such as antioxidant enzymes that rid the body of harmful oxygen radicals, but most function mainly to maintain the plasma membrane or promote changes in RBC shape. For example, the biconcave shape of an erythrocyte is maintained by a network of proteins, especially one called *spectrin,* attached to the cytoplasmic face of its plasma membrane. Because the spectrin net is deformable, it gives

17

Side view

2.5 µm

7.5 µm

Top view

FIGURE 17.3   **Structure of erythrocytes.** Cut side view above; a superficial surface view below. Notice the distinctive biconcave shape.

erythrocytes flexibility to change shape as necessary—to twist, turn, and become cup-shaped as they are carried passively through capillaries with diameters smaller than themselves—and then to resume their biconcave shape.

The erythrocyte is a superb example of complementarity of structure and function. It picks up oxygen in the capillary beds of the lungs and releases it to tissue cells across other capillaries throughout the body. It also transports some 20% of the carbon dioxide released by tissue cells back to the lungs. Each erythrocyte structural characteristic contributes to its gas transport functions: (1) Its small size and biconcave shape provide a huge surface area relative to volume (about 30% more surface area than comparable spherical cells). Because no point within its cytoplasm is far from the surface, the biconcave disc shape is ideally suited for gas exchange. (2) Discounting water content, an erythrocyte is over 97% hemoglobin, the molecule that binds to and transports respiratory gases. (3) Because erythrocytes lack mitochondria and generate ATP by anaerobic mechanisms, they do not consume any of the oxygen they are transporting, making them very efficient oxygen transporters indeed.

Erythrocytes are the major factor contributing to blood viscosity. Women typically have a lower red blood cell count than men [4.3–5.2 million cells per microliter (1 µl = 1 mm³) of blood versus 5.1–5.8 million cells/µl respectively]. When the number of red blood cells increases beyond the normal range, blood viscosity rises and blood flows more

slowly. Similarly, as the number of red blood cells drops below the lower end of the range, the blood thins and flows more rapidly.

Function

Erythrocytes are completely dedicated to their job of respiratory gas (oxygen and carbon dioxide) transport. **Hemoglobin,** the protein that makes red blood cells red, binds easily and reversibly with oxygen, and most oxygen carried in blood is bound to hemoglobin. Normal values for hemoglobin are 14–20 grams per 100 milliliters of blood (g/100 ml) in infants, 13–18 g/100 ml in adult males, and 12–16 g/100 ml in adult females.

Hemoglobin is made up of the protein **globin** bound to the red **heme** pigment. Globin consists of four polypeptide chains—two alpha (α) and two beta (β)—each bound to a ringlike heme group. Each heme group bears an atom of iron set like a jewel in its center (Figure 17.4). Since each iron atom can combine reversibly with one molecule of oxygen, a hemoglobin molecule can transport four molecules of oxygen. A single red blood cell contains about 250 million hemoglobin molecules, so each of these tiny cells can scoop up about 1 billion molecules of oxygen!

The fact that hemoglobin is contained in erythrocytes, rather than existing free in plasma, prevents it (1) from breaking into fragments that would leak out of the bloodstream (through the rather porous capillary membranes) and (2) from contributing to blood viscosity and osmotic pressure.

Oxygen loading occurs in the lungs, and the direction of transport is from lungs to tissue cells. As oxygen-deficient blood moves through the lungs, oxygen diffuses from the air sacs of the lungs into the blood and then into the erythrocytes, where it binds to hemoglobin. When oxygen binds to iron, the hemoglobin, now called **oxyhemoglobin,** assumes a new three-dimensional shape and becomes ruby red. In the tissues, the process is reversed. Oxygen detaches from iron, hemoglobin resumes its former shape, and the resulting **deoxyhemoglobin,** or *reduced hemoglobin,* becomes dark red. The released oxygen diffuses from the blood into the tissue fluid and then into the tissue cells.

About 20% of the carbon dioxide transported in the blood combines with hemoglobin, but it binds to globin's amino acids rather than to the heme group. This formation of **carbaminohemoglobin** (kar-bam″ĭ-no-he″mo-glo′bin) occurs more readily when hemoglobin is in the reduced state (dissociated from oxygen). Carbon dioxide loading occurs in the tissues, and the direction of transport is from tissues to lungs, where carbon dioxide is eliminated from the body. The mechanisms of loading and unloading these respiratory gases are described in Chapter 22.

Q *How many molecules of oxygen can a hemoglobin molecule transport?*

(a) Hemoglobin

(b) Iron-containing heme group

FIGURE 17.4 **Structure of hemoglobin. (a)** Hemoglobin is composed of the protein globin bound to the iron-containing heme pigments. Each globin molecule has four polypeptide chains: two alpha (α) chains and two beta (β) chains. Each chain is complexed with a heme group, shown as a circular green structure with iron at its center. **(b)** Structure of a heme group.

Production of Erythrocytes

Blood cell formation is referred to as **hematopoiesis** (hem″ah-to-poi-e′sis), or **hemopoiesis** (*hemo, hemato* = blood; *poiesis* = to make). This process occurs in the **red bone marrow,** which is composed largely of a soft network of reticular connective tissue bordering on wide blood capillaries called *blood sinusoids.* Within this network are immature blood cells, macrophages, fat cells, and *reticular cells* (which secrete the fibers). In adults, red marrow is found chiefly in the bones of the axial skeleton and girdles, and in the proximal epiphyses of the humerus and femur. Each type of blood cell is produced in different numbers in response to changing body needs and different regulatory factors. As they mature, they migrate through the thin walls of the sinusoids to enter the bloodstream. On average, the marrow turns out an ounce of new blood containing some 100 billion new cells each and every day.

Although the various formed elements have different functions, there are similarities in their life histories. All arise from the same type of *stem cell,* the pleuripotent **hematopoietic stem cell,** or **hemocytoblast** (*cyte* = cell, *blast* = bud), which resides in the red bone marrow. However, their maturation pathways differ; and once a cell is *committed* to a specific blood cell pathway, it cannot change. This commitment is signaled by the appearance of membrane surface receptors that respond to specific hormones or growth factors, which in turn "push" the cell toward further specialization.

Erythrocyte production, or **erythropoiesis** (ĕ-rith″ro-poi-e′sis) begins when a hemocytoblast descendant called a **myeloid stem cell** is transformed into a **proerythroblast** (Figure 17.5). Proerythroblasts, in turn, give rise to the **early (basophilic) erythroblasts** that produce huge numbers of ribosomes. During these first two phases, the cells divide many times. Hemoglobin synthesis and iron accumulation occur as the early erythroblast is transformed into a **late erythroblast** and then a

A *Four O₂ per hemoglobin molecule.*

17

Q *What does the term "committed cell" refer to?*

FIGURE 17.5 **Erythropoiesis: genesis of red blood cells.** Erythropoiesis is a sequence involving proliferation and differentiation of committed red marrow cells through the erythroblast and normoblast stages to the reticulocytes that are released into the bloodstream, and finally become erythrocytes. (The myeloid stem cell, the phase intermediate between the hemocytoblast and the proerythroblast, is not illustrated.)

normoblast. The "color" of the cell cytoplasm changes as the blue-staining ribosomes become masked by the pink color of hemoglobin. When a normoblast has accumulated almost all of its hemoglobin, it ejects most of its organelles. Additionally, its nuclear functions end and its nucleus degenerates and is pinched off, allowing the cell to collapse inward and assume the biconcave shape. The result is the **reticulocyte** (essentially a young erythrocyte), so named because it still contains a scant *reticulum* (network) of clumped ribosomes. The entire process from hemocytoblast to reticulocyte takes about 15 days. The reticulocytes, filled almost to bursting with hemoglobin, enter the bloodstream to begin their task of oxygen transport. Usually they become fully mature erythrocytes within two days of release as their ribosomes are degraded by intracellular enzymes. Reticulocytes account for 1–2% of all erythrocytes in the blood of healthy people. **Reticulocyte counts** provide a rough index of the *rate* of RBC formation—reticulocyte counts below or above this percentage range indicate abnormal rates of erythrocyte formation.

Regulation and Requirements for Erythropoiesis

The number of circulating erythrocytes in a given individual is remarkably constant and reflects a balance between red blood cell production and destruction. This balance is important because too few erythrocytes leads to tissue hypoxia (oxygen deprivation), whereas too many makes the blood undesirably viscous. To ensure that the number of erythrocytes in blood remains within the homeostatic range, new cells are produced at the incredibly rapid rate of more than 2 million per second in healthy people. This process is controlled hormonally and depends on adequate supplies of iron, amino acids, and certain B vitamins.

Hormonal Controls The direct stimulus for erythrocyte formation is provided by **erythropoietin (EPO)**, a glycoprotein hormone. Normally, a small amount of EPO circulates in the blood at all times and sustains red blood cell production at a basal rate (Figure 17.6). Although the liver produces some, the kidneys play the major role in EPO production. When certain kidney cells become hypoxic (i.e., have inadequate oxygen), they accelerate their release of erythropoietin. The drop in normal blood oxygen levels that triggers EPO formation can result from

1. Reduced numbers of red blood cells due to hemorrhage or excessive RBC destruction

2. Insufficient hemoglobin per RBC (as in iron deficiency)

3. Reduced availability of oxygen, as might occur at high altitudes or during pneumonia

Conversely, too many erythrocytes or excessive oxygen in the bloodstream depresses erythropoietin production. The easily missed point is that it is *not* the number of erythrocytes in blood that controls the rate of erythropoiesis. Control is based on their ability to transport enough oxygen to meet tissue demands.

Bloodborne erythropoietin stimulates red marrow cells that *are already committed* to becoming erythrocytes, causing them to mature more rapidly.

A A committed cell is a blood cell precursor whose path of specialization is determined. For example, the proerythroblast can only become an erythrocyte, not one of the leukocytes.

Q *How does blood doping, practiced by some athletes (see p. 656), affect the negative feedback cycle outlined here?*

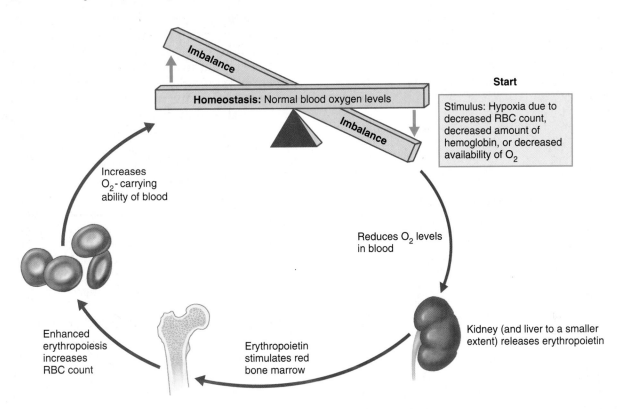

FIGURE 17.6 **Erythropoietin mechanism for regulating erythropoiesis.**
Notice that increased erythropoietin release occurs when oxygen levels in the blood become inadequate to support normal cellular activity, whatever the cause.

One to two days after erythropoietin levels rise in the blood, a marked increase in the rate of reticulocyte release (and hence reticulocyte count) occurs. Notice that hypoxia (oxygen deficit) does not activate the bone marrow directly. Instead it stimulates the kidneys, which in turn provide the hormonal stimulus that activates the bone marrow.

HOMEOSTATIC IMBALANCE

Renal dialysis patients whose kidneys have failed produce too little EPO to support normal erythropoiesis. Consequently, they routinely have red blood cell counts less than half that of healthy individuals. Genetically engineered (recombinant) EPO has helped such patients immeasurably and has also become a substance of abuse in athletes—particularly in professional bike racers and marathon runners

seeking increased stamina and performance. However, the consequences can be deadly. By injecting EPO, healthy athletes increase their normal hematocrit from 45% to as much as 65%. Then, with the dehydration that occurs in a long race, the blood concentrates even further, becoming a thick, sticky "sludge" that can cause clotting, stroke, and even heart failure. ●

The male sex hormone *testosterone* also enhances EPO production by the kidneys. Because female sex hormones do not have similar stimulatory effects, testosterone may be at least partially responsible for the higher RBC counts and hemoglobin levels seen in males. Also, a wide variety of chemicals released by leukocytes, platelets, and even reticular cells stimulates bursts of RBC production.

Dietary Requirements The raw materials required for erythropoiesis include the usual nutrients and structural materials—amino acids, lipids, and carbohydrates. Iron is essential for hemoglobin synthesis. Iron is available from the diet, and its absorption into the bloodstream is precisely controlled by

A *Blood doping, which increases the number of RBCs in the circulation and thus increases the amount of oxygen being transported, would inhibit erythropoietin release by ending the stimulus for its formation.*

Q *How would you expect blood levels of bilirubin to change in a person that has severe liver disease?*

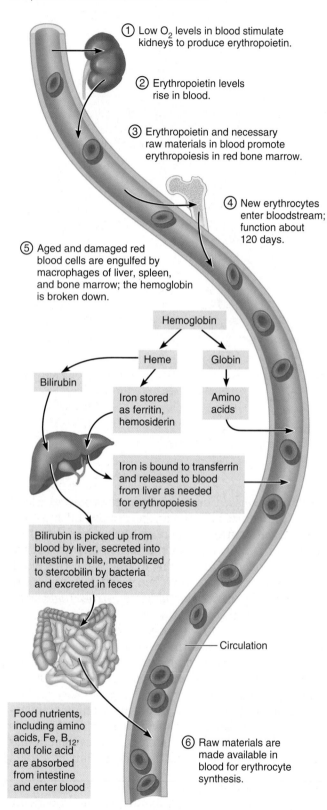

① Low O₂ levels in blood stimulate kidneys to produce erythropoietin.

② Erythropoietin levels rise in blood.

③ Erythropoietin and necessary raw materials in blood promote erythropoiesis in red bone marrow.

④ New erythrocytes enter bloodstream; function about 120 days.

⑤ Aged and damaged red blood cells are engulfed by macrophages of liver, spleen, and bone marrow; the hemoglobin is broken down.

Hemoglobin

Heme   Globin

Bilirubin

Iron stored as ferritin, hemosiderin

Amino acids

Iron is bound to transferrin and released to blood from liver as needed for erythropoiesis

Bilirubin is picked up from blood by liver, secreted into intestine in bile, metabolized to stercobilin by bacteria and excreted in feces

Circulation

Food nutrients, including amino acids, Fe, B₁₂, and folic acid are absorbed from intestine and enter blood

⑥ Raw materials are made available in blood for erythrocyte synthesis.

FIGURE 17.7   **Life cycle of red blood cells.**

intestinal cells in response to changing body stores of iron.

Approximately 65% of the body's iron supply (about 4000 mg) is in hemoglobin. Most of the remainder is stored in the liver, spleen, and (to a much lesser extent) bone marrow. Because free iron ions (Fe^{2+}, Fe^{3+}) are toxic, iron is stored inside cells as protein-iron complexes such as **ferritin** (fer′ĭ-tin) and **hemosiderin** (he″mo-sid′er-in). In blood, iron is transported loosely bound to a transport protein called **transferrin,** and developing erythrocytes take up iron as needed to form hemoglobin (Figure 17.7). Small amounts of iron are lost each day in feces, urine, and perspiration. The average daily loss of iron is 1.7 mg in women and 0.9 mg in men. In women, the menstrual flow accounts for the additional losses.

Two B-complex vitamins—vitamin B_{12} and folic acid—are necessary for normal DNA synthesis. Thus, even slight deficits jeopardize rapidly dividing cell populations, such as developing erythrocytes.

Fate and Destruction of Erythrocytes

The anucleate condition of erythrocytes carries with it some important limitations. Red blood cells are unable to synthesize new proteins, to grow, or to divide. Erythrocytes become "old" as they lose their flexibility and become increasingly rigid and fragile, and their contained hemoglobin begins to degenerate. Red blood cells have a useful life span of 100 to 120 days, after which they become trapped and fragment in smaller circulatory channels, particularly in those of the spleen. For this reason, the spleen is sometimes called the "red blood cell graveyard."

Dying erythrocytes are engulfed and destroyed by macrophages. The heme of their hemoglobin is split off from globin. Its core of iron is salvaged, bound to protein (as ferritin or hemosiderin), and stored for reuse. The balance of the heme group is degraded to **bilirubin** (bil″i-roo′bin), a yellow pigment that is released to the blood and binds to albumin for transport (Figure 17.7). Bilirubin is picked up by liver cells, which in turn secrete it (in bile) into the intestine, where it is metabolized to *urobilinogen.* Most of this degraded pigment leaves the body in feces, as a brown pigment called *stercobilin.* The protein (globin) part of hemoglobin is metabolized or broken down to amino acids, which are released to the circulation. Disposal of hemoglobin spilled from red blood cells to the blood (as occurs in sickle-cell anemia or hemorrhagic anemia) takes a similar but much more rapid course to avoid toxic buildup of

A *It would increase because the liver's processing functions are impaired.*

iron in blood. Released hemoglobin is captured by the plasma protein *haptoglobin* and the complex is phagocytized by macrophages.

Erythrocyte Disorders

Most erythrocyte disorders can be classified as anemias or polycythemias. The many varieties and causes of these conditions are described next.

Anemias Anemia (ah-ne′me-ah; "lacking blood") is a condition in which the blood has abnormally low oxygen-carrying capacity. It is a *sign* of some disorder rather than a disease in and of itself. Its hallmark is blood oxygen levels that are inadequate to support normal metabolism. Anemic individuals are fatigued, often pale, short of breath, and chilly. Common causes of anemia include the following:

1. An insufficient number of red blood cells. Conditions that reduce the red blood cell count include blood loss, excessive RBC destruction, and bone marrow failure.

Hemorrhagic anemias (hem″o-raj′ik) result from blood loss. In acute hemorrhagic anemia, blood loss is rapid (as might follow a severe stab wound); it is treated by blood replacement. Slight but persistent blood loss (due to hemorrhoids or an undiagnosed bleeding ulcer, for example) causes chronic hemorrhagic anemia. Once the primary problem is resolved, normal erythropoietic mechanisms replace the deficient blood cells.

In *hemolytic anemias* (he″mo-lit′ik), erythrocytes rupture, or lyse, prematurely. Hemoglobin abnormalities, transfusion of mismatched blood, and certain bacterial and parasitic infections are possible causes.

Aplastic anemia may result from destruction or inhibition of the red marrow by certain drugs and chemicals, ionizing radiation, or viruses. In most cases, the cause is unknown. Because marrow destruction impairs formation of *all* formed elements, anemia is just one of its signs. Defects in blood clotting and immunity are also present. Blood transfusions provide a stopgap treatment until bone marrow transplants or transfusion of umbilical blood, which contains stem cells, can be done.

2. Low hemoglobin content. When hemoglobin molecules are normal, but erythrocytes contain fewer than the usual number, a nutritional anemia is always suspected.

Iron-deficiency anemia is generally a secondary result of hemorrhagic anemias, but it also results from inadequate intake of iron-containing foods and impaired iron absorption. The erythrocytes produced, called **microcytes,** are small and pale. The obvious treatment is iron supplements, but if chronic hemorrhage is the cause, blood transfusions may also be needed.

When athletes exercise vigorously, their blood volume expands and can increase by as much as 35% over time. Since this in effect dilutes the blood components, a test for the iron content of the blood at such times would indicate iron-deficiency anemia. However, this iron deficiency illusion, called **athlete's anemia,** is reversed as blood components return to physiological levels within a week or so after resuming a normal level of activity.

Pernicious anemia is due to a deficiency of vitamin B_{12}. Because meats, poultry, and fish provide ample amounts of the vitamin, diet is rarely the problem except for strict vegetarians. A substance called **intrinsic factor,** produced by the stomach mucosa, must be present for vitamin B_{12} to be absorbed by intestinal cells. In most cases of pernicious anemia, intrinsic factor is deficient. Consequently, the developing erythrocytes grow but do not divide, and large, pale cells called **macrocytes** result. Pernicious anemia, an autoimmune disease in which the stomach mucosa atrophies, most often affects the elderly. Treatment involves regular intramuscular injections of vitamin B_{12} or application of a B_{12}-containing gel (Nascobal) to the nasal lining once a week.

3. Abnormal hemoglobin. Production of abnormal hemoglobin usually has a genetic basis. Two such examples, thalassemia and sickle-cell anemia, can be serious, incurable, and sometimes fatal diseases. In both diseases the globin part of hemoglobin is abnormal and the erythrocytes produced are fragile and rupture prematurely.

Thalassemias (thal″ah-se′me-ahs; "sea blood") are typically seen in people of Mediterranean ancestry, such as Greeks and Italians. One of the globin chains is absent or faulty, and the erythrocytes are thin, delicate, and deficient in hemoglobin. There are many subtypes of thalassemia, classified according to which hemoglobin chain is affected and where, ranging in severity from mild to so severe that monthly blood transfusion is required.

In **sickle-cell anemia,** the havoc caused by the abnormal hemoglobin, *hemoglobin S (HbS)*, results from a change in just *one* of the 287 amino acids in a beta chain of the globin molecule! This alteration causes the beta chains to link together under low-oxygen conditions, forming stiff rods so that hemoglobin S becomes spiky and sharp. This, in turn, causes the red blood cells to become crescent shaped (Figure 17.8) when they unload oxygen molecules or when the oxygen content of the blood is lower than normal, as during vigorous exercise and other activities that increase metabolic rate. The stiff, deformed erythrocytes rupture easily and tend to dam up in small blood vessels. These events interfere with oxygen delivery, leaving the victims gasping for air and

FIGURE 17.8 **Comparison of (a) a normal erythrocyte to (b) a sickled erythrocyte.** (6700×)

(a)

(b)

in extreme pain. Bone and chest pain are particularly severe; infection and stroke are common sequels. Blood transfusion is still the standard treatment for an acute sickle-cell crisis, but preliminary results using inhaled nitric oxide to dilate blood vessels are promising.

Sickle-cell anemia occurs chiefly in black people who live in the malaria belt of Africa and among their descendants. It strikes nearly one of every 400 black newborns in the United States. Globally, 300–500 million people are infected with malaria and more than a million die each year. Apparently, the gene that causes sickling of red blood cells also causes erythrocytes infected by the malaria-causing parasite to stick to capillary walls. Then, during oxygen deficit, these abnormal erythrocytes lose potassium, an essential ingredient for survival of the parasite. Thus, individuals with the sickle-cell gene have a better chance of surviving in regions where malaria is prevalent. Only those carrying two copies of the defective gene have sickle-cell anemia. Those carrying only one sickling gene have sickle-cell trait; they generally do not display the symptoms, but can transmit the gene to their offspring.

Since fetal hemoglobin (HbF) does not "sickle," even in those destined to have sickle-cell anemia, investigators have been looking for ways to switch the fetal hemoglobin gene back on. *Hydroxyurea,* a drug used to treat chronic leukemia, does just that. This drug dramatically reduces the excruciating pain and overall severity and complications of sickle-cell anemia (by 50%). A number of other approaches are now being tested, including oral arginine to stimulate nitric oxide production and dilate blood vessels, bone marrow transplants, and gene therapy using a small portion of the HIV virus as a vector to deliver therapeutic beta A globin genes for synthesizing normal beta chains.

Polycythemia Polycythemia (pol″e-si-the′me-ah; "many blood cells") is an abnormal excess of erythrocytes that increases blood viscosity, causing it to sludge, or flow sluggishly. *Polycythemia vera,* a bone marrow cancer, is characterized by dizziness and an exceptionally high RBC count (8–11 million cells/µl).

The hematocrit may be as high as 80% and blood volume may double, causing the vascular system to become engorged with blood and severely impairing circulation.

Secondary polycythemias result when less oxygen is available or EPO production increases. The secondary polycythemia that appears in individuals living at high altitudes is a normal physiological response to the reduced atmospheric pressure and lower oxygen content of the air in such areas. RBC counts of 6–8 million/µl are common in such people. Severe polycythemia is treated by blood dilution, that is, removing some blood and replacing it with saline.

Blood doping, practiced by some athletes competing in aerobic events, is artificially induced polycythemia. Some of the athlete's red blood cells are drawn off and then reinjected a few days before the event. Because the erythropoietin mechanism is triggered shortly after blood removal, the erythrocytes are quickly replaced. Then, when the stored blood is reinfused, a temporary polycythemia results. Since red blood cells carry oxygen, the additional infusion should translate into increased oxygen-carrying capacity due to a higher hematocrit, and hence greater endurance and speed. Other than problems that might derive from increased blood viscosity, such as temporary high blood pressure or reduced blood delivery to body tissues, blood doping seems to work. However, the practice is considered unethical and has been banned from the Olympic Games.

Leukocytes

General Structural and Functional Characteristics

Leukocytes (*leuko* = white), or **white blood cells (WBCs),** are the only formed elements that are complete cells, with nuclei and the usual organelles. Accounting for less than 1% of total blood volume, leukocytes are far less numerous than red blood cells. On average, there are 4800–10,800 WBCs/µl (mm^3) of blood.

Leukocytes are crucial to our defense against disease. They form a mobile army that helps protect the body from damage by bacteria, viruses, parasites, toxins, and tumor cells. As such, they have some special functional characteristics. Red blood cells are confined to the bloodstream, and they carry out their functions in the blood. But white blood cells are able to slip out of the capillary blood vessels—a process called **diapedesis** (di"ah-pĕ-de'sis; "leaping across")—and the circulatory system is simply their means of transport to areas of the body (mostly loose connective tissues or lymphoid tissues) where they are needed to mount inflammatory or immune responses. As explained in more detail in Chapter 21, the signals that prompt WBCs to leave the bloodstream at specific locations are adhesion molecules *(selectins)* displayed by endothelial cells forming the capillary walls at sites of inflammation. Once out of the bloodstream, leukocytes move through the tissue spaces by **amoeboid motion** (they form flowing cytoplasmic extensions that move them along). By following the chemical trail of molecules released by damaged cells or other leukocytes, a phenomenon called **positive chemotaxis,** they can pinpoint areas of tissue damage and infection and gather there in large numbers to destroy foreign substances or dead cells.

Whenever white blood cells are mobilized for action, the body speeds up their production and twice the normal number may appear in the blood within a few hours. A *white blood cell count* of over 11,000 cells/µl is **leukocytosis.** This condition is a normal homeostatic response to an infection in the body.

Leukocytes are grouped into two major categories on the basis of structural and chemical characteristics: *Granulocytes* contain obvious membrane-bound cytoplasmic granules; *agranulocytes* lack obvious granules. General information about the various leukocytes is provided next. More details appear in Figure 17.9 and Table 17.2.

Students are often asked to list the leukocytes in order from most abundant to least abundant. The following phrase may help you with this task: **N**ever **l**et **m**onkeys **e**at **b**ananas (neutrophils, lymphocytes, monocytes, eosinophils, basophils).

Granulocytes

Granulocytes (gran'u-lo-sīts), which include neutrophils, basophils, and eosinophils, are all roughly spherical in shape. They are larger and much shorter lived (in most cases) than erythrocytes. They characteristically have lobed nuclei (rounded nuclear masses connected by thinner strands of nuclear material), and their membrane-bound cytoplasmic granules stain quite specifically with Wright's stain. Functionally, all granulocytes are phagocytes to a greater or lesser degree.

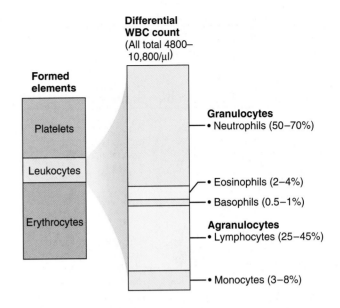

FIGURE 17.9 Types and relative percentages of leukocytes in normal blood. (The relationship of the formed elements in the left column is not shown to scale because erythrocytes comprise nearly 98% of the formed elements whereas leukocytes and platelets together account for the remaining 2+%.)

Neutrophils **Neutrophils** (nu'tro-filz), the most numerous of the white blood cells, account for 50–70% of the WBC population. Neutrophils are about twice as large as erythrocytes.

The neutrophil cytoplasm stains pale lilac and contains very fine granules (of two varieties) that are difficult to see (see Table 17.2 and Figure 17.10a). They are called neutrophils (literally, "neutral-loving") because their granules take up both *basic* (blue) and *acidic* (red) *dyes.* Together, the two types of granules give the cytoplasm a lilac color. Some of these granules contain hydrolytic enzymes, and are regarded as lysosomes. Others, especially the smaller granules, contain a potent "brew" of antimicrobial proteins, called **defensins.** Neutrophil nuclei consist of three to six lobes. Because of this nuclear variability, they are often called **polymorphonuclear leukocytes (PMNs)** or simply **polys** (*polymorphonuclear* = many shapes of the nucleus). (However, some authorities use this term to refer to all granulocytes.)

Neutrophils are chemically attracted to sites of inflammation and are active phagocytes. They are especially partial to bacteria and some fungi, and bacterial killing is promoted by a process called a respiratory burst. In the **respiratory burst,** oxygen is actively metabolized to produce potent germ-killer oxidizing substances such as bleach and hydrogen peroxide, and defensin-mediated lysis occurs. It appears that when the granules containing defensins are merged with a microbe-containing phagosome, the defensins form peptide "spears" that pierce holes

TABLE 17.2   Summary of Formed Elements of the Blood

CELL TYPE	ILLUSTRATION	DESCRIPTION*	CELLS/μl (mm³) OF BLOOD	DURATION OF DEVELOPMENT (D) AND LIFE SPAN (LS)	FUNCTION
Erythrocytes (red blood cells, RBCs)		Biconcave, anucleate disc; salmon-colored; diameter 7–8 μm	4–6 million	D: about 15 days LS: 100–120 days	Transport oxygen and carbon dioxide
Leukocytes (white blood cells, WBCs)		Spherical, nucleated cells	4800–10,800		
Granulocytes					
▪ Neutrophil		Nucleus multilobed; inconspicuous cytoplasmic granules; diameter 10–12 μm	3000–7000	D: about 14 days LS: 6 hours to a few days	Phagocytize bacteria
▪ Eosinophil		Nucleus bilobed; red cytoplasmic granules; diameter 10–14 μm	100–400	D: about 14 days LS: about 5 days	Kill parasitic worms; destroy antigen-antibody complexes; inactivate some inflammatory chemicals of allergy
▪ Basophil		Nucleus lobed; large purplish-black cytoplasmic granules; diameter 10–14 μm	20–50	D: 1–7 days LS: a few hours to a few days	Release histamine and other mediators of inflammation; contain heparin, an anticoagulant
Agranulocytes					
▪ Lymphocyte		Nucleus spherical or indented; pale blue cytoplasm; diameter 5–17 μm	1500–3000	D: days to weeks LS: hours to years	Mount immune response by direct cell attack or via antibodies
▪ Monocyte		Nucleus U or kidney shaped; gray-blue cytoplasm; diameter 14–24 μm	100–700	D: 2–3 days LS: months	Phagocytosis; develop into macrophages in the tissues
Platelets		Discoid cytoplasmic fragments containing granules; stain deep purple; diameter 2–4 μm	150,000–400,000	D: 4–5 days LS: 5–10 days	Seal small tears in blood vessels; instrumental in blood clotting

*Appearance when stained with Wright's stain.

in the membrane of the ingested "foe." Neutrophils are our body's bacteria slayers, and their numbers increase explosively during acute bacterial infections such as meningitis and appendicitis.

Eosinophils   Eosinophils (e"o-sin'o-filz) account for 2–4% of all leukocytes and are approximately the size of neutrophils. Their deep red nucleus usually resembles an old-fashioned telephone receiver; that is, it has two lobes connected by a broad band of nuclear material (see Table 17.2 and Figure 17.10b).

Large, coarse granules that stain from brick red to crimson with acid (eosin) dyes pack the cytoplasm. These granules are lysosome-like and filled with a unique variety of digestive enzymes. However, unlike typical lysosomes, they lack enzymes that specifically digest bacteria.

The most important role of eosinophils is to lead the counterattack against parasitic worms, such as flatworms (tapeworms and flukes) and roundworms (pinworms and hookworms) that are too large to be phagocytized. These worms are ingested in food

(a)

(b)

(c)

FIGURE 17.10 **Leukocytes. (a)** Neutrophil. **(b)** Eosinophil. **(c)** Basophil. **(d)** Small lymphocyte. **(e)** Monocyte. In each case the leukocytes are surrounded by erythrocytes. Note also the three platelets above the lymphocyte in (d). (All 1600×)

(d)

(e)

(especially raw fish) or invade the body via the skin and then typically burrow into the intestinal or respiratory mucosae. Eosinophils reside in the loose connective tissues at the same body sites, and when a parasitic worm "prey" is encountered, they gather around and release the enzymes from their cytoplasmic granules onto the parasite's surface, digesting it away. Eosinophils may also lessen the severity of allergies by inactivating certain inflammatory chemicals released during allergic reactions.

Basophils **Basophils** are the rarest white blood cells, averaging only 0.5–1% of the leukocyte population. Their cytoplasm contains large, coarse, histamine-containing granules that have an affinity for the basic dyes (*basophil* = "base loving") and stain purplish-black. *Histamine* is an inflammatory chemical that acts as a vasodilator (makes blood vessels dilate) and attracts other white blood cells to the inflamed site; drugs called antihistamines counter this effect. The deep purple nucleus is generally U or S shaped with two or three conspicuous constrictions.

Granulated cells similar to basophils, called *mast cells*, are found in connective tissues. Although mast cell nuclei tend to be more oval than lobed, the cells are similar microscopically, and both cell types bind to a particular antibody (immunoglobulin E) that causes the cells to release histamine. However, they arise from different cell lines.

Agranulocytes

The **agranulocytes** include lymphocytes and monocytes, WBCs that lack *visible* cytoplasmic granules. Although they are similar structurally, they are functionally distinct and unrelated cell types. Their nuclei are typically spherical or kidney shaped.

Lymphocytes **Lymphocytes,** accounting for 25% or more of the WBC population, are the second most numerous leukocytes in the blood. When stained, a typical lymphocyte has a large, dark-purple nucleus that occupies most of the cell volume. The nucleus is usually spherical but may be slightly indented, and it is surrounded by a thin rim of pale-blue cytoplasm (see Table 17.2 and Figure 17.10d). Lymphocyte diameter ranges from 5 to 17 μm, but they are often classified according to size as small (5–8 μm), medium (10–12 μm), and large (14–17 μm).

Although large numbers of lymphocytes exist in the body, only a small proportion of them (mostly the small lymphocytes) is found in the bloodstream. In fact, lymphocytes are so called because most are firmly enmeshed in lymphoid tissues (lymph nodes, spleen, etc.), where they play a crucial role in immunity. **T lymphocytes (T cells)** function in the immune response by acting directly against virus-infected cells and tumor cells. **B lymphocytes (B cells)** give rise to *plasma cells*, which produce **antibodies** (immunoglobulins) that are released to the blood. (B and T lymphocyte functions are described in Chapter 21.)

Monocytes **Monocytes,** which account for 3–8% of WBCs, have an average diameter of 18 μm and are the largest leukocytes. They have abundant pale-blue cytoplasm and a darkly staining purple nucleus, which is distinctively U or kidney shaped (see Table 17.2 and Figure 17.10e). When circulating monocytes leave the bloodstream and enter the tissues, they differentiate into highly mobile **macrophages** with prodigious appetites. Macrophages are actively phagocytic, and they are crucial in the body's defense against viruses, certain intracellular bacterial parasites, and *chronic* infections such as tuberculosis. As explained in Chapter 21, macrophages are also important in activating lymphocytes to mount the immune response.

Production and Life Span of Leukocytes

Like erythropoiesis, **leukopoiesis,** or the production of white blood cells, is stimulated by chemical messengers. These messengers, which can act either as paracrines or hormones, are glycoproteins that fall into two families of hematopoietic factors, **interleukins** and **colony-stimulating factors,** or **CSFs.** The interleukins are numbered (e.g., IL-3, IL-5), whereas most CSFs are named for the leukocyte population they stimulate—thus *granulocyte-CSF (G-CSF)* stimulates production of granulocytes. Hematopoietic factors, released by supporting cells of the bone marrow and mature WBCs, not only prompt the white blood cell precursors to divide and mature, but also enhance the protective potency of mature leukocytes.

Many of the hematopoietic hormones (EPO and several of the CSFs) are used clinically to stimulate the bone marrow of cancer patients who are receiving chemotherapy (which suppresses the marrow) and of those who have received marrow transplants, and to beef up the protective responses of AIDS patients.

Figure 17.11 shows the pathways of leukocyte differentiation. An early branching of the pathway divides the **lymphoid stem cells,** which produce lymphocytes, from the **myeloid stem cells,** which give rise to all other formed elements. In each granulocyte line, the committed cells, called **myeloblasts** (mi′ĕ-lo-blasts″), accumulate lysosomes, becoming **promyelocytes.** The distinctive granules of each granulocyte type appear next in the **myelocyte** stage and then cell division stops. In the subsequent stage, the nuclei arc, producing the **band cell** stage. Just before granulocytes leave the marrow and enter the circulation, their nuclei constrict, beginning the process of nuclear segmentation. The bone marrow stores mature granulocytes and usually contains about ten times more granulocytes than are found in the blood. The normal ratio of granulocytes to erythrocytes produced is about 3:1, which reflects the much shorter life span (0.5 to 9.0 days) of the granulocytes, most of which die combating invading microorganisms.

Despite their similar appearances, the two types of agranulocytes have very different lineages. Monocytes diverge from a myeloblast that can become either a neutrophil or a monocyte. Cells following the monocyte line pass through the **promonocyte** stage (see Figure 17.11) before leaving the bone marrow and becoming monocytes. Lymphocytes derive from the lymphoid stem cell and progress through the **lymphoblast** and **prolymphocyte** stages. The prolymphocytes leave the bone marrow and travel to the lymphoid tissues, where their further differentiation occurs (as described in Chapter 21). Monocytes may live for several months, whereas the life span of lymphocytes varies from a few days to decades.

Leukocyte Disorders

Overproduction of abnormal leukocytes occurs in leukemia and infectious mononucleosis. At the opposite pole, **leukopenia** (loo″ko-pe′ne-ah) is an abnormally low white blood cell count (*penia = poverty*), commonly induced by drugs, particularly glucocorticoids and anticancer agents.

Leukemias   The term *leukemia*, literally "white blood," refers to a group of cancerous conditions involving white blood cells. As a rule, the renegade leukocytes are members of a single *clone* (descendants of a single cell) that remain unspecialized and proliferate out of control, impairing normal bone marrow function. The leukemias are named according to the abnormal cell type primarily involved. For example, *myelocytic leukemia* involves myeloblast descendants, whereas *lymphocytic leukemia* involves the lymphocytes. Leukemia is *acute* (quickly advancing) if it derives from blast-type cells like lymphoblasts, and *chronic* (slowly advancing) if it involves proliferation of later cell stages like myelocytes. The more serious acute forms primarily affect children. Chronic leukemia is seen more often in elderly people. Without therapy, all leukemias are fatal; only the time course differs.

In all leukemias, the bone marrow becomes almost totally occupied by cancerous leukocytes and immature WBCs flood into the bloodstream. Because the other blood cell lines are crowded out, severe anemia and bleeding problems also result. Other symptoms include fever, weight loss, and bone pain. Although tremendous numbers of leukocytes are produced, they are nonfunctional and cannot defend the body in the usual way. The most common causes of death are internal hemorrhage and overwhelming infections.

FIGURE 17.11 **Leukocyte formation.** Leukocytes arise from ancestral stem cells called hemocytoblasts. **(a–c)** Granular leukocytes develop via a sequence involving myeloblasts. **(d–e)** Monocytes, like granular leukocytes, are progeny of the myeloid stem cell and diverge from a myeloblast that can become either a neutrophil or a monocyte. Only lymphocytes arise via the lymphoid stem cell line.

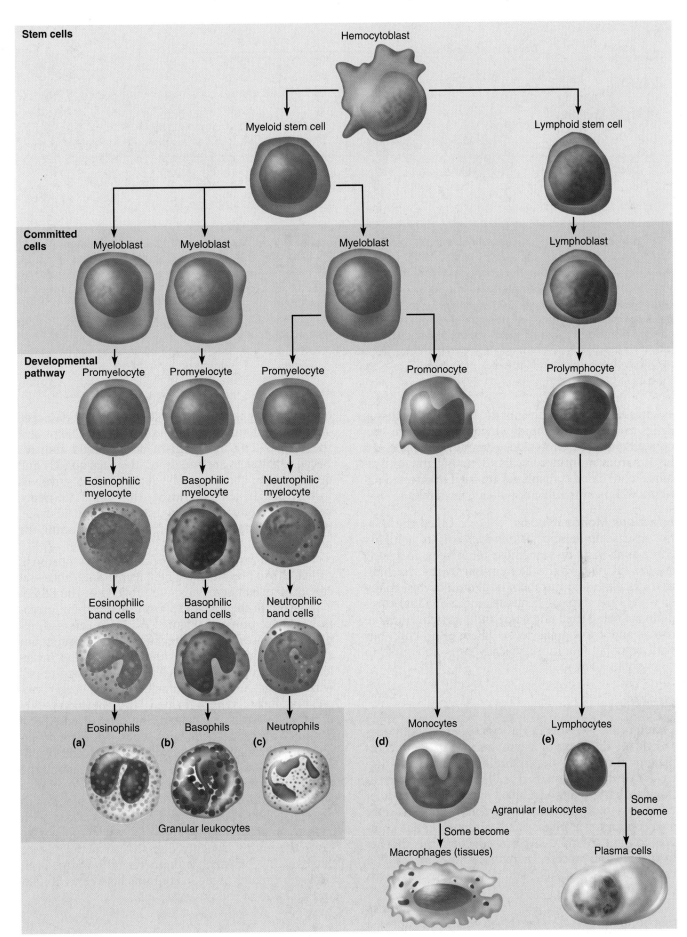

Stem cells

Hemocytoblast

Myeloid stem cell

Lymphoid stem cell

Committed cells

Myeloblast   Myeloblast   Myeloblast   Lymphoblast

Developmental pathway
Promyelocyte   Promyelocyte   Promyelocyte   Promonocyte   Prolymphocyte

Eosinophilic   Basophilic   Neutrophilic
myelocyte   myelocyte   myelocyte

Eosinophilic   Basophilic   Neutrophilic
band cells   band cells   band cells

Eosinophils   Basophils   Neutrophils   Monocytes   Lymphocytes
(a)   (b)   (c)   (d)   (e)

Agranular leukocytes

Granular leukocytes

Some become

Some become

Macrophages (tissues)   Plasma cells

17

FIGURE 17.12   Genesis of platelets. The hemocytoblast gives rise to cells that undergo several mitotic divisions unaccompanied by cytoplasmic division to produce megakaryocytes. The cytoplasm of the megakaryocyte becomes compartmentalized by membranes, and the plasma membrane then fragments, liberating the platelets. (Intermediate stages between the hemocytoblast and megakaryoblast are not illustrated.)

Irradiation and administration of antileukemic drugs to destroy the rapidly dividing cells have successfully induced remissions (symptom-free periods) lasting from months to years. Bone marrow or umbilical cord blood transplants are used in selected patients when compatible donors are available.

Infectious Mononucleosis   Once called the kissing disease, *infectious mononucleosis* is a highly contagious viral disease most often seen in young adults. Caused by the Epstein-Barr virus, its hallmark is excessive numbers of agranulocytes, many of which are atypical. The affected individual complains of being tired and achy, and has a chronic sore throat and a low-grade fever. There is no cure, but with rest the condition typically runs its course to recovery in a few weeks.

Platelets

Platelets are not cells in the strict sense. About one-fourth the diameter of a lymphocyte, they are cytoplasmic fragments of extraordinarily large cells (up to 60 μm in diameter) called **megakaryocytes** (meg″ah-kar′e-o-sītz). In blood smears, each platelet exhibits a blue-staining outer region and an inner area containing granules that stain purple. The granules contain an impressive array of chemicals that act in the clotting process, including serotonin, Ca^{2+}, a variety of enzymes, ADP, and platelet-derived growth factor (PDGF).

Platelets are essential for the clotting process that occurs in plasma when blood vessels are ruptured

or their lining is injured. By sticking to the damaged site, platelets form a temporary plug that helps seal the break. (This mechanism is explained shortly.) Because platelets are anucleate, they age quickly and degenerate in about ten days if they are not involved in clotting. In the meantime, they circulate freely, kept mobile but inactive by molecules (nitric oxide, prostacyclin) secreted by endothelial cells lining the blood vessels.

Platelet formation is regulated by a hormone called **thrombopoietin.** Their immediate ancestral cells, the megakaryocytes, are progeny of the hemocytoblast and the myeloid stem cell, but their formation is quite unusual (Figure 17.12). In this line, repeated mitoses of the **megakaryoblast** occur, but cytokinesis does not. The final result is the megakaryocyte (literally "big nucleus cell"), a bizarre cell with a huge, multilobed nucleus and a large cytoplasmic mass. When formed, the megakaryocyte presses up against a sinusoid (the specialized type of capillary in the marrow) and sends cytoplasmic extensions through the sinusoid wall into the bloodstream. These extensions rupture, releasing the platelet fragments like stamps being torn from a sheet of postage stamps and seeding the blood with platelets. The plasma membranes associated with each fragment quickly seal around the cytoplasm to form the grainy, roughly disc-shaped platelets (see Table 17.2), each with a diameter of 2–4 μm. Each cubic millimeter of blood contains between 150,000 and 400,000 of the tiny platelets.

TABLE 17.3	**Blood Clotting Factors (Procoagulants)**		
FACTOR NUMBER	**FACTOR NAME**	**NATURE/ORIGIN**	**FUNCTION OR PATHWAY**
I	Fibrinogen	Plasma protein; synthesized by liver	Common pathway; converted to fibrin, insoluble weblike substance of clot
II	Prothrombin	Plasma protein; synthesized by liver; formation requires vitamin K	Common pathway; converted to thrombin, which enzymatically converts fibrinogen to fibrin
III	Tissue factor (TF) or tissue thromboplastin	Glycoprotein in plasma membrane of cells underneath the endothelium	Activates extrinsic pathway
IV	Calcium ions (Ca^{2+})	Inorganic ion present in plasma; acquired from diet or released from bone	Needed for essentially all stages of coagulation process
V	Proaccelerin, labile factor, or platelet accelerator	Plasma protein; synthesized in liver; also released by platelets	Common pathway
VI	Number no longer used; substance now believed to be same as factor V		
VII	Proconvertin or convertin	Plasma protein; synthesized in liver in process that requires vitamin K	Both extrinsic and intrinsic mechanisms
VIII	Antihemophilic factor (AHF)	Plasma protein synthesized in liver; deficiency causes hemophilia A	Intrinsic mechanism
IX	Plasma thromboplastin component (PTC) or Christmas factor	Plasma protein; synthesized in liver; deficiency results in hemophilia B; synthesis requires vitamin K	Intrinsic mechanism
X	Stuart factor, Stuart-Prower factor, or thrombokinase	Plasma protein; synthesized in liver; synthesis requires vitamin K	Common pathway
XI	Plasma thromboplastin antecedent (PTA)	Plasma protein; synthesized in liver; deficiency results in hemophilia C	Intrinsic mechanism
XII	Hageman factor, glass factor	Plasma protein; synthesized in liver; activated by negatively charged surfaces (e.g., glass)	Intrinsic mechanism; activates plasmin; initiates clotting in vitro; activation initiates inflammation
XIII	Fibrin stabilizing factor (FSF)	Plasma protein; synthesized in liver and bone marrow	Cross-links fibrin, forming a strong, stable clot

17

Hemostasis

Normally, blood flows smoothly past the intact blood vessel lining (endothelium). But if a blood vessel wall breaks, a whole series of reactions is set in motion to accomplish **hemostasis** (he″mo-sta′sis), or stoppage of bleeding (*stasis* = halting). Without this plug-the-hole defensive reaction, we would quickly bleed out our entire blood volume from even the smallest cuts.

The hemostasis response, which is fast, localized, and carefully controlled, involves many blood coagulation factors (Table 17.3) normally present in plasma as well as some substances that are released by platelets and injured tissue cells. During hemostasis, three steps occur in rapid sequence: (1) vascu-lar spasms, (2) platelet plug formation, and (3) coagulation, or blood clotting (Figure 17.13a). Blood loss at the site is permanently prevented when fibrous tissue grows into the clot and seals the hole in the blood vessel.

Vascular Spasms

The immediate response to blood vessel injury is constriction of the damaged blood vessel (vasocon-striction). Factors that trigger this **vascular spasm** include direct injury to vascular smooth muscle, chemicals released by endothelial cells and platelets, and reflexes initiated by local pain receptors. The spasm mechanism becomes more and more efficient as the amount of tissue damage increases, and is

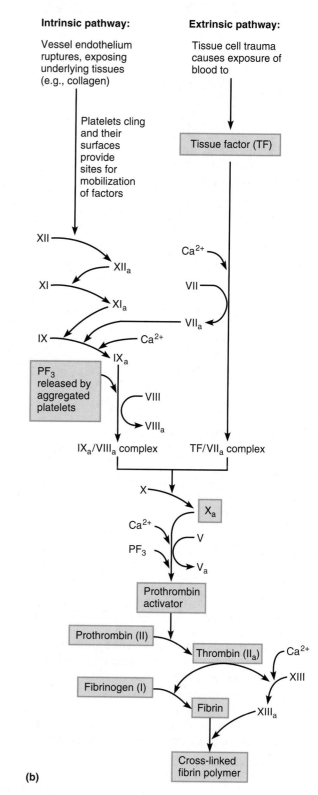

FIGURE 17.13 **Events of hemostasis. (a)** Simplified schematic of events. The steps of hemostasis are illustrated as **steps 1–3.** ①–③ are the major phases of coagulation. The color of the arrows indicates their source or destination: red from tissue, purple from platelets, and yellow to fibrin. **(b)** Detailed flowchart indicating the intermediates and events involved in platelet plug formation and the intrinsic and extrinsic mechanisms of blood clotting (coagulation). (The subscript "a" indicates the activated procoagulant.)

17

most effective in the smaller blood vessels. The value of the spasm response is obvious: A strongly constricted artery can significantly reduce blood loss for 20–30 minutes, allowing time for platelet plug formation and blood clotting to occur.

Platelet Plug Formation

Platelets play a key role in hemostasis by forming a plug that temporarily seals the break in the vessel wall. They also help to orchestrate subsequent events that lead to blood clot formation. These events are shown in simplified form in Figure 17.13a.

As a rule, platelets do not stick to each other or to the smooth endothelial linings of blood vessels. However, when the endothelium is damaged and underlying collagen fibers are exposed, platelets, with the help of a large plasma protein called von Willebrand factor (VWF) synthesized by endothelial cells, adhere tenaciously to the collagen fibers and undergo some remarkable changes. They swell, form spiked processes, and become sticky.

Once attached, the platelets are activated and their granules begin to break down and release several chemicals. Some, like **serotonin,** enhance the vascular spasm. Others, like **adenosine diphosphate (ADP),** are potent aggregating agents that attract more platelets to the area and cause them to release their contents. **Thromboxane A$_2$** (throm-boks'ān), a short-lived prostaglandin derivative that is generated and released, stimulates both events.

Thus, a positive feedback cycle that activates and attracts greater and greater numbers of platelets to the area begins and, within one minute, a platelet plug is built up, which further reduces blood loss. Limiting the platelet plug to the immediate area where it is needed is the task of **prostacyclin** (also called *PGI$_2$*), a prostaglandin produced by intact endothelial cells that is a strong inhibitor of platelet aggregation. Platelet plugs are loosely knit, but when reinforced by fibrin threads to act as a "molecular glue" for the aggregated platelets, they are quite effective in sealing the small tears in a blood vessel that occur with normal activity. Once the platelet plug is formed, the next stage, coagulation, comes into play.

Coagulation

Coagulation or **blood clotting** (Figure 17.13a), during which blood is transformed from a liquid to a gel, is a multistep process that leads to its critically important last three phases:

① A complex substance called *prothrombin activator* is formed.

② Prothrombin activator converts a plasma protein called *prothrombin* into *thrombin,* an enzyme.

③ Thrombin catalyzes the joining of *fibrinogen* molecules present in plasma to a *fibrin mesh,* which traps blood cells and effectively seals the hole until the blood vessel can be permanently repaired.

The complete coagulation process is much more complicated, however. Over 30 different substances are involved. Factors that enhance clot formation are called **clotting factors** or **procoagulants.** Although vitamin K is not directly involved in coagulation, this fat-soluble vitamin is required for the synthesis of four of the procoagulants made by the liver (see Table 17.3). Factors that inhibit clotting are called **anticoagulants.** Whether or not blood clots depends on a delicate balance between these two groups of factors. Normally, anticoagulants dominate and clotting is prevented; but when a vessel is ruptured, procoagulant activity in that area increases dramatically and clot formation begins. The procoagulants are numbered I to XIII (Table 17.3) according to the order of their discovery; hence the numerical order does *not* reflect the reaction sequence. Tissue factor (III) and Ca^{2+} (IV) are usually indicated by their names, rather than by numerals. Most of these factors are plasma proteins made by the liver that circulate in an inactive form in blood until mobilized.

Phase 1: Two Pathways to Prothrombin Activator

Clotting may be initiated by either the **intrinsic** or the **extrinsic pathway** (Figure 17.13b), and in the body both pathways are usually triggered by the same tissue-damaging events. Clotting of blood outside the body (such as in a test tube) is initiated *only* by the intrinsic mechanism. Let's examine the "why" of these differences.

Pivotal components in both mechanisms are negatively charged membranes, particularly those on platelets containing phosphatidylserine, also known as **PF$_3$** (platelet factor 3). Many intermediates of both pathways can be activated only in the presence of PF$_3$. In the slower intrinsic pathway, all factors needed for clotting are present in (intrinsic to) the blood. By contrast, when blood is exposed to an additional factor in tissues underneath the damaged endothelium called **tissue factor (TF), factor III,** or **tissue thromboplastin,** the "shortcut" extrinsic mechanism, which bypasses several steps of the intrinsic pathway, is triggered.

Each pathway requires ionic calcium and involves the activation of a *series* of procoagulants, each functioning as an enzyme to activate the next procoagulant in the sequence. The intermediate steps of each pathway cascade toward a common intermediate, factor X (Figure 17.13b). Once factor X has been activated, it complexes with calcium ions, PF$_3$, and factor V to form **prothrombin activator.**

FIGURE 17.14 **Scanning electron micrograph of erythrocytes trapped in a fibrin mesh.** (3000×)

This is usually the slowest step of the blood clotting process, but once prothrombin activator is present, the clot forms in 10 to 15 seconds.

Phase 2: Common Pathway to Thrombin

Prothrombin activator catalyzes the transformation of the plasma protein **prothrombin** to the active enzyme **thrombin.**

Phase 3: Common Pathway to the Fibrin Mesh

Thrombin catalyzes the polymerization of **fibrinogen** (another plasma protein made by the liver). As the fibrinogen molecules are aligned into long, hairlike, insoluble **fibrin** strands, they glue the platelets together and make a web that forms the structural basis of the clot. In the presence of fibrin, plasma becomes gel-like and traps formed elements that try to pass through it (Figure 17.14).

In the presence of calcium ions, thrombin also activates **factor XIII (fibrin stabilizing factor),** a cross-linking enzyme that binds the fibrin strands tightly together and strengthens and stabilizes the clot. Clot formation is normally complete within 3 to 6 minutes after blood vessel damage. Because the extrinsic pathway involves fewer steps it is more rapid than the intrinsic pathway; in cases of severe tissue trauma it can promote clot formation within 15 seconds.

Clot Retraction and Repair

Within 30 to 60 minutes, the clot is stabilized further by a platelet-induced process called **clot retraction.** Platelets contain contractile proteins (actin and myosin), and they contract in much the same manner as muscle cells. As the platelets contract, they pull on the surrounding fibrin strands, squeezing **serum** (plasma minus the clotting proteins) from the mass, compacting the clot and drawing the ruptured edges of the blood vessel more closely together. Even as clot retraction is occurring, vessel healing is taking place. **Platelet-derived growth factor (PDGF)** released by platelet degranulation stimulates smooth muscle cells and fibroblasts to divide and rebuild the wall. As fibroblasts form a connective tissue patch in the injured area, endothelial cells, stimulated by vascular endothelial growth factor (VEGF), multiply and restore the endothelial lining.

Fibrinolysis

A clot is not a permanent solution to blood vessel injury, and a process called **fibrinolysis** removes unneeded clots when healing has occurred. Because small clots are formed continually in vessels throughout the body, this cleanup detail is crucial. Without fibrinolysis, blood vessels would gradually become completely blocked.

The critical natural "clot buster" is a fibrin-digesting enzyme called **plasmin,** which is produced when the plasma protein **plasminogen** is activated. Large amounts of plasminogen are incorporated into a forming clot, where it remains inactive until appropriate signals reach it. The presence of a clot in and around the blood vessel causes the endothelial cells to secrete **tissue plasminogen activator (tPA).** Activated factor XII and thrombin released during clotting also serve as plasminogen activators. As a result, most plasmin activity is confined to the clot, and any plasmin that strays into the plasma is quickly destroyed by circulating enzymes. Fibrinolysis begins within two days and continues slowly over several days until the clot is finally dissolved.

Factors Limiting Clot Growth or Formation

Factors Limiting Normal Clot Growth

Once the clotting cascade has begun, it continues until a clot is formed. Normally, two homeostatic mechanisms prevent clots from becoming unnecessarily large: (1) swift removal of clotting factors, and (2) inhibition of activated clotting factors. For clotting to occur in the first place, the concentration of activated procoagulants must reach certain critical levels. Clot formation in rapidly moving blood is usually curbed because the activated clotting factors are diluted and washed away. For the same reasons, further growth of a forming clot is hindered when it contacts blood flowing normally.

Other mechanisms block the final step in which fibrinogen is polymerized into fibrin by restricting thrombin to the clot or by inactivating it if it escapes into the general circulation. As a clot forms, almost all of the thrombin produced is bound onto the fibrin threads. This is an important safeguard because thrombin also exerts positive feedback effects on the coagulation process prior to the common pathway. Not only does it speed up the production of prothrombin activator by acting indirectly through factor V, but it also accelerates the earliest steps of the intrinsic pathway by activating platelets. Thus, fibrin effectively acts as an anticoagulant to prevent enlargement of the clot and prevents thrombin from acting elsewhere. Thrombin not bound to fibrin is quickly inactivated by **antithrombin III,** a protein present in plasma. Antithrombin III and **protein C,** another protein produced in the liver, also inhibit the activity of other intrinsic pathway procoagulants.

Heparin, the natural anticoagulant contained in basophil and mast cell granules, is also found on the surface of endothelial cells. It inhibits thrombin by enhancing the activity of antithrombin III. Like most other clotting inhibitors, heparin also inhibits the intrinsic pathway.

Factors Preventing Undesirable Clotting

As long as the endothelium is smooth and intact, platelets are prevented from clinging and piling up. Also, antithrombic substances—nitric oxide and prostacyclin—secreted by the endothelial cells normally prevent platelet adhesion. Additionally, it has been found that vitamin E quinone, a molecule formed in the body when vitamin E reacts with oxygen, is a potent anticoagulant.

Disorders of Hemostasis

Blood clotting is one of nature's most elegant creations, but it sometimes goes awry. The two major disorders of hemostasis are at opposite poles. **Thromboembolic disorders** result from conditions that cause undesirable clot formation. **Bleeding disorders** arise from abnormalities that prevent normal clot formation. **Disseminated intravascular coagulation (DIC)** involves both wide spread clotting and severe bleeding.

Thromboembolic Conditions

Despite the body's many safeguards, undesirable intravascular clotting, called "hemostasis in the wrong place" by some, sometimes occurs. A clot that develops and persists in an *unbroken* blood vessel is called a **thrombus.** If the thrombus is large enough, it may block circulation to the cells beyond the occlusion and lead to death of those tissues. For example, if the blockage occurs in the coronary circulation of the heart (coronary thrombosis), the consequences may be death of heart muscle and a fatal heart attack. If the thrombus breaks away from the vessel wall and floats freely in the bloodstream, it becomes an **embolus** (plural: *emboli*). An embolus ("wedge") is usually no problem until it encounters a blood vessel too narrow for it to pass through; then it becomes an **embolism,** obstructing the vessel. For example, emboli that become trapped in the lungs (pulmonary embolisms) dangerously impair the ability of the body to obtain oxygen. A cerebral embolism may cause a stroke. Drugs that dissolve blood clots (such as tPA) and innovative medical techniques for removing clots are described in *A Closer Look* in Chapter 19.

Conditions that roughen the vessel endothelium, such as atherosclerosis or inflammation, cause thromboembolic disease by allowing platelets to gain a foothold. Slowly flowing blood or blood stasis is another risk factor, particularly in bedridden patients and those taking a long flight in economy-class seats. In this case, clotting factors are *not* washed away as usual and accumulate so that clot formation finally becomes possible.

A number of drugs, most importantly aspirin, heparin, and warfarin, are used clinically to prevent undesirable clotting in patients at risk for heart attack or stroke. **Aspirin** is an antiprostaglandin drug that inhibits thromboxane A_2 formation (hence, it blocks platelet aggregation and platelet plug formation). Clinical studies of men taking low-dose aspirin (one aspirin every two days) over several years demonstrated a 50% reduction in incidence of heart attack. Heparin (see above) is also prescribed as an anticoagulant drug, as is warfarin, an ingredient in rat poison. Administered in injectable form, heparin is the anticoagulant most used clinically (i.e., for preoperative and postoperative cardiac patients and for those receiving blood transfusions). Taken orally, **warfarin** (Coumadin) is a mainstay in the treatment of those prone to atrial fibrillation, a condition in which blood pools in the heart, to reduce the risk of stroke. It works via a different mechanism than heparin; it interferes with the action of vitamin K in the production of some procoagulants (see Impaired Liver Function below).

Disseminated Intravascular Coagulation

DIC is a situation in which widespread clotting occurs in intact blood vessels and the residual blood becomes unable to clot. Blockage of blood flow accompanied by severe bleeding follows. DIC is most commonly encountered as a complication of pregnancy or a result of septicemia or incompatible blood transfusions.

Bleeding Disorders

Anything that interferes with the clotting mechanism can result in abnormal bleeding. The most common causes are platelet deficiency (thrombocytopenia) and deficits of some procoagulants, which can result from impaired liver function or certain genetic conditions.

Thrombocytopenia   A condition in which the number of circulating platelets is deficient, **thrombocytopenia** (throm″bo-si″to-pe′ne-ah) causes spontaneous bleeding from small blood vessels all over the body. Even normal movement leads to widespread hemorrhage, evidenced by many small purplish blotches, called *petechiae* (pe-te′ke-e), on the skin. Thrombocytopenia can arise from any condition that suppresses or destroys the bone marrow, such as bone marrow malignancy, exposure to ionizing radiation, or certain drugs. A platelet count of under 50,000/μl of blood is usually diagnostic for this condition. Transfusions of concentrated platelets provide temporary relief from bleeding.

Impaired Liver Function   When the liver is unable to synthesize its usual supply of procoagulants, abnormal, and often severe, bleeding occurs. The causes can range from an easily resolved vitamin K deficiency (common in newborns and after taking systemic antibiotics) to nearly total impairment of liver function (as in hepatitis or cirrhosis). Vitamin K is required by the liver cells for production of the clotting factors, and because vitamin K is produced by bacteria that reside in the intestines, dietary deficiencies are rarely a problem. However, vitamin K deficiency can occur if fat absorption is impaired, because vitamin K is a fat-soluble vitamin that is absorbed into the blood along with fats. In liver disease, the nonfunctional liver cells fail to produce not only the procoagulants but also bile, which is required for fat and vitamin K absorption.

Hemophilias   The term **hemophilia** refers to several different hereditary bleeding disorders that have similar signs and symptoms. *Hemophilia A*, or *classical hemophilia*, results from a deficiency of **factor VIII (antihemophilic factor)**. It accounts for 77% of cases. *Hemophilia B* results from a deficiency of factor IX. Both types are X-linked conditions occurring primarily in males. *Hemophilia C*, a less severe form of hemophilia seen in both sexes, is due to a lack of factor XI. The relative mildness of this form, as compared to the A and B forms, reflects the fact that the procoagulant (factor IX) that factor XI

activates may also be activated by factor VII (see Figure 17.13b).

Symptoms of hemophilia begin early in life; even minor tissue trauma causes prolonged bleeding into tissues that can be life threatening. Commonly, the person's joints become seriously disabled and painful because of repeated bleeding into the joint cavities after exercise or trauma. Hemophilias are managed clinically by transfusions of fresh plasma or injections of the appropriate purified clotting factor. These therapies provide relief for several days but are expensive and inconvenient. In addition, the dependence of hemophiliacs on blood transfusions or factor injections has caused other problems. In the past, many became infected by the hepatitis virus and, beginning in the early 1980s, by HIV, a blood-transmitted virus that depresses the immune system and causes AIDS. (See Chapter 21.) New infections are now avoided as a result of new testing methods for HIV, availability of genetically engineered factor VIII, and hepatitis vaccines.

Transfusion and Blood Replacement

The human cardiovascular system is designed to minimize the effects of blood loss by (1) reducing the volume of the affected blood vessels, and (2) stepping up the production of red blood cells. However, the body can compensate for only so much blood loss. Losses of 15–30% cause pallor and weakness. Loss of more than 30% of blood volume results in severe shock, which can be fatal.

Transfusion of Red Blood Cells

Whole blood transfusions are routine when blood loss is rapid and substantial. In all other cases, infusions of **packed red cells** (whole blood from which most of the plasma has been removed) are preferred for restoring oxygen-carrying capacity. The usual blood bank procedure involves collecting blood from a donor and then mixing it with an anticoagulant, such as certain citrate or oxalate salts, which prevents clotting by binding with calcium ions. The shelf life of the collected blood at 4°C is about 35 days. Because blood is such a valuable commodity, it is most often separated into its component parts so that each component can be used when and where it is needed.

Human Blood Groups

People have different blood types and transfusion of incompatible blood can be fatal. RBC plasma membranes, like those of all body cells, bear highly specific

TABLE 17.4	ABO Blood Groups							
BLOOD GROUP	**FREQUENCY (% U.S. POPULATION)**				**RBC ANTIGENS (AGGLUTINOGENS)**	**ILLUSTRATION**	**PLASMA ANTIBODIES (AGGLUTININS)**	**BLOOD THAT CAN BE RECEIVED**
	WHITE	**BLACK**	**ASIAN**	**NATIVE AMERICAN**				
AB	4	4	5	<1	A B		None	A, B, AB, O (Universal recipient)
B	11	20	27	4	B		Anti-A (a)	B, O
A	40	27	28	16	A		Anti-B (b)	A, O
O	45	49	40	79	None		Anti-A (a) Anti-B (b)	O (Universal donor)

glycoproteins (antigens) at their external surfaces, which identify each of us as unique from all others. One person's RBC proteins may be recognized as foreign if transfused into someone with a different red blood cell type, and the transfused cells may be agglutinated (clumped together) and destroyed. Since these RBC antigens promote agglutination, they are more specifically called **agglutinogens** (ag"loo-tin'o-jenz).

At least 30 varieties of naturally occurring RBC antigens are common in humans. Besides these, perhaps 100 others occur in individual families ("private antigens") rather than in the general population. The presence or absence of each antigen allows each person's blood cells to be classified into several different blood groups. Antigens determining the ABO and Rh blood groups cause vigorous transfusion reactions (in which the foreign erythrocytes are destroyed) when they are improperly transfused. Thus, blood typing for these antigens is *always* done before blood is transfused. Other antigens (such as the MNS, Duffy, Kell, and Lewis factors) are mainly of legal or academic importance. Because these factors cause weak or no transfusion reactions, blood is not specifically typed for them unless the person is expected to need several transfusions, in which case the many weak transfusion reactions could have cumulative effects. Only the ABO and Rh blood groups are described here.

ABO Blood Groups   As shown in Table 17.4, the **ABO blood groups** are based on the presence or absence of two agglutinogens, type A and type B. Depending on which of these a person inherits, his or her ABO blood group will be one of the following: A, B, AB, or O. The O blood group, which has neither agglutinogen, is the most common ABO blood group in white, black, Asian, and Native Americans; AB, with both antigens, is least prevalent. The presence of either the A or the B agglutinogen results in group A or B, respectively.

Unique to the ABO blood groups is the presence in the plasma of *preformed antibodies* called **agglutinins.** The agglutinins act against RBCs carrying ABO antigens that are *not* present on a person's own red blood cells. A newborn lacks these antibodies, but they begin to appear in the plasma within two months and reach adult levels between 8 and 10 years of age. As indicated in Table 17.4, a person with neither the A nor the B antigen (group O) possesses both anti-A and anti-B antibodies, also called *a* and *b* agglutinins respectively. Those with group A blood have anti-B antibodies, while those with group B have anti-A antibodies. Neither antibody is produced by AB individuals.

Rh Blood Groups   There are 45 different types of Rh agglutinogens, each of which is called an **Rh factor.** Only three of these, the C, D, and E antigens, are fairly common. The Rh blood typing system is so named because one Rh antigen (agglutinogen D) was originally identified in *rhesus* monkeys. Later, the same antigen was discovered in humans. Most Americans (about 85%) are Rh^+ (Rh positive), meaning that their RBCs carry the D antigen. As a rule, a person's ABO and Rh blood groups are reported together, for example, O^+, A^-, and so on.

Unlike the ABO system antibodies, anti-Rh antibodies are not spontaneously formed in the blood of Rh^- (Rh negative) individuals. However, if an Rh^- person receives Rh^+ blood, the immune system becomes sensitized and begins producing anti-Rh antibodies against the foreign antigen soon after the transfusion. Hemolysis does not occur after the first such transfusion because it takes time for the body to react and start making antibodies. But the second time, and every time thereafter, a typical transfusion reaction occurs in which the recipient's antibodies attack and rupture the donor RBCs.

◤ HOMEOSTATIC IMBALANCE

An important problem related to the Rh factor occurs in pregnant Rh^- women who are carrying Rh^+ babies. The first such pregnancy usually results in the delivery of a healthy baby. But, when bleeding occurs as the placenta detaches from the uterus, the mother may be sensitized by her baby's Rh^+ antigens that pass into her bloodstream. If so, she will form anti-Rh antibodies unless treated with RhoGAM before or shortly after she has given birth. (The same precautions are taken in women who have miscarried or aborted the fetus.) RhoGAM is a serum containing anti-Rh agglutinins. Because it agglutinates the Rh factor, it blocks the mother's immune response and prevents her sensitization. If the mother is not treated and becomes pregnant again with an Rh^+ baby, her antibodies will cross through the placenta and destroy the baby's RBCs, producing a condition known as **hemolytic disease of the newborn,** or **erythroblastosis fetalis.** The baby becomes anemic and hypoxic. In severe cases, brain damage and even death may result unless transfusions are done *before* birth to provide the fetus with more erythrocytes for oxygen transport. Additionally, one or two *exchange transfusions* (see Related Clinical Terms, p. 673) are done after birth. The baby's Rh^+ blood is removed, and Rh^- blood is infused. Within six weeks, the transfused Rh^- erythrocytes have been broken down and replaced with the baby's own Rh^+ cells. ●

Transfusion Reactions: Agglutination and Hemolysis

When mismatched blood is infused, a **transfusion reaction** occurs in which the donor's red blood cells are attacked by the recipient's plasma agglutinins.

(Note that the donor's plasma antibodies may also be agglutinating the host's RBCs, but they are so diluted in the recipient's circulation that this does not usually present a serious problem.)

The initial event, agglutination of the foreign red blood cells, clogs small blood vessels throughout the body. During the next few hours, the clumped red blood cells begin to rupture or are destroyed by phagocytes, and their hemoglobin is released into the bloodstream. (When the transfusion reaction is exceptionally severe, the RBCs are lysed almost immediately.) These events lead to two easily recognized problems: (1) The oxygen-carrying capability of the transfused blood cells is disrupted, and (2) the clumping of red blood cells in small vessels hinders blood flow to tissues beyond those points. Less apparent, but more devastating, is the consequence of hemoglobin escaping into the bloodstream. Circulating hemoglobin passes freely into the kidney tubules, causing cell death and renal shutdown. If shutdown is complete (acute renal failure), the person may die.

Transfusion reactions can also cause fever, chills, low blood pressure, rapid heartbeat, nausea, vomiting, and general toxicity; but in the absence of renal shutdown, these reactions are rarely lethal. Treatment of transfusion reactions is directed toward preventing kidney damage by administering fluid and diuretics to increase urine output, diluting and washing out the hemoglobin.

As indicated in Table 17.4, group O red blood cells bear neither the A nor the B antigen; thus, theoretically this blood group is the **universal donor.** Indeed, some laboratories are developing methods to enzymatically convert other blood types to type O by clipping off the extra (A- or B-specific) sugar residue. Since group AB plasma is devoid of antibodies to both A and B antigens, group AB people are theoretically **universal recipients** and can receive blood transfusions from any of the ABO groups. However, these classifications are misleading, because they do not take into account the other agglutinogens in blood that can trigger transfusion reactions.

Because pooled blood transfusions carry the risk of transfusion reactions and transmission of life-threatening infections (particularly with HIV), public interest in **autologous transfusions** has risen. Autologous (*auto* = self) transfusions are particularly sought by those considering elective surgery when they are in no immediate danger. The patient *predonates* his or her own blood, and it is stored and immediately available if needed during or after the operation. Iron supplements are given, and as long as the patient's preoperative hematocrit is at least 30%, one unit (400–500 ml) of blood can be collected every 4 days, with the last unit taken 72 hours prior to surgery.

Blood Typing

The importance of determining the blood group of both the donor and the recipient *before* blood is transfused is glaringly obvious. The general procedure for determining ABO blood type is briefly outlined in Figure 17.15. Because it is critical that blood groups be compatible, cross matching is also done. *Cross matching* tests for agglutination of donor RBCs by the recipient's serum, and of the recipient's RBCs by the donor serum. Typing for the Rh factors is done in the same manner as ABO blood typing.

Restoring Blood Volume

When a patient's blood volume is so low that death from shock is imminent, there may not be time to type blood, or appropriate whole blood may be unavailable. Such emergencies demand that blood *volume* be replaced immediately to restore adequate circulation.

Fundamentally, blood consists of proteins and cells suspended in a salt solution. Replacing lost blood volume essentially consists of replacing that isotonic salt solution. *Normal saline* or a *multiple electrolyte solution* that mimics the electrolyte composition of plasma (for example, *Ringer's solution*) are the preferred choices. You might think that it would be important to add materials to mimic the osmotic properties of albumin in blood, and indeed this has been widely practiced. However, studies have shown that **plasma expanders** such as *purified human serum albumin, hetastarch,* and *dextran* provide no benefits over much cheaper electrolyte solutions and are associated with significant complications of their own. Volume replacement restores adequate circulation but cannot, of course, replace the oxygen-carrying capacity of the lost red blood cells. Research on ways to replace that capability is ongoing, as described in *A Closer Look* on pp. 672–673.

Diagnostic Blood Tests

A laboratory examination of blood yields information that can be used to evaluate a person's current state of health. For example, in some anemias, the blood is pale and yields a low hematocrit. A high fat content *(lipidemia)* gives blood plasma a yellowish hue and forecasts possible problems in those with heart disease. How well a diabetic is controlling diet and blood sugar levels is routinely determined by blood glucose tests. Infections are signaled by leukocytosis and, if severe, larger than normal buffy coats in the hematocrit.

Microscopic studies of blood can reveal variations in the size and shape of erythrocytes that pre-

FIGURE 17.15 **Blood typing of ABO blood types.** When serum containing anti-A or anti-B agglutinins is added to a blood sample diluted with saline, agglutination will occur between the agglutinin and the corresponding agglutinogen (A or B). As illustrated, agglutination occurs with both sera in blood group AB, with anti-B serum in blood group B, with anti-A serum in blood group A, and with neither serum in blood group O.

dict iron deficiency or pernicious anemia. Furthermore, a determination of the relative proportion of individual leukocyte types, a **differential white blood cell count,** is a valuable diagnostic tool. For example, a high eosinophil count may indicate a parasitic infection or an allergic response somewhere in the body.

A number of tests provide information on the status of the hemostasis system. The amount of prothrombin present in blood is assessed by determining the **prothrombin time,** and a **platelet count** is done when thrombocytopenia is suspected.

Two batteries of tests—a SMAC (SMA20, CHEM-20, or similar series) and a **complete blood count (CBC)**—are routinely ordered during physical

Concocting Blood: Artificial Blood Substitutes

The term "blood substitute" is somewhat misleading. Blood has many components and plays such a wide variety of roles—from fighting infection to transporting oxygen—that no single artificial substitute yet engineered can fulfill all those functions. However, substitute liquids are available that can transport oxygen from the lungs through the body and can "stretch" a limited blood supply, while sidestepping transfusion reactions. An important benefit of these blood substitutes is that the recipient is not at risk for transmission of bloodborne disease factors.

Modified Hemoglobin

Let's pretend to be biomedical engineers for a moment. If you wanted a substance to transport oxygen in the blood, what would you use? Like many researchers, you'd probably start with hemoglobin, the blood's own oxygen carrier. You could obtain hemoglobin from human red blood cells too old for transfusion, from readily available cow blood, or by genetic engineering. Unfortunately, hemoglobin by itself is unusable—it spontaneously splits in half in the plasma, and is rapidly cleared by the kidneys (which can lead to renal shutdown). Chemically linking hemoglobin subunits together so that they don't come apart or tying hemoglobin molecules together into long chains reduces clearance by the kidneys. Some types of these hemoglobin chains can stay in the blood for as long as 24 hours.

Another problem with free human hemoglobin is that it binds oxygen much more tightly (has a higher affinity) than hemoglobin contained inside a red blood cell, only reluctantly giving up oxygen to needy tissues. Cow hemoglobin, on the other hand, naturally binds oxygen less tightly. This solution has its own problems: the possible transmission of mad cow disease and the risk of immune reactions. Nevertheless, a cow-based product is licensed for use in South Africa where the high prevalence of HIV has made collecting uninfected blood extremely difficult. It's also possible to modify the hemoglobin with chemicals (such as pyridoxal phosphate) which mimic chemicals that lower oxygen affinity in the normal red blood cell. Hemoglobin's affinity for oxygen can also be lowered by genetically engineering its oxygen binding pocket. Each of these modified hemoglobins has undergone clinical trials with varying degrees of success.

A common problem in these trials is an increase in blood pressure when the hemoglobin compound is infused into the patient's blood. Blood vessels are normally held in a relaxed state by the action of the chemical messenger nitric oxide. Hemoglobin mops up nitric oxide, causing blood vessels to constrict and blood pressure to rise. Normally, hemoglobin in red blood cells is too far away from the source of nitric oxide to mop up much of it. The small free hemoglobin chains, however, slip close to the walls of the blood vessel where the concentration of nitric oxide is very high, and so absorb it in large quantities.

A miniature artificial cell (called a liposome) enclosing our modified hemoglobin would keep it away from blood vessel walls. Unfortunately, liposomes are cleared very rapidly by macrophages of the immune system.

---

examinations and before hospital admissions. SMAC is a blood *chemistry* profile. The CBC includes counts of the different types of formed elements, a hematocrit, measurements of hemoglobin content, and size of RBCs. Together these tests provide a comprehensive picture of one's general health status in relation to normal blood values.

A listing of the normal values for selected blood tests is provided in Appendix F.

Developmental Aspects of Blood

Early in fetal development there are many sites of blood cell formation—the fetal yolk sac, liver, and spleen, among others—but by the seventh month, the red marrow has become the primary hematopoietic area and remains so (barring serious illness) throughout life. If there is a severe need for blood cell production, however, the liver and the spleen may resume their fetal blood-forming roles. Additionally, inactive yellow bone marrow regions (essentially fatty tissue) may reconvert to active red marrow.

Blood cells develop from collections of mesenchymal cells, called *blood islands*, derived from the mesoderm germ layer. The fetus forms a unique hemoglobin, **hemoglobin F,** that has a higher affinity for oxygen than does adult hemoglobin (hemoglobin A). It contains two alpha and two gamma (γ) polypeptide chains per globin molecule, instead of the paired alpha and beta chains typical of hemoglobin A. After birth, fetal erythrocytes carrying hemoglobin F are rapidly destroyed by the liver, and the baby's erythroblasts begin producing hemoglobin A.

The most common blood diseases that appear during aging are chronic leukemias, anemias, and clotting disorders. However, these and most other age-related blood disorders are usually precipitated by disorders of the heart, blood vessels, or immune system. For example, the increased incidence of leukemias in old age is believed to result from the waning efficiency of the immune system, and abnormal thrombus and embolus formation reflects the

Instead, we could make the hemoglobin itself physically bigger by tying on long chains of polyethylene glycol (PEG). Think of it as hemoglobin floating down a river in a big inner tube, bouncing off the banks. Such a molecule is currently undergoing clinical trials and appears not to have the hypertensive effects seen with other modified hemoglobins.

And Now for Something Completely Different . . .

Some engineers have asked, "If hemoglobin has all of these problems, why use it? If you want a product with long shelf life, no biological contamination, and available in industrial quantities, why not use industrial chemistry?" Enter perfluorinated hydrocarbon chains (PFCs). These compounds, chemically similar to Teflon used in nonstick cookware, can hold large amounts of dissolved oxygen, much more than plasma. In the 1960s, researchers were amazed to discover that they could fully immerse mice for up to 30 minutes in liquid PFCs. (Mice happily breathing liquid PFCs rather than air led researchers to try ventilating humans with PFCs. Premature newborns who would ordinarily be breathing amniotic fluid are

obvious candidates, but liquid ventilation of adults with severe lung dysfunction is also currently in clinical trials.)

As artificial blood, PFCs have a serious shortcoming—they don't dissolve in plasma. Combining detergent and phospholipids with PFCs produces an emulsion of small droplets that can be suspended in the watery plasma. In order to load sufficient amounts of oxygen into PFCs, patients must breathe 70–100% oxygen by mask. The developers claim that oxygen transported by PFCs is used more easily by the body tissues because the slippery particles are much smaller than erythrocytes and glide through the capillaries at a faster rate. PFCs are cleared from the circulation and stored in the spleen and liver until they are exhaled as vapor by the lungs over several days. Side effects include hypertension, loss of gastric motility, and flu-like symptoms. Currently, one PFC is approved in the U.S. for use during cardiac catheterization.

Because each of these blood substitutes has both advantages and disadvantages, it's unlikely that we will soon come up with one universal blood substitute. Rather, it will be a matter of choosing the substitute that best fits the patient's clinical needs. Although the FDA has encouraged the development of artificial blood for over 30 years, no product, including those described above, has been approved in the U.S. for anything but experimental use in humans. Blood still remains a priceless commodity, and its beautiful complexity has yet to be replaced by modern medical technology. ■

progress of atherosclerosis, which roughens the blood vessel walls.

■ ■ ■

Because blood serves as the vehicle that the cardiovascular system uses to transport substances throughout the body, it could be considered the servant of the cardiovascular system. On the other hand, without blood, the normal functions of the heart and blood vessels are impossible. So perhaps the organs of the cardiovascular system, described in Chapters 18 and 19, are subservient to blood. The point of this circular thinking is that blood and the cardiovascular system organs are vitally intertwined in their common functions—to see that nutrients, oxygen, and other vital substances reach all tissue cells of the body and to relieve the cells of their wastes.

Related Clinical Terms

Blood chemistry tests Chemical analysis of substances in the blood, e.g., glucose, iron, or calcium determinations, protein tests, bilirubin content, and pH.

Blood fraction Any one of the components of whole blood that has been separated out from the other blood components, such as platelets or clotting factors.

Bone marrow biopsy A sample of red bone marrow is obtained by needle aspiration (typically from the anterior or posterior iliac crest), and is examined to diagnose disorders of blood-cell formation, leukemia, various marrow infections, and anemias resulting from damage to or failure of the marrow.

Exchange transfusion A technique of alternating removal of patient's blood and infusion of donor blood until a large fraction of the patient's blood has been replaced; used to treat fetal blood incompatibilities and poisoning victims.

Hematology (hem″ah-tol′o-je) Study of blood.

17

Hematoma (hem"ah-to'mah) Accumulated, clotted blood in the tissues usually resulting from injury; visible as "black and blue" marks or bruises; eventually absorbed naturally unless infections develop.

Hemochromatosis (he"mo-kro"mah-to'sis) An inherited disorder of iron overload in which the intestine absorbs too much iron from the diet. The iron builds up in body tissues, where it oxidizes to form compounds that poison those organs (especially joints, liver, and pancreas).

Myeloproliferative disorder All-inclusive term for a group of proliferative disorders including leukoerythroblastic anemia involving fibrosis of the bone marrow, polycythemia vera, and leukemia.

Plasmapheresis (plaz"mah-fe-re'sis) A process in which plasma is removed, separated from formed elements, and the formed elements are returned to the patient or donor. Most important application is removal of antibodies or immune complexes from the blood of individuals with autoimmune disorders (multiple sclerosis, myasthenia gravis, and others). Also used by blood banks to collect plasma for burn victims and for obtaining plasma components for therapeutic use.

Septicemia (sep"ti-se'me-ah; *septos* = rotten) Situation of excessive and harmful levels of bacteria or their toxins in the blood; also called blood poisoning.

Chapter Summary

Media study tools that could provide you additional help in reviewing specific key topics of Chapter 17 are referenced below.
IP = *InterActive Physiology*

Overview: Blood Composition and Functions (pp. 647–648)

Components (pp. 647–648)

1. Blood is composed of formed elements and plasma. The hematocrit is a measure of one formed element, erythrocytes, as a percentage of total blood volume.

Physical Characteristics and Volume (p. 648)

2. Blood is a viscous, slightly alkaline fluid representing about 8% of total body weight. Blood volume of a normal adult is about 5 L.

Functions (p. 648)

3. Distribution functions include delivery of oxygen and nutrients to body tissues, removal of metabolic wastes, and transport of hormones.

4. Regulation functions are maintenance of body temperature, of constant blood pH, and of adequate fluid volume.

5. Protective functions include hemostasis and prevention of infection.

Blood Plasma (pp. 648–649)

1. Plasma is a straw-colored, viscous fluid and is 90% water. The remaining 10% is solutes, such as nutrients, respiratory gases, salts, hormones, and proteins. Plasma makes up 55% of whole blood.

2. Plasma proteins, most made by the liver, include albumin, globulins, and fibrinogen. Albumin is an important blood buffer and contributes to the osmotic pressure of blood.

Formed Elements (pp. 649–662)

1. Formed elements, accounting for 45% of whole blood, are erythrocytes, leukocytes, and platelets. All formed elements arise from hemocytoblasts in red bone marrow.

Erythrocytes (pp. 649–656)

2. Erythrocytes (red blood cells) are small, biconcave cells containing large amounts of hemoglobin. They have no nucleus and few organelles. Spectrin allows the cells to change shape as they pass through tiny capillaries.

3. Oxygen transport is the major function of erythrocytes. In the lungs, oxygen binds to iron atoms in hemoglobin molecules, producing oxyhemoglobin. In body tissues, oxygen dissociates from iron, producing deoxyhemoglobin.

4. Red blood cells begin as hemocytoblasts and, through erythropoiesis, proceed from the proerythroblast (committed cell) stage to the erythroblast (early and late), normoblast, and reticulocyte stages. During this process, hemoglobin accumulates and the organelles and nucleus are extruded. Differentiation of reticulocytes is completed in the bloodstream.

5. Erythropoietin and testosterone enhance erythropoiesis.

6. Iron, vitamin B_{12}, and folic acid are essential for production of hemoglobin.

7. Red blood cells have a life span of approximately 120 days. Old and damaged erythrocytes are removed from the circulation by macrophages of the liver and spleen. Released iron from hemoglobin is stored as ferritin or hemosiderin to be reused. The balance of the heme group is degraded to bilirubin and secreted in bile. Amino acids of globin are metabolized or recycled.

IP Respiratory System; Topic: Gas Transport, pp. 3–5, 11–17.

8. Erythrocyte disorders include anemias and polycythemia.

Leukocytes (pp. 656–662)

9. Leukocytes are white blood cells. All are nucleated, and all have crucial roles in defending against disease. Two main categories exist: granulocytes and agranulocytes.

10. Granulocytes include neutrophils, basophils, and eosinophils. Basophils contain histamine, which enhances migration of leukocytes to inflammatory sites and promotes vasodilation. Neutrophils are active phagocytes. Eosinophils attack parasitic worms and their numbers increase during allergic reactions.

11. Agranulocytes have crucial roles in immunity. They include lymphocytes, the "immune cells," and monocytes which differentiate into macrophages.

12. Leukopoiesis is directed by colony-stimulating factors and interleukins released by supporting cells of the bone marrow and mature WBCs.

13. Leukocyte disorders include leukemias and infectious mononucleosis.

Platelets (p. 662)

14. Platelets are fragments of large, multinucleate megakaryocytes formed in red marrow. When a blood vessel is damaged, platelets form a plug to help prevent blood loss and play a central role in the clotting cascade.

Hemostasis (pp. 663–668)

1. Hemostasis is prevention of blood loss. The three major phases of hemostasis are vascular spasms, platelet plug formation, and blood coagulation.

Vascular Spasms and Platelet Plug Formation (pp. 663–665)

2. Spasms of smooth muscle in blood vessel walls and accumulation of platelets (platelet plug) at the site of vessel injury provide a temporary means of stopping or slowing blood loss until coagulation occurs.

Coagulation (pp. 665–666)

3. Coagulation of blood may be initiated by either the intrinsic or the extrinsic pathway. Platelet phospholipid (PF_3) is crucial to both pathways. Tissue factor (thromboplastin) exposed by tissue injury allows the extrinsic pathway to bypass many steps of the intrinsic pathway. A series of activated procoagulants oversees the intermediate steps of each cascade. The pathways converge as prothrombin is converted to thrombin.

Clot Retraction and Repair (p. 666)

4. After a clot is formed, clot retraction occurs. Serum is squeezed out and the ruptured vessel edges are drawn together. The vessel is repaired by smooth muscle, connective tissue, and endothelial cell proliferation and migration.

Fibrinolysis (p. 666)

5. When healing is complete, clot digestion (fibrinolysis) occurs.

Factors Limiting Clot Growth or Formation (pp. 666–667)

6. Abnormal expansion of clots is prevented by removal of coagulation factors in contact with rapidly flowing blood and by inhibition of activated blood factors. Prostacyclin (PGI_2) and nitric oxide secreted by the endothelial cells help prevent undesirable (unnecessary) clotting.

Disorders of Hemostasis (pp. 667–668)

7. Thromboembolytic disorders involve undesirable clot formation, which can occlude vessels. DIC is a condition of bodywide clotting in undamaged blood vessels and subsequent hemorrhages.

8. Thrombocytopenia, a deficit of platelets, causes spontaneous bleeding from small blood vessels. Hemophilia is caused by a genetic deficiency of certain coagulation factors.

Liver disease can also cause bleeding disorders because many coagulation proteins are formed by the liver.

Transfusion and Blood Replacement (pp. 668–671)

Transfusion of Red Blood Cells (pp. 668–671)

1. Whole blood transfusions are given to replace severe and rapid blood loss. Packed RBCs are given to replace lost O_2-carrying capacity.

2. Blood group is based on agglutinogens (antigens) present on red blood cell membranes.

3. When mismatched blood is transfused, the recipient's agglutinins (plasma antibodies) clump the foreign RBCs; the clumped cells are then lysed. Blood vessels may be blocked by clumped RBCs. Released hemoglobin may precipitate in the kidney tubules, causing renal shutdown.

4. Before whole blood can be transfused, it must be typed and cross matched so that transfusion reactions are avoided. The most important blood groups for which blood must be typed are the ABO and Rh groups.

Restoring Blood Volume (p. 671)

5. Plasma volume can be replaced with balanced electrolyte solutions, and these are generally preferred over plasma expanders.

Diagnostic Blood Tests (pp. 671–672)

1. Diagnostic blood tests can provide large amounts of information about the current status of the blood and of the body as a whole.

Developmental Aspects of Blood (pp. 672–673)

1. Fetal hematopoietic sites include the yolk sac, liver, and spleen. By the seventh month of development, the red bone marrow is the primary blood-forming site.

2. Blood cells develop from blood islands derived from mesoderm. Fetal blood contains hemoglobin F. After birth, hemoglobin A is formed.

3. The major blood-related problems associated with aging are leukemia, anemia, and thromboembolytic disease.

Review Questions

Multiple Choice/Matching

(Some questions have more than one correct answer. Select the best answer or answers from the choices given.)

1. The blood volume in an adult averages approximately (a) 1 L, (b) 3 L, (c) 5 L, (d) 7 L.

2. The hormonal stimulus that prompts red blood cell formation is (a) serotonin, (b) heparin, (c) erythropoietin, (d) thrombopoietin.

3. All of the following are true of RBCs except (a) biconcave disc shape, (b) life span of approximately 120 days, (c) contain hemoglobin, (d) contain nuclei.

4. The most numerous WBC is the (a) eosinophil, (b) neutrophil, (c) monocyte, (d) lymphocyte.

5. Blood proteins play an important part in (a) blood clotting, (b) immunity, (c) maintenance of blood volume, (d) all of the above.

6. The white blood cell that releases histamine and other inflammatory chemicals is the (a) basophil, (b) neutrophil, (c) monocyte, (d) eosinophil.

7. The blood cell that can become an antibody-secreting cell is the (a) lymphocyte, (b) megakaryocyte, (c) neutrophil, (d) basophil.

8. Which of the following does not promote multiple steps in the clotting pathway? (a) PF_3, (b) factor XI, (c) thrombin, (d) Ca^{2+}.

9. The normal pH of the blood is about (a) 8.4, (b) 7.8, (c) 7.4, (d) 4.7.

10. Suppose your blood was found to be AB positive. This means that (a) agglutinogens A and B are present on your red blood cells, (b) there are no anti-A or anti-B agglutinins in your plasma, (c) your blood is Rh^+, (d) all of the above.

Short Answer Essay Questions

11. (a) Define formed elements and list their three major categories. (b) Which is least numerous? (c) Which comprise(s) the buffy coat in a hematocrit tube?

12. Discuss hemoglobin relative to its chemical structure, its function, and the color changes it undergoes during loading and unloading of oxygen.

13. If you had a high hematocrit, would you expect your hemoglobin determination to be low or high? Why?

14. What nutrients are needed for erythropoiesis?

15. (a) Describe the process of erythropoiesis. (b) What name is given to the immature cell type released to the circulation? (c) How does it differ from a mature erythrocyte?

16. Besides the ability to move by amoeboid motion, what other physiological attributes contribute to the function of white blood cells in the body?

17. (a) If you had a severe infection, would you expect your WBC count to be closest to 5000, 10,000, or 15,000/μl? (b) What is this condition called?

18. (a) Describe the appearance of platelets and state their major function. (b) Why should platelets not be called "cells"?

19. (a) Define hemostasis. (b) List the three major steps of coagulation. Explain what initiates each step and what the step accomplishes. (c) In what general way do the intrinsic and extrinsic mechanisms of clotting differ? (d) What ion is essential to virtually all stages of coagulation?

20. (a) Define fibrinolysis. (b) What is the importance of this process?

21. (a) How is clot overgrowth usually prevented? (b) List two conditions that may lead to unnecessary (and undesirable) clot formation.

22. How can liver dysfunction cause bleeding disorders?

23. (a) What is a transfusion reaction and why does it happen? (b) What are its possible consequences?

24. How can poor nutrition lead to anemia?

25. What blood-related problems are most common in the aged?

Critical Thinking and Clinical Application Questions

1. Cancer patients being treated with chemotherapeutic drugs designed to destroy rapidly dividing cells are monitored closely for changes in their red and white blood counts. Why so?

2. Mary Healy, a young woman with severe vaginal bleeding, is admitted to the emergency room. She is three months pregnant, and the physician is concerned about the volume of blood she is losing. (a) What type of transfusion will probably be given to this patient? (b) What blood tests will be performed before starting the transfusion?

3. Alan Forsythe, a middle-aged college professor from Boston, is in the Swiss Alps studying astronomy during his sabbatical leave. He has been there for two days and plans to stay the entire year. However, he notices that he is short of breath when he walks up steps and tires easily with any physical activity. His symptoms gradually disappear, and after two months he feels fine. Upon returning to the United States, he has a complete physical exam and is told that his erythrocyte count is higher than normal. (a) Attempt to explain this finding. (b) Will his RBC count remain at this higher-than-normal level? Why or why not?

4. A young child is diagnosed as having acute lymphocytic leukemia. Her parents cannot understand why infection is a major problem for Janie when her WBC count is so high. Can you provide an explanation for Janie's parents?

5. Mrs. Ryan, a middle-aged woman, appears at the clinic complaining of multiple small hemorrhagic spots in her skin and severe nosebleeds. While taking her history, the nurse notes that Mrs. Ryan works as a rubber glue applicator at a local factory. Rubber glue contains benzene, which is known to be toxic to red marrow. Using your knowledge of physiology, explain the connection between the bleeding problems and benzene.

6. A reticulocyte count indicated that 5% of Tyler's red blood cells were reticulocytes. His blood test also indicated he had polycythemia and a hematocrit of 65%. Explain the connection between these three facts.

7. In 1998, the U.S. Food and Drug Administration approved the nation's first commercial surgical glue to control bleeding during certain surgeries. Called Tisseel, it forms a flexible mesh over an oozing blood vessel to help stem bleeding within five minutes. This sealant is made from two blood proteins that naturally cause blood to clot when they latch together. Name these proteins.

8. Jenny, a healthy young woman, had a battery of tests during a physical for a new job. Her RBC count was at the higher end of the normal range at that time, but four weeks later it was substantially elevated beyond that. When asked if any circumstances had changed in her life, she admitted to taking up smoking. How might her new habit explain her higher RBC count?

9. Mr. Chu has been scheduled for surgery to have his arthritic hip replaced. His surgeon tells him he must switch from aspirin to acetaminophen for pain control before his surgery. Why?

LOOKING FOR MORE STUDY HELP?
A wide variety of quiz questions, tutorials, and learning exercises are available online at the Anatomy & Physiology Place (www.anatomyandphysiology.com) and, if your instructor has provided you with a MyA&P Course ID number, in MyA&P (www.myaandp.com).

17

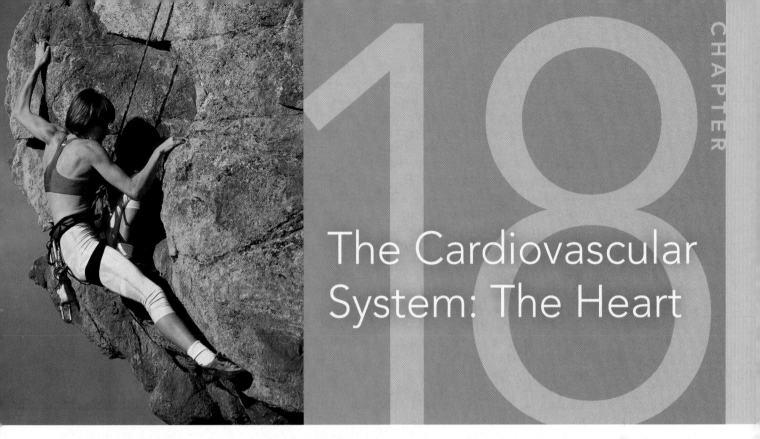

The Cardiovascular System: The Heart

Heart Anatomy (pp. 678–689)

1. Describe the size, shape, location, and orientation of the heart in the thorax.

2. Name the coverings of the heart.

3. Describe the structure and function of each of the three layers of the heart wall.

4. Describe the structure and functions of the four heart chambers. Name each chamber and provide the name and general route of its associated great vessel(s).

5. Trace the pathway of blood through the heart.

6. Name the major branches and describe the distribution of the coronary arteries.

7. Name the heart valves and describe their location, function, and mechanism of operation.

Properties of Cardiac Muscle Fibers (pp. 689–692)

8. Describe the structural and functional properties of cardiac muscle, and explain how it differs from skeletal muscle.

9. Briefly describe the events of cardiac muscle cell contraction.

Heart Physiology (pp. 692–705)

10. Name the components of the conduction system of the heart, and trace the conduction pathway.

11. Draw a diagram of a normal electrocardiogram tracing; name the individual waves and intervals, and indicate what each represents. Name some abnormalities that can be detected on an ECG tracing.

12. Describe the timing and events of the cardiac cycle.

13. Describe normal heart sounds, and explain how heart murmurs differ.

14. Name and explain the effects of various factors regulating stroke volume and heart rate.

15. Explain the role of the autonomic nervous system in regulating cardiac output.

Developmental Aspects of the Heart (pp. 705–709)

16. Describe fetal heart formation, and indicate how the fetal heart differs from the adult heart.

17. Provide examples of age-related changes in heart function.

The ceaselessly beating heart in the chest has intrigued people for centuries. The ancient Greeks believed the heart was the seat of intelligence. Others thought it was the source of emotions. While these theories have proved false, we do know that emotions affect heart rate. When your heart pounds or occasionally skips a beat, you become acutely aware of how much you depend on this dynamic organ for your very life.

Despite its vital importance, the heart does not work alone. Indeed, it is part of the cardiovascular system, which also includes the miles of blood vessels that run through the body. Day and night, tissue cells take in nutrients and oxygen and excrete wastes. Because cells can make such exchanges only with their immediate environment, some means of changing and renewing that environment is necessary to ensure a continual supply of nutrients and to prevent a buildup of wastes. The cardiovascular system provides the transport system "hardware" that keeps blood continuously circulating to fulfill this critical homeostatic need.

Stripped of its romantic cloak, the **heart** is no more than the transport system pump; the hollow blood vessels are the delivery routes. Using blood as the transport medium, the heart continually propels oxygen, nutrients, wastes, and many other substances into the interconnecting blood vessels that service body cells. Blood and blood vessels are considered separately in Chapters 17 and 19, respectively. This chapter focuses on the structure and function of the heart.

Heart Anatomy

Size, Location, and Orientation

The modest size and weight of the heart belie its incredible strength and endurance. About the size of a fist, the hollow, cone-shaped heart (Figure 18.1) has a mass of between 250 and 350 grams—less than a pound.

Snugly enclosed within the **mediastinum** (me″de-ah-sti′num), the medial cavity of the thorax, the heart extends obliquely for 12 to 14 cm (about 5 inches) from the second rib to the fifth intercostal space (Figure 18.1). As it rests on the superior surface of the diaphragm, the heart lies anterior to the vertebral column and posterior to the sternum. The lungs flank the heart laterally and partially obscure it. Approximately two-thirds of its mass lies to the left of the midsternal line; the balance projects to the right. Its broad, flat **base,** or posterior surface, is about 9 cm (3.5 in) wide and directed toward the right shoulder. Its **apex** points inferiorly toward the left hip. If you press your fingers between the fifth and sixth ribs just below the left nipple, you can easily feel your heart beating where the apex contacts the chest wall. Hence, this site is referred to as the **point of maximal intensity (PMI).**

Coverings of the Heart

The heart is enclosed in a double-walled sac called the **pericardium** (per″ĭ-kar′de-um; *peri* = around, *cardi* = heart) (Figure 18.2). The loosely fitting superficial part of this sac is the **fibrous pericardium.** This tough, dense connective tissue layer (1) protects the heart, (2) anchors it to surrounding structures, and (3) prevents overfilling of the heart with blood.

Deep to the fibrous pericardium is the **serous pericardium,** a thin, slippery, two-layer serous membrane. Its **parietal layer** lines the internal surface of the fibrous pericardium. At the superior margin of the heart, the parietal layer attaches to the large arteries exiting the heart, and then turns inferiorly and continues over the external heart surface as the **visceral layer,** also called the **epicardium** ("upon the heart"), which is an integral part of the heart wall.

Between the parietal and visceral layers is the slitlike **pericardial cavity,** which contains a film of serous fluid. The serous membranes, lubricated by the fluid, glide smoothly past one another during heart activity, allowing the mobile heart to work in a relatively friction-free environment.

◤ **HOMEOSTATIC IMBALANCE**

Pericarditis, inflammation of the pericardium, roughens the serous membrane surfaces. Consequently, as the beating heart rubs against its pericardial sac, it creates a creaking sound *(pericardial friction rub)* that can be heard with a stethoscope. Pericarditis is characterized by pain deep to the sternum. Over time, it may lead to adhesions in which the visceral and parietal pericardia stick together and impede heart activity. In severe cases, the situation changes and *large* amounts of inflammatory fluid seep into the pericardial cavity. This excess fluid compresses the heart, limiting its ability to pump blood. This condition in which the heart is compressed by fluid is called *cardiac tamponade* (tam″pŏ-nād′), literally, "heart plug." Physicians treat it by inserting a syringe into the pericardial cavity and draining off the excess fluid. ●

Layers of the Heart Wall

The heart wall, richly supplied with blood vessels, is composed of three layers (Figure 18.2).

Q   *The title for this figure points out that the heart is in the mediastinum. Just what is the mediastinum?*

FIGURE 18.1   **Location of the heart in the mediastinum. (a)** Relationship of the heart to the sternum, ribs, and diaphragm in a person who is lying down (the heart is slightly inferior to this position in a standing person). **(b)** Cross-sectional view showing the heart's relative position in the thorax. **(c)** Relationship of the heart and great vessels to the lungs.

Midsternal line

2nd rib

Sternum

Diaphragm

Point of maximal intensity (PMI)

(a)

Right lung

Heart

(b)   *Anterior*

Superior vena cava

Left lung

Aorta

Parietal pleura (cut)

Pulmonary trunk

Pericardium (cut)

Apex of heart

Diaphragm

(c)

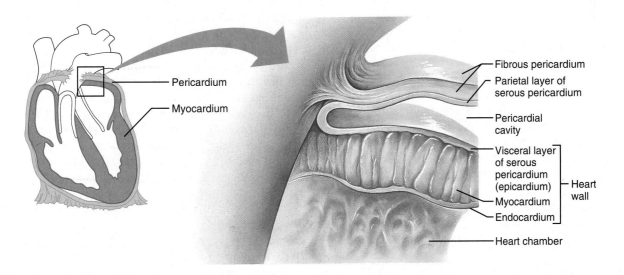

Pericardium

Myocardium

Fibrous pericardium

Parietal layer of serous pericardium

Pericardial cavity

Visceral layer of serous pericardium (epicardium)

Myocardium

Endocardium

Heart wall

Heart chamber

FIGURE 18.2   **The pericardial layers and layers of the heart wall.**

A   *The medial cavity of the thorax within which the heart, great vessels, and trachea are found.*

Cardiac
muscle
bundles

FIGURE 18.3 **The circular and spiral arrangement of cardiac muscle bundles in the myocardium of the heart.**

The superficial *epicardium* is the visceral layer of the serous pericardium. It is often infiltrated with fat, especially in older people.

The middle layer, the **myocardium** ("muscle heart"), is composed mainly of cardiac muscle and forms the bulk of the heart. It is the layer that contracts. In this layer, the branching cardiac muscle cells are tethered to one another by crisscrossing connective tissue fibers and arranged in spiral or circular *bundles* (Figure 18.3). These interlacing bundles effectively link all parts of the heart together. The connective tissue fibers form a dense network, the **fibrous skeleton of the heart,** that reinforces the myocardium internally and anchors the cardiac muscle fibers. This network of collagen and elastin fibers is thicker in some areas than others. For example, it constructs ropelike rings that provide additional support where the great vessels issue from the heart and around the heart valves (see Figure 18.8a, p. 687). Without this support, the vessels and valves might eventually become stretched because of the continuous stress of blood pulsing through them. Additionally, because connective tissue is not electrically excitable, the fibrous skeleton limits the direct spread of action potentials across the heart to specific pathways.

The third layer, the **endocardium** ("inside the heart"), is a glistening white sheet of endothelium (squamous epithelium) resting on a thin connective tissue layer. Located on the inner myocardial surface, it lines the heart chambers and covers the fibrous skeleton of the valves. The endocardium is continuous with the endothelial linings of the blood vessels leaving and entering the heart.

Chambers and Associated Great Vessels

The heart has four chambers (Figure 18.4e)—two superior **atria** (a'tre-ah) and two inferior **ventricles** (ven'trĭ-klz). The internal partition that divides the heart longitudinally is called the **interatrial septum** where it separates the atria, and the **interventricular septum** where it separates the ventricles. The right ventricle forms most of the anterior surface of the heart. The left ventricle dominates the inferoposterior aspect of the heart and forms the heart apex. Two grooves visible on the heart surface indicate the boundaries of its four chambers and carry the blood vessels supplying the myocardium. The **coronary sulcus** (Figure 18.4b, d), or *atrioventricular groove*, encircles the junction of the atria and ventricles like a crown (*corona* = crown). The **anterior interventricular sulcus,** cradling the anterior interventricular artery, marks the anterior position of the septum separating the right and left ventricles. It continues as the **posterior interventricular sulcus,** which provides a similar landmark on the heart's posteroinferior surface.

Atria: The Receiving Chambers

Except for small, wrinkled, protruding appendages called **auricles** (or'ĭ-klz; *auricle* = little ear), which increase the atrial volume somewhat, the right and left atria are remarkably free of distinguishing surface features. Internally, the right atrium has two basic parts (Figure 18.4c): a smooth-walled posterior part and an anterior portion in which the walls are ridged by bundles of muscle tissue. Because these bundles look like the teeth of a comb, these muscle bundles are called **pectinate muscles** (*pectin* = comb). The posterior and anterior regions of the right atrium are separated by a C-shaped ridge called the *crista terminalis* ("terminal crest"). In contrast, the left atrium is mostly smooth and undistinguished internally. The interatrial septum bears a shallow depression, the **fossa ovalis** (o-vă'lis), that marks the spot where an opening, the *foramen ovale*, existed in the fetal heart (Figure 18.4c,e).

Functionally, the atria are receiving chambers for blood returning to the heart from the circulation (*atrium* = entryway). Because they need contract only minimally to push blood "downstairs" into the ventricles, the atria are relatively small, thin-walled chambers. As a rule, they contribute little to the propulsive pumping activity of the heart.

Q *Which heart chamber has the thickest walls? What is the significance of this structural difference?*

FIGURE 18.4   **Gross anatomy of the heart.** In diagrammatic views, vessels transporting oxygen-rich blood are red; those transporting oxygen-poor blood are blue. **(a)** Photograph of anterior aspect (pericardium removed). **(b)** Anterior view. (See *A Brief Atlas of the Human Body,* Figure 57.)

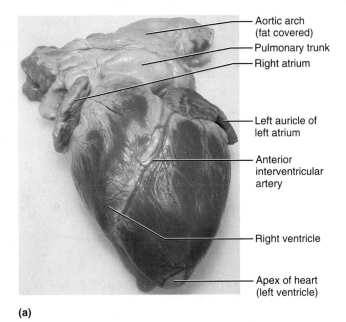

- Aortic arch (fat covered)
- Pulmonary trunk
- Right atrium
- Left auricle of left atrium
- Anterior interventricular artery
- Right ventricle
- Apex of heart (left ventricle)

(a)

- Brachiocephalic trunk
- Superior vena cava
- Right pulmonary artery
- Ascending aorta
- Pulmonary trunk
- Right pulmonary veins
- Right atrium
- Right coronary artery (in coronary sulcus)
- Anterior cardiac vein
- Right ventricle
- Marginal artery
- Small cardiac vein
- Inferior vena cava

- Left common carotid artery
- Left subclavian artery
- Aortic arch
- Ligamentum arteriosum
- Left pulmonary artery
- Left pulmonary veins
- Left atrium
- Auricle
- Circumflex artery
- Left coronary artery (in coronary sulcus)
- Left ventricle
- Great cardiac vein
- Anterior interventricular artery (in anterior interventricular sulcus)
- Apex

(b)

18

A *Left ventricle. It's the systemic pump that has to pump blood through the entire systemic circulation against high resistance.*

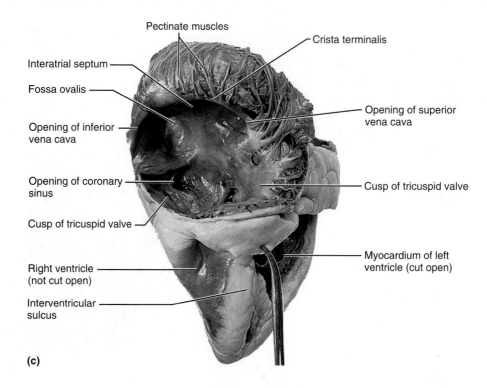

Pectinate muscles

Crista terminalis

Interatrial septum

Fossa ovalis

Opening of inferior vena cava

Opening of superior vena cava

Opening of coronary sinus

Cusp of tricuspid valve

Cusp of tricuspid valve

Right ventricle (not cut open)

Myocardium of left ventricle (cut open)

Interventricular sulcus

(c)

Aorta

Left pulmonary artery

Left pulmonary veins

Auricle of left atrium

Left atrium

Great cardiac vein

Posterior vein of left ventricle

Left ventricle

Apex

Superior vena cava — vein

Right pulmonary artery

Right pulmonary veins

Right atrium

Inferior vena cava — vein

Right coronary artery (in coronary sulcus)

Coronary sinus — vein

Posterior interventricular artery (in posterior interventricular sulcus)

Middle cardiac vein

Right ventricle

(d)

FIGURE 18.4 *(continued)* **Gross anatomy of the heart. (c)** Right anterior view of the internal aspect of the right atrium. The anterior wall of the atrium has been opened and folded superiorly. **(d)** Posterior surface view.

(See *A Brief Atlas of the Human Body,* Figure 59.)

18

Handwritten annotations: brachial cephalic a., Lt common carotida, Ascending aorta artery, Lt subclaviana, descending A.A, Aorta Arch.

Superior vena cava

Right pulmonary artery

Pulmonary trunk

Right atrium

Right pulmonary veins

Fossa ovalis

Pectinate muscles

Tricuspid valve

Right ventricle

Chordae tendineae

Trabeculae carneae

Inferior vena cava

(e)

Aorta

Left pulmonary artery

Left atrium

Left pulmonary veins

Mitral (bicuspid) valve

Aortic valve

Pulmonary valve

Left ventricle

Papillary muscle

Interventricular septum

Myocardium

Visceral pericardium

Endocardium

Blood enters the *right atrium* via three veins (Figure 18.4c–e): (1) The **superior vena cava** returns blood from body regions superior to the diaphragm; (2) the **inferior vena cava** returns blood from body areas below the diaphragm; and (3) the **coronary sinus** collects blood draining from the myocardium. Four **pulmonary veins** enter the *left atrium*, which makes up most of the heart's base. These veins, which transport blood from the lungs back to the heart, are best seen in a posterior view (Figure 18.4d).

Ventricles: The Discharging Chambers

Together the ventricles (*ventr* = underside) make up most of the volume of the heart. As already mentioned, the right ventricle forms most of the heart's anterior surface and the left ventricle dominates its posteroinferior surface. Marking the internal walls of the ventricular chambers are irregular ridges of muscle called **trabeculae carneae** (trah-bek'u-le kar'ne-e; "crossbars of flesh"). Still other muscle bundles, the conelike **papillary muscles,** which play a role in valve function, project into the ventricular cavity.

The ventricles are the discharging chambers or actual pumps of the heart (the difference in function

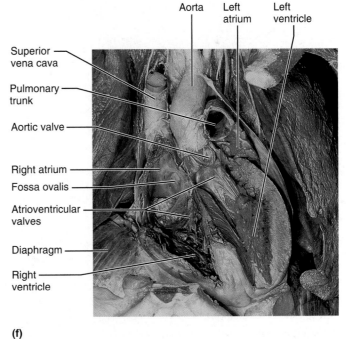

Aorta

Left atrium

Left ventricle

Superior vena cava

Pulmonary trunk

Aortic valve

Right atrium

Fossa ovalis

Atrioventricular valves

Diaphragm

Right ventricle

(f)

FIGURE 18.4 *(continued)* **Gross anatomy of the heart. (e)** Frontal section showing interior chambers and valves. **(f)** Photograph of a cadaver heart comparable to diagrammatic view of Figure 18.4e but with part of the pulmonary trunk removed.

18

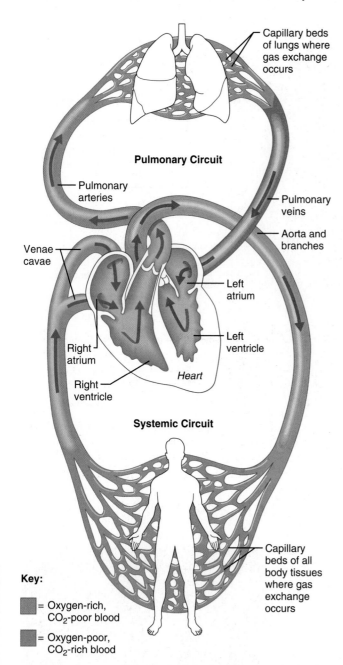

Pulmonary Circuit

Capillary beds of lungs where gas exchange occurs

Pulmonary arteries

Pulmonary veins

Venae cavae

Aorta and branches

Left atrium

Left ventricle

Right atrium

Heart

Right ventricle

Systemic Circuit

Capillary beds of all body tissues where gas exchange occurs

Key:

■ = Oxygen-rich, CO_2-poor blood

■ = Oxygen-poor, CO_2-rich blood

FIGURE 18.5 **The systemic and pulmonary circuits.** The right side of the heart pumps blood through the pulmonary circuit* (to the lungs and back to the left side of the heart). The left side of the heart pumps blood via the systemic circuit to all body tissues and back to the right side of the heart. Blood flowing through the pulmonary circuit gains oxygen and loses carbon dioxide, indicated by the color change from blue to red. Blood flowing through the systemic circuit loses oxygen and picks up carbon dioxide (red to blue color change).

*For simplicity, the actual number of two pulmonary arteries and four pulmonary veins has been reduced to one each.

between atria and ventricles is reflected in the much more massive ventricular walls; Figure 18.4e). When the ventricles contract, blood is propelled out of the heart into the circulation. The right ventricle pumps blood into the **pulmonary trunk,** which routes the blood to the lungs where gas exchange occurs. The left ventricle ejects blood into the **aorta** (a-or'tah), the largest artery in the body.

Pathway of Blood Through the Heart

Until the sixteenth century, it was believed that blood moved from one side of the heart to the other by seeping through pores in the septum. We now know that the heart passages open not from one side to the other but vertically and that the heart is actually two side-by-side pumps, each serving a separate blood circuit (Figure 18.5). The blood vessels that carry blood to and from the lungs form the **pulmonary circuit** (*pulmonos* = lung), which serves gas exchange. The blood vessels that carry the functional blood supply to and from all body tissues constitute the **systemic circuit.**

The right side of the heart is the *pulmonary circuit pump.* Blood returning from the body is relatively oxygen-poor and carbon dioxide–rich. It enters the right atrium and passes into the right ventricle, which pumps it to the lungs via the pulmonary trunk (Figure 18.4e). In the lungs, the blood unloads carbon dioxide and picks up oxygen. The freshly oxygenated blood is carried by the pulmonary veins back to the left side of the heart. Notice how unique this circulation is. Typically, we think of veins as vessels that carry blood that is relatively oxygen-poor to the heart and arteries as transporters of oxygen-rich blood from the heart to the rest of the body. Exactly the opposite condition exists in the pulmonary circuit.

The left side of the heart is the *systemic circuit pump.* Freshly oxygenated blood leaving the lungs is returned to the left atrium and passes into the left ventricle, which pumps it into the aorta. From there the blood is transported via smaller systemic arteries to the body tissues, where gases and nutrients are exchanged across the capillary walls. Then the blood, once again loaded with carbon dioxide and depleted of oxygen, returns through the systemic veins to the right side of the heart, where it enters the right atrium through the superior and inferior venae cavae. This cycle repeats itself continuously.

Although equal volumes of blood are pumped to the pulmonary and systemic circuits at any moment, the two ventricles have very unequal workloads. The pulmonary circuit, served by the right ventricle, is a short, low-pressure circulation, whereas the systemic circuit, associated with the left ventricle, takes a long pathway through the entire body and encounters about five times as much friction, or resistance to blood flow. This functional difference is revealed in the anatomy of the two ventricles (Figures 18.4e and 18.6). The walls of the left ventricle are three times as thick as those of the right ventricle, and its cavity is nearly circular. The right ventricular cavity is flattened into a crescent shape that partially encloses the left ventricle, much the way a hand might loosely grasp a clenched fist. Consequently, the left ventricle can generate much more pressure than the right and is a far more powerful pump.

Coronary Circulation

Although the heart is more or less continuously filled with blood, this blood provides little nourishment to heart tissue. (The myocardium is too thick to make diffusion a practical means of nutrient delivery.) The **coronary circulation,** the functional blood supply of the heart, is the shortest circulation in the body. The arterial supply of the coronary circulation is provided by the *right* and *left coronary arteries,* both arising from the base of the aorta and encircling the heart in the coronary sulcus (Figure 18.7a). The **left coronary artery** runs toward the left side of the heart and then divides into its major branches: the **anterior interventricular artery** (also known clinically as the *left anterior descending artery*), which follows the anterior

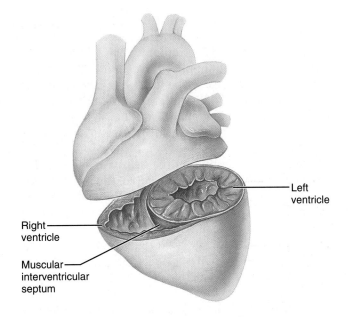

FIGURE 18.6 **Anatomical differences in right and left ventricles.** The left ventricle has a thicker wall and its cavity is basically circular; the right ventricle cavity is crescent shaped and wraps around the left ventricle.

interventricular sulcus and supplies blood to the interventricular septum and anterior walls of both ventricles; and the **circumflex artery,** which supplies the left atrium and the posterior walls of the left ventricle.

The **right coronary artery** courses to the right side of the heart, where it also divides into two

(a)

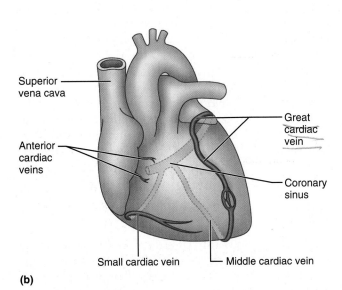

(b)

FIGURE 18.7 **Coronary circulation. (a)** The main coronary arteries. **(b)** The major cardiac veins. (In both drawings, lighter-tinted vessels are more posterior in the heart.)

branches: the **marginal artery,** which serves the myocardium of the lateral right side of the heart, and the **posterior interventricular artery,** which runs to the heart apex and supplies the posterior ventricular walls. Near the apex of the heart, this artery merges (anastomoses) with the anterior interventricular artery. Together the branches of the right coronary artery supply the right atrium and nearly all the right ventricle.

The arterial supply of the heart varies considerably. For example, in 15% of people, the left coronary artery gives rise to *both* the anterior and posterior interventricular arteries; in about 4% of people, a single coronary artery supplies the whole heart. Additionally, there may be both right and left marginal arteries. There are many anastomoses among the coronary arterial branches. These fusing networks provide additional *(collateral)* routes for blood delivery to the heart muscle, but are not robust enough to supply adequate nutrition when a coronary artery is suddenly occluded. Complete blockage leads to tissue death and heart attack.

The coronary arteries provide an intermittent, pulsating blood flow to the myocardium. These vessels and their main branches lie in the epicardium and send branches inward to nourish the myocardium. They deliver blood when the heart is relaxed, but are fairly ineffective when the ventricles are contracting because they are compressed by the contracting myocardium. Although the heart represents only about 1/200 of the body's weight, it requires about 1/20 of the body's blood supply. As might be expected, the left ventricle receives the most plentiful blood supply.

After passing through the capillary beds of the myocardium, the venous blood is collected by the **cardiac veins,** whose paths roughly follow those of the coronary arteries. These veins join together to form an enlarged vessel called the **coronary sinus,** which empties the blood into the right atrium. The coronary sinus is obvious on the posterior aspect of the heart (Figure 18.7b). The sinus has three large tributaries: the **great cardiac vein** in the anterior interventricular sulcus; the **middle cardiac vein** in the posterior interventricular sulcus; and the **small cardiac vein,** running along the heart's right inferior margin. Additionally, several **anterior cardiac veins** empty directly into the right atrium anteriorly.

HOMEOSTATIC IMBALANCE

Blockage of the coronary arterial circulation can be serious and sometimes fatal. **Angina pectoris** (an-ji'nah pek'tor-is; "choked chest") is thoracic pain caused by a fleeting deficiency in blood delivery to the myocardium. It may result from stress-induced spasms of the coronary arteries or from increased physical demands on the heart. The myocardial cells are weakened by the temporary lack of oxygen but do not die. Far more serious is prolonged coronary blockage, which can lead to a **myocardial infarction (MI),** commonly called a **heart attack** (see *A Closer Look* on pp. 706–707). Because adult cardiac muscle is essentially amitotic, most areas of cell death are repaired with noncontractile scar tissue. Whether or not a person survives a myocardial infarction depends on the extent and location of the damage. Damage to the left ventricle, which is the systemic pump, is most serious. ●

Heart Valves

Blood flows through the heart in one direction: from atria to ventricles and out the great arteries leaving the superior aspect of the heart. This one-way traffic is enforced by four valves (Figures 18.4e and 18.8) that open and close in response to differences in blood pressure on their two sides.

Atrioventricular Valves

The two **atrioventricular (AV) valves,** one located at each atrial-ventricular junction, prevent backflow into the atria when the ventricles are contracting. The right AV valve, the **tricuspid valve** (tri-kus'pid), has three flexible cusps (flaps of endocardium reinforced by connective tissue cores). The left AV valve, with two flaps, is called the **mitral valve** (mi'tral) because of its resemblance to the two-sided bishop's miter or hat. It is sometimes called the *bicuspid valve.* Attached to each AV valve flap are tiny white collagen cords called **chordae tendineae** (kor'de ten"dĭ'ne-e; "tendonous cords"), "heart strings" which anchor the cusps to the papillary muscles protruding from the ventricular walls.

When the heart is completely relaxed, the AV valve flaps hang limply into the ventricular chambers below and blood flows into the atria and then through the open AV valves into the ventricles. When the ventricles contract, compressing the blood in their chambers, the intraventricular pressure rises, forcing the blood superiorly against the valve flaps. As a result, the flap edges meet, closing the valve (Figure 18.9). The chordae tendineae and the papillary muscles serve as guy-wires to anchor the valve flaps in their *closed* position. If the cusps were not anchored in this manner, they would be blown upward into the atria, in the same way an umbrella is blown inside out by a gusty wind. The papillary muscles contract *before* the other ventricular musculature so that they take up the slack on the chordae tendineae before the full force of ventricular contraction hurls the blood against the AV valve flaps.

Q *What is the function of the papillary muscles and chordae tendineae?*

(a)

Pulmonary valve
Aortic valve
Area of cutaway
Mitral valve
Tricuspid valve

Myocardium
Tricuspid (right atrioventricular) valve
Mitral (left atrioventricular) valve
Aortic valve
Pulmonary valve
Fibrous skeleton

Anterior

(b)

(c)

Chordae tendineae attached to tricuspid valve flap
Papillary muscle

(d)

Opening of superior vena cava
Tricuspid valve
Myocardium of right ventricle
Papillary muscles
Mitral valve
Chordae tendineae
Interventricular septum
Myocardium of left ventricle

FIGURE 18.8   Heart valves. (a) Superior view of the two sets of heart valves (atria removed). The paired atrioventricular valves are located between atria and ventricles; the two semilunar valves are located at the junction of the ventricles and the arteries issuing from them. **(b)** Photograph of the heart valves, superior view. **(c)** Photograph of the tricuspid valve. This bottom-to-top view begins in the right ventricle and faces toward the right atrium. **(d)** Coronal section of the heart. (See *A Brief Atlas of the Human Body*, Figures 58 and 60.)

A *They keep the AV valve flaps from everting into the atria as the ventricles contract.*

18

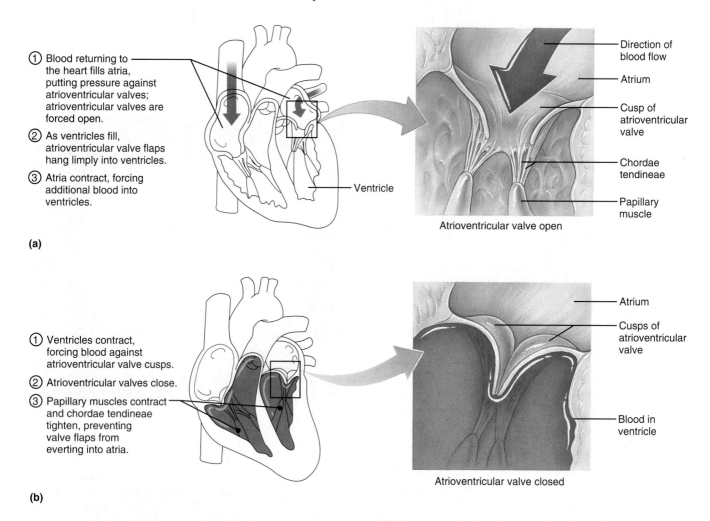

1. Blood returning to the heart fills atria, putting pressure against atrioventricular valves; atrioventricular valves are forced open.
2. As ventricles fill, atrioventricular valve flaps hang limply into ventricles.
3. Atria contract, forcing additional blood into ventricles.

Ventricle

Direction of blood flow

Atrium

Cusp of atrioventricular valve

Chordae tendineae

Papillary muscle

Atrioventricular valve open

(a)

1. Ventricles contract, forcing blood against atrioventricular valve cusps.
2. Atrioventricular valves close.
3. Papillary muscles contract and chordae tendineae tighten, preventing valve flaps from everting into atria.

Atrium

Cusps of atrioventricular valve

Blood in ventricle

Atrioventricular valve closed

(b)

FIGURE 18.9 **The atrioventricular valves. (a)** The valves open when the blood pressure exerted on their atrial side is greater than that exerted on their ventricular side. **(b)** The valves are forced closed when the ventricles contract and intraventricular pressure rises, moving the contained blood superiorly. The action of the papillary muscles and chordae tendineae keeps the valve flaps closed.

Semilunar Valves

The **aortic** and **pulmonary (semilunar, SL) valves** guard the bases of the large arteries issuing from the ventricles (aorta and pulmonary trunk, respectively) and prevent backflow into the associated ventricles. Each SL valve is fashioned from three pocketlike cusps, each shaped roughly like a crescent moon (*semilunar* = half-moon). Like the AV valves, the SL valves open and close in response to differences in pressure. In the SL case, when the ventricles are contracting and intraventricular pressure *rises above* the pressure in the aorta and pulmonary trunk, the SL valves are forced open and their cusps flatten against the arterial walls as the blood rushes past them (Figure 18.10). When the ventricles relax, and the blood (no longer propelled forward by the pressure of ventricular contraction) flows backward toward the heart, it fills the cusps and closes the valves.

We complete the valve story by mentioning what seems to be an important omission—there are no valves guarding the entrances of the venae cavae and pulmonary veins into the right and left atria, respectively. Small amounts of blood *do* spurt back into these vessels during atrial contraction, but backflow is minimal because of the inertia of the blood and because as it contracts, the atrial myocardium compresses (and collapses) these venous entry points.

HOMEOSTATIC IMBALANCE

Heart valves are simple devices, and the heart—like any mechanical pump—can function with "leaky" valves as long as the impairment is not too great. However, severe valve deformities can seriously hamper cardiac function. An *incompetent valve* forces the heart to repump the same blood over and over because the valve does not close properly and

18

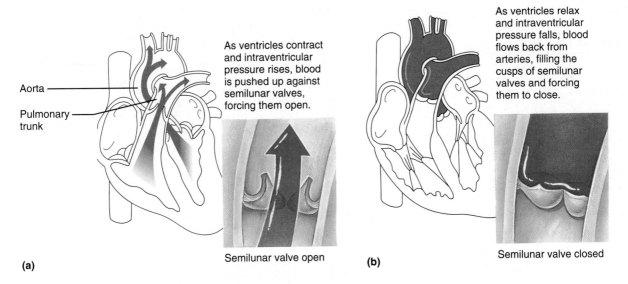

Aorta

Pulmonary trunk

As ventricles contract and intraventricular pressure rises, blood is pushed up against semilunar valves, forcing them open.

Semilunar valve open

(a)

As ventricles relax and intraventricular pressure falls, blood flows back from arteries, filling the cusps of semilunar valves and forcing them to close.

Semilunar valve closed

(b)

FIGURE 18.10 **The semilunar valves. (a)** During ventricular contraction, the valves are open. **(b)** When the ventricles relax, the backflowing blood closes the valves.

blood backflows. In valvular *stenosis* ("narrowing"), the valve flaps become stiff (typically because of scar tissue formation following endocarditis or calcium salt deposit) and constrict the opening. This stiffness compels the heart to contract more forcibly than normal. In both instances, the heart's workload increases and, ultimately, the heart may be severely weakened. Under such conditions, the faulty valve (most often the mitral valve) is replaced with a mechanical valve, a pig heart valve chemically treated to prevent rejection, or cryopreserved valves from human cadavers. Heart valves tissue-engineered from a patient's own cells grown on a biodegradable scaffold are being developed. ●

Properties of Cardiac Muscle Fibers

Although similar to skeletal muscle, cardiac muscle displays some special anatomical features that reflect its unique blood-pumping role.

Microscopic Anatomy

Cardiac muscle, like skeletal muscle, is striated, and it contracts by the sliding filament mechanism. However, in contrast to the long, cylindrical, multinucleate skeletal muscle fibers, cardiac cells are short, fat, branched, and interconnected. Each fiber contains one or at most two large, pale, *centrally* located nuclei (Figure 18.11a). The intercellular spaces are filled with a loose connective tissue matrix (the *endomysium*) containing numerous capillaries. This delicate matrix is connected to the fibrous skeleton,

which acts both as a tendon and as an insertion, giving the cardiac cells something to pull or exert their force against.

Skeletal muscle fibers are independent of one another both structurally and functionally. By contrast, the plasma membranes of adjacent cardiac cells interlock like the ribs of two sheets of corrugated cardboard at dark-staining junctions called **intercalated discs** (in-ter'kah-la"ted; *intercala* = insert) (Figure 18.11b). These discs contain anchoring *desmosomes* and *gap junctions* (cell junctions discussed in Chapter 3). The desmosomes prevent adjacent cells from separating during contraction, and the gap junctions allow ions to pass from cell to cell, transmitting current across the entire heart. Because cardiac cells are electrically coupled by the gap junctions, the myocardium *behaves* as a single coordinated unit, or **functional syncytium.**

Large mitochondria account for 25–35% of the volume of cardiac cells (compared with only 2% in skeletal muscle) and give cardiac cells a high resistance to fatigue. Most of the remaining volume is occupied by myofibrils composed of fairly typical sarcomeres. The sarcomeres have Z discs, A bands, and I bands that reflect the arrangement of the thick (myosin) and thin (actin) filaments composing them. However, in contrast to what is seen in skeletal muscle, the myofibrils of cardiac muscle cells vary greatly in diameter and branch extensively, accommodating the abundant mitochondria that lie between them. This produces a banding pattern less dramatic than that seen in skeletal muscle.

The system for delivering Ca^{2+} is less elaborate in cardiac muscle cells. The T tubules are wider and fewer than in skeletal muscle and they enter the cells once per sarcomere at the Z discs. (Remember that T

18

(a)

(b)

FIGURE 18.11 **Microscopic anatomy of cardiac muscle. (a)** Photomicrograph of cardiac muscle (700×). Notice that the cardiac muscle cells are short, branched, and striated. The dark-staining areas are intercalated discs, or junctions, between adjacent cells. **(b)** Cardiac cell relationships at the intercalated discs and relationships of cell components.

tubules are invaginations of the sarcolemma. In skeletal muscle, the T tubules invaginate twice per sarcomere, at the A-I junctions.) The cardiac sarcoplasmic reticulum is simpler and lacks the large terminal cisternae seen in skeletal muscle. Hence, no *triads* are seen in cardiac muscle fibers.

Mechanism and Events of Contraction

Although heart muscle and skeletal muscle are contractile tissues, they have some fundamental differences:

1. **Means of stimulation.** Each skeletal muscle fiber must be stimulated to contract by a nerve ending, but some cardiac muscle cells are self-excitable and can initiate their own depolarization, and that of the rest of the heart, in a spontaneous and rhythmic way. This property, called **automaticity,** or **autorhythmicity,** is described in the next section.

2. **Organ versus motor unit contraction.** In skeletal muscle, all cells of a given motor unit (but not necessarily all motor units of the muscle) are stimulated and contract at the same time. Impulses do not spread from cell to cell. In cardiac muscle, the heart either contracts as a unit or doesn't contract at all.

This is ensured by the transmission of the depolarization wave across the heart from cell to cell via ion passage through gap junctions, which tie all cardiac muscle cells together into a single contractile unit.

3. Length of absolute refractory period. The absolute refractory period (the inexcitable period when Na$^+$ channels are still open or inactivated) lasts approximately 250 ms in cardiac muscle cells, nearly as long as the contraction (Figure 18.12a). Contrast this to the refractory periods of 1–2 ms in skeletal muscle fibers, in which contractions last 15–100 ms. The long cardiac refractory period normally prevents tetanic contractions, which would stop the heart's pumping action.

Having probed their major differences, let's now look at cardiac and skeletal muscle similarities. As with skeletal muscle, cardiac muscle contraction is triggered by action potentials that sweep across cell membranes. Although about 1% of cardiac fibers are *autorhythmic* ("self-rhythm") and have the special ability to depolarize spontaneously and thus pace the heart, the bulk of heart muscle is composed of *contractile muscle fibers* responsible for the heart's pumping activity. In these contractile cells, the sequence of electrical events is similar to that in skeletal muscle fibers:

1. Depolarization opens a few **voltage-gated fast Na$^+$ channels** in the sarcolemma allowing extracellular Na$^+$ to enter. This initiates a positive feedback cycle that causes the rising phase of the action potential (and reversal of the membrane potential from −90 mV to nearly +30 mV; see Figure 18.12). The period of increased Na$^+$ permeability is very brief, because the sodium channels are quickly inactivated and the Na$^+$ influx stops.

2. Transmission of the depolarization wave down the T tubules (ultimately) causes the sarcoplasmic reticulum (SR) to release Ca^{2+} into the sarcoplasm.

3. Excitation-contraction coupling occurs as Ca^{2+} provides the signal (via troponin binding) for cross bridge activation and couples the depolarization wave to the sliding of the myofilaments.

Although these three steps are common to both skeletal and cardiac muscle cells (see Figure 9.10), how the SR is stimulated to release Ca^{2+} differs in the two muscle types. Let's take a look.

Some 10–20% of the Ca^{2+} needed for the calcium pulse that triggers contraction enters the cardiac cells from the extracellular space. Once inside, it stimulates the SR to release the other 80% of the Ca^{2+} needed. Ca^{2+} is barred from entering nonstimulated cardiac fibers, but when Na$^+$-dependent membrane depolarization occurs, the voltage change *also* opens channels that allow Ca^{2+} entry from the extracellular space. These channels are called **slow**

(b)

FIGURE 18.12   Changes in membrane potential and permeability during action potentials of contractile cardiac muscle cells. (a) Relationship between the action potential, period of contraction, and absolute refractory period in a single ventricular cell. (The tracing for an atrial contractile cell is similar but the plateau phase is shorter.) **(b)** Membrane permeability changes during the action potential. (The Na$^+$ permeability rises to a point off the scale during the action potential spike.)

Ca^{2+} channels because their opening is delayed a bit (Figure 18.12b). The local influxes of Ca^{2+} through these channels trigger opening of nearby Ca^{2+}-sensitive channels in the SR tubules, which liberate bursts of Ca^{2+} ("calcium sparks") that dramatically increase the intracellular Ca^{2+} concentration.

Although Na$^+$ permeability has plummeted to its resting levels and repolarization has begun by this point, the calcium surge across the sarcolemma prolongs the depolarization potential briefly, producing a **plateau** in the action potential tracing (Figure 18.12a). At the same time, K^+ permeability decreases, which also prolongs the plateau and prevents rapid repolarization. As long as Ca^{2+} is entering, the cells continue to contract. Notice in Figure 18.12a that muscle tension develops during the plateau, and peaks just after the plateau ends. Notice also that the duration of the action potential and contractile phase is much greater in cardiac muscle than in skeletal muscle. In skeletal muscle, the action potential typically lasts 1–2 ms and the contraction (for a single stimulus) 15–100 ms. In cardiac muscle, the action potential lasts 200 ms or more (because of the plateau), and tension development persists for 200 ms or more, providing the sustained contraction needed to eject blood from the heart.

After about 200 ms, the slope of the action potential tracing falls rapidly. This results from closure of Ca^{2+} channels and opening of voltage-gated K^+ channels, which allows a rapid loss of potassium from the cell that restores the resting membrane potential. During repolarization, Ca^{2+} is pumped back into the SR and the extracellular space.

Energy Requirements

Cardiac muscle has more mitochondria than skeletal muscle does, reflecting its greater dependence on oxygen for its energy metabolism. Unlike skeletal muscle, which can contract for prolonged periods, even during oxygen deficits, by carrying out anaerobic respiration, the heart relies almost exclusively on aerobic respiration. Hence, cardiac muscle cannot incur much of an oxygen debt and still operate effectively.

Both types of muscle tissue use multiple fuel molecules, including glucose and fatty acids. But cardiac muscle is much more adaptable and readily switches metabolic pathways to use whatever nutrient supply is available, including lactic acid generated by skeletal muscle activity. Thus, the real danger of an inadequate blood supply to the myocardium is lack of oxygen, not of nutrient fuels.

⬧ HOMEOSTATIC IMBALANCE

When a region of heart muscle is deprived of blood (is ischemic), the oxygen-starved cells begin to metabolize anaerobically, producing lactic acid. The rising H^+ level that results hinders the cardiac cells' ability to produce the ATP they need to pump Ca^{2+} into the extracellular fluid. The resulting increase in intracellular H^+ and Ca^{2+} levels causes the gap junctions (which are usually open) to close, electrically isolating the damaged cells and forcing generated action potentials to find alternate routes to the cardiac cells

beyond them. If the ischemic area is large, the pumping activity of the heart as a whole may be severely impaired, leading to a heart attack. ●

Heart Physiology

Electrical Events

The ability of cardiac muscle to depolarize and contract is intrinsic; that is, it is a property of heart muscle and does not depend on the nervous system. Even if all nerve connections to the heart are severed, the heart continues to beat rhythmically, as demonstrated by transplanted hearts. Nevertheless, the healthy heart is amply supplied with autonomic nerve fibers that can alter the basic rhythm of heart activity set by intrinsic factors.

Setting the Basic Rhythm: The Intrinsic Conduction System

The independent, but coordinated, activity of the heart is a function of (1) the presence of gap junctions, and (2) the activity of the heart's "in-house" conduction system. The latter, called the **intrinsic cardiac conduction system**, consists of noncontractile cardiac cells specialized to initiate and distribute impulses throughout the heart, so that it depolarizes and contracts in an orderly, sequential manner. Thus, the heart beats as a coordinated unit. Let's look at how this system works.

Action Potential Initiation by Autorhythmic Cells
Unlike unstimulated contractile cells of the heart (and neurons and skeletal muscle fibers), the **autorhythmic cells** making up the intrinsic conduction system do *not* maintain a stable resting membrane potential. Instead, they have an *unstable resting potential* that continuously depolarizes, drifting slowly toward threshold. These spontaneously changing membrane potentials, called **pacemaker potentials** or **prepotentials**, initiate the action potentials that spread throughout the heart to trigger its rhythmic contractions (Figure 18.13). The pacemaker potential is due to the special properties of the ion channels in the sarcolemma. In these cells, hyperpolarization at the end of an action potential leads to both closing of K^+ channels and opening of slow Na^+ channels. The Na^+ influx alters the balance between K^+ loss and Na^+ entry, and the membrane interior becomes less and less negative (more positive). Ultimately, at threshold (approximately −40 mV), **Ca^{2+} channels** open, allowing explosive entry of Ca^{2+} from the extracellular space. Thus, in autorhythmic cells, it is the influx of Ca^{2+} (rather than Na^+) that produces the rising phase of the action potential and reverses the membrane potential.

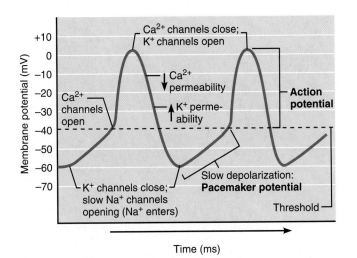

FIGURE 18.13 **Pacemaker and action potentials of autorhythmic cells of the heart.**

As in other excitable cells, the falling phase of the action potential and repolarization reflect increased K^+ permeability and efflux from the cell. Once repolarization is complete, K^+ channels close, K^+ permeability declines, and the slow depolarization to threshold begins again.

Sequence of Excitation   Autorhythmic cardiac cells are found in the following areas (Figure 18.14): sinoatrial (si"no-a'tre-al) node, atrioventricular node, atrioventricular bundle, right and left bundle branches, and ventricular walls (as Purkinje fibers). Impulses pass across the heart in the same order.

① **Sinoatrial node.** The crescent-shaped sinoatrial (SA) node is located in the right atrial wall, just inferior to the entrance of the superior vena cava. A minute cell mass with a mammoth job, the SA node typically generates impulses about 75 times every minute. (However, its inherent rate in the absence of extrinsic neural and hormonal factors is closer to 100 times per minute.) Because no other region of the conduction system or the myocardium has a faster depolarization rate, the SA sets the pace for the heart as a whole. Hence, it is the heart's **pacemaker,** and its characteristic rhythm, called **sinus rhythm,** determines heart rate.

② **Atrioventricular node.** From the SA node, the depolarization wave spreads via gap junctions throughout the atria and via the *internodal pathway* to the atrioventricular (AV) node, located in the inferior portion of the interatrial septum immediately above the tricuspid valve. At the AV node, the impulse is delayed for about 0.1 s, allowing the atria to respond and complete their contraction before the ventricles contract. This delay reflects the smaller diameter of the fibers here and the fact that they have fewer gap junctions for current flow. Thus, the AV node conducts impulses more slowly than other parts of the system, just as traffic slows when cars are forced to merge into two lanes from four. Once through the AV node, the signaling impulse passes rapidly through the rest of the system.

③ **Atrioventricular bundle.** From the AV node, the impulse sweeps to the atrioventricular (AV) bundle (also called the **bundle of His**) in the superior part of the interventricular septum. Although the atria and ventricles abut each other, they are *not* connected by gap junctions. The AV bundle is the *only* electrical connection between them. The balance of the AV junction is insulated by the nonconducting fibrous skeleton of the heart.

④ **Right and left bundle branches.** The AV bundle persists only briefly before splitting into two pathways—the right and left bundle branches, which course along the interventricular septum toward the heart apex.

⑤ **Purkinje fibers.** Essentially long strands of barrel-shaped cells with few myofibrils, the Purkinje (pur-kin'je) fibers complete the pathway through the interventricular septum, penetrate into the heart apex, and then turn superiorly into the ventricular walls. The bundle branches excite the septal cells, but the bulk of ventricular depolarization depends on the large Purkinje fibers and, ultimately, on cell-to-cell transmission of the impulse via gap junctions between the ventricular muscle cells. Because the left ventricle is much larger than the right, the Purkinje network is more elaborate in that side of the heart.

Interestingly, the Purkinje fibers directly supply the papillary muscles, which are excited to contract before the rest of the ventricular muscles. As mentioned, the papillary muscles are already tightening the chordae tendineae before the full force of the ventricular contraction pushes blood against the AV valve flaps.

The total time between initiation of an impulse by the SA node and depolarization of the last of the ventricular muscle cells is approximately 0.22 s (220 ms) in a healthy human heart.

Ventricular contraction almost immediately follows the ventricular depolarization wave. A wringing contraction begins at the heart apex and moves toward the atria, following the direction of the excitation wave through the ventricle walls. This ejects some of the contained blood *superiorly* into the large arteries leaving the ventricles.

The various autorhythmic cardiac cells have different rates of spontaneous depolarization. Although the SA node normally drives the heart at a rate of 75 beats per minute, the AV node depolarizes only about 50 times per minute, the AV bundle and the Purkinje fibers (though they conduct very rapidly) depolarize at the rate of only about 30 times per minute. However,

18

Q *What ionic event produces the plateau in the AP of the contractile muscle cells?*

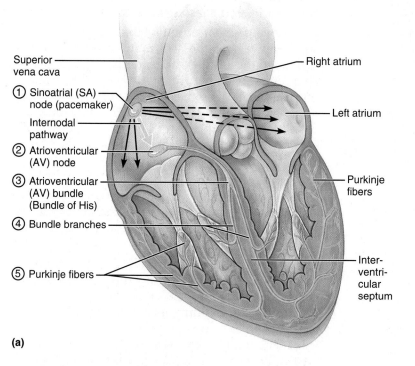

Superior vena cava

① Sinoatrial (SA) node (pacemaker)

Internodal pathway

② Atrioventricular (AV) node

③ Atrioventricular (AV) bundle (Bundle of His)

④ Bundle branches

⑤ Purkinje fibers

Right atrium

Left atrium

Purkinje fibers

Inter-ventricular septum

(a)

SA node

Atrial muscle

AV node

Ventricular muscle

0   100   200   300   400

Milliseconds

(b)

FIGURE 18.14 **Cardiac intrinsic conduction system and action potential succession during one heartbeat. (a)** The depolarization wave initiated by the SA node passes successively through the atrial myocardium to the AV node, the AV bundle, the right and left bundle branches, and the Purkinje fibers in the ventricular myocardium. **(b)** Comparison of the tracings of membrane potentials generated at various locations in the heart is shown from top to bottom beginning with the pacemaker potential generated by the SA node and ending with an action potential (with a broad plateau) typical of the contractile cardiac cells of the ventricles.

these slower "pacemakers" cannot dominate the heart unless faster pacemakers become nonfunctional.

The cardiac conduction system coordinates and synchronizes heart activity. Without it, the impulse would travel much more slowly through the myocardium—at the rate of 0.3 to 0.5 m/s as opposed to several meters per second in most parts of the conduction system. This slower rate would allow some muscle fibers to contract well before others, resulting in reduced pumping effectiveness.

⬥ HOMEOSTATIC IMBALANCE

Defects in the intrinsic conduction system can cause irregular heart rhythms, or **arrhythmias** (ah-rith′me-ahz), uncoordinated atrial and ventricular contractions, and even **fibrillation,** a condition of rapid and irregular or out-of-phase contractions in which control of heart rhythm is taken away from the SA node by rapid activity in other heart regions. The heart in fibrillation has been compared with a squirming bag of worms. Fibrillating ventricles are useless as pumps; and unless the heart is defibrillated quickly, circulation stops and brain death occurs. Defibrillation is accomplished by electrically shocking the heart, which interrupts its chaotic twitching by depolarizing the entire myocardium. The hope is that "with the slate wiped clean" the SA node will begin to function normally and sinus rhythm will be reestablished. Implantable cardioverter defibrillators (ICDs) are now available that continually monitor heart rhythms and can slow an abnormally fast heart rate or emit an electrical shock if the heart begins to fibrillate.

A defective SA node may have several consequences. An **ectopic focus** (ek-top′ik), which is an abnormal pacemaker, may appear and take over the pacing of heart rate, or the AV node may become the pacemaker. The pace set by the AV node **(junctional rhythm)** is 40 to 60 beats per minute, slower than sinus rhythm but still adequate to maintain circulation. Occasionally, ectopic pacemakers appear even when the SA node is operating normally. A small region of the heart becomes hyperexcitable, sometimes

A *Calcium entry.*

as a result of too much caffeine (several cups of coffee) or nicotine (excessive smoking), and generates impulses more quickly than the SA node. This leads to a *premature contraction* or **extrasystole** (ek"strah-sis'to-le) before the SA node initiates the next contraction. Then, because the heart has a longer time for filling, the next (normal) contraction is felt as a thud. As you might guess, premature *ventricular* contractions (PVCs) are most problematic.

Because the only route for impulse transmission from atria to ventricles is through the AV node, any damage to the AV node, referred to as a **heart block,** interferes with the ability of the ventricles to receive pacing impulses. In total heart block no impulses get through and the ventricles beat at their intrinsic rate, which is too slow to maintain adequate circulation. In partial heart block, only some of the atrial impulses reach the ventricles. In both cases, pacemakers are used to recouple the atria to the ventricles as necessary. These programmable devices speed up in response to increased physical activity just as a normal heart would, and many can send diagnostic information to the patient's doctor via the telephone. ●

Modifying the Basic Rhythm: Extrinsic Innervation of the Heart

Although the basic heart rate is set by the intrinsic conduction system, fibers of the autonomic nervous system modify the marchlike beat and introduce a subtle variability from one beat to the next. The sympathetic nervous system (the "accelerator") increases both the rate and the force of heartbeat; parasympathetic activation (the "brakes") slows the heart. These neural controls are explained later. Here we discuss the anatomy of the nerve supply to the heart.

The cardiac centers are located in the medulla oblongata. The **cardioacceleratory center** projects to sympathetic neurons in the T_1–T_5 level of the spinal cord. These preganglionic neurons, in turn, synapse with ganglionic neurons in the cervical and upper thoracic sympathetic trunk (Figure 18.15). From there, postganglionic fibers run through the cardiac plexus to the heart where they innervate the SA and AV nodes, heart muscle, and the coronary arteries. The **cardioinhibitory center** sends impulses to the parasympathetic dorsal vagus nucleus in the medulla, which in turn sends inhibitory impulses to the heart via branches of the vagus nerves. Most parasympathetic ganglionic motor neurons lie in ganglia in the heart wall and their fibers project most heavily to the SA and AV nodes.

Electrocardiography

The electrical currents generated in and transmitted through the heart spread throughout the body and can be detected with an **electrocardiograph.** A

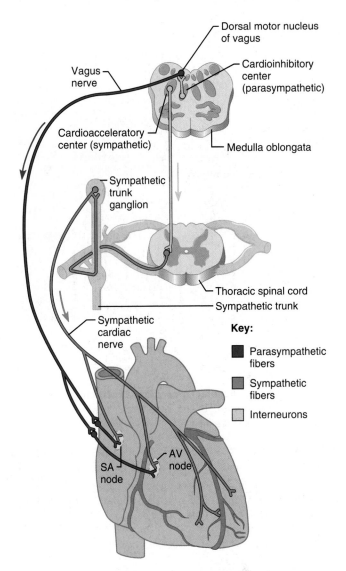

FIGURE 18.15 **Autonomic innervation of the heart.**

graphic record of heart activity is called an **electrocardiogram** (**ECG** or **EKG;** *kardio* is Greek for "heart"). An ECG is a composite of all the action potentials generated by nodal and contractile cells at a given time and *not*, as sometimes assumed, a tracing of a single action potential. Recording electrodes (leads) are positioned at various sites on the body surface; typically in a clinical setting, 12 leads are used. Three are bipolar leads that measure the voltage difference either between the arms or between an arm and a leg, and nine are unipolar leads. Together the 12 leads provide a fairly comprehensive picture of the heart's electrical activity.

A typical ECG has three distinguishable waves or *deflections* (Figure 18.16). The first, the small **P wave,** lasts about 0.08 s and results from movement of the depolarization wave from the SA node through the atria. Approximately 0.1 s after the P wave begins, the atria contract.

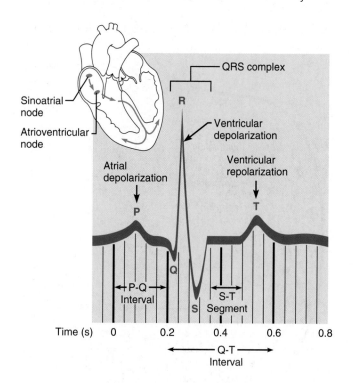

Atrial depolarization — P

Ventricular depolarization

Ventricular repolarization — T

QRS complex — R

Q, S

P-Q Interval

S-T Segment

Q-T Interval

Time (s): 0, 0.2, 0.4, 0.6, 0.8

Sinoatrial node, Atrioventricular node

FIGURE 18.16 **An electrocardiogram tracing (lead I).** The three normally recognizable deflections (waves) and the important intervals are labeled.

Q *Knowing that ventricular contraction follows the pattern of ventricular excitation, describe the path you expect the contraction wave to follow across the ventricles.*

The large **QRS complex** results from ventricular depolarization and precedes ventricular contraction. It has a complicated shape because the paths of the depolarization waves through the ventricular walls change continuously, producing corresponding changes in current direction. Additionally, the time required for each ventricle to depolarize depends on its size relative to the other ventricle. Average duration of the QRS complex is 0.08 s.

The **T wave** is caused by ventricular repolarization and typically lasts about 0.16 s. Repolarization is slower than depolarization, so the T wave is more spread out and has a lower amplitude (height) than the QRS wave. Because atrial repolarization takes place during the period of ventricular excitation, the wave representing atrial repolarization is normally obscured by the large QRS complex being recorded at the same time.

The **P-Q interval** is the time (about 0.16 s) from the beginning of atrial excitation to the beginning of ventricular excitation. Sometimes called the **P-R interval** because the Q wave tends to be very small, it includes atrial depolarization (and contraction) as well as the passage of the depolarization wave through the rest of the conduction system. During the **S-T segment** of the ECG, when the action potential is in its plateau phase, the entire ventricular myocardium is depolarized. The **Q-T interval**, lasting about 0.38 s, is the period from the beginning of ventricular depolarization through ventricular repolarization. The relationship of the parts of an ECG to movement of the action potential over the heart is illustrated in Figure 18.17.

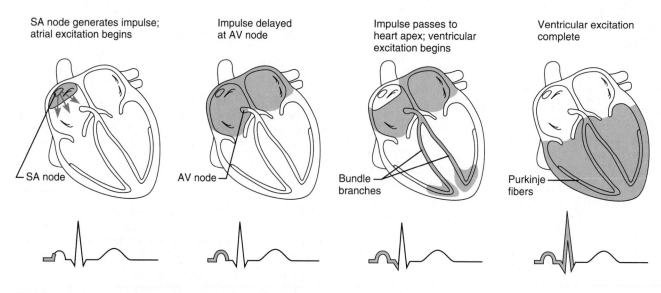

SA node generates impulse; atrial excitation begins — SA node

Impulse delayed at AV node — AV node

Impulse passes to heart apex; ventricular excitation begins — Bundle branches

Ventricular excitation complete — Purkinje fibers

FIGURE 18.17 **The sequence of excitation of the heart related to the deflection waves of an ECG tracing.**

A *From the apex of the heart superiorly toward the atria.*

(a)

(b)

(c)

(d)

FIGURE 18.18 **Normal and abnormal ECG tracings.**
(a) Normal sinus rhythm. **(b)** Junctional rhythm. The SA node is nonfunctional, P waves are absent, and heart rate is paced by the AV node at 40–60 beats/min. **(c)** Second-degree heart block. Some P waves are not conducted through the AV node; hence more P than QRS waves are seen. In this tracing, the ratio of P waves to QRS waves is mostly 2:1. In total (third degree) heart block, there is no whole number ratio between P and QRS waves, and the ventricles are no longer paced by the SA node. **(d)** Ventricular fibrillation. These chaotic, grossly irregular ECG deflections are seen in acute heart attack and electrical shock.

In a healthy heart, the size, duration, and timing of the deflection waves tend to be consistent. Thus, changes in the pattern or timing of the ECG may reveal a diseased or damaged heart or problems with the heart's conduction system (Figure 18.18). For example, an enlarged R wave hints of enlarged ventricles, an S-T segment that is elevated or depressed indicates cardiac ischemia, and a prolonged Q-T interval reveals a repolarization abnormality that increases the risk of ventricular arrhythmias.

Heart Sounds

During each heartbeat, two sounds can be distinguished when the thorax is auscultated (listened to) with a stethoscope. These **heart sounds,** often described as lub-dup, are associated with closing of heart valves. (The timing of heart sounds in the cardiac cycle is shown in Figure 18.20a.)

The basic rhythm of the heart sounds is lub-dup, pause, lub-dup, pause, and so on, with the pause indicating the quiescent period. The first sound, which occurs as the AV valves close, signifies the point when ventricular pressure rises above atrial pressure (the beginning of ventricular systole, discussed in the next section). The first sound tends to be louder, longer, and more resonant than the second, which is a short, sharp sound heard as the SL valves snap shut at the beginning of ventricular relaxation (diastole). Because the mitral valve closes slightly before the tricuspid valve does, and the aortic SL valve generally snaps shut just before the pulmonary valve, it is possible to distinguish the individual valve sounds by auscultating four specific regions of the thorax (Figure 18.19). Notice that these four points, while

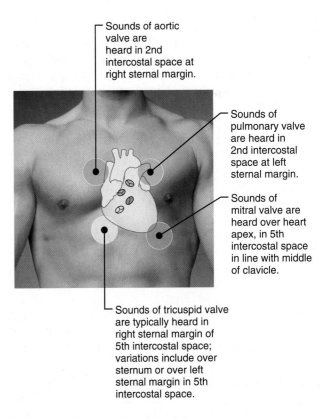

Sounds of aortic valve are heard in 2nd intercostal space at right sternal margin.

Sounds of pulmonary valve are heard in 2nd intercostal space at left sternal margin.

Sounds of mitral valve are heard over heart apex, in 5th intercostal space in line with middle of clavicle.

Sounds of tricuspid valve are typically heard in right sternal margin of 5th intercostal space; variations include over sternum or over left sternal margin in 5th intercostal space.

FIGURE 18.19 **Areas of the thoracic surface where the heart sounds can be best detected.**

18

not directly superficial to the valves (because the sounds take oblique paths to reach the chest wall), do handily define the four corners of the normal heart. Knowing normal heart size and location is essential for recognizing an enlarged (and often diseased) heart.

◢ HOMEOSTATIC IMBALANCE

Abnormal heart sounds are called **heart murmurs.** Blood flows silently as long as the flow is smooth and uninterrupted. If it strikes obstructions, however, its flow becomes turbulent and generates heart murmurs that can be heard with a stethoscope. Heart murmurs are fairly common in young children (and some elderly people) with perfectly healthy hearts, probably because their heart walls are relatively thin and vibrate with rushing blood. Most often, however, murmurs indicate valve problems. If a valve is *incompetent*, a swishing sound is heard as the blood backflows or regurgitates through the partially open valve, *after* the valve has (supposedly) closed. A stenotic valve, in which the valvular opening is narrowed, restricts blood flow *through* the valve. In a stenotic aortic valve, for instance, a high-pitched sound or click can be detected when the valve should be wide open during systole, but is not. ●

Mechanical Events: The Cardiac Cycle

The heart undergoes some dramatic writhing movements as it alternately contracts, forcing blood out of its chambers, and then relaxes, allowing its chambers to refill with blood. The terms **systole** (sis′to-le) and **diastole** (di-as′to-le) refer respectively to these *contraction* and *relaxation* periods. The **cardiac cycle** includes *all* events associated with the blood flow through the heart during one complete heartbeat, that is, atrial systole and diastole followed by ventricular systole and diastole. These mechanical events always *follow* the electrical events seen in the ECG.

The cardiac cycle is marked by a succession of pressure and blood volume changes in the heart. Because blood circulates endlessly, we must choose an arbitrary starting point for one turn of the cardiac cycle. As shown in Figure 18.20, which outlines what happens in the left side of the heart, we begin our explanation with the heart in total relaxation: Atria and ventricles are quiet, and it is mid-to-late diastole.

① **Ventricular filling: mid-to-late diastole.** Pressure in the heart is low, blood returning from the circulation is flowing passively through the atria and the open AV valves into the ventricles, and the aortic and pulmonary valves are closed. Approximately 80% of

ventricular filling occurs during this period, and the AV valve flaps begin to drift toward the closed position. (The remaining 20% is delivered to the ventricles when the atria contract toward the end of this phase.) Now the stage is set for atrial systole. Following depolarization (P wave of ECG), the atria contract, compressing the blood in their chambers. This causes a sudden slight rise in atrial pressure, which propels residual blood out of the atria into the ventricles. At this point the ventricles are in the last part of their diastole and have the maximum volume of blood they will contain in the cycle, a volume called the *end diastolic volume (EDV)*. Then the atria relax and the ventricles depolarize (QRS complex). Atrial diastole persists through the rest of the cycle.

② **Ventricular systole.** As the atria relax, the ventricles begin contracting. Their walls close in on the blood in their chambers, and ventricular pressure rises rapidly and sharply, closing the AV valves. Because, for a split second, the ventricles are completely closed chambers and blood volume in the chambers remains constant, this is called the **isovolumetric contraction phase** (i″so-vol″u-met′rik). Ventricular pressure continues to rise and when it finally exceeds the pressure in the large arteries issuing from the ventricles, the isovolumetric stage ends as the SL valves are forced open and blood is expelled from the ventricles into the aorta and pulmonary trunk. During this **ventricular ejection phase,** the pressure in the aorta normally reaches about 120 mm Hg.

③ **Isovolumetric relaxation: early diastole.** During this brief phase following the T wave, the ventricles relax. Because the blood remaining in their chambers, referred to as the *end systolic volume (ESV)*, is no longer compressed, ventricular pressure drops rapidly and blood in the aorta and pulmonary trunk backflows toward the heart, closing the SL valves. Closure of the aortic valve causes a brief rise in aortic pressure as backflowing blood rebounds off the closed valve cusps, an event beginning at the **dicrotic notch.** Once again the ventricles are totally closed chambers.

All during ventricular systole, the atria have been in diastole; they have been filling with blood and the intra-atrial pressure has been rising. When blood pressure on the atrial side of the AV valves exceeds that in the ventricles, the AV valves are forced open and ventricular filling, phase 1, begins again. Atrial pressure drops to its lowest point and ventricular pressure begins to rise, completing the cycle.

Assuming the average heart beats 75 times each minute, the length of the cardiac cycle is about 0.8 s, with atrial systole accounting for 0.1 s and ventricular systole 0.3 s. The remaining 0.4 s is a period of total heart relaxation, the **quiescent period.**

Notice two important points: (1) blood flow through the heart is controlled entirely by pressure

Q *Are the ventricular cardiac cells in isotonic or isometric contraction during phase 2a of part (b)?*

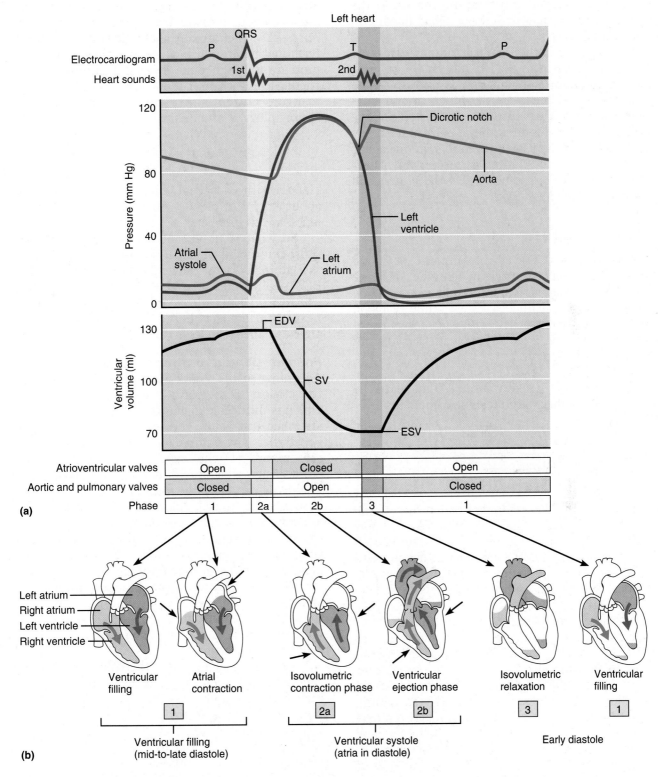

FIGURE 18.20   **Summary of events during the cardiac cycle. (a)** An ECG tracing correlated with graphs of pressure and volume changes in the left side of the heart. Pressures are lower in the right side of the heart. Timing of heart sounds is also indicated. **(b)** Events of phases 1 through 3 of the cardiac cycle.

A *They are contracting isometrically until ventricular pressure rises above the pressure in the aorta.*

changes and (2) blood flows down a pressure gradient through any available opening. The pressure changes, in turn, reflect the alternating contraction and relaxation of the myocardium and cause the heart valves to open, which keeps blood flowing in the forward direction.

The situation in the right side of the heart is essentially the same as in the left side *except* for pressure. The pulmonary circulation is a low-pressure circulation as evidenced by the much thinner myocardium of its right ventricle. Hence, typical systolic and diastolic pressures for the pulmonary artery are 24 and 8 mm Hg as compared to systemic aortic pressures of 120 and 80 mm Hg, respectively. However, the two sides of the heart eject the same blood volume with each heartbeat.

Cardiac Output

Cardiac output (CO) is the amount of blood pumped out by *each* ventricle in 1 minute. It is the product of heart rate (HR) and stroke volume (SV). **Stroke volume** is defined as the volume of blood pumped out by one ventricle with each beat. In general, stroke volume is correlated with the force of ventricular contraction.

Using normal resting values for heart rate (75 beats/min) and stroke volume (70 ml/beat), the average adult cardiac output can be computed:

$$CO = HR \times SV = \frac{75 \text{ beats}}{\text{min}} \times \frac{70 \text{ ml}}{\text{beat}}$$
$$= \frac{5250 \text{ ml}}{\text{min}} = \frac{5.25 \text{ L}}{\text{min}}$$

The normal adult blood volume is about 5 L (a little more than 1 gallon). Thus, the entire blood supply passes through each side of the heart once each minute. Notice that cardiac output varies directly with SV and HR. Thus CO increases when the stroke volume increases or the heart beats faster or both, and decreases when either or both of these factors decrease.

Cardiac output is highly variable and increases markedly in response to special demands, such as running to catch a bus. The difference between resting and maximal CO is referred to as **cardiac reserve**. In nonathletic people, cardiac reserve is typically four to five times resting CO (20–25 L/min), but CO in trained athletes during competition may reach 35 L/min (seven times resting). To understand how the heart accomplishes such tremendous increases in output, let's look at how stroke volume and heart rate are regulated.

Regulation of Stroke Volume

Essentially, SV represents the difference between **end diastolic volume (EDV)**, the amount of blood

that collects in a ventricle during diastole, and **end systolic volume (ESV)**, the volume of blood remaining in a ventricle *after* it has contracted. The EDV, determined by how long ventricular diastole lasts and by venous pressure (an increase in either factor *raises* EDV), is normally about 120 ml. The ESV, determined by arterial blood pressure (the higher the pressure the higher the ESV) and the force of ventricular contraction, is approximately 50 ml. Thus, to figure normal stroke volume, these values are simply plugged into this equation:

$$SV = EDV - ESV = \frac{120 \text{ ml}}{\text{beat}} - \frac{50 \text{ ml}}{\text{beat}} = \frac{70 \text{ ml}}{\text{beat}}$$

Hence, with each beat, each ventricle pumps out about 70 ml of blood, which is about 60% of the blood in its chambers.

So what is important here—how do we make sense out of this alphabet soup (SV, ESV, EDV)? Although many factors affect SV by causing changes in EDV or ESV, the three most important are *preload, contractility,* and *afterload*. As described in detail next, preload affects EDV, whereas contractility and afterload affect the ESV.

Preload: Degree of Stretch of Heart Muscle

According to the **Frank-Starling law of the heart**, the critical factor controlling SV is the **preload**, which is the degree to which cardiac muscle cells are stretched just before they contract (Figure 18.21a). Recall that at an *optimal length* of muscle fibers (and sarcomeres) (1) the maximum number of active cross bridge attachments is possible between actin and myosin, and (2) the force of contraction is maximal. Cardiac muscle, like skeletal muscle, exhibits a *length-tension relationship*. Resting skeletal muscle fibers are kept at or near optimal length for developing maximal tension while resting cardiac cells are normally *shorter* than optimal length. Therefore, stretching cardiac cells can produce dramatic increases in contractile force. The most important factor stretching cardiac muscle is the amount of blood returning to the heart and distending its ventricles, called **venous return.**

Anything that increases the volume or speed of venous return, such as a slow heart rate or exercise, increases EDV and, consequently, SV and contraction force. A slow heartbeat allows more time for ventricular filling. Exercise speeds venous return because of an increased heart rate and the squeezing action of the skeletal muscles on the veins returning blood to the heart. During vigorous exercise, SV may double as a result of these factors. Conversely, low venous return, such as might result from severe blood loss or an extremely rapid heart rate, decreases EDV, causing the heart to beat less forcefully and the SV to drop (see Figure 18.23 on p. 703).

Q *What problem might ensue relative to cardiac output if the heart beats far too rapidly for an extended period, that is, if tachycardia occurs? Why?*

(a) Preload   **(b) Afterload**

FIGURE 18.21   **Preload and afterload influence stroke volume. (a)** Preload is proportional to the amount of ventricular myocardial fiber stretch (chamber blood volume) just before systole. **(b)** Afterload is the pressure that the ventricles must overcome to force open the aortic and pulmonary valves. Black arrows indicate the direction the ventricular walls are moving.

Because the systemic and pulmonary circulations are in series, the intrinsic mechanism just described ensures equal outputs of the two ventricles and proper distribution of blood volume between the two circuits. If one side of the heart suddenly begins to pump more blood than the other, the increased venous return to the opposite ventricle forces that ventricle to pump out an equal volume, thus preventing backup or accumulation of blood in the circulation.

Contractility   Although EDV is the major *intrinsic factor* influencing SV, the latter can also be enhanced by *extrinsic factors* that increase heart muscle contractility. **Contractility** is defined as the contractile strength achieved at a given muscle length. Notice that contractility is *independent* of muscle stretch and EDV. An increase in contractility is due to a greater Ca^{2+} influx into the cytoplasm from the extracellular fluid and the SR. Enhanced contractility results in ejection of more blood from the heart (greater SV), hence a lower ESV. Increased sympathetic stimulation increases contractility of the heart. As noted on p. 695, sympathetic fibers serve not only the intrinsic conduction system but the entire heart, and one effect of

A *Pathological increase in heart rate results in too little time for ventricular filling. Therefore, CO declines and the heart beats feebly.*

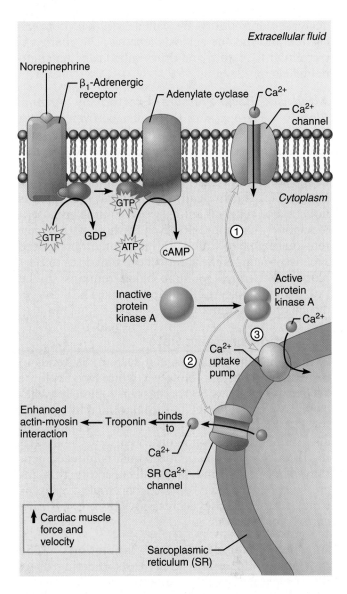

FIGURE 18.22   **Mechanism by which norepinephrine influences heart contractility.** Cyclic AMP activation of protein kinases phosphorylates ① Ca^{2+} channels in the plasma membrane, promoting entry of more Ca^{2+} from the extracellular space; and ② SR Ca^{2+} channels, causing the SR to release more Ca^{2+}. ③ In addition, phosphorylation of SR calcium uptake pumps removes Ca^{2+} more rapidly from the sarcoplasm, thus speeding relaxation and making more Ca^{2+} available for release on the next beat.

norepinephrine or epinephrine binding is to initiate a cyclic AMP second-messenger system that increases Ca^{2+} entry, which in turn promotes more cross bridge binding and enhances ventricular contractility (Figure 18.22).

A battery of other chemicals also influence contractility. For example, contractility is enhanced by Ca^{2+}, by the hormones glucagon, thyroxine, and epinephrine, and by the drug digitalis. Factors that increase contractility are called *positive inotropic agents* (*ino* = muscle, fiber). Those that impair or

18

decrease contractility are called *negative inotropic agents,* and include acidosis (excess H^+), rising extracellular K^+ levels, and drugs called calcium channel blockers.

Afterload: Back Pressure Exerted by Arterial Blood The pressure that must be overcome for the ventricles to eject blood is called **afterload.** It is essentially the back pressure exerted on the aortic and pulmonary valves by arterial blood, about 80 mm Hg in the aorta and 8 mm Hg in the pulmonary trunk (Figure 18.21b). In healthy individuals, afterload is not a major determinant of stroke volume because it is relatively constant. However, in those with hypertension (high blood pressure), it is important indeed because it reduces the ability of the ventricles to eject blood. Consequently, more blood remains in the heart after systole, resulting in increased ESV and reduced stroke volume.

Regulation of Heart Rate

Given a healthy cardiovascular system, SV tends to be relatively constant. However, when blood volume drops sharply or when the heart is seriously weakened, SV declines and CO is maintained by increasing HR and contractility. Temporary stressors can also influence HR—and consequently CO—by acting through homeostatic mechanisms induced neurally, chemically, and physically. Factors that increase HR are called *positive chronotropic (chrono = time)* factors; those decreasing HR are *negative chronotropic* factors.

Autonomic Nervous System Regulation The most important extrinsic controls affecting heart rate are exerted by the autonomic nervous system. When the sympathetic nervous system is activated by emotional or physical stressors, such as fright, anxiety, or exercise (Figure 18.23), sympathetic nerve fibers release norepinephrine at their cardiac synapses. Norepinephrine binds to β_1-adrenergic receptors in the heart, causing threshold to be reached more quickly and accelerating relaxation. As a result, the pacemaker fires more rapidly and the heart responds by beating faster. Sympathetic stimulation also enhances contractility by enhancing Ca^{2+} entry into the contractile cells as described above and in Figure 18.22. Because ESV falls as a result of this increased contractility, SV does not decline, as it would if only heart *rate* were increased. (Remember, when the heart beats faster, there is less time for ventricular filling and so a lower EDV.)

The parasympathetic division opposes sympathetic effects and effectively reduces heart rate when a stressful situation has passed. Parasympathetic-initiated cardiac responses are mediated by acetylcholine, which hyperpolarizes the membranes of its effector cells by *opening* K^+ channels. Because vagal innervation of the ventricles is sparse, parasympathetic activity has little or no effect on cardiac contractility.

Under resting conditions, both autonomic divisions continuously send impulses to the SA node of the heart, but the *dominant* influence is inhibitory. Thus, the heart is said to exhibit **vagal tone,** and heart rate is generally slower than it would be if the vagal nerves were not innervating it. Cutting the vagal nerves results in an almost immediate increase in heart rate of about 25 beats/min, reflecting the inherent rate (100 beats/min) of the pacemaking SA node.

When either division of the autonomic nervous system is stimulated more strongly by sensory inputs relayed from various parts of the cardiovascular system, the other division is temporarily inhibited. Most such sensory input is generated by *baroreceptors* which respond to changes in systemic blood pressure, as we will discuss in Chapter 19. Another example, the **atrial (Bainbridge) reflex,** is a sympathetic reflex initiated by increased venous return and increased atrial filling. Stretching the atrial walls increases heart rate by stimulating both the SA node and the atrial stretch receptors, which trigger reflexive adjustments that result in increased sympathetic stimulation of the heart.

Because increased CO results in increased systemic blood pressure and vice versa, blood pressure regulation often involves reflexive controls of heart rate. Neural mechanisms that regulate blood pressure are described in more detail in Chapter 19.

Chemical Regulation Chemicals normally present in the blood and other body fluids may influence heart rate, particularly if they become excessive or deficient.

1. **Hormones.** *Epinephrine,* liberated by the adrenal medulla during sympathetic nervous system activation, produces the same cardiac effects as norepinephrine released by the sympathetic nerves; that is, it enhances heart rate and contractility.

Thyroxine is a thyroid gland hormone that increases metabolic rate and body heat production. When released in large quantities, it causes a slower but more sustained increase in heart rate than that caused by epinephrine. Because thyroxine also *enhances* the effect of epinephrine and norepinephrine on the heart, chronically hyperthyroid individuals may develop a weakened heart.

2. **Ions.** Physiological relationships between intracellular and extracellular ions must be maintained for normal heart function. Plasma electrolyte imbalances pose real dangers to the heart.

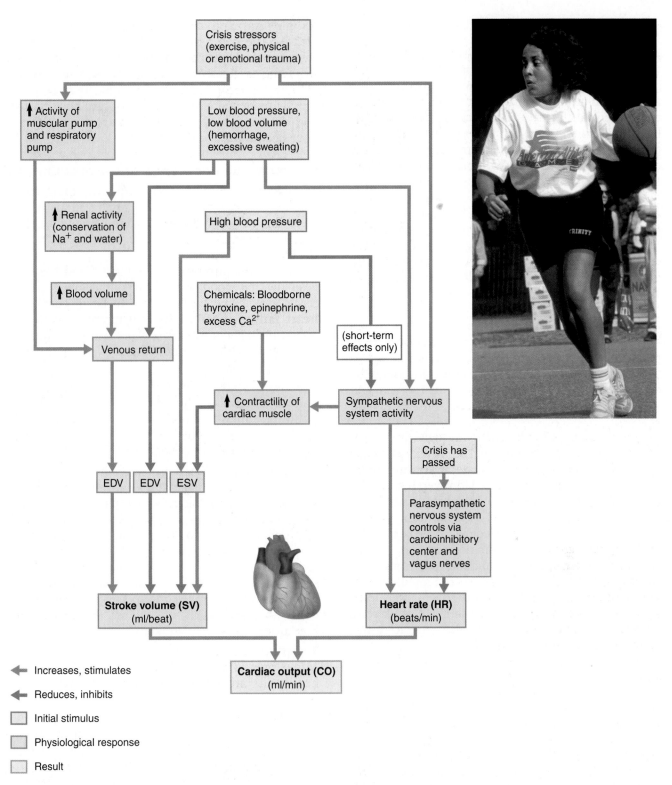

FIGURE 18.23 **Factors involved in regulation of cardiac output.**

⬛ HOMEOSTATIC IMBALANCE

Reduced Ca^{2+} blood levels *(hypocalcemia)* depress the heart. Conversely, above-normal levels *(hypercalcemia)* tightly couple the excitation-contraction mechanism and prolong the plateau phase of the action potential. These events dramatically increase heart irritability, which can lead to spastic heart contractions that permit the heart little rest. Many drugs used to treat heart conditions focus on calcium transport into cardiac cells.

High or low blood K^+ levels are particularly dangerous and arise in a number of clinical conditions. Excessive K^+ *(hyperkalemia)* interferes with depolarization by lowering the resting potential, and may lead to heart block and cardiac arrest. *Hypokalemia* is also life threatening, in that the heart beats feebly and arrhythmically. ●

Other Factors Although less important than neural factors, age, gender, exercise, and body temperature also influence HR. Resting heart rate is fastest in the fetus (140–160 beats/min) and gradually declines throughout life. Average heart rate is faster in females (72–80 beats/min) than in males (64–72 beats/min).

Exercise raises HR by acting through the sympathetic nervous system (Figure 18.23). Exercise also increases systemic blood pressure and routes more blood to the working muscles. However, resting HR in the physically fit tends to be substantially lower than in those who are out of condition, and in trained athletes it may be as slow as 40 beats/min. This apparent paradox is explained below.

Heat increases HR by enhancing the metabolic rate of cardiac cells. This explains the rapid, pounding heartbeat you feel when you have a high fever and also accounts, in part, for the effect of exercise on HR (remember, working muscles generate heat). Cold directly decreases heart rate.

⬛ HOMEOSTATIC IMBALANCE

Although HR varies with changes in activity, marked and persistent rate changes usually signal cardiovascular disease. **Tachycardia** (take-kar′de-ah; "heart hurry") is an abnormally fast heart rate (more than 100 beats/min) that may result from elevated body temperature, stress, certain drugs, or heart disease. Because tachycardia occasionally promotes fibrillation, persistent tachycardia is considered pathological.

Bradycardia (brade-kar′de-ah; *brady* = slow) is a heart rate slower than 60 beats/min. It may result from low body temperature, certain drugs, or parasympathetic nervous activation. It is a known, and desirable, consequence of endurance training.

As physical and cardiovascular conditioning increases, the heart hypertrophies and SV increases; thus, resting heart rate can be lower and still provide the same cardiac output. However, persistent bradycardia in poorly conditioned people may result in grossly inadequate blood circulation to body tissues, and bradycardia is often a warning of brain edema after head trauma. ●

Homeostatic Imbalance of Cardiac Output

The heart's pumping action ordinarily maintains a balance between cardiac output and venous return. Were this not so, a dangerous damming up of blood (blood congestion) would occur in the veins returning blood to the heart.

When the pumping efficiency (CO) of the heart is so low that blood circulation is inadequate to meet tissue needs, the heart is said to be in **congestive heart failure (CHF)**. This progressively worsening condition reflects weakening of the myocardium by various conditions which damage it in different ways. Let's take a look.

1. Coronary atherosclerosis. This condition, essentially a clogging of the coronary vessels with fatty buildup, impairs blood and oxygen delivery to the cardiac cells. The heart becomes increasingly hypoxic and begins to contract ineffectively.

2. Persistent high blood pressure. Normally, pressure in the aorta during diastole is 80 mm Hg, and the left ventricle exerts only slightly over that amount of force to eject blood from its chamber. When aortic diastolic blood pressure rises to 90 mm Hg or more, the myocardium must exert more force to open the aortic valve and pump out the same amount of blood. If this situation of enhanced afterload becomes chronic, the ESV rises and the myocardium hypertrophies. Eventually, the stress takes its toll and the myocardium becomes progressively weaker.

3. Multiple myocardial infarcts. A succession of MIs depresses pumping efficiency because the dead heart cells are replaced by noncontractile fibrous (scar) tissue.

4. Dilated cardiomyopathy (DCM) (kar″de-o-my-ah′path-e). The cause of this condition, in which the ventricles stretch and become flabby and the myocardium deteriorates, is often unknown. Drug toxicity (alcohol, cocaine, excess catecholamines, chemotherapeutic agents), hyperthyroidism, and inflammation of the heart following an infection are implicated in some cases. The heart's attempts to work harder result in increasing levels of Ca^{2+} in the cardiac cells. The Ca^{2+} activates calcineurin, a calcium-sensitive enzyme that initiates a cascade which switches on genes that cause heart enlargement. Because ventricular contractility is

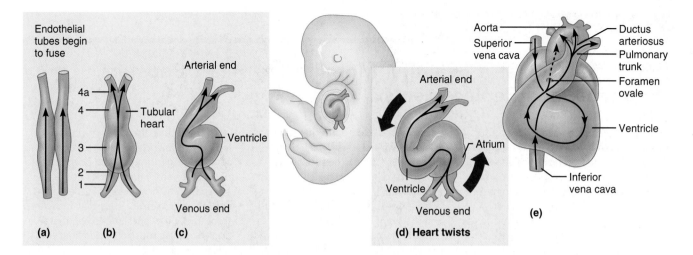

FIGURE 18.24   **Development of the human heart during week 4.** Ventral view, with the cranial direction toward the top of the figures. Arrows show the direction of blood flow. **(a)** Around day 21. **(b)** Day 22: 1 is the sinus venosus; 2, the atrium; 3, the ventricle; 4, the bulbus cordis; and 4a, the truncus arteriosus. **(c)** Day 23. **(d)** Day 24. **(e)** Day 28.

impaired, CO is poor and the condition progressively worsens.

Because the heart is a double pump, each side can initially fail independently of the other. If the left side fails, **pulmonary congestion** occurs. The right side continues to propel blood to the lungs, but the left side does not adequately eject the returning blood into the systemic circulation. Blood vessels in the lungs become engorged with blood, the pressure in them increases, and fluid leaks from the circulation into the lung tissue, causing pulmonary edema. If the congestion is untreated, the person suffocates.

If the right side of the heart fails, **peripheral congestion** occurs. Blood stagnates in body organs, and pooled fluids in the tissue spaces impair the ability of body cells to obtain adequate amounts of nutrients and oxygen and to rid themselves of wastes. The resulting edema is most noticeable in the extremities (feet, ankles, and fingers).

Failure of one side of the heart puts a greater strain on the other side, and ultimately the whole heart fails. A seriously weakened, or *decompensated,* heart is irreparable. Treatment is directed primarily toward (1) removing the excess leaked fluid with *diuretics* (drugs that increase excretion of Na$^+$ and water by the kidneys), (2) reducing afterload with drugs that drive down blood pressure, and (3) conserving heart energy with digitalis derivatives (which reduce HR). However, heart transplants and other surgical or mechanical remedies to replace damaged heart muscle are providing additional hope for some cardiac patients (see *A Closer Look* on pp. 706–707).

Developmental Aspects of the Heart

The human heart, derived from mesoderm and guided by powerful signaling molecules, begins as two simple endothelial tubes that quickly fuse to form a single chamber or heart tube that is busily pumping blood by the 23rd day of gestation (Figure 18.24). One or two days later, the tube develops four slightly bulged areas that represent the earliest heart chambers. From tail to head, following the direction of blood flow, the four chambers developed by day 25 are the following:

1. Sinus venosus (ven-o'sus). This chamber initially receives all the venous blood of the embryo. It will become the smooth-walled part of the right atrium and the coronary sinus. It also gives rise to the sinoatrial node, which takes the "baton" and sets heart rate early in embryonic development.

2. Atrium. This embryonic chamber eventually becomes the pectinate muscle-ridged parts of the atria.

3. Ventricle. The strongest pumping chamber of the early heart, the ventricle gives rise to the *left* ventricle.

4. Bulbus cordis. This chamber, plus its cranial extension, the *truncus arteriosus,* give rise to the pulmonary trunk, the first part of the aorta, and most of the *right* ventricle.

During the next three weeks, the heart "tube" exhibits dramatic contortions as it undergoes rightward looping, and major structural changes convert it into a four-chambered organ capable of acting as a double pump—all without missing a beat! The ventricle moves caudally and the atrium cranially, assuming their adult positions. The heart divides into

18

A CLOSER LOOK

From "Oh, What a Beautiful Morning" to Heart Boosters, Retreads, and Replacements

Getting up can be hazardous to your health! Even if you are a morning person, your risk of dropping dead from a heart attack is twice as high the first two hours after you climb out of bed as at any other time of the day or night. Plasma levels of stress hormones (epinephrine and others) increase right after you arise, and this makes your platelets stickier.

Some heart attacks strike like a lightning bolt with sudden, crushing chest pain. Others, particularly in women, start more subtly with shortness of breath, nausea, cold sweat, or vague discomfort in the chest, shoulder, jaw, or arm. Several million Americans will suffer a heart attack this year. Perhaps one-third of them will die almost immediately; half will be dead within the year.

But exactly what is a heart attack? Basically, it is an interruption of oxygen delivery to part of the myocardium. This is usually caused by blockage of a coronary artery by a thrombus or embolus, or occasionally by irregular and unexplainable spasms of the coronary vessels. Atherosclerosis of the coronary arteries, known as coronary artery disease (CAD), creates locations where clots can form and block the artery.

At the cellular level, oxygen deprivation, if it lasts long enough, leads to a myocardial infarction (MI), a situation in which heart muscle dies and is (eventually) replaced by scar tissue. Although it was once presumed that the lack of oxygen itself injured the myocardial cells, this is apparently not so. The trouble starts when the ischemic area is reperfused with blood, and lymphocytes and other inflammatory cells congregate in the area. These "immigrants" release cytokines (signaling chemicals) that prod

macrophages and neutrophils to release a deluge of free radicals, including superoxide. These toxic substances depress cardiac contractility ("stunned myocardium"), and also appear to cause most of the local tissue damage.

If the heart is not "tipped" into fibrillation, the patient generally survives unless damage to the myocardium is massive. Heart attack victims lucky enough to reach the hospital quickly are routinely treated with tPA or other clot-dissolving drugs, which stop many heart attacks in progress and help prevent loss of viable heart muscle.

The greater the damage to the heart, the less efficiently it pumps blood and the more likely it is that the patient begins a downward spiral toward congestive heart failure and death. So, how do we deal with a damaged heart? Our first line of treatment is drug therapy. The drug strategies for patients in congestive heart failure (p. 705) are useful here. Two classes of blood pressure–lowering drugs, beta-blockers and ACE inhibitors, are particularly important. When norepinephrine (or epinephrine) attaches to beta receptors, heart rate and force increase. Because beta-blockers inhibit this activation by the sympathetic nervous system and successfully prevent increases in blood pressure, they reduce the strain on the heart. ACE (angiotensin-converting enzyme) inhibitors lower blood pressure by preventing the formation of angiotensin II. However, ACE also has a second function—it breaks down chemicals called kinins, particularly bradykinin. Kinins protect the heart from ischemia, and blocking their breakdown improves heart function.

In the future, therapies might be aimed at coaxing the body to repair itself. Although for years the dogma has been that heart muscle does not regenerate, it is now clear that there is some mitotic activity in cardiac muscle throughout life, and limited regeneration of cardiac muscle occurs after an MI. However, this is not enough to recover from "the big one." Since the heart lacks the ability to heal itself, researchers are trying to implant stem cells derived from the patient's own blood or bone marrow into the heart in the hope that they will differentiate into new heart muscle. Clinical trials have shown some improved heart function following stem cell infusion after MI. What's not clear is whether the injected stem cells turn into myocytes or the improvement is due to some other action of the injected cells, or to the procedure itself.

Currently, the gold standard of treatment for a dying heart is heart transplant surgery. Even so, this procedure is riddled with problems. First, an acceptable tissue match must be found. Then, after complicated and traumatic surgery, the heart recipient must take drugs that suppress the immune system to thwart rejection of the donor heart. After about a year of survival, a new type of rejection may develop, in which antibodies attack the inner layer of the coronary vessels, possibly leading to a fatal MI. This rejection does not respond to any known immunosuppressive treatment. Despite the complications, heart transplants are becoming more and more successful and it is now clear that transplanted hearts incorporate muscle and blood vessel cells of the recipient. Over

its four definitive chambers (via a number of stages), the midline septum forms, and the bulbus cordis splits into the pulmonary trunk and ascending aorta. After the second month, few changes other than growth occur until birth.

The interatrial septum of the fetal heart is incomplete. The **foramen ovale** (literally, "oval door") connects the two atria and allows blood entering the right heart to bypass the pulmonary circuit and the collapsed, nonfunctional fetal lungs. Another lung bypass, the **ductus arteriosus,** exists between the pulmonary trunk and the aorta. At or shortly after birth, these shunts close, completing the separation between the right and left sides of the heart. In the three-quarters of transplant patients now survive for 2 years, and half of them survive for more than 12 years.

The severe shortage of donor hearts contrasts with the great demand for them (fully one-third of patients awaiting a heart transplant in North America die without receiving one). This unmet demand has created tremendous pressure to develop alternative treatment procedures:

■ **Left ventricular reconstruction.** Small, well-defined areas of damaged heart tissue can be surgically removed from an enlarged left ventricle. The heart, restored to its proper size, can beat more efficiently and with reduced tension on the ventricular wall. Once regarded as a last resort, this treatment is best performed before excessive stretching of the myocardium has done permanent damage.

■ **Left ventricular assist devices (LVADs).** These mechanical pumps are implanted into the abdomen, connected to the left ventricle through a hole in the diaphragm, and powered by an external battery carried in a backpack or shoulder holster (see illustration). LVADs take over part of the workload from an ailing heart, giving it the opportunity for rest and recovery. They can be used either to "bridge" a patient waiting for transplant or as a permanently implanted device in those ineligible for transplant. Compared with a 25% survival after one year for patients receiving standard medical therapy alone, about 50% of patients with LVADs survive. The primary problem with these devices is infection around the power tube that passes through the skin. Other problems include device failure, and the tendency for clots to form within the pump.

■ **Artificial hearts.** Despite over 40 years of intense development, artificial hearts are not yet ready for prime time. They are so bulky that they are only suitable for large males, and their recipients are susceptible to strokes, infections, and kidney failure. Because of these disappointing results, U.S. regulations presently allow use of an artificial heart only as a lifesaving stopgap measure while the patient awaits a permanent organ transplant.

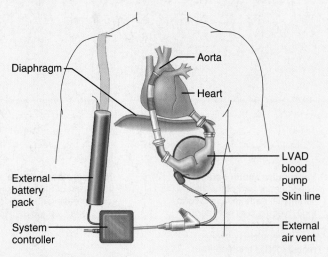

The HeartMate LVAD

Another surgical treatment is available for a slightly different population of patients with CAD. These are patients who, in spite of conventional medical (and often surgical) treatment, continue to have angina (a sharp squeezing chest pain) on exertion. Often, they are not good candidates for other, more demanding surgical techniques. *Transmyocardial laser revascularization (TMR)* uses a laser to zap 15 to 20 small channels into the wall of the left ventricular myocardium. The procedure seems to work by stimulating the coronary vessels to send more branches into the myocardium. Clinical studies indicate that TMR reduces chest pain and improves blood flow in over 40% of those treated.

A noninvasive treatment for CAD used in China for the past 20 years, *external enhanced counterpulsation (EECP)*, is now being adopted in the West. EECP consists of 35 one-hour sessions. The patient lies down while wearing three inflatable pressure cuffs on the upper and lower thighs and calves. The cuffs inflate sequentially during diastole, starting with those on the calves and moving upward, then deflate during systole. These rhythmic waves of compression push blood toward the heart, increasing cardiac output and coronary perfusion while also relieving cardiac workload. Most patients who finish the seven-week regimen report more energy and less angina. Doctors are not sure why EECP helps; it may stimulate the formation of new blood vessels, the release of growth factors that enhance blood vessel function, or the production of the vasodilator nitric oxide.

Even with all this advanced medical technology, your best bet is still to prevent CAD in the first place by decreasing the risk factors, many of which are related to lifestyle: excess weight, high cholesterol and saturated fat in the diet, smoking, and excess stress. In addition, a diet rich in antioxidant-containing fruits and vegetables is recommended. Some studies link tea drinking—the more the better—with lower cardiovascular mortality. So take care of yourself, relax with a nice cup of tea (chock-full of antioxidants), and let the stress of your anatomy and physiology course wash away! ■

adult heart, the position of the foramen ovale is revealed by the fossa ovalis, and the **ligamentum arteriosum** is the fibrous remnant of the ductus arteriosus (see Figure 18.4b). A more complete description of the fetal and newborn circulation is given in Chapter 28 (see Figure 28.13).

◣ HOMEOSTATIC IMBALANCE

Building a perfect heart is difficult. Each year about 30,000 infants are born in the U.S. with one or more of 30 different **congenital heart defects,** making them the most common of all birth defects. Most congenital heart problems are traceable to environmental

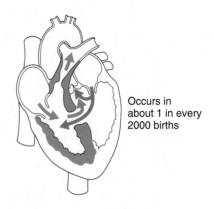

Occurs in about 1 in every 500 births

Narrowed aorta

Occurs in about 1 in every 1500 births

Occurs in about 1 in every 2000 births

(a) Ventricular septal defect. The superior part of the interventricular septum fails to form; thus, blood mixes between the two ventricles, but because the left ventricle is stronger, more blood is shunted from left to right.

(b) Coarctation of the aorta. A part of the aorta is narrowed, increasing the workload on the left ventricle.

(c) Tetralogy of Fallot. Multiple defects (*tetra* = four): Pulmonary trunk too narrow and pulmonary valve stenosed, resulting in a hypertrophied right ventricle; ventricular septal defect; aorta opens from both ventricles; wall of right ventricle thickened from overwork.

FIGURE 18.25 **Three examples of congenital heart defects.** Purple indicates heart areas where the defects are present.

influences, such as maternal infection or drug intake during month 2 when the major events of heart formation occur.

The most prevalent abnormalities produce two basic kinds of disorders in the newborn. They either (1) lead to mixing of oxygen-poor systemic blood with oxygenated pulmonary blood (so that inadequately oxygenated blood reaches the body tissues) or (2) involve narrowed valves or vessels that greatly increase the workload on the heart. Examples of the first type of defect are *septal defects* (Figure 18.25a) and *patent ductus arteriosus,* in which the connection between the aorta and pulmonary trunk remains open. *Coarctation of the aorta* (Figure 18.25b) is an example of the second type of problem. *Tetralogy of Fallot* (te-tral'o-je ov fal-o'), a serious condition in which the baby becomes cyanotic within minutes of birth, encompasses both types of disorders (Figure 18.25c). Modern surgical techniques can correct most of these heart defects. ●

In the absence of congenital heart problems, the heart functions admirably throughout a long lifetime for most people. Homeostatic mechanisms are normally so efficient that people rarely notice when the heart is working harder. In people who exercise regularly and vigorously, the heart gradually adapts to the increased demand by increasing in size and becoming a more efficient and more powerful pump. Consequently, SV increases and resting heart rate declines. Aerobic exercise also helps to clear fatty deposits from blood vessel walls throughout the body, thus retarding atherosclerosis and coronary heart disease.

Barring some chronic illnesses, this beneficial cardiac response to exercise persists into ripe old age.

The key word on benefiting from exercise is *regularity.* Regular exercise gradually enhances the myocardial endurance and strength. For example, 30 minutes a day of moderately vigorous exercise (brisk walking, biking, or yard work) offers significant health benefits to most adults. However, intermittent vigorous exercise, enjoyed by weekend athletes, may push an unconditioned heart beyond its ability to respond to the unexpected demands and bring on a myocardial infarct.

Because of the incredible amount of work the heart does over the course of a lifetime, certain structural changes are inevitable. These age-related changes affecting the heart include

1. Sclerosis and thickening of valve flaps. This occurs particularly where the stress of blood flow is greatest (mitral valve). Thus, heart murmurs are more common in elderly people.

2. Decline in cardiac reserve. Although the passing years seem to cause few changes in resting heart rate, the aged heart is less able to respond to both sudden and prolonged stressors that demand increased output. Sympathetic control of the heart becomes less efficient (in part because the amount of cAMP produced on stimulation decreases with age). HR gradually becomes more variable and there is a decline in maximum HR. These changes are less of a problem in physically active seniors.

3. Fibrosis of cardiac muscle. As one ages, more and more cardiac cells die and are replaced with fibrous tissue. As a result, the heart stiffens and its filling in preparation for the next heartbeat is less efficient, resulting in reduced stroke volume. Additionally, the nodes of the heart's conduction system sometimes become fibrosed (scarred) with age, which increases the incidence of arrhythmias and other conduction problems.

4. Atherosclerosis. Although the insidious progress of atherosclerosis begins in childhood, it is accelerated by inactivity, smoking, and stress. The most serious consequences to the heart are hypertensive heart disease and coronary artery occlusion, both of which increase the risk of heart attack and stroke. Although the aging process itself leads to changes in blood vessel walls that result in atherosclerosis, many investigators feel that diet, not aging, is the single most important contributor to cardiovascular disease. There is some agreement that risk is lowered if people consume less animal fat, cholesterol, and salt.

■ ■ ■

The heart is an exquisitely engineered double pump that operates with precision to propel blood into the large arteries leaving its chambers. However, continuous circulation of blood also depends critically on the pressure dynamics in the blood vessels. Chapter 19 considers the structure and function of these vessels and relates this information to the work of the heart to provide a complete picture of cardiovascular functioning.

Related Clinical Terms

Asystole (a-sis'to-le) Situation in which the heart fails to contract.

Cardiac catheterization Diagnostic procedure involving passage of a fine catheter (tubing) through a blood vessel into the heart; blood samples are withdrawn, allowing oxygen content, blood flow, and pressures within the heart to be measured. Findings help to detect valve problems, heart deformities, and other heart malfunctions.

Commotio cordis ("concussion of the heart") Situation in which a relatively mild blow to the chest causes heart failure and sudden death because it occurs during a vulnerable interval (2 ms) when the heart is repolarizing. Explains those rare instances when youngsters drop dead on the playing field after being hit in the chest by a ball.

Cor pulmonale (kor pul-mun-nă'le; *cor* = heart, *pulmo* = lung) A condition of right-sided heart failure resulting from elevated blood pressure in the pulmonary circuit (pulmonary hypertension). Acute cases may develop suddenly due to a pulmonary embolism; chronic cases are usually associated with chronic lung disorders such as emphysema.

Endocarditis (en"do-kar-di'tis) Inflammation of the endocardium, usually confined to the endocardium of the heart valves. Endocarditis often results from infection by bacteria that have entered the bloodstream but may result from fungal infection or an autoimmune response. Drug addicts may develop endocarditis by injecting themselves with contaminated needles.

Heart palpitation A heartbeat that is unusually strong, fast, or irregular so that the person becomes aware of it; may be caused by certain drugs, emotional pressures ("nervous heart"), or heart disorders.

Hypertrophic cardiomyopathy (HCM) The leading cause of sudden death in young athletes, this condition, which is usually inherited, causes the cardiac muscle cells to enlarge, thickening the heart wall. The heart pumps strongly but doesn't relax well during diastole when the heart is filling.

Mitral valve prolapse Valve disorder affecting up to 1% of the population; most often seen in young women. It appears to have a genetic basis resulting in abnormal chordae tendineae or a malfunction of the papillary muscles; one or more of the flaps of the mitral valve become incompetent and billow into the left atrium during ventricular systole, allowing blood regurgitation. Occasionally requires valve replacement surgery.

Myocarditis (mi"o-kar-di'tis; *myo* = muscle, *card* = heart, *itis* = inflammation) Inflammation of the cardiac muscle layer (myocardium) of the heart; sometimes follows an untreated streptococcal infection in children. May weaken the heart and impair its ability to act as an effective pump.

Paroxysmal atrial tachycardia (PAT) Bursts of atrial contractions with little pause between them.

Ventricular tachycardia (VT or V-tac) Rapid ventricular contractions that are not coordinated with atrial activity.

Chapter Summary

Media study tools that could provide you additional help in reviewing specific key topics of Chapter 18 are referenced below.
IP = *InterActive Physiology*

Heart Anatomy   (pp. 678–689)

Size, Location, and Orientation   (p. 678)

1. The human heart, about the size of a clenched fist, is located obliquely within the mediastinum of the thorax.

Coverings of the Heart   (p. 678)

2. The heart is enclosed within a double sac made up of the outer fibrous pericardium and the inner serous pericardium (parietal and visceral layers). The pericardial cavity between the serous layers contains lubricating serous fluid.

Layers of the Heart Wall   (pp. 678–680)

3. Layers of the heart wall, from the interior out, are the endocardium, the myocardium (reinforced by a fibrous skeleton), and the epicardium (visceral layer of the serous pericardium).

Chambers and Associated Great Vessels (pp. 680–684)

4. The heart has two superior atria and two inferior ventricles. Functionally, the heart is a double pump.

5. Entering the right atrium are the superior vena cava, the inferior vena cava, and the coronary sinus. Four pulmonary veins enter the left atrium.

6. The right ventricle discharges blood into the pulmonary trunk; the left ventricle pumps blood into the aorta.

Pathway of Blood Through the Heart (pp. 684–685)

7. The right heart is the pulmonary circuit pump. Oxygen-poor systemic blood enters the right atrium, passes into the right ventricle, through the pulmonary trunk to the lungs, and back to the left atrium via the pulmonary veins.

8. The left heart is the systemic circuit pump. Oxygen-laden blood entering the left atrium from the lungs flows into the left ventricle and then into the aorta, which provides the functional supply of all body organs. Systemic veins return the oxygen-depleted blood to the right atrium.

Coronary Circulation (pp. 685–686)

9. The right and left coronary arteries branch from the aorta and via their main branches (anterior and posterior interventricular, marginal, and circumflex arteries) supply the heart itself. Venous blood, collected by the cardiac veins (great, middle, and small), is emptied into the coronary sinus.

10. Blood delivery to the myocardium occurs during heart relaxation.

Heart Valves (pp. 686–689)

11. The atrioventricular valves (tricuspid and mitral) prevent backflow into the atria when the ventricles are contracting; the pulmonary and aortic valves (semilunar valves) prevent backflow into the ventricles when the ventricles are relaxing.

IP Cardiovascular System; Topic: Anatomy Review: The Heart, pp. 1–8.

Properties of Cardiac Muscle Fibers (pp. 689–692)

Microscopic Anatomy (pp. 689–690)

1. Cardiac muscle cells are branching, striated, generally uninucleate cells. They contain myofibrils consisting of typical sarcomeres.

2. Adjacent cardiac cells are connected by intercalated discs containing desmosomes and gap junctions. The myocardium behaves as a functional syncytium because of electrical coupling provided by gap junctions.

Mechanism and Events of Contraction (pp. 690–692)

3. As in skeletal muscle, the membrane depolarization of contractile myocytes causes opening of sodium channels and sodium entry, which is responsible for the rising phase of the action potential curve. Depolarization also opens slow Ca^{2+} channels; Ca^{2+} entry prolongs the period of depolarization (creates the plateau). The action potential is coupled to sliding of the myofilaments by Ca^{2+} released by the SR and entering from the extracellular space. Compared to skeletal muscle, cardiac muscle has a prolonged refractory period that prevents tetany.

IP Cardiovascular System; Topic: Cardiac Action Potential, pp. 11–18.

Energy Requirements (p. 692)

4. Cardiac muscle has abundant mitochondria and depends almost entirely on aerobic respiration to form ATP.

Heart Physiology (pp. 692–705)

Electrical Events (pp. 692–697)

1. Certain noncontractile cardiac muscle cells exhibit automaticity and rhythmicity and can independently initiate action potentials. Such cells have an unstable resting potential called a pacemaker potential that gradually depolarizes, drifting toward threshold for firing. These cells compose the intrinsic conduction system of the heart.

2. The conduction system of the heart consists of the SA and AV nodes, the AV bundle and bundle branches, and the Purkinje fibers. This system coordinates the depolarization of the heart and ensures that the heart beats as a unit. The SA node has the fastest rate of spontaneous depolarization and acts as the heart's pacemaker; it sets the sinus rhythm.

3. Defects in the intrinsic conduction system can cause arrhythmias, fibrillation, and heart block.

4. The heart is innervated by the autonomic nervous system. Cardiac centers in the medulla include the cardioacceleratory center, which projects to the T_1–T_5 region of the spinal cord, which in turn projects to the cervical and upper thoracic sympathetic trunk. Postganglionic fibers innervate the SA and AV nodes and the cardiac muscle fibers. The cardioinhibitory center exerts its influence via the parasympathetic vagus nerves (X), which project to the heart wall. Most parasympathetic fibers serve the SA and AV nodes.

5. An electrocardiogram is a graphic representation of the cardiac conduction cycle. The P wave reflects atrial depolarization. The QRS complex indicates ventricular depolarization; the T wave represents ventricular repolarization.

IP Cardiovascular System; Topic: Intrinsic Conduction System, pp. 1–7; Topic: Cardiac Action Potential, pp. 1–10.

Heart Sounds (pp. 697–698)

6. Normal heart sounds arise chiefly from turbulent blood flow during the closing of heart valves. Abnormal heart sounds, called murmurs, usually reflect valve problems.

Mechanical Events: The Cardiac Cycle (pp. 698–700)

7. A cardiac cycle consists of the events occurring during one heartbeat. During mid-to-late diastole, the ventricles fill and the atria contract. Ventricular systole consists of the isovolumetric contraction phase and the ventricular ejection phase. During early diastole, the ventricles are relaxed and are closed chambers until increasing atrial pressure forces the AV valves open and the cycle begins again. At a normal heart rate of 75 beats/min, a cardiac cycle lasts 0.8 s.

8. Pressure changes promote blood flow and valve opening and closing.

IP Cardiovascular System; Topic: Cardiac Cycle, pp. 1–19.

Cardiac Output (pp. 700–705)

9. Cardiac output, typically 5 L/min, is the amount of blood pumped out by each ventricle in 1 minute. Stroke volume is the amount of blood pumped out by a ventricle with each contraction. Cardiac output = heart rate × stroke volume.

10. Stroke volume depends to a large extent on the degree of stretch of cardiac muscle by venous return. Approximately 70 ml, it is the difference between end diastolic volume (EDV) and end systolic volume (ESV). Anything that influences heart rate or blood volume influences venous return, hence stroke volume.

18

11. Activation of the sympathetic nervous system increases heart rate and contractility; parasympathetic activation decreases heart rate but has little effect on contractility. Ordinarily, the heart exhibits vagal tone.

12. Chemical regulation of the heart is effected by hormones (epinephrine and thyroxine) and ions (particularly potassium and calcium). Imbalances in ions severely impair heart activity.

13. Other factors influencing heart rate are age, sex, exercise, and body temperature.

14. Congestive heart failure occurs when the pumping ability of the heart is inadequate to provide normal circulation to meet body needs. Right heart failure leads to systemic edema; left heart failure results in pulmonary edema.

IP Cardiovascular System; Topic: Cardiac Output, pp. 1–10.

Developmental Aspects of the Heart (pp. 705–709)

1. The heart begins as a simple (mesodermal) tube that is pumping blood by the fourth week of gestation. The fetal heart has two lung bypasses: the foramen ovale and the ductus arteriosus.

2. Congenital heart defects are the most common of all birth defects. The most common of these disorders lead to inadequate oxygenation of blood or increase the workload of the heart.

3. Age-related changes include sclerosis and thickening of the valve flaps, declines in cardiac reserve, fibrosis of cardiac muscle, and atherosclerosis.

4. Risk factors for cardiac disease include dietary factors, excessive stress, cigarette smoking, and lack of exercise.

Review Questions

Multiple Choice/Matching

(Some questions have more than one correct answer. Select the best answer or answers from the choices given.)

1. When the semilunar valves are open, which of the following are occurring? (a) 2, 3, 5, 6, (b) 1, 2, 3, 7, (c) 1, 3, 5, 6, (d) 2, 4, 5, 7.

(1) coronary arteries fill	(5) blood enters aorta
(2) AV valves are closed	(6) blood enters
(3) ventricles are in systole	pulmonary arteries
(4) ventricles are in diastole	(7) atria contract

2. The portion of the intrinsic conduction system located in the interventricular septum is the (a) AV node, (b) SA node, (c) AV bundle, (d) Purkinje fibers.

3. An ECG provides information about (a) cardiac output, (b) movement of the excitation wave across the heart, (c) coronary circulation, (d) valve impairment.

4. The sequence of contraction of the heart chambers is (a) random, (b) left chambers followed by right chambers, (c) both atria followed by both ventricles, (d) right atrium, right ventricle, left atrium, left ventricle.

5. The fact that the left ventricular wall is thicker than the right reveals that it (a) pumps a greater volume of blood, (b) pumps blood against greater resistance, (c) expands the thoracic cage, (d) pumps blood through a smaller valve.

6. The chordae tendineae (a) close the atrioventricular valves, (b) prevent the AV valve flaps from everting, (c) contract the papillary muscles, (d) open the semilunar valves.

7. In the heart, which of the following apply? (1) Action potentials are conducted from cell to cell across the myocardium via gap junctions, (2) the SA node sets the pace for the heart as a whole, (3) spontaneous depolarization of cardiac cells can occur in the absence of nerve stimulation, (4) cardiac muscle can continue to contract for long periods in the absence of oxygen. (a) all of the above, (b) 1, 3, 4, (c) 1, 2, 3, (d) 2, 3.

8. The activity of the heart depends on intrinsic properties of cardiac muscle and on neural factors. Thus, (a) vagus nerve stimulation of the heart reduces heart rate, (b) sympathetic nerve stimulation of the heart decreases time available for ventricular filling, (c) sympathetic stimulation of the heart increases its force of contraction, (d) all of the above.

9. Freshly oxygenated blood is first received by the (a) right atrium, (b) left atrium, (c) right ventricle, (d) left ventricle.

Short Answer Essay Questions

10. Describe the location and position of the heart in the body.

11. Describe the pericardium and distinguish between the fibrous and the serous pericardia relative to histological structure and location.

12. Trace one drop of blood from the time it enters the right atrium until it enters the left atrium. What is this circuit called?

13. (a) Describe how heart contraction and relaxation influence coronary blood flow. (b) Name the major branches of the coronary arteries, and note the heart regions served by each.

14. The refractory period of cardiac muscle is much longer than that of skeletal muscle. Why is this a desirable functional property?

15. (a) Name the elements of the intrinsic conduction system of the heart in order, beginning with the pacemaker. (b) What is the important function of this conduction system?

16. Draw a normal ECG pattern. Label and explain the significance of its deflection waves.

17. Define cardiac cycle, and follow the events of one cycle.

18. What is cardiac output, and how is it calculated?

19. Discuss how the Frank-Starling law of the heart helps to explain the influence of venous return on stroke volume.

20. (a) Describe the common function of the foramen ovale and the ductus arteriosus in a fetus. (b) What problems result if these shunts remain patent (open) after birth?

Critical Thinking and Clinical Application Questions

1. A gang member was stabbed in the chest during a street fight. He was cyanotic and unconscious from lack of blood delivery to the brain. The diagnosis was cardiac tamponade. What is cardiac tamponade and how does it cause the observed symptoms?

18

2. You have been called upon to demonstrate the technique for listening to valve sounds. (a) Explain where you would position your stethoscope to auscultate (1) the aortic valve of a patient with severe aortic valve incompetence and (2) a stenotic mitral valve. (b) During which period(s) would you hear these abnormal valve sounds most clearly? (During atrial diastole, ventricular systole, ventricular diastole, or atrial systole?) (c) What cues would you use to differentiate between an incompetent and a stenosed valve?

3. Florita Santos, a middle-aged woman, is admitted to the coronary care unit with a diagnosis of left ventricular failure resulting from a myocardial infarction. Her history indicated that she was aroused in the middle of the night by severe chest pain. Her skin is pale and cold, and moist sounds are heard over the lower regions of both lungs. Explain how failure of the left ventricle can cause these signs and symptoms.

4. Heather, a newborn baby, needs surgery because she was born with an aorta that arises from the right ventricle and a pulmonary trunk that issues from the left ventricle, a condition called transposition of the great vessels. What are the physiological consequences of this defect?

5. Gabriel, a heroin addict, feels tired, is weak and feverish, and has vague aches and pains. Terrified that he has AIDS, he goes to a doctor and is informed that he is suffering not from AIDS, but from a heart murmur accompanied by endocarditis. What is the most likely way that Gabriel contracted endocarditis?

6. As Cara worked at her dissection, she became frustrated that several of the structures she had to learn about had more than one common name. Provide another name for each of these structures: (a) atrioventricular groove, (b) tricuspid valve, (c) bicuspid valve (give two synonyms), and (d) atrioventricular bundle.

LOOKING FOR MORE STUDY HELP?

A wide variety of quiz questions, tutorials, and learning exercises are available online at the Anatomy & Physiology Place (www.anatomyandphysiology.com) and, if your instructor has provided you with a MyA&P Course ID number, in MyA&P (www.myaandp.com).

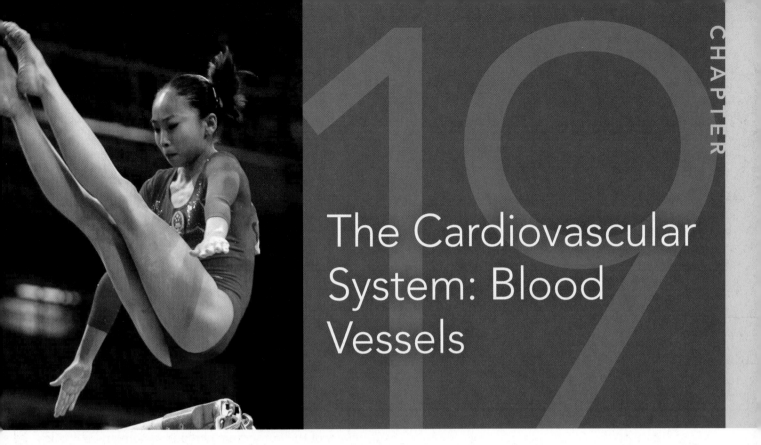

The Cardiovascular System: Blood Vessels

PART 1: OVERVIEW OF BLOOD VESSEL STRUCTURE AND FUNCTION (pp. 714–723)

1. Describe the three layers that typically form the wall of a blood vessel, and state the function of each.

2. Define vasoconstriction and vasodilation.

3. Compare and contrast the structure and function of the three types of arteries.

4. Describe the structure and function of a capillary bed.

5. Describe the structure and function of veins, and explain how veins differ from arteries.

PART 2: PHYSIOLOGY OF CIRCULATION (pp. 723–742)

6. Define blood flow, blood pressure, and resistance, and explain the relationships between these factors.

7. List and explain the factors that influence blood pressure, and describe how blood pressure is regulated.

8. Define hypertension. Describe its manifestations and consequences.

9. Explain how blood flow is regulated in the body in general and in its specific organs.

10. Outline factors involved in capillary dynamics, and explain the significance of each.

11. Define circulatory shock. List several possible causes.

PART 3: CIRCULATORY PATHWAYS: BLOOD VESSELS OF THE BODY (pp. 742, 744–766)

12. Trace the pathway of blood through the pulmonary circuit, and state the importance of this special circulation.

13. Describe the general functions of the systemic circuit. Name and give the location of the major arteries and veins in the systemic circulation.

14. Describe the structure and special function of the hepatic portal system.

Developmental Aspects of Blood Vessels (p. 743)

15. Explain how blood vessels develop in the fetus.

16. Provide examples of changes that often occur in blood vessels as a person ages.

Although blood vessels are sometimes compared to a system of pipes within which the blood circulates, this analogy is only a starting point. Unlike rigid pipes, blood vessels are dynamic structures that pulsate, constrict, relax, and even proliferate. This chapter examines the structure and function of these important circulatory passageways.

The **blood vessels** of the body form a closed delivery system that begins and ends at the heart. The idea that blood circulates in the body dates back to the 1620s with the inspired experiments of William Harvey, an English physician. Prior to that time, it was thought, as proposed by the ancient Greek physician Galen, that blood moved through the body like an ocean tide, first moving out from the heart and then ebbing back in the same vessels.

PART 1: OVERVIEW OF BLOOD VESSEL STRUCTURE AND FUNCTION

The three major types of blood vessels are *arteries, capillaries,* and *veins.* As the heart contracts, it forces blood into the large arteries leaving the ventricles. The blood then moves into successively smaller arteries, finally reaching their smallest branches, the *arterioles* (ar-te're-ōlz; "little arteries"), which feed into the capillary beds of body organs and tissues. Blood drains from the capillaries into *venules* (ven'ūlz), the smallest veins, and then on into larger and larger veins that merge to form the large veins that ultimately empty into the heart. Altogether, the blood vessels in the adult human stretch for about 100,000 km (60,000 miles) through the internal body landscape!

Because **arteries** carry blood *away from* the heart, they are said to "branch," "diverge," or "fork" as they form smaller and smaller divisions. **Veins,** by contrast, carry blood *toward* the heart and so are said to "join," "merge," and "converge" into the successively larger vessels approaching the heart. In the systemic circulation, arteries always carry oxygenated blood and veins always carry oxygen-poor blood. The opposite is true in the pulmonary circulation, where the arteries, still defined as the vessels leading away from the heart, carry oxygen-poor blood to the lungs, and the veins carry oxygen-rich blood from the lungs to the heart. The special umbilical vessels of a fetus also differ in the roles of veins and arteries.

Of all the blood vessels, only the capillaries have intimate contact with tissue cells and directly serve cellular needs. Exchanges between the blood and tissue cells occur primarily through the gossamer-thin capillary walls.

Structure of Blood Vessel Walls

The walls of all blood vessels, except the very smallest, have three distinct layers, or *tunics* ("coverings"), that surround a central blood-containing space, the vessel **lumen** (Figure 19.1).

The innermost tunic is the **tunica intima** (in'tĭ-mah; formerly called the *tunica interna*). The name is easy to remember once you know that this tunic is in *intimate* contact with the blood in the lumen. This tunic contains the *endothelium*, the simple squamous epithelium that lines the lumen of all vessels. The endothelium is a continuation of the endocardial lining of the heart, and its flat cells fit closely together, forming a slick surface that minimizes friction as blood moves through the lumen. In vessels larger than 1 mm in diameter, a *subendothelial layer*, consisting of a basement membrane and loose connective tissue, supports the endothelium.

The middle tunic, the **tunica media** (me'de-ah), is mostly circularly arranged smooth muscle cells and sheets of elastin. The activity of the smooth muscle is regulated by sympathetic *vasomotor nerve fibers* of the autonomic nervous system and a whole battery of chemicals. Depending on the body's needs at any given moment, either **vasoconstriction** (reduction in lumen diameter as the smooth muscle contracts) or **vasodilation** (increase in lumen diameter as the smooth muscle relaxes) can be effected. Because small changes in vessel diameter greatly influence blood flow and blood pressure, the activities of the tunica media are critical in regulating circulatory dynamics. Generally, the tunica media is the bulkiest layer in arteries, which bear the chief responsibility for maintaining blood pressure and continuous blood circulation.

The outermost layer of a blood vessel wall, the **tunica externa** (formerly called the *tunica adventitia*; ad"ven-tish'e-ah; "coming from outside"), is composed largely of loosely woven collagen fibers that protect and reinforce the vessel, and anchor it to surrounding structures. The tunica externa is infiltrated with nerve fibers, lymphatic vessels, and, in larger veins, a network of elastin fibers. In larger vessels, the tunica externa contains a system of tiny blood vessels, the **vasa vasorum** (va'sah vasor'um)—literally, "vessels of the vessels" that nourish the more external tissues of the blood vessel wall. The innermost or luminal portion of the vessel obtains its nutrients directly from blood in the lumen.

The three vessel types vary in length, diameter, relative wall thickness, and tissue makeup (Table 19.1). The relationship of the various blood vascular channels to one another and to vessels of the lymphatic system (which recovers fluids that leak from the circulation) is summarized in Figure 19.2a.

Q *What is the functional value of having capillaries that consist of a single layer of squamous cells underlain by sparse connective tissue?*

FIGURE 19.1   **Generalized structure of arteries, veins, and capillaries. (a)** Light photomicrograph of a muscular artery and the corresponding vein in cross section (30×). **(b)** The walls of arteries and veins are composed of the tunica intima (endothelium underlain by loose connective tissue), the tunica media (smooth muscle cells and elastic fibers), and the tunica externa (largely collagen fibers). Capillaries are composed of only the endothelium and a basement membrane. The tunica media is thick in arteries and thin in veins, while the tunica externa is thin in arteries and relatively thicker in veins.

Artery   Vein

(a)

Tunica intima
• Endothelium
• Subendothelial layer

Internal elastic lamina

Tunica media

External elastic lamina

Tunica externa

Valve

Lumen

Artery

Lumen

Vein

Capillary network

Endothelial cells

Capillary

(b)

TABLE 19.1	Summary of Blood Vessel Anatomy	
VESSEL TYPE/ ILLUSTRATION*	**AVERAGE LUMEN DIAMETER (D) AND WALL THICKNESS (T)**	**RELATIVE TISSUE MAKEUP** (Endothelium / Elastic Tissues / Smooth Muscles / Fibrous (Collagenous) Tissues)
Elastic artery	D : 1.5 cm T : 1.0 mm	
Muscular artery	D : 6.0 mm T : 1.0 mm	
Arteriole	D : 37.0 μm T : 6.0 μm	
Capillary	D : 9.0 μm T : 0.5 μm	
Venule	D : 20.0 μm T : 1.0 μm	
Vein	D : 5.0 mm T : 0.5 mm	

*Size relationships are not proportional. Smaller vessels are drawn relatively larger so detail can be seen. See column 2 for actual dimensions.

Arterial System

In terms of relative size and function, arteries can be divided into three groups—elastic arteries, muscular arteries, and arterioles.

Elastic (Conducting) Arteries

Elastic arteries are the thick-walled arteries near the heart—the aorta and its major branches. These arteries are the largest in diameter, ranging from 2.5 cm to 1 cm, and the most elastic (Table 19.1). Because their large lumens make them low-resistance pathways that conduct blood from the heart to medium-sized arteries, elastic arteries are sometimes referred to as **conducting arteries** (Figure 19.2a). They contain more elastin than any other vessel type. It is present in all three tunics, but the tunica media contains the most. There the elastin constructs concentric "holey" laminae (sheets) of elastic connective tissue that look like slices of Swiss cheese interspersed between the layers of smooth muscle cells. Although elastic arteries also contain substantial amounts of smooth muscle, they are relatively inactive in vasoconstriction. Thus, in terms of function, they can be visualized as simple elastic tubes.

Elastic arteries are pressure reservoirs, expanding and recoiling as blood is ejected from the heart. Consequently, blood flows fairly continuously rather than starting and stopping with the pulsating rhythm of the heartbeat. If the blood vessels become hard and unyielding, as in arteriosclerosis, blood flows more intermittently, similar to the way water flows through a hard rubber garden hose attached to a faucet. When the faucet is on, the high pressure makes the water gush out of the hose. But when the faucet is shut off, the water flow abruptly becomes a trickle and then stops, because the hose walls cannot recoil to keep the water under pressure. Also, without the pressure-smoothing effect of the elastic arteries, the walls of arteries throughout the body experience higher pressures. Battered by high pressures, the arteries eventually weaken and may balloon out or even burst. (These problems are discussed in *A Closer Look* on pp. 718–719.)

Muscular (Distributing) Arteries

Distally the elastic arteries give way to the **muscular, or distributing, arteries,** which deliver blood to specific body organs and account for most of the named arteries studied in the anatomy laboratory. Their internal diameter ranges from that of a little finger (1 cm) to that of a pencil lead (about 0.3 mm). Proportionately, they have the thickest media of all vessels.

Q *Which contains more blood, the systemic or pulmonary circulation? In the systemic circulation, which contains more blood, arteries or veins?*

(a)

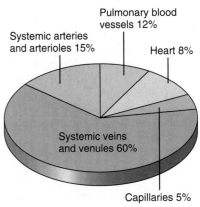

(b)

FIGURE 19.2 **Overview of vascular components and blood distribution. (a)** Schematic showing the relationship of vessels of the blood vascular system to one another and to lymphatic vessels. **(b)** Relative proportion of blood volume in the various portions of the cardiovascular system. Pulmonary blood vessels supply the lungs; systemic blood vessels supply the rest of the body.

Their tunica media contains relatively more smooth muscle and less elastic tissue than do elastic arteries (Table 19.1); therefore, they are more active in vaso-constriction and less distensible. In muscular arteries, however, there *is* an *elastic lamina* on each face of the tunica media.

Arterioles

The smallest of the arteries, **arterioles** have a lumen diameter ranging from 0.3 mm down to 10 μm.

Larger arterioles have all three tunics, but their tunica media is chiefly smooth muscle with a few scattered elastic fibers. Smaller arterioles, which lead into the capillary beds, are little more than a single layer of smooth muscle cells spiraling around the endothelial lining.

As described shortly, minute-to-minute blood flow into the capillary beds is determined by arteriole diameter, which varies in response to changing neural, hormonal, and local chemical influences. When arterioles constrict, the tissues served are largely bypassed. When arterioles dilate, blood flow into the local capillaries increases dramatically.

A The systemic circulation contains more blood and most of that blood is in the veins.

(Text continues on p. 720.)

A CLOSER LOOK

Atherosclerosis? Get Out the Cardiovascular Drāno

When pipes get clogged, it is usually because we've dumped something down the drain that shouldn't be there—a greasy mass or a hairball. Sometimes, pipes get blocked when something is growing inside them (tree roots, for example), trapping the normal sludge coming through (see top photo). In **arteriosclerosis,** the walls of our arteries become thicker and stiffer, and hypertension results. In **atherosclerosis,** the most common form of arteriosclerosis, small, patchy thickenings called *atheromas* form that can intrude into the vessel lumen, making it easy for arterial spasms or a roaming blood clot to close the vessel completely.

Although all blood vessels are susceptible to atherosclerosis, the aorta and the coronary arteries are most often affected. The condition progresses through many stages before the arterial walls actually approach the rigid tube system described in the text, but some of the earlier stages are just as lethal.

Atherosclerosis: Onset and Stages

What triggers this scourge of blood vessels that indirectly causes half of the deaths in the Western world? According to the *response to injury* hypothesis, the initial event is damage to the tunica intima caused by bloodborne chemicals, hypertension, chronic ingestion of contaminants such as arsenic, physical factors such as blows, or viral or bacterial infections. The bacterium *Chlamydia pneumoniae*, known primarily as a cause of sexually transmitted disease; *cytomegalovirus (CMV)*, which causes respiratory infections; oral bacteria from infected gums; and even *Helicobacter pylori*, the ulcer-causing bacterium, have all been found in vascular lesions. Indeed, researchers suspect that almost any type of chronic infection—including

respiratory, periodontal, and urinary tract problems—could set the stage for atherosclerosis.

Irritation to the endothelium sets off the alarm summoning the immune system and the inflammatory process to repair the damage. If it's a one-time injury, when it's over it's over, but most plaques grow slowly. The plaque gradually enlarges as injured endothelial cells release chemotactic agents and growth (mitosis-inducing) factors, and begin to transport and modify greater amounts of lipids picked up from the blood, particularly low-density lipoproteins (LDLs). LDLs are the type that deliver cholesterol to tissue cells via the bloodstream. When the sequestered LDL becomes oxidized (this seems to be a common event), it not only damages neighboring cells but also acts as a chemotactic agent to attract macrophages. Normally macrophages protect the body by ingesting invading microorganisms and toxic substances including oxidized proteins and lipids. But in a particularly fatty plaque they can become so engorged with the oxidized LDLs in the intima that they are transformed into lipid-laden *foam cells* and lose their scavenging ability.

The macrophages are joined by smooth muscle cells migrating from the tunica media. These also take up lipids and become foam cells. The accumulating foam cells initiate the **fatty streak stage.** The smooth muscle cells also deposit collagen and elastin fibers, thickening the intima and producing fibrous lesions with a core of dead and dying foam cells called **fibrous** or **atherosclerotic plaques.** At first the vessel walls accommodate the growing plaque by expanding outward, but eventually these fatty mounds begin to protrude into the vessel lumen, producing full-blown atherosclerosis (see bottom photo).

Additionally, impaired endothelial function accounts for at least some

cases of coronary artery spasms. Healthy endothelial cells release nitric oxide and prostacyclin—chemicals that promote vasodilation and inhibit platelet aggregation. Atherosclerosis impairs release of these vasodilators and antiaggregating factors. Indeed, this may be one cause of the increased thrombus formation in those with atherosclerosis.

If you add another ingredient—*lipoprotein (a)*—to the picture, the disease course accelerates. Lipoprotein (a) is a special LDL found in varying amounts in different people. It delivers cholesterol to sites where tissue is being repaired, such as areas of damaged endothelium. Although it is presumed to assist healing, it backfires when present in excess. Lipoprotein (a) is similar to a common growth factor, and it is thought to promote mitosis of the cells in the vessel wall. Because it resembles plasminogen, it can stand in for it at sites where clots have formed. However, it lacks plasminogen's clot-dissolving ability, so by competing successfully with that clot buster, it may *prevent* disposal of unneeded or undesirable clots.

As enlarging plaques hinder diffusion of nutrients from the blood to deeper tissues of the artery wall, smooth muscle cells in the tunica media die and the elastic fibers deteriorate. These elements are replaced by nonelastic scar tissue, and calcium salts are deposited in the lesions, now called **complicated plaques.** These events constrict the vessel and cause the arterial walls to fray and ulcerate, conditions that encourage blood sludging and backup, platelet adhesion, and thrombus formation. The vessels' increased rigidity leads to hypertension. Together, these events increase the risk of myocardial infarcts, strokes, and aneurysms, and are responsible for the pain (angina) that occurs when heart muscle is ischemic.

19

However, the popular view that most heart attacks are the consequence of severe vessel narrowing and hardening is now being challenged, particularly since some 70% of heart attacks are caused by much smaller obstructions, too small to be seen on an arteriogram or to cause any symptoms in most cases. It now appears that the body's defense system betrays it. The inflammatory process that occurs in the still soft, unstable, cholesterol-rich plaques changes the biology of the vessel wall and makes these vulnerable plaques susceptible to rupture, exploding off fragments that trigger massive clots that can cause lethal heart attacks. The victim appears perfectly healthy until he or she drops dead!

Treatment and Prevention

Although this theory of *vulnerable plaque* has attracted many medical converts, the question of what to do about it remains. Medical centers now test heart patients for elevated levels of cholesterol and C-reactive protein, a marker of inflammation. Electron beam computed tomography (EBCT) scans may be able to identify those at risk for heart attack by detecting calcium deposits in their coronary arteries. New classes of anti-inflammatory and antioxidant drugs are being tested as preventive measures. Even the humble aspirin is gaining new respect; the American Heart Association recommends that people at high risk for heart attack or stroke take one baby aspirin (81 mg) daily. As yet, however, there is no Drāno for clogged vessels.

When your sewer pipes are blocked, you have two choices: dig them up and replace them, or call Roto-Rooter to drill through the obstruction. Stenosis in coronary arteries is treated in much the same way. In *coronary bypass surgery*, veins removed from the legs or small arteries removed from the thoracic cavity are implanted in the heart to restore myocardial circulation. In *balloon angioplasty*, a catheter with a balloon tightly packed into its tip is

Top A pipe clogged by accumulated deposits. **Bottom** Atherosclerotic plaques nearly close a human artery.

threaded through the vessels. When the catheter reaches the obstruction, the balloon is inflated to compress the fatty mass against the vessel wall.

Although angioplasty is faster, cheaper, and much less risky than coronary bypass surgery, it has the same major shortcoming: It does nothing to stop the underlying disease, and in time *restenoses* (new blockages) occur in 30–50% of cases. Insertion of *stents*, short metal-mesh tubes that look much like a ziti noodle, into newly dilated vessels has helped solve the restenosis problem. Bursts of radiation to inhibit reclogging of arteries, a procedure called *brachytherapy*, have reduced restenosis by 50–80% in patients tested.

Even more exciting is a gel that is smeared on the area treated by

angioplasty to form a translucent film over the wall. Composed of chemicals called *antisense agents*, the gel blocks the function of specific genes that are essential for smooth muscle proliferation. Another technique is to bathe bypass graft vessels in a solution containing DNA segments targeted to limit smooth muscle proliferation after vascular injury. Researchers are also testing nitric oxide (NO) donor drugs, which enhance NO activity. NO inhibits the cell proliferation and migration necessary for plaque formation.

It was hoped that cholesterol-lowering drugs (statins) would act as cardiovascular Drāno and wash the fatty plaques off the walls. They do work to some extent, but a significant part of their action is their unexpected side benefit—anti-inflammatory activity.

When an atheroma ruptures and induces clot formation, *thrombolytic (clot-dissolving) agents* are used. These revolutionary drugs include *tissue plasminogen activator (tPA)*, a natural substance produced by genetic engineering techniques. Injecting tPA directly into the heart restores blood flow quickly and puts an early end to many heart attacks in progress. Cardiac patients receiving vessel-opening drugs appear to have a lower incidence of ventricular tachycardia and sudden death following a heart attack.

Of course, it's best to prevent atherosclerosis from progressing in the first place—by quitting smoking, losing weight to reduce blood lipid (triglyceride) levels, eating a healthy diet rich in antioxidants, and exercising regularly to increase blood levels of high-density lipoprotein (HDL, the "good" lipoprotein that removes cholesterol from vessel walls and carries it to the liver for elimination). Americans like their burgers and butter. But if heart disease can be prevented by reversing atherosclerosis, many people with diseased arteries may be willing to trade lifelong habits for a healthy old age! ■

19

(a)

(b)

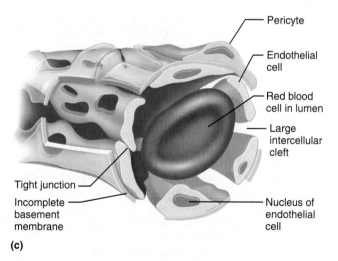

(c)

FIGURE 19.3   **Capillary structure.** Three-dimensional views of **(a)** continuous capillary, **(b)** fenestrated capillary, **(c)** sinusoidal capillary. [Note: The basement membrane is incomplete only in (c).]

Capillaries

The microscopic **capillaries** are the smallest blood vessels. Their exceedingly thin walls consist of just a thin tunica intima (see Figure 19.1b). In some cases, one endothelial cell forms the entire circumference of the capillary wall. Here and there along the outer surface of the capillaries are spider-shaped *pericytes,* smooth muscle-like cells that stabilize the capillary wall.

Average capillary length is 1 mm and average lumen diameter is 8–10 μm, just large enough for red blood cells to slip through in single file. Most tissues have a rich capillary supply, but there are exceptions. Tendons and ligaments are poorly vascularized. Cartilage and epithelia lack capillaries, but receive nutrients from blood vessels in nearby connective tissues, and the avascular cornea and lens of the eye receive nutrients from the aqueous humor.

If blood vessels are compared to a system of expressways and roads, the capillaries are the back alleys and driveways that provide direct access to nearly every cell in the body. Given their location and the thinness of their walls, capillaries are ideally suited for their role—exchange of materials (gases, nutrients, hormones, and so on) between the blood and the interstitial fluid (Figure 19.2a and Table 19.1). The mechanisms of these exchanges are described later in this chapter; here we focus on capillary structure.

Types of Capillaries

Structurally, there are three types of capillaries—*continuous, fenestrated,* and *sinusoidal.* **Continuous capillaries,** abundant in the skin and muscles, are most common. They are continuous in the sense that their endothelial cells provide an uninterrupted lining, adjacent cells being joined laterally by *tight junctions.* However, these junctions are usually incomplete and leave gaps of unjoined membrane called **intercellular clefts** (Figure 19.3a), which are just large enough to allow limited passage of fluids and small solutes. Typically, the endothelial cell cytoplasm contains numerous pinocytotic vesicles believed to ferry fluids across the capillary wall. However, brain capillaries are unique. There the tight junctions of the continuous capillaries are complete and extend around the entire perimeter of the endothelial cells, constituting the structural basis of the *blood-brain barrier* described in Chapter 12.

Fenestrated capillaries (fen′es-tra-tid) are similar to the continuous variety except that some of the endothelial cells in fenestrated capillaries are riddled with oval *pores,* or *fenestrations (fenestra = window)* (Figure 19.3b). The fenestrations are usually covered by a delicate membrane, or diaphragm (probably condensed basal lamina material), but even so, fenestrated capillaries are much more permeable to fluids and small solutes than continuous capillaries are. Fenestrated capillaries are found wherever active capillary absorption or filtrate formation occurs. For example, fenestrated capillaries in the small intestine receive nutrients from digested food, and those in endocrine organs allow hormones rapid entry into the blood. Fenestrated capillaries with perpetually open pores occur in the kidneys, where rapid filtration of blood plasma is essential.

Sinusoids (si'nŭ-soyds), or **sinusoidal capillaries,** are highly modified, leaky capillaries found only in the liver, bone marrow, lymphoid tissues, and some endocrine organs. Sinusoids have large, irregularly shaped lumens and are usually fenestrated. Their endothelial lining has fewer tight junctions and larger intercellular clefts than ordinary capillaries (Figure 19.3c). These structural adaptations allow large molecules and even blood cells to pass between the blood and surrounding tissues. In the liver, the endothelium of the sinusoids is *discontinuous* and large macrophages called **Kupffer cells,** which remove and destroy any contained bacteria, form part of the lining. In other organs, such as the spleen, phagocytes located just outside the sinusoids stick cytoplasmic extensions through the intercellular clefts into the sinusoidal lumen to get at their "prey." Blood flows sluggishly through the tortuous sinusoid channels, allowing time for it to be modified in various ways.

Capillary Beds

Capillaries do not function independently. Instead they tend to form interweaving networks called **capillary beds.** The flow of blood from an arteriole to a venule—that is, through a capillary bed—is called the **microcirculation.** In most body regions, a capillary bed consists of two types of vessels: (1) a *vascular shunt* (metarteriole–thoroughfare channel), a short vessel that directly connects the arteriole and venule at opposite ends of the bed, and (2) *true capillaries,* the actual *exchange vessels* (Figure 19.4). The **terminal arteriole** feeding the bed leads into a **metarteriole** (a vessel structurally intermediate between an arteriole and a capillary), which is continuous with the **thoroughfare channel** (intermediate between a capillary and a venule). The thoroughfare channel, in turn, joins the **postcapillary venule** that drains the bed.

The **true capillaries** number 10 to 100 per capillary bed, depending on the organ or tissues served. They usually branch off the metarteriole (proximal end of the shunt) and return to the thoroughfare channel (the distal end), but occasionally they spring

Q *Assume the capillary bed depicted is in your calf muscle. Which condition would the bed be in—(a) or (b)—if you were doing calf raises at the gym?*

(a) Sphincters open

(b) Sphincters closed

FIGURE 19.4 **Anatomy of a capillary bed.** When precapillary sphincters are constricted, the metarteriole–thoroughfare channel acts as a shunt to bypass the true capillaries.

from the terminal arteriole and empty directly into the venule. A cuff of smooth muscle fibers, called a **precapillary sphincter,** surrounds the root of each true capillary at the metarteriole and acts as a valve to regulate blood flow into the capillary. Blood flowing through a terminal arteriole may go either through the true capillaries or through the shunt. When the precapillary sphincters are relaxed (open), blood flows through the true capillaries and takes part in exchanges with tissue cells. When the

A *Condition (a): The true capillaries would be flushed with blood to ensure that the working calf muscles could receive the needed nutrients and dispose of their metabolic wastes.*

19

sphincters are contracted (closed), blood flows through the shunts and bypasses the tissue cells.

The relative amount of blood entering a capillary bed is regulated by local chemical conditions and arteriolar vasomotor nerve fibers. A bed may be flooded with blood or almost completely bypassed, depending on conditions in the body or in that specific organ. For example, suppose you have just eaten and are sitting relaxed, listening to your favorite musical group. Food digestion is going on, and blood is circulating freely through the true capillaries of your gastrointestinal organs to receive the breakdown products of digestion. However, most of these same capillary pathways are closed between meals. To take another example, when you are exercising vigorously blood is rerouted from the digestive organs (food or no food) to the capillary beds of your skeletal muscles where it is more immediately needed. This helps explain why vigorous exercise right after a meal can cause indigestion or abdominal cramps.

Venous System

Blood is carried from the capillary beds toward the heart by veins. Along the route, the diameter of successive venous vessels increases, and their walls gradually thicken as they progress from venules to the larger and larger veins.

Venules

Ranging from 8 to 100 μm in diameter, **venules** are formed when capillaries unite. The smallest venules, the *postcapillary venules*, consist entirely of endothelium around which a few pericytes congregate. They are extremely porous (more like capillaries than veins in this way), and fluid and white blood cells move easily from the bloodstream through their walls. Indeed, a well-recognized sign of an inflamed area is adhesion of white blood cells to the postcapillary venule endothelium, followed by their migration through the wall into the inflamed tissue. The larger venules have one or two layers of smooth muscle cells (a scanty tunica media) and thin externa as well.

Veins

Venules join to form *veins*. Veins usually have three distinct tunics, but their walls are always thinner and their lumens larger than those of corresponding arteries (Figure 19.1 and Table 19.1). Consequently, in the view seen in routine histological preparations, veins are usually collapsed and their lumens appear slitlike. There is relatively little smooth muscle or elastin in the tunica media, which is poorly developed and tends to be thin even in the largest veins.

The tunica externa is the heaviest wall layer. Consisting of thick longitudinal bundles of collagen fibers and elastic networks, it is often several times thicker than the tunica media. In the largest veins— the venae cavae, which return blood directly to the heart—the tunica externa is further thickened by longitudinal bands of smooth muscle.

With their large lumens and thin walls, veins can accommodate a fairly large blood volume. Because up to 65% of the body's blood supply is found in the veins at any time, veins are called **capacitance vessels** and **blood reservoirs** (Figure 19.2b). Even so, they are normally only partially filled.

Because the blood pressure in veins is low, the walls of these vessels can be much thinner than arterial walls without danger of bursting. However, the low-pressure condition demands some adaptations to ensure that blood is returned to the heart at the same rate it was pumped into the circulation. The large-diameter lumens of veins (which offer relatively little resistance to blood flow) are one structural adaptation. Another is valves that prevent blood from flowing backward. **Venous valves** are formed from folds of the tunica intima (Figure 19.1), and resemble the semilunar valves of the heart in both structure and function. Venous valves are most abundant in the veins of the limbs, where the upward flow of blood is opposed by gravity. They are absent in veins of the ventral body cavity.

A simple experiment demonstrates the effectiveness of venous valves. Hang one hand by your side until the blood vessels on its dorsal aspect distend with blood. Next place two fingertips against one of the distended veins, and pressing firmly, move the superior finger proximally along the vein and then release that finger. The vein will remain flattened and collapsed, despite the pull of gravity. Finally, remove the distal fingertip and watch the vein refill with blood.

◤ HOMEOSTATIC IMBALANCE

Varicose veins are veins that have become tortuous and dilated because of incompetent (leaky) valves. More than 15% of adults suffer from varicose veins, usually in the lower limbs. Several factors contribute, including heredity and conditions that hinder venous return, such as prolonged standing in one position, obesity, or pregnancy. Both the "potbelly" of an overweight person and the enlarged uterus of a pregnant woman exert downward pressure on vessels of the groin, and restrict return of blood to the heart. Consequently, blood pools in the lower limbs, and with time, the valves weaken and the venous walls stretch and become floppy. Superficial veins, which receive little support from surrounding tissues, are especially susceptible. Another cause of varicose veins is elevated venous pressure. For example, straining to deliver a baby or have a bowel movement raises intra-abdominal pressure, preventing blood from draining from the veins of the anal canal. The resulting varicosities in the anal veins are called *hemorrhoids* (hem′ŏ-roidz). ●

Venous sinuses, such as the *coronary sinus* of the heart and the *dural sinuses* of the brain, are highly specialized, flattened veins with extremely thin walls composed only of endothelium. They are supported by the tissues that surround them, rather than by any additional tunics. The dural sinuses, which receive cerebrospinal fluid and blood draining from the brain, are reinforced by the tough dura mater that covers the brain surface.

Vascular Anastomoses

Where vascular channels unite, they form **vascular anastomoses** (ah-nas″to-mo′sēz; "coming together"). Most organs receive blood from more than one arterial branch, and arteries supplying the same territory often merge, forming **arterial anastomoses.** These anastomoses provide alternate pathways, called **collateral channels,** for blood to reach a given body region. If one branch is cut or blocked by a clot, the collateral channel can often provide the area with an adequate blood supply. Arterial anastomoses occur around joints, where active movement may hinder blood flow through one channel. They are also common in abdominal organs, the brain, and the heart. Arteries that do not anastomose or that have a poorly developed collateral circulation supply the retina, kidneys, and spleen. If their blood flow is interrupted, cells supplied by such vessels die.

The metarteriole–thoroughfare channel shunts of capillary beds that connect arterioles and venules are examples of **arteriovenous anastomoses.** Veins interconnect much more freely than arteries, and **venous anastomoses** are common. (You may be able to see venous anastomoses through the skin on the dorsum of your hand.) Because venous anastomoses are abundant, occlusion of a vein rarely blocks blood flow or leads to tissue death.

PART 2: PHYSIOLOGY OF CIRCULATION

Have you ever climbed a mountain? Well, get ready to climb a hypothetical mountain as you learn about circulatory dynamics. Like scaling a mountain, tackling blood pressure regulation and other topics of cardiovascular physiology is challenging while you're doing it, and exhilarating when you succeed. Let's begin the climb.

To sustain life, blood must be kept circulating. By now, you are aware that the heart is the pump, the arteries are pressure reservoirs and conduits, the arterioles are resistance vessels that control distribution, the capillaries are exchange sites, and the veins are conduits and blood reservoirs. Now for the dynamics of this system.

Introduction to Blood Flow, Blood Pressure, and Resistance

First we need to define three physiologically important terms—blood flow, blood pressure, and resistance—and examine how these factors relate to the physiology of blood circulation.

Definition of Terms

1. **Blood flow** is the volume of blood flowing through a vessel, an organ, or the entire circulation in a given period (ml/min). If we consider the entire vascular system, blood flow is equivalent to cardiac output (CO), and under resting conditions, it is relatively constant. At any given moment, however, blood flow through *individual* body organs may vary widely and is intimately related to their immediate needs.

2. **Blood pressure (BP),** the force per unit area exerted on a vessel wall by the contained blood, is expressed in millimeters of mercury (mm Hg). For example, a blood pressure of 120 mm Hg is equal to the pressure exerted by a column of mercury 120 mm high. Unless stated otherwise, the term *blood pressure* means systemic arterial blood pressure in the largest arteries near the heart. It is the pressure gradient—the *differences* in blood pressure within the vascular system—that provides the driving force that keeps blood moving, always from an area of higher pressure to an area of lower pressure, through the body.

3. **Resistance** is opposition to flow and is a measure of the amount of friction blood encounters as it passes through the vessels. Because most friction is encountered in the peripheral (systemic) circulation, well away from the heart, we generally use the term **peripheral resistance.** There are three important sources of resistance: blood viscosity, vessel length, and vessel diameter.

- ***Blood viscosity.*** *Viscosity* (vis-kos′ĭ-te) is the internal resistance to flow that exists in all fluids and is related to the thickness or "stickiness" of a fluid. The greater the viscosity, the less easily molecules slide past one another and the more difficult it is to get and keep the fluid moving. Because it contains formed elements and plasma proteins, blood is much more viscous than water; hence it flows more slowly under the same conditions. Blood viscosity is fairly constant, but infrequent conditions such as polycythemia (excessive numbers of red blood cells) can increase blood viscosity and, hence, resistance. On the other hand, if the red blood cell count is low, as in some anemias, blood is less viscous and peripheral resistance declines.

- **Total blood vessel length.** The relationship between total blood vessel length and resistance is straightforward: the longer the vessel, the greater the resistance. An extra pound or two of fat requires that miles of small vessels be added to service it. This significantly increases the peripheral resistance.

- **Blood vessel diameter.** Because blood viscosity and vessel length are normally unchanging, the influence of these factors can be considered constant in healthy people. Changes in blood vessel diameter are frequent, however, and significantly alter peripheral resistance. How so? The answer lies in principles of fluid flow. Fluid close to the wall of a tube or channel is slowed by friction as it passes along the wall, whereas fluid in the center of the tube flows more freely and faster. You can verify this by watching the flow of water in a river. Water close to the bank hardly seems to move, while that in the middle of the river flows quite rapidly.

In a tube of a given size, the relative speed and position of fluid in the different regions of the tube's cross section remain constant, a phenomenon called *laminar flow* or *streamlining*. The smaller the tube, the greater the friction, because relatively more of the fluid contacts the tube wall, where its movement is impeded. Resistance varies *inversely* with the *fourth power* of the vessel radius (one-half the diameter). This means, for example, that if the radius of a vessel is doubled, the resistance drops to one-sixteenth of its original value ($r^4 = 2 \times 2 \times 2 \times 2 = 16$ and $1/r^4 = 1/16$). Thus, the large arteries close to the heart, which do not change dramatically in diameter, contribute little to peripheral resistance, and the small-diameter arterioles, which can enlarge or constrict in response to neural and chemical controls, are the major determinants of peripheral resistance.

When blood encounters either an abrupt change in the tube size or rough or protruding areas of the tube wall (such as the fatty plaques of atherosclerosis), the smooth laminar blood flow is replaced by *turbulent flow*, that is, irregular fluid motion where blood from the different laminae mixes. Turbulence dramatically increases resistance.

Relationship Between Flow, Pressure, and Resistance

Now that we have defined these terms, let us summarize briefly the relationships between them. Blood flow (F) is *directly* proportional to the difference in blood pressure (ΔP) between two points in the circulation, that is, the blood pressure, or hydrostatic pressure, gradient. Thus, when ΔP increases, blood flow speeds up, and when ΔP decreases, blood flow declines. Blood flow is *inversely* proportional to the peripheral resistance (R) in the systemic circulation; if R increases, blood flow decreases. These relationships are expressed by the formula

$$F = \frac{\Delta P}{R}$$

Of these two factors influencing blood flow, R is far more important than ΔP in influencing local blood flow. This is because when the arterioles serving a particular tissue dilate (thus decreasing the resistance), blood flow to that tissue increases, even though the systemic pressure is unchanged or may actually be falling.

Systemic Blood Pressure

Any fluid driven by a pump through a circuit of closed channels operates under pressure, and the nearer the fluid is to the pump, the greater the pressure exerted on the fluid. The dynamics of blood flow in blood vessels is no exception, and blood flows through the blood vessels along a pressure gradient, always moving from higher- to lower-pressure areas. Fundamentally, *the pumping action of the heart generates blood flow. Pressure results when flow is opposed by resistance.*

As illustrated in Figure 19.5, systemic blood pressure is highest in the aorta and declines throughout the pathway to finally reach 0 mm Hg in the right atrium. The steepest drop in blood pressure occurs in the arterioles, which offer the greatest resistance to blood flow. However, as long as a pressure gradient exists, no matter how small, blood continues to flow until it completes the circuit back to the heart.

Arterial Blood Pressure

Arterial blood pressure reflects two factors: (1) how much the elastic arteries close to the heart can be stretched (their *compliance* or *distensibility*) and (2) the volume of blood forced into them at any time. If the amounts of blood entering and leaving the elastic arteries in a given period were equal, arterial pressure would be constant. Instead, as Figure 19.5 reveals, blood pressure rises and falls in a regular fashion in the elastic arteries near the heart, that is, it is obviously *pulsatile*.

As the left ventricle contracts and expels blood into the aorta, it imparts kinetic energy to the blood, which stretches the elastic aorta as aortic pressure reaches its peak. Indeed, if the aorta were opened during this period, blood would spurt upward 5 or 6 feet! This pressure peak, called the **systolic pressure** (sis-tah'lik), averages 120 mm Hg in healthy adults. Blood moves forward into the arterial bed because the pressure in the aorta is higher than the pressure in the more distal vessels. During diastole, the aortic valve closes, preventing blood from flowing back into the heart, and the walls of the aorta (and other elastic arteries) recoil, maintaining sufficient pressure to keep the blood flowing forward into the smaller vessels. During this time, aortic pressure drops to its lowest level (approximately 70 to 80 mm Hg in healthy adults), called the **diastolic pressure** (di-as-tah'lik). Thus, you can picture the elastic arteries as pressure reservoirs that operate as auxiliary pumps to keep blood circulating throughout the period of diastole, when the heart is relaxing. Essentially, the volume and energy of blood stored in the elastic arteries during systole are given back during diastole.

The difference between the systolic and diastolic pressures is called the **pulse pressure.** It is felt as a throbbing pulsation in an artery (a *pulse*) during systole, as the elastic arteries are expanded by the blood being forced into them by ventricular contraction. Increased stroke volume and faster blood ejection from the heart (a result of increased contractility) cause *temporary* increases in the pulse pressure. Pulse pressure is chronically increased by arteriosclerosis because the elastic arteries become less stretchy. Because aortic pressure fluctuates up and down with each heartbeat, the important pressure figure to consider is the **mean arterial pressure (MAP)**; it is this pressure that propels the blood to the tissues. Because diastole usually lasts longer than systole, the MAP is not simply the value halfway between systolic and diastolic pressures. Instead, it is roughly equal to the diastolic pressure plus one-third of the pulse pressure.

$$\text{MAP} = \text{diastolic pressure} + \frac{\text{pulse pressure}}{3}$$

Thus, for a person with a systolic blood pressure of 120 mm Hg and a diastolic pressure of 80 mm Hg:

$$\text{MAP} = 80 \text{ mm Hg} + \frac{40 \text{ mm Hg}}{3} = 93 \text{ mm Hg}$$

MAP and pulse pressure both decline with increasing distance from the heart. The MAP loses ground to the never-ending friction between the blood and the vessel walls, and the pulse pressure is gradually phased out in the less elastic muscular arteries, where elastic rebound of the vessels ceases to occur. At the end of the arterial tree, blood flow is steady and the pulse pressure has disappeared.

Q *In which class of blood vessels does the greatest drop in blood pressure occur?*

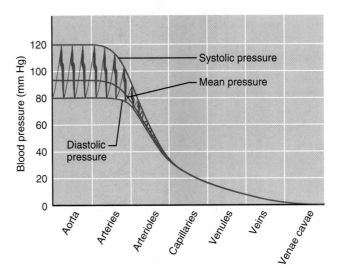

FIGURE 19.5 Blood pressure in various blood vessels of the systemic circulation.

Capillary Blood Pressure

As Figure 19.5 shows, by the time blood reaches the capillaries, blood pressure has dropped to approximately 35 mm Hg and by the end of the capillary beds is only around 15 mm Hg. Such low capillary pressures are desirable because (1) capillaries are fragile and high pressures would rupture them, and (2) most capillaries are extremely permeable and thus even the low capillary pressure forces solute-containing fluids (filtrate) out of the bloodstream into the interstitial space. As described later in this chapter, these fluid flows are important for continuously refreshing the interstitial fluid.

Venous Blood Pressure

Unlike arterial pressure, which pulsates with each contraction of the left ventricle, venous blood pressure is steady and changes very little during the cardiac cycle. The pressure gradient in the veins, from venules to the termini of the venae cavae, is only about 15 mm Hg (that from the aorta to the ends of the arterioles is about 60 mm Hg). This pressure difference between arteries and veins becomes very clear when the vessels are cut. If a vein is cut, the blood flows evenly from the wound; a lacerated artery spurts blood. The very low pressure in the

A *Arterioles, because this is the site of greatest resistance. Arterioles control the distribution of blood to the tissues by changing their resistance.*

19

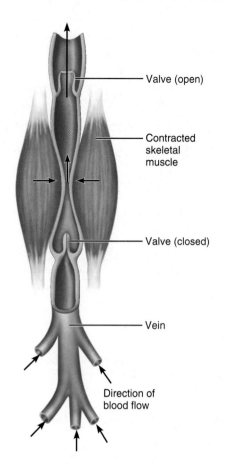

Valve (open)

Contracted skeletal muscle

Valve (closed)

Vein

Direction of blood flow

FIGURE 19.6 **The muscular pump.** When contracting skeletal muscles press against a vein, the valves proximal to the area of contraction are forced open and blood is propelled toward the heart. The valves distal to the area of contraction are closed by the backflowing blood.

venous system reflects the cumulative effects of peripheral resistance, which dissipates most of the energy of blood pressure (as heat) during each circuit.

Despite the structural modifications of veins (large lumens and valves), venous pressure is normally too low to promote adequate venous return. Hence, three functional adaptations are critically important to venous return. The first is the **respiratory "pump."** Pressure changes occurring in the ventral body cavity during breathing create the respiratory pump that moves blood up toward the heart. As we inhale, abdominal pressure increases, squeezing the local veins and forcing blood toward the heart. At the same time, the pressure in the chest decreases, allowing thoracic veins to expand and speeding blood entry into the right atrium. The second adaptation is the **muscular "pump."** Skeletal muscle activity, or the so-called muscular pump, is the more important pumping mechanism. As the skeletal muscles surrounding the deep veins contract and relax, they "milk" blood toward the heart, and once blood passes each successive valve, it cannot flow back (Figure 19.6). People who earn their living in "standing professions," such as hairdressers and dentists, often have swollen ankles

because blood pools in the feet and legs during prolonged periods of skeletal muscle inactivity. The third adaptation is the layer of smooth muscle around the veins that constricts under sympathetic control, increasing venous return. This is yet another way in which the sympathetic nervous system increases cardiac output.

Maintaining Blood Pressure

Maintaining a steady flow of blood from the heart to the toes is vital for proper organ function. But making sure a person jumping out of bed in the morning does not keel over from inadequate blood flow to the brain requires the finely tuned cooperation of the heart, blood vessels, and kidneys—all supervised by the brain. Central among the homeostatic mechanisms that regulate cardiovascular dynamics are those that maintain blood pressure, principally *cardiac output, peripheral resistance,* and *blood volume.* If we rearrange the formula pertaining to blood flow presented on p. 724, we can see how cardiac output (blood flow of the entire circulation) and peripheral resistance relate to blood pressure.

$$F = \Delta P/R \quad \text{or} \quad CO = \Delta P/R \quad \text{or} \quad \Delta P = CO \times R$$

Because CO depends on blood volume (the heart can't pump out what doesn't enter its chambers), it is clear that blood pressure varies *directly* with CO, R, and blood volume. Thus, in theory, a change (increase or decrease) in any of these variables causes a corresponding change in blood pressure. However, what *really* happens in the body is that changes in one variable that threaten blood pressure homeostasis are quickly compensated for by changes in the other variables.

As described in Chapter 18, CO is equal to *stroke volume* (ml/beat) times *heart rate* (beats/min), and normal CO is 5.0 to 5.5 L/min. Figure 19.7 shows the main factors determining cardiac output—venous return and the neural and hormonal controls. Remember that the cardioinhibitory center in the medulla is "in charge" of heart rate most of the time and, via the parasympathetic vagus nerves, maintains the *resting heart rate.* During "resting" periods, stroke volume is controlled mainly by venous return (end diastolic volume). During stress, the cardioacceleratory center takes over, activating the sympathetic nervous system and increasing both heart rate (by acting on the SA node) and stroke volume (by enhancing cardiac muscle contractility, which decreases end systolic volume). The enhanced CO, in turn, results in an increase in MAP.

The following discussion focuses on factors that regulate blood pressure by altering peripheral resistance and blood volume, but a flowchart showing the influence of nearly all other important factors is provided in Figure 19.10 (p. 731).

Short-Term Mechanisms: Neural Controls

The *short-term controls* of blood pressure, mediated by the nervous system and bloodborne chemicals, counteract moment-to-moment fluctuations in blood pressure by altering peripheral resistance (and CO).

Neural controls of peripheral resistance are directed at two main goals: (1) Maintaining adequate MAP by altering blood vessel diameter. (Remember, very small changes in blood vessel diameter cause substantial changes in peripheral resistance, and hence in systemic blood pressure.) Under conditions of low blood volume, all vessels except those supplying the heart and brain are constricted to allow as much blood as possible to flow to those two vital organs. (2) Altering blood distribution to respond to specific demands of various organs. For example, during exercise blood is shunted temporarily from the digestive organs to the skeletal muscles.

Most neural controls operate via reflex arcs involving *baroreceptors* and associated afferent fibers, the vasomotor center of the medulla, vasomotor fibers, and vascular smooth muscle. Occasionally, inputs from *chemoreceptors* and higher brain centers also influence the neural control mechanism.

Role of the Vasomotor Center

The neural center that oversees changes in the diameter of blood vessels is the **vasomotor center,** a cluster of neurons in the medulla. This center plus the cardiac centers described earlier make up the **cardiovascular center** that integrates blood pressure control by altering cardiac output and blood vessel diameter. The vasomotor center transmits impulses at a fairly steady rate along sympathetic efferents called **vasomotor fibers,** which exit from the T_1 through L_2 levels of the spinal cord and run to innervate the smooth muscle of blood vessels, mainly arterioles. As a result, the arterioles are almost always in a state of moderate constriction, called **vasomotor tone.**

The degree of tonic vasoconstriction varies from organ to organ. Generally, arterioles of the skin and digestive viscera receive vasomotor impulses more frequently and tend to be more strongly constricted than those of skeletal muscles. Any increase in sympathetic activity produces generalized vasoconstriction and a rise in blood pressure. Decreased sympathetic activity allows the vascular muscle to relax somewhat and causes blood pressure to decline to basal levels. Most vasomotor fibers release norepinephrine, which is a potent vasoconstrictor. In skeletal muscle, however, some vasomotor fibers release acetylcholine, causing vasodilation. Though they may influence local blood flow, such vasodilator fibers are *not* important to overall regulation of systemic blood pressure.

Vasomotor activity is modified by inputs from (1) baroreceptors (pressure-sensitive mechanoreceptors

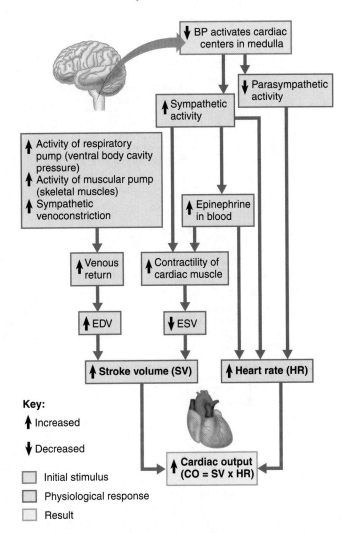

Key:

⬆ Increased

⬇ Decreased

☐ Initial stimulus

☐ Physiological response

☐ Result

FIGURE 19.7 **Major factors enhancing cardiac output.** (Efferent impulses from cardiac centers travel along autonomic nerves. EDV = end diastolic volume, ESV = end systolic volume.)

that respond to changes in arterial pressure and stretch), (2) chemoreceptors (receptors that respond to changes in blood levels of oxygen, carbon dioxide, and H^+), and (3) higher brain centers. Let's take a look.

Baroreceptor-Initiated Reflexes

When arterial blood pressure rises, it stretches **baroreceptors,** neural receptors located in the *carotid sinuses* (dilations in the internal carotid arteries, which provide the major blood supply to the brain), in the *aortic arch,* and in the walls of nearly every large artery of the neck and thorax. When stretched, baroreceptors send a rapid stream of impulses to the vasomotor center. This input inhibits the vasomotor center, resulting in vasodilation of not only arterioles but also veins, and a decline in blood pressure (Figure 19.8). While dilation of the arterioles substantially reduces peripheral resistance, venodilation shifts blood to the venous reservoirs,

Q *Which part of this feedback loop occurs when you rise from a seated position?*

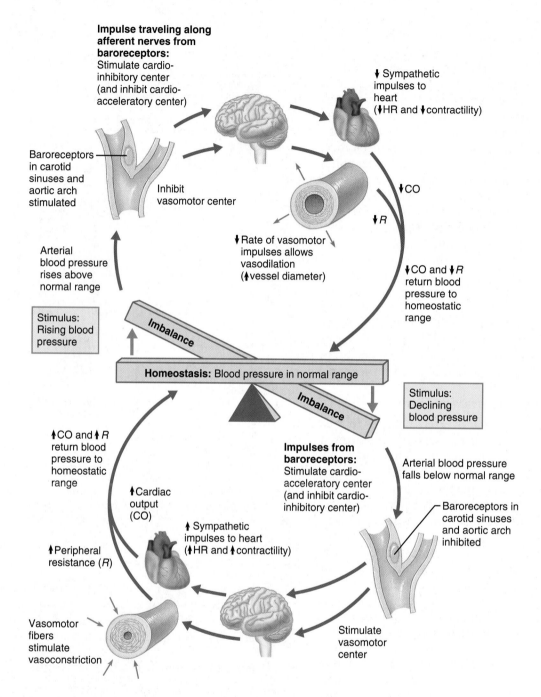

FIGURE 19.8 **Baroreceptor reflexes that help maintain blood pressure homeostasis.** CO = cardiac output; *R* = peripheral resistance; HR = heart rate; BP = blood pressure.

A *The bottom part of the figure applies because arterial blood pressure initially drops, resulting in stimulation of the vasomotor and cardioaccelleratory centers. The result is increased heart rate and vasoconstriction, which increases arterial pressure, restoring homeostasis.*

TABLE 19.2	Influence of Selected Hormones on Variables Affecting Blood Pressure			
VARIABLE AFFECTING BP	**EFFECT ON VARIABLE**	**HORMONE(S)**	**SITE OF ACTION**	**RESULT**
Cardiac output	↑(↑ HR and contractility)	Epinephrine and norepinephrine (NE)	Heart (β_1 receptors)	↑ BP
Peripheral resistance	↑ (via vasoconstriction)	Angiotensin II	Arterioles	↑ BP
		Antidiuretic hormone (ADH)	Arterioles	↑ BP
		Epinephrine and NE	Arterioles (α receptors)	↑ BP
		Atrial natriuretic peptide	Arterioles	↓ BP
Blood volume	↓ (salt and water loss)	Atrial natriuretic peptide	Kidney tubule cells	↓ BP
	↑ (salt and water retention)	Aldosterone	Kidney tubule cells	↑ BP
		Cortisol	Kidney tubule cells	↑ BP
	↑ (water retention)	ADH	Kidney tubule cells	↑ BP

causing a decline in both venous return and cardiac output. Afferent impulses from the baroreceptors also reach the cardiac centers, where the impulses stimulate parasympathetic activity and inhibit the cardioacceleratory center, reducing heart rate and contractile force. A decline in MAP initiates reflex vasoconstriction and increases cardiac output, causing blood pressure to rise. Thus, peripheral resistance and cardiac output are regulated in tandem so that changes in blood pressure are minimized.

The function of rapidly responding baroreceptors is to protect the circulation against short-term (acute) changes in blood pressure, such as those occurring when you change your posture. For example, blood pressure falls (particularly in the head) when one stands up after reclining. Baroreceptors taking part in the **carotid sinus reflex** protect the blood supply to the brain, whereas those activated in the **aortic reflex** help maintain adequate blood pressure in the systemic circuit as a whole. Baroreceptors are relatively *ineffective* in protecting us against sustained pressure changes, as evidenced by the fact that some people do have chronic hypertension. In such cases, the baroreceptors are "reprogrammed" (adapt) to monitor pressure changes at a higher set point.

Chemoreceptor-Initiated Reflexes

When the oxygen content or pH of the blood drops sharply or the carbon dioxide levels rise, **chemoreceptors** in the aortic arch and large arteries of the neck transmit impulses to the cardioacceleratory center, which then increases cardiac output, and to the vasomotor center, which causes reflex vasoconstriction. The rise in blood pressure that follows speeds the return of blood to the heart and lungs.

The most prominent chemoreceptors are the *carotid* and *aortic bodies* located close by the baro-receptors in the carotid sinus and aortic arch. Because chemoreceptors are more important in regulating respiratory rate than blood pressure, their function is considered in Chapter 22.

Influence of Higher Brain Centers

Reflexes that regulate blood pressure are integrated in the medulla of the brain stem. Although the cerebral cortex and hypothalamus are not involved in routine controls of blood pressure, these higher brain centers can modify arterial pressure via relays to the medullary centers. For example, the fight-or-flight response mediated by the hypothalamus has profound effects on blood pressure. (Even the simple act of speaking can make your blood pressure jump if the person you are talking to makes you anxious.) The hypothalamus also mediates the redistribution of blood flow and other cardiovascular responses that occur during exercise and changes in body temperature.

Short-Term Mechanisms: Hormonal Controls

As we have seen, changing levels of oxygen and carbon dioxide help regulate blood pressure via the chemoreceptor reflexes. Hormones, too, help regulate blood pressure, both in the short term via changes in peripheral resistance and in the long term via changes in blood volume (Table 19.2). Paracrines (local chemicals), on the other hand, primarily serve to match the amount of blood flow to the metabolic need of a particular tissue. In rare instances, massive release of paracrines can affect blood pressure. We will discuss these paracrines later—here we will examine the short-term effects of hormones.

- **Adrenal medulla hormones.** During periods of stress, the adrenal gland releases norepinephrine (NE) and epinephrine to the blood, and both hormones enhance the sympathetic fight-or-flight response. As noted earlier, NE has a vasoconstrictive action. Epinephrine increases cardiac output and promotes generalized vasoconstriction (except in skeletal and cardiac muscle, where it generally causes vasodilation). It is interesting to note that *nicotine*, an important chemical in tobacco and one of the strongest toxins known, causes intense vasoconstriction not only by directly stimulating ganglionic sympathetic neurons but also by prompting release of large amounts of epinephrine and NE.

- **Atrial natriuretic peptide (ANP).** The atria of the heart produce the hormone atrial natriuretic peptide, which causes blood volume and blood pressure to decline. As noted in Chapter 16, ANP antagonizes aldosterone and prods the kidneys to excrete more sodium and water from the body, causing blood volume to drop. It also causes generalized vasodilation.

- **Antidiuretic hormone (ADH, vasopressin).** This hormone is produced by the hypothalamus and stimulates the kidneys to conserve water. It is not usually important in short-term blood pressure regulation, but when blood pressure falls to dangerously low levels (as during severe hemorrhage), much more ADH is released and helps restore arterial pressure by causing intense vasoconstriction.

- **Angiotensin II.** When renal perfusion is inadequate, the kidneys release the hormone renin. Renin acts as an enzyme, ultimately generating angiotensin II (an"je-o-ten'sin), which stimulates intense vasoconstriction, promoting a rapid rise in systemic blood pressure. It also stimulates release of aldosterone and ADH, which act in long-term regulation of blood pressure by enhancing blood volume.

Long-Term Mechanisms: Renal Regulation

The long-term controls of blood pressure, mediated by renal mechanisms, counteract fluctuations in blood pressure not by altering peripheral resistance (as in short-term controls) but rather by altering blood volume.

Although baroreceptors respond to short-term changes in blood pressure, they quickly adapt to prolonged or chronic episodes of high or low pressure. This is where the kidneys step in to restore and maintain blood pressure homeostasis by regulating blood volume. Although blood volume varies with

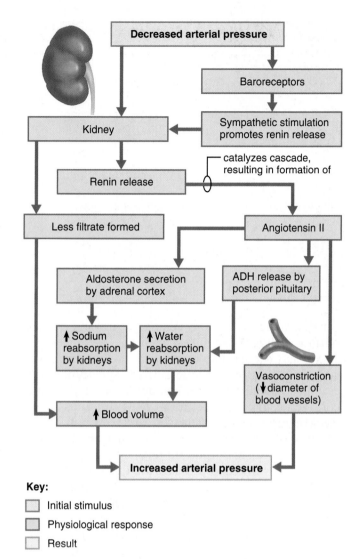

FIGURE 19.9 **Direct and indirect (hormonal) mechanisms for renal control of blood pressure.** Sympathetic nervous system stimulation and action, both part of the more rapidly acting short-term control pathway, also participate in this system by triggering renin release.

age, body size, and sex, renal mechanisms usually maintain it at close to 5 L.

As noted earlier, blood volume is a major determinant of cardiac output (via its influence on venous return, EDV, and stroke volume). An increase in blood volume is followed by a rise in blood pressure, and anything that increases blood volume—such as excessive salt intake, which promotes water retention—raises MAP because of the greater fluid load in the vascular tree. By the same token, decreased blood volume translates to a fall in blood pressure. Blood loss and the garden-variety dehydration that occurs during vigorous exercise are common causes of reduced blood volume. A sudden drop in blood pressure often signals internal bleeding and blood volume too low to support normal circulation.

19

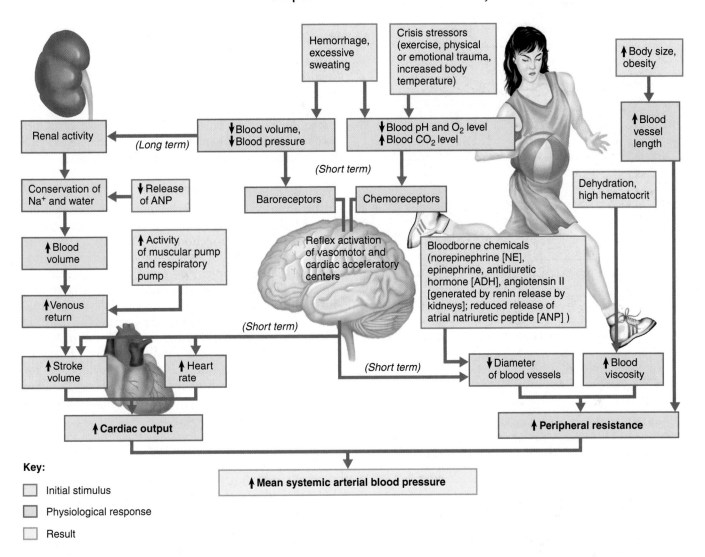

Key:

☐ Initial stimulus

☐ Physiological response

☐ Result

FIGURE 19.10   **Factors causing an increase in MAP.**

However, these assertions—increased blood volume increases BP and decreased blood volume decreases BP—do not tell the whole story because we are dealing with a dynamic system. Increases in blood volume that cause a rise in blood pressure also stimulate the kidneys to eliminate water, which reduces blood volume and consequently blood pressure. Likewise, falling blood volume triggers renal mechanisms that increase blood volume and blood pressure. As you can see, blood pressure can be stabilized or maintained within normal limits only when blood volume is stable.

The kidneys act both directly and indirectly to regulate arterial pressure and provide the major long-term mechanism of blood pressure control. The *direct renal mechanism* alters blood volume independently of hormones. When either blood volume or blood pressure rises, the rate at which fluid filters from the bloodstream into the kidney tubules is speeded up. In such situations, the kidneys cannot process the filtrate rapidly enough, and more of it

leaves the body in urine. As a result, blood volume and blood pressure fall. When blood pressure or blood volume is low, water is conserved and returned to the bloodstream, and blood pressure rises (Figures 19.9 and 19.10). As blood volume goes, so goes the arterial blood pressure.

The *indirect renal mechanism* is the **renin-angiotensin mechanism.** When arterial blood pressure declines, the kidneys release the enzymatic hormone *renin* into the blood. Renin triggers a series of reactions that produce angiotensin II, as mentioned previously. *Angiotensin II* is a potent vasoconstrictor, increasing blood pressure by increasing peripheral resistance. It also stimulates the adrenal cortex to secrete **aldosterone,** a hormone that enhances renal reabsorption of sodium, and prods the posterior pituitary to release ADH, which promotes more water reabsorption (Figure 19.9). As sodium moves into the bloodstream, water follows; thus, both blood volume and blood pressure rise.

Temporal artery

Facial artery

Common carotid artery

Brachial artery

Radial artery

Femoral artery

Popliteal artery

Posterior tibial artery

Dorsalis pedis artery

FIGURE 19.11 **Body sites where the pulse is most easily palpated.** (The specific arteries indicated are discussed on pp. 746–757.)

Monitoring Circulatory Efficiency

The efficiency of a person's circulation can be assessed by taking pulse and blood pressure measurements. These measurements, along with measurements of respiratory rate and body temperature, are referred to collectively as the body's **vital signs.** Let's examine how vital signs are determined or measured.

Taking a Pulse

The alternating expansion and recoil of arteries during each cardiac cycle allow us to feel a pressure wave—a **pulse**—that is transmitted through the arterial tree. You can feel a pulse in any artery that lies close to the body surface by compressing the artery against firm tissue, and this provides an easy way to count heart rate. Because it is so accessible, the point where the radial artery surfaces at the wrist, the *radial pulse*, is routinely used to take a pulse measurement, but there are several other clinically important arterial pulse points (Figure 19.11). Because these same points are compressed to stop blood flow into distal tissues during hemorrhage, they are also called **pressure points.** For example, if you seriously lacerate your hand, you can slow or stop the bleeding by compressing the radial or the brachial artery.

Monitoring pulse rate is an easy way to assess the effects of activity, postural changes, and emotions on heart rate. For example, the pulse of a healthy man may be around 66 beats per minute when he is lying down, rise to 70 when he sits up, and rise to 80 when he suddenly stands. During vigorous exercise or emotional upset, pulse rates between 140 and 180 are not unusual because of sympathetic nervous system effects on the heart.

Measuring Blood Pressure

Most often, systemic arterial blood pressure is measured indirectly in the brachial artery of the arm by the **auscultatory method** (aw-skul'tah-to"re). The *blood pressure cuff,* or *sphygmomanometer* (sfig"mo-mah-nom'ĕ-ter; *sphygmo* = pulse), is wrapped snugly around the arm just superior to the elbow and inflated until the cuff pressure exceeds systolic pressure. At this point, blood flow into the arm is stopped and a brachial pulse cannot be felt or heard. As the cuff pressure is gradually reduced, the examiner listens (auscultates) with a stethoscope for sounds in the brachial artery. The pressure read when the first soft tapping sounds are heard (the first point at which a small amount of blood is spurting through the constricted artery) is systolic pressure. As the cuff pressure is reduced further, these sounds, called the *sounds of Korotkoff,* become louder and more distinct, but when the artery is no longer constricted and blood flows freely, the sounds can no longer be heard. The pressure at which the sounds first disappear is the diastolic pressure.

In normal adults at rest, systolic pressure varies between 110 and 140 mm Hg, and diastolic pressure between 70 and 80 mm Hg. Blood pressure also cycles over a 24-hour period, peaking in the morning in response to waxing and waning levels of various hormones (epinephrine, glucocorticoids, and perhaps retinoic acid). These hormones can either bind directly to receptors that control vasoconstriction or increase the number of receptors available.

Extrinsic factors also play a role: Blood pressure varies with age, sex, weight, race, mood, physical activity, posture, and socioeconomic status. What is "normal" for you may not be normal for your grandfather or your neighbor. Nearly all of these variations can be explained in terms of the factors affecting blood pressure discussed earlier.

Alterations in Blood Pressure

Hypotension

Hypotension, or low blood pressure, is a systolic pressure below 100 mm Hg. In many cases, hypotension simply reflects individual variations and is no cause for concern. In fact, low blood pressure is often associated with long life and an old age free of cardiovascular illness.

 HOMEOSTATIC IMBALANCE

Elderly people are prone to *orthostatic hypotension*— temporary low blood pressure and dizziness when they rise suddenly from a reclining or sitting position. Because the aging sympathetic nervous system does not respond as quickly as it once did to postural changes, blood pools briefly in the lower limbs, reducing blood pressure and consequently blood delivery to the brain. Making postural changes slowly to give the nervous system time to adjust usually prevents this problem.

Chronic hypotension may hint at poor nutrition because poorly nourished people are often anemic and have inadequate levels of blood proteins. Because blood viscosity is low, their blood pressure is also lower than normal. Chronic hypotension also warns of Addison's disease (inadequate adrenal cortex function), hypothyroidism, or severe tissue wasting. *Acute hypotension* is one of the most important signs of circulatory shock (p. 740) and a threat to patients undergoing surgery and those in intensive care units. ●

Hypertension

Hypertension, high blood pressure, may be transient or persistent. Transient elevations in systolic pressure occur as normal adaptations during fever, physical exertion, and emotional upset. Persistent hypertension is common in obese people because the total length of their blood vessels is relatively greater than that in thinner individuals.

 HOMEOSTATIC IMBALANCE

Chronic hypertension is a common and dangerous disease that warns of increased peripheral resistance. An estimated 30% of people over the age of 50 years are hypertensive. Although this "silent killer" is usually asymptomatic for the first 10 to 20 years, it slowly but surely strains the heart and damages the arteries. Prolonged hypertension is the major cause of heart failure, vascular disease, renal failure, and stroke. Because the heart is forced to pump against greater resistance, it must work harder, and in time the myocardium enlarges. When finally strained beyond its capacity to respond, the heart weakens and its walls become flabby. Hypertension also ravages the blood vessels, accelerating the progress of atherosclerosis (see *A Closer Look* on pp. 718–719). As the vessels become increasingly blocked, blood flow to the tissues becomes inadequate and vascular complications appear in the brain, heart, kidneys, and retinas of the eyes.

Although hypertension and atherosclerosis are often linked, it is often difficult to blame hypertension on any distinct anatomical pathology. Hypertension is defined physiologically as a condition of sustained arterial pressure of 140/90 or higher, and the higher the pressure, the greater the risk for serious cardiovascular problems. As a rule, elevated diastolic pressures are more significant medically, because they always indicate progressive occlusion and/or hardening of the arterial tree.

About 90% of hypertensive people have **primary,** or **essential, hypertension,** in which no underlying cause has been identified. However, the following factors are believed to be involved:

1. Diet. Dietary factors that contribute to hypertension include high intakes of sodium, saturated fat, and cholesterol and deficiencies in certain metal ions (K^+, Ca^{2+}, and Mg^{2+}).

2. Obesity.

3. Age. Clinical signs of the disease usually appear after age 40.

4. Diabetes mellitus.

5. Heredity. Hypertension runs in families. Children of hypertensive parents are twice as likely to develop hypertension as are children of normotensive parents. More blacks than whites are hypertensive, and the course of the disease varies in different population groups.

6. Stress. Particularly at risk are "hot reactors," people whose blood pressure zooms upward during every stressful event.

7. Smoking. Nicotine enhances the sympathetic nervous system's vasoconstrictor effects.

Primary hypertension cannot be cured, but most cases can be controlled by restricting salt, fat, and cholesterol intake, losing weight, stopping smoking, managing stress, and taking antihypertensive drugs. Drugs commonly used are diuretics, beta-blockers, calcium channel blockers, and angiotensin-converting enzyme (ACE) inhibitors. Inhibiting ACE suppresses the renin-angiotensin mechanism.

Secondary hypertension, which accounts for 10% of cases, is due to identifiable disorders, such as obstruction of the renal arteries, kidney disease, arteriosclerosis, and endocrine disorders such as hyperthyroidism and Cushing's disease. Treatment for secondary hypertension is directed toward correcting the causative problem. ●

Blood Flow Through Body Tissues: Tissue Perfusion

Blood flow through body tissues, or **tissue perfusion,** is involved in (1) delivery of oxygen and nutrients to, and removal of wastes from, tissue cells, (2) gas exchange in the lungs, (3) absorption of

Q *Why is blood delivery to the skin vasculature increased during strenuous exercise?*

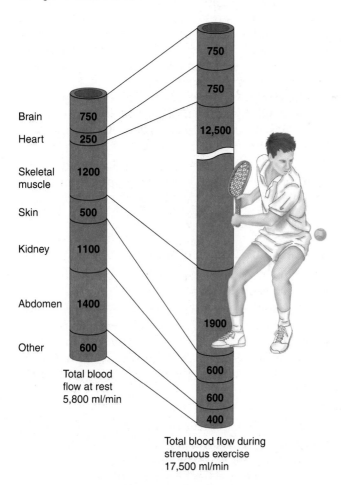

	Total blood flow at rest 5,800 ml/min	Total blood flow during strenuous exercise 17,500 ml/min
Brain	750	750
Heart	250	750
Skeletal muscle	1200	12,500
Skin	500	1900
Kidney	1100	600
Abdomen	1400	600
Other	600	400

FIGURE 19.12 Distribution of blood flow at rest and during strenuous exercise.

nutrients from the digestive tract, and (4) urine formation in the kidneys. The rate of blood flow to each tissue and organ is almost exactly the right amount to provide for proper function—no more, no less. When the body is at rest, the brain receives about 13% of total blood flow, the heart 4%, kidneys 20%, and abdominal organs 24%. Skeletal muscles, which make up almost half of body mass, normally receive about 20% of total blood flow. During exercise, however, nearly all of the increased cardiac output flushes into the skeletal muscles and blood flow to the kidneys and digestive organs is reduced (Figure 19.12).

A *Muscle activity generates heat, which must be dissipated if homeostasis is to be maintained. The skin is the body's heat exchange site.*

Velocity of Blood Flow

Have you ever watched a swift river emptying into a large lake? The water's speed decreases as it enters the lake until it becomes almost imperceptible. This is because the total cross-sectional area of the lake is much larger than that of the river. Velocity in this case is *inversely* related to cross-sectional area. The same thing happens with blood flow inside our blood vessels. As shown in Figure 19.13, the speed or velocity of blood flow changes as blood travels through the systemic circulation. It is fastest in the aorta and other large arteries (the river), slowest in the capillaries (whose large total cross-sectional area make them analogous to the lake), and then picks up speed again in the veins (the river again).

Just as in our analogy of the river and lake, blood flows fastest where the total cross-sectional area is least. As the arterial system branches, the total cross-sectional area of the vascular bed increases, and the velocity of blood flow declines proportionately. Even though the individual branches have smaller lumens, their *combined* cross-sectional areas and thus the volume of blood they can hold are much greater than that of the aorta. For example, the cross-sectional area of the aorta is 2.5 cm² but that of all the capillaries is 4500 cm². This difference in cross-sectional area results in a fast blood flow in the aorta (40–50 cm/s) and a slow blood flow in the capillaries (about 0.03 cm/s). Slow capillary flow is beneficial because it allows adequate time for exchanges between the blood and tissue cells.

As capillaries combine to form first venules and then veins, total cross-sectional area declines and velocity increases. The cross-sectional area of the venae cavae is 8 cm², and the velocity of blood flow varies from 10 to 30 cm/s in those vessels, depending on the activity of the skeletal muscle pump.

Autoregulation: Local Regulation of Blood Flow

Autoregulation is the automatic adjustment of blood flow to each tissue in proportion to the tissue's requirements at any instant. This process is regulated by local conditions and is largely independent of systemic factors. The MAP is the same everywhere in the body and homeostatic mechanisms adjust cardiac output as needed to maintain that constant pressure. Changes in blood flow through individual organs are controlled *intrinsically* by modifying the diameter of local arterioles feeding the capillaries. You can compare blood flow autoregulation to water use in your home. To get water in a sink, or a garden hose, you have to turn on a faucet. Whether you have several taps open or none, the pressure in the main water pipe in the street remains

Q *Does the speed of blood flow vary directly or inversely with the cross-sectional area of the vascular bed?*

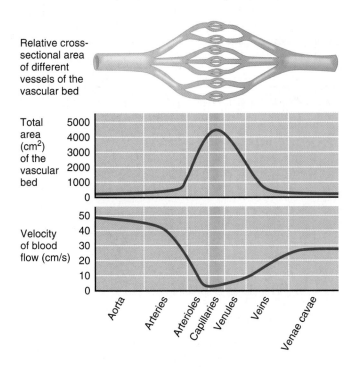

Relative cross-sectional area of different vessels of the vascular bed

Total area (cm²) of the vascular bed

Velocity of blood flow (cm/s)

Aorta Arteries Arterioles Capillaries Venules Veins Venae cavae

FIGURE 19.13 **Relationship between blood flow velocity and total cross-sectional area in various blood vessels of the systemic circulation.**

relatively constant, as it does in the even larger water lines closer to the pumping station. Similarly, what is happening in the arterioles feeding the capillary beds of a given organ has little effect on pressure in the muscular artery feeding the organ, or in the large elastic arteries. The pumping station is, of course, the heart. The beauty of this system is that as long as the water company (circulatory feedback mechanisms) maintains a relatively constant water pressure (MAP), local demand regulates the amount of fluid (blood) delivered to various areas.

Thus, organs regulate their own blood flows by varying the resistance of their arterioles. As described next, these intrinsic control mechanisms may be classed as *metabolic* or *myogenic* (Figure 19.14).

Metabolic Controls

In most tissues, declining levels of oxygen and nutrients are the strongest stimuli for autoregulation. Certain other substances released by metabolically active tissues (such as K^+, H^+, adenosine, lactic

acid, and prostaglandins) also serve as autoregulation stimuli. The relative importance of these factors is not clear. Many of them act directly to relax vascular smooth muscle, but some may act by causing the release of nitric oxide from vascular endothelial cells. **Nitric oxide (NO)** is a powerful vasodilator which acts via a cyclic GMP second-messenger system. NO is quickly destroyed and its potent vasodilator effects are very brief. However, some researchers believe that NO can be transported over longer distances by being bound to chemical buffers in the blood and that it is released where vasodilation is needed. Until recently the sympathetic nervous system was thought to rule blood vessel diameter, but we now know that its primary vascular role is to produce vasoconstriction, and that NO plays the major role in causing vasodilation. The endothelium also releases potent vasoconstrictors, including the family of peptides called **endothelins,** which are among the most potent vasoconstrictors known.

Inflammatory chemicals (such as histamine, kinins, and prostaglandins) released in injury, infection, or allergic reactions also cause vasodilation. The net result of metabolically controlled autoregulation is immediate vasodilation of the arterioles serving the capillary beds of the "needy" tissues, and therefore a temporary increase in blood flow to the area. This is accompanied by relaxation of the precapillary sphincters, which allows blood to surge through the true capillaries and become available to the tissue cells.

Myogenic Controls

Fluctuations in systemic blood pressure would cause problems for individual organs were it not for the **myogenic responses** (*myo* = muscle; *gen* = origin) of vascular smooth muscle. Inadequate blood perfusion through an organ is quickly followed by a decline in the organ's metabolic rate and, if prolonged, organ death. Likewise, excessively high arterial pressure and tissue perfusion can be dangerous because the combination may rupture more fragile blood vessels. Fortunately, vascular smooth muscle prevents these problems by responding directly to passive stretch (increased intravascular pressure) with increased tone, which resists the stretch and causes vasoconstriction. Reduced stretch promotes vasodilation and increases blood flow into the tissue. Hence, the myogenic mechanism keeps tissue perfusion fairly constant despite most variations in systemic pressure.

Generally, both chemical (metabolic) and physical (myogenic) factors determine the final autoregulatory response of a tissue. For example, **reactive hyperemia** (hi"per-e'me-ah) refers to the dramatically increased blood flow into a tissue that occurs

A *Inversely: As cross-sectional area of the vascular bed increases, flow velocity decreases.*

19

Q *Suppose you were in a bicycle race. What would happen to the smooth muscle in the arterioles supplying your quadriceps femoris muscle? What are the key mechanisms in this case?*

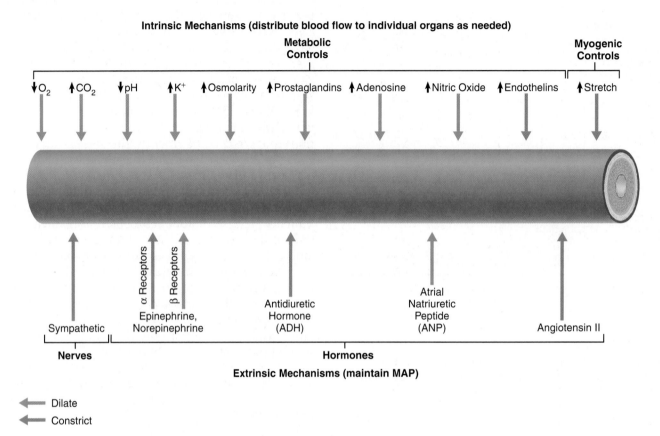

Intrinsic Mechanisms (distribute blood flow to individual organs as needed)

Metabolic Controls — **Myogenic Controls**

$\downarrow O_2$ $\uparrow CO_2$ $\downarrow pH$ $\uparrow K^+$ $\uparrow$Osmolarity $\uparrow$Prostaglandins $\uparrow$Adenosine $\uparrow$Nitric Oxide $\uparrow$Endothelins $\uparrow$Stretch

α Receptors   β Receptors

Sympathetic   Epinephrine, Norepinephrine   Antidiuretic Hormone (ADH)   Atrial Natriuretic Peptide (ANP)   Angiotensin II

Nerves   **Hormones**

Extrinsic Mechanisms (maintain MAP)

← Dilate
← Constrict

FIGURE 19.14 **Summary of control of arteriolar smooth muscle in the systemic circulation.** Arteriolar smooth muscle is under both intrinsic (local) and extrinsic control. Intrinsic mechanisms (metabolic and myogenic) control the distribution of blood flow to each organ and tissue according to its needs. Extrinsic mechanisms primarily maintain mean arterial pressure (MAP) but also redistribute blood during exercise and thermoregulation. α-Adrenergic receptors (smooth muscle contraction, arteriolar constriction) are located in arterioles supplying most tissues, whereas β-adrenergic receptors (smooth muscle relaxation, arteriolar dilation) are located primarily in arterioles supplying skeletal and heart muscle.

after the blood supply to the area has been temporarily blocked. It results both from the myogenic response and from an accumulation of metabolic wastes in the area during occlusion. The various intrinsic (local) and extrinsic controls of arteriolar diameter are summarized in Figure 19.14.

Long-Term Autoregulation

If the nutrient requirements of a tissue are greater than the short-term autoregulatory mechanism can easily supply, a long-term autoregulatory mechanism may evolve over a period of weeks or months to enrich the local blood flow still more. The number of blood vessels in the region increases, and existing vessels enlarge. This phenomenon, called *angiogenesis*, is particularly common in the heart when a coronary vessel is partially occluded. It occurs throughout the body in people who live in high-altitude areas, where the air contains less oxygen.

Blood Flow in Special Areas

Each organ has special requirements and functions that are revealed in its pattern of autoregulation. Autoregulation in the brain, heart, and kidneys is extraordinarily efficient. In those organs, adequate perfusion is maintained even when MAP is fluctuating.

A *Intrinsic metabolic controls cause arteriolar smooth muscle to relax, dilating the vessel and supplying more O_2 and nutrients. Epinephrine from the adrenal medulla may reinforce these mechanisms via β_2 receptors.*

Skeletal Muscles

Blood flow in skeletal muscle varies with fiber type and muscle activity. Generally speaking, capillary density and blood flow is greater in red (slow oxidative) fibers than in white (fast glycolytic) fibers. Resting skeletal muscles receive about 1 L of blood per minute, and only about 25% of their capillaries are open. During such periods, myogenic and general neural mechanisms predominate. When muscles become active, blood flow increases *(hyperemia)* in direct proportion to their greater *metabolic* activity, a phenomenon called **active** or **exercise hyperemia.**

This form of autoregulation occurs almost entirely in response to the decreased oxygen concentration and accumulation of metabolic factors that result from the "revved-up" metabolism of working muscles. However, systemic adjustments mediated by the vasomotor center must also occur to ensure that blood delivery to the muscles is both faster and more abundant. During exercise, sympathetic nervous system activity increases. Norepinephrine released from sympathetic nerve endings causes vasoconstriction of the vessels of blood reservoirs such as those of the digestive viscera and skin, diverting blood away from these regions temporarily and ensuring that more blood reaches the muscles. In skeletal muscles, the sympathetic nervous system and local metabolic controls have opposing effects on arteriolar diameter. During exercise, local controls override sympathetic vasoconstriction. Consequently, blood flow can increase tenfold or more during physical activity (see Figure 19.12), and virtually all capillaries in the active muscles open to accommodate the increased flow.

Epinephrine acting at beta (β) adrenergic receptors and acetylcholine acting at cholinergic receptors were once thought to contribute to arteriolar dilation during exercise. However, these appear to have little physiological importance in the control of human skeletal muscle blood flow. Without question, strenuous exercise is one of the most demanding conditions the cardiovascular system faces. Ultimately, the major factor determining how long muscles can continue to contract vigorously is the ability of the cardiovascular system to deliver adequate oxygen and nutrients and remove waste products.

The Brain

Blood flow to the brain averages 750 ml/min and is maintained at a relatively constant level. The necessity for constant cerebral blood flow becomes crystal clear when one takes into account that neurons are totally intolerant of ischemia.

Although the brain is the most metabolically active organ in the body, it is the least able to store essential nutrients. Cerebral blood flow is regulated by one of the body's most precise autoregulatory systems and is tailored to local neuronal need. Thus, when you make a fist with your right hand, the neurons in the left cerebral motor cortex controlling that movement receive a more abundant blood supply than the adjoining neurons. Brain tissue is exceptionally sensitive to declining pH, and increased blood carbon dioxide levels (resulting in acidic conditions in brain tissue) cause marked vasodilation. Oxygen deficit is a much less potent stimulus for autoregulation. However, very high carbon dioxide levels abolish autoregulatory mechanisms and severely depress brain activity.

Besides metabolic controls, the brain also has a myogenic mechanism that protects it from possibly damaging changes in blood pressure. When MAP declines, cerebral vessels dilate to ensure adequate brain perfusion. When MAP rises, cerebral vessels constrict, protecting the small, more fragile vessels farther along the pathway from rupture due to excessive pressure. Under certain circumstances, such as brain ischemia caused by rising intracranial pressure (as with a brain tumor), the brain (via the medullary cardiovascular centers) regulates its own blood flow by triggering a rise in systemic blood pressure. However, when systemic pressure changes are extreme, the brain becomes vulnerable. Fainting, or *syncope* (sin'cuh-pe; "cutting short"), occurs when MAP falls below 60 mm Hg. Cerebral edema is the usual result of pressures over 160 mm Hg, which dramatically increase brain capillary permeability.

The Skin

Blood flow through the skin (1) supplies nutrients to the cells, (2) aids in body temperature regulation, and (3) provides a blood reservoir. The first function is served by autoregulation in response to the need for oxygen; the second and third require neural intervention. The primary function of the cutaneous circulation is to help maintain body temperature, so we will concentrate on the skin's temperature regulation function here.

Below the skin surface are extensive venous plexuses, through which the blood flow can change from 50 ml/min to as much as 2500 ml/min, depending on body temperature. This capability reflects neural adjustments of blood flow through arterioles and through unique coiled arteriovenous anastomoses. These tiny A-V shunts are located mainly in the fingertips, palms of the hands, toes, soles of the feet, ears, nose, and lips. They are richly supplied with sympathetic nerve endings (a characteristic that sets them apart from the shunts of most other capillary beds), and are controlled by reflexes initiated by temperature receptors or signals from higher CNS centers. The arterioles, in addition, are responsive to metabolic autoregulatory stimuli.

19

When the skin surface is exposed to heat, or body temperature rises for other reasons (such as vigorous exercise), the hypothalamic "thermostat" signals for reduced vasomotor stimulation of the skin vessels. As a result, warm blood flushes into the capillary beds and heat radiates from the skin surface. Vasodilation of the arterioles is enhanced even more when we sweat, because an enzyme in perspiration acts on a protein present in tissue fluid to produce *bradykinin*, which stimulates the vessel's endothelial cells to release the potent vasodilator NO.

When the ambient temperature is cold and body temperature drops, superficial skin vessels are strongly constricted. Hence, blood almost entirely bypasses the capillaries associated with the arteriovenous anastomoses, diverting the warm blood to the deeper, more vital organs. Paradoxically, the skin may stay quite rosy because some blood gets "trapped" in the superficial capillary loops as the shunts swing into operation; also, the chilled skin cells take up less O_2.

The Lungs

Blood flow through the pulmonary circuit to and from the lungs is unusual in many ways. The pathway is relatively short, and pulmonary arteries and arterioles are structurally like veins and venules. That is, they have thin walls and large lumens. Because resistance to blood flow is low in the pulmonary arterial system, less pressure is needed to propel blood through those vessels. Consequently, arterial pressure in the pulmonary circulation is much lower than in the systemic circulation (24/8 versus 120/80 mm Hg).

Another unusual feature of the pulmonary circulation is that the autoregulatory mechanism is the *opposite* of what is seen in most tissues: Low pulmonary oxygen levels cause vasoconstriction, and high levels promote vasodilation. While this may seem odd, it is perfectly consistent with the gas exchange role of this circulation. When the air sacs of the lungs are flooded with oxygen-rich air, the pulmonary capillaries become flushed with blood and ready to receive the oxygen load. If the air sacs are collapsed or blocked with mucus, the oxygen content in those areas is low, and blood largely bypasses those nonfunctional areas.

The Heart

Movement of blood through the smaller vessels of the coronary circulation is influenced by aortic pressure and by the pumping activity of the ventricles. When the ventricles contract and compress the coronary vessels, blood flow through the myocardium stops. As the heart relaxes, the high aortic pressure forces blood through the coronary circulation. Under normal circumstances, the myoglobin in cardiac cells stores sufficient oxygen to satisfy the cells' oxygen needs during systole. However, an abnormally rapid heartbeat seriously reduces the ability of the myocardium to receive adequate oxygen and nutrients during diastole.

Under resting conditions, blood flow through the heart is about 250 ml/min and is probably controlled by a myogenic mechanism. Consequently, blood flow remains fairly constant despite wide variations (50 to 140 mm Hg) in coronary perfusion pressure. During strenuous exercise, the coronary vessels dilate in response to local accumulation of carbon dioxide (leading to acidosis), and blood flow may increase three to four times (see Figure 19.12). Additionally, any event that decreases the oxygen content of the blood releases vasodilators that adjust the O_2 supply to the O_2 demand. This enhanced blood flow during increased heart activity is important because under resting conditions, cardiac cells use as much as 65% of the oxygen carried to them in blood. (Most other tissue cells use about 25% of the delivered oxygen.) Thus, increasing the blood flow is the only way to make sufficient additional oxygen available to a more vigorously working heart.

Blood Flow Through Capillaries and Capillary Dynamics

Blood flow through capillary networks is slow and intermittent. This phenomenon, called **vasomotion,** reflects the on/off opening and closing of precapillary sphincters in response to local autoregulatory controls.

Capillary Exchange of Respiratory Gases and Nutrients

Oxygen, carbon dioxide, most nutrients, and metabolic wastes pass between the blood and interstitial fluid by diffusion. Recall that in **diffusion,** movement always occurs along a concentration gradient—each substance moving from an area of its higher concentration to an area of its lower concentration. Hence, oxygen and nutrients pass from the blood, where their concentration is fairly high, through the interstitial fluid to the tissue cells. Carbon dioxide and metabolic wastes leave the cells, where their content is higher, and diffuse into the capillary blood. There are four different routes across capillaries for different types of molecules (Figure 19.15). ① Lipid-soluble molecules, such as respiratory gases, diffuse through the lipid bilayer of the endothelial cell plasma membranes. Small water-soluble solutes, such as amino acids and sugars, pass through ② fluid-filled intercellular capillary clefts or ③ fenestrations. ④ Some larger molecules, such as proteins, are actively transported in pinocytotic vesicles or caveolae. As mentioned earlier, capillaries differ in their "leakiness," or permeability. Liver capillaries, for instance, have large fenestrations that allow even proteins to pass freely, whereas brain capillaries are impermeable to most substances.

Fluid Movements: Bulk Flow

All the while nutrient and gas exchanges are occurring across the capillary walls by diffusion, bulk fluid flows are also going on. Fluid is forced out of the capillaries through the clefts at the arterial end of the bed, but most of it returns to the bloodstream at the venous end. While relatively unimportant to capillary exchange, bulk flow is extremely important in determining the relative fluid volumes in the bloodstream and the extracellular space. (Approximately 20 L of fluid are filtered out of the capillaries each day before being returned to the blood—almost seven times the total plasma volume!) As described next, the *direction and amount* of fluid that flows across the capillary walls reflect the balance between two dynamic and opposing forces—hydrostatic and colloid osmotic pressures (Figure 19.16).

Hydrostatic Pressures   **Hydrostatic pressure** is the force exerted by a fluid pressing against a wall. In capillaries, hydrostatic pressure is the same as *capillary blood pressure*—the pressure exerted by blood on the capillary walls. **Capillary hydrostatic pressure (HP_c)** tends to force fluids through the capillary walls (a process called *filtration*), leaving behind cells and most proteins. Because blood pressure drops as blood flows along the length of a capillary bed, HP_c is higher at the arterial end of the bed (35 mm Hg) than at the venous end (17 mm Hg). In theory, blood pressure—which forces fluid out of the capillaries—is opposed by the **interstitial fluid hydrostatic pressure (HP_{if})** acting outside the capillaries and pushing fluid in. Thus, the *net* hydrostatic pressure acting on the capillaries at any point is the difference between HP_c and HP_{if}. However, there is usually very little fluid in the interstitial space, because the lymphatic vessels constantly withdraw it. Although HP_{if} may vary from slightly negative to slightly positive, traditionally it is assumed to be zero. For simplicity, that is the value we use here. The *net effective hydrostatic pressures* at the arterial and venous ends of the capillary bed are essentially equal to HP_c (in other words, to blood pressure) at those locations. This information is summarized in Figure 19.16.

Colloid Osmotic Pressures   **Colloid osmotic pressure,** the force opposing hydrostatic pressure, is created by the presence in a fluid of large nondiffusible molecules, such as plasma proteins, that are unable to cross the capillary wall. Such molecules draw water toward themselves; that is, they encourage osmosis whenever the water concentration in their vicinity is lower than it is on the opposite side of the capillary

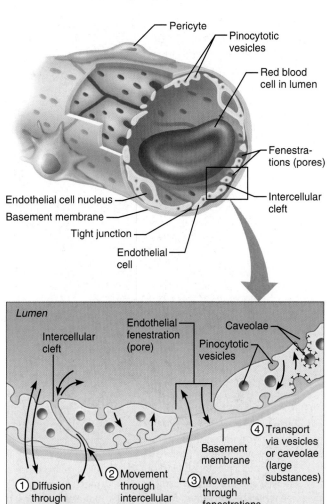

FIGURE 19.15   Capillary transport mechanisms. The four possible pathways or routes of transport across the endothelial cell wall of a fenestrated capillary. (The endothelial cell is drawn as if cut in cross section.)

membrane. The abundant plasma proteins in capillary blood (primarily albumin molecules) develop a **capillary colloid osmotic pressure (OP_c)**, also called *oncotic pressure*, of approximately 26 mm Hg. Because interstitial fluid contains few proteins, its colloid osmotic pressure (OP_{if}) is substantially lower—from 0.1 to 5 mm Hg. We use a value of 1 mm Hg for the OP_{if} in Figure 19.16. Unlike HP, OP does not vary significantly from one end of the capillary bed to the other. Thus, in our example, the *net osmotic pressure* that pulls fluid back into the capillary blood is $OP_c - OP_{if}$ = 26 mm Hg − 1 mm Hg = 25 mm Hg.

Hydrostatic-Osmotic Pressure Interactions   To determine whether there is a net gain or net loss of fluid from the blood, we have to calculate the **net filtration pressure (NFP)**, which considers all the forces acting at the capillary bed. At any point along a capillary, fluids

Q *How would fluid flows change if the OP of the interstitial fluid rose dramatically—say because of a severe bacterial infection in the surrounding tissues?*

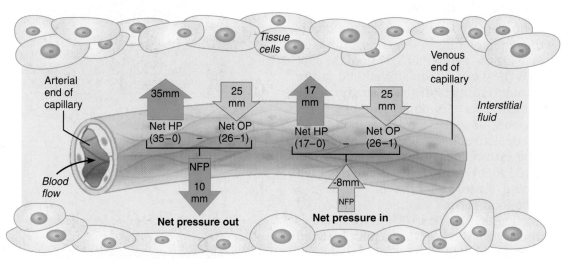

Key to pressure values:
HP$_c$ at arterial end = 35 mm Hg   HP$_{if}$ = 0 mm Hg   OP$_{if}$ = 1 mm Hg
HP$_c$ at venous end = 17 mm Hg   OP$_c$ = 26 mm Hg

FIGURE 19.16 **Fluid flows at capillaries.** The direction of fluid movement depends on the difference between net hydrostatic pressure (HP), the force that tends to push fluid out of the capillary, and net colloid osmotic pressure (OP), the force that draws fluid back into the capillary. Because HP$_{if}$ is taken to be zero, net HP (HP$_c$ − HP$_{if}$) is equal to the hydrostatic pressure of the blood (HP$_c$), which varies along the length of the capillary. Net OP (OP$_c$ − OP$_{if}$) reflects the fact that blood has a much higher content of nondiffusible solutes (proteins) than does interstitial fluid. At the arterial end of the capillary bed, net HP forcing fluid outward exceeds OP drawing water inward, resulting in a NFP (net filtration pressure) that promotes a net fluid loss from the capillary: NFP = 10 mm Hg. At the venule end of the bed, HP is overpowered by OP (NFP = −8 mm Hg), and fluid returns to the bloodstream.

will leave the capillary if net HP is greater than net OP, and fluids will enter the capillary if net OP exceeds net HP. As shown in Figure 19.16, hydrostatic forces dominate at the arterial end (all values are mm Hg):

$$NFP = (HP_c - HP_{if}) - (OP_c - OP_{if})$$
$$= (35 - 0) - (26 - 1)$$
$$= (35 - 25) = 10 \text{ mm Hg}$$

Thus, in this example, a pressure of 10 mm Hg (net excess of HP) is forcing fluid out of the capillary. At the other, venous end, osmotic forces dominate:

$$NFP = (17 - 0) - (26 - 1)$$
$$= 17 - 25 = -8 \text{ mm Hg}$$

The negative pressure value we see here indicates that the NFP (due to net excess of OP) is driving fluid *into*

the capillary bed (a process called *reabsorption*). Thus, net fluid flow is *out* of the circulation at the arterial ends of capillary beds and *into* the circulation at the venous ends. However, more fluid enters the tissue spaces than is returned to the blood, resulting in a net loss of fluid from the circulation of about 1.5 ml/min. This fluid and any leaked proteins are picked up by the lymphatic vessels and returned to the vascular system, which accounts for the relatively low levels of both fluid and proteins in the interstitial space. Were this not so, this "insignificant" fluid loss would empty your blood vessels of plasma in about 24 hours!

Circulatory Shock

Circulatory shock is any condition in which blood vessels are inadequately filled and blood cannot circulate normally. This results in inadequate blood flow to meet tissue needs. If the condition persists, cells die and organ damage follows.

The most common form of shock is **hypovolemic shock** (hi"po-vo-le'mik; *hypo* = low, deficient; *volemia* = blood volume), which results from large-scale loss of blood, as might follow acute hemorrhage,

A *Fluid that would ordinarily reenter the circulation at the venous end of the capillary bed would remain in the tissue spaces, held by the elevated OP of the interstitial fluid.*

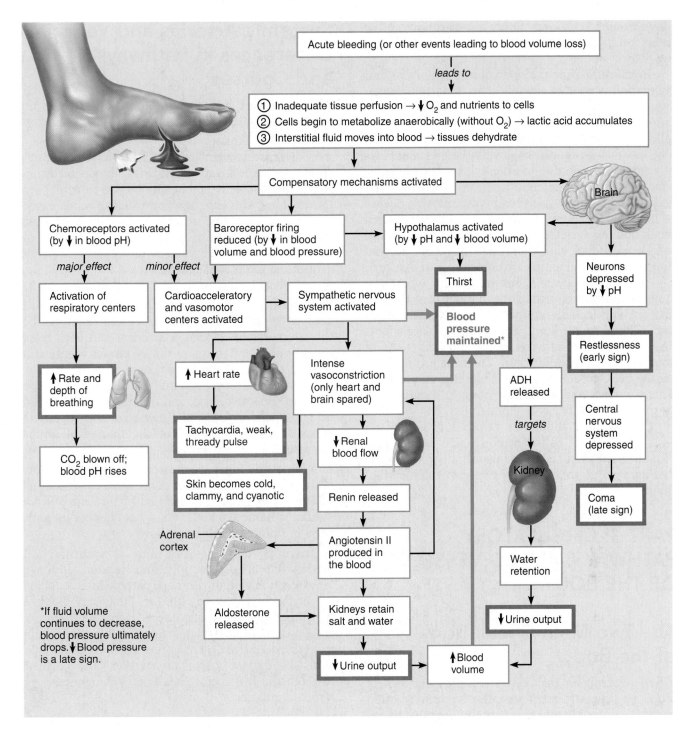

FIGURE 19.17 **Events and signs of compensated (nonprogressive) hypovolemic shock.** (Recognizable clinical signs are shown in *red-bordered boxes*.)

severe vomiting or diarrhea, or extensive burns. If blood volume drops rapidly, heart rate increases in an attempt to correct the problem. Thus, a weak, "thready" pulse is often the first sign of hypovolemic shock. Intense vasoconstriction also occurs, which shifts blood from the various blood reservoirs into the major circulatory channels and enhances venous return. Blood pressure is stable at first, but eventually drops if blood loss continues. A sharp drop in blood

pressure is a serious, and late, sign of hypovolemic shock. The key to managing hypovolemic shock is to replace fluid volume as quickly as possible.

Although you have not yet explored all of the body systems that respond to hypovolemic shock, acute bleeding is such a threat to life that it seems important to have a comprehensive flowchart of its recognizable signs and symptoms and an accounting of the body's attempt to restore homeostasis. Figure 19.17

provides such a resource. Study it in part now, and in more detail later once you have studied the remaining body systems.

In **vascular shock,** blood volume is normal, but circulation is poor as a result of an abnormal expansion of the vascular bed caused by extreme vasodilation. The huge drop in peripheral resistance that follows is revealed by rapidly falling blood pressure. The most common causes of vascular shock are loss of vasomotor tone due to anaphylaxis (anaphylactic shock), a systemic allergic reaction in which body-wide vasodilation is triggered by the massive release of histamine; failure of autonomic nervous system regulation (also referred to as *neurogenic shock*); and septicemia *(septic shock),* a severe systemic bacterial infection (bacterial toxins are notorious vasodilators).

Transient vascular shock may occur when you sunbathe for a prolonged time. The heat of the sun on your skin causes cutaneous blood vessels to dilate. Then, if you stand up abruptly, blood pools briefly (because of gravity) in the dilated vessels of your lower limbs rather than returning promptly to the heart. Consequently, your blood pressure falls. The dizziness you feel at this point is a signal that your brain is not receiving enough oxygen.

Cardiogenic shock, or pump failure, occurs when the heart is so inefficient that it cannot sustain adequate circulation. Its usual cause is myocardial damage, as might follow numerous myocardial infarcts.

PART 3: CIRCULATORY PATHWAYS: BLOOD VESSELS OF THE BODY

The Two Main Circulations of the Body

When referring to the body's complex network of blood vessels, the term **vascular system** is often used. However, the heart is actually a double pump that serves two distinct circulations, each with its own set of arteries, capillaries, and veins. The *pulmonary circulation* is the short loop that runs from the heart to the lungs and back to the heart. The *systemic circulation* routes blood through a long loop to all parts of the body before returning it to the heart. Both circuits are shown schematically in Table 19.3 on pp. 744–745.

Systemic Arteries and Veins: Differences in Pathways and Courses

Although there are many similarities between the systemic arteries and veins, there are also important differences:

1. Whereas the heart pumps all of its blood into a single systemic artery—the aorta—blood returning to the heart is delivered largely by two terminal systemic veins, the superior and inferior venae cavae. The single exception to this is the blood draining from the myocardium of the heart, which is collected by the cardiac veins and reenters the right atrium via the coronary sinus.

2. All arteries run deep and are well protected by body tissues along most of their course, but both deep and superficial veins exist. Deep veins parallel the course of the systemic arteries, and with a few exceptions, the naming of these veins is identical to that of their companion arteries. Superficial veins run just beneath the skin and are readily seen, especially in the limbs, face, and neck. Because there are no superficial arteries, the names of the superficial veins do not correspond to the names of any of the arteries.

3. Unlike the fairly clear arterial pathways, venous pathways tend to have numerous interconnections, and many veins are represented by not one but two similarly named vessels. As a result, venous pathways are more difficult to follow.

4. In most body regions, there is a similar and predictable arterial supply and venous drainage. However, the venous drainage pattern in at least two important body areas is unique. First, venous blood draining from the brain enters large *dural sinuses* rather than typical veins. Second, blood draining from the digestive organs enters a special subcirculation, the *hepatic portal circulation,* and perfuses through the liver before it reenters the general systemic circulation.

Principal Vessels of the Systemic Circulation

Except for special vessels and shunts of the fetal circulation (described in Chapter 28), the principal arteries and veins of the systemic circulation are described in Tables 19.4 through 19.13.

Notice that by convention, oxygen-rich blood is shown red, while blood that is relatively oxygen-poor is depicted blue, regardless of vessel types. A unique convention used in the schematic flowcharts (pipe diagrams) that accompany each table is that the vessels that would be closer to the viewer are shown in brighter, more intense colors than those deeper or farther from the viewer—for example, for veins, the darker blue vessels would be closer to the viewer in the body region shown.

Developmental Aspects of the Blood Vessels

The endothelial lining of blood vessels is formed by mesodermal cells, which collect in little masses called **blood islands** throughout the microscopic embryo. These then form fragile sprouting extensions that reach toward one another and toward the forming heart to lay down the rudimentary vascular tubes. Meanwhile, adjacent mesenchymal cells, stimulated by platelet-derived growth factor, surround the endothelial tubes, forming the stabilizing muscular and fibrous coats of the vessel walls. It appears that, in arteries at least, the pattern of vessel branching is orchestrated by vascular endothelial growth factor released by nearby nerves, and forming arteries snuggle closely to those nerves. As noted in Chapter 18, the heart is pumping blood through the rudimentary vascular system by the fourth week of development.

In addition to the fetal shunts that bypass the nonfunctional lungs (the *foramen ovale* and *ductus arteriosus*), other vascular modifications are found in the fetus. A special vessel, the *ductus venosus*, largely bypasses the liver. Also important are the *umbilical vein* and *arteries*, large vessels that circulate blood between the fetal circulation and the placenta where gas and nutrient exchanges occur with the mother's blood (see Chapter 28). Once the fetal circulatory pattern is laid down, few vascular changes occur until birth, when the umbilical vessels and shunts are occluded.

In contrast to congenital heart diseases, congenital vascular problems are rare, and blood vessels are remarkably trouble-free during youth. Vessel formation occurs as needed to support body growth, wound healing, and to rebuild vessels lost each month during a woman's menstrual cycle. As we age, signs of vascular disease begin to appear. In some, the venous valves weaken, and purple, snake-like varicose veins appear. In others, more insidious signs of inefficient circulation appear: tingling in the fingers and toes and cramping of muscles.

Although the degenerative process of atherosclerosis begins in youth, its consequences are rarely apparent until middle to old age, when it may precipitate a myocardial infarct or stroke. Until puberty, the blood vessels of boys and girls look alike, but from puberty to about age 45, women have strikingly less atherosclerosis than men because of the protective effects of estrogen, the beneficial effects of which are well documented. By enhancing nitric oxide production, inhibiting endothelin release, and blocking voltage-gated Ca^{2+} channels, estrogen's effect on blood vessels is to reduce resistance to blood flow. Estrogen also stimulates the liver to produce enzymes that speed up catabolism of LDLs and increase the production of HDLs, thus reducing the risk of atherosclerosis (see *A Closer Look*). Between the ages of 45 and 65, when estrogen production wanes in women, this "gap" between the sexes closes, and males and females above age 65 are equally at risk for cardiovascular disease. You might expect that giving postmenopausal women supplementary estrogen would maintain this protective effect. Surprisingly, clinical trials have shown that this is not the case.

Blood pressure changes with age. In a newborn baby, arterial pressure is about 90/55. Blood pressure rises steadily during childhood to finally reach the adult value (120/80). In old age, normal blood pressure averages 150/90, which is hypertensive in younger people. After age 40, the incidence of hypertension increases dramatically. Unlike atherosclerosis, which is increasingly important in old age, hypertension claims many youthful victims and is the single most important cause of sudden cardiovascular death in men in their early 40s and 50s.

At least some vascular disease is a product of our modern technological culture. "Blessed" with high-protein, lipid-rich diets, empty-calorie snacks, energy-saving devices, and high-stress jobs, many of us are struck down prematurely. Cardiovascular disease can be prevented somewhat by diet modifications, regular aerobic exercise, and eliminating cigarette smoking. Poor diet, lack of exercise, and smoking are probably more detrimental to your blood vessels than aging itself could ever be!

■ ■ ■

Now that we have described the structure and function of blood vessels, our survey of the cardiovascular system is complete. The pump, the plumbing, and the circulating fluid form a dynamic organ system that ceaselessly services every other organ system of the body, as summarized in *Making Connections* on pp. 768–769. However, our study of the *circulatory system* is still unfinished because we have yet to examine the lymphatic system, which acts with the cardiovascular system to ensure continuous circulation and to provide sites from which lymphocytes can police the body and provide for immunity. These are the topics of Chapter 20.

19

TABLE 19.3	Pulmonary and Systemic Circulations

Pulmonary Circulation

The pulmonary circulation (Figure 19.18a) functions only to bring blood into close contact with the alveoli (air sacs) of the lungs so that gases can be exchanged. It does not directly serve the metabolic needs of body tissues.

Oxygen-poor, dark red blood enters the pulmonary circulation as it is pumped from the right ventricle into the large **pulmonary trunk** (Figure 19.18b), which runs diagonally upward for about 8 cm and then divides abruptly to form the **right** and **left pulmonary arteries.** In the lungs, the pulmonary arteries subdivide into the **lobar arteries** (lo'bar) (three in the right lung and two in the left lung), each of which serves one lung lobe. The lobar arteries accompany the main bronchi into the lungs and then branch profusely, forming first arterioles and then the dense networks of **pulmonary capillaries** that surround and cling to the delicate air sacs. It is here that oxygen moves from the alveolar air to the blood and carbon dioxide moves from the blood to the alveolar air. As gases are exchanged and the oxygen content of the blood rises, the blood becomes bright red. The pulmonary capillary beds drain into venules, which join to form the two **pulmonary veins** exiting from each lung. The four pulmonary veins complete the circuit by unloading their precious cargo into the left atrium of the heart. Note that any vessel with the term *pulmonary* or *lobar* in its name is part of the pulmonary circulation. All others are part of the systemic circulation.

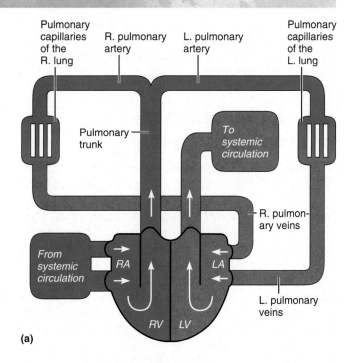

(a)

FIGURE 19.18 **Pulmonary circulation. (a)** Schematic flowchart. **(b)** Illustration. The arterial system is shown in blue to indicate that the blood carried is oxygen-poor; the venous drainage is shown in red to indicate that the blood transported is oxygen-rich.

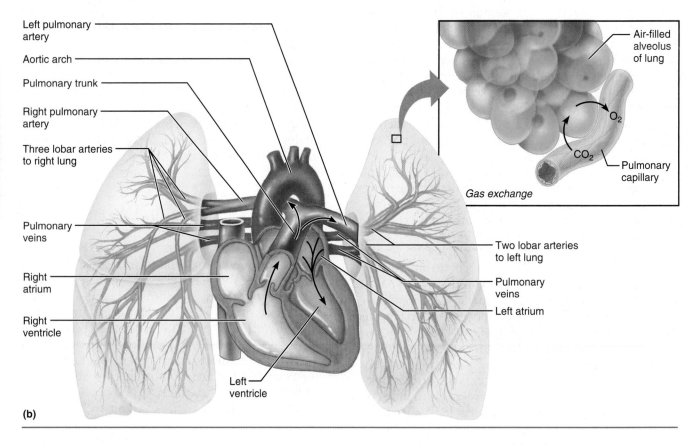

(b)

TABLE 19.3   *(continued)*

Pulmonary arteries carry oxygen-poor, carbon dioxide–rich blood, and pulmonary veins carry oxygen-rich blood.* This is opposite the situation in the systemic circulation, where arteries carry oxygen-rich blood and veins carry carbon dioxide–rich, relatively oxygen-poor blood.

Systemic Circulation

The systemic circulation provides the *functional blood supply* to all body tissues; that is, it delivers oxygen, nutrients, and other needed substances while carrying away carbon dioxide and other metabolic wastes. Freshly oxygenated blood* returning from the pulmonary circuit is pumped out of the left ventricle into the aorta (Figure 19.19). From the aorta, blood can take various routes, because essentially all systemic arteries branch from this single great vessel. The aorta arches upward from the heart and then curves and runs downward along the body midline to its terminus in the pelvis, where it splits to form the two large arteries serving the lower extremities. The branches of the aorta continue to subdivide to produce the arterioles and, finally, the capillaries that ramify through the organs. Venous blood draining from organs inferior to the diaphragm ultimately enters the inferior vena cava.[†] Except for some coronary and thoracic venous drainage (which enters the azygos system of veins), body regions above the diaphragm are drained by the superior vena cava. The venae cavae empty the carbon dioxide–laden blood into the right atrium of the heart.

Two points concerning the two major circulations must be emphasized: (1) Blood passes from systemic veins to systemic arteries only after first moving through the pulmonary circuit (Figure 19.18a), and (2) although the entire cardiac output of the right ventricle passes through the pulmonary circulation, only a small fraction of the output of the left ventricle flows through any single organ (Figure 19.19). The systemic circulation can be viewed as multiple circulatory channels functioning in parallel to distribute blood to all body organs.

As you examine the tables that follow and locate the various systemic arteries and veins in the illustrations, be aware of cues that make your memorization task easier. In many cases, the name of a vessel reflects the body region traversed (axillary, brachial, femoral, etc.), the organ served (renal, hepatic, gonadal), or the bone followed (vertebral, radial, tibial). Also, notice that arteries and veins tend to run together side by side and, in many places, they also run with nerves. Finally, be alert to the fact that the systemic vessels do not always match on the right and left sides of the body. Thus, while almost all vessels in the head and limbs are bilaterally symmetrical, some of the large, deep vessels of the trunk region are asymmetrical or unpaired.

FIGURE 19.19   Schematic flowchart showing an overview of the systemic circulation. The pulmonary circulation is shown in gray for comparison.

---

*By convention, oxygen-rich blood is shown *red* and oxygen-poor blood is shown *blue.*
[†]Venous blood from the digestive viscera passes through the hepatic portal circulation (liver and associated veins) before entering the inferior vena cava.

TABLE 19.4 **The Aorta and Major Arteries of the Systemic Circulation**

The distribution of the aorta and major arteries of the systemic circulation is diagrammed in flowchart form in Figure 19.20a and illustrated in Figure 19.20b. Fine points about the various vessels arising from the aorta are provided in Tables 19.5 through 19.8.

The **aorta** is the largest artery in the body. In adults, the aorta (a-or′tah) is approximately the size of a garden hose where it issues from the left ventricle of the heart. Its internal diameter is 2.5 cm, and its wall is about 2 mm thick. It decreases in size slightly as it runs to its terminus. The aortic valve guards the base of the aorta and prevents backflow of blood during diastole. Opposite each aortic valve cusp is an *aortic sinus,* which contains baroreceptors important in reflex regulation of blood pressure.

Different portions of the aorta are named according to shape or location. The first portion, the **ascending aorta,** runs posteriorly and to the right of the pulmonary trunk. It persists for only about 5 cm before curving to the left as the aortic arch. The only branches

of the ascending aorta are the **right** and **left coronary arteries,** which supply the myocardium. The **aortic arch,** deep to the sternum, begins and ends at the sternal angle (T$_4$ level). Its three major branches (R to L) are: (1) the **brachiocephalic trunk** (bra′ke-o-sě-fal″ik; "armhead"), which passes superiorly under the right clavicle and branches into the **right common carotid artery** (kah-rot′id) and the **right subclavian artery,** (2) the **left common carotid artery,** and (3) the **left subclavian artery.** These three vessels provide the arterial supply of the head, neck, upper limbs, and part of the thorax wall. The **thoracic,** or **descending, aorta** runs along the anterior spine from T$_5$ to T$_{12}$, sending off numerous small arteries to the thorax wall and viscera before piercing the diaphragm. As it enters the abdominal cavity, it becomes the **abdominal aorta.** This portion supplies the abdominal walls and viscera and ends at the L$_4$ level, where it splits into the **right** and **left common iliac arteries,** which supply the pelvis and lower limbs.

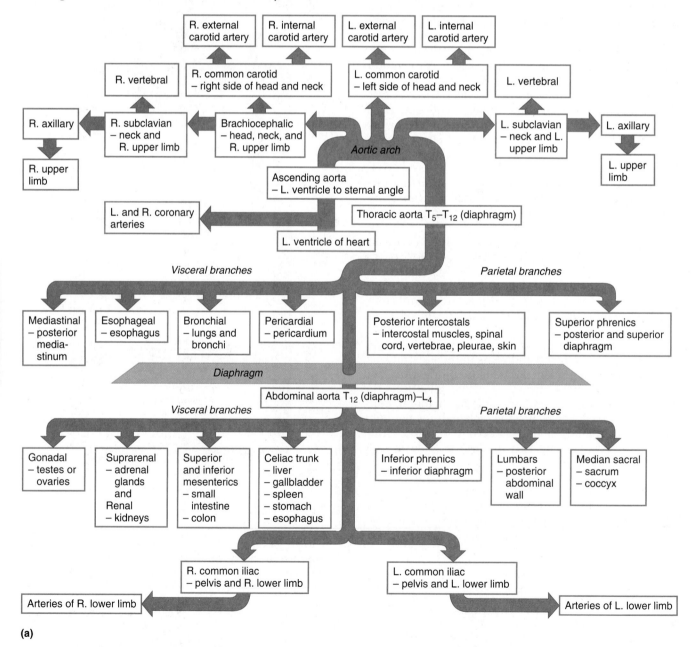

(a)

TABLE 19.4 *(continued)*

FIGURE 19.20 **Major arteries of the systemic circulation. (a)** Schematic flowchart. **(b)** Illustration, anterior view.

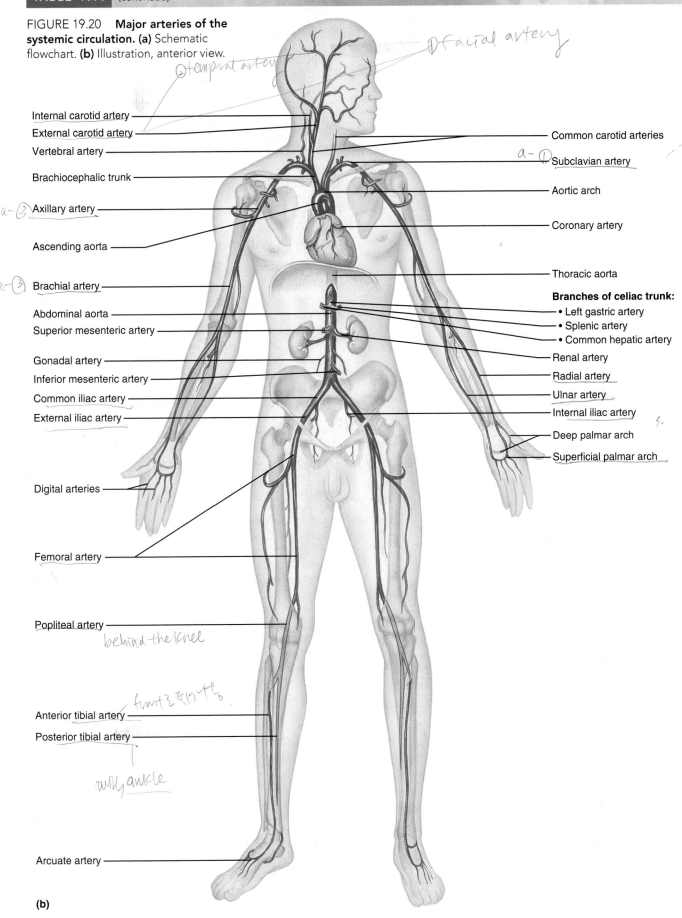

Internal carotid artery

External carotid artery

Vertebral artery

Brachiocephalic trunk

Axillary artery

Ascending aorta

Brachial artery

Abdominal aorta

Superior mesenteric artery

Gonadal artery

Inferior mesenteric artery

Common iliac artery

External iliac artery

Digital arteries

Femoral artery

Popliteal artery

Anterior tibial artery

Posterior tibial artery

Arcuate artery

Common carotid arteries

Subclavian artery

Aortic arch

Coronary artery

Thoracic aorta

Branches of celiac trunk:
• Left gastric artery
• Splenic artery
• Common hepatic artery

Renal artery

Radial artery

Ulnar artery

Internal iliac artery

Deep palmar arch

Superficial palmar arch

(b)

| TABLE 19.5 | Arteries of the Head and Neck |

Four paired arteries supply the head and neck. These are the common carotid arteries, plus three branches from each subclavian artery: the vertebral arteries, the thyrocervical trunks, and the costocervical trunks (Figure 19.21b). Of these, the common carotid arteries have the broadest distribution (Figure 19.21a).

Each common carotid divides into two major branches (the internal and external carotid arteries). At the division point, each internal carotid artery has a slight dilation, the **carotid sinus,** that contains baro-receptors that assist in reflex blood pressure control. The **carotid bodies,** chemoreceptors involved in the control of respiratory rate, are located close by. Pressing on the neck in the area of the carotid sinuses can cause unconsciousness (*carot* = stupor) because the pressure created mimics high blood pressure, eliciting vasodilation, which interferes with blood delivery to the brain.

Description and Distribution

Common carotid arteries. The origins of these two arteries differ: The right common carotid artery arises from the brachiocephalic trunk; the left is the second branch of the aortic arch. The common carotid arteries ascend through the lateral neck, and at the superior border of the larynx (the level of the "Adam's apple"), each divides into its two major branches, the *external* and *internal carotid arteries.*

The **external carotid arteries** supply most tissues of the head except for the brain and orbit. As each artery runs superiorly, it sends branches to the thyroid gland and larynx (**superior thyroid artery**), the tongue (**lingual artery**), the skin and muscles of the anterior face (**facial artery**), and the posterior scalp (**occipital artery**). Each external carotid artery terminates by splitting into a **superficial temporal artery,** which supplies the parotid salivary gland and most of the scalp, and a **maxillary artery,** which supplies the upper and lower jaws and chewing muscles, the teeth, and the nasal cavity. A clinically important branch of the maxillary artery is the *middle meningeal artery* (not illustrated). It enters the skull through the foramen spinosum and supplies the inner surface of the parietal bone, squamous region of the temporal bone, and the underlying dura mater.

The larger **internal carotid arteries** supply the orbits and more than 80% of the cerebrum. They assume a deep course and enter the skull through the carotid canals of the temporal bones. Once inside the cranium, each artery gives off one main branch, the ophthalmic artery, and then divides into the anterior and middle cerebral arteries. The **ophthalmic arteries** (of-thal'mik) supply the eyes, orbits, forehead, and nose. Each **anterior cerebral artery** supplies the medial surface of the frontal and parietal lobes of the cerebral hemisphere on its side and also anastomoses with its partner on the opposite side via a short arterial shunt called the **anterior communicating artery** (Figure 19.21d). The **middle cerebral arteries** run in the lateral sulci of their respective cerebral hemispheres and supply the lateral parts of the temporal, parietal, and frontal lobes.

Vertebral arteries. These vessels spring from the subclavian arteries at the root of the neck and ascend through foramina in the transverse processes of the cervical vertebrae to enter the skull through the foramen magnum. En route, they send branches to the vertebrae and cervical spinal cord and to some deep structures of the neck. Within the cranium, the right and left vertebral arteries join to form the **basilar artery** (bas'ĭ-lar),

(a)

19

TABLE 19.5 *(continued)*

which ascends along the anterior aspect of the brain stem, giving off branches to the cerebellum, pons, and inner ear (Figure 19.21b and d). At the pons-midbrain border, the basilar artery divides into a pair of **posterior cerebral arteries,** which supply the occipital lobes and the inferior parts of the temporal lobes.

Arterial shunts called **posterior communicating arteries** connect the posterior cerebral arteries to the middle cerebral arteries anteriorly. The two posterior and single anterior communicating arteries complete the formation of an arterial anastomosis called the **cerebral arterial circle (circle of Willis).** This structure encircles the pituitary gland and optic chiasma and unites the brain's anterior and posterior blood supplies. It also equalizes blood pressure in the two brain areas and provides alternate routes for blood to reach the brain tissue if a carotid or vertebral artery becomes occluded.

Thyrocervical and costocervical trunks. These short vessels arise from the subclavian artery just lateral to the vertebral arteries on each side (Figures 19.21b and Figure 19.22). The thyrocervical trunk mainly supplies the thyroid gland, portions of the cervical vertebrae and spinal cord, and some scapular muscles. The costocervical trunk serves deep neck and superior intercostal muscles.

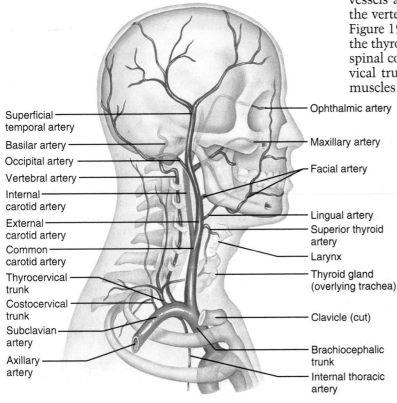

(b)

FIGURE 19.21   **Arteries of the head, neck, and brain. (a)** Schematic flowchart. **(b)** Arteries of the head and neck, right aspect. **(c)** Colorized arteriograph of the arterial supply of the brain. **(d)** Major arteries serving the brain and cerebral arterial circle (circle of Willis). In this inferior view of the brain, the right side of the cerebellum and part of the right temporal lobe have been removed to show the distribution of the middle and posterior cerebral arteries.

(c)

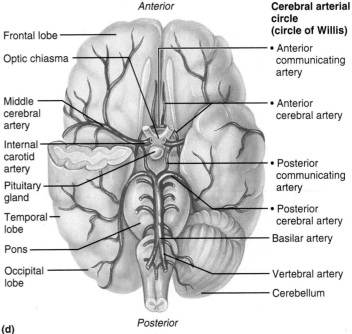

(d)

TABLE 19.6	Arteries of the Upper Limbs and Thorax

The upper limbs are supplied entirely by arteries arising from the **subclavian arteries** (Figure 19.22a). After giving off branches to the neck, each subclavian artery courses laterally between the clavicle and first rib to enter the axilla, where its name changes to axillary artery. The thorax wall is supplied by an array of vessels that arise either directly from the thoracic aorta or from branches of the subclavian arteries. Most visceral organs of the thorax receive their functional blood supply from small branches issuing from the thoracic aorta. Because these vessels are so small and tend to vary in number (except for the bronchial arteries), they are not illustrated in Figures 19.22a and b, but several of them are listed at the end of this table.

(a)

Description and Distribution

Arteries of the Upper Limb

Axillary artery. As it runs through the axilla accompanied by cords of the brachial plexus, each axillary artery gives off branches to the axilla, chest wall, and shoulder girdle. These branches include the **thoracoacromial artery** (tho"rah-ko-ah-kro'me-al), which supplies the deltoid muscle and pectoral region; the **lateral thoracic artery,** which serves the lateral chest wall and breast; the **subscapular artery** to the scapula, dorsal thorax wall, and part of the latissimus dorsi muscle; and the **anterior** and **posterior circumflex humeral arteries,** which wrap around the humeral neck and help supply the shoulder joint and the deltoid muscle. As the axillary artery emerges from the axilla, it becomes the brachial artery.

Brachial artery. The brachial artery runs down the medial aspect of the humerus and supplies the anterior flexor muscles of the arm. One major branch, the **deep artery of the arm,** serves the posterior triceps brachii muscle. As it nears the elbow, the brachial artery gives off several small branches that contribute to an anastomosis serving the elbow joint and connecting it to the arteries of the forearm. As the brachial artery crosses the anterior midline aspect of the elbow, it provides an easily palpated pulse point (brachial pulse) (see Figure 19.11). Immediately beyond the elbow, the brachial artery splits to form the radial and ulnar arteries, which more or less follow the course of similarly named bones down the length of the anterior forearm.

Radial artery. The radial artery runs from the median line of the cubital fossa to the styloid process of the radius. It supplies the lateral muscles of the forearm, the wrist, and the thumb and index finger. At the root of the thumb, the radial artery provides a convenient site for taking the radial pulse.

Ulnar artery. The ulnar artery supplies the medial aspect of the forearm, fingers 3–5, and the medial aspect of the index finger. Proximally, the ulnar artery gives off a short branch, the **common interosseous artery** (in"ter-os'e-us), which runs between the radius and ulna to serve the deep flexors and extensors of the forearm.

Palmar arches. In the palm, branches of the radial and ulnar arteries anastomose to form the **superficial** and **deep palmar arches.** The **metacarpal arteries** and the

TABLE 19.6   (continued)

Vertebral artery

Thyrocervical trunk

Costocervical trunk

Suprascapular artery

Thoracoacromial artery

Axillary artery

Subscapular artery

Posterior circumflex humeral artery

Anterior circumflex humeral artery

Brachial artery

Deep artery of arm

Common interosseous artery

Radial artery

Ulnar artery

Deep palmar arch

Superficial palmar arch

Digitals

(b)

Common carotid arteries

Right subclavian artery

Left subclavian artery

Left axillary artery

Brachiocephalic trunk

Posterior intercostal arteries

Anterior intercostal artery

Internal thoracic artery

Lateral thoracic artery

Descending aorta

FIGURE 19.22   Arteries of the right upper limb and thorax. (a) Schematic flowchart. **(b)** Illustration.

digital arteries that supply the fingers arise from these palmar arches.

Arteries of the Thorax Wall

Internal thoracic arteries. The internal thoracic arteries, also called the mammary arteries, arise from the subclavian arteries and supply blood to most of the anterior thorax wall. Each of these arteries descends lateral to the sternum and gives off **anterior intercostal arteries,** which supply the intercostal spaces anteriorly. The internal thoracic artery also sends superficial branches to the skin and mammary glands and terminates in

twiglike branches to the anterior abdominal wall and diaphragm.

Posterior intercostal arteries. The superior two pairs of posterior intercostal arteries are derived from the **costocervical trunk.** The next nine pairs issue from the thoracic aorta and course around the rib cage to anastomose anteriorly with the anterior intercostal arteries. Inferior to the 12th rib, a pair of **subcostal arteries** emerges from the thoracic aorta (not illustrated). The posterior intercostal arteries supply the posterior intercostal spaces, deep muscles of the back, vertebrae, and spinal cord. Together, the posterior and anterior intercostal arteries supply the intercostal muscles.

Superior phrenic arteries. One or more paired superior phrenic arteries serve the posterior superior aspect of the diaphragm surface.

Arteries of the Thoracic Viscera

Pericardial arteries. Several tiny branches supply the posterior pericardium.

Bronchial arteries. Two left and one right bronchial arteries supply systemic (oxygen-rich) blood to the lungs, bronchi, and pleurae.

Esophageal arteries. Four to five esophageal arteries supply the esophagus.

Mediastinal arteries. Many small mediastinal arteries serve the posterior mediastinum.

19

TABLE 19.7 Arteries of the Abdomen

The arterial supply to the abdominal organs arises from the abdominal aorta (Figure 19.23a). Under resting conditions, about half of the entire arterial flow is found in these vessels. Except for the celiac trunk, the superior and inferior mesenteric arteries, and the median sacral artery, all are paired vessels. These arteries supply the abdominal wall, diaphragm, and visceral organs of the abdominopelvic cavity. The branches are given here in order of their issue.

FIGURE 19.23 **Arteries of the abdomen. (a)** Schematic flowchart.

TABLE 19.7   *(continued)*

Description and Distribution

Inferior phrenic arteries.   The inferior phrenics emerge from the aorta at T_{12}, just inferior to the diaphragm. They serve the inferior diaphragm surface.

Celiac trunk.   This very large unpaired branch of the abdominal aorta divides almost immediately into three branches: the common hepatic, splenic, and left gastric arteries (Figure 19.23b). The **common hepatic artery** (hĕ-pat'ik) gives off branches to the stomach, duodenum, and pancreas. Where the **gastroduodenal artery** branches off, it becomes the **hepatic artery proper,** which splits into right and left branches that serve the

liver. As the **splenic artery** (splen'ik) passes deep to the stomach, it sends branches to the pancreas and stomach and terminates in branches to the spleen. The **left gastric artery** (*gaster* = stomach) supplies part of the stomach and the inferior esophagus. The **right** and **left gastroepiploic arteries** (gas"tro-ep"ĭ-plo'ik), branches of the gastroduodenal and splenic arteries, respectively, serve the greater curvature of the stomach. A **right gastric artery,** which supplies the stomach's lesser curvature, may arise from the common hepatic artery or from the hepatic artery proper.

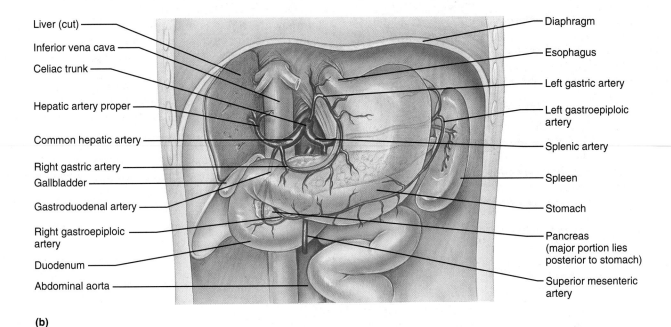

(b)

FIGURE 19.23 *(continued)*   **Arteries of the abdomen. (b)** The celiac trunk and its major branches. To make these arteries visible, the left half of the liver has been removed.

19

TABLE 19.7   **Arteries of the Abdomen** *(continued)*

Superior mesenteric artery (mes-en-ter′ik).   This large, unpaired artery arises from the abdominal aorta at the L_1 level immediately below the celiac trunk (Figure 19.23d). It runs deep to the pancreas and then enters the mesentery, where its numerous anastomosing branches serve virtually all of the small intestine via the **intestinal arteries,** and most of the large intestine—the appendix, cecum, ascending colon (via the **ileocolic artery**), and part of the transverse colon (via the **right** and **middle colic arteries**).

Suprarenal arteries (soo″prah-re′nal).   The **middle suprarenal arteries** flank the origin of the superior mesenteric artery as they emerge from the abdominal aorta (Figure 19.23c). They supply blood to the adrenal (suprarenal) glands overlying the kidneys. The adrenal glands also receive two sets of branches not illustrated: *superior suprarenal* branches from the nearby inferior phrenic arteries, and *inferior suprarenal* branches from the nearby renal arteries.

Renal arteries.   The short but wide renal arteries, right and left, issue from the lateral surfaces of the aorta slightly below the superior mesenteric artery (between L_1 and L_2). Each serves the kidney on its side.

Gonadal arteries (go-nă′dul).   The paired gonadal arteries are called the **testicular arteries** in males and the **ovarian arteries** in females. The ovarian arteries extend into the pelvis to serve the ovaries and part of the uterine tubes. The much longer testicular arteries descend through the pelvis and inguinal canal to enter the scrotal sac, where they serve the testes.

Inferior mesenteric artery.   This final major branch of the abdominal aorta is unpaired and arises from the anterior aortic surface at the L_3 level. It serves the distal part of the large intestine—from the midpart of the transverse colon to the midrectum—via its **left colic, sigmoidal,** and **superior rectal branches** (Figure 19.23d). Looping anastomoses between the superior and inferior mesenteric arteries help ensure that blood will continue to reach the digestive viscera in cases of trauma to one of these abdominal arteries.

Lumbar arteries.   Four pairs of lumbar arteries arise from the posterolateral surface of the aorta in the lumbar region. These segmental arteries supply the posterior abdominal wall.

Median sacral artery.   The unpaired median sacral artery issues from the posterior surface of the abdominal aorta at its terminus. This tiny artery supplies the sacrum and coccyx.

Common iliac arteries.   At the L_4 level, the aorta splits into the right and left common iliac arteries, which supply blood to the lower abdominal wall, pelvic organs, and lower limbs (Figure 19.23c).

TABLE 19.7   *(continued)*

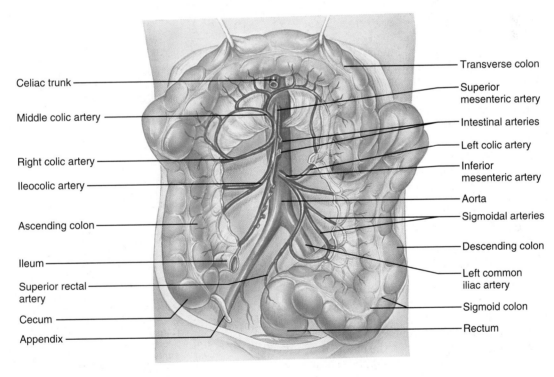

(c)

(d)

FIGURE 19.23 *(continued)*   **Arteries of the abdomen. (c)** Major branches of the abdominal aorta. **(d)** Distribution of the superior and inferior mesenteric arteries. (The transverse colon has been reflected superiorly to provide a better view of these arteries.)

19

TABLE 19.8 Arteries of the Pelvis and Lower Limbs

At the level of the sacroiliac joints, the **common iliac arteries** divide into two major branches, the internal and external iliac arteries (Figure 19.24a). The internal iliacs distribute blood mainly to the pelvic region. The external iliacs serve the lower limbs; they also send some branches to the abdominal wall.

Description and Distribution

Internal iliac arteries. These paired arteries run into the pelvis and distribute blood to the pelvic walls and viscera (bladder, rectum, uterus, and vagina in the female and prostate gland and ductus deferens in the male). Additionally they serve the gluteal muscles via the **superior** and **inferior gluteal arteries,** adductor muscles of the medial thigh via the **obturator artery,** and external genitalia and perineum via the **internal pudendal artery** (not illustrated).

External iliac arteries. These arteries supply the lower limbs (Figure 19.24b). As they course through the pelvis, they give off branches to the anterior abdominal wall. After passing under the inguinal ligaments to enter the thigh, they become the femoral arteries.

Femoral arteries. As each of these arteries passes down the anteromedial thigh, it gives off several branches to the thigh muscles. The largest of the deep branches is the **deep artery of the thigh** (also called the **deep femoral artery**), which is the main supply to the thigh muscles (hamstrings, quadriceps, and adductors). Proximal branches of the deep femoral artery, the **lateral** and **medial circumflex femoral arteries,** encircle the neck of the femur. The medial circumflex artery supplies the head and neck of the femur. A long descending branch of the lateral circumflex artery supplies the vastus lateralis muscle. Near the knee the femoral artery passes posteriorly and through a gap in the adductor magnus muscle, the *adductor hiatus,* to enter the popliteal fossa, where its name changes to popliteal artery.

Popliteal artery. This posterior vessel contributes to an arterial anastomosis that supplies the knee region and then splits into the anterior and posterior tibial arteries of the leg.

Anterior tibial artery. The anterior tibial artery runs through the anterior compartment of the leg, supplying the extensor muscles along the way. At the ankle, it becomes the **dorsalis pedis artery,** which supplies the ankle and dorsum of the foot, and gives off a branch, the **arcuate artery,** which issues the **metatarsal arteries** to the metatarsus of the foot. The superficial dorsalis pedis ends by penetrating into the sole where it forms the medial part of the **plantar arch.** The dorsalis pedis artery provides a clinically important pulse point, the pedal pulse. If the pedal pulse is easily felt, it is fairly certain that the blood supply to the leg is good.

Posterior tibial artery. This large artery courses through the posteromedial part of the leg and supplies the flexor muscles. Proximally, it gives off a large branch, the **fibular (peroneal) artery,** which supplies the lateral

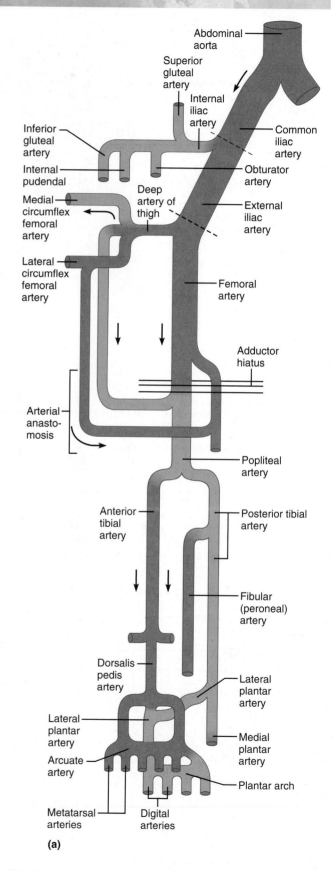

FIGURE 19.24 Arteries of the right pelvis and lower limb. (a) Schematic flowchart.

TABLE 19.8   *(continued)*

Common iliac artery

Internal iliac artery

Superior gluteal artery

External iliac artery

Deep artery of thigh

Lateral circumflex
femoral artery

Medial circumflex
femoral artery

Obturator artery

Femoral artery

Adductor hiatus

Popliteal artery

Anterior tibial artery

Posterior tibial artery

Fibular artery

Dorsalis pedis artery

Arcuate artery

Metatarsal arteries

(b)

fibularis (peroneal) muscles of the leg. At the ankle, the posterior tibial artery divides into **lateral** and **medial plantar arteries** that serve the plantar surface of the foot. The lateral plantar artery forms the lateral end of the plantar arch. The **digital arteries** serving the toes arise from the plantar arch formed by the lateral plantar artery.

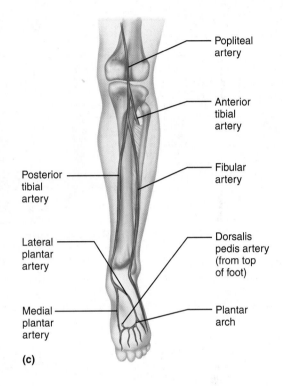

Popliteal
artery

Anterior
tibial
artery

Fibular
artery

Posterior
tibial
artery

Dorsalis
pedis artery
(from top
of foot)

Lateral
plantar
artery

Medial
plantar
artery

Plantar
arch

(c)

FIGURE 19.24 *(continued)*   **Arteries of the right pelvis and lower limb.**
(b) Illustration, anterior view. **(c)** Posterior view of the leg and foot.

19

In our survey of the systemic veins, the major tributaries (branches) of the venae cavae are noted first in Figure 19.25, followed by a description in Tables 19.10 through 19.13 of the venous pattern of the various body regions. Because veins run toward the heart, the most distal veins are named first and those closest to the heart last. Because deep veins generally drain the same areas served by their companion arteries, they are not described in detail.

Description and Areas Drained

Superior vena cava. This great vein receives systemic blood draining from all areas superior to the diaphragm, except the heart wall. It is formed by the union of the **right** and **left brachiocephalic veins** and empties into the right atrium (Figure 19.25b). Notice that there are two brachiocephalic veins, but only one brachiocephalic artery (trunk). Each brachiocephalic vein is formed by the joining of the **internal jugular** and **subclavian veins** on its side. In most of the flowcharts that follow, only the vessels draining blood from the right side of the body are followed (except for the azygos circulation of the thorax).

Inferior vena cava. The widest blood vessel in the body, this vein returns blood to the heart from all body regions below the diaphragm. The abdominal aorta lies directly to its left. The distal end of the inferior vena cava is formed by the junction of the paired **common iliac veins** at L_5. From this point, it courses superiorly along the anterior aspect of the spine, receiving venous blood draining from the abdominal walls, gonads, and kidneys. Immediately above the diaphragm, the inferior vena cava ends as it enters the inferior aspect of the right atrium.

FIGURE 19.25 **Major veins of the systemic circulation. (a)** Schematic flowchart.

19

(a)

TABLE 19.9 *(continued)*

FIGURE 19.25 *(continued)* **Major veins of the systemic circulation. (b)** Illustration, anterior view. The vessels of the pulmonary circulation are not illustrated, accounting for the incomplete appearance of the circulation from the heart.

Dural sinuses

External jugular vein
Vertebral vein
Internal jugular vein

Superior vena cava
Axillary vein

Great cardiac vein

Hepatic veins

Hepatic portal vein
Superior mesenteric vein
Inferior vena cava
Ulnar vein
Radial vein
Common iliac vein
External iliac vein
Internal iliac vein

Digital veins

Femoral vein
Great saphenous vein

Popliteal vein

Posterior tibial vein

Anterior tibial vein

Fibular vein

Dorsal venous arch

Subclavian vein

Right and left brachiocephalic veins
Cephalic vein
Brachial vein

Basilic vein

Splenic vein
Median cubital vein
Renal vein
Inferior mesenteric vein

Dorsal digital veins

(b)

19

TABLE 19.10 Veins of the Head and Neck

Most blood draining from the head and neck is collected by three pairs of veins: the external jugular veins, which empty into the subclavians, the internal jugular veins, and the vertebral veins, which drain into the brachiocephalic vein (see Figure 19.26a). Although most extracranial veins have the same names as the extracranial arteries, their courses and interconnections differ substantially.

Most veins of the brain drain into the **dural sinuses,** an interconnected series of enlarged chambers located between the dura mater layers. The **superior** and **inferior sagittal sinuses** are in the falx cerebri, which dips down between the cerebral hemispheres. The inferior sagittal sinus drains into the **straight sinus** posteriorly (Figure 19.26a and c). The superior sagittal and straight sinuses then empty into the **transverse sinuses,** which run in shallow grooves on the internal surface of the occipital bone. These drain into the S-shaped **sigmoid sinuses,** which become the *internal jugular veins* as they leave the skull through the jugular foramen. The **cavernous sinuses,** which

flank the sphenoid body, receive venous blood from the **ophthalmic veins** of the orbits and the facial veins, which drain the nose and upper lip area. The internal carotid artery and cranial nerves III, IV, VI, and part of V, all run *through* the cavernous sinus on their way to the orbit and face.

Description and Area Drained

External jugular veins. The right and left external jugular veins drain superficial scalp and face structures served by the external carotid arteries. However, their tributaries anastomose frequently, and some of the superficial drainage from these regions enters the internal jugular veins as well. As the external jugular veins descend through the lateral neck, they pass obliquely over the sternocleidomastoid muscles and then empty into the subclavian veins.

Vertebral veins. Unlike the vertebral arteries, the vertebral veins do not serve much of the brain. Instead they drain the cervical vertebrae, the spinal cord, and some small neck muscles. They run inferiorly through the transverse foramina of the cervical vertebrae and join the brachiocephalic veins at the root of the neck.

Internal jugular veins. The paired internal jugular veins, which receive the bulk of blood draining from the brain, are the largest of the paired veins draining the head and neck. They arise from the dural venous sinuses, exit the skull via the *jugular foramina,* and then descend through the neck alongside the internal carotid arteries. As they move inferiorly, they receive blood from some of the deep veins of the face and neck—branches of the **facial** and **superficial temporal veins** (Figure 19.26b). At the base of the neck, each internal jugular vein joins the subclavian vein on its own side to form a brachiocephalic vein. As already noted, the two brachiocephalic veins unite to form the superior vena cava.

(a)

FIGURE 19.26 **Venous drainage of the head, neck, and brain. (a)** Schematic flowchart.

TABLE 19.10 *(continued)*

Ophthalmic vein

Superficial temporal vein

Facial vein

Occipital vein

Posterior auricular vein

External jugular vein

Vertebral vein

Internal jugular vein

Superior and middle thyroid veins

Brachiocephalic vein

Subclavian vein

Superior vena cava

(b)

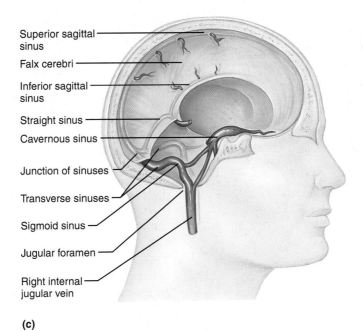

Superior sagittal sinus

Falx cerebri

Inferior sagittal sinus

Straight sinus

Cavernous sinus

Junction of sinuses

Transverse sinuses

Sigmoid sinus

Jugular foramen

Right internal jugular vein

(c)

FIGURE 19.26 *(continued)* **Venous drainage of the head, neck, and brain.**
(b) Veins of the head and neck, right superficial aspect. **(c)** Dural sinuses of the brain, right aspect.

19

TABLE 19.11 **Veins of the Upper Limbs and Thorax**

The deep veins of the upper limbs follow the paths of their companion arteries and have the same names (Figure 19.27a). However, except for the largest, most are paired veins that flank their artery. The superficial veins of the upper limbs are larger than the deep veins and are easily seen just beneath the skin. The median cubital vein, crossing the anterior aspect of the elbow, is commonly used to obtain blood samples or administer intravenous medications.

Blood draining from the mammary glands and the first two to three intercostal spaces enters the **brachiocephalic veins.** However, the vast majority of thoracic tissues and the thorax wall are drained by a complex network of veins called the **azygos system** (az'ĭ-gos). The branching nature of the azygos system provides a collateral circulation for draining the abdominal wall and other areas served by the inferior vena cava, and there are numerous anastomoses between the azygos system and the inferior vena cava.

Description and Areas Drained

Deep Veins of the Upper Limbs

The most distal deep veins of the upper limb are the radial and ulnar veins. The deep and superficial **palmar venous arches** of the hand empty into the **radial** and **ulnar veins** of the forearm, which then unite to form the **brachial vein** of the arm. As the brachial vein enters the axilla, it becomes the **axillary vein,** which becomes the **subclavian vein** at the level of the first rib.

Superficial Veins of the Upper Limbs

The superficial venous system begins with the **dorsal venous arch** (not illustrated), a plexus of superficial veins in the dorsum of the hand. In the distal forearm, this plexus drains into three major superficial veins—the cephalic and basilic veins and the median antebrachial vein of the forearm—which anastomose frequently as they course upward (see Figure 19.27b). The **cephalic vein** bends around the radius as it travels superiorly and then continues up the lateral superficial aspect of the arm to the shoulder, where it runs in the groove between the deltoid and pectoralis muscles to join the axillary vein. The **basilic vein** courses along the posteromedial aspect of the forearm, crosses the elbow, and then takes a deep course. In the axilla, it joins the brachial vein, forming the axillary vein. At the anterior aspect of the elbow, the **median cubital vein** connects the basilic and cephalic veins. The **median antebrachial vein** of the forearm lies between the radial and ulnar veins in the forearm and terminates (variably) at the elbow by entering either the basilic or the cephalic vein.

The Azygos System

The azygos system consists of the following vessels which flank the vertebral column laterally:

Azygos vein. Located against the right side of the vertebral column, the **azygos vein** (*azygos* = unpaired) originates in the abdomen, from the **right ascending lumbar vein** that drains most of the right abdominal cavity wall and from the **right posterior intercostal veins** (except the first) that drain the chest muscles. At the T_4 level, it arches over the great vessels that run to the right lung and empties into the superior vena cava.

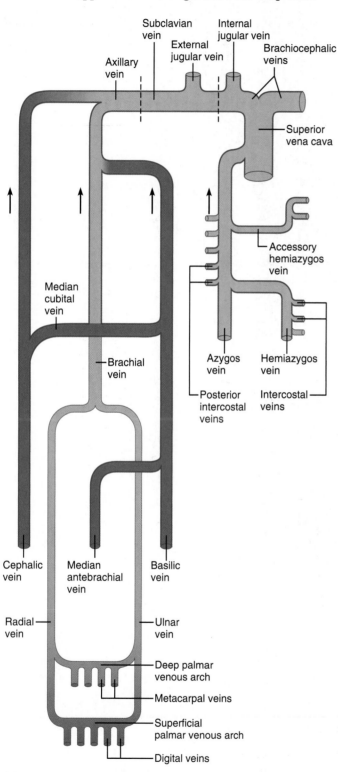

Subclavian vein
External jugular vein
Internal jugular vein
Brachiocephalic veins
Axillary vein
Superior vena cava
Accessory hemiazygos vein
Median cubital vein
Brachial vein
Azygos vein
Hemiazygos vein
Posterior intercostal veins
Intercostal veins
Cephalic vein
Median antebrachial vein
Basilic vein
Radial vein
Ulnar vein
Deep palmar venous arch
Metacarpal veins
Superficial palmar venous arch
Digital veins

(a)

TABLE 19.11   *(continued)*

Hemiazygos vein (hĕ′me-a-zi′gus; "half the azygos"). This vessel ascends on the left side of the vertebral column. Its origin, from the **left ascending lumbar vein** and the lower (9th–11th) **posterior intercostal veins,** mirrors that of the inferior portion of the azygos vein on the right. About midthorax, the hemiazygos vein passes in front of the vertebral column and joins the azygos vein.

Accessory hemiazygos vein.   The accessory hemiazygos completes the venous drainage of the left (middle) thorax and can be thought of as a superior continuation of the hemiazygos vein. It receives blood from the 4th–8th posterior intercostal veins and then crosses to the right to empty into the azygos vein. Like the azygos, it receives venous blood from the lungs *(bronchial veins).*

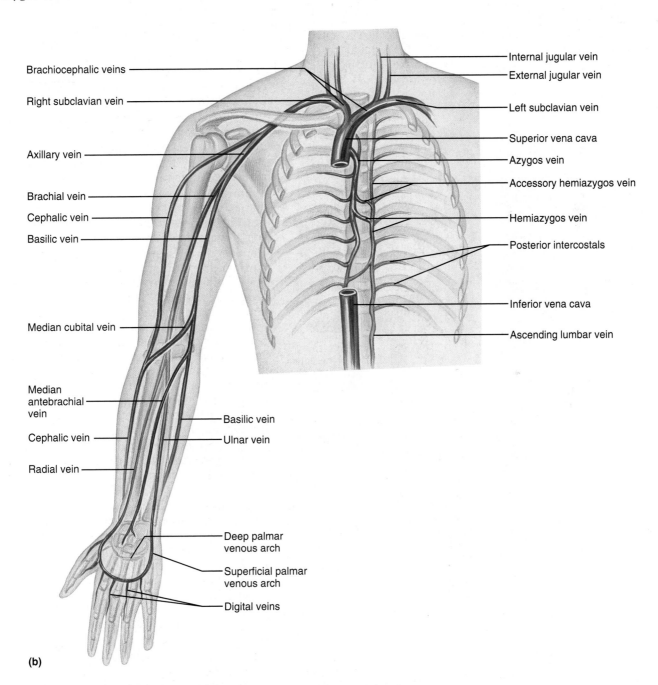

(b)

FIGURE 19.27   **Veins of the right upper limb and shoulder. (a)** Schematic flowchart. **(b)** Illustration. For clarity, the abundant branching and anastomoses of these vessels are not shown.

19

TABLE 19.12 **Veins of the Abdomen**

Blood draining from the abdominopelvic viscera and abdominal walls is returned to the heart by the **inferior vena cava** (Figure 19.28a). Most of its venous tributaries have names that correspond to the arteries serving the abdominal organs.

Veins draining the digestive viscera empty into a common vessel, the *hepatic portal vein,* which transports this venous blood into the liver before it is allowed to enter the major systemic circulation via the hepatic veins (Figure 19.28b). Such a venous system—veins to capillaries (or sinusoids) to veins—is called a *portal system* and always serves very specific regional tissue needs. The **hepatic portal system** carries nutri-

ent-rich blood from the digestive organs to the liver. As the blood percolates slowly through the liver sinusoids, hepatocytes remove the nutrients they need for their various metabolic functions, and phagocytic cells lining the sinusoids rid the blood of bacteria and other foreign matter that has penetrated the digestive mucosa. The veins of the abdomen are listed in inferior to superior order.

Description and Areas Drained

Lumbar veins. Several pairs of lumbar veins drain the posterior abdominal wall. They empty both directly into the inferior vena cava and into the ascending lumbar veins of the azygos system of the thorax.

Gonadal (testicular or ovarian) veins. The right gonadal vein drains the ovary or testis on the right side of the body and empties into the inferior vena cava. The left member drains into the left renal vein superiorly.

Renal veins. The right and left renal veins drain the kidneys.

Suprarenal veins. The right suprarenal vein drains the adrenal gland on the right and empties into the inferior vena cava. The left suprarenal vein drains into the left renal vein.

Hepatic portal system. Like all portal systems, the hepatic portal system is a series of vessels in which two separate capillary beds lie between the arterial supply and the final venous drainage. In this case, the first capillary beds are in the stomach and intestines and drain into tributaries of the **hepatic portal vein,** which brings them to the second capillary bed in the liver. The short hepatic portal vein begins at the L_2 level. Numerous tributaries from the stomach and pancreas contribute to the hepatic portal system (Figure 19.28c), but the major vessels are as follows:

- **Superior mesenteric vein:** Drains the entire small intestine, part of the large intestine (ascending and transverse regions), and stomach.
- **Splenic vein:** Collects blood from the spleen, parts of the stomach and pancreas, and then joins the superior mesenteric vein to form the hepatic portal vein.
- **Inferior mesenteric vein:** Drains the distal portions of the large intestine and rectum and joins the splenic vein just before that vessel unites with the superior mesenteric vein to form the hepatic portal vein.

Hepatic veins. The right and left hepatic veins carry venous blood from the liver to the inferior vena cava.

Cystic veins. The cystic veins drain the gallbladder and join the hepatic veins.

Inferior phrenic veins. The inferior phrenic veins drain the inferior surface of the diaphragm.

(a)

TABLE 19.12   *(continued)*

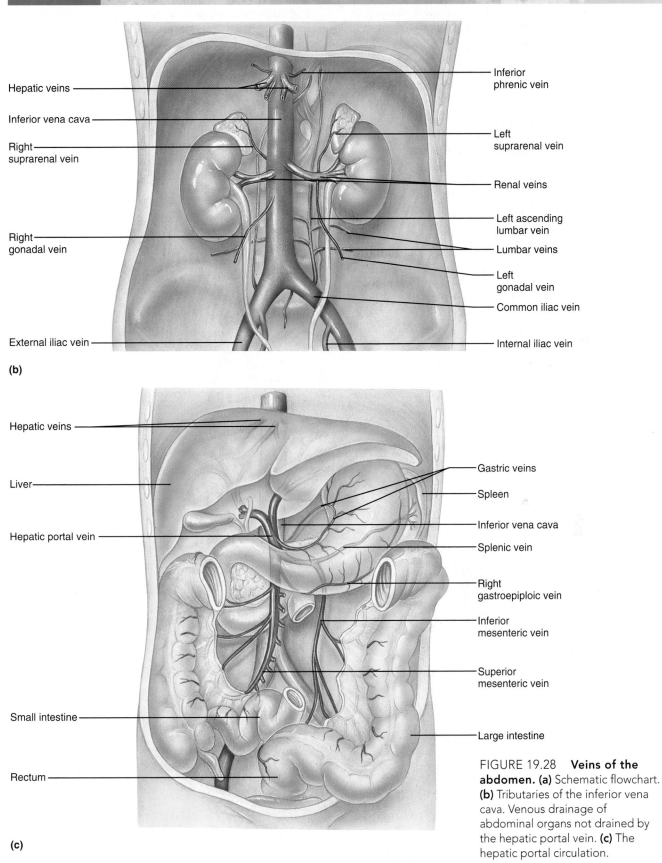

Hepatic veins

Inferior vena cava

Right suprarenal vein

Right gonadal vein

External iliac vein

Inferior phrenic vein

Left suprarenal vein

Renal veins

Left ascending lumbar vein

Lumbar veins

Left gonadal vein

Common iliac vein

Internal iliac vein

(b)

Hepatic veins

Liver

Hepatic portal vein

Small intestine

Rectum

Gastric veins

Spleen

Inferior vena cava

Splenic vein

Right gastroepiploic vein

Inferior mesenteric vein

Superior mesenteric vein

Large intestine

(c)

FIGURE 19.28   **Veins of the abdomen. (a)** Schematic flowchart. **(b)** Tributaries of the inferior vena cava. Venous drainage of abdominal organs not drained by the hepatic portal vein. **(c)** The hepatic portal circulation.

19

TABLE 19.13   Veins of the Pelvis and Lower Limbs

As in the upper limbs, most deep veins of the lower limbs have the same names as the arteries they accompany and many are double. The two superficial saphenous veins (great and small) are poorly supported by surrounding tissues, and are common sites of varicosities. The great saphenous (*saphenous* = obvious) vein is frequently excised and used as a coronary bypass vessel.

Description and Areas Drained

Deep veins. After being formed by the union of the **medial** and **lateral plantar veins**, the **posterior tibial vein** ascends deep in the calf muscle (Figure 19.29) and receives the **fibular (peroneal) vein**. The **anterior tibial vein,** which is the superior continuation of the **dorsalis pedis vein** of the foot, unites at the knee with the posterior tibial vein to form the **popliteal vein,** which crosses the back of the knee. As the popliteal vein emerges from the knee, it becomes the **femoral vein,** which drains the deep structures of the thigh. The femoral vein becomes the **external iliac vein** as it enters the pelvis. In the pelvis, the external iliac vein unites with the **internal iliac vein** to form the **common iliac vein.** The distribution of the internal iliac veins parallels that of the internal iliac arteries.

Superficial veins. The **great** and **small saphenous veins** (sah-fe′nus) issue from the **dorsal venous arch** of the foot (Figure 19.29b and c). These veins anastomose frequently with each other and with the deep veins along their course. The great saphenous vein is the longest vein in the body. It travels superiorly along the medial aspect of the leg to the thigh, where it empties into the femoral vein just distal to the inguinal ligament. The small saphenous vein runs along the lateral aspect of the foot and then through the deep fascia of the calf muscles, which it drains. At the knee, it empties into the popliteal vein.

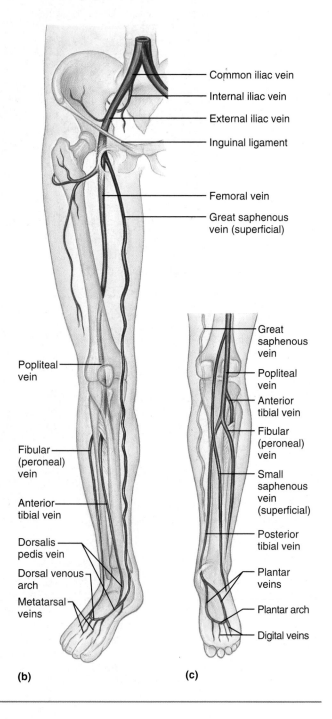

FIGURE 19.29   Veins of the right lower limb.
(a) Schematic flowchart of anterior and posterior vessels.
(b) Anterior view of the lower limb. **(c)** Posterior view of the leg and foot.

19

Related Clinical Terms

Aneurysm (an'u-rizm; *aneurysm* = a widening) A balloon-like outpocketing of an artery wall that places the artery at risk for rupture; most often reflects gradual weakening of the artery by chronic hypertension or arteriosclerosis. The most common sites of aneurysm formation are the abdominal aorta and arteries feeding the brain and kidneys.

Angiogram (an'je-o-gram"; *angio* = a vessel; *gram* = writing) Diagnostic technique involving the infusion of a radiopaque substance into the circulation for X ray examination of specific blood vessels; the major technique for diagnosing coronary artery occlusion and risk of a heart attack.

Diuretic (*diure* = urinate) A chemical that promotes urine formation, thus reducing blood volume; diuretic drugs are frequently prescribed to manage hypertension.

Phlebitis (flĕ-bi'tis; *phleb* = vein; *itis* = inflammation) Inflammation of a vein accompanied by painful throbbing and redness of the skin over the inflamed vessel; most often caused by bacterial infection or local physical trauma.

Phlebotomy (flĕ-bot'o-me; *tomy* = cut) A venous incision made for the purpose of withdrawing blood or bloodletting.

Sclerotherapy Procedure used for removing varicose or spider veins; tiny needles are used to inject hardening agents into the abnormal vein; the vein scars, closes down, and is absorbed by the body.

Thrombophlebitis Condition of undesirable intravascular clotting initiated by a roughening of a venous lining; often follows severe episodes of phlebitis. An ever-present danger is that the clot may detach and form an embolus.

Chapter Summary

Media study tools that could provide you additional help in reviewing specific key topics of Chapter 19 are referenced below.
IP *= InterActive Physiology*

PART 1: OVERVIEW OF BLOOD VESSEL STRUCTURE AND FUNCTION

1. Blood is transported throughout the body via a continuous system of blood vessels. Arteries transport blood away from the heart; veins carry blood back to the heart. Capillaries carry blood to tissue cells and are exchange sites.

Structure of Blood Vessel Walls   (pp. 714–716)

1. All blood vessels except capillaries have three layers: tunica intima, tunica media, and tunica externa. Capillary walls are composed of the tunica intima only.

Arterial System   (pp. 716–719)

1. Elastic (conducting) arteries are the large arteries close to the heart that expand during systole, acting as pressure reservoirs, and then recoil during diastole to keep blood moving. Muscular (distributing) arteries carry blood to specific organs; they are less stretchy and more active in vasoconstriction. Arterioles regulate blood flow into capillary beds.

2. Arteriosclerosis is a degenerative vascular disease that decreases the elasticity of arteries. Atherosclerosis is the formation of fatty subendothelial lesions.

Capillaries   (pp. 720–722)

1. Capillaries are microscopic vessels with very thin walls. Most exhibit clefts, which aid in the exchange between the blood and interstitial fluid.

2. The most permeable capillaries are sinusoids (wide, tortuous channels). Fenestrated capillaries with pores are next most permeable. Least permeable are continuous capillaries, which lack pores.

3. Vascular shunts (metarteriole–thoroughfare channels) connect the terminal arteriole and venule at opposite ends of a capillary bed. Most true capillaries arise from and rejoin the shunt channels. The amount of blood flowing into the true capillaries is regulated by precapillary sphincters.

Venous System   (pp. 722–723)

1. Veins have comparatively larger lumens than arteries, and a system of valves prevents backflow of blood.

2. Normally most veins are only partially filled; thus, they can serve as blood reservoirs.

Vascular Anastomoses   (p. 723)

1. The joining together of arteries to provide alternate channels for blood to reach the same organ is called an anastomosis. Vascular anastomoses also form between veins and between arterioles and venules.

IP Cardiovascular System; Topic: Anatomy Review: Blood Vessel Structure and Function, pp. 1–28.

PART 2: PHYSIOLOGY OF CIRCULATION

Introduction to Blood Flow, Blood Pressure, and Resistance   (pp. 723–724)

1. Blood flow is the amount of blood flowing through a vessel, an organ, or the entire circulation in a given period of time. Blood pressure is the force per unit area exerted on a vessel wall by the contained blood. Resistance is opposition to blood flow; blood viscosity and blood vessel length and diameter contribute to resistance.

2. Blood flow is directly proportional to blood pressure and inversely proportional to resistance.

IP Cardiovascular System; Topic: Factors that Affect Blood Pressure, pp. 1–15.

Systemic Blood Pressure   (pp. 724–726)

1. Systemic blood pressure is highest in the aorta and lowest in the venae cavae. The steepest drop in BP occurs in the arterioles, where resistance is greatest.

2. Arterial BP depends on compliance of the elastic arteries and on how much blood is forced into them. Arterial blood pressure is pulsatile, and peaks during systole; this is measured as systolic pressure. During diastole, as blood is forced distally in the circulation by the rebound of elastic arteries, arterial BP drops to its lowest value, called the diastolic pressure.

19

MAKING CONNECTIONS

SYSTEM CONNECTIONS: Homeostatic Interrelationships Between the Cardiovascular System and Other Body Systems

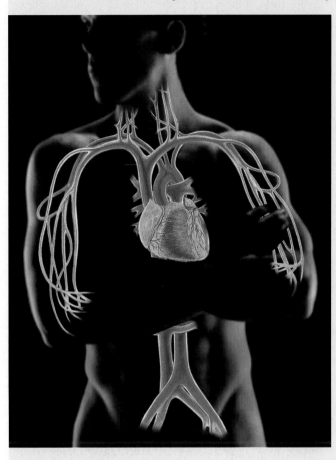

Integumentary System

- The cardiovascular system delivers oxygen and nutrients; carries away wastes
- The skin vasculature is an important blood reservoir and provides a site for heat loss from the body

Skeletal System

- The cardiovascular system delivers oxygen and nutrients; carries away wastes
- Bones are the sites of hematopoiesis; protect cardiovascular organs by enclosure; and provide a calcium depot

Muscular System

- The cardiovascular system delivers oxygen and nutrients; carries away wastes
- The muscle "pump" aids venous return; aerobic exercise enhances cardiovascular efficiency and helps prevent atherosclerosis

Nervous System

- The cardiovascular system delivers oxygen and nutrients; carries away wastes

- The ANS regulates cardiac rate and force; sympathetic division maintains blood pressure and controls blood flow to skin for thermoregulation

Endocrine System

- The cardiovascular system delivers oxygen and nutrients; carries away wastes; blood serves as a transport vehicle for hormones
- Various hormones influence blood pressure (epinephrine, ANP, angiotensin II, thyroxine, ADH); estrogen maintains vascular health in women

Lymphatic System/Immunity

- The cardiovascular system delivers oxygen and nutrients to lymphatic organs, which house immune cells; provides transport medium for lymphocytes and antibodies; carries away wastes
- The lymphatic system picks up leaked fluid and plasma proteins and returns them to the cardiovascular system; its immune cells protect cardiovascular organs from specific pathogens

Respiratory System

- The cardiovascular system delivers oxygen and nutrients; carries away wastes
- The respiratory system carries out gas exchange: loads oxygen and unloads carbon dioxide from the blood; respiratory "pump" aids venous return

Digestive System

- The cardiovascular system delivers oxygen and nutrients; carries away wastes
- The digestive system provides nutrients to the blood including iron and B vitamins essential for RBC (and hemoglobin) formation

Urinary System

- The cardiovascular system delivers oxygen and nutrients; carries away wastes; blood pressure allows filtration in the kidneys
- The urinary system helps regulate blood volume and pressure by altering urine volume and releasing renin

Reproductive System

- The cardiovascular system delivers oxygen and nutrients; carries away wastes
- Estrogen maintains vascular and osseous health in women

19

CLOSER CONNECTIONS

THE CARDIOVASCULAR SYSTEM and Interrelationships with the Muscular, Nervous, and Urinary Systems

The cardiovascular system is the "king of systems." No body system can live without the blood that surges ceaselessly through cardiovascular channels. Likewise, it is nearly impossible to find a system that does not influence the cardiovascular system in some way. The respiratory and digestive systems enrich blood with oxygen and nutrients, respectively, and in turn take a share of the various riches the blood has to offer. By returning leaked plasma fluid to the vascular system, the lymphatic system helps to keep those vessels filled with blood so that circulation is possible. However, the three cardiovascular system partnerships that we will look at more closely here are those it has with the muscular, nervous, and urinary systems.

Muscular System

Talk about one hand washing the other—that's a pretty fair analogy for the interaction between the cardiovascular and muscular systems. Muscles cramp and become nonfunctional when deprived of an adequate supply of oxygen-rich blood, and their capillary supply expands (or atrophies) along with changes in muscle mass. The arterioles of skeletal muscle even have special beta-adrenergic receptors so that they can be dilated by circulating epinephrine when most other body arterioles are responding to vasoconstrictor "orders." When muscles are active and healthy, so too is the cardiovascular system. Without exercise, the heart weakens and loses mass; but when we exercise aerobically, the heart increases in size and strength. Heart rate goes down as stroke volume rises, and a lower HR means that the heart relaxes more and beats hundreds of thousands times less in a lifetime. Aerobic exercise also enhances HDL blood levels and reduces LDL levels—helping to clear fatty deposits from the vascular walls and deferring atherosclerosis, hypertension, and heart disease. Not a bad trade!

Nervous System

The brain must have absolutely continuous oxygen and glucose delivery; thus it should come as no surprise that the brain has the body's most precise autoregulatory circulation mechanism. Acting on acutely sensitive arterioles, this mechanism protects the brain. For this we can be profoundly thankful, for when neurons die, an important part of us dies as well. The cardiovascular system is just as dependent on the nervous system. Although an intrinsic pacemaker sets sinus rhythm, it does not even begin to adapt to stimuli that mobilize the cardiovascular system to peak efficiency in maintaining blood pressure during position changes and delivering blood faster during times of stress. This is the job of the autonomic nervous system, which initiates reflexes as necessary to increase or decrease cardiac output and peripheral resistance, and to redirect blood from one organ to others to serve specific needs and protect vital organs.

Urinary System

Like the lymphatic system, the urinary system (primarily the kidneys) helps maintain blood volume and circulatory dynamics, but in a much more complicated way. The kidneys use blood pressure (courtesy of the cardiovascular system) to form the filtrate which the kidney tubule cells then process. Essentially this processing involves reclaiming needed nutrients and water while allowing metabolic waste and excess ions (including H^+) to leave the body in urine. As a result, blood is continually refreshed and blood composition and volume are carefully regulated. So dedicated are the kidneys to preserving blood volume that urine output stops entirely when blood volume is severely depressed. On the other hand, the kidneys can increase systemic BP by releasing renin when the blood pressure becomes inadequate.

19

CLINICAL CONNECTIONS

Cardiovascular System

Case study: Mr. Hutchinson, another middle-aged victim of the collision on Route 91, has a tourniquet around his thigh when admitted in an unconscious state to Noble Hospital. The emergency technician who brings him in states that his right lower limb was pinned beneath the bus for at least 30 minutes. He is immediately scheduled for surgery. Admission notes include the following:

- Multiple contusions of lower limbs
- Compound fracture of the right tibia; bone ends covered with sterile gauze
- Right leg blanched and cold, no pulse

- Blood pressure 90/48; pulse 140/min and thready; patient diaphoretic (sweaty)

1. Relative to what you have learned about tissue requirements for oxygen, what is the condition of the tissues in the right lower limb?

2. Will the fracture be attended to, or will Mr. Hutchinson's other homeostatic needs take precedence? Explain your answer choice and predict his surgical treatment.

3. What do you conclude regarding Mr. Hutchinson's cardiovascular measurements (pulse and BP), and what measures do you expect will be taken to remedy the situation before commencing surgery?

(Answers in Appendix G)

3. Pulse pressure is systolic pressure minus diastolic pressure. The mean arterial pressure (MAP) = diastolic pressure plus one-third of pulse pressure and is the pressure that keeps blood moving throughout the cardiac cycle.

4. Low capillary pressure (35 to 15 mm Hg) protects the delicate capillaries from rupture while still allowing adequate exchange across the capillary walls.

5. Venous pressure is nonpulsatile and low (declining to zero) because of the cumulative effects of resistance. Venous valves, large lumens, functional adaptations (muscular and respiratory pumps), and sympathetic nervous system activity promote venous return.

Maintaining Blood Pressure (pp. 726–733)

1. Blood pressure varies directly with CO, peripheral resistance (*R*), and blood volume. Vessel diameter is the major factor determining resistance, and small changes in vessel (chiefly arteriolar) diameter significantly affect blood pressure.

IP Cardiovascular System; Topic: Measuring Blood Pressure, pp. 1–13.

2. BP is regulated by autonomic neural reflexes involving baroreceptors or chemoreceptors, the vasomotor center (a medullary center that regulates blood vessel diameter), and sympathetic vasomotor fibers, which act on vascular smooth muscle.

3. Activation of the receptors by falling BP (and to a lesser extent by a rise in blood CO_2, or falling blood pH or O_2 levels) stimulates the vasomotor center to increase vasoconstriction and the cardioacceleratory center to increase heart rate and contractility. Rising BP inhibits the vasomotor center (permitting vasodilation) and activates the cardioinhibitory center.

4. Higher brain centers (cerebrum and hypothalamus) may modify neural controls of BP via medullary centers.

5. Hormones that increase BP by promoting vasoconstriction include epinephrine and NE (these also increase heart rate and contractility), ADH, and angiotensin II (generated in response to renin release by kidney cells). Hormones that reduce BP by promoting vasodilation include atrial natriuretic peptide, which also causes a decline in blood volume.

6. The kidneys regulate blood pressure by regulating blood volume. Rising BP directly enhances filtrate formation and fluid losses in urine; falling BP causes the kidneys to retain more water, increasing blood volume.

7. Indirect renal regulation of blood volume involves the renin-angiotensin mechanism, a hormonal mechanism. When BP falls, the kidneys release renin, which triggers the formation of angiotensin II (a vasoconstrictor) and release of aldosterone, which causes salt and water retention.

IP Cardiovascular System; Topic: Blood Pressure Regulation, pp. 1–31.

8. Pulse and blood pressure measurements are used to assess cardiovascular efficiency.

9. The pulse is the alternating expansion and recoil of arterial walls with each heartbeat. Pulse points are also pressure points.

10. Blood pressure is routinely measured by the auscultatory method. Normal blood pressure in adults is 120/80 (systolic/diastolic). Hypotension is rarely a problem. Hypertension is the major cause of myocardial infarct, stroke, and renal disease.

IP Cardiovascular System; Topic: Measuring Blood Pressure, pp. 11, 12.

11. Hypotension, or low blood pressure (systolic pressure below 100 mm Hg), is a sign of health in the well conditioned. In other individuals it warns of poor nutrition, disease, or circulatory shock.

12. Chronic hypertension (high blood pressure) is persistent BP readings of 140/90 or higher. It indicates increased peripheral resistance, which strains the heart and promotes vascular complications of other organs, particularly the eyes and kidneys. Risk factors are high-fat, high-salt diet, obesity, diabetes mellitus, advanced age, smoking, stress, and being a member of the black race or a family with a history of hypertension.

IP Cardiovascular System; Topic: Measuring Blood Pressure, pp. 11, 12.

Blood Flow Through Body Tissues: Tissue Perfusion (pp. 733–742)

1. Blood flow is involved in delivering nutrients and wastes to and from cells, gas exchange, absorbing nutrients, and forming urine.

2. Blood flows fastest where the cross-sectional area of the vascular bed is least (aorta), and slowest where the total cross-sectional area is greatest (capillaries). The slow flow in capillaries allows time for nutrient-waste exchanges.

3. Autoregulation is the local adjustment of blood flow to individual organs based on their immediate requirements. It involves myogenic controls that maintain flow despite changes in blood pressure, and local chemical factors. Vasodilators include increased CO_2, H^+, and nitric oxide. Decreased O_2 and nutrient concentrations also cause vasodilation. Other factors, including endothelins, decrease blood flow.

IP Cardiovascular; Topic: Autoregulation and Capillary Dynamics, pp. 1–13.

4. In most instances, autoregulation is controlled by oxygen deficits and accumulation of local metabolites. However, autoregulation in the brain is controlled primarily by a drop in pH and by myogenic mechanisms; and vasodilation of pulmonary circuit vessels occurs in response to high levels of oxygen.

5. Nutrients, gases, and other solutes smaller than plasma proteins cross the capillary wall by diffusion. Water-soluble substances move through the clefts or fenestrations; fat-soluble substances pass through the lipid portion of the endothelial cell membrane; larger molecules are actively transported via pinocytotic vesicles or caveolae.

6. Bulk flow of fluids at capillary beds determines the distribution of fluids between the bloodstream and the interstitial space. It reflects the relative effect of outward (net hydrostatic pressure) forces minus the effect of inward (net osmotic pressure) forces. In general, fluid flows out of the capillary bed at the arterial end and reenters the capillary blood at the venule end.

IP Cardiovascular; Topic: Autoregulation and Capillary Dynamics, pp. 14–38.

7. The small net loss of fluid and protein into the interstitial space is collected by lymphatic vessels and returned to the cardiovascular system.

8. Circulatory shock occurs when blood perfusion of body tissues is inadequate. Most cases of shock reflect low blood volume (hypovolemic shock), abnormal vasodilation (vascular shock), or pump failure (cardiogenic shock).

PART 3: CIRCULATORY PATHWAYS: BLOOD VESSELS OF THE BODY

The Two Main Circulations of the Body   (p. 742)

1. The pulmonary circulation transports O_2-poor, CO_2-laden blood to the lungs for oxygenation and carbon dioxide unloading. Blood returning to the right atrium of the heart is pumped by the right ventricle to the lungs via the pulmonary trunk. Blood issuing from the lungs is returned to the left atrium by the pulmonary veins. (See Table 19.3 and Figure 19.18.)

2. The systemic circulation transports oxygenated blood from the left ventricle to all body tissues via the aorta and its branches. Venous blood returning from the systemic circuit is delivered to the right atrium via the venae cavae.

Systemic Arteries and Veins: Differences in Pathways and Courses   (p. 742)

3. All arteries are deep while veins are both deep and superficial. Superficial veins tend to have numerous interconnections. Dural sinuses and the hepatic portal circulation are unique venous drainage patterns.

Principal Vessels of the Systemic Circulation (pp. 742–743)

4. Tables 19.3 to 19.13 and Figures 19.19 to 19.29 illustrate and describe vessels of the systemic circulation.

Developmental Aspects of Blood Vessels   (p. 743)

1. The fetal vasculature develops from embryonic blood islands and mesenchyme and is functioning in blood delivery by the fourth week.

2. Fetal circulation differs from circulation after birth. The pulmonary and hepatic shunts and special umbilical vessels are normally occluded shortly after birth.

3. Blood pressure is low in infants and rises to adult values. Age-related vascular problems include varicose veins, hypertension, and atherosclerosis. Hypertension is the most important cause of sudden cardiovascular death in middle-aged men. Atherosclerosis is the most important cause of cardiovascular disease in the aged.

Review Questions

Multiple Choice/Matching

(Some questions have more than one correct answer. Select the best answer or answers from the choices given.)

1. Which statement does not accurately describe veins? (a) They have less elastic tissue and smooth muscle than arteries, (b) they contain more fibrous tissue than arteries, (c) most veins in the extremities have valves, (d) they always carry deoxygenated blood.

2. Smooth muscle in the blood vessel wall (a) is found primarily in the tunica intima, (b) is mostly circularly arranged, (c) is most abundant in veins, (d) is usually innervated by the parasympathetic nervous system.

3. Peripheral resistance (a) is inversely proportional to the length of the vascular bed, (b) increases in anemia, (c) is decreased in obesity, (d) is inversely related to the diameter of the arterioles.

4. Which of the following can lead to decreased venous return of blood to the heart? (a) an increase in blood volume, (b) an increase in venous pressure, (c) damage to the venous valves, (d) increased muscular activity.

5. Arterial blood pressure increases in response to (a) increasing stroke volume, (b) increasing heart rate, (c) arteriosclerosis, (d) rising blood volume, (e) all of these.

6. Which of the following would *not* result in the dilation of the feeder arterioles and opening of the precapillary sphincters in systemic capillary beds? (a) a decrease in local tissue O_2 content, (b) an increase in local tissue CO_2, (c) a local increase in histamine, (d) a local increase in pH.

7. The structure of a capillary wall differs from that of a vein or an artery because (a) it has two tunics instead of three, (b) there is less smooth muscle, (c) it has a single tunic—only the tunica intima, (d) none of these.

8. The baroreceptors in the carotid sinus and aortic arch are sensitive to (a) a decrease in CO_2, (b) changes in arterial pressure, (c) a decrease in O_2, (d) all of these.

9. The myocardium receives its blood supply directly from (a) the aorta, (b) the coronary arteries, (c) the coronary sinus, (d) the pulmonary arteries.

10. Blood flow in the capillaries is steady despite the rhythmic pumping of the heart because of the (a) elasticity of the large arteries, (b) small diameter of capillaries, (c) thin walls of the veins, (d) venous valves.

11. Tracing the blood from the heart to the right hand, we find that blood leaves the heart and passes through the aorta, the right subclavian artery, the axillary and brachial arteries, and through either the radial or ulnar artery to arrive at the hand. Which artery is missing from this sequence? (a) coronary, (b) brachiocephalic, (c) cephalic, (d) right common carotid.

12. Which of the following do not drain directly into the inferior vena cava? (a) inferior phrenic veins, (b) hepatic veins, (c) inferior mesenteric vein, (d) renal veins.

13. In atherosclerosis, which layer of the vessel wall thickens most? (a) tunica media, (b) tunica intima, (c) tunica adventitia, (d) tunica externa.

14. Suppose that at a given point along a capillary, the following forces exist: capillary hydrostatic pressure (HP_c) = 30 mm Hg, interstitial fluid hydrostatic pressure (HP_{if}) = 0 mm Hg, capillary colloid osmotic pressure (OP_c) = 25 mm Hg and interstitial fluid colloid osmotic pressure (OP_{if}) = 2 mm Hg. The net filtration pressure at this point in the capillary is (a) 3 mm Hg, (b) −3 mm Hg, (c) −7 mm Hg, (d) 7 mm Hg.

15. Using the letters from column B, match the artery descriptions in column A. (Note that some require more than a single choice.)

Column A	Column B
____ **(1)** unpaired branch of abdominal aorta	**(a)** right common carotid
____ **(2)** second branch of aortic arch	**(b)** superior mesenteric
____ **(3)** branch of internal carotid	**(c)** left common carotid
____ **(4)** branch of external carotid	**(d)** external iliac
____ **(5)** origin of femoral arteries	**(e)** inferior mesenteric
	(f) superficial temporal
	(g) celiac trunk
	(h) facial
	(i) ophthalmic
	(j) internal iliac

Short Answer Essay Questions

16. How is the anatomy of capillaries and capillary beds well suited to their function?

17. Distinguish between elastic arteries, muscular arteries, and arterioles relative to location, histology, and functional adaptations.

18. Write an equation showing the relationship between peripheral resistance, blood flow, and blood pressure.

19. (a) Define blood pressure. Differentiate between systolic and diastolic blood pressure. (b) What is the normal blood pressure value for a young adult?

20. Describe the neural mechanisms responsible for controlling blood pressure.

21. Explain the reasons for the observed changes in blood flow velocity in the different regions of the circulation.

22. How does the control of blood flow to the skin for the purpose of regulating body temperature differ from the control of nutrient blood flow to skin cells?

23. Describe neural and chemical (both systemic and local) effects exerted on the blood vessels when one is fleeing from a mugger. (Be careful, this is more involved than it appears at first glance.)

24. How are nutrients, wastes, and respiratory gases transported to and from the blood and tissue spaces?

25. (a) What blood vessels contribute to the formation of the hepatic portal circulation? (b) What is the function of this circulation? (c) Why is a portal circulation a "strange" circulation?

26. Physiologists often consider capillaries and postcapillary venules together. (a) What functions do these vessels share? (b) Structurally, how do they differ?

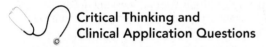

Critical Thinking and Clinical Application Questions

1. Mrs. Johnson is brought to the emergency room after being involved in an auto accident. She is hemorrhaging and has a rapid, thready pulse, but her blood pressure is still within normal limits. Describe the compensatory mechanisms that are acting to maintain her blood pressure in the face of blood loss.

2. A 60-year-old man is unable to walk more than 100 yards without experiencing severe pain in his left leg; the pain is relieved by resting for 5–10 minutes. He is told that the arteries of his leg are becoming occluded with fatty material and is advised to have the sympathetic nerves serving that body region severed. Explain how such surgery might help to relieve this man's problem.

3. Your friend Joanie, who knows little about science, is reading a magazine article about a patient who had an "aneurysm at the base of his brain that suddenly grew much larger." The surgeons' first goal was to "keep it from rupturing," and the second goal was to "relieve the pressure on the brain stem and cranial nerves." The surgeons were able to "replace the aneurysm with a section of plastic tubing," so the patient recovered. Joanie asks you what all this means. Explain. (Hint: Check this chapter's Related Clinical Terms, p. 767.)

4. The Agawam High School band is playing some lively marches while the coaches are giving pep talks to their respective football squads. Although it is September, it is unseasonably hot (88°F/31°C) and the band uniforms are wool. Suddenly, Harry the tuba player becomes light-headed and faints. Explain his fainting in terms of vascular events.

5. When one is cold or the external temperature is low, most venous blood returning from the distal part of the arm travels in the deep veins where it picks up heat (countercurrent mechanism) from the nearby brachial artery en route. However, when one is hot, and especially during exercise, venous return from the distal arm travels in the superficial veins and those veins tend to bulge superficially in a person who is working out. Explain why venous return takes a different route in the second situation.

6. Edema (swelling due to an increase in interstitial fluid) is a common clinical problem. On one of your first days of an introductory clinical experience, you encounter four patients who all have severe edema for different reasons. Your challenge is to explain the cause of the edema. In each case, try to explain the edema in terms of either an increase or a decrease in one of the four pressures that causes bulk flow at capillaries (see Figure 19.16).

(1) First you encounter Mrs. Taylor in the medical ward awaiting a liver transplant. What is the connection between liver failure and her edema? (Hint: Think about the liver's role in producing plasma proteins.)

(2) Next you follow a resident to the obstetric ward, where Mrs. So is experiencing premature labor. Which of the pressures that drive bulk flow might be altered here? (Hint: What might the expanding uterus be pressing on?)

(3) Then you are called to emergency, where Mr. Herrera is in anaphylactic shock. In anaphylactic shock, the capillaries become leaky, allowing plasma proteins that are normally kept inside the blood vessels to escape into the interstitial fluid. Which of the pressures driving bulk flow is altered in this case and in what direction is the change?

(4) Finally, you go to the oncology ward where Mrs. O'Leary is recovering from surgery for advanced breast cancer that had infiltrated her right breast and axillary lymph nodes. All of her axillary lymph nodes were removed and unfortunately, this severed most of the lymphatic vessels draining her right arm. You notice that her right arm is quite edematous. Why? Mrs. O'Leary is given a compression sleeve to wear on this arm to help relieve the edema. Which of the pressures driving bulk flow at the capillaries will be altered by the compression sleeve?

19

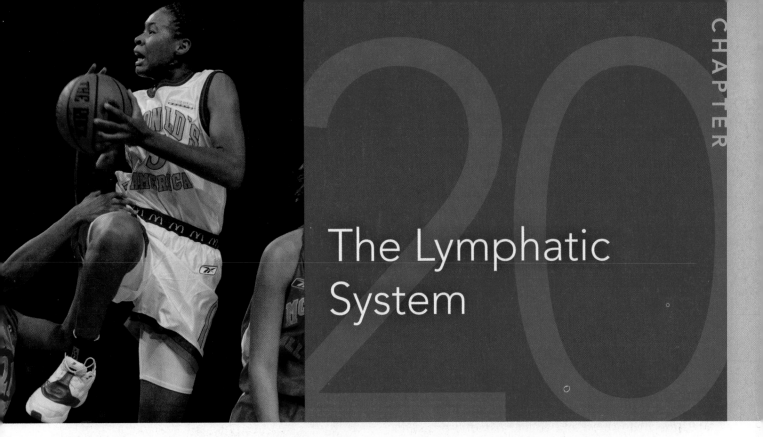

The Lymphatic System

CHAPTER 20

1. List the functions of the lymphatic system.

Lymphatic Vessels
(pp. 774–777)

2. Describe the structure and distribution of lymphatic vessels, and note their important functions.

3. Describe the source of lymph and mechanism(s) of lymph transport.

Lymphoid Cells and Tissues
(p. 777)

4. Describe the basic structure and cellular population of lymphoid tissue. Differentiate between diffuse and fallicular lymphoid tissues.

Lymph Nodes (pp. 778–779)

5. Describe the general location, histological structure, and functions of lymph nodes.

Other Lymphoid Organs
(pp. 779–782)

6. Name and describe the other lymphoid organs of the body. Compare and contrast them with lymph nodes, structurally and functionally.

Developmental Aspects of the Lymphatic System
(p. 783)

7. Outline lymphatic system development.

They can't all be superstars! When we mentally tick off the names of the body's organ systems, the lymphatic (lim-fat'ik) system is probably not the first to come to mind. Yet without this quietly working system, our cardiovascular system would stop working and our immune system would be hopelessly impaired. The **lymphatic system** actually consists of two semi-independent parts: (1) a meandering network of *lymphatic vessels* and (2) various *lymphoid tissues* and *organs* scattered throughout the body. The lymphatic vessels transport back to the blood any fluids that have escaped from the blood vascular system. The lymphoid organs house phagocytic cells and lymphocytes, which play essential roles in the body's defense mechanisms and its resistance to disease.

Lymphatic Vessels

As blood circulates through the body, nutrients, wastes, and gases are exchanged between the blood and the interstitial fluid. As explained in Chapter 19, the hydrostatic and colloid osmotic pressures operating at capillary beds force fluid out of the blood at the arterial ends of the beds ("upstream") and cause most of it to be reabsorbed at the venous ends ("downstream"). The fluid that remains behind in the tissue spaces, as much as 3 L daily, becomes part of the interstitial fluid. This leaked fluid, plus any plasma proteins that escape from the bloodstream, must be carried back to the blood to ensure that the cardiovascular system has sufficient blood volume to operate properly. This problem of circulatory dynamics is resolved by the **lymphatic vessels,** or **lymphatics,** an elaborate system of drainage vessels that collect the excess protein-containing interstitial fluid and return it to the bloodstream. Once interstitial fluid enters the lymphatics, it is called **lymph** (*lymph* = clear water).

Distribution and Structure of Lymphatic Vessels

The lymphatic vessels form a one-way system in which lymph flows only toward the heart. This transport system begins in microscopic blind-ended **lymphatic capillaries** (Figure 20.1a), which weave between the tissue cells and blood capillaries in the

FIGURE 20.1 **Distribution and special structural features of lymphatic capillaries. (a)** Structural relationship between a capillary bed of the blood vascular system and lymphatic capillaries. Arrows indicate direction of fluid movement. **(b)** Lymphatic capillaries begin as blind-ended tubes. Adjacent endothelial cells in a lymphatic capillary overlap each other, forming flaplike minivalves.

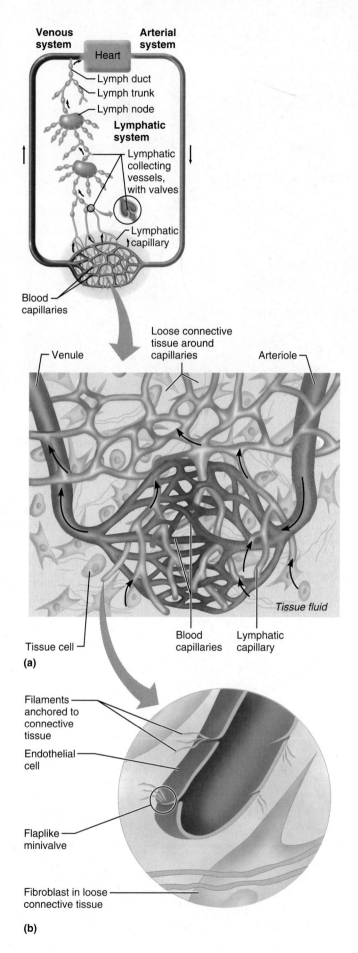
(a)

(b)

20

loose connective tissues of the body. Lymphatic capillaries are widespread; however, they are absent from bones and teeth, bone marrow, and the entire central nervous system (where the excess tissue fluid drains into the cerebrospinal fluid).

Although similar to blood capillaries, lymphatic capillaries are so remarkably permeable that they were once thought to be open at one end like a straw. We now know that they owe their permeability to two unique structural modifications:

1. The endothelial cells forming the walls of lymphatic capillaries are not tightly joined; instead, the edges of adjacent cells overlap each other loosely, forming easily opened, flaplike *minivalves* (Figure 20.1b).

2. Collagen filaments anchor the endothelial cells to surrounding structures so that any increase in interstitial fluid volume opens the minivalves, rather than causing the lymphatic capillaries to collapse.

So, what we have is a system analogous to one-way swinging doors in the lymphatic capillary wall. When fluid pressure in the interstitial space is greater than the pressure in the lymphatic capillary, the minivalve flaps gape open, allowing fluid to enter the lymphatic capillary. However, when the pressure is greater *inside* the lymphatic capillary, the endothelial minivalve flaps are forced closed, preventing lymph from leaking back out as the pressure moves it along the vessel.

Proteins in the interstitial space are unable to enter blood capillaries, but they enter lymphatic capillaries easily. In addition, when tissues are inflamed, lymphatic capillaries develop openings that permit uptake of even larger particles such as cell debris, pathogens (disease-causing microorganisms such as bacteria and viruses), and cancer cells. The pathogenic agents and cancer cells can then use the lymphatics to travel throughout the body. This threat to the body is partly resolved by the fact that the lymph takes "detours" through the lymph nodes, where it is cleansed of debris and "examined" by cells of the immune system.

Highly specialized lymphatic capillaries called **lacteals** (lak'te-alz) are present in the fingerlike villi of the intestinal mucosa. The lymph draining from the digestive viscera is milky white (*lacte* = milk) rather than clear because the lacteals play a major role in absorbing digested fats from the intestine. This fatty lymph, called **chyle** ("juice"), is also delivered to the blood via the lymphatic stream.

From the lymphatic capillaries, lymph flows through successively larger and thicker-walled channels—first collecting vessels, then trunks, and finally the largest of all, the ducts (Figure 20.2). The **lymphatic collecting vessels** have the same three tunics as veins, but the collecting vessels are thinner-walled, have more internal valves, and anastomose more. In general, lymphatics in the skin travel along with superficial *veins*, while the deep lymphatic vessels of the trunk and digestive viscera travel with the deep *arteries*. The exact anatomical distribution of lymphatic vessels varies greatly between individuals, even more so than it does for veins.

The **lymphatic trunks** are formed by the union of the largest collecting vessels, and drain fairly large areas of the body. The major trunks, named mostly for the regions from which they collect lymph, are the paired **lumbar, bronchomediastinal, subclavian,** and **jugular trunks,** and the single **intestinal trunk** (Figure 20.2b).

Lymph is eventually delivered to one of two large *ducts* in the thoracic region. The **right lymphatic duct** drains lymph from the right upper arm and the right side of the head and thorax (Figure 20.2a). The much larger **thoracic duct** receives lymph from the rest of the body. It arises anterior to the first two lumbar vertebrae as an enlarged sac, the **cisterna chyli** (sis-ter'nah ki'li), that collects lymph from the two large lumbar trunks that drain the lower limbs and from the intestinal trunk that drains the digestive organs. As the thoracic duct runs superiorly, it receives lymphatic drainage from the left side of the thorax, left upper limb, and the head region. Each terminal duct empties its lymph into the venous circulation at the junction of the internal jugular vein and subclavian vein on its own side of the body (Figure 20.2b).

HOMEOSTATIC IMBALANCE

Like the larger blood vessels, the larger lymphatics receive their nutrient blood supply from a branching vasa vasorum. When lymphatic vessels are severely inflamed, the related vessels of the vasa vasorum become congested with blood. As a result, the pathway of the associated superficial lymphatics becomes visible through the skin as red lines that are tender to the touch. This unpleasant condition is called *lymphangitis* (lim"fan-ji'tis; *angi* = vessel). ●

Lymph Transport

The lymphatic system lacks an organ that acts as a pump. Under normal conditions, lymphatic vessels are low-pressure conduits, and the same mechanisms that promote venous return in blood vessels act here as well—the milking action of active skeletal muscles, pressure changes in the thorax during breathing, and valves to prevent backflow. Lymphatics are usually bundled together in connective tissue sheaths along with blood vessels, and pulsations of nearby arteries also promote lymph flow. In addition to these mechanisms, smooth muscle in the walls of

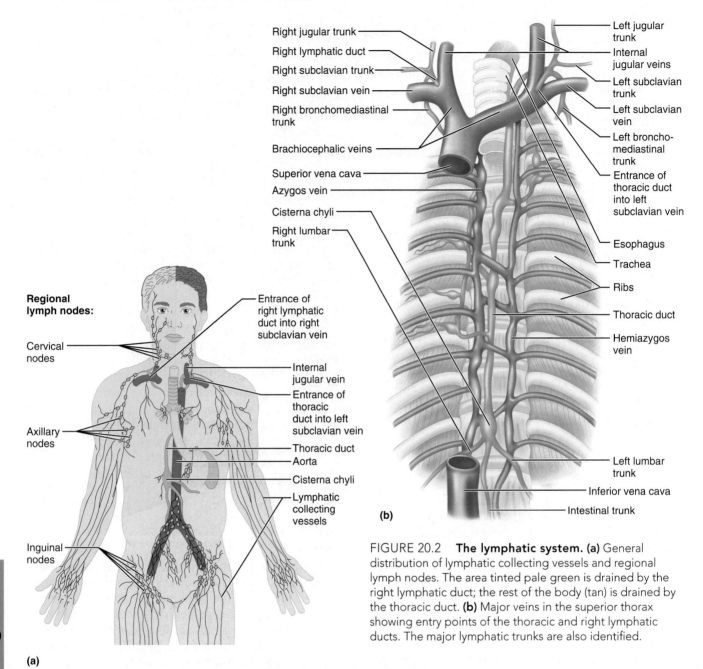

Right jugular trunk

Right lymphatic duct

Right subclavian trunk

Right subclavian vein

Right bronchomediastinal trunk

Brachiocephalic veins

Superior vena cava

Azygos vein

Cisterna chyli

Right lumbar trunk

Left jugular trunk

Internal jugular veins

Left subclavian trunk

Left subclavian vein

Left broncho-mediastinal trunk

Entrance of thoracic duct into left subclavian vein

Esophagus

Trachea

Ribs

Thoracic duct

Hemiazygos vein

Left lumbar trunk

Inferior vena cava

Intestinal trunk

(b)

Regional lymph nodes:

Cervical nodes

Axillary nodes

Inguinal nodes

Entrance of right lymphatic duct into right subclavian vein

Internal jugular vein

Entrance of thoracic duct into left subclavian vein

Thoracic duct

Aorta

Cisterna chyli

Lymphatic collecting vessels

(a)

FIGURE 20.2 The lymphatic system. (a) General distribution of lymphatic collecting vessels and regional lymph nodes. The area tinted pale green is drained by the right lymphatic duct; the rest of the body (tan) is drained by the thoracic duct. **(b)** Major veins in the superior thorax showing entry points of the thoracic and right lymphatic ducts. The major lymphatic trunks are also identified.

the lymphatic trunks and thoracic duct contracts rhythmically, helping to pump the lymph along. Even so, lymph transport is sporadic and slow. About 3 L of lymph enters the bloodstream every 24 hours, a volume almost exactly equal to the amount of fluid lost to the tissue spaces from the bloodstream in the same time period. Movement of adjacent tissues is extremely important in propelling lymph through the lymphatics. When physical activity or passive movements increase, lymph flows much more rapidly (balancing the greater rate of fluid loss from the blood in such situations). Hence, it is a good idea to immobilize a badly infected body part to hinder flow of inflammatory material from that region.

◤ HOMEOSTATIC IMBALANCE

Anything that prevents the normal return of lymph to the blood, such as blockage of the lymphatics by tumors or removal of lymphatics during cancer surgery, results in short-term but severe localized edema *(lymphedema)*. Usually, however, lymphatic drainage is eventually reestablished by regrowth from the vessels remaining in the area. ●

This completes the description of the lymphatic vessels. To summarize their functions, they (1) return excess tissue fluid to the bloodstream, (2) return leaked proteins to the blood, and (3) carry absorbed fat from the intestine to the blood (through lacteals).

Lymphoid Cells and Tissues

In order to understand the basic aspects of the lymphatic system's role in the body, we investigate the components of lymphoid organs—lymphoid cells and lymphoid tissues—before considering the organs themselves.

Lymphoid Cells

Infectious microorganisms that manage to penetrate the body's epithelial barriers quickly proliferate in the underlying loose connective tissues. These invaders are fought off by the inflammatory response, by phagocytes (macrophages), and by lymphocytes.

Lymphocytes, the main warriors of the immune system, arise in red bone marrow (along with other formed elements). They then mature into one of the two main varieties of immunocompetent cells—**T cells (T lymphocytes)** or **B cells (B lymphocytes)**—that protect the body against antigens. (*Antigens* are anything the body perceives as foreign, such as bacteria and their toxins, viruses, mismatched RBCs, or cancer cells.) Activated T cells manage the immune response, and some of them directly attack and destroy infected cells. B cells protect the body by producing **plasma cells,** daughter cells that secrete antibodies into the blood (or other body fluids). Antibodies immobilize antigens until they can be destroyed by phagocytes or other means. The precise roles of the lymphocytes in immunity are explored in Chapter 21.

Lymphoid **macrophages** play a crucial role in body protection and in the immune response by phagocytizing foreign substances and by helping to activate T cells. So, too, do the spiny-looking **dendritic cells** that capture antigens and bring them back to the lymph nodes. Last but not least are the **reticular cells,** fibroblast-like cells that produce the reticular fiber **stroma** (stro'mah), which is the network that supports the other cell types in the lymphoid organs (Figure 20.3).

Lymphoid Tissue

Lymphoid (lymphatic) tissue is an important component of the immune system, mainly because it (1) houses and provides a proliferation site for lymphocytes and (2) furnishes an ideal surveillance vantage point for lymphocytes and macrophages. Lymphoid tissue, largely composed of a type of loose connective tissue called **reticular connective tissue,** dominates all the lymphoid organs except the thymus. Macrophages live on the fibers of the reticular network, and in the spaces of the network are huge

Q *How is reticular connective tissue classified?*

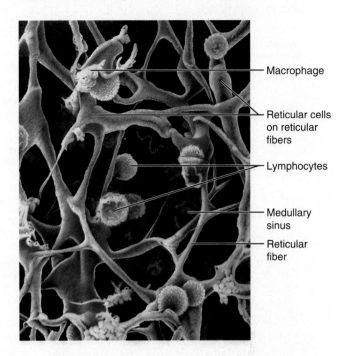

Macrophage

Reticular cells on reticular fibers

Lymphocytes

Medullary sinus

Reticular fiber

FIGURE 20.3 **Reticular tissue in a human lymph node.** Scanning electron micrograph (1100×).

numbers of lymphocytes that have squeezed through the walls of postcapillary venules coursing through this tissue. The lymphocytes reside temporarily in the lymphoid tissue (Figure 20.3), and then leave to patrol the body again. The cycling of lymphocytes between the circulatory vessels, lymphoid tissues, and loose connective tissues of the body ensures that lymphocytes reach infected or damaged sites quickly.

Lymphoid tissue comes in various "packages." **Diffuse lymphatic tissue,** consisting of a few scattered reticular tissue elements, is found in virtually every body organ, but larger collections appear in the lamina propria of mucous membranes and in lymphoid organs. **Lymphoid follicles (nodules)** represent another way lymphoid tissue is organized. Like diffuse lymphatic tissue, they lack a capsule, but follicles are solid, spherical bodies consisting of tightly packed reticular elements and cells. Follicles often have lighter-staining centers, called **germinal centers.** Follicular dendritic cells and B cells predominate in germinal centers, and these centers enlarge dramatically when the B cells are dividing rapidly and producing plasma cells. In many cases, the follicles are found forming part of larger lymphoid organs, such as lymph nodes. However, isolated aggregations of lymphoid follicles occur in the intestinal wall as Peyer's patches and in the appendix.

A Loose connective tissue proper.

Q *What is the benefit of having fewer efferent than afferent lymphatics in lymph nodes?*

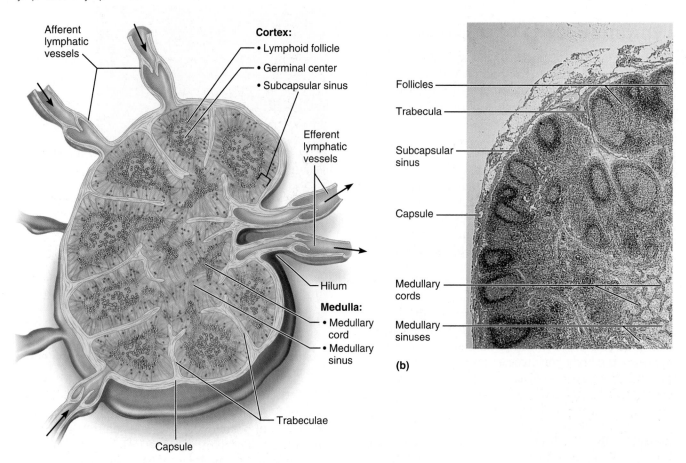

FIGURE 20.4 **Lymph node.**
(a) Longitudinal view of the internal structure of a lymph node and associated lymphatics. Notice that several afferent lymphatics converge on its convex side, whereas fewer efferent lymphatics exit at its hilum. Arrows indicate the direction of lymph flow into and out of the node. **(b)** Photomicrograph of part of a lymph node (60×).

Lymph Nodes

The principal lymphoid organs in the body are the **lymph nodes,** which cluster along the lymphatic vessels of the body. As lymph is transported back to the bloodstream, it is filtered through the lymph nodes. There are hundreds of these small organs, but because they are usually embedded in connective tissue, they are not ordinarily seen. Large clusters of lymph nodes occur near the body surface in the inguinal, axillary, and cervical regions, places where the lymphatic collecting vessels converge to form trunks (see Figure 20.2a).

Lymph nodes have two basic functions, both concerned with body protection. (1) They act as lymph "filters." Macrophages in the nodes remove and destroy microorganisms and other debris that enter the lymph from the loose connective tissues, effectively preventing them from being delivered to the blood and spreading to other parts of the body. (2) They help activate the immune system. Lymphocytes, also strategically located in the lymph nodes, monitor the lymphatic stream for the presence of *antigens* and mount an attack against them. Let's look at how the structure of a lymph node supports these defensive functions.

Structure of a Lymph Node

Lymph nodes vary in shape and size, but most are bean shaped and less than 2.5 cm (1 inch) in length. Each node is surrounded by a dense fibrous **capsule** from which connective tissue strands called **trabeculae** extend inward to divide the node into a number of compartments (Figure 20.4). The node's internal framework or stroma of reticular fibers

A *Having fewer efferents causes lymph to accumulate in lymph nodes, allowing more time for its cleansing.*

physically supports the ever-changing population of lymphocytes.

A lymph node has two histologically distinct regions, the **cortex** and the **medulla.** The superficial part of the cortex contains densely packed follicles, many with germinal centers heavy with dividing B cells. Dendritic cells nearly encapsulate the follicles and abut the deeper part of the cortex, which primarily houses T cells in transit. The T cells circulate continuously between the blood, lymph nodes, and lymph, performing their surveillance role.

Medullary cords, which are thin inward extensions from the cortical lymphoid tissue, contain both types of lymphocytes plus plasma cells and they define the medulla. Throughout the node are **lymph sinuses,** large lymph capillaries spanned by crisscrossing reticular fibers. Numerous macrophages reside on these reticular fibers and phagocytize foreign matter in the lymph as it flows by in the sinuses. Additionally, some of the lymph-borne antigens in the percolating lymph leak into the surrounding lymphoid tissue, where they activate lymphocytes to mount an immune attack against them.

Circulation in the Lymph Nodes

Lymph enters the convex side of a lymph node through a number of **afferent lymphatic vessels.** It then moves through a large, baglike sinus, the **subcapsular sinus,** into a number of smaller sinuses that cut through the cortex and enter the medulla. The lymph meanders through these sinuses and finally exits the node at its **hilum** (hi′lum), the indented region on the concave side, via **efferent lymphatic vessels.** Because there are fewer efferent vessels draining the node than afferent vessels feeding it, the flow of lymph through the node stagnates somewhat, allowing time for the lymphocytes and macrophages to carry out their protective functions. Lymph passes through several nodes before it is completely cleansed.

◣ HOMEOSTATIC IMBALANCE

Sometimes lymph nodes are overwhelmed by the agents they are trying to destroy. For example, when large numbers of bacteria are trapped in the nodes, the nodes become inflamed, swollen, and tender to the touch, a condition often referred to (erroneously) as swollen glands. Such infected lymph nodes are called *buboes* (bu′boz). (Buboes are the most obvious symptom of bubonic plague, the "Black Death" that killed much of Europe's population in the late Middle Ages.) Lymph nodes can also become secondary cancer sites, particularly in metastasizing cancers that enter lymphatic vessels and become trapped there. The fact that cancer-infiltrated lymph nodes

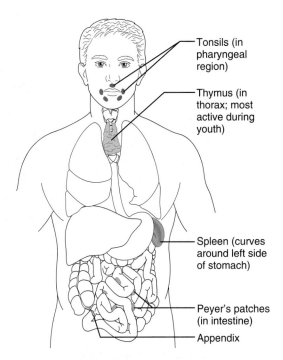

FIGURE 20.5   **Lymphoid organs.** Locations of the tonsils, spleen, thymus, Peyer's patches, and appendix.

are swollen but usually not painful helps distinguish cancerous lymph nodes from those infected by microorganisms. ●

Other Lymphoid Organs

Lymph nodes are just one example of the many types of **lymphoid organs** or aggregates of lymphatic tissue in the body. Others are the spleen, thymus, tonsils, and Peyer's patches of the intestine (Figure 20.5), as well as bits of lymphatic tissue scattered in the connective tissues. Except for the thymus, the common feature of all these organs is their tissue makeup: All are composed of *reticular connective tissue.* Although all lymphoid organs help protect the body, only the lymph nodes filter lymph. The other lymphoid organs and tissues typically have efferent lymphatics draining them, but lack afferent lymphatics.

Spleen

The soft, blood-rich **spleen** is about the size of a fist and is the largest lymphoid organ. Located in the left side of the abdominal cavity just beneath the diaphragm, it curls around the anterior aspect of the stomach (Figures 20.5 and 20.6). It is served by the large *splenic artery* and *vein,* which enter and exit the *hilum* on its slightly concave anterior surface.

The spleen provides a site for lymphocyte proliferation and immune surveillance and response. But perhaps even more important are its blood-cleansing

FIGURE 20.6 **The spleen. (a)** Gross structure. **(b)** Diagram of the histological structure. **(c)** Photograph of the spleen in its normal position in the abdominal cavity, anterior view. **(d)** Photomicrograph of spleen tissue showing white and red pulp regions (30×).

functions. Besides extracting aged and defective blood cells and platelets from the blood, its macrophages remove debris and foreign matter from blood flowing through its sinuses. The spleen also performs three additional, and related, functions.

1. It stores some of the breakdown products of red blood cells for later reuse (for example, it salvages iron for making hemoglobin) and releases others to the blood for processing by the liver.

2. It is a site of erythrocyte production in the fetus (a capability that normally ceases after birth).

3. It stores blood platelets.

Like lymph nodes, the spleen is surrounded by a fibrous capsule, has trabeculae that extend inward, and contains both lymphocytes and macrophages. Consistent with its blood-processing functions, it also contains huge numbers of erythrocytes. Areas composed mostly of lymphocytes suspended on reticular fibers are called **white pulp.** The white pulp clusters or forms "cuffs" around the *central arteries* (small branches of the splenic artery) in the organ and forms what appear to be islands in a sea of red pulp. **Red pulp** is essentially all remaining splenic tissue, that is, the venous sinuses (blood sinusoids) and the **splenic cords,** regions of reticular connective tissue exceptionally rich in macrophages. Red pulp is most concerned with disposing of worn-out red blood cells and bloodborne pathogens, whereas white pulp is involved with the immune functions of the spleen. The naming of the pulp regions reflects their appearance in fresh spleen tissue rather than their staining properties. Indeed, as can be seen in the photomicrograph in Figure 20.6d, the white pulp sometimes appears darker than the red pulp due to the darkly staining nuclei of the densely packed lymphocytes.

FIGURE 20.7 **The thymus.** The photomicrograph of a portion of the thymus shows part of a lobule with cortical and medullary regions (70×).

HOMEOSTATIC IMBALANCE

Because the spleen's capsule is relatively thin, a direct blow or severe infection may cause it to rupture, spilling blood into the peritoneal cavity. Once, removal of the ruptured spleen (a procedure called a *splenectomy*) was the standard treatment and thought necessary to prevent life-threatening hemorrhage and shock. During the past 20 years, surgeons have discovered that, if left alone, the spleen can often repair itself. At major trauma centers, the frequency of emergency splenectomies has decreased from 70% to 40%. If the spleen is removed, the liver and bone marrow take over most of its functions. In children younger than 12, the spleen will regenerate if a small part of it is left in the body. ●

Thymus

The bilobed **thymus** (thi'mus) has important functions primarily during the early years of life. It is found in the inferior neck and extends into the superior thorax, where it partially overlies the heart deep to the sternum (see Figures 20.5 and 20.7). By secreting the hormones thymopoietin and the thymosins, the thymus causes T lymphocytes to become immunocompetent; that is, it enables them to function against specific pathogens in the immune response. Prominent in newborns, the thymus continues to increase in size during the first year, when it is highly active. After puberty, it starts to atrophy gradually and by old age it has been replaced almost entirely by fibrous and fatty tissue and is difficult to distinguish from surrounding connective tissue.

To understand thymic histology, it helps to compare the thymus to a cauliflower head—the flowerets represent *thymic lobules*, each containing an outer cortex and an inner medulla (Figure 20.7). Most thymic cells are lymphocytes. In the cortical regions the rapidly dividing lymphocytes are densely packed, but a few macrophages are scattered among them. The lighter-staining medullary areas contain fewer lymphocytes plus some bizarre structures called **thymic (Hassall's) corpuscles.** Consisting of concentric whorls of keratinized epithelial cells, they are sites of T cell destruction. Because the thymus lacks B cells, it has no follicles.

The thymus differs from other lymphoid organs in two other important ways. First, it functions strictly in T lymphocyte maturation and thus is the only lymphoid organ that does not *directly* fight antigens. In fact, the so-called *blood-thymus barrier* keeps bloodborne antigens from leaking into the cortical regions to prevent premature activation of the immature lymphocytes. Second, the stroma of the thymus consists of epithelial cells rather than reticular fibers. These epithelial cells secrete the hormones that stimulate the lymphocytes to become immunocompetent.

Tonsils

The **tonsils** are the simplest lymphoid organs. They form a ring of lymphatic tissue around the entrance to the pharynx (throat), where they appear as swellings of the mucosa (Figures 20.5 and 22.3). The tonsils are named according to location. The paired **palatine tonsils** are located on either side at the posterior end of the oral cavity. These are the largest of the tonsils and the ones most often infected. A lumpy collection of lymphoid follicles at the base of the tongue is referred to collectively as the **lingual tonsil.** The **pharyngeal tonsil** (referred to as the *adenoids* if enlarged) is in the posterior wall of the

20

FIGURE 20.8   **Histology of the palatine tonsil.** The exterior surface of the tonsil is covered by squamous epithelium, which invaginates deeply to form tonsillar crypts (60×).

nasopharynx. The tiny **tubal tonsils** surround the openings of the auditory tubes into the pharynx. The tonsils gather and remove many of the pathogens entering the pharynx in food or in inhaled air.

The lymphoid tissue of the tonsils contains follicles with obvious germinal centers surrounded by diffusely scattered lymphocytes. The tonsils are not fully encapsulated, and the epithelium overlying them invaginates deep into their interior, forming blind-ended **tonsillar crypts** (Figure 20.8). The crypts trap bacteria and particulate matter, and the bacteria work their way through the mucosal epithe-

lium into the lymphoid tissue, where most are destroyed. It seems a bit dangerous to "invite" infection this way, but this strategy produces a wide variety of immune cells that have a "memory" for the trapped pathogens. Thus, the body takes a calculated risk early on (during childhood) for the benefits of heightened immunity and better health later.

Aggregates of Lymphoid Follicles

Peyer's patches (pi'erz) are large isolated clusters of lymphoid follicles, structurally similar to the tonsils, that are located in the wall of the distal portion of the small intestine (Figures 20.5 and 20.9). Lymphoid follicles are also heavily concentrated in the wall of the **appendix,** a tubular offshoot of the first part of the large intestine. Peyer's patches and the appendix are in an ideal position (1) to destroy bacteria (which are present in large numbers in the intestine), thereby preventing these pathogens from breaching the intestinal wall, and (2) to generate many "memory" lymphocytes for long-term immunity. Peyer's patches, the appendix, and the tonsils—all located in the digestive tract—and lymphoid follicles in the walls of the bronchi (organs of the respiratory tract) and in the mucosa of genitourinary organs, are part of the collection of small lymphoid tissues referred to as **mucosa-associated lymphatic tissue (MALT).** MALT protects passages that are open to the exterior from the never-ending onslaughts of foreign matter entering them.

FIGURE 20.9   **Peyer's patches.** Histological structure of aggregated lymphoid follicles—Peyer's patches (P)—in the wall of the ileum of the small intestine (SM = submucosa) (20×).

Developmental Aspects of the Lymphatic System

By the fifth week of embryonic development, the beginnings of the lymphatic vessels and the main clusters of lymph nodes are apparent. These arise from the budding of **lymph sacs** from developing veins. The first of these, the *jugular lymph sacs*, arise at the junctions of the internal jugular and subclavian veins and form a branching system of lymphatic vessels throughout the thorax, upper extremities, and head. The two main connections of the jugular lymph sacs to the venous system are retained and become the right lymphatic duct and, on the left, the superior part of the thoracic duct. Caudally the elaborate system of abdominal lymphatics buds largely from the primitive inferior vena cava. The lymphatics of the pelvic region and lower extremities form from sacs on the iliac veins.

Except for the thymus, which is an endodermal derivative, the lymphoid organs develop from mesodermal mesenchymal cells that migrate to particular body sites and develop into reticular tissue. The thymus, the first lymphoid organ to appear, forms as an outgrowth of the lining of the primitive pharynx. It then detaches and migrates caudally to the thorax where it becomes infiltrated with immature lymphocytes derived from hematopoietic tissues elsewhere in the embryo's body. Except for the spleen and tonsils, the lymphoid organs are poorly developed before birth. Shortly after birth, they become heavily populated by lymphocytes, and their development parallels the maturation of the immune system. There is some evidence that the embryonic thymus produces hormones that control the development of the other lymphoid organs.

■ ■ ■

Although the functions of the lymphatic vessels and lymphoid organs overlap, each helps maintain body homeostasis in unique ways, as summarized in *Making Connections* (pp. 784–785). The lymphatic vessels help maintain blood volume. The macrophages of lymphoid organs remove and destroy foreign matter in lymph and blood. Additionally, lymphoid organs and tissues provide sites from which the immune system can be mobilized. In Chapter 21, we continue this story as we examine the inflammatory and immune responses that allow us to resist a constant barrage of pathogens.

Related Clinical Terms

Elephantiasis (el″lĕ-fan-ti′ah-sis) Typically a tropical disease in which the lymphatics (particularly those of the lower limbs and scrotum) become clogged with parasitic roundworms, an infectious condition called filariasis; swelling (due to edema) reaches enormous proportions.

Hodgkin's disease A malignancy of lymphoid tissue; symptoms include swollen, nonpainful lymph nodes, fatigue, and often intermittent fever and night sweats. Characterized by presence of giant Reed-Sternberg cells, which are malignantly transformed B cells. Infection with Epstein-Barr virus (see mononucleosis below) and genetic susceptibility appear to be predisposing factors. Treated with chemotherapy and radiation; high cure rate.

Lymphadenopathy (lim-fad″ĕ-nop′ah-the; *adeno* = a gland; *pathy* = disease) Any disease of the lymph nodes.

Lymphangiography (lim-fan″je-og′rah-fe) Diagnostic procedure in which the lymphatic vessels are injected with radiopaque dye and then visualized with X rays.

Lymphoma Any neoplasm (tumor) of the lymphoid tissue, whether benign or malignant.

Mononucleosis A viral disease common in adolescents and young adults; symptoms include fatigue, fever, sore throat, and swollen lymph nodes. Caused by the Epstein-Barr virus, which is transmitted in saliva ("kissing disease") and specifically attacks B lymphocytes. This attack leads to a massive activation of T lymphocytes, which in turn attack the virus-infected B cells. Large numbers of oversized T lymphocytes circulate in the bloodstream. (These lymphocytes were originally misidentified as monocytes: *mononucleosis* = a condition of monocytes.) Usually lasts four to six weeks.

Non-Hodgkin's lymphoma Includes all cancers of lymphoid tissues except Hodgkin's disease. Involves uncontrolled multiplication and metastasis of undifferentiated lymphocytes, with swelling of the lymph nodes, spleen, and Peyer's patches; other organs may eventually become involved. The fifth most common cancer. A high-grade type, which primarily affects young people, grows quickly but is responsive to chemotherapy; up to a 75% remission rate. A low-grade type, which affects the elderly, is resistant to chemotherapy and so is often fatal.

Sentinel node The first node that receives lymph drainage from a body area suspected of being cancerous. When examined for presence of cancer cells, this node gives the best indication of whether metastasis through the lymph vessels has occurred.

Splenomegaly (sple″no-meg′ah-le; *mega* = big) Enlargement of the spleen due to accumulation of infectious microorganisms; typically caused by septicemia, mononucleosis, malaria, or leukemia.

Tonsillitis (ton″sĭ-li′tis; *itis* = inflammation) Inflammation of the tonsils, typically due to bacterial infection; they become red, swollen, and sore.

20

SYSTEM CONNECTIONS: Homeostatic Interrelationships Between the Lymphatic System/Immunity and Other Body Systems

Nervous System

- Lymphatic vessels pick up leaked plasma fluid and proteins in PNS structures; immune cells protect PNS structures from specific pathogens
- The nervous system innervates larger lymphatics; opiate neuropeptides influence immune functions; the brain helps regulate immune response

Endocrine System

- Lymphatic vessels pick up leaked fluids and proteins; lymph distributes hormones; immune cells protect endocrine organs
- The thymus produces hormones that promote development of lymphatic organs and "program" T cells; stress hormones depress immune activity

Cardiovascular System

- Lymphatic vessels pick up leaked plasma and proteins; spleen removes and destroys aged RBCs and debris, and stores iron and platelets; immune cells protect cardiovascular organs from specific pathogens
- Blood is the source of lymph; lymphatics develop from veins; blood circulates immune elements

Respiratory System

- Lymphatic vessels pick up leaked fluids and proteins from respiratory organs; immune cells protect respiratory organs from specific pathogens; the tonsils and plasma cells in the respiratory mucosa (which secrete the antibody IgA) prevent pathogen invasion
- The lungs provide O_2 needed by lymphoid/immune cells and eliminate CO_2; the pharynx houses the tonsils; respiratory "pump" aids lymph flow

Digestive System

- Lymphatic vessels pick up leaked fluids and proteins from digestive organs; lymph transports some products of fat digestion to the blood; lymphoid follicles in the intestinal wall prevent invasion of pathogens
- The digestive system digests and absorbs nutrients needed by cells of lymphoid organs; gastric acidity inhibits pathogens' entry into blood

Urinary System

- Lymphatic vessels pick up leaked fluid and proteins from urinary organs; immune cells protect urinary organs from specific pathogens
- Urinary system eliminates wastes and maintains homeostatic water/acid-base/electrolyte balance of the blood for lymphoid/immune cell functioning; urine flushes some pathogens out of the urinary tract

Reproductive System

- Lymphatic vessels pick up leaked fluid and proteins; immune cells protect against pathogens
- Reproductive organs' hormones may influence immune functioning; acidity of vaginal secretions is bacteriostatic

Integumentary System

- Lymphatic vessels pick up leaked plasma fluid and proteins from the dermis; lymphocytes in lymph enhance the skin's protective role by defending against specific pathogens via the immune response
- The skin's keratinized epithelium provides a mechanical barrier to pathogens; epithelial dendritic cells and dermal macrophages act as antigen presenters in the immune response; acid pH of skin secretions inhibits growth of bacteria on the skin

Skeletal System

- Lymphatic vessels pick up leaked plasma fluid and proteins from the periostea; immune cells protect bones from pathogens
- The bones house hematopoietic tissue which produces the lymphocytes (and macrophages) that populate lymphoid organs and provide immunity

Muscular System

- Lymphatic vessels pick up leaked fluids and proteins; immune cells protect muscles from pathogens
- The skeletal muscle "pump" aids the flow of lymph; heat produced during muscle activity initiates fever-like effects

THE LYMPHATIC SYSTEM: Immunity and Interrelationships with the Cardiovascular System

All living body cells are bathed by lymph. Nonetheless, the lymphatic system with its ghostly vessels and well-hidden (for the most part) organs and tissues is elusive and hard to pin down. Like a ground mole that tunnels throughout your yard, you know it's there, but you never see it as it quietly goes about its business. Since hormones made by endocrine organs are released into the extracellular space, and lymphatic vessels take up the fluid containing them, there is little question that lymph is an important medium for delivering hormones throughout the body. Lymph plays a similar delivery role as it delivers fats absorbed by the digestive organs.

Our immune system, charged with protecting the body from specific pathogens, is often considered a separate and independent functional system. However, it is impossible to divorce the immune system from the lymphatic system because lymphoid organs are the programming sites and seedbeds for the immune cells and provide crucial vantage points for monitoring blood and lymph for the presence of foreign substances. Less understood are the intimate interactions between the immune cells that populate the lymphoid tissues and the nervous and endocrine systems, but this interesting topic is deferred to Chapter 21 to give you the opportunity to consider the immune system in detail.

Although the lymphatic system serves the entire body, its chief "master" is the cardiovascular system. It is this relationship that we will explore further here.

Cardiovascular System

By now you are probably fairly comfortable with the fact that the lymphatic system picks up and returns leaked fluid and proteins to the blood vascular system.

So, what's the big deal? We ingest water in virtually everything we eat and drink—lost water is replaceable in a few minutes, right? The answer, of course, is "true." But what would still be missing is the leaked proteins, and these plasma proteins (most made by the liver) take time and energy to make. Since plasma proteins play a *major* role in keeping fluid in blood vessels (or encouraging its return), without them our blood vessels would contain too little fluid to support blood circulation. And without blood circulation, the whole body would die for lack of oxygen and nutrients and drown in its own wastes. Lymphoid organs also help to maintain the health and purity of blood—lymph nodes filter microorganisms and other debris from lymph before it is allowed to reenter the blood, and the spleen performs the same cleansing service for blood. In addition, the spleen disposes of inefficient, deformed, or aged erythrocytes.

However, this relationship is not entirely one-way. Lymphatic vessels spring from veins of the cardiovascular system, and blood delivers oxygen and nutrients to all body organs, including lymphoid ones. Blood also provides a means for (1) rapid transport of lymphocytes (immune cells) that continuously patrol the body for foreign substances and (2) broad distribution of antibodies (made by B cells and plasma cells), which bind to foreign substances and immobilize them until they can be disposed of by phagocytosis or other means. Furthermore, the endothelial cells of capillaries express surface protein "signals" (integrins/adhesion molecules) that lymphocytes can recognize when the surrounding area is injured or infected. Hence, capillaries guide immune cells to the sites where their protective services are needed, and the extremely porous walls of the postcapillary venules allow them to slip through the vessel wall to get there.

Lymphatic System/Immunity

Case study: Back to following the progress of Mr. Hutchinson, we learn that the routine complete blood count (CBC) performed on admission revealed that his leukocyte count is dangerously low and follow-up lab tests show that his lymphocytes are deficient. One day postsurgery, he complains of pain in his right ring finger (that hand had a crush injury). When examined, it was noted that the affected finger and the dorsum of the right hand were edematous, and red streaks radiated superiorly on his right forearm. Higher than normal doses of antibiotics are prescribed, and a sling is applied to the affected arm. Nurses are instructed to apply gloves and gown when giving Mr. Hutchinson his care.

Relative to these observations:

1. What do the red streaks emanating from the bruised finger indicate? What would you conclude his problem was if there were no red streaks but the right arm was very edematous?

2. Why is it important that Mr. Hutchinson not move the affected arm excessively (i.e., why was the sling ordered)?

3. How might the low lymphocyte count, megadoses of antibiotics, and orders for additional clinical staff protection be related?

4. Do you predict that Mr. Hutchinson's recovery will be uneventful or problematic? Why?

(Answers in Appendix G)

Chapter Summary

1. Lymphatic vessels, lymph nodes, and other lymphoid organs and tissues make up the lymphatic system. This system returns fluids that have leaked from the blood vascular system back to the blood, protects the body by removing foreign material from the lymph stream, and provides a site for immune surveillance.

Lymphatic Vessels (pp. 774–777)

Distribution and Structure of Lymphatic Vessels (pp. 774–775)

1. Lymphatic vessels form a one-way network—lymphatic capillaries, collecting vessels, trunks, and ducts—in which fluid flows only toward the heart. The right lymphatic duct drains lymph from the right arm and right side of the upper body; the thoracic duct receives lymph from the rest of the body. These ducts empty into the blood vascular system at the junction of the internal jugular and subclavian veins in the neck.

Lymph Transport (pp. 775–777)

2. The flow of lymphatic fluid is slow; it is maintained by skeletal muscle contraction, pressure changes in the thorax, and contractions of the lymphatic vessels. Backflow is prevented by valves.

3. Lymphatic capillaries are exceptionally permeable, admitting proteins and particulate matter from the interstitial space.

4. Pathogens and cancer cells may spread through the body via the lymphatic stream.

Lymphoid Cells and Tissues (p. 777)

Lymphoid Cells (p. 777)

1. The cells in lymphoid tissues include lymphocytes (immunocompetent cells called T cells or B cells), plasma cells (antibody-producing offspring of B cells), macrophages and dendritic cells (phagocytes and cells that initiate an immune response), and reticular cells that form the lymphoid tissue stroma.

Lymphoid Tissue (p. 777)

2. Lymphoid tissue is reticular connective tissue. It houses macrophages and a continuously changing population of lymphocytes. It is an important element of the immune system.

3. Lymphoid tissue may be diffuse or packaged into dense follicles. Follicles often display germinal centers (areas where B cells are proliferating).

Lymph Nodes (pp. 778–779)

1. Lymph nodes, the principal lymphoid organs, are discrete encapsulated structures containing both diffusely arranged and dense reticular tissue. Clustered along lymphatic vessels, lymph nodes filter lymph and help activate the immune system.

Structure of a Lymph Node (pp. 778–779)

2. Each lymph node has a fibrous capsule, a cortex, and a medulla. The cortex contains mostly lymphocytes, which act in immune responses; the medulla contains macrophages, which engulf and destroy viruses, bacteria, and other foreign debris, as well as lymphocytes and plasma cells.

Circulation in the Lymph Nodes (p. 779)

3. Lymph enters the lymph nodes via afferent lymphatic vessels and exits via efferent vessels. There are fewer efferent vessels; therefore, lymph flow stagnates within the lymph node, allowing time for its cleansing.

Other Lymphoid Organs (pp. 779–782)

1. Unlike lymph nodes, the spleen, thymus, tonsils, and Peyer's patches do not filter lymph. However, most lymphoid organs contain both macrophages and lymphocytes.

Spleen (pp. 779–781)

2. The spleen provides a site for lymphocyte proliferation and immune function, and destroys aged or defective red blood cells and bloodborne pathogens. It also stores and releases the breakdown products of hemoglobin as necessary, stores platelets, and acts as a hematopoietic site in the fetus.

Thymus (p. 781)

3. The thymus is most functional during youth. Its hormones cause T lymphocytes to become immunocompetent.

Tonsils and Aggregates of Lymphoid Follicles (pp. 781–782)

4. Peyer's patches of the intestinal wall, lymphoid follicles of the appendix, tonsils of the pharynx and oral cavity, and follicles in the genitourinary and respiratory tract mucosae are known as MALT (mucosa-associated lymphatic tissue). They prevent pathogens in these passages from penetrating the mucous membrane lining.

Developmental Aspects of the Lymphatic System (p. 783)

1. Lymphatics develop as outpocketings of developing veins. The thymus develops from endoderm; the other lymphoid organs derive from mesenchymal cells of mesoderm.

2. The thymus, the first lymphoid organ to appear, plays a role in the development of other lymphoid organs.

3. Lymphoid organs are populated by lymphocytes, which arise from hematopoietic tissue.

Review Questions

Multiple Choice/Matching

(Some questions have more than one correct answer. Select the best answer or answers from the choices given.)

1. Lymphatic vessels (a) serve as sites for immune surveillance, (b) filter lymph, (c) transport leaked plasma proteins and fluids to the cardiovascular system, (d) are represented by vessels that resemble arteries, capillaries, and veins.

2. The saclike initial portion of the thoracic duct is the (a) lacteal, (b) right lymphatic duct, (c) cisterna chyli, (d) lymph sac.

3. Entry of lymph into the lymphatic capillaries is promoted by which of the following? (a) one-way minivalves formed by overlapping endothelial cells, (b) the respiratory pump, (c) the skeletal muscle pump, (d) greater fluid pressure in the interstitial space.

4. The structural framework of lymphoid organs is (a) areolar connective tissue, (b) hematopoietic tissue, (c) reticular tissue, (d) adipose tissue.

5. Lymph nodes are densely clustered in all of the following body areas *except* (a) the brain, (b) the axillae, (c) the groin, (d) the cervical region.

6. The germinal centers in lymph nodes are largely sites of (a) macrophages, (b) proliferating B lymphocytes, (c) T lymphocytes, (d) all of these.

7. The red pulp areas of the spleen are sites of (a) venous sinuses, macrophages, and red blood cells, (b) clustered lymphocytes, (c) connective tissue septa.

8. The lymphoid organ that functions primarily during youth and then begins to atrophy is the (a) spleen, (b) thymus, (c) palatine tonsils, (d) bone marrow.

9. Collections of lymphoid tissue (MALT) that guard mucosal surfaces include all of the following *except* (a) appendix follicles, (b) the tonsils, (c) Peyer's patches, (d) the thymus.

Short Answer Essay Questions

10. Compare and contrast blood, interstitial fluid, and lymph.

11. Compare the structure and functions of a lymph node to those of the spleen.

12. (a) What anatomical characteristic ensures that the flow of lymph through a lymph node is slow? (b) Why is this desirable?

13. Why doesn't the absence of lymphatic *arteries* represent a problem?

Critical Thinking and Clinical Application Questions

1. Mrs. Jackson, a 59-year-old woman, has undergone a left radical mastectomy (removal of the left breast and left axillary lymph nodes and vessels). Her left arm is severely swollen and painful, and she is unable to raise it to more than shoulder height. (a) Explain her signs and symptoms. (b) Can she expect to have relief from these symptoms in time? How so?

2. A friend tells you that she has tender, swollen "glands" along the left side of the front of her neck. You notice that she has a bandage on her left cheek that is not fully hiding a large infected cut there. Exactly what are her swollen "glands," and how did they become swollen?

3. Once almost a rite of childhood, tonsillectomy (surgical removal of the tonsils) is now rarely performed. Similarly, while ruptured spleens were once routinely removed, they are now conserved whenever possible. Why should these lymphoid organs be preserved when possible?

LOOKING FOR MORE STUDY HELP?

A wide variety of quiz questions, tutorials, and learning exercises are available online at the Anatomy & Physiology Place (www.anatomyandphysiology.com) and, if your instructor has provided you with a MyA&P Course ID number, in MyA&P (www.myaandp.com).

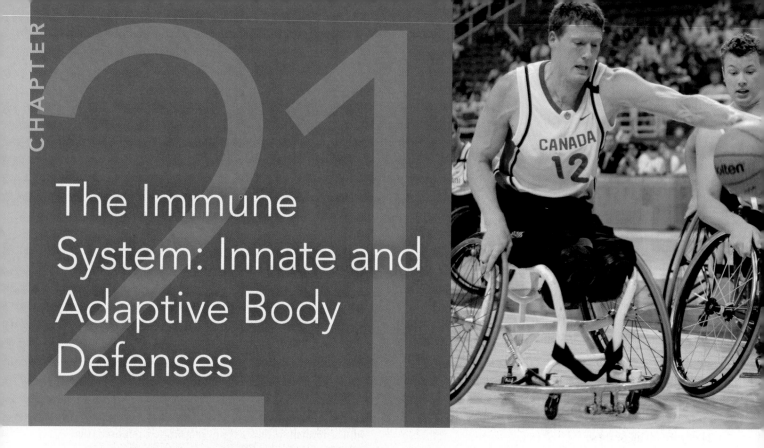

CHAPTER 21

The Immune System: Innate and Adaptive Body Defenses

PART 1: INNATE DEFENSES

Surface Barriers: Skin and Mucosae (pp. 789–790)

1. Describe surface membrane barriers and their protective functions.

Internal Defenses: Cells and Chemicals (pp. 790–798)

2. Explain the importance of phagocytosis and natural killer cells in innate body defense.

3. Describe the inflammatory process. Identify several inflammatory chemicals and indicate their specific roles.

4. Name the body's antimicrobial substances and describe their function.

5. Explain how fever helps protect the body.

PART 2: ADAPTIVE DEFENSES

Antigens (pp. 799–800)

6. Define antigen and describe how antigens affect the immune system.

7. Define complete antigen, hapten, and antigenic determinant.

8. Follow antigen processing in the body.

Cells of the Adaptive Immune System: An Overview (pp. 800–803)

9. Compare and contrast the origin, maturation process, and general function of B and T lymphocytes.

10. Define immunocompetence and self-tolerance, and describe their development in B and T lymphocytes.

11. Name several antigen-presenting cells and describe their roles in adaptive defenses.

Humoral Immune Response (pp. 804–810)

12. Define humoral immunity.

13. Describe the process of clonal selection of a B cell.

14. Recount the roles of plasma cells and memory cells in humoral immunity.

15. Compare and contrast active and passive humoral immunity.

16. Describe the structure of an antibody monomer, and name the five classes of antibodies.

17. Explain the function(s) of antibodies and describe clinical uses of monoclonal antibodies.

Cell-Mediated Immune Response (pp. 810–820)

18. Define cell-mediated immunity and describe the process of activation and clonal selection of T cells.

19. Describe T cell functions in the body.

20. Indicate the tests ordered before an organ transplant is done, and methods used to prevent transplant rejection.

Homeostatic Imbalances of Immunity (pp. 820–825)

21. Give examples of immune deficiency diseases and of hypersensitivity states.

22. Cite factors involved in autoimmune disease.

Developmental Aspects of the Immune System (pp. 825–826)

23. Describe changes in immunity that occur with aging.

24. Briefly describe the role of the nervous system in regulating the immune response.

Every second of every day, an army of hostile bacteria, fungi, and viruses swarms on our skin and yet we stay amazingly healthy most of the time. The body seems to have evolved a single-minded approach to such foes—if you're not with us, you're against us! To implement that stance, it relies heavily on two intrinsic defense systems that act both independently and cooperatively to provide resistance to disease, or **immunity** (*immun* = free).

1. The **innate (nonspecific) defense system,** like a lowly foot soldier, is always prepared, responding within minutes to protect the body from all foreign substances. This system has two "barricades." The *first line of defense* is the external body membranes—intact skin and mucosae. The *second line of defense,* called into action whenever the first line has been penetrated, uses antimicrobial proteins, phagocytes, and other cells to inhibit the invaders' spread throughout the body. The hallmark of the second line of defense is inflammation.

2. The **adaptive** (or **specific**) **defense system** * is more like an elite fighting force equipped with high-tech weapons that attacks *particular* foreign substances and provides the body's *third line of defense.* This defensive response takes considerably more time to mount than the innate response. Although we consider them separately, the adaptive and innate systems always work hand in hand. An overview of these two systems is shown in Figure 21.1.

Although certain organs of the body (notably lymphoid organs) are intimately involved in the immune response, the **immune system** is a *functional system* rather than an organ system in an anatomical sense. Its "structures" are a diverse array of molecules plus trillions of immune cells (especially lymphocytes) that inhabit lymphoid tissues and circulate in body fluids.

When the immune system is operating effectively, it protects the body from most infectious microorganisms, cancer cells, and transplanted organs or grafts. It does this both directly, by cell attack, and indirectly, by releasing mobilizing chemicals and protective antibody molecules.

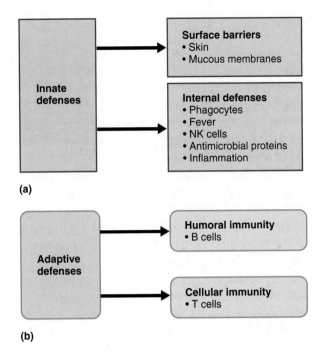

(a)

(b)

FIGURE 21.1 Overview of innate and adaptive defenses. Innate defenses include surface barriers and internal defenses. The distinct but overlapping areas of adaptive immunity are humoral (primarily involving B lymphocytes) and cellular (involving T lymphocytes). For simplicity, the many interactions between innate and adaptive defenses are not shown here. Portions of this diagram will reappear in subsequent figures to remind you of this overall scheme.

cover body surfaces and the cells and chemicals that act on the initial internal battlefronts are in place at birth, ready to ward off invading **pathogens** (harmful or disease-causing microorganisms) and infection. Many times, our innate defenses alone are able to destroy pathogens and ward off infection. In other cases, the adaptive immune system is called into action to reinforce and enhance the innate mechanisms. Either way, the innate defenses reduce the workload of the adaptive system by preventing the entry and spread of microorganisms in the body.

PART 1: INNATE DEFENSES

Because they are part and parcel of our anatomy, you could say we come fully equipped with innate or nonspecific defenses. The mechanical barriers that

Surface Barriers: Skin and Mucosae

The body's first line of defense—the *skin* and the *mucous membranes,* along with the secretions these membranes produce—is highly effective. As long as the epidermis is unbroken, this heavily keratinized epithelial membrane presents a formidable physical barrier to most microorganisms that swarm on the skin. Keratin is also resistant to most weak acids and bases and to bacterial enzymes and toxins. Intact mucosae provide similar mechanical barriers within

---

*Sometimes the term *immune system* is equated with the adaptive defense system only. However, recent research has shown that (1) many defensive molecules are released and recognized by both the innate and adaptive arms; (2) the innate responses are not as nonspecific as once thought and may have specific pathways to target certain foreign substances; and (3) proteins released during innate responses alert cells of the adaptive system to the presence of specific foreign molecules in the body.

the body. Recall that mucous membranes line all body cavities that open to the exterior: the digestive, respiratory, urinary, and reproductive tracts. Besides serving as physical barriers, these epithelial membranes produce a variety of protective chemicals:

1. The acidity of skin secretions (pH 3 to 5) inhibits bacterial growth, and sebum contains chemicals that are toxic to bacteria. Vaginal secretions of adult females are also very acidic.

2. The stomach mucosa secretes a concentrated hydrochloric acid solution and protein-digesting enzymes. Both kill microorganisms.

3. Saliva, which cleanses the oral cavity and teeth, and lacrimal fluid of the eye contain **lysozyme,** an enzyme that destroys bacteria.

4. Sticky mucus traps many microorganisms that enter the digestive and respiratory passageways.

The respiratory tract mucosae also have structural modifications that counteract potential invaders. Tiny mucus-coated hairs inside the nose trap inhaled particles, and cilia on the mucosa of the upper respiratory tract sweep dust- and bacteria-laden mucus toward the mouth, preventing it from entering the lower respiratory passages, where the warm, moist environment provides an ideal site for bacterial growth.

Although the surface barriers are quite effective, they are breached occasionally by small nicks and cuts resulting, for example, from brushing your teeth or shaving. When this happens and microorganisms invade deeper tissues, the *internal* innate defenses come into play.

Internal Defenses: Cells and Chemicals

The body uses an enormous number of nonspecific cellular and chemical devices to protect itself, including phagocytes, natural killer cells, antimicrobial proteins, and fever. The inflammatory response enlists macrophages, mast cells, all types of white blood cells, and dozens of chemicals that kill pathogens and help repair tissue. All these protective ploys identify potentially harmful substances by recognizing surface carbohydrates unique to infectious organisms (bacteria, viruses, and fungi).

Phagocytes

Pathogens that get through the skin and mucosae into the underlying connective tissue are confronted by *phagocytes* (*phago* = eat). The chief phagocytes are **macrophages** ("big eaters"), which derive from white blood cells called **monocytes** that leave the bloodstream, enter the tissues, and develop into macrophages.

Free macrophages, like the alveolar macrophages of the lungs, wander throughout the tissue spaces in search of cellular debris or "foreign invaders." *Fixed macrophages* like *Kupffer cells* in the liver and microglia of the brain are permanent residents of particular organs. Whatever their mobility, all macrophages are similar structurally and functionally.

Neutrophils, the most abundant type of white blood cell, become phagocytic on encountering infectious material in the tissues. **Eosinophils,** another type of white blood cell, are only weakly phagocytic, but they are important in defending the body against parasitic worms. When they encounter such parasites, eosinophils position themselves against the worm and discharge the destructive contents of their large cytoplasmic granules all over their prey.

Mechanism of Phagocytosis

A phagocyte engulfs particulate matter much the way an amoeba ingests a food particle. Flowing cytoplasmic extensions bind to the particle and then pull it inside, enclosed within a membrane-lined vacuole. The **phagosome** thus formed is then fused with a *lysosome* to form a **phagolysosome** (steps ①–③ in Figure 21.2b).

Phagocytic attempts are not always successful. In order for a phagocyte to accomplish ingestion, **adherence** must occur. The phagocyte must first *adhere* or cling to the pathogen, a feat made possible by recognizing the pathogen's carbohydrate "signature." Recognition is particularly difficult with microorganisms such as pneumococcus, which have an external capsule made of complex sugars. These pathogens can sometimes elude capture because phagocytes cannot bind to their capsules. Adherence is both more probable and more efficient when complement proteins or antibodies coat foreign particles, a process called **opsonization** ("to make tasty"), because the coating provides "handles" to which phagocyte receptors can bind.

Sometimes the way neutrophils and macrophages kill ingested prey is more than simple digestion by lysosomal enzymes. For example, pathogens such as the tuberculosis bacillus and certain parasites are resistant to lysosomal enzymes and can even multiply within the phagolysosome. However, when the macrophage is stimulated by chemicals released by immune cells, additional enzymes are activated that produce the **respiratory burst,** an event that liberates a deluge of free radicals (including nitric oxide and superoxide), which have potent cell-killing ability. More widespread cell killing is caused by oxidizing chemicals (H_2O_2 and a substance identical to household bleach). In yet another mechanism of killing triggered by the respiratory burst, K^+ enters the phagolysosome, the pH rises, and the phagolysosome becomes hyperosmotic.

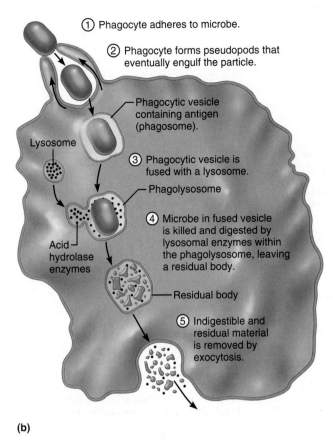

① Phagocyte adheres to microbe.

② Phagocyte forms pseudopods that eventually engulf the particle.

Phagocytic vesicle containing antigen (phagosome).

Lysosome

③ Phagocytic vesicle is fused with a lysosome.

Phagolysosome

④ Microbe in fused vesicle is killed and digested by lysosomal enzymes within the phagolysosome, leaving a residual body.

Acid hydrolase enzymes

Residual body

⑤ Indigestible and residual material is removed by exocytosis.

Innate defenses ⟶ Internal defenses

(a)

(b)

FIGURE 21.2 **Phagocytosis. (a)** In this scanning electron micrograph (2600×), a macrophage uses its long cytoplasmic extensions to pull sausage-shaped *E. coli* bacteria toward it. **(b)** Events of phagocytosis.

This activates protein-digesting enzymes that digest the invader. Neutrophils also produce antimicrobial chemicals, called *defensins* (see p. 833), that pierce the pathogen's membrane.

When phagocytes are unable to ingest their targets (because of size, for example), they can release their toxic chemicals into the extracellular fluid. Whether killing ingested or extracellular targets, neutrophils rapidly destroy themselves in the process, whereas macrophages are more robust and can go on to kill another day.

Natural Killer Cells

Natural killer (NK) cells, which "police" the body in blood and lymph, are a unique group of defensive cells that can lyse and kill cancer cells and virus-infected body cells before the adaptive immune system is activated. Sometimes called the "pit bulls" of the defense system, NK cells are part of a small group of *large granular lymphocytes.* Unlike lymphocytes of the adaptive immune system, which recognize and react only against *specific* virus-infected or tumor cells, NK cells are far less picky. They can eliminate a variety of infected or cancerous cells by detecting the lack of "self" cell surface receptors and by recognizing certain surface sugars on the target cell. The name "natural" killer cells reflects this nonspecificity of NK cells.

NK cells are not phagocytic. Their mode of killing, which involves direct contact and induces the target cell to undergo apoptosis (programmed cell death), uses the same killing mechanisms used by cytotoxic T cells (described fully on p. 815). NK cells also secrete potent chemicals that enhance the inflammatory response.

Inflammation: Tissue Response to Injury

The **inflammatory response** is triggered whenever body tissues are injured by physical trauma (a blow), intense heat, irritating chemicals, or infection by viruses, fungi, or bacteria. The inflammatory response has several beneficial effects:

1. Prevents the spread of damaging agents to nearby tissues

2. Disposes of cell debris and pathogens

3. Sets the stage for repair

21

Q *Why is it important that the capillaries become leaky during the inflammatory response?*

Innate defenses ⟶ Internal defenses

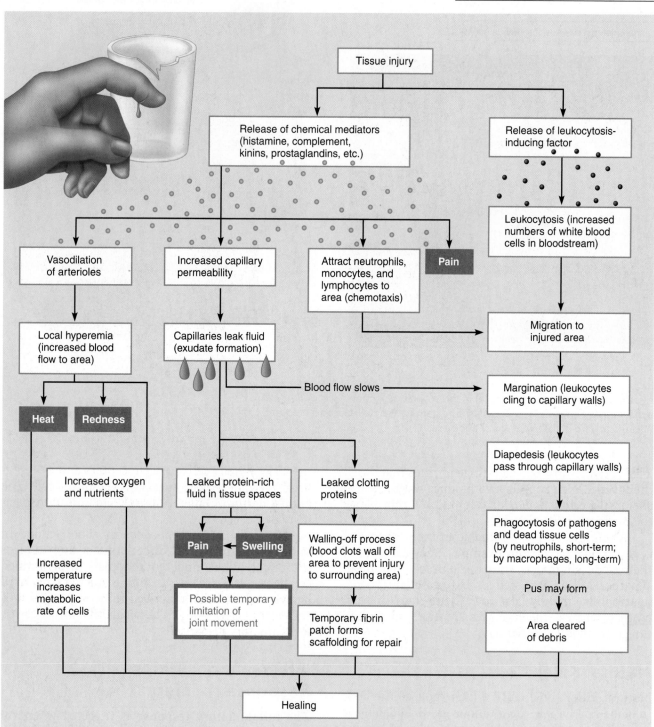

FIGURE 21.3 **Flowchart of events in inflammation.** The four cardinal signs of acute inflammation are shown in red boxes, as is limitation of joint movement, which in some cases constitutes a fifth cardinal sign (impairment of function).

A *This allows more filtrate containing blood-clotting proteins, antibodies, and complement to enter the inflamed area.*

21

TABLE 21.1	Inflammatory Chemicals	
CHEMICAL	**SOURCE**	**PHYSIOLOGICAL EFFECTS**
Histamine	Granules of basophils and mast cells; released in response to mechanical injury, presence of certain microorganisms, and chemicals released by neutrophils	Promotes vasodilation of local arterioles; increases permeability of local capillaries, promoting exudate formation
Kinins (bradykinin and others)	A plasma protein, kininogen, is cleaved by the enzyme kallikrein found in plasma, urine, saliva, and in lysosomes of neutrophils and other types of cells; cleavage releases active kinin peptides	Same as for histamine; also induce chemotaxis of leukocytes and prompt neutrophils to release lysosomal enzymes, thereby enhancing generation of more kinins; induce pain
Prostaglandins	Fatty acid molecules produced from arachidonic acid—found in all cell membranes; generated by enzymes of neutrophils, basophils, mast cells, and others	Sensitize blood vessels to effects of other inflammatory mediators; one of the intermediate steps of prostaglandin generation produces free radicals, which themselves can cause inflammation; induce pain
Platelet-derived growth factor (PDGF)	Secreted by platelets and endothelial cells	Stimulates fibroblast activity and repair of damaged tissues
Complement	See Table 21.2 (p. 796)	
Cytokines	See Table 21.4 (pp. 817–818)	

The four *cardinal signs* of short-term, or acute, inflammation are *redness*, *heat* (*inflam* = set on fire), *swelling*, and *pain* (Figure 21.3). If the inflamed area is a joint, joint movement may be hampered temporarily. This forces the injured part to rest, which aids healing. Some authorities consider *impairment of function* to be the fifth cardinal sign of acute inflammation.

Vasodilation and Increased Vascular Permeability

The inflammatory process begins with a chemical "alarm" as a flood of inflammatory chemicals are released into the extracellular fluid. Macrophages (and cells of certain boundary tissues such as epithelial cells lining the gastrointestinal and respiratory tracts) bear surface membrane receptors, called **Toll-like receptors (TLRs)**, that play a central role in triggering immune responses. So far ten types of human TLRs have been identified, each recognizing a specific class of attacking microbe. For example, one type responds to a glycolipid in cell walls of the tuberculosis bacterium and another to a component of gram-negative bacteria such as *Salmonella*. Once activated, a TLR triggers the release of chemicals called *cytokines* that promote inflammation and attract WBCs to the scene. But macrophages are not the only sort of recognition "tool" in the innate system. **Mast cells,** a key component of the inflammatory response, release the potent inflammatory chemical **histamine** (his'tah-mēn). In addition, injured and stressed tissue cells, phagocytes, lymphocytes, basophils, and blood proteins are all sources of inflammatory mediators. These include not only

histamine and cytokines, but **kinins** (ki'ninz), **prostaglandins** (pros"tah-glan'dinz), **leukotrienes,** and **complement.** Though some of these mediators have individual inflammatory roles as well (see Table 21.1), they all cause small blood vessels in the injured area to dilate. As more blood flows into the area, local **hyperemia** (congestion with blood) occurs, accounting for the *redness* and *heat* of an inflamed region.

The liberated chemicals also increase the permeability of local capillaries. Consequently, **exudate**—fluid containing clotting factors and antibodies—seeps from the blood into the tissue spaces. This exudate causes the local edema *(swelling)* that presses on adjacent nerve endings, contributing to a sensation of *pain*. Pain also results from the release of bacterial toxins, and the sensitizing effects of released prostaglandins and kinins. Aspirin and some other anti-inflammatory drugs produce their analgesic (pain-reducing) effects by inhibiting prostaglandin synthesis.

Although edema may seem detrimental, it isn't. The surge of protein-rich fluids into the tissue spaces helps to dilute harmful substances that may be present and delivers important proteins such as complement and clotting factors to the interstitial fluid (Figure 21.3). The clotting proteins form a gel-like fibrin mesh that forms a scaffold for permanent repair. This isolates the injured area and prevents the spread of bacteria and other harmful agents into surrounding tissues. Walling off the injured area is such an important defense mechanism that some bacteria (such as *Streptococcus*) have evolved enzymes that break down the clot,

21

FIGURE 21.4 **Phagocyte mobilization.** When leukocytosis-inducing factors are released by injured cells at an inflamed site, ① neutrophils are released from the bone marrow to the blood. Because blood at the inflammatory site loses fluid, blood flow slows locally and the neutrophils roll along the vascular endothelium. ② Margination begins as neutrophil cell adhesion molecules (CAMs) cling to those of the capillary endothelial cells, and then ③ diapedesis occurs as the neutrophils squeeze through the capillary walls. ④ Positive chemotaxis is the continued migration toward the site where inflammatory chemicals are present. Once at the inflamed site, the neutrophils help rid the area of pathogens and cellular debris.

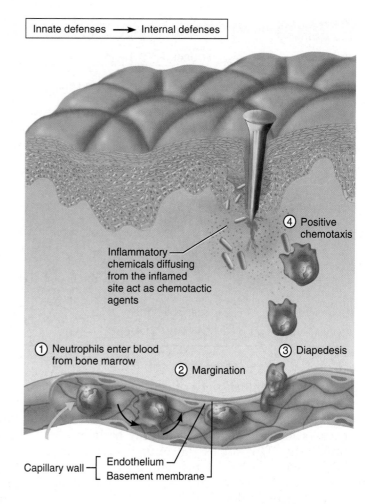

Innate defenses ⟶ Internal defenses

④ Positive chemotaxis

Inflammatory chemicals diffusing from the inflamed site act as chemotactic agents

① Neutrophils enter blood from bone marrow

② Margination

③ Diapedesis

Capillary wall { Endothelium
Basement membrane }

allowing the bacteria to spread rapidly into adjacent tissues.

At inflammatory sites where an epithelial barrier has been breached, additional chemicals enter the battle—β-defensins. These broad-spectrum antimicrobial chemicals are continuously present in epithelial mucosal cells in small amounts and help maintain the sterile environment of the body's internal passageways (urinary tract, respiratory bronchi, etc.). However, when the mucosal surface is abraded or penetrated and the underlying connective tissue becomes inflamed, β-defensin output increases dramatically, helping to control bacterial and fungal colonization in the exposed area.

Phagocyte Mobilization

Soon after inflammation begins, the damaged area is invaded by more phagocytes—neutrophils lead, followed by macrophages. If the inflammation was provoked by pathogens, a group of plasma proteins known as complement (discussed shortly) is activated and elements of adaptive immunity (lymphocytes and antibodies) also invade the injured site. The process by which phagocytes are mobilized to infiltrate the injured site is illustrated in Figure 21.4.

① **Leukocytosis.** Chemicals called **leukocytosis-inducing factors** released by injured cells promote rapid release of neutrophils from red bone marrow, and within a few hours the number of neutrophils in blood increases four- to fivefold. This increase in WBCs, called **leukocytosis,** is a characteristic of inflammation.

② **Margination.** Because of the tremendous outpouring of fluid from the blood into the injured area, blood flow in the region slows and the neutrophils begin to roll along the capillary endothelium as if "tasting" the local environment. In inflamed areas, the endothelial cells sprout cell adhesion molecules (CAMs) called *selectins.* These provide footholds (signal that "this is the place") for other CAMs (integrins) on the surfaces of the neutrophils to bind. When the complementary CAMs unite, the neutrophils cling to the inner walls of the capillaries and postcapillary venules. This phenomenon is known as **margination.**

③ **Diapedesis.** The continued chemical signaling prompts the neutrophils to squeeze through the capillary walls, a process called **diapedesis** or **emigration.**

④ **Chemotaxis.** Neutrophils usually migrate randomly, but inflammatory chemicals act as homing devices, or more precisely **chemotactic agents,** that attract the neutrophils and other white blood cells to the site of the injury. Within an hour after the inflammatory response has begun, neutrophils have collected at the site and are devouring any foreign material present.

As the counterattack continues, monocytes follow neutrophils into the injured area. Monocytes are fairly poor phagocytes, but within 12 hours of leaving the blood and entering the tissues, they swell and develop large numbers of lysosomes, becoming macrophages with insatiable appetites. These late-arriving macrophages replace the neutrophils on the battlefield. Macrophages are the central actors in the final disposal of cell debris as an acute inflammation subsides, and they predominate at sites of prolonged, or *chronic,* inflammation. The ultimate goal of an inflammatory response is to clear the injured area of pathogens, dead tissue cells, and any other debris so that tissue can be repaired. Once this is accomplished, healing usually occurs quickly.

▶ HOMEOSTATIC IMBALANCE

In severely infected areas, the battle takes a considerable toll on both sides, and creamy, yellow **pus,** a mixture of dead or dying neutrophils, broken-down tissue cells, and living and dead pathogens, may accumulate in the wound. If the inflammatory mechanism fails to clear the area of debris, the sac of pus may be walled off by collagen fibers, forming an *abscess.* Surgical drainage of abscesses is often necessary before healing can occur.

Bacteria, such as tuberculosis bacilli, that are resistant to digestion by macrophages escape the effects of prescription antibiotics by remaining snugly enclosed within their macrophage hosts. In such cases, *infectious granulomas* form. These tumorlike growths contain a central region of infected macrophages surrounded by uninfected macrophages and an outer fibrous capsule. A person may harbor pathogens walled off in granulomas for years without displaying any symptoms. However, if the person's resistance to infection is ever compromised, the bacteria may be activated and break out, leading to clinical disease symptoms. ●

Antimicrobial Proteins

A variety of **antimicrobial proteins** enhance the innate defenses by attacking microorganisms directly or by hindering their ability to reproduce. The most important of these are interferons and complement proteins (Table 21.2).

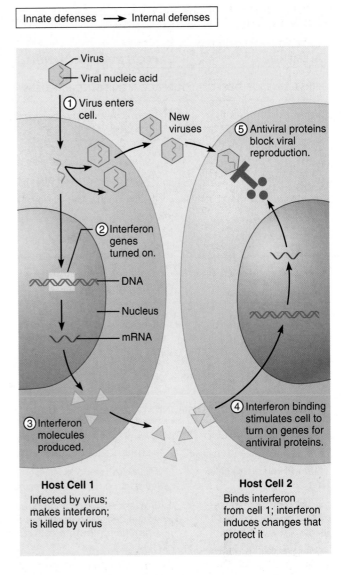

FIGURE 21.5 **The interferon mechanism against viruses.**

Interferons

Viruses—essentially nucleic acids surrounded by a protein coat—lack the cellular machinery to generate ATP or synthesize proteins. They do their "dirty work" or damage in the body by invading tissue cells and taking over the cellular metabolic machinery needed to reproduce themselves. Although the infected cells can do little to save themselves, some can secrete small proteins called **interferons (IFNs)** (in"ter-fēr'onz) to help protect cells that have not yet been infected. The IFNs diffuse to nearby cells, where they stimulate synthesis of proteins which then "interfere" with viral replication in the still-healthy cells by blocking protein synthesis and degrading viral RNA (Figure 21.5). Because IFN protection is not *virus specific*, IFNs produced against a particular virus protect against a variety of other viruses.

TABLE 21.2	Summary of Nonspecific Body Defenses
CATEGORY/ASSOCIATED ELEMENTS	**PROTECTIVE MECHANISM**

FIRST LINE OF DEFENSE: SURFACE MEMBRANE BARRIERS

Intact skin epidermis	Forms mechanical barrier that prevents entry of pathogens and other harmful substances into body
▪ Acid mantle	Skin secretions (perspiration and sebum) make epidermal surface acidic, which inhibits bacterial growth; sebum also contains bactericidal chemicals
▪ Keratin	Provides resistance against acids, alkalis, and bacterial enzymes
Intact mucous membranes	Form mechanical barrier that prevents entry of pathogens
▪ Mucus	Traps microorganisms in respiratory and digestive tracts
▪ Nasal hairs	Filter and trap microorganisms in nasal passages
▪ Cilia	Propel debris-laden mucus away from lower respiratory passages
▪ Gastric juice	Contains concentrated hydrochloric acid and protein-digesting enzymes that destroy pathogens in stomach
▪ Acid mantle of vagina	Inhibits growth of most bacteria and fungi in female reproductive tract
▪ Lacrimal secretion (tears); saliva	Continuously lubricate and cleanse eyes (tears) and oral cavity (saliva); contain lysozyme, an enzyme that destroys microorganisms
▪ Urine	Normally acid pH inhibits bacterial growth; cleanses the lower urinary tract as it flushes from the body

SECOND LINE OF DEFENSE: INNATE, CELLULAR AND CHEMICAL DEFENSES

Phagocytes	Engulf and destroy pathogens that breach surface membrane barriers; macrophages also contribute to immune response
Natural killer (NK) cells	Promote apoptosis (cell suicide) by direct cell attack against virus-infected or cancerous body cells; do not require specific antigen recognition; do not exhibit a memory response
Inflammatory response	Prevents spread of injurious agents to adjacent tissues, disposes of pathogens and dead tissue cells, and promotes tissue repair; chemical mediators released attract phagocytes (and immunocompetent cells) to the area
Antimicrobial proteins ▪ Interferons (α, β, γ)	Proteins released by virus-infected cells and certain lymphocytes that protect uninfected tissue cells from viral takeover; mobilize immune system
▪ Complement	Lyses microorganisms, enhances phagocytosis by opsonization, and intensifies inflammatory and immune responses
Fever	Systemic response initiated by pyrogens; high body temperature inhibits microbial multiplication and enhances body repair processes

The IFNs are a family of related proteins produced by a variety of body cells, each having a slightly different physiological effect. Lymphocytes secrete gamma (γ), or immune, interferon, but most other leukocytes secrete alpha (α) interferon. Beta (β) interferon is secreted by fibroblasts. IFN-β and -α reduce inflammation. Besides their antiviral effects, interferons activate macrophages and mobilize NK cells. Because both macrophages and NK cells can act directly against malignant cells, the interferons play some anticancer role.

Genetically engineered IFNs have found a niche as antiviral agents. *IFN-α* is used to treat genital warts (caused by human papillomavirus) and is the first drug to have some success in combating hepatitis C (spread via blood and sexual intercourse), the most common and most dreaded form of hepatitis. *IFN-β* is used to treat patients with multiple sclerosis, a devastating demyelinating disease.

Complement

The term **complement system,** or simply **complement,** refers to a group of at least 20 plasma proteins that normally circulate in the blood in an inactive state. These proteins include C1 through C9, factors

Q *Which pathway can occur without the need for an adaptive immune response?*

FIGURE 21.6 **Complement activation.** The classical pathway, mediated by 11 complement proteins designated C1–C9 (C1 incorporates three proteins), requires antigen-antibody interactions. The alternative pathway occurs when plasma proteins called factors B, D, and P interact with polysaccharides on the cell walls of certain bacteria and fungi. The two pathways converge to activate C3 (cleaving it into C3a and C3b), a step that initiates a common terminal sequence. Once bound to the target cell's surface, C3b initiates the remaining steps of complement activation. These steps result in the incorporation of MAC, the membrane attack complex (components C5b, and C6 to C9), into the target cell's membrane, creating a funnel-shaped pore that causes cell lysis. Bound C3b also enhances phagocytosis. Released C3a, C5a, and other products of complement activation promote the events of inflammation.

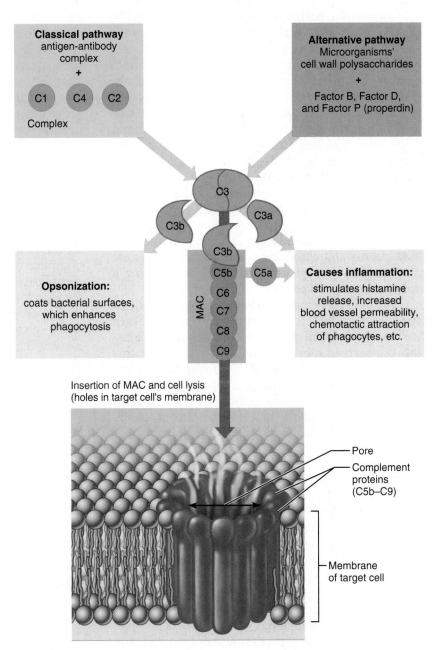

B, D, and P, plus several regulatory proteins. Complement provides a major mechanism for destroying foreign substances in the body. Its activation unleashes chemical mediators that amplify virtually all aspects of the inflammatory process. Another effect of complement activation is that certain bacteria and other cell types are killed by cell lysis. (Luckily our own cells are equipped with proteins that inactivate complement.) Although complement is a nonspe-

cific defensive mechanism, it "complements" (enhances) the effectiveness of *both* innate and adaptive defenses.

Complement can be activated by the two pathways outlined in Figure 21.6. The **classical pathway** involves *antibodies*, water-soluble protein molecules that the adaptive immune system produces to fight off foreign invaders. The classical pathway depends on the binding of antibodies to the invading

A *The alternative pathway.*

organisms and the subsequent binding of C1 to the microorganism-antibody complexes, a step called *complement fixation* (described on pp. 809–810). The **alternative pathway** is triggered when factors B, D, and P interact with polysaccharide molecules present on the surface of certain microorganisms.

Like the blood clotting cascade, complement activation by either pathway involves a cascade in which proteins are activated in an orderly sequence—each step catalyzing the next. The two pathways converge on C3, cleaving it into C3a and C3b. This event initiates a common terminal pathway that causes cell lysis, promotes phagocytosis, and enhances inflammation.

The lytic events begin when C3b binds to the target cell's surface, triggering the insertion of a group of complement proteins called **MAC (membrane attack complex)** into the cell's membrane. MAC forms and stabilizes a hole in the membrane that ensures lysis of the target cell by inducing a massive influx of water.

The C3b molecules that coat the microorganism provide "handles" that receptors on macrophages and neutrophils can adhere to, allowing them to engulf the particle more rapidly. As noted earlier, this process is called *opsonization*. C3a and other cleavage products formed during complement fixation amplify the inflammatory response by stimulating mast cells and basophils to release histamine and by attracting neutrophils and other inflammatory cells to the area.

C-reactive protein (CRP), produced by the liver in response to inflammatory molecules, is used as a clinical marker to assess for the presence of an acute infection or an inflammatory condition and its response to treatment. Because it binds with a variety of physiological ligands, it has multiple roles in immunity. By binding to certain surface molecules of pathogens and exposed self-antigens of damaged body cells, it plays a surveillance role that results in their targeting for disposal by phagocytes and complement. CRP binding to C1 of the classical complement pathway activates complement and results in the deposit of C3 on the surface of bacteria (opsonization).

Fever

Inflammation is a localized response to infection, but sometimes the body's response to the invasion of microorganisms is more widespread. **Fever,** or abnormally high body temperature, is a systemic response to invading microorganisms. As described further in Chapter 24, body temperature is regulated by a cluster of neurons in the hypothalamus, commonly referred to as the body's thermostat. Normally set at approximately 37°C (98.6°F), the thermostat is reset upward in response to chemicals called **pyrogens** (*pyro* = fire), secreted by leukocytes and macrophages exposed to foreign substances in the body.

High fevers are dangerous because excess heat denatures enzymes. Mild or moderate fever, however, is an adaptive response that seems to benefit the body. In order to multiply, bacteria require large amounts of iron and zinc, but during a fever the liver and spleen sequester these nutrients, making them less available. Fever also increases the metabolic rate of tissue cells in general, speeding up repair processes.

PART 2: ADAPTIVE DEFENSES

Most of us would find it wonderfully convenient if we could walk into a single clothing store and buy a complete wardrobe—hat to shoes—that fit perfectly regardless of any special figure problems. We know that such a service would be next to impossible to find. And yet, we take for granted our **adaptive immune system,** the body's built-in *specific defensive system* that stalks and eliminates with nearly equal precision almost any type of pathogen that intrudes into the body.

When it operates effectively, the adaptive immune system protects us from a wide variety of infectious agents, as well as from abnormal body cells. When it fails, or is disabled, the result is such devastating diseases as cancer and AIDS. The activity of the adaptive immune system tremendously amplifies the inflammatory response and is responsible for most complement activation. At first glance, the adaptive system seems to have a major shortcoming. Unlike the innate system, which is always ready and able to react, the adaptive system must "meet" or be primed by an initial exposure to a specific foreign substance (antigen) before it can protect the body against that substance, and this priming takes precious time.

The basis of this specific immunity was revealed in the late 1800s, when researchers demonstrated that animals surviving a serious bacterial infection have in their blood protective factors (the proteins we now call *antibodies*) that defend against future attacks by the same pathogen. Furthermore, it was shown that if antibody-containing serum from the surviving animals was injected into animals that had *not* been exposed to the pathogen, those injected animals would also be protected. These landmark experiments were exciting because they revealed three important aspects of the adaptive immune response:

1. It is specific: It recognizes and is directed against *particular* pathogens or foreign substances that initiate the immune response.

2. It is systemic: Immunity is not restricted to the initial infection site.

3. It has "memory": After an initial exposure, it recognizes and mounts even stronger attacks on the previously encountered pathogens.

At first antibodies were thought to be the sole artillery of the adaptive immune system, but in the mid-1900s it was discovered that injection of antibody-containing serum did *not* always protect the recipient from diseases the serum donor had survived. In such cases, however, injection of the donor's lymphocytes *did* provide immunity. As the pieces fell into place, two separate but overlapping arms of adaptive immunity were recognized, each using a variety of attack mechanisms that vary with the intruder.

Humoral immunity (hu'mor-ul), also called **antibody-mediated immunity,** is provided by antibodies present in the body's "humors," or fluids (blood, lymph, etc.). Though they are produced by lymphocytes (or their offspring), antibodies circulate freely in the blood and lymph, where they bind primarily to bacteria, to bacterial toxins, and to free viruses, inactivating them temporarily and marking them for destruction by phagocytes or complement.

When lymphocytes themselves rather than antibodies defend the body, the immunity is called **cellular** or **cell-mediated immunity** because the protective factor is living cells. Cellular immunity also has cellular targets—virus-infected or parasite-infected tissue cells, cancer cells, and cells of foreign grafts. The lymphocytes act against such targets either *directly*, by killing the foreign cells, or *indirectly*, by releasing chemical mediators that enhance the inflammatory response or activate other lymphocytes or macrophages. Thus, as you can see, although both arms of the adaptive immune system respond to virtually the same foreign substances, they do it in very different ways.

Before describing the humoral and cell-mediated responses, we will consider the *antigens* that trigger the activity of the remarkable cells involved in these immune responses.

Antigens

Antigens (an'tĭ-jenz) are substances that can mobilize the immune system and provoke an immune response. As such, they are the ultimate targets of all immune responses. Most antigens are large, complex molecules (both natural and synthetic) that are not normally present in the body. Consequently, as far as our immune system is concerned, they are intruders, or **nonself.**

Complete Antigens and Haptens

Antigens can be *complete* or *incomplete*. **Complete antigens** have two important functional properties:

1. Immunogenicity, which is the ability to stimulate proliferation of specific lymphocytes and antibodies. (*Antigen* is a contraction of "*anti*body *gen*erating," which refers to this particular antigenic property.)

2. Reactivity, which is the ability to react with the activated lymphocytes and the antibodies released by immunogenic reactions.

An almost limitless variety of foreign molecules can act as complete antigens, including virtually all foreign proteins, many large polysaccharides, and some lipids and nucleic acids. Of these, proteins are the strongest antigens. Pollen grains and microorganisms—such as bacteria, fungi, and virus particles—are all immunogenic because their surfaces bear many different foreign macromolecules.

As a rule, small molecules—such as peptides, nucleotides, and many hormones—are not immunogenic. But, if they link up with the body's own proteins, the adaptive immune system may recognize the combination as foreign and mount an attack that is harmful rather than protective. (These reactions, called *hypersensitivities*, are described later in the chapter.) In such cases, the troublesome small molecule is called a **hapten** (hap'ten; *haptein* = grasp) or **incomplete antigen.** Unless attached to protein carriers, haptens have reactivity but not immunogenicity. Besides certain drugs (particularly penicillin), chemicals that act as haptens are found in poison ivy, animal dander, detergents, cosmetics, and a number of common household and industrial products.

Antigenic Determinants

The ability of a molecule to act as an antigen depends on both its size and its complexity. Only certain parts of an entire antigen, called **antigenic determinants,** are immunogenic. Free antibodies or lymphocyte receptors bind to these sites in much the same manner an enzyme binds to a substrate.

Most naturally occurring antigens have a variety of antigenic determinants (Figure 21.7) on their surfaces, some more potent than others in provoking an immune response. Because different antigenic determinants are "recognized" by different lymphocytes, a single antigen may mobilize several lymphocyte populations and may stimulate formation of many kinds of antibodies. Large proteins have hundreds of chemically different antigenic determinants, which accounts for their high immunogenicity and reactivity. However, large simple molecules such as plastics,

21

FIGURE 21.7 **Antigenic determinants.** Antibodies (and related receptors on lymphocytes) bind to antigenic determinants on the antigen surface. Most antigens have several different antigenic determinants, which means that different antibodies can bind to a given antigen. In this example, three types of antibodies react with different antigenic determinants on the same antigen molecule. (On a real antigen molecule, each antigenic determinant would be represented many times.)

which have many identical, regularly repeating units (and thus are not chemically complex), have little or no immunogenicity. Such substances are used to make artificial implants because the substances are not seen as foreign and rejected by the body.

Self-Antigens: MHC Proteins

The external surfaces of all our cells are dotted with a huge variety of protein molecules. Assuming our immune system has been properly "programmed," these **self-antigens** are not foreign or antigenic to us, but they are strongly antigenic to other individuals. (This is the basis of transfusion reactions and graft rejection.) Among the cell surface proteins that mark a cell as *self* is a group of glycoproteins called **MHC proteins,** coded for by genes of the **major histocompatibility complex (MHC).** Because millions of combinations of these genes are possible, it is unlikely that any two people except identical twins have the same MHC proteins.

There are two major groups of MHC proteins, distinguished by location. Class I MHC proteins are found on virtually *all* body cells, but class II MHC proteins are found *only on certain cells* that act in the immune response.

Each MHC molecule has a deep groove that typically displays a peptide. In healthy cells, peptides displayed by class I MHC come from the breakdown of cellular proteins during normal protein recycling and tend to be quite diverse. However, in infected cells, class I MHC also binds to fragments of foreign antigens that come from within the infected cell. Peptides displayed by class II MHC come from outside the cell. As described shortly, these displayed

peptides play a crucial role in mobilizing the immune system.

Cells of the Adaptive Immune System: An Overview

The three crucial cell types of the adaptive immune system are two distinct populations of lymphocytes, and *antigen-presenting cells (APCs)*. **B lymphocytes** or **B cells** oversee humoral immunity. **T lymphocytes** or **T cells** are non-antibody-producing lymphocytes that constitute the cell-mediated arm of adaptive immunity. Unlike the lymphocytes, APCs do not respond to specific antigens but instead play essential auxiliary roles.

Lymphocytes

Like all other blood cells, lymphocytes originate in red bone marrow from hematopoietic stem cells. During development, lymphocytes are "educated." The aim of this education is twofold: (1) Each lymphocyte must become able (competent) to recognize its one specific antigen by binding to it. This ability is called **immunocompetence.** (2) Each lymphocyte must be relatively unresponsive to self-antigens so that it does not attack the body's own cells. This is called **self-tolerance.**

B and T cells are educated in different parts of the body. T cells undergo this two- to three-day maturation process in the thymus under the direction of thymic hormones. B cells become immunocompetent and self-tolerant in the bone marrow. The lymphoid organs where the lymphocytes become immunocompetent (thymus and bone marrow) are called **primary lymphoid organs** (Figure 21.8). All other lymphoid organs are referred to as **secondary lymphoid organs.**

Development of Immunocompetence and Self-Tolerance

When B or T cells become immunocompetent, they display a unique type of receptor on their surface. These receptors (some 10^5 per cell) enable the lymphocyte to recognize and bind to a specific antigen. Once these receptors appear, the lymphocyte is committed to react to one distinct antigenic determinant, and one only, because *all* of its antigen receptors are the same. The receptors on B cells are in fact membrane-bound antibodies, while the receptors on T cells are not antibodies but are products of the same gene superfamily. These similar structures have similar functions, and both cell types are capable of responding to the same antigens.

For T cells, the education in the thymus ensures that they meet two essential criteria for life

Q *What is the advantage of having lymphocytes that are mobile rather than fixed in the lymphoid organs?*

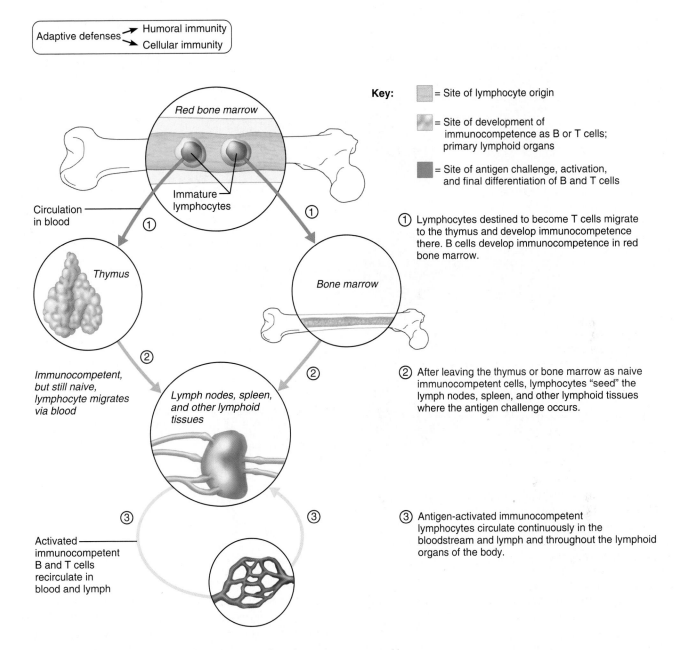

FIGURE 21.8 **Lymphocyte traffic.** Immature lymphocytes arise in red bone marrow. (Note that red marrow is not found in the medullary cavity of the diaphysis of long bones in adults.)

as a successful T cell. First, the T cell must be able to bind MHC molecules, since it is on these molecules that antigens are presented to the T cell for recognition. Second, the T cell must not react strongly to self-antigens that are normally found in

the body. In order to ensure that all T cells meet these criteria, their education consists of positive and negative selection (Figure 21.9). **Positive selection,** which occurs in the thymic cortex, is essentially an **MHC restriction process.** It identifies T cells whose receptors are capable of recognizing self-MHC molecules, thus producing an army of self-MHC-restricted T cells. T cells that make it through positive selection are then tested to make

A *It allows them to come into contact with a broader spectrum of antigens and other body cells.*

Q *What cell types act as APCs?*

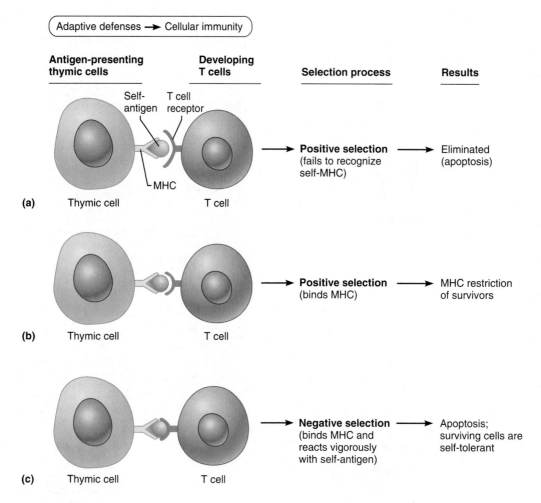

FIGURE 21.9   T cell selection in the thymus. (a, b) During positive selection, T cells must show the ability to recognize self-MHC in order to continue maturing. Those that survive the self-MHC test are later tested for reaction to self-antigen. **(c)** In negative selection, the trait of reacting strongly to self-antigens causes the T cell to be eliminated.

21

sure that they do not react vigorously to self-antigens bound to self-MHC. If they do, they are eliminated by apoptosis (programmed cell death). This is **negative selection,** and it occurs in the inner edge of the thymic cortex. Negative selection ensures immunologic self-tolerance, making sure that T cells don't attack the body's own cells, which would cause autoimmune disorders. This education of T cells is expensive indeed—only about 2% of T cells survive it and continue on to become successful immunocompetent, self-tolerant T cells.

Less is known about the factors that control B cell maturation in humans. In the bone marrow,

self-reactive B cells are either eliminated by apoptosis *(clonal deletion),* or are given a chance to change their self-reactive antigen receptor by *receptor editing,* in which there is a secondary rearrangement of the antigen-binding part of the receptor. Nevertheless, some self-reacting B cells do leave the bone marrow. In the periphery, these self-reactive B cells are inactivated (a phenomenon called *anergy).*

Immunocompetent T and B cells that have not yet been exposed to antigen are called *naive.* Naive T cells and B cells are exported to the lymph nodes, spleen, and other secondary lymphoid organs, where the encounters with antigens occur (Figure 21.8). Then, when the lymphocytes bind with recognized antigens, the lymphocytes complete their differentiation into fully functional T cells and B cells.

A *Dendritic cells, macrophages, and B cells, to name a few.*

Generation of Antigen Receptor Diversity in Lymphocytes

We know that lymphocytes become immunocompetent *before* meeting the antigens they may later attack. Thus, *it is our genes, not antigens, that determine what specific foreign substances our immune system will be able to recognize and resist.* Another way of saying the same thing is that the immune cell receptors represent our genetically acquired knowledge of the microbes that are likely to be in our environment. An antigen simply determines which of the existing T or B cells will proliferate and mount the attack against it. Only some of the antigens our lymphocytes are programmed to resist will ever invade our bodies. Consequently, only some members of our army of immunocompetent cells are mobilized in our lifetime. The others are forever idle.

Our lymphocytes make over a billion different types of antigen receptors. Because these receptors, like all other proteins, are specified by genes, it would seem that an individual must have billions of genes. Not so; each body cell contains perhaps 25,000 genes that code for all the proteins the cell must make.

How can a limited number of genes generate a seemingly limitless number of different antigen receptors? Molecular genetic studies have shown that the genes that dictate the structure of each antigen receptor are not present as such in embryonic cells. Instead of a complete set of "antigen receptor genes," embryonic cells contain a few hundred genetic bits and pieces that can be thought of as a "Lego set" for antigen receptor genes. These gene segments are shuffled and combined in different ways (a process called **somatic recombination**) by each lymphocyte as it becomes immunocompetent. The information of the newly assembled genes is then expressed as the surface receptors of B and T cells and as the antibodies later released by the B cell's "offspring."

Antigen-Presenting Cells

The major role of **antigen-presenting cells (APCs)** in immunity is to engulf antigens and then present fragments of them, like signal flags, on their own surfaces where they can be recognized by T cells—that is, they *present antigens* to the cells that will deal with the antigens. The major types of cells acting as APCs are *dendritic cells* (present in connective tissues and in the epidermis, where they are also called *Langerhans' cells*), *macrophages*, and *B lymphocytes.*

Notice that all these cell types are in sites that make it easy to encounter and process antigens. Dendritic cells are at the body's frontiers, best situated to act as mobile sentinels. Macrophages are widely distributed throughout the lymphoid organs and connective tissues. When they present antigens, dendritic cells and macrophages activate T cells. Activated T cells, in turn, release chemicals that rev up the mobilization and maturation of dendritic cells and prod macrophages to become *activated macrophages*, true "killers" that are insatiable phagocytes and secrete bactericidal chemicals. As you will see, interactions between various lymphocytes, and between lymphocytes and APCs, underlie virtually all phases of the immune response.

Macrophages tend to remain fixed in the lymphoid organs, as if waiting for antigens to come to them. But lymphocytes, especially the T cells (which account for 65–85% of bloodborne lymphocytes), circulate continuously throughout the body. This circulation greatly increases a lymphocyte's chance of coming into contact with antigens located in different parts of the body, as well as with huge numbers of macrophages and other lymphocytes. Although lymphocyte recirculation appears to be random, the lymphocyte emigration to the tissues where their protective services are needed is highly specific, regulated by homing signals (CAMs) displayed on vascular endothelial cells.

Because lymphatic capillaries pick up proteins and pathogens from nearly all body tissues, immune cells in lymph nodes are in a strategic position to encounter a large variety of antigens. Lymphocytes and APCs in the tonsils act primarily against microorganisms that invade the oral and nasal cavities, whereas the spleen acts as a filter to trap bloodborne antigens.

In addition to T cell recirculation and passive delivery of antigens to lymphoid organs by lymphatics, a third delivery mechanism—migration of dendritic cells to secondary lymphoid organs—may be an even more important way of ensuring that the immune cells encounter invading antigens. With their long veil-like extensions, dendritic cells are very efficient antigen catchers, and once they have internalized antigens by phagocytosis, they enter nearby lymphatics to get to the lymphoid organ where they will present the antigens to T and B cells. Indeed, dendritic cells are the most effective antigen presenters known—it's their only job. Dendritic cells are a key link between innate and adaptive immunity, initiating adaptive immune responses particularly tailored to the type of pathogen that they have encountered.

In summary, the two-fisted adaptive immune system uses lymphocytes, APCs, and specific molecules to identify and destroy all substances—both living and nonliving—that are in the body but not recognized as self. The system's response to such threats depends on the ability of its cells (1) to recognize antigens in the body by binding to them and (2) to communicate with one another so that the whole system mounts a response specific to those antigens.

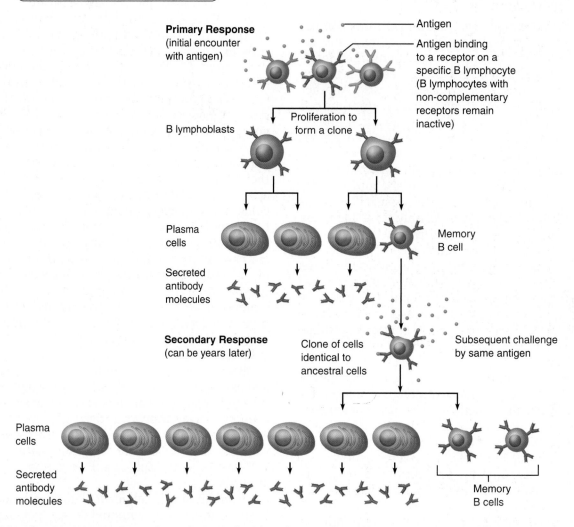

FIGURE 21.10   **Clonal selection of a B cell.** The initial meeting between a B cell and antigen stimulates the primary response in which the B cell proliferates rapidly, forming many identical B cells (a clone), most of which differentiate into antibody-producing plasma cells. (Though not indicated in the figure, the production of mature plasma cells takes about 5 days and 12 cell generations.) Cells that do not differentiate into plasma cells become memory cells primed to respond to subsequent exposures to the same antigen. Should such a meeting occur, the memory cells quickly produce more memory cells and larger numbers of effector plasma cells with the same antigen specificity. Responses generated by memory cells are called secondary responses.

Humoral Immune Response

The **antigen challenge,** the first encounter between an immunocompetent but naive lymphocyte and an invading antigen, usually takes place in the spleen or in a lymph node, but it may happen in any lymphoid tissue. If the lymphocyte is a B cell, the challenging antigen provokes the *humoral immune response,* in which antibodies are produced against the challenger.

Clonal Selection and Differentiation of B Cells

An immunocompetent but naive B lymphocyte is *activated* (stimulated to complete its differentiation) when antigens bind to its surface receptors and cross-link adjacent receptors together. Antigen binding is quickly followed by receptor-mediated endocytosis of the cross-linked antigen-receptor complexes. These events (plus some interactions with T cells described shortly) trigger **clonal selection** (klo′nul). That is, the events stimulate the B cell to grow and then multiply rapidly to form an army of cells all exactly like itself and bearing the same antigen-specific receptors (Figure 21.10). The resulting family of identical cells, all descended from the *same* ancestor cell, is called a **clone.** It is the antigen that does the selecting in clonal selection by "choosing" a lymphocyte with complementary receptors.

Most cells of the clone become **plasma cells,** the antibody-secreting effector cells of the humoral response. Although B cells secrete limited amounts of antibodies, plasma cells develop the elaborate internal machinery (largely rough endoplasmic reticulum) needed to secrete antibodies at the unbelievable rate of about 2000 molecules per second. Each plasma cell functions at this breakneck pace for 4 to 5 days and then dies. The secreted antibodies, each with the same antigen-binding properties as the receptor molecules on the surface of the parent B cell, circulate in the blood or lymph, where they bind to free antigens and mark them for destruction by other innate or adaptive mechanisms. Clone cells that do not differentiate into plasma cells become long-lived **memory cells** that can mount an almost immediate humoral response if they encounter the same antigen again at some future time (see Figure 21.10).

Immunological Memory

The cellular proliferation and differentiation just described constitute the **primary immune response,** which occurs on first exposure to a particular antigen. The primary response typically has a lag period of 3 to 6 days after the antigen challenge. This lag period mirrors the time required for the few B cells specific for that antigen to proliferate and for their offspring to differentiate into plasma cells. After the mobilization period, plasma antibody levels rise, reach peak levels in about 10 days, and then decline (Figure 21.11).

If (and when) someone is reexposed to the same antigen, whether it's the second or the twenty-second time, a **secondary immune response** occurs. Secondary immune responses are faster, more prolonged, and more effective, because the immune system has already been primed to the antigen, and sensitized memory cells are already in place "on alert." These memory cells provide what is commonly called **immunological memory.**

Within hours after recognition of the "old enemy" antigen, a new army of plasma cells is being generated. Within 2 to 3 days the antibody titer (concentration) in the blood rises steeply to reach much higher levels than were achieved in the primary response. Secondary response antibodies not only bind with greater affinity (more tightly), but their blood levels remain high for weeks to months. (Hence, when the appropriate chemical signals are present, plasma cells can keep functioning for much longer than the 4 to 5 days seen in primary responses.) Memory cells persist for long periods in humans and many retain their capacity to produce powerful secondary humoral responses for life.

The same general phenomena occur in the cellular immune response: A primary response sets up a pool of activated lymphocytes (in this case, T cells) and generates memory cells that can then mount secondary responses.

Adaptive defenses ➞ Humoral immunity

FIGURE 21.11 Primary and secondary humoral responses. The blue graph line shows a primary and a secondary response to antigen X. In the primary response, there is a 5-day time lag followed by a rapid rise and fairly rapid decline in the level of antibodies in the blood. A second exposure to antigen X on day 28 elicits a secondary response that has a very short lag time and is both more rapid and more intense. Additionally, antibody levels remain high for a much longer time. If a second antigen, antigen Y, were also encountered at day 28, the reaction to that antigen would be a primary response, not a secondary one, and its graph line (red) would show a pattern similar to that seen during the primary response to antigen X. (Time shown on the horizontal axis is given for example only. The time for response to different antigens varies greatly.)

Active and Passive Humoral Immunity

When your B cells encounter antigens and produce antibodies against them, you are exhibiting **active humoral immunity** (Figure 21.12). Active immunity is (1) *naturally acquired* when you get a bacterial or viral infection, during which time you may develop symptoms of the disease and suffer a little (or a lot), and (2) *artificially acquired* when you receive **vaccines.** Indeed, once it was realized that secondary responses are so much more vigorous than primaries, the race was on to develop vaccines to "prime" the immune response by providing a first meeting with the antigen.

Q *Why is no immunological memory established in passive forms of immunity?*

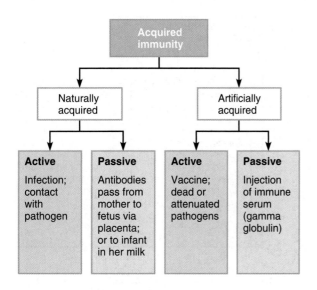

FIGURE 21.12 **Types of acquired immunity.**
Immunological memory is established via active immunity, never via passive immunity.

Most vaccines contain dead or *attenuated* (living, but extremely weakened) pathogens, or their components. Vaccines provide two benefits:

1. They spare us most of the symptoms and discomfort of the disease that would otherwise occur during the primary response.

2. Their weakened antigens provide functional antigenic determinants that are both immunogenic and reactive.

Vaccine *booster shots*, which may intensify the immune response at later meetings with the same antigen, are also available.

Vaccines have wiped out smallpox and have substantially lessened the illness caused by such former childhood killers as whooping cough, polio, and measles. Although vaccines have dramatically reduced hepatitis B, tetanus, and pneumonia in adults, immunization of adults in the U.S. has a much lower priority than that of children and as a result more than 50,000 Americans die each year from vaccine-preventable infections (pneumonia, influenza, and hepatitis).

Conventional vaccines have shortcomings. Although it was originally believed that the immune response was about the same regardless of how an antigen got into the body (under its own power or via a vaccine), that has proved not to be the case. Apparently vaccines mainly target the type of helper T cell (more details shortly) that revs up B cell defenses and antibody formation (the T_H2 cell) as opposed to the type (T_H1) that generates strong cell-mediated responses. As a result, lots of antibodies are formed that provide immediate protection, but cellular immunological memory is only poorly established. (The immune system is deprived of the learning experience that comes with clearing an infection via a T_H1-mediated response.) In extremely rare cases, vaccines cause the very disease they are trying to prevent because the attenuated virus isn't weakened enough. In other cases, contaminating proteins (e.g., egg albumin) cause allergic responses to the vaccine. The new "naked DNA" antiviral vaccines, blasted into the skin with a gene gun, and *edible* vaccines taken orally appear to circumvent these problems.

Passive humoral immunity differs from active immunity, both in the antibody source and in the degree of protection it provides (see Figure 21.12). Instead of being made by your plasma cells, the antibodies are harvested from the serum of an immune human or animal donor. As a result, your B cells are *not* challenged by antigens, immunological memory does *not* occur, and the protection provided by the "borrowed" antibodies ends when they naturally degrade in the body.

Passive immunity is conferred *naturally* on a fetus or infant when the mother's antibodies cross the placenta or are ingested with the mother's milk. For several months after birth, the baby is protected from all the antigens to which the mother has been exposed. Passive immunity is *artificially* conferred via a serum such as *gamma globulin*, which is administered after exposure to hepatitis. Other immune sera are used to treat poisonous snake bites (antivenom), botulism, rabies, and tetanus (antitoxin) because these rapidly fatal diseases would kill a person before active immunity could be established. The donated antibodies provide immediate protection, but their effect is short-lived (two to three weeks).

Antibodies

Antibodies, also called **immunoglobulins (Igs)** (im"u-no-glob'u-linz), constitute the **gamma globulin** part of blood proteins. As mentioned earlier, antibodies are proteins secreted by activated B cells or plasma cells in response to an antigen, and they are capable of binding specifically with that antigen. They are formed in response to an incredible number of different antigens. Despite their variety, all antibodies can be grouped into one of five Ig classes, each slightly different in structure and function. Before seeing how these Ig classes differ from one another, let's take a look at how all antibodies are alike.

A *Because sensitization does not occur and no memory cells are generated. The antibody protection provided by passive immunity is donated and temporary.*

Adaptive defenses → Humoral immunity

Antigen-binding site

Heavy chain

Light chain

Key:

= Heavy chain variable region

= Heavy chain constant region

= Light chain variable region

= Light chain constant region

= Disulfide bond

Complement binding site

Macrophage binding site

Hinge region

Stem region

(a) Antibody molecule

(b)

FIGURE 21.13 Antibody structure. (a) Basic antibody structure (based on IgG) consists of four polypeptide chains joined together by disulfide bonds (S—S). Two of the chains are short *light chains;* the other two are long *heavy chains.* Each chain has a V (variable) region (different in antibodies from different cells) and a C (constant) region (essentially identical in different antibodies of the same class). Because the variable regions are the antigen-binding sites, each antibody monomer has two antigen-binding sites. **(b)** Computer-generated image of antibody structure. The tiny dots show the surface of the molecule.

Basic Antibody Structure

Regardless of its class, each antibody has a basic structure consisting of four looping polypeptide chains linked together by disulfide (sulfur-to-sulfur) bonds (Figure 21.13). Two of these chains, the **heavy (H) chains,** are identical to each other and contain more than 400 amino acids each. The other two chains, the **light (L) chains,** are also identical to each other, but only about half as long as each H chain. The heavy chains have a flexible *hinge* region at their approximate "middles." The "loops" on each chain are created by disulfide bonds between amino acids that are in the same chain but about 60–70 amino acids apart; the bonds cause the intervening parts of the polypeptide chains to loop out. The four chains combined form a molecule, called an **antibody monomer** (mon′o-mer), with two identical halves, each consisting of a heavy and a light chain. The molecule as a whole is T or Y shaped.

Each chain forming an antibody has a **variable (V) region** at one end and a much larger **constant (C) region** at the other end. Antibodies responding to different antigens have very different V regions, but their C regions are the same (or nearly so) in all antibodies of a given class. The V regions of the heavy and light chains in each arm of the monomer combine to form an **antigen-binding site** shaped to "fit" a specific antigenic determinant. Hence, each antibody monomer has two such antigen-binding regions.

The C regions that form the *stem* of the antibody monomer determine the antibody class and serve common functions in all antibodies: These are the *effector regions* of the antibody that dictate (1) the cells and chemicals the antibody can bind to, and (2) how the antibody class functions in antigen elimination. For example, some antibodies can fix complement, some circulate in blood and others are found primarily in body secretions, some cross the placental barrier, and so on.

Antibody Classes

The five major immunoglobulin classes are designated IgM, IgA, IgD, IgG, and IgE, on the basis of the C regions in their heavy chains. (Remember the name MADGE to recall the five Ig types.) As illustrated in Table 21.3, IgD, IgG, and IgE have the same basic Y-shaped structure and thus are *monomers.* IgA occurs in both monomer and *dimer* (two linked monomers) forms. (Only the dimer is shown in the table.) Compared to the other antibodies, IgM is a huge antibody, a *pentamer* (*penta* = five) constructed from five linked monomers.

The antibodies of each class have different biological roles and locations in the body. IgM is the first antibody class *released* to the blood by plasma cells. IgG is the most abundant antibody in plasma and the only Ig class that crosses the placental barrier. Hence, the passive immunity that a mother transfers to her fetus is courtesy of her IgG antibodies.

TABLE 21.3	Immunoglobulin Classes
 IgD *(monomer)*	IgD is virtually always attached to the external surface of a B cell, where it functions as the antigen receptor of the B cell; important in B cell activation.
 IgM *(pentamer)*	IgM exists in monomer and pentamer (five united monomers) forms. The monomer, which is attached to the B cell surface, serves as an antigen receptor. The pentamer (illustrated) circulates in blood plasma and is the first Ig class released by plasma cells during the primary response. (This fact is diagnostically useful because presence of IgM in plasma usually indicates current infection by the pathogen eliciting IgM's formation.) Because of its numerous antigen-binding sites, IgM is a potent agglutinating agent and readily fixes and activates complement.
 IgG *(monomer)*	IgG is the most abundant and diverse antibody in plasma, accounting for 75–85% of circulating antibodies. It protects against bacteria, viruses, and toxins circulating in blood and lymph, readily fixes complement, and is the main antibody of both secondary and late primary responses. It crosses the placenta and confers passive immunity from the mother to the fetus.
 IgA *(dimer)*	IgA monomer exists in limited amounts in plasma. The dimer (illustrated), referred to as secretory IgA, is found in body secretions such as saliva, sweat, intestinal juice, and milk, and helps prevent attachment of pathogens to epithelial cell surfaces (including mucous membranes and the epidermis).
 IgE *(monomer)*	IgE is slightly larger than the IgG antibody. It is secreted by plasma cells in skin, mucosae of the gastrointestinal and respiratory tracts, and tonsils. Its stem region becomes bound to mast cells and basophils, and when its receptor ends are triggered by an antigen, it causes the cells to release histamine and other chemicals that mediate inflammation and an allergic reaction. Typically only traces of IgE are found in plasma, but levels rise during severe allergic attacks or chronic parasitic infections of the gastrointestinal tract.

Only IgM and IgG can fix complement. The IgA dimer, also called **secretory IgA,** is found primarily in mucus and other secretions that bathe body surfaces. It plays a major role in preventing pathogens from gaining entry into the body. IgD is always bound to a B cell surface; hence it acts as a B cell receptor. IgE antibodies, found in minute quantities in blood, are the "troublemaker" antibodies involved in some allergies. These and other characteristics unique to each immunoglobulin class are summarized in Table 21.3.

Mechanisms of Antibody Diversity

Recall from p. 803 that the billions of different kinds of antibodies produced by plasma cells come about as the result of somatic recombination of a limited number of genes. The genes for the heavy and light chains occur on separate chromosomes, but for each chain, the sections of coding DNA (exons) are separated by chunks of noncoding DNA (introns); this structure is essential for somatic recombination. The L and H chains are manufactured separately and then joined to form the antibody monomer. The events forming the chains are similar, but the process for the heavy chains is more complex because of the larger variety of gene segments needed for the C regions of the H chains (remember, the C regions of heavy chains determine antibody class).

The random mixing of gene segments to make unique antibody genes specifying the H and L chains accounts for only part of the huge variability seen in antibodies. Certain areas of the V gene segments in activated B cells, the so-called *hypervariable regions,* are "hot spots" for somatic mutations that enormously increase antibody variation.

A single plasma cell can switch from making one kind of H chain to making another kind, thereby producing two or more different antibody classes having the same antigen specificity. For example, the first antibody released in the primary response is IgM; then the plasma cell begins to secrete IgG. During secondary responses, almost all of the Ig protein is IgG.

Antibody Targets and Functions

Though antibodies cannot themselves destroy antigens, they can inactivate them and tag them for destruction (Figure 21.14). The common event in all antibody-antigen interactions is formation of **antigen-antibody** (or **immune**) **complexes.** Defensive mechanisms used by antibodies include neutralization, agglutination, precipitation, and complement fixation, with the first two most important.

Neutralization, the simplest effector mechanism, occurs when antibodies block specific sites on viruses or bacterial exotoxins (toxic chemicals secreted by bacteria). As a result, the virus or exotoxin

Q *Both complement fixation and agglutination aid phagocytosis, but they do so in different ways. What is this difference?*

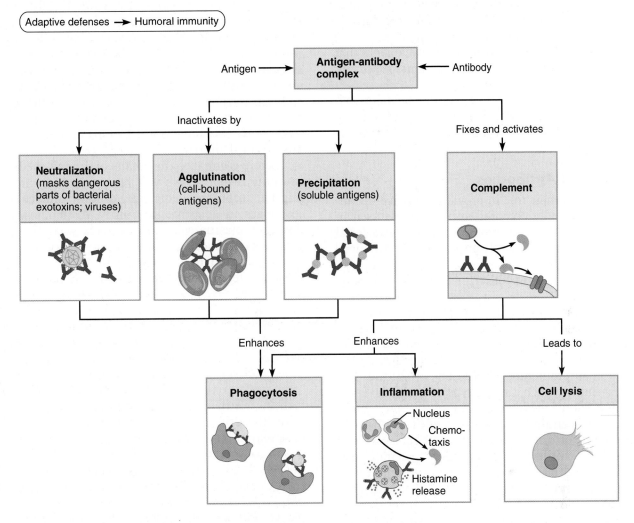

Adaptive defenses → Humoral immunity

Antigen → **Antigen-antibody complex** ← Antibody

Inactivates by

Fixes and activates

Neutralization (masks dangerous parts of bacterial exotoxins; viruses)

Agglutination (cell-bound antigens)

Precipitation (soluble antigens)

Complement

Enhances

Enhances

Leads to

Phagocytosis

Inflammation
- Nucleus
- Chemo-taxis
- Histamine release

Cell lysis

FIGURE 21.14   **Mechanisms of antibody action.** Antibodies act against free viruses, red blood cell antigens, bacterial toxins, intact bacteria, fungi, and parasitic worms.

loses its toxic effect because it cannot bind to receptors on tissue cells to cause injury. The antigen-antibody complexes are eventually destroyed by phagocytes.

Because antibodies have more than one antigen-binding site, they can bind to the same determinant on more than one antigen at a time; consequently, antigen-antibody complexes can be cross-linked into large lattices. When cell-bound antigens are cross-linked the process causes clumping, or **agglutination,**

of the foreign cells. IgM, with ten antigen-binding sites (see Table 21.3), is an especially potent agglutinating agent. Recall from Chapter 17 that this type of reaction occurs when mismatched blood is transfused (the foreign red blood cells are clumped) and is the basis of tests used for blood typing.

In **precipitation,** soluble molecules (instead of cells) are cross-linked into large complexes that settle out of solution. Like agglutinated bacteria, precipitated antigen molecules are much more easily captured and engulfed by phagocytes than are freely moving antigens.

Complement fixation and activation is the chief antibody ammunition used against cellular antigens, such as bacteria or mismatched red blood cells. When antibodies bind to cells, the antibodies change shape to expose complement-binding sites

A *With complement fixation, C3b molecules coat the cellular antigen surface, providing rough spots to which phagocytes can bind. Agglutination forms large clumps of antigen which can't go anywhere, making the clumps fair game for the phagocytes.*

on their stem regions (see Figure 21.13a). This triggers complement fixation into the antigenic cell's surface, followed by cell lysis. Additionally, as described earlier, molecules released during complement activation tremendously amplify the inflammatory response and promote phagocytosis via opsonization. Hence, a positive feedback cycle that enlists more and more defensive elements is set into motion.

A quick and dirty way to remember how antibodies work is to remember they have a PLAN of action—**p**recipitation, **l**ysis (by complement), **a**gglutination, and **n**eutralization.

Monoclonal Antibodies

In addition to their role in providing passive immunity, commercially prepared antibodies are used in research, clinical testing, and treatment. **Monoclonal antibodies,** used for such purposes, are produced by descendants of a single cell, and are pure antibody preparations specific for a single antigenic determinant.

Monoclonal antibodies are made by fusing tumor cells and B lymphocytes. The resulting cell hybrids, called **hybridomas** (hi″brĭ-do′mahz), have desirable traits of both parent cells. Like tumor cells, hybridomas proliferate indefinitely in culture; like B cells, they produce a single type of antibody.

Monoclonal antibodies are used to diagnose pregnancy, certain sexually transmitted diseases, some types of cancer, hepatitis, and rabies. These monoclonal antibody tests are more specific, more sensitive, and faster than their conventional counterparts. Monoclonal antibodies are also being used to treat leukemia and lymphomas, cancers that are present in the circulation and thus easily accessible to injected antibodies. They also serve as "guided missiles" to deliver anticancer drugs only to cancerous tissue, and to treat certain autoimmune diseases (as discussed later).

Cell-Mediated Immune Response

Despite their immense versatility, antibodies provide only partial immunity. Their prey is the *obvious* pathogen. They are fairly useless against infectious microorganisms like viruses and the tuberculosis bacillus that quickly slip inside body cells to multiply there. In these cases, the cell-mediated arm of adaptive immunity comes into play.

The T cells that mediate cellular immunity are a diverse lot, much more complex than B cells in both classification and function. There are two major populations of effector T cells based on which of a pair of structurally related *cell differentiation glycoproteins*—CD4 or CD8—is displayed by a mature T cell (Figure 21.15). These glycoprotein surface receptors, which are distinct from the T cell antigen receptors, play a role in interactions between T cells and other cells or foreign antigens. **CD4 cells** are primarily **helper T cells (T_H)**, whereas most **CD8 cells** are **cytotoxic T cells (T_C)**, whose role is to destroy any cells in the body that harbor anything foreign. In addition to these two major groups of T cells, there are regulatory T cells (T_{Reg}), memory T cells, and some fairly rare subgroups. Details of T cells' roles are provided shortly.

Before going into the details of the cell-mediated immune response, we will recap and compare the relative importance of the humoral and cellular responses in adaptive immunity. Antibodies, produced by plasma cells, are in many ways the simplest ammunition of the immune response. They are specialized to latch onto intact bacteria and soluble foreign molecules *in extracellular environments*—that is, free in body secretions and tissue fluid and circulating in blood and lymph. Antibodies never invade solid tissues unless a lesion is present. At the most basic level, antibody production and pathogen multiplication are in a race against each other and the fate of antibody targets is a case of "the quick or the dead." Remember, however, that forming antibody-antigen complexes does *not* destroy the antigens; instead, it prepares them for destruction by innate defenses.

In contrast to B cells and antibodies, T cells cannot "see" either free antigens or antigens that are in their natural state. T cells can recognize and respond only to *processed* fragments of protein antigens displayed on body cell surfaces (APCs and others) and then only under specific circumstances. Consequently, T cells are best suited for cell-to-cell interactions, and most of their direct attacks on antigens (mediated by the cytotoxic T cells) target body cells infected by viruses or bacteria; abnormal or cancerous body cells; and cells of infused or transplanted foreign tissues.

Clonal Selection and Differentiation of T Cells

The stimulus for clonal selection and differentiation is the same in B cells and T cells—binding of antigen. However, the mechanism by which T cells recognize "their" antigen is very different than that seen in B cells and has some unique restrictions.

Antigen Recognition and MHC Restriction

Like B cells, immunocompetent T cells are activated when the variable regions of their surface receptors

Adaptive defenses ➝ Cellular immunity

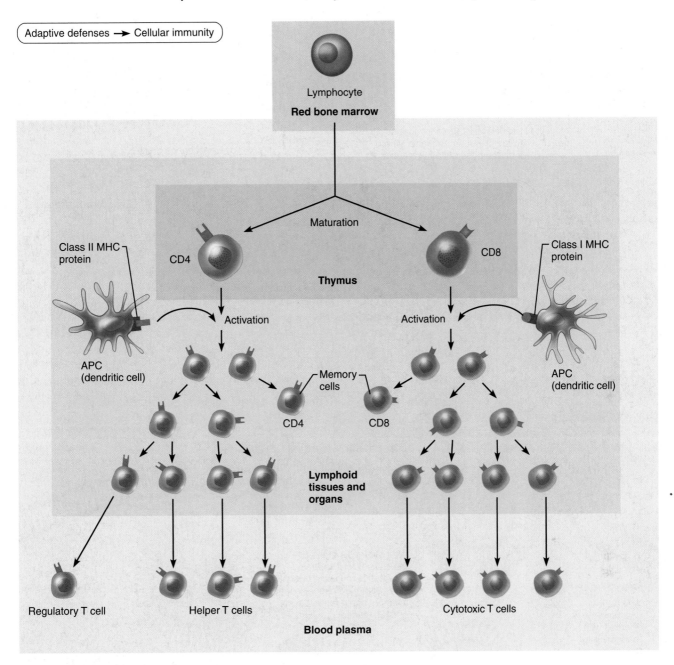

FIGURE 21.15   **Major types of T cells based on displayed cell differentiation glycoproteins (CD4, CD8).** (Regulatory T cells that do not express CD4 also exist but are not shown here.)

bind to a "recognized" antigen. However, T cells must accomplish *double recognition:* They must simultaneously recognize nonself (the antigen) and self (an MHC protein of a body cell).

Two types of MHC proteins are important to T cell activation. **Class I MHC proteins** are displayed by virtually all body cells except red blood cells and are recognized by cytotoxic (CD8) T cells. After being synthesized at the endoplasmic reticulum (Figure 21.16a), a class I MHC protein binds with a peptide 8 or 9 amino acids long ferried into

the ER from the cytosol by transport proteins aptly called TAPs (**t**ransporter **a**ssociated with **a**ntigen **p**rocessing). The "loaded" class I MHC protein then migrates to the plasma membrane to display its attached protein fragment. This attached fragment is always part of some protein synthesized *in the cell*—either a bit of a cellular (self) protein or a peptide derived from an endogenous antigen that is broken down to peptides within a proteasome. **Endogenous antigens** are foreign proteins synthesized in a body cell. Two examples are the viral proteins produced by

(a)

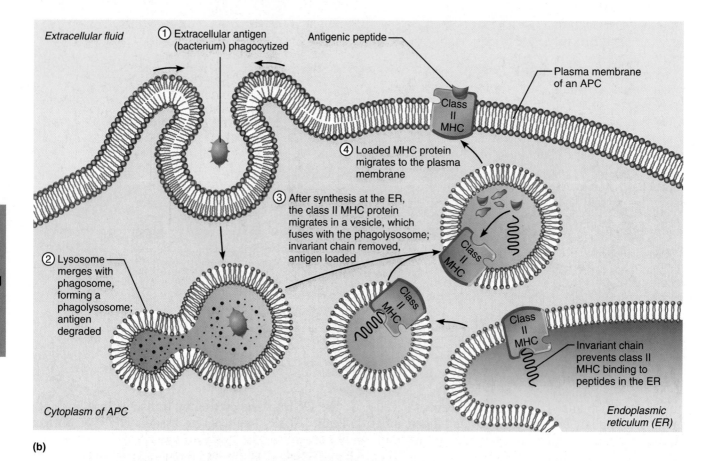

(b)

FIGURE 21.16 MHC proteins, and antigen processing and display. (a) Class I MHC proteins pick up peptide fragments in the ER. These peptides may be derived from self-proteins or from foreign (viral or cancer) proteins made within the cell. The latter are called endogenous antigens. **(b)** Class II MHC proteins pick up peptide fragments from endocytosed vesicles where phagocytized foreign debris is degraded. Both MHC classes display the peptides at the cell surface.

virus-infected cells and alien (mutated) proteins made by a body cell that has become cancerous.

The role of class I MHC proteins in the immune response is crucially important—they provide the means for signaling to cytotoxic T cells that infectious microorganisms are hiding in body cells. Without such a mechanism, viruses and certain bacteria that thrive in cells could multiply unnoticed and unbothered. When class I MHC proteins are bound to fragments of our own (self) proteins, cytotoxic T cells passing by get the signal "Leave this cell alone, it's ours!" and ignore them. When class I MHC proteins are bound to antigenic peptides, they betray the invaders and "sound a molecular alarm" that signals invasion by (1) acting as antigen holders and (2) forming the self part of the self-nonself complexes that cytotoxic T cells must recognize in order to kill.

Unlike the widely distributed class I proteins, **class II MHC proteins** are typically found only on the surfaces of cells that present antigens to helper T cells: dendritic cells, macrophages, and B cells. Like their class I MHC counterparts, class II MHC proteins are synthesized at the ER and bind to peptide fragments (Figure 21.16b). However, the peptides they bind are longer (14–17 amino acids) and come from **exogenous antigens** (foreign antigens) that have been engulfed and broken down in the phagolysosome vesicle. While still in the ER, each class II MHC molecule binds a protein called an *invariant chain*, a coupling that prevents the MHC molecule from binding to a peptide while in the ER. The class II MHC protein then moves from the ER through the Golgi apparatus and into a phagolysosome. It is there that the invariant chain loosens its hold on the MHC molecule, allowing the "jaws" of MHC to close around a degraded protein fragment. Vesicles are then recycled to the cell surface, where the class II MHC proteins display their booty for recognition by (and possibly activation of) helper T cells.

T Cell Activation

T cell activation is actually a two-step process involving antigen binding and co-stimulation. Both steps usually occur on the surface of the same antigen-presenting cell (APC). As described earlier, dendritic cells are the most potent APCs, displaying very small parts of antigens attached to their surface MHC proteins for recognition. In addition, dendritic cells actually migrate to the lymph nodes and other lymphoid tissues to present their antigens to T cells. As a result of this early alert, the body is spared a good deal of tissue damage that might otherwise occur.

Antigen Binding This first step mostly entails what has already been described: T cell antigen receptors (**TCRs**) bind to an antigen-MHC complex on

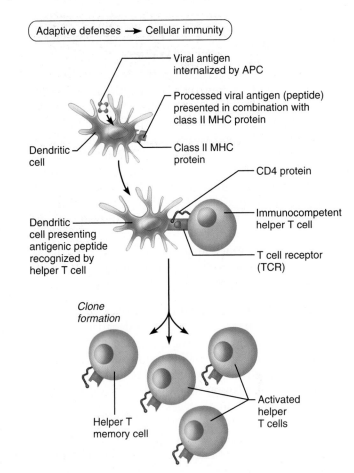

FIGURE 21.17 Clonal selection of T$_H$ and T$_C$ cells involves simultaneous recognition of self and nonself. Both T$_H$ and T$_C$ cells are stimulated to proliferate (clone) and complete their differentiation when they bind to parts of foreign antigens complexed to MHC proteins. Immunocompetent T$_H$ cells are activated when they bind to exogenous antigens (nonself)—part of a free virus in this example—complexed to a class II MHC protein. Activation of T$_C$ cells is similar, except that the processed antigen is complexed with a class I MHC protein and it often requires T$_H$ cell help.

the surface of an APC. Like B cell receptors, a TCR has variable and constant regions, but it consists of two rather than four polypeptide chains.

Helper and cytotoxic T cells have different requirements for the class of MHC protein that helps deliver the activation signal. This constraint, acquired during the education process in the thymus, is called *MHC restriction*. Helper T cells (CD4) can bind only to antigens linked to class II MHC proteins, which are typically displayed on APC surfaces (Figure 21.17). Cytotoxic T cells (CD8) are activated by antigen fragments complexed with class I MHC proteins, also found on the surface of APCs. Recall that in all other body cells, class I MHC proteins only display endogenous or self-antigens. Dendritic cells, however, have the special ability to take up

21

exogenous antigens (from, for example, dying virus-infected or tumor cells) and display them on class I MHCs in addition to class II MHCs.

The TCR that recognizes the nonself-self complex is linked to multiple intracellular signaling pathways. Besides the TCR, other T cell surface proteins are involved in this first step. For example, the CD4 and CD8 proteins used to identify the two major T cell groups (T_H and T_C) are adhesion molecules that help maintain the coupling during antigen recognition. Additionally, the CD4 and CD8 proteins are associated with kinase enzymes located inside the T cells that phosphorylate cell proteins, activating some and inactivating others when antigen binding occurs. Once antigen binding has occurred, the T cell is stimulated but is still "idling," like a car that has been started but not put into gear.

Co-stimulation The story isn't over yet because step 2 comes next. Before a T cell can proliferate and form a clone, it must recognize one or more **co-stimulatory signals.** This requires T cell binding to still other surface receptors on an APC. For example, dendritic cells and macrophages begin to sprout *B7 proteins* on their surfaces when the nonspecific defenses are being mobilized. B7 binding to the CD28 receptor on a T cell is a crucial co-stimulatory signal. After co-stimulation, cytokine chemicals such as interleukin 1 and 2 released by APCs or T cells themselves nudge the activated cells to proliferate and differentiate. As you might guess, there are several types of cytokines, each type promoting a different response in the activated T cells.

A T cell that binds to antigen without receiving the co-stimulatory signal becomes tolerant to that antigen and is unable to divide or to secrete cytokines. This state of unresponsiveness to antigen is called **anergy.** The two-signal sequence acts as a safeguard to prevent the immune system from destroying healthy cells. Without this safeguard, class I MHC proteins, which are found on all body cells and which display peptides from within the cell, could activate cytotoxic T cells, leading to widespread damage of healthy cells. The important thing to understand is that along with antigen binding, co-stimulation is crucial for T cell activation. To go back to our idling car analogy, the car will not go anywhere unless the car has both (1) been started and (2) put into gear.

Once activated, a T cell enlarges and proliferates to form a clone of cells that differentiate and perform functions according to their T cell class. This primary response peaks within a week of exposure to the triggering antigen. A period of apoptosis then occurs between days 7 and 30, during which time the activated T cells die off and effector activity wanes as the amount of antigen declines. This wholesale disposal of T cells has a critical protective role because activated T cells are potential hazards. They produce huge amounts of inflammatory cytokines, which contribute to infection-driven hyperplasia, and may promote malignancies in chronically inflamed tissue. Additionally, once they've done their job, the effector T cells are unnecessary and thus disposable. Thousands of clone members become memory T cells, persisting perhaps for life, and providing a reservoir of T cells that can later mediate secondary responses to the same antigen.

Cytokines

The chemical messengers involved in cellular immunity belong to a group of molecules called **cytokines,** a general term for mediators that influence cell development, differentiation, and responses in the immune system. Cytokines include interferons and interleukins. In Table 21.4 (pp. 817–818), you can see that there are a large variety of these molecules with myriad effects on target cells. They include hormone-like or paracrine-like glycoproteins released by a variety of cells. As mentioned previously, some cytokines act to promote T cell proliferation. For example, **interleukin 1 (IL-1),** released by macrophages, stimulates bound T cells to liberate **interleukin 2 (IL-2)** and to synthesize more IL-2 receptors. IL-2 is a key growth factor. Acting on the cells that release it, it sets up a positive feedback cycle that encourages activated T cells to divide even more rapidly. (Therapeutically IL-2 is used to treat melanoma and kidney cancers.)

Additionally, all activated T cells secrete one or more other cytokines that help amplify and regulate a variety of adaptive and innate immune responses. Some (such as tumor necrosis factor) are cell toxins; others (e.g., interferon) enhance the killing power of macrophages; and still others are inflammatory factors.

Specific T Cell Roles

Helper T Cells

Helper T cells play a central role in adaptive immunity (Figure 21.18). Once T_H cells have been primed by APC presentation of antigen, they activate macrophages, help activate B and T cells, and induce B and T cell proliferation. In fact, without the "director" T_H cells, there is *no* adaptive immune response. Their cytokines furnish the chemical help needed to recruit other immune cells to fight off intruders.

Helper T cells interact directly with B cells displaying antigen fragments bound to class II MHC receptors (Figure 21.18b), prodding the B cells into more rapid division and then, like the boss of an assembly line, signaling for antibody formation to begin. Whenever a T_H cell binds to a B cell, the T cell releases interleukin 4 and other cytokines. Although B cells may be activated solely by binding to certain antigens called **T cell–independent antigens,** most antigens require T cell help to activate the B cells to which they bind. This more common variety of antigens is called **T cell–dependent antigens.** In general, T cell–independent antigen responses are weak and short-lived. B cell division continues as long as it is stimulated by the T_H cell. Thus, helper T cells help unleash the protective potential of B cells.

Cytokines released by T_H cells not only mobilize lymphocytes and macrophages but also attract other types of white blood cells into the area and tremendously amplify innate defenses. As the released chemicals summon more and more cells into the battle, the immune response gains momentum, and the antigens are overwhelmed by the sheer numbers of immune elements acting against them.

It is interesting, but not surprising, that different subsets of helper T cells exist. The subset that develops during T_H cell differentiation depends on the type of antigen and the site at which it is encountered as well as the cytokine exposure of the differentiating T_H cell. For example, IL-12 induces T_H1 differentiation, while IL-4 drives T_H2 differentiation. Generally speaking, the T_H1 cells stimulate inflammation, activate macrophages, and promote differentiation of cytotoxic T cells. That is, they mediate classical cell-mediated immunity. By contrast, T_H2 cells mainly promote the migration of eosinophils to the battlefield and activate immune responses that depend on B cells and antibody formation.

Cytotoxic T Cells

Cytotoxic T cells are the only T cells that can directly attack and kill other cells. Activated T_C cells roam the body, circulating in and out of the blood and lymph and through lymphoid organs in search of body cells displaying antigens to which the T_C cells have been sensitized. Their main targets are virus-infected cells, but they also attack tissue cells infected by certain intracellular bacteria or parasites, cancer cells, and foreign cells introduced into the body by blood transfusions or organ transplants. Because of their ability to kill target cells by causing their lysis, T_C cells are often called **cytolytic T cells.**

Before the onslaught can begin, the cytotoxic T cell must "dock" on the target cell by binding to a self-nonself complex. Remember, all body cells display class I MHC antigens, so all infected or abnormal body cells can be destroyed by these T cells. The attack on foreign human cells, such as those of a graft, is more difficult to explain because here *all* of the antigens are nonself. However, apparently the T_C cells sometimes "see" the foreign class I MHC

(a)

(b)

FIGURE 21.18 The central role of T_H cells. Helper T cells mobilize both arms (cellular and humoral) of the immune response. **(a)** Co-stimulatory molecules required for T_C cell activation are expressed by dendritic cells in response to T_H cell binding. (Some types of antigens induce these co-stimulatory molecules themselves, in which case T_H cell help may not be needed.) The activated T_C cell produces interleukin 2 (not shown), which acts on its own interleukin 2 receptors, causing the cell to proliferate and differentiate. **(b)** T_H and B cells usually must interact directly for full B cell activation. In such cases, T_H cells bind with the self-nonself complexes on activated B cell surfaces, and then release interleukins as co-stimulatory signals.

antigens as a combination of self class I MHC protein bound to foreign antigen.

Once cytotoxic T cells recognize their targets, there are two major mechanisms by which they can deliver a **lethal hit.** One mechanism proceeds as follows:

Adaptive defenses → Cellular immunity

(a)

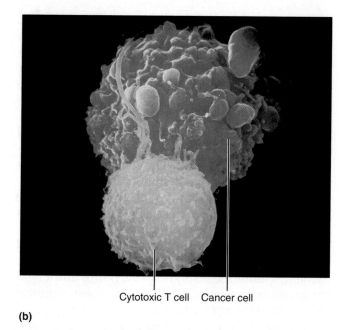

(b)

FIGURE 21.19 **Cytotoxic T cells attack infected and cancerous cells. (a)** A proposed mechanism of target cell killing by T_C cells. The initial event is the tight binding of the cytotoxic cell to the target cell. During this binding period, granules in the T_C cell fuse with its plasma membrane and release perforin molecules which insert into the target cell membrane and later polymerize, forming cylindrical holes. The pores allow granzymes, also contained in the T_C granules, to enter the target cell. **(b)** Scanning electron micrograph of a T_C cell killing a cancer cell. (8300×).

1. The T_C cell binds tightly to the target cell and, during this period, the chemicals **perforin** and **granzymes** are released from the T cell's granules. The perforins insert into the plasma membrane of the target cell (Figure 21.19a).

2. In the presence of Ca^{2+}, the perforin molecules in the target cell membrane polymerize and create transmembrane pores very much like those produced by complement activation.

3. Granzymes enter the target cell via the pores. Once inside, these proteases degrade cellular contents, stimulating apoptosis.

4. The T_C cell then detaches and searches for another prey.

Another mechanism of killing by cytotoxic cells involves binding to a specific membrane receptor (a **Fas receptor**) on the target cell, an event that stimulates the target cell to undergo apoptosis. Cytokines released by T_C cells also contribute to T_C cells' killing ability. **Tumor necrosis factor beta (TFN-β)** and **gamma interferon** activate macrophages and indirectly enhance the killing process.

NK cells use the same key mechanisms for killing their target cells. NK cells, however, do not look for foreign antigen displayed on class I MHC proteins. Instead they search for other signs of abnormality, including the *lack* of class I MHC or the presence of antibody coating the target cell. Stressed cells also often express different surface markers (such as some belonging to a family called MIC), which can activate NK cells. Thus, NK cells stalk abnormal or foreign cells in the body that T_C cells can't "see." NK and T_C lymphocytes roam the body, adhering to and crawling over the surfaces of other cells, examining them for markers they might recognize, a process called **immune surveillance.** NK cells check to make sure each cell has "identity flags" (class I MHC proteins *inhibit* NK cell attack), whereas T_C cells check the "identity flags" to see if they look the way they are supposed to (foreign antigens *stimulate* T_C cell attack).

Other T Cells

In contrast to the role of T_H cells in activating adaptive immunity, related T cells called **regulatory T (T_{Reg}) cells** (formerly known as suppressor T cells)

TABLE 21.4   Cells and Molecules of the Adaptive Immune Response

ELEMENT	FUNCTION IN IMMUNE RESPONSE
CELLS	
B cell	Lymphocyte that matures in bone marrow. Induced to replicate by antigen binding, usually followed by helper T cell interactions in lymphoid tissues. Its progeny (clone members) form memory cells and plasma cells
Plasma cell	Antibody-producing "machine"; produces huge numbers of antibodies (immunoglobulins) with the same antigen specificity. Specialized B cell clone descendant
Helper T cell (T_H)	A CD4 T cell that is central to both humoral and cellular immunity. After binding with a specific antigen presented by an APC, it stimulates production of cytotoxic T cells and B cells to help fight invader, activates macrophages, and acts both directly and indirectly by releasing cytokines
Cytotoxic T cell (T_C)	A CD8 cell; also called a cytolytic (CTL) T cell. Activated by antigen presented by an antigen-presenting cell, often with helper T cell involvement. Its specialty is killing virus-invaded body cells and cancer cells; also involved in rejection of foreign tissue grafts
Regulatory T cell (T_{Reg})	Formerly called suppressor T cell; slows or stops activity of immune system. Thought to be important in controlling autoimmune diseases; likely several different populations exist
Memory cell	Descendant of activated B cell or any class of T cell; generated during initial immune response (primary response); may exist in body for years after, enabling it to respond quickly and efficiently to subsequent infections or meetings with same antigen
Antigen-presenting cell (APC)	Any of several cell types (dendritic cell, macrophage, B cell) that engulfs and digests antigens that it encounters, presenting parts of them on its plasma membrane (bound to an MHC protein) for recognition by T cells bearing receptors for same antigen. This function, antigen presentation, is essential for normal cell-mediated responses. Macrophages also release chemicals (cytokines) that activate T cells
MOLECULES	
Antibody (immunoglobulin)	Protein produced by B cell or by plasma cell. Antibodies produced by plasma cells are released into body fluids (blood, lymph, saliva, mucus, etc.), where they attach to antigens, causing complement fixation, neutralization, precipitation, or agglutination, which "mark" the antigens for destruction by complement or phagocytes
Perforin, granzymes	Released by T_C cells. Perforin creates large pores in the target cell's membrane, allowing entry of apoptosis-inducing granzymes
Complement	Group of bloodborne proteins activated after binding to antibody-covered antigens or certain molecules on the surface of microorganisms; enhances inflammatory response and causes lysis of some microorganisms
Antigen	Substance capable of provoking an immune response. Typically a large complex molecule (e.g., protein or modified protein) not normally present in the body

dampen the immune response either by direct contact or by releasing inhibitory cytokines such as IL-10 and TGF-β. T_{Reg} cells are important in preventing autoimmune reactions because they suppress self-reactive lymphocytes in the periphery. The function and development of these cells and their subpopulations is currently a hot research topic. For example, researchers hope to use T_{Reg} cells to induce tolerance to transplanted tissue.

Gamma delta T ($T_{\gamma\delta}$) cells represent about 5% of all T cells and are found mostly in the intestinal epithelium. These oddball T cells have a different type of T cell receptor (with γ and δ subunits rather than α and β subunits) and recognize markers expressed by stressed or damaged cells (such as the MIC family and phospholipids). This and their large granular appearance makes them more similar to NK cells than other T cell types.

■ ■ ■

In summary, each type of T cell has unique roles to play in the immune response, yet is heavily enmeshed in interactions with other immune cells and elements as summarized in Table 21.4 and in the overview of the entire primary response in Figure 21.20. The lesson to take away with you is that without helper T cells, *there is no adaptive immune response* because the helper cells direct or help complete the activation of *all* other immune cells. Their crucial role in immunity is painfully evident when they are destroyed, as in AIDS (see pp. 820–821).

21

TABLE 21.4	Cells and Molecules of the Adaptive Immune Response *(continued)*
ELEMENT	**FUNCTION IN IMMUNE RESPONSE**
CYTOKINES	
Interferons (IFNs)	
▪ Alpha (α) and beta (β)	Secreted by leukocytes, fibroblasts, and other cells; antiviral effects; activate macrophages and NK cells
▪ Gamma (γ)	Secreted by lymphocytes; activates macrophages; stimulates synthesis and expression of more class I and II MHC proteins; promotes differentiation of T_H cells into T_H1
Interleukins (ILs)	
▪ IL-1	Secreted by activated macrophages; promotes inflammation and T cell activation; causes fever (a pyrogen that resets the thermostat of the hypothalamus)
▪ IL-2	Secreted by T cells; stimulates proliferation of T cells; activates NK cells
▪ IL-3	Stimulates production of leukocytes and mast cells
▪ IL-4	Secreted by T_H cells; promotes differentiation to T_H2; promotes B cell activation; switches antibody production to IgE
▪ IL-5	Secreted by some T_H cells and mast cells; attracts and activates eosinophils; causes plasma cells to secrete IgA antibodies
▪ IL-6	Induces lymphocyte activation and increases antibody production; stimulates liver to secret C-reactive protein, which binds certain bacteria, resulting in complement activation and opsonization
▪ IL-7	Induces lymphocyte proliferation and maturation
▪ IL-8 (also called CXCL8)	Stimulates chemotaxis of neutrophils, basophils, and T cells; promotes angiogenesis
▪ IL-10	Inhibits macrophages and dendritic cells; turns down cellular and innate immune response
▪ IL-12	Secreted by dendritic cells and macrophages; stimulates T_C and NK cell activity; promotes T_H1 differentiation
▪ IL-13	Secreted by T_H cells; switches antibody production to IgE
Migration inhibitory factor (MIF)	Inhibits macrophage migration and keeps them in the area of antigen deposition; a generic term for a number of cytokines
Suppressor factors	A generic term for a number of cytokines that suppress the immune system, for example TGF-β and IL-10
Transforming growth factor beta (TGF-β)	A suppressor factor similar to IL-10
Tumor necrosis factors (TNFs)	Produced by lymphocytes and in large amounts by macrophages. Enhance nonspecific killing; slow tumor growth by selectively damaging tumor blood vessels; enhance granulocyte chemotaxis; help activate T cells, phagocytes, and eosinophils; promote cell death by apoptosis

Organ Transplants and Prevention of Rejection

Organ transplants, a viable treatment option for many patients with end-stage cardiac or renal disease, have been done with mixed success for over 30 years. Immune rejection presents a particular problem when the goal is to provide such patients with functional organs from a living or recently deceased donor.

Essentially, there are four major varieties of grafts:

1. Autografts are tissue grafts transplanted from one body site to another in the *same person*.

2. Isografts are grafts donated to a patient by a *genetically identical individual*, the only example being identical twins.

FIGURE 21.20 The primary immune response.
Activities of the humoral and cellular arms of adaptive immunity are indicated by different colored backgrounds. Co-stimulation usually requires direct cell-cell interactions; cytokines enhance these and many other events, only some of which are shown here. Although complement, NK cells, and phagocytes are innate defenses, they are enlisted in the fight by cytokines. (For simplicity, only B cell receptors are illustrated, and only a few of the myriad interactions between innate and adaptive immunity are shown.)

Q What happens when antigens are bound in the absence of co-stimulators?

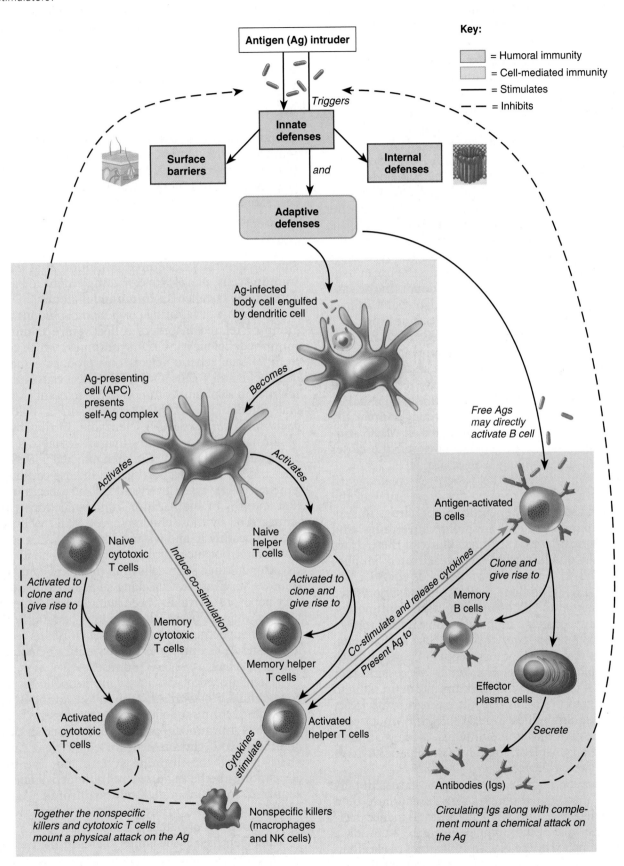

Antigen (Ag) intruder

Triggers

Innate defenses

Surface barriers

and

Internal defenses

Adaptive defenses

Key:
= Humoral immunity
= Cell-mediated immunity
= Stimulates
= Inhibits

Ag-infected body cell engulfed by dendritic cell

Ag-presenting cell (APC) presents self-Ag complex

Becomes

Free Ags may directly activate B cell

Activates

Activates

Naive cytotoxic T cells

Naive helper T cells

Activated to clone and give rise to

Activated to clone and give rise to

Antigen-activated B cells

Induce co-stimulation

Memory cytotoxic T cells

Co-stimulate and release cytokines

Clone and give rise to

Memory B cells

Memory helper T cells

Present Ag to

Activated cytotoxic T cells

Effector plasma cells

Activated helper T cells

Secrete

Cytokines stimulate

Together the nonspecific killers and cytotoxic T cells mount a physical attack on the Ag

Nonspecific killers (macrophages and NK cells)

Antibodies (Igs)

Circulating Igs along with complement mount a chemical attack on the Ag

21

A A lymphocyte becomes unresponsive to that antigen, a state called anergy.

3. **Allografts** are grafts transplanted from individuals that are *not genetically identical* but belong to the *same species*.

4. **Xenografts** are grafts taken *from another animal species*, such as transplanting a baboon heart into a human being.

Transplant success depends on the similarity of the tissues because T cells, NK cells, macrophages, and antibodies act vigorously to destroy any foreign tissue in the body. Autografts and isografts are the ideal donor tissues. Given an adequate blood supply and no infection, they are always successful because the MHC-encoded proteins are identical. Successful xenografts from genetically engineered animals are still just a promise on the horizon. Consequently, the problematic graft type, and also the type most frequently used, is the allograft, with the organ usually obtained from a living human donor (in the case of kidney, liver, bone marrow) or harvested from a human donor who has just died (heart or lung).

Before an allograft is attempted, the ABO and other blood group antigens of donor and recipient must be determined, because these antigens are also present on most body cells. Next, recipient and donor tissues are typed to determine their MHC antigen match. MHC variation among human tissues is tremendous, so matching for all MHC antigens is impossible. In general, however, the closer the match the less likely is rejection.

Following surgery the patient is treated with *immunosuppressive therapy* involving drugs of the following categories: (1) corticosteroid drugs to suppress inflammation; (2) antiproliferative drugs, and (3) immunosuppressant drugs. Many of these drugs kill rapidly dividing cells (such as activated lymphocytes), and all of them have severe side effects.

The major problem with immunosuppressive therapy is that the patient's suppressed immune system cannot protect the body against other foreign agents. As a result, overwhelming bacterial and viral infection remains the most frequent cause of death in transplant patients. The key to successful graft survival is to provide enough immunosuppression to prevent graft rejection but not enough to be toxic, and to use antibiotics to keep infection under control. Even with the best conditions, by ten years after receiving a transplant, roughly 50% of patients have rejected the donor organ.

In rare cases, transplant patients have naturally achieved a state of immune tolerance and have been able to "ditch the drugs." Finding a way to induce tolerance is the goal of the Immune Tolerance Network, a project launched by the National Institutes of Health in 1999. Currently their surgeons are temporarily suppressing the recipient's bone marrow and then dousing it with bone marrow from the same donors as the new organ in the hope that the transplanted marrow cells will establish themselves and create a **chimeric immune system** (**chimer** = monster) that treats the transplanted organ as self.

Homeostatic Imbalances of Immunity

Certain circumstances can cause the immune system to become depressed, to fail, or to act in a way that damages the body. Most such problems can be classified as immunodeficiencies, autoimmune diseases, or hypersensitivities.

Immunodeficiencies

Any congenital or acquired condition that causes immune cells, phagocytes, or complement to behave abnormally is called an **immunodeficiency.**

The most devastating *congenital conditions* are a group of related disorders called **severe combined immunodeficiency (SCID) syndromes,** which result from various genetic defects that produce a marked deficit of B and T cells. One SCID defect causes abnormalities in a subunit common to the receptors for several interleukins. Another results in a defective *adenosine deaminase (ADA)* enzyme. In the absence of normal ADA, metabolites that are lethal to T cells accumulate in the body. Children afflicted with SCID have little or no protection against disease-causing organisms of any type. Interventions must begin in the first months of life because minor infections easily shrugged off by most children cause SCID victims to become deathly ill and wasted. Untreated, this condition is fatal, but successful transplants of bone marrow tissue or cultured stem cells from umbilical cord blood improve survival rates. Lacking such a treatment, the only hope for survival has been living behind protective barriers that keep out all infectious agents. Recent genetic engineering techniques using viruses as vectors to transfer ADA minigenes to the victim's hematopoietic stem cells have shown promise.

There are various *acquired immunodeficiencies.* For example, *Hodgkin's disease,* cancer of the B cells, can lead to immunodeficiency by depressing lymph node cells. Immunosuppressive drugs used in transplantation and certain drugs used to treat cancer also suppress the immune system. But the most devastating of the acquired immunodeficiencies is **acquired immune deficiency syndrome (AIDS),** which cripples the immune system by interfering with the activity of helper T cells.

First identified in the United States in 1981 among homosexual men and intravenous drug users, AIDS is characterized by severe weight loss, night sweats, swollen lymph nodes, and increasingly frequent opportunistic infections, including a rare type of pneumonia called *pneumocystis pneumonia,* and the bizarre malignancy *Kaposi's sarcoma*, a cancer of the blood vessels evidenced by purple skin lesions. Some AIDS victims develop severe dementia. The course of AIDS is often grim, finally ending in complete debilitation and death from cancer or overwhelming infection.

AIDS is caused by a virus transmitted in body secretions—especially blood, semen, and vaginal secretions. The virus commonly enters the body via blood transfusions or blood-contaminated needles and during sexual intercourse. It is also present in saliva and tears, and there are documented cases of transmission by oral sex. Early in the epidemic, hemophiliacs were also at particular risk because the blood factors they need were isolated from pooled blood donations. Although manufacturers began taking measures to kill the virus in 1984 and new genetically engineered factors became available, an estimated 60% of the hemophiliacs in the U.S. were already infected.

The virus, **HIV (human immunodeficiency virus)**, destroys T_H cells, thus depressing cell-mediated immunity. Although B cells and T_C cells initially mount a vigorous response to viral exposure, in time a profound deficit of antibodies develops and the cytotoxic T cell activity is impaired. The whole immune system is turned topsy-turvy. It is now clear that the virus multiplies steadily in the lymph nodes throughout most of the asymptomatic period, which averages ten years. Symptoms appear when the lymph nodes can no longer contain the virus and the immune system collapses. The virus also invades the brain (which accounts for the dementia of some AIDS patients). Most victims die within a few months to eight years.

The infectious specificity of HIV reflects the fact that CD4 proteins provide the avenue of attack. Researchers have identified an HIV coat glycoprotein complex (gp120/gp41) that fits into the CD4 receptor like a plug fits into a socket. However, HIV also needs a *second* receptor (e.g., CXCR4) on the target cell. Once all these proteins have connected, gp41 fuses the virus to the target cell. Once inside, HIV "sets up housekeeping," using the viral enzyme *reverse transcriptase* to produce DNA from the information encoded in its (viral) RNA. This DNA copy, now called a *provirus*, then inserts itself into the target cell's DNA and directs the cell to crank out new copies of viral RNA and proteins so that the virus can multiply and infect other cells. Although T_H cells are the main HIV targets, other body cells displaying CD4 proteins (macrophages, monocytes, and dendritic cells) are also at risk. The HIV reverse transcriptase enzyme is not very accurate and produces errors rather frequently, causing HIV's relatively high mutation rate and thus its changing resistance to drugs.

The years since 1981 have witnessed a global AIDS epidemic. By the end of 2003, 20 million people had died of AIDS since it was first identified, and about 40 million people were infected worldwide, almost 90% of them in the developing countries of Asia and sub-Saharan Africa. Half of the victims are women, a case distribution indicating that in the most heavily hit countries, most HIV transmission occurs via heterosexual contacts. The virus can also be transmitted from an infected mother to her fetus.

By 2004, the estimated number of Americans infected with HIV was fast approaching one million. Of these, a quarter didn't yet know that they were infected, either because anti-HIV antibodies were not yet detectable in the blood (this may take as long as six months after infection), or because (for one reason or another) they had not yet been tested. The "face of AIDS" is changing too. Though homosexual men still account for the bulk of cases transmitted by sexual contact, more and more heterosexuals are contracting this disease. Particularly disturbing is the number of diagnosed cases among teenagers and young adults, with AIDS now the fifth leading killer of all Americans ages 25 to 44.

No cure for AIDS has yet been found. Over 30 clinical trials of HIV vaccines are under way around the world. Disappointingly, the two largest trials testing the effectiveness of a vaccine targeting gp120 have failed to show any effect in blocking HIV infection, and it is unlikely that an approved vaccine will be available soon. Fortunately, a number of antiviral drugs are available, and these fall into three broad classes. *Reverse transcriptase inhibitors*, such as AZT and ddC, were early on the scene, followed by *protease inhibitors* (saquinavir, ritonavir, and others). These first two classes of drugs inhibit important viral enzymes after the virus has gained entry into the target cell. New to the scene are *fusion inhibitors* (such as enfuvirtide) that block gp41 and thereby prevent entry of the virus into the cell in the first place. Combination therapy using three drugs at once delivers a one-two punch to the virus; that is, it postpones drug resistance and causes the *viral load* (amount of HIV virus per milliliter of blood) to plummet while boosting the number of T_H cells. Sadly, even combination drug therapies fail as the virus becomes resistant. New hope comes from a class of drugs now being developed that blocks the viral enzyme integrase, responsible for integration of the HIV provirus into the target cell's DNA. However, drug research is slow and laborious and the clock is ticking.

Autoimmune Diseases

Occasionally the immune system loses its ability to distinguish friend (self) from foe (foreign antigens). When this happens, the artillery of the immune system, like friendly fire, turns against itself. The body produces antibodies *(autoantibodies)* and sensitized T_C cells that destroy its own tissues. This puzzling phenomenon is called **autoimmunity**. If a disease state results, it is referred to as **autoimmune disease**.

Some 5% of adults in North America—two-thirds of them women—are afflicted with autoimmune disease. Most common are

- *Multiple sclerosis,* which destroys the white matter of the brain and spinal cord (see p. 407)

- *Myasthenia gravis,* which impairs communication between nerves and skeletal muscles (see p. 289)

- *Graves' disease,* which prompts the thyroid gland to produce excessive amounts of thyroxine (see p. 624)

- *Type 1 (insulin-dependent) diabetes mellitus,* which destroys pancreatic beta cells, resulting in a deficit of insulin and inability to use carbohydrates (see p. 636)

- *Systemic lupus erythematosus (SLE),* a systemic disease that particularly affects the kidneys, heart, lungs, and skin (see Related Clinical Terms)

- *Glomerulonephritis,* a severe impairment of renal function

- *Rheumatoid arthritis,* which systematically destroys joints (see p. 274)

One line of therapy depresses certain aspects of the immune response. For example, antibodies against TNF-α have provided dramatic results in the treatment of rheumatoid arthritis. *Thalidomide,* used in the 1950s to alleviate morning sickness in pregnancy until it was found to cause tragic birth defects, has been given a second chance in treating autoimmune disease because it blocks TNF production. Another therapeutic approach uses antibodies against cell adhesion molecules on T lymphocytes, preventing them from exiting blood vessels into target areas. This approach shows promise in helping victims of a variety of autoimmune disorders, including multiple sclerosis.

How do autoimmune diseases arise? As you recall, lymphocytes undergo an extensive education in the bone marrow and thymus that weeds out self-reactive cells. This weeding is thorough, but not too thorough, since there are pathogens that look somewhat like self. Weakly self-reactive lymphocytes that can detect these kinds of pathogens are allowed into the periphery, where they may cause autoimmune disease if they become activated. Recall that activation of a T cell requires a co-stimulatory signal on an APC (see p. 814), and that these co-stimulatory signals are only present if the APC has received "danger" signals alerting it to the presence of damage or invaders. This is an important safety check that generally keeps both humoral and cellular immunity under control. In addition, regulatory T (T_{Reg}) cells also inhibit autoimmune reactions. Normally, these mechanisms are sufficient, but sometimes these self-reactive lymphocytes slip out of control. It appears that one of the following events may trigger this:

1. Foreign antigens resemble self-antigens. If the determinants on a self-antigen resemble those on a foreign antigen, antibodies made against the foreign antigen can cross-react with the self-antigen. For instance, antibodies produced during a streptococcal infection react with heart antigens, causing lasting damage to the heart muscle and valves, as well as to joints and kidneys. This age-old disease is called *rheumatic fever.*

2. New self-antigens appear. Self-proteins not previously exposed to the immune system may appear in the circulation. They may be generated by (1) gene mutations that cause new proteins to appear at the external cell surface, (2) changes in the structure of self-antigens by hapten attachment or as a result of infectious damage, or (3) release by trauma of novel self-antigens normally hidden behind barriers such as the blood-brain barrier. These newly generated proteins then become immune system targets.

Hypersensitivities

At first, the immune response was thought to be purely protective. However, it was not long before its dangerous potentials were discovered. **Hypersensitivities** result when the immune system causes tissue damage as it fights off a perceived threat (such as pollen or animal dander) that would otherwise be harmless to the body. People rarely die of hypersensitivities; they are just miserable with them.

The different types of hypersensitivity reactions are distinguished by (1) their time course, and (2) whether antibodies or T cells are involved. Hypersensitivities mediated by antibodies are the *immediate* and *subacute hypersensitivities.* T cells cause *delayed hypersensitivity.*

Immediate Hypersensitivities

The **immediate hypersensitivities,** also called **acute** or **type I hypersensitivities,** are simply what most of us would call **allergies** (*allo* = altered; *erg* = reaction). An **allergen** is an antigen that causes an allergic reaction. Allergic reactions begin within seconds after contact with the allergen and last about half an hour.

The initial meeting with an allergen produces no symptoms but it sensitizes the person. APCs digest the allergen and present its fragments to T_H cells as usual. In susceptible individuals, an abnormally large number of these T_H cells differentiate into IL-4-secreting T_H2 cells. IL-4 stimulates B cells to mature into IgE-secreting plasma cells, which spew out huge amounts of antibody specific for the allergen. When the IgE molecules attach to *mast cells* and *basophils,* sensitization is complete. An allergic reaction is triggered by later encounters with the same allergen, which promptly binds and cross-links the IgE antibodies on the surfaces of the mast cells and basophils. This event induces an enzymatic cascade that causes the mast cells and basophils to degranulate, releasing a flood of *histamine* and other inflammatory chemicals that together induce the inflammatory response typical of allergy (Figure 21.21).

Allergic reactions may be local or systemic. Mast cells are abundant in connective tissues of the skin and beneath the mucosa of respiratory passages and the gastrointestinal tract, and these areas are common sites of local allergic reactions. Histamine causes blood vessels to become dilated and leaky, and is largely to blame for the best recognized symptoms of allergy: runny nose, itching reddened skin (hives), and watery eyes. When the allergen is inhaled, symptoms of *asthma* appear because smooth muscle in the walls of the bronchioles contracts, constricting those small passages and restricting air flow. When the allergen is ingested in food or via drugs, gastrointestinal discomfort (cramping, vomiting, or diarrhea) occurs. Over-the-counter antiallergy drugs contain antihistamines that counteract these effects.

The bodywide or systemic response known as **anaphylactic shock** is fairly rare. It typically occurs when the allergen directly enters the blood and circulates rapidly through the body, as might happen with certain bee stings or spider bites. It may also follow injection of a foreign substance (such as penicillin or other drugs which act as haptens). The mechanism of anaphylactic shock is essentially the same as that of local responses; but when mast cells and basophils are enlisted throughout the entire body, the outcome is life threatening. The bronchioles constrict (and the tongue may swell), making it difficult to breathe, and the sudden vasodilation and fluid loss from the bloodstream may cause circulatory collapse (hypotensive shock) and death within minutes. Epinephrine is the drug of choice to reverse these histamine-mediated effects.

Subacute Hypersensitivities

Like the immediate types, **subacute hypersensitivities** are caused by antibodies (IgG and IgM rather than IgE) and can be transferred via blood plasma or serum. However, their onset is slower (1–3 hours after antigen exposure) and the duration of the reaction is longer (10–15 hours).

Cytotoxic (type II) reactions occur when antibodies bind to antigens on specific body cells and subsequently stimulate phagocytosis and complement-mediated lysis of the cellular antigens. Type II hypersensitivity may occur after a patient has received a transfusion of mismatched blood and the foreign red blood cells are lysed by complement.

Immune-complex (type III) hypersensitivity results when antigens are widely distributed through the body or blood and the insoluble antigen-antibody complexes formed cannot be cleared from a particular area. (This may reflect a persistent infection or a situation in which huge amounts of antigen-antibody complexes are formed.) An intense inflammatory

Adaptive defenses   Humoral immunity

Sensitization stage

① Antigen (allergen) invades body.

② Plasma cells produce large amounts of class IgE antibodies against allergen.

③ IgE antibodies attach to mast cells in body tissues (and to circulating basophils).

— Mast cell with fixed IgE antibodies
— IgE
— Granules containing histamine

Subsequent (secondary) responses

④ More of same antigen invades body.

— Antigen

⑤ Antigen combines with IgE attached to mast cells (and basophils), which triggers degranulation and release of histamine (and other chemicals).

— Mast cell granules release contents after antigen binds with IgE antibodies

— Histamine

⑥ Histamine causes blood vessels to dilate and become leaky, which promotes edema; stimulates secretion of large amounts of mucus; and causes smooth muscles to contract (if respiratory system is site of antigen entry, asthma may ensue).

Outpouring of fluid from capillaries   Release of mucus   Constriction of small respiratory passages (bronchioles)

FIGURE 21.21 **Mechanism of an acute allergic (immediate hypersensitivity) response.**

A CLOSER LOOK

Too Clean for Our Own Good?

Ah, spring is here! You can tell by the sound of the wheezing and sneezing, not to mention the advertisements for hay fever medications. It seems that just about everyone is allergic to something. A century ago, this wasn't the case. Allergies were rare—a disease of rich city folk who had the best food, water, and medical care that money could buy. In cities of North America and Europe, allergies are now commonplace, and asthma is a serious problem for many children.

Asthma is a chronic inflammation of the small bronchioles of the lung. In allergic asthma, allergens trigger constriction of bronchiolar smooth muscle, making it difficult to breathe. This is uncomfortable, to say the least, and can be fatal. Eventually, this chronic inflammation leads to permanent damage. Over the past 20 years, the occurrence of asthma has increased by about 75% in the U.S. and Canada, yet asthma and allergy are still rare in developing countries and the former Communist bloc.

What is behind this? The cause can't be genetic because the increase in allergy and asthma has been much too rapid. Furthermore, children born in the U.S. to recent immigrants from developing countries have the same rates of allergy and asthma as do children whose parents have lived here for generations. Clearly, there is something about living in an industrialized society that increases the risk of allergy. The observation that the increase in allergy is correlated with the decrease in childhood diseases has led to the advent of the *hygiene hypothesis*. The twentieth century saw remarkable advances in public health, particularly in industrialized countries. Children no longer contract the serious diseases of the past: smallpox, polio, whooping cough, diphtheria, measles, cholera. Improvements in public sanitation and water supplies together with universal vaccination and the judicious use of antibiotics have kept us living longer, healthier lives and have drastically reduced infant mortality in the industrialized world. The cost? Allergy.

Allergy is caused by an overactive T_H2 response and a correspondingly underdeveloped T_H1 response. We all enter the world with stronger T_H2 than T_H1 responses. Cytokines secreted by the placenta seem to suppress T_H1 and T_C responses so that the fetus doesn't reject the mother (and vice versa). This is a good thing, naturally. During the first year of life, a strong T_H2 response also seems to reduce the destructive potential of novel viral infections, such as influenza. This is also a good thing because an overly aggressive T_H1 response could do irreparable damage to fragile, immature organs.

Back in the "good old days" when we lived in squalor, newborns fell prey to a wide variety of childhood diseases that would stimulate proliferation of T_H1 cells and shift the balance away from the T_H2 cells as the immune system matured. Those that survived the childhood diseases ended up with an immune system that had received a well-rounded education. Today, children are immunized against childhood infections and are often given antibiotics that wipe out beneficial symbiotic bacteria of the gut. Kept inside houses sterilized by antiseptic soaps, children don't play in (and eat) dirt as much as they used to. According to the hygiene hypothesis, the result is that children's immune systems aren't exposed to the large numbers of pathogens and toxins they once were and so retain a strong T_H2 response and a weak T_H1 response. As the T_H2 cells proliferate, they induce B cells to secrete excessive amounts of IgE, which in turn leads to histamine release from mast cells. Voilà! Allergy.

This simple story doesn't tell all, though. First, it isn't quite true that people in the third world don't get allergies—although they make plenty of IgE, they don't respond when exposed to allergens. It turns out that most people in developing countries are infected by parasites, particularly intestinal worms. When cured of their worm infections, they get allergies. Worms actively suppress the immune system,

reaction occurs, complete with complement-mediated cell lysis and cell killing by neutrophils that severely damages local tissues. One example of type III hypersensitivity is *farmer's lung* (induced by inhaling moldy hay). Additionally, many immune complex responses are involved in autoimmune disorders, such as glomerulonephritis, systemic lupus erythematosus, and rheumatoid arthritis.

Delayed Hypersensitivities

Delayed hypersensitivity (type IV) reactions are slower to appear (1–3 days) than antibody-mediated hypersensitivity reactions. The mechanism is basically that of a cell-mediated immune response, which depends on T_H1 and T_C cells. Inflammation and tissue damage comes about through the action of T_C cells and cytokine-activated macrophages. Delayed hypersensitivity to antigens can be passively transferred from one person to another by transfusions of whole blood containing the T cells that initiate the response. Cytokines released by activated T cells are the major mediators of these inflammatory responses; thus antihistamine drugs are not helpful. Corticosteroid drugs are used to provide relief.

The most familiar examples of delayed hypersensitivity reactions are those classified as **allergic contact dermatitis** which follow skin contact with poison ivy, some metals (nickel in jewelry), and certain cosmetic and deodorant chemicals. These agents act as haptens, and after diffusing through the skin and causing the release of IL-10 and TGF-β. To prove the connection between worms and allergy suppression, Professor Koichiro Fujita at Tokyo Medical and Dental University has gone so far as to eat tapeworm eggs and is the proud host to three or four of these parasites (which can grow up to 10 m long). Fujita claims that his tapeworms have cleared up his hay fever and that he's even lost some weight.

A second problem with the hygiene hypothesis is that allergy isn't the only immune disorder on the rise. Autoimmune diseases in children and young adults, such as type 1 diabetes and multiple sclerosis, have also increased in industrial societies. These diseases are caused by activation of T_H1 cells, exactly the opposite of what the hygiene hypothesis predicts.

In science studies, these contradictions would usually be enough to doom a hypothesis. However, sometimes it is possible to look more deeply and arrive at a mechanism that can explain such seemingly contradictory observations. We know the immune system swings too far in one direction or the other, but what controls the swing? Special regulatory T (T_{Reg}) cells, capable of suppressing both T_H1 and T_H2 activity, develop in the gut and the respiratory tract upon exposure to antigens. Bacterial endotoxin and hepatitis A virus are two potent stimulators. Antigens in food and air are taken up by mucosal dendritic cells. These cells then make contact with precursor T_H cells in the presence

HE WAS RAISED BY **WOLVES** SO HIS **SOCIAL SKILLS** ARE A LITTLE **WEAK**. ON THE OTHER HAND HE'S **FREE** OF **ALLERGIES** OR **ASTHMA**.

ADOPTION Agency

NEWS ITEM— STUDY FINDS GROWING UP WITH PETS BUILDS IMMUNITY...

of IL-10, causing the precursors to differentiate into T_{Reg} cells. As these T_{Reg} cells become established, the host becomes *tolerant* to the antigen, preventing allergy and autoimmune disorders. T_{Reg} development may also depend on the presence of the very bacteria depleted by antibiotics and excessive cleanliness. Thus, allergy and autoimmune disorders may be the result of faulty T_{Reg} cell development.

Perhaps, in our haste to rid ourselves of household dust, dirt, bacteria, and parasites, we have eliminated the signals our immune systems need to fully mature. Scientists are now seeking ways to imitate these lost signals. In one method, they inject patients with allergens linked to synthetic bacteria-like DNA (oligodeoxynu-

cleotides). These activate the innate immune system's Toll-like receptors, setting off our alarm system to signal the presence of an invader. Innate immune system cells (APCs, NK cells, etc.), in turn, release a flood of cytokines that shift the immune system away from the allergy-producing T_H2 response and toward a more healthy T_H1 response.

Instead of relying on injections of synthetic "dirt," perhaps we need to rethink our obsession with cleanliness. Clearly, no one wants to return to the "good old days" of 25% infant mortality, but it may be that allowing babies to get a little dirtier early in life should be looked at as a golden opportunity to prevent allergy and asthma later on! ■

attaching to self-proteins, they are perceived as foreign by the immune system. The *Mantoux* and *tine tests*, two skin tests for tuberculosis, depend on delayed hypersensitivity reactions. When the tubercle antigens are introduced just under the skin, a small hard lesion forms that persists for days if the person has been sensitized to the antigen.

Delayed hypersensitivity reactions also involve a large number of protective reactions including (1) protection against viruses, bacteria, fungi, and protozoa; (2) resistance against cancer; and (3) rejection of foreign grafts or transplanted organs. They are particularly effective against **facultative intracellular pathogens (FIPs),** which include salmonella bacteria and some yeasts. FIPs are readily phagocytized by

macrophages but are not killed and may multiply in a host unless the macrophages are activated to killer status by gamma interferon and certain other cytokines. Thus, the enhanced release of cytokines during delayed hypersensitivity reactions plays an important protective role.

Developmental Aspects of the Immune System

Stem cells of the immune system originate in the liver and spleen during weeks 1–9 of embryonic development. Later the bone marrow becomes the predominant source of stem cells, and it persists in this role into adult life. In late fetal life and shortly after birth, the young lymphocytes develop self-tolerance and immunocompetence in their "programming organs" (thymus and bone marrow) and then populate the other lymphoid tissues. When challenged by an antigen, the naive T and B cells further differentiate into effector cells and memory cells.

The newborn's immune system depends primarily on antibodies, and hence on T_H2 lymphocytes. The T_H1 system is educated and gets stronger as a result of encounters with microbes—both harmful and harmless. If such "exercise" does *not* occur, immune balance is upset and the T_H2 system flourishes, causing the immune system to teeter toward allergies. Unhappily, our desire to keep our children squeaky clean with antibiotics that kill off both harmful and harmless bacteria may derail normal immune development (see *A Closer Look*).

The ability of the immune system to recognize foreign substances is controlled by genes. However, the nervous system also plays a role in the immune response, and studies of psychoneuroimmunology—a brain-twisting term coined to describe links between the brain and the immune system—have begun to reveal some answers. For example, the immune response is definitely impaired in individuals who are depressed or under severe stress, such as those mourning the death of a beloved family member or friend.

Our immune system normally serves us very well until late in life. Then its efficiency begins to wane, and its ability to fight infection declines. Old age is also accompanied by greater susceptibility to both immune deficiency and autoimmune diseases. The greater incidence of cancer in the elderly is assumed to be an example of the progressive failure of the immune system. Why the immune system begins to fail is not known, but we do know that the thymus begins to atrophy after puberty and the production of naive T and B cells declines with age, possibly because progenitor cells reach the limits of their ability to further divide.

■ ■ ■

The adaptive immune system provides remarkable defenses against disease. These amazingly diverse defenses are regulated by cellular interactions and a flood of chemicals. T cells and antibodies make perfect partners. Antibodies respond swiftly to toxins and molecules on the outer surfaces of foreign organisms, and T cells destroy foreign antigens hidden inside cells and our own cells that have become mutinous (cancer cells). The innate immune system exhibits a different arsenal for body defense, an arsenal that is simpler perhaps and more easily understood. However, these innate and adaptive defenses are tightly interlocked, each providing what the other cannot and amplifying each other's effects.

Related Clinical Terms

Congenital thymic aplasia An immune deficiency disease in which the thymus fails to develop. Affected individuals have no T cells, hence little or no immune protection; fetal thymic and bone marrow transplants have been helpful in some cases.

Eczema (ek'zĕ-mah) A type of immediate hypersensitivity response that results in "weeping" skin lesions and intense itching. Onset is in the first five years of life in 90% of cases. The allergen is uncertain, but familial predisposition is strong.

Hashimoto's thyroiditis An autoimmune disease in which the thyroid gland is attacked by both B and T lymphocytes. It is the most common cause of hypothyroidism, affecting mostly middle-aged and elderly women. Genetic factors associated with this autoimmune disease (certain MHC variants) make individuals susceptible to environmental triggers (possibly iodine, irradiation, or trauma).

Immunization The process of rendering a subject immune (by vaccination or injection of antiserum).

Immunology The study of immunity.

Immunopathology Disease of the immune system.

Septic shock (sepsis) A dangerous condition in which the inflammatory response goes out of control. Kills 175,000 people a year in the U.S. Results from especially severe bacterial infections or more ordinary infections that grow rapidly worse in patients with weakened defenses, such as the hospitalized elderly recovering from surgery. In an inflammatory response, neutrophils and other white blood cells leave the capillaries and enter the infected connective tissue, secreting cytokines that increase capillary permeability. Secretion of cytokines is normally moderate, but in sepsis, continued cytokine release makes capillaries so leaky that the bloodstream is depleted of fluid. Blood pressure falls and the body organs shut down, causing death in 50% of all cases. Sepsis has proven difficult to control and its incidence remains high.

Systemic lupus erythematosus (SLE) (er"ĭ-the'mah-to'sus) A systemic autoimmune disorder that occurs mainly in young females. Diagnosis is helped by finding antinuclear (anti-DNA) antibodies in the patient's serum. DNA–anti-DNA complexes (typical of type III hypersensitivity) localize in the kidneys (the capillary filters, or glomeruli), in blood vessels, in the brain, and in the synovial membranes of joints, resulting in glomerulonephritis, vascular problems, loss of memory and mental sharpness, and painful arthritis. Reddened skin lesions, particularly a "butterfly rash" (the sign of the wolf, or *lupus*) on the face, are common.

Chapter Summary

PART 1: INNATE DEFENSES

Surface Barriers: Skin and Mucosae   (pp. 789–790)

1. Skin and mucous membranes constitute the first line of defense. Their role is to prevent pathogens from entering the body. Protective membranes line all body cavities and organs exposed to the exterior.

2. Surface membranes provide mechanical barriers to pathogens. Some have structural modifications and produce secretions that enhance their defensive effects: The skin's acidity, lysozyme, mucus, keratin, and ciliated cells are examples.

Internal Defenses: Cells and Chemicals (pp. 790–798)

1. The innate cellular and chemical defenses provide the body's second line of defense.

Phagocytes   (pp. 790–791)

2. Phagocytes (macrophages, neutrophils, and the like) engulf and destroy pathogens that breach epithelial barriers. This process is facilitated when antibodies or complement to which the phagocyte's receptors can bind attach to the pathogen's surface. Cell killing is enhanced by the respiratory burst.

Natural Killer Cells   (p. 791)

3. Natural killer cells are large granular lymphocytes that act nonspecifically to kill virus-infected and malignant cells.

Inflammation: Tissue Response to Injury   (pp. 791–795)

4. The inflammatory response prevents the spread of harmful agents, disposes of pathogens and dead tissue cells, and promotes healing. Exudate is formed; protective leukocytes enter the area; the area is walled off by fibrin; and tissue repair occurs.

5. The cardinal signs of inflammation are swelling, redness, heat, and pain. These result from vasodilation and increased permeability of blood vessels induced by inflammatory chemicals. If the inflamed area is a joint, movement may be impaired.

Antimicrobial Proteins   (pp. 795–798)

6. Interferons are a group of related proteins synthesized by virus-infected cells and certain immune cells that prevent viruses from multiplying in other body cells.

7. When complement (a group of plasma proteins) is fixed on a foreign cell's membrane, lysis of the target cell occurs. Complement also enhances phagocytosis and the inflammatory and adaptive immune responses.

8. C-reactive protein indicates the level of infection or inflammation in the body. It also activates complement, facilitates phagocytosis, and targets cells for disposal.

Fever   (p. 798)

9. Fever enhances the body's fight against pathogens by increasing metabolism, which speeds up defensive actions and repair processes, and by prompting the liver and spleen to sequester iron and zinc needed for bacterial multiplication.

PART 2: ADAPTIVE DEFENSES

1. The adaptive immune system recognizes something as foreign and acts to immobilize, neutralize, or remove it. The adaptive immune response is antigen-specific, systemic, and has memory. It provides the body's third line of defense.

Antigens   (pp. 799–800)

1. Antigens are substances capable of generating an immune response.

Complete Antigens and Haptens   (p. 799)

2. Complete antigens have both immunogenicity and reactivity. Incomplete antigens or haptens must combine with a body protein before becoming immunogenic.

Antigenic Determinants   (pp. 799–800)

3. Antigenic determinants are the portions of antigen molecules that are recognized as foreign. Most antigens have many such sites.

Self-Antigens: MHC Proteins   (p. 800)

4. Major histocompatibility complex (MHC) proteins are membrane-bound glycoproteins that mark our cells as "self." Class I MHC proteins are found on all body cells (except RBCs); the class II variety is found on surfaces of cells that function in the adaptive immune response.

Cells of the Adaptive Immune System: An Overview   (pp. 800–803)

Lymphocytes   (p. 800–803)

1. Lymphocytes arise from the hemocytoblasts of the bone marrow and are educated to develop immunocompetence and self-tolerance. T cells are educated in the thymus and confer cell-mediated immunity. B cells are educated in the bone marrow and provide humoral immunity. Immunocompetence is signaled by the appearance of antigen-specific receptors on the surface of the lymphocyte. Immunocompetent lymphocytes seed the lymphoid organs, where the antigen challenge occurs, and circulate between the blood, lymph, and lymphoid organs.

2. In both B and T lymphocytes, antigen receptor diversity is generated by shuffling gene fragments.

Antigen-Presenting Cells   (p. 803)

3. Antigen-presenting cells (APCs) include dendritic cells, macrophages, and B lymphocytes. They internalize antigens and present antigenic determinants on their surfaces for recognition by T cells.

Humoral Immune Response   (pp. 804–810)

Clonal Selection and Differentiation of B Cells   (pp. 804–805)

1. Clonal selection and differentiation of B cells occur when antigens bind to their receptors, causing them to proliferate. Most of the clone members become plasma cells, which secrete antibodies. This is the primary adaptive immune response.

Immunological Memory   (p. 805)

2. Other clone members become memory B cells, capable of mounting a rapid attack against the same antigen in subsequent encounters (secondary immune responses). The memory cells provide humoral immunological memory.

Active and Passive Humoral Immunity   (pp. 805–806)

3. Active humoral immunity is acquired during an infection or via vaccination and provides immunological memory. Passive immunity is conferred when a donor's antibodies are injected into the bloodstream, or when the mother's antibodies cross the placenta. Its protection is short-lived; immunological memory is not established.

21

Antibodies (pp. 806–810)

4. The antibody monomer consists of four polypeptide chains, two heavy and two light, connected by disulfide bonds. Each chain has both a constant and a variable region. Constant regions determine antibody function and class. Variable regions enable the antibody to recognize its appropriate antigen.

5. Five classes of antibodies exist: IgM, IgA, IgD, IgG, and IgE. They differ structurally and functionally.

6. Antibody functions include complement fixation and antigen neutralization, precipitation, and agglutination.

7. Monoclonal antibodies are pure preparations of a single antibody type useful in diagnostic tests and in treatment for some types of cancer. They are prepared by fusing B cells with tumor cells to produce hybridomas.

Cell-Mediated Immune Response (pp. 810–820)

Clonal Selection and Differentiation of T Cells (pp. 810–814)

1. Immunocompetent helper (T_H) and cytotoxic (T_C) T cells are activated by binding to an antigen-containing MHC protein displayed on the surface of an APC. A costimulatory signal is also essential. Clonal selection occurs and the clone members differentiate into the appropriate effector T cells that mount the primary immune response. Some clone members become memory T cells.

Specific T Cell Roles (pp. 814–818)

2. Helper T cells are required for full activation of most B and T cells, activate macrophages, and release essential cytokines. Cytotoxic T cells directly attack and kill infected cells and cancer cells. Regulatory (T_{Reg}) T cells help to maintain tolerance in the periphery. $T_{\gamma\delta}$ cells, found in the intestinal mucosae, recognize damaged cells and pathogens in a number of novel ways.

3. The immune response is enhanced by cytokines such as interleukin 1 released by macrophages, and interleukin 2, gamma interferon, and others released by activated T cells.

Organ Transplants and Prevention of Rejection (pp. 818–820)

4. Grafts or foreign organ transplants are rejected by cell-mediated responses unless the patient is immunosuppressed. Infections are major complications in such patients.

Homeostatic Imbalances of Immunity (pp. 820–825)

Immunodeficiencies (pp. 820–821)

1. Immunodeficiency diseases include severe combined immunodeficiency (SCID) syndromes and acquired immune deficiency syndrome (AIDS). Overwhelming infections are fatal because the immune system is unable to combat them.

Autoimmune Diseases (pp. 821–822)

2. Autoimmune disease occurs when the body regards its own tissues as foreign and mounts an immune attack against them. Examples include rheumatoid arthritis and multiple sclerosis.

Hypersensitivities (pp. 822–825)

3. Hypersensitivity is an abnormally intense reaction to an otherwise harmless antigen. Immediate hypersensitivities (allergies) are mounted by IgE antibodies. Subacute hypersensitivities, involving both antibodies and complement, include antibody-mediated cytotoxic and immune-complex hypersensitivities. Cell-mediated hypersensitivity is called delayed hypersensitivity.

Developmental Aspects of the Immune System (pp. 825–826)

1. Development of the immune response occurs around the time of birth. The ability of the immune system to recognize foreign substances is genetically determined.

2. The nervous system plays an important role in regulating immune responses, possibly through common mediators. Depression impairs immune function.

3. With aging, the immune system becomes less responsive. The elderly more often suffer from immune deficiency, autoimmune diseases, and cancer.

Review Questions

Multiple Choice/Matching

(Some questions have more than one correct answer. Select the best answer or answers from the choices given.)

1. All of the following are considered innate or nonspecific body defenses *except* (a) complement, (b) phagocytosis, (c) antibodies, (d) lysozyme, (e) inflammation.

2. The process by which neutrophils squeeze through capillary walls in response to inflammatory signals is called (a) diapedesis, (b) chemotaxis, (c) margination, (d) opsonization.

3. Antibodies released by plasma cells are involved in (a) humoral immunity, (b) immediate hypersensitivity reactions, (c) autoimmune disorders, (d) all of the above.

4. Which of the following antibodies can fix complement? (a) IgA, (b) IgD, (c) IgE, (d) IgG, (e) IgM.

5. Which antibody class is abundant in body secretions? (Use the choices from question 4.)

6. Small molecules that must combine with large proteins to become immunogenic are called (a) complete antigens, (b) kinins, (c) antigenic determinants, (d) haptens.

7. Lymphocytes that develop immunocompetence in the bone marrow are (a) T lymphocytes, (b) B lymphocytes, (c) NK cells, (d) B and T lymphocytes.

8. Cells that can directly attack target cells include all of the following *except* (a) macrophages, (b) cytotoxic T cells, (c) helper T cells, (d) natural killer cells.

9. Which of the following is involved in the activation of a B cell? (a) antigen, (b) helper T cell, (c) cytokine, (d) all of the above.

10. The cell type most often invaded by HIV is a(n) (a) eosinophil, (b) cytotoxic T cell, (c) natural killer cell, (d) helper T cell, (e) B cell.

11. Complement fixation promotes all of the following except (a) cell lysis, (b) inflammation, (c) opsonization, (d) interferon release, (e) chemotaxis of neutrophils and other cells.

12. Using the letters from column B, match the cell description in column A. (Note that all require more than a single choice.)

21

Column A

_____ (1) phagocyte
_____ (2) releases histamine
_____ (3) releases perforins
_____ (4) lymphocyte
_____ (5) can differentiate
         to form memory cells
_____ (6) antigen-presenting cell

Column B

(a) natural killer cells
(b) neutrophil
(c) dendritic cells
(d) mast cell
(e) cytotoxic T cell
(f) B cell
(g) macrophage
(h) helper T cell
(i) basophil

Short Answer Essay Questions

13. Besides acting as mechanical barriers, the skin epidermis and mucosae of the body have other attributes that contribute to their protective roles. Cite the common body locations and the importance of mucus, lysozyme, keratin, acid pH, and cilia.

14. Explain why attempts at phagocytosis are not always successful; cite factors that increase the likelihood of success.

15. What is complement? How does it cause bacterial lysis? What are some of the other roles of complement?

16. Interferons are referred to as antiviral proteins. What stimulates their production, and how do they protect uninfected cells? What cells of the body secrete interferons?

17. Differentiate between humoral and cell-mediated adaptive immunity.

18. Although the adaptive immune system has two arms, it has been said, "no T cells, no immunity." Explain.

19. Define immunocompetence. What event (or observation) signals that a B or a T cell has developed immunocompetence?

20. Describe the process of activation of a helper T cell.

21. Differentiate between a primary and a secondary immune response. Which is more rapid and why?

22. Define antibody. Using an appropriately labeled diagram, describe the structure of an antibody monomer. Indicate and label variable and constant regions, heavy and light chains.

23. What is the role of the variable regions of an antibody? Of the constant regions?

24. Name the five antibody classes and describe where each is most likely to be found in the body.

25. How do antibodies help defend the body?

26. Do vaccines produce active or passive humoral immunity? Explain your answer. Why is passive immunity less satisfactory?

27. Describe the specific roles of helper, regulatory, and cytotoxic T cells in normal cell-mediated immunity.

28. Name several cytokines and describe their role in the immune response.

29. Define hypersensitivity. List three types of hypersensitivity reactions. For each, note whether antibodies or T cells are involved and provide two examples.

30. What events can result in autoimmune disease?

31. What accounts for the declining efficiency of the immune system with age?

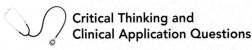

Critical Thinking and Clinical Application Questions

1. Jenny, a 6-year-old child who has been raised in a germ-free environment from birth, is a victim of one of the most severe examples of an abnormal immune system. Jenny also suffers from cancer caused by the Epstein-Barr virus. Relative to this case: (a) What is the usual fate of children with Jenny's condition and similar circumstances if no treatment is attempted? (b) Why is Jenny's brother chosen as the bone marrow donor? (c) Why is her physician planning to use umbilical cord blood as a source of stem cells for a bone marrow transplant if transplant of her brother's marrow fails (what are the hoped-for results)? (d) Attempt to explain Jenny's cancer. (e) What similarities and dissimilarities exist between Jenny's illness and AIDS?

2. Some people with a deficit of IgA exhibit recurrent respiratory tract infections. Explain this observation.

3. Explain the underlying mechanisms responsible for the cardinal signs of acute inflammation: heat, pain, redness, swelling.

4. Costanza was picking grapes in her father's arbor when she felt a short prickling pain in her finger. She ran crying to her father, who removed an insect stinger and calmed her with a glass of lemonade. Twenty minutes later Costanza's finger was red, swollen, and throbbing where she had been stung. What type of immune response was she exhibiting? What treatment would relieve her discomfort?

5. Caroline, a pregnant 29-year-old, has been HIV-positive for at least 10 years, dating back to when she was homeless and injecting heroin on a regular basis. While she currently has no symptoms of AIDS, she is taking several medications and is worried about the possibility that her baby might be infected. How do you think the HIV virus might be transferred from a mother to her offspring? Which of Caroline's cells are infected by the virus and why is the viral attack on these cells so devastating? Why is Caroline taking medication even though she has no symptoms? What types of medications might she be taking and how do they affect the virus and its replication?

21

The Respiratory System

Functional Anatomy of the Respiratory System (pp. 831–846)

1. Identify the organs forming the respiratory passageway(s) in descending order until the alveoli are reached. Distinguish between conducting and respiratory zone structures.
2. List and describe several protective mechanisms of the respiratory system.
3. Describe the makeup of the respiratory membrane, and relate structure to function.
4. Describe the gross structure of the lungs and pleurae.

Mechanics of Breathing (pp. 846–854)

5. Relate Boyle's law to events of inspiration and expiration.
6. Explain the relative roles of the respiratory muscles and lung elasticity in producing the volume changes that cause air to flow into and out of the lungs.
7. Explain the functional importance of the partial vacuum that exists in the intrapleural space.
8. List several physical factors that influence pulmonary ventilation.

9. Explain and compare the various lung volumes and capacities. Indicate types of information that can be gained from pulmonary function tests.
10. Define dead space.

Gas Exchanges Between the Blood, Lungs, and Tissues (pp. 854–858)

11. State Dalton's law of partial pressures and Henry's law.
12. Describe how atmospheric and alveolar air differ in composition, and explain these differences.
13. Relate Dalton's and Henry's laws to events of external and internal respiration.

Transport of Respiratory Gases by Blood (pp. 858–863)

14. Describe how oxygen is transported in the blood, and explain how oxygen loading and unloading is affected by temperature, pH, BPG, and P_{CO_2}.
15. Describe carbon dioxide transport in the blood.

Control of Respiration (pp. 863–869)

16. Describe the neural controls of respiration.

17. Compare and contrast the influences of lung reflexes, volition, emotions, arterial pH, and arterial partial pressures of oxygen and carbon dioxide on respiratory rate and depth.

Respiratory Adjustments (pp. 869–870)

18. Compare and contrast the hyperpnea of exercise with hyperventilation.
19. Describe the process and effects of acclimatization to high altitude.

Homeostatic Imbalances of the Respiratory System (pp. 870–873)

20. Compare the causes and consequences of chronic bronchitis, emphysema, asthma, tuberculosis, and lung cancer.

Developmental Aspects of the Respiratory System (pp. 873–875)

21. Trace the embryonic development of the respiratory system.
22. Describe normal changes that occur in the respiratory system from infancy to old age.

Far from self-sustaining, the body depends on the external environment, both as a source of substances the body needs to survive and as a catch basin for its wastes. The trillions of cells making up the body require a continuous supply of oxygen to carry out their vital functions. We cannot do without oxygen for even a little while, as we can without food or water. As cells use oxygen, they give off carbon dioxide, a waste product the body must get rid of. They also generate dangerous free radicals, the inescapable by-products of living in a world full of oxygen. But let's get to the topic of this chapter, the respiratory system.

The major function of the **respiratory system** is to supply the body with oxygen and dispose of carbon dioxide. To accomplish this function, at least four processes, collectively called **respiration,** must happen:

1. Pulmonary ventilation: movement of air into and out of the lungs so that the gases there are continuously changed and refreshed (commonly called breathing).

2. External respiration: movement of oxygen from the lungs to the blood and of carbon dioxide from the blood to the lungs.

3. Transport of respiratory gases: transport of oxygen from the lungs to the tissue cells of the body, and of carbon dioxide from the tissue cells to the lungs. This is accomplished by the cardiovascular system using blood as the transporting fluid.

4. Internal respiration: movement of oxygen from blood to the tissue cells and of carbon dioxide from tissue cells to blood.*

Only the first two processes are the special responsibility of the respiratory system, but it cannot accomplish its primary goal of obtaining oxygen and eliminating carbon dioxide unless the third and fourth processes also occur. Thus, the respiratory and circulatory systems are closely coupled, and if either system fails, the body's cells begin to die from oxygen starvation.

Because it moves air, the respiratory system is also involved with the sense of smell and with speech.

Functional Anatomy of the Respiratory System

The respiratory system includes the *nose* and *nasal cavity, pharynx, larynx, trachea, bronchi* and their smaller branches, and the *lungs,* which contain the

*The actual use of oxygen and production of carbon dioxide by tissue cells, that is, *cellular respiration,* is the cornerstone of all energy-producing chemical reactions in the body. Cellular respiration, which occurs in all body cells, is discussed more appropriately in the metabolism section of Chapter 24.

terminal air sacs, or *alveoli* (Figure 22.1). Functionally, the system consists of two zones. The **respiratory zone,** the actual site of gas exchange, is composed of the respiratory bronchioles, alveolar ducts, and alveoli, all microscopic structures. The **conducting zone** includes all other respiratory passageways, which provide fairly rigid conduits for air to reach the gas exchange sites. The conducting zone organs also cleanse, humidify, and warm incoming air. Thus, air reaching the lungs has fewer irritants (dust, bacteria, etc.) than when it entered the system, and it is warm and damp, like the air of the tropics. The functions of the major organs of the respiratory system are summarized in Table 22.1 on p. 838.

In addition to these organs, some authorities also include the respiratory muscles (diaphragm, etc.) as part of this system. Although we will consider how these skeletal muscles bring about the volume changes that promote ventilation, we continue to classify them as part of the *muscular system.*

The Nose and Paranasal Sinuses

The nose is the only externally visible part of the respiratory system. Unlike the eyes and lips, facial features often referred to poetically, the nose is usually an irreverent target. We are urged to keep our nose to the grindstone and to keep it out of other people's business. However, considering its important functions, it deserves more esteem. The nose (1) provides an airway for respiration, (2) moistens and warms entering air, (3) filters and cleans inspired air, (4) serves as a resonating chamber for speech, and (5) houses the olfactory (smell) receptors.

The structures of the nose are divided into the *external nose* and the internal *nasal cavity* for ease of consideration. The surface features of the external nose (Figure 22.2a) include the *root* (area between the eyebrows), *bridge,* and *dorsum nasi* (anterior margin), the latter terminating in the *apex* (tip of the nose). Just inferior to the apex is a shallow vertical groove called the *philtrum* (fil'trum). The external openings of the nose, the *nostrils* or *nares* (na'rez), are bounded laterally by the flared *alae.* The skeletal framework of the external nose is fashioned by the nasal and frontal bones superiorly (forming the bridge and root, respectively), the maxillary bones laterally, and flexible plates of hyaline cartilage (the lateral, septal, and alar cartilages) inferiorly (Figure 22.2b). Noses vary a great deal in size and shape, largely because of differences in the nasal cartilages. The skin covering the nose's dorsal and lateral aspects is thin and contains many sebaceous glands.

The internal **nasal cavity** lies in and posterior to the external nose. During breathing, air enters the cavity by passing through the **nostrils,** or **nares**

Q *Which of the organs shown contains both conducting zone and respiratory zone structures?*

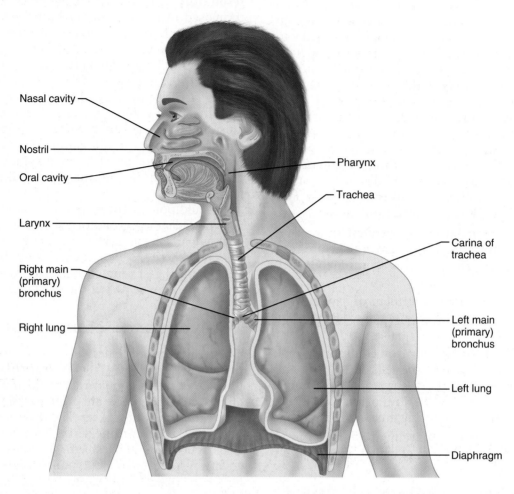

FIGURE 22.1 **The major respiratory organs in relation to surrounding structures.**

(Figure 22.2a and Figure 22.3b). The nasal cavity is divided by a midline **nasal septum,** formed anteriorly by the septal cartilage and posteriorly by the vomer bone and perpendicular plate of the ethmoid bone (see Figure 7.10b, p. 215). The nasal cavity is continuous posteriorly with the nasal portion of the pharynx through the **posterior nasal apertures,** also called the *choanae* (ko-a'ne; "funnels").

The roof of the nasal cavity is formed by the ethmoid and sphenoid bones of the skull. The floor is formed by the *palate,* which separates the nasal cavity from the oral cavity below. Anteriorly, where the palate is supported by the maxillary processes and palatine bones, it is called the **hard palate.** The unsupported posterior portion is the muscular **soft palate.**

The part of the nasal cavity just superior to the nostrils, called the **nasal vestibule,** is lined with skin containing sebaceous and sweat glands and numerous hair follicles. The hairs, or **vibrissae** (vi-bris'e; *vibro* = to quiver), filter coarse particles (dust, pollen) from inspired air. The rest of the nasal cavity is lined with two types of mucous membrane. The **olfactory mucosa,** lining the slitlike superior region of the nasal cavity, contains smell receptors. The balance of the nasal cavity mucosa, the **respiratory mucosa,** is a pseudostratified ciliated columnar epithelium, containing scattered *goblet cells,* that rests on a lamina propria richly supplied with *mucous* and *serous glands.* (Mucous cells secrete mucus, and serous cells secrete a watery fluid containing enzymes.) Each day, these glands secrete about a quart of mucus containing *lysozyme,* an antibacterial enzyme. The sticky mucus traps inspired dust, bacteria, and other debris, while lysozyme attacks and destroys bacteria chemically. The epithelial cells of the

A *The lungs.*

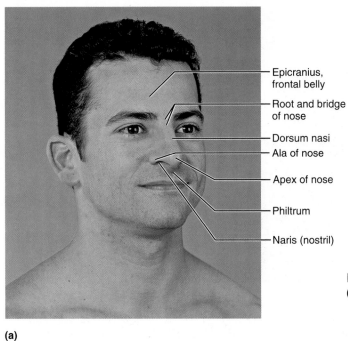

Epicranius,
frontal belly

Root and bridge
of nose

Dorsum nasi

Ala of nose

Apex of nose

Philtrum

Naris (nostril)

(a)

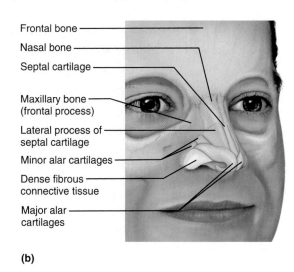

Frontal bone

Nasal bone

Septal cartilage

Maxillary bone
(frontal process)

Lateral process of
septal cartilage

Minor alar cartilages

Dense fibrous
connective tissue

Major alar
cartilages

(b)

FIGURE 22.2 **The external nose. (a)** Surface anatomy.
(b) External skeletal framework.

respiratory mucosa also secrete *defensins,* natural antibiotics that help get rid of invading microbes. Additionally, the high water content of the mucus film acts to humidify the inhaled air.

The ciliated cells of the respiratory mucosa create a gentle current that moves the sheet of contaminated mucus posteriorly toward the throat, where it is swallowed and digested by stomach juices. We are usually unaware of this important action of our nasal cilia, but when exposed to cold air they become sluggish, allowing mucus to accumulate in the nasal cavity and then dribble out the nostrils. This along with the fact that water vapor in expired air tends to condense at lower temperatures helps explain why you might have a "runny" nose on a crisp, wintry day.

The nasal mucosa is richly supplied with sensory nerve endings, and contact with irritating particles (dust, pollen, and the like) triggers a sneeze reflex. The sneeze forces air outward in a violent burst—a somewhat crude way of expelling irritants from the nose.

Rich plexuses of capillaries and thin-walled veins underlie the nasal epithelium and warm incoming air as it flows across the mucosal surface. When the inspired air is cold, the vascular plexus becomes engorged with blood, thereby intensifying the air-heating process. Because of the abundance and superficial location of these blood vessels, nosebleeds are common and often profuse.

Protruding medially from each lateral wall of the nasal cavity are three scroll-like mucosa-covered projections, the *superior, middle,* and *inferior nasal conchae* (kong'ke) (Figure 22.3). The groove inferior to each concha is a *nasal meatus* (me-a'tus). The

curved conchae greatly increase the mucosal surface area exposed to the air and enhance air turbulence in the cavity. The gases in inhaled air swirl through the twists and turns, but heavier, nongaseous particles tend to be deflected onto the mucus-coated surfaces, where they become trapped. As a result, few particles larger than 6 μm make it past the nasal cavity.

The conchae and nasal mucosa not only function during inhalation to filter, heat, and moisten the air, but also act during exhalation to reclaim this heat and moisture. That is, the inhaled air cools the conchae, then during exhalation these cooled conchae precipitate moisture and extract heat from the humid air flowing over them. This reclamation mechanism minimizes the amount of moisture and heat lost from the body through breathing, helping us to survive in dry and cold climates.

The nasal cavity is surrounded by a ring of **paranasal sinuses** (Figure 22.3b) located in the frontal, sphenoid, ethmoid, and maxillary bones (see also Figure 7.11, p. 218). The sinuses lighten the skull, and together with the nasal cavity they warm and moisten the air. The mucus they produce ultimately flows into the nasal cavity, and the suctioning effect created by nose blowing helps drain the sinuses.

▨ HOMEOSTATIC IMBALANCE

Cold viruses, streptococcal bacteria, and various allergens can cause *rhinitis* (ri-ni'tis), inflammation of the nasal mucosa accompanied by excessive mucus production, nasal congestion, and postnasal drip. The nasal mucosa is continuous with that of the rest

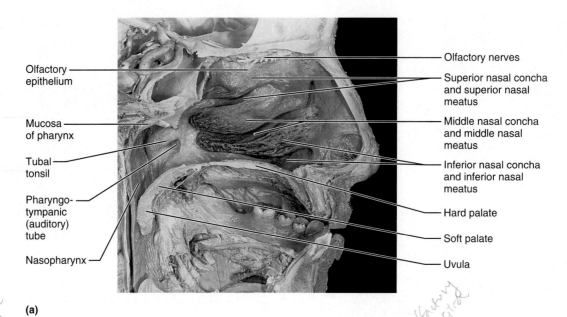

Olfactory epithelium

Mucosa of pharynx

Tubal tonsil

Pharyngo-tympanic (auditory) tube

Nasopharynx

Olfactory nerves

Superior nasal concha and superior nasal meatus

Middle nasal concha and middle nasal meatus

Inferior nasal concha and inferior nasal meatus

Hard palate

Soft palate

Uvula

(a)

Sphenoidal sinus

Nasal meatuses (superior, middle, and inferior)

Pharyngeal tonsil (adenoid)

Opening of pharyngotympanic (auditory) tube

Nasopharynx

Posterior nasal aperture

Uvula

Palatine tonsil

Isthmus of the fauces

Oropharynx

Laryngopharynx

Vestibular fold

Vocal fold

Esophagus

Frontal sinus

Cribriform plate of ethmoid bone

Nasal conchae (superior, middle and inferior)

Nasal vestibule

Nostril

Hard palate

Soft palate

Tongue

Lingual tonsil

Epiglottis

Hyoid bone

Thyroid cartilage

Cricoid cartilage

Laryngeal cartilages

Thyroid gland

Trachea

(b)

FIGURE 22.3   The upper respiratory tract. Midsagittal section of the head and neck: **(a)** Photograph. (See *A Brief Atlas of the Human Body,* Figure 47.) **(b)** Illustration.

of the respiratory tract, explaining the typical nose to throat to chest progression of colds. Because the mucosa extends tentacle-like into the nasolacrimal (tear) ducts and paranasal sinuses, nasal cavity infections often spread to those regions, causing **sinusitis** (inflamed sinuses). When the passageways connecting the sinuses to the nasal cavity are blocked with mucus or infectious material, the air in the sinus cavities is absorbed. The result is a partial vacuum and a *sinus headache* localized over the inflamed areas. ●

The Pharynx

The funnel-shaped **pharynx** (far'ingks) connects the nasal cavity and mouth superiorly to the larynx and esophagus inferiorly. Commonly called the *throat*, the pharynx vaguely resembles a short length of garden hose as it extends for about 13 cm (5 inches) from the base of the skull to the level of the sixth cervical vertebra (Figure 22.1).

From superior to inferior, the pharynx is divided into three regions—the *nasopharynx, oropharynx,* and *laryngopharynx* (Figure 22.3b). The muscular pharynx wall is composed of skeletal muscle throughout its length (see Table 10.3, pp. 340–341), but the cellular composition of its mucosa varies from one pharyngeal region to another.

The Nasopharynx

The **nasopharynx** is posterior to the nasal cavity, inferior to the sphenoid bone, and superior to the level of the soft palate. Because it lies above the point where food enters the body, it serves *only* as an air passageway. During swallowing, the soft palate and its pendulous *uvula* (u'vu-lah; "little grape") move superiorly, an action that closes off the nasopharynx and prevents food from entering the nasal cavity. (When we giggle, this sealing action fails and fluids being swallowed can end up spraying out the nose.)

The nasopharynx is continuous with the nasal cavity through the posterior nasal apertures (see Figure 22.3b), and its pseudostratified ciliated epithelium takes over the job of propelling mucus where the nasal mucosa leaves off. High on its posterior wall is the **pharyngeal tonsil** (far-rin'je-al) (or *adenoids*), which traps and destroys pathogens entering the nasopharynx in air.

HOMEOSTATIC IMBALANCE

Infected and swollen adenoids block air passage in the nasopharynx, making it necessary to breathe through the mouth. As a result, the air is not properly moistened, warmed, or filtered before reaching the lungs. When the adenoids are chronically enlarged, both speech and sleep may be disturbed. ●

The *pharyngotympanic (auditory) tubes,* which drain the middle ear cavities and allow middle ear pressure to equalize with atmospheric pressure, open into the lateral walls of the nasopharynx (Figure 22.3a). A ridge of pharyngeal mucosa, referred to as a *tubal tonsil,* arches over each of these openings. Because of their strategic location, the tubal tonsils help protect the middle ear against infections likely to spread from the nasopharynx. The pharyngeal tonsil, superoposterior and medial to the tubal tonsils, also plays this protective role.

The Oropharynx

The **oropharynx** lies posterior to the oral cavity and is continuous with it through an archway called the **isthmus of the fauces** (faw'sēz; "throat") (see Figure 22.3b). Because the oropharynx extends inferiorly from the level of the soft palate to the epiglottis, both swallowed food and inhaled air pass through it.

As the nasopharynx blends into the oropharynx, the epithelium changes from pseudostratified columnar to a more protective stratified squamous epithelium. This structural adaptation accommodates the increased friction and greater chemical trauma accompanying food passage.

Two kinds of tonsils lie embedded in the oropharyngeal mucosa. The paired **palatine tonsils** lie in the lateral walls of the fauces. The **lingual tonsil** covers the base of the tongue.

The Laryngopharynx

Like the oropharynx above it, the **laryngopharynx** (lah-ring"go-far'ingks) serves as a passageway for food and air and is lined with a stratified squamous epithelium. It lies directly posterior to the upright epiglottis and extends to the larynx, where the respiratory and digestive pathways diverge. At that point the laryngopharynx is continuous with the esophagus posteriorly. The esophagus conducts food and fluids to the stomach; air enters the larynx anteriorly. During swallowing, food has the "right of way," and air passage temporarily stops.

The Larynx

Basic Anatomy

The **larynx** (lar'ingks), or voice box, extends for about 5 cm (2 inches) from the level of the third to the sixth cervical vertebra. Superiorly it attaches to the hyoid bone and opens into the laryngopharynx. Inferiorly it is continuous with the trachea (Figure 22.3b).

The larynx has three functions. Its two main tasks are to provide a *patent* (open) airway and to act as a switching mechanism to route air and food into the proper channels. Because it houses the vocal cords, the third function of the larynx is voice production.

Q Which structure seals the larynx when we swallow?

(a)

(b)

(c)

(d)

FIGURE 22.4 **The larynx.** (a) Anterior superficial view. (b) Sagittal view; anterior surface to the right. (c) Photograph of the cartilaginous framework of the larynx, posterior view. (d) Photograph of posterior aspect.

The framework of the larynx is an intricate arrangement of nine cartilages connected by membranes and ligaments (Figure 22.4). Except for the epiglottis, all laryngeal cartilages are hyaline cartilages. The large, shield-shaped **thyroid cartilage** is formed by the fusion of two cartilage plates. The midline **laryngeal prominence** (lah-rin'je-al), which marks the fusion point, is obvious externally as the *Adam's apple*. The thyroid cartilage is typically larger in males than in females because male sex hormones stimulate its growth during puberty. Inferior to the thyroid cartilage is the ring-shaped **cricoid cartilage** (kri'koid), perched atop and anchored to the trachea inferiorly.

A The epiglottis.

Base of tongue
Epiglottis
False vocal cord
True vocal cord
Glottis
Inner lining of trachea
Corniculate cartilage

(a)   (b)

FIGURE 22.5 **Movements of the vocal cords.** Superior views of the larynx and vocal cords, mucous membranes in place. **(a)** Vocal cords in closed position. **(b)** Vocal cords in open position.

Three pairs of small cartilages, **arytenoid** (ar″ĭ-te′noid), **cuneiform** (ku-ne′ĭ-form), and **corniculate cartilages,** form part of the lateral and posterior walls of the larynx. The most important of these are the pyramid-shaped arytenoid cartilages, which anchor the vocal cords.

The ninth cartilage, the flexible, spoon-shaped **epiglottis** (ep″ĭ-glot′is; "above the glottis"), is composed of elastic cartilage and is almost entirely covered by a taste bud–containing mucosa. The epiglottis extends from the posterior aspect of the tongue to its anchoring point on the anterior rim of the thyroid cartilage (see Figure 22.4b and c). When only air is flowing into the larynx, the inlet to the larynx is open wide and the free edge of the epiglottis projects upward. During swallowing, the larynx is pulled superiorly and the epiglottis tips to cover the laryngeal inlet. Because this action keeps food out of the lower respiratory passages, the epiglottis has been called the guardian of the airways. Anything other than air entering the larynx initiates the cough reflex, which acts to expel the substance. Because this protective reflex does not work when we are unconscious, it is never a good idea to administer liquids when attempting to revive an unconscious person.

Lying under the laryngeal mucosa on each side are the **vocal ligaments,** which attach the arytenoid cartilages to the thyroid cartilage. These ligaments, composed largely of elastic fibers, form the core of mucosal folds called the **vocal folds,** or **true vocal cords,** which appear pearly white because they lack blood vessels (Figure 22.5). The vocal folds vibrate, producing sounds as air rushes up from the lungs. The vocal folds and the medial opening between them through which air passes are called the **glottis.** Superior to the vocal folds is a similar pair of mucosal folds called the **vestibular folds,** or **false vocal cords.** These play no part in sound production but help to close the glottis when we swallow.

The superior portion of the larynx, an area subject to food contact, is lined by stratified squamous epithelium. Below the vocal folds the epithelium is a pseudostratified ciliated columnar type that acts as a dust filter. The power stroke of its cilia is directed upward toward the pharynx so that mucus is continually moved *away* from the lungs. We help to move mucus up and out of the larynx when we "clear our throat."

Voice Production

Speech involves the intermittent release of expired air and the opening and closing of the glottis. The length of the true vocal cords and the size of the glottis change with the action of the intrinsic laryngeal muscles that clothe the cartilages. Most of these muscles move the arytenoid cartilages. As the length and tension of the cords change, the pitch of the sound varies. Generally, the tenser the cords, the faster they vibrate and the higher the pitch. The glottis is wide (Figure 22.5b) when we produce deep tones and narrows to a slit for high-pitched sounds. As a boy's larynx enlarges during puberty, his true vocal cords become longer and thicker. Because this causes them to vibrate more slowly, his voice becomes deeper. Until the young man learns to control his newly enlarged true vocal cords, his voice "cracks."

Loudness of the voice depends on the force with which the airstream rushes across the vocal cords. The greater the force, the stronger the vibration and the louder the sound. The vocal cords do not move at all when we whisper, but they vibrate vigorously when we yell. The power source for creating the airstream is the muscles of the chest, abdomen, and back.

The vocal folds actually produce buzzing sounds. The perceived quality of the voice depends on the coordinated activity of many structures above the glottis. For example, the entire length of the pharynx acts as a resonating chamber, to amplify and enhance

TABLE 22.1	Principal Organs of the Respiratory System	
STRUCTURE	DESCRIPTION, GENERAL AND DISTINCTIVE FEATURES	FUNCTION
Nose	Jutting external portion supported by bone and cartilage; internal nasal cavity divided by midline nasal septum and lined with mucosa	Produces mucus; filters, warms, and moistens incoming air; resonance chamber for speech
	Roof of nasal cavity contains olfactory epithelium	Receptors for sense of smell
	Paranasal sinuses around nasal cavity	Same as for nasal cavity; also lighten skull
Pharynx	Passageway connecting nasal cavity to larynx and oral cavity to esophagus; three subdivisions: nasopharynx, oropharynx, and laryngopharynx	Passageway for air and food
	Houses tonsils (lymphoid tissue masses involved in protection against pathogens)	Facilitates exposure of immune system to inhaled antigens
Larynx	Connects pharynx to trachea; framework of cartilage and dense connective tissue; opening (glottis) can be closed by epiglottis or vocal folds	Air passageway; prevents food from entering lower respiratory tract
	Houses vocal folds (true vocal cords)	Voice production
Trachea	Flexible tube running from larynx and dividing inferiorly into two main bronchi; walls contain C-shaped cartilages that are incomplete posteriorly where connected by trachealis muscle	Air passageway; cleans, warms, and moistens incoming air
Bronchial tree	Consists of right and left main bronchi, which subdivide within the lungs to form lobar and segmental bronchi and bronchioles; bronchiolar walls contain complete layer of smooth muscle; constriction of this muscle impedes expiration	Air passageways connecting trachea with alveoli; cleans, warms, and moistens incoming air
Alveoli	Microscopic chambers at termini of bronchial tree; walls of simple squamous epithelium underlain by thin basement membrane; external surfaces intimately associated with pulmonary capillaries	Main sites of gas exchange
	Special alveolar cells produce surfactant	Reduces surface tension; helps prevent lung collapse
Lungs	Paired composite organs located within pleural cavities of thorax; composed primarily of alveoli and respiratory passageways; stroma is fibrous elastic connective tissue, allowing lungs to recoil passively during expiration	House respiratory passages smaller than the main bronchi
Pleurae	Serous membranes; parietal pleura lines thoracic cavity; visceral pleura covers external lung surfaces	Produce lubricating fluid and compartmentalize lungs

the sound quality. The oral, nasal, and sinus cavities also contribute to vocal resonance. In addition, good enunciation depends on the "shaping" of sound into recognizable consonants and vowels by muscles in the pharynx, tongue, soft palate, and lips.

HOMEOSTATIC IMBALANCE

Inflammation of the vocal folds, or **laryngitis,** causes the vocal folds to swell, interfering with their vibration. This produces a change in the voice tone, hoarseness, or in severe cases inability to speak above a whisper. Laryngitis is also caused by overuse of the voice, very dry air, bacterial infections, tumors on the vocal folds, and inhalation of irritating chemicals. ●

Sphincter Functions of the Larynx

Under certain conditions, the vocal folds act as a sphincter that prevents air passage. During abdominal straining associated with defecation, the glottis closes to prevent exhalation and the abdominal muscles contract, causing the intra-abdominal pressure to rise. These events, collectively known as **Valsalva's maneuver,** help empty the rectum and can also splint (stabilize) the body trunk when one lifts a heavy load.

The Trachea

The **trachea** (tra′ke-ah), or *windpipe,* descends from the larynx through the neck and into the mediastinum. It ends by dividing into the two main

FIGURE 22.6 **Tissue composition of the tracheal wall.**
(a) Cross-sectional view of the trachea, illustrating its relationship to the esophagus, the position of the supporting
hyaline cartilage rings, and the trachealis muscle connecting
the free ends of the cartilage rings. **(b)** Photomicrograph of
a portion of the tracheal wall (cross-sectional view; 225×).
(c) Scanning electron micrograph of cilia in the trachea
(13,500×). The cilia appear as yellow, grasslike projections.
Mucus-secreting goblet cells (orange) with short microvilli
are interspersed between the ciliated cells.

bronchi at midthorax (see Figure 22.1). In humans,
it is 10–12 cm (about 4 inches) long and 2 cm
(3/4 inch) in diameter, and very flexible and mobile.
Interestingly, early anatomists mistook the trachea
for a rough-walled artery (*trachea* = rough).

The tracheal wall consists of several layers that
are common to many tubular body organs—the
mucosa, submucosa, and *adventitia* (Figure 22.6).
The **mucosa** has the same goblet cell–containing
pseudostratified epithelium that occurs throughout
most of the respiratory tract. Its cilia continually
propel debris-laden mucus toward the pharynx. This
epithelium rests on a fairly thick lamina propria that
has a rich supply of elastic fibers.

HOMEOSTATIC IMBALANCE

Smoking inhibits and ultimately destroys cilia, after
which coughing is the only means of preventing mucus from accumulating in the lungs. For this reason,
smokers with respiratory congestion should avoid
medications that inhibit the cough reflex. ●

The **submucosa,** a connective tissue layer deep
to the mucosa, contains seromucous glands that
help produce the mucus "sheets" within the tra-

chea. The outermost **adventitia** layer is a connective tissue layer reinforced internally by 16 to 20
C-shaped rings of hyaline cartilage (Figure 22.6).
Because of its elastic elements, the trachea is flexible enough to stretch and move inferiorly during inspiration and recoil during expiration, but the cartilage rings prevent it from collapsing and keep the
airway patent despite the pressure changes that occur during breathing. The open posterior parts of
the cartilage rings, which abut the esophagus (see
Figure 22.6a), are connected by smooth muscle
fibers of the **trachealis muscle** and by soft connective tissue. Because this portion of the tracheal wall
is not rigid, the esophagus can expand anteriorly as
swallowed food passes through it. Contraction of
the trachealis muscle decreases the trachea's diameter, causing expired air to rush upward from the
lungs with greater force. This action helps to expel

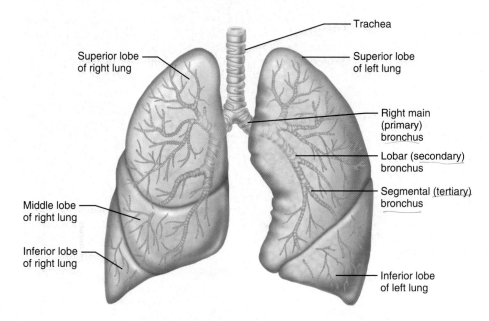

FIGURE 22.7 **Conducting zone passages.** The air pathway inferior to the larynx consists of the trachea and the main, lobar, and segmental bronchi, which branch into the smaller bronchi and bronchioles until the terminal bronchioles of the lungs are reached.

mucus from the trachea when we cough by accelerating the exhaled air to speeds of 100 mph! The last tracheal cartilage is expanded, and a spar of cartilage, called the **carina** (kar-ri'nah; "keel"), projects posteriorly from its inner face, marking the point where the trachea branches into the two *main bronchi*. The mucosa of the carina is highly sensitive and violent coughing is triggered when a foreign object makes contact with it.

◣ HOMEOSTATIC IMBALANCE

Tracheal obstruction is life threatening. Many people have suffocated after choking on a piece of food that suddenly closed off their trachea. The **Heimlich maneuver,** a procedure in which air in the victim's lungs is used to "pop out," or expel, an obstructing piece of food, has saved many people from becoming victims of "café coronaries." The maneuver is simple to learn and easy to do. However, it is best learned by demonstration because cracked ribs are a distinct possibility when it is done incorrectly. ●

The Bronchi and Subdivisions: The Bronchial Tree

The bronchial tree (Figure 22.7) is the site where conducting zone structures give way to respiratory zone structures (Figure 22.8).

Conducting Zone Structures

The **right** and **left main (primary) bronchi** (brong'ki) are formed by the division of the trachea approximately at the level of T_7 in an erect (standing) person. Each bronchus runs obliquely in the mediastinum before plunging into the medial depression (hilum) of the lung on its own side (Figure 22.7). The right main bronchus is wider, shorter, and more vertical than the left and is the more common site for an inhaled foreign object to become lodged. By the time incoming air reaches the bronchi, it is warm, cleansed of most impurities, and saturated with water vapor.

Once inside the lungs, each main bronchus subdivides into **lobar (secondary) bronchi**—three on the right and two on the left—each supplying one lung lobe. The lobar bronchi branch into third-order **segmental (tertiary) bronchi,** which divide repeatedly into smaller and smaller bronchi (fourth-order, fifth-order, etc.). Overall, there are about 23 orders of branching air passageways in the lungs. Passages smaller than 1 mm in diameter are called **bronchioles** ("little bronchi"), and the tiniest of these, the **terminal bronchioles,** are less than 0.5 mm in diameter. Because of this branching pattern, the conducting network within the lungs is often called the **bronchial** or **respiratory tree.**

The tissue composition of the walls of the main bronchi mimics that of the trachea, but as the

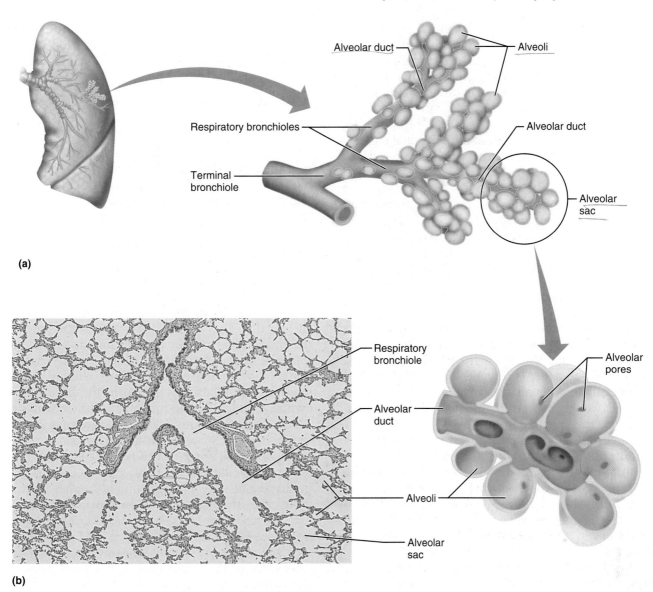

(a)

(b)

FIGURE 22.8 **Respiratory zone structures. (a)** Diagrammatic view of respiratory bronchioles, alveolar ducts, alveolar sacs, and alveoli. **(b)** Photomicrograph of a section of human lung, showing the respiratory structures that form the final divisions of the bronchial tree (40×). Notice the thinness of the alveolar walls.

conducting tubes become smaller, the following structural changes occur:

1. Support structures change. The cartilage rings are replaced by irregular *plates* of cartilage, and by the time the bronchioles are reached, supportive cartilage is no longer present in the tube walls. However, elastic fibers are found in the tube walls throughout the bronchial tree.

2. Epithelium type changes. The mucosal epithelium thins as it changes from pseudostratified columnar to columnar and then to cuboidal in the terminal bronchioles. Cilia are sparse, and mucus-producing cells are absent in the bronchioles. Thus, most airborne debris found at or below the level of the bronchioles is removed by macrophages in the alveoli.

3. Amount of smooth muscle increases. The relative amount of smooth muscle in the tube walls increases as the passageways become smaller. A complete layer of circular smooth muscle in the bronchioles and the lack of supporting cartilage (which would hinder constriction) allows the bronchioles to provide substantial resistance to air passage under certain conditions (described later).

Respiratory Zone Structures

Defined by the presence of thin-walled air sacs called **alveoli** (al-ve′o-li; *alveol* = small cavity), the respiratory zone begins as the terminal bronchioles feed into **respiratory bronchioles** within the lung (Figure 22.8). Protruding from these smallest bronchioles are scattered alveoli. The respiratory bronchioles lead into winding **alveolar ducts,** whose walls consist of diffusely arranged rings of smooth muscle cells, connective tissue fibers, and outpocketing alveoli. The alveolar ducts lead into terminal clusters of alveoli called **alveolar sacs.** Many people mistakenly equate alveoli, the site of gas exchange, with alveolar sacs, but they are not the same thing. The alveolar sac is analogous to a bunch of grapes, and the alveoli are the individual grapes. The 300 million or so gas-filled alveoli in the lungs account for most of the lung volume and provide a tremendous surface area for gas exchange.

The Respiratory Membrane The walls of the alveoli are composed primarily of a single layer of squamous epithelial cells, called **type I cells,** surrounded by a flimsy basement membrane. The thinness of their walls is hard to imagine, but a sheet of tissue paper is much thicker. The external surfaces of the alveoli are densely covered with a "cobweb" of pulmonary capillaries (Figure 22.9). Together, the alveolar and capillary walls and their fused basement membranes form the **respiratory membrane,** a 5-μm-thick *air-blood barrier* that has gas on one side and blood flowing past on the other (Figure 22.9d). Gas exchanges occur readily by simple diffusion across the respiratory membrane—O_2 passes from the alveolus into the blood, and CO_2 leaves the blood to enter the gas-filled alveolus.

Scattered amid the type I squamous cells that form the major part of the alveolar walls are cuboidal **type II cells** (Figure 22.9c). The type II cells secrete a fluid containing surfactant that coats the gas-exposed alveolar surfaces. (Surfactant's role in reducing the surface tension of the alveolar fluid is described later in this chapter.)

The alveoli have three other significant features: (1) They are surrounded by fine elastic fibers of the same type that surround the entire bronchial tree. (2) Open **alveolar pores** connecting adjacent alveoli allow air pressure throughout the lung to be equalized and provide alternate air routes to any alveoli whose bronchi have collapsed due to disease. (3) Remarkably efficient **alveolar macrophages** crawl freely along the internal alveolar surfaces. Although huge numbers of infectious microorganisms are continuously carried into the alveoli, alveolar surfaces are usually sterile. Because the alveoli are "dead ends," aged and dead macrophages must be prevented from accumulating in them. Most macrophages simply get swept up by the ciliary current of superior regions

and carried passively to the pharynx. In this manner, we clear and swallow over 2 million alveolar macrophages per hour!

The Lungs and Pleurae

Gross Anatomy of the Lungs

The paired **lungs** occupy all of the thoracic cavity except the mediastinum, which houses the heart, great blood vessels, bronchi, esophagus, and other organs (Figure 22.10). Each cone-shaped lung is suspended in its own pleural cavity and connected to the mediastinum by vascular and bronchial attachments, collectively called the lung **root.** The anterior, lateral, and posterior lung surfaces lie in close contact with the ribs and form the continuously curving **costal surface.** Just deep to the clavicle is the **apex,** the narrow superior tip of the lung. The concave, inferior surface that rests on the diaphragm is the **base.** On the mediastinal surface of each lung is an indentation, the **hilum,** through which pulmonary and systemic blood vessels enter and leave the lungs. Each main bronchus also plunges into the hilum on its own side and begins to branch almost immediately. All conducting and respiratory passageways distal to the main bronchi are found in the lungs.

Because the apex of the heart is slightly to the left of the median plane, the two lungs differ slightly in shape and size. The left lung is smaller than the right, and the **cardiac notch**—a concavity in its medial aspect—is molded to and accommodates the heart (see Figure 22.10a). The left lung is subdivided into superior and inferior **lobes** by the *oblique fissure,* whereas the right lung is partitioned into superior, middle, and inferior lobes by the *oblique* and *horizontal fissures.* Each lobe contains a number of pyramid-shaped **bronchopulmonary segments** separated from one another by connective tissue septa. Each segment is served by its own artery and vein and receives air from an individual segmental (tertiary) bronchus. Initially each lung contains ten bronchopulmonary segments arranged in similar (but not identical) patterns (Figure 22.11), but subsequent fusion of adjacent segmental arteries reduces the number in the left lung to eight or nine segments. The bronchopulmonary segments are clinically important because pulmonary disease is often confined to one or a few segments. Their connective tissue partitions allow diseased segments to be surgically removed without damaging neighboring healthy segments or impairing their blood supply.

The smallest subdivisions of the lung visible with the naked eye are the **lobules,** which appear at the lung surface as hexagons ranging from the size of a pencil eraser to the size of a penny (Figure 22.10b). Each lobule is served by a large bronchiole and its

(Text continues on p. 845.)

Q *Which cell produces surfactant and what does it do?*

(a)

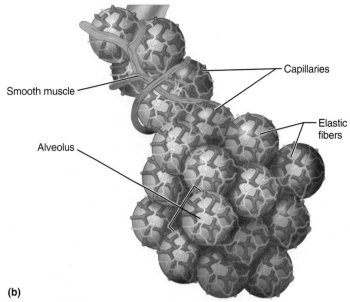

Smooth muscle

Capillaries

Alveolus

Elastic fibers

(b)

Type II (surfactant-secreting) cell

Type I cell of alveolar wall

Epithelial cell nucleus

Endothelial cell nucleus

Capillary

Alveolus

Macrophage

Respiratory membrane

Alveoli (gas-filled air spaces)

Red blood cell in capillary

Alveolar pores

(c)

Red blood cell

Capillary

O₂ CO₂

Alveolus

(d)

Nucleus of type I (squamous epithelial) cell

Alveolar epithelium

Fused basement membranes of the alveolar epithelium and the capillary endothelium

Capillary endothelium

22

FIGURE 22.9 The respiratory membrane. (a) Scanning electron micrograph of casts of alveoli and associated pulmonary capillaries (1100×). **(b)** Diagrammatic view of the pulmonary capillary-alveoli relationship. **(c, d)** Detailed anatomy of the respiratory membrane composed of the alveolar squamous epithelial cells (type I cells), the capillary endothelium, and the scant basement membranes between. Type II (surfactant-secreting) alveolar cells are also shown.

A *Type II alveolar cell; reduces the surface tension of the watery film in the alveoli.*

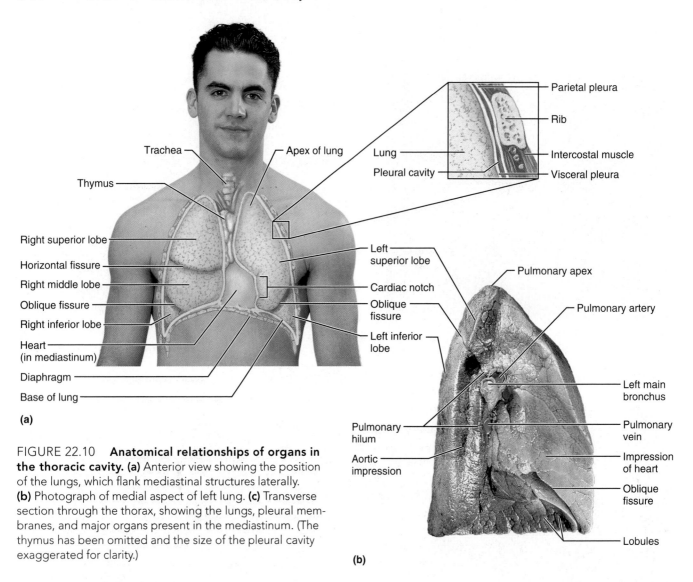

Trachea
Thymus
Apex of lung
Right superior lobe
Horizontal fissure
Right middle lobe
Oblique fissure
Right inferior lobe
Heart (in mediastinum)
Diaphragm
Base of lung

Parietal pleura
Rib
Lung
Pleural cavity
Intercostal muscle
Visceral pleura

Left superior lobe
Cardiac notch
Oblique fissure
Left inferior lobe

(a)

FIGURE 22.10 **Anatomical relationships of organs in the thoracic cavity. (a)** Anterior view showing the position of the lungs, which flank mediastinal structures laterally. **(b)** Photograph of medial aspect of left lung. **(c)** Transverse section through the thorax, showing the lungs, pleural membranes, and major organs present in the mediastinum. (The thymus has been omitted and the size of the pleural cavity exaggerated for clarity.)

Pulmonary apex
Pulmonary artery
Pulmonary hilum
Aortic impression
Left main bronchus
Pulmonary vein
Impression of heart
Oblique fissure
Lobules

(b)

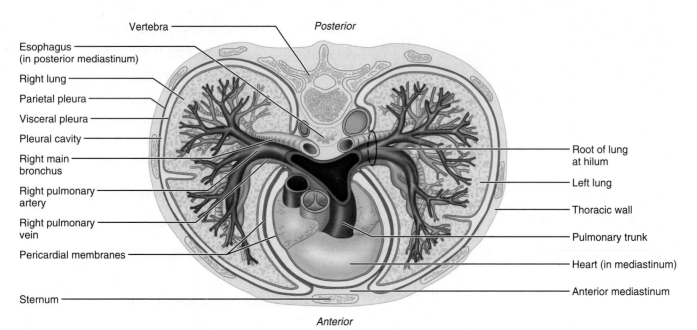

Vertebra
Posterior
Esophagus (in posterior mediastinum)
Right lung
Parietal pleura
Visceral pleura
Pleural cavity
Right main bronchus
Right pulmonary artery
Right pulmonary vein
Pericardial membranes
Sternum

Root of lung at hilum
Left lung
Thoracic wall
Pulmonary trunk
Heart (in mediastinum)
Anterior mediastinum

Anterior

(c)

22

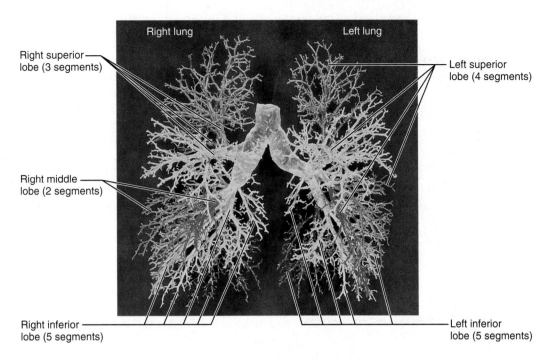

Right lung | Left lung

Right superior lobe (3 segments)

Left superior lobe (4 segments)

Right middle lobe (2 segments)

Right inferior lobe (5 segments)

Left inferior lobe (5 segments)

FIGURE 22.11 **A cast of the bronchial tree.** The individual bronchopulmonary segments have been painted different colors.

branches. In most city dwellers and in smokers, the connective tissue that separates the individual lobules is blackened with carbon.

As mentioned earlier, the lungs consist largely of air spaces. The balance of lung tissue, or its **stroma** (literally "mattress" or "bed"), is mostly elastic connective tissue. As a result, the lungs are soft, spongy, elastic organs that together weigh just over 1 kg (2.2 lb). The elasticity of healthy lungs helps to reduce the work of breathing, as described shortly.

Blood Supply and Innervation of the Lungs

The lungs are perfused by two circulations, the pulmonary and the bronchial, which differ in size, origin, and function. Systemic venous blood that is to be oxygenated in the lungs is delivered by the **pulmonary arteries,** which lie anterior to the main bronchi (Figure 22.10c). In the lungs, the pulmonary arteries branch profusely along with the bronchi and finally feed into the **pulmonary capillary networks** surrounding the alveoli (see Figure 22.9a). Freshly oxygenated blood is conveyed from the respiratory zones of the lungs to the heart by the **pulmonary veins,** whose tributaries course back to the hilum both with the corresponding bronchi and in the connective tissue septa separating the bronchopulmonary segments.

The large-volume, low-pressure venous blood entering the lungs via the pulmonary arteries contrasts with the small-volume, high-pressure input

via the bronchial arteries. The **bronchial arteries,** which provide systemic blood to lung tissue, arise from the aorta, enter the lungs at the hilum, and then run along the branching bronchi, supplying all lung tissues except the alveoli (these are supplied by the pulmonary circulation). Although some systemic venous blood is drained from the lungs by the tiny bronchial veins, there are multiple anastomoses between the two circulations, and most venous blood returns to the heart via the pulmonary veins.

Because *all* of the body's blood passes through the lungs about once each minute, the lung capillary endothelium is an ideal location for enzymes that act on materials in the blood. Examples include *angiotensin converting enzyme,* which activates an important blood pressure hormone, and enzymes that inactivate certain prostaglandins.

The lungs are innervated by parasympathetic and sympathetic motor fibers, and visceral sensory fibers. These nerve fibers enter each lung through the **pulmonary plexus** on the lung root and run along the bronchial tubes and blood vessels in the lungs. Parasympathetic fibers constrict the air tubes, whereas the sympathetic nervous system dilates them.

The Pleurae

The **pleurae** (ploo're; "sides") form a thin, double-layered serosa (see Figure 22.10). The layer called the **parietal pleura** covers the thoracic wall and superior face of the diaphragm. It continues around the

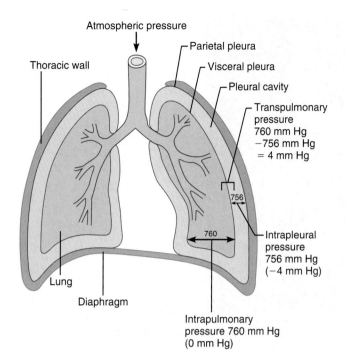

Atmospheric pressure

Thoracic wall

Parietal pleura

Visceral pleura

Pleural cavity

Transpulmonary
pressure
760 mm Hg
−756 mm Hg
= 4 mm Hg

756

760

Intrapleural
pressure
756 mm Hg
(−4 mm Hg)

Lung

Diaphragm

Intrapulmonary
pressure 760 mm Hg
(0 mm Hg)

FIGURE 22.12   Intrapulmonary and intrapleural pressure relationships. Differences in pressure relative to atmospheric pressure (760 mm Hg) are given in parentheses. Values shown are at the end of a normal expiration. For illustration, the size of the pleural cavity has been greatly exaggerated.

heart and between the lungs, forming the lateral walls of the mediastinal enclosure and snugly enclosing the lung root. From here, the pleura extends as the layer called the **visceral pleura** to cover the external lung surface, dipping into and lining its fissures.

The pleurae produce **pleural fluid,** which fills the slitlike **pleural cavity** between them. This lubricating secretion allows the lungs to glide easily over the thorax wall during our breathing movements. Although the pleurae slide easily across each other, their separation is strongly resisted by the surface tension of the pleural fluid. Consequently, the lungs cling tightly to the thorax wall and are forced to expand and recoil passively as the volume of the thoracic cavity alternately increases and decreases during breathing.

The pleurae also help divide the thoracic cavity into three chambers—the central mediastinum and the two lateral pleural compartments, each containing a lung. This compartmentalization helps prevent one mobile organ (for example, the lung or heart) from interfering with another. It also limits the spread of local infections.

◤ HOMEOSTATIC IMBALANCE

Pleurisy (ploo'rĭ-se), inflammation of the pleurae, often results from pneumonia. Inflamed pleurae

become rough, resulting in friction and stabbing pain with each breath. As the disease progresses, the pleurae may produce an excessive amount of fluid. This increased fluid relieves the pain caused by pleural surfaces rubbing together, but may exert pressure on the lungs and hinder breathing movements.

Other fluids that may accumulate in the pleural cavity include blood (leakage from damaged blood vessels) and blood filtrate (the watery fluid that oozes from the lung capillaries when right-sided heart failure occurs). The general term for fluid accumulation in the pleural cavity is *pleural effusion.* ●

Mechanics of Breathing

Breathing, or **pulmonary ventilation,** consists of two phases: **inspiration,** the period when air flows into the lungs, and **expiration,** the period when gases exit the lungs.

Pressure Relationships in the Thoracic Cavity

Before we can begin to describe the breathing process, it is important to understand that *respiratory pressures are always described relative to* **atmospheric pressure** (P_{atm}), which is the pressure exerted by the air (gases) surrounding the body. At sea level, atmospheric pressure is 760 mm Hg (the pressure exerted by a column of mercury 760 mm high). This pressure can also be expressed in atmosphere units: atmospheric pressure = 760 mm Hg = 1 atm. A negative respiratory pressure in any respiratory area, such as −4 mm Hg, indicates that the pressure in that area is lower than atmospheric pressure by 4 mm Hg (760 − 4 = 756 mm Hg). A positive respiratory pressure is higher than atmospheric pressure and zero respiratory pressure is equal to atmospheric pressure. Now we are ready to examine the pressure relationships that normally exist in the thoracic cavity.

Intrapulmonary Pressure

The **intrapulmonary** (intra-alveolar) **pressure** (P_{pul}) is the pressure in the alveoli. Intrapulmonary pressure rises and falls with the phases of breathing, but it *always* eventually equalizes with the atmospheric pressure (Figure 22.12).

Intrapleural Pressure

The pressure in the pleural cavity, the **intrapleural pressure** (P_{ip}), also fluctuates with breathing phases, but is always about 4 mm Hg less than P_{pul}. That is, P_{ip} is *always* negative relative to P_{pul}.

The question often asked is "How is this negative intrapleural pressure established?" or "What causes it?" Let's examine the forces that exist in the thorax to see if we can answer these questions. First of all, we know there are opposing forces. Two forces act to pull the lungs (visceral pleura) away from the thorax wall (parietal pleura) and cause lung collapse:

1. The lungs' natural tendency to recoil. Because of their elasticity, lungs always assume the smallest size possible.

2. The surface tension of the alveolar fluid. The surface tension of the alveolar fluid constantly acts to draw the alveoli to their smallest possible dimension.

However, these lung-collapsing forces are opposed by the natural elasticity of the chest wall, a force that tends to pull the thorax outward and to enlarge the lungs.

So which force wins? The answer is neither in a healthy person, because of the strong adhesive force between the parietal and visceral pleura. Pleural fluid secures the pleurae together in the same way a drop of water holds two glass slides together. The pleurae slide from side to side easily, but they remain closely apposed, and separating them requires extreme force. The net result of the dynamic interplay between these forces is a negative P_{ip}.

The amount of pleural fluid in the pleural cavity must remain minimal in order for the negative P_{ip} to be maintained. Active pumping of the pleural fluid out of the pleural cavity into the lymphatics occurs continuously. If it didn't, fluid would accumulate in the intrapleural space (remember, fluids move from high to low pressure), producing a positive pressure in the pleural cavity.

The importance of negative pressure in the intrapleural space and the tight coupling of the lungs to the thorax wall cannot be overemphasized. Any condition that equalizes P_{ip} with the intrapulmonary (or atmospheric) pressure causes *immediate lung collapse*. It is the **transpulmonary pressure**—the difference between the intrapulmonary and intrapleural pressures ($P_{pul} - P_{ip}$)—that keeps the air spaces of the lungs open or, phrased another way, keeps the lungs from collapsing. Moreover, it is the size of the transpulmonary pressure that determines the size of the lungs at any time—the greater the transpulmonary pressure, the larger the lungs.

⬛ HOMEOSTATIC IMBALANCE

Atelectasis (at″ĕ-lik′tah-sis), or lung collapse, occurs when a bronchiole becomes plugged (as may follow pneumonia). Its associated alveoli then absorb all of their air and collapse. Atelectasis can also occur when air enters the pleural cavity either through a chest wound, or due to rupture of the visceral pleura, which allows air to enter the pleural cavity from the respiratory tract. The presence of air in the intrapleural space is referred to as a **pneumothorax** (nu″mo-tho′raks; "air thorax"). The condition is reversed by closing the "hole" and drawing air out of the intrapleural space with chest tubes, which allows the lung to reinflate and resume its normal function. Note that because the lungs are in separate cavities, one lung can collapse without interfering with the function of the other. ●

Pulmonary Ventilation: Inspiration and Expiration

Pulmonary ventilation is a mechanical process that depends on volume changes in the thoracic cavity. A rule to keep in mind throughout the following discussion is that *volume changes* lead to *pressure changes*, and pressure changes lead to the *flow of gases* to equalize the pressure.

The relationship between the pressure and volume of a gas is given by **Boyle's law:** At constant temperature, the pressure of a gas varies inversely with its volume. That is,

$$P_1V_1 = P_2V_2$$

where P is the pressure of the gas, V is its volume, and subscripts 1 and 2 represent the initial and resulting conditions respectively.

Gases always *fill* their container. Therefore, in a large container, the molecules in a given amount of gas will be far apart and the pressure will be low. But if the volume of the container is reduced, the gas molecules will be forced closer together and the pressure will rise. A good example is an inflated automobile tire. The tire is hard and strong enough to bear the weight of the car because air is compressed to about one-third of its atmospheric volume in the tire, providing the high pressure. Now let us see how this relates to inspiration and expiration.

Inspiration

Visualize the thoracic cavity as a gas-filled box with a single entrance at the top, the tubelike trachea. The volume of this box is changeable and can be increased by enlarging all of its dimensions, thereby decreasing the gas pressure inside it. This drop in pressure causes air to rush into the box from the atmosphere, because gases always flow down their pressure gradients.

The same thing happens during normal quiet inspiration, when the **inspiratory muscles**—the diaphragm and external intercostal muscles—are activated. Here's how quiet inspiration works:

22

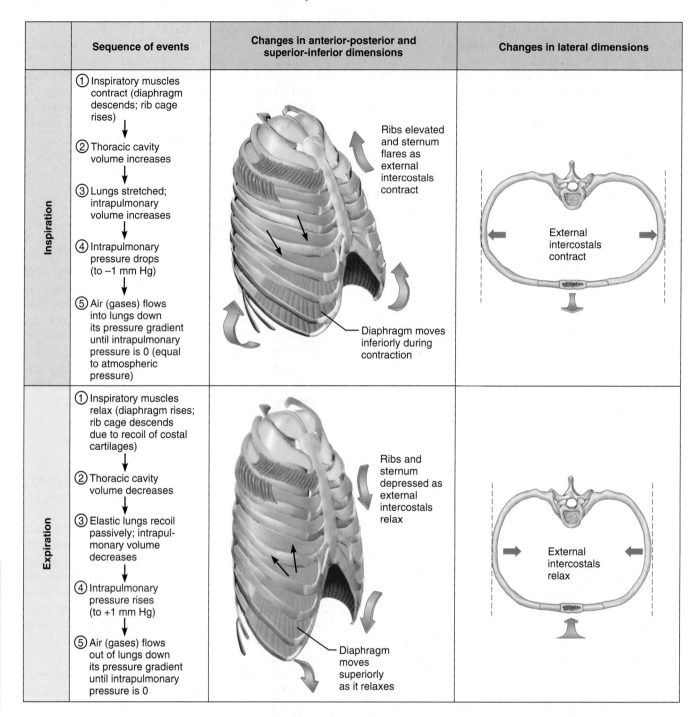

	Sequence of events	Changes in anterior-posterior and superior-inferior dimensions	Changes in lateral dimensions
Inspiration	① Inspiratory muscles contract (diaphragm descends; rib cage rises) ② Thoracic cavity volume increases ③ Lungs stretched; intrapulmonary volume increases ④ Intrapulmonary pressure drops (to –1 mm Hg) ⑤ Air (gases) flows into lungs down its pressure gradient until intrapulmonary pressure is 0 (equal to atmospheric pressure)	Ribs elevated and sternum flares as external intercostals contract Diaphragm moves inferiorly during contraction	External intercostals contract
Expiration	① Inspiratory muscles relax (diaphragm rises; rib cage descends due to recoil of costal cartilages) ② Thoracic cavity volume decreases ③ Elastic lungs recoil passively; intrapulmonary volume decreases ④ Intrapulmonary pressure rises (to +1 mm Hg) ⑤ Air (gases) flows out of lungs down its pressure gradient until intrapulmonary pressure is 0	Ribs and sternum depressed as external intercostals relax Diaphragm moves superiorly as it relaxes	External intercostals relax

FIGURE 22.13 Changes in thoracic volume during inspiration (top) and expiration (bottom). The sequence of events in the left column includes volume changes during inspiration and expiration. The lateral views in the middle column show changes in the superior-inferior dimension (as the diaphragm alternately contracts and relaxes) and in the anterior-posterior dimension (as the external intercostal muscles alternately contract and relax). The superior views of transverse thoracic sections in the right column show lateral dimension changes resulting from alternate contraction and relaxation of the external intercostal muscles.

1. Action of the diaphragm. When the dome-shaped diaphragm contracts, it moves inferiorly and flattens out (Figure 22.13, top). As a result, the superior-inferior dimension (height) of the thoracic cavity increases.

2. Action of the intercostal muscles. Contraction of the external intercostal muscles lifts the rib cage and pulls the sternum superiorly (Figure 22.13, top). Because the ribs curve downward as well as forward around the chest wall, the broadest lateral and anteroposterior dimensions of the rib cage are normally directed obliquely downward. But when the ribs are raised and drawn together, they swing outward, expanding the diameter of the thorax both laterally and in the anteroposterior plane. This is much like the action that occurs when a curved bucket handle is raised.

Although these actions expand the thoracic dimensions by only a few millimeters along each plane, this is enough to increase thoracic volume by almost 500 ml—the usual volume of air that enters the lungs during a normal quiet inspiration. Of the two types of inspiratory muscles, the diaphragm is far more important in producing the volume changes that lead to normal quiet inspiration.

As the thoracic dimensions increase during inspiration, the lungs are stretched and the intrapulmonary volume increases. As a result, P_{pul} drops about 1 mm Hg relative to P_{atm}. Anytime the intrapulmonary pressure is less than the atmospheric pressure ($P_{pul} < P_{atm}$), air rushes into the lungs along the pressure gradient. Inspiration ends when $P_{pul} = P_{atm}$. During the same period, P_{ip} declines to about −6 mm Hg relative to P_{atm} (Figure 22.14).

During the *deep* or *forced inspirations* that occur during vigorous exercise and in some chronic obstructive pulmonary diseases, the thoracic volume is further increased by activity of accessory muscles. Several muscles, including the scalenes and sternocleidomastoid muscles of the neck and the pectoralis minor of the chest, raise the ribs even more than occurs during quiet inspiration. Additionally, the back extends as the thoracic curvature is straightened by the erector spinae muscles.

Expiration

Quiet expiration in healthy individuals is a passive process that depends more on lung elasticity than on muscle contraction. As the inspiratory muscles relax and resume their resting length, the rib cage descends and the lungs recoil. Thus, both the thoracic and intrapulmonary volumes decrease. This volume decrease compresses the alveoli, and P_{pul} rises to about 1 mm Hg above atmospheric pressure (see Figure 22.14). When $P_{pul} > P_{atm}$, the pressure gradient forces gases to flow out of the lungs.

Forced expiration is an active process produced by contraction of abdominal wall muscles, primarily the oblique and transversus muscles. These contractions (1) increase the intra-abdominal pressure, which forces the abdominal organs superiorly against the diaphragm, and (2) depress the rib cage. The internal intercostal muscles also help to depress the rib cage and decrease thoracic volume.

Control of accessory muscles of expiration is important when precise regulation of air flow from the lungs is desired. For instance, the ability of a trained vocalist to hold a musical note depends on the coordinated activity of several muscles normally used in forced expiration.

Q *As thoracic volume increases, what happens to the intrapulmonary pressure? To the intrapleural pressure?*

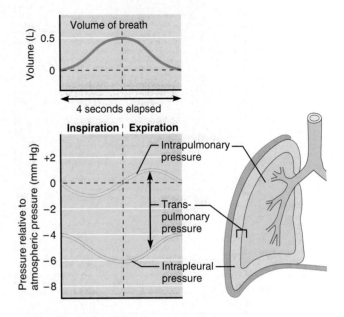

FIGURE 22.14 **Changes in intrapulmonary and intrapleural pressures during inspiration and expiration.** Notice that normal atmospheric pressure (760 mm Hg) is given a value of 0 on the scale.

Physical Factors Influencing Pulmonary Ventilation

As we have seen, the lungs are stretched during inspiration and recoil passively during expiration. The inspiratory muscles consume energy to enlarge the thorax. Energy is also used to overcome various factors that hinder air passage and pulmonary ventilation. These factors are examined next.

Airway Resistance

The major *nonelastic* source of resistance to gas flow is friction, or drag, encountered in the respiratory passageways. The relationship between gas flow (F), pressure (P), and resistance (R) is given by the following equation:

$$F = \frac{\Delta P}{R}$$

Notice that the factors determining gas flow in the respiratory passages and blood flow in the cardiovascular system are equivalent. The amount of gas flowing into and out of the alveoli is directly proportional to ΔP, the *difference* in pressure, or the pressure gradient,

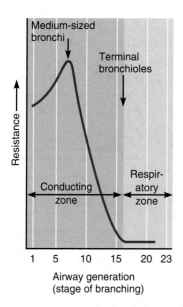

FIGURE 22.15 **Resistance in respiratory passage-ways.** Airway resistance peaks in the medium-sized bronchi and then declines sharply as the total cross-sectional area of the airway increases rapidly.

between the external atmosphere and the alveoli. Normally, very small differences in pressure produce large changes in the volume of gas flow. The average pressure gradient during normal quiet breathing is 2 mm Hg or less, and yet it is sufficient to move 500 ml of air in and out of the lungs with each breath.

But, as the equation also indicates, gas flow changes *inversely* with resistance. That is, gas flow decreases as resistance increases. As with the cardiovascular system, resistance in the respiratory tree is determined mostly by the diameters of the conducting tubes. However, as a rule, airway resistance is insignificant for two reasons:

1. Airway diameters in the first part of the conducting zone are huge, relative to the low viscosity of air.

2. As the airways get progressively smaller, there are progressively more branches. As a result, although individual bronchioles are tiny, there are an enormous number of them in parallel, so the total cross-sectional area is huge.

Hence, as shown in Figure 22.15, the greatest resistance to gas flow occurs in the medium-sized bronchi. At the terminal bronchioles, gas flow stops and diffusion takes over as the main force driving gas movement, so resistance is no longer an issue.

HOMEOSTATIC IMBALANCE

Smooth muscle of the bronchiolar walls is exquisitely sensitive to neural controls and certain chemicals. For example, inhaled irritants activate a reflex of the parasympathetic division of the nervous system that causes vigorous constriction of the bronchioles and dramatically reduces air passage. During an *acute asthma attack*, histamine and other inflammatory chemicals can cause such strong bronchoconstriction that pulmonary ventilation almost completely stops, regardless of the pressure gradient. Conversely, epinephrine released during sympathetic nervous system activation or administered as a drug dilates bronchioles and reduces airway resistance. Local accumulations of mucus, infectious material, or solid tumors in the passageways are important sources of airway resistance in those with respiratory disease.

Whenever airway resistance rises, breathing movements become more strenuous, but such compensation has its limits. When the bronchioles are severely constricted or obstructed, even the most magnificent respiratory efforts cannot restore ventilation to life-sustaining levels. ●

Alveolar Surface Tension

At any gas-liquid boundary, the molecules of the liquid are more strongly attracted to each other than to the gas molecules. This unequal attraction produces a state of tension at the liquid surface, called **surface tension**, that (1) draws the liquid molecules closer together and reduces their contact with the dissimilar gas molecules, and (2) resists any force that tends to increase the surface area of the liquid.

Water is composed of highly polar molecules and has a very high surface tension. Because water is the major component of the liquid film that coats the alveolar walls, it is always acting to reduce the alveoli to their smallest possible size. If the film was pure water, the alveoli would collapse between breaths. But the alveolar film contains **surfactant** (ser-fak′tant), a detergent-like complex of lipids and proteins produced by the type II alveolar cells. Surfactant decreases the cohesiveness of water molecules, much the way a laundry detergent reduces the attraction of water for water, allowing water to interact with and pass through fabric. As a result, the surface tension of alveolar fluid is reduced, and less energy is needed to overcome those forces to expand the lungs and discourage alveolar collapse. Breaths that are deeper than normal stimulate type II cells to secrete more surfactant.

HOMEOSTATIC IMBALANCE

When too little surfactant is present, surface tension forces can collapse the alveoli. Once this happens, the alveoli must be completely reinflated during each inspiration, an effort that uses tremendous amounts of energy. This is the problem faced by newborns with **infant respiratory distress syndrome (IRDS)**, a condition peculiar to premature babies. Since inadequate pulmonary surfactant is produced until the last two months of fetal development, babies born prematurely often are unable to keep their alveoli inflated between breaths. IRDS is treated with positive-pressure respirators that force air into the alveoli, keeping them open between breaths. Spraying natural or synthetic surfactant into the newborn's respiratory passageways also helps.

Many IRDS survivors suffer from *bronchopulmonary dysplasia*, a chronic lung disease, during childhood and beyond. This condition is believed to result from inflammatory injury to respiratory zone structures caused by use of the respirator on the newborn's delicate lungs. ●

Lung Compliance

Healthy lungs are unbelievably stretchy, and this distensibility is referred to as **lung compliance.** Specifically, lung compliance (C_L) is a measure of the change in lung volume (ΔV_L) that occurs with a given change in the transpulmonary pressure [$\Delta(P_{pul} - P_{ip})$]. This is stated as

$$C_L = \frac{\Delta V_L}{\Delta(P_{pul} - P_{ip})}$$

The more a lung expands for a given rise in transpulmonary pressure, the greater its compliance. Said another way, the higher the lung compliance, the easier it is to expand the lungs at any given transpulmonary pressure.

Lung compliance is determined largely by two factors: (1) distensibility of the lung tissue, and (2) alveolar surface tension. Because lung distensibility is generally high and alveolar surface tension is kept low by surfactant, the lungs of healthy people tend to have high compliance, which favors efficient ventilation.

Lung compliance is diminished by a decrease in the natural resilience of the lungs. Chronic inflammation, or infections such as tuberculosis, can cause nonelastic scar tissue to replace normal lung tissue (*fibrosis*). Another factor that can decrease lung compliance is a decrease in production of surfactant. The lower the lung compliance, the more energy is needed just to breathe.

Since the lungs are contained within the thoracic cavity, we also need to consider the compliance (distensibility) of the thoracic wall. Factors that decrease the compliance of the thoracic wall hinder the expansion of the lungs. The total compliance of the respiratory system is comprised of lung compliance and thoracic wall compliance.

HOMEOSTATIC IMBALANCE

Deformities of the thorax, ossification of the costal cartilages (common during old age), and paralysis of the intercostal muscles all reduce total respiratory compliance by hindering thoracic expansion. ●

Respiratory Volumes and Pulmonary Function Tests

The amount of air flushed in and out of the lungs depends on the conditions of inspiration and expiration. Consequently, several respiratory volumes can be described. Specific combinations of these respiratory volumes, called *respiratory capacities*, are measured to gain information about a person's respiratory status.

Respiratory Volumes

The four **respiratory volumes** of interest are tidal, inspiratory reserve, expiratory reserve, and residual. The values recorded in Figure 22.16a (and used in the following text) represent normal values for a healthy 20-year-old male weighing about 70 kg (155 lb). Figure 22.16b provides average values for males and females.

During normal quiet breathing, about 500 ml of air moves into and then out of the lungs with each breath. This respiratory volume is the **tidal volume (TV)**. The amount of air that can be inspired forcibly beyond the tidal volume (2100 to 3200 ml) is called the **inspiratory reserve volume (IRV).**

The **expiratory reserve volume (ERV)** is the amount of air—normally 1000 to 1200 ml—that can be evacuated from the lungs after a tidal expiration. Even after the most strenuous expiration, about 1200 ml of air remains in the lungs; this is the **residual volume (RV)**, which helps to keep the alveoli patent (open) and to prevent lung collapse.

Respiratory Capacities

The **respiratory capacities** include inspiratory capacity, functional residual capacity, vital capacity, and total lung capacity (Figure 22.16). As noted, the respiratory capacities always consist of two or more lung volumes.

The **inspiratory capacity (IC)** is the total amount of air that can be inspired after a tidal expiration; thus, it is the sum of TV and IRV. The **functional residual capacity (FRC)** is the combined RV and ERV and represents the amount of air remaining in the lungs after a tidal expiration.

Vital capacity (VC) is the total amount of exchangeable air. It is the sum of TV, IRV, and ERV. In healthy young males, VC is approximately 4800 ml. The **total lung capacity (TLC)** is the sum of all lung volumes and is normally around 6000 ml. As

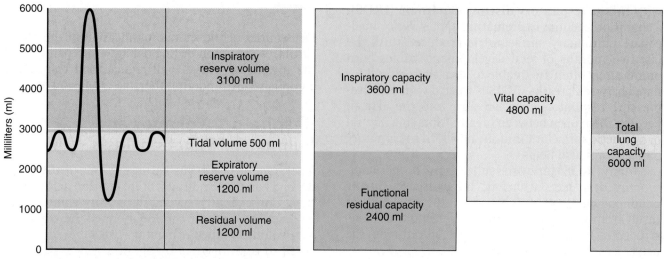

(a) Spirographic record for a male

	Measurement	Adult male average value	Adult female average value	Description
Respiratory volumes	Tidal volume (TV)	500 ml	500 ml	Amount of air inhaled or exhaled with each breath under resting conditions
	Inspiratory reserve volume (IRV)	3100 ml	1900 ml	Amount of air that can be forcefully inhaled after a normal tidal volume inhalation
	Expiratory reserve volume (ERV)	1200 ml	700 ml	Amount of air that can be forcefully exhaled after a normal tidal volume exhalation
	Residual volume (RV)	1200 ml	1100 ml	Amount of air remaining in the lungs after a forced exhalation
Respiratory capacities	Total lung capacity (TLC)	6000 ml	4200 ml	Maximum amount of air contained in lungs after a maximum inspiratory effort: TLC = TV + IRV + ERV + RV
	Vital capacity (VC)	4800 ml	3100 ml	Maximum amount of air that can be expired after a maximum inspiratory effort: VC = TV + IRV + ERV (should be 80% TLC)
	Inspiratory capacity (IC)	3600 ml	2400 ml	Maximum amount of air that can be inspired after a normal expiration: IC = TV + IRV
	Functional residual capacity (FRC)	2400 ml	1800 ml	Volume of air remaining in the lungs after a normal tidal volume expiration: FRC = ERV + RV

(b) Summary of respiratory volumes and capacities for males and females

22

FIGURE 22.16   **Respiratory volumes and capacities. (a)** Idealized spirographic record of respiratory volumes, in a healthy young 70-kg adult male. **(b)** Respiratory volumes and capacities for males and females.

indicated in Figure 22.16b, lung volumes and capacities (with the possible exception of TV) tend to be smaller in women than in men because of women's smaller size.

Dead Space

Some of the inspired air fills the conducting respiratory passageways and never contributes to gas exchange in the alveoli. The volume of these conducting zone conduits, which make up the **anatomical dead space**, typically amounts to about 150 ml. (The rule of thumb is that the anatomical dead space volume in a healthy young adult is equal to 1 ml per pound of ideal body weight.) This means that if TV is 500 ml, only 350 ml of it is involved in alveolar ventilation. The remaining 150 ml of the tidal breath is in the anatomical dead space.

If some alveoli cease to act in gas exchange (due to alveolar collapse or obstruction by mucus, for example), the **alveolar dead space** is added to the anatomical dead space, and the sum of the

TABLE 22.2	Effects of Breathing Rate and Depth on Alveolar Ventilation of Three Hypothetical Patients					
BREATHING PATTERN OF HYPOTHETICAL PATIENT	DEAD SPACE VOLUME (DSV)	TIDAL VOLUME (TV)	RESPIRATORY RATE*	MINUTE VENTILATION (MVR)	ALVEOLAR VENTILATION (AVR)	% EFFECTIVE VENTILATION (AVR/MVR)
I—Normal rate and depth	150 ml	500 ml	20/min	10,000 ml/min	7000 ml/min	70%
II—Slow, deep breathing	150 ml	1000 ml	10/min	10,000 ml/min	8500 ml/min	85%
III—Rapid, shallow breathing	150 ml	250 ml	40/min	10,000 ml/min	4000 ml/min	40%

*Respiratory rate values are artificially adjusted to provide equivalent minute respiratory volumes as a baseline for comparison of alveolar ventilation.

nonuseful volumes is referred to as **total dead space.**

Pulmonary Function Tests

Because the various lung volumes and capacities are often abnormal in people with pulmonary disorders, they are routinely measured in such patients. The original clinical measuring device, a **spirometer** (spi-rom′ĕ-ter), was a simple instrument utilizing a hollow bell inverted over water. Now patients simply blow into a small electronic measuring device. Spirometry is most useful for evaluating losses in respiratory function and for following the course of certain respiratory diseases. Although it cannot provide a specific diagnosis, it can distinguish between *obstructive pulmonary disease* involving increased airway resistance (such as chronic bronchitis) and *restrictive disorders* involving a reduction in total lung capacity resulting from structural or functional changes in the lungs (due to diseases such as tuberculosis, or to fibrosis due to exposure to certain environmental agents such as asbestos). Increases in TLC, FRC, and RV may occur as a result of hyperinflation of the lungs in obstructive disease, whereas VC, TLC, FRC, and RV are reduced in restrictive diseases, which limit lung expansion.

More information can be obtained about a patient's ventilation status by assessing the rate at which gas moves into and out of the lungs. The **minute ventilation** is the total amount of gas that flows into or out of the respiratory tract in 1 minute. During normal quiet breathing, the minute ventilation in healthy people is about 6 L/min (500 ml per breath multiplied by 12 breaths per minute). During vigorous exercise, the minute ventilation may reach 200 L/min.

Two other useful tests are FVC and FEV. **FVC,** or **forced vital capacity,** measures the amount of gas expelled when a subject takes a deep breath and then forcefully exhales maximally and as rapidly as possible. **FEV,** or **forced expiratory volume,** determines the amount of air expelled during specific time intervals of the FVC test. For example, the volume exhaled during the first second is FEV_1. Those with healthy lungs can exhale about 80% of the FVC within 1 second. Those with obstructive pulmonary disease exhale considerably less than 80% of the FVC within 1 second, while those with restrictive disease can exhale 80% or more of FVC in 1 second even though their FVC is reduced.

Alveolar Ventilation

Minute ventilation values provide a rough yardstick for assessing respiratory efficiency, but the **alveolar ventilation rate (AVR)** is a better index of effective ventilation. The AVR takes into account the volume of air wasted in the dead space and measures the flow of fresh gases in and out of the alveoli during a particular time interval. AVR is computed with this equation:

$$\underset{\text{(ml/min)}}{\text{AVR}} \quad = \quad \underset{\text{(breaths/min)}}{\text{frequency}} \quad \times \quad \underset{\text{(ml/breath)}}{\text{(TV} - \text{dead space)}}$$

In healthy people, AVR is usually about 12 breaths per minute times the difference of $500 - 150$ ml per breath, or 4200 ml/min.

Because anatomical dead space is constant in a particular individual, increasing the volume of each inspiration (breathing depth) enhances AVR and gas exchange more than raising the respiratory rate. AVR drops dramatically during rapid shallow breathing because most of the inspired air never reaches the exchange sites. Furthermore, as tidal volume approaches the dead space value, effective ventilation approaches zero, regardless of how fast a person is breathing. The effects of breathing rate and breathing depth on alveolar ventilation are summarized for three hypothetical patients in Table 22.2.

22

TABLE 22.3	Nonrespiratory Air (Gas) Movements
MOVEMENT	**MECHANISM AND RESULT**
Cough	Taking a deep breath, closing glottis, and forcing air superiorly from lungs against glottis; glottis opens suddenly and a blast of air rushes upward; can dislodge foreign particles or mucus from lower respiratory tract and propel such substances superiorly
Sneeze	Similar to a cough, except that expelled air is directed through nasal cavities as well as through oral cavity; depressed uvula routes air upward through nasal cavities; sneezes clear upper respiratory passages
Crying	Inspiration followed by release of air in a number of short expirations; primarily an emotionally induced mechanism
Laughing	Essentially same as crying in terms of air movements produced; also an emotionally induced response
Hiccups	Sudden inspirations resulting from spasms of diaphragm; believed to be initiated by irritation of diaphragm or phrenic nerves, which serve diaphragm; sound occurs when inspired air hits vocal folds of closing glottis
Yawn	Very deep inspiration, taken with jaws wide open; not believed to be triggered by levels of oxygen or carbon dioxide in blood; ventilates all alveoli (not the case in normal quiet breathing)

Nonrespiratory Air Movements

Many processes other than breathing move air into or out of the lungs, and these processes may modify the normal respiratory rhythm. Most of these **nonrespiratory air movements** result from reflex activity, but some are produced voluntarily. The most common of these movements are described in Table 22.3.

Gas Exchanges Between the Blood, Lungs, and Tissues

As you've discovered, during *external respiration* oxygen enters and carbon dioxide leaves the blood in the lungs. At the body tissues, where the process is called *internal respiration*, the same gases move in opposite directions by the same mechanism (diffusion). To understand these processes, we must examine some of the physical properties of gases and consider the composition of alveolar gas.

Basic Properties of Gases

Two more gas laws provide most of the information we need—*Dalton's law of partial pressures* reveals how a gas behaves when it is part of a mixture of gases, and *Henry's law* will help us understand movement of gases into and out of solution.

Dalton's Law of Partial Pressures

Dalton's law of partial pressures states that the total pressure exerted by a mixture of gases is the sum of the pressures exerted independently by each gas in the mixture. Further, the pressure exerted by each gas—its **partial pressure**—is directly proportional to the percentage of that gas in the gas mixture.

As indicated in Table 22.4, nitrogen makes up about 79% of air, and the partial pressure of nitrogen (P_{N_2}) is 78.6% × 760 mm Hg, or 597 mm Hg. Oxygen gas, which accounts for nearly 21% of the atmosphere, has a partial pressure (P_{O_2}) of 159 mm Hg (20.9% × 760 mm Hg). Thus, nitrogen and oxygen together contribute about 99% of the total atmospheric pressure. Air also contains 0.04% carbon dioxide, up to 0.5% water vapor, and insignificant amounts of inert gases (such as argon and helium).

At high altitudes, where the atmosphere is less influenced by gravity, partial pressures decline in direct proportion to the decrease in atmospheric pressure. For example, at 10,000 feet above sea level where the atmospheric pressure is 523 mm Hg, P_{O_2} is 110 mm Hg. Moving in the opposite direction, atmospheric pressure increases by 1 atm (760 mm Hg) for each 33 feet of descent (in water) below sea level. Thus, at 99 feet below sea level, the total pressure exerted on the body is equivalent to 4 atm, or 3040 mm Hg, and the partial pressure exerted by each component gas is also quadrupled.

Henry's Law

According to **Henry's law,** when a mixture of gases is in contact with a liquid, each gas will dissolve in the liquid in proportion to its partial pressure. Thus the greater the concentration of a particular gas in the gas phase, the more and the faster that gas will go into solution in the liquid. At equilibrium, the gas partial pressures in the two phases are the same. If, however, the partial pressure of one of the gases later becomes greater in the liquid than in the adjacent gas phase, some of the dissolved gas molecules will reenter the gaseous phase. So the direction and amount of movement of each gas is determined by its partial pressure in the two phases. This flexible situation is exactly

TABLE 22.4	Comparison of Gas Partial Pressures and Approximate Percentages in the Atmosphere and in the Alveoli				
	ATMOSPHERE (SEA LEVEL)			**ALVEOLI**	
GAS	APPROXIMATE PERCENTAGE	PARTIAL PRESSURE (mm Hg)		APPROXIMATE PERCENTAGE	PARTIAL PRESSURE (mm Hg)
N_2	78.6	597		74.9	569
O_2	20.9	159		13.7	104
CO_2	0.04	0.3		5.2	40
H_2O	0.46	3.7		6.2	47
	100.0%	760		100.0%	760

what occurs when gases are exchanged in the lungs and tissues.

How much of a gas will dissolve in a liquid at any given partial pressure also depends on the solubility of the gas in the liquid and on the temperature of the liquid. The gases in air have very different solubilities in water (and in plasma). Carbon dioxide is most soluble. Oxygen is only 1/20 as soluble as CO_2, and N_2 is only half as soluble as O_2. Thus, at a given partial pressure, much more CO_2 than O_2 dissolves in water, and practically no N_2 goes into solution. The effect of increasing the liquid's temperature is to decrease gas solubility. Think of club soda, which is produced by forcing CO_2 gas to dissolve in water under high pressure. If you take the cap off a refrigerated bottle of club soda and allow it to stand at room temperature, in just a few minutes you will have plain water—all the CO_2 gas will have escaped from solution.

Hyperbaric oxygen chambers provide clinical applications of Henry's law. These chambers contain O_2 gas at pressures higher than 1 atm and are used to force greater-than-normal amounts of O_2 into the blood of patients suffering from carbon monoxide poisoning or tissue damage following radiation therapy. Hyperbaric therapy is also used to treat individuals with gas gangrene, because the anaerobic bacteria causing this infection cannot live in the presence of high O_2 levels. Scuba diving provides another illustration of Henry's law (see *A Closer Look* on pp. 868–869).

⬛ HOMEOSTATIC IMBALANCE

Although breathing O_2 gas at 2 atm is not a problem for short periods, **oxygen toxicity** develops rapidly when P_{O_2} is greater than 2.5–3 atm. Excessively high O_2 concentrations generate huge amounts of harmful free radicals, resulting in profound CNS disturbances, coma, and death. ●

Composition of Alveolar Gas

As shown in Table 22.4, the gaseous makeup of the atmosphere is quite different from that in the alveoli. The atmosphere is almost entirely O_2 and N_2; the alveoli contain more CO_2 and water vapor and much less O_2. These differences reflect the effects of (1) gas exchanges occurring in the lungs (O_2 diffuses from the alveoli into the pulmonary blood and CO_2 diffuses in the opposite direction), (2) humidification of air by conducting passages, and (3) the mixing of alveolar gas that occurs with each breath. Because only 500 ml of air is inspired with each tidal inspiration, gas in the alveoli is actually a mixture of newly inspired gases and gases remaining in the respiratory passageways between breaths.

The alveolar partial pressures of O_2 and CO_2 are easily changed by increasing breathing depth and rate. A high AVR brings more O_2 into the alveoli, increasing alveolar P_{O_2}, and rapidly eliminates CO_2 from the lungs.

External Respiration: Pulmonary Gas Exchange

During external respiration, dark red blood flowing through the pulmonary circuit is transformed into the scarlet river that is returned to the heart for distribution by systemic arteries to all body tissues. Although this color change is due to O_2 uptake and binding to hemoglobin in red blood cells (RBCs), CO_2 exchange (unloading) is occurring equally fast.

The following three factors influence the movement of oxygen and carbon dioxide across the respiratory membrane:

22

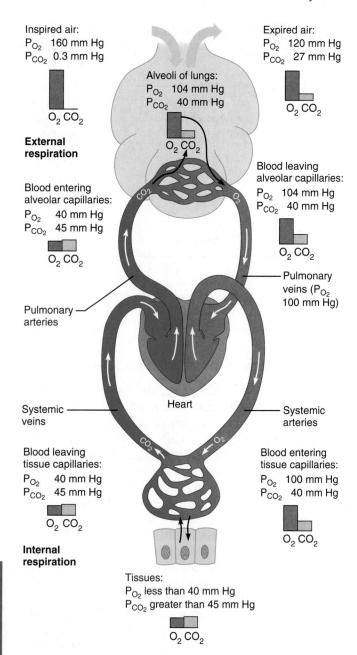

Inspired air:
P_{O_2} 160 mm Hg
P_{CO_2} 0.3 mm Hg

External respiration

Blood entering alveolar capillaries:
P_{O_2} 40 mm Hg
P_{CO_2} 45 mm Hg

Pulmonary arteries

Systemic veins

Blood leaving tissue capillaries:
P_{O_2} 40 mm Hg
P_{CO_2} 45 mm Hg

Internal respiration

Expired air:
P_{O_2} 120 mm Hg
P_{CO_2} 27 mm Hg

Alveoli of lungs:
P_{O_2} 104 mm Hg
P_{CO_2} 40 mm Hg

Blood leaving alveolar capillaries:
P_{O_2} 104 mm Hg
P_{CO_2} 40 mm Hg

Pulmonary veins (P_{O_2} 100 mm Hg)

Heart

Systemic arteries

Blood entering tissue capillaries:
P_{O_2} 100 mm Hg
P_{CO_2} 40 mm Hg

Tissues:
P_{O_2} less than 40 mm Hg
P_{CO_2} greater than 45 mm Hg

FIGURE 22.17   **Partial pressure gradients promoting gas movements in the body.** Top: Gradients promoting O_2 and CO_2 exchange across the respiratory membrane in the lungs. Bottom: Gradients promoting gas movements across systemic capillary membranes in body tissues. (Note that the composition of alveolar air and expired air are different because some dead space air mixes with the air being expired. The small decrease in P_{O_2} in pulmonary venous blood is due to partial dilution of pulmonary capillary blood with less oxygenated blood.)

1. Partial pressure gradients and gas solubilities

2. Matching of alveolar ventilation and pulmonary blood perfusion

3. Structural characteristics of the respiratory membrane

FIGURE 22.18   **Oxygenation of blood in the pulmonary capillaries at rest.** Note that the time from blood entering the pulmonary capillaries (indicated by 0) until the P_{O_2} is 104 mm Hg is approximately 0.25 second.

Partial Pressure Gradients and Gas Solubilities

Because the P_{O_2} of venous blood in the pulmonary arteries is only 40 mm Hg, as opposed to a P_{O_2} of approximately 104 mm Hg in the alveoli, a steep oxygen partial pressure gradient exists, and O_2 diffuses rapidly from the alveoli into the pulmonary capillary blood (Figure 22.17). Equilibrium—that is, a P_{O_2} of 104 mm Hg on both sides of the respiratory membrane—usually occurs in 0.25 second, which is about one-third the time a red blood cell is in a pulmonary capillary (Figure 22.18). The lesson here is that the blood can flow through the pulmonary capillaries three times as quickly and still be adequately oxygenated. Carbon dioxide moves in the opposite direction along a much gentler partial pressure gradient of about 5 mm Hg (45 mm Hg to 40 mm Hg) until equilibrium occurs at 40 mm Hg. Carbon dioxide is then expelled gradually from the alveoli during expiration. Even though the O_2 pressure gradient for oxygen diffusion is much steeper than the CO_2 gradient, equal amounts of these gases are exchanged because CO_2 is 20 times more soluble in plasma and alveolar fluid than O_2.

Ventilation-Perfusion Coupling

For gas exchange to be efficient, there must be a close match, or coupling, between *ventilation* (the amount of gas reaching the alveoli) and *perfusion* (the blood flow in pulmonary capillaries). As explained in Chapter 19 and illustrated in Figure 22.19, local autoregulatory mechanisms continuously respond to alveolar conditions.

Q *Suppose a patient is receiving oxygen by mask. What is the condition of the arterioles leading into O$_2$-enriched alveoli? What is the advantage of this response?*

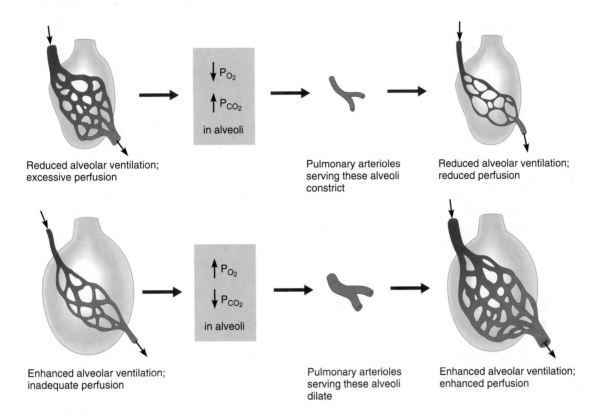

FIGURE 22.19 Ventilation-perfusion coupling. Autoregulatory events that result in local matching of blood flow (perfusion) through the pulmonary capillaries and conditions of alveolar ventilation.

In alveoli where ventilation is inadequate, P$_{O_2}$ is low. As a result, the terminal arterioles constrict, and blood is redirected to respiratory areas where P$_{O_2}$ is high and oxygen pickup may be more efficient. In alveoli where ventilation is maximal, pulmonary arterioles dilate, increasing blood flow into the associated pulmonary capillaries. Notice that the autoregulatory mechanism controlling pulmonary vascular muscle is the opposite of the mechanism controlling most arterioles in the systemic circulation.

While changes in alveolar P$_{O_2}$ affect the diameter of pulmonary blood vessels (arterioles), changes in alveolar P$_{CO_2}$ cause changes in the diameters of the *bronchioles*. Passageways servicing areas where alveolar CO$_2$ levels are high dilate, allowing CO$_2$ to be eliminated from the body more rapidly, while those serving areas where P$_{CO_2}$ is low constrict.

As a result of modifications made by these two systems, alveolar ventilation and pulmonary perfusion are synchronized. Poor alveolar ventilation results in low oxygen and high carbon dioxide levels in the alveoli; consequently, the pulmonary arterioles constrict and the airways dilate, bringing air flow and blood flow into closer physiological match. High P$_{O_2}$ and low P$_{CO_2}$ in the alveoli cause respiratory passageways serving the alveoli to constrict, and promote flushing of blood into the pulmonary capillaries. Although these homeostatic mechanisms provide appropriate conditions for efficient gas exchange, they never completely balance ventilation and perfusion in every alveolus because (1) gravity causes regional variations in both blood and air flow in the lungs, and (2) the occasional alveolar duct plugged with mucus creates unventilated areas. These factors, together with the shunting

A *They would be dilated. This response allows matching of blood flow to availability of oxygen.*

of blood from bronchial veins, account for the slight drop in P_{O_2} from alveolar air (104 mm Hg) to pulmonary venous blood (100 mm Hg), as shown in Figure 22.17.

Thickness and Surface Area of the Respiratory Membrane

In healthy lungs, the respiratory membrane is only 0.5 to 1 mm thick, and gas exchange is usually very efficient.

 HOMEOSTATIC IMBALANCE

If the lungs become waterlogged and edematous (as in pneumonia or left heart failure, see p. 705), the exchange membrane thickens dramatically. Under such conditions, even the total time (0.75 s) that red blood cells are in transit through the pulmonary capillaries may not be enough for adequate gas exchange, and body tissues begin to suffer from oxygen deprivation. ●

The greater the surface area of the respiratory membrane, the more gas can diffuse across it in a given time period. The alveolar surface area is enormous in healthy lungs. Spread flat, the total gas exchange surface of these tiny sacs in an adult male's lungs is about 90 m^2, approximately 40 times greater than the surface area of his skin!

 HOMEOSTATIC IMBALANCE

In certain pulmonary diseases, the alveolar surface area actually functioning in gas exchange is drastically reduced. This occurs in emphysema, when the walls of adjacent alveoli break through and the alveolar chambers become larger. It also occurs when tumors, mucus, or inflammatory material blocks gas flow into the alveoli. ●

Internal Respiration: Capillary Gas Exchange in the Body Tissues

In internal respiration, the partial pressure and diffusion gradients are reversed from the situation described for external respiration and pulmonary gas exchange. However, the factors promoting gas exchanges between the systemic capillaries and the tissue cells are essentially identical to those acting in the lungs (Figure 22.17). Tissue cells continuously use O_2 for their metabolic activities and produce CO_2. Because P_{O_2} in the tissues is always lower than that in the systemic arterial blood (40 mm Hg versus 100 mm Hg), O_2 moves rapidly from the blood into the tissues until equilibrium is reached, and CO_2 moves quickly along its pressure gradient into the blood. As a result, venous blood

draining the tissue capillary beds and returning to the heart has a P_{O_2} of 40 mm Hg and a P_{CO_2} of 45 mm Hg.

In summary, the gas exchanges that occur between the blood and the alveoli and between the blood and the tissue cells take place by simple diffusion driven by the partial pressure gradients of O_2 and CO_2 that exist on the opposite sides of the exchange membranes.

Transport of Respiratory Gases by Blood

Oxygen Transport

External and internal respiration have been considered consecutively to emphasize their similarities, but keep in mind that it is the blood that transports O_2 and CO_2 between these two exchange sites.

Molecular oxygen is carried in blood in two ways: bound to hemoglobin within red blood cells and dissolved in plasma (see Figure 22.22, p. 862). Oxygen is poorly soluble in water, so only about 1.5% of the oxygen transported is carried in the dissolved form. Indeed, if this were the *only* means of oxygen transport, a P_{O_2} of 3 atm or a cardiac output of 15 times normal would be required to provide the oxygen levels needed by body tissues! This problem, of course, has been solved by hemoglobin, and 98.5% of the oxygen ferried from the lungs to the tissues is carried in a loose chemical combination with hemoglobin.

Association of Oxygen and Hemoglobin

As described in Chapter 17, hemoglobin (Hb) is composed of four polypeptide chains, each bound to an iron-containing heme group (see Figure 17.4). Because the iron atoms bind oxygen, each hemoglobin molecule can combine with four molecules of O_2, and oxygen loading is rapid and reversible.

The hemoglobin-oxygen combination, called **oxyhemoglobin** (ok″sĭ-he″mo-glo′bin), is written **HbO₂**. Hemoglobin that has released oxygen is called **reduced hemoglobin**, or **deoxyhemoglobin**, and is written **HHb**. Loading and unloading of O_2 can be indicated by a single reversible equation:

$$\text{HHb} + O_2 \underset{\text{Tissuess}}{\overset{\text{Lungs}}{\rightleftharpoons}} \text{HbO}_2 + \text{H}^+$$

After the first O_2 molecule binds to iron, the Hb molecule changes shape. As a result, it more readily takes up two more O_2 molecules, and uptake of the fourth is even more facilitated. When all four heme groups are bound to O_2, a hemoglobin molecule is said to be *fully saturated*. When one, two, or three oxygen molecules are bound, hemoglobin is *partially saturated*. By the same token, unloading of one oxygen molecule enhances the unloading of the next, and so on. Thus, the *affinity* (binding strength) of hemoglobin for oxygen changes with the extent of oxygen saturation, and both loading and unloading of oxygen are very efficient.

The rate at which Hb reversibly binds or releases O_2 is regulated by P_{O_2}, temperature, blood pH, P_{CO_2}, and blood concentration of an organic chemical called BPG. These factors interact to ensure adequate deliveries of O_2 to tissue cells.

Influence of P_{O_2} on Hemoglobin Saturation

Because the affinity of hemoglobin for O_2 changes with O_2 binding as just described, the relationship between the degree of hemoglobin saturation and the P_{O_2} of blood is not linear, as the **oxygen-hemoglobin dissociation curve** of Figure 22.20 shows. This S-shaped curve has a steep slope for P_{O_2} values between 10 and 50 mm Hg and then flattens out (plateaus) between 70 and 100 mm Hg.

Under normal resting conditions (P_{O_2} = 100 mm Hg), arterial blood hemoglobin is 98% saturated, and 100 ml of systemic arterial blood contains about 20 ml of O_2. This *oxygen content* of arterial blood is written as 20 vol % (volume percent). As arterial blood flows through the systemic capillaries, about 5 ml of O_2 per 100 ml of blood is released, yielding an Hb saturation of 75% (and an O_2 content of 15 vol %) in venous blood.

The nearly complete saturation of Hb in arterial blood explains why breathing deeply (which increases both the alveolar and arterial blood P_{O_2}) causes very little increase in the O_2 saturation of hemoglobin. Remember, P_{O_2} measurements indicate only the amount of O_2 dissolved in plasma, not the amount bound to hemoglobin. However, P_{O_2} values are a good index of lung function, and when arterial P_{O_2} is significantly less than alveolar P_{O_2}, some degree of respiratory impairment exists.

A hemoglobin saturation curve (Figure 22.20) reveals two other important facts. First, Hb is almost completely saturated at a P_{O_2} of 70 mm Hg, and further increases in P_{O_2} produce only small increases in O_2 binding. The adaptive value of this is that O_2 loading and delivery to the tissues can still be adequate when the P_{O_2} of inspired air is well below its usual levels, a situation common at higher altitudes and in those with cardiopulmonary disease. Moreover, because most O_2 *unloading* occurs on the steep portion of the curve, a small drop in P_{O_2} will cause a large increase in unloading. Normally, only 20–25% of bound oxygen is unloaded during one systemic circuit, and substantial amounts of O_2 are still avail-

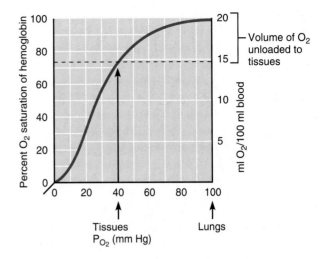

FIGURE 22.20 Oxygen-hemoglobin dissociation curve. Changes in Hb saturation and blood O_2 content as P_{O_2} changes. Notice that hemoglobin is almost completely saturated at a P_{O_2} of 70 mm Hg. Rapid loading and unloading of O_2 to and from hemoglobin occur at P_{O_2} values in the steep portion of the curve. In the systemic circuit, approximately 25% of Hb-bound O_2 is unloaded to the tissues (that is, approximately 5 ml of the 20 ml of O_2 per 100 ml of blood is released). Thus, hemoglobin of venous blood is still about 75% saturated with oxygen after one round through the body.

able in venous blood (the *venous reserve*). Thus, if O_2 drops to very low levels in the tissues, as might occur during vigorous exercise, much more O_2 will dissociate from hemoglobin to be used by the tissue cells without any increase in respiratory rate or cardiac output.

Influence of Other Factors on Hemoglobin Saturation

Temperature, blood pH, P_{CO_2}, and the amount of BPG in the blood all influence hemoglobin saturation at a given P_{O_2}. BPG (2,3-bisphosphoglycerate), which binds reversibly with hemoglobin, is produced by red blood cells (RBCs) as they break down glucose by the anaerobic process called glycolysis.

All of these factors influence Hb saturation by modifying hemoglobin's three-dimensional structure, and thereby its affinity for O_2. Generally speaking, an *increase* in temperature, P_{CO_2}, H^+ content of the blood (Figure 22.21), or BPG levels in blood decreases Hb's affinity for O_2 and causes the oxygen-hemoglobin dissociation curve to shift to the right. This enhances oxygen unloading from the blood. Conversely, a *decrease* in any of these factors increases hemoglobin's affinity for oxygen and shifts the dissociation curve to the left.

If you give a little thought to how these factors might be related, you'll realize that they all tend to

Q *Do increasing temperature and P_{CO_2} affect O_2 unloading in the same or opposite directions?*

(a)

(b)

FIGURE 22.21 **Effect of temperature, P_{CO_2}, and blood pH on the oxygen-hemoglobin dissociation curve.** Oxygen unloading is accelerated at conditions of **(a)** increased temperature, **(b)** increased P_{CO_2}, and/or hydrogen ion concentration (decreased pH), causing the dissociation curve to shift to the right. This response is called the Bohr effect.

be at their highest levels in the systemic capillaries where oxygen unloading is the goal. As cells metabolize glucose and use O_2, they release CO_2, which increases the P_{CO_2} and H^+ levels in the capillary

blood. Both declining blood pH (acidosis) and increasing P_{CO_2} weaken the Hb-O_2 bond, a phenomenon called the **Bohr effect.** As a result, oxygen unloading is enhanced where it is most needed. Additionally, heat is a by-product of metabolic activity, and active tissues are usually warmer than less active ones. A rise in temperature affects hemoglobin's affinity for O_2 both directly and indirectly (via its influence on RBC metabolism and BPG synthesis). Collectively, these factors see to it that Hb unloads much more O_2 in the vicinity of hard-working tissue cells.

The Hemoglobin–Nitric Oxide Partnership in Gas Exchange

Nitric oxide (NO), secreted by vascular endothelial cells, is a well-known vasodilator. Hemoglobin, on the other hand, has a formidable reputation as a NO scavenger—its iron-containing heme group destroys NO, which should result in vasoconstriction. Yet—and here's the paradox—local vessels dilate where gases are being unloaded and loaded. Some researchers believe that this is because hemoglobin transports NO (attached not to the heme, which would destroy it, but to the globin) along with O_2, and unloads both at the tissues. The vasodilation that would follow NO unloading could resolve the paradox. Other researchers believe that hemoglobin inside red blood cells is too far away from the endothelium to either scavenge or donate NO and that vasodilation is due only to NO release by local endothelial cells. The evidence either way is not yet conclusive.

◢◤ HOMEOSTATIC IMBALANCE

Whatever the cause, inadequate oxygen delivery to body tissues is called **hypoxia** (hi-pok'se-ah). This condition is observed more easily in fair-skinned people because their skin and mucosae take on a bluish cast (become *cyanotic*) when Hb saturation falls below 75%. In dark-skinned individuals, this color change can be observed only in the mucosae and nail beds.

Classification of hypoxia based on cause is as follows:

1. **Anemic hypoxia** reflects poor O_2 delivery resulting from too few RBCs or from RBCs that contain abnormal or too little Hb.

2. **Ischemic (stagnant) hypoxia** results when blood circulation is impaired or blocked. Congestive heart failure may cause bodywide ischemic hypoxia, whereas emboli or thrombi block oxygen delivery only to tissues distal to the obstruction.

A The same direction.

3. Histotoxic hypoxia occurs when body cells are unable to use O_2 even though adequate amounts are delivered. This variety of hypoxia is the consequence of metabolic poisons, such as cyanide.

4. Hypoxemic hypoxia is indicated by reduced arterial P_{O_2}. Possible causes include disordered or abnormal ventilation-perfusion coupling, pulmonary diseases that impair ventilation, and breathing air containing scant amounts of O_2.

Carbon monoxide poisoning is a unique type of hypoxemic hypoxia, and a leading cause of death from fire. Carbon monoxide (CO) is an odorless, colorless gas that competes vigorously with O_2 for heme binding sites. Moreover, because Hb's affinity for CO is more than 200 times greater than its affinity for oxygen, CO is a highly successful competitor. Even at minuscule partial pressures, carbon monoxide can displace oxygen.

CO poisoning is particularly dangerous because it does not produce the characteristic signs of hypoxia—cyanosis and respiratory distress. Instead the victim is confused and has a throbbing headache. In rare cases, fair skin becomes cherry red (the color of the Hb-CO complex), which the eye of the beholder interprets as a healthy "blush." Those with CO poisoning are given hyperbaric therapy (if available) or 100% O_2 until the CO has been cleared from the body. ●

Carbon Dioxide Transport

Normally active body cells produce about 200 ml of CO_2 each minute—exactly the amount excreted by the lungs. Blood transports CO_2 from the tissue cells to the lungs in three forms (Figure 22.22):

1. Dissolved in plasma (7–10%). The smallest amount of CO_2 is transported simply dissolved in plasma.

2. Chemically bound to hemoglobin (just over 20%). In this form, CO_2 is carried in the RBCs as **carbaminohemoglobin** (kar-bam″ĭ-no-he″mo-glo′bin):

$$CO_2 + Hb \rightleftharpoons HbCO_2$$
$$\text{carbaminohemoglobin}$$

This reaction is rapid and does not require a catalyst. Because carbon dioxide binds directly to the amino acids of *globin* (and not to the heme), carbon dioxide transport in RBCs does not compete with the oxyhemoglobin transport mechanism.

CO_2 loading and unloading to and from Hb are directly influenced by the P_{CO_2} and the degree of Hb oxygenation. Carbon dioxide rapidly dissociates from hemoglobin in the lungs, where the P_{CO_2} of alveolar air is lower than that in blood. Carbon dioxide is loaded in the tissues, where the P_{CO_2} is higher than that in the blood. Deoxygenated hemoglobin combines more readily with carbon dioxide than does oxygenated hemoglobin (see the discussion of the Haldane effect on p. 863).

3. As bicarbonate ion in plasma (about 70%). Most carbon dioxide molecules entering the plasma quickly enter the RBCs, where most of the reactions that prepare carbon dioxide for transport as **bicarbonate ions** (HCO_3^-) in plasma occur. As illustrated in Figure 22.22a, when CO_2 diffuses into the RBCs, it combines with water, forming carbonic acid (H_2CO_3). H_2CO_3 is unstable and quickly dissociates into hydrogen ions and bicarbonate ions:

$$\underset{\substack{\text{carbon} \\ \text{dioxide}}}{CO_2} + \underset{\text{water}}{H_2O} \rightleftharpoons \underset{\substack{\text{carbonic} \\ \text{acid}}}{H_2CO_3} \rightleftharpoons \underset{\substack{\text{hydrogen} \\ \text{ion}}}{H^+} + \underset{\substack{\text{bicarbonate} \\ \text{ion}}}{HCO_3^-}$$

Although this reaction also occurs in plasma, it is thousands of times faster in RBCs because they (and not plasma) contain **carbonic anhydrase** (kar-bon′ik an-hi′drās), an enzyme that reversibly catalyzes the conversion of carbon dioxide and water to carbonic acid. Hydrogen ions released during the reaction (as well as CO_2 itself) bind to Hb, triggering the Bohr effect; thus, O_2 release is enhanced by CO_2 loading. Because of the buffering effect of Hb, the liberated H^+ causes little change in pH under resting conditions. Hence, blood becomes only slightly more acidic (the pH declines from 7.4 to 7.34) as it passes through the tissues.

Once generated, HCO_3^- moves quickly from the RBCs into the plasma, where it is carried to the lungs. To counterbalance the rapid outrush of these anions from the RBCs, chloride ions (Cl^-) move from the plasma into the RBCs. This ion exchange process, called the **chloride shift**, occurs via facilitated diffusion through an RBC membrane protein.

In the lungs, the process is reversed (Figure 22.22b). As blood moves through the pulmonary capillaries, its P_{CO_2} declines from 45 mm Hg to 40 mm Hg. For this to occur, CO_2 must first be freed from its "bicarbonate housing." HCO_3^- reenters the RBCs (and Cl^- moves into the plasma) and binds with H^+ to form carbonic acid, which is then split by carbonic anhydrase to release CO_2 and water. This CO_2, along with that released from hemoglobin and from solution in plasma, then diffuses along its partial pressure gradient from the blood into the alveoli.

Q *Rapidly metabolizing tissues generate large amounts of CO_2 and H^+. How does this affect O_2 unloading?*

(a) Oxygen release and carbon dioxide pickup at the tissues

(b) Oxygen pickup and carbon dioxide release in the lungs

FIGURE 22.22 **Transport and exchange of CO_2 and O_2.** Gas exchanges occurring **(a)** at the tissues and **(b)** in the lungs. CO_2 is transported primarily as bicarbonate ion (HCO_3^-) in plasma (70%); smaller amounts are transported bound to hemoglobin (indicated as $HbCO_2$) in the red blood cells (22%) or in solution in plasma (7%). Nearly all O_2 transported in blood is bound to Hb as oxyhemoglobin (HbO_2) in RBCs. Very small amounts (about 1.5%) are carried dissolved in plasma. (Reduced hemoglobin is HHb.) Relative sizes of the transport arrows indicate the proportionate amounts of O_2 and CO_2 moved by each method.

A *Both CO_2 and H^+ increase O_2 unloading by binding to Hb. This is called the Bohr effect.*

The Haldane Effect

The amount of carbon dioxide transported in blood is markedly affected by the degree of oxygenation of the blood. The lower the P_{O_2} and the lower the extent of Hb saturation with oxygen, the more CO_2 that can be carried in the blood (Figure 22.23). This phenomenon, called the **Haldane effect,** reflects the greater ability of reduced hemoglobin to form carbaminohemoglobin and to buffer H^+ by combining with it. As CO_2 enters the systemic bloodstream, it causes more oxygen to dissociate from Hb (Bohr effect), which allows more CO_2 to combine with Hb and more HCO_3^- to be formed (Haldane effect).

In the pulmonary circulation (Figure 22.22b), the situation is reversed—uptake of O_2 facilitates release of CO_2. As Hb becomes saturated with O_2, the H^+ released combines with HCO_3^-, helping to unload CO_2 from the pulmonary blood. The Haldane effect encourages CO_2 exchange in both the tissues and lungs.

Influence of CO_2 on Blood pH

Typically, the H^+ released during carbonic acid dissociation is buffered by Hb or other proteins within the RBCs or in plasma. The HCO_3^- generated in the red blood cells diffuses into the plasma, where it acts as the *alkaline reserve* part of the blood's carbonic acid–bicarbonate buffer system. The **carbonic acid–bicarbonate buffer system** is very important in resisting shifts in blood pH (see the equation in point 3 on p. 861 concerning CO_2 transport). For example, if the hydrogen ion concentration in blood begins to rise, excess H^+ is removed by combining with HCO_3^- to form carbonic acid (a weak acid that dissociates very little at either physiological or acidic pH). If H^+ concentration drops below desirable levels in blood, carbonic acid dissociates, releasing hydrogen ions and lowering the pH again.

Changes in respiratory rate or depth can produce dramatic changes in blood pH by altering the amount of carbonic acid in the blood. Slow, shallow breathing allows CO_2 to accumulate in the blood. As a result, carbonic acid levels increase and blood pH drops. Conversely, rapid, deep breathing quickly flushes CO_2 out of the blood, reducing carbonic acid levels and increasing blood pH. Thus, respiratory ventilation can provide a fast-acting system to adjust blood pH (and P_{CO_2}) when it is disturbed by metabolic factors. Respiratory adjustments play a major role in the acid-base balance of the blood, as discussed in Chapter 26.

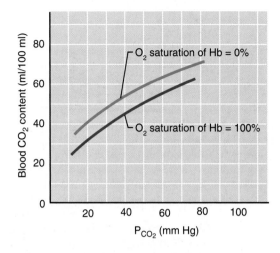

FIGURE 22.23 **The Haldane effect.** Equilibrium curves for blood CO_2 content relative to fully oxygenated hemoglobin (O_2 saturation of Hb = 100%) and deoxygenated Hb. The lower the degree of Hb saturation, the greater the amount of CO_2 that can be transported by the blood.

Control of Respiration

Neural Mechanisms and Generation of Breathing Rhythm

Although our tidelike breathing seems so beautifully simple, its control is fairly complex, involving neurons in the reticular formation of the medulla and pons. Because the medulla sets the respiratory rhythm, we will begin there.

Medullary Respiratory Centers

Clustered neurons in two areas of the medulla oblongata appear to be critically important in respiration. These are (1) the **dorsal respiratory group (DRG)**, located dorsally near the root of cranial nerve IX, and (2) the **ventral respiratory group (VRG)**, a network of neurons that extends in the ventral brain stem from the spinal cord to the pons-medulla junction. The VRG appears to be a rhythm-generating and integrative center. It contains groups of neurons that fire during inspiration and others that fire during expiration in a dance of mutual inhibition. When its inspiratory neurons fire, a burst of impulses travels along the **phrenic** and **intercostal nerves** to excite the diaphragm and external intercostal muscles, respectively (Figure 22.24). As a result, the thorax expands and air rushes into the lungs. When the VRG's expiratory neurons fire, the output stops, and expiration occurs passively as the inspiratory muscles relax and the lungs recoil. This cyclic on/off activity of the inspiratory and expiratory neurons repeats continuously and produces a respiratory rate of 12–15

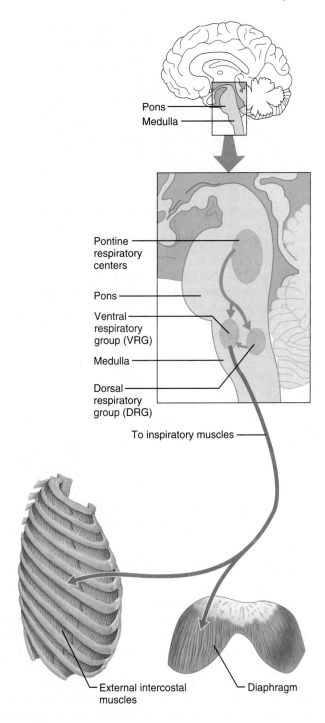

FIGURE 22.24 **Locations of respiratory centers and their postulated connections.** The ventral respiratory group (VRG) contains rhythm generators whose output drives respiration. During normal quiet breathing, a group of VRG inspiratory neurons fire, activating respiratory motor neurons that cause inspiratory muscles to contract. Passive expiration occurs when a group of expiratory neurons fire, inhibiting the VRG output and allowing the inspiratory muscles to relax. Neurons of the dorsal respiratory group (DRG) integrate peripheral sensory input and modify the rhythms generated by the VRG. The pontine respiratory centers interact with the medullary centers to smooth the breathing pattern. (The efferent pathway is incomplete. Medullary neurons communicate with lower motor neurons in the spinal cord. For simplicity, the lower motor neurons, which innervate the muscles of respiration, are not illustrated.)

Until recently, it was thought that the DRG acts as an inspiratory center, performing many of the tasks now known to be performed by the VRG. We now know that in almost all mammals including humans, the DRG integrates input from peripheral stretch and chemoreceptors (described shortly) and communicates this information to the VRG. It may seem surprising, but many of the details of this system so essential to life are still being worked out.

Pontine Respiratory Centers

Although the VRG generates the basic respiratory rhythm, the pontine respiratory centers influence and modify the activity of medullary neurons. For example, pontine centers appear to smooth out the transitions from inspiration to expiration, and vice versa; and when lesions are made in its superior region, inspirations become very prolonged, a phenomenon called *apneustic breathing*.

The **pontine respiratory group** [formerly called the *pneumotaxic center* (noo"mo-tak′sik)] and other pontine centers transmit impulses to the VRG of the medulla (Figure 22.24). This modifies and fine-tunes the breathing rhythms generated by the VRG during certain activities such as vocalization, sleep, and exercise. As you would expect from these functions, the pontine respiratory centers, like the DRG, receive input from higher brain centers and from various sensory receptors in the periphery.

Genesis of the Respiratory Rhythm

Although there is little question that breathing is rhythmic, we still cannot fully explain the origin of its rhythm. One hypothesis is that there are *pacemaker neurons*, which have intrinsic (automatic) rhythmicity like the pacemaker cells found in the heart. Though pacemaker activity has been demonstrated in rostral VRG neurons in newborns,

breaths per minute, with inspiratory phases lasting about 2 seconds followed by expiratory phases lasting about 3 seconds. This normal respiratory rate and rhythm is referred to as **eupnea** (ūp-ne′ah; *eu* = good, *pne* = breath). During severe hypoxia, VRG networks generate gasping (perhaps in a last-ditch effort to restore O_2 to the brain). When a certain cluster of VRG neurons is completely suppressed, as by an overdose of morphine, or alcohol, respiration stops completely.

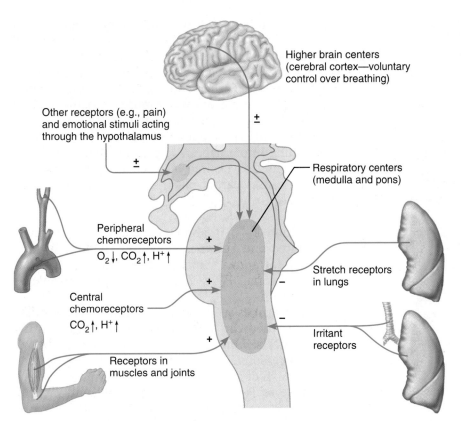

FIGURE 22.25 **Neural and chemical influences on brain stem respiratory centers.** Excitatory influences (+) increase the frequency of impulses sent to the muscles of respiration and recruit additional motor units, resulting in deeper, faster breathing. Inhibitory influences (−) have the reverse effect. In some cases, the impulses may be excitatory or inhibitory (±), depending on which receptors or brain regions are activated. The cerebral cortex also directly innervates respiratory muscle motor neurons.

no such activity has been found in adults. This leads us to the second (and most popular) hypothesis: Normal respiratory rhythm is a result of reciprocal inhibition of interconnected neuronal networks in the medulla. Rather than a single set of pacemaker neurons, there are two sets that inhibit each other and so cycle their activity to generate the rhythm.

Factors Influencing Breathing Rate and Depth

Inspiratory depth is determined by how actively the respiratory center stimulates the motor neurons serving the respiratory muscles. The greater the stimulation, the greater the number of motor units excited and the greater the force of respiratory muscle contractions. Respiratory rate is determined by how long the inspiratory center is active or how quickly it is switched off.

Depth and rate of breathing can be modified in response to changing body demands. The respiratory centers in the medulla and pons are sensitive to both excitatory and inhibitory stimuli. These stimuli are described next and summarized in Figure 22.25.

Chemical Factors

Among the factors that influence breathing rate and depth, the most important are changing levels of CO_2, O_2, and H^+ in arterial blood. Sensors respond-

ing to such chemical fluctuations, called **chemoreceptors,** are found in two major body locations. The **central chemoreceptors** are located bilaterally in the ventrolateral medulla. The **peripheral chemoreceptors** are found in the aortic arch and carotid arteries.

Influence of P_{CO_2} Of all the chemicals influencing respiration, CO_2 is the most potent and the most closely controlled. Normally, arterial P_{CO_2} is 40 mm Hg and is maintained within ±3 mm Hg of this level by an exquisitely sensitive homeostatic mechanism that is mediated mainly by the effect that rising CO_2 levels have on the central chemoreceptors of the brain stem (Figure 22.26). CO_2 diffuses easily from the blood into the cerebrospinal fluid, where it is hydrated and forms carbonic acid. As the acid dissociates, H^+ is liberated. This is the same reaction that occurs when CO_2 enters RBCs (see pp. 861–862). Unlike RBCs or plasma, however, cerebrospinal fluid contains virtually no proteins that can buffer the added H^+. Thus, as P_{CO_2} levels rise, a condition referred to as **hypercapnia** (hi″per-kap′ne-ah), the cerebrospinal fluid pH drops, exciting the central chemoreceptors, which make abundant synapses with the respiratory regulatory centers. As a result, the depth and rate of breathing are increased. This enhanced alveolar ventilation quickly flushes CO_2 out of the blood, increasing blood pH. An elevation of only 5 mm Hg in arterial P_{CO_2} results in a doubling of alveolar ventilation, even when arterial O_2 levels and pH are

22

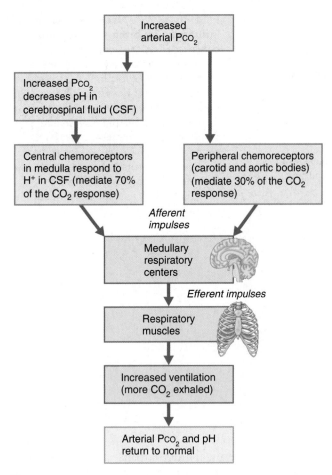

Key:

▢ Initial stimulus

▢ Physiological response

▢ Result

FIGURE 22.26 **Negative feedback mechanism by which changes in P_{CO_2} and blood pH regulate ventilation.**

unchanged. When P_{O_2} and pH are below normal, the response to elevated P_{CO_2} is even greater. Increased ventilation is normally self-limiting, ending when homeostatic blood P_{CO_2} levels are restored.

Notice that while rising CO_2 levels act as the initial stimulus, it is rising H^+ levels that prod the *central* chemoreceptors into activity. In the final analysis, control of breathing during rest is aimed primarily at *regulating the H^+ concentration in the brain.*

◢ HOMEOSTATIC IMBALANCE

Hyperventilation is an increase in the rate and depth of breathing that exceeds the body's need to remove CO_2. A person experiencing an anxiety attack may hyperventilate involuntarily to the point where he or she becomes dizzy or faints. This happens because low CO_2 levels in the blood (**hypocapnia**) cause cerebral blood vessels to constrict, reducing brain perfusion and producing cerebral ischemia. Earlier symptoms of hyperventilation are tingling and involuntary muscle spasms (tetany) in the hands and face caused by blood Ca^{2+} levels falling as pH rises. Such attacks may be averted by breathing into a paper bag because then the air being inspired is expired air, rich in carbon dioxide, which causes carbon dioxide to be retained in the blood. ●

When P_{CO_2} is abnormally low, respiration is inhibited and becomes slow and shallow. In fact, periods of **apnea** (breathing cessation) may occur until arterial P_{CO_2} rises and again stimulates respiration.

Sometimes swimmers voluntarily hyperventilate so that they can hold their breath longer during swim meets. This is incredibly dangerous for the following reasons. Blood O_2 content rarely drops much below 60% of normal during regular breath-holding, because as P_{O_2} drops, P_{CO_2} rises enough to make breathing unavoidable. However, strenuous hyperventilation can lower P_{CO_2} so much that a lag period occurs before it rebounds enough to stimulate respiration again. This lag may allow oxygen levels to fall well below 50 mm Hg, causing the swimmer to black out (and perhaps drown) before he or she has the urge to breathe.

Influence of P_{O_2}   Cells sensitive to arterial O_2 levels are found in the peripheral chemoreceptors, that is, in the **aortic bodies** of the aortic arch and in the **carotid bodies** at the bifurcation of the common carotid arteries (Figure 22.27). Those in the carotid bodies are the main oxygen sensors.

Under normal conditions, the effect of declining P_{O_2} on ventilation is slight and mostly limited to enhancing the sensitivity of peripheral receptors to increased P_{CO_2}. Arterial P_{O_2} must drop *substantially*, to at least 60 mm Hg, before O_2 levels become a major stimulus for increased ventilation. This is not as strange as it may appear. Remember, there is a huge reservoir of O_2 bound to Hb, and Hb remains almost entirely saturated unless or until the P_{O_2} of alveolar gas and arterial blood falls below 60 mm Hg. The central chemoreceptors then begin to suffer from O_2 starvation, and their activity is depressed. At the same time, the peripheral chemoreceptors become excited and stimulate the respiratory centers to increase ventilation, even if P_{CO_2} is normal. Thus, the peripheral chemoreceptor system can maintain ventilation when alveolar O_2 levels are low even though brain stem centers are depressed by hypoxia.

▶ HOMEOSTATIC IMBALANCE

In people who retain CO_2 because of pulmonary disease (e.g., emphysema and chronic bronchitis), arterial P_{CO_2} is chronically elevated and, as a result, chemoreceptors adapt to this chemical stimulus. In such cases, a declining P_{O_2} acting on the oxygen-sensitive peripheral chemoreceptors provides the principal respiratory stimulus, the **hypoxic drive.** Thus, gas mixtures administered to such patients during respiratory distress are only slightly enriched with O_2 because inspiration of pure oxygen would slow their breathing, further elevating their P_{CO_2}. ●

Influence of Arterial pH   Changes in arterial pH can modify respiratory rate and rhythm even when CO_2 and O_2 levels are normal. Because little H^+ diffuses from the blood into the cerebrospinal fluid, the direct effect of arterial H^+ concentration on central chemoreceptors is insignificant compared to the effect of H^+ generated by elevations in P_{CO_2}. The increased ventilation that occurs in response to falling arterial pH is mediated through the peripheral chemoreceptors.

Although changes in P_{CO_2} and H^+ concentration are interrelated, they are distinct stimuli. A drop in blood pH may reflect CO_2 retention, but it may also result from metabolic causes, such as accumulation of lactic acid during exercise or of fatty acid metabolites (ketone bodies) in patients with poorly controlled diabetes mellitus. Regardless of cause, as arterial pH declines, respiratory system controls attempt to compensate and raise the pH by eliminating CO_2 (and carbonic acid) from the blood; thus, respiratory rate and depth increase.

Summary of Interactions of P_{CO_2}, P_{O_2}, and Arterial pH   Although every cell in the body must have O_2 to live, the body's need to rid itself of CO_2 is the most important stimulus for breathing in a healthy person. However, CO_2 does not act in isolation, and various chemical factors enforce or inhibit one another's effects. These interactions are summarized here:

1. Rising CO_2 levels are the most powerful respiratory stimulant. As CO_2 is hydrated in cerebrospinal fluid, liberated H^+ acts directly on the central chemoreceptors, causing a reflexive increase in breathing rate and depth. Low P_{CO_2} levels depress respiration.

2. Under normal conditions, blood P_{O_2} affects breathing only indirectly by influencing chemoreceptor sensitivity to changes in P_{CO_2}. Low P_{O_2} augments P_{CO_2} effects; high P_{O_2} levels diminish the effectiveness of CO_2 stimulation.

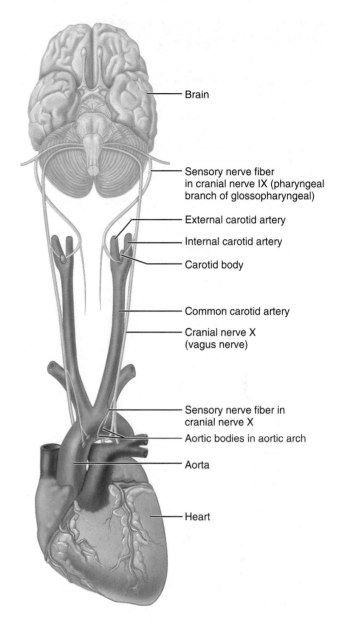

FIGURE 22.27 **Location of the peripheral chemoreceptors in the carotid and aortic bodies.** Also shown are the sensory pathways from these receptors through cranial nerves IX and X to the respiratory centers in the medulla.

Labels: Brain; Sensory nerve fiber in cranial nerve IX (pharyngeal branch of glossopharyngeal); External carotid artery; Internal carotid artery; Carotid body; Common carotid artery; Cranial nerve X (vagus nerve); Sensory nerve fiber in cranial nerve X; Aortic bodies in aortic arch; Aorta; Heart

3. When arterial P_{O_2} falls below 60 mm Hg, it becomes the major stimulus for respiration, and ventilation is increased via reflexes initiated by the peripheral chemoreceptors. This may increase O_2 loading into the blood, but it also causes hypocapnia (low P_{CO_2} blood levels) and an increase in blood pH, both of which inhibit respiration.

4. Changes in arterial pH resulting from CO_2 retention or metabolic factors act indirectly through the peripheral chemoreceptors to promote changes in ventilation, which in turn modify arterial P_{CO_2} and

A CLOSER LOOK

Dangerous Raptures of the Deep

Even the nonswimmers among us are beckoned by photos of scuba divers examining brightly colored coral and other ocean creatures as they glide effortlessly through sparkling blue water. "What a life," we think enviously. But hidden beneath that veneer of breathtaking beauty is life-threatening danger for the inexperienced, the careless, and the unlucky. In addition to the significant risk of drowning, scuba divers are exposed to the omnipresent danger of two other medical emergencies—air embolism and decompression sickness.

As divers descend to greater and greater depths underwater, the pressure on their bodies rises proportionately [1 atmosphere (760 mm Hg) of pressure for each 10 m (33 ft) of descent] because of the increasing weight of the water. **Scuba gear** (**s**elf-**c**ontained **u**nderwater **b**reathing **a**pparatus) has freed divers from air lines to the surface and heavy pressurized suits because it permits continual equalization of the air pressure (provided by the mixture of compressed air

in the tank) with the water pressure; that is, air enters the lungs at a higher-than-normal pressure. Thus descent is not usually a problem, unless divers descend below 100 feet and remain there for an extended time.

Although nitrogen ordinarily has little effect on body functioning, hyperbaric conditions for an extended time force so much nitrogen into solution in the blood that it provokes a narcotic effect called *nitrogen narcosis*. Nitrogen is far more soluble in lipids than in water, so it tends to concentrate in lipid-rich tissues such as the central nervous system, bone marrow, and fat deposits. Divers become dizzy, giddy, and appear to be intoxicated, which is why this condition is sometimes called "rapture of the deep."

Assuming divers take care to avoid these narcotizing effects, and ascend to the surface gradually (see the graph), dissolved nitrogen gas can be driven out of the tissues and eliminated by the lungs without problems. But if the ascent is rapid, the P_{N_2} decreases abruptly and the poorly soluble nitrogen gas appears to "boil"

from the tissues and out of solution in the body fluids. Gas bubbles in blood represent potentially lethal emboli, and those formed within joints, bones, and muscles can cause excruciating musculoskeletal pain, commonly called the "bends." Other signs of this *decompression sickness* are mood changes, seizures, nausea, numbness, "migrating" skin rashes, and a syndrome called *chokes*. Chokes, or cardiovascular bends, involves substernal pain, coughing, dyspnea, and, in severe cases, shock due to gas bubbles in the pulmonary capillaries. Although these signs usually appear within an hour of surfacing, they can be delayed as long as 36 hours. Even if divers experienced no apparent problems underwater, they could experience symptoms later. Decompression sickness can also strike at high altitudes, such as in unpressurized aircraft flying above 18,000 feet.

If divers ascend suddenly and without exhaling, the alveoli are likely to rupture. This situation usually occurs when they panic after aspirating seawater or encountering other

---

pH. Arterial pH does not influence the central chemoreceptors directly.

Influence of Higher Brain Centers

Hypothalamic Controls   Acting through the hypothalamus and the rest of the limbic system, strong emotions and pain send signals to the respiratory centers, modifying respiratory rate and depth. For example, have you ever touched something cold and clammy and gasped? That response was mediated through the hypothalamus. So too is the breath holding that occurs when we are angry and the increased respiratory rate that occurs when we are excited. A rise in body temperature acts to increase the respiratory rate, while a drop in body temperature produces the opposite effect; and sudden chilling of the body (a dip in the north Atlantic Ocean in late October) can cause cessation of breathing (apnea)—or at the very least, gasping.

Cortical Controls   Although breathing is normally regulated involuntarily by the brain stem respiratory centers, we can also exert conscious (volitional) control over the rate and depth of our breathing—choosing to hold our breath or to take an extra deep breath, for example. During voluntary control, the cerebral motor cortex sends signals to the motor neurons that stimulate the respiratory muscles, bypassing the medullary centers. Our ability to voluntarily hold our breath is limited, however, because the brain stem respiratory centers automatically reinitiate breathing when the blood concentration of CO_2 reaches critical levels. That explains why drowning victims typically have water in their lungs.

Pulmonary Irritant Reflexes

The lungs contain receptors that respond to an enormous variety of irritants. When activated, these receptors communicate with the respiratory

Even with modern scuba gear, divers need to know how to adjust from high underwater pressures to the lower pressures at the surface.

hazards, such as equipment failure, strong currents, or rough waters. Under such conditions, connections occur between the alveoli and the pulmonary bloodstream, and life-threatening gas emboli develop. Since divers typically ascend head-up, the emboli usually invade the cerebral circulation. Seizures, localized motor and sensory deficits, and unconsciousness are all possibilities. Indeed, many scuba-related

drownings appear to follow loss of consciousness due to arterial gas embolism.

The usual and most effective treatment for decompression sickness is hyperbaric therapy: reinstituting compression and then redoing decompression . . . slowly. When a gas embolus is suspected, oxygen and antiseizure medications are given until hyperbaric therapy can begin.

People with high body fat content or recent limb injuries are more vulnerable to decompression sickness. Consuming alcohol or exercising strenuously before a dive also increase the risk. The best therapy is to avoid the need for treatment by making sure that divers know the potential risks and are well trained in using their equipment. Assuming that is done, the vacation should be GREAT! ■

centers via vagal nerve afferents. Accumulated mucus, inhaled debris such as dust, or noxious fumes stimulate receptors in the bronchioles that promote reflex constriction of those air passages. The same irritants stimulate a cough when present in the trachea or bronchi, and a sneeze when present in the nasal cavity.

The Inflation Reflex

The visceral pleurae and conducting passages in the lungs contain numerous stretch receptors that are vigorously stimulated when the lungs are inflated. These receptors signal the medullary respiratory centers via afferent fibers of the vagus nerves, sending inhibitory impulses that end inspiration and allow expiration to occur. As the lungs recoil, the stretch receptors become quiet, and inspiration is initiated once again. This reflex, called the **inflation reflex,** or **Hering-Breuer reflex** (her'ing broy'er), is thought to be more a protective response (to prevent excessive stretching of the lungs) than a normal regulatory mechanism.

Respiratory Adjustments

Adjustments During Exercise

Respiratory adjustments during exercise are geared both to intensity and duration of the exercise. Working muscles consume tremendous amounts of O_2 and produce large amounts of CO_2; thus, ventilation can increase 10- to 20-fold during vigorous exercise. This increase in ventilation in response to metabolic needs is called **hyperpnea** (hi"perp-ne'ah). It differs from hyperventilation in that the respiratory changes in hyperpnea do not lead to significant changes in blood O_2 and CO_2 levels. By contrast, hyperventilation is excessive ventilation, and is characterized by low P_{CO_2} and alkalosis.

Exercise-enhanced ventilation does *not* appear to be prompted by rising P_{CO_2} and declining P_{O_2} and pH in the blood for two reasons. First, ventilation increases abruptly as exercise begins, followed by a gradual increase, and then a steady state of ventilation. When exercise stops, there is an initial small but abrupt decline in ventilation rate, followed by a gradual decrease to the pre-exercise value. Second, although venous levels change, arterial P_{CO_2} and P_{O_2} levels remain surprisingly constant during exercise. In fact, P_{CO_2} may decline to below normal and P_{O_2} may rise slightly because of the efficiency of the respiratory adjustments. Our present understanding of the mechanisms that produce these observations is sketchy, but the most accepted explanation is as follows.

The abrupt increase in ventilation that occurs as exercise begins reflects interaction of three neural factors:

1. Psychological stimuli (our conscious anticipation of exercise)

2. Simultaneous cortical motor activation of skeletal muscles and respiratory centers

3. Excitatory impulses reaching respiratory centers from proprioceptors in moving muscles, tendons, and joints

The subsequent gradual increase and then plateauing of respiration probably reflect the rate of CO_2 delivery to the lungs (the "CO_2 flow"). The small but abrupt decrease in ventilation that occurs as exercise ends reflects the shutting off of the three neural factors listed above. The subsequent gradual decline to baseline ventilation likely reflects a decline in the CO_2 flow that occurs as the oxygen debt is being repaid. The rise in lactic acid levels that contributes to O_2 debt is *not* a result of inadequate respiratory function, because alveolar ventilation and pulmonary perfusion are as well matched during exercise as during rest (hemoglobin remains fully saturated). Rather, it reflects cardiac output limitations or inability of the skeletal muscles to further increase their oxygen consumption. In light of this fact, the practice of inhaling pure O_2 by mask, used by some football players to replenish their "oxygen-starved" bodies as quickly as possible, is useless. The panting athlete *does* have an O_2 deficit, but inspiring extra oxygen will not help, because the shortage is in the muscles—not the lungs.

Adjustments at High Altitude

Most people live between sea level and an altitude of approximately 2400 m (8000 feet). In this range, differences in atmospheric pressure are not great enough to cause healthy people any problems when they spend brief periods in the higher-altitude areas. However, when you travel quickly from sea level to elevations above 8000 ft, where air density and P_{O_2} are lower, your body responds with symptoms of *acute mountain sickness (AMS)*—headaches, shortness of breath, nausea, and dizziness. AMS is common in travelers to ski resorts such as Vail, Colorado

(8120 ft), and Brian Head, Utah (a heart-pounding 9600 ft). In severe cases of AMS, lethal pulmonary and cerebral edema may occur.

When you move on a *long-term* basis from sea level to the mountains, your body begins to make respiratory and hematopoietic adjustments via an adaptive response called **acclimatization.** As already explained, decreases in arterial P_{O_2} cause the peripheral chemoreceptors to become more responsive to increases in P_{CO_2}, and a substantial decline in P_{O_2} directly stimulates the peripheral chemoreceptors. As a result, ventilation increases as the brain attempts to restore gas exchange to previous levels. Within a few days, the minute respiratory volume stabilizes at a level 2–3 L/min higher than the sea level rate. Because increased ventilation also reduces arterial CO_2 levels, the P_{CO_2} of individuals living at high altitudes is typically below 40 mm Hg (its value at sea level).

Because less O_2 is available to be loaded, high-altitude conditions always result in lower-than-normal hemoglobin saturation levels. For example, at about 19,000 ft above sea level, O_2 saturation of arterial blood is only 67% (compared to nearly 98% at sea level). But Hb unloads only 20–25% of its oxygen at sea level, which means that even at the reduced saturations at high altitudes, the O_2 needs of the tissues are still met adequately under resting conditions. Additionally, at high altitudes hemoglobin's affinity for O_2 is reduced because of increases in BPG concentration, with the result that more O_2 is released to the tissues during each circulatory round.

Although the tissues in a person at high altitude receive adequate oxygen under normal conditions, problems arise when all-out efforts are demanded of the cardiovascular and respiratory systems (as discovered by athletes competing in the 1968 Summer Olympics on the high mesa of Mexico City, at 7370 ft). Unless one is fully acclimatized, such conditions almost guarantee that body tissues will become severely hypoxic.

When blood O_2 levels decline, the kidneys accelerate production of erythropoietin, which stimulates bone marrow production of RBCs (see Chapter 17). This phase of acclimatization, which occurs slowly, provides long-term compensation for living at high altitudes.

Homeostatic Imbalances of the Respiratory System

The respiratory system is particularly vulnerable to infectious diseases because it is wide open to airborne pathogens. Many of these inflammatory conditions, such as rhinitis and laryngitis, were considered earlier in the chapter. Here we turn our attention to the most disabling disorders: *chronic obstructive pulmonary disease (COPD), asthma, tuberculosis,* and *lung cancer.* COPD and lung cancer are living proof of the devastating effects of cigarette smoking on the body. Long known to promote cardiovascular disease, cigarettes are perhaps even more effective at destroying the lungs.

Chronic Obstructive Pulmonary Disease

The **chronic obstructive pulmonary diseases (COPD),** exemplified best by chronic bronchitis and emphysema, are a major cause of death and disability in North America and are becoming increasingly prevalent. The key physiological feature of these diseases is an irreversible decrease in the ability to force air out of the lungs. These diseases also share other common features (Figure 22.28):

1. More than 80% of patients have a history of smoking.

2. Dyspnea (disp-ne'ah), difficult or labored breathing often referred to as "air hunger," occurs and gets progressively more severe.

3. Coughing and frequent pulmonary infections are common.

4. Most COPD victims develop respiratory failure manifested as **hypoventilation** (insufficient ventilation in relation to metabolic needs, causing CO_2 retention), respiratory acidosis, and hypoxemia.

Emphysema is distinguished by permanent enlargement of the alveoli, accompanied by destruction of the alveolar walls. Invariably the lungs lose their elasticity. This has three important consequences: (1) Accessory muscles must be enlisted to breathe, and victims are perpetually exhausted because breathing requires 15–20% of their total body energy supply (as opposed to 5% in healthy individuals). (2) For complex reasons, the bronchioles open during inspiration but collapse during expiration, trapping huge volumes of air in the alveoli. This hyperinflation leads to development of a permanently expanded "barrel chest" and flattens the diaphragm, thus reducing ventilation efficiency. (3) Damage to the pulmonary capillaries as the alveolar walls disintegrate increases resistance in the pulmonary circuit, forcing the right ventricle to overwork and consequently become enlarged. In addition to cigarette smoking, hereditary factors (e.g., alpha-1 antitrypsin deficiency) cause emphysema in some patients.

In **chronic bronchitis,** inhaled irritants lead to chronic excessive mucus production by the mucosa of the lower respiratory passageways and to inflammation and fibrosis of that mucosa. These responses obstruct the airways and severely impair lung ventilation and gas exchange. Pulmonary infections are

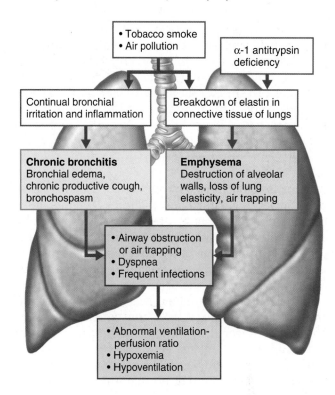

FIGURE 22.28 **The pathogenesis of COPD.**

frequent because bacteria thrive in the stagnant pools of mucus. However, the degree of dyspnea is usually moderate compared to that of emphysema sufferers. In addition to the major factor of cigarette smoking, environmental pollution may contribute to the development of chronic bronchitis.

In the clinical setting you might see two very different patterns that represent the extremes of patients with COPD. One pattern has traditionally been called the "pink puffer": these patients work so hard maintaining adequate ventilation that they lose weight, becoming thin but still having nearly normal blood gases. In contrast, "blue bloaters," commonly of stocky build, become sufficiently hypoxic that they are obviously cyanotic. The hypoxia causes constriction of pulmonary blood vessels, which leads to pulmonary hypertension and right-sided heart failure. Traditionally, "pink puffers" were associated with emphysema while "blue bloaters" were associated with chronic bronchitis. As usual, things are not that clear-cut. It turns out that patients with the same underlying disease can display either one of these two clinical patterns, and this may depend on a third factor—the strength of their innate respiratory drive. Most COPD patients fall in between these two clinical extremes.

COPD is routinely treated with bronchodilators and corticosteroids in aerosol form (inhalers). Severe dyspnea and hypoxia mandate oxygen use. Surgical treatment for COPD, called *lung volume reduction surgery*, is still highly controversial. In this procedure, part of the grossly enlarged lungs is removed to give the remaining lung tissue room to expand. While this surgery does not prolong life, it can offer certain COPD patients increased exercise capability and a higher quality of life, although at a high cost.

Asthma

Asthma is characterized by episodes of coughing, dyspnea, wheezing, and chest tightness—alone or in combination. Most acute attacks are accompanied by a sense of panic. Although sometimes classed with COPD because it is an obstructive disorder, asthma is marked by acute exacerbations followed by symptom-free periods—that is, the obstruction is *reversible*.

The cause of asthma has been hard to pin down. Initially it was viewed as a consequence of bronchospasm triggered by various factors such as cold air, exercise, or allergens. However, when it was discovered that bronchoconstriction has relatively little effect on air flow through normal lungs, researchers probed more deeply and found that in asthma, active inflammation of the airways comes first. The airway inflammation is an immune response under the control of T_H2 cells, a subset of T lymphocytes that, by secreting certain interleukins, stimulate the production of IgE and recruit inflammatory cells (notably eosinophils) to the site. Once someone has allergic asthma, the inflammation persists even during symptom-free periods and makes the airways hypersensitive to almost any irritant. (It now appears the most common triggers are in the home—the allergens from dust mites, cockroaches, cats, dogs, and fungi.) Once the airway walls are thickened with inflammatory exudate, the effect of bronchospasm is vastly magnified and can dramatically reduce air flow.

About one in ten people in North America suffer from asthma—children more than adults. Over the past 20 years, the number of cases of asthma has risen dramatically, an increase which may now be plateauing. While asthma remains a major health problem, better treatment options have begun to reduce the number of deaths due to asthma. Instead of treating the symptoms of asthma with fast-acting bronchodilators, we now treat the underlying inflammation using inhaled corticosteroids. New approaches to limiting the airway inflammation include antileukotrienes and antibodies against the patient's own IgE class of antibodies.

Tuberculosis

Tuberculosis (TB), the infectious disease caused by the bacterium *Mycobacterium tuberculosis*, is spread by coughing and primarily enters the body in inhaled air. TB mostly affects the lungs but can spread through the lymphatics to affect other organs. One-third of the world's population is infected, but most people never develop active TB because a massive inflammatory and immune response usually contains the primary infection in fibrous, or calcified, nodules (tubercles) in the lungs. However, the bacteria survive in the nodules and when the person's immunity is low, they may break out and cause symptomatic TB, involving fever, night sweats, weight loss, a racking cough, and spitting up blood.

Until the 1930s, TB was responsible for one-third of all deaths among 20- to 45-year-old adults in the U.S. With the advent of antibiotics in the 1940s, this killer was put into retreat and its prevalence declined dramatically. During the mid-1980s, there was an alarming increase in TB due to TB-infected HIV patients. This has now been brought under control and TB rates in the U.S. are again decreasing. Of potential concern are deadly strains of drug-resistant (even multidrug-resistant) TB that develop when treatment is incomplete or inadequate. Such strains are found elsewhere in the world and are becoming more common in North America. Ideal breeding grounds for such strains are shelters for the homeless with their densely packed populations. The TB bacterium grows very slowly and drug therapy entails a 12-month course of antibiotics. The transient nature of shelter populations makes it difficult to track TB patients and ensure they take their medications for the full 12 months. The threat of TB epidemics is so real that health centers in some cities are detaining such patients in sanatoriums against their will for as long as it takes to complete a cure.

Lung Cancer

Lung cancer is the leading cause of cancer death for both men and women in North America, causing more deaths than breast, prostate, and colorectal cancer combined. This is tragic, because lung cancer is largely preventable—nearly 90% of lung cancers are the result of smoking. The cure rate for lung cancer is notoriously low, with most victims dying within one year of diagnosis. The overall five-year survival of those with lung cancer is about 17%. Because lung cancer is aggressive and metastasizes rapidly and widely, most cases are not diagnosed until they are well advanced.

Lung cancer appears to follow closely the oncogene-activating steps outlined in *A Closer Look* in Chapter 4. Ordinarily, nasal hairs, sticky mucus, and cilia do a fine job of protecting the lungs from chemical and biological irritants, but when one smokes, these devices are overwhelmed and eventually stop functioning. In particular, smoking paralyzes the cilia

22

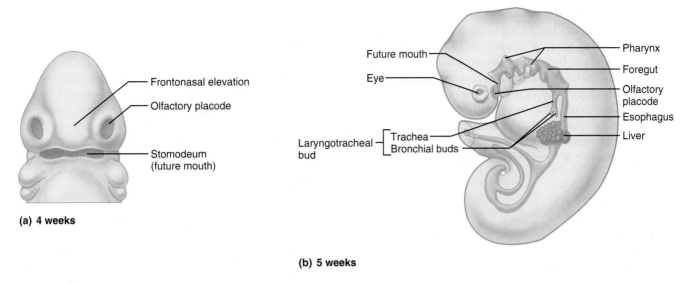

(a) 4 weeks

(b) 5 weeks

FIGURE 22.29 **Embryonic development of the respiratory system.**
(a) Anterior superficial view of the embryo's head. **(b)** Left lateral view of the
developing lower respiratory passageway mucosae.

that clear mucus from the airways, allowing irritants and pathogens to accumulate. The "cocktail" of free radicals and other carcinogens in tobacco smoke eventually translates into lung cancer.

The three most common types of lung cancer are (1) **squamous cell carcinoma** (25–30% of cases), which arises in the epithelium of the bronchi or their larger subdivisions and tends to form masses that may cavitate (hollow out) and bleed, (2) **adeno-carcinoma** (about 40%), which originates in peripheral lung areas as solitary nodules that develop from bronchial glands and alveolar cells, and (3) **small cell carcinoma** (about 20%), which contains round lymphocyte-sized cells that originate in the main bronchi and grow aggressively in small grapelike clusters within the mediastinum. Subsequent metastasis from the mediastinum is especially rapid. Some small cell carcinomas cause problems beyond their effects on the lungs because they become ectopic sites of hormone production. For example, some secrete ACTH (leading to Cushing's syndrome) or ADH (which results in diabetes insipidus, see p. 617).

Complete removal of the diseased lung has the greatest potential for prolonging life and providing a cure. However, this choice is open to few lung cancer patients because the cancer has often metastasized before it is discovered. In most cases, radiation therapy and chemotherapy are the only options, but these have low success rates. Fortunately, there are several new therapies on the horizon. These include (1) antibodies that target specific growth factors or other molecules required by the tumor or that deliver toxic agents directly to the tumor, (2) cancer vaccines to stimulate the immune system to fight the tumor, and (3) various forms of gene therapy to replace the defective genes that make tumor cells divide continuously. As clinical trials progress, we will learn which of these approaches is most effective.

Developmental Aspects of the Respiratory System

Because embryos develop in a cephalocaudal (head-to-tail) direction, the upper respiratory structures appear first. By the fourth week of development, two thickened plates of ectoderm, the **olfactory placodes** (plak′ōds), are present on the anterior aspect of the head (Figure 22.29). These quickly invaginate to form **olfactory pits** that form the nasal cavities. The olfactory pits then extend posteriorly to connect with the developing pharynx, which forms at the same time from the endodermal germ layer.

The epithelium of the lower respiratory organs develops as an outpocketing of the foregut endoderm, which becomes the pharyngeal mucosa. This protrusion, called the **laryngotracheal bud**, is present by the fifth week of development. The proximal part of the bud forms the tracheal lining, and its distal end splits and forms the mucosae of the bronchi and all their subdivisions, including (eventually) the lung alveoli. Mesoderm covers these endoderm-derived linings and forms the walls of the respiratory passageways and the stroma of the lungs. By 28 weeks, the respiratory system has developed sufficiently to allow a baby born prematurely to breathe on its own. As noted earlier, infants born before this time tend to exhibit infant respiratory distress syndrome resulting from inadequate surfactant production.

22

During fetal life, the lungs are filled with fluid and all respiratory exchanges are made by the placenta. Vascular shunts cause circulating blood to largely bypass the lungs (see Chapter 28, p. 1131). At birth, the fluid-filled pathway empties, and the respiratory passageways fill with air. As the P_{CO_2} in the baby's blood rises, the respiratory centers are excited, causing the baby to take its first breath. The alveoli inflate and begin to function in gas exchange, but it is nearly two weeks before the lungs are fully inflated.

◢ HOMEOSTATIC IMBALANCE

Important birth defects of the respiratory system include *cleft palate* (described in Chapter 7) and *cystic fibrosis*. **Cystic fibrosis (CF),** the most common lethal genetic disease in North America, strikes in one out of every 2400 births. CF causes secretion of abnormally viscous mucus that clogs the respiratory passages, providing a breeding ground for airborne bacteria that predisposes the child to respiratory infections. It appears that infection of CF victims' lungs with the bacterium *Pseudomonas aeruginosa* trips a genetic switch that causes the disabled cells to churn out oceans of abnormal mucin (the primary component of mucus). The bacteria then feed on the stagnant pools of mucus and keep sending signals to the cells to make more. Toxins released by the bacteria and the local inflammatory reaction set up by the immune response both damage the lungs. Unable to reach the bacteria embedded in the mucus, the immune cells begin to attack the lung tissue, turning the air sacs into bloated cysts. Repeated cycles of infection, chronic inflammation, and resulting tissue damage eventually result in such extensive damage that it can be treated only by a lung transplant. The disease also impairs food digestion by clogging ducts that deliver pancreatic enzymes and bile to the small intestine, and sweat glands of CF patients produce an extremely salty perspiration.

At the root of CF is a faulty gene that codes for the *CFTR* (cystic fibrosis transmembrane conductance regulator) *protein.* The normal CFTR protein works as a membrane channel to control Cl^- flow in and out of cells. In those with the mutated gene, CFTR lacks an essential amino acid and so it gets "stuck" in the endoplasmic reticulum, unable to reach the membrane and perform its normal role. Consequently, less Cl^- is secreted and less water follows, resulting in the thick mucus typical of CF.

Conventional therapy for CF has been mucus-dissolving drugs, "clapping" the chest to loosen the thick mucus, and antibiotics to prevent infection. The basic goal of CF research is to restore normal salt and water movements by (1) using disabled cold viruses to carry normal CFTR genes into respiratory tract mucosa cells, (2) prodding another channel protein to take over the duties of transporting Cl^-, and (3) developing techniques to free the CFTR protein from the ER. A drug derived from the curry spice turmeric appears to do just that, and is just beginning clinical trials. Suppressing the inflammatory response in the lungs is another goal. Among anti-inflammatory agents being tested is a fatty acid found in fish oils, docosahexanoic acid (DHA). Alone or in combination, these therapies provide new hope to patients with CF. ●

The respiratory rate is highest in newborn infants (40–80 respirations per minute). At five years of age it is around 25 per minute, and in adults it is between 12 and 18 per minute. In old age, the rate often increases again. At birth, only about one-sixth of the final number of alveoli are present. The lungs continue to mature and more alveoli are formed until young adulthood. However, if smoking begins in the early teens, the lungs never completely mature, and those additional alveoli are lost forever.

In infants, the ribs take a nearly horizontal course. Thus, infants rely almost entirely on descent of the diaphragm to increase thoracic volume for inspiration. By the second year, the ribs are positioned more obliquely, and the adult form of breathing is established.

◢ HOMEOSTATIC IMBALANCE

Most respiratory system problems that occur are the result of external factors—for example, viral or bacterial infections or obstruction of the trachea by a piece of food. For many years, bacterial pneumonia was one of the worst killers in North America. Antibiotics have greatly decreased its lethality, but it is still a dangerous disease, particularly in the elderly. By far the most problematic diseases *at present* are those described earlier: COPD, asthma, lung cancer, and multidrug-resistant tuberculosis. ●

The maximum amount of oxygen we can use during aerobic metabolism, $\dot{V}_{O_{2max}}$, declines about 9% per decade in inactive people beginning in their mid-20s. In those that remain active, $\dot{V}_{O_{2max}}$ still declines but much less. As we age, the thoracic wall becomes more rigid and the lungs gradually lose their elasticity, resulting in a decreasing ability to ventilate the lungs. Vital capacity declines by about one-third by the age of 70. Blood O_2 levels decline slightly, and many old people tend to become hypoxic during sleep and exhibit *sleep apnea* (temporary cessation of breathing during sleep).

The number of glands in the nasal mucosa decreases as does blood flow to this mucosa. Thus, the nose dries and produces a thick mucus that makes us want to clear our throat. Additionally, many of the respiratory system's protective mechanisms become less effective with age. Ciliary activity of the mucosa decreases, and the macrophages in the lungs become sluggish. The net result is that the elderly are more at risk for respiratory tract infections, particularly pneumonia and influenza.

■ ■ ■

Lungs, bronchial tree, heart, and connecting blood vessels—together, these organs fashion a remarkable system that ensures that blood is oxygenated and relieved of carbon dioxide and that all tissue cells have access to these services. Although the cooperation of the respiratory and cardiovascular systems is obvious, all organ systems of the body depend on the functioning of the respiratory system, as summarized in *Making Connections* on pp. 876–877.

Related Clinical Terms

Acute respiratory distress syndrome (ARDS) A dangerous lung condition that can develop after severe illness or injury to the body. Neutrophils leave the body's capillaries in large numbers and then secrete chemicals that increase capillary permeability. The capillary-rich lungs are heavily affected. As the lungs fill with the fluids of edema, the patient suffocates. Even with mechanical ventilation, ARDS is hard to control and often lethal.

Adenoidectomy (adenotonsillectomy) Surgical removal of an infected pharyngeal tonsil (adenoids).

Aspiration (as″pĭ-ra′shun) (1) The act of inhaling or drawing something into the lungs or respiratory passages. Pathological aspiration in which vomit or excessive mucus is drawn into the lungs may occur when a person is unconscious or anesthetized; turning the head to one side is preventive. (2) Withdrawal of fluid by suction (use of an aspirator); done during surgery to keep an area free of blood or other body fluids; mucus is aspirated from the trachea of tracheotomy patients.

Bronchoscopy (*scopy* = viewing) Use of a viewing tube inserted through the nose or mouth to examine the internal surface of the main bronchi in the lung. Forceps attached to the tip of the tube can remove trapped objects or take samples of mucus for examination.

Cheyne-Stokes breathing (chān′stōks) Abnormal breathing pattern sometimes seen just before death (the "death rattle") and in people with combined neurological and cardiac disorders. It consists of bursts of tidal volume breaths (increasing and then decreasing in depth) alternating with periods of apnea. Trauma and hypoxia of the brain stem centers, as well as P_{CO_2} imbalances between arterial blood and cerebrospinal fluid, may be causative factors.

Deviated septum Condition in which the nasal septum takes a more lateral course than usual and may obstruct breathing; often manifests in old age or from nose trauma.

Endotracheal tube A thin plastic tube threaded into the trachea through the nose or mouth; used to deliver oxygen to patients who are breathing inadequately, in a coma, or under anesthesia.

Epistaxis (ep″ĭ-stak′sis; *epistazo* = to bleed at the nose) Nosebleed; commonly follows trauma to the nose or excessive nose blowing. Most nasal bleeding is from the highly vascularized anterior septum and can be stopped by pinching the nostrils closed or packing them with cotton.

Nasal polyps Mushroomlike benign neoplasms of the nasal mucosa; sometimes caused by infections, but most often cause is unknown; may block airflow.

Orthopnea (or″thop-ne′ah; *ortho* = straight, upright) Inability to breathe in the horizontal (lying down) position.

Otorhinolaryngology (o″to-ri″no-lar″in-gol′o-je; *oto* = ear; *rhino* = nose) Branch of medicine that deals with diagnosis and treatment of diseases of the ears, nose, and throat.

Pneumonia Infectious inflammation of the lungs, in which fluid accumulates in the alveoli; the seventh most common cause of death in the United States. Most of the more than 50 different varieties of pneumonia are viral or bacterial.

Pulmonary embolism Obstruction of the pulmonary artery or one of its branches by an embolus (most often a blood clot that has been carried from the lower limbs and through the right side of the heart into the pulmonary circulation). Symptoms are chest pain, productive bloody cough, tachycardia, and rapid, shallow breathing. Can cause sudden death unless treated quickly; usual treatment is oxygen by mask, pain relievers, and anticoagulant drugs. For severe cases, clot busters (thrombolytic drugs) are also used.

Stuttering A problem of voice production in which the first syllable of words is repeated in "machine-gun" fashion. Primarily a problem with neural control of the larynx and other voice-producing structures. Many stutterers become fluent when whispering or singing, both of which involve a change in the manner of vocalization.

Sudden infant death syndrome (SIDS) Unexpected death of an apparently healthy infant during sleep. Commonly called crib death, SIDS is one of the most frequent causes of death in infants under 1 year old. Believed to be a problem of immaturity of the respiratory control centers. Most cases occur in infants placed in a prone position (on their abdomen) to sleep—a position which may result in hypoxia and hypercapnia due to rebreathing exhaled (CO_2-rich) air. Since 1992, a campaign recommending placing infants on their back to sleep has led to a decline of 40% or more in the incidence of SIDS in the U.S.

Tracheotomy (tra″ke-ot′o-me) Surgical opening of the trachea; done to provide an alternate route for air to reach the lungs when more superior respiratory passageways are obstructed (as by food or a crushed larynx).

MAKING CONNECTIONS

SYSTEMS CONNECTIONS: Homeostatic Interrelationships Between the Respiratory System and Other Body Systems

Integumentary System
- Respiratory system provides oxygen; disposes of carbon dioxide
- Skin protects respiratory system organs by forming surface barriers

Skeletal System
- Respiratory system provides oxygen; disposes of carbon dioxide
- Bones protect lungs and bronchi by enclosure

Muscular System
- Respiratory system provides oxygen needed for muscle activity; disposes of carbon dioxide
- Activity of the diaphragm and intercostal muscles essential for producing volume changes that lead to pulmonary ventilation; regular exercise increases respiratory efficiency

Nervous System
- Respiratory system provides oxygen needed for normal neuronal activity; disposes of carbon dioxide
- Medullary and pons centers regulate respiratory rate and depth; stretch receptors in lungs and chemoreceptors provide feedback

Endocrine System
- Respiratory system provides oxygen; disposes of carbon dioxide; angiotensin converting enzyme in lungs converts antiotensin I to angiotensin II
- Epinephrine dilates the bronchioles; testosterone promotes laryngeal enlargement in pubertal males; glucocorticoids promote surfactant production

Cardiovascular System
- Respiratory system provides oxygen; disposes of carbon dioxide; carbon dioxide present in blood as HCO_3^- and H_2CO_3 contributes to blood buffering
- Blood is the transport medium for respiratory gases

Lymphatic System/Immunity
- Respiratory system provides oxygen; disposes of carbon dioxide; tonsils in pharynx house immune cells
- Lymphatic system helps to maintain blood volume required for respiratory gas transport; immune system protects respiratory organs from bacteria, bacterial toxins, viruses, protozoa, fungi, and cancer

Digestive System
- Respiratory system provides oxygen; disposes of carbon dioxide
- Digestive system provides nutrients needed by respiratory system organs

Urinary System
- Respiratory system provides oxygen; disposes of carbon dioxide to provide short-term pH homeostasis
- Kidneys dispose of metabolic wastes of respiratory system organs (other than carbon dioxide) and maintain long-term pH homeostasis

Reproductive System
- Respiratory system provides oxygen; disposes of carbon dioxide

22

THE RESPIRATORY SYSTEM and Interrelationships with the Cardiovascular, Lymphatic/Immune, and Muscular Systems

Every day we inhale and exhale nearly 10,000 L of air. This accomplishes two things—it supplies the body with the oxygen it needs to oxidize food and release energy, and it expels carbon dioxide, the major waste product of that process. As crucial as breathing is, most of us don't think very often about the importance of having fresh air on call. But the phenomenon of gasping for air is familiar to every athlete. Indeed, the respiratory rate of a competitive swimmer may jump to over 40 breaths/min and the amount of air inhaled per breath may soar from the usual 500 ml to as much as 6 to 7 L.

The respiratory system is beautifully engineered for its function. Its alveoli are flushed with new air more than 15,000 times each day and the alveolar walls are so indescribably thin that red blood cells moving single-file through the pulmonary capillaries can make the gaseous "swaps" with the air-filled alveoli within a fraction of a second. Although every cell in the body depends on this system for the oxygen it needs to live, the respiratory system interactions that we will consider here are those it has with the cardiovascular, lymphatic, and muscular systems.

Cardiovascular System

The interaction between the respiratory and cardiovascular systems is so intimate that these two systems are inseparable. Respiratory system organs, as important as they are, can make only the external gas exchanges, those that occur in the lungs. Although all body cells depend on the respiratory system to provide needed oxygen, they pick up that oxygen not from the lungs but from the blood. Thus, without blood to act as the intermediary and the heart and blood vessels to act as the hardware to pump the blood around the body, all the efforts of the respiratory system would be useless.

In turn, angiotensin converting enzyme on lung capillary endothelium plays an important role in blood pressure regulation.

Lymphatic System/Immunity

Of all body systems, only the respiratory system is completely exposed to the external environment (yes, the skin is exposed but its exposed parts are all dead). Because air contains a rich mix of potentially dangerous inhabitants (bacteria, viruses, fungi, asbestos fibers, etc.), the respiratory system is continuously at risk for infection or damage from external agents. Lymphoid outposts help protect the respiratory tract and enhance the defenses (cilia, mucus) that the respiratory system itself erects. Particularly well situated to apprehend intruders at the oral-nasal-pharynx junction are the palatine, pharyngeal, lingual, and tubal tonsils. Their macrophages engulf foreign antigens and they provide sites where lymphocytes are sensitized to mount immune responses.

Muscular System

Skeletal muscle cells, like other body cells, need oxygen to live. The notable part of this interaction is that most respiratory compensations that occur service increased muscular activity. (It is difficult to think of incidents where this is not the case—the exceptions concern disease conditions.) When we are at rest, the respiratory system operates at basal levels, but any time physical activity becomes more vigorous, the respiratory rhythm picks up the beat to match supply with need and to maintain the acid-base balance of the blood.

Respiratory System

Case study: Barbara Joley was in the bus that was hit broadside. When she was freed from the wreckage, she was deeply cyanotic and her respiration had stopped. Her heart was still beating, but her pulse was fast and thready. The emergency medical technician reported that when Barbara was found, her head was cocked at a peculiar angle and it looked like she had a fracture at the level of the C_2 vertebra. The following questions refer to these observations.

1. How might the "peculiar" head position explain Barbara's cessation of breathing?

2. What procedures (do you think) should have been initiated immediately by the emergency personnel?

3. Why is Barbara cyanotic? Explain cyanosis.

4. Assuming that Barbara survives, how will her accident affect her lifestyle in the future?

Barbara survived transport to the hospital and notes recorded at admission included the following observations.

- Right thorax compressed; ribs 7 to 9 fractured
- Right lung atelectasis

Relative to these notes:

5. What is atelectasis and why is only the right lung affected?

6. How do the recorded injuries relate to the atelectasis?

7. What treatment will be done to reverse the atelectasis? What is the rationale for this treatment?

(Answers in Appendix G)

Chapter Summary

Media study tools that could provide you additional help in reviewing specific key topics of Chapter 22 are referenced below.

IP = *InterActive Physiology*

1. Respiration involves four processes: ventilation, external respiration, transport of respiratory gases in the blood, and internal respiration. Both the respiratory system and the cardiovascular system are involved in respiration.

Functional Anatomy of the Respiratory System (pp. 831–846)

2. Respiratory system organs are divided functionally into conducting zone structures (nose to bronchioles), which filter, warm, and moisten incoming air; and respiratory zone structures (respiratory bronchioles to alveoli), where gas exchanges occur.

The Nose and Paranasal Sinuses (pp. 831–835)

3. The nose provides an airway for respiration; warms, moistens, and cleanses incoming air; and houses the olfactory receptors.

4. The external nose is shaped by bone and cartilage plates. The nasal cavity, which opens to the exterior, is divided by the nasal septum. Paranasal sinuses and nasolacrimal ducts drain into the nasal cavities.

The Pharynx (p. 835)

5. The pharynx extends from the base of the skull to the level of C_6. The nasopharynx is an air conduit; the oropharynx and laryngopharynx are common passageways for food and air. Tonsils are found in the oropharynx and nasopharynx.

The Larynx (pp. 835–838)

6. The larynx, or voice box, contains the vocal folds (cords). It also provides a patent airway and serves as a switching mechanism to route food and air into the proper channels.

7. The epiglottis prevents food or liquids from entering the respiratory channels during swallowing.

The Trachea (pp. 838–840)

8. The trachea extends from the larynx to the main bronchi. The trachea is reinforced by C-shaped cartilage rings, which keep the trachea patent, and its mucosa is ciliated.

The Bronchi and Subdivisions: The Bronchial Tree (pp. 840–842)

9. The right and left main bronchi run into their respective lungs, within which they continue to subdivide into smaller and smaller passageways.

10. The terminal bronchioles lead into respiratory zone structures: respiratory bronchioles, alveolar ducts, alveolar sacs, and finally alveoli. Gas exchange occurs in the alveoli, across the respiratory membrane.

11. As the respiratory conduits become smaller, cartilage is reduced in amount and finally lost; the mucosa thins, and smooth muscle in the walls increases.

IP Respiratory System; Topic: Anatomy Review: Respiratory Structures, p. 6.

The Lungs and Pleurae (pp. 842–846)

12. The lungs, the paired organs of gas exchange, flank the mediastinum in the thoracic cavity. Each is suspended in its own pleural cavity via its root and has a base, an apex, and medial and costal surfaces. The right lung has three lobes; the left has two.

13. The lungs are primarily air passageways/chambers, supported by an elastic connective tissue stroma.

14. The pulmonary arteries carry blood returned from the systemic circulation to the lungs, where gas exchange occurs. The pulmonary veins return newly oxygenated (and most bronchial venous) blood back to the heart to be distributed throughout the body. The bronchial arteries provide the nutrient blood supply of the lungs.

15. The parietal pleura lines the thoracic wall and mediastinum; the visceral pleura covers external lung surfaces. Pleural fluid reduces friction during breathing movements.

IP Respiratory System; Topic: Anatomy Review: Respiratory Structures, pp. 1–5.

Mechanics of Breathing (pp. 846–854)

Pressure Relationships in the Thoracic Cavity (pp. 846–847)

1. Intrapulmonary pressure is the pressure within the alveoli. Intrapleural pressure is the pressure within the pleural cavity; it is always negative relative to intrapulmonary pressures.

IP Respiratory System; Topic: Pulmonary Ventilation, pp. 7–9.

Pulmonary Ventilation: Inspiration and Expiration (pp. 847–849)

2. Gases travel from an area of higher pressure to an area of lower pressure.

3. Inspiration occurs when the diaphragm and external intercostal muscles contract, increasing the dimensions (and volume) of the thorax. As the intrapulmonary pressure drops, air rushes into the lungs until the intrapulmonary and atmospheric pressures are equalized.

4. Expiration is largely passive, occurring as the inspiratory muscles relax and the lungs recoil. When intrapulmonary pressure exceeds atmospheric pressure, gases flow from the lungs.

IP Respiratory System; Topic: Pulmonary Ventilation, pp. 3–6, 11–13.

Physical Factors Influencing Pulmonary Ventilation (pp. 849–851)

5. Friction in the air passageways causes resistance, which decreases air passage and causes breathing movements to become more strenuous. The greatest resistance to air flow occurs in the midsize bronchi.

6. Surface tension of alveolar fluid acts to reduce alveolar size and collapse the alveoli. This tendency is resisted in part by surfactant.

7. Premature infants have problems keeping their lungs inflated owing to the lack of surfactant in their alveoli, resulting in infant respiratory distress syndrome (IRDS). Surfactant formation begins late in fetal development.

8. Total respiratory compliance depends on elasticity of lung tissue and flexibility of the bony thorax. When compliance is impaired, inspiration becomes more difficult.

IP Respiratory System; Topic: Pulmonary Ventilation, pp. 14–18.

Respiratory Volumes and Pulmonary Function Tests (pp. 851–853)

9. The four respiratory volumes are tidal, inspiratory reserve, expiratory reserve, and residual. The four respiratory

capacities are vital, functional residual, inspiratory, and total lung. Respiratory volumes and capacities may be measured by spirometry.

10. Anatomical dead space is the air-filled volume (about 150 ml) of the conducting passageways. If alveoli become nonfunctional in gas exchange, their volume is added to the anatomical dead space, and the sum is the total dead space.

11. Alveolar ventilation is the best index of ventilation efficiency because it accounts for anatomical dead space.

$$AVR = (TV - \text{dead space}) \times \text{respiratory rate}$$

12. The FVC and FEV tests, which determine the rate at which VC air can be expelled, are particularly valuable in distinguishing between obstructive and restrictive disease.

Nonrespiratory Air Movements (p. 854)

13. Nonrespiratory air movements are voluntary or reflex actions that clear the respiratory passageways or express emotions.

Gas Exchanges Between the Blood, Lungs, and Tissues (pp. 854–858)

Basic Properties of Gases (pp. 854–855)

1. Dalton's law states that each gas in a mixture of gases exerts pressure in proportion to its percentage in the total mixture.

2. Henry's law states that the amount of gas that will dissolve in a liquid is proportional to the partial pressure of the gas. Solubility of the gas in the liquid and the temperature are other important factors.

IP Respiratory System; Topic: Gas Exchange, pp. 1–6.

Composition of Alveolar Gas (p. 855)

3. Alveolar gas contains more carbon dioxide and water vapor and considerably less oxygen than atmospheric air.

External Respiration: Pulmonary Gas Exchange (pp. 855–858)

4. External respiration is the process of gas exchange that occurs in the lungs. Oxygen enters the pulmonary capillaries; carbon dioxide leaves the blood and enters the alveoli. Factors influencing this process include the partial pressure gradients, the thickness of the respiratory membrane, surface area available, and the matching of alveolar ventilation and pulmonary perfusion.

Internal Respiration: Capillary Gas Exchange in the Body Tissues (p. 858)

5. Internal respiration is the gas exchange that occurs between the systemic capillaries and the tissues. Carbon dioxide enters the blood, and oxygen leaves the blood and enters the tissues.

IP Respiratory System; Topic: Gas Exchange, pp. 6–11, 15–16.

Transport of Respiratory Gases by Blood (pp. 858–863)

Oxygen Transport (pp. 858–861)

1. Molecular oxygen is carried bound to hemoglobin in the blood cells. The amount of oxygen bound to hemoglobin depends on the P_{O_2} and P_{CO_2} of blood, blood pH, the presence of BPG, and temperature. A small amount of oxygen gas is transported dissolved in plasma.

2. Hypoxia occurs when inadequate amounts of oxygen are delivered to body tissues. When this occurs, the skin and mucosae may become cyanotic.

Carbon Dioxide Transport (pp. 861–863)

3. CO_2 is transported in the blood dissolved in plasma, chemically bound to hemoglobin, and (primarily) as bicarbonate ion in plasma. Loading and unloading of O_2 and CO_2 are mutually beneficial.

4. Accumulation of CO_2 leads to decreased pH; depletion of CO_2 from blood leads to increased blood pH.

IP Respiratory System; Topic: Gas Transport, pp. 1–15.

Control of Respiration (pp. 863–869)

Neural Mechanisms and Generation of Breathing Rhythm (pp. 863–865)

1. Medullary respiratory centers are the dorsal and ventral respiratory groups. The ventral respiratory group is likely responsible for the rhythmicity of breathing.

2. The pontine respiratory centers influence the activity of the medullary respiratory centers.

Factors Influencing Breathing Rate and Depth (pp. 865–869)

3. Important chemical factors modifying baseline respiratory rate and depth are arterial levels of CO_2, H^+, and O_2.

4. An increasing P_{CO_2} is the most powerful respiratory stimulant. It acts (via release of H^+ in the CSF) on the central chemoreceptors to cause a reflexive increase in the rate and depth of breathing. Hypocapnia depresses respiration and results in decreased ventilation and, possibly, apnea.

5. Arterial P_{O_2} levels below 60 mm Hg constitute the hypoxic drive.

6. Decreased pH and a decline in blood P_{O_2} act on peripheral chemoreceptors and enhance the response to CO_2.

7. Emotions, pain, body temperature changes, and other stressors can alter respiration by acting through hypothalamic centers. Respiration can also be controlled voluntarily for short periods.

8. Pulmonary irritant reflexes are initiated by dust, mucus, fumes, and pollutants.

9. The inflation (Hering-Breuer) reflex is a protective reflex initiated by extreme overinflation of the lungs; it acts to terminate inspiration.

IP Respiratory System; Topic: Control of Respiration, pp. 6–14.

Respiratory Adjustments (pp. 869–870)

Adjustments During Exercise (pp. 869–870)

1. As exercise begins, there is an abrupt increase in ventilation (hyperpnea) followed by a more gradual increase. When exercise stops, there is an abrupt decrease in ventilation followed by a gradual decline to baseline values.

2. P_{O_2}, P_{CO_2}, and blood pH remain quite constant during exercise and hence do not appear to account for changes in ventilation. Inputs from higher centers and proprioceptors may contribute.

Adjustments at High Altitude (p. 870)

3. At high altitudes, there is a decrease in arterial P_{O_2} and hemoglobin saturation levels because of the decrease in barometric pressure compared to sea level. Hyperventilation helps restore P_{O_2} to physiological levels.

4. Long-term acclimatization involves increased erythropoiesis.

Homeostatic Imbalances of the Respiratory System (pp. 870–873)

1. Two major respiratory disorders are COPD (emphysema and chronic bronchitis) and lung cancer; a significant cause is cigarette smoking. A third major disorder is asthma. Multidrug-resistant tuberculosis may become a major health problem.

Chronic Obstructive Pulmonary Disease (pp. 871–872)

2. COPD is characterized by an irreversible decrease in the ability to force air out of the lungs. Patients may become cyanotic as a result of chronic hypoxia.

3. Emphysema is characterized by permanent enlargement and destruction of alveoli. The lungs lose their elasticity, and expiration becomes an active process.

4. Chronic bronchitis is characterized by excessive mucus production in the lower respiratory passageways, which severely impairs ventilation and gas exchange.

Asthma (p. 872)

5. Asthma is a reversible obstructive condition caused by an immune response that causes its victims to wheeze and gasp for air as their inflamed respiratory passages constrict. It is marked by exacerbations and periods of relief from symptoms.

Tuberculosis (p. 872)

6. Tuberculosis (TB), an infectious disease caused by an airborne bacterium, mainly affects the lungs. Although most infected individuals remain asymptomatic by walling off the bacteria in tubercles, disease symptoms ensue when immunity is depressed. Some patients' failure to complete drug therapy have produced multidrug-resistant TB strains.

Lung Cancer (pp. 872–873)

7. Lung cancer, promoted by free radicals and other carcinogens, is extremely aggressive and metastasizes rapidly.

Developmental Aspects of the Respiratory System (pp. 873–875)

1. The superior respiratory system mucosa develops from the invagination of the ectodermal olfactory placodes; that of the inferior passageways develops from an outpocketing of the endodermal foregut lining. Mesoderm forms the walls of the respiratory conduits and the lung stroma.

2. Cystic fibrosis (CF), the most common fatal hereditary disease, results from an abnormal CFTR protein that fails to form a chloride channel. The result is thick mucus which clogs respiratory passages and invites infection.

3. With age, the thorax becomes more rigid, the lungs become less elastic, and vital capacity declines. In addition, sleep apnea becomes more common, and respiratory system protective mechanisms are less effective.

Review Questions

Multiple Choice/Matching

(Some questions have more than one correct answer. Select the best answer or answers from the choices given.)

1. Cutting the phrenic nerves will result in (a) air entering the pleural cavity, (b) paralysis of the diaphragm, (c) stimulation of the diaphragmatic reflex, (d) paralysis of the epiglottis.

2. Which of the following laryngeal cartilages is/are not paired? (a) epiglottis, (b) arytenoids, (c) cricoid, (d) cuneiform, (e) corniculate.

3. Under ordinary circumstances, the inflation reflex is initiated by (a) the inspiratory center, (b) the ventral respiratory group, (c) overinflation of the alveoli and bronchioles, (d) the pontine respiratory centers.

4. The detergent-like substance that keeps the alveoli from collapsing between breaths because it reduces the surface tension of the water film in the alveoli is called (a) lecithin, (b) bile, (c) surfactant, (d) reluctant.

5. Which of the following determines the *direction* of gas movement? (a) solubility in water, (b) partial pressure gradient, (c) temperature, (d) molecular weight and size of the gas molecule.

6. When the inspiratory muscles contract, (a) the size of the thoracic cavity is increased in diameter, (b) the size of the thoracic cavity is increased in length, (c) the volume of the thoracic cavity is decreased, (d) the size of the thoracic cavity is increased in both length and diameter.

7. The nutrient blood supply of the lungs is provided by (a) the pulmonary arteries, (b) the aorta, (c) the pulmonary veins, (d) the bronchial arteries.

8. Oxygen and carbon dioxide are exchanged in the lungs and through all cell membranes by (a) active transport, (b) diffusion, (c) filtration, (d) osmosis.

9. Which of the following would not normally be treated by 100% oxygen therapy? (Choose all that apply.) (a) anoxia, (b) carbon monoxide poisoning, (c) respiratory crisis in an emphysema patient, (d) eupnea.

10. Most oxygen carried in the blood is (a) in solution in the plasma, (b) combined with plasma proteins, (c) chemically combined with the heme in red blood cells, (d) in solution in the red blood cells.

11. Which of the following has the greatest stimulating effect on the respiratory center in the brain? (a) oxygen, (b) carbon dioxide, (c) calcium, (d) willpower.

12. In mouth-to-mouth artificial respiration, the rescuer blows air from his or her own respiratory system into that of the victim. Which of the following statements are correct?
(1) Expansion of the victim's lungs is brought about by blowing air in at higher than atmospheric pressure (positive-pressure breathing).
(2) During inflation of the lungs, the intrapleural pressure increases.
(3) This technique will not work if the victim has a hole in the chest wall, even if the lungs are intact.
(4) Expiration during this procedure depends on the elasticity of the alveolar and thoracic walls.
(a) all of these, (b) 1, 2, 4, (c) 1, 2, 3, (d) 1, 4.

13. A baby holding its breath will (a) have brain cells damaged because of low blood oxygen levels, (b) automatically start to breathe again when the carbon dioxide levels in the blood reach a high enough value, (c) suffer heart damage because of increased pressure in the carotid sinus and aortic arch areas, (d) be called a "blue baby."

14. Under ordinary circumstances, which of the following blood components is of no physiological significance? (a) bicarbonate ions, (b) carbaminohemoglobin, (c) nitrogen, (d) chloride.

15. Damage to which of the following would most likely result in cessation of breathing? (a) the pontine respiratory group, (b) the ventral respiratory group of the medulla, (c) the stretch receptors in the lungs, (d) the dorsal respiratory group of the medulla.

16. The bulk of carbon dioxide is carried (a) chemically combined with the amino acids of hemoglobin as carbaminohemoglobin in the red blood cells, (b) as the ion HCO_3^- in the plasma after first entering the red blood cell, (c) as carbonic acid in the plasma, (d) chemically combined with the heme portion of Hb.

Short Answer Essay Questions

17. Trace the route of air from the external nares to an alveolus. Name subdivisions of organs where applicable, and differentiate between conducting and respiratory zone structures.

18. (a) Why is it important that the trachea is reinforced with cartilage rings? (b) Of what advantage is it that the rings are incomplete posteriorly?

19. Briefly explain the anatomical "reason" why most men have deeper voices than boys or women.

20. The lungs are mostly passageways and elastic tissue. (a) What is the role of the elastic tissue? (b) Of the passageways?

21. Describe the functional relationships between volume changes and gas flow into and out of the lungs.

22. What is it about the structure of the respiratory membrane that makes the alveoli ideal sites for gas exchange?

23. Discuss how airway resistance, lung compliance, and alveolar surface tension influence pulmonary ventilation.

24. (a) Differentiate clearly between minute respiratory volume and alveolar ventilation rate. (b) Which provides a more accurate measure of ventilatory efficiency, and why?

25. State Dalton's law of partial pressures and Henry's law.

26. (a) Define hyperventilation. (b) If you hyperventilate, do you retain or expel more carbon dioxide? (c) What effect does hyperventilation have on blood pH?

27. Describe age-related changes in respiratory function.

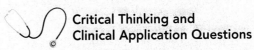

Critical Thinking and Clinical Application Questions

1. Harry, the swimmer with the fastest time on the Springfield College swim team, routinely hyperventilates before a meet, as he says, "to sock some more oxygen into my lungs so I can swim longer without having to breathe." First of all, what basic fact about oxygen loading has Harry forgotten (a lapse leading to false thinking)? Second, how is Harry jeopardizing not only his time but his life?

2. A member of the "Blues" gang was rushed into an emergency room after receiving a knife wound in the left side of his thorax. The diagnosis was pneumothorax and a collapsed lung. Explain exactly (a) why the lung collapsed, and (b) why only one lung (not both) collapsed.

3. A surgeon removed three adjacent bronchopulmonary segments from the left lung of a patient with TB. Almost half of the lung was removed, yet there was no severe bleeding, and relatively few blood vessels had to be cauterized (closed off). Why was the surgery so easy to perform?

4. After a week of scuba diving in the Bahamas, Mary Ann boards an airplane. During her flight home, she develops aching joints, nausea, and dyspnea, which resolve upon landing. During the flight, the cabin pressure was equivalent to an altitude of 8000 feet. Explain her problems.

22

CHAPTER 23

The Digestive System

PART 1: OVERVIEW OF THE DIGESTIVE SYSTEM (pp. 883–889)

1. Describe the function of the digestive system, and differentiate between organs of the alimentary canal and accessory digestive organs.

2. List and define the major processes occurring during digestive system activity.

3. Describe the location and function of the peritoneum. Define retroperitoneal and name the retroperitoneal organs.

4. Describe the tissue composition and the general function of each of the four layers of the alimentary canal.

PART 2: FUNCTIONAL ANATOMY OF THE DIGESTIVE SYSTEM (pp. 889–927)

5. Describe the anatomy and basic function of each organ and accessory organ of the alimentary canal.

6. Explain the dental formula and differentiate clearly between deciduous and permanent teeth.

7. Describe the composition and functions of saliva, and explain how salivation is regulated.

8. Describe the mechanisms of chewing and swallowing.

9. Identify structural modifications of the wall of the stomach and small intestine that enhance the digestive process in these regions.

10. Describe the composition of gastric juice, name the cell types responsible for secreting its components, and indicate the importance of each component in stomach activity.

11. Explain regulation of gastric secretion and stomach motility.

12. Describe the function of intestinal hormones and paracrines.

13. State the roles of bile and of pancreatic juice in digestion.

14. Describe how entry of pancreatic juice and bile into the small intestine is regulated.

15. List the major functions of the large intestine, and describe the regulation of defecation.

PART 3: PHYSIOLOGY OF CHEMICAL DIGESTION AND ABSORPTION (pp. 927–933)

16. List the enzymes involved in chemical digestion; name the foodstuffs on which they act and the end products of protein, fat, carbohydrate, and nucleic acid digestion.

17. Describe the process of absorption of digested foodstuffs that occurs in the small intestine.

Developmental Aspects of the Digestive System (pp. 933, 936–937)

18. Describe embryonic development of the digestive system.

19. Describe abnormalities of the gastrointestinal tract at different stages of life.

Q *Which of the internal organs depicted here have been met while studying other organ systems?*

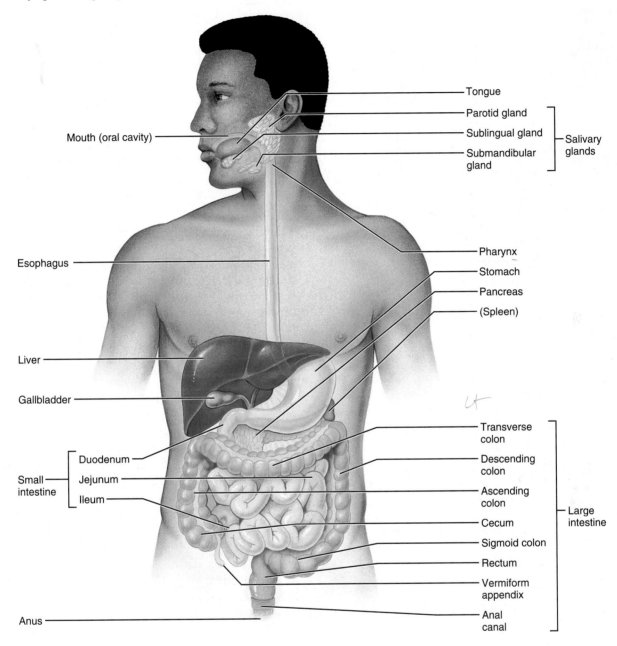

FIGURE 23.1   **Alimentary canal and related accessory digestive organs.**
(See *A Brief Atlas of the Human Body*, figure 64a.)

Children are fascinated by the workings of the digestive system. They relish crunching a potato chip, delight in making "mustaches" with milk, and giggle when their stomach "growls." As adults, we know that a healthy digestive system is essential to maintaining life, because it converts foods into the raw materials that build and fuel our body's cells. Specifically, the **digestive system** takes in food, breaks it down into nutrient molecules, absorbs these molecules into the bloodstream, and then rids the body of the indigestible remains.

PART 1: OVERVIEW OF THE DIGESTIVE SYSTEM

The organs of the digestive system (Figure 23.1) fall into two main groups: (1) those of the *alimentary canal*

A *The pancreas (part of the endocrine system), the spleen (part of the immune system and a "graveyard" for old RBCs), and the pharynx (part of the respiratory system).*

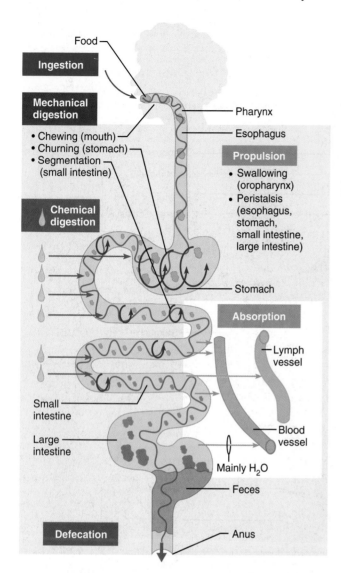

FIGURE 23.2 **Gastrointestinal tract activities.**
Gastrointestinal tract activities include ingestion, mechanical digestion, chemical (enzymatic) digestion, propulsion, absorption, and defecation. Sites of chemical digestion are also sites that produce enzymes or that receive enzymes or other secretions made by accessory organs outside the alimentary canal. The mucosa of the GI tract secretes mucus, which protects and lubricates.

(al″ĭ-men′tar-e; *aliment* = nourish) and (2) *accessory digestive organs.*

The **alimentary canal,** also called the **gastrointestinal (GI) tract** or **gut,** is the continuous, muscular digestive tube that winds through the body. It **digests** food—breaks it down into smaller fragments (*digest* = dissolved)—and **absorbs** the digested fragments through its lining into the blood. The organs of the alimentary canal are the *mouth, pharynx, esophagus, stomach, small intestine,* and *large intestine.* The large intestine leads to the terminal opening, or *anus.* In a cadaver, the alimentary canal is

approximately 9 m (about 30 ft) long, but in a living person, it is considerably shorter because of its muscle tone. Food material in this tube is technically outside the body because the canal is open to the external environment at both ends.

The **accessory digestive organs** are the *teeth, tongue, gallbladder,* and a number of large digestive glands—the *salivary glands, liver,* and *pancreas.* The teeth and tongue are in the mouth, or oral cavity, while the digestive glands and gallbladder lie outside the GI tract and connect to it by ducts. The accessory digestive glands produce a variety of secretions that contribute to the breakdown of foodstuffs.

Digestive Processes

The digestive tract can be viewed as a "disassembly line" in which food becomes less complex at each step of processing and its nutrients become available to the body. The processing of food by the digestive system involves six essential activities: ingestion, propulsion, mechanical digestion, chemical digestion, absorption, and defecation (Figure 23.2).

1. Ingestion is simply taking food into the digestive tract, usually via the mouth.

2. Propulsion, which moves food through the alimentary canal, includes *swallowing,* which is initiated voluntarily, and *peristalsis* (per″ĭ-stal′sis), an involuntary process. **Peristalsis** (*peri* = around; *stalsis* = constriction), the major means of propulsion, involves alternate waves of contraction and relaxation of muscles in the organ walls (Figure 23.3a). Its main effect is to squeeze food along the tract, but some mixing occurs as well. In fact, peristaltic waves are so powerful that, once swallowed, food and fluids will reach your stomach even if you stand on your head.

3. Mechanical digestion physically prepares food for chemical digestion by enzymes. Mechanical processes include chewing, mixing of food with saliva by the tongue, churning food in the stomach, and segmentation, or rhythmic local constrictions of the intestine (Figure 23.3b). **Segmentation** mixes food with digestive juices and increases the efficiency of absorption by repeatedly moving different parts of the food mass over the intestinal wall.

4. Chemical digestion is a series of catabolic steps in which complex food molecules are broken down to their chemical building blocks by enzymes secreted into the lumen of the alimentary canal. Chemical digestion of foodstuffs begins in the mouth and is essentially complete in the small intestine.

5. Absorption is the passage of digested end products (plus vitamins, minerals, and water) from the

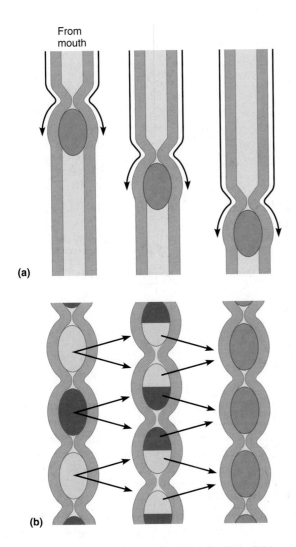

(a)

(b)

FIGURE 23.3 **Peristalsis and segmentation. (a)** In peristalsis, adjacent segments of the intestine (or other alimentary tract organs) alternately contract and relax, which moves food along the tract distally. **(b)** In segmentation, nonadjacent segments of the intestine alternately contract and relax, moving the food now forward and then backward. This results mainly in food mixing, but slow food propulsion also occurs.

lumen of the GI tract through the mucosal cells by active or passive transport into the blood or lymph. The small intestine is the major absorptive site.

6. **Defecation** eliminates indigestible substances from the body via the anus in the form of feces.

Some of these processes are the job of a single organ. For example, only the mouth ingests and only the large intestine defecates. But most digestive system activities require the cooperation of several organs and occur bit by bit as food moves along the tract. Later, we will consider which of these specific processes each GI tract organ performs and the neural or hormonal factors that regulate these processes.

Basic Functional Concepts

A theme stressed in this book is the body's efforts to maintain the constancy of its internal environment. Most organ systems respond to changes in that environment either by attempting to restore some plasma variable to its former levels or by changing their own function. The digestive system, however, creates an optimal environment for its functioning in the lumen (cavity) of the GI tract, an area that is actually *outside* the body, and essentially all digestive tract regulatory mechanisms act to control luminal conditions so that digestion and absorption can occur there as effectively as possible.

Two facts apply to these regulatory mechanisms:

1. **Digestive activity is provoked by a range of mechanical and chemical stimuli.** Sensors (mechanoreceptors and chemoreceptors) involved in controls of GI tract activity are located in the walls of the tract organs (Figure 23.4). These sensors respond to several stimuli; the most important are stretching of the organ by food in the lumen, osmolarity (solute concentration) and pH of the contents, and the presence of substrates and end products of digestion. When stimulated, these receptors initiate reflexes that (1) activate or inhibit glands that secrete digestive juices into the lumen or hormones into the blood or (2) mix lumen contents and move them along the tract by stimulating smooth muscle of the GI tract walls.

2. **Controls of digestive activity are both extrinsic and intrinsic.** Many of the controlling systems of the

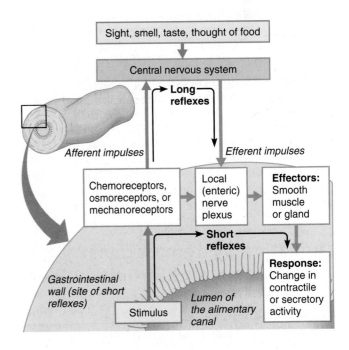

FIGURE 23.4 **Neural reflex pathways initiated by stimuli inside or outside the gastrointestinal tract.**

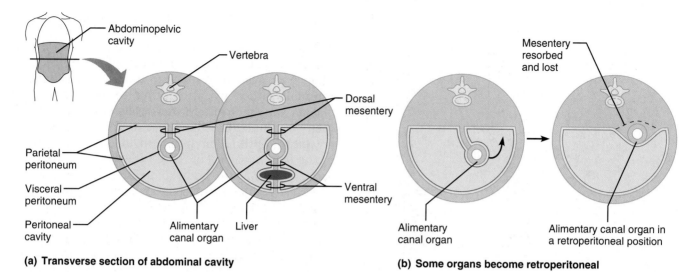

(a) Transverse section of abdominal cavity

(b) Some organs become retroperitoneal

FIGURE 23.5 **The peritoneum and the peritoneal cavity. (a)** Simplified cross sections through the abdominal cavity showing the relative locations of the visceral and parietal peritoneums, and dorsal (left) and ventral (right) mesenteries. Note that the peritoneal cavity is much smaller than depicted here. **(b)** Some alimentary canal organs lose their mesentery during development and become retroperitoneal.

digestive tract are intrinsic—a product of "in-house" nerve plexuses or hormone-producing cells. The wall of the alimentary canal contains nerve plexuses which spread like chicken wire along the entire length of the GI tract and influence each other both in the same and in different digestive organs. As a result, two kinds of reflex activity occur, short and long. *Short reflexes* are mediated entirely by the local *(enteric)* plexuses (the so-called gut brain) in response to GI tract stimuli. *Long reflexes* are initiated by stimuli arising inside or outside the GI tract and involve CNS centers and extrinsic autonomic nerves (Figure 23.4). Generally speaking, nerve fibers that excite smooth muscle secrete acetylcholine or substance P, whereas those that inhibit smooth muscle release vasoactive intestinal peptide (VIP) or nitric oxide.

The stomach and small intestine also contain hormone-producing cells that, when appropriately stimulated, release their products to the interstitial fluid in the extracellular space. These hormones are distributed via blood and interstitial fluid to their target cells in the same or different digestive tract organs, which they prod to secrete or contract.

Digestive System Organs: Relationship and Structural Plan

Relationship of the Digestive Organs to the Peritoneum

Most digestive system organs reside in the abdominopelvic cavity. Recall from Chapter 1 that all ventral body cavities contain slippery *serous membranes*. The **peritoneum** of the abdominopelvic cavity is the most extensive of these membranes (Figure 23.5a). The **visceral peritoneum** covers the external surfaces of most digestive organs and is continuous with the **parietal peritoneum** that lines the body wall. Between the two peritoneums is the **peritoneal cavity**, a slitlike potential space containing fluid secreted by the serous membranes. The serous fluid lubricates the mobile digestive organs, allowing them to glide easily across one another and along the body wall as they carry out their digestive activities.

A **mesentery** (mes'en-ter"e) is a double layer of peritoneum—a sheet of two serous membranes fused back to back—that extends to the digestive organs from the body wall. Mesenteries provide routes for blood vessels, lymphatics, and nerves to reach the digestive viscera; hold organs in place; and store fat. In most places the mesentery is *dorsal* and attaches to the posterior abdominal wall, but there are *ventral* mesenteries as well (Figure 23.5a). Some of the mesenteries, or peritoneal folds, are given specific names (such as the *omenta*), as described later.

Not all alimentary canal organs are suspended by a mesentery. For example, some parts of the small intestine adhere to the dorsal abdominal wall (Figure 23.5b). In so doing, they lose their mesentery and come to lie posterior to the peritoneum. These organs, which include most of the pancreas and parts of the large intestine, are called **retroperitoneal organs** (*retro* = behind). By contrast, digestive organs (like the stomach) that keep their mesentery and remain in the peritoneal cavity are called **intraperitoneal** or **peritoneal organs**.

FIGURE 23.6 **Basic structure of the alimentary canal.** Its four basic layers are the mucosa, submucosa, muscularis externa, and serosa.

HOMEOSTATIC IMBALANCE

Peritonitis, or inflammation of the peritoneum, can arise from a piercing abdominal wound or from a perforating ulcer that leaks stomach juices into the peritoneal cavity, but most commonly it results from a burst appendix (that sprays bacteria-containing feces all over the peritoneum). In peritonitis, the peritoneal coverings tend to stick together around the infection site. This localizes the infection, providing time for macrophages to attack to prevent the inflammation from spreading. If peritonitis becomes widespread within the peritoneal cavity, it is dangerous and often lethal. Treatment includes removing as much infectious debris as possible from the peritoneal cavity and administering megadoses of antibiotics. ●

Blood Supply: The Splanchnic Circulation

The **splanchnic circulation** includes those arteries that branch off the abdominal aorta to serve the digestive organs and the *hepatic portal circulation.* The arterial supply—the hepatic, splenic, and left gastric branches of the celiac trunk that serve the spleen, liver, and stomach, and the mesenteric arteries (superior and inferior) that serve the small and large intestines (see pp. 908 and 922)—normally receives one-quarter of the cardiac output. This percentage (blood volume) increases after a meal has been eaten. The hepatic portal circulation (described on pp. 764–765) collects nutrient-rich venous blood draining from the digestive viscera and delivers it to the liver. The liver collects the absorbed nutrients for metabolic processing or for storage before releasing them back to the bloodstream for general cellular use.

Histology of the Alimentary Canal

Each digestive organ has only a share of the work of digestion. Consequently, it helps to consider structural characteristics that promote similar functions in all parts of the alimentary canal before we consider the functional anatomy of the digestive system.

From the esophagus to the anal canal, the walls of the alimentary canal have the same four basic layers, or *tunics* (Figure 23.6)—*mucosa, submucosa, muscularis externa,* and *serosa*—each containing a predominant tissue type that plays a specific role in food breakdown.

The Mucosa

The **mucosa,** or **mucous membrane**—the innermost layer—is a moist epithelial membrane that lines the alimentary canal lumen from mouth to anus. Its major functions are (1) *secretion* of mucus, digestive enzymes, and hormones, (2) *absorption* of the end products of digestion into the blood, and (3) *protection* against infectious disease. The mucosa in a particular region of the GI tract may express one or all three of these capabilities.

More complex than most other mucosae in the body, the typical digestive mucosa consists of three sublayers: (1) a lining epithelium, (2) a lamina propria, and (3) a muscularis mucosae. Typically, the **epithelium** of the mucosa is a *simple columnar epithelium* rich in mucus-secreting *goblet cells*. The slippery mucus it produces protects certain digestive organs from being digested themselves by enzymes working within their cavities and eases food passage along the tract. In the stomach and small intestine, the mucosa also contains both enzyme-synthesizing and hormone-secreting cells. Thus, in such sites, the mucosa is a diffuse kind of endocrine organ as well as part of the digestive organ.

The **lamina propria** (*proprius* = one's own), which underlies the epithelium, is loose areolar connective tissue. Its capillaries nourish the epithelium and absorb digested nutrients. Its isolated lymphoid follicles, part of **MALT,** the mucosa-associated lymphatic tissue described on p. 782, help defend us against bacteria and other pathogens, which have rather free access to our digestive tract. Particularly large collections of lymphoid follicles occur within the pharynx (as the tonsils) and in the appendix.

External to the lamina propria is the **muscularis mucosae,** a scant layer of smooth muscle cells that produces local movements of the mucosa. For example, twitching of this muscle layer dislodges food particles that have adhered to the mucosa. In the small intestine, it throws the mucosa into a series of small folds that immensely increase its surface area.

The Submucosa

The **submucosa,** just external to the mucosa, is a moderately dense connective tissue containing blood and lymphatic vessels, lymphoid follicles, and nerve fibers. Its rich supply of elastic fibers enables the stomach to regain its normal shape after temporarily storing a large meal. Its extensive vascular network supplies surrounding tissues of the GI tract wall.

The Muscularis Externa

Just deep to the submucosa is the **muscularis externa,** also simply called the **muscularis.** This layer is responsible for segmentation and peristalsis. It typically has an inner *circular layer* and an outer *longitudinal layer* of smooth muscle cells (Figure 23.6). In several places along the tract, the circular layer thickens, forming *sphincters* that act as

valves to prevent backflow and control food passage from one organ to the next.

The Serosa

The **serosa,** the protective outermost layer of the intraperitoneal organs, is the *visceral peritoneum.* It is formed of areolar connective tissue covered with *mesothelium*, a single layer of squamous epithelial cells.

In the esophagus, which is located in the thoracic instead of the abdominopelvic cavity, the serosa is replaced by an **adventitia** (ad″ven-tish′e-ah). The adventitia is ordinary fibrous connective tissue that binds the esophagus to surrounding structures. Retroperitoneal organs have *both* a serosa (on the side facing the peritoneal cavity) and an adventitia (on the side abutting the dorsal body wall).

Enteric Nervous System of the Alimentary Canal

The alimentary canal has its own in-house nerve supply, staffed by the so-called **enteric neurons** (*enter* = gut), which communicate widely with one another to regulate digestive system activity. These semiautonomous enteric neurons constitute the bulk of the two major *intrinsic nerve plexuses* (ganglia interconnected by unmyelinated fiber tracts) found in the walls of the alimentary canal: the submucosal and myenteric nerve plexuses (Figure 23.6).

The **submucosal nerve plexus** occupies the submucosa, includes sensory as well as motor neurons, and chiefly regulates the activity of glands and smooth muscle in the mucosa. The large **myenteric nerve plexus** (mi-en′ter-ik; "intestinal muscle") lies between the circular and longitudinal muscle layers of the muscularis externa. Enteric neurons of this plexus provide the major nerve supply to the GI tract wall and control GI tract motility. Control of the patterns of segmentation and peristalsis is largely automatic, involving local reflex arcs between enteric neurons in the same or different plexuses or (even) organs.

The enteric nervous system is also linked to the central nervous system by afferent visceral fibers and by sympathetic and parasympathetic branches (motor fibers) of the autonomic nervous system that enter the intestinal wall and synapse with neurons in the intrinsic plexuses. Thus, digestive activity is also subject to extrinsic controls exerted by autonomic fibers via long reflex arcs. Generally speaking, parasympathetic inputs enhance secretory activity and motility, whereas sympathetic impulses inhibit digestive activities. But the largely independent enteric ganglia are much more than just way stations

Q *What is the protective value of having several sets of tonsils at the oral entry to the pharynx?*

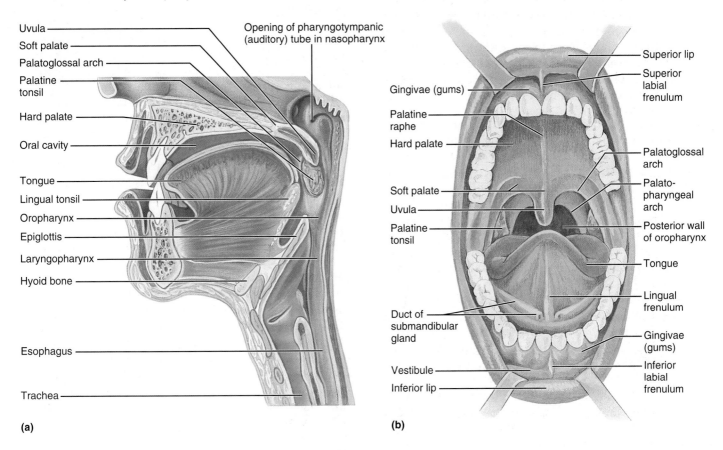

(a)

(b)

FIGURE 23.7 **Anatomy of the oral cavity (mouth). (a)** Sagittal section of the oral cavity and pharynx. **(b)** Anterior view.

for the autonomic nervous system as is the case in other organ systems. Indeed, the enteric nervous system contains over 100 million neurons, more than the entire spinal cord.

PART 2: FUNCTIONAL ANATOMY OF THE DIGESTIVE SYSTEM

Now that we have summarized some points that unify the digestive system organs, we are ready to consider the special structural and functional capabilities of each organ of this system. Most of the digestive organs are shown in their normal body positions in Figure 23.1, so you may find it helpful to refer back to that illustration from time to time as you read the following sections.

A *Tonsils contain immune cells (lymphocytes and macrophages) that can remove some foreign substances (bacteria and the like) and prevent them from reaching the stomach and intestines.*

The Mouth, Pharynx, and Esophagus

The mouth is the only part of the alimentary canal involved in ingestion. However, most digestive functions associated with the mouth reflect the activity of the related accessory organs, such as the teeth, salivary glands, and tongue, because in the mouth food is chewed and mixed with saliva containing enzymes that begin the process of chemical digestion. The mouth also begins the propulsive process of swallowing, which carries food through the pharynx and esophagus to the stomach.

The Mouth and Associated Organs

The Mouth

The **mouth,** a mucosa-lined cavity, is also called the **oral cavity,** or **buccal cavity** (buk'al). Its boundaries are the lips anteriorly, cheeks laterally, palate superiorly, and tongue inferiorly [Figure 23.7]. Its anterior opening is the **oral orifice.** Posteriorly, the oral cavity is continuous with the *oropharynx.* The walls of the mouth are lined with stratified squamous epithelium which can withstand considerable friction. The epithelium on the gums, hard palate, and dorsum of the tongue is slightly keratinized for extra protection against abrasion during eating. Like all moist surface linings, the oral mucosa responds to injury by producing antimicrobial peptides called *defensins*, which helps to explain how the mouth, a site teeming with disease-causing microbes, remains so remarkably healthy.

The Lips and Cheeks The **lips (labia)** and the **cheeks** have a core of skeletal muscle covered externally by skin. The *orbicularis oris muscle* forms the fleshy lips; the cheeks are formed largely by the *buccinators*. The lips and cheeks help keep food between the teeth when we chew and play a small role in speech. The recess bounded externally by the lips and cheeks and internally by the gums and teeth is called the **vestibule** ("porch"). The area that lies within the teeth and gums is the **oral cavity proper.**

The lips are much larger than most people think; anatomically they extend from the inferior margin of the nose to the superior boundary of the chin. The reddened area where one applies lipstick or lands a kiss is called the **red margin.** This transitional zone, where keratinized skin meets the oral mucosa, is poorly keratinized and translucent, allowing the red color of blood in the underlying capillaries to show through. The lack of sweat or sebaceous glands in this region means it must be moistened with saliva periodically to prevent it from becoming dry and cracked (chapped lips). The **labial frenulum** (fren'u-lum) is a median fold that joins the internal aspect of each lip to the gum (Figure 23.7b).

The Palate The **palate,** forming the roof of the mouth, has two distinct parts: the hard palate anteriorly and the soft palate posteriorly (see Figure 23.7). The **hard palate** is underlain by the palatine bones and the palatine processes of the maxillae, and it forms a rigid surface against which the tongue forces food during chewing. The mucosa on either side of its *raphe* (ra'fe), a midline ridge, is slightly corrugated, which helps to create friction.

The **soft palate** is a mobile fold formed mostly of skeletal muscle. Projecting downward from its free edge is the fingerlike **uvula** (u'vu-lah). The soft palate rises reflexively to close off the nasopharynx when we swallow.

■ To demonstrate this action, try to breathe and swallow at the same time.

Laterally, the soft palate is anchored to the tongue by the **palatoglossal arches** and to the wall of the oropharynx by the more posterior **palatopharyngeal arches.** These two paired folds form the boundaries of the **fauces** (faw'sēz; *fauc* = throat), the arched area of the oropharynx that contains the palatine tonsils.

The Tongue

The **tongue** occupies the floor of the mouth and fills most of the oral cavity when the mouth is closed (see Figure 23.7). The tongue is composed of interlacing bundles of skeletal muscle fibers, and during chewing, it grips the food and constantly repositions it between the teeth. The tongue also mixes food with saliva and forms it into a compact mass called a **bolus** (bo'lus; "a lump"), and then initiates swallowing by pushing the bolus posteriorly into the pharynx. The versatile tongue also helps us form consonants (k, d, t, and so on) when we speak.

The tongue has both intrinsic and extrinsic skeletal muscle fibers. The **intrinsic muscles** are confined in the tongue and are not attached to bone. Their muscle fibers, which run in several different planes, allow the tongue to change its shape (but not its position), becoming thicker, thinner, longer, or shorter as needed for speech and swallowing. The **extrinsic muscles** extend to the tongue from their points of origin on bones of the skull or the soft palate, as described in Chapter 10 (see Table 10.2 and Figure 10.7). The extrinsic muscles alter the tongue's position; they protrude it, retract it, and move it from side to side. The tongue has a median septum of connective tissue, and each half contains identical muscle groups. A fold of mucosa, called the **lingual frenulum,** secures the tongue to the floor of the mouth and limits posterior movements of the tongue.

▲ **HOMEOSTATIC IMBALANCE**

Children born with an extremely short lingual frenulum are often referred to as "tongue-tied" because of speech distortions that result when tongue movement is restricted. This congenital condition, called *ankyloglossia* ("fused tongue"), is corrected surgically by snipping the frenulum. ●

The superior tongue surface bears papillae, peglike projections of the underlying mucosa (Figure 23.8). The conical **filiform papillae** give the tongue surface a roughness that aids in licking semisolid foods (such as ice cream) and provide friction for manipulating foods in the mouth. These papillae, the smallest and most numerous type, align in parallel rows on the tongue dorsum. They contain keratin, which stiffens them and gives the tongue its whitish appearance.

The mushroom-shaped **fungiform papillae** are scattered widely over the tongue surface. Each has a vascular core that gives it a reddish hue. Ten to twelve large **circumvallate,** or **vallate, papillae** are located in a V-shaped row at the back of the tongue. They resemble the fungiform papillae but have an additional surrounding furrow. Pleatlike **foliate papillae** are located on the lateral aspects of the

Epiglottis

Palatopharyngeal arch

Palatine tonsil

Lingual tonsil

Palatoglossal arch

Sulcus terminalis

Foliate papillae

Dorsum of tongue

Circumvallate papilla

Filiform papillae

Fungiform papilla

FIGURE 23.8   **Dorsal surface of the tongue.** Also shown are the tonsils, and the locations and detailed structures of the circumvallate, fungiform, filiform, and foliate papillae. (Top right, 300×; bottom right, 100×) (See *A Brief Atlas of the Human Body,* figure 62.)

posterior tongue. The fungiform, circumvallate, and foliate papillae house taste buds; however, those on the foliate papillae function in taste primarily in infancy and early childhood.

Immediately posterior to the circumvallate papillae is the **sulcus terminalis,** a groove that distinguishes the anterior two-thirds of the tongue that lies in the oral cavity from its posterior third residing in the oropharynx. The mucosa covering the root of the tongue lacks papillae, but it is still bumpy because of the nodular *lingual tonsil,* which lies just deep to its mucosa (see Figure 23.8).

The Salivary Glands

A number of glands associated with the oral cavity secrete **saliva.** Saliva (1) cleanses the mouth, (2) dissolves food chemicals so that they can be tasted, (3) moistens food and aids in compacting it into a bolus, and (4) contains enzymes that begin the chemical breakdown of starchy foods.

Most saliva is produced by **extrinsic salivary glands** that lie outside the oral cavity and empty their secretions into it. Their output is augmented slightly by small **intrinsic salivary glands,** also called **buccal glands,** scattered throughout the oral cavity mucosa.

The extrinsic salivary glands are paired compound tubuloalveolar glands that develop from the oral mucosa and remain connected to it by ducts

(Figure 23.9). The large **parotid gland** (pah-rot'id; *par* = near, *otid* = the ear) lies anterior to the ear between the masseter muscle and the skin. The prominent parotid duct parallels the zygomatic arch, pierces the buccinator muscle, and opens into the vestibule next to the second upper molar. Branches of the facial nerve run through the parotid gland on their way to the muscles of facial expression. For this reason, surgery on this gland can result in facial paralysis.

HOMEOSTATIC IMBALANCE

Mumps, a common children's disease, is an inflammation of the parotid glands caused by the mumps virus *(myxovirus),* which spreads from person to person in saliva. If you check the location of the parotid glands in Figure 23.9a, you can understand why people with mumps complain that it hurts to open their mouth or chew. Besides that discomfort, other signs and symptoms of mumps include moderate fever and pain when swallowing acid foods (sour pickles, grapefruit juice, etc.). Mumps viral infections in adult males carry a 25% risk that the testes may become infected as well, leading to sterility. ●

About the size of a walnut, the **submandibular gland** lies along the medial aspect of the mandibular body. Its duct runs beneath the mucosa of the oral cavity floor and opens at the base of the lingual

23

FIGURE 23.9 **The salivary glands. (a)** The parotid, submandibular, and sublingual salivary glands associated with the left aspect of the oral cavity. **(b)** Photomicrograph of the sublingual salivary gland (40✕), which is a mixed salivary gland. Mucus-producing cells stain light blue and serous-secreting units stain purple. The serous cells sometimes form demilunes (caps) around the bases of the mucous cells.

frenulum (see Figure 23.7). The small **sublingual gland** lies anterior to the submandibular gland under the tongue and opens via 10–12 ducts into the floor of the mouth.

To a greater or lesser degree, the salivary glands are composed of two types of secretory cells: mucous and serous. **Serous cells** produce a watery secretion containing enzymes, ions, and a tiny bit of mucin, whereas the **mucous cells** produce **mucus,** a stringy, viscous solution. The parotid glands contain only serous cells. Submandibular and buccal glands have approximately equal numbers of serous and mucous cells. The sublingual glands contain mostly mucous cells.

Composition of Saliva

Saliva is largely water— 97 to 99.5%—and therefore is hypo-osmotic. Its osmolarity depends on the precise glands that are active and the nature of the stimulus for salivation. As a rule, saliva is slightly acidic (pH 6.75 to 7.00), but its pH may vary. Its solutes include electrolytes (Na^+, K^+, Cl^-, PO_4^-, and HCO_3^-); the digestive enzyme salivary amylase; the proteins mucin (mu′sin), lysozyme, and IgA; and metabolic wastes (urea and uric acid). In addition, secretions of the intrinsic salivary glands contain *lingual lipase*, a fat-digesting enzyme that is optimally active at an acid pH. When dissolved in water, the glycoprotein *mucin* forms thick mucus that lubricates the oral cavity and hydrates foodstuffs.

Protection against microorganisms is provided by (1) *IgA antibodies*; (2) *lysozyme*, a bacteriostatic enzyme that inhibits bacterial growth in the mouth and may help to prevent tooth decay; (3) a cyanide compound; and (4) *defensins* (see p. 657). Besides acting as a local antibiotic, defensins function as cytokines to call defensive cells (lymphocytes, neutrophils, etc.) into the mouth for battle. In addition to these four protectors, the friendly bacteria that live on the back of the tongue convert food-derived nitrates in saliva into nitrites which, in turn, are converted into *nitric oxide* in an acid environment. This transformation occurs around the gums, where acid-producing bacteria tend to cluster, and in the hydrochloric acid–rich secretions of the stomach. The highly toxic nitric oxide is believed to act as a bactericidal agent in these locations.

Control of Salivation

The intrinsic salivary glands secrete saliva continuously in amounts just sufficient to keep the mouth moist. But when food enters the mouth, the extrinsic glands are activated and copious amounts of saliva pour out. The average output of saliva is 1000–1500 ml per day.

Salivation is controlled primarily by the parasympathetic division of the autonomic nervous system.

When we ingest food, chemoreceptors and mechanoreceptors in the mouth send signals to the **salivatory nuclei** in the brain stem (pons and medulla). As a result, parasympathetic nervous system activity increases and impulses sent via motor fibers in the *facial (VII)* and *glossopharyngeal (IX) nerves* trigger a dramatically increased output of watery (serous), enzyme-rich saliva. The chemoreceptors are activated most strongly by acidic substances such as vinegar and citrus juice. The mechanoreceptors are activated by virtually any mechanical stimulus in the mouth—even rubber bands.

Sometimes just the sight or smell of food is enough to get the juices flowing. The mere thought of hot fudge sauce on peppermint stick ice cream will make many a mouth water! Irritation of the lower regions of the GI tract by bacterial toxins, spicy foods, or hyperacidity—particularly when accompanied by a feeling of nausea—also increases salivation. This response may help wash away or neutralize the irritants.

In contrast to parasympathetic controls, the sympathetic division (specifically fibers in T_1–T_3) causes release of a thick, mucin-rich saliva. Extremely strong activation of the sympathetic division constricts blood vessels serving the salivary glands and almost completely inhibits saliva release, causing a dry mouth *(xerostomia)*. Dehydration also inhibits salivation because low blood volume results in reduced filtration pressure at capillary beds.

HOMEOSTATIC IMBALANCE

Any disease process that inhibits saliva secretion causes a marked increase in dental caries (cavities) and difficulty in talking, swallowing, and eating. Because decomposing food particles are allowed to accumulate and bacteria flourish, *halitosis* (hal"ĭ-to'sis; "bad breath") can result. The odor is caused mainly by the metabolic activity of anaerobic protein-digesting bacteria at the back of the tongue that yields hydrogen sulfide (rotten egg smell), methyl mercaptan (also in feces), cadaverine (associated with rotting corpses), and others. ●

The Teeth

The **teeth** lie in sockets (alveoli) in the gum-covered margins of the mandible and maxilla. The role of the teeth in food processing needs little introduction. We *masticate*, or chew, by opening and closing our jaws and moving them from side to side while continually using our tongue to move the food between our teeth. In the process, the teeth tear and grind the food, breaking it down into smaller fragments.

Dentition and the Dental Formula Ordinarily by age 21, two sets of teeth, the **primary** and

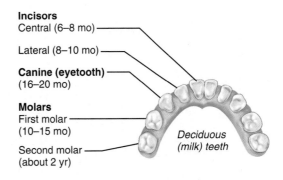

Incisors
Central (6–8 mo)
Lateral (8–10 mo)
Canine (eyetooth)
(16–20 mo)
Molars
First molar
(10–15 mo)
Second molar
(about 2 yr)

Deciduous (milk) teeth

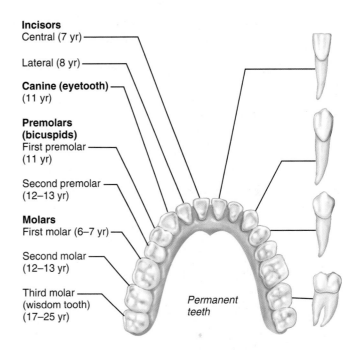

Incisors
Central (7 yr)
Lateral (8 yr)
Canine (eyetooth)
(11 yr)
Premolars (bicuspids)
First premolar
(11 yr)
Second premolar
(12–13 yr)
Molars
First molar (6–7 yr)
Second molar
(12–13 yr)
Third molar
(wisdom tooth)
(17–25 yr)

Permanent teeth

FIGURE 23.10 Human deciduous and permanent teeth of the lower jaw. Approximate age at which tooth erupts is shown in parentheses. The shapes of individual teeth are shown on the right.

permanent dentitions, have formed (Figure 23.10). The primary dentition consists of the **deciduous teeth** (de-sid'u-us; *decid* = falling off), also called **milk** or **baby teeth.** The first teeth to appear, at about age 6 months, are the lower central incisors. Additional pairs of teeth erupt at one- to two-month intervals until about 24 months, when all 20 milk teeth have emerged.

As the deep-lying **permanent teeth** enlarge and develop, the roots of the milk teeth are resorbed from below, causing them to loosen and fall out between the ages of 6 and 12 years. Generally, all the teeth of the permanent dentition but the third molars have erupted by the end of adolescence. The third molars, also called *wisdom teeth*, emerge between the ages of 17 and 25 years. There are usually 32 permanent teeth in a full set, but sometimes the wisdom teeth never erupt or are completely absent.

Q *Which material forms the bulk of the tooth?*

FIGURE 23.11 **Longitudinal section of a canine tooth within its bony alveolus.**

Labels on figure:
- Enamel
- Dentin
- Dentinal tubules
- Pulp cavity (contains blood vessels and nerves)
- Gingiva (gum)
- Cementum
- Root canal
- Periodontal ligament
- Apical foramen
- Bone
- Crown
- Neck
- Root

⬛ HOMEOSTATIC IMBALANCE

When a tooth remains embedded in the jawbone, it is said to be *impacted.* Impacted teeth can cause a good deal of pressure and pain and must be removed surgically. Wisdom teeth are most commonly impacted. ●

Teeth are classified according to their shape and function as incisors, canines, premolars, and molars (Figure 23.10). The chisel-shaped **incisors** are adapted for cutting or nipping off pieces of food. The conical or fanglike **canines** (cuspids or eye-teeth) tear and pierce. The **premolars** (bicuspids) and **molars** have broad crowns with rounded cusps (tips) and are best suited for grinding or crushing. The molars (literally, "millstones"), with four or

five cusps, are the best grinders. During chewing, the upper and lower molars repeatedly lock together, an action that generates tremendous crushing forces.

The **dental formula** is a shorthand way of indicating the numbers and relative positions of the different types of teeth in the mouth. This formula is written as a ratio, uppers over lowers, for *one-half* of the mouth. Since the other side is a mirror image, the total dentition is obtained by multiplying the dental formula by 2. The primary dentition consists of two incisors (I), one canine (C), and two molars (M) on each side of each jaw, and its dental formula is written as

$$\frac{2I, 1C, 2M \text{ (upper jaw)}}{2I, 1C, 2M \text{ (lower jaw)}} \times 2 \text{ (20 teeth)}$$

Similarly, the permanent dentition [two incisors, one canine, two premolars (PM), and three molars] is

$$\frac{2I, 1C, 2PM, 3M}{2I, 1C, 2PM, 3M} \times 2 \text{ (32 teeth)}$$

Tooth Structure   Each tooth has two major regions: the crown and the root (Figure 23.11). The enamel-covered **crown** is the exposed part of the tooth above the **gingiva** (jin'jĭ-vah), or **gum,** which surrounds the tooth like a tight collar. **Enamel,** an acellular, brittle material that directly bears the force of chewing, is the hardest substance in the body. It is heavily mineralized with calcium salts, and its densely packed hydroxyapatite (mineral) crystals are oriented in force-resisting columns perpendicular to the tooth's surface. The cells that produce enamel degenerate when the tooth erupts; consequently, any decayed or cracked areas of the enamel will not heal and must be artificially filled.

The portion of the tooth embedded in the jawbone is the **root.** Canine teeth, incisors, and premolars have one root, although the first upper premolars commonly have two. The first two upper molars have three roots, while the corresponding lower molars have two. The root pattern of the third molar varies, but a fused single root is most common.

The crown and root are connected by a constricted tooth region called the **neck.** The outer surface of the root is covered by **cementum,** a calcified connective tissue, which attaches the tooth to the thin **periodontal ligament** (per"e-o-don'tal; "around the tooth"). This ligament anchors the tooth in the bony alveolus of the jaw, forming a fibrous joint called a *gomphosis.* Where the gingiva borders on a tooth, it dips downward to form a shallow groove called the *gingival sulcus.* In youth, the gingiva

A *Dentin.*

adheres tenaciously to the enamel covering the crown. But as the gums begin to recede with age, the gingiva adheres to the more sensitive cementum covering the superior region of the root. As a result, the teeth *appear* to get longer in old age—hence the expression "long in the tooth" sometimes applied to elderly people.

Dentin, a bonelike material, underlies the enamel cap and forms the bulk of a tooth. It surrounds a central **pulp cavity** containing a number of soft tissue structures (connective tissue, blood vessels, and nerve fibers) collectively called **pulp.** Pulp supplies nutrients to the tooth tissues and provides for tooth sensation. Where the pulp cavity extends into the root, it becomes the **root canal.** At the proximal end of each root canal is an **apical foramen** that allows blood vessels, nerves, and other structures to enter the pulp cavity. The teeth are served by the superior and inferior alveolar nerves, branches of the trigeminal nerve (see Table 13.2, p. 504), and by the superior and inferior alveolar arteries, branches of the maxillary artery (see Figure 19.21, p. 749).

Dentin contains unique radial striations called *dentinal tubules* (Figure 23.11). Each tubule contains an elongated process of an **odontoblast** (o-don'to-blast; "tooth former"), the cell type that secretes and maintains the dentin. The cell bodies of odontoblasts line the pulp cavity just deep to the dentin. Dentin is formed throughout adult life and gradually encroaches on the pulp cavity. New dentin can also be laid down fairly rapidly to compensate for tooth damage or decay. Although enamel, dentin, and cementum are all calcified and resemble bone, they differ from bone in that they are avascular. Enamel also differs from cementum and dentin because it lacks collagen as its main organic component.

⬛ HOMEOSTATIC IMBALANCE

Death of a tooth's nerve and consequent darkening of the tooth is commonly caused by a blow to the jaw. Local swelling pinches off the blood supply to the tooth and the nerve dies. Typically the pulp becomes infected by bacteria sometime later and must be removed by *root canal therapy.* After the cavity is sterilized and filled with an inert material, the tooth is capped. ●

Tooth and Gum Disease **Dental caries** (kār'ēz; "rottenness"), or **cavities,** result from gradual demineralization of enamel and underlying dentin by bacterial action. Decay begins when **dental plaque** (a film of sugar, bacteria, and other mouth debris) adheres to the teeth. Bacterial metabolism of the trapped sugars produces acids, which can dissolve the calcium salts of the teeth. Once the salts are leached out, the remaining organic matrix of the tooth is readily digested by protein-digesting enzymes

released by the bacteria. Frequent brushing and flossing daily help prevent damage by removing forming plaque.

More serious than tooth decay is the effect of unremoved plaque on the gums. As dental plaque accumulates, it calcifies, forming **calculus** (kal'ku-lus; "stone") or tartar, which disrupts the seals between the gingivae and the teeth, deepening the sulcus and putting the gums at risk for infection by pathogenic anaerobic bacteria. In the early stages of such an infection, called *gingivitis* (jin"ji-vi'tis), the gums are red, sore, swollen, and may bleed. Gingivitis is reversible if the calculus is removed, but if it is neglected the bacteria eventually form pockets of infection which elicit the inflammatory response. Neutrophils and immune system cells (lymphocytes and macrophages) attack not only the intruders but also the body tissues, carving deep pockets around the teeth, destroying the periodontal ligament and activating osteoclasts which dissolve the bone away. This more serious condition, called **periodontal disease,** or **periodontitis,** affects up to 95% of all people over the age of 35 and accounts for 80–90% of tooth loss in adults.

Still, tooth loss is not inevitable. Even advanced periodontitis can be treated by scraping the teeth, cleaning the infected pockets, then cutting the gums to shrink the pockets, and following up with anti-inflammatory and antibiotic therapy. Together, these treatments alleviate the bacterial infestations and encourage reattachment of the surrounding tissues to the teeth and bone. Much less painful are (1) a new laser approach for destroying the diseased tissues and (2) a nonsurgical therapy now in clinical trials in which an antibiotic-impregnated film is temporarily glued to the exposed root surface. Clinical treatment is followed up by a home regimen of plaque removal by consistent frequent brushing and flossing and hydrogen peroxide rinses.

There may be more at risk than teeth in those with periodontal disease. Some contend that it increases the risk of heart disease and stroke in at least two ways: (1) the chronic inflammation promotes atherosclerotic plaque formation, and (2) bacteria entering the blood from infected gums stimulate clot formation that helps to clog coronary and cerebral arteries. Risk factors for periodontal disease include smoking, diabetes mellitus, and oral (tongue or lip) piercing.

The Pharynx

From the mouth, food passes posteriorly into the **oropharynx** and then the **laryngopharynx** (see Figure 23.7), both common passageways for food, fluids, and air. (The nasopharynx has no digestive role.)

Q *What is the functional significance of the epithelial change seen in part (b)?*

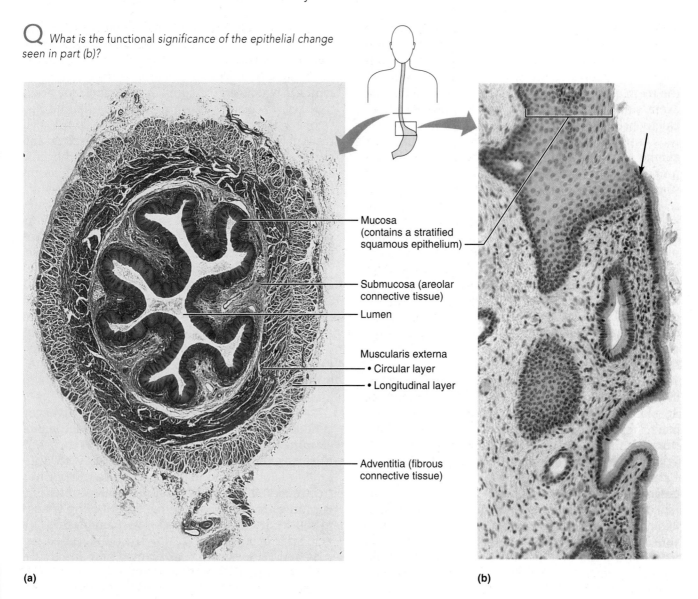

Mucosa (contains a stratified squamous epithelium)

Submucosa (areolar connective tissue)

Lumen

Muscularis externa
• Circular layer
• Longitudinal layer

Adventitia (fibrous connective tissue)

(a)

(b)

FIGURE 23.12   Microscopic structure of the esophagus. (a) Cross-sectional view of the esophagus showing its four tunics (5×). The section shown is taken from the region close to the stomach junction, so the muscularis is composed of smooth muscle. **(b)** Longitudinal section through the esophagus-stomach junction (80×). Arrow shows the point of abrupt transition from the stratified squamous epithelium of the esophagus (top) to the simple columnar epithelium of the stomach (bottom).

The histology of the pharyngeal wall resembles that of the oral cavity. The mucosa contains a friction-resistant stratified squamous epithelium well supplied with mucus-producing glands. The external muscle layer consists of two *skeletal muscle* layers. The cells of the inner layer run longitudinally. Those of the outer layer, the *pharyngeal constrictor muscles*, encircle the wall like three stacked fists (see

Figure 10.8). Contractions of these muscles propel food into the esophagus below.

The Esophagus

The **esophagus** (ĕ-sof'ah-gus; "carry food"), a muscular tube about 25 cm (10 inches) long, is collapsed when not involved in food propulsion (Figure 23.12). After food moves through the laryngopharynx, it is routed into the esophagus posteriorly as the epiglottis closes off the larynx to food entry.

As shown in Figure 23.1, the esophagus takes a fairly straight course through the mediastinum of the thorax and pierces the diaphragm at the

A *The presence of the stratified squamous epithelium indicates the esophagus is mainly a chute and thus must accommodate high friction, whereas the stomach has a secretory simple columnar epithelium, reflecting its secretory role in chemical digestion.*

esophageal hiatus (hi-a′tus; "gap") to enter the abdomen. It joins the stomach at the **cardiac orifice.** The cardiac orifice is surrounded by the **gastroesophageal** or **cardiac sphincter** (gas″tro-ĕ sof″ah-je′al) (see Figure 23.13), which is a *physiological* sphincter. That is, it acts as a valve, but the only structural evidence of this sphincter is a slight thickening of the circular smooth muscle at that point. The muscular diaphragm, which surrounds this sphincter, helps keep it closed when food is not being swallowed.

◤ HOMEOSTATIC IMBALANCE

Heartburn, the first symptom of *gastroesophageal reflux disease (GERD),* is the burning, radiating substernal pain that occurs when the acidic gastric juice regurgitates into the esophagus. Symptoms are so similar to those of a heart attack that many first-time sufferers of heartburn are rushed to the hospital emergency room. Heartburn is most likely to happen when one has eaten or drunk to excess, and in conditions that force abdominal contents superiorly, such as extreme obesity, pregnancy, and running, which causes stomach contents to splash upward with each step (runner's reflux). It is also common in those with a **hiatal hernia,** a structural abnormality (most often due to an abnormal relaxation or weakening of the gastroesophageal sphincter) in which the superior part of the stomach protrudes slightly above the diaphragm. Since the diaphragm no longer reinforces the sphincter, gastric juice may enter the esophagus, particularly when lying down. If the episodes are frequent and prolonged, *esophagitis* (inflammation of the esophagus) and *esophageal ulcers* may result. An even more threatening sequel is esophageal cancer. However, these consequences can usually be prevented or managed by avoiding late-night snacks and by using antacid preparations. ●

Unlike the mouth and pharynx, the esophagus wall has all four of the basic alimentary canal layers described earlier. Some features of interest:

1. The esophageal mucosa contains a nonkeratinized stratified squamous epithelium. At the esophagus-stomach junction, that abrasion-resistant epithelium changes abruptly to the simple columnar epithelium of the stomach, which is specialized for secretion (Figure 23.12b).

2. When the esophagus is empty, its mucosa and submucosa are thrown into longitudinal folds (Figure 23.12a). When food is in transit in the esophagus, these folds flatten out.

3. The submucosa contains mucus-secreting *esophageal glands.* As a bolus moves through the esophagus, it compresses these glands, causing them to secrete mucus that "greases" the esophageal walls and aids food passage.

4. The muscularis externa is skeletal muscle in its superior third, a mixture of skeletal and smooth muscle in its middle third, and entirely smooth muscle in its inferior third.

5. Instead of a serosa, the esophagus has a fibrous adventitia composed entirely of connective tissue, which blends with surrounding structures along its route.

Digestive Processes Occurring in the Mouth, Pharynx, and Esophagus

The mouth and its accessory digestive organs are involved in most digestive processes. The mouth (1) ingests, (2) begins mechanical digestion by chewing, and (3) initiates propulsion by swallowing. Salivary amylase, the main enzyme in saliva, starts the chemical breakdown of polysaccharides (starch and glycogen) into smaller fragments of linked glucose molecules. (If you chew a piece of bread for a few minutes, it will begin to taste sweet as sugars are released.) Lingual lipase, another enzyme in saliva, acts in the acidic environment of the stomach. Except for a few drugs that are absorbed through the oral mucosa (for example, nitroglycerine), essentially no absorption occurs in the mouth.

In contrast to the multifunctional mouth, the pharynx and esophagus merely serve as conduits to pass food from the mouth to the stomach. Their single digestive function is food propulsion, accomplished by the role they play in swallowing.

Since chemical digestion is covered in a special physiology section later in the chapter, only the mechanical processes of chewing and swallowing are discussed here.

Mastication (Chewing)

As food enters the mouth, its mechanical breakdown begins with **mastication,** or chewing. The cheeks and closed lips hold food between the teeth, the tongue mixes food with saliva to soften it, and the teeth cut and grind solid foods into smaller morsels. Mastication is partly voluntary and partly reflexive. We voluntarily put food into our mouths and contract the muscles that close our jaws. The pattern and rhythm of continued jaw movements are controlled mainly by stretch reflexes and in response to pressure inputs from receptors in the cheeks, gums, and tongue, but they can also be voluntary as desired.

Deglutition (Swallowing)

To send food on its way from the mouth, it is first compacted by the tongue into a bolus and then

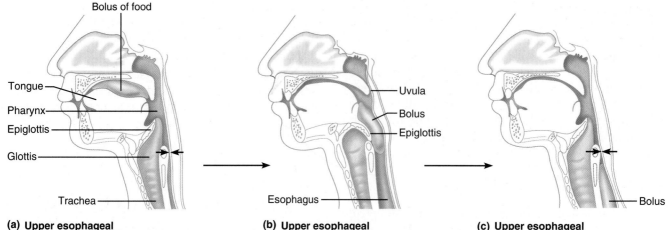

(a) Upper esophageal sphincter contracted

(b) Upper esophageal sphincter relaxed

(c) Upper esophageal sphincter contracted

FIGURE 23.13   Deglutition (swallowing). The process of swallowing consists of a voluntary (buccal) phase (a) and involuntary (pharyngeal-esophageal) phases (b–e). **(a)** During the buccal phase, the tongue rises and presses against the hard palate, forcing the food bolus into the oropharynx where the involuntary phase of swallowing begins. **(b)** The uvula and larynx rise to prevent food from entering respiratory passageways. Relaxation of the upper esophageal sphincter allows food to enter the esophagus. **(c)** The constrictor muscles of the pharynx contract, forcing food into the esophagus inferiorly, and the upper esophageal sphincter contracts after entry. **(d)** Food is moved through the esophagus to the stomach by peristalsis. **(e)** The gastroesophageal sphincter opens, and food enters the stomach.

(d)

(e)

swallowed. **Deglutition** (deg"loo-tish'un), or swallowing, is a complicated process that involves coordinated activity of over 22 separate muscle groups. It has two major phases, the buccal and the pharyngeal-esophageal.

The **buccal phase** occurs in the mouth and is voluntary. In the buccal phase, we place the tip of the tongue against the hard palate, and then contract the tongue to force the bolus into the oropharynx (Figure 23.13a). As food enters the pharynx and stimulates tactile receptors there, it passes out of our control and into the realm of involuntary reflex activity.

Triggered by that "bit of saliva" or food reaching receptors in the posterior pharynx, the involuntary **pharyngeal-esophageal phase** of swallowing is controlled by the swallowing center located in the brain stem (medulla and lower pons). Motor impulses from that center are transmitted via various cranial nerves, most importantly the vagus nerves, to the muscles of the pharynx and esophagus. Once food

enters the pharynx, respiration is momentarily inhibited and as illustrated in Figure 23.13b, all routes except the desired one—into the digestive tract—are blocked off:

- The tongue blocks off the mouth.
- The soft palate rises to close off the nasopharynx.
- The larynx rises so that the epiglottis covers its opening into the respiratory passageways, and the upper esophageal sphincter relaxes.

Food is moved along through the pharynx and into the esophagus by pressure gradients created by wavelike peristaltic contractions (Figure 23.13c–e). Solid foods pass from the oropharynx to the stomach in about 8 seconds; fluids, aided by gravity, pass in 1 to 2 seconds. Just before the peristaltic wave (and food) reaches the end of the esophagus, the gastroesophageal sphincter relaxes reflexively to allow food to enter the stomach. After food entry, that sphincter closes, preventing regurgitation.

Q *What structural modification of a tunic underlies the stomach's ability to mechanically digest food?*

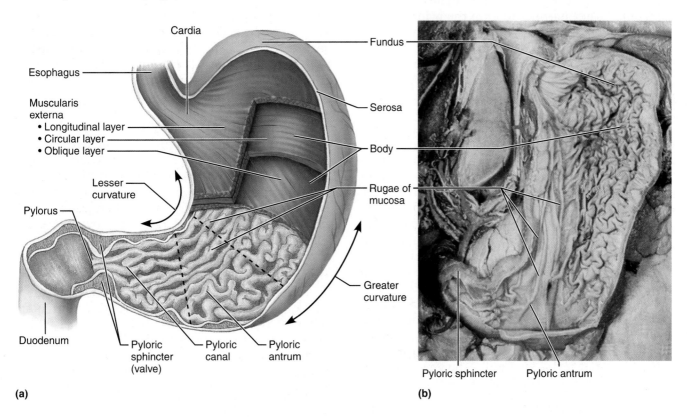

FIGURE 23.14 **Anatomy of the stomach. (a)** Gross internal anatomy (frontal section). **(b)** Photograph of internal aspect of stomach. (See *A Brief Atlas of the Human Body,* figure 69a.)

If we try to talk or inhale while swallowing, the various protective mechanisms may be short-circuited and food may enter the respiratory passageways instead. This event typically triggers the cough reflex in an attempt to expel the food.

The Stomach

Below the esophagus, the GI tract expands to form the **stomach** (see Figure 23.1), a temporary "storage tank" where chemical breakdown of proteins begins and food is converted to a creamy paste called **chyme** (kīm; "juice"). The stomach lies in the upper left quadrant of the peritoneal cavity, nearly hidden by the liver and diaphragm. Specifically, it lies in the left hypochondriac, epigastric, and umbilical regions of the abdomen. Though relatively fixed at both ends, the stomach is quite movable in between. It

tends to lie high and run horizontally in short, stout people (a steer-horn stomach) and is often elongated vertically in tall, thin people (a J-shaped stomach).

Gross Anatomy

The adult stomach varies from 15 to 25 cm (6 to 10 inches) long, but its diameter and volume depend on how much food it contains. An empty stomach has a volume of about 50 ml and a cross-sectional diameter only slightly larger than the large intestine, but when it is really distended it can hold about 4 L (1 gallon) of food and may extend nearly all the way to the pelvis! When empty, the stomach collapses inward, throwing its mucosa (and submucosa) into large, longitudinal folds called **rugae** (roo'ge; *ruga* = wrinkle, fold).

The major regions of the stomach are shown in Figure 23.14a. The small **cardiac region,** or **cardia** ("near the heart"), surrounds the cardiac orifice through which food enters the stomach from the esophagus. The **fundus** is its dome-shaped part, tucked beneath the diaphragm, that bulges superolaterally to the cardia. The **body,** the midportion of

A *The muscularis externa has a third layer of smooth muscle in which the fibers run obliquely, allowing the stomach to exhibit churning movements that physically break down the food.*

the stomach, is continuous inferiorly with the funnel-shaped **pyloric region.** The wider and more superior part of the pyloric region, the **pyloric antrum** (*antrum* = cave) narrows to form the **pyloric canal,** which terminates at the **pylorus.** The pylorus is continuous with the duodenum (the first part of the small intestine) through the **pyloric sphincter,** which controls stomach emptying (*pylorus* = gatekeeper).

The convex lateral surface of the stomach is its **greater curvature,** and its concave medial surface is the **lesser curvature.** Extending from these curvatures are two mesenteries, called *omenta* (o-men′tah), that help tether the stomach to other digestive organs and the body wall (see Figure 23.30, p. 924). The **lesser omentum** runs from the liver to the lesser curvature of the stomach, where it becomes continuous with the visceral peritoneum covering the stomach. The **greater omentum** drapes inferiorly from the greater curvature of the stomach to cover the coils of the small intestine. It then runs dorsally and superiorly, wrapping the spleen and the transverse portion of the large intestine before blending with the *mesocolon*, a dorsal mesentery that secures the large intestine to the parietal peritoneum of the posterior abdominal wall. The greater omentum is riddled with fat deposits (*oment* = fatty skin) that give it the appearance of a lacy apron. It also contains large collections of lymph nodes. The immune cells and macrophages in these nodes "police" the peritoneal cavity and intraperitoneal organs.

The stomach is served by the autonomic nervous system. Sympathetic fibers from thoracic splanchnic nerves are relayed through the celiac plexus. Parasympathetic fibers are supplied by the vagus nerve. The arterial supply of the stomach is provided by branches (gastric and splenic) of the celiac trunk (see Figure 19.23). The corresponding veins are part of the hepatic portal system (see Figure 19.28c) and ultimately drain into the hepatic portal vein.

Microscopic Anatomy

The stomach wall contains the four tunics typical of most of the alimentary canal, but its muscularis and mucosa are modified for the special roles of the stomach. Besides the usual circular and longitudinal layers of smooth muscle, the muscularis externa has an innermost smooth muscle layer that runs *obliquely* (Figure 23.14a and Figure 23.15). This arrangement allows the stomach not only to move food along the tract, but also to churn, mix, and pummel the food, physically breaking it down into smaller fragments.

The lining epithelium of the stomach mucosa is a simple columnar epithelium composed entirely of goblet cells, which produce a protective two-layer coat of alkaline mucus in which the surface layer consists of viscous mucus that traps a layer of bicarbonate-rich fluid beneath it. This otherwise smooth lining is dotted with millions of deep **gastric pits** (Figure 23.15), which lead into the **gastric glands** that produce the stomach secretion called **gastric juice.** The cells forming the walls of the gastric pits are primarily goblet cells, but those composing the gastric glands vary in different stomach regions. For example, the cells in the glands of the cardia and pylorus are primarily mucus secreting, whereas cells of the pyloric antrum produce mucus and several hormones including most of the stimulatory hormone called gastrin. Glands of the stomach fundus and body, where most chemical digestion occurs, are substantially larger and produce the majority of the stomach secretions. The glands in these regions contain a variety of secretory cells, including the four types described here:

1. **Mucous neck cells,** found in the upper, or "neck," regions of the glands, produce a thin, quite different type of mucus from that secreted by the goblet cells of the surface epithelium. It is not yet understood what special function this *acidic* mucus performs.

2. **Parietal cells,** found mainly in the middle region of the glands scattered among the chief cells (described next), simultaneously secrete *hydrochloric acid (HCl)* and *intrinsic factor*. Although the parietal cells appear spherical when viewed with a light microscope, they actually have three prongs that exhibit dense microvilli (they look like fuzzy pitchforks!). This structure provides a huge surface area for secreting H^+ and Cl^- into the stomach lumen. HCl makes the stomach contents extremely acidic (pH 1.5–3.5), a condition necessary for activation and optimal activity of pepsin. The acidity also helps in food digestion by denaturing proteins and breaking down cell walls of plant foods, and is harsh enough to kill many of the bacteria ingested with foods. Intrinsic factor is a glycoprotein required for vitamin B_{12} absorption in the small intestine.

3. **Chief cells** produce *pepsinogen* (pep-sin′o-jen), the inactive form of the protein-digesting enzyme **pepsin.** The chief cells occur mainly in the basal regions of the gastric glands. When chief cells are stimulated, the first pepsinogen molecules they release are activated by HCl encountered in the apical region of the gland (Figure 23.15c). But once pepsin is present, it also catalyzes the conversion of pepsinogen to pepsin. This positive feedback process is limited only by the amount of pepsinogen present. The activation process involves removal of a small peptide fragment from the pepsinogen molecule, causing it to change shape and expose its active site.

FIGURE 23.15 **Microscopic anatomy of the stomach.**
(a) Layers of stomach wall (longitudinal section). **(b)** Enlarged view of gastric pits. **(c)** Locations of the HCl-producing parietal cells and the pepsin-secreting chief cells in the gastric pit.

Chief cells also secrete insignificant amounts of lipases (fat-digesting enzymes).

4. Enteroendocrine cells (en"ter-o-en'do-krin; "gut endocrine") release a variety of chemical messengers directly into the interstitial fluid of the lamina propria. Some of these, for example **histamine** and **serotonin,** act locally as paracrines. Others, such as **somatostatin,** act both locally and as hormones, diffusing into the blood capillaries to influence several digestive system target organs (see Table 23.1, p. 906). **Gastrin,** a hormone, plays essential roles in regulating stomach secretion and motility, as described shortly.

The stomach mucosa is exposed to some of the harshest conditions in the entire digestive tract. Gastric juice is corrosively acidic (the H^+ concentration in the stomach can be 100,000 times that found in blood), and its protein-digesting enzymes can digest the stomach itself. However, the stomach is not a passive victim of its formidable environment. It mounts an aggressive counterattack to protect itself, producing what is called the **mucosal barrier.** Four factors create this barrier:

1. A thick coating of bicarbonate-rich mucus is built up on the stomach wall.

2. The epithelial cells of the mucosa are joined together by tight junctions that prevent gastric juice from leaking into the underlying tissue layers.

3. Damaged epithelial mucosal cells are shed and quickly replaced by division of *undifferentiated stem cells* that reside where the gastric pits join the gastric glands. The stomach surface epithelium is completely renewed every three to six days. (However, glandular cells deep within the gastric glands have a much longer life span.)

HOMEOSTATIC IMBALANCE

Anything that breaches the gel-like mucosal barrier causes inflammation of the stomach wall, a condition called *gastritis*. Persistent damage to the underlying tissues can promote **gastric ulcers,** erosions of the stomach wall. The most distressing symptom of gastric ulcers is gnawing epigastric pain that seems to bore through to your back. The pain typically occurs 1–3 hours after eating and is often relieved by eating again. The danger posed by ulcers is perforation of the stomach wall followed by peritonitis and, perhaps, massive hemorrhage.

For years, the blame for causing ulcers was put on factors that favor high HCl production or low mucus secretion such as aspirin and nonsteroidal anti-inflammatory drugs (ibuprofen), smoking, spicy food, alcohol, coffee, and stress. Although acid conditions *are* necessary for ulcer formation, acidity in and of itself is not sufficient to cause ulcer formation. Most recurrent ulcers (90%) are the work of acid-resistant, corkscrew-shaped *Helicobacter pylori* bacteria, which burrow much like a drill bit through the mucus and destroy the protective mucosal layer, leaving denuded areas. These pathological effects occur in 10–20% of infected individuals. The antimicrobial activity of gastric mucin appears to play a major role in protecting the remaining 80–90% from *H. pylori*'s invasive attacks. The bacterial causal theory has been difficult to prove because the bacterium is also found in more than 50% of healthy people. Even more troubling are studies that link this bacterium to some stomach cancers.

These bacteria release several chemicals that help them do their "dirty work," including (1) some that curb HCl production and release ammonia (the ammonia then acts as a base to neutralize some of the stomach acid in their locale), (2) a *cytotoxin* that lesions the stomach epithelium, and (3) several proteins, some that cause the epithelial cells to detach from each other and others that act as chemotactic agents to attract macrophages and other defensive cells into the area, thus promoting a chronic inflammatory response.

The presence or absence of *H. pylori* is easily detected by a breath test. In ulcers colonized by it, the goal is to kill the embedded bacteria. A one- to two-week-long course of antibiotics (preferably two antibiotics with complementary effects, such as metronidazole and tetracycline) in combination with a bismuth-containing compound, promotes healing and prevents recurrence. (Bismuth is the active ingredient in Pepto-Bismol.) For active ulcers, a H_2-receptor blocker, which inhibits HCl secretion by blocking histamine's effects (see Figure 23.17), may also help. In noninfectious cases, H_2-receptor blocker drugs such as cimetidine (Tagamet) and ranitidine (Zantac) are the therapy of choice. ●

Digestive Processes Occurring in the Stomach

Except for ingestion and defecation, the stomach is involved in the whole "menu" of digestive activities. Besides serving as a holding area for ingested food, the stomach continues the demolition job begun in the oral cavity by further degrading food both physically and chemically. It then delivers chyme, the product of its activity, into the small intestine.

Protein digestion is initiated in the stomach and is the only significant type of enzymatic digestion that occurs there. Dietary proteins are denatured by HCl produced by stomach glands in preparation for enzymatic digestion. (The unfolded amino acid chain is more accessible to the enzymes.) The most important protein-digesting enzyme produced by the gastric mucosa is pepsin. In infants, however, the stomach glands also secrete **rennin,** an enzyme that acts on milk protein (casein), converting it to a curdy substance that looks like soured milk. Additionally, lingual lipase released by the intrinsic salivary glands may digest some triglycerides in the stomach. Two common lipid-soluble substances—alcohol and aspirin—pass easily through the stomach mucosa into the blood. Alcohol and aspirin may cause gastric bleeding, so these substances should be avoided by those with gastric ulcers.

Despite the obvious benefits of preparing food to enter the intestine, the only stomach function essential to life is secretion of intrinsic factor. **Intrinsic factor** is required for intestinal absorption of vitamin B_{12}, needed to produce mature erythrocytes; in its absence, *pernicious anemia* results. However, if vitamin B_{12} is administered by injection, individuals can survive with minimal digestive problems even after total gastrectomy (stomach removal). (The stomach's activities are summarized in Table 23.2, p. 920).

Since chemical digestion and absorption are described later, here we will focus on events that (1) control secretory activity of the gastric glands and (2) regulate stomach motility and emptying.

Regulation of Gastric Secretion

Gastric secretion is controlled by both neural and hormonal mechanisms. Under normal conditions

Q *Distension of the stomach and duodenal walls have differing effects on stomach secretory activity. What are these effects?*

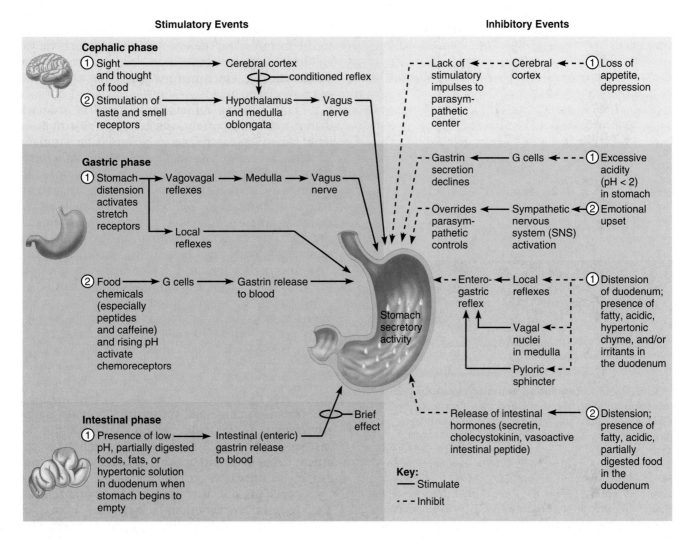

Stimulatory Events   **Inhibitory Events**

FIGURE 23.16   **Neural and hormonal mechanisms that regulate release of gastric juice.** Stimulatory factors are shown on the left; inhibitory factors are shown on the right.

the gastric mucosa pours out as much as 3 L of gastric juice—an acid brew so potent it can dissolve nails—every day. Nervous control is provided by long (vagus nerve–mediated) and short (local enteric) nerve reflexes. When the vagus nerves stimulate the stomach, secretory activity of virtually all of its glands increases. (By contrast, activation of sympathetic nerves depresses secretory activity.) Hormonal control of gastric secretion is largely the province of gastrin, which stimulates secretion of enzymes and

HCl, and of hormones produced by the small intestine, which are mostly gastrin antagonists.

Stimuli acting at three distinct sites—the head, stomach, and small intestine—provoke or inhibit gastric secretory activity and, accordingly, the three phases of gastric secretion are called the *cephalic, gastric,* and *intestinal phases* (Figure 23.16). However, the effector site is the stomach in all cases and, once initiated, one or all three phases may be occurring at the same time.

Phase 1: Cephalic (Reflex)   The **cephalic,** or **reflex, phase** of gastric secretion occurs *before* food enters the stomach. Only a few minutes long, this phase is triggered by the aroma, taste, sight, or

A *Distension of the stomach promotes increased secretory activity whereas stretching the wall of the duodenum causes hormones to be released that inhibit stomach secretory activity.*

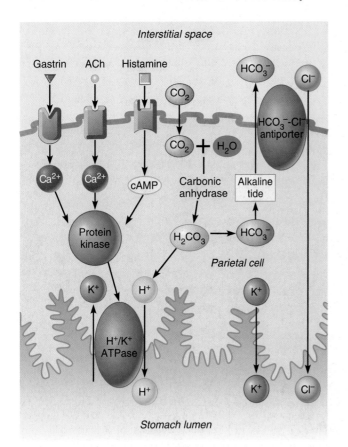

FIGURE 23.17 **Regulation and mechanism of HCl secretion.** Binding of histamine, gastrin, and acetylcholine (ACh) to parietal cell membrane receptors initiates intracellular events (mediated by second-messenger systems) that lead to HCl secretion into the stomach lumen. H^+ and HCO_3^- (bicarbonate ions) are generated from the dissociation of carbonic acid (H_2CO_3). As H^+-K^+ ATPase pumps H^+ into the lumen, K^+ enters the cell. Meanwhile, the HCO_3^--Cl^- antiporter transports HCO_3^- into the interstitial space in exchange for chloride ions (Cl^-). Cl^- and K^+ then diffuse into the lumen through membrane channels (membrane channels not depicted).

thought of food, and it gets the stomach ready for its upcoming digestive chore. Inputs from activated olfactory receptors and taste buds are relayed to the hypothalamus, which in turn stimulates the vagal nuclei of the medulla oblongata, causing motor impulses to be transmitted via the vagus nerves to parasympathetic enteric ganglia. Enteric ganglionic neurons in turn stimulate the stomach glands. The enhanced secretory activity that results when we see or think of food is a *conditioned reflex* and occurs only when we like or want the food. If we are depressed or have no appetite, this part of the cephalic reflex is suppressed.

Phase 2: Gastric Once food reaches the stomach, local neural and hormonal mechanisms initiate the **gastric phase.** This phase is three to four hours

long and provides about two-thirds of the gastric juice released. The most important stimuli are distension, peptides, and low acidity. Stomach distension activates stretch receptors and initiates both local (myenteric) reflexes and the long vagovagal reflexes. In the latter type of reflex, impulses travel to the medulla and then back to the stomach via vagal fibers. Both types of reflexes lead to acetylcholine (ACh) release, which in turn stimulates the output of more gastric juice.

Though neural influences initiated by stomach distension are important, the hormone gastrin probably plays a greater role in stimulating stomach gland secretion during the gastric phase. Chemical stimuli provided by partially digested proteins, caffeine, and rising pH directly activate gastrin-secreting enteroendocrine cells called **G cells** in the stomach antrum. Although gastrin also stimulates the release of enzymes, its main target is the HCl-secreting parietal cells, which it prods to spew out even more HCl (Figure 23.17). Highly acidic (pH below 2) gastric contents *inhibit* gastrin secretion.

When protein foods are in the stomach, the pH of the gastric contents generally rises because proteins act as buffers to tie up H^+. The rise in pH stimulates gastrin and subsequently HCl release, which in turn provides the acidic conditions needed for protein digestion. The more protein in the meal, the greater the amount of gastrin and HCl released. As proteins are digested, the gastric contents gradually become more acidic, which again inhibits the gastrin-secreting cells. This negative feedback mechanism helps maintain optimal pH and working conditions for the gastric enzymes.

G cells are also activated by the neural reflexes already described. Emotional upsets, fear, anxiety, or anything that triggers the fight-or-flight response inhibits gastric secretion because (during such times) the sympathetic division overrides parasympathetic controls of digestion (Figure 23.16).

The control of the HCl-secreting parietal cells is multifaceted. HCl secretion is stimulated by three chemicals, all of which work through second-messenger systems (Figure 23.17): *ACh* released by parasympathetic nerve fibers and *gastrin* secreted by G cells bring about their effects by increasing intracellular Ca^{2+} levels. *Histamine*, released by the so-called *enterochromaffin-like* (ECL) cells in response to gastrin (and to a lesser extent by ACh) acts through cyclic AMP (cAMP). When only one of the three chemicals binds to the parietal cells, HCl secretion is scanty, but when all three bind, HCl pours forth as if shot out by a high-pressure hose. (As noted earlier, antihistamines, such as cimetidine, which bind to and block the H_2 receptors of parietal cells, are used to treat gastric ulcers due to hyperacidity.)

The process of HCl formation within the parietal cells is complicated. The consensus is that H^+ is actively pumped into the stomach lumen against a tremendous concentration gradient by H^+-K^+ ATPases as K^+ ions are moved into the cell from the interstitial fluid. Chloride ions (Cl^-) are also pumped into the lumen to maintain an electrical balance in the stomach. The Cl^- is obtained from blood plasma, while H^+ comes from the breakdown of carbonic acid (formed by the combination of carbon dioxide and water) within the parietal cell (Figure 23.17):

$$CO_2 + H_2O \rightarrow H_2CO_3 \rightarrow H^+ + HCO_3^-$$

As H^+ is pumped from the cell and HCO_3^- (bicarbonate ion) accumulates within the cell, HCO_3^- is ejected through the basal cell membrane into the capillary blood. As a result, blood draining from the stomach is more alkaline than the blood serving it. This phenomenon is called the **alkaline tide.** Notice that HCO_3^- and Cl^- are moved by a HCO_3^--Cl^- antiporter in the basolateral membrane, and this is the means of entry of the Cl^- that moves into the lumen as the chloride part of the HCl product. K^+ and Cl^- move into the lumen by diffusing through membrane channels.

Phase 3: Intestinal

The **intestinal phase** of gastric secretion has two components—one excitatory and the other inhibitory (Figure 23.16). The *excitatory* aspect is set into motion as partially digested food fills the initial part (duodenum) of the small intestine. This stimulates intestinal mucosal cells to release a hormone that encourages the gastric glands to continue their secretory activity. The effects of this hormone mirror those of gastrin, so it has been named **intestinal (enteric) gastrin.** However, this stimulatory effect is brief because as the intestine distends with chyme containing large amounts of H^+, fats, partially digested proteins, and various irritating substances, the *inhibitory* component is triggered in the form of the **enterogastric reflex.**

The enterogastric reflex is actually a trio of reflexes that (1) inhibit the vagal nuclei in the medulla, (2) inhibit local reflexes, and (3) activate sympathetic fibers that cause the pyloric sphincter to tighten and prevent further food entry into the small intestine. As a result, gastric secretory activity declines. These "brakes" on gastric activity protect the small intestine from excessive acidity and match the small intestine's processing abilities to the amount of chyme entering it at a given time.

In addition, the factors just named trigger the release of several intestinal hormones, collectively called **enterogastrones,** which include **secretin**

(se-kre'tin), **cholecystokinin (CCK)** (ko"le-sis"to-ki'nin), and **vasoactive intestinal peptide (VIP).** All of these hormones inhibit gastric secretion when the stomach is very active and also play other roles, which are summarized in Table 23.1.

Gastric Motility and Emptying

Stomach contractions not only cause its emptying but also compress, knead, twist, and continually mix the food with gastric juice to produce chyme. Because the mixing movements are accomplished by a unique type of peristalsis (for example, in the pylorus it is bidirectional rather than unidirectional), the processes of mechanical digestion and propulsion are inseparable in the stomach.

Response of the Stomach to Filling   The stomach stretches to accommodate incoming food, but internal stomach pressure remains constant until about 1.5 L of food has been ingested. Thereafter, the pressure rises. The relatively unchanging pressure in a filling stomach is due to (1) the reflex-mediated receptive relaxation of the stomach muscle and (2) the plasticity of visceral smooth muscle.

Receptive relaxation of smooth muscle in the stomach fundus and body occurs both in anticipation of and in response to food movement through the esophagus and into the stomach. This process is coordinated by the swallowing center of the brain stem and mediated by the vagus nerves acting on serotonin and NO-releasing enteric neurons. **Plasticity** is the intrinsic ability of visceral smooth muscle to exhibit the stress-relaxation response, that is, to be stretched without greatly increasing its tension and contracting expulsively. As described in Chapter 9, this capability is very important in hollow organs, like the stomach, that must serve as temporary reservoirs.

Gastric Contractile Activity   As in the esophagus, the stomach exhibits peristalsis. After a meal, peristalsis begins near the gastroesophageal sphincter, where it produces gentle rippling movements of the thin stomach wall. But as the contractions approach the pylorus, where the stomach musculature is thicker, they become much more powerful. Consequently, the contents of the fundus and body (food storage area) remain relatively undisturbed, while foodstuffs in and around the pyloric antrum receive a truly lively pummeling and mixing.

The pyloric region of the stomach, which holds about 30 ml of chyme, acts as a "dynamic filter" that allows only liquids and small particles to pass through the barely open pyloric valve during the digestive period. Normally, each peristaltic wave reaching the pyloric muscle "spits" or squirts 3 ml or less of chyme into the small intestine. Because the

23

TABLE 23.1	Hormones and Paracrines That Act in Digestion*			
HORMONE	**SITE OF PRODUCTION**	**STIMULUS FOR PRODUCTION**	**TARGET ORGAN**	**ACTIVITY**
Gastrin	Stomach mucosa	Food (particularly partially digested proteins) in stomach (chemical stimulation); acetylcholine released by nerve fibers	Stomach	▪ Causes gastric glands to increase secretory activity; most pronounced effect is on HCl secretion ▪ Stimulates gastric emptying
			Small intestine	▪ Stimulates contraction of intestinal muscle
			Ileocecal valve	▪ Relaxes ileocecal valve
			Large intestine	▪ Stimulates mass movements
Serotonin	Stomach mucosa	Food in stomach	Stomach	▪ Causes contraction of stomach muscle
Histamine	Stomach mucosa	Food in stomach	Stomach	▪ Activates parietal cells to release HCl
Somatostatin	Stomach mucosa; duodenal mucosa	Food in stomach; stimulation by sympathetic nerve fibers	Stomach	▪ Inhibits gastric secretion of all products; inhibits gastric motility and emptying
			Pancreas	▪ Inhibits secretion
			Small intestine	▪ Inhibits GI blood flow; thus inhibits intestinal absorption
			Gallbladder	▪ Inhibits contraction and bile release
Intestinal gastrin	Duodenal mucosa	Acidic and partially digested foods in duodenum	Stomach	▪ Stimulates gastric glands and motility
Secretin	Duodenal mucosa	Acidic chyme (also partially digested proteins, fats, hypertonic or hypotonic fluids, or irritants in chyme)	Stomach	▪ Inhibits gastric gland secretion and gastric motility during gastric phase of secretion
			Pancreas	▪ Increases output of pancreatic juice rich in bicarbonate ions; potentiates CCK's action
			Liver	▪ Increases bile output
Cholecystokinin (CCK)	Duodenal mucosa	Fatty chyme, in particular, but also partially digested proteins	Liver/pancreas	▪ Potentiates secretin's actions on these organs
			Pancreas	▪ Increases output of enzyme-rich pancreatic juice
			Gallbladder	▪ Stimulates organ to contract and expel stored bile
			Hepatopancreatic sphincter (of Oddi)	▪ Relaxes sphincter to allow entry of bile and pancreatic juice into duodenum
Vasoactive intestinal peptide (VIP)	Duodenal mucosa	Chyme containing partially digested foods	Duodenum	▪ Stimulates buffer secretion; dilates intestinal capillaries
			Stomach	▪ Inhibits HCl production
			Small intestine	▪ Relaxes intestinal smooth muscle
Motilin	Duodenal mucosa	Fasting; periodic release every 1½–2 hours by neural stimuli	Proximal duodenum	▪ Stimulates migrating motility complex

*Except for somatostatin, all of these polypeptides also stimulate the growth (particularly of the mucosa) of the organs they affect.

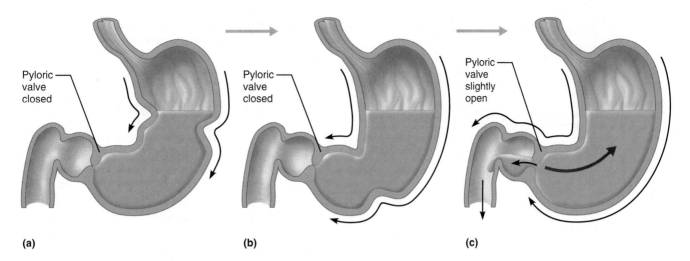

FIGURE 23.18 **Peristaltic waves in the stomach. (a)** Peristaltic waves move toward the pylorus. **(b)** The most vigorous peristalsis and mixing action occurs close to the pylorus. **(c)** The pyloric end of the stomach acts as a pump that delivers small amounts of chyme into the duodenum, simultaneously forcing most of its contained material backward into the stomach, where it undergoes further mixing.

contraction also *closes* the valve, which is normally partially relaxed, the rest (about 27 ml) is propelled backward into the stomach, where it is mixed further (Figure 23.18). This back-and-forth pumping action (retropulsion) effectively breaks up solids in the gastric contents.

Although the intensity of the stomach's peristaltic waves can be modified, their rate is constant—always around three per minute. This contractile rhythm is set by the spontaneous activity of *pacemaker cells* located in the longitudinal smooth muscle layer. The pacemaker cells, muscle-like noncontractile cells called *interstitial cells of Cajal* (ka-hal′), depolarize and repolarize spontaneously three times each minute, establishing the so-called *cyclic slow waves* of the stomach, or its **basic electrical rhythm (BER).** Since the pacemakers are electrically coupled to the rest of the smooth muscle sheet by gap junctions, their "beat" is transmitted efficiently and quickly to the entire muscularis. The pacemakers set the maximum rate of contraction, but they do not initiate the contractions or regulate their force. Instead, they generate subthreshold depolarization waves, which are then "ignited" (enhanced by further depolarization and brought to threshold) by neural and hormonal factors.

Factors that increase the strength of stomach contractions are the same factors that enhance gastric secretory activity. Distension of the stomach wall by food activates stretch receptors and gastrin-secreting cells, which both ultimately stimulate gastric smooth muscle and so increase gastric motility. Thus, the more food there is in the stomach, the more vigorous the stomach mixing and emptying movements will be—within certain limits—as described next.

Regulation of Gastric Emptying The stomach usually empties completely within four hours after a meal. However, the larger the meal (the greater the stomach distension) and the more liquid its contents, the faster the stomach empties. Fluids pass quickly through the stomach. Solids linger, remaining until they are well mixed with gastric juice and converted to the liquid state.

The rate of gastric emptying depends as much—and perhaps more—on the contents of the duodenum as on what is happening in the stomach. The stomach and duodenum act in tandem like a "coupled meter" that functions at less than full capacity. As chyme enters the duodenum, receptors in its wall respond to chemical signals and to stretch, initiating the enterogastric reflex and the hormonal (enterogastrone) mechanisms that inhibit acid and pepsin secretion as described earlier. These mechanisms inhibit gastric secretory activity and prevent further duodenal filling by reducing the force of pyloric contractions (Figure 23.19).

A carbohydrate-rich meal moves through the duodenum rapidly, but fats form an oily layer at the top of the chyme and are digested more slowly by enzymes acting in the intestine. Thus, when chyme entering the duodenum is fatty, food may remain in the stomach six hours or more.

◢◣ HOMEOSTATIC IMBALANCE

Vomiting, or **emesis,** is an unpleasant experience that causes stomach emptying by a different route. Many factors signal the stomach to "launch lunch," but the most common are extreme stretching of the stomach or intestine or the presence of irritants such

Key:

☐ Initial stimulus
☐ Physiological response
☐ Result

◄───── Stimulate
◄- - - Inhibit

FIGURE 23.19 **Neural and hormonal factors inhibiting gastric emptying.** These controls ensure that the food will be well liquefied in the stomach and prevent the small intestine from being overwhelmed.

as bacterial toxins, excessive alcohol, spicy foods, and certain drugs in those organs. Both bloodborne molecules and sensory impulses streaming from the irritated sites to the **emetic center** (e-met'ik) of the medulla initiate a number of motor responses. The diaphragm and abdominal wall muscles contract, increasing intra-abdominal pressure, the cardiac sphincter relaxes, and the soft palate rises to close off the nasal passages. As a result, the stomach (and perhaps duodenal) contents are forced upward through the esophagus and pharynx and out the mouth. Before vomiting, an individual typically is pale, feels nauseated, and salivates. Excessive vomiting can cause dehydration and may lead to severe disturbances in the electrolyte and acid-base balance of the body. Since large amounts of HCl are lost in

vomitus, the blood becomes alkaline as the stomach attempts to replace its lost acid. ●

The Small Intestine and Associated Structures

In the small intestine, usable food is finally prepared for its journey into the cells of the body. However, this vital function cannot be accomplished without the aid of secretions from the liver (bile) and pancreas (digestive enzymes). Thus, these necessary accessory organs will also be considered in this section.

The Small Intestine

The **small intestine** is the body's major digestive organ. Within its twisted passageways, digestion is completed and virtually all absorption occurs.

Gross Anatomy

The small intestine is a convoluted tube extending from the pyloric sphincter in the epigastric region to the **ileocecal valve** (il"e-o-se'kal) in the right iliac region where it joins the large intestine (see Figure 23.1). It is the longest part of the alimentary tube, but is only about half the diameter of the large intestine, ranging from 2.5 to 4 cm (1–1.6 inches). Although it is 6–7 m long (approximately 20 ft, or as tall as a two-story building) in a cadaver, the small intestine is only about 2–4 m (7–13 ft) long during life because of muscle tone.

The small intestine has three subdivisions: the duodenum, which is mostly retroperitoneal, and the jejunum and ileum, both intraperitoneal organs. The relatively immovable **duodenum** (du"o-de'num; "twelve finger widths long"), which curves around the head of the pancreas (Figure 23.20), is about 25 cm (10 inches) long. Although it is the shortest intestinal subdivision, the duodenum has the most features of interest. The bile duct, delivering bile from the liver, and the main pancreatic duct, carrying pancreatic juice from the pancreas, unite in the wall of the duodenum in a bulblike point called the **hepatopancreatic ampulla** (hep"ah-to-pan"kre-at'ik am-pul'ah; *ampulla* = flask). The ampulla opens into the duodenum via the volcano-shaped **major duodenal papilla.** The entry of bile and pancreatic juice is controlled by a muscular valve called the **hepatopancreatic sphincter,** or **sphincter of Oddi.**

The **jejunum** (jĕ-joo'num; "empty"), about 2.5 m (8 ft) long, extends from the duodenum to the ileum. The **ileum** (il'e-um; "twisted"), approximately 3.6 m (12 ft) in length, joins the large intestine at the ileocecal valve. The jejunum and ileum hang in

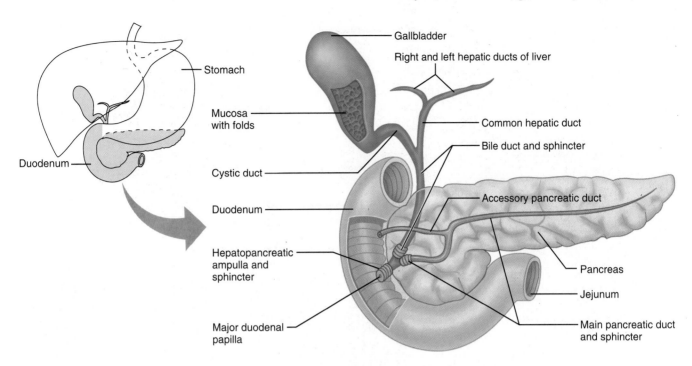

FIGURE 23.20 **The duodenum of the small intestine, and related organs.** Emptying into the duodenum are ducts from the pancreas, gallbladder, and liver.

sausagelike coils in the central and lower part of the abdominal cavity, suspended from the posterior abdominal wall by the fan-shaped *mesentery* (see Figure 23.30). These more distal parts of the small intestine are encircled and framed by the large intestine.

Nerve fibers serving the small intestine include parasympathetics from the vagus and sympathetics from the thoracic splanchnic nerves, both relayed through the superior mesenteric (and celiac) plexus. The arterial supply is primarily from the superior mesenteric artery (pp. 754–755). The veins parallel the arteries and typically drain into the superior mesenteric vein. From there, the nutrient-rich venous blood from the small intestine drains into the hepatic portal vein, which carries it to the liver.

Microscopic Anatomy

Modifications for Absorption The small intestine is highly adapted for nutrient absorption. Its length alone provides a huge surface area, and its wall has three structural modifications—plicae circulares, villi, and microvilli—that amplify its absorptive surface enormously (by a factor of more than 600 times). One estimate is that the intestinal surface area is about equal to the floor space of an average two-story house! Most absorption occurs in the proximal part of the small intestine, so these

specializations decrease in number toward its distal end.

The **circular folds,** or **plicae circulares** (pli'ke ser"ku-lar'ēs), are deep, permanent folds of the mucosa and submucosa (Figure 23.21a). Nearly 1 cm tall, these folds force chyme to spiral through the lumen, slowing its movement and allowing time for full nutrient absorption.

Villi (vil'i; "tufts of hair") are fingerlike projections of the mucosa, over 1 mm high, that give it a velvety texture, much like the soft nap of a towel (Figures 23.21b and Figure 23.22a). The epithelial cells of the villi are chiefly absorptive columnar cells. In the core of each villus is a dense capillary bed and a wide lymph capillary called a **lacteal** (lak'te-al). Digested foodstuffs are absorbed through the epithelial cells into both the capillary blood and the lacteal. The villi are large and leaflike in the duodenum (the intestinal site of most active absorption) and gradually narrow and shorten along the length of the small intestine. A "slip" of smooth muscle in the villus core allows it to alternately shorten and lengthen, pulsations that (1) increase the contact between the villus and the contents of the intestinal lumen, making absorption more efficient, and (2) "milk" lymph along through the lacteals.

Microvilli, tiny projections of the plasma membrane of the absorptive cells of the mucosa, give the mucosal surface a fuzzy appearance called the **brush**

Q *What is a lacteal and what is its function?*

FIGURE 23.21 **Structural modifications of the small intestine that increase its surface area for digestion and absorption. (a)** Enlargement of a few circular folds, showing associated fingerlike villi. **(b)** Structure of a villus. **(c)** Two absorptive cells that exhibit microvilli on their free (luminal) surface. **(d)** Photomicrograph of the mucosa, showing villi (80×). (See *A Brief Atlas of the Human Body,* figure 69b.)

border (Figures 23.21c and Figure 23.22b). The plasma membranes of the microvilli bear enzymes referred to as **brush border enzymes,** which complete the digestion of carbohydrates and proteins in the small intestine.

Histology of the Wall Externally the subdivisions of the small intestine appear to be nearly identical, but their internal and microscopic anatomies reveal some important differences. The four tunics typical of the GI tract are also seen

here, but the mucosa and submucosa are modified to reflect the intestine's functions in the digestive pathway.

The epithelium of the mucosa is largely simple columnar *absorptive cells* bound by tight junctions and richly endowed with microvilli. It also has many mucus-secreting *goblet cells;* scattered *enteroendocrine cells* (the source of the enterogastrones—secretin and cholecystokinin to name two), and interspersed T cells called *intraepithelial lymphocytes (IELs),* which represent an important immunological compartment. Unlike other T cells, IELs do *not* need "priming." Upon encountering antigens, they immediately release cytokines that cause killing of infected target cells.

A *lymphatic capillary that receives some of the fatty materials absorbed from the intestine.*

Villi

Desquamating cells

(a)

Microvilli

Absorptive cell

(b)

FIGURE 23.22 **Villi and microvilli of the small intestine.** False-color electron micrographs. **(a)** Villi (700×). Dead desquamating cells seen on the ridges of the villi are colored yellow and orange. **(b)** Microvilli (40,000×) of absorptive cells appear as red projections from the surface of the absorptive cell. Yellow granules are mucus granules.

Between the villi, the mucosa is studded with *pits* that lead into tubular intestinal glands called **intestinal crypts,** or **crypts of Lieberkühn** (le′ber-kun). The epithelial cells that line these crypts secrete *intestinal juice,* a watery mixture containing mucus that serves as a carrier fluid for absorbing nutrients from chyme. Deep in the crypts are specialized secretory cells called *Paneth cells,* which fortify the small intestine's defenses by releasing antimicrobial agents such as defensins and *lysozyme,* an antibacterial enzyme. The crypts decrease in number along the length of the small intestine, but the goblet cells become more abundant.

The various epithelial cells arise from rapidly dividing stem cells in the crypts. As the daughter cells gradually migrate up the villi, they differentiate, becoming specialized cell types. They are shed from the villus tips, renewing the villus epithelium every three to six days. The rapid replacement of intestinal (and gastric) epithelial cells has clinical as well as physiological significance. Treatments for cancer, such as radiation therapy and chemotherapy, preferentially target rapidly dividing cells. This kills cancer cells, but it also nearly obliterates the GI tract epithelium, causing nausea, vomiting, and diarrhea after each treatment.

The submucosa is typical areolar connective tissue, and it contains both individual and *aggregated lymphoid follicles,* the latter called **Peyer's patches** (pi′erz). Peyer's patches increase in abundance toward the end of the small intestine, reflecting the fact that this region of the small intestine contains huge numbers of bacteria that must be prevented from entering the bloodstream. Elaborate mucus-secreting **duodenal** *(Brunner's)* **glands** are found in the submucosa of the duodenum only. These glands (see Figure 23.21b) produce an alkaline (bicarbonate-rich) mucus that helps neutralize the acidic chyme moving in from the stomach. When this protective mucus barrier is inadequate, the intestinal wall erodes and *duodenal ulcers* result.

The muscularis is typical and bilayered. Except for the bulk of the duodenum, which is retroperitoneal and has an adventitia, the external intestinal surface is covered by visceral peritoneum (serosa).

Intestinal Juice: Composition and Control

The intestinal glands normally secrete 1 to 2 L of **intestinal juice** daily. The major stimulus for its production is distension or irritation of the intestinal mucosa by hypertonic or acidic chyme. Normally, intestinal juice is slightly alkaline (7.4–7.8), and isotonic with blood plasma. Intestinal juice is largely water but it also contains some mucus, which is secreted both by the duodenal glands and by goblet cells of the mucosa. Intestinal juice is enzyme-poor because intestinal enzymes are limited to the bound enzymes of the brush border.

23

The Liver and Gallbladder

The *liver* and *gallbladder* are accessory organs associated with the small intestine. The liver, one of the body's most important organs, has many metabolic and regulatory roles. However, its *digestive* function is to produce bile for export to the duodenum. Bile is a fat emulsifier; that is, it breaks up fats into tiny particles so that they are more accessible to digestive enzymes. We will describe bile and the emulsification process when we discuss the digestion and absorption of fats later in the chapter. Although the liver also processes nutrient-laden venous blood delivered to it directly from the digestive organs, this is a metabolic rather than a digestive role. (See Chapter 24.) The gallbladder is chiefly a storage organ for bile.

Gross Anatomy of the Liver

The ruddy, blood-rich **liver** is the largest gland in the body, weighing about 1.4 kg (3 lb) in the average adult. Shaped like a wedge, it occupies most of the right hypochondriac and epigastric regions, extending farther to the right of the body midline than to the left. Located under the diaphragm, the liver lies almost entirely within the rib cage, which provides some protection (see Figures 23.1 and 23.23c).

Typically, the liver is said to have four primary lobes. The largest of these, the *right lobe*, is visible on all liver surfaces and separated from the smaller *left lobe* by a deep fissure (Figure 23.23a). The posteriormost *caudate lobe* and the *quadrate lobe*, which lies inferior to the left lobe, are visible in an inferior view of the liver (Figure 23.23b). A mesentery, the **falciform ligament,** separates the right and left lobes anteriorly and suspends the liver from the diaphragm and anterior abdominal wall (see also Figure 23.30a and d, p. 924). Running along the inferior edge of the falciform ligament is the **round ligament,** or **ligamentum teres** (te′rēz; "round"), a fibrous remnant of the fetal umbilical vein. Except for the superiormost liver area (the *bare area*), which touches the diaphragm, the entire liver is enclosed by the visceral peritoneum. As mentioned earlier, a dorsal mesentery, the lesser omentum (see Figure 23.30b), anchors the liver to the lesser curvature of the stomach. The **hepatic artery** and the **hepatic portal vein,** which enter the liver at the **porta hepatis** ("gateway to the liver"), and the common hepatic duct, which runs inferiorly from the liver, all travel through the lesser omentum to reach their destinations. The gallbladder rests in a recess on the inferior surface of the right liver lobe.

The traditional scheme of defining liver lobes (outlined above) has been criticized because it is based on superficial features of the liver. Some anatomists emphasize that the primary lobes of the liver should be defined as the territories served by the right and left hepatic ducts. These two territories are delineated by a plane drawn from the indentation (sulcus) of the inferior vena cava to the gallbladder recess (see Figure 23.23b). Those to the right of the plane are the *right lobe* and those to its left constitute the *left lobe.* According to this scheme, the small quadrate and caudate lobes are part of the left lobe.

Bile leaves the liver through several bile ducts that ultimately fuse to form the large **common hepatic duct,** which travels downward toward the duodenum. Along its course, that duct fuses with the **cystic duct** draining the gallbladder to form the **bile duct** (Figure 23.20).

Microscopic Anatomy of the Liver

The liver is composed of sesame seed–sized structural and functional units called **liver lobules** (Figure 23.24). Each lobule is a roughly hexagonal (six-sided) structure consisting of plates of *liver cells*, or **hepatocytes** (hep′ah-to-sīts), organized like bricks in a garden wall. The hepatocyte plates radiate outward from a **central vein** running in the longitudinal axis of the lobule. To make a rough "model" of a liver lobule, open a thick paperback book until its two covers meet: The pages represent the plates of hepatocytes and the hollow cylinder formed by the rolled spine represents the central vein.

If you keep in mind that the liver's main function is to filter and process the nutrient-rich blood delivered to it, the description of its anatomy that follows will make a lot of sense. At each of the six corners of a lobule is a **portal triad** (*portal tract* region), so named because three basic structures are always present there: a branch of the *hepatic artery* (supplying oxygen-rich arterial blood to the liver), a branch of the *hepatic portal vein* (carrying venous blood laden with nutrients from the digestive viscera), and a *bile duct*. Between the hepatocyte plates are enlarged, leaky capillaries, the **liver sinusoids.** Blood from both the hepatic portal vein and the hepatic artery percolates from the triad regions through these sinusoids and empties into the central vein. From the central veins blood eventually enters the hepatic veins, which drain the liver, and empty into the inferior vena cava. Forming part of the sinusoid walls are star-shaped **hepatic macrophages,** also called **Kupffer cells** (koop′fer) (Figure 23.24d), which remove debris such as bacteria and worn-out blood cells from the blood as it flows past.

The versatile hepatocytes have large amounts of both rough and smooth ER, Golgi apparatuses, peroxisomes, and mitochondria. Thus equipped, the hepatocytes not only can produce bile but can also (1) process the bloodborne nutrients in various ways (e.g., they store glucose as glycogen and use amino

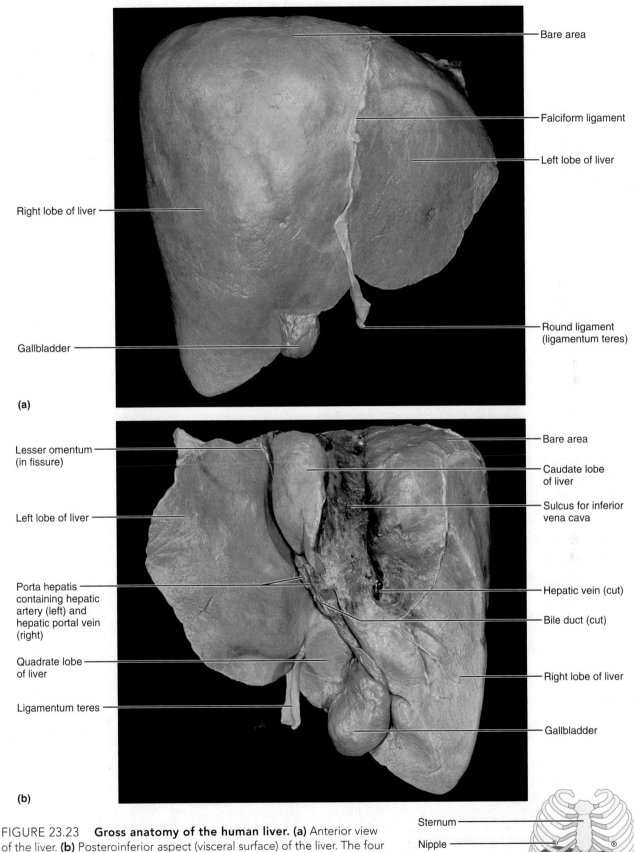

Bare area

Falciform ligament

Left lobe of liver

Right lobe of liver

Round ligament
(ligamentum teres)

Gallbladder

(a)

Lesser omentum
(in fissure)

Bare area

Caudate lobe
of liver

Sulcus for inferior
vena cava

Left lobe of liver

Porta hepatis
containing hepatic
artery (left) and
hepatic portal vein
(right)

Hepatic vein (cut)

Bile duct (cut)

Quadrate lobe
of liver

Right lobe of liver

Ligamentum teres

Gallbladder

(b)

Sternum

Nipple

Liver

(c)

FIGURE 23.23   **Gross anatomy of the human liver. (a)** Anterior view
of the liver. **(b)** Posteroinferior aspect (visceral surface) of the liver. The four
liver lobes are separated by a group of fissures in this view. The porta
hepatis is a deep fissure that contains the hepatic portal vein, hepatic
artery, hepatic duct, and lymphatics. (Note: Another scheme classifies the
caudate and quadrate lobes as part of the left liver lobe.) **(c)** Diagrammatic
view of the liver's location in the body. (See *A Brief Atlas of the Human
Body,* figures 64 and 65.)

23

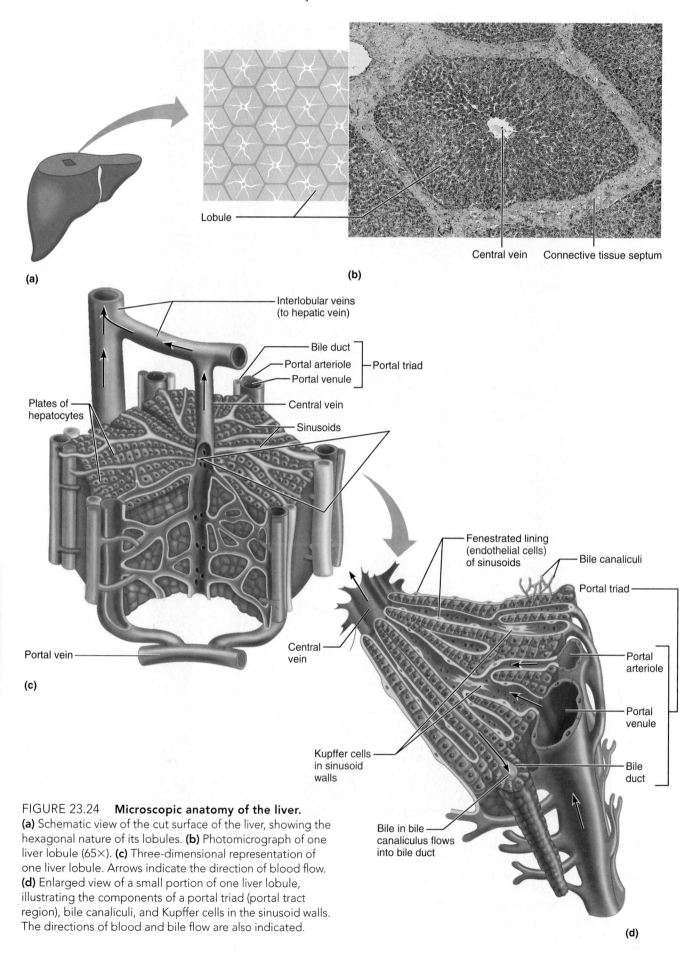

(a)

(b)

Lobule

Central vein   Connective tissue septum

Interlobular veins
(to hepatic vein)

Bile duct
Portal arteriole   Portal triad
Portal venule

Plates of
hepatocytes

Central vein

Sinusoids

Portal vein

(c)

Fenestrated lining
(endothelial cells)
of sinusoids

Bile canaliculi

Portal triad

Central
vein

Portal
arteriole

Portal
venule

Kupffer cells
in sinusoid
walls

Bile
duct

Bile in bile
canaliculus flows
into bile duct

(d)

FIGURE 23.24   **Microscopic anatomy of the liver.**
(a) Schematic view of the cut surface of the liver, showing the
hexagonal nature of its lobules. **(b)** Photomicrograph of one
liver lobule (65×). **(c)** Three-dimensional representation of
one liver lobule. Arrows indicate the direction of blood flow.
(d) Enlarged view of a small portion of one liver lobule,
illustrating the components of a portal triad (portal tract
region), bile canaliculi, and Kupffer cells in the sinusoid walls.
The directions of blood and bile flow are also indicated.

23

acids to make plasma proteins); (2) store fat-soluble vitamins; and (3) play important roles in detoxification, such as ridding the blood of ammonia by converting it to urea (Chapter 24). Thanks to these various jobs, the processed blood leaving the liver contains fewer nutrients and waste materials than the blood that entered it. The intimate relationship between the hepatocytes and their blood supply has liver growth and repair consequences in addition to its role in providing the hepatocytes with blood for processing and nutrition. During liver injury, hepatocytes secrete *vascular endothelial growth factor (VEGF)* which binds to specific receptors on endothelial cells lining the sinusoids. The endothelial cells proliferate and release other growth factors, such as hepatocyte growth factor (HGF) and interleukin 6, which in turn prompt the hepatocytes to multiply and replace dead and dying liver tissue. The regenerative capacity of the liver is exceptional; it can regenerate to its former size even after surgical removal or loss of 70% of its normal mass.

Secreted bile flows through tiny canals, called **bile canaliculi** (kan"ah-lik'u-li; "little canals"), that run between adjacent hepatocytes toward the bile duct branches in the portal triads (see Figure 23.24d). Notice that blood and bile flow in opposite directions in the liver lobule. Bile entering the bile ducts eventually leaves the liver via the common hepatic duct to travel toward the duodenum.

◢ HOMEOSTATIC IMBALANCE

Hepatitis (hep"ah-ti'tis), or inflammation of the liver, is most often due to viral infection. Thus far the catalogue of hepatitis-causing viruses numbers six—from the hepatitis A virus (HVA) to the hepatitis F virus (HVF). Of these, two (HVA and HVE) are transmitted enterically and the infections they cause tend to be self-limiting. Those transmitted via blood—most importantly HVB and HVC—are linked to chronic hepatitis and liver cirrhosis (see discussion below). HVD is a mutated virus that needs HVB to be infectious. Thus far, little is known about HVF. Nonviral causes of acute hepatitis include drug toxicity and wild mushroom poisoning.

In the United States, over 40% of hepatitis cases are due to HVB, which is transmitted via blood transfusions, contaminated needles, or sexual contact. A serious problem in its own right, hepatitis B carries with it a greater menace—an elevated risk of liver cancer. However, childhood immunization using vaccine produced in bacteria is sweeping the feet out from under HVB, and the incidence of acute hepatitis from this strain has fallen dramatically since its peak in 1985.

Hepatitis A, accounting for about 32% of cases, is a more benign form frequently observed in day-care centers. It is transmitted via sewage-contaminated food, raw shellfish, water, and by the feces-mouth route, which explains why it is important for restaurant employees to scrub their hands after using the washroom. Hepatitis E is transmitted in a similar way. It causes waterborne epidemics, largely in developing countries, and is a major cause of death in pregnant women. It is relatively insignificant in the United States.

Hepatitis C has emerged as the most important liver disease in the United States because it produces persistent or chronic liver infections (as opposed to acute infections). More than 4 milion Americans are infected and over 10,000 die annually due to sequels of HVC infection. However, the life-threatening C form of hepatitis is now being successfully treated by combination drug therapy entailing weekly injections of interferon (Pegasys, PEG-Intron) and ribavirin (Rebetol), an oral antiviral drug.

Cirrhosis (sĭr-ro'sis; "orange colored") is a progressive chronic inflammation of the liver that typically results from chronic alcoholism or severe chronic hepatitis. The alcohol-poisoned or damaged hepatocytes regenerate, but the liver's connective (scar) tissue regenerates faster. As a result, the liver becomes fatty and fibrous and its activity is depressed. As the scar tissue shrinks, it obstructs blood flow throughout the hepatic portal system, causing **portal hypertension.** Fortunately, some veins of the portal system anastomose with veins that drain into the venae cavae *(portal-caval anastomoses)*. The main ones are (1) veins in the inferior esophagus, (2) hemorrhoidal veins in the anal canal, and (3) superficial veins around the umbilicus. However, these connecting veins are small and tend to burst when forced to carry large volumes of blood. Signs of their failure include vomiting blood, and a snakelike network of distended veins surrounding the navel. This network is called *caput medusae* (kap'ut mĕ-du'se; "medusa head") after a monster in Greek mythology whose hair was made of writhing snakes. Other complications due to portal hypertension include swollen veins in the esophagus (esophageal varices) and *ascites*, an accumulation of fluid in the peritoneal cavity.

Liver transplants are the only clinically proven effective treatment for patients with end-stage liver disease. The one- and five-year survival rate of such transplants is approximately 90% and 75% respectively. However, donor organs are very scarce and many patients die while waiting for a suitable organ. ●

Composition of Bile

Bile is a yellow-green, alkaline solution containing bile salts, bile pigments, cholesterol, triglycerides, phospholipids (lecithin and others), and a variety of electrolytes. Of these, *only* bile salts and phospholipids aid the digestive process.

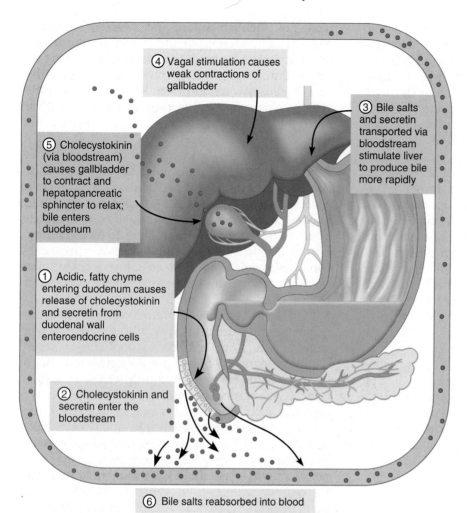

④ Vagal stimulation causes weak contractions of gallbladder

③ Bile salts and secretin transported via bloodstream stimulate liver to produce bile more rapidly

⑤ Cholecystokinin (via bloodstream) causes gallbladder to contract and hepatopancreatic sphincter to relax; bile enters duodenum

① Acidic, fatty chyme entering duodenum causes release of cholecystokinin and secretin from duodenal wall enteroendocrine cells

② Cholecystokinin and secretin enter the bloodstream

⑥ Bile salts reabsorbed into blood

FIGURE 23.25 **Mechanisms promoting secretion of bile.** When digestion is not occurring, bile is stored and concentrated in the gallbladder. When acidic fatty chyme enters the small intestine, several mechanisms are initiated that accelerate the liver's output of bile and cause the gallbladder to contract and the hepatopancreatic sphincter to relax. This allows bile (and pancreatic juice) to enter the small intestine. The single most important stimulus of bile secretion is an increased level of bile salts in the enterohepatic circulation.

Bile salts, primarily cholic and chenodeoxycholic acids, are cholesterol derivatives. Their role is to *emulsify* fats—that is, to distribute them throughout the watery intestinal contents, just as a dish detergent breaks up a pool of fat drippings in a roasting pan. (Another example of emulsification is homogenization, which distributes cream throughout the watery phase of milk.) As a result, large fat globules entering the small intestine are physically separated into millions of small, more accessible fatty droplets that provide large surface areas for the fat-digesting enzymes to work on. Bile salts also facilitate fat and cholesterol absorption (discussed later) and help solubilize cholesterol, both that contained in bile and that entering the small intestine in food. Although many substances secreted in bile leave the body in feces, bile salts are not among them. Instead, bile salts are conserved by means of a recycling mechanism called the **enterohepatic circulation.** In this process, bile salts are (1) reabsorbed into the blood by the ileum, (2) returned to the liver via the hepatic portal blood, and then (3) resecreted in newly formed bile.

The chief bile pigment is **bilirubin** (bil″ĭ-roo′bin), a waste product of the heme of hemoglobin formed during the breakdown of worn-out erythrocytes (see Chapter 17). The globin and iron parts of hemoglobin are saved and recycled, but bilirubin is absorbed from the blood by the liver cells, excreted into bile, and metabolized in the small intestine by resident bacteria. One of its breakdown products, *stercobilin* (ster′ko-bi″lin), gives feces a brown color. In the absence of bile, feces are gray-white in color and have fatty streaks (because essentially no fats are digested or absorbed).

The liver produces 500 to 1000 ml of bile daily, and production is stepped up when the GI tract contains fatty chyme. Bile salts themselves are the major stimulus for enhanced bile secretion (Figure 23.25), and when the enterohepatic circulation is returning large amounts of bile salts to the liver, its output of bile rises dramatically. *Secretin,* released by intestinal cells exposed to fatty chyme, also stimulates liver cells to secrete bile.

The Gallbladder

The **gallbladder** is a thin-walled green muscular sac about 10 cm (4 inches) long. Roughly the size of a kiwi fruit, it snuggles in a shallow fossa on the ventral surface of the liver (see Figures 23.1 and 23.23). Its rounded fundus protrudes from the inferior margin of the liver. The gallbladder stores bile that is not immediately needed for digestion and concentrates it by absorbing some of its water and ions. (In some cases, bile released from the gallbladder is ten times as concentrated as that entering it.) When empty, or when storing only small amounts of bile, its mucosa is thrown into honeycomb-like folds that, like the rugae of the stomach, allow the organ to expand as it fills. When its muscular wall contracts, bile is expelled into its duct, the *cystic duct*, and then flows into the bile duct. The gallbladder, like most of the liver, is covered by visceral peritoneum.

Regulation of Bile Release into the Small Intestine

When no digestion is occurring, the hepatopancreatic sphincter (guarding the entry of bile and pancreatic juice into the duodenum) is closed and the released bile backs up the cystic duct into the gallbladder, where it is stored until needed. Although the liver makes bile continuously, bile does not usually enter the small intestine until the gallbladder contracts. The major stimulus for gallbladder contraction is *cholecystokinin (CCK)*, an intestinal hormone (Figure 23.25) released to the blood when acidic, fatty chyme enters the duodenum. Besides causing the gallbladder to contract, CCK (1) stimulates secretion of pancreatic juice, and (2) relaxes the hepatopancreatic sphincter so that bile and pancreatic juice can enter the duodenum. CCK and the other digestive hormones are summarized in Table 23.1. Parasympathetic impulses delivered by the vagus nerves are a minor stimulus for gallbladder contraction.

◣ HOMEOSTATIC IMBALANCE

Bile is the major vehicle for cholesterol excretion from the body, and bile salts keep the cholesterol dissolved within bile. Too much cholesterol or too few bile salts leads to cholesterol crystallization, forming **gallstones**, or *biliary calculi* (bil'e-a"re kal'ku-li), which obstruct the flow of bile from the gallbladder. Then, when the gallbladder or its duct contracts, the sharp crystals cause agonizing pain that radiates to the right thoracic region. Treatments for gallstones include dissolving the crystals with drugs, pulverizing them with ultrasound vibrations (lithotripsy), vaporizing them with lasers, and the classical treatment, surgically removing the gallbladder. When the gallbladder is removed, the bile duct enlarges to assume the bile-storing role. Gallstones are easy to diagnose because they show up well with ultrasound imaging.

Bile duct blockage prevents both bile salts and bile pigments from entering the intestine. As a result, yellow bile pigments accumulate in blood and eventually are deposited in the skin, causing it to become yellow, or *jaundiced*. Jaundice caused by blocked ducts is called *obstructive jaundice*, but jaundice may also reflect liver disease (in which the liver is unable to carry out its normal metabolic duties). ●

The Pancreas

The **pancreas** (pan'kre-as; *pan* = all, *creas* = flesh, meat) is a soft, tadpole-shaped gland that extends across the abdomen from its *tail* (abutting the spleen) to its *head*, which is encircled by the C-shaped duodenum (see Figures 23.1 and 23.20). Most of the pancreas is retroperitoneal and lies deep to the greater curvature of the stomach.

An accessory digestive organ, the pancreas is important to the digestive process because it produces enzymes that break down all categories of foodstuffs, which the pancreas then delivers to the duodenum. This exocrine product, called **pancreatic juice,** drains from the pancreas via the centrally located **main pancreatic duct.** The pancreatic duct generally fuses with the bile duct just as it enters the duodenum (at the hepatopancreatic ampulla). A smaller *accessory pancreatic duct* empties directly into the duodenum just proximal to the main duct.

Within the pancreas are the **acini** (as'ĭ-ni; singular: acinus), clusters of secretory cells surrounding ducts (Figure 23.26). These cells are full of rough endoplasmic reticulum and exhibit deeply staining **zymogen granules** (zi'mo-jen; "fermenting") containing the digestive enzymes they manufacture.

Scattered amid the acini are the more lightly staining *pancreatic islets (islets of Langerhans).* These mini-endocrine glands release insulin and glucagon, hormones that play an important role in carbohydrate metabolism, as well as several other hormones (see Chapter 16).

Composition of Pancreatic Juice

Approximately 1200 to 1500 ml of clear pancreatic juice is produced daily. It consists mainly of water, and contains enzymes and electrolytes (primarily bicarbonate ions). The acinar cells produce the enzyme-rich component of pancreatic juice. The epithelial cells lining the smallest pancreatic ducts release the bicarbonate ions that make it alkaline (about pH 8). The high pH of pancreatic fluid helps neutralize acid chyme entering the duodenum and provides the optimal environment for activity of intestinal and pancreatic enzymes. Like pepsin of the stomach, pancreatic proteases (protein-digesting enzymes) are produced and released in inactive forms, which are activated in the duodenum, where they do their work. This prevents the pancreas from self-digestion. For example,

(a)

(b)

FIGURE 23.26 **Structure of the enzyme-producing tissue of the pancreas. (a)** One acinus (a secretory unit). The cell apices contain abundant zymogen (enzyme-containing) granules. **(b)** Photomicrograph of pancreatic acinar tissue (200×).

within the duodenum, *trypsinogen* is activated to **trypsin** by **enteropeptidase** (formerly called *enterokinase)*, an intestinal brush border protease. Trypsin, in turn, activates two other pancreatic proteases *(procarboxypeptidase* and *chymotrypsinogen)* to their active forms, **carboxypeptidase** (kar-bok"se-pep'tĭ-dās) and **chymotrypsin** (ky"mo-trip'sin), respectively (Figure 23.27). Other pancreatic enzymes—**amylase, lipases,** and **nucleases**—are secreted in active form, but require that ions or bile be present in the intestinal lumen for optimal activity.

Regulation of Pancreatic Secretion

Secretion of pancreatic juice is regulated both by hormones and by the parasympathetic nervous system (Figure 23.28). The more important hormonal

Q *What is the significance of the fact that pancreatic enzymes are activated in the small intestine?*

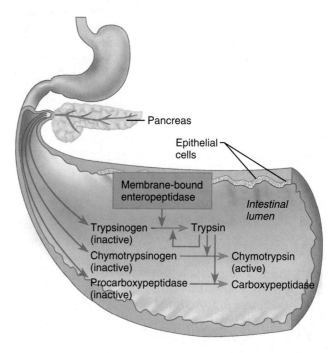

FIGURE 23.27 **Activation of pancreatic proteases in the small intestine.** Pancreatic proteases are secreted in an inactive form and are activated in the duodenum.

mechanism is exerted by two intestinal hormones. Both hormones act on the pancreas, but secretin released in response to the presence of HCl in the intestine mainly targets the duct cells, prompting their release of watery *bicarbonate-rich* pancreatic juice. CCK, released in response to the entry of proteins and fats, stimulates the acini to release *enzyme-rich* pancreatic juice, and potentiates the effect of secretin. Hence, substantially more bicarb-rich juice is secreted when both hormones are present. Vagal stimulation causes release of pancreatic juice primarily during the cephalic and gastric phases of gastric secretion.

Normally, the amount of HCl produced in the stomach is exactly balanced by the amount of bicarbonate (HCO_3^-) secreted by the pancreas, and as HCO_3^- is secreted into the pancreatic juice, H^+ enters the blood. Consequently, the pH of venous blood returning to the heart remains relatively unchanged because alkaline blood draining from the stomach is neutralized by the acidic blood draining the pancreas.

A *They are activated in the small intestine where they work and where the cells exposed to them are protected by mucus. No such protection exists in the pancreas.*

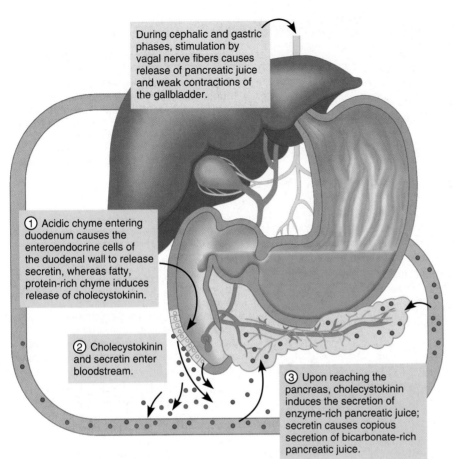

During cephalic and gastric phases, stimulation by vagal nerve fibers causes release of pancreatic juice and weak contractions of the gallbladder.

① Acidic chyme entering duodenum causes the enteroendocrine cells of the duodenal wall to release secretin, whereas fatty, protein-rich chyme induces release of cholecystokinin.

② Cholecystokinin and secretin enter bloodstream.

③ Upon reaching the pancreas, cholecystokinin induces the secretion of enzyme-rich pancreatic juice; secretin causes copious secretion of bicarbonate-rich pancreatic juice.

FIGURE 23.28 **Regulation of pancreatic juice secretion.** Hormonal controls, exerted by secretin and cholecystokinin (steps ①–③), are the main regulatory factors. Neural control is mediated by parasympathetic fibers of the vagus nerves.

Digestive Processes Occurring in the Small Intestine

Food reaching the small intestine is unrecognizable, but it is far from being digested chemically. Carbohydrates and proteins are partially degraded, but virtually no fat digestion has occurred to this point. The process of food digestion is accelerated during the chyme's tortuous journey of three to six hours through the small intestine, and it is here that absorption of most of the water and virtually all nutrients occurs. Like the stomach, the small intestine plays no part in ingestion or defecation.

Requirements for Optimal Intestinal Digestive Activity

Although a primary function of the small intestine is digestion, intestinal juice provides little of what is needed to perform this function. Most substances required for chemical digestion—bile, digestive enzymes (except for the brush border enzymes), and bicarbonate ions (to provide the proper pH for enzymatic catalysis)—are *imported* from the liver and pancreas. Hence, anything that impairs liver or pancreatic function or delivery of their juices to the small intestine severely hinders our ability to digest food and absorb nutrients. The other primary function of the small intestine—absorption—is efficiently accomplished by its absorptive cells with their rich crop of apical microvilli.

Optimal digestive activity in the small intestine also depends on a slow, measured delivery of chyme from the stomach. Why is this so? Entering chyme is usually hypertonic. Thus, if large amounts of chyme were rushed into the small intestine, the osmotic water loss from the blood into the intestinal lumen would result in dangerously low blood volume. Additionally, the low pH of entering chyme must be adjusted upward and the chyme must be well mixed with bile and pancreatic juice for digestion to continue. These modifications take time. Thus, food movement into the small intestine is carefully controlled by the pumping action of the stomach pylorus (see pp. 905 and 907) to prevent the duodenum from being overwhelmed. Since the actual chemistry of digestion and absorption is covered in detail later, next we will examine how the small intestine mixes and propels food along its length, and how its motility is regulated.

Motility of the Small Intestine

Intestinal smooth muscle mixes chyme thoroughly with bile and pancreatic and intestinal juices, and moves food residues through the ileocecal valve into

23

TABLE 23.2	Overview of the Functions of the Gastrointestinal Organs	
ORGAN	**MAJOR FUNCTIONS***	**COMMENTS/ADDITIONAL FUNCTIONS**
Mouth and associated accessory organs	■ Ingestion: food is voluntarily placed into oral cavity ■ Propulsion: voluntary (buccal) phase of deglutition (swallowing) initiated by tongue; propels food into pharynx ■ Mechanical digestion: mastication (chewing) by teeth and mixing movements by tongue ■ Chemical digestion: chemical breakdown of starch is begun by salivary amylase present in saliva produced by salivary glands	Mouth serves as a receptacle; most functions performed by associated accessory organs. Mucus present in saliva helps dissolve foods so they can be tasted and moistens food so that tongue can compact it into a bolus that can be swallowed. Oral cavity and teeth cleansed and lubricated by saliva
Pharynx and esophagus	■ Propulsion: peristaltic waves move food bolus to stomach, thus accomplishing involuntary (pharyngeal-esophageal) phase of deglutition	Primarily food chutes; mucus produced helps to lubricate food passageways
Stomach	■ Mechanical digestion and propulsion: peristaltic waves mix food with gastric juice and propel it into the duodenum ■ Chemical digestion: digestion of proteins begun by pepsin ■ Absorption: absorbs a few fat-soluble substances (aspirin, alcohol, some drugs)	Also serves as storage site for food until it can be moved into the duodenum. Hydrochloric acid produced is a bacteriostatic agent and activates protein-digesting enzymes. Mucus produced helps lubricate and protect stomach from self-digestion. Intrinsic factor produced is required for intestinal absorption of vitamin B_{12}
Small intestine and associated accessory organs (liver, gallbladder, pancreas)	■ Mechanical digestion and propulsion: segmentation by smooth muscle of the small intestine continually mixes contents with digestive juices and moves food along tract and through ileocecal valve at a slow rate, allowing sufficient time for digestion and absorption ■ Chemical digestion: digestive enzymes conveyed in from pancreas and brush border enzymes attached to villi membranes complete digestion of all classes of foods ■ Absorption: breakdown products of carbohydrate, protein, fat, and nucleic acid digestion, plus vitamins, electrolytes, and water, are absorbed by active and passive mechanisms	Small intestine is highly modified for digestion and absorption (circular folds, villi, and microvilli). Alkaline mucus produced by intestinal glands and bicarbonate-rich juice ducted in from pancreas help neutralize acidic chyme and provide proper environment for enzymatic activity. Bile produced by liver emulsifies fats and enhances (1) fat digestion and (2) absorption of fatty acids, monoglycerides, cholesterol, phospholipids, and fat-soluble vitamins. Gallbladder stores and concentrates bile; bile is released to small intestine in response to hormonal signals
Large intestine	■ Chemical digestion: some remaining food residues are digested by enteric bacteria (which also produce vitamin K and some B vitamins) ■ Absorption: absorbs most remaining water, electrolytes (largely NaCl), and vitamins produced by bacteria ■ Propulsion: propels feces toward rectum by peristalsis, haustral churning, and mass movements ■ Defecation: reflex triggered by rectal distension; eliminates feces from body	Temporarily stores and concentrates residues until defecation can occur. Copious mucus produced by goblet cells eases passage of feces through colon

*The colored boxes beside the functions correspond to the color coding of digestive functions (gastrointestinal tract activities) illustrated in Figure 23.2.

the large intestine. In contrast to the peristaltic waves of the stomach, *segmentation* is the most common motion of the small intestine.

If X-ray fluoroscopy is used to examine the small intestine after it is "loaded" with a meal, it looks like the intestinal contents are being massaged—that

is, the chyme is simply moved backward and forward in the lumen a few centimeters at a time by alternating contraction and relaxation of rings of smooth muscle. These segmenting movements of the intestine (see Figure 23.3b), like the peristalsis of the stomach, are initiated by intrinsic pacemaker

TABLE 23.3	Control of Small Intestinal Motility		
PHASE	**STIMULUS**	**MECHANISM**	**EFFECT ON MOTILITY**
Gastric	↑ Gastric motility and emptying	Long neural reflexes (gastroileal reflex)	↑ Activity in ileum
		Gastrin	↑ Segmenting movements in ileum; relaxes ileocecal sphincter
Intestinal	Distension of small intestine	Long and short neural reflexes	↑ Strength of segmentation
	Reduced intestinal volume; fasting	Long and short neural reflexes; initiated by ↑ blood levels of motilin	Initiates migrating motility complex (peristalsis); repeats until next meal

cells in the longitudinal smooth muscle layer. However, unlike the stomach pacemakers, which have only one rhythm, the pacemakers in the duodenum depolarize more frequently (12–14 contractions per minute) than those in the ileum (8 or 9 contractions per minute). As a result, segmentation moves intestinal contents slowly and steadily toward the ileocecal valve at a rate that allows ample time to complete digestion and absorption. The intensity of segmentation is altered by long and short reflexes (which parasympathetic activity enhances and sympathetic activity decreases) and hormones (Table 23.3). The more intense the contractions, the greater the mixing effect; however, the basic contractile rhythms of the various intestinal regions remain unchanged.

True peristalsis occurs late in the intestinal phase only after most nutrients have been absorbed. At this point, segmenting movements wane and the duodenal mucosa begins to release the hormone *motilin*. As motilin blood levels rise, peristaltic waves are initiated in the proximal duodenum and begin to sweep slowly along the intestine, moving 50–70 cm (about 2 ft) before dying out. Each successive wave is initiated a bit more distally, and this pattern of peristaltic activity is called the **migrating motility complex (MMC)**. A complete "trip" from duodenum to ileum takes about two hours. The process then repeats itself, sweeping the last remnants of the meal plus bacteria, sloughed-off mucosal cells, and other debris into the large intestine. This "housekeeping" function is critical for preventing the overgrowth of bacteria that migrate from the large intestine into the small intestine. As food again enters the stomach with the next meal, peristalsis is replaced by segmentation.

The local enteric neurons of the GI tract wall coordinate these intestinal motility patterns. The physiological diversity of the enteric neurons allows a variety of effects to occur depending on which neurons are activated or inhibited. For example, a given ACh-releasing (cholinergic) sensory neuron in the small intestine, once activated, may simultaneously send messages to several different interneurons in the myenteric plexus that regulate peristalsis:

- Impulses sent proximally by cholinergic effector neurons cause contraction and shortening of the circular muscle layer.

- Impulses sent distally to certain interneurons cause shortening of the longitudinal muscle layer and distension of the intestine, in response to ACh-releasing effector neurons.

As a result, as the proximal area constricts and forces chyme along the tract, the lumen of the distal part of the intestine enlarges to receive it.

Most of the time, the ileocecal sphincter is constricted and closed. However, two mechanisms—one neural and the other hormonal—cause it to relax and allow food residues to enter the cecum when ileal motility increases. Enhanced activity of the stomach initiates the **gastroileal reflex** (gas"tro-il'e-ul), a long reflex that enhances the force of segmentation in the ileum. In addition, gastrin released by the stomach increases the motility of the ileum and relaxes the ileocecal sphincter. Once the chyme has passed through, it exerts backward pressure that closes the valve's flaps, preventing regurgitation into the ileum. This reflex ensures that the contents of the previous meal are swept completely out of the stomach and small intestine as the next meal is eaten.

23

HOMEOSTATIC IMBALANCE

Injury to the intestinal wall by severe stretching, some bacterial infections, or mechanical trauma may lead to a total cessation of small intestine motility, a phenomenon called intestino-intestinal reflex. ●

The Large Intestine

The **large intestine** (see Figure 23.1) frames the small intestine on three sides and extends from the ileocecal valve to the anus. Its diameter, at about 7 cm, is greater than that of the small intestine (hence, *large* intestine), but it is less than half as long (1.5 m versus 6 m). In terms of digestive system functioning, its major function is to absorb most of the remaining water from indigestible food residues (delivered to it in a fluid state), store the residues temporarily, and then eliminate them from the body as semisolid **feces** (fe'sēz).

Gross Anatomy

The large intestine exhibits three features not seen elsewhere—teniae coli, haustra, and epiploic appendages. Except for its terminal end, the longitudinal muscle layer of its muscularis is reduced to three bands of smooth muscle called **teniae coli** (ten'ne-e ko'li; "ribbons of the colon"). Their tone causes the wall of the large intestine to pucker into pocketlike sacs called **haustra** (haw'strah; "to draw up"). Another obvious feature of the large intestine is its **epiploic appendages** (ep"ĭ-plo'ik), small fat-filled pouches of visceral peritoneum that hang from its surface (Figure 23.29a). Their significance is not known.

Subdivisions

The large intestine has the following subdivisions: cecum, appendix, colon, rectum, and anal canal. The saclike **cecum** (se'kum; "blind pouch"), which lies below the ileocecal valve in the right iliac fossa, is the first part of the large intestine (Figure 23.29a). Attached to its posteromedial surface is the blind, wormlike **vermiform appendix.** The appendix contains masses of lymphoid tissue, and as part of MALT (see p. 782), it plays an important role in body immunity. However, it has an important structural shortcoming—its twisted structure provides an ideal location for enteric bacteria to accumulate and multiply.

 HOMEOSTATIC IMBALANCE

Acute inflammation of the appendix, or **appendicitis,** results from a blockage (often by feces) that traps infectious bacteria in its lumen. Unable to empty its contents, the appendix swells, squeezing off venous drainage, which may lead to ischemia and necrosis (death and decay) of the appendix. If the appendix ruptures, feces containing bacteria spray over the abdominal contents, causing *peritonitis.* Although the symptoms of appendicitis are variable, the first is usually pain in the umbilical region. Loss of appetite, nausea and vomiting, and relocalization of pain to the lower right abdominal quadrant follow. Immediate surgical removal of the appendix (appendectomy) is the accepted treatment for suspected appendicitis. Appendicitis is most common during adolescence, when the entrance to the appendix is at its widest. ●

The **colon** has several distinct regions. As the **ascending colon,** it travels up the right side of the abdominal cavity to the level of the right kidney. Here it makes a right-angle turn—the **right colic,** or **hepatic, flexure**—and travels across the abdominal cavity as the **transverse colon.** Directly anterior to the spleen, it bends acutely at the **left colic (splenic) flexure** and descends down the left side of the posterior abdominal wall as the **descending colon.** Inferiorly, it enters the pelvis, where it becomes the S-shaped **sigmoid colon.** Except for the transverse and sigmoid parts of the colon, which are intraperitoneal and anchored to the posterior abdominal wall by mesentery sheets called **mesocolons** (see Figure 23.30c and d), the colon is retroperitoneal.

In the pelvis, at the level of the third sacral vertebra, the sigmoid colon joins the **rectum,** which runs posteroinferiorly just in front of the sacrum. The position of the rectum allows a number of pelvic organs (e.g., the prostate gland of males) to be examined digitally (with a finger) through the anterior rectal wall. This is called a **rectal exam.** Despite its name (*rectum* = straight), the rectum has three lateral curves or bends, represented internally as three transverse folds called **rectal valves** (Figure 23.29b). These valves separate feces from flatus, that is, they stop feces from being passed along with gas.

The **anal canal,** the last segment of the large intestine, lies in the perineum, entirely external to the abdominopelvic cavity. About 3 cm long, it begins where the rectum penetrates the levator ani muscle of the pelvic floor and opens to the body exterior at the **anus.** The anal canal has two sphincters, an involuntary **internal anal sphincter** composed of smooth muscle (part of the muscularis), and a voluntary **external anal sphincter** composed of skeletal muscle. The sphincters, which act rather like purse

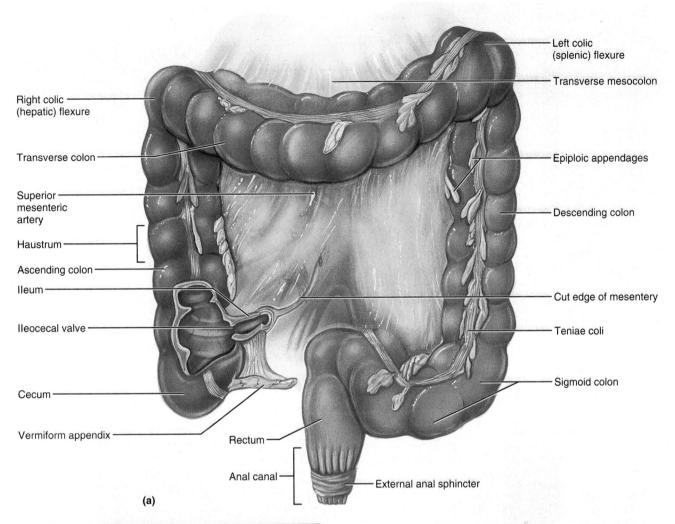

Right colic (hepatic) flexure

Transverse colon

Superior mesenteric artery

Haustrum

Ascending colon

Ileum

Ileocecal valve

Cecum

Vermiform appendix

Left colic (splenic) flexure

Transverse mesocolon

Epiploic appendages

Descending colon

Cut edge of mesentery

Teniae coli

Sigmoid colon

Rectum

Anal canal

External anal sphincter

(a)

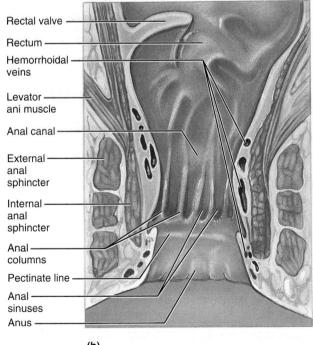

Rectal valve

Rectum

Hemorrhoidal veins

Levator ani muscle

Anal canal

External anal sphincter

Internal anal sphincter

Anal columns

Pectinate line

Anal sinuses

Anus

(b)

FIGURE 23.29 **Gross anatomy of the large intestine.**
(a) Diagrammatic view. **(b)** Structure of the anal canal.

strings to open and close the anus, are ordinarily closed except during defecation.

Microscopic Anatomy

The wall of the large intestine (Figure 23.31) differs in several ways from that of the small intestine. The colon *mucosa* is simple columnar epithelium except in the anal canal. Because most food is absorbed before reaching the large intestine, there are no circular folds, no villi, and virtually no cells that secrete digestive enzymes. However, its mucosa is thicker, its abundant crypts are deeper, and there are tremendous numbers of goblet cells in the crypts (Figure 23.31). Mucus produced by goblet cells eases the passage of feces and protects the intestinal wall from irritating acids and gases released by resident bacteria in the colon.

The mucosa of the anal canal, a stratified squamous epithelium, merges with the true skin surrounding the anus and is quite different from that of the rest of the colon, reflecting the greater abrasion that this region receives. Superiorly, it hangs in long

23

(a)

Falciform ligament
Liver
Gallbladder
Lesser omentum
Spleen
Stomach
Duodenum
Ligamentum teres
Transverse colon
Greater omentum
Small intestine
Cecum
Urinary bladder

(b)

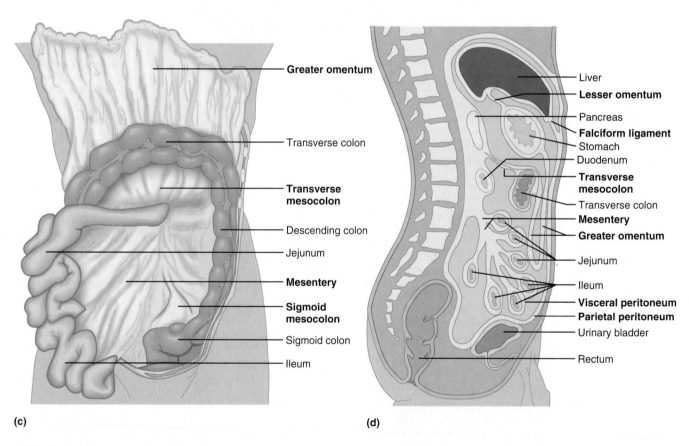

(c)

Greater omentum
Transverse colon
Transverse mesocolon
Descending colon
Jejunum
Mesentery
Sigmoid mesocolon
Sigmoid colon
Ileum

(d)

Liver
Lesser omentum
Pancreas
Falciform ligament
Stomach
Duodenum
Transverse mesocolon
Transverse colon
Mesentery
Greater omentum
Jejunum
Ileum
Visceral peritoneum
Parietal peritoneum
Urinary bladder
Rectum

FIGURE 23.30 Mesenteries of the abdominal digestive organs. (a) The greater omentum, a dorsal mesentery, is shown in its normal position covering the abdominal viscera. **(b)** The lesser omentum, a ventral mesentery attaching the liver to the lesser curvature of the stomach (the liver and gallbladder have been reflected superiorly). **(c)** The greater omentum has been reflected superiorly to reveal the mesentery attachments of the small and large intestine. **(d)** Sagittal section of the abdominopelvic cavity of a male.

23

ridges or folds called **anal columns. Anal sinuses** (Figure 23.29b), recesses between the anal columns, exude mucus when compressed by feces, which aids in emptying the anal canal. The horizontal, tooth-shaped line that parallels the inferior margins of the anal sinuses is called the *pectinate line.* Superior to this line, the mucosa is innervated by visceral sensory fibers and is relatively insensitive to pain. The area inferior to the pectinate line is very sensitive to pain, a reflection of the somatic sensory fibers serving it. Two superficial venous plexuses are associated with the anal canal, one with the anal columns and the other with the anus itself. If these (hemorrhoidal) veins are inflamed, itchy varicosities called *hemorrhoids* result.

Teniae coli and haustra are absent in the rectum and anal canal. However, consistent with its need to generate strong contractions to perform its expulsive role in defecation, the rectum's muscularis muscle layers are complete and well developed.

Bacterial Flora

Although most bacteria entering the cecum from the small intestine are dead (having been killed by the action of lysozyme, defensins, HCl, and protein-digesting enzymes), some are still "alive and kicking." Together with bacteria that enter the GI tract via the anus, these constitute the **bacterial flora** of the large intestine, over 700 species of them. These bacteria colonize the colon, metabolize some host-derived proteins (mucin, heparin, and hyaluronic acid) and ferment some of the indigestible carbohydrates (cellulose, xylan, and others), releasing irritating acids and a mixture of gases (including dimethyl sulfide, H_2, N_2, CH_4, and CO_2). Some of these gases (such as dimethyl sulfide) are quite odorous. About 500 ml of gas (flatus) is produced each day, much more when certain carbohydrate-rich foods (such as beans) are eaten. The bacterial flora also synthesize B complex vitamins and most of the vitamin K the liver requires to synthesize some of the clotting proteins.

Although the huge population of bacteria would seem to be enough (feces) inhabitants, there are more—including viruses and protozoans. Of these, at least 20 are known pathogens.

Most enteric bacteria are commensals that coexist peacefully with their host as long as they remain in the gut lumen. An elegant system keeps the commensals from breaching the mucosal barrier. In response to specific bacterial components, the epithelial cells of the gut mucosa release chemicals that recruit immune cells, particularly dendritic cells, into the mucosa. The dendritic cells pry open tight junctions between the epithelial cells and send

FIGURE 23.31 **The mucosa of the large intestine.** Light photomicrograph (500×).

- Columnar cells with striated border
- Lamina propria
- Goblet cells
- Crypt
- Muscularis mucosae

extensions into the lumen to sample the microbial antigens. They then migrate to the nearby lymphoid follicles (MALT) within the gut mucosa where they present the antigens to T cells. As a result, an IgA antibody–mediated response restricted to the gut lumen is triggered that prevents the commensals from straying beyond the mucosa where they might elicit a much more widespread systemic response.

Digestive Processes Occurring in the Large Intestine

What is finally delivered to the large intestine contains few nutrients, but it still has 12 to 24 hours more to spend there. Except for a small amount of digestion of that residue by the enteric bacteria, no further food breakdown occurs in the large intestine.

Although the large intestine harvests vitamins made by the bacterial flora and reclaims most of the remaining water and some of the electrolytes

23

(particularly sodium and chloride), absorption is not the *major* function of this organ. As mentioned, the primary concerns of the large intestine are propulsive activities that force the fecal material toward the anus and then eliminate it from the body (defecation).

While the large intestine is important for our comfort, it is not essential for life. If the colon is removed, as may be necessitated by colon cancer, the terminal ileum is brought out to the abdominal wall in a procedure called an *ileostomy* (il″e-os′to-me), and food residues are eliminated from there into a sac attached to the abdominal wall. Another surgical technique, *ileoanal juncture*, links the ileum directly to the anal canal.

Motility of the Large Intestine

The large intestine musculature is inactive much of the time, but pressure in the ileum terminus opens the ileoceal sphincter and then closes it, preventing backward movement of the chyme. When presented with food residue the colon becomes motile, but its contractions are sluggish or short lived. The movements most seen in the colon are **haustral contractions,** slow segmenting movements lasting about one minute that occur every 30 minutes or so. These contractions, which occur mainly in the transverse and descending colon, reflect local controls of smooth muscle within the walls of the individual haustra. As a haustrum fills with food residue, the distension stimulates its muscle to contract, which propels the luminal contents into the next haustrum. These movements also mix the residue, which aids in water absorption.

Mass movements (mass peristalsis) are long, slow-moving, but powerful contractile waves that move over large areas of the colon three or four times daily and force the contents toward the rectum. Typically, they occur during or just after eating, which indicates that the presence of food in the stomach activates the gastroileal reflex in the small intestine and the propulsive **gastrocolic reflex** in the colon. Bulk, or fiber, in the diet increases the strength of colon contractions and softens the stool, allowing the colon to act like a well-oiled machine.

◤ HOMEOSTATIC IMBALANCE

When the diet lacks bulk and the volume of residues in the colon is small, the colon narrows and its contractions become more powerful, increasing the pressure on its walls. This promotes formation of *diverticula* (di″ver-tik′u-lah), small herniations of the mucosa through the colon walls. This condition, called **diverticulosis,** most commonly occurs in the sigmoid colon, and affects over half of people over the age of 70. In about 20% of cases, diverticulosis progresses to **diverticulitis,** in which the diverticula become inflamed and may rupture, leaking feces into the peritoneal cavity, which can be life threatening.

Irritable bowel syndrome is a functional GI disorder not explained by anatomical or biochemical abnormalities. Affected individuals have recurring (or persistent) abdominal pain that is relieved by defecation, changes in the consistency (watery to stonelike) and frequency of their stools, and varying complaints of bloating, flatulence, nausea, and depression. Psychological and/or physiological stress are common precipitating factors, and stress management is an important aspect of treatment. ●

The semisolid product delivered to the rectum, called feces or the stool, contains undigested food residues, mucus, sloughed-off epithelial cells, millions of bacteria, and just enough water to allow its smooth passage. Of the 500 ml or so of food residue entering the cecum daily, approximately 150 ml becomes feces.

Defecation

The rectum is usually empty, but when feces are forced into it by mass movements, stretching of the rectal wall initiates the **defecation reflex** (Figure 23.32). This is a spinal cord–mediated parasympathetic reflex that causes the sigmoid colon and the rectum to contract, the internal anal sphincter to relax, and the external anal sphincter to contract (initially). As feces are forced into the anal canal, messages reach the brain allowing us to decide whether the external (voluntary) anal sphincter should be opened or remain constricted to stop feces passage temporarily. If defecation is delayed, the reflex contractions end within a few seconds, and the rectal walls relax. With the next mass movement, the defecation reflex is initiated again—and so on, until one chooses to defecate or the urge to defecate becomes unavoidable.

During defecation, the muscles of the rectum contract to expel the feces. We aid this process voluntarily by closing the glottis and contracting our diaphragm and abdominal wall muscles to increase the intra-abdominal pressure (a procedure called *Valsalva's maneuver*). We also contract the levator ani muscle (pp. 350–351), which lifts the anal canal superiorly. This lifting action leaves the feces below the anus—and outside the body. Involuntary or automatic defecation (incontinence of feces) occurs in infants because they have not yet gained control of their external anal sphincter. It also occurs in those with spinal cord transections.

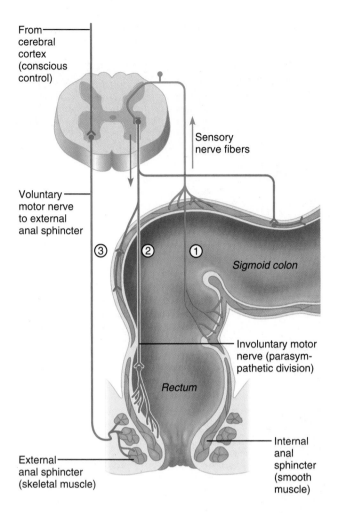

FIGURE 23.32 **Defecation reflex.** ① Distension, or stretch, of the rectal walls caused by movement of feces into the rectum triggers the depolarization of sensory (afferent) fibers, which synapse with spinal cord neurons. ② Parasympathetic motor (efferent) fibers, in turn, stimulate contraction of the rectal walls and relaxation of the internal anal sphincter. ③ If it is convenient to defecate, voluntary signals stimulate relaxation of the external anal sphincter. Defecation may be delayed temporarily by conscious (cortical) controls, which allow voluntary constriction of the external sphincter.

▲ HOMEOSTATIC IMBALANCE

Watery stools, or **diarrhea,** result from any condition that rushes food residue through the large intestine before that organ has had sufficient time to absorb the remaining water. Causes include irritation of the colon by bacteria or, less commonly, prolonged physical jostling of the digestive viscera (occurs in marathon runners). Prolonged diarrhea may result in dehydration and electrolyte imbalance (acidosis and loss of potassium). Conversely, when food remains in the colon for extended periods, too much water is absorbed and the stool becomes hard and difficult to pass. This condition, called **constipation,**

may result from lack of fiber in the diet, improper bowel habits (failing to heed the "call"), lack of exercise, emotional upset, or laxative abuse. ●

PART 3: PHYSIOLOGY OF CHEMICAL DIGESTION AND ABSORPTION

So far in this chapter, we have examined the structure and overall function of the organs that make up the digestive system. Now we will investigate the entire chemical processing (enzymatic breakdown and absorption) of each class of foodstuffs as it moves through the GI tract. These matters are summarized in Figure 23.33.

Chemical Digestion

After foodstuffs have spent even a short time in the stomach, they are unrecognizable. Nonetheless, they are still mostly the starchy, carbohydrate-rich foods, meat proteins, butter and other fats, and so on that we ingested. Only their appearance has been changed by mechanical digestive activities. By contrast, the products of chemical digestion are the chemical building blocks of the ingested foods and are very different molecules chemically. Let us look more closely at the process of chemical digestion.

Mechanism of Chemical Digestion: Enzymatic Hydrolysis

Chemical digestion is a catabolic process in which large food molecules are broken down to *monomers* (chemical building blocks), which are small enough to be absorbed by the GI tract lining. Chemical digestion is accomplished by enzymes secreted by both intrinsic and accessory glands into the lumen of the alimentary canal. The enzymatic breakdown of any type of food molecule is **hydrolysis** (hi-drol'ĭ-sis) because it involves addition of a water molecule to each molecular bond to be broken (lysed).

Chemical Digestion of Specific Food Groups

Carbohydrates

Most of us ingest between 200 and 600 grams of carbohydrate foods each day. **Monosaccharides** (simple sugars), the monomers of carbohydrates, are absorbed immediately without further ado. Only three of these are common in our diet: *glucose, fructose,* and *galactose.* The more complex carbohydrates

23

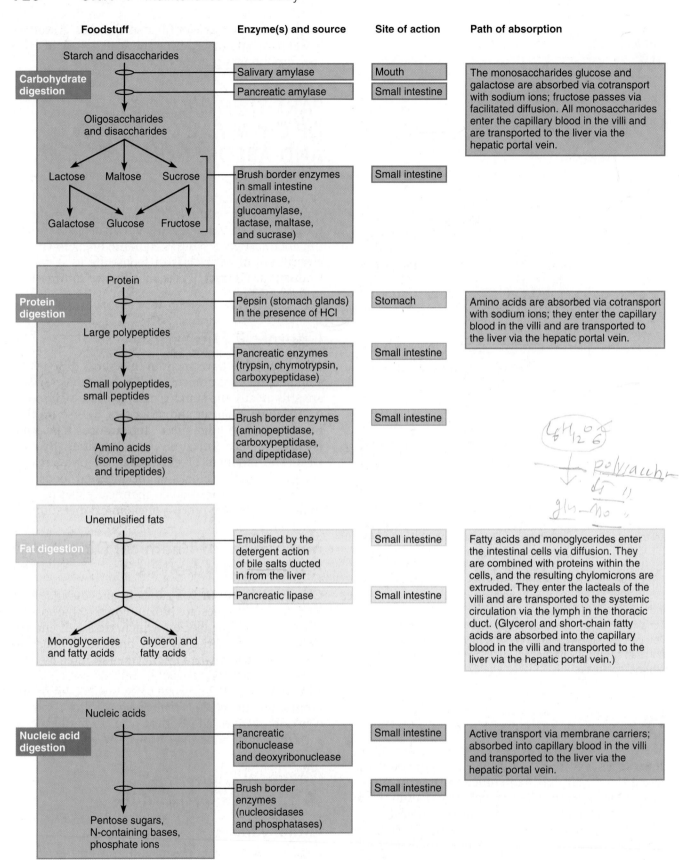

FIGURE 23.33 **Flowchart of chemical digestion and absorption of foodstuffs.**

that our digestive system is able to break down to monosaccharides are the disaccharides *sucrose* (table sugar), *lactose* (milk sugar), and *maltose* (grain sugar) and the polysaccharides *glycogen* and *starch*. In the average diet, most digestible carbohydrates are in the form of starch, with smaller amounts of disaccharides and monosaccharides. Humans lack enzymes capable of breaking down most other polysaccharides, such as cellulose. Thus, indigestible polysaccharides do not nourish us but they do help move the food along the GI tract by providing bulk, or fiber.

Chemical digestion of starch (and perhaps glycogen) begins in the mouth. **Salivary amylase,** present in saliva, splits starch into *oligosaccharides,* smaller fragments of two to eight linked glucose molecules. Salivary amylase works best in the slightly acid to neutral environment (pH of 6.75–7.00) maintained in the mouth by the buffering effects of bicarbonate and phosphate ions in saliva. Starch digestion continues until amylase is inactivated by stomach acid and broken apart by the stomach's protein-digesting enzymes. Generally speaking, the larger the meal, the longer amylase continues to work in the stomach because foodstuffs in its relatively immobile fundus are poorly mixed with gastric juices.

Starchy foods and other digestible carbohydrates that escape being broken down by salivary amylase are acted on by **pancreatic amylase** in the small intestine (see Figure 23.33). Within about ten minutes of entering the small intestine, starch is entirely converted to various oligosaccharides, mostly maltose. Intestinal brush border enzymes further digest these products to monosaccharides. The most important of the brush border enzymes are **dextrinase** and **glucoamylase,** which act on oligosaccharides composed of more than three simple sugars, and **maltase, sucrase,** and **lactase,** which hydrolyze maltose, sucrose, and lactose respectively into their constituent monosaccharides. Because the colon does not secrete digestive enzymes, chemical digestion *officially ends* in the small intestine. As noted earlier, however, resident colon bacteria do break down and metabolize the residual complex carbohydrates further, adding much to their own nutrition but essentially nothing to ours.

⬛ HOMEOSTATIC IMBALANCE

In some people, intestinal lactase is present at birth but then becomes deficient due to genetic factors. In such cases, the person becomes intolerant of milk products (the source of lactose), and undigested lactose creates osmotic gradients that not only prevent water from being absorbed in the small and large intestines but also pull water from the interstitial space into the intestines. The result is diarrhea. Bacterial metabolism of the undigested solutes produces large amounts of gas that result in bouts of bloating, flatulence, and cramping pain. The solution to this problem is simple—add lactase enzyme "drops" to your milk or take a lactase tablet before meals containing milk products. ●

Proteins

Proteins digested in the GI tract include not only dietary proteins (typically about 125 g per day), but also 15–25 g of enzyme proteins secreted into the GI tract lumen by its various glands and (probably) an equal amount of protein derived from sloughed and disintegrating mucosal cells. In healthy individuals, much of this protein is digested all the way to its **amino acid** monomers.

Protein digestion begins in the stomach when pepsinogen secreted by the chief cells is activated to **pepsin** (actually a group of protein-digesting enzymes). Pepsin functions optimally in the acidic pH range found in the stomach: 1.5–2.5. It preferentially cleaves bonds involving the amino acids tyrosine and phenylalanine so that proteins are broken into polypeptides and small numbers of free amino acids (see Figure 23.33). Pepsin, which hydrolyzes 10–15% of ingested protein, is inactivated by the high pH in the duodenum, so its proteolytic activity is restricted to the stomach. **Rennin** (the enzyme that coagulates milk protein) is not produced in adults.

Protein fragments entering the small intestine from the stomach are greeted by a host of proteolytic enzymes (Figure 23.33). **Trypsin** and **chymotrypsin** secreted by the pancreas cleave the proteins into smaller peptides, which in turn become the grist for other enzymes. The pancreatic and brush border enzyme **carboxypeptidase** splits off one amino acid at a time from the end of the polypeptide chain that bears the carboxyl group. Other brush border enzymes such as **aminopeptidase** and **dipeptidase** liberate the final amino acid products (Figure 23.34). Aminopeptidase digests a protein, one amino acid at a time, by working from the amine end. Both carboxypeptidase and aminopeptidase can independently dismantle a protein, but the teamwork between these enzymes and between trypsin and chymotrypsin, which attack the more internal parts of the protein, speeds up the process tremendously.

Lipids

Although the American Heart Association recommends a low-fat diet, the amount of lipids (fats) ingested daily varies tremendously among American adults, ranging from 30 g to 150 g or more. The small intestine is essentially the sole site of lipid digestion because the pancreas is the only significant source of fat-digesting enzymes, or **lipases** (Figure 23.33).

23

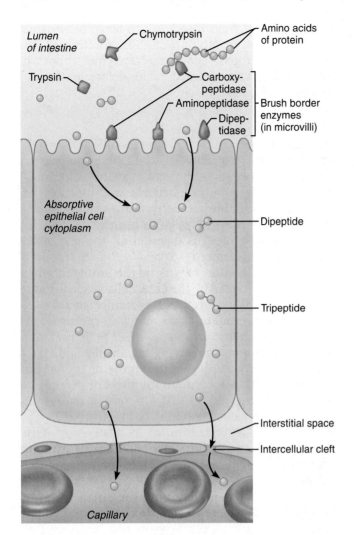

FIGURE 23.34 **Protein digestion and absorption in the small intestine.** Proteins and protein fragments are digested to amino acids by the action of pancreatic proteases (trypsin, chymotrypsin, and carboxypeptidase), and by brush border enzymes of the intestinal mucosal cells. The amino acids are then absorbed by active transport into the absorptive cells, move to their opposite side (transcytosis), and then enter the capillary via intracellular clefts.

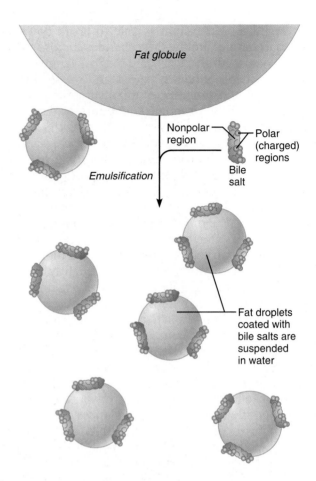

FIGURE 23.35 **Role of bile salts in fat emulsification.** As large aggregates of fats enter the small intestine, bile salts cling via their nonpolar parts to the fat molecules (triglycerides). Their polar parts, facing the aqueous phase, interact with water and repel each other, causing the fatty globule to be physically broken up into smaller fat droplets.

Triglycerides (neutral fats or triacylglycerols) are the most abundant fats in the diet.

Because triglycerides and their breakdown products are insoluble in water, fats need special "pretreatment" with bile salts to be digested and absorbed in the watery environment of the small intestine. In aqueous solutions, triglycerides aggregate to form large fat globules, and only the triglyceride molecules at the surfaces of such fatty masses are accessible to the water-soluble lipase enzymes. However, this problem is quickly resolved because as the fat globules enter the duodenum, they are coated with detergent-like bile salts (Figure 23.35). Bile salts have both nonpolar and polar regions. Their nonpolar (hydrophobic) parts cling to the fat molecules, and their polar (ionized hydrophilic) parts allow them to repel each other and to interact with water. As a result, fatty droplets are pulled off the large fat globules, and a stable *emulsion*—an aqueous suspension of fatty droplets, each about 1 mm in diameter—is formed. Emulsification does *not* break chemical bonds. It just reduces the attraction between fat molecules so that they can be more widely dispersed. This process vastly increases the number of triglyceride molecules exposed to the pancreatic lipases. Without bile, lipids would be incompletely digested in the time food is in the small intestine.

The pancreatic lipases catalyze the breakdown of fats by cleaving off two of the fatty acid chains, thus yielding free **fatty acids** and **monoglycerides** (glycerol with one fatty acid chain attached). Fat-soluble vitamins that ride with fats require no digestion.

Nucleic Acids

Both DNA and RNA, present in the nuclei of cells forming the ingested foods, are hydrolyzed to their

nucleotide monomers by **pancreatic nucleases** present in pancreatic juice. The nucleotides are then broken apart by intestinal brush border enzymes (**nucleosidases** and **phosphatases**), which release their free bases, pentose sugars, and phosphate ions (see Figure 23.33).

Absorption

Up to 10 L of food, drink, and GI secretions enter the alimentary canal daily, but only 1 L or less reaches the large intestine. Virtually all of the foodstuffs, 80% of the electrolytes, and most of the water (remember water follows salt) are absorbed in the small intestine. Although absorption occurs all along the length of the small intestine, most of it is completed by the time chyme reaches the ileum. Hence, the major absorptive role of the ileum is to reclaim bile salts to be recycled back to the liver for resecretion. It is virtually impossible to exceed the absorptive capacity of the human gut, and at the end of the ileum, all that remains is some water, indigestible food materials (largely plant fibers such as cellulose), and millions of bacteria. This debris is passed on to the large intestine.

To understand absorption, you need to remember that the fluid mosaic structure of the plasma membrane dictates that nonpolar substances, which can dissolve in the lipid core of the membrane, can be absorbed passively, and that polar substances must be absorbed by carrier mechanisms. Most nutrients are absorbed through the mucosa of the intestinal villi by *active transport* processes driven directly or indirectly (secondarily) by metabolic energy (ATP). They then enter the capillary blood in the villus to be transported in the hepatic portal vein to the liver. The exception is some lipid digestion products, which are absorbed passively by diffusion and then enter the lacteal in the villus to be carried to the blood via lymphatic fluid. Because the epithelial cells of the intestinal mucosa are joined at their luminal surfaces by tight junctions, substances cannot move *between* the cells. Consequently, materials must pass *through* the epithelial cells and into the interstitial fluid abutting their basolateral membranes (via transcytosis) if they are to enter the blood capillaries. Absorption of each nutrient class is described next and summarized on the right-hand side of Figure 23.33.

Absorption of Specific Nutrients

Carbohydrates

The monosaccharides glucose and galactose, liberated by the breakdown of starch and disaccharides, are shuttled by secondary active transport (cotransport with Na^+) into the epithelial cells by common protein carriers. They then move out of these cells by facilitated diffusion and pass into the capillaries via intercellular clefts. By contrast, fructose moves entirely by facilitated diffusion. The transport proteins, which are located very close to the disaccharidase enzymes on the microvilli, combine with the monosaccharides as soon as the disaccharides are broken down.

Proteins

Several types of carriers transport the different amino acids resulting from protein digestion. Most of these carriers, like those for glucose and galactose, are coupled to the active transport of sodium. Short chains of two or three amino acids (dipeptides and tripeptides, respectively) are also actively absorbed, but are digested to their amino acids within the epithelial cells before entering the capillary blood by diffusion (see Figure 23.34).

HOMEOSTATIC IMBALANCE

Whole proteins are not usually absorbed, but in rare cases intact proteins are taken up by endocytosis and released on the opposite side of the epithelial cell by exocytosis. This process, most common in newborn infants, reflects the immaturity of their intestinal mucosa and accounts for many early food allergies. The immune system "sees" the intact proteins as antigenic and mounts an attack. These food allergies usually disappear as the mucosa matures. This mechanism may also provide a route for IgA antibodies present in breast milk to reach an infant's bloodstream. These antibodies confer some passive immunity on the infant (temporary protection against antigens to which the mother has been sensitized). ●

Lipids

Just as bile salts accelerate lipid digestion, they are also essential for the absorption of its end products. As the water-insoluble products of fat digestion—the monoglycerides and free fatty acids—are liberated by lipase activity, they quickly become associated with bile salts and *lecithin* (a phospholipid found in bile) to form micelles. **Micelles** (mi-selz′) are collections of fatty elements clustered together with bile salts in such a way that the polar (hydrophilic) ends of the molecules face the water and the nonpolar portions form the core. Also nestled in the hydrophobic core are cholesterol molecules and fat-soluble vitamins. Although micelles are similar to emulsion droplets, they are much smaller "vehicles" and easily diffuse between microvilli to come into close contact with the luminal cell surface (Figure 23.36). The various lipid substances then leave the micelles and move

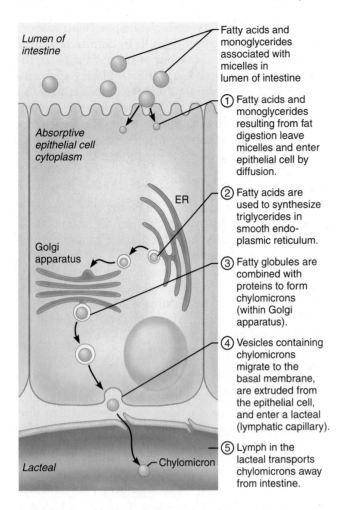

Lumen of intestine

Fatty acids and monoglycerides associated with micelles in lumen of intestine

Absorptive epithelial cell cytoplasm

ER

Golgi apparatus

① Fatty acids and monoglycerides resulting from fat digestion leave micelles and enter epithelial cell by diffusion.

② Fatty acids are used to synthesize triglycerides in smooth endoplasmic reticulum.

③ Fatty globules are combined with proteins to form chylomicrons (within Golgi apparatus).

④ Vesicles containing chylomicrons migrate to the basal membrane, are extruded from the epithelial cell, and enter a lacteal (lymphatic capillary).

⑤ Lymph in the lacteal transports chylomicrons away from intestine.

Lacteal   Chylomicron

FIGURE 23.36   Fatty acid absorption. Digestion products of fat breakdown, lecithin, and cholesterol associate with bile salts to form micelles, which serve to "ferry" them to the intestinal mucosa. They then dissociate and enter the mucosal cells by diffusion. In the mucosal epithelial cells, they are recombined to lipids and packaged with other lipoid substances and protein to form chylomicrons. The chylomicrons are extruded from the epithelial cells by exocytosis and enter the lacteal for distribution in the lymph. Free fatty acids and monoglycerides enter the capillary bed.

through the lipid phase of the plasma membrane by simple diffusion. Without the micelles, the lipids simply float on the surface of the chyme (like oil on water), inaccessible to the absorptive surfaces of the epithelial cells. Generally, fat absorption is completed in the ileum, but in the absence of bile (as might occur when a gallstone blocks the cystic duct) it happens so slowly that most of the fat passes into the large intestine and is lost in feces.

Once inside the epithelial cells, the free fatty acids and monoglycerides are resynthesized into triglycerides. The triglycerides are then combined with phospholipids and cholesterol, and coated with a "skin" of proteins to form water-soluble lipoprotein

droplets called **chylomicrons** (ki"lo-mi'kronz). These are processed by the Golgi apparatus for extrusion from the cell. This series of events is quite different from the absorption of amino acids and simple sugars, which pass through the epithelial cells unchanged.

Although a few free fatty acids enter the capillary blood, the milky-white chylomicrons are too large to pass through the basement membranes of the blood capillaries and instead enter the more permeable lacteals. Thus, most fat enters the lymphatic stream and is eventually emptied into the venous blood in the neck region via the thoracic duct, which drains the digestive viscera. While in the bloodstream, the triglycerides of the chylomicrons are hydrolyzed to free fatty acids and glycerol by **lipoprotein lipase,** an enzyme associated with the capillary endothelium. The fatty acids and glycerol can then pass through the capillary walls to be used by tissue cells for energy or stored as fats in adipose tissue. The residual chylomicron material is combined with proteins by the liver cells, and these "new" lipoproteins are used to transport cholesterol in the blood.

Nucleic Acids

The pentose sugars, nitrogenous bases, and phosphate ions resulting from nucleic acid digestion are transported actively across the epithelium by special carriers in the villus epithelium. They then enter the blood.

Vitamins

The small intestine absorbs dietary vitamins, and the large intestine absorbs some of the K and B vitamins made by its enteric bacterial "guests." As already noted, fat-soluble vitamins (A, D, E, and K) dissolve in dietary fats, become incorporated into the micelles, and move across the villus epithelium by passive diffusion. It follows that gulping pills containing fat-soluble vitamins without simultaneously eating some fat-containing food results in little or no absorption of these vitamins.

Most water-soluble vitamins (B vitamins and vitamin C) are absorbed easily by diffusion or via specific active or passive transporters. The exception is vitamin B_{12}, which is a very large, charged molecule. *Intrinsic factor*, produced by the stomach, binds to vitamin B_{12}. The vitamin B_{12}–intrinsic factor complex then binds to specific mucosal receptor sites in the terminal ileum, which trigger its active uptake by endocytosis.

Electrolytes

Absorbed electrolytes come from both ingested foods and gastrointestinal secretions. Most ions are actively absorbed along the entire length of the small intestine. However, iron and calcium absorption is largely limited to the duodenum.

As noted, absorption of sodium ions in the small intestine is coupled to active absorption of glucose and amino acids. For the most part, anions passively follow the electrical potential established by sodium transport. That is, Na^+ is actively pumped out of the epithelial cells by a Na^+-K^+ pump after entering those cells. Chloride ions are also transported actively, and in the terminus of the small intestine $HCO3^-$ is actively secreted into the lumen in exchange for Cl^-.

Potassium ions move across the intestinal mucosa passively by facilitated diffusion (or via leaky tight functions) in response to changing osmotic gradients. As water is absorbed from the lumen, the resulting rise in potassium levels in chyme creates a concentration gradient for its absorption. Thus, anything that interferes with water absorption (resulting in diarrhea) not only reduces potassium absorption but also "pulls" K^+ from the interstitial space into the intestinal lumen.

For most nutrients, the amount *reaching* the intestine is the amount absorbed, regardless of the nutritional state of the body. In contrast, absorption of iron and calcium is intimately related to the body's need for them at the time.

Ionic iron, essential for hemoglobin production, is actively transported into the mucosal cells, where it binds to the protein **ferritin** (fer′ĭ-tin). This phenomenon is called the *mucosal iron barrier*. The intracellular iron-ferritin complexes then serve as local storehouses for iron. When body reserves of iron are adequate, little is allowed to pass into the portal blood, and most of the stored iron is lost as the epithelial cells later slough off. However, when iron reserves are depleted (as during acute or chronic hemorrhage), iron uptake from the intestine and its release to the blood are accelerated. Menstrual bleeding is a major route of iron loss in females, and the intestinal epithelial cells of women have about four times as many iron transport proteins as do those of men. In the blood, iron binds to **transferrin**, a plasma protein that transports it in the circulation.

Calcium absorption is closely related to blood levels of ionic calcium. It is locally regulated by the active form of **vitamin D,** which acts as a cofactor to facilitate active calcium absorption. Decreased blood levels of ionic calcium prompt *parathyroid hormone (PTH)* release from the parathyroid glands. Besides facilitating the release of calcium ions from bone matrix and enhancing the reabsorption of calcium by the kidneys, PTH stimulates activation of vitamin D by the kidneys, which in turn accelerates calcium ion absorption in the small intestine.

Water

Approximately 9 L of water, mostly derived from GI tract secretions, enter the small intestine daily. Water is the most abundant substance in chyme, and 95% of it is absorbed in the small intestine by osmosis. The normal rate of water absorption is 300 to 400 ml per hour. Water moves freely in both directions across the intestinal mucosa, but *net osmosis* occurs whenever a concentration gradient is established by the active transport of solutes (particularly Na^+) into the mucosal cells. Thus, water uptake is effectively coupled to solute uptake and, in turn, affects the rate of absorption of substances that normally pass by diffusion. As water moves into the mucosal cells, these substances follow along their concentration gradients.

Malabsorption of Nutrients

Malabsorption, or impaired nutrient absorption, has many and varied causes. It can result from anything that interferes with the delivery of bile or pancreatic juice to the small intestine, as well as factors that damage the intestinal mucosa (severe bacterial infections and antibiotic therapy with neomycin) or reduce its absorptive surface area. A common (one in 100 people) malabsorption syndrome is *gluten-sensitive enteropathy* or *celiac disease.* This chronic genetic condition is caused by an immune reaction to gluten, a protein plentiful in some grains (wheat, rye, barley). Breakdown products of gluten interact with molecules of the immune system in the GI tract, forming complexes that activate T cells, which then mount an attack on the intestinal lining. As a result, the intestinal villi are damaged and the length of the microvilli of the brush border is reduced. The resulting bloating, diarrhea, pain, and malnutrition are usually controlled by eliminating gluten-containing grains (all grains but rice and corn) from the diet. Not many children can conceive of a world without cookies or pizza, but these are just two of the foods celiac disease victims must avoid.

Developmental Aspects of the Digestive System

As described many times before, the very young embryo is flat and consists of three germ layers, which, from top to bottom, are ectoderm, mesoderm, and endoderm. However, this flattened cell mass soon folds to form a cylindrical body, and its internal cavity becomes the cavity of the alimentary tube, which is initially closed at both ends. The epithelial lining of the developing alimentary tube, or **primitive gut,** forms from endoderm (Figure 23.37a). The rest of the wall arises from mesoderm. The anteriormost endoderm (that of the foregut) touches a depressed area of the surface ectoderm called the **stomodeum** (sto″mo-de′um; "on the way to becoming the mouth"). The two membranes fuse, forming the **oral**

(Text continues on p. 936)

MAKING CONNECTIONS

SYSTEM CONNECTIONS: Homeostatic Interrelationships Between the Digestive System and Other Body Systems

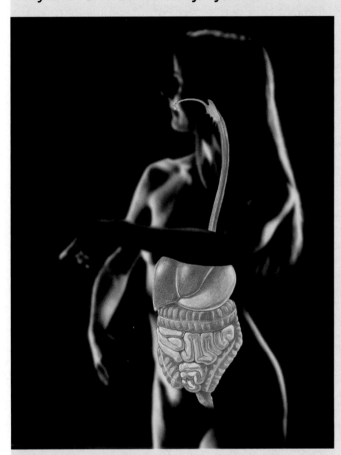

Integumentary System

- Digestive system provides nutrients needed for energy, growth, and repair; supplies fats that provide insulation in the dermis and subcutaneous tissue
- The skin synthesizes vitamin D needed for calcium absorption from the intestine; protects by enclosure

Skeletal System

- Digestive system provides nutrients needed for energy, growth, and repair; absorbs calcium needed for bone salts
- Skeletal system protects some digestive organs by bone; cavities store some nutrients (e.g., calcium, fats)

Muscular System

- Digestive system provides nutrients needed for energy, growth, and repair; liver removes lactic acid, resulting from muscle activity, from the blood
- Skeletal muscle activity increases motility of GI tract

Nervous System

- Digestive system provides nutrients needed for normal neural functioning; nutrient signals influence neural regulation of satiety
- Neural controls of digestive function; in general, parasympathetic fibers accelerate and sympathetic fibers inhibit digestive activity; reflex and voluntary controls of defecation

Endocrine System

- Liver removes hormones from blood, ending their activity; digestive system provides nutrients needed for energy, growth, and repair; pancreas, stomach, and small intestine have hormone-producing cells
- Hormones and paracrines help regulate digestive function

Cardiovascular System

- Digestive system provides nutrients to heart and blood vessels; absorbs iron needed for hemoglobin synthesis; absorbs water necessary for normal plasma volume; liver secretes bilirubin resulting from hemoglobin breakdown in bile and stores iron for reuse
- Cardiovascular system transports nutrients absorbed by alimentary canal to all tissues of body; distributes hormones of the digestive tract

Lymphatic System/Immunity

- Digestive system provides nutrients for normal functioning; lysozyme of saliva and HCl of stomach provide nonspecific protection against bacteria
- Lacteals drain fatty lymph from digestive tract organs and convey it to blood; Peyer's patches and lymphoid tissue in mesentery house macrophages and immune cells that protect digestive tract organs against infection; plasma cells provide IgA in digestive tract secretions

Respiratory System

- Digestive system provides nutrients needed for energy metabolism, growth, and repair
- Respiratory system provides oxygen to and carries away carbon dioxide produced by digestive system organs

Urinary System

- Digestive system provides nutrients for energy fuel, growth, and repair; excretes some bilirubin produced by the liver
- Kidneys transform vitamin D to its active form, which is needed for calcium absorption

Reproductive System

- Digestive system provides nutrients for energy, growth, and repair and extra nutrition needed to support fetal growth

23

THE DIGESTIVE SYSTEM and Interrelationships with the Cardiovascular, Lymphatic, and Endocrine Systems

As body systems go, the digestive system is very independent. Although the central nervous system can and does influence its activity, that is not a requirement. Indeed, most digestive system activities can be regulated entirely by local controls. Consider, for example, the following: (1) stomach and intestinal muscle is self-pacing, (2) the enteric neurons of the GI tract's intrinsic nerve plexuses carry out reflex activity that can regulate not only the organ they reside in but also adjacent and more distant GI tract organs, and (3) its enteroendocrine cells are probably even more important than neural influences in controlling digestive activity. Also unique is the fact that the digestive system operates in and regulates an environment that is actually outside the body. This is a difficult chore indeed—consider how quickly that environment can be changed by incoming foods (pizza and beer) or intestinal outflow (diarrhea).

Every cell in the body needs nutrients to stay healthy and grow, so the importance of the digestive system to virtually all body systems is clear-cut. But what systems are essential to the digestive system? If we ignore universal services, like gas exchange and renal regulation of body fluids, then the most crucial interactions are those with the cardiovascular, lymphatic, and endocrine systems. Let's take a look.

Cardiovascular and Lymphatic Systems

The important elements in this interaction are the pickup vessels. Indeed, all digestive activity would be for naught if the digested end products were not absorbed into the blood capillaries and lacteals, where they are accessible to all body cells. Besides its transport function, the lymphatic system also offers protective services via its tonsils, Peyer's patches, and individual lymphoid follicles dispersed all along the length of the alimentary tube. Again, the fact that the alimentary canal is open at both ends makes it easy prey for both pathogenic and opportunistic bacteria and fungi.

Endocrine System

The digestive tract not only has major interactions with the endocrine system, it is itself the largest and most complex endocrine organ in the body. It makes hormones that regulate GI tract motility and secretory activity of the stomach, small intestine, liver, and pancreas (e.g., secretin, CCK), as well as cause local blood vessels to dilate to receive the digested food products being absorbed (VIP). Furthermore, some digestive organ hormones (CCK and glucagon, for example) help mediate hunger or satiety, and pancreatic hormones (insulin and glucagon) are involved in bodywide regulation of carbohydrate, fat, and amino acid metabolism.

Digestive System

Case study: Remember Mr. Gutteman, the gentleman who was dehydrating? It seems that his tremendous output of urine was only one of his current problems. Today, he complains of a headache, gnawing epigastric pain, and has "the runs" (diarrhea). To pinpoint the problem, he is asked the following questions.

- Have you had these symptoms previously? (Response: "Yes, but never this bad.")

- Are you allergic to any foods? (Response: "Shellfish doesn't like me and milk gives me the runs.")

As a result of his responses, a lactose-free diet is ordered for Mr. Gutteman instead of the regular diet originally prescribed.

1. Why is the new diet prescribed? (What is believed to be his problem?)

Mr. Gutteman's problem continues despite the diet change. In fact, the frequency of diarrhea increases and by the end of the next day, he is complaining of severe abdominal pain. Again, he is asked some questions to probe his condition. One is whether he has traveled outside the country recently. He has not, reducing the possibility of infection with *Shigella* bacteria, which is associated with poor sanitation. Other questions:

- Do you drink alcohol and how much? (Response: "Little or none.")

- Have you recently eaten raw eggs or a salad containing mayonnaise at a gathering? (Response: "No.")

- Are there certain foods that seem to precipitate these attacks? (Response: "Yes, when I have coffee and a sandwich.")

2. On the basis of these responses, what do you think Mr. Gutteman's diarrhea stems from? How will it be diagnosed and treated?

(Answers in Appendix G)

23

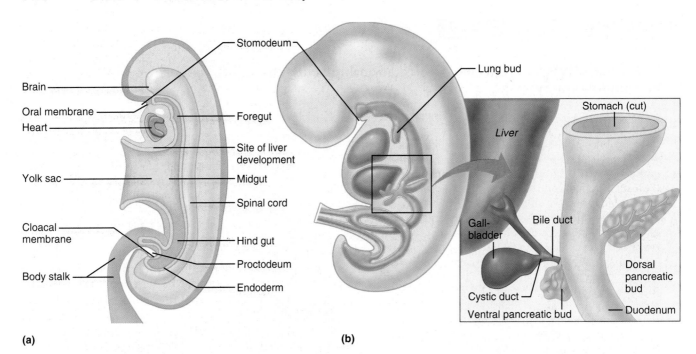

(a)

(b)

FIGURE 23.37 **Embryonic development of the digestive system. (a)** Three-week-old embryo. The endoderm has folded, and the foregut and hindgut have formed. (The midgut is still open and continuous with the yolk sac.) **(b)** By eight weeks of development, the accessory organs are budding out from the endodermal layer, as shown in the enlargement.

membrane, which shortly breaks through to form the opening of the mouth. Similarly, the end of the hindgut fuses with an ectodermal depression, called the **proctodeum** (*procto* = anus), to form the **cloacal membrane** (*cloaca* = sewer), which then breaks through to form the anus. By week 8, the alimentary canal is a continuous "tube" extending from the mouth to the anus and is open to the external environment at each end. Shortly after, the glandular organs (salivary glands, liver with gallbladder, and pancreas) bud out from the mucosa at various points along its length (Figure 23.37b). These glands retain their connections, which become ducts leading into the digestive tract.

HOMEOSTATIC IMBALANCE

The digestive system is susceptible to many congenital defects that interfere with feeding. The most common are *cleft palate*, in which the palatine bones or palatine processes of the maxillae (or both) fail to fuse, and *cleft lip,* which often occur together. Of the two, cleft palate is far more serious because the child is unable to suck properly. Another common defect is *tracheoesophageal fistula,* in which there is an opening between the esophagus and the trachea, and the esophagus often lacks a connection to the stomach. The baby chokes and becomes cyanotic during feedings because food enters the respiratory passageways. These defects are usually corrected surgically.

Cystic fibrosis (described in more detail in Chapter 22, p. 874) primarily affects the lungs, but it also impairs the activity of the pancreas. In this genetic disease, the mucous glands produce abnormally thick mucus, which blocks the ducts or passageways of involved organs. Blockage of the pancreatic duct prevents pancreatic juice from reaching the small intestine. As a result, digestion of chyme is less than optimal and most fats and fat-soluble vitamins are not digested or absorbed. Consequently the stools are bulky and fat laden. The pancreatic problems can be handled by administering pancreatic enzymes with meals. ●

During fetal life, the developing infant receives all of its nutrients through the placenta. Nonetheless, the fetal GI tract is "trained" in utero for future food digestion as the fetus naturally swallows some of the surrounding amniotic fluid. This fluid contains several chemicals that stimulate GI maturation, including gastrin and epidermal growth factor. By contrast, feeding is a newborn baby's most important activity, and several reflexes enhance the infant's ability to obtain food: The *rooting reflex* helps the infant find the nipple, and the *sucking reflex* helps the baby hold onto the nipple and swallow.

Newborn babies tend to double their birth weight within six months, and their caloric intake and food processing ability are extraordinary. For example, a 6-week-old infant weighing about 4 kg (less than 9 lb) drinks about 600 ml of milk daily. A 65-kg adult (143 lb) would have to drink 10 L of milk to ingest a corresponding volume of fluid! However, the stomach of a newborn infant is very small, so feeding must be frequent (every 3–4 hours). Peristalsis is inefficient, and vomiting of the feeding is not unusual. As the teeth break through the gums, the infant progresses to solid foods and is usually eating an adult diet by the age of 2 years.

As a rule, the digestive system operates throughout childhood and adulthood with relatively few problems. However, contaminated food or extremely spicy or irritating foods sometimes cause an inflammation of the GI tract, called **gastroenteritis** (gas″tro-en″tĕ-ri′tis). Ulcers and gallbladder problems— inflammation or **cholecystitis** (ko″le-sis-ti′tis), and gallstones—are problems of middle age.

During old age, GI tract activity declines. Fewer digestive juices are produced, absorption is less efficient, and peristalsis slows. The result is less frequent bowel movements and, often, constipation. Taste and smell are less acute, and periodontal disease often develops. Many elderly people live alone or on a reduced income. These factors, along with increasing physical disability, tend to make eating less appealing, and many of our elderly citizens are inadequately nourished.

Diverticulosis, fecal incontinence, and cancer of the GI tract are fairly common problems of the aged. Stomach and colon cancers rarely have early signs, and have often metastasized (making it inoperable) before a person seeks medical attention. Should metastasis occur, secondary cancer of the liver is almost guaranteed because of the "detour" the splanchnic venous blood takes through the liver via the hepatic portal circulation. However, when detected early, these cancers are treatable. Perhaps the best advice is to have regular dental and medical checkups. Most oral cancers are detected during routine dental examinations, 50% of all rectal cancers can be felt digitally, and nearly 80% of colon cancers can be seen and removed during a colonoscopy.

Presently, colon cancer is the second largest cause of cancer deaths (behind lung cancer) in males in the United States. Since most colorectal cancers derive from initially benign mucosal tumors called polyps, and the incidence of polyp formation increases with age, an occult blood examination once a year should be a health priority in everyone over the age of 50, and colonoscopies should be conducted at 3- to 10-year intervals depending on prior findings. As described in *A Closer Look* in Chapter 4, development of colon cancer is a gradual process that involves mutations in several regulatory genes. Recent studies have identified the mutant gene responsible for nearly 50% of all colon cancers. Dubbed *p53*, the gene normally acts as a watchdog to make sure that errors in DNA are not passed on before being corrected. When *p53* is damaged or inhibited, its tumor suppressor effect is lost and damaged DNA accumulates, resulting in carcinogenesis.

■ ■ ■

As summarized in *Making Connections*, the digestive system keeps the blood well supplied with the nutrients needed by all body tissues to fuel their energy needs and to synthesize new proteins for growth and maintenance of health. Now we are ready to examine how these nutrients are used by body cells, the topic of Chapter 24.

Related Clinical Terms

Ascites (ah-si′tēz; *asci* = bag, bladder) Abnormal accumulation of fluid within the peritoneal cavity; if excessive, causes visible bloating of the abdomen. May result from portal hypertension caused by liver cirrhosis or by heart or kidney disease.

Barrett's esophagus A pathological change in the epithelium of the lower esophagus from stratified squamous to a metaplastic columnar epithelium. A possible sequel to untreated chronic gastroesophageal reflux due to hiatal hernia, it predisposes the individual to aggressive esophageal cancer (adenocarcinoma).

Bruxism (bruck′sizm) Grinding or clenching of teeth, usually at night during sleep in response to stress. Can wear down and crack the teeth.

Bulimia (bu-lim′e-ah; *bous* = ox; *limos* = hunger) Binge-purge behavior—episodes of massive overeating are followed by some method of purging (self-induced vomiting, taking laxatives or diuretics, or excessive exercise). Most common in high school or college age women and in high school males in certain athletic activities (wrestling). Rooted in a pathological fear of being fat, and a need for control; provides a means of handling stress and depression. Consequences include erosion of tooth enamel and stomach trauma or rupture (from vomiting) and severe electrolyte disturbances which impair heart activity. Therapy includes hospitalization to control behavior, and nutritional counseling.

Dysphagia (dis-fa′je-ah; *dys* = difficult, abnormal; *phag* = eat) Difficulty swallowing; usually due to obstruction or physical trauma to the esophagus.

Endoscopy (en-dos′ko-pe; *endo* = within, inside; *scopy* = viewing) Visual examination of a ventral body cavity or the interior of a visceral organ with a flexible tubelike device called an endoscope, which contains a light source and a lens. A general term for a colonoscopy (viewing the colon), sigmoidoscopy (viewing the sigmoid colon), etc.

Enteritis (*enteron* = intestine) Inflammation of the intestine, especially the small intestine.

Hemochromatosis (he″mo-kro″mah-to′sis; *hemo* = blood; *chroma* = color; *osis* = condition of) A disorder in iron metabolism due to excessive/prolonged iron intake or a breakdown of the mucosal iron barrier; excess iron is deposited in the tissues, causing increased skin pigmentation and increased incidence of hepatic cancer and liver cirrhosis; also called *bronze diabetes* and *iron storage disease.*

Ileus (il′e-us) A condition in which all GI tract movement stops and the gut appears to be paralyzed. Can result from electrolyte imbalances and blockade of parasympathetic impulses by drugs (such as those commonly used during abdominal surgery); usually reversed when these interferences end. Restoration of motility is indicated by the reappearance of bowel (intestinal) sounds (gurgling, etc.).

Inflammatory bowel disease A noncontagious, periodic inflammation of the intestinal wall now understood to be an abnormal immune and inflammatory response to bacterial antigens that normally occur in the intestine. Affects up to two of every 1000 people. Symptoms include cramping, diarrhea, weight loss, and intestinal bleeding. Two subtypes occur: Crohn's disease, a syndrome characterized by relapsing and remitting periods, is more serious, with deep ulcers and fissures developing along the whole intestine, but mostly in the terminal ileum. Ulcerative colitis, by contrast, is characterized by a shallow inflammation of the large-intestinal mucosa, mainly in the rectum. They are treated with a special diet, reducing stress, antibiotics, and anti-inflammatory and immunosuppressant drugs.

Laparoscopy (lap″ah-ros′ko-pe; *lapar* = the flank; *scopy* = observation) Examination of the peritoneal cavity and its organs with an endoscope inserted through the anterior abdominal wall. Often used to assess the condition of the digestive organs and the pelvic reproductive organs of females.

Orthodontics (or″tho-don′tiks; *ortho* = straight) Branch of dentistry that prevents and corrects misaligned teeth.

Pancreatitis (pan″kre-ah-ti′tis) A rare but extremely serious inflammation of the pancreas. May result from excessively high levels of fat in the blood, but most often results from activation of pancreatic enzymes in the pancreatic duct, causing the pancreatic tissue and duct to be digested. This painful condition can lead to nutritional deficiencies because pancreatic enzymes are essential to food digestion in the small intestine.

Peptic ulcers Term referring to gastric and duodenal ulcers.

Proctology (prok-tol′o-je; *procto* = rectum, anus; *logy* = study of) Branch of medicine dealing with treatment of diseases of the colon, rectum, and anus.

Pyloric stenosis (pi-lor′ik stě-no′sis; *stenosis* = narrowing, constriction) Congenital abnormality in which the pyloric sphincter is abnormally constricted. There is usually no problem until the baby begins to take solid food, and then projectile vomiting begins. Corrected surgically.

Vagotomy (va-got′o-me) Cutting or severing of the vagus nerve to decrease secretion of gastric juice in those with peptic ulcers that do not respond to medication.

Xerostomia (ze″ro-sto′me-ah; *zer* = dry, *stom* = mouth) Extreme dryness of the mouth; can be caused by blockage of salivary glands by cysts or autoimmune invasion of the salivary glands or ducts (Sjögren's syndrome).

Chapter Summary

Media study tools that could provide you additional help in reviewing specific key topics of Chapter 24 are referenced below.
IP = *InterActive Physiology*

PART 1: OVERVIEW OF THE DIGESTIVE SYSTEM

1. The digestive system includes organs of the alimentary canal (mouth, pharynx, esophagus, stomach, small and large intestines) and accessory digestive system organs (teeth, tongue, salivary glands, liver, gallbladder, and pancreas).

Digestive Processes (pp. 884–885)

1. Digestive system activities include six processes: ingestion, or food intake; propulsion, or movement of food through the tract; mechanical digestion, or processes that physically mix or break foods down into smaller fragments; chemical digestion, or food breakdown by enzymatic action; absorption, or transport of products of digestion through the intestinal mucosa into the blood; and defecation, or elimination of the undigested residues (feces) from the body.

Basic Functional Concepts (pp. 885–886)

1. The digestive system controls the environment within its lumen to ensure optimal conditions for digestion and absorption of foodstuffs.

2. Receptors and hormone-secreting cells in the alimentary canal wall respond to stretch and chemical signals that result in stimulation or inhibition of GI secretory activity or motility. The alimentary canal has an intrinsic nerve supply.

IP Digestive System; Topic: Control of the Digestive System, pp. 1, 3, 4–5, 8.

Digestive System Organs: Relationship and Structural Plan (pp. 886–889)

1. The parietal and visceral layers of the peritoneum are continuous with one another via several extensions (mesenteries, falciform ligament, lesser and greater omenta), and are separated by a potential space containing serous fluid, which decreases friction during organ activity.

2. The digestive viscera is served by the splanchnic circulation, consisting of arterial branches of the celiac trunk and aorta and the hepatic portal circulation.

3. All organs of the GI tract have the same basic pattern of tissue layers in their walls; all have a mucosa, a submucosa, a muscularis, and a serosa (or adventitia). Intrinsic nerve plexuses (enteric nervous system) are found within the wall.

PART 2: FUNCTIONAL ANATOMY OF THE DIGESTIVE SYSTEM

The Mouth, Pharynx, and Esophagus (pp. 889–899)

1. Food enters the GI tract via the mouth, which is continuous with the oropharynx posteriorly. The boundaries of the mouth are the lips and cheeks, palate, and tongue.

2. The oral mucosa is stratified squamous epithelium, an adaptation seen where abrasion occurs.

3. The tongue is mucosa-covered skeletal muscle. Its intrinsic muscles allow it to change shape; its extrinsic muscles allow it to change position.

4. Saliva is produced by many small buccal glands and three pairs of major salivary glands—parotid, submandibular, and sublingual—that secrete their product into the mouth via ducts. Largely water, saliva also contains ions, proteins, metabolic wastes, lysozyme, defensins, IgA, salivary amylase, a cyanide compound, and mucin.

5. Saliva moistens and cleanses the mouth; moistens foods, aiding their compaction; dissolves food chemicals to allow for taste; and begins chemical digestion of starch (salivary amylase). Saliva output is increased by parasympathetic reflexes initiated by activation of chemical and pressure receptors in the mouth and by conditioned reflexes. The sympathetic nervous system depresses salivation.

6. The 20 deciduous teeth begin to be shed at the age of 6 and are gradually replaced during childhood and adolescence by the 32 permanent teeth.

7. Teeth are classed as incisors, canines, premolars, and molars. Each tooth has an enamel-covered crown and a cementum-covered root. The bulk of the tooth is dentin, which surrounds the central pulp cavity. A periodontal ligament secures the tooth to the bony alveolus.

8. Food propelled from the mouth passes through the oropharynx and laryngopharynx. The mucosa of the pharynx is stratified squamous epithelium; skeletal muscles in its wall (constrictor muscles) move food toward the esophagus.

9. The esophagus extends from the laryngopharynx and joins the stomach at the cardiac orifice, which is surrounded by the gastroesophageal sphincter.

10. The esophageal mucosa is stratified squamous epithelium. Its muscularis is skeletal muscle superiorly and changes to smooth muscle inferiorly. It has an adventitia rather than a serosa.

11. The mouth and associated accessory organs accomplish food ingestion and mechanical digestion (chewing and mixing), initiate the chemical digestion of starch (salivary amylase), and propel food into the pharynx (buccal phase of swallowing).

12. Teeth function to masticate food. Chewing is initiated voluntarily and is then controlled reflexively.

13. The tongue mixes food with saliva, compacts it into a bolus, and initiates swallowing (the voluntary phase). The pharynx and esophagus are primarily food conduits that conduct food to the stomach by peristalsis. The swallowing center in the medulla and pons controls this phase reflexively. When the peristaltic wave approaches the gastroesophageal sphincter, the sphincter relaxes to allow food entry to the stomach.

IP Digestive System; Topic: Motility, pp. 3–5.

The Stomach   (pp. 899–908)

1. The C-shaped stomach lies in the upper left quadrant of the abdomen. Its major regions are the cardia, fundus, body, and pyloric region. When empty, its internal surface exhibits rugae.

2. The stomach muscularis contains a third (oblique) layer of smooth muscle that allows it to churn and mix food.

3. The stomach mucosa is simple columnar epithelium dotted with gastric pits that lead into gastric glands. Secretory cells in the gastric glands include pepsinogen-producing chief cells; parietal cells, which secrete hydrochloric acid and intrinsic factor; mucous neck cells, which produce mucus; and enteroendocrine cells, which secrete hormones.

4. The mucosal barrier, which protects the stomach from self-digestion and HCl, reflects the fact that the mucosal cells are connected by tight junctions, secrete a thick mucus, and are quickly replaced when damaged.

5. Protein digestion is initiated in the stomach by activated pepsin and requires acidic conditions (provided by HCl). Few substances are absorbed.

6. Gastric secretory activity is controlled by both nervous and hormonal factors. The three phases of gastric secretion are the cephalic, gastric, and intestinal. Most stimuli acting on the head and stomach (cephalic and gastric respectively) stimulate gastric secretion. Most stimuli acting on the small intestine trigger the enterogastric reflex and release of secretin and CCK, all of which inhibit gastric secretory activity. Sympathetic activity also inhibits gastric secretion.

7. Mechanical digestion in the stomach is triggered by stomach distension and coupled to food propulsion and stomach emptying. Food movement into the duodenum is controlled by the pylorus and feedback signals from the small intestine. Pacemaker cells in the smooth muscle sheet set the maximal rate of peristalsis.

IP Digestive System; Topic: Control of the Digestive System, pp. 3, 5–6, 8.

The Small Intestine and Associated Structures   (pp. 908–922)

1. The small intestine is the major digestive and absorptive organ. It extends from the pyloric sphincter to the ileocecal valve. Its three subdivisions are the duodenum, jejunum, and ileum. The bile duct and pancreatic duct join to form the hepatopancreatic ampulla and empty their secretions into the duodenum through the hepatopancreatic sphincter (of Oddi).

2. Circular folds, villi, and microvilli increase the intestinal surface area for digestion and absorption.

3. The duodenal submucosa contains elaborate mucus-secreting duodenal glands (Brunner's glands); that of the ileum contains Peyer's patches (lymphoid follicles). The duodenum is covered not with a serosa but an adventitia.

4. Intestinal juice is largely water and is relatively enzyme-poor. The major stimuli for its release are stretch and chemicals.

5. The liver is a lobed organ overlying the stomach. Its digestive role is to produce bile, which it secretes into the common hepatic duct.

6. The structural and functional units of the liver are the liver lobules. Blood flowing to the liver via the hepatic artery and hepatic portal vein flows into its sinusoids, from which Kupffer cells remove debris and hepatocytes remove nutrients. Hepatocytes store glucose as glycogen, use amino acids to make plasma proteins, and detoxify metabolic wastes and drugs.

7. Bile is made continuously by the hepatocytes. Bile salts, secretin, and vagal stimulation stimulate bile production.

8. The gallbladder, a muscular sac that lies beneath the right liver lobe, stores and concentrates bile.

9. Bile contains electrolytes, a variety of fatty substances, bile salts, and bile pigments in an aqueous medium. Bile salts are emulsifying agents; they disperse fats and form water-soluble micelles, which solubilize the products of fat digestion.

10. Cholecystokinin released by the small intestine stimulates the gallbladder to contract and the hepatopancreatic sphincter to relax, allowing bile (and pancreatic juice) to enter the duodenum.

11. The pancreas is retroperitoneal between the spleen and small intestine. Its exocrine product, pancreatic juice, is carried to the duodenum via the pancreatic duct.

23

12. Pancreatic juice is an HCO_3^--rich fluid containing enzymes that digest all categories of foods. Its secretion of pancreatic juice is controlled by intestinal hormones and the vagus nerves.

IP Digestive System; Topic: Secretion, pp. 11–14.

13. Mechanical digestion and propulsion in the small intestine mix chyme with digestive juices and bile and force the residues, largely by segmentation, through the ileocecal valve. Pacemaker cells set the rate of segmentation. Ileocecal valve opening is controlled by the gastroileal reflex and gastrin.

The Large Intestine (pp. 922–927)

1. The subdivisions of the large intestine are the cecum (and appendix), colon (ascending, transverse, descending, and sigmoid portions), rectum, and anal canal. It opens to the body exterior at the anus.

2. The mucosa of most of the large intestine is simple columnar epithelium containing abundant goblet cells. The longitudinal muscle in the muscularis is reduced to three bands (teniae coli), which pucker its wall, producing haustra.

3. The major functions of the large intestine are absorption of water, some electrolytes, and vitamins made by enteric bacteria, and defecation (evacuation of food residues from the body).

4. The defecation reflex is triggered when feces enter the rectum. It involves parasympathetic reflexes leading to the contraction of the rectal walls and is aided by Valsalva's maneuver.

IP Digestive System; Topic: Anatomy Review, pp. 3–5.

PART 3: PHYSIOLOGY OF CHEMICAL DIGESTION AND ABSORPTION

Chemical Digestion (pp. 927–931)

1. Chemical digestion is accomplished by hydrolysis, catalyzed by enzymes.

2. Most chemical digestion is done in the small intestine by intestinal (brush border) enzymes and, more importantly, by pancreatic enzymes. Alkaline pancreatic juice neutralizes the acidic chyme and provides the proper environment for operation of the enzymes. Both pancreatic juice (the main source of lipases) and bile are necessary for fat breakdown.

Absorption (pp. 931–933)

1. Virtually all of the foodstuffs and most of the water and electrolytes are absorbed in the small intestine. Except for fat digestion products, fat-soluble vitamins, and most water-soluble vitamins (which are absorbed by diffusion), most nutrients are absorbed by active transport processes.

2. Fat breakdown products are solubilized by bile salts (in micelles), resynthesized to triglycerides in the intestinal mucosal cells, and combined with other lipids and protein as chylomicrons that enter the lacteals. Other absorbed substances enter the villus blood capillaries and are transported to the liver via the hepatic portal vein.

Developmental Aspects of the Digestive System (pp. 933, 936–937)

1. The glandular accessory organs (salivary glands, liver, pancreas, and gallbladder) form from outpocketings of the foregut endoderm. The mucosa of the alimentary canal develops from the endoderm, which folds to form a tube. The remaining three tunics of the alimentary canal wall are formed by mesoderm.

2. Important congenital abnormalities of the digestive tract include cleft palate/lip, tracheoesophageal fistula, and cystic fibrosis. All interfere with normal nutrition.

3. Various inflammations plague the digestive system throughout life. Appendicitis is common in adolescents, gastroenteritis and food poisoning can occur at any time (given the proper irritating factors), ulcers and gallbladder problems increase in middle age.

4. The efficiency of all digestive system processes declines in the elderly, and periodontal disease is common. Diverticulosis, fecal incontinence, and GI tract cancers such as stomach and colon cancer appear with increasing frequency in an aging population.

Review Questions

Multiple Choice/Matching

(Some questions have more than one correct answer. Select the best answer or answers from the choices given.)

1. The peritoneal cavity (a) is the same thing as the abdominopelvic cavity, (b) is filled with air, (c) like the pleural and pericardial cavities is a potential space containing serous fluid, (d) contains the pancreas and all of the duodenum.

2. Obstruction of the hepatopancreatic sphincter impairs digestion by reducing the availability of (a) bile and HCl, (b) HCl and intestinal juice, (c) pancreatic juice and intestinal juice, (d) pancreatic juice and bile.

3. The action of an enzyme is influenced by (a) its chemical surroundings, (b) its specific substrate, (c) the presence of needed cofactors or coenzymes, (d) all of these.

4. Carbohydrates are acted on by (a) peptidases, trypsin, and chymotrypsin, (b) amylase, maltase, and sucrase, (c) lipases, (d) peptidases, lipases, and galactase.

5. The parasympathetic nervous system influences digestion by (a) relaxing smooth muscle, (b) stimulating peristalsis and secretory activity, (c) constricting sphincters, (d) none of these.

6. The digestive juice product containing enzymes capable of digesting all four major foodstuff categories is (a) pancreatic, (b) gastric, (c) salivary, (d) biliary.

7. The vitamin associated with calcium absorption is (a) A, (b) K, (c) C, (d) D.

8. Someone has eaten a meal of buttered toast, cream, and eggs. Which of the following would you expect to happen? (a) Compared to the period shortly after the meal, gastric motility and secretion of HCl decrease when the food reaches the duodenum; (b) gastric motility increases even as the person is chewing the food (before swallowing); (c) fat will be emulsified in the duodenum by the action of bile; (d) all of these.

9. The site of production of VIP and cholecystokinin is (a) the stomach, (b) the small intestine, (c) the pancreas, (d) the large intestine.

10. Which of the following is not characteristic of the large intestine? (a) It is divided into ascending, transverse, and descending portions; (b) it contains abundant bacteria, some of which synthesize certain vitamins; (c) it is the main absorptive site; (d) it absorbs much of the water and salts remaining in the wastes.

11. The gallbladder (a) produces bile, (b) is attached to the pancreas, (c) stores and concentrates bile, (d) produces secretin.

12. The sphincter between the stomach and duodenum is (a) the pyloric sphincter, (b) the cardiac sphincter, (c) the hepatopancreatic sphincter, (d) the ileocecal sphincter.

In items 13–17, trace the path of a single protein molecule that has been ingested.

13. The protein molecule will be digested by enzymes secreted by (a) the mouth, stomach, and colon, (b) the stomach, liver, and small intestine, (c) the small intestine, mouth, and liver, (d) the pancreas and stomach.

14. The protein molecule must be digested before it can be transported to and utilized by the cells because (a) protein is only useful directly, (b) protein has a low pH, (c) proteins in the circulating blood produce an adverse osmotic pressure, (d) the protein is too large to be readily absorbed.

15. The products of protein digestion enter the bloodstream largely through cells lining (a) the stomach, (b) the small intestine, (c) the large instestine, (d) the bile duct.

16. Before the blood carrying the products of protein digestion reaches the heart, it first passes through capillary networks in (a) the spleen, (b) the lungs, (c) the liver, (d) the brain.

17. Having passed through the regulatory organ selected above, the products of protein digestion are circulated throughout the body. They will enter individual body cells as a result of (a) active transport, (b) diffusion, (c) osmosis, (d) phagocytosis.

Short Answer Essay Questions

18. Make a simple line drawing of the organs of the alimentary tube and label each organ. Then add three labels to your drawing—salivary glands, liver, and pancreas—and use arrows to show where each of these organs empties its secretion into the alimentary tube.

19. Sara was on a diet but she could not eat less and kept claiming her stomach had a mind of its own. She was joking, but indeed, there is a "gut brain" called the enteric nervous system. Is it part of the parasympathetic and sympathetic nervous system? Explain.

20. Name the layers of the alimentary tube wall. Note the tissue composition and major function of each layer.

21. What is a mesentery? Mesocolon? Greater omentum?

22. Name the six functional activities of the digestive system.

23. (a) Describe the boundaries of the oral cavity. (b) Why do you suppose its mucosa is stratified squamous epithelium rather than the more typical simple columnar epithelium?

24. (a) What is the normal number of permanent teeth? Of deciduous teeth? (b) What substance covers the tooth crown? Its root? (c) What substance makes up the bulk of a tooth? (d) What and where is pulp?

25. Describe the two phases of swallowing, noting the organs involved and the activities that occur.

26. Describe the role of these cells found in gastric glands: parietal, chief, mucous neck, and enteroendocrine.

27. Describe the regulation of the cephalic, gastric, and intestinal phases of gastric secretion.

28. (a) What is the relationship between the cystic, common hepatic, bile, and pancreatic ducts? (b) What is the point of fusion of the bile and pancreatic ducts called?

29. Explain why fatty stools result from the absence of bile or pancreatic juice.

30. Indicate the function of the Kupffer cells and the hepatocytes of the liver.

31. What are (a) brush border enzymes? (b) chylomicrons?

32. Name one inflammatory condition particularly common to adolescents, two common in middle age, and one common in old age.

33. What are the effects of aging on digestive system activity?

Critical Thinking and Clinical Application Questions

1. You are a research assistant at a pharmaceutical company. Your group has been asked to develop an effective laxative that (1) provides bulk and (2) is nonirritating to the intestinal mucosa. Explain why these requests are important by describing what would happen if the opposite conditions were present.

2. After a heavy meal rich with fried foods, Debby Collins, an overweight 45-year-old woman, was rushed to the emergency room with severe spasmodic pains in her epigastric region that radiated to the right side of her rib cage. She indicated that the attack came on suddenly, and her abdomen was found to be tender to the touch and somewhat rigid. What do you think is this patient's problem and why is her pain discontinuous (colicky)? What are the treatment options and what might happen if the problem is not resolved?

3. A baby is admitted to the hospital with a history of diarrhea and watery feces occurring over the last three days. The baby has sunken fontanels, indicating extreme dehydration. Tests indicate that the baby has a bacterium-induced colitis, and antibiotics are prescribed. Because of the baby's loss of intestinal juices, do you think that his blood pH would indicate acidosis or alkalosis? Explain your reasoning.

4. Gary Francis, a middle-aged salesman, complains of a burning pain in the "pit of his stomach," usually beginning about two hours after eating and abating after drinking a glass of milk. When asked to indicate the site, he points to his epigastric region. The GI tract is examined by X-ray fluoroscopy. A gastric ulcer is visualized, and drug therapy using an antibiotic-bismuth approach is recommended. (a) Why is this treatment suggested? (b) What are the possible consequences of nontreatment?

5. Dr. Dolan used an endoscope to view Mr. Habib's colon. He noted the presence of several polyps and removed them during the same procedure. What is an endoscope? Why did Dr. Dolan opt to remove the polyps immediately?

6. Mr. Holden has had severe diarrhea all day and is severely weakened. Explain why his nurse is concerned about his present condition.

23

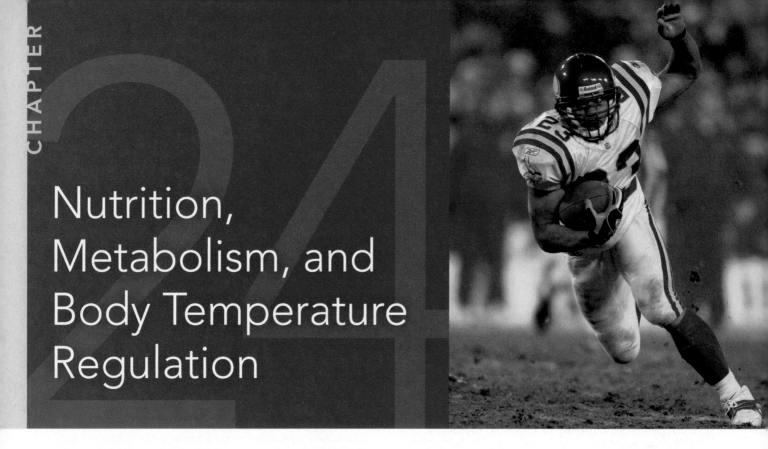

Nutrition (pp. 943–956)

1. Define nutrient, essential nutrient, and calorie.

2. List the six major nutrient categories. Note important sources and main cellular uses.

3. Distinguish between simple and complex carbohydrate sources.

4. Distinguish between saturated, unsaturated, and trans fatty acid sources.

5. Distinguish between nutritionally complete and incomplete proteins.

6. Define nitrogen balance and indicate possible causes of positive and negative nitrogen balance.

7. Distinguish between fat- and water-soluble vitamins, and list the vitamins in each group.

8. For each vitamin, list important sources, body functions, and consequences of its deficit or excess.

9. List minerals essential for health; note important dietary sources and describe how each is used.

Metabolism (pp. 956–981)

10. Define metabolism. Explain how catabolism and anabolism differ.

11. Define oxidation and reduction and indicate the importance of these reactions in metabolism. Indicate the role of coenzymes used in cellular oxidation reactions.

12. Explain the difference between substrate-level phosphorylation and oxidative phosphorylation.

13. Follow the oxidation of glucose in body cells. Summarize important events and products of glycolysis, the Krebs cycle, and electron transport.

14. Define glycogenesis, glycogenolysis, and gluconeogenesis.

15. Describe the process by which fatty acids are oxidized for energy.

16. Define ketone bodies, and indicate the stimulus for their formation.

17. Describe how amino acids are metabolized for energy.

18. Describe the need for protein synthesis in body cells.

19. Explain the concept of amino acid or carbohydrate-fat pools and describe pathways by which substances in these pools can be interconverted.

20. List important events of absorptive and postabsorptive states, and explain how these events are regulated.

21. Describe several metabolic functions of the liver.

22. Differentiate between LDLs and HDLs relative to their structures and major roles in the body.

Energy Balance (pp. 981–989)

23. Explain what is meant by body energy balance.

24. Describe some current theories of food intake regulation.

25. Define basal metabolic rate and total metabolic rate. Name factors that influence each.

26. Describe how body temperature is regulated, and indicate the common mechanisms regulating heat production/retention and heat loss from the body.

Developmental Aspects of Nutrition and Metabolism (pp. 989, 992)

27. Describe the effects of inadequate protein intake on the fetal nervous system.

28. Describe the cause and consequences of the low metabolic rate typical of the elderly.

29. List ways that medications commonly used by aged people may influence their nutrition and health.

re you a food lover? Most of us can be divided into two camps according to our reactions to food—those who live to eat and those who eat to live. The saying "you are what you eat" is true in that part of the food we eat is converted to our living flesh. In other words, some nutrients are used to build cell structures, replace worn-out parts, and synthesize functional molecules. However, most nutrients we ingest are used as metabolic fuel. That is, they are oxidized and transformed to **ATP,** the chemical energy form used by cells. The energy value of foods is measured in **kilocalories (kcal)** or "large calories (C)." One kilocalorie is the amount of heat energy needed to raise the temperature of 1 kilogram of water 1°C (1.8°F) and is the unit conscientiously counted by dieters.

In Chapter 23, we considered how foods are digested and absorbed, but what happens to these foods once they enter the blood? Why do we need bread, meat, and fresh vegetables? Why does everything we eat seem to turn to fat? This chapter will try to answer these questions as it explains both the nature of nutrients and their metabolic roles.

Nutrition

A nutrient is a substance in food used by the body to promote normal growth, maintenance, and repair. The nutrients needed for health divide neatly into six categories. Three of these—carbohydrates, lipids, and proteins—are collectively called the **major nutrients** and make up the bulk of what we eat. The fourth and fifth categories, vitamins and minerals, though equally crucial for health, are required in minute amounts. In a strict sense, water, which accounts for about 60% by volume of the food we eat, is also a major nutrient. However, because its importance in the body is described in Chapter 2, only the five nutrient categories listed above will be considered in detail here.

Most foods offer a combination of nutrients. For example, cream of mushroom soup contains all the major nutrients plus some vitamins and minerals. A diet consisting of foods from each of the five food groups—grains, fruits, vegetables, meats and fish, and milk products—normally guarantees adequate amounts of all the needed nutrients. There are several examples of food guide pyramids around; two are provided in Figure 24.1. Fresh out of the oven on April 19, 2005, the USDA's new version of the food guide pyramid—MyPyramid—is a significant departure from traditional food pyramids. MyPyramid separates the food categories vertically (rather than horizontally). Narrowing of each food group from bottom to top of the pyramid suggests moderation in selecting foods from each food group (more "picks"

Key:
- Grains
- Vegetables
- Fruits
- Oils
- Milk
- Meat and beans

(a) USDA food guide pyramid

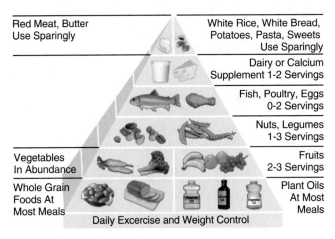

Red Meat, Butter Use Sparingly

White Rice, White Bread, Potatoes, Pasta, Sweets Use Sparingly

Dairy or Calcium Supplement 1-2 Servings

Fish, Poultry, Eggs 0-2 Servings

Nuts, Legumes 1-3 Servings

Vegetables In Abundance

Fruits 2-3 Servings

Whole Grain Foods At Most Meals

Plant Oils At Most Meals

Daily Excercise and Weight Control

(b) Healthy eating pyramid

FIGURE 24.1 **Food guide pyramids. (a)** The USDA food guide pyramid MyPyramid, issued by the U.S. Department of Agriculture in the spring of 2005. **(b)** The Healthy Eating Pyramid, presented by Walter Willett of Harvard.

from food choices at the bottom of the food band which contain less added sugar and solid fats). Also new to this food pyramid version is the emphasis on at least 30 minutes daily of physical activity as represented by the stick person climbing the steps. Considered very important is the fact that one's diet can be personalized by age, sex, and activity level by logging on to the Internet (www.mypyramid.gov) where information is available to help consumers make healthy choices and determine the size and number of servings recommended daily.

The Healthy Eating Pyramid was presented by Walter Willett of Harvard as a healthier alternative to the previous (1992) USDA food guide pyramid. It uses the traditional orientation of food groups, and emphasizes eating whole grain foods and abundant (nonstarchy) fruits and vegetables. It also recommends substituting plant oils and nuts for animal fats, and restricting red meat, sweets, and starchy foods.

24

The ability of cells, especially those of the liver, to convert one type of molecule to another is truly remarkable. These interconversions allow the body to use the wide range of chemicals found in foods and to adjust to varying food intakes. But there are limits to this ability to conjure up new molecules from old. At least 45 and possibly 50 molecules, called **essential nutrients,** cannot be made fast enough to meet the body's needs and so must be provided by the diet. As long as all the essential nutrients are ingested, the body can synthesize the hundreds of additional molecules required for life and good health. The use of the word "essential" to describe the chemicals that must be obtained from outside sources is unfortunate and misleading, because both essential and nonessential nutrients are equally vital for normal functioning.

Carbohydrates

Dietary Sources

Except for milk sugar (lactose) and negligible amounts of glycogen in meats, all the carbohydrates we ingest are derived from plants. Sugars (monosaccharides and disaccharides) come from fruits, sugar cane, sugar beets, honey, and milk. The polysaccharide starch is found in grains and vegetables. There are two varieties of polysaccharides that provide fiber. Cellulose, a polysaccharide plentiful in most vegetables, is not digested by humans but provides roughage, or *insoluble fiber,* which increases the bulk of the stool and facilitates defecation. *Soluble fiber,* or pectin, found in apples and citrus fruits, reduces blood cholesterol levels, a desirable goal in those with cardiac disease.

Uses in the Body

The monosaccharide **glucose** is the carbohydrate molecule ultimately used as fuel by body cells to produce ATP. Carbohydrate digestion also yields fructose and galactose, but these monosaccharides are converted to glucose by the liver before they enter the general circulation. Although many body cells use fats as energy sources, neurons and red blood cells rely almost entirely on glucose for their energy needs. Because even a temporary shortage of blood glucose can severely depress brain function and lead to neuron death, the body carefully monitors and regulates blood glucose levels. Any glucose in excess of what is needed for ATP synthesis is converted to glycogen or fat and stored for later use.

Other uses of monosaccharides are meager. Small amounts of pentose sugars are used to synthesize nucleic acids, and a variety of sugars are attached to externally facing plasma membrane proteins and lipids.

Dietary Requirements

The low-carbohydrate diet of the Inuit (Eskimos) and the high-carbohydrate diet of peoples in the Far East indicate that humans can be healthy even with wide variations in carbohydrate intake. The minimum requirement for carbohydrates is not known, but 100 grams per day is presumed to be the smallest amount needed to maintain adequate blood glucose levels. The recommended dietary allowance (130 g/d) is based on the amount needed to fuel the brain, not the total amount need to supply all daily activities. Recommended carbohydrate intake to maintain health is 45–65% of one's total calorie intake, with the emphasis on *complex* carbohydrates (whole grains and vegetables). When less than 50 grams per day is consumed, tissue proteins and fats are used for energy fuel.

American adults typically consume about 46% of dietary food energy in the form of carbohydrates. Because starchy foods (rice, pasta, breads) are less expensive than meat and other high-protein foods, carbohydrates make up an even greater percentage of the diet in low-income groups. Vegetables, fruits, whole grains, and milk have many valuable nutrients, such as vitamins and minerals. By contrast, highly refined carbohydrate foods such as candy and soft drinks provide concentrated energy sources only—the term "empty calories" is commonly used to describe such foods. Eating refined, sugary foods instead of more complex carbohydrates may cause nutritional deficiencies as well as obesity. Other possible consequences of excessive intake of simple carbohydrates are listed in Table 24.1.

Lipids

Dietary Sources

The most abundant dietary lipids are triglycerides, also called neutral fats or triacylglycerols (Chapter 2). We eat saturated fats in animal products such as meat and dairy foods, in a few tropical plant products such as coconut, and in hydrogenated oils (trans fats) such as margarine and solid shortenings used in baking. Unsaturated fats are present in seeds, nuts, olive oil, and most vegetable oils. Fats are digested to monoglycerides or all the way to fatty acids and glycerol, and then reconverted to triglycerides for transport in the lymph. Major sources of cholesterol are egg yolk, meats and organ meats, shellfish, and milk products. However, it is estimated that the liver produces about 85% of blood cholesterol.

Although the liver is adept at converting one fatty acid to another, it cannot synthesize *linoleic acid* (lin″o-le′ik), a fatty acid component of *lecithin* (les′ĭ-thin). Thus, linoleic acid, an omega-6 fatty acid, is an *essential fatty acid* that must be ingested.

TABLE 24.1	Summary of Carbohydrate, Lipid, and Protein Nutrients			

FOOD SOURCES	RECOMMENDED DIETARY ALLOWANCE (RDA) FOR ADULTS	PROBLEMS	
		EXCESSES	DEFICITS
CARBOHYDRATES			
Total Digestible ■ *Complex carbohydrates (starches):* bread, cereal, crackers, flour, pasta, nuts, rice, potatoes ■ *Simple carbohydrates (sugars):* carbonated drinks, candy, fruit, ice cream, pudding, young (immature) vegetables	130 g 45–65% of total caloric intake	Obesity; nutritional deficits; dental caries; gastrointestinal irritation; elevated triglycerides in plasma	Tissue wasting (in extreme deprivation); metabolic acidosis resulting from accelerated fat use for energy
Total Fiber	25–30 g		
LIPIDS			
■ *Animal sources:* lard, meat, poultry, eggs, milk, milk products ■ *Plant sources:* chocolate; corn, soy, cottonseed, olive oils; coconut; corn; peanuts	80–100 g 20–35% of total caloric intake	Obesity and increased risk of cardiovascular disease (particularly if excesses of saturated and trans fat)	Weight loss; fat stores and tissue proteins catabolized to provide metabolic energy; problems controlling heat loss (due to depletion of subcutaneous fat)
■ *Essential fatty acids:* fish oil, corn, cottonseed, soy oils; wheat germ; vegetable shortenings	10–17 g	Excess dietary intake of omega-3 fatty acid, may increase risk of stroke	Poor growth; skin lesions (eczema-like); depression
■ *Cholesterol:* organ meats (liver, kidneys, brains), egg yolks, fish roe; smaller concentrations in milk products and meat	250 mg or less	Increased levels of plasma cholesterol and LDL lipoproteins; correlated with increased risk of cardiovascular disease	Increased risk of stroke (CVA) in susceptible individuals
PROTEINS			
■ *Complete proteins:* eggs, milk, milk products, meat (fish, poultry, pork, beef, lamb) ■ *Incomplete proteins:* legumes (soybeans, lima beans, kidney beans, lentils); nuts and seeds; grains and cereals; vegetables	0.8 g/kg body weight 12–20% of total caloric intake	Obesity; enhanced calcium excretion and bone loss; high cholesterol levels in blood; kidney stones	Profound weight loss and tissue wasting; growth retardation in children; anemia; edema (due to deficits of plasma proteins) During pregnancy: miscarriage or premature birth

Linolenic acid, an omega-3 fatty acid, may also be essential. Fortunately, these two fatty acids are found in most vegetable oils.

Uses in the Body

Fats have fallen into disfavor, particularly among those for whom the "battle of the bulge" is constant. But fats make foods tender, flaky, or creamy, and make us feel full and satisfied. Furthermore, dietary fats *are* essential for several reasons. They help the body absorb fat-soluble vitamins; triglycerides are the major energy fuel of hepatocytes and skeletal muscle; and phospholipids are an integral component of myelin sheaths and cellular membranes. Fatty deposits in adipose tissue provide (1) a protective cushion around body organs, (2) an insulating layer beneath the skin, and (3) an easy-to-store concentrated source of energy fuel. Regulatory molecules called *prostaglandins* (pros"tah-glan'dinz), formed from linoleic acid via arachidonic acid (ah"rah-kǐ-don'ik), play a role in smooth muscle contraction, control of blood pressure, and inflammation.

Unlike triglycerides, cholesterol is not used for energy. It is important as a stabilizing component of plasma membranes and is the precursor from which bile salts, steroid hormones, and other essential molecules are formed.

Dietary Requirements

Fats represent over 40% of the calories in the typical American diet. There are no precise recommendations on amount or type of dietary fats, but the American Heart Association suggests that (1) fats should represent 30% or less of total caloric intake, (2) saturated fats should be limited to 10% or less of total fat intake, and (3) daily cholesterol intake should be no more than 300 mg (the amount in one egg yolk). The goal of these recommendations is to keep total blood cholesterol and triglycerides to less than 200 mg/dl. Because a diet high in saturated fats and cholesterol may contribute to cardiovascular disease, these are wise guidelines. Sources of the various lipid classes and consequences of their deficient or excessive intake are summarized in Table 24.1.

Fat Substitutes

In an attempt to reduce fat intake without losing fat's appetizing aspects, many people have turned to fat substitutes or foods prepared with them. Perhaps the oldest fat substitute is air (beaten into a product to make it fluffy). Other fat substitutes are modified starches and gums, and more recently milk whey protein (Simplesse). Except for those based on dietary fibers (gums), such products are metabolized and provide calories. One of the newest substitutes, Olestra, a fat-based product made from cottonseeds, is not metabolized because it is not digested or absorbed.

Most fat substitutes have two drawbacks: (1) They don't stand up to the intense heat needed to fry foods, and (2) although manufacturers claim otherwise, they don't taste nearly as good as the "real thing." The ones that are not absorbed tend to cause flatus (gas) or diarrhea, and may interfere with absorption of fat-soluble drugs, vitamins, and phytochemicals such as beta-carotene, a precursor of vitamin A.

Proteins

Dietary Sources

Animal products contain the highest-quality proteins, that is, those with the greatest amount and best ratios of essential amino acids (Figure 24.2). Proteins in eggs, milk, fish, and most meats (Table 24.1) are **complete proteins** that meet all the body's amino acid requirements for tissue maintenance and growth. Legumes (beans and peas), nuts, and cereals are protein-rich, but their proteins are nutritionally incomplete because they are low in one or more of the essential amino acids. Leafy green vegetables are well balanced in all essential amino acids except methionine, but contain only small amounts of protein. Strict vegetarians must carefully plan their diets to obtain all the essential amino acids and prevent protein malnutrition. When ingested together, cereal grains and legumes provide all the essential amino acids (Figure 24.2b), and some combination of these foods is found in the diets of all cultures (most obviously in the rice and beans seen on nearly every plate in a Mexican restaurant). For nonvegetarians, grains and legumes are useful as partial substitutes for more expensive animal proteins.

Uses in the Body

Proteins are important structural materials of the body, including, for example, keratin in skin, collagen and elastin in connective tissues, and muscle proteins. In addition, functional proteins such as enzymes and some hormones regulate an incredible variety of body functions. Whether amino acids are used to synthesize new proteins or are burned for energy depends on a number of factors:

1. The all-or-none rule. All amino acids needed to make a particular protein must be present in a cell at the same time and in sufficient amounts. If one is missing, the protein cannot be made. Because essential amino acids cannot be stored, those not used immediately to build proteins are oxidized for energy or converted to carbohydrates or fats.

2. Adequacy of caloric intake. For optimal protein synthesis, the diet must supply sufficient carbohydrate or fat calories for ATP production. When it doesn't, dietary and tissue proteins are used for energy.

3. Nitrogen balance. In healthy adults the rate of protein synthesis equals the rate of protein breakdown and loss. This homeostatic state is reflected in the body's **nitrogen balance.** The body is in nitrogen balance when the amount of nitrogen ingested in proteins equals the amount excreted in urine and feces.

The body is in *positive nitrogen balance* when the amount of protein being incorporated into tissue is greater than the amount being broken down and used for energy—the normal situation in growing children and pregnant women. A positive balance also occurs when tissues are being repaired following illness or injury.

In *negative nitrogen balance*, protein breakdown for energy exceeds the amount of protein being

Q *John eats nothing but baked bean sandwiches. Is he getting all the essential amino acids in this rather restricted diet?*

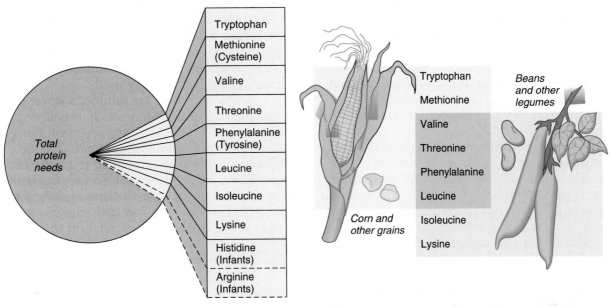

(a) Essential amino acids

(b) Vegetarian diets providing the eight essential amino acids for humans

FIGURE 24.2 **Essential amino acids.** In order for protein synthesis to occur, ten amino acids must be available simultaneously and in the correct relative amounts. **(a)** Relative amounts of the essential amino acids and total proteins needed by adults. Notice that the essential amino acids represent only a small percentage of the total recommended protein intake. Histidine and arginine are graphed with dashed lines because they are made in inadequate amounts in infants, and thus are essential in infants but not in adults. The amino acids shown in parentheses are *not* essential but can substitute in part for methionine and phenylalanine. **(b)** Vegetarian diets must be carefully constructed to provide all essential amino acids. As shown, corn has little isoleucine and lysine. Beans have ample isoleucine and lysine but little tryptophan and methionine. All essential amino acids can be obtained by consuming a meal of corn and beans.

incorporated into tissues. This occurs during physical and emotional stress (for example, infection, injury, or burns), or when the quality or quantity of dietary protein is poor, or during starvation.

4. Hormonal controls. Certain hormones, called *anabolic hormones*, accelerate protein synthesis and growth. The effects of these hormones vary continually throughout life. For example, pituitary *growth hormone* stimulates tissue growth during childhood and conserves protein in adults, and the *sex hormones* trigger the growth spurt of adolescence. Other hormones, such as the adrenal *glucocorticoids* released during stress, enhance protein breakdown and conversion of amino acids to glucose.

Dietary Requirements

Besides supplying essential amino acids, dietary proteins furnish the raw materials for making nonessential amino acids and various nonprotein nitrogen-containing substances. The amount of protein a person needs reflects his or her age, size, metabolic rate, and current state of nitrogen balance. As a rule of thumb, nutritionists recommend a daily intake of 0.8 g per kilogram of body weight. About 30 g of protein is supplied by a small serving of fish and a glass of milk. Most Americans eat far more protein than they need. Prolonged high protein consumption may lead to bone loss. This may occur because metabolizing sulfur-containing amino acids makes the blood more acidic and calcium is pulled from the bones to buffer these acids.

Vitamins

Vitamins (*vita* = life) are potent organic compounds needed in minute amounts for growth and good

A *Yes. He has both grain and beans, which together contain all the essential amino acids.*

health. Unlike other organic nutrients, vitamins are not used for energy and do not serve as building blocks, but they are crucial in helping the body use those nutrients that do. Without vitamins, all the carbohydrates, proteins, and fats we eat would be useless.

Most vitamins function as **coenzymes** (or parts of coenzymes), which act with an enzyme to accomplish a particular chemical task. For example, the B vitamins riboflavin and niacin act as coenzymes in the oxidation of glucose for energy. We will describe the roles of some vitamins in the metabolism discussion.

Because most vitamins are not made in the body, they must be taken in via foods or vitamin supplements. The exceptions are vitamin D made in the skin, and small amounts of B vitamins and vitamin K synthesized by intestinal bacteria. In addition, the body can convert *beta-carotene* (kar'o-tēn), the orange pigment in carrots and other foods, to vitamin A. (Thus, beta-carotene and substances like it are called *provitamins*.) Vitamins are found in all major food groups, but no one food contains all the required vitamins. Thus, a balanced diet is the best way to ensure a full vitamin complement.

Initially vitamins were given a convenient letter designation that indicated the order of their discovery. Although more chemically descriptive names have been assigned to the vitamins, this earlier terminology is still commonly used.

Vitamins are either **fat soluble** or **water soluble.** The water-soluble vitamins, which include B-complex vitamins and vitamin C, are absorbed along with water from the gastrointestinal tract. (The exception is vitamin B_{12}, which must bind to gastric intrinsic factor to be absorbed.) Because only insignificant amounts of water-soluble vitamins are stored in lean tissue of the body, any ingested amounts not used within an hour or so are excreted in urine. Consequently, few conditions resulting from excessive levels of these vitamins (*hypervitaminoses*) are known.

TABLE 24.2   Vitamins

VITAMIN	DESCRIPTION, COMMENTS	SOURCES AND RECOMMENDED DAILY AMOUNTS (RDA) FOR ADULTS	IMPORTANCE IN BODY	PROBLEMS	
				EXCESSES	DEFICITS
FAT-SOLUBLE VITAMINS					
A (retinol)	Group of compounds including retinol and retinal; 90% is stored in liver, which can supply body needs for a year; stable to heat, acids, alkalis; easily oxidized; rapidly destroyed by exposure to light	Formed from provitamin beta-carotene in intestine, liver, kidneys; carotene found in deep-yellow and deep-green leafy vegetables; vitamin A found in fish liver oils, egg yolk, liver, fortified foods (milk, margarine) RDA: males 900 µg, females 700 µg	Required for synthesis of photoreceptor pigments, integrity of skin and mucosae, normal tooth and bone development, normal reproductive capabilities; important antioxidant (hence, anticancer and anti-atherosclerosis effects)	Toxic when ingested in excess of 10 mg daily for months; symptoms: nausea, vomiting, anorexia, headache, hair loss, bone and joint pain, bone fragility, enlargement of liver and spleen; may increase smokers' risk of lung cancer	Night blindness; epithelial changes; dry skin and hair, skin sores; increased respiratory, digestive, urogenital infections; drying of conjunctiva; clouding of cornea; in pregnant women, developmental defects of the embryo
D (antirachitic factor)	Group of chemically distinct sterols; concentrated in liver and to lesser extent in skin, kidneys, spleen, other tissues; stable to heat, light, acids, alkalis, oxidation	Vitamin D_3 is chief form in body cells; produced in skin by irradiation of 7-dehydrocholesterol by UV light; active form (1,25-dihydroxyvitamin D_3) produced by chemical modification of vitamin D_3 in liver, then kidneys; major food sources: fish liver oils, egg yolk, fortified milk RDA: 5 µg	Functionally a hormone; increases calcium blood levels by enhancing absorption of calcium; with PTH mobilizes calcium from bones; both mechanisms serve calcium homeostasis of blood (essential for normal neuromuscular function, blood clotting, bone and tooth formation)	22–25 µg/day may be toxic to children, massive doses induce toxicity in adults; symptoms: vomiting, diarrhea, fatigue, weight loss, hypercalcemia and calcification of soft tissues, irreversible cardiac and renal damage	Faulty mineralization of bones and teeth; rickets in children, osteomalacia in adults; poor muscle tone and leg weakness; restlessness, irritability

TABLE 24.2	*(continued)*				
				PROBLEMS	
VITAMIN	**DESCRIPTION, COMMENTS**	**SOURCES AND RECOMMENDED DAILY AMOUNTS (RDA) FOR ADULTS**	**IMPORTANCE IN BODY**	**EXCESSES**	**DEFICITS**
E (antisterility factor)	Group of related compounds called tocopherols, chemically related to sex hormones; stored primarily in muscle and adipose tissues; resistant to heat, light, acids; unstable in presence of oxygen	Wheat germ and vegetable oils, nuts, whole grains, dark-green leafy vegetables RDA: 15 mg (actual RDA depends on diet; high-fat diet requires a higher RDA)	An antioxidant that disarms free radicals; helps prevent oxidation of unsaturated fatty acids and cholesterol, thus helps prevent oxidative damage to cell membranes and atherosclerosis	Few side effects even at massive doses; slow wound healing; decreased platelet adhesion and increased clotting time	Extremely rare, precise effects uncertain: possible decreased life span and hemolysis of RBCs, fragile capillaries; spinocerebellar degeneration
K (coagulation vitamin)	Number of related compounds known as quinones; small amounts stored in liver; heat resistant; destroyed by acids, alkalis, light, oxidizing agents; antagonized by certain anticoagulants and antibiotics that interfere with synthetic activity of enteric bacteria	Most synthesized by bacteria in large intestine; food sources: leafy green vegetables, broccoli, cabbage, cauliflower, pork, liver RDA: males 120 µg, females 90 µg; obtaining adequate amount is not a problem	Essential for formation of clotting proteins and some other proteins made by liver; as intermediate in electron transport chain, participates in oxidative phosphorylation in all body cells	None known, not stored in appreciable amounts	Easy bruising and bleeding (prolonged clotting time)

WATER-SOLUBLE VITAMINS

VITAMIN	DESCRIPTION, COMMENTS	SOURCES AND RECOMMENDED DAILY AMOUNTS (RDA) FOR ADULTS	IMPORTANCE IN BODY	EXCESSES	DEFICITS
C (ascorbic acid)	Simple 6-carbon crystalline compound derived from glucose; rapidly destroyed by heat, light, alkalis; about 1500 mg is stored in body, particularly in adrenal gland, retina, intestine, pituitary; when tissues are saturated, excess excreted by kidneys	Fruits and vegetables, particularly citrus, cantaloupe, strawberries, tomatoes, fresh potatoes, leafy green vegetables RDA: 75 mg for females, 90 mg for males, and an extra 35 mg for those who smoke	Antioxidant; acts in hydroxylation reactions in connective tissue formation, in conversion of tryptophan to serotonin and of cholesterol to bile salts; enhances iron absorption and use; required for activation of folacin (a B vitamin)	Result of megadoses (10 or more times RDA); diarrhea; enhanced mobilization of bone minerals and blood coagulation; high uric acid levels and exacerbation of gout, kidney stone formation	Defective formation of intercellular cement; joint pains, poor tooth and bone growth; poor wound healing, increased susceptibility to infection; extreme deficit causes scurvy (bleeding gums, anemia, degeneration of muscle and cartilage, weight loss)
B₁ (thiamin)	Rapidly destroyed by heat; very limited amount stored in body; excess eliminated in urine	Lean meats, liver, fish, eggs, whole grains, leafy green vegetables, legumes RDA: 1.2 mg	Part of coenzyme cocarboxylase, which acts in carbohydrate metabolism; required for transformation of pyruvic acid to acetyl CoA, for synthesis of pentose sugars and acetylcholine; for oxidation of alcohol	None known	Beriberi; decreased appetite, vision disturbances; unsteadiness when standing or walking, confusion, loss of memory; profound fatigue; heart enlargement, tachycardia

24

| TABLE 24.2 | **Vitamins** (continued) | | | | |

VITAMIN	DESCRIPTION, COMMENTS	SOURCES AND RECOMMENDED DAILY AMOUNTS (RDA) FOR ADULTS	IMPORTANCE IN BODY	PROBLEMS	
				EXCESSES	DEFICITS

WATER-SOLUBLE VITAMINS (continued)

B₂ (riboflavin)	Named for its similarity to ribose sugar: has green-yellow fluorescence; quickly decomposed by UV, visible light, alkalis; body stores are carefully guarded; excess eliminated in urine	Widely varying sources such as liver, yeast, egg white, whole grains, meat, poultry, fish, legumes; major source is milk RDA: 1.1–1.3 mg	Present in body as coenzymes FAD and FMN (flavin mononucleotide), which act as hydrogen acceptors in body; also is component of amino acid oxidases	None known	Dermatitis; cracking of lips at corners (cheilosis); lips and tongue become purple-red and shiny; ocular problems: light sensitivity, blurred vision; one of the most common vitamin deficiencies
B₃ (niacin, nicotinamide)	Simple organic compounds stable to acids, alkalis, heat, light, oxidation (even boiling does not decrease potency); very limited amount stored in body, day-to-day supply is desirable; excess secreted in urine	Diets with adequate protein usually provide adequate niacin because amino acid tryptophan is easily converted to niacin; preformed niacin provided by poultry, meat, fish; less important sources: liver, yeast, peanuts, potatoes, leafy green vegetables RDA: 16 mg males; 14 mg females	Constituent of NAD⁺ (nicotinamide adenine dinucleotide) coenzyme involved in glycolysis, oxidative phosphorylation, fat breakdown, DNA repair, transcriptional regulation; inhibits cholesterol synthesis; peripheral vascular dilator	Result of megadoses; hyperglycemia; vasodilation leading to flushing of skin, tingling sensations; possible liver damage; gout	Pellagra after months of deprivation (rare in U.S.); early signs—listlessness, headache, loss of appetite—progress to sore tongue and lips, nausea, vomiting, diarrhea, skin rough and ulcerated, neurological symptoms; characterized by the 4 Ds: dermatitis, diarrhea, dementia, and death (in final stage)
B₆ (pyridoxine)	Group of three pyridines occurring in both free and phosphorylated forms in body; stable to heat, acids; destroyed by alkalis, light; body stores very limited	Meat, poultry, fish, whole grains, bananas; less important sources: potatoes, sweet potatoes, tomatoes, spinach RDA: 1.3 mg	Active form is coenzyme pyridoxal phosphate, which functions with several enzymes involved in amino acid metabolism; required for conversion of tryptophan to niacin, for glycogenolysis, for formation of antibodies and hemoglobin, and for breakdown of homocysteine	Depressed deep tendon reflexes, numbness and loss of sensation in extremities; difficulty walking; nerve damage	Infants: nervous irritability, convulsions, anemia, vomiting, weakness, abdominal pain; adults: seborrhea lesions around eyes and mouth; increased risk of heart disease
B₅ (pantothenic acid)	Quite stable, little loss of activity with cooking except in acidic or alkaline solutions; liver, kidneys, brain, adrenal, heart tissues contain large amounts	Name derived from Greek *panthos* meaning "everywhere"; widely distributed in animal foods, whole grains, legumes; liver, yeast, egg yolk, meat especially good sources; some produced by enteric bacteria RDA: 5 mg	Functions in form of coenzyme A in reactions that remove or transfer acetyl group, e.g., formation of acetyl CoA from pyruvic acid, oxidation and synthesis of fatty acids; also involved in synthesis of steroids and heme of hemoglobin	None known	Symptoms vague: loss of appetite, abdominal pain, mental depression, pains in arms and legs, muscle spasms, neuromuscular degeneration (neuropathy of alcoholics is thought to be related to deficits)

24

TABLE 24.2	(continued)				
				PROBLEMS	
VITAMIN	**DESCRIPTION, COMMENTS**	**SOURCES AND RECOMMENDED DAILY AMOUNTS (RDA) FOR ADULTS**	**IMPORTANCE IN BODY**	**EXCESSES**	**DEFICITS**
Biotin	Urea derivative containing sulfur; crystalline in its free form; stable to heat, light, acids; in tissues, is usually combined with protein; stored in minute amounts, particularly in liver, kidneys, brain, adrenal glands	Liver, egg yolk, legumes, nuts; some synthesized by bacteria in gastrointestinal tract RDA: not established, probably about 0.3 mg (assumed that formation of the vitamin by enteric bacteria provides far more than is needed)	Functions as coenzyme for a number of enzymes that catalyze carboxylation, decarboxylation, deamination reactions; essential for reactions of Krebs cycle, for formation of purines and nonessential amino acids, for use of amino acids for energy	None known	Scaly skin, muscle pains, pallor, anorexia, nausea, fatigue; elevated blood cholesterol levels
B_{12} (cyanocobalamin)	Most complex vitamin; contains cobalt; stable to heat; inactivated by light and strongly acidic or basic solutions; intrinsic factor required for transport across intestinal membrane; stored principally in liver; liver stores of 2000–3000 µg sufficient to provide body needs for 3–5 years	Liver, meat, poultry, fish, dairy foods except butter, eggs; not found in plant foods RDA: 2.4 µg	Functions as coenzyme in all cells, particularly in gastrointestinal tract, nervous system, and bone marrow; in bone marrow, acts in synthesis of DNA; when absent, erythrocytes do not divide but continue to enlarge; essential for synthesis of methionine and choline	None known	Pernicious anemia, signified by pallor, anorexia, dyspnea, weight loss, neurological disturbances; most cases reflect impaired absorption rather than actual deficit
Folic acid (folacin)	Pure vitamin is bright-yellow crystalline compound; stable to heat; easily oxidized in acidic solutions and light; stored mainly in liver	Liver, orange juice, deep-green vegetables, yeast, lean beef, eggs, veal, whole grains; synthesized by enteric bacteria RDA: 400 µg	Basis of coenzymes that act in synthesis of methionine and certain other amino acids, choline, DNA; essential for formation of red blood cells and for normal neural tube development in the embryo; helps breakdown of homocysteine	None known	Macrocytic or megaloblastic anemia; gastrointestinal disturbances; diarrhea; spina bifida risk in newborn; low birth weight and neurological deficits; increased risk of heart attack and stroke

Notes
1. Because vitamin D is present in natural foods in only very small amounts, infants, pregnant and lactating women, and people who have little exposure to sunlight should use vitamin D supplements (or supplemented foods, e.g., fortified milk).
2. Vitamins A and D are toxic in excessive amounts and should be used in supplementary form only when prescribed by a physician. Because most water-soluble vitamins are excreted in urine when ingested in excess, the effectiveness of taking supplements is questionable.
3. Many vitamin deficiencies are secondary to disease (including anorexia, vomiting, diarrhea, or malabsorption diseases) or reflect increased metabolic requirements due to fever or stress factors. Specific vitamin deficiencies require therapy with the vitamins that are lacking.

24

Fat-soluble vitamins (A, D, E, and K) bind to ingested lipids and are absorbed along with their digestion products. Anything that interferes with fat absorption also interferes with the uptake of fat-soluble vitamins. Except for vitamin K, fat-soluble vitamins are stored in the body, and pathologies due to fat-soluble vitamin toxicity, particularly vitamin A hypervitaminosis, are well documented clinically. Vitamin K is filtered out by the kidneys in modest amounts.

As described in the next section, metabolism uses oxygen, and during these reactions some potentially harmful free radicals are generated. Vitamins C, E, and A (in the form of its dimer beta-carotene) and the mineral selenium are *antioxidants* that neutralize tissue-damaging free radicals. The whole story of how antioxidants interact in the body is still murky, but chemists propose that they act much like a bucket brigade to pass the dangerous free electron from one molecule to the next, until it is finally absorbed by a chemical such as glutathione and flushed from the body in urine. Broccoli, cabbage, cauliflower, and brussels sprouts are all good sources of vitamins A and C and other chemicals that, collectively, appear to have anti-cancer effects.

Controversy abounds concerning the ability of vitamins to work wonders, such as the idea that huge doses of vitamin C will prevent colds. The notion that megadoses of vitamin supplements are the road to eternal youth and glowing health is useless at best and, at worst, may cause serious health problems, particularly in the case of fat-soluble vitamins. Table 24.2 contains an overview of the roles of vitamins in the body.

Minerals

The body requires moderate amounts of seven **minerals** (calcium, phosphorus, potassium, sulfur, sodium, chlorine, magnesium) and trace amounts of about a dozen others (Table 24.3). Minerals make up about 4% of the body by weight, with calcium and phosphorus (as bone salts) accounting for about three-quarters of this amount.

Minerals, like vitamins, are not used for fuel but work with other nutrients to ensure a smoothly

TABLE 24.3	**Minerals**				

MINERAL	DISTRIBUTION IN BODY, COMMENTS	SOURCES AND RECOMMENDED DAILY AMOUNTS (RDA) FOR ADULTS	IMPORTANCE IN BODY	PROBLEMS	
				EXCESSES	DEFICITS
Calcium (Ca)	Most stored in salt form in bones; the most abundant cation in body; absorbed from intestine in presence of vitamin D; excess excreted in feces; blood levels regulated by PTH and calcitonin (during youth)	Milk, milk products, leafy green vegetables, egg yolk, shellfish RDA: 1300 mg, dropping to 1000 mg after age 25	In salt form, required for hardness of bones, teeth; ionic calcium in blood and cells essential for normal membrane permeability, transmission of nerve impulses, muscle contraction, normal heart rhythm, blood clotting; activates certain enzymes; helps prevent hypertension	Depressed neural function; lethargy and confusion; muscle pain and weakness; calcium salt deposit in soft tissues; kidney stones	Muscle tetany; osteomalacia, osteoporosis; retarded growth and rickets in children
Chlorine (Cl)	Exists in body almost entirely as chloride ion; principal anion of extracellular fluid; highest concentrations in cerebrospinal fluid and gastric juice; excreted in urine	Table salts (as for sodium); usually ingested in excess RDA: not established; normal diet contains 3–9 g	With sodium, helps maintain osmotic pressure and pH of extracellular fluid; required for HCl formation by stomach glands; activates salivary amylase; aids in transport of CO_2 by blood (chloride shift)	Vomiting	Severe vomiting or diarrhea leads to Cl loss and alkalosis; muscle cramps; apathy

| TABLE 24.3 | *(continued)* | | | | |

MINERAL	DISTRIBUTION IN BODY, COMMENTS	SOURCES AND RECOMMENDED DAILY AMOUNTS (RDA) FOR ADULTS	IMPORTANCE IN BODY	*PROBLEMS* EXCESSES	DEFICITS
Sulfur (S)	Widely distributed: particularly abundant in hair, skin, nails; excreted in urine	Meat, milk, eggs, legumes (all rich in sulfur-containing amino acids) RDA: not established; diet adequate in proteins meets body's needs	Essential constituent of many proteins (insulin), some vitamins (thiamin and biotin); found in mucopolysaccharides present in cartilage, tendons, bone	Not known	Not known
Potassium (K)	Principal intracellular cation, 97% within cells; fixed proportion of K is bound to proteins, and measurements of body K are used to determine lean body mass; K⁺ leaves cells during protein catabolism, dehydration, glycogenolysis; most excreted in urine	Widely distributed in foods; normal diet provides 2–6 g/day; avocados, dried apricots, meat, fish, fowl, cereals RDA: not established; diet adequate in calories provides ample amount, i.e., 2500 mg	Helps maintain intracellular osmotic pressure; needed for normal nerve impulse conduction, muscle contraction, glycogenesis, protein synthesis	Usually a complication of renal failure or severe dehydration, but may result from severe alcoholism; paresthesias, muscular weakness, cardiac abnormalities	Rare but may result from diuretic therapy, severe diarrhea, or vomiting; muscular weakness, paralysis, nausea, vomiting, tachycardia, heart failure
Sodium (Na)	Widely distributed: 50% found in extracellular fluid, 40% in bone salts, 10% within cells; absorption is rapid and almost complete; excretion, chiefly in urine, controlled by aldosterone	Table salt (1 tsp = 2000 mg); cured meats (ham, etc.), sauerkraut, cheese; diet supplies substantial excess RDA: not established; probably about 2500 mg	Most abundant cation in extracellular fluid: principal electrolyte maintaining osmotic pressure of extracellular fluids and water balance; as part of bicarbonate buffer system, aids in acid-base balance of blood; needed for normal neuromuscular function; part of pump for transport of glucose and other nutrients	Hypertension; edema	Rare but can occur with excessive vomiting, diarrhea, sweating, or poor dietary intake; nausea, abdominal and muscle cramping, convulsions
Magnesium (Mg)	In all cells, particularly abundant in bones; absorption parallels that of calcium; excreted chiefly in urine	Milk, dairy products, whole-grain cereals, nuts, legumes, leafy green vegetables RDA: 400 mg for males; 320 mg for females	Constituent of many coenzymes that play a role in conversion of ATP to ADP; required for normal muscle and nerve irritability	Diarrhea	Neuromuscular problems, tremors, muscle weakness, irregular heartbeat; vasospasm and hypertension; sudden cardiac death; seen in alcoholism, severe renal disease, prolonged diarrhea, and with diuretic drugs

24

TABLE 24.3 **Minerals** *(continued)*

MINERAL	DISTRIBUTION IN BODY, COMMENTS	SOURCES AND RECOMMENDED DAILY AMOUNTS (RDA) FOR ADULTS	IMPORTANCE IN BODY	PROBLEMS	
				EXCESSES	DEFICITS
Phosphorus (P)	About 80% found in inorganic salts of bones, teeth; remainder in muscle, nervous tissue, blood; absorption aided by vitamin D; about 1/3 dietary intake excreted in feces; metabolic by-products excreted in urine	Diets rich in proteins are usually rich in phosphorus; plentiful in milk, eggs, meat, fish, poultry, legumes, nuts, whole grains RDA: 700 mg	Component of bones and teeth, nucleic acids, proteins, phospholipids, ATP, phosphates (buffers) of body fluids; thus, important for energy storage and transfer, muscle and nerve activity, cell permeability	Not known, but excess in diet may depress absorption of iron and manganese	Rickets, poor growth

TRACE MINERALS*

Fluorine (F)	Component of bones, teeth, other body tissues; excreted in urine	Fluoridated water RDA: 3–4 mg	Important for tooth structure; may help prevent dental caries (particularly in children) and osteoporosis in adults	Mottling of teeth	Not known
Cobalt (Co)	Found in all cells; larger amounts in bone marrow	Liver, lean meat, poultry, fish, milk RDA: not established	A constituent of vitamin B_{12}, which is needed for normal maturation of red blood cells	Goiter, polycythemia, heart disease	See deficit of vitamin B_{12} (Table 24.2)
Chromium (Cr)	Widely distributed	Liver, meat, cheese, whole grains, brewer's yeast, wine RDA: 35 μg for males; 25 μg for females	Required for synthesis of glucose tolerance factor (GTF) needed for proper glucose metabolism; enhances effectiveness of insulin on carbohydrate metabolism; may increase blood levels of HDLs while decreasing levels of LDLs	Not known	Impairs ability of insulin to work, hence increases insulin secretion and risk of adult-onset diabetes mellitus
Copper (Cu)	Concentrated in liver, heart, brain, spleen; excreted in feces	Liver, shellfish, whole grains, legumes, meat; typical diet provides 2–5 mg daily RDA: 900 μg	Required for synthesis of hemoglobin; essential for manufacture of melanin, myelin, some intermediates of electron transport chain	Rare; abnormal storage in Wilson's disease	Rare

*Trace minerals together account for less than 0.005% of body weight.

TABLE 24.3	(continued)				

MINERAL	DISTRIBUTION IN BODY, COMMENTS	SOURCES AND RECOMMENDED DAILY AMOUNTS (RDA) FOR ADULTS	IMPORTANCE IN BODY	PROBLEMS	
				EXCESSES	DEFICITS
Iodine (I)	Found in all tissues, but in high concentrations only in thyroid gland; absorption controlled by blood levels of protein-bound iodine; excreted in urine	Cod liver oil, iodized salt, shellfish, vegetables grown in iodine-rich soil RDA: 150 µg	Required to form thyroid hormones (T_3 and T_4), which are important in regulating cellular metabolic rate	Depressed synthesis of thyroid hormones	Hypothyroidism: cretinism in infants, myxedema in adults (if less severe, simple goiter); impaired learning and motivation in children
Iron (Fe)	60–70% in hemoglobin; remainder in skeletal muscle, liver, spleen, bone marrow bound to ferritin; only 2–10% of dietary iron is absorbed because of mucosal barrier; lost from body in urine, perspiration, menstrual flow, shed hair, sloughed skin and mucosal cells	Best sources: meat, liver, also in shellfish, egg yolk, dried fruit, nuts, legumes, molasses RDA: males 8 mg, females 15–18 mg	Part of heme of hemoglobin, which binds bulk of oxygen transported in blood; component of cytochromes, which function in oxidative phosphorylation	Hemochromatosis (inherited condition of iron excess); damage to liver (cirrhosis and liver cancer), heart, pancreas (causing diabetes)	Iron-deficiency anemia; pallor, lethargy, flatulence, anorexia, paresthesias, impaired cognitive performance in children; inability to maintain body temperature; depressed killing by phagocytes (due to inability to produce the respiratory burst)
Manganese (Mn)	Most concentrated in liver, kidneys, spleen; excreted largely in feces	Nuts, legumes, whole grains, leafy green vegetables, fruit RDA: 1.8–2.3 mg	Acts with enzymes catalyzing synthesis of fatty acids, cholesterol, urea, hemoglobin; needed for normal neural function, lactation, oxidation of carbohydrates, protein hydrolysis	Appears to contribute to obsessive behavior, hallucinations, and violent behavior	Not known
Selenium (Se)	Stored in liver, kidneys	Meat, seafood, cereals RDA: 55 µg	Antioxidant; constituent of certain enzymes; spares vitamin E	Nausea, vomiting, irritability, fatigue, weight loss, loss of hair	Oxidative damage
Zinc (Zn)	Concentrated in liver, kidneys, brain; excreted in feces	Seafood, meat, cereals, legumes, nuts, wheat germ, yeast RDA: 11 mg for males; 8 mg for females	Constituent of several enzymes (e.g., carbonic anhydrase); plays a structural role in a variety of proteins (e.g., transcription factors and tumor suppressor protein p53); required for normal growth, wound healing, taste, smell, sperm production	Difficulty in walking; slurred speech; tremors; interferes with body's ability to absorb copper, which can lead to weakened immunity	Loss of taste and smell; growth retardation; learning impairment; depressed immunity

24

functioning body. Incorporation of minerals into structures gives added strength. For example, calcium, phosphorus, and magnesium salts harden the teeth and strengthen the skeleton. Most minerals are ionized in body fluids or bound to organic compounds to form phospholipids, hormones, enzymes, and other functional proteins. For example, iron is essential to the oxygen-binding heme of hemoglobin, and sodium and chloride ions are the major electrolytes in blood. The amount of a particular mineral in the body gives very few clues to its importance in body function—just a few milligrams of iodine (required for thyroid hormone synthesis) can make a critical difference to health.

A fine balance between uptake and excretion is crucial for retaining needed amounts of minerals while preventing toxic overload. The sodium present in virtually all natural and minimally processed foods poses little or no health risk. However, the large amounts added to processed foods and that sprinkled on prior to eating may contribute to fluid retention and high blood pressure. This is particularly true in American blacks, whose kidneys have a greater tendency to retain salt than do those of American whites.

Fats and sugars are practically devoid of minerals, and highly refined cereals and grains are poor sources. The most mineral-rich foods are vegetables, legumes, milk, and some meats.

Metabolism

Overview

Once inside body cells, nutrients become involved in an incredible variety of biochemical reactions known collectively as **metabolism** (*metabol* = change). During metabolism, substances are constantly being built up and torn down. Cells use energy to extract more energy from foods, and then use some of this extracted energy to drive their activities. Even at rest, the body uses energy on a grand scale.

Anabolism and Catabolism

Metabolic processes are either *anabolic* (synthetic, building up) or *catabolic* (degradative, tearing down). **Anabolism** (ah-nab'o-lizm) is the general term for all reactions in which larger molecules or structures are built from smaller ones; for example, the bonding together of amino acids to make proteins. **Catabolism** (kah-tab'o-lizm) refers to all processes that break down complex structures to simpler ones, one example being hydrolysis of foods in the digestive tract. In the group of catabolic reactions collectively called **cellular respiration,** food fuels, particularly glucose, are broken down in cells and some of the energy released is captured to form ATP, the cells'

energy currency. ATP then serves as the "chemical drive shaft" that links energy-releasing catabolic reactions to cellular work.

Recall from Chapter 2 that reactions driven by ATP are coupled. ATP is never hydrolyzed directly. Instead enzymes shift its high-energy phosphate groups to other molecules, which are then said to be **phosphorylated** (fos"for-ĭ-la'ted). Phosphorylation primes the molecule to change in a way that increases its activity, produces motion, or does work. For example, many regulatory enzymes that catalyze key steps in metabolic pathways are activated by phosphorylation.

Three major stages are involved in the processing of energy-containing nutrients in the body (Figure 24.3):

- Stage 1 is digestion in the gastrointestinal tract, described in Chapter 23. The absorbed nutrients are then transported in blood to the tissue cells.

- In stage 2, which occurs in the cell cytoplasm, newly delivered nutrients are either built into lipids, proteins, and glycogen by anabolic pathways or broken down by catabolic pathways to *pyruvic acid* (pi-roo'vik) and *acetyl CoA* (as'ĕ-til ko-a').

- Stage 3, which is almost entirely catabolic, occurs in the mitochondria, requires oxygen, and completes the breakdown of foods, producing carbon dioxide and water and harvesting large amounts of ATP.

The primary function of *cellular respiration,* which consists of glycolysis of stage 2 and all events of stage 3, is to generate ATP, which traps some of the chemical energy of the original food molecules in its own high-energy bonds. Thus, food fuels, such as glycogen and fats, *store* energy in the body, and these stores are later *mobilized to produce ATP for cellular use.*

You do not need to memorize Figure 24.3, but as you will soon see, it provides a cohesive summary of nutrient processing and metabolism in the body.

Oxidation-Reduction Reactions and the Role of Coenzymes

Many of the reactions that take place within cells are **oxidation reactions.** *Oxidation* was originally defined as the combination of oxygen with other elements. Examples are the rusting of iron (the slow formation of iron oxide) and the burning of wood and other fuels. In burning, oxygen combines rapidly with carbon, producing carbon dioxide, water, and an enormous amount of energy, which is liberated as heat and light. Later it was discovered that oxidation *also* occurs when hydrogen atoms are *removed* from compounds and so the definition was expanded to its current form: *Oxidation is the gain of oxygen or the loss of hydrogen.* As explained in Chapter 2, whichever way oxidation occurs, the oxidized substance always *loses* (or nearly loses) electrons as they move to (or toward) a substance that more strongly attracts them.

FIGURE 24.3 **Three stages of metabolism of energy-containing nutrients.** In stage 1, foods are degraded to absorbable forms by digestive enzymes in the GI tract.

In stage 2, the absorbed nutrients are transported in blood to the body cells, where they may be incorporated into molecules (anabolism) or broken down via glycolysis and other reactions to pyruvic acid and/or acetyl CoA, and then funneled into the pathways of stage 3.

Stage 3 consists of the catabolic pathways of the Krebs cycle and oxidative phosphorylation, both of which take place in the mitochondria. During the Krebs cycle, acetyl CoA is broken apart: Its carbon atoms are liberated as carbon dioxide (CO_2), and the hydrogen atoms removed are delivered to a chain of receptors (the electron transport chain), which ultimately delivers them (as protons and free electrons) to molecular oxygen so that water is formed. Some of the energy released during the electron transport chain reactions is used to form ATP. Stages 2 and 3 collectively constitute cellular respiration.

This loss of electrons can be explained by reviewing the consequences of different electron-attracting abilities of atoms (see p. 33). Consider a molecule made up of a hydrogen atom plus some other kinds of atoms. Because hydrogen is very electropositive, its lone electron usually spends more time orbiting the other atoms of the molecule. But when a hydrogen *atom* is removed, its electron goes with it, and the molecule as a whole loses that electron. Conversely, oxygen is very electron-hungry (electronegative), and so when oxygen binds with other atoms the shared electrons spend more time in oxygen's vicinity.

Again, the molecule as a whole loses electrons. As you will soon see, essentially all oxidation of food fuels involves the step-by-step removal of pairs of hydrogen atoms (and thus pairs of electrons) from the substrate molecules, eventually leaving only carbon dioxide (CO_2). Molecular oxygen (O_2) is the *final* electron acceptor. It combines with the removed hydrogen atoms at the very end of the process, to form water (H_2O).

Whenever one substance loses electrons (is oxidized), another substance gains them (is reduced). Thus, oxidation and reduction are coupled reactions and we speak of **oxidation-reduction reactions,** or

(a)

(b)

FIGURE 24.4 **Mechanisms of phosphorylation. (a)** Substrate-level phosphorylation occurs when a high-energy phosphate group is transferred directly from a substrate to ADP to form ATP. This reaction occurs both in the cytoplasm and in the mitochondrial matrix. **(b)** Oxidative phosphorylation, which occurs in mitochondria, reflects the activity of electron transport proteins that act as proton "pumps" to create a proton gradient across the cristae membranes. The source of energy for this pumping is energy released during oxidation of food molecules. As the protons flow passively back into the mitochondrial fluid matrix, the energy of the electrochemical gradient is used to bind phosphate groups to ADP.

more commonly, **redox reactions.** The key understanding about redox reactions is that "oxidized" substances *lose* energy and "reduced" substances *gain* energy as energy-rich electrons are transferred from the former to the latter. Consequently, as food fuels are oxidized, their energy is transferred to a "bucket brigade" of other molecules and ultimately to ADP to form energy-rich ATP.

Like all other chemical reactions in the body, redox reactions are catalyzed by enzymes. Those that catalyze redox reactions in which hydrogen atoms are removed are called **dehydrogenases** (de-hi′dro-jen-ās″ez), while those catalyzing the transfer of oxygen are **oxidases.** Most of these enzymes require the help of a specific coenzyme, typically derived from one of the B vitamins. Although the enzymes catalyze the removal of hydrogen atoms to oxidize a substance, they cannot *accept* the hydrogen (hold on or bond to it). Their *coenzymes,* however, act as hydrogen (or electron) acceptors, becoming reduced each time a substrate is oxidized. Two very important coenzymes of the oxidative pathways are **nicotinamide adenine dinucleotide (NAD⁺)** (nik″o-tin′ah-mīd), based on *niacin,* and **flavin adenine dinucleotide (FAD),** derived from *riboflavin.* The oxidation of succinic acid to fumaric acid and

the simultaneous reduction of FAD to $FADH_2$, an example of a coupled redox reaction, is

$$
\begin{array}{ccc}
& \text{FAD} & \text{FAD}\,\textcircled{H_2} \\
& \text{(oxidized)} & \text{(reduced)} \\
\text{COOH} & & \text{COOH} \\
\textcircled{H}\!-\!\text{C}\!-\!\text{H} & & \text{C}\!-\!\text{H} \\
& \xrightarrow{\ \ \text{oxidation } [-2H]\ \ } & \parallel \\
\textcircled{H}\!-\!\text{C}\!-\!\text{H} & & \text{C}\!-\!\text{H} \\
\text{COOH} & & \text{COOH} \\
\text{succinic} & & \text{fumaric} \\
\text{acid} & & \text{acid}
\end{array}
$$

Mechanisms of ATP Synthesis

How do our cells capture some of the energy liberated during cellular respiration to make ATP molecules? There appear to be two mechanisms—substrate-level phosphorylation and oxidative phosphorylation.

Substrate-level phosphorylation occurs when high-energy phosphate groups are transferred directly from phosphorylated substrates (metabolic intermediates such as glyceraldehyde phosphate) to ADP (Figure 24.4a). Essentially, this process occurs because the high-energy bonds attaching the phosphate groups to the substrates are even more unstable than those in ATP. ATP is synthesized by this route during one of the steps in glycolysis, and once during

FIGURE 24.5 Sites of ATP formation during cellular respiration. Glycolysis occurs in the cytosol. The Krebs cycle and the electron transport chain reactions occur in the mitochondria. During glycolysis, each glucose molecule is broken down to two molecules of pyruvic acid. The pyruvic acid enters the mitochondrial matrix, where the Krebs cycle decomposes it to CO_2. During glycolysis and the Krebs cycle, small amounts of ATP are formed by substrate-level phosphorylation. Chemical energy from glycolysis and the Krebs cycle, in the form of energy-rich electrons picked up by coenzymes, is then transferred to the electron transport chain, which is built into the membrane of the cristae. The electron transport chain carries out oxidative phosphorylation, which accounts for most of the ATP generated by cellular respiration.

each turn of the Krebs cycle (Figure 24.5). The enzymes catalyzing substrate-level phosphorylations are located in both the cytoplasm and in the watery matrix inside the mitochondria.

Oxidative phosphorylation is much more complicated, but it also releases most of the energy that is eventually captured in ATP bonds during cellular respiration. This process, which is carried out by electron transport proteins forming part of the mitochondria cristae, is an example of a chemiosmotic process. **Chemiosmotic processes** couple the movement of substances across membranes to chemical reactions. In this case, some of the energy released during the oxidation of food fuels (the "chemi" part of the term) is used to pump (*osmo* = push) protons (H^+) across the cristae membrane into the intermembrane space (Figure 24.4b). This creates a steep concentration gradient for protons across the membrane. Then, when H^+ does flow back across the membrane (through a membrane channel protein called *ATP synthase*), some of this gradient energy is captured and used to attach phosphate groups to ADP.

Carbohydrate Metabolism

Because all food carbohydrates are eventually transformed to glucose, the story of carbohydrate metabolism is really a tale of glucose metabolism. Glucose enters the tissue cells by facilitated diffusion, a process that is greatly enhanced by insulin. Immediately upon entry into the cell, glucose is phosphorylated to *glucose-6-phosphate* by transfer of a phosphate group to its sixth carbon during a coupled reaction with ATP:

$$Glucose + ATP \rightarrow glucose\text{-}6\text{-}PO_4 + ADP$$

Most body cells lack the enzymes needed to reverse this reaction, so it effectively traps glucose inside the cells. Because glucose-6-phosphate is a *different* molecule from simple glucose, the reaction also keeps intracellular glucose levels low, maintaining a concentration gradient for glucose entry. Only intestinal mucosa cells, kidney tubule cells, and liver cells have the enzymes needed to reverse this phosphorylation reaction, which reflects their central roles in glucose uptake *and* release. The catabolic and anabolic pathways for carbohydrates all begin with glucose-6-phosphate.

Oxidation of Glucose

Glucose is the pivotal fuel molecule in the oxidative (ATP-producing) pathways. Glucose is catabolized via the reaction

$$\underset{\text{glucose}}{C_6H_{12}O_6} + \underset{\text{oxygen}}{6O_2} \rightarrow \underset{\text{water}}{6H_2O} + \underset{\substack{\text{carbon} \\ \text{dioxide}}}{6CO_2} + 38\ ATP + heat$$

This equation gives few hints that glucose breakdown is complex and involves three of the pathways included in Figures 24.3 and 24.5:

Q *What would happen in this pathway if O₂ were absent and NADH + H⁺ could not transfer its "picked-up" hydrogens to pyruvic acid?*

FIGURE 24.6 **The three major phases of glycolysis.** During phase 1, glucose is activated by phosphorylation and converted to fructose-1,6-bisphosphate. In phase 2, fructose-1,6-bisphosphate is cleaved into two 3-carbon fragments (reversible isomers). In phase 3, the 3-carbon fragments are oxidized (by removal of hydrogen) and 4 ATP molecules are formed. The fate of pyruvic acid depends on whether or not molecular O₂ is available.

A *Glycolysis would come to a halt because the oxidase enzyme cannot hold onto the H⁺ removed during substrate oxidation. If all the coenzymes are already reduced and can't release hydrogen, the oxidase enzyme can't continue to function.*

1. Glycolysis (color-coded light orange throughout the chapter)

2. The Krebs cycle (color-coded pale-green)

3. The electron transport chain and oxidative phosphorylation (color-coded violet)

These metabolic pathways occur in a definite order, and we will consider them sequentially.

Glycolysis   A series of ten chemical steps by which glucose is converted to two *pyruvic acid* molecules, **glycolysis** (gli-kol′ĭ-sis; "sugar splitting") occurs in the cytosol of cells. All steps except the first, during which glucose entering the cell is phosphorylated to glucose-6-phosphate, are fully *reversible*.

Glycolysis is an *anaerobic process* (an-a′er-ōb-ik; *an* = without, *aero* = air). Although this term is sometimes mistakenly interpreted to mean the pathway occurs only in the absence of oxygen, the correct interpretation is that glycolysis *does not use oxygen and occurs whether or not oxygen is present*. Figure 24.6 shows the three major phases of the glycolytic pathway. The complete glycolytic pathway appears in Appendix D.

1. Sugar activation. In phase 1, glucose is phosphorylated and converted to fructose-6-phosphate, which is then phosphorylated again. These three steps yield fructose-1,6-bisphosphate and use two ATP molecules. The two separate reactions of the sugar with ATP provide the *activation energy* needed to prime the later stages of the pathway—hence phase 1 is sometimes called the *energy investment phase*. (The importance of activation energy is described in Chapter 2.)

2. Sugar cleavage. During phase 2, fructose-1,6-bisphosphate is split into two 3-carbon fragments that exist (reversibly) as one of two isomers: glyceraldehyde (glis″er-al′dĕ-hīd) 3-phosphate or dihydroxyacetone (dī″hi-drok″se-as′ĕ-tōn) phosphate.

3. Oxidation and ATP formation. In phase 3, consisting of six steps, two major events happen. First, the two 3-carbon fragments are oxidized by the removal of hydrogen, which is picked up by NAD⁺. Hence, some of glucose's energy is transferred to NAD⁺. Second, inorganic phosphate groups (Pᵢ) are attached to each oxidized fragment by high-energy bonds. Later, as these terminal phosphates are cleaved off, enough energy is captured to form four ATP molecules. As noted earlier, formation of ATP this way is called *substrate-level phosphorylation*.

The final products of glycolysis are two molecules of **pyruvic acid** and two molecules of reduced NAD⁺ (NADH + H⁺),* with a net gain of two ATP molecules per glucose molecule. Four ATPs are produced,

---

*NAD carries a positive charge (NAD⁺); thus, when it accepts the hydrogen pair, NADH + H⁺ is the resulting reduced product.

but remember that two are consumed in phase 1 to "prime the pump." Each pyruvic acid molecule has the formula $C_3H_4O_3$, and glucose is $C_6H_{12}O_6$. Thus, between them the two pyruvic acid molecules have lost four hydrogen atoms, which are now bound to two molecules of NAD^+. Although a small amount of ATP has been harvested, the other two products of glucose oxidation (H_2O and CO_2) have yet to appear.

The fate of pyruvic acid, which still contains most of glucose's chemical energy, depends on the availability of oxygen at the time the pyruvic acid is produced. Because the supply of NAD^+ is limited, glycolysis can continue only if the reduced coenzymes ($NADH + H^+$) formed during glycolysis are relieved of their extra hydrogen. Only then can they continue to act as hydrogen acceptors. When oxygen is readily available, this is no problem. $NADH + H^+$ delivers its burden of hydrogen atoms to the enzymes of the electron transport chain in the mitochondria, which deliver them to O_2, forming water. However, when oxygen is not present in sufficient amounts, as might occur during strenuous exercise, $NADH + H^+$ unloads its hydrogen atoms *back onto pyruvic acid*, thus reducing it. This addition of two hydrogen atoms to pyruvic acid yields **lactic acid** (see bottom right of Figure 24.6), some of which diffuses out of the cells and is transported to the liver. When oxygen is again available, lactic acid is oxidized back to pyruvic acid and enters the **aerobic pathways** (the oxygen-requiring Krebs cycle and electron transport chain within the mitochondria), and is completely oxidized to water and carbon dioxide. The liver may also convert lactic acid all the way back to glucose-6-phosphate (reverse glycolysis) and then store it as glycogen or free it of its phosphate and release it to the blood if blood sugar levels are low.

Although glycolysis generates ATP rapidly, only 2 ATP molecules are produced per glucose molecule, as compared to the 38 ATP per glucose harvested when glucose is completely oxidized. Except for red blood cells (which typically carry out *only* glycolysis), prolonged anaerobic metabolism ultimately results in acid-base problems. Consequently, *totally* anaerobic conditions resulting in lactic acid formation provide only a temporary route for rapid ATP production. It can go on without tissue damage for the longest periods in skeletal muscle, for much shorter periods in cardiac muscle, and almost not at all in the brain.

Krebs Cycle Named after its discoverer Hans Krebs, the **Krebs cycle** is the next stage of glucose oxidation. The Krebs cycle occurs in the fluid mitochondrial matrix and is fueled largely by pyruvic acid produced during glycolysis and by fatty acids resulting from fat breakdown.

After pyruvic acid enters the mitochondria, the first order of business is a transitional phase that converts it to *acetyl CoA* via a three-step process (Figure 24.7):

1. **Decarboxylation,** in which one of pyruvic acid's carbons is removed and released as carbon dioxide gas. CO_2 diffuses out of the cells into the blood to be expelled by the lungs.

2. **Oxidation** by the removal of hydrogen atoms, which are picked up by NAD^+.

3. Combination of the resulting acetic acid with *coenzyme A* to produce the final product, **acetyl coenzyme A (acetyl CoA).** Coenzyme A (CoA-SH) is a sulfur-containing coenzyme derived from pantothenic acid, a B vitamin.

Acetyl CoA is now ready to enter the Krebs cycle and be broken down completely by mitochondrial enzymes. Coenzyme A shuttles the 2-carbon acetic acid to an enzyme that condenses it with a 4-carbon acid called **oxaloacetic acid** (ok"sah-lo"ah-sēt'ik) to produce the 6-carbon **citric acid.** Because citric acid is the first substrate of the cycle, biochemists prefer to call the Krebs cycle the **citric acid cycle.**

As the cycle moves through its eight successive steps, the atoms of citric acid are rearranged to produce different intermediate molecules, most called **keto acids.** The acetic acid that enters the cycle is broken apart carbon by carbon (decarboxylated) and oxidized, simultaneously generating $NADH + H^+$ and $FADH_2$. At the end of the cycle, acetic acid has been totally disposed of and oxaloacetic acid, the *pickup molecule*, is regenerated. Because two *decarboxylations* and four *oxidations* occur, the products of the Krebs cycle are two CO_2 molecules and four molecules of reduced coenzymes (3 $NADH + H^+$ and 1 $FADH_2$). The addition of water at certain steps accounts for some of the released hydrogen. One molecule of ATP is formed (via substrate-level phosphorylation) during each turn of the cycle. The detailed events of each of the eight steps of the Krebs cycle are described in Appendix D.

Now let's account for the pyruvic acid molecules entering the mitochondria. Each pyruvic acid yields three CO_2 molecules and five molecules of reduced coenzymes—1 $FADH_2$ and 4 $NADH + H^+$ (equal to the removal of 10 hydrogen atoms). The products of glucose oxidation in the Krebs cycle are twice that (remember 1 glucose = 2 pyruvic acids): six CO_2, ten molecules of reduced coenzymes, and two ATP molecules. Notice that it is these Krebs cycle reactions that produce the CO_2 evolved during glucose oxidation. The reduced coenzymes, which carry their extra electrons in high-energy linkages, must now be oxidized if the Krebs cycle and glycolysis are to continue.

Although the glycolytic pathway is exclusive to carbohydrate oxidation, breakdown products of carbohydrates, fats, and proteins can feed into the Krebs cycle to be oxidized for energy. On the other hand, some Krebs cycle intermediates can be siphoned off

Q *What two major kinds of chemical reactions occur in this cycle, and how are these reactions indicated symbolically?*

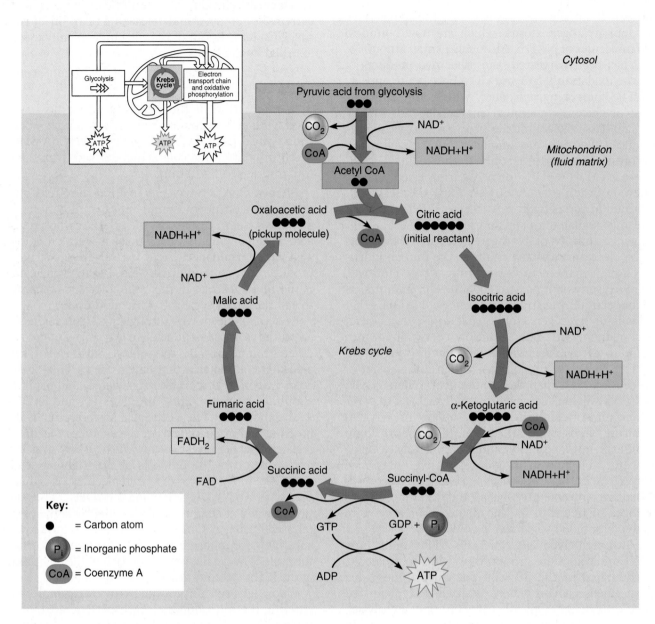

FIGURE 24.7 **Simplified version of the Krebs (citric acid) cycle.** During each turn of the cycle, two carbon atoms are removed from the substrates as CO_2 (decarboxylation reactions); four oxidations by removal of hydrogen atoms occur, producing four molecules of reduced coenzymes (3 NADH + H$^+$ and 1 FADH$_2$); and one ATP is synthesized by substrate-level phosphorylation. An additional decarboxylation and an oxidation reaction occur to convert pyruvic acid, the product of glycolysis, to acetyl CoA, the molecule that enters the Krebs cycle pathway.

A *Decarboxylation, shown as removal of CO_2, and oxidation, shown as reduction of coenzymes, e.g., NAD$^+$ → NADH + H$^+$.*

FIGURE 24.8 **Mechanism of oxidative phosphorylation.** Schematic diagram showing the flow of electrons through the three major respiratory enzyme complexes—① NADH dehydrogenase (FMN, Fe-S), ② cytochrome b-c$_1$, and ③ cytochrome oxidase (a-a$_3$)—of the electron transport chain during the transfer of two electrons from reduced NAD$^+$ to oxygen. Coenzyme Q (ubiquinone) and cytochrome c are mobile and act as carriers between the complexes.

The electron transport chain is an energy converter, transforming chemical energy to the energy of a H$^+$ gradient. As electrons flow along their energy gradient, some of the energy is used by each complex to pump H$^+$ from the mitochondrial matrix into the intermembrane space. These H$^+$ ions create an electrochemical proton gradient that drives them back across the inner membrane through the ATP synthase complex. ATP synthase uses the energy of H$^+$ flow (electrical energy) to synthesize ATP from ADP and P$_i$. Oxidation of each NADH + H$^+$ to NAD$^+$ yields 3 ATP. Because FADH$_2$ unloads its H atoms to coenzyme Q beyond the first respiratory complex, less energy (2 ATP) is captured as a result of its oxidation.

to make fatty acids and nonessential amino acids. Thus the Krebs cycle, besides serving as the final common pathway for the oxidation of food fuels, is a source of building materials for anabolic reactions.

Electron Transport Chain and Oxidative Phosphorylation   Like glycolysis, none of the reactions of the Krebs cycle use oxygen directly. This is the exclusive function of the **electron transport chain,** which oversees the final catabolic reactions that occur on the mitochondrial cristae. However, because the reduced coenzymes produced in the Krebs cycle are the substrates for the electron transport chain, these pathways are coupled, and both phases are considered to be oxygen requiring (aerobic).

In the electron transport chain, the hydrogens removed during the oxidation of food fuels are combined with O$_2$, and the energy released during those reactions is harnessed to attach P$_i$ groups to ADP. As noted earlier, this type of phosphorylation process is called *oxidative phosphorylation*. Let us peek under the hood of a cell's power plant and look more closely at this rather complicated process.

Most components of the electron transport chain are proteins that are bound to metal atoms *(cofactors)*. These proteins, which form multiprotein complexes that are firmly embedded in the mitochondrial cristae membranes, vary in composition (Figure 24.8). For example, some of the proteins, the

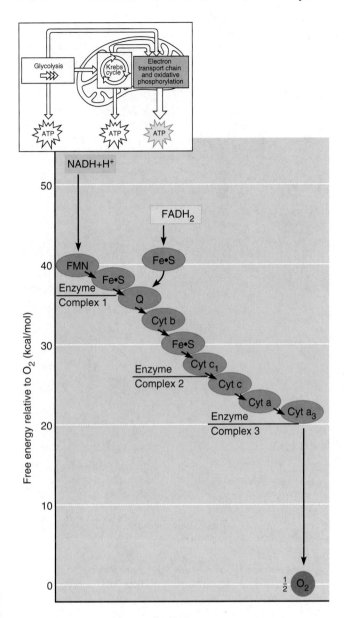

FIGURE 24.9   Electronic energy gradient in the electron transport chain. Each member of the chain (respiratory enzyme complex) oscillates between a reduced state and an oxidized state. A member becomes reduced by accepting electrons from its "uphill" neighbor and then reverts to its oxidized form as it passes electrons to its "downhill" neighbor (which has a greater affinity for the electrons). Oxygen, at the "bottom" of the chain, is *very* electronegative. The overall energy drop for electrons traveling from NADH to oxygen is 53 kcal/mol, but this fall is broken up into smaller steps by the electron transport chain.

flavins, contain flavin mononucleotide (FMN) derived from the vitamin riboflavin, and others contain both sulfur (S) and iron (Fe). Most, however, are brightly colored iron-containing pigments called **cytochromes** (si'to-krōmz; *cyto* = cell, *chrom* = color). Neighboring carriers are clustered together to form three major **respiratory enzyme complexes**

that are alternately reduced and oxidized by picking up electrons and passing them on to the next complex in the sequence. The first such complex accepts hydrogen atoms from NADH + H$^+$, oxidizing it to NAD$^+$. FADH$_2$ transfers its hydrogen atoms slightly farther along the chain to coenzyme Q (also called ubiquinone). The hydrogen atoms delivered to the electron transport chain by the reduced coenzymes are quickly split into protons (H$^+$) plus electrons. The electrons are shuttled along the crista membrane from one acceptor to the next, losing energy with each transfer. The protons escape into the watery matrix only to be picked up and deposited ("pumped") across the crista membrane into the intermembrane space by one of the three major respiratory enzyme complexes. Ultimately the electron pairs are delivered to half a molecule of O$_2$ (in other words, to an oxygen atom), creating oxygen ions (O$^-$) that strongly attract H$^+$ and form water as indicated by the reaction

$$2H^+ + 2e^- + \tfrac{1}{2}O_2 \rightarrow H_2O$$

Virtually all the water resulting from glucose oxidation is formed during oxidative phosphorylation. Because NADH + H$^+$ and FADH$_2$ are oxidized as they release their burden of picked-up hydrogen atoms, the net reaction for the electron transport chain is

$$\text{Coenzyme-2H} + \tfrac{1}{2}O_2 \rightarrow \text{coenzyme} + H_2O$$

reduced	oxidized
coenzyme	coenzyme

The transfer of electrons from NADH + H$^+$ to oxygen releases large amounts of energy. If hydrogen combined directly with molecular oxygen, the energy would be released in one big burst and most of it would be lost to the environment as heat. Instead energy is released in many small steps as the electrons stream from one electron acceptor to the next. Each successive carrier has a greater affinity for electrons than those preceding it. Therefore, the electrons cascade "downhill" from NADH + H$^+$ to progressively lower energy levels until they are finally delivered to oxygen, which has the greatest affinity of all for electrons (Figure 24.9). You could say that oxygen "pulls" the electrons down the chain.

By using the stepwise release of electronic energy to pump protons from the matrix into the intermembrane space, the electron transport chain functions as an energy converter. Because the crista membrane is nearly impermeable to H$^+$, this chemiosmotic process creates an **electrochemical proton (H$^+$) gradient** across that membrane that has potential energy. This energy source is referred to as *proton motive force* to emphasize the capacity of the gradient to do work.

The proton gradient (1) creates a pH gradient, with the H^+ concentration in the matrix much lower than that in the intermembrane space; and (2) generates a voltage across the membrane that is negative on the matrix side and positive between the mitochondrial membranes. Both conditions strongly attract H^+ back into the matrix. However, the only areas of the membrane freely permeable to H^+ are at large enzyme-protein complexes called **ATP synthases,** which lay claim to being nature's smallest rotary motors. As the protons take this "route" they create an electrical current, and ATP synthase harnesses this electrical energy to catalyze attachment of a phosphate group to ADP to form ATP (Figure 24.8). The enzyme's subunits appear to work together like gears. As the ATP synthase core rotates, ADP and inorganic phosphate are pulled in and ATP is churned out, thus completing the process of oxidative phosphorylation.

Studies of the molecular structure of ATP synthase are providing an understanding of how it works (Figure 24.10). The enzyme complex consists of two major linked parts, each with several protein subunits: (1) F_0, a *rotor* embedded in the crista membrane, and (2) F_1, a *knob* extending into the mitochondrial matrix, with a *rod* connecting the two. The current created by the downhill flow of H^+ causes the rotor and rod to rotate, just as flowing water turns a water wheel. This rotation activates catalytic sites in the knob where ADP and P_i are combined to make ATP.

Notice something here. The ATP synthase works like an ion pump running in reverse. Recall from Chapter 3 that ion pumps use ATP as their energy source to transport ions against an electrochemical gradient. Here we have ATP synthases using the energy of a proton gradient to power ATP synthesis. The proton gradient also supplies energy to pump needed metabolites (ADP, pyruvic acid, inorganic phosphate) and calcium ions across the relatively impermeable crista membrane. The outer membrane is quite freely permeable to these substances, so no "help" is needed there. However, the supply of energy from oxidation is not limitless; so when more of the proton motive force or gradient energy is used to drive these transport processes, less is available to make ATP.

HOMEOSTATIC IMBALANCE

Studies of metabolic poisons support the chemiosmotic model of oxidative phosphorylation. For example, cyanide (the gas used in gas chambers) disrupts the process by binding to cytochrome oxidase and blocking electron flow from cytochrome a_3 to oxygen. Poisons commonly called "uncouplers" abolish the proton gradient by making the crista

Intermembrane space

F_0: A **rotor** in the membrane spins clockwise when H^+ flows through it down the H^+ gradient.

Inner mitochondrial membrane

A **rod** connecting the cylindrical rotor and knob also spins, activating catalytic sites in the knob.

F_1: A protruding **knob** contains catalytic sites that join inorganic phosphate to ADP to make ATP.

ADP + P_i

ATP

Mitochondrial matrix

FIGURE 24.10 Structure of ATP synthase.

membrane permeable to H^+. Consequently, although the electron transport chain continues to deliver electrons to oxygen at a furious pace, and oxygen consumption rises, no ATP is made. ●

The stimulus for ATP production is entry of *ADP* into the mitochondrial fluid matrix. As ADP is transported in, ATP is moved out in a coupled transport process.

Summary of ATP Production   The average person at rest uses energy at the rate of roughly 100 kcal/hour, which is equal to 116 watts or slightly more than that of a standard lightbulb. This seems to be a minuscule amount, but from a biochemical standpoint it places a staggering power demand on our mitochondria. Luckily, they are up to the task. When O_2 is present, cellular respiration is remarkably efficient. Of the 686 kcal of energy present in 1 mole of glucose, as much as 262 kcal can be captured in ATP bonds. (The rest is liberated as heat.) This corresponds to an energy capture of about 38%, making cells far more efficient than any human-made machines, which use only 10–30% of the energy available to them.

During cellular respiration, most energy flows in this sequence: Glucose → NADH + H^+ → electron transport chain → proton motive force → ATP. Let's do a little bookkeeping to summarize the net energy

24

FIGURE 24.11   Energy yield during cellular respiration.

gain from one glucose molecule. Once we have tallied the net gain of 4 ATP produced directly by substrate-level phosphorylations (2 during glycolysis and 2 during the Krebs cycle), all that remains to be calculated is the number of ATP molecules produced by oxidative phosphorylation (Figure 24.11).

Each $NADH + H^+$ that transfers a pair of high-energy electrons to the electron transport chain contributes enough energy to the proton gradient to generate between 2 and 3 ATP molecules. (We will round this yield off to 3 to simplify our calculations.) The oxidation of $FADH_2$ is less efficient because it doesn't donate electrons to the "top" of the electron transport chain as does $NADH + H^+$, but to a lower energy level (at coenzyme Q). So, for each 2 H delivered by $FADH_2$, just about 2 ATPs are produced (instead of 2+ or 3). Thus, the 8 $NADH + H^+$ and the 2 $FADH_2$ produced during the Krebs cycle are "worth" 24 and 4 ATPs respectively. The 2 $NADH + H^+$ generated during glycolysis yields 6 ATP molecules. Overall, complete oxidation of 1 glucose molecule to CO_2 and H_2O yields a maximum of 38 molecules of ATP (Figure 24.11).

However, there is an uncertainty about the energy yield of reduced NAD^+ generated *outside* the mitochondria by glycolysis. The crista membrane is *not* permeable to reduced NAD^+ generated in the cytosol, so $NADH + H^+$ formed during glycolysis uses a *shuttle molecule* to deliver its extra electron pair to the electron transport chain. It appears that cells using the malate/aspartate shuttle harvest the whole 3 ATP from oxidation of reduced NAD^+, but in cells using a different shuttle (the glycerol phosphate

shuttle for example) the shuttle has an energy cost. At present, the consensus is that the net energy yield for reoxidation of reduced NAD^+ in this case is probably the same as for $FADH_2$, that is, 2 ATP per electron pair. Thus, if we deduct 2 ATP to cover the "fare" for the shuttle, our bookkeeping comes up with a grand total of 36 ATP per glucose as the maximum possible energy yield. (Actually our figures are probably still too high because, as mentioned earlier, the proton motive force is also used to do other work and the electron transport chain may not work at maximum capacity all of the time.)

Glycogenesis and Glycogenolysis

Although most glucose is used to generate ATP molecules, unlimited amounts of glucose do *not* result in unlimited ATP synthesis, because cells cannot store large amounts of ATP. When more glucose is available than can be immediately oxidized, rising intracellular ATP concentrations eventually inhibit glucose catabolism and initiate processes that store glucose as either glycogen or fat. Because the body can store much more fat than glycogen, fats account for 80–85% of stored energy.

When glycolysis is "turned off" by high ATP levels, glucose molecules are combined in long chains to form glycogen, the animal carbohydrate storage product. This process, called **glycogenesis** (*glyco* = sugar; *genesis* = origin), begins when glucose entering cells is phosphorylated to glucose-6-phosphate and then converted to its isomer, *glucose-1-phosphate*. The terminal phosphate group is cleaved off as the enzyme *glycogen synthase* catalyzes the attachment of glucose to the growing glycogen chain (Figure 24.12). Liver and skeletal muscle cells are most active in glycogen synthesis and storage.

When blood glucose levels drop, glycogen lysis (splitting) occurs. This process is known as **glycogenolysis** (gli″ko-jĕ-nol′ĭ-sis). The enzyme *glycogen phosphorylase* oversees phosphorylation and cleavage of glycogen to release glucose-1-phosphate, which is then converted to glucose-6-phosphate, a form that can enter the glycolytic pathway to be oxidized for energy.

In muscle cells and most other cells, the glucose-6-phosphate resulting from glycogenolysis is trapped because it cannot cross the cell membrane. However, hepatocytes (and some kidney and intestinal cells) contain *glucose-6-phosphatase*, an enzyme that removes the terminal phosphate, producing free glucose. Because glucose readily diffuses from the cell into the blood, the liver can use its glycogen stores to provide blood sugar for the benefit of other organs when blood glucose levels drop. Liver glycogen is also an important energy source for skeletal muscles that have depleted their own glycogen reserves.

A common misconception is that athletes need to eat large amounts of protein to improve their performance and maintain their muscle mass. Actually, a diet rich in complex carbohydrates, which stores more muscle glycogen, is much more effective in sustaining intense muscle activity than are high-protein meals. Notice that the emphasis is on *complex* carbohydrates. Eating a candy bar before an athletic event to provide "quick" energy does more harm than good because it stimulates insulin secretion, which favors glucose use and retards fat use at a time when fat use should be maximal. Building muscle protein or avoiding its loss requires not only extra protein, but also extra (protein-sparing) complex carbohydrate calories to meet the greater energy needs of the increasingly massive muscles.

Endurance athletes, long-distance runners in particular, are well aware of the practice of glycogen loading, popularly called "carbo loading," for endurance events. Glycogen loading "tricks" the muscles into storing more glycogen than they normally would. Carbo loading generally involves eating a carbohydrate-rich diet (75% of energy intake) for three to four days before an endurance event while decreasing activity. This has been shown to increase muscle glycogen stores to as much as twice the normal amount. Carbo loading is now standard practice among marathon runners and distance cyclists, because studies have shown that it improves performance and endurance. While the initial studies were of male athletes, more recent studies of females have shown less dramatic effects.

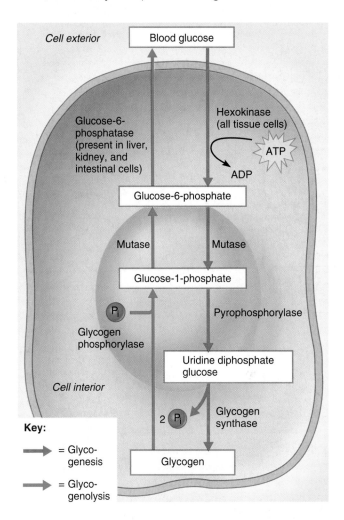

FIGURE 24.12 Glycogenesis and glycogenolysis. When glucose supplies exceed demands, glycogenesis, the conversion of glucose to glycogen for storage, occurs. Glycogenolysis, the breakdown of glycogen to release glucose, is stimulated by falling blood glucose levels. Notice that glycogen is synthesized and degraded by different enzymatic pathways.

Gluconeogenesis

When too little glucose is available to stoke the "metabolic furnace," glycerol and amino acids are converted to glucose. **Gluconeogenesis,** the process of forming new *(neo)* glucose from *noncarbohydrate* molecules, occurs in the liver. It takes place when dietary sources and glucose reserves have been depleted and blood glucose levels are beginning to drop. Gluconeogenesis protects the body, the nervous system in particular, from the damaging effects of low blood sugar *(hypoglycemia)* by ensuring that ATP synthesis can continue.

Lipid Metabolism

Fats are the body's most concentrated source of energy. They contain very little water, and the energy yield from fat catabolism is approximately twice that

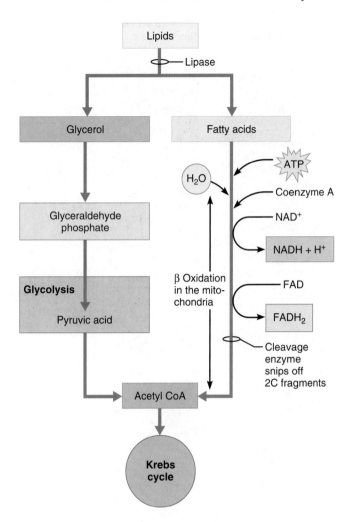

FIGURE 24.13 **Initial phase of lipid oxidation.** The glycerol portion is converted to glyceraldehyde phosphate, a glycolysis intermediate, and completes the glycolytic pathway through pyruvic acid to acetyl CoA. The fatty acids undergo beta oxidation. In this process the fatty acids are first activated by a coupled reaction with ATP and combined with coenzyme A. After being oxidized twice (reducing NAD^+ and FAD), the acetyl CoA created in β oxidation is cleaved off and the process begins again.

from either glucose or protein catabolism—9 kcal per gram of fat versus 4 kcal per gram of carbohydrate or protein. Most products of fat digestion are transported in lymph in the form of fatty-protein droplets called *chylomicrons* (see Chapter 23). Eventually, the lipids in the chylomicrons are hydrolyzed by plasma enzymes, and the resulting fatty acids and glycerol are taken up by body cells and processed in various ways.

Oxidation of Glycerol and Fatty Acids

Of the various lipids, only triglycerides are routinely oxidized for energy. Their catabolism involves the separate oxidation of their two different building blocks: glycerol and fatty acid chains (Figure 24.13).

Most body cells easily convert glycerol to glyceraldehyde phosphate, a glycolysis intermediate that enters the Krebs cycle. Glyceraldehyde is equal to half a glucose molecule, and ATP energy harvest from its complete oxidation is approximately half that of glucose (18 ATP/glycerol).

Beta oxidation, the initial phase of fatty acid oxidation, occurs in the mitochondria. Although oxidation, dehydration, and other reactions are involved, the net result is that the fatty acid chains are broken apart into two-carbon *acetic acid* fragments, and coenzymes are reduced (Figure 24.13). Each acetic acid molecule is fused to coenzyme A, forming acetyl CoA. The term "beta oxidation" reflects the fact that the carbon in the beta (third) position is oxidized during the process and cleavage of the fatty acid in each case occurs between the alpha and beta carbons. Acetyl CoA is then picked up by oxaloacetic acid and enters the aerobic pathways to be oxidized to CO_2 and H_2O.

Notice that unlike glycerol, which enters the glycolytic pathway, acetyl CoA resulting from fatty acid breakdown *cannot* be used for gluconeogenesis because the metabolic pathway is irreversible past pyruvic acid.

Lipogenesis and Lipolysis

There is a continuous turnover of triglycerides in adipose tissue. New fats are "put in the larder" for later use, while stored fats are broken down and released to the blood. That bulge of fatty tissue you see today does *not* contain the same fat molecules it did a month ago.

Glycerol and fatty acids from dietary fats not immediately needed for energy are recombined into triglycerides and stored. About 50% ends up in subcutaneous tissue; the balance is stockpiled in other fat depots of the body. Triglyceride synthesis, or **lipogenesis** (Figure 24.14), occurs when cellular ATP and glucose levels are high. Excess ATP also leads to an accumulation of acetyl CoA and glyceraldehyde-PO_4, two intermediates of glucose metabolism that would otherwise feed into the Krebs cycle. But when these two metabolites are present in excess, they are channeled into triglyceride synthesis pathways. Acetyl CoA molecules are condensed together, forming fatty acid chains that grow two carbons at a time. (This accounts for the fact that almost all fatty acids in the body contain an even number of carbon atoms.) Because acetyl CoA, an intermediate in glucose catabolism, is also the *starting point* for fatty acid synthesis, glucose is easily converted to fat. Glyceraldehyde-PO_4 is converted to glycerol, which is condensed with fatty acids to form triglycerides. Thus, even if the diet is fat-poor, carbohydrate intake can provide *all the raw materials* needed to form neutral fats. When blood sugar is high, lipogenesis is

24

Q *What is the central molecule in lipid metabolism?*

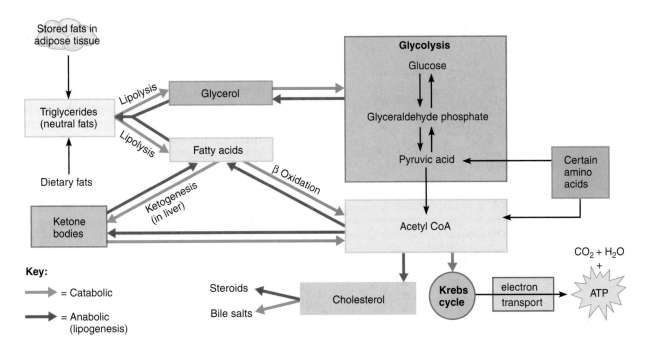

FIGURE 24.14 Metabolism of triglycerides. When needed for energy, dietary or stored fats enter the catabolic pathways. Glycerol enters the glycolytic pathway (as glyceraldehyde phosphate) and the fatty acids are broken down by beta oxidation to acetyl CoA, which enters the Krebs cycle. When fats are to be synthesized (lipogenesis) and stored in fat depots, the intermediates are drawn from glycolysis and the Krebs cycle in a reversal of the processes noted above. Likewise, excess dietary fats are stored in adipose tissues. When triglycerides are in excess or are the primary energy source, the liver releases their breakdown products (fatty acids → acetyl CoA) in the form of ketone bodies. Excessive amounts of carbohydrates and amino acids are also converted to triglycerides (lipogenesis).

the major activity in adipose tissues and is also an important liver function.

Lipolysis (lĭ-pol′ĭ-sis; "fat splitting"), the breakdown of stored fats into glycerol and fatty acids, is essentially lipogenesis in reverse. The fatty acids and glycerol are released to the blood, helping to ensure that body organs have continuous access to fat fuels for aerobic respiration. (The liver, cardiac muscle, and resting skeletal muscles actually prefer fatty acids as an energy fuel.) The meaning of the adage "fats burn in the flame of carbohydrates" becomes clear when carbohydrate intake is inadequate. Under such conditions, lipolysis is accelerated as the body attempts to fill the fuel gap with fats. However, the ability of acetyl CoA to enter the Krebs cycle depends on the availability of oxaloacetic acid to act as the pickup molecule. When carbohydrates are deficient, oxaloacetic acid is converted to glucose (to fuel the brain). Without oxaloacetic acid, fat oxidation is incomplete, acetyl CoA accumulates, and via a process called **ketogenesis,** the liver converts acetyl CoA molecules to **ketone bodies,** or **ketones,** which are released into the blood. Ketone bodies include acetoacetic acid, β-hydroxybutyric acid, and acetone, all formed from acetic acid. (The *keto acids* cycling through the Krebs cycle and the *ketone bodies* resulting from fat metabolism are quite different and should not be confused.)

HOMEOSTATIC IMBALANCE

When ketone bodies accumulate in the blood, *ketosis* results and large amounts of ketone bodies are excreted in the urine. Ketosis is a common consequence of starvation, unwise dieting (in which inadequate amounts of carbohydrates are eaten), and diabetes mellitus. Because most ketone bodies are organic acids, the outcome of ketosis is *metabolic acidosis.* The body's buffer systems cannot tie up the acids (ketones) fast enough, and blood pH drops to dangerously low levels. The person's breath smells fruity as acetone vaporizes from the lungs, and breathing becomes more rapid as the respiratory system tries to reduce blood carbonic acid by blowing off CO_2 to force the blood pH up. In severe untreated cases, the person may become comatose or even die as the acid pH depresses the nervous system. ●

A *Acetyl CoA.*

24

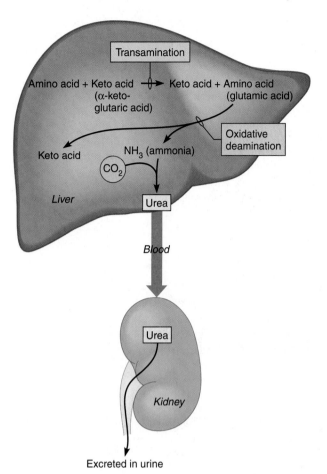

FIGURE 24.15 **Transamination and oxidative processes that occur when amino acids are oxidized for energy.** Transamination involves the switching of an amine group from an amino acid to a keto acid, usually α-ketoglutaric acid. As a result the original amino acid becomes a keto acid, and the keto acid becomes an amino acid, typically glutamic acid. In oxidative deamination the amine group of glutamic acid is released as ammonia and then combined with CO_2 by the liver cells to form urea.

Synthesis of Structural Materials

All body cells use phospholipids and cholesterol to build their membranes. Phospholipids are also important components of myelin sheaths of neurons. In addition, the liver (1) synthesizes lipoproteins for transport of cholesterol, fats, and other substances in the blood; (2) synthesizes cholesterol from acetyl CoA; and (3) uses cholesterol to form bile salts. The ovaries, testes, and adrenal cortex use cholesterol to synthesize their steroid hormones.

Protein Metabolism

Like all other biological molecules, proteins have a limited life span and must be broken down and replaced before they begin to deteriorate. As proteins are broken down, their amino acids are recycled and used in building new proteins or modified to form a different N-containing compound. Newly ingested amino acids transported in the blood are taken up by cells by active transport processes and used to *replace* tissue proteins at the rate of about 100 grams each day. Although popular opinion has it that excess protein can be stored by the body, nothing is farther from the truth. When more protein is available than is needed for these anabolic purposes, amino acids are oxidized for energy or converted to fat for future energy needs.

Oxidation of Amino Acids

Before amino acids can be oxidized for energy, they must be *deaminated*, that is, their amine group (NH_2) must be removed. (In sulfur-containing amino acids, such as methionine and cysteine, sulfur is released prior to deamination.) The resulting molecule is then converted to pyruvic acid or to one of the keto acid intermediates in the Krebs cycle [acetyl CoA, alpha (α) ketoglutaric acid, succinyl CoA, fumaric acid, or oxaloacetic acid]. The key molecule in these conversions is the nonessential amino acid *glutamic acid* (gloo-tam′ik). The events that occur (Figure 24.15) are:

1. Transamination (trans″am-ĭ-na′shun). A number of amino acids can transfer their amine group to α-ketoglutaric acid (a Krebs cycle keto acid), thereby transforming α-ketoglutaric acid to glutamic acid. In the process, the original amino acid becomes a keto acid (that is, it has an oxygen atom where the amine group formerly was). This reaction is fully reversible.

2. Oxidative deamination. In the liver, the amine group of glutamic acid is removed as **ammonia (NH_3)**, and α-ketoglutaric acid is regenerated. The liberated NH_3 molecules are combined with CO_2, yielding **urea** and water. The urea is released to the blood and removed from the body in urine. Because ammonia is toxic to body cells, the ease with which glutamic acid funnels amine groups into the **urea cycle** is extremely important. This mechanism rids the body not only of NH_3 produced during oxidative deamination, but also of bloodborne NH_3 produced by intestinal bacteria.

3. Keto acid modification. The goal of amino acid degradation is to produce molecules that can be either oxidized in the Krebs cycle or converted to glucose. Hence, keto acids resulting from transamination are altered as necessary to produce metabolites that can enter the Krebs cycle. The most important of these metabolites are pyruvic acid, acetyl CoA, α-ketoglutaric acid, and oxaloacetic acid (Figure 24.7). Because the reactions of glycolysis are reversible, deaminated amino acids that are converted to pyruvic acid can be reconverted to glucose and contribute to gluconeogenesis.

TABLE 24.4	**Thumbnail Summary of Metabolic Reactions**

CARBOHYDRATES

Cellular respiration	Reactions that together complete the oxidation of glucose, yielding CO_2, H_2O, and ATP
Glycolysis	Conversion of glucose to pyruvic acid
Glycogenesis	Polymerization of glucose to form glycogen
Glycogenolysis	Hydrolysis of glycogen to glucose monomers
Gluconeogenesis	Formation of glucose from noncarbohydrate precursors
Krebs cycle	Complete breakdown of pyruvic acid to CO_2, yielding small amounts of ATP and reduced coenzymes
Electron transport chain	Energy-yielding reactions that split H removed during oxidations to H^+ and e^- and create a proton gradient used to bond ADP to P_i (forming ATP)

LIPIDS

Beta oxidation	Conversion of fatty acids to acetyl CoA
Lipolysis	Breakdown of lipids to fatty acids and glycerol
Lipogenesis	Formation of lipids from acetyl CoA and glyceraldehyde phosphate

PROTEINS

Transamination	Transfer of an amine group from an amino acid to α-ketoglutaric acid, thereby transforming α-ketoglutaric acid to glutamic acid
Oxidative deamination	Removal of an amine group from glutamic acid as ammonia and regenerating α-ketoglutaric acid (NH_3 is converted to urea by the liver)

Protein Synthesis

Amino acids are the most important anabolic nutrients. Not only do they form all protein structures, but they form the bulk of the body's functional molecules as well. As described in Chapter 3, protein synthesis occurs on ribosomes, where ribosomal enzymes oversee the formation of peptide bonds linking the amino acids together into protein polymers. The amount and type of protein synthesized are precisely controlled by hormones (growth hormone, thyroxine, sex hormones, insulin-like growth factors, and others), and so protein anabolism reflects the hormonal balance at each stage of life.

During your lifetime, your cells will have synthesized 225–450 kg (about 500–1000 lb) of proteins, depending on your size. However, you do not need to consume anywhere near that amount of protein because nonessential amino acids are easily formed by siphoning keto acids from the Krebs cycle and transferring amine groups to them. Most of these transformations occur in the liver, which provides nearly all the nonessential amino acids needed to produce the relatively small amount of protein that the body synthesizes each day. However, a complete set of amino acids must be present for protein synthesis to take place, so all essential amino acids must be provided by the diet. If some are not, the rest are oxidized for energy even though they may be needed for anabolism. In such cases, negative nitrogen balance results because body protein is broken down to supply the essential amino acids needed.

The various metabolic reactions described thus far are summarized briefly in Table 24.4.

Catabolic-Anabolic Steady State of the Body

The body exists in a *dynamic catabolic-anabolic state* as organic molecules are continuously broken down and rebuilt—frequently at a head-spinning rate.

The blood is the transport pool for all body cells, and it contains many kinds of energy sources—glucose, ketone bodies, fatty acids, glycerol, and lactic acid. Some organs routinely use blood energy sources other than glucose, thus saving glucose for tissues with stricter glucose requirements (see Table 24.5 on p. 977).

The body **nutrient pools**—amino acid, carbohydrate, and fat stores—can be drawn on to meet its varying needs (Figure 24.16). These pools are interconvertible because their pathways are linked by key

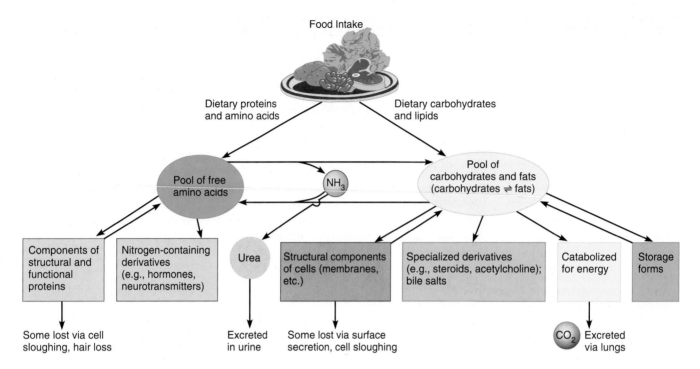

FIGURE 24.16   **Carbohydrate/fat and amino acid pools.**

intermediates (see Figure 24.17). The liver, adipose tissue, and skeletal muscles are the primary effector organs determining the amounts and direction of the conversions shown in the figure.

The **amino acid pool** is the body's total supply of free amino acids. Small amounts of animo acids and proteins are lost daily in urine and in sloughed hairs and skin cells. Typically, these lost molecules are replaced via the diet; otherwise, amino acids arising from tissue breakdown return to the pool. This pool is the source of amino acids used for protein synthesis and in the formation of amino acid derivatives. In addition, as described above, deaminated amino acids can participate in gluconeogenesis. Not all events of amino acid metabolism occur in all cells. For example, *only* the liver forms urea.

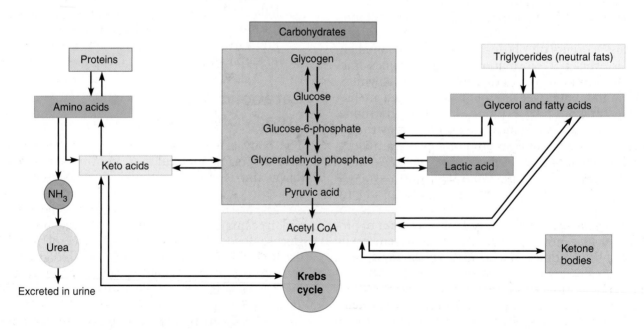

FIGURE 24.17   **Interconversion of carbohydrates, fats, and proteins.** The liver, adipose tissue, and skeletal muscles are the primary effector organs determining the amounts and direction of the conversions shown.

Nonetheless, the concept of a common amino acid pool is valid because all cells are connected by the blood.

Because carbohydrates are easily and frequently converted to fats, the **carbohydrate** and **fat pools** are usually considered together (Figures 24.16 and 24.17). There are two major differences between this pool and the amino acid pool: (1) Fats and carbohydrates are oxidized directly to produce cellular energy, whereas amino acids can be used to supply energy *only after being converted to a carbohydrate intermediate* (a keto acid). (2) Excess carbohydrate and fat can be stored as such, whereas excess amino acids are *not* stored as protein. Instead, they are oxidized for energy or converted to fat or glycogen for storage.

Absorptive and Postabsorptive States

Metabolic controls act to equalize blood concentrations of energy sources between two nutritional states. Sometimes referred to as the *fed state*, the **absorptive state** is the time during and shortly after eating, when nutrients are flushing into the blood from the gastrointestinal tract. The **postabsorptive** *(fasting)* **state** is the period when the GI tract is empty and energy sources are supplied by the breakdown of body reserves. Those who eat "three squares" a day are in the absorptive state for the four hours during and after each meal and in the postabsorptive state in the late morning, late afternoon, and all night. However, postabsorptive mechanisms can sustain the body for much longer intervals if necessary—even to accommodate weeks of fasting—as long as water is taken in.

Absorptive State

During the absorptive state (Figure 24.18) anabolism exceeds catabolism. Glucose is the major energy fuel. Dietary amino acids and fats are used to remake degraded body protein or fat, and small amounts are oxidized to provide ATP. Excess metabolites, regardless of source, are transformed to fat if not used for anabolism. We will consider the fate and hormonal control of each nutrient group during this phase.

Carbohydrates   Absorbed monosaccharides are delivered directly to the liver, where fructose and galactose are converted to glucose. Glucose, in turn, is released to the blood or converted to glycogen and fat. Glycogen formed in the liver is stored there, but most fat synthesized there is packaged with proteins as *very low density lipoproteins (VLDLs)* and released to the blood to be picked up for storage by adipose tissues. Bloodborne glucose not sequestered by the liver enters body cells to be metabolized for energy; any excess is stored in skeletal muscle cells as glycogen or in adipose cells as fat.

Triglycerides   Nearly all products of fat digestion enter the lymph in the form of chylomicrons, which are hydrolyzed to fatty acids and glycerol before they can pass through the capillary walls. *Lipoprotein lipase,* the enzyme that catalyzes fat hydrolysis, is particularly active in the capillaries of muscle and fat tissues. Adipose cells, skeletal muscle cells, and liver cells use triglycerides as their primary energy source, and when dietary carbohydrates are limited, other cells begin to oxidize more fat for energy. Although some fatty acids and glycerol are used for anabolic purposes by tissue cells, most enter adipose tissue to be reconverted to triglycerides and stored.

Amino Acids   Absorbed amino acids are delivered to the liver, which deaminates some of them to keto acids. The keto acids may flow into the Krebs cycle to be used for ATP synthesis, or they may be converted to liver fat stores. The liver also uses some of the amino acids to synthesize plasma proteins, including albumin, clotting proteins, and transport proteins. However, most amino acids flushing through the liver sinusoids remain in the blood for uptake by other body cells, where they are used for protein synthesis. Figure 24.18 has been simplified to show nonliver amino acid uptake only by muscle.

Hormonal Control   **Insulin** directs essentially all events of the absorptive state (Figure 24.19). Rising blood glucose levels after a carbohydrate-containing meal act as a humoral stimulus that prods the beta cells of the pancreatic islets to secrete more insulin. [This glucose-induced stimulation of insulin release is enhanced by the GI tract hormone glucose-dependent insulinotropic peptide (GIP) and parasympathetic stimulation.] A second important stimulus for insulin release is elevated amino acid levels in the blood. As insulin binds to membrane receptors of its target cells, it stimulates the translocation of the glucose transporter (GLUT-4 in muscle and adipose tissue) to the plasma membrane, thus enhancing the carrier-mediated facilitated diffusion of glucose into the cells. Within minutes, the rate of glucose entry into tissue cells (particularly muscle, adipose, and liver cells) increases about 20-fold. (The exception is brain cells, which take up glucose whether or not insulin is present.) Once glucose enters tissue cells, insulin enhances glucose oxidation for energy and stimulates its conversion to glycogen and, in adipose tissue, to triglycerides. Insulin also "revs up" the active transport of amino acids into cells, promotes protein synthesis, and inhibits liver export of glucose and virtually all liver enzymes that promote gluconeogenesis.

FIGURE 24.18 **Major events and principal metabolic pathways of the absorptive state.** Although not indicated in (b), amino acids are also taken up by tissue cells and used for protein synthesis, and fats (triglycerides) are the primary energy fuel of muscle, liver cells, and adipose tissue.

As you can see, insulin is a **hypoglycemic hormone** (hi″po-gli-se′mik). It sweeps glucose out of the blood into the tissue cells, thereby lowering blood glucose levels. Additionally, it enhances glucose oxidation or storage while simultaneously inhibiting any process that might increase blood glucose levels.

HOMEOSTATIC IMBALANCE

Diabetes mellitus is a consequence of inadequate insulin production or abnormal insulin receptors. Without insulin or receptors that "recognize" it, glu-cose becomes unavailable to most body cells. Thus, blood glucose levels remain high, and large amounts of glucose are excreted in urine. Metabolic acidosis, protein wasting, and weight loss occur as large amounts of fats and tissue proteins are used for energy. (Diabetes mellitus is described in more detail in Chapter 16.) ●

Postabsorptive State

In the postabsorptive state, net synthesis of fat, glycogen, and proteins ceases, and catabolism of these substances begins to occur. The primary goal

TABLE 24.5	Profiles of the Major Body Organs in Fuel Metabolism		
TISSUE	**FUEL STORES**	**PREFERRED FUEL**	**FUEL SOURCES EXPORTED**
Brain	None	Glucose (ketone bodies during starvation)	None
Skeletal muscle (resting)	Glycogen	Fatty acids	None
Skeletal muscle (during exertion)	None	Glucose	Lactate
Heart muscle	None	Fatty acids	None
Adipose tissue	Triglycerides	Fatty acids	Fatty acids, glycerol
Liver	Glycogen, triglycerides	Amino acids, glucose, fatty acids	Fatty acids, glucose, ketone bodies

Adapted from Mathews, van Holde, and Ahern, 2000, *Biochemistry* 3/e, San Francisco: Addison Wesley Longman, p. 832.

during this state, that is, between meals when blood glucose levels are dropping, is to maintain blood glucose levels within the homeostatic range (70–110 mg of glucose per 100 ml). The importance of constant blood glucose has already been explained, chiefly that the brain almost always uses glucose as its energy source. Most events of the postabsorptive state either make glucose available to the blood or save glucose for the organs that need it most by using fats for energy (Figure 24.20).

Sources of Blood Glucose   Glucose can be obtained from stored glycogen, from tissue proteins, and in limited amounts from fats (Table 24.5).

1. Glycogenolysis in the liver. The liver's glycogen stores (about 100 g) are the first line of glucose reserves. They are mobilized quickly and efficiently and can maintain blood sugar levels for about four hours during the postabsorptive state.

2. Glycogenolysis in skeletal muscle. Glycogen stores in skeletal muscle are approximately equal to those of the liver. Before liver glycogen is exhausted, glycogenolysis begins in skeletal muscle (and to a lesser extent in other tissues). However, the glucose produced is not released to the blood because, unlike the liver, skeletal muscle does not have the enzymes needed to dephosphorylate glucose. Instead, glucose is partly oxidized to pyruvic acid (or, during anaerobic conditions, lactic acid), which enters the blood, is reconverted to glucose by the liver, and is released to the blood again. Thus, skeletal muscle contributes to blood glucose homeostasis indirectly, via liver mechanisms.

3. Lipolysis in adipose tissues and the liver. Adipose and liver cells produce glycerol by lipolysis, and the liver converts the glycerol to glucose (gluconeogenesis), which is released to the blood. Because acetyl CoA, a product of the beta oxidation of fatty

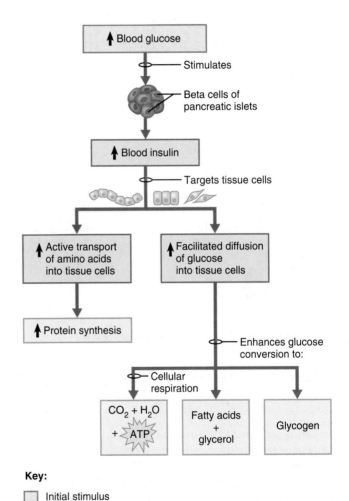

Key:
- ☐ Initial stimulus
- ☐ Physiological response
- ☐ Result

FIGURE 24.19   **Effects of insulin on metabolism.** When insulin concentrations are low (during the postabsorptive period), these normal effects of insulin are inhibited and glycogenolysis and gluconeogenesis occur, that is, the insulin-mediated intracellular reactions are reversed. (Note: Not all effects shown occur in all cells.)

FIGURE 24.20   Major events and principal metabolic pathways of the postabsorptive state.

acids, is produced beyond the *reversible* steps of glycolysis, fatty acids *cannot* be used to bolster blood glucose levels.

4. Catabolism of cellular protein. Tissue proteins become the major source of blood glucose when fasting is prolonged and glycogen and fat stores are nearly exhausted. Cellular amino acids (mostly from muscle) are deaminated and converted to glucose in the liver. During fasts lasting several weeks, the kidneys also carry out gluconeogenesis and contribute fully as much glucose to the blood as does the liver.

Even during prolonged fasting or starvation, the body sets priorities. Muscle proteins are the first to go (to be catabolized). Movement is not nearly as im-

portant as maintaining wound healing and the immune response. But as long as life continues, so does the body's ability to produce the ATP needed to drive life processes. Obviously, there are limits to the amount of tissue protein that can be catabolized before the body stops functioning. The heart is almost entirely muscle protein, and when it is severely catabolized, the result is death. In general, the amount of fat the body contains determines the time one can survive without food.

Glucose Sparing   Even collectively, all of the manipulations aimed at increasing blood glucose are not enough to provide energy supplies for prolonged fasting. Luckily, the body can adapt to burn more fats and proteins, which enter the Krebs cycle along with glucose breakdown products. The increased use of noncarbohydrate fuel molecules (especially triglycerides) to conserve glucose is called **glucose sparing.**

As the body progresses from absorptive to postabsorptive state, the brain continues to take its share of blood glucose; but virtually every other organ switches to fatty acids as its major energy source, thus sparing glucose for the brain. During this transition phase, lipolysis begins in adipose tissues and released fatty acids are picked up by tissue cells and oxidized for energy. In addition, the liver oxidizes fats to ketone bodies and releases them to the blood for use by tissue cells. If fasting continues for longer than four or five days, the brain too begins to use large quantities of ketone bodies as well as glucose as its energy fuel (Table 24.5). The survival value of the brain's ability to use an alternative fuel source is obvious—much less tissue protein has to be ravaged to form glucose.

Hormonal and Neural Controls The sympathetic nervous system and several hormones interact to control events of the postabsorptive state. Consequently, regulation of this state is much more complex than that of the absorptive state when a single hormone, insulin, holds sway.

An important trigger for initiating postabsorptive events is damping of insulin release, which occurs as blood glucose levels drop. As insulin levels decline, all insulin-induced cellular responses are inhibited as well.

Declining glucose levels also stimulate the alpha cells of the pancreatic islets to release the insulin antagonist **glucagon.** Like other hormones acting during the postabsorptive state, glucagon is a *hyperglycemic hormone*, that is, it promotes a rise in blood glucose levels. Glucagon targets the liver and adipose tissue (Figure 24.21). The hepatocytes respond by accelerating glycogenolysis and gluconeogenesis. Adipose cells mobilize their fatty stores (lipolysis) and release fatty acids and glycerol to the blood. Thus, glucagon "refurbishes" blood energy sources by enhancing both glucose and fatty acid levels. Under certain hormonal conditions and persistent low glucose levels or prolonged fasting, most of the fat mobilized is converted to ketone bodies. Glucagon release is inhibited after the next meal or whenever blood glucose levels rise and insulin secretion begins again.

Thus far, the picture is pretty straightforward. Increasing blood glucose levels trigger insulin release, which "pushes" glucose out of the blood and into the cells. This drop in blood glucose stimulates secretion of glucagon, which "pulls" glucose from

Q What hormone is glucagon's main antagonist?

FIGURE 24.21 Influence of glucagon on blood glucose levels. Negative feedback control exerted by rising plasma glucose levels on glucagon secretion is indicated by the dashed arrow.

the cells into the blood. However, there is more than a push-pull mechanism here because *both* insulin and glucagon release are strongly stimulated by rising amino acid levels in the blood. This effect is insignificant when we eat a balanced meal, but it has an important adaptive role when we eat a high-protein, low-carbohydrate meal. In this instance, the stimulus for insulin release is strong, and if it were not counterbalanced, the brain might be damaged by the abrupt onset of hypoglycemia as glucose is

A Insulin.

TABLE 24.6   Summary of Normal Hormonal Influences on Metabolism

HORMONE'S EFFECTS	INSULIN	GLUCAGON	EPINEPHRINE	GROWTH HORMONE	THYROXINE	CORTISOL	TESTOSTERONE
Stimulates glucose uptake by cells	✓				✓		
Stimulates amino acid uptake by cells	✓			✓			
Stimulates glucose catabolism for energy	✓				✓		
Stimulates glycogenesis	✓						
Stimulates lipogenesis and fat storage	✓						
Inhibits gluconeogenesis	✓						
Stimulates protein synthesis (anabolic)	✓			✓	✓		✓
Stimulates glycogenolysis		✓	✓				
Stimulates lipolysis and fat mobilization		✓	✓	✓	✓	✓	
Stimulates gluconeogenesis		✓	✓	✓		✓	
Stimulates protein breakdown (catabolic)						✓	

rushed out of the blood. Simultaneous release of glucagon modulates the effects of insulin and helps stabilize blood glucose levels.

The sympathetic nervous system also plays a crucial role in supplying fuel quickly when blood glucose levels drop suddenly. Adipose tissue is well supplied with sympathetic fibers, and epinephrine released by the adrenal medulla in response to sympathetic activation acts on the liver, skeletal muscle, and adipose tissues. Together, these stimuli mobilize fat and promote glycogenolysis—essentially the same effects prompted by glucagon. Injury, anxiety, or any other stressor that mobilizes the fight-or-flight response will trigger this control pathway, as does exercise. During exercise, large amounts of fuels must be made available for muscle use, and the metabolic profile is essentially the same as that of a fasting person when glucagon and the sympathetic nervous system are in control except that the facilitated diffusion of glucose into muscle is enhanced. (The mechanism of this enhancement is not yet understood.)

In addition to glucagon and epinephrine, a number of other hormones—including growth hormone, thyroxine, sex hormones, and corticosteroids—influence metabolism and nutrient flow. Growth hormone secretion is enhanced by prolonged fasting or rapid declines in blood glucose levels, and GH exerts important anti-insulin effects; for example, it reduces the ability of insulin to promote glucose uptake in fat and muscle. However, the release and activity of most of these hormones are not specifically related to absorptive or postabsorptive metabolic events. Typical metabolic effects of various hormones are described in Table 24.6.

The Metabolic Role of the Liver

The liver is one of the most biochemically complex organs in the body. It processes nearly every class of nutrients and plays a major role in regulating plasma cholesterol levels. While mechanical contraptions can, in a pinch, stand in for a failed heart, lungs, or kidney, the only thing that can do the versatile liver's work is a hepatocyte.

General Metabolic Functions

The hepatocytes carry out some 500 or more intricate metabolic functions. A description of all of these functions is well beyond the scope of this text, but a brief summary is provided in Table 24.7.

Cholesterol Metabolism and Regulation of Blood Cholesterol Levels

Cholesterol, though an important dietary lipid, has received little attention in this discussion so far, primarily because it is not used as an energy source. It serves instead as the structural basis of bile salts, steroid hormones, and vitamin D and as a major component of plasma membranes. Additionally, cholesterol is part of a key signaling molecule (the *hedgehog protein*) that helps direct embryonic development. About 15% of blood cholesterol comes from the diet. The other 85% is made from acetyl CoA by

TABLE 24.7	Summary of Metabolic Functions of the Liver

METABOLIC PROCESSES TARGETED	FUNCTIONS

CARBOHYDRATE METABOLISM

Particularly important in maintaining blood glucose homeostasis	<ul><li>Converts galactose and fructose to glucose</li><li>Glucose buffer function: stores glucose as glycogen when blood glucose levels are high; in response to hormonal controls, performs glycogenolysis and releases glucose to blood</li><li>Gluconeogenesis; converts amino acids and glycerol to glucose when glycogen stores are exhausted and blood glucose levels are falling</li><li>Converts glucose to fats for storage</li></ul>

FAT METABOLISM

Although most cells are capable of some fat metabolism, liver bears the major responsibility	<ul><li>Primary body site of beta oxidation (breakdown of fatty acids to acetyl CoA)</li><li>Converts excess acetyl CoA to ketone bodies for release to tissue cells</li><li>Stores fats</li><li>Forms lipoproteins for transport of fatty acids, fats, and cholesterol to and from tissues</li><li>Synthesizes cholesterol from acetyl CoA; catabolizes cholesterol to bile salts, which are secreted in bile</li></ul>

PROTEIN METABOLISM

Other metabolic functions of the liver could be dispensed with and body could still survive; however, without liver metabolism of proteins, severe survival problems ensue: many essential clotting proteins would not be made, and ammonia would not be disposed of, for example	<ul><li>Deaminates amino acids (required for their conversion to glucose or use for ATP synthesis); amount of deamination that occurs outside the liver is unimportant</li><li>Forms urea for removal of ammonia from body; inability to perform this function (e.g., in cirrhosis or hepatitis) results in accumulation of ammonia in blood</li><li>Forms most plasma proteins (exceptions are gamma globulins and some hormones and enzymes); plasma protein depletion causes rapid mitosis of the hepatocytes and actual growth of liver, which is coupled with increase in synthesis of plasma proteins until blood values are again normal</li><li>Transamination: intraconversion of nonessential amino acids; amount that occurs outside liver is inconsequential</li></ul>

VITAMIN/MINERAL STORAGE

	<ul><li>Stores vitamin A (1–2 years' supply)</li><li>Stores sizable amounts of vitamins D and B_{12} (1–4 months' supply)</li><li>Stores iron; other than iron bound to hemoglobin, most of body's supply is stored in liver as ferritin until needed; releases iron to blood as blood levels drop</li></ul>

BIOTRANSFORMATION FUNCTIONS

	<ul><li>Relative to alcohol and drug metabolism, performs synthetic reactions which yield inactive products that can be secreted by the kidneys and nonsynthetic reactions which may result in products that are more active, changed in activity, or less active</li><li>Processes bilirubin resulting from RBC breakdown and excretes bile pigments in bile</li><li>Metabolizes bloodborne hormones to forms that can be excreted in urine</li></ul>

24

the liver, and to a lesser extent other body cells, particularly intestinal cells. Cholesterol is lost from the body when it is catabolized and secreted in bile salts, which are eventually excreted in feces.

Cholesterol Transport Because triglycerides and cholesterol are insoluble in water, they do not circulate free in the blood. Instead, they are transported to and from tissue cells bound to small lipid-protein complexes called **lipoproteins.** These complexes solubilize the hydrophobic lipids, and the protein part of the complexes contains signals that regulate lipid entry and exit at specific target cells.

Lipoproteins vary considerably in their relative fat-protein composition, but they all contain triglycerides, phospholipids, and cholesterol in addition to protein (Figure 24.22). In general, the higher the percentage of lipid in the lipoprotein, the lower its density; and the greater the proportion of protein, the higher its density. On this basis, there are **high-density lipoproteins (HDLs), low-density lipoproteins (LDLs),** and **very low density lipoproteins (VLDLs).** *Chylomicrons,* which transport absorbed lipids from the GI tract, are a separate class and have the lowest density of all.

The liver is the primary source of VLDLs, which transport triglycerides from the liver to the peripheral tissues, but mostly to *adipose tissues.* Once the triglycerides are unloaded, the VLDL residues are converted to LDLs, which are cholesterol-rich. The role of the LDLs is to transport cholesterol to *peripheral tissues,* making it available to the tissue cells for membrane or hormone synthesis and for storage for later use. The LDLs also regulate cholesterol synthesis in the tissue cells. Docking of LDL to the LDL receptor triggers receptor-mediated endocytosis of the entire particle.

The major function of HDLs, which are particularly rich in phospholipids and cholesterol, is to scoop up and transport excess cholesterol *from peripheral tissues to the liver,* where it is broken down and becomes part of bile. The liver makes the protein envelopes of the HDL particles and then ejects them into the bloodstream in collapsed form, rather like deflated beach balls. Once in the blood, these still-incomplete HDL particles fill with cholesterol picked up from the tissue cells and "pulled" from the artery walls. HDL also services the needs of steroid-producing organs, like the ovaries and adrenal glands, for their raw material (cholesterol). These organs have the ability to selectively remove cholesterol from the HDL particles without engulfing them.

Recommended Total Cholesterol, HDL, and LDL Levels For adults, a total cholesterol level of 200 mg/100 ml of blood (or lower) is recommended. Blood cholesterol levels above 200 mg/100 ml have

been linked to risk of atherosclerosis, which clogs the arteries and causes strokes and heart attacks. However, it is not enough to simply measure total cholesterol. The form in which cholesterol is transported in the blood is more important clinically.

As a rule, high levels of HDLs are considered *good* because the transported cholesterol is destined for degradation. In the United States, the average HDL level in males is 40–50 and in women is 50–60. Levels below 40 are considered undesirable. HDL levels above 60 are thought to protect against heart disease.

High LDL levels (130 or above) are considered *bad* because when LDLs are excessive, potentially lethal cholesterol deposits are laid down in the artery walls. The goal for LDL levels is 100 or less, but new guidelines for those at risk for cardiac disease recommend 70 mg/100 ml or less. A good rule of thumb is that HDL levels can't be too high and LDL levels can't be too low.

If LDLs are "bad" cholesterol, then one variety of LDL—lipoprotein (a)—is "really nasty." This lipid appears to promote plaque formation that thickens and stiffens the blood vessel walls. High levels of lipoprotein (a) in the blood can double a man's risk of a heart attack before the age of 55. It is estimated that one in five males has elevated levels of this lipoprotein in the blood. (See *A Closer Look* in Chapter 19 for more information.)

Factors Regulating Plasma Cholesterol Levels A negative feedback loop partially adjusts the amount of cholesterol produced by the liver according to the amount of cholesterol in the diet. A high cholesterol intake inhibits its synthesis by the liver, but it is not a one-to-one relationship because the liver produces a certain basal amount of cholesterol (about 85%) even when dietary intake is excessive. For this reason, severe restriction of dietary cholesterol, although helpful, does not lead to a steep reduction in plasma cholesterol levels. Additionally, severe restriction of dietary cholesterol may remove important nutrients found in meats, shellfish, and dairy products from a person's diet.

The relative amounts of saturated and unsaturated fatty acids in the diet have an important effect on blood cholesterol levels. Saturated fatty acids *stimulate liver synthesis* of cholesterol and *inhibit its excretion* from the body. In contrast, unsaturated (mono- and polyunsaturated) fatty acids (found in olive oil and in most vegetable oils respectively) *enhance excretion* of cholesterol and its catabolism to bile salts, thereby reducing total cholesterol levels. The unhappy exception to this good news about unsaturated fats concerns "healthy" oils that have been

Q *Are the lipoprotein particles with the most healthy effects those with high protein and low cholesterol or those with high cholesterol and low protein?*

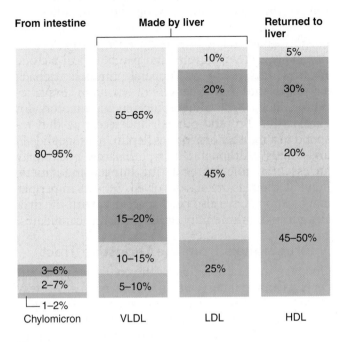

Key:

☐ = Triglyceride ☐ = Cholesterol
☐ = Phospholipid ☐ = Protein

FIGURE 24.22 **Approximate composition of lipoproteins that transport lipids in body fluids.** VLDL = very low density lipoprotein; LDL = low-density lipoprotein; HDL = high-density lipoprotein.

hardened by hydrogenation to make them more solid. Hydrogenation changes the fatty acids in the oils to *trans fatty acids*, which cause serum changes worse than those caused by saturated fats—they spark a greater increase in LDLs and a greater reduction in HDLs, thus producing the unhealthiest ratio of total cholesterol to HDL.

The unsaturated omega-3 fatty acids found in especially large amounts in some cold-water fish lower the proportions of both saturated fats and cholesterol. The omega-3 fatty acids have a powerful antiarrhythmic effect on the heart and also make blood platelets less sticky, thus helping prevent spontaneous clotting that can block blood vessels. They also appear to lower blood pressure (even in nonhypertensive people). In those with moderate to high cholesterol levels, replacing half of the lipid- and cholesterol-rich animal proteins in the diet with soy protein lowers cholesterol significantly.

A *Those with high protein and low cholesterol.*

Factors other than diet also influence blood cholesterol levels. For example, cigarette smoking, coffee drinking, and stress appear to lower HDL levels, whereas regular aerobic exercise and estrogen lower LDL levels and increase HDL levels. Interestingly, body shape, that is, the distribution of body fat, provides clues to risky blood levels of cholesterol and fats. "Apples" (people with upper body and abdominal fat distribution, seen more often in men) tend to have higher levels of cholesterol in general and higher LDLs in particular than "pears" where fat is localized in the hips and thighs, a pattern more common in women.

Most cells other than liver and intestinal cells obtain the bulk of the cholesterol they need for membrane synthesis from the blood. When a cell needs cholesterol, it makes receptor proteins for LDL and inserts them in its plasma membrane. LDL binds to the receptors and is engulfed in coated pits by endocytosis. Within 15 minutes the endocytotic vesicles fuse with lysosomes, where the cholesterol is freed for use. When excessive cholesterol accumulates in a cell, it inhibits both the cell's own cholesterol synthesis and its synthesis of LDL receptors.

◤ HOMEOSTATIC IMBALANCE

Previously, high cholesterol and LDL:HDL ratios were considered the most valid predictors of risk for atherosclerosis, cardiovascular disease, and heart attack. However, almost half of those who get heart disease have normal cholesterol levels, while others with poor lipid profiles remain free of heart disease. Presently, LDL levels and assessments of risk factors are believed to be more accurate indicators of whether treatment is needed or not, and many physicians recommend dietary changes regardless of total cholesterol or HDL levels. Cholesterol-lowering drugs such as the *statins* (e.g., lovastatin and pravastatin) are routinely prescribed for cardiac patients with LDL levels over 130. It is estimated that more than 10 million Americans are now taking statins, and tests of a vaccine that lowers LDL while raising HDL are under way. ●

Energy Balance

When any fuel is burned, it consumes oxygen and liberates heat. The "burning" of food fuels by our cells is no exception. As described in Chapter 2, energy can be neither created nor destroyed—only converted from one form to another. If we apply this principle (actually the *first law of thermodynamics*) to cell metabolism, it means that bond energy released as foods are catabolized must be precisely balanced by the total energy output of the body.

Thus, a dynamic balance exists between the body's energy intake and its energy output:

$$\text{Energy intake} = \text{energy output}$$
$$(\text{heat} + \text{work} + \text{energy storage})$$

Energy intake is the energy liberated during food oxidation. (Undigested foods are not part of the equation because they contribute no energy.) **Energy output** includes energy (1) immediately lost as heat (about 60% of the total), (2) used to do work (driven by ATP), and (3) stored as fat or glycogen. (Because losses of organic molecules in urine, feces, and perspiration are very small in healthy people, they are usually ignored in calculating energy output.) A close look at this situation reveals that *nearly all the energy derived from foodstuffs is eventually converted to heat.* Heat is lost during every cellular activity— when ATP bonds are formed and when they are cleaved to do work, as muscles contract, and through friction as blood flows through blood vessels. Though cells cannot use this energy to do work, the heat warms the tissues and blood and helps maintain the homeostatic body temperature that allows metabolic reactions to occur efficiently. Energy storage is an important part of the equation only during periods of growth and net fat deposit.

Regulation of Food Intake

When energy intake and energy output are balanced, body weight remains stable. When they are not, weight is either gained or lost. Body weight in most people is surprisingly stable. This fact indicates the existence of physiological mechanisms that control food intake (and hence, the amount of food oxidized) or heat production or both. Unhappily for many people, the body's weight-controlling systems appear to be designed more to protect against weight loss than weight gain. Some methods used by the obese to lose or control their weight are discussed in *A Closer Look* on pp. 990–991.

Control of food intake poses difficult questions to researchers. For example, what type of receptor could sense the body's total calorie content and alert one to start eating or to put down that fork? Despite heroic research efforts, no such single receptor type has been found.

It has been known for some time that the hypothalamus, particularly its *arcuate nucleus (ARC)*, releases several peptides that influence feeding behavior. Most importantly, this reflects the activity of two distinct sets of neurons. The NPY/AgRP group release neuropeptide Y (NPY) and agouti-related peptide (AgRP), which collectively enhance appetite while reducing metabolism. The other neuron group consists of the POMC/CART neurons which release pro-opiomelanocortin (POMC) and cocaine- and amphetamine-regulated transcript (CART), appetite-suppressing peptides.

Current theories of how feeding behavior and hunger are regulated focus on one or more of five factors: neural signals from the digestive tract, blood-borne signals related to body energy stores, hormones, body temperature, and psychological factors. All these factors appear to operate through feedback signals to the feeding centers of the brain. Brain receptors include thermoreceptors, chemoreceptors (for glucose, insulin, and others), and receptors that respond to a number of peptides (leptin, neuropeptide Y, and others). Although the hypothalamic nuclei play an essential role in regulating hunger and satiety, brain stem areas are also involved. Sensors in peripheral locations have also been suggested, with the liver and gut itself (alimentary canal) the prime candidates.

Neural Signals from the Digestive Tract

One way the brain evaluates the contents of the gut depends on vagal nerve fibers that carry on a two-way conversation between gut and brain. For example, clinical tests show that 2 kcal worth of protein produces a 30–40% larger and longer response in vagal afferents than does 2 kcal worth of glucose, and activation of stretch receptors ultimately inhibits appetite. Using these signals, together with others it receives, the brain can decode what is eaten and how much.

Nutrient Signals Related to Energy Stores

At any time, blood levels of glucose, amino acids, and fatty acids provide information to the brain that may help adjust energy intake to energy output. For example, nutrient signals that indicate fullness or satiety include

1. Rising blood glucose levels. When we eat, blood glucose levels rise and subsequent activation of glucose receptors in the brain ultimately depresses eating. During fasting, this signal is absent, resulting in hunger and a "turning on" of food-seeking behavior.

2. Elevated blood levels of amino acids depress eating, but the precise mechanism mediating this effect is unknown.

3. Blood concentrations of fatty acids provide a mechanism for controlling hunger. According to this theory, the greater the fat reserves, the larger the baseline amount of fatty acids released to the blood and the more eating behavior is inhibited.

Hormones

Insulin, released during food absorption, depresses hunger and is presumed to be an important satiety signal, as are cholecystokinin and PYY, gut hormones secreted during food digestion, and *leptin*

Key:

← Stimulates

← Inhibits

CCK — Cholecystokinin

Ghr — Ghrelin

Sn — Solitary nucleus

FIGURE 24.23 **Model for hypothalamic command of appetite and food intake.** The arcuate nucleus (ARC) of the brain contains two sets of neurons with opposing effects. Activation of NPY/AgRP neurons enhances appetite whereas activation of POMC/CART neurons has the opposite effect. These centers connect with interneurons in other brain centers, and signals are transmitted through the brain stem to the body. Many appetite-regulating hormones act through the ARC, though they may also exert direct effects on other brain centers as is shown for cholecystokinin (CCK) acting directly on the solitary nucleus (SN) satiety center.

("thin"), a hormone released by fat cells which serves as an indicator of the body's total energy stores in adipose tissue. In contrast, glucagon and epinephrine levels rise during fasting and stimulate hunger. Ghrelin (Ghr), produced by the stomach, is a powerful appetite stimulant.

Body Temperature

Increased body temperature may inhibit eating. Such a thermal signal would help explain why people in cold climates normally eat more than those in warm climates.

Psychological Factors

Although the mechanisms described thus far are reflexive, their final outcome may be enhanced or inhibited by psychological factors that have little to do with caloric balance. Appetite and food intake is def-initely influenced by the appearance, smell, and taste of food—what disgusts the senses will not be ingested. Stress may increase or decrease appetite.

Psychological factors are thought to be very important in obese people. However, even when psychological factors are the underlying cause of obesity, individuals do *not* continue to gain weight endlessly. Their feeding controls still operate, but they have a higher "set point," which maintains total energy content at higher-than-normal levels.

A Hypothetical Model: Interrelationship of Factors in Control of Food Intake

Whew! How does all this information fit together? So far we only have bits and pieces of the story, but the best current hypothesis based on animal studies is shown in Figure 24.23.

A key component of the long-term controls of feeding behavior and satiety appears to be **leptin.** Over a period of hours, leptin is secreted exclusively by fat tissue in response to an increase in body fat mass. Leptin binds to receptors in the choroid plexuses of the ventricles, where it gains entry to the brain. There, it acts on the hypothalamus to regulate the amount of body fat via controls of appetite and energy output by suppressing the activity of NPY/AgRP neurons and stimulating POMC neurons. Neuropeptide Y (NPY) is the most potent appetite stimulant known; hence, by blocking its action leptin decreases appetite and (subsequently) food intake while simultaneously cranking up metabolic activity and heat production, eventually promoting weight loss. When fat stores shrink, leptin blood levels drop, which directly activates the NPY/AgRP neurons and blocks the activity of the POMC/CART center. Consequently, appetite and food intake increase, metabolic rate drops, and weight gain occurs.

It initially seemed that leptin was the magic bullet that obesity researchers were looking for, but their hopes were soon dashed because while rising leptin levels promote weight loss, they do so only to a certain point, beyond which that capability ends. Furthermore, obese individuals have higher-than-normal leptin blood levels, but for some unknown reason, they are resistant to its action. Thus, now the consensus is that leptin's main role is to protect against weight loss in times of nutritional deprivation.

An important outcome of the leptin studies was elucidation of the role of the arcuate nucleus in long- and short-term weight control. Although leptin has received the most attention as a long-term appetite and metabolism regulator, there are several other players. Insulin, which acts on receptors throughout the brain, also acts on ARC receptors. Like leptin it inhibits NPY release in non-insulin-resistant individuals, but its effect is less potent.

Three peptides appear to target and control short-term food intake and satiety. Ghrelin (Ghr), a hormone that stimulates growth hormone production by the anterior pituitary, also acts on ARC neurons to stimulate appetite. In fact, it appears to be the "dinner bell" or trigger for meal initiation. Its levels peak just before mealtime, letting the brain know that it's time to eat, and then trough out after the meal. In contrast, cholecystokinin and PYY, two other peptides formed in the digestive tract, act to thwart the appetite-inducing effect of NPY.

Metabolic Rate and Heat Production

The body's rate of energy output is called the **metabolic rate.** It is the total heat produced by all the chemical reactions and mechanical work of the body.

It can be measured directly or indirectly. In the *direct method,* a person enters a chamber called a **calorimeter** and heat liberated by the body is absorbed by water circulating around the chamber. The rise in water temperature is directly related to the heat produced by the person's body. The *indirect method* uses a **respirometer** to measure oxygen consumption, which is directly proportional to heat production. For each liter of oxygen used, the body produces about 4.8 kcal of heat.

Because many factors influence metabolic rate, it is usually measured under standardized conditions. The person is in a postabsorptive state (has not eaten for at least 12 hours), is reclining, and is mentally and physically relaxed. The temperature of the room is a comfortable 20–25°C. The measurement obtained under these circumstances is called the **basal metabolic rate (BMR)** and reflects the energy the body needs to perform only its most essential activities, such as breathing and maintaining resting levels of organ function. Although named the *basal* metabolic rate, this measurement is *not* the lowest metabolic state of the body. That situation occurs during sleep, when the skeletal muscles are completely relaxed. The BMR, often referred to as the "energy cost of living," is reported in kilocalories per square meter of body surface per hour ($kcal/m^2/h$).

A 70-kg adult has a BMR of approximately 66 kcal/h. You can approximate your BMR by multiplying weight in kilograms (2.2 lb = 1 kg) by 1 if you are male and by 0.9 if you are female.

Factors influencing BMR include body surface area, age, gender, stress, and hormones. Although BMR is related to overall weight and size, the critical factor is body surface area. This reflects the fact that as the ratio of body surface area to body volume increases, heat loss to the environment increases and the metabolic rate must be higher to replace the lost heat. Hence, if two people weigh the same, the taller or thinner person will have the higher BMR.

In general, the younger a person, the higher the BMR. Children and adolescents require large amounts of energy for growth. In old age, BMR declines dramatically as skeletal muscles begin to atrophy. (This helps explain why those elderly who fail to reduce their caloric intake gain weight.) Gender also plays a role. Metabolic rate is disproportionately higher in males than in females, because males typically have more muscle, which is very active metabolically even during rest. Fatty tissue, present in greater relative amounts in females, is metabolically more sluggish than muscle. Surprisingly, physical training has little effect on BMR. Although it would appear that athletes, especially those with greatly enhanced muscle mass, should have much higher BMRs than nonathletes, there is little difference between those of the same sex and surface area.

Body temperature and BMR tend to rise and fall together. Thus, fever (hyperthermia) results in a marked increase in metabolic rate. Stress, whether physical or emotional, increases BMR by mobilizing the sympathetic nervous system. Bloodborne norepinephrine and epinephrine (released by adrenal medullary cells) provoke a rise in BMR primarily by stimulating fat catabolism.

The amount of **thyroxine** produced by the thyroid gland is probably the most important hormonal factor in determining BMR; hence, thyroxine has been dubbed the "metabolic hormone." Its direct effect on most body cells (except brain cells) is to increase O_2 consumption and heat production, presumably by accelerating the use of ATP to operate the sodium-potassium pump. As ATP reserves decline, cellular respiration accelerates. Thus, the more thyroxine produced, the higher the BMR.

◤ HOMEOSTATIC IMBALANCE

Hyperthyroidism causes a host of problems resulting from the excessive BMR it produces. The body catabolizes stored fats and tissue proteins, and, despite increased hunger and food intake, the person often loses weight. Bones weaken and muscles, including the heart, begin to atrophy. In contrast, *hypothyroidism* results in slowed metabolism, obesity, and diminished thought processes. ●

The **total metabolic rate (TMR)** is the rate of kilocalorie consumption needed to fuel *all* ongoing activities—involuntary and voluntary. BMR accounts for a surprisingly large part of TMR. For example, a woman whose total energy needs per day are about 2000 kcal may spend 1400 kcal or so supporting vital body activities. Skeletal muscle activity causes the most dramatic short-term changes in TMR, reflecting the fact that skeletal muscles make up nearly half of body mass. Even slight increases in muscular work can cause remarkable leaps in TMR and heat production. When a well-trained athlete exercises vigorously for several minutes, TMR may increase 20-fold, and it remains elevated for several hours after exercise stops. Food ingestion also induces a rapid increase in TMR. This effect, called **food-induced thermogenesis,** is greatest when proteins are eaten. The heightened metabolic activity of the liver during such periods probably accounts for the bulk of additional energy use. In contrast, fasting or very low caloric intake depresses TMR and results in a slower breakdown of body reserves.

Regulation of Body Temperature

As shown in Figure 24.24, body temperature represents the balance between heat production and heat loss. Although all body tissues produce heat, those

FIGURE 24.24 Body temperature remains constant as long as heat production and heat loss are balanced.

most active metabolically produce the greatest amounts. When the body is at rest, most heat is generated by the liver, heart, brain, and endocrine organs, with the inactive skeletal muscles accounting for only 20–30%. This situation changes dramatically with even slight alterations in muscle tone, however; and during vigorous exercise, heat production by the skeletal muscles can be 30 to 40 times that of the rest of the body. Clearly, a change in muscle activity is one of the most important means of modifying body temperature.

Body temperature averages 37°C ± 0.5°C (98.6°F) and is usually maintained within the range 35.8–38.2°C (96–101°F), despite considerable change in external (air) temperature. A healthy individual's body temperature fluctuates approximately 1°C (1.8°F) in 24 hours, with the low occurring in early morning and the high in late afternoon or early evening.

The adaptive value of this precise temperature homeostasis becomes obvious when we consider the effect of temperature on the rate of enzymatic activity. At normal body temperature, conditions are optimal for enzymatic activity. As body temperature rises, enzymatic catalysis is accelerated: With each rise of 1°C, the rate of chemical reactions increases about 10%. As the temperature spikes above the homeostatic range, neurons are depressed and proteins begin to denature. Children below the age of 5 go into convulsions when body temperature reaches 41°C (106°F), and 43°C (about 109°F) appears to be the absolute limit for life. In contrast, most body tissues can withstand marked reductions in temperature if other conditions are carefully controlled. This fact underlies the use of body cooling during open heart surgery when the heart must be stopped. Low body temperature reduces metabolic rate (and consequently nutrient requirements of body tissues and

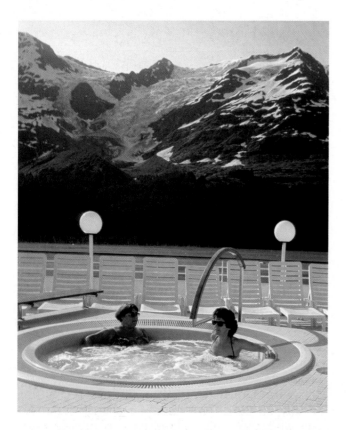

FIGURE 24.25 **Mechanisms of heat exchange.**
Passengers enjoying a hot tub on a cruise to Alaska illustrate several mechanisms of heat exchange between the body and its environment. **(1)** Conduction: Heat transfers from the hot water to the skin. **(2)** Radiation: Heat transfers from the exposed part of the body to the cooler air. **(3)** Convection: Warmed air moves away from the body via breezes. There may also be **(4)** evaporation of perspiration: Excess body heat is carried away.

the heart), allowing more time for surgery without incurring tissue damage.

Core and Shell Temperatures

Different body regions have different resting temperatures. The body's **core** (organs within the skull and the thoracic and abdominal cavities) has the highest temperature and its **shell** (essentially the skin) has the lowest temperature in most circumstances. Of the two body sites used routinely to obtain body temperature clinically, the rectum typically has a temperature about 0.4°C (0.7°F) higher than the mouth and is a better indicator of core temperature.

It is core temperature that is precisely regulated. Blood serves as the major *agent of heat exchange* between the core and shell. Whenever the shell is warmer than the external environment, heat is lost from the body as warm blood is allowed to flush into the skin capillaries. On the other hand, when heat must be conserved, blood largely bypasses the skin. This reduces heat loss and allows the shell temperature to fall toward that of the environment. Thus, while the core temperature stays relatively constant, the temperature of the shell may fluctuate substantially [between 20°C (68°F) and 40°C (104°F) for instance] as its "thickness" is adapted to changes in body activity and external temperature. (You really *can* have cold hands and a warm heart.)

Mechanisms of Heat Exchange

The mechanisms that govern heat exchange between our skin and the external environment (Figure 24.25) are the same as those governing heat exchange between inanimate objects. It helps to think of an object's temperature—whether that object is the skin or a radiator—as a guide to its heat content (*think* "heat concentration"). Then just remember that heat always flows down its concentration gradient from a warmer region to a cooler region. The body uses four mechanisms of heat transfer—radiation, conduction, convection, and evaporation.

Radiation is the loss of heat in the form of infrared waves (thermal energy). Any object that is warmer than objects in its environment—for example, a radiator and (usually) the body—will transfer heat to those objects. Under normal conditions, close to half of body heat loss occurs by radiation.

Because the direction of radiant energy flow is always from warmer to cooler, radiation explains why an initially cold room warms up shortly after it is filled with people (the "body heat furnace," so to speak). The body also gains heat by radiation, as demonstrated by the warming of the skin during sunbathing.

Conduction is the transfer of heat from a warmer object to a cooler one when the two are in direct contact with each other. For example, when we step into a hot tub, some of the heat of the water is transferred to our skin, and warm buttocks transfer heat to the seat of a chair by conduction.

The process called **convection** occurs because warm air expands and rises and cool air (being denser) falls. Thus, the warmed air enveloping the body is continually being replaced by cooler air molecules. Convection substantially enhances heat transfer from the body surface to the air because the cooler air absorbs heat by conduction more rapidly than the already-warmed air. Together, conduction and convection account for 15–20% of heat loss to the environment. These processes are enhanced by anything that moves air more rapidly across the body surface such as wind or a fan, that is, by *forced convection.*

The fourth mechanism by which the body loses heat is **evaporation.** Water evaporates because its molecules absorb heat from the environment and become energetic enough (that is, vibrate fast enough) to escape as gas (water vapor). The heat absorbed by water during evaporation is called **heat of vaporization.** Because water absorbs a great deal of heat before vaporizing, its evaporation from body surfaces removes large amounts of body heat. For every gram of water evaporated, about 0.58 kcal of heat is removed from the body.

There is a basal level of body heat loss due to the continuous evaporation of water from the lungs, from the oral mucosa, and through the skin. The unnoticeable water loss occurring via these routes is called **insensible water loss,** and the heat loss that accompanies it is called **insensible heat loss.** Insensible heat loss dissipates about 10% of the basal heat production of the body and is a constant not subject to body temperature controls. When necessary, however, the control mechanisms do initiate heat-promoting activities to counterbalance this insensible heat loss.

Evaporative heat loss becomes an active *(sensible)* process when body temperature rises and sweating produces increased amounts of water for vaporization. Extreme emotional states activate the sympathetic nervous system, causing body temperature to rise one degree or so, and vigorous exercise can thrust body temperature upward as much as 2–3°C (3.6–5.4°F). During vigorous muscular activity, 1–2 L/h of perspiration can be produced and evaporated, removing 600–1200 kcal of heat from the body each hour. This is more than 30 times the amount of heat lost via insensible heat loss!

HOMEOSTATIC IMBALANCE

When sweating is heavy and prolonged, especially in untrained individuals, losses of water and NaCl may cause painful muscle spasms called *heat cramps.* This situation is easily rectified by ingesting fluids. ●

Role of the Hypothalamus

Although other brain regions contribute, the hypothalamus, particularly its *preoptic* region, is the main integrating center for thermoregulation. Together the **heat-loss center** (located more anteriorly) and the **heat-promoting center** make up the brain's **thermoregulatory centers.**

The hypothalamus receives afferent input from (1) **peripheral thermoreceptors** located in the shell (the skin), and (2) **central thermoreceptors** sensitive to blood temperature and located in the body core including the anterior portion of the hypothalamus. Much like a thermostat, the hypothalamus responds to this input by reflexively initiating appropriate heat-promoting or heat-loss activities via autonomic effector pathways. Although the central thermoreceptors are more critically located than the peripheral ones, varying inputs from the shell probably alert the hypothalamus of the need to act to prevent temperature changes in the core; that is, they allow the hypothalamus to anticipate possible changes to be made.

Heat-Promoting Mechanisms

When the external temperature is low or blood temperature falls for any reason, the heat-promoting center is activated and triggers one or more of the following mechanisms to maintain or increase core body temperature (Figure 24.26).

1. Constriction of cutaneous blood vessels. Activation of the sympathetic vasoconstrictor fibers serving the blood vessels of the skin causes strong vasoconstriction. As a result, blood is restricted to deep body areas and largely bypasses the skin. Because the skin is separated from deeper organs by a layer of insulating subcutaneous (fatty) tissue, heat loss from the shell is dramatically reduced and shell temperature drops toward that of the external environment.

HOMEOSTATIC IMBALANCE

Restricting blood flow to the skin is not a problem for a brief period, but if it is extended (as during prolonged exposure to very cold weather), skin cells deprived of oxygen and nutrients begin to die. This extremely serious condition is called *frostbite.* ●

2. Shivering. Shivering, involuntary shuddering contractions, is triggered when brain centers controlling muscle tone are activated and muscle tone reaches sufficient levels to alternately stimulate stretch receptors in antagonistic muscles. Shivering is very effective in increasing body temperature because muscle activity produces large amounts of heat.

3. Increase in metabolic rate. Cold stimulates the release of epinephrine and norepinephrine by the adrenal medulla in reponse to sympathetic nerve stimuli, which elevates the metabolic rate and enhances heat production. This mechanism, called **chemical,** or **nonshivering, thermogenesis,** is known to occur in infants but still controversial in adults.

4. Enhanced thyroxine release. When environmental temperature decreases gradually, as in the transition from summer to winter, the hypothalamus of infants releases *thyrotropin-releasing hormone.* This activates the anterior pituitary to release *thyroid-stimulating hormone,* which induces the thyroid to liberate larger amounts of thyroid hormone to the blood. Because thyroid hormone increases metabolic rate, body heat production increases. A similar TSH response to cold exposure does not appear to occur in adults.

Beside these involuntary adjustments, we humans make a number of *behavioral modifications* to prevent overcooling of our body core:

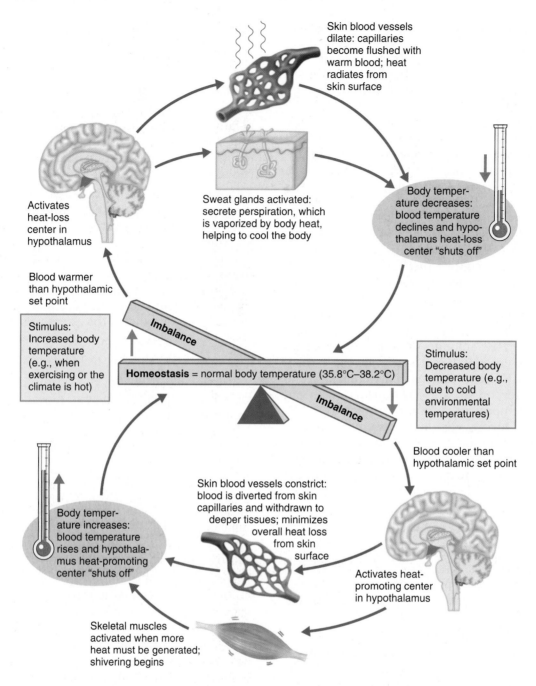

Skin blood vessels dilate: capillaries become flushed with warm blood; heat radiates from skin surface

Activates heat-loss center in hypothalamus

Sweat glands activated: secrete perspiration, which is vaporized by body heat, helping to cool the body

Body temperature decreases: blood temperature declines and hypothalamus heat-loss center "shuts off"

Blood warmer than hypothalamic set point

Stimulus: Increased body temperature (e.g., when exercising or the climate is hot)

Imbalance

Homeostasis = normal body temperature (35.8°C–38.2°C)

Imbalance

Stimulus: Decreased body temperature (e.g., due to cold environmental temperatures)

Blood cooler than hypothalamic set point

Body temperature increases: blood temperature rises and hypothalamus heat-promoting center "shuts off"

Skin blood vessels constrict: blood is diverted from skin capillaries and withdrawn to deeper tissues; minimizes overall heat loss from skin surface

Activates heat-promoting center in hypothalamus

Skeletal muscles activated when more heat must be generated; shivering begins

FIGURE 24.26   **Mechanisms of body temperature regulation.**

- Putting on more or warmer clothing to restrict heat loss (a hat, gloves, and "insulated" outer garments)
- Drinking hot fluids
- Changing posture to reduce exposed body surface area (hunching over or clasping the arms across the chest)
- Increasing physical activity to generate more heat (jumping up and down, clapping the hands)

Heat-Loss Mechanisms

Heat-loss mechanisms protect the body from excessively high temperatures. Most heat loss occurs through the skin via radiation, conduction, convection, and evaporation. How do the heat-exchange mechanisms fit into the heat-loss temperature regulation scheme? The answer is quite simple. Whenever core body temperature rises above normal, the hypothalamic heat-promoting center is inhibited. At the same time, the heat-loss center is activated and so triggers one or both of the following (Figure 24.26):

1. Dilation of cutaneous blood vessels. Inhibiting the vasomotor fibers serving blood vessels of the skin allows the vessels to dilate. As the blood vessels swell with warm blood, heat is lost from the shell by radiation, conduction, and convection.

24

2. Enhanced sweating. If the body is extremely overheated or if the environment is so hot [over 33°C (about 92°F)] that heat cannot be lost by other means, evaporation becomes necessary. The sweat glands are strongly activated by sympathetic fibers and spew out large amounts of perspiration. Evaporation of perspiration is an efficient means of ridding the body of surplus heat as long as the air is dry. However, when the relative humidity is high, evaporation occurs much more slowly. In such cases, the heat-liberating mechanisms cannot work well, and we feel miserable and irritable.

Behavioral or voluntary measures commonly taken to reduce body heat include

- Reducing activity ("laying low")

- Seeking a cooler environment (a shady spot) or using a device to increase convection (a fan) or cooling (an air conditioner)

- Wearing light-colored, loose clothing that reflects radiant energy. (This is actually cooler than being nude because bare skin absorbs most of the radiant energy striking it.)

HOMEOSTATIC IMBALANCE

Under conditions of overexposure to a hot and humid environment, normal heat-loss processes become ineffective. The **hyperthermia** (elevated body temperature) that ensues depresses the hypothalamus. At a core temperature of around 105°F, heat-control mechanisms are suspended, creating a vicious *positive feedback cycle*. Increasing temperatures increase the metabolic rate, which increases heat production. The skin becomes hot and dry and, as the temperature continues to spiral upward, multiple organ damage becomes a distinct possibility, including brain damage. This condition, called **heat stroke,** can be fatal unless corrective measures are initiated immediately (immersing the body in cool water and administering fluids).

The terms *heat exhaustion* and *exertion-induced heat exhaustion* are often used to describe the heat-associated collapse of an individual during or following vigorous physical activity accompanied by extreme sweating. This condition, evidenced by elevated body temperature and mental confusion and/or fainting, is due to dehydration and consequent low blood pressure. In contrast to heat stroke, heat-loss mechanisms are still functional in heat exhaustion; indeed, the symptoms are a direct consequence of those mechanisms. However, heat exhaustion can rapidly progress to heat stroke if the body is not cooled and rehydrated promptly.

Hypothermia (hi"po-ther'me-ah) is low body temperature resulting from prolonged uncontrolled exposure to cold. Vital signs (respiratory rate, blood pressure, and heart rate) decrease as cellular enzymes become sluggish. Drowsiness sets in and, oddly, the person becomes comfortable even though previously he or she felt extremely cold. Shivering stops at a core temperature of 30–32°C (87–90°F) when the body has exhausted its heat-generating capabilities. Uncorrected, the situation progresses to coma and finally death (by cardiac arrest), when body temperatures approach 21°C (70°F). ●

Fever

Fever is *controlled hyperthermia*. Most often, it results from infection somewhere in the body, but it may be caused by cancer, allergic reactions, or CNS injuries. Whatever the cause, macrophages and other cells release cytokines, originally called *pyrogens* (literally, "fire starters"), at least two of which are now known to be interleukins. These chemicals act on the hypothalamus, causing release of prostaglandins which reset the hypothalamic thermostat to a higher-than-normal temperature, so that heat-promoting mechanisms kick in. As a result of vasoconstriction, heat loss from the body surface declines, the skin cools, and shivering begins to generate heat. These "chills" are a sure sign body temperature is rising. The temperature rises until it reaches the new setting, and then is maintained at that setting until natural body defenses or antibiotics reverse the disease process, and chemical messengers called *cryogens* (vasopressin and others) act to prevent fever from becoming excessive and reset the thermostat to a lower (or normal) level. Then, heat-loss mechanisms swing into action; sweating begins and the skin becomes flushed and warm. Physicians have long recognized these signs as signals that body temperature is falling (aah, she has passed the crisis).

As explained in Chapter 21, fever, by increasing the metabolic rate, helps speed healing, and it also appears to inhibit bacterial growth. The danger of fever is that if the body thermostat is set too high, proteins may be denatured and permanent brain damage may occur.

Developmental Aspects of Nutrition and Metabolism

Good nutrition is essential in utero, as well as throughout life. If the mother is ill nourished, the development of her infant is affected. Most serious is the lack of adequate calories, proteins, and vitamins needed for fetal tissue growth, especially brain growth. Additionally, because brain growth continues for the first three years after birth, inadequate nutrients during this time will lead to mental deficits or learning disorders. Proteins are needed for

(Text continues on p. 992.)

A CLOSER LOOK

Obesity: Magical Solution Wanted

How fat is too fat? What distinguishes an obese person from one who is merely overweight? The bathroom scale is an inaccurate guide because body weight tells little of body composition. Dense bones and well-developed muscles can make a person technically overweight. Arnold Schwarzenegger, for example, has tipped the scales at a hefty 257 lb.

The official medical measure of obesity and body fatness is the *body mass index (BMI)*, an index of a person's weight relative to height. To estimate BMI, multiply weight in pounds by 705 and then divide by your height in inches squared:

$$BMI = wt(lb) \times 705/ht(inches)^2$$

Overweight is defined by a BMI between 25 and 30 and having some health risk; obesity is a BMI greater than 30 with markedly increased health risk. The most common view of obesity is that it is a condition of excessive triglyceride storage. We bewail our inability to rid ourselves of fat, but the real problem is that we keep refilling the storehoses by consuming too many calories. A body fat content of 18–20% of body weight (males and females respectively) is deemed normal for adults.

However it's defined, obesity is perplexing and poorly understood, and the economic toll of obesity-related disease is staggering. Despite its adverse health effects (the obese have a higher incidence of atherosclerosis, diabetes mellitus, hypertension, heart disease, and osteoarthritis), the U.S. is big and getting bigger, at least around its middle. Two out of three adults are overweight; of that, one out of three is obese and one in twelve has diabetes, a common sequel of weight problems. U.S. kids are getting fatter too: 20 years ago, 5% were overweight; today 15% are and more are headed that way. Furthermore, because they are opting for video games and nachos instead of tag or touch football and an apple, their general cardiovascular fitness is declining as well and health

risks associated with excess weight start frighteningly early. For example, obesity-related heart problems, such as an enlarged heart—a risk factor for heart attack and CHF—may start developing in the early teens or even younger.

Besides the physical toll, the social stigma and economic disadvantages of obesity are legendary. A fat person pays higher insurance premiums, is discriminated against in the job market, has fewer clothing choices, and endures frequent humiliation throughout life. It's a fair bet that few people choose to become obese. So what causes it?

Theories of Obesity Causes

1. Overeating during childhood promotes adult obesity. Some believe that the "clean your plate" order sets the stage for adult obesity by increasing the number of adipose cells formed during childhood. The more adipose cells there are, the more fat can be stored.

2. Obese people are more fuel efficient and more effective "fat storers." Although it is often assumed that the obese eat more, this is not necessarily true—many actually eat less than people of normal weight. When yo-yo dieters lose weight, their metabolic rate falls sharply. But, when they subsequently gain weight, their metabolic rate increases like a furnace being stoked. Each successive weight loss occurs more slowly, but regaining weight occurs three times as fast. Furthermore, fats pack more wallop per calorie (are more fattening) than are proteins or carbohydrates because of the way the body processes them. If 100 excess carbohydrate calories are ingested, 23 are used in metabolic processing and 77 are stored. However, if the 100 excess calories come from fat, only 3 calories are "burned" and the rest (97) are stored. These facts apply to everyone, but when you are obese the picture is even bleaker.

Adipose cells of overweight people sprout more alpha receptors, which favor fat accumulation, and enteroendocrine cells of the stomach secrete much larger amounts of ghrelin (which ratchets up the appetite just before eating) in those that have recently lost weight. Furthermore, the enzyme lipoprotein lipase, which unloads fat from the blood (usually to fat cells) is exceptionally efficient in the obese. Although it would appear that the so-called satiety chemicals (hormones and others) should prevent massive fat deposit, this seems not to be the case in the obese. It may be that excess weight promotes not only insulin resistance (the enlarged adipose cells spew out tumor necrosis factor alpha, which can act as a trigger) but leptin resistance as well.

3. Genetic predisposition. Morbid obesity is the destiny of those inheriting two obesity genes. These people, given extra calories, will always lay them down as fat, as opposed to those that lay down more muscle with some of the excess. However, a true genetic predisposition for "fatness" appears to account for only about 5% of the American obese.

Treatments—The Bad and the Good

Some so-called treatments for obesity are almost more dangerous than the disease itself. Unfortunate strategies include

1. "Water pills." Diuretics prompt the kidneys to excrete more water and may cause a few pounds of weight loss for a few hours. They can also cause serious dehydration and electrolyte imbalance.

2. Diets. Diet products and books sell well, but do any of the currently popular diets work and are they safe? At the present time there is a duel between those promoting low-carbohydrate (high-protein and -fat) diets such as the Atkins and South Beach diets, and those espousing the traditional low-fat (high–complex carbohydrates) diet. Clinical studies show that those on the low-carbohydrate diets lose weight more quickly at first, but tend to plateau at 6 months. They seem to preferentially lose fat from the body trunk, a weight distribution pattern (the "apple") associated with heart disease and diabetes mellitus. (This propensity to these diseases, called "metabolic syndrome," appears to be due to the large amounts of inflammatory cytokines released by visceral fat cells.) When dieting was continued for a year, those on the low-fat diets lost just as much weight as did those on the low-carbohydrate diets and they experienced fewer episodes of diarrhea, constipation, headache, and muscle cramps. Although there was concern that the low-carbohydrate diets would promote undesirable plasma cholesterol and lipid values, for the most part this has not been the case.

Diets that have users counting the glycemic indexes of the food they eat, such as the New Glucose Revolution diet, distinguish between good carbs (whole grains, nonstarchy vegetables and fruits) and bad carbs (starches, sugary foods, refined grains) and have the approval of many physicians. The oldie-but-goodie Weight Watcher's diet, which has dieters counting points, still works and allows virtually any food choice as long as the allowed point count isn't exceeded.

Some over-the-counter liquid high-protein diets contain such poor-quality (incomplete) protein that they are actually dangerous. The worst are those that contain collagen protein instead of milk or soybean sources.

3. Surgery. Sometimes sheer desperation prompts surgical solutions: wiring the jaws shut; reducing stomach volume by banding; gastric bypass surgery, which may involve stomach stapling and intestinal bypass surgery, or the more radical biliopancreatic diversion (BPD); and liposuction (removal of fat by suctioning).

BPD rearranges the digestive tract. Up to two-thirds of the stomach is removed and the small intestine is cut

in half and one portion is sutured to the stomach opening. Pancreatic juice and bile are diverted away from the "new intestine" so far fewer nutrients and no fats are absorbed. Many of these procedures have been remarkably effective at promoting weight loss and restoring health. (Blood pressure returns to normal in many that were originally hypertensive, and sleep apnea is reduced.) Patients can eat anything they want without gaining weight, but exceeding the stomach capacity leads to the dumping syndrome, in which nausea and vomiting occur.

Liposuction reshapes the body by suctioning off fat deposits, but it is not a good choice for losing weight. Like BPD, it carries all the risks of surgery, and unless eating habits change, fat depots elsewhere in the body overfill.

4. Diet drugs and weight-loss supplements. Currently popular weight-loss drugs include phentermine, sibutramine, and orlistat. Phentermine is one-half of the former fen-phen (Redux) combination that caused heart problems, deaths, and litigation for its producer in the 1990s. It acts via increased sympathetic nervous system activity, which increases blood pressure and heart rate. Sibutramine (Meridia) inhibits reclama-

tion of the neurotransmitters norepinephrine and serotonin and has amphetamine-like effects. It has recently come under fire because of suspected cardiovascular side effects. Orlistat (Xenical) interferes with pancreatic lipase so that part of the fat eaten is not digested or absorbed, which also interferes with the absorption of fat-soluble vitamins. Although it is effective as a weight-loss agent, its side effects, which include diarrhea and anal leakage, are unpleasant to say the least. Currently a number of drugs are being developed that act at several different CNS sites, including neuropeptide Y inhibitors.

Some over-the-counter weight-loss supplements that are claimed to increase metabolism and burn calories at an accelerated rate have proved to be very dangerous. For example:

- Capsules containing usnic acid, a chemical found in some lichens, damages hepatocytes and has led to liver failure in a few cases.

- Ephedra-containing supplements are notorious—over 100 deaths and 16,000 cases of problems including strokes, seizures, and headaches have been reported.

When it comes to such supplements, the burden of proof is on the FDA to show that the product is unsafe. Hence, the true extent of ills caused by weight-loss supplements is not known—while the worst cases attract attention, less serious ones go unreported or undiagnosed.

So are there any good treatments for obesity? The best way to lose weight—indeed the only realistic way—is to take in fewer calories and increase physical activity. Fidgeting helps and so does resistance exercise, which increases muscle mass. Furthermore, low activity levels actually stimulate eating, while physical exercise depresses appetite and increases metabolic rate not only during activity but also for some time after. The only way to keep the weight off is to make dietary and exercise changes lifelong habits. ■

24

muscle and bone growth, and calcium is required for strong bones. Although anabolic processes are less critical after growth is completed, sufficient nutrients are still essential to maintain normal tissue replacement and metabolism.

◣ HOMEOSTATIC IMBALANCE

There are many inborn errors of metabolism (or genetic disorders), but perhaps the two most common are *cystic fibrosis* and *phenylketonuria (PKU)* (fen″il-ke″to-nu′re-ah). Cystic fibrosis is described in Chapter 22. In PKU, the tissue cells are unable to use the amino acid phenylalanine (fen″il-al′ah-nīn), which is present in all protein foods. The defect involves a deficiency of the enzyme that converts phenylalanine to tyrosine. Phenylalanine cannot be metabolized, so it and its deaminated products accumulate in the blood and act as neurotoxins that cause brain damage and retardation within a few months. These consequences are uncommon today because most states require a urine or blood test to identify affected newborns, and these children are put on a low-phenylalanine diet. When this special diet should be terminated is controversial. Some believe it should be continued through adolescence; others order it discontinued when the child is 6 years old. Expectant women are sometimes encouraged to return to the controlled phenylalanine diet during their pregnancy.

There are a number of other enzyme defects, classified according to the impaired process as carbohydrate, lipid, or mineral metabolic disorders. The carbohydrate deficit *galactosemia* results from an abnormality in or lack of the liver enzymes needed to transform galactose to glucose. Galactose accumulates in the blood and leads to mental deficits. In the carbohydrate disorder *glycogen storage disease*, glycogen synthesis is normal, but one of the enzymes needed to convert it back to glucose is missing. As excessive amounts of glycogen are stored, its storage organs (liver and skeletal muscles) become glutted with glycogen and enlarge tremendously. ●

With the exception of *insulin-dependent diabetes mellitus*, children free of genetic disorders rarely exhibit metabolic problems. However, by middle age and particularly old age, *non-insulin-dependent diabetes mellitus* becomes a major problem, particularly in the obese.

Metabolic rate declines throughout the life span. In old age, muscle and bone wasting and declining efficiency of the endocrine system take their toll. Because many elderly are also less active, the metabolic rate is sometimes so low that it becomes nearly impossible to obtain adequate nutrition without gaining weight. The elderly also use more medications

than any other group, at a time of life when the liver has become less efficient in its detoxifying duties. Consequently, many of the agents prescribed for age-related medical problems influence nutrition. For example:

- Some diuretics prescribed for congestive heart failure or hypertension (to flush fluids out of the body) can cause severe hypokalemia by promoting excessive loss of potassium.
- Some antibiotics, for example, sulfa drugs, tetracycline, and penicillin, interfere with food digestion and absorption. They may also cause diarrhea, thereby decreasing nutrient absorption further.
- Although its use is discouraged by physicians because it interferes with absorption of fat-soluble vitamins, mineral oil is still a popular laxative with the elderly.
- Alcohol is used by about half the elderly population in the U.S. When it is substituted for food, nutrient stores can be depleted. Excessive alcohol intake leads to absorption problems, certain vitamin and mineral deficiencies, deranged metabolism, and damage to the liver and pancreas.

In short, the elderly are at risk not only from the declining efficiency of their metabolic processes, but also from a huge variety of lifestyle and medication factors that affect their nutrition.

Although malnutrition and a waning metabolic rate present problems to some elderly, certain nutrients—notably glucose—appear to contribute to the aging process in people of all ages. Nonenzymatic reactions (the so-called *browning reactions*) between glucose and proteins, long known to discolor and toughen foods, may have the same effects on body proteins. When enzymes attach sugars to proteins, they do so at specific sites and the glycoproteins produced play well-defined roles in the body. By contrast, nonenzymatic binding of glucose to proteins (a process that increases with age) is haphazard and eventually causes cross-links between proteins. The increase in this type of binding probably contributes to lens clouding, atherosclerotic plaque formation, and the general tissue stiffening and loss of elasticity so common in the aged.

■ ■ ■

Nutrition is one of the most overlooked areas in clinical medicine. Yet, what we eat and drink influences nearly every phase of metabolism and plays a major role in our overall health. Now that we have examined the fates of nutrients in body cells, we are ready to study the urinary system, the organ system that works tirelessly to rid the body of nitrogen wastes resulting from metabolism and to maintain the purity of our internal fluids.

Related Clinical Terms

Appetite A desire for food. A psychological phenomenon dependent on memory and associations, as opposed to hunger, which is a physiological need to eat.

Familial hypercholesterolemia (hi"per-ko-les"ter-ol-e′me-ah). An inherited condition in which the LDL receptors are absent or abnormal, the uptake of cholesterol by tissue cells is blocked, and the total concentration of cholesterol (and LDLs) in the blood is enormously elevated (e.g., 680 mg of cholesterol per 100 ml of blood). Affected individuals develop atherosclerosis at an early age, heart attacks begin in the third or fourth decade, and most die by age 60 from coronary artery disease. Treatment entails dietary modifications, exercise, and various cholesterol-reducing drugs.

Kwashiorkor (kwash"e-or′kor) Severe protein and calorie deficiency which is particularly devastating in children,

resulting in mental retardation and failure to grow. A consequence of malnutrition or starvation, it is characterized by a bloated abdomen because the level of plasma proteins is inadequate to keep fluid in the bloodstream. Skin lesions and infections likely.

Marasmus (mah-raz′mus) Protein-calorie malnutrition, accompanied by progressive wasting. Often due to ingestion of food of very poor quality. Growth for age is severely stunted.

Pica (pi′kah) Craving and eating substances not normally considered nutrients, such as clay, cornstarch, or dirt.

Skin-fold test Clinical test of body fatness. A skin fold in the back of the arm or below the scapula is measured with a caliper. A fold over 1 inch in thickness indicates excess fat. Also called the fat-fold test.

Chapter Summary

Media study tools that could provide you additional help in reviewing specific key topics of Chapter 24 are referenced below.
IP = *InterActive Physiology*

Nutrition   (pp. 943–956)

1. Nutrients include water, carbohydrates, lipids, proteins, vitamins, and minerals. The bulk of the organic nutrients is used as fuel to produce cellular energy (ATP). The energy value of foods is measured in kilocalories (kcal).

2. Essential nutrients are those that are inadequately synthesized by body cells and must be ingested in the diet.

Carbohydrates   (pp. 944–945)

3. Carbohydrates are obtained primarily from plant products. Absorbed monosaccharides other than glucose are converted to glucose by the liver.

4. Monosaccharides are used primarily for cellular fuel. Small amounts are used for nucleic acid synthesis and to glycosylate plasma membranes.

5. Recommended carbohydrate intake for adults is 45–65% of daily caloric intake.

Lipids   (pp. 944–946)

6. Most dietary lipids are triglycerides. The primary sources of saturated fats are animal products, tropical oils, and hydrogenated oils; unsaturated fats are present in plant products, nuts, and cold-water fish. The major sources of cholesterol are egg yolk, meats, and milk products.

7. Linoleic and linolenic acids are essential fatty acids.

8. Triglycerides provide reserve energy, cushion body organs, and insulate the body. Phospholipids are used to synthesize plasma membranes and myelin. Cholesterol is used in plasma membranes and is the structural basis of vitamin D, steroid hormones, and bile salts.

9. Fat intake should represent 35% or less of caloric intake, and saturated and trans fats should be replaced by mono- and polyunsaturated fats if possible. The liver makes a basal amount of cholesterol (85%) even when dietary cholesterol intake is excessive.

Proteins   (pp. 945, 946–947)

10. Animal products provide high-quality complete protein containing all (10) essential amino acids. Most plant products lack one or more of the essential amino acids.

11. Amino acids are the structural building blocks of the body and of important regulatory molecules.

12. Protein synthesis can and will occur if all essential amino acids are present and sufficient carbohydrate (or fat) calories are available to produce ATP. Otherwise, amino acids will be burned for energy.

13. Nitrogen balance occurs when protein synthesis equals protein loss.

14. A dietary intake of 0.8 g of protein per kg of body weight is recommended for most healthy adults.

Vitamins   (pp. 947–952)

15. Vitamins are organic compounds needed in minute amounts. Most act as coenzymes. The richest sources are whole grains, vegetables, legumes, and fruit.

16. Except for vitamin D and the K and B vitamins made by enteric bacteria, vitamins are not made in the body.

17. Water-soluble vitamins (B and C) are not stored to excess in the body. Fat-soluble vitamins include vitamins A, D, E, and K; all but vitamin K are stored and can accumulate to toxic amounts.

Minerals   (pp. 952–956)

18. Besides calcium, phosphorus, potassium, sulfur, sodium, chloride, and magnesium, the body requires trace amounts of at least a dozen other minerals.

19. Minerals are not used for energy. Some are used to mineralize bone; others are bound to organic compounds or exist as ions in body fluids, where they play various roles in cell processes and metabolism.

20. Mineral uptake and excretion are carefully regulated to prevent mineral toxicity. The richest sources of minerals are animal products, vegetables, seeds, and legumes.

Metabolism   (pp. 956–981)

Overview   (pp. 956–959)

1. Metabolism encompasses all chemical reactions necessary to maintain life. Metabolic processes are either anabolic or catabolic.

2. Cellular respiration refers to catabolic processes during which energy is released and some is captured in ATP bonds.

3. Energy is released when organic compounds are oxidized. Cellular oxidation is accomplished primarily by the

removal of hydrogen (electrons). When molecules are oxidized, others are simultaneously reduced by accepting hydrogen (or electrons).

4. Most enzymes catalyzing oxidation-reduction reactions require coenzymes as hydrogen acceptors. Two important coenzymes in these reactions are NAD^+ and FAD.

5. In animal cells, the two mechanisms of ATP synthesis are substrate-level phosphorylation and oxidative phosphorylation.

IP Muscular System; Topic: Muscle Metabolism, pp. 3–8.

Carbohydrate Metabolism (pp. 959–967)

6. Carbohydrate metabolism is essentially glucose metabolism.

7. Phosphorylation of glucose on entry into cells effectively traps it in most tissue cells.

8. Glucose is oxidized to carbon dioxide and water via three successive pathways: glycolysis, Krebs cycle, and electron transport chain. Some ATP is harvested in each pathway, but the bulk is captured in the electron transport chain.

9. Glycolysis is a reversible pathway in which glucose is converted to two pyruvic acid molecules; two molecules of reduced NAD^+ are formed, and there is a net gain of 2 ATP. Under aerobic conditions, pyruvic acid enters the Krebs cycle; under anaerobic conditions, it is reduced to lactic acid.

10. The Krebs cycle is fueled by pyruvic acid (and fatty acids). To enter the cycle, pyruvic acid is converted to acetyl CoA. The acetyl CoA is then oxidized and decarboxylated. Complete oxidation of two pyruvic acid molecules yields $6 CO_2$, $8 NADH + H^+$, $2 FADH_2$, and a net gain of 2 ATP. Much of the energy originally present in the bonds of pyruvic acid is now present in the reduced coenzymes.

11. In the electron transport chain, (a) reduced coenzymes are oxidized by delivering hydrogen to a series of oxidation-reduction acceptors; (b) hydrogen is split into hydrogen ions and electrons (as electrons run downhill from acceptor to acceptor, the energy released is used to pump H^+ into the mitochondrial intermembrane space, which creates an electrochemical proton gradient); (c) the energy stored in the electrochemical proton gradient drives H^+ back through ATP synthase, which uses the energy to form ATP; (d) H^+ and electrons are combined with oxygen to form water.

12. For each glucose molecule oxidized to carbon dioxide and water, there is a net gain of 38 ATP: 4 ATP from substrate-level phosphorylation and 34 ATP from oxidative phosphorylation. The shuttle for reduced NAD^+ produced in the cytosol may use 2 ATP of that amount.

13. When cellular ATP reserves are high, glucose catabolism is inhibited and glucose is converted to glycogen (glycogenesis) or to fat (lipogenesis). Much more fat than glycogen is stored.

14. Gluconeogenesis is the formation of glucose from non-carbohydrate (fat or protein) molecules. It occurs in the liver when blood glucose levels begin to fall.

IP Muscular System; Topic: Muscle Metabolism, pp. 10–22.

Lipid Metabolism (pp. 967–970)

15. End products of lipid digestion (and cholesterol) are transported in blood in the form of chylomicrons.

16. Glycerol is converted to glyceraldehyde-PO_4 and enters the Krebs cycle or is converted to glucose.

17. Fatty acids are oxidized by beta oxidation into acetic acid fragments. These are bound to coenzyme A and enter the Krebs cycle as acetyl CoA. Dietary fats not needed for energy or structural materials are stored in adipose tissue.

18. There is a continual turnover of fats in fatty depots. Breakdown of fats to fatty acids and glycerol is called lipolysis.

19. When excessive amounts of fats are used, the liver converts acetyl CoA to ketone bodies and releases them to the blood. Excessive levels of ketone bodies (ketosis) lead to metabolic acidosis.

20. All cells use phospholipids and cholesterol to build their plasma membranes. The liver forms many functional molecules (lipoproteins, bile salts, etc.) from lipids.

Protein Metabolism (pp. 970–971)

21. To be oxidized for energy, amino acids are converted to keto acids that can enter the Krebs cycle. This involves transamination, oxidative deamination, and keto acid modification.

22. Amine groups removed during deamination (as ammonia) are combined with carbon dioxide by the liver to form urea. Urea is excreted in urine.

23. Deaminated amino acids may also be converted to fatty acids and glucose.

24. Amino acids are the body's most important building blocks. Nonessential amino acids are made in the liver by transamination.

25. In adults, most protein synthesis serves to replace tissue proteins and to maintain nitrogen balance.

26. Protein synthesis requires the presence of all ten essential amino acids. If any are lacking, amino acids are used as energy fuels.

Catabolic-Anabolic Steady State of the Body (pp. 971–973)

27. The amino acid pool provides amino acids for synthesis of proteins and amino acid derivatives, ATP synthesis, and energy storage. To be stored, amino acids are first deaminated and then converted to fats or glycogen.

28. The carbohydrate-fat pool primarily provides fuels for ATP synthesis and other molecules that can be stored as energy reserves.

29. The nutrient pools are connected by the bloodstream; fats, carbohydrates, and proteins may be interconverted via common intermediates.

Absorptive and Postabsorptive States (pp. 973–978)

30. During the absorptive state (during and shortly after a meal), glucose is the major energy source; needed structural and functional molecules are made; excesses of carbohydrates, fats, and amino acids are stored as glycogen and fat.

31. Events of the absorptive state are controlled by insulin, which enhances the entry of glucose (and amino acids) into cells and accelerates its use for ATP synthesis or storage as glycogen or fat.

32. The postabsorptive state is the period when bloodborne fuels are provided by breakdown of energy reserves. Glucose is made available to the blood by glycogenolysis, lipolysis, and gluconeogenesis. Glucose sparing begins and, if fasting is prolonged (4–5 days), the brain also begins to metabolize ketone bodies.

33. Events of the postabsorptive state are controlled largely by glucagon and the sympathetic nervous system, which mobilize glycogen and fat reserves and trigger gluconeogenesis.

The Metabolic Role of the Liver (pp. 978–981)

34. The liver is the body's main metabolic organ and it plays a crucial role in processing (or storing) virtually every nutrient group. It helps maintain blood energy sources, metabolizes hormones, and detoxifies drugs and other substances.

35. The liver synthesizes cholesterol, catabolizes cholesterol and secretes it in the form of bile salts, and makes lipoproteins.

36. LDLs transport triglycerides and cholesterol from the liver to the tissues, whereas HDLs transport cholesterol from the tissues to the liver (for catabolism and elimination).

37. Excessively high LDL levels are implicated in atherosclerosis, cardiovascular disease, and strokes.

Energy Balance (pp. 981–991)

1. Body energy intake (derived from food oxidation) is precisely balanced by energy output (heat, work, and energy storage). Eventually, all of the energy intake is converted to heat.

2. When energy balance is maintained, weight remains stable. When excess amounts of energy are stored, obesity results (condition of excessive fat storage, 20% or more above the norm).

Regulation of Food Intake (pp. 982–984)

3. The hypothalamus (particularly its arcuate nucleus) and other brain centers are involved in the regulation of eating behavior.

4. Factors thought to be involved in regulating food intake include (a) neural signals from the gut to the brain, (b) nutrient signals related to total energy storage (e.g., large fatty reserves and increased plasma levels of glucose and amino acids depress hunger and eating); (c) plasma concentrations of hormones that control events of the absorptive and postabsorptive states, and hormones that provide feedback signals to brain feeding centers (leptin appears to exert the main long-term controls of appetite and energy metabolism); (d) body temperature; and (e) psychological factors.

Metabolic Rate and Heat Production (pp. 984–985)

5. Energy used by the body per hour is the metabolic rate.

6. Basal metabolic rate (BMR), reported in $kcal/m^2/h$, is the measurement obtained under basal conditions: the person is at comfortable room temperature, supine, relaxed, and in the postabsorptive state. BMR indicates energy needed to drive only the resting body processes.

7. Factors influencing metabolic rate include age, sex, size, body surface area, thyroxine levels, specific dynamic action of foods, and muscular activity.

Regulation of Body Temperature (pp. 985–989)

8. Body temperature reflects the balance between heat production and heat loss and is normally 37°C ($\pm$ 0.5°C), which is optimal for physiological activities.

9. At rest, most body heat is produced by the liver, heart, brain, kidneys, and endocrine organs. Activation of skeletal muscles causes dramatic increases in body heat production.

10. The body core (organs within the skull and the ventral body cavity) generally has the highest temperature. The shell (the skin) is the heat-exchange surface, and is usually coolest.

11. Blood serves as the major heat-exchange agent between the core and the shell. When skin capillaries are flushed with blood and the skin is warmer than the environment, heat is lost from the body. When blood is withdrawn to deep organs, heat loss from the shell is inhibited.

12. Heat-exchange mechanisms include radiation, conduction, convection, and evaporation. Evaporation, the conversion of water to water vapor, requires the absorption of heat. For each gram of water vaporized, about 0.6 kcal of heat is absorbed.

13. The hypothalamus acts as the body's thermostat. Its heat-promotion and heat-loss centers receive inputs from peripheral and central thermoreceptors, integrate these inputs, and initiate responses leading to heat loss or heat promotion.

14. Heat-promoting mechanisms include constriction of skin vasculature, increase in metabolic rate in infants (via release of norepinephrine), and shivering. If environmental cold is prolonged, the thyroid gland may be stimulated to release more thyroxine.

15. When heat must be removed from the body, dermal blood vessels are dilated, allowing heat loss through radiation, conduction, and convection. When greater heat loss is mandated (or the environmental temperature is so high that radiation and conduction are ineffective), sweating is initiated. Evaporation of perspiration is an efficient means of heat loss as long as the humidity is low.

16. Profuse sweating can lead to heat exhaustion, indicated by a rise in temperature, a drop in blood pressure, and collapse. When the body cannot rid itself of surplus heat, body temperature rises to the point where all thermoregulatory mechanisms become ineffective—a potentially lethal condition called heat stroke.

17. Fever is controlled hyperthermia, which follows thermostat resetting to higher levels by prostaglandins and initiation of heat-promotion mechanisms, evidenced by the chills. When the disease process is reversed, heat-loss mechanisms are initiated.

Developmental Aspects of Nutrition and Metabolism (pp. 989, 992)

1. Good nutrition is essential for normal fetal development and normal growth during childhood.

2. Inborn errors of metabolism include cystic fibrosis, PKU, glycogen storage disease, galactosemia, and many others. Hormonal disorders, such as lack of insulin or thyroid hormone, may also lead to metabolic abnormalities. Diabetes mellitus is the most significant metabolic disorder in middle-aged and older adults.

3. In old age, metabolic rate declines as enzyme and endocrine systems become less efficient and skeletal muscles atrophy. Reduced caloric needs make it difficult to obtain adequate nutrition without becoming overweight.

4. Elderly individuals ingest more medications than any other age group, and many of these drugs negatively affect their nutrition.

Review Questions

Multiple Choice/Matching

(Some questions have more than one correct answer. Select the best answer or answers from the choices given.)

1. Which of the following reactions would liberate the most energy? (a) complete oxidation of a molecule of sucrose to CO_2 and water, (b) conversion of a molecule of ADP to ATP, (c) respiration of a molecule of glucose to lactic acid, (d) conversion of a molecule of glucose to carbon dioxide and water.

2. The formation of glucose from glycogen is (a) gluconeogenesis, (b) glycogenesis, (c) glycogenolysis, (d) glycolysis.

3. The net gain of ATP from the complete metabolism (aerobic) of glucose is closest to (a) 2, (b) 30, (c) 38, (d) 4.

4. Which of the following *best* defines cellular respiration? (a) intake of carbon dioxide and output of oxygen by cells, (b) excretion of waste products, (c) inhalation of oxygen and exhalation of carbon dioxide, (d) oxidation of substances by which energy is released in usable form to the cells.

5. During aerobic respiration, electrons are passed down the electron transport chain and ____ is formed. (a) oxygen, (b) water, (c) glucose, (d) NADH + H$^+$.

6. Metabolic rate is relatively low in (a) youth, (b) physical exercise, (c) old age, (d) fever.

7. In a temperate climate under ordinary conditions, the greatest loss of body heat occurs through (a) radiation, (b) conduction, (c) evaporation, (d) none of the above.

8. Which of the following is *not* a function of the liver? (a) glycogenolysis and gluconeogenesis, (b) synthesis of cholesterol, (c) detoxification of alcohol and drugs, (d) synthesis of glucagon, (e) deamination of amino acids.

9. Amino acids are essential (and important) to the body for all the following *except* (a) production of some hormones, (b) production of antibodies, (c) formation of most structural materials, (d) as a source of quick energy.

10. A person has been on a hunger strike for seven days. Compared to normal, he has (a) increased release of fatty acids from adipose tissue, ketosis, and ketonuria, (b) elevated glucose concentration in the blood, (c) increased plasma insulin concentration, (d) increased glycogen synthetase (enzyme) activity in the liver.

11. Transamination is a chemical process by which (a) protein is synthesized, (b) an amine group is transferred from an amino acid to a keto acid, (c) an amine group is cleaved from the amino acid, (d) amino acids are broken down for energy.

12. Three days after removal of the pancreas from an animal, the researcher finds a persistent increase in (a) acetoacetic acid concentration in the blood, (b) urine volume, (c) blood glucose, (d) all of the above.

13. Hunger, appetite, obesity, and physical activity are interrelated. Thus, (a) hunger sensations arise *primarily* from the stimulation of receptors in the stomach and intestinal tract in response to the absence of food in these organs; (b) obesity, in most cases, is a result of the abnormally high enzymatic activity of the fat-synthesizing enzymes in adipose tissue; (c) in all cases of obesity, the energy content of the ingested food has exceeded the energy expenditure of the body; (d) in a normal individual, increasing blood glucose concentration increases hunger sensations.

14. Body temperature regulation is (a) influenced by temperature receptors in the skin, (b) influenced by the temperature of the blood perfusing the heat regulation centers of the brain, (c) subject to both neural and hormonal control, (d) all of the above.

15. Which of the following yields the greatest caloric value per gram? (a) fats, (b) proteins, (c) carbohydrates, (d) all are equal in caloric value.

Short Answer Essay Questions

16. What is cellular respiration? What is the common role of FAD and NAD$^+$ in cellular respiration?

17. Describe the site, major events, and outcomes of glycolysis.

18. Pyruvic acid is a product of glycolysis, but it is not the substance that enters the Krebs cycle. What is that substance, and what must occur if pyruvic acid is to be transformed into this molecule?

19. Define glycogenesis, glycogenolysis, gluconeogenesis, and lipogenesis. Which is (are) likely to be occurring (a) shortly after a carbohydrate-rich meal, (b) just before waking up in the morning?

20. What is the harmful result when excessive amounts of fats are burned for energy? Name two conditions that might lead to this result.

21. Make a flowchart that indicates the pivotal intermediates through which glucose can be converted to fat.

22. Distinguish between the role of HDLs and that of LDLs.

23. List some factors that influence plasma cholesterol levels. Also list the sources and fates of cholesterol in the body.

24. What is meant by "body energy balance," and what happens if the balance is not precise?

25. Explain the effect of the following on metabolic rate: thyroxine levels, eating, body surface area, muscular exercise, emotional stress, starvation.

26. Explain the terms "core" and "shell" relative to body temperature balance. What serves as the heat-transfer agent from one to the other?

27. Compare and contrast mechanisms of heat loss with mechanisms of heat promotion, and explain how these mechanisms determine body temperature.

Critical Thinking and Clinical Application Questions

1. Calculate the number of ATP molecules that can be harvested during the complete oxidation of an 18-carbon fatty acid. (Take a deep breath and think about it—you *can* do it.)

2. Every year dozens of elderly people are found dead in their unheated apartments and listed as victims of hypothermia. What is hypothermia, and how does it kill? Why are the elderly more susceptible to hypothermia than the young?

3. Frank Moro has been diagnosed as having severe atherosclerosis and high blood cholesterol levels. He is told that he is at risk for a stroke or a heart attack. First, what foods would you suggest that he avoid like the plague? What foods would you suggest he add or substitute? What activities would you recommend?

4. In the 1940s, some physicians prescribed low doses of a chemical called dinitrophenol (DNP) to help patients lose weight. This drug therapy was abandoned after a few patients died. DNP uncouples the chemiosmotic machinery. Explain how this causes weight loss.

5. While attempting to sail solo from Los Angeles to Tahiti, Simon encountered a storm that marooned him on an uninhabited island. He was able, using his ingenuity and a pocket knife, to obtain plenty of fish to eat, and roots were plentiful. However, the island was barren of fruits and soon his gums began to bleed and he started to develop several infections. Analyze his problem. (The tables might help.)

6. Gregor, a large beefy man, came home from the doctor's office and complained to his wife that his blood tests "were bad." He told her that the doctor said he would have to give up some of his steaks and butter. He went on to mourn the fact that he would have to start eating more cottage cheese and olive oil instead. What kind of problem was revealed by his "bad" blood tests? How should his wife respond to his choice of food substitutes and why? What foods should she suggest?

LOOKING FOR MORE STUDY HELP?
A wide variety of quiz questions, tutorials, and learning exercises are available online at the Anatomy & Physiology Place (www.anatomyandphysiology.com) and, if your instructor has provided you with a MyA&P Course ID number, in MyA&P (www.myaandp.com).

The Urinary System

Kidney Anatomy (pp. 998–1006)

1. Describe the gross anatomy of the kidney and its coverings.
2. Trace the blood supply through the kidney.
3. Describe the anatomy of a nephron.

Kidney Physiology: Mechanisms of Urine Formation (pp. 1007–1021)

4. List several kidney functions that help maintain body homeostasis.
5. Identify the nephron parts responsible for filtration, reabsorption, and secretion, and describe mechanisms underlying each of these functional processes.
6. Explain the role of aldosterone and of atrial natriuretic peptide in sodium and water balance.
7. Describe the mechanisms responsible for the medullary osmotic gradient.
8. Explain formation of dilute versus concentrated urine.

Urine (pp. 1021–1023)

9. Describe the normal physical and chemical properties of urine.
10. List several abnormal urine components, and name the condition characterized by the presence of detectable amounts of each.

Ureters (pp. 1023–1024)

11. Describe the general location, structure, and function of the ureters.

Urinary Bladder (pp. 1024–1026)

12. Describe the general location, structure, and function of the urinary bladder.

Urethra (p. 1026)

13. Describe the general location, structure, and function of the urethra.
14. Compare the course, length, and functions of the male urethra with those of the female.

Micturition (p. 1027)

15. Define micturition and describe its neural control.

Developmental Aspects of the Urinary System (pp. 1027–1030)

16. Trace the embryonic development of the urinary organs.
17. List several changes in urinary system anatomy and physiology that occur with age.

Every day the kidneys filter nearly 200 liters of fluid from the bloodstream, allowing toxins, metabolic wastes, and excess ions to leave the body in urine while returning needed substances to the blood. Much like a water purification plant that keeps a city's water drinkable and disposes of its wastes, the kidneys are usually unappreciated until they malfunction and body fluids become contaminated. Although the lungs and skin also participate in excretion, the kidneys are the major excretory organs.

As the kidneys perform these excretory functions, they also act as essential regulators of the volume and chemical makeup of the blood, maintaining the proper balance between water and salts and between acids and bases. Frankly, this would be tricky work for a chemical engineer, but the kidneys do it efficiently most of the time.

Other renal functions include

- Gluconeogenesis (see p. 966) during prolonged fasting.

- Producing the hormones renin and erythropoietin (see Chapter 16). *Renin* (re'nin; *ren* = kidney) acts as an enzyme to help regulate blood pressure and kidney function. *Erythropoietin* (ĕ-rith″ro-poi′ĕ-tin) stimulates red blood cell production.

- Metabolizing vitamin D to its active form (see Chapter 16).

Besides the urine-forming kidneys, the **urinary system** includes the *urinary bladder,* a temporary storage reservoir for urine, plus three tubelike organs—the paired *ureters* (u-re'terz) and the *urethra* (u-re'thrah), all three of which furnish transportation channels for urine (Figure 25.1).

Kidney Anatomy

Location and External Anatomy

The bean-shaped kidneys lie in a retroperitoneal position (between the dorsal body wall and the parietal peritoneum) in the *superior* lumbar region (Figure 25.2). Extending approximately from T_{12} to L_3, the kidneys receive some protection from the lower part of the rib cage (Figure 25.2b). The right kidney is crowded by the liver and lies slightly lower than the left. An adult's kidney has a mass of about 150 g (5 ounces) and its average dimensions are 12 cm long, 6 cm wide, and 3 cm thick—about the size of a large bar of soap. The lateral surface is convex. The medial surface is concave and has a vertical cleft called the **renal hilum** that leads into an internal space within the kidney called the *renal sinus.* The ureter, renal blood vessels, lymphatics, and nerves all join each kidney at the hilum and occupy the sinus. Atop each kidney is an *adrenal* (or *suprarenal*) *gland,* an endocrine gland that is functionally unrelated to the kidney.

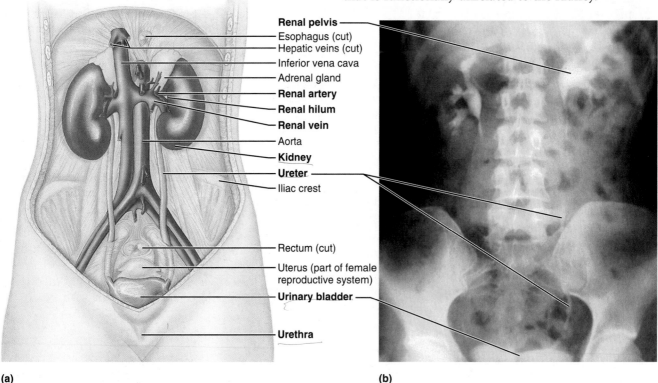

Renal pelvis
Esophagus (cut)
Hepatic veins (cut)
Inferior vena cava
Adrenal gland
Renal artery
Renal hilum
Renal vein
Aorta
Kidney
Ureter
Iliac crest
Rectum (cut)
Uterus (part of female reproductive system)
Urinary bladder
Urethra

(a)

(b)

FIGURE 25.1 **The urinary system.** Anterior view of the female urinary organs. (Most unrelated abdominal organs have been omitted.) **(a)** Diagrammatic view. **(b)** X ray of urinary organs after injection of contrast medium.

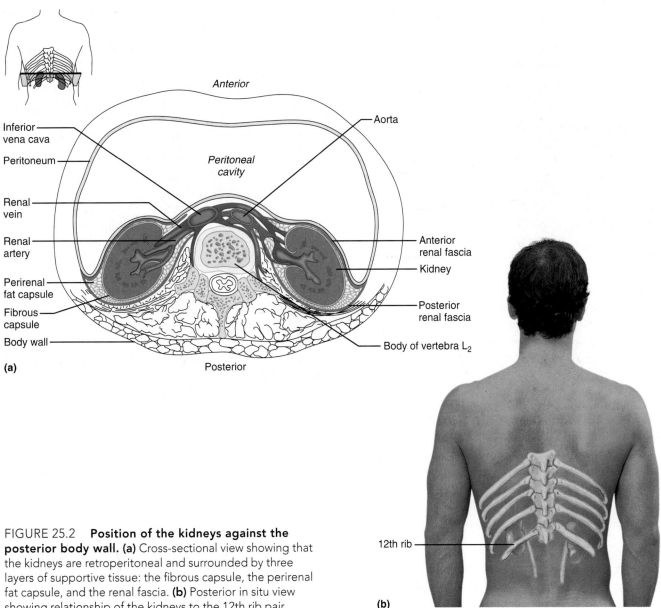

Inferior vena cava
Peritoneum
Renal vein
Renal artery
Perirenal fat capsule
Fibrous capsule
Body wall

Aorta
Anterior renal fascia
Kidney
Posterior renal fascia
Body of vertebra L₂

Anterior
Peritoneal cavity
Posterior

(a)

12th rib

(b)

FIGURE 25.2 **Position of the kidneys against the posterior body wall. (a)** Cross-sectional view showing that the kidneys are retroperitoneal and surrounded by three layers of supportive tissue: the fibrous capsule, the perirenal fat capsule, and the renal fascia. **(b)** Posterior in situ view showing relationship of the kidneys to the 12th rib pair.

Three layers of supportive tissue surround each kidney:

1. The **fibrous capsule,** a transparent capsule that prevents infections in surrounding regions from spreading to the kidneys

2. The **perirenal fat capsule,** a fatty mass that attaches the kidney to the posterior body wall and cushions it against blows

3. The **renal fascia,** an outer layer of dense fibrous connective tissue that anchors the kidney and the adrenal gland to surrounding structures

 HOMEOSTATIC IMBALANCE

The fatty encasement of the kidneys is important in holding the kidneys in their normal body position. If the amount of fatty tissue dwindles (as with extreme emaciation or rapid weight loss), one or both kidneys may drop to a lower position, an event called *renal ptosis* (to'sis; "a fall"). Renal ptosis may cause a ureter to become kinked, which creates problems because the urine, unable to drain, backs up into the kidney and exerts pressure on its tissue. Backup of urine from ureteral obstruction or other causes is called *hydronephrosis* (hi"dro-ně-fro'sis; "water in the kidney"). Hydronephrosis can severely damage the kidney, leading to necrosis (tissue death) and renal failure. ●

Internal Anatomy

A frontal section through a kidney reveals three distinct regions: *cortex, medulla,* and *pelvis* (Figures 25.3 and 25.4a). The most superficial region, the **renal cortex,** is light in color and has a granular appearance. Deep to the cortex is the darker, reddish-brown **renal medulla,** which exhibits cone-shaped tissue

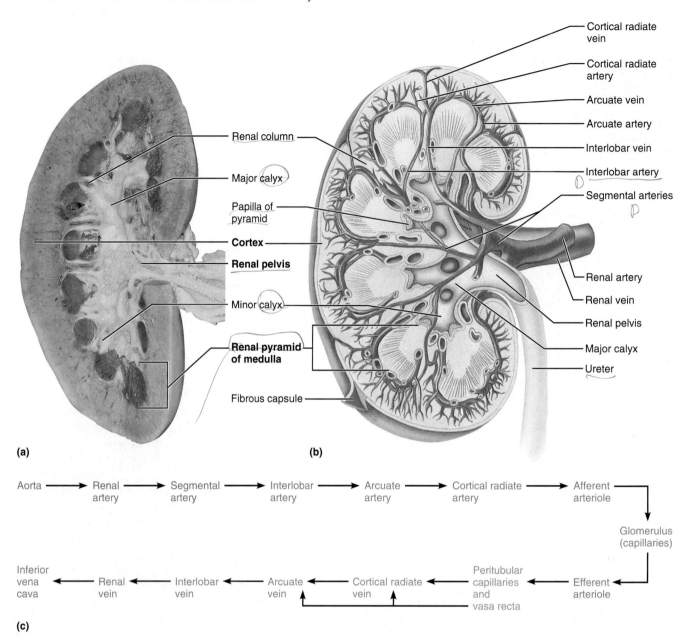

FIGURE 25.3   **Internal anatomy of the kidney. (a)** Photograph of a frontal section of a triple-injected kidney. (Arteries and veins are injected with red and blue latex respectively; pelvis and ureter are injected with yellow latex.) **(b)** Diagrammatic view of a frontally sectioned kidney, illustrating major blood vessels. **(c)** Summary of renal vasculature pathway.

masses called **medullary** or **renal pyramids.** The broad *base* of each pyramid faces toward the cortex, and its apex, or *papilla* ("nipple"), points internally. The pyramids appear striped because they are formed almost entirely of parallel bundles of microscopic urine-collecting tubules and capillaries. The **renal columns,** inward extensions of cortical tissue, separate the pyramids. Each pyramid and its surrounding cortical tissue constitutes one of approximately eight **lobes** of a kidney.

The **renal pelvis,** a funnel-shaped tube, is continuous with the ureter leaving the hilum. Branching

extensions of the pelvis form two or three **major calyces** (ka'lih-sĕz; singular: calyx), each of which subdivides to form several **minor calyces,** cup-shaped areas that enclose the papillae. The calyces collect urine, which drains continuously from the papillae, and empty it into the renal pelvis. The urine then flows through the renal pelvis and into the ureter, which moves it to the bladder to be stored. The walls of the calyces, pelvis, and ureter contain smooth muscle that contracts rhythmically to propel urine along its course by peristalsis.

HOMEOSTATIC IMBALANCE

Infection of the renal pelvis and calyces produces the condition called *pyelitis* (pi″ĕ-li′tis). Infections or inflammations that affect the entire kidney are *pyelonephritis* (pi″ĕ-lo-nĕ-fri′tis). Kidney infections in females are usually caused by fecal bacteria that spread from the anal region to the urinary tract. Less often they result from bloodborne bacteria (traveling from other infected sites) that lodge and multiply in the kidneys. In severe cases of pyelonephritis, the kidney swells, abscesses form, and the pelvis fills with pus. Untreated, the kidneys may be severely damaged, but antibiotic therapy can usually treat the infection successfully. ●

Blood and Nerve Supply

The kidneys continuously cleanse the blood and adjust its composition, and so it is not surprising that they have a rich blood supply. Under normal resting conditions, the large **renal arteries** deliver one-fourth of the total cardiac output (about 1200 ml) to the kidneys each minute. The renal arteries issue at right angles from the abdominal aorta; because the aorta lies to the left of the midline, the right renal artery is longer than the left. As it approaches a kidney, each renal artery divides into five **segmental arteries.** Within the renal sinus, each segmental artery branches further to form several **interlobar arteries.**

At the medulla-cortex junction, the interlobar arteries branch into the **arcuate arteries** (ar′ku-āt) that arch over the bases of the medullary pyramids. Small **cortical radiate arteries** radiate outward from the arcuate arteries to supply the cortical tissue (see Figure 25.3a). More than 90% of the blood entering the kidney perfuses the renal cortex.

Veins pretty much trace the pathway of the arterial supply in reverse. Blood leaving the renal cortex drains sequentially into the **cortical radiate, arcuate, interlobar,** and finally **renal veins.** (There are no segmental veins.) The renal veins issue from the kidneys and empty into the inferior vena cava. Because the inferior vena cava lies to the right of the vertebral column, the left renal vein is about twice as long as the right.

The **renal plexus,** a variable network of autonomic nerve fibers and ganglia, provides the nerve supply of the kidney and its ureter. An offshoot of the celiac plexus, the renal plexus is largely supplied by sympathetic fibers from the least thoracic and first lumbar splanchnic nerves, which course along with the renal artery to reach the kidney. These sympathetic vasomotor fibers regulate renal blood flow by adjusting the diameter of renal arterioles and also influence the urine-forming role of the nephrons.

Nephrons

Nephrons (nef′ronz) are the structural and functional units of the kidneys. Each kidney contains over 1 million of these tiny blood-processing units, which carry out the processes that form urine (Figure 25.4b). In addition, there are thousands of *collecting ducts*, each of which collects fluid from several nephrons and conveys it to the renal pelvis.

Each **nephron** consists of a **glomerulus** (glomer′u-lus; *glom* = ball of yarn), which is a tuft of capillaries, and a **renal tubule.** The cup-shaped end of the renal tubule, the **glomerular capsule** (or **Bowman's capsule**) is blind and completely surrounds the glomerulus (much as a well-worn baseball glove encloses a ball). Collectively, the glomerular capsule and the enclosed glomerulus are called the **renal corpuscle.** The endothelium of the glomerular capillaries is *fenestrated* (penetrated by many pores), which makes them exceptionally porous. This allows large amounts of solute-rich, virtually protein-free fluid to pass from the blood into the glomerular capsule. This plasma-derived fluid or **filtrate** is the raw material that the renal tubules process to form urine.

The external *parietal layer* of the glomerular capsule (Figures 25.4b, 25.6, and 25.7) is simple squamous epithelium. This layer simply contributes to the capsule structure and plays no part in forming filtrate. The *visceral layer*, which clings to the glomerular capillaries, consists of highly modified, branching epithelial cells called **podocytes** (pod′o-sīts; "foot cells"). The octopus-like podocytes terminate in **foot processes,** which intertwine as they cling to the basement membrane of the glomerulus. The clefts or openings between the foot processes are called **filtration slits.** Through these slits, filtrate enters the **capsular space** inside the glomerular capsule.

The remainder of the renal tubule is about 3 cm (1.2 inches) long and has three major parts. It leaves the glomerular capsule as the elaborately coiled **proximal convoluted tubule (PCT),** makes a hairpin loop called the **loop of Henle** (also called **Henle's loop**), and then winds and twists again as the **distal convoluted tubule (DCT)** before emptying into a collecting duct. The terms *proximal* and *distal* indicate relationship of the convoluted tubules to the renal corpuscle—filtrate from the renal corpuscle passes through the PCT first and then the DCT, which is thus "further away" from the renal corpuscle. The meandering nature of the renal tubule increases its length and enhances its filtrate processing capabilities.

The **collecting ducts,** each of which receives filtrate from many nephrons, run through the medullary pyramids and give them their striped appearance. As the collecting ducts approach the renal pelvis, they fuse together and deliver urine into the minor calyces via papillae of the pyramids.

25

FIGURE 25.4 Location and structure of nephrons. (a) Diagram showing the orientation of nephrons; such a segment contains more than 100,000 nephrons. **(b)** Schematic view of a nephron depicting the structural characteristics of epithelial cells forming its various regions. **(c)** Photomicrograph of renal cortical tissue. Notice the renal corpuscles and the sections through the various tubules. In the proximal convoluted tubules, the lumens appear "fuzzy" because they are filled with the long microvilli of the epithelial cells that form the tubule walls. In the distal tubules, by contrast, the lumens are clear (300×).

Throughout its length, the renal tubule consists of a single layer of polar epithelial cells on a basement membrane, but each of its regions has a unique cellular anatomy that reflects its role in processing filtrate. The walls of the PCT are formed by cuboidal epithelial cells with large mitochondria; their luminal (exposed) surfaces bear dense microvilli (Figure 25.4b and c). Just as in the intestine, this *brush border* dramatically increases the surface area and capacity for reabsorbing water and solutes from the filtrate and secreting substances into it.

The U-shaped *loop of Henle* has *descending* and *ascending limbs.* The proximal part of the descending limb is continuous with the proximal tubule and its cells are similar. The rest of the descending limb, called the **thin segment,** is a simple squamous epithelium freely permeable to water. The epithelium becomes cuboidal or even low columnar in the ascending part of the loop of Henle, which therefore becomes the **thick segment.** In some nephrons, the thin segment is found only in the descending limb. In others, it extends into the ascending limb as well.

The epithelial cells of the DCT, like those of the PCT, are cuboidal and confined to the cortex, but they are thinner and almost entirely lack microvilli. The transition between the DCT and the collecting duct is marked by the appearance of a heterogeneous collection of cells. The two cell types seen in the collecting ducts are *intercalated cells,* cuboidal cells with abundant microvilli, and the more numerous *principal cells,* which have sparse, short microvilli. The two varieties (type A and B) of intercalated cells play a major role in maintaining the acid-base balance of the blood. The principal cells help maintain the body's water and Na$^+$ balance.

Cortical nephrons represent 85% of the nephrons in the kidneys. Except for small parts of their loops of Henle that dip into the outer medulla, they are located entirely in the cortex. The remaining **juxtamedullary nephrons** (juks"tah-mĕ'dul-ah-re) originate close to (*juxta* = near to) the cortex-medulla junction, and they play an important role in the kidneys' ability to produce concentrated urine. Their loops of Henle deeply invade the medulla, and their thin segments are much more extensive than those of cortical nephrons (Figure 25.5).

Nephron Capillary Beds

Every nephron is closely associated with two capillary beds: the *glomerulus* and the *peritubular capillaries* (Figure 25.5). The glomerulus, in which the capillaries run in parallel, is specialized for filtration. It differs from all other capillary beds in the body in that it is both fed and drained by arterioles—the **afferent arteriole** and the **efferent arteriole,** respectively. The afferent arterioles arise from the *cortical radiate arteries* that run through the renal cortex. Because (1) arterioles are high-resistance vessels and (2) the afferent arteriole has a larger diameter than the efferent, the blood pressure in the glomerulus is extraordinarily high for a capillary bed and easily forces fluid and solutes out of the blood into the glomerular capsule. Most of this filtrate (99%) is reabsorbed by the renal tubule cells and returned to the blood in the peritubular capillary beds.

The **peritubular capillaries** arise from the efferent arterioles draining the glomeruli. These capillaries cling closely to adjacent renal tubules and empty into nearby venules. They are low-pressure, porous capillaries that readily absorb solutes and water from the tubule cells as these substances are reclaimed from the filtrate.

Notice that the efferent arterioles serving the juxtamedullary nephrons tend *not* to break up into peritubular capillaries. Instead they form bundles of long straight vessels called **vasa recta** (va'sah rek'tah; "straight vessels") that extend deep into the medulla paralleling the longest loops of Henle (Figure 25.5a). The thin-walled vasa recta play an important role in forming concentrated urine, as described shortly.

In summary, the microvasculature of the nephrons consists of two capillary beds separated by intervening efferent arterioles. The first capillary bed (glomerulus) produces the filtrate. The second (peritubular capillaries) reclaims most of that filtrate.

Vascular Resistance in the Microcirculation

Blood flowing through the renal circulation encounters high resistance, first in the afferent and then in the efferent arterioles. As a result, renal blood pressure declines from approximately 95 mm Hg in the renal arteries to 8 mm Hg or less in the renal veins. The resistance of the afferent arterioles protects the glomeruli from large fluctuations in systemic blood pressure. Resistance in the efferent arterioles reinforces the high glomerular pressure and reduces the hydrostatic pressure in the peritubular capillaries.

Juxtaglomerular Apparatus

Each nephron has a region called a **juxtaglomerular apparatus (JGA)** (juks"tah-glo-mer'u-lar), where the most distal portion of the ascending limb of the loop of Henle lies against the afferent arteriole feeding the glomerulus (and sometimes the efferent arteriole) (Figure 25.6). Both the ascending limb and the afferent arteriole are modified at the point of contact.

In the arteriole walls are the **granular cells** [also called **juxtaglomerular (JG) cells**]—enlarged, smooth muscle cells with prominent secretory granules containing renin. Granular cells act as mechanoreceptors that sense the blood pressure in the afferent

Renal corpuscle
- Glomerular capillaries (glomerulus) *(blue purple cup.)*
- Glomerular (Bowman's) capsule

inside glomerulus

Proximal convoluted tubule *twisted*

Cortex *(light green color)*
Medulla

Ureter
Kidney
Renal pelvis

Peritubular capillaries

Ascending or thick limb of the loop of Henle

Arcuate vein
Arcuate artery
Loop of Henle

Descending or thin limb of loop of Henle

Cortical nephron

model 9/23

② Efferent arteriole *out*

Cortical radiate vein
Cortical radiate artery
Afferent arteriole
Collecting duct
Distal convoluted tubule *dark green*
Afferent arteriole

Efferent arteriole

Cortico-medullary junction

Vasa recta

Juxtamedullary nephron

(a)

Glomeruli

Afferent arteriole

Efferent arteriole

Peritubular capillary bed

(b)

FIGURE 25.5 **Comparison of cortical and juxtamedullary nephron anatomy. (a)** Peritubular capillaries arise from efferent arterioles draining cortical nephrons (as shown on the left). The vasa recta dipping deep into the medulla to surround the long loops of Henle of the juxtamedullary nephrons arise from efferent arterioles of the juxtamedullary nephrons (as shown on the right). Arrows indicate direction of blood flow. **(b)** Scanning electron micrograph of a cast of blood vessels associated with nephrons (90×).

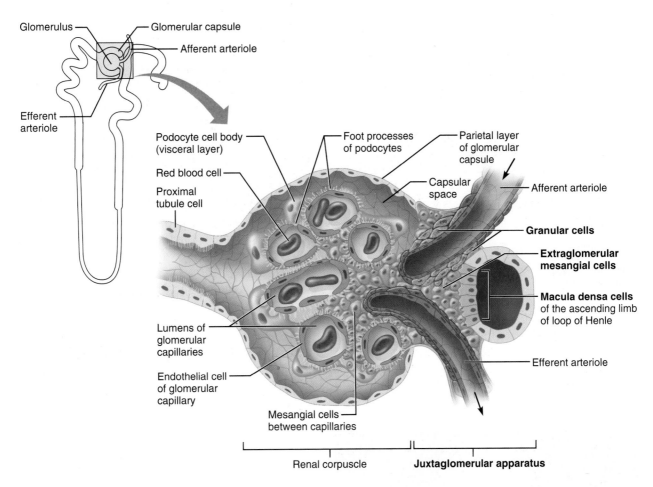

FIGURE 25.6 **Juxtaglomerular apparatus (JGA) of a nephron.** The JGA is made up of the granular cells of the arterioles, the macula densa cells of the thick ascending limb of the loop of Henle, and the extraglomerular mesangial cells. Other (glomerular) mesangial cells surround the glomerular capillaries.

arteriole. The **macula densa** (mak'u-lah den'sah; "dense spot") is a group of tall, closely packed cells of the ascending limb of the loop of Henle that lies adjacent to the granular cells (Figure 25.6). The macula densa cells are chemoreceptors that respond to changes in the NaCl content of the filtrate. These two cell populations play important roles in regulating the rate of filtrate formation and systemic blood pressure, as described shortly. *Extraglomerular mesangial cells* are also part of the JGA, but their function remains unclear.

The Filtration Membrane

The **filtration membrane** lies between the blood and the interior of the glomerular capsule (Figure 25.7). It is a porous membrane that allows free passage of water and solutes smaller than plasma proteins. Its three layers are (1) the fenestrated endothelium of the glomerular capillaries, (2) the visceral membrane of the glomerular capsule, made of podocytes, and (3) the intervening basement membrane composed of the fused basal laminae of the other layers.

The fenestrations (capillary pores) allow passage of all plasma components but not blood cells. The basement membrane restricts all but the smallest proteins while permitting most other solutes to pass. The structural makeup of the gel-like basement membrane also confers electrical selectivity on the filtration process. Most of the proteins in the membrane are negatively charged glycoproteins that repel other macromolecular anions and hinder their passage into the tubule. Because most plasma proteins also bear a net negative charge, this electrical repulsion reinforces the plasma protein blockage imposed by molecular size. Macromolecules that do manage to make it through the basement membrane may still be blocked by thin membranes *(slit diaphragms)* that extend across the filtration slits. Macromolecules that get "hung up" in the filtration membrane are engulfed and degraded by mesangial cells within the glomerulus. These *glomerular mesangial cells* can also contract, changing the total surface area of the capillaries available for filtration.

(a)

FIGURE 25.7 **The filtration membrane.** The filtration membrane is composed of three layers: the fenestrated endothelium of the glomerular capillaries, the podocyte-containing visceral layer of the glomerular capsule, and the intervening basement membrane. **(a)** Diagrammatic view of the relationship of the visceral layer of the glomerular capsule to the glomerular capillaries. The visceral epithelium is drawn incompletely to show the fenestrations in the underlying capillary wall. **(b)** Scanning electron micrograph of the visceral layer. Filtration slits between the podocyte foot processes are evident (3000×). **(c)** Diagrammatic view of a section through the filtration membrane showing all three structural elements.

Kidney Physiology: Mechanisms of Urine Formation

Of the approximately 1200 ml of blood that passes through the glomeruli each minute, some 650 ml is plasma, and about one-fifth of this (120–125 ml) is forced into the renal tubules. This is equivalent to filtering out your entire plasma volume more than 60 times each day! Considering the magnitude of their task, it is not surprising that the kidneys (which account for only 1% of body weight) consume 20–25% of all oxygen used by the body at rest.

Filtrate and urine are quite different. Filtrate contains everything found in blood plasma except proteins, but by the time filtrate flows into the collecting ducts, it has lost most of its water, nutrients, and ions. What remains, now called **urine**, contains mostly metabolic wastes and unneeded substances. The kidneys process about 180 L (47 gallons!) of blood-derived fluid daily. Of this amount, less than 1% (1.5 L) typically leaves the body as urine; the rest returns to the circulation.

Urine formation and the adjustment of blood composition involve three major processes: *glomerular filtration* by the glomeruli, and *tubular reabsorption* and *tubular secretion* in the renal tubules (Figure 25.8). In addition, the collecting ducts work in concert with the nephrons to concentrate or dilute the urine.

Step 1: Glomerular Filtration

Glomerular filtration is a passive process in which hydrostatic pressure forces fluids and solutes through a membrane (see Chapters 3 and 19). Because filtrate formation does not consume metabolic energy, the glomeruli can be viewed as simple mechanical filters. The glomerulus is a much more efficient filter than are other capillary beds because (1) its *filtration membrane* (Figure 25.7) has a large surface area and is thousands of times more permeable to water and solutes, and (2) glomerular blood pressure is much higher than that in other capillary beds (approximately 55 mm Hg as opposed to 18 mm Hg or less), resulting in a much higher *net filtration pressure*. As a result of these differences, the kidneys produce about 180 L of filtrate daily, in contrast to the 3 to 4 L formed daily by all other capillary beds of the body combined.

Molecules smaller than 3 nm in diameter—such as water, glucose, amino acids, and nitrogenous wastes—pass freely from the blood into the glomerular capsule. Hence, these substances usually show similar concentrations in the blood and the glomerular filtrate. Larger molecules pass with greater difficulty, and those larger than 5 nm are generally barred from entering the tubule. Keeping the plasma proteins *in* the capillaries maintains the colloid

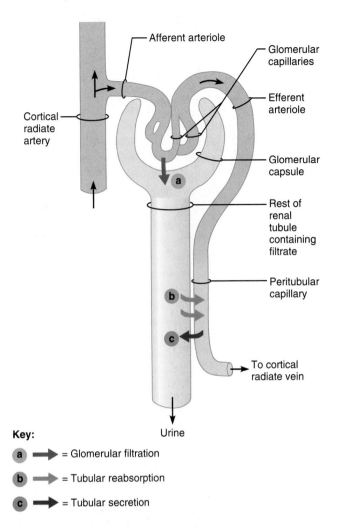

Key:
a ⟶ = Glomerular filtration
b ⟶ = Tubular reabsorption
c ⟶ = Tubular secretion

FIGURE 25.8   **The kidney depicted schematically as a single, uncoiled nephron.** A kidney actually has millions of nephrons acting in parallel. The three major mechanisms by which the kidneys adjust plasma composition are **(a)** glomerular filtration, **(b)** tubular reabsorption, and **(c)** tubular secretion.

osmotic (oncotic) pressure of the glomerular blood, preventing the loss of all its water to the renal tubules. The presence of proteins or blood cells in the urine usually indicates a problem with the filtration membrane.

Net Filtration Pressure

The **net filtration pressure (NFP)**, responsible for filtrate formation, involves forces acting at the glomerular bed (Figure 25.9). **Glomerular hydrostatic pressure (HP_g)** (essentially glomerular blood pressure) is the chief force pushing water and solutes out of the blood and across the filtration membrane. Although theoretically the colloid osmotic pressure in the intracapsular space of the glomerular capsule "pulls" the filtrate into the tubule, this pressure is essentially zero because virtually no proteins enter

Q How would liver disease affect the process shown here?

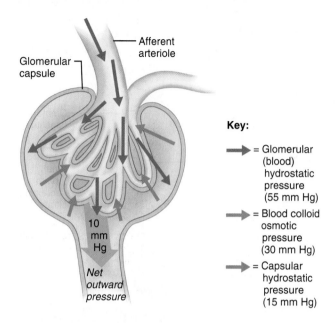

FIGURE 25.9 **Forces determining glomerular filtration and filtration pressure.** The glomerular hydrostatic (blood) pressure is the major factor forcing fluids and solutes out of the blood. This pressure is opposed by the colloid osmotic pressure of the blood and the hydrostatic pressure in the glomerular capsule. The pressure values cited in the diagram are approximate.

the capsule. The HP_g is opposed by two forces that inhibit fluid loss from glomerular capillaries. These filtration-opposing forces are (1) **colloid osmotic (oncotic) pressure of glomerular blood (OP_g)** and (2) **capsular hydrostatic pressure (HP_c)** exerted by fluids in the glomerular capsule. Thus, using the values shown in Figure 25.9, the NFP responsible for forming renal filtrate from plasma is 10 mm Hg:

$$NFP = HP_g - (OP_g + HP_c)$$

$$= 55 \text{ mm Hg} - (30 \text{ mm Hg} + 15 \text{ mm Hg})$$

$$= 10 \text{ mm Hg}$$

Glomerular Filtration Rate

The **glomerular filtration rate** or **GFR** is the volume of filtrate formed each minute by the combined activity of all 2 million glomeruli of the kidneys. Factors governing filtration rate at the capillary beds are (1) total surface area available for filtration, (2) filtration membrane permeability, and (3) NFP. In adults the normal GFR in both kidneys is 120–125 ml/min.

A With liver disease you probably wouldn't have a normal supply of plasma proteins. Hence, more filtrate would be formed due to lower osmotic pressure in the blood.

Because glomerular capillaries are exceptionally permeable and have a huge surface area (collectively equal to the surface area of the skin), huge amounts of filtrate can be produced even with the usual modest NFP of 10 mm Hg. The opposite side of this "coin" is that a drop in glomerular pressure of only 18% stops filtration altogether.

Because the GFR is *directly proportional* to the NFP, any change in any of the pressures acting at the filtration membrane (Figure 25.9) changes both the NFP and the GFR. In the absence of regulation, an increase in arterial (and glomerular) blood pressure in the kidneys increases the GFR. As we shall see in the next section however, GFR is tightly regulated.

Regulation of Glomerular Filtration

GFR is regulated by both intrinsic and extrinsic controls. These two types of controls serve two different (and sometimes opposing) needs. The kidneys need a relatively constant GFR in order to do their job and maintain extracellular homeostasis. On the other hand, the body as a whole needs a constant blood pressure, and therefore a constant blood volume. Intrinsic controls *(renal autoregulation)* act locally within the kidney to maintain GFR, while extrinsic controls by the nervous and endocrine systems maintain blood pressure. In extreme changes of blood pressure (mean arterial pressure less than 80 or greater than 180 mm Hg), extrinsic controls take precedence over intrinsic controls. Both types of control are examined next.

Intrinsic Controls: Renal Autoregulation By adjusting its own resistance to blood flow, a process called **renal autoregulation**, the kidney can maintain a nearly constant GFR despite fluctuations in systemic arterial blood pressure. Renal autoregulation entails two types of controls: (1) a *myogenic mechanism* and (2) a *tubuloglomerular feedback mechanism* (Figure 25.10).

1. **Myogenic mechanism.** The **myogenic mechanism** (mi″o-jen′ik) reflects the tendency of vascular smooth muscle to contract when stretched. Increasing systemic blood pressure causes the afferent arterioles to constrict, which restricts blood flow into the glomerulus and prevents glomerular blood pressure from rising to damaging levels. Declining systemic blood pressure causes dilation of afferent arterioles and raises glomerular hydrostatic pressure. Both responses help maintain a normal GFR.

2. **Tubuloglomerular feedback mechanism.** Autoregulation by the flow-dependent **tubuloglomerular feedback mechanism** is "directed" by the *macula densa cells* of the *juxtaglomerular apparatus* (see Figure 25.6). These cells, located in the walls of the ascending limb of Henle's loop, respond to filtrate

Q *Why are the myogenic and tubuloglomerular mechanisms called autoregulatory mechanisms?*

Key:

(+) = Stimulation

(−) = Inhibition

↑ = Increased

↓ = Decreased

| Myogenic mechanism of autoregulation | Tubuloglomerular mechanism of autoregulation | Hormonal (renin-angiotensin) mechanism | Neural controls |

↓ **Systemic blood pressure**

Myogenic mechanism of autoregulation
- ↓ Blood pressure in afferent arterioles
- ↓ Stretch of smooth muscle in walls of afferent arterioles
- Vasodilation of afferent arterioles
- ↑ **GFR**

Tubuloglomerular mechanism of autoregulation
- ↓ GFR
- ↓ Filtrate flow and ↓ NaCl in ascending limb of Henle's loop
- ⊖ Targets
- Macula densa cells of JG apparatus of kidney
- Release of ⊖ vasoactive chemical inhibited
- Vasodilation of afferent arterioles

(+)

Hormonal (renin-angiotensin) mechanism
- Granular cells of juxtaglomerular apparatus of kidney
- ⊖ Release
- Renin
- ⊖ Catalyzes cascade resulting in conversion
- Angiotensinogen ⊖ Angiotensin II
- (+) Adrenal cortex
  - ⊖ Releases
  - Aldosterone
  - ⊖ Targets
  - Kidney tubules
  - ↑ Na+ reabsorption; water follows
  - ↑ Blood volume
- (+) Systemic arterioles
  - Vasoconstriction; ↑ peripheral resistance
- ↑ **Systemic blood pressure**

Neural controls
- (−) Baroreceptors in blood vessels of systemic circulation
- (+) Sympathetic nervous system
- (+) (to Granular cells)
- (+) (to Systemic arterioles)

Intrinsic mechanisms maintain GFR despite changes in blood pressure (between 80 and 180 mm Hg mean arterial pressure).

Extrinsic mechanisms maintain systemic blood pressure, ultimately maintaining GFR.

FIGURE 25.10 **Physiological mechanisms regulating glomerular filtration rate (GFR) in the kidneys.** (Note that while the extrinsic controls are aimed at maintaining blood pressure, they also maintain GFR since blood pressure drives filtration in the kidneys.)

A *Because they are initiated by and within the kidney and allow the kidney to control its own (auto) rate of blood flow and GFR.*

25

NaCl concentration (which varies directly with filtrate flow rate). When GFR increases, there is insufficient time for reabsorption and the concentration of NaCl in the filtrate remains high. This causes the macula densa cells to release a vasoconstrictor chemical (probably ATP) that causes intense constriction of the afferent arteriole. This hinders blood flow into the glomerulus, which decreases the NFP and GFR, allowing more time for filtrate processing (NaCl absorption). On the other hand, when the macula densa cells are exposed to slowly flowing filtrate with its low NaCl concentration (Figure 25.10), ATP release is inhibited, causing vasodilation of the afferent arterioles. This allows more blood to flow into the glomerulus, thus increasing the NFP and GFR.

Autoregulatory mechanisms maintain a relatively constant blood flow through the kidneys over an arterial pressure range from about 80 to 180 mm Hg. Consequently, large changes in water and solute excretion are prevented. However, the intrinsic controls cannot handle extremely low systemic blood pressure, such as might result from serious hemorrhage (*hypovolemic shock*). Once the mean systemic blood pressure drops below 80 mm Hg, autoregulation ceases.

Extrinsic Controls: Neural and Hormonal Mechanisms

The purpose of the extrinsic controls regulating the GFR is to maintain systemic blood pressure—sometimes to the detriment of the kidneys.

1. Sympathetic nervous system controls. Neural renal controls serve the needs of the body as a whole. When the volume of the extracellular fluid is normal and the sympathetic nervous system is at rest, the renal blood vessels are maximally dilated and renal autoregulation mechanisms prevail. However, during extreme stress or emergency when it is necessary to shunt blood to vital organs, neural controls may overcome renal autoregulatory mechanisms. Norepinephrine released by sympathetic nerve fibers (and epinephrine released by the adrenal medulla) acts on alpha-adrenergic receptors on vascular smooth muscle, strongly constricting afferent arterioles, thereby inhibiting filtrate formation. This, in turn, indirectly trips the renin-angiotensin mechanism by stimulating the macula densa cells. The sympathetic nervous system also directly stimulates the granular cells to release renin, as discussed next.

2. Renin-angiotensin mechanism. The **renin-angiotensin mechanism** is triggered when various stimuli cause the granular cells to release the hormone **renin**. Renin acts enzymatically on **angiotensinogen**, a plasma globulin made by the liver, converting it to **angiotensin I**. This, in turn, is converted to **angiotensin II** by **angiotensin converting enzyme (ACE)** associated with the capillary endothelium in various body tissues, particularly the lungs.

Angiotensin II acts in five ways to stabilize systemic blood pressure and extracellular fluid volume. (1) As a potent vasoconstrictor, it activates smooth muscle of arterioles throughout the body, raising mean arterial blood pressure. (2) Angiotensin II stimulates reabsorption of sodium, both directly by acting on renal tubules and indirectly by triggering the release of aldosterone from the adrenal cortex. Because water follows sodium osmotically, blood volume and blood pressure rise (Figure 25.10). (3) Angiotensin II stimulates the hypothalamus to release antidiuretic hormone and activates the hypothalamic thirst center, both of which increase blood volume (see Chapter 26). (4) Angiotensin II also increases fluid reabsorption by decreasing peritubular capillary hydrostatic pressure. This pressure drop occurs because the efferent arterioles constrict, and the downstream drop in hydrostatic pressure allows more fluid to move back into the peritubular capillary bed. (5) Finally, angiotensin II targets the glomerular mesangial cells, causing them to contract and reduce the GFR by decreasing the total surface area of glomerular capillaries available for filtration. While this seems like a daunting list at first, it will help if you remember that all of the effects of angiotensin II are aimed at restoring blood volume and blood pressure. Of angiotensin II's many effects, the first two are the most important.

Several factors acting independently or collectively can trigger renin release.

- Reduced stretch of the granular cells. A drop in mean systemic blood pressure below 80 mm Hg (as might be due to hemorrhage, dehydration, etc.) reduces the stretch of the granular cells and stimulates them to release more renin.

- Stimulation of the granular cells by input from activated macula densa cells. When macula densa cells sense low NaCl concentration (slowly moving filtrate), they signal the granular cells to release renin. This signal may be *decreased* release of ATP (also thought to be the tubuloglomerular feedback messenger), *increased* release of the prostaglandin PGE_2, or both.

- Direct stimulation of granular cells via β_1-adrenergic receptors by renal sympathetic nerves.

Other Factors Affecting GFR

Renal cells produce a battery of chemicals, many of which act as paracrines (local signaling molecules).

1. Prostaglandin E_2 (PGE_2): The vasodilatory paracrine PGE_2, in addition to its role discussed above, counteracts vasoconstriction by norepinephrine and angiotensin II within the kidney. The adaptive value of these opposing actions is to prevent renal damage while responding to body demands to increase peripheral resistance.

FIGURE 25.11 **Transcellular and paracellular routes of tubular reabsorption.** Water and solutes move from inside the tubular lumen into the peritubular capillaries via either transcellular or paracellular routes. The transcellular route consists of four steps: ① transport across the luminal membrane, ② diffusion through the cytosol, ③ transport across the basolateral membrane, and ④ movement through the interstitial fluid and into the capillary. Transcellular transport often involves the lateral intercellular spaces because ATP-dependent pumps located on the basolateral membrane pump ions into these spaces. Water and solutes following the paracellular route move through leaky tight junctions, particularly in the PCT. (Transporters, ion channels, and aquaporins are not depicted.)

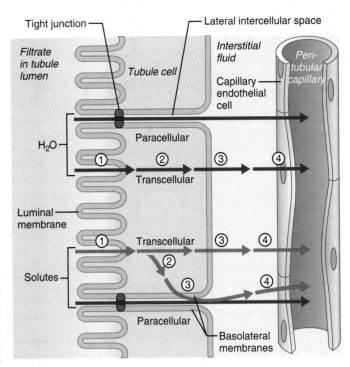

Key:

➡ Active transport ➡ Passive transport

2. Intrarenal angiotensin II: Although we usually think of angiotensin II as a hormone, the kidney has recently been shown to make its own, locally acting, angiotensin II that reinforces the effects of hormonal angiotensin II. It also dampens the resulting renal vasoconstriction by causing PGE_2 release.

3. Adenosine: Adenosine can be released as such or produced extracellularly from ATP released by macula densa cells. Although it functions as a vasodilator systemically, adenosine constricts the renal vasculature.

HOMEOSTATIC IMBALANCE

Abnormally low urinary output (less than 50 ml/day), called *anuria* (ah-nu're-ah), may indicate that glomerular blood pressure is too low to cause filtration. However, renal failure and anuria can result from situations in which the nephrons cease to function for a variety of other reasons, including acute nephritis, transfusion reactions, and crush injuries. ●

Step 2: Tubular Reabsorption

Our total plasma volume filters into the renal tubules about every 22 minutes, so all our plasma would be drained away as urine in less than 30 minutes were it not for the fact that most of the tubule contents are quickly reclaimed and returned to the blood. This reclamation process, called **tubular reabsorption**, is a selective *transepithelial process* that begins as soon as the filtrate enters the proximal tubules. To reach the blood, transported substances move through *three* barriers—the *luminal* and *basolateral membranes* of the tubule cells and the *endothelium* of the peritubular capillaries. Because the tubule cells are connected by tight junctions, movement of substances between the cells is limited, although some important ions (Ca^{2+}, Mg^{2+}, K^+, and some Na^+) may use the *paracellular pathway* (Figure 25.11).

Given healthy kidneys, virtually all organic nutrients such as glucose and amino acids are completely reabsorbed to maintain or restore normal plasma concentrations. On the other hand, the reabsorption of water and many ions is continuously regulated and adjusted in response to hormonal signals. Depending on the substances transported, the reabsorption process may be *passive* (no ATP required) or *active* (at least one of its steps is driven by ATP directly or indirectly).

Sodium Reabsorption

Sodium ions are the single most abundant cation in the filtrate, and about 80% of the energy used for active transport is devoted to their reabsorption. Sodium reabsorption is almost always active and via the transcellular (transepithelial) route. In general, two basic processes that promote active Na^+ reabsorption occur in each tubule segment: Na^+ (1) enters the tubule cells from the filtrate at the luminal membrane and then (2) is actively transported out of the tubule cell by a Na^+-K^+ ATPase pump present in the basolateral membrane (Figure 25.12). From there, Na^+ is swept along by the bulk flow of water into adjacent peritubular capillaries. This bulk flow of water and solutes into the peritubular capillaries is rapid because of that blood's low hydrostatic pressure and high osmotic pressure (remember, most proteins are not filtered out of the blood into the tubule).

Q *How are primary and secondary active transport processes (both shown here) different?*

Key:

→ = Primary active transport

- - → = Secondary active transport

→ = Passive transport (diffusion)

● = Protein carrier

╫ = Ion channel

FIGURE 25.12   Reabsorption by PCT cells. "Downhill" Na⁺ entry at the luminal surface is usually coupled to the transport of another solute (a cotransport process referred to as secondary active transport). After Na⁺ enters, it diffuses to the basolateral membrane, where it is pumped into the interstitial space by a sodium pump (a Na⁺-K⁺ ATPase). From there it diffuses into the peritubular capillary. Active pumping of Na⁺ at the basolateral membrane creates concentration and osmotic gradients that drive reabsorption of water by osmosis, of anions and fat-soluble substances by diffusion, and of organic nutrients and selected cations by secondary active transport (symport with Na⁺ at the luminal membrane). Though not illustrated here, most organic nutrients reabsorbed in the PCT move through the basolateral membrane by facilitated diffusion. (Luminal microvilli not illustrated.)

Active pumping of Na⁺ from the tubule cells results in a strong electrochemical gradient that favors its passive entry at the luminal face via cotransport (symport or antiport) carriers or via facilitated diffusion through channels. This occurs because (1) the pump maintains the intracellular Na⁺ concentration at low levels, and (2) the K⁺ pumped into the tubule cells almost immediately diffuses out into the interstitial fluid via leakage channels, leaving the interior of the tubule cell with a net negative charge.

Because each tubule segment plays a slightly different role in reabsorption, the precise mechanism by which Na⁺ is reabsorbed at the luminal membrane varies. However, the net effect is that Na⁺ reabsorption by primary active transport provides the energy and the means for reabsorbing most other solutes.

Reabsorption of Water, Ions, and Nutrients

In **passive tubular reabsorption**, which encompasses diffusion, facilitated diffusion, and osmosis, substances move along their electrochemical gradient without the use of ATP. As they move through the tubule cells into the peritubular capillary blood, Na⁺ ions establish an electrical gradient that favors passive reabsorption of anions (Cl⁻ and HCO₃⁻ for example) to restore electrical neutrality in the filtrate and plasma.

As we have seen, Na⁺ movement also establishes a strong osmotic gradient, and water moves by osmosis into the peritubular capillaries, a process aided by water-filled channels called *aquaporins*. In continuously water-permeable regions of the renal

A *In primary active transport, the energy for the process is provided directly by the cleavage of ATP. In secondary active transport, the energy for the process is provided by the Na⁺ concentration gradient established by the active pumping of Na⁺. As Na⁺ moves down its own concentration gradient, it drives the movement of another substance (e.g., glucose) against its concentration gradient.*

tubules, such as the PCT, aquaporins are constant components of the tubule cell membranes. Because these channels are always present, the body is "obliged" to absorb water in the proximal nephron regardless of its state of over- or underhydration. This water flow is referred to as **obligatory water reabsorption.** Aquaporins are virtually absent in the luminal membranes of the collecting duct unless antidiuretic hormone (ADH) is present.

As water leaves the tubules, the concentration of solutes in the filtrate increases and, if able, they too begin to follow their concentration gradients into the peritubular capillaries (Figure 25.12). This phenomenon of solutes following solvent explains the passive reabsorption of a number of solutes present in the filtrate, such as cations, fatty acids, and some urea. It also explains in part why lipid-soluble drugs and environmental toxins are difficult to excrete: Since lipid-soluble compounds can generally pass through membranes, they will follow their concentration gradients and be reabsorbed, even if this is "not desirable."

Substances reabsorbed by **secondary active transport** (the "push" comes from the gradient created by Na^+-K^+ pumping at the basolateral membrane) include glucose, amino acids, lactate, vitamins, and most cations. In nearly all these cases, a luminal carrier moves Na^+ down its concentration gradient as it cotransports (symports) another solute (Figure 25.12). Cotransported solutes diffuse (via different transport proteins) across the basolateral membrane before moving into the peritubular capillaries. Although there is some overlap of carriers, the transport systems for the various solutes are quite specific *and limited.*

Excluding Na^+, there is a **transport maximum (T_m)** for nearly every substance that is actively reabsorbed. The T_m (reported in mg/min) reflects the number of carriers in the renal tubules available to ferry each particular substance. In general, there are plenty of carriers and therefore high T_m values for substances such as glucose that need to be retained, and few or no carriers for substances of no use to the body. When the carriers are saturated—that is, all bound to the substance they transport—the excess is excreted in urine. This is what happens in individuals who become hyperglycemic because of uncontrolled diabetes mellitus. As levels of glucose approach 400 mg/100 ml of plasma, the glucose T_m of 375 mg/min is exceeded and large amounts of glucose are lost in the urine even though the renal tubules are still functioning normally.

Any plasma proteins that squeeze through the filtration membrane are removed from the filtrate in the proximal tubule by endocytosis, digested to their amino acids, and moved into the peritubular blood.

Nonreabsorbed Substances

Some substances are either not reabsorbed or are reabsorbed incompletely because they (1) lack carriers or channels, (2) are not lipid soluble, or (3) are too large to pass through tight junctions between the tubular cells. The most important of these are the nitrogenous end products of protein and nucleic acid metabolism: **urea, creatinine,** and **uric acid.** Urea handling in the nephron is complicated and will be discussed on p. 1018, but the net effect is that 50–60% of the urea present in filtrate is reclaimed. Creatinine, a large, lipid-insoluble molecule, is not reabsorbed at all. Its plasma concentration remains stable as long as muscle mass is stable, which makes it useful for measuring the GFR and glomerular function.

Absorptive Capabilities of the Renal Tubules and Collecting Ducts

Proximal Convoluted Tubule   Table 25.1 compares the reabsorptive abilities of various regions of the renal tubules and collecting ducts. Although the entire renal tubule is involved in reabsorption to some degree, the PCT cells are by far the most active "reabsorbers" and the events just described occur mainly in this tubular segment. Normally, the PCT reabsorbs all of the glucose, lactate, and amino acids in the filtrate and 65% of the Na^+ and water. Additionally, 90% of the filtered bicarbonate (HCO_3^-), 60% of the Cl^-, and about 55% of the K^+ are reclaimed in the PCT. The bulk of the reabsorption of electrolytes is accomplished by the time the filtrate reaches the loop of Henle. Nearly all of the uric acid is reabsorbed in the proximal tubule, but it is later secreted back into the filtrate.

Loop of Henle   Beyond the PCT, the permeability of the tubule epithelium changes dramatically. Here, for the first time, water reabsorption is not coupled to solute reabsorption. Water can leave the descending limb of the loop of Henle but *not* the ascending limb, where aquaporins are scarce or absent in the tubule membrane. For reasons that will be explained shortly, these permeability differences play a vital role in the kidneys' ability to form dilute and concentrated urine.

The rule for water is that it leaves the descending (but not the ascending) limb of Henle's loop; the opposite is true for solutes. Virtually no solute reabsorption occurs in the descending limb, but both active and passive reabsorption of solute occurs in the ascending limb. In the thin portion of the ascending limb, Na^+ moves passively down the concentration gradient created by water reabsorption. A Na^+-K^+-$2Cl^-$ symporter is the main means of Na^+ entry at the luminal surface in the thick portion of the ascending limb. However, this segment also has

25

TABLE 25.1	Reabsorption Capabilities of Different Segments of the Renal Tubules and Collecting Ducts	
TUBULE SEGMENT	**SUBSTANCE REABSORBED**	**MECHANISM**
PROXIMAL CONVOLUTED TUBULE		
	Sodium ions (Na^+)	Primary active transport via basolateral Na^+-K^+ pump; sets up electrochemical gradient for passive solute diffusion, osmosis, and secondary active transport (cotransport) with Na^+
	Virtually all nutrients (glucose, amino acids, vitamins)	Secondary active transport with Na^+
	Cations (K^+, Mg^{2+}, Ca^{2+}, and others)	Passive transport driven by electrochemical gradient for most; the paracellular route is important
	Anions (Cl^-, HCO_3^-)	Passive transport; paracellular diffusion driven by electrochemical gradient for Cl^-; secondary active transport (with Na^+) for HCO_3^-
	Water	Osmosis; driven by solute reabsorption (obligatory)
	Urea and lipid-soluble solutes	Passive diffusion driven by the concentration gradient created by reabsorption of water
	Small proteins	Endocytosed by tubule cells and digested to amino acids within tubule cells
LOOP OF HENLE		
Descending limb	Water	Osmosis
Ascending limb	Na^+, Cl^-, K^+	Secondary active transport of Cl^-, Na^+, and K^+ via Na^+-K^+-$2Cl^-$ cotransporter in thick portion; paracellular diffusion; Na^+-H^+ antiport
	Ca^{2+}, Mg^{2+}	Passive paracellular diffusion driven by electrochemical gradient
DISTAL CONVOLUTED TUBULE		
	Na^+, Cl^-	Primary active Na^+ transport at basolateral membrane; secondary active transport at luminal membrane via Na^+-Cl^- symporter and channels; aldosterone-regulated at distal portion
	Ca^{2+}	Passive uptake via PTH-modulated channels in luminal membrane; primary and secondary active transport (antiport with Na^+) in basolateral membrane
COLLECTING DUCT		
	Na^+, H^+, K^+, HCO_3^-, Cl^-	Primary active transport of Na^+ (requires aldosterone) and the medullary gradient create the conditions for passive transport of some HCO_3^- and Cl^- and cotransport of H^+, Cl^-, and HCO_3^-; K^+ is both reabsorbed and secreted (aldosterone dependent), usually resulting in net K^+ secretion
	Water	Osmosis; controlled (facultative) water reabsorption; ADH required to insert aquaporins
	Urea	Facilitated diffusion in response to concentration gradient in the deep medulla region; recycles and contributes to medullary osmotic gradient

Na^+-H^+ antiporters, and some 50% of Na^+ passes via the paracellular route in this region. A Na^+-K^+ ATPase operates at the basolateral membrane to create the ionic gradient that drives the symporter.

Distal Convoluted Tubule and Collecting Duct

By the time the DCT is reached, only about 10% of the originally filtered NaCl and 25% of the water remain in the tubule. Some unregulated NaCl reabsorption occurs in the DCT via Na^+-Cl^- symporters. However, most reabsorption from this point on depends on the body's needs at the time and is regulated by hormones (mainly aldosterone for Na^+, ADH for water, and PTH for Ca^{2+} as described in Chapter 26). If necessary, nearly all of the water and Na^+ reaching these regions can be reclaimed. In the absence of regulatory hormones, the DCT and collecting duct are relatively impermeable to water. Reabsorption of more water depends on the presence of antidiuretic hormone (ADH), which makes the collecting ducts more permeable to water by inserting aquaporins into the collecting duct luminal membranes.

Aldosterone "fine-tunes" reabsorption of the remaining Na^+. Decreased blood volume or blood pressure, low extracellular Na^+ concentration (hyponatremia), or high extracellular K^+ concentration (hyperkalemia) can cause the adrenal cortex to release aldosterone to the blood. Except for hyperkalemia (which directly stimulates the adrenal cortex to secrete aldosterone), these conditions promote the renin-angiotensin mechanism, which in turn prompts the release of aldosterone (see Figure 25.10). Aldosterone targets the principal cells of the collecting ducts and cells of the distal portion of the DCT (prodding them to open or synthesize more luminal Na^+ and K^+ channels, and more basolateral Na^+-K^+ ATPases). As a result, little or no Na^+ leaves the body in urine. In the absence of aldosterone, much less Na^+ is reabsorbed by these segments, resulting in Na^+ losses of about 2% of Na^+ filtered daily, an amount incompatible with life.

A second effect of aldosterone is to facilitate water reabsorption: As Na^+ is reabsorbed, water follows it back into the blood (if it can). Aldosterone also reduces blood K^+ concentrations because aldosterone-induced reabsorption of Na^+ is coupled to K^+ secretion in the principal cells, that is, as Na^+ enters, K^+ moves into the lumen.

In contrast to aldosterone, which acts to conserve Na^+, atrial natriuretic peptide (ANP) reduces blood Na^+, thereby decreasing blood volume and blood pressure. Released by cardiac atrial cells when blood volume or blood pressure is elevated, ANP exerts several effects that lower blood Na^+ levels. For example, it (1) acts directly on medullary collecting ducts to inhibit Na^+ reabsorption, (2) indirectly inhibits Na^+ reabsorption by counteracting the stimulatory effect of angiotensin II on aldosterone secretion by the adrenal cortex, and (3) indirectly stimulates an increased GFR by targeting the renal arterioles, thereby reducing water reabsorption and blood volume.

Step 3: Tubular Secretion

The failure of tubule cells to reabsorb some solutes is an important means of clearing plasma of unwanted substances. A second such mechanism is **tubular secretion**—essentially, reabsorption in reverse. Substances such as H^+, K^+, NH_4^+, creatinine, and certain organic acids either move into the filtrate from the peritubular capillaries through the tubule cells or are synthesized in the tubule cells and secreted. Thus, the urine eventually excreted contains both filtered and secreted substances. With one major exception (K^+), the PCT is the main site of secretion, but the cortical parts of the collecting ducts and the late regions of the distal tubules are also active (see Figure 25.16, p. 1020).

Tubular secretion is important for

1. Disposing of substances, such as certain drugs and metabolites, which are tightly bound to plasma proteins. Such substances are not readily filtered and so must be secreted.

2. Eliminating undesirable substances or end products that have been reabsorbed by passive processes (urea and uric acid).

3. Ridding the body of excess K^+. Because virtually all K^+ present in the filtrate is reabsorbed in the PCT and ascending loop of Henle, nearly all K^+ in urine is from aldosterone-driven active tubular secretion into the late DCT and collecting ducts.

4. Controlling blood pH. When blood pH drops toward the acidic end of its homeostatic range, the renal tubule cells actively secrete more H^+ into the filtrate and retain more HCO_3^- (a base). As a result, the blood pH rises and the urine drains off the excess H^+. Conversely, when blood pH approaches the alkaline end of its range, Cl^- is reabsorbed instead of HCO_3^-, which is allowed to leave the body in urine. The kidneys' role in pH homeostasis is discussed in more detail in Chapter 26.

Regulation of Urine Concentration and Volume

A solution's **osmolality** (oz"mo-lal'ĭ-te) is the number of solute particles dissolved in 1 kg of water and reflects the solution's ability to cause osmosis. For any solution interfacing with a semipermeable membrane, this ability, called osmotic activity, is

FIGURE 25.13 **Osmotic gradient in the renal medulla and its relationship to the loops of Henle and collecting ducts.** The osmolality of the interstitial fluid in the renal cortex is isotonic at 300 mOsm, but the osmolality of the interstitial fluid in the renal medulla increases progressively from 300 mOsm at the corticomedullary junction to 1200 mOsm at the medullary-pelvis junction. One greatly enlarged nephron and its collecting duct are depicted to show their positions relative to the medullary gradient.

determined only by the number of nonpenetrating solute particles (solute particles unable to pass through the membrane) and is independent of their type. Ten sodium ions have the same osmotic activity as ten glucose molecules or ten amino acids in the same volume of water. Because one *osmol* (equivalent to 1 mole of particles) is a fairly large unit, the **milliosmol (mOsm)** (mil″e-oz′mōl), equal to 0.001 osmol, is generally used. In the discussion that follows, we use mOsm to mean mOsm/kg.

One crucial renal function is to keep the solute load of body fluids constant at about 300 mOsm, the osmotic concentration of blood plasma, by regulating urine concentration and volume. The kidneys accomplish this feat using **countercurrent mechanisms.** In the kidneys, the term *countercurrent* means that

fluid flows through adjacent tubes in opposite directions. These countercurrent mechanisms are (1) the interaction between the flow of filtrate through the ascending and descending limbs of the long loops of Henle of juxtamedullary nephrons (the *countercurrent multiplier*), and (2) the flow of blood through the ascending and descending portions of the vasa recta blood vessels (the *countercurrent exchanger*).* The countercurrent mechanisms establish and maintain an osmotic gradient extending from the cortex through the depths of the medulla that allows the kidneys to vary urine concentration dramatically.

The osmolality of the filtrate entering the PCT is identical to that of plasma, about 300 mOsm. As described earlier, because of PCT reabsorption of water *and* solutes, the filtrate is still isosmotic with plasma by the time the descending limb of the loop of Henle is reached. However, its osmolality increases from 300 to about 1200 mOsm in the deepest part of the medulla (Figure 25.13). How does this increase in concentration occur? The answer lies in the unique workings of the long loops of Henle of the juxtamedullary nephrons, and the vasa recta. Notice in Figure 25.14 that in each case the fluids involved—filtrate in the loops of Henle and blood in the vasa recta—first descend and then ascend through parallel limbs.

The Countercurrent Multiplier

First, we will follow filtrate processing through the loop of Henle, as portrayed in Figure 25.14a, to see how the loop functions as a **countercurrent multiplier** to establish the osmotic gradient. The countercurrent multiplier functions because of three factors:

1. The descending limb of the loop of Henle is relatively impermeable to solutes and freely permeable to water. Because the osmolality of the medullary interstitial fluid increases all along the descending limb (the mechanism of this increase is explained shortly), water passes osmotically out of the filtrate all along this course. Thus, the filtrate osmolality reaches its highest point (1200 mOsm) at the bend of the loop.

2. The ascending limb is permeable to solutes, but not to water. As the filtrate rounds the bend into the ascending limb, the tubule permeability changes, becoming impermeable to water and selectively permeable to salt. The Na⁺ and Cl⁻ concentration in the filtrate entering the ascending limb is very high (and

---

* The term "countercurrent" is commonly misunderstood to mean that the direction of fluid flow in the loops of Henle is opposite that of the blood in the vasa recta. In fact, there is no one-to-one relationship between individual loops of Henle and capillaries of the vasa recta as might be suggested by two-dimensional diagrams such as Figures 25.5 and 25.14. Instead, there are many tubules and capillaries packed together. Each tubule is surrounded by many blood vessels, whose flow is not necessarily counter to flow in that tubule.

Q *What portion of the nephron acts as the countercurrent multiplier? As the countercurrent exchanger?*

Key:

→ Active transport

→ Passive transport

FIGURE 25.14 **Countercurrent mechanism for establishing and maintaining the medullary osmotic gradient. (a)** Filtrate entering the descending limb of the loop of Henle is isosmotic to both blood plasma and cortical interstitial fluid. As the filtrate flows from the cortex to the medulla in the descending limb, water leaves the tubule by osmosis and the filtrate osmolality increases from 300 to 1200 mOsm. As the filtrate flows into the ascending limb, the permeability of the tubule epithelium changes from being permeable to water and impermeable to salt to the opposite condition: water impermeable, salt permeable. Consequently, NaCl leaves the ascending limb, diluting the filtrate as it approaches the cortex. Thus the descending limb produces increasingly salty filtrate, while the ascending limb uses this high salt concentration to establish the high osmolality of the interstitial fluid in the medulla and the medullary osmotic gradient. Diffusion of urea from the lower portion of the collecting duct also contributes to the high osmolality in the medulla. **(b)** Dissipation of the medullary osmotic gradient is prevented because the blood in the vasa recta continuously becomes isosmotic to the interstitial fluid—becoming more concentrated as it descends deeper into the medulla and less concentrated as it approaches the cortical region. This occurs because of the high porosity and sluggish blood flow in the vasa recta.

A *The countercurrent multiplier is the loop of Henle of juxtamedullary nephrons. The countercurrent exchanger is the vasa recta.*

interstitial fluid concentrations of these two ions are lower). Na^+ and Cl^- reabsorption in the ascending limb is both passive (mostly in the thin segment) and active (via the Na^+-K^+-$2Cl^-$ cotransporter in the thick segment). As Na^+ and Cl^- are extruded from the filtrate into the medullary interstitial fluid, they contribute to the high osmolality there. Because it loses salt but not water, the filtrate in the ascending limb becomes increasingly dilute until, at 100 mOsm at the DCT, it is hypo-osmotic, or hypotonic, to blood plasma and cortical interstitial fluids.

Notice in Figure 25.14 that there is a constant difference in filtrate concentration (200 mOsm) between the two limbs of the loop of Henle, and between the ascending limb and the interstitial fluid. This reflects the power of the ascending limb's NaCl pumps, which are just powerful enough to create a 200 mOsm difference between the inside and outside of the ascending limb. A 200-mOsm gradient by itself would not be enough to allow excretion of very concentrated urine. The beauty of this system lies in the fact that, because of countercurrent flow, the loop of Henle is able to "multiply" these small changes in solute concentration into a gradient change along the vertical length of the loop (both inside and outside) that is closer to 900 mOsm (1200 mOsm − 300 mOsm).

Although the two limbs of the loop of Henle are not in direct contact with each other, they are close enough to influence each other's exchanges with the interstitial fluid they share. Hence, water diffusing out of the descending limb produces the increasingly "salty" filtrate that the ascending limb uses to raise the osmolality of the medullary interstitial fluid. Furthermore, the more NaCl the ascending limb extrudes, the more water diffuses out of the descending limb and the saltier the filtrate in the descending limb becomes. This establishes a positive feedback mechanism that produces the high osmolality of the fluids in the descending limb and the interstitial fluid.

3. Urea recycling contributes to the medullary osmotic gradient. In the thin limbs of the loop of Henle, urea enters the filtrate by facilitated diffusion. As the filtrate moves on, water is reabsorbed but urea is left behind because the tubule between Henle's thin limb and the collecting duct is not permeable to urea. When filtrate reaches the collecting duct in the deep medullary region, urea, now highly concentrated, is transported by facilitated diffusion out of the tubule into the interstitial fluid of the medulla, forming a pool of urea that recycles back into the thin limb of the loop of Henle. This pool of urea contributes substantially to the high osmolality in the medulla. Antidiuretic hormone (ADH), which stimulates excretion of highly concentrated urine (as we will see shortly), enhances urea transport in the medullary collecting duct. When ADH is present,

urea recycling is enhanced, the medullary osmotic gradient is enhanced, and more concentrated urine can be formed.

The Countercurrent Exchanger

As shown in Figure 25.14b, the vasa recta function as **countercurrent exchangers,** maintaining the osmotic gradient established by the cycling of salt while delivering blood to cells in the area. Because these vessels receive only about 10% of the renal blood supply, blood flow through the vasa recta is sluggish. Moreover, they are freely permeable to water and NaCl, allowing blood to make passive exchanges with the surrounding interstitial fluid and achieve equilibrium. Consequently, as the blood flows into the medullary depths, it loses water and gains salt (becomes hypertonic). Then, as it emerges from the medulla into the cortex, the process is reversed: It picks up water and loses salt. Because blood leaving and reentering the cortex via the vasa recta has the same solute concentration, the vessels of the vasa recta act as countercurrent exchangers. This system does not create the medullary gradient, but it protects it by preventing rapid removal of salt from the medullary interstitial space, and by removing reabsorbed water.

Formation of Dilute Urine

Because tubular filtrate is diluted as it travels through the ascending limb of the loop of Henle, all the kidney needs to do to secrete dilute (hypo-osmotic) urine is allow the filtrate to continue on its way into the renal pelvis (Figure 25.15a). When ADH is not being released by the posterior pituitary, that is exactly what happens. The collecting ducts remain essentially impermeable to water due to the absence of aquaporins in their luminal cell membranes, and no further water reabsorption occurs. Moreover, as noted, Na^+ and selected other ions can be removed from the filtrate by DCT and collecting duct cells so that urine becomes even more dilute before entering the renal pelvis. The osmolality of urine can plunge as low as 70 mOsm, about one-fourth the concentration of glomerular filtrate or blood plasma.

Formation of Concentrated Urine

As its name reveals, **antidiuretic hormone (ADH)** inhibits *diuresis* (di"u-re'sis), or urine output. It accomplishes this via a second-messenger system using cyclic AMP that causes insertion of aquaporins into the luminal membrane of the principal cells of the collecting ducts. Consequently water passes easily into and through the cells into the interstitial space, and the osmolality of the filtrate becomes equal to that of the interstitial fluid.

Key:

→ Active transport
→ Passive transport

FIGURE 25.15   Mechanisms for forming dilute and concentrated urine.
(a) In the absence of ADH, dilute filtrate produced by the countercurrent mechanism remains dilute as it passes through the collecting duct. **(b)** In the presence of ADH, concentrated urine is excreted. ADH causes insertion of aquaporins in luminal membranes of principal cells of the collecting duct. Consequently water rapidly leaves the filtrate in the collecting duct.

In the distal tubules, the filtrate osmolality is approximately 100 mOsm, but as the filtrate flows through the collecting ducts and is subjected to the hyperosmolar conditions in the medulla, water, followed by urea, rapidly leaves the filtrate (Figures 25.15b and 25.16e). Depending on the amount of ADH released (which is keyed to the level of body hydration), urine concentration may rise as high as 1200 mOsm, the concentration of interstitial fluid in the deepest part of the medulla. With maximal ADH secretion, up to 99% of the water in the filtrate is reabsorbed and returned to the blood, and half a liter per day of highly concentrated urine is excreted. The ability of our kidneys to produce such concentrated urine is critically tied to our ability to survive without water. Water reabsorption that depends on the presence of ADH is called **facultative water reabsorption.**

ADH is released more or less continuously unless the blood solute concentration drops too low. Release of ADH is enhanced by any event that raises plasma osmolality above 300 mOsm such as sweating or diarrhea, or greatly reduced blood volume or blood pressure (see Chapter 26). Although release of ADH is the "signal" to produce concentrated urine that opens the door for water reabsorption (through aquaporins), the kidneys' ability to respond to this signal depends on the high medullary osmotic gradient.

Diuretics

There are several types of **diuretics,** chemicals that enhance urinary output. An *osmotic diuretic* is a substance that is not reabsorbed and that carries water out with it (for example, the high blood glucose levels of a diabetes mellitus patient). Alcohol,

25

FIGURE 25.16   Summary of nephron functions. The glomerulus provides the filtrate processed by the renal tubule. The various regions of the renal tubule carry out reabsorption and secretion and maintain a gradient of osmolality within the medullary interstitial fluid. Varying osmolality at different points in the interstitial fluid is symbolized in the central figure by gradients of color. The inserts that accompany the central figure describe the main transport functions of the four regions of the nephron tubule and of the collecting duct. **(a) Proximal tubule.** Filtrate that enters the PCT from the glomerular capsule has about the same osmolality as blood plasma. The main activity of the PCT transport epithelium is reabsorption of certain solutes from the filtrate back into the blood. Nearly all nutrients and about 65% of Na^+ are actively transported out of the PCT and enter the peritubular capillaries; Cl^- and water follow passively. PCT cells also secrete ammonium and other nitrogenous wastes into the filtrate and help maintain a constant pH in blood and interstitial fluid by the secretion of H^+ and reabsorption of HCO_3^-. By the end of the proximal tubule, the filtrate volume has been reduced by 65%. **(b) Descending limb.** The descending limb of the loop of Henle is freely permeable to water but not to NaCl. As filtrate in this limb descends into the medulla, the filtrate loses water by osmosis to the interstitial fluid, which is increasingly hypertonic in that direction. Consequently, salt and other solutes become more concentrated in the filtrate. **(c) Ascending limb.** The ascending limb of the loop of Henle is impermeable to water but permeable to Na^+ and Cl^-. These ions, which became concentrated in the descending limb, move passively out of the thin portion of the ascending limb, are actively pumped out of the thick portion of the ascending limb, and contribute to the high osmolality of interstitial fluid in the inner medulla. K^+ is cotransported with Na^+ and Cl^-. The tubule epithelium here is not permeable to water, so the filtrate becomes more and more dilute as the exodus of salt from the filtrate continues. **(d) Distal tubule.** The DCT, like the PCT, is specialized for selective secretion and reabsorption. Na^+ and Cl^- are cotransported, H^+ may be secreted, and in the presence of aldosterone, more Na^+ is reabsorbed. The water permeability of the DCT is extremely low and almost no further H_2O absorption occurs there. **(e) Collecting duct.** The urine, normally quite dilute at this point, begins its journey via the collecting duct back into the medulla, with its increasing osmolality gradient. In the cortical collecting duct, K^+, H^+, and/or HCO_3^- ions may be reabsorbed or secreted depending on what is required to maintain homeostasis. The wall of the medullary region of the collecting duct is permeable to urea and is made more so by the presence of ADH. Some urea diffuses out of the collecting duct and contributes to the high osmolality of the inner medulla. In the absence of ADH, the collecting duct is nearly impermeable to water, and dilute urine is excreted. In the presence of ADH, more aquaporins are inserted into the collecting duct, and the filtrate loses water by osmosis as it passes through medullary regions of increasing osmolality. Consequently, water is conserved, and concentrated urine is excreted.

essentially a sedative, encourages diuresis by inhibiting release of ADH. Other diuretics increase urine flow by inhibiting Na^+ reabsorption and the obligatory water reabsorption that normally follows. Examples include caffeine (found in coffee, tea, and colas) and many drugs prescribed for hypertension or the edema of congestive heart failure. Common diuretics inhibit Na^+-associated symporters. "Loop diuretics" [like furosemide (Lasix)] are powerful because they inhibit formation of the medullary gradient by acting at the ascending limb of Henle's loop. Thiazides are less potent and act at the DCT.

Renal Clearance

Renal clearance refers to the volume of plasma that is cleared of a particular substance in a given time, usually 1 minute. Renal clearance tests are done to determine the GFR, which allows us to detect glomerular damage and follow the progress of renal disease (discussed in A Closer Look, p. 1022).

The renal clearance rate (RC) of any substance, in ml/min, is calculated from the equation

$$RC = UV/P$$

where

U = concentration of the substance in urine (mg/ml)

V = flow rate of urine formation (ml/min)

P = concentration of the substance in plasma (mg/ml)

Because it is freely filtered and neither reabsorbed nor secreted by the kidneys, *inulin* (in'u-lin) is the standard used to determine the GFR. A polysaccharide with a molecular weight of approximately 5000, inulin's renal clearance value is equal to the GFR. When inulin is infused such that its plasma concentration is 1 mg/ml ($P = 1$ mg/ml), then generally $U = 125$ mg/ml, and $V = 1$ ml/min. Therefore, its renal clearance is RC = $(125 \times 1)/1 = 125$ ml/min, meaning that in 1 minute the kidneys have removed (cleared) all the inulin present in 125 ml of plasma.

A clearance value less than that of inulin means that a substance is partially reabsorbed. An example is urea with an RC of 70 ml/min, meaning that of the 125 ml of glomerular filtrate formed each minute, approximately 70 ml is completely cleared of urea, while the urea in the remaining 55 ml is recovered and returned to the plasma. If the RC is zero (such as for glucose in healthy individuals), reabsorption is complete or the substance is not filtered. If the RC is greater than that of inulin, the tubule cells are secreting the substance into the filtrate.

This is the case with most drug metabolites. Knowing a drug's renal clearance value is essential because if it is high, the drug dosage must also be high and administered frequently to maintain a therapeutic level. Creatinine, which has an RC of 140 ml/min, is freely filtered but also secreted in small amounts. It is often used nevertheless to give a "quick and dirty" estimate of GFR.

Urine

Physical Characteristics

Color and Transparency

Freshly voided urine is clear and pale to deep yellow. Its yellow color is due to **urochrome** (u'ro-krōm), a pigment that results from the body's destruction of hemoglobin (via bilirubin or bile pigments). The more concentrated the urine, the deeper the yellow color. An abnormal color such as pink or brown, or a smoky tinge, may result from eating certain foods (beets, rhubarb) or may be due to the presence in the urine of bile pigments or blood. Additionally, some commonly prescribed drugs and vitamin supplements alter the color of urine. Cloudy urine may indicate a urinary tract infection.

Odor

Fresh urine is slightly aromatic, but if allowed to stand, it develops an ammonia odor as bacteria metabolize its urea solutes. Some drugs and vegetables alter the usual odor of urine, as do some diseases. For example, in uncontrolled diabetes mellitus the urine smells fruity because of its acetone content.

pH

Urine is usually slightly acidic (around pH 6), but changes in body metabolism or diet may cause the pH to vary from about 4.5 to 8.0. A predominantly *acidic* diet that contains large amounts of protein and whole wheat products produces acidic urine. A vegetarian *(alkaline)* diet, prolonged vomiting, and bacterial infection of the urinary tract all cause the urine to become alkaline.

Specific Gravity

Because urine is water plus solutes, a given volume has a greater mass than the same volume of distilled water. The ratio of the mass of a substance to the mass of an equal volume of distilled water is its **specific gravity.** The specific gravity of distilled water is 1.0 and that of urine ranges from 1.001 to 1.035, depending on its solute concentration.

25

Chronic Renal Disease: A National Health Crisis in the Making

How long has it been since you had a urinalysis? If you're like most of us, the answer is: too long. This simple, inexpensive, painless test can detect renal disease years before any symptoms appear, buying time for early treatment and preventing life-threatening complications.

Unfortunately, urinalysis is often omitted from routine medical check-ups. Unfortunate, because chronic renal disease is a major burden to the U.S. health care system. Some 10–20 million Americans—one out of every 15—have some degree of kidney dysfunction. More than 2.6 million Americans suffer major impairment, and nearly 350,000 require dialysis or a kidney transplant just to stay alive.

In addition to its physical toll on individuals, chronic renal disease creates a huge financial burden for the nation. The U.S. spends $22.8 billion annually to treat these patients, a figure that is projected to increase to $38.35 billion by 2010. Medicare spending for renal failure rises by 5–10% every year. People with chronic kidney disease make up only 0.6% of the Medicare population, but consume 6% of its budget.

Stages of Renal Disease

Renal failure can strike as an acute crisis, perhaps due to trauma, infections, or poisoning by heavy metals or organic solvents. More often, though, it develops silently and insidiously over many years. Filtrate formation decreases gradually, nitrogenous wastes accumulate in the blood, and blood pH drifts toward the acidic range.

Chronic renal disease refers to this gradual loss of kidney function, defined as either kidney damage or a GFR of less than 60 ml/min for at least three months. Kidney damage is defined as the presence of structural or functional abnormalities, or of damage markers such as abnormal components in blood and urine.

Clinicians classify chronic renal disease into five stages according to the level of kidney function:

- Stage 1: Signs of kidney damage with GFR≥90
- Stage 2: Signs of kidney damage with GFR of 60–89
- Stage 3: GFR 30–59
- Stage 4: GFR 15–29
- Stage 5: GFR <15

Patients in stage 5 are considered to be in renal failure (also called end-stage renal disease). At this point they have only 10–15% of kidney function left, and most require dialysis or a transplant to survive.

Symptoms and Risk Factors

Warning signs of kidney trouble may include high blood pressure, frequent urination, difficult or painful urination, puffy eyes, or swollen hands or feet. But all too often, there are few noticeable symptoms until advanced stages, when a significant percentage of kidney function has already been lost. Urinalysis is valuable because it can detect proteinuria, a sensitive early marker of kidney damage.

The most abundant protein found in urine is albumin. Normally urinary albumin averages less than 100 mg/day (as measured over a 24-hour period); excretion of more than 300 mg/day signals clinical proteinuria.

Other tests that can evaluate kidney function include

- Creatinine clearance, which measures filtering efficiency by comparing the creatinine level in the blood to that in the urine.
- Serum creatinine, which detects levels of creatinine in the blood.
- Blood urea nitrogen (BUN), which measures the amount of urea in the blood. Generally, if creatinine is abnormal, BUN will be too.

Where did this kidney crisis come from? In adults, chronic renal disease often develops in conjunction with other chronic health conditions. As the U.S. population ages and gains weight (see *A Closer Look* in Chapter 24), risk factors for renal problems multiply.

The leading cause is diabetes mellitus, which accounts for approximately 44% of new cases each year. Hypertension is a close second, accounting for about 28% of cases. Note that hypertension is both a cause and a symptom: High blood pressure impairs kidney function by damaging renal blood vessels and reducing circulation to the organs, even as hypertension-battered kidneys push blood pressure upward. Atherosclerosis compounds the problem by further impairing circulation.

Race and ethnicity may play a role; African Americans are nearly four times more likely to develop renal failure than Caucasian Americans. Hispanics

Chemical Composition

Water accounts for about 95% of urine volume; the remaining 5% consists of solutes. The largest component of urine by weight, apart from water, is *urea*, which is derived from the normal breakdown of amino acids. Other **nitrogenous wastes** in urine include *uric acid* (an end product of nucleic acid metabolism) and *creatinine* (a metabolite of creatine phosphate, which stores energy for the regeneration of ATP and is found in large amounts in skeletal muscle tissue). Normal solute constituents of urine, in order of decreasing concentration, are urea, Na^+, K^+, PO_4^{3-}, SO_4^{2-}, creatinine, and uric acid. Much smaller but highly variable amounts of Ca^{2+}, Mg^{2+}, and HCO_3^- are also present in urine. Unusually high concentrations of any solute, or the presence of abnormal substances such as blood proteins, WBCs and Native Americans are two times more likely, and Asians have 1.3 times the risk. Researchers ascribe this in part to the prevalence of type 2 diabetes in these populations.

Genetic factors, as yet poorly understood, may also be involved, since a family history of chronic kidney disease, diabetes, or hypertension seems to increase the risk. Studies are under way to identify genes that influence susceptibility to renal disease.

Treatments and New Research

Tight control of blood glucose and blood pressure can slow the progression of kidney disease and possibly forestall renal failure. Diabetics who maintain glucose levels within the normal range can prevent many renal complications. The National Heart, Lung and Blood Institute recommends that people in early stages of chronic renal disease keep their blood pressure below 130/80 mm Hg. Angiotensin converting enzyme (ACE) inhibitor drugs seem to be especially effective for lowering blood pressure while protecting the kidneys.

Even in early stages, a special diet can do much to relieve the kidneys' workload and control the accumulation of waste products. In particular, renal dietitians advise patients to limit their intake of protein, phosphorus, and sodium. Too much protein causes urea to build up; too much phosphorus leaches calcium from the skeleton and weakens bones; high sodium intake tends to raise blood pressure.

If renal disease progresses, hemodialysis may become necessary. In *hemodialysis*, which uses an "artificial kidney" apparatus, the patient's blood is passed

Hemodialysis.

through a membrane tubing that is permeable only to selected substances, and the tubing is immersed in a bathing solution that differs slightly from normal cleansed plasma (see illustration). As blood circulates through the tubing, substances such as nitrogenous wastes and K^+ present in the blood (but not in the bath) diffuse out of the blood into the surrounding solution, and substances to be added to the blood, mainly buffers for H^+ (and glucose for malnourished patients), move from the bathing solution into the blood. In this way, needed substances are retained in the blood or added to it, while wastes and ion excesses are removed.

Transplant surgery is the treatment of last resort, but unless the new kidney comes from an identical twin, recipients must take immunosuppressive drugs for the rest of their lives to prevent rejection. Kidney transplants in the U.S. during 2001 numbered 15,311, almost 5000 of them from living donors. But this leaves 57,000 Americans still waiting for a kidney, more than for any other organ.

If this sounds bleak, consider that 40 years ago, people who reached end-stage renal failure survived for only a few days. Today, they can live for years or even decades, and researchers are laboring to improve both life span and quality of life. Infection is a constant hazard in hemodialysis, since back filtration can accidentally return bacteria-contaminated solution into the patient. Researchers are developing a dialysis membrane of bioengineered cells capable of removing toxic solutes.

Stem cell research may provide the ultimate answer. Recently, scientists cloned kidney cells from adult cow skin cell nuclei, grew them on three-dimensional molds, and placed the molds in incubators, where the cells attached and formed tissue. When transplanted back into the cows that donated the original nuclei, the cell-mold structures excreted a urinelike fluid containing metabolic waste products, and they did not trigger an immune response. In short, they behaved tantalizingly like miniature kidneys. ■

25

(pus), or bile pigments, may indicate pathology (Table 25.2). (Normal urine values are listed in Appendix F.)

Ureters

The **ureters** are slender tubes that convey urine from the kidneys to the bladder (see Figure 25.1). Each ureter begins at the level of L_2 as a continuation of

the renal pelvis. From there, it descends behind the peritoneum and runs obliquely through the posterior bladder wall. This arrangement prevents backflow of urine during bladder filling because any increase in bladder pressure compresses and closes the distal ends of the ureters.

Histologically, the ureter wall is trilayered. The transitional epithelium of its lining *mucosa* is continuous with that of the kidney pelvis superiorly and the bladder medially. Its middle *muscularis* is

TABLE 25.2	Abnormal Urinary Constituents	
SUBSTANCE	**NAME OF CONDITION**	**POSSIBLE CAUSES**
Glucose	Glycosuria	Nonpathological; excessive intake of sugary foods Pathological: diabetes mellitus
Proteins	Proteinuria, or albuminuria	Nonpathological; excessive physical exertion; pregnancy; high-protein diet Pathological (over 250 mg/day): heart failure, severe hypertension; glomerulonephritis; often initial sign of asymptomatic renal disease
Ketone bodies	Ketonuria	Excessive formation and accumulation of ketone bodies, as in starvation and untreated diabetes mellitus
Hemoglobin	Hemoglobinuria	Various: transfusion reaction, hemolytic anemia, severe burns, etc.
Bile pigments	Bilirubinuria	Liver disease (hepatitis, cirrhosis) or obstruction of bile ducts from liver or galbladder
Erythrocytes	Hematuria	Bleeding urinary tract (due to trauma, kidney stones, infection, or neoplasm)
Leukocytes (pus)	Pyuria	Urinary tract infection

composed chiefly of two smooth muscle sheets: the internal longitudinal layer and the external circular layer. An additional smooth muscle layer, the external longitudinal layer, appears in the lower third of the ureter. The *adventitia* covering the ureter's external surface is typical fibrous connective tissue (Figure 25.17).

The ureter plays an active role in transporting urine. Incoming urine distends the ureter and stimulates its muscularis to contract, propelling urine into the bladder. (Urine does *not* reach the bladder through gravity alone.) The strength and frequency of the peristaltic waves are adjusted to the rate of urine formation. Although each ureter is innervated by both sympathetic and parasympathetic fibers,

neural control of peristalsis appears to be insignificant compared to the way ureteral smooth muscle responds to stretch.

 HOMEOSTATIC IMBALANCE

On occasion, calcium, magnesium, or uric acid salts in urine may crystallize and precipitate in the renal pelvis, forming **renal calculi** (kal'ku-li; *calculus* = little stone), or kidney stones. Most calculi are under 5 mm in diameter and pass through the urinary tract without causing problems. However, larger calculi can obstruct a ureter and block urine drainage. Increasing pressure in the kidney causes excruciating pain, which radiates from the flank to the anterior abdominal wall on the same side. Pain also occurs when the contracting ureter wall closes in on the sharp calculi as they are being eased through a ureter by peristalsis.

Predisposing conditions are frequent bacterial infections of the urinary tract, urine retention, high blood levels of calcium, and alkaline urine. Surgical removal of calculi has been almost entirely replaced by *shock wave lithotripsy*, a noninvasive procedure that uses ultrasonic shock waves to shatter the calculi. The pulverized, sandlike remnants of the calculi are then painlessly eliminated in the urine. People with a history of kidney stones are encouraged to acidify their urine by drinking cranberry juice and to ingest enough water to keep the urine dilute. ●

Urinary Bladder

The **urinary bladder** is a smooth, collapsible, muscular sac that stores urine temporarily. It is located retroperitoneally on the pelvic floor just posterior to

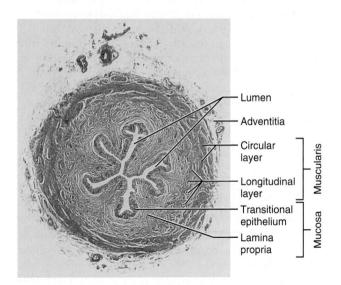

FIGURE 25.17 **Cross-sectional view of the ureter wall (15×).**

Q *How do the internal and external urethral sphincters differ structurally and functionally?*

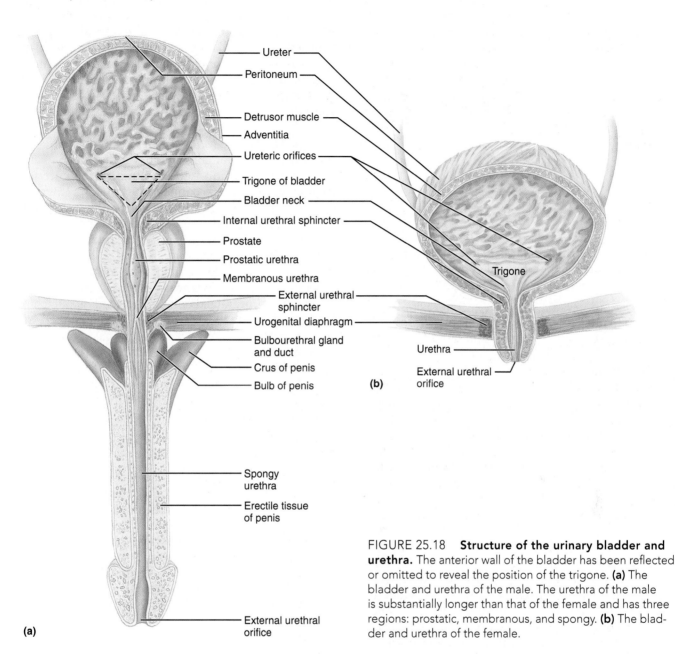

Ureter
Peritoneum
Detrusor muscle
Adventitia
Ureteric orifices
Trigone of bladder
Bladder neck
Internal urethral sphincter
Prostate
Prostatic urethra
Membranous urethra
External urethral sphincter
Urogenital diaphragm
Bulbourethral gland and duct
Crus of penis
Bulb of penis
Spongy urethra
Erectile tissue of penis
External urethral orifice

(a)

Trigone
Urethra
External urethral orifice

(b)

FIGURE 25.18 **Structure of the urinary bladder and urethra.** The anterior wall of the bladder has been reflected or omitted to reveal the position of the trigone. **(a)** The bladder and urethra of the male. The urethra of the male is substantially longer than that of the female and has three regions: prostatic, membranous, and spongy. **(b)** The bladder and urethra of the female.

the pubic symphysis. The prostate (part of the male reproductive system) surrounds the bladder neck inferiorly where it empties into the urethra. In females, the bladder is anterior to the vagina and uterus.

The interior of the bladder has openings for both ureters and the urethra (Figure 25.18). The smooth, triangular region of the bladder base outlined by these three openings is the **trigone** (tri´gōn; *trigon* = triangle), important clinically because infections tend to persist in this region.

The bladder wall has three layers: a mucosa containing transitional epithelium, a thick muscular layer, and a fibrous adventitia (except on its superior surface, where it is covered by the peritoneum). The muscular layer, called the **detrusor muscle** (de-tru´sor;

A *The internal sphincter, composed of smooth muscle, is controlled involuntarily; the external sphincter, of skeletal muscle, is controlled voluntarily.*

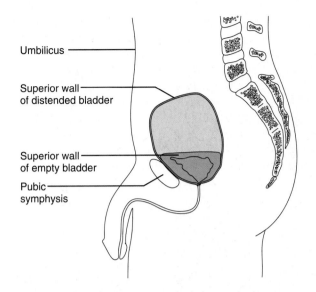

Umbilicus

Superior wall of distended bladder

Superior wall of empty bladder

Pubic symphysis

FIGURE 25.19 **Position and shape of a distended and an empty urinary bladder in an adult male.**

"to thrust out"), consists of intermingled smooth muscle fibers arranged in inner and outer longitudinal layers and a middle circular layer.

The bladder is very distensible and uniquely suited for its function of urine storage. When empty, the bladder collapses into its basic pyramidal shape and its walls are thick and thrown into folds (rugae). As urine accumulates, the bladder expands, becomes pear shaped, and rises superiorly in the abdominal cavity (Figure 25.19). The muscular wall stretches and thins, and rugae disappear. These changes allow the bladder to store more urine without a significant rise in internal pressure. A moderately full bladder is about 12 cm (5 inches) long and holds approximately 500 ml (1 pint) of urine, but it can hold nearly double that if necessary. When tense with urine, it can be palpated well above the pubic symphysis. The maximum capacity of the bladder is 800–1000 ml and when it is overdistended, it may burst. Although urine is formed continuously by the kidneys, it is usually stored in the bladder until its release is convenient.

Urethra

The **urethra** is a thin-walled muscular tube that drains urine from the bladder and conveys it out of the body. The epithelium of its mucosal lining is mostly pseudostratified columnar epithelium. However, near the bladder it becomes transitional epithelium, and near the external opening it changes to a protective stratified squamous epithelium.

At the bladder-urethra junction a thickening of the detrusor smooth muscle forms the **internal**

urethral sphincter (Figure 25.18). This involuntary sphincter keeps the urethra closed when urine is not being passed and prevents leaking between voiding. This sphincter is unusual in that contraction opens it and relaxation closes it. The **external urethral sphincter** surrounds the urethra as it passes through the *urogenital diaphragm*. This sphincter is formed of skeletal muscle and is voluntarily controlled. The *levator ani* muscle of the pelvic floor also serves as a voluntary constrictor of the urethra (see Table 10.7, p. 350).

The length and functions of the urethra differ in the two sexes. In females the urethra is only 3–4 cm (1.5 inches) long and tightly bound to the anterior vaginal wall by fibrous connective tissue. Its external opening, the **external urethral orifice,** lies anterior to the vaginal opening and posterior to the clitoris.

In males the urethra is approximately 20 cm (8 inches) long and has three regions. The **prostatic urethra,** about 2.5 cm (1 inch) long, runs within the prostate. The **membranous urethra,** which runs through the urogenital diaphragm, extends about 2 cm from the prostate to the beginning of the penis. The **spongy urethra,** about 15 cm long, passes through the penis and opens at its tip via the **external urethral orifice.** The male urethra has a double function: It carries semen as well as urine out of the body. The reproductive function of the male urethra is discussed in Chapter 27.

◤ HOMEOSTATIC IMBALANCE

Because the female's urethra is very short and its external orifice is close to the anal opening, improper toilet habits (wiping back to front after defecation) can easily carry fecal bacteria into the urethra. Actually, most urinary tract infections occur in sexually active women, because intercourse drives bacteria from the vagina and external genital region toward the bladder. The use of spermicides magnifies this problem, because the spermicide kills helpful bacteria, allowing infectious fecal bacteria to colonize the vagina. Overall, 40% of all women get urinary tract infections.

The urethral mucosa is continuous with that of the rest of the urinary tract, and an inflammation of the urethra *(urethritis)* can ascend the tract to cause bladder inflammation *(cystitis)* or even renal inflammations *(pyelitis* or *pyelonephritis)*. Symptoms of urinary tract infection include *dysuria* (painful urination), urinary *urgency* and *frequency,* fever, and sometimes cloudy or blood-tinged urine. When the kidneys are involved, back pain and a severe headache often occur. Most urinary tract infections are easily cured by antibiotics. ●

Micturition

Micturition (mik"tu-rish'un; *mictur* = urinate), also called urination or **voiding,** is the act of emptying the bladder. However, most of the time we are not micturating, but storing urine with the help of our storage reflexes. As urine accumulates, distension of the bladder walls activates stretch receptors there. Impulses from the activated receptors travel via visceral afferent fibers to the sacral region of the spinal cord, setting up spinal reflexes that (1) increase sympathetic inhibition of the bladder detrusor muscle, which keeps the internal sphincter closed (temporarily), and (2) stimulate contraction of the external urethral sphincter by activating pudendal motor fibers (Figure 25.20a).

When about 200 ml of urine has accumulated, afferent impulses are transmitted to the brain, creating the urge to void. Contractions of the bladder become more frequent and more urgent and if it is convenient to empty the bladder (a decision made by the cerebral cortex), voiding reflexes are initiated. Visceral afferent impulses activate the *micturition center* of the dorsolateral pons. Acting as an on/off switch for micturition, this center signals the parasympathetic neurons that stimulate contraction of the detrusor muscle, opening the internal sphincter. It also inhibits somatic efferents, relaxing the external sphincter, and allowing urine to flow (Figure 25.20b).

When one chooses not to void, reflex bladder contractions subside within a minute or so and urine continues to accumulate. Because the external sphincter is voluntarily controlled, we can choose to keep it closed and postpone bladder emptying temporarily. After another 200–300 ml or so has collected, the micturition reflex occurs again and, if urination is delayed again, is damped once more. The urge to void eventually becomes irresistible and micturition occurs when urine volume exceeds 500–600 ml, whether one wills it or not. After normal micturition, only about 10 ml of urine remains in the bladder.

⬛ HOMEOSTATIC IMBALANCE

After the toddler years, **incontinence** is usually a result of emotional problems, physical pressure during pregnancy, or nervous system problems. In *stress incontinence,* a sudden increase in intra-abdominal pressure (during laughing and coughing) forces urine through the external sphincter. This condition is common during pregnancy when the heavy uterus stretches the muscles of the pelvic floor and the urogenital diaphragm that support the external sphincter. In *overflow incontinence,* urine dribbles from the urethra whenever the bladder overfills.

In **urinary retention,** the bladder is unable to expel its contained urine. Urinary retention is normal after general anesthesia (it seems that it takes a little time for the detrusor muscle to regain its activity). Urinary retention in men often reflects hypertrophy of the prostate, which narrows the urethra, making it difficult to void. When urinary retention is prolonged, a slender rubber drainage tube called a **catheter** (kath'ĕ-ter) must be inserted through the urethra to drain the urine and prevent bladder trauma from excessive stretching. ●

Developmental Aspects of the Urinary System

As the kidneys develop in a young embryo, it almost seems as if they are unable to "make up their mind" how to go about it. As illustrated in Figure 25.21, three different sets of kidneys develop from the *urogenital ridges,* paired elevations of the intermediate mesoderm that give rise to both the urinary organs and the reproductive organs. Only the last set persists to become adult kidneys.

During the fourth week of development, the first tubule system, the **pronephros** (pro-nef'ros; "prekidney"), forms and then quickly degenerates as a second, lower set appears. Although the pronephros never functions and is gone by the sixth week, the **pronephric duct** that connects it to the cloaca persists and is used by the later-developing kidneys. (The cloaca is the terminal part of the gut that opens to the body exterior.) As the second renal system, the **mesonephros** (mez"o-nef'ros; "middle kidney"), claims the pronephric duct, it comes to be called the **mesonephric duct.** The mesonephric kidneys degenerate (with remnants incorporated into the male reproductive system) once the third set, the **metanephros** (met"ah-nef'ros; "after kidney"), makes its appearance.

The metanephros starts to develop at about five weeks as hollow **ureteric buds** that push superiorly from the mesonephric duct into the urogenital ridge, inducing the mesoderm there to form nephrons. The distal ends of the ureteric buds form the renal pelves, calyces, and collecting ducts; their unexpanded proximal parts, now called the **ureteric ducts,** become the ureters.

Because the kidneys develop in the pelvis and then ascend to their final position, they receive their blood supply from successively higher sources. Although the lower blood vessels usually degenerate, they sometimes persist so that multiple renal arteries are common. The metanephric kidneys are excreting urine by the third month of fetal life, and most of the amniotic fluid that surrounds a developing fetus is fetal urine. Nonetheless,

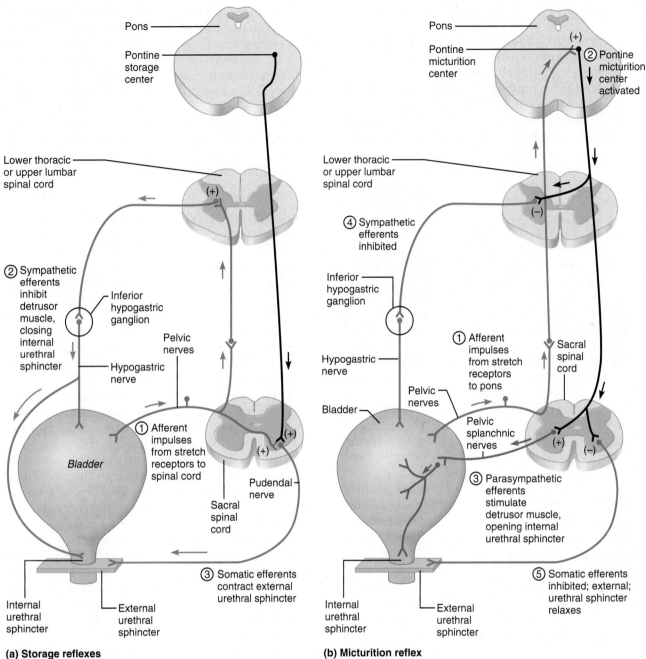

Key:

(+) Excitatory synapse
(–) Inhibitory synapse
—— Visceral afferent
—— Sympathetic
—— Somatic efferent
—— Parasympathetic
—— Interneuron

(a) Storage reflexes

(b) Micturition reflex

FIGURE 25.20 **Neural circuits controlling continence and micturition. (a)** As the bladder fills with urine, distension of the bladder wall initiates storage reflexes. **(b)** The micturition reflex is initiated either by further bladder distension, which increases afferent impulses to the pontine micturition center, or by input from higher brain centers (not shown) initiating voluntary micturition.

the fetal kidneys do not work nearly as hard as they will after birth because exchange through the placenta allows the mother's urinary system to clear most of the undesirable substances from the fetal blood.

As the metanephros is developing, the cloaca subdivides to form the future rectum and anal canal and the **urogenital sinus,** into which the urinary and genital ducts empty. The urinary bladder and the urethra then develop from the urogenital sinus.

25

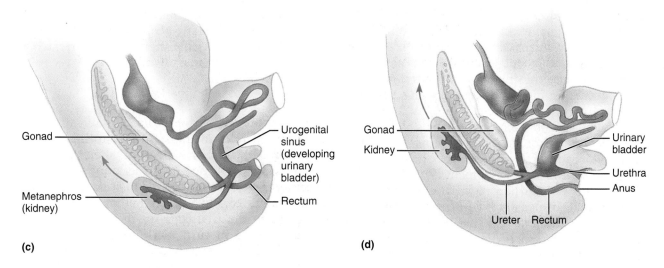

FIGURE 25.21 **Development of the urinary system of the embryo. (a)** Fifth week. **(b)** Sixth week. **(c)** Seventh week. **(d)** Eighth week. (Direction of metanephros migration as it develops is indicated by red arrows.)

25

HOMEOSTATIC IMBALANCE

Three of the most common congenital abnormalities of the urinary system are horseshoe kidney, hypospadias, and polycystic kidney.

When ascending from the pelvis the kidneys are very close together, and in 1 out of 600 people they fuse across the midline, forming a single, U-shaped *horseshoe kidney*. This condition is usually asymptomatic, but it may be associated with other kidney abnormalities, such as obstructed drainage, that place a person at risk for frequent kidney infections.

Hypospadias (hi"po-spa′de-as), found in male infants only, is the most common congenital abnormality of the urethra. It occurs when the urethral orifice is located on the ventral surface of the penis.

This problem is corrected surgically when the child is around 12 months old.

Polycystic kidney disease (PKD) is a group of disorders characterized by the presence of many fluid-filled cysts in the kidneys, which interfere with renal function, ultimately leading to renal failure. These disorders can be grouped into two general forms. The less severe form is inherited in an autosomal dominant manner and is much more common, affecting 1 in 500 people. The cysts develop so gradually that they produce no symptoms until about 40 years of age. Then both kidneys begin to enlarge as blisterlike cysts containing fluid accumulate. The damage caused by these cysts progresses slowly, and many victims live without problems until their 60s. Ultimately, however, the kidneys become "knobby" and grossly enlarged, reaching a mass of up to 14 kg (30 lb) each.

The much less common and more severe form follows an autosomal recessive pattern of inheritance. Almost half of newborns with recessive PKD die just after birth, and survivors generally develop renal failure in early childhood. Recessive PKD results from a mutation in a single huge gene, but the dominant form of PKD (described above) is usually caused by a mutation in one of two different genes, which code for proteins involved in cell signaling. It is not yet clear how defects in these proteins lead to cyst formation. As yet, the only treatments are the usual treatments for kidney failure—renal dialysis or a kidney transplant. ●

Because its bladder is very small and its kidneys are less able to concentrate urine for the first two months, a newborn baby voids 5 to 40 times daily, depending on fluid intake. By 2 months of age, the infant is voiding approximately 400 ml/day, and the amount steadily increases until adolescence, when adult urine output (about 1500 ml/day) is achieved.

Incontinence, the inability to control micturition, is normal in infants because they have not yet learned to control the external urethral sphincter. Reflex voiding occurs each time a baby's bladder fills enough to activate the stretch receptors. Control of the voluntary urethral sphincter goes hand in hand with nervous system development. By 15 months, most toddlers know when they have voided. By 18 months, they can usually hold urine for about two hours. This is the first sign that toilet training can begin. Daytime control usually is achieved first; it is unrealistic to expect complete nighttime control before age 4.

From childhood through late middle age, most urinary system problems are infectious conditions. *Escherichia coli* (esh″ĕ-rik′e-ah ko′li) bacteria are normal residents of the digestive tract and generally cause no problems there, but these bacteria account for 80% of all urinary tract infections. *Sexually transmitted diseases* can also inflame the urinary tract

and clog some of its ducts. Childhood streptococcal infections such as strep throat and scarlet fever, if not treated promptly, may cause long-term inflammatory renal damage.

Only about 3% of elderly people have histologically normal kidneys, and kidney function declines with advancing age. The kidneys shrink as the nephrons decrease in size and number, and the tubule cells become less efficient. By age 80, the GFR is only half that of middle-aged adults, possibly due to atherosclerotic narrowing of the renal arteries. Diabetics are particularly at risk for renal disease, and nearly 50% of those who have had diabetes mellitus for 20 years are in renal failure.

The bladder of an aged person is shrunken, with less than half the capacity of a young adult (250 ml versus 600 ml). Loss of bladder tone causes an annoying increase in frequency of micturition. *Nocturia* (nok-tu′re-ah), the need to get up during the night to urinate, plagues almost two-thirds of this population. Many people eventually experience incontinence, which can usually be treated with exercise, medications, or surgery.

▪ ▪ ▪

The ureters, urinary bladder, and urethra play important roles in transporting, storing, and eliminating urine from the body, but when the term "urinary system" is used, it is the kidneys that capture center stage. As summarized in *Making Connections* in Chapter 26, other organ systems of the body contribute to the well-being of the urinary system in many ways. In turn, without continuous kidney function, the electrolyte and fluid balance of the blood is dangerously disturbed, and internal body fluids quickly become contaminated with nitrogenous wastes. No body cell can escape the harmful effects of such imbalances.

Now that renal mechanisms have been described, we are ready to integrate kidney function into the larger topic of fluid and electrolyte balance in the body—the focus of Chapter 26.

Related Clinical Terms

Acute glomerulonephritis (GN) (glo-mer″u-lo-nef-ri′tis) Inflammation of the glomeruli, leading to increased permeability of the filtration membrane. In some cases, circulating immune complexes (antibodies bound to foreign substances, such as streptococcal bacteria) become trapped in the glomerular basement membranes. In other cases, immune responses are mounted against one's own kidney tissues, leading to glomerular damage. In either case, the inflammatory response that follows damages the filtration membrane, allowing blood proteins and even blood cells to pass into the renal tubules and into the urine. As the osmotic pressure of

blood drops, fluid seeps from the bloodstream into the tissue spaces, causing bodywide edema. Renal shutdown requiring dialysis may occur temporarily, but normal renal function usually returns within a few months. If permanent glomerular damage occurs, chronic GN and ultimately renal failure result.

Bladder cancer Bladder cancer, three times more common in men than in women, accounts for about 2% of all cancer deaths. It usually involves neoplasms of the bladder's lining epithelium and may be induced by carcinogens from the environment or the workplace that end up in urine. Smoking, exposure to industrial chemicals, and arsenic in drinking water also have been linked to bladder cancer. Blood in the urine is a common warning sign.

Cystocele (sis'to-sēl; *cyst* = a sac, the bladder; *cele* = hernia, rupture) Herniation of the urinary bladder into the vagina; a common result of tearing of the pelvic floor muscles during childbirth.

Cystoscopy (sis-tos'ko-pe; *cyst* = bladder; *scopy* = observation) Procedure in which a thin viewing tube is threaded into the bladder through the urethra to examine the bladder's mucosal surface.

Diabetes insipidus (in-sĭ'pĭ-dus; *insipid* = tasteless, bland) Condition in which large amounts (up to 40 L/day) of dilute urine flush from the body; results from malfunction or deficiency of aquaporins or ADH receptors in the collecting duct (nephrogenic diabetes insipidus), or little or no ADH release due to injury to, or a tumor in, the hypothalamus or posterior pituitary. Can lead to severe dehydration and electrolyte imbalances unless the individual drinks large volumes of liquids. See Chapter 16, p. 617.

Intravenous pyelogram (IVP) (pi'ĕ-lo-gram; *pyelo* = kidney pelvis; *gram* = written) An X ray of the kidney and ureter obtained after intravenous injection of a contrast medium (as in Figure 25.1b). Allows assessment for obstructions,

viewing of renal anatomy (pelvis and calyces), and determination of rate of excretion of the contrast medium.

Nephrotoxin A substance (heavy metal, organic solvent, or bacterial toxin) that is toxic to the kidney.

Nocturnal enuresis (NE) (en"u-re'sis) An inability to control urination at night during sleep; bed-wetting. In children over 6, called primary NE if control has never been achieved and secondary NE if control was achieved and then lost. Secondary NE often has psychological causes. Primary NE is more common and results from a combination of inadequate nocturnal ADH production, unusually sound sleep, or a small bladder capacity. Synthetic ADH (as tablet or nasal spray) often corrects the problem.

Renal infarct Area of dead, or necrotic, renal tissue due to blockage of the vascular supply to the kidney or hemorrhage. A common cause of localized renal infarct is obstruction of an interlobar artery. Because interlobar arteries are end arteries (do not anastomose), their obstruction leads to ischemic necrosis of the portions of the kidney they supply.

Urinalysis Analysis of urine as an aid to diagnosing health or disease. The most significant indicators of disease in urine are proteins, glucose, acetone, blood, and pus.

Urologist (u-rol'o-jist) Physician who specializes in diseases of urinary structures in both sexes and in diseases of the reproductive tract of males.

Chapter Summary

Media study tools that could provide you additional help in reviewing specific key topics of Chapter 25 are referenced below.
IP *= InterActive Physiology*

Kidney Anatomy   (pp. 998–1006)

Location and External Anatomy   (pp. 998–999)

1. The paired kidneys are retroperitoneal in the superior lumbar region.

2. A fibrous capsule, a perirenal fat capsule, and renal fascia surround each kidney. The perirenal fat capsule helps hold the kidneys in position.

Internal Anatomy   (pp. 999–1001)

3. A kidney has a superficial cortex, a deeper medulla consisting mainly of medullary pyramids, and a medial pelvis. Extensions of the pelvis (calyces) surround and collect urine draining from the apices of the medullary pyramids.

Blood and Nerve Supply   (p. 1001)

4. The kidneys receive 25% of the total cardiac output per minute.

5. The vascular pathway through a kidney is as follows: renal artery → segmental arteries → interlobar arteries → arcuate arteries → cortical radiate arteries → afferent arterioles → glomeruli → efferent arterioles → peritubular capillary beds → cortical radiate veins → arcuate veins → interlobar veins → renal vein.

6. The nerve supply of the kidneys is derived from the renal plexus.

Nephrons   (pp. 1001–1006)

7. Nephrons are the structural and functional units of the kidneys.

8. Each nephron consists of a glomerulus (a high-pressure capillary bed) and a renal tubule. Subdivisions of the renal

tubule (from the glomerulus) are the glomerular capsule, proximal convoluted tubule, loop of Henle, and distal convoluted tubule. A second capillary bed, the low-pressure peritubular capillary bed, is closely associated with the renal tubule of each nephron.

9. The more numerous cortical nephrons are located almost entirely in the cortex; only a small part of their loop of Henle penetrates into the medulla. Glomeruli of juxtamedullary nephrons are located at the cortex-medulla junction, and their loop of Henle dips deeply into the medulla. Instead of directly forming peritubular capillaries, the efferent arterioles of many of the juxtamedullary nephrons form unique bundles of straight vessels, called vasa recta, that serve tubule segments in the medulla. Juxtamedullary nephrons and the vasa recta play an important role in establishing the medullary osmotic gradient.

10. Collecting ducts receive urine from many nephrons and help concentrate urine. They form the medullary pyramids.

11. The juxtaglomerular apparatus is at the point of contact between the afferent arteriole and the most distal part of the ascending limb of the loop of Henle. It consists of the granular cells and the macula densa.

IP Urinary System; Topic: Anatomy Review, pp. 1–20.

12. The filtration membrane consists of the fenestrated glomerular endothelium, the intervening basement membrane, and the podocyte-containing visceral layer of the glomerular capsule. It permits free passage of substances smaller than (most) plasma proteins.

Kidney Physiology: Mechanisms of Urine Formation (pp. 1007–1021)

1. Functions of the nephrons include filtration, tubular reabsorption, and tubular secretion. Via these functional processes, the kidneys regulate the volume, composition, and pH of the blood, and eliminate nitrogenous metabolic wastes.

Step 1: Glomerular Filtration   (pp. 1007–1011)

2. The glomeruli function as filters. High glomerular blood pressure (55 mm Hg) occurs because the glomeruli are fed and drained by arterioles, and the afferent arterioles are larger in diameter than the efferent arterioles.

3. About one-fifth of the plasma flowing through the kidneys is filtered from the glomeruli into the renal tubules.

4. Usually about 10 mm Hg, the net filtration pressure (NFP) is determined by the relationship between forces favoring filtration (glomerular hydrostatic pressure) and forces that oppose it (capsular hydrostatic pressure and blood colloid osmotic pressure).

5. The glomerular filtration rate (GFR) is directly proportional to the net filtration pressure and is about 125 ml/min (180 L/day).

6. Renal autoregulation, which enables the kidneys to maintain a relatively constant renal blood flow and glomerular filtration rate, involves a myogenic mechanism and a tubuloglomerular feedback mechanism mediated by the macula densa.

7. Extrinsic control of GFR, via nerves and hormones, maintains blood pressure. Strong sympathetic nervous system activation causes constriction of the afferent arterioles, which decreases filtrate formation and stimulates renin release by the granular cells.

IP Urinary System; Topic: Glomerular Filtration, pp. 1–15.

8. The renin-angiotensin mechanism mediated by the granular cells raises systemic blood pressure via generation of angiotensin II, which promotes aldosterone secretion.

Step 2: Tubular Reabsorption   (pp. 1011–1015)

9. During tubular reabsorption, needed substances are removed from the filtrate by the tubule cells and returned to the peritubular capillary blood. The primary active transport of Na^+ by a Na^+-K^+ ATPase pump at the basolateral membrane accounts for Na^+ reabsorption and establishes the electrochemical gradient that drives the reabsorption of most other solutes and H_2O. Na^+ enters at the luminal surface of the tubule cell via facilitated diffusion through channels or as part of a cotransport mechanism.

10. Passive tubular reabsorption is driven by electrochemical gradients established by active reabsorption of sodium ions. Water, many anions, and various other substances (for example, urea) are reabsorbed passively by diffusion via transcellular or paracellular pathways.

11. Secondary active tubular reabsorption occurs by cotransport with Na^+ via protein carriers. Transport of such substances is limited by the number of carriers available. Actively reabsorbed substances include glucose, amino acids, and some ions.

12. Certain substances (creatinine, drug metabolites, etc.) are not reabsorbed or are reabsorbed incompletely because of the lack of carriers, their size, or non–lipid solubility.

13. The proximal tubule cells are most active in reabsorption. Most of the nutrients, 65% of the water and sodium ions, and the bulk of actively transported ions are reabsorbed in the proximal convoluted tubules.

14. Reabsorption of additional sodium ions and water occurs in the distal tubules and collecting ducts and is hormonally controlled. Aldosterone increases the reabsorption of sodium (and water that follows it); antidiuretic hormone enhances water reabsorption by the collecting ducts.

Step 3: Tubular Secretion   (p. 1015)

15. Tubular secretion is a means of adding substances to the filtrate (from the blood or tubule cells). It is an active process that is important in eliminating drugs, certain wastes, and excess ions and in maintaining the acid-base balance of the blood.

Regulation of Urine Concentration and Volume (pp. 1015–1021)

16. The graduated hyperosmolality of the medullary fluids (largely due to the cycling of NaCl and urea) ensures that the filtrate reaching the distal convoluted tubule is dilute (hypo-osmolar). This allows urine with osmolalities ranging from 70 to 1200 mOsm to be formed.

- The descending limb of the loop of Henle is permeable to water, which leaves the filtrate and enters the medullary interstitium. The filtrate and medullary fluid at the bend of the loop of Henle are hyperosmolar.
- The ascending limb is impermeable to water. Na^+ and Cl^- move out of the filtrate into the interstitial space, passively in the thin limb and actively in the thick limb. The filtrate becomes more dilute.
- As filtrate flows through the collecting ducts in the inner medulla, urea diffuses into the interstitial space. From here, urea reenters the thin limb and is recycled.
- The blood flow in the vasa recta is sluggish, and the contained blood equilibrates with the medullary interstitial fluid. Hence, blood entering and exiting the medulla in the vasa recta is isotonic to blood plasma and the high solute concentration of the medulla is maintained.

17. In the absence of antidiuretic hormone, dilute urine is formed because the dilute filtrate reaching the collecting duct is simply allowed to pass from the kidneys.

18. As blood levels of antidiuretic hormone rise, the collecting ducts become more permeable to water, and water moves out of the filtrate as it flows through the hyperosmotic medullary areas. Consequently, more concentrated urine is produced, and in smaller amounts.

IP Urinary System; Topics: Early Filtrate Processing, pp. 1–22; Late Filtrate Processing, pp. 1–13.

Renal Clearance   (p. 1021)

19. Renal clearance is the volume of plasma that is completely cleared of a particular substance per minute. Studies of renal clearance provide information about renal function or the course of renal disease.

Urine   (pp. 1021–1023)

1. Urine is typically clear, yellow, aromatic, and slightly acidic. Its specific gravity ranges from 1.001 to 1.035.

2. Urine is 95% water; solutes include nitrogenous wastes (urea, uric acid, and creatinine) and various ions (always sodium, potassium, sulfate, and phosphate).

3. Substances not normally found in urine include glucose, proteins, erythrocytes, leukocytes, hemoglobin, and bile pigments.

4. Daily urinary volume is typically 1.5–1.8 L, but this depends on the state of hydration of the body.

Ureters   (pp. 1023–1024)

1. The ureters are slender tubes running retroperitoneally from each kidney to the bladder. They conduct urine by peristalsis from the renal pelvis to the urinary bladder.

25

Urinary Bladder (pp. 1024–1026)

1. The urinary bladder, which functions to store urine, is a distensible muscular sac that lies posterior to the pubic symphysis. It has two inlets (ureters) and one outlet (urethra) that outline the trigone. In males, the prostate surrounds its outlet.

2. The bladder wall consists of a transitional epithelium-containing mucosa, a three-layered detrusor muscle, and an adventitia.

Urethra (p. 1026)

1. The urethra is a muscular tube that conveys urine from the bladder to the body exterior.

2. Where the urethra leaves the bladder, it is surrounded by an internal urethral sphincter, an involuntary smooth muscle sphincter. Where it passes through the urogenital diaphragm, the voluntary external urethral sphincter is formed by skeletal muscle.

3. In females the urethra is 3–4 cm long and conducts only urine. In males it is 20 cm long and conducts both urine and semen.

Micturition (p. 1027)

1. Micturition is emptying of the bladder.

2. Stretching of the bladder wall by accumulating urine initiates the micturition reflex, in which parasympathetic fibers, in response to signals from the micturition center of the pons, cause the detrusor muscle to contract and the internal urethral sphincter to open.

3. Because the external sphincter is voluntarily controlled, micturition can usually be delayed temporarily.

Developmental Aspects of the Urinary System (pp. 1027–1030)

1. Three sets of kidneys (pronephric, mesonephric, and metanephric) develop from the intermediate mesoderm. The metanephros is excreting urine by the third month of development.

2. Common congenital abnormalities are horseshoe kidney, polycystic kidney, and hypospadias.

3. The kidneys of newborns are less able to concentrate urine; their bladder is small and voiding is frequent. Neuromuscular maturation generally allows toilet training for micturition to begin by 18 months of age.

4. The most common urinary system problems in children and young to middle-aged adults are bacterial infections.

5. Renal failure has serious consequences: the kidneys are unable to concentrate urine, nitrogenous wastes accumulate in the blood, and acid-base and electrolyte imbalances occur.

6. With age, nephrons are lost, the filtration rate decreases, and tubule cells become less efficient at concentrating urine.

7. Bladder capacity and tone decrease with age, leading to frequent micturition and (often) incontinence. Urinary retention is a common problem of elderly men.

Review Questions

Multiple Choice/Matching

(Some questions have more than one correct answer. Select the best answer or answers from the choices given.)

1. The lowest blood concentration of nitrogenous waste occurs in the (a) hepatic vein, (b) inferior vena cava, (c) renal artery, (d) renal vein.

2. The glomerular capillaries differ from other capillary networks in the body because they (a) have a larger area of anastomosis, (b) are derived from and drain into arterioles, (c) are not made of endothelium, (d) are sites of filtrate formation.

3. Damage to the renal medulla would interfere *first* with the functioning of the (a) glomerular capsules, (b) distal convoluted tubules, (c) collecting ducts, (d) proximal convoluted tubules.

4. Which is reabsorbed by the proximal convoluted tubule cells? (a) Na^+, (b) K^+, (c) amino acids, (d) all of the above.

5. Glucose is not normally found in the urine because it (a) does not pass through the walls of the glomerulus, (b) is kept in the blood by colloid osmotic pressure, (c) is reabsorbed by the tubule cells, (d) is removed by the body cells before the blood reaches the kidney.

6. Filtration at the glomerulus is inversely related to (a) water reabsorption, (b) capsular hydrostatic pressure, (c) arterial blood pressure, (d) acidity of the urine.

7. Tubular reabsorption (a) of glucose and many other substances is a T_m-limited active transport process, (b) of chloride is always linked to the passive transport of Na^+, (c) is the movement of substances from the blood into the nephron, (d) of sodium occurs only in the proximal tubule.

8. If a freshly voided urine sample contains excessive amounts of urochrome, it has (a) an ammonia-like odor, (b) a pH below normal, (c) a dark yellow color, (d) a pH above normal.

9. Conditions such as diabetes mellitus, starvation, and low-carbohydrate diets are closely linked to (a) ketonuria, (b) pyuria, (c) albuminuria, (d) hematuria.

10. Which of the following is/are true about ADH? (a) It promotes obligatory water reabsorption, (b) it is secreted in response to an increase in extracellular fluid osmolality, (c) it causes insertion of aquaporins in the PCT, (d) it promotes Na^+ reabsorption.

Short Answer Essay Questions

11. What is the importance of the perirenal fat capsule that surrounds the kidney?

12. Trace the pathway a creatinine molecule takes from a glomerulus to the urethra. Name every microscopic or gross structure it passes through on its journey.

13. Explain the important differences between blood plasma and renal filtrate, and relate the differences to the structure of the filtration membrane.

14. Describe the mechanisms that contribute to renal autoregulation.

15. Describe the physiological role and mechanisms of extrinsic regulation of GFR.

16. Describe what is involved in active and passive tubular reabsorption.

17. Explain how the peritubular capillaries are adapted for receiving reabsorbed substances.

25

18. Explain the process and purpose of tubular secretion.

19. How does aldosterone modify the chemical composition of urine?

20. Explain why the filtrate becomes hypotonic as it flows through the ascending limb of the loop of Henle. Also explain why the filtrate at the bend of the loop of Henle (and the interstitial fluid of the deep portions of the medulla) is hypertonic.

21. How does urinary bladder anatomy support its storage function?

22. Define micturition and describe the storage and micturition reflexes.

23. Describe the changes that occur in kidney and bladder anatomy and physiology in old age.

 ### Critical Thinking and Clinical Application Questions

1. Mrs. Bigda, a 60-year-old woman, was brought to the hospital by the police after falling to the pavement. She is found to have alcoholic hepatitis. She is put on a salt- and protein-restricted diet and diuretics are prescribed to manage her ascites (accumulated fluid in the peritoneal cavity). How will diuretics reduce this excess fluid? Name and describe the mechanisms of action of three types of diuretics. Why is her diet salt-restricted?

2. While repairing a frayed utility wire, Herbert, an experienced lineman, slips and falls to the ground. Medical exami-nation reveals a fracture of his lower spine and transection of the lumbar region of the spinal cord. How will Herbert's micturition be controlled from this point on? Will he ever again feel the need to void? Will there be dribbling of urine between voidings? Explain the reasoning behind all your responses.

3. What is cystitis? Why are women more frequent cystitis sufferers than men?

4. Hattie, aged 55, is awakened by excruciating pain that radiates from her right abdomen to the loin and groin regions on the same side. The pain is not continuous but re-curs at intervals of 3 to 4 minutes. Diagnose her problem, and cite factors that might favor its occurrence. Also, ex-plain why Hattie's pain comes in "waves."

5. Why does use of a spermicide increase a woman's risk for urinary tract infection?

6. Why are renal failure patients undergoing dialysis at risk for anemia and osteoporosis? What medications or sup-plements could you give them to prevent these problems?

LOOKING FOR MORE STUDY HELP?
A wide variety of quiz questions, tutorials, and learning exercises are available online at the Anatomy & Physiology Place (www.anatomyandphysiology.com) and, if your instructor has provided you with a MyA&P Course ID number, in MyA&P (www.myaandp.com).

Fluid, Electrolyte, and Acid-Base Balance

Body Fluids (pp. 1036–1038)

1. List the factors that determine body water content and describe the effect of each factor.

2. Indicate the relative fluid volume and solute composition of the fluid compartments of the body.

3. Contrast the overall osmotic effects of electrolytes and nonelectrolytes.

4. Describe factors that determine fluid shifts in the body.

Water Balance and ECF Osmolality (pp. 1039–1043)

5. List the routes by which water enters and leaves the body.

6. Describe feedback mechanisms that regulate water intake and hormonal controls of water output in urine.

7. Explain the importance of obligatory water losses.

8. Describe possible causes and consequences of dehydration, hypotonic hydration, and edema.

Electrolyte Balance (pp. 1043–1049)

9. Indicate the routes of electrolyte entry and loss from the body.

10. Describe the importance of ionic sodium in fluid and electrolyte balance of the body, and indicate its relationship to normal cardiovascular system functioning.

11. Describe mechanisms involved in regulating sodium balance, blood volume, and blood pressure.

12. Explain how potassium, calcium, and anion balance of plasma is regulated.

Acid-Base Balance (pp. 1049–1057, 1060)

13. List important sources of acids in the body.

14. List the three major chemical buffer systems of the body and describe how they resist pH changes.

15. Describe the influence of the respiratory system on acid-base balance.

16. Describe how the kidneys regulate hydrogen and bicarbonate ion concentrations in the blood.

17. Distinguish between acidosis and alkalosis resulting from respiratory and metabolic factors. Describe the importance of respiratory and renal compensations to acid-base balance.

Developmental Aspects of Fluid, Electrolyte, and Acid-Base Balance (p. 1060)

18. Explain why infants and the aged are at greater risk for fluid and electrolyte imbalances than are young adults.

Have you ever wondered why on certain days you don't urinate for hours at a time, while on others you void every few minutes? Or why on occasion you cannot seem to quench your thirst? These situations and many others reflect one of the body's most important functions: maintaining fluid, electrolyte, and acid-base balance.

Cell function depends not only on a continuous supply of nutrients and removal of metabolic wastes, but also on the physical and chemical homeostasis of the surrounding fluids. This was recognized with style in 1857 by the French physiologist Claude Bernard, who said, "It is the fixity of the internal environment which is the condition of free and independent life." In this chapter, we first examine the composition and distribution of fluids in the internal environment and then consider the roles of various body organs and functions in establishing, regulating, and altering this balance.

Body Fluids

Body Water Content

If you are a healthy young adult, water probably accounts for about half your body mass. However, not all bodies contain the same amount of water. Total body water is a function not only of age and body mass, but also of sex and the relative amount of body fat. Because of their low body fat and low bone mass, infants are 73% or more water (this high level of hydration accounts for their "dewy" skin, like that of a freshly picked peach). After infancy total body water declines throughout life, accounting for only about 45% of body mass in old age. A healthy young man is about 60% water; a healthy young woman about 50%. This difference between the sexes reflects the fact that females have relatively more body fat and relatively less skeletal muscle than males. Of all body tissues, adipose tissue is *least* hydrated (containing up to 20% water); even bone contains more water than does fat. By contrast, skeletal muscle is about 75% water. Thus, people with greater muscle mass have proportionately more body water.

Fluid Compartments

Water occupies two main **fluid compartments** within the body (Figure 26.1). A little less than two-thirds by volume is in the **intracellular fluid (ICF) compartment,** which actually consists of trillions of tiny individual "compartments": the cells. In an adult male of average size (70 kg, or 154 lb), ICF accounts for about 25 L of the 40 L of body water. The remaining one-third or so of body water is outside

FIGURE 26.1 **The major fluid compartments of the body.** [Values are for a 70-kg (154-lb) male.]

cells, in the **extracellular fluid (ECF) compartment.** The ECF constitutes the body's "internal environment" referred to by Claude Bernard and is the external environment of each cell. The ECF compartment is divisible into two *subcompartments:* (1) **plasma,** the fluid portion of blood, and (2) **interstitial fluid (IF),** the fluid in the microscopic spaces between tissue cells. There are numerous other examples of ECF that are distinct from both plasma and interstitial fluid—lymph, cerebrospinal fluid, humors of the eye, synovial fluid, serous fluid, secretions of the gastrointestinal tract—but most of these are similar to IF and are usually considered part of it.

Composition of Body Fluids

Electrolytes and Nonelectrolytes

Water serves as the *universal solvent* in which a variety of solutes are dissolved. Solutes may be classified broadly as *electrolytes* and *nonelectrolytes.* **Nonelectrolytes** have bonds (usually covalent bonds) that prevent them from dissociating in solution; therefore, no electrically charged species are created when nonelectrolytes dissolve in water. Most nonelectrolytes are organic molecules—glucose, lipids, creatinine, and urea, for example. In contrast, **electrolytes** are chemical compounds that *do* dissociate into ions in water. (See Chapter 2 if necessary to review these concepts of chemistry.) Because ions are charged particles, they can conduct an electrical current—hence the name *electrolyte.* Typically, electrolytes include inorganic salts, both inorganic and organic acids and bases, and some proteins.

Although all dissolved solutes contribute to the osmotic activity of a fluid, electrolytes have much greater osmotic power than nonelectrolytes because each electrolyte molecule dissociates into at least two ions. For example, a molecule of sodium chloride (NaCl) contributes twice as many solute particles as glucose (which remains undissociated), and a molecule of magnesium chloride ($MgCl_2$) contributes three times as many:

$$NaCl \rightarrow Na^+ + Cl^- \qquad \text{(electrolyte; two particles)}$$

$$MgCl_2 \rightarrow Mg^{2+} + 2Cl^- \qquad \text{(electrolyte; three particles)}$$

$$glucose \rightarrow glucose \qquad \text{(nonelectrolyte; one particle)}$$

Regardless of the type of solute particle, water moves according to osmotic gradients—from an area of lesser osmolality to an area of greater osmolality. Thus, electrolytes have the greatest ability to cause fluid shifts.

Electrolyte concentrations of body fluids are usually expressed in **milliequivalents per liter (mEq/L)**, a measure of the number of electrical charges in 1 liter of solution. The concentration of any ion in solution can be computed using the equation

$$mEq/L = \frac{\text{ion concentration (mg/L)}}{\text{atomic weight of ion (mg/mmol)}} \times \begin{array}{l} \text{no. of} \\ \text{electrical} \\ \text{charges on} \\ \text{one ion} \end{array}$$

Thus, to compute the mEq/L of sodium or calcium ions in solution in plasma, we would determine the normal concentration of these ions in plasma, look up their atomic weights in the periodic table (see Appendix E), and plug these values into the equation:

$$Na^+: \frac{3300 \text{ mg/L}}{23 \text{ mg/mmol}} \times 1 = 143 \text{ mEq/L}$$

$$Ca^{2+}: \frac{100 \text{ mg/L}}{40 \text{ mg/mmol}} \times 2 = 5 \text{ mEq/L}$$

Notice that for ions with a single charge, 1 mEq is equal to 1 mOsm, whereas 1 mEq of bivalent ions (those with a double charge like calcium) is equal to 1/2 mOsm. In either case, 1 mEq provides the same amount of charge.

Comparison of Extracellular and Intracellular Fluids

A quick glance at the bar graphs in Figure 26.2 reveals that each fluid compartment has a distinctive pattern of electrolytes. Except for the relatively high protein content in plasma, however, the extracellular fluids are very similar. Their chief cation is sodium, and their major anion is chloride. However, plasma contains somewhat fewer chloride ions than interstitial fluid, because the nonpenetrating plasma proteins are normally anions and plasma is electrically neutral.

In contrast to extracellular fluids, the ICF contains only small amounts of Na^+ and Cl^-. Its most abundant cation is potassium, and its major anion is HPO_4^{2-}. Cells also contain substantial quantities of soluble proteins (about three times the amount found in plasma).

Notice that sodium and potassium ion concentrations in ECF and ICF are nearly opposite (Figure 26.2). The characteristic distribution of these ions on the two sides of cellular membranes reflects the activity of cellular ATP-dependent sodium-potassium pumps, which keep intracellular Na^+ concentrations low and K^+ concentrations high. Renal mechanisms can reinforce these ion distributions by secreting K^+ into the filtrate as Na^+ is reabsorbed from the filtrate.

Electrolytes are the most abundant solutes in body fluids and determine most of their chemical and physical reactions, but they do not constitute the *bulk* of dissolved solutes in these fluids. Proteins and some of the nonelectrolytes (phospholipids, cholesterol, and triglycerides) found in the ECF are large molecules. They account for about 90% of the mass of dissolved solutes in plasma, 60% in the IF, and 97% in the ICF.

Fluid Movement Among Compartments

The continuous exchange and mixing of body fluids are regulated by osmotic and hydrostatic pressures. Although water moves freely between the compartments along osmotic gradients, solutes are unequally distributed because of their size, electrical charge, or dependence on transport proteins. Anything that changes the solute concentration in any compartment leads to net water flows.

Exchanges between plasma and IF occur across capillary membranes. The pressures driving these fluid movements are described in detail in Chapter 19 on pp. 739–740. Here we will simply review the outcome of these mechanisms. Nearly protein-free plasma is forced out of the blood into the interstitial space by the hydrostatic pressure of blood. This filtered fluid is then almost completely reabsorbed into the bloodstream in response to the colloid osmotic (oncotic) pressure of plasma proteins. Under normal circumstances, the small net leakage that remains behind in the interstitial space is picked up by lymphatic vessels and returned to the blood.

Exchanges between the IF and ICF occur across plasma membranes and depend on the membranes' complex permeability properties. As a general rule,

26

Q *What is the major cation in ECF? In ICF? What are the intracellular anion counterparts of ECF's chloride ions?*

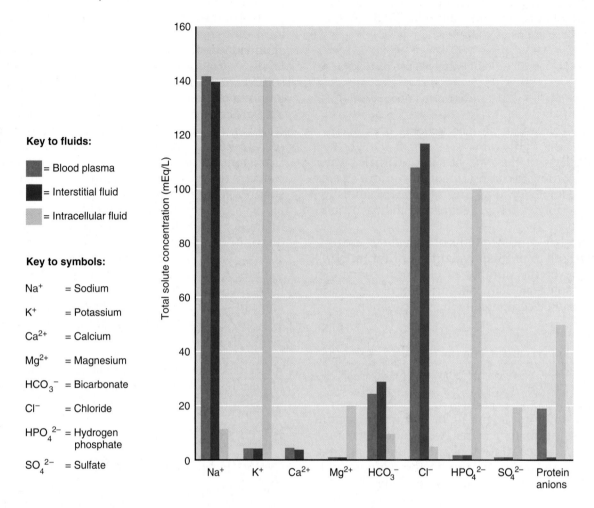

FIGURE 26.2   **Electrolyte composition of blood plasma, interstitial fluid, and intracellular fluid.** The very low intracellular Ca^{2+} concentration (10^{-7} *M*) does not include Ca^{2+} stores sequestered inside organelles. The high concentration of intracellular HPO_4^{2-} includes large amounts bound to intermediate metabolites, proteins, and lipids.

two-way osmotic flow of water is substantial. But ion fluxes are restricted and, in most cases, ions move selectively by active transport or through channels. Movements of nutrients, respiratory gases, and wastes are typically unidirectional. For example, glucose and oxygen move into the cells and metabolic wastes move out.

Plasma circulates throughout the body and links the external and internal environments (Figure 26.3). Exchanges occur almost continuously in the lungs, gastrointestinal tract, and kidneys. Although these exchanges alter plasma composition and volume, compensating adjustments in the other two fluid compartments follow quickly so that balance is restored.

Many factors can change ECF and ICF volumes. Because water moves freely between compartments, however, the osmolalities of all body fluids are equal (except during the first few minutes after a change in one of the fluids occurs). Increasing the ECF solute content (mainly the NaCl concentration) can be expected to cause osmotic and volume changes in the ICF—namely, a shift of water out of the cells. Conversely, decreasing ECF osmolality causes water to move into the cells. Thus, the ICF volume is determined by the ECF solute concentration. These concepts underlie all events that control fluid balance in the body and should be understood thoroughly.

A *Na^+; K^+; HPO_4^{2-}, protein anions.*

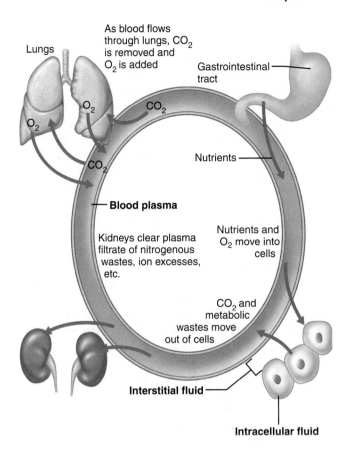

FIGURE 26.3 **The continuous mixing of body fluids.** Exchanges of nutrients and wastes between the intracellular fluid and the plasma occur through the interstitial fluid. Blood plasma transports nutrients and wastes between the cells and the external environment of the body.

Water Balance and ECF Osmolality

For the body to remain properly hydrated, water intake must equal water output. *Water intake* varies widely from person to person and is strongly influenced by habit, but it is typically about 2500 ml a day in adults (Figure 26.4). Most water enters the body through ingested liquids and solid foods. Body water produced by cellular metabolism is called **metabolic water** or **water of oxidation.**

Water output occurs by several routes. Water that vaporizes out of the lungs in expired air or diffuses directly through the skin is called **insensible water loss.** Some is lost in obvious perspiration and in feces. The balance (about 60%) is excreted by the kidneys in urine.

Healthy people have a remarkable ability to maintain the tonicity of their body fluids within very narrow limits (280–300 mOsm/kg). A rise in plasma osmolality triggers (1) thirst, which prompts us to drink water, and (2) release of antidiuretic hormone (ADH), which causes the kidneys to conserve water

Q *How would the values shown here be affected by (1) drinking a six-pack of beer? (2) a fast in which only water is ingested?*

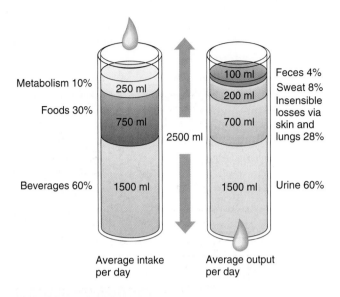

FIGURE 26.4 **Major sources of water intake and output.** When intake and output are in balance, the body is adequately hydrated.

and excrete concentrated urine. On the other hand, a decline in osmolality inhibits both thirst and ADH release, the latter followed by output of large volumes of dilute urine.

Regulation of Water Intake

The **thirst mechanism** is the driving force for water intake. An increase in plasma osmolality of only 2–3% excites the hypothalamic *thirst center*. A dry mouth also occurs because the rise in plasma oncotic pressure causes less fluid to leave the bloodstream. Because the salivary glands obtain the water they require from the blood, less saliva is produced, reinforcing the drive to drink. The same response is produced by a decline in blood volume (or pressure). However, because a substantial decrease (10–15%) is required, this is the less potent stimulus.

The hypothalamic thirst center neurons are stimulated when their *osmoreceptors* lose water by osmosis to the hypertonic ECF, or are activated by angiotensin II, by baroreceptor inputs, or other stimuli. Collectively, these events cause a subjective

A (1) *Much more water intake from beverages; much greater water output in urine (and perhaps in vomit, if too much alcohol was imbibed, an output route not illustrated). (2) Beverage intake would represent a higher percentage of water intake; water intake from foods and metabolism would drop drastically. Less urine would be made and excreted by the kidneys.*

26

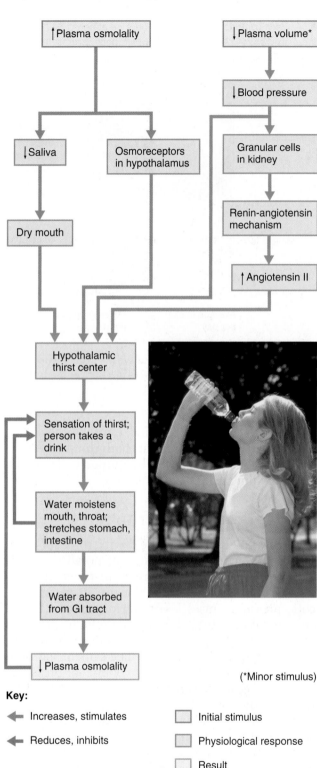

↑ Plasma osmolality

↓ Plasma volume*

↓ Blood pressure

↓ Saliva

Osmoreceptors in hypothalamus

Granular cells in kidney

Dry mouth

Renin-angiotensin mechanism

↑ Angiotensin II

Hypothalamic thirst center

Sensation of thirst; person takes a drink

Water moistens mouth, throat; stretches stomach, intestine

Water absorbed from GI tract

↓ Plasma osmolality

(*Minor stimulus)

Key:

← Increases, stimulates

← Reduces, inhibits

☐ Initial stimulus

☐ Physiological response

☐ Result

FIGURE 26.5 **The thirst mechanism for regulating water intake.** The major stimulus is increased osmolality of blood plasma. (Not all effects of angiotensin II are depicted.)

A *Because pretzels are salty, blood osmolality would increase, activating osmoreceptors in the hypothalamus, thus increasing thirst.*

26

sensation of thirst, which motivates us to get a drink (Figure 26.5). This mechanism helps explain why it is that some cocktail lounges and bars provide free *salty* snacks to their patrons.

Curiously, thirst is quenched almost as soon as we begin drinking water, even though the water has yet to be absorbed into the blood. The damping of thirst begins as the mucosa of the mouth and throat is moistened and continues as stretch receptors in the stomach and intestine are activated, providing feedback signals that inhibit the thirst center. This premature quenching of thirst prevents us from drinking more than we need and overdiluting our body fluids, and allows time for the osmotic changes to come into play as regulatory factors.

As effective as thirst is, it is not always a reliable indicator of need. This is particularly true during athletic events, when thirst can be satisfied long before sufficient liquids have been drunk to maintain the body in top form. Additionally, elderly or confused people may not recognize or heed thirst signals, and fluid-overloaded renal or cardiac patients may feel thirsty despite their condition.

Regulation of Water Output

Output of certain amounts of water is unavoidable. Such **obligatory water losses** help to explain why we cannot survive for long without drinking. Even the most heroic conservation efforts by the kidneys cannot compensate for zero water intake. Obligatory water loss includes the *insensible water losses* described above, water that accompanies undigested food residues in feces, and a minimum daily **sensible water loss** of 500 ml in urine. Obligatory water loss in urine reflects the facts that (1) when we eat an adequate diet, our kidneys must excrete 900–1200 mOsm of solutes to maintain blood homeostasis, and (2) human kidneys must flush urine solutes (end products of metabolism and so forth) out of the body in water.

Beyond obligatory water loss, the solute concentration and volume of urine excreted depend on fluid intake, diet, and water loss via other avenues. For example, if you perspire profusely on a hot day, much less urine than usual has to be excreted to maintain water balance. Normally, the kidneys begin to eliminate excess water about 30 minutes after it is ingested. This delay reflects the time required to inhibit ADH release. Diuresis reaches a peak in 1 hour after drinking and then declines to its lowest level after 3 hours.

The body's water volume is closely tied to a powerful water "magnet," ionic sodium. Moreover, our ability to maintain water balance through urinary output is really a problem of sodium *and* water balance because the two are always regulated in tandem by mechanisms that serve cardiovascular function and blood pressure. However, before dealing with Na$^+$ issues, we will recap ADH's effect on water output.

Influence of ADH

The amount of water reabsorbed in the renal collecting ducts is proportional to ADH release. When ADH levels are low, most of the water reaching the collecting ducts is not reabsorbed but simply allowed to pass through because the lack of aquaporins in the luminal membranes of the principal cells prevents the movement of water. The result is dilute urine and a reduced volume of body fluids. When ADH levels are high, aquaporins are inserted in the principal cell luminal membranes and nearly all of the filtered water is reabsorbed; a small volume of concentrated urine is excreted.

Osmoreceptors of the hypothalamus sense the ECF solute concentration and trigger or inhibit ADH release from the posterior pituitary accordingly (Figure 26.6). A decrease in ECF osmolality inhibits ADH release and allows more water to be excreted in urine, restoring normal blood osmolality. In contrast, an increase in ECF osmolality stimulates ADH release by stimulating the hypothalamic osmoreceptors.

ADH secretion is also influenced by *large* changes in blood volume or blood pressure. A decrease in BP triggers an increase in ADH secretion from the posterior pituitary either directly via baroreceptors in the atria and various blood vessels or indirectly via the renin-angiotensin mechanism. The key word here is "large" because changes in ECF osmolality are much more important as stimulatory or inhibitory factors. Factors that trigger ADH release by reducing blood volume include prolonged fever; excessive sweating, vomiting, or diarrhea; severe blood loss; and traumatic burns. Under these conditions, ADH also acts to constrict arterioles, directly increasing blood pressure—hence its other name: *vasopressin*. Figure 26.9 (p. 1046) summarizes how renal mechanisms involving aldosterone, angiotensin II, and ADH tie into overall controls of blood volume and blood pressure.

Disorders of Water Balance

Few people really appreciate the importance of water in keeping the body's "machinery" working at peak efficiency. The principal abnormalities of water balance are dehydration, hypotonic hydration, and edema, and each of these conditions presents a special set of problems for its victims.

Dehydration

When water output exceeds intake over a period of time and the body is in negative fluid balance, the

Q *ADH, by itself, cannot reduce an increase in osmolality. Why not? What other mechanism is required?*

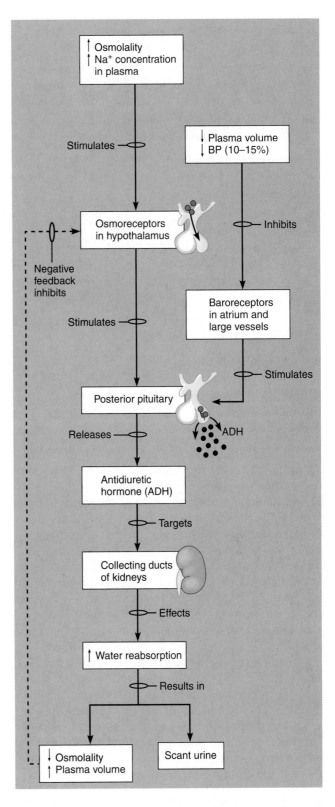

FIGURE 26.6 **Mechanisms and consequences of ADH release.** (Vasoconstrictor effects of ADH are not shown.)

A *ADH cannot add H$_2$O. It can only conserve what is already there. The thirst mechanism is required.*

(a) Mechanism of dehydration

(b) Mechanism of hypotonic hydration

FIGURE 26.7   **Disturbances in water balance.**

result is **dehydration**. Dehydration is a common sequel to hemorrhage, severe burns, prolonged vomiting or diarrhea, profuse sweating, water deprivation, and diuretic abuse. Dehydration may also be caused by endocrine disturbances, such as diabetes mellitus or diabetes insipidus (see Chapter 16). Early signs and symptoms of dehydration include a "cottony" or sticky oral mucosa, thirst, dry flushed skin, and decreased urine output *(oliguria)*. If prolonged, dehydration may lead to weight loss, fever, and mental confusion. Another serious consequence of water loss from plasma is inadequate blood volume to maintain normal circulation and ensuing *hypovolemic shock*.

In all these situations, water is lost from the ECF (Figure 26.7a). This is followed by the osmotic movement of water from the cells into the ECF, which equalizes the osmolality of the extracellular and intracellular fluids even though the total fluid volume has been reduced. Though the overall effect is called dehydration, it rarely involves only a water deficit, because most often electrolytes are lost as well.

Hypotonic Hydration

When the ECF osmolality starts to drop (usually this reflects a deficit of Na^+), several compensatory mechanisms are set into motion. ADH release is inhibited, and as a result, less water is reabsorbed and excess water is quickly flushed from the body in urine. But,

when there is renal insufficiency or when an extraordinary amount of water is drunk very quickly, a type of cellular *overhydration* called **hypotonic hydration** may occur. In either case, the ECF is diluted—its sodium content is normal, but excess water is present. Thus, the hallmark of this condition is **hyponatremia** (low ECF Na^+), which promotes net osmosis into the tissue cells, causing them to swell as they become abnormally hydrated (Figure 26.7b). This leads to severe metabolic disturbances evidenced by nausea, vomiting, muscular cramping, and cerebral edema. Hypotonic hydration is particularly damaging to neurons. Uncorrected cerebral edema quickly leads to disorientation, convulsions, coma, and death. Sudden and severe hyponatremia (as in overhydrated athletes) is treated by intravenous administration of hypertonic saline to reverse the osmotic gradient and "pull" water out of the cells.

Edema

Edema (ĕ-de′mah; "a swelling") is an atypical accumulation of fluid in the interstitial space, leading to tissue swelling. Edema may be caused by any event that steps up the flow of fluid out of the blood or hinders its return.

Factors that accelerate fluid loss from the blood include increases in capillary hydrostatic pressure and permeability. Increased capillary hydrostatic pressure can result from incompetent venous valves, localized blood vessel blockage, congestive heart failure, or high blood volume. Whatever the cause, the abnormally high capillary hydrostatic pressure intensifies filtration at the capillary beds.

Increased capillary permeability is usually due to an ongoing inflammatory response. Recall from p. 791 that inflammatory chemicals cause local capillaries to become very porous, allowing large amounts of exudate (containing not only clotting proteins but also other plasma proteins, nutrients, and immune elements) to form.

Edema caused by hindered fluid return to the blood usually reflects an imbalance in the colloid osmotic pressures on the two sides of the capillary membranes. For example, **hypoproteinemia** (hi″po-pro″te-ĭ-ne′me-ah), a condition of unusually low levels of plasma proteins, results in tissue edema because protein-deficient plasma has an abnormally low colloid osmotic pressure. Fluids are forced out of the capillary beds at the arterial ends by blood pressure as usual, but fail to return to the blood at the venous ends. Thus, the interstitial spaces become congested with fluid. Hypoproteinemia may result from protein malnutrition, liver disease, or *glomerulonephritis* (in which plasma proteins pass through "leaky" renal filtration membranes and are lost in urine).

Although the cause differs, the result is the same when lymphatic vessels are blocked or have been surgically removed. The small amounts of plasma proteins that seep out of the bloodstream are not returned to the blood as usual. As the leaked proteins accumulate in the IF, they exert an ever-increasing colloid osmotic pressure, which draws fluid from the blood and holds it in the interstitial space. Because excess fluid in the interstitial space increases the distance nutrients and oxygen must diffuse between the blood and the cells, edema can impair tissue function. However, the most serious problems resulting from edema affect the cardiovascular system. When fluid leaves the bloodstream and accumulates in the interstitial space, both blood volume and blood pressure decline and the efficiency of the circulation can be severely impaired.

Electrolyte Balance

Electrolytes include salts, acids, and bases, but the term **electrolyte balance** usually refers to the salt balance in the body. Salts are important in controlling fluid movements and provide minerals essential for excitability, secretory activity, and membrane permeability. Although many electrolytes are crucial for cellular activity, here we will specifically examine the regulation of sodium, potassium, and calcium. Acids and bases, which are more intimately involved in determining the pH of body fluids, are considered in the next section.

Salts enter the body in foods and fluids, and small amounts are generated during metabolic activity. For example, phosphates are liberated during catabolism of nucleic acids and bone matrix. Obtaining enough electrolytes is usually not a problem. Indeed, most of us have a far greater taste than need for salt. We shake table salt (NaCl) on our food even though natural foods contain ample amounts and processed foods contain exorbitant quantities. The taste for very salty foods is learned, but some liking for salt may be innate to ensure adequate intake of these two vital ions.

Salts are lost from the body in perspiration, feces, and urine. Even though sweat is normally hypotonic, large amounts of salt can be lost on a hot day simply because more sweat is produced. Gastrointestinal disorders can also lead to large salt losses in feces or vomitus. Thus, the flexibility of renal mechanisms that regulate the electrolyte balance of the blood is a critical asset. Some causes and consequences of electrolyte imbalances are summarized in Table 26.1.

◤◢ HOMEOSTATIC IMBALANCE

Severe electrolyte deficiencies may prompt a craving for salty or sour foods, such as smoked meats or pickled eggs. This is common in those with *Addison's disease*, a disorder entailing deficient mineralocorticoid hormone production by the adrenal cortex. When minerals such as iron are deficient, a person may even eat substances not usually considered foods, like chalk, clay, starch, and burnt match tips. This appetite for abnormal substances is called *pica*. ●

The Central Role of Sodium in Fluid and Electrolyte Balance

Sodium holds a central position in fluid and electrolyte balance and overall body homeostasis. Indeed, regulating the balance between sodium input and output is one of the most important renal functions. The salts $NaHCO_3$ and $NaCl$ account for 90–95% of all solutes in the ECF, and they contribute about 280 mOsm of the total ECF solute concentration (300 mOsm). At its normal plasma concentration of about 142 mEq/L, Na^+ is the single most abundant cation in the ECF and the only one exerting *significant* osmotic pressure. Additionally, cellular plasma membranes are relatively impermeable to Na^+, but some does manage to diffuse in and must be pumped out against its electrochemical gradient. These two qualities give sodium the primary role in controlling ECF volume and water distribution in the body.

It is important to understand that while the sodium content of the body may change, *its ECF concentration normally remains stable* because of immediate adjustments in water volume. Remember, *water follows salt*. Furthermore, because all body fluids are in osmotic equilibrium, a change in plasma Na^+ levels affects not only plasma volume and blood pressure, but also the ICF and IF volumes. In addition, sodium ions continuously move back and forth between the ECF and body secretions. For example, about 8 L of Na^+-containing secretions (gastric, intestinal, and pancreatic juice, saliva, bile) are spewed into the digestive tract daily, only to be almost completely reabsorbed. Finally, renal acid-base control mechanisms (discussed shortly) are coupled to Na^+ transport.

Regulation of Sodium Balance

Despite the crucial importance of sodium, receptors that specifically monitor Na^+ levels in body fluids have yet to be found. Regulation of the Na^+-water balance is inseparably linked to blood pressure and volume, and involves a variety of neural and hormonal controls. Reabsorption of Na^+ does *not* exhibit a transport maximum, and in healthy individuals nearly all Na^+ in the urinary filtrate can be reabsorbed. We will begin our coverage of sodium balance by reviewing the

26

TABLE 26.1   **Causes and Consequences of Electrolyte Imbalances**

ION	ABNORMALITY (SERUM VALUE)	POSSIBLE CAUSES	CONSEQUENCES
Sodium	Hypernatremia (Na^+ excess: >145 mEq/L)	Dehydration; uncommon in healthy individuals; may occur in infants or the confused aged (individuals unable to indicate thirst) or may be a result of excessive intravenous NaCl administration	Thirst: CNS dehydration leads to confusion and lethargy progressing to coma; increased neuromuscular irritability evidenced by twitching and convulsions
	Hyponatremia (Na^+ deficit: <135 mEq/L)	Solute loss, water retention, or both (e.g., excessive Na^+ loss through vomiting, diarrhea, burned skin, tubal drainage of stomach, and as a result of excessive use of diuretics); deficiency of aldosterone (Addison's disease); renal disease; excess ADH release; excess H_2O ingestion	Most common signs are those of neurologic dysfunction due to brain swelling. If sodium amounts are actually normal but water is excessive, the symptoms are the same as those of water excess: mental confusion; giddiness; coma if development occurs slowly; muscular twitching, irritability, and convulsions if the condition develops rapidly. In hyponatremia accompanied by water loss, the main signs are decreased blood volume and blood pressure (circulatory shock)
Potassium	Hyperkalemia (K^+ excess: >5.5 mEq/L)	Renal failure; deficit of aldosterone; rapid intravenous infusion of KCl; burns or severe tissue injuries which cause K^+ to leave cells	Nausea, vomiting, diarrhea; bradycardia; cardiac arrhythmias, depression, and arrest; skeletal muscle weakness; flaccid paralysis
	Hypokalemia (K^+ deficit: <3.5 mEq/L)	Gastrointestinal tract disturbances (vomiting, diarrhea), gastrointestinal suction; Cushing's disease; inadequate dietary intake (starvation); hyperaldosteronism; diuretic therapy	Cardiac arrhythmias, flattened T wave; muscular weakness; metabolic alkalosis; mental confusion; nausea; vomiting
Phosphate	Hyperphosphatemia (HPO_4^{2-} excess: >2.9 mEq/L)	Decreased urinary loss due to renal failure; hypoparathyroidism; major tissue trauma; increased intestinal absorption	Clinical symptoms arise because of reciprocal changes in Ca^{2+} levels rather than directly from changes in plasma phosphate concentrations
	Hypophosphatemia (HPO_4^{2-} deficit: <1.6 mEq/L)	Decreased intestinal absorption; increased urinary output; hyperparathyroidism	
Chloride	Hyperchloremia (Cl^- excess: >105 mEq/L)	Dehydration; increased retention or intake; metabolic acidosis; hyperparathyroidism	No direct clinical symptoms; symptoms generally associated with the underlying cause, which is often related to pH abnormalities
	Hypochloremia (Cl^- deficit: <95 mEq/L)	Metabolic alkalosis (e.g., due to vomiting or excessive ingestion of alkaline substances); aldosterone deficiency	
Calcium	Hypercalcemia (Ca^{2+} excess: >5.2 mEq/L or 10.5 mg%)*	Hyperparathyroidism; excessive vitamin D; prolonged immobilization; renal disease (decreased excretion); malignancy	Decreased neuromuscular excitability leading to cardiac arrhythmias and arrest, skeletal muscle weakness, confusion, stupor, and coma; kidney stones; nausea and vomiting
	Hypocalcemia (Ca^{2+} deficit: <4.5 mEq/L or 9 mg%)*	Burns (calcium trapped in damaged tissues); hypoparathyroidism; vitamin D deficiency; renal tubular disease; renal failure; hyperphosphatemia; diarrhea; alkalosis	Increased neuromuscular excitability leading to tingling of fingers, tremors, skeletal muscle cramps, tetany, convulsions; depressed excitability of the heart; osteomalacia; fractures
Magnesium	Hypermagnesemia (Mg^{2+} excess: >2.2 mEq/L)	Rare; occurs in renal failure when Mg is not excreted normally; excessive ingestion of Mg^{2+}-containing antacids	Lethargy; impaired CNS functioning, coma, respiratory depression; cardiac arrest
	Hypomagnesemia (Mg^{2+} deficit: <1.4 mEq/L)	Alcoholism; loss of intestinal contents, severe malnutrition; diuretic therapy	Tremors, increased neuromuscular excitability, tetany, convulsions

*1 mg% = 1 mg/100 ml

regulatory effect of aldosterone. Then we will examine various feedback loops that interact to regulate sodium and water balance and blood pressure.

Influence of Aldosterone

The hormone **aldosterone** "has the most to say" about renal regulation of sodium ion concentrations in the ECF. But whether aldosterone is present or not, some 65% of the Na^+ in the renal filtrate is reabsorbed in the proximal tubules of the kidneys and another 25% is reclaimed in the loops of Henle (see Chapter 25).

When aldosterone concentrations are high, essentially all the remaining filtered Na^+ is actively reabsorbed in the distal convoluted tubules and collecting ducts. Water follows if it can, that is, if the collecting duct permeability has been increased by ADH. Thus, aldosterone usually promotes both sodium and water retention. When aldosterone release is inhibited, virtually no Na^+ reabsorption occurs beyond the distal tubule. So, although urinary excretion of large amounts of Na^+ *always* results in the excretion of large amounts of water as well, the reverse is *not* true. Substantial amounts of nearly sodium-free urine can be eliminated as needed to achieve water balance.

The most important trigger for aldosterone release from the adrenal cortex is the renin-angiotensin mechanism mediated by the juxtaglomerular apparatus of the renal tubules (see Figures 26.8 and 26.9). When the juxtaglomerular (JG) apparatus responds to (1) sympathetic stimulation, (2) decreased filtrate NaCl concentration, or (3) decreased stretch (due to decreased blood pressure), the granular cells release renin. Renin catalyzes the series of reactions that produce angiotensin II, which prompts aldosterone release. Conversely, high renal blood pressure and high filtrate NaCl concentrations depress release of renin, angiotensin II, and aldosterone. The adrenal cortical cells are also directly stimulated to release aldosterone by elevated K^+ levels in the ECF (Figure 26.8).

Aldosterone brings about its effects slowly, over a period of hours to days. The principal effects of aldosterone are to diminish urinary output and increase blood volume. However, before these factors can change by more than a few percent, feedback mechanisms for blood volume control come into play. In addition to releasing aldosterone, angiotensin II also has a number of other actions, all aimed at raising blood volume and blood pressure. These were described in Chapter 25 (p. 1010).

◢ HOMEOSTATIC IMBALANCE

People with Addison's disease (hypoaldosteronism) lose tremendous amounts of NaCl and water to

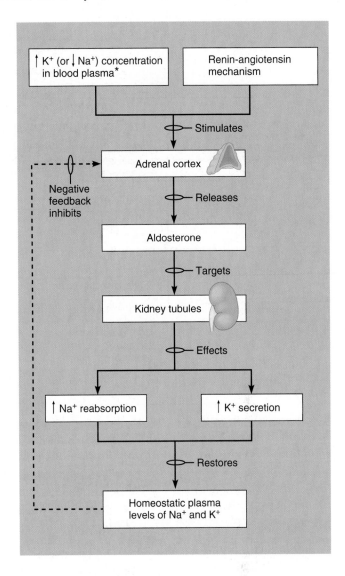

FIGURE 26.8   **Mechanisms and consequences of aldosterone release.**

*The adrenal cortex is much less sensitive to decreased plasma Na^+ than to increased plasma K^+.

urine. They are perpetually teetering on the brink of hypovolemia, but as long as they ingest adequate amounts of salt and fluids, people with this condition can avoid problems with Na^+ balance. ●

Cardiovascular Baroreceptors

Blood volume is carefully monitored and regulated to maintain blood pressure and cardiovascular function. As blood volume (hence pressure) rises, baroreceptors in the heart and in the large vessels of the neck and thorax (carotid arteries and aorta) alert the cardiovascular centers in the brain stem. Shortly after, sympathetic nervous system impulses to the kidneys decline, allowing the afferent arterioles to dilate. As the glomerular filtration rate rises, Na^+ output and water output increase. This phenomenon,

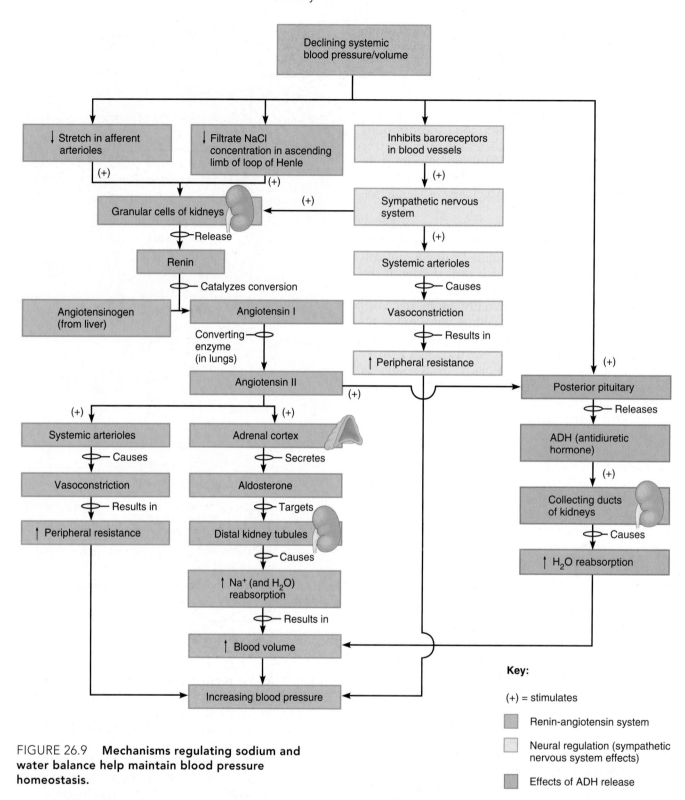

FIGURE 26.9 **Mechanisms regulating sodium and water balance help maintain blood pressure homeostasis.**

part of the baroreceptor reflex described in Chapter 19 (p. 727), reduces blood volume and blood pressure.

Drops in systemic blood pressure lead to reflex constriction of systemic arterioles including the afferent arterioles, which reduces filtrate formation and urinary output and increases systemic blood pressure (see Figure 26.9). Thus, the baroreceptors provide information on the "fullness" or volume of the circulation that is critical for maintaining cardiovascular homeostasis. Because Na^+ concentration determines fluid volume, the baroreceptors might be regarded as "sodium receptors."

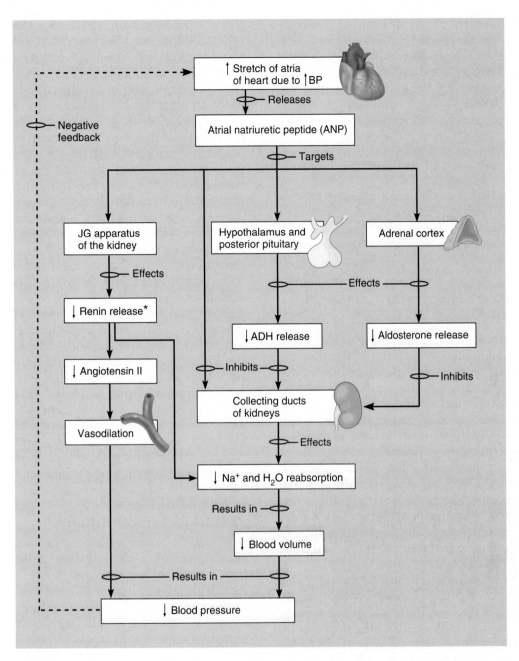

FIGURE 26.10   **Mechanisms and consequences of ANP release.**

*↓ Renin release also inhibits ADH and aldosterone release and hence the effects of those hormones.

Influence of Atrial Natriuretic Peptide

The influence of **atrial natriuretic peptide (ANP)** can be summarized in one sentence: It reduces blood pressure and blood volume by inhibiting nearly all events that promote vasoconstriction and Na^+ and water retention (Figure 26.10). A hormone that is released by certain cells of the heart atria when they are stretched by the effects of elevated blood pressure, ANP has potent diuretic and natriuretic (salt-excreting) effects. It promotes excretion of Na^+ and water by the kidneys by inhibiting the ability of the collecting duct to reabsorb Na^+ and by suppressing the release of ADH, renin, and aldosterone. Additionally, ANP acts both directly and indirectly (by inhibiting renin-induced generation of angiotensin II) to relax vascular smooth muscle; thus it causes vasodilation. Collectively, these effects reduce blood pressure.

Influence of Other Hormones

Female Sex Hormones   The **estrogens** are chemically similar to aldosterone and, like aldosterone, enhance NaCl reabsorption by the renal tubules. Because water follows, many women retain fluid as their estrogen levels rise during the menstrual cycle. The edema experienced by many pregnant women is also largely due to the effect of estrogens. **Progesterone** appears to decrease Na$^+$ reabsorption by blocking the effect aldosterone has on the renal tubules. Thus, progesterone has a diuretic-like effect and promotes Na$^+$ and water loss.

Glucocorticoids   The usual effect of **glucocorticoids**, such as cortisol and hydrocortisol, is to enhance tubular reabsorption of Na$^+$, but they also promote an increased glomerular filtration rate that may mask their effects on the tubules. However, when their plasma levels are high, the glucocorticoids exhibit potent aldosterone-like effects and promote edema.

Regulation of Potassium Balance

Potassium, the chief intracellular cation, is required for normal neuromuscular functioning as well as for several essential metabolic activities. Because the relative ICF-ECF potassium concentration directly affects a cell's resting membrane potential, even slight changes in K$^+$ concentration in the ECF have profound effects on neurons and muscle fibers that can be extremely dangerous. K$^+$ excess in the ECF decreases their membrane potential, causing depolarization, often followed by reduced excitability. Too little K$^+$ in the ECF causes hyperpolarization and nonresponsiveness. The heart is particularly sensitive to K$^+$ levels. Both too much and too little K$^+$ (hyperkalemia and hypokalemia respectively) can disrupt electrical conduction in the heart, leading to sudden death (Table 26.1).

Potassium is also part of the body's buffer system, which resists changes in the pH of body fluids. Shifts of hydrogen ions (H$^+$) into and out of cells induce corresponding shifts of K$^+$ in the opposite direction to maintain cation balance. Thus, ECF potassium levels rise with acidosis, as K$^+$ leaves and H$^+$ enters the cells, and fall with alkalosis, as K$^+$ moves into the cells and H$^+$ leaves them to enter the ECF. Although these pH-driven shifts do not change the total amount of K$^+$ in the body, they can seriously interfere with the activity of excitable cells.

Regulatory Site: The Cortical Collecting Duct

Like Na$^+$ balance, K$^+$ balance is maintained chiefly by renal mechanisms. However, there are important differences in the way this balance is achieved. The amount of Na$^+$ reabsorbed in the tubules is precisely tailored to need, and Na$^+$ is *never* secreted into the filtrate.

In contrast, the proximal tubules predictably reabsorb about 60–80% of the filtered K$^+$, and the thick ascending limb of Henle's loop absorbs another 10–20% or so, leaving about 10% to be lost in urine regardless of need. The responsibility for K$^+$ balance falls chiefly on the cortical collecting ducts, and is accomplished mainly by changing the amount of K$^+$ *secreted* into the filtrate.

As a rule, K$^+$ levels in the ECF are sufficiently high that K$^+$ needs to be excreted, and the rate at which the principal cells of the cortical collecting ducts secrete K$^+$ into the filtrate is accelerated over basal levels. (At times, the amount of K$^+$ excreted may actually exceed the amount filtered.) When ECF potassium concentrations are abnormally low, K$^+$ moves from the tissue cells into the ECF and the renal principal cells conserve K$^+$ by reducing its secretion and excretion to a minimum. Note that these principal cells are the same cells that mediate aldosterone-induced reabsorption of Na$^+$ and the ADH-stimulated reabsorption of water. Additionally, *type A intercalated cells*, a unique population of collecting duct cells, can reabsorb some of the K$^+$ left in the filtrate (in conjunction with active secretion of H$^+$), thus helping to reestablish K$^+$ (and pH) balance. However, keep in mind that the main thrust of renal regulation of K$^+$ is to *excrete* it. Because the kidneys have a limited ability to retain K$^+$, it may be lost in urine even in the face of a deficiency. Consequently, failure to ingest potassium-rich substances eventually results in a severe deficiency.

Influence of Plasma Potassium Concentration

The single most important factor influencing K$^+$ secretion is the K$^+$ concentration in blood plasma. A high-potassium diet increases the K$^+$ content of the ECF. This favors entry of K$^+$ into the principal cells of the cortical collecting duct and prompts them to secrete K$^+$ into the filtrate so that more of it is excreted. Conversely, a low-potassium diet or accelerated K$^+$ loss depresses its secretion (and promotes its limited reabsorption) by the collecting ducts.

Influence of Aldosterone

The second factor influencing K$^+$ secretion into the filtrate is aldosterone. As it stimulates the principal cells to reabsorb Na$^+$, aldosterone simultaneously enhances K$^+$ secretion (see Figure 26.8). Thus, as plasma Na$^+$ levels rise, K$^+$ levels fall proportionately.

Adrenal cortical cells are *directly* sensitive to the K$^+$ content of the ECF bathing them. When it increases even slightly, the adrenal cortex is strongly stimulated to release aldosterone, which increases K$^+$ secretion by the exchange process just described. Thus, K$^+$ controls its own concentrations in the ECF via feedback regulation of aldosterone release.

Aldosterone is also secreted in response to the renin-angiotensin mechanism previously described.

HOMEOSTATIC IMBALANCE

In an attempt to reduce NaCl intake, many people have turned to salt substitutes, which are high in potassium. However, heavy consumption of these substitutes is safe only when aldosterone release in the body is normal. In the absence of aldosterone, hyperkalemia is swift and lethal regardless of K^+ intake (Table 26.1). Conversely, when a person has an adrenocortical tumor that pumps out tremendous amounts of aldosterone, ECF potassium levels fall so low that neurons all over the body hyperpolarize and paralysis occurs. ●

Regulation of Calcium and Phosphate Balance

About 99% of the body's calcium is found in bones in the form of calcium phosphate salts, which provide strength and rigidity to the skeleton. The bony skeleton provides a dynamic reservoir from which calcium and phosphate can be withdrawn or deposited to maintain the balance of these electrolytes in the ECF. Ionic calcium in the ECF is important for normal blood clotting, cell membrane permeability, and secretory behavior, but its most important effect by far is on neuromuscular excitability. Hypocalcemia increases excitability and causes muscle tetany. Hypercalcemia is equally dangerous because it inhibits neurons and muscle cells and may cause life-threatening cardiac arrhythmias (Table 26.1).

ECF calcium ion levels are closely regulated, rarely deviating from normal limits. Under normal circumstances about 98% of the filtered Ca^{2+} is reabsorbed owing to the action of **parathyroid hormone (PTH).** * This hormone is released by the tiny parathyroid glands located on the posterior aspect of the thyroid gland in the pharynx. Declining plasma levels of Ca^{2+} directly stimulate the parathyroid glands to release PTH, which promotes an increase in calcium levels by targeting the following organs (see also Figure 16.12 on p. 625):

1. Bones. PTH activates osteoclasts (bone-digesting cells), which break down the bone matrix, resulting in the release of Ca^{2+} and HPO_4^{2-} to the blood.

2. Small intestine. PTH enhances intestinal absorption of Ca^{2+} indirectly by stimulating the kidneys to transform vitamin D to its active form, which is necessary for Ca^{2+} absorption by the small intestine.

3. Kidneys. PTH increases Ca^{2+} reabsorption by the renal tubules while decreasing phosphate ion reabsorption. Thus, calcium conservation and phosphate excretion go hand in hand. Hence, the *product* of Ca^{2+} and HPO_4^{2-} concentrations in the ECF remains constant, preventing calcium-salt deposits in bones or soft body tissues.

Most Ca^{2+} is reabsorbed passively in the PCT via diffusion through the paracellular route (a process driven by the electrochemical gradient). However, as with other ions, "fine-tuning" of Ca^{2+} reabsorption occurs in the distal nephron. PTH-regulated Ca^{2+} channels control Ca^{2+} entry into DCT cells at the luminal membrane, while Ca^{2+} pumps and antiporters export it at the basolateral membrane.

As a rule, 75% of the filtered phosphate ions (including $H_2PO_4^-$, HPO_4^{2-}, and PO_4^{3-}) are reabsorbed in the PCT by active transport. Phosphate reabsorption is set by its transport maximum. Amounts present in excess of that maximum simply flow out in urine. PTH inhibits active transport of phosphate by decreasing its T_m.

When ECF calcium levels are within normal limits (9–11 mg/100 ml of blood) or higher, PTH secretion is inhibited. Consequently, release of Ca^{2+} from bone is inhibited, larger amounts of Ca^{2+} are lost in feces and urine, and more phosphate is retained. Hormones other than PTH alter phosphate reabsorption. For example, insulin increases it while glucagon decreases it.

Regulation of Anions

Chloride is the major anion accompanying Na^+ in the ECF and, like sodium, Cl^- helps maintain the osmotic pressure of the blood. When blood pH is within normal limits or slightly alkaline, about 99% of filtered Cl^- is reabsorbed. In the PCT, it moves passively and simply follows sodium ions out of the filtrate and into the peritubular capillary blood. In most other tubule segments, Na^+ and Cl^- transport are coupled.

When acidosis occurs, less Cl^- accompanies Na^+ because HCO_3^- reabsorption is stepped up to restore blood pH to its normal range. Thus, the choice between Cl^- and HCO_3^- serves acid-base regulation. Most other anions, such as sulfates and nitrates, have transport maximums, and when their concentrations in the filtrate exceed the amount that can be reabsorbed, excesses spill into urine.

Acid-Base Balance

Because of their abundant hydrogen bonds, all functional proteins (enzymes, hemoglobin, cytochromes, and others) are influenced by H^+ concentration. It

---

* Although calcitonin is often thought of as a calcium-lowering hormone (as discussed in Chapter 16, p. 624), its effects on blood calcium levels in adults are negligible.

Q *To minimize the pH shift that occurs in situation (a), would it be better to add a strong base or a weak base? Why?*

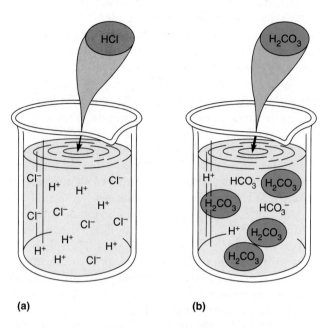

(a)   **(b)**

FIGURE 26.11   **Dissociation of strong and weak acids.**
(a) When added to water, the strong acid HCl dissociates completely into its ions (H^+ and Cl^-). **(b)** By contrast, dissociation of H_2CO_3, a weak acid, is incomplete, and some molecules of H_2CO_3 remain undissociated (symbols shown in green ovals) in solution.

follows then that nearly all biochemical reactions are influenced by the pH of their fluid environment, and the acid-base balance of body fluids is closely regulated. (For a review of the basic principles of acid-base reactions and pH, see Chapter 2.)

Optimal pH varies from one body fluid to another, but not by much. The normal pH of arterial blood is 7.4, that of venous blood and IF is 7.35, and that of ICF averages 7.0. The lower pH in cells and venous blood reflects their greater amounts of acidic metabolites and carbon dioxide, which combines with water to form carbonic acid, H_2CO_3.

Whenever the pH of arterial blood rises above 7.45, a person is said to have **alkalosis** (al″kah-lo′sis) or **alkalemia.** A drop in arterial pH to below 7.35 results in **acidosis** (as″ĭ-do′sis) or **acidemia.** Because pH 7.0 is neutral, chemically speaking 7.35 is not acidic. However, it is a higher-than-optimal H^+ concentration for most cells, so any arterial pH between 7.35 and 7.0 is called *physiological acidosis.*

Although small amounts of acidic substances enter the body via ingested foods, most hydrogen ions originate as metabolic by-products or end products. For

example, (1) breakdown of phosphorus-containing proteins releases *phosphoric acid* into the ECF, (2) anaerobic respiration of glucose produces *lactic acid,* (3) fat metabolism yields other organic acids, such as fatty acids and *ketone bodies,* and (4) the loading and transport of carbon dioxide in the blood as HCO_3^- liberates hydrogen ions. Finally, although hydrochloric acid produced by the stomach is not really *in* the body, it is a source of H^+ that must be buffered if digestion is to occur normally in the small intestine.

The H^+ concentration in blood is regulated sequentially by (1) chemical buffers, (2) the brain stem respiratory centers, and (3) renal mechanisms. Chemical buffers act within a fraction of a second to resist pH changes and are the first line of defense. Within 1–3 minutes, changes in respiratory rate and depth are occurring to compensate for acidosis or alkalosis. The kidneys, the body's most potent acid-base regulatory system, ordinarily require hours to a day or more to effect changes in blood pH.

Chemical Buffer Systems

Recall that acids are *proton donors,* and that the acidity of a solution reflects only the *free* hydrogen ions, not those bound to anions. *Strong acids,* which dissociate completely and liberate all their H^+ in water (Figure 26.11a), can dramatically change a solution's pH. By contrast, *weak acids* dissociate only partially (Figure 26.11b), and so have a much slighter effect on pH. However, weak acids are efficient at preventing pH changes, and this feature allows them to play important roles in chemical buffer systems.

Bases are *proton acceptors.* Strong bases are those that dissociate easily in water and quickly tie up H^+. Conversely, weak bases are slower to accept protons.

A **chemical buffer** is a system of one or more compounds that acts to resist changes in pH when a strong acid or base is added. They do this by binding to H^+ whenever the pH drops and releasing them when pH rises. The three major chemical buffer systems in the body are the *bicarbonate, phosphate,* and *protein buffer systems.* Anything that causes a shift in H^+ concentration in one fluid compartment simultaneously causes a change in the others. Thus, the buffer systems actually buffer one another, so that any drifts in pH are resisted by the *entire* buffer system.

Bicarbonate Buffer System

The **bicarbonate buffer system** is a mixture of carbonic acid (H_2CO_3) and its salt, sodium bicarbonate (NaHCO$_3$), in the same solution. Although it also buffers the ICF, it is the *only* important *ECF* buffer.

Carbonic acid, a weak acid, does not dissociate to any great extent in neutral or acidic solutions.

Thus, when a strong acid such as HCl is added to this buffer system, most of the existing carbonic acid remains intact. However, the bicarbonate ions of the salt act as weak bases to tie up the H^+ released by the stronger acid (HCl), forming *more* carbonic acid:

$$\underset{\text{strong acid}}{HCl} + \underset{\text{weak base}}{NaHCO_3} \rightarrow \underset{\text{weak acid}}{H_2CO_3} + \underset{\text{salt}}{NaCl}$$

Because it is converted to the weak acid H_2CO_3, HCl lowers the pH of the solution only slightly.

When a strong base such as sodium hydroxide (NaOH) is added to the same buffer solution, a weak base such as sodium bicarbonate ($NaHCO_3$) does not dissociate under the alkaline conditions and so does not contribute to the rise in pH. However, the added base forces the carbonic acid to dissociate further, donating more H^+ to tie up the OH^- released by the strong base:

$$\underset{\text{strong base}}{NaOH} + \underset{\text{weak acid}}{H_2CO_3} \rightarrow \underset{\text{weak base}}{NaHCO_3} + \underset{\text{water}}{H_2O}$$

The net result is replacement of a strong base (NaOH) by a weak one ($NaHCO_3$), so that the pH of the solution rises very little.

Although the bicarbonate salt in the example is sodium bicarbonate, other bicarbonate salts function in the same way because the HCO_3^- is the important ion, not the cation it is paired with. In cells, where little Na^+ is present, potassium and magnesium bicarbonates are part of the bicarbonate buffer system.

The buffering power of this type of system is directly related to the concentrations of the buffering substances. Thus, if acids enter the blood at such a rate that all the available HCO_3^- ions, often referred to as the **alkaline reserve,** are tied up, the buffer system becomes ineffective and blood pH changes. The bicarbonate ion concentration in the ECF is normally around 25 mEq/L and is closely regulated by the kidneys. The concentration of H_2CO_3 is just over 1 mEq/L but the supply of carbonic acid (which comes from the CO_2 released during cellular respiration) is almost limitless, so obtaining that member of the buffer pair is usually not a problem. The carbonic acid content of the blood is subject to respiratory controls.

Phosphate Buffer System

The operation of the **phosphate buffer system** is nearly identical to that of the bicarbonate buffer. The components of the phosphate system are the sodium salts of dihydrogen phosphate ($H_2PO_4^-$) and monohydrogen phosphate (HPO_4^{2-}). NaH_2PO_4 acts as a weak acid. Na_2HPO_4, with one less hydrogen atom, acts as a weak base.

Again, H^+ released by strong acids is tied up in weak acids:

$$\underset{\text{strong acid}}{HCl} + \underset{\text{weak base}}{Na_2HPO_4} \rightarrow \underset{\text{weak acid}}{NaH_2PO_4} + \underset{\text{salt}}{NaCl}$$

and strong bases are converted to weak bases:

$$\underset{\text{strong base}}{NaOH} + \underset{\text{weak acid}}{NaH_2PO_4} \rightarrow \underset{\text{weak base}}{Na_2HPO_4} + \underset{\text{water}}{H_2O}$$

Because the phosphate buffer system is present in low concentrations in the ECF (approximately one-sixth that of the bicarbonate buffer system), it is relatively unimportant for buffering blood plasma. However, it is a very effective buffer in urine and in ICF, where phosphate concentrations are usually higher.

Protein Buffer System

Proteins in plasma and in cells are the body's most plentiful and powerful source of buffers, and constitute the **protein buffer system.** In fact, at least three-quarters of all the buffering power of body fluids resides in cells, and most of this reflects the buffering activity of intracellular proteins.

As described in Chapter 2, proteins are polymers of amino acids. Some of the linked amino acids have exposed groups of atoms called *organic acid (carboxyl) groups (—COOH)*, which dissociate to release H^+ when the pH begins to rise:

$$R^{*}-COOH \rightarrow R-COO^- + H^+$$

Other amino acids have exposed groups that can act as bases and accept H^+. For example, an exposed $—NH_2$ group can bind with hydrogen ions, becoming $—NH_3^+$:

$$R-NH_2 + H^+ \rightarrow R-NH_3^+$$

Because this removes free hydrogen ions from the solution, it prevents the solution from becoming too acidic. Consequently, a single protein molecule can function reversibly as either an acid or a base depending on the pH of its environment. Molecules with this ability are called **amphoteric molecules** (am"fo-ter'ik).

Hemoglobin of red blood cells is an excellent example of a protein that functions as an intracellular buffer. As explained earlier, CO_2 released from the tissues forms H_2CO_3, which dissociates to liberate H^+ and HCO_3^- in the blood. Meanwhile, hemoglobin is unloading oxygen, becoming reduced hemoglobin, which carries a negative charge. Because H^+

---

* Note that R indicates the rest of the organic molecule, which contains many atoms.

rapidly binds to the hemoglobin anions, pH changes are minimized. In this case, carbonic acid, a weak acid, is buffered by an even weaker acid, hemoglobin.

Respiratory Regulation of H$^+$

Respiratory system regulation of acid-base balance provides a *physiological buffering system*. Although such a buffer system acts more slowly than a chemical buffer system, it has one to two times the buffering power of all the body's chemical buffers combined. As described in Chapter 22, the respiratory system eliminates CO_2 from the blood while replenishing its supply of O_2. Carbon dioxide generated by cellular respiration enters erythrocytes in the circulation and is converted to bicarbonate ions for transport in the plasma:

$$CO_2 + H_2O \underset{\text{carbonic}}{\overset{\text{carbonic anhydrase}}{\rightleftharpoons}} \underset{\substack{\text{carbonic} \\ \text{acid}}}{H_2CO_3} \rightleftharpoons H^+ + \underset{\substack{\text{bicarbonate} \\ \text{ion}}}{HCO_3^-}$$

The first set of double arrows indicates a reversible equilibrium between dissolved carbon dioxide and water on the left and carbonic acid on the right. The second set indicates a reversible equilibrium between carbonic acid on the left and hydrogen and bicarbonate ions on the right. Because of these equilibria, an increase in any of these chemical species pushes the reaction in the opposite direction. Notice also that the right side of the equation is equivalent to the bicarbonate buffer system.

In healthy individuals, CO_2 is expelled from the lungs at the same rate it is formed in the tissues. During carbon dioxide unloading, the reaction shifts to the left, and H$^+$ generated from carbonic acid is reincorporated into water. Because of the protein buffer system, H$^+$ produced by CO_2 transport is not allowed to accumulate and has little or no effect on blood pH. However, when hypercapnia occurs, it activates medullary chemoreceptors (via cerebrospinal fluid acidosis promoted by excessive accumulation of CO_2) that respond by increasing respiratory rate and depth. Additionally, a rising plasma H$^+$ concentration resulting from any metabolic process excites the respiratory center indirectly (via peripheral chemoreceptors) to stimulate deeper, more rapid respiration. As ventilation increases, more CO_2 is removed from the blood, pushing the reaction to the left and reducing the H$^+$ concentration.

When blood pH rises, the respiratory center is depressed. As respiratory rate drops and respiration becomes shallower, CO_2 accumulates; the equilibrium is pushed to the right, causing the H$^+$ concentration to increase. Again blood pH is restored to the normal range. These respiratory system–mediated corrections of blood pH are accomplished within a minute or so.

Changes in alveolar ventilation can produce dramatic changes in blood pH—far more than is needed. For example, a doubling or halving of alveolar ventilation can raise or lower blood pH by about 0.2 pH unit. Because normal arterial pH is 7.4, a change of 0.2 pH unit yields a blood pH of 7.6 or 7.2—both well beyond the normal limits of blood pH. Actually, alveolar ventilation can be increased about 15-fold or reduced to zero. Thus, respiratory controls of blood pH have a tremendous reserve capacity.

Anything that impairs respiratory system functioning causes acid-base imbalances. For example, net carbon dioxide retention (hypoventilation) leads to acidosis; hyperventilation, which causes net elimination of CO_2, causes alkalosis. When the cause of the pH imbalance is respiratory system problems, the resulting condition is either *respiratory acidosis* or *respiratory alkalosis* (see Table 26.2 on p. 1056).

Renal Mechanisms of Acid-Base Balance

Chemical buffers can tie up excess acids or bases temporarily, but they cannot eliminate them from the body. And while the lungs can dispose of the **volatile acid** carbonic acid by eliminating CO_2, only the kidneys can rid the body of other acids generated by cellular metabolism: phosphoric, uric, and lactic acids, and ketone bodies. These acids are sometimes referred to as **metabolic (fixed) acids**, but this terminology is both unfortunate and incorrect because CO_2 and hence carbonic acid are also products of metabolism. Additionally, only the kidneys can regulate blood levels of alkaline substances and renew chemical buffers that are used up in regulating H$^+$ levels in the ECF. (HCO_3^-, which helps regulate H$^+$ levels, is lost from the body when CO_2 flushes from the lungs.) Thus, the ultimate acid-base regulatory organs are the kidneys, which act slowly but surely to compensate for acid-base imbalances resulting from variations in diet or metabolism or from disease.

The most important renal mechanisms for regulating acid-base balance of the blood involve (1) conserving (reabsorbing) or generating new HCO_3^-, and (2) excreting HCO_3^-. If we look back at the equation for the operation of the carbonic acid–bicarbonate buffer system of the blood, it is obvious that losing a HCO_3^- from the body produces the same net effect as gaining a H$^+$, because it pushes the equation to the right, increasing the H$^+$ level. By the same token, generating or reabsorbing HCO_3^- is the same as losing H$^+$ because it pushes the equation to the left, decreasing the H$^+$ level. Therefore, to reabsorb bicarbonate, H^+ has to be secreted, and when we excrete excess HCO_3^-, H^+ is retained (not secreted).

Because the mechanisms for regulating acid-base balance depend on H^+ being secreted into the filtrate, we consider that process first. Secretion of H^+ occurs mainly in the PCT and in type A intercalated cells of the collecting duct. The H^+ secreted is obtained from the dissociation of carbonic acid, created from the combination of CO_2 and water within the tubule cells (Figure 26.12), a reaction catalyzed by *carbonic anhydrase*. For each H^+ secreted into the tubule lumen, one Na^+ is reabsorbed from the filtrate, maintaining the electrical balance.

The rate of H^+ secretion rises and falls with CO_2 levels in the ECF. The more CO_2 in the peritubular capillary blood, the faster the rate of H^+ secretion. Because blood CO_2 levels directly relate to blood pH, this system can respond to both rising and falling H^+ concentrations. Notice that secreted H^+ can combine with HCO_3^- in the filtrate, generating CO_2 and water. In this case, H^+ is bound in water. The rising concentration of CO_2 in the filtrate creates a steep diffusion gradient for its entry into the tubule cell, where it promotes still more H^+ secretion.

Conserving Filtered Bicarbonate Ions: Bicarbonate Reabsorption

Bicarbonate ions (HCO_3^-) are an important part of the bicarbonate buffer system, the most important inorganic blood buffer. If this reservoir of base, or *alkaline reserve*, is to be maintained, the kidneys must do more than just eliminate enough hydrogen ions to counter rising blood H^+ levels. Depleted stores of HCO_3^- have to be replenished. This is more complex than it seems because the tubule cells are almost completely impermeable to the HCO_3^- in the filtrate—they cannot reabsorb them. However, the kidneys can conserve filtered HCO_3^- in a rather roundabout way, also illustrated in Figure 26.12. As you can see, dissociation of carbonic acid liberates HCO_3^- as well as H^+. Although the tubule cells cannot reclaim HCO_3^- directly from the filtrate, they can and do shunt HCO_3^- generated within them (as a result of splitting H_2CO_3) into the peritubular capillary blood. HCO_3^- leaves the tubule cell either accompanied by Na^+ or in exchange for Cl^-. Thus, reabsorption of HCO_3^- depends on the active secretion of H^+, mostly by a Na^+-H^+ antiporter, but also by an H^+ ATPase. In the filtrate H^+ combines with filtered HCO_3^-. For each filtered HCO_3^- that "disappears," a HCO_3^- generated within the tubule cells enters the blood—a one-for-one exchange. When large amounts of H^+ are secreted, correspondingly large amounts of HCO_3^- enter the peritubular blood, and the net effect is that HCO_3^- is almost completely removed from the filtrate.

Key:

→ Primary active transport → Simple diffusion

▪▪▶ Secondary active transport ● Protein carrier

(CA) Carbonic anhydrase

FIGURE 26.12 Reabsorption of filtered HCO_3^- is coupled to H^+ secretion. (Numbers by reaction lines indicate the sequence of events.)
① CO_2 combines with water within the tubule cell, forming H_2CO_3.
② H_2CO_3 is quickly split, forming H^+ and HCO_3^-.
③ For each H^+ secreted into the filtrate, a bicarbonate ion (HCO_3^-) enters the peritubular capillary blood by cotransport (either via symport with Na^+ or via antiport with Cl^-).
④ Secreted H^+ combines with HCO_3^- present in the tubular filtrate, forming carbonic acid (H_2CO_3). Thus, HCO_3^- disappears from the filtrate at the same rate that HCO_3^- (formed within the tubule cell) enters the peritubular capillary blood.
⑤ The H_2CO_3 formed in the filtrate dissociates to release carbon dioxide and water.
⑥ Carbon dioxide then diffuses into the tubule cell, where it acts to trigger further H^+ secretion.

*The breakdown of H_2CO_3 to CO_2 and H_2O in the tubule *lumen* is catalyzed by carbonic anhydrase *only* in the PCT.

Generating New Bicarbonate Ions

Two renal mechanisms commonly carried out by the type A intercalated cells of the collecting ducts generate *new* HCO_3^- that can be added to plasma. Both mechanisms involve renal excretion of acid, *via secretion and excretion* of either H^+ or ammonium ions in urine. Let's examine how these mechanisms differ.

Key:

➡ Primary active transport	● Protein carrier
∎∎➤ Secondary active transport	╫ Ion channel
➡ Simple diffusion	CA Carbonic anhydrase
∎∎➤ Facilitated diffusion	

FIGURE 26.13 **Generation of new HCO₃⁻ via buffering of excreted H⁺ by monohydrogen phosphate (HPO₄²⁻).** H⁺ from the dissociation of H_2CO_3 is actively secreted by a H⁺ ATPase pump and combines with HPO_4^{2-} in the lumen. HCO_3^- generated at the same time leaves the basolateral membrane via an antiport carrier in a $HCO_3^- $-$Cl^-$ exchange process.

Via Excretion of Buffered H⁺

As long as *filtered bicarbonate* is reclaimed (Figure 26.12), the secreted H⁺ is *not excreted or lost* from the body in urine. Instead, the H⁺ is buffered by HCO_3^- in the filtrate and ultimately becomes part of water molecules (most of which are reabsorbed).

However, once the filtered HCO_3^- is "used up" (this has usually been accomplished by the time the collecting ducts are reached), any additional H⁺ secreted is excreted in urine. More often than not, this is the case.

Reclaiming filtered HCO_3^- simply restores the bicarbonate concentration of plasma that exists at the time. However, a normal diet introduces new H⁺ into the body, and this additional H⁺ must be balanced by the generation of new HCO_3^- (as opposed to filtered HCO_3^-) which moves into the blood to counteract acidosis. This process of alkalinizing the blood is the way the kidneys compensate for acido-

sis. The excreted H⁺ also must bind with buffers in the filtrate. Otherwise, a urine pH incompatible with life would result. (H⁺ secretion ceases when urine pH falls to 4.5.) The most important urine buffer is the *phosphate buffer system*, specifically its weak base *monohydrogen phosphate* (HPO_4^{2-}).

The components of the phosphate buffer system filter freely into the tubules, and about 75% of the filtered phosphate is reabsorbed. However, their absorption is inhibited during acidosis; therefore, the buffer pair becomes more and more concentrated as the filtrate moves through the renal tubules. As shown in Figure 26.13, the type A intercalated cells secrete H⁺ actively via a H⁺-ATPase pump and via a K⁺-H⁺ antiporter (not illustrated). The secreted H⁺ combines with HPO_4^{2-}, forming $H_2PO_4^-$ which then flows out in urine. Bicarbonate ions generated in the cells during the same reaction move into the interstitial space via a HCO_3^--Cl^- antiport process and then move passively into the peritubular capillary blood. Notice again that when H⁺ is being excreted, "brand new" bicarbonate ions are added to the blood—over and above those reclaimed from the filtrate. Thus, in response to acidosis, the kidneys generate new HCO_3^- and add it to the blood (alkalinizing the blood) while adding an equal amount of H⁺ to the filtrate (acidifying the urine).

Via NH₄⁺ Excretion

The second and more important mechanism for excreting acid uses the ammonium ion (NH_4^+) produced by glutamine metabolism in the PCT cells (Figure 26.14). Ammonium ions are weak acids that donate few H⁺ at physiological pH. For each glutamine metabolized (deaminated, oxidized, and acidified by combination with H⁺), two NH_4^+ and two HCO_3^- result. The HCO_3^- moves through the basolateral membrane into the blood. The NH_4^+, in turn, is excreted and lost in urine. As with the phosphate buffer system, this buffering mechanism replenishes the alkaline reserve of the blood, because as NH_4^+ is secreted the newly made HCO_3^- enters the blood.

Bicarbonate Ion Secretion

When the body is in alkalosis, another population of intercalated cells (type B) in the collecting ducts exhibit net HCO_3^- secretion (rather than net HCO_3^- reabsorption) while reclaiming H⁺ to acidify the blood. Overall the type B cells can be thought of as "flipped" type A cells and the HCO_3^- secretion process can be visualized as the exact opposite of the HCO_3^- reabsorption process illustrated in Figure 26.12. However, the predominant process in the nephrons and collecting ducts is HCO_3^- reabsorption, and even during alkalosis, the amount of HCO_3^- excreted is much less than the amount conserved.

26

Abnormalities of Acid-Base Balance

All cases of acidosis and alkalosis can be classed according to cause as *respiratory* or *metabolic* (Table 26.2). The methods for determining the cause of an acid-base disturbance and whether it is being compensated (whether the lungs or kidneys are taking steps to correct the imbalance) are described in *A Closer Look* on p. 1057.

Respiratory Acidosis and Alkalosis

Respiratory pH imbalances result from some failure of the respiratory system to perform its normal pH-balancing role. The partial pressure of carbon dioxide (P_{CO_2}) is the single most important indicator of the adequacy of respiratory function. When respiratory function is normal, the P_{CO_2} fluctuates between 35 and 45 mm Hg. Generally speaking, higher values indicate respiratory acidosis, and lower values indicate respiratory alkalosis.

Respiratory acidosis is the most common cause of acid-base imbalance. It most often occurs when a person breathes shallowly or when gas exchange is hampered by diseases such as pneumonia, cystic fibrosis, or emphysema. Under such conditions, CO_2 accumulates in the blood. Thus, respiratory acidosis is characterized by falling blood pH and rising P_{CO_2}.

Respiratory alkalosis results when carbon dioxide is eliminated from the body faster than it is produced, causing the blood to become more alkaline. This is called *hyperventilation* (see p. 866). While respiratory acidosis is frequently associated with respiratory system pathology, respiratory alkalosis is often due to stress or pain.

Metabolic Acidosis and Alkalosis

Metabolic pH imbalances include all abnormalities of acid-base imbalance *except* those caused by too much or too little carbon dioxide in the blood. Bicarbonate ion levels below or above the normal range of 22–26 mEq/L indicate a metabolic acid-base imbalance.

The second most common cause of acid-base imbalance, **metabolic acidosis,** is recognized by low blood pH and HCO_3^- levels. Typical causes of metabolic acidosis are ingestion of too much alcohol (which is metabolized to acetic acid) and excessive loss of HCO_3^-, as might result from persistent diarrhea. Other causes are accumulation of lactic acid during exercise or shock, the ketosis that occurs in diabetic crisis or starvation, and, infrequently, kidney failure.

Metabolic alkalosis, indicated by rising blood pH and HCO_3^- levels, is much less common than metabolic acidosis. Typical causes are vomiting of the acidic contents of the stomach (or loss of those secretions through gastrointestinal suctioning) and intake of excess base (antacids, for example).

Key:

→ Primary active transport

⬤ Protein carrier

---▶ Secondary active transport

→ Passive transport (simple diffusion)

FIGURE 26.14 Generation of new HCO_3^- via glutamine metabolism and NH_4^+ secretion. PCT cells metabolize glutamine to NH_4^+ and HCO_3^-. NH_4^+ (a weak acid) is then actively secreted by occupying the H^+ site on the H^+-Na^+ antiporter. The new HCO_3^- generated moves into the peritubular capillary blood.

Effects of Acidosis and Alkalosis

The absolute blood pH limits for life are a low of 7.0 and a high of 7.8. When blood pH falls below 7.0, the central nervous system is so depressed that the person goes into coma and death soon follows. When blood pH rises above 7.8, the nervous system is overexcited, leading to such characteristic signs as muscle tetany, extreme nervousness, and convulsions. Death often results from respiratory arrest.

Respiratory and Renal Compensations

When an acid-base imbalance is due to inadequate functioning of one of the physiological buffer systems (the lungs or kidneys), the other system tries to compensate. The respiratory system attempts to compensate for metabolic acid-base imbalances, and the kidneys (although much slower) work to correct imbalances caused by respiratory disease. These **respiratory** and **renal compensations** can be recognized by changes in plasma P_{CO_2} and bicarbonate ion

26

TABLE 26.2 Causes and Consequences of Acid-Base Imbalances

CONDITION AND HALLMARK	POSSIBLE CAUSES; COMMENTS
METABOLIC ACIDOSIS	
uncompensated (uncorrected) (HCO_3^- <22 mEq/L; pH <7.35)	**Severe diarrhea:** bicarbonate-rich intestinal (and pancreatic) secretions rushed through digestive tract before their solutes can be reabsorbed; bicarbonate ions are replaced by renal mechanisms that generate new bicarbonate ions
	Renal disease: failure of kidneys to rid body of acids formed by normal metabolic processes
	Untreated diabetes mellitus: lack of insulin or inability of tissue cells to respond to insulin, resulting in inability to use glucose; fats are used as primary energy fuel, and ketoacidosis occurs
	Starvation: lack of dietary nutrients for cellular fuels; body proteins and fat reserves are used for energy—both yield acidic metabolites as they are broken down for energy
	Excess alcohol ingestion: results in excess acids in blood
	High ECF potassium concentrations: potassium ions compete with H^+ for secretion in renal tubules; when ECF levels of K^+ are high, H^+ secretion is inhibited
METABOLIC ALKALOSIS	
uncompensated (HCO_3^- >26 mEq/L; pH >7.45)	**Vomiting or gastric suctioning:** loss of stomach HCl requires that H^+ be withdrawn from blood to replace stomach acid; thus H^+ decreases and HCO_3^- increases proportionately
	Selected diuretics: cause K^+ depletion and H_2O loss. Low K^+ directly stimulates the tubule cells to secrete H^+. Reduced blood volume elicits the renin-angiotensin mechanism, which stimulates Na^+ reabsorption and H^+ secretion.
	Ingestion of excessive sodium bicarbonate (antacid): bicarbonate moves easily into ECF, where it enhances natural alkaline reserve
	Excess aldosterone (e.g., adrenal tumors): promotes excessive reabsorption of Na^+, which pulls increased amount of H^+ into urine. Hypovolemia promotes the same relative effect because aldosterone secretion is increased to enhance Na^+ (and H_2O) reabsorption.
RESPIRATORY ACIDOSIS (HYPOVENTILATION)	
uncompensated (>45 mm Hg; pH <7.35)	**Impaired lung function** (e.g., in chronic bronchitis, cystic fibrosis, emphysema): impaired gas exchange or alveolar P_{CO_2} ventilation
	Impaired ventilatory movement: paralysis of respiratory muscles, chest injury, extreme obesity
	Narcotic or barbiturate overdose or injury to brain stem: depression of respiratory centers, resulting in hypoventilation and respiratory arrest
RESPIRATORY ALKALOSIS (HYPERVENTILATION)	
uncompensated (P_{CO_2} <35 mm Hg; pH >7.45)	**Strong emotions**: pain, anxiety, fear, panic attack
	Hypoxia: asthma, pneumonia, high altitude; represents effort to raise P_{O_2} at the expense of excessive CO_2 excretion
	Brain tumor or injury: abnormality of respiratory controls

concentrations (see *A Closer Look*). Because the compensations act to restore normal blood pH, the pH may actually be in the normal range when the patient has a significant medical problem.

Respiratory Compensations   As a rule, changes in respiratory rate and depth are evident when the respiratory system is attempting to compensate for meta-bolic acid-base imbalances. In metabolic acidosis, the respiratory rate and depth are usually elevated—an indication that the respiratory centers are stimulated by the high H^+ levels. The blood pH is low (below 7.35) and the HCO_3^- level is below 22 mEq/L. As the respiratory system "blows off" CO_2 to rid the blood of excess acid, the P_{CO_2} falls below 35 mm Hg. By contrast,

26

A CLOSER LOOK

Sleuthing: Using Blood Values to Determine the Cause of Acidosis or Alkalosis

Students, particularly nursing students, are often given blood values and asked to determine (1) whether the patient is in acidosis or alkalosis, (2) the cause of the condition (respiratory or metabolic), and (3) whether the condition is being compensated. If they are approached systematically, such determinations are not nearly as difficult as they may appear. To analyze a person's acid-base balance, scrutinize the blood values in the following order:

1. Note the pH. This tells you whether the person is in acidosis (pH below 7.35) or alkalosis (pH above 7.45), but it does *not* tell you the cause.

2. Next, check the P_{CO_2} to see if this is the cause of the acid-base imbalance. Because the respiratory system is a fast-acting system, an excessively high or low P_{CO_2} may indicate either that the condition is respiratory system—caused or that the respiratory system is compensating. For example, if the pH indicates acidosis and

   a. The P_{CO_2} is over 45 mm Hg, the respiratory system is the *cause* of the problem and the condition is a respiratory acidosis

   b. The P_{CO_2} is below normal limits (below 35 mm Hg), the respiratory system is *not the cause but is compensating*

   c. The P_{CO_2} is within normal limits, the condition is *neither caused nor compensated* by the respiratory system

3. Check the bicarbonate level. If step 2 proves that the respiratory system is not responsible for the imbalance, then the condition is metabolic and should be reflected in increased or decreased bicarbonate levels. Metabolic acidosis is indicated by HCO_3^- values below 22 mEq/L, and metabolic alkalosis by values over 26 mEq/L. Notice that whereas P_{CO_2} levels vary inversely with blood pH (P_{CO_2} rises as blood pH falls), HCO_3^- levels vary directly with blood pH (increased HCO_3^- results in increased pH).

Beyond this bare-bones approach there is something else to consider when you are assessing acid-base problems. If an imbalance is *fully* compensated, the pH may be normal even while the patient is in trouble. Hence, when the pH is normal, carefully scrutinize the P_{CO_2} or HCO_3^- values for clues to what imbalance may be occurring.

Consider the following two examples of the three-step approach.

Problem 1

Blood values: pH 7.5; P_{CO_2} 24 mm Hg; HCO_3^- 23 mEq/L

Analysis:

1. The pH is elevated: alkalosis.

2. The P_{CO_2} is very low: the cause of the alkalosis.

3. The HCO_3^- value is within normal limits.

Conclusion: This is a respiratory alkalosis not compensated by renal mechanisms, as might occur during short-term hyperventilation.

Problem 2

Blood values: pH 7.48; P_{CO_2} 46 mm Hg; HCO_3^- 33 mEq/L
Analysis:

1. The pH is elevated: alkalosis.

2. The P_{CO_2} is elevated: the cause of *acidosis,* not alkalosis; thus, the respiratory system is compensating and is not the cause.

3. The HCO_3^- is elevated: the cause of the alkalosis.

Conclusion: This is a metabolic alkalosis being compensated by respiratory acidosis (retention of CO_2 to restore blood pH to the normal range).

See the accompanying simple chart to help you in your future determinations.

Acid-base Disturbance	Normal Range in Plasma		
	pH 7.35–7.45	P_{CO_2} 35–45 mm HG	HCO_3^- 22–26 mEq/L
Respiratory acidosis	↓	↑	↑ if compensating
Respiratory alkalosis	↑	↓	↓ if compensating
Metabolic acidosis	↓	↓ if compensating	↓
Metabolic alkalosis	↑	↑ if compensating	↑

in respiratory acidosis, the respiratory rate is often depressed and *is the immediate cause of the acidosis* (with some exceptions such as pneumonia or emphysema where gas exchange is impaired).

Respiratory compensation for metabolic alkalosis involves slow, shallow breathing, which allows CO_2 to accumulate in the blood. A metabolic alkalosis being compensated by respiratory mechanisms is revealed by a pH over 7.45 at least initially, elevated bicarbonate levels (over 26 mEq/L), and a P_{CO_2} above 45 mm Hg.

Renal Compensations When an acid-base imbalance is of respiratory origin, renal mechanisms are stepped up to correct the imbalance. For example,

SYSTEM CONNECTIONS: Homeostatic Interrelationships Between the Urinary System and Other Body Systems

Integumentary System

- Kidneys dispose of nitrogenous wastes; maintain fluid, electrolyte, and acid-base balance of blood
- Skin provides external protective barrier; site of water loss (via perspiration); vitamin D synthesis site

Skeletal System

- Kidneys dispose of nitrogenous wastes; maintain fluid, electrolyte, and acid-base balance of blood
- Bones of rib cage provide some protection to kidneys; form major store of calcium and phosphate ions

Muscular System

- Kidneys dispose of nitrogenous wastes; maintain fluid, electrolyte, and acid-base balance of blood; renal regulation of Na^+, K^+, and Ca^{2+} content in ECF crucial for muscle excitability and contractility
- Muscles of pelvic diaphragm and external urethral sphincter function in voluntary control of micturition; creatinine is a nitrogenous waste product of muscle metabolism that must be excreted by the kidneys

Nervous System

- Kidneys dispose of nitrogenous wastes; maintain fluid, electrolyte, and acid-base balance of blood; renal control of Na^+, K^+, and Ca^{2+} in ECF essential for normal neural function
- Neural controls involved in micturition; sympathetic nervous system activity triggers the renin-angiotensin mechanism

Endocrine System

- Kidneys dispose of nitrogenous wastes; maintain fluid, electrolyte, and acid-base balance of blood; produce erythropoietin; renal regulation of Na^+ and water balance essential for blood pressure homeostasis and hormone transport in blood
- ADH, aldosterone, ANP, and other hormones help regulate renal reabsorption of water and electrolytes

Cardiovascular System

- Kidneys dispose of nitrogenous wastes; maintain fluid, electrolyte, and acid-base balance of blood; renal regulation of Na^+/water balance essential for blood pressure homeostasis. Na^+, K^+, and Ca^{2+} regulation maintains cardiac irritability
- Systemic arterial blood pressure is the driving force for glomerular filtration; heart secretes atrial natriuretic peptide; blood transports nutrients, oxygen, etc. to urinary organs

Lymphatic System/Immunity

- Kidneys dispose of nitrogenous wastes; maintain fluid, electrolyte, and acid-base balance of blood
- By returning leaked plasma fluid to cardiovascular system, lymphatic vessels help ensure normal systemic arterial pressure required for kidney function; immune cells protect urinary organs from infection and cancer

Respiratory System

- Kidneys dispose of nitrogenous wastes; maintain fluid, electrolyte, and long-term acid-base balance of blood
- Respiratory system provides oxygen required by kidney cells for their high metabolic activity; disposes of carbon dioxide; rapid acid-base balance of blood; lung capillary endothelial cells convert angiotensin I to angiotensin II

Digestive System

- Kidneys dispose of nitrogenous wastes; maintain fluid, electrolyte, and acid-base balance of blood; also, metabolize vitamin D to the active form needed for calcium absorption
- Digestive organs provide nutrients needed for kidney cell health; liver synthesizes urea and glutamine to transport waste nitrogen to the kidneys for excretion

Reproductive System

- Kidneys dispose of nitrogenous wastes; maintain fluid, electrolyte, and acid-base balance of blood

THE URINARY SYSTEM and Interrelationships with the Cardiovascular, Endocrine, and Nervous Systems

A drink of water—such a simple thing. It quenches a powerful thirst, but that's not all. Inadequate hydration can cause poor functioning, both mental and physical, and fatigue, illness, and even death. The body also needs water to regulate its temperature via perspiration, to wash wastes and toxins out of the body in urine, to maintain proper blood volume and pressure, and to keep the skeletal muscles well hydrated (otherwise they feel weak and tire quickly, and even stop working altogether). A drink provides that needed water, but it takes the kidneys to keep it pure so that all of these vital activities can continue to occur. Seemingly wise, the exceedingly tiny nephrons "know" which blood solutes are valuable and which disposable, and that alcohol and caffeine are diuretics and as such drain water from the body. Make no mistake about it, the kidneys are crucially important to the body—all systems, all cells. The body systems that most influence the kidneys' ability to do their life-sustaining work are the cardiovascular, endocrine, and nervous systems.

Cardiovascular System

As important as they are, and as intricate as their functioning is, the kidneys cannot work without blood to process and blood pressure to drive filtrate through the glomerular filters. When we hemorrhage severely, the GFR drops and the kidneys stop functioning altogether. When blood pressure is normal, it provides the driving force that allows the nephrons to perform their job. On the other hand, by excreting or retaining water, the kidneys maintain the blood volume that furnishes that filtration pressure.

Endocrine System and Nervous System

The kidneys have a whole "toolbox" of ways to ensure that their own blood pressure is normal. However, autoregulation can be overridden by hormonal mechanisms (the renin-angiotensin mechanism which calls aldosterone and ADH into service, and release of ANP by the heart) in order to maintain systemic blood pressure. Sympathetic activity also ensures that bodywide blood pressure is maintained within homeostatic limits so as to maintain adequate GFR. Alternatively, the kidneys' needs are overcome as necessary by the same sympathetic fibers to make sure that the heart and brain receive adequate blood perfusion in periods of dramatically falling blood pressure. Now that's flexibility!

Urinary System

Case study: Mr. Heyden, a somewhat stocky 72-year-old man, is brought in to the emergency room (ER). The paramedics report that his left arm and the left side of his body trunk were pinned beneath some wreckage, and that when he was freed, his left hypogastric and lumbar areas appeared to be compressed and his left arm was blanched and without sensation. On admission, Mr. Heyden is alert, slightly cyanotic, and complaining of pain in his left side; he loses consciousness shortly thereafter. His vital signs are taken, blood is drawn for laboratory tests, and Mr. Heyden is catheterized and immediately scheduled for a CT scan of his left abdominal region.

Analyze the information that was subsequently recorded on Mr. Heyden's chart:

■ Re vital signs: Temperature 102°F; BP 90/50 mm Hg and falling; heart rate 116 beats/min and thready; 30 respirations/min

1. Given the values above and his attendant cyanosis, what would you guess is Mr. Heyden's immediate problem? Explain your reasoning.

■ Re CT scan: CT scan reveals a ruptured spleen and a large hematoma in the upper left abdominal quadrant. Splenic repair surgery is scheduled but unsuccessful; the spleen is removed.

2. Rupture of the spleen results in massive hemorrhage. Explain this observation. What organs (if any) will compensate for the removal of Mr. Heyden's spleen?

■ Re hematology data: Most blood tests yield normal results. However, renin, aldosterone, and ADH levels are elevated.

3. Explain the cause and consequence of each of the hematology findings.

■ Re urinalysis: Some granular casts (particulate cell debris) are noted, and the urine is brownish-red in color; other values are normal, but urine output is very low. An order is given to force fluids.

4. What might account for (1) the low volume of urine output? (Name at least two possibilities.) (2) the casts and abnormal color of his urine? Can you see any possible relationship between his crush injury and these findings?

The next day, Mr. Heyden is awake and alert. He says that he now has feeling in his arm, but he is still complaining of pain. However, the pain site appears to have moved from the left upper quadrant to his lumbar region. His urine output is still low. He is scheduled once again for a CT scan, this time of his lumbar region. The order to force fluids is renewed and some additional and more specific blood tests are ordered. We will visit Mr. Heyden again shortly, but in the meantime think about what these new findings may indicate.
(Answers in Appendix G)

a hypoventilating individual will exhibit acidosis. When renal compensation is occurring, both the P_{CO_2} and the HCO_3^- levels are high. The high P_{CO_2} is the cause of the acidosis, and the rising HCO_3^- level indicates that the kidneys are retaining bicarbonate to offset the acidosis. Conversely, a person with renal-compensated respiratory alkalosis will have a high blood pH and a low P_{CO_2}. Bicarbonate ion levels begin to fall as the kidneys eliminate more HCO_3^- from the body by failing to reclaim it or by actively secreting it. Note that the kidneys cannot compensate for alkalosis or acidosis if that condition reflects a *renal* problem.

Developmental Aspects of Fluid, Electrolyte, and Acid-Base Balance

An embryo and a very young fetus are more than 90% water, but solids accumulate as fetal development continues, and at birth an infant is "only" 70–80% water. (The average value for adults is 58%.) Infants have proportionately more ECF than adults and, consequently, a much higher NaCl content in relation to K^+, Mg^{2+}, and PO_4^{3-} salts. Distribution of body water begins to change about two months after birth and achieves the adult pattern by the time the child is 2 years old. Although plasma electrolyte concentrations are similar in infants and adults, K^+ and Ca^{2+} values are higher and Mg^{2+}, HCO_3^-, and total protein levels are lower in the first few days of life than at any other time. At puberty, sex differences in body water content become obvious as males develop relatively greater amounts of skeletal muscle.

Problems with fluid, electrolyte, and particularly acid-base balance are most common in infancy, reflecting the following conditions:

1. The very low residual volume of infant lungs (approximately half that of adults relative to body weight). When respiration is altered, rapid and dramatic changes in P_{CO_2} can result.

2. The high rate of fluid intake and output in infants (about seven times higher than in adults). Infants may exchange fully half their ECF daily. Though infants have proportionately much more body water than adults, this does not protect them from excessive fluid shifts. Even slight alterations in fluid balance can cause serious problems. Further, although adults can live without water for about ten days, infants can survive for only three to four days.

3. The relatively high infant metabolic rate (about twice that of adults). The higher metabolic rate

yields much larger amounts of metabolic wastes and acids that need to be excreted by the kidneys. This, along with buffer systems that are not yet fully effective, results in a tendency toward acidosis.

4. The high rate of insensible water loss in infants because of their larger surface area relative to body volume (about three times that of adults). Infants lose substantial amounts of water through their skin.

5. The inefficiency of infant kidneys. At birth, the kidneys are immature, only about half as proficient as adult kidneys at concentrating urine, and notably inefficient at ridding the body of acids.

All these factors put newborns at risk for dehydration and acidosis, at least until the end of the first month when the kidneys achieve reasonable efficiency. Bouts of vomiting or diarrhea greatly amplify the risk.

In old age, total body water often decreases (the loss is largely from the intracellular compartment) because muscle mass progressively declines and body fat rises. Although few changes occur in the solute concentrations of body fluids, the speed with which homeostasis is restored after being disrupted declines with age. Elders may be unresponsive to thirst cues and thus are at risk for dehydration. Additionally, they are the most frequent prey of diseases that lead to severe fluid, electrolyte, or acid-base problems, such as congestive heart failure (and its attendant edema) and diabetes mellitus. Because most fluid, electrolyte, and acid-base imbalances occur when body water content is highest or lowest, the very young and the very old are the most frequent victims.

■ ■ ■

This chapter has examined the chemical and physiological mechanisms that provide the optimal internal environment for survival. Although the kidneys are the "Rolex" among homeostatic organs in regulating water, electrolyte, and acid-base balance, they do not and cannot act alone. Rather, their activity is made possible by a host of hormones and enhanced both by bloodborne buffers, which give the kidneys time to react, and by the respiratory system, which shoulders a substantial responsibility for acid-base balance of the blood. Now that we have discussed the topics relevant to renal functioning, and once you read in *Making Connections* how the urinary system interacts with other body systems, the topics in Chapters 25 and 26 should draw together in an understandable way.

Related Clinical Terms

Antacid An agent that counteracts acidity, such as sodium bicarbonate, aluminum hydroxide gel, and magnesium trisilicate. Commonly used in the management of heartburn.

Hyperaldosteronism (Conn's disease) A condition of hypersecretion of aldosterone by adrenal cortical cells accompanied by excessive loss of potassium and generalized muscular weakness, hypernatremia, and hypertension. Usual cause is adrenal tumor; usual treatment is adrenal-suppressing drugs prior to tumor removal.

Renal tubular acidosis A metabolic acidosis resulting from impaired renal reabsorption of bicarbonate; the urine is alkaline.

Syndrome of inappropriate ADH secretion (SIADH) A group of disorders associated with excessive ADH secretion in the absence of appropriate (osmotic or nonosmotic) stimuli. Characterized by hyponatremia, concentrated urine, fluid retention, and weight gain. Usual causes are ectopic secretion of ADH by cancer cells (e.g., bronchogenic cancer cells) and brain disorders or trauma affecting the ADH-secreting hypothalamic neurons. Temporary management involves water restriction.

Chapter Summary

Media study tools that could provide you additional help in reviewing specific key topics of Chapter 26 are referenced below.
IP = *InterActive Physiology*

Body Fluids   (pp. 1036–1038)

Body Water Content   (p. 1036)

1. Water accounts for 45–75% of body weight, depending on age, sex, and amount of body fat.

Fluid Compartments   (p. 1036)

2. About two-thirds (25 L) of body water is found within cells in the intracellular fluid (ICF) compartment; the balance (15 L) is in the extracellular fluid (ECF) compartment. The ECF includes plasma and interstitial fluid.

Composition of Body Fluids   (pp. 1036–1037)

3. Solutes dissolved in body fluids include electrolytes and nonelectrolytes. Electrolyte concentration is expressed in mEq/L.

4. Plasma contains more proteins than does interstitial fluid; otherwise, extracellular fluids are similar. The most abundant ECF electrolytes are sodium, chloride, and bicarbonate ions.

5. Intracellular fluids contain large amounts of protein anions and potassium, phosphate, and magnesium ions.

IP Fluid, Electrolyte, and Acid/Base Balance; Topic: Introduction to Body Fluids, pp. 1–8.

Fluid Movement Among Compartments (pp. 1037–1039)

6. Fluid exchanges between compartments are regulated by osmotic and hydrostatic pressures: (a) Filtrate is forced out of the capillaries by hydrostatic pressure and pulled back in by colloid osmotic pressure. (b) Water moves freely between the ECF and the ICF by osmosis, but solute movements are restricted by size, charge, and dependence on transport proteins. (c) Water flows always follow changes in ECF osmolality.

7. Plasma links the internal and external environments.

IP Fluid, Electrolyte, and Acid/Base Balance; Topic: Introduction to Body Fluids, pp. 19–23.

Water Balance and ECF Osmolality (pp. 1039–1043)

1. Sources of body water are ingested foods and fluids and metabolic water.

2. Water leaves the body via the lungs, skin, gastrointestinal tract, and kidneys.

Regulation of Water Intake   (pp. 1039–1040)

3. Increased plasma osmolality triggers the thirst mechanism, mediated by hypothalamic osmoreceptors. Thirst, inhibited by distension of the gastrointestinal tract by ingested water and then by osmotic signals, may be damped before body needs for water are met.

Regulation of Water Output   (pp. 1040–1041)

4. Obligatory water loss is unavoidable and includes insensible water losses from the lungs, the skin, in feces, and about 500 ml of urine output daily.

5. Beyond obligatory water loss, the volume of urinary output depends on water intake and loss via other routes and reflects the influence of antidiuretic hormone and aldosterone on the renal tubules.

Influence of ADH   (p. 1041)

6. Antidiuretic hormone causes aquaporins (water channels) to be inserted in the cell membranes of the collecting ducts, so that most filtered water is reabsorbed. ADH release is triggered if ECF osmolality is high, or if a large drop in blood volume or pressure occurs.

Disorders of Water Balance   (pp. 1041–1043)

7. Dehydration occurs when water loss exceeds water intake over time. It is evidenced by thirst, dry skin, and decreased urine output. A serious consequence is hypovolemic shock.

8. Hypotonic hydration occurs when body fluids are excessively diluted and cells become swollen by water entry. The most serious consequence is cerebral edema.

9. Edema is an abnormal accumulation of fluid in the interstitial space, which may impair blood circulation.

IP Fluid, Electrolyte, and Acid/Base Balance; Topic: Water Homeostasis, pp. 1–27.

Electrolyte Balance (pp. 1043–1049)

1. Most electrolytes (salts) are obtained from ingested foods and fluids. Salts, particularly NaCl, are often ingested in excess of need.

2. Electrolytes are lost in perspiration, feces, and urine. The kidneys are most important in regulating electrolyte balance.

The Central Role of Sodium in Fluid and Electrolyte Balance (p. 1043)

3. Sodium salts are the most abundant solutes in ECF. They exert the bulk of ECF osmotic pressure and control water volume and distribution in the body.

4. Na^+ transport by the renal tubule cells is coupled to and helps regulate K^+, Cl^-, HCO_3^-, and H^+ concentrations in the ECF.

Regulation of Sodium Balance (pp. 1043–1048)

5. Sodium ion balance is linked to ECF volume and blood pressure regulation and involves both neural and hormonal controls.

6. Aldosterone promotes Na^+ reabsorption and H_2O conservation, unless other mechanisms favor water excretion.

7. Declining blood pressure and falling filtrate osmolality stimulate the granular cells to release renin. Renin, via angiotensin II, enhances systemic blood pressure and aldosterone release.

8. Cardiovascular system baroreceptors sense changing arterial blood pressure, prompting changes in sympathetic vasomotor activity. Rising arterial pressure leads to vasodilation and enhanced Na^+ and water loss in urine. Falling arterial pressure promotes vasoconstriction and conserves Na^+ and water.

9. Atrial natriuretic peptide, released by certain atrial cells in response to rising blood pressure (or blood volume), causes systemic vasodilation and inhibits renin, aldosterone, and ADH release. Hence, it enhances Na^+ and water excretion, reducing blood volume and blood pressure.

10. Estrogens and glucocorticoids increase renal retention of sodium. Progesterone promotes enhanced sodium and water excretion in urine.

Regulation of Potassium Balance (pp. 1048–1049)

11. About 90% of filtered potassium is reabsorbed by the more proximal regions of the nephrons.

12. The main thrust of renal regulation of K^+ is to excrete it. Potassium ion secretion by the principal cells of the cortical collecting ducts is enhanced by increased plasma K^+ content and aldosterone. Type A cells of the collecting duct reabsorb small amounts of K^+ during K^+ deficit.

Regulation of Calcium and Phosphate Balance (p. 1049)

13. Calcium balance is regulated primarily by parathyroid hormone (PTH), which enhances blood Ca^{2+} levels by targeting the bones, intestine, and kidneys. PTH-regulated reabsorption occurs primarily in the DCT.

14. PTH decreases renal reabsorption of phosphate ions.

Regulation of Anions (p. 1049)

15. When blood pH is normal or slightly high, chloride is the major anion accompanying sodium reabsorption. In acidosis, chloride is replaced by bicarbonate.

16. Reabsorption of most other anions is regulated by their transport maximums (T_m).

IP Fluid, Electrolyte, and Acid/Base Balance; Topic: Electrolyte Homeostasis, pp. 1–38.

Acid-Base Balance (pp. 1049–1057, 1060)

1. Acids are proton (H^+) donors; bases are proton acceptors. Acids that dissociate completely in solution are strong acids; those that dissociate incompletely are weak acids. Strong bases are more effective proton acceptors than are weak bases.

2. The homeostatic pH range of arterial blood is 7.35 to 7.45. A higher pH represents alkalosis; a lower pH reflects acidosis.

3. Some acids enter the body in foods, but most are generated by breakdown of phosphorus-containing proteins, incomplete oxidation of fats or glucose, and the loading and transport of carbon dioxide in the blood.

4. Acid-base balance is achieved by chemical buffers, respiratory regulation, and in the long term by renal regulation of bicarbonate ion (hence, hydrogen ion) concentration of body fluids.

IP Fluid, Electrolyte, and Acid/Base Balance; Topic: Acid/Base Homeostasis, pp. 1–15.

Chemical Buffer Systems (pp. 1050–1052)

5. Chemical buffers are single or paired sets (a weak acid and its salt) of molecules that act rapidly to resist excessive shifts in pH by releasing or binding H^+.

6. Chemical buffers of the body include the bicarbonate, phosphate, and protein buffer systems.

IP Fluid, Electrolyte, and Acid/Base Balance; Topic: Acid/Base Homeostasis, pp. 16–26.

Respiratory Regulation of H^+ (p. 1052)

7. Respiratory regulation of acid-base balance of the blood utilizes the bicarbonate buffer system and the fact that CO_2 and H_2O are in reversible equilibrium with H_2CO_3.

8. Acidosis activates the respiratory center to increase respiratory rate and depth, which eliminates more CO_2 and causes blood pH to rise. Alkalosis depresses the respiratory center, resulting in CO_2 retention and a fall in blood pH.

IP Fluid, Electrolyte, and Acid/Base Balance; Topic: Acid/Base Homeostasis, pp. 27–28.

Renal Mechanisms of Acid-Base Balance (pp. 1052–1054)

9. The kidneys provide the major long-term mechanism for controlling acid-base balance by maintaining stable HCO_3^- levels in the ECF. Metabolic acids (organic acids other than carbonic acid) can be eliminated from the body only by the kidneys.

10. Secreted hydrogen ions come from the dissociation of carbonic acid generated within the tubule cells.

11. Tubule cells are impermeable to bicarbonate in the filtrate, but they can conserve filtered bicarbonate ions indirectly by absorbing HCO_3^- generated within them (by dissociation of carbonic acid to HCO_3^- and H^+). For each HCO_3^- (and Na^+) reabsorbed, one H^+ is secreted into the filtrate, where it combines with HCO_3^-.

12. To generate and add new HCO_3^- to plasma to counteract acidosis, either of two mechanisms may be used:
   - Secreted H^+, buffered by bases other than HCO_3^-, is excreted from the body in urine (the major urine buffer is the phosphate buffer system).
   - NH_4^+ (derived from glutamine catabolism) is excreted in urine.

13. To counteract alkalosis, bicarbonate ion is secreted into the filtrate and H^+ is reabsorbed.

IP Fluid, Electrolyte, and Acid/Base Balance; Topic: Acid/Base Homeostasis, pp. 29–37.

Abnormalities of Acid-Base Balance (pp. 1055–1057, 1060)

14. Classification of acid-base imbalances as metabolic or respiratory indicates the cause of the acidosis or alkalosis.

15. Respiratory acidosis results from carbon dioxide retention; respiratory alkalosis occurs when carbon dioxide is eliminated faster than it is produced.

16. Metabolic acidosis occurs when fixed acids (lactic acid, ketone bodies, and others) accumulate in the blood or when bicarbonate is lost from the body; metabolic alkalosis occurs when bicarbonate levels are excessive.

17. Extremes of pH for life are 7.0 and 7.8.

18. Compensations occur when the respiratory system or kidneys act to reverse acid-base imbalances resulting from abnormal or inadequate functioning of the alternate system. Respiratory compensations involve changes in respiratory rate and depth. Renal compensations modify blood levels of HCO_3^-.

IP Fluid, Electrolyte, and Acid/Base Balance; Topic: Acid/Base Homeostasis, pp. 38–59.

Developmental Aspects of Fluid, Electrolyte, and Acid-Base Balance (p. 1060)

1. Infants have a higher risk of dehydration and acidosis because of their low lung residual volume, high rate of fluid intake and output, high metabolic rate, relatively large body surface area, and functionally immature kidneys at birth.

2. The elderly are at risk for dehydration because of their low percentage of body water and insensitivity to thirst cues. Diseases that promote fluid and acid-base imbalances (cardiovascular disease, diabetes mellitus, and others) are most common in the aged.

Review Questions

Multiple Choice/Matching

(Some questions have more than one correct answer. Select the best answer or answers from the choices given.)

1. Body water content is greatest in (a) infants, (b) young adults, (c) elderly adults.

2. Potassium, magnesium, and phosphate ions are the predominant electrolytes in (a) plasma, (b) interstitial fluid, (c) intracellular fluid.

3. Sodium balance is regulated primarily by control of amount(s) (a) ingested, (b) excreted in urine, (c) lost in perspiration, (d) lost in feces.

4. Water balance is regulated primarily by control of amount(s) (use choices in question 3).

5–10. Answer questions 5 through 10 by choosing responses from the following:

(a) ammonium ions	(f) magnesium
(b) bicarbonate	(g) phosphate
(c) calcium	(h) potassium
(d) chloride	(i) sodium
(e) hydrogen ions	(j) water

5. Three substances regulated (at least in part) by the influence of aldosterone on the kidney tubules.

6. Two substances regulated by parathyroid hormone.

7. Two substances secreted into the proximal convoluted tubules in exchange for sodium ions.

8. Part of an important chemical buffer system in plasma.

9. Two ions produced during catabolism of glutamine.

10. Substance regulated by ADH's effects on the renal tubules.

11. Which of the following factors will enhance ADH release? (a) increase in ECF volume, (b) decrease in ECF volume, (c) decrease in ECF osmolality, (d) increase in ECF osmolality.

12. The pH of blood varies *directly* with (a) HCO_3^-, (b) P_{CO_2}, (c) H^+, (d) none of the above.

13. In an individual with metabolic acidosis, a clue that the respiratory system is compensating is provided by (a) high blood bicarbonate levels, (b) low blood bicarbonate levels, (c) rapid, deep breathing, (d) slow, shallow breathing.

Short Answer Essay Questions

14. Name the body fluid compartments, noting their locations and the approximate fluid volume in each.

15. Describe the thirst mechanism, indicating how it is triggered and terminated.

16. Explain why and how ECF osmolality is maintained.

17. Explain why and how sodium balance, ECF volume, and blood pressure are jointly regulated.

18. Describe the role of the respiratory system in controlling acid-base balance.

19. Explain how the chemical buffer systems resist changes in pH.

20. Explain the relationship of the following to renal secretion and excretion of hydrogen ions: (a) plasma carbon dioxide levels, (b) phosphate, and (c) sodium bicarbonate reabsorption.

21. List several factors that place newborn babies at risk for acid-base imbalances.

Critical Thinking and Clinical Application Questions

1. Mr. Jessup, a 55-year-old man, is operated on for a cerebral tumor. About a month later, he appears at his physician's office complaining of excessive thirst. He claims to have been drinking about 20 liters of water daily for the past week and says he has been voiding nearly continuously. A urine sample is collected and its specific gravity is reported as 1.001. What is your diagnosis of Mr. Jessup's problem? What connection might exist between his previous surgery and his present problem?

2. For each of the following sets of blood values, name the acid-base imbalance (acidosis or alkalosis), determine its cause (metabolic or respiratory), decide whether the condition is being compensated, and cite at least one possible cause of the imbalance.

Problem 1: pH 7.63; P_{CO_2} 19 mm Hg; HCO_3^- 19.5 mEq/L

Problem 2: pH 7.22; P_{CO_2} 30 mm Hg; HCO_3^- 12.0 mEq/L

3. Explain how emphysema and congestive heart failure can lead to acid-base imbalance.

26

4. Mrs. Bush, a 70-year-old woman, is admitted to the hospital. Her history states that she has been suffering from diarrhea for three weeks. On admission, she complains of severe fatigue and muscle weakness. A blood chemistry study yields the following information: Na$^+$ 142 mEq/L; K$^+$ 1.5 mEq/L; Cl$^-$ 92 mEq/L; P$_{CO_2}$ 32 mm Hg. Which electrolytes are within normal limits? Which are so abnormal that the patient has a medical emergency? Which of the following represents the greatest danger to Mrs. Bush? (a) a fall due to her muscular weakness, (b) edema, (c) cardiac arrhythmia and cardiac arrest.

5. During a routine medical checkup, Candace, a 26-year-old physiotherapy student, is surprised to hear that her blood pressure is 180/110. She also has a rumbling systolic and diastolic abdominal bruit (murmur) that is loudest at the mid-epigastric area. Her physician suspects renal artery stenosis (narrowing). She orders an abdominal ultrasound and renal artery arteriography, which confirms that Candace has a small right kidney, and that the distal part of her right renal artery is narrowed by more than 70%. Her physician prescribes diuretics and calcium channel blockers as temporary measures, and refers Candace to a cardiovascular surgeon. Explain the connection between Candace's renal artery stenosis and her hypertension. Why is her right kidney smaller than her left? What would you expect Candace's blood levels of K$^+$, Na$^+$, aldosterone, angiotensin II, and renin to be?

CHAPTER 27

The Reproductive System

1. Describe the common function of the male and female reproductive systems.

Anatomy of the Male Reproductive System (pp. 1066–1072)

2. Describe the structure and function of the testes, and explain the importance of their location in the scrotum.

3. Describe the structure of the penis, and indicate its role in the reproductive process.

4. Describe the location, structure, and function of the accessory reproductive organs of the male.

5. Discuss the sources and functions of semen.

Physiology of the Male Reproductive System (pp. 1072–1082)

6. Describe the phases of the male sexual response.

7. Define meiosis. Compare and contrast it to mitosis.

8. Outline events of spermatogenesis.

9. Discuss hormonal regulation of testicular function and the physiological effects of testosterone on male reproductive anatomy.

Anatomy of the Female Reproductive System (pp. 1082–1091)

10. Describe the location, structure, and function of the ovaries.

11. Describe the location, structure, and function of each of the organs of the female reproductive duct system.

12. Describe the anatomy of the female external genitalia.

13. Discuss the structure and function of the mammary glands.

Physiology of the Female Reproductive System (pp. 1091–1100)

14. Describe the process of oogenesis and compare it to spermatogenesis.

15. Describe ovarian cycle phases, and relate them to events of oogenesis.

16. Describe the regulation of the ovarian and uterine cycles.

17. Discuss the physiological effects of estrogens and progesterone.

18. Describe the phases of the female sexual response.

Sexually Transmitted Diseases (pp. 1100–1101)

19. Indicate the infectious agents and modes of transmission of gonorrhea, syphilis, chlamydia, trichomoniasis, genital warts, and genital herpes.

Developmental Aspects of the Reproductive System: Chronology of Sexual Development (pp. 1101–1105, 1108)

20. Discuss the determination of genetic sex and prenatal development of male and female structures.

21. Describe the significant events of puberty and menopause.

Most organ systems of the body function almost continuously to maintain the well-being of the individual. The **reproductive system,** however, appears to "slumber" until puberty. The **primary sex organs, or gonads** (go'nadz; "seeds"), are the *testes* in males and the *ovaries* in females. The gonads produce sex cells, or **gametes** (gam'ēts; "spouses"), and secrete a variety of steroid hormones commonly called **sex hormones.** The remaining reproductive structures—ducts, glands, and external genitalia (jen-ĭ-ta'le-ah)—are referred to as **accessory reproductive organs.** Although male and female reproductive organs are quite different, their common purpose is to produce offspring.

The male's reproductive role is to manufacture male gametes called *sperm* and deliver them to the female reproductive tract, where fertilization can occur. The complementary role of the female is to produce female gametes, called *ova* or *eggs.* As a result of appropriately timed intercourse, a sperm and egg may fuse to form a fertilized egg, the first cell of the new individual, from which all body cells will arise. The male and female reproductive systems are equal partners in events leading up to fertilization, but once fertilization has occurred, the female partner's uterus provides the protective environment in which the embryo develops until birth. Sex hormones—androgens in males and estrogens and progesterone in females—play vital roles both in the development and function of the reproductive organs and in sexual behavior and drives. These hormones also influence the growth and development of many other organs and tissues of the body.

Anatomy of the Male Reproductive System

The sperm-producing **testes** (tes'tez; "witnesses"), or **male gonads,** lie within the *scrotum.* From the testes, the sperm are delivered to the body exterior through a system of ducts including (in order) the *epididymis,* the *ductus deferens,* the *ejaculatory duct,* and finally the *urethra,* which opens to the outside at the tip of the *penis.* The accessory sex glands, which empty their secretions into the ducts during ejaculation, are the *seminal vesicles, prostate,* and *bulbourethral glands.* Take a moment to trace the duct system in Figure 27.1, and identify the testis and accessory glands before continuing.

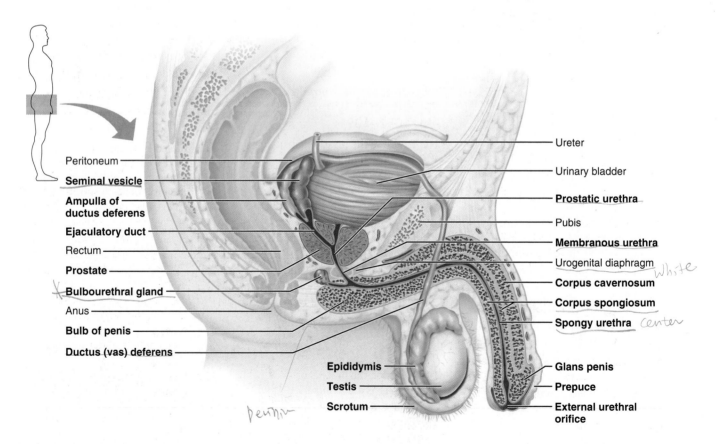

Peritoneum
Seminal vesicle
Ampulla of ductus deferens
Ejaculatory duct
Rectum
Prostate
Bulbourethral gland
Anus
Bulb of penis
Ductus (vas) deferens
Epididymis
Testis
Scrotum

Ureter
Urinary bladder
Prostatic urethra
Pubis
Membranous urethra
Urogenital diaphragm
Corpus cavernosum
Corpus spongiosum
Spongy urethra
Glans penis
Prepuce
External urethral orifice

FIGURE 27.1   Reproductive organs of the male, sagittal view. A portion of the pubis of the coxal bone has been left to show the relationship of the ductus deferens to the bony pelvis. (See *A Brief Atlas of the Human Body,* Figures 72 and 73.)

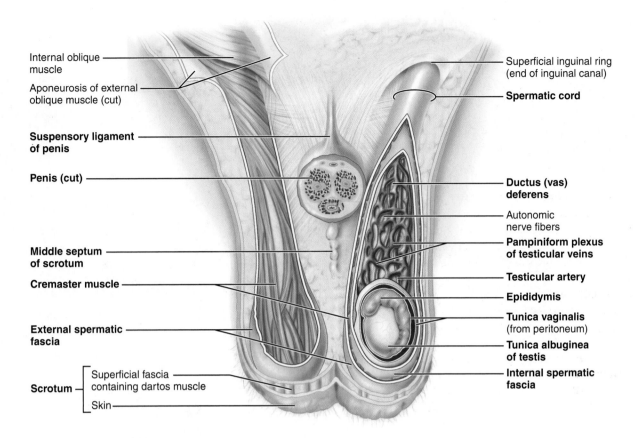

Internal oblique muscle

Aponeurosis of external oblique muscle (cut)

Suspensory ligament of penis

Penis (cut)

Middle septum of scrotum

Cremaster muscle

External spermatic fascia

Scrotum
— Superficial fascia containing dartos muscle
— Skin

Superficial inguinal ring (end of inguinal canal)

Spermatic cord

Ductus (vas) deferens

Autonomic nerve fibers

Pampiniform plexus of testicular veins

Testicular artery

Epididymis

Tunica vaginalis (from peritoneum)

Tunica albuginea of testis

Internal spermatic fascia

FIGURE 27.2 **Relationships of the testis to the scrotum and spermatic cord.** The scrotum has been opened and its anterior portion removed.

The Scrotum

The **scrotum** (skro'tum; "pouch") is a sac of skin and superficial fascia that hangs outside the abdominopelvic cavity at the root of the penis (Figure 27.2). It is covered with sparse hairs, and contains paired oval testes. A midline septum divides the scrotum, providing a compartment for each testis. This seems a rather vulnerable location for a man's testes, which contain his entire genetic heritage. However, because viable sperm cannot be produced in abundance at core body temperature (37°C), the superficial location of the scrotum, which provides a temperature about 3°C lower, is an essential adaptation. Furthermore, the scrotum responds to temperature changes. When it is cold, the testes are pulled closer to the warmth of the body wall, and the scrotum becomes shorter and heavily wrinkled, increasing its thickness to reduce heat loss. When it is warm, the scrotal skin is flaccid and loose to increase the surface area for cooling (sweating) and the testes hang lower, away from the body trunk. These changes in scrotal surface area help maintain a fairly constant intrascrotal temperature and reflect the activity of two sets of muscles. The **dartos muscle** (dar'tos; "skinned"), a layer of smooth muscle in the superficial fascia, wrinkles the scrotal skin. The

cremaster muscles (kre-mas'ter; "a suspender"), bands of skeletal muscle that arise from the internal oblique muscles of the trunk, elevate the testes.

The Testes

Each plum-sized testis is approximately 4 cm (1.5 inches) long and 2.5 cm (1 inch) in width and is surrounded by two tunics. The outer tunic is the two-layered **tunica vaginalis** (vaj"ĭ-nal'is), derived from an outpocketing of the peritoneum (see Figures 27.2 and 27.3). Deep to this serous layer is the **tunica albuginea** (al"bu-jin'e-ah; "white coat"), the fibrous capsule of the testis. Septa extending from the tunica albuginea divide the testis into 250 to 300 wedge-shaped *lobules* (Figure 27.3), each containing one to four tightly coiled **seminiferous tubules** (sem"ĭ-nif'er-us; "sperm-carrying"), the actual "sperm factories." Surrounding each seminiferous tubule are smooth muscle–like **myoid cells** (see Figure 27.3b). By contracting rhythmically, these cells may help to squeeze sperm and testicular fluids through the tubules and out of the testes.

The seminiferous tubules of each lobule converge to form a **tubulus rectus,** a straight tubule that conveys sperm into the **rete testis** (re'te), a tubular network on the posterior side of the testis. From the

27

Q *Which of the tubular structures shown here are the "sperm factories"?*

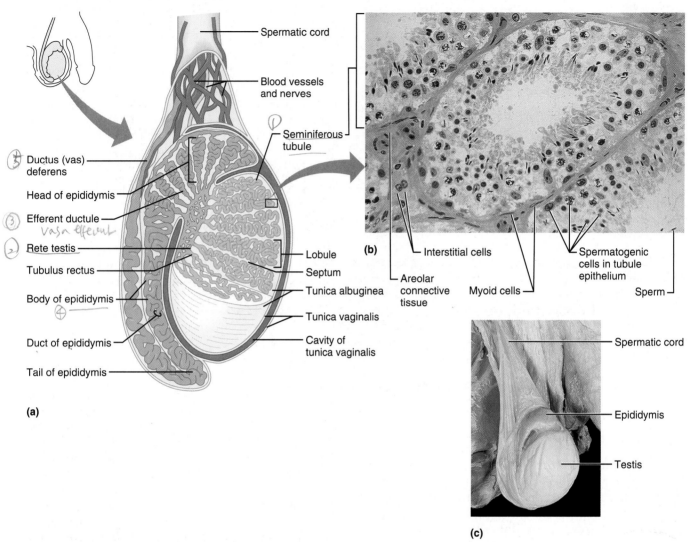

Spermatic cord

Blood vessels and nerves

Seminiferous tubule

Ductus (vas) deferens

Head of epididymis

Efferent ductule
vasa efferent

Rete testis

Tubulus rectus

Body of epididymis

Duct of epididymis

Tail of epididymis

Lobule

Septum

Tunica albuginea

Tunica vaginalis

Cavity of tunica vaginalis

(a)

(b)

Interstitial cells

Areolar connective tissue

Myoid cells

Spermatogenic cells in tubule epithelium

Sperm

Spermatic cord

Epididymis

Testis

(c)

FIGURE 27.3   **Structure of the testis. (a)** Partial sagittal section through the testis and epididymis. The anterior aspect is to the right. (See *Brief Atlas of the Human Body*, Figure 73). **(b)** Seminiferous tubule in cross section (200×). Note the spermatogenic (sperm-forming) cells in the tubule epithelium and the interstitial cells in the connective tissue between the tubules. **(c)** External view of a testis from a cadaver; same orientation as in (a).

rete testis, sperm leave the testis through the *efferent ductules* and enter the *epididymis* (ep″ĭ-did′ĭ-mis), which hugs the external testis surface.

Lying in the soft connective tissue surrounding the seminiferous tubules are the **interstitial cells,** also called *Leydig cells* (Figure 27.3). These cells produce androgens (most importantly *testosterone*), which they secrete into the surrounding interstitial fluid. Thus, the sperm-producing and hormone-producing functions of the testis are carried out by completely different cell populations.

The long **testicular arteries,** which branch from the abdominal aorta superior to the pelvis (see *gonadal arteries* in Figure 19.23c, p. 755), supply the testes. The **testicular veins** draining the testes arise from a network called the **pampiniform plexus** (pam-pin′ĭ-form; "tendril-shaped") that surrounds the portion of the testicular artery within the scrotum like a climbing vine (see Figure 27.2). The pampiniform plexus absorbs heat from the arterial blood, cooling it before it enters the testes. Thus, this plexus provides an additional way to keep the testes at their cool homeostatic temperature.

27

A *Seminiferous tubules.*

The testes are served by both divisions of the autonomic nervous system. Associated sensory nerves transmit impulses that result in agonizing pain and nausea when the testes are hit forcefully. The nerve fibers are enclosed, along with the blood vessels and lymphatics, in a connective tissue sheath called the **spermatic cord** which passes through the inguinal canal (see Figure 27.2).

▶ HOMEOSTATIC IMBALANCE

Although *testicular cancer* is relatively rare (affecting one of every 50,000 males), it is the most common cancer in young men (ages 15 to 35). A history of mumps or orchitis (inflammation of the testis) and substantial maternal exposure to environmental toxins before birth increases the risk, but the most important risk factor for this cancer is *cryptorchidism* (nondescent of the testes, see p. 1104). Because the most common sign of testicular cancer is a painless solid mass in the testis, self-examination of the testes should be practiced by every male. If detected early, it has an impressive cure rate. Over 90% of testicular cancers are cured by surgical removal of the cancerous testis *(orchiectomy)* either alone or in combination with radiation therapy or chemotherapy. ●

The Penis

The **penis** ("tail") is a copulatory organ, designed to deliver sperm into the female reproductive tract (Figures 27.1 and 27.4). The penis and scrotum, which hang suspended from the perineum, make up the external reproductive structures, or **external genitalia,** of the male. The male **perineum** (per″ĭ-ne′um; "around the anus") is the diamond-shaped region located between the pubic symphysis anteriorly, the coccyx posteriorly, and the ischial tuberosities laterally. The floor of the perineum is formed by muscles described in Chapter 10 (pp. 350–351).

The penis consists of an attached *root* and a free *shaft* or *body* that ends in an enlarged tip, the **glans penis.** The skin covering the penis is loose, and it slides distally to form a cuff called the **prepuce** (pre′pūs), or **foreskin,** around the glans. Frequently, the foreskin is surgically removed shortly after birth, a procedure called *circumcision* ("cutting around").

To understand penile anatomy, it is important to know that its dorsal and ventral surfaces are named in reference to the erect penis. Internally, the penis contains the spongy urethra and three long cylindrical bodies *(corpora)* of erectile tissue, each covered by a sheath of dense fibrous connective tissue. This *erectile tissue* is a spongy network of connective tissue and smooth muscle riddled with vascular spaces. During sexual excitement, the vascular spaces fill with blood, causing the penis to enlarge and become rigid. This event, called *erection*, enables the penis

to serve as a penetrating organ. The midventral erectile body, the **corpus spongiosum** (spon″je-o′sum; "spongy body") surrounds the urethra. It expands distally to form the glans and proximally to form the part of the root called the **bulb of the penis.** The bulb is covered externally by the sheetlike bulbospongiosus muscle and is secured to the urogenital diaphragm. The paired dorsal erectile bodies, called the **corpora cavernosa** (kor′por-ah kă-ver-no′sah; "cavernous bodies"), make up most of the penis and are bound by fibrous tunica albuginea. Their proximal ends form the **crura of the penis** (kroo′rah; "legs"; singular: crus). Each crus is surrounded by an ischiocavernosus muscle and anchors to the pubic arch of the bony pelvis.

The Male Duct System

As mentioned earlier, sperm travel from the testes to the body exterior through a system of ducts. In order (proximal to distal), the **accessory ducts** are the epididymis, the ductus deferens, the ejaculatory duct, and the urethra.

The Epididymis

The cup-shaped **epididymis** (*epi* = beside; *didym* = the testes) is about 3.8 cm (1.5 inches) long (see Figures 27.1 and 27.3a, c). Its *head*, which contains the efferent ductules, caps the superior aspect of the testis. Its *body* and *tail* are on the posterolateral area of the testis. Most of the epididymis consists of the highly coiled *duct of the epididymis* with an uncoiled length of about 6 m (20 feet). Some pseudostratified epithelium cells of the duct mucosa exhibit long, nonmotile microvilli (*stereocilia*). The huge surface area of these stereocilia allows them to absorb excess testicular fluid and to pass nutrients to the many sperm stored temporarily in the lumen.

The immature, nearly nonmotile sperm that leave the testis are moved slowly along the duct of the epididymis through fluid that contains a number of antimicrobial proteins, including several β-defensins. As they move along its tortuous course (a trip that takes about 20 days), the sperm gain the ability to swim. Sperm are ejaculated from the epididymis, not the testes as many believe, and when a male is sexually stimulated and ejaculates, the smooth muscle in the epididymis walls contracts, expelling sperm into the next segment of the duct system, the *ductus deferens*. Sperm can be stored in the epididymis for several months, but if held longer, they are eventually phagocytized by epithelial cells of the epididymis.

The Ductus Deferens and Ejaculatory Duct

The **ductus deferens** (duk′tus def′er-ens; "carrying away"), or *vas deferens*, is about 45 cm (18 inches) long. It runs upward as part of the spermatic cord

27

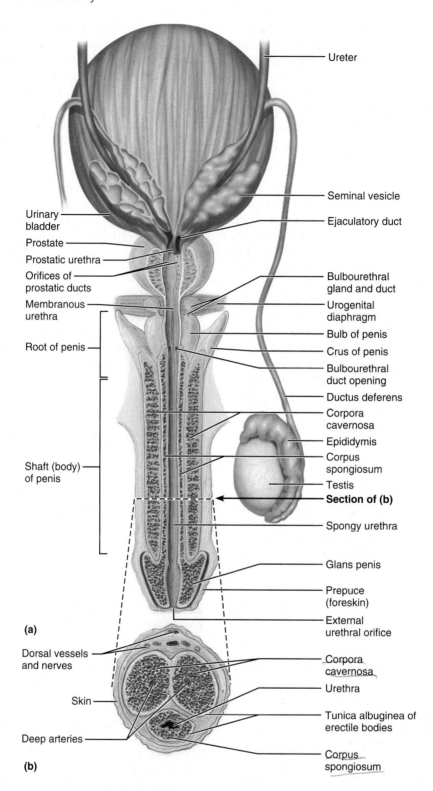

Ureter

Seminal vesicle

Ejaculatory duct

Urinary bladder

Prostate

Prostatic urethra

Orifices of prostatic ducts

Bulbourethral gland and duct

Membranous urethra

Urogenital diaphragm

Bulb of penis

Root of penis

Crus of penis

Bulbourethral duct opening

Ductus deferens

Corpora cavernosa

Epididymis

Corpus spongiosum

Shaft (body) of penis

Testis

Section of (b)

Spongy urethra

Glans penis

Prepuce (foreskin)

External urethral orifice

(a)

Dorsal vessels and nerves

Corpora cavernosa

Urethra

Skin

Tunica albuginea of erectile bodies

Deep arteries

Corpus spongiosum

(b)

FIGURE 27.4   **Male reproductive structures. (a)** Posterior view showing longitudinal (coronal) section of the penis. **(b)** Transverse section of the penis.

from the epididymis through the inguinal canal into the pelvic cavity (see Figure 27.1). Easily palpated as it passes anterior to the pubic bone, it then loops medially over the ureter and descends along the posterior bladder wall. Its terminus expands to form the **ampulla** of the ductus deferens and then joins with

the duct of the seminal vesicle (a gland) to form the short **ejaculatory duct.** Each ejaculatory duct enters the prostate; there it empties into the urethra.

Like that of the epididymis, the mucosa of the ductus deferens is pseudostratified epithelium. However, its muscular layer is extremely thick and the duct feels like a hard wire when squeezed between the fingertips. At the moment of ejaculation, the thick layers of smooth muscle in its walls create strong peristaltic waves that rapidly squeeze the sperm forward along the tract and into the urethra.

As Figure 27.3 illustrates, part of the ductus deferens lies in the scrotal sac. Some men opt to take full responsibility for birth control by having a **vasectomy** (vah-sek'to-me; "cutting the vas"). In this relatively minor operation, the physician makes a small incision into the scrotum and then cuts through and ligates (ties off) the ductus deferens. Sperm are still produced, but they can no longer reach the body exterior. Eventually, they deteriorate and are phagocytized. Vasectomy is simple and provides highly effective birth control (close to 100%). For those wishing to reverse that procedure, the success rate is about 50%.

The Urethra

The **urethra** is the terminal portion of the male duct system (see Figures 27.1 and 27.4). It conveys both urine and semen (at different times), so it serves both the urinary and reproductive systems. Its three regions are (1) the *prostatic urethra*, the portion surrounded by the prostate; (2) the *membranous (or intermediate part of the) urethra* in the urogenital diaphragm; and (3) the *spongy (penile) urethra*, which runs through the penis and opens to the outside at the *external urethral orifice*. The spongy urethra is about 15 cm (6 inches) long and accounts for 75% of urethral length. Its mucosa contains scattered *urethral glands* that secrete mucus into the lumen just before ejaculation.

Accessory Glands

The **accessory glands** include the paired seminal vesicles and bulbourethral glands and the single prostate (Figures 27.1 and 27.4). Together these glands produce the bulk of *semen* (sperm plus accessory gland secretions).

The Seminal Vesicles

The **seminal vesicles** (sem'ĭ-nul) or **seminal glands,** lie on the posterior bladder surface. Each of these fairly large, hollow glands is about the shape and length (5–7 cm) of a little finger. However, because a seminal vesicle is pouched, coiled, and folded back on itself, its uncoiled length is actually about 15 cm. Its fibrous capsule encloses a thick layer of smooth muscle which contracts during ejaculation to empty the gland. Stored within the mucosa's honeycomb of crypts and blind alleys is a yellowish viscous alkaline fluid containing fructose sugar, ascorbic acid, a coagulating enzyme *(vesiculase)*, and prostaglandins, as well as other substances that enhance sperm motility or fertilizing power. As noted, the duct of each seminal vesicle joins that of the ductus deferens on the same side to form the ejaculatory duct. Sperm and seminal fluid mix in the ejaculatory duct and enter the prostatic urethra together during ejaculation. Seminal gland secretion accounts for some 60% of the volume of semen.

The Prostate

The **prostate** (pros'tāt) is a single doughnut-shaped gland about the size of a peach pit (see Figures 27.1 and 27.4). It encircles the urethra just inferior to the bladder. Enclosed by a thick connective tissue capsule, it is made up of 20 to 30 compound tubuloalveolar glands embedded in a mass (stroma) of smooth muscle and dense connective tissue. The prostatic gland secretion enters the prostatic urethra via several ducts when prostatic smooth muscle contracts during ejaculation. It plays a role in activating sperm and accounts for up to one-third of the semen volume. It is a milky, slightly acid fluid that contains citrate (a nutrient source), several enzymes (fibrinolysin, hyaluronidase, acid phosphatase), and prostate-specific antigen (PSA).

▶ HOMEOSTATIC IMBALANCE

The prostate has a reputation as a health destroyer (perhaps reflected in the common mispronunciation "prostrate"). Hypertrophy of the prostate gland, called *benign prostatic hyperplasia (BPH)*, which affects nearly every elderly male, distorts the urethra. Although its precise cause is unknown, it may be associated with changes in hormone levels as a result of aging. The more the man strains to urinate, the more the valvelike prostatic mass blocks the opening, enhancing the risk of bladder infections (cystitis) and kidney damage. Traditional treatment has been surgical, but some newer options are gaining popularity, such as using microwaves or drugs to shrink the prostate; and inserting and inflating a small balloon to compress the prostate tissue away from the prostatic urethra. Another option is a procedure in which a catheter containing a tiny needle is inserted and burstlike releases of radio-frequency radiation are used to incinerate excess prostate tissue. Finasteride, which ratchets down production of dihydrotestosterone, the hormone linked to male pattern balding and prostate enlargement, is helpful in some cases. Additionally, several new drugs (such as doxazosin) are available that relax the smooth muscles at the bladder outlet, facilitating bladder emptying and providing relief.

Prostatitis (pros"tah-ti'tis), inflammation of the prostate, is the most common reason for a man to consult a urologist, and prostate cancer is the second

27

most common cause of cancer death in men (after lung cancer). Risk factors include fatty diet and genetic predisposition, and this cancer is twice as common in blacks as in whites, and half as common in Asians. Screening for prostate cancer typically involves digital examination of the prostate through the anterior rectal wall and assay of PSA levels in the blood. PSA, although a normal component of blood at levels below 0.4 ng/ml, is a tumor marker and its rising serum level follows BPH as well as the clinical disease course of prostate cancer. These screening procedures are followed by biopsies of suspicious prostate areas, if deemed necessary, and metastases (most commonly to the pelvic lymph nodes and the skeleton) are detected by bone or MRI scans. When possible, prostate cancer is treated surgically, alone or in conjunction with radiotherapy. Alternative therapies for metastasized cancers involve castration or therapy with drugs (flutamide) that block androgen receptors, or LHRH* analogues (such as leuprolide), which inhibit gonadotropin release. Deprived of the stimulatory effects of androgens, the prostatic tissue regresses and urinary symptoms typically decline. However, many prostate cancers are very slow growing and may never represent a threat to the patient. In such cases, frequent tests to monitor the tumor may be all that is necessary. ●

The Bulbourethral Glands

The **bulbourethral glands** (bul″bo-u-re′thral) are pea-sized glands inferior to the prostate gland (Figures 27.1 and 27.4). They produce a thick, clear mucus, some of which drains into the spongy urethra when a man becomes sexually excited and neutralizes traces of acidic urine in the urethra.

Semen

Semen (se′men) is a milky white, somewhat sticky mixture of sperm and accessory gland secretions. The liquid provides a transport medium and nutrients and contains chemicals that protect and activate the sperm and facilitate their movement. Mature sperm cells are streamlined cellular "missiles" containing little cytoplasm or stored nutrients. Catabolism of the fructose in seminal vesicle secretion provides nearly all the fuel needed for sperm ATP synthesis. Prostaglandins in semen decrease the viscosity of mucus guarding the entry (cervix) of the uterus and stimulate reverse peristalsis in the uterus, facilitating sperm movement through the female reproductive tract. The presence of the hormone *relaxin* and certain enzymes in semen enhance sperm motility. The relative alkalinity of semen as a whole (pH 7.2–7.6) helps neutralize the acid environment of the male's urethra and the female's vagina, thereby protecting the delicate sperm and enhancing their motility. Sperm are very sluggish under acidic conditions (below pH 6). Semen also contains substances that suppress the immune response in the female's reproductive tract and an antibiotic chemical called **seminalplasmin,** which destroys certain bacteria. Clotting factors found in semen coagulate it just after it is ejaculated. Soon, its contained fibrinolysin liquefies the sticky mass, enabling the sperm to swim out and begin their journey through the female duct system.

The amount of semen propelled out of the male duct system during ejaculation is relatively small, only 2–5 ml, but there are between 20 and 150 million sperm per milliliter.

Physiology of the Male Reproductive System

Male Sexual Response

Although there is more to it, the chief phases of the male sexual response are (1) *erection* of the penis, which allows it to penetrate the female vagina, and (2) *ejaculation*, which expels semen into the vagina.

Erection

Erection, enlargement and stiffening of the penis, results from engorgement of the erectile bodies with blood. When a man is not sexually aroused, arterioles supplying the erectile tissue are constricted and the penis is flaccid. However, during sexual excitement a parasympathetic reflex is triggered that promotes release of nitric oxide locally. NO relaxes vascular smooth muscle, causing these arterioles to dilate, which allows the erectile bodies to fill with blood. Expansion of the corpora cavernosa of the penis compresses their drainage veins, retarding blood outflow and maintaining engorgement. The corpus spongiosum expands but not nearly as much as the cavernosa; its main job is to keep the urethra open during ejaculation. It is important that the erect penis not kink or buckle during intercourse. This is prevented by the longitudinal and circular arrangement of collagen fibers surrounding the penis. Erection of the penis is one of the rare examples of parasympathetic control of arterioles. Another parasympathetic effect is stimulation of the bulbourethral glands, the secretion of which lubricates the glans penis.

Erection is initiated by a variety of sexual stimuli, such as touching the genital skin, mechanical stimulation of the pressure receptors in the penis,

---

* LHRH (luteinizing hormone–releasing hormone) is analogous to GnRH (gonadotropin-releasing hormone). See discussion of GnRH's effects on p. 616.

and erotic sights, sounds, and smells. The CNS responds to such stimuli by activating parasympathetic neurons that innervate the internal pudendal arteries serving the penis. Sometimes erection is induced solely by emotional or higher mental activity (the thought of a sexual encounter). Emotions and thoughts can also inhibit erection, causing vasoconstriction and resumption of the flaccid penile state. Impotence, the inability to attain erection, is considered in *A Closer Look* on p. 1074.

Ejaculation

Ejaculation (*ejac* = to shoot forth) is the propulsion of semen from the male duct system. Although erection is under parasympathetic control, *ejaculation* is under sympathetic control. When impulses provoking erection reach a certain critical level, a spinal reflex is initiated, and a massive discharge of nerve impulses occurs over the sympathetic nerves serving the genital organs (largely at the level of L_1 and L_2). As a result,

1. The reproductive ducts and accessory glands contract, emptying their contents into the urethra.

2. The bladder sphincter muscle constricts, preventing expulsion of urine or reflux of semen into the bladder.

3. The bulbospongiosus muscles of the penis undergo a rapid series of contractions, propelling semen at a speed of up to 500 cm/s (200 inches/s) from the urethra. These rhythmic contractions are accompanied by intense pleasure and many systemic changes, such as generalized muscle contraction, rapid heartbeat, and elevated blood pressure.

The entire ejaculatory event is referred to as **climax** or **orgasm.** Orgasm is quickly followed by muscular and psychological relaxation and vasoconstriction of the penile arterioles, which allows the penis to become flaccid once again. After ejaculation, there is a latent period, ranging in time from minutes to hours, during which a man is unable to achieve another orgasm. The latent period lengthens with age.

Spermatogenesis

Spermatogenesis (sper″mah-to-jen′ĕ-sis; "sperm formation") is the sequence of events in the seminiferous tubules of the testes that produces male gametes—*sperm* or *spermatozoa.* The process begins around the age of 14 years in males, and continues throughout life. Every day, a healthy adult male makes about 400 million sperm. It seems that nature has made sure that the human species will not be endangered for lack of sperm.

Before we describe the process of spermatogenesis, let's define some terms. First, having two sets of chromosomes, one from each parent, is a key factor

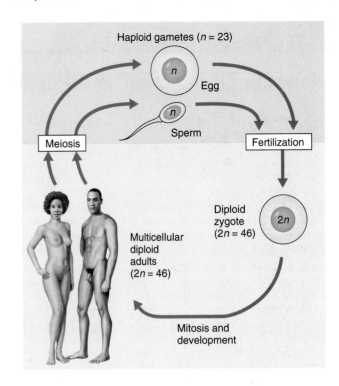

FIGURE 27.5 **The human life cycle.**

in the human life cycle (Figure 27.5). The normal chromosome number in most body cells is referred to as the **diploid chromosomal number** (dip′loid) of the organism, symbolized as **2*n*.** In humans, this number is 46, and such diploid cells contain 23 pairs of similar chromosomes called **homologous chromosomes** (ho-mol′ŏ-gus) or **homologues.** One member of each pair is from the male parent (the *paternal chromosome*); the other is from the female parent (the *maternal chromosome*). Generally speaking, the two homologues of each chromosome pair look alike and carry genes that code for the same traits, though not necessarily for identical expression of those traits. (Consider, for example, the homologous genes controlling the expression of freckles; the paternal gene might code for an ample sprinkling of freckles and the maternal gene for no freckles.) In Chapter 29, we will consider how mom's and dad's genes interact to produce our visible traits.

The number of chromosomes present in human gametes is 23, referred to as the **haploid chromosomal number** (hap′loid), or ***n;*** gametes contain only one member of each homologous pair. When sperm and egg fuse, they form a fertilized egg that reestablishes the typical diploid chromosomal number of human cells.

Gamete formation in both sexes involves **meiosis** (mi-o′sis; "a lessening"), a unique kind of nuclear division that, for the most part, occurs only in the gonads. Recall that *mitosis* (the process by which most body cells divide) distributes replicated chromosomes

27

A CLOSER LOOK

Erectile Dysfunction and Passion Pills

Erectile dysfunction (ED), a form of **impotence,** is the inability to attain an erection when desired. What is missing? In two words, nitric oxide. When males become aroused, parasympathetic nerves in the penis release nitric oxide, which activates cyclic GMP, an enzyme that causes smooth muscle in the penile blood vessel walls to relax. As it does so, blood rushes into the spongy cavernous tissue, stiffening the penis. And what blocks nitric oxide release or its effects? Psychological factors, alcohol, or certain drugs can cause temporary impotence even in healthy males. When chronic, the condition is largely the result of hormonal, vascular, or nervous system problems. The problem is not limited to older men; approximately 50% of American males over age 40 (some 32 million men) have some degree of erectile dysfunction.

For a long time, impotence was dismissed as "being in your head," but it now appears that psychological or emotional causes account for less than 20% of cases. Numerous drugs can produce impotence, including antihypertensives, antihistamines, antidepressants, the antiulcer drug cimetidine (Tagamet), and some appetite suppressants and cold remedies. Vascular problems that are common causes include arteriosclerosis, injury to penile blood vessels, or varicose veins in the penis, which create venous leaks that allow blood to leave the penis prematurely. Neural causes typically result from stroke, multiple sclerosis, tumors, physical trauma, or damage to penile nerves during surgery or radiation therapy. The single most important hormonal factor is diabetes mellitus, which leads to arterial blockages that reduce blood flow into the penis and nerve damage that makes erection difficult or impossible. Cush-

ing's disease, hypothyroidism, and elevated levels of prolactin are other possible hormone-based causes.

Let's assume the cause is determined, but the problem still exists. What's a man to do? Until recently, most remedies were unpleasant and invasive. Using a vacuum pump to suck blood into the penis and thus pump up a flaccid penis often embarrasses its user and can take the romance out of the moment. Drugs such as papaverine and alprostadil (PGE_1) dilate the penile blood vessels but require painful injections into the penis, and alprostadil gel (Muse), a soft pellet that is inserted into the urethra, is said by users to hurt more than the injections. In cases of nonresponsive vascular disease or damage to penile nerves, the usual approaches are reconstructive surgery to repair damaged arteries or a venous leak, or implanting a device in the penis that will make it erect. However, surgery is expensive and has its shortcomings even in the most capable hands, and the implantable prostheses sometimes break down, requiring still more surgery.

As you might expect then, a little blue diamond-shaped pill called Viagra (sildenafil) was greeted with great enthusiasm by men who have an erectile dysfunction that allows them some erectile ability but not enough to permit penetration. To say that Viagra has been a big hit is a vast understatement. The FDA approved the drug in March 1998; by that September, 4 million prescriptions had been filled. In late 2003, two similar drugs—tadalis (Cialis), which claims its effects last for up to 36 hours, and vardenafil (Levitra), which works faster (in 30 minutes versus one hour for Viagra)—hit the marketplace.

Viagra works, but not for everyone; its success rate is 70%. Among Viagra's advantages are that it (1) works within the hour to produce a sustained erec-

Viagra pills.

tion by increasing the concentration of nitric oxide and blood flow in the penis, (2) is taken orally, and (3) has essentially no significant side effects in healthy males (i.e., those who do not have severe vascular problems or longstanding pyschogenic impotence). Some men experience transient blue-green vision, stuffy nose, headache, temporary facial flushing, or mild stomach upset—all trade-offs that many say they are ready to put up with in exchange for erections. The major problems with Viagra and similar drugs involve men with preexisting serious health problems (heart disease or diabetes mellitus) who ignore the drug's (or their physician's) warnings that Viagra also reduces systemic blood pressure as it works its "miracle." Consequently, some fatalities have occurred, most involving men taking nitrate drugs to dilate the coronary circulation. Nonetheless, Viagra is seen as a wonder drug.

Will it work equally well for women with problems with sexual arousal? The clitoris is physiologically similar to the penis and researchers have detected nitric oxide activity in the vagina and clitoris. Clinical trials are rolling, not only on Viagra and similar feminine-oriented oral products, but on creams and hormone sprays that are applied to the skin and a sexual arousal patch. More later. ■

equally between the two daughter cells. Consequently, each daughter cell receives a set of chromosomes identical to that of the mother cell. Meiosis, on the other hand, consists of two consecutive nuclear divisions, and its product is four daughter cells instead of two, each with *half* as many chromosomes as typical body cells. Thus, meiosis reduces the chromosomal number by half (from $2n$ to n) in gametes. Mitosis and meiosis are compared in Figure 27.6.

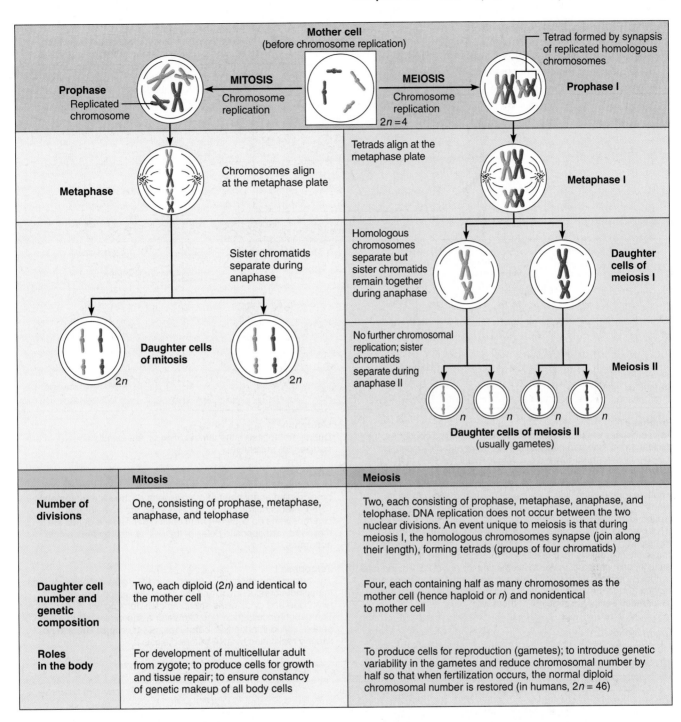

FIGURE 27.6 **Comparison of mitosis and meiosis in a mother cell with a diploid number (2n) of 4.** Mitosis is shown on the left, meiosis on the right. (Not all the phases of mitosis and meiosis are shown.)

Meiosis

The two nuclear divisions of meiosis, called *meiosis I* and *meiosis II*, are divided into phases for convenience. Although these phases are given the same names as those of mitosis (prophase, metaphase, anaphase, and telophase), some events of meiosis I are quite different from those of mitosis, as detailed next.

Recall that prior to mitosis all the chromosomes are replicated. Then the identical copies remain to-

gether as *sister chromatids* connected by a centromere throughout prophase and during metaphase. At anaphase, the centromeres split and the sister chromatids separate from each other so that each daughter cell inherits a copy of *every* chromosome possessed by the mother cell (see Figure 27.6). Let's look at how meiosis differs.

Meiosis I As in mitosis, chromosomes replicate before meiosis begins. But in prophase of meiosis I,

FIGURE 27.7   **Meiosis.** The series of events in meiotic cell division for an animal cell with a diploid number (2n) of 4. The behavior of the chromosomes is emphasized.

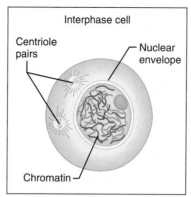

Interphase events
As in mitosis, meiosis is preceded by events occurring during interphase that lead to DNA replication and other preparations needed for the cell division process. Just before meiosis begins, the replicated chromatids, held together by centromeres, are ready and waiting.

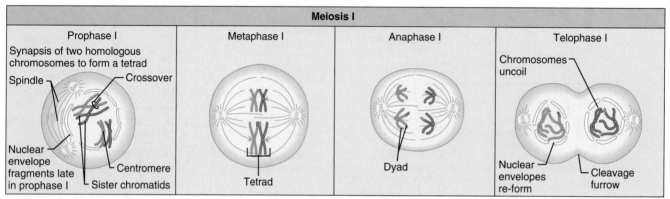

Prophase I
As in prophase of mitosis, the chromosomes coil and condense, the nuclear membrane and nucleolus break down and disappear, and the spindle is formed. However, a unique event not seen in mitosis, called synapsis, occurs in prophase I of meiosis. Synapsis involves the coming together of homologous chromosomes all along their length to form tetrads, little packets of four chromatids. While in synapsis, the "arms" of homologous chromatids become wrapped around each other, forming several points of crossover or chiasmata. (This process of crossover is shown between two of the four chromatids in one tetrad of the prophase I view, and the result of that one event of crossing over is followed through meiosis II.) Prophase I is the longest period of meiosis, accounting for about 90% of the total period. By its end, the tetrads have attached to the spindle and are moving toward the spindle equator, and the nonsister chromatids have traded segments at points of crossover.

Metaphase I
During metaphase I, the tetrads align on the spindle equator in preparation for anaphase.

Anaphase I
Unlike the anaphase events of mitosis, the centromeres do not break during anaphase I of meiosis, and so the sister chromatids (dyads) remain firmly attached. However, the homologous chromosomes do separate from each other and the dyads are moved toward opposite poles of the cell, guided by the spindle apparatus.

Telophase I
The nuclear membranes re-form around the chromosomal masses, the spindle breaks down, and the chromatin reappears as telophase and cytokinesis are completed, forming two daughter cells. The daughter cells (now haploid) enter a second interphase-like period, called interkinesis, before meiosis II occurs. There is no second replication of DNA before meiosis II.

Meiosis II begins with the products of meiosis I (two haploid daughter cells) and undergoes a mitosis-like nuclear division process referred to as the equational division of meiosis. After progressing through prophase, metaphase, anaphase, and telophase, followed by cytokinesis, the product is four haploid daughter cells each genetically different from the original mother cell. During human spermatogenesis the daughter cells remain interconnected by cytoplasmic extensions.

an event never seen in mitosis (nor in meiosis II for that matter) occurs. The replicated chromosomes seek out their homologous partners and pair up with them along their entire length (Figure 27.7). This alignment takes place at discrete spots along the length of the homologues—more like buttoning together than zipping. As a result of this process, called **synapsis**, little groups of four chromatids called **tetrads** are formed. During synapsis, a second unique event called crossover occurs. **Crossovers,** also called **chiasmata** (singular: chiasma), are formed within each tetrad as the free ends of one maternal and one paternal chromatid wrap around each other at one or more points. Crossover allows an exchange of genetic material between the paired maternal and paternal chromosomes.

During metaphase I, the tetrads line up randomly at the spindle equator; that is, either the paternal or maternal chromosome can be on a given side of the equator. During anaphase I, the sister chromatids representing each homologue behave as a unit—almost as if replication had not occurred—and the *homologous chromosomes* (each still composed of two joined sister chromatids) are distributed to opposite ends of the cell.

Thus, when meiosis I is completed, the following conditions exist: Each daughter cell has (1) *two* copies of one member of each homologous pair (either the paternal or maternal) and none of the other, and (2) a *haploid* chromosomal number (because the still-united sister chromatids are considered to be a single chromosome) but twice the amount of DNA. Because meiosis I reduces the chromosome number from 2n to n, it is sometimes called the **reduction division of meiosis.**

Meiosis II

Meiosis II The second meiotic division, meiosis II, mirrors mitosis in every way, except that the chromosomes are *not* replicated before it begins. Instead, the sister chromatids in the two daughter cells of meiosis I are simply parceled out among four cells. Because the chromatids are distributed equally to the daughter cells (as in mitosis), meiosis II is sometimes referred to as the **equational division of meiosis** (Figure 27.7).

Meiosis accomplishes two important tasks: (1) It reduces the chromosomal number by half and (2) it introduces genetic variability. The random alignment of the homologous pairs during meiosis I provides tremendous variability in the resulting gametes by scrambling genetic characteristics of the two parents in different combinations. Variability is increased further by crossover—during late prophase I, the homologues break at crossover points and exchange chromosomal segments (see Figure 27.7). (This process is described in Chapter 29.) As a result, it is likely that no two gametes are exactly alike, and all are different from the original mother cells.

Spermatogenesis: Summary of Events in the Seminiferous Tubules

A histological section of an adult testis shows that most cells making up the epithelial walls of the seminiferous tubules are in various stages of cell division (Figure 27.8). These cells, collectively called **spermatogenic cells** (*spermatogenic* = sperm forming), give rise to sperm in the following series of cellular divisions and transformations.

Mitosis of Spermatogonia: Forming Spermatocytes   The outermost tubule cells, which are in direct contact with the epithelial basal lamina, are stem cells called **spermatogonia** (sper″mah-to-go′ne-ah; "sperm seed"). The spermatogonia divide more or less continuously by *mitosis* and, until puberty, all their daughter cells become spermatogonia.

Spermatogenesis begins during puberty, and from then on, each mitotic division of a spermatogonium results in two distinctive daughter cells—*types A* and *B*. The **type A daughter cell** remains at the basement membrane to maintain the germ cell line. The **type B cell** gets pushed toward the lumen, where it becomes a **primary spermatocyte** destined to produce four sperm. (To keep these cell types straight, remember that just as the letter A is always at the beginning of our alphabet, a type A cell is always at the tubule basement membrane ready to begin a new generation of gametes.)

Meiosis: Spermatocytes to Spermatids   Each primary spermatocyte generated during the first phase undergoes meiosis I, forming two smaller haploid cells called **secondary spermatocytes.** The secondary spermatocytes continue on rapidly into meiosis II, and their daughter cells, called **spermatids** (sper′mah-tidz), are small round cells with large spherical nuclei seen closer to the lumen of the tubule. Midway through spermatogenesis, the developing sperm "turn off" nearly all their genes and compact their DNA into dense pellets.

Spermiogenesis: Spermatids to Sperm   Each spermatid has the correct chromosomal number for fertilization *(n)*, but is nonmotile. It still must undergo a streamlining process called **spermiogenesis,** during which it elongates, sheds its excess cytoplasmic baggage, and forms a tail. Details of this process appear in Figure 27.9a. The resulting **sperm,** or **spermatozoon** (sper″mah-to-zo′on; "animal seed"), has a head, a midpiece, and a tail, which correspond roughly to *genetic, metabolic,* and *locomotor regions,* respectively. Sperm "pack" lightly. The **head** of a sperm consists almost entirely of its flattened nucleus, which contains the compacted DNA. Adhering to the top of the nucleus is a helmetlike **acrosome** (ak′ro-sōm; "tip piece"). The lysosome-like acrosome is produced by the Golgi apparatus

27

Q *What cell type results from meiosis?*

(a)

FIGURE 27.8 **Spermatogenesis. (a)** Scanning electron micrograph of a cross-sectional view of a seminiferous tubule (350×). **(b)** Events of spermatogenesis, showing the relative position of various spermatogenic cells. **(c)** Enlarged view of a portion of the wall of the seminiferous tubule, showing the spermatogenic cells surrounded by sustentacular cells (colored gold). (*Note:* The process of spermatogenesis encompasses the phases through the production of sperm. Conversion of the haploid spermatids to sperm cells is specifically called spermiogenesis.)

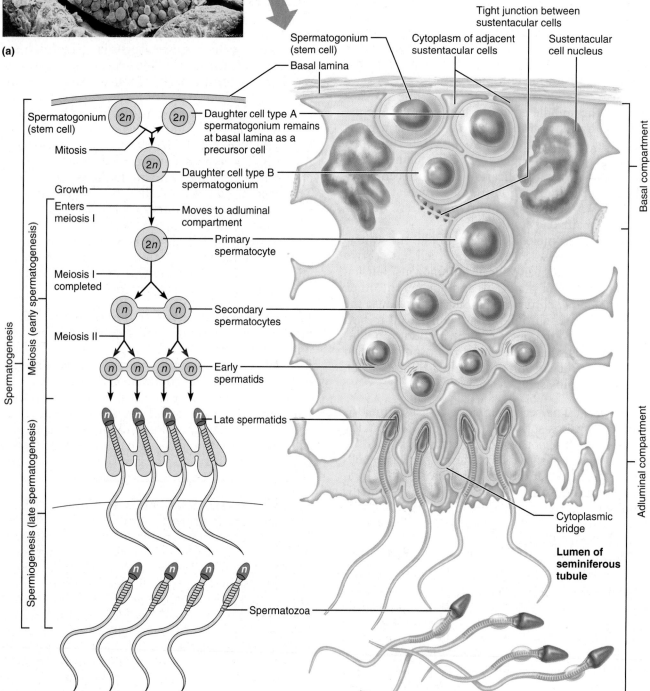

(b)

(c)

A *Spermatids.*

27

FIGURE 27.9 **Spermiogenesis: transformation of a spermatid into a functional sperm. (a)** The stepwise process of spermiogenesis consists of ① packaging of the acrosomal enzymes by the Golgi apparatus, ② forming the acrosome at the anterior end of the nucleus and positioning the centrioles at the opposite end of the nucleus, ③ elaboration of microtubules to form the flagellum, ④ mitochondrial multiplication and their positioning around the proximal portion of the flagellum, and ⑤ sloughing off excess cytoplasm. ⑥ Structure of an immature sperm that has just been released from a sustentacular cell. ⑦ Structure of a fully mature sperm. **(b)** Scanning electron micrograph of mature sperm (600×).

and contains hydrolytic enzymes that enable the sperm to penetrate and enter an egg. The sperm **midpiece** contains mitochondria spiraled tightly around the contractile filaments of the tail. The long **tail** is a typical flagellum produced by the centriole near the nucleus. The mitochondria provide the metabolic energy (ATP) needed for the whiplike movements of the tail that will propel the sperm along its way in the female reproductive tract.

Role of the Sustentacular Cells Throughout spermatogenesis, descendants of the same spermatogonium remain closely attached to one another by cytoplasmic bridges (see Figure 27.8). They are also surrounded by and connected to supporting cells of a special type, called **sustentacular cells** or **Sertoli cells,** which extend from the basal lamina to the lumen of the tubule. The sustentacular cells, bound to each other laterally by tight junctions, divide the seminiferous tubule into two compartments. The **basal compartment** extends from the basal lamina to their tight junctions and contains spermatogonia and the earliest primary spermatocytes. The **adluminal compartment** lies internal to the tight junctions and includes the meiotically active cells and the tubule lumen.

The tight junctions between the sustentacular cells form the **blood-testis barrier.** This barrier prevents the membrane antigens of differentiating sperm from escaping through the basal lamina into the bloodstream where they would activate the immune system. Because sperm are not formed until puberty, they are absent when the immune system is being programmed to recognize one's own tissues early in life. The spermatogonia, which are recognized as "self," are outside the barrier and thus can be influenced by bloodborne chemical messengers that prompt spermatogenesis. Following mitosis of the spermatogonia, the tight junctions of the sustentacular cells open to allow primary spermatocytes to pass into the adluminal compartment—much as locks in a canal open to allow a boat to pass.

27

In the adluminal compartment, spermatocytes and spermatids are nearly enclosed in recesses in the sustentacular cells (see Figure 27.8), anchored there by a particular glycoprotein on the spermatogenic cell's surface. The sustentacular cells provide essential signals and nutrients to the dividing cells, move them along to the lumen, secrete **testicular fluid** (rich in androgens and metabolic acids) that provides the transport medium for sperm in the lumen, and phagocytize the excess cytoplasm sloughed off the spermatids as they transform into sperm. The sustentacular cells also produce chemical mediators (inhibin and androgen-binding protein) that help regulate spermatogenesis as described below.

Spermatogenesis—from formation of a primary spermatocyte to release of immature sperm into the lumen—takes 64 to 72 days. Sperm in the lumen are unable to "swim" and are incapable of fertilizing an egg. They are pushed by the pressure of the testicular fluid through the tubular system of the testes into the epididymis, where they gain increased motility and fertilizing power.

◥ HOMEOSTATIC IMBALANCE

Roughly one in seven American couples seek treatment for infertility, mostly because of problems with sperm quality or quantity. According to some studies, a gradual decline in male fertility has been occurring in the past 50 years. Some believe the main cause is *xenobiotics*, alien molecules that have invaded our lives in a variety of forms including environmental toxins, PVCs, phthalates (oily solvents that make plastics flexible), certain components in pesticides and herbicides, and especially compounds with estrogenic effects. These estrogen-like compounds, which block the action of male sex hormones as they program sexual development, are now found in our meat supply as well as in the air. Common antibiotics such as tetracycline may suppress sperm formation; and radiation, lead, marijuana, lack of selenium, and excessive alcohol can cause abnormal (two-headed, multiple-tailed, etc.) sperm to be produced. Male infertility may also be caused by the lack of a specific type of Ca^{2+} channel (Ca^{2+} is needed for normal sperm motility), anatomical obstructions, hormonal imbalances, and oxidative stress (which contributes to DNA fragmentation in sperm). A low sperm count accompanied by a high percentage of immature sperm may hint that a man has a *varicocele* (var′ĭ-ko-sēl″), a condition that hinders drainage of the testicular vein, resulting in an elevated temperature in the scrotum that interferes with normal sperm development. ●

Hormonal Regulation of Male Reproductive Function

The Brain-Testicular Axis

Hormonal regulation of spermatogenesis and testicular androgen production involves interactions between the hypothalamus, anterior pituitary gland, and testes, a relationship sometimes called the **brain-testicular axis.** The sequence of regulatory events, shown schematically in Figure 27.10, is as follows:

① The hypothalamus releases **gonadotropin-releasing hormone (GnRH),** which controls the release of the two anterior pituitary gonadotropins: **follicle-stimulating hormone (FSH)** and **luteinizing hormone (LH).** (Both FSH and LH were named for their effects on the female gonad.) GnRH reaches the anterior pituitary cells via the blood of the hypophyseal portal system.

② Binding of GnRH to pituitary cells (gonadotrophs) prompts them to secrete FSH and LH into the blood.

③ FSH stimulates spermatogenesis indirectly by stimulating the sustentacular cells to release **androgen-binding protein (ABP).** ABP prompts the spermatogenic cells to bind and concentrate **testosterone,** which in turn stimulates spermatogenesis. Thus, FSH makes the cells receptive to testosterone's stimulatory effects.

④ LH binds to the interstitial cells, prodding them to secrete testosterone (and a small amount of estrogen). Locally, testosterone serves as the final trigger for spermatogenesis. Testosterone entering the bloodstream exerts a number of effects at other body sites.

⑤ Testosterone inhibits hypothalamic release of GnRH and acts directly on the anterior pituitary to inhibit gonadotropin release. **Inhibin** (in-hib′in), a protein hormone produced by the sustentacular cells, serves as a "barometer" of the normalcy of spermatogenesis. When the sperm count is high, inhibin release increases and it inhibits anterior pituitary release of FSH and hypothalamic release of GnRH. When sperm count falls below 20 million/ml, inhibin secretion declines steeply.

As you can see, the amount of testosterone and sperm produced by the testes reflects a balance among three sets of hormones: (1) GnRH, which indirectly stimulates the testes via its effect on FSH and LH release; (2) gonadotropins, which directly stimulate the testes; and (3) testicular hormones (testosterone and inhibin), which exert negative feedback controls on the hypothalamus and anterior pituitary. Because the hypothalamus is also influenced by input from other brain areas, the whole axis is under CNS control. In the absence of GnRH and gonadotropins, the testes atrophy, and sperm and testosterone production ceases.

Development of male reproductive structures (discussed later in the chapter) depends on prenatal secretion of male hormones, and for a few months after birth, a male infant has plasma gonadotropin and testosterone levels nearly equal to those of a midpubertal boy. Soon thereafter, blood levels of these hormones recede and they remain low throughout childhood. As puberty nears, much higher levels of testosterone are required to suppress hypothalamic release of GnRH. So as more GnRH is released, more testosterone is secreted by the testes, but the threshold for hypothalamic inhibition keeps rising until the adult pattern of hormone interaction is achieved, evidenced by the presence of mature sperm in the semen. Maturation of the brain-testicular axis takes about three years, and once established, the balance between the interacting hormones remains relatively constant. Consequently, an adult male's sperm and testosterone production also remains fairly stable.

Mechanism and Effects of Testosterone Activity

Testosterone, like all steroid hormones, is synthesized from cholesterol and exerts its effects by activating specific genes, which results in enhanced synthesis of certain proteins in the target cells. (See Chapter 16 for mechanisms of steroid hormone action.) In some target cells, testosterone must be transformed into another steroid to exert its effects. In the prostate, testosterone is converted to *dihydrotestosterone (DHT)* before it can bind in the nucleus, and in certain neurons of the brain, testosterone is converted to *estradiol* (es'trah-di-ol) to bring about its stimulatory effects.

As puberty ensues, testosterone not only prompts spermatogenesis but has multiple anabolic effects throughout the body (see Table 27.1, p. 1099). It targets accessory reproductive organs—ducts, glands, and the penis—causing them to grow and assume adult size and function. In adult males, normal plasma levels of testosterone maintain these organs: When the hormone is deficient or absent, all accessory organs atrophy, semen volume declines markedly, and erection and ejaculation are impaired. Thus, a man becomes both sterile and impotent. This situation is easily remedied by testosterone replacement therapy.

Male secondary sex characteristics—that is, features induced in the *nonreproductive* organs by the male sex hormones (mainly testosterone)—make their appearance at puberty. These include the appearance of pubic, axillary, and facial hair, enhanced hair growth on the chest or other body areas in some men, and a deepening of the voice as the larynx enlarges. The skin thickens and becomes oilier

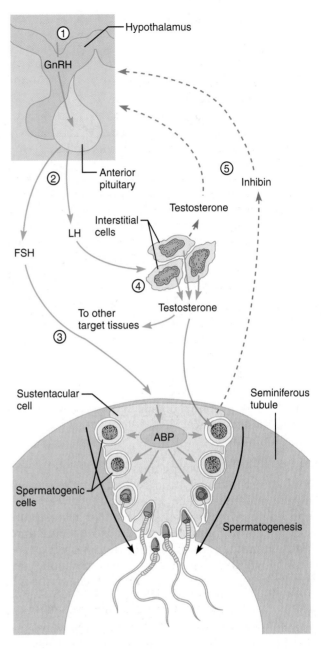

Key:

———▶ = Stimulates

- - - -▶ = Inhibits

FIGURE 27.10 Hormonal regulation of testicular function, the brain-testicular axis. The hypothalamus releases gonadotropin-releasing hormone (GnRH). GnRH stimulates the anterior pituitary to release gonadotropins— follicle-stimulating hormone (FSH) and luteinizing hormone (LH). FSH causes the sustentacular cells to release androgen-binding protein (ABP). LH acts on the interstitial cells, stimulating their release of testosterone. ABP binding of testosterone then enhances spermatogenesis. Rising levels of testosterone and inhibin (released by the sustentacular cells) exert feedback inhibition on the hypothalamus and pituitary. (Only one sustentacular cell is depicted so that its structural relationship to the spermatogenic cells it encloses is clearly seen. However, it would be flanked by sustentacular cells on each side.)

27

Peritoneum
Uterosacral ligament
Perimetrium
Rectouterine pouch
Rectum
Posterior fornix
Cervix
Anterior fornix
Vagina
Anus
Urogenital diaphragm

Suspensory ligament of ovary
Infundibulum
Uterine tube
Ovary
Fimbriae
Uterus
Round ligament
Vesicouterine pouch
Urinary bladder
Pubic symphysis
Mons pubis
Urethra
Clitoris
External urethral orifice
Hymen
Labium minus
Labium majus

FIGURE 27.11 **Internal organs of the female reproductive system, midsagittal section.** (See *A Brief Atlas of the Human Body,* Figure 74.)

(which predisposes young men to acne), bones grow and increase in density, and skeletal muscles increase in size and mass. The last two effects are often referred to as the *somatic effects* of testosterone (*soma* = body). Epiphyseal plate closure occurs in response to rising estrogen levels late in puberty.

Testosterone also boosts basal metabolic rate and influences behavior. It is the basis of the sex drive (libido) in males and to some extent in females, be they heterosexual or homosexual. Thus, although testosterone is called a "male" sex hormone, it should not be specifically tagged as a promoter of male sexual activity. In embryos, the presence of testosterone masculinizes the brain. Testosterone also appears to continue to shape certain regions of the male brain well into adult life, as indicated by the differences in males' and females' brain areas involved in sexual arousal (for example, the amygdala).

The testes are not the only source of androgens; the adrenal glands of both sexes also release androgens. However, the relatively small amounts of adrenal androgens are unable to support normal testosterone-mediated functions when the testes fail to produce androgens, so we can assume that it is the testosterone production by the testes that supports male reproductive function. However, as noted later (p. 1100), the adrenal androgen DHEA appears to be more important than testosterone in helping to determine the *female* libido.

Anatomy of the Female Reproductive System

The reproductive role of the female is far more complex than that of a male. Not only must she produce gametes, but her body must prepare to nurture a developing embryo for a period of approximately nine months. **Ovaries, the female gonads,** are the primary reproductive organs of a female, and like the male testes, ovaries serve a dual purpose: They produce the female gametes (ova) and sex hormones, the **estrogens*** and **progesterone** (pro-ges'tĕ-rōn). The accessory ducts (uterine tubes, uterus, and vagina) transport or otherwise serve the needs of the reproductive cells and a developing fetus.

As illustrated in Figure 27.11, the ovaries and duct system, collectively known as the **internal genitalia,** are mostly located in the pelvic cavity. The female's accessory ducts, from the vicinity of the ovary to the body exterior, are the *uterine tubes,* the *uterus,* and the *vagina.* The external sex organs of females are referred to as the **external genitalia.**

---

*The ovaries produce several different estrogens (*estradiol, estrone,* and *estriol*). Estradiol is the most abundant and is most responsible for estrogenic effects.

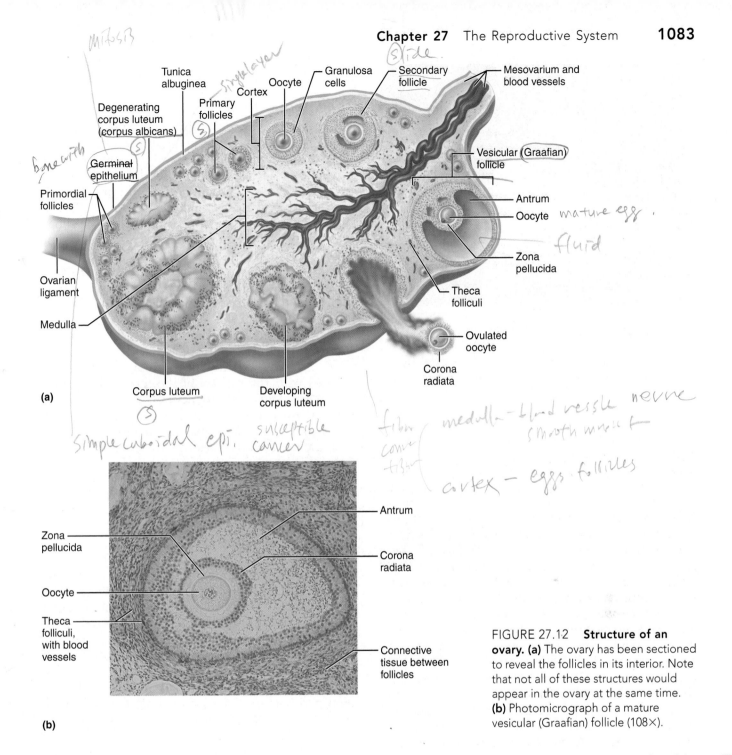

FIGURE 27.12   **Structure of an ovary. (a)** The ovary has been sectioned to reveal the follicles in its interior. Note that not all of these structures would appear in the ovary at the same time. **(b)** Photomicrograph of a mature vesicular (Graafian) follicle (108×).

The Ovaries

The paired ovaries flank the uterus on each side (see Figure 27.11). Shaped like an almond and about twice as large, each ovary is held in place in the fork of the iliac blood vessels within the peritoneal cavity by several ligaments. The **ovarian ligament** anchors the ovary medially to the uterus; the **suspensory ligament** anchors it laterally to the pelvic wall; and the **mesovarium** (mez″o-va′re-um) suspends it in between (see Figures 27.11 and 27.14a). The suspensory ligament and the mesovarium are part of the **broad ligament,** a peritoneal fold that "tents" over the uterus and supports the uterine tubes, uterus,

and vagina. The ovarian ligaments are enclosed by the broad ligament.

The ovaries are served by the **ovarian arteries,** branches of the abdominal aorta (see Figure 19.23c), and by the *ovarian branch of the uterine arteries*. The ovarian blood vessels reach the ovaries by traveling through the suspensory ligaments and mesovaria.

Like each testis, each ovary is surrounded externally by a fibrous **tunica albuginea** (Figure 27.12), which is in turn covered externally by a layer of cuboidal epithelial cells called the *germinal epithelium,* actually a continuation of the peritoneum. The ovary has an outer cortex, which houses the

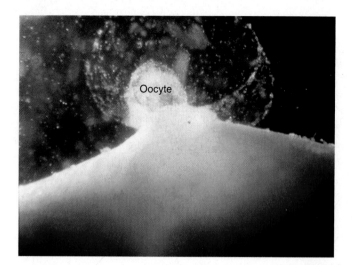

Oocyte

FIGURE 27.13 **Ovulation.** A secondary oocyte is re-leased from a follicle at the surface of the ovary (30×). The orange mass below the ejected oocyte is part of the ovary. (Primary and secondary oocytes are explained in Figure 27.19 on p. 1091.)

forming gametes, and an inner medullary region, containing the largest blood vessels and nerves, but the relative extent of each region is poorly defined.

Embedded in the highly vascular connective tissue of the ovary cortex are many tiny saclike structures called **ovarian follicles.** Each follicle consists of an immature egg, called an **oocyte** (o'o-sīt; *oo* = egg), encased by one or more layers of very different cells. The surrounding cells are called **follicle cells** if a single layer is present, and **granulosa cells** when more than one layer is present. Follicles at different stages of maturation are distinguished by their structure. In a **primordial follicle,** one layer of squamouslike follicle cells surrounds the oocyte. A **primary follicle** has two or more layers of cuboidal or columnar-type granulosa cells enclosing the oocyte; it becomes a **secondary follicle** when fluid-filled spaces appear between the granulosa cells and then coalesce to form a central fluid-filled cavity called an *antrum.* At the mature **vesicular follicle,** or **Graafian follicle** (graf'e-an), stage, the follicle bulges from the surface of the ovary. The oocyte of the vesicular follicle "sits" on a stalk of granulosa cells at one side of the antrum. Each month in adult women, one of the ripening follicles ejects its oocyte from the ovary, an event called **ovulation** (Figure 27.13). After ovulation, the ruptured follicle is transformed into a very different looking glandular structure called the **corpus luteum** (lu'te-um; plural: corpora lutea), which eventually degenerates. As a rule, most of these structures can be seen within the same ovary. In older women, the surfaces of the ovaries are scarred and pitted, revealing that many oocytes have been released.

The Female Duct System

The Uterine Tubes

The **uterine tubes** (u'ter-in), also called **fallopian tubes** or **oviducts,** form the initial part of the female duct system (Figures 27.11 and 27.14a). They receive the ovulated oocyte and are the site where fertilization generally occurs. Each uterine tube is about 10 cm (4 inches) long and extends medially from the region of an ovary to empty into the super-olateral region of the uterus via a constricted region called the **isthmus** (is'mus). The distal end of each uterine tube expands as it curves around the ovary, forming the **ampulla;** fertilization usually occurs in this region. The ampulla ends in the **infundibulum** (in"fun-dib'u-lum), an open, funnel-shaped structure bearing ciliated, fingerlike projections called **fimbriae** (fim'bre-e; "fringe") that drape over the ovary. Unlike the male duct system, which is continuous with the tubules of the testes, the uterine tubes have little or no actual contact with the ovaries. An ovulated oocyte is cast into the peritoneal cavity, and many oocytes are lost there. However, the uterine tube performs complex movements to capture oocytes—it bends to drape over the ovary while the fimbriae stiffen and sweep the ovarian surface. The beating cilia on the fimbriae then create currents in the peritoneal fluid that tend to carry an oocyte into the uterine tube, where it begins its journey toward the uterus.

The uterine tube contains sheets of smooth muscle, and its thick, highly folded mucosa contains both ciliated and nonciliated cells. The oocyte is carried toward the uterus by a combination of muscular peristalsis and the beating of the cilia. Nonciliated cells of the mucosa have dense microvilli and produce a secretion that keeps the oocyte (and sperm, if present) moist and nourished.

Externally, the uterine tubes are covered by visceral peritoneum and supported along their length by a short mesentery (part of the broad ligament) called the **mesosalpinx** (mez"o-sal'pinks; "mesentery of the trumpet"; *salpin* = trumpet), a reference to the trumpet-shaped uterine tube it supports (see Figure 27.14a).

HOMEOSTATIC IMBALANCE

The fact that the uterine tubes are not continuous with the ovaries places women at risk for *ectopic pregnancy* in which a zygote, fertilized in the peritoneal cavity or distal portion of the uterine tube, begins developing there. Because the tube lacks adequate mass and vascularization to support the full term of pregnancy, such pregnancies naturally abort, often with substantial bleeding. Another potential problem is infection spreading into the peritoneal

27

FIGURE 27.14 **Internal reproductive organs of a female. (a)** Posterior view of the female reproductive organs. The posterior walls of the vagina, uterus, and uterine tubes and the broad ligament (a peritoneal fold) have been removed on the right side to reveal the shape of the lumen of these organs. **(b)** Anterior view of the reproductive organs of a female cadaver. (See *A Brief Atlas of the Human Body,* Figure 75.)

cavity from other parts of the reproductive tract. Gonorrhea bacteria and other sexually transmitted microorganisms sometimes infect the peritoneal cavity in this way, causing an extremely severe inflammation called **pelvic inflammatory disease (PID)**. Unless treated promptly with broad-spectrum antibiotics, PID can cause scarring of the narrow uterine tubes and of the ovaries, causing sterility. Indeed, scarring and closure of the uterine tubes, which have an internal diameter as small as the width of a human hair in some regions, is one of the major causes of female infertility. ●

The Uterus

The **uterus** (Latin for "womb") is located in the pelvis, anterior to the rectum and posterosuperior to the bladder (see Figures 27.11 and 27.14). It is a hollow, thick-walled, muscular organ that functions to receive, retain, and nourish a fertilized ovum. In a premenopausal woman who has never been pregnant, the uterus is about the size and shape of an inverted pear, but it is usually somewhat larger in women who have borne children. Normally, the uterus flexes anteriorly where it joins the vagina, causing the uterus as a whole to be inclined forward, or *anteverted*. However, the organ is frequently turned backward, or *retroverted*, in older women.

The major portion of the uterus is referred to as the **body** (see Figures 27.11 and 27.14). The rounded region superior to the entrance of the uterine tubes is the **fundus**, and the slightly narrowed region between the body and the cervix is the *isthmus*. The **cervix** of the uterus is its narrow neck, or outlet, which projects into the vagina inferiorly. The cavity of the cervix, called the **cervical canal**, communicates with the vagina via the *external os* (os = mouth) and with the cavity of the uterine body via the *internal os*. The mucosa of the cervical canal contains *cervical glands* that secrete a mucus that fills the cervical canal and covers the external os, presumably to block the spread of bacteria from the vagina into the uterus. Cervical mucus also blocks the entry of sperm, except at midcycle, when it becomes less viscous and allows sperm to pass through.

⬛ HOMEOSTATIC IMBALANCE

Cancer of the cervix strikes about 450,000 women worldwide each year, killing about half. It is most common among women between the ages of 30 and 50. Risk factors include frequent cervical inflammations, sexually transmitted diseases including genital warts, and multiple pregnancies. The cancer cells arise from the epithelium covering the cervical tip. In a *Papanicolaou (Pap) smear*, or cervical smear test, some of these cells are scraped away and then examined for abnormalities. A Pap smear is the most effective way to detect this slow-growing cancer, and American Cancer Society guidelines advise women to have one yearly until the age of 70, when this monitoring can be stopped if there have been no abnormal results in the past 10 years. When results are inconclusive, a test for the sexually transmitted human papillomavirus (the cause of virtually all cervical cancer) can be done from the same Pap sample. New on the treatment horizon is a vaccine against that virus which appears to be 100% effective in clinical tests. ●

Supports of the Uterus   The uterus is supported laterally by the **mesometrium** ("mesentery of the uterus") portion of the broad ligament (Figure 27.14a). More inferiorly, the **lateral cervical (cardinal) ligaments** extend from the cervix and superior vagina to the lateral walls of the pelvis, and the paired **uterosacral ligaments** secure the uterus to the sacrum

posteriorly. The uterus is bound to the anterior body wall by the fibrous **round ligaments**, which run through the inguinal canals to anchor in the subcutaneous tissue of the labia majora. These ligaments allow the uterus a good deal of mobility, and its position changes as the rectum and bladder fill and empty.

⬛ HOMEOSTATIC IMBALANCE

Despite the many anchoring ligaments, the principal support of the uterus is provided by the muscles of the pelvic floor, namely the muscles of the urogenital and pelvic diaphragms (Table 10.7). These muscles are sometimes torn during childbirth. Subsequently, the unsupported uterus may sink inferiorly, until the tip of the cervix protrudes through the external vaginal opening. This condition is called **prolapse of the uterus.** ●

The undulating course of the peritoneum produces several cul-de-sacs, or blind-ended peritoneal pouches. The most important of these are the *vesicouterine pouch* (ves"i-ko-u'ter-in) between the bladder and uterus, and the *rectouterine pouch* between the rectum and uterus (see Figure 27.11).

The Uterine Wall   The wall of the uterus is composed of three layers (Figure 27.14a). The **perimetrium**, the incomplete outermost serous layer, is the peritoneum. The **myometrium** (mi"o-me'tre-um; "muscle of the uterus") is the bulky middle layer, composed of interlacing bundles of smooth muscle, that contracts rhythmically during childbirth to expel the baby from the mother's body. The **endometrium** is the mucosal lining of the uterine cavity (Figure 27.15); it is a simple columnar epithelium underlain by a thick lamina propria. If fertilization occurs, the young embryo burrows into the endometrium (implants) and resides there for the rest of its development.

The endometrium has two chief *strata* (layers). The **stratum functionalis** (fungk-shun-a'lis), or **functional layer,** undergoes cyclic changes in response to blood levels of ovarian hormones and is shed during menstruation (approximately every 28 days). The thinner, deeper **stratum basalis** (ba-sǎ'lis), or **basal layer,** forms a new functionalis after menstruation ends. It is unresponsive to ovarian hormones. The endometrium has numerous *uterine glands* that change in length as endometrial thickness changes.

To understand the cyclic changes of the uterine endometrium (discussed later in the chapter), it is essential to understand the vascular supply of the uterus. The **uterine arteries** arise from the *internal iliacs* in the pelvis, ascend along the sides of the uterus, and send branches into the uterine wall (Figure 27.14a). These branches break up into several

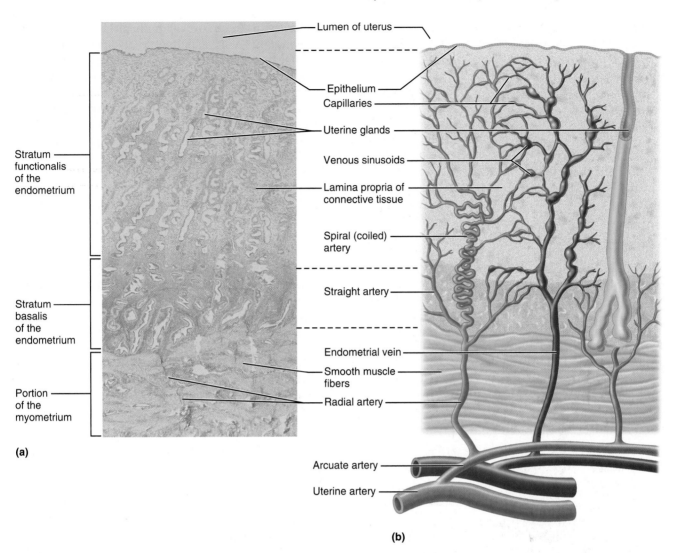

FIGURE 27.15 The endometrium and its blood supply. (a) Photomicrograph of the endometrium, longitudinal section, showing its functionalis and basalis regions (35×). **(b)** Diagrammatic view of the endometrium, showing the straight arteries that serve the stratum basalis and the spiral arteries that serve the stratum functionalis. The thin-walled veins and venous sinusoids are also illustrated.

arcuate arteries (ar′ku-āt) within the myometrium. The arcuate arteries send **radial branches** into the endometrium, where they in turn give off **straight arteries** to the stratum basalis and **spiral (coiled) arteries** to the stratum functionalis. The spiral arteries repeatedly degenerate and regenerate, and it is their spasms that actually cause the functionalis layer to be shed during menstruation. Veins in the endometrium are thin-walled and form an extensive network with occasional sinusoidal enlargements.

The Vagina

The **vagina** ("sheath") is a thin-walled tube, 8–10 cm (3–4 inches) long. It lies between the bladder and the rectum and extends from the cervix to the body exterior (see Figure 27.11). The urethra is embedded in its anterior wall. Often called the *birth canal*, the

vagina provides a passageway for delivery of an infant and for menstrual flow. Since it receives the penis (and semen) during sexual intercourse, it is the *female organ of copulation.*

The distensible wall of the vagina consists of three coats: an outer fibroelastic *adventitia*, a smooth muscle *muscularis*, and a *mucosa* marked by transverse ridges or *rugae*, which stimulate the penis during intercourse. The mucosa is a stratified squamous epithelium adapted to stand up to friction. Certain mucosal cells *(dendritic cells)* act as antigen-presenting cells and are thought to provide the route of HIV transmission from an infected male to the female during sexual intercourse. (AIDS, the immune deficiency disease caused by HIV, is described in Chapter 21.) The vaginal mucosa has no glands; it is lubricated by the cervical mucous

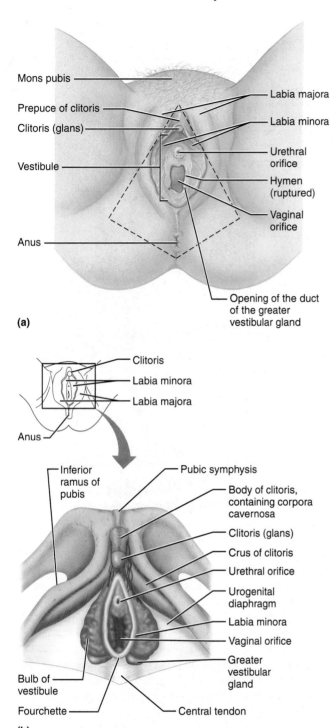

(a)

(b)

FIGURE 27.16   **The external genitalia (vulva) of the female. (a)** Superficial structures. The region enclosed by the dashed lines is the perineum. **(b)** Deep structures. The labia majora and associated skin have been removed to show the underlying erectile bodies. For the associated superficial muscles, see Figure 10.12 on p. 351.

glands. Its epithelial cells release large amounts of glycogen, which is anaerobically metabolized to lactic acid by resident bacteria. Consequently, the pH of a woman's vagina is normally quite acidic. This

acidity helps keep the vagina healthy and free of infection, but it is also hostile to sperm. Although vaginal fluid of *adult* females is acidic, it tends to be alkaline in adolescents, predisposing sexually active teenagers to sexually transmitted diseases.

In virgins (those who have never participated in sexual intercourse), the mucosa near the distal **vaginal orifice** forms an incomplete partition called the **hymen** (hi'men) (Figure 27.16). The hymen is very vascular and tends to bleed when it is ruptured during the first coitus (sexual intercourse). However, its durability varies. In some females, it is ruptured during a sports activity, tampon insertion, or pelvic examination. Occasionally, it is so tough that it must be breached surgically if intercourse is to occur.

The upper end of the vaginal canal loosely surrounds the cervix of the uterus, producing a vaginal recess called the **vaginal fornix.** The posterior part of this recess, the *posterior fornix*, is much deeper than the *lateral* and *anterior fornices* (see Figures 27.11 and 27.14a). Generally, the lumen of the vagina is quite small and, except where it is held open by the cervix, its posterior and anterior walls are in contact with one another. The vagina stretches considerably during copulation and childbirth, but its lateral distension is limited by the ischial spines and the sacrospinous ligaments.

◤ **HOMEOSTATIC IMBALANCE**

The uterus tilts away from the vagina. Hence, attempts by untrained persons to induce an abortion by entering the uterus with a surgical instrument may result in puncturing of the posterior wall of the vagina, followed by hemorrhage and—if the instrument is unsterile—peritonitis. ●

The External Genitalia

As mentioned earlier, the female reproductive structures that lie external to the vagina are called the *external genitalia* (see Figure 27.16). The external genitalia, also called the **vulva** (vul'vah; "covering") or **pudendum** ("shameful"), include the mons pubis, labia, clitoris, and structures associated with the vestibule.

The **mons pubis** (mons pu'bis; "mountain on the pubis") is a fatty, rounded area overlying the pubic symphysis. After puberty, this area is covered with pubic hair. Running posteriorly from the mons pubis are two elongated, hair-covered fatty skin folds, the **labia majora** (la'be-ah mah-jor'ah; "larger lips"). These are the female counterpart, or *homologue*, of the male scrotum (that is, they derive from the same embryonic tissue). The labia majora enclose the **labia minora** (mi-nor'ah; "smaller"), two thin, hair-free skin folds, homologous to the ventral penis. The

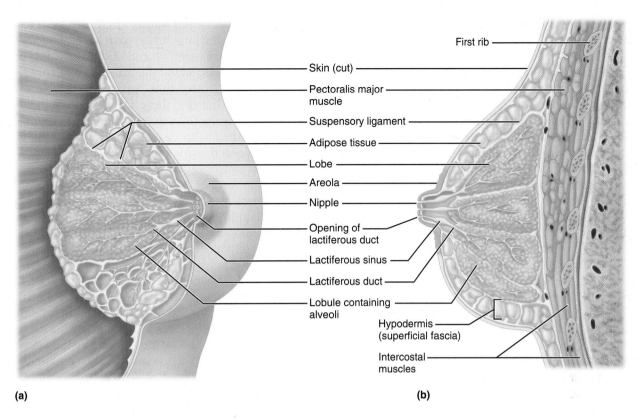

First rib

Skin (cut)

Pectoralis major
muscle

Suspensory ligament

Adipose tissue

Lobe

Areola

Nipple

Opening of
lactiferous duct

Lactiferous sinus

Lactiferous duct

Lobule containing
alveoli

Hypodermis
(superficial fascia)

Intercostal
muscles

(a)

(b)

FIGURE 27.17 **Structure of lactating mammary glands. (a)** Anterior view of a
partially dissected breast. **(b)** Sagittal section of a breast.

labia minora enclose a recess called the **vestibule**
("entrance hall"), which contains the external openings of the urethra and the vagina. Flanking the vaginal opening are the pea-size **greater vestibular
glands,** homologous to the bulbourethral glands of
males. These glands release mucus into the
vestibule and help to keep it moist and lubricated, facilitating intercourse. At the extreme posterior end
of the vestibule the labia minora come together to
form a ridge called the **fourchette.**

Just anterior to the vestibule is the **clitoris**
(klit′ o-ris; "hill"), a small, protruding structure
composed largely of erectile tissue, which is homologous to the penis of the male. Its exposed portion
is called the **glans of the clitoris.** It is hooded by a
skin fold called the **prepuce of the clitoris,** formed
by the junction of the labia minora folds. The
clitoris is richly innervated with sensory nerve
endings sensitive to touch, and it becomes swollen
with blood and erect during tactile stimulation,
contributing to a female's sexual arousal. Like the
penis, the body of the clitoris has dorsal erectile
columns (corpora cavernosa) attached proximally
by crura, but it lacks a corpus spongiosum that
conveys a urethra. In males the urethra carries both
urine and semen and runs through the penis, but
the female urinary and reproductive tracts are
completely separate. Instead, the **bulbs of the**

vestibule, which lie along each side of the vaginal
orifice and deep to the bulbospongiosus muscle, are
the homologues of the single penile bulb and
corpus spongiosum of the male, and during sexual
stimulation the bulbs of the vestibule engorge with
blood. This may help grip the penis within the
vagina and also squeezes the urethral orifice shut,
which prevents semen (and bacteria) from traveling
superiorly into the bladder during intercourse.

The female **perineum** is a diamond-shaped region located between the pubic arch anteriorly, the
coccyx posteriorly, and the ischial tuberosities laterally. The soft tissues of the perineum overlie the
muscles of the pelvic outlet, and the posterior ends
of the labia majora overlie the *central tendon,* into
which most muscles supporting the pelvic floor insert (see Table 10.7).

The Mammary Glands

The **mammary glands** are present in both sexes, but
they normally function only in females (Figure 27.17).
The biological role of the mammary glands is to produce milk to nourish a newborn baby, so they are
important only when reproduction has already been
accomplished.

Developmentally, mammary glands are modified
sweat glands that are really part of the *skin,* or

27

integumentary system. Each mammary gland is contained within a rounded skin-covered breast within the hypodermis (superficial fascia), anterior to the pectoral muscles of the thorax. Slightly below the center of each breast is a ring of pigmented skin, the **areola** (ah-re′o-lah), which surrounds a central protruding **nipple.** Large sebaceous glands in the areola make it slightly bumpy and produce sebum that reduces chapping and cracking of the skin of the nipple. Autonomic nervous system controls of smooth muscle fibers in the areola and nipple cause the nipple to become erect when stimulated by tactile or sexual stimuli and when exposed to cold.

Internally, each mammary gland consists of 15 to 25 **lobes** that radiate around and open at the nipple. The lobes are padded and separated from each other by fibrous connective tissue and fat. The interlobar connective tissue forms **suspensory ligaments** that attach the breast to the underlying muscle fascia and to the overlying dermis. As suggested by their name, the suspensory ligaments provide natural support for the breasts, like a built-in brassiere. Within the lobes are smaller units called **lobules,** which contain glandular **alveoli** that produce milk when a woman is lactating. These compound alveolar glands pass the milk into the **lactiferous ducts** (lak-tif′er-us), which open to the outside at the nipple. Just deep to the areola, each duct has a dilated region called a **lactiferous sinus** where milk accumulates during nursing. The process and regulation of lactation are described in Chapter 28.

The description of mammary glands given here applies only to nursing women or women in the last trimester of pregnancy. In nonpregnant women, the glandular structure of the breast is largely undeveloped and the duct system is rudimentary; hence breast size is largely due to the amount of fat deposits.

Breast Cancer

Invasive breast cancer is the most common malignancy and the second most common cause of cancer death of U.S. women. Thirteen percent of women in the general population (132 out of 1000 individuals) will develop this condition. Breast cancer usually arises from the epithelial cells of the smallest ducts, not from the alveoli. A small cluster of cancer cells grows into a lump in the breast from which cells eventually metastasize.

Known risk factors for developing breast cancer include (1) early onset menses and late menopause; (2) no pregnancies or first pregnancy later in life and no or short periods of breast feeding; (3) family history of breast cancer (especially in a sister or mother), and (4) postmenopausal estrogen-progesterone replacement. Some 10% of breast cancers stem from

hereditary defects and half of these can be traced to dangerous mutations in a pair of genes, dubbed *BRCA1* (breast cancer 1) and *BRCA2*, which cause 80% of those who carry the altered gene to develop breast cancer. Notice that, with the possible exception of family history, these factors reflect increased lifelong exposure to estrogen. However, more than 70% of women who develop breast cancer have no known risk factors for the disease.

Breast cancer is often signaled by a change in skin texture, puckering, or leakage from the nipple. Since most breast lumps are discovered by women themselves in routine monthly breast exams, this simple examination should be a health maintenance priority in every woman's life. The American Cancer Society had recommended scheduling **mammography**—X-ray examination that detects breast cancers too small to feel (less than 1 cm)—every two years for women between 40 and 49 years old and yearly thereafter (Figure 27.18); however, some authorities suggest that yearly is too frequent. A new study suggests that at-risk women who carry a BRCA gene should preferably have diagnostic MRI scans.

Once diagnosed, breast cancer is treated in various ways depending on specific characteristics of the lesion. Current therapies include (1) radiation therapy, (2) chemotherapy, and (3) surgery, often followed by irradiation or chemotherapy to destroy stray cancer cells. Drug therapies include trastuzumab (Herceptin), a drug containing bioengineered antibodies that jam estrogen receptors that control aggressive growth in breast cancer cells; tamoxifen, an antiestrogen compound that blocks estrogen's effects and significantly improves the outcome for those (premenopausal women) with early- or late-stage breast cancer; and letrozole (Femara), which disables the enzyme needed to make estrogen and reduces breast cancer recurrences in women (particularly postmenopausal women) who have exhausted the usefulness of tamoxifen.

Until the 1970s, the standard treatment was **radical mastectomy** (mas-tek′to-me; "breast cutting"), removal of the entire affected breast, plus all underlying muscles, fascia, and associated lymph nodes. Most physicians now recommend **lumpectomy,** less extensive surgery in which only the cancerous part (lump) is excised, or **simple mastectomy,** removal of the breast tissue only (and perhaps some of the axillary lymph nodes). Many mastectomy patients opt for breast reconstruction to replace the excised tissue. Currently tissue "flaps," containing muscle, fat, and skin taken from the patient's abdomen or back, are providing acceptable alternatives for "sculpting" a natural-looking breast.

27

Malignancy

(a)
(b)
(c)

FIGURE 27.18 **Mammograms. (a)** Photograph of a woman undergoing mammography. **(b)** Normal breast. **(c)** Breast with tumor.

Physiology of the Female Reproductive System

Oogenesis

Gamete production in males begins at puberty and continues throughout life, but the situation is quite different in females. It has been assumed that a female's total supply of eggs is already determined by the time she is born, and the time span during which she releases them extends only from puberty to menopause (about the age of 50). However, a recent study in adult mice has indicated that germ stem cells are alive and generating little "egglets" throughout life and there are hints that egg stem cells also exist in adult women. Although these findings seem to overturn the assumption that the number of oocytes (thus, potential eggs) is limited—an idea that has been part of the bedrock of biology—it is still too early to retire the "no new eggs" doctrine.

Meiosis, the specialized nuclear division that occurs in the testes to produce sperm, also occurs in the ovaries. In this case, female sex cells are produced, and the process is called **oogenesis** (o"o-gen'e-sis; "the beginning of an egg"). The process of oogenesis (Figure 27.19) takes years to complete. First, in the fetal period the **oogonia,** the diploid stem cells of the ovaries, multiply rapidly by mitosis and then enter a growth phase and lay in nutrient reserves. Gradually, *primordial follicles* begin to appear as the oogonia are transformed into **primary oocytes** and become surrounded by a single layer of flattened follicle cells. The primary oocytes begin the first meiotic division,

but become "stalled" late in prophase I and do not complete it. By birth, a female has been presumed to have her lifetime supply of primary oocytes; of the original 7 million oocytes approximately 2 million of them escape programmed death and are already in place in the cortical region of the immature ovary. Since they remain in their state of suspended animation all through childhood, the wait is a long one—10 to 14 years at the very least!

At puberty, perhaps 250,000 oocytes remain and beginning at this time a small number of primary oocytes are recruited (activated) each month in response to the LH surge midcycle (see Figure 27.22). However, only one is "selected" each time to continue meiosis I, ultimately producing two haploid cells (each with 23 replicated chromosomes) that are quite dissimilar in size. The smaller cell is called the **first polar body.** The larger cell, which contains nearly all the cytoplasm of the primary oocyte, is the **secondary oocyte.** The events of this first maturation division are interesting. A spindle forms at the very edge of the oocyte (see Figure 27.19, left), and a little "nipple," into which the polar body chromosomes will be cast, appears at that edge. This ensures that the polar body receives almost no cytoplasm or organelles.

The first polar body may continue its development and undergo meiosis II, producing two even smaller polar bodies. However, in humans, the secondary oocyte arrests in metaphase II and it is this cell (not a functional ovum) that is ovulated. If an ovulated secondary oocyte is not penetrated by a sperm, it simply deteriorates. But, if sperm penetration *does* occur, it quickly completes meiosis II, yielding one large **ovum** and a tiny **second polar**

27

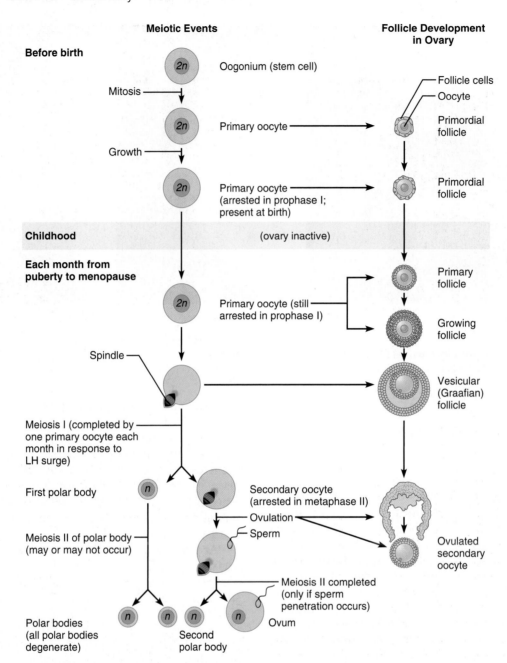

Meiotic Events

Before birth

Mitosis

Growth

Oogonium (stem cell)

Primary oocyte

Primary oocyte
(arrested in prophase I;
present at birth)

Childhood

**Each month from
puberty to menopause**

Spindle

Primary oocyte (still
arrested in prophase I)

Meiosis I (completed by
one primary oocyte each
month in response to
LH surge)

First polar body

Secondary oocyte
(arrested in metaphase II)

Ovulation

Sperm

Meiosis II of polar body
(may or may not occur)

Meiosis II completed
(only if sperm
penetration occurs)

Polar bodies
(all polar bodies
degenerate)

Second
polar body

Ovum

**Follicle Development
in Ovary**

Follicle cells

Oocyte

Primordial
follicle

Primordial
follicle

(ovary inactive)

Primary
follicle

Growing
follicle

Vesicular
(Graafian)
follicle

Ovulated
secondary
oocyte

FIGURE 27.19 **Events of oogenesis.** Left, flowchart of meiotic events. Right, correlation with follicle development and ovulation in the ovary.

body (see Figure 27.19). The union of the egg and sperm nuclei, described in Chapter 28, constitutes fertilization. What you should realize now is that the potential end products of oogenesis are three tiny polar bodies, nearly devoid of cytoplasm, and one large ovum. All of these cells are haploid, but only the ovum is a *functional gamete*. This is quite different from spermatogenesis, where the product is four viable gametes—spermatozoa.

The unequal cytoplasmic divisions that occur during oogenesis ensure that a fertilized egg has ample nutrients for its six- to seven-day journey to the uterus. Without nutrient-containing cytoplasm the polar bodies degenerate and die. Since the reproduc-

tive life of a female is at most about 40 years (from the age of 11 to approximately 51) and typically only one ovulation occurs each month, fewer than 500 oocytes out of her estimated pubertal potential of 250,000 are released during a woman's lifetime. Again, nature has provided us with a generous oversupply of sex cells.

Perhaps the most striking difference between male and female meiosis is the error rate. As many as 20% of oocytes but only 3–4% of sperm have the wrong number of chromosomes, a situation that often results from failure of the homologues to separate during meiosis I. Thus, it appears that faced with meiotic disruption, meiosis in males grinds to a halt but in females it marches on.

Q *Which of the follicles shown contain a primary oocyte?*
Which contain a secondary oocyte?

FIGURE 27.20 **Schematic view of the ovarian cycle: development and fate of ovarian follicles.** The numbers on the diagram indicate the sequence of events in follicle development, *not* the movement of a developing follicle within the ovary. ① Primordial follicle containing a primary oocyte surrounded by flattened cells. ② A primary follicle containing a primary oocyte surrounded by cuboidal follicle cells. ③ and ④ The growing primary follicle, which is secreting estrogen as it continues to mature. ⑤ The secondary follicle with its forming antrum. ⑥ The mature vesicular follicle, ready to be ovulated. Meiosis I, producing the secondary oocyte and first polar body, occurs in the mature follicle. ⑦ The ruptured follicle and ovulated secondary oocyte surrounded by its corona radiata of granulosa cells. ⑧ The corpus luteum, formed from the ruptured follicle under the influence of LH, produces progesterone (and estrogens). ⑨ The scarlike corpus albicans.

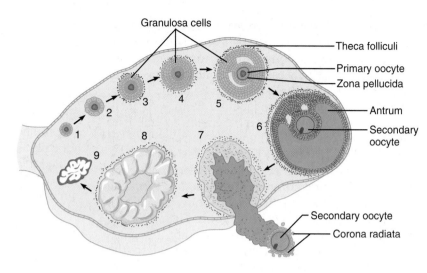

Granulosa cells

Theca folliculi
Primary oocyte
Zona pellucida
Antrum
Secondary oocyte

Secondary oocyte
Corona radiata

The Ovarian Cycle

The monthly series of events associated with the maturation of an egg is called the **ovarian cycle.** The ovarian cycle is best described in terms of two consecutive phases. The **follicular phase** is the period of follicle growth, typically indicated as lasting from the first to the fourteenth day of the cycle. The **luteal phase** is the period of corpus luteum activity, days 14–28. The so-called typical ovarian cycle repeats at intervals of 28 days, with *ovulation* occurring midcycle. However, only 10–15% of women naturally have 28-day cycles; cycles as long as 40 days or as short as 21 days are fairly common. In such cases, the length of the follicular phase and timing of ovulation vary, but the luteal phase remains constant: It is 14 days between the time of ovulation and the end of the cycle.

The Follicular Phase

Maturation of a primordial follicle to the mature state occupies the first half of the cycle and involves several events as shown in Figure 27.20, steps 1–6.

A Primordial Follicle Becomes a Primary Follicle

When a primordial follicle ① is activated (a process

directed by the oocyte), the squamouslike cells surrounding the primary oocyte grow, becoming cuboidal cells, and the oocyte enlarges. The follicle is now called a primary follicle ②.

A Primary Follicle Becomes a Secondary Follicle

Next, follicular cells proliferate, forming a stratified epithelium around the oocyte ③. As soon as more than one cell layer is present, the follicle cells take on the name *granulosa cells.* The granulosa cells are connected to the developing oocyte by gap junctions, through which ions, metabolites, and signaling molecules can pass, and from this point on, bidirectional "conversations" occur between the oocyte and granulosa cells, so they guide one another's development. One of the signals passing from the granulosa cells to the oocyte "tells" the oocyte to grow. Others dictate asymmetry (polarity) in the future egg.

In the next stage ④, a layer of connective tissue condenses around the follicle, forming the **theca folliculi** (the'kah fah-lik'u-li; "box around the follicle"). As the follicle grows, the thecal and granulosa cells cooperate to produce estrogens (the inner thecal cells produce androgens, which the granulosa cells convert to estrogens). At the same time, the oocyte secretes a glycoprotein-rich substance that forms a thick transparent membrane, called the **zona pellucida** (pĕ-lu'sid-ah), that encapsulates it (see Figure 27.12). In phase ⑤, clear liquid accumulates between the granulosa cells and eventually coalesces to

A *1–5 contain a primary oocyte; 6 contains a secondary oocyte.*

27

form a fluid-filled cavity called the **antrum** ("cave"). The presence of an antrum distinguishes the new secondary follicle from the primary follicle.

A Secondary Follicle Becomes a Vesicular Follicle

The antrum continues to expand with fluid until it isolates the oocyte, along with its surrounding capsule of granulosa cells called a **corona radiata** ("radiating crown"), on a stalk on one side of the follicle. When a follicle is full size (about 2.5 cm, or 1 inch, in diameter), it becomes a vesicular follicle and bulges from the external ovarian surface like an "angry boil." This usually occurs by day 14.

As one of the final events of follicle maturation, the primary oocyte completes meiosis I to form the secondary oocyte and first polar body (see Figure 27.19). Once this has occurred (⑥ in Figure 27.20), the stage is set for ovulation. At this point, the granulosa cells send another important signal to the oocyte that says, in effect, "Wait, do not complete meiosis yet!"

Ovulation

Ovulation occurs when the ballooning ovary wall ruptures and expels the secondary oocyte (still surrounded by its *corona radiata*) into the peritoneal cavity ⑦. Some women experience a twinge of pain in the lower abdomen when ovulation occurs. This episode, called *mittelschmerz* (mit'el-shmārts; German for "middle pain"), is caused by the intense stretching of the ovarian wall during ovulation.

In the ovaries of adult females, there are always several follicles at different stages of maturation. As a rule, one follicle outstrips the others to become the *dominant follicle* and is at the peak stage of maturation when the hormonal (LH) stimulus is given for ovulation. How this follicle is selected, or selects itself, is still uncertain, but it is probably the one that attains the greatest FSH sensitivity the quickest. The others degenerate (undergo programmed cell death, or apoptosis) and are reabsorbed.

In 1–2% of all ovulations, more than one oocyte is ovulated. This phenomenon, which increases with age, can result in multiple births. Since, in such cases, different oocytes are fertilized by different sperm, the siblings are *fraternal*, or nonidentical, twins. *Identical twins* result from the fertilization of a single oocyte by a single sperm, followed by separation of the fertilized egg's daughter cells in early development. Additionally, it now appears that in some women, oocytes may be released at times unrelated to the woman's hormone levels, which may help to explain why a rhythm method of contraception sometimes fails and why some fraternal twins have different conception dates.

The Luteal Phase

After ovulation, the ruptured follicle collapses, and the antrum fills with clotted blood. This *corpus hemorrhagicum* is eventually absorbed. The remaining granulosa cells increase in size and along with the internal thecal cells they form a new, quite different endocrine gland, the *corpus luteum* ("yellow body") (see Figure 27.20, step ⑧), that begins to secrete progesterone and some estrogen. If pregnancy does not occur, the corpus luteum starts degenerating in about ten days and its hormonal output ends. In this case, all that ultimately remains is a scar ⑨ called the *corpus albicans* (al'bĭ-kans; "white body"). On the other hand, if the oocyte is fertilized and pregnancy ensues, the corpus luteum persists until the placenta is ready to take over its hormone-producing duties in about three months. The last two or three days of the luteal phase, when the endometrium is just beginning to erode, is sometimes called the *luteolytic* or *ischemic phase*.

Hormonal Regulation of the Ovarian Cycle

Ovarian events are much more complicated than those occurring in the testes, but the hormonal controls set into motion at puberty are similar in the two sexes. Gonadotropin-releasing hormone (GnRH), the pituitary gonadotropins, and, in this case, ovarian estrogen and progesterone interact to produce the cyclic events occurring in the ovaries. However, in females another hormone plays an important role in stimulating the hypothalamus to release GnRH. The onset of puberty in females is linked to adiposity, and the messenger from fatty tissue to the hypothalamus is *leptin*. If blood levels of lipids and leptin (better known for its role in energy production and appetite) are low, puberty is delayed.

Establishing the Ovarian Cycle

During childhood, the ovaries grow and continuously secrete small amounts of estrogens, which inhibit hypothalamic release of GnRH. As puberty nears, the hypothalamus becomes less sensitive to estrogen and begins to release GnRH in a rhythmic pulselike manner. GnRH, in turn, stimulates the anterior pituitary to release FSH and LH, which prompt the ovaries to secrete hormones (primarily estrogens).

Gonadotropin levels continue to increase for about four years and, during this time, pubertal girls are still not ovulating and thus are incapable of getting pregnant. Eventually, the adult cyclic pattern is achieved, and hormonal interactions stabilize. These events are heralded by the young woman's first menstrual period, referred to as **menarche** (mĕ-nar'ke; *men* = month, *arche* = first). Usually, it is

Q *Which of the events illustrated here is an example of positive feedback?*

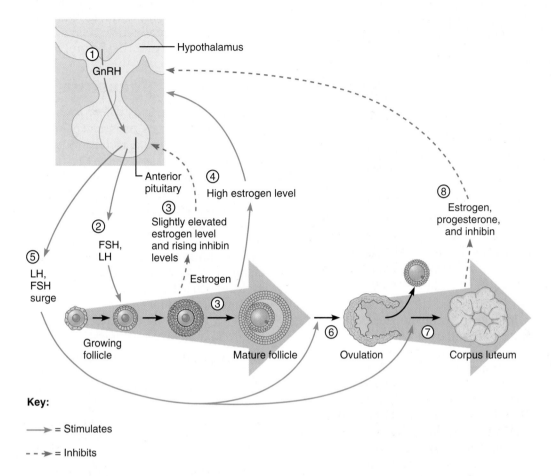

Key:

⟶ = Stimulates

- - -➤ = Inhibits

FIGURE 27.21   **Feedback interactions in the regulation of ovarian function.** Numbers refer to events listed in the text. Events that follow step 8 (negative feedback inhibition of the hypothalamus and anterior pituitary by progesterone and estrogens) are not depicted, but involve a gradual deterioration of the corpus luteum and, therefore, a decline in ovarian hormone production. Ovarian hormones reach their lowest blood levels around day 28.

not until the third year postmenarche that the cycles become regular and all are ovulatory.

Hormonal Interactions During the Ovarian Cycle

The waxing and waning of anterior pituitary gonadotropins (FSH and LH) and ovarian hormones and the positive and negative feedback interactions that regulate ovarian function are as described next. Notice that events 1–8 in the following discussion directly correspond to the same-numbered steps in Figure 27.21. A 28-day cycle is assumed.

A *Stimulation of LH (and FSH) surges by rising estrogen levels, steps 4 and 5.*

① On day 1 of the cycle, rising levels of GnRH from the hypothalamus stimulate increased production and release of follicle-stimulating hormone (FSH) and luteinizing hormone (LH) by the anterior pituitary.

② FSH and LH stimulate follicle growth and maturation and estrogen secretion. FSH exerts its main effects on the follicle cells, whereas LH (at least initially) targets the thecal cells. (Why only *some* follicles respond to these hormonal stimuli is still a mystery. However, there is little doubt that enhanced responsiveness is due to formation of more gonadotropin receptors.) As the follicles enlarge, LH prods the thecal cells to produce androgens. These diffuse through the basement membrane, where they are converted to estrogens by the granulosa cells. Only tiny amounts of ovarian androgens enter the blood, because they are almost completely converted to estrogens within the ovaries.

③ The rising estrogen levels in the plasma exert *negative feedback* on the anterior pituitary, inhibiting its release of FSH and LH, while simultaneously prodding it to synthesize and accumulate these gonadotropins. Within the ovary, estrogen increases estrogen output by intensifying the effect of FSH on follicle maturation. *Inhibin*, released by the granulosa cells, also exerts negative feedback controls on FSH release during this period.

④ Although the initial small rise in estrogen blood levels inhibits the hypothalamic-pituitary axis, high estrogen levels have the opposite effect. Once estrogen reaches a critical blood concentration, it exerts *positive feedback* on the brain and anterior pituitary.

⑤ High estrogen levels set a cascade of events into motion. There is a sudden burstlike release of accumulated LH (and, to a lesser extent, FSH) by the anterior pituitary about midcycle (also see Figure 27.22a).

⑥ The LH surge stimulates the primary oocyte of the dominant follicle to complete the first meiotic division, forming a secondary oocyte that continues on to metaphase II. LH also triggers ovulation at or around day 14. Whatever the mechanism, blood stops flowing through the protruding part of the follicle wall and within 5 minutes, that region of the follicle wall bulges out, thins, and then ruptures. The role (if any) of FSH in this process is unknown. Shortly after ovulation, estrogen levels decline. This probably reflects the damage to the dominant estrogen-secreting follicle during ovulation.

⑦ The LH surge also transforms the ruptured follicle into a corpus luteum (hence the name "luteinizing" hormone), and stimulates the newly formed endocrine gland to produce progesterone and estrogen almost immediately after it is formed.

⑧ Rising progesterone and estrogen blood levels exert a powerful negative feedback effect on anterior pituitary release of LH and FSH. Corpus luteum release of inhibin enhances this inhibitory effect. Declining gonadotropin levels inhibit the development of new follicles and prevent additional LH surges that might cause additional oocytes to be ovulated.

As LH blood levels fall, the stimulus for luteal activity ends, and the corpus luteum degenerates. As goes the corpus luteum, so go the levels of ovarian hormones, and blood estrogen and progesterone levels drop sharply. The marked decline in ovarian hormones at the end of the cycle (days 26–28) ends their blockade of FSH and LH secretion, and the cycle starts anew.

Although the ovarian events are described as if we are following one follicle through the 28-day cycle, this is not really the case. What is happening is that the increase of FSH at the beginning of each cycle activates several follicles to mature. Then, with the midcycle LH surge, one (or more) Graafian follicles undergo ovulation. However, the ovulated oocyte would actually have been activated about 110 days (some three months) before, not 14 days before.

The Uterine (Menstrual) Cycle

Although the uterus is where the young embryo implants and develops, it is receptive to implantation for only a short period each month. Not surprisingly, this brief interval is exactly the time when a developing embryo would normally begin implanting, six to seven days after ovulation. The **uterine,** or **menstrual** (men'stroo-al), **cycle** is a series of cyclic changes that the uterine endometrium goes through each month as it responds to the waxing and waning of ovarian hormones in the blood. These endometrial changes are coordinated with the phases of the ovarian cycle, which are dictated by gonadotropins released by the anterior pituitary.

The events of the uterine cycle, depicted in Figure 27.22d, are as follows:

1. Days 1–5: Menstrual phase. In this phase, **menstruation** (men"stroo-a'shun), the uterus sheds all but the deepest part of its endometrium. (At the beginning of this stage, ovarian hormones are at their lowest normal levels and gonadotropins are beginning to rise. Then FSH levels begin to rise.) The thick, hormone-dependent functional layer of the endometrium detaches from the uterine wall, a process that is accompanied by bleeding for 3–5 days. The detached tissue and blood pass out through the vagina as the menstrual flow. By day 5, the growing ovarian follicles are starting to produce more estrogen (see Figure 27.22b).

2. Days 6–14: Proliferative (preovulatory) phase. In this phase, the endometrium rebuilds itself: Under the influence of rising blood levels of estrogens, the basal layer of the endometrium generates a new functional layer. As this new layer thickens, its glands enlarge and its spiral arteries increase in number (also see Figure 27.15). Consequently, the endometrium once again becomes velvety, thick, and well vascularized. During this phase, estrogens also induce synthesis of progesterone receptors in the endometrial cells, readying them for interaction with progesterone.

Normally, cervical mucus is thick and sticky, but rising estrogen levels cause it to thin and become crystalline, forming channels that facilitate the passage of sperm into the uterus. *Ovulation*, which takes less than five minutes, occurs in the ovary at the end of the proliferative stage (day 14) in response to the sudden release of LH from the anterior pituitary. LH also converts the ruptured follicle to a corpus luteum.

27

FIGURE 27.22   **Correlation of anterior pituitary and ovarian hormones with structural changes of the ovary and uterus.** The time bar at the bottom of the figure, reading Days 1 to 28, applies to all four parts of this figure. **(a)** The fluctuating levels of pituitary gonadotropins in the blood (FSH = follicle-stimulating hormone; LH = luteinizing hormone). These hormones regulate the events of the ovarian cycle. **(b)** The fluctuating levels of ovarian hormones (estrogens and progesterone) that cause the endometrial changes of the uterine cycle. The high estrogen levels are also responsible for the LH/FSH surge in (a). **(c)** Structural changes in the ovarian follicles during the 28-day ovarian cycle are correlated with **(d)** changes in the endometrium of the uterus during the uterine cycle. **(d)** The three phases of the uterine cycle: menstrual, proliferative, and secretory. Basically, the first phase is a shedding and the second is a rebuilding of the functional zone of the endometrium. Both of these events occur before ovulation and together they correspond to the follicular phase of the ovarian cycle. The third phase, the secretory phase which begins immediately after ovulation, enriches the blood supply and provides the nutrients that prepare the endometrium to receive an embryo. It corresponds in time to the luteal phase of the ovarian cycle.

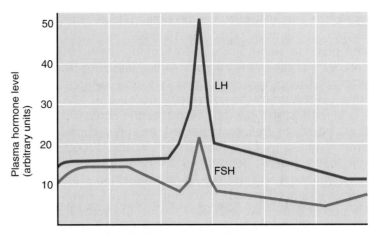

(a) Fluctuation of gonadotropin levels

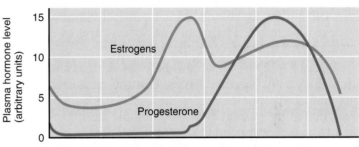

(b) Fluctuation of ovarian hormone levels

(c) Ovarian cycle

(d) Uterine cycle

3. Days 15–28: Secretory (postovulatory) phase. This 14-day phase is the most constant timewise. During the secretory phase the endometrium prepares for implantation of an embryo. Rising levels of progesterone from the corpus luteum act on the estrogen-primed endometrium, causing the spiral arteries to elaborate and converting the functional layer to a secretory mucosa. The uterine glands enlarge, coil, and begin secreting nutritious glycogen into the uterine cavity. These nutrients sustain the embryo until it has implanted in the blood-rich endometrial lining. Increasing progesterone levels also cause the cervical mucus to become viscous again, forming the *cervical plug*, which blocks sperm entry and plays an important role in keeping the uterus "private" in the event an embryo has begun to implant. Rising progesterone (and estrogen) levels inhibit LH release by the anterior pituitary.

If fertilization has not occurred, the corpus luteum begins to degenerate toward the end of the secretory phase as LH blood levels decline. Progesterone levels fall, depriving the endometrium of hormonal support, and the spiral arteries kink and go into spasms. Denied oxygen and nutrients, the ischemic endometrial cells die, setting the stage for menstruation to begin on day 28. The spiral arteries constrict one final time and then suddenly relax and open wide. As blood gushes into the weakened capillary beds, they fragment, causing the functional layer to slough off. The menstrual cycle starts over again on this first day of menstrual flow.

Figure 27.22 also illustrates how the ovarian and uterine cycles fit together. Notice that the menstrual and proliferative phases overlap the follicular stage and ovulation in the ovarian cycle, and that the uterine secretory phase corresponds to the ovarian luteal phase.

Extremely strenuous activity can delay menarche in girls and can disrupt the normal menstrual cycle in adult women, even causing *amenorrhea* (a-men"o-re'ah), cessation of menses. Female athletes have little body fat, and fat deposits help convert adrenal androgens to estrogens and are the source of leptin which, as noted above, plays a critical permissive role in the onset of puberty in females. In mature females, leptin keeps the hypothalamus informed about whether energy stores are sufficient to support the high energy demands of reproduction. If not, the reproductive cycles are shut down. These effects are usually totally reversible when the athletic training is discontinued, but a worrisome consequence of amenorrhea in young, healthy adult women is that they suffer dramatic losses in bone mass normally seen only in old age. Once estrogen levels drop and the menstrual cycle stops (regardless of cause), bone loss begins.

Although menses has traditionally been viewed as a somewhat messy way of discarding a uterine lining "fattened" in anticipation of a baby that was never conceived, its adaptive value and expense to the female body in terms of tissue, blood, and nutrient (particularly iron) loss have been questioned. Why not just keep the prepared endometrium for the next cycle? A controversial view of menses is that the uterus is a hospitable receptacle for bacteria and viruses delivered via the male penis and piggy-backing in semen. This being so, menses is an aggressive way of cleaning house. Bleeding rids the body of the uterine lining where pathogens are likely to linger, and menstrual blood is loaded with macrophages which provide active protection.

Extrauterine Effects of Estrogens and Progesterone

With a name meaning "generators of sexual activity," estrogens are analogous to testosterone, the male steroid. As estrogen levels rise during puberty, they (1) promote oogenesis and follicle growth in the ovary and (2) exert anabolic effects on the female reproductive tract (see Table 27.1). Consequently, the uterine tubes, uterus, and vagina grow larger and become functional—ready to support a pregnancy. The uterine tubes and uterus exhibit enhanced motility; the vaginal mucosa thickens; and the external genitalia mature.

Estrogens also support the growth spurt at puberty that makes girls grow much more quickly than boys during the ages of 12 and 13. But this growth is short lived because rising estrogen levels also cause the epiphyses of long bones to close sooner, and females reach their full height between the ages of 15 and 17 years. In contrast, the aggressive growth of males continues until the age of 19 to 21 years, at which point rising estrogen levels cause epiphyseal closure.

The estrogen-induced secondary sex characteristics of females include (1) growth of the breasts; (2) increased deposit of subcutaneous fat, especially in the hips and breasts; and (3) widening and lightening of the pelvis (adaptations for childbirth). Estrogens have several metabolic effects, including maintaining low total blood cholesterol levels (and high HDL levels) and facilitating calcium uptake, which helps sustain the density of the skeleton. (These metabolic effects, though initiated under estrogen's influence during puberty, are not true secondary sex characteristics.)

Progesterone works with estrogen to establish and then help regulate the uterine cycle and promotes changes in cervical mucus (see Table 27.1). Its other effects are exhibited largely during pregnancy, when it inhibits uterine motility and takes up where estrogen leaves off in preparing the breasts for lactation. Indeed, progesterone is named for these important roles (*pro* = for; *gestation* = pregnancy). However, the source of progesterone and estrogen during most of pregnancy is the placenta, not the ovaries.

Female Sexual Response

The **female sexual response** is similar to that of males in most respects. During sexual excitement, the clitoris, vaginal mucosa, and breasts engorge with blood; the nipples erect; and increased activity of the vestibular glands lubricates the vestibule and facilitates entry of the penis. These events, though more widespread, are analogous to the *erection* phase in men. Sexual excitement is promoted by touch and psychological stimuli and is mediated along the same autonomic nerve pathways as in males.

TABLE 27.1	Summary of Hormonal Effects of Gonadal Estrogens, Progesterone, and Testosterone		
SOURCE, STIMULUS, EFFECTS	**ESTROGENS**	**PROGESTERONE**	**TESTOSTERONE**
Major source	Ovary: developing follicles and corpus luteum	Ovary: mainly the corpus luteum	Testes: interstitial cells
Stimulus for release	FSH (and LH)	LH	LH and declining levels of inhibin produced by the sustentacular cells
Feedback effects exerted	Both negative and positive feedback exerted on anterior pituitary release of gonadotropins	Negative feedback exerted on anterior pituitary release of gonadotropins	Negative feedback suppresses release of LH by the anterior pituitary (and perhaps release of GnRH by the hypothalamus)
Effects on reproductive organs	Stimulate growth and maturation of reproductive organs and breasts at puberty and maintain their adult size and function. Promote the proliferative phase of the uterine cycle; stimulate production of watery (crystalline) cervical mucus and activity of fimbriae and uterine tube cilia	Cooperates with estrogen in stimulating growth of breasts and in regulating the uterine cycle (promotes the secretory phase of the uterine cycle); stimulates production of viscous cervical mucus	Stimulates formation of male reproductive ducts, glands, and external genitalia. Promotes descent of the testes. Stimulates growth and maturation of the internal and external genitalia at puberty; maintains their adult size and function
	Promote oogenesis and ovulation by stimulating formation of FSH and LH receptors on follicle cells. Stimulate capacitation of sperm in the female reproductive tract by affecting vaginal and uterine secretions	During pregnancy, quiets the myometrium and acts with estrogen to cause mammary glands to achieve their mature milk-producing state	Required for normal spermatogenesis via effects promoted by its binding to ABP on spermatogenic cells; suppresses mammary gland development
	During pregnancy stimulate growth of the uterus and enlargement of the external genitalia and mammary glands		
Promotion of secondary sex characteristics and somatic effects	Promote lengthening of long bones and feminization of the skeleton (particularly the pelvis); inhibit bone reabsorption and then stimulate epiphyseal closure; promote hydration of the skin and stimulate female pattern of fat deposit		Stimulates the growth spurt at puberty; promotes increased skeletal mass during adolescence; promotes growth of the larynx and vocal cords and deepening of the voice; enhances sebum secretion and hair growth, especially on the face, axillae, genital region, and chest
	During pregnancy act with relaxin (placental hormone) to induce softening and relaxation of the pelvic ligaments and pubic symphysis		
Metabolic effects	Generally anabolic; stimulate Na$^+$ reabsorption by the renal tubules, hence inhibit diuresis; enhance HDL (and reduce LDL) blood levels (cardiovascular sparing effect)	Promotes diuresis (antiestrogenic effect); increases body temperature	Generally anabolic; stimulates hematopoiesis; enhances the basal metabolic rate
Neural effects	Feminize the brain; along with DHEA (an androgen produced by the adrenal cortex) are partially responsible for sex drive (libido) in females		Responsible for libido in males; masculinizes the brain; promotes aggressiveness

The final phase of the female sexual response, *orgasm*, is not accompanied by ejaculation, but muscle tension increases throughout the body, pulse rate and blood pressure rise, and the uterus begins to contract rhythmically. As in males, orgasm is accompanied by a sensation of intense pleasure and followed by relaxation. Orgasm in females is not followed by a refractory period, so females may experience multiple orgasms during a single sexual experience. A man must achieve orgasm and ejaculate if fertilization is to occur, but female orgasm is not required for conception. Indeed, some women never experience orgasm, yet are perfectly able to conceive.

Although the female libido was formerly believed to be prompted by testosterone, new studies indicate that dehydroepiandrosterone (DHEA), an androgen produced by the adrenal cortex, is in fact the male sex hormone associated with desire or lack of it in females.

Sexually Transmitted Diseases

Sexually transmitted diseases (STDs), also called *venereal diseases (VDs),* are infectious diseases spread through sexual contact. The United States has the highest rates of infection among developed countries. Over 12 million people in the United States, a quarter of them adolescents, get STDs each year.

As a group, STDs are the single most important cause of reproductive disorders. Until recently, the bacterial infections gonorrhea and syphilis were the most common STDs, but now viral diseases have taken center stage. AIDS, the most notorious STD, is caused by HIV, the virus that cripples the immune system. AIDS is described in Chapter 21; the other important bacterial and viral STDs are described here. Condoms are effective in helping to prevent the spread of STDs, and their use is strongly urged, particularly since the advent of AIDS.

Gonorrhea

The causative agent of **gonorrhea** (gon"o-re'ah) is *Neisseria gonorrhoeae,* which invades the mucosae of the reproductive and urinary tracts. These bacteria are spread by contact with genital, anal, and pharyngeal mucosal surfaces. Commonly called "the clap," gonorrhea occurs most frequently in adolescents and young adults.

The most common symptom of gonorrhea in males is *urethritis,* accompanied by painful urination and discharge of pus from the penis (penile "drip"). Symptoms vary in women, ranging from none (about 20% of cases) to abdominal discomfort, vaginal discharge, abnormal uterine bleeding, and occasionally, urethral symptoms similar to those seen in males.

Untreated gonorrhea can cause urethral constriction and inflammation of the entire male duct system. In women, it causes pelvic inflammatory disease and sterility. These consequences declined with the advent in the 1950s of penicillin, tetracycline, and certain other antibiotics. However, strains resistant to those antibiotics are becoming increasingly prevalent. Currently, ceftriaxone is the antibiotic used most often to treat gonorrhea.

Syphilis

Syphilis (sif'ĭ-lis), caused by *Treponema pallidum,* a corkscrew-shaped bacterium, is usually transmitted sexually, but it can be contracted congenitally from an infected mother. Indeed, an increasing number of women trading sex for "crack" (a cocaine derivative) are passing syphilis on to their fetuses. Fetuses infected with syphilis are usually stillborn or die shortly after birth. The bacterium easily penetrates intact mucosae and abraded skin. Within a few hours of exposure, an asymptomatic bodywide infection is in progress. After an incubation period of two to three weeks, a red, painless primary lesion called a *chancre* (shang'ker) appears at the site of bacterial invasion. In males, this is typically the penis, but in females the lesion often goes undetected within the vagina or on the cervix. The chancre ulcerates and becomes crusty; then it heals spontaneously and disappears within a few weeks.

If syphilis is untreated, its secondary signs appear several weeks later. A pink skin rash all over the body is one of the first symptoms. Fever and joint pain are common. These signs and symptoms disappear spontaneously in three to twelve weeks. Then the disease enters the *latent period* and is detectable only by a blood test. The latent stage may last a person's lifetime (or the bacteria may be killed by the immune system), or it may be followed by the signs of *tertiary syphilis.* Tertiary syphilis is characterized by *gummas* (gum'ahs), destructive lesions of the CNS, blood vessels, bones, and skin. Penicillin is still the treatment of choice for all stages of syphilis.

Chlamydia

Chlamydia (klah-mid'e-ah; *chlamys* = cloak) is a largely undiagnosed, silent epidemic that infects perhaps 4–5 million people yearly, making it the most common bacterial sexually transmitted disease in the United States. Chlamydia is responsible for 25–50% of all diagnosed cases of pelvic inflammatory disease (and, consequently, at least a 1 in 4 chance of ectopic pregnancy), and each year more than 150,000 infants are born to infected mothers. About 20% of men and 30% of women infected with gonorrhea are also infected by *Chlamydia trachomatis,* the causative agent of chlamydia.

Chlamydia is a bacterium with a viruslike dependence on host cells. Its incubation period within the body cells is about one week. Symptoms include urethritis (involving painful, frequent urination and a thick penile discharge); vaginal discharge; abdominal, rectal, or testicular pain; painful intercourse; and irregular menses. In men, it can cause arthritis as well as widespread urogenital tract infection. In women, 80% of whom suffer *no* symptoms from the

27

infection, it is a major cause of sterility. Newborns infected in the birth canal tend to develop conjunctivitis (or *trachoma*, a painful eye infection that leads to corneal scarring if untreated, often the case in third world countries) and respiratory tract inflammations including pneumonia. The disease can be diagnosed by cell culture techniques and is easily treated with tetracycline.

Trichomoniasis

Trichomoniasis is the most common *curable* STD in sexually active young women in the U.S. Accounting for about 7.4 million new cases of STD infections per year, this parasitic infection is easily and inexpensively treated once diagnosed. Trichomoniasis is indicated by a yellow-green vaginal discharge with a strong odor, however, many of its victims exhibit no symptoms.

Genital Warts

Genital warts due to the *human papillomavirus (HPV)*—actually a group of about 60 viruses—is the second most common STD in the United States. About 6.2 million new cases of genital warts develop in Americans each year, and it appears that HPV infection increases the risk for cancers in infected regions. Indeed, the virus is linked to 80% of all cases of invasive cervical cancer.

Treatment is difficult and controversial, and the warts tend to disappear. Some clinicians prefer to leave the warts untreated unless they become widespread, whereas others recommend their removal by cryosurgery, or laser therapy, and/or treatment with alpha interferon.

Genital Herpes

The common cause of **genital herpes** is the *human herpes virus type 2,* and these viruses are among the most difficult human pathogens to control. They remain silent for weeks or years and then suddenly flare up, causing a burst of blisterlike lesions. Direct transmission of the virus is via infectious secretions. The painful lesions that appear on the reproductive organs of infected adults are usually more of a nuisance than a threat. However, congenital herpes infections can cause severe malformations of a fetus. Most people who have genital herpes do not know it, and it has been estimated that one-quarter to one-half of all adult Americans harbor the type 2 herpes simplex virus. Only about 15% of that population displays signs of infection. The antiviral *acyclovir,* which speeds healing of the lesions and reduces the frequency of flare-ups, is the drug of choice for treatment. Once contracted, genital herpes never leaves; it just goes into periodic remissions.

Developmental Aspects of the Reproductive System: Chronology of Sexual Development

Thus far, we have described the reproductive organs as they exist and operate in adults. Now we are ready to look at events that cause us to become reproductive individuals. These events begin long before birth and end, at least in women, in late middle age.

Embryological and Fetal Events

Determination of Genetic Sex

Aristotle believed that the "heat" of lovemaking determined maleness. Not so! Genetic sex is determined at the instant the genes of a sperm combine with those of an ovum, and the determining factor is the **sex chromosomes** each gamete contains. Of the 46 chromosomes in the fertilized egg, two (one pair) are sex chromosomes. The other 44 are called **autosomes**. Two types of sex chromosomes, quite different in size, exist in humans: the large **X chromosome** and the much smaller **Y chromosome**. The body cells of females have two X chromosomes and are designated XX; the ovum resulting from normal meiosis in a female always contains an X chromosome. Males have one X chromosome and one Y in each body cell (XY). Approximately half of the sperm produced by normal meiosis in males contain an X and the other half a Y. If the fertilizing sperm delivers an X chromosome, the fertilized egg and its daughter cells will contain the female (XX) composition, and the embryo will develop ovaries. If the sperm bears the Y, the offspring will be male (XY) and will develop testes. A single gene on the Y chromosome— the *SRY* gene—is the master switch that initiates testes development and hence maleness. Thus, the father determines the genetic sex of the offspring, and all subsequent events of sexual differentiation depend on which gonads are formed during embryonic life. Mutation of the *SRY* gene can result in XY females with the male chromosome but female sex characteristics.

◤ HOMEOSTATIC IMBALANCE

When meiosis distributes the sex chromosomes to the gametes improperly, an event called **nondisjunction**, abnormal combinations of sex chromosomes occur in the zygote and cause striking abnormalities in sexual and reproductive system development. For example, females with a single X chromosome (XO), a condition called *Turner's syndrome*, never develop ovaries. Males with no X chromosome (YO) die during embryonic development. Although most XXX

FIGURE 27.23   Development of the internal reproductive organs.

females have normal intelligence, females carrying four or more X chromosomes as a rule are mentally retarded and have underdeveloped ovaries and limited fertility. *Klinefelter's syndrome,* which affects one out of 500 live male births, is the most common sex chromosome abnormality. Affected individuals usually have a single Y chromosome, two or more X chromosomes, and are sterile males. Although XXY males are normal (or only slightly below normal) intellectually, the incidence of mental retardation increases as the number of X chromosomes rises. ●

Sexual Differentiation of the Reproductive System

The gonads of both males and females begin their development during week 5 of gestation as masses of mesoderm called the **gonadal ridges** (Figure 27.23). The gonadal ridges form bulges on the dorsal abdominal wall just medial to the mesonephros (a transient kidney system, see p. 1027). The **paramesonephric,** or **Müllerian, ducts** (future female ducts) develop lateral to the **mesonephric (Wolffian) ducts** (future male ducts), and both sets of ducts empty into a common chamber called the *cloaca.* At this stage of development, the embryo is said to be in the **sexually indifferent stage,** because the gonadal ridge tissue can develop into either male or female gonads and both duct systems are present.

Shortly after the gonadal ridges appear, **primordial germ cells** migrate to them from a different region of the embryo [presumably guided by a gradient of chemical signals (chemokines)], and seed the developing gonads with stem cells destined to become spermatogonia or oogonia. Once these cells are in residence, the gonadal ridges form testes or ovaries, depending on the genetic makeup of the embryo. The process begins in week 7 in male embryos. Seminiferous tubules form in the internal part of the gonadal ridges and join the mesonephric duct via the efferent ductules. Further development of the mesonephric duct produces the duct system of the male. The paramesonephric ducts play no part in male development and degenerate unless the tiny testes fail to secrete a hormone called *anti-Müllerian hormone (AMH).* [AMH causes the breakdown of the paramesonephric (Müllerian) ducts, which give rise to the female duct system (oviducts and uterus).]

In female embryos the process begins about a week later. The outer, or cortical, part of the immature ovaries forms follicles, and the paramesonephric ducts differentiate into the structures of the female duct system. The mesonephric ducts degenerate.

Like the gonads, the external genitalia arise from the same structures in both sexes (Figure 27.24). During the indifferent stage, all embryos exhibit a small projection called the **genital tubercle** on their external body surface. The urogenital sinus, which develops from subdivision of the cloaca (future urethra and bladder), lies deep to the tubercle. The **urethral groove,** the external opening of the urogenital sinus, is on the tubercle's inferior surface. The urethral groove is flanked laterally by the **urethral folds** and then the **labioscrotal swellings.**

During week 8, the external genitalia begin to develop rapidly. In males, the genital tubercle enlarges, forming the penis. The urethral folds fuse in the midline, forming the spongy urethra in the penis. Only the tips of the folds remain unfused to form the *urethral orifice* at the tip of the penis. The labioscrotal swellings also fuse in the body midline to form the scrotum. In females, the genital tubercle gives rise to the clitoris and the urethral groove persists as the vestibule. The unfused urethral folds become the labia minora, and the unfused labioscrotal folds become the labia majora.

Differentiation of accessory structures and the external genitalia as male or female structures depends on the presence or absence of testosterone. When testes are formed, they quickly begin to release testosterone, which continues until four to five days after birth and which causes the development of male accessory ducts and external genitalia. In the absence of testosterone, the female ducts and external genitalia develop.

◤ HOMEOSTATIC IMBALANCE

Any interference with the normal pattern of sex hormone production in the embryo results in bizarre abnormalities. For example, if the embryonic testes do not produce testosterone, a genetic male develops the female accessory structures and external genitalia. If the testes fail to produce AMH, both the female and male duct systems form, but the external genitalia are those of the male. On the other hand, if a genetic female is exposed to testosterone (as might happen if the mother has an androgen-producing tumor of her adrenal gland), the embryo has ovaries but develops the male ducts and glands, as well as a penis and an empty scrotum. It appears that the female pattern of reproductive structures has an intrinsic ability to develop (is the default condition), and in the absence of testosterone it proceeds to do so, regardless of the embryo's genetic makeup.

Individuals with accessory reproductive structures that do not "match" their gonads are called *pseudohermaphrodites* (soo-do-her-maf'ro-dīts). (True *hermaphrodites* are rare and possess both ovarian and testicular tissue.) Many pseudohermaphrodites have sought sex-change operations to match their outer selves (external genitalia) with their inner selves (gonads). ●

27

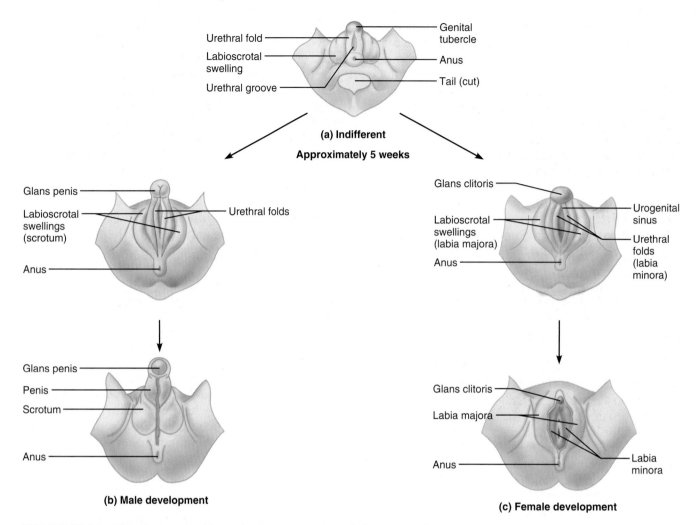

(a) Indifferent

Approximately 5 weeks

(b) Male development

(c) Female development

FIGURE 27.24   **Development of homologous structures of the external genitalia in both sexes.** The two pictures at the bottom of the figure show the fully developed perineal region.

Descent of the Gonads

About two months before birth, the testes begin their descent toward the scrotum, dragging their supplying blood vessels and nerves along behind them (Figure 27.25). They finally exit from the pelvic cavity via the inguinal canals and enter the scrotum. This migration is stimulated by testosterone made by the male fetus's testes, and is guided mechanically by a strong fibrous cord called the **gubernaculum** ("governor"), which extends from the testis to the floor of the scrotal sac. The *tunica vaginalis* covering of the testis that is pulled into the scrotum with the testis is derived from a fingerlike outpocketing of the parietal peritoneum, the *vaginal process*. The accompanying blood vessels, nerves, and fascial layers form part of the *spermatic cord*, which helps suspend the testis within the scrotum.

Like the testes, the ovaries descend during fetal development, but in this case only to the pelvic brim, where their progress is stopped by the tentlike broad ligament. Each ovary is guided in its descent by a gubernaculum (anchored in the labium majus) that later divides, becoming the ovarian and round ligaments that help support the internal genitalia in the pelvis.

▲ HOMEOSTATIC IMBALANCE

Failure of the testes to make their normal descent leads to *cryptorchidism* (*crypt* = hidden, concealed; *orchi* = testicle). Because this condition causes sterility and increases the risk of testicular cancer, surgery is usually performed during early childhood to rectify this problem. ●

Puberty

FSH and LH levels, elevated at birth, fall to low levels within a few months and remain low throughout the prepubertal years. Between the ages of 10 and 15 years, a host of interacting hormones bring on the changes of puberty. **Puberty** is the period of life when the reproductive organs grow to adult size and become functional. These changes occur in response to rising levels of gonadal hormones (testosterone in males and estrogen in females). The secondary sex characteristics and regulatory events of puberty were described earlier. But it is important to remember that puberty represents the earliest time that reproduction is possible.

The events of puberty occur in the same sequence in all individuals, but the age at which they occur varies widely. In males, secretion of adrenal androgens [particularly dehydroepiandrosterone (DHEA)] begins to rise several years before the testosterone surge of puberty and initiates facial, pubic, and axillary hair growth and other pubertal events. The major event that signals puberty's onset in males is enlargement of the testes and scrotum between the ages of 8 and 14. Growth of the penis goes on over the next two years, and sexual maturation is evidenced by the presence of mature sperm in the semen. In the meantime, the young man has unexpected, and often embarrassing, erections and frequent nocturnal emissions ("wet dreams") as his hormones surge and the hormonal control axis struggles to achieve a normal balance.

The first sign of puberty in females is budding breasts, apparent between the ages of 8 and 13 years, followed by the appearance of axillary and pubic hair. Menarche usually occurs about two years later. Dependable ovulation and fertility await the maturation of the hormonal controls, which takes nearly two more years.

Menopause

Most women reach the peak of their reproductive abilities in their late 20s. After that, ovarian function declines gradually, presumably because the ovaries become less and less responsive to gonadotropin signals. At the age of 30, there are still some 100,000 oocytes in the ovaries but the quality (hence fertility) has begun to decline; by the age of 50, there are probably 3 eggs left (the pantry is nearly bare). As estrogen production declines, many ovarian cycles become anovulatory, while in others 2 to 4 oocytes per month are ovulated, a sign of declining control. These increasingly frequent multiple ovulations explain why twins and triplets are more common in women who have deferred childbearing until their 30s. Menstrual periods become erratic and increasingly shorter. Eventually, ovulation and menses cease entirely. This normally occurs between the ages of 46 and 54 years, an event called menopause. **Menopause** is considered to have occurred when a whole year has passed without menstruation. As mentioned earlier, recent findings indicate that adult women generate new germ line stem cells through-

(a) 3-month fetus

(b) 7-month fetus

(c) 1-month-old infant

FIGURE 27.25 **Descent of the testes.** Sagittal sections through the pelvis of a male fetus and infant. **(a)** At 3 months, a testis begins to descend behind the peritoneum toward the inguinal region, and the vaginal process (a peritoneal extension) pushes caudally into the future scrotum (scrotal swellings). **(b)** By 7 months, the testis, accompanied by the vaginal process, descends rapidly into the scrotum via the inguinal canal. **(c)** In the one-month-old infant, descent is complete. The caudal part of the vaginal process has become the tunica vaginalis covering of the testis. The proximal portion of the vaginal process is obliterated.

out their reproductive life. If so, the question to be answered next is why these stem cells stop replenishing the oocyte supply as menopause nears. Is it simply declining levels of estrogen? Learning the answer to this question may allow menopause to be delayed if the stem cells can be stimulated to remain actively dividing in some way.

MAKING CONNECTIONS

SYSTEM CONNECTION: Homeostatic Interrelationships Between the Reproductive System and Other Body Systems

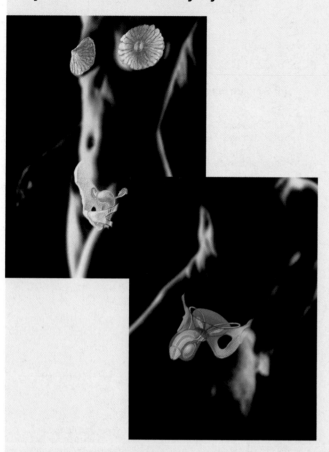

Nervous System

- Sex hormones masculinize or feminize the brain and influence sex drive
- Hypothalamus regulates timing of puberty; neural reflexes regulate events of sexual response

Endocrine System

- Gonadal hormones exert feedback effects on hypothalamic-pituitary axis; placental hormones promote maternal hypermetabolism
- Gonadotropins (and GnRH) help regulate function of gonads; leptin signals the hypothalamus about the body's state of energy availability (in fat stores)

Cardiovascular System

- Estrogens lower blood cholesterol levels and promote cardiovascular health in premenopausal women; pregnancy increases workload of the cardiovascular system
- Cardiovascular system transports needed substances to organs of reproductive system; local vasodilation involved in erection; blood transports sex hormones

Lymphatic System/Immunity

- Developing embryo/fetus escapes immune surveillance (not rejected)
- Lymphatic vessels drain leaked tissue fluids; transport sex hormones; immune cells protect reproductive organs from disease; IgA is present in breast milk

Respiratory System

- Pregnancy impairs descent of the diaphragm, promotes dyspnea
- Respiratory system provides oxygen; disposes of carbon dioxide; vital capacity and respiratory rate increase during pregnancy

Digestive System

- Digestive organs crowded by developing fetus; heartburn, constipation common during pregnancy
- Digestive system provides nutrients needed for health

Urinary System

- Hypertrophy of the prostate inhibits urination; compression of bladder during pregnancy leads to urinary frequency and urgency
- Kidneys dispose of nitrogenous wastes and maintain acid-base balance of blood of mother and fetus; semen discharged through the urethra of the male

Integumentary System

- Androgens activate oil glands that lubricate skin and hair; gonadal hormones stimulate characteristic fat distribution and appearance of pubic and axillary hair; estrogen increases skin hydration, and during pregnancy it enhances facial skin pigmentation
- Skin protects all body organs by external enclosure; mammary gland secretions (milk) nourish the infant

Skeletal System

- Androgens masculinize the skeleton and increase bone density; estrogen feminizes the skeleton and maintains bone mass in females
- The bony pelvis encloses some reproductive organs; if narrow, the bony pelvis may hinder vaginal delivery of an infant

Muscular System

- Androgens promote increase in muscle mass
- Abdominal muscles active during childbirth; muscles of the pelvic floor support reproductive organs and aid erection of penis/clitoris

THE REPRODUCTIVE SYSTEM and Interrelationships with the Endocrine, Skeletal, and Muscular Systems

The reproductive system seems to be a particularly "selfish" system—interested only in its own well-being. But when we reflect on the importance of reproduction and continuity in the scheme of things, that selfishness is a benefit, not a drawback. Indeed, the reproductive system ensures (or tries to) that a person's gene pool passes on and, rather than directing its main energy to other body systems, it builds a whole new organism. Quite an incredible feat, don't you think?

Though reproductive system interactions with other body systems are relatively meager, one—that with the endocrine system—stands out and will receive the bulk of our attention. Indeed, these two systems are difficult to divorce from one another, particularly since the gonads themselves function as endocrine organs. Most other reproductive system interactions, such as those with the nervous and cardiovascular systems, are mediated through its hormones. For example, testosterone and estrogen imprint the brain as male or female, respectively, and estrogens help stave off atherosclerosis and help keep a woman's cardiovascular system (particularly her blood vessels) youthful. The gonadal hormones also play major roles in somatic development, particularly at puberty, and these are explored below.

Endocrine System

First of all, specific endocrine organs of the body—the hypothalamus via its gonadotropin-releasing hormones and the anterior pituitary gland via FSH and LH—help orchestrate virtually all reproductive functions. Without them, the gonads would never mature to adult functional status during adolescence, gametes would not be produced, and subsequent effects mediated by gonadal hormones would fail to occur. We would forever remain sexually infantile with a childlike reproductive system. On the other hand, if testosterone were not secreted by the tiny male fetal testes, the male reproductive tract would not be formed to begin with. Furthermore, gonadal hormones produced in response to gonadotropins also help to regulate gonadotropin release (via negative and positive feedback mechanisms), as well as that of GnRH. So what we have here is an interlocking cycle in which one part cannot function without the other. On the other hand, leptin should not be forgotten because that hormonal messenger from adipose tissue alerts the hypothalamus when the young woman's body is ready for reproduction.

Skeletal and Muscular Systems

Once the reproductive system gonads are "up and running," they in turn start producing hormones that not only cause maturation of their own system's accessory organs and help maintain gametogenesis, but also are crucial for the incredible growth spurt that occurs during puberty and converts the child's body to an adult's. The most important effects are the anabolic effects exerted on bone and skeletal muscle. The skeleton becomes taller, heavier, and denser, and in females its pelvis is shaped to accommodate birth. All through a woman's reproductive years, estrogen helps maintain a healthy bone mass. (Its lack is quickly obvious after menopause.) The skeletal muscles, too, increase in size and mass, and become capable of great strength. Testosterone in particular is the muscle builder. Although the gonadal hormones do not act alone, and their effects are superimposed on those of growth hormone and thyroid hormone, they certainly promote adult stature and are responsible for the musculoskeletal changes that distinguish the sexes anatomically.

Reproductive System

Case study: We are back to look in on Mr. Heyden today. Since we last saw him (Chapter 26), he has had an X ray to try to determine the cause of his back pain, and his blood test results have come in. According to the note recorded from radiology:

- X irradiation of skeleton displays numerous carcinomatous metastases in his skull and lumbar vertebrae.

The hematology note of interest here reads:

- Serum acid phosphatase levels abnormally high.

1. What is carcinoma? What do you suppose is the primary source of the secondary carcinoma lesions in his skull and spine?

2. On what basis did you come to this conclusion?

3. What other tests might be of some diagnostic help here?

4. What type of therapy do you predict Mr. Heyden will be given to treat his carcinoma? Why?

(Answers in Appendix G)

Although ovarian estrogen production continues for a while after menopause, the ovaries finally stop functioning as endocrine organs. Without sufficient estrogen the reproductive organs and breasts begin to atrophy, the vagina becomes dry, and vaginal infections become increasingly common. Other sequels due to lack of estrogen include irritability and depression (in some); intense vasodilation of the skin's blood vessels, which causes uncomfortable, sweat-drenching "hot flashes"; gradual thinning of the skin, and loss of bone mass. Slowly rising total blood cholesterol levels and falling HDL levels place postmenopausal women at risk for cardiovascular disorders. At one time physicians prescribed low-dose estrogen-progesterone preparations to help women through this often difficult period and to prevent the skeletal and cardiovascular complications. These seemed like great bonuses and until July 2002, some 14 million American women were taking some form of estrogen-containing hormone replacement therapy (HRT). Then, on July 9, the Women's Health Initiative (WHI) abruptly ended a clinical trial of 16,000 postmenopausal women, reporting that in those taking a popular progesterone-estrogen hormone combination there was an increase of 51% in heart disease, 24% in invasive breast cancer, 31% in stroke, and a doubling of the risk of dementia compared to those taking placebos. The backlash of this finding is still spreading through physicians' offices and research labs and is restricting funding and the ability to find new volunteers for future studies. Why the effects seen in humans failed to match the lab animal studies remains to be determined, but in the meantime it has dampened enthusiasm for HRT in both the medical community and postmenopausal women.

There is no equivalent of menopause in males. While aging men do exhibit a steady decline in testosterone secretion and a longer latent period after orgasm, a male's reproductive capability seems unending. Healthy men are able to father offspring well into their eighth decade of life thanks to their small but enduring population of germ line stem cells (spermatogonia). However, there is a noticeable difference in sperm motility with aging. Sperm of a young man can make it up the uterine tubes in 20–50 minutes, whereas those of a 75-year-old take 2½ days for the same trip.

■ ■ ■

The reproductive system is unique among organ systems in at least two ways: (1) It is nonfunctional during the first 10–15 years of life, and (2) it is capable of interacting with the complementary system of another person—indeed, it *must* do so to carry out its biological function—pregnancy and birth. To be sure, having a baby is not always what the interacting partners have in mind, and we humans have devised a variety of techniques for preventing this outcome (see *A Closer Look* on p. 1128).

The major goal of the reproductive system is ensuring the healthy function of its own organs so that conditions are optimal for producing offspring. However, as illustrated in *Making Connections*, gonadal hormones do influence other body organs, and the reproductive system depends on other body systems for oxygen and nutrients and to carry away and dispose of its wastes.

Now that we know how the reproductive system functions to prepare itself for childbearing, we are ready to consider the events of pregnancy and prenatal development of a new living being, the topics of Chapter 28.

Related Clinical Terms

Dysmenorrhea (dis"men-ŏ-re'ah; *dys* = bad; *meno* = menses, a month) Painful menstruation; may reflect abnormally high prostaglandin activity during menses.

Endometrial cancer (en"do-me'tre-al; *endo* = within; *metrio* = the uterus, womb) Cancer which arises from the uterine endometrium (usually from uterine glands); the fourth most common cancer of women. Most important sign is vaginal bleeding, which allows early detection. Risk factors include obesity and HRT.

Endometriosis (en"do-me"tre-o'sis) An inflammatory condition in which endometrial tissue occurs and grows atypically in the pelvic cavity. Characterized by abnormal uterine or rectal bleeding, dysmenorrhea, and pelvic pain. May cause sterility.

Gynecology (gi"nĕ-kol'o-je; *gyneco* = woman; *ology* = study of) Specialized branch of medicine that deals with the diagnosis and treatment of female reproductive system disorders.

Gynecomastia (gi"nĕ-ko-mas'te-ah) Development of breast tissue in the male; a consequence of adrenal cortex hypersecretion of estrogens, certain drugs (cimetidine, spironolactone, and some chemotherapeutic agents), and marijuana use.

Hysterectomy (his"tĕ-rek'to-me; *hyster* = uterus; *ectomy* = cut out) Surgical removal of the uterus.

Inguinal hernia Protrusion of part of the intestine into the scrotum or through a separation in the abdominal muscles in the groin region. Since the inguinal canals represent weak points in the abdominal wall, inguinal hernia may be caused by heavy lifting or other activities that increase intra-abdominal pressure.

Laparoscopy (lap"ah-ros'ko-pe; *lapar* = the flank, *scopy* = observation) Examination of the abdominopelvic cavity with a laparoscope, a viewing device at the end of a thin tube inserted through the anterior abdominal wall. Laparoscopy is often used to assess the condition of the pelvic reproductive organs of females.

Oophorectomy (o"of-o-rek'to-me; *oophor* = ovary) Surgical removal of the ovary.

Orchitis (or-ki'tis; *orcho* = testis) Inflammation of the testes, sometimes caused by the mumps virus.

Ovarian cancer Malignancy that typically arises from the cells in the germinal epithelial covering of the ovary. The fifth most common reproductive system cancer, its incidence increases with age. Called the "disease that whispers" because early symptoms are nondescript and easily mistaken for other disorders (back pain, abdominal discomfort, nausea, bloating, and flatulence). Diagnosis may involve palpating a mass during a physical exam, visualizing it with an ultrasound probe, or conducting blood tests for a protein marker for ovarian cancer (CA-125). However, medical assessment is often delayed until after metastasis has occurred; five-year survival rate is 90% if the condition is diagnosed before metastasis.

Ovarian cysts The most common disorders of the ovary; some are tumors. Types include (1) *simple follicle retention cysts* in which single or clustered follicles become enlarged with a clear fluid; (2) *dermoid cysts,* which are filled with a thick yellow fluid and contain partially developed tissues of hair, teeth, bone, etc.; and (3) *chocolate cysts* filled with dark gelatinous material, which are the result of endometriosis of the ovary. None of these is malignant, but the latter two may become so.

Polycystic ovary syndrome (PCOS) The most common endocrinopathy in women and the most common cause of anovulatory infertility. Affects 5–10% of women; characterized by signs of androgen excess, increased cardiovascular risk (evidenced by high blood pressure, decreased HDL cholesterol levels, and high triglycerides); and linked to extreme obesity and some degree of insulin resistance. Treatment with insulin-sensitizing drugs results in a decrease in signs and symptoms of PCOS.

Salpingitis (sal"pin-ji'tis; *salpingo* = uterine tube) Inflammation of the uterine tubes.

Chapter Summary

1. The function of the reproductive system is to produce offspring. The gonads produce gametes (sperm or ova) and sex hormones. All other reproductive organs are accessory organs.

Anatomy of the Male Reproductive System (pp. 1066–1072)

The Scrotum (p. 1067)

1. The scrotum contains the testes. It provides a temperature slightly lower than that of the body, as required for viable sperm production.

The Testes (pp. 1067–1069)

2. Each testis is covered externally by a tunica albuginea that extends internally to divide the testis into many lobules. Each lobule contains sperm-producing seminiferous tubules and interstitial cells that produce androgens.

The Penis (p. 1069)

3. The penis, the male copulatory organ, is largely erectile tissue (corpus spongiosum and corpora cavernosa). Engorgement of the erectile tissue with blood causes the penis to become rigid, an event called erection.

4. The male perineum is the region encompassed by the pubic symphysis, ischial tuberosities, and coccyx.

The Male Duct System (pp. 1069–1071)

5. The epididymis hugs the external surface of the testis and serves as a site for sperm maturation and storage.

6. The ductus (vas) deferens, extending from the epididymis to the ejaculatory duct, propels sperm into the urethra by peristalsis during ejaculation. Its terminus fuses with the duct of the seminal vesicle, forming the ejaculatory duct, which empties into the urethra within the prostate.

7. The urethra extends from the urinary bladder to the tip of the penis. It conducts semen and urine to the body exterior.

Accessory Glands (pp. 1071–1072)

8. The accessory glands produce the bulk of the semen, which contains fructose from the seminal vesicles, activating fluid from the prostate, and mucus from the bulbourethral glands.

Semen (p. 1072)

9. Semen is an alkaline fluid that dilutes and transports sperm. Important chemicals in semen are nutrients, prostaglandins, and seminalplasmin. An ejaculation contains 2–5 ml of semen, with 20–150 million sperm/ml in normal adult males.

Physiology of the Male Reproductive System (pp. 1072–1082)

Male Sexual Response (pp. 1072–1073)

1. Erection is controlled by parasympathetic reflexes.

2. Ejaculation is expulsion of semen from the male duct system, promoted by the sympathetic nervous system. Ejaculation is part of male orgasm, which also includes pleasurable sensations and increased pulse and blood pressure.

Spermatogenesis (pp. 1073–1080)

3. Spermatogenesis, the production of male gametes in the seminiferous tubules, begins at puberty.

4. Meiosis, the basis of gamete production, consists of two consecutive nuclear divisions without DNA replication in between. Meiosis reduces the chromosomal number by half and introduces genetic variability. Events unique to meiosis include synapsis and crossover of homologous chromosomes.

5. Spermatogonia divide by mitosis to maintain the germ cell line. Some of their progeny become primary spermatocytes, which undergo meiosis I to produce secondary spermatocytes. Secondary spermatocytes undergo meiosis II, each producing a total of four haploid (*n*) spermatids.

6. Spermatids are converted to functional sperm by spermiogenesis, during which superfluous cytoplasm is stripped away and an acrosome and a flagellum (tail) are produced.

27

7. Sustentacular cells form the blood-testis barrier, nourish spermatogenic cells, move them toward the lumen of the tubules, and secrete fluid for sperm transport.

Hormonal Regulation of Male Reproductive Function (pp. 1080–1082)

8. GnRH, produced by the hypothalamus, stimulates the anterior pituitary gland to release FSH and LH. FSH causes sustentacular cells to produce androgen-binding protein (ABP). LH stimulates interstitial cells to release testosterone, which binds to ABP, stimulating spermatogenesis. Testosterone and inhibin (produced by sustentacular cells) feed back to inhibit the hypothalamus and anterior pituitary.

9. Maturation of hormonal controls occurs during puberty and takes about three years.

10. Testosterone stimulates maturation of the male reproductive organs and triggers the development of the secondary sex characteristics of the male. It exerts anabolic effects on the skeleton and skeletal muscles, stimulates spermatogenesis, and is responsible for sex drive.

Anatomy of the Female Reproductive System (pp. 1082–1091)

1. The female reproductive system produces gametes and sex hormones and houses a developing infant until birth.

The Ovaries   (pp. 1083–1084)

2. The ovaries flank the uterus laterally and are held in position by the ovarian and suspensory ligaments and mesovaria.

3. Within each ovary are oocyte-containing follicles at different stages of development and corpora lutea.

The Female Duct System   (pp. 1084–1088)

4. The uterine tube, supported by the mesosalpinx, extends from near the ovary to the uterus. Its fimbriated and ciliated distal end creates currents that help move an ovulated oocyte into the uterine tube. Cilia of the uterine tube mucosa help propel the oocyte toward the uterus.

5. The uterus has fundus, body, and cervical regions. It is supported by the broad, lateral cervical, uterosacral, and round ligaments.

6. The uterine wall is composed of the outer perimetrium, the myometrium, and the inner endometrium. The endometrium consists of a functional layer (stratum functionalis), which sloughs off periodically unless an embryo has implanted, and an underlying basal layer (stratum basalis), which rebuilds the functional layer.

7. The vagina extends from the uterus to the exterior. It is the copulatory organ and allows passage of the menstrual flow and a baby.

The External Genitalia   (pp. 1088–1089)

8. The female external genitalia (vulva) include the mons pubis, labia majora and minora, clitoris, and the urethral and vaginal orifices. The labia majora house the mucus-secreting greater vestibular glands.

The Mammary Glands   (pp. 1089–1091)

9. The mammary glands lie over the pectoral muscles of the chest and are surrounded by adipose and fibrous connective tissue. Each mammary gland consists of many lobules, which contain milk-producing alveoli.

Physiology of the Female Reproductive System (pp. 1091–1100)

Oogenesis   (pp. 1091–1092)

1. Oogenesis, the production of eggs, begins in the fetus. Oogonia, the diploid stem cells of female gametes, are converted to primary oocytes before birth. The infant female's ovaries contain about 2 million primary oocytes arrested in prophase of meiosis I. This view of limited oocyte potential is now being questioned.

2. At puberty, meiosis resumes. Each month, one primary oocyte completes meiosis I, producing a large secondary oocyte and a tiny first polar body. Meiosis II of the secondary oocyte produces a functional ovum and a second polar body, but does not occur unless the secondary oocyte is penetrated by a sperm.

3. The ovum contains most of the primary oocyte's cytoplasm. The polar bodies are nonfunctional and degenerate.

The Ovarian Cycle   (pp. 1093–1094)

4. During the follicular phase (days 1–14), several primary follicles begin to mature. The follicle cells proliferate and produce estrogens, and a connective tissue capsule (theca) is formed around the maturing follicle. Generally, only one follicle per month completes the maturation process and protrudes from the ovarian surface. Late in this phase, the oocyte in the dominant follicle completes meiosis I. Ovulation occurs, usually on day 14, releasing the secondary oocyte into the peritoneal cavity. Other developing follicles deteriorate.

5. In the luteal phase (days 15–28), the ruptured follicle is converted to a corpus luteum, which produces progesterone and estrogen for the remainder of the cycle. If fertilization does not occur, the corpus luteum degenerates after about ten days.

Hormonal Regulation of the Ovarian Cycle (pp. 1094–1096)

6. Beginning at puberty, the hormones of the hypothalamus, anterior pituitary, and ovaries interact to establish and regulate the ovarian cycle. Establishment of the mature cyclic pattern, indicated by menarche, takes about four years.

7. The hormonal events of each ovarian cycle are as follows: (1) GnRH stimulates the anterior pituitary to release FSH and LH, which stimulate follicle maturation and estrogen production. (2) When blood estrogen reaches a certain level, positive feedback exerted on the hypothalamic-pituitary axis causes a sudden release of LH that stimulates the primary oocyte to continue meiosis and triggers ovulation. LH then causes conversion of the ruptured follicle to a corpus luteum and stimulates its secretory activity. (3) Rising levels of progesterone and estrogen inhibit the hypothalamic-pituitary axis, the corpus luteum deteriorates, ovarian hormones drop to their lowest levels, and the cycle begins anew.

The Uterine (Menstrual) Cycle   (pp. 1096–1098)

8. Varying levels of ovarian hormones in the blood trigger events of the uterine cycle.

9. During the menstrual phase of the uterine cycle (days 1–5), the functional layer sloughs off in menses. During the proliferative phase (days 6–14), rising estrogen levels stimulate its regeneration, making the uterus receptive to implantation about one week after ovulation. During the secretory phase (days 15–28), the uterine glands secrete glycogen, and endometrial vascularity increases further.

10. Falling levels of ovarian hormones during the last few days of the ovarian cycle cause the spiral arteries to become spastic and cut off the blood supply of the functional layer, and the uterine cycle begins again with menstruation.

Extrauterine Effects of Estrogens and Progesterone (p. 1098)

11. Estrogen promotes oogenesis. At puberty, it stimulates the growth of the reproductive organs and the growth spurt and promotes the appearance of the secondary sex characteristics.

12. Progesterone cooperates with estrogen in breast maturation and regulation of the uterine cycle.

Female Sexual Response   (pp. 1098–1100)

13. The female sexual response is similar to that of males. Orgasm in females is not accompanied by ejaculation and is not necessary for conception.

Sexually Transmitted Diseases   (pp. 1100–1101)

1. Sexually transmitted diseases (STDs) are infectious diseases spread via sexual contact. Gonorrhea, syphilis, chlamydia, and some forms of vaginitis are bacterial diseases; if untreated, they can cause sterility. Syphilis has broader consequences than most other sexually transmitted bacterial diseases since it can infect organs throughout the body. Trichomoniasis is a parasitic infection. Genital herpes and genital warts are viral infections implicated in cervical cancer. AIDS, a condition of immune suppression, can also be transmitted sexually.

Developmental Aspects of the Reproductive System: Chronology of Sexual Development (pp. 1101–1105, 1108)

Embryological and Fetal Events   (pp. 1101–1104)

1. Genetic sex is determined by the sex chromosomes: an X from the mother, an X or a Y from the father. If the fertilized egg contains XX, it is a female and develops ovaries; if it contains XY, it is a male and develops testes.

2. Gonads of both sexes arise from the mesodermal gonadal ridges. The mesonephric ducts produce the male accessory ducts and glands. The paramesonephric ducts produce the female duct system.

3. The external genitalia arise from the genital tubercle and associated structures. The development of male accessory structures and external genitalia depends on the presence of testosterone produced by the embryonic testes. In its absence, female structures develop.

4. The testes form in the abdominal cavity and descend into the scrotum.

Puberty   (pp. 1104–1105)

5. Puberty is the interval when reproductive organs mature and become functional. It begins in males with penile and scrotal growth and in females with breast development. Leptin serves a permissive role in puberty's onset, stimulating the hypothalamus when adipose tissue is sufficient for the energy requirements of reproduction.

Menopause   (pp. 1105, 1108)

6. During menopause, ovarian function declines, and ovulation and menstruation cease. Hot flashes and mood changes may occur. Postmenopausal events include atrophy of the reproductive organs, bone mass loss, and increasing risk for cardiovascular disease.

Review Questions

Multiple Choice/Matching

(Some questions have more than one correct answer. Select the best answer or answers from the choices given.)

1. The structures that draw an ovulated oocyte into the female duct system are (a) cilia, (b) fimbriae, (c) microvilli, (d) stereocilia.

2. The usual site of embryo implantation is (a) the uterine tube, (b) the peritoneal cavity, (c) the vagina, (d) the uterus.

3. The male homologue of the female clitoris is (a) the penis, (b) the scrotum, (c) the penile urethra, (d) the testis.

4. Which of the following is correct relative to female anatomy? (a) The vaginal orifice is the most dorsal of the three openings in the perineum, (b) the urethra is between the vaginal orifice and the anus, (c) the anus is between the vaginal orifice and the urethra, (d) the urethra is the more ventral of the two orifices in the vulva.

5. Secondary sex characteristics are (a) present in the embryo, (b) a result of male or female sex hormones increasing in amount at puberty, (c) the testis in the male and the ovary in the female, (d) not subject to withdrawal once established.

6. Which of the following produces the male sex hormones? (a) seminal vesicles, (b) corpus luteum, (c) developing follicles of the testes, (d) interstitial cells.

7. Which will occur as a result of nondescent of the testes? (a) Male sex hormones will not be circulated in the body, (b) sperm will have no means of exit from the body, (c) inadequate blood supply will retard the development of the testes, (d) viable sperm will not be produced.

8. The normal diploid number of human chromosomes is (a) 48, (b) 47, (c) 46, (d) 23, (e) 24.

9. Relative to differences between mitosis and meiosis, choose the statements that apply *only* to events of meiosis. (a) tetrads present, (b) produces two daughter cells, (c) produces four daughter cells, (d) occurs throughout life, (e) reduces the chromosomal number by half, (f) synapsis and crossover of homologues occur.

10. Match the key choices with the descriptive phrases below.

Key: **(a)** androgen-binding protein   **(e)** inhibin
(b) estrogens   **(f)** LH
(c) FSH   **(g)** progesterone
(d) GnRh   **(h)** testosterone

_____ **(1)** Hormones that directly regulate the ovarian cycle

_____ **(2)** Chemicals in males that inhibit the pituitary-testicular axis

_____ **(3)** Hormone that makes the cervical mucus viscous

_____ **(4)** Potentiates the activity of testosterone on spermatogenic cells

_____ **(5)** In females, exerts feedback inhibition on the hypothalamus and anterior pituitary

_____ **(6)** Stimulates the secretion of testosterone

11. The menstrual cycle can be divided into three continuous phases. Starting from the first day of the cycle, their consecutive order is (a) menstrual, proliferative, secretory, (b) menstrual, secretory, proliferative, (c) secretory, menstrual, proliferative, (d) proliferative, menstrual, secretory, (e) secretory, proliferative, menstrual.

12. Spermatozoa are to seminiferous tubules as oocytes are to (a) fimbriae, (b) corpus albicans, (c) ovarian follicles, (d) corpora lutea.

13. Which of the following does not add a secretion that makes a major contribution to semen? (a) prostate, (b) bulbourethral glands, (c) testes, (d) vas deferens.

14. The corpus luteum is formed at the site of (a) fertilization, (b) ovulation, (c) menstruation, (d) implantation.

15. The sex of a child is determined by (a) the sex chromosome contained in the sperm, (b) the sex chromosome contained in the oocyte, (c) the number of sperm fertilizing the oocyte, (d) the position of the fetus in the uterus.

16. FSH is to estrogen as estrogen is to (a) progesterone, (b) LH, (c) FSH, (d) testosterone.

17. A drug that "reminds the pituitary" to produce gonadotropins might be useful as (a) a contraceptive, (b) a diuretic, (c) a fertility drug, (d) an abortion stimulant.

Short Answer Essay Questions

18. Why is the term *urogenital system* more applicable to males than to females?

19. The spermatid is haploid, but it is not a functional gamete. Name and describe the process during which a spermatid is converted to a motile sperm, and describe the major structural (and functional) regions of a sperm.

20. Oogenesis in the female results in one functional gamete—the egg, or ovum. What other cells are produced? What is the significance of this rather wasteful type of gamete production—that is, production of a single functional gamete instead of four, as seen in males?

21. List three secondary sex characteristics of females.

22. Describe the events and possible consequences of menopause.

23. Define menarche. What does it indicate?

24. Trace the pathway of a sperm from the male testes to the uterine tube of a female.

25. In menstruation, the stratum functionalis is shed from the endometrium. Explain the hormonal and physical factors responsible for this shedding. (Hint: See Figure 27.22.)

26. Both the epithelium of the vagina and the cervical glands of the uterus help prevent the invasion and spread of vaginal pathogens. Explain how each of these mechanisms works.

27. Some anatomy students were saying that the bulbourethral glands of males act like city workers who come around and clear parked cars from the street before a parade. What did they mean by this analogy?

28. A man swam in a cold lake for an hour and then noticed that his scrotum was shrunken and wrinkled. His first thought was that he had lost his testicles. What had really happened?

Critical Thinking and Clinical Application Questions

1. Gina Marciano, a 44-year-old mother of eight children, visited her physician complaining of a "bearing down" sensation in her pelvis, low backache, and urinary incontinence. A vaginal examination showed that the external os of her cervix was just inside the vaginal orifice and her perineum exhibited large keloids. Her history revealed that she was a member of a commune located in the nearby mountains that shunned hospital births (if at all possible). What do you think Gina's problem is and what caused it? (Be anatomically specific.)

2. Harry, a sexually active adolescent, appeared in the emergency room complaining of a penile "drip" and pain in urination. An account of his recent sexual behavior was requested and recorded. (a) What do you think Harry's problem is? (b) What is the causative agent of this disorder? (c) How is the condition treated, and what may happen if it isn't treated?

3. A 36-year-old mother of four is considering tubal ligation as a means of ensuring that her family gets no larger. She asks the physician if she will become "menopausal" after the surgery. (a) How would you answer her question and explain away her concerns? (b) Explain what a tubal ligation is.

4. Mr. Scanlon, a 76-year-old gentleman, is interested in a much younger woman. Concerned because of his age, he asks his urologist if he will be able to father a child. What questions would a physician ask of this man, and what diagnostic tests would be ordered?

5. Lucy had both her left ovary and her right uterine tube removed surgically at age 17 because of a cyst and a tumor in these organs. Now, at age 32, she remains healthy and is expecting her second child. How could Lucy conceive a child with just one ovary and one uterine tube, widely separated on opposite sides of the pelvis like this?

> **LOOKING FOR MORE STUDY HELP?**
> A wide variety of quiz questions, tutorials, and learning exercises are available online at the Anatomy & Physiology Place (www.anatomyandphysiology.com) and, if your instructor has provided you with a MyA&P Course ID number, in MyA&P (www.myaandp.com).

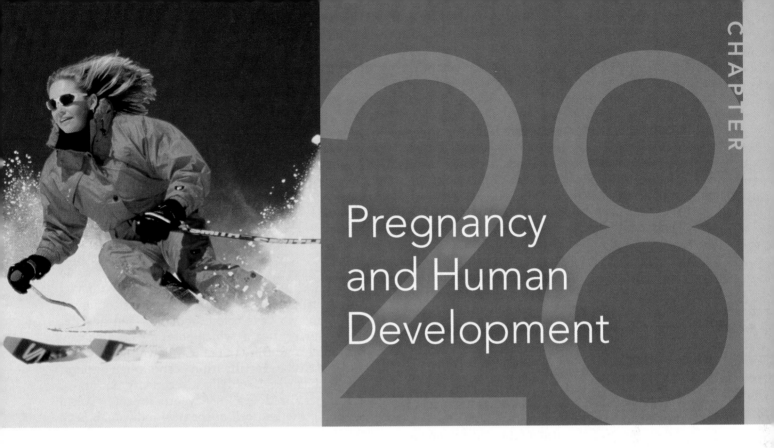

CHAPTER 28

Pregnancy and Human Development

From Egg to Zygote (pp. 1114–1117)

1. Describe the importance of sperm capacitation.
2. Explain the mechanism of the slow block to polyspermy.
3. Define fertilization.

Events of Embryonic Development: Zygote to Blastocyst Implantation (pp. 1117–1122)

4. Explain the process and product of cleavage.
5. Describe implantation and placenta formation, and list placental functions.

Events of Embryonic Development: Gastrula to Fetus (pp. 1122–1132)

6. Describe gastrulation and its consequence.
7. Name and describe the formation, location, and function of the extraembryonic membranes.

8. Define organogenesis and indicate the important roles of the three primary germ layers in this process.
9. Describe unique features of the fetal circulation.

Events of Fetal Development (p. 1133)

10. Indicate the duration of the fetal period, and note the major events of fetal development.

Effects of Pregnancy on the Mother (pp. 1133–1135)

11. Describe functional changes in maternal reproductive organs and in the cardiovascular, respiratory, and urinary systems during pregnancy.
12. Indicate the effects of pregnancy on maternal metabolism and posture.

Parturition (Birth) (pp. 1135–1137)

13. Explain how labor is initiated, and describe the three stages of labor.

Adjustments of the Infant to Extrauterine Life (pp. 1137–1138)

14. Outline the events leading to the first breath of a newborn.
15. Describe changes that occur in the fetal circulation after birth.

Lactation (pp. 1138–1139)

16. Explain how the breasts are prepared for lactation.

Assisted Reproductive Technology and Reproductive Cloning (pp. 1139–1140)

17. Describe some techniques of ART including IVF, ZIFT, and GIFT.

Because the birth of a baby is such a familiar event, we tend to lose sight of the wonder of this accomplishment: How does a single cell, the fertilized egg, grow to become a complex human being consisting of trillions of cells? The details of this process can fill a good-sized book. Our intention here is simply to outline the important events of gestation and to consider briefly the events occurring immediately after birth.

To get started, we need to define some terms. The term **pregnancy** refers to events that occur from the time of fertilization (conception) until the infant is born. The pregnant woman's developing offspring is called the **conceptus** (kon-sep′tus; "that which is conceived"). The time during which development occurs is referred to as the **gestation period** (*gestare* = to carry) and extends by convention from the last menstrual period (a date the woman is likely to remember) until birth, approximately 280 days. Thus, at the moment of fertilization, the mother is officially (but illogically) two weeks pregnant! From fertilization through week 8, the *embryonic period,* the conceptus is called an **embryo,** and from week 9 through birth, the *fetal period,* the conceptus is called a **fetus** ("the young in the womb"). At birth, it is an infant. Figure 28.1 shows the changing size and shape of the conceptus as it progresses from fertilization to the early fetal stage.

From Egg to Zygote

Accomplishing Fertilization

Before fertilization can occur, sperm must reach the ovulated secondary oocyte. The oocyte is viable for 12 to 24 hours after it is cast out of the ovary; the chance of pregnancy drops to almost zero the next day. Most sperm retain their fertilizing power for 24 to 48 hours after ejaculation. Consequently, for successful fertilization to occur, coitus must occur no more than two days before ovulation and no later than 24 hours after, at which point the oocyte is approximately one-third of the way down the length of the uterine tube. **Fertilization** occurs when a sperm fuses with an egg (actually a secondary oocyte) to form a fertilized egg, or **zygote** (zi′gōt; "yoked together"), the first cell of the new individual. Let's look at the events leading to fertilization.

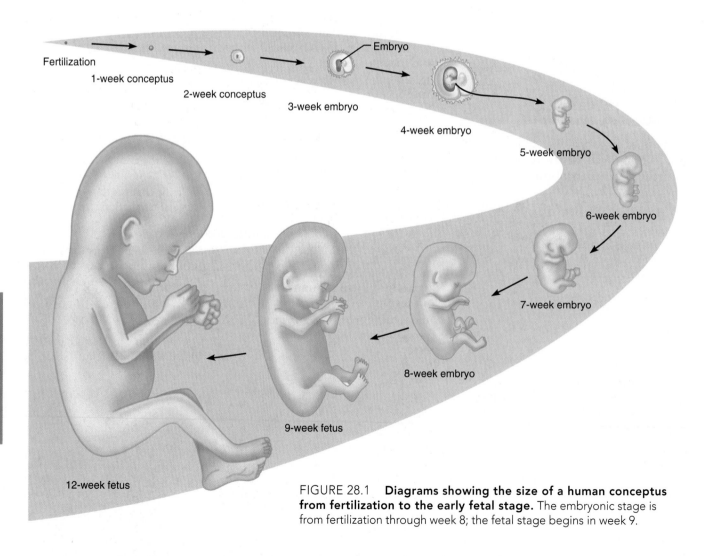

Fertilization

1-week conceptus

2-week conceptus

3-week embryo

Embryo

4-week embryo

5-week embryo

6-week embryo

7-week embryo

8-week embryo

9-week fetus

12-week fetus

FIGURE 28.1 **Diagrams showing the size of a human conceptus from fertilization to the early fetal stage.** The embryonic stage is from fertilization through week 8; the fetal stage begins in week 9.

Sperm Transport and Capacitation

During copulation, a man expels millions of sperm with considerable force into his partner's vaginal canal. Despite this "head start," most sperm don't reach the oocyte, even though it is only about 5 inches away. Millions of sperm leak from the vagina almost immediately after being deposited there. Of those remaining, millions more are destroyed by the vagina's acidic environment and, unless the thick "curtain" of cervical mucus has been made fluid by estrogens, millions more fail to make it through the cervix. Those that do reach the uterus by their whip-like tail movements are then subjected to forceful uterine contractions that act in a washing machine-like manner to disperse them throughout the uterine cavity, where thousands more are destroyed by resident phagocytes. Only a few thousand (and sometimes fewer than 200) sperm, out of the millions in the male ejaculate, are conducted by reverse peristalsis into and up the uterine tubes, where the oocyte may be moving leisurely toward the uterus.

These difficulties aside, there is still another hurdle to overcome. Sperm freshly deposited in the vagina are incapable of penetrating an oocyte. They must first be **capacitated** over the next 6 to 8 hours; that is, their mobility is enhanced and their membranes must become fragile so that the hydrolytic enzymes in their acrosomes can be released. As sperm swim through the cervical mucus, uterus, and uterine tubes, secretions of the female tract cause some of their membrane proteins to be removed, and the cholesterol that keeps their acrosomal membranes "tough" and stable is depleted. Thus, even though the sperm may reach the oocyte within a few minutes, they must "wait around" (so to speak) for capacitation to occur. This is an elaborate mechanism for preventing the spilling of acrosomal enzymes. But consider the alternative—fragile acrosomal membranes in the male reproductive tract could rupture prematurely, causing some degree of autolysis (self-digestion) of the male reproductive system.

How sperm navigate to find a released oocyte in the uterine tube is an area of active research. It now appears that they "sniff" their way to the oocyte. Sperm are known to bear proteins called *olfactory receptors* that respond to chemical stimuli and it is presumed that the oocyte or its surrounding cells release signaling molecules that direct the sperm.

Acrosomal Reaction and Sperm Penetration

The ovulated oocyte is encapsulated by the corona radiata and the deeper zona pellucida, a transparent layer of glycoprotein-rich extracellular matrix secreted by the oocyte, and both must be breached before the oocyte can be penetrated. Once a sperm gets to the immediate vicinity of the oocyte, it penetrates the corona radiata, assisted by a cell-surface hyaluronidase that digests the intercellular cement between the granulosa cells in the immediate area, causing them to fall away from the oocyte. After breaching the corona, the sperm head binds to the ZP3 glycoprotein of the zona pellucida, which functions as a sperm receptor and helps trigger the acrosomal (ak′ro-som-al) reaction. The **acrosomal reaction** involves the breakdown of the plasma membrane and the acrosomal membrane, and release of acrosomal enzymes (acrosin, proteases, and others) which digest holes through the zona pellucida (Figure 28.2). Hundreds of acrosomes must undergo exocytosis to digest holes in the zona pellucida. This is one case that does not bear out the adage, "The early bird catches the worm." A sperm that comes along later, after hundreds of sperm have undergone acrosomal reactions to expose the oocyte membrane, is in the best position to be *the* fertilizing sperm.

Once a path has been cleared and a single sperm fuses with the oocyte's membrane receptors, its nucleus is pulled into the oocyte cytoplasm (Figure 28.2a). Each sperm carries a special two-part binding apparatus on its surface. The *beta protein* part acts first as it binds to a receptor on the oocyte membrane. This event engages the *alpha protein* part, causing it to insert into the membrane. This somehow causes the egg and sperm membranes to open and fuse together with such perfect contact that the contents of both cells are combined within a single membrane—all without spilling a drop. Interestingly, the region of the oocyte where the sperm enters determines the future right and left axes of the embryo's body.

Blocks to Polyspermy

Polyspermy (entry of several sperm into an egg) occurs in some animals, but in humans only one sperm is allowed to penetrate the oocyte, ensuring **monospermy,** the one-sperm-per-oocyte condition. Once the sperm has entered the oocyte, waves of Ca^{2+} are released by the oocyte's endoplasmic reticulum into its cytoplasm, which activates the oocyte to prepare for cell division. These calcium surges also cause the **cortical reaction** (see Figure 28.2a), in which granules located just inside the plasma membrane spill their enzymes into the extracellular space beneath the zona pellucida. These enzymes, called *zonal inhibiting proteins (ZIPs)*, destroy the sperm receptors, preventing further sperm entry. Additionally, the spilled material binds water, and as it swells it detaches all sperm still bound to receptors on the oocyte membrane, accomplishing the so-called *slow block to polyspermy*. In rare cases of polyspermy that do occur, the embryos contain too much genetic material and are nonviable (die).

Completion of Meiosis II and Fertilization

After a sperm enters the oocyte it loses its tail and midpiece, and the centrosome in its midpiece elaborates microtubules which the sperm uses to find the oocyte nucleus. The sperm then locomotes its

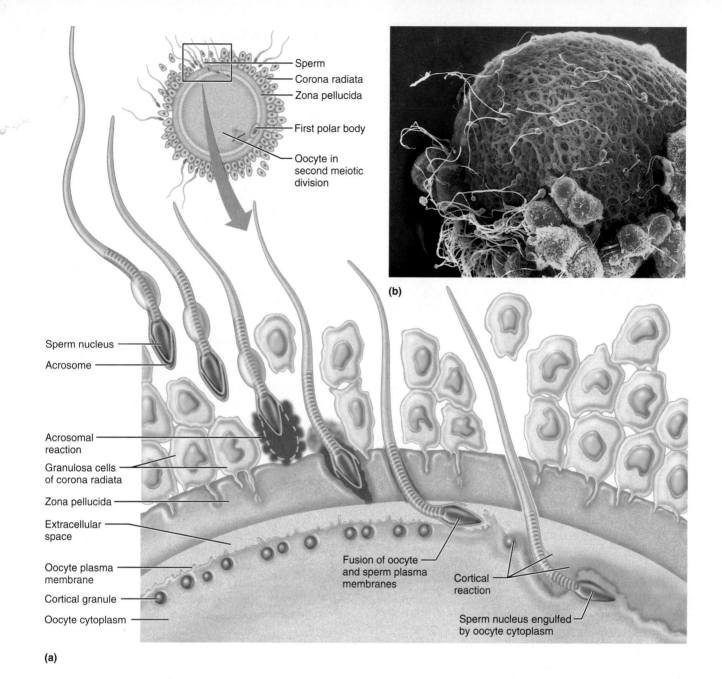

Sperm
Corona radiata
Zona pellucida

First polar body

Oocyte in
second meiotic
division

(b)

Sperm nucleus
Acrosome

Acrosomal
reaction

Granulosa cells
of corona radiata

Zona pellucida

Extracellular
space

Oocyte plasma
membrane

Cortical granule

Oocyte cytoplasm

Fusion of oocyte
and sperm plasma
membranes

Cortical
reaction

Sperm nucleus engulfed
by oocyte cytoplasm

(a)

FIGURE 28.2 **Sperm penetration and the cortical reaction (slow block to polyspermy). (a)** The sequential steps of oocyte penetration by a sperm are depicted from left to right. Sperm penetration through the corona radiata and zona pellucida is accomplished by a surface-bound hyaluronidase, and by release of acrosomal enzymes by many sperm. Fusion of the plasma membrane of a single sperm with the oocyte membrane is followed by engulfment of the sperm by the oocyte cytoplasm and the cortical reaction (release of cortical granules' contents into the extracellular space) preventing the entry of more than one sperm. **(b)** Scanning electron micrograph of human sperm surrounding a human oocyte (650×). The smaller spherical cells are granulosa cells of the corona radiata.

DNA-rich nucleus toward the oocyte, its nucleus swelling to about five times its normal size to form the **male pronucleus** (pro-nu'kle-us; *pro* = before) on the way. Meanwhile the secondary oocyte, stimulated into activity by the calcium surges, completes meiosis II, forming the ovum nucleus and the second polar body (Figure 28.3a and b). This accomplished, the ovum nucleus swells, becoming the **female pronucleus,** and the two pronuclei approach each other. A mitotic spindle develops between them (Figure 28.3c), and the pronuclei membranes rupture,

releasing their chromosomes into the immediate vicinity of the newly formed spindle. The true moment of fertilization occurs as the maternal and paternal chromosomes combine and produce the diploid *zygote,* or fertilized egg (Figure 28.3d).* Almost as soon as the male and female pronuclei

---

* Some sources define the term *fertilization* simply as the act of oocyte penetration by the sperm. However, unless the chromosomes in the male and female pronuclei are actually joined, the zygote is never formed in humans.

come together, their chromosomes replicate. Then, the first mitotic division of the conceptus begins (Figure 28.3d–f).

Events of Embryonic Development: Zygote to Blastocyst Implantation

Embryonic development begins with fertilization and continues as the embryo travels through the uterine tube, floats free in the cavity of the uterus, and finally implants in the uterine wall. Significant events of this early embryonic period are *cleavage,* which produces a structure called a blastocyst, and *implantation* of the blastocyst.

Cleavage and Blastocyst Formation

Cleavage is a period of fairly rapid mitotic divisions of the zygote following fertilization (Figure 28.4). Cleavage produces small cells with a high surface-to-volume ratio, which enhances their uptake of nutrients and oxygen and the disposal of wastes. It also provides a large number of cells to serve as building blocks for constructing the embryo. Consider, for a moment, the difficulty of trying to construct a building from one huge block of granite. If you now consider how much easier it would be if instead you could use hundreds of bricks, you will quickly grasp the importance of cleavage.

Some 36 hours after fertilization, the first cleavage division has produced two identical cells called *blastomeres.* These divide to produce four cells, then eight, and so on. By 72 hours after fertilization, a loose collection of cells that form a berry-shaped cluster of 16 or more cells called the **morula** (mor′u-lah; "little mulberry") has been formed. All the while, transport of the embryo toward the uterus continues. By day 3 or 4 after fertilization, the embryo consists

FIGURE 28.3 **Events immediately following sperm penetration. (a)** Once a sperm has entered the secondary oocyte, the oocyte completes meiosis II, forming the ovum nucleus and casting out the second polar body. The first polar body formed in the first meiotic division may also undergo division, producing two more polar bodies. **(b, c)** The ovum nucleus formed during meiosis II swells, and the sperm and egg nuclei (pronuclei) approach each other. **(d–g)** As the male and female pronuclei come together (fertilization), their DNA replicates. Chromosomes then form, attach to the mitotic spindle, and undergo a mitotic division. This division is the first cleavage division and results in two daughter cells. **(h)** Scanning electron micrograph of a fertilized egg (zygote). Notice the second polar body protruding at the right. A single sperm is seen against the zygote's surface (500×).

(a)

- Sperm
- Extracellular space
- Second meiotic division of oocyte
- Second meiotic division of first polar body
- Corona radiata
- Zona pellucida

(b)

- Detached sperm tail
- Sperm pro-nucleus
- Ovum nucleus
- Polar bodies

(c)

- Male pronucleus
- Mitotic spindle
- Centriole
- Female pronucleus

(d)

- Zygote

(e)

- Sperm and ovum chromosomes

(f)

- Anaphase of first cleavage division

(g)

- Daughter cells

(h)

28

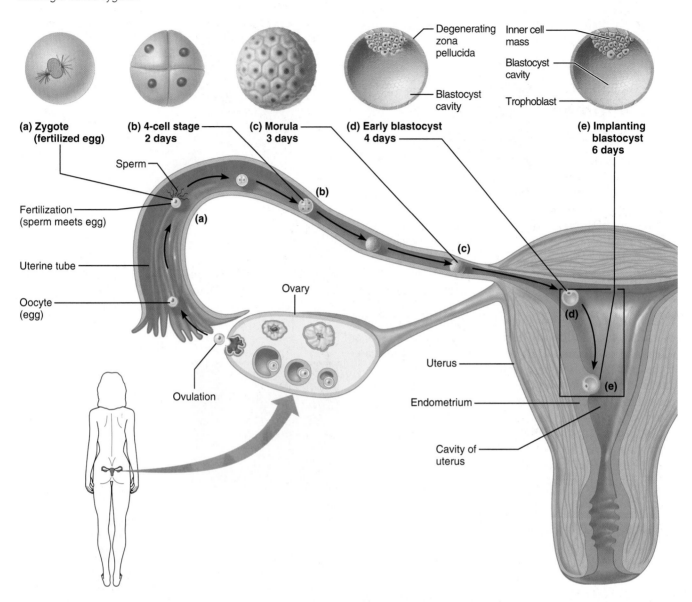

(a) Zygote (fertilized egg)

(b) 4-cell stage 2 days

(c) Morula 3 days

(d) Early blastocyst 4 days

Degenerating zona pellucida

Blastocyst cavity

Inner cell mass

Blastocyst cavity

Trophoblast

(e) Implanting blastocyst 6 days

Sperm

Fertilization (sperm meets egg)

(a)

(b)

Uterine tube

Oocyte (egg)

Ovary

Ovulation

(c)

(d)

(e)

Uterus

Endometrium

Cavity of uterus

FIGURE 28.4 **Cleavage from zygote to blastocyst.** The zygote begins to divide about 24 hours after fertilization, and continues the rapid mitotic divisions of cleavage as it travels down the uterine tube. Three to four days after ovulation, the embryo reaches the uterus and floats freely for two to three days, nourished by secretions of the endometrial glands. At the late blastocyst stage, the embryo is implanting into the endometrium; this begins at about day 7 after ovulation. **(a)** Zygote. **(b)** Four-cell stage. **(c)** Morula, a solid ball of blastomeres. **(d)** Early blastocyst; the morula hollows out, fills with fluid, and "hatches" from the zona pellucida. **(e)** Late blastocyst, composed of an outer sphere of trophoblast cells and an eccentric cell cluster called the inner cell mass.

of about 100 cells and floats free in the uterus. By this time, it has tightened its connections between neighboring cells (a process called *compaction*) and begins accumulating fluid within an internal cavity. The zona pellucida now starts to break down and the inner structure, now called a blastocyst, "hatches" from it. The **blastocyst** (blas'to-sist) is a fluid-filled hollow sphere composed of a single layer of large, flattened cells called **trophoblast cells** (trof'o-blast) and a small cluster of 20 to 30 rounded cells, called the **inner cell mass,** located at one side (Figure 28.4e). Trophoblast cells begin to display L-selectin (adhesion) molecules on their surface soon after the blastocyst hatching. They also take part in placenta formation, a fact hinted at by the literal translation of "trophoblast" (nourishment generator), and secrete and display several factors with immunosuppressive effects that protect the trophoblast (hence the developing embryo)

A *Because virtually no growth occurs between the successive divisions of cleavage.*

FIGURE 28.5 **Implantation of the blastocyst. (a)** View of a blastocyst that has just adhered to the uterine endometrium. **(b)** Slightly later stage of an implanting embryo (approximately seven days after ovulation), depicting the cytotrophoblast and syncytiotrophoblast of the eroding trophoblast. **(c)** Light micrograph of an implanted blastocyst (approximately 12 days after ovulation) (60×).

from attack by the mother's cells. The inner cell mass becomes the **embryonic disc,** which forms the embryo proper (and the extraembryonic membranes except the chorion, a trophoblast derivative).

Implantation

While the blastocyst floats in the uterine cavity for two to three days, it receives nourishment from glycogen-rich uterine secretions. Then, some six to seven days after ovulation, given a properly prepared endometrium, **implantation** begins. The receptivity of the endometrium to implantation—the so-called *window of implantation*—is opened by the surging levels of ovarian hormones (estrogens and progesterone) in the blood. If the mucosa is properly prepared, integrin and selectin proteins on the trophoblast cells bind respectively to the extracellular matrix components (collagen, fibronectin, laminin, and others) of the endometrial cells and to selectin-binding carbohydrates on the inner uterine wall, and the blastocyst implants high in the uterus. If the endometrium is not yet optimally mature, the blastocyst detaches and floats to a lower level, implanting when it finds a site with the proper receptors and chemical signals. The trophoblast cells overlying the inner cell mass adhere to the endometrium (Figure 28.5a) and secrete digestive enzymes and growth factors against

the endometrial surface. The endometrium quickly thickens at the point of contact and takes on characteristics of an acute inflammatory response—the uterine blood vessels become more permeable and leaky, and inflammatory cells including lymphocytes, natural killer cells, and macrophages invade the area. The trophoblast then proliferates and forms two distinct layers (Figure 28.5b). The cells in the inner layer, collectively called the **cytotrophoblast** (si"to-trof'o-blast) or **cellular trophoblast,** retain their cell boundaries. The cells in the outer layer lose their plasma membranes and form a multinuclear cytoplasmic mass called the **syncytiotrophoblast** (sin-sit"e-o-trof'o-blast; *syn* = together, *cyt* = cell) or **syncytial trophoblast,** which invades the endometrium and rapidly digests the uterine cells it contacts. As the endometrium is eroded, the blastocyst burrows into this thick, velvety lining and is surrounded by a pool of blood leaked from degraded endometrial blood vessels. Shortly, the implanted blastocyst is covered over and sealed off from the uterine cavity by proliferation of the endometrial cells (Figure 28.5c).

In cases where implantation fails to occur, a receptive uterus becomes nonreceptive once again. It is estimated that a minimum of two-thirds of all zygotes formed fail to implant by the end of the first week or spontaneously abort. Moreover, an estimated 30% of implanted embryos later miscarry.

28

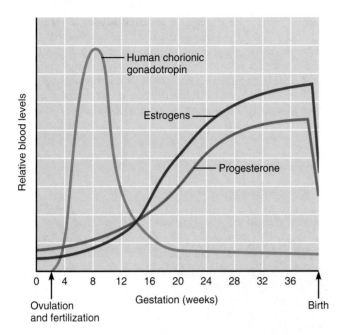

FIGURE 28.6   Hormonal changes during pregnancy.
The relative changes in maternal blood levels of three hormones that maintain pregnancy are depicted, rather than actual blood concentrations.

luteum to continue secreting progesterone and estrogen. The *chorion*, which develops from the trophoblast after implantation, continues this hormonal stimulus; thus, the developing conceptus takes over the hormonal control of the uterus during this early phase of development. Usually detectable in the mother's blood one week after fertilization, blood levels of hCG rise until the end of the second month and then decline sharply by four months to reach a low value, which persists for the remainder of gestation (Figure 28.6). Between the second and third month, the placenta (described next) assumes the role of progesterone and estrogen production for the remainder of the pregnancy. The corpus luteum then degenerates and the ovaries remain inactive until after birth. All pregnancy tests used today are antibody tests that detect hCG in a woman's blood or urine.

Initially, the implanted embryo obtains its nutrition by digesting the endometrial cells, but by the second month, the placenta is providing nutrients and oxygen to the embryo and carrying away embryonic metabolic wastes. Since placenta formation is a continuation of the events of implantation, we will consider it next, although we will be getting ahead of ourselves a little as far as embryonic development is concerned.

Placentation

Placentation (plas″en-ta′shun) refers to the formation of a **placenta** ("flat cake"), a temporary organ that originates from both embryonic and maternal (endometrial) tissues. Cells from the original inner cell mass give rise to a layer of extraembryonic mesoderm that lines the inner surface of the trophoblast (Figure 28.7b); together these become the **chorion.** The chorion develops fingerlike **chorionic villi**

When successful, implantation takes about five days and is usually completed by the 12th day after ovulation—just before the endometrium normally begins to slough off in menses. Obviously, menses would flush away the embryo as well and must be prevented if the pregnancy is to continue. Viability of the corpus luteum is maintained by an LH-like hormone called **human chorionic gonadotropin (hCG)** (ko″re-on′ik go-nad″o-trōp′in) secreted by the trophoblast cells. hCG bypasses pituitary-ovarian controls at this critical time and prompts the corpus

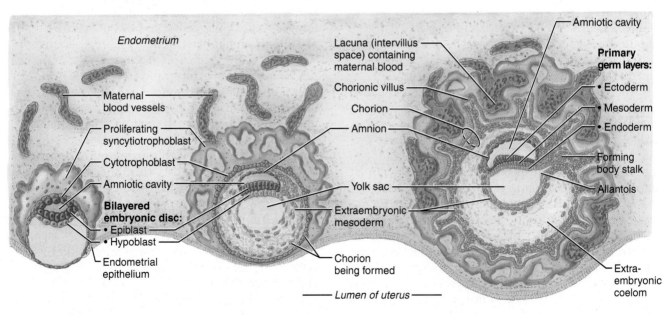

(a) 7½-day implanting blastocyst   **(b) 12-day implanted blastocyst**   **(c) 16-day embryo**

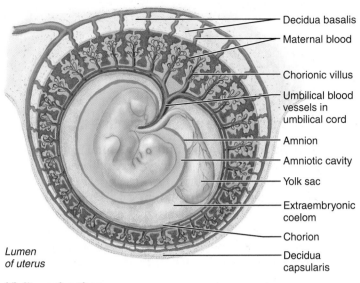

(d) 4½-week embryo

Labels for (d):
- Decidua basalis
- Maternal blood
- Chorionic villus
- Umbilical blood vessels in umbilical cord
- Amnion
- Amniotic cavity
- Yolk sac
- Extraembryonic coelom
- Chorion
- Decidua capsularis
- Lumen of uterus

(e) 7-week embryo

Labels for (e):
- Amniotic sac
- Umbilical cord
- Umbilical vein
- Chorionic villi
- Yolk sac
- Cut edge of chorion

(f) 13-week fetus

Labels for (f):
- Placenta
- Decidua basalis
- Chorionic villi
- Yolk sac
- Amnion
- Amniotic cavity
- Umbilical cord
- Decidua capsularis
- Extraembryonic coelom
- Uterus
- Lumen of uterus

(g)

Labels for (g):
- Maternal arteries
- Maternal veins
- Myometrium
- Stratum basalis of endometrium
- Maternal portion of placenta (decidua basalis)
- Fetal portion of placenta (chorion)
- Chorionic villus containing fetal capillaries
- Maternal blood in lacuna (intervillus space)
- Fetal arteriole
- Fetal venule
- Amnion
- Umbilical cord
- Umbilical arteries
- Umbilical vein
- Connection to yolk sac

FIGURE 28.7 **Events of placentation, early embryonic development, and extraembryonic membrane formation.** Times given refer to the age of the conceptus, which is typically 2 weeks "younger" than the gestation age. **(a)** Implanting blastocyst. Endometrial erosion by the syncytiotrophoblast is ongoing, and cells of the embryonic disc are now separated by a fluid-filled space from the amnion. **(b)** Implantation is completed by day 12 and extraembryonic mesoderm is forming a discrete layer beneath the cytotrophoblast. **(c)** By day 16, the cytotrophoblast and associated mesoderm have become the chorion, and chorionic villi are elaborating. The embryo exhibits all three germ layers, a yolk sac (formed by endodermal cells), and an allantois, an outpocketing abutting the yolk sac that forms the structural basis of the body stalk, or umbilical cord. **(d)** At 4½ weeks, the decidua capsularis and decidua basalis are well formed. The chorionic villi lie in blood-filled intervillus spaces within the endometrium. Organogenesis is occurring in the embryo, which is now receiving its nutrition via the umbilical vessels that connect it (via the body stalk) to the placenta. The amnion and yolk sac are well developed. **(e)** A 7-week embryo and the extraembryonic membranes that will contribute to the placenta (at right). **(f)** 13-week fetus. **(g)** Detailed anatomy of the vascular relationships in the mature decidua basalis. This state of development has been accomplished by the end of the third month of development.

28

(Figure 28.7c), which are especially elaborate where they are in contact with maternal blood. Soon the mesodermal cores of the chorionic villi become richly vascularized by newly forming blood vessels, which extend to the embryo via the allantois as the umbilical arteries and vein. The continuing erosion produces large, blood-filled **lacunae,** or **intervillus spaces,** in the stratum functionalis of the endometrium (see Figure 27.15, p. 1087), and the villi come to lie in these spaces totally immersed in maternal blood (Figure 28.7d). The part of the endometrium that lies between the chorionic villi and the stratum basalis becomes the **decidua basalis** (de-sid′u-ah), whereas that surrounding the uterine cavity face of the implanted embryo forms the **decidua capsularis** (Figure 28.7d and f). Together, the chorionic villi and the decidua basalis form the disc-shaped placenta.

The fetal side of the placenta is easily recognized because it is slick and smooth, and the umbilical cord projects from its surface. In contrast, the maternal side is "bumpy," revealing the shape of the chorionic villus masses.

The placenta detaches and sloughs off after the infant is born, so the name of the maternal portion—*decidua* ("that which falls off")—is appropriate. The decidua capsularis expands to accommodate the fetus, which eventually fills and stretches the uterine cavity. As the developing fetus grows, the villi in the decidua capsularis are compressed and degenerate, and the villi in the decidua basalis increase in number and branch even more profusely.

The placenta is usually fully functional as a nutritive, respiratory, excretory, and endocrine organ by the end of the third month of pregnancy. However, well before this time, oxygen and nutrients are diffusing from maternal to embryonic blood, and embryonic metabolic wastes are passing in the opposite direction. The barriers to free passage of substances between the two blood supplies are embryonic barriers—the membranes of the chorionic villi and the endothelium of embryonic capillaries. Although the maternal and embryonic blood supplies are very close, they normally do not intermix.

While the placenta secretes hCG from the beginning, the ability of its syncytiotrophoblast cells (the "hormone manufacturers") to produce the estrogens and progesterone of pregnancy matures much more slowly. If, for some reason, placental hormones are inadequate when hCG levels wane, the endometrium degenerates and the pregnancy is aborted. Throughout pregnancy, blood levels of estrogens and progesterone continue to increase (see Figure 28.6), encouraging growth and further differentiation of the mammary glands and readying them for lactation. The placenta also produces other hormones, such as *human placental lactogen, human chorionic thyrotropin,* and *relaxin.* The effects of these hormones on the mother are described shortly.

Events of Embryonic Development: Gastrula to Fetus

Having followed placental development into the fetal stage, we will now backtrack and consider development of the embryo during and after implantation. Even while implantation is occurring, the blastocyst is being converted to a **gastrula** (gas′troo-lah), in which the three primary germ layers form, and the extraembryonic membranes develop. Before becoming three-layered, the inner cell mass first subdivides into two layers—the upper *epiblast* and the lower *hypoblast.*

Formation and Roles of the Extraembryonic Membranes

The **extraembryonic membranes** that form during the first two to three weeks of development include the amnion, yolk sac, allantois, and chorion (see Figure 28.7c). The **amnion** (am′ne-on) develops when cells of the epiblast fashion themselves into a transparent membranous sac. This sac, the amnion, becomes filled with **amniotic fluid.** Later, as the embryonic disc curves to form the tubular body, the amnion curves with it. Eventually, the sac extends all the way around the embryo, broken only by the umbilical cord (see Figure 28.7d).

Sometimes called the "bag of waters," the amnion provides a buoyant environment that protects the developing embryo against physical trauma, and helps maintain a constant homeostatic temperature. The fluid also prevents the rapidly growing embryonic parts from adhering and fusing together and allows the embryo considerable freedom of movement. Initially, the fluid is derived from the maternal blood, but as the fetal kidneys become functional later in development, fetal urine contributes to amniotic fluid volume.

The **yolk sac** forms from cells of the primitive gut (see below), which arrange themselves into a sac that hangs from the ventral surface of the embryo (see Figure 28.7b). Thus, the amnion and yolk sac resemble two balloons touching one another with the embryonic disc at the point of contact. In many species, the yolk sac is the main source of nutrition for the embryo, but human eggs contain very little yolk and nutritive functions have been taken over by the placenta. Nevertheless, the yolk sac is important in humans because it (1) forms part of the *gut* (digestive tube), and (2) produces the earliest blood cells and blood vessels.

The **allantois** (ah-lan′to-is) forms as a small outpocketing of embryonic tissue at the caudal end of the yolk sac (see Figure 28.7c). In animals that develop in shelled eggs, the allantois is a disposal site for solid metabolic wastes (excreta). In humans, the allantois is the structural base for the **umbilical cord** that links the embryo to the placenta, and becomes part of the urinary bladder. The fully formed umbilical cord contains a core of embryonic connective tissue (Wharton's jelly), the umbilical arteries and vein, and is covered externally by amniotic membrane.

The *chorion*, which helps to form the placenta, has already been described (see Figure 28.7c). As the outermost membrane, the chorion encloses the embryonic body and all other membranes.

Gastrulation: Germ Layer Formation

During week 3, the two-layered embryonic disc transforms into a three-layered *embryo* in which the **primary germ layers**—*ectoderm, mesoderm*, and *endoderm*—are present. This process, called **gastrulation** (gas″troo-la′shun), involves cellular rearrangements and migrations.

Gastrulation begins when a groove with raised edges called the **primitive streak** appears on the dorsal surface of the embryonic disc and establishes the longitudinal axis of the embryo (Figure 28.8e and f). Surface (epiblast) cells of the embryonic disc then migrate medially across other cells and enter the primitive streak. The first cells to enter the groove displace the hypoblast cells of the yolk sac and form the most inferior germ layer, the **endoderm.** Those that follow push laterally between the cells at the upper and lower surfaces, forming the **mesoderm** (see Figure 28.8g and h). The cells that remain on the embryo's dorsal surface are the **ectoderm.** The mesodermal cells immediately beneath the early primitive streak aggregate, forming a rod of mesodermal cells called the **notochord** (no′to-kord), the first axial support of the embryo (see Figure 28.9a). At this point, the embryo is about 2 mm long.

The three primary germ layers serve as the *primitive tissues* from which all body organs will derive. Ectoderm ("outer skin") fashions structures of the nervous system and the skin epidermis. Endoderm ("inner skin") forms the epithelial linings of the digestive, respiratory, and urogenital systems, and associated glands. Mesoderm ("middle skin") forms virtually everything else. Both ectoderm and endoderm consist mostly of cells that are securely joined to each other and are *epithelia.* Mesoderm, by contrast, is a *mesenchyme* [literally, "poured into the middle (of the embryo)"]. Notice, however, that the term **mesenchyme** indicates *any* embryonic tissue with star-shaped cells that are free to migrate

widely within the embryo. Table 28.1 (p. 1130) lists the germ layer derivatives; some of the details of the differentiation processes are described next.

Organogenesis: Differentiation of the Germ Layers

Gastrulation lays down the basic structural framework of the embryo and sets the stage for the rearrangements of **organogenesis** (or″gah-no-jen′ĕ-sis), formation of body organs and organ systems. By the end of the embryonic period, when the embryo is about 22 mm (slightly less than 1 inch) long from head to buttocks (referred to as the *crown-rump measurement*), all the adult organ systems are recognizable. It is truly amazing how much organogenesis occurs in such a short time in such a small amount of living matter.

Specialization of the Ectoderm

The first major event in organogenesis is **neurulation,** the differentiation of ectoderm that produces the brain and spinal cord (Figure 28.9). This process is *induced* (stimulated to happen) by chemical signals from the *notochord,* the rod of mesoderm that defines the body axis, mentioned earlier. The ectoderm overlying the notochord thickens, forming the **neural plate** (Figure 28.9a), and then starts to fold inward as a **neural groove,** which forms prominent **neural folds** as it deepens (Figure 28.9b, c). By day 22, the superior margins of the neural folds fuse, forming a **neural tube,** which soon pinches off and becomes covered by surface ectoderm (Figure 28.9d). As described in Chapter 12, the anterior end of the neural tube becomes the brain and the rest becomes the spinal cord. The associated **neural crest cells** migrate widely and give rise to the cranial, spinal, and sympathetic ganglia (and associated nerves), to the medulla of the adrenal gland, and to pigment cells, and contribute to some connective tissues.

By the end of the first month of development, the three primary brain vesicles (fore-, mid-, and hindbrain) are obvious. By the end of the second month, all brain flexures are evident, the cerebral hemispheres cover the top of the brain stem (see Figure 12.3), and brain waves can be recorded. Most of the remaining ectoderm forming the surface layer of the embryonic body differentiates into the epidermis of the skin. Other ectodermal derivatives are indicated in Table 28.1.

Specialization of the Endoderm

As noted, the embryo starts off as a flat plate, but as it grows, it folds to achieve a cylindrical body shape which lifts off the yolk sac and protrudes into the

28

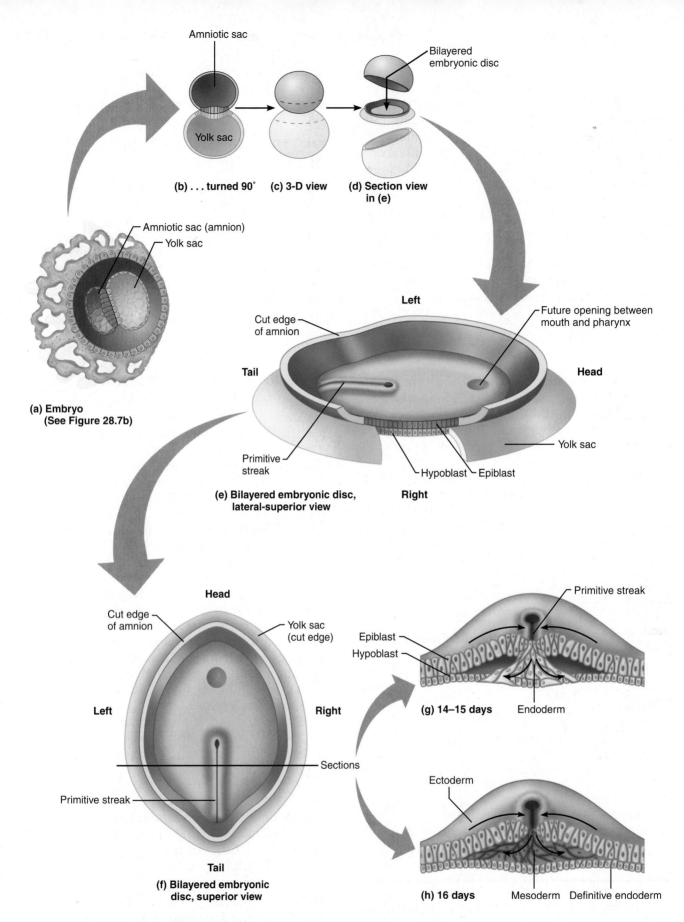

(b) . . . turned 90° **(c) 3-D view** **(d) Section view in (e)**

Amniotic sac

Yolk sac

Bilayered embryonic disc

Amniotic sac (amnion)

Yolk sac

(a) Embryo (See Figure 28.7b)

Left

Cut edge of amnion

Future opening between mouth and pharynx

Tail

Head

Primitive streak

Yolk sac

Hypoblast Epiblast

Right

(e) Bilayered embryonic disc, lateral-superior view

Head

Cut edge of amnion

Yolk sac (cut edge)

Left

Right

Sections

Primitive streak

Tail

(f) Bilayered embryonic disc, superior view

Primitive streak

Epiblast
Hypoblast

Endoderm

(g) 14–15 days

Ectoderm

Mesoderm Definitive endoderm

(h) 16 days

FIGURE 28.8 **Formation of the three primary germ layers. (a–d)** Orienting diagrams. **(e, f)** Surface views of an embryonic disc, amnion and yolk sac removed. **(g, h)** Cross sections of the embryonic disc, showing the germ layers resulting from cell migration. The first epiblast cells that migrate medially into the primitive streak (g) become endoderm. Those that follow (h) become mesoderm. The epiblast surface is now called ectoderm.

28

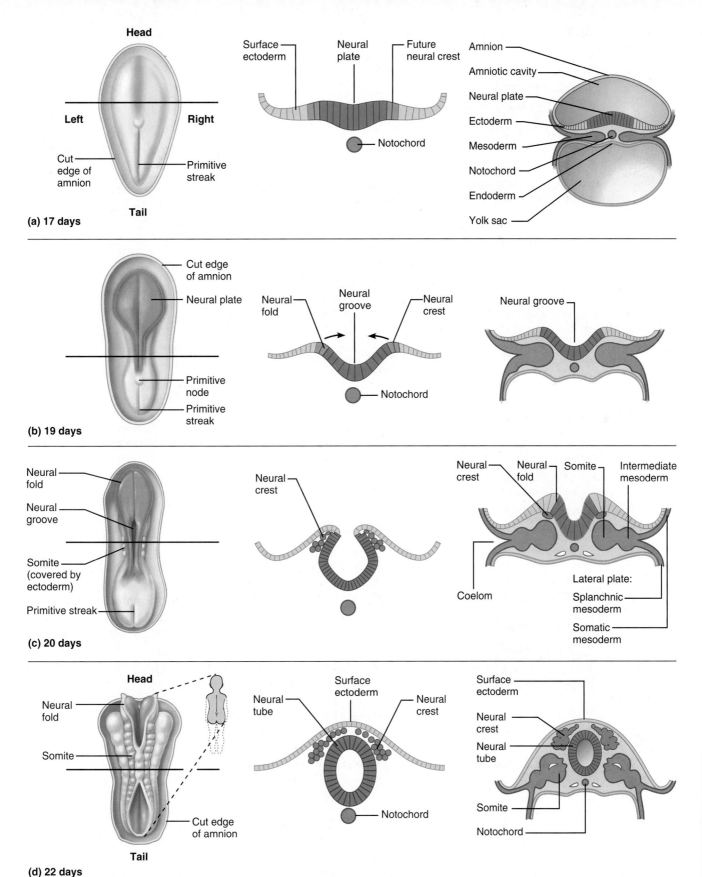

(a) 17 days

Head · Left · Right · Tail

Cut edge of amnion · Primitive streak

Surface ectoderm · Neural plate · Future neural crest · Notochord

Amnion · Amniotic cavity · Neural plate · Ectoderm · Mesoderm · Notochord · Endoderm · Yolk sac

(b) 19 days

Cut edge of amnion · Neural plate · Primitive node · Primitive streak

Neural fold · Neural groove · Neural crest · Notochord

Neural groove

(c) 20 days

Neural fold · Neural groove · Somite (covered by ectoderm) · Primitive streak

Neural crest

Neural crest · Neural fold · Somite · Intermediate mesoderm · Coelom · Lateral plate: Splanchnic mesoderm · Somatic mesoderm

(d) 22 days

Head · Neural fold · Somite · Cut edge of amnion · Tail

Surface ectoderm · Neural tube · Neural crest · Notochord

Surface ectoderm · Neural crest · Neural tube · Somite · Notochord

FIGURE 28.9 **Neurulation.** Dorsal surface views on the left; frontal sections on the right. **(a)** The flat three-layered embryo, which has accomplished gastrulation. The notochord and neural plate have formed. **(b)** The neural folds form by folding of the neural plate. **(c)** The neural folds begin to close. **(d)** The newly formed neural tube has detached from the surface ectoderm and lies between the surface ectoderm and the notochord; the neural crest is evident and the embryonic body is beginning to fold.

28

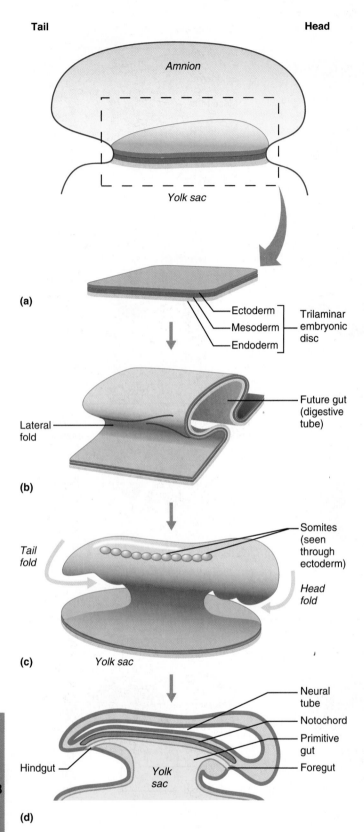

Tail **Head**

(a)

Ectoderm ⎤
Mesoderm ⎬ Trilaminar embryonic disc
Endoderm ⎦

(b)

Lateral fold

Future gut (digestive tube)

(c)

Tail fold

Head fold

Somites (seen through ectoderm)

Yolk sac

(d)

Hindgut

Yolk sac

Neural tube
Notochord
Primitive gut
Foregut

FIGURE 28.10 **Folding of the embryonic body.** Views are lateral, with the head on the right. **(a)** Model of the flat three-layered embryo as three sheets of paper. **(b, c)** Folding begins with lateral folds, then head and tail folds appear. **(d)** A 24-day embryo in sagittal section. Notice the primitive gut, which derives from the yolk sac, and the notochord and neural tube dorsally.

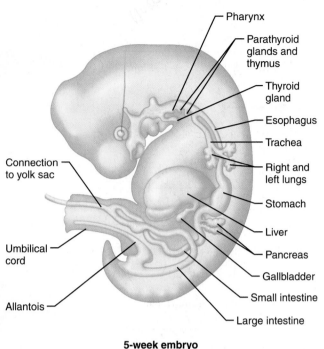

5-week embryo

FIGURE 28.11 **Endodermal differentiation to form the epithelial linings of the digestive and respiratory tracts and associated glands.**

amniotic cavity (Figure 28.10). In the simplest sense, this process resembles three stacked sheets of paper folding laterally into a tube. At the same time, the head and tail regions fold under as shown in Figure 28.10c. The folding occurs from both ends, and progresses toward the central part of the embryonic body, where the yolk sac and umbilical vessels protrude. As the endoderm undercuts and its edges come together and fuse, it encloses part of the yolk sac. The tube of endoderm formed, called the **primitive gut,** forms the epithelial lining (mucosa) of the gastrointestinal tract (Figure 28.11). The organs of the GI tract (pharynx, esophagus, etc.) quickly become apparent, and then the oral and anal openings perforate. The mucosal lining of the respiratory tract forms as an outpocketing from the *foregut* (pharyngeal endoderm), and glands arise as endodermal outpocketings at various points further along the tract. For example, the epithelium of the thyroid, parathyroids, and thymus forms from the pharyngeal endoderm, and that of the liver and pancreas arises from the intestinal mucosa *(midgut)* more inferiorly.

Specialization of the Mesoderm

The first evidence of mesodermal differentiation is the appearance of the notochord in the embryonic disc (see Figure 28.9a). Although the notochord is eventually replaced by the vertebral column, its remnants persist in the springy *nucleus pulposus* of the intervertebral discs. Shortly thereafter, three mesodermal

FIGURE 28.12 **Early mesodermal differentiation.**
(a) Segregation of the mesoderm (with the exception of notochord formation, which occurs earlier) takes place as neurulation is occurring. The notochord becomes flanked bilaterally by a somite, intermediate mesoderm, and lateral mesoderm successively. **(b)** Schematic view of the undercutting of the lateral folds showing how the lateral mesodermal plates move ventrally, forming the coelom. **(c)** Mesodermal divisions and relationships in an undercut (folded) embryo. The sclerotome, dermatome, and myotome of each somite contribute to the formation of the vertebrae, skin dermis, and skeletal muscles, respectively. The intermediate mesoderm forms the kidneys, gonads, and associated structures. The somatic mesoderm portion of the lateral mesoderm forms the limb buds, parietal serosa, and contributes to the dermis. The splanchnic mesoderm forms the muscle, connective tissues, and serosae of the walls of the visceral organs, and the heart and blood vessels.

(a)

(b)

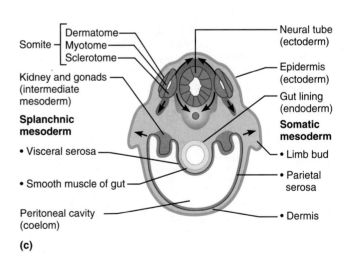

(c)

aggregates appear on either side of the notochord (Figures 28.9 b–d and 28.12a). The largest of these, the *somites* (so'mīts), are paired mesodermal blocks that hug the notochord on either side. All 40 pairs of somites are present by the end of week 4. Flanking the somites laterally are small clusters of segmented mesoderm called *intermediate mesoderm* and then double sheets of *lateral mesoderm*.

Each **somite** has three functional parts—*sclerotome, dermatome,* and *myotome.* Cells of the **sclerotome** (skle'ro-tōm; "hard piece") migrate medially, gather around the notochord and neural tube, and produce the vertebra and rib at the associated level. The **dermatome** ("skin piece") cells, which form the outer wall of each somite, help form the dermis of the skin in the dorsal part of the body. The **myotome** (mi'o-tōm; "muscle piece") consists of somite cells that remain behind and develop in conjunction with the vertebrae. They form the skeletal muscles of the neck, body trunk, and, via their **limb buds,** the muscles of the limbs.

Cells of the **intermediate mesoderm** form the gonads and kidneys. The **lateral mesoderm** consists of paired mesodermal plates: the *somatic mesoderm* and the *splanchnic mesoderm.* Cells of the **somatic mesoderm** (1) help to form the dermis of the skin in the ventral body region; (2) form the parietal serosa that lines the ventral body cavity; and (3) migrate into the forming limbs and produce the bones, ligaments, and dermis of the limbs (see Figure 28.12c). **Splanchnic mesoderm** provides the mesenchymal cells that form the heart and blood vessels and most connective tissues of the body. Splanchnic mesodermal cells also collect around the endodermal mucosal linings, where they form the smooth muscle, connective tissues, and serosal coverings (in other words, nearly the entire wall) of the digestive and respiratory organs. Thus the lateral mesodermal layers cooperate to form the serosae of the **coelom** (se'lom) or ventral body cavity.

By the end of the embryonic period, the bones have begun to ossify and the skeletal muscles are well formed and contracting spontaneously. Metanephric kidneys are developing, gonads are formed, and the lungs and digestive organs are attaining their final shape and body position. Blood delivery to and from

28

A CLOSER LOOK

Contraception: To Be or Not To Be

In a society such as ours, where many women opt for professional careers or work for economic reasons, **contraception** (*contra* = against; *cept* = taking), or birth control, is often seen as a necessity. Scientists are making headway in the search for a male contraceptive. Clinical tests of monthly injections of androgens and androgen-containing transdermal patches and implants, which suppress testicular testosterone production and subsequently spermatogenesis, are ongoing, and an effective antisperm vaccine exists. However, none of these male contraceptive methods have yet been approved for widespread use. Consequently, thus far the burden for birth control has fallen on women's shoulders, and most birth control products are female directed.

The key to birth control is dependability. As the red arrows in the accompanying flowchart show, the birth control techniques currently available have many sites of action for blocking reproduction. Let's examine a few of them more closely.

Coitus interruptus, or withdrawal of the penis just before ejaculation, is simply against nature, and control of ejaculation is never assured. *Rhythm* or *temporary abstinence methods* involve avoiding intercourse during periods of ovulation or fertility. This may be accomplished by (1) recording daily basal body temperatures (body temperature drops slightly immediately prior to ovulation and then rises slightly after ovulation) or (2) more simply by buying the over-the-counter *Ovulite Microscope,* which is the size of a lipstick. On awakening, a drop of saliva is placed on the microscope slide and examined for a particular pattern of crystals that indicate the optimal days

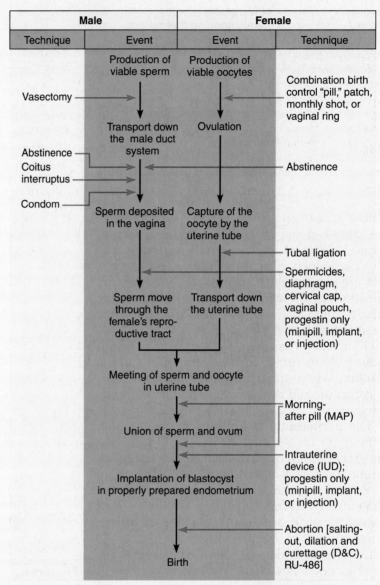

Male		Female	
Technique	Event	Event	Technique
	Production of viable sperm	Production of viable oocytes	Combination birth control "pill," patch, monthly shot, or vaginal ring
Vasectomy			
	Transport down the male duct system	Ovulation	
Abstinence			Abstinence
Coitus interruptus			
Condom			
	Sperm deposited in the vagina	Capture of the oocyte by the uterine tube	
			Tubal ligation
			Spermicides, diaphragm, cervical cap, vaginal pouch, progestin only (minipill, implant, or injection)
	Sperm move through the female's reproductive tract	Transport down the uterine tube	
	Meeting of sperm and oocyte in uterine tube		
	Union of sperm and ovum		Morning-after pill (MAP)
			Intrauterine device (IUD); progestin only (minipill, implant, or injection)
	Implantation of blastocyst in properly prepared endometrium		
			Abortion [salting-out, dilation and curettage (D&C), RU-486]
	Birth		

Flowchart of the events that must occur to produce a baby. Techniques or products that interfere with the process are indicated by colored arrows at the site of interference and act to prevent the next step from occurring.

for fertilization. These techniques require accurate record keeping for several cycles before they can be used

with confidence, but have a high success rate for those willing to take the time necessary. With a failure rate of

the placenta via the umbilical vessels is constant and efficient. The heart and the liver are competing for space and form a conspicuous bulge on the ventral surface of the embryo's body. All this by the end of eight weeks in an embryo about 1 inch long from crown to rump!

Development of the Fetal Circulation

Embryonic development of the cardiovascular system lays the groundwork for the fetal circulatory pattern, which is converted to the adult pattern at birth. The first blood cells arise in the yolk sac. Before week 3 of development, tiny spaces appear in

10–20%, it is obvious that some people are willing and some are not.

Barrier methods, such as diaphragms, cervical caps, male and female condoms, spermicidal foams, gels, and sponges, are quite effective, especially when used in combination—for example, condoms and spermicides. But many avoid them because they can reduce the spontaneity of sexual encounters, and sperm may be present in male secretions that precede ejaculation.

For several years, the second most used contraceptive method was the *intrauterine device (IUD),* and it is still one of the most commonly used methods in the world, largely because of its economy. Developed in 1909, this plastic or metal device is inserted into the uterus and prevents the fertilized egg from implanting in the endometrial lining. Although IUDs' failure rate was nearly as low as that of the pill, they were taken off the U.S. market because of occasional contraceptive failure, uterine perforation, or pelvic inflammatory disease. New IUD products that provide sustained local delivery of synthetic progesterone to the endometrium are particularly recommended for women who have given birth and are in monogamous relationships (i.e., who have a lower risk of developing PID).

The most-used contraceptive product in the United States is the *birth control pill,* or simply "the pill," first marketed in 1960. Supplied in 28-tablet packets, the first 20 or 21 tablets contain minute amounts of estrogens and progestins (progesterone-like hormones) taken daily; the last seven tablets are hormone free. The pill tricks the hypothalamic-pituitary axis and "lulls it to sleep," because the relatively constant blood levels of ovarian hormones make it appear that the woman is pregnant (both estrogen and progesterone are produced through-out pregnancy). Ovarian follicles do not develop, ovulation ceases, and menstrual flow is much reduced. However, since hormonal balance is one of the most precisely controlled body functions, some women cannot tolerate these changes—they become nauseated and/or hypertensive. The pill has adverse cardiovascular effects in a small number of users and there is still debate about whether it increases the risk of uterine, ovarian, or (particularly) breast cancer. Presently, well over 50 million women use the pill, and its failure rate is less than 1%.

Other delivery methods using the combination hormone approach include two slow-release products approved in 2001, a vaginal ring and a transdermal patch. *NuvaRing,* a flexible polymer ring that is inserted into the vagina, is left in place for three consecutive weeks, and then removed for one week to allow menstruation. *Ortho Evra,* a transdermal patch, delivers continuous levels of estrogen and progestin into the bloodstream. It is replaced each week for three consecutive weeks, followed by one week with no patch. Failure rates and side effects of NuvaRing and Ortho Evra are comparable to those of the pill, although in clinical trials the patch was less effective in women weighing more than 198 pounds.

Combination birth control pills with substantially higher hormone concentrations (marketed under various names including Ovral, Tetragynon, and Triphasil) are being used for *postcoital contraception.* Taken within three days of unprotected intercourse, these *morning-after pills (MAPs)* "mess up" normal hormonal signals enough to prevent a fertilized egg from implanting or prevent fertilization altogether.

Other hormonal approaches to contraception use progestin-only products which act by causing the cervical mucus to become thick, thus blocking sperm entry into the uterus, and make the endometrium inhospitable to implantion. These include the *minipill,* a tablet form; *Norplant,* which consists of two (originally six) tiny silicone rods implanted just under the skin that release progestin over a five-year period; and *Depo-Provera,* an injectible form that lasts for three months. The failure rates of Norplant and Depo-Provera are even less than that of the "pill."

Abortion is the termination of a pregnancy that is in progress. Spontaneous abortion, also called miscarriage, is common and frequently occurs before a woman is aware that she has conceived. Additionally, over a million American women choose to undergo abortions performed by physicians. *Mifepristone (RU-486),* the so-called abortion pill developed in France, enables a woman to end a pregnancy during the first 7 weeks and has a 96–98% success rate with few side effects. RU-486 is an antihormone that, when taken along with a tiny amount of prostaglandin to stimulate uterine contractions, induces miscarriage by blocking progesterone's quieting effect on the uterus.

Sterilization techniques, such as *tubal ligation* or *vasectomy* (cutting or cauterizing the uterine tubes or vas deferens, respectively,) are nearly foolproof and are the choice of approximately 33% of couples of childbearing age in the United States. Both procedures can be done in the physician's office. However, these techniques are usually permanent, making them unpopular with individuals who still plan to have children but want to select the time.

This summary doesn't even begin to touch on the experimental birth control drugs now awaiting clinical trials, and other methods are sure to be developed in the near future. In the final analysis, however, the only 100% effective means of birth control is the age-old one—*total abstinence.* ∎

the splanchnic mesoderm. These are quickly lined by endothelial cells, covered with mesenchyme, and linked together into rapidly spreading vascular networks, destined to form the heart, blood vessels, and lymphatics. By the end of week 3, the embryo has a system of paired blood vessels, and the two vessels forming the heart have fused and bent into an S shape (see Figure 18.24). By 3½ weeks, the miniature heart is pumping blood for an embryo less than a quarter inch long.

Unique cardiovascular modifications seen only during prenatal development include the **umbilical**

TABLE 28.1	Derivatives of the Primary Germ Layers	
ECTODERM	**MESODERM**	**ENDODERM**
All nervous tissue	Skeletal, smooth, and cardiac muscle	Epithelium of digestive tract (except that of oral and anal cavities)
Epidermis of skin and epidermal derivatives (hairs, hair follicles, sebaceous and sweat glands, nails)	Cartilage, bone, and other connective tissues	Glandular derivatives of digestive tract (liver, pancreas)
Cornea and lens of eye	Blood, bone marrow, and lymphoid tissues	Epithelium of respiratory tract, auditory tube, and tonsils
Epithelium of oral and nasal cavities, of paranasal sinuses, and of anal canal	Endothelium of blood vessels and lymphatics	Thyroid, parathyroid, and thymus glands
Tooth enamel	Serosae of ventral body cavity	Epithelium of reproductive ducts and glands
Epithelium of pineal and pituitary glands and adrenal medulla	Fibrous and vascular tunics of eyes	Epithelium of urethra and bladder
Melanocytes	Synovial membranes of joint cavities	
Some cranial bones and branchial cartilages (derived from neural crest)	Organs of urogenital system (ureters, kidneys, gonads, and reproductive ducts)	

arteries and vein and three *vascular shunts* (Figure 28.13). All of these structures are occluded at birth. As you read about these vessels, keep in mind that the heart the blood is flowing from and to is the fetal heart. The large umbilical vein carries freshly oxygenated blood returning from the placenta into the embryonic body, where it is conveyed to the liver. There, some of the returning blood percolates through the liver sinusoids and out the hepatic veins. Most of the blood coursing through the umbilical vein, however, enters the **ductus venosus** (duk'tus ve-no'sus), a venous shunt that bypasses the liver sinusoids. Both the hepatic veins and the ductus venosus empty into the inferior vena cava where the placental blood mixes with deoxygenated blood returning from the lower parts of the fetus's body. The vena cava in turn conveys this "mixed load" of blood directly to the right atrium of the heart. After birth, the liver plays an important role in nutrient processing, but during embryonic life these functions are performed by the mother's liver. Consequently, blood flow through the liver during development is important only to ensure viability of the liver cells.

Blood entering and leaving the heart encounters two more shunt systems, each serving to bypass the nonfunctional lungs. Some of the blood entering the right atrium flows directly into the left atrium via the **foramen ovale** ("oval hole"), an opening in the interatrial septum loosely closed by a flap of tissue. Blood that enters the right ventricle is pumped out into the pulmonary trunk. However, the second shunt, the **ductus arteriosus,** transfers most of that blood directly into the aorta, again bypassing the pulmonary circuit. (The lungs *do* receive adequate blood to maintain their growth.) Blood enters the two pulmonary bypass shunts because the heart chamber or vessel on the other side of each shunt is a lower-

pressure area, owing to the low volume of venous return from the lungs. Blood flowing distally through the aorta eventually reaches the umbilical arteries, which are branches of the internal iliac arteries serving the pelvis. From here the largely deoxygenated blood, laden with metabolic wastes, is delivered back to the capillaries in the chorionic villi of the placenta. The changes in the circulatory plan that occur at birth are illustrated in Figure 28.13b.

HOMEOSTATIC IMBALANCE

Because many potentially harmful substances can cross placental barriers and enter the fetal blood, a pregnant woman should be aware of what she is taking into her body, particularly during the embryonic period when the body's foundations are laid down. **Teratogens** (ter'ah-to-jenz; *terato* = monster), factors that may cause severe congenital abnormalities or even fetal death, include alcohol, nicotine, many drugs (anticoagulants, sedatives, antihypertensives, and some antibiotics), and maternal infections, particularly German measles. For example, when a woman drinks alcohol, her fetus becomes inebriated as well. However, the fetal consequences may be much more lasting and result in the *fetal alcohol syndrome (FAS)* typified by microcephaly (small head), mental retardation, and abnormal growth. Nicotine hinders oxygen delivery to the fetus, impairing normal growth and development. The sedative **thalidomide** (thah-lid'o-mīd) was used by thousands of pregnant women in the 1960s to alleviate morning sickness. When taken during the period of limb bud differentiation (days 26–56), it sometimes resulted in tragically deformed infants with short flipperlike legs and arms. ●

Fetus

Newborn

Aortic arch
Superior vena cava
Ductus arteriosus
Lung
Ligamentum arteriosum
Pulmonary artery
Pulmonary veins
Heart
Foramen ovale
Fossa ovalis
Liver
Ductus venosus
Ligamentum venosum
Hepatic portal vein
Umbilical vein
Ligamentum teres
Inferior vena cava
Umbilicus
Abdominal aorta
Common iliac artery
Umbilical arteries
Medial umbilical ligaments
Urinary bladder
Umbilical cord

(b)

Placenta

Key:

= High oxygenation

= Moderate oxygenation

= Low oxygenation

= Very low oxygenation

(a)

28

FIGURE 28.13 **Circulation in fetus and newborn.** Arrows indicate direction of blood flow. **(a)** Special adaptations for embryonic and fetal life. The umbilical vein carries oxygen- and nutrient-rich blood from the placenta to the fetus; the umbilical arteries carry waste-laden blood from the fetus to the placenta; the ductus arteriosus and foramen ovale bypass the nonfunctional lungs; and the ductus venosus allows blood to partially bypass the liver. **(b)** Changes in the cardiovascular system at birth. The umbilical vessels are occluded, as are the liver and lung bypasses (ductus venosus and arteriosus, and the foramen ovale).

TABLE 28.2	**Developmental Events of the Fetal Period**

TIME	CHANGES AND ACCOMPLISHMENTS
8 weeks (end of embryonic period) 8 weeks	Head nearly as large as body; all major brain regions present; first brain waves in brain stem Liver disproportionately large and begins to form blood cells Limbs present; digits are initially webbed, but fingers and toes are free by the end of this interval Ossification just begun; weak, spontaneous muscle contractions occur Cardiovascular system fully functional (heart has been pumping blood since the fourth week) All body systems present in at least rudimentary form Approximate crown-to-rump length: 22 mm (0.9 inches); weight: 2 grams (0.06 ounce)
9–12 weeks (month 3) 12 weeks	Head still dominant, but body elongating; brain continues to enlarge, shows its general structural features; cervical and lumbar enlargements apparent in spinal cord; retina of eye is present Skin epidermis and dermis obvious; facial features present in crude form Liver prominent and bile being secreted; palate is fusing; most glands of endodermal origin are developed; walls of hollow visceral organs gaining smooth muscle Blood cell formation begins in bone marrow Notochord degenerating and ossification accelerating; limbs well molded Sex readily detected from the genitals Approximate crown-to-rump length at end of interval: 90 mm
13–16 weeks (month 4) 16 weeks	Cerebellum becoming prominent; general sensory organs differentiated; eyes and ears assume characteristic position and shape; blinking of eyes and sucking motions of lips occur Face looks human and growth of the body beginning to outpace that of the head Glands developed in GI tract; meconium is collecting Kidneys attain typical structure Most bones are now distinct and joint cavities are apparent Approximate crown-to-rump length at end of interval: 140 mm
17–20 weeks (month 5)	Vernix caseosa (fatty secretions of sebaceous glands) covers body; lanugo (silklike hair) covers skin Fetal position (body flexed anteriorly) assumed because of space restrictions Limbs reach near-final proportions Quickening occurs (mother feels spontaneous muscular activity of fetus) Approximate crown-to-rump length at end of interval: 190 mm
21–30 weeks (months 6 and 7) *turn head to d-wn*	Period of substantial increase in weight (may survive if born prematurely at 27–28 weeks, but hypothalamic temperature regulation and lung production of surfactant are still inadequate) Myelination of cord begins; eyes are open Distal limb bones are beginning to ossify Skin is wrinkled and red; fingernails and toenails are present; tooth enamel is forming on deciduous teeth Body is lean and well proportioned Bone marrow becomes sole site of blood cell formation Testes reach scrotum in seventh month (in males) Approximate crown-to-rump length at end of interval: 280 mm
30–40 weeks (term) (months 8 and 9) At birth	Skin whitish pink; fat laid down in subcutaneous tissue (hypodermis) Approximate crown-to-rump length at end of interval: 360 mm (14 inches); weight: 3.2 kg (7 lb)

28

(a)   (b)

FIGURE 28.14 **Photographs of a developing fetus. (a)** Fetus in month 3, about 6 cm long. **(b)** Fetus late in month 5, about 19 cm long. By birth, the fetus is typically 36 cm long from crown to rump.

Events of Fetal Development

The main events of the fetal period—weeks 9 through 38—are listed chronologically in Table 28.2. The fetal period is a time of rapid growth of the body structures that were established in the embryo. During the first half of this period, cells are still differentiating into specific cell types to form the body's distinctive tissues and are completing the fine details of body structure. During the fetal period, the developing fetus grows from a crown-to-rump length of about 22 mm (slightly less than 1 inch) and a weight of approximately 2 g (0.06 ounce) to about 360 mm (14 inches) and 3.2 kg (7 lb) or more. (Total body length at birth is about 550 mm, or 22 inches.) As you might expect with such tremendous growth, the changes in fetal appearance are quite dramatic (Figure 28.14). Nevertheless, the greatest amount of growth occurs in the first 8 weeks of life, when the embryo grows from one cell to a fetus of 1 inch.

Effects of Pregnancy on the Mother

Pregnancy can be a difficult time for the mother. Not only are there anatomical changes, but striking changes in her metabolism and physiology occur as well.

Anatomical Changes

As pregnancy progresses, the female reproductive organs become increasingly vascular and engorged with blood, and the vagina develops a purplish hue *(Chadwick's sign)*. The enhanced vascularity increases vaginal sensitivity and sexual intensity, and some women achieve orgasm for the first time when they are pregnant. The breasts, too, engorge with blood and, prodded by rising levels of estrogen and progesterone, they enlarge and their areolae darken. Some women develop increased pigmentation of facial skin of the nose and cheeks, a condition called *chloasma* (klo-az'mah; "to be green") or the "mask of pregnancy."

The degree of uterine enlargement during pregnancy is remarkable. Starting as a fist-sized organ, the uterus fills most of the pelvic cavity by 16 weeks (Figure 28.15b). Though the fetus is only about 140 mm long (crown-to-rump) at this time, the placenta is fully formed, uterine muscle is hypertrophied, and amniotic fluid volume is increasing. As pregnancy continues, the uterus pushes higher into the abdominal cavity, exerting pressure on both abdominal and pelvic organs (Figure 28.15c). As birth nears, the uterus reaches the level of the xiphoid process and occupies most of the abdominal cavity (Figure 28.15d). The crowded abdominal organs press superiorly against the diaphragm, which intrudes on the

28

Q *Using this figure as a reference, explain why many pregnant women complain of being "short-winded."*

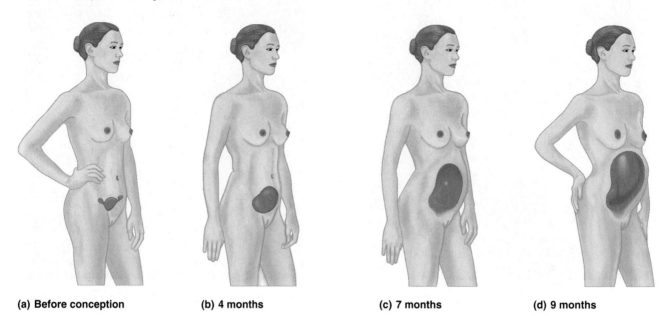

(a) Before conception   (b) 4 months   (c) 7 months   (d) 9 months

FIGURE 28.15   **Relative size of the uterus before conception and during pregnancy. (a)** Before conception, the uterus is the size of a fist and resides within the pelvis. **(b)** At 4 months, the fundus of the uterus is halfway between the pubic symphysis and the umbilicus. **(c)** At 7 months, the fundus is well above the umbilicus. **(d)** At 9 months, the fundus reaches the xiphoid process.

thoracic cavity. As a result, the ribs flare, causing the thorax to widen.

The increasing bulkiness of the anterior abdomen changes the woman's center of gravity, and many women develop lordosis (accentuated lumbar curvature) and backaches during the last few months of pregnancy. Placental production of the hormone **relaxin** causes pelvic ligaments and the pubic symphysis to relax, widen, and become more flexible. This increased motility eases birth passage, but it may result in a waddling gait in the meantime. Additionally, relaxin relaxes the springy ligaments supporting the bones of the foot and many women need to buy larger shoes during pregnancy.

Considerable weight gain occurs during a normal pregnancy. Because some women are over- or underweight before pregnancy begins, it is almost impossible to state the ideal or desirable weight gain. However, summing up the weight increases resulting from fetal and placental growth, growth of the maternal reproductive organs and breasts, and increased blood volume during pregnancy, a weight gain of approximately 13 kg (about 28 lb) usually occurs.

Obviously, good nutrition is necessary all through pregnancy if the developing fetus is to have all the building materials (especially proteins, calcium, and iron) needed to form its tissues. Additionally, multivitamins containing folic acid reduce the risk of having a baby with neurological problems, including such birth defects as spina bifida and anencephaly. However, a pregnant woman needs only 300 additional calories daily to sustain proper fetal growth. The emphasis should be on eating high-quality food, not just more food. Not surprisingly, effects of the fetal environment may not show up until decades later. Below-normal birth weight, for instance, places females at risk for gestational diabetes and increases the general risk of cardiovascular disease later in life.

Metabolic Changes

As the placenta enlarges, it secretes increasing amounts of **human placental lactogen (hPL)**, also called **human chorionic somatomammotropin (hCS)**, which works cooperatively with estrogens and progesterone to stimulate maturation of the breasts for lactation. hPL also promotes growth of the fetus and exerts a glucose-sparing effect in the mother. Consequently, maternal cells metabolize more fatty acids and less glucose than usual, sparing glucose for use by the fetus. Gestational diabetes mellitus occurs in

A *As the pregnancy advances, the uterus pushes higher in the abdomen, eventually pressing on the diaphragm and inhibiting its downward movement.*

about 10% of pregnancies, but over half of those women go on to develop type II diabetes later in life. The placenta also releases **human chorionic thyrotropin (hCT)**, a glycoprotein hormone similar to thyroid-stimulating hormone of the anterior pituitary. hCT activity increases the rate of maternal metabolism throughout the pregnancy, causing hypermetabolism. Because plasma levels of parathyroid hormone and activated vitamin D rise, pregnant women tend to be in positive calcium balance throughout pregnancy. This ensures that the developing fetus will have adequate calcium to mineralize its bones.

Physiological Changes

Gastrointestinal System

Many women suffer nausea, commonly called *morning sickness*, during the first few months of pregnancy, until their system adjusts to the elevated levels of progesterone and estrogens. (Nausea is also a side effect of many birth control pills.) *Heartburn*, due to reflux of stomach acid into the esophagus, is common because the esophagus is displaced and the stomach is crowded by the growing uterus. *Constipation* occurs because motility of the digestive tract declines during pregnancy.

Urinary System

The kidneys produce more urine during pregnancy because they have the additional burden of disposing of fetal metabolic wastes. As the growing uterus compresses the bladder, urination becomes more frequent, more urgent, and sometimes uncontrollable *(stress incontinence)*.

Respiratory System

The nasal mucosa responds to estrogens by becoming edematous and congested. Thus, nasal stuffiness and occasional nosebleeds may occur. Tidal volume and respiratory rate increase during pregnancy. But residual volume declines, and many women exhibit *dyspnea* (disp-ne'ah), or difficult breathing, during the later stages of pregnancy.

Cardiovascular System

The most dramatic physiological changes occur in the cardiovascular system. Total body water rises; blood volume increases 25–40% by the 32nd week to accommodate the additional needs of the fetus. The rise in blood volume also safeguards against blood loss during birth. Blood pressure and pulse typically rise and increase cardiac output by 20–40% at various stages of pregnancy. This helps propel the greater circulatory volume around the body. Because the uterus presses on the pelvic blood vessels, venous return from the lower limbs may be impaired, resulting in *varicose veins*.

▲ HOMEOSTATIC IMBALANCE

A dangerous complication of pregnancy called *preeclampsia* results in an insufficient placental blood supply, which can starve a fetus of oxygen. The pregnant woman becomes edematous and hypertensive and proteinuria occurs. This condition, which affects one in ten pregnancies, is believed to be due to immunological abnormalities in some cases, because its occurrence seems to be positively correlated with the number of fetal cells that enter the maternal circulation. ●

Parturition (Birth)

Parturition (par″tu-rish′un; "bringing forth young") is the culmination of pregnancy—giving birth to the baby. It usually occurs within 15 days of the calculated due date (280 days from the last menstrual period). The series of events that expel the infant from the uterus are collectively called **labor.**

Initiation of Labor

Several events and hormones interlock to trigger labor. During the last few weeks of pregnancy, estrogens reach their highest levels in the mother's blood.* This has two important consequences: It stimulates the myometrial cells of the uterus to form abundant oxytocin receptors (Figure 28.16) and it

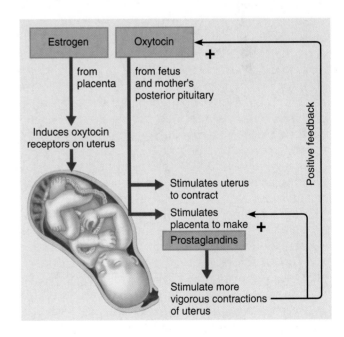

FIGURE 28.16 **Hormonal induction of labor.**

---

* Studies indicate that the fetus determines its own birth date. Rising levels of fetal adrenocortical hormones (especially cortisol) late in pregnancy are a major stimulus for the placenta to release such large amounts of estrogens.

(a)

- Umbilical cord
- Placenta
- Uterus
- Cervix
- Vagina

(b)

- Pubic symphysis
- Sacrum

(c)

- Perineum

(d)

- Uterus
- Placenta (detaching)
- Umbilical cord

antagonizes progesterone's quieting influence on uterine muscle. As a result, the myometrium becomes increasingly irritable, and weak, irregular uterine contractions begin to occur. These contractions, called *Braxton Hicks contractions*, have caused many women to go to the hospital, only to be told that they were in **false labor** and sent home.

As birth nears, two more chemical signals cooperate to convert these false labor pains into the real thing. Certain fetal cells begin to produce **oxytocin** (ok″sĭ-to′sin), which causes the placenta (Figure 28.16) to release **prostaglandins** (pros″tah-glan′dinz). Both hormones are powerful uterine muscle stimulants, and since the myometrium is now highly sensitive to oxytocin, contractions become more frequent and more vigorous. At this point, the increasing emotional and physical stresses activate the mother's hypothalamus, which signals for oxytocin release by the posterior pituitary. Together the elevated levels of oxytocin and prostaglandins trigger the rhythmic expulsive contractions of true labor. Once the hypothalamus is involved, a *positive feedback mechanism* is propelled into action—greater contractile force causes the release of more oxytocin, which causes greater contractile force, and so on (Figure 28.16). These expulsive contractions are aided by the fact that *fetal fibronectin*, a natural "stickum" (adhesive protein) that binds the fetal and maternal tissues of the placenta together throughout pregnancy, changes to a lubricant just before true labor begins. Increased production of *surfactant protein A (SF-A)* by the fetal lungs in the weeks before delivery appears to trigger an inflammatory response in the cervix that triggers its softening in preparation for labor.

Both oxytocin and prostaglandins are essential for initiating labor in humans. Untimely spurts of oxytocin may provoke some instances of premature birth, and interfering with production of either of these hormones will hinder onset of labor. For example, antiprostaglandin drugs such as ibuprofen can inhibit the early stages of labor and such drugs are used occasionally to prevent preterm births.

FIGURE 28.17 **Parturition. (a)** Dilation stage (early). The baby's head is engaged in the true pelvis. The widest head dimension is along the left-right axis. **(b)** Late dilation. The baby's head rotates so that its greatest dimension is in the anteroposterior axis as it moves through the pelvic outlet. Dilation of the cervix is nearly complete. **(c)** Expulsion stage. The baby's head extends as it reaches the perineum and is delivered. **(d)** Placental stage. After the baby is delivered, the placenta is detached by the continuing uterine contractions and removed.

Stages of Labor

Stage 1: Dilation Stage

The **dilation stage** (Figure 28.17a) is the time from labor's onset until the cervix is fully dilated by the baby's head (about 10 cm in diameter). As labor starts, weak but regular contractions begin in the upper part of the uterus and move toward the vagina. At first, only the superior uterine muscle is active, the contractions are 15–30 minutes apart, and they last for 10–30 seconds. As labor progresses, the contractions become more vigorous and rapid, and the lower uterine segment gets involved. As the infant's head is forced against the cervix with each contraction, the cervix softens and thins *(effaces)*, and dilates. Eventually the amnion ruptures, releasing the amniotic fluid, an event commonly called "breaking the water." The dilation stage is the longest part of labor, lasting 6–12 hours or more. Several events happen during this phase. *Engagement* occurs when the infant's head enters the true pelvis. As descent continues through the birth canal, the baby's head rotates so that its greatest dimension is in the anteroposterior line (Figure 28.17b), which allows it to navigate the narrow dimensions of the pelvic outlet.

Stage 2: Expulsion Stage

The **expulsion stage** (Figure 28.17c) lasts from full dilation to delivery of the infant, or actual childbirth. By the time the cervix is fully dilated, strong contractions are occurring every 2–3 minutes and lasting about 1 minute; a mother undergoing labor without local anesthesia has an increasing urge to push or bear down with the abdominal muscles. Although this phase may last 2 hours, it is typically 50 minutes in a first birth and around 20 minutes in subsequent births.

Crowning occurs when the largest dimension of the baby's head distends the vulva. At this point, an *episiotomy* (e-piz"e-ot'o-me) may be done to reduce tissue tearing. An episiotomy is an incision made to widen the vaginal orifice. The baby's neck extends as the head exits from the perineum, and once the head has been delivered, the rest of the baby's body is delivered much more easily. After birth, the umbilical cord is clamped and cut.

When the infant is in the usual *vertex*, or head-first, *presentation*, the skull (its largest diameter) acts as a wedge to dilate the cervix. The head-first presentation also allows the baby to be suctioned free of mucus and to breathe even before it has completely exited from the birth canal (Figure 28.17c). In *breech* (buttock-first) and other nonvertex presentations, these advantages are lost and delivery is much more difficult, often requiring the use of forceps.

◥ HOMEOSTATIC IMBALANCE

If a woman has a deformed or malelike pelvis, labor may be prolonged and difficult. This condition is called *dystocia* (dis-to'se-ah; *dys* = difficult; *toc* = birth). Besides extreme maternal fatigue, another possible consequence of dystocia is fetal brain damage, resulting in cerebral palsy or epilepsy. To prevent these outcomes, a *cesarean (C-) section* (se-sa're-an) is performed in many such cases. A C-section is delivery of the infant through an incision made through the abdominal and uterine walls. ●

Stage 3: Placental Stage

The **placental stage** (Figure 28.17d), or the delivery of the placenta, is usually accomplished within 30 minutes after birth of the infant. The strong uterine contractions that continue after birth compress uterine blood vessels, limit bleeding, and shear the placenta off the uterine wall (cause placental detachment). The placenta and its attached fetal membranes, collectively called the **afterbirth,** are then easily removed by a gentle tug on the umbilical cord. It is very important that all placental fragments be removed to prevent continued uterine bleeding after birth *(postpartum bleeding).*

Adjustments of the Infant to Extrauterine Life

The **neonatal period** is the four-week period immediately after birth. Here we will be concerned with the events of just the first few hours after birth in a normal infant. As you might suspect, birth represents quite a shock to the infant. Exposed to physical trauma during the birth process, it is suddenly cast out of its watery, warm environment and its placental life supports are severed. Now it must do for itself all that the mother had been doing for it— respire, obtain nutrients, excrete, and maintain its body temperature.

At 1 and 5 minutes after birth, the infant's physical status is assessed based on five signs: heart rate, respiration, color, muscle tone, and reflexes (tested by response to catheter in nostril). Each observation is given a score of 0 to 2, and the total is called the **Apgar score.** An Apgar score of 8 to 10 indicates a healthy baby. Lower scores reveal problems in one or more of the physiological functions assessed.

Taking the First Breath and Transition

The crucial first requirement is to breathe. Once carbon dioxide is no longer removed by the placenta, it accumulates in the baby's blood, causing central

28

acidosis. This excites respiratory control centers in the baby's brain and triggers the first inspiration. The first breath requires a tremendous effort—the airways are tiny, and the lungs are collapsed. However, once the lungs have been inflated in full-term babies, surfactant in alveolar fluid reduces surface tension in the alveoli, and breathing is easier. The rate of respiration is rapid (about 45 respirations/min) during the first two weeks and then gradually declines to normal levels.

Keeping the lungs inflated is much more difficult for premature infants (those weighing less than 2500 g, or about 5.5 lb, at birth) because surfactant production occurs during the last months of prenatal life. Consequently, preemies are usually put on respiratory assistance (a ventilator) until their lungs are mature enough to function on their own.

For 6–8 hours after birth, infants pass through an unstable **transitional period** marked by alternating periods of increased activity and sleep, and during which they adjust to extrauterine life. During the activity periods vital signs are irregular and the baby gags frequently as it regurgitates mucus and debris. After this, the infant stabilizes, with waking periods (dictated by hunger) occurring every 3–4 hours.

Occlusion of Special Fetal Blood Vessels and Vascular Shunts

After birth the special umbilical blood vessels and fetal shunts are no longer necessary (see Figure 28.13b). The umbilical arteries and vein constrict and become fibrosed. The proximal parts of the umbilical arteries persist as the *superior vesical arteries* that supply the urinary bladder; their distal parts become the **medial umbilical ligaments.** The remnant of the umbilical vein becomes the **round ligament of the liver,** or **ligamentum teres,** that attaches the umbilicus to the liver. The ductus venosus collapses as blood stops flowing through the umbilical vein and is eventually converted to the **ligamentum venosum** on the liver's undersurface.

As the pulmonary circulation becomes functional, left heart pressure increases and right heart pressure decreases, causing the pulmonary shunts to close. The flap of the foramen ovale is pushed to the shut position, and its edges fuse to the septal wall. Ultimately, only a slight depression, the **fossa ovalis,** marks its position. The ductus arteriosus constricts and is converted to the cordlike **ligamentum arteriosum,** connecting the aorta and pulmonary trunk.

Except for the foramen ovale, all of the special circulatory adaptations of the fetus are functionally occluded within 30 minutes after birth. Closure of the foramen ovale is usually complete within the year. As described in Chapter 18, failure of the ductus arteriosus or foramen ovale to close leads to congenital heart defects.

Lactation

Lactation is production of milk by the hormone-prepared mammary glands. Rising levels of (placental) estrogens, progesterone, and lactogen toward the end of pregnancy stimulate the hypothalamus to release prolactin-releasing hormone (PRH). The anterior pituitary gland responds by secreting **prolactin.** (This mechanism is described below.) After a delay of two to three days, true milk production begins. Serotonin, a well-known neurotransmitter, is synthesized by the mammary glands. Its role there appears to be to send feedback signals to the hypothalamus that slow down prolactin release (and milk production) once the mammary glands are full of milk.

During the initial delay (and during late gestation), a yellowish fluid called **colostrum** (ko-los'trum) is secreted. Colostrum has less lactose than milk and almost no fat, but it contains more protein, vitamin A, and minerals than true milk. Like milk, colostrum is rich in IgA antibodies. Since these antibodies are resistant to digestion in the stomach, they may help to protect the infant's digestive tract against bacterial infection. Additionally, these IgA antibodies are absorbed by endocytosis and subsequently enter the bloodstream to provide even broader immunity.

After birth, prolactin release gradually wanes, and continual milk production depends on mechanical stimulation of the nipples, normally provided by the sucking infant. Mechanoreceptors in the nipple send afferent nerve impulses to the hypothalamus, stimulating secretion of PRH. This results in a burstlike release of prolactin, which stimulates milk production for the next feeding. The same afferent impulses also prompt hypothalamic release of oxytocin from the posterior pituitary via a *positive feedback mechanism.* Oxytocin causes the **let-down reflex,** the actual ejection of milk from the alveoli of the mammary glands (Figure 28.18). Let-down occurs when oxytocin binds to myoepithelial cells surrounding the glands, after which milk is ejected from *both* breasts, not just the suckled one. During nursing oxytocin also stimulates the recently emptied uterus to contract, helping it to return to (nearly) its prepregnant size.

Breast milk has advantages for the infant: (1) Its fats and iron are better absorbed and its amino acids are metabolized more efficiently than those of cow's milk. (2) Besides IgA, it has a host of other beneficial chemicals, including complement, lysozyme,

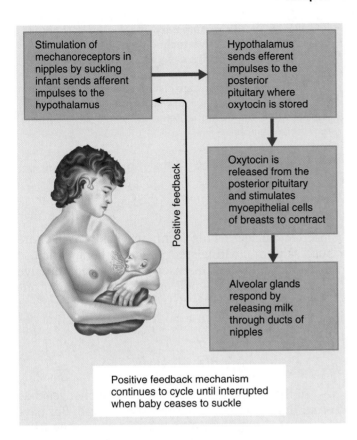

Stimulation of mechanoreceptors in nipples by suckling infant sends afferent impulses to the hypothalamus

Hypothalamus sends efferent impulses to the posterior pituitary where oxytocin is stored

Oxytocin is released from the posterior pituitary and stimulates myoepithelial cells of breasts to contract

Alveolar glands respond by releasing milk through ducts of nipples

Positive feedback

Positive feedback mechanism continues to cycle until interrupted when baby ceases to suckle

FIGURE 28.18 **Positive feedback mechanism of the milk let-down reflex.**

interferon, and lactoperoxidase, that protect infants from life-threatening infections. Mother's milk also contains interleukins and prostaglandins that prevent overzealous inflammatory responses, and a glycoprotein that deters the ulcer-causing bacterium (H. pylori) from attaching to the stomach mucosa. (3) Its natural laxative effect helps to cleanse the bowels of **meconium** (mĕ-ko′ne-um), a tarry green-black paste containing sloughed-off epithelial cells, bile, and other substances. Since meconium, and later feces, provides the route for eliminating bilirubin from the body, clearing meconium as quickly as possible helps to prevent *physiological jaundice* (see the Related Clinical Terms section). It also encourages bacteria (the source of vitamin K and some B vitamins) to colonize the large intestine.

When nursing is discontinued, the stimulus for prolactin release and milk production ends, and the mammary glands stop producing milk. Women who nurse their infants for six months or more lose a significant amount of calcium from their bones, but those on sound diets usually replace lost bone calcium after weaning the infant. While prolactin levels are high, the normal hypothalamic-pituitary controls of the ovarian cycle are damped, probably because

stimulation of the hypothalamus by sucking causes it to release beta endorphin, a peptide hormone that inhibits hypothalamic release of GnRH and hence the release of gonadotropins by the pituitary. Because of this prolactin-induced inhibition of ovarian function, nursing has been called natural birth control. Nonetheless, there is a good deal of "slippage" in these controls, and most women begin to ovulate even while continuing to nurse their infants.

Assisted Reproductive Technology and Reproductive Cloning

So far we have been describing how babies are made. But if a couple lacks that capability for some reason, what recourse do they have? Hormone therapy may increase sperm or egg production in cases where that is the problem, and surgery can open blocked uterine tubes. Beyond that is *assisted reproductive technology (ART)*, procedures that entail surgical removal of oocytes from a woman's ovaries following hormone stimulation, fertilizing the oocytes, and then returning them to the woman's body. Unused oocytes, sperm, and embryos can be frozen for later attempts at accomplishing pregnancy.

In the most common ART process, *in vitro fertilization (IVF)*, harvested oocytes are incubated with sperm in culture dishes for several days to allow fertilization to occur. In cases where the quality or number of sperm is low, the oocytes are injected with sperm (Figure 28.19). Embryos reaching the two-cell or blastocyst stage are then carefully transferred into the woman's uterus in the hope that implantation will occur. In *zygote intrafallopian transfer (ZIFT)*, oocytes fertilized in vitro are immediately transferred to the woman's uterine (fallopian) tubes with the goal of development to the blastocyst stage there and normal implantation in the uterus. In *gamete intrafallopian transfer (GIFT)*, no in vitro procedures are used; instead sperm and harvested oocytes are transferred together into the woman's uterine tubes in the hope that fertilization will occur there. These procedures, now performed worldwide in major medical centers, have produced thousands of infants, but they are expensive, emotionally draining, and painful for the oocyte donor.

Although there is a great deal of hubbub in the scientific community about using cloning as another possible avenue to produce offspring, human beings have proved notoriously difficult to create and sustain past very early (blastocyst) development. Cloning entails insertion of a somatic cell nucleus into an oocyte and then an incubation period to dedifferentiate the

28

Mature secondary oocyte surrounded by corona radiata (harvested from ovary)

Polar body

Normal sperm

When number or quality of sperm is low

In vitro fertilization (oocyte incubated with sperm)

Micro-pipette

Intracyto-plasmic sperm injection (injection of sperm)

Pronuclei

Fertilized egg

Day 2

2-cell stage

Extra embryos formed

Embryo transfer

4-cell stage

Cryopreservation

Morula

Day 5

Blastocyst

FIGURE 28.19 **Brief summary of selected techniques of assisted reproductive technology (ART).** Mature oocytes harvested from the ovary are incubated with sperm to allow natural fertilization to occur or are injected with sperm. The fertilized eggs are cultured in vitro to achieve the two-cell or blastocyst stage, at which time the embryo(s) is transferred to the receptive uterus. Extra embryos are frozen for future attempts.

inserted nucleus. This technique has proved more successful in creating stem cells for therapeutic use in treating selected diseases than for reproductive cloning to produce whole and healthy human offspring. Furthermore, human reproductive cloning is currently fraught with legal, moral, ethical, and political roadblocks.

■ ■ ■

In this chapter, we have focused on changes that occur during human development in utero. But having a baby is not always what the interacting partners have in mind, and we humans have devised a variety of techniques for preventing this outcome (see *A Closer Look* on p. 1128).

Getting back to human embryonic development, we must admit that the description here has fallen short because the phenomenon of differentiation has barely been touched upon. How does an unspecialized cell that can become *anything* in the body develop into a specific *something* (a heart cell, for example)? And what paces the developmental sequence, so that if a particular process fails to occur at a precise time, it never occurs at all? Scientists are beginning to believe that there are master switches in the genes. Chapter 29, the final chapter of this book, describes a small part of the "how" as it examines the interaction of genes that determine who we finally become.

Related Clinical Terms

Abortion (*abort* = born prematurely) Premature removal of the embryo or fetus from the uterus; may be spontaneous or induced.

Ectopic pregnancy (ek-top'ik; *ecto* = outside) A pregnancy in which the embryo implants in any site other than the uterus; most often the site is a uterine tube (tubal pregnancy). Since the uterine tube (as well as most other ectopic sites) is unable to establish a placenta or accommodate growth, the uterine tube ruptures unless the condition is diagnosed early, or the pregnancy spontaneously aborts.

Hydatid (hydatidiform) mole (hi'dah-tid; *hydat* = watery) Developmental abnormality of the placenta; the conceptus degenerates and the chorionic villi convert into a mass of vesicles that resemble tapioca. Signs include vaginal bleeding, which contains some of the grapelike vesicles.

Physiological jaundice (jawn'dis) Jaundice sometimes occurring in normal newborns within three to four days after birth. Fetal erythrocytes are short-lived, and they break down rapidly after birth; the infant's liver may be unable to process the bilirubin (breakdown product of hemoglobin pigment) fast enough to prevent its accumulation in blood and subsequent deposit in body tissues.

Placenta abruptio (ah-brup'she-o; *abrupt* = broken away from) Premature separation of the placenta from the uterine wall; if this occurs before labor, it can result in fetal death due to anoxia.

Placenta previa (pre've-ah) Placental formation adjacent to or across the internal os of the uterus. Represents a problem because as the uterus and cervix stretch, tearing of the placenta may occur. Additionally, the placenta precedes the infant during labor.

Ultrasonography (ul"trah-son-og'rah-fe) Noninvasive technique that uses sound waves to visualize the position and size of the fetus and placenta (see *A Closer Look*, Chapter 1).

Chapter Summary

1. The gestation period of approximately 280 days extends from the woman's last menstrual period to birth. The conceptus undergoes embryonic development for 8 weeks after fertilization, and fetal development from week 9 to birth.

From Egg to Zygote (pp. 1114–1117)

Accomplishing Fertilization (pp. 1114–1117)

1. An oocyte is fertilizable for up to 24 hours; most sperm are viable within the female reproductive tract for one to two days.

2. Sperm must survive the hostile environment of the vagina and become capacitated (capable of reaching and fertilizing the oocyte).

3. Hundreds of sperm must release their acrosomal enzymes to break down the egg's corona radiata and zona pellucida.

4. When one sperm binds to receptors on the egg, it triggers the slow block to polyspermy (release of cortical granules).

5. Following sperm penetration, the secondary oocyte completes meiosis II. Then the ovum and sperm pronuclei fuse (fertilization), forming a zygote.

Events of Embryonic Development: Zygote to Blastocyst Implantation (pp. 1117–1122)

Cleavage and Blastocyst Formation (pp. 1117–1119)

1. Cleavage, a rapid series of mitotic divisions without intervening growth, begins with the zygote and ends with a blastocyst. The blastocyst consists of the trophoblast and an inner cell mass. Cleavage produces a large number of cells with a favorable surface-to-volume ratio.

Implantation (pp. 1119–1120)

2. The trophoblast adheres to, digests, and implants in the endometrium. Implantation is completed when the blastocyst is entirely surrounded by endometrial tissue, about 12 days after ovulation.

3. hCG released by the blastocyst maintains hormone production by the corpus luteum, preventing menses. hCG levels decline after four months.

Placentation (pp. 1120–1122)

4. The placenta acts as the respiratory, nutritive, and excretory organ of the fetus and produces the hormones of pregnancy. It is formed from embryonic (chorionic villi) and maternal (endometrial decidua) tissues. The chorion develops when the trophoblast becomes associated with extraembryonic mesoderm. Typically, the placenta is functional as an endocrine organ by the third month.

Events of Embryonic Development: Gastrula to Fetus (pp. 1122–1132)

Formation and Roles of the Extraembryonic Membranes (pp. 1122–1123)

1. The fluid-filled amnion forms from cells of the superior surface (epiblast) of the embryonic disc. It protects the embryo from physical trauma and adhesion formation, provides a constant temperature, and allows fetal movements.

2. The yolk sac forms from the hypoblast of the embryonic disc; it is the source of early blood cells.

3. The allantois, a caudal outpocketing adjacent to the yolk sac, forms the structural basis of the umbilical cord.

4. The chorion is the outermost membrane and takes part in placentation.

Gastrulation: Germ Layer Formation (p. 1123)

5. Gastrulation involves cellular migrations that ultimately transform the inner cell mass into a three-layered embryo (gastrula) containing ectoderm, mesoderm, and endoderm. Cells that move through the midline primitive streak become endoderm if they form the most inferior layer of the embryonic disc and mesoderm if they ultimately occupy the middle layer. Cells remaining on the superior surface become ectoderm.

Organogenesis: Differentiation of the Germ Layers (pp. 1123–1132)

6. Ectoderm forms the nervous system and the epidermis of the skin and its derivatives. The first event of organogenesis is neurulation, which produces the brain and spinal cord. By the eighth week, all major brain regions are formed.

28

7. Endoderm forms the mucosa of the digestive and respiratory systems, and the epithelial cells of all associated glands (thyroid, parathyroids, thymus, liver, pancreas). It becomes a continuous tube when the embryonic body undercuts and fuses ventrally.

8. Mesoderm forms all other organ systems and tissues. It segregates early into (1) a dorsal superior notochord, (2) paired somites that form the vertebrae, skeletal trunk muscles, and part of the dermis, and (3) paired masses of intermediate and lateral mesoderm. The intermediate mesoderm forms the kidneys and gonads. The somatic layer of the lateral mesoderm forms the dermis of skin, parietal serosa, and bones and muscles of the limbs; the splanchnic layer forms the cardiovascular system and the visceral serosae.

9. The fetal cardiovascular system is formed in the embryonic period. The umbilical vein delivers nutrient- and oxygen-rich blood to the embryo; the paired umbilical arteries return oxygen-poor, waste-laden blood to the placenta. The ductus venosus allows most of the blood to bypass the liver; the foramen ovale and ductus arteriosus are pulmonary shunts.

Events of Fetal Development (p. 1133)

1. All organ systems are laid down during the embryonic period; growth and tissue/organ specialization are the major events of the fetal period.

2. During the fetal period, fetal length increases from about 22 mm to 360 mm, and weight increases from less than an ounce to 7 pounds or more.

Effects of Pregnancy on the Mother (pp. 1133–1135)

Anatomical Changes (pp. 1133–1134)

1. Maternal reproductive organs and breasts become increasingly vascularized during pregnancy, and the breasts enlarge.

2. The uterus eventually occupies nearly the entire abdominopelvic cavity. Abdominal organs are pushed superiorly and encroach on the thoracic cavity, causing the ribs to flare.

3. The increased abdominal mass changes the woman's center of gravity; lordosis and backache are common. A waddling gait occurs as pelvic ligaments and joints are loosened by placental relaxin.

4. A typical weight gain during pregnancy in a woman of normal weight is 28 pounds.

Metabolic Changes (pp. 1134–1135)

5. Human placental lactogen has anabolic effects and promotes glucose sparing in the mother. Human chorionic thyrotropin results in maternal hypermetabolism.

Physiological Changes (p. 1135)

6. Many women suffer morning sickness, heartburn, and constipation during pregnancy.

7. The kidneys produce more urine, and pressure on the bladder may cause frequency, urgency, and stress incontinence.

8. Tidal volume and respiratory rate increase, but residual volume decreases. Dyspnea is common.

9. Total body water and blood volume increase dramatically. Heart rate and blood pressure rise, resulting in enhancement of cardiac output in the mother.

Parturition (Birth) (pp. 1135–1137)

1. Parturition encompasses a series of events called labor.

Initiation of Labor (pp. 1135–1136)

2. When estrogen levels are sufficiently high, they induce oxytocin receptors on the myometrial cells and inhibit progesterone's quieting effect on uterine muscle. Weak, irregular contractions begin.

3. Fetal cells produce oxytocin, which stimulates prostaglandin production by the placenta. Both hormones stimulate contraction of uterine muscle. Increasing stress activates the hypothalamus, causing oxytocin release from the posterior pituitary; this sets up a positive feedback loop resulting in true labor.

Stages of Labor (p. 1137)

4. The dilation stage is from the onset of rhythmic, strong contractions until the cervix is fully dilated. The head of the fetus rotates as it descends through the pelvic outlet.

5. The expulsion stage extends from full cervical dilation until birth of the infant.

6. The placental stage is the delivery of the afterbirth (the placenta and attached fetal membranes).

Adjustments of the Infant to Extrauterine Life (pp. 1137–1138)

1. The infant's Apgar score is recorded immediately after birth.

Taking the First Breath and Transition (pp. 1137–1138)

2. After the umbilical cord is clamped, carbon dioxide accumulates in the infant's blood, causing respiratory centers in the brain to trigger the first inspiration.

3. Once the lungs are inflated, breathing is eased by the presence of surfactant, which decreases the surface tension of the alveolar fluid.

4. During transition, the first 8 hours after birth, the infant is physiologically unstable and adjusting. After stabilizing, the infant wakes approximately every 3–4 hours in response to hunger.

Occlusion of Special Fetal Blood Vessels and Vascular Shunts (p. 1138)

5. Inflation of the lungs causes pressure changes in the circulation; as a result, the umbilical arteries and vein, ductus venosus, and ductus arteriosus collapse, and the foramen ovale closes. The occluded blood vessels are converted to fibrous cords; the site of the foramen ovale becomes the fossa ovalis.

Lactation (pp. 1138–1139)

1. The breasts are prepared for lactation during pregnancy by high blood levels of estrogen, progesterone, and placental lactogen.

2. Colostrum, a premilk fluid, is a fat-poor fluid that contains more protein, vitamin A, and minerals than true milk. It is produced toward the end of pregnancy and for the first two to three days after birth.

3. True milk is produced around day 3 in response to suckling, which stimulates the hypothalamus to prompt anterior pituitary release of prolactin and posterior pituitary release of oxytocin. Prolactin stimulates milk production. Serotonin inhibits prolactin release when the mammary glands are full of milk, and oxytocin triggers milk let-down. Continued breast-feeding is required for continued milk production.

4. At first, ovulation and menses are absent or irregular during nursing, but in most women the ovarian cycle is eventually reestablished while still nursing.

Assisted Reproductive Technology and Reproductive Cloning   (pp. 1139–1140)

1. Assisted reproductive technology (ART) procedures assist infertile couples to bear children. Among the most used techniques are IVF, ZIFT, and GIFT. IVF and ZIFT attempt to fertilize harvested oocytes in vitro and then return the embryo or zygote to the woman's body. GIFT utilizes in vivo methods—sperm and oocytes are transferred together to the woman's uterine tubes.

2. Reproductive cloning in humans has proved difficult to achieve and the practice has met several roadblocks.

Review Questions

Multiple Choice/Matching

(Some questions have more than one correct answer. Select the best answer or answers from the choices given.)

1. Indicate whether each of the following statements is describing (a) cleavage or (b) gastrulation.

_____ **(1)** period during which a morula forms
_____ **(2)** period when vast amounts of cell migration occur
_____ **(3)** period when the three embryonic germ layers appear
_____ **(4)** period during which the blastocyst is formed

2. Most systems are operational in the fetus by four to six months. Which system is the exception to this generalization, affecting premature infants? (a) the circulatory system, (b) the respiratory system, (c) the urinary system, (d) the digestive system.

3. The zygote contains chromosomes from (a) the mother only, (b) the father only, (c) both the mother and father, but half from each, (d) each parent and synthesizes others.

4. The outer layer of the blastocyst, which later attaches to the uterus, is the (a) decidua, (b) trophoblast, (c) amnion, (d) inner cell mass.

5. The fetal membrane that forms the basis of the umbilical cord is the (a) allantois, (b) amnion, (c) chorion, (d) yolk sac.

6. In the fetus, the ductus arteriosus carries blood from (a) the pulmonary artery to the pulmonary vein, (b) the liver to the inferior vena cava, (c) the right ventricle to the left ventricle, (d) the pulmonary trunk to the aorta.

7. Which of the following changes occur in the baby's cardiovascular system after birth? (a) Blood clots in the umbilical vein, (b) the pulmonary vessels dilate as the lungs expand, (c) the ductus venosus becomes obliterated, as does the ductus arteriosus, (d) all of these.

8. Following delivery of the infant, the delivery of the afterbirth includes the (a) placenta only, (b) placenta and decidua, (c) placenta and attached (torn) fetal membranes, (d) chorionic villi.

9. Identical twins result from the fertilization of (a) one ovum by one sperm, (b) one ovum by two sperm, (c) two ova by two sperm, (d) two ova by one sperm.

10. The umbilical vein carries (a) waste products to the placenta, (b) oxygen and food to the fetus, (c) oxygen and food to the placenta, (d) oxygen and waste products to the fetus.

11. The germ layer from which the skeletal muscles, heart, and skeleton are derived is the (a) ectoderm, (b) endoderm, (c) mesoderm.

12. Which of the following cannot pass through placental barriers? (a) blood cells, (b) glucose, (c) amino acids, (d) gases, (e) antibodies.

13. The most important hormone in initiating and maintaining lactation after birth is (a) estrogen, (b) FSH, (c) prolactin, (d) oxytocin.

14. The initial stage of labor, during which the neck of the uterus is stretched, is the (a) dilation stage, (b) expulsion stage, (c) placental stage.

15. Match each embryonic structure in Column A with its adult derivative in Column B.

Column A	Column B
_____ **(1)** notochord	**(a)** kidney
_____ **(2)** ectoderm (not neural tube)	**(b)** peritoneal cavity
_____ **(3)** intermediate mesoderm	**(c)** pancreas, liver
_____ **(4)** splanchnic mesoderm	**(d)** parietal serosa, dermis
_____ **(5)** sclerotome	**(e)** nucleus pulposus
_____ **(6)** coelom	**(f)** visceral serosa
_____ **(7)** neural tube	**(g)** hair and epidermis
_____ **(8)** somatic mesoderm	**(h)** brain
_____ **(9)** endoderm	**(i)** ribs

Short Answer Essay Questions

16. Fertilization involves much more than a mere restoration of the diploid chromosome number. (a) What does the process of fertilization entail on the part of both the egg and sperm? (b) What are the effects of fertilization?

17. Cleavage is an embryonic event that mainly involves mitotic divisions. How does cleavage differ from mitosis occurring during life after birth, and what are its important functions?

18. The life span of the ovarian corpus luteum is extended for nearly three months after implantation, but otherwise it deteriorates. (a) Explain why this is so. (b) Explain why it is important that the corpus luteum remain functional following implantation.

19. The placenta is a marvelous, but temporary, organ. Starting with a description of its formation, show how it is an intimate part of both fetal and maternal anatomy and physiology during the gestation period.

20. Why is it that only one sperm out of the hundreds (or thousands) available enters the oocyte?

21. What is the function of gastrulation?

22. (a) What is a breech presentation? (b) Cite two problems with this type of presentation.

23. What factors are believed to bring about uterine contractions at the termination of pregnancy?

24. Explain how the flat embryonic disc takes on the cylindrical shape of a tadpole.

28

Critical Thinking and Clinical Application Questions

1. Jennie, a freshman in your dormitory, tells you she just discovered that she is three months pregnant. She recently bragged that since she came to college she has been drinking alcohol heavily and experimenting with every kind of recreational drug she could find. From the following, select the advice you would give her, and explain why it is the best choice. (a) She must stop taking drugs, but they could not have affected her fetus during these first few months of her pregnancy. (b) Harmful substances usually cannot pass from mother to embryo, so she can keep using drugs. (c) There could be defects in the fetus, so she should stop using drugs and visit a doctor as soon as possible. (d) If she has not taken any drugs in the last week, she is okay.

2. During Mrs. Jones's labor, the obstetrician decided that it was necessary to perform an episiotomy. What is an episiotomy, and why is it done?

3. A woman in substantial pain called her doctor and explained (between sobs) that she was about to have her baby "right here." The doctor calmed her and asked how she had come to that conclusion. She said that her water had broken and that her husband could see the baby's head. (a) Was she right? If so, what stage of labor was she in? (b) Do you think that she had time to make it to the hospital 60 miles away? Why or why not?

4. Mary is a heavy smoker and has ignored a friend's advice to stop smoking during her pregnancy. On the basis of what you know about the effect of smoking on physiology, describe how Mary's smoking might affect her fetus.

5. While Mortimer was cramming for his anatomy test, he read that some parts of the mesoderm become segmented. He suddenly realized that he could not remember what segmentation is. Define segmentation, and give two examples of segmented structures in the embryo.

6. Assume a sperm has penetrated a polar body and their nuclei fuse. Why would it be unlikely for the resulting cell to develop into a healthy embryo?

LOOKING FOR MORE STUDY HELP?

A wide variety of quiz questions, tutorials, and learning exercises are available online at the Anatomy & Physiology Place (www.anatomyandphysiology.com) and, if your instructor has provided you with a MyA&P Course ID number, in MyA&P (www.myaandp.com).

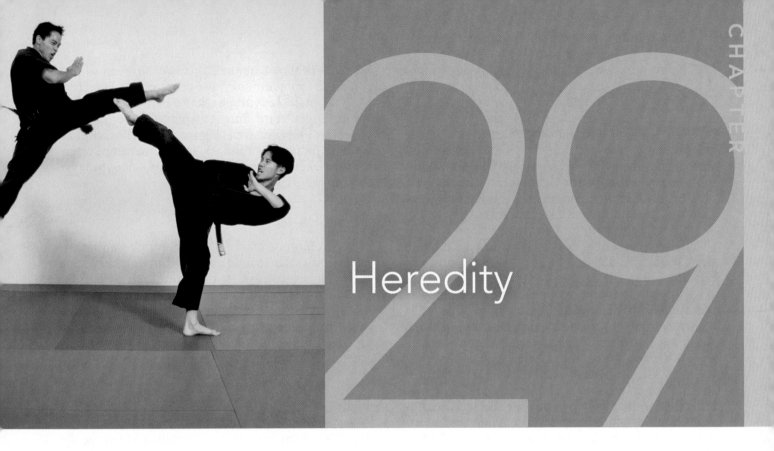

Heredity

The Vocabulary of Genetics (pp. 1146–1147)

1. Define allele.

2. Differentiate between genotype and phenotype.

Sexual Sources of Genetic Variation (pp. 1147–1149)

3. Describe events that lead to genetic variability of gametes.

Types of Inheritance (pp. 1149–1153)

4. Compare and contrast dominant-recessive inheritance with incomplete dominance and codominance.

5. Describe the mechanism of sex-linked inheritance.

6. Explain how polygene inheritance differs from that resulting from the action of a single pair of alleles.

Environmental Factors in Gene Expression (p. 1153)

7. Provide examples illustrating how gene expression may be modified by environmental factors.

Nontraditional Inheritance (pp. 1153–1154)

8. Describe how RNA-only genes and epigenetic marks affect gene expression.

9. Describe the basis of extranuclear (mitochondria-based) genetic disorders.

Genetic Screening, Counseling, and Therapy (pp. 1154–1157)

10. List and explain several techniques used to determine or predict genetic diseases.

11. Describe briefly some approaches of gene therapy.

The wondrous growth and development of a new individual is guided by the gene-bearing chromosomes it receives from its parents in egg and sperm. As described in Chapter 3, individual *genes*, or DNA segments, contain the "recipes" or genetic blueprints for proteins, many of which are enzymes that dictate the synthesis of virtually all the body's molecules. Consequently, genes are ultimately expressed in your hair color, sex, blood type, and so on. However, genes do not act as free agents. As you will see, a gene's ability to prompt the development of a specific trait is enhanced or inhibited by interactions with other genes, as well as by environmental factors.

Although the science of **genetics,** which studies the mechanism of heredity (*genes* = give birth to), is relatively young, our understanding of how human genes act and interact has advanced considerably since the basic principles of heredity were first proposed by Gregor Mendel in the mid-1800s. Part of the problem in unraveling the story of human genetics is that, unlike the pea plants Mendel studied, humans have long life spans, produce relatively few offspring, and cannot be mated experimentally just to examine the nature of their offspring. Furthermore, Mendel studied characteristics that vary in an either-or fashion rather than those that vary in a more-or-less fashion the way many human traits do. The urge to understand human inheritance is a powerful one, however, and recent advances provided by the *Human Genome Project*, which scanned and determined the human DNA sequence, are enabling geneticists to manipulate and engineer human genes to examine their expression. This research has tremendous promise for more sophisticated genetic screening, and for drug development to treat or cure disease. For example, by using viruses to introduce bioengineered genes into human cells, specific disease-causing genes can be silenced. Although we touch upon some of these newer topics, we will concentrate on the principles of heredity discovered by Mendel more than a century ago.

The Vocabulary of Genetics

The nuclei of all human cells except gametes contain the diploid number of chromosomes (46), consisting of 23 pairs of homologous chromosomes.* Two of the 46 are **sex chromosomes** (X and Y), which determine genetic sex (male = XY; female =

XX). The other 44 are the 22 pairs of **autosomes** that guide the expression of most other traits. The complete human **karyotype** (kar′e-o-tīp), or diploid chromosomal complement displayed in homologous pairs, is illustrated in Figure 29.1. The diploid **genome** (je′nōm), or genetic (DNA) makeup, represents two sets of genetic instructions—one from the egg and the other from the sperm.

Gene Pairs (Alleles)

Because chromosomes are paired, it follows that the genes in them are paired as well. Consequently, each of us receives two genes, one from each parent (for the most part), that interact to dictate a particular trait. Any two matched genes, which are at the same *locus* (location) on homologous chromosomes, are called **alleles** (ah-lēlz′) of each other. Alleles may code for the same or for alternative forms of a given trait. For example, of the alleles that dictate whether or not you have loose thumb ligaments, one variant might code for tight ligaments and the other for loose ligaments (the double-jointed thumb condition). When the two alleles controlling a trait are the same, a person is said to be **homozygous** (ho-mo-zi′gus) for that trait. When the two alleles are different, the individual is **heterozygous** (het″er-o-zi′gus) for the trait.

Sometimes, one allele masks or suppresses the expression of its partner. Such an allele is said to be **dominant,** whereas the allele that is masked is said to be **recessive.** By convention, a dominant allele is represented by a capital letter (for example, *J*), and a recessive allele by the lowercase form of the same letter (*j*). Dominant alleles are expressed, or make themselves "known," when they are present in either single or double dose. For recessive alleles to be expressed, they must be present in double dose, that is, the homozygous condition. Returning to our thumb example, a person whose genetic makeup includes either the gene pair *JJ* (the homozygous dominant condition) or the gene pair *Jj* (the heterozygous condition) will have double-jointed thumbs. The combination *jj* (the homozygous recessive condition) is needed to produce tight thumb ligaments.

A common misconception is that dominant traits will be seen more often because they are expressed whether the allele is present in single or double dose. However, dominance and recessiveness alone do not determine the frequency of a trait in a population; this also depends on the relative abundance of the respective dominant or recessive alleles in that population. For example, five fingers per hand is recessive to six fingers per hand, yet we certainly see a lot more people with five fingers on each hand.

---

* Recall that homologous chromosomes are chromosome pairs— one from the father (sperm) and one from the mother (egg)—that look similar and carry genes for the same traits, but do not necessarily convey the same expressions of those traits.

Q *When a geneticist orders a karyotype, why are cells in metaphase studied instead of those in interphase?*

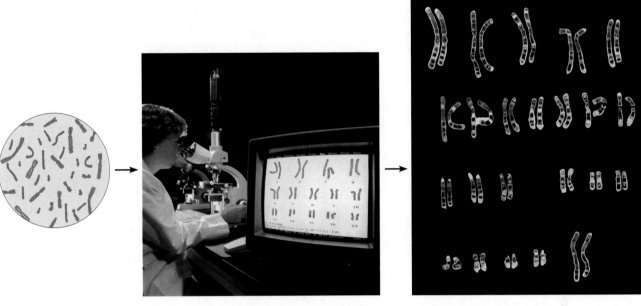

(a) The slide is viewed with a microscope, and the chromosomes are photographed.

(b) The photograph is entered into a computer, and the chromosomes are electronically rearranged into pairs according to size and structure.

(c) The resulting display is the karyotype.

FIGURE 29.1 **Preparing a karyotype.** After lymphocytes are stimulated to divide and grow in culture for several days, they are treated with a drug that arrests mitosis in metaphase, a stage when the chromosomes are easily identified. The cells are harvested, treated with a solution that makes their chromosomes spread out, and **(a)** transferred to a microscope for photography. **(b)** The photograph is entered into a computer for analysis and arrangement of the chromosomes into homologous pairs. **(c)** The karyotype is displayed for examination of chromosomal structure and number. The patterns of stained bands help to identify specific chromosomes and parts of chromosomes.

Genotype and Phenotype

A person's genetic makeup is referred to as his or her **genotype** (jen′o-tīp). The way that genotype is expressed in the body is called one's **phenotype** (fe′no-tīp). Thus, the double-jointed condition is the phenotype produced by a genotype of *JJ* or *Jj*.

Sexual Sources of Genetic Variation

Before we examine how genes interact, let us consider why (with the possible exception of identical siblings) each of us is one of a kind, with a unique genotype and phenotype. This variability reflects three events that occur before we are even a twinkle in our parents' eyes: independent assortment of chromosomes, crossover of homologues, and random fertilization of eggs by sperm.

Chromosome Segregation and Independent Assortment

As described in Chapter 27, each pair of homologous chromosomes synapses during meiosis I, forming a tetrad. This happens during both spermatogenesis and oogenesis. Because chance determines how the tetrads align on the meiosis I metaphase spindle, maternal and paternal chromosomes are randomly distributed to daughter nuclei. As illustrated in Figure 29.2, this simple event leads to an amazing amount of variation in gametes. The cell in our example has a diploid number of 6, and so three tetrads form. As you can see, the possible combinations of

A *The genetic material is more dispersed as chromatin during interphase, so no individual chromosomes are visible (or identifiable).*

29

Q *What event leads to the variability seen here?*

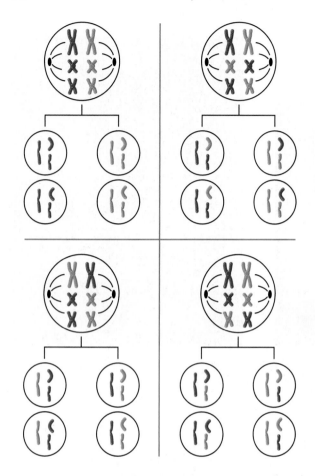

FIGURE 29.2   **Gamete variability resulting from independent assortment.** During metaphase of meiosis I, the tetrads of homologous chromosomes (two originals each with its replica) align independently of other tetrads. The large circles depict the possible alignments in a mother cell having a diploid number of 6 (paternal homologues purple; maternal, green). The small circles show the gametes arising from each alignment. Some gametes contain all maternal or all paternal chromosomes; others have maternal and paternal chromosomes in various combinations.

alignments of the three tetrads result in eight gamete possibilities. Because the way each tetrad aligns is random, and because many mother cells are undergoing meiosis simultaneously, each alignment and each type of gamete occurs with the same frequency as all others.

Two important points about meiosis I metaphase: (1) The two alleles determining each trait are **segregated,** which means that they are distributed to different gametes. (2) Alleles on different pairs of homologous chromosomes are distributed independently

of each other. The net result is that each gamete has a single allele for each trait, and that allele represents only one of the four possible parental alleles.

The number of different gamete types resulting from **independent assortment** of homologues during meiosis I can be calculated for any genome from the formula 2^n, where *n* is the number of homologous pairs. In our example, $2^n = 2^3$ $(2 \times 2 \times 2)$, for a total of eight different gamete types. The number of gamete types increases dramatically as chromosome number increases. A cell with six pairs of homologues would produce 2^6, or 64, kinds of gametes. In a man's testes, the number of gamete types that can be produced on the basis of independent assortment alone is 2^{23}, or about 8.5 million—an incredible variety. Because a human female's ovaries complete at most 500 reduction divisions in her lifetime, the number of different gamete types produced simultaneously is significantly less. Still, each ovulated oocyte will most likely be novel genetically because of independent assortment.

Crossover of Homologues and Gene Recombination

Additional gamete variation results from the crossing over and exchange of chromosomal parts during meiosis I. Genes are arranged linearly along a chromosome's length, and genes on the same chromosome are said to be **linked** because they are physically connected and transmitted as a unit to daughter cells during mitosis. However, during meiosis, chromosomes can break and precisely exchange gene segments with their homologous counterparts, giving rise to **recombinant chromosomes** that have mixed contributions from each parent.

In the hypothetical example shown in Figure 29.3, the genes for hair and eye color are linked. The paternal chromosome contains alleles coding for blond hair and blue eyes, and the maternal alleles code for brown hair and brown eyes. In the **crossover,** or **chiasma,** shown, the break occurs between these linked genes, resulting in some gametes with alleles for blond hair and brown eyes and others with alleles for brown hair and blue eyes. As a result of the crossover, two of the four chromatids present in the tetrad end up with a mixed set of alleles— some maternal and some paternal. This means that when the chromatids segregate, each gamete will receive a unique combination of parental genes.

All four chromatids in a tetrad may take part in crossing over and recombination, and these may make many crossovers while synapsed. Furthermore, each crossover causes many genes to recombine, not just two as shown in our example. In general, crossovers occur at random points, and tend to occur nearer the medial regions of the chromatid arms.

A ▶ *Random alignment of the tetrads on the metaphase spindle.*

Because humans have 23 tetrads, with crossovers going on in most of them during meiosis I, the variability resulting from this factor alone is tremendous.

Random Fertilization

At any point in time, gametogenesis is turning out gametes with all variations possible from independent assortment and random crossovers. Compounding this variety is the fact that a single human egg will be fertilized by a single sperm on a totally haphazard or random basis. If we consider variation resulting only from independent assortment and random fertilization, any offspring represents one out of the close to 72 trillion (8.5 million × 8.5 million) zygotes possible. The additional variation introduced by crossovers increases this number exponentially. Perhaps now you can understand why brothers and sisters are so different, and marvel at how they can also be so alike in many ways.

Once these sources of variability are understood, it is easy to see that the concept most people have of inheritance is inaccurate. We often hear something like "I'm one-half German, one-quarter Scottish, and one-quarter Italian," which reveals a belief that genes from both sides of the family are parceled out in mathematically precise combinations. While it is true that we receive half of our genes from each parent, these genes do not contain one-quarter from each grandparent, one-eighth from each great grandparent, and so on. Additionally, there are no such things as German, Scottish, or Italian genes.

Types of Inheritance

Although a few human phenotypes can be traced to a single gene pair (as described shortly), most such traits are very limited in nature, or reflect variation in a single enzyme. Most human traits are determined by multiple alleles or by the interaction of several gene pairs.

Dominant-Recessive Inheritance

Dominant-recessive inheritance reflects the interaction of dominant and recessive alleles. A simple diagram, called the **Punnett square,** is used to figure

FIGURE 29.3 **Crossover and genetic recombination.** These meiosis I events increase genetic variability in the gametes formed. For simplicity, only two chromatids are shown taking part in crossover. Multiple crossovers result in more complex patterns.

Q *What would be the result if the crossover occurred at a different location?*

Hair color genes   Eye color genes

Homologous chromosomes synapse during prophase of meiosis I; each chromosome consists of two sister chromatids.

Chiasma

One chromatid segment exchanges positions with a homologous chromatid segment; that is, crossing over occurs, forming a chiasma.

The chromatids forming the chiasma break and the broken-off ends join their corresponding homologues.

Gamete 1
Gamete 2
Gamete 3
Gamete 4

At the conclusion of meiosis, each haploid gamete has one of the four chromosomes shown; two of the chromosomes are recombinant (they carry new combinations of genes).

Key

H = allele for brown hair   *E* = allele for brown eyes
h = allele for blond hair   *e* = allele for blue eyes

▮ = Paternal chromosome
▮ = Maternal chromosome ⎱ Homologous pair

A *There would be a different selection of linked genes in the resulting gametes.*

29

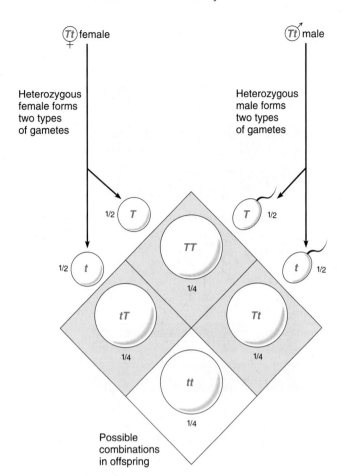

FIGURE 29.4   Genotype and phenotype probabilities resulting from a mating of two heterozygous parents. The Punnett square shows all possible combinations of a set of alleles in the zygote. In this example, the *T* allele is dominant and determines tongue-rolling ability; the *t* allele is recessive.

out, for a single trait, the possible gene combinations that would result from the mating of parents of known genotypes (Figure 29.4). In the example shown, both parents can roll their tongue into a U because both are heterozygous for the dominant allele *(T)* that confers this ability. In other words, each parent has the genotype *Tt*. The alleles of one parent are written along one side of the Punnett square, and the alleles for the other parent are shown along an adjacent side. The alleles are then combined down and across to determine the possible gene combinations (genotypes) and their expected frequency in the offspring of these two parents. As the completed Punnett square shows, the probability of these parents producing a homozygous dominant child *(TT)* is 25% (1 out of 4); of producing a heterozygous child *(Tt)*, 50% (2 out of 4); and of producing a homozygous recessive child, 25% (1 out of 4). The *TT* and *Tt* offspring will be tongue rollers; only the *tt* offspring will not be able to roll their tongues.

The Punnett square predicts only the *probability* of having a certain percentage of offspring with a particular genotype (and phenotype). The larger the number of offspring, the greater the likelihood that the ratios will conform to the predicted values—just as the chances of getting heads half the time and tails half the time increase with the number of tosses of a coin. If we toss only twice, we may well get heads both times. Likewise, if the couple in our example had only two children, it would not be surprising if both children had the genotype *Tt*.

What are the chances of having two children of the same genotype? To determine the probability of two events happening in succession, we must multiply the probabilities of the separate events happening. The probability of getting heads in one coin toss is ½, so the probability of getting two heads in a row is ½ × ½ = ¼. Now consider the chances of our couple's having two children who are both non–tongue rollers *(tt)*. The probability that one child will be *tt* is ¼, so the probability that both children will be *tt* is ¼ × ¼ = ⅟₁₆, only slightly better than 6%. Remember though that the production of each child, like each coin toss in a series, is an *independent event* that does not influence the production of any other child by the same couple. If you get heads on the first toss, the chance of getting heads the second time is still ½. Likewise, if our couple's first child is a *tt*, they still have a ¼ chance of getting a *tt* the next time.

Dominant Traits

Human traits dictated by dominant alleles include widow's peaks, dimples, and freckles.

Genetic disorders caused by dominant genes are uncommon because *lethal dominant genes* are almost always expressed and result in the death of the embryo, fetus, or child. Thus, the deadly genes are not usually passed along to successive generations. However, in some dominant disorders the person is less impaired or at least survives long enough to reproduce. One example is *achondroplasia* (a-kon″dro-pla′ze-ah), a rare type of dwarfism resulting from a fetus's inability to form cartilage (endochondral) bone. Another is *Huntington's disease,* a fatal nervous system disease involving degeneration of the basal nuclei. The latter involves a *delayed-action gene* that is expressed when the affected individual is about 40. Offspring of a parent with Huntington's disease have a 50% chance of inheriting the lethal gene. (The parent is heterozygous, because the dominant homozygous condition is lethal to the fetus.) Many informed offspring of such parents are opting not to become parents themselves. These and other dominant gene–determined traits are listed in Table 29.1.

29

TABLE 29.1	Traits Determined by Simple Dominant-Recessive Inheritance

PHENOTYPE DUE TO EXPRESSION OF:

DOMINANT GENES (ZZ OR Zz)	RECESSIVE GENES (zz)
Tongue roller	Inability to roll tongue into a U shape
Astigmatism	Normal vision
Freckles	Absence of freckles
Dimples in cheeks	Absence of dimples
Feet with normal arches	Flat feet
PTC* taster	PTC nontaster
Widow's peak	Straight hairline
Double-jointed thumb	Tight thumb ligaments
Broad lips	Thin lips
Polydactyly (extra fingers and toes)	Normal number of fingers and toes
Syndactyly (webbed digits)	Normal digits
Achondroplasia (heterozygous: dwarfism; homozygous: lethal)	Normal cartilage bone formation
Huntington's disease	Absence of Huntington's disease
Normal skin pigmentation	Albinism
Absence of Tay-Sachs disease	Tay-Sachs disease
Absence of cystic fibrosis	Cystic fibrosis

*PTC is phenylthiocarbamide, a harmless bitter chemical.

Recessive Traits

Some examples of recessive inheritance are the more desirable genetic condition. For example, normal vision is dictated by recessive alleles, whereas astigmatism is prescribed by dominant alleles. However, many if not most genetic disorders are inherited as simple recessive traits. These include conditions as different as *albinism* (lack of skin pigmentation); *cystic fibrosis,* a condition of excessive mucus production that impairs lung and pancreatic functioning; and *Tay-Sachs disease,* a disorder of brain lipid metabolism, caused by an enzyme deficit that shows itself a few months after birth.

Recessive genetic disorders are more frequent than those caused by dominant alleles because those who carry a *single* recessive allele for a recessive genetic disorder do not themselves express the disease. However, they can pass the gene on to offspring and so are called *carriers* of the disorder. Conversely, as explained above, few individuals with dominant genetic disorders get a chance to pass on the detrimental gene.

Incomplete Dominance

In dominant-recessive inheritance, one allele variant completely masks the other. Some traits, however, exhibit **incomplete dominance.** In such instances, the heterozygote has a phenotype intermediate between those of homozygous dominant and homozygous recessive individuals. Incomplete dominance is uncommon in humans.

Perhaps the best human example is inheritance of the *sickling gene (s),* which causes a substitution of one amino acid in the beta chain of hemoglobin. Hemoglobin molecules containing the abnormal polypeptide chains crystallize when blood oxygen tension is low, causing the erythrocytes to assume a sickle shape (see Figure 17.8b, p. 656). Individuals with a double dose of the sickling allele *(ss)* have **sickle-cell anemia,** and any condition that lowers their blood oxygen level, such as respiratory difficulty or excessive exercise, can precipitate a *sickle-cell crisis.* The deformed erythrocytes jam up and fragment in small capillaries, causing intense pain.

Individuals heterozygous for the sickling gene *(Ss)* have **sickle-cell trait.** They make both normal and sickling hemoglobin. As a rule, these individuals are healthy, and do not display the signs and symptoms. However, they can suffer a crisis if there is prolonged reduction in blood oxygen levels, as might happen when traveling in high-altitude areas, and they can transmit the sickling gene to their offspring.

Multiple-Allele Inheritance

Although we inherit only two alleles for each gene, some genes exhibit more than two allele forms, leading to a phenomenon called **multiple-allele inheritance.** For example, three alleles determine the ABO blood types in humans: I^A, I^B, and i. Each of us receives two of these. The I^A and I^B alleles are *codominant,* and both are expressed when present. The i allele is recessive to the other two. Genotypes determining the four possible ABO blood groups are shown in Table 29.2 below.

TABLE 29.2	ABO Blood Groups			
		FREQUENCY (% OF U.S. POPULATION)		
BLOOD GROUP (PHENOTYPE)	**GENOTYPE**	**WHITE**	**BLACK**	**ASIAN**
O	*ii*	45	49	40
A	I^AI^A or I^Ai	40	27	28
B	I^BI^B or I^Bi	11	20	27
AB	I^AI^B	4	4	5

29

Sex-Linked Inheritance

Inherited traits determined by genes on the sex chromosomes are said to be **sex-linked.** The X and Y sex chromosomes are not homologous in the true sense. The Y, which contains the gene (or genes) that determines maleness, is only about one-third as large as the X. The X bears over 2500 genes, and a disproportionately large number of them code for proteins important to brain function. The Y carries only 78 genes as of the last count. Hence the Y chromosome lacks many of the genes present on the X. For example, genes coding for certain clotting factors, cone pigments, and even testosterone receptors are present on X but not on Y. A gene found only on the X chromosome is said to be **X-linked.** Only relatively short regions at either end of the Y chromosome (corresponding to about 5% of the Y's DNA) code for nonsexual characteristics corresponding to those on the X, and those regions are the only areas that can participate in crossovers with the X. The balance of the Y chromosome contains eight stretches of DNA with sequences that are essentially mirror images of each other, creating what are called *genetic palindromes*—the equivalents of the sentence "MADAM I'M ADAM." The benefit of such a condition seems to be that if one of these sections bends in the middle, it can donate a gene to fix a defective copy in its neighboring area.

When a male inherits an X-linked recessive allele—for example, for hemophilia or for red-green color blindness—its expression is never masked or damped, because there is no corresponding allele on his Y chromosome. Consequently, the recessive gene is always expressed, even when present only in single dose. In contrast, females must have two X-linked recessive alleles to express such a disorder; as a result, very few females exhibit any X-linked conditions.

X-linked traits are typically passed from mother to son, never from father to son, because males receive no X chromosome from their father. Of course, the mother can also pass the recessive allele to her daughter, but unless the daughter receives another such allele from her father, she will not express the trait.

It should also be noted that some segments of the Y chromosome have no counterpart on the X chromosome. Traits coded for by genes in these segments (including the *SRY* gene necessary for proper male development and the gene for hairy ear pinnae) appear only in males and are passed from fathers to sons. This type of sex-linked gene transmission is referred to as **Y-linked inheritance.**

Polygene Inheritance

So far, we have considered only traits inherited by mechanisms of classical Mendelian genetics, which are fairly easily understood. Such traits typically have two, or perhaps three, alternate forms. However, many phenotypes depend on several gene pairs at different locations acting in tandem. Such **polygene inheritance** results in *continuous*, or *quantitative*, phenotypic variation between two extremes and explains many human characteristics. Examples of polygene traits in humans include skin color, height, and intelligence.

Skin color, for instance, is controlled by three separately inherited genes, each existing in two allelic forms: *A, a; B, b; C, c.* The *A, B,* and *C* alleles confer dark skin pigment, and their effects are additive. The *a, b,* and *c* alleles confer pale skin tone. Hence, an individual with an *AABBCC* genotype would be about as dark-skinned as a human can get, while an *aabbcc* person would be very fair. However, when individuals heterozygous for at least one of these gene pairs mate, a broad range of pigmentation is possible in their offspring. Such polygene inheritance results in a distribution of genotypes and phenotypes that, when plotted, yields a bell-shaped curve (Figure 29.5).

Height is controlled by four gene pairs, and different combinations of the tallness or shortness alleles are reflected in differences in stature in much the same way as described for inheritance of skin tone. The phenomenon of polygene inheritance helps explain why parents of average height can produce very tall or very short offspring.

Environmental Factors in Gene Expression

In many situations environmental factors override or at least influence gene expression. Although our genotype (discounting mutations) is as unchanging as the Rock of Gibraltar, our phenotype is more like clay. If this were not the case, we would never get a tan, women bodybuilders would never develop bulging muscles, and there would be no hope for treating genetic disorders.

Sometimes, such maternal factors as drugs or pathogens alter normal gene expression during embryonic development. Take, for example, the case of the "thalidomide babies" (discussed on p. 1130). As a result of their mothers taking that sedative, the embryos developed phenotypes (flipperlike appendages) not directed by their genes. Such environmentally produced phenotypes that mimic conditions that may be caused by genetic mutations (permanent transmissible changes in the DNA) are called **phenocopies.**

Equally significant are environmental factors that may influence genetic expression after birth, such as the effect of poor infant nutrition on brain growth, general body development, and height. In this way, a person with "tall genes" can be stunted by insufficient nutrition. Furthermore, hormonal deficits during childhood can lead to abnormal skeletal growth and proportions as exemplified by cretinism, a type of dwarfism resulting from hypothyroidism. This is an example of genes (or genetic abnormalities) other than those dictating height having an influence on the height phenotype. Hence, part of a gene's environment consists of the influence of other genes.

Nontraditional Inheritance

Mendel's writings underlie mainstream thinking about heredity, but some genetic outcomes fail to fit his rules. Among these nontraditional types of inheritance are influences due to RNA-only genes, to chemical groups attached to DNA or histone proteins, and to *extranuclear inheritance* conferred by mitochondrial DNA.

Beyond DNA: Regulation of Gene Expression

Our genome is a biochemical system of awesome complexity, with three basic levels of controls. The protein-coding genes that we have been describing to this point only make up the first level and account for less than 2% of the DNA of a human cell. This is the part of the genome traditionally considered to be a "blueprint" for protein structure.

Since the 1960s, scientists have been locating information important in directing development elsewhere—in the noncoding DNA and even totally outside the DNA sequences. They found, in many cases, that these second and third layers of information can account for certain cancers in cells that don't harbor mutations and for illnesses that run in families but pop up unpredictably, even differing in identical twins. For example, when one identical twin develops type 1 diabetes or schizophrenia, the other twin usually does not. So what are these other regulatory systems?

Small RNAs

The second layer appears to be the double-stranded RNA (dsRNA) product of the abundant "RNA-only genes" (see p. 109), formerly believed to be "junk," that are sequestered in the non-protein-coding DNA. They form a parallel regulatory or signaling system that consists of microRNAs (miRNAs) and short interfering RNAs (siRNAs), which can tame or inacti-

FIGURE 29.5   Simplified model for polygenic inheritance of skin color based on three gene pairs. Alleles for dark skin are incompletely dominant over those for light skin. Each dominant gene (*A, B, C*) contributes one "unit" of darkness (indicated by a dark dot) to the phenotypes. Here the parents are homozygotes at opposite ends of the phenotype range. Each child inherits 3 "units" of darkness (is a heterozygote) and has intermediate pigmentation. When they grow up and mate with those with a different gene pool, their offspring (second generation) may have a wide variation in pigmentation, as shown by the plotted distribution of skin colors.

vate aggressive (jumping) genes, called *transposons*, that tend to replicate themselves and then insert the copies into distant DNA sites, disabling or hyperactivating those genes. Small RNAs control timing of programmed cell death during development and can also prevent translation of another gene—for example, when invading viruses try to commandeer a cell's protein-making machinery to make viral proteins. Mutations in these RNA-only areas have already been linked to several conditions including prostate and lung cancers and schizophrenia. These small RNA molecules can act directly on DNA, other RNAs, or proteins and so they have an edge over proteins for transmitting information and regulating activity within the genome itself. As a result of the genome project, nucleotide sequences of these RNA-specifying DNA areas are now worked out and biochemical companies are investing heavily in gene therapy research. They are especially hot on synthesizing RNA-interfering drugs to silence or shut down particular genes to treat age-related macular degeneration, Parkinson's disease, cancer, hepatitis C, and a host of other disorders.

Epigenetic Marks

Epigenetic marks form the third layer of gene controls. This continually changing information is stored in the proteins and chemical groups that bind to and surround the DNA and in the manner in which chromatin is packaged in the cell. Epigenetic marks may even be passed from parent to child, yet they do not alter the associated DNA. Within cells, chemical tags such as methyl and acetyl groups bound to DNA segments and to histones determine whether the DNA is available for transcription (acetylation) or silenced (methylation), and recent evidence indicates that it is the small RNA molecules (see above) that direct the placement of chromatin tags. Epigenetic marks also account for the inactivation (by methylation) of one of the female's X chromosomes in the early embryo. Because tumor cell chromatin tends to be methyl-deficient, there is some consensus that epigenetic marks or lack of them may predispose for cell transformation from normal to cancerous. Beyond this, we now know that even slight deviations in the epigenetic marks on specific chromosomes can result in devastating human illness.

Epigenetic marks also underlie the phenomenon called genomic imprinting. For most genes, the maternal and paternal genes turn on or off at the same time. This balance is upset during gametogenesis when certain genes in both sperm and eggs are modified by the addition of methyl ($-CH_3$) groups. This process, called **genomic imprinting,** somehow tags the genes as paternal or maternal and confers important functional differences in the resulting embryo; this is essential for normal development. The developing embryo "reads" these tags, and then either expresses the mother's gene while the father's version remains idle or vice versa. The methylation process is reversible. In each generation, the old imprints are "erased" when new gametes are produced and all the chromosomes are newly imprinted according to the sex of the parents. Mutations of imprinted genes may lead to pathology. For example, victims of Prader-Willi syndrome are mildly to moderately retarded, short, and grossly obese. Children with Angelman syndrome are severely retarded, unable to speak coherently, laugh uncontrollably, and exhibit jerky, lurching movements as if tied to a pup-

peteer's strings (the French name for this condition is *marionette joyeuse*). The symptoms of these two disorders are very different, but the genetic cause is the same—deletion of a particular region of chromosome 15. If the defective chromosome comes from the father, the result is Prader-Willi syndrome; the mother's defective chromosome confers Angelman syndrome. Thus, it seems that the same allele can have different effects depending on which parent it comes from. Losing imprints in certain DNA segments may explain differences in the expression of schizophrenia and other inherited diseases seen in identical twins.

The power of these three levels of genetic expression and regulation is seen in a research study on a particular trait in sheep. The recipe for the trait and pedigree was seen to involve a standard protein-specifying gene, one or more RNA-only genes, and two epigenetic effects. It is now clear that protein-coding genes are not the only instructions to which cells refer. RNA matters, and so do the tiny chemical tags that attach to the chromatin.

Extranuclear (Mitochondrial) Inheritance

Although we have focused on the chromosomal basis of inheritance, remember that not all genes are in the cell's nucleus. Some 37 genes (referred to as mtDNA) are in mitochondria. Because the ovum donates essentially all the cytoplasm in the fertilized egg, mitochondrial genes are transmitted to the offspring almost exclusively by the mother. A growing list of disorders, all rare, is now being linked to errors (mutations) in mitochondrial genes. Most involve problems with oxidative phosphorylation within the mitochondria, or more rarely unusual degenerative muscle disorders or neurological problems. Some researchers suggest that Alzheimer's and Parkinson's disease may be among them.

Genetic Screening, Counseling, and Therapy

Genetic screening and *genetic counseling* provide information and options for prospective parents not even dreamed of 100 years ago. Newborn infants are routinely screened for a number of anatomical disorders (congenital hip dysplasia, imperforate anus, and others), and testing for phenylketonuria (PKU) and other metabolic diseases is mandated by law in many states. These tests are performed much too late to allow parental choice concerning whether or not to have the child, but they do alert the new parents that treatment is necessary to ensure the well-being of their infant. Anatomical defects are usually treated surgically, and PKU is managed by strict dietary measures that exclude most phenylalanine-containing foods.

Adult children of parents with Huntington's disease are obvious candidates for these services, but many other genetic conditions also place babies at risk. For example, a woman pregnant at age 35 may wish to know if her baby has trisomy-21 or Down syndrome (see Related Clinical Terms, p. 1157), a chromosome abnormality with a high incidence in children of older mothers.

Depending on the condition being investigated, screening can occur before conception, by carrier recognition, or during fetal testing.

Carrier Recognition

When a prospective parent displays a recessive genetic disorder but his or her partner does not, it is important to find out if the partner is heterozygous for the same recessive gene. If not, the offspring will receive only one such gene and will not express the trait. If the partner *is* a carrier, the child's chance of having two harmful genes is 50%.

There are two major avenues for identifying carriers: pedigrees and blood tests. A **pedigree** traces a genetic trait through several generations and helps predict the future. For prospective parents, a genetic counselor collects phenotype information on as many family members as possible and uses it to construct the pedigree. Figure 29.6a uses the rare woolly hair trait of northern Europeans to illustrate how a pedigree is constructed and read. Woolly hair, resulting from the presence of a dominant allele *(W)*, is fuzzy-textured and breaks easily. Individuals with the woolly hair phenotype (purple symbols) have at least one dominant gene *(WW or Ww)*, while those with normal hair must be homozygous recessive *(ww)*. By working backward from the bottom row and applying the rules of dominant-recessive inheritance, the counselor can deduce the genotypes of the parents (middle row). That three of their six offspring have normal hair *(ww)* tells the counselor that each parent must have at least one recessive gene. The mother has woolly hair, determined by the *W* gene, and so her genotype must be *Ww*. The father with normal hair must be homozygous recessive. You should be able to take it from here and figure out the genotypes of the offspring. (Try it!)

Figure 29.6b illustrates a pedigree analysis for albinism, a recessive trait. See what you can deduce from it. These pedigrees represent two of the simplest cases. Many human traits are controlled by multiple alleles or polygenes and are much more difficult to work out.

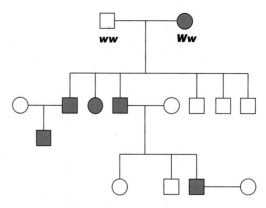

(a) Pedigree of a dominant trait

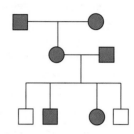

(b) Pedigree of a recessive trait

FIGURE 29.6   **Pedigree analysis to detect carriers of particular genes.** Circles represent females; squares represent males. Horizontal lines indicate a mating of connected individuals; vertical lines show offspring of a mating. **(a)** Pedigree tracing the dominant woolly hair gene in three generations of a family. Purple symbols represent individuals expressing the dominant woolly hair trait. White symbols represent those not expressing the trait; these individuals are homozygous recessive *(ww)*. **(b)** Pedigree tracing the recessive trait albinism (lack of skin pigmentation) through three generations (P = pigmented skin, dominant; p = albinism, recessive). Both parents in the second generation have pigmented skin (purple symbols), and yet two of their four children have the albino trait (white symbols). We can deduce that both these parents are heterozygous and have pigmented skin because the allele for that trait is dominant.

Simple blood tests are used to screen for the sickling gene in heterozygotes, and sophisticated *blood chemistry tests* and *DNA probes* can detect the presence of other unexpressed recessive genes. At present, carriers of the Tay-Sachs and cystic fibrosis genes can be identified with such tests.

Fetal Testing

Fetal testing is used when there is a known risk of a genetic disorder. The most common type of fetal testing is **amniocentesis** (am″ne-o-sen-te′sis). In this fairly simple procedure, a wide-bore needle is inserted into the amniotic sac through the mother's

Q *What noninvasive imaging technique is used to determine some aspects of fetal development? (You might want to check A Closer Look in Chapter 1 for this.)*

(a) Amniocentesis

(b) Chorionic villi sampling

FIGURE 29.7   Fetal testing. (a) In amniocentesis, ultrasound is used to locate the fetus, and a small amount of amniotic fluid is extracted. Physicians can diagnose some disorders from chemicals in the fluid, and other disorders may show up in tests performed on cells cultured from fetal cells present in the fluid. These tests include biochemical tests to detect the presence of certain enzymes, and karyotyping, to determine whether fetal chromosomes are normal in number and appearance. **(b)** In chorionic villi sampling, a physician inserts a narrow tube through the cervix and suctions out a tiny sample of fetal tissue (chorionic villi) from the placenta. The fetal tissue sample is used immediately for karyotyping.

abdominal wall (Figure 29.7a), and about 10 ml of fluid is withdrawn. Because there is a chance of injuring the fetus before ample amniotic fluid is present, this procedure is not normally done before the 14th week of pregnancy. Using ultrasound to visualize the position of the fetus and the amniotic sac has dramatically reduced the risk of this procedure. Although the fluid is checked for enzymes and other chemicals that serve as markers for specific diseases, most tests are done on the sloughed-off fetal cells in the fluid. These cells are isolated and cultured in laboratory dishes over a period of several weeks. Then the cells are examined for DNA markers of genetic disease and karyotyped (see Figure 29.1) to check for chromosomal abnormalities.

Chorionic villi sampling (CVS) suctions off bits of the chorionic villi from the placenta for examination (Figure 29.7b). A small tube is inserted through the vagina and cervical canal and guided by ultrasound to an area where a piece of placental tissue can be removed. CVS allows testing at eight weeks (but waiting until after the tenth week is usually recommended) and is much faster than amniocentesis. Karyotyping can be done almost immediately on the rapidly dividing chorionic cells.

Because both of these procedures are invasive, they carry with them an inherent risk to both fetus and mother. (For example, increased fetal risk of finger and toe defects is linked to CVS.) Although these tests are routinely ordered for pregnant women over 35 (because of the enhanced risk of Down syndrome), they are performed on younger women only when the probability of finding a severe fetal disorder is greater than the probability of doing

A *Ultrasound scanning.*

harm during the procedure. If a serious genetic or congenital defect is detected in the developing fetus, the parents must decide whether or not to continue the pregnancy.

Human Gene Therapy

As indicated earlier, the genome project has opened an exciting world to scientists investigating gene expression. As advances have been made in diagnosing human genetic diseases, new applications of "gene therapy" to alleviate or even cure the disorders have been quick to follow, particularly in cases traced to a single defective gene or protein. Indeed, genetic engineering has the potential to replace a defective gene with a normal version. One approach (used successfully in treatment of SCID) is to "infect" the defective cells with a virus into which a functional gene has been inserted; another is to inject the "corrected" DNA directly into the patient's cells. Such therapies have had mixed results in treating cystic fibrosis and muscular dystrophy. However, genetic engineering processes are prohibitively expensive and raise some thorny ethical, religious, and societal questions: Who will pay? Who determines who will be treated with the new therapies? Are we playing God?

∎ ∎ ∎

In this chapter, we have explored some of the basic principles of genetics, the manner in which genes are expressed, and the means by which gene expression can be modified. Considering the precision required to make perfect copies of genes and chromosomes, and considering the incredible mechanical events of meiotic division, it is amazing that genetic defects are as rare as they are. Perhaps, after reading this chapter, you have a greater sense of wonder that you turned out as well as you did.

Related Clinical Terms

Deletion Chromosomal aberration in which part of a chromosome is lost.

Down syndrome Formerly called mongolism, this condition usually reflects the presence of an extra autosome (trisomy of chromosome 21); the child has slightly slanted eyes, flattened facial features, a large tongue, and a tendency toward short stature and stubby fingers. Some, but not all, affected people are mentally retarded. Down syndrome individuals have mitochondrial defects, which have been associated with neurodegeneration in other disorders. A distinctive feature of Down syndrome is early onset of Alzheimer's disease. The most important risk factor appears to be advanced maternal (or paternal) age.

Mutation (*mutare* = change) A permanent structural change in a gene; the mutation may or may not affect function, depending on the precise site and nature of the alteration.

Nondisjunction Abnormal segregation of chromosomes during meiosis, resulting in gametes receiving two or no copies of a particular parental chromosome; more common in female meiosis than in male meiosis. If the abnormal gamete participates in fertilization, the resulting zygote will have an abnormal chromosomal complement (monosomy or trisomy) for that particular chromosome (as in Down syndrome).

Chapter Summary

1. Genetics is the study of heredity and mechanisms of gene transmission.

The Vocabulary of Genetics   (pp. 1146–1147)

1. A complete diploid set of chromosomes is called the karyotype of an organism; the complete genetic complement is the genome. A person's genome consists of two sets of instructions, one from each parent.

Gene Pairs (Alleles)   (p. 1146)

2. Genes coding for the same trait and found at the same locus on homologous chromosomes are called alleles.

3. Alleles may be the same or different in expression. When the allele pair is identical, the person is homozygous for that trait; when the alleles differ, the person is heterozygous.

Genotype and Phenotype   (p. 1147)

4. The actual genetic makeup of cells is the genotype; phenotype is the manner in which those genes are expressed.

Sexual Sources of Genetic Variation (pp. 1147–1149)

Chromosome Segregation and Independent Assortment (pp. 1147–1148)

1. During meiosis I of gametogenesis, tetrads align randomly on the metaphase plate, and chromatids are randomly distributed to the daughter cells. This is called independent assortment of the homologues. Each gamete receives only one allele of each gene pair.

2. Each different metaphase I alignment produces a different assortment of parental chromosomes in the gametes, and all combinations of maternal and paternal chromosomes are equally possible.

Crossover of Homologues and Gene Recombination (pp. 1148–1149)

3. During meiosis I, two to four of the four chromatids of each tetrad may cross over at one or more points and exchange corresponding gene segments. The recombinant

chromosomes contain new gene combinations, adding to the variability arising from independent assortment.

Random Fertilization (p. 1149)

4. The third source of genetic variation is random fertilization of eggs by sperm.

Types of Inheritance (pp. 1149–1153)

Dominant-Recessive Inheritance (pp. 1149–1151)

1. Dominant genes are expressed when present in single or double dose; recessive genes must be present in double dose to be expressed.

2. For traits following the dominant-recessive pattern, the laws of probability predict the outcome of a large number of matings.

3. Genetic disorders more often reflect the homozygous recessive condition than the homozygous dominant or heterozygous condition because dominant genes are expressed and, if they are lethal genes, the pregnancy usually results in miscarriage. Genetic disorders caused by dominant alleles include achondroplasia and Huntington's disease; recessive disorders include cystic fibrosis and Tay-Sachs disease.

4. Carriers are heterozygotes who carry a deleterious recessive gene (but do not express the trait) and have the potential of passing it on to offspring.

Incomplete Dominance (p. 1151)

5. In incomplete dominance, the heterozygote exhibits a phenotype intermediate between those of the homozygous dominant and recessive individuals. Inheritance of sickle-cell trait is an example of incomplete dominance.

Multiple-Allele Inheritance (p. 1151)

6. Multiple-allele inheritance involves genes that exist in more than two allelic forms in a population. Only two of the alleles are inherited, but on a random basis. Inheritance of ABO blood types is an example of multiple-allele inheritance in which the I^A and I^B alleles are codominant.

Sex-Linked Inheritance (p. 1152)

7. Traits determined by genes on the X and Y chromosomes are said to be sex-linked. The small Y chromosome lacks most genes present on the X chromosome. Recessive genes located only on the X chromosome are expressed in single dose in males. Examples of such X-linked conditions, passed from mother to son, include hemophilia and red-green color blindness. There are a few Y-linked genes, passed from father to son only.

Polygene Inheritance (pp. 1152–1153)

8. Polygene inheritance occurs when several gene pairs interact to produce phenotypes that vary quantitatively over a broad range. Height, intelligence, and skin pigmentation are examples.

Environmental Factors in Gene Expression (p. 1153)

1. Environmental factors may influence the expression of genotype.

2. Maternal factors that cross the placenta may alter expression of fetal genes. Environmentally provoked phenotypes that mimic genetically determined ones are called phenocopies. Nutritional deficits or hormonal imbalances may alter anticipated growth and development during childhood.

Nontraditional Inheritance (pp. 1153–1154)

Beyond DNA: Regulation of Gene Expression (pp. 1153–1154)

1. Three levels encompass the genome: protein-coding genes, RNA-only genes, and epigenetic marks. The latter two account for many cases of inherited disease that fail to follow traditional genetics.

2. The product of the RNA-only genes (siRNA and miRNA) may silence genes or prevent their expression and appear to play a role in directing apoptosis during development.

3. Epigenetic marks encompass the attachment of small chemical groups (methyl or acetyl) to DNA or histone proteins. In general, methylation prevents access to the DNA whereas acetylation provides access to the DNA. Genomic imprinting, which involves methylation of certain genes during gametogenesis, confers different effects and phenotypes on maternal and paternal genes. It is reversible, and occurs anew each generation.

Extranuclear (Mitochondrial) Inheritance (p. 1154)

4. Cytoplasmic (mitochondrial) genes pass to offspring via the ovum and help to determine certain characteristics. Deletions or mutations in mitochondrial genes are responsible for some problems with oxidative phosphorylation and some rare genetic diseases.

Genetic Screening, Counseling, and Therapy (pp. 1154–1157)

Carrier Recognition (p. 1155)

1. The likelihood of an individual carrying a deleterious recessive gene may be assessed by constructing a pedigree. Some of these genes can be deduced by various blood tests and DNA probes.

Fetal Testing (pp. 1155–1157)

2. Amniocentesis is fetal testing based on aspirated samples of amniotic fluid. Fetal cells in the fluid are cultured for several weeks, then examined for chromosomal defects (karyotyped) or for DNA markers of genetic disease. Amniocentesis cannot be performed until the 14th week of pregnancy.

3. Chorionic villi sampling is fetal testing based on a sample of the chorion. This tissue is rapidly mitotic, so karyotyping can be done almost immediately. Samples may be obtained by the eighth week.

Human Gene Therapy (p. 1157)

4. The Human Genome Project has allowed research on diagnosis of genetic disease and on its treatment to surge forward. Thus far, gene therapy has been particularly useful for correcting single-gene disorders. The most common approach involves transferring a corrected gene via a virus (or some other vector) to the affected cells to restore normal function.

Review Questions

Multiple Choice/Matching

(Some questions have more than one correct answer. Select the best answer or answers from the choices given.)

1. Match one of the following terms (a–i) with each of the appropriate descriptions below:

Key: (a) alleles   **(f)** homozygote
      (b) autosomes   **(g)** phenotype
      (c) dominant allele **(h)** recessive allele
      (d) genotype   **(i)** sex chromosomes
      (e) heterozygote

____ **(1)** genetic makeup
____ **(2)** how genetic makeup is expressed
____ **(3)** chromosomes that dictate most body characteristics
____ **(4)** alternate forms of the same gene
____ **(5)** an individual bearing two alleles that are the same for a particular trait
____ **(6)** an allele that is expressed whether in single or double dose
____ **(7)** an individual bearing two alleles that differ for a particular trait
____ **(8)** an allele that must be present in double dose to be expressed

2. Match the following types of inheritance (a–e) with the descriptions below:

Key: **(a)** dominant-recessive   **(d)** polygene
     (b) incomplete dominance **(e)** sex-linked
     (c) multiple-allele   **(f)** extranuclear

____ **(1)** only sons show the trait
____ **(2)** homozygotes and heterozygotes have the same phenotype
____ **(3)** heterozygotes exhibit a phenotype intermediate between those of the homozygotes
____ **(4)** phenotypes of offspring may be more varied than those of the parents
____ **(5)** inheritance of ABO blood types
____ **(6)** inheritance of stature
____ **(7)** reflects activity of mitochondrial DNA

Short Answer Essay Questions

3. Describe the important mechanisms that lead to genetic variations in gametes.

4. The ability to taste PTC (phenylthiocarbamide) depends on the presence of a dominant gene *T*; nontasters are homozygous for the recessive gene *t*. This is a situation of classical dominant-recessive inheritance. (a) Consider a mating between heterozygous parents producing three offspring. What proportion of the offspring will be tasters? What is the chance that all three offspring will be tasters? Nontasters? What is the chance that two will be tasters and one will be a nontaster? (b) Consider a mating between *Tt* and *tt* parents. What is the anticipated percentage of tasters? Nontasters? What proportion can be expected to be homozygous recessive? Heterozygous? Homozygous dominant?

5. Most albino children are born to normally pigmented parents. Albinos are homozygous for the recessive gene *(aa)*. What can you conclude about the genotypes of the nonalbino parents?

6. A woman with blood type A has two children. One has type O blood and the other has type B blood. What is the genotype of the mother? What are the genotype and phenotype of the father? What is the genotype of each child?

7. In skin color inheritance, what will be the relative range of pigmentation in offspring arising from the following parental matches? (a) *AABBCC × aabbcc*, (b) *AABBCC × AaBbCc*, (c) *Aabbcc × aabbcc*.

8. Compare and contrast amniocentesis and chorionic villi sampling as to the time at which they can be performed and the techniques used to obtain information on the fetus's genetic status.

Critical Thinking and Clinical Application Questions

1. A color-blind man marries a woman with normal vision. The woman's father was also color-blind. (a) What is the chance that their first child will be a color-blind son? A color-blind daughter? (b) If they have four children, what is the chance that two will be color-blind sons? (Be careful on this one.)

2. Brian is a college student. His genetics assignment is to do a family pedigree for dimples in the cheeks. Absence of dimples is recessive; presence of dimples reflects a dominant allele. Brian has dimples, as do his three brothers. His mother and maternal grandmother are dimple free, but his father and all other grandparents have dimples. Construct a pedigree spanning three generations for Brian's family. Show the phenotype and genotype for each person.

3. Mr. and Mrs. Lehman have sought genetic counseling. Mrs. Lehman is concerned because she is unexpectedly pregnant and her husband's brother died of Tay-Sachs disease. She can recall no incidence of Tay-Sachs disease in her own family. Do you think biochemical testing should be recommended to detect the deleterious gene in Mrs. Lehman? Explain your answer.

4. The Browns are both carriers of the recessive allele that causes the metabolic disorder called phenylketonuria. What is the probability of each of the following occurring? (a) All three children will have the disorder. (b) None of their three children will have the disorder. (c) One or more of their children will have the disorder. (d) At least one of their children will be phenotypically normal.

29

Appendix A
The Metric System

MEASUREMENT	UNIT AND ABBREVIATION	METRIC EQUIVALENT	METRIC TO ENGLISH CONVERSION FACTOR	ENGLISH TO METRIC CONVERSION FACTOR
Length	1 kilometer (km)	$= 1000\ (10^3)$ meters	1 km = 0.62 mile	1 mile = 1.61 km
	1 meter (m)	$= 100\ (10^2)$ centimeters = 1000 millimeters	1 m = 1.09 yards 1 m = 3.28 feet 1 m = 39.37 inches	1 yard = 0.914 m 1 foot = 0.305 m
	1 centimeter (cm)	$= 0.01\ (10^{-2})$ meter	1 cm = 0.394 inch	1 foot = 30.5 cm 1 inch = 2.54 cm
	1 millimeter (mm)	$= 0.001\ (10^{-3})$ meter	1 mm = 0.039 inch	
	1 micrometer (μm) [formerly micron (μ)]	$= 0.000001\ (10^{-6})$ meter		
	1 nanometer (nm)	$= 0.000000001\ (10^{-9})$ meter		
	1 angstrom (Å)	$= 0.0000000001\ (10^{-10})$ meter		
Area	1 square meter (m^2)	= 10,000 square centimeters	$1\ m^2$ = 1.1960 square yards $1\ m^2$ = 10.764 square feet	1 square yard = $0.8361\ m^2$ 1 square foot = $0.0929\ m^2$
	1 square centimeter (cm^2)	= 100 square millimeters	$1\ cm^2$ = 0.155 square inch	1 square inch = $6.4516\ cm^2$
Mass	1 metric ton (t)	= 1000 kilograms	1 t = 1.103 ton	1 ton = 0.907 t
	1 kilogram (kg)	= 1000 grams	1 kg = 2.205 pounds	1 pound = 0.4536 kg
	1 gram (g)	= 1000 milligrams	1 g = 0.0353 ounce 1 g = 15.432 grains	1 ounce = 28.35 g
	1 milligram (mg)	= 0.001 gram	1 mg = approx. 0.015 grain	
	1 microgram (μg)	= 0.000001 gram		
Volume (solids)	1 cubic meter (m^3)	= 1,000,000 cubic centimeters	$1\ m^3$ = 1.3080 cubic yards $1\ m^3$ = 35.315 cubic feet	1 cubic yard = $0.7646\ m^3$ 1 cubic foot = $0.0283\ m^3$
	1 cubic centimeter (cm^3 or cc)	= 0.000001 cubic meter = 1 milliliter	$1\ cm^3$ = 0.0610 cubic inch	1 cubic inch = $16.387\ cm^3$
	1 cubic millimeter (mm^3)	= 0.000000001 cubic meter		
Volume (liquids and gases)	1 kiloliter (kl or kL)	= 1000 liters	1 kL = 264.17 gallons	1 gallon = 3.785 L
	1 liter (l or L)	= 1000 milliliters	1 L = 0.264 gallon 1 L = 1.057 quarts	1 quart = 0.946 L
	1 milliliter (ml or mL)	= 0.001 liter = 1 cubic centimeter	1 ml = 0.034 fluid ounce 1 ml = approx. $\frac{1}{5}$ teaspoon 1 ml = approx. 15–16 drops (gtt)	1 quart = 946 ml 1 pint = 473 ml 1 fluid ounce = 29.57 ml 1 teaspoon = approx. 5 ml
	1 microliter (μl or μL)	= 0.000001 liter		
Time	1 second (s)	$= \frac{1}{60}$ minute		
	1 millisecond (ms)	= 0.001 second		
Temperature	Degrees Celsius (°C)		°F = $\frac{9}{5}$(°C) + 32	°C = $\frac{5}{9}$(°F − 32)

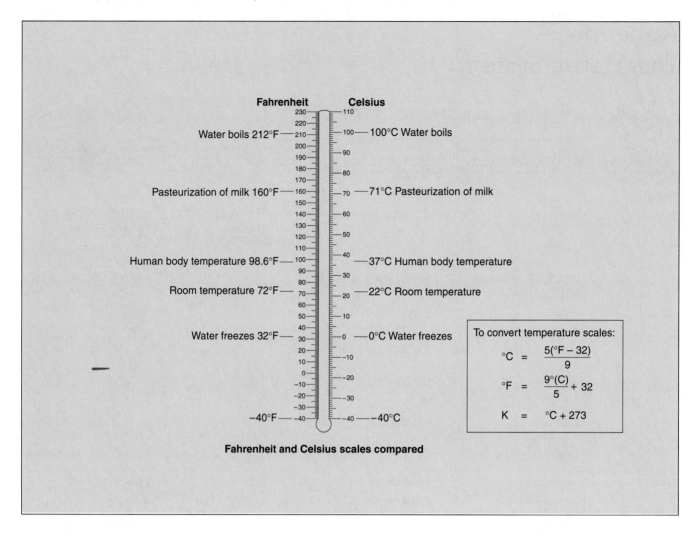

Fahrenheit and Celsius scales compared

Appendix B
Functional Groups in Organic Molecules

Functional group	General formula	Name of compounds	Example	Where else found
Hydroxyl —OH (or HO—)	—O—H	Alcohols	Ethanol	Sugars; water-soluble vitamins
Carbonyl CO	(aldehyde formula)	Aldehydes	Propanal	Some sugars; formaldehyde (a preservative)
	(ketone formula)	Ketones	Acetone	Some sugars; "ketone bodies" in urine (from fat breakdown)
Carboxyl —COOH	(carboxyl formula)	Carboxylic acids	Acetic acid	Amino acids; proteins; some vitamins; fatty acids
Amino —NH₂ (or H₂N—)	(amine formula)	Amines	Methylamine	Amino acids; proteins; urea in urine (from protein breakdown)

Appendix C
The Amino Acids

Appendix D
Two Important Metabolic Pathways

Step 1 Glucose enters the cell and is phosphorylated by the enzyme hexokinase, which catalyzes the transfer of a phosphate group, indicated as P_i, from ATP to the number six carbon of the sugar, producing glucose-6-phosphate. The electrical charge of the phosphate group traps the sugar in the cell because of the impermeability of the plasma membrane to ions. Phosphorylation of glucose also makes the molecule more chemically reactive. Although glycolysis is supposed to *produce* ATP, in step 1 ATP is actually consumed—an energy investment that will be repaid with dividends later in glycolysis.

Step 2 Glucose-6-phosphate is rearranged and converted to its isomer, fructose-6-phosphate. Isomers, remember, have the same number and types of atoms but in different structural arrangements.

Step 3 In this step, still another molecule of ATP is used to add a second phosphate group to the sugar, producing fructose-1,6-bisphosphate. So far, the ATP ledger shows a debit of −2. With phosphate groups on its opposite ends, the sugar is now ready to be split in half.

Step 4 This is the reaction from which glycolysis gets its name. An enzyme cleaves the sugar molecule into two different 3-carbon sugars: glyceraldehyde 3-phosphate and dihydroxyacetone phosphate. These two sugars are isomers of one another.

Step 5 The isomerase enzyme interconverts the 3-carbon sugars, and if left alone in a test tube, the reaction reaches equilibrium. This does not happen in the cell, however, because the next enzyme in glycolysis uses only glyceraldehyde phosphate as its substrate and is unreceptive to dihydroxyacetone phosphate. This pulls the equilibrium between the two 3-carbon sugars in the direction of glyceraldehyde phosphate, which is removed as fast as it forms. Thus, the net result of steps 4 and 5 is cleavage of a 6-carbon sugar into two molecules of glyceraldehyde phosphate; each will progress through the remaining steps of glycolysis.

Step 6 An enzyme now catalyzes two sequential reactions while it holds glyceraldehyde phosphate in its active site. First, the sugar is oxidized by the transfer of H from the number one carbon of the sugar to NAD, forming $NADH + H^+$. Here we see in metabolic context the oxidation-reduction reaction described in Chapter 24. This reaction releases substantial amounts of energy, and the enzyme capitalizes on this by coupling the reaction to the creation of a high-energy phosphate bond at the number one carbon of the oxidized substrate. The source of the phosphate is inorganic phosphate (P_i) always present in the cytosol. The enzyme releases $NADH + H^+$ and 1,3-bisphosphoglyceric acid as products. Notice in the figure that the new phosphate bond is symbolized with a squiggle (~), which indicates that the bond is at least as energetic as the high-energy phosphate bonds of ATP.

THE TEN STEPS OF GLYCOLYSIS Each of the ten steps of glycolysis is catalyzed by a specific enzyme found dissolved in the cytoplasm. All steps are reversible. An abbreviated version of the three major phases of glycolysis appears in the lower right-hand corner of the second page.

Step 7 Finally, glycolysis produces ATP. The phosphate group, with its high-energy bond, is transferred from 1,3-bisphosphoglyceric acid to ADP. For each glucose molecule that began glycolysis, step 7 produces two molecules of ATP, because every product after the sugar-splitting step (step 4) is doubled. Of course, two ATPs were invested to get sugar ready for splitting. The ATP ledger now stands at zero. By the end of step 7, glucose has been converted to two molecules of 3-phosphoglyceric acid. This compound is not a sugar. The sugar was oxidized to an organic acid back in step 6, and now the energy made available by that oxidation has been used to make ATP.

Step 8 Next, an enzyme relocates the remaining phosphate group of 3-phosphoglyceric acid to form 2-phosphoglyceric acid. This prepares the substrate for the next reaction.

Step 9 An enzyme forms a double bond in the substrate by removing a water molecule from 2-phosphoglyceric acid to form phosphoenolpyruvic acid, or PEP. This results in the electrons of the substrate being rearranged in such a way that the remaining phosphate bond becomes very unstable; it has been upgraded to high-energy status.

Step 10 The last reaction of glycolysis produces another molecule of ATP by transferring the phosphate group from PEP to ADP. Because this step occurs twice for each glucose molecule, the ATP ledger now shows a net gain of two ATPs. Steps 7 and 10 each produce two ATPs for a total credit of four, but a debt of two ATPs was incurred from steps 1 and 3. Glycolysis has repaid the ATP investment with 100% interest. In the meantime, glucose has been broken down and oxidized to two molecules of pyruvic acid, the compound produced from PEP in step 10.

Step 1   Two-carbon acetyl CoA is combined with oxaloacetic acid, a 4-carbon compound. The unstable bond between the acetyl group and CoA is broken as oxaloacetic acid binds and CoA is freed to prime another 2-carbon fragment derived from pyruvic acid. The product is the 6-carbon citric acid, for which the cycle is named.

Step 2   A molecule of water is removed, and another is added back. The net result is the conversion of citric acid to its isomer, isocitric acid.

Step 3   The substrate loses a CO_2 molecule, and the remaining 5-carbon compound is oxidized, forming an α-ketoglutaric acid and reducing NAD^+.

Step 4   This step is catalyzed by a multienzyme complex very similar to the one that converts pyruvic acid to acetyl CoA. CO_2 is lost; the remaining 4-carbon compound is oxidized by the transfer of electrons to NAD^+ to form $NADH+H^+$ and is then attached to CoA by an unstable bond. The product is succinyl CoA.

Step 5   Substrate-level phosphorylation occurs in this step. CoA is displaced by a phosphate group, which is then transferred to GDP to form guanosinetriphosphate (GTP). GTP is similar to ATP, which is formed when GTP donates a phosphate group to ADP. The products of this step are succinic acid and ATP.

Step 6   In another oxidative step, two hydrogens are removed from succinic acid, forming fumaric acid, and transferred to FAD to form $FADH_2$. The function of this coenzyme is similar to that of $NADH+H^+$, but $FADH_2$ stores less energy. The enzyme that catalyzes this oxidation-reduction reaction is the only enzyme of the cycle that is embedded in the mitochondrial membrane. All other enzymes of the citric acid cycle are dissolved in the mitochondrial matrix.

Step 7   Bonds in the substrate are rearranged in this step by the addition of a water molecule. The product is malic acid.

Step 8   The last oxidative step reduces another NAD^+ and regenerates oxaloacetic acid, which accepts a 2-carbon fragment from acetyl CoA for another turn of the cycle.

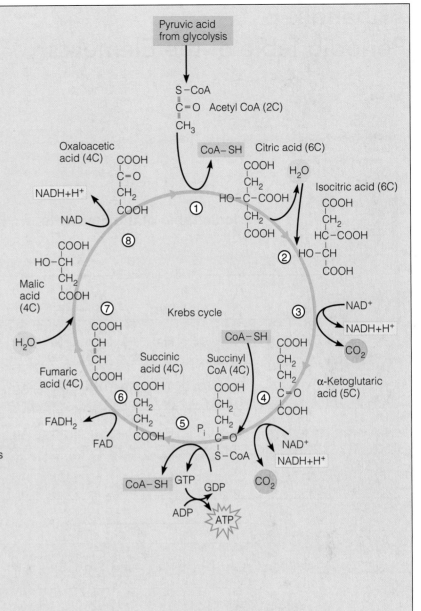

Krebs Cycle (Citric Acid Cycle) All but one of the steps (step 6) occur in the mitochondrial matrix. The preparation of pyruvic acid (by oxidation, decarboxylation, and reaction with coenzyme A) to enter the cycle as acetyl CoA is shown above the cycle. Acetyl CoA is picked up by oxaloacetic acid to form citric acid; and as it passes through the cycle, it is oxidized four more times [forming three molecules of reduced NAD ($NADH + H^+$) and one of reduced FAD ($FADH_2$)] and decarboxylated twice (releasing 2 CO_2). Energy is captured in the bonds of GTP, which then acts in a coupled reaction with ADP to generate one molecule of ATP by substrate-level phosphorylation.

Appendix E
Periodic Table of the Elements

Periodic Table of the Elements

Representative (main group) elements

Representative (main group) elements

Transition metals

	IA																VIIIA
1	**1** H 1.0079	IIA											IIIA	IVA	VA	VIA	VIIA	**2** He 4.003
2	**3** Li 6.941	**4** Be 9.012											**5** B 10.811	**6** C 12.011	**7** N 14.007	**8** O 15.999	**9** F 18.998	**10** Ne 20.180
3	**11** Na 22.990	**12** Mg 24.305	IIIB	IVB	VB	VIB	VIIB	VIIIB			IB	IIB	**13** Al 26.982	**14** Si 28.086	**15** P 30.974	**16** S 32.066	**17** Cl 35.453	**18** Ar 39.948

4	**19** K 39.098	**20** Ca 40.078	**21** Sc 44.956	**22** Ti 47.88	**23** V 50.942	**24** Cr 51.996	**25** Mn 54.938	**26** Fe 55.845	**27** Co 58.933	**28** Ni 58.69	**29** Cu 63.546	**30** Zn 65.39	**31** Ga 69.723	**32** Ge 72.61	**33** As 74.922	**34** Se 78.96	**35** Br 79.904	**36** Kr 83.8
5	**37** Rb 85.468	**38** Sr 87.62	**39** Y 88.906	**40** Zr 91.224	**41** Nb 92.906	**42** Mo 95.94	**43** Tc 98	**44** Ru 101.07	**45** Rh 102.906	**46** Pd 106.42	**47** Ag 107.868	**48** Cd 112.411	**49** In 114.82	**50** Sn 118.71	**51** Sb 121.76	**52** Te 127.60	**53** I 126.905	**54** Xe 131.29
6	**55** Cs 132.905	**56** Ba 137.327	**57** La 138.906	**72** Hf 178.49	**73** Ta 180.948	**74** W 183.84	**75** Re 186.207	**76** Os 190.23	**77** Ir 192.22	**78** Pt 195.08	**79** Au 196.967	**80** Hg 200.59	**81** Tl 204.383	**82** Pb 207.2	**83** Bi 208.980	**84** Po 209	**85** At 210	**86** Rn 222
7	**87** Fr 223	**88** Ra 226.025	**89** Ac 227.028	**104** Rf 261	**105** Db 262	**106** Sg 263	**107** Bh 262	**108** Hs 265	**109** Mt 266	**110** Ds 269	**111** Rg 272	**112** Uub 277	**113** Uut	**114** Uuq	**115** Uup	**116** Uuh		

Rare earth elements

	58 Ce 140.115	**59** Pr 140.908	**60** Nd 144.24	**61** Pm 145	**62** Sm 150.36	**63** Eu 151.964	**64** Gd 157.25	**65** Tb 158.925	**66** Dy 162.5	**67** Ho 164.93	**68** Er 167.26	**69** Tm 168.934	**70** Yb 173.04	**71** Lu 174.967
Lanthanides														
Actinides	**90** Th 232.038	**91** Pa 231.036	**92** U 238.029	**93** Np 237.048	**94** Pu 244	**95** Am 243	**96** Cm 247	**97** Bk 247	**98** Cf 251	**99** Es 252	**100** Fm 257	**101** Md 258	**102** No 259	**103** Lr 262

The periodic table arranges elements according to atomic number and atomic weight into horizontal rows called periods and 18 vertical columns called groups or families. The elements in the groups are classified as being in either A or B classes.

Elements of each group of the A series have similar chemical and physical properties. This reflects the fact that members of a particular group have the same number of valence shell electrons, which is indicated by the number of the group. For example, group IA elements have one valence shell electron, group IIA elements have two, and group VA elements have five. In contrast, as you progress across a period from left to right, the properties of the elements change in discrete steps, varying gradually from the very metallic properties of groups IA and IIA elements to the nonmetallic properties seen in group VIIA (chlorine and others), and finally to the inert elements (noble gases) in group VIIIA. This change reflects the continual increase in the number of valence shell electrons seen in elements (from left to right) within a period.

Class B elements are referred to as transition elements. All transition elements are metals, and in most cases they have one or two valence shell electrons. (In these elements, some electrons occupy more distant electron shells before the deeper shells are filled.)

In this periodic table, the colors are used to convey information about the phase (solid, liquid, or gas) in which a pure element exists under standard conditions (25 degrees centigrade and 1 atmosphere of pressure). If the element's symbol is solid black, then the element exists as a solid. If its symbol is red, then it exists as a gas. If its symbol is dark blue, then it is a liquid. If the element's symbol is green, the element does not exist in nature and must be created by some type of nuclear reaction.

Appendix F
Reference Values for Selected Blood and Urine Studies

The reference values listed for the selected blood and urine studies are common ranges for adults, but specific "normals" are established by the laboratory performing the analysis. The values may be affected by a wide range of circumstances, including testing methods and equipment used, client age, body mass, sex, diet, activity level, medications, and extent of disease processes.

Reference values are identified in both standard or conventional units and in the system of international (SI) units. SI units (given in parentheses) are measurements of amount per volume and are used in most countries and scientific journals. SI units are often given as moles or millimoles per liter. Most clinical laboratories and textbooks in the United States use conventional or standard units, which measure mass per volume. These values are given as grams, milligrams, or milliequivalents per deciliter or liter. It is anticipated that the United States will eventually use SI units exclusively.

For enzymes, 1 international unit (IU) represents an arbitrary but defined amount of activity, whereas 1 katal (kat) is the amount of enzyme required to consume 1 mol of substrate per second.

Sample types in column 1 are serum (S), plasma (P), arterial whole blood (A), and whole blood (WB).

TEST (SAMPLE)	REFERENCE VALUES: CONVENTIONAL (SI)	PHYSIOLOGICAL INDICATION AND CLINICAL IMPLICATIONS
Blood Chemistry Studies		
Ammonia (P)	15–120 µg/dl (9–70 µmol/L)	Liver and renal function. Increased values in liver disease, renal failure, newborn hemolytic disease, heart failure, cor pulmonale. Decreased values in hypertension.
Amylase (S)	56–190 IU/L (0.4–2.1 µkat/L)	Pancreatic function. Increased values in pancreatitis, mumps, obstruction of pancreatic duct, ketoacidosis. Decreased values in kidney disease, pancreatic damage or cancer, toxemia of pregnancy.
Aspartate aminotransferase (AST, or SGOT) (S)	≤40 U/ml (≤0.7 µkat/L)	Cellular damage. Increased after myocardial infarction, acute liver disease, drug toxicity, muscle trauma. Decreased in pyridoxine (vitamin B_6) deficiency.
Bilirubin (S)	Total: 0.1–1.0 mg/dl (1.7–17.1 µmol/L) Direct: <0.4 mg/dl (<6.8 µmol/L) Indirect: 0.1–1.0 mg/dl (1.7–17.1 µmol/L) Newborn: <13.0 mg/dl (<222 µmol/L)	Liver function and red cell breakdown. Increased levels of direct in liver disease and biliary obstruction. Increased levels of indirect in hemolysis of red blood cells.
Blood urea nitrogen (S)	7–26 mg/dl (2.5–9.3 mmol/L)	Kidney function. Increased values in renal disease, dehydration, urinary obstruction, congestive heart failure, myocardial infarction, burns. Decreased values in liver failure, overhydration, impaired protein absorption, pregnancy.
Cholesterol	<200 mg/dl (<5.2 mmol/L)	Metabolism—fat utilization. Increased values in diabetes mellitus, pregnancy, use of oral contraceptives or anabolic steroids.
High-density lipoprotein (HDL) cholesterol (S)	20–30% of total >40 mg/dl (>1.0 mmol/L)	Increased levels in liver disease, aerobic exercise. Decreased levels in atherosclerotic heart disease, malnutrition.
Low-density lipoprotein (LDL) cholesterol (S)	60–70% of total <130 mg/dl (<3.4 mmol/L)	Increased values in hyperlipidemia, atherosclerotic heart disease. Decreased values in fat malabsorption and malnutrition.
Very low density lipoprotein cholesterol (VLDL) (S)	10–15% of total	Same as LDL.

▶

TEST (SAMPLE)	REFERENCE VALUES: CONVENTIONAL (SI)	PHYSIOLOGICAL INDICATION AND CLINICAL IMPLICATIONS
Creatine kinase (CK) (S)	Female: ≤190 U/L (≤3.2 μkat/L) Male: ≤235 U/L (≤3.9 μkat/L)	Cellular damage. Increased values in myocardial infarction, muscular dystrophy, hypothyroidism, pulmonary infarction, cerebrovascular accident (CVA), shock, tissue damage, and trauma.
Creatinine (S)	0.5–1.2 mg/dl (44–106 μmol/L)	Renal function. Increased values in renal disease and acromegaly. Decreased in muscular dystrophy.
Gases (A)		Acid-base balance.
Bicarbonate	22–26 mEq/L (22–26 mmol/L)	Increased values in metabolic alkalosis and respiratory acidosis. Decreased values in metabolic acidosis and respiratory alkalosis.
Carbon dioxide content	Arterial: 19–24 mEq/L (19–24 mmol/L) Venous: 22–30 mEq/L (22–30 mmol/L)	
Carbon dioxide partial pressure (P_{CO_2})	Arterial: 35–45 mm Hg Venous: 45 mm Hg	
Oxygen (O_2) saturation	95–98% (same)	Values increased slightly in hyperventilation. Decreased values (hypoxia) in pulmonary disease, hypoventilation, high altitude.
Oxygen partial pressure (P_{O_2})	80–105 mm Hg	
pH	7.35–7.45 (same)	Increased values in metabolic and respiratory alkalosis. Decreased values in metabolic and respiratory acidosis.
Glucose (S)	70–120 mg/dl (3.9–6.7 mmol/L)	Metabolic function. Increased values in diabetes mellitus, Cushing's syndrome, liver disease, acute stress, and acromegaly. Decreased levels in Addison's disease, insulinomas.
Immunoglobulins (S)		
IgG	560–1800 mg/dl (5.6–18 g/L)	Immune response. Increased levels in chronic infections, rheumatic fever, liver disease, rheumatoid arthritis. Decreased levels in amyloidosis, leukemia, and preeclampsia.
IgE	<43.2 μg/dl (<432 μg/L)	Allergic responses. Increased values in allergic responses. Decreased values in agammaglobulinemia.
IgA	85–563 mg/dl (0.85–5.6 g/L)	Immune integrity. Increased values in liver disease, rheumatic fever, chronic infection, inflammatory bowel disease. Decreased values in immunodeficiency disorders and immunosuppression.
IgM	55–375 mg/dl (0.5–3.8 g/L)	Immune integrity. Increased in autoimmune disease (e.g., rheumatoid arthritis), acute infections. Decreased in amyloidosis and leukemia.
IgD	0.5–14 mg/dl (5–140 mg/L)	Immune integrity. Increased values in myelomas.
Ketone bodies (S or P)	Negative Toxic level >20 mg/dl (0.2 g/L)	Fatty acid catabolism. Increased values (ketosis, ketoacidosis) in starvation, low-carbohydrate diet, uncontrolled diabetes mellitus, aspirin overdose.
Lactate dehydrogenase (LDH) (S)	105–333 U/L (1.7–5.6 μkat/L)	Tissue damage of organs or striated muscle. Increased in myocardial infarction, pulmonary infarction, liver disease, cerebrovascular accident, infectious mononucleosis, muscular dystrophy, fractures.
Lactic acid (lactate) (P)	9–16 mg/dl (1.0–1.8 mmol/L)	Anaerobic tissue metabolism. Increased values in congestive heart failure, shock, hemorrhage, strenuous exercise.
Osmolality (S)	280–300 mOsm/kg H_2O (280–300 mmol/kg H_2O)	Fluid and electrolyte balance. Increased levels in hypernatremia, dehydration, kidney disease, alcohol ingestion. Decreased levels in hyponatremia, overhydration, and syndrome of inappropriate ADH secretion (SIADH).

TEST (SAMPLE)	REFERENCE VALUES: CONVENTIONAL (SI)	PHYSIOLOGICAL INDICATION AND CLINICAL IMPLICATIONS
Phosphate (S) (phosphorus)	2.5–4.5 mg/dl (0.8–1.5 mmol/L)	Parathyroid function; bone disease. Increased levels in hypoparathyroidism, renal failure, bone metastasis, hypocalcemia. Decreased values in hyperparathyroidism, hypercalcemia, alcoholism, vitamin D deficiency, ketoacidosis, osteomalacia.
Potassium (S)	3.5–5.5 mEq/L (3.5–5.5 mmol/L)	Fluid and electrolyte balance. Increased levels in renal disease, Addison's disease, ketoacidosis, burns, and crush injuries. Decreased levels in vomiting, diarrhea, Cushing's syndrome, alkalosis, diuretics.
Protein (S)		
Total	6.0–8.5 g/dl (60–85 g/L)	Osmotic pressure; immune system integrity. Increased values in multiple myeloma, dehydration, myxedema. Decreased values in protein malnutrition, burns, diarrhea, renal failure, liver failure.
Albumin	3.2–5.0 g/dl (32–50 g/L)	Osmotic pressure. Increased levels in dehydration. Decreased levels in liver disease, malnutrition, Crohn's disease, nephrotic syndrome, systemic lupus erythematosus.
Sodium (S)	135–145 mEq/L (135–145 mmol/L)	Fluid and electrolyte balance. Increased values in dehydration, diabetes insipidus, Cushing's syndrome. Decreased values in vomiting, diarrhea, burns, Addison's disease, myxedema, congestive heart failure, overhydration, syndrome of inappropriate ADH secretion (SIADH).
Triglycerides	10–150 mg/dl (0.1–1.5 g/L)	Increased values in diabetes mellitus, liver disease, nephrotic syndrome, pregnancy.
Uric acid (S)	Female: 2.0–7.3 mg/dl (119–434 μmol/L) Male: 2.1–8.5 mg/dl (125–506 μmol/L)	Renal function. Increased in lead poisoning, impaired renal function, gout, alcoholism, hematologic cancers. Decreased in Wilson's disease.

Hematology Studies

TEST (SAMPLE)	REFERENCE VALUES: CONVENTIONAL (SI)	PHYSIOLOGICAL INDICATION AND CLINICAL IMPLICATIONS
Hemoglobin (S)	Female: 12–16 g/dl (120–160 g/L) Male: 13–18 g/dl (130–180 g/L)	Oxygenation status. Increased values in dehydration, polycythemia, congestive heart failure, chronic obstructive pulmonary disease, high altitudes. Decreased levels in anemia, hemorrhage, bone marrow cancer, renal disease, systemic lupus erythematosus, nutritional deficiency.
Hematocrit (WB)	Female: 37–47% (same) Male: 42–52% (same)	Oxygenation status. Increased levels in polycythemia, dehydration, congestive heart failure, shock, surgery. Decreased levels in anemia, hemorrhage, bone marrow disease, malnutrition, cirrhosis, rheumatoid arthritis.
Partial thromboplastin time (activated) (PTT or aPTT)	20–36 s (same)	Clotting mechanisms. Increased values in clotting factor deficiencies, cirrhosis, vitamin K deficiency, disseminated intravascular coagulation (DIC). Decreased values in early DIC, extensive cancer.
Platelet count (WB)	150,000–400,000/μl (150–400 $\times$ 10^9/L)	Clotting mechanisms. Increased values in polycythemia, cancers, rheumatoid arthritis, trauma. Decreased values in liver disease, hemolytic uremic syndrome, disseminated intravascular coagulation (DIC), idiopathic thrombocytopenic purpura (ITP), systemic lupus erythematosus (SLE).
Prothrombin time (PT) (WB)	11–12.5 s (same) 1.5–2 $\times$ control (evaluating anticoagulant treatment)	Clotting mechanisms. Increased values in liver disease, vitamin K deficiency, salicylate intoxication. Decreased values in disseminated intravascular coagulation (DIC).

TEST (SAMPLE)	REFERENCE VALUES: CONVENTIONAL (SI)	PHYSIOLOGICAL INDICATION AND CLINICAL IMPLICATIONS

Hematology Studies (continued)

TEST (SAMPLE)	REFERENCE VALUES: CONVENTIONAL (SI)	PHYSIOLOGICAL INDICATION AND CLINICAL IMPLICATIONS
Red blood cell count (RBC) (WB)	Female: 4.2–5.4 million/μl ($4.2–5.4 \times 10^{12}$/L) Male: 4.7–6.1 million/μl ($4.7–6.1 \times 10^{12}$/L)	Oxygenation status. Increased values in high altitudes, polycythemia, hemoconcentration, cor pulmonale. Decreased values in hemorrhage, hemolysis, anemias, chronic illness, nutritional deficiencies, leukemia, overhydration.
Reticulocyte count (WB)	0.5–2.0% (same)	Bone marrow function. Increased values in hemolytic anemia, sickle-cell anemia, leukemia, pregnancy. Decreased values in pernicious anemia, folic acid deficiency, cirrhosis, chronic infection, bone marrow depression or failure.
White blood cell count (WBC) (WB)		
Total (males)	4800–10,800 μl ($4.8–10.8 \times 10^9$/L)	Immune system integrity. Increased values in infection, trauma, stress, tissue necrosis, inflammation. Decreased values in bone marrow depression or failure, drug toxicity, overwhelming infection, malnutrition.
White blood cell count, differential (WB)		
Neutrophils	50–70% (same)	Immune system integrity. Increased values in acute bacterial infections, stress, Cushing's syndrome, inflammatory disorders, ketoacidosis, gout. Decreased levels in aplastic anemia, bone marrow suppression, and overwhelming bacterial infections.
Lymphocytes	25–40% (same)	Immune system integrity. Increased values in viral infections (e.g.), mumps, rubella, infectious mononucleosis, hepatitis), lymphocytic leukemia, certain bacterial infections. Decreased levels in leukemia, immunodeficiency, lupus erythematosus, bone marrow depressive drugs.
Eosinophils	1–4% (same)	Immune system integrity. Increased levels in allergic reactions, parasitic infections, leukemia. Decreased levels in excess adrenosteroid production.
Monocytes	3–8% (same)	Immune system integrity. Increased levels in certain infections (e.g., tuberculosis, malaria), inflammatory disorders.
Basophils	0.5–1.0% (same)	Immune system integrity. Increased levels in myeloproliferative disorders, leukemia. Decreased levels in allergic reactions, hyperthyroidism, stress.

Urine Tests

TEST (SAMPLE)	REFERENCE VALUES: CONVENTIONAL (SI)	PHYSIOLOGICAL INDICATION AND CLINICAL IMPLICATIONS
Amylase (24 h)	<6000 Somogyi units/24 h 0–500 U/24 h (0–8.3 μkat/24h)	Pancreatic function. Increased values in pancreatic disease or obstruction, inflammation of the parotid or salivary glands, and cholecystitis.
Bilirubin (random)	Negative (same)	Liver function. Increased values in liver disease, extrahepatic obstruction (gallstones, tumor, inflammation).
Blood (hemoglobin) (random)	Negative (same)	Urinary system function. Increased values in cystitis, renal disease, hemolytic anemia, transfusion reaction, prostatitis, burns.
Osmolality (random or fasting)	Random: 50–1200 mOsm/kg H_2O (50–1200 mmol/kg H_2O) Fluid restriction: $\geq$850 mOsm/kg H_2O ($\geq$850 mmol/kg H_2O)	Fluid and electrolyte balance, renal function, and endocrine function. Increased levels in hypernatremia, syndrome of inappropriate ADH secretion (SIADH), congestive heart failure, metabolic acidosis. Decreased levels in diabetes insipidus, water intoxication, pyelonephritis, renal tubular necrosis, aldosteronism.
Phosphate (24 h)	0.9–1.3g/24 hr (same)	Parathyroid function. Increased levels in hyperparathyroidism, osteomalacia, certain renal diseases, vitamin D deficiency. Decreased levels in hypoparathyroidism.

TEST (SAMPLE)	REFERENCE VALUES: CONVENTIONAL (SI)	PHYSIOLOGICAL INDICATION AND CLINICAL IMPLICATIONS
Urine Tests (continued)		
Potassium (24 h)	25–120 mEq/24 h (25–120 mmol/24 h)	Fluid and electrolyte balance. Increased values in renal tubular necrosis, metabolic acidosis, dehydration, aldosteronism, Cushing's syndrome. Decreased values in Addison's disease, malabsorption, acute renal failure.
Protein (random)	<8 mg/dl (<80 mg/L)	Renal function. Increased levels in nephrotic syndrome, renal trauma, hyperthyroidism, diabetic nephropathy, lupus erythematosus.
Sodium (24 h)	40–220 mEq/24 h (40–220 mmol/24 h)	Fluid and electrolyte balance. Increased values in dehydration, ketoacidosis, syndrome of inappropriate ADH secretion (SIADH), adrenocortical insufficiency. Decreased levels in congestive heart failure, renal failure, diarrhea, aldosteronism.
Uric acid (24 h)	250–750 mg/24 h (1.5–4.5 mmol/24 h)	Renal function and metabolism. Increased in gout, leukemia, liver disease, ulcerative colitis. Decreased in renal disease, alcoholism, lead toxicity, folic acid deficiency.
Urinalysis (random)		
Color	Straw, yellow, amber	Fluid balance and renal function. Darker in dehydration. Lighter in overhydration, diabetes insipidus. Color varies with disease states, diet, and medications.
Odor	Aromatic	Metabolic function, infection. Abnormal odors in infection, ketonuria, rectal fistula, hepatic failure, phenylketonuria.
Specific gravity	1.005–1.035	An indirect measurement of urine concentration (osmolality). Same physiological indications and clinical implications as osmolality.
Urobilinogen (24 h)	0.2–1.0 mg/dl (2–10 mg/L)	Liver function. Increased in hemolytic anemias, hepatitis, cirrhosis, biliary disease. Decreased in common bile duct obstruction.
Volume (24 h)	800–2000 ml/24 h (0.8–2.0 L/24 h)	Fluid and electrolyte balance, renal function. Increased values in diabetes insipidus, diabetes mellitus, renal disease. Decreased values in dehydration, syndrome of inappropriate ADH secretion (SIADH), renal disease.

Appendix G
Answers to Clinical Connections, Multiple Choice, and Matching Questions

Chapter 1
1. c; **2.** a; **3.** e; **4.** a, d; **5.** (a) wrist (b) hip bone (c) nose (d) toes (e) scalp; **6.** neither c nor d would be visible in the median sagittal section; **7.** (a) dorsal (b) ventral (c) dorsal (d) ventral; **8.** b; **9.** b; **10.** c

Chapter 2
1. b, d; **2.** d; **3.** b; **4.** a; **5.** b; **6.** a; **7.** a; **8.** b; **9.** d; **10.** a; **11.** b; **12.** a, c; **13.** (1)a, (2)c; **14.** c; **15.** d; **16.** e; **17.** d; **18.** d; **19.** a; **20.** b; **21.** b; **22.** c

Chapter 3
1. d; **2.** a, c; **3.** b; **4.** d; **5.** b; **6.** e; **7.** c; **8.** d; **9.** a; **10.** a; **11.** b; **12.** d; **13.** c; **14.** b; **15.** d; **16.** a; **17.** b; **18.** d; **19.** c

Chapter 4
1. a, c, d, b; **2.** c, e; **3.** b, f, a, d, g, d; **4.** b; **5.** c; **6.** b

Chapter 5
Clinical Connections **1.** The skin separates and protects the internal environment of the body from potentially dangerous elements in the external environment. Mrs. DeStephano's chart indicates epidermal abrasions, which represent the loss of this barrier. Epidermal loss will also cost Mrs. DeStephano the acid mantle of her skin, protection against UV radiation, and Langerhans' cells, which protect against invasion by microorganisms. **2.** Macrophages found in the dermis can act as a backup system against bacterial and viral invasion when the epidermis is damaged. **3.** Suturing brings the edges of wounds close together and promotes faster healing because smaller amounts of granulation tissue need to be formed. This is termed *healing by first intention.* **4.** Cyanosis signals a decrease in the amount of oxygen carried by hemoglobin in the blood. Respiratory system and/or cardiovascular system impairments can lead to cyanosis.
Review Questions **1.** a; **2.** c; **3.** d; **4.** d; **5.** b; **6.** b; **7.** c; **8.** c; **9.** b; **10.** b; **11.** a; **12.** d; **13.** b

Chapter 6
Clinical Connections **1.** Mrs. DeStephano's broken leg has a transverse fracture of the open variety because the broken ends of the bone are protruding through the skin. **2.** The laceration of the skin caused by the broken end of the bone creates a breach in the protective barrier created by the skin, providing an entry point for bacteria and other microorganisms. In addition, the protruding ends of the bone have now been exposed to the nonsterile external environment. This could result in the development of osteomyelitis, a bacterial infection, which can be treated with antibiotics. **3.** Reduction of a fracture is the clinical term for "setting the bone." Mrs. DeStephano's physician chose internal reduction, in which surgery is performed and the broken ends of the bone are secured together by pins or wires. A cast was applied to keep the aligned ends of the bone immobile until healing of the fracture has occurred. **4.** Healing of Mrs. DeStephano's fracture will begin as bony callus formation fills the break in the bone with bony tissue. This process begins 3–4 weeks after the break occurs and is completed within 2–3 months. **5.** Nutrient arteries supply blood to the bone tissue. In order for Mrs. DeStephano's break to heal normally, the bony tissue must be supplied with oxygen (to generate ATP for energy) and nutrients in order to rebuild the bone. Damage to a nutrient artery will decrease the delivery of these building materials and could slow the process of healing. **6.** For a fracture that is slow to heal, new techniques that promote healing include electrical stimulation, which promotes the deposition of new bone tissue; ultrasound treatments, known to speed healing; and possibly the addition of bone substitutes to the fractured area. **7.** At age 45, Mrs. DeStephano will most likely not regenerate her knee cartilage. (Cartilage growth typically ends during adolescence.) Cartilage damage that occurs during adulthood is slow to heal, due to the avascular nature of cartilage, and is usually irreparable. Surgical removal of torn cartilage to allow improved movement of the joint is the usual treatment for this type of damage.
Review Questions **1.** e; **2.** b; **3.** c; **4.** d; **5.** e; **6.** b; **7.** c; **8.** b; **9.** e; **10.** c; **11.** b; **12.** c; **13.** a; **14.** b

Chapter 7
1. (1)b, g; (2)h; (3)d; (4)d, f; (5)e; (6)c; (7)a, b, d, h; (8)i; **2.** (1)g, (2)f, (3)b, (4)a, (5)b, (6)c, (7)d, (8)e; **3.** (1)b, (2)c, (3)e, (4)a, (5)h, (6)e, (7)f

Chapter 8
1. (1)c, (2)a, (3)a, (4)b, (5)c, (6)b, (7)b, (8)a, (9)c; **2.** b; **3.** d; **4.** d; **5.** b; **6.** d; **7.** d

Chapter 9
Clinical Connections **1.** The first reaction to tissue injury is the initiation of the inflammatory response. The inflammatory chemicals increase the permeability of the capillaries in the injured area, allowing white blood cells, fluid, and other substances to reach the injured area. The next step in healing involves the formation of granulation tissue, in which the vascular supply for the injured area is regenerated and collagen fibers to knit the torn edges of the tissue together are formed. Skeletal muscle does not regenerate well, so the damaged areas of Mrs. DeStephano's muscle tissue will probably be repaired primarily by the formation of fibrous tissue, creating scar tissue. **2.** Healing is aided by good circulation of blood within the injured area. Vascular damage compromises healing because the supply of oxygen and nutrients to the tissue is reduced. **3.** Under normal circumstances, skeletal muscles receive electrical signals from the nervous system continuously. These signals help to maintain muscle tone and readiness. Severing of the sciatic nerve removes this continuous nervous input to the muscles and will lead to muscle atrophy. Immobility of muscles will lead to a replacement of contractile muscle tissue with noncontractile fibrous connective tissue. Distal to the point of transection, the muscle will begin to decrease in size within 3–7 days of becoming immobile. This process can be delayed by electrically stimulating the tissues. Passive range-of-motion exercises also help prevent loss of muscle tone and joint range, and improve circulation in the injured areas. **4.** Mrs. DeStephano's physician wants to supply her damaged tissues with the necessary building materials to encourage healing. A high-protein diet will provide plenty of amino acids to rebuild or replace damaged proteins, carbohydrates will provide the fuel molecules needed to generate the required ATP, and vitamin C is important for the regeneration of connective tissue.
Review Questions **1.** c; **2.** b; **3.** (1)b, (2)a, (3)b, (4)a, (5)b, (6)a; **4.** c; **5.** a; **6.** a; **7.** d; **8.** a; **9.** (1)a, (2)a, c, (3)b, (4)c, (5)b, (6)b; **10.** a; **11.** c; **12.** c; **13.** c; **14.** b

Chapter 10
1. c; **2.** c; **3.** (1)e, (2)c, (3)g, (4)f, (5)d; **4.** a; **5.** c; **6.** d; **7.** c; **8.** c; **9.** b; **10.** d; **11.** b; **12.** a; **13.** c; **14.** d; **15.** a, b; **16.** a

Chapter 11
1. b; **2.** (1)d, (2)b, (3)f, (4)c, (5)a; **3.** b; **4.** c; **5.** a; **6.** c; **7.** b; **8.** d; **9.** c; **10.** c; **11.** a; **12.** (1)d, (2)b, (3)a, (4)c

Chapter 12
1. a; **2.** d; **3.** c; **4.** a; **5.** (1)d, (2)f, (3)e, (4)g, (5)b, (6)f, (7)i, (8)a; **6.** b; **7.** c; **8.** a; **9.** (1)a, (2)b, (3)a, (4)a, (5)b, (6)a, (7)b, (8)b, (9)a; **10.** d; **11.** (1)d, (2)e, (3)d, (4)a

Chapter 13

1. b; **2.** c; **3.** d; **4.** c; **5.** e; **6.** c; **7.** (1)d, (2)c, (3)f, (4)b, (5)e, (6)a; **8.** (1)f, (2)i, (3)b, (4)g, h, (5)e, (6)i, (7)c, (8)k, (9)l, (10)c, d, f, k; **9.** (1)b 6; (2)d 8; (3)c 2; (4)c 5; (5)a 4; (6)a 3, 9; (7)a 7; (8)a 7; (9)d 1; (10)a 3, 4, 7, 9; **10.** (1)a, 1 and 5; (2)a, 3 and 5; (3)a, 4; (4)a, 2; (5)c, 2; (6)b, 2; **11.** c

Chapter 14

Clinical Connections 1. The location of Jimmy's lacerations and bruises and his inability to rise led the paramedics to suspect a head, neck, or back injury. They immobilized his head and torso to prevent any further damage to the brain and spinal cord. **2.** The worsening neurological signs indicate a probable intracranial hemorrhage. The blood escaping from the ruptured blood vessel(s) will begin to compress Jimmy's brain and increase his intracranial pressure. Jimmy's surgery will involve repair of the damaged vessel(s) and removal of the mass of clotted blood pressing on his brain. **3.** The blow to Jimmy's head caused his brain and spinal cord to swell (cerebral and spinal edema) as part of the inflammatory response to tissue injury. Dexamethasone is an anti-inflammatory drug that will decrease swelling and relieve intracranial pressure. **4.** Loss of motor and sensory function below the level of the nipples indicates a lesion at T_4. See Figure 13.12. **5.** Jimmy is suffering from spinal shock, which occurs as a result of injury to the spinal cord. Spinal shock is a temporary condition in which all reflex and motor activities caudal to the level of spinal cord injury are lost, so Jimmy's muscles are paralyzed, his blood pressure is low due to the loss of sympathetic tone in his vasculature. **6.** Jimmy's exaggerated reflexes are caused by damaged upper motor neuron axons in the spinal cord. These upper motor neurons normally inhibit spinal reflexes. He is incontinent because there are no longer pathways to support voluntary control of bowel and bladder emptying. **7.** This condition is called *autonomic dysreflexia* (or *autonomic hyperreflexia*). This is a condition in which a normal stimulus triggers a massive activation of autonomic neurons. **8.** Extremely high arterial blood pressure can cause a rupture of the cerebral blood vessels (as well as other blood vessels in the body) and put Jimmy's life at risk.

Review Questions 1. d; **2.** (1)S, (2)P, (3)P, (4)S, (5)S, (6)P, (7)P, (8)S, (9)P, (10)S, (11)P, (12)S; **3.** b; **4.** c; **5.** a

Chapter 15

1. c; **2.** d; **3.** a; **4.** b; **5.** c; **6.** d; **7.** b; **8.** a; **9.** b; **10.** b; **11.** b; **12.** d; **13.** d; **14.** a; **15.** d; **16.** c; **17.** d; **18.** b; **19.** b; **20.** c; **21.** d; **22.** b; **23.** b; **24.** e; **25.** b; **26.** c; **27.** c; **28.** c; **29.** c

Chapter 16

Clinical Connections 1. Rationale for orders: As Mr. Gutteman is unconscious, the level of damage to his brain is unclear. Monitoring his responses and vital signs every hour will provide information for his care providers about the extent of his injuries. Turning him every 4 hours and providing careful skin care will prevent decubitus ulcers (bedsores) as well as stimulating his proprioceptive pathways. **2.** Mr. Gutteman's condition is termed *diabetes insipidus*, a condition in which insufficient quantities of antidiuretic hormone (ADH) are produced or released. Diabetes insipidus patients excrete large volumes of urine but do not have glucose or ketones present in the urine. The head trauma could have damaged Mr. Gutteman's hypothalamus, which produces the hormone, or injured his posterior pituitary gland, which releases ADH into the bloodstream. **3.** Diabetes insipidus is not life threatening for most individuals with normal thirst mechanisms, as they will be thirsty and drink to replenish the lost fluid. However, Mr. Gutteman is comatose, so his fluid output must be monitored closely so that the volume lost can be replaced by IV line. His subsequent recovery may be complicated if he has suffered damage to his hypothalamus, which houses the thirst center neurons.

Review Questions 1. b; **2.** a; **3.** c; **4.** d; **5.** (1)c, (2)a and b, (3)f, (4)d, (5)e, (6)g, (7)a, (8)h, (9)b and e, (10)a; **6.** d; **7.** c; **8.** b; **9.** d; **10.** b; **11.** d; **12.** b; **13.** c; **14.** d

Chapter 17

1. c; **2.** c; **3.** d; **4.** b; **5.** d; **6.** a; **7.** a; **8.** b; **9.** c; **10.** d

Chapter 18

1. a; **2.** c; **3.** b; **4.** c; **5.** b; **6.** b; **7.** c; **8.** d; **9.** b

Chapter 19

Clinical Connections 1. The tissues in Mr. Hutchinson's right leg were deprived of oxygen and nutrients for at least one-half hour. When tissues are deprived of oxygen, tissue metabolism decreases and eventually ceases, so these tissues may have died due to anoxia. **2.** Mr. Hutchinson's vital signs (low BP; rapid, thready pulse) indicate that he is facing a life-threatening problem that must be stabilized before other, less vital problems can be addressed. As for surgery, he may be scheduled for open reduction of his crushed bone, depending upon the condition of the tissues in his crushed right leg. If tissue death has occurred in his leg, he may undergo amputation of that limb. **3.** Mr. Hutchinson's rapid, thready pulse and falling blood pressure are indications of hypovolemic shock, a type of shock resulting from decreased blood volume. Because his blood volume is low, his heart rate is elevated to increase cardiac output in an effort to maintain the blood supply to his vital organs. Mr. Hutchinson's blood volume must be increased as quickly as possible with blood transfusions or intravenous saline. This will stabilize his condition and allow his physicians to continue with his surgery.

Review Questions 1. d; **2.** b; **3.** d; **4.** c; **5.** e; **6.** d; **7.** c; **8.** b; **9.** b; **10.** a; **11.** b; **12.** c; **13.** b; **14.** d; **15.** (1)b, e, g; (2)c; (3)i; (4) f, h; (5) d

Chapter 20

Clinical Connections 1. The red streaks radiating from Mr. Hutchinson's finger indicate that his lymphatic vessels are inflamed. This inflammation may be caused by a bacterial infection. If Mr. Hutchinson's arm had exhibited edema without any accompanying red streaks, the problem would likely have been impaired lymph transport from his arm back to his trunk, due to injury or blockage of his lymphatic vessels. **2.** Mr. Hutchinson's arm was placed in a sling to immobilize it, slowing the drainage of lymph from the infected area in an attempt to limit the spread of the inflammation. **3.** Mr. Hutchinson's low lymphocyte count indicates that his body's ability to fight infection by bacteria or viruses is impaired. The antibiotics and additional staff protection will protect Mr. Hutchinson until his lymphocyte count increases again. Gloving and gowning also protect the staff caring for Mr. Hutchinson from any body infection he might have. **4.** Mr. Hutchinson's recovery may be problematic, as he probably already has an ongoing bacterial infection and his ability to raise a defense to this infection is impaired.

Review Questions 1. c; **2.** c; **3.** a, d; **4.** c; **5.** a; **6.** b; **7.** a; **8.** b; **9.** d

Chapter 21

1. c; **2.** a; **3.** d; **4.** d, e; **5.** a; **6.** d; **7.** b; **8.** c; **9.** d; **10.** d; **11.** d; **12.** (1)b, g; (2)d, i; (3)a, e; (4)a, e, f, h; (5)e, f, h; (6)c, f, g

Chapter 22

Clinical Connections 1. Spinal cord injury from a fracture at the level of the C_2 vertebra would interrupt the normal transmission of signals from the brain stem down the phrenic nerve to the diaphragm, and Barbara would be unable to breathe due to paralysis of the diaphragm. **2.** Barbara's head, neck, and torso should have been immobilized to prevent further damage to the spinal cord. In addition, she required assistance to breathe, so her airway was probably intubated to permit ventilation of her lungs. **3.** Cyanosis is a decrease in the degree of oxygen saturation of hemoglobin. As Barbara's respiratory efforts cease, her alveolar P_{O_2} will fall, so there is less diffusion of oxygen between the lungs and the bloodstream. In addition, her arterial P_{CO_2} will increase. Both of these conditions will promote the unloading of oxygen from hemoglobin. **4.** Injury to the spinal cord at the level of the C_2 vertebra will cause quadriplegia (paralysis of all four limbs). **5.** Atelectasis is the collapse of a lung. Because it is the right thorax that is compressed, only her right lung is affected. Because the lungs are in separate pleural cavities, only the right lung collapsed. **6.** Barbara's fractured ribs probably punctured her lung tissue and allowed air within the lung to enter the pleural cavity. **7.** The atelectasis will be reversed by closing the tear in her lung tissue, then removing the air from the pleural cavity using chest tubes. This will allow her lung to re-inflate.

Review Questions **1.** b; **2.** a and c; **3.** c; **4.** c; **5.** b; **6.** d; **7.** d; **8.** b; **9.** c, d; **10.** c; **11.** b; **12.** b; **13.** b; **14.** c; **15.** b; **16.** b

Chapter 23

Clinical Connections **1.** Mr. Gutteman's statement about the effects of milk on his digestive tract suggests that he may be deficient in lactase, a brush border enzyme that breaks down lactose (milk sugar). **2.** His responses to the questions reduced the possibility that he has gastric ulcers. Mr. Gutteman's diarrhea may be due to gluten enteropathy. To verify this diagnosis, Mr. Gutteman's diet should be restricted by eliminating all grains but rice and corn and he should have a follow-up examination to see if his condition has improved.

Review Questions **1.** c; **2.** d; **3.** d; **4.** b; **5.** b; **6.** a; **7.** d; **8.** d; **9.** b; **10.** c; **11.** c; **12.** a; **13.** d; **14.** d; **15.** b; **16.** c; **17.** a

Chapter 24

1. a; **2.** c; **3.** c; **4.** d; **5.** b; **6.** c; **7.** a; **8.** d; **9.** d; **10.** a; **11.** b; **12.** d; **13.** c; **14.** d; **15.** a

Chapter 25

1. d; **2.** b; **3.** c; **4.** d; **5.** c; **6.** b; **7.** a; **8.** c; **9.** a; **10.** b

Chapter 26

Clinical Connections **1.** Mr. Heyden's vital signs suggest that he is in hypovolemic shock, which is probably due to an internal hemorrhage. **2.** The spleen is a highly vascular organ due to its role as a blood filtering organ. The macrophages in Mr. Heyden's liver and bone marrow will help compensate for the loss of his spleen. **3.** Elevation of renin, aldosterone, and antidiuretic hormone indicate that Mr. Heyden's body is trying to compensate for his falling blood pressure and blood loss. *Renin:* released when renal blood flow is diminished and blood pressure falls. The angiotensin-aldosterone response is initiated by renin. The formation of angiotensin II leads to vasoconstriction, which will increase blood pressure, and to the release of aldosterone. *Aldosterone:* increases Na^+ reabsorption by the kidney. The movement of this reabsorbed Na^+ into the bloodstream will promote the movement of water from the interstitial fluid, resulting in an increase in blood volume. *Antidiuretic hormone (ADH):* released when the hypothalamic osmoreceptors sense an increase in osmolality. ADH has two consequences: it is a potent vasoconstrictor and will increase blood pressure, and it promotes water retention by the kidney, increasing blood volume. **4.** Mr. Heyden's urine production

may be decreased for several reasons. The severe drop in his blood pressure would reduce renal blood flow, thus reducing glomerular blood pressure and decreasing his glomerular filtration rate. The elevation in his ADH levels can reduce urine output due to increased water reabsorption by the kidney. He may also have damage to the kidney due to his crush injury in the left lumbar region. The presence of casts and a brownish-red color in his urine are probably damaged cells and blood. If he has suffered kidney damage due to being crushed, he may have nephron damage that would include disruption of the filtration membrane, allowing red blood cells to pass into the filtrate and therefore the urine. He may also have damaged renal tubules and peritubular capillaries, allowing entry of blood and damaged renal tubule epithelial cells into the filtrate.

Review Questions **1.** a; **2.** c; **3.** b; **4.** b; **5.** h, i, j; **6.** c, g; **7.** a, e; **8.** b; **9.** a, b; **10.** j; **11.** b, d; **12.** a; **13.** c

Chapter 27

Clinical Connections **1.** *Carcinoma* is the term for cancer originating from epithelial tissue. The primary source of Mr. Heyden's cancer is likely to be the prostate. **2.** Elevation of serum acid phosphatase levels is diagnostic for carcinoma of the prostate. (In addition, Mr. Heyden's age places him in a group that is at relatively higher risk for this type of cancer.) **3.** Digital examination of Mr. Heyden's prostate should detect the presence of carcinoma in this tissue. In addition, serum levels of prostate-specific antigen (PSA) should be checked, as an increase in this antigen is specific for prostate cancer. **4.** Mr. Heyden's carcinoma has advanced to the point of metastasis. He will probably undergo a treatment that reduces the levels of androgens in his body, as androgens promote growth of the prostate-derived tissue. These treatments could include castration or administration of drugs that block the production and/or effects of androgens.

Review Questions **1.** a and b; **2.** d; **3.** a; **4.** d; **5.** b; **6.** d; **7.** d; **8.** c; **9.** a, c, e, f; **10.** (1)c, f; (2)e, h; (3)g; (4)a; (5)b, g, and e; (6)f; **11.** a; **12.** c; **13.** d; **14.** b; **15.** a; **16.** b; **17.** c

Chapter 28

1. (1)a, (2)b, (3)b, (4)a; **2.** b; **3.** c; **4.** b; **5.** a; **6.** d; **7.** d; **8.** c; **9.** a; **10.** b; **11.** c; **12.** a; **13.** c; **14.** a; **15.** (1)e, (2)g, (3)a, (4)f, (5)i, (6)b, (7)h, (8)d, (9)c

Chapter 29

1. (1)d, (2)g, (3)b, (4)a, (5)f, (6)c, (7)e, (8)h; **2.** (1)e, (2)a, (3)b, (4)d, (5)c, (6)d, (7)f

Glossary

Abdomen (ab′do-men) Portion of the body between the diaphragm and the pelvis.

Abduct (ab-dukt′) To move away from the midline of the body.

Absolute refractory period Period following stimulation during which no additional action potential can be evoked.

Absorption Process by which the products of digestion pass through the alimentary tube mucosa into the blood or lymph.

Accessory digestive organs Organs that contribute to the digestive process but are not part of the alimentary canal; include the tongue, teeth, salivary glands, pancreas, liver.

Accommodation The process of increasing the refractive power of the lens of the eye; focusing.

Acetabulum (as″ĕ-tab′u-lum) Cuplike cavity on lateral surface of the hip bone that receives the femur.

Acetylcholine (ACh) (as″ĕ-til-ko′lēn) Chemical transmitter substance released by some nerve endings.

Acetylcholinesterase (AChE) (as″ĕ-til-ko″lin-es′ter-ās) Enzyme present at the neuromuscular junction and synapses that degrades acetylcholine and terminates its action.

Achilles tendon. *See* Calcaneal tendon.

Acid A substance that releases hydrogen ions when in solution (compare with Base); a proton donor.

Acid-base balance Situation in which the pH of the blood is maintained between 7.35 and 7.45.

Acidosis (as″ĭ-do′sis) State of abnormally high hydrogen ion concentration in the extracellular fluid.

Actin (ak′tin) A contractile protein of muscle.

Action potential A large transient depolarization event, including polarity reversal, that is conducted along the membrane of a muscle cell or a nerve fiber.

Activation energy The amount of energy required to push a reactant to the level necessary for action.

Active immunity Immunity produced by an encounter with an antigen; provides immunological memory.

Active site Region on the surface of a functional (globular) protein where it binds and interacts chemically with other molecules of complementary shape and charge.

Active transport Membrane transport processes for which ATP is provided, e.g., solute pumping and endocytosis.

Adaptation (1) Any change in structure or response to suit a new environment; (2) decline in the transmission of a sensory nerve when a receptor is stimulated continuously and without change in stimulus strength.

Adduct (a-dukt′) To move toward the midline of the body.

Adenine (A) (ad′ĕ-nēn) One of the two major purines found in both RNA and DNA; also found in various free nucleotides of importance to the body, such as ATP.

Adenohypophysis (ad″ĕ-no-hi-pof′ĭ-sis) Anterior pituitary; the glandular part of the pituitary gland.

Adenoids (ad′en-noids) Pharyngeal tonsil.

Adenosine triphosphate (ATP) (ah-den′o-sēn tri″fos′fāt) Organic molecule that stores and releases chemical energy for use in body cells.

Adipocyte (ad′ĭ-po-sīt) An adipose, or fat cell.

Adipose tissue (ad′ĭ-pōs) Areolar connective tissue modified to store nutrients; a connective tissue consisting chiefly of fat cells.

Adrenal glands (uh-drē′nul) Hormone-producing glands located superior to the kidneys; each consists of medulla and cortex areas.

Adrenergic fibers (ad″ren-er′jik) Nerve fibers that release norepinephrine.

Adrenocorticotropic hormone (ACTH) (ah-dre′no-kor″tĭ-ko-trō′pik) Anterior pituitary hormone that influences the activity of the adrenal cortex.

Adventitia (ad″ven-tish′e-ah) Outermost layer or covering of some organs.

Aerobic (a′er-ōb″ik) Oxygen-requiring.

Aerobic endurance The length of time a muscle can continue to contract using aerobic pathways.

Aerobic respiration Respiration in which oxygen is consumed and glucose is broken down entirely; water, carbon dioxide, and large amounts of ATP are the final products.

Afferent (af′er-ent) Carrying to or toward a center.

Afferent (sensory) nerve Nerve that contains processes of sensory neurons and carries nerve impulses to the central nervous system.

Afferent (sensory) neuron Nerve cell that carries impulses toward the central nervous system; initiates nerve impulses following receptor stimulation.

Agglutination (ah-gloo″tĭ-na′shun) Clumping of (foreign) cells; induced by cross-linking of antigen-antibody complexes.

Agonist (ag′o-nist) Muscle that bears the major responsibility for effecting a particular movement; a prime mover.

AIDS Acquired immune deficiency syndrome; caused by human immunodeficiency virus (HIV); symptoms include severe weight loss, night sweats, swollen lymph nodes, opportunistic infections.

Albumin (al-bu′min) The most abundant plasma protein.

Aldosterone (al-dos′ter-ōn) Hormone produced by the adrenal cortex that regulates Na^+ reabsorption and K^+ secretion by the kidneys.

Alimentary canal (al″ĭ-men′tar-e) The continuous hollow tube extending from the mouth to the anus; its walls are constructed by the oral cavity, pharynx, esophagus, stomach, and small and large intestines.

Alkalosis (al″kah-lo′sis) State of abnormally low hydrogen ion concentration in the extracellular fluid.

Allantois (ah″lan′to-is) Embryonic membrane; its blood vessels develop into blood vessels of the umbilical cord.

Alleles   Genes coding for the same trait and found at the same locus on homologous chromosomes.

Allergy   A type of hypersensitivity (overzealous immune response to an otherwise harmless antigen) that involves IgE antibodies and histamine release.

Alopecia (al″o-pe′she-ah)   Baldness.

Alpha (α)-helix   The most common type of secondary structure of the amino acid chain in proteins; resembles the coils of a telephone cord.

Alveolar (acinar) gland (al-ve′o-lar)   A gland whose secretory cells form small, flasklike sacs.

Alveolar ventilation rate (AVR)   An index of respiratory efficiency; measures volume of fresh air that flows in and out of alveoli.

Alveolus (al-ve′o-lus)   (1) One of the microscopic air sacs of the lungs; (2) tiny milk-producing glandular sac in the breast; (3) tooth socket.

Alzheimer's disease (altz′hi-merz)   Degenerative brain disease resulting in progressive loss of memory and motor control, and increasing dementia.

Amino acid (ah-me′no)   Organic compound containing nitrogen, carbon, hydrogen, and oxygen; building block of protein.

Ammonia (NH_3)   Common waste product of protein breakdown in the body; a colorless volatile gas, very soluble in water and capable of forming a weak base; a proton acceptor.

Amniocentesis   A common form of fetal testing in which a small sample of fluid is removed from the amniotic cavity.

Amnion (am′ne-on)   Fetal membrane that forms a fluid-filled sac around the embryo.

Amoeboid motion (ah-me′boyd)   The flowing movement of the cytoplasm of a phagocyte.

Amphiarthrosis (am″fe-ar-thro′sis)   A slightly movable joint.

Ampulla (am-pul′lah)   A localized dilation of a canal or duct.

Amylase   Digestive system enzyme that breaks down starchy foods.

Anabolism (ah-nab′o-lizm)   Energy-requiring building phase of metabolism in which simpler substances are combined to form more complex substances.

Anaerobic (an-a′er-ōb-ik)   Not requiring oxygen.

Anaerobic glycolysis (gli-kol′ĭ-sis)   Energy-yielding conversion of glucose to lactic acid in various tissues, notably muscle, when sufficient oxygen is not available.

Anaerobic threshold   The point at which muscle metabolism converts to anaerobic glycolysis.

Anaphase   Third stage of mitosis in which a full set of daughter chromosomes move toward each pole of a cell.

Anastomosis (ah-nas″to-mo′sis)   A union or joining of nerves, blood vessels, or lymphatics.

Anatomy   Study of the structure of living organisms.

Androgen (an′dro-jen)   A hormone such as testosterone that controls male secondary sex characteristics.

Anemia (ah-ne′me-ah)   Reduced oxygen-carrying ability of blood resulting from too few erythrocytes or abnormal hemoglobin.

Aneurysm (an′u-rizm)   Blood-filled sac in an artery wall caused by dilation or weakening of the wall.

Angina pectoris (an′jĭ-nah pek′tor-is)   Severe suffocating chest pain caused by brief lack of oxygen supply to heart muscle.

Angiotensin II (an″je-o-ten′sin)   A potent vasoconstrictor activated by renin; also triggers release of aldosterone.

Anion (an′i-on)   An ion carrying one or more negative charges and therefore attracted to a positive pole.

Anoxia (ah-nŏk′se-ah)   Deficiency of oxygen.

Antagonist (an-tag′o-nist)   (1) Muscle that reverses, or opposes, the action of another muscle. (2) Hormone that opposes the action of another hormone.

Anterior pituitary.   *See* Adenohypophysis.

Antibody   A protein molecule that is released by a plasma cell (a daughter cell of an activated B lymphocyte) and that binds specifically to an antigen; an immunoglobulin.

Anticodon (an″ti-ko′don)   The three-base sequence complementary to the messenger RNA (mRNA) codon.

Antidiuretic hormone (ADH, also called **vasopressin)** (an″tĭ-dī″yer-eh′tik)   Hormone produced by the hypothalamus and released by the posterior pituitary; stimulates the kidneys to reabsorb more water, reducing urine volume.

Antigen (Ag) (an′tĭ-jen)   A substance or part of a substance (living or nonliving) that is recognized as foreign by the immune system, activates the immune system, and reacts with immune cells or their products.

Anucleate cell (a-nu′kle-āt)   A cell without a nucleus.

Anus (a′nus)   Distal end of digestive tract; outlet of rectum.

Aorta (a-or′tah)   Major systemic artery; arises from the left ventricle of the heart.

Aortic body   Receptor in the aortic arch sensitive to changing oxygen, carbon dioxide, and pH levels of the blood.

Apgar score   Evaluation of an infant's physical status at 1 and 5 minutes after birth by assessing five criteria: heart rate, respiration, color, muscle tone, and reflexes.

Apnea   Breathing cessation.

Apocrine sweat gland (ap′o-krin)   The less numerous type of sweat gland; produces a secretion containing water, salts, proteins, and fatty acids.

Apoenzyme (ap′ō-en-zīm)   The protein portion of an enzyme.

Aponeurosis (ap″o-nu-ro′sis)   Fibrous or membranous sheet connecting a muscle and the part it moves.

Apoptosis   A process of controlled cellular suicide; eliminates cells that are unneeded, stressed, or aged.

Appendicitis (ă-pen′dĭ-si′tis)   Inflammation of the appendix (wormlike sac attached to the cecum of the large intestine).

Appendicular   Relating to the limbs; one of the two major divisions of the body.

Appositional growth   Growth accomplished by the addition of new layers onto those previously formed.

Aqueous humor (a′kwe-us)   Watery fluid in the anterior segment of the eye.

Arachnoid (ah-rak-noid)   Weblike; specifically, the weblike arachnoid mater, the middle layer of the three meninges.

Areola (ah-re′o-lah)   Circular, pigmented area surrounding the nipple; any small space in a tissue.

Areolar connective tissue   A type of loose connective tissue.

Arrector pili (ah-rek′tor pi′li)   Tiny, smooth muscles attached to hair follicles; contraction causes the hair to stand upright.

Arrhythmia (a-rith′me-ah)   Irregular heart rhythm, often caused by defects in the intrinsic conduction system.

Arteries   Blood vessels that conduct blood away from the heart and into the circulation.

Arteriole (ar-tēr′e-ōl)   A minute artery.

Arteriosclerosis (ar-tēr′e-o-skler-o′sis)   Any of a number of proliferative and degenerative changes in the arteries leading to their decreased elasticity.

Arthritis   Inflammation of the joints.

Arthroscopic surgery (ar-thro-skop′ik)   Procedure enabling a surgeon to repair the interior of a joint through a small incision.

Articular capsule   Double-layered capsule composed of an outer fibrous capsule lined by synovial membrane; encloses the joint cavity of a synovial joint.

Articular cartilage   Hyaline cartilage covering bone ends at movable joints.

Articulation (joint)   The junction of two or more bones.

Association areas   Functional areas of the cerebral cortex that act mainly to integrate diverse information for purposeful action.

Astigmatism (ah-stig′mah-tizm)   A condition in which unequal curvatures in different parts of the cornea or lens of the eye lead to blurred vision.

Astrocyte (as′tro-sīte)   A type of CNS supporting cell; assists in exchanges between blood capillaries and neurons.

Ataxia (ah-tak′se-ah)   Disruption of muscle coordination resulting in inaccurate movements.

Atelectasis (at″ĕ-lik′tah-sis)   Lung collapse.

Atherosclerosis (a″ther-o″skler-o′sis)   Changes in the walls of large arteries consisting of lipid deposits on the artery walls; the early stage of arteriosclerosis.

Atmospheric pressure   Force that air exerts on the surface of the body (760 mm Hg at sea level).

Atom   Smallest particle of an elemental substance that exhibits the properties of that element; composed of protons, neutrons, and electrons.

Atomic mass number   Sum of the number of protons and neutrons in the nucleus of an atom.

Atomic number   The number of protons in an atom.

Atomic symbol   The one- or two-letter symbol used to indicate an element; usually the first letter(s) of the element's name.

Atomic weight   The average of the mass numbers of all the isotopes of an element.

ATP (adenosine triphosphate) (ah-den′o-sēn tri″fos′fāt)   Organic molecule that stores and releases chemical energy for use in body cells.

Atria (a′tre-ah)   The two superior receiving chambers of the heart.

Atrial natriuretic peptide (ANP) (a′tre-al na″tre-u-ret′ik)   A hormone released by certain cells of the heart atria that reduces blood pressure and blood volume by inhibiting nearly all events that promote vasoconstriction and Na^+ and water retention.

Atrioventricular (AV) bundle (a″tre-o-ven-tri′kyoo-ler)   Bundle of specialized fibers that conduct impulses from the AV node to the right and left ventricles; also called bundle of His.

Atrioventricular (AV) node   Specialized mass of conducting cells located at the atrioventricular junction in the heart.

Atrioventricular (AV) valve   Valve that prevents backflow into the atrium when the connected ventricle is contracting.

Atrophy (at′ro-fe)   Reduction in size or wasting away of an organ or cell resulting from disease or lack of use.

Auditory ossicles (ah′sih-kulz)   The three tiny bones serving as transmitters of vibrations and located within the middle ear: the malleus, incus, and stapes.

Auditory tube   *See* Pharyngotympanic tube.

Autoimmunity   Production of antibodies or effector T cells that attack a person's own tissue.

Autolysis (aw″tol′ĭ-sis)   Process of autodigestion (self-digestion) of cells, especially dead or degenerate cells.

Autonomic ganglion   Collection of sympathetic or parasympathetic ganglionic neuronal cell bodies.

Autonomic nervous system (ANS)   Efferent division of the peripheral nervous system that innervates cardiac and smooth muscles and glands; also called the involuntary or visceral motor system.

Autonomic (visceral) reflexes   Reflexes that activate smooth or cardiac muscle and/or glands.

Autoregulation   The automatic local adjustment of blood flow to a particular body area in response to its current requirements.

Autosomes   Chromosomes number 1 to 22; do not include the sex chromosomes.

Avogadro's number (av″o-gad′rōz)   The number of molecules in one mole of any substance, 6.02×10^{23}.

Axial   Relating to the head, neck, and trunk; one of the two major divisions of the body.

Axolemma (ak″so-lem′ah)   The plasma membrane of an axon.

Axon   Neuron process that carries impulses away from the nerve cell body; efferent process; the conducting portion of a nerve cell.

Axon terminals (synaptic knobs, boutons)   The bulbous distal endings of the terminal branches of an axon.

B cells   Also called B lymphocytes; oversee humoral immunity; their descendants differentiate into antibody-producing plasma cells.

Baroreceptor (bayr″o-re-sep′tor)   A sensory nerve ending in the wall of the carotid sinus or aortic arch sensitive to vessel stretching.

Basal body (ba′sal)   An organelle structurally identical to a centriole and forming the base of a cilium or flagellum.

Basal ganglia   *See* Basal nuclei.

Basal lamina (lam′ĭ-nah)   Noncellular, adhesive supporting sheet consisting largely of glycoproteins secreted by epithelial cells.

Basal metabolic rate (BMR)   Rate at which energy is expended (heat produced) by the body per unit time under controlled (basal) conditions: 12 hours after a meal, at rest.

Basal nuclei (basal ganglia)   Specific gray matter areas located deep within the white matter of the cerebral hemispheres.

Basal surface   The surface near the base or interior of a structure; nearest the lower side or bottom of a structure.

Base   A substance capable of binding with hydrogen ions; a proton acceptor.

Basement membrane   Extracellular material consisting of a basal lamina secreted by epithelial cells and a reticular lamina secreted by underlying connective tissue cells.

Basophil (ba′zo-fil)   White blood cell whose granules stain purplish-black and nucleus purple with basic dye.

Benign (be-nīn′)   Not malignant.

Biceps (bi′seps)   Two-headed, especially applied to certain muscles.

Bile   Greenish-yellow or brownish fluid produced in and secreted by the liver, stored in the gallbladder, and released into the small intestine.

Bilirubin (bil″i-roo′bin)   Yellow pigment of bile.

Bipolar neuron   Neuron with axon and dendrite that extend from opposite sides of the cell body.

Blastocyst (blas′to-sist)   Stage of early embryonic development; the product of cleavage.

Blood pressure (BP)   Force exerted by blood against a unit area of the blood vessel walls; differences in blood pressure between different areas of the circulation provide the driving force for blood circulation.

Blood-brain barrier   Mechanism that inhibits passage of materials from the blood into brain tissues; reflects relative impermeability of brain capillaries.

Bolus (bo′lus)   A rounded mass of food prepared by the mouth for swallowing; any soft round mass.

Bone marrow   Fat- or blood-forming tissue found within bone cavities; called yellow and red bone marrow, respectively.

Bone (osseous tissue) (os′e-us)   A connective tissue that forms the bony skeleton.

Bone remodeling   Process involving bone formation and destruction in response to hormonal and mechanical factors.

Bone resorption   The removal of osseous tissue; part of the continuous bone remodeling process.

Bowman's capsule (bo-manz′)   *See* Glomerular capsule.

Boyle's law   States that when the temperature is constant, the pressure of a gas varies inversely with its volume.

Bradycardia (brad″e-kar′deah)   A heart rate below 60 beats per minute.

Brain death   State of irreversible coma, even though life-support measures may have restored other body organs.

Brain stem   Collectively the midbrain, pons, and medulla of the brain.

Brain ventricle   Fluid-filled cavity of the brain.

Branchial groove (brang′ke-al)   An indentation of the surface ectoderm in the embryo; the external acoustic meatus develops from these.

Bronchioles   Smaller (<1 mm in diameter) branching air passageways inside the lungs.

Bronchus (brong′kus)   One of the two large branches of the trachea that leads to the lungs.

Buffer   Chemical substance or system that minimizes changes in pH by releasing or binding hydrogen ions.

Burn   Tissue damage inflicted by intense heat, electricity, radiation, or certain chemicals, all of which denature cell proteins and cause cell death in the affected areas.

Bursa (ber′sa)   A fibrous sac lined with synovial membrane and containing synovial fluid; occurs between bones and muscle tendons (or other structures), where it acts to decrease friction during movement.

Bursitis   Inflammation of a bursa.

Calcaneal tendon (kal-ka′ne-al)   Tendon that attaches the calf muscles to the heelbone (calcaneus); also called the Achilles tendon.

Calcitonin (kal″sih-to′nin)   Hormone released by the thyroid that promotes a decrease in calcium levels in the blood.

Calculus (kal′ku-lus)   A stone formed within various body parts.

Callus (kal′lus)   (1) Localized thickening of skin epidermis resulting from physical trauma; (2) repair tissue (fibrous or bony) formed at a fracture site.

Calorie (cal)   Amount of energy needed to raise the temperature of 1 gram of water 1° Celsius. Energy exchanges associated with biochemical reactions are usually reported in kilocalories (1 kcal = 1000 cal), also called large calories (Cal).

Calyx (ka′liks)   A cuplike extension of the pelvis of the kidney.

Canaliculus (kan″ah-lik′u-lus)   Extremely small tubular passage or channel.

Cancer   A malignant, invasive cellular neoplasm that has the capability of spreading throughout the body or body parts.

Capillaries (kap′il-layr″ēs)   The smallest of the blood vessels and the sites of exchange between the blood and tissue cells.

Carbohydrate (kar″bo-hi′drāt)   Organic compound composed of carbon, hydrogen, and oxygen; includes starches, sugars, cellulose.

Carbonic acid–bicarbonate buffer system   Chemical system that helps maintain pH homeostasis of the blood.

Carbonic anhydrase (kar-bon′ik an-hi′dras)   Enzyme that facilitates the combination of carbon dioxide with water to form carbonic acid.

Carcinogen (kar″sĭ′no-jin)   Cancer-causing agent.

Cardiac cycle   Sequence of events encompassing one complete contraction and relaxation of the atria and ventricles of the heart.

Cardiac muscle   Specialized muscle of the heart.

Cardiac output (CO)   Amount of blood pumped out of a ventricle in one minute.

Cardiac reserve   The difference between resting and maximal cardiac output.

Cardiogenic shock   Pump failure; the heart is so inefficient that it cannot sustain adequate circulation.

Cardiovascular system   Organ system that distributes the blood to deliver nutrients and remove wastes.

Carotene (kar′o-tēn)   Yellow to orange pigment that accumulates in the stratum corneum epidermal layer and in fatty tissue of the hypodermis.

Carotid body (kar-rot′id)   A receptor in the common carotid artery sensitive to changing oxygen, carbon dioxide, and pH levels of the blood.

Carotid sinus (si-nus)   A dilation of a common carotid artery; involved in regulation of systemic blood pressure.

Carrier   A transmembrane protein that changes shape to envelop and transport a polar substance across the cell membrane.

Cartilage (kar′tĭ-lij)   White, semiopaque connective tissue.

Cartilage bone (endochondral bone)   Bone formed by using hyaline cartilage structures as models for ossification.

Cartilaginous joints (kar″ti-laj′ĭ-nus)   Bones united by cartilage; no joint cavity is present.

Catabolism (kat-tab′o-lizm)   Process in which living cells break down substances into simpler substances.

Catalyst (kat′ah-list)   Substance that increases the rate of a chemical reaction without itself becoming chemically changed or part of the product.

Cataract   Clouding of the eye's lens; often congenital or age-related.

Catecholamines (kat″ĕ-kol′ah-menz)   Epinephrine, norepinephrine, and dopamine; a class of amines that act as chemical transmitters.

Cation (kat′i-on)   An ion with a positive charge.

Caudal (kaw′dul)   Literally, toward the tail; in humans, the inferior portion of the anatomy.

Cecum (se′kum)   The blind-end pouch at the beginning of the large intestine.

Cell   Structural unit of all living things.

Cell differentiation   The development of specific and distinctive features in cells, from a single cell (the fertilized egg) to all the specialized cells of adulthood.

Cell division period   One of two major periods in the cell life cycle; involves the division of the nucleus (mitosis) and the division of the cytoplasm (cytokinesis).

Cell life cycle   Series of changes a cell goes through from the time it is formed until it reproduces itself.

Cell-mediated immunity   Immunity conferred by activated T cells, which directly lyse infected or cancerous body cells or cells of foreign grafts and release chemicals that regulate the immune response.

Cell membrane.   *See* Plasma membrane.

Cellular respiration   Metabolic processes in which ATP is produced.

Cellulose (sel′u-lōs)   A fibrous carbohydrate that is the main structural component of plant tissues.

Central (Haversian) canal (hah-ver′zhan)   The canal in the center of each osteon that contains minute blood vessels and nerve fibers that serve the needs of the osteocytes.

Central nervous system (CNS)   Brain and spinal cord.

Centriole (sen′tre-ol)   Minute body found near the nucleus of the cell; active in cell division.

Centrosome (cell center)   A region near the nucleus which contains paired organelles called centrioles.

Cerebellum (ser″ĕ-bel′um)   Brain region most involved in producing smooth, coordinated skeletal muscle activity.

Cerebral aqueduct (ser′ĕ-bral, sĕ-re′bral)   The slender cavity of the midbrain that connects the third and fourth ventricles.

Cerebral arterial circle (circle of Willis)   An arterial anastomosis at the base of the brain.

Cerebral cortex   The outer gray matter region of the cerebral hemispheres.

Cerebral dominance   Designates the hemisphere that is dominant for language.

Cerebral palsy   Neuromuscular disability in which voluntary muscles are poorly controlled or paralyzed as a result of brain damage.

Cerebral white matter   Consists largely of myelinated fibers bundled into large tracts; provides for communication between cerebral areas and lower CNS centers.

Cerebrospinal fluid (CSF) (ser″ĕ-bro-spi′nal)   Plasmalike fluid that fills the cavities of the CNS and surrounds the CNS externally; protects the brain and spinal cord.

Cerebrovascular accident (CVA) (ser″ĕ-bro-vas′ku-lar)   Condition in which brain tissue is deprived of a blood supply, as in blockage of a cerebral blood vessel; a stroke.

Cerebrum (ser′ĕ-brum)   The cerebral hemispheres and the structures of the diencephalon.

Cervical vertebrae   The seven vertebrae of the vertebral column located in the neck.

Cervix   Lower outlet of the uterus extending into the vagina.

Channel   A transmembrane protein that helps form aqueous channels that transport substances from one side of the membrane to the other.

Chemical bond   An energy relationship holding atoms together; involves the interaction of electrons.

Chemical digestion   A series of catabolic steps in which complex food molecules are broken down to their building blocks by enzymes.

Chemical energy   Energy stored in the bonds of chemical substances.

Chemical equilibrium   A state of apparent repose created by two reactions proceeding in opposite directions at equal speed.

Chemical reaction   Process in which molecules are formed, changed, or broken down.

Chemoreceptor (ke″mo-re-sep′ter)   Receptor sensitive to various chemicals in solution.

Chemotaxis (ke″mo-tak′sis)   Movement of a cell, organism, or part of an organism toward or away from a chemical substance.

Cholecystokinin (CCK) (ko″le-sis″to-ki′nin)   An intestinal hormone that stimulates gallbladder contraction and pancreatic juice release.

Cholesterol (ko-les′ter-ol″) Steroid found in animal fats as well as in most body tissues; made by the liver.

Cholinergic fibers (ko″lin-er′jik) Nerve endings that, upon stimulation, release acetylcholine.

Chondroblast (kon′dro-blast) Actively mitotic cell of cartilage.

Chondrocyte (kon′dro-sīt) Mature cell of cartilage.

Chorion (kor′e-on) Outermost fetal membrane; helps form the placenta.

Chorionic villi sampling (ko″re-on′ik vil′i) Fetal testing procedure in which bits of the chorionic villi from the placenta are snipped off and the cells karyotyped. This procedure can be done as early as 8 weeks into the pregnancy.

Choroid (ko′roid) The vascular middle layer of the eye.

Choroid plexus (ko′roid plex′sus) A capillary knot that protrudes into a brain ventricle; involved in forming cerebrospinal fluid.

Chromatin (kro′mah-tin) Structures in the nucleus that carry the hereditary factors (genes).

Chromosomes (kro′mo-somz) Barlike bodies of tightly coiled chromatin; visible during cell division.

Chronic obstructive pulmonary disease (COPD) Collective term for progressive, obstructive respiratory disorders; includes emphysema, chronic bronchitis.

Chyme (kīm) Semifluid, creamy mass consisting of partially digested food and gastric juice.

Cilia (sil′e-ah) Tiny, hairlike projections on cell surfaces that move in a wavelike manner.

Circumduction (ser″kum-duk′shun) Movement of a body part so that it outlines a cone in space.

Cirrhosis (sĭ-ro′sis) Chronic disease of the liver, characterized by an overgrowth of connective tissue or fibrosis.

Cisterna chyli (sis-ter′nah ki′li) An enlarged sac at the base of the thoracic duct; the origin of the thoracic duct.

Cisternae (sis-ter′ne) Any cavity or enclosed space serving as a reservoir.

Cleavage An early embryonic phase consisting of rapid mitotic cell divisions without intervening growth periods; product is a blastocyst.

Clonal selection (klo′nul) Process during which a B cell or T cell becomes sensitized through binding contact with an antigen.

Clone Descendants of a single cell.

Coagulation Process in which blood is transformed from a liquid to a gel; blood clotting.

Cochlea (kok′le-ah) Snail-shaped chamber of the bony labyrinth that houses the receptor for hearing [the spiral organ (of Corti)].

Codon (ko′don) The three-base sequence on a messenger RNA molecule that provides the genetic information used in protein synthesis.

Coenzyme (ko-en′zīm) Nonprotein substance associated with and activating an enzyme, typically a vitamin.

Cofactor Metal ion or organic molecule that is required for enzyme activity.

Collagen fiber The most abundant of the three fibers found in the matrix of connective tissue.

Colloid (kol′oid) A mixture in which the solute particles (usually proteins) do not settle out readily. Colloid in the thyroid gland contains thyroglobulin protein.

Colloid osmotic pressure (kol′oid ahz-mah′tik) Pressure created in a fluid by large nondiffusible molecules, such as plasma proteins that are prevented from moving through a (capillary) membrane. Such substances tend to draw water to them.

Colon Regions of the large intestine; includes ascending, transverse, descending, and sigmoid portions.

Combination (synthesis) reaction Chemical reaction in which larger, more complex atoms or molecules are formed from simpler ones.

Complement A group of bloodborne proteins, which, when activated, enhance the inflammatory and immune responses and may lead to cell lysis.

Complementarity of structure and function The relationship between a structure and its function; i.e., structure determines function.

Complementary base Refers to the ability of a nitrogenous base of DNA or RNA to bond to another nitrogenous base. For example, adenine (A) is the complementary base of thymine (T). The result is base pairing.

Complete blood count (CBC) Clinical test that includes counts of all formed elements, a hematocrit, and measurements of erythrocyte size and hemoglobin content.

Compound Substance composed of two or more different elements, the atoms of which are chemically united.

Concentration gradient The difference in the concentration of a particular substance between two different areas.

Conducting zone Includes all respiratory passageways that provide conduits for air to reach the sites of gas exchange (the respiratory zone).

Conductivity Ability to transmit an electrical impulse.

Cones One of the two types of photoreceptor cells in the retina of the eye; provide for color vision.

Congenital (kun-jeh′nih-tul) Existing at birth.

Congestive heart failure (CHF) Condition in which the pumping efficiency of the heart is depressed so that circulation is inadequate to meet tissue needs.

Conjunctiva (kon″junk-ti′vah) Thin, protective mucous membrane lining the eyelids and covering the anterior surface of the eye itself.

Connective tissue A primary tissue; form and function vary extensively. Functions include support, storage, and protection.

Connexons (kŏ-nek′sonz) Hollow cylinders made of transmembrane proteins that connect adjacent cells at gap junctions, allowing chemical substances to pass through.

Consciousness The ability to perceive, communicate, remember, understand, appreciate, and initiate voluntary movements.

Contraception The prevention of conception; birth control.

Contractility Muscle cell's ability to move by shortening.

Contraction To shorten or develop tension, an ability highly developed in muscle cells.

Contralateral Relating to the opposite side.

Control center One of three interdependent components of homeostatic control mechanisms; determines the set point.

Cornea (kor′ne-ah) Transparent anterior portion of the eyeball; part of the fibrous layer.

Corona radiata (kor-o′nah ra-de-ah′tah) (1) Arrangement of elongated follicle cells around a mature ovum; (2) crownlike arrangement of nerve fibers radiating from the internal capsule of the brain to every part of the cerebral cortex.

Coronary circulation The functional blood supply of the heart; shortest circulation in the body.

Cortex (kor′teks) Outer surface layer of an organ.

Corticosteroids (kor″tĭ-ko-stĕ′roidz) Steroid hormones released by the adrenal cortex.

Cortisol (hydrocortisone) (kor′tih-sol) Glucocorticoid produced by the adrenal cortex.

Covalent bond (ko-va′lent) Chemical bond created by electron sharing between atoms.

Cranial nerves The 12 nerve pairs that arise from the brain.

Craniosacral division Another name for the parasympathetic division of the autonomic nervous system.

Cranium (cranial bones) (kra′ne-um) Bony protective encasement of the brain and organs of hearing and equilibrium; also called the skull.

Creatine kinase (kre′ah-tin) Enzyme that catalyzes the transfer of phosphate from creatine phosphate to ADP, forming creatine and ATP; important in muscle contraction.

Creatine phosphate (CP) (fos-fāt) Compound that serves as an alternative energy source for muscle tissue.

Creatinine (kre-at′ĭ-nin) A nitrogenous waste molecule which is not reabsorbed by the kidney; this characteristic makes it useful for measurement of the GFR and glomerular function.

Crista ampullaris   Sensory receptor organ within the ampulla of each semicircular canal of the inner ear; dynamic equilibrium receptor.

Cross section   A cut running horizontally from right to left, dividing the body into superior and inferior parts.

Crystals   A highly ordered 3-D lattice; formed when an element or compound solidifies or is in a dry state.

Cutaneous (ku-ta′ne-us)   Pertaining to the skin.

Cutaneous sensory receptors   Receptors located throughout the skin that respond to stimuli arising outside the body; part of the nervous system.

Cyclic AMP   Intracellular second messenger that mediates the effects of the first (extracellular) messenger (hormone or neurotransmitter); formed from ATP by a plasma membrane enzyme (adenylate cyclase).

Cystic fibrosis (CF)   Genetic disorder in which secretion of overly viscous mucus clogs the respiratory passages, predisposes to fatal respiratory infections.

Cytochromes (si′to-krōmz)   Brightly colored iron-containing proteins that form part of the inner mitochondrial membrane and function as electron carriers in oxidative phosphorylation.

Cytokines   Chemical mediators involved in cellular immunity.

Cytokinesis (si″to-ki-ne′sis)   The division of cytoplasm that occurs after the cell nucleus has divided.

Cytoplasm (si′to-plazm)   The cellular material surrounding the nucleus and enclosed by the plasma membrane.

Cytosine (C) (si′to-sēn)   Nitrogen-containing base that is part of a nucleotide structure.

Cytoskeleton   Literally, cell skeleton. An elaborate series of rods running through the cystol, supporting cellular structures and providing the machinery to generate various cell movements.

Cytosol   Viscous, semitransparent fluid substance of cytoplasm in which other elements are suspended.

Cytotoxic T cell (T_C cell)   Effector T cell that directly kills (lyses) foreign cells, cancer cells, or virus-infected body cells. Also called a cytolytic T cell.

Deamination (de′am″ih-na′shun)   Removal of an amine group from an organic compound.

Decomposition reaction   Chemical reaction in which a molecule is broken down into smaller molecules or its constituent atoms.

Defecation (def″ih-ka′shun)   Elimination of the contents of the bowels (feces).

Deglutition (deg″loo-tish′un)   Swallowing.

Dehydration (de″hi-dra′shun)   Condition of excessive water loss.

Dehydration synthesis   Process by which a large molecule is synthesized by removing water and covalently bonding smaller molecules together.

Dendrite (den′drīt)   Branching neuron process that serves as a receptive, or input, region; transmits an electrical signal toward the cell body.

Dendritic cells   Protective cells that phagocytize antigens, migrate to lymph nodes, and present the antigen to T cells, causing them to activate and mount an immune response; called Langerhans′ cells in the skin.

Depolarization (de-po″ler-ah-za′shun)   Loss of a state of polarity; loss or reduction of negative membrane potential.

Dermatome (der′mah-tōm)   Portion of somite mesoderm that forms the dermis of the skin; also the area of skin innervated by the cutaneous branches of a single spinal nerve.

Dermis   Layer of skin deep to the epidermis; composed of dense irregular tissue.

Desmosome (dez′muh-sōm)   Cell junction composed of thickened plasma membranes joined by filaments.

Diabetes insipidus (di″ah-be′tez in-sih′pih-dus)   Disease characterized by passage of a large quantity of dilute urine plus intense thirst and dehydration caused by inadequate release of antidiuretic hormone (ADH).

Diabetes mellitus (DM) (meh-li′tus)   Disease caused by deficient insulin release or by insulin resistance, leading to inability of the body cells to use carbohydrates.

Dialysis (di-al′ah-sis)   Diffusion of solute(s) through a semipermeable membrane.

Diapedesis (di″ah-pĕ-de′sis)   Passage of white blood cells through intact vessel walls into tissue.

Diaphragm (di′ah-fram)   (1) Any partition or wall separating one area from another; (2) a muscle that separates the thoracic cavity from the lower abdominopelvic cavity.

Diaphysis (di-af′ĭ-sis)   Elongated shaft of a long bone.

Diarthrosis (di″ar-thro′sis)   Freely movable joint.

Diastole (di-as′to-le)   Period of the cardiac cycle when either the ventricles or the atria are relaxing.

Diastolic pressure (di-as-tah′lik)   Arterial blood pressure reached during or as a result of diastole; lowest level of any given cardiac cycle.

Diencephalon (interbrain) (di″en-seh′fuh-lon)   That part of the forebrain between the cerebral hemispheres and the midbrain including the thalamus, the third ventricle, and the hypothalamus.

Differential white blood cell count   Diagnostic test to determine relative proportion of individual leukocyte types.

Diffusion (dĭ-fu′zhun)   The spreading of particles in a gas or solution with a movement toward uniform distribution of particles.

Digestion   Chemical or mechanical process of breaking down foodstuffs to substances that can be absorbed.

Digestive system   System that processes food into absorbable units and eliminates indigestible wastes.

Dipeptide   A combination of two amino acids united by means of a peptide bond.

Diploë (dip′lo-e)   The internal layer of spongy bone in flat bones.

Diploid chromosomal number   The chromosomal number characteristic of an organism, symbolized as $2n$; twice the chromosomal number (n) of the gamete; in humans, $2n = 46$.

Diplopia (dĭ-plo′pe-ah)   Double vision.

Dipole (polar molecule)   Nonsymmetrical molecules that contain electrically unbalanced atoms.

Disaccharide (di-sak′ah-rīd″, di-sak′ah-rid)   Literally, double sugar; e.g., sucrose, lactose.

Dislocation (luxation)   Occurs when bones are forced out of their normal alignment at a joint.

Displacement (exchange) reaction   Chemical reaction in which bonds are both made and broken; atoms become combined with different atoms.

Distal (dis′tul)   Away from the attached end of a limb or the origin of a structure.

Diuretics (di″u-ret′iks)   Chemicals that enhance urinary output.

Diverticulum (di″ver-tik′u-lum)   A pouch or sac in the walls of a hollow organ or structure.

DNA (deoxyribonucleic acid) (de-ok″sĭ-ri″bo-nu-kla′ik)   A nucleic acid found in all living cells; it carries the organism′s hereditary information.

DNA replication   Process that occurs before cell division; ensures that all daughter cells have identical genes.

Dominant traits   Occurs when one allele masks or suppresses the expression of its partner.

Dominant-recessive inheritance   Reflects the interaction of dominant and recessive alleles.

Dorsal (dor′sul)   Pertaining to the back; posterior.

Dorsal root ganglion   Peripheral collection of cell bodies of first-order afferent neurons whose central axons enter the spinal cord.

Double helix   The secondary structure assumed by two strands of DNA, held together throughout their length by hydrogen bonds between bases on opposite strands.

Duct (dukt)   A canal or passageway; a tubular structure that provides an exit for the secretions of a gland, or for conducting any fluid.

Ductus (vas) deferens   Extends from the epididymis to the urethra; propels sperm into the urethra by peristalsis during ejaculation.

Duodenum (du″o-de′num)   First part of the small intestine.

Dura mater (du′rah ma′ter)   Outermost and toughest of the three membranes (meninges) covering the brain and spinal cord.

Dynamic equilibrium Sense that reports on angular (rotatory) acceleration or deceleration of the head in space.

Dyskinesia (dis-kĭ-ne′ze-ah) Disorders of muscle tone, posture, or involuntary movements.

Dyspnea (disp-ne′ah) Difficult or labored breathing; air hunger.

Eccrine glands (ek′rin) Sweat glands abundant on the palms, soles of feet, and the forehead.

Ectoderm (ek′to-derm) Embryonic germ layer; forms the epidermis of the skin and its derivatives, and nervous tissues.

Edema (ĕ-de′mah) Abnormal increase in the amount of interstitial fluid; causes swelling.

Effector (ef-ek′ter) Organ, gland, or muscle capable of being activated by nerve endings.

Efferent (ef′er-ent) Carrying away or away from, especially a nerve fiber that carries impulses away from the central nervous system.

Elastic cartilage Cartilage with abundant elastic fibers; more flexible than hyaline cartilage.

Elastic fiber Fiber formed from the protein elastin, which gives a rubbery and resilient quality to the matrix of connective tissue.

Electrical energy Energy formed by the movement of charged particles across cell membranes.

Electrocardiogram (ECG or EKG) (e-lek″tro-car′de-o-gram″) Graphic record of the electrical activity of the heart.

Electrochemical gradient The combined difference in concentration and charge; influences the distribution and direction of diffusion of ions.

Electroencephalogram (EEG) (e-lek″tro-en-sef′ah-lo-gram″) Graphic record of the electrical activity of nerve cells in the brain.

Electrolyte (e-lek′tro-līt) Chemical substances, such as salts, acids, and bases, that ionize and dissociate in water and are capable of conducting an electrical current.

Electrolyte balance Refers to the balance between input and output of salts (sodium, potassium, calcium, magnesium) in the body.

Electromagnetic radiation Emitted photons (wave packets) of energy, e.g., light, X ray, infrared.

Electron Negatively charged subatomic particle; orbits the atom's nucleus.

Electron shells (energy levels) Regions of space that consecutively surround the nucleus of an atom.

Element One of a limited number of unique varieties of matter that composes substances of all kinds; e.g., carbon, hydrogen, oxygen.

Embolism (em′bo-lizm) Obstruction of a blood vessel by an embolus (blood clot, fatty mass, bubble of air, or other debris) floating in the blood.

Embryo (em′bre-o) Developmental stage extending from fertilization to the end of the eighth week.

Emesis Reflexive emptying of the stomach through the esophagus and pharynx; also known as vomiting.

Encephalitis (en″seh-fuh-lī′tis) Inflammation of the brain.

Endergonic reaction Chemical reaction that absorbs energy, e.g., an anabolic reaction.

Endocardium (en″do-kar′de-um) Endothelial membrane that lines the interior of the heart.

Endochondral ossification (en″do-kon′dral) Embryonic formation of bone by the replacement of calcified cartilage; most skeletal bones are formed by this process.

Endocrine glands (en′do-krin) Ductless glands that empty their hormonal products directly into the blood.

Endocrine system Body system that includes internal organs that secrete hormones.

Endocytosis (en″do-si-to′sis) Means by which fairly large extracellular molecules or particles enter cells, e.g., phagocytosis, pinocytosis, receptor-mediated endocytosis.

Endoderm (en′do-derm) Embryonic germ layer; forms the lining of the digestive tube and its associated structures.

Endogenous (en-doj′ĕ-nŭs) Originating or produced within the organism or one of its parts.

Endometrium (en″do-me′tre-um) Mucous membrane lining of the uterus.

Endomysium (en″do-mis′e-um) Thin connective tissue surrounding each muscle cell.

Endoplasmic reticulum (ER) (en″do-plaz′mik rĕ-tik′u-lum) Membranous network of tubular or saclike channels in the cytoplasm of a cell.

Endosteum (en-dos′te-um) Connective tissue membrane covering internal bone surfaces.

Endothelium (en″do-the′le-um) Single layer of simple squamous cells that line the walls of the heart, blood vessels, and lymphatic vessels.

Energy The capacity to do work; may be stored (potential energy) or in action (kinetic energy).

Energy intake Energy liberated during food oxidation.

Energy output Sum of energy lost as heat, as work, and as fat or glycogen storage.

Enzyme (en′zīm) A protein that acts as a biological catalyst to speed up a chemical reaction.

Eosinophil (e″o-sin′o-fil) Granular white blood cell whose granules readily take up an acid stain called eosin.

Ependymal cell (ĕ-pen′dĭ-mul) A type of CNS supporting cell; lines the central cavities of the brain and spinal cord.

Epidermis (ep″ĭ-der′mis) Superficial layer of the skin; composed of keratinized stratified squamous epithelium.

Epididymis (ep″ĭ-dĭ′dĭ-mis) That portion of the male duct system in which sperm mature. Empties into the ductus (or vas) deferens.

Epidural space Area between the bony vertebrae and the dura mater of the spinal cord.

Epiglottis (eh″puh-glah′tis) Elastic cartilage at the back of the throat; covers the opening of the larynx during swallowing.

Epileptic seizures Abnormal electrical discharges of groups of brain neurons, during which no other messages can get through.

Epimysium (ep″ĭ-mis′e-um) Sheath of fibrous connective tissue surrounding a muscle.

Epinephrine (ep″ĭ-nef′rin) Chief hormone produced by the adrenal medulla. Also called adrenaline.

Epiphyseal plate (e″pĭ-fis′e-ul) Plate of hyaline cartilage at the junction of the diaphysis and epiphysis that provides for growth in length of a long bone.

Epiphysis (e-pif′ĭ-sis) The end of a long bone, attached to the shaft.

Epithalamus Most dorsal portion of the diencephalon; forms the roof of the third ventricle with the pineal gland extending from its posterior border.

Epithelium (epithelial tissue) (ep″ĭ-the′le-ul) Pertaining to a primary tissue that covers the body surface, lines its internal cavities, and forms glands.

Erythrocytes (e-rith′ro-sīts) Red blood cells.

Erythropoiesis (ĕ-rith″ro-poi-e′sis) Process of erythrocyte formation.

Erythropoietin (EPO) (ĕ-rith″ro-poi′ĕ-tin) Hormone that stimulates production of red blood cells.

Esophagus (ĕ-sof′ah-gus) Muscular tube extending from the laryngopharynx through the diaphragm to join the stomach; collapses when not involved in food propulsion.

Estrogens (es′tro-jenz) Hormones that stimulate female secondary sex characteristics; female sex hormones.

Eupnea (ūp-ne′ah) Normal respiratory rate and rhythm.

Exchange (displacement) reaction Chemical reaction in which bonds are both made and broken; atoms become combined with different atoms.

Excitation-contraction (E-C) coupling Sequence of events by which transmission of an action potential along the sarcolemma leads to the sliding of myofilaments.

Excitatory postsynaptic potential (EPSP) Depolarizing graded potential in a postsynaptic neuron.

Excretion (ek-skre′shun) Elimination of waste products from the body.

Exergonic reaction Chemical reaction that releases energy, e.g., a catabolic or oxidative reaction.

Exocrine glands (ek′so-krin) Glands that have ducts through which their secretions are carried to a particular site.

Exocytosis (ek″so-si-to′sis) Mechanism by which substances are moved from the cell interior to the extracellular space as a secretory vesicle fuses with the plasma membrane.

Exogenous (ek-sah′jeh-nus) Developing or originating outside an organ or part.

Exons Amino acid–specifying informational sequences (separated by introns) in the genes of higher organisms.

Extension Movement that increases the angle of a joint, e.g., straightening a flexed knee.

Exteroceptor (ek″ster-o-sep′tor) Sensory end organ that responds to stimuli from the external world.

Extracellular fluid (ECF) Internal fluid located outside cells; includes plasma and interstitial fluid.

Extracellular materials Substances found outside the cell; include interstitial fluid, blood plasma, and cerebrospinal fluid.

Extracellular matrix Nonliving material in connective tissue consisting of ground substance and fibers that separates the living cells.

Extrasystole (ek″strah-sis′to-le) Premature heart contraction.

Extrinsic (ek-strin′sik) Of external origin.

Extrinsic eye muscles The six skeletal muscles which attach to and move each eye.

Facilitated diffusion Passive transport process used by certain molecules, e.g., glucose and other simple sugars too large to pass through plasma membrane pores. Involves movement through channels or movement facilitated by a membrane carrier.

Fallopian tube (fah-lō′pē-un). *See* Uterine tube.

Fascia (fash′e-ah) Layers of fibrous tissue covering and separating muscle.

Fascicle (fas′ĭ-kl) Bundle of nerve or muscle fibers bound together by connective tissues.

Fatty acids Linear chains of carbon and hydrogen atoms (hydrocarbon chains) with an organic acid group at one end. A constituent of fat.

Feces (fe′sēz) Material discharged from the bowel; composed of food residue, secretions, bacteria.

Fenestrated (fen′es-tra-tid) Pierced with one or more small openings.

Fertilization Fusion of the sperm and egg nuclei.

Fetus Developmental stage extending from the ninth week of development to birth.

Fiber A slender threadlike structure or filament. *See also* Nerve fiber, Muscle fiber.

Fibrillation Condition of rapid and irregular or out-of-phase heart contractions.

Fibrin (fi′brin) Fibrous insoluble protein formed during blood clotting.

Fibrinogen (fi-brin′o-jin) A soluble blood protein that is converted to insoluble fibrin during blood clotting.

Fibrinolysis Process that removes unneeded blood clots when healing has occurred.

Fibroblast (fi′bro-blast) Young, actively mitotic cell that forms the fibers of connective tissue.

Fibrocartilage The most compressible type of cartilage; resistant to stretch. Forms vertebral discs and knee joint cartilages.

Fibrocyte (fi′bro-sīt) Mature fibroblast; maintains the matrix of fibrous types of connective tissue.

Fibrosis Proliferation of fibrous connective tissue called scar tissue.

Fibrous joints Bones joined by fibrous tissue; no joint cavity is present.

Filtrate A plasma-derived fluid that is processed by the renal tubules to form urine.

Filtration Passage of a solvent and dissolved substances through a membrane or filter.

First-degree burn A burn in which only the epidermis is damaged.

Fissure (fih′zher) (1) A groove or cleft; (2) the deepest depressions or inward folds on the brain.

Fixator (fix′a-ter) Muscle that immobilizes one or more bones, allowing other muscles to act from a stable base.

Flagellum (flah-jel′lum) Long, whiplike extension of the plasma membrane of some bacteria and of sperm; propels the cell.

Flexion (flek′shun) Movement that decreases the angle of the joint, e.g., bending the knee from a straight to an angled position.

Flexor (withdrawal) reflex Reflex initiated by a painful stimulus (actual or perceived); causes automatic withdrawal of the threatened body part from the stimulus.

Fluid mosaic model A depiction of the structure of the membranes of a cell as phospholipid bilayers in which proteins are dispersed.

Follicle (fah′lih-kul) (1) Ovarian structure consisting of a developing egg surrounded by one or more layers of follicle cells; (2) colloid-containing structure of the thyroid gland.

Follicle-stimulating hormone (FSH) Hormone produced by the anterior pituitary that stimulates ovarian follicle production in females and sperm production in males.

Fontanels (fon″tah-nelz′) Fibrous membranes at the angles of cranial bones that accommodate brain growth in the fetus and infant.

Foramen (fo-ra′men) Hole or opening in a bone or between body cavities.

Forebrain (prosencephalon) Anterior portion of the brain consisting of the telencephalon and the diencephalon.

Formed elements Cellular portion of blood.

Fossa (fos′ah) A depression, often an articular surface.

Fovea (fo′ve-ah) A pit.

Fracture A break in a bone.

Free radicals Highly reactive chemicals with unpaired electrons that can scramble the structure of proteins, lipids, and nucleic acids.

Frontal (coronal) plane Longitudinal (vertical) plane that divides the body into anterior and posterior parts.

Fulcrum The fixed point on which a lever moves when a force is applied.

Fundus (fun′dus) Base of an organ; part farthest from the opening of the organ.

G protein Protein that relays signals between extracellular first messengers (hormones or neurotransmitters) and intracellular second messengers (such as cyclic AMP) via an effector enzyme.

Gallbladder Sac beneath the right lobe of the liver used for bile storage.

Gallstones (biliary calculi) Crystallized cholesterol that obstructs the flow of bile from the gallbladder.

Gamete (gam′ēt) Sex or germ cell.

Gametogenesis (gam″eh-to-jen′eh-sis) Formation of gametes.

Ganglion (gang′gle-on) Collection of nerve cell bodies outside the CNS.

Ganglionic neuron (gan″gle-ah′nik) Autonomic motor neuron that has its cell body in a peripheral ganglion and projects its (postganglionic) axon to an effector.

Gap junction A passageway between two adjacent cells; formed by transmembrane proteins called connexons.

Gastrin Hormone secreted in the stomach; regulates gastric juice secretion by stimulating HCl production.

Gastroenteritis Inflammation of the gastrointestinal tract.

Gastrulation (gas″troo-la′shun) Developmental process that produces the three primary germ layers (ectoderm, mesoderm, and endoderm).

Gene One of the biological units of heredity located in chromatin; transmits hereditary information.

Genetic code Refers to the rules by which the base sequence of a DNA gene is translated into protein structures (amino acid sequences).

Genitalia (jen″i-ta′le-ă) The internal and external reproductive organs.

Genome The complete set of chromosomes derived from one parent (the haploid genome); or the two sets of chromosomes, i.e., one set from the egg, the other from the sperm (the diploid genome).

Genotype (jen′o-tīp) One's genetic makeup or genes.

Germ layers Three cellular layers (ectoderm, mesoderm, and endoderm) that represent the initial specialization of cells in the embryonic body and from which all body tissues arise.

Gestation period (jes-ta′shun)   The period of pregnancy; about 280 days for humans.

Gland   Organ specialized to secrete or excrete substances for further use in the body or for elimination.

Glaucoma (glaw-ko′mah)   Condition in which intraocular pressure increases to levels that cause compression of the retina and optic nerve; results in blindness unless detected early.

Glial cells (gle′al)   *See* Neuroglia.

Glomerular capsule (glō-mer′yoo-ler)   Double-walled cup at end of a renal tubule; encloses a glomerulus. Also called Bowman's capsule.

Glomerular filtration rate (GFR)   Rate of filtrate formation by the kidneys.

Glomerulus (glo-mer′u-lus)   (1) Cluster of capillaries forming part of the nephron; forms filtrate; (2) odor-specific processing unit in olfactory bulb.

Glottis (glah′tis)   Opening between the vocal cords in the larynx.

Glucagon (gloo′kah-gon)   Hormone formed by alpha cells of pancreatic islets; raises the glucose level of blood.

Glucocorticoids (gloo″ko-kor′tĭ-koidz)   Adrenal cortex hormones that increase blood glucose levels and aid the body in resisting long-term stressors.

Gluconeogenesis (gloo″ko-ne″o-jen′ĕ-sis)   Formation of glucose from noncarbohydrate molecules.

Glucose (gloo′kōs)   Principal blood sugar; a hexose.

Glycerol (glis′er-ol)   A modified simple sugar (a sugar alcohol); a building block of fats.

Glycocalyx (cell coat) (gli″ko-kal′iks)   A layer of externally facing glycoproteins on a cell's plasma membrane that determines blood type; involved in the cellular interactions of fertilization, embryonic development, and immunity, and acts as an adhesive between cells.

Glycogen (gli′ko-jin)   Main carbohydrate stored in animal cells; a polysaccharide.

Glycogenesis (gli″ko-jen′ĕ-sis)   Formation of glycogen from glucose.

Glycogenolysis (gli″ko-jĕ-nol′ĭ-sis)   Breakdown of glycogen to glucose.

Glycolipid (gli″ko-lip′id)   A lipid with one or more covalently attached sugars.

Glycolysis (gli-kol′ĭ-sis)   Breakdown of glucose to pyruvic acid—an anaerobic process.

Goblet cells   Individual cells (unicellular glands) that produce mucus.

Golgi apparatus (gol′je)   Membranous system close to the cell nucleus that packages protein secretions for export, packages enzymes into lysosomes for cellular use, and modifies proteins destined to become part of cellular membranes.

Golgi tendon organs   Proprioceptors located in tendons; monitor muscle tension to prevent tearing and help smooth onset and termination of muscle contraction.

Gonad (go′nad)   Primary reproductive organ; i.e., the testis of the male or the ovary of the female.

Gonadocorticoids (gon″ah-do-kor′tĭ-koidz)   Sex hormones, primarily androgens, secreted by the adrenal cortex.

Gonadotropins (gon″ah-do-trōp′inz)   Gonad-stimulating hormones produced by the anterior pituitary.

Graafian follicle (graf′e-an).   *See* Vesicular follicle.

Graded muscle responses   Variations in the degree of muscle contraction by changing either the frequency or strength of the stimulus.

Graded potential   A local change in membrane potential that varies directly with the strength of the stimulus, declines with distance.

Graves' disease   Disorder resulting from hyperactive thyroid gland.

Gray matter   Gray area of the central nervous system; contains neuronal cell bodies and their dendrites.

Growth hormone (GH)   Hormone that stimulates growth in general; produced in the anterior pituitary; also called somatotropin (STH).

Guanine (G) (gwan′ēn)   One of two major purines occurring in all nucleic acids.

Gustation (gus-ta′shun)   Taste.

Gyrus (ji′rus)   An outward fold of the surface of the cerebral cortex.

Hair follicle   Structure with outer and inner root sheaths extending from the epidermal surface into the dermis and from which new hair develops.

Hapten (hap′ten)   An incomplete antigen; has reactivity but not immunogenicity.

Haversian system (hah-ver′zhen).   *See* Osteon.

Heart attack (coronary).   *See* Myocardial infarction.

Heart block   Impaired transmission of impulses from atrium to ventricle resulting in abnormally slow heart rhythms.

Heart murmur   Abnormal heart sound (usually resulting from valve problems).

Heimlich maneuver   Procedure in which the air in a person's own lungs is used to expel an obstructing piece of food.

Helper T cell   Type of T lymphocyte that orchestrates cellular immunity by direct contact with other immune cells and by releasing chemicals called cytokines; also helps to mediate the humoral response by interacting with B cells.

Hematocrit (he-mat′o-krit)   The percentage of total blood volume occupied by erythrocytes.

Hematoma (he″mah-to′mah)   Mass of clotted blood that forms at an injured site.

Hematopoiesis (hem″ah-to-poi-e′sis)   Blood cell formation; hemopoiesis.

Heme (hēm)   Iron-containing pigment that is essential to oxygen transport by hemoglobin.

Hemocytoblast (he″mo-si′to-blast)   Bone marrow cell that gives rise to all the formed elements of blood; hematopoietic stem cell.

Hemoglobin (he′muh-glo-bin)   Oxygen-transporting protein of erythrocytes.

Hemolysis (he-mah′lĕ-sis)   Rupture of erythrocytes.

Hemophilia (he″mo-fil′e-ah)   A term loosely applied to several different hereditary bleeding disorders that exhibit similar signs and symptoms.

Hemopoiesis (he″mo-poi-e′sis)   *See* Hematopoiesis.

Hemorrhage (hem′or-ij)   Loss of blood from the vessels by flow through ruptured walls; bleeding.

Hemostasis (he″mo-sta′sis)   Stoppage of bleeding.

Heparin   Natural anticoagulant secreted into blood plasma.

Hepatic portal system (hĕ-pat′ik)   Circulation in which the hepatic portal vein carries dissolved nutrients to the liver tissues for processing.

Hepatitis (hep″ah-ti′tis)   Inflammation of the liver.

Hernia (her′ne-ah)   Abnormal protrusion of an organ or a body part through the containing wall of its cavity.

Heterozygous (het″er-o-zi′gus)   Having different allelic genes at a given locus or (by extension) many loci.

Hilton's law   Any nerve serving a muscle that produces movement at a joint also innervates the joint and the skin over the joint.

Hilum (hi′lum)   The indented region of an organ from which blood and/or lymph vessels and nerves enter and exit.

Hippocampus   Limbic system structure that plays a role in converting new information into long-term memories.

Histamine (his′tuh-mēn)   A chemical messenger (neurotransmitter or paracrine); causes vasodilation and increased capillary permeability; in stomach causes acid secretion.

Histology (his-tol′o-je)   Branch of anatomy dealing with the microscopic structure of tissues.

HIV (human immunodeficiency virus)   Virus that destroys helper T cells, thus depressing adaptive immunity; symptomatic AIDS gradually appears when lymph nodes can no longer contain the virus.

Holocrine glands (hol′o-krin)   Glands that accumulate their secretions within their cells; secretions are discharged only upon rupture and death of the cell.

Homeostasis (ho″me-o-sta′sis)   A state of body equilibrium or stable internal environment of the body.

Homologous (ho-mol'ŏ-gus) Parts or organs corresponding in structure but not necessarily in function.

Homozygous (ho-mo-zi'gus) Having identical genes at one or more loci.

Hormones Steroidal or amino acid–based molecules released to the blood that act as chemical messengers to regulate specific body functions.

Humoral immunity (hu'mer-ul) Immunity conferred by antibodies present in blood plasma and other body fluids.

Huntington's disease Hereditary disorder leading to degeneration of the basal nuclei and the cerebral cortex.

Hyaline cartilage (hi'ah-līn) The most abundant cartilage type in the body; provides firm support with some pliability.

Hydrochloric acid (HCl) (hi"dro-klor'ik) Acid that aids protein digestion in the stomach; produced by parietal cells.

Hydrogen bond Weak bond in which a hydrogen atom forms a bridge between two electron-hungry atoms. An important intramolecular bond.

Hydrogen ion (H^+) A hydrogen atom minus its electron and therefore carrying a positive charge (i.e., a proton).

Hydrolysis (hi"drah'lă-sis) Process in which water is used to split a substance into smaller particles.

Hydrophilic (hi"dro-fil'ik) Refers to molecules, or portions of molecules, that interact with water and charged particles.

Hydrophobic (hi"dro-fo'bik) Refers to molecules, or portions of molecules, that interact only with nonpolar molecules.

Hydrostatic pressure (hi"dro-stă'tic) Pressure of fluid in a system.

Hydroxyl ion (OH^-) (hi-drok'sil) An ion liberated when a hydroxide (a common inorganic base) is dissolved in water.

Hyperalgesia Pain amplification.

Hypercapnia (hi"per-kap'ne-ah) High carbon dioxide levels in the blood.

Hyperemia An increase in blood flow into a tissue or organ; congested with blood.

Hyperglycemic (hi"per-gli-se'mik) Term used to describe hormones such as glucagon that elevate blood glucose level.

Hyperopia (hi"per-o'pe-ah) A condition in which visual images are routinely focused behind rather than on the retina; commonly known as farsightedness.

Hyperplasia (hi"per-pla'ze-ah) Accelerated growth, e.g., in anemia, the bone marrow produces red blood cells at a faster rate.

Hyperpnea (hi"perp-ne'ah) An increase in ventilation in response to metabolic need (e.g., during exercise).

Hyperpolarization An increase in membrane potential in which the membrane becomes more negative than resting membrane potential.

Hypersensitivity Overzealous immune response to an otherwise harmless antigen.

Hypertension (hi"per-ten'shun) High blood pressure.

Hypertonic (hi"per-ton'ik) Excessive, above normal, tone or tension.

Hypertonic solution A solution that has a higher concentration of nonpenetrating solutes than the reference cell; having greater osmotic pressure than the reference solution (blood plasma or interstitial fluid).

Hypertrophy (hi-per'trah-fe) Increase in size of a tissue or organ independent of the body's general growth.

Hyperventilation An increase in the depth and rate of breathing that is in excess of the body's need for removal of carbon dioxide.

Hypocapnia Low carbon dioxide levels in the blood.

Hypodermis (superficial fascia) Subcutaneous tissue just deep to the skin; consists of adipose plus some areolar connective tissue.

Hypoglycemic (hi"po-gli-se'mik) Term used to describe hormones such as insulin that decrease blood glucose level.

Hyponatremia Abnormally low concentrations of sodium ions in extracellular fluid.

Hypoproteinemia (hi"po-pro"te-ĭ-ne'me-ah) A condition of unusually low levels of plasma proteins causing a reduction in colloid osmotic pressure; results in tissue edema.

Hypotension Low blood pressure.

Hypothalamic-hypophyseal tract (hi"po-thah-lam'ik–hi"po-fiz'-e-al) Nerve bundles that run through the infundibulum and connect the neurohypophysis and the hypothalamus.

Hypothalamus (hi"po-thal'ah-mus) Region of the diencephalon forming the floor of the third ventricle of the brain.

Hypotonic (hi"po-ton'ik) Below normal tone or tension.

Hypotonic solution A solution that is more dilute (containing fewer nonpenetrating solutes) than the reference cell. Cells placed in hypotonic solutions plump up rapidly as water rushes into them.

Hypoventilation A decrease in the depth and rate of breathing; characterized by an increase in blood carbon dioxide.

Hypovolemic shock (hi"po-vo-le'mik) Most common form of shock; results from extreme blood loss.

Hypoxia (hi-pok'se-ah) Condition in which inadequate oxygen is available to tissues.

Ileocecal valve (il"e-o-se'kal) Site where the small intestine joins the large intestine.

Ileum (il'e-um) Terminal part of the small intestine; between the jejunum and the cecum of the large intestine.

Immune system A functional system whose components attack foreign substances or prevent their entry into the body.

Immunity (im'ūn'ĭ-te) Ability of the body to resist many agents (both living and nonliving) that can cause disease; resistance to disease.

Immunocompetence Ability of the body's immune cells to recognize (by binding) specific antigens; reflects the presence of plasma membrane-bound receptors.

Immunodeficiency Any congenital or acquired condition causing a deficiency in the production or function of immune cells or certain molecules (complement, antibodies, etc.) required for normal immunity.

In vitro (in ve'tro) In a test tube, glass, or artificial environment.

In vivo (in ve'vo) In the living body.

Incompetent valve Valve which does not close properly.

Incontinence Inability to control micturition voluntarily.

Infarct (in'farkt) Region of dead, deteriorating tissue resulting from a lack of blood supply.

Infectious mononucleosis Highly contagious viral disease; marked by excessive agranulocytes.

Inferior (caudal) Pertaining to a position near the tail end of the long axis of the body.

Inferior vena cava Vein that returns blood from body areas below the diaphragm.

Inflammation (in"flah-ma'shun) An innate (nonspecific) defensive response of the body to tissue injury; includes dilation of blood vessels and an increase in vessel permeability; indicated by redness, heat, swelling, and pain.

Infundibulum (in"fun-dib'u-lum) (1) A stalk of tissue that connects the pituitary gland to the hypothalamus; (2) the distal end of the uterine (fallopian) tube.

Inguinal (ing'wĭ-nal) Pertaining to the groin region.

Inhibitory postsynaptic potential (IPSP) A graded potential in a postsynaptic neuron that inhibits action potential generation; usually hyperpolarizing.

Inner cell mass Accumulation of cells in the blastocyst from which the embryo develops.

Innervation (in"er-va'shun) Supply of nerves to a body part.

Inorganic compound Chemical substances that do not contain carbon, including water, salts, and many acids and bases.

Insertion Movable attachment of a muscle.

Insula Lobe of the cerebral cortex that is buried in the lateral sulcus beneath portions of the parietal, frontal, and temporal lobes.

Insulin A hormone that enhances the carrier-mediated diffusion of glucose into tissue cells, thus lowering blood glucose levels.

Insulin resistance State in which a greater than normal amount of insulin is required to maintain normal glucose blood levels.

Integration The process by which the nervous system processes and interprets sensory input and makes decisions about what should be done at each moment.

Integumentary system (in-teg″u-men′tar-e) Skin and its derivatives; provides the external protective covering of the body.

Intercalated discs (in-ter′kah-la″ted) Specialized connections between myocardial cells containing gap junctions and desmosomes.

Interferons (IFNs) (in-ter-fēr′ons) Proteins released from virus-infected (and other) cells that protect uninfected cells from viral takeover. Also inhibit some cancers.

Internal capsule Band of projection fibers that runs between the basal nuclei and the thalamus.

Internal respiration Exchange of gases between blood and tissue fluid and between tissue fluid and cells.

Interneuron (association neuron) Nerve cell located between motor and sensory neurons that shuttles signals through CNS pathways where integration occurs.

Interoceptor (in″ter-o-sep′tor) Sensory receptor nerve ending in the viscera, which is sensitive to changes and stimuli within the body's internal environment; also called visceroceptor.

Interphase One of two major periods in the cell life cycle; includes the period from cell formation to cell division.

Interstitial cells Cells located in the loose connective tissue surrounding the seminiferous tubules; they produce androgens (most importantly testosterone), which are secreted into the surrounding interstitial fluid.

Interstitial fluid (IF) (in″ter-stish′al) Fluid between the cells.

Interstitial lamellae Incomplete lamellae that lie between intact osteons, filling the gaps between forming osteons, or representing the remnants of an osteon that has been cut through by bone remodeling.

Intervertebral discs (in″ter-ver′teh-brul) Discs of fibrocartilage between vertebrae.

Intracapsular ligament Ligament located within and separate from the articular capsule of a synovial joint.

Intracellular fluid (ICF) (in″trah-sel′u-ler) Fluid within a cell.

Intrinsic factor Substance produced by the stomach that is required for vitamin B_{12} absorption.

Intron Noncoding segment or portion of DNA that ranges from 60 to 100,000 nucleotides long.

Involuntary muscle Muscle that cannot ordinarily be controlled voluntarily.

Involuntary nervous system The autonomic nervous system.

Ion (ī′on) Atom with a positive or negative electric charge.

Ionic bond (ī-ah′nik) Chemical bond formed by electron transfer between atoms.

Ipsilateral (ip″sih-la′ter-ul) Situated on the same side.

Irritability Ability to respond to stimuli.

Ischemia (is-ke′me-ah) Local decrease in blood supply.

Isograft Tissue graft donated by an identical twin.

Isomer (i′so-mer) One of two or more substances that has the same molecular formula but with its atoms arranged differently.

Isometric contraction (i″so-mě′trik) Contraction in which the muscle does not shorten (the load is too heavy) but its internal tension increases.

Isotonic contraction (i″so-tah′nik) Contraction in which muscle tension remains constant at a given joint angle and load, and the muscle shortens.

Isotonic solution A solution with a concentration of nonpenetrating solutes equal to that found in the reference cell.

Isotopes (i′so-tōps) Different atomic forms of the same element, vary only in the number of neutrons they contain; the heavier species tend to be radioactive.

Jejunum (jě-joo′num) The part of the small intestine between the duodenum and the ileum.

Joint (articulation) The junction of two or more bones.

Joint kinesthetic receptor (kin″es-thet′ik) Receptor that provides information on joint position and motion.

Juxtaglomerular apparatus (JGA) (juks″tah-glo-mer′ular) Cells of the distal part of the ascending limb of the loop of Henle and afferent arteriole located close to the glomerulus; involved in blood pressure regulation (via release of the hormone renin) and autoregulation of GFR.

Karyotype (kar′e-o-tīp) The diploid chromosomal complement, typically shown as homologous chromosome pairs arranged from longest to shortest (X and Y are arranged by size rather than paired).

Keratin (ker′ah-tin) Fibrous protein found in the epidermis, hair, and nails that makes those structures hard and water-repellent; precursor is keratohyaline.

Ketones (ketone bodies) (ke′tōnz) Fatty acid metabolites; strong organic acids.

Ketosis (kē-tō′sis) Excess levels of ketone bodies in blood. Called ketoacidosis if blood pH is low.

Killer T cell *See* Cytotoxic T cell.

Kilocalories (kcal) *See* Calorie.

Kinetic energy (ki-net′ik) The energy of motion or movement, e.g., the constant movement of atoms, or the push given to a swinging door that sets it into motion.

Krebs cycle Aerobic metabolic pathway occurring within mitochondria, in which food metabolites are oxidized and CO_2 is liberated, and coenzymes are reduced. Also called the citric acid cycle.

Labia (la′be-ah) Lips; singular: labium.

Labor Collective term for the series of events that expel the infant from the uterus.

Labyrinth (lab′ĭ-rinth″) Bony cavities and membranes of the inner ear.

Lacrimal (lak′ri-mal) Pertaining to tears.

Lactation (lak-ta′shun) Production and secretion of milk.

Lacteal (lak′te-al) Special lymphatic capillaries of the small intestine that take up lipids.

Lactic acid (lak′tik) Product of anaerobic metabolism, especially in muscle.

Lacunae (lah-ku′ne) A small space, cavity, or depression; lacunae in bone or cartilage are occupied by cells.

Lamella (lah-mel′ah) A layer, such as of bone matrix in an osteon of compact bone.

Lamina (lam′ĭ-nah) (1) A thin layer or flat plate; (2) the portion of a vertebra between the transverse process and the spinous process.

Large intestine Portion of the digestive tract extending from the ileocecal valve to the anus; includes the cecum, appendix, colon, rectum, and anal canal.

Larynx (lar′ingks) Cartilaginous organ located between the trachea and the pharynx; voice box.

Latent period Period of time between stimulation and the onset of muscle contraction.

Lateral Away from the midline of the body.

Leptin Hormone released by fat cells that signals satiety.

Leukemia Refers to a group of cancerous conditions of white blood cells.

Leukocytes (loo′ko-sīts) White blood cells; formed elements involved in body protection that take part in inflammatory and immune responses.

Leukocytosis An increase in the number of leukocytes (white blood cells); usually the result of a microbiological attack on the body.

Leukopenia (loo″ko-pe′ne-ah) Abnormally low white blood cell count.

Leukopoiesis The production of white blood cells.

Lever system Consists of a lever (bone), effort (muscle action), resistance (weight of object to be moved), and fulcrum (joint).

Ligament (lig′ah-ment) Band of regular fibrous tissue that connects bones.

Ligands Signaling chemicals that bind specifically to membrane receptors.

Limbic system (lim′bik) Functional brain system involved in emotional response and memory formation.

Lipid (lih′pid) Organic compound formed of carbon, hydrogen, and oxygen; examples are fats and cholesterol.

Lipolysis (li-pol′ĭ-sis) The breakdown of stored fats into glycerol and fatty acids.

Liver Lobed accessory organ that overlies the stomach; produces bile to help digest fat, and serves other metabolic and regulatory functions.

Lumbar (lum'bar) Portion of the back between the thorax and the pelvis.

Lumbar vertebrae The five vertebrae of the lumbar region of the vertebral column, commonly called the small of the back.

Lumen (loo'min) Cavity inside a tube, blood vessel, or hollow organ.

Luteinizing hormone (LH) (lu'te-in-ī z"ing) Anterior pituitary hormone that aids maturation of cells in the ovary and triggers ovulation in females. In males, causes the interstitial cells of the testis to produce testosterone.

Lymph (limf) Protein-containing fluid transported by lymphatic vessels.

Lymph node Small lymphoid organ that filters lymph; contains macrophages and lymphocytes.

Lymphatic system (lim-fat'ik) System consisting of lymphatic vessels, lymph nodes, and other lymphoid organs and tissues; drains excess tissue fluid from the extracellular space and provides a site for immune surveillance.

Lymphatics General term used to designate the lymphatic vessels that collect and transport lymph.

Lymphocyte Agranular white blood cell that arises from bone marrow and becomes functionally mature in the lymphoid organs of the body.

Lymphokines (lim'fo-kīnz) Proteins involved in cell-mediated immune responses that enhance immune and inflammatory responses.

Lysosomes (li'so-sōmz) Organelles that originate from the Golgi apparatus and contain strong digestive enzymes.

Lysozyme (li'so-zīm) Enzyme in sweat, saliva, and tears that is capable of destroying certain kinds of bacteria.

Macromolecules Large, complex molecules containing from 100 to over 10,000 amino acids.

Macrophage (mak'ro-fāj") Protective cell type common in connective tissue, lymphoid tissue, and many body organs; phagocytizes tissue cells, bacteria, and other foreign debris; important as an antigen presenter to T cells in the immune response.

Macula (mak'u-lah) (1) Static equilibrium receptor within the vestibule of the inner ear; (2) a colored area or spot.

Malignant (muh-lig'nent) Life threatening; pertains to neoplasms that spread and lead to death, such as cancer.

Malignant melanoma (mel"ah-no'mah) Cancer of the melanocytes; can begin wherever there is pigment.

Mammary glands (mam'mer-e) Milk-producing glands of the breast.

Mandible (man'dĭ-bl) Lower jawbone; U-shaped, largest bone of the face.

Mast cells Immune cells that function to detect foreign substances in the tissue spaces and initiate local inflammatory responses against them; typically found clustered deep to an epithelium or along blood vessels.

Mastication (mas"tĭ-ka'shun) Chewing.

Meatus (me-a'tus) External opening of a canal.

Mechanical advantage (power lever) Condition that occurs when the load is close to the fulcrum and the effort is applied far from the fulcrum; allows a small effort exerted over a relatively large distance to move a large load over a small distance.

Mechanical disadvantage (speed lever) Condition that occurs when the load is far from the fulcrum and the effort is applied near the fulcrum; the effort applied must be greater than the load to be moved.

Mechanical energy The energy directly involved in moving matter; e.g., in bicycle riding, the legs provide the mechanical energy that moves the pedals.

Mechanoreceptor (meh"kĕ-no-rē-sep'ter) Receptor sensitive to mechanical pressure such as touch, sound, or exerted by muscle contraction.

Medial (me'de-ahl) Toward the midline of the body.

Median (midsagittal) plane Specific sagittal plane that lies exactly in the midline.

Mediastinum (me"de-ah-sti'num) A subdivision of the thoracic cavity containing the pericardial cavity.

Medulla (mĕ-dul'ah) Central portion of certain organs.

Medulla oblongata (mĕ-dul'ah ob"long-gah'tah) Inferiormost part of the brain stem.

Medullary cavity Central cavity of a long bone. Contains yellow or red (bone) marrow.

Meiosis (mi-o'sis) Nuclear division process that reduces the chromosomal number by half and results in the formation of four haploid (n) cells; occurs only in certain reproductive organs.

Melanin (mel'ah-nin) Dark pigment formed by cells called melanocytes; imparts color to skin and hair.

Melatonin (mel"ah-to'nin) A hormone secreted by the pineal gland; secretion peaks at night and helps set sleep-wake cycles; also a powerful antioxidant.

Membrane potential Voltage across the plasma membrane.

Membrane receptors A large, diverse group of integral proteins and glycoproteins that serve as binding sites.

Memory cells Members of T cell and B cell clones that provide for immunological memory.

Menarche (mĕ-nar'ke) Establishment of menstrual function; the first menstrual period.

Meninges (mĕ-nin'jē z) Protective coverings of the central nervous system; from the most external to the most internal, the dura mater, arachnoid, and pia mater.

Meningitis (mĕ-nin-ji'tis) Inflammation of the meninges.

Menopause Period of life when, prompted by hormonal changes, ovulation and menstruation cease.

Menstruation (men"stroo-a'shun) The periodic, cyclic discharge of blood, secretions, tissue, and mucus from the mature female uterus in the absence of pregnancy.

Merocrine glands (mer'o-krin) Glands that produce secretions intermittently; secretions do not accumulate in the gland.

Mesencephalon (mes"en-sef'ah-lon) One of the three primary vesicles of the developing brain; becomes the midbrain.

Mesenchyme (meh'zin-kīm) Common embryonic tissue from which all connective tissues arise.

Mesenteries (mes"en-ter'ēz) Double-layered extensions of the peritoneum that support most organs in the abdominal cavity.

Mesoderm (mez'o-derm) Primary germ layer that forms the skeleton and muscles of the body.

Mesothelium (mez"o-the'le-um) The epithelium found in serous membranes lining the ventral body cavity and covering its organs.

Messenger RNA (mRNA) Long nucleotide strands that reflect the exact nucleotide sequences of the genetically active DNA and carry the message of the latter.

Metabolic (fixed) acid Acid generated by cellular metabolism that must be eliminated by the kidneys.

Metabolic rate (mĕt"ah-bol'ik) Energy expended by the body per unit time.

Metabolic water (water of oxidation) Water produced from cellular metabolism (about 10% of our body's water).

Metabolism (mĕ-tab'o-lizm) Sum total of the chemical reactions occurring in the body cells.

Metaphase Second stage of mitosis.

Metastasis (mĕ-tas'tah-sis) The spread of cancer from one body part or organ into another not directly connected to it.

Metencephalon (afterbrain) A secondary brain vesicle; anterior portion of the rhombencephalon of the developing brain; becomes the pons and the cerebellum.

MHC (major histocompatibility complex) proteins Molecules on the outer plasma membrane of all cells; help the immune system distinguish self from nonself. T cells recognize antigens only when combined with these proteins.

Microfilaments (mi"kro-fil'ah-ments) Thin strands of the contractile protein actin.

Microglia (mi-kro'gle-ah) A type of CNS supporting cell; can transform into phagocytes in areas of neural damage or inflammation.

Microtubules (mi″kro-tu′būlz) One of three types of rods in the cytoskeleton of a cell; hollow tubes made of spherical protein that determine the cell shape as well as the distribution of cellular organelles.

Microvilli (mi″kro-vil′i) Tiny projections on the free surfaces of some epithelial cells; increase surface area for absorption.

Micturition (mik″tu-rish′un) Urination, or voiding; emptying the bladder.

Midbrain (mesencephalon) Region of the brain stem between the diencephalon and the pons.

Midsagittal (median) plane Specific sagittal plane that lies exactly in the midline.

Milliequivalents per liter (mEq/L) The units used to measure electrolyte concentrations of body fluids; a measure of the number of electrical charges in 1 liter of solution.

Mineralocorticoid (min″er-al′ō-kor′tih-koyd) Steroid hormone of the adrenal cortex that regulates Na^+ and K^+ metabolism and fluid balance.

Minerals Inorganic chemical compounds found in nature; salts.

Mitochondria (mi″to-kon′dre-ah) Cytoplasmic organelles responsible for ATP generation for cellular activities.

Mitosis Process during which the chromosomes are redistributed to two daughter nuclei; nuclear division. Consists of prophase, metaphase, anaphase, and telophase.

Mitral (bicuspid) valve (mi′tral) The left atrioventricular valve.

Mixed nerves Nerves containing the processes of motor and sensory neurons; their impulses travel to and from the central nervous system.

Molar (mo′lar) A solution concentration determined by mass of solute—1 liter of solution contains an amount of solute equal to its molecular weight in grams.

Molarity (mo-lar′ĭ-te) A way to express the concentration of a solution; moles per liter of solution.

Mole (mōl) A mole of any element or compound is equal to its atomic weight or its molecular weight (sum of atomic weights) measured in grams.

Molecule Particle consisting of two or more atoms joined together by chemical bonds.

Monoclonal antibodies (mon″o-klo′nal) Pure preparations of identical antibodies that exhibit specificity for a single antigen.

Monocyte (mon′o-sīt) Large single-nucleus white blood cell; agranular leukocyte.

Monokines Chemical mediators that enhance the immune response; secreted by macrophages.

Monosaccharide (mon″o-sak′ah-rīd) Literally, one sugar; building block of carbohydrates; e.g., glucose.

Morula (mor′u-lah) The mulberry-like solid mass of blastomeres resulting from cleavage in the early conceptus.

Motor areas Functional areas in the cerebral cortex that control voluntary motor functions.

Motor end plate Troughlike part of a muscle fiber's sarcolemma that helps form the neuromuscular junction.

Motor (efferent) nerves Nerves that carry impulses leaving the brain and spinal cord, and destined for effectors.

Motor unit A motor neuron and all the muscle cells it stimulates.

Mucous membranes (mucosae) Membranes that form the linings of body cavities open to the exterior (digestive, respiratory, urinary, and reproductive tracts).

Mucus (myoo′kus) A sticky, thick fluid secreted by mucous glands and mucous membranes; keeps the free surface of membranes moist.

Multinucleate cell (mul″tĭ-nu′kle-āt) Cell with more than one nucleus, e.g., skeletal muscle cells, liver cells.

Multiple sclerosis (MS) Demyelinating disorder of the CNS; causes hardened patches (sclerosis) in the brain and spinal cord.

Multipolar neurons Neurons with three or more processes; most common neuron type in the CNS.

Muscarinic receptors (mus″kah-rin′ik) Acetylcholine-binding receptors of the autonomic nervous system's target organs; named for activation by the mushroom poison muscarine.

Muscle fiber A muscle cell.

Muscle spindle (neuromuscular spindle) Encapsulated receptor found in skeletal muscle that is sensitive to stretch.

Muscle tension The force exerted by a contracting muscle on some object.

Muscle tone Low levels of contractile activity in relaxed muscle; keeps the muscle healthy and ready to act.

Muscle twitch The response of a muscle to a single brief threshold stimulus.

Muscular dystrophy A group of inherited muscle-destroying diseases.

Muscular system The organ system consisting of the skeletal muscles of the body and their connective tissue attachments.

Myelencephalon (spinal brain) A secondary brain vesicle; lower part of the developing hindbrain, especially the medulla oblongata.

Myelin sheath (mi′ĕ-lin) Fatty insulating sheath that surrounds all but the smallest nerve fibers.

Myoblasts Embryonic mesoderm cells from which all muscle fibers develop.

Myocardial infarction (MI) (mi″o-kar′de-al in-fark′shun) Condition characterized by dead tissue areas in the myocardium; caused by interruption of blood supply to the area. Commonly called heart attack.

Myocardium (mi″o-kar′de-um) Layer of the heart wall composed of cardiac muscle.

Myofibril (mi″o-fi′bril) Rodlike bundle of contractile filaments (myofilaments) found in muscle fibers (cells).

Myofilament (mi″o-fil′ah-ment) Filament that constitutes myofibrils. Of two types: actin and myosin.

Myoglobin (mi″o-glo′bin) Oxygen-binding pigment in muscle.

Myogram A graphic recording of mechanical contractile activity produced by an apparatus that measures muscle contraction.

Myometrium (mi″o-me′tre-um) Thick uterine musculature.

Myopia (mi-o′pe-ah) A condition in which visual images are focused in front of rather than on the retina; nearsightedness.

Myosin (mi′o-sin) One of the principal contractile proteins found in muscle.

Myxedema (mik″sĕ-de′mah) Condition resulting from underactive thyroid gland.

Nares (na′rez) Nostrils.

Natural killer (NK) cell Defensive cell (a type of lymphocyte) that can lyse and kill cancer cells and virus-infected body cells before the adaptive immune system is activated.

Necrosis (nĕ-kro′sis) Death or disintegration of a cell or tissues caused by disease or injury.

Negative feedback mechanisms The most common homeostatic control mechanism. The net effect is that the output of the system shuts off the original stimulus or reduces its intensity.

Neonatal period The four-week period immediately after birth.

Neoplasm (ne′o-plazm) An abnormal mass of proliferating cells. Benign neoplasms remain localized; malignant neoplasms are cancers, which can spread to other organs.

Nephron (nef′ron) Structural and functional unit of the kidney; consists of the glomerulus and renal tubule.

Nerve A bundle of axons in the peripheral nervous system.

Nerve fiber Axon of a neuron.

Nerve growth factor (NGF) Protein that promotes survival and development of sympathetic and sensory neurons; secreted by the target cells of postganglionic axons.

Nerve impulse A self-propagating wave of depolarization; also called an action potential.

Nerve plexuses Interlacing nerve networks that occur in the cervical, brachial, lumbar, and sacral regions and primarily serve the limbs.

Nervous system Fast-acting control system that triggers muscle contraction or gland secretion.

Neural tube Fetal tissue which gives rise to the brain, spinal cord, and associated neural structures; formed from ectoderm by day 23 of embryonic development.

Neuroglia (nu-rog'le-ah) Nonexcitable cells of neural tissue that support, protect, and insulate the neurons; glial cells.

Neurohypophysis (nu"ro-hi-pof'ĭ-sis) Posterior pituitary plus infundibulum; portion of the pituitary gland derived from the brain.

Neuromuscular junction Region where a motor neuron comes into close contact with a skeletal muscle cell.

Neuron (nerve cell) (nu'ron) Cell of the nervous system specialized to generate and transmit electrical signals (action potentials and graded potentials).

Neuron cell body The biosynthetic center of a neuron; also called the perikaryon, or soma.

Neuronal pools Functional groups of neurons that process and integrate information.

Neuropeptides (nu"ro-pep'tĭds) A class of neurotransmitters including beta endorphins and enkephalins (which act as euphorics and reduce perception of pain) and gut-brain peptides.

Neurotransmitter Chemical messenger released by neurons that may, upon binding to receptors of neurons or effector cells, stimulate or inhibit those neurons or effector cells.

Neutral fats Consist of fatty acid chains and glycerol; also called triglycerides or triacylglycerols. Commonly known as oils when liquid.

Neutralization reaction Displacement reaction in which mixing an acid and a base forms water and a salt.

Neutron (nu'tron) Uncharged subatomic particle; found in the atomic nucleus.

Neutrophil (nu'tro-fil) Most abundant type of white blood cell.

Nicotinic receptors (nik"o-tin'ik) Acetylcholine-binding receptors of all autonomic ganglionic neurons and skeletal muscle neuromuscular junctions; named for activation by nicotine.

Nitric oxide (NO) A gaseous chemical messenger; diverse functions include participation in memory formation in the brain, and causing vasodilation throughout the body.

Nociceptor (no"se-sep'tor) Receptor sensitive to potentially damaging stimuli that result in pain.

Nondisjunction Failure of sister chromatids to separate during mitosis or failure of homologous pairs to separate during meiosis; results in abnormal numbers of chromosomes in the resulting daughter cells.

Nonpolar molecules Electrically balanced molecules.

Norepinephrine (NE) (nor"ep-ĭ-nef'rin) A catecholamine neurotransmitter and adrenal medullary hormone, associated with sympathetic nervous system activation.

Nuclear envelope The double membrane barrier of a cell nucleus.

Nucleic acid (nu-kle'ik) Class of organic molecules that includes DNA and RNA.

Nucleoli (nu-kle'o-li) Dense spherical bodies in the cell nucleus involved with ribosomal subunit synthesis and storage.

Nucleosome (nu'kle-o-sōm) Fundamental unit of chromatin; consists of a strand of DNA wound around a cluster of eight histone proteins.

Nucleotide (nu'kle-o-tīd) Building block of nucleic acids; consists of a sugar, a nitrogen-containing base, and a phosphate group.

Nucleus (nu'kle-is) (1) Control center of a cell; contains genetic material; (2) clusters of nerve cell bodies in the CNS.

Nutrients Chemical substances taken in via the diet that are used for energy and cell building.

Oblique section A cut made diagonally between the horizontal and vertical plane of the body or an organ.

Occlusion (ah-kloo'zhun) Closure or obstruction.

Octet rule (rule of eights) (ok-tet') The tendency of atoms to interact in such a way that they have eight electrons in their valence shell.

Olfaction (ol-fak'shun) Smell.

Oligodendrocyte (ol'ĭ-go-den'dro-sīt) A type of CNS supporting cell that composes myelin sheaths.

Oocyte (o'o-sīt) Immature female gamete.

Oogenesis (o"o-jen'ĕ-sis) Process of ovum (female gamete) formation.

Ophthalmic (op-thal'mik) Pertaining to the eye.

Optic (op'tik) Pertaining to the eye or vision.

Optic chiasma (op'tik ki-az'muh) The partial crossover of fibers of the optic nerves.

Organ A part of the body formed of two or more tissues and adapted to carry out a specific function; e.g., the stomach.

Organ system A group of organs that work together to perform a vital body function; e.g., the nervous system.

Organelles (or"gah-nelz') Small cellular structures (ribosomes, mitochondria, and others) that perform specific metabolic functions for the cell as a whole.

Organic compound Any compound composed of atoms (some of which are carbon) held together by covalent (shared electron) bonds.

Organic Pertaining to carbon-containing molecules, such as proteins, fats, and carbohydrates.

Organism The living animal (or plant), which represents the sum total of all its organ systems working together to maintain life.

Origin Attachment of a muscle that remains relatively fixed during muscular contraction.

Osmolality The number of solute particles dissolved in 1 kilogram (1000 g) of water; reflects the solution's ability to cause osmosis.

Osmolarity (oz"mo-lar'ĭ-te) The number of solute particles present in 1 liter of a solution.

Osmoreceptor (oz"mo-re-sep'tor) Structure sensitive to osmotic pressure or concentration of a solution.

Osmosis (oz-mo'sis) Diffusion of a solvent through a membrane from a dilute solution into a more concentrated one.

Osmotic pressure A measure of the tendency of water to move into a more concentrated solution.

Ossicles (os'sik-kilz). *See* Auditory ossicles.

Ossification (os"ĭ-fi-ka'shun). *See* Osteogenesis.

Osteoblasts (os-'te-o-blasts) Bone-forming cells.

Osteoclasts (os'te-o-klasts) Large cells that resorb or break down bone matrix.

Osteocyte (os'te-o-sīt) Mature bone cell.

Osteogenesis (os"te-o-jen'e-sis) The process of bone formation; also called ossification.

Osteoid (os'te-oid) Unmineralized bone matrix.

Osteomalacia (os"te-o-mah-la'she-ah) Disorder in which bones are inadequately mineralized; soft bones.

Osteon (os'te-on) System of interconnecting canals in the microscopic structure of adult compact bone; unit of bone; also called Haversian system.

Osteoporosis (os"te-o-po-ro'sis) Decreased density and strength of bone resulting from a gradual decrease in rate of bone formation.

Ovarian cycle (o-vayr'e-an) Monthly cycle of follicle development, ovulation, and corpus luteum formation in an ovary.

Ovary (o'var-e) Female reproductive organ in which ova (eggs) are produced; female gonad.

Ovulation (ov"u-la'shun) Ejection of an immature egg (oocyte) from the ovary.

Ovum (o'vum) Female gamete; egg.

Oxidases Enzymes that catalyze the transfer of oxygen in oxidation-reduction reactions.

Oxidation (oks'ĭ-da"shun) Process of substances combining with oxygen or the removal of hydrogen.

Oxidation-reduction (redox) reaction A reaction that couples the oxidation (loss of electrons) of one substance with the reduction (gain of electrons) of another substance.

Oxidative phosphorylation (ok'sĭ-da"tiv fos"for-ĭ-la'shun) Process of ATP synthesis during which an inorganic phosphate group is attached to ADP; occurs via the electron transport chain within the mitochondria.

Oxygen debt The volume of oxygen required after exercise to replenish stores of O_2, ATP, creatine phosphate, and glycogen and oxidize the lactic acid formed during exercise.

Oxyhemoglobin (ok″sĭ-he″mo-glo′bin)　Oxygen-bound form of hemoglobin.

Oxytocin (ok″sĭ-to′sin)　Hormone synthesized in the hypothalamus and secreted by the posterior pituitary; stimulates contraction of the uterus during childbirth and the ejection of milk during nursing.

Paget's disease (paj′ets)　Disorder characterized by excessive bone breakdown and abnormal bone formation.

Palate (pal′at)　Roof of the mouth.

Pancreas (pan′kre-us)　Gland located behind the stomach, between the spleen and the duodenum; produces both endocrine and exocrine secretions.

Pancreatic juice (pan″kre-at′ik)　Bicarbonate-rich secretion of the pancreas containing enzymes for digestion of all food categories.

Papilla (pah-pil′ah)　Small, nipplelike projection; e.g., dermal papillae are projections of dermal tissue into the epidermis.

Paracrine (par″ah-krin′)　A chemical messenger that acts locally within the same tissue and is rapidly destroyed. Examples are prostaglandins and nitric oxide.

Parasagittal planes　All sagittal planes offset from the midline.

Parasympathetic division　The division of the autonomic nervous system that oversees digestion, elimination, and glandular function; the resting and digesting subdivision.

Parasympathetic tone　Normal (background) level of parasympathetic output; sustains normal gastrointestinal and urinary tract activity, lowers heart rate.

Parathyroid glands (par″ah-thi′roid)　Small endocrine glands located on the posterior aspect of the thyroid gland.

Parathyroid hormone (PTH)　Hormone released by the parathyroid glands that regulates blood calcium level.

Parietal (pah-ri′ĕ-tal)　Pertaining to the walls of a cavity.

Parietal serosa　The part of the double-layered membrane that lines the walls of the ventral body cavity.

Parkinson's disease　Neurodegenerative disorder of the basal nuclei due to insufficient secretion of the neurotransmitter dopamine; symptoms include tremor and rigid movement.

Partial pressure　The pressure exerted by a single component of a mixture of gases.

Parturition (par″tu-rish′un)　Culmination of pregnancy; giving birth.

Passive immunity　Short-lived immunity resulting from the introduction of "borrowed antibodies" obtained from an immune animal or human donor; immunological memory is not established.

Passive (transport) processes　Membrane transport processes that do not require cellular energy (ATP), e.g., diffusion, which is driven by kinetic energy.

Pathogen (path′o-jen)　Disease-causing microorganism.

Pectoral (pek′tor-al)　Pertaining to the chest.

Pectoral (shoulder) girdle　Bones that attach the upper limbs to the axial skeleton; includes the clavicle and scapula.

Pedigree　Traces a particular genetic trait through several generations and helps predict the genotype of future offspring.

Pelvic girdle (hip girdle)　Consists of the paired coxal bones that attach the lower limbs to the axial skeleton.

Pelvis (pel′vis)　(1) Basin-shaped bony structure composed of the pelvic girdle, sacrum, and coccyx; (2) funnel-shaped tube within the kidney continuous with the ureter.

Penis (pe′nis)　Male organ of copulation and urination.

Pepsin　Enzyme capable of digesting proteins in an acid pH.

Peptide bond (pep′tid)　Bond joining the amine group of one amino acid to the acid carboxyl group of a second amino acid with the loss of a water molecule.

Perforating canals　Canals that run at right angles to the long axis of the bone, connecting the vascular and nerve supplies of the periosteum to those of the central canals and medullary cavity; also called Volkmann's canals.

Pericardium (per″ĭ-kar′de-um)　Double-layered sac enclosing the heart and forming its superficial layer; has fibrous and serous layers.

Perichondrium (per″ĭ-kon′dre-um)　Fibrous, connective-tissue membrane covering the external surface of cartilaginous structures.

Perimysium (per″ĭ-mis′e-um)　Connective tissue enveloping bundles of muscle fibers.

Perineum (per″ĭ-ne′um)　That region of the body spanning the region between the ischial tuberosities and extending from the pubic arch to the coccyx.

Periosteum (per″e-os′te-um)　Double-layered connective tissue that covers and nourishes the bone.

Peripheral congestion　Condition caused by failure of the right side of the heart; results in edema in the extremities.

Peripheral nervous system (PNS)　Portion of the nervous system consisting of nerves and ganglia that lie outside of the brain and spinal cord.

Peripheral resistance　A measure of the amount of friction encountered by blood as it flows through the blood vessels.

Peristalsis (per″i-stal′sis)　Progressive, wavelike contractions that move foodstuffs through the alimentary tube organs (or that move other substances through other hollow body organs).

Peritoneum (per″ĭ-to-ne′um)　Serous membrane lining the interior of the abdominal cavity and covering the surfaces of abdominal organs.

Peritonitis (per″ĭ-to-ni′tis)　Inflammation of the peritoneum.

Permeability　That property of membranes that permits passage of molecules and ions.

Peroxisomes (pĕ-roks′ĭ-sōmz)　Membranous sacs in cytoplasm containing powerful oxidase enzymes that use molecular oxygen to detoxify harmful or toxic substances, such as free radicals.

Petechiae (pe-te′ke-ah)　Small, purplish skin blotches caused by widespread hemorrhage due to thrombocytopenia.

Peyer's patches (pi′erz)　Lymphoid organs located in the small intestine.

pH unit (pe-āch)　The measure of the relative acidity or alkalinity of a solution.

Phagocytosis (fag″o-si-to′sis)　Engulfing of foreign solids by (phagocytic) cells.

Phagosome (fag′o-sōm)　Vesicle formed as a result of phagocytosis.

Pharmacological dose　A drug dose that is dramatically higher than normal levels of that substance (e.g., hormone) in the body.

Pharyngotympanic tube　Tube that connects the middle ear and the pharynx. Also called auditory tube, eustachian tube.

Pharynx (fayr′inks)　Muscular tube extending from the region posterior to the nasal cavities to the esophagus.

Phenotype (fe′no-tīp)　Observable expression of the genotype.

Phospholipid (fos″fo-lip′id)　Modified lipid, contains phosphorus.

Phosphorylation　A chemical reaction in which a phosphate molecule is added to a molecule; for example, phosphorylation of ADP yields ATP.

Photoreceptor (fo″to-re-sep′tor)　Specialized receptor cells that respond to light energy; rods and cones.

Physiological acidosis (as″ĭ-do′sis)　Arterial pH lower than 7.35 resulting from any cause.

Physiological dose　A drug dose that replicates normal levels of that substance (e.g., hormone) in the body.

Physiology (fiz″e-ol′o-je)　Study of the function of living organisms.

Pineal gland (body) (pin′e-al)　A hormone-secreting part of the diencephalon of the brain thought to be involved in setting the biological clock and influencing reproductive function.

Pinocytosis (pe″no-si-to′sis)　Engulfing of extracellular fluid by cells.

Pituitary gland (pĭ-tu′ih-tayr″e)　Neuroendocrine gland located beneath the brain that serves a variety of functions including regulation of gonads, thyroid, adrenal cortex, lactation, and water balance.

Placenta (plah-sen′tah)　Temporary organ formed from both fetal and maternal tissues that provides nutrients and oxygen to the developing fetus, carries away fetal metabolic wastes, and produces the hormones of pregnancy.

Plasma (plaz′mah)　The nonliving fluid component of blood within which formed elements and various solutes are suspended and circulated.

Plasma cells Members of a B cell clone; specialized to produce and release antibodies.

Plasma membrane Membrane, composed of phospholipids, cholesterol, and proteins, that encloses cell contents; outer limiting cell membrane.

Platelet (plăt′let) Cell fragment found in blood; involved in clotting.

Pleura (ploo′rah) Two-layered serous membrane that lines the thoracic cavity and covers the external surface of the lung.

Pleural cavity (ploo′ral) A potential space between the two layers of pleura; contains a thin film of serous fluid.

Plexus (plek′sus) A network of converging and diverging nerve fibers, blood vessels, or lymphatics.

Polar molecules Nonsymmetrical molecules that contain electrically unbalanced atoms.

Polarized State of a plasma membrane of an unstimulated neuron or muscle cell in which the inside of the cell is relatively negative in comparison to the outside; the resting state.

Polycythemia (pol″e-si-the′me-ah) An abnormally high number of erythrocytes.

Polymer A substance of high molecular weight with long, chainlike molecules consisting of many similar (repeated) units.

Polypeptide (pol″e-pep′tīd) A chain of amino acids.

Polyps Benign mucosal tumors.

Polysaccharide (pol″e-sak′ah-rīd) Literally, many sugars, a polymer of linked monosaccharides; e.g., starch, glycogen.

Pons (1) Any bridgelike structure or part; (2) the part of the brain stem connecting the medulla with the midbrain, providing linkage between upper and lower levels of the central nervous system.

Pore The surface opening of the duct of a sweat gland.

Positive feedback mechanisms Feedback that tends to cause the level of a variable to change in the same direction as an initial change.

Posterior pituitary. *See* Neurohypophysis.

Postganglionic axon (fiber) (post″gang-gle-ah′nik) Axon of a ganglionic neuron, an autonomic motor neuron that has its cell body in a peripheral ganglion; the axon projects to an effector.

Potential energy Stored or inactive energy.

Preganglionic neuron Autonomic motor neuron that has its cell body in the central nervous system and projects its axon to a peripheral ganglion.

Presbyopia (pres″be-o′pe-ah) A condition that results in the loss of near focusing ability; typical onset is around age 40.

Pressure gradient Difference in hydrostatic pressure that drives filtration.

Primary active transport A type of active transport in which the energy needed to drive the transport process is provided directly by hydrolysis of ATP.

Prime mover Muscle that bears the major responsibility for effecting a particular movement; an agonist.

Process (1) Prominence or projection; (2) series of actions for a specific purpose.

Progesterone (pro-jes′ter-ōn) Hormone partly responsible for preparing the uterus for the fertilized ovum.

Prolactin (PRL) (pro-lak′tin) Adenohypophyseal hormone that stimulates the breasts to produce milk.

Pronation (pro-na′shun) Inward rotation of the forearm causing the radius to cross diagonally over the ulna—palms face posteriorly.

Prophase The first stage of mitosis, consisting of coiling of the chromosomes accompanied by migration of the two daughter centrioles toward the poles of the cell, and nuclear membrane breakdown.

Proprioceptor (pro″pre-o-sep′tor) Receptor located in a joint, muscle, or tendon; concerned with locomotion, posture, and muscle tone.

Prostaglandin (PG) (pros″tah-glan′din) A lipid-based chemical messenger synthesized by most tissue cells that acts locally as a paracrine.

Prostate Accessory reproductive gland; produces one-third of semen volume, including fluids that activate sperm.

Protein (pro′tēn) Complex substance containing carbon, oxygen, hydrogen, and nitrogen; composes 10–30% of cell mass.

Prothrombin time Diagnostic test to determine status of hemostasis system.

Proton (pro′ton) Subatomic particle that bears a positive charge; located in the atomic nucleus.

Proton acceptor A substance that takes up hydrogen ions in detectable amounts. Commonly referred to as a base.

Proton donor A substance that releases hydrogen ions in detectable amounts; an acid.

Proximal (prok′si-mul) Toward the attached end of a limb or the origin of a structure.

Pseudounipolar neuron (soo″do-u″nĭ-po′lar) Another term for unipolar neuron.

Puberty Period of life when reproductive maturity is achieved.

Pulmonary (pul′muh-nayr-e) Pertaining to the lungs.

Pulmonary arteries Vessels that deliver blood to the lungs to be oxygenated.

Pulmonary circuit System of blood vessels that serves gas exchange in the lungs; i.e., pulmonary arteries, capillaries, and veins.

Pulmonary edema (ĕ-de′muh) Leakage of fluid into the air sacs and tissue of the lungs.

Pulmonary veins Vessels that deliver freshly oxygenated blood from the respiratory zones of the lungs to the heart.

Pulmonary ventilation Breathing; consists of inspiration and expiration.

Pulse Rhythmic expansion and recoil of arteries resulting from heart contraction; can be felt from outside the body.

Pupil Opening in the center of the iris through which light enters the eye.

Purkinje fibers (pur-kin′je) Modified ventricular muscle fibers of the conduction system of the heart.

Pus Fluid product of inflammation composed of white blood cells, the debris of dead cells, and a thin fluid.

Pyloric sphincter (pi-lor′ik sfink′ter) Valve of the distal end of the stomach that controls food entry into the duodenum.

Pyramidal (corticospinal) tracts Major motor pathways concerned with voluntary movement; descend from pyramidal cells in the frontal lobes of each cerebral hemisphere.

Pyruvic acid An intermediate compound in the metabolism of carbohydrates.

Radioactivity The process of spontaneous decay seen in some of the heavier isotopes, during which particles or energy is emitted from the atomic nucleus; results in the atom becoming more stable.

Radioisotope (ra″de-o-i′so-tōp) Isotope that exhibits radioactive behavior.

Ramus (ra′mus) Branch of a nerve, artery, vein, or bone.

Rapid eye movement (REM) sleep Stage of sleep in which rapid eye movements, an alert EEG pattern, and dreaming occur.

Reactant A substance taking part in a chemical reaction.

Receptor (re-sep′tor) (1) A cell or nerve ending of a sensory neuron specialized to respond to particular types of stimuli; (2) protein that binds specifically with other molecules, e.g., neurotransmitters, hormones, paracrines, antigens.

Receptor-mediated endocytosis One of three types of endocytosis in which engulfed particles attach to receptors before endocytosis occurs.

Receptor potential A graded potential that occurs at a sensory receptor membrane.

Recessive traits A trait due to a particular allele that does not manifest itself in the presence of other alleles that generate traits dominant to it; must be present in double dose to be expressed.

Reduction Chemical reaction in which electrons and energy are gained by a molecule (often accompanied by gain of hydrogen ions) or oxygen is lost.

Referred pain Pain felt at a site other than the area of origin.

Reflex Automatic reaction to stimuli.

Refraction The bending of a light ray when it meets a different surface at an oblique rather than right angle.

Regeneration Replacement of destroyed tissue with the same kind of tissue.

Regulatory T cells (T_{Reg} cells) Population of T cells (usually expressing CD4) that suppress the immune response.

Relative refractory period Follows the absolute refractory period; interval when a threshold for action potential stimulation is markedly elevated.

Renal (re'nal) Pertaining to the kidney.

Renal autoregulation Process the kidney uses to maintain a nearly constant glomerular filtration rate despite fluctuations in systemic blood pressure.

Renal clearance The volume of plasma from which a particular substance is completely removed in a given time, usually 1 minute; provides information about renal function.

Renin (re'nin) Hormone released by the kidneys that is involved with raising blood pressure.

Rennin Stomach-secreted enzyme that acts on milk protein; not produced in adults.

Repolarization Movement of the membrane potential to the initial resting (polarized) state.

Reproductive system Organ system that functions to produce offspring.

Resistance exercise High-intensity exercise in which the muscles are pitted against high resistance or immovable forces and, as a result, muscle cells increase in size.

Respiration The processes involved in supplying the body with oxygen and disposing of carbon dioxide.

Respiratory system Organ system that carries out gas exchange; includes the nose, pharynx, larynx, trachea, bronchi, lungs.

Resting membrane potential The voltage that exists across the plasma membrane during the resting state of an excitable cell; ranges from −90 to −20 millivolts depending on cell type.

Reticular activating system (RAS) Diffuse brain stem neural network that receives a wide variety of sensory input and maintains wakefulness of the cerebral cortex.

Reticular fibers (ret-tik'u-lar) Fine network of connective tissue fibers that form the internal supporting framework of lymphoid organs.

Reticular formation Functional system that spans the brain stem; involved in regulating sensory input to the cerebral cortex, cortical arousal, and control of motor behavior.

Reticular lamina A layer of extracellular material containing a fine network of collagen protein fibers; together with the basal lamina it is a major component of the basement membrane.

Reticulocyte (rĕ-tik'u-lo-sīt) Immature erythrocyte.

Retina (ret'ĭ-nah) Neural layer of the eyeball; contains photoreceptors (rods, cones).

Rhombencephalon (hindbrain) (romb"en-sef'ah-lon) Caudal portion of the developing brain; constricts to form the metencephalon and myelencephalon; includes the pons, cerebellum, and medulla oblongata.

Ribosomal RNA (rRNA) A constituent of ribosome; exists within the ribosomes of cytoplasm and assists in protein synthesis.

Ribosomes (ri'bo-sōmz) Cytoplasmic organelles at which proteins are synthesized.

RNA (ribonucleic acid) (ri'bo-nu-kle'ik) Nucleic acid that contains ribose and the bases A, G, C, and U. Carries out DNA's instructions for protein synthesis.

Rods One of the two types of photosensitive cells in the retina.

Rotation The turning of a bone around its own long axis.

Rugae (ru'ge) Elevations or ridges, as in stomach mucosa.

Rule of nines Method of computing the extent of burns by dividing the body into a number of areas, each accounting for 9% (or a multiple thereof) of the total body area.

S (synthetic) phase The part of the interphase period of the cell life cycle in which DNA replicates itself, ensuring that the two future cells will receive identical copies of genetic material.

Sagittal plane (sa'jih-tul) A longitudinal (vertical) plane that divides the body or any of its parts into right and left portions.

Saliva Secretion of the salivary glands; cleanses and moistens the mouth and begins chemical digestion of starchy foods.

Saltatory conduction Transmission of an action potential along a myelinated fiber in which the nerve impulse appears to leap from node to node.

Sarcolemma The plasma membrane surface of a muscle fiber.

Sarcomere (sar'ko-mēr) The smallest contractile unit of muscle; extends from one Z disc to the next.

Sarcoplasm The nonfibrillar cytoplasm of a muscle fiber.

Sarcoplasmic reticulum (SR) (sar"ko-plaz'mik rĕ-tik'u-lum) Specialized endoplasmic reticulum of muscle cells.

Schwann cell A type of supporting cell in the PNS; forms myelin sheaths and is vital to peripheral nerve fiber regeneration.

Sclera (skle'rah) White opaque portion of the fibrous layer of the eyeball.

Scrotum (skro'tum) External sac enclosing the testes.

Sebaceous glands (oil glands) (se-ba'shus) Epidermal glands that produce an oily secretion called sebum.

Sebum (se'bum) Oily secretion of sebaceous glands.

Second-degree burn A burn in which the epidermis and the upper region of the dermis are damaged.

Second messenger Intracellular molecule generated by the binding of a chemical (hormone or neurotransmitter) to a plasma membrane receptor; mediates intracellular responses to the chemical messenger.

Secondary sex characteristics Anatomic features, not directly involved in the reproductive process, that develop under the influence of sex hormones, e.g., male or female pattern of muscle development, bone growth, body hair distribution, etc.

Secretion (se-kre'shun) (1) The passage of material formed by a cell to its exterior; (2) cell product that is transported to the exterior of a cell.

Secretory vesicles (granules) Vesicles containing proteins that migrate to the plasma membrane of a cell and discharge their contents from the cell by exocytosis.

Section A cut through the body (or an organ) that is made along a particular plane; a thin slice of tissue prepared for microscopic study.

Segregation During meiosis, the distribution of the members of the allele pair to different gametes.

Selectively permeable membrane A membrane that allows certain substances to pass while restricting the movement of others; also called differentially permeable membrane.

Semen (se'men) Fluid mixture containing sperm and secretions of the male accessory reproductive glands.

Semilunar valves (sĕ"me-loo'ner) Valves that prevent blood return to the ventricles after contraction; aortic and pulmonary valves.

Seminiferous tubules (sem"ĭ-nif'er-us) Highly convoluted tubes within the testes; form sperm.

Sense organs Localized collections of many types of cells working together to accomplish a specific receptive process.

Sensory (afferent) nerves Nerves that contain processes of sensory neurons and carry impulses to the central nervous system.

Sensory areas Functional areas of the cerebral cortex that provide for conscious awareness of sensation.

Sensory receptor Dendritic end organs, or parts of other cell types, specialized to respond to a stimulus.

Serosa (serous membrane) (se-ro'sah) The moist membrane found in closed ventral body cavities.

Serous fluid (sēr'us) Clear, watery fluid secreted by cells of a serous membrane.

Serum (sēr'um) Amber-colored fluid that exudes from clotted blood as the clot shrinks; plasma without clotting factors.

Sesamoid bones (ses'ah-moid) Short bones embedded in tendons, variable in size and number, many of which influence the action of muscles; largest is the patella (kneecap).

Severe combined immunodeficiency syndromes (SCIDs) Congenital conditions resulting in little or no protection against disease-causing organisms of any type.

Sex chromosomes The chromosomes, X and Y, that determine genetic sex (XX = female; XY = male); the 23rd pair of chromosomes.

Sex-linked inheritance Inherited traits determined by genes on the sex chromosomes, e.g., X-linked genes are passed from mother to son, Y-linked genes are passed from father to son.

Sexually transmitted disease (STD) Infectious disease spread through sexual contact.

Signal sequence A short peptide segment present in a protein being synthesized that causes the associated ribosome to attach to the membrane of rough ER.

Simple diffusion The unassisted transport across a plasma membrane of a lipid-soluble or very small particle.

Sinoatrial (SA) node (si"no-a'tre-al) Specialized myocardial cells in the wall of the right atrium; pacemaker of the heart.

Sinus (si'nus) (1) Mucous-membrane-lined, air-filled cavity in certain cranial bones; (2) dilated channel for the passage of blood or lymph.

Skeletal cartilage Composes most of the skeleton in early fetal life; articular cartilage, nasal cartilage in the adult skeleton.

Skeletal muscle Muscle composed of cylindrical multinucleate cells with obvious striations; the muscle(s) attached to the body's skeleton; voluntary muscle.

Skeletal system System of protection and support composed primarily of bone and cartilage.

Skull Bony protective encasement of the brain and the organs of hearing and equilibrium; includes the facial bones. Also called the cranium.

Small intestine Convoluted tube extending from the pyloric sphincter to the ileocecal valve where it joins the large intestine; the site where digestion is completed and virtually all absorption occurs.

Smooth muscle Spindle-shaped cells with one centrally located nucleus and no externally visible striations (bands). Found mainly in the walls of hollow organs.

Sodium-potassium (Na$^+$-K$^+$) pump A primary active transport system that simultaneously drives Na$^+$ out of the cell against a steep gradient and pumps K$^+$ back in.

Sol-gel transformation Reversible change of a colloid from a fluid (sol) to a more solid (gel) state.

Solute (sol'yoot) The substance that is dissolved in a solution.

Solute pump Enzyme-like protein carrier that mediates active transport of solutes such as amino acids and ions uphill against their concentration gradients.

Somatic nervous system (so-ma'tik) Division of the peripheral nervous system that provides the motor innervation of skeletal muscles; also called the voluntary nervous system.

Somatic reflexes Reflexes that activate skeletal muscle.

Somatosensory system That part of the sensory system dealing with reception in the body wall and limbs; receives inputs from exteroceptors, proprioceptors, and interoceptors.

Somite (so'mīt) A mesodermal segment of the body of an embryo that contributes to the formation of skeletal muscles, vertebrae, and dermis of skin.

Spatial discrimination The ability of neurons to identify the site or pattern of stimulation.

Special senses The senses of taste, smell, vision, hearing, and equilibrium.

Specific gravity Term used to compare the weight of a substance to the weight of an equal volume of distilled water.

Sperm (spermatozoon) Male gamete.

Spermatogenesis (sper"mah-to-jen'ĕ-sis) The process of sperm (male gamete) formation; involves meiosis.

Sphincter (sfink'ter) A circular muscle surrounding an opening; acts as a valve.

Spinal cord The bundle of nervous tissue that runs from the brain to the first to third lumbar vertebrae and provides a conduction pathway to and from the brain.

Spinal nerves The 31 nerve pairs that arise from the spinal cord.

Splanchnic circulation (splangk'nik) The blood vessels serving the digestive system.

Spleen Largest lymphoid organ; provides for lymphocyte proliferation, immune surveillance and response, and blood-cleansing functions.

Spongy bone Internal layer of skeletal bone. Also called cancellous bone.

Sprain Ligaments reinforcing a joint are stretched or torn.

Static equilibrium Sense of head position in space with respect to gravity.

Stenosis (stě-no'sis) Abnormal constriction or narrowing.

Steroids (stě'roidz) Group of chemical substances including certain hormones and cholesterol; they are fat soluble and contain little oxygen.

Stimulus (stim'u-lus) An excitant or irritant; a change in the environment that evokes a response.

Stomach Temporary reservoir in the gastrointestinal tract where chemical breakdown of proteins begins and food is converted into chyme.

Stressor Any stimulus that directly or indirectly causes the hypothalamus to initiate stress-reducing responses, such as the fight-or-flight response.

Stroke. *See* Cerebrovascular accident.

Stroke volume (SV) Amount of blood pumped out of a ventricle during one contraction.

Stroma (stro'mah) The basic internal structural framework of an organ.

Structural (fibrous) proteins Consist of extended, strandlike polypeptide chains forming a strong, ropelike structure that is linear, insoluble in water, and very stable; e.g., collagen.

Subcutaneous (sub"kyu-ta'ne-us) Beneath the skin.

Substrate A reactant on which an enzyme acts to cause a chemical action to proceed.

Sudoriferous gland (su"do-rif'er-us) Epidermal gland that produces sweat.

Sulcus (sul'kus) A furrow on the brain, less deep than a fissure.

Summation Accumulation of effects, especially those of muscular, sensory, or mental stimuli.

Superficial Located close to or on the body surface.

Superior Refers to the head or upper body regions.

Superior vena cava Vein that returns blood from body regions superior to the diaphragm.

Supination (soo"pĭ-na'shun) The outward rotation of the forearm causing palms to face anteriorly.

Surfactant (ser-fak'tant) Secretion produced by certain cells of the alveoli that reduces the surface tension of water molecules, thus preventing the collapse of the alveoli after each expiration.

Suspension Heterogeneous mixtures with large, often visible solutes that tend to settle out.

Suture (soo'cher) An immovable fibrous joint; with one exception, all bones of the skull are united by sutures.

Sweat gland. *See* Sudoriferous gland.

Sympathetic division The division of the autonomic nervous system that prepares the body for activity or to cope with some stressor (danger, excitement, etc.); the fight, fright, and flight subdivision.

Sympathetic (vasomotor) tone State of partial vasoconstriction of the blood vessels maintained by sympathetic fibers.

Symphysis (sim'fĭh-sis) A joint in which the bones are connected by fibrocartilage.

Synapse (sin'aps) Functional junction or point of close contact between two neurons or between a neuron and an effector cell.

Synapsis (sĭ-nap'sis) Pairing of homologous chromosomes during the first meiotic division.

Synaptic cleft (si-nap'tik) Fluid-filled space at a synapse.

Synaptic delay Time required for an impulse to cross a synapse between two neurons.

Synaptic vesicles Small membranous sacs containing neurotransmitter.

Synarthrosis (sin″ar-thro′sis) Immovable joint.

Synchondrosis (sin″kon-dro′sis) A joint in which the bones are united by hyaline cartilage.

Syndesmosis (sin″des-mo′sis) A joint in which the bones are united by a ligament or a sheet of fibrous tissue.

Synergist (sin′er-jist) (1) Muscle that aids the action of a prime mover by effecting the same movement or by stabilizing joints across which the prime mover acts to prevent undesirable movements. (2) Hormone that amplifies the effect of another hormone at a target cell.

Synostosis (sin″os-to′sis) A completely ossified joint; a fused joint.

Synovial fluid Fluid secreted by the synovial membrane; lubricates joint surfaces and nourishes articular cartilages.

Synovial joint Freely movable joint exhibiting a joint cavity; also called a diarthrosis.

Synthesis (combination) reaction A chemical reaction in which larger, more complex atoms or molecules are formed from simpler ones.

Systemic (sis-tem′ik) Pertaining to the whole body.

Systemic circuit System of blood vessels that serves gas exchange in the body tissues.

Systole (sis′to-le) Period when either the ventricles or the atria are contracting.

Systolic pressure (sis-tah′lik) Pressure exerted by blood on the blood vessel walls during ventricular contractions.

T cells Lymphocytes that mediate cellular immunity; include helper, cytotoxic, regulatory, and memory cells. Also called T lymphocytes.

T tubule (transverse tubule) Extension of the muscle cell plasma membrane (sarcolemma) that protrudes deeply into the muscle cell.

Tachycardia (tak″e-kar′de-ah) A heart rate over 100 beats per minute.

Taste buds Sensory receptor organs that house gustatory cells, which respond to dissolved food chemicals.

Telencephalon (endbrain) (tel″en-seh′fuh-lon) Anterior subdivision of the primary forebrain that develops into olfactory lobes, cerebral cortex, and basal nuclei.

Telophase The final phase of mitosis; begins when migration of chromosomes to the poles of the cell has been completed and ends with the formation of two daughter nuclei.

Tendon (ten′dun) Cord of dense fibrous tissue attaching muscle to bone.

Tendonitis Inflammation of tendon sheaths, typically caused by overuse.

Terminal branches Branching ends of an axon that allow it to form many axon terminals; telodendria.

Testis (tes′tis) Male primary reproductive organ that produces sperm; male gonad.

Testosterone (tes-tos′tĕ-rōn) Male sex hormone produced by the testes; during puberty promotes virilization, and is necessary for normal sperm production.

Tetanus (tet′ah-nus) (1) A smooth, sustained muscle contraction resulting from high-frequency stimulation; (2) an infectious disease caused by an anaerobic bacterium.

Thalamus (tha′luh-mis) A mass of gray matter in the diencephalon of the brain.

Thermogenesis (ther″mo-jen′ĕ-sis) Heat production.

Thermoreceptor (ther″mo-re-sep′ter) Receptor sensitive to temperature changes.

Third-degree burn A burn that involves the entire thickness of the skin; also called a full-thickness burn. Usually requires skin grafting.

Thoracic cage (bony thorax) Bones that form the framework of the thorax; includes sternum, ribs, and thoracic vertebrae.

Thoracic duct Large duct that receives lymph drained from the entire lower body, the left upper extremity, and the left side of the head and thorax.

Thorax (tho′raks) That portion of the body trunk above the diaphragm and below the neck.

Threshold stimulus Weakest stimulus capable of producing a response in an irritable tissue.

Thrombin (throm′bin) Enzyme that induces clotting by converting fibrinogen to fibrin.

Thrombocyte (throm′bo-sīt) Platelet; cell fragment that participates in blood coagulation.

Thrombocytopenia (throm″bo-si″to-pe′ne-ah) A reduction in the number of platelets circulating in the blood.

Thrombus (throm′bus) A clot that develops and persists in an unbroken blood vessel.

Thymine (T) (thi′mēn) Single-ring base (a pyrimidine) in DNA.

Thymus (thi′mus) Lymphoid organ and endocrine gland active in immune response; site of maturation of T lymphocytes.

Thyroid gland (thi′roid) One of the largest of the body's endocrine glands; straddles the anterior trachea.

Thyroid hormone (TH) The major hormone secreted by thyroid follicles; stimulates enzymes concerned with glucose oxidation.

Thyroid-stimulating hormone (TSH) Adenohypophyseal hormone that regulates secretion of thyroid hormones.

Thyroxine (T_4) (thi-rok′sin) Iodine-containing hormone secreted by the thyroid gland; accelerates cellular metabolic rate in most body tissues.

Tight junction Area where plasma membranes of adjacent cells are fused.

Tissue A group of similar cells and their intercellular substance specialized to perform a specific function; primary tissue types of the body are epithelial, connective, muscle, and nervous tissue.

Tissue perfusion Blood flow through body tissues or organs.

Tonicity (to-nis′ĭ-te) A measure of the ability of a solution to cause a change in cell shape or tone by promoting osmotic flows of water.

Tonsils A ring of lymphoid tissue around the entrance to the pharynx. *See also* adenoids.

Trabecula (trah-bek′u-lah) (1) Any of the fibrous bands extending from the capsule into the interior of an organ; (2) strut or thin plate of bone in spongy bone.

Trachea (tra′ke-ah) Windpipe; cartilage-reinforced tube extending from larynx to bronchi.

Tract A collection of axons in the central nervous system having the same origin, termination, and function.

Transcription One of the two major steps in the transfer of genetic code information involving the transfer of information from a DNA gene's base sequence to the complementary base sequence of an mRNA molecule.

Transduction (trans-duk′shun) The conversion of the energy of a stimulus into an electrical event.

Transepithelial transport (trans-ep″ĭ-the′le-al) Movement of substances through, rather than between, adjacent epithelial cells connected by tight junctions, such as absorption of nutrients in the small intestine.

Transfer RNA (tRNA) Short-chain RNA molecules that transfer amino acids to the ribosome.

Transfusion reaction Agglutination and destruction of red blood cells following transfusion of incompatible blood.

Translation One of the two major steps in the transfer of genetic code information, in which the information carried by mRNA is decoded and used to assemble polypeptides.

Transverse (horizontal) plane A plane running from right to left, dividing the body into superior and inferior parts.

Tricuspid valve (tri-kus′pid) The right atrioventricular valve.

Triglycerides (tri-glis′er-īdz) Fats and oils composed of fatty acids and glycerol; are the body's most concentrated source of energy fuel; also known as neutral fats.

Triiodothyronine (T_3) (tri″i-o″do-thi′ro-nēn) Thyroid hormone; secretion and function similar to those of thyroxine (T_4).

Tripeptide A combination of three amino acids united by means of peptide bonds.

Trophoblast (tro′fo-blast) Outer sphere of cells of the blastocyst.

Tropic hormone (trōp'ik) A hormone that regulates the secretory action of another endocrine organ.

Trypsin Proteolytic enzyme secreted by the pancreas.

Tubular reabsorption The movement of filtrate components from the renal tubules into the blood.

Tubular secretion The movement of substances (such as drugs, urea, excess ions) from blood into filtrate.

Tumor An abnormal growth of cells; a swelling; may be cancerous.

Tunica (too'nĭ-kah) A covering or tissue coat; membrane layer.

Tympanic membrane (tim-pan'ik) Eardrum.

Ulcer (ul'ser) Lesion or erosion of the mucous membrane, such as gastric ulcer of stomach.

Umbilical cord (um-bĭ'lĭ-kul) Structure bearing arteries and veins connecting the placenta and the fetus.

Umbilicus (um-bĭ'lĭ-kus) Navel; marks site where umbilical cord was attached in fetal stage.

Unipolar neuron Neuron in which embryological fusion of the two processes leaves only one process extending from the cell body.

Unmyelinated fibers (un-mi'ĕ-lĭ-nāt″ed) Axons lacking a myelin sheath and therefore conducting impulses quite slowly.

Uracil (U) (u'rah-sil) A smaller, single-ring base (a pyrimidine) found in RNA.

Urea (u-re'ah) Main nitrogen-containing waste excreted in urine.

Ureter (u-re'ter) Tube that carries urine from kidney to bladder.

Urethra (u-re'thrah) Canal through which urine passes from the bladder to outside the body.

Uric acid The nitrogenous waste product of nucleic acid metabolism; component of urine.

Urinary bladder A smooth, collapsible, muscular sac that stores urine temporarily.

Urinary system System primarily responsible for water, electrolyte, and acid-base balance and removal of nitrogenous wastes.

Uterine tube (u'ter-in) Tube through which the ovum is transported to the uterus. Also called fallopian tube.

Uterus (u'ter-us) Hollow, thick-walled organ that receives, retains, and nourishes fertilized egg; site where embryo/fetus develops.

Uvula (u'vu-lah) Tissue tag hanging from soft palate.

Vaccine Preparation that provides artificially acquired active immunity.

Vagina Thin-walled tube extending from the cervix to the body exterior; often called the birth canal.

Valence shell (va'lens) Outermost electron shell (energy level) of an atom that contains electrons.

Varicosities Knoblike swellings of certain autonomic axons containing mitochondria and synaptic vesicles.

Vas (vaz') A duct; vessel.

Vasa recta (va'sah rek'tah) Capillary branches that supply loops of Henle in the medulla region of the kidney.

Vascular Pertaining to blood vessels or richly supplied with blood vessels.

Vascular spasm Immediate response to blood vessel injury; results in constriction.

Vasoconstriction (vas″o-kon-strik'shun) Narrowing of blood vessels.

Vasodilation (vas″o-di-la'shun) Relaxation of the smooth muscles of the blood vessels, producing dilation.

Vasomotion (vas″o-mo'shun) Intermittent contraction or relaxation of the precapillary sphincters, resulting in a staggered blood flow when tissue needs are not extreme.

Vasomotor center (vas″o-mo'ter) Brain area concerned with regulation of blood vessel resistance.

Vasomotor fibers Sympathetic nerve fibers that cause the contraction of smooth muscle in the walls of blood vessels, thereby regulating blood vessel diameter.

Veins (vānz″) Blood vessels that return blood toward the heart from the circulation.

Ventral Pertaining to the front; anterior.

Ventricle (1) Paired, inferiorly located heart chambers that function as the major blood pumps; (2) cavities in the brain.

Venule (ven'ūl) A small vein.

Vertebral column (spine) (ver'ti-brul) Formed of a number of individual bones called vertebrae and two composite bones (sacrum and coccyx).

Vesicle (vĕ'sĭ-kul) A small liquid-filled sac or bladder.

Vesicular (bulk) transport The movement of large particles and macromolecules across a plasma membrane.

Vesicular follicle Mature ovarian follicle.

Vestibule An enlarged area at the beginning of a canal, i.e., inner ear, nose, larynx.

Villus (vil'us) Fingerlike projections of the small intestinal mucosa that tremendously increase its surface area for absorption.

Visceral (vis'er-al) Pertaining to an internal organ of the body or the inner part of a structure.

Visceral muscle Type of smooth muscle; its cells contract as a unit and rhythmically, are electrically coupled by gap junctions, and often exhibit spontaneous action potentials.

Visceral organs (viscera) A group of internal organs housed in the ventral body cavity.

Visceral serosa (se-ro'sah) The part of the double-layered membrane that lines the outer surfaces of organs within the ventral body cavity.

Viscosity (vis'kos'ĭ-te) State of being sticky or thick.

Visual field The field of view seen when the head is still.

Vital capacity (VC) The volume of air that can be expelled from the lungs by forcible expiration after the deepest inspiration; total exchangeable air.

Vital signs Includes pulse, blood pressure, respiratory rate, and body temperature measurements.

Vitamins Organic compounds required by the body in minute amounts.

Vocal folds Mucosal folds that function in voice production (speech); also called the true vocal cords.

Volatile acid An acid that can be eliminated by the lungs; carbonic acid is converted to CO_2, which diffuses into the alveoli.

Volkmann's canals *See* Perforating canals.

Voluntary muscle Muscle under strict nervous control; skeletal muscle.

Voluntary nervous system The somatic nervous system.

Vulva (vul'vuh) Female external genitalia.

Wallerian degeneration (wal-er'ē-an) A process of disintegration of an axon that occurs when it is crushed or severed and cannot receive nutrients from the cell body.

White matter White substance of the central nervous system; myelinated nerve fibers.

Xenograft Tissue graft taken from another animal species.

Yolk sac (yōk) One of the extraembryonic membranes; involved in early blood cell formation.

Zygote (zi'gōt) Fertilized egg.

Photo and Illustration Credits

Photo Credits

Critical Thinking icon: Brand X Pictures/Getty Images.
A Closer Look icon: Photodisc Blue/Getty Images.
Making Connections icon: Photodisc Green/Getty Images.
Table background: Photodisc Green/Getty Images.

Chapter 1
Chapter Opener: Jorge Silva/Corbis.
1.1: Photodisc.
1.8, 1: Jenny Thomas/Addison Wesley Longman.
1.8a: Howard Sochurek.
1.8b: Science Photo Library/Photo Researchers.
1.8c: CNRI/Science Photo Library/Photo Researchers.
1.11a: From Martini, Timmons, McKinley, *Human Anatomy*, 3e, F1.9a (Benjamin Cummings).
A Closer Look, a: Clinique Ste Catherine/CNRI/Science Photo Library/Photo Researchers.
b: Custom Medical Stock Photography.

Chapter 2
Chapter Opener: Comstock Images.
2.6, 1: Chip Clark.
2, 3: Stephen Frisch/Benjamin Cummings.
2.10b: Animals Animals/Earth Scenes.
2.22c: Computer Graphics Laboratory, University of California, San Francisco.
A Closer Look: Geoff Tomkinson/SPL/Photo Researchers.

Chapter 3
Chapter Opener: Duomo/Corbis.
3.9a–c: David M. Philips/Visuals Unlimited.
3.12b: Birgit H. Satir, Dept. of Anatomy and Structural Biology, Albert Einstein College of Medicine.
3.14: John Heuser, Heuser Lab.
3.17b: Don Fawcett/Visuals Unlimited.
3.18b: Barry King, University of California, Davis School of Medicine.
3.20b: Don Fawcett/Visuals Unlimited.
3.22: K. G. Murti/Visuals Unlimited.
3.24a: Mary Osborn, Max Planck Institute.
3.24b: Frank Solomon and J. Dinsmore, Massachusetts Institute of Technology.

3.24c: Mark S. Ladinsky and J. Richard McIntosh, University of Colorado.
3.26c: David M. Philips/Visuals Unlimited.
3.28b1: From L. Orci and A. Perrelet, *Freeze-Etch Histology*. (Heidelberg: Springer-Verlag, 1975) © 1975 Springer-Verlag.
2: From A. C. Faberge, *Cell Tiss. Res.* 151 (1974):403. © 1974 Springer-Verlag.
3: U. Aebi et al. *Nature* 323 (1996):560–564, figure 1a. Used by permission.
3.29a: Ada Olins/Biological Photo Services.
3.29b: GF Bahr, Armed Forces Institute of Pathology.
3.32, 1–6: Conly Rieder.
3.37b: E. Kiselva/D. Fawcett/Visuals Unlimited.

Chapter 4
Chapter Opener: Getty Images.
4.2a: G. W. Willis/Visuals Unlimited.
4.2b: Allen Bell, University of New England/Benjamin Cummings.
4.2c: Cabisco/Visuals Unlimited.
4.2d: R. Calentine/Visuals Unlimited.
4.2e: Nina Zanetti, Benjamin Cummings Publishers, Pearson Ed.
4.2f: Allen Bell, University of New England/Benjamin Cummings.
4.3a: CNRI/SPL.
4.9a: Ed Reschke.
4.9b: Nina Zanetti, Benjamin Cummings Publishers, Pearson Ed.
4.9c: Allen Bell, University of New England/Benjamin Cummings.
4.9d: Ed Reschke/Peter Arnold.
4.9e,f: Ed Reschke.
4.9g: Nina Zanetti, Benjamin Cummings Publishers, Pearson Ed.
4.9h: Allen Bell, University of New England/Benjamin Cummings.
4.9i,j: Ed Reschke.
4.10: Biophoto Associates/Photo Researchers.
4.11a: Eric Graves/Photo Researchers.
4.11b: Ed Reschke.
4.11c: Allen Bell, University of New England/Benjamin Cummings.

Chapter 5
Chapter Opener: David R. Stoecklein Photography/Corbis.
5.2a: Dennis Strete/Fundamental Photographs.
5.3a: Cabisco/Visuals Unlimited.
5.3b: John D. Cunningham/Visuals Unlimited.

5.4: CNRI/Science Photo Library/Photo Researchers.
5.5b: Carolina Biological Supply/Phototake.
5.5d: Manfred Kage/Peter Arnold.
5.7a: Bart's Medical Library/Phototake.
5.7b: P. Marazzi/SPL/Photo Researchers.
5.7c: Zeva Oelbaum/Peter Arnold.
5.8b: Myrleen Ferguson/PhotoEdit.
5.8c: P. Marazzi/Science Photo Library/Photo Researchers.
5.8d: John Meyer/Custom Medical Stock Photography.
A Closer Look: Thinkstock/Getty Images.

Chapter 6
Chapter Opener: Comstock Images.
6.6c: Allen Bell, University of New England/Benjamin Cummings.
6.9: Ed Reschke.
6.14a,b: P. Motta, Department of Anatomy, University "La Sapienza," Rome/Science Photo Library/Photo Researchers.
6.15: Carolina Biological Supply.
Table 6.2, 1: Lester Bergman/Corbis.
2: ISM/Phototake.
3: SIU/Peter Arnold.
4: SIU/Visuals Unlimited.
5,6: University of Iowa's Virtual Hospital.

Chapter 7
Chapter Opener: Getty Images.
7.5, 3: R.T. Hutchings.
7.6c: Dave Roberts/Science Photo Library/Photo Researchers.
7.7, 3: R.T. Hutchings.
7.9a: R.T. Hutchings.
7.20c: R. T. Hutchings.
7.24c: Lester Bergman/Corbis.
7.25, 1–6: R.T. Hutchings.
7.26b: Department of Anatomy and Histology, University of California, San Francisco.
7.28a: From *A Stereoscopic Atlas of Human Anatomy* by David L. Bassett.
7.29b: Biophoto Associates/Science Source/Photo Researchers.
7.30: R.T. Hutchings.
7.34: Center for Cranialfacial Anomalies, University of California, San Francisco.
Table 7.4, 3–6: From *A Stereoscopic Atlas of Human Anatomy* by David L. Bassett.

Chapter 8
Chapter Opener: Getty Images.
8.3b: Mark Neilsen, University of Utah/Addison Wesley Longman.

8.5a–g: John Wilson White/Addison Wesley Longman.
8.6a–e: John Wilson White/Addison Wesley Longman.
8.8d: L. Bassett/Visuals Unlimited.
8.10c: From *A Stereoscopic Atlas of Human Anatomy* by David L. Bassett.
8.11c: VideoSurgery/Photo Researchers.
8.12b: From *A Stereoscopic Atlas of Human Anatomy* by David L. Bassett.
8.14: Elaine Marieb.
8.15: CNRI/Science Photo Library/Photo Researchers.
A Closer Look, 1: Lawrence Livermore National Laboratory/Photo Researchers.
2: Elaine Marieb.

Chapter 9
Chapter Opener: Getty Images.
9.1: Thomas S. Leeson.
9.2b: John D. Cunningham/Visuals Unlimited.
9.3a: Marian Rice.
9.4e: John Heuser.
9.6, 1–3: H. E. Huxley, Brandeis University, Waltham, MA.
9.13b: Eric Graves/Photo Researchers.
Table 9.3, 4: Eric Graves/Photo Researchers.
5: Marian Rice.
6: Department of Anatomy and Histology, University of California, San Francisco.
A Closer Look: Thinkstock/PictureQuest.

Chapter 10
Chapter Opener: Comstock Images.
10.4a: John Wilson White/Benjamin Cummings.
10.5a: John Wilson White/Benjamin Cummings.
10.9c: From *A Stereoscopic Atlas of Human Anatomy* by David L. Bassett.
10.10c: From *A Stereoscopic Atlas of Human Anatomy* by David L. Bassett.
10.13b, 1: From *A Stereoscopic Atlas of Human Anatomy* by David L. Bassett.
10.16c: L. Bassett/Visuals Unlimited.
10.25c: Charles Thomas, Kansas University Medical Center.

Chapter 11
Chapter Opener: Getty Images.
11.4a: Manfred Kage/Peter Arnold.
11.5d: Don W. Fawcett/ Photo Researchers.

11.17b: Oliver Meckes/Ottawa/ Photo Researchers.
A Closer Look: Brookhaven National Laboratory/ PictureQuest.

Chapter 12
Chapter Opener: Getty Images.
12.6b: Robert A. Chase.
12.6c: A. Glauberman/Photo Researchers.
12.7: Volker Steger/Peter Arnold.
12.10b: Peter J. Ocello, Office of Intellectual Properties, Michigan State University.
12.11b, 1: Pat Lynch/Photo Researchers.
12.14: Leonard Lessin/Peter Arnold.
12.17a,c: L. Bassett/Visuals Unlimited
12.17d: Biophoto Associates/Photo Researchers.
12.20a: Alexander Tsiara/Photo Researchers.
12.24b: From *A Stereoscopic Atlas of Human Anatomy* by David L. Bassett.
12.27: Carroll H. Weiss.
12.29b,c,d: L. Bassett/Visuals Unlimited.
12.36: Biophoto Associates/Science Source/Photo Researchers.
A Closer Look: Frederick C. Skvara, M.D.

Chapter 13
Chapter Opener: Associated Press, AP.
13.03a: From *Tissues and Organs: A Text Atlas of Scanning Electron Microscopy* by R. Kessel and R. Kardon, © W. H. Freeman, 1979.
Table 13.2c: William Thompson/ Addison Wesley Longman.

Chapter 14
Chapter Opener: Getty Images.

Chapter 15
Chapter Opener: Image Bank.
15.01a: Richard Tauber/Benjamin Cummings.
15.4b: From *A Stereoscopic Atlas of Human Anatomy* by David L Bassett.
15.6c: Ed Reschke/Peter Arnold.
15.7: A. L. Blum/Visuals Unlimited.
15.9: NMSB/Custom Medical Stock Photography.
15.11: Charles D. Wintrer/Photo Researchers.
15.19b: Stephen Spector/Benjamin Cummings.
15.23d: Carolina Biological Supply Company/Phototake, NYC.
15.28d: P. Motta/Department of Anatomy/University "La Sapienza," Rome/Science Photo Library/Photo Researchers.
15.33: *Science* Vol.279 March 1998, p. 1870.
15.37c: I. M. Hunter-Duvar, Department of Otolaryngology, The Hospital for Sick Children, Toronto.

Chapter 16
Chapter Opener: David R. Stoecklein Photography/Corbis.
16.8b: Ed Reschke.
16.10a,b: Photo Researchers.
16.11b: From *Color Atlas of Histology* by Leslie P. Garner and James L. Hiatt, © Williams and Wilkins, 1990.
16.13b: Ed Reschke.
16.15a,b: Charles B. Wilson, Neurological Surgery, University of California Medical Center, San Francisco.
16.17: Carolina Biological Supply/Phototake.
A Closer Look: Saturn Stills/ Science Photo Library/Photo Researchers.

Chapter 17
Chapter Opener: Getty Images.
17.2: Ed Reshke/Peter Arnold.
17.8a,b: Stan Flegler/Visuals Unlimited.
17.10a: J. O. Ballard.
17.10b: Ed Reschke/Peter Arnold.
17.10c,d: J. O. Ballard.
17.10e: Carden Jennings Publishing Ltd.
17.14: Meckes/Ottawa/Photo Researchers.
17.15, 1–4: Jack Scanlon, Holyoke Community College.
A Closer Look: Ed Eckstein/Phototake.

Chapter 18
Chapter Opener: Duomo/Corbis.
18.4a: A. & F. Michler/Peter Arnold.
18.4c: L. Bassett/Visuals Unlimited.
18.4f: A. & F. Michler/Peter Arnold.
18.8b: From *A Stereoscopic Atlas of Human Anatomy* by David L. Bassett.
18.8c: Lennart Nilsson, *The Body Victorious*, New York: Dell, © Boehringer Ingelheim International GmbH.
18.8d: L. Bassett/Visuals Unlimited.
18.11a: Ed Reschke.
18.19: Phil Jude/Science Photo Library/Photo Researchers.
18.23: Robert Brenner/PhotoEdit.

Chapter 19
Chapter Opener: Associated Press, AP.
19.1a: Gladden Willis/Visuals Unlimited.
19.21c: Science Photo Library/Photo Researchers.
A Closer Look, 1: ISM/Phototake— All rights reserved.
2: Sheila Terry/Science Photo Library/Photo Researchers.

Chapter 20
Chapter Opener: Getty Images.
20.3: Francis Leroy, Biocosmos/ Science Photo Library/ Photo Researchers.
20.4b: Biophoto Associates/Photo Researchers.
20.6c: Mark Neilsen/Benjamin Cummings.
20.6d: Victor Eroschenko, University of Idaho; Benjamin Cummings.
20.7: Astrid and Hanss-Freider Michler/Science Photo Library/ Photo Researchers.
20.8: John Cunningham/Visuals Unlimited.
20.9: Biophoto Associates/Science Source/Photo Researchers.

Chapter 21
Chapter Opener: Getty Images.
21.2a: Lennart Nilsson, *The Body Victorious*, New York: Dell, © Boehringer Ingelheim International GmbH.
21.13b: Arthur J. Olsen, The Scripps Research Institute.
21.19b: Andrejs Liepins/Science Photo Library/Photo Researchers.
A Closer Look: Vance Rodewald/ Calgary Herald.

Chapter 22
Chapter Opener: Associated Press, AP.
22.2a: Jenny Thomas/Benjamin Cummings.
22.3a: From *A Stereoscopic Atlas of Human Anatomy* by David L. Bassett.
22.4c,d: From *A Stereoscopic Atlas of Human Anatomy* by David L. Bassett.
22.6b: University of San Francisco.
22.6c: Science Photo Library/Photo Researchers.
22.8b: Carolina Biological Supply/ Phototake.
22.9a: R. Kessel/Visuals Unlimited.
22.10a: Richard Tauber/Benjamin Cummings.
22.10b: From *A Stereoscopic Atlas of Human Anatomy* by David L. Bassett.
22.11: Science Photo Library/Photo Researchers.
A Closer Look: Fred Bavendam/ Peter Arnold.

Chapter 23
Chapter Opener: Getty Images.
23.8, 2,3: From *Tissues and Organs* by R. Kessel and R. Kardon, © W. H. Freeman, 1979.
23.9b: Science Photo Library/Photo Researchers.
23.12a: Biophoto Associates/Photo Researchers.
23.12b: From *Color Atlas of Histology* by Leslie P. Garner and James L. Hiatt, © Williams and Wilkins, 1990.
23.14b: From *Color Atlas of Histology* by Leslie P. Garner and James L. Hiatt, © Williams and Wilkins, 1990.
23.21d: LUMEN Histology, Loyola University Medical Education Network, http://www.lumen .luc.edu/ lumen/MedEd/ Histo/frames/histo_frames.html.
23.22a: P. Motta/Department of Anatomy/University "La Sapienza," Rome/Science Photo Library/Photo Researchers.
23.22b: Secchi-Lecaque-Roussel-UCLAF/CNRI/Science Photo Library/Photo Researchers.
23.23a,b: From *A Stereoscopic Atlas of Human Anatomy* by David L. Bassett.
23.24b: From *A Stereoscopic Atlas of Human Anatomy* by David L. Bassett.
23.26b: Victor Eroschenko, University of Idaho/Benjamin Cummings.
23.30a: From *A Stereoscopic Atlas of Human Anatomy* by David L. Bassett.
23.31: Ed Reschke/Peter Arnold.

Chapter 24
Chapter Opener: Getty Images.
24.25: Omni-Photo.
A Closer Look: Stone/Getty Images.

Chapter 25
Chapter Opener: Getty Images.
25.1b: L. Bassett/Visuals Unlimited.
25.2b: Richard Tauber/Benjamin Cummings.
25.3a: From *A Stereoscopic Atlas of Human Anatomy* by David L. Bassett.
25.4c: Biophoto Associates/Photo Researchers.
25.5b: From *Tissues and Organs* by R. Kessel and R. Kardon, © W. H. Freeman, 1979.
25.7b: P. Motta and M. Castellucci/ Science Photo Library/ Photo Researchers.
25.17: Biophoto Associates/Photo Researchers.
A Closer Look: AJ Photo/Photo Researchers.

Chapter 26
Chapter Opener: Taxi/Getty Images.
26.5: Spencer Grant/Stock Boston.

Chapter 27
Chapter Opener: Getty Images.
27.3c: Ed Reschke.
27.8a: From *Tissues and Organs* by R. Kessel and R. Kardon, © W. H. Freeman, 1979.
27.9b: Manfred Kage/Peter Arnold.
27.12b: Ed Reschke.
27.13: C. Edelman/La Vilette/ Photo Researchers.
27.14b: From *A Stereoscopic Atlas of Human Anatomy* by David L. Bassett.
27.15a: Victor Eroschenko, University of Idaho/Benjamin Cummings.
27.18a: Spencer Grant/Stock Boston.
27.18b,c: Richard D'Amico/ Custom Medical Stock Photography.
A Closer Look: AFP/Corbis.

Chapter 28
Chapter Opener: David Stoecklein Photography/Corbis.
28.2b: Lennart Nilsson, *A Child Is Born*, New York: Dell, © Boehringer Ingelheim International GmbH.

28.3h: C. A. Ziomek, Worcester Fund for Experimental Biology, Shewsbury, MA.
28.5c: Allen C. Enders, University of California, Davis/Carnegie Collection.
28.7e: From *A Stereoscopic Atlas of Human Anatomy* by David L. Bassett.
28.14a,b: From Lennart Nilsson/ Albert Bonniers Forlag.

Chapter 29
Chapter Opener: Getty Images.
29.1b: Lester Lefkowitz/Corbis.
29.1c: L.Williatt, East Anglian Regional Genetics/SPL/Photo Researchers.

Illustration Credits

All illustrations by Imagineering STA Media Services unless otherwise noted.

Chapter 1 1.1: Jeanne Koelling.
1.2: Adapted from Campbell, Reece, and Mitchell, *Biology*, 5e, F40.10a, © Benjamin Cummings, 1999.
1.3: Vincent Perez/Wendy Hiller Gee.
1.10a: Adapted from Seeley, Stephens, and Tate, *Anatomy & Physiology*, 4e, F1.15a, New York: WCB/McGraw-Hill, © McGraw-Hill, 1998.
1.10b: Adapted from Marieb and Mallatt, *Human Anatomy*, 3e, F1.9, © Benjamin Cummings, 2003.
1.13: Adapted from Marieb and Mallatt, *Human Anatomy*, 3e, F1.10, © Benjamin Cummings, 2003.

Chapter 2 2.5b: Adapted from Campbell, Reece, and Mitchell, *Biology*, 5e, F2.13, © Benjamin Cummings, 1999.

Chapter 3 3.2: Tomo Narashima.
3.5: Tomo Narashima.
3.5b,c: Adapted from Lodish, et al., *Molecular Cell Biology*, 3e, F24-35, F24-38, New York: Freeman, © Scientific American Books, 1995.
3.17a: Tomo Narashima.
3.18a: Tomo Narashima.
3.18c: Adapted from Marieb, Mallatt, and Wilhelm, *Human Anatomy*, 4e, F2.5c, © Benjamin Cummings, 2005.
3.20: Tomo Narashima.
3.21: Tomo Narashima.
3.23: Adapted from Campbell, Reece, and Mitchell, *Biology*, 5e, F7.16, © Benjamin Cummings, 1999.
3.24: Tomo Narashima.
3.25: Adapted from Campbell, *Biology*, 4e, F7.21, © Benjamin Cummings, 1996.
3.26: Tomo Narashima.
3.28a: Tomo Narashima.
3.32: Adapted from Campbell, Reece, and Mitchell, *Biology*, 5e, F12.5, © Benjamin Cummings, 1999.

Chapter 4 4.3b: Adapted from Marieb, Mallatt, and Wilhelm, *Human Anatomy*, 4e, F4.5, © Benjamin Cummings, 2005.
4.7: From Mathews, Van Holde, and Ahern, *Biochemistry*, 3e, F9.24, © Benjamin Cummings, 2000.

Chapter 5 5.1: Tomo Narashima.
Making Connections: Vincent Perez/Wendy Hiller Gee.

Chapter 6 6.2: Adapted from Tortora and Grabowski, *Principles of Anatomy and Physiology*, 9e, F7.2, New York: Wiley, © Biological Sciences Textbooks and Sandra Reynolds Grabowski, 2000.
A Closer Look: Adapted from Ranier I. Kotz, Reinhard Windhager, et al., *Nature*, Fig 1, Vol 406:143, 13 July 2000, © Macmillan Publishers Ltd.
Making Connections: Vincent Perez/Wendy Hiller Gee.

Chapter 7 7.1: Nadine Sokol.
7.2: Nadine Sokol.
7.3: Nadine Sokol.
7.4: Nadine Sokol.
7.5: Nadine Sokol.
7.6a,b: Nadine Sokol.
7.7: Nadine Sokol.
7.8: Nadine Sokol. Adapted from Marieb, Mallatt, and Wilhelm, *Human Anatomy*, 4e, F7.8, © Benjamin Cummings, 2005.
7.9b: Nadine Sokol.
7.10: Nadine Sokol.
7.12: Nadine Sokol.
7.13: Kristin Otwell.
7.14: Laurie O'Keefe.
7.15: Laurie O'Keefe.
7.16: Laurie O'Keefe.
7.17: Laurie O'Keefe.
7.20a,b: Laurie O'Keefe.
7.21: Nadine Sokol.
7.22: Laurie O'Keefe.
7.23: Laurie O'Keefe.
7.24a,b: Laurie O'Keefe.
7.26: Laurie O'Keefe.
7.27: Laurie O'Keefe.
7.28b: Laurie O'Keefe.
7.29a,b: Laurie O'Keefe.
7.31: Kristin Otwell.
7.33: Nadine Sokol.
Table 7.2: Kristin Otwell.
Table 7.3: Kristin Otwell.
Table 7.4: Laurie O'Keefe.
Table 7.5: Kristin Otwell.

Chapter 8 8.1: Adapted from Marieb, Mallatt, and Wilhelm, *Human Anatomy*, 4e, F9.1, © Benjamin Cummings, 2005.
8.2: Carla Simmons and Kristin Mount. Adapted from Marieb, Mallatt, and Wilhelm, *Human Anatomy*, 4e, F9.2, © Benjamin Cummings, 2005.
8.4: Barbara Cousins.
8.7: Adapted from Marieb, *Human Anatomy & Physiology Laboratory Manual, Main Version*, 7e, F13.4, © Benjamin Cummings, 2005.
8.8a–c: Barbara Cousins.

8.8e: Carla Simmons and Kristin Mount. Adapted from Marieb, Mallatt, and Wilhelm, *Human Anatomy*, 4e, F9.14d, © Benjamin Cummings, 2005.
8.10a,b,d: Barbara Cousins.
8.11a,b: Barbara Cousins.
8.12a,c,d: Barbara Cousins.
8.13: Adapted from Marieb, Mallatt, and Wilhelm, *Human Anatomy*, 4e, F9.9 © Benjamin Cummings, 2005.

Chapter 9 9.2a: Raychel Ciemma.
9.3: Adapted from Marieb and Mallatt, *Human Anatomy*, 3e, F10.4, © Benjamin Cummings, 2003.
9.19: Adapted from Martini, *Fundamentals of Anatomy & Physiology*, 4e, F10.14, Upper Saddle River, NJ: Prentice-Hall, © Frederic H. Martini, 1998.
9.24: Adapted from Marieb and Mallatt, *Human Anatomy*, 3e, F10.12, © Benjamin Cummings, 2003.
Making Connections: Vincent Perez/Imagineering.

Chapter 10 10.1: Adapted from Martini, *Fundamentals of Anatomy & Physiology*, 4e, F11.1, Upper Saddle River, NJ: Prentice-Hall, © Frederic H. Martini, 1998.

Chapter 12 12.8: Adapted from Marieb and Mallatt, *Human Anatomy*, 3e, F13.10, © Benjamin Cummings, 2003.
12.11: Adapted from Marieb, Mallatt, and Wilhelm, *Human Anatomy*, 4e, F13.14, © Benjamin Cummings, 2005.
12.15: Adapted from Marieb and Mallatt, *Human Anatomy*, 3e, F13.20, © Benjamin Cummings, 2003.
12.19: Adapted from Marieb and Mallatt, *Human Anatomy*, 3e, F13.24, © Benjamin Cummings, 2003.
12.31: Stephanie McCann.
12.35: Adapted from Marieb and Mallatt, *Human Anatomy*, 3e, F13.34, © Benjamin Cummings, 2003.

Chapter 13 13.3b: Charles W. Hoffman.
13.7: Stephanie McCann. Adapted from Marieb, Mallatt, and Wilhelm, *Human Anatomy*, 4e, F14.10, © Benjamin Cummings, 2005.
13.9: Adapted from Marieb, Mallatt, and Wilhelm, *Human Anatomy*, 4e, F14.12, © Benjamin Cummings, 2005.
Table 13.2, 4, 5: Adapted from Marieb, Mallatt, and Wilhelm, *Human Anatomy*, 4e, T14.2, 4, 5, © Benjamin Cummings, 2005.

Chapter 14 14.3: Adapted from Marieb, Mallatt, and Wilhelm, *Human Anatomy*, 4e, F15.3, © Benjamin Cummings, 2005.
14.5: Adapted from Marieb, Mallatt, and Wilhelm, *Human Anatomy*, 4e, F15.7, © Benjamin Cummings, 2005.
14.6a: Adapted from Marieb, Mallatt, and Wilhelm, *Human Anatomy*, 4e, F15.8a, © Benjamin Cummings, 2005.
Making Connections: Vincent Perez/Wendy Hiller Gee.

Chapter 15 15.2: Charles W. Hoffman.
15.23c,d: Adapted from Marieb and Mallatt, *Human Anatomy*, 3e, F16.1, © Benjamin Cummings, 2003.
15.24: Adapted from Marieb and Mallatt, *Human Anatomy*, 3e, F16.2, © Benjamin Cummings, 2003.
15.25: Adapted from Marieb and Mallatt, *Human Anatomy*, 3e, F16.17, © Benjamin Cummings, 2003.
15.37: Charles W. Hoffman.

Chapter 16 16.1: Adapted from Marieb, *Essentials of Human Anatomy & Physiology*, 7e, F9.3, © Benjamin Cummings, 2003.
Making Connections: Vincent Perez/Wendy Hiller Gee.

Chapter 17 17.4: Nadine Sokol.

Chapter 18 18.1: Wendy Hiller Gee.
18.2: Barbara Cousins.
18.3: Barbara Cousins.
18.4b,d,e: Barbara Cousins.
18.6: Barbara Cousins.
18.8a: Barbara Cousins.
18.9: Barbara Cousins.
18.10: Barbara Cousins.
18.14a: Barbara Cousins.
18.25: Adapted from Marieb, Mallatt, and Wilhelm, *Human Anatomy*, 4e, F18.17, © Benjamin Cummings, 2005.

Chapter 19 19.1: Adapted from Tortora and Grabowski, *Principles of Anatomy and Physiology*, 9e, F21.1, New York: Wiley, © Biological Sciences Textbooks and Sandra Reynolds Grabowski, 2000.
19.18b: Barbara Cousins.
19.20b: Barbara Cousins.
19.21b,d: Barbara Cousins.
19.22b: Barbara Cousins.
19.23b–d: Barbara Cousins.
19.24b,c: Barbara Cousins.
19.25b: Barbara Cousins.
19.26b,c: Barbara Cousins.
19.27b: Barbara Cousins.
19.28b,c: Barbara Cousins.
19.29b,c: Barbara Cousins.
Making Connections: Vincent Perez/Wendy Hiller Gee.

Chapter 20 20.1, 1: Adapted from Marieb and Mallatt, *Human Anatomy*, 3e, F20.1, © Benjamin Cummings, 2003.
Making Connections: Vincent Perez/Wendy Hiller Gee.

Chapter 21 21.15: Adapted from Johnson, *Human Biology*, 2e, F9.13, © Benjamin Cummings, 2003.

Index

Note: Page numbers in **boldface** indicate a definition. A *t* following a page number indicates tabular material, an *f* indicates an illustration, and a *b* indicates boxed material.

A (adenine), **55–57**, 56*f*, 57*t*
A bands (dark bands), **284**, 285*f*, 689, 690*f*
ABCD rule, **166**
Abdomen
  arteries, 752–755*t*
  blood flow at rest/during exercise, 734, 734*f*
  innervation, 514, 541
    aortic plexus, 539*f*, **541**
    wall, 509*f*, 510*f*, 515*f*, 515*t*
  muscles, 331*f*, 348*t*, 349*f*
    wall, 348–349*t*, 349*f*
  reflexes, 527
  veins, 758*t*, **764–765*t***
Abdominal cavity, **15**, 17*f*
Abdominopelvic cavity, **15**, 17*f*
  peritoneum of, 886, 886*f*
  quadrants, **19**, 19*f*
  regions, 18, 18*f*
  serosae of, 142*f*, 143
Abdominopelvic organs
  muscles that compress, 348*t*, 349*f*
  muscles that support, **350*t***, 351*f*
Abducens nerve (VI), 448*f*, 451, **500**, 501*f*
  muscles served by, 558, 559*f*
  origin/course/function, 505*f*, **505*t***
Abduction (movement), **261**, 262*f*
  of lower limbs, 379–380*t*, 380*f*
  of upper limbs, 362–363*t*, 363*f*
Abductor digiti minimi muscles
  of foot, **381*t***, 382*f*
  of hand, **364*t***, 365*f*
Abductor hallucis muscle, **381*t***, 382*f*
Abductor pollicis brevis muscle, **364*t***, 365*f*
Abductor pollicis longus muscle, **360*t***, 361*f*
  actions of (summary), 362*t*, 363*f*
ABO blood groups, **669**, 669*t*
  genotypes determining, 1151, 1151*t*
Abortion, 1129*b*, **1141**
ABP (androgen-binding protein), **1080**, 1081*f*
Absence seizures, 457
Absolute refractory periods, 406–407, 406*f*
  in cardiac muscle, 691, 691*f*
Absorption, **884–885**, 884*f*, 920*t*, **931–933**
  active transport mechanisms, 931
  of carbohydrates, 928*f*, 931
  flowchart, 928*f*
  of lipids, 928*f*, 931–932, 932*f*
  malabsorption of nutrients and, 933
  of proteins, 928*f*, 930*f*, 931

Absorptive cells, of small intestine, 910, 910*f*
Absorptive (fed) state, **973–974**
  major events/metabolic pathways, 974*f*
Accessory nerve (XI), 448*f*, 449*f*, **500**, 501*f*
  cervical plexus in relation to, 511*f*
  muscles served by, 342*t*, 352*t*
  origin/course/function, 508*f*, **508*t***
Acclimatization, **870**
Accommodation, 567*f*, **568**
Accommodation pupillary reflex, **568**
ACE (angiotensin converting enzyme), 845, 1009*f*, **1010**
Acetabular labrum, **270**, 270*f*
Acetabulum, **237**, 238*f*, 243*f*
  in females vs. males, 240*f*, 240*t*
Acetic acid, 41
  in muscle contraction, 289, 290*f*
Acetone breath, 635*f*
Acetylcholine (ACh), **289**, 290*f*, **417–418**
  as ANS neurotransmitter, 543, 544*t*
  Botox injections and, 156*b*
  excitatory effect of, 534
  receptors, **289**, 290, 290*f*, 312, 415*t*
  secretion sites/effects, 415*t*
  smooth muscle contraction and, 312
Acetylcholinesterase (AChE), **289**, 290*f*, **417**, 519
  inhibitors, 545*t*
Acetyl coenzyme A (acetyl CoA)
  in glycolysis, 956, 957*f*
  in Krebs cycle, 961, 962*f*, 963
  in lipolysis, 969, 969*f*
AChE. *See* Acetylcholinesterase
Achilles tendon. *See* Calcaneal (Achilles) tendon
Achondroplasia, **199**, 1150
ACh. *See* Acetylcholine
Acid-base balance, **1049–1057**, 1060
  abnormalities, 1055–1060
    blood values to assess, 1057*b*
    causes/consequences, 1056*t*
    compensations, 1055–1057, 1060
    metabolic, 1055, 1056*t*
    respiratory, 1055, 1056*t*
  aging and, 1060
  buffer systems, 43, 52*t*
    chemical, 863, 1050–1052
    physiological, 1052
    renal, 1052–1054
    respiratory, 1052
  compensations
    renal, 1057, 1060
    respiratory, 1056–1057

developmental aspects, 1060
  in diabetes mellitus, 635*f*
Acidemia, **1050**
Acid group of amino acids, 49, 49*f*
Acid hydrolases, 88*f*, 89
Acidic solutions, 42
Acid mantle
  of skin, **164**, 796*t*
  of vagina, 796*t*
Acidosis, **60**, **1050**
  metabolic, 1055, 1056*t*
  physiological, 1050
  respiratory, **1055**, 1056*t*
  using blood values to assess, 1057*b*
Acids, **41–43**, 42*f*, 52*t*
  in buffer systems, 1050–1052
  metabolic (fixed), **1052**
  pH scale, 42, 42*f*
  strong/weak, **43**
    dissociation of, 1050, 1050*f*
  volatile, 1052
Acinar cells/acini, **125**, 632, **917**, 918*f*
ACL (anterior cruciate ligament) injuries, 267, 267*f*, 268
Acne, 159, 170
Acoustic meatus
  external, 206*f*, **207**, 208*f*, 209*f*, **216*t***, 584*f*, **585**
    in relation to temporomandibular joint, 271*f*
  internal, 206*f*, 208*f*, **209**, 216*t*
Acquired immune deficiency syndrome (AIDS), **820–821**
Acquired immunity, 805–806, 806*f*
Acromegaly, **615**, 618*t*
Acromial end (clavicle), **229**, 230*f*, 234*f*, 236*t*
Acromioclavicular joint, 230*f*, **231**, 258*t*
Acromion, 230*f*, **231**, 234*f*, 236*t*, 257*f*, 269*f*
  joint of, 258*t*
Acrosomal reaction, **1115**, 1116*f*
Acrosome, **1077**, 1079, 1079*f*, 1116*f*
ACTH. *See* Adrenocorticotropic hormone
Actin, 52*t*, 90, 139, 282*t*, 285*f*, **286–287**, 286*f*
  in muscle contraction, 293–294, 293*f*–295*f*
Action potentials (APs), **288**, **402**
  as all-or-none event, 406
  in autorhythmic cells, 692–694, 694*f*
  in cardiac muscle, 689–692, 691*f*
  conduction distance in, 414*t*
  conduction velocity of, 407–408, 407*f*
  end plate potential and, 290

function, 414*t*
  generation of, 290–291, 291*f*, 401*f*, 402–404
  neuromuscular junction and, 289–290, 290*f*
  peak membrane potential and, 414*t*
  as positive feedback mechanism, 404, 414*t*
  postsynaptic potentials vs., 414*t*
  propagation of, 290–291, 291*f*, 404–405, 405*f*
    impairment, 408
  refractory periods in, 406–407, 406*f*, 414*t*
  repolarization in, 414*t*
  sarcolemma permeability and, 291, 291*f*
  sliding of myofilaments and, 291–293, 292*f*
  stimulus intensity and, 406, 406*f*
Activation energy in chemical reactions, 54, 54*f*
Active humoral immunity, **805–806**, 806*f*
Active membrane transport, **70**
  active transport, **75–77**
    in absorption of nutrients, 931
    primary, 76*f*, 77
    secondary, 77, 77*f*
    in tubular reabsorption, 1012*f*, **1013**
  energy source/description/ examples, 80*t*
  vesicular transport, **77–81**
    endocytosis, 78–81
    exocytosis, 77–78
Active sites, **52**, 53*f*, 54, 55*f*
Acute respiratory distress syndrome (ARDS), **875**
AD (Alzheimer's disease), 462, **469**
Adaptation, **495**
  to light/dark, 574–575
  olfactory, 580
Adaptive body defenses, 789*f*, **798–799**. *See also* Immune system
Addiction, 424–425*b*
Addison's disease, 158, 627*t*, 629, **630**, 1043, 1045
Adduction (movement), **261**, 262*f*
  of lower limbs, 379–380*t*, 380*f*
  of upper limbs, 362–363*t*, 363*f*
Adductor brevis muscle, 368*f*, **369*t***
  actions of (summary), 379–380*t*, 380*f*
Adductor hallucis muscle, 383*f*, **383*t***
Adductor hiatus, 756*f*, 756*t*, 757*f*
Adductor longus muscle, 331*f*, 368*f*, **369*t***

continues

Adductor longus muscle (*cont.*)
actions of (summary), 379–380*t*, 380*f*
Adductor magnus muscles, 333*f*, 368*f*, 369*t*, 371*f*
actions of (summary), 379–380*t*, 380*f*
tendon, 266*f*
Adductor muscles, 330*f*, **367**, 368*f*, 369*t*
Adductor pollicis muscle, 364*t*, 365*f*
Adductor tubercle, **241**, 241*f*, 243*f*
Adenine (A), **55–57**, 56*f*, 57*t*
Adenocarcinoma, 148
lung, **873**
Adenohypophysis, **612**, 613*f*
Adenoidectomy (adenotonsillectomy), **875**
Adenoids (pharyngeal tonsil), **781–782**, 834*f*, **835**, 875
Adenoma, **148**
colorectal, 146*b*
Adenosine, **418**
Adenosine diphosphate (ADP), 57, 57*f*, **665**
in aerobic cellular respiration, 85
cellular work and, 59, 59*f*
in exchange reaction of ATP and glucose, 38, 38*f*
in muscle contraction, 293, 295*f*, 301–302
in platelet plug formation, 665
in sodium-potassium pump, 76*f*
Adenosine monophosphate (AMP), 57*f*, 59, 59*f*
Adenosine triphosphate (ATP), **57**. *See also* ATP
Adenotonsillectomy (adenoidectomy), **875**
Adenylate cyclase, **607**, 607*f*
Adherence, **790**
Adhesions, scar tissue and, 145
ADH. *See* Antidiuretic hormone
Adipocyte, 131*f*, **132**
Adiponectin, 637*b*
Adipose (fat) cell, 131*f*, **132**
Adipose tissue, **132–133**, 132*f*
ANS effects, 546*t*
brown, **133**
cholesterol and, 980
as connective tissue, 128*f*, 132–133
hormones produced by, 638, 638*t*
in hypodermis, 152, 153*f*
preferred fuel source of, 975*t*
water content, 1036
white, 133
Adolescence
bone growth in, 186–187, 186*f*, 187*f*
body proportions and, 247–248, 248*f*
cartilage growth and, 176
skin changes during, 170
ADP. *See* Adenosine diphosphate
Adrenal cortex. *See* Adrenal glands
Adrenal glands, **626–632**
adrenal cortex, **626–631**
hormones, 627–631, 627*t*
microscopic, 626*f*
adrenal medulla, **626**, 631–632
as an ANS structure, 536*f*, 539*f*, 542, 546*t*, 626, 631–632

hormones, 627*t*, 631–632
microscopic, 626*f*
aging and, 639
kidneys in relation to, 998, 998*f*
stress and, 631, 631*f*, 639
structure of, 626–627, 626*f*
Adrenaline. *See* Epinephrine
Adrenal medulla. *See* Adrenal glands
Adrenergic fibers, **543**
Adrenergic receptors, **543**
locations/effects, 544*t*
thyroid hormone and, 621
Adrenocortical hormones, 48*t*, 626, 627*t*
Adrenocorticotropic hormone (ACTH), **616**
aldosterone release and, 628–629, 628*f*
regulation/effects (summary), 618*t*
Adrenogenital syndrome, 630–631
Adventitia
esophageal, 888, 896*f*
tracheal, 839, 839*f*
ureter, 1024, 1024*f*
vaginal, 1087
Aerobic (cellular) respiration, **302**, 303*f*, 315*t*
Aerobic endurance, **303**
exercise, 307, 309
of skeletal muscle, 303
Aerobic pathways, 306–307, 306*t*, **961**
Afferent arterioles, nephron, **1003**, 1004*f*
Afferent division of PNS. *See* Sensory (afferent) division
Afferent lymphatic vessels, 778*f*, **779**
Afferent pathways, 9*f*, 10
Afferent (sensory) neurons, **395**, 396–397*t*
Afterbirth, **1137**
After-hyperpolarization, **404**
Afterload, 701*f*, **702**
Age-related macular degeneration (ARMD), **599**
Ageusia, **599**
Agglutination, **809**, 809*f*
Agglutinins, **669**, 669*t*
Agglutinogens, **669**, 669*t*
Aging
bone resorption rate, 198
calcified cartilage and, 176
cancer risk and, 145, 146–147*b*
diabetes mellitus risk and, 637*b*
fractures and, 191, 192*t*
muscles and, 318, 320
osteoporosis and, 193–194
skin and, 170–171
smell sense disorders and, 583
"Aging pigment" in neurons, 392
Agonist (prime mover) muscles, **325**
Agranulocytes, 657*f*, **659–660**
summary, 658*t*
Agrin, 316–317
AHF (antihemophilic factor), 663*t*, **668**
AIDS (acquired immune deficiency syndrome), **820–821**
Air-blood barrier, 842, 843*f*
Air cells (mastoid sinuses), **207**
Airway resistance, **849–850**

Alae
ilium, **225**, 225*f*, **237**, 238*f*
nasal, 831, 833*f*
sacral, **225**, 225*f*
Alar plate, **470**, 470*f*
Albinism, **171**
Albumin, 52*t*, **648**, 649*t*
Albuminuria, 1024*t*
Alcohol
blood-brain barrier and, 467
as diuretic, 1021
fetus and, 1130
metabolic acidosis and, 1056*t*
stomach absorption of, 902, 920*t*
Aldosterone, 48*t*, **627–629**, **731**
blood pressure and, 729*t*, 730*f*, 731
in potassium balance, 1048–1049
regulation of, 628–629, 628*f*, 1045*f*
summary, 627*t*
in sodium balance, 1045, 1045*f*
in sodium reabsorption, 1014*t*, 1015
in water reabsorption, 1014*t*, 1015
Aldosteronism, 627*t*, 629
Alertness (consciousness state), 458
Alimentary canal, 883*f*, **884**. *See also* Gastrointestinal (GI) tract
Alkalemia, **1050**
Alkaline phosphatase, 188
Alkaline reserve, **1051**
Alkaline solutions, 42
Alkaline tide, **905**
Alkalosis, 60, **1050**
metabolic, **1055**, 1056*t*
respiratory, **1055**, 1056*t*
using blood values to assess, 1057*b*
Allantois, 1120*f*, **1123**
Alleles, **1146**
dominant, 1150–1151
recessive, 1151
Allergen, **822**
Allergies, **822–823**, 823*f*
hygiene hypothesis of, 824–825*b*
Allografts, **820**
All-or-none phenomenon, **406**
All-*trans* isomer, **571–572**, 571*f*
Alopecia, **162**, 163
Alpha-blocker drugs, 545
Alpha brain waves, **456**, 457*f*, 459, 459*f*
Alpha cells, **632**, 632*f*
Alpha efferent fibers, **522–523**, 522*f*
Alpha globulin, 649*t*
Alpha helix, **50**, 51*f*
Alpha motor neurons, **522–523**, 522*f*–524*f*, 525
Alpha particles, 29–30
Alpha receptors, **543**
ALS (amyotrophic lateral sclerosis), 481
Altitude adjustments in breathing, 870
Alveolar margins
mandible, 206*f*, **211**, 212*f*
maxilla, 206*f*, **212**, 212*f*, 215*f*

Alveolar secretory units of glands, **125**, 126*f*
Alveolar ventilation rate (AVR), **853**, 853*t*
Alveoli (dental), 211, **217***t*
Alveoli (mammary gland), 1089*f*, **1090**
Alveoli (pulmonary), 838*t*, **841–842**, 843*f*
composition of gas in, 855, 855*t*
dead space, 852
ducts, 841*f*, **842**
macrophages, **842**, 843*f*
pores, 841*f*, **842**, 843*f*
sacs, 841*f*, **842**
surface tension of, 850–851
Alzheimer's disease (AD), 426, **469**
Amacrine cells, retinal, 562*f*
Amenorrhea, 1098
Amino acids
absorption of, 928*f*, 930*f*, 931
digestion of, 928*f*, 929
essential, 946, 947*f*
fate in absorptive state, 973–974, 974*f*
functional groups of, 49, 49*f*
hormones based on, 606
metabolism of, 957*f*
as neurotransmitters, 416*t*, 418
nutrient pools, 972–973, 972*f*
oxidation of, 970, 970*f*
peptide bonds and, 49, 49*f*
in protein synthesis, 37, 38*f*, 49, 49*f*, 971
vs. energy expenditure, 946–947
reabsorption of, 1014*t*
structure, 49, 49*f*
Aminoacyl-tRNA synthetase, 108*f*
Aminopeptidase, 928*f*, **929**
Amitotic cells, 391
Ammonia, **41–42**, **970**, 970*f*
Ammonium ions, 42, 1054, 1055*f*
Ammonium salts, in blood plasma, 649*t*
Amniocentesis, **1155–1156**, 1156*f*
Amnion, 1120*f*, 1121*f*, **1122**, 1124*f*, 1125*f*, 1126*f*
Amniotic cavity, 1120*f*, 1121*f*, 1125*f*
Amniotic fluid, **1122**
Amniotic sac, 1121*f*, 1124*f*
Amoeboid motion, 80, 91, **657**
AMP (adenosine monophosphate), 57*f*, 59, 59*f*
Amphetamines, 424–425*b*
Amphiarthroses, **253**, 258*t*, 259*f*
Amphipathic molecules, 47
Amphoteric molecules, **1051**
Amplitude (sound), **589**, 589*f*, 590*f*
Ampulla
semicircular canal, 586*f*, **587**
uterine tube, **1084**, 1085*f*
vas deferens, 1066*f*, **1070**
Amygdala, **454**, 455*f*
memory and, 455
pleasure centers and, 424*b*
Amylase, **918**
Amyotrophic lateral sclerosis (ALS), **481**
Anabolic hormones, 52*t*, 947
Anabolic processes, 37, **956**, 957*f*
Anabolic steroids, misuse/abuse of, **308***b*
Anabolism, 7, **956**

Anaerobic (cellular) respiration, 302, 303f, 315t
Anaerobic glycolysis, 302, 303, 303f, 306, 306f
Anaerobic pathways
  of glycolysis, 960–961, 960f
  of muscle metabolism, 302, 303f
Anaerobic threshold, 303
Anal canal, 922, 923f
Anal columns, 923f, 925
Analgesia, 527
Anal sinuses, 923f, 925
Anal sphincters, 922, 923f, 924
Anaphase, 101, 103f, 1075f, 1076f
Anaphylactic shock, 742, 823
Anaplasia, 112
Anastomoses, 685f, 686, 723, 750f, 756f, 915
Anatomical dead space, 852–853
Anatomical neck of humerus, 231f, 232, 234f
Anatomical position, 12, 13t, 14f
Anatomical terminology, 12–19
  body cavities/membranes, 15, 17–19, 17f–19f
  body planes/sections, 15, 16f
  direction/orientation, 12, 13t
  regional, 12, 14, 14f
Anatomy, 2–3
Anconeus muscle, 356f, 357, 357t, 361f
  actions (summary), 362t
Androgen-binding protein (ABP), 1080, 1081f
Androgens, 630
  adrenal, 1082
  brain-testicular axis and, 1080–1081, 1081f
  hyper-/hyposecretion, 627t, 630–631
  sebum secretion and, 158, 159
  terminal hair response to, 162
Androstenedione, 308b, 630
Anemias, 655, 902
  sickle-cell, 655–656, 656f, 1151
Anemic hypoxia, 860
Anencephaly, 483
Anergy, 802, 814
Anesthetics
  blood-brain barrier and, 467
  propagation of nerve impulses and, 408
Aneurysm, 767
Angina pectoris, 686
Angiogenesis, 736
Angiogram, 767
Angiotensin converting enzyme (ACE), 845, 1009f, 1010
Angiotensin I, 1010
Angiotensin II, 628, 628f, 1010
  blood pressure and, 729t, 730
Angiotensinogen, 628, 628f, 1010
Angle, sternal, 226f, 227
Angular movements, 259, 260–261, 260–262f
Anions, 33
  acids and, 41
  in blood plasma/IF/ICF, 1038f
  reabsorption of, 1014t
  regulation of, 1049
Ankle (talus bone), 244, 245f, 246f, 246t
  joint, 259t
  muscles, 373–378t, 379–380t, 380f

Ankyloglossia, 890
Ankylosing spondylitis, 276
Ankylosis, 274
Annular ligament, 268, 268f
Annular ring, 558, 559f
Anopsias, 502t
Anosmias, 502t, 583
ANP. See Atrial natriuretic peptide
Ansa cervicalis, 340t, 511f, 511t
ANS. See Autonomic nervous system
Antacid, 1061
Antagonist hormones, 611
Antagonist muscles, 325
Antebrachial veins, 762f, 762t, 763f
Antebrachium. See Forearm
Anterior association area. See Prefrontal cortex
Anterior orientation/direction, 13t
Anterior segment (cavity) of eye, 559, 560f, 564f
  chambers of, 564, 564f
Anterograde amnesia, 463
Anterograde movement, 393
Anterolateral pathways, 475–477, 476f, 477t
Antibodies (immunoglobulins), 659, 806–810
  active immunity and, 805–806, 806f
  antigen-binding sites and, 807, 807f
  as blood proteins, 52t, 806
  classes of, 807–808
    characteristics unique to, 808t
  complement activation and, 797–798, 797f
  diversity mechanisms, 808
  functions (summary), 817t
  mechanisms of action, 808–810, 809f
  monoclonal, 810
  as monomer molecules, 807, 807f
  passive immunity and, 806, 806f
  plasma cells as source of, 777, 806
  structure, 807, 807f
  targets, 808–810, 809f
Antibody-mediated immunity. See Humoral immunity
Anticoagulants, 665
Anticodons, 107, 108f, 109, 110f
Antidiuretic hormone (ADH), 10, 613, 613f, 617–620
  blood pressure and, 729t, 730
  concentrated urine and, 1018–1019, 1019f
  hypersecretion, 619–620, 619t
  hyposecretion, 617–619, 619t
  summary of regulation/effects, 619t
  water balance and, 1041, 1041f
Antigen-antibody complex, 797f, 808–809, 809f
Antigen-presenting cells (APCs), 164, 800, 803, 813, 813f
  functions (summary), 817t
Antigens, 799
  antigenic determinants, 799–800, 800f
  binding sites and, 807, 807f
  complete, 799
  endogenous, 811, 812f, 813

exogenous, 813, 813f
  first encounters (antigen challenge), 804
  functions (summary), 817t
  humoral immune response to, 804–810
  immunological memory and, 805
  incomplete, 799
  mechanisms of action against, 797f, 808–809, 809f
  self-antigens, 800
  T cell-independent/dependent, 815
Antihemophilic factor (AHF), 663t, 668
Antimicrobial proteins, 795–798, 796t
  complement, 796–798
  interferons, 795–796
Antioncogenes, 146b
Antioxidants, 952
Antiport system, 76t, 77
Antirachitic factor. See Vitamin D
Antisense RNAs/agents, 109, 719b
Antisterility factor (vitamin E), 48t, 667, 949t
Antithrombin III, 667
Antivenom serum, 806
Antiviral agents, interferons as, 795–796, 795f, 796t
Antrum, 1093f, 1094
Anucleate cells, 95
  erythrocytes as, 649
  platelets as, 662
Anulus fibrosus, 220, 220f
Anuria, 1011
Anus, 883f, 922, 923f
Aorta, 679f, 682f, 683f, 684, 685f
  abdominal, 745f, 746f, 746t, 747f
  ascending, 681f, 746f, 746t, 747f
  blood flow velocity in, 735f
  blood pressure in, 724–725, 725f
  descending (thoracic), 745f, 746f, 746t, 747f
Aortic arch, 681f, 727, 728f, 745f, 746t
Aortic bodies, 729, 866–867, 867f
Aortic impression, 844f
Aortic plexus (abdominal), 538, 539f
Aortic reflex, 728f, 729
Aortic valve, 683f, 687f, 688, 689f
APCs (antigen-presenting cells), 800
Apertures
  cerebral, 434, 434f, 466f
  nasal (choanae), 832, 834f
Apgar score, 1137
Aphasias, 460, 527
Apical foramen, 894f, 895
Apical surface of epithelia, 119, 120f
Aplastic anemia, 655
Apnea, 866
  sleep, 460, 874
Apocrine sweat glands, 126, 158
Apoenzyme, 53
Aponeuroses, 135, 284
  of abdominal wall, 348, 349f
Apoptosis, 111, 146b, 425
  after brain injury, 468
Appendicitis, 922

Appendicular region of body, 12
  lower limbs. See Lower limbs
  upper limbs. See Upper limbs
Appendicular skeleton, 176, 228
  pectoral girdle/upper limbs, 229–237
  pelvic girdle/lower limbs, 237–246
Appendix, 779f, 782, 883f, 922, 923f
  abdominal arteries in relation to, 755f
  inflamed or ruptured, 887, 922
Appetite, 982–984, 983f, 993
Appositional growth of cartilage, 176
APs. See Action potentials
Aquaporin (AQP), 73, 1012–1013
Aqueous humor, 564, 564f
Arachnoid mater (arachnoid), 464–465, 464f
  CSF in relation to, 466f
  spinal, 470, 471f, 473f
Arachnoid villi, 464f, 465
  CSF in relation to, 466f
Arbor vitae, 445f, 453
ARC (arcuate nucleus), 445f, 982, 983f, 984
Arches of foot, 244–245, 245f
  muscles that support, 381–383t
Arcuate arteries, 747f, 756f, 756t, 1000f, 1001, 1004f, 1087, 1087f
Arcuate line, 237, 238f
Arcuate nucleus (ARC), 445f, 982, 983f, 984
Arcuate veins, 1000f, 1001, 1004f
ARDS (acute respiratory distress syndrome), 875
Areola, 1089f, 1090
Areolar connective tissue, 128f, 130f, 131–132, 131f
  "tissue fluid" and, 132–133
Arginine, 947f
Arm
  bone, 231, 231f, 234f, 236f, 236t
  innervation, 513f, 514t
  muscles
    acting on, 353f, 354–356t, 356f, 362–363t, 363f
    superficial, 331f, 333f
ARMD (age-related macular degeneration), 599
Arrector pili muscles, 153f, 161f, 162
  ANS effects, 539f, 546t
Arrhythmias, 694
ART (assisted reproductive technology), 1139–1140, 1140f
Arterial anastomoses, 723
Arteries, 714, 716–723
  blood flow velocity in, 735f
  blood pressure in, 724–725, 725f
  elastic (conducting), 716, 716f, 716t
  major, of systemic circulation, 746t–757t
  muscular (distributing), 716–717, 716f, 717f
  of pulmonary circulation, 744f, 744–745f
  role in blood circulation, 647, 714
  veins vs., 742

Arterioles, 714, 716t, **717**, 717f
blood flow velocity in, 735f
blood pressure in, 725, 725f
nephron, **1003**, 1004f
role in tissue perfusion, 734–736
terminal, 717f, **721**, 721f
Arteriosclerosis, **718**b
Arteriovenous anastomoses, 717f, **723**
Arthritis, **273**–274, 276
gouty, 274, 276
osteoarthritis, 273–274
rheumatoid, 274, 275b, 822
Arthrology, **276**
Arthroscopic surgery, 272, 273f
Articular cartilage, **135**, 176, 177f, 180f, 270f, 271f
in endochondral ossification, 185f, 186
of synovial joints, 255–256, 255f, 268f
Articular discs (menisci), **256**
Articular facets, 221, 222, 222f, 227f
Articular (joint) capsule, 255f, **256**, 257f
Articular processes
sacral, **225**, 225f
vertebral, 220f–224f, **221**, 224t, 258t
Articulations, **253**. See also Joints
Artifacts (tissue specimen), 118
Artificial joints, 275b
Artificially acquired immunity, 805–806, 806f
Arytenoid cartilages, 836f, **837**
Arytenoid muscles, 836f
Ascending (sensory) pathways to brain, 475–478
conscious awareness and, 495–496
general characteristics, 474–475
major spinal cord tracts
ascending and descending, 475f
location/origin/termination/function, 477t
nonspecific, **475**, 476f, 477t
specific, 476f, 477t, **478**
neural integration and, 495–498, 495f
perception and, 494, 495f, 496–498
spinocerebellar tracts and, 475, 475f, 477t
types of neurons in, 475, 476f
Ascites, 915, **937**
Ascorbic acid (vitamin C), **949**t, 952
Aspartate, **418**
Aspiration, **875**
Aspiration pneumonia, 247
Aspirin, **667**, 902, 920t
Assisted reproductive technology (ART), 1139–1140, 1140f
Association areas of cerebral cortex, 436, 437f, 440–441
Association fibers, in white matter, 442f, **443**
Association neurons (interneurons), **395**, 396–397t, 397
Aster, 102f
Asthma, 823, 824–825b, **872**
Astigmatism, **568**
Astrocytes, **390**–391, 390f

Asystole, **709**
Atelectasis, **847**
Atherosclerosis, **709**
fibrous plaques, 718b
onset/stages, 718–719b
therapy/prevention, 719b
Athlete's anemia, **655**
Atlanto-axial joint, 258t
Atlanto-occipital joint, 258t
Atlas (C1), **221**, 222f, 223f, 258t
Atmospheric pressure, 8, **846**
alveolar gases vs., 854, 855t
Atomic mass unit, 28
Atomic number, **28**–29
Atomic symbol, **27**
Atomic weight, **29**
Atoms, 3, **27**–30, 27f
chemically inert, 32–33, 32f
structure, 27–30, 27f, 28f
orbital vs. planetary model, 27f, **28**
Atonic bladder, **551**
ATP, 57, 418, **943**
aerobic respiration and, 85, 302, 303f
in cellular metabolism, 7, 38, 38f, 39, 57, 59, 59f
as chemical energy, 25
dietary carbohydrates and, 46
in DNA translation, 107, 108f
in exchange reactions, 38, 38f, 39
glucose and, 72
major pathways of forming, 306–307, 306t
in membrane transport, 70, 75, 76f, 77, 77f, 78, 80t
as metabolic fuel, **943**
overview, 956–959, 957f
motor proteins and, 92, 92f
in muscle contraction
skeletal, 292f, 293–294, 295f, 300–304, 303f
smooth, 311–312, 313f
as neurotransmitter, 416t, 418
protein degradation reactions and, 110
regeneration methods, 301–304, 303f
sodium-potassium pump and, 76f, 77, 77f
stored, 300–301
structure of, 57, 57f
summary of production, 965–966, 966f
synthesis
by oxidative phosphorylation, 958f, **959**, 959f, 966, 966f
sites of, 85, 94t, 959f
by substrate-level phosphorylation, **958**–960, 958f–960f
summary, 965–966, 966f
ATP synthases, 958f, 959, **965**, 965f
Atria, 680, 681f–683f, 683, 684f, 685f
Atrial (Bainbridge) reflex, **702**
Atrial natriuretic peptide (ANP), 628f, **629**, 637, 638f
blood pressure and, 729t, 730, 731f
sodium balance influenced by, 1047, 1047f
source/trigger/effects, 638t
Atrioventricular (AV) bundle, **693**–694, 694f

Atrioventricular (AV) node, **693**–694, 694f
Atrioventricular (AV) valves, 683f, **686**, 687f, 688f
Atrioventricular groove (coronary sulcus), 680, 681f, 682f
Atrium (embryonic), **705**
Atrophy, **111**, 309
Attachments (muscle), 283–284
Auditory association area, 437f, **440**
Auditory canal, 584f, **585**
Auditory cortex (primary), 437f, **440**, 592f, **593**
Auditory nerve. See Vestibulocochlear nerve
Auditory ossicles, **217**t, 584f, **585**–586, 585f
Auditory (pharyngotympanic) tube, 584f, **585**, 585f, 834f, 835
Auditory reflex center, 592f, 593
Auras
olfactory, 583
seizure, **457**
Auricle
ear, 583, 584f, 585
heart, **680**, 681f, 682f
Auricular nerve, 511f, 511t
Auricular surface
iliac, **237**, 238f, 243f
sacral, **225**, 225f
Auricular veins, 761f
Auscultation, 2–3
to measure blood pressure, **732**
Autism, **485**
Autocrines, **606**
Autografts, **818**, 820
Autoimmune diseases, **821**–822
Autoimmunity, **821**
Autologous transfusions, **670**
Autolysis, **89**
Automaticity of cardiac muscle contraction, **690**–692
Autonomic dysreflexia, 551
Autonomic nervous system (ANS), **388**, 389t, 532–554, **533**
aging and, 551
control hierarchy in, 547, 547f, 550
developmental aspects, 551
embryonic, 1123–1128, 1130t
fetal, 1132t, 1133
disorders, 550–551
hypothalamus and, 446, 547, 547f, 550
interactions of divisions, 544–547, 550
as involuntary system, 388, 389f, 533
parasympathetic division, **389**, **535**. See also Parasympathetic division
physiology, 543–547, 550
somatic nervous system vs., 533–534, 534f
sympathetic division, **388**, **535**. See also Sympathetic division
Autonomic (visceral) reflexes, **521**–522, 542, 542f
Autopsy, 148
Autoregulation of blood flow, **734**–736, 736f
Autorhythmic cardiac cells, **692**–694, 693f, 694f
Autorhythmicity, **690**

Autosomes, **1101**, **1146**
AV (atrioventricular) bundle, **693**–694, 694f
AV (atrioventricular) node, **693**–694, 694f
AV (atrioventricular) valves, 683f, **686**, 687f
Avogadro's number, **31**
Axial skeleton, **176**, **203**–228, 204f
bony thorax, **226**–228
joints of, 253
skull, 203–218
vertebral column, **218**–225
Axillary arteries, 746f, 747f, 749f, 750f, **750**t, 751f
Axillary nerve, **512**, 513f, 514t
muscles served by, 355t
Axillary veins, 758f, 759f, 762f, **762**t, 763f
Axis (C2), **222**, 222f, 223f, 258t
Axis of body, 12
Axoaxonic synapses, 408, 409f
Axodendritic synapses, **408**, 409f
Axolemma, **393**
Axon, 139, 289, 392, 392f, **393**
anterograde transport and, 393
autonomic motor, 519
in bipolar/multipolar/unipolar neurons, 396t
diameter variations in, 407
in motor unit, 296–297, 296f
myelinated fibers and, **394**–395, 394f
conduction speed and, 408
in neuromuscular junctions, 289, 290f, 296f
retrograde transport and, 393–394
Schwann cells in relationship to, 394, 394f
Axon collateral, **393**
Axon hillock, 392f, **393**
Axon terminal, 290f, 292f, 296f, 315t, **393**
in chemical synapses, 409–411, 410f
peripheral motor endings and, 519
Axosomatic synapses, **408**, 409f
Azygos system, 745f, 758f, **762**f, 763f
Azygos vein, 762f, **762**t

Babinski's sign, **527**
Baby (deciduous) teeth, 893, 893f
Back
innervation, 511f, 511t
muscles
intrinsic, 343f, 343–344t, 345f
superficial, 332f, 342
Bainbridge (atrial) reflex, **702**
Balance sense. See Equilibrium
Baldness, 162
Ball-and-socket joint, 258t, 259t, 264f, **265**
Balloon angioplasty, 719b
"Bandage" muscle, 343f
Band cells, **660**, 661f
Baroreceptors, 702, **727**
locations, 727, 728f
reflexes initiated by, 727–729, 728f, 731f
role in sodium balance, 1045–1046
Barrett's esophagus, **937**

Basal bodies (centrioles), 66*f*, 85, **92**–**93**, 92*f*, **93**
  structure/functions (summary), 94*t*
Basal cell carcinoma, **165**, 166*f*
Basal cells
  gustatory, **581**–**582**, 581*f*
  olfactory, **578**, 579*f*
Basal ganglia. *See* Basal nuclei
Basal lamina of epithelia, **119**
Basal layer of skin, **153**–**154**, 154*f*
Basal metabolic rate (BMR), **984**–**985**
  aging and, 639
  ANS effects, 546*t*
  problems with fast/slow, 985
  testosterone's effects, 1082
  thyroid hormone's effects, 621, 621*t*, 985
Basal nuclei, **443**, 444*f*
  disorders, 443
  embryonic origins, 432*f*, 433
  functions (summary), 453*t*
  memory and, 462*f*, 463
  sensorimotor integration/control and, **520**–**521**, 520*f*
  substantia nigra and, 449
Basal plate (embryonic spinal cord), **470**, 470*f*
Basal surface of epithelia, **119**, 120*f*
Basement membrane, 70*f*, **119**, 121*f*–124*f*
Bases, **41**–**43**
  in buffer systems, 1050–1052
  pH scale, 42, 42*f*
  strong/weak, **43**
Basic electrical rhythm (BER), **907**
Basilar artery, 748*f*, **748**–**749***t*, 749*f*
Basilar membrane, **587**, 588*f*
  resonance of, 591, 591*f*
Basilic vein, 762*f*, **762***t*, 763*f*
Basioccipital plate, 207, 208*f*
Basket cells, **452**, 452*f*
Basophils, 657*f*, 659*f*
  in allergies, 822, 823*f*
  summary, 658*t*
B cells. *See* B lymphocytes
Bell's palsy, 505*t*
Benign prostatic hyperplasia (BPH), **1071**
BER (basic electrical rhythm), 907
Beta amyloid peptide, 469
Beta brain waves, **456**, 457*f*
Beta-carotene, 948
Beta cells, **632**, 632*f*
Beta endorphin, **418**
Beta globulin, as blood plasma protein, 649*t*
Beta oxidation, **968**, 968*f*, 969*f*, 971*t*
Beta particle emissions, 29–30
Beta-pleated sheet, **50**, 51*f*
Beta receptors, **543**
Biaxial body movement, **259**
Bicarbonate buffer system, 863, **1050**–**1051**
Bicarbonate ions, **41**, **861**, 862*f*
  in blood plasma/IF/ICF, 1038*f*
  in chemical buffer systems, 1050–1052
  generating new, 1053–1054, 1054*f*
  reabsorption, 1053, 1053*f*
  respiratory regulation of, 1052
  secretion, 1054

Biceps brachii muscle, 356*f*, **357**, 357*t*, 359*f*
  actions (summary), 362–363*t*, 363*f*
  superficial, 330*f*, 331*f*
Biceps femoris muscle, 371*f*, 372*t*
  actions of (summary), 379*t*
  superficial, 332*f*, 333*f*
Bicipital groove, 231*f*, **232**, 234*f*, 236*t*
Bicuspid (mitral) valve, 683*f*, **686**, 687*f*
  prolapse, **709**
Bile, **915**, 920*t*
  gallbladder storage/release, 916–917
  mechanisms promoting secretion, 916*f*
  in urine, 1024*t*
Bile canaliculi, 914*f*, **915**
Bile duct, 909*f*, **912**, 913*f*, 914*f*
Bile salts, **916**, 916*f*
  location/function in body, 48*t*
  role in fat emulsification, 930, 930*f*
Biliary calculi (gallstones), **917**
Bilirubin, **654**–**655**, 654*f*, **916**
Bilirubinuria, 1024*t*
Biochemistry, **40**–**59**
  inorganic compounds, **40**–**43**
  organic compounds, **40**, **43**–**59**
Biofeedback techniques, **550**
Biogenic amines, 415*t*, **418**
Biological clock, 446, 459, 635
Biological colloids, 40
Biologic response modifiers, 274
Biology, molecular, 2
Biopsy, **147***b*
Bipennate muscle, 326, 327*f*
Bipolar cells, retinal, **562**, 562*f*, 570*f*
Bipolar neurons, **395**, 396–397*t*
Birth canal. *See* Vagina
Birth control, 1128–1129*b*
  lactation and, 1139
Birth (parturition), **1135**–**1137**, 1135*f*, 1136*f*
Blanching (pallor), 158
Blastocyst, **1118**, 1118*f*
  formation, 1117–1119, 1118*f*
Bleaching of the pigment, 571*f*, **572**
Bleeding disorders, **667**, 668
Blepharitis, **599**
Blepharospasm, 156*b*
Blindness
  color, **572**
  night, 575
Blind spot (optic disc), 560*f*, **562**–**563**, 562*f*, 563*f*
Blisters, 157
Blood, **137**–**139**, 138*f*, 646–676, **647**
  as agent of heat exchange, 649, 738, 986
  aging and, 672–673
  artificial, 672–673*b*
  as biological colloid, 40
  components, 647–648, 647*f*
    erythrocytes, **649**–**656**
    leukocytes, **656**–**662**
    plasma, **648**–**649**
    platelets, **662**
  as connective tissue, 127, 128*f*, 137, 647
  developmental aspects, 672–673
  embryonic, 128*f*, 672

diagnostic tests of, 671–672
distribution functions of, 648
fibers of, 139
formed elements, 647, 647*f*, 649–662
  summary, 658*t*
functions, 127, 128*f*, 139, 648
interstitial fluid derived from, 70
matrix components, 128*f*, 137, 138*f*
oxygen transport by, 858–861
pH variations and, 43
physical characteristics, 648
poisoning, 674
protective functions of, 648
regulatory functions of, 648
role in circulation, 647
substitutes, 672–673*b*
transfusions, 668–671, 823
viscosity of, 650, **723**–**724**
Blood-brain barrier, **467**, 720
Blood chemistry tests, **673**
Blood clotting (coagulation), **665**–**667**
  ANS effects, 546*t*
  anticoagulants, **665**
  clot retraction/repair, 666
  clotting factors, **665**
    nature/origin/function/pathway, 663*t*
  events of, 664*f*
  extrinsic/intrinsic pathways, 664*f*, 665–666
  factors limiting clot formation, 666–667
  fibrinolysis, **666**
  positive feedback mechanism regulating, 10–11, 12*f*
Blood doping, **656**
Blood flow, **723**. *See also* Tissue perfusion
  blood pressure, resistance and, 724
  to brain, 734*f*, 737
  heart and, 738
  lungs and, 738
  at rest/during exercise, 734, 734*f*
  to skeletal muscles, 734*f*, 737
  skin and, 737–738
  through capillaries, 738–740
  velocity of, 734, 735*f*
Blood fraction, **673**
Blood groups
  ABO, **669**, 669*t*, 1151, 1151*t*
  Rh, **669**–**670**
Blood islands, 672, **743**
Blood pressure (BP), **723**, 724–733
  aging and, 743
  antidiuretic hormone release and, 730, 730*f*, 1041, 1041*f*
  arterial, **724**–**725**, 725*f*, 731*f*
  blood flow, peripheral resistance and, 724
  capillary, **725**, 725*f*
  circulatory efficiency and, 732
  developmental aspects, 743
  diastolic, **725**, 725*f*
  extrinsic factors affecting, 732
  high (hypertension), **733**
  low (hypotension), 732–733
  maintaining
    blood volume and, 726–731
    cardiac output and, 726–731
    factors causing increase in MAP, 731*f*

hormonal controls, 729–730, 729*t*
  influence of higher brain centers on, 729
  long-term control mechanisms, 730–731
  neural controls, 727–729
  peripheral resistance and, 726–731
  peripheral resistance and, blood flow and, 724
  reflexes that regulate, 727–729
  renal regulation, 730–731, 1010–1011
  short-term control mechanisms, 727–730
  vasomotor center role in, 727–729
  measuring, **732**
    cuff (sphygmomanometer), 732
  pulse pressure and, **725**, 732, 732*f*
  systolic, **725**, 725*f*
  thyroid hormone's effects on, 621, 621*t*
  venous, **725**–**726**, 726*f*
Blood reservoirs, 717*f*, **722**
Blood sinusoids, 651
Blood sugar. *See* Glucose
Blood-testis barrier, **1079**
Blood-thymus barrier, 781
Blood vessels, 713–772, **714**
  aging and, 743
  anatomy, 714–723
    diameters/tissue makeup, 716*t*
    arteries, **714**, 715*f*, 716–723
      of pulmonary circulation, 744*f*, 744–745*t*
      of systemic circulation, 746*t*–757*t*
  in bone, 137
  developmental aspects, 743
    embryonic, 1122, 1130*t*
  length of, 731*f*
  lymphatic vessel relationship to, 717*f*
  parasympathetic effects, 546*t*
  peripheral resistance and, 723–724
  in pregnancy, 1135
  relationship of vessels to one another, 717*f*
  relative proportion of blood volume, 717*f*
  sympathetic effects, 539*f*, 546*t*, 714
  tissue perfusion and, 733–742
  veins, **714**, 715*f*, 722–723
    of pulmonary circulation, 744*f*, 744–745*t*
    of systemic circulation, 758*t*–766*t*
  wall structure, 714, 715*f*
Blood volume, 10, 648
  antidiuretic hormone release and, 1041, 1041*f*
  blood pressure and, 726–731, 731*f*
  dermal vascular supply and, 165
  hormones influencing, 729*t*
  hypovolemic shock and, **740**–**742**, 741*f*, 1042
  restoring, 671
B lymphocytes (B cells), **777**, **800**
  antigen challenge and, 804
  as antigen-presenting cells, 803
         continues

B lymphocytes (B cells) (cont.)
  development of
    immunocompetence in,
      800–802, 801f
  functions (summary), 817t
  in humoral immune response,
    804–810
BMI (body mass index), 990b
BMP (bone morphogenic protein),
  179, 195b
BMR. See Basal metabolic rate
Body cavities, 15, 17f, 18f, 19, 19f
Body defense systems, 52t,
  788–829. See also Immune
  system
  adaptive, 798–825
  innate, 789–798
  overview, 789f
Body fluids, 41, 111. See also
  Fluids of body
Body heat, 164. See also Body
  temperature
  blood as agent of, 649, 738, 986
  distributed by plasma, 649
  generated by muscle
    contraction, 281, 985
  heat exhaustion, 989
  thyroid hormone's role in, 621
Body mass index (BMI), 990b
Body planes/sections, 15, 16f
Body temperature
  BMR and, 985
  core, 986
  food ingestion/fasting and,
    983, 985
  mechanisms of heat exchange,
    986–987, 986f
  muscle contraction's role in,
    281, 985
  normal, 8, 985
  oxygen-hemoglobin
    dissociation curve and,
      859–860, 860f
  regulation
    heat-loss mechanisms,
      988–989, 988f
    heat-promoting mechanisms,
      987–988, 988f
    hypothalamic, 446,
      987–989, 988f
  at rest/during activity, 985
  shell, 987
  thyroid hormone effects, 621t
Bohr effect, 860
Boils, 171
Bolus of food, 890
Bone morphogenic protein (BMP),
  179, 195b
Bone (osseous tissue), 137, 138f
  blood vessels in, 137, 138f
  calcium (bone) salts in, 137
  collar, 180, 184f, 185, 185f
  as connective tissue, 127, 128f,
    137, 138f
  embryonic origins, 127, 128f
  functions, 127, 137
  marrow, 180, 180f, 181,
    183f, 651
    biopsy, 673
    as primary lymphoid organ,
      800, 801f
  matrix, 128f, 137, 138f, 179,
    181–182
    in bone resorption, 188
    in endochondral ossification,
      185, 185f

    in intramembranous
      ossification, 184f
    in osteoporosis, 193
    Pagetic, 195
    resorption processes, 188
Bones
  aging and, 192t, 193–194, 198
  of appendicular skeleton,
    176–178, 177f
  artificial, 195b
  of axial skeleton, 176–178,
    176, 177f
  chemical composition of,
    182–184
  classes of, 177, 178f
  density of
    leptin and, 190
    osteoporosis, 193–195,
      193f, 248
    statin drugs and, 194
  deposit, 188, 193–195, 198
  developmental schedule,
    198, 198f
  formation of, 184–186,
    198, 198f
  functions of, 178–179
  growth
    hormonal regulation, 187
    over lifetime, 247, 248f
    postnatal, 184, 186–187
  homeostasis, 187–193
    imbalances, 193–195, 198
    remodeling, 188–190, 193
    repair, 190–191, 193
    repair, clinical advances in,
      194–195b
    repair, fracture types,
      190–191, 192t, 193
  markings, 179, 179t
  responses to mechanical stress,
    190, 190f
  structure of, 179–184
Bony (hard) callus, 191,
  191f, 193
Bony (osseous) labyrinth,
  586–587, 586f
Bony pelvis, 237, 238f
Bony spur, 199
Bony thorax (thoracic cage), 203,
  204f, 226–228
Botulism
  immunity and, 806
  wrinkle therapy and, 156b
Boutons, 393. See also
  Axon terminal
Bovine spongiform encephalopathy
  (BSE), 482–483b
Bowman's (glomerular) capsule,
  1001, 1002f, 1004f
Boyle's law, 847
BPH (benign prostatic
  hyperplasia), 1071
Brachial arteries, 747f, 750f,
  750t, 751f
Brachialis muscle, 356f, 357,
  357t, 357t
  actions (summary), 362–363t,
    363f
  superficial, 331f, 333f
Brachial plexus, 509f,
  512–514, 513f
  nerves/structures served, 514t
Brachial veins, 759f, 762f,
  762t, 763f
Brachiocephalic trunk, 681f,
  746f–751f, 746t

Brachiocephalic veins, 758f, 758t,
  759f, 761f, 762f, 762t, 763f
Brachioradialis muscle, 356f, 357,
  357t, 359f, 361f
  actions (summary),
    362–363t, 363f
  superficial, 330f, 331f, 333f
Brachytherapy, 719b
Bradycardia, 704
Bradykinins, 496b
  source/effects, 793t
Brain, 388, 389f, 431–456
  arteries, 748–749t, 749f
  blood-brain barrier and, 467
  blood flow through, 737
  brain stem, 447–451
  cerebellum, 451–454
  cerebral hemispheres, 434–443
  in CNS's arrangement of
    gray/white matter,
    433, 433f
  cranial cavity and, 203
  developmental aspects, 481
    embryonic, 431–433
  diencephalon, 443–447
  disorders
    degenerative, 469–470
    functional, 485
    traumatic, 467–469
  fasting's effects on, 977
  higher mental functions
    brain wave patterns, 456–457
    consciousness, 457–458
    language, 460
    sleep, 458–460
  injuries, 467, 468
  insulin's role in, 633
  limbic system, 454–455
  preferred fuel source of, 975t
  protective devices
    blood-brain barrier, 467
    cerebrospinal fluid, 465–467
    cranial bones, 203–211
    meninges, 463–464
  regions, 432f, 433
  reticular formation, 455–456
  spinal cord pathways to,
    475–478
    ascending, 475f, 476f, 477t
    descending, 475f, 478, 479t
  thermoregulatory centers, 987
  veins, 758f, 758t, 760f,
    760–761t, 761f
  ventricles, 433–434
Brain death, 457, 458
Brain stem, 445f, 447–451
  in ANS control hierarchy, 547,
    547f, 550
  cerebral hemispheres in relation
    to, 435f
  diencephalon in relation to,
    448–449f
  embryonic origins, 432f, 433
  functions (summary), 453t
  gray matter and, 447
  gray/white matter arrangement
    in, 433, 433f
  injuries, hypoventilation
    and, 1056t
  medulla oblongata, 447,
    449f, 451
  midbrain, 445f, 447, 447f,
    448–449, 449f, 450f, 453t
  nuclei of importance, 450f
  pons, 447, 449, 449f,
    450f, 451

Brain-testicular axis,
  1080–1081, 1081f
Brain vesicles
  primary, 431, 432f, 433
  secondary, 432f, 433
Brain wave patterns,
  456–457, 457f
Branchial groove, 599
BRCA1/BRCA2 genes, 1090
Breast milk, advantages,
  1138–1139
Breasts, 1089–1090, 1089f
  cancer, 1090
Breathing, 846–854
  airway resistance, 849–850, 850f
  alveolar surface tension and,
    850–851
  apneurstic, 864
  atmospheric pressure and,
    846–847, 846f
  Cheyne-Stokes, 875
  conscious controls over, 868
  exercise adjustments, 869–870
  first breath, 874, 1137–1138
  forced, 346, 849
  high altitude adjustments, 870
  hypothalamic controls, 868
  inflation reflex and, 869
  influences on rate/depth,
    865–869
  irritants and, 868–869
  lung compliance and, 851
  muscles of, 346t, 347f, 847–849
  neural controls, 863–865
  nonrespiratory air movements,
    854, 854t
  physical factors influencing,
    849–850
  pressure relationships,
    846–847, 846f
  pulmonary function tests, 853
  respiratory volumes and,
    851–853
  rhythm of, 864–865
  scuba diving and, 868–869b
  thoracic volume changes
    during, 848f
Breech presentation, 1137
Brittle bone disease, 199
Broad ligament, 1083, 1085f
Broca's area, 437f, 439
  language and, 460
Brodmann areas, 436, 437f
Bronchi, 844f
  primary, 832f, 840–841, 840f
  secondary (lobar), 840–841, 840f
  tertiary (segmental),
    840–841, 840f
Bronchial arteries, 746f, 751t, 845
Bronchial tree, 840–842, 845f
  features/functions, 838t
  structures
    conducting zone,
      840–841, 840f
    respiratory zone,
      841–842, 841f
Bronchial veins, 763t
Bronchioles, 841f, 842
  terminal, 841f, 842
Bronchitis, chronic, 871
Bronchomediastinal lymphatic
  trunks, 775, 776f
Bronchopulmonary dysplasia, 851
Bronchopulmonary segments, of
  lung lobes, 842, 844f
Bronchoscopy, 875

Bronzing of skin, 158
Brown fat (adipose) tissue, **133**
Bruises, 158
Brunner's glands (duodenal glands), 910*f*, **911**
Brush border, 119, **909–910**, 910*f*, 911*f*
Brush border enzymes, **910**
    in chemical digestion, 928*f*, 929
Bruxism, **937**
BSE (bovine spongiform encephalopathy), 482–483*b*
Buboes, 779
Buccal cavity. *See* Oral cavity
Buccal glands. *See* Salivary glands
Buccal phase of deglutition, **898**, 898*f*
Buccinator muscles, 336*t*, 337*f*, **338**, 338*t*, 339*f*, 890
    chewing and, 336*t*, 339*f*
    swallowing and, 340, 341*f*
Buffers, 43, 52*t*
    chemical, **1051**
Buffer systems
    bicarbonate, 863, 1050–1051
    phosphate, 1051
    physiological, 1052
    protein, 1051–1052
Buffy coat, **647**, 647*f*
Bulbar conjunctiva, 557, 557*f*, 564*f*
Bulbospongiosus muscle, **350**, 350*t*, 351*f*
Bulbourethral glands/ducts, 1066, 1066*f*, 1070*f*, **1072**
Bulbs of vestibule, 1088*f*, **1089**
Bulbus cordis, **705**
Bulimia, **937**
Bundle branches, 693, 694*f*
Bundle of His (AV bundle), **693**, 694*f*
Burns, **166–167**, 167*f*, 170
Bursae, **257**, 257*f*, 265, 266*f*, 267
Bursitis, **273**

Cadherins, 83
Caffeine, 1021
Calcaneal (Achilles) tendon, 244, 245*f*, 333*f*, 377*f*, 378*f*, 382*f*
    rupture of, **384**
Calcaneal tuberosity, **244**, 245*f*, 382*f*
Calcaneus, **244**, 245*f*, 246*f*, 246*t*, 377*f*, 378*f*
Calcarine sulcus, 437*f*, 440
Calcification zone, 186–187, 186*f*
Calcitonin, **188–189**, 189*f*, **624**
Calcitriol, 625, **638**
Calcium, 26*t*, 952*t*
    amount recycled in adult skeleton/day, 187
    blood clotting and, 663*t*
    in blood plasma/IF/ICF, 1038*f*
    bone as storage reservoir for, 179
    in bone matrix, 137, 183, 293
    in bone remodeling, 188–189, 189*f*
    bone salts, 41
    in cardiac/skeletal/smooth muscle, 315*t*
    channels, 409–410, 410*f*
    dietary, 193, 952*t*
        absorption of, 932, 933
        problems with excesses/deficits, 952*t*
        recommended daily amounts, 952*t*
        vitamin D and, 933, 952*t*

    in electrolyte balance, 1044*t*, 1049
    in heart conduction system, 692–694, 694*f*
    importance in body, 188, 293, 952*t*
    membrane transport mechanisms and, 77
    in muscle contraction, 289–295, 294*f*, 297
        smooth muscle, 310, 312, 313*f*
        treppe and, 299
    percentage of body mass, 26*t*
    reabsorption of, 1014*t*
    as second messenger, 420, 420*f*
Calcium blood levels, 188–189, 189*f*
    after brain injury, 468–469
    imbalances in, 704, 1044*t*
Calculus, **895**
Callus
    in fracture healing, **191**, 191*f*
    friction, 152
Calmodulin, **293**, 312, 313*f*, 315*t*, 608*f*, **609**
Calories (kilocalories), **943**
Calorigenic effect, **621**
Calorimeter, **984**
Calsequestrin, **293**
Calvaria (cranial vault), 203
Calyces, **1000**, 1000*f*
cAMP response-element binding protein (CREB), 463
CAMs (cell adhesion molecules), 68*f*, **83**, 91, 127, 794
Canaliculi, **182**, 183*f*
    bile, 914*f*, **915**
Canal of Schlemm (scleral venous sinus), 560*f*, **564**, 564*f*
Cancellous (spongy) bone, **179–180**, 187
    as connective tissue, 128*f*
    in endochondral ossification, 185–186, 185*f*
    in flat bones, 181, 181*f*
    structure, 180*f*, 181*f*, 182, 183*f*
Cancer
    adenocarcinoma, 148, 873
    aging tissues and, 145, 146–147*b*
    basal cell carcinoma, **165**, 166*f*
    bladder, **1030–1031**
    cellular contact inhibition and, 101
    cervical, 1086
    colon, development of, 147*b*
    diagnosis, 146–147*b*
    endometrial, **1108**
    lung, 872–873
    mechanisms of, 146*b*
    melanoma, **166**, 166*f*
    prevalence, 146*b*
    skin, 165–166, 165*f*
    squamous cell carcinoma, **166**, 166*f*
    staging, 146–147*b*
    testicular, 1069
    therapies, 147*b*
    vaccine, 147*b*
Canine teeth, 893*f*, **894**
Canthi (commissures), **556**, 557*f*
Capacitance current, 401–402
Capacitance vessels, 717*f*, **722**
Capacitation, **1115**

Capillaries, 714, 715*f*, 716*t*, 717*f*, **720–723**
    blood flow through, 738–740
    blood pressure in, 725, 725*f*
    colloid osmotic pressure and, 739–740
    exchange of
        nutrients/respiratory gases in, 738–740, 856*f*, 858
        fluid flows, 740*f*
        transport mechanisms, 739*f*
    fenestrated, **720–721**, 720*f*
    hydrostatic pressure and, 75, 75*t*, 739–740, 1042
    lymphatic, 717*f*, **774–775**, 774*f*
        blood capillaries and, 774*f*
    in respiratory membrane, 843*f*
    role in circulation of blood, 647, 720
    structure, 720, 720*f*
    true, **721**, 721*f*
    types of, 720–721, 720*f*
    velocity of blood flow in, 735*f*
Capillary beds, **721–722**, 721*f*, 745*f*
    glomerulus, 1003, 1004*f*
    peritubular, **1003**, 1004*f*
    pulmonary circuit and, 684*f*
    systemic circuit and, 684*f*
Capillary plexuses, 613*f*, **614**
Capitate bone, **235**, 235*f*, 236*f*, 236*t*
Capitulum, 231*f*, **232**, 234*f*, 236*t*
Capsular hydrostatic pressure, **1008**, 1008*f*
Capsular (intrinsic) ligaments, **256**
Capsular space, glomerular, **1001**, 1002*f*, 1005*f*
Caput medusae, 915
Carbaminohemoglobin, 650, **861**, 862*f*
Carbides, 43–44
Carbohydrates, **44–46**
    absorption, 928*f*, 931
    as cellular fuel source, 46
    classification of, 44, 45*f*
    dietary requirements, 944, 945*t*
    digestion, 927, 928*f*, 929
    fate in absorptive (fed) state, 973–974, 974*f*
    food/dietary sources, 944, 945*t*
    functions, 46
    metabolism, 956–967
        gluconeogenesis, 967
        glucose oxidation, 959–966
        glycogenesis, 966–967
        glycogenolysis, 967
        interconversion and, 972*f*, 973
        summary, 971*t*
        thyroid hormone's effects, 621*t*
    nutrient pools of, 971, 972*f*, **973**
    problems with excesses/deficits, 945*t*
    recommended dietary allowance, 945*t*
    uses in body, 46, 944
Carbon
    electroneutrality of, 44
    functions in body, 26*t*
    isotopes, 29
    organic/inorganic compounds and, 43–44
    percentage of body mass, 26*t*
    as reactive element, 32, 32*f*
Carbon dioxide
    in cellular respiration, 38, 1052
    influence on blood pH, 863, 1052

    influence on breathing rate/depth, 865–866
    as inorganic compound, 43–44
    molecular models of, 36*f*
    transport and exchange, 71, 75*t*, 861–862, 862*f*
        erythrocytes and, 650
        Haldane effect and, **863**, 863*f*
        summary, 862*f*
Carbonic acid, 41, 1050–1051
    renal controls of, 1052–1054
    respiratory controls of, 1052
Carbonic acid–bicarbonate buffer system, 863, **1050–1051**
Carbonic anhydrase, **861**, 862*f*
Carbon monoxide, 43–44
    as neurotransmitter, 417*t*, **419**
    poisoning, 861
Carboxypeptidase, **918**, 918*f*, 928*f*, **929**
Carbuncles, **171**
Carcinoembryonic antigen (CEA), 147*b*
Carcinogenesis, mechanisms of, 146*b*
Carcinogens, 146*b*
Carcinoma, **148**
    adenocarcinoma, 148
    basal cell, **165**, 166*f*
    colon, 146*b*
    small cell, 873
    squamous cell, **166**, 166*f*, **873**
Cardia (cardiac region) of stomach, **899–900**, 899*f*
Cardiac catheterization, **709**
Cardiac centers, medullary, 451, 550
Cardiac conduction system, 315*t*, **692–695**, 694*f*
Cardiac cycle, **698**, 699*f*, 700
Cardiac (gastroesophageal) sphincter, **897**, 898, 898*f*
Cardiac muscle, **139**, 140*f*, 141
    age-related changes in, 708–709
    autorhythmicity of, 690–692
    contraction mechanisms, 690–692, 691*f*
        regulation of, 315*t*
    embryonic origins, 317
    energy requirements, 692
    fibrosis, 708–709
    microscopic anatomy, 314*t*, 690*f*
    myofibrils and, 314*t*, 689
    organ vs. motor unit contraction in, 690–691
    preferred fuel source of, 975*t*
    properties of, 689–690, 690*f*
    refractory periods of, 691, 691*f*
    regenerative capacity, 144, 317
    stretch and, 700–701, 701*f*
    tissue, **280**
    T tubules and, 314*t*, 689–690, 690*f*
    vs. skeletal muscle, 314–315*t*, 689–692
    vs. smooth muscle, 314–315*t*
Cardiac notch, **842**, 844*f*
Cardiac orifice, **897**
Cardiac output, **700–703**
    blood pressure and, 726–731
    disorders, 704–705
    factors influencing, 703*f*, 726, 727*f*, 729*t*
Cardiac plexuses, 537*f*, **538**, 539*f*

Cardiac region (cardia), of stomach, **899**–900, 899f
Cardiac reserve, **700**, 708
Cardiac tamponade, 678
Cardiac veins, 681f, 682f, 685f, **686**, 759f
Cardinal (cervical) ligaments of uterus, 1085f, **1086**
Cardioacceleratory center, **695**, 695f
Cardioinhibitory center, **695**, 695f
Cardiovascular center, 451
　blood pressure and, **727**–729, 728f
Cardiovascular system, 6, 6f
　aging, 708–709, 743
　blood vessels, 713–772. *See also* Blood vessels
　　anatomy, 714–723
　　circulatory dynamics, 723–742
　　major arteries/veins, 742–766
　developmental aspects
　　blood vessels, 743
　　embryonic, 1128–1130, 1130t
　　fetal, 1128–1130, 1131f, 1132t, 1133
　　heart, 705–709
　digestive system and, 934b, 935b
　endocrine system and, 640b
　heart, 677–712. *See also* Heart
　　anatomy, 678–692
　　physiology, 692–705
　homeostatic interrelationships, 768b
　integumentary system and, 168b, 169b
　lymphatic system/immunity and, 784b, 785b
　muscular system and, 318b, 319b
　nervous system and, 548b
　physiology, 3, 723–742
　in pregnancy, 1135
　reproductive system and, 1106b
　respiratory system and, 876b, 877b
　skeletal system and, 196b
　skin and, 168b, 169b
　thyroid hormone's effects, 621t
　urinary system and, 1058b, 1059b
Carina, 832f, **840**
Carotene, **157**
Carotid arteries, 681f, 745f–751f, **746t**, 748t
Carotid bodies, 729, **748t**, **866**–867, 867f
Carotid canal, 208f, **209**, 216t
Carotid sinuses, 727, 728f, **748t**
Carotid sinus reflex, 728f, **729**
Carpals (carpal bones), 228f, **233**, 235f, 236f, 236t
　joints of, 258t
Carpal tunnel syndrome, 235
Carpometacarpal joints, 258t
Carpus. *See* Wrist
Carrier proteins, 52t, 68, **71**
　in active transport mechanisms, 75–77, 76f
　in passive transport mechanisms, 71–72, 72f
Cartilage, **135**–137, 136f, 137f
　articular, 135
　blast cell type in, 128f, 129, 135
　calcified, 176, 185, 186–187

cartilaginous joints and, 254f, 255
　as connective tissue, 127, 128f, 129, 135
　elastic, 136f, **137**
　　skeletal, **176**, 177f
　embryonic origins, 128f
　in endochondral ossification, 185–186
　fibrocartilage, **137**, 137f
　　skeletal, **176**, 177f
　fragments (loose bodies), 272
　functions, 127, 128f
　growth of, 176, 186–187
　hyaline, **135**, 136f
　　skeletal, **176**, 177f
　injuries to, 272, 273f
　matrix components, 128f
　regenerative capacity of, 144
　　skeletal, **176**, 177f
Cartilage (endochondral) bone, **184**
Cartilaginous joints, 253, 254f, **255**
　articulating bones/movements allowed, 258t, 259t
Cascades, 10
Caspases, 111
Catabolic-anabolic steady state, 971–973
Catabolism, 6–7, 37, **956**
Catalysts, **39**–40. *See also* Enzymes
　globular proteins as, 52t, 53
Cataplexy, 460
Cataract, **565**, 565f
Catecholamines, **418**, 631, 631f
Cathelicidins, 164
Cations, **33**
　bases and, 41
　reabsorption of, 1014t
CAT. *See* Computed tomography
Cauda equina, **470**, 471f, 472f, 509, 509f
Caudal orientation/direction, 13t
Caudate nucleus, **443**, 444f
Caveoli, 80t, **81**, 310, 311f
Caveolin-coated vesicles, 81, 81f
Cavernous sinuses, 465f, **760t**, 761f
Cavities (dental caries), **895**
CBC (complete blood count), **671**–672
C cells (parafollicular cells), 620, 620f, **624**
CCK. *See* Cholecystokinin
C (cytosine), **55**–57, 56f, 57t
CD4 T cells, **810**, 811f
CD8 T cells, **810**, 811f
Cdks (cyclin-dependent kinases), **101**
CEA (carcinoembryonic antigen), 147b
Cecum, 755f, 883f, **922**, 923f, 924f
Celiac disease, 933
Celiac ganglia, 539f, **541**
Celiac plexus, 537f, 900
Celiac trunk, 746f, 747f, 752f, 753f, **753t**, 755f
Cell adhesion molecules (CAMs), 68f, **83**, 91, 127, 794
Cells, 3, 64–116, **64**, 66f
　aging, 111–112
　anucleate, 95
　composition of, 65–66
　developmental aspects, 111–112
　differentiation, 111
　excitotoxicity and, 468
　extracellular materials, 111

growth and reproduction, 97–111
　cell division, 99, 99f, **101**, 102–103f
　cell life cycle, 97–101
　protein synthesis, 101, 104–111
　junctions, 69, 70f
　lysis and, 797f, 798
　motility of, 90, 92, 92f
　multinucleate, 95
　polarized state of, 81–82
　principle of complementarity and, 65
　programmed death of, 111, 425
　signaling processes, 68, 83–84
　specialization of, 111, 118
　steady state of, 82
　stem, 111, 145
　structures of, 65–98. *See also* individual structures
　　cellular extensions, 93, 95
　　cytoplasm, 84–95
　　generalized or composite, **66**, 66f
　　nucleus, 95–98
　　plasma membrane, 66–84
　　summary, 94–95t
　theories, 65
　types of, 65, 65f
Cellular immune response, **799**, 810–820
　antigen recognition/MHC restriction, 810–813
　co-stimulatory signals, 814
　cytokines, 814
　helper T cells' role, 814–815, 815f
　humoral immune response vs., 810
　immunological memory in, 804f, 805, 805f
　t cell activation, 813–814, 813f
Cellular respiration, 7, 57, 59, 59f, **956**, 957f
　aerobic, 302, 303f
　anaerobic, 302, 303f
　as catabolic process, 956
　energy yield during, 965, 965f
　oxidation-reduction reactions of, 38–39
　primary function of, 956
　site of, 85, 959f
　summary, 971t
Cellulose, 46
　indigestibility of, 929
Cementum, **894**, 894f
Central artery of retina, 560f, 562f, **563**
Central canal (of spinal cord)
　brain ventricles and, 433, 434f
　CSF in relation to, 466f
　embryonic origins, 432f, 433
　gray commissure enclosure of, 472, 473f
Central (Haversian) canal, 137, 138f, **182**, 182f, 183f
Central nervous system (CNS), **388**, 389f, 430–489, **431**
　aging and, 484
　brain, 388, 389f, 431–456
　　protection of, 463–470
　developmental aspects, 481–484
　　embryonic, 1123–1128, 1130t
　　fetal, 1132t, 1133
　　neurulation and, 1123, 1125f
　diagnostic procedures, 481

disorders, 447, 460, 463, 467–470, 480–481
　enteric nervous system and, 888–889
　mental functions, 456–463
　regenerative capacity, 500
　role in ANS control hierarchy, 547, 547f, 550
　role within nervous system, 388, 389f
　spinal cord, 388, 389f, 470–481
Central pattern generators (CPGs), **519**, 520f
Central sulcus, **434**, 435f, 436, 437f
Central tendon of diaphragm, 347f
Central tendon of perineum, **350**, 351f, 1089
Central vein of liver, **912**, 914f
Central vein of retina, 560f, 562f, **653**
Centrioles (basal bodies), 66f, 85, **92**–93, 92f, **93**
　in mitosis, 92–93, 102f
　structure/functions (summary), 94t
Centromeres, 102f, 103f
Centrosome (cell center), 90, **92**
　matrix, 66f, 92–93, 92f
Centrum, vertebral, 220f, **221**, 221f, 224f, 224t
Cephalic reflex phase, **903**–904, 903f
Cephalic vein, 759f, 762f, **762t**, 763f
Cephalin, 48t
Cephalization, **431**
Cerebellar hemispheres, **452**, 452f
Cerebellar peduncles, 448, 448f, 449f, 450f, 451, **454**
Cerebellum, 445f, **451**–454, 452f
　cognitive functions of, 454
　embryonic origins, 432f, 433
　functions (summary), 453t
　gray/white matter arrangement in, 433, 433f
　hemispheres, **452**–454, 452f
　injury to, 454
　motor activity processing of, 454
　muscle contractions and, 451
　neural integration and, 495f
　peduncles, 448, 448f–450f, 451, **454**
　sensorimotor integration/control and, 520–521, 520f
　spinal cord tracts and, 476f
　vestibular nuclei in, 597, 597f
Cerebral angiography, 481
Cerebral aqueduct, **434**, 434f, 445f, 448, 450f
　CSF in relation to, 466f
　embryonic origins, 432f, 433
Cerebral arterial circle (circle of Willis), 749f, **749t**
Cerebral arteries, 748f, **748t**, 749f, **749t**
Cerebral cortex, **436**–441, 437f
　embryonic origins, 432f, 433
　functional areas, 437f
　　association, 440–441
　　motor, 436–439
　　sensory, 439–440
　functions (summary), 453t
　position in ANS control hierarchy, 547, 547f, 550

voluntary control of visceral activities and, 550
Cerebral dominance, **441**
Cerebral edema, **468**
Cerebral fissures, **434**, 435f
Cerebral hemispheres, **434**–443
 basal nuclei, **443**, 444f
 convolutions of, 433
 cortex, **436**–441
 embryonic origins, 432f, 433
 fissures of, 435f, 436
 functions (summary), 453t
 lobes of, 435f, 436
 white matter, **441**–443
Cerebral palsy, **482**–483
Cerebral peduncles, **448**, 450f, 480f
 crus cerebri of, 448f
Cerebral vein, 466f
Cerebrospinal fluid (CSF), **465**–467, 466f
 as biological colloid, 40
 cushioning role of water in, 41
 formation/location/circulation, 465, 466f
Cerebrovascular accidents (CVAs), **468**
 cerebral angiography to diagnose, 481
 nitric oxide and, 419
Cerebrum, **433**. See also Cerebral hemispheres
Cerumen, **585**
Ceruminous glands, **158**, **585**
Cervical canal, 1085f, **1086**
Cervical (cardinal) ligaments of uterus, 1085f, **1086**
Cervical curvatures, **219**, 219f, 247
Cervical enlargement, 471f, **472**, 509f
Cervical ganglia, 539f, **541**
Cervical glands, 1086
Cervical nerves, 471f, 509f
 muscles served by, 340t, 342t, 343t, 353t
Cervical plexus, 509f, **511**–512, 511f
 branches/nerves/structures served by, 511t
 muscles served by, 340t
Cervical plug, 1098
Cervical vertebrae, **219**, 219f
 articulated, 223f
 curvatures, **219**, 219f
 features, 221–222, 222f
 summary, 224f, 224t
 movements allowed, 224t
 transverse foramen, 221, 222f
Cervix, 1082f, 1085f, **1086**
Cesarean (C-) section, 1137
CF (cystic fibrosis), **874**
Chadwick's sign, 1133
Chalazion, 556
Chambers of eye, **564**, 564f
Chancre, 1100
Channel-linked receptors, **419**–420, 420f
Channel proteins, 52t, 68, **72**, 72f
 leakage, 72
 voltage-sensitive, 84
Chaperonins, **52**–53
Charley horse, **384**
Cheeks, **890**
Chemical bonds, **31**–36
 covalent bonds, 34–36, 35f, 36f
 electron's role in, 32–33
 hydrogen bonds, 36, 37f

intramolecular, 36
 ionic bonds, 33–34, 33f, 34f
Chemical digestion, **884**, 885f, 920t, **927**–931
 of carbohydrates, 927, 928f, 929
 enzymatic hydrolysis and, 927
 flowchart, 928f
 of lipids, 928f, **929**–930
 of proteins, 928f, 929
Chemical energy, **25**
Chemical equilibrium, **39**
Chemical level, of body's structure, 3–4, 4f
Chemically-gated ion channels, 83, 290, 290f, **398**–399, 398f
Chemical (nonshivering) thermogenesis, **987**
Chemical reactions, **36**–40
 chemical equilibrium and, 39
 energy flow in, 38–39
 equations to symbolize, 36–37
 exergonic reactions, 38
 factors influencing rate of, 39–40
 reversibility of, 39
 types of, 37–38, 38f
Chemical senses, **578**. See also Smell sense; Taste sense
Chemical synapses, **409**
 integrating/modifying events of, 411–413, 413f
 postsynaptic potentials, 411–413
 action potentials vs., 411, 414t
 steps in, 409–411, 410f
 synaptic delay, 411
Chemiosmotic processes, 958f, **959**, 964
Chemistry, 25–40
 atoms and elements, 27–30
 biochemistry, 40–59
 chemical reactions, 36–40
 matter and energy, 25–27
 molecules and mixtures, 30–31
Chemoreceptors, **491**, 493t, **578**, **729**
 in blood pressure regulation, 729, 731f
 in breathing regulation, 865–868
 central, **865**, 865f
 peripheral, **865**, 865f
Chemotactic agents, **795**
Chemotaxis, **794**, **795**
 positive, **657**
Chemotherapy, cancer, 147b
Chewing (mastication), 884f, **897**, 920t
 muscles, **338**–339t, 339f
Cheyne-Stokes breathing, **875**
CHF (congestive heart failure), **704**
Chiasma (crossover), 1076f, **1077**, 1148–1149, 1149f
Chiasmatic groove, 210, 210f
Chief cells, 624f, **625**, **900**–901, 901f
Chimeric immune system, **820**
Chiropractic, **248**
Chlamydia, **1100**–1101
Chloasma, 1133
Chloride
 in blood plasma/IF/ICF, 1038f
 imbalances (causes/ consequences), 1044t
 regulation of, 1049

Chloride shift, **861**
Chlorine, **26t**, **952t**
 in table salt, 33–34, 33f, 34f
Chokes (cardiovascular bends), 868b
Cholecalciferol, **638**, 638t
Cholecystitis, **937**
Cholecystokinin (CCK), **905**
 functional class/secretion sites/effects, 417t
 gallbladder contraction and, 916f, 917
 production site/stimuli/target/ actions, 906t
 in regulation of pancreatic juice secretion, 918, 919f
 source/trigger/effects, 638t
Cholesterol, 47, **978**, 980
 factors regulating blood levels, 980–981
 food sources/dietary requirements, 945t
 location/function in body, 48t
 molecular structure, 47f
 in plasma membrane, 67, 67f
 problems with excesses/ deficits, 945t
 recommended levels, 980
 in steroid hormone synthesis, 970
 synthesis of, 970
 transport, 980, 981f
 uses in body, 946
Choline, 289, 290f
Choline acetyltransferase, 417
Cholinergic fibers, **543**
Cholinergic receptors, **543**
 locations/effects, 544t
Chondroblasts, 128f, **129**, 135
Chondrocytes, 128f, **129**–130, **135**, 136f, 176
 autologous implantation, 275b
Chondroitin sulfate, 128, 129f
Chondromalacia patellae, **276**
Chordae tendineae, 683f, **686**, 687f
Chorda tympani, 582
Chorea, 470
Chorion, **1120**, 1120f, 1121f, 1123
Chorionic villi, **1120**, 1120f, 1121f
Chorionic villi sampling, **1156**–1157, 1156f
Choroid, 560f, **561**, 562f
Choroid plexuses, 445f, 449f, 450f, **465**
 CSF formation, 465, 466f
Christmas factor, 663t
Chromaffin cells, **631**
Chromatids, 98f, **99**, 102f
Chromatin, 66f, 95f, 96f, **97**, 98f, 102f
Chromatophilic substance (Nissl bodies), **391**, 392f
Chromium, 26t, **954t**
Chromosomes, **97**, 98f
 maternal, 1073
 in mitosis, 102f
 paternal, 1073
Chromosome segregation, 1147–1148
Chronic obstructive pulmonary diseases (COPD), **871**–872, 871f
Chyle, **775**
Chylomicrons, **932**, 932f, 968, 980
Chyme, **899**, 920t
 impact on small intestine, 919

Chymotrypsin, **918**, 918f, 928f, **929**
Chymotrypsinogen, 918, 918f
Cilia, **93**, 93f, 95, **119**
 flagella vs., 93
 motion of, 93f, 95
 olfactory, **578**, 579f
 protective mechanisms of, 796t
 structure/functions (summary), 95t
 tracheal wall, 839, 839f
Ciliary body, 560f, **561**, 564f
Ciliary ganglia, 503f, **537**, 537f
Ciliary glands, 556
Ciliary muscles, 546t, 560f, **561**, 564f
Ciliary processes, 560f, **561**, 564f
Ciliary vein, 564f
Ciliary zonule (suspensory ligament), 560f, **561**, 564f
Cingulate gyrus, 437f, **454**, 455f
Circadian rhythm, 459
Circle of Willis (cerebral arterial circle), 749f, **749t**
Circuit level processing, in neural integration, 494–495, 495f
Circuit patterns in neuronal pools, 421–422, 422f
Circular fascicle pattern, **326**, 327f
Circular folds (plicae circulares), **909**, 910f
Circulation
 of cerebrospinal fluid, 465–467, 466f
 coronary, **685**–686, 685f
 enterohepatic, **916**, 916f
 fetal, 1128–1130, 1131f
 of lymph, 775–777, 776f
 monitoring efficiency of, 732
 pulmonary, 742, 744f, 744–745t
 systemic, 742, 745f, 745t
  major arteries/veins, 746t–766t
Circulatory dynamics
 arterial system, 716–722
 blood pressure, 724–733
 tissue perfusion, 733–742
 venous system, 722–723
Circulatory shock, 733, **740**–742, 741f
Circumcision, 1069
Circumduction (movement), **261**, 262f
Circumferential lamellae, **182**, 183f
Circumflex arteries
 coronary, 681f, **685**, 685f
 femoral, 756f, **756t**, 757f
 humeral, 750f, **750t**, 751f
Circumvallate papillae, **581**, 581f, **890**, 891f
Cirrhosis, **915**
cis face, 87, 88f
11-cis isomer, **571**, 571f
Cisternae, **86**, 87f, 88f, 96f
 chyli, **775**, 776f
Citric acid, **961**, 962f
Citric acid cycle, **961**–963, 962f
 summary, 971t
CJD (Creutzfeldt-Jakob disease), 483b
Clathrin, **79**, 79f
Clathrin-coated vesicles, **78**–79, 79f
Clavicle, 228f, **229**, 230f, 234f, 236f, 236t
 joint of, 258t
 muscles of neck/spine and, 343f
 scapular movements and, 353f

Clavicular notch, **226**, 226f
Claw hand, 513
Clear layer of skin (stratum lucidum), 154f, **155**
Cleavage, **1117**–1119, 1118f
Cleavage furrow, **101**, 103f
Cleavage (tension) lines, 156
Cleft lip, 936
Cleft palate, 246–247, 247f, 874, 936
Climax (orgasm), **1073**, 1099–1100
Clinoid processes, 208f, **209**, 210f
Clitoris, 1082f, 1088f, **1089**
    ANS effects, 546t
Cloacal membrane, **936**, 936f
Clonal selection of B cells, **804**–805, 804f
Clone, **804**, 804f
Cloning research, 67
    reproductive, 1139–1140
Clot retraction, **666**
Clotting factors (procoagulants), 663f, **665**. See also Blood clotting
Clubfoot, **248**
CNS. See Central nervous system
Coagulation, 664f, **665**. See also Blood clotting
Coagulation vitamin (vitamin K), 48t, 665, 920t, 925, 932, **949t**
Coarctation of aorta, 708, 708f
Coated pit, 78–79, 79f
Coatomer-coated transport vesicles, 87f, 88f
Coatomer (COP1 and COP2) proteins, **81**
Cobalt, 26t, **954t**
Cocaine addiction, 424–425b
Coccygeal nerve, 509f
Coccygeus muscle, **350**, 350t, 351f
Coccyx, 204f, 218, **219**, 219f, **225**, 225f
    female vs. male, 240f, 240t
    as part of bony pelvis, 237, 238f
Cochlea, 584f, 586f, **587**, 588f
Cochlear division, of vestibulocochlear nerve (VIII), 505f, 506t
Cochlear duct, 586f, 587, **587**, 588f
Cochlear hair cells, 588f, **591**, 591f, 592f
Cochlear nerve, 586f, 587, 588f
    disorders, 594
    in hearing, 591–592, 591f, 592f
Cochlear nuclei, 450f, **451**, **592**–593, 592f
Cochlear (round) window, 584f, **585**
Coding strand, 105, 106f
Codons, **105**, 107, 107f, 108f, 109, 110f
Coelom, 1125f, **1127**, 1127f
Coenzymes, **53**, **948**, 956–958
    Q (ubiquinone), 964
Cofactor, enzyme, **53**
Cognition, 455, 456
    cerebellum's role in, 454
    limbic system and, 455
Cohesin, 99, 102f, 103f
Cold sores (fever blisters), **171**
Cold (temperature)
    body temperature and, 987–988, 988f
    hypothermia, 989
    metabolic rate increased by, 987

propagation of nerve impulses and, 408
    receptors, 491, 493t, **987**
Colic arteries, 752f, **754t**, 755f
Colic (hepatic) flexure, **922**, 923f
Colic (splenic) flexure, **922**, 923f
Collagenase, 165
Collagen fibers, **129**, 134f
    of bone, 182–183
    of connective tissue, **129**, 130f, 131f
    in fibrocartilage, 137, 137f
    functions/examples from body, 52t
    in hyaline cartilage, 176
    in skin, cleavage lines and, 156
Collateral channels, **723**
Collateral ligaments
    forearm, 268, 268f
    leg, 266f, **267**
Collateral (prevertebral) ganglia, **538**
    pathways with synapses in, 540f, 541–542
Collecting ducts, **1001**, 1002f, 1003, 1004f
    absorptive capabilities, 1013, 1014t, 1015
    cell types, 1002f, 1003
    functions (summary), 1020f
    in potassium balance regulation, 1048
    reabsorptive capabilities, 1014t, 1015
Colle's fracture, **232**, 233f
Colliculi, 448f, **449**, 449f, 450f, **575**, 576f
    hearing and, 592f, **593**
Colloid, thyroid, **620**, 622, 622f, 623
Colloid osmotic (oncotic) pressure
    capillary, **739**–740, 740f
    of glomerular blood, **1008**
    in hypoproteinemia, 1042–1043
Colloids (emulsions), **31**
    biological, 40
Colon, 883f, **922**, 923f, 924f. See also Large intestine
    abdominal arteries in relation to, 755f
    cancer, 147b, 937
Colony-stimulating factors (CSFs), **660**
Color blindness, **572**
Colostrum, **1138**
Columnar epithelia, **119**
    functions/locations, 122f
    pseudostratified, 122f, **123**
    simple, **120**, 122f
    stratified, **124**
Coma, **458**
    cortical contusions and, 468
    reticular activating system and, 456
    sleep vs., 458
Combination reactions, **37**, 38f
Comminuted fractures, **192t**
Commissures (canthi), **556**, 557f
Commissures (commissural fibers), 442f, **443**, 445f, 455f, 474, 475f
Common fibular (peroneal) nerve, **516**, 517f, 517t
    muscles served by, 372t
Commotio cordis, **709**

Communicating arteries, 748f, **748t**, 749f, **749t**
Compact bone, 128f, **179**, 184f, 187
    in flat bones, 181f
    in long bones, 180f
    osteon of, **181**, 182f, 183f
    structure, 181–182, 183f
Complementarity principle, 2, **3**
    erythrocyte as example of, 650
Complementary bases, **56**, 56f
Complement (complement system), 52t, **796**–798
    activation pathways
        alternative, 797f, **798**
        classical, **797**–798, 797f
    fixation, 798, 809–810, 809f
    functions (summary), 817t
    as inflammatory chemicals, **793**, 793t
    MAC proteins and, 798
    protective mechanism (summary), 796t
Complete blood count (CBC), **671**–672
Compounds, **30**
    vs. mixtures, 31
Compression fractures, **192t**
Computed tomography (CT), **20b**
    to assess CNS dysfunction, 481
Computerized axial tomography (CAT). See Computed tomography
Concentration gradients, **71**, 72, 73, 73f
    electrochemical gradient and, 83, 393, 398, **399**
    nerve impulses and, 398–400, 399f
Concentration of solutions, 30–31
    in chemical reactions, 39
Concentric muscle contraction, **300**, 301f
Conceptus, **1114**
Conchae, nasal. See Nasal conchae
Concussion, **468**
Condoms, STDs and, 1100
Conducting (elastic) arteries, **716**, 716f, 717f
Conducting regions of neurons, compared, 396t
Conducting zone (respiratory system), **831**
    structures, 840–841, 840f
Conduction
    continuous, **407**
    heat, **986**
    saltatory, **407**, 407f
Conduction deafness, **593**
Conductors (electrical), 398
Condyle (bone marking), **179t**
Condyloid (ellipsoidal) joint, 259t, 264f, **265**
Cones, 562f, **563**, 570f
    excitation of, **572**
    visual pigments and, 569–571
Congenital disorders
    heart defects, **707**–708, 708f
    hip dysplasia, 247–248
    immunodeficiency disorders, **820**
    spina bifida, **248**
    thymic aplasia, **826**
Congestive heart failure (CHF), **704**
Conjunctiva, **557**, 557f, 559f
Conjunctival sac, **557**, 557f
Conjunctivitis, 557

Connective tissue, **126**–139
    characteristics, 127
    classes/subclasses, 126–127, 128f, 131–139
    embryonic origins, 127, 128f, 145, 145f
    functions, 127, 148
    regenerative capacity of, 144
    structural elements, 127–129
    vascularity of, 127
Connective tissue proper, 126, **131**–135
Connective tissue root sheath, **160**, 161f
Connexons, 69, 70f
Conn's disease, **1061**
Conscious mind, 436. See also Cerebral cortex
Consciousness, **457**–458
    epileptic seizures and, 457
    loss of, 458
Conscious proprioception, 475
Consensual light reflex, 575
Constant (C) regions of antibodies, **807**, 807f
Constipation, **927**
    in pregnancy, 1135
Contact dermatitis, **171**
    allergic, **824**–825
Contact inhibition, as property of normal cells, 101
Contact signaling of cells, 83
Continuous capillaries, **720**
Contraception, **1128**–1129b
    lactation and, 1139
Contractile myofilaments, 282f, 282t
Contractile proteins, 282f, 282t
    ATP as energy source, 59, 59f
Contractile ring, 101, 103f
Contractile unit, of skeletal muscle, 282f, 282t
Contractility, 5, **280**
    of cardiac muscle, **701**–702, 701f
Contraction, of muscles. See Muscle contraction
Contractions (labor)
    Braxton Hicks, 1136
    as positive feedback mechanism, 10, 1135–1136
Contractures, **303**
    muscle, post-CVA, 468
Contrecoup injury, 468
Control center, in homeostatic systems, 9–10, 9f, 11f
Contusion, **468**
Conus medullaris, **470**, 471f
Convection, **986**
Convergence (eyeball), **568**
Convergent fascicle pattern, **326**, 327f
Converging circuits, **421**–422, 422f
Convertin, nature/origin/function/pathway, 663t
COP1 and COP2 (coatomer proteins), **81**
COPD (chronic obstructive pulmonary diseases), **871**–872, 871f
Copper, 26t, **954t**
Coracoacromial ligament, 257f, 269f
Coracobrachialis muscle, 353f, **354**, 355t, 356f
    actions of (summary), 362t

Coracohumeral ligament, **269**, 269f
Coracoid process, 230f, **231**, 236t
Cordotomy, **485**
Cords of brachial plexus, **512**, 513f, 514t
Core body temperature, **986**
Cornea, 557f, **560–561**, 560f, 564f
Corneal endothelium, 560, 564f
Corneal epithelium, 564f
Corniculate cartilages, 836f, **837**
Cornified (horny) cells, 155
Cornua (horns), of hyoid bone, 218, 218f
Coronal (frontal) plane, **15**, 16f
Coronal suture, 203, 206f, **207**
Corona radiata, 442f, **443**, 444f, 1093f, **1094**, 1116f
Coronary arteries, 681f, 682f, **685–686**, 685f, 746f, **746t**, 747f
Coronary bypass surgery, 719b
Coronary circulation, **685–686**, 685f
ANS effects, 546t
Coronary sinus, 682f, **683**, 685f, **686**, 723
Coronary sulcus (atrioventricular groove), **680**, 681f, 682f
Coronoid fossa, humerus, 231f, **232**, 234f, 236t
Coronoid process
mandible, 206f, 212f, **217t**
ulna, **232**, 233f, 234f, 236t, 268f
Corpora cavernosa, **1069**, 1088f
Corpora quadrigemina, 445f, **449**, 449f
Cor pulmonale, **709**
Corpus albicans, 1093f, **1094**
Corpus callosum, 437f, 442f, **443**, 445f, 455f, 466f
gender differences in, 481
Corpus cavernosum, 1066f
Corpus hemorrhagicum, 1094
Corpus luteum, 1083f, **1084**, 1093f, 1094
Corpus spongiosum, 1066f, **1069**, 1070f
Corpus striatum, **443**, 444f
Corrugator supercilii muscle, **335t**, 337f
Cortical nephrons, **1003**
juxtamedullary nephrons vs., 1003, 1004f
Cortical radiate arteries, 1000f, **1001**, 1004f
Cortical radiate veins, 1000f, **1001**, 1004f
Cortical reaction, **1115**, 1116f
Corticospinal (pyramidal) tracts, **438**, 450f, 475f, **478**, 480f
location/origin/termination/function, 479t
Corticosteroids, **626**, 627t
Corticosterone, **629**
Corticotropin, **616**, 618t
Corticotropin-releasing hormone (CRH), **616**, 618t
Cortisol (hydrocortisone), **629–630**
blood pressure and, 729t
gluconeogenesis and, 629
influences on metabolism, 978t
location/function, 48t
structure/regulation/effects, 627t
Cortisone, **629**

Costal cartilages, 176, 177f, 204f, 226f, 227f
sternocostal joint and, 254f, 255
Costal margin, 226f, **228**
Costal surface, lung, 842, 844f
Co-stimulatory signals, **814**
Costocervical trunk, 749f, **749t**, 750f, 751f, **751t**
Coughing
mechanism/result, 854t
regulatory centers, 451
Countercurrent mechanisms, **1016**, 1017f, 1018
exchanger, **1018**
multiplier, **1016**, 1018
Coup injury, 468
Covalent bonds, **34–36**
ionic vs., 36, 36f
Coxal (hip) bone, **237**, 238f, 243f, 246f, 246t
at hip joint, 259t, 270, 270f
CP (creatine phosphate), **301–303**, 303f
CPGs (central pattern generators), **519**, 520f
Cranial base/floor, 203
Cranial bones (cranium), **203–211**, 205f, 206f
at birth, 247
joints of, 258t
Cranial cavity, **15**, 17f, 203
Cranial fossae, 203, 204, **207**, 208f, **209**
Cranial nerves, 388, 389f, 499, **500**
location/function of, 501f
muscles served by, 335–339t, 338–339t
origin/course/function, 502–508t
Cranial orientation/direction, 13t
Cranial parasympathetics, **537–538**, 537f
Cranial sensory ganglia, **501**
Cranial vault (calvaria), 203
Craniosacral division, **536**. See also Parasympathetic division (ANS)
Cranium (cranial bones), **203–211**, 205f, 206f
at birth, 247
joints of, 258t
Creatine phosphate (CP), **301–303**, 303f
Creatinine, 649t, **1013**
CREB (cAMP response-element binding protein), 463
Cremaster muscles, **1067**, 1067f
Crenated cells, 74, 74f
Crest (bone marking), 179t
Cretinism, 618t, **624**
Creutzfeldt-Jakob disease (CJD), 483b
CRH. See Corticotropin-releasing hormone
Cribriform plate, 208f, **210**, 215f, **217t**, 834f
olfactory nerve and, 502t
olfactory receptors and, 578, 579f
Cricoarytenoid muscle, 836f
Cricoid cartilage, **836**, 836f
Cricothyroid ligament, 836f
Cricotracheal ligament, 836f
Cristae, mitochondrial, **85**, 85f
Cristae ampullares, 586f, 587
in equilibrium, **595–597**, 596f

Crista galli, 208f, **211**, 211f, 215f, **217t**
Crista terminalis, 680, 682f
Cross bridges, **286**
in muscle contraction, 287–288, 293–294, 295f
of smooth muscle, 311, 311f, 313f
Crossed-extensor reflex, **526**, 526f
Crossover of meiosis I, 1076f, **1077**, 1148–1149, 1149f
Crown, tooth, 894, 894f
Crowning, in labor, 1137
Crown-rump measurement, 1123
CRP (C-reactive protein), **798**
Cruciate ligament, 266f, **267**
injuries, 267–268, 267f
Crura of penis, **1069**, 1070f
Crus cerebri of cerebral peduncles, 448f
Crying, mechanism/result, 854t
Cryogens, **989**
Cryptorchidism, 1069
Crypts of Lieberkühn (intestinal crypts), 910f, **911**
Crystallins, 565
Crystals, 33f, **34**
CSFs (colony-stimulating factors), **660**
CSF. See Cerebrospinal fluid
CT. See Computed tomography
Cubital veins, 759f, 762f, **762t**, 763f
Cuboidal epithelia, **119**
simple, **120**, 121f
stratified, **123**
Cuboid bone, **244**, 245f, 246f, 246t
Cuneiform bones, **244**, 245f, 246f, 246t
Cuneiform cartilages, 836f, **837**
Cupula, **596**, 596f
Current, capacitance, 401–402
Current (electrical), **397–398**
Curvatures
primary, **247**
secondary, **247**
spinal, 218–219, 219f
stomach, 899f, **900**
Cushingoid signs, 629–630, 630f
Cushing's disease, 618t, **629**
Cushing's syndrome, 627t, **629**
Cutaneous (cervical) nerve, 511f, 511t
Cutaneous membrane, 141, 142f. See also Skin
glands, 158–159, 159f
Cutaneous nerves, **511**
dermatomes and, 516, 518f
Cutaneous plexus, 155–156
Cutaneous sensory receptors, **164–165**
Cuticle
hair, **160**, 160f, 161f
nail (eponychium), 163
CVAs (cerebrovascular accidents), **468**
Cyanocobalamin. See Vitamin B12
Cyanosis, 157
Cyclic AMP signaling mechanism, 84, 84f
by gustatory receptors, 582
by hormones, **607–608**, 607f
by neurotransmitters, **420–421**, 420f
by olfactory receptors, 580, 580f
Cyclic GMP, 419, **420–421**

Cyclic GMP (cGMP), **572**, 573f
Cyclin-dependent kinases (Cdks), **101**
Cyclins, **101**
Cysteine, 947t
Cystic duct, 909f, **912**, 917
Cystic fibrosis (CF), **874**, 936, 992
Cystic veins, 764f, **764t**
Cystitis, 1026
Cystocele, **1031**
Cystoscopy, **1031**
Cytochromes, **964**
Cytokines, 793, 814, 818t
Cytokinesis, 99f, **101**, 103f
Cytology, **2**
Cytolytic T cells, **815**
Cytoplasm, 66, 66f, 67f, **84–93**
muscle fiber. See Sarcoplasm
as site of translation, 107
structure/function (summary), **94t**
Cytoplasmic organelles, 3, 66, **84–93**
membranous vs. nonmembranous, 85
structure/function (summary), **94t**
Cytosine (C), **55–57**, 56f, 57t
Cytoskeleton, **90–92**, 91f
membrane proteins and, 68, 68f, 69
of smooth muscle fibers, 310–311, 311f
Cytosol, 31, 66f, **84**, 94t
Cytotoxic T cells, 810, 811f, **815–816**, 816f
functions (summary), 817t
lethal hit mechanisms, 815–816, 816f
Cytotoxic (type II) hypersensitivity, **823**
Cytotrophoblast, **1119**, 1119f, 1120f

DAG (diacylglycerol), **420–421**, 608f, **609**
Dalton's law of partial pressures, **854**, 855t
Dark adaptation, **574–575**
Dark bands (A bands), **284**, 285f, 689, 690f
Dartos muscle, **1067**, 1067f
Daughter chromosomes, 103f, 1075f, 1076f
Daughter strand in DNA replication, 100f
dB (decibels), **589**
DCM (dilated cardiomyopathy), 704–705
DCT (distal convoluted tubule), **1001**, 1002f, 1003
Dead space
alveolar, **852**
anatomical, **852**
total, **853**
Deafness, **593**
central, 506t
conduction, **593**
nerve, 506t
sensorineural, **593**
Death
brain, 457, **458**
cell (programmed), 111, 425
rigor, 294
sudden infant, 875
Decarboxylation, **961**, 962f

Decibels (dB), **589**
Decidua basalis, 1121f, **1122**
Decidua capsularis, 1121f, **1122**
Deciduous (milk) teeth, **893**, 893f
Declarative (fact) memory, **461**, 462f
Decomposition reactions, 37, 38f
 hydrolysis reactions, 41, 44, 45f
Decompression sickness, 868–869b
Decubitus ulcer, 171
Decussation of pyramids, 442f, 448f, **451**, 480f
Deep artery of arm, 750f, 750t, 751f
Deep femoral artery (deep artery of thigh), 756, 756f, 757f
Deep orientation/direction, 13t
Defecation, 884f, **885**, 920t
Defecation reflex, **926–927**, 927f
Defense system, body's. *See* Immune system
Defensins, **657**, 791, 833, 890
 in saliva, 892
Defibrillation, 694
Degenerative disorders, 469–470
Deglutition (swallowing), **884**, 884f, **897–899**, 898f, 920t
 hyoid bone and, 218
 muscles that promote, 340–341t, 341f
 regulatory centers, 451
Dehydration, 1041–**1042**, 1042f
 blood pressure and, 731b
Dehydration synthesis, 41, 44, 45f, 49, 49f
Dehydroepiandrosterone (DHEA), 630, 1082, 1100
Dehydrogenases, **958**
Delayed hypersensitivity (Type IV) reactions, **824–825**
Deletion, **1157**
Delta brain waves, **456**, 457f, 459, 459f
Deltoid muscle, 330f–333f, **354**, **355t**, 356f
 actions of (summary), 362t
 arm movements and, 354, 355t
Deltoid tuberosity, 231f, **232**, 234f, 236t
Demifacets, 222, 223f
Denatured proteins, **50**, 52, 53f, 54
Dendrites, 139, 392, 392f, **393**, 396f
 unmyelinated nature of, 394
Dendritic cells (Langerhans' cells)
 as antigen-presenting cells, 803, 813, 813f, 1087
 as lymphoid cells, **777**
Dendritic spine, 392f, 393
Dendrodendritic synapses, 408
Dendrosomatic synapses, 408
Dense bodies, **310–311**, 311f
Dense connective tissue, **131**
 elastic, 135
 in intramembranous ossification, 184–185, 184f
 irregular, 134f, **135**
 regular, **133–134**, 134f
Dens (odontoid process), **222**, 222f, 223f
Dental caries (cavities), **895**
Dental formula, **894**
Dental plaque, **895**
Dentate gyrus, 454, 455f
Dentate nuclei, 452
Denticulate ligaments, 471f, **472**

Dentin, **895**
Dentinal tubules, 894f, 895
Dentitions
 permanent, **893–894**, 894f
 primary, **893**, 893f
Deoxyhemoglobin, **650**, 858–859
Deoxyribonucleic acid. *See* DNA
Deoxyribose, as a monosaccharide, 44, 45f
Depolarization, **290–291**, 291f, **400–401**, 400f
 in chemical synapses, 409–411, 410f
 generation of action potentials and, 401f, 402–404
 graded potentials and, 401, 401f, 402f
 refractory periods and, 406–407, 406f
Depressed fractures, 192t
Depression, 485
 gastric secretions and, 903f, 904
Depression (movement), **262**, 263f
Depressor anguli oris muscle, 336t, 337f
Depressor labii inferioris muscle, 336t, 337f
Depth perception, **575**, 576f
Dermal papillae, 153f, **155**
Dermal ridges, 155
Dermatitis, **170**
 contact, **171**
Dermatology, **171**
Dermatomes, **516**, 518f, 527, **1127**, 1127f
Dermicidin, 158
Dermis, 152, 153f, 154f, **155**
 as blood reservoir, 165
 blood vessels of, 152f, 155–156
 papillary layer, 153f, **155**
 reticular layer, 153f, 155–156
 tissue type, 135, 155
Descending (motor) pathways to brain, 478–480
 major spinal cord tracts, 475, 475f, 479t, 480f
 direct (pyramidal), **478**, 479t, 480f
 indirect (extrapyramidal), **478**, 479t, 480f
Desmosomes, **69**, 70f, 154f
 of cardiac muscle, 689, 690f
 of epithelia, 119
Detrusor muscle, **1025–1026**, 1025f
Deuterium, 29f
Developmental anatomy, **2**
Development of bone, 184–187
Deviated septum, **875**
Dextrinase, 928f, **929**
DHEA (dehydroepiandrosterone), 630, 1082, 1100
DHT (dihydrotestosterone), 1081
Diabetes insipidus, **617–619**, **1031**
Diabetes mellitus (DM), **634**, 974
 as autoimmune disease, 822
 gestational, 1134–1135
 metabolic acidosis and, 1056t
 type 1/type 2/therapies, 636–637b
Diacylglycerol (DAG), **420–421**, 608f, **609**
Diapedesis (emigration), **657**, 794, 794f

Diaphragm, 15, 17f, **346**, 347f
 abdominal arteries in relation to, 753f
 in breathing, 847–849, 848f
 central tendon of, 347f
 description/action/nerve supply, 346t
 heart in relation to, 679f
 innervation of, 511f, 511t
 as muscle of breathing, 346
 origin/insertion, 346t
 phrenic nerve and, 512
 respiratory organs in relation to, 832f
 in thoracic cavity, 844f
Diaphragm (pelvic), **350**, 351f
 muscles, **350t**, 351f
Diaphragm (urogenital), **350**, 351f
 muscles, **350t**, 351f
Diaphysis, **180**, 180f
 in endochondral ossification, 185f, 186
Diarrhea, **927**, 1056t
Diarthroses, **253**, 258t
Diastole, **698**, 699f, 700
Diastolic blood pressure, **725**, 725f
DIC (disseminated intravascular coagulation), 667–668
Diencephalon, **443–447**, 445f
 brain stem in relation to, 448–449f
 embryonic origins, 432f, 433
 epithalamus, 445f, **447**, 448f
 functions (summary), 453t
 hypothalamus, 445f, **446–447**
 thalamus, **443**, 445f, 446
Diets
 vegetarian, 947f
 weight-loss, 990–991b
Differentially (selectively) permeable barrier, **70**, 71
Differential white blood cell count, **671**
Diffuse endocrine system, 125
Diffuse junctions, **310**, 311f
Diffusion, **71**, 71f
 capillary exchange and, 738–740, 740f
 electrochemical gradient, ions and, 83
 facilitated, 71–72, 72f
 influence of membrane permeability on, 73, 73f
 simple, 71, 72f
Digastric muscle, **340t**, 341f, 343f
Digestion, 5–6, **884**, 884f
 of carbohydrates, 927, 928f, 929
 chemical, **884**, 885f, 920t, **927–931**
 in esophagus, 897–899
 as first stage of metabolism, 957f
 flowchart, 927f
 in large intestine, 925–927
 of lipids, 928f, 929–930
 mechanical, **884**, 885f, 920t
 in mouth, 897–899, 928f
 neural reflexes controlling, 885–886, 885f
 in pharynx, 897–899
 of proteins, 928f, 929
 in small intestine, 919–922, 928f
 stimuli provoking, 885–886, 885f
 in stomach, 902–907, 928f
Digestive cavity, **19**, 19f

Digestive system, **7**, 7f, 882–941, **883**
 age-related changes in, 937
 cardiovascular system and, 768b
 congenital defects, 936
 developmental aspects, 933, 936–937
 embryonic, 1123–1128, 1130t
 fetal, 1132t, 1133
 digestive processes
 overview, 884–886, 884f
 in stomach, 902–908
 disorders, 917
 endocrine system and, 640b
 homeostatic interrelationships, 934b, 935b
 integumentary system and, 168b
 lymphatic system/immunity and, 784b
 muscular system and, 318b
 nervous system and, 548b, 549b
 overview of, 883–884, 883f
 functions of GI organs, 920t
 in pregnancy, 1135
 reproductive system and, 1106b
 respiratory system and, 876b
 skeletal system and, 196b
 skin and, 168b
 splanchnic circulation of, 887
 urinary system and, 1058b
Digital arteries, 747f, 750f, 750t, 751f, 756f, 757f, **757t**
Digital subtraction angiography (DSA), **20b**
Digital veins, 759f, 762f, 763f, 766f
Digits. *See* Fingers; Toes
Dihydrotestosterone (DHT), 1081
Diiodotyrosine (DIT), **622**, 622f
Dilated cardiomyopathy (DCM), 704–705
Dilation stage of labor, 1136f, **1137**
Dilator pupillae muscles, 561, 561f
Dimers, 165, 807, 808t
Dipeptidase, 928f, **929**, 930f
Dipeptide, 49, 49f
Diploë, **181**, 181f, 184f
Diploid chromosomal number, **1073**
Diplopia (double vision), **558–559**
Dipole, **35–36**
Direct (fleshy) muscle attachments, **284**
Directional anatomy terms, 13t
Direct phosphorylation, 301–302, 303f
Direct (pyramidal) system, **478**, 479t, 480f
Disaccharides (double sugars), **44**, 45f
Discrimination, spatial, **439**
Discriminative touch, 475
Dislocation (luxation) of joints, **273**
Displacement reactions, 37–38, 38f
Disseminated intravascular coagulation (DIC), 667–668
Dissociation reaction, 40, 40f
Distal convoluted tubule (DCT), **1001**, 1002f, 1003, 1004f
 functions (summary), 1020f
 reabsorptive capabilities, 1014t, 1015
Distal orientation/direction, 13t
Distributing (muscular) arteries, **716–717**, 716t, 717f
Disuse atrophy, 309
DIT (diiodotyrosine), **622**, 622f

Diuresis, 617, 1018
  osmotic, 635f
Diuretics, 617, 705, **767**, **1019**, 1021
  as diet pills, 990b
  metabolic alkalosis and, 1056t
Diverging circuits, **421**, 422f
Diverticulitis, **926**
Diverticulosis, **926**
Divisions of brachial plexus, **512**, 513f, 514t
DMD (Duchenne muscular dystrophy), **317**
DM. See Diabetes mellitus
DNA, **55–56**, 56f
  antisense RNAs and, 109
  as biological barrier to skin penetration, 164
  as blueprint for protein synthesis, 101, 104
  cellular site of, 55, 57t
  in chromatin, 97
  coding strand, 105, 106f
  fingerprinting, **58–59b**
  function of, 55, 57t
  helix, 98f, 99
  information transfer to RNA, 109, 110f
  "junk," 104, 105, 109–110
  linker, 97, 98f
  microRNAs and, 110
  mitochondrial, 58b, 85, 85f
  mutations
    cancer risk and, 145, 146–147b
    by carcinogens, 146b
  photodamaged, repair of, 157, 165
  replication of, **98–99**, 100f
    environmental toxins and, 112
  riboswitches and, **110**
  RNA compared to, 55, 57t, 104
  structure of, 55–56, 56f, 57t
  template, 99, 100f, 105, 106f
  termination signal, 105, 106f
  transcription, 104–105, 105f, 106f
  triplets and, 104
  UV radiation and, 157, 165
DNA ligase, 99, 100f
DNA polymerase III, 99, 100f
DNA probe, 58b
Domains, of cerebral cortex, 436
Dominance, cerebral, **441**
Dominant allele, **1146**
Dominant traits, 1150–1151, 1151f
  lethal, 1151
Dopa decarboxylase, 418f
Dopamine
  cocaine addiction and, 424–425b
  functional class/secretion sites/effects, 415t
  Huntington's disease and, 470
  memory and, 462f
  Parkinson's disease and, 469
  synthesis of, 418, 418f
Dopamine beta-hydroxylase, 418f
Dorsal body cavity, **15**, 17f
Dorsal horns, of spinal cord, **472**, 473f
Dorsal interosseous muscles
  of foot, 383f, **383t**
  of hand, 365f, **366t**
Dorsalis pedis artery, 756f, **756t**, 757f
Dorsalis pedis vein, 766f, **766t**

Dorsal orientation/direction, 13t
Dorsal rami, **509**, 510f, 540f
  muscles served by, 343t, 344t
Dorsal respiratory group (DRG), **863–864**, 864f
Dorsal root ganglia, 473f, 474f, 499, 509, 510f, 540f
  of embryonic spinal cord, 470, 470f
Dorsal roots, 449f, 471f, 473f, 474f, **509**, 510f
  sympathetic trunks in relation to, 540f
Dorsal scapular nerve, muscles served by, 353t
Dorsal venous arch, 759f, **762t**, 766f, **766t**
Dorsiflexion (movement), **261**, 261f
  muscles involved in, 379–380t, 380f
Dorsum sellae, 208f, **209**, 210f
Double helix, 56, 56f, 99
Double sugars (disaccharides), 44, 45f
Double vision (diplopia), **558–559**
Double zipper of integral proteins, 287
Dowager's hump, 248
Down-regulation, by hormone receptors, **610**
Down syndrome, **1157**
Dreaming, REM sleep and, 458
DRG (dorsal respiratory group), **863–864**, 864f
Drowsiness (consciousness state), 458
Drugs
  blood-brain barrier and, 467
  penetration enhancers, 164
  that influence ANS activity, 543–544, 545t
DSA (digital subtraction angiography), **20b**
DSR (dynamic spatial reconstruction), **20b**
Dual innervation, **535**, 544
Duchenne muscular dystrophy (DMD), **317**
Duct, 125, 126f
Ductless glands. See Endocrine glands
Ductules, efferent (testes), 1068, 1068f
Ductus arteriosus, **706**, **1130**, 1131f
Ductus (vas) deferens, 1066, 1066f–1068f, **1069–1071**, 1070f
Ductus venosus, **1130**, 1131f
Duodenal glands (Brunner's glands), 910f, **911**
Duodenum, 753f, 883f, **908**, 909f, 920t, 924f
  hormones produced by, 638t, 906t
Dural septa, **464**, 465f
Dural sinuses, **464**, 464f, 723, 758f, 759f, **760t**, 761f
Dura mater, 64, **463–464**, 464f, 466f
  spinal, 466f, **470**, 471f, 473f
Dwarfism, 187
  pituitary, **616**, 618t
  psychosocial, **642**
Dynamic equilibrium, 9, **594**
  activating receptors, 595–597, 596f

Dynamic spatial reconstruction (DSR), **20b**
Dynein, ciliary motion and, 93f, 95
Dyneins, 90
Dynorphin, **418**
Dysarthria, **527**
Dyslexia, 441
Dysmenorrhea, **1108**
Dysphagia, **937**
Dysphasia, **527**
Dysplasia, **112**
  hip (congenital), 247–248
Dyspnea, **871**
  in pregnancy, 1135
Dystocia, 1137
Dystonia, **527**
Dystrophin, **287**
  functions/examples from body, 52t
Dysuria, 1026

Ear
  anatomy, 583–587
  auditory pathway to brain, 592–593, 592f
  hearing and, 583–598
  inner (internal/labyrinth), 584f, **586–587**, 586f
    cochlea, 584f, 586f, **587**
    disorders, 594
    semicircular canals, 584f, 586f, **587**
    vestibule, 584f, **586–587**, 586f
  innervation of, 511f, 511t
  middle (tympanic cavity), **585–586**
  outer (external), 207, **583**, 584f, 585
    acoustic meatus, **585**
    auricle, **583**
    elastic cartilage of, 137, 176, 177f
  route of sound waves through, 590, 590f
Ear cavity. See Tympanic cavity
Eardrum (tympanic membrane), 584f, **585**, 590f
  perforated (ruptured), 593
EB (epidermolysis bullosa), **171**
Eccentric muscle contraction, **300**, 301f
Eccrine (merocrine) sweat glands, **126**, 127f, 153f, **158**, 159f
E-C (excitation-contraction) coupling, **291**
  of skeletal muscle, 288, 291–293, 292f
  of smooth muscle, 310, 312, 313f
ECG (electrocardiogram), **695–696**, 696f, 697f
ECM (extracellular matrix), 68f
Ectoderm, 145, 145f, 1120f, **1123**, 1124f, 1126f
  derivatives, 431, 431f, **1123**, 1125f, 1130t
Ectopic focus, **694–695**
Ectopic pregnancy, 1084–1085, **1141**
Eczema, **826**
Edema, **132**, **1042**
  cerebral, **468**
  in inflammatory response, 792f, 793
ED (erectile dysfunction), **1074b**
Edinger-Westphal oculomotor nuclei, 537

EDV (end diastolic volume), **700**, 703f, 727f
EEG (electroencephalogram), **456–457**, 457f
  sleep stages and patterns of, 458, 459f
Effectors, 9f, **10**, 11f
  in reflex arcs, **521**, 521f
  in somatic vs. autonomic nervous systems, 533, 534f
Efferent arterioles, nephron, **1003**, 1004f
Efferent division (PNS). See Motor (efferent) division
Efferent lymphatic vessels, 778f, **779**
Efferent (motor) neurons, **395**, 396–397t
Efferent pathways, 9f, 10
Effort, **326–328**, 328f, 329f
Eicosanoids, **48**, 48t, **606**
Ejaculation, 1072, **1073**
Ejaculatory duct, 1066, 1066f, **1070**, 1070f
EKG (electrocardiogram), **695–696**, 696f, 697f
Elastic cartilages, 128f, 135, 136f, **137**
  skeletal, **176**, 177f
Elastic (conducting) arteries, **716**, 716f, 716t
  blood pressure and, 724–725
Elastic connective tissue, 135
Elastic fibers, **129**, 130f, 131f
Elasticity of muscle tissue, **280**
Elastic lamina, of muscular arteries, 717
Elastic (titin) filaments, 284, 285f, 286, **287**
Elastin, 129, 137
  functions/examples in body, 52t
Elbow
  joint, **268**, 268f
    articulating bones/movements allowed, 258t
    muscles acting on, 362–363t, 363f
    muscles crossing, 356f, **357t**
  olecranon process, **232**, 233f, 234f, 268f
Electrical energy, **25–26**
Electrical gradients, 399
Electrical signaling
  bone remodeling and, 190
  of cells, 84
Electrical synapses, **408–409**
Electricity, principles of/definitions, 397–399
Electrocardiogram (ECG or EKG), **695–696**, 696f, 697f
Electrocardiography, **695–697**
Electrochemical gradient, **83**, 398, **399**
Electrochemical proton gradient, **964–965**
Electroencephalogram (EEG), **456–457**, 457f
  brain death and, 457
  sleep stages and patterns of, 458, 459f
Electrolysis, 162
Electrolyte balance, 1043–1049
  aging and, 1060
  of calcium, 1049

Electrolyte balance (*cont.*)
central role of sodium in, 1043
developmental aspects, 1060
of phosphate, 1049
of potassium, 1048–1049
of sodium, 1043, 1044*t*, 1045–1048
Electrolytes, 41, 920*t*, **1036–1037**, 1038*f*
absorption of, 932
in blood plasma, 649*t*, 1037–1038, 1038*f*
in extracellular fluid, 1037
imbalances
causes/consequences, 1044*t*
heart rate and, 702
in interstitial fluid, 1037, 1038*f*
in intracellular fluid, 1037, 1038*f*
osmotic power of, 1036–1037
Electromagnetic (radiant) energy, 26
Electromagnetic radiation, **565**, 566*f*
Electromagnetic spectrum, 26
Electromyography, **384**
Electron acceptors, 33, 33*f*
Electron cloud, 27*f*, 28, 32
Electron donors, 33, 33*f*, 38
Electronegativity of atoms, **34–36**, 36*f*
Electroneutrality, **44**
Electron microscopy
scanning (SEM), 118
transmission, 118
Electrons, 27*f*, **28–30**
in chemical bonding, 32–33, 32*f*
Electron shell (energy level), 32
Electron transport chain, 957*f*, 959*f*, **963–965**, 963*f*
summary, 971*t*
Electrophoresis, DNA, 58*b*
Electropositivity of atoms, **34–36**, 36*f*
Elements, **27**
chemically inert/reactive, 32, 32*f*
of human body, 26*t*
trace, 26*t*, 27
Elephantiasis, **783**
Elevation (movement), **262**, 263*f*
Ellipsoidal (condyloid) joint, 259*t*, 264*f*, **265**
Embolism, **667**
scuba diving and, 868–869*b*
Embryo, **1114**
Embryology, 2
Embryonic development, 1117–1130
brain, 431–433, 431*f*, 432*f*
cleavage/blastocyst formation, 1117–1119
of digestive system, 933, 936, 936*f*
early, 1117–1118
events (summary), 1121*f*
formation of bony skeleton, 184–186
implantation, 1119–1120
nervous tissue, 408–409
of peripheral nervous system, 527
placentation, 1120–1122
primary germ layers, **145**, 145*f*
respiratory system, 873–874, 873*f*
size/shape changes during, 1114*f*
skeleton, 176
of skin, 170

Embryonic disc, **1119**, 1120*f*, 1123, 1124*f*, 1126*f*
Embryonic tissue implants, 469, 470
Emesis (vomiting), 451, **907–908**
Emetic center, of medulla, **908**
Emigration (diapedesis), **657**, **794**, 794*f*
Emmetropic eye, **567**, 569*f*
Emotions
gastric secretions and, 903*f*, 904
hyperventilation and, 1056*t*
hypothalamus and, 446, 550
limbic system and, 454–455
pain tolerance and, 496*b*
psychosomatic illnesses, 455
Emphysema, 858, **871**
Emulsification of fats, 916, 916*f*, 930, 930*f*
Emulsions (colloids), 31
Enamel, tooth, **894**, 894*f*
Encapsulated dendritic endings, **492–494**, 493*t*
Encephalitis, 465
Encephalopathy, **485**
End diastolic volume (EDV), **700**, 703*f*, 727*f*
Endemic (colloidal) goiter, **623**, 623*f*
Endergonic reactions, **38–39**
Endocarditis, **709**
Endocardium, 679*f*, **680**, 683*f*
Endochondral (cartilage) bone, **184**
Endochondral ossification, 184, **185–186**
steps of, 185, 185*f*, 186
Endocrine glands, **124–125**, **605**, 605*f*
developmental aspects, 639
hormone synthesis/release
nervous system modulation, 611–612
stimuli types, 611, 611*f*
major, of body, 612–636
negative feedback systems and, 10, 611
Endocrine system, 6, 6*f*, **604–645**
age-related changes in, 639
cardiovascular system and, 768*b*
developmental aspects, 639
embryonic, 1123–1128, 1130*t*
fetal, 1132*t*, 1133
diffuse, 125
digestive system and, 934*b*, 935*b*
homeostatic interrelationships, 640*b*, 641*b*
hypothalamus as part of, 446, 605
integumentary system and, 168*b*
lymphatic system/immunity and, 784*b*
major organs, 612–636
locations, 605*f*
muscular system and, 318*b*, 319*b*
nervous system and, 548*b*
hormonal release adjustments, 611–612
overview, 605–606, 605*f*
reproductive system and, 1106*b*, 1107*b*
respiratory system and, 876*b*
skeletal system and, 196*b*, 197*b*
skin and, 168*b*
urinary system and, 1058*b*, 1059*b*
Endocrinology, **605**

Endocytosis, **78–81**
microfilament's role in, 91
Endoderm, 145, 145*f*, 1120*f*, **1123**, 1124*f*, 1125*f*, 1126*f*
organs derived from, 1123, 1126, 1126*f*, 1130*t*
Endogenous antigens, **811**, 812*f*, 813
Endolymph, **586**, 594, 596–597, 596*f*
Endomembrane system, **89–90**, 90*f*
cytoplasmic organelles and, 85
Endometrial cancer, **1108**
Endometriosis, **1108**
Endometrium, 1085*f*, **1086**, 1087*f*
in cardiac and skeletal muscle, 314*t*
in smooth muscle, 309, 311, 314*t*
Endoneurium, **498**, 498*f*
Endoplasmic reticulum (ER), **86**
endomembrane system interactions, 89–90, 90*f*
rough, 66*f*, **86–87**, 86*f*, 87*f*
smooth, 66*f*, 86*f*, **87**
Endorphins, 417*t*, **418**
pain and, 497*b*
Endoscopy, **937**
Endosome, 79, 79*f*
Endosteum, 180*f*, **181**, 183*f*
Endothelins, **735**
Endothelium, **120**
of blood vessel wall, 714, 715*f*
Endotracheal tube, **875**
End systolic volume (ESV), **700**, 703*f*, 727*f*
Endurance (aerobic) exercise, 303, **307**, 309
skeletal muscle fiber type and, 306*t*
Energy, **25**
activation, 54
cellular, 25, 26*t*
conversions, 26–27
food fuels catabolized for, 25, 38, 956
forms of, 25–26
stored, 25, 48*t*
Energy balance of body, 981–989
body temperature and, 985–989
energy intake/output, **982**, 984
metabolic rate and, 984–985
first law of thermodynamics in, 981
food intake and, 982–984
Energy level (electron shell), 32
Engagement (labor stage), 1137
Enkephalins, **418**
pain and, 497*b*
Enteric nervous system, 542, 887*f*, **888–889**
Enteric neurons, **888**, 921
Enteritis, **837**
Enteroendocrine cells, 637, **901**, 901*f*, 904, 910
Enterogastric reflex, **905**
Enterogastrones, **905**, 908*f*
Enterohepatic circulation, **916**, 916*f*
Enteropeptidase, **918**
Enucleation, **599**
Enzymes, **53**
activation energy and, 54, 54*f*
as biological catalysts, 39–40, 53–55, 55*f*
characteristics, 53–54

denaturation and, 50, 52, 53*f*, 54
digestive, 89
functions, 52, 53–54, 53*f*, 54*f*
"immortality," 112
inhibitors of, 54
mechanism of action, 54, 54*f*, 55*f*
restriction, 58*b*
substrates of, **55**, 55*f*
Eosinophils, 657*f*, **658–659**, 659*f*, 790
summary, 658*t*
Ependymal cells, 390*f*, **391**, 433, 466*f*
Ephedra, 991*b*
Epiblast, 1122, 1124*f*
Epicanthic fold, 556
Epicardium, **678**, 679*f*, 680
Epicondyle (bone marking), 179*t*
Epicranius muscle, **335**, 335*t*, 337*f*
frontal belly, 335*t*, 337*f*, 833*f*
superficial, 331*f*, 333*f*
Epidermal dendritic cell. *See* Langerhans' cell
Epidermal ridges, 155
Epidermis, 123, **152**, 153*f*
cells, 152–153, 154*f*
hormone produced by, 638*t*
layers of, 153–155, 154*f*
metabolic functions, 165
protective mechanisms, 789–790, 796*t*
Epidermolysis bullosa (EB), **171**
Epididymis, 1066, 1066*f*–1068*f*, 1068, **1069**
Epidural space, 470, 473*f*
Epigastric region, **18**, 18*f*
Epigenetic marks, 1154
Epiglottis, 834*f*, 836*f*, **837**, 889*f*, 891*f*
elastic cartilage of, 137, 176, 177*f*
Epileptic seizures, **457**
Epimysium, 282*f*, 282*t*, **283**, 283*f*
Epinephrine, **631**
adrenal medulla secretion of, 542, 627*t*, 631
as adrenergic receptor, 544*t*
blood pressure and, 729*t*, 730
BMR and, 985, 985*f*
heart rate and, 702
influences on metabolism, 978*t*
synthesis of, 418*f*
Epineurium, **498**, 498*f*
Epiphyseal fractures, **192**t
Epiphyseal line, **180**, 180*f*
Epiphyseal plate, **180**, 185*f*, 186
closure of, 187
in postnatal bone growth, 186–187, 186*f*, 187*f*
as temporary joint, 254*f*, 255
Epiphyses, **180**, 180*f*
in endochondral ossification, 185*f*, 186
Epiploic appendages, **922**, 923*f*
Episiotomy, 1137
Epistaxis, **875**
Epithalamus, 445*f*, **447**, 448*f*
embryonic origins, 432*f*, 433
Epithelial root sheath, of hair follicle, **160**, 161*f*
Epithelial tissue (epithelium), **118**
avascularity, 119
classification, 119–120, 120*f*
embryonic origins, 145, 145*f*
functions, 118, 121*f*–124*f*, 148

of GI mucosa, **888**, 888*f*
glandular, 118, 124–126, 127*f*
innervation of, 119
polarity of, 119
regenerative capacity, 119, 143–144
simple, **119**, 120–123, 120*f*, 121*f*–122*f*
special characteristics, 118–119
specialized contacts/ junctions, 119
stomach, 901–902
stratified, **119**, 120*f*, 123–124, 123*f*, 124*f*
underlying connective tissue of, 119
Epitympanic recess, **585**, 585*f*
Eponychium (cuticle), **163**
EPSPs (excitatory postsynaptic potentials), **411**–413, 412*f*
action potentials compared to, 414*t*
Equational division of meiosis, **1077**
Equations, chemical, 36–37
Equilibrium sense, 556, 594–598
chemical, **39**
cortical processing, 440, 597, 597*f*
dynamic, 9, **595**–597, 596*f*
motor pathways and, 478
pathways to brain, 597–598, 597*f*
static, **594**–595, 594*f*, 595*f*
vestibulocochlear nerve and, 506*f*, 506*t*
Equilibrium (vestibular) cortex, **440**
Erectile dysfunction (ED), **1074***b*
Erection, 1069, **1072**–1073
Erector spinae muscles, **342**, **344***t*, 345*f*
superficial, 332*f*
ER. *See* Endoplasmic reticulum
Erythema, 157
Erythroblastosis fetalis, **670**
Erythroblasts
early (basophilic), **651**, 652*f*
late, **651**–652, 652*f*
Erythrocytes, 138*f*, 647, 647*f*, **649**–656, 649*f*
dietary requirements, 653–654
disorders, 655–656
fate/destruction of, 654–655
life cycle, 654*f*
function, 650
hormonal controls, 652–653
production of, 651–652, 652*f*
structure, 649–650, 650*f*
summary, 658*t*
in urine, 1024*t*
Erythropoiesis, **651**–652, 652*f*
Erythropoietin (EPO), **638**, **652**, 998
erythropoiesis and, 652–653, 652*f*
source/trigger/effects, 638*t*
Eschar, 170
Esophageal arteries, 746*f*, **751***t*
Esophageal (cardiac) sphincters, **897**, 898, 898*f*
Esophageal glands, 897
Esophageal hiatus, **897**
Esophageal plexuses, **538**
Esophageal ulcers, 897
Esophageal varices, 915

Esophagitis, 897
Esophagus, 883*f*, 889*f*, **896**–897, 896*f*
abdominal arteries in relation to, 753*f*
digestive processes occurring in, 897–899, 898*f*
major functions (overview), 920*t*
upper respiratory tract in relation to, 834*f*
Essential amino acids, 946, 947*f*
Essential nutrients, **944**
Estradiol, 1081, 1082
Estriol, 1082
Estrogen replacement therapy, 194
Estrogens, 634–635, **1082**
in early pregnancy, 1120, 1120*f*
in late pregnancy, 1135, 1135*f*
location/function in body, 48*t*
in ovarian cycle, 1094–1096, 1095*f*
in puberty, 1098
regulation/effects, 627*t*
sodium balance influenced by, 1047–1048
source/stimulus/effects (summary), 1099*t*
in uterine cycle, 1096–1098, 1097*f*
Estrone, 1082
ESV (end systolic volume), **700**, 703*f*, 727*f*
Ethmoid bone, 205*f*, 206*f*, **210**–211, 211*f*
nasal cavity and, 213, 215*f*, 834*f*
orbits and, 211, 211*f*, 213, 214*f*
summary/important markings, **217***t*
Ethmoid sinuses, **211**, 211*f*, 218, 218*f*
Eupnea, **864**
Evaporation, **986**
body temperature and, 986–987
water and, 40, 986–987
Eversion (movement), **262**, 263*f*
muscles involved in, 379–380*t*, 380*f*
Exchange reactions, **37**–38, 38*f*
Exchange transfusion, 670, **673**
Excitability (responsiveness/ irritability), **280**
Excitation-contraction (E-C) coupling, **291**
of skeletal muscle, 288, 291–293, 292*f*
of smooth muscle, 310, 312, 313*f*
Excitation vs. inhibition, in cardiac/skeletal/smooth muscle, 315*t*
Excitatory postsynaptic potentials (EPSPs), **411**–413, 412*f*
action potentials compared to, 414*t*
Excitotoxin, 468
Excreta, 8
Excretion, **8**
Exercise
adaptations to, 307, 309
aerobic (endurance), 303, **307**, 309
blood flow during, 734, 734*f*
body heat increased by, 985
bone benefits, 197*b*
effects on muscle, 305, 307, 309

endurance (aerobic), 303, **307**, 309
energy systems used during, 300–304, 303*f*
heart benefits, 708
heat produced during, 304
lactic acid and, 302, 303*f*
metabolic rate and, 985
overload principle, 309
overuse injuries, 309
oxygen debt caused by, 304
resistance, **307**, 309
respiratory adjustments during, 869–870
skeletal muscle fiber type and, 306*t*
stored ATP and, 300–301
stored CP and, 301–302
Exergonic reactions, **38**
Exocrine glands, 124, **125**, 605
compound, 126*f*
multicellular, **125**–126, 126*f*, 127*f*
unicellular, **125**, 125*f*
Exocytosis, **77**–78, 78*f*, 91
Exogenous antigens, **813**, 813*f*
Exons, **104**, 105
Exophthalmos, **599**, 624
Expiration, **846**, 848*f*, 849
forced, 849
muscles of, 346*t*, 347*f*, 849
Expiratory reserve volume (ERV), **851**, 852*f*
Expulsion stage of labor, 1136*f*, **1137**
Extensibility of muscle tissue, **280**
Extension (movement), **260**–261, 260*f*, 261*f*
of lower limbs, 379–380*t*, 380*f*
of upper limbs, 362–363*t*, 363*f*
Extensor carpi radialis brevis muscle, **360***t*, 361*f*
actions (summary), 362*t*
tendon, 361*f*
Extensor carpi radialis longus muscle, 333*f*, 359*f*, **360***t*, 361*f*
actions (summary), 362*t*
tendon, 361*f*
Extensor carpi ulnaris muscle, 333*f*, **360***t*, 361*f*
actions (summary), 362*t*
Extensor digiti minimi muscle, 361*f*
Extensor digitorum brevis muscle, 374*f*, 375*f*, **381***t*
origin/insertion, **381***t*
Extensor digitorum longus muscle, 331*f*, **373**, 373*t*, 374*f*, 375*f*
actions of (summary), 379*t*
description/action/nerve supply, **373***t*
Extensor digitorum muscle, 333*f*, **360***t*, 361*f*
actions (summary), 362*t*
tendon, 361*f*
Extensor hallucis brevis muscle, 374*f*, 375*f*
Extensor hallucis longus muscle, **373**, 373*t*, 374*f*, 375*f*
actions of (summary), 379*t*
Extensor indicis muscle, 361*f*, **361***t*
actions (summary), 362*t*
Extensor pollicis brevis muscle, **360***t*, 361*f*
actions (summary), 362*t*

Extensor pollicis longus muscle, **360***t*, 361*f*
actions (summary), 362*t*
Extensor retinacula
of ankle, **373**, 374*f*, 375*f*
of wrist, **358**, 360*t*
External orientation/ direction, 13*t*
Exteroceptors, 164, **491**–492, 493*f*
Extracapsular ligaments, **256**
of knee joint, 266*f*, 267
Extracellular fluid (ECF), 66, 67*f*, 111
buffer systems and, 1050–1052
composition of, **1036**, 1036*f*
osmolality and, 1039–1043
Extracellular matrix (ECM)
of bone tissue, 181
of connective tissue, **127**
as membrane protein's anchor, 68*f*
skeletal cartilages and, 176
Extraembryonic coelom, 1121*f*
Extraembryonic membranes, **1122**–1123
Extraembryonic mesoderm, 1120*f*
Extrafusal muscle fibers, **522**–523, 524*f*
Extraglomerular mesangial cells, 1005, 1005*f*
Extranuclear (mitochondrial) inheritance, 1154
Extrapyramidal (indirect) tracts/system, **478**, 479*t*, 480*f*
Extrasystole, **695**
Extrinsic eye muscles, **558**–559, 559*f*
innervation, 558, 559*f*
Extrinsic tongue muscles, **338**, 339*t*
Exudate, 792*f*, **793**
Eyebrows, 556, 557*f*
Eye (eyeball), **556**–578, 559, 560*f*
accessory structures, 556–559, 557*f*
muscles, extrinsic, 558–559, 559*f*
orbits and, 203, 204
parasympathetic fibers, 536*f*, 537*f*
structure, 559–565
chambers, 564, 564*f*
layers, 559–563
poles, 559, 560*f*
segments, 559, 560*f*, 563–565
sympathetic fibers, 536*f*, 539*f*
vision and, 565–578. *See also* Vision
"watery," 558
Eyelashes, **556**, 557*f*
Eyelids (palpebrae), **556**, 557*f*
Eyestrain, 568

Face
arteries, 748*f*, **748***t*
bones, 211–218
at birth, 247, 248*f*
joints of, 258*t*
summary, 217*t*
muscles
of facial expression, 335–336*t*, 337*f*
superficial, 331*f*
Facet (bone marking), 179*t*
Facial arteries, 748*f*, **748***t*, 749*f*

Facial nerve (VII), 448f, 449f, 451, **500**, 501f
  gustatory pathway and, **582**, 583f
  inner ear and, 586f
  muscles served by, 335–336t, 338t, 340t
  origin/course/function, 505f, **505**–506t, 506f
  parasympathetic fibers, 537, 537f
Facial veins, 760f, **760**t, 761f
Facilitated diffusion, **71**
  carrier-mediated, 71–72, 72f
  channel-mediated, 72, 72f
  concentration gradients and, 77
  energy source/description/ examples, 75t
  selectivity of, 75
F actin (fibrous actin), 286
Factor III (tissue factor), 663t, 664f, **665**
Factor VIII (antihemophilic factor), 663t, **668**
Factor XIII (fibrin stabilizing factor), 663t, 664f, **666**
Facultative intracellular pathogens (FIPs), **825**
Facultative water reabsorption, **1019**
Failure to thrive, 447, 642
Fainting (syncope), **458**, 737
  orthostatic hypotension, **551**
  vasovagal syncope, **551**
Falciform ligament, **912**, 913f, 924f
Fallopian (uterine) tubes, **1084**–1085, 1085f
False pelvis, **239**
False (vertebrochondral) ribs, 226f, 227f, **228**
False vocal cords (vestibular folds), 834f, 836f, **837**, 837f
Falx cerebelli, **464**, 465f
Falx cerebri, **464**, 464f, 465f, 761f
Familial hypercholesterolemia, **993**
Familial predispositions, to type 2 diabetes mellitus, 637b
Farmer's lung, 824
Far point of vision, **567**, 567f
Fascia lata, 370t
Fascicles
  arrangement/patterns, **326**, 327f
  of muscles, 282t, **283**, 283f
  of nerves, **498**, 498f
Fasciculus cuneatus, 448f, 449f, 475f, 476f, 477t, **478**
Fasciculus gracilis, 448f, 449f, 475f, 476f, 477t, **478**
FAS (fetal alcohol syndrome), 1130
Fas receptor, **816**
Fast glycolytic fibers, 305–307, **306**, 306t
Fast oxidative fibers, 305–307, **306**, 306t
Fat (adipose) cells, 126, 130, 130f, 131, 131f, **132**
  brown vs. white, 133
  as energy site, 127, 133
  in epidural space of spinal cord, 470, 473f
  insulation function, 127, 133
  in marrow cavity of long bones, 180
  subcutaneous, 152, 153f
Fat capsule, perirenal, **999**, 999f
Fat-fold test, **993**

Fatigue
  central, 303
  muscle, **303**–304
  psychological, 303
Fat-soluble vitamins, 48t, **948**, 948–949t, 952
Fats (triglycerides), **46**–47
  absorption, 931–932, 932f
  dietary requirements, 945t, 946
  digestion, 920t, 928f, 929–930, 930f
  fate in absorptive (fed) state, 973–974, 974f
  functions in body, 48t
  metabolism, 957f, 967–969, 969f
    insulin's influence, 633
    summary, 971t
  molecular structure, 47f
  nutrient pools of, 971, 972f, **973**
  oxidation of, 968, 968f
  saturated/unsaturated, **46**
  substitutes for, 946
  synthesis of, 46, 47f
  trans fats/fatty acids, 46–47, 981
  transport processes, 71, 75t
  uses in body, 945–946
Fatty acids, 46, 47f
  absorption, 931–932, 932f
  digestion and, 928f, **930**
  essential, 944–945, 945t
  omega-3, 47
  oxidation of, 968, 968f
Fatty pad, **256**
  of elbow joint, 268f
  of knee joint, 266f
  laryngeal, 836f
Fatty streak stage (atherosclerosis), **718**b
Fauces, **890**
Feces, 920t, **922**
Feedback control
  mechanisms, 10, 11f
  negative. See Negative feedback mechanisms
  positive. See Positive feedback mechanisms
Female reproductive system, 7, 7f, 1082–1100
  age-related changes in, 1108
  anatomy, 1082–1091, 1082f
    female duct system, 1084–1085, 1085f
  cancer, cervical, 1086
  contraceptive techniques, 1128–1129b
  developmental aspects
    chronology, 1102f, 1103
    embryonic, 1123–1128, 1130t
    fetal, 1132t, 1133
    genetic sex, 1101, 1103
    menopause, 1105, 1108
    puberty, 1104–1105
    sex differentiation, 1102f, 1103–1104
  endocrine system and, 640b, 641b
  estrogen's role in, 634–635, 1099t
  nervous system and, 548b
  oogenesis, **1091**–1092, 1092f
  pelvis, in males vs., 240f, 240t
  progesterone's role in, 634–635
Female sexual response, **1098**–1100

Femoral arteries, 747f, 756f, **756**t, 757f
Femoral condyles, 241, 241f, 243f, 266f
Femoral cutaneous nerve, 515f, 515t
Femoral epicondyles, 241, 241f, 243f
Femoral head, **239**, 241, 241f, 243f, 270f
Femoral neck, 239, 241, 241f, 243f
Femoral nerve, **514**, 515f, 515t
  muscles served by, 367t, 369t, 370t
Femoral vein, 759f, 766f, **766**t
Femoropatellar joint, **265**, 266f
  articulating bones/movements allowed, 259t
Femur, 228f, **239**, 241, 241f, 243f, 246f, 246t
  "broken hip" fracture, 241
  at hip joint, 259t, 270, 270f
  at knee joint, 259t, 265, 266f, 267
Fenestrated capillaries, **720**–721, 720f
Fenestrations (pores), 720, 720f
  of nephrons, 1005, 1006f
Ferritin, 654, 654f, **933**
Fertilization, **1114**
  events before/after, 1115–1117, 1116f, 1117f
  random nature of, 1149
Fetal alcohol syndrome (FAS), 1130
Fetal development, 1114, 1114f, 1133
  of bones/skeleton, 198, 198f
  chronology of events, 1132t
  circulation, 1128–1130, 1131f
  of skin, 170
  of skull, 246, 247f
Fetal fibronectin, 1136
Fetal tissue implants
  in Huntington's disease, 470
  in Parkinson's disease, 469
Fetus, **1114**
Fever, 796t, **798**, **989**
  as controlled hyperthermia, 989
  increased metabolic rate and, 985
Fever blisters (cold sores), **171**
FEV (forced expiratory volume), **853**
Fiber, dietary, insoluble vs. soluble, 944
Fibers, of connective tissue, 127, 129, 176
Fibril, 282f, 282t
Fibrillation, **694**, 697f
Fibrin, 664f, **666**
Fibrin mesh, 665
Fibrinogen, 649t, 663t, 664f, 665, **666**
Fibrinolysis, **666**
Fibrin stabilizing factor (FSF), 663t, 664f, **666**
Fibroblasts, 128f, **129**, 130f, 134f
  in areolar connective tissue, 131, 131f
Fibrocartilage, 128f, **137**, 137f
  of intervertebral joints, 254f, 255
  skeletal, **176**, 177f
Fibrocartilaginous callus, **191**, 191f
Fibrocytes, 128f, 129–130
Fibromyalgia (fibromyositis), **320**

Fibromyositis (fibromyalgia), **320**
Fibronectin, fetal, 1136
Fibrosis
  cardiac muscle, 708–709
  lung, 851
  in tissue repair, **143**, 144, 144f
Fibrous capsule
  joint, 125, 255f, **256**, 257f
  kidney, **999**, 999f, 1000f
Fibrous connective tissues. See Dense connective tissues
Fibrous joints, **253**–254, 253f
  articulating bones/movements allowed, 253, 258t, 259t
Fibrous layer of eye, **559**–560, 560f
Fibrous pericardium, **678**, 679f
Fibrous skeleton of heart, **680**, 687f
Fibrous (structural) proteins, **50**
  functions/examples from body, 52t
Fibula, 228f, 242f, 243f, **244**, 246f, 246t
  collateral ligaments, 266f, **267**
  head, 242f, 243f, **244**, 377f
  joints, 259t
  knee joint and, 265, 266f, 267
  leg implant for damaged, 194b
  muscles and, 373–378f
Fibularis brevis muscle, 375f, **376**t, 377f, 378f
  actions of (summary), 379t
Fibularis longus muscle, 374f, 375f, **376**t, 377f, 378f
  actions of (summary), 379t
  superficial, 331f, 333f
  tendon, 375f, 382f, 383f
Fibularis (peroneus) longus muscle, **376**t
Fibularis tertius muscle, 373, 373t, 374f, 375f
  actions of (summary), 379t
Fibular malleolus, 242f, 243f
Fibular nerve, muscles served by, 373t, 376t, 381t
Fibular notch, **244**
Fibular (peroneal) artery, 756f, **756**–757t
Fibular (peroneal) vein, 759f, 766f, **766**t
Fibular retinacula, of ankle, **373**, 375f
Fight-or-flight response, 449, 550, 631, 631f
  gastric secretions and, 903f, 904
Filaments, of muscle. See Myofilaments
Filiform papillae, **890**, 891f
Filopodia, 424
Filtrate, 75, 75t, **1001**, 1006f
  urine vs., 1007
Filtration, 71, **75**
  in capillary exchange, 739
  energy source/description/ examples, 75t
  glomerular, 1007–1011
  selectivity of, 75
Filtration membrane, **1005**, 1006f
Filtration slits, **1001**, 1005, 1006f
Filum terminale, 466f, **470**, 471f, 472f
Fimbriae, 1082f, **1084**, 1085f
Fingerprints, 155
Fingers (digits)
  bones, 228f, 233, 235f, 236f, 236t, **237**

innervation of, 513f, 514t
joints, 258t
muscles acting on, 358–361t
actions (summary), 362–363t, 363f
muscles of fine movements, 364–366t
FIPs (facultative intracellular pathogens), **825**
First-class levers, **328**, 329f
First-degree burns, 167f, **170**
First law of thermodynamics, 981
First messengers, **607**, 607f
First-order neurons, **475**, 476f, 495
Fission, mitochondrial, 85
Fissure (bone marking), 179t
Fissures
of cerebral hemisphere, **434**, 435f
of lung, 844f
of spinal cord, **472**, 473f
Fixators, synergist muscles functioning as, **325**
Fixed tissue specimen, **118**
Flaccid paralysis, **478**
Flagella, **93**, 95
cilia vs., 93
structure/functions (summary), 95t
Flat bones, **178**, 178f
of skull, 203
structure, 181, 181f
typical rib as, 227f, 228
Flavins, **964**
Fleshy (direct) muscle attachments, **284**
Flexion (movement), **260**, 260f, 261f
of lower limbs, 379–380t, 380f
of upper limbs, 362–363t, 363f
Flexor accessorius (quadratus plantae) muscle, **381t**, 382f, 383f
Flexor carpi radialis muscle, 331f, **358t**, 359f
actions (summary), 362t
tendon, 365f
Flexor carpi ulnaris muscle, 333f, **358t**, 361f
actions (summary), 362t
tendon, 359f, 365f
Flexor digiti minimi brevis muscle
of foot, 382f, **383t**
of hand, **364t**, 365f
Flexor digitorum brevis muscle, **381t**, 382f
Flexor digitorum longus muscle, **373**, 376t, 378f
actions of (summary), 379t
tendon, 382f, 383f
Flexor digitorum profundus muscle, 359f, **359t**, 365f
actions (summary), 362t
tendon, 359f, 365f
Flexor digitorum superficialis muscle, 359f, **359t**, 365f
actions (summary), 362t
tendon, 359f, 365f
Flexor hallucis brevis muscle, 382f, **383t**
Flexor hallucis longus muscle, **373**, 375f, **376t**, 378f
actions of (summary), 379t
tendon, 382f, 383f
Flexor pollicis brevis muscle, **364t**, 365f

Flexor pollicis longus muscle, 359f, **359t**
actions (summary), 362t
tendon, 359f, 365f
Flexor retinacula
of ankle, **373**, 382f
of wrist, **358**, 359f, 365f, **373**
Flexor (withdrawal) reflex, **525–526**, 526f
Flexure lines, 156–157
Flexures
colic (hepatic), **922**, 923f
colic (splenic), **922**, 923f
Flexures (embryonic brain)
cervical, 432f, 433
midbrain, 432f, 433
Floating (vertebral) ribs, 226f, **228**
Flocculonodular lobes, **452**, 454
Fluid compartments, 1036, 1036f
Fluid mosaic model, **67**, 67f
Fluid-phase endocytosis (pinocytosis), **80**–81, 80t
Fluids of body
age-related changes in, 1060
capillary exchange and, 739–740, 740f
cerebrospinal, 465–467
compartments, 1036
extra-/intracellular, 1036, 1036f
composition of
electrolytes, **1036**–1038, 1038f
nonelectrolytes, **1036**
continuous mixing/exchanges of, 1038, 1039f
developmental aspects, 1060
disturbances of, 1041–1043
extracellular, 66, 67f, 111, **1036**, 1036f
interstitial, 70, 127, 1036, 1036f
intracellular, 66, **1036**, 1036f
lymph, 774
pleural, 846
pressure of. See Hydrostatic pressure
serous, 17, 17f, 143
synovial, 255f, 256
water, 1036
Fluorine, 26t, **954t**
Focal point, **566**, 567f
Folacin (folic acid), **951t**
erythrocytes and, 654
Folate, ultraviolet radiation and, 157
Folia, **452**
Foliate papillae, **581**, 581f, **890–891**, 891f
Folic acid (folacin), **951t**
erythrocytes and, 654
Follicles
hair, 153f, **160**, 161f, 162, 171
lymphoid, **777**, 778f, 911
ovarian, 1083f, **1084**, 1093, 1093f
thyroid gland, **620**, 620f
Follicle-stimulating hormone (FSH), **616**
in menstrual cycle, 1096, 1097f
in ovarian cycle, 1094–1096, 1095f
in spermatogenesis regulation, **1080**–1081, 1081f
summary of regulation/effects, 618t
Follicular phase, ovarian cycle, **1093**–1094, 1093f
Fontanels, **246**, 247f

Food
allergies in newborns, 931
energy value of, 85, 943
nutrient categories, 943
swallowing muscles and, 340–341t, 341f
Food guide pyramids, 943, 943f
Food-induced thermogenesis, **985**
Food intake regulation, 982–984
body temperature, 983
hormonal, 982–983
hypothalamic controls, 446f, 982
model, 983–984, 983f
neural signals from GI tract, 982
nutrient signals related to energy stores, 982
psychological factors, 983
Foot
arches, 244–245, 245f
bones, 244–245, 245f, 246f, 246t
innervation of, 515f, 515t, 516, 517f, 517t
muscles acting on, 373–378t
summary, 379–380t
muscles of (intrinsic), 381–383t
transverse arch of, **244**–245, 245f
Footdrop, 373t, 516
Foot processes of podocytes, **1001**, 1005f, 1006f
Foot proteins, 287
Foramen (bone marking), 179t
Foramen lacerum, 208f, **209**
Foramen magnum, **207**, 208f, **216t**
Foramen of Monro (interventricular foramen), **434**, 434f, 445f, 466f
Foramen ovale, 208f, **210**, 210f, **216t**, 680, **706–707**, **1130**
Foramen rotundum, 208f, **210**, 210f, **216t**
Foramen spinosum, 208f, **210**, 210f, **216t**
Force, applied, 326–327, 328f
Forced expiratory volume (FEV), 853
Forced vital capacity (FVC), **853**
Force (mechanical)
bone remodeling and, 190, 190f
muscle contraction and, 295–296, 299, 304–305, 304f
Forearm
arteries, 746f, 747f, 750–751t
bones, 232, 233f, 234f, 236t
innervation of, 513f, 514t
muscles acting on, 356f, **357t**
summary, 362–363t, 363f
muscles of, 358–361t
superficial, 331f, 333f
veins, 758f, 758t, 762–763t
Forebrain (prosencephalon), **431**, 432f
Forehead. See Frontal squama
Forensic medicine, 58b
Foreskin (prepuce), 1066f, **1069**
Formed elements of blood, 647, 647f, **649**
erythrocytes, 649–656
leukocytes, 656–662
platelets, 662
summary, 658t
unusual features, 649

Fornix
cerebral, 437f, 442f, 445f, **454**, 455f
vaginal, 1082f, 1085f, **1088**
Fossa (bone marking), 179t
Fossa ovalis, 680, 682f, 683f, **1138**
Fourchette, 1088f, **1089**
Fourth ventricle, **434**, 434f, 449f
CSF in relation to, 466f
diencephalon in relation to, 445f
lateral/median apertures, 434, 434f
Fovea capitis, **239**, 241f
Fovea centralis, 560f, **563**
Fractures, **190**–193
pathologic, **199**
Pott's, 242f, 244
stages of healing, 191, 191f, 193
traction to treat, **199**
treatment advances, 194–195b
types of, **192t**
Frank-Starling law of the heart, **700**
Fraternal twins, 1094
FRC (functional residual capacity), **851**, 852f
Freckles, 157
Free (naked) nerve endings, 153f, **492**, 495f
functional classes/body location, 493t
pain and, 155, 165, 492, 493t
Free radicals, **90**, 112, 952
after brain injury, 468
peroxisome's role in neutralizing, 90, 112
Frenulum
labial, 889f, **890**
lingual, 889f
Frequency (sound waves), **589**, 590f
Frontal bone, **203**–204, 205f, 206f, 208f
summary/important markings, 216t
Frontal (coronal) plane, **15**, 16f
Frontal eye field of cerebral cortex, 437f, **439**
Frontal lobe, 434, 435f, **436**, 445f, 501f
in ANS control hierarchy, 547, 547f
Frontal processes, maxillary, 212f, **213**, **217t**, 833f
Frontal sinuses, **204**, 215f, 218, 218f, 834f
Frontal squama (forehead), 204, 205f
Frontonasal suture, 204, 205f
Fructose
absorption of, 931
as a monosaccharide, 44, 45f
chemical digestion of, 927, 928f
FSF (fibrin stabilizing factor), 663t, 664f, **666**
FSH. See Follicle-stimulating hormone
Fulcrum, in bone-muscle lever systems, **326**–328, 328f, 329f
Full-thickness burns, 170
Functional brain disorders, **485**
Functional (globular) proteins, **50**
active sites, 52, 53f
enzymes, 53–54, 53f, 54f
functions/examples from body, 52t
molecular chaperones, 52–53, 52t

Functional groups, in biochemical reactions, 44
Functional MRI, **21***b*
Functional residual capacity (FRC), **851**, 852*f*
Functional syncytium, **689**
Fundus
  of eye, **562–563**, 563*f*
  of stomach, 899–900, 899*f*
  uterus, 1085*f*, **1086**
Fungiform papillae, **581**, 581*f*, **890**, 891*f*
Funiculi (white columns), 473*f*, **474**, 475*f*
Fusiform muscles, **326**
Fusion inhibitors, 821
FVC (forced vital capacity), **853**

G₀ phase of cell life cycle, **98**, 99*f*
G₁ phase of cell life cycle, **98**, 99*f*
GABA (gamma-aminobutyric acid), 416*t*, **418**, 469
G actin (globular actin), 286
GAGs (glycosaminoglycans), 121*f*, 129*f*
Galactose
  absorption of, 928*f*, 931
  as a monosaccharide, 44, 45*f*
  chemical digestion of, 927, 928*f*
Galactosemia, 992
Galea aponeurotica, 335*t*, 337*f*
Gallbladder, 753*f*, 883*f*, 913*f*, **916–917**, 920*t*, 924*f*
  ANS fibers/effects, 536*f*, 537*f*, 539*f*, 546*t*
  disorders, 917, 937
  major functions (overview), 920*t*
  regulation of bile release, 916*f*, 917
  small intestine in relation to, 909*f*
  vagus nerve and, 917, 919*f*
Gallstones (biliary calculi), **917**
Gamete, **1066**
  production
    female, 1091–1092
    male, 1073, 1077–1080
  meiosis of, 1073–1077
  variability sources, 1147–1148, 1148*f*, 1149*f*
Gamete intrafallopian transfer (GIFT), 1139
Gamma-aminobutyric acid (GABA), 416*t*, **418**, 469
Gamma delta T cells, **817**
Gamma efferent fibers, **522–523**, 522*f*
Gamma globulin, 649*t*, **806**
  passive immunity and, 806
Gamma interferon, **816**
Gamma motor neurons, 524*f*, 525
Gamma rays, 29, 30
Ganglia, **392**, 491, **499**
  autonomic, **533**, 534*f*
  cranial sensory, **501**
  dorsal root, 499
  location in parasympathetic *vs.* sympathetic divisions, 536*f*
Ganglion cells, retinal, 562, 562*f*
Ganglionic neurons, **533**, 534*f*
Gap junctions (nexus), **69**, 70*f*
  of cardiac muscle, 315*t*, 689, 690*f*
  of smooth muscle, 311, 315*t*, 316

Gas embolism, scuba diving and, 868–869*b*
Gases, **25**
  basic properties, 854–855, 855*t*
  as neurotransmitters, 417*t*, 419
  noble, 32, 32*f*
Gas exchange, 854–858
  capillary, 856*f*, 858
  pulmonary, 855–858, 856*f*
  pulmonary circuit and, 684, 684*f*, 855
  systemic circuit and, 684, 684*f*
Gasserian (semilunar/trigeminal) ganglia, 504*t*
Gastric arteries, 747*f*, 752*f*, 753*f*, **753***t*
Gastric glands, **900**, 901*f*
Gastric juice, 796*t*, **900**, 902–905, 903*f*
Gastric phase, of gastric secretions, 903*f*, **904–905**
Gastric pits, **900**, 901*f*
Gastric ulcers, **902**
Gastric veins, 765*f*
Gastrin, 312, **901**, 904
  intestinal, **905**, 906*t*
  production site/stimuli/target/ actions, 906*t*
  in small intestine motility, 921, 921*t*
  source/trigger/effects, 638*t*
Gastritis, 902
Gastrocnemius muscle, **373**, 374*f*, 375*f*, **376***t*, 377*f*, 378*f*
  actions of (summary), 379*f*
  knee joint and, 266*f*
  superficial, 331*f*–333*f*
  tendon, 377*f*
Gastrocolic reflex, **926**
Gastroduodenal artery, 752*f*, 753*f*
Gastroenteritis, **937**
Gastroepiploic arteries, 752*f*, 753*f*, **753***t*
Gastroepiploic veins, 765*f*
Gastroesophageal (cardiac) sphincter, **897**, 898, 898*f*
Gastroesophageal reflux disease (GERD), **897**
Gastroileal reflex, **921**, 921*t*
Gastrointestinal (GI) tract, 883*f*, **884**
  accessory organs, 884
  activities, 884–886, 884*f*
  ANS effects, 546*t*
  enteric nervous system of, 887*f*, **888–889**
  as food intake regulator, 982
  histology, 887–888, 888*f*
  hormones produced by, 637, 638*t*, 906*t*
  motility, thyroid hormone's effects, 621*t*
  neural reflex pathways, 885–886, 885*f*
  organs (overview), 883*f*, 884
  paracrines produced by, 906*t*
Gastrula, **1122**
Gastrulation, **1123**, 1124*f*
Gate control theory of pain, 497*b*
G cells, 903*t*, **904**
G-CSF (granulocyte-CSF), 660
Gel electrophoresis, 58*b*
Gemellus muscle, 371*f*, **372***t*
  actions of (summary), 379*t*
Gender differences, in CNS development, 481

Generator potentials, 401, **494–495**
Genes, 55, **104**, 1146
  cell aging programming of, 112
  delayed-action, 1150
  linked, **1148**
  role in cancer, 146*b*
  type 1 diabetes and, 636*b*
Genetic palindromes, 1152
Genetic recombination, **1148–1149**, 1149*f*
Genetics, **1146**
  DNA segments as our genetic material, 55
  dominant/recessive traits, 1150–1151, 1151*t*
  environmental factors influencing, 1152–1153
  gene therapy, 1157
    for Parkinson's disease, 469
  genetic code, **104**, 105, 106*f*
  nontraditional inheritance, 1153–1154
  regulation of gene expression, 1153–1154
  screening tests, 1154–1157
    amniocentesis, **1155–1156**, 1156*f*
    carrier recognition, 1155
    chorionic villi sampling, **1156–1157**, 1156*f*
    pedigree analysis, 1155, 1155*f*
  sex determination, 1101, 1103
  sources of genetic variation, 1147–1149
  types of inheritance, 1149–1152
  vocabulary of, 1146–1147
Geniculate bodies, 445*f*, 446, 449*f*, **575**, 576*f*, 592*f*
Geniculate ganglia, 505*f*, 505*t*
Genioglossus muscle, 339*f*, **339***t*
Geniohyoid muscle, 339*f*, **340***t*, 341*f*
Genital herpes, **1101**
Genitalia
  external, **1082**
    female, **1088–1089**, 1088*f*
    male, **1069**
  female, internal, **1082**, 1082*f*
  parasympathetic fibers, 536*f*
  sympathetic fibers, 536*f*, 539*f*
Genital tubercle, 1102*f*, **1103**
Genital warts, **1101**
Genitofemoral nerve, 515*f*, 515*t*
Genome, 55, **1146**
Genomic imprinting, **1154**
Genotype, **1147**
GERD (gastroesophageal reflux disease), **897**
Germinal centers
  lymph node, 777, 778*f*
  in lymphoid follicles, 782*f*
Germinal epithelium, 1083, 1083*f*
Germ layers (embryonic), 145, 145*f*, **1123**
  formation, 1123, 1124*f*
  organogenesis, **1123**, 1126–1132
Gestation period, **1114**, 1114*f*
GFR. *See* Glomerular filtration rate
G (globular) actin, 286
G (guanine), 55–57, 56*f*, 57*t*
GHIH. *See* Growth hormone-inhibiting hormone
Ghrelin, appetite and, 983, 983*f*, 984

GHRH. *See* Growth hormone-releasing hormone
GH. *See* Growth hormone
GIFT (gamete intrafallopian transfer), 1139
Gigantism, 187, **615**, 618*t*
Gingivae (gums), 889*f*, **894–895**, 894*f*
GI tract. *See* Gastrointestinal (GI) tract
Glabella, **204**, 205*f*
Glands, **124**
  ductless, 124
  endocrine, **124–125**
  exocrine, **124**, 125–126, 125*f*–127*f*
  holocrine, **126**, 127*f*
  merocrine, **126**, 127*f*
  sweat, 153*f*
Glans of clitoris, 1088*f*, **1089**
Glans penis, **1069**
Glass factor, origin/function, 663*t*
Glaucoma, **564–565**
Glenohumeral (shoulder) joint, 257*f*, **269–270**, 269*f*
  articulating bones/movements allowed, 258*t*
  ligaments, **269**, 269*f*
Glenoid cavity, **229**, 230*f*, 234*f*, 236*t*, 257*f*, 269*f*
Glenoid labrum, **269**, 269*f*
Glial cells (neuroglia), **389–390**
  in CNS, 390–391, 390*f*
  in PNS, 390*f*, 391
Gliding movements (translation), 259, **260**, 260*f*
Globin, 650, 651*f*
Globular (functional) proteins, **50**
  active sites, **52**, 53*f*
  enzymes, 53–54, 53*f*, 54*f*
  functions/examples from body, 52*t*
  molecular chaperones, 52–53, 52*t*
Globulins, as blood plasma proteins, 649*t*
Globus pallidus, **443**, 444*f*
Glomerular (Bowman's) capsule, **1001**, 1002*f*, 1004*f*, 1005*f*
Glomerular capillaries (glomerulus), **1001**, 1002*f*, 1004*f*–1006*f*
  arterioles serving, **1003**, 1004*f*
Glomerular filtration, **1007–1008**
Glomerular filtration rate (GFR), **1008**, 1009*f*
  regulation
    extrinsic, 1010–1011
    intrinsic, 1008–1010
Glomerular hydrostatic pressure, **1007–1008**, 1008*f*
Glomerular mesangial cells, 1005, 1005*f*
Glomeruli (olfactory), 579*f*, **580**
Glomerulonephritis, 822, 1042
  acute, **1030**
Glomerulus (glomerular capillaries), **1001**, 1002*f*, 1004*f*–1006*f*
  arterioles serving, **1003**, 1004*f*
Glossopharyngeal nerve (IX), 448*f*, 449*f*, 451, **500**, 501*f*
  gustatory pathway and, **582**, 583*f*
  origin/course/function, **506–507***t*, 507*f*

parasympathetic fibers, 537, 537f
Glottis, 836f, **837**
Glucagon, **632**, **977**
    as hyperglycemic hormone, 632,
        633f, 977
    influences on blood glucose,
        632, 633f, 977, 977f
    influences on metabolism, 978t
Glucoamylase, 928f, **929**
Glucocorticoids, **629**–630
    hyper-/hyposecretion, 627t,
        629–630
    location/functions, 48t
    sodium balance and, 1048
    structure/regulation/effects, 627t
Gluconeogenesis, 632, 635f,
    967, 971t
    cortisol and, 629
Glucose
    absorption, 928f, 931
    age-related changes in, 639, 992
    as a monosaccharide, 44, 45f
    blood levels
        aging and, 639
        measuring, 637b
        in postabsorptive state,
            975–979, 977f
        regulation by insulin/glucagon,
            632–634, 633f
        sources of, 975–976, 975t
    in cellular respiration, 38,
        38f, 959f
    digestion, 927, 928f
    glucose sparing, 976–**977**
    insulin and, 632–634, 633f
        in diabetes mellitus, 635f
    metabolism, 38, 38f, 959–967
        glycogenesis, 966–967
        glycogenolysis, 967
        oxidation, 959–966
    in mitochondrial matrix, 85
    reabsorption of, 1014t
    sources of, 975–976
    transport processes, 72, 72f, 75,
        75t, 77, 77f
    in urine, 1024t
Glucose-phosphate, 38, 38f
Glucose tolerance, aging and, 639
Glutamate
    addiction and, 425b
    after brain injury, 468–469
    functional class/secretion
        sites/effects, 416t
    pain impulse transmission
        and, 496b
    role as neurotransmitter, **418**
Glutamic acid, 970, 970f
Gluteal arteries, 756f, **756**f, 757f
Gluteal lines, **237**, 238f, 243f
Gluteal nerves, 516, 517f, 517t
    muscles served by, 370t
Gluteal surface, **237**
Gluteal tuberosity, **241**, 241f
Gluten-sensitive enteropathy
    (celiac disease), 933
Gluteus muscles, 332f, 333f, **367**,
    370t, 371f
    actions of (summary), 379–380t
Glycerol, **46**, 47f
    metabolism and, 957f
    oxidation of, 968, 968f
Glycine, 416t, **418**
Glycocalyx, 67f, **69**, 83, 85
Glycogen
    as a polysaccharide, 44, 45f, 46
    chemical digestion and, 928f, 929

in decomposition reaction,
    37, 38f
metabolism and, 957f
as storage carbohydrate, 46
stores of in skeletal muscle fiber
    types, 306t
Glycogenesis, **966**–967,
    967f, 971t
Glycogenolysis, 632, 635f, **967**,
    967f, 971t
    in liver, 975
    in skeletal muscle, 975
Glycogen storage disease, 992
Glycolipids, **67**–68, 67f
Glycolysis, **302**, 303f
    anaerobic, **302**, 303f, 306, 306t
    in carbohydrate metabolism,
        959f, **960**–961,
        960f, 971t
Glycolytic fibers, fast, **306**–307
    activities best suited for, 306t
    metabolic/structural
        properties, 306t
Glycoproteins, 67f, **68**–69
    as binding cites (membrane
        receptors), 83–84
    as cell adhesive, 69, 83
Glycosaminoglycans (GAGs),
    128, 129f
Glycosomes, 284
Glycosuria, 634, 635f, 1024t
GnRH. *See* Gonadotropin-releasing
    hormone
Goblet cells, **120**, 122f
    as a unicellular exocrine gland,
        125, 125f
    of GI mucosa, 888
    of large intestine, 920t
    large intestine mucosa, 925f
    of respiratory mucosa, 832
    of small intestine, 910, 910f
    of stomach mucosa, 900
Goiter, **623**–624, 623f
Golgi apparatus, 66f, **87**–89, 88f
    endomembrane system
        interactions, 89–90, 90f
    structure/functions
        (summary), 94t
Golgi tendon organs, **494**,
    522, 522f
    functional classes/body
        location, 493t
Golgi tendon reflexes, **525**, 525f
Gomphoses, **254**, 894
Gonadal arteries, 746f, 747f,
    752f, **754**t
Gonadal ridges, 1102f, **1103**
Gonadal veins, 758f, 764f,
    764t, 765f
Gonadocorticoids (sex hormones),
    630–631, **1066**
    location/functions, 48t
    sources/stimuli/effects, 1099t
    structure/regulation/
        effects, 627t
Gonadotrophs, **616**
Gonadotropin-releasing hormone
    (GnRH), **616**, 618t, 619t
    in ovarian cycle,
        1094–1096, 1096f
    in spermatogenesis regulation,
        1080–1081, 1081f
Gonadotropins, **616**, 618t, 619t
Gonads (primary sex organs), 605f,
    634–635, **1066**
    aging and, 639

female. *See* Ovaries
male. *See* Testes
Gonorrhea, **1100**
Gouty arthritis (gout), **274**, 276
G protein, **84**, 84f
    hormone signaling and,
        607–608, 607f
G protein-linked receptors, **84**, 84f,
    420–421, 420f
    smell sense and, 580
    vision and, 572
Graafian (vesicular) follicle, 1083f,
    1084, 1092f
Gracilis muscle, 331f, 368f,
    369t, 371f
    actions of (summary), 379–380t
Graded muscle responses,
    297–299, 298f–300f
Graded potentials, **401**–402,
    401f, 402f
    dendrites and, 393
    stimulus energy processing and,
        494–495, 495f
Grafts
    allografts, **820**
    autografts, **818**
    bone, 194b
    isografts, **818**, 820
    ligament, 268, 272
    osteochondral, 275b
    rejection, 818, 820
    self-antigens and, 800
    skin, 170
    xenografts, **820**
Grand mal seizures, 457
Granular (juxtaglomerular) cells,
    1003, 1005, 1005f
Granular layer of skin (stratum
    granulosum), 154f, **155**
Granulation tissue
    in fracture repair, 191, 191f
    in tissue repair, **143**, 144f
Granule cells, 452, 452f, 580
Granules (secretory vesicles), **87**,
    88f, 89
Granulocyte-CSF (G-CSF), 660
Granulocytes, **657**–659, 657f
    summary, 658t
Granulomas, infectious, 795
Granulosa cells, 1083f, **1084**,
    1093, 1093f, 1116f
Granzymes, **816**, 816f
    functions (summary), 817t
Graves' disease, 618t, **624**, 822
Gravitational pull, balance and,
    594–595, 595f
Gravity
    body's center of, 225
    bone's response to, 190
Gray commissure, **472**, 473f
Gray matter, **395**
    arrangement in CNS, 433, 433f
    brain stem and, 447
    somatic motor zone, **474**, 474f
    somatic sensory zone, **474**, 474f
    spinal cord, 433, 433f,
        472–474, 473f, 510f
    organization in, 474, 474f
    visceral motor zone, **474**, 474f
    visceral sensory zone, **474**, 474f
    white matter fiber tracts
        and, 442f
Gray rami communicantes, 536t,
    540f, **541**
Gonads (primary sex organs), 605f,
Greater curvature (stomach),
    899f, **900**

Greater omentum, **900**, 924f
Greater sciatic notch, **237**,
    238f, 243f
Greater trochanter of femur,
    241, 241f
Greater tubercle of humerus, 231f,
    232, 234f
Greater wing of sphenoid
    bone, **209**
Greenstick fractures, 192t
Gristle. *See* Hyaline cartilage
Groove (bone marking), 179t
Gross anatomy, **2**
    histology and, 118
Ground substance, **127**–129, 129f
Group A, B, and C nerve fibers, **408**
Growth, **8**
Growth cone (axon), **423**–424
Growth cycles of hair follicles, 162
Growth factors
    agrin and, 316
    stored in bone matrix, 179
Growth hormone (GH), **614**–616
    in epiphyseal plate activity, 187
    functions of, 52t, 618t
    hyper-/hyposecretion, 615,
        616, 618t
    influences on metabolism, 978t
    metabolic actions of, 615f
    summary of regulation/
        effects, 618t
Growth hormone-inhibiting
    hormone (GHIH), **614**–615,
    615f, 618t
Growth hormone-releasing
    hormone (GHRH), **614**–615,
    615f, 618t
Growth phase/metabolic phase of
    cell life cycle, 98
Growth (proliferation) zone of long
    bones, 186, 186f
GTP (guanosine triphosphate), 78,
    107, 607, 607f
Guanine (G), **55**–57, 56f, 57t
Guanosine triphosphate (GTP), 78,
    107, 607
Guanylyl cyclase, 419
Gummas, 1100
Gums (gingivae), 889f, **894**, 894f
Gustatory cortex, 437f, 440, **440**,
    582, 583f
Gustatory hairs, **581**, 581f
Gustatory (taste) cells, **581**, 581f
Gustducin, 582
Gut, 883f, **884**. *See also*
    Gastrointestinal (GI) tract
Gut brain, 886
Gut-brain peptides, **418**
Gynecology, **1108**
Gynecomastia, **1108**
Gyri, **434**, 435f
    postcentral, 435f, **436**
    precentral, 435f, **436**

Hageman factor, 663t
Hair cells
    cochlear, 588f, **591**, 591f, 592f
    maculae, 594–595, 594f, 595f
Hair follicle receptors (root hair
    plexus), 153f, **160**, 161f, 164,
    492, 493t
Hair follicles, 153f, **160**, 161f, 162
    aging and, 171
Hairs (pili), **159**
    baldness/thinning, 162–163, 171
    color, 160, 171

continues

Hairs (pili) (cont.)
  growth, 162
  structure, 153f, 159–160
  types, 162
Hairs (stereocilia), 588f
Haldane effect, 863, 863f
Half-life of radioisotopes, 29
Hallux, 244, 245f, 246f
Hamate bone, 235, 235f, 236f, 236t
Hamstring muscles, 333f,
  367, 372t
  actions of (summary),
    379–380t, 380f
  strains, 384
Hand
  bones, 233, 235, 235f, 236t, 237
  innervation, 513f, 514t
  muscles acting on,
    358–361t, 362t
  muscles of (intrinsic), 364–366t
Haploid chromosomal
  number, 1073
Hapten (incomplete antigen), 799
Haptoglobin, 655
Hashimoto's thyroiditis, 826
Haustra, 922, 923f
  contractions, 920t, 926
Haversian (central) canal of osteon,
  137, 138f, 182, 182f, 183f
Haversian system (osteon), 137,
  181, 182f, 183f
Hb. See Hemoglobin
HbS (hemoglobin S), 655–656
hCG (human chorionic
  gonadotropin), 1120, 1120f
HCL. See Hydrochloric acid
HCM (hypertrophic
  cardiomyopathy), 709
hCS (human chorionic
  somatomammotropin),
  1134–1135
HDLs (high-density lipoproteins),
  48t, 980, 981f
Head
  arteries, 746f, 748–749t, 749f
  equilibrium and, 594–598
  innervation, 511f, 511t
    sympathetic, 541
  muscles, 342–345t, 343f, 345f
    of facial expression,
      335–337t, 337f
    of mastication, 338–339t, 339f
  of sperm, 1077, 1079f
  traumatic injuries to, 468
  veins, 758f, 758t, 760f,
    760–761t, 761f
Headache, sinus, 835
Head (bone marking), 179t
Healing by first intention, 148
Healing by second intention, 148
Hearing, 556, 583–598
  age-related changes in, 599
  auditory association area,
    437f, 440
  auditory pathway to brain,
    592–593, 592f
  congenital abnormalities, 599
  developmental aspects, 599
  disorders, 593–594
  ear anatomy, 583–587
  physiology, 587–593
    auditory pathway to brain,
      592–593, 592f
    cortical processing, 593
    excitation of hair cells,
      591–592, 591f, 592f

resonance of basilar
    membrane, 591, 591f
  transmission of sound,
    590, 590f
  primary auditory cortex, 437f,
    440, 592f, 593
Heart, 677–712, 678
  age-related changes in, 708–709
  anatomy, 678–689, 681–683f
  artificial, 707b
  autorhythmic cells of,
    692–694, 694f
  blood flow through, 738
  blood supply of, 685–686, 685f
  chambers, 679f, 680–684
  contractility of, 701–702, 701f
  coverings, 678, 679f
  decompensated, 705
  developmental aspects, 705–709
  embryonic origins, 1127
  fetal, 705–707
  hormone produced by, 637, 638t
  innervation, 536f, 537f, 538f,
    541, 541t, 546t, 695, 695f,
    701, 701f
  intrinsic conduction system of,
    692–695, 694f
    disorders, 694–695
  location, 678, 679f
  murmurs, 698
  muscle, 689–690. See also
    Cardiac muscle
    contraction mechanism,
      690–692
  as organ in thoracic cavity, 844f
  pacemaker of, 693, 694f
  palpitations, 709
  pathways of blood through,
    684–685
  physiology, 692–705
    cardiac cycle, 698–700
    cardiac output, 700–705
    electrical events, 692–697
  point of maximal intensity,
    678, 679f
  in pregnancy, 1135
  role in circulation of blood, 647
  size, 678
  sounds, 697–698, 697f
  thyroid hormone and, 621t
  transplants, 706–707b
  valves, 686–689, 687f
    disorders, 688–689, 709
  wall layers, 678–680, 679f
Heart attack (myocardial
  infarction), 686, 692
  congestive heart failure and, 704
  etiology and therapies, 706–707b
Heart block, 695, 697f
Heartburn, 897
  in pregnancy, 1135
Heart failure
  cyanotic skin and, 157
  left-sided, 705
  right-sided, 705, 871
Heart rate, 702, 704
  age factors, 704
  ANS and, 702
  blood pressure and, 726–731,
    731f
  cardiac output and, 726, 727f
  disorders, 704
  exercise and, 704
  hormones that influence,
    621t, 702
  sinus rhythm and, 693

Heat exhaustion, 989
Heat-loss center, hypothalamic, 987
Heat-loss mechanisms,
  988–989, 988f
Heat (metabolic). See also Body
  temperature
  distributed by blood plasma, 649
  evaporation and, 986–987
  generated by muscle
    contraction, 281, 304, 985
  in inflammatory response,
    792f, 793
  lost in cellular activity, 982
  metabolic rate and, 984–985
  thyroxine's role in, 621, 986
Heat-promoting center,
  hypothalamic, 987
Heat-promoting mechanisms,
  987–988, 988f
Heat shock proteins (hsp), 53
Heat stroke, 989
Heat (temperature)
  blood flow to skin and, 738, 986
  body's response to, 547,
    986–989, 988f
  energy conversions liberating, 27
  exchange mechanisms,
    986–987, 986f
  water's capacity for, 40
Heavy (H) chains of antibody
  molecule, 807, 807f
Heavy metals, 60
  skin penetrated by, 164
Heimlich maneuver, 840
Helicase enzyme, 99
Helicobacter pylori bacteria, gastric
  ulcers and, 902
Helicotrema, 587, 588f
Helium, 27f, 28, 28f, 32, 32f
Helix
  double, 56, 56f
  ear, 584f, 585
Helper T cells, 810, 811f,
  814–815, 815f
  functions (summary), 817t
Hematocrit, 647–648
Hematology, 673
Hematoma, 674
  beneath the skin, 158
  at fracture sites, 191, 191f
Hematopoiesis (hemopoiesis), 651
  site of, 179, 181
Hematopoietic stem cell, 128f,
  129, 651
Hematuria, 1024t
Heme, 650, 651f
Hemiazygos vein, 762f, 763f, 763t
Hemiplegia, 479
  CVAs and, 468
Hemochromatosis, 674, 938
Hemocytoblasts, 651, 662f
Hemodialysis, 1023b
Hemoglobin F, 672
Hemoglobin (hB), 649, 650
  abnormal, 655–656
  as a globular protein, 52t
  as an intracellular buffer,
    1051–1052
  iron in, 654
  modified, 672–673b
  molecule, 51f
  nitric oxide and, 860
  in oxygen transport, 858–861
  skin color and, 157
  structure, 650, 651f
  in urine, 1024t

Hemoglobin S (HbS), 655–656
Hemoglobinuria, 1024t
Hemolytic anemias, 655
Hemolytic disease of newborn, 670
Hemophilias, 668
Hemopoiesis. See Hematopoiesis
Hemorrhagic anemias, 655
Hemorrhoidal veins, 923f, 925
Hemorrhoids, 723, 925
Hemosiderin, 654, 654f
Hemostasis, 663–668
  blood clotting factors, 663t, 665
  disorders, 667–668
  events of, 664f
    clot retraction/repair, 666
    coagulation stage, 665–667
    fibrinolysis, 666
    platelet plug formation, 665
    vascular spasm, 663, 665
Henle's loop. See Loop of Henle
Henry's law, 854–855
Heparin, 130, 667
Hepatic arteries, 747f, 752f, 753f,
  753t, 912, 913f
Hepatic colic flexure, 922, 923f
Hepatic ducts, 909f, 912, 913f
Hepatic macrophages (Kupffer
  cells), 912, 914f
Hepatic portal system, 764t, 887,
  900
Hepatic portal vein, 759f, 764f,
  764t, 765f, 900, 912, 913f
Hepatic veins, 758f, 759f, 764f,
  764t, 765f, 912, 913f
Hepatitis, 915
Hepatocytes, 912, 914f
Hepatopancreatic ampulla,
  908, 909f
Hepatopancreatic sphincter
  (sphincter of Oddi), 908, 909f
Herceptin (trastuzumab), 147b
Heredity, 1146. See also Genetics
Hering-Breuer (inflation) reflex, 869
Hermaphrodites, 1103
Hernia, 320, 384
  inguinal, 1108
Herniated (prolapsed) disc,
  220–221, 220f
Herpes virus, 1101
Hertz (Hz), 589
Heterogeneous substances, 31
Heterozygous, 1146
Hexose sugars, 44, 45f
Hiatal hernia, 897
Hiatus, 755f
Hiccups, 451, 512
  mechanism/result, 854t
Hierarchy of structural
  organization, 2
High-density lipoproteins (HDLs),
  48t, 980, 981f
Hilton's law, 516, 518
Hilum
  lymph node, 778f, 779
  pulmonary, 842, 844f
  renal, 998, 998f
  spleen, 779, 780f
Hindbrain (rhombencephalon),
  431, 432f
Hinge joint, 258t, 259t, 264f, 265
Hip (coxal) bone, 237, 238f, 243f,
  246f, 246t
Hip (coxal) joint, 237, 270–271,
  270f
  articulating bones/movements
    allowed, 259t

congenital hip dysplasia, 247–248
innervation of, 515f, 515t
muscles acting on (summary), 379–380t, 380f
muscles crossing, 333f, 367–372t
stability of, 271
total replacement, 275b
Hip (pelvic) girdle, 229, **237**
bones, 237–239, 238f, 243f, 246f, 246t
Hippocampus, 454, **455**, 455f
memory and, 462, 462f, 463
Hirsutism, 162, **642**
Histamine, 130f, **793**, 793t, **901**, 904
allergies and, 822–823, 823f
functional class/secretion sites/effects, 415t
production site/stimuli/target/ actions, 906t
source/effects, 793t
stomach and, 901
synthesized from histidine, 418
Histidine, 947f
histamine synthesized from, 418
Histology, **2**, **118**
Histone proteins, **97**, 98f
Histotoxic hypoxia, **861**
HIV (human immunodeficiency virus) infection, **821**, 1087
Hodgkin's disease, **783**, 820
Holocrine glands, **126**, 127f, 159
Holoenzyme, **53**
Homeostasis, 2, 8–12, **9**
control systems, 9–11, 9f
imbalances, 11–12
Homogeneous substances, 30
Homologous chromosomes (homologues), **1073**, 1146
Homozygous, **1146**
Homunculi
motor, **438**–439, 438f
somatosensory, 438f, **439**
Horizontal cell, retina, 562f
Horizontal plate, of palatine bone, 208f, **213**, 215f
Horizontal (transverse) plane, **15**, 16f
Hormonal stimuli, of endocrine glands, 611, 611f
Hormone replacement therapy (HRT), 194, 1108
Hormones, **605**, **606**
amino-acid based, **606**
anabolic, 52t, 947
antagonistic interactions of, 611
calcium blood levels and, 188–189, 189f
chemistry of, 606
of digestion, **906t**
duration of action, 610
endocrine glands and, **124**–125
food intake regulation and, 982–983
found in blood plasma, 649t
half-life of, 610
hormonal stimuli and, 611, 611f
humoral stimuli and, 611, 611f
hyper-/hypoglycemic, 632
inhibiting, **614**
lipid-soluble, 606
mechanisms of action, 606–610
direct gene activation, 609–610, 609f

PIP-calcium signaling, 608–609, 608f
second-messenger systems, 607–609, 607f
metabolism and, 48t, 978t
negative feedback mechanisms, 10, 11f, 611–612, 623, 629
neural stimuli and, 611, 611f
onset of action, 610
permissive interactions of, 611
pituitary, 614–620
produced by non-endocrine organs, 636–638, 638t
prohormones and, 614
releasing, **614**
sex. See Sex hormones
as signaling chemical, 83
steroid, **606**
synergistic interactions of, 611
target cell specificity, 610
tropic, **614**
typical changes produced by, 606
water-soluble, 606
Horner's syndrome, **551**
Horns (cornua), of hyoid bone, 218, 218f
Horny layer of skin (stratum corneum), 154f, **155**
Housemaid's knee, 273
hPL (human placental lactogen), 1122, **1134**–1135
HRT (hormone replacement therapy), 194, 1108
Human blood groups, **668**–670
ABO blood groups, **669**, 669t
Human body
anatomical variability and, 14–15
elements composing, 26t
homeostasis, 8–12
necessary life functions, 4–8, 5f
structural organization, 3–4, 4f
survival needs, 8
Human chorionic gonadotropin (hCG), **1120**, 1120f
Human chorionic somatomammotropin (hCS), **1134**–1135
Human chorionic thyrotropin (hCT), 1122, **1135**
Human defensin, secreted by skin cells, 164
Human development
embryonic, 1117–1132
fertilization, 1114–1117
fetal, 1132–1133
gestation period and, 1114
life cycle and, 1073, 1073f
neonatal, 1137–1139
partition (birth), 1135–1137
Human Genome Project, 55, 1146
Human immunodeficiency virus (HIV) infection, **821**
Human life cycle, 1073, 1073f
Human placental lactogen (hPL), 1122, **1134**–1135
Humeral ligament, 269f
Humerus, 228f, **231**–232, 231f, 234f, 236f, 236t
anatomical vs. surgical neck, 231f, **232**, 234f
elbow joint and, 268, 268f
joint of, 258t
transverse humeral ligament, 269f
Humoral immune response, **799**, 804–810

active immunity in, 805–806, 806f
antibodies of, 806–810. See also Antibodies
cellular immune response vs., 810
clonal selection/differentiation, 804–805, 804f
immunological memory, 805, 805f
mechanism of, 808–810, 809f
passive immunity in, 806, 806f
primary, **805**, 805f, 819f
secondary, **805**, 805f
Humoral immunity, **799**
active, **805**–806, 806f
passive, **806**, 806f
Humoral stimuli, of endocrine glands, 611, 611f
Humors, eyeball, 559
Hunger sensation, hypothalamic regulation of, 446
Huntington's disease, **469**–470, 1150
Hyaline cartilages, 128f, **135**, 136f
in endochondral ossification, 185, 185f
skeletal, **176**, 177f
Hyaluronic acid, 128, 129f
Hydatid (hydatidiform) mole, **1141**
Hydration layers of water, **40**
Hydrocephalus, 467, 467f
Hydrochloric acid (HCL), 900, 901f, 920t
in bone resorption, 188
regulation/mechanism of secretion, 904–905, 904f
vomiting and, 908
Hydrocortisone. See Cortisol
Hydrogen
atomic structure, 28, 28f
in formation of single covalent bonds, 35f
functions in body, 26t
isotopes, 29, 29f
percentage of body mass, 26t
as reactive element, 32, 32f
Hydrogen bonds, 36, 37f
Hydrogen ions, **41**
acidity and, 42
regulation of
chemical buffers, 1050–1052
renal, 1052–1054
respiratory, 1052
Hydrogen peroxide, 90
Hydrogen phosphate, 1038f
Hydrolases, 53–54
Hydrolysis reactions, **41**, 44, 45f
enzymatic, in digestion, **927**
hydrolases and, 53–54
peptide bonds and, 49f
Hydronephrosis, 999
Hydrophilic molecules, 67
Hydrophobic molecules, 67
Hydrostatic pressure, **73**, **739**
body fluids exchange regulated by, 1037–1038, 1038f
capillary, 75, 75t, **739**–740, 740f, 1042
in filtration, 75, 75t
glomerular, 1007–1008, 1008f
in osmosis, 73–74
Hydroxides, 41
Hydroxyapatites (mineral/bone salts), 183, 195b

Hydroxyl ions, **41**
alkalinity and, 42
Hydroxyurea, 656
Hygiene hypothesis of allergies, 824–825b
Hymen, 1082f, **1088**, 1088f
Hyoglossus muscle, 339f, **339t**, 341f
Hyoid bone, **218**, 218f, 339f, 341f, 834f, 836f, 889f
swallowing and, 340
Hyperaldosteronism (Conn's disease), **1061**
Hyperalgesia, 497b
Hyperbaric oxygen chambers, 855
Hypercalcemia, 189, 704, 1044t
Hypercapnia, **865**–866, 866f
Hyperchloremia, 0144t
Hyperemia, 792f, **793**
active, **737**
exercise, **737**
reactive, **735**
Hyperextension (movement), **261**, 261f
Hyperglycemia, 634, 635f, 636b
Hyperglycemic hormones, 632, 634, 977
Hyperinsulinism, 634
Hyperkalemia, 704, 1044t
Hypermagnesemia, 1044t
Hypernatremia, 1044t
Hyperopia (farsightedness), **568**, 569f
Hyperparathyroidism, 625
Hyperphosphatemia, 1044t
Hyperplasia, **111**
of smooth muscle fibers, 316
Hyperpnea, 635f, **869**
Hyperpolarization, 400f, **401**, 401f, 402–404
Hypersensitivity disorders, **822**–825
acute (immediate), **822**–823, 823f
allergies, **822**–823, 823f
subacute, 823–824
Hypersomnia, 485
Hypertension, **733**
as ANS imbalance, 550
congestive heart failure and, 704
portal, **915**
primary (essential), **733**
secondary, **733**
Hyperthermia, 989, **989**
Hyperthyroidism, 618t, 985
Hypertonic solutions, 74, 74f, 75
Hypertrophic cardiomyopathy (HCM), **709**
Hypertrophic zone of long bones, 186, 186f
Hypertrophy, **112**
Hyperventilation, 866, 1055, 1056t
Hypervitaminoses, 948, 952
Hypoblast, 1122, 1124f
Hypocalcemia, 704, 1044t
Hypocapnia, **866**
Hypochloremia, 1044t
Hypochondriac regions (right and left), **18**, 18f
Hypodermis (superficial fascia), **152**, 153f
Hypogastric ganglia, **541**
Hypogastric (pelvic) plexus, 537f, **538**
Hypogastric plexuses, 539f
Hypogastric (pubic) region, **18**, 18f
Hypoglossal canal, **207**, 208f, 216t

Hypoglossal nerve (XII), 448f, 451, **500**, 501f
  cervical plexus in relation to, 511f
  muscles served by, 339t, 340t, 341t
  origin/course/function, 508f, **508t**
Hypoglossal nuclei, 450f
Hypoglycemia, **634**
Hypoglycemic hormones, 632, **974**
Hypokalemia, 704, 1044t
Hypomagnesemia, 1044t
Hyponatremia, **1042**, 1042f, 1044t
Hyponychium, **163**
Hypoparathyroidism, 625
Hypophyseal fossa, 208f, **209**, 210f
Hypophyseal portal system, 613f, **614**
Hypophyseal portal veins, 613f, **614**
Hypophysectomy, **642**
Hypophysis, **612**–620. See also Pituitary gland
Hypoproteinemia, **1042**–1043
Hypotension, **732**–733
  acute, 733
  chronic, 733
  orthostatic, 733
Hypothalamic-hypophyseal tract, **613**, 613f
Hypothalamic nucleus, 445f
Hypothalamus, 445f, **446**–447, 448f
  in ANS control hierarchy, 547, 547f, 550
  disorders, 447
  embryonic origins, 432f, 433
  as endocrine system organ, 605, 605f
  functions (summary), 453t
  growth hormone secretion regulated by, 614–616, 615f
  homeostatic roles of, 446
  as limbic structures, 454, 455f
  as neuroendocrine organ, **605**
  nuclei of, 445f, 446
  in pain pathway, 496b
  pituitary relationships, 445f, 446, 613–614, 613f
  sleep and, 459
  in spermatogenesis regulation, 1080–1081, 1081f
  thermoregulatory centers of, **987**
Hypothenar eminence, 364
  muscles, 364t, 365f
Hypothermia, **989**
Hypothyroidism, 985
Hypotonic hydration, **1042**, 1042f
Hypotonic solutions, **74**, 74f
Hypoventilation, **871**, 1056t
Hypovolemic shock, **740**–742, 741f, 1042
Hypoxemic hypoxia, **861**
Hypoxia, **860**–861
  respiratory alkalosis and, 1056t
Hypoxic drive, **867**
Hysterectomy, **1108**
Hz (hertz), 589
H zone, **284**, 285f, 288f, 289f

I bands, **284**, 285f, 288f, 289f, 689, 690f
ICF. See Intracellular fluid
"Icon molecule," 147b
Identical twins, 1094
IFNs. See Interferons
IF. See Interstitial fluid

IgA to IgM immunoglobulins, 807–808, 808t, 892
IgA in breast milk, 1138–1139
IGFs (insulin-like growth factors), 179, **614**, 615f, 618t
Ileoanal juncture surgery, 926
Ileocecal valve, **908**, 923f
Ileocolic artery, 752f, **754t**, 755f
Ileostomy, 926
Ileum, 755f, 883f, **908**–909, 909f, 923f, 924f
Ileus, **938**
Iliac arteries, 746f, **746t**, 747f, 752f, **754t**, 755f–757f, **756t**, 1086f
Iliac crest, **237**, 238f, 243f
Iliac fossa, **237**, 238f
Iliac/inguinal regions (right and left), **18**, 18f
Iliac spine, **237**, 238f, 243f, 270f
Iliac veins, 758f, **758t**, 759f, 765f, 766f, **766t**
Iliococcygeus muscle, 350t, 351f
Iliocostalis muscles, 344t, 345f
Iliofemoral ligament, **270**, 270f
Iliohypogastric nerve, 515f, 515t
Ilioinguinal nerve, 515f, 515t
Iliopsoas muscle, **367**, 367t, 368f
  actions (summary), 370–380t
  superficial, 331f
Iliotibial tract, 333f, 370t, 371f
Ilium, **237**, 238f, 240f, 243f
ILs (interleukins), **814**, 818t
Imaging techniques, 3, 20–21b, 147b, 481
Immune-complex (type III) hypersensitivity, **823**–824
Immune response
  antibody-mediated. See Humoral immune response
  cell-mediated. See Cellular immune response
  primary (overview), 819f
Immune surveillance, **816**
Immune system, 788–829, **789**
  adaptive defenses, 789f, **798**–820
    cellular, 810–820
    humoral, 804–810
  age-related changes in, 826
  antigens overview, 799–800, 800f
  burn injury and, 167
  cell aging theories and, 112
  chimeric, **820**
  developmental aspects, 825–826
    embryonic, 1123–1128, 1130t
    fetal, 1132f, 1133
  disorders
    autoimmune diseases, 821–822
    hypersensitivities, **822**–825
    immunodeficiencies, 820–821
  innate defenses, 789–798, 789f
    antimicrobial proteins, 795–798
    fever, 798
    inflammatory response, 791–795
    NK cells, 791
    phagocytes, 790–791
    summary, 796t
    surface barriers, mucosae, 789–790
    surface barriers, skin, 789–790
    surface barriers, summary, 796t

Immunity, **789**
  acquired, 805–806, 806f
  active, 805–806, 806f
  cellular, 789f, **799**
  colostrum's boost to, 1138
  humoral, 789f, **799**, 805–806, 806f
  passive, 806, 806f
Immunization, **826**
Immunocompetence, **800**–803, 801f, 802f
Immunodeficiency disorders, **820**–821
Immunogenicity, of complete antigens, **799**
Immunoglobulins (Igs), **806**–810
  active immunity and, 805–806, 806f
  antigen-binding sites and, 807, 807f
  as blood proteins, 52t, 806
  classes of, 807–808
    characteristics unique to, 808t
  complement activation and, 797–798, 797f
  diversity mechanisms, 808
  mechanisms of action, 808–810, 809f
  monoclonal antibodies and, 810
  as monomer molecules, 807, 807f
  passive immunity and, 806, 806f
  plasma cells as source of, 777, 806
  structure, 807, 807f
  targets, 808–810, 809f
Immunological memory, **805**
  active vs. passive immunity and, 805–806, 806f
  time lags in, 805f
Immunology, **826**
Immunopathology, **826**
Immunosuppressive therapy, 820
Impacted teeth, 894
Implantation of blastocyst, **1119**–1120, 1119f, 1120f
Impotence, 1073, **1074b**
Incisive fossa, 206f, 208f, **212**, **217t**
Incisor teeth, 893f, **894**
Inclusions (cytoplasmic), 84, **94t**
Incompetent heart valve, 688–689, 698
Incomplete antigen (hapten), **799**
Incomplete dominance, **1151**
Incontinence, **1027**
  in pregnancy, 1135
  stress vs. overflow, 1027
Incus bone, **217t**, 584f, **585**, 585f
Independent assortment, 1147–1148, 1148f
Indirect (extrapyramidal) system/tracts, **478**, 479t, 480f
Indirect muscle attachments, **284**
Indolamines, **418**
Inert vs. reactive elements, 32–33, 32f
Infant period, 1114
Infant respiratory distress syndrome (IRDS), **851**
Infants
  adjustments to extrauterine life, 1137–1139
  transitional period of, **1138**
Infections
  in burn patients, 167
  tissue repair in, 143

Infectious granulomas, 795
Infectious mononucleosis, **662**
Inferior orientation/direction, 13t
Infertility, 1080
Inflammation
  enhanced by antibody action, 809f, 810
  pain and, 496b
Inflammatory bowel disease, **938**
Inflammatory response, 143, 144f, **791**–795, 796t
  cardinal signs, 793
  events of (flowchart), 792f
Inflation (Hering-Breuer) reflex, **869**
Infrahyoid muscles, **340**, 340–341t, 341f
  swallowing and, 340, 340–341t
  as synergists, 342
Infraorbital foramen, 205f, 208f, 212f, **213**, 214f, **217t**
Infraorbital groove, 214f
Infrapatellar bursa, 266f
Infrapatellar fat pad, 266f
Infraspinatus muscle, 353f, **354**, **355t**, 356f
  actions of (summary), 362t
  superficial, 333f
Infraspinous fossa, of scapula, 230f, 231, 234f, 236t
Infratemporal fossa, 271f, 272
Infundibulum
  hypothalamus, 445f, **446**, 448f
  pituitary, **612**
  uterine tube, 1082f, **1084**, 1085f
Ingestion, **884**, 884f, 920t
Inguinal hernia, **1108**
Inguinal/iliac regions (right and left), **18**, 18f
Inguinal ligament, 349f
  iliopsoas muscle in relation to, 367t
  pelvic veins in relation to, 766f
Inheritance
  dominant-recessive, **1149**–1151, 1150f, 1151t
  dominant traits, 1150
  recessive traits, 1151
  extranuclear (mitochondrial), 1154
  incomplete dominance, **1151**
  multiple-allele inheritance, **1151**, 1151t
  polygene, **1152**, 1153f
  sex-linked, **1152**
Inhibin, **1080**, 1081f, 1096
Inhibiting hormones, **614**
Inhibitory postsynaptic potentials (IPSPs), **411**–413, 412f
  action potentials compared to, 414t
Initiator tRNA, **107**, 109
Injuries
  cartilage, 272, 273f
  hemostasis and, 663–668
  knee, 267–268, 267f
  ligaments, 272
Inner cell mass, **1118**, 1118f, 1119f
Inner layer of eye, **561**. See also Retina
Inorganic compounds, **40**–43
  salts, 40f, 41
  water, 40–41, 40f
Inositol triphosphate (IP), 608f, **609**
Insanity, 485
Insensible heat loss, **987**

Insensible water loss, **987**, **1039**, 1040
Insertion (muscle), **259**, **283**–284, 325
Insomnia, **460**
Inspiration, **846**, 847–849
abdominal muscles during, 348
diaphragm and, 346, 346t, 847, 848
forced, 849
intercostal muscles and, 848–849, 848f
as mechanical process, 847
muscles of, 346, 346t, 847–849
sequence of events, 848–849, 848f
Inspiratory capacity (IC), **851**, 852f
Inspiratory muscles, 346t, 347f
Inspiratory reserve volume (IRV), **851**, 852f
Insula, 435f, **436**, 440, 583f
Insulators (electrical), 398
Insulin, 52t, **632**, **973**
blood glucose levels and, 632–634, 633f, 973–974, 975f
summary, 978t
deficiency, 634, 635f
excess, 634
food intake regulation and, 982
as hypoglycemic hormone, 632, 633f, **974**
manufactured, 637b
metabolism and, 973–974, 975f, 978t
Insulin-like growth factors (IGFs), 179, **614**, 615f, 618t
Insulin resistance, **637b**
Integral proteins, 67f, **68**, 68f, 71
membrane receptors, 83–84
Integration, as nervous system function, 388, 388f
Integration centers, of reflex arcs, **521**, 521f
Integrins, 83
Integumentary system, 5, **6**, 6f, 151–174, **152**. See also Skin
aging and, 170–171
cardiovascular system and, 768b
developmental aspects, 170–171
embryonic, 1123–1128, 1130t
fetal, 1132t, 1133
digestive system and, 934b
embryonic development, 1123–1128, 1130t
endocrine system and, 640b
functions of, 163–165
homeostatic interrelationships with other body systems, 168b, 169b
lymphatic system/immunity and, 784b
muscular system and, 318b
nervous system and, 548b
reproductive system and, 1106b
respiratory system and, 876b
skeletal system and, 196b, 197b
skin, 152–158
appendages, 158–163
thyroid hormone's effects, 621t
urinary system and, 1058b
Interatrial septum, **680**, 682f
Intercalated cells, of collecting ducts, 1002f, 1003
Intercalated discs, 140f, **141**, **689**, 690f

Intercarpal joints, 258t
Intercellular clefts, **720**, 720f
Intercondylar eminence, **242**, 242f, 243f
Intercondylar fossa, **241**, 241f
Intercostal arteries, 746f, 750f, 751f, **751t**
Intercostal muscles, 331f, 540f
in breathing, 847–849, 848f
external, **346**, **346t**, 347f
as inspiratory muscles, 346, 347f
internal, **346**, **346t**, 347f
as expiratory muscles, 346, 347f
Intercostal nerves, 509f, 510f, **511**, 540f
breathing and, **863**, 864f
muscles served by, 346t, 348t
Intercostal spaces, 226, 226f
Intercostal veins, 762f, **762t**, 763f, **763t**
Interferons (IFNs), 795–796
alpha, 818t
beta, 818t
as cytokines, 814
functions (summary), 818t
gamma, **816**, 818t
protective mechanism, 795f, 796t
Interleukins (ILs), **660**, **814**, 818t
Interlobar arteries, 1000f, **1001**
Interlobar veins, 1000f, **1001**
Interlobular veins, 914f
Intermediate filaments, 66f, 70f, **91**–92, 91f
other names for, 92
of smooth muscle fibers, 310–311, 311f
structure/functions (summary), 94t
Intermediate mass (interthalamic adhesion), **443**, 445f
Intermediate orientation or direction, 13t
Intermittent claudication, 320
Internal capsule, 442f, **443**, 444f, 480f
Internal orientation or direction, 13t
Interneurons (association neurons), **395**, 396–397t, 397
Internodal pathway, 693, 694f
Interoceptors (visceroceptors), **492**, 493t
Interosseous arteries, **750t**, 751f
Interosseous membrane, **232**, 233f, 234f, 242, 242f
Interosseous muscles
of foot, 383f, **383t**
of hand, 361f, **364**, **366t**
Interosseous nerve, muscles served by, 360t, 361t
Interosseus arteries, 750f
Interphalangeal joint, articulating bones/movements allowed, 259t
Interphase, 97, **98**–99, 99f, 101, 102f
Interspinales muscle, 345f
Interspinous ligament, 220f
Interstitial cells of Cajal, 907
Interstitial fluid (IF), **70**, **1036**, 1036f
in connective tissue's ground substance, 127
electrolyte composition of, 1038f
hydrostatic pressure of, **739**, 740f
as lymph, 774

Interstitial growth of cartilage, **176**
Interstitial lamellae, **182**, 183f
Interstitial (Leydig) cells, **1068**, 1068f
Intertarsal joints
articulating bones/movements allowed, 259t
muscles acting on, 373–378t
Interthalamic adhesion (intermediate mass), **443**, 445f
Intertransversarius muscle, 345f
Intertrochanteric crest, **241**, 241f
Intertrochanteric line, **241**, 241f, 243f
Intertubercular sulcus, 231f, **232**, 234f, 236t
Interventricular arteries, 681f, 682f, **685**, 685f, 686
Interventricular foramen (foramen of Monro), **434**, 434f, 445f, 466f
Interventricular septum, **680**, 683f, 687f, 694f
Interventricular sulci, **680**, 681f, 682f
Intervertebral disc, in relation to rib, 227f
Intervertebral discs, 218, 219f, **220**–221, 220f, 223f
fibrocartilage in, 137, 137f, 176, 177f
herniated, 516
Intervertebral foramen, 219f, 220f, **221**
Intervertebral joints, 254f, 255, 258t
Intervillus space (lacuna), 1121f
Intestinal arteries, 752f, **754t**, 755f
Intestinal crypts (crypts of Lieberkühn), 910f, **911**
Intestinal gastrin, **905**
source/trigger/effects, 638t
Intestinal glands, 126f
Intestinal juice, **911**
Intestinal lymphatic trunk, **775**, 776f
Intestinal phase of gastric secretion, 903f, **905**
Intestino-intestinal reflex, 922
Intra-abdominal pressure, 350
Intracapsular ligaments, **256**
of knee joint, 266f, 267
Intracellular fluid (ICF), 66, **1036**
buffer systems and, 1050–1052
compartment, **1036**, 1036f
electrolyte composition of, 1038f
Intraepithelial lymphocytes, 910f
Intrafusal muscle fibers, 494, **522**, 522f, 524–525, 524f
Intramembranous ossification, **184**–185, 184f
Intramolecular bonds, 36
Intramural ganglia, 538
Intraperitoneal organs, **886**
Intrapleural pressure, **846**–847, 846f
changes during inspiration/expiration, 849, 849f
Intrapulmonary pressure, **846**–847, 846f
changes during inspiration/expiration, 849, 849f
Intravenous pyelogram (IVP), **1031**
Intrinsic (capsular) ligaments, **256**
Intrinsic cardiac conduction system, 315f, **692**–695, 694f
disorders, 694–695
Intrinsic factor, **655**, 900, **902**, 920t, 932, 951t

Intron DNA ("junk" DNA), **104**, 105, 109–110
Inulin, 1021
Inversion (movement), **262**, 263f
muscles involved in, 379–380t, 380f
In vitro fertilization (IVF), 1139, 1140f
Involuntary nervous system, **388**, **533**. See also Autonomic nervous system
involuntary vs. voluntary muscle, **141**, 280, 315t
Iodine, 26t, **954t**
in thyroid hormone synthesis, 622, 622f
Ion channels, **398**–399
in chemical synapses, 409–411, 410f
gated/nongated, 398–399, 398f
Ionic bonds, **33**–34, 33f, 34f
dissociation and, 40, 40f
redox reactions and, 38
vs. polar/nonpolar, 36, 36f
Ionizing radiation, 30, **60**
Inotropic receptors, 420
Ions, **33**
diffusion of, 83
as electrical energy, 25
as electrolytes, 41
Iotropic agents, 701–702
Ipsilateral fiber distribution, **454**
Ipsilateral reflexes, **524**
IPSPs (inhibitory postsynaptic potentials), **411**–413, 412f
action potentials compared to, 414t
IRDS (infant respiratory distress syndrome), **851**
Iris, 546t, 557f, 560f, **561**
Iron, 26t, **954t**, 956
absorption, 932, 933
red blood cell formation and, 653–654, 933
Iron-deficiency anemia, 655
Irregular bones, **178**, 178f
structure, 181
Irritability (excitability/responsiveness), 5, **280**, 397
Irritable bowel syndrome, 926
IRV (inspiratory reserve volume), **851**, 852f
Ischemia, **468**
Ischemic (stagnant) hypoxia, **860**
Ischial body, **237**, 238f
Ischial ramus, **237**, 238f, 243f
Ischial spine, **237**, 238f, 243f
Ischial tuberosity, **237**, 238f, 239, 243f
Ischiocavernosus muscle, **350**, **350t**, 351f
Ischiofemoral ligament, **270**–271, 270f
Ischium, **237**, 238f, 239, 270f
Islets of Langerhans (pancreatic islets), **917**
Isografts, **818**, 820
Isoleucine, 947f
Isomers, **44**, 45f
Isometric muscle contractions, 296, **300**, 301f
Isotonic muscle contractions, 296, **300**, 301f
Isotonic solutions, **74**
Isotopes, **29**, 29f

Isthmus
　thyroid gland, 620, 620f
　uterine tube, **1084**, 1085f
　uterus, 1085f, 1086
Isthmus of the fauces, 834f, **835**
Itch receptors, 492
IVP (intravenous pyelogram), **1031**

Jaundice, 158, 917
　physiological, 1139, **1141**
Jaw
　bones
　　lower. See Mandible
　　upper. See Maxilla
　joint. See Temporomandibular
　　joint
　muscles, 338–339t, 339f
Jejunum, 883f, **908**–909, 909f, 924f
JGA. See Juxtaglomerular
　apparatus
JG (juxtaglomerular) cells, **1003**,
　1005, 1005f
Joint cavities, 19, 19f, 255f, **256**
Joint kinesthetic receptors,
　494, 495f
　functional classes/body location,
　　493t
Joints, 252–278, **253**
　aging and, 276
　artificial, 275b
　bones articulated/type/movements
　　allowed, 258–259t
　cartilaginous, 253, 254f, **255**
　　summary, 256t
　classification
　　by function, 253, 256t
　　by structure, 253, 256t
　developmental aspects, 276
　dislocation (luxation), **273**
　exercise and, 276
　fibrous, **253**–254, 253f
　　summary, 256t
　homeostatic imbalances,
　　272–274, 276
　inflammatory/degenerative
　　conditions, 273–274, 276
　injuries common to, 272–273,
　　273f
　innervation of, 516, 518
　intervertebral, 254f, 255
　replacement, 275b
　replacement therapy, 275b
　sternocostal, 254f, 255
　synovial, **255**. See also Synovial
　　joints
Joint stretch receptors (propri-
　oceptors), pathways to, 476f
Jugular foramen, 208f, **209**, 216t,
　760, 761f
Jugular lymphatic trunks, **775**, 776f
Jugular lymph sacs, 783
Jugular (suprasternal) notch,
　226f, **227**
Jugular veins, 758f, **758t**, 759f,
　760f, **760t**, 761f, 762f, 763f
Junctional folds, of sarcolemma,
　289, 290f
Junctional rhythm, **694**–695, 697f
Junctions, cell
　anchoring, 69, 70f
　desmosomes, **69**, 70f
　gap, **69**, 70f
　impermeable, 69, 70f
　tight, **69**, 70f
　types of, 69, 70f
Juxtaglomerular apparatus (JGA),
　1003, 1005, 1005f

tubuloglomerular feedback in,
　1008, 1009f, 1010
Juxtaglomerular (granular) cells,
　1003, 1005, 1005f
Juxtamedullary nephrons, **1003**
　cortical nephrons vs., 1003, 1004f

Kaposi's sarcoma, 821
Karyotype, **1146**, 1147f
Kcal (kilocalories), **943**
Keloid, **148**
Keratan sulfate, 128, 129f
Keratin, **152**
　epidermal, 123
　functions/examples from body,
　　52t
　in hair, 163
　hard vs. soft, 160, 163
　in nails, 163
　protective mechanism, 796t
Keratinized cells, 123
Keratinocytes, **152**, 154f, 165
Keratohyaline granules, 155
Ketoacidosis, **634**, 635f, 636b, 637b
Keto acids, 961, 962f, 970
Ketogenesis, 635f, **969**, 969f
Ketones (ketone bodies), **634**, **969**,
　1024t, 1050
Ketonuria, 634, 635f, 1024t
Ketosis, **60**, 969
Kidneys, **998**
　in acid-base balance,
　　1052–1054
　　compensations, 1057, 1060
　aging and, 1030
　anatomy, 998–1006
　blood pressure regulation by,
　　730–731
　blood supply, 1000f, 1001
　　in nephrons, 1003, 1004f
　chronic renal disease,
　　1022–1023b
　diagnostic tests, 1022b
　hemodialysis, 1023b
　hormones produced by, 638, 638t
　innervation, 1001
　　ANS effects, 539f, 541t,
　　　546t, 547
　lobes, **1000**, 1000f
　renal calculi, 1024
　transplant surgery, 1023b
Kilocalories (kcal), **943**
Kinase enzymes, 312, 313f
Kinesins, 90, 103f
Kinetic energy, **25**
　in passive membrane transport
　　processes, 75t
Kinetochores, 102f, 103f
Kinins, **793**
　source/effects, 793t
Kinocilium, 594f, 595, 595f
Klinefelter's syndrome, 1103
Knee
　bones, 239, 241, 241f
　injuries, 267, 267f
　ligaments, 265, 266f, 267
Kneecap (patella), 228f, 239, 241,
　241f, **242**, 246f, 246f
Knee-jerk (patellar) reflex, 265,
　523–524, 523f
Knee joint, **265**–268, 266f
　articulating bones/movements
　　allowed, 259t
　femoropatellar, **265**, 266f
　inflammatory conditions, 273
　innervation of, 515f, 515t, 516,
　　517f, 617t

muscles acting on (summary),
　379–380t, 380f
　muscles crossing, 367–372t
　replacement/prosthetic, 275b
　tibiofemoral, **265**, 266f
Knee replacements, 275b
Knuckle joints, 258t
Knuckles, 235, 235f
Krebs cycle, 957f, 959f, **961**–963,
　962f
　summary, 971t
Kupffer cells, **721**, 790, **912**, 914f
Kuru disease, 482–483b
Kwashiorkor, **993**
Kyphosis, 219, 248

Labia, mouth, 889f, **890**
Labial frenulum, 889f, **890**
Labia majora, **1088**, 1088f
Labia minora, **1088**–1089, 1088f
Labioscrotal swellings, 1102f, **1103**
Labor, **1135**
　false, **1136**
　hormonal induction,
　　1135–1136, 1135f
　oxytocin and, 10, 1135–**1136**,
　　1135f
　as positive feedback mechanism,
　　10, 1135f, 1136
　stages, 1136f, 1137
Labyrinth (inner ear), 584f,
　586–587, 586f
　bony (osseous), **586**–587, 586f
　disorders, 594
　membranous, **586**, 586f
Labyrinthitis, 599
Lacrimal apparatus, **557**–558, 558f
Lacrimal bones, 205f, 206f, **213**
　orbits and, 213, 214f
　summary/important markings,
　　217t
Lacrimal canaliculi, **557**, 558f
Lacrimal caruncle, **556**, 557f
Lacrimal fossa, 206f, **213**, 217t
Lacrimal glands, **557**, 558f
　ANS effects, 546t
　orbits and, 213
　parasympathetic fibers, 537f
　sympathetic fibers, 539f
Lacrimal nuclei, 537
Lacrimal puncta, **557**, 558f
Lacrimal sac, 213, **557**, 558f
Lacrimal secretions (tears), **557**
　lysozyme and, 558, 790
　as protective mechanism, 796t
Lactase, 928f, **929**
Lactation, **1138**–1139, 1139f
Lacteals, **775**, **909**, 910f, 932, 932f
Lactic acid, **302**, 303f, 960f, **961**,
　1050
　formation, 302, 303f
Lactiferous ducts, 1089f, **1090**
Lactiferous sinus, 1089f, **1090**
Lactose
　as a disaccharide, 44, 45f
　chemical digestion of, 928f, 929
Lactotrophs, **616**
Lacunae, 135, 136f, 138f, **182**, 183f
Lacunae (intervillus spaces),
　1121f, **1122**
Lagging strand, in DNA
　replication, 99, 100f
Lambdoid suture, 203, 205f,
　206f, **207**

Lamellae, 137, 138f, **179**, 183f
Lamellar bone, **181**–182
Lamellated granules, 155
Lamellated (Pacinian) corpuscles,
　493f
Laminae, vertebral, **221**, 221f,
　222f, 223f
Lamina propria, 131f, 132, **142**
　of large intestine mucosa, 925f
　stomach, 901f
Laminar flow (streamlining), 724
Laminectomy, 248
Lamins, 96f, 97
Langerhans' cell (dendritic cell),
　152, 154f
　as antigen-presenting cell, 803
　as biological barrier, 164
　as lymphoid cell, **777**
Language, 436, 460
　cerebral dominance and, 441
Lanugo coat, 170
Laparoscopy, **938**, **1109**
Large intestine, 883f, **922**–927
　abdominal veins in relation to,
　　765f
　anatomy, gross, 922–923, 923f
　bacterial flora, **925**
　blood supply, 754t, 764t, 923f
　digestive processes, 925–927
　disorders, 922, 926, 927
　functions, 920t, 922
　mucosa, 925, 925f
　parasympathetic fibers, 536f, 537f
　sympathetic fibers, 539f
　sympathetic innervation, 541t
Laryngeal cartilages, 341f, 834f,
　836–837, 836f
Laryngeal prominence, **836**, 836f
Laryngitis, **838**
Laryngopharynx, 834f, **835**, 889f,
　895–896
Laryngotracheal bud, **873**
Larynx, 832f, **835**–838
　cartilage skeleton of, 176, 177f
　features/functions, 838t
　hyoid bone and, 218
　sphincter functions, 838
　swallowing and, 340
Latent period of muscle twitch,
　297, 297f
Lateral excursion, of mandible,
　271f, 272
Lateral horns, **472**, 473f, **538**, 540f
Lateralization, 441
Lateral ligament, of temporo-
　mandibular joint, 271f, **272**
Lateral masses
　of atlas (C1), 221, 222f
　of ethmoid bone, **211**, 211f
Lateral orientation/direction, 13t
Lateral (small cell) nuclear group,
　450f, **455**
Lateral thalamic nuclei, 445f, 446
Lateral ventricles (brain), **434**, 434f
　white matter fiber tracts and, 442f
Latissimus dorsi muscle, **354**,
　354t, 356f
　actions of (summary), 362t
　arm movements and,
　　354, 354t
　as posterior thorax muscles,
　　352, 353f
　superficial, 332f, 333f
Laughing, mechanism/result,
　854f
LDLs (low-density lipoproteins),
　48t, **980**, 981f

L-Dopa, 469
    pathway for synthesis of, 418f
Lead, 164
Leading strand, in DNA
    replication, 99, 100f
Leakage (nongated) ion channels,
    72, **398**
Learning, hyperalgia and, 497b
Lecithin, 931, 944
Left lower quadrant (LLQ), **19**, 19f
Left upper quadrant (LUQ), **19**, 19f
Left ventricular assist devices
    (LVADs), 707b
Leg
    bones, 242–244, 242f, 243f,
        246f, 246t
    innervation of, 515f, 515t
    muscles, 373–378t
        acting on, 367–372t
        actions of (summary),
            379t, 380f
        superficial, 331f, 333f
Lemniscal system/tract, 476f, 477t,
    478, 592f, **593**
Lens, 560f, 564f, **565**
    refraction and, 565–566, 567f
Lens epithelium, 564f, **565**
Lens fibers, **565**
Lens vesicle, **598**
Lentiform nucleus, **443**, 444f
Leptin, 190, **638**, 982–983,
    983f, **984**
    female puberty onset and,
        1094, 1098
    source/trigger/effects, 638t
Lesion, **148**
Lesser curvature (stomach),
    899f, **900**
Lesser omentum, **900**, 913f, 924f
Lesser sciatic notch, of ischium,
    237, 238f, 243f
Lesser trochanter, of femur, **241**,
    241f, 243f
Lesser tubercle, of humerus, 231f,
    232, 234f, 236t
Let-down reflex, 617, **1138**, 1139f
    as positive-feedback mechanism,
        1138
Lethal dominant genes, 1150
Lethal hit mechanisms, by
    cytotoxic T cells, 815–816,
    816f
Lethargy, 458
Leucine, 947t
Leukemias, 660
Leukocytes, **130**, 138f, 647, 647f,
    656–662
    disorders, 660, 662
    production of, 660, 661f
    structure, 656–657
    types of/percentages, 657,
        657f, 659f
        agranulocytes, **659**–660
        granulocytes, **657**–659
        summary, 658t
    in urine, 1024t
Leukocytosis, **657**, **794**, 794f
Leukopenia, **660**
Leukoplakia, 146b
Leukopoiesis, **660**, 661f
Leukotrienes, 606, **793**, 793t
    location/function in body, 48t
Levator ani muscle, **350**, 350t,
    351f, 923f, 1026
Levator labii superioris muscle,
    336t, 337f

Levator palpebrae superioris
    muscle, 503t, **556**, 557f
Levator scapulae muscle, **352**,
    353f, 353t
Levator veli palatini, 340, 341f
Levers, **326**
Lever systems (bone-muscle),
    326–330
    effort, muscle contraction as,
        327, 328f
    fulcrum, joints as, 327, 328f
    lever
        bone as, 326–327
        first/second/third class,
            328, 329f
        power, 327–328, 328f
        speed, 327–328, 328f
        load, bone (plus weight) as,
            326–327, 328f
    mechanical
        advantage/disadvantage
            and, **327**–330, 328f
Leydig (interstitial) cells, **1068**,
    1068f
LH. See Luteinizing hormone
Libido
    DHEA and, 630, 1082, 1100
    estrogens and, 1099t
    testosterone and, 1082, 1099t,
        1100
Life cycle
    cell, 97–101
    functions essential to, 4–8
    survival needs for, 8
Ligamenta flava, 135
Ligament of head of femur, 239,
    270f, **271**
Ligaments, **256**
    artificial, 272
    capsular, **256**, 268
    as connective tissue proper, 126
    elastic connective tissue of, 135
    extracapsular, **256**
    grafts, 268, 272
    intracapsular, **256**
    intrinsic, **256**
    joint stability and, 257
    longitudinal, **220**, 220f
    sprain injuries, 272
    syndesmoses and, 253–254, 253f
Ligamentum arteriosum, 681f,
    707, **1138**
Ligamentum flavum, 220,
    220f, 472f
Ligamentum nuchae, 135, 207,
    216t, 343, 343t
    back muscles in relation to, 345f
Ligamentum teres
    of femur, 270f, **271**
    of liver, **912**, 913f, 924f, **1138**
Ligamentum venosum, **1138**
Ligand-gated ion channels, 290,
    290f, **398**–399, 398f
    mechanism of action, 419–420,
        420f
Ligands, **83**, 83f, 290
Light, properties of, 565–567,
    566f, 567f
Light adaptation, **574**–575
Light (L) chains of antibody
    molecule, **807**, 807f
Limb buds, **1127**, 1127f
Limbic association area, **441**
Limbic system, 440, **454**–455, 455f
    in ANS control hierarchy, 547,
        547f, 550

communication between
    cerebral cortex and, 455
    functions (summary), 453t
    hypothalamic nuclei and, 446
Limbs (appendages), 12. See also
    Lower limbs; Upper limbs
Limbus (corneal-scleral junction),
    564f
Linea alba, **348**, 349f
Linea aspera, **241**, 241f
Line (bone marking), 179t
Lingual artery, 748f, **748t**, 749f
Lingual frenulum, 889f, **890**
Lingual lipase, 892
Lingual tonsil, **781**, 834f, 889f,
    891, 891f
Linked genes, 1148
Linker DNA segment, 97, 98f
Linker proteins, 69, 70f
Linoleic acid, 944–945
Lipases, **918**, 928f, **929**
Lipid bilayer of plasma membrane,
    67, 67f
    passive transport processes and,
        71–75, 72f
Lipidemia, 635f, 671
Lipid rafts, **68**
Lipids, **46**, 48t
    absorption, 928f, 931–932, 932f
    digestion, 928f, 929–930, 930f
    food/dietary sources, 944–945,
        945t
    lipoid substances, 48, 48t
    metabolism, 621t, 967–970
        summary, 971t
    molecular structure, 47f
    phospholipids, 47, 47f, 48t
    in plasma membrane, 67, 67f
    problems with excesses/deficits,
        945t
    recommended dietary allowance,
        945t
    steroids, 47–48, 47f, 48t
    triglycerides, 46–47, 47f, 48t
    uses in body, 945–946
Lipofuscin, 392
Lipogenesis, **968**–969, 969f, 971t
Lipolysis, 635f, 968–**969**,
    969f, 971t
    in adipose tissues, 975–976
Lipoprotein (a), 980
    atherosclerosis and, 718b
Lipoproteins, **980**, 981f
    functions as a globular protein,
        52f
    location/functions in body, 48t
Liposomes, **112**
Lips (labia), 889f, **890**
    cleft lip, 936
Liquids, **25**
Lithium, atomic structure, 28, 28f
Liver, 883f, **912**–916, 924f
    abdominal veins in relation to,
        765f
    as accessory organ to small
        intestine, 912
    anatomy
        gross, 912, 913f
        microscopic, 912, 914f, 915
    ANS effects, 546t
    blood supply, 753t, 764t, 912
    in cholesterol synthesis, 970
    disorders, 668, 915
    glycogenolysis in, 975
    ligaments of, 912, 913f
    lipolysis in, 975–976

in lipoprotein synthesis, 970
    lobes, 912, 913f
    major functions (overview), 920t
    mesentery of, 912, 913f
    metabolic functions, 978–981
        summary, 979t
    optimal intestinal digestive
        activity and, 919
    parasympathetic fibers, 536f,
        537f
    preferred fuel source, 975t
    as site of glucagon activities,
        632, 633
    sympathetic fibers, 536f, 539f
    sympathetic innervation,
        541t, 632
Liver cells (hepatocytes), **912**, 914f
Liver lobules, **912**, 914f
Liver sinusoids, **912**, 914f
LLQ. See Left lower quadrant
Load, **296**, **326**
    in bone-muscle lever systems,
        326–330, 328f, 329f
    influence on muscle
        contraction, 307, 307f
Lobar arteries, 744f, **744t**
Lobes
    cerebellar, **452**, 452f, 453
    cerebral, 434, 435f, **436**
    of glands, 125
    kidney, **1000**, 1000f
    liver, **912**, 913f
    lung, **842**, 844f
    mammary gland, 1089f, **1090**
    thyroid gland, 620, 620f
Lobules
    ear, 584f, **585**
    liver, **912**, 914f
    lung, 842, 844f, 845
    mammary gland, 1089f, **1090**
    testes, 1067, 1068f
Locus on homologous
    chromosomes, 1146
Long bones, **178**, 178f
    developmental schedule,
        198, 198f
    formation of, 185–186, 185f
    growth (postnatal), 186–187
        in length, 186–187, 186f
        in width (thickness), 187, 187f
    structure of, 180–181, 180f
Longissimus muscles, 344t, 345f
Longitudinal arches, of foot,
    244, 245f
Longitudinal fissure (cerebral
    hemisphere), **434**, 435f
    white matter fiber tracts and, 442f
Longitudinal ligaments, **220**, 220f
Long reflexes of GI tract, 886,
    908f, 921, 921t
Long-term memory (LTM),
    461, 461f
Long-term potentiation (LTP), 413
    memory formation and, 463
Loop of Henle, **1001**, 1002f, 1003,
    1004f
    functions (summary), 1020f
    reabsorptive abilities, 1013,
        1014t, 1015
Loose bodies, 272
Loose connective tissues, **131**
    areolar/adipose/reticular,
        131–133, 131f–133f
Lordosis, 219, 247
Loudness of sound, **589**, 590f
    detection of, 593

Low-density lipoproteins (LDLs), **980**, 981*f*
function in body, 48*t*
Lower limbs
arteries, **746***t*, 756–757*t*
bones, 239–246
summary, 246*f*, 246*t*
innervation, sympathetic, 541*t*
innervation of, 514–517
distribution of major peripheral nerves in, 515*f*
skin, 516, 518*f*
veins, 758*f*, 758*t*, 766*f*, **766***t*
LTP (long-term potentiation), 413
in excitotoxicity, 468
memory formation and, 463
Lubrication, weeping, 256
Lumbar arteries, 746*f*, 752*f*, **754***t*, 755*f*
Lumbar curvatures, **219**, 219*f*, 247
Lumbar enlargement, 471*f*, **472**, 509*f*
Lumbar lymphatic trunks, **775**, 776*f*
Lumbar nerves, 471*f*, 509*f*
muscles served by, 344*t*
Lumbar plexus, 509*f*, **514**–516, 515*f*
nerves/spinal roots/structures served, 515*t*
Lumbar puncture (tap), **470**, 472*f*
Lumbar veins, 758*f*, 762*f*, **762***t*, 763*f*, **763***t*, 764*f*, **764***t*, 765*f*
Lumbar vertebrae, 204*f*, **219**, 219*f*
curvatures, **219**, 219*f*
features, 223, 223*f*
summary, 224*f*, 224*t*
movements allowed, 224*t*
Lumbosacral plexus, **514**. *See also* Lumbar plexus; Sacral plexus
Lumbosacral trunk, **514**, 515*f*, 516
Lumbrical muscles
of foot, 381*t*, 382*f*
of hand, 359*f*, **364**, 365*f*, **366***t*
Lumen
of blood vessels, **714**, 715*f*
of esophagus, 896*f*
of small intestine, 910*f*
of uterus, 1085*f*, 1087*f*
Lumpectomy, **1090**
Lunate bone, **235**, 235*f*, 236*f*, 236*t*
Lungs, 832*f*, **842**, 845*f*
ANS effects, 546*t*
blood flow to and from, 738
blood supply of, 845
cancer of, 872–873
features/functions, 838*t*
fibrosis, 851
heart in relation to, 679*f*
innervation of, 845
lung compliance, **851**
in neonatal period, 1137–1138
nonrespiratory air (gas) movements, **854**, 854*t*
parasympathetic fibers, 536*f*, 537*f*
sympathetic fibers, 536*f*, 539*f*
Lung volume reduction surgery, 871–872
Lunula, of nail matrix, 163
LUQ. *See* Left upper quadrant
Luteal phase, ovarian cycle, **1093**, 1093*f*, 1094
Luteinizing hormone (LH), **616**
in ovarian cycle, 1094–1096, 1095*f*

in spermatogenesis regulation, **1080**–1081, 1081*f*
summary of regulation/effects, 619*t*
in uterine cycle, 1096–1098, 1097*f*
Luxation (dislocation), **273**
LVADs (left ventricular assist devices), 707*b*
Lyme disease, **276**
Lymph, **774**
circulation/transport of, 775–777, 776*f*
Lymphadenopathy, **783**
Lymphangitis, 775
Lymphatic (lymphoid) tissue, **777**
diffuse, **777**
Lymphatic system/immunity, 7, 7*f*, 773–787, **774**
cardiovascular system and, 768*b*
developmental aspects, 783
embryonic, 1123–1128, 1130*t*
fetal, 1132*t*, 1133
digestive system and, 934*b*, 935*b*
endocrine system and, 640*b*
homeostatic interrelationships, 784*b*, 785*b*
integumentary system and, 168*b*, 169*b*
muscular system and, 318*b*, 319*b*
nervous system and, 548*b*
reproductive system and, 1106*b*
respiratory system and, 876*b*, 877*b*
skeletal system and, 196*b*
skin and, 168*b*, 169*b*
urinary system and, 1058*b*
Lymphatic vessels (lymphatics)
afferent, 778*f*, **779**
blood vessels in relation to, 717*f*, 774*f*
capillaries, 717*f*, 774–775, 774*f*
collecting vessels, 775, 776*f*
ducts
right, **775**, 776*f*
thoracic, **775**, 776*f*
efferent, 778*f*, **779**
functions of, 776–777
general distribution of, 776*f*
trunks, **775**, 776*f*
Lymphedema, 776
Lymph nodes, **778**–779, 778*f*
blood vessels in relation to, 717*f*
regional, 776*f*
Lymphoblasts, **660**, 661*f*
Lymphocytes, 649*f*, 657*f*, 658*t*, **659**, 659*f*, **777**, 777*f*
generation of antigen receptor diversity in, 803
granular, 791
immunocompetence and, **800**–803
naive, 802
somatic recombination and, 803
Lymphocytic leukemia, 660
Lymphoid follicles (nodules), **777**
in appendix, **782**
in Peyer's patches, **782**, 782*f*
Lymphoid (lymphatic) tissue, **777**
Lymphoid organs, 779–782
appendix, 779*f*, **782**
cells of, 777, 777*f*
lymph nodes, **778**–779, 778*f*
Peyer's patches, 779*f*, **782**, 782*f*
primary, **800**, 801*f*

secondary, **800**
spleen, 779–781, 779*f*, 780*f*
thymus, 779*f*, **781**, 781*f*
tissue of, 777, 777*f*
tonsils, 779*f*, **781**, 782*f*
Lymphoid stem cells, **660**, 661*f*
Lymphoma, **783**
Lymph sacs, **783**
Lysed cells, 74, 74*f*
Lysine, 947*f*
Lysis, cell, in antibody actions, 809–810, 809*f*
Lysosomal enzymes, in bone resorption, 188
Lysosomes, 66*f*, 79, 79*f*, 88*f*, **89**, 89*f*
endomembrane system interactions, 89–90, 90*f*
secretory, 89
structure/functions (summary), 94*t*
Lysozyme, **558**, **790**, 911
of respiratory mucosa, **832**
in saliva, 892

M2A Swallowable Imaging Capsule, 21*b*
MAC (membrane attack complex), 797*f*, **798**
Macrocytes, **655**
Macromolecules, **49**
Macrophages, **660**, **790**
as antigen-presenting cells, **803**
as biological barriers, 164
in connective tissue, **130**, 130*f*
free vs. fixed, 790
as lymphoid cells, 777
Macroscopic anatomy, **2**
Macula densa, **1005**, 1005*f*
in tubuloglomerular feedback, 1008, 1009*f*, 1010
Maculae, 586*f*, 587
in equilibrium, **594**–595, 594*f*, 595*f*
Macula lutea, 560*f*, **563**, 563*f*
Mad cow disease, 482–483*b*
Magnesium, 26*t*, **953***t*
in blood plasma/IF/ICF, 1038*f*
causes/consequences of imbalances, 1044*t*
Magnetic resonance imaging (MRI), 20–21*b*
to assess CNS dysfunction, 481
functional, 21*b*
Magnetic resonance spectroscopy (MRS), 21*b*
Major histocompatibility complex (MHC), **800**–802, 802*f*
Malabsorption, **933**
Male pattern baldness, **162**
Male reproductive system, 7, 7*f*
aging and, 1108
anatomy, 1066–1072
accessory ducts, 1069–1071
accessory glands, 1071–1072
contraceptive techniques, 1128–1129*b*
developmental aspects
chronology, 1102*f*, 1103
embryonic, 1123–1128, 1130*t*
fetal, 1132*t*, 1133
genetic sex, 1101, 1103
gonad descent, 1104, 1105*f*
puberty, 1104–1105
sex determination, 1103
endocrine system and, 640*b*, 641*b*

hormonal regulation of, 1080–1082, 1081*f*
nervous system and, 548*b*
pelvis compared to female, 240*t*
physiology, 1072–1082
effects of testosterone on, 635, 1099*t*
spermatogenesis, 1073–1080
Male sexual response, 1072–1073
Malleolus, 375*f*
fibular, 242*f*, 243*f*, **244**
lateral, 375*f*, 377*f*
medial, 377*f*, 378*f*
tibial, 242*f*, 243*f*
Malleus bone, **217***t*, 584*f*, **585**, 585*f*
Maltase, 928*f*, **929**
MALT (mucosa-associated lymphatic tissue), **782**, 887*f*, **888**, 922
Maltose
as a disaccharide, 44, 45*f*
chemical digestion of, 928*f*, 929
Mammary arteries, 751*t*
Mammary glands, **158**, **1089**–1090, 1089*f*
Mammillary bodies, 445*f*, **446**, 448*f*, 455*f*
Mammograms/mammography, 146*b*, **1090**, 1091*f*
Mandible, 205*f*, 206*f*, **211**–212, 212*f*
lateral movements of, 271*f*, 272
summary/important markings, **217***t*
temporomandibular joint, 258*t*, **271**–272, 271*f*
Mandibular angle, 206*f*, **211**, 212*f*
Mandibular body, **211**, 212*f*
Mandibular condyle, 206*f*, **211**, 212*f*
Mandibular condyles, **217***t*
Mandibular division, of trigeminal nerve (V), 504*f*, 504*t*
Mandibular foramen, 206*f*, **211**–212, 212*f*, **217***t*
Mandibular fossa, **207**, 208*f*, 209*f*, 212*f*, **216***t*, 271*f*
Mandibular neck, 271*f*
Mandibular notch, 206*f*, **211**, 212*f*
Mandibular rami, 206*f*, 211, 212*f*
Mandibular symphysis, 205*f*, **211**, **217***t*
in relation to tongue muscles, 339*f*
Manganese, 26*t*, **955***t*
Manic-depressive disease, 485
Manipulation, as tool for studying anatomy, 2–3
Manubrium, **226**, 226*f*
first rib and, synchondrosis at, 254*f*, 255
muscles of neck/spine and, 343*f*
Manus region, 14*f*
MAP (mean arterial pressure), **725**, 725*f*
factors causing increase in, 731*f*
Marasmus, **993**
Marfan's syndrome, **148**
Marginal artery, 681*f*, 685*f*, **686**
Margination, 792*f*, **794**, 794*f*
Marrow, bone, 180, 180*f*, 181, 183*f*
Marrow (medullary) cavity, **180**, 180*f*, 183*f*
Masculinization, 630
Mass, 25

Masseter muscle, 337f, **338**, 339f
  description/action/nerve supply,
    338t
  origin/insertion, 338t
  superficial, 331f
Mass movements (mass
    peristalsis), 920t, **926**
Mass number, **29**
Mast cells, 793, 793t
  in allergies, 822, 823f
  found in connective tissue,
    130, 130f
Mastectomy
  radical, **1090**
  simple, **1090**
Mastication (chewing), 884f,
    897, 920t
  muscles, 338–339t, 339f
Mastoid air cells, 585
Mastoid antrum, **585**
Mastoiditis, 207
Mastoid process, 205f, 206f, 207,
    208f, 209f, **216**t
Mastoid region of temporal bone,
    207, 209f
Mastoid sinuses (air cells), **207**
Matrix
  of blood, 137, 138f
  of bone, 137, 138f, 179, 181,
    182, 184, 185
  of cartilage, 135, 136f, 137f
  of connective tissue, 131–132
  of dermis, 156
  of hair, 160, 161f, 162
  of mitochondria, 85, 85f
  of nail bed, **163**
  of skeletal hyaline cartilage, 176
  in tissue repair, 143, 144f
Matter, **25**
Maxilla (maxillary bones), 205f,
    206f, 208f, **212–213**, 212f
  frontal process, 212f, **213**, 214f,
    217t, 833f
  orbital surface, 214f
  sinuses, 213, 218, 218f
  summary/important markings,
    217t
Maxillary arteries, 748f,
    748t, 749f
Maxillary division, of trigeminal
    nerve (V), 504f, 504t
Maximal stimulus, **298–299**, 299f
Mean arterial pressure (MAP),
    725, 725f
  factors causing increase in,
    730–731, 730f
Meatus (bone marking), 179t
  of nasal cavity, 213, 215f
Mechanical advantage, in lever
    systems, 327–328, 329f
Mechanical disadvantage, in lever
    systems, **328**, 329f
Mechanical energy, **26**
Mechanically-gated ion channels,
    398
Mechanoreceptors, **491**, 493t
Meconium, **1139**
Medial (large cell) nuclear group,
    450f, **455**
Medial lemniscal system/tracts,
    451, 476f, 477t, **478**
Medial orientation/direction, 13t
Median (midsagittal) plane, **15**, 16f
Median nerve, **512**, 513f, 514t
  muscles served by, 358f, 359f,
    360t, 364t, 366t

Median sulcus, posterior, 449f
Mediastinal arteries, 746f, **751**t
Mediastinum, **15**, 17f, **678**, 679f
  in thoracic cavity, 844f
Medical imaging techniques, 3,
    20–21b
  to assess CNS dysfunction, 481
  to diagnosis cancer, 147b
Medulla
  of hair, 160, 161f
  lymph node, 778f, **779**
Medulla oblongata (medulla),
    445f, **451**
  cardiac centers in, 695, 695f
  cerebral hemispheres in relation
    to, 435f
  cranial nerves in relation to, 501f
  embryonic origins, 432f, 433
  functions (summary), 453t
  hypothalamus in relation to, 451
  meninges in relation to, 464f
  neural integration and, 495f
  nuclei of importance, 450f, 451
    in visceral homeostasis, 451
  respiratory centers in, 451,
    863–864, 864f
  terminus, 471f
  white matter fiber tracts and,
    442f
Medullary cords, lymph node,
    778f, **779**
Medullary (marrow) cavity, **180**,
    180f, 183f
  in endochondral ossification,
    185f, 186
Medullary (renal) pyramids, **1000**,
    1000f
Medullary sinus, lymph node,
    778f, **779**
Megakaryoblasts, **662**, 662f
Megakaryocytes, **662**, 662f
Meibomian (tarsal) glands,
    556, 557f
Meiosis, **1073**
  error rate in female vs. male,
    1092
  mitosis vs., 101, 1074, 1075f
  in oogenesis, 1091–1092
  phases of, 1075–1077
    flowchart, 1076f
  in spermatogenesis, 1077–1079
Meissner's (tactile) corpuscles,
    153f, 155, 164, **492**
  functional classes/body location,
    493t
Melanin, 152, 154f, **157**
  as chemical pigment shield, 164
  as natural sunscreen, 157
Melanocytes, 152, 154f, 157
Melanocyte-stimulating hormone
    (MSH), 614
Melanoma, **166**, 166f
Melanopsin, 575
Melanosomes, 152, 157
Melatonin, 447, **635–636**
Membrane, of cell. See Plasma
    membrane
Membrane attack complex (MAC),
    797f, **798**
Membrane bone, **184**
Membrane potential
  acting as signals
    action potentials, 402–408
    graded potentials, 401–402
  action, **402–408**
  depolarization of, **400–401**, 400f

graded, **401–402**, 401f
  hyperpolarization of, 400f, **401**
  resting, 399–400, 399f
Membrane potential (voltage) of
    plasma membrane, **81**
Membrane receptors of plasma
    membrane, **83–84**
Membranes, of long bones,
    180–181, 180f
Membranes of body
  cutaneous, **141**, 142f
  mucous, **141**, 142f
  serous, **17–18**, 17f, **142–143**,
    142f
Membrane transport mechanisms,
    70–81
  active, **70**, 75–81
  passive, **70**, 71–75
  summaries, 75t, 80t
Membranous labyrinth, **586**, 586f
Membranous urethra, 1025f,
    1026, 1066f, 1070f, 1071
Memory, 436, **460–463**
  Alzheimer's disease and,
    462, 469
  amnesia and, 463
  brain structures involved in,
    462–463, 462f
  categories of, 461–462
  consolidation, 461, 462, 463
  declarative (fact), **461**
    flowchart, 462f
  disorders, 463
  emotions and, 461
  factors affecting, 461
  immunological, 804f, 805, 805f
  limbic system structures and,
    455
  mechanisms of, 463
  motor, **461**
  procedural (skills), **461**
    flowchart, 462f
  research on enhancing, 463
  stages of, 461, 461f
  working, versus long-term,
    461, 461f
Memory cells, 804f, **805**
  functions (summary), 817t
Menarche, **1095**
Ménière's syndrome, **594**
Meningeal artery, middle,
    210, 748t
Meningeal branch, of spinal rami,
    509
Meningeal dura mater, 464, 464f
  CSF in relation to, 466f
Meninges, **463–465**, 464f
  spinal, 473f
Meningitis, 465
Meningocele, 484
Menisci (articular discs), **256**, 265
  fibrocartilage of, 137, 176, 177f
  of knee, **265**, 266f
    torn, 267, 267f, 272, 273f
Menopause, **1105**, 1108
Menstrual (uterine) cycle,
    1096–1098, 1097f
Mental foramina, 205f, 206f,
    212, 212f
Mental functions
  brain waves and, 456–457
  consciousness, 457–458
  cortical domains and, 436, 437f
  language, 460
  memory, 436, 460–463
  sleep-wake cycles, 458–460

Mentalis muscle, **336**t, 337f
Men vs. women on muscle
    strength, 317
Merkel cells, **152–153**, 154f, 492
Merkel (tactile) discs, 153, 164, **492**
  functional classes/body location,
    493t
Merocrine (eccrine) sweat glands,
    126, 127f, 153f, **158**, 159f
Mesangial cells, glomerular, 1005,
    1005f
Mesencephalon (midbrain),
    431, 432f, **433**
Mesenchymal cells, 131, 184f,
    185, 198
Mesenchymal stem cell
    regeneration, 275b
Mesenchyme, **1123**
  connective tissues arising from,
    127, 128f, **131**
  in intramembranous
    ossification, 184f
Mesenteric arteries, 746f, 747f,
    752f, 753f, **754**t, 755f, 923f
Mesenteric ganglia, 539f, **541**
Mesenteric veins, 759f, 764f,
    764t, 765f
Mesenteries, **886**, 886f, 923f, 924f
Mesocolons, 900, **922**, 923f, 924f
Mesoderm, 145, 145f, 1120f,
    1123, 1124f, 1125f, 1126f
  derivatives, 1126–1130
  intermediate, **1127**, 1127f
Mesometrium, 1085f, **1086**
Mesonephric duct, **1027**, 1029f
Mesonephric (Wolffian) ducts,
    1102f, **1103**
Mesonephros, **1027**, 1029f
Mesosalpinx, 1084, 1085f
Mesothelium, **120**
Mesovarium, **1083**, 1083f, 1085f
Messenger RNA (mRNA), 57,
    104–105, 105f, 107, 109
  signal sequence and, 87, 87f
Metabolic acidosis, 969, **1055**,
    1056t
Metabolic alkalosis, **1055**, 1056t
Metabolic (fixed) acids, **1052**
Metabolic pathways, used to
    regenerate ATP, 301–303, 303f
Metabolic rate, **984–985**
  aging and, 992
  ANS effects, 546t
  basal, **984–985**
  thyroid hormone and, 621,
    621t, 985
  total, **985**
Metabolic water, **1039**
Metabolism, 6–7, **956–981**
  absorptive state, **973–974**,
    974f
  aging and, 992
  anabolic, **956**, 957f
  carbohydrate, 959–967
  catabolic, **956**, 957f
  catabolic-anabolic steady state,
    971–973
  cellular, 90, 649, 1039
  developmental aspects, 989, 992
  disorders, 992
  effects of insulin on, 973–974,
    975f
  energy balance
    body temperature, 985–989
    food intake regulation,
      982–984

continues

Metabolism (cont.)
  heat production, 984–985
  metabolic rate, 984–985
free radicals as byproduct of, 90
globular proteins in regulation
    of, 52t
gluconeogenesis, 967
heat as by-product of, 649
hormonal influences on, 978t
hydrogen peroxide as by-product
    of, 90
inborn errors, 992
lipids, 967–970, 969f
metabolic rate, 984
nutrient pools and, 971–973,
    971f
overview, 956–959
postabsorptive state, 973–978
protein, 970–971
reactions in (summary), 971t
water as by-product of, 1039
Metabotropic receptors, 421
Metacarpal arteries, 750f, 750t
Metacarpal bones, 228f, 235, 235f,
    236f, 236t
  joints of, 258t
Metacarpal veins, 762f
Metacarpophalangeal (knuckle)
    joints, 258t
Metacarpus (palm), 233, 235, 235f,
    236f, 236t, 237
Metanephros, 1027, 1029f
Metaphase, 98f, 101, 103f, 1075f,
    1076f
Metaphysis, 180
Metarteriole, 717f, 721, 721f
Metarteriole-thoroughfare channel
    (vascular shunt), 721, 721f
Metastasis of malignant
    neoplasms, 146
Metastatic calcification, 625
Metatarsal arteries, 756f, 756t, 757f
Metatarsal bones, 228f, 244, 245f,
    246f, 246t
  joints, 259t
Metatarsal veins, 766f
Metatarsophalangeal joint,
    articulating
  bones/movements allowed,
    259t
Metatarsus, 244
Metencephalon, 432f, 433
Methamphetamine ("speed"), 424b
Methane gas, 35f
Methane gas molecule, 35f
Methionine, 947t
MHC (major histocompatibility
    complex), 800
  restriction process, 801–802,
    802f
MHC proteins, 800, 811–813, 812f
Micelles, 931, 932f
Microcirculation, 721
Microcytes, 655
Microfilaments, 66f, 90–91, 91f
  interaction of motor proteins
    with, 92, 92f
  structure/functions (summary),
    94t
Microglia, 390f, 391
MicroRNAs (miRNAs), 57, 110
Microscopic anatomy, 2
  preparing tissue for, 118
Microtubules, 66f, 90, 91f
  centrosome matrix and, 90, 92

doublets, 93, 93f
interaction of motor proteins
    with, 92, 92f
kinetochore, 102f
polar, 102f
structure/functions (summary),
    94t
triplets, 93
Microvilli, 66f, 69, 70, 119
  of small intestine, 909–910,
    910f, 911f
  structure/functions (summary),
    95t
Micturition, 1027
Micturition reflex, 1027, 1028f
Midbrain, 445f, 447f, 448
  diencephalon in relation to,
    448–449f
  embryonic origins, 431,
    432f, 433
    mesencephalon, 431
  functions (summary), 453t
  nuclei of importance, 449, 450f
  oculomotor nerve originating in,
    503f, 503t
  spinal cord tracts and, 476f
Middle ear, auditory ossicles of,
    217t
Middle ear cavities, 19, 19f
Midpalmar muscles, 366t
Midpiece, sperm, 1079, 1079f
Midsagittal (median) plane, 15, 16f
MIF (migration inhibitory factor),
    818t
Migrating motility complex
    (MMC), 921, 921t
Migration inhibitory factor (MIF),
    818t
Milia, 170
Milk (deciduous) teeth, 893, 893f
Milliosmol (mOsm), 1016
MI (myocardial infarction), 686
Mind, 456
Mineralocorticoids, 627–629
  structure/regulation/effects, 627t
Minerals, 952, 956
  bone as storage reservoir for, 179
  roles in body (overview),
    952–955t
Mineral salts (hydroxyapatites), 183
Minute ventilation, 853
miRNAs (microRNAs), 57, 110
MIT (monoiodotyrosine), 622, 622f
Mitochondria, 66f, 85, 85f
  in cardiac muscle cells, 689, 690f
  fission process and, 85
  as site of cellular respiration, 85,
    956, 957f
  skeletal muscle fiber, 288f, 290f
  structure/functions (summary),
    94t
Mitosis, 99, 99f, 101, 102–103f,
    1073–1074
  centriole's role in, 92–93, 102f
  meiosis vs., 101, 1074, 1075f
Mitotic spindle, 102f
  centrioles and, 93
Mitral (bicuspid) valve, 683f,
    686, 687f
  prolapse, 709
Mitral cells, 579f, 580
Mittelschmerz, 1094
Mixed nerves, 499
  cranial nerves and, 500–501
Mixtures, 30–31
  vs. compounds, 31

M line, 284, 285f, 288f
MMC (migrating motility
    complex), 921, 921t
Modiolus, 587, 588f
Molarity, 30–31
Molar teeth, 893f, 894
Mole, 30–31
Molecular biology, 2
Molecular chaperones, 52–53, 52t
Molecular formula, 37
Molecular mimicry, 636b
Molecular "Velcro," 83
Molecular weight, 30–31
Molecules, 3, 30–31
  amphipathic, 47
  amphoteric, 1051
  nonpolar vs. polar, 34–36,
    35f, 36f
Moles
  changes in, 166
  pigmented, 157
Molybdenum, 26t
Mongolian spot, 171
Monoclonal antibodies, 810
Monocytes, 649f, 657f, 659–660,
    659f, 790
  summary, 658t
Monoglycerides, digestion and,
    928f, 930
Monohydrogen phosphate, 1054,
    1054f
Monoiodotyrosine (MIT or T1),
    622, 622f
Monomers, 807, 927
Mononucleosis, 783
Monosaccharides, 927
Monosaccharides (simple sugars),
    44, 45f
Monospermy, 1115
Monosynaptic reflexes, 521, 524
Monounsaturated fats, 46
Mons pubis, 1082f, 1088, 1088f
Morning sickness, 1135
Morula, 1117, 1118f
Motilin
  production site/stimuli/
    target/actions, 906t
  in small intestine motility,
    921, 921t
Motility
  gastric, 905–907, 907f
  large intestine, 926
  small intestine, 919–922
  stomach, 905, 907
Motion sickness, 598
Motor areas of cerebral cortex,
    436, 437f
  Broca's, 437f, 439
  cerebellar processing and, 454
  frontal eye field, 437f, 439
  premotor, 437f, 439
  primary motor, 437f, 438–439,
    438f
Motor cortex (primary), 437f,
    438–439, 438f
  damage to, 439
  major descending pathways,
    479t, 480f
  neural integration and, 495f
Motor (efferent) division of PNS,
    388, 389f
  ANS division, 388, 389f
  somatic nervous system
    division, 388, 389f
Motor (efferent) nerves, 499
  of ventral roots, 509, 510f

Motor (efferent) neurons, 395,
    396–397t
Motor endings
  autonomic, 519
  peripheral, 289, 290f, 491, 519
Motor homunculi
  cerebellar, 452f, 453
  cortical, 438–439, 438f
Motor integration, hierarchy,
    519–520, 520f
Motor neurons
  in motor unit, 296–297, 296f
  muscle contraction and,
    288–289, 296–297, 296f
  myelinated axons and, 290f
  in reflex arcs, 521, 521f
Motor output, 388, 388f
Motor proteins, 90, 92f
Motor speech area of cerebral
    cortex, 439
Motor unit, 296–297, 296f
  force of muscle contraction and,
    304
Mountain sickness, 870
Mouth (oral cavity), 19, 19f, 832f,
    883f, 889–895, 889f
  digestive processes occurring in,
    897–899, 898f
  major functions (overview), 920t
  muscles forming floor of,
    340t, 341f
Movement
  anterograde, 393
  retrograde, 393
Movements, body, 5, 259–263
  agonist muscles and, 325, 326
  allowed by synovial joints
    angular, 260–261, 260–262f
    rotation, 261–262, 262f
    special movements, 262–263,
      263f
  allowed by vertebrae, 221, 224t
  antagonist muscles and,
    325, 326
  biaxial, 259
  contraction of muscles and, 281
  fixator muscles and, 325, 326
  multiaxial, 259
  muscle's origin/insertion and,
    259, 325
  nonaxial, 259
  prime mover muscles for
    specific kinds of, 325
  role of bones in, 179
  synergist muscles and, 325, 326
  types of, 259–263, 260–263f
  uniaxial, 259
MPF (M-phase promoting factor),
    101
M phase of cell life cycle,
    90, 103f
M-phase promoting factor (MPF),
    101
MRI. See Magnetic resonance
    imaging
mRNA (messenger RNA), 57,
    104–105
  polyribosomes and, 109, 109f
  signal sequence and, 87, 87f
  synthesis of, 105, 106f
  in translation, 107,
    108f, 109
MRS (magnetic resonance
    spectroscopy), 21b
MSH (melanocyte-stimulating
    hormone), 614

MS (multiple sclerosis), **407**–408, 822
Mucin, **125**, 125*f*, 874, 892
Mucosa-associated lymphatic tissue (MALT), **782**, 887*f*, **888**, 922
Mucosal barrier of stomach, **901**–902
Mucosal iron barrier, 933
Mucous cells, of salivary glands, **892**
Mucous membranes (mucosae), **141**, 142*f*
   of GI tract, **887**–888, 887*f*
      esophageal, 896*f*, 897
      stomach, 899*f*, 900, 901*f*
   in immunity, 789–790, 796*t*
   respiratory, 214, **832**–833
   tracheal, **839**, 839*f*
   ureter, 1023–1024
Mucous neck cells, **900**, 901*f*
Mucus, 93*f*, **125**, 796*t*, **892**, 920*t*
Multiaxial movement, **259**
Multicellular exocrine glands, **125**–126, 126*f*
   modes of secretion, 126, 127*f*
   simple or compound, 125, 126*f*
   structural classification, 125, 126*f*
Multifidus muscle, 345*f*
Multimodal association areas, **440**–441
Multineuronal motor pathways, **478**
Multinucleate cells, **95**
Multipennate muscle, 326, 327*f*
Multiple motor unit summation (recruitment), **298**–299, 299*f*
Multiple sclerosis (MS), **407**–408, 822
Multipolar neurons, **395**
   bipolar/unipolar neurons vs., 396–397*t*
Mumps, 891
Muscarinic ACh receptors, 415*t*
Muscarinic agents, effects on ANS activity, 545*t*
Muscarinic receptors, **543**
Muscle contraction
   in cardiac muscle, 690–692, 691*f*
   in cardiac vs. skeletal vs. smooth muscle, 315*t*
   categories
      concentric, 300, 301*f*
      eccentric, 300, 301*f*
      isometric, 300, 301*f*
      isotonic, 300, 301*f*
   contractures and, **303**
   duration of, 304*f*, 305–307, 306*t*
   energy sources for
      aerobic respiration, 302, 303*f*
      anaerobic mechanism, 302, 303*f*
      direct phosphorylation, 301–302, 303*f*
      during sports activities, 302–303
      fatigue and, 298, 303–304
      oxygen debt, 304
      size principle and, 299, 299*f*
      stored ATP, 300–301
   force of, 295–296, 304–305, 304*f*
      lever systems and, 326–330, 328*f*

frequency of stimulation and, 305
   graded contractions, **297**
      by recruitment, **297**–299, 299*f*, 307
      treppe and, 299–300, 300*f*
      by wave summation/tetanus, **297**–298, 298*f*
   heat produced during, 304
   influence of load on, 307, 307*f*
   length-tension relationships and, 305
   lever systems and, **326**–330, 328*f*, 329*f*
   mechanics of, 295–296, 326–330
   metabolic pathways for, 300–303, 303*f*
   myofilaments and, 280
   nerve stimulus for, 288–289, 290*f*
   regulation in cardiac vs. skeletal vs. smooth, 315*t*
   regulation of, 315*t*
   rhythmicity of, in cardiac vs. skeletal vs. smooth muscle, 315*t*
   size of muscle fibers stimulated, 305
   of skeletal muscle
      fiber, 288–294
      of whole muscle, 295–300
   sliding filament theory of, 287–**288**, 289*f*
   of smooth muscle, 311–313, 311*f*, 315*t*, 316
   speed of, 305–306, 306*f*, 307*f*
   stimulus frequency and, 297–298, 298*f*
   stimulus strength and, 298–299, 299*f*
   tension (force) and, **295**–296, 299*f*, 305, 305*f*
   tetanus/tetanic contractions, **298**, 298*f*, 305
   twitch contractions, **297**, 297*f*
   velocity of, 305–307, 306*t*
   vs. relaxation of muscle fiber, 287–**288**, 289*f*
   wave summation, **297**–298, 298*f*
Muscle disorders, Botox to treat dystonia, 156*b*
Muscle fatigue, **303**–304
   of oxidative vs. glycolytic fibers, 306*t*
   prolonged tetanus and, 298
Muscle fibers (cells), **139**, 140*f*, **280**
Muscle mechanics
   fascicle arrangement/patterns, 326, 327*f*
   lever systems, 326–330, 328*f*, 329*f*
Muscle metabolism, 300–304. See also Muscle contraction
Muscle spindles, **494**, 495*f*
   adjusting sensitivity in, 524–525
   anatomy, 522–523, 522*f*
   functional classes/body location, 493*t*
   operation of, 524*f*
   stretch and, 523–524, 523*f*
Muscle tendons. See also Tendons
   of shoulder joint, 269, 269*f*

that cross joints, joint stability and, 257, 257*f*, 259
Muscle tension, **295**–296
   external, **305**
   internal, **305**
   in isotonic and isometric contractions, 300, 301*f*
   length-tension relationships and, 305, 305*f*
   in smooth muscle, 316
   stimulus intensity and, 298–299, 299*f*
Muscle tissue, **139**–141
   ability to transform chemical energy (ATP) into mechanical energy and, 280
   characteristics, 280
   contractile proteins of, and ATP-driven cellular work, 59, 59*f*
   developmental aspects, 316–318, 320
   embryonic origins, 145, 145*f*, 316–317
   functions, 280–281
   types
      cardiac, **139**, 140*f*, 280
      skeletal, **139**, 140*f*, 280
      smooth, **141**, 141*f*, 280
   vascularity, 139
Muscle tone, **300**
   joint stability and, 257, 259, 300
   of smooth muscle, 312
Muscle twitch, **297**, 297*f*
Muscular arteries, 716–717, 716*f*, 717*f*
Muscular dystrophy, **317**
Muscularis externa (muscularis), 887*f*, **888**, 896*f*
   circular layer, 887*f*, 888, 896*f*, 899*f*, 901*f*
   large intestine, 925*f*
   longitudinal layer, 887*f*, 888, 896*f*
   oblique layer (stomach), 899*f*, 900, 901*f*
   small intestine, 910*f*
   stomach, 901*f*
   ureter, 1023, 1024*f*
   vaginal, 1087
Muscular "pump," **726**, 726*f*, 727*f*, 731*f*
Muscular system, **6**, 6*f*, 324–386. See also Skeletal muscles
   cardiac muscle. See Cardiac muscle
   cardiovascular system and, 768*b*, 769*b*
   developmental aspects, 316–318, 320, 1132*t*, 1133
      embryonic, 1123–1128, 1130*t*
   digestive system and, 934*b*
   endocrine system and, 640*b*
   homeostatic interrelationships with other body systems, 318*b*, 319*b*
      between skeletal muscles in body, 325
   integumentary system and, 168*b*
   lymphatic system/immunity and, 784*b*
   nervous system and, 548*b*, 549*b*

reproductive system and, 1106*b*, 1107*b*
   respiratory system and, 876*b*, 877*b*
   skeletal system and, 196*b*, 197*b*
   skin and, 168*b*
   smooth muscle. See Smooth muscle
   thyroid hormone's effects, 621*t*
   urinary system and, 1058*b*
Musculocutaneous nerve, **512**, 513*f*, 514*t*
   muscles served by, 355*t*, 357*t*
Mutation (DNA), **112**, **1157**
   caused by carcinogens, 146*b*
Myalgia, **320**
Myasthenia gravis, 289, 822
Myelencephalon, 432*f*, **433**
Myelinated nerve fibers, **394**–395, 394*f*
   conduction velocity and, 407, 407*f*
Myelin sheath, 390*f*, 391, **394**–395, 394*f*
   in multiple sclerosis, 408
   in PNS, 394, 394*f*
Myelitis, **485**
Myeloblasts, **660**, 661*f*
Myelocytes, **660**, 661*f*
Myelocytic leukemia, 660
Myelogram, **485**
Myeloid stem cell, **651**, 652*f*
Myeloid stem cells, **660**, 661*f*
Myelomeningocele, 484
Myeloproliferative disorder, **674**
Myenteric nerve plexus, 887*f*, **888**, 901*f*
Mylohyoid muscle, 340*t*, 341*f*, 343*f*
Myoblasts, **316**–317
Myoblast transfer therapy, 317
Myocardial infarction (MI), **686**, 692, 706–707*b*
Myocarditis, **709**
Myocardium, **680**, 681*f*, 682*f*, 683*f*, 687*f*
Myoclonus, **485**
Myofascial pain syndrome, **320**
Myofibrils, 282*f*, 282*t*, **284**, 285*f*, 286, 288*f*
   neuromuscular junction and, 290*f*
Myofilaments, **139**, 282*f*, 282*t*, **284**, 285*f*, 286, 286*f*
   of smooth muscle, 310
Myogenic responses
   in renal autoregulation, **1008**, 1009*f*
   of vascular smooth muscle, **735**–736, 736*f*
Myoglobin, **284**
   content in skeletal muscle fiber, 306*t*
Myogram, **297**, 297*f*
Myoid cells, **1067**, 1068*f*
Myomesin, 287
Myometrium, 1085*f*, **1086**, 1087*f*
Myopathy, **320**
Myopia (nearsightedness), **568**, 569*f*
Myosin, 52*t*, 139, 282*t*, 285*f*, **286**, 286*f*
   in skeletal muscle contraction, 286, 293–294, 293*f*–295*f*, 306*t*

continues

Myosin (cont.)
  in smooth muscle contraction,
    310, 311–312, 313f
  unconventional, 90
Myosin kinase, 312, 313f
Myosin light chain kinase,
  312, 313f
Myotome, 1127, 1127f
Myotubes, 316
Myringotomy, 585
Myxedema, 618t, 623–624

Na⁺–K⁺ ATPase, 76f, 77
NAD+, 960, 960f
NAD+ (nicotinamide adenine
  dinucleotide), 958
Nails, 163, 163f
Naked nerve endings. See Free
  (naked) nerve endings
Na⁺–K⁺ gated ion channel,
  operation of, 398f
Nanobiotechnology, in bone repair,
  194b
Narcolepsy, 460
Narcotic overdose, respiratory
  acidosis and, 1056t
Nares (nostrils), 831–832, 834f
Nasal apertures (choanae), 832, 834f
Nasal bones, 205f, 206f, 213,
  215f, 833f
  summary/important markings,
    217t
Nasal cartilages, 176, 177f
Nasal cavity, 19, 19f, 213–214,
  831–835, 832f
  features/functions, 838t
  paranasal sinuses, 214,
    218, 218f
  special characteristics, 213–214,
    215f
Nasal conchae
  inferior, 834f
  superior, 834f
Nasal conchae (turbinates)
  inferior, 205f, 213, 215f, 217t
  middle, 205f, 211, 211f, 215f,
    217t
  olfactory receptors and,
    579–580, 579f
  respiratory functions, 833, 834f
  superior, 211, 215f, 217t
Nasal glands, ANS effects, 546t
Nasal hairs (vibrissae), 832
  protective mechanisms of, 796t
Nasal meatus, 833, 834f
  inferior, 834f
  middle, 834f
Nasal meatuses, 213, 834f
Nasal mucosa
  parasympathetic fibers, 537f
  sympathetic fibers, 539f
Nasal polyps, 875
Nasal septum, 213–214, 832, 838t
Nasal spine, anterior, 212,
  212f, 215f
Nasal vestibule, 832, 834f
Nasolacrimal duct, 557, 558f
Nasopharynx, 834f, 835
Natural killer (NK) cells, 791, 796t
  immune surveillance and, 816
Navicular bone, 244, 245f,
  246f, 246t
N-CAM (nerve cell adhesion
  molecule), 423–424

Near point of vision, 568
Nearsightedness (myopia), 568, 569f
Nebulin, 287
Neck
  arteries, 746f, 748–749t, 749f
  innervation, 511–512,
    511f, 511t
    sympathetic, 541, 541t
  muscles
    of head/trunk movements,
      342–344t, 343f, 345f
    lateral, 337f
    superficial, 331f, 333f
    of swallowing, 340–341t, 341f
  veins, 671f, 758t, 758f, 760f,
    760–761t
Neck (bone marking)
  of femur, 239, 241, 241f
  of radius, 233f, 234f
  of rib, 227f, 228
Neck of tooth, 894, 894f
Necropsy, 148
Necrosis, 112
Negative feedback mechanisms,
  10, 11f
  in blood calcium level control,
    188–190, 189f
  of estrogens, 1099t
  glucagon and blood glucose
    levels, 977, 977f
  glucocorticoid secretion, 629
  hormone release regulation,
    611–612, 612f
  in ovarian cycle, 1094–1096,
    1095f
  of progesterone, 1099t
  in regulating ventilation,
    865–866, 866f
  of testosterone, 1099t
  thyroid hormones and, 623
Negative selection, of T cells,
  802, 802f
NE (nocturnal enuresis), 1031
Neon, as inert element, 32, 32f
Neonatal period, 1137–1139
  cardiovascular changes at birth,
    1131f
  fetal blood vessels/shunts,
    1138
  lactation and, 1138–1139
  transitional period of, 1138
Neoplasms, benign vs. malignant,
  146b
Neostigmine, 544
Nephrons, 1001, 1002f
  anatomy, 1001–1006
  capillary beds, 1003
  cortical, 1003, 1004f
  functions (summary), 1020f
  juxtaglomerular apparatus,
    1003, 1005, 1005f
  juxtamedullary, 1003, 1004f
Nephrotoxin, 1031
Nerve cell adhesion molecule
  (N-CAM), 423–424
Nerve cell. See Neurons
Nerve conduction studies, 527
Nerve endings, encapsulated/
  unencapsulated, 492–494,
  493t
Nerve fiber, 393
  myelinated, 394–395, 394f
  somatic afferent, 388
  unmyelinated, 394–395
  visceral afferent, 388
Nerve fibers, diameter of, 408

Nerve growth factor, 551
Nerve growth factor (NGF), 423
Nerve impulse, 397, 402. See also
  Action potentials
  as electrical energy, 25
Nerve plexuses of spinal cord
  nerves, 509f, 510
Nerves, 491, 498
  mixed, 499
  regeneration of, 499–500, 499f
  structure, 498–499, 498f
Nerve stimulus, in muscle
  contraction, 288–289, 290f
Nervous system, 6f, 388
  autonomic. See Autonomic
    nervous system
  cardiovascular system and,
    768b, 769b
  central. See Central Nervous
    System
  developmental aspects
    embryonic, 1123–1128, 1130t
    fetal, 1132t, 1133
    neurulation and, 1123, 1125f
  digestive system and, 934b
  embryonic development, 423,
    431, 1123–1128, 1130t
  endocrine activity modulation
    by, 611–612
  endocrine system and, 640b,
    641b
  enteric (GI tract), 542, 887f,
    888–889
  homeostatic interrelationships,
    548b, 549b
  integration function, 388, 388f
  integumentary system and,
    168b, 169b
  involuntary, 388–389, 389f
  lymphatic system/immunity
    and, 784b
  motor output function,
    388, 388f
  muscular system and, 318b
  neurophysiology principles,
    397–421
  organizational overview,
    388–389, 389f
  peripheral. See Peripheral
    nervous system
  reproductive system and, 1106b
  respiratory system and, 876b
  sensory input function,
    388, 388f
  skeletal system and, 196b
  somatic. See Somatic nervous
    system
  thyroid hormone's effects, 621t
  urinary system and, 1058b,
    1059b
  voluntary, 388, 389f
Nervous tissue, 139, 139f, 388.
  See also Neurons
  cell types
    neuroglia, 389–391
    neurons, 391–397
  embryonic origins, 145, 145f
  embryonic synapses, 408–409
  regenerative capacity of, 144
  supporting cells of, 389–391,
    390f
Net filtration pressure (NFP),
  739–740, 740f, 1007–1008,
  1008f
Neural crest, 423, 431, 431f, 551,
  1123, 1124f, 1125f

Neural folds, 431, 431f, 1123,
  1124f, 1125f
Neuralgia, 527
Neural groove, 431, 431f, 1123,
  1124f, 1125f
Neural integration, 421
  circuit patterns, 421–422, 422f
  neuronal pools, 421, 421f
  parallel input processing, 423
  of postsynaptic potentials,
    411–413, 413f
  at receptor level, 494–495, 495f
  reflex role in, 423
  serial input processing,
    422–423, 423f
  in somatosensory system, at
    circuit level, 495–496,
    495f
Neural layer of retina, 561, 562f
Neural plate, 431, 431f, 1123,
  1124f, 1125f
Neural stimuli, of endocrine
  glands, 611, 611f
Neural tube, 423, 431, 1123,
  1124f, 1126f
  ANS embryonic development,
    551
  CNS structures derived from,
    431, 432f, 433
  spinal cord development,
    470, 470f
Neurilemma (sheath of Schwann),
  392f, 394, 394f
Neuritis, 528
Neuroblastoma, 426
Neuroblasts, 423
Neurocardiogenic syncope, 551
Neuroendocrine organs, 605
Neuroepithelial cells, in CNS
  formation, 423
Neurofibrillary tangles, 469
Neurofibril node (node of Ranvier),
  392f, 394
Neurofibrils, 391
Neurofilaments. See Neurofibrils
Neurogenic shock, 742
Neuroglia (glial cells), 389–390
  in CNS, 390–391, 390f
  in PNS, 390f, 391
Neurohormones, 612
Neurohypophysis, 612, 613f
Neurolemmocytes (Schwann cells),
  390f, 391
Neurologists, 426
Neuromodulators, 419
Neuromuscular junctions,
  289–290, 290f, 519
  in cardiac vs. skeletal vs.
    smooth muscle, 315t
  peripheral motor endings and,
    519
  vs. diffuse junctions, 310, 311f
Neuron cell body, 391–392, 392f
  in CNS (nuclei), 392
  in PNS (ganglia), 392
Neuron processes, 139f, 392–395,
  392f
  in CNS (tracts), 392
  in PNS (nerves), 392
  types of
    axons, 392f, 393–394
    dendrites, 392f, 393
Neurons (nerve cells), 139, 139f,
  391–397
  afferent (sensory) neurons, 395,
    396–397t

continues

Neurons (nerve cells) (cont.)
  amitotic nature of, 391
  anatomy
    cell body, 139f, 391–392,
      392f, 396t
    processes, 392–395
  biosynthetic center of, 391
  classes of, 395, 397
    compared, 396–397t
  conducting region, 392f, 393
  conduction velocity of, 407
  developmental aspects, 423–425
  glucose requirements of, 391
  impulse generating region of,
    392f, 393
  interneurons (association
    neurons), 395, 396–397t,
    397
  longevity of, 391
  membrane potentials
    measuring, 399, 399f
    resting, 399–400, 399f
  motor (efferent), 395, 396–397t
  neuronal pools and, 421, 421f
  oxygen requirements of, 391
  physiology of, 397–421
  plasma membrane of, as site of
    electrical signaling, 391
  receptive (input) region of, 392,
    392f, 393
  relative abundance/location in
    body, 396t
  secretory region, 393
  sensory (afferent), 395,
    396–397t
  structural variations, 396t
Neuropathy, 426
Neuropeptides, 418
Neuropharmacology, 426
Neurophysiology, 3, 397–421
  electricity principles, 397–399
  membrane potentials
    action, 402–408
    graded, 401–402
    resting, 399–400
Neuroses, 485
Neurotoxin, 426
Neurotransmitters, 413–421
  axon terminals and, 393
  in chemical synapses, 409–411,
    410f
  classes of
    by chemical structure,
      414–419
    by function, 419
    overview, 415–417t
  direct vs. indirect mechanism of
    action, 419
  excitatory versus inhibitory,
    415–417t, 419
  mechanism of action, 419
  in parasympathetic division,
    534f, 536f
  postsynaptic potentials and,
    411–413
  receptors for
    channel-linked, 419–420, 420f
    G protein-linked, 420–421,
      420f
  released by ANS neurons, 543
  as signaling chemical, 83
  smooth muscles and, 312
  varicosities, 310, 311f
  in somatic nervous system vs.
    ANS, 534, 534f
  in sympathetic division, 534f, 536f

Neurotrophins, 423
Neurulation, 431, 431f, 1123, 1125f
Neutral fats. See Fats
Neutralization, by antibodies,
  808–809, 809f
Neutralization reaction, 42–43
Neutrons, 27–30, 27f
Neutrophils, 130f, 138f, 649f,
  657–658, 657f, 659f, 790
  Neutrophils, summary, 658t
Nexus (gap junction), 69, 70f
NFP. See Net filtration pressure
NGF (nerve growth factor), 423
NH3 (ammonia), 970, 970f
Niacin/nicotinamide (vitamin B3),
  950t, 958
Nicotinamide adenine dinucleotide
  (NAD+), 958
Nicotinamide/niacin (vitamin B3),
  950t, 958
Nicotine
  adrenal medulla hormones and,
    730
  blood-brain barrier and, 467
Nicotinic agents, effects on ANS
  activity, 545t
Nicotinic receptors, 415t, 543
Night blindness, 575
Nipple, 1089f, 1090
Nissl bodies (chromatophilic
  substance), 391, 392f
Nitric oxide, saliva and, 892
Nitric oxide (NO), 419, 735
  as a signaling molecule, 84, 417
  brain injury and, 468
  hemoglobin and, 860
  as neurotransmitter, 417t, 419
  vasodilation and, 735
Nitric oxide synthase (NOS), 419
Nitrogen, atomic symbol/
  percentage body mass/
  functions in body, 26t
Nitrogen balance, protein synthesis
  and, 946–947
Nitrogen gas, molecule of, 35f
Nitrogenous wastes, 1022
  in urine, 1022–1023
NK (natural killer) cells, 791, 796t
  immune surveillance and, 816
NMDA (N-methyl-D-aspartate)
  receptors
    after brain injury, 468–469
    long-lasting pain and, 497b
    memory and, 463
  N-methyl-D-aspartate (NMDA)
    receptors, 412–413
Nobel gases, 32, 32f
Nociceptors, 491, 493t
Nocturia, 1030
Nocturnal enuresis (NE), 1031
Node of Ranvier (neurofibril node),
  392f, 394
Noise, 589, 590f, 593
  physiologic consequences, 599
Nonaxial movement, 259
Nondisjunction, 1101–1102,
  1157
Nonelectrolytes, vs. electrolytes,
  1036–1037
Nongated (leakage) ion channels,
  72, 398
Non-Hodgkin's lymphoma, 783
Nonpolar tails/polar heads of
  phospholipids, 67–68, 67f
Nonpolar vs. polar molecules,
  34–36, 35f, 36f

Non-rapid eye movement (NREM)
  sleep, 458, 459f
Nonself molecules, 799
Nonshivering (chemical)
  thermogenesis, 987
Nonspecific ascending pathways/
  tracts, 475–477, 476f, 477t
Noradrenaline. See
  Norepinephrine
Norepinephrine (NE), 631
  adrenal medulla secretion of,
    542, 627t, 631
  as ANS neurotransmitter, 543,
    544, 544t
  blood pressure and, 729f, 730
  BMR and, 985, 985f
  effect variability in ANS,
    534, 534f
  functional class/secretion
    sites/effects, 415t
  heart contractility and, 701, 701f
  heart rate and, 701f, 702
  memory processing and, 461
  in smooth muscle contraction,
    312
  synthesis of, 418, 418f, 631
Norian SRS (bone cement), 195b
Normoblasts, 652, 652f
Nose, 831–835
  external, 831, 833f
    alae, 833f
    bridge, 833f
    cartilage of, 176, 177f
    dorsum nasi, 833f
    nostrils (nares), 833f
    philtrum
    root, 833f
  features/functions, 838t
  internal (nasal cavity), 831–835
NOS (nitric oxide synthase), 419
Nostrils (nares), 831–832,
  832f, 834f
Notochord, 1123, 1125f, 1126f
NREM (non-rapid eye movement)
  sleep, 458, 459f
Nuchal lines
  inferior, 205f, 207, 208f, 216t
  superior, 205f, 207, 208f, 216t
Nuclear envelope (membrane), 66f,
  95, 96f
  endomembrane system
    interactions, 89–90, 90f
  endoplasmic reticulum and,
    86, 86f
  in mitosis, 102f, 103f
  structure/functions (summary),
    95t
Nuclear group
  anterior, 445f
  lateral, 450f
  medial, 450f
Nuclear lamina, 96f, 97
Nuclear membrane. See Nuclear
  envelope
Nuclear pore, 96f, 108f
Nucleases, 918
Nuclei, 392
Nucleic acid digestion, 920t
Nucleic acids, 54–57, 57t
  absorption, 928f, 932
  digestion, 928f, 930–931
  DNA, 55–57
  RNA, 55–57
Nucleoli, 66f, 96f, 97, 102f, 103f
  structure/functions (summary),
    95t

Nucleolus, of neuron cell body, 392f
Nucleoplasm of nuclear
  envelope, 97
Nucleosidases, 928f, 931
Nucleosides, 55
Nucleosomes, 97, 98f
Nucleotides, 54–57, 56f
  chemical digestion and, 928f,
    931
  in DNA replication, 99, 100f
Nucleus
  of atom, 27–28, 27f
  of cell, 66, 66f, 95–97, 96f, 98f
    structure/functions
      (summary), 95t
  of neuron cell body, 392f
Nucleus accumbens, 424b
Nucleus ambiguus, 450f
Nucleus cuneatus, 451, 476f
Nucleus gracilis, 451, 476f
Nucleus pulposus, 220, 220f, 1126
Nutrients, 8, 943
  ATP's relationship to, 943
  in blood plasma, 649t
  capillary exchange of, 738–740,
    739f, 740f
  carbohydrates, 944, 945t
  energy value of, 943
  essential, 944
  lipids, 944–945, 945t
  major, 943
  membrane transport processes,
    75t
  minerals, 952–955
  nutrient pools, 971–973, 971f
  proteins, 945t, 946–947
  reabsorption of, 1014t
  stages of processing, 956, 957f
  vitamins, 947–952
  water as major, 943
Nutrition, 943–956
  essential for life, 944
  food guide pyramids, 943–944,
    943f
  hypothalamic regulation and,
    446
  major nutrients. See Nutrients
Nyctalopia, 575

OA (osteoarthritis), 273–274
Obesity, 990–991b
  measures of, 990b
  theories/treatments, 990–991b
Obligatory water loss, 1040
Obligatory water reabsorption,
  1013
Oblique muscles
  external, 345f, 348, 349f
    aponeurosis of, 349f
    description/action/nerve
      supply, 348t
    origin/insertion, 348t
    superficial, 330f, 331f
  internal, 331f, 348, 349f
    description/action/nerve
      supply, 348t
    origin/insertion, 348t
Oblique muscles (eye), 503f,
  558, 559f
Oblique section, 15, 16f
Observation, as tool for studying
  anatomy, 2–3
Obturator artery, 756f, 756t, 757f
Obturator externus muscle, 371f
  actions of (summary),
    379–380t, 380f

continues

Obturator externus muscle (*cont.*)
description/action/nerve supply, **371***t*
origin/insertion, **371***t*
Obturator foramen, 238*f*, **239**, 243*f*
Obturator internus muscle, 351*f*, 371*f*
actions of (summary), 379–380*t*, 380*f*
description/action/nerve supply, **372***t*
origin/insertion, **372***t*
Obturator nerve, 515*f*, 515*t*
muscles served by, 369*t*, 371*t*
Occipital artery, 748*f*, **748***t*, 749*f*
Occipital belly, epicranius muscle, 335*t*, 337*f*
Occipital bone, 205*f*, 206*f*, **207**, 208*f*
summary/important markings, 216*t*
Occipital condyles, 205*f*, **207**, 208*f*, 216*t*
Occipital crest, external, 205*f*, 207, 208*f*, 216*t*
Occipital lobe, 437*f*
meninges in relation to, 464*f*
Occipital lobe of cerebral hemisphere, 434, 435*f*, **436**, 445*f*
Occipital nerve, 511*f*, 511*t*
Occipital protuberance, external, 205*f*, 206*f*, **207**, 208*f*, **216***t*
Occipital vein, 761*f*
Occipitofrontalis muscle, **335***t*, 337*f*. *See also* Epicranius muscle
Occipitomastoid suture, 205*f*, 206*f*, 207
Octet rule (rule of eights), 33
Oculomotor nerve (III), 448*f*, **500**, 501*f*
muscles served by, 558, 559*f*
origin/course/function, 502*f*, **503***t*
parasympathetic fibers, 537, 537*f*
Oculomotor nuclei, 449, 450*f*, 537, 550
Odontoblast, 895
Odontoid process (dens), **222**, 222*f*
Odors, limbic system and, 454
Off-center fields, 577, 577*f*
Ohm's law, **398**
Oil (sebaceous) glands, 153*f*, **159**, 159*f*
Oils (triglycerides), 46–47, 47*f*
Old age, skeleton and, 248
Olecranon bursitis, 273
Olecranon fossa, 231*f*, **232**, 236*f*
Olecranon process (elbow bone), **232**, 233*f*, 234*f*, 268*f*, 356*f*, 361*f*
Oleoresins, 164
Olfactory adaptation, 580
Olfactory auras, 583
Olfactory bulbs, 437*f*, 455*f*, 579*f*, **580**
olfactory nerve and, 501*f*, 502*f*
Olfactory cilia, **578**, 579*f*
Olfactory cortex (primary), 437*f*, **440**
Olfactory epithelium, **578**, 579*f*, 834*f*
Olfactory foramina, 208*f*, 210

Olfactory gland, 579*f*
Olfactory hallucinations, 583
Olfactory mucosa, of nasal cavity, **832**
Olfactory nerve (I), **500**, 501*f*, 834*f*
filaments of, **578**, 579*f*
origin/course/function, 502*f*, 502*t*
Olfactory pits, **873**
Olfactory placodes, 873, 873*f*
Olfactory receptor cells, **578**, 579*f*
activation of, 579–580, 580*f*
Olfactory receptors
specificity of, 578–579
in sperm, 1115
Olfactory tracts, 437*f*, 579*f*, **580**
olfactory nerve and, 501*f*, 502*f*
Oligodendrocytes, 390*f*, **391**
Oligosaccharides, in chemical digestion of starch, 928*f*, 929
Oliguria, 1042
Olivary nuclei, inferior, 450*f*, **451**
Olivary nucleus, 592*f*, **593**
Olives, 448*f*, **451**
Omega-3 fatty acids, 47
Omenta, 886
stomach, **900**
Omohyoid muscle, 341*f*, **341***t*, 343*f*
On-center fields, 577, 577*f*
Oncogenes, **146***b*
Oncotic pressure, 739–740, 740*f*
Oocytes, 1083*f*, **1084**, 1084*f*
in events of fertilization, 1115–1117, 1116*f*, 1117*f*
primary, **1091**, 1092*f*
secondary, **1091**, 1092*f*
Oogenesis, **1091**–1092, 1092*f*
Oogonia, **1091**, 1092*f*
Oophorectomy, **1109**
Ophthalmic arteries, 748*f*, **748***t*, 749*f*
Ophthalmic division, of trigeminal nerve (V), 504*f*, 504*t*
Ophthalmic veins, 760*f*, **760***t*, 761*f*
Ophthalmology, **600**
Opponens digiti minimi muscle, 365*f*
description/action/nerve supply, **364***t*
origin/insertion, **364***t*
Opponens pollicis muscle, 365*f*
description/action/nerve supply, **364***t*
origin/insertion, **364***t*
Opposition (movement), 237, **262**–263, 263*f*
Opsins, 570*f*, **571**–572, 571*f*
Opsonization, **790**, 797*f*, 798
Optic canals, 205*f*, 208*f*, **210**, 210*f*, 214*f*, 216*t*
Optic chiasma, 445*f*, 448*f*, **575**, 576*f*
optic nerve in relation to, 501*f*, 502*t*
Optic cups, **598**
Optic disc (blind spot), 560*f*, **562**–563, 562*f*, 563*f*
Optic nerve (II), 448*f*, **500**, 501*f*, 526*f*, 560*f*
extrinsic eye muscles and, 559*f*
origin/course/function, 502*f*, **502***t*
vision and, **575**, 576*f*
Optic radiation, 502*f*, 502*t*, **575**, 576*f*

Optics, light and, 565–568
Optic tract, 448*f*
optic nerve in relation to, 501*f*, 502*t*
Optic tracts, **575**, 576*f*
Optic vesicles, **598**
Optometrist, **600**
Oral cavity (mouth), 19, 19*f*, 832*f*, 883*f*, **889**–895, 889*f*
digestive processes occurring in, 897–899, 898*f*
major functions (overview), 920*t*
muscles forming floor of, 340*f*, 341*f*
Oral cavity proper, **890**
Oral membrane, **936**, 936*f*
Ora serrata, 560*f*, **561**
Orbicularis oculi muscle, 331*f*, **335***t*, 337*f*, 557*f*
Orbicularis oris muscle, 331*f*, **336***t*, 337*f*, 339*f*, 890
Orbital cavities. *See* Orbits
Orbital fissures
inferior, 205*f*, 213, 214*f*, **217***t*
superior, 205*f*, 210, 210*f*, 214*f*, **216***t*, 503*f*, 505*f*
Orbital model of atomic structure, 27*f*, **28**
Orbital plates, **211**, 214*f*
Orbital process, of palatine bone, 214*f*
Orbitals, atomic, 27*f*, **28**
Orbital surface of zygomatic bone, 214*f*
Orbitofrontal cortex, 437*f*
Orbits (orbital cavities), 19, 19*f*, **213**, 214*f*
frontal bone and, 204
as skull cavities, 203
special characteristics, **213**, 214*f*
Orchiectomy, 1069
Orchitis, **1109**
Organelles, 94*t*. *See also* Cytoplasmic organelles
Organic acid (carboxyl) groups (—COOH), 1051
Organic compounds, **40**, 43–59
carbohydrates, 44–46
functional groups and, 44
inorganic compounds vs., 43–44
Organic solvents, 164
Organismal level, **4**, 4*f*
Organs, 3–4, 4*f*
bones as, 179
skin as, 152
Organ systems, 3–4, 4*f*
interrelationships among, 5*f*, 6–7*f*
summary of body's, 6–7*f*
Organ transplants, 818, 820
heart, 706–707*b*
Orgasm (climax), **1073**, 1099–1100
Orientation anatomical terms, 13*t*
Origin (muscle), **259**, 284, 325
Oropharynx, 834*f*, **835**, 889, 889*f*, 895
Orthodontics, **938**
Orthopedist/orthopedic surgeon, **248**
Orthopnea, 875
Orthostatic hypotension, 551, 733
Os, uterine, 1085*f*, 1086
Oscillating (reverberating) circuits, **422**, 422*f*
Os coxae. *See* Coxal (hip) bone

Osmolality, **1015**–1016, 1016*f*
extracellular fluid and, 1039–1043, 1040*f*, 1041*f*
Osmolarity, **73**, 73*f*
vs. tonicity, 74
Osmoreceptors, 446, 1039–1041, 1040*f*, 1041*f*
Osmosis, 71, **72**
aquaporins and, 73
energy source/description/ examples, 75*t*
hydrostatic pressure, 73–74
membrane permeability and, 73, 73*f*
osmotic pressure, 73–74
selectivity of, 74–75
tonicity and, 74
Osmotic gradients, in urine concentration/volume, 1016, 1017*f*, 1018
Osmotic pressure, **73**–74
body fluids exchanges regulated by, 1037–1038, 1038*f*
plasma proteins and, 649*t*
Osseous spiral lamina, **587**, 588*f*
Osseous tissue (bone), **137**, 138*f*. *See also* bone
Ossicles, auditory, **217***t*, 584*f*, **585**–586, 585*f*
Ossification centers
fetal, 246, 247*f*
primary/secondary, **185**–186, 185*f*, 198, 198*f*
sutural bones and, 211
Ossification (osteogenesis), **184**–187
bone growth form of, 184
endochondral, 184
intramembranous, 184–185, 184*f*
Ossification (osteogenic) zone of long bones, 186–187, 186*f*
Ostealgia, **199**
Osteitis, **199**
Osteitis fibrosa cystica, 625
Osteoarthritis (OA), **273**–274
Osteoblasts, 128*f*, **129**, 137, **181**
in intramembranous ossification, 184*f*
Osteochondral grafting, 275*b*
Osteoclasts, **181**
Osteocytes, 128*f*, **129**–130, **137**, 138*f*, **182**, 183*f*
Osteogenesis imperfecta, **199**
Osteogenesis (ossification), **184**–187
Osteogenic cells, **181**
Osteogenic layer of periosteum of long bones, 181
Osteoid, **182**–183
in intramembranous ossification, 184*f*
Osteoid seam, 188
Osteomalacia, **193**
Osteomyelitis, **199**
Osteon (Haversian system), 137, **181**, 182*f*, 183*f*
Osteoporosis, **193**–195, 193*f*, 248
Osteoprogenitor cells, **181**
Osteosarcoma, **199**
Otalgia, **600**

Otic ganglia, 506t, **537**, 537f
Otic pit, **599**
Otic placodes, **599**
Otic vesicle, **599**
Otitis externa, **600**
Otitis media, **585**
Otoacoustic emissions, 592
Otolithic membrane, **594–595**, 594f, 595f
Otoliths, 594f, **595**
Otorhinolaryngology, **875**
Otosclerosis, **593**
Outer hair cells, 588f
Ova (eggs), 1066
   in oogenesis, 1091–1092, 1092f
Oval (vestibular) window, 584f, **585**, 586f, 588f
Ovarian cancer, **1109**
Ovarian cycle, **1093–1096**, 1093f
   establishing, 1094–1095
   hormonal regulation, 1094–1096, 1095f
   uterine cycle and, 1097f, 1098
Ovarian cysts, **1109**
Ovarian follicles, 1083f, **1084**, 1093, 1093f
Ovarian (gonadal) arteries, 746f, 747f, 752f, **754t**, **1083**, 1085f
Ovarian (gonadal) veins, 758f, 764f, **764t**, 765f, 1085f
Ovarian ligament, **1083**, 1083f, 1085f
Ovaries, 1066, **1082**, 1082f, 1085f
   as endocrine organ, 605f
   estrogens and, 634–635
   progesterone and, 634–635
   structure, 1083–1084, 1083f
Overuse injuries, **309**
Oviducts. See Uterine (fallopian) tubes
Ovulation, **1084**, 1084f, 1093, **1094**, 1096
Ovum, **1091**, 1092f
Oxaloacetic acid, **961**, 962f
Oxidases, **958**
   detoxifying functions, 90
   free radicals and, 90
   as globular protein, 52t
   reaction type catalyzed by, 54
Oxidation, 8
   of amino acids, 970, 970f
   of food fuels, 956–958
   of lipids, 968, 968f
Oxidation-reduction (redox) reactions, 33f, **38**, 956–**958**, 957f
Oxidative deamination, **970**, 970f, 971t
Oxidative fibers, **305–307**, 306t
Oxidative phosphorylation, 957f, 958f, **959**, 959f
   energy yield of, 965, 965f
   mechanism of, 963–965, 963f
Oxycodone (OxyContin), 425b
Oxygen, **8**
   atomic symbol/percentage of body mass/functions in body, 26t
   in formation of double covalent bond, 35f
   influences on breathing rate/depth, 866–868
   as reactive element, 32, 32f
   transport processes, 71, 72, 75t
Oxygen debt, muscle contraction and, **304**

Oxygen gas, molecule of, 35f
Oxygen-hemoglobin dissociation curve, 859, 859f
Oxygen toxicity, **855**
Oxygen transport and exchange, 858–861
   erythrocytes and, 650
   hemoglobin saturation and, 858–860, 859f
   summary, 862f
Oxyhemoglobin, **650**, **858–859**
Oxyphil cells, 624f, 625
Oxytocin, 10, 613, 613f, **617**
   let-down reflex and, **1138**, 1139f
   summary of regulation/effects, 619t

p16 gene, 146b
p53 gene, 146b, 937
   UV radiation and, 165
Pacemaker cells
   breathing and, 864–865
   in cardiac vs. skeletal vs. smooth muscle, 315t
   smooth muscle fiber contractions and, 311
   in stomach, 907
Pacemaker potentials, **692–693**, 693f
Pacinian corpuscles, 153f
   as pressure receptors, 164–165
Pacinian (lamellated) corpuscles, **492**, 494
   functional classes/body location, 493t
Packed red cell blood transfusions, **668**
Pagetic bone, 195
Paget's disease, **195**, 198
Pain, **496–497b**
   amplification of, 497b
   gate control theory of, 497b
   in inflammatory response, 792f, 793
   modulating techniques, 497b
   myofascial pain syndrome, 320
   periaqueductal gray matter and, 449, 497b
   phantom limb, 497b
   receptors, 153f, 155, 165, 492, 496b
   referred, 496b, **542**, 543f
   somatic vs. visceral, 496b
   spinal cord pathways, 476f, 477
   substance P and, **418**, 496b, 497b
   threshold, **496b**
   tolerance, **496b**
Pain receptors
   in cornea, 561
   smell sense and, 579
Palate, **890**
   cleft, 246–247, 247f, 874, 936
   hard, 208f, **832**, 834f, 889f, **890**
   soft, **832**, 834f, 889f, **890**
Palatine bones, 206f, **213**, 215f
   horizontal plate, 208f, **213**, 215f
   orbital process, 214f
   perpendicular plate, 215f
   summary/important markings, **217t**
Palatine process, maxilla, 206f, 208f, **212**, 212f, 215f, **217t**
Palatine raphe, 889f
Palatine suture, medial, 208f
Palatine tonsils, **781**, 782f, 834f, **835**, 889f, 891f

Palatoglossal arches, 889f, **890**, 891f
Palatopharyngeal arches, 889f, **890**, 891f
Pallidectomy, **485**
Pallor, 158
Palmar aponeurosis, 359f
Palmar arches, 747f, 750f, **750t**, 751f
Palmar interosseous muscles
   of foot, 383f, **383t**
   of hand, 365f, **366t**
Palmaris longus muscle, 331f, 359f
   actions of (summary), 362t
   description/action/nerve supply, **358t**
   origin/insertion, 358t
   tendon, 365f
Palmar venous arches, 762f, **762t**, 763f
Palm of hand (metacarpus)
   arteries, 747f, 750f, **750t**, 751f
   bones, 233, **235**, 235f, 236f, 236t, 237
   muscles, 331f, **358t**, 359f, 362t, 365f, **366t**
   tendons, 365f
   transverse ligament, 359f
Palpation, 2–3
Palpebrae (eyelids), **556**, 557f
Palpebral conjunctiva, 557, 557f
Palpebral fissure, **556**, 557f
Pampiniform plexus, 1067f, **1068**
Pancreas, **632–634**, 883f, 909f, **917–918**
   abdominal arteries in relation to, 753f
   as an accessory digestive organ, 917
   location, 605f
   major functions (overview), 920t
   microscopic tissue, 632f
   parasympathetic fibers, 536f, 537f
   sympathetic fibers, 536f
   sympathetic innervation, 541t
Pancreatic amylase, 928f, **929**
Pancreatic ducts, 909f, **917**
Pancreatic islets (islets of Langerhans), **632**, 632f, 917
Pancreatic juice, **917**, 920t
   composition, 917–918
   secretion regulation, 918, 919f
Pancreatic nucleases, nucleic acid digestion and, 928f, **931**
Pancreatic polypeptide (PP), 632
Pancreatitis, **938**
Paneth cells, 911
Pannus, **274**
Panoramic vision, 575
Pantothenic acid (vitamin B5), **950t**
Papanicolaou (Pap) smear, 1086
Papillae
   dermal, 153f, **155**
   duodenal, 909f
   hair, 160, 161f
   of renal pyramids, 1000, 1000f
   tongue, 581, 581f, **890–891**, 891f
Papillary muscles, **683**, 683f, 687f
Papilledema, **600**
Paracrines, **606**
   blood pressure and, 729
   as signaling chemical, 83
   that act in digestion, 906t

Parafollicular cells (C cells), 620, 620f, **624**
Parahippocampal gyrus, 437f, 454, 455f
Parallel after-discharge circuits, **422**, 422f
Parallel fascicle pattern, **326**, 327f
Parallel neural processing, **423**
Paralysis, 478–479
Paramesonephric (Müllerian) ducts, 1102f, **1103**
Paranasal sinuses, 214, **218**, 218f, **833–834**, 834f
Paraneurons, 637
Paraplegia, **478–479**
Parasagittal plane, **15**
Parasympathetic division (ANS), **389**, 535, 537f
   antagonistic interactions, 544
   cooperative ANS effects, 545–546
   cranial outflow, 537–538, 537f
   effects on target organs, 546t
   functional role of, 536f
   heart rate regulation by, 701f, 702
   localized vs. diffuse effects, 547
   position within nervous system structure, 389, 389f, 533, 533f
   sacral outflow, 537f, **538**
   sympathetic division vs., 534f, 536f, 536t
      interactions, 544–547, 550
   tone and, **545**
Parasympathetic fibers, in cranial nerves, 501f
Parasympathetic nervous system. See Parasympathetic division (ANS)
Parasympathomimetic agents, effects on ANS activity, 545t
Parathormone. See Parathyroid glands
Parathyroid glands, 605f, **624**, 624f
   aging and, 639
   disorders, 625
   effect on bone/intestine/kidney, 625, 625f
   hormone secreted, 625
Parathyroid hormone (PTH), **188**, **625**, 933
   calcium balance and, 188–189, 189f, 1049
Paraventricular nuclei, 445f, 446, **613**, 613f
Paravertebral ganglia, 538
Paresthesia, **528**
Parietal bones, **205**, 205f, 206f, 207, 208f
   summary/important markings, 216t
Parietal cells, of stomach glands, **900**, 901f
Parietal layer of serous pericardium, 17f, 18, 142f, **678**, 679f
Parietal lobe of cerebral hemisphere, 434, 435f, **436**, 437f, 445f
Parietal peritoneum, 18, **886**, 886f, 924f
Parietal pleura, 18, 679f, 844f, **845–846**
Parietal serosa, **17**, 17f
Parieto-occipital sulcus, 437f

Parkinson's disease, 449, **459**
Parotid gland, 883f, **891**, 892f
parasympathetic fibers, 537f
Paroxysmal atrial tachycardia (PAT), **709**
Partial pressures, **854**–855, 855t
Partial-thickness burns, 170
Particle size, in chemical reactions, 39
Parturition (birth), **1135**–1137, 1135f, 1136f
Passive humoral immunity, **806**, 806f
Passive membrane transport processes, **70**
  diffusion, **71**–75, 75t
  filtration, 71, **75**, 75t
  summary, 75t
Patella, 228f, 241, 241f, **242**, 246f, 246t, 266f
  joint, 259t
  leg muscles and, 375f
  thigh muscles and, 368f
Patellar (knee-jerk) reflex, 265, **523**–524, 523f
Patellar ligament, **265**, 266f, 368f
Patellar retinacula, **265**, 266f
Patellar surface, **241**, 241f, 243f
Patent ductus arteriosus, 708
Pathogens, **789**
Pathological anatomy, 2
Pathologic fracture, **199**
Pathology, **148**
PAT (paroxysmal atrial tachycardia), **709**
PCOS (polycystic ovary syndrome), **1109**
PCT (proximal convoluted tubule), **1001**, 1002f, 1003
PDGF (platelet-derived growth factor), **666**
  source/effects, 793t
Pectinate line, 923f, 925
Pectinate muscles, **680**, 682f, 683f
Pectineus muscle, 331f, 368f
  actions of (summary), **379**–380t
  description/action/nerve supply, **369**t
  origin/insertion, **369**t
Pectoralis major muscle, 352, **354**, 356f
  actions of (summary), 362t
  description/action/nerve supply, **354**t
  origin/insertion, **354**t
  shoulder movements and, 352, 353f
  superficial, 330f, 331f
Pectoralis minor muscle, 352, 353f
  description/action/nerve supply, **352**t
  origin/insertion, **352**t
  superficial, 331f
Pectoral nerves, muscles served by, 352, 354t
Pectoral (shoulder) girdle, 228, **229**
  articulated, 230f
  bones
    clavicles, **229**, 230f, 234f, 236f
    scapulae, **229**, 230f
    summary, 236t
  muscles acting on, **352**–353t, 353f
  upper limbs and, 231–237
Pedicles, vertebral, **221**, 221f, 222f, 223f, 471f

Pedigree analysis, **1155**, 1155f
Pelvic brim/inlet, 237, **239**
  female vs. male, 240f, 240t
Pelvic cavity, **15**, 17f
Pelvic floor/diaphragm, muscles, 350t, 351f
Pelvic (hip) girdle, 229, **237**
  bones, 237–239, 238f, 243f, 246f, 246t
Pelvic inflammatory disease (PID), **1085**
  gonorrhea and, 1101
Pelvic outlet, **239**, 240f
  female vs. male, 240f, 240t
Pelvic splanchnic nerves, 537f, **538**
Pelvimetry, **248**
Pelvis
  arteries, 756–757t
  bony, **237**, 238f
  in childbearing, 239, 240t
  false, **239**
  female vs. male, 239, 240f, 240t
  innervation of, 514
  muscles, 331f
  sympathetic innervation, 541–542
  true, 237, **239**
  veins, 758f, 758t, 766f, 766t
Penis, 1066, 1066f, **1069**, 1070f
  ANS effects, 541
  sympathetic fibers, 539f
Pennate fascicle pattern, **326**, 327f
Pentamers, 807, 808t
Pentose sugars, 44, 45f
Pepsin, **900**, 901f, 920t, 928f, **929**
Pepsinogen, 001f, 900
Peptic ulcers, **938**
Peptide bond, **49**, 49f
Peptide hormones, functions of, 52t
Peptides
  gut-brain, **418**
  neuropeptides, **418**
  as neurotransmitters, 417t
Perception (sensory), 491, **494**
  cerebral cortex as site of, 496–497
  estimating stimulus intensity, 406f, 497
  feature abstraction in, **498**
  pattern recognition in, 498
  qualities of, 497–498
  role in neural integration, 494, 496–498
  somatosensory system and, 494
  spacial discrimination and, 497–498
  stimulus detection and, 497
Perfluorinated hydrocarbon chains (PFCs), 673b
Perforated (ruptured) eardrum, 593
Perforating (Sharpey's) fibers, 180f, 181, 183f
Perforating (Volkmann's) canals, **182**, 183f
Perforin, **816**
  functions (summary), 817t
Perforins, **816**, 816f
Periaqueductal gray matter, 449, 450f
  pain and, 497b
Pericardial arteries, 746f, **751**t
Pericardial cavity, **15**, 17f, **678**, 679f

Pericardial friction rub, 678
Pericardial membranes, 844f
Pericardial sac, 347f, 678, 679f
Pericarditis, 678
Pericardium, 142f, **143**, **678**, 679f
  fibrous, **678**, 679f
  serous, **678**, 679f
    parietal layer, 17f, 18, 142f, **678**, 679f
    visceral layer, 17f, 18, 142f, **678**, 679f
Perichondrium, 176
Pericytes, 720, 720f
Perikaryon, **391**. *See also* Neuron cell body
Perilymph, 586, 591f, 594
Perimetrium, 1082f, 1085f, **1086**
Perimysium, 282f, 282t, **283**, 283f
Perineal muscles, 350, 351f
  deep transverse, **350**t, 351f
  description/action/nerve supply, **350**t
  origin/insertion, **350**t
  superficial transverse, **350**t, 351f
Perineum, 350
  female, **1089**
  innervation of, 516, 517f, 517t
  male, **1069**
  muscles of, 350t, 351f, 1069
Perineurium, **498**, 498f
Periodic table, 27
Period of contraction, of muscle twitch, **297**, 297f
Period of relaxation, of muscle twitch, **297**, 297f
Periodontal disease, 895
Periodontal ligament, **894**, 894f
Periodontal ligaments, 254
Periodontitis, **895**
Periosteal blood vessel, 183f
Periosteal bud, **185**–186, 185f
Periosteal dura mater, 464, 464f
  CSF in relation to, 466f
Periosteum, **180**–181, 180f, 183f
  dura mater in relation to, 464, 464f
  in intramembranous ossification, 184f
Peripheral congestion, **705**
Peripheral motor endings, **289**, 290f, 491, **519**
Peripheral nervous system (PNS), **388**–389, 389f, 490–531, **491**
  aging and, 527
  cranial nerves, 388, 389f, 499, **500**–501, 502–508t
  developmental aspects, 527
    embryonic, 1123–1128, 1130t
    fetal, 1132t, 1133
  motor division, **388**, 389f
  in nervous system's structural organization, 491, 491f
  reflex activity, 521–527
  sensory division, **388**, 389f
  spinal nerves, 388, 389f, 499, **508**–518
Peripheral process of unipolar neurons, 395, 396f
Peripheral proteins, 67f, **68**–69
Peripheral resistance, **723**
  blood pressure and, 726–731
  hormones influencing, 729t
  major determinants of, 724
Perirenal fat capsule, kidney, **999**, 999f

Peristalsis, **309**–310, **884**, 884f, 885f, 920t
  in esophagus, 898, 898f
  mass movements, **926**
  in stomach, 905, 907, 907f
Peritoneal cavity, **886**, 886f
Peritoneal organs, 886
Peritoneum, 142f, **143**, **886**, 886f, 1066f
  parietal, 18, 142f, 886, 886f
  relationship of digestive organs to, 886–887, 886f
  visceral, 18, 142f, 886, 886f
Peritonitis, 18, 887, 922
Peritubular capillaries, **1003**, 1004f
Pernicious anemia, 655, 902
Peroneal (fibular) artery, 756f, **756**–757t
Peroneal (fibular) vein, 766f, 766t
Peroneal muscles, **373**
Peroneus muscles. *See* Fibularis muscles
Peroxisomes, 66f, **90**
  structure/functions (summary), 94t
Perpendicular plate
  of ethmoid bone, 205f, 206f, **211**, 211f
  of palatine bone, 215f
Perpendicular (vertical) plates, of palatine bones, 213, 215f
Perspiration, water and, 40
Pepsinogen, 900
Petechiae, 668
Petit mal seizures, 457
PET (positron emission tomography), **20**b
Petrous region of temporal bone, 208f, **209**
Peyer's patches, **782**, 782f
  of small intestine, 911
PF3 (platelet factor 3), 664f, 665
PFCs (perfluorinated hydrocarbon chains), 673b
PGI2 (prostacyclin), 665
pH, **42**, 42f, 52t
  imbalances, 867–868, 1050, 1055–1058
    in acidosis/alkalosis, 1055
  regulation, 1050–1054
    buffer systems, 1050–1052
    by kidneys, 1052–1054
    by lungs, 1052
Phagocytes
  in body's defense systems, 790–791, 796t
  lysosomes and, 89
  mobilization of, 794–795, 794f
Phagocytosis, **79**–80, 79f
  enhanced by antibody action, 809f, 810
  mechanism, 790–791, 791f
Phagolysosomes, **790**, 791f
Phagosomes, **79**, 88f, **790**, 791f
Phalanges
  fingers, 228f, 233, 235f, 236f, 236t, **237**
    joints of, 258t
  toes, 228f, **244**, 245f, 246f, 246t
    joints of, 259t
Phantom limb pain, 497b
Pharyngeal constrictor muscles, **340**, 341f, 896
  description/action/nerve supply, **341**t
  origin/insertion, **341**t

Pharyngeal-esophageal phase of deglutition, 898, 898f
Pharyngeal plexus, muscles served by, 341t
Pharyngeal pouches, 599
Pharyngeal tonsil (adenoids), 781–782, 834f, **835**, 875
Pharyngeal tubercle, 207, 208f
Pharyngotympanic (auditory) tube, 584f, **585**, 585f, 834f, 835
   opening in nasopharynx, 889f
Pharynx, 832f, **835**, 883f, **895–896**
   digestive processes occurring in, 897–899, 898f
   features/functions, 838t
   major functions (overview), 920t
   mucosa, 834f
   swallowing and, 340
Phasic receptors, **495**
Phenocopies, **1152**
Phenotype, **1147**
Phenylalanine, 947f
Phenylethanolamine N-methyltransferase, 418f
Phenylketonuria (PKU), 992
Pheochromocytoma, 632
Philtrum, 831, 833f
Phlebitis, **767**
Phlebotomy, **767**
Phosphatases, in chemical digestion, 928f, **931**
Phosphate, 1044t
   balance regulation, 1049
   bone as storage reservoir for, 179
   monohydrogen, 1054, 1054f
Phosphate buffer system, **1051**, 1054, 1054f
Phosphatidylcholine, 47f, 48t
Phosphatidyl inositol biphosphate (PIP), **608–609**, 608f
Phosphodiesterase, **608**
Phospholipase C, 608f, **609**
Phospholipids, 46, 47, 47f, 48t
   in lipid bilayer of plasma membrane, 67, 67f
   polar heads/nonpolar tails, 67, 67f
   in synthesis of structural materials, 970
Phosphoric acid, 1050
Phosphorus, 26t, **954t**
Phosphorylation, **956**, 958f
   direct, in muscle metabolism, 301–302, 303f
   oxidative, 957f, 958f, **959**
   in sodium-potassium pump, 76f, 77
   substrate-level, **958**, 958f
Photo-aging, 171
Photons, **565**
Photopigments (visual pigments), **569–570**, 570f
   capture of light by, 571–572, 571f
Photoreceptors, **491**, 561, 562f, 570f
   functional anatomy, 569–571
   inner/outer segments, **569**, 570f
   light and dark adaptation, 574–575
   light transduction reactions, 572–574
   sensitivities to different wavelengths, 565, 566f
   stimulation of, 572
   visual pigments and, 569–572

Photosensitivity, 157
Phototransduction, **569**
   events of, 572–575, 574f
Phrenic arteries, 746f, **751t**, 752f, **753t**, 755f
Phrenic nerve, 511f, 511t, **512**
   breathing and, **863**, 864f
   muscles served by, 346t
Phrenic veins, 764f, **764f**, 765f
Physiological jaundice, 1139, **1141**
Physiology, **2**
   topics of, 3
Pia mater, 464f, **465**, 466f
   spinal, 470, 473f
Pica, **993**, 1043
PID (pelvic inflammatory disease), **1085**
Piezoelectric effect, 194b
Pigment, hair, 160
Pigmented layer of retina, **561**, 562f
Pigmented moles, 157
Pili. See Hairs
Pineal gland, 445f, **447**, 449f, 605f, **635–636**
Pinealocytes, **635**
Pinkeye, 557
Pinna (auricle), **583**, 584f, 585, 590f
Pinocytosis (fluid-phase endocytosis), **80–81**, 80t
Pinocytotic vesicles, 720f
PIP2, 608f, **609**
PIP-calcium signal mechanism, **608–609**, 608f
PIP (phosphatidyl inositol bisphosphate), 608, 608f, **609**
Piriformis muscle, 351f, 371f
   actions of (summary), 379–380t
   description/action/nerve supply, **370t**
   origin/insertion, **370t**
Piriform lobe, 437f, 440
Pisiform bone, **235**, 235f, 236f, 236t
   hand muscles in relation to, 365f
Pitch (sound), **589**
   perception of, 593
Pituitary dwarfism, **616**, 618t
Pituitary gland, 445f, **446**, 448f, 605f, **612–620**
   aging and, 639
   anterior lobe, **612**, 613f
      hormones, 614–617, 618–619t
      in spermatogenesis regulation, 1080–1081, 1081f
   blood supply, 613
   CSF in relation to, 466f
   hypothalamic relationships, 445f, 446, 613–614, 613f
   posterior lobe, **612**, 613f
      hormones, 617–620, 619t
Pivot joint, 258t, 264f, **265**
PKU (phenylketonuria), 992
Placenta, **1120**
   hormones produced by, 637, 1122
Placenta abruptio, **1141**
Placental stage of labor, 1136f, **1137**
Placenta previa, **1141**
Placentation, **1120**, 1122
   events of, 1121f
Plane joint, 258t, 259t, **263**, 264f, 265
Planes, body, 15, 16f

Planetary model of atomic structure, 27f, **28**
Plantar arch, 756f, **756t**, 757f, 766f
Plantar arteries, 756f, 757f, **757t**
Plantar flexion (movement), **261**, 261f
   muscles involved in, 379–380t
Plantar interosseous muscles, 383f, **383t**
Plantaris muscle, 376t, 377f, 378f
   actions of (summary), 379–380t
   tendon, 377f
Plantar nerve, muscles served by, 381t
Plantar nerves, **516**, 517f, 517t
Plantar reflex, **527**
Plantar veins, 766f, **766t**
Plaque
   atherosclerotic, 718–719b
   in desmosome junctions, 69, 70f
Plasma (blood), 52t, 128f, 137, 138f, 139, 647, 647f, **648–649**
   composition, 649t
      electrolyte, 1038f
   continuous mixing with other body fluids, 1037–1038, 1039f
   electrolyte composition of, 1038f
   as extracellular fluid, 1036, 1036f
   metabolic heat distributed by, 649
   plasma expanders, **671**
   proteins, 52t, 648, 649t
Plasma cells, **777**, **804**
   antibodies and, 777, 806
   in areolar connective tissue, **130**, 130f
   functions (summary), 817t
   in humoral immune response, 659, 777, 804–805, 804f
Plasma expanders, **671**
Plasma membrane, **66**, 66f
   cell adhesion molecules and, 83
   endomembrane system and, 90, 90f
   fluid mosaic model, **67**, 67f
   functions, 70–84
      of its receptors, 83–84, 84f
      resting potential and, 81–83
      summary, 94t
      in transport processes, 70–81.
      See also Membrane transport mechanisms
      voltage-sensitive channel proteins and, 84
   junctions, 69, 70f
   of muscle fibers. See Sarcolemma
   in neurons, as site of electrical signaling, 391
   permeability, 70, 71, 81–82
   specializations of, 69, 70f
   structure, 67–69, 67f
      lipids in, 48t, 67–68, 67f
      microvilli, 66f, 69
      proteins in, 68–69, 68f
      summary, 94t
   summary of structure/function, 67f, 94t
Plasmapheresis, **674**
Plasma thromboplastin antecedent (PTA), nature/origin/function/pathway, 663t

Plasma thromboplastin component (PTC), nature/origin/function/pathway, 663t
Plasmin, **666**
Plasminogen, **666**
Plasticity of stomach smooth muscle, **905**
Platelet accelerator, nature/origin/function/pathway, 663t
Platelet count, **671**
Platelet-derived growth factor (PDGF), **666**
   source/effects, 793t
Platelets, 647, 647f, 649f, **662**
   formation, 662, 662f
   in hemostasis, platelet plugs, 664f, 665
   summary, 658t
Platysma muscle, 337f
   back muscles in relation to, 343f
   description/action/nerve supply, **336t**
   origin/insertion, **336t**
   role in facial expression, 336t
   superficial, 331f
Pleura/pleurae, 142f, **143**, 838t, 844f, **845–846**
   parietal, 18, 142f, 838t, 844f
   visceral, 18, 142f, 838t, 844f
Pleural cavity, **15**, 17f, 844f, **846**, 846f
Pleural effusion, 846
Pleural fluid, **846**
Pleurisy, 18, **846**
Plicae circulares (circular folds), **909**, 910f
PMI (point of maximal intensity), **678**, 679f
PMNs (polymorphonuclear leukocytes), **657**
Pneumocystis pneumonia, 820
Pneumonia, **875**
   aspiration, 247
   bacterial, 874
Pneumothorax, **847**
PNS. See Peripheral nervous system
Podocytes, **1001**, 1002f, 1005f, 1006f
Point of maximal intensity (PMI), **678**, 679f
Poisonous snake bites, immunity and, 806
Poisons, metabolic, 965
Polar body
   first, **1091**, 1092f
   second, **1091–1092**, 1092f
Polar heads/nonpolar tails of phospholipids, 67–68, 67f
Polarized cells, **81**
Polar microtubules, 102f, 103f
Polar molecules, 34–36, 35f, 36f
   water and, 40
Poles of eye, **559**, 560f
Poliomyelitis, 481
Pollex (thumb), 235, 235f, 236f, **237**
Polyatomic ions, 41
Polycystic ovary syndrome (PCOS), **1109**
Polycythemias, **656**
Polydipsia, **634**, 635f
Polygene inheritance, **1152**, 1153f
Polymers, **44**
   DNA as, 55, 56f

Polymorphonuclear leukocytes (PMNs or polys), **657**
Polypeptides, 49
Polyphagia, **634**, 635*f*
Polyps, 146*b*
Polyribosomes, 109, 109*f*
Polysaccharides, 44, 45*f*, 46
Polyspermy, **1115**
Polys (polymorphonuclear leukocytes PMNs), **657**
Polysynaptic reflex, **521**
Polyunsaturated fats, **46**
Polyuria, **634**, 635*f*
POMC (pro-opiomelanocortin), **614**
Pons, 445*f*, 448*f*, **449**, 449*f*
    cerebral hemispheres in relation to, 435*f*
    embryonic origins, 432*f*, 433
    functions (summary), 453*t*
    neural integration and, 495*f*
    nuclei of importance, 450*f*, 451
    respiratory centers of, **864**, 864*f*
    spinal cord tracts and, 476*f*
    white matter fiber tracts and, 442*f*
Pontine nuclei, 449, 450*f*
Pontine respiratory group, **864**, 864*f*
Popliteal artery, 747*f*, 756*f*, **756*t***, 757*f*
Popliteal ligaments
    arcuate, 266*f*, **267**
    oblique, 266*f*, **267**
Popliteal vein, 759*f*, 766*f*, **766*t***
Popliteus muscle, **373**, 377*f*, 378*f*
    actions of (summary), 379*t*
    description/action/nerve supply, **376*t***
    knee joint and, 266*f*, 379*t*
    origin/insertion, **376*t***
Pore
    complexion, 153*f*, 158
    sweat, 158, 159*f*
Pore complexes, of nuclear envelope, 96*f*, **97**
Pores (fenestrations), 720, 720*f*
Porphyria, **171**
Porta hepatis, **912**, 913*f*
Portal-caval anastomoses, 915
Portal hypertension, **915**
Portal system, 614, 764*t*
Portal triad, **912**, 914*f*
Positive chemotaxis, **657**
Positive feedback mechanisms, **10–11**, 12*f*
    in action potentials, 404
    in heat stroke, 989
    of ovarian cycle, 1096
    oxytocin and, 617
Positive selection, T cells and, **801–802**, 802*f*
Positron emission tomography (PET), **20*b***
Postabsorptive (fasting) state, **973**, 974–978
    basal metabolic rate in, 984
    hormonal controls, 977–978, 978*t*
    major events/metabolic pathways, 976*f*
    neural controls, 977–978
Postcapillary venules, 717*f*, **721**, 721*f*, 722
Posterior direction/orientation, 13*t*
Posterior segment (cavity) of eye, 559, 560*f*, **563–564**, 564*f*

vitreous humor in, 560*f*, **563–564**, 564*f*
Posterior thalamic nuclei, 445*f*, 446
Postganglionic axons, **533**, 534*f*
Postmortem examination, 148
Postpartum bleeding, 1137
Postpolio syndrome, **481**
Postsynaptic neuron, **409**
    in chemical synapses, 409–411
    summation by, 411–413, 413*f*
Postsynaptic potentials, **401**, **411**
    action potentials compared to, 414*t*
    conduction distance, 414*t*
    excitatory, **411–413**, 414*t*
    function (summary), 414*t*
    as graded event, 401, 414*t*
    inhibitory, **411–413**, 414*t*
    peak membrane potential, 414*t*
    refractory period in, 414*t*
    repolarization in, 414*t*
    stimulus for opening ionic gates, 414*t*
    summation and, 411–412, 413*f*
Posture
    erect or seated, skeletal muscles and, 281
    motor pathways regulating, 478
    muscles, 342–344*t*, 343*f*, 345*f*
Potassium, 26*t*, 953*t*, **1048**
    absorption, 932
    in action potentials, 402–404, 403*f*
    balance regulators, 1048–1049
        causes/consequences of imbalances, 1044*t*
    in blood plasma/IF/ICF, 1038*f*
    metabolic acidosis and, 1056*t*
    in muscle contraction, 290, 290*f*, 291, 291*f*
    reabsorption, 1014*t*
    resting membrane potential and, 82–83, 82*f*, 399*f*
    in salt substitutes, 1049
    in sodium-potassium pump, 76*f*, 77, 77*f*, 82, 82*f*
Potassium chloride, as body salt, 41
Potential, in measuring voltage, 397
Potential energy, **25**
Pott's fracture, 242*f*, 244
Power and recovery strokes of cilia, 93*f*, 95
PP (pancreatic polypeptide), 632
P-Q interval, **696**, 696*f*, 697*f*
Precapillary sphincter, 717*f*, **721–722**, 721*f*
Precipitation, by antibodies, **809**, 809*f*
Precommand areas of motor control hierarchy, **520–521**, 520*f*
Preeclampsia, 1135
Prefrontal cortex, 437*f*, **441**
    memory and, 462*f*
Preganglionic axons, **533**, 534*f*
Preganglionic neurons, **533**, 534*f*
Pregnancy, **1114**
    ectopic, 1084–1085, **1141**
    effects on mother, 1133–1135, 1134*f*
    fertilization, 1114–1117
    flowchart of events of, 1128*b*
    hormonal changes during, 1120, 1120*f*
Preload, stroke volume and, **700–701**, 701*f*

Premature ventricular contractions (PVCs), 695
Premolar (bicuspid) teeth, 893*f*, **894**
Premotor cortex, 437*f*, **439**
    damage to, 439
    memory and, 462*f*
pre-mRNA (primary transcript), 105, 105*f*
Preoptic nucleus, 445*f*
    sleep-wake cycle and, 459
Prepatellar bursa, inflammation, 273
Prepotentials, **692**
Prepuce (foreskin), 1066*f*, **1069**
Prepuce of clitoris, 1088*f*, **1089**
Presbycusis, **599**
Presbyopia, **568**
Pressure gradient, **75**, 75*t*
Pressure points, **732**, 732*f*
Prestriate cortices. *See* Visual association areas
Presynaptic inhibition, **413**
Presynaptic neurons, **408**
    axon terminal and, 409, 410*f*
    in chemical synapses, 409–411, 410*f*
Pretectal nuclei, 575, 576*f*
Prevertebral ganglia. *See* Collateral (prevertebral) ganglia
PRH. *See* Prolactin-releasing hormone
Prickle cells, 155
Prickly layer of skin (stratum spinosum), **154–155**, 154*f*
Primary auditory cortex, 592*f*
Primary germ layers, 1120*f*, **1123**
    gastrulation, 1123, 1124*f*
    organogenesis, 1123, 1126–1132
Primary motor area. *See* Motor cortex
Primary ossification center, **185**, 185*f*
Primary sex organs (gonads), **1066**
Primary somatosensory cortex, 437*f*, **439**
Primary transcript (pre-mRNA), 105, 105*f*
Primary visual cortex, 575, 576*f*
    processing of retinal inputs, 578
Primase, 100*f*
Prime mover (agonist) muscles, **325**
Primitive gut, **933**, 936, 936*f*, 1122, **1126**, 1126*f*
Primitive node, 1125*f*
Primitive streak, **1123**, 1124*f*, 1125*f*
Primordial follicle, 1083*f*, **1084**
Primordial germ cells, 1102*f*, **1103**
Principal cells, of collecting ducts, 1002*f*, 1003
Principle of complementarity, 2, **3**, 65
P-R interval, **696**, 696*f*, 697*f*
Prion proteins/disorders, 482–483*b*
PRL. *See* Prolactin
Proaccelerin, nature/origin/ function/pathway, 663*t*
Procarboxypeptidase, 918, 918*f*
Procedural (skills) memory, **461**, 462*f*

Process (bone marking), 179*t*
Procoagulants (clotting factors), 663*t*, **665**. *See also* Blood clotting
Proconvertin, nature/origin/ function/pathway, 663*t*
Proctodeum, **936**, 936*f*
Proctology, **938**
Product(s), in chemical equations, 36, **37**
Proerythroblast, **651**, 652*f*
Progesterone, levels in late pregnancy, 1136
Progesterone, **634–635**, **1082**
    in early pregnancy, 1120, 1120*f*
    location/function in body, 48*t*
    in ovarian cycle, 1094–1096, 1095*f*
    in puberty, 1098
    sodium balance and, 1048
    source/stimulus/effects (summary), 1099*t*
    in uterine cycle, 1096–1098, 1097*f*
Prohormones, 614
Proinsulin, **632**
Projection, **497**
Projection fibers, in white matter, 442*f*, **443**
Projection level of motor hierarchy, **520**, 520*f*
Prolactin, **1138**
Prolactin-inhibiting hormone (PIH), **616**, 619*t*
Prolactinoma, **642**
Prolactin (PRL), **616**
    hypersecretion, 616–617
    summary of regulation/effects, 619*t*
Prolactin-releasing hormone (PRH), **616**, 619*t*
Prolapsed (herniated) disc, **220–221**, 220*f*
Prolymphocytes, **660**, 661*f*
Promegakaryocytes, 662*f*
Promonocytes, **660**, 661*f*
Promoter, DNA, 105, 106*f*
Promyelocytes, **660**, 661*f*
Pronation (movement), **262**, 263*f*
    muscles involved in, 362*f*
Pronator quadratus muscle, **358**, 359*f*
    actions (summary), 362*t*
    description/action/nerve supply, **360*t***
    origin/insertion, **360*t***
Pronator teres muscle, 358, 359*f*
    actions (summary), 362–363*t*, 363*f*
    description/action/nerve supply, **358*t***
    origin/insertion, **358*t***
    superficial, 331*f*
Pronephric duct, **1027**, 1029*f*
Pronephros, **1027**, 1029*f*
Pronucleus
    female, **1116**, 1117*f*
    male, **1116**, 1117*f*
Pro-opiomelanocortin (POMC), **614**
Pro Osteon, 195*b*
Prophase, **101**, 102*f*, 1075*f*, 1076*f*
Proprioception, conscious, 475
Proprioceptors, **492**, 493*t*
    pathways to, 476*f*
Propulsion, **884**, 884*f*
    in mouth (oral cavity), 920*t*

Prosencephalon (forebrain), **431**, 432f
Prostacyclin, **665**
Prostaglandins, 606, **793**, 793t, 945–946, 1135f, **1136**
  location/function in body, 48t
  as pain-producing chemical, 496b
  source/effects, 793t
Prostate, 1066, 1066f, 1070f, **1071**
  cancer, 1072
Prostate-specific antigen (PSA), 1071, 1072
Prostatic urethra, 1025f, **1026**, 1066f, 1070f, 1071
Prostatitis, 1071–1072
Prostheses, joint, 275b
Protease inhibitors, 821
Proteases, 130f
Proteasomes, 111
Protein, metabolism, thyroid hormone's effects, 621t
Protein buffer system, **1051–1052**
Protein C, **667**
Protein (dietary)
  absorption, 928f, 930f, 931
  digestion, 902, 920t, 928f, 929, 930f
  essential amino acids, 946, 947f
  food sources, 945t, 946
  metabolism, 957f, 970–971
    insulin's influence, 633
    summary, 971t
    thyroid hormone's effects, 621t
  problems with excesses/deficits, 945t
Proteins, 48
  carrier, 52t, 68, **71**–72, 72f
  channel, 52t, 68
  complement, 52t
  complete, 945t, **946**
  contractile, 282f, 282t
    ATP and, 59f
  cytosolic degradation of, 110–111
  denaturation, 50, 52, 53f
  fibrous, 50, 52t
  functions, 49, 50, 52, 52t
  globular, **50**, 52t
  heat shock (hsp), 53
  histone, **97**
  integral, 67f, 68
  kinases, **607**, 607f
  linker, 69, 70f
  in lipid bilayer of plasma membrane, 67, 67f
  as macromolecules, 49
  motor, **90**
  percent of cell mass, 48
  peripheral, 67f, **68**
  plasma, 52t, 796–798
  stress, 53
  structure of, 37, 38f, 49, 49f
  synthesis. See Protein synthesis
  transmembrane, 68
  transport, 52t, 68
  types found in body, 52t
  in urine, 1024t
  uses in body, 946–947
Protein synthesis
  amino acids and, 37, 38f
  cytosolic degradation and, 110–111

dietary factors influencing, 946–947
DNA's role in (overview), 55, 101, 104, 105f
  ribosomes as site of, 85, 94t
RNA's role in (overview), 55, 104, 105f
  sequence of events/final distribution, 88f
  steps of, 104–109
    signal mechanisms, 87, 87f
    transcription, 104–106
    translation, 107–109
Proteinuria, 1024t
Proteoglycans, 127–128, 129f
Proteome, 48
Prothrombin, 665
Prothrombin activator, 664f, **665**, **665–666**
Prothrombin, 664f, **666**
  nature/origin/function/pathway, 663t
Prothrombin time, **671**
Proton acceptors, 41, 49, 1050
Proton donors, 41, 49, 1050
Protons, 27–30, 27f
ProTon-oncogenes, 146b
Protraction (movement),**262**, 263f
Provirus, 821
Provitamin D3 (cholecalciferol), 638, 638f
Provitamins, 948
Proximal convoluted tubule (PCT), **1001**, 1002f, 1003, 1004f
  functions (summary), 1020f
  reabsorptive abilities, 1013, 1014t
Proximal orientation/direction, 13t
PSA (prostate-specific antigen), 1071, 1072
Pseudohermaphrodites, 1103
Pseudopods, 79
Pseudostratified columnar epithelium, 122f, **123**
  functions/location, 122f
Pseudounipolar neurons, 395, 396–397t
Psoas major muscle, 347f, 368f
  description/action/nerve supply, **367**t
  origin/insertion, 367t
Psoas minor muscle, 368f
Psoriasis, **171**
Psychological factors, regulating food intake, 983
Psychoses, 485
Psychosocial dwarfism, **642**
Psychosomatic illnesses, **455**
PTA (plasma thromboplastin antecedent), origin/function, 663t
ptc gene, 165
PTC (plasma thromboplastin component), origin/function, 663t
Pterygoid muscles, 338, 339f
  description/action/nerve supply, **338**
  origin/insertion, **338**t
Pterygoid processes, 206f, **210**, 210f, 215f

Pterygopalatine ganglia, 505f, 505t, **537**, 537f
PTH (parathyroid hormone), **188**, **625**
  blood calcium levels and, 188–189, 189f
Ptosis, 503t
Puberty, **1104–1105**
  apocrine secretion in, 158
  estrogen levels during, 1098
  estrogen's influence on, 1099t
  hormonal regulation of bone growth and, 187
  leptin and onset in females, 1094, 1098
  male secondary sex characteristics, 1081–1082
  oocyte count during, 1091
  ovarian cycle in, 1094–1095
  sebum secretion in, 159
  skeletal changes in, 248
  spermatogenesis during, 1077
  testosterone'e influence on, 1099t
Pubic arch/angle, 238f, **239**
  in females vs. males, 240f, 240t
Pubic body, **239**, 243f
Pubic bone (pubis), 238f, **239**
Pubic bones, joint, 259t
Pubic crest, 238f, **239**
Pubic (hypogastric) region, 18, 18f
Pubic rami, 238f, **239**, 243f
Pubic symphysis joint, 177f, **239**, 243f, 255
  articulating bones/movements allowed, 259t
Pubic tubercle, 238f, **239**, 243f
Pubis (pubic bone), 238f, **239**
Pubococcygeus muscle, 350t, 351f
Pubofemoral ligament, **270**, 270f
Pudendal artery, **756**, 756f
Pudendal nerve, 516, 517f, 517t
  muscles served by, 350t
Pudendum (vulva), **1088**, 1088f
"Pulled groin" injury, 369t
"Pulled hamstrings" injury, 372t
Pulmonary arteries, 681f–683f, 744f, **744t**, 844f, **845**
Pulmonary capillaries, 744f, **744t**, 844f, **845**
Pulmonary circuit, **684**–685, 684f
Pulmonary circulation, 744f, **744–745**t
Pulmonary congestion, **705**
Pulmonary embolism, **875**
Pulmonary function tests, 853
Pulmonary gas exchange, 855–858
  gas solubilities, 856, 856f
  partial pressure gradients, 856, 856f
  ventilation-perfusion coupling, 856–858, 857f
Pulmonary heart valve, 683f, 687f, **688**, 689f
Pulmonary plexuses, 537f, 538, 539f, **845**
Pulmonary trunk, 679f, 681f, 683f, **684**, 685f, **744**, 844f
Pulmonary veins, 681f–683f, **683**, 744f, **744t**, 844f, **845**
Pulmonary ventilation, 831, 846–854. See also Breathing
Pulp, tooth, 895
Pulp cavity, 894f, **895**

Pulse, 725, **732**
  body sites, 732f
Pulse pressure, **725**
Pulvinar nuclei, 445f, 446
Punnett square, **1149**–1150, 1150f
Pupillary light reflex, 575
Pupils, 557f, 560f, **561**
  constriction of, 561, 568
Purines, 55, 416t, 418
Purkinje cells, 396t, **452–453**, 452f
Purkinje fibers, **693**–694, 694f
Pus, 148, 795
  in urine, 1024t
Putamen, **443**, 444f
P Wave, **695**, 696f, 697f
Pyelitis, 1001, 1026
Pyelonephritis, 1001, 1026
Pyloric antrum, 899f, **900**
Pyloric canal, 899f, **900**
Pyloric region (stomach), 899f, **900**
Pyloric sphincter, 899f, **900**
Pyloric stenosis, 938
Pylorus, 899f, **900**
Pyramid, 448f
  of medulla oblongata, 450f
Pyramidal cells, 396t, **438**
Pyramidal (corticospinal) tracts, **438**, 450f, 478, 479t, 480f
Pyramidal (direct) system, **478**, 479t, 480f
Pyramids, 451, 480f
Pyridoxine (vitamin B6), **950**t
Pyrimidines, 55
Pyrogens, **798**, 989
Pyruvic acid, 302, 303f, 956, 957f, **960**–961, 960f
Pyuria, 1024t

QRS complex, **696**, 696f, 697f
Q-T interval, **696**, 696f, 697f
Quadratus femoris muscle, 371f
  actions of (summary), 379t
  description/action/nerve supply, **372**t
  origin/insertion, 372t
Quadratus lumborum muscle, 345f, 347f, 368f
  description/action/nerve supply, **344**t
  origin/insertion, 344t
Quadratus plantae (flexor accessorius) muscle, 381t, 382f, 383f
Quadriceps femoris muscle, 367, 368f, 371f
  description/action/nerve supply, **369**t
  knee joint and, 266f
  origin/insertion, 369t
  strains, **384**
  tendon, 266f, 267, 368f, 369t
Quadriplegia, **479**
Quality (sound), **589**
Quanta, **565**
Quarks, 29

Rabies, **426**
  immunity and, 806
Radial arteries, 747f, 750f, **750**t, 751f
  uterine wall, **1087**, 1087f
Radial collateral ligament, **268**, 268f
Radial fossa, of humerus, 231f, **232**

Radial groove, of humerus, 231f, **232**, 236t
Radial keratotomy, 568
Radial nerve, **513–514**, 513f, 514t
  muscles served by, 357t, 360t
Radial notch, of ulna, **232**, 233f, 234f, 236t
Radial pulse, 732, 732f
Radial tuberosity, **232**, 233f, 234f, 236t
Radial veins, 759f, 762f, **762t**, 763f
Radiant (electromagnetic) energy, **26**
Radiation
  body heat loss/gain and, 986
  ionizing, 30
Radiation sickness, **60**
Radiation therapy, cancer, 147b
Radioactivity, 29
Radiocarpal (wrist) joint, 258t
Radiographic anatomy, 2
Radiograph (X ray), **20b**
Radioisotopes, **29–30**
Radioulnar joints, proximal/distal, **232**, 233f, 234f, 258t
Radius, 228f, **232**, 233f, 234f, 236f, 236t
  at elbow joint, 258t, 268f
  at radioulnar joints, 258t
Radon, 30
Raloxifene, to treat osteoporosis, 194
Rami communicantes, **509**, 510f, 536f, **538**, 539f
Ramus (bone marking), 179t
  ischial, **237**, 238f
  pubic, 238f, **239**
Random fertilization, 1149
Range of motion, 259
  fascicular patterns and, 326
  at major joints, 258–259t
Raphe nuclei, 450f, **455**
Rapid eye movement (REM) sleep, **458**, 459f
RA (rheumatoid arthritis), **274**, 274f, 275b, 822
RAS (reticular activating system), 455f, **456**
  injury to, 468
Rathke's pouch, 613–614
Raynaud's disease, 551
RBCs (red blood cells). See Erythrocytes
Reactants
  in chemical equations, 36, **37**
  oxidized, **38**
Reactions, chemical, 36–40
Reactive hyperemia, 735–736
Reactive vs. inert elements, 32–33, 32f
Reactivity, of complete antigens, **799**
Real image, **566**, 567f
Receptive endings, of unipolar neurons, 395, 396f
Receptive region of neurons, compared, 396t
Receptive relaxation of stomach smooth muscle, **905**
Receptor, in reflex arcs, **521**, 521f
Receptor-mediated endocytosis, 80t, **81**
Receptor potentials, 401, **494–495**, 495f
Receptor region, of postsynaptic neurons, 409, 410f

Receptors (sensors), **9**, 9f, 11f
  general sensory, **492–494**, 493t
  special vs., **556**
Recessive allele, **1146**
Recessive gene-determined traits, **1151**, 1151t
Reciprocal activation, **525**
Reciprocal inhibition, 523f, **524**
Recombinant chromosomes, **1148–1149**, 1149f
Recovery and power strokes of cilia, 93f, 95
Recruitment (multiple motor unit summation), **298–299**, 299f, 306t, 307
Rectal arteries, 752f, **754t**, 755f
Rectal exam, **922**
Rectal nerve, 350t
Rectal valves, **922**, 923f
Rectouterine pouch, 1082f
Rectum, 883f, **922**, 923f, 924f
  abdominal arteries in relation to, 755f
  abdominal veins in relation to, 765f
  parasympathetic fibers, 536f, 537f
  sympathetic fibers, 539f
Rectus abdominis muscles, **348**, 349f
  description/action/nerve supply, **348t**
  origin/insertion, 348t
  superficial, 330f
Rectus femoris muscle, 367, 368f
  actions of (summary), 379–380t, 380f
  description/action/nerve supply, **369t**
  origin/insertion, **369t**
  superficial, 330f, 331f
  tendon, 368f
Rectus muscles, eye, 503f, 505f, **558**, 559f
Red blood cells (RBCs). See Erythrocytes
Red bone marrow, 180, **181**, **651**
Red margin, **890**
Red marrow cavities, **181**, 183f, 184f
Redness, in inflammatory response, 792f, 793
Red nucleus, **449**, 450f, 480f
Redox (oxidation-reduction) reactions, 33f, **38**, **956–958**, 957f
Red pulp, **780**, 780f
Reduced reactants, **38**
Reduction division of meiosis, **1077**
Reduction of dislocations, 273
Reduction of fractures, 191
Reference man/woman, 2
Referred pain, 496b, **542**, 543f
Reflection of light, **565–566**
Reflex
  letdown, 617
  monosynaptic, **521**
  polysynaptic, **521**
Reflex arcs, **423**, 423f, **521**
  components, 521, 521f
Reflex (cephalic) phase of gastric secretion, **903–904**, 903f
Reflexes, **423**
  abdominal, **527**
  atrial (Bainbridge), **702**

  autonomic, **521–522**, **542**, 542f
  Babinski's sign, **527**
  flexor, **525–526**, 526f
  inborn (intrinsic), 521
  knee-jerk, 265
  learned (acquired), 521
  plantar, **527**
  somatic, **521**
  startle, 449
  superficial, **526–527**
  thyroid hormone's effects, 621t
  visceral, **521–522**, **542**, 542f
  withdrawal, **525–526**, 526f
Refraction, **566**
  lens and, 565–566, 566f
  problems, 568, 569f
Refractory periods, **291**, 406–407, 406f
  in cardiac muscle, 691, 691f
Regeneration, tissue, **143**, 144, 144f
Regeneration of nerves, 499–500, 499f
Regional anatomy, **2**
  terminology, 14, 14f
Regulatory T cells, **816–817**
  functions (summary), 817t
Relative refractory periods, 406–407, 406f
Relaxation, vs. contraction of muscle fibers, 287–288, 289f
Relaxin, 1072, 1122, **1134**
Releasing hormones, **614**
Remodeling, bone, 184, **188–190**, 189f
REM (rapid eye movement) sleep, **458–460**, 459f
Renal arteries, 747f, 752f, **754t**, 755f, 998, 1000f, **1001**
Renal autoregulation, **1008**, 1010
  myogenic, 735–736, **1008**, 1009f
  tubuloglomerular feedback, **1008**, 1009f, 1010
Renal calculi, **1024**
Renal circulation, vascular resistance in microcirculation of, 1003
Renal clearance, **1021**
Renal columns, **1000**, 1000f
Renal corpuscle, **1001**, 1002f, 1004f, 1005f
Renal cortex, **999**, 1000f
Renal failure, 1022–1023b
Renal fascia, 999, 999f
Renal hilum, 998, 998f
Renal infarct, **1031**
Renal medulla, **999–1000**, 1000f
Renal (medullary) pyramids, **1000**, 1000f
Renal pelvis, 998f, **1000**, 1000f, 1004f
Renal physiology, **3**
Renal plexus, **1001**
Renal ptosis, 999
Renal sinus, 998
Renal tubular acidosis, **1061**
Renal tubules, **1001**, 1002f, 1003
  reabsorptive capabilities, 1013, 1014t, 1015
Renal veins, 758f, 759f, 764f, **764t**, 765f, 998f, 1000f, **1001**
Renin, 628, 628f, 638, 638t, 998, **1010**
  source/trigger/effects, 638t
  sympathetic impulses and, 547

Renin-angiotensin mechanism, **628**, 628f, 731, **1010**
Rennin, 902, 928f, **929**
Replicase, 100f
Replication bubble, 99, 100f
Replication fork, 99, 100f
Replication of DNA, **99**, 100f
Replisome, 99, 100f
Repolarization, **290–291**, 291f, 402–**404**, 403f
  refractory periods and, 406–407, 406f
Reproduction, 7f, **8**
Reproductive organs, sympathetic innervation, 541t
Reproductive system, 7, 7f, **1066**. See also Female reproductive system; Male reproductive system
  accessory organs, **1066**
  aging and, 1108
  cardiovascular system and, 768b
  contraceptive techniques, 1128–1129b
  developmental aspects
    embryonic, 1123–1128, 1130t
    fetal, 1132t, 1133
    puberty, 1104–1105
    sex differentiation, 1102f, 1103–1104
    sexual, 1101–1105, 1108
  digestive system and, 934b
  endocrine system and, 640b, 641b
  female, 7, 7f
  homeostatic interrelationships with other systems, 1106b, 1107b
  integumentary system and, 168b
  lymphatic system/immunity and, 784b
  male, 7, 7f
  muscular system and, 318b
  nervous system and, 548b
  primary sex organs (gonads) of, **1006**
  respiratory system and, 876b
  sex hormones of, **1066**
  skeletal system and, 196b
  skin and, 168b
  thyroid hormone's effects, 621t
  urinary system and, 1058b
Residual volume (RV), **851**, 852f
Resistance, **723**
  electrical, **398**
  peripheral, **723**
Resistance exercises, 307, 309
Resistin, 638
  source/trigger/effects, 638t
Resonance, 591
Respiration, **831**
  external, **831**, 855–858
  internal, **831**, 856f, 858
  muscles of, 346, 347f
Respiratory acidosis, 1052, **1055**, 1056t
Respiratory alkalosis, 1052, **1055**, 1056t
Respiratory bronchioles, 841f, **842**
Respiratory burst, 657–658, **790**
Respiratory capacities, **851–852**, 852f
Respiratory cartilages, 176, 177f
Respiratory centers, medullary, 451, 863–864, 864f

Respiratory disorders, cyanotic skin and, 157
Respiratory enzyme complexes, **964**
Respiratory gases
 capillary exchanges, 738–740, 739f, 740f, 856f, 858
 found in blood plasma, 649t
 pulmonary gas exchange, 856–858
 transport by blood, 831, 858–863
  erythrocytes and, 650
  oxygen, 858–861
Respiratory membrane, 842, 843f
 thickness/surface area, gas exchange and, 858
Respiratory muscles, 346t, **346t**, 347f, 831
Respiratory passageway (larynx), swallowing and, 340
Respiratory "pump," **726**, 727f, 731f
Respiratory rate, in newborns vs. adults, 874
Respiratory system, 7, 7f, 830–881, **831**
 in acid-base balance, 1052, 1055, 1056t
  compensations, 1056–1057
 aging and, 874–875
 birth defects, 874
 cardiovascular system and, 768b
 conducting zone, **831**
 developmental aspects, 873–875
 digestive system and, 934b
 disorders, 870–873
 embryonic development, 1123, 1126, 1126f
 endocrine system and, 640b
 homeostatic interrelationships, 876b, 877b
 integumentary system and, 168b
 lymphatic system/immunity and, 784b
 muscular system and, 318b
 in neonatal period, 1137–1138
 nervous system and, 548b, 549b
 in pregnancy, 1135
 principal organs of, 831, 838t
 reproductive system and, 1106b
 respiratory zone, **831**
 skeletal system and, 196b
 skin and, 168b
 urinary system and, 1058b
Respiratory tract, upper, 834f
Respiratory tree. See Bronchial tree
Respiratory volumes, 851–853, 852f
Respiratory zone (respiratory system), **831**
 structures, **841–842**, 841f
Respirometer, **984**
Responsiveness (excitability/irritability), **280**
Responsiveness (irritability), **5**
Restenoses, 719b
Resting membrane potential, 81, **399–400**, 399f
 depolarization of, 400–401, 400f
 generating/maintaining, 81–83, 82f
 hyperpolarization of, 400f, 401
Resting (quiescent) zone, of long bones when growing, 186, 186f
Restriction enzymes, 58b

Restriction point, 101
Rete testis, **1067–1068**, 1068f
Reticular activating system (RAS), 455f, **456**
 injury to, 468
Reticular cells, **133**, 133f, 651
 as lymphoid cells, **777**
Reticular connective tissue, 128f, **133**, 133f, 135, **777**, 777f
Reticular fibers, **129**, 130f, 133, 133f
Reticular formation, 449, 450f, **455–456**, 455f
 in ANS control hierarchy, 547, 547f, 550
 functions (summary), 453t
 neural integration and, 495f
Reticular lamina, 119
Reticular layer of dermis, 153f, 155–156
Reticulocyte counts, **652**
Reticulocytes, 562f, **652**
Reticulospinal tracts, 475f, **478**, 479t
 of reticular formation, 456
Retina, 560f, **561–563**, 562f, 563f
 embryonic origins, 432f, 433
 focusing of light on, 566–568
 neural layer, **561**
 optic nerve and, 502f, 502t
 photoreceptors of, 569–571, 570f
 pigmented layer, **561**, 562f
 signal transmission in, 572–574, 573f
 visual processing and, 576–577, 577f
Retinal, **571–572**, 571f
Retinal detachment, 563
Retinitis pigmentosa, 575
Retinol (vitamin A), 48t, **947t**
Retraction (movement), **262**, 263f
Retrograde amnesia, 463
Retrograde movement, 393
Retroperitoneal organs, **886**, 886f
Reverberating (oscillating) circuits, **422**, 422f
Reverse transcriptase, 821
Reverse transcriptase inhibitors, 821
R group of amino acids, 49, 49f
Rheumatic fever, 822
Rheumatism, 276
Rheumatoid arthritis (RA), **274**, 274f, 822
 joint prostheses for, 275b
Rh factor, **669–670**
Rhinencephalon
 limbic system and, 440, 454
 olfactory cortex and, 440
Rhinitis, 833, 835
Rhodopsin, 571f, **572**, 574–575
 light/dark adaptation and, 574–575
Rhombencephalon (hindbrain), **431**, 432f
Rhomboid muscles, 333f, **352**, 353f
 description/action/nerve supply, **353t**
 origin/insertion, **353t**
Riboflavin (vitamin B2), **950t**, 958
Ribonucleic acid. See RNA
Ribose
 as a monosaccharide, 44, 45f
 as sugar of RNA, 56, 57t

Ribosomal RNA (rRNA), 57, 85, **104**
Ribosomal subunits, 95t, 97, 107, 108f
Ribosomes, 66f, **85–86**, 86f
 free vs. membrane-bound, 85–86
 protein synthesis and, 85, 87, 87f, 107, 108f, 109, 109f
 in rough ER, 86, 86f, 87, 87f
 structure/functions (summary), 94t
Ribs, 204f, **227–228**, 227f
 false, 226f
 floating, 226f
 joints of, 258t
 as structures in thoracic cavity, 844f
 true, 226f
RICE treatment, **320**
Rickets, **193**
Right lower quadrant (RLQ), **19**, 19f
Right upper quadrant (RUQ), **19**, 19f
Rigor mortis, 294
Ringer's solution, to restore blood volume, 671
Risorius muscle, 336t, 337f
RLQ. See Right lower quadrant
RNA (ribonucleic acid), 55, 56–57, 56f, 57t
 antisense, **109**
 arising from "junk" DNA, 109–110
 in chromatin, 97
 DNA compared to, 55, 57t, 104
 information transfer from DNA to, 109, 110f
 messenger, 104
 microRNAs (miRNAs), 57
 mitochondrial, 85
 polymerase, 105, 106f
 primers, 99, 100f
 in protein synthesis, 55, 104, 105f
 ribosomal, 85, 104
 role of, 55
 small, 1153–1154
 structure, 56–57
 transfer, 104
 varieties of, 57
Rods, 562f, **563**, 570f
 excitation of, 570f, 571f, **572**
 visual pigments and, 569–571
Root
 lung, **842**, 844f
 penis, 1069, 1070f
 tooth, **894**, 894f
Root canal, tooth, 894f, **895**
Root hair plexus (hair follicle receptor), 153f, **160**, 161f
Rooting reflex, 936
Rootlets of spinal nerves, 509, 510f
Root sheaths of hair follicles, **160**, 161f
Roots of brachial plexus, 512, 513f, 514t
Rotation (movement), 259, **261–262**, 262f
 of lower limbs, 379–380t, 380f
 of upper limbs, 362–363t, 363f
 vestibular nystagmus and, 597
Rotator cuff, **269–270**
 muscles, 354, **355**, 356f

Rotatores muscle, 345f
Rough ER (endoplasmic reticulum), 66f, 85, **86–87**, 86f–88f
 endomembrane system interactions, 89–90, 90f
 structure/function (summary), 94t
Round (cochlear) window, 584f, **585**, 586f, 588f
Round ligament of liver (ligamentum teres), **912**, 913f, 924f, **1138**
Round ligament of uterus, 1082f, 1085f
rRNA (ribosomal RNA), 57, **104**
Rubrospinal tracts, 475f, **478**, 480f
 location/origin/termination/function, 479t
Ruffini endings, **494**
 functional classes/body location, 493t
Rugae
 stomach, **899**, 899f
 vaginal, 1087
Rule of eights (octet rule), 33
Rule of nines, 167, 167f
Ruptured (perforated) eardrum, 593
RUQ. See Right upper quadrant
RV (residual volume), **851**, 852f

Saccule, 586f, **587**
 equilibrium and, 594–595, 594f
Sacral artery, 746f, 752f, **754t**, 755f
Sacral canal, 225, 225f
Sacral crests, 225, 225f
Sacral curvatures, **219**, 219f, 247
Sacral foramen, **225**, 225f
Sacral hiatus, **225**, 225f
Sacral nerves, 471f, 509f
Sacral parasympathetics, 537f, **538**
Sacral plexus, 509f, **516**, 517f
 injury to, 516
 nerves/spinal roots/structures served, 517t
Sacral promontory, **225**, 225f, 238f
Sacroiliac joint, 225, 237, 238f
 articulating bones/movements allowed, 259t
Sacrospinalis muscles. See Erector spinae muscles
Sacrospinous ligament, 237
Sacrotuberous ligament, 239
Sacrum, 204f, 218, **219**, 219f, **225**, 225f
 female vs. male, 240f, 240t
 joint, 259t
 as part of bony pelvis, 237, 238f
 transverse ridges of, 225, 225f
Saddle joint, 258t, 264f, **265**
Sagittal sinuses, 464f, 465, **760**, 760f, **760t**, 761f
Sagittal plane, **15**, 16f
Sagittal suture, 203, 205f, **207**
Saliva, **891**, 920t
 composition, 892
 as protective mechanism, 796t
Salivary amylase, 928f, **929**
 as a globular protein, 52t
Salivary glands, 883f, **891–893**, 892f
 parasympathetic fibers, 536f
 sympathetic fibers, 536f, 539f

Salivation, ANS control of, 892–893
Salivatory nuclei, 537, **893**
Salpingitis, **1109**
Saltatory conduction, 404
Salts, 34, 40*f*, **41**
    commonly found in body, 26*t*, 41
    dissociation in water and, 40, 40*f*, 41
    electrolyte balance and, 1043
Salt substitutes, 1049
Saphenous nerve, 515*f*
Saphenous veins, 759*f*, 766*f*, **766***t*
Sarcolemma, 280, 282*f*, 282*t*, **284**, 285*f*, 288*f*
    action potentials and, 290–291, 290*f*, 291*f*
    in cardiac muscle, 690*f*
Sarcomeres, 282*f*, 282*t*, **284**, 285*f*
    in cardiac muscle cells, 689–690, 690*f*
Sarcopenia, 318
Sarcoplasm, 280, **284**, 285*f*
Sarcoplasmic reticulum (SR), **287**, 288*f*
    in cardiac and skeletal muscle, 314*t*, 690*f*
    of smooth muscle fibers, 310, 313*f*, 314*t*
Sartorius muscle, 331*f*, **367**, 368*f*
    actions of (summary), 379–380*t*
    description/action/nerve supply, **367***t*
    origin/insertion, **367***t*
SA (sinoatrial) node, **693**, 694*f*, 696*f*
Satellite cells, 317, 390*f*, **391**
Satiety, 982, 983*f*, 984
    hypothalamic regulation of, 446
Saturated fats, 46
Scab, in tissue repair, 143, 144*f*
Scalae, cochlear, **587**, 588*f*
Scala media, **587**, 588*f*
Scala tympani, **587**, 588*f*
Scala vestibuli, **587**, 588*f*
Scalene muscles, 342, 343*f*
    description/action/nerve supply, **342***t*
    head/neck movements and, 342
    origin/insertion, 342*t*
Scalp
    meninges in relation to, 464*f*
    muscles, **335***t*, 337*f*
Scaphoid bone, **233**, 235*f*, 236*f*, 236*t*
Scapulae, **229–231**, 230*f*
    muscles that move, 352*t*, 353*f*
    as part of appendicular skeleton, 228*f*
    illus./location/markings, 236*f*, 236*t*
    photograph, 234*f*
    at shoulder joint, 258*t*, 269, 269*f*
Scapular (dorsal) nerve, 513*f*, 514*t*
Scar tissue, **143**, 144, 144*f*
    adhesions and, 145
Schizophrenia, 485
Schwann cells (neurolemmocytes), 390*f*, **391**, 392*f*
    axons in relationship to, 394, 394*f*
    in nerve regeneration, 499, 499*f*
Sciatica, 516
Sciatic nerve, **516**, 517*f*, 517*t*
    muscles served by, 369*t*, 372*t*

Sciatic notch
    greater, **237**
    lesser, **237**, 238*f*
SCID (severe combined immunodeficiency disorders) syndromes, 820
Sclera, 557*f*, **560**, 560*f*, 562*f*, 564*f*
Scleral venous sinus (Canal of Schlemm), 560*f*, **564**, 564*f*
Scleroses, 408
Sclerotherapy, **767**
Sclerotome, **1127**, 1127*f*
Scoliosis, 219, 247
Scotoma, **600**
Scrotum, 1066, 1066*f*, **1067**, 1067*f*
    septum, 1067*f*
Scuba diving, 868–869*b*
Scurvy, **148**
Sebaceous (oil) glands, 153*f*, **159**, 159*f*, 161*f*
    inflammation, 159
    overactive, 159
Seborrhea, 159
Sebum, **159**
    bactericidal properties, 159
Secondary follicle, 1083*f*, **1084**
Secondary ossification center, 185*f*, **186**
Secondary sex characteristics
    female, 1098, 1099*t*
    male, **1081–1082**, 1099*t*
Second-class levers, 328, 329*f*
Second-degree burns, 167*f*, **170**
Second-messenger molecules, neurotransmitters and, 419
Second messengers, 84, 84*f*, 420–421, 420*f*
Second-messenger systems, **607–608**, 607*f*
Second-order neurons, 475, 476*f*, 495
Secretin, **905**
    bile secretion and, 916
    production site/stimuli/target/ actions, 906*t*
    in regulation of pancreatic juice secretion, 918, 919*f*
    source/trigger/effects, 638*t*
Secretion (glandular), **124**
Secretory cells, 125
Secretory IgA, **808**, 808*t*
Secretory lysosomes, 89
Secretory region of neurons, compared, 396*f*
Secretory unit (acinus) of exocrine glands, 125
    types of, 125, 126, 126*f*, 127*f*
Secretory vesicles (granules), **87**, 88*f*, 89
    interactions in endomembrane system, 89–90, 90*f*
Section
    cross, **15**, 16*f*
    oblique, **15**, 16*f*
    of tissue specimen, **118**
    transverse, **15**, 16*f*
Segmental arteries, 1000*f*, **1001**
Segmental level of motor hierarchy, **419**, 520*f*
Segmental nerve, 511*f*, 511*t*
Segmentation, **884**, 884*f*, 885*f*, 920*t*
Segments, bronchopulmonary, **842**, 844*f*
Seizures, epileptic, **457**

Selectins, 657, 794
Selective estrogen receptor modulators (SERMs), 194
Selectively permeable barrier, **70**
    plasma membrane as, 70, 71
Selenium, 26*t*, **955***t*
Self-antigens, 800
Self-extending endoprostheses, 194*b*
Self-tolerance, **800–803**
Sella turcica, 206*f*, 208*f*, **209**, 215*f*, **216***t*
Semen, **1072**
Semicircular canals, 584*f*, 586*f*, **587**
Semicircular duct, 586*f*, **587**
Semiconservative replication, **99**, 100*f*
Semilunar cartilages. *See* Menisci
Semilunar (gasserian/trigeminal) ganglia, 504*f*
Semilunar (SL) valves, **688**, 689*f*
Semimembranosus muscle, 333*f*, 371*f*
    actions of (summary), 379*f*
    description/action/nerve supply, **372***t*
    origin/insertion, 372*t*
    tendon, 266*f*
Seminalplasmin, **1072**
Seminal vesicles (glands), 1066, 1066*f*, 1070*f*, **1071**
Seminiferous tubules, **1067**, 1068*f*
Semispinalis muscle, 345*f*
    description/action/nerve supply, **344***t*
    origin/insertion, 344*t*
Semitendinosus muscle, 333*f*, 371*f*
    actions of (summary), 379*t*
    description/action/nerve supply, **372***t*
    origin/insertion, 372*t*
SEM (scanning electronic microscopy), 118
Sensation, 491, **494**
    to perception (overview), 494–498
Sense organs, **492**
Sensible water loss, **1040**
Sensorineural deafness, **593**
Sensor (receptor), in homeostatic control systems, 9–10, 9*f*, 11*f*
Sensory (afferent) division of PNS, 388, 389*f*
Sensory (afferent) nerves, **499**
    of dorsal roots, **509**, 510*f*
Sensory (afferent) neurons, **395**, 396–397*t*
Sensory areas of cerebral cortex, 437*f*, 439–440
Sensory (ascending) spinal cord tracts
    major pathways/tracts, 475–478, 476*f*, 477*t*
    specific/nonspecific, 475–478, 476*f*, 477*t*
    types of neurons in, 475, 476*f*
Sensory cortex, somatic, 438*f*
Sensory input, 388, 388*f*
Sensory nerve ending/fiber, 153*f*, 154*f*, 388, 389*f*
    hair follicle receptor as, 160, 161*f*
Sensory neurons, in reflex arcs, **521**, 521*f*

Sensory receptors, 491, **491–494**
    adaptation and, 495
    classification
        by location, 491–492
        by stimulus type, 491
        by structural complexity, 492, 494
    complex. *See* Sense organs
    general, **492–494**, 493*t*
        encapsulated, 492, 493*t*, 494
        special vs., 556
        unencapsulated, 492, 493*t*
    processing (neural integration) of, 494–495, 495*f*
    simple vs. complex, 492
    special, **556**
Sentinel node, **783**
Separase, 103*f*
Sepsis (septic shock), **826**
Septal cartilage, 214, 215*f*, 833*f*
Septal nuclei, 454, 455*f*
Septicemia, **674**
Septic shock, 742
Septic shock (sepsis), **826**
Septum
    deviated, **875**
    interarterial, **680**
    interventricular, **680**, 683*f*
    nasal, 213–214, **832**, 838*t*
    scrotal, 1067*f*
    testes, 1068*f*
Septum pellucidum, **434**, 434*f*, 445*f*, 455*f*, 466*f*
Serratus anterior muscle, 352, 353*f*
    description/action/nerve supply, **352***t*, 353*f*
    origin/insertion, 352*t*, 353*f*
Serial neural processing, **422–423**, 423*f*
Series elastic components, 283
SERMs (selective estrogen receptor modulators), 194
Serotonin, **901**
    functional class/secretion sites/effects, 415*t*
    in platelet plug formation, 665
    production site/stimuli/target/ actions, 906*t*
    stomach and, 901
    synthesis of, 418
Serous cells, of salivary glands, **892**
Serous fluid, 17, 17*f*, 143
Serous membranes (serosae), **17–18**, 17*f*, **142–143**, 142*f*
    of GI tract, 886, 886*f*, 887*f*, **888**
        stomach, 901*f*
    parietal, 17, 17*f*
    of pericardium, **678**, 679*f*
    of pleurae, 844*f*, 845–846
    visceral, 17, 17*f*
Serratus anterior muscle, 331*f*, **352**, 353*f*
    abdominal wall and, 349*f*
    description/action/nerve supply, **352***t*
    origin/insertion, 352*t*
Sertoli (sustentacular) cells, 1078*f*, **1079–1080**
Serum, **666**
Sesamoid bones, **178**, 178*f*
Set point, 10, 11*f*
Severe combined immunodeficiency disorders (SCID) syndromes, **820**

Sex characteristics (secondary)
female, 1098, 1099t
male, **1081**–1082, 1099t
Sex chromosomes, **1101**, 1103, **1146**
Sex hormones, location/function in body, 48t
Sex hormones (gonadocorticoids), **630**–631, **1066**, **1082**
gonads and, 166, 634–635, 1082
location/functions, 48t
sources/stimuli/effects, 1099t
structure/regulation/effects, 627t
Sex-linked inheritance, **1152**
Sexual development
genetic sex, 1101, 1103
gonad descent, 1104, 1105f
menopause, 1105, 1108
puberty, 1104–1105
sex differentiation, 1102f, 1103–1104
Sexually transmitted diseases (STDs), 1030, **1100**–1101
Sexual response
female, **1098**–1100
male, 1072–1073
Shaft
of humerus, 234f
of penis, 1069, 1070f
of rib, 227f, 228
Sharpey's (perforating) fibers, 180f, 181, 183f
Sheath of Schwann (neurilemma), 392f, **394**, 394f
Shell body temperature, **986**
Shingles, **426**
Shin splints, 373t, **384**
Shivering, **987**
low core temperatures and, 989
Shock
anaphylactic, 742, **823**
cardiogenic, **742**
circulatory, 733, **740**–742, 741f
hypovolemic, **740**–742, 741f
neurogenic, 742
septic, 742, **826**
spinal, **479**, 522
vascular, **742**
Shock wave lithotripsy, 1024
Short bones, **178**, 178f
structure, 181
Short reflexes of GI tract, 886, 908f, 921, 921t
Short-term memory (STM), **461**, 461f
Shoulder (glenohumeral) joint, 257f, **269**–270, 269f
articulating bones/movements allowed, 258t
dislocations, 270
innervation of, 513f, 514t
muscles crossing, **354**–355t, 356f
Shoulder (pectoral) girdle, 228, **229**
arteries, 746f, 747f, 750–751t
articulated, 230f
bones, **229**, 230f, 231, 234f, 236f
summary, 236t
innervation of, 511f, 511t, 512, 513f, 514t
muscles acting on, **352**–353t, 353f
superficial muscles, 331f, 333f
veins, 762–763t, 763f
SIADH (syndrome of inappropriate ADH secretion), 619t, 620, **1061**

Sickle-cell anemia, **655**–656, 656f, **1151**
Sickle-cell trait, **1151**
Sight sense. *See* Eye; Vision
Sigmoidal arteries, 752f, **754t**, 755f
Sigmoid sinuses, **760**, 760t, 761f
Signal-recognition particle (SRP), **87**, 87f
Signal sequence, 87, 87f
Signal transduction, 68, 68f
Silicon, 26t
Simple alveolar exocrine glands, 126f
Simple diffusion, 71, 72f
energy source/described/ examples in body, 75t
selectivity of, 74–75
Simple epithelia, 119, 120f
columnar, **120**, 122f
cuboidal, **120**, 121f
functions/locations, 121f, 122f
squamous, **120**, 121f
Simple multicellular glands, **125**, 126f
Simple sugars (monosaccharides), 44, 45f
Simple tubular exocrine glands, 126f
Sinoatrial (SA) node, **693**, 694f
Sinus (bone marking), 179t
Sinuses
dural, **464**, 464f
ethmoid, **211**, 211f, 218f
frontal, **204**, 218f, 834f
lymph, 778f, **779**
mastoid, **207**
maxillary, **213**, 218f
paranasal, 214, **218**, 218f, **833**–834, 834f
of skull bones, 203
sphenoid, **206**f, **209**, 218f
Sinus headache, 835
Sinusitis, **835**
Sinusoidal capillaries (sinusoids), 651, 717f, 720f, **721**
of liver, **912**, 914f
Sinus rhythm, **693**, 697f
Sinus venosus, **705**
Size principle, in recruitment of motor neurons, 299, 299f
Skeletal cartilages, **176**, 177f
appositional vs. interstitial growth of, 176
developmental aspects, 198
locations, 176, 177f
Skeletal muscle, **281**, 282f
aging and, 318, 320
atrophy, 111, 309, 318
attachments, 283–284, 325
cardiac muscle vs., 314–315t
contraction
duration of, 305–307
force of, 295–296, 304–305
metabolic pathways, 300–304, 315t
of muscle fibers, 288–294, 292f, 294f, 295f, 306t
nerve stimulus and, 288–289, 290f, 315t
regulation of, 315t
velocity of, 305–307, 315t
of whole muscle, 139, 281, 282t, 295–300
developmental aspects, 317–318, 320

disorders, 320
embryonic origins, 145, 145f, 316–317
exercise and its effect on, 307, 309
fibers (cells), **139**, 140f, 282f, 282t
fast vs. slow, 305–307, 306f
metabolic properties, 306t
microscopic anatomy, myofibrils, 283–285, 284f
microscopic anatomy, myofilaments, 286–287, 286f
microscopic anatomy, sarcoplasmic reticulum, 287, 288f
microscopic anatomy, T tubules, 287, 288f
motor unit and, 296–297, 296f
structural properties, 306t
genetic disorders, 317
gross anatomy
blood supply, 281, 281f, 282t, 283f
connective tissue sheaths, 281, 282t, 283, 283f
nerve supply, 281, 282t
structural/organizational levels, 282t
muscle mechanics and, 295–296
overload principle, 309
percent of body mass, in men vs. women, 317
regenerative capacity, 144, 317
smooth muscle vs., 314–315t
somatic reflexes and, 521
as type of tissue, **139**, 140f, 280
as voluntary muscle, **280**
vs. cardiac muscle, 314–315t
vs. smooth muscle, 314–315t
Skeletal muscles, 325
blood flow through, 737
functional groups
antagonists, **325**
fixators, **325**
prime movers (agonists), **325**
synergists, **325**
interactions to achieve movement, 325
major, 330–383
superficial, 330f–333f
naming criteria, 325–326
preferred fuel source, 975t
Skeletal muscle tissue, water content, 1036
Skeletal system, **6**, 6f
cardiovascular system and, 768b
digestive system and, 934b
endocrine system and, 640b
homeostatic interrelationships with other body systems, 196b, 197b
integumentary system and, 168b
lymphatic system/immunity and, 784b
muscular system and, 318b, 319b
nervous system and, 548b
reproductive system and, 1106b, 1107b
respiratory system and, 876b

thyroid hormone's effects, 621t
urinary system and, 1058b
Skeleton
aging and, 198, 248
appendicular, **176**, 177f, **228**, 228f
pectoral girdle/upper limb, 229–237
pelvic girdle/lower limb, 237–246
summary, 236f, 246t
axial, **176**, 177f, **203**, 204f
skull, 203–218
skull, summary, 216–217t
spine, 218–225
thoracic cage, 226–228
bone remodeling and, 184, **188**–190, 189f
cartilages of, **176**, 177f, 203
developmental aspects, 198, 198f, 246–248
embryonic, 1123–1128, 1130t
fetal, 1132t, 1133
embryonic, 176, 198, 198f
functions of, 178–179
homeostatic imbalances of bone, 193–195, 198
skin and, 168b
Skin, 152–174
aging and, 170–171
appendages
hair, 159–163
nails, 163
sebaceous glands, 159
sweat glands, 158, 159f
as biological barrier, 164
blood flow to, 737–738, 986
in thermoregulation, 987, 988
as blood reservoir, 165
body temperature regulation by, 164
bronzing, 158
bruising, 158
burns, 166–167, 167f, 170
cancer, 165–166, 165f
cardiovascular system and, 168b, 169b
as chemical barrier, 164
color, 157–158
as cutaneous membrane, **141**, 142f
developmental aspects of, 170–171
digestive system and, 168b
endocrine system and, 168b
excretion function of, 165
functions, 163–165
body temperature regulation, 164
cutaneous sensation, 164–165
metabolic, 165
protection, 163–164
grafting, 170
hematomas, 157
homeostatic imbalances, 165
burns, 166–167, 170
cancers, 165–166
homeostatic interrelationships, 168b, 169b, 171
hormone produced by, 638, 638t
innervation of, 516, 518f
lymphatic system/immunity and, 168b, 169b
markings, 156–157, 156b
metabolic functions, 165
muscular system and, 168b

continues

Skin (cont.)
  nerve supply, 511f, 511t
  nervous system and, 168b, 169b
  pallor, 158
  as physical barrier, 164, 790
  properties of, 152
  protective functions, 163–164,
    789–790, 796f
  redness or erythema, 157
  regeneration after burns, 170
  reproductive system and, 168b
  respiratory system and, 168b
  secretions of as chemical barrier,
    164
  sensory (cutaneous) receptors of,
    164–165
  shell body temperature and, 987
  skeletal system and, 168b
  stratified epithelia of, 123
  structure, 152, 153f
    dermis, 152, 153f, 154–157
    epidermis, 152–155,
      153f, 154f
    hypodermis, 152, 153f
  substances that penetrate, 164
  sympathetic fibers, 536f, 539f
  synthetic, 170
  thick, 153
  urinary system and, 168b
  vacuum-assisted closure for
    wounds/ulcers, 148
  vascularity of, 152
  wound repair, 143–145, 144f
  yellow cast, 158
Skin cancer, sun exposure and, 157
Skin-fold test, 993
Skull, 203–218, 204f–206f, 208f
  bones
    cranial, 203–211
    facial, 211–218
    as flat bone, 181, 181f, 203
    summary, 216–217t
  fetal, 246, 247f
  fractures, 192t
  geographic overview, 203
  joints (sutures), 203, 205f,
    206f, 258t
  meninges in relation to, 464, 464f
Sleep
  coma vs., 458
  delta brain waves and, 456, 457f
  disorders, 460
  hypothalamus and, 459
  importance of, 459–460
  patterns, 459
  RAS nuclei and, 456, 459
  types of, 458, 459f
  unconsciousness and, 458
Sleep apnea, 460, 874
Sleep-wake cycle
  hypothalamic regulation of, 446
  pineal gland and, 447
SLE (systemic lupus erythematosus),
    822, 826
Sliding filament theory of muscle
    contraction, 287–288, 289f
"Slipped" (herniated) disc,
    220–221, 220f
Slit diaphragm, 1005, 1006f
Slow Ca2+ channels, 691–692
Slow oxidative fibers, 305–307,
    306
  activities best suited for, 306t
  metabolic/structural properties,
    306t
Slow-wave sleep, 458

SL (semilunar) valves, 688, 689f
Small cell carcinoma, lung, 873
Small intestine, 883f, 908–911,
    924f
  bile release into, 917
  blood supply, 754t, 764t, 765f,
    909
  chyme in, 919–920
  digestive processes, 919–922
    liver's role, 919
  innervation, 536f, 537f, 539f,
    541t, 909
  major functions (overview), 920t
  modifications for absorption,
    909–910, 910f
  motility, 919–922
    control mechanisms, 921t
    peristalsis, 921, 921t
    segmentation, 920–921, 921t
  wall
    histology, 910–911, 911f
    smooth muscle arrangement,
      309, 310f
Smell sense, 556, 578–580
  aging and, 598
  developmental aspects, 598
  disorders, 583
  limbic system and, 454
  olfactory cortex, 437f, 440
  olfactory pathway, 580
  physiology of, 579–580, 580f
  taste sense and, 583
  transduction, 580, 580f
Smiling, muscles of, 336t, 337f
Smoking, chronic obstructive
    pulmonary diseases and,
    871–872
Smooth ER (endoplasmic
    reticulum), 66f, 86f, 87
  endomembrane system
    interactions, 89–90, 90f
  structure/function (summary),
    94t
Smooth muscle, 309–316
  body location of, 314t
  cardiac muscle vs., 314–315t
  contraction
    hormonal regulation, 312
    length and tension changes,
      316
    mechanism of, 311–312,
      311f
    neural regulation, 312
    peristalsis and, 309–310
    regulation of, 315t
    response to stretch, 312, 313,
      315t, 316
  developmental aspects,
    317–318, 320
  embryonic origins, 317
  energy requirements, 312
  fibers (cells)
    calcium ions and, 310
    connective tissue
      components, 314t
    layers of, 309, 310f
    microscopic structure,
      309–311, 310f, 314t
    shape and appearance, 314t
    vs. cardiac muscle fibers, 314t
    vs. skeletal muscle fibers,
      309–311
  hyperplasia of, 316
  innervation, 310, 311f
    diffuse junctions, 310, 311f
    varicosities, 310, 311f

layers
  circular, 309, 310f
  longitudinal, 309, 310f
  multiunit, 316
  regeneration of, 317
  single-unit, 316
  skeletal muscle vs., 314–315t
  stress-relaxation response and,
    313, 316
  tone, 312
  varicosities and, 519
  vascular, myogenic responses of,
    735–736
  visceral (single-unit), 316
  vs. cardiac muscle, 314–315t
  vs. skeletal muscle, 314–315t
Smooth muscle tissue, 141, 141f,
    280
  fibers (cells), 280
    contraction, 280
  hair follicles and, 162
  regenerative capacity of, 144
Sneezing
  mechanism/result, 854t
  regulatory centers, 451
Sodium, 26t, 953t
  absorption, 933
  in action potentials, 402–404,
    403f
  aldosterone and, 628–629, 628f
  in blood plasma/IF/ICF, 1040f
  in chemically-gated ion
    channels, 398f
  importance to body, 26t, 953t
  in fluid/electrolyte balance,
    1043
  loss via sweating, 165
  membrane transport processes
    and, 76f, 77, 77f
  in muscle contraction,
    290–291, 290f, 291f
  problems with excesses/deficits,
    953t, 956
  reabsorption, 1011–1012,
    1012f, 1014t
  as reactive element, 32, 32f
  resting membrane potential and,
    82–83, 82f, 399f
  in table salt, 33–34, 33f, 34f
Sodium balance regulation, 1043
  by aldosterone, 1045
  by atrial natriuretic peptide, 1047
  blood pressure homeostasis and,
    1046f
  by cardiovascular baroreceptors,
    1045–1046
  causes/consequences of
    imbalances in, 1044t
  by female sex hormones,
    1047–1048
  by glucocorticoids, 1048
Sodium-potassium pump, 76f, 77,
    77f, 291, 404
  action potentials and, 402–404,
    403f
  resting membrane potential and,
    399–400, 399f
Soleus muscle, 331f–333f, 373,
    374f, 375f, 377f, 378f
  actions of (summary), 379t
  description/action/nerve supply,
    376t
  origin/insertion, 376t
Sol-gel transformations, 31
Solids, 25
Solitary nucleus, 450f, 582, 583f

Solute pumps, 76f, 77, 80t
Solutes, 30–31
  electrolytes/nonelectrolytes, 1036
Solutions, 30
  acidic/alkaline, 42
  concentration of, 30–31
  true, 30
Solvents, 30
  organic, skin penetration by, 164
  water as universal, 30, 40, 1036
Soma, 391. See also Neuron cell
    body
Somatic afferent sensory nerve
    fibers, 388, 389f
Somatic mesoderm, 1127, 1127f
Somatic motor neurons, 288–289
Somatic motor zone, of spinal gray
    matter, 474, 474f
Somatic nervous system, 388, 389f
  ANS compared to, 533–535, 534f
Somatic pain, superficial or deep,
    496b
Somatic reflexes, 521
Somatic sensation areas, in
    cerebral cortex, 437f,
    439–440
Somatic sensory cortex, 438f
Somatic sensory zone, of spinal
    gray matter, 474, 474f
Somatomedins, 614, 615f
Somatosensory system
  association cortex, 437f,
    439–440
  circuit level processing in,
    495–496, 495f
  homunculi, 438f, 439
  organization of, 494, 495f
  perceptual processing in, 494,
    496–498
  primary cortex, 437f, 439
  spinal cord tracts and, 476f
  receptor level processing in,
    494–495, 495f
Somatostatin, 614–615, 615f,
    618t, 632, 901
  functional class/secretion
    sites/effects, 417t
  insulin release and, 634
  production site/stimuli/target/
    actions, 906t
  stomach and, 901
Somatotopy, 438, 438f, 475
Somatotrophs, 614, 615f
Somites, 1125f, 1127, 1127f
Sonography (ultrasound imaging),
    20b
Sound, 587, 589f
  bones of, 217t
  high-pitched, 599
  localization of, 593
  properties of, 589, 590f
  source and propagation,
    587–589, 589f
Sounds of Korotkoff, 732
Soy protein, to treat osteoporosis,
    194
Spasm, 320
Spastic paralysis, 478
Spatial discrimination, 439,
    497–498
  two-point discrimination test,
    498
Spatial summation, 412, 413f
Special senses, 492, 556–603. See
    also Balance; Hearing; Smell
    sense; Taste sense; Vision

Specific ascending pathways, 476f, 477t, **478**
Specific gravity, **1021**
Spectrin, 649–650
  functions/examples from body, 52t
Speech
  hyoid bone and, 218
  tongue muscles involved in, 338, 339f, 340–341, 341f
Speed levers, **328**, 329f
"Speed" (methamphetamine), 424b
Spermatic cord, 1067f, 1068f, **1069**
Spermatic fascia, 1067f
Spermatids, **1077**, 1078f, 1079, 1079f
Spermatocytes, primary/secondary, **1077**, 1078f
Spermatogenesis, **1073**–1080
  summary of events, 1077–1080, 1078f, 1079f
  sustentacular cell's role, 1078f, 1079–1080
Spermatogenic cells, **1077**
Spermatogonia, **1077**, 1078f
Spermiogenesis, **1077**, 1079f
Sperm (spermatozoa), 1066, 1073, **1077**, 1079f
  in events of fertilization, 1115–1117, 1116f, 1117f
S phase, 98, 99f
Sphenoidal sinus, 834f
Sphenoid bone, 205f, **209**–210, 210f, 215f
  body, **209**, 210f, 214f
  greater wing, 205f, 206f, 208f, **209**, 210f, 214f
  lesser wing, 208f, **209**, 210f, 214f
  summary/important markings, 216f
Sphenoid sinuses, 206f, **209**, **210**, 215f, 218, 218f
Sphenomandibular muscle, 338
Sphincter muscles, urethral, **350**t, 351f
Sphincter of Oddi (hepatopancreatic sphincter), **908**, 909f
Sphincter pupillae muscles, 561, 561f
Sphincters
  circular fascicles of, 326
  of muscularis, 888
Sphygmomanometer, 732
Spina bifida, **248**, **483**–484
Spinal accessory nerve. *See* Accessory nerve
Spinal column, 14f
Spinal cord, 388, 389f, **470**–481
  in ANS control hierarchy, 547, 547f, 550
  brain stem in relation to, 448–449f
  developmental aspects, 481–484
  diencephalon in relation to, 448–449f
  disorders, 481
  embryonic origins, 432f, 433, 470
  gray matter, 472–474
    arrangement in CNS, 433, 433f
    organization, 474f
  pathways/tracts to brain
    ascending, 475–478
    descending, 478–480

protective devices
  cerebrospinal fluid, 465–467
  dura mater, 466f, 470, 471f
  vertebral column, 218–225
structure
  cross-sectional, 472–478
  gross, 470–472
  trauma, 478–479
  white matter, 472, 474, 475f
    arrangement in CNS, 433, 433f
Spinal fusion, **248**
Spinalis muscles, 345f
  description/action/nerve supply, **344**t
  origin/insertion, **344**t
Spinal nerve root, 220f
Spinal nerves, 388, 389f, **508**–518
  cervical, 471f
    muscles served by, 340t, 342t, 343t, 353t
  distribution, 508–510, 509f
  formation of, 509–510, 510f
  innervation of specific body regions, 509–510
  intervertebral foramen and, 219f, 221
  lumbar, 471f
    muscles served by, 344t
  muscles served by, 344t, 510
  nerve plexuses, 509f, **510**
    brachial, 509f, **512**–514, 513f, 514f
    cervical, **511**–512, 511f, 511t
    lumbar, 509f, **514**–516, 515f, 515t
    sacral, 509f, **516**, 517f
  thoracic, 471f
Spinal reflexes, **522**–527
Spinal roots, 471f, 472–474, 473f, 508t
Spinal shock, **479**, 522
Spinal (vertebral) cavity, **15**, 17f
Spine (bone marking), 179t
  iliac, **237**, 238f
  ischial, **237**, 238f
  scapular, **229**, 230f, 231, 234f, 236t
Spine (vertebral column), 203, 204f, **218**–225, 219f
  aging and, 248
  curvatures, 219, 219f, 247
  divisions, 218–219, 219f
  muscles of, 342–344t, 345f
Spinocerebellar pathways/tracts, 475, 475f, 476f, 477t, **478**
  proprioceptive impulses and, 496
Spinothalamic pathways/tracts, 475f, 476f, **477**, 477t
  pain impulses via, 497b
Spinous process, of rib, 227f
Spinous processes, 219f–223f, 221, **221**
  bifid, 221, 223f
  of cervical/thoracic/lumbar vertebrae, compared, 224f, 224t
  of lumbar vertebrae, 471f
  of vertebra prominens, 221, 223f
Spiral (coiled) arteries, **1087**, 1087f
Spiral fractures, **192**t
Spiral ganglia, 506f, 506t, 588f, **592**, 592f
Spiral organ (of Corti), 586f, **587**, 588f, 592f
Spirometer, **853**

Splanchnic circulation, **887**
Splanchnic mesoderm, 1125f, **1127**, 1127f
Splanchnic nerves, **538**
  lumbar, 539f, **541**
  sacral, **541**
  thoracic, 540f, **541**
Spleen, **779**–781, 779f, 780f, 883f, 924f
  abdominal arteries in relation to, 753f
  abdominal veins in relation to, 765f
  sympathetic fibers, 539f
  sympathetic innervation, 541t
Splenectomy, 781
Splenic arteries, 752f
Splenic artery, 747f, 752f, 753f, **753**t, 779, 780f
Splenic colic flexure, **922**, 923f
Splenic cords, 780, 780f
Splenic vein, 759f, 764f, **764**t, 765f, 779, 780f
Splenius muscles, **342**, 343f
  description/action/nerve supply, **343**t
  origin/insertion, **343**t
Splenomegaly, **783**
Spliceosomes, 105
Spongy (cancellous) bone, **179**–180, 187
  as connective tissue, 128f
  in endochondral ossification, 185–186, 185f
  in flat bones, 181, 181f
  structure, 180f, 181f, 182, 183f
Spongy urethra, 1025f, **1026**
Sports injuries, knee, 267, 267f
Sprains, **272**
Squamous cell carcinoma, **166**, 166f
  lung, 873
Squamous epithelia, **119**
  functions/locations, 121f
  simple, **120**, 121f
  stratified, **123**, 123f
Squamous region of temporal bone, **207**, 209f
Squamous (squamosal) suture, 203, 206f, **207**
SRP (signal-recognition particle), **87**, 87f
SR. *See* Sarcoplasmic reticulum
Staging cancer prognosis, 147b
Stapedius muscle, 585f, **586**
Stapes bone, 217t, 584f, **585**, 585f, 586f
Starch, 44, 46
  chemical digestion of, 928f, 929
Startle reflex, 449
Starvation, 1056t
Static equilibrium, **594**–595, 594f, 595f
Statins drugs, bone density and, 194
STDs (sexually transmitted diseases), 1030, **1100**–1101
Stellate cells, 452, 452f
Stem cells, 111, 145
Stenosis, valvular, 689
Stents, 719b
Stercobilin, 654, 654f, 816
Stereocilia, 1069
Stereocilia (hairs), 588f
Sterility, STDs and, 1100, 1101
Sternal angle, 226f, **227**

Sternal end, of clavicles, **229**, 230f, 234f, 236t
Sternoclavicular joint, 258t
Sternocleidomastoid muscles, **342**, 343f
  description/action/nerve supply, **342**t
  head movements and, 342, 343f
  origin/insertion, **342**t
  shoulder movements and, 353f
  as superficial muscles, 330f–331f, 333f, 337f, 341f
Sternocostal joints, 254f, 255, 258t
Sternohyoid muscle, 331f, **340**t, 341f, 343f
Sternothyroid muscle, **340**t, 341f
Sternum, 204f, **226**–227, 226f, 227f
  first rib and, synchondrosis at, 254f, 255
  heart in relation to, 679f
  joints of, 258t
  shoulder movements and, 353f
  in thoracic cavity, 844f
Stereocilia, 594f, 595f
Steroid diabetes, 629–630, 630f
Steroid hormones, **605**
  direct gene activation mechanism of, 609–610, 609f
Steroids, 46, **47**–48, 48t
  anabolic, **208**b
  cholesterol, 47, 47f, 48t
  location/function in body, 48t
Stimuli, **491**
  in homeostatic control systems, 9–10, 9f, 11f
  intensity of, and action potentials, 406, 406f
  magnitude estimation in perception of, 497
  maximal, **298**–299, 299f
  muscle response to, 298–299, 299f, 315t
  neural integration of, 494–495, 495f
  sensory receptor classes and, 491
  sensory receptors and, 491–494
  threshold, **298**–299, 299f
STM (short-term memory), **461**, 461f
Stomach, 883f, **899**–908, 924f
  blood supply, 753f, 753t, 764t, 900
  curvatures, 899f, **900**
  emptying of, 907–908, 908f
  hormone produced by, 638t
  innervation, 536f, 537f, 539f, 541, 541t, 900
  major functions (overview), 920t
  motility, 905, 907
  mucosal barrier of, **901**–902
  omenta, **900**
  regions, 899–900, 899f
  secretions regulation, 902–905
  ulcers, 902
Stomodeum, **933**, 936, 936f
Strabismus, 503t, 505t, **559**
  Botox to treat, 156b
Straight arteries, uterine wall, **1087**, 1087f
Straight sinus, 465f, 760f, **760**t, 761f
  CSF in relation to, 466f

Strain, **320**
Stratified epithelia, **119**, 120*f*
  columnar, **124**
  cuboidal, **123**
  functions/locations, 123–124, 123*f*, 124*f*
  squamous, **123**, 123*f*
  transitional, **124**, 124*f*
Stratum basale (basal layer of skin), **153**–154, 154*f*
Stratum basalis (basal layer), uterine wall, **1086**, 1087*f*
Stratum corneum (horny layer of skin), 154*f*, **155**
Stratum functionalis, of endometrium, **1086**, 1087*f*, 1121*f*, 1122
Stratum germinativum. *See* Stratum basale
Stratum granulosum (granular layer of skin), 154*f*, **155**
Stratum lucidum (clear layer of skin), **155**
Stratum spinosum (prickly layer of skin), **154**–155, 154*f*
Streamlining (laminar flow), 724
Stress incontinence, 1027
Stress (physical), increased BMR and, 985
Stress proteins, 53, 636*b*
Stress-relaxation response, in smooth muscle contraction, **313**, 316
Stress response
  cortisol and, 629
  increased BMR and, 985
  mechanics of, 631, 631*f*
  psychosomatic illness and, 455
  short/long-term effects, 631, 631*f*
Stretch
  joint stretch pathways, 476*f*
  muscle spindles and, 523–524, 523*f*
  as regulator of muscle contraction, 315*t*
  response to, in cardiac vs. skeletal vs. smooth muscle, 315*t*
Stretch receptors, 491, 493*t*, 523*f*
Stretch reflex, **523**–524, 523*f*
Striae, 157
Striate cortex. *See* Visual cortex (primary)
Striated muscle cells, 139
Striations, muscle, 280, 282*f*, 282*t*, **284**, 285*f*
Stria vascularis, **587**, 588*f*
Stroke. *See* Cerebrovascular accidents
Stroke volume, **700**–703, 701*f*, 703*f*, 726, 727*f*, 731*f*
Stroma, **133**, 777, 845
Strong acids, **43**
Strong bases, **43**
Structural (fibrous) proteins, **50**
  functions/examples from body, 52*t*
Structural hierarchy of human body, 3–4, 4*f*
S-T segment, **696**, 696*f*, 697*f*
Stuart factor, nature/origin/function/pathway, 663*t*
Stuart-Prower factor, nature/origin/function/pathway, 663*t*
Student's elbow, 273

Stupor, as state of consciousness, 458
Sty, 556
Styloglossus muscle, 339*f*, 339*t*
Stylohyoid ligaments, 218
Stylohyoid muscle, 339*f*, **340***t*, 341*f*
Styloid process
  of radius, **232**, 233*f*, 234*f*, 236*t*
  in relation to muscles of neck and throat, 341*f*
  in relation to tongue muscles, 339*f*
  of temporal bone, 206*f*, **207**, 208*f*, 209*f*, 216*t*
  of ulna, **232**, 233*f*, 236*t*
Stylomastoid foramen, **207**, 208*f*, 216*t*
Stylopharyngeus muscle, 506*t*
Subacromial bursa, 257*f*, 269*f*
Subacute hypersensitivities, **823**–824
Subarachnoid space, 464*f*, **465**, 472*f*, 473*f*
  CSF in relation to, 466*f*
Subcapillary plexus of dermal papillae, 155
Subcapsular sinus, lymph node, 778*f*, **779**
Subclavian arteries, 681*f*, 745*f*–751*f*, **746***t*, 750*t*
Subclavian lymphatic trunks, **775**, 776*f*
Subclavian veins, 758*f*, **758***t*, 759*f*, 761*f*, 762*f*, 762*t*
Subclavius muscle, 352, 353*f*
  description/action/nerve supply, **352***t*
  origin/insertion, 352*t*
Subcostal arteries, 751*t*
Subcostal nerves, **511**
Subcutaneous prepatellar bursa, 265, 266*f*, 267
Subdural space, 464*f*, **465**, 473*f*
Subendothelial layer, of blood vessel wall, 714, 715*f*
Sublingual gland, 883*f*, **892**, 892*f*
  parasympathetic fibers, 537*f*
Subluxation, **273**
Submandibular ganglia, 505*f*, 505*t*, **537**
Submandibular gland, 343*f*, 883*f*, 889*f*, **891**–892, 892*f*
  parasympathetic fibers, 537*f*
Submucosa
  of GI tract, 887*f*, **888**, 896*f*
  small intestine, 910*f*
  stomach, 901*f*
  tracheal, 839, 839*f*
Submucosal nerve plexus, 887*f*, **888**, 901*f*
Subpubic angle (pubic arch), **239**, 240*f*, 240*t*
Subscapular arteries, 751*f*
Subscapular artery, 750*f*, **750***t*, 751*f*
Subscapular fossa, 230*f*, 231, 234*f*, 236*t*
Subscapularis muscle, 353*f*, **354**, 356*f*
  actions of (summary), 362*t*
  description/action/nerve supply, **355***t*
  origin/insertion, 355*t*
Subscapular nerve, muscles served by, 355*t*

Substance or vesicular trafficking, 78, 81
Substance P, **418**
Substantia nigra, 443, **449**, 450*f*
  memory and, 462*f*
  Parkinson's disease and, 469
Substrate-level phosphorylation, **958**–959, 958*f*
Substrates of enzymes, **54**, 55*f*
Subthalamic nuclei, 443
Sucking reflex, 936
Sucrase, 928*f*, **929**
Sucrose
  as a disaccharide, 44, 45*f*
  chemical digestion of, 928*f*, 929
Sudden infant death syndrome (SIDS), 875
Sudoriferous (sweat) glands, 153*f*, **158**, 159*f*
Sugars
  double (disaccharides), 44, 45*f*
  simple (monosaccharides), 44, 45*f*
Sulci, **434**, 435*f*
  central, **434**, 435*f*, 436, 437*f*
  lateral, 435*f*, **436**
  parieto-occipital, 435*f*, **436**
  posterior median of spinal cord, 471*f*, 473*f*
Sulcus terminalis, **891**, 891*f*
Sulfate, in blood plasma/IF/ICF, 1038*f*
Sulfur, 26*t*, 953*t*
Summation
  in action vs. postsynaptic potentials, 414*t*
  multiple motor unit, **298**–299, 299*f*
  by postsynaptic neuron, 411–413, 413*f*
  spatial, **412**, 413*f*
  temporal, **412**, 413*f*
  wave, **297**–298, 298*f*
Sun exposure, skin damage and, 157
Superficial fascia (hypodermis), **152**, 153*f*
Superficial muscles of body, 330*f*–333*f*
Superficial orientation/direction, 13*t*
Superficial reflexes, **526**–527
Superficial space muscles, 350, 351*f*
  description/action/nerve supply, **350***t*
  origin/insertion, 350*t*
Superior orientation/direction, 13*t*
Supination (movement), **262**, 263*f*
  muscles involved in, 362*t*
Supinator muscle, 358, 359*f*, 361*f*
  actions (summary), 362*t*
  description/action/nerve supply, **360***t*
  origin/insertion, 360*t*
Supporting cells
  maculae, 594, 594*f*
  of olfactory receptors, **578**, 579*f*
Suppressor factors in immune response, 818*t*
Suprachiasmatic nucleus, 445*f*, 446, **575**, 576*f*, 635
  sleep-wake cycle and, 446, 459, 635
Supraclavicular nerves, 511*f*, 511*t*
Supracondylar lines, **241**, 241*f*

Supracondylar ridges, of humerus, 231*f*, **232**
Suprahyoid muscles, 340, 341*f*
  description/action/nerve supply, **340***t*
  origin/insertion, 340*t*
  swallowing and, 340–341*t*, 341*f*
  as synergists, 342
Supraoptic nuclei, **613**, 613*f*
Supraoptic nucleus, 445*f*, 446
Supraorbital foramen (notch), **204**, 205*f*, 214*f*, **216***t*
Supraorbital margins, 204, 205*f*
Suprapatellar bursa, 266*f*
Suprarenal arteries, 746*f*, 752*f*, **754***t*, 755*f*
Suprarenal glands. *See* Adrenal glands
Suprarenal veins, 758*f*, 764*f*, **764***t*, 765*f*
Suprascapular artery, 750*f*, 751*f*
Suprascapular nerve, 513*f*, 514*t*
  muscles served by, 355*t*
Suprascapular notch, 230*f*, **231**
Supraspinatus muscle, 353*f*, **354**, 356*f*
  actions of (summary), 362*t*
  description/action/nerve supply, **355***t*
  origin/insertion, 355*t*
Supraspinous fossa, of scapula, 230*f*, 231, 234*f*, 236*t*
Supraspinous ligament, 220*f*, 472*f*
Suprasternal (jugular) notch, 226*f*, **227**
Sural nerve, **516**, 517*f*, 517*t*
Surface anatomy, 2
Surface tension, 36, 37*f*
Surfactant, **850**–851
Surfactant protein A, 1136
Surgical neck of humerus, 231*f*, **232**, 234*f*
Survival factors needed to maintain life, 8
Suspensions, **31**
Suspensory ligament (ciliary zonule), 560*f*, **561**, 564*f*
Suspensory ligament of mammary glands, 1089*f*, **1090**
Suspensory ligament of ovary, 1082*f*, **1083**, 1083*f*, 1085*f*
Suspensory ligament of penis, 1067*f*
Sustentacular (Sertoli) cells, 1078*f*, **1079**–1080
Sustentaculum tali, **244**, 245*f*
Sutural bones, 205*f*, **211**
Sutures, **207**, 253
  bones articulated/movements allowed, 258*t*
  coronal, 203, 206*f*, 207
  as fibrous joints, 253, 253*f*
  lambdoid, 203, 205*f*, 206*f*, 207
  sagittal, 203, 205*f*, 207
  squamous, 203, 206*f*, 207
Swallowing (deglutition), **884**, 884*f*, **897**–899, 898*f*, 920*t*
  hyoid bone and, 218
  muscles that promote, 340–341*t*, 341*f*
  regulatory centers, 451
Sweat and sweating, 158
  bactericidal action of, 158
  as excretion route for nitrogen-containing wastes, 165
  as heat-loss mechanism, 989

Sweat glands
    ANS effects, 546t
    sympathetic fibers, 539f
Sweating, enhanced, as heat-loss
    mechanism, 989
Sweat (sudoriferous) glands, 153f,
    158, 159f
Swelling, in inflammatory
    response, 792f, 793
Sympathectomy, 551
Sympathetic division (ANS),
    388–389, **538**, 539f
    antagonistic interactions, 544
    blood pressure and, 727–729,
        727f
    cooperative ANS effects, 545–546
    heart rate regulation by, 701f, 702
    localized vs. diffuse effects, 547
    metabolic effects promoted by,
        547
    in nervous system structure,
        533, 533f
    organs affected by, 546t
    parasympathetic division vs.,
        534f, 536f, 536t
        interactions, 544–547, 550
    renal mechanisms and, 1010
    thyroid hormone's effects, 621t
    unique roles, 535, 546–567
    vasomotor tone and, 7727, 545
Sympathetic trunk (chain) ganglia,
    510f, **538**, 539f
    pathways with synapses in,
        540–541, 540f
Sympathetic trunks, **538**, 540f
Sympathetic (vasomotor) tone, **545**
Sympatholytic agents, effects on
    ANS activity, 545t
Sympathomimetic agents, effects
    on ANS activity, 545t
Symphyses, 254f, **255**
Symphysis joint, 259t
Symphysis pubis, 351f
Symport system, **77**
Synapses, **408**–411
    axoaxonic, 408
    axodendritic, **408**, 409f
    axosomatic, **408**, 409f
    chemical, **409**, **409**–411, 410f
        integrating/modifying events
            of, 411–413, 413f
        postsynaptic potentials and,
            411–413, 414t
        steps of, 409–411, 410f
        synaptic delay, 411
    dendrodendritic, 408
    dendrosomatic, 408
    developmental aspects,
        424–425
    electrical, 408–409, **408**–409
    integrating/modifying events of,
        411–413, 413f
    potentiation and, 412–413
    presynaptic inhibition and, **413**
    synapses en passant, 519
Synapses en passant, 519
Synapsis, 1076f, **1077**
Synaptic cleft, **289**, 290f, **409**, 410f
    of smooth muscle (diffuse
        junction), 310, 311f
Synaptic delay, **411**
Synaptic knob. See Axon terminal
Synaptic potentiation, **412**–413
Synaptic terminals of
    photoreceptors, 569, 570f,
    572–573, 573f

Synaptic vesicles, **289**, 290f, 291f,
    409–411, 410f
    autonomic, 519
    of smooth muscle, 310, 311f
Synaptotagmin, 410
Synarthroses, **253**, 258f, 259t
Synchondroses, 254f, **255**, 258t
Synchrotriophoblast, **1119**, 1119f,
    1120f
Syndesmoses, **253**–254, 253f, 259t
Syndrome of inappropriate ADH
    secretion (SIADH), 619t,
    620, **1061**
Synergism, of hormones, **611**
Synergist muscles, **325**
Synostoses, **253**
Synovial fluid, 255f, 256
Synovial (joint) cavity, 19, 19f,
    255f, **256**
    of elbow, 268f
    of knee, 266f
Synovial joints, 253, **255**–272
    articular capsule, 255f, **256**
    articular cartilage, 255f, **256**
    articulating bones/movements
        allowed, 258t, 259t
    cavity, 19, 19f, 255f, **256**,
        266f, 268f
    distinguishing features,
        255–256, 255f, 256t
    factors influencing stability,
        257, 259
    fatty pads, **256**
    fluid, 255f, **256**
    friction-reducing structures
        bursae, **257**, 257f
        tendon sheath, **257**, 257f
    ligaments, 255f, **256**
    membrane, 255f, **256**, 257f
    menisci, **256**
    movements allowed by,
        259–263, 260–262f
    selected
        elbow joint, **268**, 268f
        knee joint, **265**–268
    types of, 263–265, 264f
Synovial membrane, 255f,
    256, 257f
    of elbow joint, 268f
Synovitis, 274, **276**
Synthesis reactions, **37**, 38f
Synthetic skin, 170
Syphilis, **1100**
Systemic anatomy, **2**
Systemic blood pressure, 724–733.
    See also Blood pressure
Systemic circuit, **684**–685, 684f
    gas exchange and, 684, 684f
Systemic circulation
    arteries and veins, compared,
        742
    blood pressure in various blood
        vessels, 725, 725f
    major pathways
        arteries, 746t–757t
        flowchart overview, 745f
Systemic lupus erythematosus
    (SLE), 822, **826**
Systole, **698**, 699f, 700
Systolic blood pressure, **725**, 725f

T1 (monoiodotyrosine), **622**, 622f
T2 (diiodotyrosine), **622**, 622f
T3 (triiodothyronine), **621**–622,
    622f

T4 (thyroxine), **620**, 622–623,
    622f
Tabes dorsalis, **528**
Tachycardia, **704**
Tachykinins, functional class/
    secretion sites/effects, 417t
Tactile (Meissner's) corpuscles,
    153f, 155, 164, **492**
    functional classes/body location,
        493t
Tail, sperm, **1079**, 1079f
Talar shelf, 244
Talus bone (ankle), **244**, 245f,
    246f, 246t
    joint, 259t
Tanning, skin, 157
Target cells, of hormones, **606**
Tarsal bones, 228f, **244**, 245f,
    246f, 246t
    joints, 259t
Tarsal (meibomian) glands,
    556, 557f
Tarsal plates, **556**, 557f
Tarsometatarsal joint, articulating
    bones/movements allowed,
    259t
Tarus, **244**
Tastant, 582
Taste buds, **580**–582, 581f
Taste pore, **581**, 581f
Taste sense, 556, 578, **580**–583
    activation of receptors, 582
    aging and, 598
    basic taste sensations, 582
    developmental aspects, 598
    disorders, 583
    gustatory cortex, 437f, 440, **440**,
        582, 583f
    gustatory pathway, 582, 583f
    influence of other sensations on,
        583
    transduction mechanism, 582
Tau (protein), 469
Tay-Sachs disease, 89
TBGs (thyroxine-binding
    globulins), 623
TB (tuberculosis), **872**
T cell-dependent antigens, **815**
T cell-independent antigens, **815**
T cells. See T lymphocytes
Tears (lacrimal secretions), 557
    lysozyme and, 558, 790
    as protective mechanism, 796t
Tectorial membrane, 588f, **592**
Tectospinal tracts, 475f, **478**
    location/origin/termination/
        function, 479t
Tectum, 448, 449f
Teeth, **893**–895, 893f, 920t
    deciduous, 893, 893f
    structure, 894–895, 894f
Telencephalon, 432f, **433**
Telodendria (terminal branches) of
    axons, **393**
Telomerase, 112
Telomeres, **112**
Telophase, **101**, 103f, 1076f
Temperature, chemical reactions
    and, 39
Temperature receptors, spinal cord
    pathways for, 476f, 477
Temperature stimuli, nerve
    endings responding to, 492
Template, DNA, 99, 100f, 105,
    106f, 108f
Temporal arteries, 748f, **748t**, 749f

Temporal bone, meninges in
    relation to, 464f
Temporal bones, 205f, 206f, **207**,
    208f, 209f
    summary/important markings,
        216t
    temporomandibular joint, 258t,
        271–272, 271f
Temporalis muscle, 337f, **338**, 339f
    description/action/nerve supply,
        338t
    origin/insertion, 338t
    superficial, 331f
Temporal lobe, role in memory
    consolidation/access, 462,
    463
Temporal lobe of cerebral
    hemisphere, 434, 435f, **436**,
    437f, 445f
    cranial nerves in relation to, 501f
Temporal summation, **412**, 413f
Temporal veins, 760f, **760t**, 761f
Temporomandibular joint (TMJ),
    207, 211, 212f, **271**–272,
    271f
    dislocation, 272
    movements allowed by, 258t,
        271f, 272
Tendon, **284**
    central, of diaphragm, 347f
    as in indirect muscle
        attachment, 284
    in relation to connective tissue
        sheath, 282f, 283, 283f
Tendonitis, **273**
Tendon of adductor magnus, 266f
Tendon of biceps muscle, 268,
    268f, 359f
Tendon of long head of biceps
    brachii muscle, 257f,
    269, 269f
Tendon of quadriceps femoris
    muscle, knee joint and, 266f
Tendon of quadriceps muscle,
    265, 266f
Tendon of semimembranosus
    muscle, 266f
Tendon of subscapularis muscle,
    269f
Tendon of triceps muscle,
    268, 268f
Tendons
    dense regular connective tissue
        of, 135
    of knee, 266f, 267
    of rotator cuff, 269
    synovial joint stability and, 257,
        257f, 259
Tendon sheath, **257**, 257f, 269f
    inflammation, 273
Teniae coli, **922**, 923f
Tennis elbow, **384**
Tension (cleavage) lines, 156
Tensor fasciae latae muscle, 331f,
    367, 368f
    actions of (summary),
        379–380t, 380f
    description/action/nerve supply,
        370t
    origin/insertion, **370t**
Tensor muscle, 340
Tensor tympani muscle, 585f,
    586
Tensor veli palatini, 341f
TENS (transcutaneous electrical
    nerve stimulation), 497b

Tentorium cerebelli, **464**, 464f, 465f
  CSF in relation to, 466f
Teratogens, **1130**
Teres major muscle, 353f, **354**, 356f
  actions of (summary), 362t
  description/action/nerve supply, **355**t
  origin/insertion, **355**t
  superficial, 333f
Teres minor muscle, 353f, **354**, 356f
  actions of (summary), 362t
  description/action/nerve supply, **355**t
  origin/insertion, **355**t
Terminal arterioles, 717f, **721**, 721f
Terminal branches (telodendria) of axon, 392f, **393**
Terminal bronchioles, 841f, 842
Terminal cisternae, **287**, 288f
Terminal ganglia, **536**
Terminal hair, **162**
Termination signal, 105, 106f
Testes, **1066**, 1066f, 1067f
  in brain-testicular axis, 1080–1081, 1081f
  as endocrine system organ, 605f, 635
  as primary sex organ, 1066
  structure, 1067–1069, 1068f
Testicular cancer, 1069
Testicular fluid, **1080**
Testicular (gonadal) arteries, 746f, 747f, 752f, **754**t, 1067f, **1068**
Testicular (gonadal) veins, 758f, 764f, **764**t, 765f, **1068**
Testosterone, **635**, 1068, **1080**
  in brain-testicular axis, 1080–1081, 1081f
  CNS gender-specific development and, 481
  EPO production and, 653
  in "juice" (anabolic steroids), **308**b
  location/functions, 48t
  mechanisms/effects, 1081–1082
  source/stimulus/effects (summary), 1099t
  structure/regulation/effects, 627t
  terminal hair response to, 162
Tetanus (disease), 298, **320**
  immunity and, 806
Tetanus/tetanic muscle contractions, **298**, 298f
  frequency of stimulation and, 305
  fused/complete, **298**, 298f
  unfused/incomplete, **298**, 298f
Tetany, 625
Tetrads, 1076f, **1077**
Tetrahydrogestrinone (THG), 308b
Tetralogy of Fallot, 708, 708f
TF (tissue factor), 663t, 664f, **665**
Thalamic nuclei, 443, **445**f, 446, 583f
  anterior, as limbic structure, 454, 455f
  functions (summary), 453t
Thalamic nucleus, 445f, 446
Thalamus, **443**, 445f, 446, 448f, 449f
  basal nuclei in relation to, 444f
  embryonic origins, 432f, 433

internal capsule and, 442f, 443, 446
  memory and, 462f
  as memory circuit, 462f
  neural integration and, 495f
  nuclei of, 443, 445f, 446
  in pain pathway, 496b
  spinal cord tracts and, 476f
Thalassemias, **655**
Thalidomide, **1130**
Theca folliculi, **1093**, 1093f
Thenar eminence, 364
Thenar muscles, 359f, **364**t, 365f
Theory of spontaneous generation, 65
Thermogenesis
  chemical (nonshivering), **987**
  food-induced, **985**
Thermoreceptors, **491**, 493t
  central, **987**
  peripheral, **987**
Thermoregulation
  brain centers for, **987**
  heat-loss mechanisms, 988–989, 988f
  heat-promoting mechanisms, 987–988, 988f
  sympathetic ANS responses, 547
Theta brain waves, **456**, 457f, 459, 459f
THG (tetrahydrogestrinone), 308b
Thiamin (vitamin B1), **949**t
Thick (myosin) filaments, 282f, 282t, **284**–286, 285f, 286f
  in muscle contraction, 293–294, 295f
Thick segment, loop of Henle, 1002f, **1003**, 1004f
Thick skin, **153**
Thigh
  bone, 239, 241, 241f, 246f, 246t
  innervation of, 515f, 515t
  muscles, 367–372t
    actions of (summary), 379–380t
    superficial, 331f, 333f
Thin (actin) filaments, 282f, 282t, **284**, 285f, 286–287, 286f
  globular, 286
  in muscle contraction, 293–294, 295f
Thinking
  Alzheimer's disease and, 469
  memory processing circuits, 462f
Thin segment, loop of Henle, 1002f, **1003**, 1004f
Third-class levers, **328**, 329f
Third-degree burns, 167f, **170**
Third-order neurons, **475**, 476f, 495
Third ventricle (brain), **434**, 434f, 449f
  CSF in relation to, 466f
  white matter fiber tracts and, 442f
Thirst center, hypothalamic, 446, 1039
Thirst mechanism, **1039**–1040, 1040f
  aging and, 1060
Thoracic arteries, 750f, **750**t, 751f, **751**t

Thoracic cage (bony thorax), 203, 204f, **226**
  in relation to spine, 226, 226f
  ribs, 226f, 227–228, 227f
  sternum, **226**–227, 226f
Thoracic cavity, **15**, 17f
  anatomical relationships of organs in, 844f
Thoracic curvatures, **219**, 219f, 247
Thoracic lymphatic duct, **775**
Thoracic nerves, 471f, 509, 509f, 513f
  muscles served by, 352t
  rami communicantes and, 509, 510f
Thoracic splanchnic nerves, 540f
Thoracic vertebrae, **219**, 219f
  articulated, 223f
  curvatures, **219**, 219f, 247
  features, 222, 223f
    summary, 224f, 224t
  movements allowed, 224t
  in relation to ribs, 227f
Thoracic viscera arteries, 751t
Thoracoacromial arteries, 750f, **750**t, 751f
Thoracodorsal nerve, muscles served by, 354t
Thoracolumbar division of ANS, **538**. See also Sympathetic division
Thorax
  arteries, 746f, 747f, 750–751t
  veins, 758f, 758t
Thorax (bony thorax/thoracic cage), 226–228
  aging and, 248
  innervation, 509, 510f, 511, 511t, 512, 513f
    sympathetic, 539f, 541, 541t
  muscles, 331f, **352**–353t, 353f
    of breathing, 346t, 347f
    superficial, 356f
  vertebral column in relation to, 226f
Thoroughfare channel, 717f, **721**, 721f
Three-dimensional vision, **575**, 576f
Threonine, 947f
Threshold, **404**, 406f
  all-or-none phenomenon and, 405–406
  stimuli, **298**–299, 299f, 405–406, 406f
Throat, muscles that promote swallowing, 340–341t, 341f
Thrombin, 664f, 665, **666**
Thrombocytopenia, **668**
Thromboembolic disorders, **667**
Thrombokinase, nature/origin/ function/pathway, 663t
Thrombolytic agents, 719b
  TPA, 469, 481, **666**, 706b
Thrombophlebitis, **767**
Thrombopoietin, **662**
Thromboxanes
  location/functions, 48t
  thromboxane A2, **665**
Thrombus, **667**
TH. See Thyroid hormone
Thumb (pollex), 235, 235f, 236f, **237**
  joint, 264f, 265
  muscles, 359f, 362t
Thymic factor, **636**

Thymic (Hassall's) corpuscles, **781**, 781f
Thymine (T), **55**–57, 56f, 57t
Thymopoietins, **636**
Thymosins, **636**
Thymus, in thoracic cavity, 844f
Thymus gland, 605f, **636**, 779f, **781**, 781f
  T cell immunocompetence and, 800–802, 801f, 802f
Thyrocervical trunk, 749f, **749**t, 750f, 751f
Thyroglobulin, **620**
  formation/storage of, 621–622, 622f
Thyrohyoid membrane, 341f, 836f
Thyrohyoid muscle, 339f, 341f, **341**t
Thyroid arteries, 620, 620f, 748f, **748**t, 749f
Thyroid cartilage, 341f, 834f, **836**, 836f
  tongue muscles in relation to, 339f
Thyroid gland, **620**–624, 834f
  aging and, 639
  blood supply, 620, 620f
  disorders, 623–624
  hormone secreted by, 620–623
  location, 605f, 620, 620f
  muscles proximal to, 341f
  structure, 620, 620f
Thyroid hormone (TH), **620**–624
  calorigenic effect, **621**
  hyper-/hyposecretion, 621t, 623–624
  major effects on body systems, 621t
  regulation, 623
  synthesis, 621–623, 622f
  transport, 623
Thyroid-stimulating hormone (TSH), **616**, 623
  summary of regulation/effects, 618t
Thyroid storm (thyroid crisis), **642**
Thyroid veins, 761f
Thyrotrophs, **616**
Thyrotropin-releasing hormone (TRH), **616**, 618f, 623
Thyrotropin. See Thyroid-stimulating hormone
Thyroxine (T4), **620**, **985**
  body heat production and, 985, 987
  heart rate and, 702
  influences on BMR, 985, 985f
  influences on metabolism, 978t
  synthesis of, 621–623, 622f
  thyroxine-binding globulins (TBGs), 623
TIAs (transient ischemic attacks), **468**
Tibia, 228f, **242**, 242f, 243f, 244, 246f, 246t
  collateral ligaments, 266f, **267**
  joints of, 259t
  knee and, 265, 266f, 267
  muscles and, 373–378t
Tibial arteries, 382f, 747f, 756f, **756**t, 757f
Tibial borders, 243f, **244**
Tibial condyles, **242**, 242f, 243f, 266f
Tibialis anterior muscle, 331f, **373**, 374f, 375f

actions of (summary),
379–380t, 380f
description/action/nerve supply,
373t
origin/insertion, **373**t
tendon, 382f
Tibialis posterior muscle, **373**
actions of (summary), 379t
description/action/nerve supply,
376t
origin/insertion, **376**t
tendon, 377f, 378f, 382f
Tibial malleolus, 243f, **244**
Tibial nerve, **516**, 517f, 517t
muscles served by, 372t, 376t
Tibial tuberosity, **242**, 242f, 243f
Tibial veins, 759f, 766f, **766**t
Tibiofemoral joint, **265**, 266f
articulating bones/movements
allowed, 259t
Tibiofibular joint, **242**, 242f,
243f, 244
articulating bones/movements
allowed, 259t
Tic douloureux, 504t
Tidal volume (TV), **851**, 852f
Tight junctions, **69**, 70f
of blood-brain barrier, 467
continuous capillaries, 720, 720f
of epithelia, 119
Tin, 26t
Tinnitus, **594**
Tip-links, 592, 592f
Tissue factor (TF), 663t, 664f,
665
Tissue perfusion, **733–742**
autoregulation, 734–736, 736f
long-term, 736
in the brain, 737
in the heart, 738
in the lungs, 738
metabolic controls, 735
myogenic response and,
735–736, 736f
in skeletal muscles, 737
in the skin, 737–738
ventilation-perfusion coupling
and, 856–858, 857f
Tissue plasminogen activator (tPA),
469, 481, **666**, 706b, 719b
Tissues, 3, 117–150, **118**
aging and, 145, 148
bone, **137**, 138f
connective, 118, **126–139**
developmental aspects, 145,
145f, 148
epithelial, 118, **118–126**
functions (overview), 118, 148
granulation, **143**, 144f
growth, thyroid hormone and,
621
microscopy preparations, 118
muscle, 118, **139–141**
nervous, 118, **139**, 389–397
regenerative capacity, 143–144
repair of, 143–145, 144f
scar, **143**, 144, 144f
in structural organization of
human body, **3–4**, 4f
wasting, 146b
Tissue thromboplastin, 664f, **665**
nature/origin/function/pathway,
663t
Tissue thromboplastin (Factor III),
663t, 664f, **665**
Titin, 52t, 284, 285f, 286, **287**

TLC (total lung capacity),
851–852, 852f
TLRs (toll-like receptors), **793**
T lymphocytes (T cells), **659**,
777, **800**
activation, 813–814
antigen recognition/MHC
restriction, 810–813
CD4/CD8 cells and,
810, 811f
cytotoxic T cells, **810**, 811f,
815–816, 816f
development of
immunocompetence/self-
tolerance, 800–802,
801f, 802f
gamma delta, **817**
helper T cells, **810**, 811f,
814–815, 815f
regulatory, **816–817**
thymus gland hormones and,
636
TMJ. See Temporomandibular
joint
TMR (total metabolic rate),
985
TNFs (tumor necrosis factors),
637b, **816**, 818t
Toes (digits)
bones, 228f, **244**, 245f, 246f
joints
articulating bones/movements
allowed, 259t
muscles acting on, 373–378t,
381–383t
muscles acting on, summary,
379–380t
Toll-like receptors (TLRs), **793**
Tongue, 834f, 883f, 889f, **890**,
891f, 920t
movements, 339f, 339t
muscles, **338**, 339f, 339t
extrinsic, 339f, **339**t, 890
intrinsic, **338**, 890
swallowing and, 340
Tonic-clonic seizures, 457
Tonicity, **74**, 74f
vs. osmolarity, 74
Tonic receptors, **495**
Tonsillar crypts, **782**, 782f
Tonsillitis, **783**
Tonsils, **781–782**, 782f
lingual, **781**, 834f, **835**, 889f,
891, 891f
palatine, **781**, 782f, 834f, **835**,
889f, 891f
pharyngeal (adenoids),
781–782, 834f, **835**, 875
tubal, **782**, 834f, 835
Torticollis (wryneck), 342t, **384**
Total dead space, 853
Total lung capacity (TLC),
851–852, 852f
Total metabolic rate (TMR), **985**
Touch
crude, spinal cord pathways for,
476f
discriminative, **475**, 492
Touch receptors, 492
hair follicle receptors as,
160, 164
Merkel disc on epidermis,
154f
pathways to, 476f
tPA (tissue plasminogen activator),
469, 481, **666**, 706b, 719b

Trabeculae
in intramembranous
ossification, 184f
lymph node, **778**, 778f
spleen, 780f
of spongy bone, 180, 183f
Trabeculae carneae, **683**, 683f
Trace elements, 26t, 954–955t
Trace minerals, 26t, 954–955t
Trachea, 832f, 834f, **838–840**,
889f
cartilage of, 176, 177f
features/functions, 838t
in thoracic cavity, 844f
tissue composition of wall,
839, 839f
Tracheal cartilages, 836f
Trachealis muscle, **839**, 839f
Tracheoesophageal fistula, 936
Tracheotomy, **875**
Trachoma, **600**, 1101
Traction, **199**
Transamination, **970**, 971t
Transcription factor, 105, 106f
Transcription (genetic), **104–105**,
105f
overview, 106f
Transcutaneous electrical nerve
stimulation (TENS), 497b
Transcytosis, 78, 79
Transducin, **572**, 573f
Transduction, **494–495**, 495f
light, 572–574, 574f
sound, 592
trans face, 87, 87f
Trans fats/fatty acids, 46–47, 981
Trans fatty acids, 980
Transferrin, **654**, 654f, 933
Transfer RNA (tRNA), 57, **104**
Transforming growth factor, 179
Transforming growth factor beta,
818t
Transfusions (blood), **668–671**
blood typing, 671, 671f
reactions to, 670, 823
self-antigens and, 800
restoring blood volume, 671
Transient ischemic attacks (TIAs),
468
Translation, **107–109**, 108f
information flow from DNA
gene to protein structure,
105
Translation (gliding movements),
259, **260**, 260f
Transmembrane proteins, 68
Transmissible spongiform
encephalopathies (TSEs),
482–483b
Transmission electron microscopy,
118
Transplantation (organ), 818, 820
Transplants
heart, 706–707b
liver, 915
Transport proteins, in carbohydrate
absorption, 928f, 931
Transport vesicles, 87f, 88f,
90, 90f
Transposons, 1153
Transpulmonary pressure, **847**
Transverse (horizontal) plane,
15, 16f
Transverse processes, 219f, 220f,
221, 221f, 223f
compared, 224f, 224t

Transverse sinuses, 760f,
760t, 761f
Transversus abdominis muscle,
331f, **348**, 349f
description/action/nerve supply,
348t
origin/insertion, **348**t
Trapezium bone, **235**, 235f, 236f,
236t
Trapezius muscles, **352**, 353f
description/action/nerve supply,
352t
head extension and, 342
origin/insertion, **352**t
as superficial muscle,
330f–333f, 337f
Trapezoid bone, **235**, 235f, 236f,
236t
Trastuzumab (Herceptin), 147b
Treppe, **299**, 300f
TRH. See Thyrotropin-releasing
hormone
Triads, **287**, 288f
Triceps brachii muscle, 356f,
357, 359f
actions (summary), 362–363t,
363f
description/action/nerve supply,
357t
origin/insertion, **357**t
superficial, 331f–333f
Triceps surae muscles, **376**t,
377f, 380f
Trichomoniasis, **1101**
Trichosiderin, 160
TRICOM (cancer vaccine), 147b
Tricuspid valve, 682f, 683f,
686, 687f
Trigeminal (gasserian/semilunar)
ganglia, 504t
Trigeminal nerve (V), 448f, 450f,
451, **500**, 501f
mandibular division, 340t,
504f, 504t
maxillary division, 504f, 504t
muscles served by, 338–339t,
340t
ophthalmic division, 504f, 504t
origin/location/function,
504f, **504**t
parasympathetic fibers, 537
Trigeminal nuclei
motor, 450f
sensory, 450f
Trigger zone in neurons, 393
location, compared, 396t
Triglycerides (fats), **46–47**
absorption, 931–932, 932f
digestion, 920t, 928f, 929–930,
930f
fate in absorptive (fed) state,
973–974, 974f
location/function in body, 48t
metabolism, 957f, 967–969,
969f
insulin's influence, 633
interconversion and, 972f, 973
summary, 971t
molecular structure, 47f
monounsaturated/polyunsaturat
ed, 46
nutrient pools of, 971, 972f, **973**
saturated/unsaturated, 46
trans fats/fatty acids, **46–47**,
981
Trigone, **1025**, 1025f

Triiodothyronine (T3), **621**
  synthesis of, 621–623, 622f
Tripeptide, 49
Triplets (genetic), **104**, 109, 110f
Triplets (microtubule), 93
Triquetral bone, **235**, 235f,
  236f, 236t
Tritium, 29f
tRNA (transfer RNA), **104**
  initiator, **107**, 108f
  in translation process, 107,
    108f, 109, 110f
Trochanter (bone marking), 179t
Trochlea
  eye, 503f, **558**, 559f
  humerus, 231f, **232**, 234f,
    236t, 268f
  talus, 244, 245f
Trochlear nerve (IV), 448f, 449f,
  500, 501f
  muscles served by, 558, 559f
  origin/course/function, 503f,
    503t
Trochlear notch, of ulna, **232**,
  233f, 234f, 236t, 268f
Trochlear nuclei, 449
Trophoblast cells, **1118**, 1118f,
  1119f
Tropic hormones (tropins), **614**
Tropins (tropic hormones), **614**
Tropomyosin, 286f, **287**, 292f, 294f
Troponin, 286f, **287**, 292f,
  294f, 315t
True capillaries, **721**, 721f
True pelvis, 237, **239**
True solutions, 30
True (vertebrosternal) ribs, 226f,
  227f, **228**
True vocal cords (vocal folds), 834f,
  836f, **837**, 837f
Trunk
  arteries, 746f
  innervation of, 511f, 511t
  movements, 342–345t,
    343f, 345f
  muscles, 342–344t, 343f, 345f
    abdominal wall, 348t, 349f
    superficial, 330f–333f
  veins, 758f, 758t
Trunks of brachial plexus, **512**,
  513f, 514t
Trypsin, **918**, 918f, 928f, **929**
Trypsinogen, 918, 918f
Tryptophan, 418, 947f
TSH. See Thyroid-stimulating
  hormone
t-SNAREs, 78, 78f
T (thymine), **55**–57, 56f, 57t
T tubules, **287**, 288f, 290f
  in cardiac muscle, 314t, 690f
  as modified sarcolemma, 284
Tubal tonsils, **782**, 834f, 835
Tubercle (bone marking), 179t
  of atlas (C1), 222f
  of humerus, 231f, **232**
  of iliac crest, **237**, 238f
  of rib, 222, 227f, 228
Tuberculosis (TB), **872**
Tuberculum sellae, 208f, **209**
Tuberosity (bone marking), 179t
  deltoid (of humerus), 231f, **232**
  radial, **232**, 233f
Tubular reabsorption, **1011**
  nonreabsorbed substances, 1013
  paracellular pathway, 1011,
    1011f

passive, **1012**–1013
  of sodium, 1011–1012, 1012f
  transport maximum, **1013**
  of water, 1012–1013
Tubular secretory units, **125**, 126f
Tubulins, 91f
Tubuloalveolar secretory units,
  125, 126f
Tubuloglomerular feedback
  mechanism, **1008**, 1009f,
  1010
Tubulus rectus, **1067**, 1068f
Tumor necrosis factors (TNFs),
  637b, **816**, 818t
Tumor suppressor genes, **146b**
Tunica adventitia. See Tunica
  externa
Tunica albuginea
  ovary, **1083**, 1083f
  testis, **1067**, 1067f, 1068f,
    1070f
Tunica externa, **714**, 715f
Tunica interna. See Tunica
  intima
Tunica intima, **714**, 715f
Tunica media, **714**, 715f
Tunica vaginalis, **1067**, 1067f,
  1068f
Tunics of blood vessels, 714, 715f
Turbinates. See Nasal conchae
Turbulence in blood flow,
  resistance and, 724
Turner's syndrome, 1101
TV (tidal volume), **851**, 852f
Twins, fraternal/identical, 1094
Two-point discrimination test, **498**
Tympanic cavity (middle ear),
  585–586, 585f
Tympanic membrane (eardrum),
  584f, **585**, 585f, 590f
Tympanic region of temporal bone,
  207, 209f
Type 1 diabetes mellitus, **636**–637b
Type 2 diabetes mellitus,
  636–637b
Type A daughter cell, **1077**, 1078f
Type A delta fibers, pain and,
  496b, 497f
Type B daughter cell, **1077**, 1078f
Type C fibers, pain and, 496b, 497f
Type Ia fibers, **522**–523, 522f
Type I cells, **842**, 843f
Type I hypersensitivities, **822**–823,
  823f
Type II cells, **842**, 843f
Type II fibers, **522**–523, 522f
Type II hypersensitivity, **823**
Type III hypersensitivity,
  823–824
Type IV hypersensitivity,
  824–825
Tyrosine, 418f, 947f
Tyrosine hydroxylase, 418f
Tyrosine kinase, 609

Ubiquinone (coenzyme Q), 964
Ubiquitins, 110–111
Ulcers
  decubitus, **171**
  esophageal, 897
  peptic, **938**
Ulna, 228f, **232**, 233f, 234f, 236f,
  236t
  at elbow joint, 258t, 268f
  at radioulnar joint, 258t

Ulnar arteries, 747f, 750f,
  750t, 751f
Ulnar collateral ligament,
  268, 268f
Ulnar nerve, **512**–513, 513f, 514t
  muscles served by, 358t, 359t,
    364t, 366t
Ulnar notch, of radius, **232**,
  233f, 236t
Ulnar veins, 759f, 762f, **762t**, 763f
Ultrasonography, **1141**
Ultrasound imaging (sonography),
  20b
Ultraviolet radiation
  DNA and, 157
  melanin in skin and, 164
  skin cancer and, 165
Umbilical arteries, **1129**–1130,
  1131f
Umbilical cord, 1121f, **1123**, 1131f
Umbilical ligaments, **1138**
Umbilical vein, 1121f, **1130**, 1131f
Uncinate fits, 583
Unconventional myosin, **90**
Uncus, 437f, 440
Undershoot (after-
  hyperpolarization), **404**
Unencapsulated dendritic endings,
  492, 493t
Uniaxial movement, **259**
Unicellular exocrine glands,
  125, 125f
Unipennate muscle, 326, 327f
Unipolar neurons, **395**, 396f,
  396–397t
  bipolar/multipolar neurons vs.,
    396–397t
Universal solvent, 30, **40**, 1036
Unmyelinated axon/nerve fiber,
  394–395, 394f
Unsaturated fats, **46**
Upper limbs
  arteries, 746f, 747f, 750–751t
  bones, 231–237
    summary, 236f, 236t
  distribution of major peripheral
    nerves in, 513f
  innervation, 512–514, 513f, 514t
    skin, 516, 518f
    sympathetic, 541, 541t
  veins, 758f, 758t, 762–763t
Up-regulation, by hormone
  receptors, **610**
Uracil (U), **55**–57, 56f, 57t
Urea, **970**, 970f, **1013**, 1018
  in blood plasma, 649t
  as component of urine, 1022
  reabsorption of, 1014t
Urea cycle, **970**
Ureteric buds, **1027**, 1029f
Ureteric ducts, **1027**, 1029f
Ureters, 998f, 1000f, **1023**–1024,
  1024f
  abdominal arteries in relation
    to, 755f
  parasympathetic fibers, 537f
  sympathetic innervation, 541t
Urethra, 998f, 1025f, **1026**
  ANS effects, 546t
  male, 1066, 1066f, 1070f, **1071**
    membranous, 1025f, **1026**,
      1066f, 1071
    prostatic, 1025f, **1026**, 1066f,
      1071
    spongy, 1025f, **1026**, 1066f,
      1071

Urethral folds, 1102f, **1103**
Urethral glands, 1071
Urethral groove, 1102f, **1103**
Urethral orifice, 1025f, **1026**
  male, 1066f, 1071
Urethral sphincters
  external, **350**, 351f, 1025f, **1026**
    description/action/nerve
      supply, 350t
    origin/insertion, 350t
  internal, 1025f, **1026**
Urethritis, 1026, 1100
Uric acid, **1013**
  in blood plasma, 649t
  gouty arthritis and, 274
Urinalysis, 1022b, **1031**
Urinary bladder, 924f, 998f,
  1024–1026, 1025f
  aging and, 1030
  ANS effects, 546t
  atonic, 551
  cancer, **1030**–1031
  continence, 1027, 1028f
  disorders, 1027
  empty vs. distended, 1026,
    1026f
  incontinence, 1027
  micturition and, 1027, 1028f
  parasympathetic fibers,
    536f, 537f
  sympathetic fibers, 536f, 539f
  sympathetic innervation, 541t
Urinary retention, **1028**
Urinary system, 7, 7f, 997–1034,
  998, 998f
  aging and, 1030
  cardiovascular system and,
    768b, 769b
  developmental aspects,
    1027–1030
    embryonic, 1123–1128, 1130t
    fetal, 1132t, 1133
  digestive system and, 934b
  endocrine system and, 640b
  homeostatic interrelationships
    with other body systems,
    1058b, 1059b
  integumentary system and, 168b
  lymphatic system/immunity
    and, 784b
  muscular system and, 318b
  nerve supply, 1001
  nervous system and, 548b
  organs
    kidneys, 998–1021
    ureters, 1023–1024
    urethra, 1026
    urinary bladder, 1024–1026
  in pregnancy, 1135
  reproductive system and, 1106b
  respiratory system and, 876b
  skeletal system and, 196b
  skin and, 168b
  vasculature pathway (summary),
    1000, 1000f
Urinary tract infections, 1026
Urination (voiding), **1027**
  neural circuits controlling,
    1027, 1028f
Urine, **1007**
  abnormal constituents, 1024t
  antidiuretic hormone and,
    1018–1019
  chemical composition,
    1022–1023
  concentrated, 1018, 1019f

continues

Urine, (cont.)
  dilute, 1018, 1019f
  mechanisms of formation
    glomerular filtration,
      1007–1011
    tubular reabsorption,
      1011–1015
    tubular secretion, **1015**
  phosphate buffer system and,
    1051, 1054
  physical characteristics, 1021
  protective mechanisms of,
    796t
  regulation of concentration/
    volume, 1015–1021
Urobilinogen, 654
Urochrome, **1021**
Urogenital diaphragm, **350**, 1025f,
  1026, 1066f, 1070f
  female, 1082f, 1088f
  muscles, 350t, 351f
Urogenital ridges, 1027, 1029f
Urogenital sinus, **1027**–1028,
  1029f
Urologist, **1031**
Uterine arteries, 1085f, **1086**,
  1087f
  ovarian branch, 1083
Uterine (fallopian) tubes, 1082f,
  1084–1085, 1085f
Uterine glands, 1086, 1087f
Uterine (menstrual) cycle,
  1096–1098, 1097f
  ovarian cycle and, 1097f, 1098
Uterine veins, 1085f
Uterosacral ligaments, 1082f,
  1085f, **1086**
Uterus, 1082f, **1085**–1086, 1085f
  ligaments of, 1082f, 1085f, 1086
  in pregnancy, 1133–1134, 1134f
  prolapse, 1086
  sympathetic fibers, 539f
  wall layers, 1085f, **1086**–1087,
    1087f
Utricle, 586f, **587**
  equilibrium and, 594–595, 594f
Utrophin, 317
Uvea (vascular layer of eye),
  560f, **561**
Uvula, 834f, 835, 889f, **890**

Vaccines, **805**–806, 806f
  cancer, 147b
  edible, 806
Vacuole, 90f
Vacuum-assisted closure (VAC), **148**
Vagal tone, **702**
Vagal trunks, anterior/posterior,
  538
Vagina, 1082f, 1085f, **1087**–1088
  ANS effects, 546t
  sympathetic fibers, 539f
Vaginal fornix, 1082f, 1085f, **1088**
Vaginal orifice, **1088**, 1088f
Vagotomy, **551**, **938**
Vagus nerve (X), 448f, 449f, 451,
  500, 501f
  gallbladder contractions and,
    917, 919f
  gustatory pathway and, **582**,
    582f, 583f
  muscles served by, 341t
  origin/course/function, 507f,
    507t
  pancreatic juice secretion and,
    918, 919f

parasympathetic fibers,
  537–538, 537f
pharyngeal plexus branch, 341t
  stimulator, 457
  stomach and, 900
Vagus nuclei, 450f
Valence shell, **32**–33, 33f
Valine, 947f
Vallate papillae, **581**, 581f,
  890, 891f
Valsalva's maneuver, 348, **838**, 926
Valvular stenosis, 689
Vanadium, 26t
Vanilloid receptor, 492
Vaporization, water and, 40
Variable, in homeostasis, **9**, 9f
Variable (V) regions of antibodies,
  807, 807f
variant Creutzfeldt-Jakob disease
  (vCJD), **482**–483b
Varicocele, 1080
Varicose veins, **722**–723, 1135
Varicosities, **310**, 311f, 519
Vasa recta, **1003**, 1004f
Vasa vasorum, 714
Vascular anastomoses, **723**
Vascular endothelial growth factor
  (VEGF)
  to build new bone tissue, 194b
  in liver injury, 915
Vascularity of connective tissue,
  127
Vascular layer (uvea) of eye,
  561, 561f
Vascular resistance, renal
  circulation and, 1003
Vascular shock, **742**
Vascular shunt (metarteriole-
  thoroughfare channel),
  721, 721f
  fetal, 1130, 1131f, 1138
Vascular spasm, in hemostasis,
  663, 664f, 665
Vascular system, **742**
Vas deferens. See Ductus (vas)
  deferens
Vasectomy, **1071**
Vasoactive intestinal peptide (VIP),
  905
  production site/stimuli/target/
    actions, 906t
Vasoconstriction, **714**
  endothelins as, 735
Vasodilation, **714**
  nitric oxide and, 735
Vasomotion, **738**
Vasomotor center, **727**–729, 728f
Vasomotor centers, medullary,
  451, 550
Vasomotor fibers, **545**, **727**, 728f
Vasomotor nerve fibers, in tunica
  media, 714
Vasomotor (sympathetic) tone, **545**
Vasomotor tone, **727**
Vasopressin. See Antidiuretic
  hormone
Vasovagal syncope, **551**
Vastus muscles, 330f, 331f, 368f
  actions of (summary),
    379–380t, 380f
  description/action/nerve supply,
    369t, **370**t
  origin/insertion, 369t, 370t
vCJD (variant Creutzfeldt-Jakob
  disease), **482**–483b
VC (vital capacity), **851**, 852f

VDs (venereal diseases),
  1100–1101
Vegetarian diets, 947f
VEGF. See Vascular endothelial
  growth factor
Veins, **714**, 715f, 716t, **722**–723
  arteries vs., 742
  blood flow velocity in, 735f
  blood pressure in, 725–726,
    725f, 726f
  major, of systemic circulation,
    758t–766t
  in pulmonary circulation, 744f,
    744–745t
  role in blood circulation, 647
  walls of, 715f, 716t, 722
Vellus hair, **162**
Venae cavae
  areas drained by, **758**–759t
  blood flow velocity in, 735f
  blood pressure in, 725f
  inferior, 681f–683f, **683**, 758f,
    758t, 763f–766f, **764**t
  superior, 679f, 681f–683f, **683**,
    685f, 687f, 745f, **758**t
Venereal diseases (VDs),
  1100–1101
Venous anastomoses, **723**
Venous arch, foot, 759f
Venous blood pressure, **725**–726,
  726f
Venous return, **700**, 727f, 731f
  adaptations that promote, 726
Venous sinuses, **723**
Venous system, **722**–723
Venous valves, 715f, **722**
Ventilation
  minute, **853**
  negative feedback mechanisms
    and, 865–866, 866f
  pulmonary, **831**, 846–854. See
    also Breathing
Ventilation-perfusion coupling,
  856–858, 857f
Ventral body cavity, **15**, 17f
  membranes in, 17–18, 17f,
    142, 142f
Ventral horns, of spinal cord,
  472, 473f
Ventral orientation/direction, 13t
Ventral rami, **509**–510, 510f,
  511, 540f
  muscles served by, 342t, 344t,
    367t
Ventral respiratory group (VRG),
  863–864, 864f
Ventral roots, 448f, **472**, 473f,
  474f, **509**, 510f
  sympathetic trunks in relation
    to, 540f
Ventral tegmental area (VTA), 424b
Ventral thalamic nuclei, 445f, 446
Ventricles
  brain, **433**–434, 434f
    embryonic origins, 432f, 433
  heart, **680**, 681f–685f, **683**–684
    anatomical differences in
      right/left, 684–685, 685f
    embryonic, 705
Ventricular septal defects,
  708, 708f
Ventricular tachycardia (VT or
  V-tac), **709**
Ventromedial nucleus, 445f
Venules, **714**, 716t, **722**, 725f
  blood flow velocity in, 735f

Vermiform appendix, 779f, **782**,
  883f, **922**, 923f
  abdominal arteries in relation
    to, 755f
  inflamed or ruptured, 887, 922
Vermis, **452**, 452f
Vernix caseosa, 170
Vertebrae, **218**
  cervical, 204f, **219**, 219f,
    221–222, 222f–224f, 224t
  joints of, 258t
  lumbar, 204f, **219**, 219f, 223,
    223f, 224f, 224t
  regional characteristics,
    221–223, 224f, 224t
  spinal cord in relation to, 473f
  structure of typical, 221, 221f
  thoracic, 204f, **219**, 219f, 222,
    223f, 224f, 224t
Vertebral arches, **221**, 221f, 471f
  lumbar, 471f
Vertebral arteries, 746f–751f,
  748t
Vertebral body (centrum), 220f,
  221, 221f
  intervertebral joints, 258t
  spinal cord in relation to,
    473f
Vertebral canal, **221**, 221f
Vertebral column, **218**. See also
  Spine
Vertebral (floating) ribs, **228**
Vertebral foramen, **221**, 221f
  in cervical/thoracic/lumbar,
    compared, 224f, 224t
Vertebral (spinal) cavity, **15**, 17f
Vertebral spinous process,
  219f, 220f
Vertebral veins, 758f, 759f, 760f,
  760t, 761f
Vertebra prominens, **221**
Vertebrocostal joint, 258t
Vertebrosternal (true) ribs, 226f,
  227f, **228**
Vertex presentation of infants,
  1137
Very low density lipoproteins
  (VLDLs), 973, **980**, 981f
Vesicles, **78**, 78f
  caveolin-coated, 81, 81f
  clathrin-coated, 78–79, 79f
  coatomer-coated, 87f, 88f
  secretory, 87, 88f, 89
  transport, 87f, 88f
Vesicouterine pouch, 1082f, 1086
Vesicular (Graafian) follicle, 1083f,
  1084, 1092f
Vesicular trafficking, 78, 80t, 81
Vesicular transport, **77**–81
Vesiculase, 1071
Vestibular apparatus, **594**
Vestibular division, of
  vestibulocochlear nerve, 506f,
  506t
Vestibular (equilibrium) cortex,
  440
Vestibular folds (false vocal cords),
  834f, 836f, **837**, 837f
Vestibular ganglia, 506f, 506t, 586f
Vestibular glands, greater, 1088f,
  1089
Vestibular membrane, **587**, 588f
Vestibular nerve, 586f, 594f,
  595, 596f
Vestibular nuclear complex, 450f,
  451, 597–598, 597f

Vestibular nystagmus, **597**
Vestibular (oval) window, 584f, **585**
Vestibule, 584f, **586**–587, 586f
   oral cavity, 889f, **890**
   of vagina, 1088f, **1089**
Vestibulocochlear nerve (VIII),
      448f, 449f, 451, **500**, 501f
   auditory pathway and, 592f
   cochlea and, 587
   origin/course/function, 506f, **506t**
Vestibulospinal tracts, 475f, **478**
   location/origin/termination/
      function, 479t
Viagra, 1074b
Vibrissae (nasal hairs), **832**
Visceral peritoneum, 924f
Villi, of small intestine, **909**,
      910f, 911f
Vimentin, 287
VIP. *See* Vasoactive intestinal
      peptide
Viral load, 821
Viruses, interferons and, 795–796,
      795f, 796t
Viscera, **15**, 17f
Visceral afferent nerve fibers,
      388, 389f
Visceral (autonomic) reflexes,
      521–522
Visceral layer of serous pericardium
      (epicardium), 17f, 18, 142f,
      143, 678, 679f, 680, 683f
Visceral motor functions, reticular
      formation and, 456
Visceral motor nuclei, in medulla,
      451
Visceral motor system, general,
      533. *See also* Autonomic
      nervous system
Visceral motor zones, 473f, **474**,
      474f, **538**, 540f
Visceral muscle (single-unit
      smooth muscle), **316**
Visceral organs, **15**, 17f
   ANS nerve fibers serving, 389f
   dual innervation by both ANS
      divisions, 544
Visceral pain, 496b
Visceral peritoneum, 18, 142f,
      143, 886, 886f
Visceral pleura, 844f, **846**
Visceral reflex arcs, **542**, 542f
Visceral reflexes, **521**–522,
      542, 542f
Visceral sensory area of cerebral
      cortex, **440**
Visceral sensory neurons,
      542, 542f
Visceral sensory zone, of spinal
      gray matter, **474**, 474f
Visceral serosa, **17**, 17f, 142f, 143
Visceroceptors (interoceptors),
      492, 493t
Viscosity of blood, **723**–724, 731f
Visible light, **565**, 566f
Visible spectrum, **565**, 566f
Vision, **565**–578
   adaptation to light/dark,
      574–575
   aging and, 598–599
   association area, 437f, **440**
   congenital disorders, 598
   cortical processing, 578
   developmental aspects, 598–599
   double, 558–559

focusing, 565–568
   far vs. near, 567–568
   light properties, 565–566
   panoramic, 575
   pathways to brain, 575
   phototransduction, 568–575
   primary visual cortex, 437f,
      440
   retinal processing and, 576–577
   thalamic processing, 577–578
Visual association areas, 437f, **440**
   damage to, 440
   processing of retinal inputs, 578
Visual cortex (primary), 437f, **440**,
      575, 576f
   damage to, 440
   processing of retinal inputs, 578
Visual fields, 575, 576f
Visual pigments (photopigments),
      569–570, 570f
   capture of light by, 571–572,
      571f
Vital capacity (VC), **851**, 852f
Vitamin A (retinol), 48t, **947t**
Vitamin B1 (thiamin), **949t**
Vitamin B2 (riboflavin), **950t**
Vitamin B3 (niacin/nicotinamide),
      950t
Vitamin B5 (pantothenic acid),
      950t
Vitamin B6 (pyridoxine), **950t**
Vitamin B12 (cyanocobalamin),
      902, 920t, **951t**
   erythrocytes and, 654
   intrinsic factor and, 655, 900,
      902, 920t, 932, 951t
Vitamin C (ascorbic acid),
      949t, 952
Vitamin D (antirachitic factor),
      48t, **933**, 948t, 998
   bones and, 196b, 197b
   calcium absorption and, 196b,
      197b, 933
   deficiency, 193, 948t
   parathyroid hormone and, 625
   provitamin D3 (cholecalciferol),
      638, 638f
   skin synthesis of, 165, 196t,
      197b, 948t
Vitamin E (antisterility factor),
      48t, **949t**
   as anticoagulant, 667
Vitamin K (coagulation vitamin),
      48t, 920t, 925, **949t**
   absorption of, 932
   clotting factors and, 665
Vitamins, 920t, **947**–952
   absorption of, 932
   acting as coenzymes, **948**
   fat-soluble, **948**, 952
   made in body, 948
   reabsorption of, 1014t
   roles in body (overview),
      949–951t
   water-soluble, **948**, 949–951t
Vitiligo, **171**
Vitreous humor, 560f, **563**–564,
      564f
VLDLs (very low density
      lipoproteins), 973, **980**, 981f
Vocal cords, true/false, 834f, 836f,
      837, 837f
Vocal folds (true vocal cords), 834f,
      836f, **837**, 837f
Vocal ligaments, **837**, 837f
Voice, paranasal sinuses and, 218

Voice production, 837–838, 837f
Voiding (urination), **1027**
Volatile acids, **1052**
Volkmann's (perforating) canals,
      182, 183f
Voltage, **397**
   cell membrane potential and, **81**
   channel proteins sensitive to, 84
   volts/millivolts as measures, 397
Voltage-gated ion channels, 84,
      398–399, 398f
   calcium, 289, 409
   in cardiac muscle contraction,
      691–692
   role in action potentials,
      402–404, 403f
Voluntary movement, cortical
      motor areas that control,
      436–439
Voluntary nervous system
   somatic nervous system and,
      388, 389f
   voluntary vs. involuntary
      muscle, **141**, 280, 315t
Vomer bone, 205f, 206f, 208f,
      213, 215f
   summary/important markings,
      217t
Vomiting (emesis), 451, **907**–908
   metabolic acidosis and, 1056t
VRG (ventral respiratory group),
      863–864, 864f
v-SNAREs, 78, 78f
V-tac (ventricular tachycardia), **709**
VTA (ventral tegmental area), 424b
VT (ventricular tachycardia), **709**
Vulnerable plaque theory of
      atherosclerosis, 719b
Vulva (pudendum), **1088**, 1088f

Wallerian degeneration, **499**, 499f
Warfarin, **667**
Warts, 165
   genital, **1101**
Water, **8**, **40**
   absorption, 920t, 922, 933
   in blood plasma, 649t
   body content in infants/females/
      males, 1036
   cushioning of body organs by, 41
   environmental temperature
      and, 40
   evaporation and, 40
   exchanges among fluid
      compartments,
      1037–1038, 1038f
   hydrogen bonding and, 36, 37f
   insensible loss, **987**
   intake, 1039
   membrane transport processes
      (diffusion/osmosis) and,
      72–73, 72f, 73f
   metabolic, **1039**
   molecular model, 36f
   movement between fluid
      compartments,
      1037–1038, 1039f
   perspiration and, 40
   polarity and, 35–36, 36f
   properties of, 40–41, 40f
   reabsorption, 1012–1013,
      1014t, 1019, 1019f, 1041,
      1041f
   as reactant in chemical
      reactions, 40–41
   tonicity and, 74

as universal solvent, 30, 40, 1036
   in urine, 1022
   vaporization, heat and, 987
Water balance
   antidiuretic hormone and, 1041,
      1041f
   aquaporins and, 73
   blood pressure homeostasis
      and, 1046f
   disturbances in, 1041–1043,
      1042f
   intake, 1039
      major sources, 1039f
      regulation, 446, 1039–1040
   output, 1039
      major sources, 1039f
      regulation, 1040–1041, 1041f
Water loss
   insensible, 987, **1039**, 1040
   obligatory, **1040**
   sensible, **1040**
   from sweating, 165
Water of oxidation, **1039**
Water on the knee, 273
Water output, 1039
Water-soluble vitamins, **948**,
      949–951t
Wavelength of sound, 589, 590f
Wave summation muscle
      contractions, 297–298, 298f
WBCs (white blood cells). *See*
      Leukocytes
Weak acids, **43**
Weak bases, **43**
Weber's test, **600**
Weeping lubrication, 256
Wernicke's area, 437f
   language and, **460**
White blood cells (WBCs). *See*
      Leukocytes
White columns (funiculi), 473f,
      474, 475f, 477f, **478**, 540f
White fat (adipose) tissue, 133
White fibers. *See* Collagen fibers
Whitehead, 159
White matter, **395**, **441**–443
   arrangement in CNS, 433, 433f
   embryonic origins, 432f
   spinal, 472, 473f, 474, 510f
      ascending/descending tracts,
         474, 475f
      types of fiber tracts in, 442f, 443
White pulp, **780**, 780f
White rami communicantes, 536t,
      538, 540f
Whole blood transfusions, **668**
Withdrawal (flexor) reflex,
      525–526, 526f
Withdrawal reflex, 10
Wolff's law, 190
Wound repair, 143–145, 144f, 148
   cathelicidins released by injured
      skin, 164
Wrinkles, 156b, 170, 171
Wrist
   bone (carpus), **233**, 235,
      235f, 236f
   joint (radiocarpal), 258t
   muscles acting on, 358–361t
      actions (summary),
         362–363t, 363f
Wryneck (torticollis), 342t, **384**

X chromosome, **1101**, 1103
Xenobiotics, 1080
Xenon computed tomography, **20b**

Xerostomia, 893, **938**
Xiphisternal joint, 226f, **227**
Xiphoid process, **226**–227, 226f
X-linked inheritance, **1152**
X ray (radiograph), **20**b

Yawning, mechanism/result, 854t
Y chromosome, **1101**, 1103
Yellow bone marrow, 180, 180f
Yellow bone marrow cavity, **180**
Yellow cast to skin, 158
Yellow fibers. *See* Elastic fibers

Y-linked inheritance, **1152**
Yolk sac, 1102f, 1121f, **1122**,
    1124f, 1125f, 1126f

Z disc (Z line), **284**, 285f, 288f,
    289f, 689, 690f
ZIFT (zygote intrafallopian
    transfer), 1139
Zinc, 26t, **955**t
ZIPs (zonal inhibiting proteins),
    1115
Zona fasiculata, **626**, 626f

Zona glomerulosa, **626**, 626f
Zonal inhibiting proteins
    (ZIPs), 1115
Zona pellucida, **1093**, 1093f,
    1116f
Zona reticularis, **626**–627, 626f
Zygomatic arch, **207**
Zygomatic bones, 205f, 206f, 208f,
    213, 214f
  orbital surface, 214f
  summary/important markings,
    217t

Zygomatic process, 206f, **207**, 209f,
    212f, **213**, 214f, **216**t, **217**t
  in relation to temporomandibular
    joint, 271f
Zygomaticus muscle, 337f
  description/action/nerve supply,
    336t
  superficial, 331f
Zygote, **1114**, 1116, 1117f
Zygote intrafallopian transfer
    (ZIFT), 1139
Zymogen granules, **917**, 918f